What is

McGraw Hill Edge Courseware is a versatile learning and assessment solution, that uses credible content and innovative pedagogies to make the readers' exam preparation journey holistic and adaptive to changing examination trends. By blending the strengths of authoritative McGraw Hill books with cutting-edge digital resources and latest updates, this Courseware offers a dynamic content solution for exam aspirants. It provides the students a thorough understanding of the subject matter, enhances learning and retention, and shares deep insights about their performance, ultimately boosting their confidence. This Courseware is at the forefront of innovation; revolutionising learning to guide learners on their path to success!

Unlock Your Potential with

McGraw Hill Edge Courseware

Conceptual Videos

To transform complex ideas into engaging visual storytelling!

Study Aids

To simplify learning with visual summaries, mind maps, flash cards, infographics etc.

Knowledge Enrichment Content

To craft your path to success with exclusive reading materials

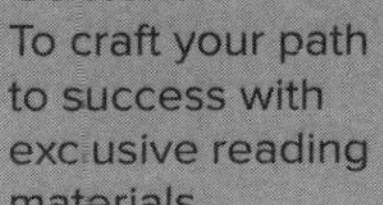

Previous Years' Questions

To practice from an extensive collection of PYQs with detailed explanations

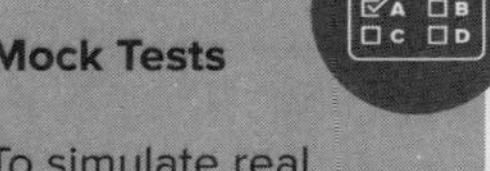

Mock Tests

To simulate real exam conditions and boost confidence

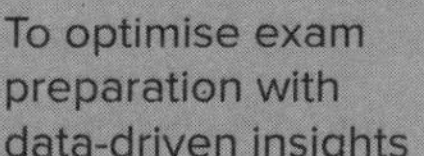

Performance Analytics

To optimise exam preparation with data-driven insights

Live Interactive Sessions

To gain valuable insights from the author through interactive sessions

eBook Access

To conveniently access study materials anytime, anywhere

What do you get with Courseware on Quantitative Aptitude for CAT?

The **Courseware on Quantitative Aptitude for CAT** is an end-to-end learning solution meticulously designed for CAT and management entrance exam applicants:

- **Previous Years' Questions:** Access to CAT 2020–2024 QA questions with detailed solutions and analytics
- **Problem-solving Videos:** Over 200 assisted problem-solving videos to simplify challenging concepts
- **Practice Questions:** 4000+ practice questions with detailed explanations
- **Mock Test Papers:** 2 CAT (full-length) and 11 QA solved mock tests for knowledge assessment and confidence building
- **Sectional Tests:** Exclusive access to 3 sectional tests with detailed explanations to refine your understanding and give you an advantage!
- **Live Interactive Sessions:** Interactive author sessions on the right approach and preparation strategy for CAT 2025

COUNTER THE COUNTERFEIT & BUILD A STRONG FOUNDATION FOR SUCCESS

Books are our best friends, is the adage we have grown up with. However, the pirates of piracy are continuously forging 'our best friends'. Our books and their supplementary online resources are copyrighted, and we don't lend any right-to-copy. Piracy is synonymous to stealing books.

Knowledge comes real, let's not encourage its counterfeit. Therefore, we appeal all our readers to discourage pirated books and **choose authentic ones**.

HOW TO IDENTIFY THE PIRATED BOOKS?

1 TRANSPARENCY CODE ON THE BOOK

Congratulations! The book you have purchased is protected by Transparency. Transparency by Amazon is a unit-level product serialization service that verifies a unit's authenticity and enables you to view rich information about the product you purchased. Please look for the Transparency logo and code on the book back cover (Transparency barcode is a square code that can be found next to the "T" symbol). You can scan the barcode with the Transparency app to verify the book's authenticity. Simply download the Transparency app from the App Store or Google Play. Scan the barcode with the app. The app will display a green checkmark when the book has been verified as authentic.

2 COVER AND SPINE

- Look and feel (new or used book)
- Blurred images on the cover
- Hologram pasted on front
- Defective spine (wrinkles) or air pocket at its bottom
- Unclear ISBN/bar codes
- Missing/non-operational Unique Coupon Code for exclusive access to McGraw Hill Edge

3 TEXT/PRINTING/BINDING

- Uneven inking of pages
- Poor quality or blurred photographs/images/charts
- Substandard paper quality and opacity

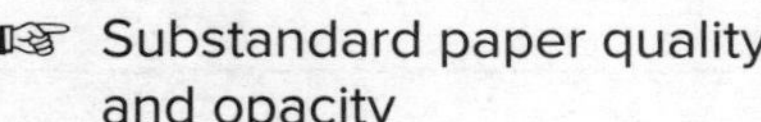

- Misaligned pages
- Missing pages
- Inferior binding quality

You can further watch this video on How to identify a pirated book

For more information about identifying piracy, visit **https://www.mheducation.co.in/piracy**

To report a pirated book, send 'Hi' on WhatsApp code given on the back cover or write to us at **support.india@mheducation.com**.

Reported pirated books are examined to combat their piracy.

Let's fight the Pirates of Piracy and resolve to go for original!

12e
2025

COURSEWARE ON

QUANTITATIVE APTITUDE

for

CAT

Common Admission Test & Other Management Examinations

Arun Sharma

McGraw Hill Education (India) Private Limited

Published by McGraw Hill Education (India) Private Limited
Registered Office: Anjana Complex No: 5/90 A, Butt Road, St. Thomas Mount, Chennai – 600016,

Courseware on Quantitative Aptitude for CAT 2025, 12e

First reprint 2025

Print Edition:
ISBN (13): 978-93-6444-776-8
ISBN (10): 93-6444-776-X

E-Book Edition:
ISBN (13): 978-93-6444-923-6
ISBN (10): 93-6444-923-1

02 03 04 05 06 RAJ 29 28 27 26 25

Typeset at CoKrator Content Solutions Private Limited, Delhi-110092 and printed and bound at Rajkamal Electric Press, Kundli, Haryana-131028.

Cover Designer: Yaman

Visit us at: www.mheducation.co.in
Write to us at: support.india@mheducation.com
CIN: U80302TN2010PTC111532
Toll Free Number: 1800 103 5875

Dedicated to

My Father (Mr MK Sharma), Mother (Mrs Renu Sharma)
and Brother (Mr Ravi Sharma)
who have instilled in me the courage to have my convictions
and to stand by them

About the Author

Arun Sharma is a postgraduate from the prestigious Indian Institute of Management, Bangalore. He has been training corporate houses and CAT aspirants since 1996 and has personally trained thousands of students in IIMs and other top B Schools. Besides, he holds the unique distinction of clearing CAT 22 times in a row, with many scores of percentile 99.99.

Preface to the Twelfth Edition

Creating the 12th edition of this highly successful book has been an exciting journey—primarily because technology has enabled us to achieve what few other books around the world have done. The introduction of QR codes, granting access to videos, learning materials, and tests, is a game changer. As an author, this innovation enhances my ability to connect with you in new ways. We have embraced this opportunity wholeheartedly, transforming this work from a traditional book into comprehensive Courseware. By integrating learning materials and videos, we aim to help you grasp concepts more effectively and enrich your learning experience.

Across its 20 chapters and five blocks, QR codes are strategically placed at key points in the text and exercises. By scanning them, you'll gain access to following types of explanatory videos:

Throughout the 20 chapters across the five blocks you would go through, you would find QR codes inserted at strategic and important junctures of the text/exercises. Scanning these QR codes will take you to access content in the form of explanatory videos, in the following categories:

1. **Chapter Launchpad:** Introductory and descriptive videos at the start of each chapter to set the foundation
2. **Going Beyond the Book:** Assisted problem-solving videos that tackle examples and miscellaneous questions
3. **Knowledge Enrichment Corner:** Additional problem-solving videos provided before the main exercise
4. **Concept Explainer:** Deep-dive videos designed to enhance conceptual understanding and mastery
5. **High Yield Questions (in chapters and mock tests):** Guided walkthroughs of select LOD questions to sharpen your problem-solving skills

Besides, across the years, with the evolution of CAT in its online avatar and with the continuous evolution of the CAT paper from year to year, I felt the need to create a comprehensive and updated book that caters to CAT aspirants. We have kept in mind the following facts while designing the book you now hold in your hands:

1. Questions from this book: Over the past two decades, it has been noticed that a minimum of 10–20% questions in CAT every year as also in all major management entrance examinations like XAT, IIFT, NMAT etc. have been directly taken from the questions provided in this book. Besides, the logic contained in the questions in this book historically has taken care of over 80% of the questions that the CAT has asked in every year for the past 20 years. Furthermore, all other management entrance and aptitude-based exams like UPSC CSAT, Bank PO, SSC, placement exams at graduation levels, GMAT, GRE and the entire gamut of aptitude exams at the graduate and post graduate levels have seen to have taken questions/question ideas directly from this book's question banks. This trend has been observed for close to a couple of decades, which is perhaps one of the reasons why this book has become one of the most important resources that every student at these levels uses.

CAT having gone online saw no change in this trend. Many questions in each of the test papers that CAT has administered in its decade long online avatar since 2009, are covered in this book.

In fact, 2009 onwards, the onset of CAT online pattern has created a significant shift in terms of the CAT preparation process. This is because 2009 was the first year when there were multiple CAT papers to study, analyse and base our writing and preparation process on. In subsequent years, with the increase of CAT window, the number of papers every year had gone up to around 30–40 papers. CAT between 2015 to 2019, however, went back to a two-slot test and hence, had a total of only 2 test papers. CAT 2017 was also a significant shift point, in this journey –as for the first time in the history of the Online CAT, the actual test paper was released for the students who took the exam. Of course, due to the Pandemic and due to the need for social distancing CAT 2020 and CAT 2021 became a 3-slot examination. This trend of 3 slots for the exam continued in CAT 2022 and CAT 2024.

Thus, all said, overall, I am richer by the experience of 150 plus test papers, when it comes to understanding what I need to provide to my readers for their preparation. It is on the basis of this rather rich insight that I have based the changes in this edition (Note: Similar changes have been incorporated in my other books *How to Prepare for Verbal Ability and Reading Comprehension for CAT, How to Prepare for Data Interpretation for CAT, How to Prepare for Logical Reasoning for CAT* and *Previous Years' Solved CAT Papers.*

2. The History of the CAT and the implications for your preparation cycle: The CAT changed its stripes in 2015, when it moved being from a 2 section examination to a 3-section examination. Before 2015 it used to be a 2 section exam, with the sections being Section 1: Quantitative Aptitude and Data Interpretation and Section 2:Verbal Ability/Reading Comprehension and Logical Reasoning. In 2015, the CAT became a 3-section examination with the three sections being: Quantitative Aptitude, Verbal Ability and Reading Comprehension, Data Interpretation and Logical Reasoning.

This change altered preparation requirements drastically, since the two-section exam pattern which the aspirant to take a strategy of doing very well in the Logical Reasoning questions in Section 2 and hence get through that section without being too good at Verbal Ability/Reading Comprehension. Likewise, aspirants could get through Section 1, by being really good at DI and moderately skilled in Quantitative Aptitude or vice versa. The 3-section exam does not provide the aspirant with that luxury any longer. You would need to display competence in each of the three areas of the exam in order to get a good percentile. Hence, this created a significant change in terms of preparation strategies for CAT. The selective skills development approach, became redundant and students have simply no option of taking preparation short cuts of not preparing any one of the three sections.

The Introduction of TITA questions - questions having no options: CAT 2015 onwards, the CAT has had on average had as many as 30% plus questions without options – something that is described as Type in The Answer (TITA). The presence of such a large number of questions without options clearly meant that students were tested for the clarity of their concepts in each area — especially in the QA section. Since this trend is supposed to continue, it is quite clear that you would need to know the exact answer for every question that you are trying to solve — gone are the days where an 'educated' guess would take you through a few questions in the exam.

However, you need to understand an important point in this context that the QA section is not a test of your mathematical knowledge. A closer look at the kind of questions (in which no options are given) reveals that these are pretty much solvable using simple numeric logic rather than using hard-core mathematical process and formula. There has not been a single question in this category that forced you to follow the hard-core mathematical way, of solving such questions.

The need for greater variety in your preparation: Prior to the CAT going online, preparing for QA used to be a battle for Blocks I, III, IV and V – as defined in this book. Even out of these, if someone did Blocks I and IV well, he stood a strong chance at the QA section, since over 60% of the questions asked in the papers were from these areas (and solving 60% questions in QA, normally guarantees you a 99+ percentile).

However, as explained below, the latest changes of this exam requires the aspirant to be much more balanced in the context of portion coverage.

As per the scheme followed in this book, the QA portion can be divided into 5 major parts (or blocks as I call them in this book).

The underlying constant that used to exist in the paper-and-pen version (through the entire decade prior to the first online CAT) was the prominence of Block I and Block IV. (Block I comprising Number Systems and Progressions and Block IV comprising the chapters on Functions, Inequalities, Quadratic and other Equations and Logarithms.)

In each of the years from 1999 to 2008, the QA section required you to get a net score of approximately 30 – 40% of the total marks in order to score a high 90+ percentile in this section.

In the light of this fact, the importance of Block I and Block IV can be gauged from the table below:

Block	*Weightage (as a % of total marks)*
Block I	30–50%
Block IV	15–50%
Combined weightage of Blocks I & IV	60–80%

Add to this, the chapter on Time, Speed and Distance with a minimum weightage of 5–10% and you pretty much had the QA section well covered. In a nutshell, QA for CAT preparation had become "do 10 chapters well".

However, this scenario has changed in the context of the online version of the exam – and something that we have seen consistently over the 15 years of the Online CAT.

The balance of weightage of questions shifted and each of the five blocks have become important. Between 2009 to 2023, aspirants of CAT online version saw a weightage distribution of the kind illustrated below:

Block	*Percentage of Questions*
Block I	15–20
Blocks II	40–50
Block III	10–20
Block IV	15–30
Block V	5–10

Note: In the 2-hour CAT test that was taken in 2020, the number of questions were brought down to 22 and the sectional timing was brought down to 40 minutes (from 60 minutes and 34 questions of the 2017–2018–2019 pattern). This pattern of 22 questions in the QA section of the exam has continued as a constant up until 2023. The proportion of questions from various parts of the portion has remained by and large constant in the 2-hour exam. However, it does influence a few aspects in terms of time available per question and speed of solving required (I will talk about it later in this preface).

Qualifying scores and attempts required at various accuracy levels: Over the past 4 years the CAT has become a 2 hour exam with a time limit of 40 minutes per section. The QA section has settled down to become a 22 questions section – with a total marks of 66. In this context one of the things you should know is the significantly higher level of difficulty of the CAT 2023 paper. Going forward, the exam might revert back to the difficulty level of CAT 2020–22 or remain as difficult as CAT 2023. Hence, you should clearly know your targets for what you would need to be trying to achieve in this section. The following table would give you a clear idea about your targets based on the percentile you are targeting in the QA section:

	CAT 20, 21 and 22 2 Hour 66 question exam: QA 40 minutes 22 questions		*CAT 2023 2 hour 66 question exam: QA 40 minutes 22 questions*		*CAT 2024 2 hours 68 question exam QA 40 minutes 22 questions*	
To score	*Number of attempts required at 100% accuracy*	*Number of attempts required at 85–95% accuracy*	*Number of attempts required at 100% accuracy*	*Number of attempts required at 85–95% accuracy*	*Number of attempts required at 100% Accuracy*	*Number of attempts required at 85–95% accuracy*
99.8+ percentile	16–18	20–22	11–12	17–18	13–14	17–18
99 percentile	12–13	16–19	8–10	12–14	10–11	13–14
98 percentile	10–11	13–15	7–8	9–10	9–10	12–13
95 percentile	7–8	11–13	6	7–8	7–8	9–10
90 percentile	5–6	8–9	5	6–7	5–6	8–9
80 percentile	4+	6–7	3	5–6	4+	6–7

A few trends you can see from this table:

(i) For a 99 percentile you need to be able to solve approximately half the paper (for a difficulty level similar to CAT 20–22; while for the significantly higher level of difficulty associated with CAT 2023, you would need to solve only about 40% of the paper (if you are solving all correct), to get the coveted 99 percentile in the exam. In CAT 2024, the difficulty level was a bit lower than 2023.

(ii) A difficult paper gives you more choice in terms of leaving questions, while your choice is significantly reduced in an easier paper – simply because if you want to remain in the same league of percentile score, you would be required to do much more.

(iii) **Accuracy is more important than speed:** This is a clear trend indication, if you take a look at say the attempts required for 98 percentile in CAT 2024: At 100% accuracy it is 9–10 out of 22, while at 85–95% accuracy you would need to attempt 12–13 questions out of 22. From having a choice of leaving 12–13 questions in the test, your choice has gone down to barely 9–10. This effectively means that instead of being able to solve 5 questions in every 10, you would need to be able to solve 6+ out of 10, if your accuracy is down. Naturally, the pressure on you to solve every question that appears in front of you is much higher in such a case.

Hence, the key learning for you while preparing is to focus on improving your accuracy as well as the belief in your process of solving. This is especially true while preparing for the QA section. While solving a QA question, you should be able to know that if your process is correct then your answer would also be correct. The need to check the answer to a QA question is something that is only required for minds weak in Quantitative Aptitude. This is where an under-prepared aspirant loses out to the best—in the knowledge of whether what they are solving is correct or not. Unfortunately, most students I see are more interested in seeing the answer to the question as soon as they solve the same. This is a habit I would strongly discourage you from. The ideal preparation process for you should be:

(a) solve the question,
(b) review your process and tell yourself, "if your process is correct, so is your answer", and
(c) only check your answer after you have reviewed your process.

This is important, because when you are solving a QA question inside CAT, you would not have the cushion to 'look' at the answer. The only thing you have is the question and the process you use in solving the same. Your mind should be able to tell you whether the answer you have got is correct or not. This is a key difference in solving questions in practice and solving them under exam pressure.

Hence, developing more confidence in your QA problem-solving processes becomes a key ingredient and objective of your preparation process for this section.

Tougher level of CAT exam: As already stated above, the quality of questions asked in the CAT over the past 4–5 of years has become extremely good with 2023 becoming a kind of a watershed year for level of difficulty and 2024 following on that path (though there were more sitters in the 2024 exam than in 2023—requiring an upgradation of your grasp of concepts and understanding of each particular topic to a level not required before. In fact a trend observed especially in CAT 2022 and 2023 was the high usage of multidisciplinary questions in the test. This shift has necessitated that we do more through this book and in this light the LOD 2 and 3's especially of the chapters of Number Systems, Arithmetic and Algebra become extremely important for you to cover. With the inputs gathered from CAT 2022–2023, we have in fact tightened the question banks for more than half the chapters in the book – removing repetitive and/or irrelevant questions while adding the kind of question patterns that the exam has introduced in the last 2 years. We have also curated a set of questions in the most important topics, that would be an extremely valuable resource for you to understand where the CAT might of – going forward.

A story you simply need to hear and a lesson you simply must take: Students appearing for CAT 2018 got a dual shock- The CAT 2018 exam was a 34 questions exam with a 1 hour time frame. Good students aiming for 99+ percentiles went into the paper with a target of solving about 22–23 questions in the exam. This attempt target would mean a flexibility of around 11–12 questions which one could leave out of 34. Thus, out of every 5 questions, one would need to solve on average just above 3 in order to get the required score.

During the preparation phase of the examination, a majority of the students had taken the Logarithms chapter lightly during their preparation – as somehow it had gained a reputation of not having too many questions in the exam. Also, Arithmetic was one of the most critically prepared areas of QA for most students – as it had a high rate of questions appearing in the exam over the past decade. The dual shock students faced in Slot 1 was: 3 questions from Logarithms all of Level of Difficulty 1. Anyone who had studied the topic for a few hours and knew the Logarithm chapters would easily get these questions. Naturally, those who had not studied Logarithms had no chance in these questions. Hence, they were effectively solving the exam out of 31 questions & hence their flexibility of leaving questions was down to 8. The second aspect of this double whammy was that the arithmetic questions had a very high level of difficulty – and even the well prepared aspirant found it difficult to solve at least 6–8 questions out of the 14 arithmetic questions in the exam. Naturally, the majority of students who had 'left' Logarithms, had their elbow room completely taken away in the exam, with the result that the panic that this caused created a complete chaos for these students. A similar story was repeated in Slot 2. These kind of happenings are very common in the CAT exam and hence the all important lesson that you should learn is that **'Do not do selective studying'.** If you are planning to do anything of the sort as a preparation strategy, you are leaving yourself open to a lot of risks which you would ideally want to minimise.

Preparation for other Management Entrance Exams: I have also come to know that many readers use this book for their preparation of other important management entrance exams (like XAT, CMAT, MAT, SNAP, etc). So now, I have also included/modified the contents so that aspirants of the above exams need not look for any other resource beyond this book for strengthening their hold on the quantitative aptitude section.

Apart from management entrance examinations, the book also has relevance for aspirants of UPSC and state civil services, Bank PO exams, CUET, IPMAT, CLAT, GATE, Engineering Placement exams, etc. In short the scope of this book has considerably widened to cover the entire subject of quantitative aptitude that finds a resonance in all aptitude exams for all career aspirants.

The book you now hold in your hand has always been written keeping in mind the avowed objective of developing your quantitative intelligence to a point where you can quickly scale the height of preparation in each chapter of the portion.

KEY FEATURES:

1. **Comprehensive solutions** (wherever relevant) to questions in all LODs of all chapters. Note: Most of LOD 3 is unsolved, because I feel that once someone has reached the LOD 3 level of solving and is aspiring to be able to solve LOD 3's of chapters, he should be in a self-solve mode rather than an assisted solving mode. Anyways, you only need to solve the LOD3's in case you are looking to score a high 99.5+ percentile.
2. Tighter more uptodate question banks: The question banks contained in the previous editions of this book, have been combed through in detail and we have weeded out repetitive or irrelevant questions. At the same time, we have introduced close to a thousand new questions in this edition – mapped to the latest CAT Papers and based on our reading of where the CAT is heading towards. This has been done in at least 75% of the chapters of the book.
3. At some places, the need was felt to introduce an entire additional exercise on concepts of a chapter. This too has been accomplished in this revision.

4. **Rewriting of the theory:** For a lot of the chapters, we have taken a deep look at the theory write ups and improved or updated them with fresh thoughts wherever required.
   The CAT Experience: We recognise the need for an aspirant to test his preparation. In this context, we have introduced the most important part of this book –THE CAT EXPERIENCE, which is a series of 11 mock tests which have been carefully curated. The questions for these 11 tests have been carefully created in order to map the exact CAT experience. I can confidently state that when you are taking these mocks, you will get a feeling that is very close to the actual CAT exam. I would advise you to make sure that you make the time to solve the CAT EXPERIENCE tests after you have completed the portion. **Take the following inputs from this section:**
   (i) How are you performing in the tests?
   (ii) Which chapters are working well for you and more importantly which chapters are not working well for you? Hence, in which topics do you need to improve your knowledge and ability to solve questions correctly? And in which topics do you need to work on your efficiency and speed?
   (iii) Based on the feedback you get from your performance in these tests, you might want to cover some topics again with a focus on ability and some topics with a focus on speed and efficiency.
5. Introduction of a critical section within each block called 'Taste of the Exams' that covers the questions asked in the CAT, for the last two decades, updated till 2019. What's more, these sections are completely solved, with illustrative thought processes as well as thought short cuts that you would not find in any other book of this type
6. Introduction of questions without options in each of the relevant chapters of the book. This is in keeping with the latest trends introduced in the last CAT examination.
7. Completely revamped question banks at Level of Difficulty 1 and Level of Difficulty 2 for many chapters. We felt the need to update the chapter LODs in various critical chapters, based on the latest trends in the exam.
   The book is you hold in your hands is totally in sync with the new trend and pattern of the examination.
   Ultimately the endeavour is to provide a one-stop solution for CAT and MBA exam aspirants to tackle the QA section of all major management entrance exams—an endeavour I feel I have managed to do pretty well.
   Through this book, I am confident of giving you—the reader—an invaluable resource for enhancing your QA section score drastically. Contained in this book is the very best advisory for each and every question type. Your job is simple— to ensure that you follow the process contained in this advisory.

KEY POINTS FOR YOUR PREPARATION

Outline and Strategy

The first aspect I would like to deal with here is to focus on helping you with the formulation of your strategy with respect to the portion to be covered for the Quantitative Aptitude section of the various management entrance exams including CAT, XAT, CMAT, NMAT, SNAP, MHCET and other examinations.

Let us start by trying to understand some of the key areas in Quantitative Aptitude (QA).

Tackling each portion

My experience shows that very often students look at the vast number of chapters and concepts to be studied for QA and get disheartened. This is especially true for students who do not have a strong traditional background in Mathematics. Indeed if you were to look at it with a chapter-wise approach, you can easily define the course to be studied by dividing it into 20+ chapters— preparation for which is such a long-drawn effort that it ends up draining the student's energy enthusiasm and motivation.

It is in this context and for this precise reason that I have divided this book into five manageable blocks—the approach being rationalising the chapters and grouping them according to the amount of shared concepts these chapters have amongst each other.

The outline as defined in the contents to this book would divide your work into 5 major areas to prepare for. For your convenience and strategising I have put down the relative importance of each of these five blocks into perspective:

Block I: Number Systems and Progressions

Importance: **Very High** for CAT, XAT, NMAT, SNAP, CUET, IPMAT, SSC, Banking etc.

Block II: Averages and Alligations, Percentages, Ratio, Proportion and Variation, Time and Work, Time, Speed and Distance. Interest and Profit & Loss.

Importance: **Very High** for CAT, XAT, NMAT, SNAP, CUET, IPMAT, SSC, Banking, CMAT etc.

Also High for Data Interpretation as a lot of questions in DI are based on the concepts of Averages and Alligations, Percentages and Ratio & Proportions.

Note: *The chapter on "Time, Speed and Distance" is extremely important for these exams (especially for the CAT as questions from this chapter have been asked every year in the CAT examinations for the last two decades.)*

Block III: Geometry, Mensuration and Coordinate Geometry

Importance: **Very High** for CAT, XAT, IIFT. **Average** for NMAT, MAT, CMAT, SNAP, etc.

Block IV: Functions, Inequalities, Logs and Quadratic Equations

Importance: **Very High** for CAT, XAT. **Low** for SNAP, NMAT, MAT, CMAT etc.

Block V: Permutations and Combinations, Probability and Set Theory

Importance: **Moderate** for CAT, XAT, IIFT, etc. **Average** for other exams

Based on the experience of the online CAT, the strategic preparation imperative for you should be to do at least three blocks and if possible up to five blocks really well.

What does it mean to prepare a block "really well"? This is something I feel needs emphasis here.

Well what I mean to say is that do not just focus on studying the theory in each of these areas but develop an intuitive knowledge of all problem scenarios which emerge out of each block.

Only then would you be able to reach a situation in the exam—that when the question presents itself to you in the exam— you would have had the logic for the same worked out before-hand. This is something that can make a huge difference to your chances in CAT.

Analysing Your Knowledge Level

The first thing you need to focus on is an analysis of your knowledge level in each of these five parts. In each of the above areas, first analyse your level of knowledge/ability. In order to do so the typical question you should ask yourself is: For the next 100 questions I face in each of these areas, how many would I be able to handle comfortably?

Think of a number as an answer to this question for each of the five blocks.

Based on your answer, the following analysis would provide you a thumb rule which would tell you how much of a knowledge issue you have:

1. 90+: You know pretty much every question type and variant in the area. You should focus your energies on other aspects rather than knowledge improvement in the area.
2. 80+: Maybe you need to increase your exposure to questions a little bit; around 200–300 more questions in that area would be sufficient.
3. 60–80+: You have a significant knowledge issue in the area. You might need to go back to the basics, but it is less likely to be a theory issue but more of an exposure to questions issue.
4. <60: You need to work on both theory and exposure to questions.

Needless to say, the target and objective for preparations has to be to reach the 90+ range as explained above in any block you intend to do "really well".

Looking beyond Ability (Quick Reflexes)

A common frustrating experience for test-takers while taking the test is to not being able to solve a known question/logic and subsequently, not being able to score marks in questions which they knew.

In order to handle this problem, you would need to work on your reactions and reflexes when faced with QA questions. Once you have solved your knowledge/ability issue in a particular block, your next step is to improve your reactions and reflexes while solving a question. Needless to say you would need to do this block wise.

So obviously the main issue is how to improve reflexes and reactions.

(a) For every block, once you have solved the LODs, the most crucial exercise in this context would be a comprehensive revision and review of each and every question you have solved in that block. Solve every question of every LOD again and review the logic/process of problem solving used. This needs to be done to the point where you almost "recollect" the logic of the question and are able to recognise the same if it is used again in a different context/ problem.

(b) A thorough revision on the theory of the block.

1. Improve your ability to select what you know and leave what you do not

In the context of an examination where the required scores for 99 percentile would be 60–70% attempts with 100% accuracy, it is easy to see that perfect knowledge is perhaps not needed in order to crack CAT. Hence, even if you have around 60–70% knowledge of the questions in an average test, you are perhaps good enough to crack the exam. A good way to test whether you have sufficient knowledge would be to pick up 10–20 test papers and divide your QA section into blocks of 5 questions each. Then test your knowledge by looking at the average number of questions you know. If on an average for every 5 QA test questions that you pick up, if you know more than 3, then the prognosis would be that you have adequate knowledge for cracking CAT. Thus, while you may want to move towards knowing 5 out of 5 in this context, there are other things that you should focus on—developing your ability to decide on whether you are going to be able to solve a question while reading it for the first time. This would help you stop fishing during the test. (Fishing can be described as the activity of trying to solve a question without knowing whether you would actually complete the question.)

Your mind should give you a clear indication of whether you would be able to do the last step in a question, before you start doing it. In that sense you should be able to clearly define four types of outcomes when you finish reading a question for the first time:

(a) I see a clear flowchart and the steps are manageable—Obviously you need to go on and solve these questions.

(b) I see a clear flowchart but the steps are too lengthy—In this case, you need to see where you stand in your test-time and attempt-wise.

(c) I do not see a clear flowchart but I can try as I see a starting point—This is potentially the most dangerous situation for you in the duration of the test, as once you get sucked into a question, there is a strong tendency to lose track of the time you are using up while trying the question. My advice is that while taking the test, you should not even start doing such questions. However, you can only avoid these, if you have a sufficient population of the first two reactions listed above.

(d) I see no flowchart and no starting point to the question—Obviously you should leave such questions and in fact if these are limited to around 10–15% of the paper there is no problem and you need not worry about them. Of course in the longer term, you might want to fill in this knowledge/ability gap.

2. Focus on thorough knowledge of 'problem scenarios' rather than theoretical learning

To illustrate this, I would like to start with a few examples.

Consider the following string of 3 questions. Before I come to my main point here, I would like you to start by solving these questions before looking at the explanations provided:

1. A boy starts adding consecutive natural numbers starting from 1. After some time he reaches a total of 1000 when he realises that he has double counted a number. Find the number double counted.
2. A boy starts adding consecutive natural numbers starting from 1. He reaches a total of 575 when he realises that he has missed a number. What can be said about the number missed?
3. Find the 288th term of the series: ABBCCCDDDDEEEEEFFFFFFG....

We can now start to look at each of these 3 questions:

1. Consider the fact that when you add numbers as stated above (1 + 2 + 3 + 4 +) the result is known as a triangular number. Hence, numbers like 1, 1 + 2 = 3, 1 + 2 + 3 = 6 and so on are triangular numbers. This question asks us to consider the possibility of making the mistake of double counting a number. So instead of 1 + 2 + 3 + 4 if you were to do by error 1 + 2 + 3 + 3 + 4, you would realise that the number you would get would be 13 which would be more than 10 (which should have been your correct addition) and less than 15 (the sum of 1 to 5) which is the next triangular number. The double counted value could be achieved by spotting 10 as the immediately lower value—and the difference between 10 and 13 would give you the required double counted number.
   To carry forward this logic into the given question, we should realise that we are just bothered about finding the last triangular number below 1000, and in trying to work this out is where we really apply our intelligence.
   Before one writes about that though, one fully realises that a lot of readers (especially aspirants with an engineering background) at this point are thinking about $n \times (n + 1)/2$. Knowing that process, one chooses to write about the alternate way to think about in this question.

$$1 + 2 + 3 + 4 \ldots + 10 = 55$$

Hence, we can easily see that 11 + 12 + 13 + 14 + 15 + ... + 20 would equal 155 and the sum of 21 to 30 would equal 255 and so on.

Thus, in trying to find the last triangular number below 1000 we can just do: 55 + 155 + 255 + 355 = 820 (which is the sum of the first 40 natural numbers) and since we have still not reached close to 1000, we start by adding more numbers as: 820 + 41 + 42 + 43 + 44 = 990 and the difference between 990 and 1000 is 10 which is the required answer.

2. For this question, we would just need to carry the learning from the previous question forward and realise that when we miss a number, we actually get a total which is lower than the correct total. Hence, if we want to find the number missed, all we need to do is to find the first triangular number greater than 575. This can be got simply by, 55 + 155 + 255 + 31 + 32 + 33 + 34 = 595, so the number missed has to be 20.

3. In this question all you would need to notice is that in the series ABBCCCDDDDEEEEEF...

A ends after the first term; B ends after the third (1 + 2) term; C ends after the sixth (1 + 2 + 3) term and so on. So we can infer that what we are looking at is how many numbers need to be added before we get to a number just below 288. So 55 + 155 + 21 + 22 + 23 gives us 276 which pretty much means that the 24th alphabet (i.e., x) would be running in this series when we reach the 288th term.

So looking at the three questions above and the solutions, one wants the reader to only answer one specific question: How much does knowing the first question and developing your thought ability and your intelligence help you in solving the second and the third one? I hope you see the connection. For your information, the three questions presented above were asked in three consecutive years in the CAT (2001–2002–2003) -and questions based on this logic have been often asked in the online CAT too. What is more, you will find such strings of questions with repeated logic in all the recent CAT exams too.

So the big message and take away for you is that the majority of learning that you would acquire in your CAT prep journey would be by learning through questions (as against by studying theory). It is here that the question banks contained in this book will be your constant guide and companion in this journey.

CONCLUDING NOTE

You sit in front of your CAT question paper and the first question comes in front of you. If you have identified the logic of the question or seen the question itself earlier, your entire QA preparation is fructified. In fact, every question/logic (that you would face in your test) which you have seen earlier represents a triumph of your preparation process. It is for this very reaction that you prepare for an aptitude exam like CAT. Any other preparation is quite worthless.

Your battle for CAT would be won if you get a "YES I KNOW THIS PATTERN/LOGIC" reaction to 50–60% of the questions in your test.

Contained in this book is detailed theory, short cut thoughts and the finest collection of questions which you would hope to find anywhere. Remember, each question solved needs to be a learning experience—one that is to be kept in your mind for future problem solving. Adopt this approach with the problems contained in this book and I am quite confident that you would KNOW over 70% of your actual CAT test paper since you have already solved something like that before!!

I can be reached through my youtube channels Arun Sharma & The Arun Sharma Academy. You can also follow me on Instagram (handle: arunsharmaiimb) and LinkedIn (https://www.linkedin.com/in/arun-sharma-5450a713/). Do follow me on social media to get regular videos and updates from my side about how to use this book, problem solving short cut methods and strategy and career related advice. I wish you all the best in your journey.

All the Best!

Arun Sharma

Preface to the First Edition

Over the last few years, as a trainer of CAT and other aptitude tests, I have felt the need for a comprehensive book on the subject. Students appearing for the CAT and other aptitude tests usually struggle for appropriate study material to prepare for this vital section of the examination.

This book comes as a humble attempt to fulfil this gap.

Structure of the book

The book is divided into 19 chapters and five test papers. Each chapter is divided into three broad parts:

(a) Theory
(b) Solved examples
(c) Chapter end exercises (LODs I, II & III), with answer key

The questions in the chapter end exercises have been categorised into three levels of difficulty, viz, Level of Difficulty I, Level of Difficulty II and Level of Difficulty III.

Level of Difficulty I (LOD I): These are the basic types of questions pertaining to the chapter. A majority of the MBA entrance tests would test the student with LOD I questions. Tests which ask LOD I questions include MAT, IMT, IRMA, IIFT, NIFT, CET Maharashtra, Bank PO examinations, BBA, BCA, Law, and so on. Besides, there are about 10 questions of LOD I type in the CAT nowadays.

Level of Difficulty II (LOD II): These are questions, which are more advanced than the LOD I questions. These questions test all basic as well as applied concepts in the chapter. *LOD II questions are closest to the difficulty levels of the CAT.* Hence, the objective of LOD II questions should be to:

(a) Clearly understand the concept which underlies the question.
(b) Create a judgment of time required for different mental processes.
(c) Identify the time guzzlers.
(d) Reinforce application of a method in mental processes through the question.
(e) Learn to flowchart complex questions.

Level of Difficulty III (LOD III): LOD III questions build on the previous questions and are a step beyond the LOD II questions. Although they are also normally more difficult than the average CAT question, approximately 5–10 LOD III questions could be asked in the CAT every year. Hence, the learning objectives at LOD III are to:

(a) Learn applications of the basic concepts at the highest level.
(b) Sharpen the flowcharting skills learnt at LOD II.
(c) Use each question as a learning opportunity.

One should not be disheartened if he/she is unable to solve LOD III questions. These questions are extremely tough and uncommon in the CAT and other aptitude tests. Questions in actual tests will appear very simple and elementary if one can solve LOD III questions.

Approach Taken in Writing This Book

In my experience, the 'math skill' of students appearing for CAT can be classified into three levels:

Level 1: Students who are weak at Mathematics
Level 2: Students who are average at Mathematics
Level 3: Students who are strong at Mathematics

This book has been written keeping in mind all the three kinds of students.

From my experience I have given below my perspective of what one should aim for (based on the category that he/she belongs to). It is important to clearly understand the starting level and accordingly define strategy for the QA section.

Level 1: Students who are weak at mathematics: Typically, these are students who were weak at mathematics in school and/or have left mathematics after their 10th or 12th class. They face a mental block in mathematics and have problems in writing equations. They also have severe problems in understanding mathematical language and are unable to convert the mathematical language into mathematical equations. They make mistakes even in interpretation of the most basic statements in mathematics (leave alone the complex statements). Besides, these students also have problems in solving equations. They suffer from the insecurity of knowing that they are unable to solve most problems which they face.

Level 2: Students who are average at mathematics: These students lie between the Level 1 and Level 3 students.

Level 3: Students who are strong at mathematics: These are the students who have got strong, structured and logical thinking ability. They not only understand the basic repetitive statements in mathematics but also complex statements. They are able to create their own flowcharts to arrive at solutions of these complex mathematical situations.

There are two alternative approaches that a student can take in solving this book.

Approach 1: "Start with basic concepts, solved examples then move on to LOD I, then LOD II in the chapter. Do not go into LOD III in the chapter in the first go. Complete all 19 chapters and then re-start with Chapter 1 — review the basic concepts, resolve LOD I and LOD II, then move on to LOD III. This approach is advocated for students who are weak to average in mathematics (i.e., students of Level 1 and Level 2).

After completing the theory and practice exercises of the book for a second time, go to the practice sets 1–5 provided at the end of book. Set a time limit of 40 minutes for each set and take the tests. The questions contained in the sets are questions which have appeared in the CAT over the last 5 years (based on memory)."

Approach 2: "Start with the basic concepts, solved examples and then go through the exercises of LOD I, LOD II and LOD III. This is recommended for students who have strong concepts in mathematics (Level 3 students)."

Then go to the 5 practice tests given at the end of the book and take them one by one (time limit of 40 minutes for each test)."

An Important Point

Each of the questions contained in the LOD I, LOD II and LOD III exercises in the chapters have immense learning value. Hence, the approach that one takes while solving the questions should be one of learning. The reader should try to clearly understand the interpretation of each sentence used in the construction of the questions.

In other words the learning in every chapter should not be restricted to the solved examples or the theory contained in the chapter, but should continue through each of the questions contained in the exercises.

In conclusion, this is a book which is unique in approach and coverage. Any CAT aspirant who goes through the questions contained in this book in the manner advised in this book would get a distinct advantage when he/she faces the CAT.

Arun Sharma

Acknowledgements

The text and questions contained in this book is the manifestation of a learning process that began for me over 28 years ago. During the intervening period I have come across some wonderful people in the form of relatives, friends or acquaintances from whom I have learnt immensely. While it is not possible to name them individually, I would like to express a deep sense of gratitude towards them.

I would also like to express my heartfelt thanks to my wonderful students due to whom I have had a wonderful opportunity to live a highly fulfilled life. This book would not have been possible in the absence of this opportunity. This work would not have been possible but for the support and encouragement from McGraw-Hill, India. My sincere thanks and words of appreciation to them. I would like to make specific mention of Tanmoy Roychowdhury, Tanweer Ahmad, Nikhil Wadhera, Pankaj Dwivedi, Aarooshi Garg-Khattar, Atul Gupta and Anjali Nair from McGraw Hill.

I would also like to thank my colleagues who have supported me through thick and thin during the last few years. These include my colleagues at Mindworkzz - Arun Chaturvedi, Renu Rai, Koushik Rai, Sanjeeta Girotra, Ritika Sharma, Sumika Bhatt, Sapna Singh, Sundus Fatima, Kavita Jindal, Vaishali Sharma, Deepak Sharma, Jyoti Bisht, Sanjay, Jeetu Singh Tapesh and Ishtiaque Rahi. Besides, a special mention of thanks to Pallav Jalan who has worked as hard as me (if not harder) on this book. This book would not have been possible but for his technical inputs and unyielding efforts.

My mind also gets reminded of the multitude of people who have worked on the previous editions of this book – and I would like to mention a special word of thanks and appreciation to each of them.

To my Parents M.K.Sharma & Renu Sharma and my brother Ravi Sharma who have brought me up to be the person I am – instilling in me the courage of my convictions, the gift of curiosity, the ability to learn and transform myself and embedded the importance of humility and love in my mind.

No amount of thanks can ever repay the great debt that I owe my wife Meenakshi who has provided me with the constant inspiration over the past few years. In fact, this book would not have been possible but for the direct and indirect support, inspiration and guidance from Meenakshi who has been a constant partner in all my efforts over the past years. Last but not the least, a special mention of my son Shaurya, who has now become an integral contributor to my books and their revisions. His hard work and detailed inputs have contributed immensely to the contents of this edition of the book.

Arun Sharma

Contents

BLOCK STARTER

Scan this QR code to access a video on this block's chapters, the time needed to cover them and their weightage in the examination.

BLOCK I

NUMBERS

Block I is one of the most important areas in quantitative aptitude for a CAT aspirant. Besides, it is also important for other MBA entrance exams like XAT, IIFT, NMAT, SNAP and a host of other aptitude exams. Over the last few years, this section has had various patterns - 34 questions in 1 hour; 26 questions in 40 minutes and 22 questions in 40 minutes. In each of these patterns of the exam, the block has always contributed to around 15–30 percent of the questions. The importance of this group of chapters is also increased due to the fact that the concepts learnt in these chapters (especially in Number Systems) would be utilised across various chapters of other blocks that you would need to learn.

Thus, my advice to you is: Go through this block indepth and try to gain clarity of concepts as well as exposure to questions for honing your ability to do well in this area.

BACK TO SCHOOL...

- **Chapters in this Block: Number Systems and Progressions**
- **Block Importance-20–25%**

The importance of this block can be gauged from the table below:

Year	*% of Marks from Block I*	*Qualifying Score (approx. score for 96 percentile)*
2000	48%	35%
2001	36%	35%
2002	36%	35%
2003 (cancelled)	30%	32%
2003 (retest)	34%	35%
2004	32%	35%
2005	40%	35%
2006	32%	40%
2007	24%	32%
2008	40%	35%
Online CAT 2009–2021	15–30%	60% with no errors
CAT 2022	15–20%	40%
CAT 2023	15–20%	30%

As you can see from the table above, doing well in this block alone could give you a definite edge and take you a long way to qualifying the QA section. Although the online CAT has significantly reduced the relative importance to this block, the importance of this block remains high, since you would still expect between 15 to 30% questions in a normal CAT paper.

Hence, understanding the concepts involved in these chapters properly and strengthening your problem-solving experience could go a long way towards a good score.

THE NUMBER LINE

Core Concepts

I. The concept of the number line is one of the most crucial concepts in basic numeracy.

The number line is a line that starts from zero and goes towards positive infinity when it moves to the right and towards negative infinity when it moves to the left.

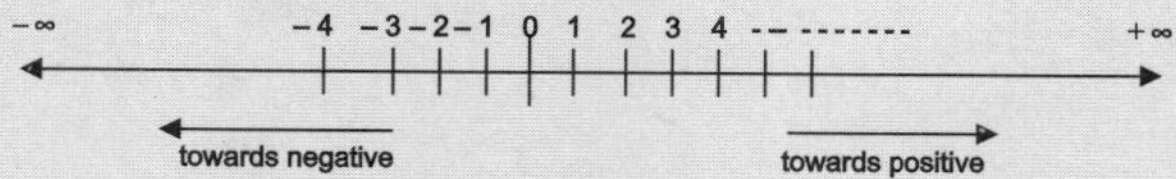

Important concept: Distance between two points on the number line = difference between the numbers. Thus, for example if we look at the distance between the points + 3 and – 2, it will be given by their difference. $3 - (-2) = 3 + 2 = 5$.

II. Types of numbers—

We will be looking at the types of numbers in detail again when we go into the chapter of Number Systems. Let us first work out in our minds, the various types of numbers. While doing so, do not fail to notice that most of these number types occur in pairs (i.e. the definition of one of them, defines the other automatically).

(Note: Here the number line is one of the most critical concepts in understanding and grasping quantitative aptitude and indeed mathematics.)

Multiples on the Number Line

All tables and multiples of every number can be visualised on the number line. Thus, multiples of 7 on the number line would be seen as follows:

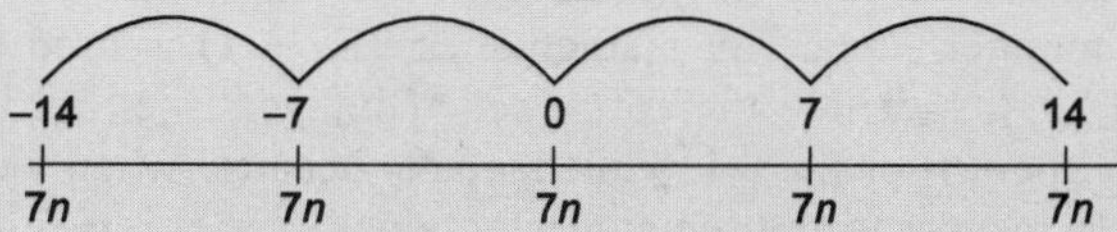

In order to visualise this you can imagine a frog jumping consistently 7 units every time. If it lands on –14, the next landing would be on –7, then on 0, then 7 and finally at 14. This is how you can visualise the table of 7 (in mathematical terms we can also refer to this as $7n$ – meaning the set of numbers which are multiples of 7 or in other words the set of numbers which are divisible by 7).

You can similarly visualise $5n$, $4n$, $8n$ and so on—practically all tables on the number line as above.

What do We Understand by $7n + 1$ and Other such Notations and the Equivalence of $7n + 1$ and $7n - 6$

Look at the following figure closely:

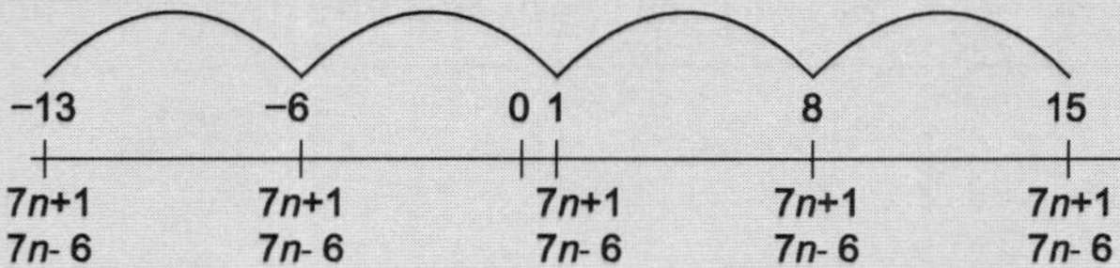

Concept Explainer

Scan this QR code to access a conceptual video on $7n + 1$ and other such notations

Our $7n$ frog is made to first land on –13 and then asked to keep doing its stuff (jumping 7 to the right everytime). What is the result? It lands on –6, + 1, 8, 15 and its next landing would be on 22, 29 and so forth. These numbers cannot be described as $7n$, but rather they all have a single property which is constant for all numbers.

They can be described as: "One more than a multiple of 7" and in mathematical terms such numbers are also called as $7n + 1$. Alternately these numbers also have the property that they are "6 less than multiples of 7" and in mathematical terms such numbers can also be called as $7n - 6$.

That is why in mathematics, we say that the set of numbers represented by $7n + 1$ is the same as the set of numbers represented by $7n - 6$.

The Implication in Terms of Remainders

This concept can also be talked about in the context of remainders.

When a number which can be described as $7n + 1$ or $7n - 6$ (like the numbers 8, 15, –6, –13, –20, –27, –34, –41…) is divided by 7, the remainder in every case is seen to be 1. For some people, reconciling the fact that the remainder when –27 is divided by 7 the remainder is 1, seems difficult on the surface. (**Note:** This needs to be done because remainders are always non-negative.

However, the following thinking would give you the remainder in every case:

27/7, remainder is 6.

–27/7, remainder is –6. In the context of dividing by 7, a remainder of –6 means a remainder of 7 – 6 = 1.

Let us look at another example:

What is the remainder when –29 is divided by 8.

First reaction 29/8 → remainder 5, –29/8 → remainder –5, hence actual remainder is 8 – 5 = 3.

The student is advised to practice more such situations and get comfortable in converting positive remainders to negative remainders and vice versa.

Even and Odd Numbers

The Meaning of 2n and 2n + 1: $2n$ means a number which is a multiple of the number 2. Since, this can be visualised as a frog starting from the origin and jumping 2 units to the right in every jump, you can also say that this frog represents $2n$.

(**Note**: Multiples of 2 are even numbers. Hence, $2n$ is also used to denote even numbers.)

So, what does $2n + 1$ mean?

Well, simply put, if you place the above frog on the point represented by the number 1 on the number line, then the frog will reach points such as 3, 5, 7, 9, 11...and so on. This essentially means that the points the frog now reaches are displaced by 1 unit to the right of the $2n$ frog. In mathematical terms, this is represented as $2n + 1$.

In other words, $2n + 1$ also represents numbers which leave a remainder of 1, when divided by 2. (**Note**: This is also the definition of an odd number. Hence, in mathematics, $(2n + 1)$ is used to denote an odd number. Also note that taken together $2n$ and $2n + 1$ denote the entire set of integers, i.e., all integers from $-\infty$ to $+\infty$ on the number line can be denoted by either $2n$ or $2n + 1$. This happens because when we divide any integer by 2, there are only two results possible with respect to the remainder obtained, viz: a remainder of zero $(2n)$ or a remainder of one $(2n + 1)$.

This concept can be expanded to represent integers with respect to any number. Thus, in terms of 3, we can only have three types of integers $3n$, $3n + 1$ or $3n + 2$ (depending on whether the integer leaves a remainder 0, 1 or 2 respectively when divided by 3.) Similarly, with respect to 4, we have 4 possibilities –$4n$, $4n + 1$, $4n + 2$ or $4n + 3$.

Needless to say, from these representations above, the representations $2n$ and $2n + 1$ (which can also be represented as $2n - 1$) have great significance in Mathematics as they represent even and odd numbers respectively. Similarly, we use the concept of $4n$ to check whether a year is a leap year or not.

These representations can be seen on the number line as follows:

Representation of $2n$ and $2n + 1$:

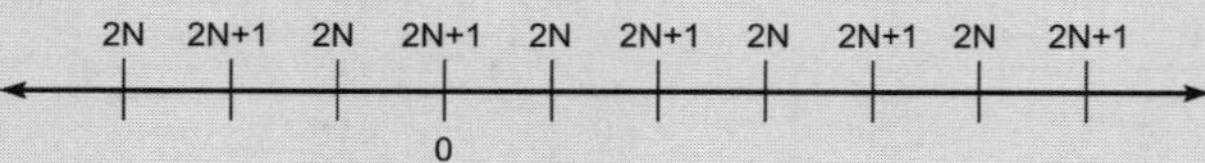

Representation of $3n$, $3n + 1$ and $3n + 2$:

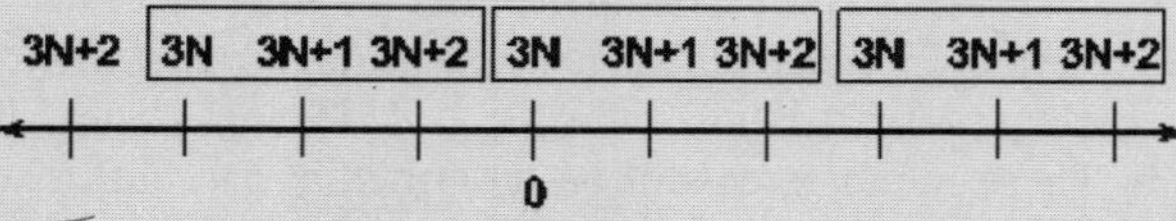

Representation of $4n$, $4n + 1$, $4n + 2$ and $4n + 3$:

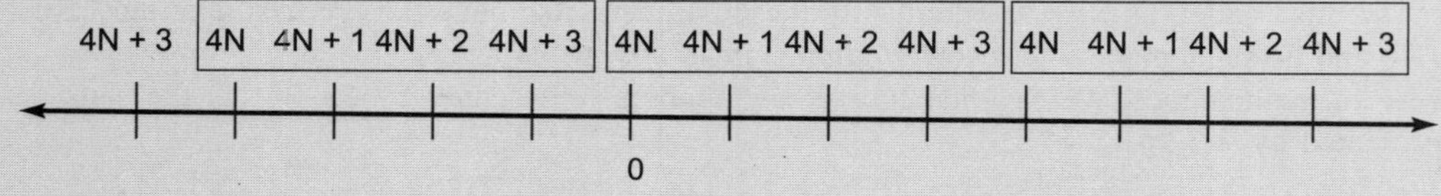

One Particular Number can be a Multiple of more than 1 Number—The Concept of Common Multiples

Of course, one of the things you should notice as you go through the above discussion is that individual numbers can indeed be multiples of more than 1 number—and actually often are.

Thus, for instance the number 14 is a multiple of both 7 and 2—hence 14 can be called as a common multiple of 2 and 7. Obviously, I think you can visualise more such numbers which can be classified as common multiples of 2 and 7?? 28, 42, 56 and in fact the list is infinite—i.e. the numbers never end. Thus, the common multiples of 2 and 7 can be represented by the infinite set:

{14, 28, 42, 56, 70...1400...14000...140000...and so on}

LCM and Its Significance

From the above list, the number 14 (which is the lowest number in the set of common multiples of 2 and 7) has a lot of significance in mathematics. It represents what is commonly known as the **Least Common Multiple (LCM)** of 2 and 7. It is the first number which is a multiple of both 2 and 7 and there are a variety of questions in quantitative aptitude which you would come across—not only when you solve questions based on number systems (where the LCM has its dedicated set of questions), but applications of the LCM are seen even in chapters like Time, Speed, Distance, Time and Work, etc.

So what did school teach us about the process of finding LCM?

Before you start to review/relearn that process, you first need to know about prime factors of a number.

I hope at this point you recognise the difference between finding factors of a number and prime factors of a number. Simply put, finding factors of a number means finding the divisors of the number. Thus, for instance the factors of the number 80 would be the numbers 1, 2, 4, 5, 8, 10, 16, 20, 40 and 80. On the other hand, finding the prime factors of the same number would mean writing the number 80 as $2^4 \times 5^1$. This form of writing the number is also called the **STANDARD FORM** or the **CANONICAL FORM** of the number.
The school process of writing down the standard form of a number:
Now this is something I would think most of you would remember and recognise:
Finding the prime factors of the number 80.

Concept Explainer
Scan this QR code to access a conceptual video on Standard Form

2	80
2	40
2	20
2	10
5	5
	1

The prime factors of the number 80 are: $2 \times 2 \times 2 \times 2 \times 5 = 2^4 \times 5^1$.

EXERCISE FOR SELF-PRACTICE

Write down the standard form of the following numbers.

(a) 20 (b) 44 (c) 142 (d) 200
(e) 24 (f) 324 (g) 120 (h) 84
(i) 371 (j) 143 (k) 339 (l) 147
(m) 1715

Finding the LCM of two or more numbers: The school process

Step 1: Write down the prime factor form of all the numbers.
Let us say that you have 3 numbers whose standard forms are:

$$2^4 \times 3^2 \times 5^3 \times 7^1$$

$$2^3 \times 3^1 \times 5^2 \times 11^2$$

$$2^4 \times 3^2 \times 5^1 \times 13^1$$

To write down the LCM of these numbers, write down all the prime numbers and multiply them with their highest available powers. The resultant number would be the LCM of these numbers.

Thus, in the above case the LCM would be:

$$2^4 \times 3^2 \times 5^3 \times 7^1 \times 11^2 \times 13^1$$

(**Note:** Short cuts to a lot of these processes have been explained in the main chapters of the book.)

Divisors (Factors) of a Number

As we already mentioned, finding the factors or divisors of a number are one and the same thing. In order to find factors of a number, the key is to spot the factors below the square root of the number. Once you have found them, the factors above the square root would be automatically seen. Consider this for factors of the number 80.

Factors below the square root *of 80 (8.xxx) Hence, factors up to and including 8*	
1	
2	
4	
5	
8	

Once you can visualise the list on the left, the factors on the right would be seen automatically.

Factors below the square root *of 80 (8.xxx)* *Hence, factors up to and including 8*	Factors above the square root
1	80
2	40
4	20
5	16
8	10
	(**Note:** These will be seen automatically the moment you have the list on the left.

Common Divisors Between Two Numbers

List of Common Divisors

When we write down the factors of two numbers, we can look for the common elements within the two lists.

For instance, the factors of 80 are (1, 2, 4, 5, 8, 10, 16, 20, 40 and 80) while the factors of 144 are (1, 2, 3, 4, 6, 8, 9, 12, 16, 18, 24, 36, 48, 72 and 144).

If you observe the two lists closely, you will get the following list of common factors or common divisors between the two:

List of common factors of 80 and 144: (1, 2, 4, 8, 16)

The number 16 being the highest in this list of common factors (or divisors) is also called the Highest Common Factor or the Greatest Common Divisor. In short, it is denoted as HCF or GCD. It has a lot of significance in terms of quantitative thinking—as the HCF is used in a multitude of problems and hence being able to spot the HCF of two or more numbers is one of the critical operations in Mathematics. You would be continuously seeing applications of the HCF in problems in the chapter of Number systems and right through the chapters of Arithmetic (defined as wordbased chapters in this book).

Rounding off and its use for approximation

One of the important things that we learnt in school was the use of approximation in order to calculate.

Thus, 72×53 can be approximated to 70×50 and hence seen as 3500.

Similarly, the addition of $48 + 53 + 61 + 89$ can be taken as $50 + 50 + 60 + 90 = 250$.

Number Types You Should Know

Integers and Decimals: All numbers that do not have a decimal in them are called integers. Thus, –3, –17, +4, +13, +1473, 0, etc., are all integers.

Obviously, decimal numbers are numbers which have a decimal value attached to them. Thus, 1.3, 14.76, –12.24, etc., are all decimal numbers, since they have certain values after the decimal point.

Before we move ahead, let us pause a brief while, to further understand decimals. As you shall see, the concept of decimals is closely related to the concept of division and divisibility. Suppose, I have four pieces of bread which I want to divide equally between two people. It is easy for me to do this, since I can give two whole pieces to each of them.

However, if we alter the situation in such a way, that I now have five pieces of bread to distribute equally amongst two people. What do I do?

I give two whole pieces each, to each of them. The fifth piece has to be divided equally between the two. I can no longer do this, without in some way breaking the fifth piece into two parts. This is the elementary situation that gives rise to the need for decimals in Mathematics.

Going back to the situation above, my only option is to divide the fifth piece into two equal parts (which in quants are called as halves).

This concept has huge implications for problem solving especially once you recognise that a half (i.e. a '.5' in the decimal) only comes when you divide a whole into two parts.

Thus, in fact, all standard decimals emerge out of certain fixed divisors.

Hence, for example, the divisor 2, gives rise to the decimal .5.

Similarly the divisor 3 gives rise to the decimals .33333 and .66666, etc.

Prime numbers and Composite numbers: Amongst natural numbers, there are three broad divisions–

1. Unity: It is representative of the number 1.
2. Prime numbers: These are numbers which have no divisors/factors apart from 1 and itself.
3. Composite numbers: On the other hand, these are numbers, which have at least one more divisor apart from 1 and itself.

(Note: A brief word about factors/division—A number X is said to divide Y (or is said to be a divisor or factor of Y) when the division of Y/X leaves no remainder.)

All composite numbers have the property that they can be written as a product of their prime factors.

Thus, for instance, the number 40 can be represented as: $40 = 2 \times 2 \times 2 \times 5$ or $40 = 2^3 \times 5^1$

This form of writing is called as the **standard form** of the composite number.

Difference between Rational and Irrational Numbers: This difference is one of the critical but unfortunately one of the less well understood differences in elementary Mathematics.

Definition of Rational Numbers: Numbers which can be expressed in the form p/q where $q \neq 0$ are called rational numbers.

Obviously, numbers which cannot be represented in the form p/q are called as irrational numbers. To put it in short, the test of whether a number is rational or not, is simply about whether it can be represented as a fraction or not. Numbers that can be represented as a fraction would be called rational, while those that cannot be represented as a fraction would be called irrational.

However, one of the less well understood issues in this regard is what does this mean?

The difference becomes clear when the values of decimals are examined in details:

Consider the following numbers.

(1) 4.2,
(2) 4.333....,
(3) 4.1472576345.......

What is the difference between the decimal values of the three numbers above?

To put it simply, the first number has what can be described as a finite decimal value. Such numbers can be expressed in the form p/q easily. Since 4.2 can be first written as 42/10 and then converted to 21/5.

Similarly, numbers like 4.5732 can be represented as 45732/10000. Thus, numbers having a finite terminating decimal value are rational.

Now, let us consider the decimal value: 4.3333........

Such decimal values will continue endlessly, i.e. they have no end. Hence, they are called **infinite decimals** (or non-terminating decimals).

But, we can easily see that the number 4.333.... can be represented as 13/3. Hence, this number is also rational. In fact, all numbers which have infinite decimal values, but have any recurring form within them can be represented in the p/q form.

For example, the value of the number: 1.14814814814.... is 93/81.

(What I mean to say is that whenever you have any recurring decimal number, even if the value of 'q' might not be obvious, but it will always exist.)

Thus, we can conclude that all numbers whose decimal values are infinite (non-terminating) but which have a recurring pattern within them are rational numbers.

This leaves us with the third kind of decimal values, viz. **infinite non-recurring decimal values**. These decimals neither have a recurring pattern, nor do they have an end—they go on endlessly. For such numbers, it is not possible to find the value of a denominator 'q' which can be used in order to represent them as p/q. Hence, such numbers are called as irrational numbers.

In day-to-day mathematics, we come across numbers like $\sqrt{3}$, $\sqrt{5}$, $\sqrt[3]{7}$, π, e, etc., which are irrational numbers since they do not have a p/q representation (i.e. they cannot be written as a fraction).

(**Note:** $\sqrt{3}$ can also be represented as $3^{1/2}$, just as $\sqrt[3]{7}$ can be represented as $7^{1/3}$.)

An Important Tip

Rational and Irrational numbers do not mix.: This means that in case you get a situation where an irrational number has appeared while solving a question, it will remain till the end of the solution. It can only be removed from the solution if it is multiplied or divided by the same irrational number.

Consider an example: The area of an equilateral triangle is given by the formula $(\sqrt{3}/4) \times a^2$ (where a is the side of the equilateral triangle). Since, $\sqrt{3}$ is an irrational number, it remains in the answer till the end. Hence, the area of an equilateral triangle will always have a $\sqrt{3}$ as part of the answer.

Before we move ahead, we need to understand one final thing about recurring decimals.

As I have already mentioned, recurring decimals have the property of being able to be represented in the p/q form. The question that arises is—Is there any process to convert a recurring decimal into a proper fraction?

Yes, there is. In fact, in order to understand how this operates, you first need to understand that there are two kinds of recurring decimals. The process for converting an infinite recurring decimal into a fraction basically varies for both of these types. Let's look at these one by one.

Type 1—Pure recurring decimals: These are recurring decimals where the recurrence starts immediately after the decimal point.

For example: $0.5555\ldots = 0.\overline{5}$

$3.242424\ldots = 3.\overline{24}$

$5.362362\ldots = 5.\overline{362}$

The process of converting these decimals to fractions can be illustrated as:

$0.5555 = 5/9$

$3.242424 = 3 + (24/99)$

$5.362362 = 5 + (362/999)$

A little bit of introspection will tell you that what we have done is nothing but to put down the recurring part of the decimal as it is and dividing it by a group of 9's. Also the number of 9's in this group equals the number of digits in the recurring part of the decimal.

Thus, in the second case, the fraction is derived by dividing 24 by 99 (24 being the recurring part of the decimal and 99 having 2 nines because the number of digits in 24 is 2).

Similarly, $0.43576254357625\ldots = \dfrac{4357625}{9999999}$

Type 2—Impure recurring decimals: Unlike pure recurring decimals, in these decimals, the recurrence occurs after a certain number of digits in the decimal. The process to convert these into a fraction is also best illustrated by an example:

Consider the decimal 0.435424242

$= 0.435\overline{42}$

The fractional value of the same will be given by: (43542 – 435)/99000. This can be understood in two steps.

Step 1: Subtract the non-recurring initial part of the decimal (in this case, it is 435) from the number formed by writing down the starting digits of the decimal value up to the digit where the recurring decimals are written for the first time;

Expanding the meaning—

(**Note**: For 0.435424242, subtract 435 from 43542)

Step 2: The number, thus, obtained, has to be divided by a number formed as follows; Write down as many 9's as the number of digits in the recurring part of the decimal. (in this case, since the recurring part '42' has 2 Digits, we write down two 9's.) These nines have to be followed by as many zeroes as the number of digits in the non-recurring part of the decimal value. (In this case, the non-recurring part of the decimal value is '435'. Since, 435 has 3 digits, attach three zeroes to the two nines to get the number to divide the result of the first step.)

Hence divide 43542 – 435 by 99000 to get the fraction.

Similarly, for 3.436213213 we get $\dfrac{436213 - 436}{999000}$

Mixed Fractions

A *mixed number* is a whole number plus a fraction. Here are a few mixed numbers:

$$1\frac{1}{2},\quad 1\frac{1}{4},\quad 2\frac{1}{3},\quad 2\frac{2}{7},\quad 5\frac{4}{5}$$

In order to convert a mixed fraction to a proper fraction, you do the following conversion process.

$$1\frac{1}{2} = (1 \times 2 + 1)/2 = 3/2$$

$$2\frac{1}{3} = (2 \times 3 + 1)/3 = 7/3$$

Similiarly, $1\frac{1}{4} = 5/4$

$$2\frac{2}{7} = 16/7$$

$5\frac{4}{5} = 29/5$ and so on.

i.e. multiply the whole number part of the mixed number by the denominator of the fractional part and add the resultant to the numerator of the fractional part to get the numerator of the proper fraction. The denominator of the proper fraction would be the same as the denominator of the mixed fraction.

OPERATIONS ON NUMBERS

Exponents and Powers

Exponents or powers are an important part of Maths as they are necessary to indicate that a number is multiplied by itself for a given number of times.

When a number is multiplied by itself, it gives the 'square of the number'.

Thus, $n \times n = n^2$ (for example $3 \times 3 = 3^2$)

If the same number is multiplied by itself twice, we get the cube of the number.

Thus, $n \times n \times n = n^3$ (for example $3 \times 3 \times 3 = 3^3$)

$n \times n \times n \times n = n^4$ and so on.

With respect to powers of numbers, there are five basic rules which you should know. These are referred to commonly in Mathematics as the **Rules of Indices**.

For any number 'n' the following rules would apply:

Rule 1: $n^a \times n^b = n^{(a+b)}$. Thus, $4^3 \times 4^5 = 4^8$.

Rule 2: $n^a / n^b = n^{a-b}$. Thus, $3^9/3^4 = 3^5$.

Rule 3: $(n^a)^b = n^{ab}$. Thus, $(3^2)^4 = 3^8$.

Rule 4: $n^{(-a)} = 1/n^a$. Thus, $3^{-4} = 1/3^4$.

Rule 5: $n^0 = 1$. Thus, $5^0 = 1$.

These are also popularly known as the rules of indices.

General Form of Writing 2–3 Digit Numbers: The Place Value system

In Mathematics, many a times we have to use algebraic equations in order to solve questions. In such cases, an important concept is the way we represent two or three digit numbers in equation form.

For instance, suppose we have a 2 digit number with the digits 'AB'.

In order to write this in the form of an equation, we have to use:

$10A + B$. This is because in the number 'AB', the digit A is occupying the tens place. Hence, in order to represent the value of the number 'AB' in the form of an equation — we can write $10A + B$.

Thus, the number $29 = 2 \times 10 + 9 \times 1$

Similarly, for a three digit number with the digits A, B and C respectively — the number 'ABC' can be represented as below:

$$ABC = 100\,A + 10\,B + C$$

Thus, $243 = 2 \times 100 + 4 \times 10 + 3 \times 1$

BODMAS Rule: It is used for the ordering of mathematical operations in a mathematical situation:

In any mathematical situation, the first thing to be considered is Brackets followed by Division, Multiplication, Addition and Subtraction in that order.

Thus, $3 \times 5 - 2 = 15 - 2 = 13$

Also, $3 \times 5 - 6 \div 3 = 15 - 2 = 13$

Also, $3 \times (5 - 6) \div 3 = 3 \times (-1) \div 3 = -1$.

Operations on Odd and Even numbers

Odds

Odd × Odd	= Odd
Odd + Odd	= Even
Odd – Odd	= Even
Odd ÷ Odd	= Odd

Evens

Even × Even	= Even
Even + Even	= Even
Even – Even	= Even
Even ÷ Even	= Even or Odd

Odds & Evens

Odd × Even	= Even
Odd + Even	= Odd
Odd – Even	= Odd
Even ÷ Odd	= Even

Odd ÷ Even → Not divisible

SERIES OF NUMBERS

In many instances in Mathematics, we are presented with a series of numbers formed simply when a group of numbers is written together. The following are examples of series:

1. 3, 5, 8, 12, 17…
2. 3, 7, 11, 15, 19…(Such series where the next term is derived by adding a certain fixed value to the previous number are called as Arithmetic Progressions).
3. 5, 10, 20, 40 …..(Such series where the next term is derived by multiplying the previous term by a fixed value are called as Geometric Progressions).
   (**Note**: You will study AP and GP in details in the chapter of Progressions which is Chapter 2 of this block.)
4. 2, 7, 22, 67 ….
5. 1/3, 1/5, 1/7, 1/9, 1/11…
6. $1/1^2$, $1/2^2$, $1/3^2$, $¼^2$, $1/5^2$…
7. $1/1^3$, $1/3^3$, $1/5^3$…

Remember the following points at this stage:

1. AP and GP are two specific instances of series. They are studied in details only because they have many applications and have defined rules.
2. Based on the behaviour of their sums, series can be classified as:

Divergent: These are series whose sum to '*n*' terms keeps increasing and reaches infinity for infinite terms.

Convergent: Convergent series have the property that their sum tends to approach an upper limit/lower limit as you include more terms in the series. They have the additional property that even when infinite terms of the series are included they will only reach that value and not cross it.

For example consider the series;

$1/1^2 + 1/3^2 + 1/5^2 + 1/7^2$ …

It is evident that subsequent terms of this series keep getting smaller. Hence, their value becomes negligible after a few terms of the series are taken into account.

If taken to infinite terms, the sum of this series will reach a value which it will never cross. Such series are called convergent, because their sum converges to a limit and only reaches that limit for infinite terms.

(**Note:** Questions on finding infinite sums of convergent series are very commonly asked in most aptitude exams and you can find a detailed discussion of the same in the Chapter 2 (on Progressions) in this block. These question types are a favorite of the CAT as well as the XAT exam.)

NOTE TO THE READER: NOW THAT YOU ARE THROUGH WITH THE *BACK TO SCHOOL* SECTION, YOU ARE READY TO PROCEED INTO THE CHAPTERS OF THIS BLOCK. HAPPY LEARNING!!

CHAPTER 1

Number Systems

Chapter Launchpad

Scan this QR code to access a video on 'Introduction to Number Systems' and this chapter's importance for CAT

INTRODUCTION

The chapter on Number Systems is amongst the most important chapters in the entire syllabus of Quantitative Aptitude for the CAT examination (and also for other parallel MBA entrance exams). Students are advised to go through this chapter with utmost care; understanding each concept and question type on this topic. The CAT has consistently contained anything between 20–40 percent of the marks based on questions taken from this chapter. Naturally, this chapter becomes one of the most crucial as far as your quest to reach close to the qualification score in the section of Quantitative Aptitude is concerned.

Hence, going through this chapter and its concepts properly is imperative for you. It would be a good idea to first go through the basic definitions of all types of numbers. Also, closely follow the solved examples based on various concepts discussed in the chapter. Also, the approach and attitude while solving questions on this chapter is to try to maximise your learning experience out of every question. Hence, do not just try to solve the questions but also try to think of alternative processes in order to solve the same question. Refer to hints or solutions only as a last resort.

To start off, the following pictorial representation of the types of numbers will help you improve your quality of comprehension of different types of numbers.

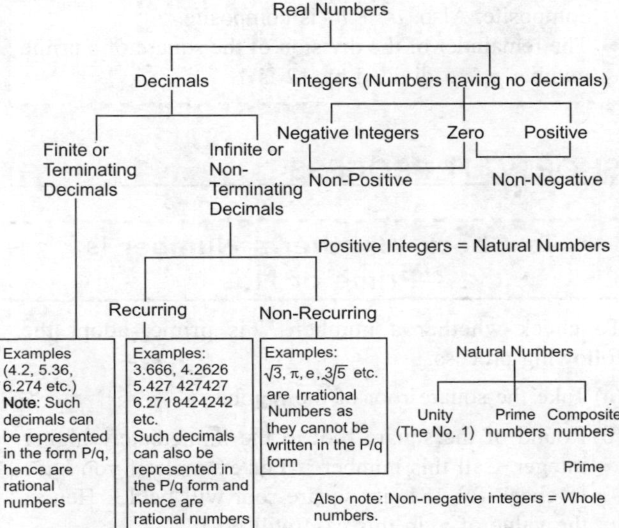

DEFINITION

Natural Numbers These are the numbers (1, 2, 3, etc.) that are used for counting. In other words, all positive integers are natural numbers.

There are infinite natural numbers and the number 1 is the least natural number.

Examples of natural numbers: 1, 2, 4, 8, 32, 23, 4321 and so on.

The following numbers are examples of numbers that are not natural: –2, –31, 2.38, 0 and so on.

Based on divisibility, there could be two types of natural numbers: *Prime* and *Composite*.

Prime Numbers A natural number larger than unity is a prime number if it does not have other divisors except for itself and unity.

Note: Unity (i.e., 1) is not a prime number.

Some Properties of Prime Numbers

- The lowest prime number is 2.
- Number 2 is also the only even prime number.
- The lowest odd prime number is 3.
- The remainder when a prime number $p \geq 5$ is divided by 6 is 1 or 5. However, if a number on being divided by 6 gives a remainder of 1 or 5, the number need not be prime. Thus, this can be referred to as a necessary but not sufficient condition. In mathematical and algebraic writing, this logic is represented as: Prime numbers after 3, would always be of the form $6n + 1$ or $6n + 5$. It can also be referred to as: Prime numbers after 3 would always be of the form: $6n \pm 1$.

- The remainder of the division of the square of a prime number $p \geq 5$ divided by 24 is 1.
- For prime numbers $p > 3$, $p^2 - 1$ is divisible by 24.
- Prime numbers between 1 to 100 are: 2, 3, 5, 7, 11, 13, 17, 19, 23, 29, 31, 37, 41, 43, 47, 53, 59, 61, 67, 71, 73, 79, 83, 89, 97.
- Prime numbers between 100 to 200 are: 101, 103, 107, 109, 113, 127, 131, 137, 139, 149, 151, 157, 163, 167, 173, 179, 181, 191, 193, 197, 199.
- If a and b are any two odd primes then $a^2 - b^2$ is composite. Also, $a^2 + b^2$ is composite.
- The remainder of the division of the square of a prime number $p \geq 5$ divided by 12 is 1.

SHORT-CUT PROCESS

To Check Whether a Number is Prime or Not

To check whether a number N is prime, adopt the following process.

(a) Take the square root of the number.

(b) Round of the square root to the immediately higher integer. Call this number z. For example if you have to check for 181, its square root will be 13. Hence, the value of z, in this case will be 14.

(c) Check for divisibility of the number N by all prime numbers below z. If there is no prime number below the value of z which divides N then the number N will be prime.

To illustrate :-

The value of $\sqrt{239}$ lies between 15 to 16. Hence, take the value of z as 16.

Prime numbers less than or equal to 16 are 2, 3, 5, 7, 11 and 13, 239 is not divisible by any of these. Hence you can conclude that 239 is a prime number.

A Brief Look into Why this Works?

Suppose you are asked to find the factors of the number 40.

An untrained mind will find the factors as : 1, 2, 4, 5, 8, 10, 20 and 40.

The same task will be performed by a trained mind as follows:

	1	×	40
	2	×	20
	4	×	10
and	5	×	8

i.e., The discovery of one factor will automatically yield the other factor. In other words, factors will appear in terms of what can be called as factor pairs. The locating of one factor, will automatically pinpoint the other one for you. Thus, in the example above, when you find 5 as a factor of 40, you will automatically get 8 too as a factor.

Now take a look again at the pairs in the example above. If you compare the values in each pair with the square root of 40 (i.e. 6.xxx) you will find that for each pair the number in the left column is lower than the square root of 40, while the number in the right column is higher than the square root of 40.

This is a property for all numbers and is always true.

Hence, we can now phrase this as: Whenever you have to find the factors of any number N, you will get the factors in pairs (i.e., factor pairs). Further, the factor pairs will be such that in each pair of factors, one of the factors will be lower than the square root of N while the other will be higher than the square root of N.

As a result of this fact, one need not make any effort to find the factors of a number above the square root of the number. These come automatically. All you need to do is to find the factors below the square root of the number.

Extending this logic, we can say that if we are not able to find a factor of a number up to the value of its square root, we will not be able to find any factor above the square root and the number under consideration will be a prime number. This is the reason why when we need to check whether a number is prime, we have to check for factors only below the square root.

But, we have said that you need to check for divisibility only with the prime numbers below (and including) the square root of the number.

Let us look at an example to understand why you need to look only at prime numbers below the square root.

Uptil now, we have deduced that in order to check whether a number is prime, we just need to do a factor search below (and including) the square root.

Thus, for example, in order to find whether 181 is a prime number, we need to check for it's divisibility with the numbers = 2, 3, 4, 5, 6, 7, 8, 9, 10, 11, 12, and 13.

The first thing you will realise, when you first look at the list above is that all even numbers will get eliminated automatically (since no even number can divide an odd number and of course you will check a number for being prime only if it is odd!)

This will leave you with the numbers 3, 5, 7, 9, 11 and 13 to check 181.

Why do we not need to check with composite numbers below the square root? This will again be understood best if explained in the context of the example above. The only composite number in the list above is 9. You do not need to check with 9, because when you checked N for divisibility with 3 you would get either of two cases:

Case 1: If N is divisible by 3: In such a case, N will automatically become non-prime and you can stop your checking. Hence, you will not need to check for the divisibility of the number by 9.

Case 2: N is not divisible by 3: If N is not divisible by 3, it is obvious that it will not be divisible by 9. Hence, you will not need to check for the divisibility of the number by 9.

Thus, in either case, checking for divisibility by a composite number (9 in this case) is an unnecessary step. This will be true for all composite numbers.

Hence, when we have to check whether a number N is prime or not, we need to only check for its divisibility by prime factors below the square root of N.

Finding Prime Numbers: The Short Cut

Using the logic that we have to look at only the prime numbers below the square root in order to check whether a number is prime, we can actually cut short the time for finding whether a number is prime drastically.

Before I start to explain this, you should perhaps realise that in an examination like the CAT, or any other aptitude test for that matter whenever you would need to be checking for whether a number is prime or not, you would typically be checking 2-digit or maximum 3-digit numbers in the range of 100 to 200.

Also, one would never really need to check with the prime number 5, because divisibility by 5 would automatically be visible and thus, there is no danger of anyone ever declaring a number like 35 to be prime. Hence, in the list of prime numbers below the square root, we would never include 5 as a number to check with.

Checking Whether a Number is Prime (For Numbers below 49)

The only number you would need to check for divisibility with is the number 3. Thus, 47 is prime because it is not divisible by 3.

Checking Whether a Number is Prime (For Numbers above 49 and below 121)

Naturally, you would need to check this with 3 and 7. But if you remember that 77, 91 and 119 are not prime, you would be able to spot the prime numbers below 121 by just checking for divisibility with the number 3.

Why? Well, the odd numbers between 49 and 121 which are divisible by 7 are 63, 77, 91, 105 and 119. Out of these, perhaps 91 and 119 are the only numbers that you can mistakenly declare as prime. The numbers 77 and 105 are so obviously not-prime that you would never be in danger of declaring them prime.

Thus, for numbers between 49 and 121, you can find whether a number is prime or not by just dividing by 3 and checking for its divisibility.

For example:

61 is prime because it is not divisible by 3 and it is neither 91 nor 119.

Checking Whether a Number is Prime (For Numbers above 121 and below 169)

Naturally you would need to check this with 3, 7 and 11. But if you remember that 133,143 and 161 are not prime, you would be able to spot the prime numbers between 121 to 169 by just checking for divisibility with the number 3.

Why? The logic is same as explained above. The odd numbers between 121 and 169 which are divisible by either 7 or 11 are 133, 143, 147, 161 and 165. Out of these 133, 143 and 161 are the only numbers that you can mistakenly declare as prime if you do not check for 7 or 11. The number 147 would be found not to be prime when you check its divisibility by 3 while the number 165 you would never need to check for, for obvious reasons.

Thus, for numbers between 121 and 169 you can find whether a number is prime or not by just dividing by 3 and checking for its divisibility.

For example:

149, is prime because it is not divisible by 3 and it is neither 133, 143 nor 161.

Thus, we have been able to go all the way till 169 with just checking for divisibility with the number 3.

This logic can be represented on the number line as follows:

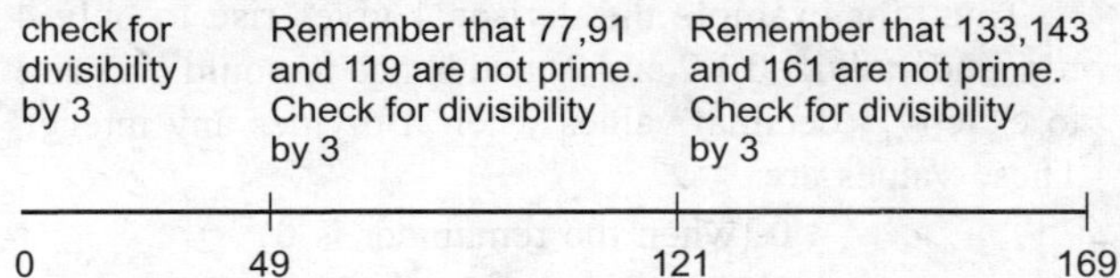

I would encourage you to build this logic further till 200 at least, if not till 289.

Integers A set which consists of natural numbers, negative integers (–1, –2, –3…–*n*…) and zero is known as the set of integers. The numbers belonging to this set are known as integers.

Integers can be visualised on the number line:

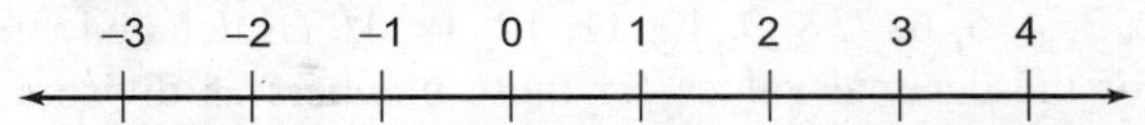

Note: Positive integers are the same thing as natural numbers.

The moment you define integers, you automatically define **decimals.**

Decimals

A *decimal* number is a number with a *decimal point* in it, for example, 1.5, 3.21, 4.173, 5.1, etc.

The number to the left of the decimal is an ordinary whole number. The first number to the right of the decimal is the number of tenths (1/10's). The second is the number of hundredths (1/100's) and so on. So, for the number 5.1, this is a shorthand way of writing the mixed number $5\frac{1}{10}$. The number 3.27 is the same as 3 + 2/10 + 7/100.

A word on where decimals originate from

Consider the situation where there are 5 children and you have to distribute 10 chocolates between them in such a way that all the chocolates should be distributed and each child should get an equal number of chocolates. How would you do it? Well, simple—divide 10 by 5 to get 2 chocolates per child.

Now consider what if you had to do the same thing with 9 chocolates amongst 5 children. In such a case, you would not be able to give an integral number of chocolates to each person. You would give 1 chocolate each to all the 5 and the 'remainder' 4 would have to be divided into 5 parts. 4 out of 5 would give rise to the decimal 0.8 and hence you would give 1.8 chocolates to each child. That is how the concept of decimals enters mathematics in the first place.

Taking this concept further, you can realise that the decimal value of any fraction essentially emerges out of the remainder when the numerator of the fraction is divided by the denominator. Also, since we know that each divisor has a few defined remainders possible, there would be a limited set of decimals that each denominator gives rise to.

Thus, for example the divisor 4 gives rise to only 4 remainders (viz. 0,1,2 and 3) and hence it would give rise to exactly 4 decimal values when it divides any integer. These values are:

0 (when the remainder is 0)
0.25 (when the remainder is 1)
0.50 (when the remainder is 2)
0.75 (when the remainder is 3)

There would be similar connotations for all integral divisors—although the key is to know the decimals that the following divisors give you:

Primary list:
2, 3, 4, 5, 6, 7, 8, 9, 10, 11, 12, 15, 16 (A detailed table for the decimal values for these numbers as divisors is provided in the chapter on Percentages in this book)

Secondary list:
18, 20, 24, 25, 30, 40, 50, 60, 80, 90, 120

A detailed discussion of some of these decimals is given in the chapter on Percentages in this book.

Composite Numbers It is a natural number that has at least one divisor different from unity and itself.

Every composite number n can be factored into its prime factors. (This is sometimes called the canonical form of a number.)

In mathematical terms: $n = p_1^m \cdot p_2^n \ldots p_k^s$, where $p_1, p_2 \ldots p_k$ are prime numbers called factors and $m, n \ldots k$ are natural numbers.

Thus, $24 = 2^3 \cdot 3$, $84 = 7 \cdot 3 \cdot 2^2$, etc.

This representation of a composite number is known as the standard form of a composite number. It is an extremely useful form of seeing a composite number as we shall see.

Whole Numbers The set of numbers that includes all natural numbers and the number zero are called whole numbers. Whole numbers are also called as non-negative integers.

Concept of the Number Line The number line is a straight line between negative infinity on the left to positive infinity to the right.

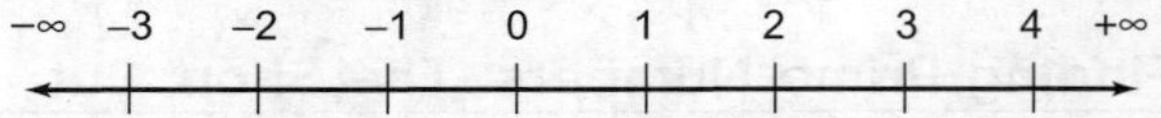

The distance between any two points on the number line is obtained by subtracting the lower value from the higher value. Alternately, we can also start with the lower number and find the required addition to reach the higher number. This is an important method to replace your need to follow the standard process for subtraction. Instead of using the carryover method we learnt in school, whenever you face a A-B subtraction, try to add an appropriate number to B, to get to A. You can think about this on the number line. For instance, if you wanted to subtract 28 from 82, think of what you would add to 28 to get to 82. Thus, 28 + 4 = 32 and 32 + 50 = 82. Hence, 54 would be the answer if you were to subtract 28 from 82.

Likewise, for subtracting 287 from 711, think like this: 287 + 13 = 300 and 300 + 411 = 711. Hence, the answer of 711 – 287 = 411 + 13 = 424.

Real Numbers All numbers that can be represented on the number line are called real numbers. Every real number can be approximately replaced with a terminating decimal.

The following operations of addition, subtraction, multiplication and division are valid for both whole numbers and real numbers: [For any real or whole numbers a, b and c]–

(a) Commutative property of addition: $a + b = b + a$
(b) Associative property of addition: $(a + b) + c = a + (b + c)$
(c) Commutative property of multiplication: $a \cdot b = b \cdot a$
(d) Associative property of multiplication: $(a \cdot b) \cdot c = a \cdot (b \cdot c)$
(e) Distributive property of multiplication with respect to addition: $(a + b)\, c = ac + bc$
(f) Subtraction and division are defined as the inverse operations to addition and multiplication respectively

Thus, if $a + b = c$, then $c - b = a$ and if $q = a/b$ then $b \cdot q = a$ (where $b \neq 0$).

Division by zero is not possible since there is no number q for which $b \cdot q$ equals a, non zero number a if b is zero.

Rational Numbers A rational number is defined as a number of the form a/b where a and b are integers and $b \neq 0$.

The set of rational numbers encloses the set of integers and fractions. The rules given above for addition, subtraction, multiplication and division also apply on rational numbers.

Rational numbers that are not integral will have decimal values. These values can be of two types:

(a) **Terminating (or finite) decimal fractions:** For example, 17/4 = 4.25, 21/5 = 4.2 and so forth.

(b) **Non-terminating decimal fractions:** Amongst non-terminating decimal fractions there are two types of decimal values:

(i) *Non-terminating periodic fractions*: These are non-terminating decimal fractions of the type $x \cdot a_1a_2a_3a_4 \ldots a_na_1a_2a_3a_4 \ldots a_na_1a_2a_3a_4 \ldots a_n$. For example $\frac{16}{3}$ = 5.3333, 15.23232323, 14.287628762 876 … and so on.

(ii) *Non-terminating non-periodic fractions*: These are of the form $x \cdot b_1b_2b_3b_4 \ldots b_nc_1c_2c_3 \ldots c_n$. For example: 5.2731687143725186....

Of the above categories, terminating decimal and non-terminating periodic decimal fractions belong to the set of rational numbers.

Irrational Numbers Fractions, that are non-terminating, non-periodic fractions, are irrational numbers.

Some examples of irrational numbers are $\sqrt{2}$, $\sqrt{3}$, etc. In other words, all square and cube roots of natural numbers that are not squares and cubes of natural numbers are irrational. Other irrational numbers include π, e and so on. Every positive irrational number has a negative irrational number corresponding to it.

All operations of addition, subtraction, multiplication and division applicable to rational numbers are also applicable to irrational numbers.

As briefly stated in the Back to School section, whenever an expression contains a rational and an irrational number together, the two have to be carried together till the end. In other words, an irrational number once it appears in the solution of a question will continue to appear till the end of the question. This concept is particularly useful in Geometry. For example: If you are asked to find the ratio of the area of a circle to that of an equilateral triangle, you can expect to see a $\pi/\sqrt{3}$ in the answer. This is because the area of a circle will always have a π component in it, while that of an equilateral triangle will always have $\sqrt{3}$.

You should realise that once an irrational number appears in the solution of a question, it can only disappear if it is multiplied or divided by the same irrational number.

CONCEPT OF GCD (GREATEST COMMON DIVISOR OR HIGHEST COMMON FACTOR)

Consider two natural numbers n_1 and n_2.

If the numbers n_1 and n_2 are exactly divisible by the same number x, then x is a common divisor of n_1 and n_2.

The highest of all the common divisors of n_1 and n_2 is called as the GCD or the HCF. This is denoted as GCD (n_1, n_2).

Rules for Finding the GCD of Two Numbers n_1 and n_2

(a) Find the standard form of the numbers n_1 and n_2.

(b) Write out all prime factors that are common to the standard forms of the numbers n_1 and n_2.

(c) Raise each of the common prime factors listed above to the lesser of the powers in which it appears in the standard forms of the numbers n_1 and n_2.

(d) The product of the results of the previous step will be the GCD of n_1 and n_2.

Illustration: Find the GCD of 150, 210, 375.

Step 1: Writing down the standard form of numbers

$$150 = 5 \times 5 \times 3 \times 2$$
$$210 = 5 \times 2 \times 7 \times 3$$
$$375 = 5 \times 5 \times 5 \times 3$$

Step 2: Writing prime factors common to all the three numbers is $5^1 \times 3^1$

Step 3: This will give the same result, i.e., $5^1 \times 3^1$

Step 4: Hence, the HCF will be 5 × 3 = 15

For practice, find the HCF of the following:

(a) 78, 39, 195
(b) 440, 140, 390
(c) 198, 121, 1331

SHORTCUT FOR FINDING THE HCF

The above 'school' process of finding the HCF (or the GCD) of a set of numbers is, however, extremely cumbersome and time-taking. Let us take a look at a much faster way of finding the HCF of a set of numbers.

Suppose you were required to find the HCF of 39,78 and 195.

Logic The HCF of these numbers would necessarily have to be a factor (divisor) of the difference between any pair of numbers from the above 3, i.e., the HCF has to be a factor of (78 – 39 = 39) as well as of (195 – 39 = 156) and (195 – 78 = 117). Why?

Well the logic is simple if you were to consider the tables of numbers on the number line.

For any two numbers on the number line, a common divisor would be one which divides both. However, for any number to be able to divide both the numbers, it can only do so if it is a factor of the difference between the two numbers. Got it?

Take an example:

Let us say, we take the numbers 68 and 119. The difference between them being 51, it is not possible for any number outside the factor list of 51 to divide both 68 and 119. Thus, for example a number like 4, which divides 68 can never divide any number which is 51 away from 68– because 4 is not a factor of 51.

Only factors of 51, i.e., 51, 17, 3 and 1 'could' divide both these numbers simultaneously.

Hence, getting back to the HCF problem we were trying to tackle—take the difference between any two numbers of the set—of course, if you want to reduce your calculations in the situation, take the difference between the two closest numbers. In this case, that would be the difference between 78 and 39 = 39.

'You can of course realise that in case you see a prime number difference between two of the numbers, you would prefer the prime number difference even if it is not the smallest difference—as in such a case, either the prime number itself would be the HCF of all the numbers or in case it does not divide even one of the numbers, 1 would become the HCF. For example: If you had to find the HCF of 122, 144, 203 and 253, the difference between 144 and 203 can be seen to be 59 and it is evident that 59 is not the HCF here and hence the HCF of the given numbers would be 1.'

The HCF has then to be a factor of this number. In order to find the factors quickly, remember to use the fact we learnt in the back to school section of this part of the book—that whenever we have to find the list of factors/divisors for any number we have to search the factors below the square root and the factors above the square root would be automatically visible).

A factor search of the number 39 yields the following factors:

1×39

3×13

Hence, one of these 4 numbers has to be the HCF of the numbers 39,78 and 195. Since we are trying to locate the **highest** common factor—we would begin our search from the highest number (viz:39).

Check for divisibility by 39 Any one number out of 39 and 78 and also check the number 195 for divisibility by 39. You would find all the three numbers are divisible by 39 and hence 39 can be safely taken to be the correct answer for the HCF of 39, 78 and 195.

Suppose the numbers were:

39, 78 and 182.

The HCF would still be a factor of 78 – 39 = 39. The probable candidates for the HCF's value would still remain 1,3,13 and 39.

When you check for divisibility of all these numbers by 39, you would realise that 182 is not divisible and hence 39 would not be the HCF in this case.

The next check would be with the number 13. It can be seen that 13 divides 39 (hence would automatically divide 78—no need to check that) and also divides 182. Hence, 13 would be the required HCF of the three numbers.

Typical questions where HCF is used directly

Example 1: The sides of a hexagonal field are 216, 423, 1215, 1422, 2169 and 2223 metres. Find the greatest length of tape that would be able to exactly measure each of these sides without having to use fractions/parts of the tape.

Solution: In this question, we are required to identify the HCF of the numbers 216, 423, 1215, 1422, 2169 and 2223.

In order to do that, we first find the smallest difference between any two of these numbers. It can be seen that the difference between 2223 – 2169 = 54. Thus, the required HCF would be a factor of the number 54.

The factors of 54 are:

1×54

2×27

3×18

6×9

One of these 8 numbers has to be the HCF of the 6 numbers. Number 54 cannot be the HCF because the numbers 423 and 2223 being odd numbers would not be divisible by any even number. Thus, we do not need to check any even numbers in the list.

Number 27 does not divide 423 and hence, cannot be the HCF. Number 18 can be skipped as it is even.

Checking for 9:

9 divides 216, 423, 1215, 1422 and 2169. Hence, it would become the HCF. (**Note:** we do not need to check 2223, once we know that 2169 is divisible by 9)

Example 2: A nursery has 363, 429 and 693 plants respectively of 3 distinct varieties. It is desired to place these plants in straight rows of plants of 1 variety only so that the number of rows required is the minimum. What is the size of each row and how many rows would be required?

Solution: The size of each row would be the HCF of 363, 429 and 693. Difference between 363 and 429 = 66. Factors of 66 are 66, 33, 22, 11, 6, 3, 2, 1.

Number 66 need not be checked as it is even and 363 is odd. Number 33 divides 363, hence would automatically divide 429 and also divides 693. Hence, 33 is the correct answer for the size of each row.

For how many rows would be required, we need to follow the following process:

Minimum number of rows required = 363/33 + 429/33 + 693/33 = 11 + 13 + 21 = 45 rows.

CONCEPT OF LCM (LEAST COMMON MULTIPLE)

Let n_1 and n_2 be two natural numbers distinct from each other. The smallest natural number n that is exactly divisible by n_1 and n_2 is called the Least Common Multiple (LCM) of n_1 and n_2 and is designated as LCM (n_1, n_2).

Rule for Finding the LCM of Two Numbers n_1 and n_2

(a) Find the standard form of the numbers n_1 and n_2.
(b) Write out all the prime factors, which are contained in the standard forms of either of the numbers.
(c) Raise each of the prime factors listed above to the highest of the powers in which it appears in the standard forms of the numbers n_1 and n_2.
(d) The product of results of the previous step will be the LCM of n_1 and n_2.

Illustration: Find the LCM of 150, 210, 375.

Step 1: Writing down the standard form of numbers

$$150 = 5 \times 5 \times 3 \times 2$$
$$210 = 5 \times 2 \times 7 \times 3$$
$$375 = 5 \times 5 \times 5 \times 3$$

Step 2: Write down all the prime factors: that appear at least once in any of the numbers: 5, 3, 2, 7.

Step 3: Raise each of the prime factors to their highest available power (considering each to the numbers).

The LCM = $2^1 \times 3^1 \times 5^3 \times 7^1 = 5250$

Important Rule:

GCD (n_1, n_2). LCM $(n_1, n_2) = n_1 \cdot n_2$
i.e., the product of the HCF and the LCM equals the product of the numbers.

Note: This rule is applicable only for two numbers

SHORT CUT FOR FINDING THE LCM

The LCM (least common multiple) again has a much faster way of doing it than what we learnt in school.

The process has to do with the use of co-prime numbers.

Before we look at the process, let us take a fresh look at what co-prime numbers are.

Co-prime numbers are any two numbers which have an HCF of 1, i.e., when two numbers have no common prime factor apart from the number 1, they are called co-prime or relatively prime to each other.

Some Rules for Co-primes

Two Numbers being Co-prime

(i) Two consecutive natural numbers are always co-prime (Examples: 5, 6; 82, 83; 749, 750 and so on)
(ii) Two consecutive odd numbers are always co-prime (Examples: 7, 9; 51, 53; 513, 515 and so on)
(iii) Two prime numbers are always co-prime (Examples: 13, 17; 53, 71 and so on)
(iv) One prime number and another composite number (such that the composite number is not a multiple of the prime number) are always co-prime (Examples: 17, 38; 23, 49 and so on, but note that 17 and 51 are not co-prime)
(v) Two odd numbers with a difference that is equal to any power of 2. (Examples: 17, 21; 33, 97; 21, 85; 33, 65)
(vi) Two numbers that have a difference of 3, but are themselves not multiples of 3 (Examples: 32, 35; 43, 46; 71, 74 and so on)

Three or more numbers being co-prime with each other means that all possible pairs of the numbers would be co-prime with each other.

Thus, 47, 49, 51 and 52 are co-prime since each of the 6 pairs (47, 49); (47, 51); (47, 52); (49, 51); (49, 52) and (51, 52) are co-prime.

Rules for Spotting Three Co-prime Numbers

(i) Three consecutive odd numbers are always co-prime (Examples: 15, 17, 19; 51, 53, 55 and so on)
(ii) Three consecutive natural numbers with the first one being odd (Examples: 15, 16, 17; 21, 22, 23; 41, 42, 43 and so on). (**Note:** 22, 23, 24 are not co-prime.)
(iii) Two consecutive natural numbers along with the next odd number such that the first number. is even (Examples: 22, 23, 25; 52, 53, 55; 68, 69, 71 and so on). Please note that this would not be true in case the first and the last number would be a multiple of 3.
(iv) Three prime numbers (Examples: 17, 23, 29; 13, 31, 43 and so on)
(v) Two prime numbers and one composite number such that the composite number is not a multiple of either of the primes (Examples: 23, 31 and 42; 17, 23 and 28; 13, 23 and 27 and so on)
(vi) Three odd numbers for which the pairwise difference for each of the three pairs of numbers taken two at a time is a power of 2 (Examples: 21, 25, 29; 55, 63, 71 and so on)

So what do co-prime numbers have to do with LCMs?

By using the logic of co-prime numbers, you can actually bypass the need to take out the prime factors of the set of numbers for which you are trying to find the LCM. How?

The following process will make it clear:

Let us say that you were trying to find the LCM of 9, 10, 12 and 15.

The LCM can be directly written as: 9 × 10 × 2. The thinking that gives you the value of the LCM is as follows:

Step 1: If you can see a set of 2 or more co-prime numbers in the set of numbers for which you are finding the LCM write them down by multiplying them.

So in the above situation, since we can see that 9 and 10 are co-prime to each other, we can start off writing the LCM by writing 9 × 10 as the first step.

Step 2: For each of the other numbers, consider what part of them have already been taken into the answer and what part remains outside the answer. In case, you see any part of the other numbers such that it is not a part of the value of the LCM you are writing—such a part would need to be taken into the answer of the LCM.

The process will be clear once you see what we do (and how we think) with the remaining 2 numbers in the above problem.

At this point, when we have written down 9 × 10 we already have taken into account the numbers 9 and 10 leaving us to account for 12 and 15.

Thought about 12: 12 is 2 × 2 × 3

9 × 10 already has a 3 and 2 in its prime factors. However, the number 12 has two 2's. This means that one of the two 2's of the number 12 is still not accounted for in our answer. Hence, we need to modify the LCM by multiplying the existing 9 × 10 by a 2. With this change, the LCM now becomes:

9 × 10 × 2

Thought about 15: 15 is 5 × 3

9 × 10 × 2 already has a 5 and a 3. Hence, there is no need to add anything to the existing answer.

Thus, 9 × 10 × 2 would become the correct answer for the LCM of the numbers 9, 10, 12 and 15.

What if the numbers were: 9, 10, 12 and 25

Step 1: 9 and 10 are co-prime

Hence, the starting value is 9 × 10

Thought about 12: 12 is 2 × 2 × 3

9 × 10 already has a 3 and one 2 in it prime factors. However, the number 12 has two 2's. This means that one of the two 2's of the number 12 is still not accounted for in our answer. Hence, we need to modify the LCM by multiplying the existing 9 × 10 by a 2. With this change, the LCM now becomes:

9 × 10 × 2

Thought about 25: 25 is 5 × 5

9 × 10 × 2 has only one 5. Hence, we need to add another 5 to the answer.

Thus, 9 × 10 × 2 × 5 would become the correct answer for the LCM of the numbers 9, 10, 12 and 25.

Rule for Finding out HCF and LCM of Fractions

(a) HCF of two or more fractions is given by:

$$\frac{\text{HCF of Numerators}}{\text{LCM of Denominators}}$$

(b) LCM of two or more fractions is given by:

$$\frac{\text{LCM of Numerators}}{\text{HCF of Denominators}}$$

Note: Make sure that you reduce the fractions to their lowest forms before you use these formulae, otherwise you may get the wrong answer.

You would be able to see most of the standard questions on LCMs in the practice exercise on HCF and LCM given below.

HCF and LCM

Practice Exercise 1

(Typical questions asked in Exams)

1. Find the common factors for the numbers
   (a) 24 and 64 (b) 42, 294 and 882
   (c) 60, 120 and 220
2. Find the HCF of
   (a) 420 and 1782 (b) 36 and 48
   (c) 54, 72, 198 (d) 62, 186 and 279
3. Find the LCM of
   (a) 13, 23 and 48 (b) 24, 36, 44 and 62
   (c) 22, 33, 45, and 72 (d) 13, 17, 21 and 33
4. Find the series of common multiples of (a) 54 and 36, (b) 33, 45 and 60
   [*Hint*: Find the LCM and then create an arithmetic progression with the first term as the LCM and the common difference also as the LCM.]
5. The LCM of two numbers is 936. If their HCF is 4 and one of the numbers is 72, the other is:
   (a) 42 (b) 52
   (c) 62 (d) None of these
   [Answer: (b). Use HCF × LCM = product of numbers.]
6. Two alarm clocks ring their alarms at regular intervals of 50 seconds and 48 seconds. If they first beep together at noon, at what time will they beep again for the first time?
   (a) 12:10 p.m. (b) 12:12 p.m.
   (c) 12:11 p.m. (d) None of these
7. Four Bells toll together at 9:00 a.m. They toll after 7, 8, 11 and 12 seconds respectively. How many times will they toll together again in the next 3 hours?
   (a) 3 (b) 4
   (c) 5 (d) 6

8. On Ashok Marg, three consecutive traffic lights change after 36, 42 and 72 seconds, respectively. If the lights are first switched on at 9:00 a.m. sharp, at what time will they change simultaneously?

(a) 9 : 08 : 04 (b) 9 : 08 : 24
(c) 9 : 08 : 44 (d) None of these

[Answer (b). The LCM of 36, 42 and 72 is 504. Hence, the lights will change simultaneously after 8 minutes and 24 seconds.]

9. The HCF of 2472, 1284 and a third number '*N*' is 12. If their LCM is $2^3 \times 3^2 \times 5^1 \times 103 \times 107$, then the number '*N*' could be

(a) $2^2 \times 3^2 \times 7^1$ (b) $2^2 \times 3^3 \times 103$
(c) $2^2 \times 3^2 \times 5^1$ (d) None of these

[Answer: (c)]

10. Two equilateral triangles have the sides of lengths 34 and 85, respectively.

(a) The greatest length of tape that can measure both of them exactly is

[Answer: HCF of 34 and 85 is 17.]

(b) How many such equal parts can be measured?

[Answer: $\frac{34}{17} \times 3 + \frac{85}{17} \times 3 = 2 \times 3 + 5 \times 3 = 21$]

11. Two numbers are in the ratio 17:13. If their HCF is 15, what are the numbers?

(Answer: 17 × 15 and 13 × 15 i.e., 255 and 195 respectively.) (**Note:** This can be done when the numbers are co-prime.)

12. A forester wants to plant 44 apple trees, 66 banana trees and 110 mango trees in equal rows (in terms of number of trees). Also, he wants to make distinct rows of trees (i.e., only one type of tree in one row). The number of rows (minimum) that are required are

(a) 2 (b) 3
(c) 10 (d) 11

[Answer: (c) 44/22 + 66/22 + 110/22 (Since 22 is the HCF)]

13. Three runners running around a circular track can complete one revolution in 2, 4 and 5.5 hours, respectively. When will they meet at the starting point?

(a) 22 (b) 33
(c) 11 (d) 44

[Answer: (d). The LCM of 2, 4 and 11/2. This will give you 44 as the answer].

14. The HCF and LCM of two numbers are 20 and 120, respectively. When the first number is divided by 2, the quotient is 20. The other number is

[Answer: 20 × 120 = 40 × *n*. Hence, *n* = 60.]

15. The greatest number which will divide 4003, 4126 and 4249 is

(a) 43 (b) 41
(c) 45 (d) None of these

The answer will be the HCF of the three numbers. (1 in this case)

16. Which of the following represents the largest 4-digit number which can be added to 7249 in order to make the derived number divisible by each of 12, 14, 21, 33, and 54?

(a) 9123 (b) 9383
(c) 8727 (d) None of these

[Answer: The LCM of the numbers 12, 14, 21, 33 and 54 is 8316. Hence, in order for the condition to be satisfied we need to get the number as:

$$7249 + n = 8316 \times 2$$

Hence, $n = 9383$]

17. Find the greatest number of 5 digits, that will give us a remainder of 5, when divided by 8 and 9, respectively.

(a) 99931 (b) 99941
(c) 99725 (d) None of these

[Answer: The LCM of 8 and 9 is 72. The largest 5 digit multiple of 72 is 99936. Hence, the required answer is 99941.]

18. The least perfect square number which is divisible by 3, 4, 6, 8, 10 and 11 is

[Answer: The number should have at least one 3, three 2's, one 5 and one 11 for it to be divisible by 3, 4, 6, 8, 10 and 11.]

Further, each of the prime factors should be having an even power in order to be a perfect square. Thus, the correct answer will be: 3 × 3 × 2 × 2 × 2 × 2 × 5 × 5 × 11 × 11

19. Find the greatest number of 4-digits which when divided by 10, 11, 15 and 22 leaves 3, 4, 8 and 15 as remainders, respectively.

(a) 9907 (b) 9903
(c) 9893 (d) None of these

[Answer: First find the greatest 4-digit multiple of the LCM of 10, 11, 15 and 22. (In this case it is 9900). Then, subtract 7 from it to give the answer.]

20. Find the HCF of $(3^{125} - 1)$ and $(3^{35} - 1)$.

[Answer: The solution of this question is based on the rule that:

The HCF of $(a^m - 1)$ and $(a^n - 1)$ is given by $(a^{\text{HCF of } m,\, n} - 1)$

Thus, in this question the answer is: $(3^5 - 1)$. Since 5 is the HCF of 35 and 125.]

Practice Exercise 2

21. What will be the least possible number of the planks, if three pieces of timber 42 m, 49 m and 63 m long have to be divided into planks of the same length?

(a) 7 (b) 8
(c) 22 (d) None of these

22. Find the greatest number, which will divide 215, 167 and 135 so as to leave the same remainder in each case.

(a) 64 (b) 32
(c) 24 (d) 16

23. Find the LCM of 2.5, 0.5 and 0.175.
(a) 2.5 (b) 5
(c) 7.5 (d) 17.5

24. The LCM of 4.5; 0.009; and 0.18 = ?
(a) 4.5 (b) 45
(c) 0.225 (d) 2.25

25. The LCM of two numbers is 1890 and their HCF is 30. If one of them is 270, the other will be
(a) 210 (b) 220
(c) 310 (d) 320

26. What is the smallest number which when increased by 6 is divisible by 36, 63 and 108?
(a) 750 (b) 752
(c) 754 (d) 756

27. The smallest square number, which is exactly divisible by 2, 3, 4, – 9, 6, 18, 30 and 60, is
(a) 900 (b) 1600
(c) 3600 (d) None of these

28. The HCF of two numbers is 11, and their LCM is 616. If one of the numbers is 88, find the other.
(a) 77 (b) 87
(c) 97 (d) None of these

29. What is the greatest possible rate at which a man can walk 51 km and 85 km in an exact number of minutes?
(a) 11 km/min (b) 13 km/min
(c) 17 km/min (d) None of these

30. The HCF and LCM of two numbers are 12 and 144 respectively. If one of the numbers is 36, the other number is
(a) 4 (b) 48
(c) 72 (d) 432

31. HCF of (9000, X) = 60; where X is a natural number less than 9000. Find the number of possible values of X.
(a) 24 (b) 40
(c) 30 (d) 36

32. The sum of two numbers is 2800 and 7 is their HCF, how many pairs of such numbers are possible?
(a) 80 (b) 160
(c) 60 (d) 100

33. There are three positive integers a, b and c such that HCF of each possible pair is 11 and product of all three numbers is 13310. How many sets of $\{a, b, c\}$ is possible?
(a) 2 (b) 6
(c) 3 (d) 9

34. The HCF and LCM of two numbers are 75 and 920 respectively. If one of the numbers is 600, find the other number.
(a) 115 (b) 230
(c) 23 (d) Data inconsistent

35. If the LCM of 1, 2, 3, ..., 120 is n, find the LCM of 1, 2, 3, ..., 125.
(a) n (b) $5n$
(c) $11n$ (d) $55n$

36. The sum of two numbers is 112 and the sum and the difference of their LCM and HCF are 208 and 176 respectively. Then the smaller number is
(a) 92 (b) 24
(c) 48 (d) 64

ANSWER KEY

21. (c)	22. (d)	23. (d)	24. (a)	25. (a)
26. (a)	27. (a)	28. (a)	29. (c)	30. (b)
31. (b)	32. (a)	33. (b)	34. (d)	35. (d)
36. (c)				

Going Beyond the Book

Scan this QR code to access video explanations of complex questions in Exercise 2 (Q 31, 32, 33)

SOLUTIONS AND SHORTCUTS

Practice Exercise 1

4. (a) The first common multiple is also the LCM. The LCM of 36 and 54 would be 108. The next common multiple would be 216, 324 and so on. Thus, the required series would be 108, 216, 324, 432, 540, 648....
   (b) The LCM of 33, 45 and 60 = 60 × 3 × 11 = 1980. Thus, the required series is: 1980, 3960, 5940...
5. LCM × HCF = 936 × 4 = $N_1 \times N_2 \rightarrow$ $936 \times 4 = 72 \times N_2 \rightarrow N_2 = 13 \times 4 = 52$. Option (b) is correct.
6. The first time the alarm clocks would ring together would be after a time that is equal to the LCM of 50 and 48. The LCM of 50 and 48 is 50 × 24 = 1200. Hence, the first time they would ring together after noon would be exactly 1200 seconds or 20 minutes later. Option (d) is correct.
7. The LCM of 7, 8, 11 and 12 is given by 12 × 11 × 2 × 7 = 264 × 7 = 1848. 1848 seconds is 30 minutes 48 seconds. Hence, the 4 bells would toll together every 30 minutes 48 seconds.
   The number of times they would toll together in the next 3 hours would be given by the quotient of the division: 3 × 60 × 60 /1848 → 5 times.
   Alternately, by thinking of 1848 seconds as 30 minutes 48 seconds you can also solve the same question by thinking as follows:

Noon	12:30:48	Just after 1	Just after 1:30	Just after 2	Just after 2:30	After 3 p.m.
	first ring	second ring	third ring	fourth ring	fifth ring	sixth ring

Since the sixth ring is after 3 p.m., we can say that the bells would toll 5 times in the next 3 hours

9. $2472 = 2^3 \times 103 \times 3$; $1284 = 2^2 \times 107 \times 3$. Since the HCF is 12, the number must have a component of $2^2 \times 3^1$ at the very least in it. Also, since the LCM is $2^3 \times 3^2 \times 5^1 \times 103 \times 107$ we can see that the minimum requirement in the required number has to be $3^2 \times 5^1$. Combining these two requirements, we get that the number should have $2^2 \times 3^2 \times 5^1$ at the minimum and the power of 2 could also be 2^3 while we could also have either one of 103^1 and/or 107^1 as a part of the required number.

Thus, for instance, the number could also be $2^3 \times 3^2 \times 5^1 \times 103^1 \times 107^1$. The question has asked us- what ***'could'*** the number be?

Option (c) gives us a possible value of the number. Hence, option (c) the correct answer.

Practice Exercise 2

21. The least possible number of planks would occur when we divide each plank into a length equal to the HCF of 42, 49 and 63. The HCF of these numbers is clearly 7 – and this should be the size of each plank. Number of planks in this case would be: 42/7 + 49/7 + 63/7 = 6 + 7 + 9 = 22 planks. Hence, option (c) is correct.
22. The difference between 135 and 167 is 32, while the difference between 167 and 215 is 48. The answer to this question would be the HCF of these differences. Hence, HCF of 32 and 48 = 16. Hence, option (d) is correct.
23. The numbers are 5/2, ½ and 175/1000 = 7/40. The LCM of three fractions is given by the formula:

    LCM of numerators/HCF of denominators = (LCM of 5, 1 and 7)/(HCF of 2 and 40) = 35/2 = 17.5
24. Use the same process as for question 23 for the numbers 9/2; 9/1000 and 9/50.

    (LCM of 9,9,9)/(HCF of 2,1000 & 50) = 9/2 = 4.5
25. $1890 \times 30 = 270 \times N_2 \rightarrow N_2 = 210$. Hence, option (a) is correct.
26. The LCM of 36, 63 and 108 is 756. Hence, the required number is 750. Option (a) is correct.
27. The LCM of the given numbers is 180. Hence, all multiples of 180 would be divisible by all of these numbers. Checking the series 180, 360, 540, 720, 900 we can see that 900 is the first perfect square in the list. Option (a) is correct.
28. Using the property HCF × LCM = product of the numbers, we get:

    $616 \times 11 = 88 \times N_2 \rightarrow N_2 = 77$. Option (a) is correct.
29. The answer would be given by the HCF of 51 and 85 – which is 17. Hence, option (c) is correct.
30. Using the property HCF × LCM = product of the numbers, we get:

    $12 \times 144 = 36 \times N_2 \rightarrow N_2 = 48$. Option (b) is correct.
31. The numbers would be of the form $60 \times a$ and $60 \times b$, where 'a' and 'b' are co-prime numbers.

    (**Note:** This is a general property of HCFs, where if H is the HCF of 3 numbers x, y, z, then the numbers can be denoted as $H \times a$, $H \times b$ and $H \times c$, where a, b and c are co-prime numbers. In this question, since the first number is given to us as 9000, the value of a can be calculated as: $60 \times a = 9000$. Hence, $a = 150$. We need to find values of b that are co-prime to 150 – and are below 150. To find this, we need to look for numbers below 150, that can be constructed using prime numbers other than 2,3, and 5 (since 150 has 2's, 3's and 5's in it). There are 22 prime numbers below 100, other than 2, 3 and 5. Between 100 and 150, there are an additional 10 prime numbers. Besides this, numbers like 7^2, 11^2, 7×11, 7×13, 7×17, 7×19, 11×13. This makes a total of 22 + 10 + 7 = 39 numbers. Besides, this we also need to visualise that if we take the value of b as 1, then again we would get the HCF of 60 and 9000 as 60. Thus, there are a total of 40 such numbers below 9000, that would have an HCF of 60 along with the number 9000. Option (b) is correct.
32. In this question, we can again think of the numbers are $7 \times a$ and $7 \times b$, where a and b should be co-prime. Since the sum of the numbers is 2800, we have $7 \times a + 7 \times b = 2800$, which means that $a + b = 400$. Thus, a and b should fulfill two conditions – they should add up to 400 and they should be co-prime. Since, $400 = 2^4 \times 5^2$, all numbers below 400 that are not multiples of 2 or 5, would be co-prime. If we take the value of a = 1, 3, 7 or 9; the value of b would come out as 399, 397, 393 and 391. Going forward between every set of numbers from 11 to 20, 21 to 30 and so on, we will find 4 such numbers that would not be a multiple of 2 or 5. Thus, there would be a total of 20 × 4 = 80 such pairs of numbers, whose HCF is 7 and sum is 2800. Option (*a*) is correct.
33. The numbers can be taken as $11x$, $11y$ and $11z$, where x, y, z are co-prime. The product of the three numbers would be $11 \times 11 \times 11 \times xyz = 1331 \times xyz$. For this to be equal to 13310, the product xyz needs to be 10. There is only one way of making a product of 10 using three distinct numbers – viz: 1 × 2 × 5. However, these three values can be used interchangeably between x, y and z in 6 ways (3! = 6). Hence, there are 6 sets of $\{a, b, c\}$ possible. Option (*b*) is correct.
34. Normally, students would solve this question as $75 \times 920 = 600 \times n \rightarrow n = 115$. But this is not correct in this situation. The reason for the same is that it is not possible to have the LCM of two numbers such that it is not the product of their HCF. The LCM would always necessarily be a product of the HCF. Hence, the correct answer for this question is Data inconsistent. Hence, option (*d*) is correct.
35. Going forward from 121 to 125, the number 121 being 11^2 would alter the LCM to $11 \times n$ (since, the

LCM is got by multiplying all the prime factors using their highest powers.). Also, 125 being 5^3, would necessitate a multiplication by 5 for the LCM. Thus, the correct LCM would be $11 \times 5 \times n = 55 \times n$. Hence, option (*d*) is correct.

36. LCM + HCF = 208 and LCM – HCF = 176 → LCM = 192 and HCF = 16. Thus, the two numbers are $16a$ and $16b$ with a and b as co-prime. Also, since $16a + 16b = 112$, we get that $a + b = 7$. Trial and error with different values of a and b, gives us that the numbers would be 48 and 64 (using $a = 3$ and $b = 4$). Hence, the correct answer is option (*c*).

DIVISIBILITY

A number x is said to be divisible by another number 'y' if it is completely divisible by y (i.e., it should leave no remainder).

In general, it can be said that any integer N, when divided by a natural number D, there exists a unique pair of numbers Q and R which are called the quotient and remainder respectively.

Thus, $N = QD + R$.

Where Q is an integer and D is a natural number or zero and $0 \le R < N$ (i.e., remainder has to be a whole number less than N.)

If the remainder is zero, we say that the number N is divisible by D.

When $R > 0$, we say that the number N is divisible by D with a remainder.

Thus, 25/8 can be written as: $25 = 3 \times 8 + 1$ (3 is the quotient and 1 is the remainder)

While, –25/7 will be written as $-25 = 7 \times (-4) + 3$ (–4 is the quotient and 3 is the remainder)

Note: An integer $b > 0$ is said to divide an integer a if there exists another integer c such that:

$$a = bc$$

It is important to explain at this point a couple of concepts with respect to the situation, when we divide a negative number by a natural number N.

Suppose, we divide – 32 by 7. Contrary to what you might expect, the remainder in this case is + 3 (and not – 4). This is because the remainder is always non negative.

Thus, –32/7 gives quotient as – 5 and remainder as + 3.

The relationship between the remainder and the decimal:

1. Suppose we divide 42 by 5. The result has a quotient of 8 and remainder of 2.

   But 42/5 = 8.4. As you can see, the answer has an integer part and a decimal part. The integer part being 8 (equals the quotient), the decimal part is 0.4 (and is given by 2/5).

   Since, we have also seen that for any divisor N, the set of remainders obeys the inequality $0 \le R < N$, we should realise that any divisor N, will yield exactly N possible remainders. (For example, if the divisor is 3, we have 3 possible remainders 0, 1 and 2. Further, when 3 is the divisor, we can have only 3 possible decimal values 0.00, 0.333 and 0.666 corresponding to remainders of 0, 1 or 2. Remember this concept when you study the fraction to percentage conversion table in the chapter on percentages.)

2. In the case of –42 being divided by 5, the value is – 8.4. In this case, the interpretation should be thus: The integer part is – 9 (which is also the quotient of this division) and the decimal part is 0.6 (corresponding to 3/5). Notice that since the remainder cannot be negative, the decimal too cannot be negative.

Theorems of Divisibility

(a) If a is divisible by b, then ac is also divisible by b.

(b) If a is divisible by b and b is divisible by c, then a is divisible by c.

(c) If a and b are natural numbers such that a is divisible by b and b is divisible by a, then $a = b$.

(d) If n is divisible by d and m is divisible by d then $(m + n)$ and $(m - n)$ are both divisible by d. This has an important implication. Suppose 28 and 742 are both divisible by 7. Then (742 + 28) as well as (742 – 28) are divisible by 7 (and in fact so is + 28 – 742).

(e) If a is divisible by b and c is divisible by d then ac is divisible by bd.

(f) The highest power of a prime number p, which divides $n!$ exactly is given by

$$[n/p] + [n/p^2] + [n/p^3] + \ldots$$

where $[x]$ denotes the greatest integer less than or equal to x.

As we have already seen earlier—

Any composite number can be written down as a product of its prime factors (also called standard form).

Thus, for example the number 1240 can be written as $2^3 \times 31^1 \times 5^1$.

The standard form of any number has a huge amount of information stored in it. The best way to understand the information stored in the standard form of a number is to look at concrete examples. As a reader you must understand each of the processes defined below and use them to solve similar questions given in the exercise that follows and beyond:

1. **Using the standard form of a number to find the sum and the number of factors of the number:**

   (a) Sum of factors of a number:

   Suppose, we have to find the sum of factors and the number of factors of 240.

$$240 = 2^4 \times 3^1 \times 5^1$$

   The sum of factors will be given by:

$$(2^0 + 2^1 + 2^2 + 2^3 + 2^4)(3^0 + 3^1)(5^0 + 5^1)$$
$$= 31 \times 4 \times 6 = 744$$

Note: This is a standard process, wherein you create the same number of brackets as the number of distinct prime factors the number contains and then each bracket is filled with the sum of all the powers of the respective prime number starting from 0 to the highest power of that prime number contained in the standard form.

Thus, for 240, we create 3 brackets—one each for 2, 3 and 5. Further in the bracket corresponding to 2, we write $(2^0 + 2^1 + 2^2 + 2^3 + 2^4)$.

Hence, for example for the number $40 = 2^3 \times 5^1$, the sum of factors will be given by: $(2^0 + 2^1 + 2^2 + 2^3)(5^0 + 5^1)$ {2 brackets since 40 has 2 distinct prime factors 2 and 5}

(b) Number of factors of the number:

Let us explore the sum of factors of 40 in a different context.

$$(2^0 + 2^1 + 2^2 + 2^3)(5^0 + 5^1)$$
$$= 2^0 \times 5^0 + 2^0 \times 5^1 + 2^1 \times 5^0 + 2^1 \times 5^1 + 2^2 \times 5^0 + 2^2 \times 5^1 + 2^3 \times 5^0 + 2^3 \times 5^1$$
$$= 1 + 5 + 2 + 10 + 4 + 20 + 8 + 40 = 90$$

A clear look at the numbers above will make you realise that it is nothing but the addition of the factors of 40. Hence, we realise that the number of terms in the expansion of $(2^0 + 2^1 + 2^2 + 2^3)(5^0 + 5^1)$ will give us the number of factors of 40. Hence, 40 has $4 \times 2 = 8$ factors.

Note: The moment you realise that $40 = 2^3 \times 5^1$ the answer for the number of factors can be obtained by $(3 + 1)(1 + 1) = 8$

2. Sum and number of even and odd factors of a number:

Suppose, you are trying to find out the number of factors of a number represented in the standard form by: $2^3 \times 3^4 \times 5^2 \times 7^3$

As you are already aware, the answer to the question is $(3 + 1)(4 + 1)(2 + 1)(3 + 1)$ and is based on the logic that the number of terms will be the same as the number of terms in the expansion: $(2^0 + 2^1 + 2^2 + 2^3)(3^0 + 3^1 + 3^2 + 3^3 + 3^4)(5^0 + 5^1 + 5^2)(7^0 + 7^1 + 7^2 + 7^3)$.

Now, suppose you have to find out the sum of the even factors of this number. The only change you need to do in this respect will be evident below. The answer will be given by:

$(2^1 + 2^2 + 2^3)(3^0 + 3^1 + 3^2 + 3^3 + 3^4)(5^0 + 5^1 + 5^2)(7^0 + 7^1 + 7^2 + 7^3)$

Note: We have eliminated 2^0 from the original answer. By eliminating 2^0 from the expression for the sum of all factors, you are ensuring that you have only even numbers in the expansion of the expression.

Consequently, the number of even factors will be given by: $(3)(4 + 1)(2 + 1)(3 + 1)$

i.e., since 2^0 is eliminated, we do not add 1 in the bracket corresponding to 2.

Let us now try to expand our thinking to try to think about the number of odd factors for a number.

In this case, we just have to do the opposite of what we did for even numbers. The following step will make it clear:

Odd factors of the number whose standard form is : $2^3 \times 3^4 \times 5^2 \times 7^3$

Sum of odd factors $= (2^0)(3^0 + 3^1 + 3^2 + 3^3 + 3^4)(5^0 + 5^1 + 5^2)(7^0 + 7^1 + 7^2 + 7^3)$

i.e., ignore all powers of 2. The result of the expansion of the above expression will be the complete set of odd factors of the number. Consequently, the number of odd factors for the number will be given by the number of terms in the expansion of the above expression.

Thus, the number of odd factors for the number $2^3 \times 3^4 \times 5^2 \times 7^3 = 1 \times (4 + 1)(2 + 1)(3 + 1)$.

3. Sum and number of factors satisfying other conditions for any composite number:

These are best explained through examples:

(i) Find the sum and the number of factors of 1200 such that the factors are divisible by 15.

Solution : $1200 = 2^4 \times 5^2 \times 3^1$.

For a factor to be divisible by 15 it should compulsorily have 3^1 and 5^1 in it. Thus, sum of factors divisible by 15 $= (2^0 + 2^1 + 2^2 + 2^3 + 2^4) \times (5^1 + 5^2) \times (3^1)$ and consequently the number of factors will be given by $5 \times 2 \times 1 = 10$.

(What we have done is ensured that in every individual term of the expansion, there is a minimum of $3^1 \times 5^1$. This is done by removing powers of 3 and 5 which are below 1.)

Task for the student: Physically verify the answers to the question above and try to convert the logic into a mental algorithm.

<u>NOTE FROM THE AUTHOR:</u> The need for thought algorithms:

I have often observed that the key difference between understanding a concept and actually applying it under examination pressure, is the presence or absence of a mental thought algorithm which clarifies the concept to you in your mind. The thought algorithm is a personal representation of a concept—and any concept that you read/understand in this book (or elsewhere) will remain an external concept till it remains in someone else's words. The moment the thought becomes internalised, the concept becomes yours to apply and use.

Practice Exercise on Factors

For the number 2450, find

1. The sum and number of all factors
2. The sum and number of even factors
3. The sum and number of odd factors
4. The sum and number of factors divisible by 5
5. The sum and number of factors divisible by 35
6. The sum and number of factors divisible by 245

For the number 7200, find

7. The sum and number of all factors
8. The sum and number of even factors
9. The sum and number of odd factors
10. The sum and number of factors divisible by 25
11. The sum and number of factors divisible by 40
12. The sum and number of factors divisible by 150
13. The sum and number of factors not divisible by 75
14. The sum and number of factors not divisible by 24
15. Find the number of divisors of 1728.
    (a) 18 (b) 30
    (c) 28 (d) 20
16. Find the number of divisors of 1080 excluding the divisors, which are perfect squares.
    (a) 28 (b) 29
    (c) 30 (d) 31
17. Find the number of divisors of 544 excluding 1 and 544.
    (a) 12 (b) 18
    (c) 11 (d) 10
18. Find the number of divisors of 544 which are greater than 3.
    (a) 15 (b) 10
    (c) 12 (d) None of these
19. Find the sum of divisors of 544 excluding 1 and 544.
    (a) 1089 (b) 545
    (c) 589 (d) 1134
20. Find the sum of divisors of 544 which are perfect squares.
    (a) 32 (b) 64
    (c) 42 (d) 21
21. Let $d_1, d_2, ... d_k$ be all the factors of a positive integer n, in ascending order including 1 and n. Suppose $d_1 + d_2 + ... d_k = 72$. Then the value of $1/d_1 + 1/d_2 + ... + 1/d_k$ is
    (a) $n^2/72$ (b) $n/72$
    (c) $72/n$ (d) $36/n$
22. How many factors of $4^5 \times 5^4 \times 6^3$ are perfect squares but not perfect cubes?
    (a) 6 (b) 24
    (c) 30 (d) 39
23. How many of the following statements are true?
    (i) Only squares of prime numbers have three factors
    (ii) If a number has 4 factors, the number must be a perfect cube
    (iii) If a number has 5 factors, the number must be a fourth power of a natural number
    (a) None of these (b) One
    (c) Two (d) All three
24. n is the smallest positive integer such that $n/2$ is a perfect square, $n/3$ is a perfect cube and $n/5$ is a perfect fifth power. If n is represented in its factorised form as $p^a \times q^b \times r^c \times .....$, where $p, q, r, ...$ are all distinct prime numbers, then find the minimum sum $a + b + c + ...$
    (a) 31 (b) 37
    (c) 54 (d) 56
25. n is the smallest positive integer such that $2n$ is a perfect square, $3n$ is a perfect cube and $5n$ is a perfect fifth power. If n is represented in its factorised form as $p^a \times q^b \times r^c \times ......$, where $p, q, r, ...$ are all distinct prime numbers, then find the minimum sum $a + b + c + ...$
    (a) 31 (b) 37
    (c) 54 (d) 59
26. N^2 has 13 factors smaller than N. Find the maximum number of factors of N^3.
    (a) 40 (b) 52
    (c) 64 (d) None of these

ANSWER KEY

15. (c)	16. (a)	17. (d)	18. (b)	19. (c)
20. (d)	21. (c)	22. (d)	23. (c)	24. (a)
25. (d)	26. (c)			

SOLUTIONS AND SHORTCUTS

Solutions for Questions 1 to 6:

$2450 = 50 \times 49 = 2^1 \times 5^2 \times 7^2$

1. Sum and number of all factors:
   Sum of factors = $(2^0 + 2^1)(5^0 + 5^1 + 5^2)(7^0 + 7^1 + 7^2)$
   Number of factors = $2 \times 3 \times 3 = 18$
2. Sum of all even factors:
   $(2^1)(5^0 + 5^1 + 5^2)(7^0 + 7^1 + 7^2)$
   Number of even factors = $1 \times 3 \times 3 = 9$
3. Sum of all odd factors:
   $(2^0)(5^0 + 5^1 + 5^2)(7^0 + 7^1 + 7^2)$
   Number of odd factors = $1 \times 3 \times 3 = 9$
4. Sum of factors divisible by 5:
   $(2^0 + 2^1)(5^1 + 5^2)(7^0 + 7^1 + 7^2)$
   Number of factors divisible by 5 = $2 \times 2 \times 3 = 12$

5. Sum of factors divisible by 35:
$(2^0 + 2^1)(5^1 + 5^2)(7^1 + 7^2)$
Number of factors divisible by 35 = 2 × 2 × 2 = 8
6. Sum of all factors divisible by 245:
$(2^0 + 2^1)(5^1 + 5^2)(7^2)$
Number of factors divisible by 245 = 2 × 2 × 1 = 4

Solutions for Questions 7 to 14:

$7200 = 72 \times 100 = 12 \times 6 \times 100 = 2^5 \times 3^2 \times 5^2$

7. **Sum and number of all factors:**
Sum of factors = $(2^0 + 2^1 + 2^2 + 2^3 + 2^4 + 2^5)(3^0 + 3^1 + 3^2)(5^0 + 5^1 + 5^2)$
Number of factors = 6 × 3 × 3 = 54
8. **Sum and number of even factors:**
Sum of even factors = $(2^1 + 2^2 + 2^3 + 2^4 + 2^5)(3^0 + 3^1 + 3^2)(5^0 + 5^1 + 5^2)$
Number of even factors = 5 × 3 × 3 = 45
9. **Sum and number of odd factors:**
Sum of odd factors = $(2^0)(3^0 + 3^1 + 3^2)(5^0 + 5^1 + 5^2)$
Number of odd factors = 1 × 3 × 3 = 9
10. **Sum and number of factors divisible by 25:**
Sum of factors divisible by 25 = $(2^0 + 2^1 + 2^2 + 2^3 + 2^4 + 2^5)(3^0 + 3^1 + 3^2)(5^2)$
Number of factors divisible by 25 = 6 × 3 × 1 = 18
11. **Sum and number of factors divisible by 40:**
Sum of factors divisible by 40 = $(2^3 + 2^4 + 2^5)(3^0 + 3^1 + 3^2)(5^1 + 5^2)$
Number of factors = 3 × 3 × 2 = 18
12. **Sum and number of factors divisible by 150:**
Sum of factors divisible by 150 = $(2^1 + 2^2 + 2^3 + 2^4 + 2^5)(3^1 + 3^2)(5^2)$
Number of factors divisible by 150 = 5 × 2 × 1 = 10
13. **Sum and number of factors not divisible by 75:**
Sum of factors not divisible by 75 = Sum of all factors – Sum of factors divisible by 75 = $(2^0 + 2^1 + 2^2 + 2^3 + 2^4 + 2^5)(3^0 + 3^1 + 3^2)(5^0 + 5^1 + 5^2) - (2^0 + 2^1 + 2^2 + 2^3 + 2^4 + 2^5)(3^1 + 3^2)(5^2)$
Number of factors not divisible by 75 = Number of factors of 7200 – Number of factors of 7200 which are divisible by 75 = 6 × 3 × 3 – 6 × 2 × 1 = 54 – 12 = 42
14. **Sum and number of factors not divisible by 24:**
Sum of factors not divisible by 24 = Sum of all factors – Sum of factors divisible by 24 = $(2^0 + 2^1 + 2^2 + 2^3 + 2^4 + 2^5)(3^0 + 3^1 + 3^2)(5^0 + 5^1 + 5^2) - (2^3 + 2^4 + 2^5)(3^1 + 3^2)(5^0 + 5^1 + 5^2)$
Number of factors not divisible by 24 = Number of factors of 7200 – Number of factors of 7200 which are divisible by 24 = 6 × 3 × 3 – 3 × 2 × 3 = 54 – 18 = 36
15. **Number of divisors of 1728**
$1728 = 4 \times 432 = 16 \times 108 = 64 \times 27 = 2^6 \times 3^3$
Number of factors = 7 × 4 = 28. Option (c) is correct.
16. $1080 = 108 \times 10 = 27 \times 4 \times 10 = 3^3 \times 2^3 \times 5^1$
Number of factors = 4 × 4 × 2 = 32
In order to see the number of factors of 1080 which are perfect squares we need to visualise the structure for writing down the sum of perfect square factors of 1080.
This would be given by:
Sum of all perfect square factors of 1080 = $(2^0 + 2^2)(3^0 + 3^2)(5^0)$.
From the above structure, it is clear that the number of perfect square factors is going to be 2 × 2 × 1 = 4.
Thus, the number of factors of 1080 which are not perfect squares are equal to 32 – 4 = 28.
Option **(a)** is correct.
17. $544 = 17^1 \times 2^5$. Hence, the total number of factors of 544 is 2 × 6 = 12. But we have to count factors excluding 1 and 544. Thus, we need to remove 2 factors from this. The required answer is 12 – 2 = 10. Option **(d)** is correct.
18. Using the fact that 544 has a total of 12 factors and the numbers 1 and 2 are the two factors which are lower than 3, we would get a total of 10 factors greater than 3. Option **(b)** is correct.
19. The required answer would be given by: Sum of all factors of 544 – 1 – 544 = $(2^0 + 2^1 + 2^2 + 2^3 + 2^4 + 2^5)(17^0 + 17^1) - 545 = 63 \times 18 - 545 = 589$. Option **(c)** is correct.
20. Sum of divisors of 544 which are perfect squares is: $(2^0 + 2^2 + 2^4)(17^0) = 21$. Option **(d)** is correct.
21. Since the sum of factors of n are given as 72, we can visualise that n would be a number like $2^1 \times 3^1 \times 5^1 = 30$.
(**Note:** For this visualise 72 as 3 × 4 × 6 and then visualise 3 × 4 × 6 as $(2^0 + 2^1) \times (3^0 + 3^1) \times (5^0 + 5^1)$] The factors of 30 are: 1, 2, 3, 5, 6, 10, 15 and 30. The value of:
$1/d_1 + 1/d_2 + ... + 1/d_k = 72/30$. Hence, option **(c)** is correct.)
22. The number is: $2^{13} \times 3^3 \times 5^4$. Sum of the factors that are perfect squares would be given by the expression: $(2^0 + 2^2 + 2^4 + \ldots 2^{12}) \times (3^0 + 3^2) \times (5^0 + 5^2 + 5^4)$. For the number of factors, we would need to look at the number of terms in the expansion of this expression. There are: 7 × 2 × 3 = 42 terms in this expansion. Hence, the given number has 42 factors that are perfect squares. Out of these, three factors viz: $2^0 \times 3^0 \times 5^0$; $2^6 \times 3^0 \times 5^0$ and $2^{12} \times 3^0 \times 5^0$ are perfect cubes too. Hence, the required answer is 42 – 3 = 39. Option (*d*) is correct.

23. The first statement would always be true – as we cannot make 3 by multiplying any two numbers. Thus, only numbers like 2^2, 3^2, 5^2, 7^2,11^2 would give us 3 factors. The second statement need not be true, since we can easily visualise that numbers like: $2^1 \times 3^1$ would also give us 4 factors. The third statement would again be true since only numbers like 2^4, 3^4 11^4 would give us 5 factors. Hence, the correct answer would be **(c)**.
24. First visualise the number in its general form as: $2^{2m+1} \times 3^{3x+1} \times 5^{5y+1}$ with $2m + 1$, simultaneously being a multiple of 3 and 5, $3x + 1$ being a multiple of 2 as well as a multiple of 5 and $5y + 1$ being a multiple of 2 and 3. Thus, the minimum values with these constraints would be: $2^{15} \times 3^{10} \times 5^6$. In such a case, the number on division by 2, becomes a perfect square, on division by 3 becomes a perfect cube and on division by 5 becomes a perfect fifth power. In this case, the sum of the powers on 2, 3 and 5 are 15 + 10 + 6 = 31. Option (*a*) is correct.
25. First visualise the number in its general form as: $2^{2m-1} \times 3^{3x-1} \times 5^{5y-1}$ with $2m - 1$, simultaneously being a multiple of 3 and 5, $3x - 1$ being a multiple of 2 as well as a multiple of 5 and $5y - 1$ being a multiple of 2 and 3. Thus, the minimum values with these constraints would be: $2^{15} \times 3^{20} \times 5^{24}$. In such a case, the number on multiplication by 2 becomes a perfect square, on multiplication by 3 becomes a perfect cube and on multiplication by 5 becomes a perfect fifth power. In this case, the sum of the powers on 2, 3 and 5 are 15 + 20 + 24 = 59. Option (*d*) is correct.
26. From the given information, we can see that N^2 would have 13 pairs of factors apart from its square root N. Thus, N^2 has 27 factors. 27 factors for a number would occur if the number N^2 is of the form: $p_1{}^8 \times p_2{}^2$ or $p_1{}^2 \times p_2{}^2 \times p_3{}^2$. In the first case: N would be: $p_1{}^4 \times p_2{}^1$. Thus, N^3 would be $p_1{}^{12} \times p_2{}^3$. This number would have 13 × 4 = 52 factors. In the second case: N would be: $p_1{}^1 \times p_2{}^1 \times p_3{}^1$ and consequently N^3 would be: $p_1{}^3 \times p_2{}^3 \times p_3{}^3$. In this case, the number of factors would be 4 × 4 × 4 = 64 factors. Option (*c*) is correct. (**Note:** p^{26} can also be the form of the number N^2. In such a case, $N = p^{13}$ and $N^3 = P^{39}$. This would have only 40 factors.)

NUMBER OF ZEROES IN AN EXPRESSION

Suppose you have to find the number of zeroes in a product: 24 × 32 × 17 × 23 × 19 = $(2^3 \times 3^1) \times (2^5) \times 17^1 \times 23 \times 19$

As you can notice, this product will have no zeroes because it has no 5 in it.

However, if you have an expression like: 8 × 15 × 23 × 17 × 25 × 22

The above expression can be rewritten in the standard form as:

$$2^3 \times 3^1 \times 5^1 \times 23 \times 17 \times 5^2 \times 2^1 \times 11^1$$

Zeroes are formed by a combination of 2 × 5. Hence, the number of zeroes will depend on the number of pairs of 2's and 5's that can be formed.

In the above product, there are four twos and three fives. Hence, we shall be able to form only three pairs of (2 × 5). Hence, there will be 3 zeroes in the product.

Finding the Number of Zeroes in a Factorial Value

Suppose you had to find the number of zeroes in 6!

6! = 6 × 5 × 4 × 3 × 2 × 1 = (3 × 2) × (5) × (2 × 2) × (3) × (2) × (1)

The above expression will have only one pair of 5 × 2, since there is only one 5 and an abundance of 2's.

It is clear that in any factorial value, the number of 5's will always be lesser than the number of 2's. Hence, all we need to do is to count the number of 5's. The process for this is explained in Solved Examples 1.1 to 1.3.

Exercise for Self-practice

Find the number of zeroes in the following cases:

1. 47!
2. 58!
3. 13 × 15 × 22 × 125 × 44 × 35 × 11
4. 12 × 15 × 5 × 24 × 13 × 17
5. 173!
6. 144! × 5 × 15 × 22 × 11 × 44 × 135
7. 148!
8. 1093!
9. 1132!
10. 1142! × 348! × 17!

SOLUTIONS AND SHORTCUTS

1. 47/5 → Quotient 9. 9/5 → Quotient → 1. 9 + 1 = 10 zeroes.
2. 58/5 → Quotient 11. 11/5 → Quotient → 2. 11 + 2 = 13 zeroes.
3. The given expression has five 5's and three 2's. Thus, there would be three zeroes in the expression.
4. The given expression has two 5's and five 2's. Thus, there would be two zeroes in the expression.
5. 173/5 → Quotient 34. 34/5 → Quotient 6. 6/5 → Quotient 1. 34 + 6 + 1 = 41 zeroes.
6. 144! Would have 28 + 5 + 1 = 34 zeroes and the remaining part of the expression would have three zeroes. A total of 34 + 3 = 37 zeroes.
7. 148/5 → Quotient 29. 29/5 → Quotient 5. 5/5 → Quotient 1. 29 + 5 + 1 = 35 zeroes.
8. 1093/5 → Quotient 218. 218/5 → Quotient 43. 43/5 → Quotient 8. 8/5 → Quotient 1. 218 + 43 + 8 + 1 = 270 zeroes.
9. 1132/5 → Quotient 226. 226/5 → Quotient 45. 45/5 → Quotient 9. 9/5 → Quotient 1. 226 + 45 + 9 + 1 = 281 zeroes.

10. 1142/5 → Quotient 228. 228/5 → Quotient 45. 45/5 → Quotient 9. 9/5 → Quotient 1. 228 + 45 + 9 + 1 = 283 zeroes.

348/5 → Quotient 69. 69/5 → Quotient 13. 13/5 → Quotient 2. 69 + 13 + 2 = 84 zeroes.

17/5 → Quotient 3 → 3 zeroes.

Thus, the total number of zeroes in the expression is: 283 + 84 + 3 = 370 zeroes.

A special implication: Suppose you were to find the number of zeroes in the value of the following factorial values:

45!, 46!, 47!, 48!, 49!

What do you notice? The number of zeroes in each of the cases will be equal to 10. Why does this happen? It is not difficult to understand that the number of fives in any of these factorials is equal to 10. The number of zeroes will only change at 50! (It will become 12).

In fact, this will be true for all factorial values between two consecutive products of 5.

Thus, 50!, 51!, 52!, 53! and 54! will have 12 zeroes (since they all have 12 fives).

Similarly, 55!, 56!, 57!, 58! and 59! will each have 13 zeroes.

Apart from this fact, did you notice another thing? That while there are 10 zeroes in 49!, there are directly 12 zeroes in 50!. This means that there is no value of a factorial which will give 11 zeroes. This occurs because to get 50!, we multiply the value of 49! by 50. When you do so, the result is that we introduce two 5's in the product. Hence, the number of zeroes jumps by two (since we never had any paucity of twos.)

Note: At 124! you will get 24 + 4 ⇒ 28 zeroes

At 125!, you will get 25 + 5 + 1 = 31 zeroes (A jump of 3 zeroes.)

Exercise for Self-practice

1. $n!$ has 23 zeroes. What is the maximum possible value of n?
2. $n!$ has 13 zeroes. The highest and least values of n are
3. Find the number of zeroes in the product $1^1 \times 2^2 \times 3^3 \times 4^4 \times 5^5 \times 6^6 \times \ldots \times 49^{49}$
4. Find the number of zeroes in $100^1 \times 99^2 \times 98^3 \times 97^4 \times \ldots\ldots \times 1^{100}$
5. Find the number of zeroes in $1^{1!} \times 2^{2!} \times 3^{3!} \times 4^{4!} \times 5^{5!} \times \ldots\ldots 10^{10!}$
6. Find the number of zeroes in the value of $2^2 \times 5^4 \times 4^6 \times 10^8 \times 6^{10} \times 15^{12} \times 8^{14} \times 20^{16} \times 10^{18} \times 25^{20}$
7. What is the number of zeroes in the following?
   (a) 3200 + 1000 + 40000 + 32000 + 15000000
   (b) 3200 × 1000 × 40000 × 32000 × 16000000

SOLUTIONS AND SHORTCUTS

1. This can never happen because at 99!, number of zeroes is 22 and at 100!, the number of zeroes is 24.
2. 59 and 55, respectively.
3. The 5's will be less than the 2's. Hence, we need to count only the 5's.
   Thus : $5^5 \times 10^{10} \times 15^{15} \times 20^{20} \times 25^{25} \times 30^{30} \times 35^{35} \times 40^{40} \times 45^{45}$
   gives us: 5 + 10 + 15 + 20 + 25 + 25 + 30 + 35 + 40 + 45 fives. Thus, the product has 250 zeroes.
4. Again the key here is to count the number of fives. This can get done by:
   $100^1 \times 95^6 \times 90^{11} \times 85^{16} \times 80^{21} \times 75^{26} \times \ldots\ldots 5^{96}$
   (1 + 6 + 11 + 16 + 21 + 26 + 31 + 36 + 41 + 46 + …….. + 96) + (1 + 26 + 51 + 76)
   = 20 × 48.5 + 4 × 38.5 (Using sum of A.P. explained in the next chapter.)
   = 970 + 154 = 1124
5. The answer will be the number of 5's. Hence, it will be 5! + 10!
6. The number of 5's is again lesser than the number of 2's.
   The number of 5's will be given by the power of 5 in the product:
   $$5^4 \times 10^8 \times 15^{12} \times 20^{16} \times 10^{18} \times 25^{20}$$
   $$= 4 + 8 + 12 + 16 + 18 + 40 = 98$$
7. (a) The number of zeroes in the sum will be two, since:

```
    3200
    1000
   40000
   32000
15000000
--------
15076200
```

   Thus, in such cases the number of zeroes will be the least number of zeroes amongst the numbers.
   Exception: 3200 + 1800 = 5000 (three zeroes, not two).
   (b) The number of zeroes will be:
   2 + 3 + 4 + 3 + 6 = 18

An extension of the process for finding the number of zeroes.

Consider the following questions:

1. Find the highest power of 5 which is contained in the value of 127!
2. When 127! is divided by 5^n the result is an integer. Find the highest possible value for n.
3. Find the number of zeroes in 127!

In each of the above cases, the value of the answer will be given by:

$$[127/5] + [127/25] + [127/125]$$
$$= 25 + 5 + 1 = 31$$

This process can be extended to questions related to other prime numbers. For example:
Find the highest power of:

1. 3 which completely divides 38!
   Solution: $[38/3] + [38/3^2] + [38/3^3] = 12 + 4 + 1 = 17$
2. 7 which is contained in 57!
   $[57/7] + [57/7^2] = 8 + 1 = 9$

This process changes when the divisor is not a prime number. You are first advised to go through worked out problems 1.4, 1.5, 1.6 and 1.19.

Now try to solve the following exercise:

1. Find the highest power of 7 which divides 81!
2. Find the highest power of 42 which divides 122!
3. Find the highest power of 84 which divides 342!
4. Find the highest power of 175 which divides 344!
5. Find the highest power of 360 which divides 520!

SOLUTIONS AND SHORTCUTS

1. 81/7 → Quotient 11. 11/7 → Quotient 1. Highest power of 7 in 81! = 11 + 1 = 12.
2. In order to check for the highest power of 42, we need to realise that 42 is 2 × 3 × 7. In 122! the least power between 2,3 and 7 would obviously be for 7. Thus, we need to find the number of 7's in 122! (or in other words— the highest power of 7 in 122!).
   This can be done by:
   122/7 → Quotient 17. 17/7 → Quotient 2. Highest power of 7 in 122! = 17 + 2 = 19.
3. 84 = 2 × 2 × 3 × 7. This means we need to think of which amongst 2^2, 3 and 7 would appear the least number of times in 342! It is evident that there would be more 2^2s and 3's than 7's in any factorial value (Because if you write any factorial 1 × 2 × 3 × 4 × 5 × 6 × **7** × 8 × 9 × 10 × 11 × 12 × 13 × 14 × 15... you can clearly see that before a 7 or it's multiple appears in the multiplication, there are at least two 2's and one 3 which appear beforehand.)
   Hence, in order to solve this question we just need to find the power of 7 in 342!
   This can be done as:
   342/7 → Quotient 48. 48/7 → Quotient 6. 6/7 → Quotient 0. Highest power of 7 in 342! = 48 + 6 = 54.
4. 175 = 5 × 5 × 7. This means we need to think of which amongst 5^2 and 7 would appear the least number of times in 175! In this case, it is not immediately evident that whether there would be more 5's or more 7's, in any factorial value (Because if you write any factorial 1 × 2 × 3 × 4 × 5 × 6 × **7** × 8 × 9 × 10 × 11 × 12 × 13 × 14 × 15...you can clearly see that although the 5's appear more frequently than the 7's it is not evident that we would have at least two fives before the 7 appears.) Hence, in this question we would need to check for both the number of 5's and the number of 7's.
   Number of 7's in 344!
   344/7 → Quotient 49. 49/7 → Quotient 7. 7/7 → Quotient 1. Highest power of 7 in 344! = 49 + 7 + 1 = 57.
   In order to find the number of 5^2s in 344!, we first need to find the number of 5's in 344!
   344/5 → Quotient 68. 68/5 → Quotient 13. 13/5 → Quotient 2. Number of 5's in 344! = 68 + 13 + 2 = 83.
   83 fives would obviously mean [83/2] = 41, 5 squares.
   Thus, there are 41, 5 squares and 57, 7's in 344!
   Since, the number of 5 squares are lower, they would determine the highest power of 175 that would divide 344!
   The answer is 41.
5. 360 = 5 × 2 × 2 × 2 × 3 × 3. This means we need to think of which amongst 2^3, 3^2 and 5 would appear the least number of times in 520! In this case, it is not immediately evident which of these three would appear least number of times. Hence, in this question we would need to check for all three – 2^3s, 3^2s and 5's.
   Number of 5's in 520!
   520/5 → Quotient 104. 104/5 → Quotient 20. 20/5 → Quotient 4. Highest power of 5 in 520! = 104 + 20 + 4 = 128.
   In order to find the number of 3^2s in 520! we first need to find the number of 3's in 520!
   520/3 → Quotient 173. 173/3 → Quotient 57. 57/3 → Quotient 19. 19/3 → Quotient 6. 6/3 → Quotient 2. 2/3 → Quotient 0. Number of 3's in 520! = 173 + 57 + 19 + 6 + 2 = 257.
   257 threes would obviously mean [257/2] = 128 3^2s.
   In order to find the number of 2^3s in 520!, we first need to find the number of 2's in 520!
   520/2 → Quotient 260. 260/2 → Quotient 130. 130/2 → Quotient 65. 65/2 → Quotient 32. 32/2 → Quotient 16. 16/2 → Quotient 8. 8/2 → Quotient 4. 4/2 → Quotient 2. 2/2 → Quotient 1. 1/2 → Quotient 0.
   Number of 2's in 520! = 260 + 130 + 65 + 32 + 16 + 8 + 4 + 2 + 1 = 518. 518 twos would obviously mean [518/3] = 172 2^3s.
   Thus, there are 128 3^2s, 128 5's and 172 2^3's in 520!
   The highest power of 360 that would divide 520! would be the least of 128, 128 and 172.
   The answer is 128.

Exercise for Self-practice

1. Find the maximum value of n such that 157! is perfectly divisible by 10^n.
   (a) 37 (b) 38
   (c) 16 (d) 31
2. Find the maximum value of n such that 157! is perfectly divisible by 12^n.

(a) 77 (b) 76
(c) 75 (d) 78

3. Find the maximum value of n such that 157! is perfectly divisible by 18^n.
(a) 37 (b) 38
(c) 39 (d) 40

4. Find the maximum value of n such that 50! is perfectly divisible by 2520^n.
(a) 6 (b) 8
(c) 7 (d) None of these

5. Find the maximum value of n such that 50! is perfectly divisible by 12600^n.
(a) 7 (b) 6
(c) 8 (d) None of these

6. Find the maximum value of n such that 77! is perfectly divisible by 720^n.
(a) 35 (b) 18
(c) 17 (d) 36

7. Find the maximum value of n such that 42 × 57 × 92 × 91 × 52 × 62 × 63 × 64 × 65 × 66 × 67 is perfectly divisible by 42^n.
(a) 4 (b) 3
(c) 5 (d) 6

8. Find the maximum value of n such that 570 × 60 × 30 × 90 × 100 × 500 × 700 × 343 × 720 × 81 is perfectly divisible by 30^n.
(a) 12 (b) 11
(c) 14 (d) 13

9. Find the maximum value of n such that 77 × 42 × 37 × 57 × 30 × 90 × 70 × 2400 × 2402 × 243 × 343 is perfectly divisible by 21^n.
(a) 9 (b) 11
(c) 10 (d) 6

Find the number of consecutive zeroes at the end of the following numbers.

10. 72!
(a) 17 (b) 9
(c) 8 (d) 16

11. 77! × 42!
(a) 24 (b) 9
(c) 27 (d) 18

12. 100! + 200!
(a) 73 (b) 24
(c) 11 (d) 22

13. 57 × 60 × 30 × 15625 × 4096 × 625 × 875 × 975
(a) 6 (b) 16
(c) 17 (d) 15

14. 1! × 2! × 3! × 4! × 5! × .... × 50!
(a) 235 (b) 12
(c) 262 (d) 105

15. $1^1 \times 2^2 \times 3^3 \times 4^4 \times 5^5 \times 6^6 \times 7^7 \times 8^8 \times 9^9 \times 10^{10}$.
(a) 25 (b) 15
(c) 10 (d) 20

16. 100! × 200!
(a) 49 (b) 73
(c) 132 (d) 33

ANSWER KEY

1. (b)	2. (c)	3. (a)	4. (b)	5. (b)
6. (c)	7. (b)	8. (b)	9. (d)	10. (d)
11. (c)	12. (b)	13. (d)	14. (c)	15. (b)
16. (b)				

SOLUTIONS AND SHORTCUTS

1. [157/5] = 31. [31/5] = 6. [6/5] = 1. 31 + 6 + 1 = 38. Option **(b)** is correct.

2. Number of 2's in 157! = [157/2] + [157/4] + [157/8]... + [157/128] = 78 + 39 + 19 + 9 + 4 + 2 + 1 = 152. Hence, the number of 2^2s would be [152/2] = 76. Number of 3's in 157! = 52 + 17 + 5 + 1 = 75. The answer would be given by the lower of these values. Hence, 75 Option **(c)** is correct.

3. From the above solution:
Number of 2's in 157! = 152
Number of 3^2s in 157! = [75/2] = 37.
Hence, option **(a)** is correct.

4. $2520 = 7 \times 3^2 \times 2^3 \times 5$
The value of n would be given by the value of the number of 7s in 50!
This value is equal to [50/7] + [50/49] = 7 + 1 = 8
Option **(b)** is correct.

5. $12600 = 7 \times 3^2 \times 2^3 \times 5^2$
The value of 'n' would depend on which of number of 7's and number of 5^2s is lower in 50!.
Number of 7's in 50! = 8. (**Note:** If we check for 7's we do not need to check for 3^2s as there would be at least two 3's before a 7 comes in every factorial's value. Similarly, there would always be at least three 2's before a 7 comes in any factorial's value. Thus, the number of 3^2s and the number of 2^3s can never be lower than the number of 7's in any factorial's value.)
Number of 5s in 50! = 10 + 2 = 12. Hence, the number of 5^2s in 50! = [12/2] = 6.
6 will be the answer as the number of 5^2s is lower than the number of 7's.
Option **(b)** is correct.

6. $720 = 2^4 \times 5^1 \times 3^2$
In 77! there would be 38 + 19 + 9 + 4 + 2 + 1 = 73 twos → hence [73/4] = 18 2^4s
In 77! there would be 25 + 8 + 2 = 35 threes → hence [35/2] = 17 3^2s
In 77! there would be 15 + 3 = 18 fives
Since 17 is the least of these values, option **(c)** is correct.

7. In the expression given, there are three 7's and more than three 2's and 3's. Thus, option **(b)** is correct.
8. Checking for the number of 2's, 3's and 5's in the given expression, you can see that the minimum is for the number of 3's (there are 11 of them while there are 12, 5's and more than 11, 2's) Hence, option **(b)** is correct.
9. The number of 7's in the number is 6, while there are more than six 3's. Hence, option **(d)** is correct.
10. The number of zeroes would depend on the number of 5's in the value of the factorial.
    $72! \rightarrow 14 + 2 = 16$. Option **(d)** is correct.
11. The number of zeroes would depend on the number of 5's in the value of the factorial.
    $77! \times 42! \rightarrow 15 + 3 = 18$ (for 77!) and $8 + 1 = 9$ (for 42!).
    Thus, the total number of zeroes in the given expression would be $18 + 9 = 27$. Option **(c)** is correct.
12. The number of zeroes would depend on the number of 5's in the value of the factorial.
    100! would end in $20 + 4 = 24$ zeroes
    200! Would end in $40 + 8 + 1 = 49$ zeroes.
    When you add the two numbers (one with 24 zeroes and the other with 49 zeroes at its end), the resultant total would end in 24 zeroes. Option **(b)** is correct.
13. The given expression has fifteen 2's and seventeen 5's. The number of zeroes would be 15 as the number of 2's is lower in this case. Option **(d)** is correct.
14. 1! to 4! would have no zeroes while 5! to 9! all the values would have 1 zero. Thus, a total of 5 zeroes till 9!. Going further 10! to 14! would have two zeroes each — so a total of 10 zeroes would come out of the product of $10! \times 11! \times 12! \times 13! \times 14!$.
    Continuing this line of thought further we get:
    Number of zeroes between $15! \times 16! ... \times 19! = 3 + 3 + 3 + 3 + 3 = 3 \times 5 = 15$
    Number of zeroes between $20! \times 21! ... \times 24! = 4 \times 5 = 20$
    Number of zeroes between $25! \times 26! ... \times 29! = 6 \times 5 = 30$
    Number of zeroes between $30! \times 31! ... \times 34! = 7 \times 5 = 35$
    Number of zeroes between $35! \times 36! ... \times 39! = 8 \times 5 = 40$
    Number of zeroes between $40! \times 41! ... \times 44! = 9 \times 5 = 45$
    Number of zeroes between $45! \times 46! ... \times 49! = 10 \times 5 = 50$
    Number of zeroes for $50! = 12$
    Thus, the total number of zeroes for the expression $1! \times 2! \times 3! .... \times 50! = 5 + 10 + 15 + 20 + 30 + 35 + 40 + 45 + 50 + 12 = 262$ zeroes. Option **(c)** is correct.
15. The number of 5's is 15 while the number of 2's is much more. Option **(b)** is correct.
16. The number of zeroes would depend on the number of 5's in the value of the factorial.
    100! would end in $20 + 4 = 24$ zeroes
    200! would end in $40 + 8 + 1 = 49$ zeroes.
    When you multiply the two numbers (one with 24 zeroes and the other with 49 zeroes at its end), the resultant total would end in $24 + 49 = 73$ zeroes. Option **(b)** is correct.

Co-Prime or Relatively Prime Numbers Two or more numbers that do not have a common factor are known as co-prime or relatively prime. In other words, these numbers have a highest common factor of unity.

If two numbers m and n are relatively prime and the natural number x is divisible by both m and n independently then the number x is also divisible by mn.

Key Concept 1: The spotting of two numbers as co-prime has a very important implication in the context of the two numbers being in the denominators of fractions.

The concept is again best understood through an example:

Suppose, you are doing an operation of the following format — $M/8 + N/9$ where M and N are integers.

What are the chances of the result being an integer, if M is not divisible by 8 and N is not divisible by 9? A little bit of thought will make you realise that the chances are zero. The reason for this is that 8 and 9 are co-prime and the decimals of co-prime numbers never match each other.

Note: This will not be the case in the case of:

$$M/3 + N/27$$

In this case, even if 3 and 27 are not dividing M and N respectively, there is a possibility of the values of M and N being such that you have an integral answer.

For instance: $5/3 + 36/27 = 81/27 = 3$

The result will never be integral if the two denominators are co-prime.

Note: This holds true even for expressions of the nature $A/7 - B/6$, etc.

This has huge implications for problem solving especially in the case of solving linear equations related to word based problems. Students are advised to try to use these throughout Blocks I and II of this book.

Example: Find all 5-digit numbers of the form $34x5y$ that are divisible by 36.

Solution: 36 is a product of two co-primes 4 and 9. Hence, if $34x5y$ is divisible by 4 and 9, it will also be divisible by 36. Hence, for divisibility by 4, we have that the value of y can be 2 or 6. Also, if y is 2 the number becomes $34x52$. For this to be divisible by 9, the addition of $3 + 4 + x + 5 + 2$ should be divisible by 9. For this, x can be 4.

Hence, the number 34452 is divisible by 36.

Also for $y = 6$, the number $34x56$ will be divisible by 36 when the addition of the digits is divisible by 9. This will happen when x is 0 or 9. Hence, the numbers 34056 and 34956 will be divisible by 36.

Key Concept 2: The prime factors of the numbers, is another way to check whether the numbers under consideration are co-prime or not. For two or more co-prime numbers, their prime factors would have no commonality between themselves. Thus, if we have A and B co-prime, and $A = 2^n \times 3^m$, then it necessarily follows that in the prime factors of B, there would be no 2 or 3. In other words, B would be created out of prime numbers like 5, 7, 11 and so on, but cannot have a 2 or 3 in it.

Exercise for Self-practice

1. Find all numbers of the form $56x3y$ that are divisible by 36.
2. Find all numbers of the form $72xy$ that are divisible by 45.
3. Find all numbers of the form $135xy$ that are divisible by 45.
4. Find all numbers of the form $517xy$ that are divisible by 89.

Divisibility Rules

Divisibility by 2 or 5: A number is divisible by 2 or 5 if the last digit is divisible by 2 or 5.

Divisibility by 3 or 9: all such numbers, the sum of whose digits are divisible by 3 (or 9) are divisible by 3 (or 9).

Divisibility by 4: A number is divisible by 4 if the last 2-digits are divisible by 4.

Divisibility by 6: A number is divisible by 6 if it is simultaneously divisible by 2 and 3.

Divisibility by 8: A number is divisible by 8 if the last 3-digits of the number are divisible by 8.

Divisibility by 11: A number is divisible by 11, if the difference of the sum of the digits in the odd places and the sum of the digits in the even places is zero or is divisible by 11.

Divisibility by 12: All numbers divisible by 3 and 4 are divisible by 12.

Divisibility by 7, 11 or 13: The integer n is divisible by 7, 11 or 13 if and only if the difference of the number of its thousands and the remainder of its division by 1000 is divisible by 7, 11 or 13.

For example: 473312 is divisible by 7 since the difference between $473 - 312 = 161$ is divisible by 7.

Even Numbers: All integers that are divisible by 2 are even numbers. They are also denoted by $2n$.

Example: 2, 4, 6, 12, 122, –2, –4, –12.

Also note that zero is an even number.

2 is the lowest positive even number.

Odd Numbers: All integers that are not divisible by 2 are odd numbers. Odd numbers leave a remainder of 1 on being divided by 2. They are denoted by $2n + 1$ or $2n - 1$.

Lowest positive odd number is 1.

Example: –1, –3, –7, –35, 3, 11, etc.

Complex Numbers: The arithmetic combination of real numbers and imaginary numbers are called complex numbers.

Alternately: All numbers of the form $a + ib$, where $i = \sqrt{-1}$ are called complex numbers.

Twin Primes: A pair of prime numbers are said to be twin prime when they differ by 2.

Example: 3 and 5 are twin primes, so also are 11 and 13.

Perfect Numbers: A number n is said to be a perfect number if the sum of all the divisors of n (including n) is equal to $2n$.

Example: $6 = 1 \times 2 \times 3$ sum of the divisors $= 1 + 2 + 3 + 6 = 12 = 2 \times 6$

$28 = 1, 2, 4, 7, 14, 28, = 56 = 2 \times 28$

Task for student: Find all perfect numbers below 1000.

Mixed Numbers: A number that has both an integral and a fractional part is known as a mixed number.

Triangular Numbers: A number which can be represented as the sum of consecutive natural numbers starting with 1 are called as triangular numbers.

e.g.: $1 + 2 + 3 + 4 = 10$. So, 10 is a triangular number.

Certain Rules

1. Of n consecutive whole numbers $a, a + 1 \ldots a + n - 1$, one and only one is divisible by n.
2. *Mixed numbers:* A number that has both the integral and fractional parts is known as mixed number.
3. If a nu mber n can be represented as the product of two numbers p and q, that is, $n = p \cdot q$, then we say that the number n is divisible by p and by q and each of the numbers p and q is a divisor of the number n. Also, each factor of p and q would be a divisor of n.
4. Any number n can be represented in the decimal system of numbers as
   $N = a_k \times 10^k + a_{k-1} \times 10^{k-1} + \ldots + a_i \times 10 + a_0$
   Example: 2738 can be written as: $2 \times 10^3 + 7 \times 10^2 + 3 \times 10^1 + 8 \times 10^0$
5. 3^n will always have an even number of tens. (Example: 2 in 27,8 in 81,24 in 243,72 in 729 and so on.)
6. A sum of 5 consecutive whole numbers will always be divisible by 5.

7. The difference between 2 two digit numbers: $(xy) - (yx)$ will be divisible by 9
8. The square of an odd number when divided by 8 will always leave a remainder of 1.
9. The product of 3 consecutive natural numbers is divisible by 6.
10. The product of 3 consecutive natural numbers the first of which is even is divisible by 24.
11. Products:
    Odd × odd = odd
    Odd × even = even
    Even × even = even
12. All numbers not divisible by 3 have the property that their square will have a remainder of 1 when divided by 3.
13. $(a^2 + b^2)/(b^2 + c^2) = (a^2/b^2)$ if $a/b = b/c$.
14. The product of any r consecutive integers (numbers) is divisible by $r!$
15. If m and n are two integers then $(m + n)!$ is divisible by $m!n!$
16. Difference between any number and the number obtained by writing the digits in reverse order is divisible by 9. (for any number of digits)
17. Any number written in the form $10^n - 1$ is divisible by 3 and 9.
18. If a numerical expression contains no parentheses, first the operations of the third stage (involution or raising a number to a power) are performed, then the operations of the second stage (multiplication and division) and, finally, the operations of the first stage (addition and subtraction) are performed. In this case, the operations of one and the same stage are performed in the sequence indicated by the notation. If an expression contains parentheses, then the operation indicated in the parentheses are to be performed first and then all the remaining operations. In this case, operations of the numbers in parentheses as well as standing without parentheses are performed in the order indicated above.

    If a fractional expression is evaluated, then the operations indicated in the numerator and denominator of the function are performed and the first result is divided by the second.
19. $(a)^n/(a + 1)$ leaves a remainder of
    a if n is odd
    1 if n is even
20. $(a + 1)^n/a$ will always give a remainder of 1.
21. For any natural number n, n^5 has the same units digit as n has.
22. For any natural number: $n^3 - n$ is divisible by 6.
23. The expression $\frac{1\times2\times3\times4\times\cdots(n-1)}{n}$ gives a remainder of $(n - 1)$ if n is prime.

    In case n is composite, the remainder would be 0.

REMAINDER THEOREM

Consider the following question:

$$17 \times 23$$

Concept Explainer
Scan this QR code to access conceptual videos on Remainder Theorem

Suppose you have to find the remainder of this expression when divided by 12.

We can write this as:

$$17 \times 23 = (12 + 5) \times (12 + 11)$$

Which when expanded gives us:

$$12 \times 12 + 12 \times 11 + 5 \times 12 + 5 \times 11$$

You will realise that, when this expression is divided by 12, the remainder will only depend on the last term above:

Thus, $\frac{12\times12+12\times11+5\times12+5\times11}{12}$ gives the same remainder as $\frac{5\times11}{12}$

Hence, 7.

This is the remainder when 17 × 23 is divided by 12.

Learning Point: In order to find the remainder of 17 × 23 when divided by 12, you need to look at the individual remainders of 17 and 23 when divided by 12. The respective remainders (5 and 11) will give you the remainder of the original expression when divided by 12.

Mathematically, this can be written as:

The remainder of the expression $[A \times B \times C + D \times E]/M$, will be the same as the remainder of the expression $[A_R \times B_R \times C_R + D_R \times E_R]/M$.

Where A_R is the remainder when A is divided by M,
B_R is the remainder when B is divided by M,
C_R is the remainder when C is divided by M,
D_R is the remainder when D is divided by M and
E_R is the remainder when E is divided by M.

We call this transformation as the remainder theorem transformation and denote it by the sign $\xrightarrow{R}$

Thus, the remainder of 1421 × 1423 × 1425 when divided by 12 can be given as:

$$\frac{1421\times1423\times1425}{12} \xrightarrow{R} \frac{5\times7\times9}{12} = \frac{35\times9}{12} \xrightarrow{R} \frac{11\times9}{12}$$

$\xrightarrow{R}$ gives us a remainder of 3.

In the above question, we have used a series of remainder theorem transformations (denoted by $\xrightarrow{R}$) and equality transformations to transform a difficult looking expression into a simple expression.

Try to solve the following questions on remainder theorem:

Find the remainder in each of the following cases:

1. 17 × 23 × 126 × 38 divided by 8.

2. 243 × 245 × 247 × 249 × 251 divided by 12.

3. $\frac{173 \times 261}{13} + \frac{248 \times 249 \times 250}{15}$

4. $\frac{1021 \times 2021 \times 3021}{14}$

5. $\frac{37 \times 43 \times 51}{7} + \frac{137 \times 143 \times 151}{9}$

USING NEGATIVE REMAINDERS

Consider the following question:

Find the remainder when: 14 × 15 is divided by 8.

The obvious approach in this case would be

$$\frac{14 \times 15}{8} \xrightarrow{R} \frac{6 \times 7}{8} = \frac{42}{8} \xrightarrow{R} 2$$

However there is another option by which you can solve the same question:

When 14 is divided by 8, the remainder is normally seen as + 6. However, there might be times when using the negative value of the remainder might give us more convenience. Which is why you should know the following process:

Concept Note: Remainders by definition are always non-negative. Hence, even when we divide a number like –27 by 5 we say that the remainder is 3 (and not –2). However, looking at the negative value of the remainder—it has its own advantages in mathematics as it results in reducing calculations.

Thus, when a number like 13 is divided by 8, the remainder being 5, the negative remainder is – 3.

Note: It is in this context that we mention numbers like 13, 21, 29, etc., as $8n + 5$ or $8n - 3$ numbers.

Thus, $\frac{14 \times 15}{8}$ will give us $\frac{-2 \times -1}{8}$ $R \rightarrow 2$.

Consider the advantage this process will give you in the following question:

$$\frac{51 \times 52}{53} \xrightarrow{R} \frac{-2 \times -1}{53} \xrightarrow{R} 2$$

(The alternative will involve long calculations. Hence, the principle is that you should use negative remainders wherever you can. They can make life much simpler!)

What if the Answer Comes Out Negative?

For instance, $\frac{62 \times 63 \times 64}{66} \xrightarrow{R} \frac{-4 \times -3 \times -2}{66}$ $R \rightarrow \frac{-24}{66}$

But, we know that a remainder of –24, equals a remainder of 42 when divided by 66. Hence, the answer is 42.

Of course, nothing stops you from using positive and negative remainders at the same time in order to solve the same question—

Thus, $\frac{17 \times 19}{9} \xrightarrow{R} \frac{(-1) \times (1)}{9}$ $R \rightarrow -1$ $R \rightarrow 8$

Dealing with Large Powers There are two tools which are effective in order to deal with large powers—

(a) If you can express the expression in the form $\frac{(ax+1)^n}{a}$, the remainder will become 1 directly. In such a case, no matter how large the value of the power n is, the remainder is 1.

For instance, $\frac{(37^{12635})}{9} \xrightarrow{R} \frac{(1^{12635})}{9} \xrightarrow{R} 1.$

In such a case, the value of the power does not matter.

(b) $\frac{(ax-1)^n}{a}$. In such a case using –1 as the remainder, it will be evident that the remainder will be +1 if n is even and it will be –1 (Hence a – 1) when n is odd.

e.g.: $\frac{31^{127}}{8} \xrightarrow{R} \frac{(-1)^{127}}{8} \xrightarrow{R} \frac{(-1)}{8} \xrightarrow{R} 7$

ANOTHER IMPORTANT POINT

Suppose you were asked to find the remainder of 14 divided by 4. It is clearly visible that the answer should be 2.

But consider the following process:

$14/4 = 7/2 \xrightarrow{R} 1$ (The answer has changed!!)

What has happened?

We have transformed 14/4 into 7/2 by dividing the numerator and the denominator by 2. The result is that the original remainder 2 is also divided by 2 giving us 1 as the remainder. In order to take care of this problem, we need to reverse the effect of the division of the remainder by 2. This is done by multiplying the final remainder by 2 to get the correct answer.

Note: In any question on remainder theorem, you should try to cancel out parts of the numerator and denominator as much as you can, since it directly reduces the calculations required.

APPLICATION OF REMAINDER THEOREM

Finding the last 2-digits of an expression:

Suppose you had to find the last 2-digits of the expression:

22 × 31 × 44 × 27 × 37 × 43

The remainder the above expression will give when it is divided by 100 is the answer to the above question.

Hence, to answer the question above, find the remainder of the expression when it is divided by 100.

Solution: $\frac{22 \times 31 \times 44 \times 27 \times 37 \times 43}{100}$

$= \frac{22 \times 31 \times 11 \times 27 \times 37 \times 43}{25}$ (on dividing by 4)

$$\xrightarrow{R} \frac{22\times6\times11\times2\times12\times18}{25} = \frac{132\times22\times216}{25}$$

$$\xrightarrow{R} \frac{7\times22\times16}{25}$$

$$= \frac{154\times16}{25} \xrightarrow{R} \frac{4\times16}{25} \xrightarrow{R} 14$$

Thus, the remainder being 14, (after division by 4). The actual remainder should be 56.

[Do not forget to multiply by 4 !!]

Hence, the last 2-digits of the answer will be 56.

Using negative remainders here would have helped further.

Note: Similarly finding the last 3-digits of an expression means finding the remainder when the expression is divided by 1000.

THE PRIME NUMBER DIVISOR RULE

This rule states that: If '*P*' is a prime number then:

The remainder of the expression $\frac{A^{P-1}}{P}$ is 1. (Provided *A* is not a multiple of *P*)

For example: The remainder of $\frac{24^{82}}{83} = 1$

SPLITTING THE DENOMINATOR INTO CO-PRIME NUMBERS:

This is also sometimes referred to as the 'Chinese Remainder Theorem'. It is useful when you have to find the remainder when there is a large denominator, and no other short cuts are working. It is best explained through an example.

Suppose you were trying to find the remainder of $\frac{107^{1444}}{136}$. You can split the denominator into two co-prime numbers as 17 and 8.

First find the remainder of $\frac{107^{1444}}{17} \rightarrow \frac{5^{1444}}{17} = \frac{5^{16n}\times5^4}{17} \rightarrow \frac{1\times5^4}{17} \rightarrow$ Remainder = 13. This means that 107^{1444} is a $17n + 13$ number.

Next, find the remainder of $\frac{107^{1444}}{8} \rightarrow \frac{3^{1444}}{8} = \frac{3^{2n}}{8} \rightarrow$ Remainder = 1. This means that 107^{1444} is a $8n + 1$ number.

The next step is to find a number below 136 that is both a $17n + 13$ as well as an $8n + 1$ number. That number would be the answer.

The list of $17n + 13$ numbers below 136 is: 13, 30, 47, 64, 81, 98, 115 and 132. 81 can be seen to be an $8n + 1$ number too.

Thus, the correct answer is 81.

Exercise for Self-practice

1. Find the remainder when 73 + 75 + 78 + 57 + 197 is divided by 34.
(a) 32 (b) 4
(c) 15 (d) 28
2. Find the remainder when 73 × 75 × 78 × 57 × 197 is divided by 34.
(a) 22 (b) 30
(c) 15 (d) 28
3. Find the remainder when 73 × 75 × 78 × 57 × 197 × 37 is divided by 34.
(a) 32 (b) 30
(c) 15 (d) 28
4. Find the remainder when 43^{197} is divided by 7.
(a) 2 (b) 4
(c) 6 (d) 1
5. Find the remainder when 51^{203} is divided by 7.
(a) 4 (b) 2
(c) 1 (d) 6
6. Find the remainder when 59^{28} is divided by 7.
(a) 2 (b) 4
(c) 6 (d) 1
7. Find the remainder when 67^{99} is divided by 7.
(a) 2 (b) 4
(c) 6 (d) 1
8. Find the remainder when 75^{80} is divided by 7.
(a) 4 (b) 3
(c) 2 (d) 6
9. Find the remainder when 41^{77} is divided by 7.
(a) 2 (b) 1
(c) 6 (d) 4
10. Find the remainder when 21^{875} is divided by 17.
(a) 8 (b) 13
(c) 16 (d) 9
11. Find the remainder when 54^{124} is divided by 17.
(a) 4 (b) 5
(c) 13 (d) 15
12. Find the remainder when 83^{261} is divided by 17.
(a) 13 (b) 9
(c) 8 (d) 2
13. Find the remainder when 25^{102} is divided by 17.
(a) 13 (b) 15
(c) 4 (d) 2

ANSWER KEY

1. (b)	2. (a)	3. (a)	4. (d)	5. (a)
6. (b)	7. (d)	8. (a)	9. (c)	10. (b)
11. (a)	12. (d)	13. (c)		

SOLUTIONS AND SHORTCUTS

1. The remainder would be given by: (5 + 7 + 10 + 23 + 27)/34 = 72/34 → remainder = 4. Option (b) is correct.

2. The remainder would be given by: $(5 \times 7 \times 10 \times 23 \times 27)/34 \rightarrow 35 \times 230 \times 27/34 \rightarrow 1 \times 26 \times 27/34 = 702/34 \rightarrow$ remainder = 22. Option (a) is correct.
3. The remainder would be given by: $(5 \times 7 \times 10 \times 23 \times 27 \times 3)/34 \rightarrow 35 \times 230 \times 27 \times 3/34 \rightarrow 1 \times 26 \times 81/34 \rightarrow 26 \times 13/34 = 338/34 \rightarrow$ remainder = 32. Option (a) is correct.
4. $43^{197}/7 \rightarrow 1^{197}/7 \rightarrow$ remainder = 1. Option (d) is correct.
5. $51^{203}/7 \rightarrow 2^{203}/7 = (2^3)^{67} \times 2^2/7 = 8^{67} \times 4/7 \rightarrow$ remainder = 4. Option (a) is correct.
6. $59^{28}/7 \rightarrow 3^{28}/7 = (3^6)^4 \times 3^4/7 = 729^6 \times 81/7 \rightarrow$ remainder = 4. Option (b) is correct.
7. $67^{99}/7 \rightarrow 4^{99}/7 = (4^3)^{33}/7 = 64^{33}/7 \rightarrow$ remainder = 1. Option (d) is correct.
8. $75^{80}/7 \rightarrow 5^{80}/7 = (5^6)^{13} \times 5^2/7 \rightarrow 1^{13} \times 25/7 \rightarrow$ remainder = 4. Option (a) is correct.
9. $41^{77}/7 \rightarrow 6^{77}/7 \rightarrow$ remainder = 6 (as the expression is in the form $a^n/(a+1)$. Option (c) is correct.
10. $21^{875}/17 \rightarrow 4^{875}/17 = (4^4)^n \times 4^3/17 = 256^n \times 64/17 \rightarrow 1^n \times 13/17 \rightarrow$ remainder = 13. Option (b) is correct.
11. $54^{124}/17 \rightarrow 3^{124}/17$. At this point, like in each of the other questions solved above, we need to plan the power of 3 which would give us a convenient remainder of either 1 or –1. As we start to look for remainders that powers of 3 would have when divided by 17, we get that at the power 3^6 the remainder is 15. If we convert this to –2, we will get that at the fourth power of 3^6, we should get a 16/17 situation (as $-2 \times -2 \times -2 \times -2 = 16$). This means that at a power of 3^{24}, we are getting a remainder of 16 or –1. Naturally then if we double the power to 3^{48}, the remainder would be 1.
With this thinking, we can restart solving the problem: $3^{124}/17 = 3^{48} \times 3^{48} \times 3^{24} \times 3^4/17 \rightarrow 1 \times 1 \times 16 \times 81/17 \rightarrow 16 \times 13/17 = 208/17 \rightarrow$ remainder = 4. Option (a) is correct.
(**Note:** That if we are dividing a number by 17 and if we see the remainder as 15, we can logically say that the remainder is –2 — even though negative remainders are not allowed in mathematics)
12. Using the logic developed in Question 11 above, we have $83^{261}/17 \rightarrow 15^{261}/17 \rightarrow$
$(-2)^{261}/17 \rightarrow (-2^4)^{65} \times (-2)/17 \rightarrow 16^{65} \times (-2)/17 \rightarrow (-1) \times (-2)/17 \rightarrow$ remainder = 2. Option (d) is correct.
13. $25^{102}/17 \rightarrow 8^{102}/17 = 2^{306}/17 = (2^4)^{76} \times 2^2/17 \rightarrow 16^{76} \times 4/17 \rightarrow 1 \times 4/17 \rightarrow$ remainder = 4. Option (c) is correct.

BASE SYSTEM

All the work that we carry out with numbers is called as the decimal system. In other words, we work in the decimal system. Why is it called decimal? It is because there are 10 digits in the system 0–9.

However, depending on the number of digits contained in the base system other number systems are also possible. Thus, a number system with base 2 is called the binary number system and will have only 2-digits 0 and 1. Some of the most commonly used systems are: Binary (base 2), Octal (base 8), Hexadecimal (base 16).

Binary system has 2-digits : 0, 1. Octal has 8 digits : – 0, 1, 2, 3, … 7.

Hexadecimal has 16 digits – 0, 1, 2, … 9, *A*, *B*, *C*, *D*, *E*, *F*. Where *A* has a value 10, *B* = 11 and so on.

Before coming to the questions asked under this category, let us first look at a few issues with regard to converting numbers between different base systems.

1. Conversion from any base system into decimal:

Suppose you have to write the decimal equivalent of the base 8 number 146_8.

In such a case, follow the following structure for conversion:

$$146_8 = 1 \times 8^2 + 4 \times 8^1 + 6 \times 8^0 = 64 + 32 + 6 = 102$$

Note: If you remember the process, for writing the value of any random number, say 146, in our decimal system (base 10), we use: $1 \times 10^2 + 4 \times 10^1 + 6 \times 10^0$. All you need to change, in case you are trying to write the value of the number in base 8, is that you replace 10 with 8 in every power.

Try to write the decimal equivalents of the following numbers:

143_5, 143_6, 143_7, 143_8, 143_9

1256_7, 1256_8, 1256_9

2. Conversion of a number in decimals into any base:

Suppose you have to find out the value of the decimal number 347 in base 6. The following process is to be adopted:

Step 1: Find the highest power of the base (6 in this case) that is contained in 347. In this case, you will realise that the value of $6^3 = 216$ is contained in 347, while the value of $6^4 = 1296$ is not contained in 347. Hence, we realise that the highest power of 6 contained in 347 is 3. This should make you realise that the number has to be constructed by using the powers 6^0, 6^1, 6^2, 6^3 respectively. Hence, a 4-digit number.

Structure of number: – – – –

Step 2: We now need to investigate, how many times each of the powers of 6 is contained in 347. For this, we first start with the highest power as found above. Thus we can see that 6^3 (216) is contained in 347 once. Hence, our number now becomes:

1 – – –

That is, we now know that the first digit of the number is 1. Besides, when we have written the number 1 in this place, we have accounted for a value of 216 out of 347. This leaves us with 131 to account for.

We now need to look for the number of times 6^2 is contained in 131. We can easily see that $6^2 = 36$ is contained in 131 three times. Thus, we write 3 as the next digit of our number which will now look like:

1 3 – –

In other words, we now know that the first 2-digits of the number are 13. Besides, when we have written the number 3 in this place, we have accounted for a value of 108 out of 131 which was left to be accounted for. This leaves us with 131–108 = 23 to account for.

We now need to look for the number of times 6^1 is contained in 23. We can easily see that $6^1 = 6$ is contained in 23 three times. Thus, we write 3 as the next digit of our number which will now look like:

1 3 3 –

In other words, we now know that the first 3-digits of the number are 133. Besides, when we have written the number 3 in this place, we have accounted for a value of 18 out of the 23 which was left to be accounted for. This leaves us with 23 – 18 = 5 to account for.

The last digit of the number corresponds to $6^0 = 1$. In order to make a value of 5 in this place, we will obviously need to use this power of 6, 5 times, thus, giving us the final digit as 5. Hence, our number is:

1 3 3 5

A few points you, should know about base systems:

(i) In single digits there is no difference between the value of the number—whichever base we take. For example, the equality $5_6 = 5_7 = 5_8 = 5_9 = 5_{10}$.

(ii) Suppose you have a number in base x. When you convert this number into its decimal value, the value should be such that when it is divided by x, the remainder should be equal to the units digit of the number in base x.

In other words, 342_8 will be a number of the form $8n + 2$ in base 10. You can use this principle for checking your conversion calculations.

Illustrations

1. The number of x digit numbers in nth base system will be

(a) n^x (b) $n^x - 1$
(c) $n^x - n$ (d) $n^x - n^{(x-1)}$

Solution: Base $\rightarrow n$, digit $\rightarrow x$

So, required number of numbers = $n^x - n^{(x-1)}$

2. The number of 2-digit numbers in binary system is

(a) 2 (b) 90
(c) 10 (d) 4

Solution: By using the formula, we get the required number of numbers = $2^2 - 2^1 = 2$

$\Rightarrow$ Option (a)

3. The number of 5 digit numbers in binary system is

(a) 48 (b) 16
(c) 32 (d) 20

Solution: Required number of numbers = $2^5 - 2^4 = 32 - 16 = 16$

$\Rightarrow$ Option (b)

4. I celebrate my birthday on 12th January on earth. On which date would I have to celebrate my birthday if I were on a planet where binary system is being used for counting. (The number of days, months and years are same on both the planets.)

(a) 11th Jan (b) 111th Jan
(c) 110th Jan (d) 1100th Jan

Solution: On earth (decimal system is used).

12th Jan $\Rightarrow$ 12th Jan

The 12th day on the planet where binary system is being used will be called

$(12)_{10} = (?)_2$

$$= \frac{1}{2^3}\ \frac{1}{2^2}\ \frac{0}{2^1}\ \frac{0}{2^0}$$

i.e., 1100th day on that planet

So, 12th January on earth = 1100th January on that planet

$\Rightarrow$ Option (d)

5. My year of birth is 1982. What would the year have been instead of 1982 if base 12 were used (for counting) instead of decimal system?

(a) 1182 (b) 1022
(c) 2082 (d) 1192

Solution: The required answer will be equal to $(1982)_{10} = (?)_{12}$.

$$= \frac{1}{12^3}\ \frac{1}{12^2}\ \frac{9}{12^1}\ \frac{2}{12^0} \rightarrow$$

$1 \times 12^3 + 1 \times 12^2 + 9 \times 12^1 + 2 \times 9^0 = 1728 + 144 + 108 + 2 = 1982$

Hence, the number $(1192)_{12}$ represents 1982 in our base system.

$\Rightarrow$ Option (d)

6. 203 in base 5 when converted to base 8, becomes

(a) 61 (b) 53
(c) 145 (d) 65

Solution: $(203)_5 = (?)_{10}$

$= 2 \times 5^2 + 0 \times 5^1 + 3 \times 5^0$

$= 50 + 0 + 3 = 53$

Now,

$(53)_{10} = (?)8$

$$= \frac{6}{8^1}\ \frac{5}{8^0}$$

$= (203)_5 = (65)_8$

$\Rightarrow$ Option (d)

7. $(52)_7 + 46_8 = (?)_{10}$

(a) $(75)_{10}$ (b) $(50)_{10}$
(c) $(39)_{39}$ (d) $(28)_{10}$

Solution: $(52)_7 = (5 \times 7^1 + 2 \times 7^0)_{10} = (37)_{10}$
also, $(46)_8 = (4 \times 8^1 + 6 \times 8^0)_{10} = (38)_{10}$
sum $= (75)_{10}$

$\Rightarrow$ Option (a)

8. $(23)_5 + (47)_9 = (?)_8$
(a) 70 (b) 35
(c) 64 (d) 18

Solution: $(23)_5 = (2 \times 5^1 + 3 \times 5^0)_{10} = (13)_{10}$
also, $(47)_9 = (4 \times 9^1 + 7 \times 9^0)_{10} = (43)_{10}$
sum $= (13)_{10} + (43)_{10} = (56)_{10} \rightarrow (70)_8$

$\Rightarrow$ Option (a)

9. $(11)_2 + (22)_3 + (33)_4 + (44)_5 + (55)_6 + (66)_7 + (77)_8 + (88)_9 = (?)_{10}$
(a) 396 (b) 276
(c) 250 (d) 342

Solution: $(11)_2 = (1 \times 2^1 + 1 \times 2^0)_{10} = (3)_{10}$
$(22)_3 = (2 \times 3^1 + 2 \times 3^0)_{10} = (8)_{10}$
$(33)_4 = (3 \times 4^1 + 3 \times 4^0)_{10} = (15)_{10}$
$(44)_5 = (4 \times 5^1 + 4 \times 5^0)_{10} = (24)_{10}$
$(55)_6 = (5 \times 6^1 + 5 \times 6^0)_{10} = (35)_{10}$
$(66)_7 = (6 \times 7^1 + 6 \times 7^0)_{10} = (48)_{10}$
$(77)_8 = (7 \times 8^1 + 7 \times 8^0)_{10} = (63)_{10}$
$(88)_9 = (8 \times 9^1 + 8 \times 9^0)_{10} = (80)_{10}$
sum $= (276)_{10}$

$\Rightarrow$ Option (b)

10. $(24)_5 \times (32)_5 = (?)_5$
(a) 1423 (b) 1422
(c) 1420 (d) 1323

Solution: $(24)_5 = 14_{10}$ and $32_5 = 17_{10}$. Hence, the required answer can be obtained by $14 \times 17 = 238_{10} = 1 \times 5^3 + 4 \times 5^2 + 2 \times 5^1 + 3 \times 5^0 \rightarrow 1423$ as the correct answer.

Alternately, you could multiply directly in base 5 as follows:

$$\begin{array}{r} (2\ 4) \\ \times\ (3\ 2) \\ \hline (1\ 4\ 2\ 3) \end{array}$$

Unit's digit of the answer would correspond to: $4 \times 2 = 8 \rightarrow 13_5$. Hence, we write 3 in the units place and carry over 1.

(**Note:** That in this process when we are doing 4×2, we are effectively multiplying individual digits of one number with individual digits of the other number. In such a case, we can write $4 \times 2 = 8$ by assuming that both the numbers are in decimal system as the value of a single digit in any base is equal.)

The tens digit will be obtained by: $2 \times 2 + 4 \times 3 = 16 + 1 = 17 \rightarrow 32_5$

Hence, we write 2 in the tens place and carry over 3 to the hundreds place.

Where we get $3 \times 2 + 3 = 9 \rightarrow 14$

Hence, the answer is 14.

$\Rightarrow$ Option (a)

11. In base 8, the greatest 4-digit perfect square is
(a) 9801 (b) 1024
(c) 8701 (d) 7601

Solution: In base 10, the greatest 4-digit perfect square = 9801

In base 9, the greatest 4-digits perfect square = 8701

In base 8, the greatest 4-digits perfect square = 7601

Alternately, multiply $(77)_8 \times (77)_8$ to get 7601 as the answer.

I would encourage the student to try to multiply these two numbers in base 8 to get the value.

Unit's Digit

(A) The unit's digit of an expression can be calculated by getting the remainder while the expression is divided by 10.

Thus, for example if we have to find the units digit of the expression:

$$17 \times 22 \times 36 \times 54 \times 27 \times 31 \times 63$$

We try to find the remainder –

$$\frac{17 \times 22 \times 36 \times 54 \times 27 \times 31 \times 63}{10} \xrightarrow{R} \frac{7 \times 2 \times 6 \times 4 \times 7 \times 3}{10}$$

$$= \frac{14 \times 24 \times 21}{10} \xrightarrow{R} \frac{4 \times 4 \times 1}{10} = \frac{16}{10} \xrightarrow{R} 6$$

Hence, the required answer is 6.

This could have been directly obtained by multiplying: $7 \times 2 \times 6 \times 4 \times 7 \times 1 \times 3$ and only accounting for the unit's digit.

(B) Unit's digits in the contexts of powers — Study the following table carefully.

Unit's digit when 'N' is raised to a power

Number Ending With	*Value of power* 1	2	3	4	5	6	7	8	9
1	1	1	1	1	1	1	1	1	1
2	2	4	8	6	2	4	8	6	2
3	3	9	7	1	3	9	7	1	3
4	4	6	4	6	4	6	4	6	4
5	5	5	5	5	5	5	5	5	5
6	6	6	6	6	6	6	6	6	6
7	7	9	3	1	7	9	3	1	7
8	8	4	2	6	8	4	2	6	8
9	9	1	9	1	9	1	9	1	9
0	0	0	0	0	0	0	0	0	0

In the table above, if you look at the columns corresponding to the power 5 or 9 you will realise that the unit's digit for all numbers is repeated (i.e., it is 1 for 1, 2 for, 3 for 3….9 for 9).

This means that whenever we have any number whose unit's digit is '*x*' and it is raised to a power of the form $4n + 1$, the value of the unit's digit of the answer will be the same as the original units digit.

Illustrations: $(1273)^{101}$ will give a unit's digit of 3. $(1547)^{25}$ will give a unit's digit of 7 and so forth.

Thus, the above table can be modified into the form –

Value of Power

Number Ending in	*If the value of the Power is* $4n + 1$	$4n + 2$	$4n + 3$	$4n$
1	1	1	1	1
2	2	4	8	6
3	3	9	7	1
4	4	6	4	6
5	5	5	5	5
6	6	6	6	6
7	7	9	3	1
8	8	4	2	6
9	9	1	9	1

[Remember, at this point that we had said (in the Back to School section of Part 1) that all natural numbers can be expressed in the form $4n + x$. Hence, with the help of the logic that helps us build this table, we can easily derive the units digit of any number when it is raised to a power.]

A Special Case

Question: What will be the unit's digit of $(1273)^{122!}$?

Solution: 122! is a number of the form $4n$. Hence, the answer should be 1. [**Note:** 1 here is derived by thinking of it as 3 (for $4n + 1$), 9 (for $4n + 2$), 7 (for $4n + 3$), 1(for $4n$)]

Exercise for Self-practice

Find the unit's digit in each of the following cases:

1. $2^2 \times 4^4 \times 6^6 \times 8^8$

2. $1^1 \times 2^2 \times 3^3 \times 4^4 \times 5^5 \times 6^6 \dots \times 100^{100}$

3. $17 \times 23 \times 51 \times 32 + 15 \times 17 \times 16 \times 22$

4. $13 \times 17 \times 22 \times 34 + 12 \times 6 \times 4 \times 3 - 13 \times 33$

5. $37^{123} \times 43^{144} \times 57^{226} \times 32^{127} \times 52^{5!}$

6. $67 \times 37 \times 43 \times 91 \times 42 \times 33 \times 42$

(a) 2 (b) 6
(c) 8 (d) 4

7. $67 \times 35 \times 43 \times 91 \times 47 \times 33 \times 49$

(a) 1 (b) 9
(c) 5 (d) 6

8. $67 \times 35 \times 45 \times 91 \times 42 \times 33 \times 81$

(a) 2 (b) 4
(c) 0 (d) 8

9. $67 \times 35 \times 45 + 91 \times 42 \times 33 \times 82$

(a) 8 (b) 7
(c) 0 (d) 5

10. $(52)^{97} \times (43)^{72}$

(a) 2 (b) 6
(c) 8 (d) 4

11. $(55)^{75} \times (93)^{175} \times (107)^{275}$

(a) 7 (b) 3
(c) 5 (d) 0

12. $(173)^{45} \times (152)^{77} \times (777)^{999}$

(a) 2 (b) 4
(c) 8 (d) 6

13. $81 \times 82 \times 83 \times 84 \times 86 \times 87 \times 88 \times 89$

(a) 0 (b) 6
(c) 2 (d) 4

14. $82^{43} \times 83^{44} \times 84^{97} \times 86^{98} \times 87^{105} \times 88^{94}$

(a) 2 (b) 6
(c) 4 (d) 8

15. $432 \times 532 + 532 \times 974 + 537 \times 531 + 947 \times 997$

(a) 5 (b) 6
(c) 9 (d) 8

ANSWER KEY

6. (d)	7. (c)	8. (c)	9. (b)	10. (a)
11. (c)	12. (c)	13. (b)	14. (b)	15. (d)

SOLUTIONS AND SHORTCUTS

1. The unit's digit would be given by the unit's digit of the multiplication of $4 \times 6 \times 6 \times 6 = 4$
2. 0
3. $7 \times 3 \times 1 \times 2 + 0 \rightarrow 2 + 0 = 2$
4. $8 + 4 - 9 \rightarrow 3$
5. $3 \times 1 \times 9 \times 8 \times 6 = 6$
6. $7 \times 7 \times 3 \times 1 \times 2 \times 3 \times 2 = 4$
7. Since we have a 5 multiplied with odd numbers, the units digit would naturally be 5.
8. $5 \times 2 \rightarrow 0$
9. $5 + 2 \rightarrow 7$
10. $2 \times 1 \rightarrow 2$
11. $5 \times 7 \times 3 \rightarrow 5$
12. $3 \times 2 \times 3 \rightarrow 8$
13. $2 \times 3 \times 4 \times 6 \times 7 \times 8 \times 9 \rightarrow 6$
14. $8 \times 1 \times 4 \times 6 \times 7 \times 4 \rightarrow 6$
15. $4 + 8 + 7 + 9 \rightarrow 8$

WORKED-OUT PROBLEMS

Problem 1.1: Find the number of zeroes in the factorial of the number 18.

Solution: 18! contains 15 and 5, which combined with one even number give zeroes. Also, 10 is also contained in 18!, which will give an additional zero. Hence, 18! contains 3 zeroes and the last digit will always be zero.

Problem 1.2: Find the numbers of zeroes in 27!

Solution: $27! = 27 \times 26 \times 25 \times \ldots \times 20 \times \ldots \times 15 \times \ldots \times 10 \times \ldots \times 5 \times \ldots \times 1$

A zero can be formed by combining any number containing 5 multiplied by any even number. Similarly, everytime a number ending in zero is found in the product, it will add an additional zero. For this problem, note that $25 = 5 \times 5$ will give 2 zeroes and zeroes will also be obtained by 20, 15, 10 and 5. Hence 27! will have 6 zeroes.

Short-cut method: Number of zeroes is $27! \rightarrow [27/5] + [27/25]$ where $[x]$ indicates the integer just lower than the fraction Hence, $[27/5] = 5$ and $[27/5^2] = 1$, 6 zeroes

Problem 1.3: What exact power of 5 divides 87!?

Solution: $[87/5] + [87/25] = 17 + 3 = 20$

Problem 1.4: What power of 8 exactly divides 25!?

Solution: If 8 were a prime number, the answer should be $[25/8] = 3$. But since 8 is not prime, use the following process.

The prime factors of 8 is $2 \times 2 \times 2$. For divisibility by 8, we need three twos. So, everytime we can find 3 twos, we add one to the power of 8 that divides 25! To count how we get 3 twos, we do the following. All even numbers will give one 'two' at least $[25/2] = 12$

Also, all numbers in 25! divisible by 2^2 will give an additional two $[25/2^2] = 6$

Further, all numbers in 25! divisible by 2^3 will give a third two. Hence $[25!/2^3] = 3$

And all numbers in 25! divisible by 2^4 will give a fourth two. Hence $[25!/2^4] = 1$

Hence, total number of twos in 25! is 22. For a number to be divided by 8, we need three twos. Hence, since 25! has 22 twos, it will be divided by 8 seven times.

Exercise for Self-practice

(a) What is the highest power of 30 that will exactly divide 128!
Hint: $[128/5] + [128/5^2] + [128/5^3]$

(b) What is the highest power of 210 that will exactly divide 142!

Problem 1.5: Find the last digit in the expression $(36472)^{123!} \times (34767)^{76!}$.

Solution: If we try to formulate a pattern for 2 and its powers and their units digit, we see that the units digit for the powers of 2 goes as: 2, 4, 8, 6, 2, 4, 8, 6, 2, 4, 8, 6 and so on. The number 2 when raised to a power of $4n + 1$ will always give a units digit of 2. This also means that the units digit for 2^{4n} will always end in 6. The power of 36472 is 123! . 123! can be written in the form $4n$. Hence, $(36472)^{123!}$ will end in 6.

The second part of the expression is $(34767)^{76!}$. The units digit depends on the power of 7. If we try to formulate a pattern for 7 and its powers and their units digit, we see that the units digit for the powers of 7 go as: 7 9 3 1 7 9 3 1 and so on. This means that the units digit of the expression 7^{4n} will always be 1.

Since 76! can be written as a multiple of 4 as $4n$, we can conclude that the unit's digit in $(34767)^{76!}$ is 1.

Hence, the units digit of $(36472)^{123!} \times (34767)^{76!}$ will be 6.

Counting

Problem 1.6: Find the number of numbers between 100 to 200 if

(i) Both 100 and 200 are counted
(ii) Only one of 100 and 200 is counted
(iii) Neither 100 nor 200 is counted

Solution:

(i) Both ends included-Solution: $200 - 100 + 1 = 101$
(ii) One end included-Solution: $200 - 100 = 100$
(iii) Both ends excluded-Solution: $200 - 100 - 1 = 99$

Problem 1.7: Find the number of even numbers between 122 and 242 if

(i) Both ends are included
(ii) Only one end is included
(iii) Neither end is included

Solution:

(i) Both ends included—Solution: $(242 - 122)/2 = 60 + 1 = 61$
(ii) One end included-Solution: $(242 - 122)/2 = 60$
(iii) Both ends excluded-Solution: $(242 - 122)/2 - 1 = 59$

Exercise for Self-practice

Problem 1.8: Find the number of numbers between 300 to 400 (both included), that are not divisible by 2, 3, 4, and 5.

Solution: Total numbers: 101

Step 1: Not divisible by 2 = All even numbers rejected: 51
Numbers left: 50

Step 2: Of which: divisible by 3 = first number 300, last number 399. But even numbers have already been removed,

hence count out only odd numbers between 300 and 400 divisible by 3. This gives us that:
First number 303, last number 399, common difference 6

So, remove: [(399 – 303)/6] + 1 = 17

∴ 50 – 17 = 33 numbers left.

We do not need to remove additional terms for divisibility by 4 since this would eliminate only even numbers (which have already been eliminated).

Step 3: Remove from 33 numbers left all odd numbers that are divisible by 5 and not divisible by 3.

Between 300 to 400, the first odd number divisible by 5 is 305 and the last is 395 (since both ends are counted, we have 10 such numbers as: [(395 – 305)/10 + 1 = 10].

However, some of these 10 numbers have already been removed to get to 33 numbers.

Operation left: Of these 10 numbers, 305, 315…395, reduce all numbers that are also divisible by 3. Quick perusal shows that the numbers start with 315 and have common difference 30.

Hence, [(Last number – First number)/Difference + 1] = [(375 – 315)/30 + 1] = 3

These 3 numbers were already removed from the original 100. Hence, for numbers divisible by 5, we need to remove only those numbers that are odd, divisible by 5 but not by 3. There are 7 such numbers between 300 and 400.

So numbers left are: 33 – 7 = 26.

Exercise for Self-practice

Find the GCD, and the LCM of the following numbers:

(i) 360, 8400 (ii) 120, 144
(iii) 275, 180, 372, 156 (iv) 70, 112
(v) 75, 114 (vi) 544, 720

Problem 1.9: The ratio of the factorial of a number x to the square of the factorial of another number, which when increased by 50% gives the required number, is 1.25. Find the number x.

(a) 6 (b) 5
(c) 9 (d) None of these

Solution: Solve through options: Check for the conditions mentioned. When we check for option (a) we get 6 ! = 720 and $(4!)^2$ = 576 and we have 6 !$/(4!)^2$ = 1.25, which is the required ratio.

Hence, the answer is (a)

Problem 1.10: Three numbers A, B and C are such that the difference between the highest and the second highest two-digit numbers formed by using two of A, B and C is 5. Also, the smallest two two-digit numbers differ by 2. If $B > A > C$, then what is the value of B?

(a) 1 (b) 6 (c) 7 (d) 8

Solution: Since B is the largest digit, option (a) is rejected. Check for option (b).

If B is 6, then the two largest two-digit numbers are 65 and 60 (Since, their difference is 5) and we have $B = 6$, $A = 5$ and $C = 0$.

But with this solution, we are unable to meet the second condition. Hence (b) is not the answer. We also realise here that C cannot be 0.

Check for option (c).

B is 7, then the numbers. are 76 and 71 or 75 and 70. In both these cases, the smallest two two-digit numbers do not differ by 2.

Hence, the answer is not (c).
Hence, option (d) is the answer.
[To confirm, put $B = 8$, then the solution $A = 6$ and $C = 1$ satisfies the 2nd condition.]

Problem 1.11: Find the GCD and the LCM of the numbers P and Q where $P = 2^3 \times 5^3 \times 7^2$ and $Q = 3^3 \times 5^4$.

Solution: GCD or HCF is given by the lowest powers of the common factors.

Thus, GCD = 5^3.

LCM is given by the highest powers of all factors available.

Thus, LCM = $2^3 \times 3^3 \times 5^4 \times 7^2$

Problem 1.12: A school has 378 girl students and 675 boy students. The school is divided into strictly boys or strictly girls sections. All sections in the school have the same number of students. Given this information, what are the minimum number of sections in the school?

Solution: The answer will be given by the HCF of 378 and 675.

$$378 = 2 \times 3^3 \times 7$$
$$675 = 3^3 \times 5^2$$

Hence, HCF of the two is $3^3 = 27$

Hence, the number of sections is given by: $\frac{378}{27} + \frac{675}{27} =$ 14 + 25 = 39 sections.

Problem 1.13: The difference between the number of numbers from 2 to 100 which are not divisible by any other number except 1 and itself and the numbers which are divisible by at least one more number along with 1 and itself.

(a) 25 (b) 50
(c) 49 (d) can not be determined

Solution: From 2 to 100.

The number of numbers which are divisible by 1 and itself only = 25

Also, the number of numbers which are divisible by at least one more number except 1 and itself (i.e., composite numbers) 99 – 25 = 74

So, required difference = 74 – 25 = 49

⇒ Option (c)

Problem 1.14: If the sum of $(2n + 1)$ prime numbers where n N is an even number, then one of the prime numbers must be

(a) 2 (b) 3
(c) 5 (d) 7

Solution: For any n N, $2n + 1$ is odd.
Also, it is given in the problem that the sum of an odd number of prime numbers = even. Since all prime numbers except 2 are odd, the above condition will only be fulfilled if we have an (odd + odd + even) structure of addition. Since, the sum of the three prime numbers is said to be even, we have to include one even prime number. Hence, 2 being the only even prime number must be included.

If we add odd number of prime numbers, not including 2 (two), we will always get an odd number, because

$$\frac{\text{odd} + \text{odd} + \text{odd} + \text{-----} + \text{odd}}{\text{(an odd number of times)}} = \text{odd number}$$

⇒ Option (a)

Problem 1.15: A long part of wood of some length when cut into equal pieces each of 242 cms, leaves a small piece of length 98 cms. If this part were cut into equal pieces each of 22 cms, the length of the leftover wood would be

(a) 76 cm (b) 12 cm
(c) 11 cm (d) 10 cm

Solution: As 242 is divisible by 22, so the required length of left wood will be equal to the remainder when 98 is divided by 22:
Hence, 10 [98/22; remainder 10]
⇒ Option (d)

Problem 1.16: Find the number of numbers from 1 to 100 which are not divisible by 2.

(a) 51 (b) 50
(c) 49 (d) 48

Solution: The 1st number from 1 to 100, not divisible by 2 is 1 and the last number from 1 to 100, not divisible by 2 is 99.

Every alternate number (i.e, at the gap of 2) will not be divisible by 2 from 1 to 99. (1, 2, 3, - - - - , 95, 97, 99)

$$\text{So, the required number of nos} = \frac{\text{last no.} - \text{first no.}}{\text{gap (or step)}} + 1$$

$$= \frac{99-1}{2} + 1 = 50$$

⇒ Option (b)

Alternate method

Total number of numbers from 1 to 100 = 100 (1)

Now, if we count number of numbers from 1 to 100 which are divisible by 2 and subtract that from the total number of numbers from 1 to 100, as a result we will find the number of numbers from 1 to 100 which are not divisible by 2.

To count the number of numbers from 1 to 100 which are divisible by 2:

The 1st number which is divisible by 2 = 2
The last number which is divisible by 2 = 100
(2, 4, 6, ... , 96, 98, 100)
Gap/step between two consecutive numbers = 2
So, the number of numbers which are divisible by 2

$$= \frac{\text{last no.} - \text{first no.}}{\text{gap (or step)}} + 1 = \frac{100-2}{2} + 1 = 50 \quad (2)$$

So, from (1) & (2)
Required number of numbers = 100 – 50 = 50
⇒ Option (b)

Problem 1.17: Find the number of numbers from 1 to 100 which are not divisible by any one of 2 and 3.

(a) 16 (b) 17
(c) 18 (d) 33

Solution: From 1 to 100
Number of numbers not divisible by 2 and 3 = Total number of numbers–number of numbers divisible by either 2 or 3. (1)
Now, total number of numbers = 100 (2)
For number of numbers divisible by either 2 or 3:

$$\text{Number of numbers divisible by } 2 = \frac{\text{last no.} - \text{first no.}}{\text{gap (or step)}} + 1$$

$$= \frac{100-2}{2} + 1 = 50 \quad (3)$$

Now, the number of numbers divisible by 3 (but not by 2, as it has already been counted)

1st such number = 3 and the gap will be 6. Hence 2nd such number will be 9, 3rd number would be 15 and the last number would be 99. Hence this series is 3, 9, 15, ..., 93, 99.
So, the number of numbers divisible by 3 (but not by 2) =

$$\frac{\text{last such no.} - \text{first such no.}}{\text{gap/step}} + 1 = \frac{99-3}{6} + 1 = 17$$

Hence, the number of numbers divisible by either 2 or 3 = 50 + 17 = 67

So, from (1), (2) & (3) required number of numbers = 100 – 67 = 33
⇒ Option (d)

Problem 1.18: Find the number of numbers from 1 to 100 which are not divisible by any one of 2, 3, and 5.

(a) 26 (b) 27
(c) 29 (d) 32

Solution: From the above question, we have found out that from 1 to 100, number of numbers divisible by 2 = 50 (1)
Number of numbers divisible by 3 (but not by 2) = 17 (2)

Now, we have to find out the number of numbers which are divisible by 5 (but not by 2 and 3). Numbers which are divisible by 5

(5) 10 15 20 (25) 30 (35) 40 45 50 (55) 60 (65) 70 75 80 (85) 90 (95) 100

That is, there are 7 such numbers. (iii)

Another way to find out the number of numbers that are divisible by 5 but not 2 and 3 is to first only consider odd multiples of 5.

You will get the series of 10 numbers: 5, 15, 25, 35, 45, 55, 65, 75, 85 and 95.

From amongst these, we need to exclude multiples of 3. In other words, we need to find the number of common elements between the above series and the series of odd multiples of 3, viz, 3, 9, 15, 21 .... 99.

This situation is the same as finding the number of common elements between the two series for which we need to first observe that the first such number is 15. Then the common terms between these two series will themselves form an arithmetic series and this series will have a common difference which is the LCM of the common differences of the two series. (In this case, the common difference of the two series are 10 and 6 respectively and their LCM being 30, the series of common terms between the two series will be 15, 45 and 75.) Thus, there will be 3 terms out of the 10 terms of the series 5, 15, 25...95 which will be divisible by 3 and hence, need to be excluded from the count of numbers which are divisible by 5 but not 2 or 3.

Hence, the required answer would be: 100 – 50 – 17 – 7 = 26

$\Rightarrow$ Option (a)

Problem 1.19: Find the number of numbers from 1 to 100 which are not divisible by any one of 2, 3, 5 and 7.

(a) 22 (b) 24
(c) 23 (d) 27

Solution: From the above question, we have seen that from 1 to 100

Number of numbers divisible by 2 = 50 (1)

Number of numbers divisible by 3 but not by 2 = 17 (2)

Number of numbers divisible by 5 but not by 2 and 3 = 7 (3)

Number of numbers divisible by 7 but not by 2, 3 and 5; such numbers are 7, 49, 77, 91 = 4 numbers (4)

Required number of numbers = Total number of numbers from 1 to 100 – {(1) + (2) + (3) + (4)}

= 100 – (50 + 17 + 7 + 4)

= 22

$\Rightarrow$ Option (a)

Problem 1.22: What will be the value of x for $\frac{(100^{17}-1)+(10^{34}+x)}{9}$; the remainder = 0

(a) 3 (b) 6
(c) 9 (d) 8

Solution: $\frac{(100^{17}-1)+(10^{34}+x)}{9}$

$100^{17}-1 = \underbrace{1000\ldots00}_{17\text{ zeroes}}-1 = \underbrace{9999\ldots99}_{16\text{ nines}} \Rightarrow$ divisible by 9 $\Rightarrow R = 0$

Since the first part of the expression is giving a remainder of 0, the second part should also give 0 as the remainder if the entire remainder of the expression has to be 0. Hence, we now evaluate the second part of the numerator.

$10^{34}+x = \underbrace{1000\ldots00}_{34\text{ zeroes}}+x = \underbrace{1000\ldots00x}_{33\text{ zeroes}}$

with x at the right most place. In order for this number to be divisible by 9, the sum of digits should be divisible by 9.

$\Rightarrow 1 + 0 + 0 \ldots + 0 + x$ should be divisible by 9.

$\Rightarrow 1 + x$ should be divisible by 9 $\Rightarrow x = 8$

$\Rightarrow$ Option (d)

KNOWLEDGE ENRICHMENT CORNER

Scan this QR code to access a video on three 'must know' questions before heading into the LOD exercises

Space for Rough Work

LEVEL OF DIFFICULTY (I)

1. The last digit of the number obtained by multiplying the numbers 121 × 132 × 143 × 154 × 165 × 176 × 187 × 198 × 209 will be?
   (a) 0 (b) 9
   (c) 6 (d) 2
2. The sum of the digits of a two-digit number is 10, while when the digits are reversed, the number decreases by 54. Find the changed number.
   (a) 28 (b) 19
   (c) 37 (d) 46
3. When we multiply a certain 2-digit number by the sum of it's digits, the answer is 567. However, when the 2-digit number is reversed and then multiplied by the sum of the digits, the product is 324. Find the number.
   (a) 71 (b) 63
   (c) 81 (d) 36
4. The sum of two numbers is 15 and their geometric mean is 20% lower than their arithmetic mean. Find the numbers.
   (a) 11, 4 (b) 12, 3
   (c) 13, 2 (d) 10, 5
5. The difference between 2 numbers (both less than 100) is 80 and the difference between their Arithmetic Mean and Geometric Mean is two more than half of 1/3rd of 180. Find the numbers?
6. If $A381$ is divisible by 11, find the value of the smallest natural number A.
   (a) 5 (b) 6
   (c) 7 (d) 9
7. Find the ratio of the LCM and HCF of 12,18 and 30.
   (a) 15 : 1 (b) 60 : 1
   (c) 15 : 2 (d) 30 : 1
8. What will be the remainder obtained when $(9^6 + 1)$ will be divided by 8?
   (a) 0 (b) 3
   (c) 7 (d) 2
9. If 573A is divisible by 9, then find the value of the smallest natural number A.
10. Find the LCM of 5/2, 8/9, 11/14.
    (a) 280 (b) 360
    (c) 420 (d) None of these
11. If the number A is even, which of the following will be true?
    (a) $3A$ will always be divisible by 6
    (b) $3A + 5$ will always be divisible by 11
    (c) $(A^2 + 3)/4$ will be divisible by 7
    (d) All of these
12. A five-digit number is taken. Sum of the first 4-digits (excluding the number at the units digit) equals sum of all the five digits. Which of the following will not divide this number necessarily?
    (a) 10 (b) 2
    (c) 4 (d) 5
13. The number P4351Q is divisible by 72, where P and Q are single digit numbers. Find the value of $P + Q$.
14. Difference between a two-digit number ab and the number obtained by reversing its digits is a perfect cube, then how many values of ab are possible

Directions for Questions 15 to 17: Given two different prime numbers P and Q, find the number of divisors of the following:

15. $P.Q$
    (a) 2 (b) 4
    (c) 6 (d) 8
16. P^2Q
    (a) 2 (b) 4
    (c) 6 (d) 8
17. P^3Q^2
    (a) 2 (b) 4
    (c) 6 (d) 12
18. The sides of a pentagonal field (not regular) are 1737 metres, 2160 metres, 2358 metres, 1422 metres and 2214 metres respectively. Find the greatest length of the tape by which the five sides may be measured completely.
    (a) 7 (b) 13
    (c) 11 (d) 9
19. There are 576 boys and 448 girls in a school that are to be divided into equal sections of either boys or girls alone. Find the minimum total number of sections thus formed.
    (a) 24 (b) 32
    (c) 16 (d) 20
20. A milkman has three different qualities of milk. 403 gallons of 1st quality, 465 gallons of 2nd quality and 496 gallons of 3rd quality. Find the least possible number of bottles of equal size in which different milk of different qualities can be filled without mixing.
    (a) 34 (b) 46
    (c) 26 (d) 44
21. What is the greatest number of 4-digits that when divided by any of the numbers 6, 9, 12, 17 leaves a remainder of 1?
    (a) 9997 (b) 9793
    (c) 9895 (d) 9487

22. Find the least number that when divided by 16, 18 and 20 leaves a remainder 4 in each case, but is completely divisible by 7.
(a) 364 (b) 2254
(c) 2964 (d) 2884

23. Four bells ring at the intervals of 6, 8, 12 and 18 seconds. They start ringing together at 12'O' clock. After how many seconds will they ring together again?
(a) 72 (b) 84
(c) 60 (d) 48

24. For Question 23, find how many times will they ring together during the next 12 minutes. (including the 12 minute mark).
(a) 9 (b) 10
(c) 11 (d) 12

25. If $AB + XY = 1XP$, where $A > 0$ and all the letters signify different digits from 0 to 9, then the value of A is
(a) 6 (b) 7
(c) 9 (d) 8

26. Find the number of divisors of 720 (including 1 and 720).
(a) 25 (b) 28
(c) 29 (d) 30

27. How many values are possible for a three-digit number *ABC*, such that *AB* and *BC* are perfect squares?

28. If $n = 1 + x$, where x is the product of four consecutive positive integers, then which of the following is/are true?
(i) n is odd
(ii) n is prime
(iii) n is a perfect square
(a) (i) and (iii) only (b) (i) and (ii) only
(c) (i) only (d) None of the above

29. The number A is not divisible by 3. Which of the following will not be divisible by 3?
(a) $9 \times A$ (b) $2 \times A$
(c) $18 \times A$ (d) $24 \times A$

30. Find the remainder when the number 9^{100} is divided by 8.
(a) 1 (b) 2
(c) 0 (d) 4

31. Find the remainder of 2^{1000} when divided by 3.
(a) 1 (b) 2
(c) 4 (d) 6

32. Decompose the number 20 into two terms such that their product is the greatest.
(a) $x_1 = x_2 = 10$ (b) $x_1 = 5, x_2 = 15$
(c) $x_1 = 16, x_2 = 4$ (d) $x_1 = 8, x_2 = 12$

33. Find the number of zeroes at the end of 50!
(a) 13 (b) 11
(c) 5 (d) 12

34. Which of the following can be a number divisible by 24?
(a) 4,32,15,604 (b) 25,61,284
(c) 13,62,480 (d) All of these

35. For a number to be divisible by 88, it should be
(a) Divisible by 22 and 8
(b) Divisible by 11 and 8
(c) Divisible by 11 and thrice by 2
(d) All of these

36. Find the number of divisors of 10800.
(a) 57 (b) 60
(c) 72 (d) 64

37. Difference between a two-digit number *ab* and the number obtained by reversing its digits is a perfect square, then how many values of *ab* are possible?

38. There are 5 prime numbers such that $P_1 < P_2 < P_3 < P_4 < P_5$ and $P_1 + P_2 + P_3 + P_4 + P_5 = 350$. Find the value of $(P_1)^5$.
(a) 243 (b) 32
(c) 55 (d) Can't be determined

39. Some birds settled on the branches of a tree. First, they sat one to a branch and there was one bird too many. Next they sat two to a branch and there was one branch too many. How many branches were there?
(a) 3 (b) 4
(c) 5 (d) 6

40. The square of a number greater than 1000 that is not divisible by three, when divided by three, leaves a remainder of
(a) 1 always (b) 2 always
(c) 0 (d) either 1 or 2

41. The value of the expression $(15^3 \cdot 21^2)/(35^2 \cdot 3^4)$ is
(a) 3 (b) 15
(c) 21 (d) 12

42. If $A = \left(\frac{-3}{4}\right)^3$, $B = \left(\frac{-2}{5}\right)^2$, $C = (0.3)^2$, $D = (-1.2)^2$ then
(a) $A > B > C > D$
(b) $D > A > B > C$
(c) $D > B > C > A$
(d) $D > C > A > B$

43. If $2 < x < 4$ and $1 < y < 3$, then find the ratio of the upper limit for $x + y$ and the lower limit of $x - y$.
(a) 6 (b) 7
(c) 8 (d) None of these

44. Find the pairs of natural numbers whose least common multiple is 78 and the greatest common divisor is 13.

45. Find two natural numbers whose sum is 85 and the least common multiple is 102.
(a) 30 and 55 (b) 17 and 68
(c) 35 and 55 (d) 51 and 34

46. Find the pairs of natural numbers the difference of whose squares is 55.

47. Which of these is greater?

(a) 54^4 or 21^{12} (b) $(0.4)^4$ or $(0.8)^3$

48. Is it possible for a common fraction whose numerator is less than the denominator to be equal to a fraction whose numerator is greater than the denominator?

(a) Yes (b) No

49. What digits should be put in place of c in $38c$ to make it divisible by

(a) 2 (b) 3
(c) 4 (d) 5
(e) 6 (f) 9
(g) 10

50. Find the LCM and HCF of the following numbers: (54, 81, 135 and 189), (156, 195) and (1950, 5670 and 3900).

51. The last digit in the expansions of the 3-digit number $(34x)^{43}$ and $(34x)^{44}$ are 7 and 1, respectively. What can be said about the value of x?

(a) $x = 5$ (b) $x = 3$
(c) $x = 6$ (d) $x = 2$

Directions for Questions 52 and 53: Amitesh buys a pen, a pencil and an eraser for ₹41. If the least cost of any of the three items is ₹12 and it is known that a pen costs less than a pencil and an eraser costs more than a pencil, answer the following questions:

52. What is the cost of the pen?

(a) 12 (b) 13
(c) 14 (d) 15

53. If it is known that the eraser's cost is not divisible by 4, the cost of the pencil could be

(a) 12 (b) 13
(c) 14 (d) 15

54. A naughty boy Amrit watches an innings of Sachin Tendulkar and acts according to the number of runs he sees Sachin scoring. The details of these are given below.

1 run Place an orange in the basket
2 runs Place a mango in the basket
3 runs Place a pear in the basket
4 runs Remove a pear and a mango from the basket

One fine day, at the start of the match, the basket is empty. The sequence of runs scored by Sachin in that innings are given as 11232411234232341121314. At the end of the above innings, how many more oranges were there compared to mangoes inside the basket? (The basket was empty initially)

(a) 4 (b) 5
(c) 6 (d) 7

55. In the famous Bel Air Apartments in Ranchi, there are three watchmen meant to protect the precious fruits in the campus. However, one day a thief got in without being noticed and stole some precious mangoes. On the way out however, he was confronted by the three watchmen, the first two of whom asked him to part with 1/3rd of the fruits and one more. The last asked him to part with 1/5th of the mangoes and 4 more. As a result he had no mangoes left. What was the number of mangoes he had stolen?

(a) 12 (b) 13
(c) 15 (d) None of these

56. A hundred and twenty digit number is formed by writing the first x natural numbers in front of each other as 12345678910111213… Find the remainder when this number is divided by 8.

(a) 6 (b) 7
(c) 2 (d) 0

57. A test has 80 questions. There is one mark for a correct answer, while there is a negative penalty of –1/2 for a wrong answer and –1/4 for an unattempted question. What is the number of questions answered correctly, if the student has scored a net total of 34.5 marks?

(a) 45 (b) 48
(c) 54 (d) Cannot be determined

58. For Question 57, if it is known that he has left 10 questions unanswered, the number of correct answers are

(a) 45 (b) 48
(c) 54 (d) Cannot be determined

59. Three mangoes, four guavas and five watermelons cost ₹750. Ten watermelons, six mangoes and nine guavas cost ₹1580. What is the cost of six mangoes, ten watermelons and four guavas?

(a) 1280 (b) 1180
(c) 1080 (d) Cannot be determined

60. From a number M subtract 1. Take the reciprocal of the result to get the value of 'N'. Then which of the following is necessarily true?

(a) $0 \le M^N \le 2$ (b) $M^N > 3$
(c) $1 < M^N < 3$ (d) $1 < M^N < 5$

61. The cost of four mangoes, six guavas and sixteen watermelons is ₹500, while the cost of seven magoes, nine guavas and nineteen watermelons is ₹620. What is the cost of one mango, one guava and one watermelon?

(a) 120 (b) 40
(c) 150 (d) Cannot be determined

62. For the question above, what is the cost of a mango?

(a) 20 (b) 14
(c) 15 (d) Cannot be determined

63. The following is known about three real numbers, x, y and z.
$-4 \le x \le 4$, $-8 \le y \le 2$ and $-8 \le z \le 2$. Then the range of values that $M = xz/y$ can take is best represented by
(a) $-\infty < x < \infty$ (b) $-16 \le x \le 8$
(c) $-8 \le x \le 8$ (d) $-16 \le x \le 16$

64. A man sold 38 pieces of clothing (combined in the form of shirts, trousers and ties). If he sold at least 11 pieces of each item and he sold more shirts than trousers and more trousers than ties, then the number of ties that he must have sold is
(a) Exactly 11 (b) At least 11
(c) At least 12 (d) Cannot be determined

65. For Question 64, find the number of shirts he must have sold.
(a) At least 13 (b) At least 14
(c) At least 15 (d) At most 16

66. Find the least number which when divided by 12, 15, 18 or 20 leaves in each case a remainder 4.
(a) 124 (b) 364
(c) 184 (d) None of these

67. What is the least number by which 2800 should be multiplied so that the product may be a perfect square?
(a) 2 (b) 7
(c) 14 (d) None of these

68. The least number of 4-digits which is a perfect square is
(a) 1064 (b) 1040
(c) 1024 (d) 1012

69. The least multiple of 7 which leaves a remainder of 4 when divided by 6, 9, 15 and 18 is
(a) 94 (b) 184
(c) 364 (d) 74

70. What is the least 3-digit number that when divided by 2, 3, 4, 5 or 6 leaves a remainder of 1?
(a) 131 (b) 161
(c) 121 (d) None of these

71. A certain number, when divided by 899, leaves a remainder 63. Find the remainder when the same number is divided by 29.
(a) 5 (b) 4
(c) 1 (d) Cannot be determined

72. Find the least number, which must be subtracted from 7147 to make it a perfect square.
(a) 86 (b) 89
(c) 91 (d) 93

73. Find the least square number which is divisible by 6, 8 and 15.
(a) 2500 (b) 3600
(c) 4900 (d) 4500

74. Find the least number by which 30492 must be multiplied or divided so as to make it a perfect square.
(a) 11 (b) 7
(c) 3 (d) 2

75. The greatest 4-digit number exactly divisible by 88 is
(a) 8888 (b) 9768
(c) 9944 (d) 9988

76. What is the remainder when $7^{22} \times 5^{17}$ is divided by 100?
(a) 25 (b) 75
(c) 45 (d) 55

77. If 5625 plants are to be arranged in such a way that there are as many rows as there are plants in a row, the number of rows will be
(a) 95 (b) 85
(c) 65 (d) None of these

78. A boy took a seven digit number ending in 9 and raised it to an even power greater than 2000. He then took the number 17 and raised it to a power which leaves the remainder 1 when divided by 4. If he now multiplies both the numbers, what will be the unit's digit of the number he so obtains?
(a) 7 (b) 9
(c) 3 (d) Cannot be determined

79. Two friends were discussing their marks in an examination. While doing so they realised that both the numbers had the same prime factors, although Raveesh got a score which had two more factors than Harish. If their marks are represented by one of the options as given below, which of the following options would correctly represent the number of marks they got?
(a) 30,60 (b) 20,80
(c) 40,80 (d) 20,60

80. A number is such that when divided by 3, 5, 6, or 7 it leaves the remainder 1, 3, 4, or 5 respectively. Which is the largest number below 4000 that satisfies this property?
(a) 3358 (b) 3988
(c) 3778 (d) 2938

81. A number when divided by 2,3 and 4 leaves a remainder of 1. Find the least number (after 1) that satisfies this requirement.
(a) 25 (b) 13
(c) 37 (d) 17

82. A number when divided by 2, 3 and 4 leaves a remainder of 1. Find the second lowest number (not counting 1) that satisfies this requirement.
(a) 25 (b) 13
(c) 37 (d) 17

83. A number when divided by 2, 3 and 4 leaves a remainder of 1. Find the highest 2-digit number that satisfies this requirement.
(a) 91 (b) 93
(c) 97 (d) 95

84. A number when divided by 2, 3 and 4 leaves a remainder of 1. Find the highest 3-digit number that satisfies this requirement.
(a) 991 (b) 993
(c) 997 (d) 995

85. A frog is sitting on vertex *A* of a square *ABCD*. It starts jumping to the immediately adjacent vertex on either side in random fashion and stops when it reaches point *C*. In how many ways, can it reach point *C* if it makes exactly 7 jumps?
(a) 1 (b) 3
(c) 5 (d) 0

86. Three bells ring at intervals of 5 seconds, 6 seconds and 7 seconds respectively. If they toll together for the first time at 9 a.m. in the morning, after what interval of time will they together ring again for the first time?
(a) After 30 seconds (b) After 42 seconds
(c) After 35 seconds (d) After 210 seconds

87. For the question above, how many times would they ring, together in the next 1 hour?
(a) 17 (b) 18
(c) 19 (d) None of these

88. A garrison has three kinds of soldiers. There are 66 soldiers of the first kind, 110 soldiers of the second kind and 242 soldiers of the third kind. It is desired to be arranging these soldiers in equal rows such that each row contains the same number of soldiers and there is only 1 kind of soldier in each row. What is the maximum number of soldiers who can be placed in each row?
(a) 11 (b) 1
(c) 22 (d) 33

89. For the question above, what are the minimum number of rows that would be required to be formed?
(a) 11 (b) 19
(c) 18 (d) None of these

90. A milkman produces three kinds of milk. On a particular day, he has 170 litres, 102 litres and 374 litres of the three kinds of milk. He wants to bottle them in bottles of equal sizes- so that each of the three varieties of milk would be completely bottled. How many bottle sizes are possible such that the bottle size in terms of litres is an integer?
(a) 1 (b) 2
(c) 4 (d) 34

91. For the above question, what is the size of the largest bottle which can be used?
(a) 1 (b) 2
(c) 17 (d) 34

92. For Question 90, what are the minimum number of bottles that would be required?
(a) 11 (b) 19
(c) 18 (d) None of these

93. Find the number of zeroes at the end of 100!
(a) 20 (b) 23
(c) 24 (d) 25

94. Find the number of zeroes at the end of 122!
(a) 20 (b) 23
(c) 24 (d) 28

95. $53!/3^n$ is an integer. Find the highest possible value of *n* for this to be true.
(a) 19 (b) 21
(c) 23 (d) 24

96. $155!/20^n$ is an integer. Find the highest possible value of *n* for this to be true.
(a) 77 (b) 38
(c) 75 (d) 37

97. Find the remainder when 5^{59} is divided by 13.
(a) 5 (b) 8
(c) 0 (d) 12

98. Find the sum of all 2-digit natural numbers which leave a remainder of 3 when divided by 7.
(a) 650 (b) 663
(c) 676 (d) 702

99. How many numbers between 1 and 200 are exactly divisible by exactly two of 3, 9 and 27?
(a) 14 (b) 15
(c) 16 (d) 17

100. A number *N* is squared to give a value of *S*. The minimum value of *N* + *S* would happen when *N* is
(a) –0.3 (b) –0.5
(c) –0.7 (d) None of these

101. $L = x + y$ where *x* and *y* are prime numbers. Which of the following statement/s is/are true?
(i) The unit's digit of *L* cannot be 5
(ii) The unit's digit of *L* cannot be 0
(iii) *L* cannot be odd.
(a) All three (b) Only (iii)
(c) only (ii) (d) None of these

102. *XYZ* is a 3-digit number such that when we calculate the difference between the two 3-digit numbers *XYZ* – *YXZ* the difference is exactly 90. How many possible values exist for the digits *X* and *Y*?
(a) 9 (b) 8
(c) 7 (d) 6

103. What is the sum of all even numbers between 1 and 100 (both included)?
(a) 2450 (b) 2500
(c) 2600 (d) 2550

104. The least number which can be added to 763 so that it is completely divisible by 57 is
(a) 35 (b) 22
(c) 15 (d) 25

105. The least number which can be subtracted from 763 so that it is completely divisible by 57 is
(a) 35 (b) 22
(c) 15 (d) 25

106. The least number which can be added to 8441 so that it is completely divisible by 57 is
(a) 42 (b) 15
(c) 5 (d) 52

107. The least number which can be subtracted from 8441 so that it is completely divisible by 57 is
(a) 3 (b) 4
(c) 5 (d) 6

108. Find the least number of 5 digits that is exactly divisible by 79.
(a) 10003 (b) 10033
(c) 10043 (d) None of these

109. Find the maximum number of 5 digits that is exactly divisible by 79.
(a) 99925 (b) 99935
(c) 99945 (d) 99955

110. The nearest integer to 773 which is exactly divisible by 12 is
(a) 768 (b) 772
(c) 776 (d) None of these

111. A number when divided by 84 leaves a remainder of 57. What is the remainder when the same number is divided by 12?
(a) 7 (b) 8
(c) 9 (d) Cannot be determined

112. A number when divided by 84 leaves a remainder of 57. What is the remainder when the same number is divided by 11?
(a) 2 (b) 7
(c) 8 (d) Cannot be determined

113. 511 and 667 when divided by the same number, leave the same remainder. How many numbers can be used as the divisor in order to make this occur?
(a) 14 (b) 12
(c) 10 (d) 8

114. How many numbers between 200 and 400 are divisible by 13?
(a) 14 (b) 15
(c) 16 (d) 17

115. A boy was trying to find 5/8th of a number. Unfortunately, he found out 8/5th of the number and realised that the difference between the answer he got and the correct answer is 39. What was the number?
(a) 38 (b) 39
(c) 40 (d) 52

116. The sum of two numbers is equal to thrice their difference. If the smaller of the numbers is 10, find the other number.
(a) 15 (b) 20
(c) 40 (d) None of these

117. $4^{11} + 4^{12} + 4^{13} + 4^{14} + 4^{15}$ is divisible by which of the following?
(a) 11 (b) 31
(c) 341 (d) All of these

118. The product of two numbers is 7168 and their HCF is 16. How many pairs of numbers are possible such that the above conditions are satisfied?
(a) 2 (b) 3
(c) 4 (d) 6

119. When 876 is added to another 3-digit number 2P3, we get a 4-digit number 10Q9 and 10Q9 is divisible by 11 then the value of P – Q is

120. There is a 22- digit number which consists of only one digit – from 1, 2, 3, 4, 5 or 6, e.g. 11111111.....11, 2222222....22, ...6666.....66. Such a number is always divisible by

121. The product of the factors of 72 is

122. The number of ways of expressing 72 as a product of 2 factors is

123. In how many ways can 144 be expressed as a product of two distinct factors?

124. How many numbers lie between 100 and 1000 which when divided by 7 leaves remainder 3 and when divided by 11 leaves remainder 4?

125. HCF of $3^{15} - 1$ and $3^{25} - 1$ is

126. LCM and HCF of 10! and 15! are respectively
(a) 5! and 25! (b) 5! and 30!
(c) 10! and 30! (d) 15! and 10!

127. Given that $7x + y$ is a prime number for natural numbers x and y, then what is the minimum value of $(x + y)$?

128. If n is an odd digit then unit's digit of the product $171n \times 1414 \times 729 \times 2015$ will be

129. If unit's digit of the product $171n \times 1413 \times 729 \times 2015$ is 0 then the maximum number of values that 'n' may take will be

130. The first two, 2-digit numbers that divide $(21^{12346} - 1)$ are

131. What is the unit's digit of 1! + 2! + 3! + 4!+ 5! + 6! + 7! + ...+ 1000?

132. How many zeroes are there at the end of $(34!)^{6!}$?

133. The unit's digit of $7^{51!^{31!}}$ is

134. If $N^2 = 1234567654321$, then $N = ?$

135. The LCM of two numbers is 421. What is the HCF of these two numbers?

136. Which of the following is greatest?

$$3^{50}, 4^{40}, 5^{30}, 6^{20}$$

137. What is the value of $M \times N$ if $M39048458N$ is divisible by 8 and 11, where M and N are single digit integers?

138. How many times does the digit 4 appear when we count from 21 to 500?

139. Find the remainder when the sum of 15 consecutive natural numbers starting from 3671 is divided by 3670.

140. X is a number formed by writing 9 for 99 times. What will be the remainder of this number when divided by 7?

141. Find the remainder of $\frac{2^{41}}{41}$.

142. Find the remainder when 40! is divided by 41.

143. Find the remainder when $x^4 + 3x^3 + 4$ is divided by $x + 3$.

144. If X is a prime number then for how many values of X, $X^2 + 7$ is also a prime number?

145. If $X = 99^3 - 63^3 - 36^3$ then the number of factors of X is

146. If x is a natural number and $4 < x < 50$, then the largest n, such that $n!$ would always divide: $x(x^2 - 1)(x^2 - 4)(x^2 - 9)(x + 4)$ is

147. If X is a natural number and $X!$ ends with Y zeros then number of zeros at the end of $(5X)$ is

148. There are 90 questions in a test. Each correct answer fetches 1 mark, each wrong answer and unanswered question attract a penalty of 1/4 marks and 1/8 marks respectively. Bilbo scored 23 marks in the test. What is the minimum possible number of the questions wrongly answered by him?

149. If $A = n^{2n^n}$, $B = n^{n^{2n}}$, $C = (n^{2n})^n$, $D = (n^n)^{n^2}$ when n is a natural number and $n \neq 1$.
Then arrange them in terms of their values.

150. How many numbers in the form of $2^n - 1$, which are less than 5000 are prime?

Space for Rough Work

LEVEL OF DIFFICULTY (II)

1. Find the remainder when $[(1!)^3 + (2!)^3 + (3!)^3 + ... + (20!)^3]$ is divided by 1000.
2. Which of the following is the largest number which is always a factor of the product of any ten consecutive natural numbers?
   (a) 1 (b) 10^2
   (c) 10^3 (d) 10^1
3. What is the difference between the highest and lowest 2-digit value of n for which $2^{3n} - 1$ is divisible by 7?
4. The LCM and the HCF of two numbers p and q, are x and y respectively. If $x = p$ and $p > q$, q is equal to
   (a) x/p (b) p/q
   (c) y (d) y/p
5. A 4-digit number when divided by 5, 6, 7 and 8 leave a remainder of 4, 5, 6 and 7. What is the difference between the highest and lowest such numbers?
6. If $X = 100!/5^n$ and it is an integer, find the largest value of the natural number n.
   (a) 20 (b) 22
   (c) 23 (d) 24
7. If the LCM of 18^6, 8^8 and 'x' is 12^{12}, how many values can 'x' take?
8. Outside a shop, its name "Basant Raj Enterprises" is displayed using blinking lights. Each word flashes at a regular interval and remains lit for 1 second. After remaining lit for 1 second, "Basant" lights up again after 3 seconds, "Raj" lights up again after 5 seconds and "Enterprises" lights up again after 9 seconds. If all the words flash together at 8:00 p.m. sharp, find the minimum time interval between the time when the first two words flash together for the second time and the last two words flash together for the third time.
   (a) 6 (b) 40
   (c) 112 (d) 66
9. Find the least value of LCM for two numbers whose product is 540.
10. If a number has 3 factors apart from 1 and the number itself, Then how many such numbers are there between 1 and 1000?
11. In a charity event, a collection box is designed to receive donations in the form of coins of ₹5, ₹10, and ₹20. Later, the collection box was discovered to hold exactly 150 coins, at least 1 coin of each denomination with a total value of ₹2,100. What is the highest possible count of ₹20 coins that could be in the collection box?
12. When two natural numbers are divided by 7, they leave a remainder of 3 and 5 respectively. The remainder is C when their sum is divided by 7. Find the value of (3C – 7) / 4.
13. At the National Sports Academy, 77 students played football, and 105 students played cricket. All the 182 students are assigned into 91 pairs. In exactly 32 of these pairs, both Students played football. In how many pairs were both students playing cricket?
14. In a jar, there are four different flavours of candies: 6 strawberry, 8 chocolate, 7 mint, and 5 caramel. Shaurya is selecting candies from the jar. What is the minimum number of candies he must select to guarantee that he has at least four candies of the same flavor?
15. In a jar, there are four different flavors of candies: 6 strawberry, 8 chocolate, 7 mint, and 5 caramel. Pallav is selecting candies from the jar. What is the minimum number of candies he must select to guarantee that he has at least 1 candy of each flavour?
16. Pallav meets 100 people sitting in chairs 1 to 100 in a line. From every third person, starting with the first person Pallav collects 200 coins. From the coins taken from the Nth person, he gives away 50% of the coins to the $(N + 10)^{th}$ person. How much money does Pallav have after he meets the 41st person, assuming he started with no coins and there are no give and takes of coins other than those mentioned?
17. At a Bus Terminal 12 men and 17 women boarded an empty bus, but at the next stop half of the men and 7 women got down and a total 8 people boarded the bus. As a result, the number of men became greater than the number of women in the bus. What is the difference between the maximum possible number of women and the maximum possible number of men in the bus now?
18. Find out the unit's digit of the expression $(2018^{2018} + 2019^{2019} + 2020^{2020} + 2021^{2021} + 2022^{2022})$
19. Find the number of numbers between 200 and 300, both included, which are not divisible by 2, 3, 4 and 5.
   (a) 27 (b) 26
   (c) 25 (d) 28
20. Find the units digit of the expression: $(1^1 + 2^2 + 3^3 + ... + 2020^{2020} + 2021^{2021} + 2022^{2022})$
21. The unit digit in the expression $36^{234} \times 33^{512} \times 39^{180} - 54^{29} \times 25^{123} \times 31^{512}$ will be
   (a) 8 (b) 0
   (c) 6 (d) 5
22. The difference of $10^{25} - 7$ and $10^{24} + x$ is divisible by 3 for x = ?
   (a) 3 (b) 2
   (c) 4 (d) 6

23. If $P = (1^1 + 2^2 + 3^3 + ... + 2020^{2020} + 2021^{2021} + 2022^{2022})$; the unit's digit of $(P^P)^P$

24. $F_n(p, q)$ gives the remainder of p when divided by q^n Find out the value of $F_1(F_2(P, 10), F_1(S, 10))$ where $P = (1^1 + 2^2 + 3^3 + ... + 2020^{2020} + 2021^{2021} + 2022^{2022})$; $S = P - 2022^{2022}$

25. $125^{5}/3^{11} + 8^{48}/16^{18}$ will give the digit at units place as

(a) 4 (b) 6
(c) 8 (d) 0

26. The mean of 1, 2, 2^2.... 2^{31} lies in between

(a) 2^{24} to 2^{25} (b) 2^{25} to 2^{26}
(c) 2^{26} to 2^{27} (d) 2^{29} to 2^{30}

27. xy is a number that is divided by ab where $xy < ab$ and gives a result $0.xyxyxy$... then ab equals

(a) 11 (b) 33
(c) 99 (d) 66

28. A number xy is multiplied by another number ab and the result comes as pqr, where $r = 2y$, $q = 2(x + y)$ and $p = 2x$ where $x, y < 5$, $q > 0$. The value of ab may be

(a) 11 (b) 13
(c) 31 (d) 22

29. $[x]$ denotes the greatest integer value just below x and $\{x\}$ its fractional value. The sum of $[x]^3$ and $\{x\}^2$ is –7.91. Find x.

(a) –2.03 (b) –1.97
(c) –2.97 (d) –1.7

30. $16^5 + 2^{15}$ is divisible by

(a) 31 (b) 13
(c) 27 (d) 33

31. Find out the smallest 4-digit number which when divided by 5, 7, 13 gives a remainder of 3, 5, 11 respectively.

Directions for Questions 32 and 33: Find the possible integral values of x.

32. $|x - 3| + 2|x + 1| = 4$

(a) 1 (b) –1
(c) 3 (d) 2

33. $x^2 + |x - 1| = 1$

(a) 1 (b) –1
(c) 0 (d) 1 or 0

34. If $4^{2n+1} + x$ and $4^{2n} - x$ are divisible by 5, n being an even integer, find the least value of x.

(a) 1 (b) 2
(c) 3 (d) 0

35. If the sum of the numbers $(a25)^2$ and a^3 is divisible by 9, then which of the following may be a value for a ?

(a) 1 (b) 7
(c) 9 (d) There is no value

36. If $|x - 4| + |y - 4| = 4$, then how many integer values can the set (x, y) have?

(a) Infinite (b) 5
(c) 16 (d) 9

37. $[3^{32}/50]$ gives a remainder and {.} denotes the fractional part of that. The fractional part is of the form $(0 \cdot bx)$. The value of x could be

(a) 2 (b) 4
(c) 6 (d) 8

38. The highest power on 990 that will exactly divide 1090! is

(a) 101 (b) 100
(c) 108 (d) 109

Directions for Questions 39 to 42: At the annual Drone meet in the Republic of Arkana, Indian drones were using codewords to communicate with each other. There were 100 drones from India ($A_1, A_2, A_3 ... A_{100}$) who went for a drill at night, each in one drone carrier. Every drone carrier had 100 switches ($S_1, S_2, S_3 ... S_{100}$). Once a switch is kept on/off by any drone carrier, that switch will be in the same situation (on/off) in all other drone carriers. **Example–** If DC 1 keeps S_n in off position, then S_n will be in the off position in all the carriers until anyone changes the position. Initially, all the switches were in off position. A_1 puts all the switches in on position. A_2 changes the position of those switches (puts it in on mode if is presently in off mode & vice versa) whose subscripts were divisible by 2. A_3 changes the position of all the switches whose subscripts were divisible by 3 and so on till A_{100}. Every switch in the on position represents an alphanumeric code as shown below–

$A_1 = a_1$, $A_2 = b_1$, $A_3 = c_1$, ... $A_{26} = z_1$, $A_{27} = a_2$, $A_{28} = b_2$ ... $A_{53} = a_3$ and so on. These codes are visible in the control room.

If a drone carrier goes out of range, then that drone in that drone carrier cannot change the code.

39. If all the drone carriers remain in range throughout, then what will be the message the control room will receive from the switches pressed by the drones?

(a) $a_1, b_1, c_1, i_1, w_1, z_1, m_2, w_2, j_3, c_4, k_4$
(b) $a_1, b_1, d_1, i_1, w_1, z_1, c_2, y_2, c_3, j_3, a_4, k_4$
(c) $a_1, d_1, i_1, p_1, y_1, j_2, w_2, l_3, c_4, v_4$
(d) $a_1, d_1, c_1, z_1, c_2, y_2, j_3, a_4, v_4$

40. The normal code signal is denoted as N which is a set of all the alphanumeric codes when none of the drones have gone out of range. Find out the minimum subscript of drone carriers which went out of range if the control room received the code as [N + $\{s_1, e_3, q_4\}$]. If multiple drone carriers went out of range, then write the sum of the subscripts of the drones that went out of range in the answer.

41. All the drone carriers are divided across 4 regiments- North ($A_1, A_2, A_3, ... A_{25}$), South ($A_{26}, A_{27}, A_{28}, ... A_{50}$), East ($A_{51}, A_{52}, A_{53}, ... A_{75}$), West ($A_{76}, A_{77}, A_{78}, ... A_{100}$). If all the drone carriers of the East

Regiment went out of range, then find the number of alphanumeric signals in the code received by the control room?

42. All the drone carriers are divided across 4 regiments- North (A_1, A_2, A_3, ... A_{25}), South (A_{26}, A_{27}, A_{28}, ... A_{50}), East (A_{51}, A_{52}, A_{53}, ... A_{75}), West (A_{76}, A_{77}, A_{78}, ... A_{100}). If all the drone carriers in the South regiment went out of range, then find the number of alphanumeric signals in the code received by the control room?

43. $[x]$ denotes the greatest integer value just below x and $\{x\}$ its fractional value. The sum of $[x]^2$ and $\{x\}^1$ is 25.16. Find x.

(a) 5.16 (b) −4.84
(c) Both (a) and (b) (d) 4.84

44. If we add the square of the digit in the tens place of a positive two-digit number to the product of the digits of that number, we shall get 52, and if we add the square of the digit in the units place to the same product of the digits, we shall get 117. Find the two-digit number.

45. $S = 1 + 11 + 111 + \ldots$ 20 terms. What will be the sum of the digits of S?

(a) 37 (b) 60
(c) 75 (d) 11

46. The sum of the digits of a three-digit number is 17, and the sum of the squares of its digits is 109. If we subtract 495 from that number, we shall get a number consisting of the same digits written in the reverse order. Find the number.

47. Find the number of zeros in the product: $1^1 \times 2^2 \times 3^3 \times 4^4 \times \ldots\ldots 98^{98} \times 99^{99} \times 100^{100}$.

(a) 1200 (b) 1300
(c) 1050 (d) 1225

48. How many pairs of natural numbers exist such that their HCF is 5 and their LCM is 105.

49. Kaku has written all the numbers from 1 to 100 on the board. His brother Chiku is removing all the numbers which are having a GCD of more than 1 with 100. How many numbers are left on the board?

50. Had Chiku removed all the numbers which are giving a GCD > 1 with 120, intead of 100. Then how many numbers would have been left on the board?

51. The sum of the squares of the digits constituting a two-digit positive number is 2.5 times as large as the sum of its digits. It is also larger by unity, than the trebled product of its digits. There are 2 numbers that satisfy this condition for a 2-digit number. Can you find them?

52. Three numbers are such that the second is as much lesser than the third as the first is lesser than the second. If the product of the two smaller numbers is 85 and the product of two larger numbers is 115. Find the middle number.

(a) 9 (b) 8
(c) 12 (d) 10

53. Find the smallest natural number n such that $n!$ is divisible by 990.

(a) 3 (b) 5
(c) 11 (d) 12

54. $\sqrt{x}\sqrt{y} = \sqrt{xy}$ is true only when

(a) $x > 0, y > 0$ (b) $x > 0$ and $y < 0$
(c) $x < 0$ and $y > 0$ (d) All of these

Directions for Questions 55 to 72: Read the instructions below and solve the questions based on this.

In an examination situation, always solve the following type of questions by substituting the given options, to arrive at the solution.

However, as you can see, there are no options given in the questions here since these are meant to be an exercise in equation writing (which I believe is a primary skill required to do well in aptitude exams testing mathematical aptitude). Indeed, if these questions had options for them, they would be rated as LOD 1 questions. But since the option-based solution technique is removed here, these are placed in the LOD 2 category.

55. The product of the digits of a two-digit number is twice as large as the sum of its digits. If we subtract 27 from the required number, we get a number consisting of the same digits written in the reverse order. Find the number.

56. The product of the digits of a two-digit number is one-third that number. If we add 18 to the required number, we get a number consisting of the same digits written in the reverse order. Find the number.

57. The sum of the squares of the digits of a two-digit number is 13. If we subtract 9 from that number, we get a number consisting of the same digits written in the reverse order. Find the number.

58. A two-digit number is thrice as large as the sum of its digits, and the square of that sum is equal to the trebled required number. Find the number.

59. Find a two-digit number that exceeds by 12 the sum of the squares of its digits and by 16 the doubled product of its digits.

60. The sum of the squares of the digits constituting a two-digit number is 10, and the product of the required number by the number consisting of the same digits written in the reverse order is 403. Find the 2 numbers that satisfy these conditions.

61. If we divide a two-digit number by the sum of its digits, we get 4 as a quotient and 3 as a remainder. Now, if we divide that two-digit number by the product of its digits, we get 3 as a quotient and 5 as a remainder. Find the two-digit number.

62. There is a natural number that becomes equal to the square of a natural number when 100 is added to it, and to the square of another natural number when 169 is added to it. Find the number.

63. Find two natural numbers whose sum is 85 and whose least common multiple is 102.

64. Find 2 three -digit numbers whose sum is a multiple of 504 and the quotient is a multiple of 6.

65. The difference between the digits in a two-digit number is equal to 2, and the sum of the squares of the same digits is 52. Find all the possible numbers.

66. If we divide a given two-digit number by the product of its digits, we obtain 3 as a quotient and 9 as a remainder. If we subtract the product of the digits constituting the number, from the square of the sum of its digits, we obtain the given number. Find the number.

67. Find the three-digit number if it is known that the sum of its digits is 17 and the sum of the squares of its digits is 109. If we subtract 495 from this number, we obtain a number consisting of the same digits written in reverse order.

68. The sum of the cubes of the digits constituting a two-digit number is 243 and the product of the sum of its digits by the product of its digits is 162. Find the 2 two-digit numbers.

69. The difference between two numbers is 16. What can be said about the total numbers divisible by 7 that can lie in between these two numbers.

70. Arrange the following in descending order:

111^4, 110.109.108.107, 109.110.112.113

71. If $3 \le x \le 5$ and $4 \le y \le 7$. Find the greatest value of xy and the least value of x/y.

72. Which of these is greater?
(a) 200^{300} or 300^{200} or 400^{150}
(b) 5^{100} and 2^{200}
(c) 10^{20} and 40^{10}

73. Define a number K such that it is the sum of the squares of the first M natural numbers. (i.e., $K = 1^2 + 2^2 + ... + M^2$) where $M < 55$. How many values of M exist such that K is divisible by 4?
(a) 10 (b) 11
(c) 12 (d) None of these

74. M is a 2-digit number which has the property that: the product of factorials of its digits > sum of factorials of its digits
How many values of M exist?
(a) 56 (b) 64
(c) 63 (d) None of these

75. A natural number when increased by 50% has its number of factors unchanged. However, when the value of the number is reduced by 75%, the number of factors is reduced by 66.66%. One such number could be
(a) 32 (b) 84
(c) 126 (d) None of these

76. Find the 28383rd term of the series: 123456789101112....
(a) 3 (b) 4
(c) 9 (d) 7

77. If you form a subset of integers chosen from between 1 to 3000, such that no two integers add up to a multiple of nine, what can be the maximum number of elements in the subset. (Include both 1 and 3000.)
(a) 1668 (b) 1332
(c) 1333 (d) 1336

78. The series of numbers (1,1/2,1/3,1/4 ....1/1972) is taken. Now two numbers are taken from this series (the first two) say x, y. Then the operation $x + y + x.y$ is performed to get a consolidated number. The process is repeated. What will be the value of the set after all the numbers are consolidated into one number?
(a) 1970 (b) 1971
(c) 1972 (d) None of these

79. K is a 3-digit number such that the ratio of the number to the sum of its digits is least. What is the difference between the hundreds and the tens digits of K?
(a) 9 (b) 8
(c) 7 (d) None of these

80. In Question 79, what can be said about the difference between the tens and the units digit?
(a) 0 (b) 1
(c) 2 (d) None of these

81. For the above question, for how many values of K will the ratio be the highest?
(a) 9 (b) 8
(c) 7 (d) None of these

82. A triangular number is defined as a number which has the property of being expressed as a sum of consecutive natural numbers starting with 1. How many triangular numbers less than 1000, have the property that they are the difference of squares of two consecutive natural numbers?
(a) 20 (b) 21
(c) 22 (d) 23

83. x and y are two positive integers. Then what will be the sum of the coefficients of the expansion of the expression $(x + y)^{44}$?
(a) 2^{43} (b) $2^{43} + 1$
(c) 2^{44} (d) $2^{44} - 1$

84. What is the remainder when $9 + 9^2 + 9^3 + ...9^{2n+1}$ is divided by 6?
(a) 1 (b) 2
(c) 3 (d) 4

85. The remainder when the number 123456789101112 ......484950 is divided by 16 is
(a) 3 (b) 4
(c) 5 (d) 6

86. What is the highest power of 3 available in the expression 58! – 38!?

(a) 17 (b) 18
(c) 19 (d) None of these

87. Find the remainder when the number represented by 22334 raised to the power $(1^2 + 2^2 + ... + 66^2)$ is divided by 5?

(a) 2 (b) 4
(c) 1 (d) None of these

88. What is the total number of divisors of the number $12^{33} \times 34^{23} \times 2^{70}$?

(a) 4658 (b) 9316
(c) 2744 (d) None of these

89. For Question 88, which of the following will represent the sum of factors of the number (such that only odd factors are counted)?

(a) $\frac{(3^{34}-1)}{2} \times \frac{(17^{24}-1)}{16}$ (b) $(3^{34}-1) \times (17^{24}-1)$

(c) $\frac{(3^{34}-1)}{33}$ (d) None of these

90. What is the remainder when $(1!)^3 + (2!)^3 + (3!)^3 + (4!)^3 + \ldots(1152!)^3$ is divided by 1152?

(a) 125 (b) 225
(c) 325 (d) 205

91. A set S is formed by including some of the first one thousand natural numbers. S contains the maximum number of numbers such that they satisfy the following conditions:

1. No number of the set S is prime.
2. When the numbers of the set S are selected two at a time, we always see co-prime numbers.

What is the number of elements in the set S?

(a) 11 (b) 12
(c) 13 (d) 7

Find the last 2-digits of the following numbers.

92. 101 × 102 × 103 × 197 × 198 × 199

(a) 54 (b) 74
(c) 64 (d) 84

93. 65 × 29 × 37 × 63 × 71 × 87

(a) 05 (b) 95
(c) 15 (d) 25

94. 65 × 29 × 37 × 63 × 71 × 87 × 85

(a) 25 (b) 35
(c) 75 (d) 85

95. Arun, Bikas and Chetakar have a total of 80 coins among them. Arun triples the number of coins with the others by giving them some coins from his own collection. Next, Bikas repeats the same process. After this, Bikas now has 20 coins. Find the number of coins he had at the beginning.

(a) 22 (b) 20
(c) 18 (d) 24

96. The super computer at Ram Mohan Roy Seminary takes an input of a number N and a X where X is a factor of the number N. In a particular case N is equal to $83p796161q$ and X is equal to 11 where $0 < p < q$. Find the sum of remainders when N is divided by $(p + q)$ and p successively.

(a) 6 (b) 3
(c) 2 (d) 9

97. On 1 March 2016, Sherry saved ₹1. Everyday starting from 2 March 2016, he saved ₹1 more than the previous day. Find the first date after 1 March 2016 at the end of which his total savings will be a perfect square.

(a) 17 March 2016 (b) 18 April 2016
(c) 26 March 2016 (d) None of these

98. What is the rightmost digit preceding the zeroes in the value of 20^{53}?

(a) 2 (b) 8
(c) 1 (d) 4

99. What is the remainder when 2(8!) – 21(6!) divides 14(7!) + 14(13!)?

(a) 1 (b) 7!
(c) 8! (d) 9!

100. How many integer values of x and y are there such that $4x + 7y = 3$, while $|x| < 500$ and $|y| < 500$?

(a) 144 (b) 141
(c) 143 (d) 142

101. If $n = 1 + m$, where m is the product of four consecutive positive integers, then which of the following is/are true?

(A) n is odd (B) n is not a multiple of 3
(C) n is a perfect square

(a) All three (b) A and B only
(c) A and C only (d) None of these

102. How many two-digit numbers less than or equal to 50, have the product of the factorials of their digits less than or equal to the sum of the factorials of their digits?

(a) 18 (b) 16
(c) 15 (d) None of these

103. A candidate takes a test and attempts all the 100 questions in it. While any correct answer fetches 1 mark, wrong answers are penalised as follows; one-tenth of the questions carry 1/10 negative marks each, one-fifth of the questions carry 1/5 negative marks each and the rest of the questions carry ½ negative mark each. Unattempted questions carry no marks. What is the difference between the maximum and the minimum marks that he can score?

(a) 100 (b) 120
(c) 140 (d) None of these

Directions for Questions 104 to 106: A mock test is taken at Mindworkzz. The test paper comprises of questions in three levels of difficulty—LOD1, LOD2 and LOD 3.

The following table gives the details of the positive and negative marks attached to each question type:

Difficulty level	*Positive marks for answering the question correctly*	*Negative marks for answering the question wrongly*
LOD 1	4	2
LOD 2	3	1.5
LOD 3	2	1

The test had 200 questions with 80 on LOD 1 and 60 each on LOD 2 and LOD 3.

104. If a student has solved 100 questions exactly and scored 120 marks, the maximum number of incorrect questions that he/she might have marked is
(a) 44 (b) 56
(c) 60 (d) None of these

105. If Amit attempted the least number of questions and got a total of 130 marks, and if it is known that he attempted at least one of every type, then the number of questions he must have attempted is
(a) 34 (b) 35
(c) 36 (d) None of these

106. In the above question, what is the least number of questions he might have got incorrect?
(a) 0 (b) 1
(c) 2 (d) None of these

107. Amitabh has a certain number of toffees, such that if he distributes them amongst ten children he has nine left, if he distributes amongst nine children he would have eight left, if he distributes amongst eight children he would have seven left ... and so on until if he distributes amongst five children he should have four left. What is the second lowest number of toffees he could have with him?
(a) 2519 (b) 7559
(c) 8249 (d) 5039

108. If a positive integer '*n*' is subtracted from the squares of three consecutive terms of an arithmetic progression, the numbers obtained are 108, 220 and 364 respectively. What is the sum of the digits of '*n*'?

109. How many integers exist such that not only are they multiples of 904^{2008} but also are factors of 904^{2015}?

110. What is the remainder when $1^5 + 2^5 + 3^5 + ...+ 96^5$ is divided by 194?

111. If $\left[\frac{s}{2}\right]+\left[\frac{s}{3}\right]+\left[\frac{s}{7}\right]=\frac{41}{42}s$ where[*s*] is the greatest integer less than or equal to '*s*' and $0 < s < 1000$, then find the number of possible values of '*s*'.

Directions for Questions 112 to 114:

In a zoo with 100 rabbits, there are three kinds of rabbits, weight-wise viz. 1 kg rabbits, 2 kg rabbits and 5 kg rabbits. There are a minimum of 10 and a maximum of 60 of each kind of rabbit. On a particular day, the zoo director transfers 40 rabbits from his stock and sends them off to the neighbouring zoo. On weighing these rabbits, it was found that the total weight of these 40 rabbits, was 148 kgs. It was also found that the weight of the remaining rabbits was 212 kgs.

112. What is the minimum number of 1 kg rabbits that were transferred?

113. What is the maximum possible number of 5 kg rabbits that remain?

114. If, a total of 26 5-kg rabbits were transferred, then what is the maximum possible numbers of 1 kg rabbits that remain in the zoo?

115. Let *A* be a two-digit number. The sum of the number *A*, the number formed by reversing the digits of *A* and the value of the product of the digits of *A* is found to equal 117. Then what is the sum of the digits of *A*?

116. Let *M* be the product of all natural numbers between 35 and 250 that have an odd number of factors. Find the highest power of 12 in *M*.

117. *x* and *y* are natural numbers such that they satisfy the equation $x + y + 21 = 3xy$. Find the maximum possible integral power of 6 in $(xy)!$.[$n!$ is the product of the first '*n*' natural numbers.]

118. Let *X* is the set of all the natural numbers each of which is equal to the number of its factors and *Y* is the set of all natural numbers from 1 to 100, each of which differ from the sum of its factors 1. Also, let *x* and *y* represent the number of elements in the sets respectively. Then find the value of $[y/x]$, where [] represents the greatest integer function.

119. A 4-digit number *X* has 15 factors. What is the number of factors of X^2?

120. How many four- digit odd numbers are possible such that the hundreds digit is two more than the tens digit?

121. Three natural numbers *X*, *Y*, *Z* are prime numbers less than 20 and are in arithmetic progression. If $X > Y > Z$, then how many possible values can we get for $X + Y + Z$?

122. A 100-digit number is multiplied by a 200-digit number and the product is multiplied with a 300-digit number and this product is again multiplied with a 400-digits number. What is the least number of digits in the product?

123. What are the last 2-digits of the number 3^{400}?

124. The unit digit in $1^7 \times 2^7 \times 3^7 \times .....\times 9^7 \times 11^7 \times 12^7.....19^7 \times 21^7......99^7$ is

125. How many 2-digit numbers have their squares as 1 more than a multiple of 24?

126. There are 80 questions in a test. Each correct answer fetches 1 mark, each wrong answer and unanswered question attract a penalty of 1/4 mark and 1/8 mark respectively each. Frodo scored 23 marks in the test. What is the minimum possible number of the question wrongly answered by him?

127. 1777 has exactly 5 digits when converted to base 'x' from the decimal system. What is the minimum possible value of x?

(a) 3 (b) 4
(c) 6 (d) None of these

128. What will be the sum of all natural numbers between 101 and 1000 which on division by 2, 4, 6, 8, 10 leave remainders 1, 3, 5, 7, 9, respectively?

129. Units digit of which of the following is the same as the units digits of $a^{17} + b^{17}$ for any positive integer value of a, b?

(a) $a^2 + b^2$ (b) $a^{12} + b^{12}$
(c) $a^{13} + b^{13}$ (d) $a^{10} + b^{10}$

130. How many 4-digit numbers are there in the decimal system, which have exactly 4-digits when expressed in base 6, base 7 and base 8?

(a) 158 (b) 248
(c) 296 (d) 368

131. What is the difference between the highest and the least 4-digit natural numbers that have exactly 4-digits when expressed in base 6 and base 7.

132. If n is a natural number, then what is the sum of all the possible distinct remainders when $9^n + 6^n + 4^n + 11^n$ is divided by 10?

133. If x, y, z and w are natural numbers, then what is the sum of all the possible remainders when $9^x + 6^y + 4^z + 11^z$ is divided by 10?

134. What is the maximum possible sum of the number of Mondays and Thursdays in two consecutive years?

135. In the previous question, find the minimum possible sum of the number of Mondays and Thursdays.

136. What will be the value of remainder when (11111111..........64terms) × (22222222......... 55terms) is divided by 18?

(a) 0 (b) 1
(c) 2 (d) 17

137. Find the number of solutions of the equation: $x^2 - y^2 = 777314$:

Directions for Questions 138 and 139: There was a table in a room and there were 100 coins (coin 1 to coin 100) in a row on the table. All the coins were heads up initially. You entered the room and turned all the coins, the second time you entered the room and turned every 2nd coin (coin 2, coin 4, ...), the 3rd time you entered the room and turned every 3rd coin (coin 3, coin 6, coin 9, ...) and so on. If you visited the room 100 times and continued this sequence every time, then answer the following questions.

138. What were the states of 54th and 91st coin after the 100th visit? Type 1, if both are heads; Type 2, if the first one is head and the other is tail; Type 3, if the first one is tail and the second is tail; Type 4, if both are tails.

139. After your 100th visit, how many coins were in the heads-up position?

140. What is the digit at the hundredths place of the number $(225)^{40}$?

(a) 2 (b) 4
(c) 6 (d) 8

141. Consider the set of the first 14 natural numbers. Three numbers a, b, c are selected from this set such that $a > 3b > 4c$. How many such distinct triplets (a, b, c) are possible?

(a) 32 (b) 26
(c) 22 (d) 18

142. How many four-digit numbers having distinct digits using the first five natural numbers (1 to 5) can be formed such that the numbers formed are divisible by each of the digits used in the number?

(a) 0 (b) 1
(c) 2 (d) 3

High Yield Questions

Scan this QR code to access assisted problem solving videos on questions 17, 77, 103 and 112-114 from LOD 2

Space for Rough Work

LEVEL OF DIFFICULTY (III)

1. If a four-digit natural number is 7083 more than the number formed by reversing the order of its digits, then how many such natural numbers are possible?
2. When a certain number of tracksuits were distributed equally among a group of four athletes or another group of six athletes, two suits were left in each case. What is the difference between the smallest and highest two-digit number of suits distributed in the first group among each athlete?
(a) 87 (b) 84
(c) 85 (d) 86
3. The product of the digits of a three-digit number N is 24. If the digits of N + 1 are such that they reach the maximum possible value as a product of the three digits for N + 1, then find the difference between the maximum and second lowest possible values of N + 1.
4. If A = 1! + 2! + 3! + 4!.....12345! and A = B. Find the remainder when A^B is divided by 5.
5. If the LCM of 16! × 20! and 18! × 19! is $x!y!/z!$, where x and y are two digit integers and z is a single digit integer. What is the value of $x + y + z$?
(a) 38 (b) 39
(c) 40 (d) 41
6. Abhijit Roy wrote down several distinct positive integers, not exceeding 60 on a blackboard. Their product was not divisible by 36. At most how many numbers could he have written?
(a) 40 (b) 30
(c) 41 (d) 34
7. Let $a_1, a_2, a_3, \ldots$ be a geometric progression having more than 9 terms and $a_1 + a_2 + a_3 + \ldots + a_9 = 4k$. If $a_1 < 0$, $a_1 + a_2 = 4$ and $a_3 + a_4 = 16$, then find the value of |k|.
8. If a, b, x and y are natural numbers such that $a, b > 1$. If $a^x \times b^y = 75^{232}$, then minimum value of $|x - y|$ is?
9. On Christmas, Santa numbered his gifts for the children from 1 to N. While adding up the box numbers, Santa mistakenly added a number twice and instead of adding a number he subtracted the number, resulting in an incorrect sum of 448. In how many ways could Santa have made these errors (in terms of using distinct double counted and subtracted numbers) and achieved the incorrect sum of 448?
10. For the above question, if we consider all the ways in which Santa could have made these errors (in terms of using distinct double counted and subtracted numbers) and achieved the incorrect sum of 448, what is the maximum addition of the two numbers which contributed to the error?
11. For natural numbers x, y and z, if $xy + yz = 19$ and $yz + xz = 51$, then the minimum possible value of xyz is?
12. Let $3^{P!} \times n = m!$ where P, n and m are natural numbers and n is not divisible by 3. If $n \geq 100$, then what is the smallest possible value of $P + n + m$?
13. Let N = abbbd, be a 5-digit number which is a multiple of 3. If $a + b + d = 18$ and each of a, b, d is a natural number, then how many possible values can N take?
14. abc, cba and $pq4$ are three digit number such that $abc - cba = pq4$, then how many factors does the resultant number have?
15. If N is the smallest number that can be written both as $2a^5$ and $3b^2$, where both a and b are natural numbers, what is the least possible value of $a + b$?
16. For two non-negative integers x and y, $2x + 3y = 80$. What is the maximum possible value of $x + y + z$, where z is the sum of factors of the number 80?
17. If $ab^2 + b^2c = 13$ and $bc + ca = 33$, where a, b, c are distinct natural numbers, the difference between maximum and minimum possible values of $a \times b \times c$ is
18. If $4^{6n+1} + x$ and $6^{12n} - x$ are divisible by 5, then find the sum of all values of x, where x lies between –10 and 10.
19. For three distinct natural numbers whose sum is 14, what is the difference between maximum and minimum value of sum of their product and all possible pair wise product?
20. How many integers x are there such that $\frac{x+95}{x+5}$ is an integer?
21. abc is a three-digit number such that none of the digits is 0 and $abc = 5\,(ab + bc + ca)$. What is the difference between the highest and lowest possible values for abc?
22. How many numbers between 1 and 250 have exactly 4 factors apart from 1 and itself?
23. A natural number x^2 has exactly five of its factors more than x. What is the number of factors of x^5 ?
24. Let N = abbbd, be a 5-digit number which is a multiple of 3. If $a + b + d = 18$ and each of a, b and d are distinct natural numbers, then how many possible values can N take?
25. The expression $7^{4n} - 5^{4n}$, where n is an even number, is always divisible by which of the following number?
(i) 2 (ii) 23
(iii) 111 (iv) 37

(a) Only (i) (b) Only (ii)
(c) (i) and (iii) (d) (i), (iii) and (iv)

26. If the LCM of 3^{12}, 8^8 and x is 12^{12}, then how many values are possible for x?

27. 'X' is a set of three numbers such that the sum and HCF of the three numbers in it are 105 and 5 respectively. If at least one number in X is less than or equal to 15, then how many such sets are possible?

28. Find the last 2-digits of: $15 \times 37 \times 63 \times 51 \times 97$ 17.
(a) 35 (b) 45
(c) 55 (d) 85

Directions for Questions 29 and 30: $15x\ 3y\ 7z$, a seven-digit number, is completely divisible by 44. 'x', 'y' and 'z' are single digit whole numbers.

29. Find the distinct possible values of $y + z - x$.

30. What is the maximum possible value of $(y + z - x)$.

Directions for Questions 31 and 32: If 'a' is an even natural number and 'b' is an odd natural number & $ab - 3a - 2b - 594 = 0$, then answer the following questions:

31. Find the total number of solutions of the given equation $ab - 3a - 2b - 594 = 0$.

32. Maximum possible value of $a + b$

Directions for Questions 33 and 34: 'x' is a 2-digit number more than 40 such that the tens digit of the number is a factor of x.

33. How many values are possible for x?

34. Find the sum of all values of x.

35. How many distinct five digit multiples of 11 can be formed using the digits 2, 3, 4, 5 and 6 ?

36. N is a 2-digit number, $N < 98$. When 910 is divided by N and $N + 2$ the remainder is 'x' in both cases. Then, the values of 'x' for maximum possible value of N =?

37. If P be the product of all the natural numbers between 50 and 290 that have an odd number of factors, what is the highest power of 6 in P?

38. Find the number of composite odd natural numbers less than 100 and relatively prime to 70.

39. If 51!/10! is completely divisible by 12^x, where x is a natural number, then what is the maximum possible value of x?

Directions for Questions 40 and 41: The sum of number of factors of N and N^2 is 60. If N is a three-digit number. Then answer the following questions:

40. How many values can N have?

41. What is the largest possible value of N?

42. If P and Q are two natural numbers such that
$P^2 + 3Q^2 = 1376$
How many solutions are possible for the above mentioned equation?

43. The last two-digits in the multiplication $122 \times 123 \times 125 \times 127 \times 129$ will be
(a) 20 (b) 50
(c) 30 (d) 40

44. A 2-digit number is divided by the sum of its digits. What is the maximum possible remainder?

45. X is the set of all the integers from –100 to 100. How many subsets of X having exactly 199 elements can be formed such that the sum of all the elements in each subset is either 1 or –1?

46. a, b, c, d, e, f, g and h are eight integers from the sets (–10, 10). Find the minimum possible value of $ab + bc + cd + de + ef + fg + gh + ha$.

47. The remainder obtained when $43^{101} + 23^{101}$ is divided by 66 is
(a) 2 (b) 10
(c) 5 (d) 0

48. Both the HCF and the difference of two numbers is 6. If the LCM of the two numbers is a 4-digit number, then what is the maximum possible value of the bigger number?

49. Both the HCF and the difference of two numbers is 6. If the LCM of the two numbers is a 4-digit number, then how many such pairs are possible?

Directions for Questions 50 and 51: N is a natural number which has 6 factors. If $1 \le N \le 50$, then answer the following questions:

50. How many values are possible for N?

51. Find the maximum possible value of N.

52. The numbers $(6 - p)$, $(6 - q)$, $(6 - r)$, $(6 - s)$ and $(6 - t)$ are all distinct integers whose product is equal to 6720. What is the value of $(p + q + r + s + t)$?

53. For how many positive integer values of x, will the expression $87y - 264x = 60$ be valid, if x and y are positive integers less than 100?

Directions for Questions 54 to 56: A two-digit number 'ab' having distinct digits when divided by the sum of the digits gives the same remainder as when a two-digit number that is formed by reversing the digits of original number is divided by the sum of the digits.

54. How many such two-digit numbers are possible?

55. Find the maximum value of the 2-digit number 'ab'.

56. Find the minimum value of 'ab'.

57. 'X' is a 62-digit number. All the digits except the 26th digit from the right are the same. If 'X' is divisible by 13, then which of the following can never be the unit's digit of 'X'?
(a) 4 (b) 1
(c) 5 (d) 6

58. $P = \{2, 3, 5, 10, 20, 40, 80, 160, 320\}$. How many distinct values of 'S' are possible, if 'S' is defined as the sum of one or more elements of the set 'P'?

59. Given that p, q, r and s are positive integers such that $q^{\frac{1}{2}} = p$ and $s^{\frac{7}{4}} = r$ If $s - q = 17$, then find the value of $p + r$.

60. $\frac{32^{32^{32}}}{9}$ will leave a remainder
(a) 4 (b) 7
(c) 1 (d) 2

Directions for Questions 61 to 63: *abc* is a 3-digit number and accb is a 4-digit number (*a, b, c* are single digit natural numbers). If *ab* × *ac* = *abc*, then answer the following questions:

61. What is the value of *b*?
(a) 2 (b) 1
(c) 0 (d) Cannot be determined

62. What is the remainder when *bc* × *accaaa* is divided by *ac*?

63. If *abc* is divisible by 17, then what is the remainder when *abcbac* is divided by 14?

64. The remainder of $\frac{32^{32^{32}}}{7}$ is equal to:
(a) 4 (b) 2
(c) 1 (d) 3

65. *n* is a number, such that 2*n* has 28 factors and 3*n* has 30 factors. 6*n* has
(a) 35 (b) 32
(c) 28 (d) None of these

66. Suppose the sum of *n* consecutive integers is $x + (x + 1) + (x + 2) + (x + 3) + \ldots + (x + (n - 1))$ = 1000, then which of the following cannot be true about the number of terms *n*
(a) The number of terms can be 16
(b) The number of terms can be 5
(c) The number of terms can be 25
(d) The number of terms can be 20

67. The remainder when $2^2 + 22^2 + 222^2 + 2222^2 + \ldots\ldots.(222\ldots..49 \text{ twos})^2$ is divided by 9 is
(a) 2 (b) 5
(c) 6 (d) 7

68. $N = 202 \times 20002 \times 200000002 \times 2000000000000002 \times 200000000\ldots.2$ (31 zeroes) The sum of digits in this multiplication will be
(a) 112 (b) 160
(c) 144 (d) Cannot be determined

69. Twenty-five sets of problems on Data Interpretation–one each for the DI sections of 25 CATALYST tests were prepared by the Mindworkzz research team. The DI section of each CATALYST contained 50 questions of which exactly 35 questions were unique, i.e., they had not been used in the DI section of any of the other 24 CATALYSTs. What could be the maximum possible number of questions prepared for the DI sections of all the 25 CATALYSTs put together?
(a) 1100 (b) 975
(c) 1070 (d) 1055

70. In the above question, what could be the minimum possible number of questions prepared?
(a) 890 (b) 875
(c) 975 (d) None of these

Directions for Questions 71 to 73: At a particular time in the twenty-first century, there were seven bowlers in the Indian cricket team's list of 16 players short-listed to play the next world cup. Statisticians discovered that that if you looked at the number of wickets taken by any of the 7 bowlers of the current Indian cricket team, the number of wickets taken by them had a strange property. The numbers were such that for any team selection of 11 players (having 1 to 7 bowlers) by using the number of wickets taken by each bowler and attaching coefficients of +1, 0, or –1 to each value available and adding the resultant values, any number from 1 to 1093, both included could be formed. If we denote W_1, W_2, W_3, W_4, W_5, W_6 and W_7 as the 7 values in the ascending order what could be the answer to the following questions?

71. Find the value of $W_1 + 2W_2 + 3W_3 + 4W_4 + 5W_5 + 6W_6$.
(a) 2005 (b) 1995
(c) 1985 (d) None of these

72. Find the index of the largest power of 3 contained in the product $W_1 W_2 W_3 W_4 W_5 W_6 W_7$.
(a) 15 (b) 10
(c) 21 (d) 6

73. If the sum of the seven coefficients is 0, find the smallest number that can be obtained.
(a) – 1067 (b) – 729
(c) – 1040 (d) – 1053

Directions for Questions 74 and 75: Answer these questions on the basis of the information given below.

In the ancient game of Honololo, the task involves solving a puzzle asked by the chief of the tribe. Anybody answering the puzzle correctly is given the hand of the most beautiful maiden of the tribe. Unfortunately, for the youth of the tribe, solving the puzzle is not a cakewalk since the chief is the greatest mathematician of the tribe.

In one such competition the chief called everyone to attention and announced openly:

"A three-digit number '*mnp*' is a perfect square and the number of factors it has, is also a perfect square. It is also known that the digits *m*, *n* and *p* are all distinct. Now answer my questions and win the maiden's hand."

74. If $(m + n + p)$ is also a perfect square, what is the number of factors of the six-digit number *mnpmnp*?
(a) 36 (b) 72
(c) 48 (d) Cannot be determined

75. If the fourth power of the product of the digits of the number *mnp* is not divisible by 5, what is the number of factors of the nine-digit number, *mnpmnpmnp*?

(a) 36 (b) 72
(c) 48 (d) Cannot be determined

76. In a cricket tournament organised by the ICC, a total of 15 teams participated. Australia, as usual, won the tournament by scoring the maximum number of points. The tournament is organised as a single round robin tournament—where each team plays with every other team exactly once. Three points are awarded for a win, 2 points are awarded for a tie/washed out match and 1 point is awarded for a loss. Zimbabwe had the lowest score (in terms of points) at the end of the tournament. Zimbabwe scored a total of 21 points. All the 15 national teams got a distinct score (in terms of points scored). It is also known that at least, one match played by the Australian team was tied/washed out. Which of the following is always true for the Australian team?

(a) It had at least two ties/washouts
(b) It had a maximum of 3 losses
(c) It had a maximum of 9 wins
(d) All of these

77. What is the remainder when 128^{1000} is divided by 153?
(a) 103 (b) 145
(c) 118 (d) 52

78. Find the remainder when $50^{51^{52}}$ is divided by 11.
(a) 6 (b) 4
(c) 7 (d) 3

79. Find the remainder when $32^{33^{34}}$ is divided by 11.
(a) 5 (b) 4
(c) 10 (d) 1

80. Find the remainder when $30^{72^{87}}$ is divided by 11.
(a) 5 (b) 9
(c) 6 (d) 3

81. Find the remainder when $50^{56^{52}}$ is divided by 11.
(a) 7 (b) 5
(c) 9 (d) 10

82. Find the remainder when $33^{34^{35}}$ is divided by 7.
(a) 5 (b) 4
(c) 6 (d) 2

83. Let S_m denote the sum of the squares of the first m natural numbers. For how many values of $m < 100$, is S_m a multiple of 4?
(a) 50 (b) 25
(c) 36 (d) 24

84. For the above question, for how many values will the sum of cubes of the first m natural numbers be a multiple of 5 (if $m < 50$)?
(a) 20 (b) 21
(c) 22 (d) None of these

85. How many integer values of x and y satisfy the expression $4x + 7y = 3$ where $|x| < 1000$ and $|y| < 1000$?
(a) 284 (b) 285
(c) 286 (d) None of these

86. $N = 7777..................7777$, where the digit 7 repeats itself 603 times. What is the remainder left when N is divided by 1144?

87. How many factors of 19! are there, whose unit digit is 5?

88. $N = 1! - 2! + 3! - 4! + ... + 47! - 48! + 49!, - 50! + 51!$ Then what is the unit digit of N^N?

89. How many numbers less than 100 have exactly four factors?

90. Two odd numbers have 36 factors each and the HCF of these two numbers is 225. What is the minimum possible LCM of these two numbers if the power of any prime factor in these two numbers is not more than 3?

91. Find the remainder when $[(7!)^{6!}]^{17777}$ is divided by 17?

92. A 4-digit number $wxyz$ is such that $x + y = 2w$ and $y + 6z = 2(w + x)$ & $w + 5z = 2y$. Find the sum of such 4-digit numbers which satisfy the given conditions.

93. Find the remainder when (17)(9!)+2 (18!) is divided by (9!)17408.

94. X is a number formed by writing the first 1002 natural numbers one after another from left to right then find the remainder when X is divided by 9.

95. X is a number formed by writing the first 1002 whole numbers one after another from left to right then a vertical line is drawn which divides the number such that the number of digits on either side of line is the same. Find the remainder when the number formed by the digits on the left of the vertical line, is divided by 625.

96. Amongst all the 4-digit natural numbers divisible by 24, how many have the number 24 in them?

97. If X is a natural number and $X < 100$ then the number of values of X for which $18X + 2$ & $12X + 1$ are relatively prime?

98. P is a natural number of at least 6 digits and its leftmost digit is 7. When this leftmost digit is removed from P, the number thus obtained is found to be 1/21 times of P. What is the product of the all the nonzero digits of P?
(a) 126 (b) 105
(c) 60 (d) 72

99. $X!$ is completely divisible by11^{51} but not by 11^{52}. What is the sum of digits of largest such number X?

100. If 'a' is a natural number and HCF of a, $a + 5$ is 5. If the LCM of the two numbers is a three-digit number, then what is the difference between the maximum and minimum possible values of the smaller number?
(a) 25 (b) 35
(c) 40 (d) 45

101. How many times would 1 be used while writing all the natural numbers from 8 to 127 in the binary number system?

(a) 212 (b) 218
(c) 424 (d) 436

102. What is the maximum number of elements that one can pick from the set of natural numbers from 1 to 20 such that the product of no two of them results in a perfect square or perfect cube?

103. *abcdefghij* is a ten digit number with distinct digits such that $a > b > c, d > e > f, g > h > i > j$. a, b, c are consecutive even digits and g, h, i, j are consecutive odd digits. If $d + e + f = 9$, then what is the value of $\left[\frac{a \times b \times c \times d}{h}\right]$ (where [] denotes greatest integer function)?

(a) 42 (b) 0
(c) 54 (d) 66

104. $N = abc$ is a 3-digit number, the sum of whose digits is $1/7^{th}$ of the product of its digits. Then how many possible non-ordered sets of (a, b, c) are possible?

105. $(3132!)_{10} = (x)_{34}$, then what will be the number of consecutive zeroes at the end of 'x'?

(a) 124 (b) 167
(c) 194 (d) None of these

High Yield Questions

Scan this QR code to access assisted problem solving videos on questions 64, 76, 104 and 105 from LOD 3

Space for Rough Work

ANSWER KEY

Level of Difficulty (I)

1. (a)	2. (a)	3. (b)	4. (b)
5. 1 and 81	6. (c)	7. (d)	8. (d)
9. 3	10. (d)	11. (a)	12. (c)
13. 6	14. 13	15. (b)	16. (c)
17. (d)	18. (d)	19. (c)	20. (d)
21. (b)	22. (d)	23. (a)	24. (b)
25. (c)	26. (d)	27. 4	28. (a)
29. (b)	30. (a)	31. (a)	32. (a)
33. (d)	34. (c)	35. (d)	36. (b)
37. 29	38. (b)	39. (a)	40. (a)
41. (b)	42. (c)	43. (d)	
44. 13, 78 & 26, 39		45. (d)	
46. 27, 28 & 3, 8		47. (a) → 21^{12}	(b) → 0.8^3
48. (b)			

49. a. → 0, 2, 4, 6, 8
  b. → 1, 4, 7
  c. → 0, 4, 8
  d. → 0, 5
  e. → 4
  f. → 7
  g. → 0

50. LCM → 5670
  HCF → 27
  LCM → 780
  HCF → 39
  LCM → 737100
  HCF → 30

51. (b)	52. (a)	53. (c)	54. (c)
55. (c)	56. (a)	57. (d)	58. (b)
59. (b)	60. (a)	61. (b)	62. (d)
63. (a)	64. (a)	65. (b)	66. (c)
67. (b)	68. (c)	69. (c)	70. (c)
71. (a)	72. (c)	73. (b)	74. (b)
75. (c)	76. (a)	77. (d)	78. (a)
79. (c)	80. (b)	81. (b)	82. (a)
83. (c)	84. (c)	85. (d)	86. (d)
87. (a)	88. (c)	89. (b)	90. (c)
91. (d)	92. (b)	93. (c)	94. (d)
95. (c)	96. (b)	97. (b)	98. (c)
99. (b)	100. (b)	101. (d)	102. (b)
103. (d)	104. (a)	105. (b)	106. (d)
107. (c)	108. (b)	109. (b)	110. (a)
111. (c)	112. (d)	113. (b)	114. (b)
115. (c)	116. (b)	117. (d)	118. (a)
119. 7	120. 11	121. 72^6	122. 6
123. 7	124. 12	125. 242	126. (d)
127. 5	128. 0	129. 5	
130. 10 and 11		131. 3	132. 5040
133. 1	134. 1111111	135. 1	136. 4^{40}
137. 24	138. 198	139. 120	140. 5
141. 2	142. 40	143. 4	144. 1
145. 96	146. 8	147. $X + Y$	148. 5
149. $B \geq A > D \geq C$		150. 4	

Level of Difficulty (II)

1. 49	2. (b)	3. 899	4. (c)
5. 7560	6. (d)	7. 325	8. (d)
9. 90	10. 4	11. 89	12. –1
13. 46	14. 13	15. 22	16. 1700
17. 3	18. 8	19. (b)	20. 9
21. (c)	22. (b)	23. 9	24. 4
25. (d)	26. (c)	27. (c)	28. (d)
29. (d)	30. (d)	31. 1363	32. (b)
33. (d)	34. (a)	35. (d)	36. (c)
37. (a)	38. (c)	39. (c)	40. 57
41. 33	42. 71	43. (c)	44. 49
45. (c)	46. 863	47. (b)	48. 2
49. 40	50. 26	51. 13 and 31	52. (d)
53. (c)	54. (a)	55. 63	56. 24
57. 32	58. 27	59. 64	60. 13, 31
61. 23	62. 1056	63. 51, 34	
64. 144, 864	65. 46, 64		
66. 63	67. 863	68. 36, 63	

69. may be 2 or 3 depending upon the numbers

70. $111^4 > 109.110.112.113 > 110.109.108.107$

71. greatest → 35 least 3/7

72. (a) 200^{300} (b) 5^{100} (c) 10^{20}

73. (c)	74. (c)	75. (b)	76. (a)
77. (d)	78. (c)	79. (b)	80. (a)
81. (a)	82. (b)	83. (c)	84. (c)
85. (d)	86. (a)	87. (b)	88. (d)
89. (a)	90. (b)	91. (b)	92. (c)
93. (b)	94. (c)	95. (b)	96. (d)
97. (d)	98. (a)	99. (b)	100. (c)
101. (a)	102. (a)	103. (c)	104. (b)
105. (a)	106. (a)	107. (d)	108. 9
109. 176	110. 0	111. 23	112. 1
113. 37	114. 10	115. 9	116. 8
117. 4	118. 12	119. 45	120. 360
121. 4	122. 997	123. 01	124. 0
125. 30	126. 6	127. (d)	128. 4312
129. (c)	130. 296	131. 295	132. 4
133. 8	134. 209	134. 208	136. (c)
137. 0	138. 1	139. 90	140. (c)
141. (c)	142. (a)		

Level of Difficulty (III)

1. 27	2. (a)	3. 586	4. 3
5. (b)	6. (c)	7. 171	8. 0
9. 22	10. 52	11. 34	12. 569
13. 57	14. 16	15. 78	16. 226
17. 8	18. –6	19. 96	20. 24
21. 220	22. 31	23. 26	24. 42
25. (d)	26. 325	27. 22	28. (a)
29. 12	30. 14	31. 12	32. 307
33. 12	34. 827	35. 12	36. 11
37. 8	38. 11	39. 19	40. 4 values

41. 784	42. 0	43. 50	44. 15
45. 200	46. –800	47. (d)	48. 246
49. 28	50. 8	51. 50	52. 0
53. 1	54. 16	55. 84	56. 12
57. (a)	58. 384	59. 2195	60. 4
61. (d)	62. 0	63. 8	64. 4
65. (a)	66. (d)	67. (c)	68. (b)
69. (d)	70. (a)	71. (a)	72. (c)
73. (c)	74. (c)	75. (a)	76. (b)
77. (d)	78. (a)	79. (c)	80. (a)
81. (b)	82. (d)	83. (d)	84. (d)
85. (b)	86. 777	87. 1296	88. 1
89. 32	90. $3^3 \times 5^2 \times 7^2 \times 11 \times 13$		91. 1
92. 9723	93. 17.9!	94. 6	95. 601
96. 25	97. 99	98. (b)	99. 14
100. (d)	101. 436	102. 14	103. (c)
104. 2	105. (c)		

SOLUTIONS AND SHORTCUTS

Level of Difficulty (I)

2. When you read the sentence "when the digits are reversed, the number decreases by 54, you should automatically get two reactions going in your mind.
   (i) The difference between the digits would be $54/9 = 6$.
   (ii) Since the number 'decreases'- the tens digit of the number would be larger than the units digit.

   Also, since we know that the sum of the digits is 10, we get that the digits must be 8 and 2 and the number must be 82. Thus, the changed number is 28.
3. If we look at the factors of 567, the factors are 1, 567; 3, 189; 7, 81; 9, 63; 21, 27. Out of these, only the 9,63 pair has the property expressed by the first statement in the question – i.e., product of the number and the sum of its digits is 567. You do not even need to check the second condition provided in the question. However, if you were to check it (with 63 as the number), reversing the number would make it 36 and multiplying 36 by the sum of its digits gives us 324. Hence, option (b) is correct.
4. You can solve this question by using options. It can be seen that Option (b) 12,3 fits the situation perfectly as their arithmetic mean = 7.5 and their geometric mean = 6 and the geometric mean is 20% less than the arithmetic mean.
5. Since the difference between GM and AM is an integer = two more than half of 1/3rd of 180 = two more than half of 60 = two more than 30 = 32, it means that their GM will also be an integer. We can conclude that the numbers must be such that their product is a perfect square (for its square root to be an integer). A little bit of numerical thinking gives us 1 and 81 as the only pair of numbers that have a difference of 80, are below 100 and have their produce as a perfect square. Hence, the numbers are 1 and 81.
6. For the number A381 to be divisible by 11, the sum of the even placed digits and the odds placed digits should be either 0 or a multiple of 11. This means that $(A + 8) – (3 + 1)$ should be a multiple of 11 – as it is not possible to make it zero. Thus, the smallest value that A can take (and in fact the only value it can take) is 7. Option (c) is correct.
7. The HCF of 12, 18 and 30 is 6, while the LCM is 180. Hence, the required ratio is 30 : 1.
8. 9^6 when divided by 8, would give a remainder of 1. Hence, the required answer would be 2.
9. The sum of the digits of the number should be a multiple of 9. This occurs when we use $A = 3$. Hence, the correct answer is 3.
10. LCM of 5/2, 8/9 and 11/14 would be given by: (LCM of numerators)/(HCF of denominators) = 440/1 = 440
11. Only the first option can be verified to be true in this case. If A is even, 3A would always be divisible by 6 as it would be divisible by both 2 and 3. Options (b) and (c) can be seen to be incorrect by assuming the value of A as 4.
12. The essence of this question is in the fact that the last digit of the number is 0. Naturally, the number is necessarily divisible by 2, 5 and 10. Only 4 does not necessarily divide it.
13. For P4351Q to be divisible by 72, it should be divisible by 8 and 9. Divisibility by 8 is determined through the last 3-digits. Hence, Q can only be 2. P can only be 3, giving $P + 4 + 3 + 5 + 1 + Q = 18$. Thus, $P + Q = 6$.
14. In difference between a 2-digit number and the number obtained by reversing its digits is always 9 × d, where 'd' is the difference between the digits of the number. For 9 × d to be a perfect cube, d has to be necessarily 3. The 2-digit numbers that satisfy this quality are: 30, 41–14; 52–25; 63–36; 74–47; 85–58; 96–69. A total of 13 numbers. Hence, the correct answer is 13.
15. Since both P and Q are prime numbers, the number of factors would be $(1 + 1)(1 + 1) = 4$.
16. Since both P and Q are prime numbers, the number of factors would be $(2 + 1)(1 + 1) = 6$.
17. Since both P and Q are prime numbers, the number of factors would be $(3 + 1)(2 + 1) = 12$.
18. The sides of the pentagon being 1422, 1737, 2160, 2214 and 2358, the least difference between any two numbers is 54. Hence, the correct answer will be a factor of 54.

Further, since there are some odd numbers in the list, the answer should be an odd factor of 54.

Hence, check with 27, 9 and 3 in that order. You will get 9 as the HCF.

19. The HCF of 576 and 448 is 64. Hence, each section should have 64 children. The number of sections would be given by: 576/64 + 448/64 = 9 + 7 = 16. Option (c) is correct.
20. The HCF of the given numbers is 31 and hence the number of bottles required would be
 403/31 + 465/31 + 496/31 = 13 + 15 + 16 = 44. Option (d) is correct.
21. The LCM of the 4 numbers is 612. The highest 4-digit number which would be a common multiple of all these 4 numbers is 9792. Hence, the correct answer is 9793.
22. The LCM of 16, 18 and 20 is 720. The numbers which would give a remainder of 4, when divided by 16, 18 and 20 would be given by the series: 724, 1444, 2164, 2884 and so on. Checking each of these numbers for divisibility by 7, it can be seen that 2884 is the least number in the series that is divisible by 7 and hence is the correct answer. Option (d) is correct.
23. They will ring together again after a time which would be the LCM of 6, 8, 12 and 18. The required LCM = 72. Hence, they would ring together after 72 seconds. Option (a) is correct.
24. 720/72 = 10 times. Option (b) is correct.
25. The interpretation of the situation $AB + XY = 1XP$ is that the tens digit in XY is repeated in the value of the solution (i.e., $1XP$). Thus, for instance if X was 2, it would mean we are adding a 2-digit number AB to a number in the 20's to get a number in the 120's. This can only happen if AB is in the 90's which means that A is 9.
26. $720 = 2^4 \times 3^2 \times 5^1$. Number of factors = 5 × 3 × 2 = 30. Option (d) is correct.
27. There are 4 such numbers viz: 164; 364; 649 and 816. Hence, the correct answer is 4.
28. Since x will be an even number, $x + 1$ will be an odd number. Also, through trial and error, we can remove the possibility of $x + 1$ being a prime number (1 × 2 × 3 × 4 = 24. 24 + 1 = 25. Hence, we can reject conclusion (ii). If we try other numerical products of 4 consecutive numbers, we see that on adding 1 to the answer, we always get a perfect square. Hence, we can conclude that option (a) is correct.
29. If A is not divisible by 3, it is obvious that 2A would also not be divisible by 3, as 2A would have no '3' in it.
30. $9^{100}/8 = (8 + 1)^{100}/8 \rightarrow$ Since this is of the form $(a + 1)^n/a$, the Remainder = 1. Option (a) is correct.
31. $2^{1000}/3$ is of the form $(a)^{\text{EVEN POWER}}/(a + 1)$. The remainder = 1 in this case as the power is even. Option (a) is correct.
32. The condition for the product to be the greatest is if the two terms are equal. Thus, the break up in option (a) would give us the highest product of the two parts. Option (a) is correct.
33. 50/5 = 10, 10/5 = 2.
 Thus, the required answer would be 10 + 2 = 12. Option (d) is correct.
34. For a number to be divisible by 24, it should be divisible by 3 and 8. Only option (c) has this property.
35. Any number divisible by 88, has to be necessarily divisible by 11, 2, 4, 8, 44 and 22. Thus, each of the first three options is correct.
36. $10800 = 108 \times 100 = 3^3 \times 2^4 \times 5^2$.
 The number of divisors would be: (3 + 1) (4 + 1) (2 + 1) = 4 × 5 × 3 = 60 divisors. Option (b) is correct.
37. The difference between a two-digit number and the number formed by reversing the digits, is always a multiple of 9. For it to be a perfect square, this difference should be either 9, 36 or 81. For the difference to be 9, the difference between the digits of the number has to be 1. The numbers pairs that exhibit this requirement are: 12–21; 23–32; 34–43; 45–54; 56–65; 67–76; 78–87; 89–98 a total of 16 numbers. Also, the number 10, when reversed becomes the single-digit number 1, and also shows a difference of 9, so it should also be counted. For the difference to be 36, we need to use 15–51; 26–62; 37–73; 48–84; 59–95. Besides, 40 also exhibits this property. For the difference to be 81, the difference between the digits should be 9. This only happens for the number 90. Hence, there are a total of 16 + 1 + 10 + 1 + 1 = 29 such numbers. Hence, the correct answer is 29.
38. Since the sum of 5 prime numbers is even, it must be the case that the even prime number 2 must have been included in it. Also, since 2 is the smallest prime number, P1 has to have a value of 2. Thus, the required answer is option (b).
39. When the birds sat one on a branch, there was one extra bird. When they sat 2 to a branch, one branch was extra.
 To find the number of branches, go through options. Checking option (a), if there were 3 branches, there would be 4 birds. (this would leave one bird without branch as per the question.)
 When 4 birds would sit 2 to a branch there would be 1 branch free (as per the question). Hence, the answer (a) is correct.
40. The number would either be $(3n + 1)^2$ or $(3n + 2)^2$. In the expansion of each of these, the only term which would not be divisible by 3 would be the square of 1 and 2 respectively. When divided by 3, both of these give 1 as remainder.

41. The given expression can be written as: $5^3 \times 3^3 \times 3^2 \times 7^2/5^2 \times 7^2 \times 3^4 = 5^3 \times 3^5 \times 7^2/5^2 \times 7^2 \times 3^4 = 15$. Option (b) is correct.
42. $D = 1.44$, $C = 0.09$, $B = 0.16$, while the value of A is negative.
Thus, $D > B > C > A$ is the required order. Option (c) is correct.
43. The upper limit for $x + y = 4 + 3 = 7$. The lower limit of $x - y = 2 - 3 = -1$. Required ratio $= 7/-1 = -7$.
Option (d) is correct.
44. Since the HCF is 13, the numbers can be thought of as $13a$ and $13b$, where a and b are co-prime numbers. Also, the product of $13 \times a \times b$ should be equal to 78. Thus, $a \times b = 6$ and a,b should be co-prime. There are two possible values for $a \times b$ viz: 1×6 and 2×3. Accordingly, the pairs of numbers are 13 and 78 or 26 and 39.
45. Solve using options. Option (d) 51 and 34 satisfies the required conditions.
46. For the difference of squares to be 55, $a^2 - b^2 = 55$, we should have the conditions $(a - b) \times (a + b) = 55$. The factors of 55 are: 1×55 giving a and b as 28 and 27 respectively; 5×11 giving a and b as 8 and 3 respectively. Thus, the required pairs are 27, 28 & 3, 8.
47. (a) $21^{12} = (21^3)^4$
Since $21^3 > 54$, $21^{12} > 54^4$.
(b) $(0.4)^4 = (4/10)^4 = 1024/10000 = 0.1024$
$(0.8)^3 = (8/10)^3 = 512/1000 = 0.512$
Hence, $(0.8)^3 > (0.4)^4$
48. This is never possible.
49. (a) $c = 0, 2, 4, 6$ or 8 would make $38c$ as even and hence divisible by 2.
(b) $c = 1, 4$ or 7 are possible values to make $38c$ divisible by 3.
(c) $c = 0, 4$ or 8 would make the number end in 80, 84 or 88 and would hence be divisible by 4.
(d) $c = 0$ or 5 would make the number 380 or 385 – in which case it would be divisible by 5.
(e) For the number to become divisible by 6, it should be even and divisible by 3. From the values 1, 4 and 7 which make the number divisible by 3, we only have $c = 4$ making it even. Thus, $c = 4$.
(f) For the number to be divisible by 9, $3 + 8 + c$ should be a multiple of 9. $c = 7$ is the only value of c which can make the number divisible by 9.
(g) Obviously $c = 0$ is the correct answer.
50. Use the standard process to solve for LCM and HCF.
51. For $34x^{43}$ to be ending in 7, x has to be 3 (as $43 = 4n + 3$). Option (b) is correct.

Solutions for Questions 52 and 53:

The given condition says that Pen<Pencil<Eraser. Also, since the least cost of the three is ₹12, if we allocate a minimum of 12 to each we use up 36 out of the 41 available. The remaining 5 can be distributed as 0, 1, 4 or 0, 2 and 3 giving possible values of **Case 1 :** 12, 13 and 16 or **Case 2:** 12, 14 and 15.

52. In both cases, the cost of the pen is 12.
53. If the cost of the eraser is not divisible by 4, it means that **Case 2** holds true. For this case, the cost of the pencil is 14.
54. Amrit would place eight oranges in the basket (as there are eight 1's).
For the mangoes, he would place six mangoes (number of 2's) and remove four mangoes (number of 4's) from the basket. Thus, there would be 2 mangoes and 8 oranges in the basket.
A total of $8 - 2 = 6$ extra oranges in the basket. Option (c) is correct.
55. Solve using trial and error – Option (c) fits the situation as if we start with 15 mangoes, the following structure would take place:
Start with 15 mangoes → First watchman takes 1/3rd + 1 more = 5 + 1 = 6 mangoes → 9 mangoes left.
Second watchman takes → 1/3rd + 1 more = 3 + 1 = 4 mangoes → 5 mangoes left.
Third watchman takes → 1/5th + 4 more = 1 + 4 = 5 mangoes → 0 mangoes left.
56. The last 3-digits of the number would determine the remainder when it is divided by 8. The number up to the 120th digit would be 1234567891011... 646. 646 divided by 8 gives us a remainder of 6.
57. There would be multiple ways of scoring 34.5 marks. Think about this as follows:
If he solves 80 and gets all 80 correct, he would end up scoring 80 marks.
With every question that would go wrong, his score would fall down by 1.5 marks (he would lose the 1 mark he is gaining and further attract a penalty of 0.5 marks).
Also, for every question he does not attempt, his score would fall down by: 1.25 marks (he would lose the 1 mark he is gaining and further attract a penalty of 0.25 marks).
Thus, his score would drop @ 1.5 and @1.25 marks for every wrong and every unattempted question respectively.
Also, to get a total of 34.5 marks overall, he has to lose 45.5 marks.
There are many possible combinations of non-attempts and wrongs through which he can possibly lose 45.5 marks—for example:

17 wrongs (loses 25.5 marks) and 16 non-attempts (loses 20 marks)
12 wrongs (loses 18 marks) and 22 non-attempts (loses 27.5 marks)
Hence, we cannot answer this question uniquely and the answer is Option (d).

58. Continuing the thought process for the previous question our thinking would go as follows:
10 questions unanswered → loses 12.5 marks
To lose another 33 marks, he needs to get 22 incorrects.
Thus, the number of corrects would be 80 – 10 – 22 = 48. Option (b) is correct.

59. $3M + 4G + 5W = 750$ (1)
$6M + 9G + 10W = 1580$ (2)
Adding the two equations we get:
$9M + 13G + 15W = 2330$ (3)
Dividing this expression by 3, we get:
$3M + 4.33G + 5W = 776.666$ (4)
(4) – (1) → $0.33\ G = 26.666 \rightarrow G = 80$
Now, if we look at the equation (1) and multiply it by 2, we get: $6M + 8G + 10W = 1500$. If we subtract the cost of 4 guavas from this we would get:
$6M + 4G + 10W = 1500 - 320 = 1180$
Option (b) is correct.

60. If you try a value of M as 5, N would become ¼. It can be seen that $5^{1/4}$ (which would be the value of M^N) would be around 1.4 and hence, less than 2.
If you try for possible values of M^N by increasing the value of M, you would get $6^{1/5}$, $7^{1/6}$, $8^{1/7}$, $9^{1/8}$ and so on. In each of these cases, you can clearly see that the value of M^N would always be getting consecutively smaller than the previous value.
If you tried to go for values of M such that they are lower than 5, you would get the following values for M^N:
$4^{1/3}$, $3^{1/2}$ and the last value would be $2^{1/1}$. In this case, we can clearly see that the value of the expression M^N is increasing. However, it ends at the value of 2 (for $2^{1/1}$) and hence that is the maximum value that M^N can take. Option (a) is correct.

61. (7M + 9G + 19W) – (4M + 6G + 16W) = 120.
Hence, 1M + 1G + 1W = 40

62. The cost of a mango cannot be uniquely determined here because we have only 2 equations between 3 variables, and there is no way to eliminate one variable.

63. Since the value of y varies between –8 to 2, it is evident that if we take a very small value for y, say 0.0000000000000000000000001, and we take normal integral values for x and z, the expression xz/y would become either positive or negative infinity (depending on how you manage the signs of the numbers x, y and z).

64. Ties < Trousers < Shirts. Since each of the three is minimum 11, the total would be a minimum of 33 (for all 3). The remaining 5 need to be distributed amongst ties, trousers and shirts so that they can maintain the inequality, Ties < Trousers < Shirts.
This can be achieved with 11 ties, and the remaining 27 pieces of clothing distributed between trousers and shirts such that the shirts are greater than the trousers.
This can be done in at least 2 ways: 12 trousers and 15 shirts; 13 trousers and 14 shirts.
If you try to go for 12 ties, the remaining 26 pieces of clothing need to be distributed amongst shirts and trousers such that the shirts are greater than the trousers and both are greater than 12.
With only 26 pieces of clothing to be distributed between shirts and trousers, this is not possible. Hence, the number of ties has to be exactly 11. Option (a) is correct.

65. The number of shirts would be at least 14 as the two distributions possible are: 11, 12, 15 and 11, 13, 14. Option (b) is correct.

66. The LCM of 12, 15, 18 and 20 is 180. Thus, the least number would be 184.
Option (c) is correct.

67. 2800 = 20 × 20 × 7. Thus, we need to multiply or divide with 7 in order to make it a perfect square.

68. The answer is given by $\sqrt{1024} = 32$.
This can be experimentally verified as $30^2 = 900$, $31^2 = 961$ and $32^2 = 1024$. Hence, 1024 is the required answer. Option (c) is correct.

69. First find the LCM of 6, 9, 15 and 18. Their LCM = 18 × 5 = 90.
The series of numbers which would leave a remainder of 4 when divided by 6, 9, 15 and 18 would be given by:
LCM + 4; 2 × LCM + 4; 3 × LCM + 4; 4 × LCM + 4; 5 × LCM + 4 and so on.
Thus, this series would be:
94, 184, 274, 364, 454….
The other constraint in the problem is to find a number which also has the property of being divisible by 7. Checking each of the numbers in the series above for their divisibility by 7, we see that 364 is the least value which is also divisible by 7. Option (c) is correct.

70. LCM of 2, 3, 4, 5 and 6 = 6 × 5 × 2 = 60 (Refer to the shortcut process for LCM given in the chapter notes).
Thus, the series 61, 121, 181, etc., would give us a remainder 1 when divided by 2, 3, 4, 5 and 6.
The least 3-digit number in this series is 121. Option (c) is correct.

71. The number is of the form $899n + 63$. Since 899 is a multiple of 29, it means that the remainder of

899n + 63 when divided by 29, will be equal to the remainder of 63 divided by 29. The required remainder would be 63/29 = 5.

72. 7056 is the closest perfect square below 7147. Hence, 7147 – 7056 = 91 is the required answer. Option (c) is correct.

73. The LCM of 6, 8 and 15 is 120 = $2^3 \times 3 \times 5$. For a number to be a perfect square, all the prime factors should have even powers. Thus, if we multiply the above number by 2 × 3 × 5 = 30, we will get the required smallest perfect square. Thus, the correct answer is 120 × 30 = 3600.

74. 30492 = $2^2 \times 3^2 \times 7^1 \times 11^2$.

For a number to be a perfect square, each of the prime factors in the standard form of the number needs to be raised to an even power. Thus, we need to multiply or divide the number by 7 so that we either make it: $2^2 \times 3^2 \times 7^2 \times 11^2$ (if we multiply the number by 7) or

We make it: $2^2 \times 3^2 \times 11^2$ (if we divide the number by 7).

Option (b) is correct.

75. 88 × 113 = 9944 is the greatest 4-digit number exactly divisible by 88. Option (c) is correct.

76. The last 2-digits of 7^{22} = 49. When multiplied by any power of 5 that is 2 or greater than 2, the resultant calculation is 49 × 25, whose resultant last 2-digits are always 25. Hence, option (a) is correct.

77. The correct arrangement would be 75 plants in a row and 75 rows since 5625 is the square of 75.

78. $9^{\text{EVEN POWER}} \times 7^{4n+1} \rightarrow 1 \times 7 = 7$ as the units digit of the multiplication.

Option (a) is correct.

79. It can be seen that for 40 and 80 the number of factors are 8 and 10, respectively. Thus, option (c) satisfies the condition.

80. In order to solve this question, you need to realise that remainders of 1, 3, 4 and 5 in the case of 3, 5, 6 and 7, respectively, means remainders of –2 in each case. In order to find the number which leaves remainder –2 when divided by these numbers, you need to first find the LCM of 3, 5, 6 and 7 and subtract 2 from them. Since the LCM is 210, the first such number which satisfies this condition is 208. However, the question has asked us to find the largest such number below 4000. So you need to look at multiples of the LCM and subtract 2. The required number is 3990 – 2 = 3988

81. The number would be given by the (LCM of 2, 3 and 4) +1 → which is 12 + 1 = 13. Option (b) is correct.

82. The number would be given by the 2 × (LCM of 2, 3 and 4) +1 → which is 24 + 1 = 25. Option (a) is correct.

83. In order to solve this, you need to find the last 2-digit number in the series got by the logic: (LCM of 2, 3, 4) + 1; 2 × (LCM of 2, 3, 4) + 1; 3 × (LCM of 2, 3, 4) + 1 …

i.e., you need to find the last 2-digit number in the series:

13, 25, 37, 49….

In order to do so, you can do one of the following:

(a) Complete the series by writing the next numbers as: 61, 73, 85, 97 to see that 97 is the required answer.

(b) Complete the series by adding a larger multiple of 12 so that you reach closer to 100 faster.

Thus, if you have seen 13, 25, 37,,,,, you can straightaway add any multiple of 12 to get a number close to 100 in the series in one jump.

Thus, if you were to add 12 × 4 = 48 to 37, you would reach a value of 85 (and because you have added a multiple of 12 to 37, you can be sure that 85 would also be on the same series.)

Thus, the thinking in this case would go as follows: 13, 25, 37, …, 85, 97. Hence, the number is 97.

If you look at the two processes above– it would seem that there is not much difference between the two, but the real difference would be seen and felt if you would try to solve a question which might have asked you to find the last 3-digit number in the series. (as you would see in the next question). In such a case, getting to the number would be much faster if you use a multiple of 12 to jump ahead on the series rather than writing each number one by one.

(c) For the third way of solving this, you can see that all the numbers in the series:

13, 25, 37… are of the form 12n + 1. Thus, you are required to find a number which is of the form 12n + 1 and is just below 100.

For this purpose, you can try to first see what is the remainder when 100 is divided by 12.

Since the remainder is 4, you can realise that the number 100 is a number of the form 12n + 4.

Obviously then, if 100 is of the form 12n + 4, the largest 12n + 1 number just below 100 would occur at a value which would be 3 less than 100. (This occurs because the distance between 12n + 4 and 12n + 1 on the number line is 3.)

Thus, the answer is 100 – 3 = 97.

Hence, Option (c) is correct.

84. In order to solve this, you need to find the last 3-digit number in the series obtained by the logic: (LCM of 2, 3, 4) +1; 2 × (LCM of 2, 3, 4) +1; 3 × (LCM of 2, 3, 4) + 1 …

i.e., you need to find the last 3-digit number in the series:

13, 25, 37, 49….

In order to do so, you can do one of the following:

(a) Try to complete the series by writing the next numbers as:

61, 73, 85, 97, 109… However, you can easily see that this process would be unnecessarily too long and hence infeasible to solve this question.

(b) Complete the series by adding a larger multiple of 12 so that you reach closer to 1000 faster.

This is what we were hinting at in the previous question. If we use a multiple of 12 to write a number which will come later in the series, then we can reach close to 1000 in a few steps. Some of the ways of doing this are shown below:

(i) 13, 25, 37, …….. 997 (we add 12 × 80 = 960 to 37 to get to 37 + 960 = 997 which can be seen as the last 3-digit number as the next number would cross 1000).

(ii) 13, 25, 37, …… (add 600)….637, …(add 120)… 757,,,,, (add 120),,,, 877, ….(add 120)….997. This is the required answer.

(iii) 13, 25, 37, ……(add 120)….157, …(add 120)...277……(add 120)…..397….(add 120)……517…. (add 120)...637……(add 120)...757,,,,, (add 120),,,, 877, ….(add 120)….997. This is the required answer.

What you need to notice is that all the processes shown above are correct. So while one of them might be more efficient than the other, as far as you ensure that you add a number which is a multiple of 12 (the common difference), you would always be correct.

(c) Of course, you can also do this by using remainders. For this, you can see that all the numbers in the series:

13, 25, 37….are of the form $12n + 1$. Thus, you are required to find a number which is of the form $12n + 1$ and is just below 1000.

For this purpose, you can try to first see what is the remainder when 1000 is divided by 12.

Since the remainder is 4, you can realise that the number 1000 is a number of the form $12n + 4$.

Obviously then, if 1000 is of the form $12n + 4$, the largest $12n + 1$ number just below 1000 would occur at a value which would be 3 less than 1000. (This occurs because the distance between $12n + 4$ and $12n + 1$ on the number line is 3.)

Thus, the answer is 1000 – 3 = 997.

Hence, Option (c) is correct.

85. The logic of this question is that the frog can never reach point C if it makes an odd number of jumps. Since, the question has asked us to find out in how many ways can the frog reach point C in exactly 7 jumps, the answer would naturally be 0. Option (d) is correct.

86. They would ring together again after a time interval which would be the LCM of 5, 6 and 7. Since the LCM is 210, option (d) is the correct answer.

87. Since they would ring together every 210 seconds, their ringing together would happen at time intervals denoted by the following series- 210, 420, 630, 840, 1050, 1260, 1470, 1680, 1890, 2100, 2310, 2520, 2730, 2940, 3150, 3360, 3570 – a total of 17 times. This answer can also be calculated by taking the quotient of 3600/210 = 17. Option (a) is correct.

88. The maximum number of soldiers would be given by the HCF of 66, 110 and 242. The HCF of these numbers can be found to be 22 and hence, option (c) is correct.

89. The minimum number of rows would happen when the number of soldiers in each row is the maximum. Since, the HCF is 22 the number of soldiers in each row is 22. Then the total number of rows would be given by:

66/22 + 110/22 + 242/22 = 3 + 5 + 11 = 19 rows

Option (b) is correct.

90. The number of bottle sizes possible would be given by the number of factors of the HCF of 170, 102 and 374. Since, the HCF of these numbers is 34, the bottle sizes that are possible would be the divisors of 34 which are 1 litre, 2 litres, 17 litres and 34 litres, respectively. Thus, a total of 4 bottle sizes are possible. Option (c) is correct.

91. The size of the largest bottle that can be used is obviously 34 litres (HCF of 170, 102 and 374). Option (d) is correct.

92. The minimum number of bottles required would be: 170/34 + 102/34 + 374/34 = 5 + 3 + 11 = 19. Option (b) is correct.

(**Note:** The logic of how to think about Questions 93 to 103 has been given in the theory in the chapter. Please have a relook at that in case you have doubts about any of the solutions till Question 103.)

93. The answer would be given by the quotients of 100/5 + 100/25 = 20 + 4 = 24. Option (c) is correct.

94. 24 + 4 = 28. Option (d) is correct.

95. 17 + 5 + 1 = 23. Option (c) is correct.

96. The power of 20 which would divide 155! would be given by the power of 5's which would divide 155! since $20 = 2^2 \times 5$ and the number of 2^2s in any factorial would always be greater than the number of 5s in the factorial. 31 + 6 + 1 = 38. Option (b) is correct.

97. $5^{59} = 5 \times (5^2)^{29}$. The remainder of 5^2 by 13 is –1 (= 12). Thus, $(5^2)^{29}$, will also give a remainder of 12. Hence, $5^{59}/13$ will give us a remainder of $12 \times 5/13 =$ 8. Hence, option (b) is correct.

98. The 2-digit numbers that would leave a remainder of 3 when divided by 7 would be the numbers 10, 17, 24, 31, 38, 45, …94. The sum of these numbers would be given by the formula
(number of numbers × average of the numbers) = ?
There are 13 numbers in the series and their average is 52. Thus, the required answer is 13 × 52 = 676. Option (c) is correct.
(**Note:** The logic used here is that of sum of an Arithmetic Progression and is explained in details in the next chapter).

99. All numbers divisible by 27 would also be divisible by 3 and 9. Numbers divisible by 9 but not by 27 would be divisible by 3 and 9 only and need to be counted to give us our answer.
The numbers which satisfy the given condition are: 9, 18, 36, 45, 63, 72, 90, 99, 117, 126, 144, 153, 171, 180 and 198. There are 15 such numbers.
Alternately, you could also think of this as:
Between 1 to 200, there are 22 multiples of 9. But not all these 22 have to be counted as multiples of 27 need to be excluded from the count. There are 7 multiples of 27 between 1 and 200. Thus, the answer would be given by 22 – 7 = 15. Option (b) is correct.

100. The required minimum happens when we use (–0.5) as the value of N. $(-0.5)^2 + (-0.5) = 0.25 - 0.5 = -0.25$ is the least possible value for the sum of any number and its square. Option (b) is correct.

101. Each of the statements are false as we can have the sum of 2 prime numbers ending in 5, 0 and the sum can also be odd. Option (d) is correct.

102. This occurs for values such as: 213 – 123; 324 – 234, etc., where it can be seen that the value of X is 1 more than Y. The possible pairs of X and Y are: 2,1; 3,2… 9,8 – a total of eight pairs of values. Option (b) is correct.

103. The required sum would be given by the formula $n(n + 1)$ for the first n even numbers. In this case, it would be 50 × 51 = 2550. Option (d) is correct.

104. 763/57 leaves a remainder of 22 when it is divided by 57. Thus, if we were to add 35 to this number, the number we obtain would be completely divisible by 57. Option (a) is correct.

105. Since, 763/57 leaves a remainder of 22, we would need to subtract 22 from 763 in order to get a number divisible by 57. Option (b) is correct.

106. 8441/57 leaves a remainder of 5. Thus, if we were to add 52 to this number, the number we obtain would be completely divisible by 57. Option (d) is correct.

107. Since, 8441/57 leaves a remainder of 5. We would need to subtract 5 from 8441 in order to get a number divisible by 57. Option (c) is correct.

108. 10000 divided by 79 leaves a remainder of 46. Hence, if we were to add 33 to 10000 we would get a number divisible by 79. The correct answer is 10033. Option (b) is correct.

109. 100000 divided by 79 leaves a remainder of 65. Hence, if we were to subtract 65 from 100000, we would get a number divisible by 79. The correct answer is 99935. Option (b) is correct.

110. It can be seen that in the multiples of 12, the number closest to 773 is 768. Option (a) is correct.

111. Since 12 is a divisor of 84, the required remainder would be obtained by dividing 57 by 12. The required answer is 9. Option (c) is correct.

112. Since 11 does not divide 84, there are many possible answers for this question and hence we cannot determine one unique value for the answer. Option (d) is, thus, correct.

113. The numbers that can do so are going to be factors of the difference between 511 and 667, i.e., 156. The factors of 156 are 1, 2, 3, 4, 6, 12, 13, 26, 39, 52, 78, 156. There are 12 such numbers. Option (b) is correct.

114. The multiples of 13 between 200 and 400 would be represented by the series:
208, 221, 234, 247, 260, 273, 286, 299, 312, 325, 338, 351, 364, 377 and 390
There are a total of 15 numbers in the above series. Option (b) is correct.
(**Note:** The above series is an Arithmetic Progression. The process of finding the number of terms in an Arithmetic Progression are defined in the chapter on Progressions.)

115. $8n/5 - 5n/8 = 39n/40 = 39$. Solve for n to get the value of $n = 40$. Option (c) is correct.

116. $x + y = 3(x - y) \rightarrow 2x = 4y$. If we take y as 10, we would get the value of x as 20. Option (b) is correct.

117. $4^{11} + 4^{12} + 4^{13} + 4^{14} + 4^{15} = 4^{11}(1 + 4^1 + 4^2 + 4^3 + 4^4) = 4^{11} \times 341$. The factors of 341 are:
1, 11, 31 and 341. Thus, we can see that the values in each of the three options would divide the expression. $4^{11} + 4^{12} + 4^{13} + 4^{14} + 4^{15}$. Thus, option (d) is correct.

118. Since the numbers have their HCF as 16, both the numbers have to be multiples of 16 (i.e., 2^4).
$$7168 = 2^{10} \times 7^1$$
In order to visualise the required possible pairs of numbers, we need to look at the prime factors of 7168 in the following fashion:
$7168 = 2^{10} \times 7^1 = (2^4 \times 2^4) \times 2^2 \times 7^1 = (16 \times 16) \times 2 \times 2 \times 7$. It is then a matter of distributing the 2 extra twos and the 1 extra seven in $2^2 \times 7^1$ between the two numbers given by 16 and 16 inside the bracket. The possible pairs are:
32 × 224; 64 × 112; 16 × 448. Thus, there are 3 distinct pairs of numbers which are multiples of 16 and whose product is 7168. However, out of these,

the pair 32 × 224 has its HCF as 32 and hence does not satisfy the given conditions. Thus, there are two pairs of numbers that would satisfy the condition that their HCF is 16 and their product is 7168. Option (a) is correct.

119. 876 + 2*P*3 = 10*Q*9,
It is clear that there is no carryover obtained in the addition of the unit's digit, while the sum of hundredth digit of the numbers is same as the hundredths digit of the sum. It means $7 + P = Q$.
10*Q*9 is divisible by 11, so $(9 + 0) - (1 + Q) = 11n$, where $n = 0, 1, 2, 3, 4, \ldots$
$$Q = 8 \;\&\; P = Q - 7 = 1.$$
Therefore, $P - Q = 7$

120. Since a number is divisible by 11 if the difference of the sum of digits in the odd places and sum of digits in the even places is 0 or divisible by 11. In the 22 digit number as described above, it is evident that there are 11 digits in the even place and 11 digits in the odd place. Since all the digits are equal, it means that the difference between these digits would be 0. Hence, the given numbers would be always divisible by 11.

121. $72 = 2^3 \times 3^2$
Total number of factors = (3 + 1)(2 + 1) = 12. This would mean that there are 6 pairs of factors, each of which pair would have a product of 72.
So the product of all the factors = $(72)^{\frac{12}{2}} = (72)^6$

122. $72 = 2^3 \times 3^2$
Total number of factors of 72 = (3 + 1)(2 + 1) = 12
Total number of ways of expressing 72 as a product of two factors = $\dfrac{12}{2} = 6$

123. $144 = 2^4 \times 3^2$
Total number of factors = (4 + 1)(2 + 1) = 15
Number of ways of expressing 144 as a product of two factors = $\dfrac{15+1}{2} = 8$
But the factors must be distinct, so we exclude the 12×12 case.
So the correct answer = 8 – 1 = 7

124. Let the number be *N*. According to the question:
$N = 7k + 3 = 11n + 4$ (where $k, n = 0, 1, 2, 3, 4, 5, \ldots$)
$$k = \frac{11n+1}{7}$$
Now put the minimum possible value of *n* for which *k* is an integer.
For $n = 5$, $k = 8$. So minimum possible value of *N* $= 7 \times 8 + 3 = 59$
Adding the LCM of 11 and 7 to 59, would get the next number. Thus, the next number would be 59 + 77 = 136. Further numbers would be numbers belonging to the Arithmetic Progression, 136, 213, 290, ... 829, 906, 983. There are a total of 12 numbers which fulfill the given condition.

125. The HCF of $a^m - 1$, $a^n - 1 = a^{\text{HCF of } m,n} - 1$
The required HCF = $3^{\text{HCF of } 15,25} - 1 = 3^5 - 1 = 242$

126. 10! is contained in 15!, so the LCM of 10! and 15! is 15!. By the same logic, their HCF is 10!.

127. For $x = 1$, $y = 4$, $7x + y = 11$, which is a prime number. $x + y = 1 + 4 = 5$.

128. 1414 has 2 as a factor and 2015 has 5 as a factor so the unit's digit of the product must 0.

129. The unit's digit of the product $1413 \times 729 \times 2015$ is 5. So if the product has 0 as its unit's digit then *n* must be either 0 or even. So '*n*' may take maximum 5 values.

130. The given number is divisible by 10, 11.
Remainder when we divide the number by 10 = $1^{12346} - 1 = 0$
Remainder when we divide the number by 11 = $(-1)^{12346} - 1 = 1 - 1 = 0$

131. In the given expression, after 5! all the values would have a units' digit of 0. Thus, the units digit of the given expression just depends on the units' digit of 1! + 2! + 3! + 4!
1! + 2! + 3! + 4! = 1 + 2 + 6 + 24 = 33
So unit's digit of 1! + 2! + 3! + 4! + 5!+ …..+ 1000! = 3

132. Number of zeroes at the end of 34! = [34/5] + [34/25] = 6 + 1 = 7
So number of zeroes at the end of $(34!)^{6!} = 7 \times 6! = 5040$.

133. $51!^{31!}$ is divisible by 4 & unit's digit of 7^{4k} is 1. So unit's digit of $7^{51!^{31!}}$ is 1.

134. $11^2 = 121$
$111^2 = 12321$
$1111^2 = 1234321$
$11111^2 = 123454321$
So $1234567654321 = (1111111)^2$

135. 421 is a prime number so 421 = 1 × 421. So HCF of the numbers is 1.

136. $3^{50} = (243)^{10}$, $4^{40} = (256)^{10}$, $5^{30} = (125)^{10}$, $6^{20} = (36)^{10}$,
So 4^{40} is greatest of all.

137. A number is divisible by 8, if the number formed by the last 3-digits is divisible by 8, i.e., 58*N* is divisible by 8 ⇒ $N = 4$.
Again a number is divisible by 11, if the difference between the sum of digits at even places and sum of digits at the odd places is either 0 or divisible by 11, i.e., $(M + 9 + 4 + 4 + 8) - (3 + 0 + 8 + 5 + N) = M - N + 9 = M + 5$ (since $N = 4$) It cannot be zero hence, $M + 5 = 11 \Rightarrow M = 6$.
Hence, $M \times N = 24$.

138. We can check for the appearance of 4 in the units place, the tens place and the hundreds place separately. So, 4 in the units place would occur once in each number of the arithmetic series: 24, 34, 44, 54, …494 → A total of 48 times. Further, 4 would appear once in each number of the series': 40, 41, 42, …49 (Thus, 10 times); Similarly, it would appear 10 times in the tens place in the 140s, the 240s, the 340s and the 440s. Thus, a total of 50 appearances of 4, in the tens place. Also, 4 would appear in the hundreds' place exactly 100 times from 400 to 499. Thus, the correct answer would be: 48 + 50 + 100 = 198.

139. Here, we want the remainder of $\frac{3671+3672+3673+\ldots+3685}{3670}$

$\Rightarrow 1 + 2 + 3 + \ldots + 15 = 120$

140. 999999 is divisible by 7. It means 999999……99 (6 × 16) times is divisible by 7.

So the required remainder = Remainder of $\frac{999}{7} \Rightarrow 5$

141. We know that $A^{p-1} \div p$, leaves a remainder of 1, when p is a prime number.

Here, 41 is a prime number. Hence, $\frac{2^{40}}{41}$ leaves a remainder 1. Thus, the remainder of $2^{41} \div 41$ would be equal to the remainder of $2^1 \div 41 \rightarrow 2$ (required remainder).

142. According to the Wilson theorem, if p is a prime number then $(p - 1)! + 1$ is a multiple of p.

Here 41 is a prime number so 40! + 1 is completely divisible by 41. This means that 40! leaves a remainder –1 when we divide it by 41 or it leaves a remainder 41 – 1 = 40.

143. $x + 3 = 0$ for $x = -3$

So the required remainder $= (-3)^4 + 3(-3)^3 + 4 = 4$

144. For any odd X, $X^2 + 7$ will be an even number. So for any odd X, $X^2 + 7$ cannot be a prime number. Only even prime number is 2 for which $2^2 + 7 = 11$ is also a prime number.

So required number of values = 1.

145. $X = 99^3 - 63^3 - 36^3$ or $99^3 + (-63)^3 + (-36)^3$

As we know that $a^3 + b^3 + c^3 = 3abc$ (if $a + b + c = 0$)

So $X = 3(99)(-63)(-36) = 2^2 \times 3^7 \times 7^1 \times 11^1$

Number of factors of $X = (2 + 1)(7 + 1)(1 + 1)(1 + 1) = 3 \times 8 \times 2 \times 2 = 96$

146. The given expression can be written as

$x(x^2 - 1)(x^2 - 4)(x^2 - 9)(x + 4) = (x - 3)(x - 2)(x - 1)x(x + 1)(x + 2)(x + 3)(x + 4)$

It is the product of eight consecutive natural numbers, so this product should be divisible by 8! Hence, the largest n, would be $n = 8$.

147. Number of zeroes at the end of

$$X! = \left[\frac{X}{5}\right] + \left[\frac{X}{25}\right] + \left[\frac{X}{125}\right] + \ldots = Y$$

Number of zeroes at the end of

$$5X! = \left[\frac{5X}{5}\right] + \left[\frac{5X}{25}\right] + \left[\frac{5X}{125}\right] + \ldots \text{ or}$$

$$[X] + \left[\frac{X}{5}\right] + \left[\frac{X}{25}\right] + \ldots$$

So the number of zeros at the end of $5X!$ is $X + Y$. Alternately, you could also solve this question through trial and error. Suppose, you take X as 10 and $5X$ as 50: You can see that in this case $Y = 2$ and the number of zeroes in $5X!$ is 12 which is also equal to $X + Y$. The relationship is maintained if you were to take $X = 20$ and $5X = 100$. Thus, 20! has 4 zeroes and 100! has 24 zeroes (again equal to $X + Y$).

148. He is losing a total of 67 marks in the test (from the all correct situation). Further, we know that if he answers a question wrongly, his score would drop by 1.25 marks from the maximum possible. The only other way for him to lose marks is if he leaves a question unanswered. In such a case, he is losing 1.125 marks (when he leaves a question unanswered, he gets a negative score of –0.125 marks instead of getting +1). Once we realise this, we need to check whether 0 wrong answers are possible. In such a case, we can think of the following table to find the correct answer to the question.

Marks lost by wrong questions	Marks required to be lost by unanswered questions	Is that possible?
0 (0 wrong answers)	67	67/1.125 is not an integer. Hence, No.
1.25 (1 wrong answers)	65.75	65.75/1.125 is not an integer. Hence, No.
2.5 (2 wrong answers)	64.5	64.5/1.125 is not an integer. Hence, No.
3.75 (3 wrong answers)	63.25	63.25/1.125 is not an integer. Hence, No.
5 (4 wrong answers)	62	62/1.125 is not an integer. Hence, No.
6.25 (5 wrong answers)	60.75	60.75/1.125 is an integer. Hence, Yes.

Thus, the minimum number of wrong answers is 5.

149. For $n = 2$, $A = 2^{4^2} = 2^{16}$, $B = 2^{2^4} = 2^{16}$ So $A = B$ in this case. Also, for $n = 2$, $C = 2^8$ & D is 2^8. However, if we go for values of n greater than 2, (3 for instance), we see that $B = 3^{729}$, $A = 3^{216}$, $D = 3^{27}$ and $C = 3^{18}$. We notice that this relationship continues for $n = 4$ too.

We can, thus, conclude that $B \geq A > D \geq C$

150. The numbers we need to check for are: 1, 3, 7, 15, 31, 63, 127, 255, 511, 1023, 2047 and 4095. Out of these, the prime numbers are: 3, 7, 31 and 127. Hence, 4 numbers.

Level of Difficulty (II)

1. The remainder when any number is divided by 1000 is the last three digits of that number. In the expression given in the question, we'll get values only for numbers till 4! As every number after that will give 0 as its last three digits.
So, $1!^3 + 2!^3 + 3!^3 + 4!^3 = 1 + 8 + 216 + 13824 = 14049$. Hence, 49 is the correct answer.
2. Any 10 consecutive natural numbers will always contain two 5s. Hence, we can make 2 10s from these 5s. So product of any ten consecutive natural numbers will always contain 2 0s. Hence, it will always 100 as its factor. Hence, Option (b) is the correct answer.
3. 2^{3n} can be written as 8^n which will always leave a remainder of 1 and from the second term we get a remainder of –1. From these two we can see that the net remainder will be 0. Hence, for all values of n the given expression will be divisible by 7. This means that the value of n will have no bearing on the outcome. Since the constraint in the question is for 3 digit numbers, the lowest value of n possible is 100 and the highest possible is 999. Hence, the required difference is 899. The correct answer is 899.
4. It is given that $p = x$. This means that p is the LCM which indicates that p is a multiple of q. Hence, q has to be the HCF of the two numbers which is y. Hence, q is equal to y. Hence, Option (c) is the correct answer.
5. In the question we see that each remainder is 1 short of the actual number. So we need to find a number which is 1 less than the number which is a multiple of 5, 6, 7 and 8. Since the LCM of 5, 6, 7 and 8 is 840, the required number should be of the form $840x - 1$. The lowest and highest numbers that satisfy this are 1679 and 9239. Hence, the required difference is 7560.
6. In 100!, we need to find the number of 5s. For each multiple of 5 we'll get 1 5 and for each mutiple of 25, we'll get 1 extra 5. So we have 20 + 4 = 24 5s in 100!. Hence, 24 is the correct answer.
7. $18^6 = 2^6 \times 3^{12}$
$8^8 = 2^{24}$
$12^{12} = 2^{24} \times 3^{12}$
Our x can contain any power of 3 from 0 to 12 and can have any power of 2 from 0 to 24. So total possible values of x is 13 × 25 = 325. The correct answer is 325.
8. The first two words would blink together in the interval of LCM of (1 + 3, 1 + 5) at 12s. Second time would be at 24 seconds. The last two words would blink together in the interval of LCM of (1 + 5, 1 + 9) at 30 seconds. The last two words would blink together for the third time after 90 seconds. The required difference in the time is (90 – 24) = 66 seconds. Hence, Option (d) is the correct answer.
9. 540 = 2 × 5 × 2 × 3 × 3 × 3. In order to minimize the LCM, we need to distribute these factors equally between the two numbers.
The two numbers can be 2 × 3 × 5 (30), 2 × 3 × 3 (18) or 2 × 3 and 2 × 3 × 3 × 5. Hence, the LCM would be 2 × 3 × 3 × 5 = 90. Alternately, one can also solve this question using factor pairs of 540. If we visualize these we will see: 1 × 540; 2 × 270; 31 × 80; 4 × 135; 5 × 108; 6 × 90; 10 × 54; 12 × 45; 15 × 36; 18 × 30; 20 × 27. In the cases of 6 × 90 and 18 × 30, the LCM is 90 in each case. This is the least value possible for the LCM. The correct answer is 90.
10. Since the number has 3 factors apart from 1 and number itself. It has a total of 5 factors. From the formula for number of factors, $a^x \times b^y \times c^z$ has $(1 + x)(1 + y)(1 + z)$ factors. So 5 can be expressed as 1 × 5. Hence, our number has to be of the form a^4. So all numbers of this form will have 3 factors apart from 1 and itself. The fourth powers of 2, 3, 4 and 5 satisfy this requirement in the range of 1 and 1000. Hence, the correct answer is 4.
11. Let the number of 5, 10 and 20 rupee coins be x,y and z respectively.
$x + y + z = 150$
$5x + 10y + 20z = 2100 \rightarrow x + 2y + 4z = 420$.
Subtracting, we get $y + 3z = 270$.
In order to maximize z, we need to minimize y. Since, there is at least 1 coin of each denomination, the minimum value of $3z$ = 3 and y's maximum value is 89. The highest value of z = 89. Hence, the correct answer is 89.
12. The numbers are of the form $7x + 3$ and $7y + 5$. Sum = $7(x + y) + 8$. When this is divided by 7, the first part will be completely divisible and the second part will give a remainder of 1. Hence, C = 1. Hence, our required answer is –1.
13. Since 182 students are being divided into pairs, this means that students who play football and cricket are exclusive. It is given that 32 pairs have both footballers. This means that we have accommodated 64 football players. Remaining 13 players would form pairs with cricketers. That leaves us with 92 cricketers. This means that there would be 46 pairs with both cricketers. The correct answer is 46.
14. In order to guarantee the given condition, we need to maximize the number of candies even after which the condition won't be satisfied. This is possible if there are 3 candies of each type. So 12 candies (3 of each type). So, when we pick the 13th candy it will guarantee that we have at least 4 candies of 1 flavor. The correct answer is 13.

15. In order to guarantee the given condition, we need to maximize the number of candies even after which the condition will not be satisfied. This is possible if we pick the maximum number of candies and still not have all the flavors. This is possible if we first pick 8 chocolate, 7 mint and then 6 strawberry flavored candies. So, a total of 21 candies can be picked without having all the four flavors. So the next candy we pick will guarantee that we have at least 1 candy of each flavor. Hence, 22 is the correct answer.
16. Pallav will take 200 coins from person 1, 4, 7, 10, … 40. A total of 14 × 200 = 2800 coins. He will give 100 coins to persons sitting on chairs 11, 14, 17, 20, 23, 26, 29, 32, 35, 38 and 41. Hence, we would give away 100 × 11 = 1100 coins. Thus after meeting the 41st person he would have 2800 – 1100 = 1700 coins. The correct answer is 1700.
17. Part 1 → 12 Men, 17 Women.
After Deboarding, 6 Men, 10 Women.
After the 8 people board there will be 24 people in the bus. For Men to be more than women, we have 2 cases: 14 men and 10 women or 13 men and 11 women. Maximum number of women = 11. Maximum number of men = 14. Hence, the required difference = 3. The correct answer is 3
18. Unit's digit of $(2018^{2018} + 2019^{2019} + 2020^{2020} + 2021^{2021} + 2022^{2022})$ is x (let's say). Then–
$x = 818 + 919 + 11 + 222$
$x = 4 + 9 + 1 + 4 = 8$
19. Use the principle of counting given in the theory of the chapter. Start with 101 numbers (i.e., all numbers between 200 and 300 both included) and subtract the number of numbers which are divisible by 2 (viz. [(300 – 200)/2] + 1 = 51 numbers), the number of numbers which are divisible by 3 but not by 2 (**Note**: This would be given by the number of terms in the series 201, 207, … 297. This series has 17 terms) and the number of numbers which are divisible by 5 but not by 2 and 3. (The numbers are 205, 215, 235, 245, 265, 275, 295. A total of 7 numbers). Thus, the required answer is given by 101 – 51 – 17 – 7 = 26. Option (b) is correct.
20. Unit's digit of $(1^1 + 2^2 + 3^3 + \ldots + 2020^{2020} + 2021^{2021} + 2022^{2022})$ is y (let's say).
We need to first find out the last digit of $(1^1 + 2^2 + \ldots + 20^{20})$ as the last digit of 3^{23} is same as 3^3
The last digit of $(1^1 + 2^2 + \ldots + 20^{20}) = 1 + 4 + 7 + 6 + 5 + 6 + 3 + 6 + 9 + 0 + 1 + 6 + 3 + 6 + 5 + 6 + 7 + 4 + 9 + 0 = 4$
Now $(1^1 + 2^2 + \ldots + 20^{20})$ will be repeated 101 times in $(1^1 + 2^2 + 3^3 + \ldots + 2020^{2020})$. So, the last digit of $(1^1 + 2^2 + 3^3 + \ldots + 2020^{2020})$ is 101 × 4 = 4
So, $y = 4 + 1^1 + 2^2 = 9$
21. It can be seen that the first expression is larger than the second one. Hence, the required answer would be given by the (units digit of the first expression – units digit of the second expression) = 6 – 0 = 6. Option (c) is correct.
22. Suppose you were to solve the same question for $10^3 – 7$ and $10^2 + x$.
$10^3 – 7 = 993$ and $10^2 + x = 100 + x$
Difference = $893 – x$
For $10^4 – 7$ and $10^3 + x$
The difference would be $9993 – (1000 + x)$
$= (8993 – x)$
For $10^5 – 7$ and $10^4 + x$
Difference: $99993 – (10000 + x) = 89993 – x$
You should realise that the difference for the given question would be 8999 . . . . 9 3 – x. For this difference to be divisible by 3, x must be 2 (since that is the only option which will give you a sum of digits divisible by 3).
23. Last digit of $P = (1^1 + 2^2 + 3^3 + \ldots + 2020^{2020} + 2021^{2021} + 2022^{2022})$ is 9. Also, in $(P^P)^P$ the power of the base P is P^2, which is an odd number. Hence, the unit digit of $(P^P)^P$, will be equivalent to the unit digit of $9^{\text{Odd Power}}$, which would be 9.
24. $F_2(P, 10) = x9$ where $x9$ is a 2-digit number having ten's digit as x and $F_1(S, 10) = 5$
So, $F_1(F_2(P, 10), F_1(S, 10)) = F_1(x9, 5) = 4$
25. $12^{55}/3^{11} = 3^{44}.4^{55}$ → 4 as units place.
Similarly, $8^{48}/16^{18} = 2^{72}$ → 6 as the units place.
Hence, 0 is the answer.
26. $1 + 2 + 2^2 + \ldots + 2^{31} = 2^{32} – 1$
Hence, the average will be: $\frac{2^{32}-1}{32} = 2^{27} - 1/2^5$
which lies between 2^{26} and 2^{27}.
Hence, the answer will be (c).
27. The denominator 99 has the property that the decimals it gives rise to are of the form 0.$xyxyxy$. This question is based on this property of 99. Option (c) is correct.
28. The value of b has to be 2 since, $r = 2y$. Hence, option (d) is the only choice.
29. For $[x]^3 + \{x\}^2$ to give – 7.91,
$[x]^3$ should give – 8 (hence, $[x]$ should be –2]
Further, $\{x\}^2$ should be + 0.09.
Both these conditions are satisfied by –1.7.
Hence option (d) is correct.
30. $16^5 + 2^{15} = 2^{20} + 2^{15} = 2^{15}(2^5 + 1)$ → Hence, is divisible by 33.
31. The LCM of 5, 7, 13 is 455
The gap between the respective divisors and the remainders are constant (2)

So, we need to find the number (or set of numbers) which when divided by 5, 7, 13 give a remainder of –2

The smallest number is 455 – 2 = 453

Any number which gives a remainder of –2 when divided by 5, 7, 13 are in the form of $455n - 2$ where n is a natural number.

So, the smallest 4-digit number which when divided by 5, 7, 13 gives a remainder of 3 is 455 × 3 – 2 = 1363

32. $|x - 3| + 2|x + 1| = 4$ can happen under three broad conditions.
   (a) When $2|x + 1| = 0$, then $|x - 3|$ should be equal to 4.
   Putting $x = -1$, both these conditions are satisfied.
   (b) When $2|x + 1| = 2$, x should be 0, then $|x - 3|$ should also be 2. This does not happen.
   (c) When $2|x + 1| = 4$, x should be + 1 or – 3, in either case $|x - 3|$ which should be zero does not give the desired value.

33. At a value of $x = 0$, we can see that the expression $x^2 + |x - 1| = 1 \rightarrow 0 + 1 = 1$. Hence, $x = 0$ satisfies the given expression. Also at $x = 1$, we get 1 + 0 = 1. Option (d) is correct.

34. 4^{2n+1} represents an odd power of 4 (and hence would end in 4). Similarly, 4^{2n} represents an even power of 4 (and hence would end in 6). Thus, the least number 'x' that would make both $4^{2n+1} + x$ and $4^{2n} - x$ divisible by 5 would be for $x = 1$.

35. Check for each value of the options to see that the expression does not become divisible by 9 for any of the initial options. Thus, there is no value that satisfies the divisibility by 9 case.

36. The expression would have solutions based on a structure of:
   4 + 0; 3 + 1; 2 + 2; 1 + 3 or 0 + 4.
   There will be 2 × 1 = 2 solutions for 4 + 0 as in this case x can take the values of 8 and 0, while y can take a value of 4;
   Similarly there would be 2 × 2 = 4 solutions for 3 + 1 as in this case x can take the values of 7 or 1, while y can take a value of 5 or 3;
   Thus, the total number of solutions can be visualised as: 2 (for 4 + 0) + 4 (for 3 + 1) + 4 (for 2 + 2) + 4 (for 1 + 3) + 2 (for (0 + 2) = 16 solutions for the set (x, y) where both x and y are integers.

37. The numerator of $3^{32}/50$ would be a number that would end in 1. Consequently, the decimal of the form $.bx$ would always give us a value of x as 2.

38. $990 = 11 \times 3^2 \times 2 \times 5$. The highest power of 990 which would divide 1090! would be the power of 11 available in 1090. This is given by [1090/11] + [1090/121] = 99 + 9 = 108.

39. If all the drone carriers are in range, then only those switches will be in "on mode" whose subscripts are perfect squares as perfect squares have an odd number of factors.
   So, $S_1, S_4, S_9, S_{16}, S_{25}, S_{36}, S_{49}, S_{64}, S_{81}, S_{100}$ will be in on mode. Hence, the right answer is $a_1, d_1, i_1, p_1, y_1, j_2, w_2, l_3, c_4, v_4$. Option (c) is correct.

40. If $\{s_1, e_3, q_4\}$ codes are visible apart from the normal code $N = \{a_1, d_1, i_1, p_1, y_1, j_2, w_2, l_3, c_4, v_4\}$ then S_{19}, S_{57}, S_{95} switches are in on position. This clearly indicates that these 3 switches are in an on position – which is because, they were toggled an odd number of times. This can only happen if the drone carrier 19, goes out of range. But if only the 19th drone carrier goes out of range, then 38th & 76th switches should also have been in the on position and signals l_2 and X_3 would also be visible. As the control room did not get the signals for 38th and 76th switches, it means that these switches were toggled an even number of times. This can only happen if drone carrier 38 also goes out of range. So, A_{38} also went out of range. Thus, the sum of the subscripts is (19 + 38) = 57

41. If all the drone carriers in the Eastern regiment is taken down then A_{51} to A_{75} cannot alter their switches. So, the number of switches that will remain on are = number of perfect squares from 1 to 50 + Number of perfect squares from 76 to 100 + number of non-perfect squares from 51 to 75
   = 7 + 2 + (25 – 1) = 33.

42. If all the drone carriers in the South regimes go out of range, then the number of on switches are = Number of perfect squares from 1 to 25 + Number of non-perfect squares from 26 to 50 + (Number of non-perfect squares between 51 and 100 – Number of numbers between 51 and 100 that are having 2 factors between 26 to 50)
   = 5 + (25 – 2) + (47 – 4) = 71.
   (**Note:** the switches for 78, 84, 90 and 96 will remain off and not send any signals as they will lose two toggles – giving them an even number of toggles.)
   For example: 78 has the factors: 1, 78, 2, 39, 3, 26, 6, 13. So if all the 100 drone carriers had operated without going out of range, then these switches would have been in off position (as it is toggled 8 times), not sending any signals to the control room. However, since the drone carriers 26 to 50 have gone out of range, it means that 78 will get toggled only 6 times and get back to the off position. A similar thing occurs for 84,90 and 96 too.

43. Both the values of options (a) and (b) satisfy the given expression. As for 5.16, the value of $[x]^2$ = 25 and the value of $\{x\}$ = 0.16. Thus, $[x]^2 + \{x\}^1$ = 25.16.

Similarly for a value of $x = -4.84$, the value of $[x] = -5$ and hence $[x]^2 = 25$ and the value of $\{x\} = 0.16$. Thus, $[x]^2 + \{x\}^1 = 25.16$

44. The given conditions can be seen to be true for the number 49.
45. If $a + b = c$ then the D(D(a) + D(b)) = D(c) where D(a) is the digital sum of a.
D(1) = 1
D(11) = 2
...
D(1111.. upto 20 terms) = 2
So, D(1) + D(11) +... D(1111... upto 20 terms) = (1 + 2 + 3 + ... + 9) + (1 + 2 + 3 ... + 9) + (1 + 2) = 93
D(93) = D(12) = 3
Only option (c) has a digital sum of 3. Thus, (c) is the right answer.
46. 863 satisfies each of the conditions and can be spotted using trial and error.
47. The number of zeroes would be given by counting the number of 5's. The relevant numbers for counting the number of 5's in the product would be given by: 5^5; 10^{10}, 15^{15}, 20^{20}, 25^{25}...and so on till 100^{100}.
The number of 5's in these values would be given by: (5 + 10 + 15 + 20 + 50 + 30 + 35 + 40 + 45 + 100 + 55 + 60 + 65 + 70 + 150 + 80 + 85 + 90 + 95 + 200)
This can also be written as:
(5 + 10 + 15 + 20 + 25 + 30 + 35 + 40 + 45 + 50 + 55 + 60 + 65 + 70 + 75 + 80 + 85 + 90 + 95 + 100) + (25 + 50 + 75 + 100)
= 1050 + 250 = 1300
48. Since the numbers have their HCF as 5, we can think of the numbers as $5a$ and $5b$, where a and b should be co-prime. Also, $5 \times a \times b = 105$. Hence, $a \times b = 21$. a, b can only be 1×21 or 3×7 where both the conditions get matched. Hence, there are two pairs that have this property – HCF 5 and LCM 105. These are 5×1, 5×21 viz: 5 and 105; 5×3, 5×7 viz 15 and 35.
49. Chiku has removed all the numbers which are having a GCD of more than 1 with 100. So only co-primes with 100 are left.
Number of numbers which are co-prime to 100 and less than it is 100 × (1/2) × (1 – 1/5) = 40. The logic of doing this is to first remove all even numbers & then remove all numbers that are divisible by 5 from the remaining.
So, only 40 numbers will be left.
50. 120 has 2,3,5 as its factors. Find the maximum number (under 100) which is a multiple of the LCM of 2, 3, 5. It will be 90.
Number of numbers which are co-prime to 90 and are less than 90 = 90 × (1/2) × (1 – 1/3) × (1 – 1/5) = 24
Between 90 & 100, manually find the numbers that are co-prime to 120. There are two such numbers viz: 91 & 97.
So, the answer will be (24 + 2) = 26
51. There needs to be a little trial and error while solving this question. Firstly, the algebraic equations that exist for a number like 'ab' are: $a^2 + b^2 = 2.5 \times (a + b)$. The squares of the digits from 1 to 9 are 1, 4, 9, 16, 25, 36, 49, 64, 81. The first condition we are looking for is that the sum of the squares divided by 2.5 should give us an integer. Also, the maximum value of $a + b$ is 18 (since the sum of the digits of a 2-digit number cannot cross 18). So the maximum sum of the squares of the digits would be 18 × 2.5 = 45. Hence, 7, 8, 9 cannot be one of the digits. Looking at the squares from 1 to 6, we get only 1 + 9 = 10 or 4 + 16 = 20 or 9 + 36 = 45 as the three cases where the sum of squares of the digits is a multiple of 2.5 and limited in value to being maximum 45. Considering these three cases, we can reject the third basis the thought that if $a^2 + b^2 = 45$, then a and b are respectively 3 and 6. But then the sum of $a + b = 9$ and 45 is not a 2.5 times multiple of 9. The second possibility is rejected on the basis of the second condition. If $a^2 + b^2 = 20$, $a = 2$, $b = 4$. The second condition is that $a^2 + b^2 = 3a \times b + 1$. This is only true for a, b being 1 and 3. Hence, the possible values of the number are 13 or 31.
52. The first sentence means that the numbers are in an arithmetic progression. From the statements and a little bit of visualisation, you can see that 8.5, 10 and 11.5 can be the three values we are looking for – and hence the middle value is 10.
53. $990 = 11 \times 3^2 \times 5 \times 2$. For $n!$ to be divisible by 990, the value of $n!$ should have an 11 in it. Since, 11 itself is a prime number, hence the value of n should be at least 11.
54. For the expression to hold true, x and y should both be positive.

Solutions for Questions 55 to 59:

Write simple equations for each of the questions and solve.

60. Since the sum of squares of the digits of the 2-digit number is 10, the only possibility of the numbers are 31 and 13.
61. If the number is 'ab', we have the following equations:
$(10a + b) = 4\,(a + b) + 3 \rightarrow 6a - 3b = 3$
$(10a + b) = 3\,(a \times b) + 5$
Obviously, we would need to solve these two equations in order to get the values of the digits (a) and (b) respectively. However, it might not be a very prudent decision to try to follow this process- as it might turn out to be too cumbersome.

A better approach to think here is:
From the first statement, we know that the number is of the form $4n + 3$. Thus, the number has to be a term in the series 11, 15, 19, 23, 27…
Also from the second statement, we know that the number must be a $3n + 5$ number.
Thus, the numbers could be 11, 14, 17, 20, 23….
Common terms of the above two series would be probable values of the number.
It can be seen that the common terms in the two series are: 11, 23, 35, 47, 59, 71, 83 and 95. One of these numbers has to be the number we are looking for.
If we try these values one by one, we can easily see that the value of the 2-digit number should be 23 since → 23/ (2 + 3) → Quotient as 4 and remainder = 3.

Similarly, if we look at the other condition given in the problem we would get the following-

23/6 → quotient as 3 and remainder = 5.

Thus, the value of the number would be 23.

62. We can see from the description that the number (say X) must be such that $X + 100$ and $X + 169$ both must be perfect squares. Thus, we are looking for two perfect squares which are 69 apart from each other. This would happen for 34^2 and 35^2 since their difference would be $(35 - 34)(35 + 34) = 69$.

63. Since their least common multiple is 102, we need to look for two factors of 102 such that they add up to 85. 51 and 34 can be easily spotted as the numbers.

64. If one number is x, the other should be $6x$ or $12x$ or $18x$ or $24x$ and so on. Also, their sum should be either 504 or 1008 or 1512. (**Note**: the next multiple of 504 = 2016 cannot be the sum of two 3-digit numbers.) Trial and error gives us 144 and 864 as the values.

65. Obviously 46 and 64 are the possible numbers.

66. The key here is to look for numbers which are more than three times but less than four times the product of their digits. Also, the product of the digits should be greater than 9 so as to leave a remainder of 9 when the number is divided by the product of its digits.

In the 10s, 20s and 30s, the numbers 14,15,23 and 33 give us a quotient of 3, when divided by the product of their digits, but do not give us the required remainder. In the 40s, 43 is the only number which has a quotient of 3 when divided by 12 (product of its digits). But 43/12 does not give us a remainder of 9 as required.

In the 50s, the number 53 divided by 15 leaves a remainder of 8, while in the 60s, 63 divided by 18 gives us a remainder of 9 as required.

67. The first thing to use while solving this question is to look at the information that the sum of squares of the 3-digits is 109. A little bit of trial and error shows us that this can only occur if the digits are 8, 6 and 3. Using the other information, we get that the number must be 863 since, 863 – 495 = 368.

68. It is obvious that the only condition where the cubes of 3 numbers add up to 243 is when we add the cubes of 3 and 6. Hence, the numbers possible are 36 and 63.

69. There would definitely be two numbers and in case we take the first number as $7n - 1$, there would be three numbers – (as can be seen when we take the first number as 27 and the other number is 43).

70. Between 111^4, $110 \times 109 \times 108 \times 107$, $109 \times 110 \times 112 \times 113$.

It can be easily seen that

$111 \times 111 \times 111 \times 111 > 110 \times 109 \times 108 \times 107$

also $109 \times 110 \times 112 \times 113 > 109 \times 110 \times 108 \times 107$

Further the product $111 \times 111 \times 111 \times 111 > 109 \times 110 \times 112 \times 113$ (since, the sum of the parts of the product are equal on the LHS and the RHS and the numbers on the LHS are closer to each other than the numbers on the RHS).

71. Both x and y should be highest for xy to be maximum. Similarly x should be minimum and y should be maximum for x/y to be minimum.

72. $200^{300} = (200^6)^{50}$
$300^{200} = (300^4)^{50}$
$400^{150} = (400^3)^{50}$
Hence 200^{300} is greater.

73. The sum of squares of the first n natural numbers is given by $n(n + 1)(2n + 1)/6$.
For this number to be divisible by 4, the product of $n(n + 1)(2n + 1)$ should be a multiple of 8. Out of n, $(n + 1)$ and $(2n + 1)$ only one of n or $(n + 1)$ can be even and $(2n + 1)$ would always be odd.
Thus, either n or $(n + 1)$ should be a multiple of 8. This happens if we use n = 7, 8, 15, 16, 23, 24, 31, 32, 39, 40, 47, 48. Hence, 12 such numbers.

74. In the 20s, the numbers are: 23 to 29
In the 30s, the numbers are: 32 to 39
Subsequently the numbers are 42 to 49, 52 to 59, 62 to 69, 72 to 79, 82 to 89 and 92 to 99.
A total of 63 numbers.

75. You need to solve this question using trial and error.
For 32, option (a):
$32 = 2^5$. Hence, 6 factors. On increasing by 50%, $48 = 2^4 \times 3^1$ has 10 factors. Thus, the number of factors is increasing when the number is increased by 50% which is not what the question is defining for the number. Hence, 32 is not the correct answer.
Checking for option (b) 84.

$84 = 2^2 \times 3^1 \times 7^1 \rightarrow (2+1)(1+1)(1+1) = 12$ factors

On increasing by 50% → $126 = 2^1 \times 3^2 \times 7^1 \rightarrow (1+1)(2+1)(1+1) = 12$ factors. (no change in number of factors).

Second Condition: When the value of the number is reduced by 75% → 84 would become 21 $(3^1 \times 7^1)$ and the number of factors would be $2 \times 2 = 4$ – a reduction of 66.66% in the number of factors.

76. There will be 9 single digit numbers using 9 digits, 90 two digit numbers using 180 digits, 900 three digit numbers using 2700 digits. Thus, when the number 999 would be written, a total of 2889 digits would have been used up. Thus, we would need to look for the 25494th digit when we write all 4-digit numbers. Since, 25494/4 = 6373.5 we can conclude that the first 6373 four digit numbers would be used up for writing the first 25492-digits. The second digit of the 6374th four digit number would be the required answer. Since, the 6374th four digit number is 7373, the required digit is 3.

77. In order to solve this question, think of the numbers grouped in groups of 9 as:

{1, 2, 3, 4, 5, 6, 7, 8, 9} {10, 11, 12…..18} and so on till {2989, 2990…2997} – A total of 333 complete sets. From each set, we can take 4 numbers giving us a total of 333 × 4 = 1332 numbers.

Apart from this, we can also take exactly 1 multiple of 9 (any one) and also the last 3 numbers viz 2998, 2999 and 3000. Thus, there would be a total of 1332 + 4 = 1336 numbers.

78. It can be seen that for only 2 numbers (1 and 1/2), the consolidated number would be 1 + 1/2 + 1/2 = 2. For 3 numbers (1, 1/2 , 1/3), the number would be 3. Thus, for the given series the consolidated number would be 1972.

79. The value of K would be 199 and hence, the required difference is 9 – 1 = 8.

80. 9 – 9 = 0 would be the difference between the units and the tens digits.

81. The highest ratio would be a ratio of 100 in the numbers, 100, 200, 300, 400, 500, 600, 700, 800 and 900. Thus a total of 9 numbers.

82. Basically every odd triangular number would have this property, that it is the difference of squares of two consecutive natural numbers. Thus, we need to find the number of triangular numbers that are odd.

3, 15, 21, 45, 55, 91, 105, 153, 171, 231, 253, 325, 351, 435, 465, 561, 595, 703, 741, 861, 903 – a total of 21 numbers.

83. The coefficients would be ${}^{44}C_0$, ${}^{44}C_1$, ${}^{44}C_2$ and so on till ${}^{44}C_{44}$. The sum of these coefficients would be 2^{44} (since the value of ${}^nC_0 + {}^nC_1 + {}^nC_2 + \ldots {}^nC_n = 2^n$).

84. The remainder of each power of 9 when divided by 6 would be 3. Thus, for $(2n + 1)$ powers of 9, there would be an odd number of 3's. Hence, the remainder would be 3.

85. The remainder when a number is divided by 16 is given by the remainder of the last 4-digits divided by 16 (because 10000 is a multiple of 16. This principle is very similar in logic to why we look at last 2-digits for divisibility by 4 and the last 3-digits for divisibility by 8). Thus, the required answer would be the remainder of 4950/16 which is 6.

86. 58! – 38! = 38! (58 × 57 × 56 × 55 × …. × 39 – 1) → 38! $(3n - 1)$ since the expression inside the bracket would be a $3n - 1$ kind of number. Thus, the number of 3's would depend only on the number of 3's in 38! → 12 + 4 + 1 = 17.

87. The given expression can be seen as $(22334^{\text{ODD POWER}})/5$, since the sum of $1^2 + 2^2 + 3^2 + 4^2 + \ldots + 66^2$ can be seen to be an odd number. The remainder would always be 4 in such a case.

88. $12^{33} \times 34^{23} \times 2^{70} = 2^{159} \times 3^{33} \times 17^{23}$. The number of factors would be 160 × 34 × 24 = 130560. Thus, option (d) is correct.

89. Option (a) is correct.

90. $1152 = 2 \times 2 \times 2 \times 2 \times 2 \times 2 \times 2 \times 3 \times 3 = 2^7 \times 3^2$. Essentially every number starting from $4!^3$ would be divisible perfectly by 1152 since each number after that would have at least 7 twos and 2 threes. Thus, the required remainder is obtained by the first three terms:

(1 + 8 + 216)/1152 = 225/1152 gives us 225 as the required remainder.

91. We can take only perfect squares of prime numbers and the number 1. Thus, for instance we can take numbers like 1, 4, 9, 25, 49, 121, 169, 289, 361, 529, 841 and 961. A total of 12 such numbers can be taken.

92. (101 × 102 × 103 × 197 × 198 × 199)/100 → [1 × 2 × 3 × (–3) × (–2) × (–1)]/100 → –36 as remainder → remainder is 64.

93. [65 × 29 × 37 × 63 × 71 × 87]/100 → [–35 × 29 × 37 × –37 × –29 × –13]/100 → [35 × 29 × 37 × 37 × 29 × 13]/100 = [1015 × 1369 × 377]/100 → 15 × 69 × 77/100 → remainder as 95.

94. [65 × 29 × 37 × 63 × 71 × 87 × 85]/100 → [–35 × 29 × 37 × –37 × –29 × –13 × –15]/100 → [35 × 29 × 37 × 37 × 29 × 13 × –15]/100 = [1015 × 1369 × 377 × –15]/100 → [15 × 69 × 77 × – 15]/100 → remainder as 75.

95. Bikas's movement in terms of the number of coins would be:

B → 3B (when Arun triples everyone's coins) → B.

Think of this as: When Bikas triples everyone's coins, and is left with 20 it means that the other 3 have 60 coins after their coins are tripled. This means that before the tripling by Bikas, the other three must have had 20 coins—meaning Bikas must have had 60 coins. But 60 = 3B → B = 20.

96. For $83p796161q$ to be a multiple of 11 (here X is 11), we should have the difference between the sum of odd placed digits and even placed digits should be 0 or a multiple of 11.

$(8 + p + 9 + 1 + 1) - (3 + 7 + 6 + 6 + q) = (19 + p) - (22 + q)$. For this difference to be 0, p should be 3 more than q which cannot occur since $0 < p < q$.

The only way in which $(19 + p) - (22 + q)$ can be a multiple of 11 is if we target a value of –11 for the expression. One such possibility is if we take p as 1 and q as 9.

The number would be 8317961619. On successive division by $(p + q) = 10$ and 1 the sum of remainders would be 9.

97. $n(n + 1)/2$ should be a perfect square. The first value of n when this occurs would be for $n = 8$. Thus, on the 8 March, the required condition would come true.

98. We have to find the unit's digit of $2^{53} \rightarrow 2^{4n+1} \rightarrow 2$ as the units digit.

99. $[7!\ (14 + 14 \times 13 \times 12 \times 11 \times 10 \times 9 \times 8)]/[7!\ (16 - 3)] = [(14 + 14 \times 13 \times 12 \times 11 \times 10 \times 9 \times 8)]/[(13)] \rightarrow$ remainder 1.

Hence, the original remainder must be 7! (because for the sake of simplification of the numbers in the question, we have cut the 7! from the numerator and the denominator in the first step).

100. $x = 6$ and $y = -3$ is one pair of values where the given condition is met.

After that you should be able to spot that if you were to increase x by 7, y would decrease by 4. The number of such pairs would depend on how many terms are there in the series.

–498, –491, ….. –1, 6, 13, 20, … 489, 496. The series has 994/7 + 1 = 143 terms and hence there would be 143 pairs of values for (x, y) which would satisfy the equation.

101. All three conditions can be seen to be true.

102. Product of factorials < Sum of factorials would occur for any number that has either 0 or 1 in it.

The required numbers uptil and including 50 are: 10 to 19, 20, 21, 30, 31, 40, 41, 50. Besides for the number 22, the product of factorials of the digits would be equal to the sum of factorials of the digits. Thus, a total of 18 numbers.

103. The maximum marks he can score is: 100 (if he gets all correct).

The minimum marks he can score would be given by: $10 \times (-0.1) + 20 \times (-0.2) + 70 \times (-0.5) = -40$.

The difference between the two values would be $100 - (-40) = 140$ marks.

Solutions for Questions 104 to 106:

If a student solved 200 questions and got everything correct, he would score a total of 620 marks. By getting a LOD 1 question wrong, he would lose 4 + 2 = 6 marks, while by not solving an LOD 1 question, he would lose 4 marks.

Similarly for LOD 2 questions, loss of marks = 4.5 (for wrong answers) and loss of marks = 3 (for not solved).

Similarly for LOD 3 questions, loss of marks = 3 (for wrong answers) and loss of marks = 2 (for not solved)

Since, he has got 120 marks from 100 questions solved he has to lose 500 marks (from the maximum possible total of 620) by combining to lose marks through 100 questions not solved and some questions wrong.

104. It can be seen through a little bit of trial and error with the options, that if he got 44 questions of LOD 1 correct and 56 questions of LOD 3 wrong he would end up scoring $44 \times 4 - 56 \times 1 = 176 - 56 = 120$. In such a case, he would have got the maximum possible incorrects with the given score.

105. $32 \times 4 + 1 \times 3 - 1 \times 1 = 130$ (in this case, he has solved 32 corrects from LOD 1, 1 correct from LOD 2 and 1 incorrect from LOD 3). Thus, a total of 34 attempts.

106. In the above case, he gets 1 question incorrect. However, he can also get 130 marks by $30 \times 4 + 2 \times 3 + 2 \times 2$ where he gets 30 LOD 1 questions correct, and 2 questions correct each from LOD 2 and LOD 3).

The least number of incorrects would be 0.

107. The least number would be (LCM of 10, 9, 8, 7, 6 and 5 – 1) = 2519. The second least number = $2520 \times 2 - 1 = 5039$.

108. A quick scan of squares above the given numbers tells us that the required perfect squares are: 144, 256 and 400, which would be the squares of the numbers 12, 16 and 20 respectively. Hence, n would be 144 −108 = 36. The sum of digits of n is 3 + 6 = 9.

109. The number $904 = 8 \times 113 = 2^3 \times 113$. This means that $904^{2008} = 2^{6024} \times 113^{2008}$. Also, $904^{2015} = 2^{6045} \times 113^{2015}$. Multiples of 904^{2008} would be numbers that would have $2^{6024 \text{ or more}}$ and $113^{2008 \text{ or more}}$. Also, factors of 904^{2015} would have $2^{6045 \text{ or less}}$ and $113^{2015 \text{ or less}}$. This means that the number of numbers that would be multiples of the first number and simultaneously be factors of the other number would be $22 \times 8 = 176$.

110. The expression $1^5 + 2^5 + 3^5 + \ldots\ldots + 96^5$ can be written as $(1 + 2 + \ldots + 96)(1^4 + \ldots\ldots)$. The first bracket in this expression would have a value of $96 \times 97 \div 2 = 48 \times 97$ (Using the formula for the sum of the first n natural numbers.). Since, 48×97 is a multiple of 194, the required remainder would be 0.

111. Since, the LHS of the above expression would always be an integer, the RHS too needs to be an integer. This condition is satisfied when s is a multiple of 42. Also, on checking for values of s as 42, 84, etc., we realise that for all values of s, the RHS gives a value that is equal to the LHS. So, in order to answer the question, we need to find out the number of multiples of 42 below 1000. We start from 42 × 1 and end at 42 × 23. Hence, there are 23 such numbers.

Solutions for Questions 112 to 114:

The list of possible number of rabbits that were transferred for each weight category would be:

1 kg rabbits	2 kg rabbits	5 kg rabbits
1	16	23
4	12	24
7	8	25
10	4	26
13	0	27

Possible number of rabbits remaining in the zoo:

1 kg rabbits	2 kg rabbits	5 kg rabbits
1	28	31
4	24	32
7	20	33
10	16	34
13	12	35
16	8	36
19	4	37
22	0	38

The answers can be read off the tables:

112. The minimum number of 1 kg rabbits that were transferred was 1.

113. The maximum possible numbers of 5 kg rabbits that remain were 37. (**Note**: 38 is not possible, since the minimum number of 5 kg rabbits transferred out was 23 – and 23 + 38 would cross 60, which is not allowed in the question)

114. If 26, five kg rabbits were transferred, it means that there can be a maximum of 34, five kg rabbits that remain in the zoo. In such a case, we would get the highest numbers of 1 kg rabbits that remain in the zoo as 10. Hence, the correct answer for this question is '10'.

115. The best way to solve such questions is to do a selective trial and error. Scanning numbers, the first thing that becomes clear is that we cannot have both the digits of the number as even, in this context. This means that we need to scan only odd numbers. Scanning through the odd numbers, we find 36 and its reverse 63 giving us the required value as 36 + 63 + 3 × 6 = 117. Also, we can see that even 63 + 36 + 18 gives us the same value. In both cases, the sum of the digits turns out to be 9.

116. The numbers that have an odd number of factors are the perfect squares. Thus, $M = 36 \times 49 \times 64 \times 81 \times 100 \times 121 \times 144 \times 169 \times 196 \times 225 = 2^{16} \times 3^8 \times 5^4 \times 7^4 \times 11^2 \times 13^2$. 12 is a number consisted only of 2's and 3's. Also, $12 = 2^2 \times 3^1 \rightarrow$ In the number M, we have eight 2^2s and eight 3^1s. Hence, the highest power of 12 in M is 8.

117. First through trial and error identify the two values of x and y that satisfy this. The first one that satisfies are the values 3 and 3, the next pair is 11 and 1. (This will also be the last pair!! Think why??) Further, since we are looking for the maximum possible integral power of 6, we will use the pair 11 and 1. We need to find the highest power of 6 in 11! which is given by [11/3] + [11/9] = 3 + 1 = 4.

118. X has only 2 elements 1, 2 (so $x = 2$) and Y consists all the prime numbers. The prime numbers below 100 are 2,3,5,7,11,13,17,19,23,29,31,37,41,43,47, 53,59,61,67,71,73,79,83,89 and 97 $\rightarrow Y = 25$. So the value of $[y/x] = [25/2] = 12$

119. If X has 15 factors, then it should either be of the form a^{14} or $b^2 \times c^4$ where a, b, c are prime numbers.
Case 1: When the number is of the form a^{14}, in this case the smallest possible number is $2^{14} = 16384$ which is a five digit number so this case is not possible.
Case 2: When the number is of the form $b^2 \times c^4$, the minimum possible number $3^2 \times 2^4 = 144$

$$X^2 = b^4 \times c^8$$

So the square of the number has (4 + 1).(8 + 1) = 5 × 9 = 45 factors.

120. If $wxyz$ is the 4-digit number then according to the question:
$x = y + 2$, therefore, y can take any value from 0 to 7 for which x can take the respective values from 2 to 9. Since the number is odd, z can take five values (1, 3, 5, 7, 9). Now we have total 8 possibilities for x, y and five possibilities for z. For w, we have a total of 9 possibilities (from 1 to 9). So, the total possible numbers = 9 × 8 × 5 = 360.

121. X, Y, Z are in A.P. Let the common difference between them is d then following cases are possible.
Case 1: When $d = 1$, no triplet possible
Case 2: When $d = 2$, possible triplet is (3, 5, 7). Sum = 15
Case 3: When $d = 3$, no triplet possible
Case 4: When $d = 4$, possible triplet is (3, 7, 11). Sum = 21
Case 5: When $d = 5$, no triplet possible
Case 6: When $d = 6$, possible triplet is (5, 11, 17), (7, 13, 19). Sum = 33, 39
Case 7: When $d = 7$, no triplet possible
Case 8: When $d = 8$, possible triplet is (3, 11, 19). Sum = 33

For $d > 8$, no triplet possible. Hence, we see that the possible sums for X, Y and Z are 15, 21, 33 and 39 respectively. Hence, a total of 4 possibilities.

122. When a 'x' digit number is multiplied by a 'y' digit number, the product would have either '$x + y$' or '$x + y - 1$' digits.
So when we multiply a 100-digits number by a 200-digits number then the product will have 100 + 200 or 100+ 200 – 1 = 300 or 299 digits. Further, when this number is again multiplied by a 300 digit number, we get a 598 to 600 digit number. Finally, when this number is further multiplied by a 400 digit number, the answer would have a minimum of 997 digits to a maximum of 1000 digits. Hence, the correct answer is 997.

123. $3^{400} \Rightarrow (3^4)^{100} \Rightarrow (81)^{100}$
$\Rightarrow (1 + 80)^{100} \Rightarrow 1^{100} + 80^{100}$
Now we can easily see that in 80^{100} last 2-digits will always be 00.
Hence, 1 + 00 = 01.

124. This problem can be easily solved through Cyclicity principle. The units digits of all numbers starting from 1^7up to 9^7 will be repeated ten times each for every range of ten numbers. Hence, we have to check out the units digit of $1^7 \times 2^7 \times .... 9^7$, i.e.,
1^7 end in 1
2^7 end in 8
3^7 end in 7
4^7 end in 4
5^7ends in 5.... Hence, $1^7 \times 2^7 \times .... 9^7$ would end in 0. Hence, the units digits would be 0 for the entire expression.

125. On division by 24, the square of a natural number, would leave a remainder of 1, only if the number is of the form $6n \pm 1$, where $n \in N$ (since n must not be divisible by 2 or 3).
In the 2-digit numbers, we have 15 numbers of the form $6n$ (6×2, 6×3 till 6×16). Hence, there are a total of 30 2-digit numbers of the form ($6n \pm 1$) [15 of the form $6n + 1$, 15 of the form of $6n - 1$].

126. Logical Solution: The maximum total marks, in the exam are 80 (if he gets all questions correct). From this number, he has two mechanisms for losing marks – For a wrong answer, he loses 1.25 marks for each wrong answer. For an unanswered question, he loses 1.125 marks per question. Since he has scored a total of only 23 marks, he has lost 57 marks (from the maximum possible total of 80). Since, we are trying to look for the minimum possible wrong answers, we can start trying to put the number of wrong answers as 0. In that case, we would need to lose the entire 57 marks due to not attempting questions. However, $57 \div 1.125$ is not an integer, hence 0 wrong answers is not possible. Going for 1 wrong answer, marks lost due to wrong answers = 1.25. Marks to be lost due to un-attempted questions = 57 – 1.25 = 55.75. Going further in this direction, we realise that if we put 6 incorrect questions, we would need 49.5 marks to be lost due to un-attempted questions. $49.5 \div 1.125 = 44$. Hence, we get 6 as the required answer.

127. In base-3, the decimal value of a five digit number must lie from 81 to 242.
$[(10000)_3 = 81 \ \& \ (22222)_3 = 242]$
Similarly in the base-4, the decimal value of a five-digit number must lie from 256 to 1023.
In base 5, the decimal value of the five-digit number must lie from 625 to 3124. Hence $x = 5$
Option (d) is correct.

128. Difference between the divisor and the remainder is 1 in each division. [2 –1 = 4 – 3 = 6 – 5 = 8 – 7 = 10 – 9 = 1]
So the general form of the number will be LCM of [2, 4, 6, 8, 10] – 1 = $120k - 1$ where 'k' is a natural number.
There are 8 such numbers between 101 to 1000: 119, 239, 359, 479, 599, 719, 839, 959.
So the required sum = 119 + 239 + 359 + 479 + 599 + 719 + 839 + 959 = 4312

129. Any digit (from 0 to 9) raised to the power of the type $4k + 1$ ($k \in N$) will always end in the same digit. It means for all possible values of x, x^{4k+1} has same unit digit as unit digit of x. So a has same unit digit as unit digit of $a^5, a^9, a^{13}, a^{17}, a^{21}, ...$ similarly b has same unit digit as $b^5, b^9, b^{13}, b^{17}, b^{21}, ...$ So $a^{13} + b^{13}$ has same unit digit as $a^{17} + b^{17}$.

130. The number of 4-digit numbers in decimal system will be from $10^3 = 1000$ to $10^4 - 1 = 9999$, i.e., 9000 numbers.
The number of 4-digit numbers in base 8 will be from $8^3 = 512$ to $8^4 - 1 = 4095$, i.e., 3584 numbers.
The number of 4-digit numbers in base 7 will be from $7^3 = 343$ to $7^4 - 1 = 2400$, i.e., 2058 numbers.
The number of 4-digit numbers in base 6 will be from $6^3 = 216$ to $6^4 - 1 = 1295$, i.e., 1080 numbers.
So the numbers from 1000 to 1295, would have 4-digits in each of base 6, 7 and 8. So, there are a total of 296 numbers possible.

131. The number of 4-digit numbers in decimal system will be from $10^3 = 1000$ to $10^4 - 1 = 9999$.
The number of 4-digit numbers in base 7 will be from $7^3 = 343$ to $7^4 - 1 = 2400$.
The number of 4-digit numbers in base 6 will be from $6^3 = 216$ to $6^4 - 1 = 1295$.
So the common numbers are from 1000 to 1295. So, the required difference = 1295 – 1000 = 295.

132. $9^n + 11^n$ is divisible by 10 when n is odd but when n is even then it would leave a remainder of 2 (last digit of $9^2 + 11^2$).
$6^n + 4^n$ is divisible by 10 when n is odd but when n is even then it would leave a remainder of 2. (Last digit

of $6^2 + 4^2$). Hence, whenever n is odd, there would be no remainder when 10 divides the expression. When n is even, then the remainder would be $2 + 2 = 4$.

So the sum of all possible remainders in this case will be 4.

133. There are four possible scenarios for the units' digit combination of the four numbers. These essentially arise from the even/odd combinations taking x and z:

Scenario 1: Both even: $1 + 6 + 6 + 1 \rightarrow$ Remainder $= 4$;

Scenario 2: Both odd: $9 + 6 + 4 + 1 \rightarrow$ Remainder $= 0$

Scenario 3: x odd, z even: $9 + 6 + 6 + 1 \rightarrow$ Remainder $= 2$

Scenario 4: x even, z odd: $1 + 6 + 4 + 1 \rightarrow$ Remainder $= 2$

Thus, the sum of all remainders $= 4 + 0 + 2 + 2 = 8$.

134. In order to think of the maximum possible Mondays and Thursdays, we will need to consider one of the two years to be a leap year. In such a case, there are 104 weeks and 3 extra days in 2 years.

But these three extra days must be consecutive so if Monday is one of these three days then Thursday cannot be one of three days and vice-versa.

So maximum possible number of Mondays and Thursdays $= 104 \times 2 + 1 = 209$.

135. In order to think of the minimum possible Mondays and Thursdays, we will need to consider none of the two years to be a leap year. In such a case, there are 104 weeks and 2 extra days in 2 years.

So minimum possible number of Mondays and Thursdays $= 104 \times 2 = 208$. (In the event, that neither of these extra days is a Monday or a Thursday).

136. Remainder of

$$\frac{[(111111111.........64\,terms)\times(22222222.........55\,terms)]}{18}$$

$= 2 \times$ Remainder of

$$\frac{[(111111111.........64\,terms)\times(111111.........55\,terms)]}{9}$$

$\rightarrow$ Remainder $= 1$

So required remainder $= 2 \times 1 = 2$

137. We can see from the expression that $(x - y)(x + y)$ is an even number. Both $x - y$ and $x + y$ are even numbers, so product of $(x - y)(x + y)$ must be divisible by 4. But 777314 is not divisible by 4. So it has no solution. The correct answer would be 0.

Solutions for Questions 138 and 139: Coin 1 was turned only once, coin 2 was turned twice, coin 3 was turned twice, coin 4 was turned thrice, coin 5 was turned twice, coin 6 was turned 4 times, coin 7 was turned twice, coin 8 was turned 4 times, while coin 9 was turned 3 times as so on.

We can easily see that each of the coins would be turned a number of times that would be equal to the number of factors the number on the coin has. Thus, it would be the coins having perfect square numbers that would be turned an odd number of times (hence show tails) and the rest of the coins were turned an even number of times (Hence, would be showing heads). There are a total 10 coins having perfect square numbers and these would be showing tails.

138. After the 100th visit, coin numbers 54 and 91 were in heads-up state.

139. After the 100th visit, there were $100 - 10 = 90$ coins in heads-up state.

140. The last 3-digits of any number are the same as the remainder when we divide the number by 1000.

$$\frac{(225)^{40}}{1000} = \frac{5^{80}\cdot 9^{40}}{1000} = \frac{5^{77}\cdot 9^{40}}{8}$$

$9^{40} = (8 + 1)^{40}$ gives remainder 1 when we divide it by 8.

$\frac{5^{77}}{8} = \frac{5\cdot(24+1)^{38}}{8}$ leaves a remainder 5.

So last 3-digits of $(225)^{40} = 125 \times 5 = 625$.

So the value of 100th digit is 6.

141. 'c' cannot be greater than 3 because if $c \geq 4$ then 'a' should be greater than or equal to 16 which is not possible. Similarly 'b' cannot be greater than 4.

c	b	a	Number of triplets
3	No possible values as $3b$ can be 13 or 14 only, but that gives us no value for b (as neither of these numbers is a multiple of 3)	No values possible	0
2	4	13, 14	2
2	3	10-14	5
1	2	7-14	8
1	3	10-14	5
1	4	13, 14	2

Total possible triplets $= 0 + 2 + 5 + 8 + 5 + 2 = 22$.

142. There are two cases in this situation:

If we include 5: If this number consists of the digit 5, then we would need to use at least one of the even digits between 2 and 4. In this case, the number would need to be even and also divisible by 5. For this to occur, the number should end in 0 – which is not a possibility in the given case. So 5 cannot be one of these 4-digits.

If we do not include 5: In this case the number, would be consisting of the digits 1,2,3 and 4. In such a case, we can easily realise that such a number cannot be a multiple of 3, since the sum of digits of the number is 10.

Level of Difficulty (III)

1. We can express our 4 digit number as $1000a + 100b + 10c + d$. According to question, $999(a-d) + 90(b-c) = 7083 \rightarrow 111(a-d) + 10(b-c) = 787$. Since the maximum value of the term containing $(b-c)$ can be 90, the minimum value of $(a-d)$ will be 7 and it cannot exceed 7 as $(b-c)$ has to be positive.
   $(a-d) = 7 \rightarrow (b-c) = 1$
   For a & d, we have 3 possibilities (9, 2; 8, 1; 7,0). For $b-c$ we have 9 possibilites (9, 8; 8, 7; 7, 6…1, 0). Hence, we have a total of 27 such numbers. The correct answer is 27.
2. From the question we can deduce that the number of tracksuits is 2 more than a number which is a multiple of both 4 and 6. So the required total number of suits is of the form $12x + 2$. Lowest possible number for suits with each person is 12 with total suits being 50. The highest possible number of suits with each person is 99 with total suits being 398. Hence, required difference is 87. Hence, Option (a) is the correct answer.
3. The possibility for the digits of a three digit number giving a product of 24 are: (8, 3, 1); (6, 4, 1); (6, 2, 2); (4, 3, 2). The digits in N + 1 can be visualized based on which of the cases we take and in each case, what is the units digit we have taken for the original number. For instance, for (8, 3, 1) if we take the value of N as 831, the number N + 1 would become 832. On the other hand if we take N as 138, N + 1 would be 139. Visualising these cases, we see that the digits possible for N + 1 would be: (8, 3, 2); (8, 4, 1); (9, 3, 1); (7, 4, 1); (6, 5, 1); (6, 4, 2); (6, 2, 3); (7, 2, 2); (5, 3, 2); (4, 4, 2); (4, 3, 3). The maximum product in this case is 48 and is got using the cases of (N + 1) having the digits (8, 3, 2) or (6, 4, 2). N + 1 has a maximum value of 832 and a second least value of 246. The correct answer is 586.
4. The units digit of the number will determine the remainder. For the given expression A, our units digit will be equal to 3 (The unit's digit of 5! onwards will always be 0). So we need to find the units digit of $(\ldots\ldots3)^{(\ldots.3)}$. Now we know that the cyclicity of 3 is 4. When we divide A by 4, we will get a remainder of either 1 or 3 depending on the value of the tens digit (1 for odd and 3 for even). So we need to find the tens digit of A to check which of these cases is being used here. Till 4!, the sum is 33. For numbers 10! onwards we will get tens digit as 0 for all numbers. Hence, we need to find the sum till 9!. So for different factorials from 5! to 9! we will get tens digit as 2, 2, 4, 2, 8. Hence, the tens digit of A would be got by adding (3 + 2 + 2 + 4 + 2 + 8 = 1). Hence, our required expression A^B will be $(\ldots..13)^{(\ldots..13)}$. So the units digit of this number would be 3. Hence, when this number is divided by 5, the remainder will be 3. The correct answer is 3.
5. LCM of the two given numbers is equal to $16!^2 \times (18 \times 17)^2 \times 19 \times 20$. This can be rewritten as $18! \times 20! \rightarrow$ So, $x, y = 18, 20$ and $z = 1$. Hence, $x + y + z = 39$. Hence, Option (b) is the correct answer.
6. To make a product of 36, we need 2 2s and 2 3s. To maximize the number of integers, we need to remove one of the 3s. So till 60, we have 40 numbers which are not a multiple of 3. However we can include one number which is a multiple of 3. Hence, the maximum number of integers he wrote is 41. The correct answer is 41.
7. Let a and r be the first term and common ratio of the Geometric Progression respectively.
   So, $a + ar = 4$, $ar^2 + ar^3 = 16 \rightarrow a(1 + r) = 4$, $ar^2(1 + r) = 16$. On dividing both the equations we get $r^2 = 4 \rightarrow r = \pm 2$. If $r = +2$, $a = 4/3$ but $a < 0$. Hence, $r = -2$. So $a = -4$. So sum of a_1 to a_9 is using $a = -4$, $r = -2$ and $n = 9$ in the formula for sum of a Geometric Progression as: $a\left(\frac{r^n - 1}{r - 1}\right) = -4\left(\frac{-2^9 - 1}{-2 - 1}\right) = -684.$ It is given that $-684 = 4k \rightarrow k = -171$. Hence, the value of $|k| = 171$. The correct answer is 171.
8. It is given that $a^x \times b^y = 75^{232} = 3^{232} \times 5^{464}$. However, these two numbers can be expressed as some number raised to power 1. It seems that the required difference is $454 - 232 = 232$. But actually we can think of 3^{232} itself as some natural number $N_1^{\,1}$ and likewise for 5^{464}. Hence, the minimum value of difference will be $1 - 1 = 0$. The correct answer is 0.

Solutions for Questions 9 and 10:

We solve this question using hit and trial method. If first number is less than second, our actual sum has to be more than what Santa got. Sums of first N natural numbers above 448 are 465 (Sum of 1 to 30); 496 (Sum of 1 to 31); 528 (Sum of 1 to 32) and so on. If we think of the double counted number as x and the subtracted number as y, 448 will be less than the correct sum of 1 to N by a value of $2y - x$. From here we will look at going through a trial and error solution for the question. If we take N as 30, the correct sum should have been 1 + 2 + 3 +…+ 3 0 = 465. Thus, in this case $2y - x = 17$, which gives us multiple answers for y and x (while keeping both distinct and between 1 and 31). These values can be listed as: 23, 29; 22, 27; 21, 25….;9, 1 (a total of 15 cases).

If we take N as 31, the correct sum should have been $1 + 2 + 3 + \ldots + 31 = 496$. Thus, in this case $2y - x = 48$, which gives us multiple answers for y and x (while keeping both distinct and between 1 and 31). These values can be listed as: 25, 2; 26, 4; 27, 6….; 31, 14 (a total of 7 cases).

If we take N as 32, the correct sum should have been $1 + 2 + 3 + \ldots + 32 = 528$. Thus, in this case $2y - x = 80$, which gives us no values for y and x (while keeping both distinct and between 1 and 32).

Thus, there are a total of $15 + 7 = 22$ possible ways in which this could happen.

The second question in the set can be solved by looking at the various pairs in the solution. The highest sum happens if we take y as 23 and x as 29 and is equal to 52.

The correct answers are 22 and 52.

11. $y(x + z) = 19$, $z(x + y) = 51$. Since x, y and z are natural numbers, from equation 1, $y = 1$ and $(x + z) = 19$. From the second equation we have, $z(x + 1) = 3 \times 17$. Hence, on comparing, $z = 3$ and $x = 16$ or $z = 17$ and $x = 2$. The product xyz can be $16 \times 1 \times 3 = 48$ or $2 \times 1 \times 17 = 34$. The minimum possible value of xyz is hence equal to 34. The correct answer is 34.

12. In order to solve this question, we first need to find the value of m. Minimum value of n is 100 and in the LHS of the equation it is also getting multiplied by a power of 3.. So the minimum value of m! is 300. Starting a trial and error process from this point, we see that the Minimum value of m is $6 \rightarrow 3^{P!} \times n = 720$. Since n is not a multiple of 3, it can take a maximum value of 80 but $n \geq 100$. So m cannot take a value of 6. Checking for $m = 7$. $3^{P!} \times n = 5040$. In this $n = 560$. This means that $3^{P!} = 9 \rightarrow P = 2$. So our required sum is 569. The correct answer is 569.

13. For a number to be a multiple of 3, $a + d + 3b$ should be multiple of 3. It is given that $a + b + d = 18$ which is a multiple of 3. So $2b$ has to be a multiple of 3. This means that b = 3, 6, 9. So $a + d$ = 15, 12, 9.

For $a + d = 15$, 4 possibilities for a and d from 6, 9; 7, 8; 8, 7 and 9, 6. Hence, $4 \times 3 = 12$ possibilities for the combination of a, b, d.

For $a + d = 12$, 7 possibilities for a and d (3 + 9; 4 + 8 ;…; 9 + 3), giving us 21 combinations for a, b, d.

For $a + d = 9$, 8 possibilities for a and d (8 + 1; 7 + 2; …1 + 8), giving us 24 combinations for a, b, d.

So there are a total of $19 \times 3 = 57$ possible values for N. The correct answer is 57.

14. The numbers can be expressed as $100a + 10b + c - 100c - 10b - a = pq4 \rightarrow 99(a - c) = pq4$. Since the highest value of $a - c$ is 9, to get a units digit of 4 when it is multiplied by 99, we need to use the value of $(a - c)$ as 6. Thus, $pq4 = 594 = 3 \times 3 \times 11 \times 2 \times 3. \rightarrow 2 \times 3^3 \times 11$. The number of factors for this number are $2 \times 4 \times 2 = 16$. Hence, the correct answer is 16.

15. It is given that $2a^5 = 3b^2 \rightarrow a^5/b^2 = 3/2$. This means that a is a multiple of 3 and b is a multiple of 2. To have such a case possible, we need 2s and 3s in both numerator and denominator. This means that both a and b are multiples of 6. So, if a is 6, we'll have to eliminate 5 2s and 4 3s, from the numerator when is it divided by b^2. This means that we have 6 2s and 4 3s in denominator. $\rightarrow$ value of $b^2 = 72^2$. Hence, 6 and 72 are our values of a and b respectively. Hence, the smallest value of $a + b = 78$.

16. The sum of factors of $80 = (2^0 + 2^1 + 2^2 + 2^3 + 2^4) \times (5^0 + 5^1) = 31 \times 6 = 186$

Possible values of x and y are (40, 0; 37, 2; 34, 4; … 1, 26). The maximum sum of $x + y + z = 40 + 0 + 186 = 226$. The correct answer is 226.

17. $b^2(a + c) = 13$, $c(b + a) = 33$. Since a, b and c are natural numbers, from equation 1, $b = 1$ and $(a + c) = 13$. From 2, $c(a + 1) = 3 \times 11$. Hence, on comparing, $c = 3$ and $a = 10$ or $c = 11$ and $a = 2$. The products for $a \times b \times c$ are 30 and 22 respectively. Hence, 8 is the correct answer.

18. Let's take one number at a time.

According to the question, $4^{6n+1} + x$ is divisible by 5. In this number the first term will leave a remainder of 4 when it is divided by 5, as the power of 4 is odd. This has to be negated by x. So x has to be among (–9, –4, 1, 6).

Also, $6^{12n} - x$ is divisible by 5. In this number the first term will leave a remainder of 1 when divided by 5. This has to be negated by x. So x has to be among (– 9, –4, 1, 6).

Since all 4 values are common to both the equations, we'll consider all values of x. Hence, the required sum is $-9 - 4 + 1 + 6 = -6$. The correct answer is –6.

19. Let the three numbers be x, y and z. So we need to maximize the value of $xyz + xy + yz + zx$. To maximize the product of integers for a given sum, we need to place the numbers as close to each other as possible. There are 2 cases (3, 4, 7 or 3, 5, 6) in which values are as close as they can get. We need to check the value of $xyz + xy + xz + yz$ in each case.

Case 1: $84 + 12 + 28 + 21 = 145$

Case 2: $90 + 15 + 30 + 18 = 153$

Hence the maximum possible sum is 153.

The nine possibilities for x, y, z in any order are (11, 2, 1); (10, 3, 1); (9, 3, 2); (9, 4, 1); (8, 5, 1); (7, 6, 1); (7, 5, 2); (7, 4, 3); (6, 5, 3).

In each of these cases, we need to check the value of $xyz + xy + xz + yz$: In the first case (11, 2, 1);, we get a value of $22 + 22 + 11 + 2 = 57$ for the expression. This is the least value of $xyz + xy + xz$

+ yz. The maximum value of $xyz + xy + xz + yz$ can be seen to occur when we use (6, 5, 3) – the value of $xyz + xy + xz + yz$ in this case is 90 + 15 + 30 + 18 = 153. The difference between the maximum and minimum possible values of the expression is 153 – 57 = 96. Hence, the correct answer is 96.

20. The given expression can be rewritten as $\frac{x+5}{x+5} + \frac{90}{x+5}$
So $x + 5$ has to be factor of 90.
As 90 has 12 factors, the value of $x + 5$ can be equal to any of these factors (viz: 1, 2, 3, 5, 6, 9, 10, 15, 18, 30, 45 and 90). Thus, from here we get 12 values for x. (example if $x + 5 = 1 \rightarrow x = -4$; if $x + 5 = 2 \rightarrow x = -3 \ldots x + 5 = 90 \rightarrow x = 85$ and so on). However, we also need to take into account cases where $x + 5$ is equal to –1, –2, –3, –5, –6, –9, –10… –90. So there will be another 12 values possible for x. So, there will be a total of 24 possible values of x. Hence, the correct answer is 24.

21. The expression can be rewritten as $100a + 10b + c = 5(10a + b + 10b + c + 10c + a) \rightarrow 100a + 10b + c = 55a + 55b + 55c \rightarrow 45a = 45b + 54c \rightarrow a = b + 6c/5$. Since a is a single digit number, $6c$ has to be a multiple of 5. c is not equal to 0 so the only value for c is 5. So $a = b + 6$. The possibilities are (715, 825 and 935). Hence, the required difference is 220.

22. For a number to have 4 factors apart from 1 and itself, it should have a total of 6 factors. The prime representation of such a number has to be a^5 or $a^1 b^2$. Between 1 and 250, there are exactly 2 numbers that are fifth powers of a prime number (Viz: 2^5 & 3^5). Next we need to identify numbers that can be expressed as $a^1 b^2$. If $a = 2$, b can be any prime number between 3 and 11. (Possible values for b are 3, 5, 7, 11). If $a = 3$, b can be 2, 5, 7. For a = 5 and 7 also we can see three values possible for b such that ab^2 is less than 250. After that all prime numbers from 11 to 23 (11, 13, 17, 19, 23) will have exactly two values of b as 2 and 3. For a = 29, 31, 37, 41, 43, 47, 53 and 59, the only value possible for b would be 2. Thus, there are a total of 4 + 3 + 3 + 3 + 2 + 2 + 2 + 2 + 2 + 8 = 31 numbers. The correct answer is 31 + 2 = 33.

23 Since, x^2 has 5 factors more than x, it would necessarily have 5 factors less than x. Also, x itself would be a factor of x^2. Hence, x^2 has a total of 11 factors. This is only possible when it is of the form p^{10}, where p is a prime number. So, $x^2 = p^{10} \rightarrow x = p^5 \rightarrow x^5 = p^{25}$. So x^5 has 26 factors. Hence, 26 is the correct answer.

24. For a number to be a multiple of 3, $a + d + 3b$ should be multiple of 3. It is given that $a + b + d = 18$ which is a multiple of 3. So $2b$ has to be a multiple of 3. This means that b = 3, 6, 9. So $a + d$ = 15, 12, 9. We also need to remember that we need to keep a, b, d as distinct from each other.
For $a + d = 15$, possible combinations of 4 possibilities for a and d from 6, 9; 7, 8; 8, 7 and 9, 6. Hence, 4 × 3 = 12 possibilities for the combination of a, b, d. However, we need to remove combinations where each digit is not distinct. When a, d 6, 9; b can only be 3. For 7, 8 and 8, 7 b can be any of 3, 6 or 9. For a, d as 9, 6 b can again only be 3. Thus, in this case there are a total of 8 possible values of the 5 digit number abbbd.
For $a + d = 12$, Possibilities for a and d (3 + 9, b can only be 6; 4 + 8, b can be 3, 6, 9; 5 + 7, b can be 3, 6, 9; 7 + 5, b can be 3, 6, 9; 8 + 4, b can be 3, 6, 9; 9 + 3, b can only be 6), giving us 14 combinations for a, b, d.
For $a + d = 9$, the following possibilities emerge: a + d = 8 + 1, b can be 3, 6, 9; $a + d = 7 + 2$, b can be 3, 6, 9; $a + d = 6 + 3$, b can only be 9; $a + d = 5 + 4$, b can be 3, 6, 9; $a + d = 4 + 5$, b can be 3, 6, 9; $a + d = 3 + 6$, b can only be 9; $a + d = 2 + 7$, b can be 3, 6, 9; $a + d = 1 + 8$, b can be 3, 6, 9, giving us a total of 20 combinations.
So there are a total of 8 + 14 + 20 = 42 possible values for N. The correct answer is 42.

25. $a^n - b^n$ is always divisible by $(a - b)$. Also, if n is even then $a^n - b^n$ is divisible by $(a + b)$.
$7^{4n} - 5^{4n}$ is divisible by $(7 - 5) = 2$, $7^4 - 5^4 = 1776$ and $7^4 + 5^4 = 3026$
1776 is divisible by 37 and 111.
Hence, the given expression is divisible by 2, 111 and 37. Hence, option (d) is correct.

26. LCM of 3^{12}, 2^{24} and x is $2^{24} \times 3^{12}$.
x can take 25 powers of 2 from 2^0 to 2^{24} and thirteen powers of 3, from 3^0 to 3^{12}.
Hence, total possible values are 25 × 13 = 325.

27. The numbers would be $5a, 5b, 5c$ adding up to 105. Hence, $a + b + c = 21$, with a, b, c having an HCF of 1. Since we do not need ordered pairs we can look just find pairs of a, b, c assuming $a \le b \le c$. The sets can be thought of by fixing a as the smallest number and checking how many cases occur for b and c. For example if $a = 1$, we get: (1, 1, 19); (1, 2, 18); (1, 3, 17); (1, 4, 16) … (1, 10, 10) – a total of 10 values.
For $a = 2$, we get: (2, 2, 17); (2, 3, 16) … (2, 9, 10) – a total of 8 values. When $a = 3$, we get: (3, 3, 15); (3, 4, 14); (3, 5, 13); (3, 6, 12); (3, 7, 11); (3, 8, 10); (3, 9, 9) – a total of 7 values, but we need to be careful here since a, b, c as 3, 3, 15 do not have an HCF 1 and hence the numbers $5a$, $5b$ and $5c$ (which would be 15, 15, 75 in this case) would not have an HCF of 5. Hence, we need to reject the cases: (3, 3, 15); (3, 6, 12) and (3, 9, 9). Thus, we have only 4 instances in this case. With a as 4, all three numbers $5a$, $5b$ and $5c$ would become greater than 15 and hence we do not need to consider these

as part of our answer. Hence, the correct answer is $10 + 8 + 4 = 22$.

28. $15 \times 37 \times 63 \times 51 \times 97 \times 17$ on division by 100 would give us a remainder that would be equal to its last 2-digits. First we can divide the numerator and the denominator by 5 to get the expression: $\frac{3\times37\times63\times51\times97\times17}{20}$ using remainder theorem $\rightarrow \frac{3\times17\times3\times11\times17\times17}{20} = \frac{51\times33\times289}{20}$ using remainder theorem $\rightarrow \frac{11\times13\times9}{20} = \frac{143\times9}{20} \rightarrow \frac{3\times9}{20} = \frac{27}{20} \rightarrow$ Remainder = 7. Hence, the required remainder = $7 \times 5 = 35$, which would also be the last 2-digits of the given number.
Hence, option (a) is correct.

Solutions for Questions 29 and 30:

29. Since the number is divisible by 44, then the number must be divisible by 4 and 11.
For the number to be divisible by 4, then z must be 2 or 6.
For the number to be divisible by 11, $(1 + x + y + z) - (5 + 3 + 7) = x + y + z - 14$ must be divisible by 11.
Case 1: $z = 2$
Then, $x + y + z - 14 = x + y - 12$ must be divisible by 11. Since, x and y are single digit whole numbers, this is only possible if $x + y - 12 = 0$ or if $x + y - 12 = -11$.
Thus, we get: $x + y = 12$ or $x + y = 1$
The following solutions would work for the above situations with x, y as

x	y	$y + z - x$
3	9	8
4	8	6
5	7	4
6	6	2
7	5	0
8	4	–2
9	3	–4
0	1	3
1	0	1

Case 2: When, $z = 6$
Then $x + y + z - 14$ or $x + y - 8$ must be a multiple of 11. For this to occur, $x + y - 8$ can again be 0.
(**Note:** $x + y - 8$ cannot reach 11, because the maximum value of $x + y$ can be 18. It cannot also reach –11, because $x + y$ would need to be –3 to get to –11, which is again not possible, since x and y are whole numbers.)

x	y	$y + z - x$
1	7	12
2	6	10
3	5	8
4	4	6
5	3	4
6	2	2
7	1	0
8	0	–2
0	8	14

Hence, $y + z - x$ can take total 12 values.

30. Maximum possible value of $y + z - x$ is 14.

Solutions for Questions 31 and 32:

31. $ab - 3a - 2b + 6 = 600$
$(a - 2)(b - 3) = 600$
As a is an even number and b is an odd number, $(a - 2)$ and $(b - 3)$ both must be even numbers. The following sets satisfy the given equation: (2, 300), (4, 150), (6, 100), (10, 60), (12, 50) and (20, 30).
Hence, there are total $6 \times 2 = 12$ solutions of the given equation.

32. Maximum possible value of a + b = 2 + 2 + 300 + 3 = 4 + 303 = 307.

Solutions for Questions 33 and 34:

Let $x = ab = 10a + b$, as x is more than 40 so a ≥ 4.
According to the question 'a' is a factor of $10a + b$ then b must be divisible by 'a'.
In the 40s, there would be two such numbers 44 and 48. Likewise, 50 and 55; 60 and 66; 70 and 77; 80 and 88 and 90 and 99.

33. Twelve values are possible for x.

34. 99 + 88 + 48 + 77 + 66 + 55 + 44 + 90 + 80 + 70 + 60 + 50 = 827

35. Let the five digit number be *abcde*.
According to the question: $a + c + e - b - d = 0, 11$.
However, a closer inspection shows us that the value of 11 is not achievable, no matter what you try to do with the numbers. It can be numerically visualised that $a + c + e - b - d = 0$ can be achieved only if we share 2, 3, 5 between a, c and e. b and d need to be allocated 4 and 6 amongst them. This can be thought out algebraically also as follows:
For $a + c + e - b - d = 0$
$a + c + e + b + d = 2(b + d)$
$2 + 3 + 4 + 5 + 6 = 2(b + d)$
$2(b + d) = 20$ or $b + d = 10$
It is possible only when $b = 4$ or 6 and $d = 6$ or 4.
a, c and e can take total $3! = 6$ values by distributing 2, 3 and 5 amongst them.
Hence, total possible numbers $= 2 \times 6 = 12$.
Hence, there are only twelve such numbers are possible.

36. $910 = Na + x$
$910 = (N + 2)\ b + x$, where 'a' and 'b' are natural numbers.
To maximise the value of 'N', the value of 'a' and 'b' must be equal to '$N + 2$' and 'N' respectively.
$910 = N(N + 2) + x$
$N(N + 2) = 910 - x$
$$N^2 + 2N + 1 = 911 - x$$
$$(N + 1)^2 = 911 - x$$
To maximise the value of N, x must be equal to 11.
$$(N + 1)^2 = 911 - 11 = 900$$
$N = 29$. Hence, the required answer would be the remainder of 910 divided by 29, which is 11.

37. Only perfect squares have odd number of factors. Hence, the required value of $P = 64 \times 81 \times 100 \times 121 \times 144 \times 169 \times 196 \times 225 \times 256 \times 289 = 2^{22} \times 3^8 \times 5^4 \times 11^2 \times 13^2 \times 17^2 \times 7^2$
Hence, the maximum power of 6 = minimum of (22, 8) = 8.

38. $70 = 2 \times 5 \times 7$
Hence, the number must be in the form of $3^p \times 11^q \times 13^r \times 17^s \times 19^t \times 23^u \times 29^v \times 31^w$...
On substituting the values of p, q, r, s, ….. we get the following composite numbers: 9, 27, 33, 39, 51, 57, 69, 81, 87, 93 and 99. Hence, there are a total of 11 numbers.

39. $51! = 2^{47} \times 3^{23} \times P$
$10! = 2^8 \times 3^4 \times Q$
$$\frac{51!}{10!} = \frac{2^{47} \times 3^{23} \times P}{2^8 \times 3^4 \times Q} = 2^{39} \times 3^{19} \times \left(\frac{P}{Q}\right)$$
As 51! is divisible by 10! completely so P/Q must be an integer and 51! must be divisible by $2^{2x} \times 3^x$.
Maximum possible value of $x = 19$.

Solutions for Questions 40 and 41:

40. As the number of factors of N^2 is odd. Hence, the number of factors of N must be odd. (Odd + Odd = even). So N must be a perfect square.
For $N = 2^4 \times 3^2$, number of factors = (4 + 1) (2 + 1) = 15. $N^2 = 2^8 \times 3^4$, number of factors = (8 + 1) (4 + 1) = 45
Hence, the total number of factors = 15 + 45 = 60
For $N = 3^4 \times 2^2$, number of factors = (4 + 1) (2 + 1) = 15, $N^2 = 3^8 \times 2^4$ number of factors = (8 + 1) (4 + 1) = 45
Hence, the total number of factors = 15 + 45 = 60
Similarly for $N = 5^2 \times 2^4$ and for $N = 2^4 \times 7^2$, number of factors of N and N^2 would be 15 + 45 = 60.
Thus, possible values of N = 144, 324, 400 and 784.
Hence, four values are possible for N.

41. 784.

42. $3Q^2 = 1376 - P^2$
$1376 - P^2$ must be a multiple of 3, which is not possible for any real value of P. Hence, the correct answer is 0.

43. Divide the given expression by 100 and find the remainder to get the answer. 50 would be the last 2-digits here.

44. The remainder will always be less than 18, since the sum of the digits (which would be the divisor) would at the maximum be 18. We would need to adopt a trial and error approach.
When the sum of digits is 18 then, only possible remainder is 9 (for 99).
When the sum of digits is 17 then, the largest possible remainder is 13 (for 98).
When the sum of digits is 16 then, the largest possible remainder is 15 (for 79).
When the sum of digits is 15 or below, we would not be able to get a remainder that is less greater than 15.
Hence, the maximum possible remainder is 15.

45. X has exactly 201 elements and the sum of all elements of X is equal to 0. As the subsets of X have exactly 199 elements. Hence, we have to leave rest of the two elements whose sum in either +1 or –1 out of that subset.
Sum '–1' for 199 elements can be obtained by removing two elements whose sum is 1.
This can be done by removing any of the following pairs of numbers: (0, 1), (–1, 2), (–2, 3),.....,(–99, 100). Similarly we can sum '+1' in 100 ways.
Hence, the required answer = 100 + 100 = 200.

46. The value of $ab + bc + cd + de + ef + gh + hi + ij + ja$ will be minimum when all the $a, b, c, d, e, f, g, h, i$ and j are 10, –10, 10, –10, ... –10 (As it is not given that all the integers are distinct or same). Hence, minimum possible value of $ab + bc + cd + de + ef + fg + gh + ha = 10 \times -10 + -10 \times 10 + ... + 10 \times -10 = -800$

47. $43^{101} + 23^{101}$ is of the form $a^n + b^n$ with n odd. Such a number can be written to be a multiple of $(a + b)$. Thus, the given expression is a multiple of (43 + 23) = 66. Hence, the required remainder would be 0.

48. Let the numbers are $6k$ and $6(k + 1)$.
For the HCF to be 6, k and $k + 1$ are always co-prime.
LCM of 6k and $6(k + 1)$ is $6\ k\ (k + 1)$.
$6\ k\ (k + 1)$ is a 5-digit number for $k \geq 41$.
Hence, the maximum possible value of k is 40 for which the LCM is a 4– digit number.
Hence, the required number = $6(k + 1) = 6 \times 41 = 246$.

49. Let the numbers be $6k$ and $6(k + 1)$.
For the HCF to be 6, k and $k + 1$ are always co-prime.
LCM of $6k$ and $6(k + 1)$ is $6\ k\ (k + 1)$.
$6\ k\ (k + 1)$ is a 4-digit number for $40 \geq k \geq 13$.

Hence, the required number of pairs = 40 – 13 + 1 = 28.

50. N would have 6 factors if its standard form appears as any one of these: **Case 1:** $a \times b^2$ or **Case 2:** c^5 Where a, b and c are prime numbers.

Case 1: N = $a \times b^2$

Possible values: when $a = 2$, $b = 3, 5$: and $N =$ **18, 50**

$a = 3, b = 2 – N =$ **12**

$a = 5, b = 2, 3 – N =$ **20, 45**

$a = 7, b = 2 – N =$ **28**

$a = 11, b = 2 – N =$ **44**

Case 2: $N = c^5$

$c = 2 – N =$ **32**

Hence, total number of possible values of N are 8.

51. 50

52. $(6 – p) \times (6 – q) \times (6 – r) \times (6 – s) \times (6 – t) = 6720$
$= (6 – 2)\ (6 – 1)\ (6 + 0)\ (6 + 1)\ (6 + 2)$
$p = 2, q = 1, r = 0, s = –1, t = –2.$
$p + q + r + s + t = 2 + 1 + 0 – 1 – 2 = 0$

53. $87y – 264x = 60$
$87y – 60 = 264x \rightarrow 87y – 60 = (87 \times 3 + 3)x$
$87\ (y – 3x) = 60 + 3x$
As x and y are integers hence, $y – 3x$ must be integer.
For $y – 3x = 1$ $x = 9, y = 28$
For $y – 3x = 2$ $x = 38$ and $y = 116$ (not possible as x and y should both be below 100).
Hence, only one solution is possible.

Solutions for Questions 54 to 56:

Let the number be $10a + b$. Then, the number formed by reversing the digits would be $10b + a$. According to the question, when both these numbers are divided by their sum of digits (viz: $a + b$), the remainder is the same in both cases. This can be represented algebraically as:

$10a + b = p(a + b) + r$, $10b + a = q(a + b) + r$

By subtracting the second equation from the first we get: $9(a – b) = (a + b)\ (p – q)$

Or: $p – q = 9(a – b)/(a + b)$

Since $p – q$, $(a – b)$ and $(a + b)$ are all integers, $(a + b)$ must be a multiple of 3.

By this logic, we get that the possible values of $(a + b) = 3, 6, 9, 12, 15, 18$. Of these $a + b = 15$ is not possible because if $a + b = 15$ then in order for $(p – q)$ to be an integer, $(a – b)$ must be 5. We get from $a + b = 15$ and $a – b = 5$, $a = 10$ and $b = 5$ which is not possible. Also for $a + b$ to be equal to 18, both a and b must be 9 each, which does not make sense in this question since we are talking about reversing of digits here.

Hence, using $a + b = 3, 6, 9$ or 12 we get the possible values of a and b as given in the following table.

Note: In order to make this table, we have to also check the same remainder condition being fulfilled when the digits are reversed:

Value of b	Value of a	Total possible values of the number
1	2, 5, 8	21, 51, 81
2	1, 4, 7	12, 42, 72
3	6	63
4	2, 5, 8	24, 54, 84
5	1, 4	15, 45
6	3	36
7	2	27
8	1, 4	18, 48
9	No values possible	
0	Reversal does not make sense	

54. There are 16 such numbers (8 such pairs).

55. Maximum possible value of ‘ab’ = 84

56. Minimum possible value of ‘ab’ = 12

57. Visualise the 62 digit number as X = pppppp.......(36 times) qp pppppp....24 times.
We know that if a digit is written 6 times side by side, then such a six digit number is always divisible by 7, 11 and 13.
∴ pppppp.......(36 times) and pppppp....24 times are divisible by 13.
For X to be divisible by 13, qp must be divisible by 13. Since, no 2-digit multiple of 13 has either 4 or 7 as its units digit. Hence, option (a) is correct.

58. Using the numbers (2, 3, 5), we can form distinct sum as 2, 3, 5, 2 + 5 = 7, 3 + 5 = 8 and 2 + 3 + 5 = 10 (6 – distinct sums)
If we include 10, we could not only obtain the above mentioned sum but also the following sums:
10 + 2 = 12, 10 + 3 = 13, 10 + 5 = 15, 10 + 7 = 17, 10 + 8 = 18, 10 + 10 = 20. In other words, we can obtain 6 + 6 = 12 different sums if we use 2, 3, 5 and 10.
Similarly if we use 2, 3, 5, 10 and 20 we can obtain 12 + 12 = 24 different sums. Continuing with this logic, we can conclude that there will be a total of 384 distinct sums.

59. It is given that p and r are integers then q must be a perfect square and s must be a 4th power of a natural number.
$q = x^2$ and $s = y^4$
$$y^4 – x^2 = 17$$
$$(–x + y^2)\ (x + y^2) = 1 \times 17$$
On solving the above equation, we get $x = 8$ and $y = 3$.
$q = 64$ and $s = 81$

$64^{\frac{1}{2}} = 8, r = 81^{\frac{7}{4}} = 2187$

$p + r = 8 + 2187 = 2195$

60. $32^{32^{32}} \div 9 \rightarrow 5^{32^{32}} \div 9 = 5^{6n+x} \div 9$. We write this in the form of 5^{6n+x} because 5^6 leaves a remainder of 1 when divided by 9. When we try to see 32^{32} as $6n + x$, we can find the value of x as the remainder of 2^{32} when divided by 6. The following thought process would help us find this value:
$2^{32} \div 6 = 2^{31} \div 3 \rightarrow$ Remainder = 2 (by the $a^n \div (a + 1)$ rule). Thus, $2^{32} \div 6$ would have a remainder of $2 \times 2 = 4$.
Hence, the required remainder would be $5^4 \div 9$, which is 4.

Solutions for Questions 61 to 63:

61. We are given that: $ab \times ac = abc$
This can be written as: $ab \times ac = ab \times 10 + c$
$ab\ (ac - 10) = c$
The right hand side of the above equation is a single digit number and the left hand side of the above equation can never be a single digit number. Hence, c must be equal to 0 and ac must be equal to 10. Hence, $a = 1$ and $c = 0$ we can not determine the exact value of b. Hence, option (*d*) is correct.
62. As $ac = 10$ and the last digit of bc must be 0 hence, $bc \times accaaa$ is perfectly divisible by ac. Hence, the required remainder is equal to 0.
63. $abc = 1b0$ and abc is divisible by 17 if and only if $b = 7$.
$abcbac = 170710$. If we divide 170710 by 14, we get 8 as the remainder.
64. $32^{32^{32}} \div 7 \rightarrow 4^{32^{32}} \div 7 = 4^{3n+x} \div 7$. We write this in the form of 4^{3n+x} because 4^3 leaves a remainder of 1 when divided by 7. When we try to see 32^{32} as $3n + x$, we can find the value of x as the remainder of 2^{32} when divided by 3. The following thought process would help us find this value:
$2^{32} \div 3 = 1$. (remainder)
Hence, the required remainder would be $4^1 \div$, 7 which is 4.
65. If we visualise the number as $2^p \times 3^q$, the number of factors would be $(p + 1)(q + 1)$; For $2n$, we realise that $2n = 2^{P+1} \times 3^q$ and its number of factors would be $(p + 2)(q + 1) = 28$. This has multiple possibilities based on the factors of 28. These are: 1×28; 2×14 and 4×7. Also, $3n = 2^p \times 3^{q+1}$ would have $(p + 1)(q + 2) = 30$ factors. Looking through the factor pairs of 30, we see 1×30, 2×15, 3×10 and 5×6. Considering both these lists, we can see that if we take p as 5 and q as 3, we get both the conditions fulfilled. Thus, $6n = 2^{p+1} \times 3^{q+1} = 2^6 \times 3^4$ would give us $7 \times 5 = 35$ factors.
66. Solve this question through the options. For n terms being 16 option (a), we would need an AP with 16 terms and common difference 1, that would add up to 1000. Since, the average value of a term of this AP turns out to be $1000 \div 16 = 62.5$, we can create a 16 term AP as 55,56,57….62,63,64…70 that adds up to 1000. Hence, 16 terms is possible. Likewise, 5 terms gives the average as 200 and the 5 terms can be taken as 198,199,200,201,202. It is similarly possible for 25 terms with an average of 40, but is not possible for 20 terms with an average of 50. Hence, option (d) is correct.
67. The first remainder would be 4, the second one would be given by $4 \times 4 = 16/9 \rightarrow 7$, the third one $6 \times 6 = 36/9 \rightarrow 0$. The fourth one, $8 \times 8 = 64/9 \rightarrow 1$. Subsequent, remainders would be 1, 0, 7, 4, 0. This cycle would repeat for the next 9 numbers each time. Thus, the remainder for the first 45 numbers = $(4 + 7 + 0 + 1 + 1 + 0 + 7 + 4 + 0)$ repeated 5 times $\rightarrow 120/9 \rightarrow$ remainder = 3. The last 4 terms would then add $4 + 7 + 0 + 1$ to the remainder. Thus, the final remainder = $15/9 \rightarrow 6$.
68. The product would be 32323232…repeated 32 times. Hence, the sum of digits would be 160.
69. For the maximum number of questions, we would need to keep the 15 questions that are not unique, to be shared between the least number of tests (i.e., 2 each). This would give us 12 sets of 15 questions each that are not unique. Also, the number of unique questions would be $35 \times 25 = 875$. Thus, the required maximum number of questions would be $875 + 180 = 1055$.
70. For the minimum number of questions, we would need to share the 15 non-unique questions amongst the entire 25 sets. The number of questions in this case would be: $35 \times 25 + 15 = 875 + 15 = 890$.

Solutions for Questions 71 to 73:

The given condition in the problem is a property of the numbers in the geometric series of the powers of 3. The numbers from W_1 to W_7 would be 1,3,9,27,81,243 and 729. The answers can be got according to these values.

71. $1 + 2 \times 3 + 3 \times 9 + 4 \times 27 + 5 \times 81 + 6 \times 243 = 1 + 6 + 27 + 108 + 405 + 1458 = 2005$.
72. $3^0 \times 3^1 \times 3^2 \times 3^3 \times 3^4 \times 3^5 \times 3^6 = 3^{21}$.
73. We would need to use the coefficients as 1,1,1,0, –1, –1 and –1 to W_1 to W_7 in that order to get: $1 + 3 + 9 + 0 - 81 - 243 - 729 = -1040$. (**Note:** In this question, we have to take the coefficients as defined in the problem as +1, 0 or –1 only).

Solutions for Questions 74 and 75:

There are two 3-digit perfect square numbers that obey the factors are perfect squares rule - viz. 196 and 256. However, questions 74 and 75, both rule out the use of 256. Hence, for question 50, we are looking for the number of factors of $196196 = 2 \times 2 \times 7 \times 7 \times 7 \times 13 \times 11$. This number would have $3 \times 4 \times 2 \times 2 = 48$ factors. Hence, option (c) is correct. For question 75, we need the number of factors of $196196196 = 2 \times 2 \times 3 \times 7 \times 7 \times 333667$. This number gives us $3 \times 2 \times 3 \times 2 = 36$ factors.

(**Note:** The number 333667 is a prime number.)

76. Since each team scored a different number of points, it follows that the points scored by the 15 teams would be 21,22,23,24,...till 35. This is because, the total number of matches in the tournament is ${}^{15}C_2 = 105$ and there are 4 points for each match (either 3 + 1 or 2 + 2). Thus, the total number of points in the tournament is $105 \times 4 = 420$. The only way to fit in 420 points amongst 15 teams with each team getting different number of points and the least value for any team being 21 points would be to use the Arithmetic Progression 21,22,23,24...till 35. Once, we realise this, we know that Australia scored 35 points out of a maximum possible $14 \times 3 = 42$ (14 wins). This means that Australia is dropping 7 points. Each loss makes you drop 2 points as instead of 3 for a win, you receive only 1 point for a loss. Hence, it is not possible for Australia to lose 4 matches. The maximum losses Australia could have had is 3.

77. We can solve this by splitting the denominator into two co-prime numbers 9 and 17. First find the remainder of 128^{1000} on division by 9.

$128^{1000} \div 9 \xrightarrow{R} 2^{1000} \div 9 = (2^6)^{166} \times 2^4 \div 9 \rightarrow$ Remainder = 7. This means that 128^{1000} is a $9n + 7$ number.

Next find the remainder of 128^{1000} on division by 17.

$128^{1000} \div 17 \rightarrow 9^{1000} \div 17 = [(9^{16})^{62} \times 9^8] \div 17 \rightarrow$ Remainder = 1. This means that 128^{1000} is a $17n + 1$ number.

If we try to look for a number below 153, that is both $17n + 1$ as well as $9n + 7$, we would see that the number 52 fulfills this requirement. Hence, 52 is the required remainder of $128^{1000} \div 153$.

78. $\dfrac{50^{51^{52}}}{11} \rightarrow \dfrac{6^{51^{52}}}{11} = \dfrac{6^{10x} \times 6^1}{11} \rightarrow$ Remainder = 6

79. Use the –1 remainder rule for odd powers. Thus,

$\dfrac{32^{33^{34}}}{11} \rightarrow \dfrac{10^{\text{Odd Power}}}{11} \rightarrow$ Remainder = 10

80. $\dfrac{30^{72^{87}}}{11} \rightarrow \dfrac{8^{72^{87}}}{11} = \dfrac{8^{10x} \times 8^{2^{87}}}{11} \rightarrow \dfrac{1 \times 8^{2^{87}}}{11} \rightarrow \dfrac{8^{10x} \times 8^8}{11} \rightarrow$

Remainder = 5

81. $\dfrac{50^{56^{62}}}{11} \rightarrow \dfrac{6^{56^{62}}}{11} = \dfrac{6^{10x} \times 6^6}{11} \rightarrow$ Remainder = 5

82. $\dfrac{33^{34^{35}}}{7} \rightarrow \dfrac{5^{34^{35}}}{7} = \dfrac{5^{6x} \times 5^4}{7} \rightarrow$ Remainder = 2

83. We need the expression $\dfrac{n(n+1)(2n+1)}{6}$ to be a multiple of 4. For this to occur, the numerator of the above expression should be a multiple of 8. In the expression $n(n + 1)(2n + 1)$, $2n + 1$ would always be an odd number. Also, amongst n and $(n + 1)$ one number would be odd and the other would be even. Since, we need $n(n + 1)(2n + 1)$ to be a multiple of 8, we would need either n or $(n + 1)$ to be a multiple of 8 (while at the same time it should be below 100). Thus, we get the number series n = 7, 8, 15, 16, 23, 24, ...95, 96. Since there are 12 multiples of 8 below 100, the required answer is $12 \times 2 = 24$.

84. We need the expression $\dfrac{[n(n+1)]^2}{2^2}$ to be a multiple of 5. For this to occur, the numerator of the above expression should be a multiple of 5. Either n or $n + 1$ should be a multiple of 5. Below 50, there are 19 such instances. Hence, the correct answer is 19.

85. The first solution easily visible here would be at $x = -1$, and $y = 1$. In such equations, we should know that the value of x would change with the coefficient of y, while the value of y would change with the coefficient of x (and the two values would move in the opposite directions since there is a 'plus' sign in the middle). Thus, the series of values of x from its highest positive value below 1000 to the lower limit of being just above –1000 would be 993, 986 ,...... 13, 6, –1,–8, –15,... –995. The number of terms in this series $= \dfrac{1988}{7} + 1 = 285$.

86. 1144 can be written as a product of three co-prime numbers – viz: $13 \times 8 \times 11$. Further, the given number when divided by 11, leaves a remainder of 7, when divided by 13 leaves a remainder of 10 (because, if you divide 777777 by 13, there is no remainder. Hence, when you divide the given number by 13, the remainder would only depend on the remainder of the last three 7's. i.e., 777 ÷ 13). Also, the given number when divided by 8, leaves a remainder of 1. Hence, the given number is a number that is simultaneously $13n + 10$, $8n + 1$ and $11n + 7$. If we create a series of $13n + 10$, we can see that the series would be: 10, 23, 36, 49, 62... At 62, the number is $13n + 10$ as well as an $11n + 7$ number. The next such number would be 62 + 143 (because 143 is the LCM of 13 and 11). Thus, writing down the series of numbers that belong to $13n + 10$ and $11n + 7$ and checking when it also simultaneously becomes $8n + 1$, we can see that the series would be:

62, 205, 348, 491, 634, 777. The number 777 is also an $8n + 1$ number. Hence, the correct remainder is 777.

87. In order to solve this question, you would need to find the odd factors of 19! that are also multiples of 5. $19! = 2^{16} \times 3^8 \times 5^3 \times 7^2 \times 11^1 \times 13^1 \times 17^1 \times 19^1$. The required answer would be $1 \times 9 \times 3 \times 3 \times 2 \times 2 \times 2 \times 2 = 81 \times 16 = 1296$.

88. From 5! onwards, each of the numbers would have a units digit of 0. Hence, the units digit of the given number would depend on the units digit of 1! – 2! + 3! – 4!, which would be 1 (1 – 2 + 6 – 4). Since N is a number that has a unit's digit of 1, when it is raised to any power, the units digit would not change. Hence, the correct answer would be 1.

89. Exactly four factors would occur for numbers that can be represented by a single prime factor as p^3. Also, any number that can be represented by a product of two prime factors $p^1 \times q^1$ would also have four factors. There are four perfect cubes below 100. Besides, numbers like $2^1 \times 3^1$; $2^1 \times 5^1$; ....$2^1 \times 47^1$ (a total of 14 numbers). Next we consider numbers with the lower prime factor as 3. These would be $3^1 \times 5^1; 3^1 \times 7^1; ...3^1 \times 31^1$ (a total of 9 numbers). Next, we consider numbers with their lower prime factor as 5. These would be $5^1 \times 7^1$; $5^1 \times 11^1$; ...$5^1 \times 19^1$ (a total of 5 numbers). For numbers starting with 7, we would get $7^1 \times 11^1$; $7^1 \times 13^1$; (a total of 2 numbers). But, out of the four perfect cubes, 1 and 64 do not have four factors. Hence, there are a total of 32 such numbers, below 100 that would have exactly 4 factors.

90. Since both the numbers are odd, there are no 2's in their prime factors. Since, their HCF is 225, both these numbers would necessarily have $3^2 \times 5^2$ inside them. From the information, that both these numbers have 36 factors, we can realise that 36 factors can only occur in cases where the prime factors of the numbers look as follows: $p^8 \times q^3$; $p^{11} \times q^2$; $p^2 \times q^3 \times r^2$ and $p^2 \times q^2 \times r \times s$. Amongst these, the best strategy to make smaller numbers satisfying the criteria would obviously be to use the structures: $p^2 \times q^3 \times r^2$ and $p^2 \times q^2 \times r \times s$. Since, the third prime factor of the two numbers cannot be the same (else it would change the HCF), we would need to introduce 7 and 11. Also, we would not try to increase the powers of 7 and 11 as they are comparatively larger as compared to 3 and 5. Thus, we can visualise the numbers: $3^2 \times 5^2 \times 11 \times 13$, $3^3 \times 5^2 \times 7^2$. The required smallest LCM would be $3^3 \times 5^2 \times 7^2 \times 11 \times 13$.

91. 7! = 5040. When we divide 7! by 17, it leaves a remainder 8. When $[(7!)^{6!}]^{17777}$ is divided by 17 it leaves a remainder that is the same as when we divide $[(8)^{6!}]^{17777}$ or $[(8)^{720}]^{17777}$ or $[(16)^{540}]^{17777}$ by 17. The remainder when $[(16)^{540}]^{17777}$ or $[(17-1)^{540}]^{17777}$ divided by 17 is 1 (since the power on 16 is even).

92. $x + y = 2w$ (1)
$y + 6z = 2(w + x)$ (2)
$w + 5z = 2y$ (3)

From equation (2) – equation (1), we get: $6z - x = 2x$ or $x = 2z$

Substituting $x = 2z$ in equation (1), we get : $2w - y = 2z$ (4)

Solving equation (3) and (4), we get $w = 3z$ and $y = 4z$

$z: y: x: w = 1: 4: 2: 3$

So 3241 and 6482 are two possible values of *wxyz*.

So the required sum = 3241+ 6482 = 9723.

Alternately, once you have the relationship $x = 2z$, you can think of values and try to fit in the conditions of the other equations. z and x can take only 4 feasible values: viz 1, 2; 2, 4;3, 6 and 4, 8. This gives us four possibilities for the numbers: _2_1; _4_2; _6_3; _8_4. The fourth of these, with $z = 4$ can be eliminated by looking at the third equation ($w + 5z = 2y$) as it would need y to be greater than 10.

For $z = 3$ and $x = 6$; we get $w = 1$ and $y = 8$ or $w = 3$ and $y = 9$ from the third equation. Both these values do not match the second equation.

For $z = 2$ and $x = 4$; we get $w = 2$ and $y = 6$ or $w = 4$ and $y = 7$ or $w = 6$ and $y = 8$ or $w = 8$ and $y = 9$. Checking for the second equation, only the values of $w = 6$ and $y = 8$ matches. Hence, we get the number 6482.

Likewise, when you check for $z = 1$ and $x = 2$, you would be able to find the number 3241.

93. $$\frac{[17(9!)+2(18!)]}{9!.17408} = \frac{17.9!}{9!17.2^{10}} + \frac{2.18!}{9!.17.2^{10}}$$

$$\frac{17.9!}{9!17.2^{10}} = \frac{1}{2^{10}} \text{ and remainder of } \frac{1}{2^{10}} = 1$$

Hence, the Remainder of $\left(\frac{17.9!}{9!17.2^{10}}\right) = 17.9!$

2.18! = 2.18.17.16.15.14.13.12.11.10.9!

In 18, 16, 14, 12, 10 the number of 2*s* are 1, 4, 1, 2 and 1, respectively.

So 2.18! = 2.18.17.16.15.14.13.12.11.10.9! = $2^{10}.17k.9!$ = Where k is an integer.

Remainder $\left(\frac{2^{10}.17k.9!}{9!(17)2^{10}}\right) = 0$

So the required remainder is 17.9! + 0 = 17.9!.

94. Remainder when X is divided by 9, is same as remainder when sum of digits of X is divided by 9. Sum of digits of first 999 natural numbers is 13500, which is divisible by 9.

Now sum of digits of 1000, 1001, 1002 are 1, 2 and 3, respectively.

Sum of digits of X is $9n + (1 + 2 + 3) = 9n + 6$. So the required remainder is 6.

95. X = 0123456789.........1001

X has a total of $10 + 2 \times 90 + 3 \times 900 + 2 \times 4 = 2898$ digits.

So there are total 1449 digits on the left of the vertical line, out of these 1449 numbers there are total 1449 – (10 + 180)= 1259 digits are digits of 3-digit numbers.

$$1259 = 419 \times 3 + 2$$

On the left side of the vertical line, there are 419 3-digit numbers and 2 more digits.

419th 3-digit number = 518 and next 2-digits are 5, 1. Hence last 4-digits are 1851.

The remainder of any number divided by 625 is the remainder when last 4-digits of the number is divided by 625.

Required remainder = Remainder of (1851/625) = 601

96. If the 4- digit number is *abcd,* then three cases are possible for the number to have 24 in it.

Case 1: If $cd = 24$ then the numbers are of the form $ab24$

$$ab24 = 100ab + 24$$

24 is divisible by 24 and $100 \times ab$ must be divisible by 24. 100 is divisible so 4 then ab must be divisible by 6. Possible values of ab = 12, 18, 24, …., 96. So there are 15 such numbers possible.

Case 2: If $bc = 24$ then the number is of the form $a24b$.

$a24b$ must be divisible by 3 and 8. If $a24b$ is divisible by 8 then $24b$ is divisible by 8. Possible values of b = 0, 8.

Similarly $a + 2 + 4 + b = (a + b) + 6$ must be divisible by 3.

When $b = 0$ then a = 3, 6, 9 (3 possible cases)

When $b = 8$ then a = 1, 4, 7 (3 possible cases)

So there are total 6 possible cases.

Case 3: $ab = 24$ so the number should be of the form $24cd$.

$$\mathbf{24cd = 2400 + cd}$$

2400 is divisible by 24, cd divisible by 24 when cd = 00, 24, 48, 72, 96 (5 possible cases).

However, the number 2424 occurred in cases 1 and 3 both. So the total possible numbers = 5 + 6 + 15 – 1 = 25.

97. If N divides both $18X + 2$, $12X + 1$ then their difference $6X + 1$ will also be divisible by N and difference of $12X + 1$ and $6X + 1$, i.e., $6X$ will also be divisible by N. If $6X$ is divisible by N then N can also divide $12X$. It means N divides both $12X$, $12X + 1$. Since $12X$ and $12X + 1$ both are consecutive numbers so $N = 1$. So the given numbers are relatively prime for all values of X, i.e., X would have 99 values.

98. Let $P = 7 \times 10^{5+n} + k$ where n, k are whole numbers. After removal of the leftmost digit, the new number will be k.

According to the question:

$$7 \times 10^5 \times 10^n + k = 21k$$

$$7 \times 10^5 \times 10^n = 20k$$

$$\frac{7 \times 10^5 \times 10^n}{20} = k$$

$$k = 35000 \times 10^n$$

$$P = 735000 \times 10^n$$

The required product = 7 × 3 × 5 = 105

99. $X!$ is completely divisible by 11^{51}. So the value of X should be less than 11 × 51 = 561

Highest power of 11 in 561! $\left[\frac{561}{11}\right] + \left[\frac{561}{11^2}\right] + \ldots$

= 51 + 4 = 55

If we subtract 11 × 3 = 33 from 561, we get 561 – 33 = 528. Highest power of 11 in 528! is

$$\left[\frac{528}{11}\right] + \left[\frac{528}{11^2}\right] = 52$$

Highest power of 11 in 528 – 1 = 527! is

$$= \left[\frac{527}{11}\right] + \left[\frac{527}{11^2}\right] = 47 + 4 = 51$$

So the required number is 527.

Sum of the digits = 5 + 2 + 7 = 14.

100. Let $a = 5k$ then $a + 5 = 5(k + 1)$. Both k, $k + 1$ are co-prime.

LCM of a, $a + 5 = 5.k.(k + 1)$

For $k = 4$, $5k(k + 1) = 100$.

So minimum possible value of smaller number is 20.

Maximum value of k for which the LCM is a three-digit number is 13.

Maximum possible value of the smaller number = 65

So the required difference = 65 – 20 = 45.

101. We need to look at writing the binary number system from 8 = $(1000)_2$ to 127 = $(1111111)_2$

There are 64 seven digit numbers in binary system are from 1000000 to 1111111. There are six digits after the leftmost 1. Each of these 6 digits can be filled by either 0 or 1 and both are equally probable in any position. So the number of 1 from 1000000 to 1111111 = $64 + 64 \times \frac{1}{2} \times 6 = 64 + 192 = 256$.

There are 32 six digit numbers in binary system are from 100000 to 111111. There are five digits after the leftmost 1. Each of these 5 digits can be filled by either 0 or 1 and both are equally probable in any position. So the number of 1 from 100000 to 111111 $= 32 + 32 \times \frac{1}{2} \times 5 = 32 + 80 = 112$.

Similarly, from 10000 to 11111, there are $16 + \frac{16}{2} \times 4 = 16 + 32 = 48$.

Similarly, from 1000 to 1111, there are $8 + 8 \times \frac{1}{2} \times 3 = 20$

So total 1's = 20 + 48 + 112 + 256 = 436.

102. First of all pick all the prime numbers, i.e., {2, 3, 5, 7, 11, 13, 17, 19}. We cannot pick perfect square numbers, i.e., 4, 9, 16 and perfect cube numbers i.e., 8.

Now we are left with the numbers 6, 10, 12, 14, 15, 18, 20 out of which 12 and 18 will give perfect square numbers when we multiply them with 3 and 2, respectively. Also, we would need to take 1 into this list. So we have a total 14 such numbers {1, 2, 3, 5, 6, 7, 10, 11, 13, 14, 15, 17, 19, 20}. (**Note:** If you try to improve this solution, by taking the perfect squares and the perfect cubes in, you would first need to get rid of 1, in the list. Also, you can take only one perfect square number (as if you were to take two perfect squares, their product would be a perfect square too). With respect to the perfect cube 8, we can see that $8 \times 2 = 16$ is a perfect square. Hence, if we try to take in 8, we would need to remove 2 from our list. Thus, you can see that you can take this list to a maximum of 14 numbers.)

103. It is given that $d + e + f = 9$, now two cases are possible.

Case 1: When all three of them are odd. This case is not possible because if all three of them are odd then g, h, i, j cannot be odd digits.

Case 2: When only one number is odd. This case is possible and the digit which is odd among d, e, f can be 1 only. So the sum of rest of the 2-digits is 8 which is possible as 0 + 8 only.

$g = 9$, $h = 7$, $i = 5$ and $j = 3$ & $d = 8$, $f = 0$. So $e = 1$.

$a = 6$, $b = 4$ and $c = 2$

$$\left[\frac{a \times b \times c \times d}{h}\right] = \left[\frac{2 \times 4 \times 6 \times 8}{7}\right] = 54$$

104. If $N = abc$, then $a + b + c = abc/7$

As the product is divisible by 7 so one of the digits must be 7.

$a + b + 7 = ab.7/7$

$a + b + 7 = ab$

$ab - a - b = 7$

$ab - a - b + 1 = 8$

$a(b - 1) - (b - 1) = 8$

$(a - 1)(b - 1) = 8$. There are two possible ways to get 8 as a product of 2-digits. These are: 4×2 and 1×8

This gives us: $a = 5$, $b = 3$ and $a = 2$, $b = 9$

Possible sets of digits used in the numbers are (2, 9, 7), (3, 5, 7). Hence, the correct answer is 2 (i.e., 2 sets are possible)

105. In base 34, 10 means 34. In base 10, 10 is obtained by multiplying 2 and 5. In base 34, it is obtained by multiplying 2 and 17. Number of consecutive zeroes in base 34 at the end of the number is same as the number of 2's and 17's in 3132!. Since the number of 2's is much more than number of 17's, so we count number of 17's in 3132!

Maximum power of 17 in 3132! = $\left[\frac{3132}{17}\right] + \left[\frac{3132}{17^2}\right]$
$= 184 + 10 = 194$.

CHAPTER 2

Progressions and Series

Chapter Launchpad

Scan this QR code to access a video on 'Introduction to Progressions and Series' and this chapter's importance for CAT and how to study the chapter effectively.

The chapter on progressions essentially yields commonsense based questions in examinations.

Questions in the CAT and other aptitude exams mostly appear from either Arithmetic Progressions (A.P.) (more common) or from Geometric Progressions.

The chapter of progressions is a logical and natural extension to the chapter on Number Systems since there is such a lot of commonality of logic between the problems associated with these two chapters. Let us start by looking at the definitions and the mathematics with regards to various kinds of Progressions and Series.

ARITHMETIC PROGRESSIONS

Quantities are said to be in arithmetic progression when they increase or decrease by a common difference.

Thus, each of the following series forms an arithmetic progression:

$$3, 7, 11, 15, \ldots$$
$$8, 2, -4, -10, \ldots$$
$$a, a + d, a + 2d, a + 3d, \ldots$$

The common difference is found by subtracting any term of the series from the next term.

That is, common difference of an *A.P.* = $(t_N - t_{N-1})$.

In the first of the above examples, the common difference is 4; in the second it is –6; in the third it is d.

If we examine the series $a, a + d, a + 2d, a + 3d, \ldots$ we notice that *in any term, the coefficient of d is always less by one than the position of that term in the series.*

Thus, the rth term of an arithmetic progression is given by $T_r = a + (r - 1)d$.

If n be the number of terms, and if L denotes the last term or the nth term, we have

$$L = a + (n - 1)d$$

To Find the Sum of the Given Number of Terms in an Arithmetic Progression

Let a denote the first term d, the common difference, and n the total number of terms. Also, let L denote the last term, and S the required sum; then

$$S = \frac{n(a+L)}{2} \quad (1)$$
$$L = a + (n - 1)d \quad (2)$$
$$S = \frac{n}{2} \times [2a + (n - 1)d] \quad (3)$$

If any two terms of an arithmetical progression is given, the series can be completely determined; for this data results in two simultaneous equations, the solution of which will give the first term and the common difference.

When three quantities are in arithmetic progression, the middle one is said to be the **arithmetic mean** of the other two.

Thus, a is the arithmetic mean between $a - d$ and $a + d$. So, when it is required to arbitrarily consider three numbers in A.P. Take $a - d$, a and $a + d$ as the three numbers as this reduces one unknown, thereby, making the solution easier.

To Find the Arithmetic Mean Between any Two Given Quantities

Let a and b be two quantities and A be their arithmetic mean. Then, since a, A, b, are in A.P. We must have

$$b - A = A - a$$

Each being equal to the common difference;

this gives us $A = \frac{(a+b)}{2}$

Between two given quantities, it is always possible to insert any number of terms such that the whole series thus formed shall be in A.P. The terms, thus, inserted are called the **arithmetic means**.

To Insert a Given Number of Arithmetic Means between Two Given Quantities

Let a and b be the given quantities and n be the number of means.

Including the extremes, the number of terms will then be $n + 2$ so that we have to find a series of $n + 2$ terms in A.P., of which a is the first, and b is the last term.

Let d be the common difference,

then $b =$ the $(n + 2)^{th}$ term $= a + (n + 1)d$

hence, $d = \frac{(b-a)}{(n+1)}$

and the required means are

$$a + \frac{(b-a)}{n-1}, a + \frac{2(b-a)}{n+1}, \cdots a + \frac{n(b-a)}{n+1}$$

Math Simplified

Scan this QR code to access a video that simplifies this equation and shows you how to apply it in questions

Till now we have studied A.P.s in their mathematical context. This was important for you to understand the basic mathematical construct of A.P.s. However, you need to understand that questions on A.P. are seldom solved on a mathematical basis (especially under the time pressure that you are likely to face in the CAT and other aptitude exams). In such situations, the mathematical processes for solving progressions based questions are likely to fail or at the very least, be very tedious. Hence, understanding the following logical aspects about Arithmetic Progressions is likely to help you solve questions based on A.P.s in the context of an aptitude exam.

Let us look at these issues one by one:

1. Process for finding the nth term of an A.P.

Suppose you have to find the 17th term of the A.P. 3, 7, 11.......

The conventional mathematical process for this question would involve using the formula.

$$T_n = a + (n - 1)\, d$$

Thus, for the 17th term we would do

$$T_{17} = 3 + (17 - 1) \times 4 = 3 + 16 \times 4 = 67$$

Most students would mechanically insert the values for a, n and d and get this answer.

However, if you replace the above process with a thought algorithm, you will get the answer much faster.

The algorithm goes like this:

In order to find the 17th term of the above sequence, add the common difference to the first term, sixteen times.

Note: Sixteen, since it is one less than seventeen.

Similarly, in order to find the 37th term of the A.P. 3, 11 ..., all you need to do is add the common difference (8 in this case), 36 times.

Thus, the answer is 288 + 3 = 291.

Note: You ultimately end up doing the same thing, but you are at an advantage since the entire solution process is reactionary.

2. Average of an A.P. and corresponding terms of the A.P.

Consider the A.P., 2, 6, 10, 14, 18, 22. If you try to find the average of these six numbers you will get: Average = (2 + 6 + 10 + 14 + 18 + 22)/6 = 12

Notice that 12 is also the average of the first and the last terms of the A.P. In fact, it is also the average of 6 and 18 (which correspond to the second and 5th terms of the A.P.). Further, 12 is also the average of the 3rd and 4th terms of the A.P.

Note: In this A.P. of six terms, the average was the same as the average of the 1st and 6th terms. It was also given by the average of the 2nd and the 5th terms, as well as that of the 3rd and 4th terms.

We can call each of these pairs as "CORRESPONDING TERMS" in an A.P.

What you need to understand is that every A.P. has an average.

And for any A.P., the average of any pair of corresponding terms will also be the average of the A.P.

If you try to notice the sum of the term numbers of the pair of corresponding terms given above:

1st and 6th (hence, 1 + 6 = 7)
2nd and 5th (hence, 2 + 5 = 7)
3rd and 4th (hence, 3 + 4 = 7)

Note: In each of these cases, the sum of the term numbers for the terms in a corresponding pair is one greater than the number of terms of the A.P.

This rule will hold true for all A.P.s.

For example, if an A.P. has 23 terms then for instance, you can predict that the 7th term will have the 17th term as its corresponding term, or for that matter the 9th term will have the 15th term as its corresponding term. (Since 24 is one more than 23 and 7 + 17 = 9 + 15 = 24.)

3. Process for finding the sum of an A.P.

Once you can find a pair of corresponding terms for any A.P., you can easily find the sum of the A.P. by using the property of averages:

i.e., Sum = Number of terms × Average

In fact, this is the best process for finding the sum of an A.P. It is much more superior than the process of finding the sum of an A.P. using the expression $\frac{n}{2}(2a + (n - 1)\, d)$.

4. Finding the common difference of an A.P., given two terms of an A.P.

Suppose you were given that an A.P. had its 3rd term as 8 and its 8th term as 28. You should visualise this A.P. as

–, –, 8, –, –, –, –, 28.

From the above figure, you can easily visualise that to move from the third term to the eighth term, (8 to 28) you need to add the common difference five times. The net addition being 20, the common difference should be 4.

Illustration: Find the sum of an A.P. of 17 terms, whose 3rd term is 8 and 8th term is 28.

Solution: Since we know the third term and the eighth term, we can find the common difference as 4 by the process illustrated above.

The total = 17 × Average of the A.P.

Our objective now shifts into the finding of the average of the A.P. In order to do so, we need to identify either the 10th term (which will be the corresponding term for the

8th term) or the 15th term (which will be the corresponding term for the 3rd term.)

Again: Since the 8th term is 28 and $d = 4$, the 10th term becomes $28 + 4 + 4 = 36$.

Thus, the average of the A.P.

= Average of 8th and 10th terms

= $(28 + 36)/2 = 32$

Hence, the required answer is sum of the A.P. = $17 \times 32 = 544$.

The logic that has applied here is that the difference in the term numbers will give you the number of times the common difference is used to get from one to the other term.

For instance, if you know that the difference between the 7th term and 12th term of an A.P. is –30, you should realise that 5 times the common difference will be equal to –30 (Since $12 - 7 = 5$).

Hence, $d = -6$.

Note: Replace this algorithmic thinking in lieu of the mathematical thinking of:

$$12^{th} \text{ term} = a + 11d$$

$$7^{th} \text{ term} = a + 6d$$

$$\text{Hence, difference} = -30 = (a + 11d) - (a + 6d)$$

$$-30 = 5d$$

$$\therefore \quad d = -6$$

---

5. Types of A.P.s: Increasing and Decreasing A.P.s.

Depending on whether '*d*' is positive or negative, an A.P. can be increasing or decreasing.

Let us explore these two types of A.P.s further:

(A) Increasing A.P.s:

Every term of an increasing A.P. is greater than the previous term.

Depending on the value of the first term, we can construct two graphs for sum of an increasing A.P.

Case 1: When the first term of the increasing A.P. is positive. In such a case, the sum of the A.P. will show a continuously increasing graph which will look like the one shown in the figure below.

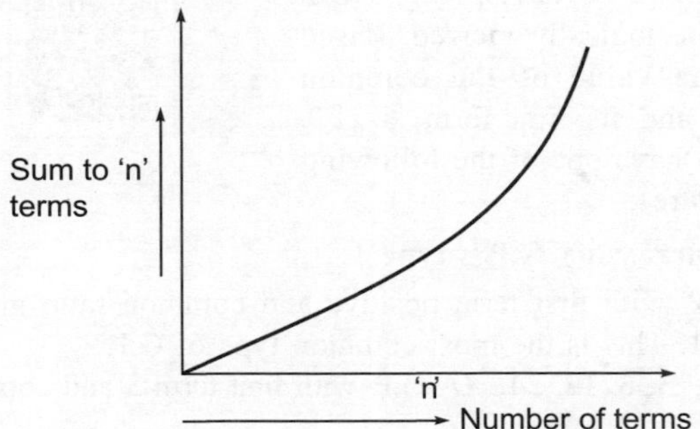

Case 2: When the first term of the increasing A.P. is negative. In such a case, the sum of the A.P. plotted against the number of terms will give the following figure:

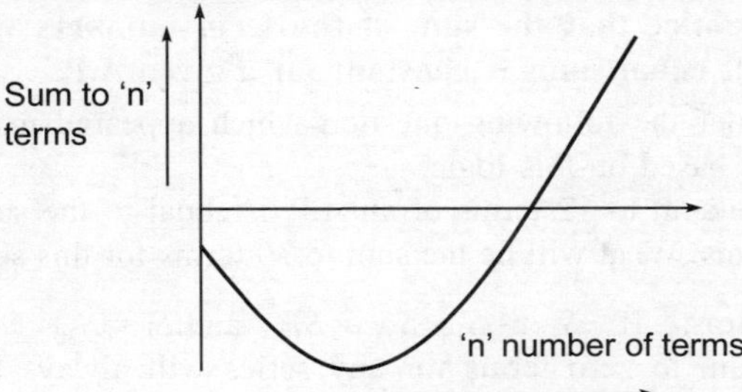

The specific case of the sum to n_1 terms being equal to the sum to n_2 terms.

In the series case 2 above, there is a possibility of the sum to '*n*' terms being repeated for 2 values of '*n*'. However, this will not necessarily occur.

Concept Explainer

Scan this QR code to access a conceptual video on Increasing A.P.s

This issue will get clear through the following example:

Consider the following series:

Series 1: –12, –8, –4, 0, 4, 8, 12

As is evident, the sum to 2 terms and the sum to 5 terms in this case is the same. Similarly, the sum to 3 terms is the same as the sum to 4 terms. This can be written as:

$$S_2 = S_5 \text{ and } S_3 = S_4$$

In other words, the sum to n_1 terms is the same as the sum to n_2 terms.

Such situations arise for increasing A.P.s where the first term is negative. But as we have already stated that this does not happen for all such cases.

Consider the following A.P.s.

Series 2 : –8, –3, +2, + 7, + 12…

Series 3 : –13, –7, –1, + 5, + 11…

Series 4 : –12, –6, 0, 6, 12 …

Series 5 : –15, –9, –3, + 3, 9, 15 …

Series 6 : –20, –12, –4, 4 , 12, …

If you check the series listed above, you will realise that this occurrence happens in the case of series 4, series 5 and series 6 while in the case of series 1, series 2 and series 3 the same value is not repeated for the sum of the series.

A clear look at the two series will reveal that this phenomenon occurs in series which have what can be called a balance about the number zero.

Another issue to notice is that in series 4,

$$S_2 = S_3 \text{ and } S_1 = S_4$$

While in series 5,

$$S_1 = S_5 \text{ and } S_2 = S_4$$

In the first case (where '0' is part of the series), the sum is equal for two terms such that one of them is odd and the other is even.

In the second case, on the other hand (when '0' is not part of the series) the sum is equal for two terms such that both are odd or both are even.

Also notice that the sum of the term numbers which exhibit equal sums is constant for a given A.P.

Consider the following question which appeared in CAT and is based on this logic:

The sum to 12 terms of an A.P. is equal to the sum to 18 terms. What will be the sum to 30 terms for this series?

Solution: If $S_{12} = S_{18}$, $S_{11} = S_{19...}$ and $S_0 = S_{30}$

But sum to zero terms for any series will always be 0. Hence, $S_{30} = 0$.

Note: The solution to this problem does not take more than ten seconds if you know this logic.

(B) Decreasing A.P.s.

Similar to the cases of the increasing A.P.s, we can have two cases for decreasing A.P.s. —

Case 1: Decreasing A.P. with first term negative

Case 2: Decreasing A.P. with first term positive

I leave it to the reader to understand these cases and deduce that whatever was true for increasing A.P.s with first term negative will also be true for decreasing A.P.s with first term positive.

GEOMETRIC PROGRESSION

Quantities are said to be in geometric progression when they increase or decrease by a constant factor.

The constant factor is also called the *common ratio* and it is found by dividing any term by the term immediately preceding it.

If we examine the series $a, ar, ar^2, ar^3, ar^4, \ldots$ *we notice that in any term the index of r is always less by one than the number of the term in the series.*

If n be the number of terms and if l denote the last, or n^{th} term, we have

$$l = ar^{n-1}$$

When three quantities are in geometrical progression, the middle one is called the geometric mean between the other two. While arbitrarily choosing three numbers in G.P., we take a/r, a and ar. This makes it easier since we come down to two variables for the three terms.

To Find the Geometric Mean Between Two Given Quantities

Let a and b be the two quantities; G the geometric mean. Then since a, G, b are in G.P.,

$$b/G = G/a$$

Each being equal to the common ratio

$$G^2 = ab$$

Hence, $$G = \sqrt{ab}$$

To Insert a Given Number of Geometric Means Between Two Given Quantities

Let a and b be the given quantities and n the required number of means to be inserted. In all, there will be $n + 2$ terms so that we have to find a series of $n + 2$ terms in G.P. of which a is the first and b the last.

Let r be the common ratio;

Then $b = \text{the } (n+2)^{th} \text{ term} = ar^{n+1}$;

$$\therefore \quad r^{(n+1)} = \frac{b}{a}$$

$$\therefore \quad r = \left(\frac{b}{a}\right)^{\frac{1}{n+1}} \quad (1)$$

Hence, the required number of means are $ar, ar^2, \ldots ar^n$, where r has the value found in (1).

To Find the Sum of a Number of Terms in a Geometric Progression

Let a be the first term, r the common ratio, n the number of terms, and S_n be the sum to n terms.

If $r > 1$, then

$$S_n = \frac{a(r^n - 1)}{(r-1)} \quad (1)$$

If $r < 1$, then

$$S_n = \frac{a(1 - r^n)}{(1-r)} \quad (2)$$

Note: It will be convenient to remember both forms given above for S.

Sum of an infinite geometric progression when $r < 1$

$$S_\infty = \frac{a}{(1-r)}$$

Obviously, this formula is used only when the common ratio of the G.P. is less than one.

Math Simplified

Scan this QR code to access a video that simplifies this equation and shows you how to apply it in questions

Similar to A.P.s, G.P.'s can also be logically viewed. Based on the value of the common ratio and its first term, a G.P. might have one of the following structures:

(1) Increasing G.P.'s type 1:

A G.P. with first term positive and common ratio greater than 1. This is the most common type of G.P.,

e.g: 3, 6, 12, 24…(A G.P. with first term 3 and common ratio 2).

The plot of the sum of the series with respect to the number of terms in such a case will appear as follows:

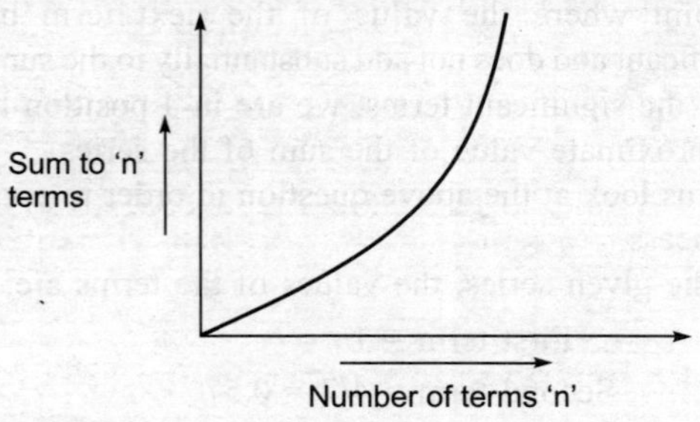

(2) Increasing G.P.s type 2:

A G.P. with first term negative and common ratio less than 1.

e.g: –8, –4,–2, –1, – ……

As you can see in this G.P., all terms are greater than their previous terms.

[The following figure will illustrate the relationship between the number of terms and the sum to '*n*' terms in this case]

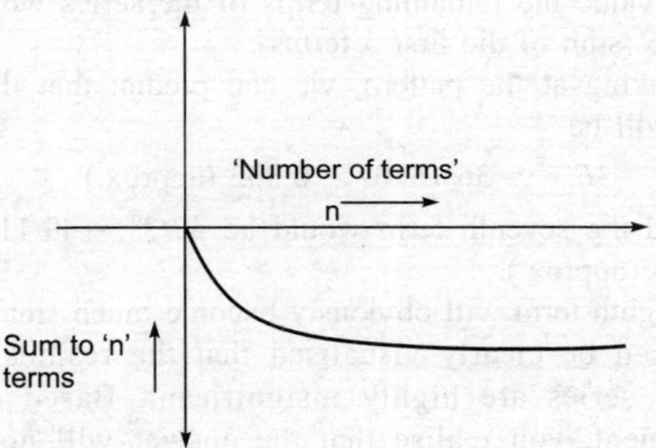

(3) Decreasing G.P.'s type 1:

These G.P.'s have their first term positive and common ratio less than 1.

e.g: 12, 6, 3, 1.5, 0.75 ……

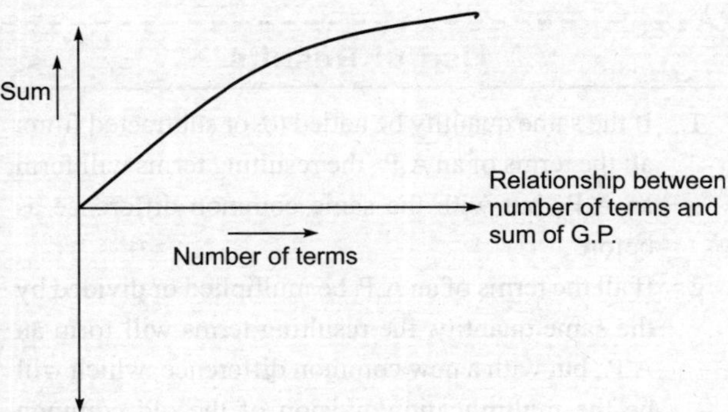

(4) Decreasing G.P.'s type 2:

First term negative and common ratio greater than 1.

e.g: –2, –6, –18 ….

In this case, the relationship looks like

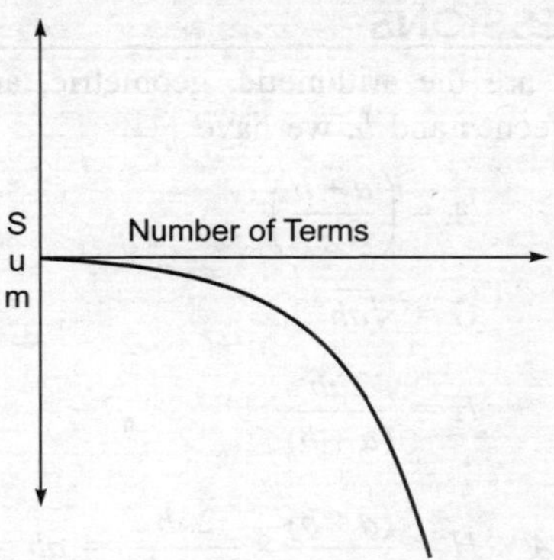

HARMONIC PROGRESSION

Three quantities a, b, c are said to be in harmonic progression when $a/c = \dfrac{(a-b)}{(b-c)}$.

In general, if a, b, c, d are in A.P. then $1/a$, $1/b$, $1/c$ and $1/d$ are all in H.P.

Any number of quantities are said to be in harmonic progression when every three consecutive terms are in harmonic progression.

The reciprocals of quantities in harmonic progression are in arithmetic progression. This can be proved as:

By definition, if a, b, c are in harmonic progression,

$$\frac{a}{c} = \frac{(a-b)}{(b-c)}$$

$$\therefore \quad a(b-c) = c(a-b),$$

dividing every term by abc, we get

$$\left[\frac{1}{c} - \frac{1}{b} = \frac{1}{b} - \frac{1}{a}\right]$$

which proves the proposition.

Note: There is no general formula for the sum of any number of quantities in H.P. Questions in H.P. are generally solved by inverting the terms, and making use of the properties of the corresponding A.P.

To Find the Harmonic Mean Between Two Given Quantities

Let a, b be the two quantities, H their harmonic mean; then $1/a$, $1/H$ and $1/b$ are in A.P.;

$$\therefore \quad \frac{1}{H} - \frac{1}{a} = \frac{1}{b} - \frac{1}{H}$$

$$\frac{2}{H} = \frac{1}{a} + \frac{1}{b}$$

i.e. $$H = \frac{2ab}{(a+b)}$$

THEOREMS RELATED WITH PROGRESSIONS

If A, G, H are the arithmetic, geometric, and harmonic means between a and b, we have

$$A = \left(\frac{a+b}{2}\right) \quad (1)$$

$$G = \sqrt{ab} \quad (2)$$

$$H = \frac{2ab}{(a+b)} \quad (3)$$

Therefore, $A \times H = \frac{(a+b)}{2} \times \frac{2ab}{(a+b)} = ab = G^2$, that is,

G is the geometric mean between A and H.

From these results, we see that

$$A - G = \frac{a+b}{2} - \sqrt{ab} = \frac{(a+b-2\sqrt{ab})}{2}$$

$$= \left[\frac{(\sqrt{a}-\sqrt{b})}{\sqrt{2}}\right]^2$$

which is positive if a and b are positive. Therefore, the arithmetic mean of any two positive quantities is greater than their geometric mean.

Also from the equation $G^2 = AH$, we see that G is intermediate in value between A and H; and it has been proved that $A > G$, therefore $G > H$ and $A > G > H$.

The arithmetic, geometric, and harmonic means between any two positive quantities are in descending order of magnitude.

As we have already seen in the 'Back to School' section of this block, there are some number series which have a continuously decreasing value from one term to the next — and such series have the property that they have what can be defined as the sum of infinite terms. Questions on such series are very common in most aptitude exams. Even though they cannot be strictly said to be under the domain of progressions, we choose to deal with them here.

Consider the following question which appeared in CAT 2003.

Find the infinite sum of the series:

$$1 + \frac{4}{7} + \frac{9}{7^2} + \frac{16}{7^3} + \frac{25}{7^4} + \cdots$$

(a) 27/14 (b) 21/13
(c) 49/27 (d) 256/147

Solution: Such questions have two alternative widely divergent processes to solve them.

The first relies on mathematics using algebraic solving. Unfortunately, this process being overly mathematical requires a lot of writing and hence is not advisable to be used in an aptitude exam.

The other process is one where we try to predict the approximate value of the sum by taking into account the first few significant terms. (This approach is possible to use because of the fact that in such series, we invariably reach the point where the value of the next term becomes insignificant and does not add substantially to the sum). After adding the significant terms, we are in a position to guess the approximate value of the sum of the series.

Let us look at the above question in order to understand the process.

In the given series, the values of the terms are:

First term = 1
Second term = 4/7 = 0.57
Third term = 9/49 = 0.183
Fourth term = 16/343 = 0.04
Fifth term = 25/2401 = 0.01

Addition up to the fifth term is approximately 1.76.

Options (b) and (d) are smaller than 1.76 in value and hence, cannot be correct.

That leaves us with options (a) and (c).

Option 1 has a value of 1.92 approximately while option 3 has a value of 1.81 approximately.

At this point, you need to make a decision about how much value the remaining terms of the series would add to 1.76 (sum of the first 5 terms).

Looking at the pattern, we can predict that the sixth term will be

$36/7^5 = 36/16807 = 0.002$ (approx.)

And the seventh term would be $49/7^6 = 49/117649 = 0.0004$ (approx.).

The eighth term will obviously become much smaller.

It can be clearly visualised that the residual terms in the series are highly insignificant. Based on this judgement, you realise that the answer will not reach 1.92 and will be restricted to 1.81. Hence, the answer will be option (c).

Try using this process to solve other questions of this nature whenever you come across them. (There are a few such questions inserted in the LOD exercises of this chapter)

Useful Results

1. If the same quantity be added to, or subtracted from, all the terms of an A.P., the resulting terms will form an A.P., but with the same common difference as before.
2. If all the terms of an A.P. be multiplied or divided by the same quantity, the resulting terms will form an A.P., but with a new common difference, which will be the multiplication/division of the old common difference (as the case may be).
3. If all the terms of a G.P. be multiplied or divided by the same quantity, the resulting terms will form a G.P. with the same common ratio as before

4. If $a, b, c, d, \ldots$ are in G.P., they are also in continued proportion, since, by definition,

$$a/b = b/c = c/d = \ldots = 1/r$$

Conversely, a series of quantities in continued proportion may be represented by $x, xr, xr^2, \ldots$

5. If you have to assume 3 terms in A.P., assume them as

$$a - d, a, a + d \quad \text{or} \quad \text{as } a, a + d \text{ and } a + 2d$$

For assuming 4 terms of an A.P., we use: $a - 3d$, $a - d$, $a + d$ and $a + 3d$.

For assuming 5 terms of an A.P., take them as: $a - 2d, a - d, a, a + d, a + 2d$.

These are the most convenient in terms of problem solving.

6. For assuming three terms of a G.P., assume them as

$$a, ar \text{ and } ar^2 \quad \text{or} \quad \text{as } a/r, a \text{ and } ar$$

7. To find the sum of the first n natural numbers

Let the sum be denoted by S; then

$S = 1 + 2 + 3 + \ldots + n$, is given by

$$S = \frac{n(n+1)}{2}$$

8. To find the sum of the squares of the first n natural numbers

Let the sum be denoted by S; then

$$S = 1^2 + 2^2 + 3^2 + \ldots + n^2$$

This is given by : $S = \left\{\frac{n(n+1)(2n+1)}{6}\right\}$

9. To find the sum of the cubes of the first n natural numbers.

Let the sum be denoted by S; then

$$S = 1^3 + 2^3 + 3^3 + \ldots + n^3$$

$$S = \left[\frac{n(n+1)}{2}\right]^2$$

Thus, the sum of the cubes of the first n natural numbers is equal to the square of the sum of these numbers.

10. To find the sum of the first n odd natural numbers.

$$S = 1 + 3 + 5 + \ldots + (2n - 1) \rightarrow n^2$$

11. To find the sum of the first n even natural numbers.

$$S = 2 + 4 + 6 + \ldots + 2n \rightarrow n(n + 1) = n^2 + n$$

12. To find the sum of odd numbers $\leq n$ where n is a natural number:

Case 1: If n is odd $\rightarrow [(n + 1)/2]^2$

Case 2: If n is even $\rightarrow [n/2]^2$

13. To find the sum of even numbers $\leq n$ where n is a natural number:

Case 1: If n is even $\rightarrow \{(n/2)[(n/2) + 1]\}$

Case 2: If n is odd $\rightarrow [(n - 1)/2][(n + 1)/2]$

14. Number of terms in an Arithmetic Progression:

The best way to count the number of terms in an Arithmetic Progression is to use the logic of what I call as $\frac{\text{Difference}}{\text{difference}} + 1$ or $\frac{D}{d} + 1$.

Let me explain. Take the difference between the first term and the last term. Call it 'D'. Identify the common difference of the series (d). Use these to calculate the number of terms in the series = $\frac{D}{d} + 1$

Example: For finding the number of terms in the arithmetic series 76, 83, 90, …, 237:

- (D = 237 – 76 = 161)
- (d = 7)

Hence, 161/7 + 1 = 23 + 1 = 24.

What if the common difference is 1? That is, we are counting all natural numbers between two numbers. For example, how many numbers are there from 18 to 53? In this case, we are looking at the set of numbers 18, 19, 20, 21, …, 53. Since the value of (d = 1) in this case, the answer will simply be (D + 1). So,

- (D = 53 – 18 = 35)
- Number of terms = (D + 1 = 35 + 1 = 36).

The student is advised to try and experiment on these principles to get a clear picture.

WORKED-OUT PROBLEMS

Problem 2.1 Two persons—Ramu Dhobi and Kalu Mochi have joined Donkey-Work Associates. Ramu Dhobi and Kalu Mochi started with an initial salary of ₹500 and ₹640, respectively with annual increments of ₹25 and ₹20 each respectively. In which year will Ramu Dhobi start earning more salary than Kalu Mochi?

Solution The current difference between the salaries of the two is ₹140. The annual rate of reduction of this dfference is ₹5 per year. At this rate, it will take Ramu Dhobi 28 years to equalise his salary with Kalu Dhobi's salary.

Thus, in the 29th year, he will earn more.

This problem should be solved while reading and the thought process should be 140/5 = 28. Hence, answer is 29th year.

Problem 2.2 Find the value of the expression

1 – 6 + 2 – 7 + 3 – 8 +……… to 100 terms.

(a) –250 (b) –500
(c) –450 (d) –300

Solution The series (1 – 6 + 2 – 7 + 3 – 8 +……… to 100 terms) can be rewritten as:

⇒ (1 + 2 + 3 + … to 50 terms) – (6 + 7 + 8 + … to 50 terms)

Both these are *A.P.*s with values of *a* and *d* as →

$a = 1$, $n = 50$ and $d = 1$ and $a = 6$, $n = 50$ and $d = 1$, respectively.

Using the formula for sum of an A.P., we get:

$\rightarrow 25(2 + 49) - 25(12 + 49)$

$\rightarrow 25(51 - 61) = -250$

Alternatively, we can do this faster by considering (1 – 6), (2 – 7), and so on as one unit or one term.

1 – 6 = 2 – 7 = … = –5. Thus, the above series is equivalent to a series of fifty –5's added to each other.

So, (1 – 6) + (2 – 7) + (3 – 8) + … 50 terms = –5 × 50 = –250

Problem 2.3 Find the sum of all numbers divisible by 6 in between 100 to 400.

Solution Here 1st term = a = 102 (which is the 1st term greater than 100 and divisible by 6).

The last term less than 400, which is divisible by 6 is 396.

The number of terms in the *A.P.;* 102, 108, 114…396 is given by [(396 – 102)/6] + 1 = 50 numbers.

Common difference = d = 6

So, $S = 25\ (204 + 294) = 12450$

Problem 2.4 If x, y, z are in G.P., then $1/(1 + \log_{10}x)$, $1/(1 + \log_{10}y)$ and $1/(1 + \log_{10}z)$ will be in

(a) A.P. (b) G.P.
(c) H.P. (d) Cannot be determined

Solution Go through the options.

Checking option (a), the three will be in A.P. if the 2nd expression is the average of the 1st and 3rd expressions. This can be mathematically written as

$$2/(1 + \log_{10}y) = [1/(1 + \log_{10}x)] + [1/(1 + \log_{10}z)]$$

$$= \frac{[1 + (1 + \log_{10} x) + 1 + (1 + \log_{10} z)]}{[(1 + \log_{10} x)(1 + \log_{10} z)}$$

$$= \frac{[2 + \log_{10} xz]}{(1 + \log_{10} x)\ (1 + \log_{10} z)}$$

Applying our judgement, there seems to be no indication that we are going to get a solution.

Checking option (b),

$$[1/(1 + \log_{10}y)]^2 = [1/(1 + \log_{10}x)]\ [1/(1 + \log_{10}z)]$$

$$= [1/(1 + \log_{10}(x + z) + \log_{10}xz)]$$

Again we are trapped and any solution is not in sight.

Checking option (c),

$1/(1 + \log_{10}x)$, $1/(1 + \log_{10}y)$ and $1/(1 + \log_{10}z)$ are in *H.P.* then $1 + \log_{10}x$, $1 + \log_{10}y$ and $1 + \log_{10}z$ will be in A.P.

So, $\log_{10}x$, $\log_{10}y$ and $\log_{10}z$ will also be in A.P.

Hence, $2 \log_{10}y = \log_{10}x + \log_{10}z$

⇒ $y^2 = xz$ which is given

So, (c) is the correct option.

Alternatively, you could have solved through the following process.

x, y and z are given in a G.P.

Assume $x = 1$, $y = 10$ and $z = 100$ as x, y, z are in G.P.

So, $1 + \log_{10}x = 1$, $1 + \log_{10}y = 2$ and $1 + \log_{10}z = 3$

⇒ Thus, we find that since 1, 2 and 3 are in A.P., we can assume that

$1 + \log_{10}x$, $1 + \log_{10}y$ and $1 + \log_{10}z$ are in A.P.

⇒ Hence, by definition of an H.P., we have that $1/(1 + \log_{10}x)$, $1/(1 + \log_{10}y)$ and $1/(1 + \log_{10}z)$ are in H.P. Hence, option (c) is the required answer.

Author's Note: In my experience, I have always found that the toughest equations and factorisations get solved very easily when there are options, by assuming values in place of the variables in the equation. The values of the variables should be taken in such a manner that the basic restrictions put on the variables should be respected. For example, if an expression in three variables *a*, *b* and *c* is given and it is mentioned that $a + b + c = 0$ then the values that you assume for *a*, *b* and *c* should satisfy this restriction. Hence, you should look at values like 1, 2 and –3 or 2, –1, –1, etc.

This process is especially useful in the case where the question as well as the options both contain expressions. Factorisation and advanced techniques of Maths are then not required. This process will be very beneficial for students who are weak at Mathematics.

Problem 2.5 Find t_{10} and S_{10} for the following series:

1, 8, 15,...

Solution This is an A.P. with first term 1 and common difference 7.

$$t_{10} = a + (n - 1)\, d = 1 + 9 \times 7 = 64$$

$$S_{10} = \frac{10 \times 65}{2} = 325$$

Problem 2.6 Find t_{18} and S_{18} for the following series:

2, 8, 32, ...

Solution This is a G.P. with first term 2 and common ratio 4.

$$t_{18} = ar^{n-1} = 2.4^{17}$$

$$S_{18} = \frac{a(r^n - 1)}{r - 1} = \frac{2(4^{18} - 1)}{(4 - 1)}$$

Problem 2.7 Is the series 1, 4,... to *n* terms an A.P., or a G.P., or an H.P., or a series which cannot be determined?

Solution *To determine any progression, we should have at least three terms.*

If the series is an A.P., then the next term of this series will be 7.

Again, if the next term is 16, then this will be a G.P. series (1, 4, 16 ...).

So, *we cannot determine* the nature of the progression of this series.

Problem 2.8 Find the sum to 200 terms of the series $1 + 4 + 6 + 5 + 11 + 6 + \ldots$

(a) 30,200 (b) 29,800
(c) 30,200 (d) None of these

Solution Spot that the above series is a combination of two A.P.s.

The 1st A.P. is (1 + 6 + 11 +...) and the 2nd A.P. is (4 + 5 + 6 +...).

Since the terms of the two series alternate, $S = (1 + 6 + 11 + \ldots \text{ to 100 terms}) + (4 + 5 + 6 + \ldots \text{ to 100 terms})$

$$= \frac{100[2 \times 1 + 99 \times 5]}{2} + \frac{100[2 \times 4 + 99 \times 1]}{2} \rightarrow \text{(Using}$$

the formula for the sum of an *A.P.*)

$= 50[497 + 107] = 50[604] = 30200$

Alternatively, we can treat every two consecutive terms as one.

So we will have a total of 100 terms of the nature:

$(1 + 4) + (6 + 5) + (11 + 6) \ldots \rightarrow 5, 11, 17\ldots$

Now, $a = 5$, $d = 6$ and $n = 100$

Hence, the sum of the given series is

$$S = \frac{100}{2} \times [2 \times 5 + 99 \times 6]$$

$$= 50[604] = 30200$$

Problem 2.9 How many terms of the series –12, –9, –6,... must be taken that the sum may be 54?

Solution Here $S = 54$, $a = -12$, $d = 3$, *n* is unknown and has to be calculated. To do so, we use the formula for the sum of an *A.P.* and get

$$54 = \frac{[2(-12) + (n - 1)3]n}{2}$$

or $\quad 108 = -24n - 3n + 3n^2$ or $3n^2 - 27n - 108 = 0$

or $\quad n^2 - 9n - 36 = 0$, or $n^2 - 12n + 3n - 36 = 0$

$$n(n - 12) + 3(n - 12) = 0 \Rightarrow (n + 3)\,(n - 12) = 0$$

The value of *n* (the number of terms) cannot be negative. Hence, –3 is rejected.

So we have $n = 12$

Alternatively, we can directly add up individual terms and keep adding manually till we get a sum of 54. We will observe that this will occur after adding 12 terms (In this case, as also in all cases where the number of terms is mentally manageable, mentally adding the terms till we get the required sum will turn out to be much faster than the equation-based process).

Problem 2.10 Find the sum of n terms of the series 1.2.4 + 2.3.5 + 3.4.6 + ...

(a) $n(n + 1)(n + 2)$
(b) $(n(n + 1)/12)(3n^2 + 19n + 26)$
(c) $((n + 1)(n + 2)(n + 3))/4$
(d) $(n^2\,(n + 1)(n + 2)(n + 3))/3$

Solution In order to solve such problems in the examination, the option-based approach is the best. Even if you can find out the required expression mathematically, it is advisable to solve through the options as this will end up saving a lot of time for you. Use the options as follows:

If we put $n = 1$, we should get the sum as 1.2.4 = 8. By substituting $n = 1$ in each of the four options, we will get the following values for the sum to 1 term:

Option (a) gives a value of: 6
Option (b) gives a value of: 8
Option (c) gives a value of: 6
Option (d) gives a value of: 8

From this check, we can reject the options (a) and (c).

Now put $n = 2$. You can see that up to 2 terms, the expression is 1.2.4 + 2.3.5 = 38.

The correct option should also give 38 if we put $n = 2$ in the expression. Since, (a) and (c) have already been rejected, we only need to check for options (b) and (d).

Option (b) gives a value of 38.
Option (d) gives a value of 80.

Hence, we can reject option (d) and get (b) as the answer.

Note: The above process is very effective for solving questions having options. The student should try to keep an eye open for the possibility of solving questions through options. In my opinion, approximately 50–75% of the questions asked in CAT in the QA section can be solved with options (at least partially).

Space for Rough Work

LEVEL OF DIFFICULTY (I)

1. There is an AP 11, 13, 15.... Which term of this AP is 65?
   (a) 25th (b) 26th
   (c) 27th (d) 28th
2. Find the 25th term of the sequence 50, 45, 40, ...
   (a) −55 (b) −65
   (c) −70 (d) −75
3. If Ajit saves ₹400 more each year than he did the year before and if he saves ₹2000 in the first year, after how many years will his savings be more than ₹100000 altogether?
   (a) 19 years (b) 20 years
   (c) 21 years (d) 18 years
4. The 6th and 20th terms of an AP are 8 and −20 respectively. Find the 30th term.
   (a) −34 (b) −40
   (c) −32 (d) −30
5. How many terms are there in the AP 10, 15, 20, 25,... 120?
   (a) 21 (b) 22
   (c) 23 (d) 24
6. Find the number of terms of the series 1/27, 1/9, 1/3,... 729.
   (a) 10 (b) 11
   (c) 12 (d) 13
7. If the fifth term of a G.P. is 80 and first term is 5, what will be the 4th term of the G.P.?
   (a) 20 (b) 15
   (c) 40 (d) 25
8. Binay was appointed to Mindworkzz in the pay scale of 12000–1500–22,500. Find how many years he will take to reach the maximum of the scale.
   (a) 7 years (b) 8 years
   (c) 9 years (d) 10 years
9. How many natural numbers between 100 to 500 are multiples of 9?
   (a) 44 (b) 48
   (c) 47 (d) 50
10. The sum of the first 20 terms of an AP whose first term and third term are 25 and 35, respectively is
    (a) 1200 (b) 1250
    (c) 1400 (d) 1450
11. A number 39 is divided into three parts which are in A.P. and the sum of their squares is 515. Find the largest number.
    (a) 17 (b) 15
    (c) 13 (d) 11
12. Sushil agrees to work at the rate of 10 rupee on the first day, 20 rupees on the second day, 40 rupees on the third day and so on. How much will Sushil get if he starts working on the 1st of April and finishes on the 20th of April?
    (a) 10.2^{20} (b) $10.2^{20} - 10$
    (c) $10.2^{20} - 1$ (d) 2^{19}
13. Find the sum of all numbers in between 1–100 excluding all those numbers which are divisible by 7. (Include 1 and 100 for counting.)
    (a) 4315 (b) 4245
    (c) 4320 (d) 4160
14. The 3rd and 8th term of a GP are 1/3 and 81, respectively. Find the 2nd term.
    (a) 3 (b) 1
    (c) 1/27 (d) 1/9
15. The sum of 5 numbers in AP is 35 and the sum of their squares is 285. Which of the following is the third term?
    (a) 5 (b) 7
    (c) 6 (d) 8
16. The number of terms of the series 26 + 24 + 22 +... such that the sum is 182 is
    (a) 13 (b) 14
    (c) Both a and b (d) 15
17. Find the lowest number in an AP such that the sum of all the terms is 105 and greatest term is 6 times the least.
    (a) 5 (b) 10
    (c) 15 (d) (a), (b) & (c)
18. Find the general term of the GP with the third term 1 and the seventh term 8.
    (a) $(2^{3/4})^{n-3}$ (b) $(2^{3/2})^{n-3}$
    (c) $(2^{3/4})^{3-n}$ (d) $(2^{3/4})^{2-n}$
19. The sum of the first and the third term of a geometric progression is 15 and the sum of its first three terms is 21. Find the progression.
    (a) 3,6,12… (b) 12, 6, 3...
    (c) Both of these (d) None of these
20. Ishita's salary is ₹5000 per month in the first year. She has joined in the scale of 5000-500-10000. After how many years will her expenses be 64,800?
    (a) 8 years (b) 7 years
    (c) 6 years (d) Cannot be determined
21. A sum of money kept in a bank amounts to ₹1500 in 5 years and ₹2000 in 10 years at simple interest. Find the sum.
    (a) ₹1250 (b) ₹1200
    (c) ₹1150 (d) ₹1000
22. The sum of three numbers in a G.P. is 13 and the sum of their squares is 91. Find the smallest number.
    (a) 1 (b) 3
    (c) 4 (d) 12

23. Find the 1st term of an AP whose 8th and 12th terms are respectively 60 and 80.
(a) 15 (b) 20
(c) 25 (d) 30

24. The first term of an arithmetic progression is 13 and the common difference is 4. Which of the following will be a term of this AP?
(a) 4003 (b) 10091
(c) 7881 (d) 13631

25. Anuj receives ₹600 for the first week and ₹30 more each week than the preceding week. How much does he earn by the 30th week?
(a) 31050 (b) 32320
(c) 32890 (d) 32900

26. A number of squares are described whose areas are in G.P. Then their sides will be in
(a) A.P. (b) G.P.
(c) H.P. (d) Nothing can be said

27. How many terms are there in the G.P. 5, 10, 20, 40,... 1280?
(a) 6 (b) 8
(c) 9 (d) 10

28. The least value of n for which the sum of the series 5 + 10 + 15... n terms is not less than 765 is
(a) 17 (b) 18
(c) 19 (d) 20

29. Four geometric means are inserted between 5 and 160. Find the 2nd geometric mean.
(a) 80 (b) 40
(c) 10 (d) 20

30. The seventh term of a GP is 4 times the 5th term. What will be the first term when its 4th term is 40?
(a) 4 (b) 5
(c) 3 (d) 2

31. How many terms are identical in the two A.P.s 21, 23, 25,... up to 120 terms and 23, 26, 29,... up to 80 terms?
(a) 39 (b) 40
(c) 41 (d) None of these.

32. The sum of the first four terms of an A.P. is 56 and sum of the first eight terms of the same A.P. is 176. Find the sum of the first 16 terms of the A.P.?
(a) 646 (b) 640
(c) 608 (d) 536

33. X and Y are two numbers whose A.M. is 41 and G.M. is 9. Which of the following may be a value of X?
(a) 125 (b) 49
(c) 81 (d) 25

34. Two numbers A and B are such that $A > B$ and their G.M. is 40% lower than their A.M. Find the ratio between the numbers.
(a) 4 : 3 (b) 9 : 1
(c) : 1 (d) 3 : 1

35. A man saves ₹1000 in January 2015 and increases his saving by ₹500 every month over the previous month. What is the annual saving for the man in the year 2015?
(a) ₹40000 (b) ₹45000
(c) ₹42000 (d) ₹41000

36. Find the 23rd term of the sequence: 1, 4, 5, 8, 9, 12, 13, 16, 17, ...
(a) 33 (b) 39
(c) 45 (d) 43

37. If log$a$, log$b$, log$c$ are in A.P., then the GM of a & c is
(a) b (b) b^2
(c) b^4 (d) None of these.

38. Each of the series 1 + 3 + 5 + 7 +.... and 4 + 7 + 10 +... is continued to 1000 terms. Find how many terms are identical between the two series.
(a) 335 (b) 334
(c) 332 (d) 333

39. Find the sum of the series till 23rd terms for the series: 1, 4, 5, 8, 9, 12, 13, 16, 17, ...
(a) 585 (b) 560
(c) 540 (d) 520

40. What is the maximum sum of the terms in the arithmetic progression 25, 24, 23, 22......?
(a) 325 (b) 345
(c) 332.5 (d) 350

41. If 8th term of an A.P. is the geometric mean of the 1st and 22nd terms of the same A.P. Find the common difference of the A.P., given that the sum of the first twenty-two terms of the A.P. is 770.
(a) Either 1 or 1/2 (b) 2
(c) 1 (d) Either 1 or 2

42. How many terms of the series 1 + 3 + 5 + 7 + ... amount to 1234567654321?
(a) 1110111 (b) 1111011
(c) 1011111 (d) 111111

43. Tom and Jerry were playing mathematical puzzles with each other. Jerry drew a square of sides 32 cm and then kept on drawing squares inside the squares by joining the mid points of the squares. She continued this process indefinitely. Jerry asked Tom to determine the sum of the areas of all the squares that she drew. If Tom answered correctly then what would be his answer?
(a) 2048 (b) 1024
(c) 512 (d) 4096

44. The sum of the first two terms of an infinite geometric series is 36. Also, each term of the series is equal to the sum of all the terms that follow. Find the sum of the series
(a) 48 (b) 54
(c) 72 (d) 96

45. An equilateral triangle is drawn by joining the mid-points of the sides of another equilateral triangle. A third equilateral triangle is drawn inside the second one joining the midpoints of the sides of the second equilateral triangle, and the process continues infinitely. Find the sum of the areas of all the equilateral triangles, if the side of the largest equilateral triangle is 8 units.

(a) $32\sqrt{3}$ units (b) $64\sqrt{3}$ units
(c) 64 units (d) $64/\sqrt{3}$ units

46. After striking a floor a rubber ball rebounds (5/6)th of the height from which it has fallen. Find the total distance (in metres) that it travels before coming to rest, if it is gently dropped from a height of 210 metres.

(a) 2960 (b) 2310
(c) 2080 (d) 2360

For questions 47 to 56, there are no options. Kindly solve these and put down your answer to the question asked.

47. In an infinite geometric progression, each term is equal to 3 times the sum of the terms that follow. If the first term of the series is 4, find the product of first three terms of the series?

48. A student takes a test consisting of 100 questions with differential marking is told that each question after the first is worth 5 marks more than the preceding question. If the 5th question of the test is worth 25 marks, What is the maximum score that the student can obtain by attempting 90 questions?

49. In Narora nuclear power plant a technician is allowed an interval of maximum 100 minutes. A timer with a bell rings at specific intervals of time such that the minutes when the timer rings are not divisible by 2, 3, 5 and 7. The last alarm rings with a buzzer to give time for decontamination of the technician. How many times will the bell ring within these 100 minutes and what is the value of the last minute when the bell rings for the last time in a 100 minute shift?

50. The internal angles of a plane polygon are in AP. The smallest angle is 100° and the common difference is 10°. Find the number of sides of the polygon.

51. If $\dfrac{a^{n+1}+b^{n+1}}{a^n+b^n}$ is the arithmetic mean of a and b then find the value of n.

52. If $\dfrac{a^{n+1}+b^{n+1}}{a^n+b^n}$ is the harmonic mean of a and b then find the value of n.

(a) –1 (b) 0
(c) 1 (d) None of these.

53. If a, b are two numbers such that $a, b > 0$. If harmonic mean of a, b is equals to geometric mean of a, b then what can be said about the relationship between a and b.

54. Product of 36 positive integers is 1. Their sum is ≥

55. If we have two numbers a, b. A.M. of a, b is 12 and H.M. is 3. Find the value of ab

56. If $x+\dfrac{1}{yz}, y+\dfrac{1}{zx}, z+\dfrac{1}{xy}$ are in A.P. then x, y, z are in:

Space for Rough Work

LEVEL OF DIFFICULTY (II)

1. If a times the ath term of an A.P. is equal to b times the bth term, find the $(a + b)^{th}$ term.
(a) 0 (b) $a^2 - b^2$
(c) $a - b$ (d) 1

2. A number 28 is divided into four parts that are in AP such that the product of the first and fourth is to the product of the second and third is 5: 6. Find the smallest part.
(a) 2 (b) 4
(c) 8 (d) 6

3. Find the value of the expression: 1 – 3 + 5 – 7... to 100 terms.
(a) –150 (b) –100
(c) –50 (d) 75

4. If a clock strikes once at 12 A.M., twice at 1 A.M., thrice at 2 A.M. and so on, how many times will the clock be struck in the course of 3 days? (Assume a 24 hour clock)
(a) 756 (b) 828
(c) 678 (d) 1288

5. What will be the maximum sum of 54, 52, 50, ... ?
(a) 702 (b) 704
(c) 756 (d) 700

6. Find the sum of the integers between 100 and 300 that are multiples of 7.
(a) 10512 (b) 5586
(c) 10646 (d) 10546

7. If x > 1, y > 1, z > 1 are in G.P., then $\frac{1}{1+\log x}$, $\frac{1}{1+\log y}$, $\frac{1}{1+\log z}$ are in
(a) A.P. (b) H.P.
(c) G.P. (d) None of the above

8. Find the sum of all odd numbers lying between 1000 and 2000.
(a) 7,50,000 (b) 7,45,000
(c) 7,55,000 (d) 7,65,000

9. Find the sum of all integers of 3 digits that are divisible by 11.
(a) 49,335 (b) 41,338
(c) 44,550 (d) 47,300

10. The first and the last terms of an A.P. are 113 and 253. If there are six terms in this sequence, find the sum of sequence.
(a) 980 (b) 910
(c) 1098 (d) 920

11. Find the value of 1 – 2 – 3 + 2 – 3 – 4 +... + upto 100 terms.
(a) –694 (b) –626
(c) –624 (d) –660

12. What will be the sum to n terms of the series 7 + 77 + 777 +...?
(a) $7(10^n - 9n)/81$ (b) $7(10^{n+1} - 10 - 9n)/81$
(c) $7(10^{n-1} - 10)$ (d) $7(10^{n+1} - 10)$

13. If log a, log b, log c are in A.P., then a, b, c are in
(a) A.P. (b) G.P.
(c) H.P. (d) None of these

14. After striking the floor, a rubber ball rebounds to 3/5th of the height from which it has fallen. Find the total distance that it travels before coming to rest if it has been gently dropped from a height of 20 metres.
(a) 40 metres (b) 60 metres
(c) 80 metres (d) 120 metres

15. If x be the first term, y be the nth term and p be the product of n terms of a G.P., then the value of p^2 will be
(a) $(xy)^{n-1}$ (b) $(xy)^n$
(c) $(xy)^{1-n}$ (d) $(xy)^{n/2}$

16. The sum of an infinite G.P. whose common ratio is positive and is numerically less than 1 is 36 and the sum of the first two terms is 32. What will be the third term?
(a) 1/3 (b) 4/3
(c) 8 /3 (d) 2

17. What will be the value of $2^{1/3}.2^{1/6}.2^{1/12}$... to infinity.
(a) 2^2 (b) $2^{2/3}$
(c) $2^{3/2}$ (d) 8

18. In an infinite G.P. the first term is A and the infinite sum 5, then A belongs to
(a) $A < -10$ (b) $0 < A < 10$
(c) $0 < A \leq 10$ (d) None of these

19. Determine the fourth term of the geometric progression, the sum of whose first term and third term is 50 and the sum of the second term and fourth term is 150.
(a) 120 (b) 125
(c) 135 (d) 45

20. What is the 13th term of 2/9, 1/4, 2/7, 1/3 ....?
(a) –2 (b) 1
(c) –3/13 (d) –2/3

21. The sum of the third and the fourth term of an A.P. is 19 and that of the first and the seventh term is 22. Find the 9th term.
(a) 26 (b) 17
(c) 15 (d) 16

22. How many terms of an A.P. must be taken for their sum to be equal to 200 if its third term is 16 and the difference between the 6th and the 1st term is 30?
(a) 6 (b) 9
(c) 7 (d) 8

23. Four numbers are inserted between the numbers 4 and 34 such that an A.P. results. Find the smallest of these four numbers.

(a) 11.5 (b) 11
(c) 12 (d) 10

24. Find the sum of all three-digit natural numbers, which on being divided by 7, leave a remainder equal to 6.
(a) 70,208 (b) 70,780
(c) 70,680 (d) 71,270

25. The sum of the first three terms of the arithmetic progression is 24 and the sum of the squares of the first term and the second term of the same progression is 80. Find the 8th term of the progression if its fifth term is known to be exactly divisible by 10.
(a) 32 (b) 36
(c) 40 (d) 42

26. Anita and Babita set out to meet each other from two places 200 km apart. Anita travels 20 km the first day, 19 km the second day, 18 km the third day and so on. Babita travels 8 km the first day, 10 km the second day, 12 km the third day and so on. On which day will they meet?
(a) 9th day (b) 8th day
(c) 7th day (d) 6th day

27. If a man saves ₹1000 each year and invests at the end of the year at 5% compound interest, how much will the amount be at the end of 15 years?
(a) ₹21,478 (b) ₹21,578
(c) ₹22,578 (d) ₹22,478

28. If sum to n terms of a series is given by $(2n + 7)$ then its second term will be given by
(a) 10 (b) 9
(c) 8 (d) 2

29. If A is the sum of the n terms of the series 2 + 1/2 + 1/8 + ... and B is the sum of $2n$ terms of the series 2 + 1 + 1/2 + ..., then find the value of B/A.
(a) 1/3 (b) 2
(c) 2/3 (d) 3/2

30. Aman receives a pension starting with ₹1000 for the first year. Each year he receives 80% of what he received the previous year. Find the maximum total amount he can receive even if he lives forever.
(a) 4000 (b) 5000
(c) 1500 (d) 4900

31. The sum of the series $\frac{1}{1\times 5}+\frac{1}{5\times 9}+\frac{1}{9\times 13}+\ldots+\frac{1}{221\times 225}$ is
(a) 28/221 (b) 56/221
(c) 56/225 (d) None of these

32. The sum of the series $\frac{1}{\sqrt{3}+\sqrt{4}}+\frac{1}{\sqrt{4}+\sqrt{5}}+\ldots+\frac{1}{\sqrt{224}+\sqrt{225}}$ is:
(a) $15-\sqrt{3}$ (b) $\sqrt{15}-2$
(c) 12 (d) None of these

33. Find the infinite sum of the series 1/1 + 1/3 + 1/6 + 1/10 + 1/15 ....
(a) 2 (b) 2.25
(c) 3 (d) 4

34. The sum of the series $3 \times 5 + 5 \times 7 + 7 \times 9 + \ldots$ upto n terms will be:
(a) $\frac{n(4n^2+18n+23)}{3}$ (b) $\frac{n(4n^2+18n+23)}{6}$
(c) $n(4n^2+18n+23)$ (d) None of these.

35. The sum of the series: 1/3 + 4/15 + 4/35 + 4/63 + ... upto 6 terms is:
(a) 12/13 (b) 13/14
(c) 14/13 (d) None of these

36. For the above question 35, what is the sum of the series if taken to infinite terms:
(a) 1.1 (b) 1
(c) 14/13 (d) None of these

Directions for Questions 37 to 39: Answer these questions based on the following information. There are 250 integers a_1, a_2,... a_{250}, not all of them necessarily different. Let the greatest integer of these 250 integers be referred to as Max, and the smallest integer be referred to as Min. The integers a_1 through a_{124} form sequence A and the rest form sequence B. Each member of A is less than or equal to each member of B.

37. All values in A are changed in sign, while those in B remain unchanged. Which of the following statements is true?
(a) Every member of A is greater than or equal to every member of B.
(b) Max is in A.
(c) If all numbers originally in A and B had the same sign, then after the change of sign, the largest number of A and B is in A.
(d) None of these

38. Elements of A are in ascending order, and those of B are in descending order. a_{124} and a_{125} are interchanged. Then which of the following statements is true?
(a) A continues to be in ascending order.
(b) B continues to be in descending order.
(c) A continues to be in ascending order and B in descending order.
(d) None of the above

39. Every element of A is made greater than or equal to every clement of B by adding to each element of A an integer x. Then, x cannot be less than:
(a) 2^{10} (b) the smallest value of B
(c) the largest value of B
(d) (Maximm-Minimum)

40. Rahul drew a rectangular grid of 625 cells, arranged in 25 Rows and 25 columns, and filled each cell with a number. The numbers with which he filled each cell were such that the numbers of each row taken from left to right formed an arithmetic series and the numbers of each column taken from top to bottom also formed an arithmetic series. The 6th and the 20th numbers of the fifth row were 37 and 73 respectively, while the 6th and the 20th numbers of the 25th row were 63 and 87, respectively. What is the sum of all the numbers in the grid?

(a) 32798 (b) 65596
(c) 52900 (d) None of these

41. How many four digit numbers have the property that their digits taken from left to right form an Arithmetic or a Geometric Progression?

(a) 15 (b) 21
(c) 20 (d) 23

Directions for Questions 42 and 43: These questions are based on the following data. At Goli - Vadapav—a famous fast food centre in Andheri in Mumbai, vadapavs are made only on an automatic vadapav making machine. The machine continuously makes different sorts of vadapavs by adding different sorts of fillings on a common bread. The machine makes the vadapavs at the rate of 1 vadapav per half a minute. The various fillings are added to the vadapavs in the following manner. The 1st, 3rd, 5th, 7th,...vadapavs are filled with a chicken patty; the 1st, 5th, 9th, ...vadapavs with vegetable patty; the 1st, 8th, 17th, ...vadapavs with mushroom patty; and the rest with plain cheese and tomato fillings. The machine makes exactly 500 vadapavs per day.

42. How many vadapavs per day are made with cheese and tomato as fillings?

43. How many vadapavs are made with all three fillings Chicken, vegetable and mushroom?

44. An arithmetic progression P consists of n terms. From the progression three different progressions P_1, P_2 and P_3 are created such that P_1 is obtained by the 1st, 4th ,7th terms of P, P_2 has the 2nd, 5th, 8th, terms of P and P_3 has the 3rd, 6th, 9th, terms of P. It is found that of P_1, P_2 and P_3, two progressions have the property that their average is itself a term of the original Progression P. Which of the following can be a possible value of n?

(a) 20 (b) 26
(c) 36 (d) Both (a) and (b)

45. For the above question, if the Common Difference between the terms of P_1 is 6, what is the common difference of P?

(a) 2 (b) 3
(c) 6 (d) Cannot be determined

Directions for Questions 46 to 48:
If $S = a, b, b, c, c, c, d, d, d, d, ...z, z, z.$

46. Find the number of terms in the above series:

47. Find 144th term of the above series:

48. If $a = 1, b = 3, c = 5, d = 7, ...,z = 51$ then find the sum of all terms of S:

49. If $f(4x) = 8x + 1$. Then for how many positive real values of x , $f(2x)$ will be G.M. of $f(x)$ and $f(4x)$:

50. If x, y, z, w are positive real numbers such that x, y, z, w form an increasing A.P. and x, y, w form an increasing G.P. then w/x =?

(a) 1 (b) 2
(c) 3 (d) 4

51. If x, y, z are the mth, nth and pth terms, respectively of a G.P. then $(n - p) \log x + (p - m) \log y + (m - n) \log z$ =?

52. Find the sum of first n groups of 1 + (1 + 2) + (1 + 2 + 3) + ...

(a) $\frac{n(n+1)(n+2)}{6}$

(b) $\frac{n(n+1)(n+2)}{12}$

(c) $\frac{n(n+1)(n+2)(n+3)}{6}$

(d) None of these.

53. If $A = 1 + x + x^2 + x^3 + ...$ & $B = 1 + y + y^2 + y^3 + ...$ and $0 < x, y < 1$, then the value of $1 + xy + x^2y^2 + x^3y^3 + ...$is:

(a) $AB/(A + B)$ (b) $AB/(A + B - 1)$
(c) $(AB - 1)/(A + B)$ (d) AB

54. If all the angles of a quadrilateral are in G.P. and all the angles and the common ratio are natural numbers. Exactly two angles are acute and two are obtuse then find the largest angle.

55. The sum to 16 groups of the series (1) + (1 + 3) + (1 + 3 + 5) + (1 + 3 + 5 + 7)+ .....

56. Sum of 16 terms of the series 1 + 1 + 3 + 1 + 3 + 5 + 1 + 3 + 5 + 7 + ...

57. If the sum of n terms of a progression is $2n^2 + 3$. Then which term is equals to 78?

58. Sum of 17 terms of the series $1^2 - 2^2 + 3^2 - 4^2 + 5^2 - 6^2 + ...$

59. Find the sum of 20 terms of the series 3 + 6 + 10 + 15 + ...

60. If $1^n + 2^n + 3^n + ... + x^n$ is always divisible by 1 + 2 + 3 + ...+ x then n is

(a) Even (b) odd
(c) Multiple of 2 (d) None of these.

61. Find the 12th term of the series 3, 14, 61, 252, ...

High Yield Questions

Scan this QR code to access assisted problem solving videos on questions 6, 14, 26, 31, 40 and 57 from LOD 2

LEVEL OF DIFFICULTY (III)

1. If in any decreasing arithmetic progression, sum of all its terms, except for the first term, is equal to –36, the sum of all its terms, except for the last term, is zero, and the difference of the tenth and the sixth term is equal to –16, then what will be first term of this series?
(a) 16 (b) 20
(c) –16 (d) –20
2. The sum of all terms of the arithmetic progression having ten terms except for the first term, is 99, and except for the sixth term, 89. Find the third term of the progression if the sum of the first and the fifth term is equal to 10.
(a) 15 (b) 5
(c) 8 (d) 10
3. Product of the fourth term and the fifth term of an arithmetic progression is 456. Division of the ninth term by the fourth term of the progression gives quotient as 11 and the remainder as 10. Find the first term of the progression.
(a) –52 (b) –42
(c) –56 (d) –66
4. A number of saplings are lying at a place by the side of a straight road. These are to be planted in a straight line at a distance interval of 10 metres between two consecutive saplings. Mithilesh, the country's greatest forester, can carry only one sapling at a time and has to move back to the original point to get the next sapling. In this manner, he covers a total distance of 1.32 km. How many saplings does he plant in the process if he ends at the starting point?
(a) 11 (b) 14
(c) 13 (d) 12
5. A geometric progression consists of 500 terms. Sum of the terms occupying the odd places is P_1 and the sum of the terms occupying the even places is P_2. Find the common ratio.
(a) P_2/P_1 (b) P_1/P_2
(c) $P_2 + P_1/P_1$ (d) $P_2 + P_1/P_2$
6. The sum of the first ten terms of the geometric progression is S_1 and the sum of the next ten terms (11th through 20th) is S_2. Find the common ratio.
(a) $(S_1/S_2)^{1/10}$ (b) $-(S_1/S_2)^{1/10}$
(c) $\pm\sqrt[10]{S_2/S_1}$ (d) $(S_1/S_2)^{1/5}$
7. The first and the third terms of an arithmetic progression are equal, respectively, to the first and the third term of a geometric progression, and the second term of the arithmetic progression exceeds the second term of the geometric progression by 0.25. Calculate the sum of the first five terms of the arithmetic progression if its first term is equal to 2.
(a) 2.25 or 25 (b) 2.5
(c) 1.5 (d) 3.25
8. If (2 + 4 + 6 +... 50 terms)/(1 + 3 + 5 +... *n* terms) = 51/2, then find the value of *n*.
(a) 12 (b) 13
(c) 9 (d) 10
9. (666.... *n* digits)^2 + (888... *n* digits) is equal to
(a) $(10^n - 1) \times \frac{4}{9}$ (b) $(10^{2n} - 1) \times \frac{4}{9}$
(c) $\frac{4(10^n - 10^{n-1} - 1)}{9}$ (d) $\frac{4(10^n + 1)}{9}$
10. The interior angles of a polygon are in *A.P.*. The smallest angle is 120° and the common difference is 5°. Find the number of sides of the polygon.
(a) 7 (b) 8
(c) 9 (d) 10
11. Find the sum to *n* terms of the series 11 + 103 + 1005 + ...
(a) $\frac{10(10^n - 1)}{9} + 1$ (b) $\frac{10(10^n - 1)}{9} + n$
(c) $\frac{10(10^n - 1)}{9} + n^2$ (d) $\frac{10(10^n + 1)}{11} + n^2$
12. The sum of the first term and the fifth term of an *A.P.* is 26 and the product of the second term by the fourth term is 160. Find the sum of the first seven terms of this *A.P.*.
(a) 110 (b) 114
(c) 112 (d) 116
13. The sum of the third and the ninth term of an *A.P.* is 10. Find a possible sum of the first 11 terms of this *A.P.*
(a) 55 (b) 44
(c) 66 (d) 48
14. The sum of the squares of the fifth and the eleventh term of an *A.P.* is 3 and the product of the second and the fourteenth term is equal to *P*. Find the product of the first and the fifteenth term of the *A.P.*.
(a) $(58P - 39)/45$ (b) $(98P + 39)/72$
(c) $(116P - 39)/90$ (d) $(98P + 39)/90$
15. If the ratio of harmonic mean of two numbers to their geometric mean is 12 : 13, find the ratio of the numbers.
(a) 4/9 or 9/4 (b) 2/3 or 3/2
(c) 2/5 or 5/2 (d) None of these
16. Find the sum of the series $1.2 + 2.2^2 + 3.2^3 + \ldots + 100.\ 2^{100}$.
(a) $100.2^{101} + 2$ (b) $99.2^{100} + 2$
(c) $99.2^{101} + 2$ (d) None of these

17. The sequence $[x_n]$ is a $G.P.$ with $x_2/x_4 = 1/4$ and $x_1 + x_4 = 108$. What will be the value of x_3?
(a) 42 (b) 48
(c) 44 (d) 56

18. If x, y, z are in G.P. and a^x, b^y and c^z are equal, then a, b, c are in
(a) A.P. (b) G.P.
(c) H.P. (d) None of these

19. Find the sum of all possible whole number divisors of 720.
(a) 2012 (b) 2624
(c) 2210 (d) 2418

20. Sum to n terms of the series $\log m + \log m^2/n + \log m^3/n^2 + \log m^4/n^3 \ldots$ is
(a) $\log\left(\frac{m^{n+1}}{n^{n-1}}\right)^{\frac{n}{2}}$ (b) $\log\left(\frac{n^{n-1}}{m^{n+1}}\right)^{\frac{n}{2}}$
(c) $\log\left(\frac{m^n}{n^n}\right)^{\frac{n}{2}}$ (d) $\log\left(\frac{m^{1-n}}{n^{1-m}}\right)^{\frac{n}{2}}$

21. The sum of first 20 and first 50 terms of an A.P. is 420 and 2550. Find the eleventh term of a G.P. whose first term is the same as the A.P. and the common ratio of the G.P. is equal to the common difference of the A.P.
(a) 560 (b) 512
(c) 1024 (d) 2048

22. If three positive real numbers x, y, z are in $A.P.$ such that $xyz = 4$, then what will be the minimum value of y?
(a) $2^{1/3}$ (b) $2^{2/3}$
(c) $2^{1/4}$ (d) $2^{3/4}$

23. If a_n be the nth term of an $A.P.$ and if $a_7 = 15$, then the value of the common difference that would make $a_2a_7a_{12}$ greatest is
(a) 3 (b) 3/2
(c) 7 (d) 0

24. Sum of the series $\frac{1^3}{1} + \frac{1^3+2^3}{1+3} + \frac{1^3+2^3+3^3}{1+3+5} + \ldots$ to 10 terms

25. If the first two terms of a $H.P.$ are 2/5 and 12/13, respectively, which of the following terms is the largest term?
(a) 4th term (b) 5th term
(c) 6th term (d) 2nd term

26. One side of a staircase is to be closed in by rectangular planks from the floor to each step. The width of each plank is 9 inches and their heights are successively 6 inches, 12 inches, 18 inches and so on. There are 24 planks required in total. Find the area in square feet.
(a) 112.5 (b) 107
(c) 118.5 (d) 105

27. The middle points of the sides of a triangle are joined forming a second triangle. Again a third triangle is formed by joining the middle points of this second triangle and this process is repeated infinitely. If the perimeter and area of the outer triangle are P and A respectively, what will be the sum of perimeters of triangles thus formed?
(a) $2P$ (b) P^2
(c) $3P$ (d) $P^2/2$

28. In problem 27, find the sum of areas of all the triangles.
(a) $\frac{4}{5}$A (b) $\frac{4}{3}$A
(c) $\frac{3}{4}$A (d) $\frac{5}{4}$A

29. A square has a side of 40 cm. Another square is formed by joining the mid-points of the sides of the given square and this process is repeated infinitely. Find the perimeter of all the squares thus formed.
(a) $160\,(1 + \sqrt{2})$
(b) $160\,(2 + \sqrt{2})$
(c) $160\,(2 - \sqrt{2})$
(d) $160\,(1 - \sqrt{2})$

30. In problem 29, find the area of all the squares thus formed.
(a) 1600 (b) 2400
(c) 2800 (d) 3200

31. The sum of the first n terms of the arithmetic progression is equal to half the sum of the next n terms of the same progression. Find the ratio of the sum of the first $3n$ terms of the progression to the sum of its first n terms.
(a) 5 (b) 6
(c) 7 (d) 8

32. In a certain colony of cancerous cells, each cell breaks into two new cells every hour. If there is a single productive cell at the start and this process continues for 9 hours, how many cells will the colony have at the end of 9 hours? It is known that the life of an individual cell is 20 hours.
(a) $2^9 - 1$ (b) 2^{10}
(c) 2^9 (d) $2^{10} - 1$

33. Find the sum of all three-digit whole numbers less than 500 that leave a remainder of 2 when they are divided by 3.
(a) 49637 (b) 39767
(c) 49634 (d) 39770

34. If a be the arithmetic mean and b, c be the two geometric means between any two positive numbers, then $(b^3 + c^3)\,/abc$ equals
(a) $(ab)^{1/2}/c$
(b) 1
(c) a^2c/b
(d) None of these

35. If p, q, r are three consecutive distinct natural numbers then the expression $(q + r - p)(p + r - q)(p + q - r)$ is
(a) Positive (b) Negative
(c) Non-positive (d) Non-negative

36. If $S=\left[1+\left(-\frac{1}{3}\right)\right]\left[1+\left(-\frac{1}{3}\right)^2\right]\left[1+\left(-\frac{1}{3}\right)^4\right]\left[1+\left(-\frac{1}{3}\right)^8\right.\ldots\ldots$ till n terms. Then S = ?
(a) $4(10^{2n} - 1)$ (b) $4/3(10^n - 1)$
(c) $2/3(10^n - 1)$ (d) None of these

37. The number 7777….77 (total 133 digits) is
(a) Divisible by 3
(b) A prime Number
(c) A composite Number
(d) None of these

38. First term of an A.P. of consecutive integers is $n^2 + 1$ (n is a positive integer). Sum of 1st $2n$ terms of the series will be
(a) $n(2n^2 + 2n + 1)$ (b) $(2n^2 + 2n + 3)$
(c) $n(2n^2 + 2n + 3)$ (d) None of these

39. $S=\frac{1}{1!+2!}+\frac{1}{2!+3!}+\frac{1}{3!+4!}+\ldots..+\frac{1}{19!+20!}$, then S=?
(a) $\frac{1}{2!}-\frac{1}{21!}$ (b) $\frac{1}{2!}-\frac{1}{20!}$
(c) None of these

40. a, b, c are in H.P. and $n > 1$ then $a^n + c^n$ is
(a) Less than $2b^n$
(b) Less than or equal to $2b^n$
(c) More than $2b^n$
(d) More than or equal to $2b^n$

41. The sum to 17 terms of the series
$\frac{3}{1^2.2^2}+\frac{5}{2^2.3^2}+\frac{7}{3^2.4^2}+\ldots.$ is

42. Find the value of S if
$S=\frac{4}{11}+\frac{44}{11^2}+\frac{444}{11^3}+\frac{4444}{11^4}+\ldots\infty$

43. Find the value of S if $S=\frac{1}{2.5}+\frac{1}{5.8}+\frac{1}{8.11}+\ldots..+\infty$
(a) 1/3 (b) 1/2
(c) 1/6 (d) None of these

44. $A = a + A_1 + A_2 + \ldots..+ A_N + b$
$B = a + G_1 + G_2 + \ldots.+ G_N + b$
A is the sum of $n + 2$ terms of an A.P. with first term a and last term b.
B is the sum of $n + 2$ terms of a G.P. with first term a and last term b.
Then, what can be said about the relative values of A and B?

45. $\frac{9}{2}+\frac{25}{6}+\frac{49}{12}+\ldots.+\frac{9801}{2450}$ =?

46. Two series X (x_1, x_2, x_3, x_4, …x_n) and Y (y_1, y_2, y_3, y_4, ….., y_n) are in A.P., such that $x_n - y_n = n - 2$. It is also known that $x_3 = b_5$. Find the value of $x_{99} - y_{197}$.
(a) 47 (b) 48
(c) 49 (d) 50

47. From the first 12 natural numbers, how many arithmetic progressions of 4 terms can be formed such that the common difference is a factor of the 4th term?

48. The product of 1st five terms of an increasing A.P. is 3840. If the 1st, 2nd and 4th terms of the A.P. are in G.P. Find 10th term of the series.

49. If
$$S=\left[1+\left(-\frac{1}{3}\right)\right]\left[1+\left(-\frac{1}{3}\right)^2\right]\left[1+\left(-\frac{1}{3}\right)^4\right]\left[1+\left(-\frac{1}{3}\right)^8\ldots..\right]$$
then S = ?

50. Let the positive numbers a, b, c, d be in A.P. Then the type of progression for the numbers abc, abd, acd, bcd is

High Yield Questions

Scan this QR code to access assisted problem solving videos on questions 1, 4, 29, 30, 31 and 43 from LOD 3

Space for Rough Work

ANSWER KEY

Level of Difficulty (I)

1. (d)	2. (c)	3. (a)	4. (b)
5. (c)	6. (a)	7. (c)	8. (a)
9. (a)	10. (d)	11. (b)	12. (b)
13. (a)	14. (d)	15. (b)	16. (c)
17. (d)	18. (a)	19. (c)	20. (d)
21. (d)	22. (a)	23. (c)	24. (c)
25. (a)	26. (b)	27. (c)	28. (a)
29. (d)	30. (b)	31. (b)	32. (c)
33. (c)	34. (b)	35. (b)	36. (c)
37. (a)	38. (d)	39. (c)	40. (a)
41. (b)	42. (d)	43. (a)	44. (a)
45. (d)	46. (b)	47. 1	48. (d)
49. 22,97	50. 8	51. 0	52. −1
53. a = b	54. 36	55. 36	56. A.P.

Level of Difficulty (II)

1. (a)	2. (b)	3. (b)	4. (b)
5. (c)	6. (b)	7. (b)	8. (a)
9. (c)	10. (c)	11. (b)	12. (b)
13. (b)	14. (c)	15. (b)	16. (c)
17. (b)	18. (b)	19. (c)	20. (d)
21. (a)	22. (d)	23. (d)	24. (a)
25. (a)	26. (c)	27. (b)	28. (d)
29. (d)	30. (b)	31. (c)	32. (a)
33. (a)	34. (a)	35. (d)	36. (b)
37. (d)	38. (a)	39. (d)	40. (d)
41. (d)	42. 214	43. 18	44. (d)
45. (a)	46. 351	47. q	48. 12051
49. 0	50. (d)	51. 0	52. (a)
53. (b)	54. 192degrees	55. 1496	56. 56
57. 20	58. 153	59. 1770	60. (b)
61. 4^{12}-12			

Level of Difficulty (III)

1. (a)	2. (b)	3. (d)	4. (d)
5. (a)	6. (c)	7. (b)	8. (d)
9. (b)	10. (c)	11. (c)	12. (c)
13. (a)	14. (c)	15. (a)	16. (c)
17. (b)	18. (b)	19. (d)	20. (a)
21. (d)	22. (b)	23. (d)	24. 126.25
25. (d)	26. (a)	27. (a)	28. (b)
29. (b)	30. (d)	31. (b)	32. (c)
33. (b)	34. (d)	35. (d)	36. (d)
37. (c)	38. (a)	39. (a)	40. (c)
41. $\frac{323}{324}$	42. 22/5	43. (c)	44. A > B
45. 9849/50	46. (b)	47. 13	48. 24
49. 3/4	50. Harmonic Progression		

SOLUTIONS AND SHORTCUTS

Level of Difficulty (I)

1. The number of terms in a series are found by: $\frac{\text{Difference between first and last terms}}{\text{Common Difference}}+1=$ $\frac{65-11}{2}+1 = 27+1 = 28^{\text{th}}$ term. Option (d) is correct.
2. The first term is 50 and the common difference is −5, thus the 25th term is: $50 + 24\,x\,(-5) = -70$. Option (c) is correct.
3. We need the sum of the series 2000 + 2400 + 2800 to cross 100000. Trying out the options, we can see that in 20 years the sum of his savings would be: 2000 + 2400 + 2800 +...+ 9600. The sum of the series would be 20 × 5800 = 116000. If we remove the 20th year we will get the saving for 19 years. The series would be 2000 + 2400 + 2800 + ... + 9200. Sum of the series would be 116000 – 9600 = 106400. If we remove the 19th year's savings the savings would be 106400 – 9200 which would go below 100000. Thus, after 19 years his savings would cross 100000. Option (a) is correct.
4. $a + 5d = 8$ and $a + 19d = -20$. Solving we get $14d = -28 \rightarrow d = -2$. 30th term = 20th term + $10d$ = $-20 + 10 \times (-2) = -40$. Option (b) is correct.
5. In order to count the number of terms in the AP, use the shortcut: [(last term – first term)/ common difference] + 1. In this case it would become: [(120 – 10)/5] + 1 = 23. Option (c) is correct.
6. $r = 3$. $729 = \frac{1}{27}(3)^{n-1}$, $n - 1 = 9$ or $n = 10$ option (a) is correct.
7. $5r^4 = 80 \rightarrow r^4 = 80/5 \rightarrow r = 2$. Thus, 4th term $= ar^3 = 5 \times (2)^3 = 40$. Option (c) is correct.
8. 12000 – 1500 – 22500 means that the starting scale is 12000 and there is an increment of 1500 every year. Since, the total increment required to reach the top of his scale is 10500, the number of years required would be 10500/1500 = 7. Option (a) is correct.
9. The series will be 108, 117, 126,…. 495. Hence, Answer = $\frac{495-108}{9}+1 = 44$. Option (a) is correct.
10. $a = 25$, $a + 2d = 35$ means $d = 5$. The 20th term would be $a + 19d = 25 + 95 = 120$. The sum of the series would be given by: [20/2] × [25 + 120] = 1450. Option (d) is correct.
11. The three parts are 11, 13 and 15 since $11^2 + 13^2 + 15^2 = 515$. Since, we want the largest number, the answer would be 15. Option (b) is correct.

12. Sum of a G.P. with first term 10 and common ratio 2 and no. of terms 20. $\frac{10\times(2^{20}-1)}{2-1}=10(2^{20}-1)$. Option (b) is correct.
13. The answer will be given by:
[1 + 2 + 3 +...+ 100]— [7 + 14 + 21 +... + 98]
= 50 × 101 – 7 × 105
= 5050 – 735 = 4315. Option (a) is correct.
14. 3rd term $ar^2 = 1/3$, 8th term $ar^7 = 81$
$r^5 = 243$ Gives us: $r = 3$.
Hence, the second term will be given by (3rd term/r)
= 1/3 1/3 = 1/9. Option (d) is correct.
[Note: To go forward in a G.P. you multiply by the common ratio, to go backward in a G.P. you divide by the common ratio.]
15. Since the sum of 5 numbers in AP is 35, their average would be 7. The average of 5 terms in an AP is also equal to the value of the 3rd term (logic of the middle term of an AP). Hence, the third term's value would be 7. Option (b) is correct.
16. Use trial and error by using various values from the options.
If you find the sum of the series till 13 terms the value is 182. The 14th term of the given series is 0, so also for 14 terms the value of the sum would be 182. Option (c) is correct.
17. Trying Option (a),
We get least term 5 and largest term 30 (since the largest term is 6 times the least term).
The average of the A.P becomes (5 + 30)/2 = 17.5
Thus, 17.5 × n = 105 gives us:
to get a total of 105 we need $n = 6$ i.e. 6 terms in this A.P. That means the A.P. should look like: 5, _, _, _, _, 30.
It can be easily seen that the common difference should be 5. The A.P, 5, 10, 15, 20, 25, 30 fits the situation.
The same process used for option (b) gives us the A.P. 10, 35, 60. (10 + 35 + 60 = 105) and in the third option 15, 90 (15 + 90 = 105).
Hence, all the three options are correct.
18. Go through the options. The correct option should give value as 1, when $n = 3$ and as 8 when $n = 7$. Only option (a) satisfies both conditions.
19. The answer to this question can be seen from the options. Both 3, 6, 12 and 12, 6, 3 satisfy the required conditions— viz, GP with sum of first and third terms as 15. Thus, option (c) is correct.
20. The answer to this question cannot be determined because the question is talking about income and asking about expenses. You cannot solve this unless you know the value of the expenditure she incurs over the years. Thus, "Cannot be Determined" is the correct answer.
21. The difference between the amounts at the end of 5 years and 10 years will be the simple interest on the initial capital for 5 years.
Hence, (2000 – 1500)/5 = 100 (simple interest.)
Also, the Simple Interest for 5 years when added to the sum gives 1500 as the amount.
Hence, the original sum must be 1000. Option (d) is correct.
22. Visualising the squares below 91, we can see that the only way to get the sum of 3 squares as 91 is: $1^2 + 3^2 + 9^2 = 1 + 9 + 81 = 91$. The smallest number is 1. Option (a) is correct.
23. Since the 8th and the 12th terms of the AP are given as 60 and 80, respectively, the difference between the two terms would equal 4 times the common difference. Thus we get $4d = 80 – 60 = 20$. This gives us $d = 5$. Also, the 8th term in the AP is represented by $a + 7d$, we get:
$a + 7d = 60 \rightarrow a + 7 \times 5 = 60 \rightarrow a = 25$. Option (c) is correct.
24. The series would be given by: 13, 17, 21... which essentially means that all the numbers in the series are of the form $4n + 13$ or $4k + 1$(Where $k = n + 3$). Only the value in option (c) is a $4k + 1$ number and is hence the correct answer.
25. His total earnings would be 600 + 630 + 660 + ... + 1470 = ₹31050. Option (a) is correct.
26. If we take the square of the side we get the area of the squares. Thus, if the side of the respective squares are a_1, a_2, a_3, a_4... their areas would be a_1^2 a_2^2, a_3^2, a_4^2. Since the areas are in GP, the sides would also be in GP.
27. $1280 = 5.\ 2^{n-1}$ or $n – 1 = 8$ or $n = 9$. Thus, there are total of 9 terms in the series. Option (c) is correct.
28. Solve this question through trial and error by using values of n from the options:
For 16 terms, the series would be 5 + 10 + 15 + ... + 80 which would give us a sum for the series as 8 × 85 = 680. The next term (17th term of the series) would be 85. Thus, 680 + 85 = 765 would be the sum to 17 terms. It can thus be concluded that for 17 terms the value of the sum of the series is not less than 765. Option (a) is correct.
29. $5 \times r^5 = 160 \rightarrow r^5 = 32 \Rightarrow r = 2$.
Thus, the series would be 5, 10, 20, 40, 80, 160. The second geometric mean between 5 and 160 in this case would be 20. Option (d) is correct.
30. In the case of a G.P. the 7th term is derived by multiplying the 5th term twice by the common ratio. (Note: this is very similar to what we had seen in the case of an A.P.) Since, the seventh term is derived by multiplying the 5th term by 4, the relationship.

$r^2 = 4$ must be true.
Hence, $r = 2$
If the 4th term is 40, the series in reverse from the 4th to the first term will look like:
40, 20, 10, 5. Hence, option (b) is correct.

31. The first common term is 23, the next will be 29 (Notice that the second common term is exactly 6 away from the first common term. 6 is also the LCM of 2 and 3 which are the respective common differences of the two series.)
Thus, the common terms will be given by the A.P 23, 29, 35 ....., last term. To find the answer you need to find the last term that will be common to the two series.
The first series is 23, 25, 27 ... 259
While the second series is 23, 26, 29 ..... 260.
Hence, the last common term is 257.
Thus our answer becomes $\frac{257-23}{6}+1=40$. Option (b) is correct.

32. Think like this:
The average of the first 4 terms is 14, while the average of the first 8 terms must be 22.
Now visualise this:
1st $\underbrace{\text{2nd 3rd}}_{\text{average}=14}$ $\underbrace{\text{4th 5th}}_{\text{average}=22}$ 6th 7th 8th
Hence, $d = 8/2 = 4$ [Note: understand this as a property of an A.P.]
Hence, the average of the 8th and 9th term = 22 + 4.4 = 38 But this 38 also represents the average of the 16 term A.P.
Hence, required answer = 16 × 38 = 608. Option (c) is correct.

33. AM = 41 means that their sum is 82 and GM = 9 means their product is 81. The numbers can only be 81 and 1. Option (c) is correct.

34. Trial and error gives us that for option (b):
With the ratio 9:1, the numbers can be taken as $9x$ and $1x$. Their AM would be $5x$ and their GM would be $3x$. The GM can be seen to be 40% lower than the AM. Option (b) is thus the correct answer.

35. The total savings would be given by the sum of the series: 1000 + 1500 + 2000 +.....+ 6500 = 12 × 3750 = 45000. Option (b) is correct.

36. The 23rd term of the sequence would be the 12th term of the sequence 1, 5, 9, 13, ...
The 12th term of the sequence would be 1 + 4 × 11 = 45. Option (c) is correct.

37. log a, log b, log c are in A.P then 2log b = log a+ log c or log b^2 = log ac or $b^2 = ac$
So G.M. of a and c is b.
Option (a) is correct.

38. The two series till their 1000th terms are 1, 3, 5, 7....1999 and 4, 7, 10...3001. The common terms of the series would be given by the series 7, 13, 19,...1999. The number of terms in this series of 333. Option (d) is correct.

39. The sum to 23 terms of the sequence would be:
The sum to 12 terms of the sequence 1, 5, 9, 13, ... + The sum to 11 terms of the sequence 4, 8, 12, 16,....
The required sum would be
$\frac{12}{2}(2.1+(12-1)4)+\frac{11}{2}[2.4+(11-1)4]$ = 6 × 46 + 11 × 24 = 276 + 264 = 540. Option (c) is correct.

40. The maximum sum would occur when we take the sum of all the positive terms of the series. The series 25, 24, 23,... 1, 0 has 26 terms. The sum of the series would be given by:
n × average = 26 × 12.5 = 325
Option (a) is correct.

41. Since the sum of 22 terms of the AP is 770, the average of the numbers in the AP would be 770/22 = 35. This means that the sum of the first and last terms of the AP would be 2 × 35 = 70. Trial and error gives us the terms of the required GP as 14, 28, 56. Thus, the common difference of the $AP=\frac{28-14}{7}=2$.

42. It can be seen that for the series the average of first two terms is 2, for first 3 terms the average is 3 and so on. Thus, the sum of first 2 terms is 2^2, of first 3 terms it is 3^2 and so on. For 1111111 terms it would be $1111111^2 = 1234567654321$. Option (d) is correct.

43. The area of the first square would be 1024 sq cm. the second square would give 512, the third one 256 and so on. The infinite sum of the geometric progression 1024 + 512 + 256 + 128... = 2048. Option (a) is correct.

44. $a=\frac{ar}{1-r}$ or $1 - r = r$ or $r = 1/2$ $a + \underline{ar} = 36$ or $a = 24$
Required sum $=\frac{24}{1-\frac{1}{2}}=48$. Option (a) is correct.

45. The side of the first equilateral triangle being 8 units, the first area is $16\sqrt{3}$ square units. The second area would be 1/4 of area of largest triangle and so on.
$16\sqrt{3}$, $4\sqrt{3}$, $\sqrt{3}$, $\frac{\sqrt{3}}{4}$, $\frac{\sqrt{3}}{16}$,.....
The infinite sum of this series — $16\sqrt{3}/(1 - 1/4)$ = $64/\sqrt{3}$ square units.
Option (d) is correct.

46. The sum of the total distance it travels would be given by the infinite sum of the series:
$$210+2\left[210\times\left(\frac{5}{6}\right)+210\times\left(\frac{5}{6}\right)^2+210\times\left(\frac{5}{6}\right)^3+.....\right]$$

$210 + 2\cdot 210\cdot\left(\frac{5}{6}\right)\left[1+\frac{5}{6}+\left(\frac{5}{6}\right)^2+.....\right]$

$210 + 350\left[\frac{1}{1-\frac{5}{6}}\right] = 210 + 350 \times 6 = -210 + 2100$

= 2310 metres.

Option (b) is correct.

47. Let the series be $a, ar, ar^2, ar^3,....$
According to the question $a = 3ar/(1 - r)$ or $r = 1/4$. The series would be 4, 4/4, 4/16,..... and so on. The product of first three terms of the series would be $4\cdot 1\cdot\frac{1}{4}=1$.

48. 5th term= 25. 1st term = 25 – (4 × 5) = 5, 11th term = 5 + 10 × 5 = 55, 100th term = 5 + 99 × 5 = 500
Student will score maximum marks if he attempts question 11 to 100. The maximum score would be the sum of the series 55 + 60 + ... + 495 + 500 = (90 × 555)/2 = 24975.

49. In order to find how many times the alarm rings we need to find the number of numbers below 100, which are not divisible by 2, 3, 5 or 7. This can be found by:
100 — (numbers divisible by 2) – (numbers divisible by 3 but not by 2) — (numbers divisible by 5 but not by 2 or 3) — (numbers divisible by 7 but not by 2 or 3 or 5).
Numbers divisible by 2 up to 100 would be represented by the series 2, 4, 6, 8, 10...100 → A total of 50 numbers.
Numbers divisible by 3 but not by 2 up to 100 would be represented by the series 3, 9, 15, 21...99 → A total of 17 numbers. Note use short cut for finding the number of number in this series :
[(last term — first term)/ common difference] + 1 = [(99 — 3)/6] + 1 = 16 + 1 = 17.
Numbers divisible by 5 but not by 2 or 3: Numbers divisible by 5 but not by 2 up to 100 would be represented by the series 5, 15, 25, 35...95 → A total of 10 numbers. But from these numbers, the numbers 15, 45 and 75 are also divisible by 3. Thus, we are left with 10 — 3 = 7 new numbers which are Divisible by 5 but not by 2 and 3.
Numbers divisible by 7, but not by 2, 3 or 5: numbers divisible by 7 but not by 2 upto 100 would be represented by the series 7, 21, 35, 49, 63, 77, 91 → A total of 7 numbers. But from these numbers we should not count 21, 35 and 63 as they are divisible by either 3 or 5. Thus a total of 7 — 3 = 4 numbers are divisible by 7 but not by 2, 3 or 5.
Thus we get a total of 100 – 78 = 22 times. Also, the last time the bell would ring would be in the 97th minute (as 98, 99 and 100 are divisible by at least one of the numbers).

50. Smallest interior angle = 100, largest exterior angle = 180 – 100 = 80
Similarly other exterior angles are 70, 60, 50, ...
Sum of all the exterior angles = 360
So $\frac{n(2.80+(n-1)(-10))}{2} = 360$ or $n(17 - n) = 72$
We can see that the above equation is true for both $n = 8, 9$. But for $n = 9$, the 9th exterior angle must be 0 which is not possible so only 8 is possible.

51. $\frac{a^{n+1}+b^{n+1}}{a^n+b^n}=\frac{a+b}{2}$
For $n = 0$ the above equality is true. So n must be 0.

52. $\frac{a^{n+1}+b^{n+1}}{a^n+b^n}=\frac{2ab}{a+b}$
For $n = -1$ the above equality is true so $n = -1$.

53. According to the question $\frac{2ab}{a+b} = \sqrt{ab}$, this equality will be true only for $a = b$. Hence, $a = b$.

54. A.M. of n positive integers is always greater than or equals to G.M. of the numbers. Then according to the question,
Sum of the numbers ≥ n (product of n positive integers)$^{1/n}$
Sum of the numbers ≥ n

55. G.M.^{2} = A.M. × H.M. = 12 × 3 = 36.

56. We can solve this problem by checking for values. If we assume that x, y, z are in A.P. & $x = 1, y = 2, z = 3$.

$$x+\frac{1}{yz}=1+\frac{1}{6}=\frac{7}{6}$$

$$y+\frac{1}{zx}=2+\frac{1}{3}=\frac{7}{3}$$

$$z+\frac{1}{xy}=3+\frac{1}{2}=\frac{7}{2}$$

We can see if x, y, z are in A. P. then $x+\frac{1}{yz}, y+\frac{1}{zx}, z+\frac{1}{xy}$ are also in A.P.

Level of Difficulty (II)

1. Identify an AP which satisfies the given condition. Suppose we are talking about the second and third terms of the AP.
Then an AP with second term 3 and third term 2 satisfies the condition.
A times the $\underline{a}^{th}$ term = b times the bth term.
In this case the value of $a = 2$ and $b = 3$.
Hence, for the $(a + b)^{th}$ term, we have to find the 5th term.
It is clear that the 5th term of the AP must be zero.
Check the other three options to see whether any option gives 0 when $a = 2$ and $b = 3$.

Since none of the options b, c or d gives zero for this particular value, option (a) is correct.

2. Since the four parts of the number are in AP and their sum is 28, the average of the four parts must be 7. Looking at the options for the smallest part, only the value of 4 fits in, as it leads us to think of the AP 4, 6, 8, 10. In this case, the ratio of the product of the first and fourth (4 × 10) to the product of the first and second (6 × 8) are in 5: 6 ratio.
3. View: 1 – 3 + 5 – 7 + 9 – 11 ..... 100 terms as (1 – 3) + (5 – 7) + (9 – 11) ...... 50 terms. Hence, –2 + –2 + –2 ... 50 terms = 50 × –2 = –100. Option (b) is correct.
4. In a period of 1 day or 24 hours the clock would strike 1 + 2 + 3 + ...+ 23 = 276 times. In the course of 3 days the clock would strike 276 × 3 = 828 times. Option (b) is correct.
5. Since this is a decreasing A.P. with first term positive, the maximum sum will occur upto the point where the progression remains non-negative. 54, 52, 50, ... 0 Hence, 28 terms × 27 = 756. Option (c) is correct.
6. The sum of the required series of integers would be given by 105 + 112 + 119 + ...294 = 28 × 199.5 = 5586. Option (b) is correct.
7. $y^2 = xz$, 1 + log x, 1 + log y, 1 + log z are in A.P. if 2 log y= log x + log z or $y^2 = xz$, Option (b) is right.
8. 1001 + 1003 + 1005 + ... 1999 = 1500 × 500 = 750000.
9. The required sum would be given by the sum of the series 110, 121, 132, ... 990. The number of terms in this series = (990 – 110)/11 + 1 = 80 + 1 = 81. The sum of the series = 81 × 550 (average of 110 and 990) = 44550. Option (c) is correct.
10. 6 × average of 113 and 253 = 6 × 183 = 1098. Option (c) is correct.
11. The first 100 terms of this (1 – 2 – 3) + (2 – 3 – 4) + ... + (33 – 34 – 35) + 34

    The first 33 terms of the above series (indicated inside the brackets) will give an AP.:

    –4, –5, –6.... –36 = 33 × –20 = –660 (sum of this A.P.). The required answer would be

    –660 + 34 = –626.
12. Solve this one through trial and error. For $n = 2$ terms the sum upto 2 terms is equal to 84. Putting n in the options it can be seen that for option (b) the sum to two terms would be given by

    7 × (1000 – 10 – 18)/81 = 7 × 972/81 = 7 × 12 = 84.
13. 2log b = log a+ log c or log b^2 = log ac or $b^2 = ac$, so a, b, c are in GP. Option (b) is correct.
14. The path of the rubber ball is:

    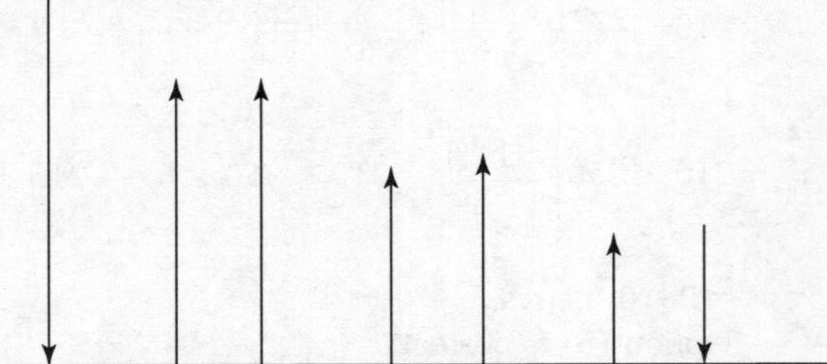

    In the figure above, every bounce is 3/5th of the previous drop.

    In the above movement, there are two infinite G.Ps (The GP representing the falling distances and the GP representing the rising distances.)

    The required answer: (Using $a/(1 – r)$ formula)

    $\frac{20}{2/5} + \frac{12}{2/5} = 80$ metres. Option (c) is correct.
15. Solve this for a sample GP. Let us say we take the GP as 2, 6, 18, 54. x, the first term is 2, let $n = 3$ then the 3rd term y = 18 and the product of 3 terms $p = 2 \times 6 \times 18 = 216 = 6^3$. The value of $p^2 = 216 \times 216 = 6^6$.

    Putting these values in the options we have:

    Option (a) gives us $(xy)^{n-1} = 36^2$ which is not equal to the value of p^2 we have from the options

    Option (b) gives us $(xy)^n = 36^3 = 6^6$ which is equal to the value of p^2 we have from the options.

    It can be experimentally verified that the other options yield values of p^2 which are different from 6^6 and hence we can conclude that option (b) is correct.
16. Trying to plug in values we can see that the infinite sum of the GP 24, 8, 8/3... is 36. Hence the third term is 8/3.
17. The expression can be written as $2^{1/3+1/6+1/12+....} = 2^{\text{INFINTE SUM OF THE GP}} = 2^{2/3}$. Option (b) is correct.
18. $\frac{A}{1-r} = 5$ then $r = 1 - \frac{A}{5}$

    Now since it is an infinite G.P. $|r|<|$, implies

    $-1 < 1 - \frac{A}{5} < 1$ or $0 < A < 10$
19. From the facts given in the question it is self evident that the common ratio of the GP must be 3 (as the sum of the 2nd and 4th term is thrice the sum of the first and third term).

    $a + ar^2 = 50$ or $a = 50/(1 + 9) = 5$

    Largest term = $5.(3)^3 = 135$. Option (c) is correct.
20. 2/9, 1/4, 2/7, 1/3 ....

    This is an HP series. The corresponding AP will be:

    9/2, 4/1, 7/2, 3/1, ...

    or 4.5, 4, 3.5, 3 ....

    i.e., this is an AP with first term 4.5 and common difference –0.5.

Hence $T_{13} = 4.5 + 12\ (-0.5) = -1.5$
The corresponding T_{13} HP is $1/-1.5 = 1 \times -2/3 = -2/3$

21. Third term = $a + 2d$, Fourth term = $a + 3d$; 1st term = a, seventh term = $a + 6d$.
Thus $2a + 5d = 19$ and $2a + 6d = 22 \rightarrow d = 3$ and $a = 2$.
The 9th term = $a + 8d = 2 + 24 = 26$. Thus, option (a) is correct.
22. If the difference between the 6th and the 1st term is 30, it means that the common difference is equal to 6. Since, the third term is 16, the AP would be 4, 10, 16, 22, 28, 34, 40, 46 and the sum to 8 terms for this AP would be 200. Thus, option (d) is correct.
23. $5d = 30 \rightarrow d = 6$. Thus, the numbers are 4, 10, 16, 22, 28, 34. The smallest number is 10. Option (d) is correct.
24. Find sum of the series: 104, 111, 118,...993
Average × $n = \frac{104+993}{2} \times 128 = 70208$. Option (a) is correct.
25. Since the sum of the first three terms of the AP is 24, the average of the AP till 3 terms would he 24/3 = 8. Value of the second term would be equal to this average and hence the second term is 8. Using the information about the sum of squares of the first and second terms being 80, we have that the first term must be 4. Thus, the AP has a first term of 4 and a common difference of 4. The eighth term would be 32. Thus option (a) is correct.
26. The combined travel would be 28 on the first day, 29 on the second day, 30 on the third day, 31 on the fourth day, 32 on the fifth day and 33 on the sixth day, 34 on 7th day. They meet after 7 days. Option (c) is correct.
27. This is an intensive calculation, problem and you are not supposed to know how to do the calculations in this question mentally. The problem has been put here to test your concepts about whether you recogsize how this is a question of GPs. If you feel like, you can use a calculator/computer spreadsheet to get the answer to this question.
The logic of the question would hinge on the fact that the value of the investment of the fifteenth year would be 1000. At the end of the 15th year, the investment of the 14th year would be equal to 1000×1.05, the 13th year's investment would amount to 1000×1.05^2 and so on till the first year's investment which would amount to 1000×1.05^{14} after 15 years. Thus, you need to calculate the sum of the GP: 1000, 1000×1.05, 1000×1.05^2, 1000×1.05^3 for 15 terms.
28. Since, sum to n terms is given by $(2n + 7)$,
Sum to 1 terms = 9
Sum to 2 terms = 11
Thus, the 2nd term must be 2,
29. Solve this question by looking at hypothetical values for n and $2n$ terms. Suppose, we take the sum to 1 (n = 1) term of the first series and the sum to 2 terms ($2n$ = 2) of the second series we would get B/A as 3/2
For $n = 2$ and $2n = 4$ we get $A = 5/2$ and $B = 15/4$ and $B/A = 15/4/5/2 = 3/2$
Thus, we can conclude that the required ratio is always constant at 3/2 and hence the correct option is (d).
30. We need to find the infinite sum of the GP: 1000, 800, 640..... (first term = 1000 and common ratio = 0.8) We get: infinite sum of the series as 1000/(1 – 0.8) = 5000, Thus option (b) is correct.
31. Questions such as these have to be solved on the basis of a reading of the pattern of the question. The sum upto the first term is: 1/5. Upto the second term it is 2/9 and upto the third term it is 3/12. It can be easily seen that for the first term, second term and third term the numerators are 1, 2 and 3 respectively. Also, for 1/5 — the 5 is the second value in the denominator of 1/1 × 5 (the first term); for 2/9 also the same pattern is followed— as 9 comes out of the denominator of the second term of series and tar 3/13 the 13 comes out of the denominator of the third term of the series and so on. The given series has 56 terms and hence the correct answer would be 56/225.
32. Solve this on the same pattern as Question 31 and you can easily see that for the first term sum of the series is $2-\sqrt{3}$, for 2 terms we have the sum as $\sqrt{5}-\sqrt{3}$ and so on. For the given series of 120 terms the sum would be $\sqrt{225}-\sqrt{3}=15-\sqrt{3}$. Option (a) is correct.
33. If you look for a few more terms in the series, the series is: 1, 1/3, 1/6, 1/10, 1/15, 1/21, 1/28, 1/36, 1/45, 1/55, 1/66, 1/78, 1/91, 1/105, 1/120, 1/136. 1/153 and so on. If you estimate the values of the individual terms it can be seen that the sum would tend to 2 and would not be good enough to reach even 2.25. Thus, option (a) is correct.
34. Solve this using trial and error. For 1 term the sum should be 15 and we get 15 only from the first option when we put is $n = 1$. Thus, option (a) is correct.
35. For this question too you would need to read the pattern of the values being followed. The given sum has 6 terms.
It can be seen that the sum to 1 term = 1/3
Sum to 2 terms = 3/5
Sum to 3 terms = 5/7
Hence, the sum to 6 terms would be 11/13.
36. The sum to infinite terms would tend to 1 because we would get (infinity)/(infinity + 2).
37. All members of A are smaller than all members of B. In order to visualise the effect of the change in sign

in k assume that A is {1, 2, 3...124} and B is {126, 12.7...250}. It can be seen that for this assumption of values neither options (a), (b) or (c) is correct.

38. If elements of A are in ascending order a_{124} would be the largest value in A. Also a_{125} would be the largest value in B. On interchanging a_{124} and a_{125}, A continues to be in ascending order, but B would lose its descending order arrangement since a_{124} would be the least value in B. Hence, option (a) is correct.

39. Since the minimum is in A and the maximum is in B, the value of x cannot be less than Maximum – Minimum.

40. It is evident that the whole question is built around Arithmetic progressions. The 5th row has an average of 55, while the 25th row has an average of 75. Since even column wise each column is arranged in an AP we can conclude the following:
1st row - average 51 - total = 25 × 51
2nd row - average 52 - total 25 × 52.....
25th row - average 75 - total 25 × 75
The overall total can be got by using averages as: 25 (51 + 52 + 53 + …..+ 75)= 25.1575 = 39375

41. The numbers forming an AP would be:
1234, 1357, 2345, 2468, 3210, 3456, 3579, 4321, 4567, 5432, 5678, 6543, 6420, 6789, 7654, 7531, 8765, 8642, 9876, 9753, 9630.
A total of 21 numbers.
If we count the GPs we get: 1248, 8421-a total of 2 numbers.
Hence, we have a total of 23, 4-digit numbers where the digits are either APs or GPs.
Thus, option (d) is correct.

42. Total vadapavs made = 500
Vadapavs with chicken patty = 250 (Number of terms in the series 1, 3, 5, 7, 9...499) out of which half of the vadapavs also have vegetable patty.
Vadapavs with only mushroom patty = 36 (Number of terms of the series 8, 22, 36, ….)
Vadapavs with chicken, mushroom and vegetable patty = 18 (Number of terms in the series 1, 29, 57... .
Required answer = 500 – 250 – 36 = 214.

43. From the above question, we have 18 such vadapavs.

44. The key to this question is what you understand from the statement— 'for two progressions out of P_1, P_2 and P_3 the average is itself a term of the original progression P.' For option (a) which tells us that the Progression P has 20 terms, we can see that P_1 would have 7 terms, P_2 would have 7 terms and P_3 would have 6 terms. Since, both P_1 and P_2 have an odd number of terms we can see that for P_1 and P_2 their 4th terms (being the middle terms for an AP with 7 terms) would be equal to their average. Since, all the terms of P_1, P_2 and P_3 have been taken out of the original AP P, we can see that for P_1 and P_2 their average itself would be a term of the original progression P. This would not occur for P_3 as P_3, has an even number of terms. Thus, 20 is a correct value for n.
Similarly, if we go for $n = 26$ from the second option we get:
P_1, P_2 and P_3 would have 9, 9 and 8 terms, respectively and the same condition would be met here too.
For n = 36 from the third option, the three progressions would have 12 terms each and none of them would have an odd number of terms.
Thus, option (d) is correct as both options (a) and (b) satisfy the conditions given in the problem.

45. Since, P_1 is formed out of every third term of P, the common difference of P_1 would be three times the common difference of P. Thus, the common difference of P would be 2.

46. S consists one a, two b's, three c's and so on. So total number of terms = 1 + 2 + 3 + …..+ 26 = $\frac{26}{2}(1+26) = 13 \times 27 = 351.$

47. For 16th alphabet total number of terms of S = 136. So 144th term of S will be 17th alphabet, which is q.

48. Let S' be the sum of all terms of the series S then according to the question:
$S' = 1a + 2b + 3c + 4d + 5e + \ldots + 26z = 1.1 + 2.3 + 3.5 + 4.7 + \ldots + 26.51 = \sum_{n=1}^{26} n(2n-1) =$
$\sum_{n=1}^{26} 2n^2 - n = 12051$

49. If $f(4x) = 8x + 1$ then $f(x) = 2x + 1$ & $f(2x) = 4x + 1$
$(4x + 1)^2 = (8x + 1)(2x + 1)$
$x = 0$
So for no positive value of x, $f(2x)$ is the G.M. of $f(x)$, $f(4x)$.

50. If $y = x + d$, $z = x + 2d$, $w = x + 3d$ then
$(x + d)^2 = x(x + 3d)$ or $d = x$
$w/x = 4x/x = 4$

51. Let the G.P. be 1, 3, 9, 27, 81,…
Let $m = 2$, $n = 3$, $p = 5$ then $(n - p) \log x + (p - m) \log y + (m - n) \log z = (3 - 5)\log 3 + (5 - 2)\log 9 + (2 - 3)\log 81 = -2\log 3 + 6 \log 3 - 4\log 3 = 0$

52. Go through options.
Option (a) $\frac{n(n+1)(n+2)}{6}$ for $n = 1$, sum = 1
For $n = 2$, Sum = 4
So option (a) is correct.

53. $A = 1/(1 - x)$ & $B = 1/(1 - y)$
$x = (A - 1)/A$ & $y = (B - 1)/B$
$1 + xy + x^2y^2 + x^3y^3 + \ldots =$
$$\frac{1}{1-xy} = \frac{1}{1-\frac{A-1}{A}\cdot\frac{B-1}{B}} = \frac{AB}{A+B-1}$$

54. Let the angles are x, xr, xr^2, xr^3
$x + xr + xr^2 + xr^3 = 360^0$.
The angles are 24^0, 48^0, 96^0, 192^0. Largest angle = 192^0

55. $S = 1 + 4 + 9 + 16 + ...$
$$S_n = \sum n^2 = \frac{1}{6}n(n+1)(2n+1)$$
$$S_{16} = \frac{1}{6}.16.17.33 = 1496$$

56. $S_{16} = 1 + (1 + 3) + (1 + 3 + 5) + (1 + 3 + 5 + 7) + (1 + 3 + 5 + 7 + 9) + 1$
$$S_{16} = \frac{1}{6}5(5+1)(2.5+1)+1 = 56$$

57. Going through the trial and error = $2(20)^2 + 3 - 2(19)^2 - 3 = 78$

58. $1^2 - 2^2 + 3^2 - 4^2 + 5^2 - 6^2 + ... = (1 - 2)(1 + 2) + (3 - 4)(3 + 4) + ... + (15 - 16)(15 + 16) + 17^2 = -(1 + 2 + 3 + 4 + ... + 16) + 17^2 = 289 - 136 = 153$

59. $3 + 6 + 10 + 15 + ...$
$(1 + 2) + (1 + 2 + 3) + (1 + 2 + 3 + 4) + ... = 1 + (1 + 2) + (1 + 2 + 3) + (1 + 2 + 3 + 4) + ... -1$
Required sum = Sum of 21 terms of series $1 + (1 + 2) + (1 + 2 + 3) + ,.... -1 = \sum_{n=21} \frac{(n+1)n}{2} - 1 = 1771 - 1 = 1770$

60. If we take $x = 4$ and $n = 1$ then $1^1 + 2^1 + 3^1 = 6$ is divisible by $1 + 2 + 3 = 6$. But for $n = 2$
$1^2 + 2^2 + 3^2 = 14$ is not divisible by 6 again for $n = 3$, $1^n + 2^n + 3^n$ divisible by 6 and so on. So for every odd value of n, $1^n + 2^n + 3^n + ... + x^n$ is always divisible by $1 + 2 + 3 + ...+ x$.

61. $3 = 4^1 - 1$
$14 = 4^2 - 2$
$61 = 4^3 - 3$
$252 = 4^4 - 4$
So 12th term = $4^{12} - 12$

Level of Difficulty (III)

1. Since the difference between the tenth and the sixth terms is −16, the common difference would be −4. Using a trial and error approach with the options, we can see that if we take the first term as 16, we will get the series 16,12,8,4,0,−4,−8,−12,−16,−20. We can see that both the conditions given in the question are met by this series. Hence, the first term would be 16.
2. Any sub-part of an A.P. is also an A.P.. Thus, the third term would be the average of the first and the fifth term. Hence, the third term would be 5.
3. A factor search for factor pairs of 456 give us the following possibilities. 1,456; 2,228; 3,152; 4,114; 6,76; 8,57; 12,38 and 19,24. A check of the conditions given in the problem, tells us that if we take 12 as the 4th term and 38 as the 5th term, we would get the series till 9 terms as: −66, −40, −14, 12, 38, 64, 90, 116, 142. In this series, we can see that the division of the 9th term by the 4th term gives us a quotient of 11 and a remainder of 10. Hence, the required first term is −66.
4. The distances covered by him (to and fro) would be 20, 40, 60, 80, 100, 120, 140, 160, 180, 200 and 220 to get a total distance of 1.32 km. There are 11 terms in this A.P. However, he must also have planted one sapling at the starting point and hence the number of saplings planted would be 12.
5. The answer would directly be P_2/P_1. Assume a series having a few number of terms, e.g. 1, 2, 4, 8, 16, 32. The value of P_2 here = 42, while P_1 = 21. The common ratio can be seen to be $P_2/P_1 = 2$.
6. Solve on the same pattern as above. The correct answer is option (c).
7. Solve this question using options. The average of the sum of the first 5 terms of the A.P. can be used to get the value of the third term of the A.P. If we try to use the options, in option 2, if the sum of the first 5 terms is 2.5, the third term must be 2.5/5 = 0.5. This means our A.P. is 2,1.25,0.5,−0.25,−1. The corresponding G.P. with the same 1st and 3rd terms is 2,1,0.5,0.25... The condition for the second term is also matched here.
8. Use the options to get the answer. For $n = 10$, we get the required ratio as 51/2.
9. For 1 digit, the sum would be $6^2 + 8$, for 2 digits, the sum would be $66^2 + 88$ and so on. Checking the options gives us option (b) as the correct answer.
10. The sum of the interior angles of any polygon of n sides is given by
$(n - 2) \times 180$. This needs to match the sum of the A.P. 120 + 125 + 130 +...n terms. For $n = 9$, we get the two sums equal and hence option (c) is correct.
11. Solve this one using options to check the correct answer.
12. Tracing the second and fourth terms through factor pairs of 160, we get the numbers that fit in the requirements of the problem as: 7, 10, 13, 16, 19, 22, 25. The sum of the series is 112.
13. The third and ninth terms of an 11 term A.P. are a pair of corresponding terms of the A.P. Hence, their average would be the average of the A.P. This gives us the required sum of the A.P. as $11 \times 5 = 55$.
14. $(a + 4d)^2 + (a + 10d)^2 = 3 \rightarrow a^2 + 14ad + 58d^2 = 1.5$. Also, $(a + d)(a + 13d) = P \rightarrow a^2 + 14ad + 13d^2 = P$. Further, we need to find the value of $a^2 + 14ad$ (product of the first and fifteenth terms of the A.P.). From the above two equations, we get that $45d^2 = \frac{3}{2} - P \rightarrow 13d^2 = \frac{(39-26P)}{90}$

Thus, $a^2 + 14ad = P - \frac{(39-26P)}{90} = (116P - 39)/90$.
Option (c) is correct.

15. Solve using options. The values in option (a) give you the required 12:13 ratio between the HM and the GM. Hence, option (a) is correct.
16. Solve this based on pattern of the options. The given series has 100 terms. For n = 100, the options can be converted as:
Option (a) = $n \times 2^{(n+1)} + 2$. This means that for 1 term, the sum should be $1 \times 2^2 + 2 = 6$. But we can see that for 1 term, the series has a sum of only $1 \times 2 = 2$. Hence, this option can be rejected. Option (c) satisfies the conditions.
Option (b) = $(n - 1) \times 2^n + 2$. For 1 term, this gives us a value of 2. For 2 terms, this gives us a value of 6, which does not match the actual value in the question. Hence, this option can be rejected.
17. Since the ratio of the second to the fourth term is given as ¼, we can conclude that the common ratio of the G.P. is 2. Also, $a + 8a = 108 \rightarrow 9a = 108 \rightarrow a = 12$. Thus, $x_3 = 48$.
18. You can try to fit in values to get the correct answer. a,b,c would be in G.P. If we take x, y and z as 1,2,4, we get a,b,c as 4,2 and 1, respectively to keep a^x, b^y and c^z equal.
19. The prime factors of 720 are: $2^4 \times 3^2 \times 5^1$. The required sum of factors would be: $(1 + 2 + 2^2 + 2^3 + 2^4)(1 + 3 + 3^2)(1 + 5) = 31 \times 13 \times 6 = 2418$.
20. Check the options to get option (a) as the correct answer.
21. The first term of the given A.P. is 2 and the common difference is also 2. Thus, the 11th term of the G.P. $= 2 \times 2^{10} = 2048$.
22. The minimum value of y would occur when all the three values are equal. Thus, $y^3 = 4 \rightarrow y = 2^{2/3}$.
23. For the product to be the maximum, since the sum of a_2, a_7 and a_{12} would be fixed; we would need to keep each of the three numbers as equal. Thus, the value of the common difference would be 0.
24. n^{th} term $= \frac{\sum n^3}{\sum(2n-1)} = \frac{1}{4}(n^2+2n+1)$
Sum of n terms of the given series =
$$\frac{1}{4}\left(\frac{1}{6}n(n+1)(2n+1)+n(n+1)+n\right)$$
For n = 10, the required sum = $\frac{1}{4}[505] = 126.25$
25. The corresponding A.P. would be 2.5, 1.0833,... This gives us a common difference of −1.4166. From the third term onwards, the A.P. and its reciprocal H.P. would both become negative. Hence, the largest term of the H.P. is the second term itself.
26. The series of plank sizes would be: 0.75 × 0.5, 0.75 × 1, 0.75 × 1.5....0.75 × 12. The sum of this A.P. is 112.5.
27. Each subsequent triangle would have the sum of sides halved from the previous triangle. Thus, the sum of the perimeters would be given by $P + P/2 + P/4 + P/8 + \ldots$ till infinite terms. Hence, the sum of all the perimeters of the infinite triangles would be $2P$.
28. The areas would be $A + A/4 + A/16 + \ldots$till infinite terms. The infinite sum of all the perimeters would be $4A/3$.
29. The first perimeter is 160, the second one is $\frac{160}{\sqrt{2}}$, the third one would be 80 and so on till infinite terms.
The infinite sum would be equal to $160(2+\sqrt{2})$.
30. The areas would consecutively get halved. So, the first area being 1600, the next one would be 800, then 400 and so on till infinite terms. Thus, the infinite sum would be 3200.
31. If the sum of the first n terms is 'x', the sum of the next n terms is given as '$2x$' (as defined in the problem). Naturally, the sum of the next n terms would be '$3x$' (When you add the same number of terms of an A.P. consecutively, you get another A.P.). Thus, the required ratio is $6x/x = 6$.
32. Since, the problem says that the cell breaks into two new cells, it means that the original cell no longer exists. Hence, after 1 hour there would be 2^1 cells, after 2 hours there would be 2^2 cells and so on. After 9 hours there would be 2^9 cells. Hence, option (c) is correct.
33. We need the sum of the A.P.: 101, 104, 107,... 497 = 133 × 299 = 39767.
34. Solve by taking values and checking with the options. If we take the numbers as 1 and 8, we would get $a = 4.5$ and b and c as 2 and 4 respectively. Then $(b^3 + c^3)/abc = 2$. None of the first three options gives us a value equal to 2. Hence, the correct answer is option (d).
35. This can be checked using any values of p, q, r. If we try with 1,2,3, we get the value as 0. If we try values of p, q, r as 2,3,4, we get the expression as positive. Hence, we conclude that the expression's value would always be non-negative.
36. For n = 1 sum = 2/3
For n = 2 sum = 20/27
For n = 3 sum = 1640/2187
None of the options matches these numbers and hence option (d) is correct.
37. $77777\ldots7777 = 7(10^{132} + \ldots + 10^2 + 10^1 + 1) = \frac{7(10^{133}-1)}{10-1} = \frac{7(10^{133}-1)}{9}$
$10^{133} - 1$ is divisible by 9. Hence the given number is a composite number. Option (c) is correct.
38. $S = n^2 + 1 + n^2 + 2 + \ldots + n^2 + 2n = 2n^3 + n(2n + 1) = n(2n^2 + 2n + 1)$

Option (a) is correct.

Alternative method: Suppose $n = 2$ then 1st term of the series will be $2^2 + 1 = 5$. Now we want to find the sum of first $2n = 4$ terms. First 4 terms of the series will be 5, 6, 7, 8. Sum = 26.

If we put $n = 2$ in the above options then only option (a) satisfies.

39. m^{th} term of the series $= \frac{1}{m! + (m+1)!}$

$$= \frac{1}{(m+1)!} - \frac{1}{(m+2)!}$$

$$S = \frac{1}{2!} - \frac{1}{3!} + \frac{1}{3!} - \frac{1}{4!} + \ldots + \frac{1}{20!} - \frac{1}{21!} = \frac{1}{2!} - \frac{1}{21!}.$$

Option (a) is correct.

40. $\frac{a^n + c^n}{2} > \left(\frac{a+c}{2}\right)^n$, if n does not lie between 0 and 1.

But we know that A.M. > H.M.

b is the H.M. of a and c.

$$\frac{a+c}{2} > b$$

As $n > 1$ $\left(\frac{a+c}{2}\right)^n > b^n$

$$\frac{a^n + c^n}{2} > \left(\frac{a+c}{2}\right)^n > b^n$$

$a^n + c^n > 2b^n$. Option (c) is correct.

41. $S = \frac{3}{1^2.2^2} + \frac{5}{2^2.3^2} + \frac{7}{3^2.4^2} + \ldots$

$$= \left(1 - \frac{1}{2^2}\right) + \left(\frac{1}{2^2} - \frac{1}{3^2}\right) + \left(\frac{1}{3^2} - \frac{1}{4^2}\right) + \ldots + \left(\frac{1}{17^2} - \frac{1}{18^2}\right)$$

$$= 1 - \frac{1}{18^2} = \frac{323}{324}$$

42. $S = \frac{4}{11} + \frac{44}{11^2} + \frac{444}{11^3} + \frac{4444}{11^4} + \ldots$

$$\frac{S}{11} = \frac{4}{11^2} + \frac{44}{11^3} + \frac{444}{11^4} + \ldots$$

$$S - \frac{S}{11} = \frac{4}{11} + \frac{40}{11^2} + \frac{400}{11^3} + \ldots$$

$$\frac{10S}{11} = \frac{4}{11}\left(1 + \frac{10}{11} + \frac{100}{11^2} + \ldots\right)$$

$$\frac{10S}{11} = \frac{4}{11}\left(\frac{1}{1 - \frac{10}{11}}\right) = 4$$

$S = 44/10 = 22/5$

43. $S = \frac{1}{2.5} + \frac{1}{5.8} + \frac{1}{8.11} + \ldots + \infty$

$$S = \frac{1}{3}\left(\frac{1}{2} - \frac{1}{5} + \frac{1}{5} - \frac{1}{8} + \frac{1}{8} - \frac{1}{11} + \ldots - \frac{1}{\infty}\right)$$

$$= \frac{1}{3} \times \frac{1}{2} = \frac{1}{6}$$

44. We can easily solve these problems by considering suitable values.

Let G.P. be 1, 2, 4, 8, 16, 32 and A.P. be 1, 7.2, 13.4, 19.6, 25.8, 32.

$A = 99$, $B = 63$. So $A > B$.

45. $4 + \frac{1}{2} + 4 + \frac{1}{6} + 4 + \frac{1}{12} + \ldots 4 + \frac{1}{2450}$

$$= 4 + \left(1 - \frac{1}{2}\right) + 4 + \left(\frac{1}{2} - \frac{1}{3}\right) + 4 + \left(\frac{1}{3} - \frac{1}{4}\right) + \ldots$$

$$+ 4 + \left(\frac{1}{49} - \frac{1}{50}\right)$$

$$= 49 \times 4 + \left(1 - \frac{1}{2} + \frac{1}{2} - \frac{1}{3} + \frac{1}{3} - \ldots + \frac{1}{49} - \frac{1}{50}\right)$$

$$= 196 + \frac{49}{50} = \frac{9849}{50}$$

46. Let the common difference of the series X be d_1 and that of Y be d_2.

Since $x_n - y_n = n - 2$, $x_1 - y_1 = -1$ or $y_1 = x_1 + 1$

$x_3 = y_5$

$x_1 + 2d_1 = y_1 + 4d_2$

$x_1 + 2d_1 = x_1 + 1 + 4d_2$

$2d_1 - 4d_2 = 1$

$x_{99} - y_{197} = x_1 + 98d_1 - y_1 - 196d_2 = -1 + 49(2d_1 - 4d_2)$

$= -1 + 49 = 48$. Option (b) is correct.

47. If a be the 1st term and d be the common difference of the A.P., the 4th term of the series will be $a + 3d$. If $a + 3d$ is divisible by d then a should be divisible by d. Hence the cases are:

$d = 1$, $a = 1, 2, 3, 4, 5, 6, 7, 8, 9$

$d = 2$, $a = 2, 4, 6$

$d = 3$, $a = 3$

So the required answer is $9 + 3 + 1 = 13$

48. If $a - 2d$ be the first term and d be the common difference of A.P., then according to the question:

$(a - 2d)(a - d)a(a + d)(a + 2d) = 3840$ (1)

$$\frac{a-d}{a-2d} = \frac{a+d}{a-d}$$

$$d(3d - a) = 0$$

$$a = 3d$$

By putting $a = 3d$ in equation 1 we get:

$d \times 2d \times 3d \times 4d \times 5d = 3840$

By solving we get $d = 2$ and $a = 6$

10th term $= 6 + 9.2 = 24$.

49. Let $x = -1/3$

$S = (1 + x)(1 + x^2)(1 + x^4)....$

$(1 - x)S = (1 - x)(1 + x)(1 + x^2)(1 + x^4)...$

$(1 - x)S = (1 - x^2)(1 + x^2)(1 + x^4)(1 + x^8).....$

$(1 - x)S = (1 - x^4)(1 + x^4)(1 + x^8).....$

Since $x < 0$ and $|x| < 1$ so the value of RHS would be equal to 1.

$(1 - x)\ S = 1$ or $S = 1/(1 - x)$ or $1/(1 - (-1/3)) = 3/4$.

50. a, b, c, d are in A.P.

$\frac{a}{abcd}, \frac{b}{abcd}, \frac{c}{abcd}, \frac{d}{abcd}$ are also in A.P.

$\frac{1}{bcd}, \frac{1}{acd}, \frac{1}{abd}, \frac{1}{abc}$ are also in A.P.

Hence, their reciprocals are in H.P.

Space for Rough Work

SERIES

Questions based on mixed and infinite series are quite common in the CAT and XAT examinations. You would also see a fair presence of the same in other Management entrance examinations like SNAP and NMAT. After getting the process to solve the infinite series summation of geometric progression, we need to understand the process to calculate the summation of mixed series using different methods. Let's now take a look at the most commonly asked questions in various examinations.

Example 1: Find the value of S, where $S = 4/3 + 10/9 + 28/27 + 82/81 + \ldots 99$ terms.

Solution: To solve these kinds of questions, we need to break the series in the below mentioned manner:

$S = 4/3 + 10/9 + 28/27 + 82/81 + \ldots$

$S = 1 + 1/3 + 1 + 1/9 + 1 + 1/27 + 1 + 1/81 + \ldots$

$S = [1 + 1 + 1 + \ldots 99 \text{ terms}] + [1/3 + 1/9 + 1/27 + 1/81 + \ldots 99 \text{ terms}]$

$$S = 99 + \frac{\frac{1}{3}\left[1-\left(\frac{1}{3}\right)^{99}\right]}{\left[1-\frac{1}{3}\right]} = 99 + \frac{1}{2}\left[1-\left(\frac{1}{3}\right)^{99}\right]$$

Example 2: Find the value of S, where

$$S = \frac{1}{2}+\frac{1}{6}+\frac{1}{12}+\frac{1}{20}+\ldots$$

Solution: When the numerators of all the terms are the same, the following process is adopted:

$$S = \frac{1}{1\times 2}+\frac{1}{2\times 3}+\frac{1}{3\times 4}+\ldots = 1-\frac{1}{2}+\frac{1}{2}-\frac{1}{3}+\frac{1}{3}-\frac{1}{4}+\frac{1}{4}-\frac{1}{5}+\ldots$$

$$-\frac{1}{\infty} = 1-\frac{1}{\infty} = 1$$

What we have done here is first rewrite each term by re-writing its' denominator. Next, we break each term as the difference of two terms such that the second part of each term would get cancelled with the first part of the next term. In such a manner, only the first and the last term would remain at the end.

Example 3: Find the value of S, where

$$S = 1+\frac{1}{11}+\frac{3}{11^2}+\frac{5}{11^3}+\frac{7}{11^4}+\ldots$$

Solution: When the numerators of the series are forming an arithmetic progression and the denominator form a geometric series, then we can solve the series in the following manner.

$$S = 1+\frac{1}{11}+\frac{3}{11^2}+\frac{5}{11^3}+\frac{7}{11^4}+\ldots \quad (1)$$

Multiply the given series by 1/11

$$\left(\frac{1}{11}S\right) = \frac{1}{11}+\frac{1}{11^2}+\frac{3}{11^3}+\frac{5}{11^4}+\ldots \quad (2)$$

Equation 1-Equation 2 gives:

$$\frac{10S}{11} = 1+\left[\frac{2}{11^2}+\frac{2}{11^3}+\frac{2}{11^4}+\frac{2}{11^5}+\ldots\right] = 1+\frac{2}{11^2}\left(\frac{1}{1-\frac{1}{11}}\right) = \frac{56}{55}$$

Note: The series in the bracket in the above expression is an infinite geometric progression with common ratio as 1/11.

$$S = \frac{56}{55}\times\frac{11}{10} = \frac{56}{50} = \frac{28}{25}.$$

Practice Exercise

1. $S = 3/2 + 5/4 + 9/8 + 17/16 + \ldots$ 99 terms
   $S = ?$
   (a) $100-\frac{1}{2^{99}}$ (b) $99-\frac{1}{2^{99}}$
   (c) $10-\frac{1}{2^{99}}$ (d) None of these

2. Find the value of S, where
   $$S = 1+\frac{1}{11}+\frac{3}{11^2}+\frac{5}{11^3}+\frac{7}{11^4}+\ldots$$

3. $$S = 1+\frac{2}{11}+\frac{5}{11^2}+\frac{10}{11^3}+\frac{17}{11^4}+\ldots$$
   What is the value of S?
   (a) 154/125 (b) 154/135
   (c) 145/125 (d) None of these

4. $$M = \left(1+\left(-\frac{2}{3}\right)\right)\left(1+\left(-\frac{2}{3}\right)^2\right)\left(1+\left(-\frac{2}{3}\right)^4\right)\left(1+\left(-\frac{2}{3}\right)^8\right)\ldots$$
   ..infinite terms
   Find the value of M.

5. If $a_1 = 1/(2 \times 5)$, $a_2 = 1/(5 \times 8)$, $a_3 = 1/(8 \times 11)$, ……, then $a_1, + a_2, + a_3, + \ldots\ldots\ldots a_{100}$ is
   (a) 25/151 (b) 1/2
   (c) 1/4 (d) 111/55

6. Find the value of S, where
   $$S = \left(\frac{\sqrt{3}}{\sqrt{3}+3}+\frac{\sqrt{5}}{\sqrt{15}+5}+\frac{\sqrt{7}}{\sqrt{35}+7}+\ldots+\frac{\sqrt{25}}{\sqrt{575}+25}\right)$$

7. Find the value of S, where
   $$S = \frac{1}{1!+2!}+\frac{1}{2!+3!}+\frac{1}{3!+4!}+\ldots+\frac{1}{19!+20!}$$
   (a) $2\left(\frac{1}{2!}-\frac{1}{21!}\right)$ (b) $1-\frac{1}{20!}$
   (c) $\frac{1}{2!}-\frac{1}{19!}$ (d) None of these

8. What is the value of the following expression?

$$\frac{1}{(2^2-1)}+\frac{1}{(4^2-1)}+\frac{1}{(6^2-1)}+\ldots\ldots\ldots+\frac{1}{(20^2-1)}$$

(a) $\frac{9}{19}$ (b) $\frac{10}{19}$
(c) $\frac{10}{21}$ (d) $\frac{11}{21}$

9. Find the sum of the following series:

$$\frac{2}{1!}+\frac{3}{2!}+\frac{6}{3!}+\frac{11}{4!}+\frac{18}{5!}+\ldots$$

(a) 3e (b) 3e – 1
(c) 3(e – 1) (d) 3e + 1

10. Evaluate $\frac{1}{3^2-1}+\frac{1}{5^2-1}+\frac{1}{7^2-1}+\ldots+\frac{1}{99^2-1}$

(a) $\frac{49}{100}$ (b) $\frac{49}{200}$
(c) $\frac{51}{200}$ (d) $\frac{51}{200}$

11. The value of 1/6 + 1/12 + 1/20 +……………… 1/90 is equal to
(a) 0.4 (b) 0.7
(c) 0.9 (d) 0.75

12. Find the value of *S*, where

$$S=\frac{1}{2}+\frac{1}{6}+\frac{1}{12}+\frac{1}{20}+\ldots\frac{1}{9900}$$

13. Find the value of *S*, where

$$S=\frac{1}{3}+\frac{1}{15}+\frac{1}{35}+\frac{1}{63}+\ldots\frac{1}{195}$$

(a) 7/15 (b) 6/7
(c) 6/13 (d) None of these

14. Find the value of *S*, where

$$S=\frac{1}{12}+\frac{1}{60}+\frac{1}{140}+\frac{1}{196}+\ldots+\frac{1}{1020}$$

15. Find the value of *S*, where

$$S=\frac{1}{4}+\frac{1}{28}+\frac{1}{70}+\frac{1}{130}+\ldots+\frac{1}{700}$$

16. $S=\frac{1}{9}+\frac{1}{153}+\frac{1}{425}+\frac{1}{825}=?$

ANSWER KEY

1. (a)	2. 28/25	3. (a)	4. 3/5
5. (a)	6. 2	7. (d)	8. (c)
9. (c)	10. (a)	11. (a)	12. 0.99
13. (a)	14. 2/17	15. 9/28	16. 4/33

SOLUTIONS AND SHORTCUTS

1. *S* = 3/2 + 5/4 + 9/8 + 17/16 + ….. 99 terms
S = (1 + ½) + (1 + ¼) + (1 + 1/8) + (1 + 1/16) + ….. 99 terms
S = (1 + 1 + 1 + …. 99 terms) + (1/2 + ¼ + 1/8 + 1/16 + ….. 99 terms)

$$S=99+(\frac{1}{2}+\frac{1}{2^2}+\frac{1}{2^3}+\ldots+99 \text{ terms})$$

$$S=99+\frac{\left(\frac{1}{2}\right)\left(1-\frac{1}{2^{99}}\right)}{1-\frac{1}{2}}=99+1-\frac{1}{2^{99}}=100-\frac{1}{2^{99}}.$$

Hence, option (a) is correct.

2. $$S=1+\frac{1}{11}+\frac{3}{11^2}+\frac{5}{11^3}+\frac{7}{11^4}+\ldots \quad (1)$$

$$\left(\frac{1}{11}S\right)=\frac{1}{11}+\frac{1}{11^2}+\frac{3}{11^3}+\frac{5}{11^4}+\ldots \quad (2)$$

Subtracting (2) from (1) gives us:

$$\frac{10S}{11}=1+\frac{2}{11^2}+\frac{2}{11^3}+\frac{2}{11^4}+\frac{2}{11^5}+\ldots=1+\frac{2}{11^2}\left(\frac{1}{1-\frac{1}{11}}\right)=\frac{56}{55}$$

$$S=\frac{56}{55}\times\frac{11}{10}=\frac{56}{50}=\frac{28}{25}.$$

3. $$S=1+\frac{2}{11}+\frac{5}{11^2}+\frac{10}{11^3}+\frac{17}{11^4}+\ldots \quad (1)$$

Multiplying by 1/11, we get:

$$S/11=\frac{1}{11}+\frac{2}{11^2}+\frac{5}{11^3}+\frac{10}{11^4}+\ldots \quad (2)$$

$$S-\frac{S}{11}=\frac{10S}{11}=1+\frac{1}{11}+\frac{3}{11^2}+\frac{5}{11^3}+\frac{7}{11^4}+\ldots \quad (3)$$

Again multiplying by 1/11, we get:

$$\frac{10}{11^2}S=\frac{1}{11}+\frac{1}{11^2}+\frac{3}{11^3}+\frac{5}{11^4}+\frac{7}{11^5}+\ldots \quad (4)$$

Subtracting (4) from (3):

$$\frac{10}{11}\left(\frac{10}{11}S\right)=1+\frac{2}{11^2}+\frac{2}{11^3}+\frac{2}{11^4}+\ldots$$

$$\frac{100}{121}S=1+\frac{2}{11^2}\left(\frac{1}{1-\frac{1}{11}}\right)=\frac{56}{55}$$

S = 154/125
Hence, option (a) is correct.

4. $\left(1-\left(-\frac{2}{3}\right)\right) M=\left(1-\left(-\frac{2}{3}\right)\right)\left(1+\left(-\frac{2}{3}\right)\right)\left(1+\left(-\frac{2}{3}\right)^2\right)\left(1+\left(-\frac{2}{3}\right)^4\right)\left(1+\left(-\frac{2}{3}\right)^8\right)\ldots..$

$\frac{5}{3} M=\left(1-\left(-\frac{2}{3}\right)^2\right)\left(1+\left(-\frac{2}{3}\right)^2\right)\left(1+\left(-\frac{2}{3}\right)^4\right)\left(1+\left(-\frac{2}{3}\right)^8\right)\ldots$

$\frac{5}{3} M=\left(1-\left(-\frac{2}{3}\right)^4\right)\left(1+\left(-\frac{2}{3}\right)^4\right)\left(1+\left(-\frac{2}{3}\right)^8\right)\left(1+\left(-\frac{2}{3}\right)^{16}\right)..$

The expression on the RHS can be rewritten as: $\left(1-\left(-\frac{2}{3}\right)^{\infty}\right)$

$\left(-\frac{2}{3}\right)^{\infty}$ can be approximated as 0.

Hence, $\frac{5}{3}M = 1$ OR $M = 3/5$

5. $a_1=\frac{1}{2\times 5}=\frac{1}{3}\left(\frac{1}{2}-\frac{1}{5}\right)$

$a_2=\frac{1}{5\times 8}=\frac{1}{3}\left(\frac{1}{5}-\frac{1}{8}\right)$

.
.
.
.

$a_{100}=\frac{1}{299\times 302}=\frac{1}{3}\left(\frac{1}{299}-\frac{1}{302}\right)$

The required sum $= a_1 + a_2 + a_3 + a_4 + a_5 \ldots.. + a_{100}$

$=\frac{1}{3}\left(\frac{1}{2}-\frac{1}{5}\right)+\frac{1}{3}\left(\frac{1}{5}-\frac{1}{8}\right)+\ldots..+\frac{1}{3}\left(\frac{1}{299}-\frac{1}{302}\right)=$

$=\frac{1}{3}\left(\frac{1}{2}-\frac{1}{302}\right)=\frac{1}{3}\times\frac{300}{604}=\frac{100}{604}=\frac{25}{151}$

Hence, option (a) is correct.

6. $S=\left(\frac{\sqrt{3}}{\sqrt{3}+3}+\frac{\sqrt{5}}{\sqrt{15}+5}+\frac{\sqrt{7}}{\sqrt{35}+7}+\ldots+\frac{\sqrt{25}}{\sqrt{575}+25}\right)$

$S=\left(\frac{\sqrt{3}}{\sqrt{3}\left(1+\sqrt{3}\right)}+\frac{\sqrt{5}}{\sqrt{5}\left(\sqrt{3}+\sqrt{5}\right)}+\frac{\sqrt{7}}{\sqrt{7}(\sqrt{5}+\sqrt{7}}\right)+\ldots+\frac{\sqrt{25}}{\sqrt{25}(\sqrt{23}+\sqrt{25})}\Bigg)$

$S=\frac{1}{1+\sqrt{3}}+\frac{1}{\sqrt{3}+\sqrt{5}}+\frac{1}{\sqrt{5}+\sqrt{7}}+\ldots+\frac{1}{\sqrt{23}+\sqrt{25}}$

$S=\frac{\sqrt{3}-1}{3-1}+\frac{\sqrt{5}-\sqrt{3}}{5-3}+\frac{\sqrt{7}-\sqrt{5}}{7-5}+\ldots+\frac{\sqrt{25}-\sqrt{23}}{\sqrt{25}+\sqrt{23}}$

$=\frac{\sqrt{25}-1}{2}=\frac{5-1}{2}=2.$

7. Any expression of the sort: $1/[(n! + (n + 1)!]$ can be rewritten as

$=\frac{1}{n!(n+2)}=\frac{(n+1)}{(n+2)!}=\frac{1}{(n+1)!}-\frac{1}{(n+2)!}$

Put n= 1, 2, 3, …..19 to get:

$\left[\frac{1}{2!}-\frac{1}{3!}\right]+\left[\frac{1}{3!}-\frac{1}{4!}\right]+\ldots+\left[\frac{1}{20!}-\frac{1}{21!}\right]=\frac{1}{2!}-\frac{1}{20!}$

Hence, option (d) is correct.

8. The series can be simplified as

$\frac{1}{(2^2-1)}+\frac{1}{(4^2-1)}+\frac{1}{(6^2-1)}+\ldots\ldots\ldots\ldots.+\frac{1}{(20^2-1)}$

$=\frac{1}{3}+\frac{1}{15}+\frac{1}{35}+\ldots\ldots\ldots\ldots\ldots\ldots+\frac{1}{399}$

$=\frac{1}{1\times 3}+\frac{1}{3\times 5}+\frac{1}{5\times 7}+\ldots\ldots\ldots\ldots\ldots\ldots+\frac{1}{19\times 21}$

$=\frac{1}{2}\left(1-\frac{1}{3}\right)+\frac{1}{2}\left(\frac{1}{3}-\frac{1}{5}\right)+\frac{1}{2}\left(\frac{1}{5}-\frac{1}{7}\right)+\ldots\ldots\ldots\ldots\ldots\ldots$

$+\frac{1}{2}\left(\frac{1}{19}-\frac{1}{21}\right)$

$=\frac{1}{2}-\frac{1}{42}=\frac{10}{21}$. Hence, option (c) is correct.

9. $S=\frac{2}{1!}+\frac{3}{2!}+\frac{6}{3!}+\frac{11}{4!}+\frac{18}{5!}+\ldots..$

Let T_n be the nth term of S.

We can observe that $T_n=\frac{n^2-2n+3}{n!}$

$S=\sum_{n=1}^{\infty}\frac{n^2}{n!}-\frac{2n}{n!}+\frac{3}{n!}$

$S=\sum\frac{n^2}{n!}-\sum\frac{2n}{n!}+\sum\frac{3}{n!}$. Evaluating these components individually, we see that:

$\sum\frac{n^2}{n!}=\sum\frac{n}{(n-1)!}=\sum\frac{n-1+1}{(n-1)!}=\sum_{n=2}^{\infty}\frac{1}{(n-2)!}+$

$\sum_{n=1}^{\infty}\frac{1}{(n-1)!}=e+e=2e$

$$\left(Since, e = 1 + \frac{1}{1!} + \frac{1}{2!} + \frac{1}{3!} + \frac{1}{4!} + ...\infty\right)$$

$$\sum_{n=1}^{\infty}\frac{2n}{n!} = 2\sum_{n=1}^{\infty}\frac{1}{(n-1)!} = 2e$$

$$\sum_{n=1}^{\infty}\frac{3}{n!} = 3\sum_{n=1}^{\infty}\frac{1}{(n)!} = 3(e-1)$$

$$S = \sum_{n=1}^{\infty}\frac{n^2}{n!} - \frac{2n}{n!} + \frac{3}{n!} = 2e - 2e + 3e - 3 = 3(e-1)$$

Hence, option (c) is correct.

10. $S = \frac{1}{3^2-1} + \frac{1}{5^2-1} + \frac{1}{7^2-1} + ... + \frac{1}{99^2-1}$

$= \frac{1}{2\times4} + \frac{1}{4\times6} + \frac{1}{6\times8} + ... + \frac{1}{98\times100}$

$= \frac{1}{2}\left(\frac{1}{2} - \frac{1}{4} + \frac{1}{4} - \frac{1}{6} + \frac{1}{6} - \frac{1}{8} + ... + \frac{1}{98} - \frac{1}{100}\right)$

$= \frac{1}{2}\left(\frac{1}{2} - \frac{1}{100}\right) = \frac{49}{200}$. Hence, option (a) is correct.

11. Consider $S = 1/6 + 1/12 + 1/20 .... + 1/90$
$= 1/2 \times 3 + 1/3 \times 4 + 1/4 \times 5 + ... + 1/9 \times 10$
$= 1/2 - 1/3 + 1/3 - 1/4 + 1/4 - 1/5 + ... + 1/9 - 1/10$
$= 1/2 - 1/10 = 0.4$. Hence, option (a) is correct.

12. $S = \frac{1}{2} + \frac{1}{6} + \frac{1}{12} + \frac{1}{20} + ... \frac{1}{9900} = 1 - \frac{1}{2} + \frac{1}{2} - \frac{1}{3} + \frac{1}{3} - \frac{1}{4} +$

$... + \frac{1}{99} - \frac{1}{100} = 1 - \frac{1}{100} = 0.99$

13. $S = \frac{1}{3} + \frac{1}{15} + \frac{1}{35} + \frac{1}{63} + ... \frac{1}{195} = [\frac{1}{1\times3} + \frac{1}{3\times5} + \frac{1}{5\times7} + ...]$

$= \frac{1}{2}\left[1 - \frac{1}{3} + \frac{1}{3} - \frac{1}{5} + \frac{1}{5} - \frac{1}{7} + \frac{1}{7} - \frac{1}{9} + ... + \frac{1}{13} - \frac{1}{15}\right]$

$= \frac{1}{2} \times \left[1 - \frac{1}{15}\right] = \frac{7}{15}$

Hence, option (a) is correct.

14. $S = \frac{1}{12} + \frac{1}{60} + \frac{1}{140} + \frac{1}{252} + ... + \frac{1}{1020} = \frac{1}{4}\left[\frac{4}{12} + \frac{4}{60} +\right.$

$\left.\frac{4}{140} + \frac{4}{252} + ... + \frac{4}{1020}\right] = \frac{1}{4}\left[\frac{1}{2} - \frac{1}{6} + \frac{1}{6} - \frac{1}{10} + \frac{1}{10} - \frac{1}{14}\right.$

$\left.+ \frac{1}{14} - \frac{1}{18} + ... + \frac{1}{30} - \frac{1}{34}\right] = \frac{1}{4}\left[\frac{1}{2} - \frac{1}{34}\right] = \frac{1}{4} \times \frac{32}{68} = \frac{8}{68}$

$= \frac{2}{17}$

15. $S = \frac{1}{4} + \frac{1}{28} + \frac{1}{70} + \frac{1}{130} + ... + \frac{1}{700} = \frac{1}{3}\left[\frac{3}{4} + \frac{3}{28} + \frac{3}{70} +\right.$

$\left.... + \frac{3}{700}\right] = \frac{1}{3}\left[1 - \frac{1}{4} + \frac{1}{4} - \frac{1}{7} + \frac{1}{7} - \frac{1}{10} + ... + \frac{1}{25} - \frac{1}{28}\right]$

$= \frac{1}{3}\left[1 - \frac{1}{28}\right] = \frac{9}{28}$

16. $S = \frac{1}{9} + \frac{1}{153} + \frac{1}{425} + \frac{1}{825} = \frac{1}{8}\left[\frac{8}{9} + \frac{8}{153} + \frac{8}{425} + \frac{8}{825}\right]$

$= \frac{1}{8}\left[1 - \frac{1}{9} + \frac{1}{9} - \frac{1}{17} + \frac{1}{17} - \frac{1}{25} + \frac{1}{25} - \frac{1}{33}\right] = \frac{1}{8}\left[1 - \frac{1}{33}\right]$

$= \frac{4}{33}$

Note on how to think in Questions 11 to 16: Observe the progression of the denominators and how the denominators can be constructed as a product of 2 numbers. For example, in question 11: $1/2 + 1/6 + 1/12$, we can see that $2 = 1 \times 2$, $6 = 2 \times 3$, $12 = 3 \times 4$, $20 = 4 \times 5$ and so on. Hence, we rewrite the expression as: $1/2 \times 3 + 1/3 \times 4 + 1/4 \times 5 + ... + 1/9 \times 10$ $= 1/2 - 1/3 + 1/3 - 1/4 + 1/4 - 1/5 + ...+ 1/9 - 1/10$ and solve. Question 12 is solved on a similar process and pattern.

In question 13, however, we are given the expression $\frac{1}{3} + \frac{1}{15} + \frac{1}{35} + \frac{1}{63} + ... \frac{1}{195}$.

In such an expression, the denominators being 3, 15, 35 and so on, they can be visualised as: $3 = 1 \times 3$; $15 = 3 \times 5$; $35 = 5 \times 7$ and so on. We can observe that the difference between the multipliers is 2 for each denominator. In this case, when we rewrite the expression as: $\left[\frac{1}{1\times3} + \frac{1}{3\times5} + \frac{1}{5\times7} + ...\right]$, the next transformation requires as 1/2 to multiply the expression. Hence, we can rewrite this as:

$\frac{1}{2}\left[1 - \frac{1}{3} + \frac{1}{3} - \frac{1}{5} + \frac{1}{5} - \frac{1}{7} + \frac{1}{7} - \frac{1}{9} + ... + \frac{1}{13} - \frac{1}{15}\right]$

Similarly, in question 16, looking through the denominators, we see that:
9, 153, 425, etc., are the denominators and hence they can be written as: $9 = 1 \times 9$; $153 = 9 \times 17$; $425 = 17 \times 25$ and so on. Hence, when we do the last step in the question, we use a 1/8 to multiply the expression as we see in:

$\frac{1}{8}\left[1 - \frac{1}{9} + \frac{1}{9} - \frac{1}{17} + \frac{1}{17} - \frac{1}{25} + \frac{1}{25} - \frac{1}{33}\right]$

TASTE OF THE EXAMS—BLOCK I

CAT

1. If a and b are integers of opposite signs such that $(a + 3)^2 : b^2 = 9 : 1$ and $(a - 1)^2 : (b - 1)^2 = 4 : 1$, then the ratio $a^2 : b^2$ is **(CAT 2017)**
(a) 9 : 4 (b) 81 : 4
(c) 1 : 4 (d) 25 : 4

2. If $x + 1 = x^2$ and $x > 0$, then $2x^4$ is **(CAT 2017)**
(a) $6 + 4\sqrt{5}$ (b) $3 + 5\sqrt{5}$
(c) $5 + 3\sqrt{5}$ (d) $7 + 3\sqrt{5}$

3. The number of solutions (x, y, z) to the equation $x - y - z = 25$, where x, y, and z are positive integers such that $x \le 40$, $y \le 12$, and $z \le 12$ is **(CAT 2017)**
(a) 101 (b) 99
(c) 87 (d) 105

4. For how many integers n, will the inequality $(n - 5)(n - 10) - 3(n - 2) \le 0$ be satisfied? **(CAT 2017)**

5. If the square of the 7th term of an arithmetic progression with positive common difference equals the product of the 3rd and 17th terms, then the ratio of the first term to the common difference is **(CAT 2017)**
(a) 2 : 3 (b) 3 : 2
(c) 3 : 4 (d) 4 : 3

6. Let $a_1, a_2, \ldots\ldots\ldots a_{3n}$ be an arithmetic progression with $a_1 = 3$ and $a_2 = 7$. If $a_1 + a_2 + \ldots. + a_{3n} = 1830$, then what is the smallest positive integer 'm' such that $m \times (a_1 + a_2 + \ldots. + a_n) > 1830$? **(CAT 2017)**
(a) 8 (b) 9
(c) 10 (d) 11

7. If the product of three consecutive positive integers is 15600 then the sum of the squares of these integers is **(CAT 2017)**
(a) 1777 (b) 1785
(c) 1875 (d) 1877

8. Let a_1, a_2, a_3, a_4, a_5 be a sequence of five consecutive odd numbers. Consider a new sequence of five consecutive even numbers ending with $2a_3$. If the sum of the numbers in the new sequence is 450, then a_5 is **(CAT 2017)**

9. How many different pairs (a, b) of positive integers are there such that $a \le b$ and $\frac{1}{a} + \frac{1}{b} = \frac{1}{9}$? **(CAT 2017)**

10. An infinite geometric progression $a_1, a_2, a_3 \ldots$ has the property that $a_n = 3(a_{n+1} + a_{n+2} + \ldots.)$ for every $n \ge 1$. If the sum $a_1 + a_2 + a_3 + \ldots.. = 32$, then a_5 is **(CAT 2017)**
(a) 1/32 (b) 2/32
(c) 3/32 (d) 4/32

11. If $a_1 = 1/2 \times 5$, $a_2 = 1/5 \times 8$, $a_3 = 1/8 \times 11$, ……, then $a_1 + a_2 + a_3 + \ldots\ldots\ldots. a_{100}$ is **(CAT 2017)**
(a) 25/151 (b) 1/2
(c) 1/4 (d) 111/55

12. While multiplying three real numbers, Ashok took one of the numbers as 73 instead of 37. As a result, the product went up by 720. Then the minimum possible value of the sum of squares of the other two numbers is **(CAT 2018)**

13. If $u^2 + (u - 2v - 1)^2 = -4v(u + v)$, then what is the value of $u + 3v$? **(CAT 2018)**
(a) $\frac{1}{4}$ (b) $\frac{1}{2}$
(c) 0 (d) –1/4

14. Let x, y, z be three positive real numbers in a geometric progression such that $x < y < z$. If $5x$, $16y$, and $12z$ are in an arithmetic progression then the common ratio of the geometric progression is **(CAT 2018)**

15. The number of integers x such that $0.25 < 2^x < 200$, and $2^x + 2$ is perfectly divisible by either 3 or 4, is **(CAT 2018)**

16. Given that $x^{2018}y^{2017} = \frac{1}{2}$ and $x^{2016}y^{2019} = 8$ the value of $x^2 + y^3$ is **(CAT 2018)**
(a) 37/4 (b) 31/4
(c) 35/4 (d) 33/4

17. Let $a_1, a_2, \ldots, a_{52}$ be positive integers such that $a_1 < a_2 < \ldots < a_{52}$. Suppose, their arithmetic mean is one less than the arithmetic mean of $a_2, a_3, \ldots, a_{52}$. If $a_{52} = 100$, then the largest possible value of a_1 is **(CAT 2018)**
(a) 48 (b) 20
(c) 45 (d) 23

18. Let $t_1, t_2, \ldots$ be real numbers such that $t_1 + t_2 + \ldots + t_n = 2n^2 + 9n + 13$, for every positive integer $n \ge 2$. If $t_k = 103$, then k equals **(CAT 2018)**

19. If N and x are positive integers such that $N^N = 2^{160}$ and $N^2 + 2^N$ is an integral multiple of 2^x, then the largest possible x is **(CAT 2018)**

20. The smallest integer n for which $4^n > 17^{19}$ holds, is closest to **(CAT 2018)**
(a) 33 (b) 39
(c) 37 (d) 35

21. The smallest integer n such that $n^3 - 11n^2 + 32n - 28 > 0$ is **(CAT 2018)**

22. How many two-digit numbers, with a non-zero digit in the units place, are there, which are more than thrice the number formed by inter-changing the positions of its digits? **(CAT 2018)**
(a) 6 (b) 8
(c) 7 (d) 5

23. If the sum of squares of two numbers is 97, then which one of the following cannot be their product? **(CAT 2018)**

(a) 48 (b) 64
(c) −32 (d) 16

24. The value of the sum 7 × 11 + 11 × 15 + 15 × 19 + ...+ 95 × 99 is **(CAT 2018)**
(a) 80707 (b) 80730
(c) 80751 (d) 80773

25. If $A = \{6^{2n} - 35n - 1;\ n = 1, 2, 3....\}$ and $B = 35(n - 1);\ n = 1, 2, 3, ...$ then which of the following is true? **(CAT 2018)**
(a) Neither every member of A is in B, nor is every member of B in A
(b) Every member of A is in B, and at least one member of B is not in A
(c) Every member of B is in A
(d) At least one member of A is not in B

26. If the population of a town is p in the beginning of any year then it becomes $3 + 2p$ in the beginning of the next year. If the population in the beginning of 2019 is 1000, then the population in the beginning of 2034 will be **(CAT 2019)**
(a) $(1003)^{15} + 6$ (b) $(977)^{15} - 3$
(c) $(1003) \times 2^{15} - 3$ (d) $(977) \times 2^{14} + 3$

27. The product of two positive numbers is 616. If the ratio of the difference of their cubes to the cube of their difference is 157 : 3, then the sum of the two numbers is **(CAT 2019)**
(a) 50 (b) 85
(c) 95 (d) 58

28. If $a_1 + a_2 + a_3 + ... + a_n = 3(2^{n+1} - 2)$, then a_{11} equals **(CAT 2019)**

29. If $a_1, a_2, a_3, ...$ are in A.P., then $\frac{1}{\sqrt{a_1}+\sqrt{a_2}} + \frac{1}{\sqrt{a_2}+\sqrt{a_3}} + ...+ \frac{1}{\sqrt{a_n}+\sqrt{a_{n-1}}}$ is equal to **(CAT 2019)**
(a) $\frac{n}{\sqrt{a_1}+\sqrt{a_{n-1}}}$ (b) $\frac{n-1}{\sqrt{a_n}+\sqrt{a_1}}$
(c) $\frac{n}{\sqrt{a_1}-\sqrt{a_{n+1}}}$ (d) $\frac{n-1}{\sqrt{a_1}+\sqrt{a_{n-1}}}$

30. If m and n are integers such that $(\sqrt{2})^{19} \times 3^4 \times 4^2 \times 9^m \times 8^n = 3^n \times 16^m \times (\sqrt[4]{64})$, then m is **(CAT 2019)**

31. Let a, b, x, y be real numbers such that $a^2 + b^2 = 25$, $x^2 + y^2 = 169$ and $ax + by = 65$. If $k = ay - bx$, then **(CAT 2019)**
(a) $k = 0$ (b) $k > 5/13$
(c) $k = 5/13$ (d) $0 < k \leq 5/13$

32. Let a_1, a_2 be integers such that $a_1 - a_2 + a_3 - a_4 + ... + (-1)^{n-1} a_n = n$, for $n \geq 1$. Then $a_{51} + a_{52} + ... + a_{1023}$ equals **(CAT 2019)**
(a) −1 (b) 1
(c) 0 (d) 10

33. How many factors of $2^4 \times 3^5 \times 10^4$ are perfect squares which are greater than 1? **(CAT 2019)**

34. How many pairs of positive integers (m, n) satisfy the equation $m^2 + 105 = n^2$ **(CAT 2019)**

35. In a six-digit number, the sixth, that is, the rightmost digit is the sum of the first three digits, the fifth digit is the sum of first two digits, the third digit is equal to the first digit, the second digit is twice the first digit and the fourth digit is the sum of fifth and sixth digits. Then, the largest possible value of the fourth digit is **(CAT 2019)**

36. The number of common terms in the two sequences: 15, 19, 23, 27, ... , 415 and 14, 19, 24, 29, ..., 464 is **(CAT 2019)**
(a) 20 (b) 18
(c) 21 (d) 19

37. If $(2n + 1) + (2n + 3) + (2n + 5) + ... + (2n + 47) = 5280$, then what is the value of $1 + 2 + 3 + ... + n$? **(CAT 2019)**

38. If $x = (4096)^{7+4\sqrt{3}}$, then which of the following equals 64? **(CAT 2020)**
(a) $\frac{x^{\frac{7}{2}}}{x^{\frac{4}{\sqrt{3}}}}$ (b) $\frac{x^{\frac{7}{2}}}{x^{2\sqrt{3}}}$
(c) $\frac{x^7}{x^{4\sqrt{3}}}$ (d) $\frac{x^7}{x^{2\sqrt{3}}}$

39. An alloy is prepared by mixing three metals A, B and C in the proportion 3 : 4 : 7 by volume, Weights of the same volume of the metals A, B and C are in the ratio 5 : 2 : 6. In 130 kg of the alloy, the weight, in kg of the metal C is **(CAT 2020)**
(a) 48 (b) 70
(c) 96 (d) 84

40. If a, b and c are positive integers such that $ab = 432$, $bc = 96$ and $c < 9$, then the smallest possible value of $a + b + c$ is **(CAT 2020)**
(a) 49 (b) 46
(c) 59 (d) 56

41. A gentleman decided to treat a few children in the following manner. He gives half of his total stock of toffees and one extra to the first child, and then the half of the remaining stock along with one extra to the second and continues giving away in this fashion. His total stock exhausts after he takes care of 5 children. How many toffees were there in his stock initially? **(CAT 2020)**

42. Let the mth and nth terms of a geometric progression be $\frac{3}{4}$ and 12, respectively, where $m < n$. If the common ratio of the progression is an integer r, then smallest possible value of $r + n - m$ is **(CAT 2020)**
(a) 2 (b) −2
(c) −4 (d) 6

43. Aron bought some pencils and sharpeners. Spending the same amount of money as Aron, Aditya bought twice as many pencils and 10 less sharpeners. If the cost of one sharpener is ₹2 more than the cost of a pencil, then the minimum possible number of pencils bought by Aron and Aditya together is **(CAT 2020)**

(a) 27 (b) 36
(c) 33 (d) 30

44. How many of the integers 1, 2, … , 120 are divisible by none of 2, 5 and 7? **(CAT 2020)**

(a) 43 (b) 40
(c) 41 (d) 42

45. If a, b, c are non-zero and $14^a = 36^b = 84^c$, then $6b\left(\frac{1}{c}-\frac{1}{a}\right)$ is equal to **(CAT 2020)**

46. Let N, x and y be positive integers such that $N = x + y$, $2 < x < 10$ and $14 < y < 23$. If $N > 25$, then how many distinct values are possible for N? **(CAT 2020)**

47. How many pairs (a, b) of positive integers are there such that $a \le b$ and $ab = 4^{2017}$? **(CAT 2020)**

(a) 2020 (b) 2019
(c) 2017 (d) 2018

48. Let m and n be natural numbers such that n is even and $0.2 < \frac{m}{20}, \frac{n}{m}, \frac{n}{11} < 0.5$. Then $m - 2n$ equals **(CAT 2020)**

(a) 3 (b) 4
(c) 1 (d) 2

49. How many three-digit numbers are greater than 100 and increase by 198 when the three digits are arranged in the reverse order? **(CAT 2021)**

50. The natural numbers are divided into groups as (1), (2, 3, 4), (5, 6, 7, 8, 9), ….. and so on. Then, the sum of the numbers in the 15th group is equal to **(CAT 2021)**

(a) 7471 (b) 4941
(c) 6090 (d) 6119

51. For all possible integers n satisfying $2.25 \le 2 + 2^{n+2} \le 202$, the number of integer values of $3 + 3^{n+1}$ is **(CAT 2021)**

52. For a 4-digit number, the sum of its digits in the thousands, hundreds and tens places is 14, the sum of its digits in the hundreds, tens and units places is 15, and the tens place digit is 4 more than the units place digit. Then the highest possible 4- digit number satisfying the above conditions is **(CAT 2021)**

53. If n is a positive integer such that $\left(\sqrt[7]{10}\right)\left(\sqrt[7]{10}\right)^2 \ldots\ldots\left(\sqrt[7]{10}\right)^n > 999$, then the smallest value of n is **(CAT 2021)**

54. Consider a sequence of real numbers $x_1\ x_2, x_3, \ldots..$ such that $x_{n+1} = x_n + n - 1$ for all $n \ge 1$. If $x_1 = -1$ then x_{100} is equal to **(CAT 2021)**

(a) 4850 (b) 4949
(c) 4950 (d) 4849

55. For any natural number n, suppose the sum of the first n terms of an arithmetic progression is $(n + 2n^2)$. If the nth term of the progression is divisible by 9, then the smallest possible value of n is **(CAT 2022)**

(a) 7 (b) 4
(c) 8 (d) 9

56. Let A be the largest positive integer that divides all the numbers of the form $3^k + 4^k + 5^k$, and B be the largest positive integer that divides all the numbers of the form $4^k + 3(4^k) + 4^{k+2}$, where k is any positive integer. Then $(A + B)$ equals? **(CAT 2022)**

57. For natural numbers x, y and z, if $xy + yz = 19$ and $yz + xz = 51$, then the minimum possible value of xyz is? **(CAT 2022)**

58. Pinky is standing in a queue at a ticket counter. Suppose the ratio of the number of persons standing ahead of Pinky to the number of persons standing behind her in the queue is 3 : 5. If the total number of persons in the queue is less than 300, then the maximum possible number of persons standing ahead of Pinky is? **(CAT 2022)**

59. Let a and b be natural numbers. If $a^2 + ab + a = 14$ and $b^2 + ab + b = 28$, then $(2a + b)$ equals **(CAT 2022)**

(a) 8 (b) 9
(c) 7 (d) 10

60. Consider the arithmetic progression 3, 7, 11,... and let A_n denote the sum of the first n terms of this progression. Then the value of $\frac{1}{25}\sum_{n=1}^{25} A_n$ is **(CAT 2022)**

(a) 442 (b) 415
(c) 404 (d) 455

61. For some natural number n, assume that (15,000)! is divisible by $(n!)!$. The largest possible value of n is **(CAT 2022)**

(a) 5 (b) 4
(c) 6 (d) 7

62. The average of a non-decreasing sequence of N numbers $a_1\ a_2, \ldots, a_N$ is 300. If a_1 is replaced by $6a_1$, the new average becomes 400. Then, the number of possible values of a_1 is? **(CAT 2022)**

63. On day one, there are 100 particles in a laboratory experiment. On day n, where $n \ge 2$, one out of every n particles produces another particle. If the total number of particles in the laboratory experiment increases to 1000 on day m, then m equals **(CAT 2022)**

(a) 18 (b) 19
(c) 16 (d) 17

64. In an examination, there were 75 questions. 3 marks were awarded for each correct answer, 1 mark was deducted for each wrong answer and 1 mark was awarded for each unattempted question. Rayan scored a total of 97 marks in the examination. If the number of unattempted questions was higher than the number of attempted questions, then the maximum number of correct answers that Rayan could have given in the examination is? **(CAT 2022)**

65. If $\left(\sqrt{\frac{7}{5}}\right)^{3x-y} = \frac{875}{2401}$ and $\left(\frac{4a}{b}\right)^{6x-y} = \left(\frac{2a}{b}\right)^{y-6x}$, for all non-zero real values of a and b, then the value of $x + y$ is? **(CAT 2022)**

66. A school has less than 5000 students and if the students are divided equally into teams of either 9 or 10 or 12 or 25 each, exactly 4 are always left out. However, if they are divided into teams of 11 each, no one is left out. The maximum number of teams of 12 each that can be formed out of the students in the school is? **(CAT 2022)**

67. The average of all 3-digit terms in the arithmetic progression 38, 55, 72,..., is? **(CAT 2022)**

High Yield Questions

Scan this QR code to access assisted problem solving videos on questions 24, 38, 51, 62 and 65 from Taste of the Exams- Block 1

ANSWER KEY

1. (d)	2. (d)	3. (b)	4. 11
5. (a)	6. (b)	7. (d)	8. 51
9. 3	10. (c)	11. (a)	12. 40
13. (d)	14. 5/2	15. 5	16. (d)
17. (d)	18. 24	19. 10	20. (b)
21. 8	22. (a)	23. (b)	24. (a)
25. (b)	26. (c)	27. (a)	28. 6144
29. (b)	30. –12	31. (a)	32. (b)
33. 44	34. 4	35. 7	36. (a)
37. 4851	38. (b)	39. (d)	40. (b)
41. 62	42. (b)	43. (c)	44. (c)
45. 3	46. 6	47. (d)	48. (c)
49. 70	50. (d)	51. 7	52. 4195
53. 6	54. (a)	55. (a)	56. 82
57. 34	58. 111	59. (a)	60. (d)
61. (d)	62. 14	63. (b)	64. 24
65. 14	66. 150	67. 548	

SOLUTIONS AND SHORTCUTS

1. $(a + 3)^2 : b^2 = 9 : 1$ and $(a - 1)^2 : (b - 1)^2 = 4 : 1$

   $(a + 3) : b = \pm 3$, $\frac{a-1}{b-1} = \pm 2$

   Four cases are possible:

   $a + 3 = 3b$, $a - 1 = 2b - 2$; $(a, b) = (3, 2)$ (Rejected, since the integers a, b are of opposite signs)

   $a + 3 = 3b$, $a - 1 = -2b + 2$; a, b are non integers. (Rejected)

   $a + 3 = -3b$, $a - 1 = 2b - 2$; a, b are non integers. (Rejected)

   $a + 3 = -3b$, $a - 1 = -2b + 2$; $a = 15$, $b = -6$.

   $a^2 : b^2 = \left(\frac{15}{6}\right)^2 = 25:4$

2. $x^2 - x - 1 = 0$ on solving we get: $x = \frac{1+\sqrt{5}}{2}$

   $2x^4 = 2(x + 1)^2 = 2x^2 + 4x + 2 = 2x + 2 + 4x + 2 = 6x + 4 = 6 \times \frac{1+\sqrt{5}}{2} + 4 = 7 + 3\sqrt{5}$

3. $x - y - z = 25$

   $x = 25 + y + z$

   Maximum possible value of $y + z = 12 + 12 = 24$, Minimum possible value of $y + z = 1 + 1 = 2$.

   For $y + z = 2$, $x = 25 + 2 = 27$. $(x, y, z) = (27, 1, 1)$ one value.

   For $y + z = 3$, $x = 25 + 3 = 28$, $(x, y, z) = (28, 1, 2)$, $(25, 2, 1)$. Two possible values.

   For $y + z = 4$, $x = 25 + 4 = 29$, $(x, y, z) = (29, 1, 3)$, $(29, 3, 1)$, $(29, 2, 2)$. Three possible values.

   Similarly for $y + z = 5$, Four possible values.

   For $y + z = 6$, five possible values.

   ⋮

   For $y + z = 13$, twelve possible values.

   For $y + z = 14$, $x = 39$, eleven possible values.

   For $y + z = 15$, $x = 40$, ten possible values.

   The number of solutions = 1 + 2 + 3 + 4 + 5 + ….. + 12 + 11 + 10 = 99.

4. $(n - 5)(n - 10) - 3(n - 2) \le 0$

   $n^2 - 15n + 50 - 3n + 6 \le 0$

   $n^2 - 18n + 56 \le 0$

   $n^2 - 14n - 4n + 56 \le 0$

   $n \in [4, 14]$

   Total 11 values are possible.

5. Let 'a' and 'd' are the first term and the common difference of the A.P.

   $[a + 6d]^2 = (a + 2d)(a + 16d)$

   $a^2 + 36d^2 + 12ad = a^2 + 18ad + 32d^2$

   $4d^2 = 6ad$, $a : d = 2 : 3$

6. Common difference = 7 – 3 = 4.

   $a_1 + a_2 + \cdots + a_{3n} = 1830$,

   $3 + 7 + 11 + \ldots..3n$ terms = 1830.

   $\frac{3n}{2}[2.3 + (3n - 1)4] = 1830$

   $\frac{3n}{2}[2 + 12n] = 1830$

   $3n(1 + 6n) = 1830 = 30 \times 61$

   $3n = 30$ or $n = 10$.

   $a_1 + a_2 + \ldots. + a_n = 3 + 7 + 11 + \ldots..10$ terms = 210

   $210m > 1830$

   $m > 8.7$. Hence, the smallest integer value of $m = 9$.

7. $15600 = 24 \times 25 \times 26$
Sum of squares $= 24^2 + 25^2 + 26^2 = 1877$

8. Five consecutive even numbers ending with $2a_3$. Hence, the numbers are $2a_3 - 8$, $2a_3 - 6$, $2a_3 - 4$, $2a_3 - 2$, $2a_3$.
Required sum $= 2a_3 - 8 + 2a_3 - 6 + 2a_3 - 4 + 2a_3 - 2 + 2a_3 = 450$
$10a_3 - 20 = 450$ or $a_3 = 47$. Since, we are looking for 5 consecutive odd integers, we get $a_5 = 51$

9. You can experimentally verify that there would be only three pairs of values that would satisfy this- viz: (18, 18) ; (12, 36) and (10, 90). No other pair would satisfy this condition.

10. Let the first term be 'a' and the common ratio be 'r'.
$a_n = 3(a_{n+1} + a_{n+2} + \cdots)$
$ar^{n-1} = 3(ar^n + ar^{n+1} + \cdots)$
$ar^{n-1} = 3\left(\frac{ar^n}{1-r}\right)$ or $3r = 1 - r$ or $r = \frac{1}{4}$
$a_1 + a_2 + a_3 + \ldots = 32$
$a + ar + ar^2 + \ldots = 32$
$\frac{a}{1-r} = 32$
$a = 24$
$a_5 = ar^4 = 24 \cdot (1/4)^4 = 3/32$

11. $a_1 = \frac{1}{2\times 5} = \frac{1}{3}\left(\frac{1}{2} - \frac{1}{5}\right)$

$a_2 = \frac{1}{5\times 8} = \frac{1}{3}\left(\frac{1}{5} - \frac{1}{8}\right)$

⋮

$a_{100} = \frac{1}{299\times 302} = \frac{1}{3}\left(\frac{1}{299} - \frac{1}{302}\right)$

The required sum $= a_1 + a_2 + a_3 + a_4 + a_5 \ldots + a_{100} =$
$\frac{1}{3}\left(\frac{1}{2} - \frac{1}{5}\right) + \frac{1}{3}\left(\frac{1}{5} - \frac{1}{8}\right) + \ldots + \frac{1}{3}\left(\frac{1}{299} - \frac{1}{302}\right)$
$= \frac{1}{3}\left(\frac{1}{2} - \frac{1}{302}\right) = \frac{1}{3} \times \frac{300}{604} = \frac{100}{604} = \frac{25}{151}$

12. Let other two numbers are 'a' and 'b'.
$73 \times a \times b - 37 \times a \times b = 720$
$36 \times a \times b = 720$
$a \times b = 20$
To minimise the sum of squares of two numbers 'a' must be equal to 'b'.
$a = b = \sqrt{20}$
Required sum $= a^2 + b^2 = 20 + 20 = 40$.

13. $(u - 2v - 1)^2 + u^2 \rightarrow u^2 + 4v^2 + 1 - 4uv + 4v - 2u + u^2 = -4vu - 4v^2$
$2u^2 + 8v^2 + 1 + 4v - 2u = 0$

$$2\left(u^2 - u + \frac{1}{4}\right) + 2\left(4v^2 + 2v + \frac{1}{4}\right) = 0$$

$$2\left(u - \frac{1}{2}\right)^2 + 2\left(2v + \frac{1}{2}\right)^2 = 0$$

$u = \frac{1}{2}$ and $v = -\frac{1}{4}$

$u + 3v = \frac{1}{2} - \frac{3}{4} = -\frac{1}{4}$

Hence, option (d) is correct.

14. $16y = \frac{5x + 12z}{2}$ or $32y = 5x + 12z$
x, y and z are a/r, a, ar, respectively.
$32a = \frac{5a}{r} + 12ar$
$32 = \frac{5}{r} + 12r$
$12r^2 - 32r + 5 = 0$
On solving the above equation, we get $r = 1/6, 5/2$
As $x < y < z$, the Geometric Progression has to be an increasing GP. $r = 5/2$ is the only possible value that satisfies this requirement. Hence, 5/2 is the correct answer.

15. $0.25 < 2^x < 200$ for $-2 < x < 8$. Between these values, for ($x = 0, 1, 2, 4, 6$), $2^x + 2$ would be divisible by 3 or 4. Hence, there are total five integers.

16. $\frac{x^{2018}y^{2017}}{x^{2016}y^{2019}} = \frac{1}{16}$ or $\frac{x^2}{y^2} = \frac{1}{16}$ or $\frac{x}{y} = \frac{1}{4}$
$y = 4x$
Put $y = 4x$ in $x^{2018}\ y^{2017} = \frac{1}{2}$ or $x^{2018}\ (4x)^{2017} = \frac{1}{2}$
or $x^{4035} = \frac{1}{2^{4035}}$ or $x = \frac{1}{2}$
Consequently, $y = 2$
Value of $x^2 + y^3 = \left(\frac{1}{2}\right)^2 + 8 = \frac{33}{4}$. Hence, option (d) is correct.

17. Let 'x' is the average of all the 52 positive integers $a_1, a_2, \ldots\ldots, a_{52}$.
$a_1 + a_2 + a_3 + \ldots + a_{52} = 52x$ (1)
Therefore, the average of $a_2, a_3, a_4, a_5, \ldots a_{52} = x + 1$
Or $a_2 + a_3 + a_4 + a_5 + \ldots\ a_{52} = 51(x + 1)$ (2)
From (1) and (2), we get:
$a_1 = x - 51$. a_1 will be maximum when 'x' is maximum. The maximum value of 'x' will happen if the numbers from a_{52}, a_{51}, a_{50} are taken as 100, 99, 98 etc. Thus, the numbers from a_1 to a_{52} would be 49, 50, 51,..100 in order to maximise the value of x. With these values, the average of these 52 numbers turns out as 74.5. So, the maximum value of a_1 would be $74.5 - 51 = 23.5$. But since a_1 is an integer, its value should turn out to be 23. Hence, option (d) is correct.

18. Let $S_n = t_1 + t_2 + ... + t_n$
$t_k = S_k - S_{k-1} = 2k^2 + 9k + 13 - 2(k-1)^2 - 9(k-1)$
$- 13 = 4k + 7 = 103$
$k = 24$

19. $N^N = 2^{160}$ is possible only for $N = 32$
For $N^2 + 2^N = 32^2 + 2^{32} = 2^{10} + 2^{32}$ to be an integral multiple of 2^x, then the maximum possible value of $x = 10$.

20. $4^n > 17^{19}$
$4^{38} = 16^{19} < 17^{19}$. Hence, for $n = 38$, $4^n < 17^{19}$
Hence, option (a), (c) and (d) are incorrect. Only option (b) is correct.

21. $n^3 - 11n^2 + 32n - 28 > 0$. You would need to do a trial-and-error with values to check for the smallest value of 'n' where the expression becomes positive. The first thing that should be evident, should be that at $n = 0$, the expression is negative and for negative values of n, the value of the expression would always be negative (since each of the four terms of the expression would be negative). So, your check needs to start with positive integral values of x. Checking by inserting values of n as 1, 2, 3,...we see that at $n = 7$, the value becomes equal to 0. And at $n = 8$ we get: $n^3 - 11n^2 + 32n - 28 = 36$
Hence, the smallest possible integer is 8.

22. Let the number be 'ab' where b is not equal to 0.
According to the question:
$(10a + b) > 3(10b + a)$
$7a > 29b$
The above condition is possible when $a = 5$ and $b = 1$. $a = 6$ and $b = 1$. $a = 7$ and $b = 1$. $a = 8$, $b = 1$, $a = 9$ and $b = 1, 2$. Hence, six such numbers are possible. Option (a) is correct.

23. Let a and b are the given numbers.
According to the question: $a^2 + b^2 = 97$
$$a^2 + b^2 - 2ab = 97 - 2ab$$
$$(a - b)^2 = 97 - 2ab$$
$97 - 2ab$ must be non-negative, since the LHS is non-negative. This is not possible for $ab = 64$.

24. $S = 7 \times 11 + 11 \times 15 + 15 \times 19 + ..., + 95 \times 99$th term of the series:
$$S = \sum_{n=1}^{n=23} (4n+3)\times(4n+7) =$$
$$\sum_{n-1}^{n=23} 16n^2 + 40n + 21 = \frac{16\times23\times24\times47}{6} + 40\times\frac{23\times24}{2}$$
$+ 21 \times 23 = 80707$
Hence, option (a) is correct.

25. The value of A for $n = 1$, would be 0 and for $n = 2$ would be 1225. B, on the other hand is the set of all multiples of 35 (starting from 0). It can also be observed that every member of A would be a multiple of 35, but obviously not all multiples of 35. Hence, clearly every member of A is in B, while every member of B is not in A.

26. Let the population of the town in 2019 is 1000.
Population in 2020 (2nd year) is $3 + 2 \times 1000 = 1003 \times 2^1 - 3 = 2003$
Population in 2021 (3rd year) $= 3 + 2 \times 2003 = (1003) \times 2^2 - 3$
Population in 2022 (4th year) $= (1003) \times 2^3 - 3$
Similarly, population in 2034 will be $(1003) \times 2^{15} - 3$.
Hence, option (c) is correct.

27. Do a quick factor search of 616.
1×616; 2×308; 4×154; 7×88; 8×77; 11×56; 14×44; 22×28
The pairs to consider are: 22 & 28 (for option a); 77 and 8 for option (b); 7 and 88 for option (c); and 44 and 14 for option (d). Also one needs to understand that the targeted ratio of 157 : 3 has a value of 52.33. For option (a), we can see that difference of cubes $28^3 - 22^3 = (28 - 22)(28^2 + 28 \times 22 + 22^2)$, while the cube of the difference $= 6^3$. So the effective thought would go as follows:
$$\frac{(28-22)(28^2+28\times22+22^2)}{6\times6\times6} = \frac{784+616+484}{36} = \frac{1884}{36}$$
$= 52.33$
Hence, this option is correct.
Just for your information, the mathematical process goes like this:
Let the numbers are 'a' and 'b'.
$ab = 616 = 23 \times 7 \times 11$
$$\frac{a^3 - b^3}{(a-b)^3} = \frac{157}{3}$$
$3a^3 - 3b^3 = 157a^3 - 157b^3 - 157 \times 3 \times ab(a - b)$
$154a^3 - 154b^3 + 3 \times 616 \times 157(a - b) = 0$
$a^3 - b^3 + 3 \times 4 \times 157(a - b) = 0$
$(a - b)(a^2 + b^2 + ab) + 3 \times 4 \times 157(a - b) = 0$
$a^2 + b^2 + ab = 3 \times 4 \times 157$
$a^2 + b^2 + 2ab = 3 \times 4 \times 157 + ab$
$= 3 \times 4 \times 157 + 616 = 2500$
$(a + b)^2 = 2500$ or $a + b = 50$
Hence, option (a) is correct.

28. $S_n = a_1 + a_2 + a_3 + ... + a_n$
$a_n = S_n - S_{n-1}$
$a_{11} = S_{11} - S_{10} = 3 \times (2^{12} - 2) - 3 \times (2^{11} - 2) = 3 \times (2^{12} - 2^{11}) = 3 \times 2^{11} = 6144$.

29. Let the common difference of the AP be d.
$$\frac{1}{\sqrt{a_1}+\sqrt{a_2}} = \frac{1}{\sqrt{a_1}+\sqrt{a_2}} \times \frac{\sqrt{a_2}-\sqrt{a_1}}{\sqrt{a_2}-\sqrt{a_1}} = \frac{\sqrt{a_2}-\sqrt{a_1}}{d}$$
$$\frac{1}{\sqrt{a_2}+\sqrt{a_3}} = \frac{\sqrt{a_3}-\sqrt{a_2}}{d}$$
$$\frac{1}{\sqrt{a_1}+\sqrt{a_2}} + \frac{1}{\sqrt{a_2}+\sqrt{a_3}} + ... + \frac{1}{\sqrt{a_n}+\sqrt{a_{n-1}}}$$

$$= \frac{\sqrt{a_2}-\sqrt{a_1}}{d}+\frac{\sqrt{a_3}-\sqrt{a_2}}{d}+.....+\frac{\sqrt{a_n}-\sqrt{a_{n-1}}}{d}$$

$$= \frac{\sqrt{a_n}-\sqrt{a_1}}{d}$$

$$\frac{\sqrt{a_n}-\sqrt{a_1}}{d} = \frac{\sqrt{a_n}-\sqrt{a_1}}{d} \times \frac{\sqrt{a_n}+\sqrt{a_1}}{\sqrt{a_n}+\sqrt{a_1}}$$

$$= \frac{a_n - a_1}{d\left(\sqrt{a_n}+\sqrt{a_1}\right)} = \frac{n-1}{\left(\sqrt{a_n}+\sqrt{a_1}\right)}$$

Hence, option (b) is correct.

30. $(\sqrt{2})^{19} \times 3^4 \times 4^2 \times 9^m \times 8^n = 3^n \times 16^m \times (\sqrt[4]{64})$
$\sqrt{2} \times 2^9 \times 3^4 \times 2^4 \times 3^{2m} \times 2^{3n} = 3^n \times 2^{4m} \times 2 \times \sqrt{2}$
$2^{13+3n} \times 3^{4+2m} = 2^{4m+1} \times 3^n$
On comparing RHS with LHS, we get:
$13 + 3n = 4m + 1$ and $4 + 2m = n$
On solving the above two equations, we get: $m = -12$, $n = -20$

31. $a^2 + b^2 = 25$ and $x^2 + y^2 = 169$
$(a^2 + b^2)(x^2 + y^2) = a^2x^2 + b^2y^2 + a^2y^2 + b^2x^2$
$= 25 \times 169 = 5^2 \times 13^2$ (1)
$ax + by = 65$ & $(ax + by)^2 = a^2x^2 + b^2y^2 + 2abxy$
$= 65^2 = 13^2 \times 5^2$ (2)
equation (1) – equation (2):
$a^2y^2 + b^2x^2 - 2abxy = 0$
$(ay - bx)^2 = 0$ *or* $ay - bx = 0$
Hence, option (a) is correct.

32. $a_1 - a_2 = 2$, $a_1 - a_2 + a_3 = 3$
On solving the above two equations, we get $a_3 = 1$.
$a_1 - a_2 + a_3 - a_4 = 4$, $a_4 = -1$
Similarly, $a_n = 1$ for odd value of n and $a_n = -1$ for even value of n.
$a_{51} + a_{52} + ... + a_{1023} = 1 - 1 + 1 - 1 + ... + 1 = 1.$
Hence, option (b) is correct.

33. $2^4 \times 3^5 \times 10^4 = 2^4 \times 3^5 \times 2^4 \times 5^4 = 2^8 \times 3^5 \times 5^4$
For the factor to be a perfect square, all the prime factors should be even powers of the number.
In 2^8, the factors which are perfect squares are 2^0, 2^2, 2^4, 2^6, 2^8. Five values.
In 3^5 the factors which are perfect squares are 3^0, 3^2, 3^4. Three values.
In 5^4 the factors which are perfect squares are 5^0, 5^2, 5^4. Three values.
Number of perfect squares which are greater than 1 $= 5 \times 3 \times 3 - 1 = 44$

34. $n^2 - m^2 = (n - m)(n + m) = 105$
We need to find factor pairs of 105 and check for values of n and m. Thus, for
$105 \times 1 = 105 \rightarrow n - m = 1, n + m = 105; n = 53, m = 52$
$35 \times 3 = 105 \rightarrow n - m = 3, n + m = 35; n = 19, m = 16$
$21 \times 5 = 105 \rightarrow n - m = 5, n + m = 21; n = 13, m = 8$
$15 \times 7 = 105 \rightarrow n - m = 7, n + m = 15; n = 11, m = 4$
Thus, only four possible pairs can be found.

35. Let the six digit number be *pqrstu*.
$u = p + q + r, t = p + q, r = p, q = 2p, s = t + u$
Therefore, $s = 2p + 2q + r = 2p + 4p + p = 7p.$
p cannot be 0 as the number is a six-digit number. p cannot be more than *1,* as s would become a two-digit number. Therefore, $p = 1$ and $s = 7$. Hence, the correct answer is 7.

36. First common term = 19
Common difference = LCM of 5, 4 = 20. We will need to find the number of terms of the series, 19, 39, 59,...399. The number of terms in the series is: 380/20 + 1 = 20.
Hence, option (a) is correct.

37. $(2n + 1) + (2n + 3) + (2n + 5) + ... + (2n + 47) = 5280$
There are total $\frac{47-1}{2}+1 = 24$ terms in the above series.
$(2n + 1) + (2n + 3) + (2n + 5) + ... + (2n + 47) = 5280$
$48n + (1 + 3 + 5 + ...+ 47) = 5280$
$48n + 576 = 5280$
On solving, we get $n = 98$
$1 + 2 + 3 + ...+ 98 = \frac{98\times99}{2} = 4851.$

38. $x = 4096^{7+4\sqrt{3}} = (2^{12})^{7+4+\sqrt{3}} = 2^{84+48\sqrt{3}}$
Checking the options we see that
$x^{7/2} = 2^{294+168\sqrt{3}}$ Also $x^{2\sqrt{3}} = 2^{168\sqrt{3}+288}$
Option (b) gives us : $\frac{2^{294+168\sqrt{3}}}{2^{168\sqrt{3}+288}} = 64$

39. The weights of the three alloys would be in the ratio: 3 × 5 : 4 × 2 : 7 × 6 = 15:8:42. Since, the total weight is 130 kg, it means that the weight of the heaviest piece would be 42 × 2 = 84 kg. Option (d) is correct.

40. We can form the following possibilities for a, b, c. Note: We start with $bc = 96$ to find pairs of values of b and c, using $c < 9$ as a constraint and then try to calculate the value of a using $ab = 432$

a	b	c	$a + b + c$
Not integral	96	1	NA
9	48	2	59
Not integral	32	3	NA
18	24	4	46
27	16	6	49
36	12	8	56

Hence, option (b) is correct.

41. Before the 5th child is given toffees, the gentleman would have 2 toffees. Only then, would he be left with 0, if he gives half of his stock and one extra. Prior to the 4th child, the gentleman would be left with 6 toffees – from 6 if you were to give half the stock + one extra you would give out 4 toffees and be left with 2. Prior to the 3rd child the gentleman would have 14 toffees (14/2 = 7 plus 1 = 8 and 14 – 8 = 6). The series of numbers in reverse order for toffees left would be:

Toffees at the end	0
Toffees left after 4th child	2
Toffees left after 3rd child	6
Toffees left after 2nd child	14
Toffees left after 1st child	30
Toffees left before 1st child	62

Hence, the correct answer is 62.

42. The GP to minimise $r + n - m$, can be visualised as $\frac{3}{4}$, –3, 12. In this case, $r = -4$, $m = 1$ and $n = 3$.
$r + n - m = -4 + 3 - 1 = -2$.
Option (b) is correct.

43. Let Aron buy P pencils and S sharpeners at prices of x and $(x + 2)$. Then, we have Aditya would buy 2P pencils and S – 10 sharpeners at the same prices. It is also given to us that the amount spent by both are equal. Hence,
$Px + S(x + 2) = 2Px + (S - 10)(x + 2)$
$\Rightarrow Px + Sx + 2S = 2Px + Sx + 2S - 10x - 20$
$\Rightarrow Px = 10x + 20$
$x(P - 10) = 20$
The, minimum value of P for this expression to hold would be P = 11. Hence, the combined number of pencils they would have bought would be 3P = 33. Hence, option (c) is correct.

44. The required answer will be got using the logic: All numbers – (Number of numbers divisible by 2) – (Number of numbers divisible by 5, but not 2) – (Number of numbers divisible by 7, but not by 2 or 5).
In this case, all numbers = 120 and number of numbers divisible by 2 = number of terms in the series 2, 4, 6, 8,…120 = 60.
The Number of numbers divisible by 5, but not 2 = number of terms in the series: 5, 15, 25, 35, 45,…115 = 12.
The number of numbers divisible by 7, but not by 2 or 5 = 7, 21, 49, 63, 77, 91 and 119 = 7.
Hence, the required answer = 120 – 60 – 12 – 7 = 41. Option (c) is correct.

45. Let $14^a = 36^b = 84^c = k$. Using the definition of logs, we can write:
$\log_{14}k = a$; $\log_{36}k = b$; $\log_{84}k = c$.

$$6b\left(\frac{1}{c}-\frac{1}{a}\right) = 6\log_{36} k\left(\log_k 84 - \log_k 14\right)$$

$$\Rightarrow \frac{6}{\log_k 36}\times \log 6 = \frac{6}{2\times \log_k 6}\times(\log_k 6) = 3$$

46. Since, the value of N > 25, The values that N can be taken to can be visualised if we keep y maximised at 22. For $y = 22$, if we take x as 4, 5, 6, 7, 8 or 9, we will get values of N as 26, 27, 28, 29, 30, 31. If we try to take values of y as 21, x with values of 5, 6, 7, 8 or 9 will only be able to reach values like 26, 27, 28, 29, 30. We should realise through this thinking that there are only 6 values that N can take. Hence, the correct answer is 6.

47. $4^{2017} = 2^{4034}$. Pairs of a, b can be visualized as 2^0 & 2^{4034}; 2^1 & 2^{4033}; 2^2 & 2^{4032}…2^{2017}& 2^{2017}. Hence, there are a total of 2018 pairs possible for the values of a, b. Option (d) is correct.
Note: When we take the value of $a = 2^0$, the value of a turns out to be 1 and hence it obeys the requirement that a and b are positive integers. A lot of students made the mistake of missing 2^0 as a counting case and came up with an answer of 2017 and got this question incorrect.

48. $0.2 < \frac{m}{20}, \frac{n}{m}, \frac{n}{11} < 0.5$

$$\frac{1}{5} < \frac{m}{20}, \frac{n}{m}, \frac{n}{11} < \frac{1}{2}$$

$$\frac{1}{5} < \frac{m}{20} < \frac{1}{2} \Rightarrow 5,6,7,8,9$$

Since, at $m = 4$, the LHS inequality is not obeyed and for $m = 10$, the RHS inequality is disobeyed. So, the possible values that m can take = {5, 6, 7, 8, 9}
Thinking, in the same way, we get that the possible values of $n = 3, 4, 5$. However, since n is even, we have $n = 4$.

If $n = 4 \frac{n}{m}$ will be greater than $\frac{1}{5}$ if m is less than 20.

Similarly at $n = 4$; $\frac{n}{m}$ will be lesser than $\frac{1}{2}$ if m is greater than 8.
So, for $n = 4$; $8 < m < 20$.
m can only take one of the values in {5, 6, 7, 8, 9}
Hence, m = **9**.
$m - 2n = 9 - 2(4) = 9 - 8 = 1$.
Option (c) is correct.

49. For three–digit numbers say 'abc' the difference between '*abc*' and '*cba*' would be 99 × $|a - c|$. This difference is given to us as 198. Hence, we can conclude that $|a - c| = 2$. Further, since the numbers

increase on reversal, $c > a$. Thus, we would have numbers of the form: 1_3; 2_4; 3_5;....7_9 → a total of 7 sets. In each of these sets numbers, the middle digit can be between 0 to 9 – thus, there will be 10 instances in each set. Thus, the total number of such numbers would be 7 × 10 = 70.

50. The first group is (1); the second group is (2, 3, 4); the third group is (5, 6, 7, 8, 9) and so on. You can observe two things here:
    (i) The first group ends with the number 1^2, the second group with 2^2, third group with 3^2 and so on. The 14th group would end on 196.
    (ii) The first group has 1 number, the second has 3, the third has 5, and thus the nth group would have $2n - 1$ numbers. Thus, the 15th group starts from 197 to 225. It's sum can be got using: $29 \times \frac{197+225}{2} = 6119$.

51. n can take the values of –4, –3,–2, –1, 0, 1, 2, 3, 4, 5 in order to satisfy the inequality. $3 + 3^{n+1}$, will be an integer if n = –1, 0, 1, 2, 3, 4 or 5. Thus, the correct answer is 7.

52. Let the four digit number be represented by '*abcd*'. $a + b + c = 14$ and $b + c + d = 15 \rightarrow d = (a + 1)$. Also, it is given to us that $c = (a + 5)$. The largest number that can be formed would need to maximise the value of a. Since $(a + 5)$ also needs to be a single-digit number, we can take a's maximum value as 4. Thus, the number would be 4*b*95. From $a + b + c$ = 14, we get b = 1. Hence, the required number is 4195.

53. The expression on the LHS of the inequality can be rewritten as:
$10^{1/7} \times 10^{2/7} \times 10^{3/7} \times 10^{4/7} \times \ldots\ 10^{n/7} > 999$.
$\rightarrow 10^{(1+2+3+\ldots+n)/7} > 999$.
For n = 6, we have the LHS becoming 10^3 and is greater than the RHS of the inequality. Hence, 6 is the correct answer.

54. The value of $X_1 = -1$; $X_2 = -1$; $X_3 = 0$; $X_4 = 0 + 2 = 2$; $X_5 = 2 + 3 = 5$; $X_6 = 5 + 4 = 9$. So $X_{100} = 0 + 2 + 3 + 4 + \ldots 98 = 50 \times 97 = 4850$. Option (a) is correct.

55. We can try to see what the value of a particular term would be, when we take different values of n from the option. The problem tells us that the sum of the first n terms is $n + 2n^2$. Let's first try to check for n = 4. In order to find the 4th term, we will find the sum to 3 terms and then the sum of 4 terms and we can find the value of the 4th term by taking the difference. $S_3 = 21$, $S_4 = 36$. Hence, $t_4 = 15$, which is not divisible by 9. $S_7 = 105$, $S_6 = 78$. Hence, $T_7 = 105 - 78 = 27$, which is divisible by 9. Hence, the correct answer is option (a).
Alternately, since it is given to us that it's an arithmetic progression, we can see that $t_1 = S_1 = 3$ and $t_2 = S_2 - S_1 = 7$. Hence, the next terms are 11, 15, 19, 23 and 27 (which is the 7th term). Hence, option (a) is correct.

56. The value of $3^k + 4^k + 5^k$ at $k = 1$, is 12. Thus, any factor of 12 (12, 6, 4, 3, 2, 1) could be the value of A (the largest positive integer that divides $3^k + 4^k + 5^k$ for any k. At $k = 2$, $3^k + 4^k + 5^k = 50$. Since, this is not divisible by any of 12, 6, 4 or 3, we can reject these values for A. Thus, A is either 2 or 1. Also, if we consider that $3^k + 4^k + 5^k$ will always be of the form Odd + Even + Odd, we know that $3^k + 4^k + 5^k$ is always an even number. Thus, we conclude that the value of $A = 2$. To find the value of B, we look at the expression: $4^k + 3 \times 4^k + 4^{k+2} = 4^k + 3 \times 4^k + 16 \times 4^k = 20 \times 4^k$. At $k = 1$, 80 or any of it's factors would divide this number. As we take k to larger values, we can see that 80 would still divide the number. Hence, $B = 80$. The value of $(A + B) = 82$.

57. $y \times (x + z) = 19$ can only mean that $y = 1$ and $x + z = 19$. $z \times (x + y) = 51$, gives us two possibilities for z and x: 17 and 2 or 3 and 16. The least possible value of $x \times y \times z = 2 \times 1 \times 17 = 34$, since the other value we get is $16 \times 1 \times 3 = 48$.

58. The number of people ahead of Pinky is $3x$, the number behind her is $5x$. Thus, the total number of people in the queue is $8x + 1 < 300 \rightarrow$ Maximum value of $x = 37$. Hence, the maximum number of people ahead of Pinky is 37 × 3 = 111.

59. We have $a \times (a + b + 1) = 14$ and $b \times (b + a + 1) = 28$. The factors that fit the situation are based on $a = 2$ and $b = 4$, giving 2 × 7 = 14 and 4 × 7 = 28. Hence, $2a + b = 8$. Hence, option (a) is correct.

60. The series to be added is
$$\frac{1}{25} \times [3 + (3+7) + (3+7+11) + \ldots (3+7+11+99)$$
The sum of the expression is given by
$$\frac{1}{25} \times \sum_1^{25} \frac{n}{2} \times (2a + (n-1)d$$
$$= \frac{1}{25} \times \sum_1^{25} 3n + \sum_1^{25} 2n \times (n-1)$$
$$= \frac{1}{25} \times \sum_1^{25} n + \frac{1}{25} \times 2 \times \sum_1^{25} n^2$$
$$= \frac{1}{25} \times \left[\frac{25 \times 26}{2} + 2 \times \frac{25 \times 26 \times 51}{6}\right] = 13 + 442 = 455.$$
Option (d) is correct.

61. For 15000! to be divisible by $(n!)!$, the value of $n!$ should be lower than 15000. At $n = 8$, the value of $n!$ becomes equal to 40320, which is larger than 15000. At $n = 7$, the value of $n!$ is 5040, and we can see that 15000! would be divisible by 5040! but not by 40320!. Hence, the largest possible value of n is 7. Option (d) is correct.

62. Let the number of numbers be n. Then $6a_1 - a_1 = 5a_1 = 400 \times n - 300 \times n = 100n$ OR $a_1 = 20n$. In this situation, the lowest possible value of n is 2, in which case the two terms would be a_1 and a_2 and these would be 40 and 560 respectively to give us an average of 300 for 2 terms. At $n = 3$, $a_1 = 60$ and sum of 3 terms should be $3 \times 300 = 900$, which can also be structured as a non-decreasing sequence of numbers. $n = 4, 5, 6\ldots$ all work as possible values of n and we need to think of the limiting case. At $n = 15$, the value of $a_1 = 300$ and a non-decreasing sequence of 15 terms with an average of 300 can only be possible if all the terms are 300 each. It can be seen that $n = 16$ is not possible, since at $n = 16$, $a_1 = 20 \times n = 320$, we cannot create a non-decreasing sequence of numbers that have an average of 300. Thus, between 2 and 15 (both inclusive) there are 14 possible values of n.

63. On day 2, one out of every 2 particles will produce a particle, which means that 50 out of 100 particles will produce a particle. Thus, on day 2, the total number of particles would be 100 + 50 = 150. On day 3, one out of every 3 particles will produce a particle, which means that 50 out of 150 particles will produce a particle. Thus, on day 3, the total number of particles would be 150 + 50 = 200. This is an arithmetic progression 100, 150, 200...with $a = 100$ and $d = 50$.

Using $a + (m - 1) \times d = 1000 \rightarrow 100 + (m - 1) \times 50 = 1000$ we get $m = 19$. Option (b) is correct.

64. Since, the number of un-attempted questions are greater than the number of attempted questions, the limiting case is 37 attempted, 38 un-attempted. In this scenario he scores $38 \times 1 = 38$ marks due to un-attempted questions. Thus, he has to score a total of 59 marks from 37 attempted questions. The maximum marks he can score out of 37 attempted questions is $37 \times 3 = 111$ (if all questions are correct). For every wrong answer he would lose 4 marks from this maximum. To get 59 marks he has to lose $111 - 59 = 52$ marks. This happens when $111 - 13 \times 4 = 59$, which means that he gets 13 wrong answers and 24 correct answers in this case. There are other ways to score 97 marks overall, and can be identified as follows:

Attempted, un-attempted: 36, 39. Marks from un-attempted $= 39 \times 1 = 39$. Balance marks from attempted $= 97 - 39 = 58$. Maximum possible marks in case of all correct $= 36 \times 3 = 108$. Marks to be lost due to wrong answers $= 108 - 58 = 50$. Not possible since 50 is not a multiple of 4.

Attempted, un-attempted: 35, 40. Marks from un-attempted $= 40 \times 1 = 40$. Balance marks from attempted $= 97 - 40 = 57$. Maximum possible marks in case of all correct $= 35 \times 3 = 105$. Marks to be lost due to wrong answers $= 105 - 57 = 48$. Number of incorrect answers $= 48/4 = 12$. Number of corrects $= 35 - 12 = 23$.

As we can see, the number of correct answers goes down in this case. Since, we have to find the maximum possible number of correct answers we do not need to find other possibilities as the number would always be lower than the 24 we found in the first case. Hence, the correct answer is 24.

65. $\dfrac{7^{\frac{3x-y}{2}}}{5^{\frac{3x-y}{2}}} = \dfrac{5^3}{7^3} = \dfrac{7^{-3}}{5^{-3}}$

Hence, $\dfrac{3x-y}{2} = -3 \rightarrow 3x - y = -6$.

From the powers of b in the second equation, we know $6x - y = y - 6x$ or $y = 6x$.

Hence, $x = 2$ and $y = 12$. The value of $x + y = 14$.

66. The LCM of 9, 10, 12 or 25 is 900. So, numbers that leave a remainder of 4, when divided by each of these would be 904, 1804, 2704 and so on. Checking for divisibility by 11, we see that 1804 is the smallest number divisible by 11 in this series (and it is the only number below 5000 that has this property). Hence, the school has 1804 students and the maximum number of teams of 12 that can be formed will be the quotient when 1804 is divided by 12 = 150.

67. The first three digit term in the expression would be 106 and the last would be 990. In three digits the arithmetic series would be 106, 123, 140,...990. The average of an arithmetic series is given by the average of the first and last terms $\rightarrow$ average of 106 and 990 = 548.

BLOCK STARTER

Scan this QR code to access a video on this block's chapters, the time needed to cover them, and their weightage in the examination.

BLOCK

ARITHMETIC

BACK TO SCHOOL...

As you are already aware, this block consists of the following chapters:
Averages,
Alligations and Mixtures,
Percentages,
Profit and Loss,
Interest,
Ratio, Proportion and Variation,
Time and Work,
Time, Speed and Distance

These chapters are also sometimes referred to as Word Based Chapters in Quantitative Aptitude. To put it very simply, the reason for these seemingly diverse chapters to be under one block of chapters is **Linear Equations.**

Yes, the solving of linear equations is the common thread that binds all the chapters in this block.

But before we start going through what a linear equation is, let us first understand the concept of a variable and its need in the context of solving mathematical expressions.

Let us start off with a small exercise first:

Think of a number.
Add 2 to it.
Double the number to get a new number.
Add half of this new number to itself.
Divide the number by 3.
Take away the original number from it.
The number you now have is .... 2!!
How do I know this result?

The answer is pretty simple. Take a look. I am assuming that you had taken the initial number as 5 to show you what has happened in this entire process.

Instruction	*You*	*Me*
Think of a number	5	X
Add 2 to it	$5 + 2 = 7$	$X + 2$
Double the number to get a new number	$7 \times 2 = 14$	$2X + 4$
Add half of this new number to itself	$14 + 7 = 21$	$3X + 6$
Divide the result by 3	$21/3 = 7$	$X + 2$
Take away the original number from it	$7 - 5 = 2$	$X + 2 - X = 2$
The number you now have is..... 2 and is independent of the value again	The number you now have is..... 2!	The number you now have is..... 2!

The above is a perfect illustration of what a variable is and how it operates.

In this entire process, it does not matter to me as to what number you have assumed. All I set up is a kind of a parallel world wherein the number in your mind is represented by the variable X in my mind.

By ensuring that the final value does not have an X in it, I have ensured that the answer is independent of the value you would have assumed. Thus, even if someone had assumed 7 as the original value, his values would go as: 7, 9, 18, 27, 9, 2.

What you need to understand is that in Mathematics, whenever we have to solve for the value of an unknown, we represent that unknown by using some letter (like x, y, a, etc.) These letters are then called as the variable representations of the unknown quantity.

Thus, for instance, if you come across a situation where a question says: The temperature of a city increases by 1°C on Tuesday from its value on Monday, you assume that if Monday's temperature was t, then Tuesday's temperature will be $t + 1$.

Thus, although you do not have the actual value in your mind, you can still move ahead in the question by assuming a variable to represent the value of the unknowns. All problems in Mathematics ultimately take you to a point which will give the value of the unknown—which then becomes the answer to the question.

The opposite of a variable is a constant. Thus, if it is said in the same problem that the temperature on Wednesday is 34° C, then 34 becomes a constant value in the context of the problem.

As a trainer and mentor to lacs of students over the past 25 odd years, one of the things that has interested me a lot has been to identify exactly what goes wrong in the thinking of a student when he/she is not able to solve a question. This has particularly intrigued me, since in the answer to this question lies the path to changing the skills of solving quants for my readers and my students. In order to explain my point of view, I would first discuss what it takes to solve a question in a word-based chapter (like the ones in block II and III).

Any quants question elicits a reaction from the solver. If you are solving a question in QA and you can come up with the correct reactions (and not make any errors in the calculations), you should largely be able to solve any question you come across. This then that if you are solving a question and the question requires a particular reaction at a particular time/step during the solution, and you are not able to come up with that particular reaction – then you would not be able to get an answer to the question. I refer to these points in any question that elicit a reaction from you as **'triggers'. Improving your ability in QA, then means improving the quality and precision of the reactions that your mind has – at various trigger points during the solving of the questions.**

Language triggers: The beauty of QA and Mathematics, and the ease of these subjects, emerges from the fact that reactions and processes of solving questions are standardised – throughout the subject. And since they are standardised, each process and/or reaction has to be learnt only once. Unfortunately, a vast majority of students never see the subject for the essential simplicity it has – but rather look at the subject with a great deal of suspicion and fear.

If instead, you were able to bring yourself around to trying to discover in a systematic fashion what these standard triggers are and what their reactions are, skilling yourself up in solving QA problems could become child's play.

A closer look at problem-solving situations would show you that there are two kinds of triggers that you face in QA questions:

Language triggers: As the name itself suggests, a language trigger is essentially a trigger in the question, that is completely communicated in language terms to the solver. Consider the following question from CAT 2017, which would clarify for you, what a language trigger is:

Of the total number of shirts produced, in a factory, 15% of the shirts are defective. (*Language trigger 1: Your thought: Assume 100 shirts produced, 15 are defective).* Of the remaining shirts, 20% are sold in the domestic market. (*Language trigger 2: Your thought: I was left with 85 shirts – and 20% of those are defective. Thus, 20% of 85 = 17 are defective. That leaves me with 100-15-17 = 68 shirts).* The remaining 8840 shirts are exported. (*Language trigger 3: Your thought: Out of 100, 68 shirts are exported. Given: 8840 shirts are exported. Means that the 68 in the context of the assumption of 100 shirts produced, is actually 8840. If 68 is 8840, it means that 1 is 130.)* Find the number of shirts produced. (*Question statement: Your thought: 1 is 130, hence 100 is 100 × 130 = 13000.)*

As you could see in the above question, what is required to successfully solve the question, is the reaction with each language trigger the question was throwing at you. If you can react to each of the language triggers, you would get to the answer of the question automatically.

Situation triggers: However, many a times, while solving a question in Mathematics/Quants, just reacting to language triggers is not sufficient. In such questions, during the process of solving, one reaches a specific point/s in the question, where the quantitative situation you are faced with tells you what to do (i.e. the language of the question would not tell you what to do next). In such situations, you need your mind to be equipped to think correctly from that situation and come up with the correct thoughts that would take you to the answer.

Thus, in summary, there are only two reasons that you are not able to solve a question in QA:

1. You are not able to react to a language trigger in the question;
2. You are not able to react to a situation trigger in the question.

There is simply no third reason, for not being able to solve a question.

Hence, the focus of your preparation as you start to enter the remaining part of this book (and not just this block) has to be to focus on (i) identifying and programming your reactions for the language triggers in the chapter;

(ii) identifying and programming your reactions for the situation triggers in the chapter.

Once, the programs are done – allow the beauty of repetitions and practice to carry you to the skill level of someone who is well-equipped with Mathematical and quantitative thinking.

Thus, your progress while studying any chapter in this book should be:

Learning objective 1: Get control of the language of the chapter;

Learning objective 2: Get control of the quantitative situations that questions in the chapter throw up regularly;

Learning objective 3: Get control of the typical mathematical equations that the chapter throws up – learn to write them and solve them;

Learning objective 4: Get control of the calculations.

While what we have talked about in the above discussion applies to all chapters of this book, an interesting observation arises when you think of the equations that emerge in the chapters of Block II. A majority of the times, when you are solving questions from chapters of these blocks, you would be dealing with linear equations. Hence, when we are talking about Learning objective 3 above, the focus for these blocks of chapters has to be on linear equations.

One of the first things you need to realise when you are trying to improve your Quantitative Aptitude, is to understand that Math questions are always about variables. A variable emerges in a math problem depending on what is being talked about. So if I make a statement 'I was driving from Delhi to Lucknow at 60 kmph' the statement gives rise to three variables – speed (whose value has got defined in the context of the problem being set up as 60 kmph and automatically two unnamed and hidden variables emerge in this scenario, since when I have made this statement, one automatically realises that there is some time and some distance involved, whose values have not been provided in the statement. This is where we can think mathematically by saying that let the time be 't' and the distance be 'd'. The multiplication operator of math will then connect these to give you an equation: $60 \times t = d$. This is a linear equation with 2 unknowns. In general, variables might be embedded in a problem either explicitly stated (like speed in the above case) or as hidden in the story (like time and distance, which needed to be inferred). Also, even the stated variables in the problem could be without a value.

So, if it is said: 'I was driving from Delhi to Lucknow at a certain speed' the problem is not giving you a value for the speed. You will assume a letter to denote it and the problem will be structured further in such a way that it would allow you to get to the values of the unknown values.

Depending upon the number of variables in a problem, a linear equation might have one variable, two variables or even three or more variables. The only thing you should know is that in order to get the value of a variable, the number of equations needed is always equal to the number of variables. In other words, if you have more variables in a system of equations than the number of equations, you cannot solve for the individual values of the variables.

The basic mathematical principle goes like this:

For a system of equations to be solvable, the number of equations should be equal to the number of variables in the equations. Thus for instance, if you have two variables, you need two equations to get the values of the two variables, while if you have three variables, you will need three equations.

The Multiple Possibility situation:

What happens if there are more unknowns than equations? Understanding this is crucial for you since, one of the favourite ways for question setters to make difficult questions is to give you more unknowns than equations.

Concept Explainer

Scan this QR code to access two videos, where I have explained solving linear equation in 1 variable and linear equation in 2 variables.

This leads to not solving, but analysis of the situation. The situation is best exemplified by the situation where you might have the following equation: $x + y = 7$. If it is known that both x and y are natural numbers, it yields a set of possibilities for the values of x and y as follows: (1, 6), (2, 5), (3, 4), (4, 3), (5, 2), (6, 1). One of these possibilities has to be the answer.

In fact, it might be a good idea to think of all linear equation situations in this fashion. Hence, before you go ahead to read about the next equation, you should set up this set of possibilities based on the first equation.

Over the past few years setting up maxima minima type questions using this structure has become one of the favourite go-to approaches for exams like CAT, when they are setting tough problems.

Consider the following situation where a question yields a set of possibilities:

Four enemies A, B, C and D gather together for a picnic in a park with their wives. A's wife consumes 5 times as many glasses of juice as A.

B's wife consumes 4 times as many glasses of juice as *B*. *C*'s wife consumes 3 times as many glasses of juice as *C* and *D*'s wife consumes 2 times as many glasses of juice as *D*. In total, the wives of the four enemies consume a total of 44 glasses of juice. If *A* consumes at least 5 glasses of juice while each of the other men have at least one glass, find the least number of drinks that could have been consumed by the 4 enemies together.

(1) 9 (2) 12
(3) 11 (4) 10

In the question above, we have 8 variables—A, B, C, D and a, b, c, d — the number of glasses consumed by the four men and the number of glasses consumed by the four wives.

Also, the question gives us five informations which can be summarised into five equations as follows.

$a = 5A$
$b = 4B$
$c = 3C$
$d = 2D$
and $a + b + c + d = 44$
Also, $A \geq 5$.

Under this condition, you do not have enough information to get all values and hence you will get a set of possibilities.

Since the minimal value of A is 5, 'a' can take the values 25, 30, 35 and 40 when A takes the values 5, 6, 7 and 8, respectively. Based on these, and on the realisation that b has to be a multiple of 4, c a multiple of 3 and d a multiple of 2, the following possibilities emerge:

At $A = 5$

a	(multiple of 5)	*25*	*25*	*25*	*25*	*25*
b	(multiple of 4)	12	8	8	4	4
c	(multiple of 3)	3	9	3	3	9
d	(multiple of 2)	4	2	8	12	6
	$a + b + c + d$	44	44	44	44	44

a		$A = 6$, $a = 30$	$A = 7$, $a = 35$	$A = 8$, $a = 40$
b	(multiple of 4)	4	4	No solution
c	(multiple of 3)	6	3	
d	(multiple of 2)	4	2	
	$a + b + c + d$	44	44	

In this case, the answer will be 10, since in the case of $a = 35$, $b = 4$, $c = 3$ and $d = 2$, the values for A,B,C and D will be respectively 7,1,1 and 1. This solution is the least number of drinks consumed by the four enemies together as in all the other possibilities the number of glasses is greater than 10.

Such utilisations of linear equations are very common in CAT and top-level aptitude examinations.

CHAPTER 3

Averages

Chapter Launchpad

Scan this QR code to access a video on 'Introduction to Averages' and this chapter's importance for CAT

THEORY

For any group of given numbers, we are often interested in finding the value of the central tendency of the group of numbers. Statistics provides us with three basic measures of the central tendency for any group of numbers. These are: Mean (also referred to as Arithmetic Mean), Median and Mode. Let us take a look at the definitions for all these three measures of central tendency:

1. **Arithmetic Mean** (also referred to as Mean or Average):

$$\text{Arithmetic Mean} = \frac{\textit{Sum of the given numbers}}{\textit{Number of numbers}} = \frac{Sum}{n}$$

This formula has three variants in which it is normally used – the first of it is what you see above. This is used obviously when you are given (or can find) the value of the sum of the numbers and also know the number of numbers. For example, consider the following statements, which you would come across regularly in this chapter: 'The sum of 8 numbers is 96'. 'A batsman has scored 1240 runs in 80 innings.' ' 40 children in a class have scored a total of 800 marks in an examination'. In each of these cases, you would use the Average = $\frac{Sum}{n}$ formula. Thus, we would have: 1240/80 = 15.5; 800/40 = 20 as the calculated averages in the above two cases.

Consider the following statements: 'The average age of 12 students is 20 years.' 'The average reading in seven experiments is 22.1 grams.' 'A batsman has an average of 55 runs per innings in 6 innings.' In each of these cases, we will use the: $Sum = n \times average$ formula. Thus, we would have: The sum total of ages of the 12 students in the first example as 12 × 20 = 240; the sum total of the seven readings would be: 7 × 22.1 = 154.7; total runs scored by the batsman = 55 × 6 = 330.

The third variant in which form this formula is used is $n = \frac{Sum}{Average}$. This is used if we are provided information like: 'A class of students scored a total of 800 marks with an average score of 40 marks per student.' With information of this kind, we can work out the number of students in the class using 800/40 = 20.

2. **Median:** The median is the number that has the central value in the group of numbers whose central tendency we are looking for.

   Thus, for example if we have a group of numbers like 13, 22, 34, 54, 72. In this case, since 34 has the middle value for this group of numbers, the median of this group would be 34. In cases, where there are two middle values, we take the average of the two middle values to identify the value of the median.

   For example: The median of: 3, 5, 6 and 10, would be the average of 5 and 6 = 5.5.

Note: While the median is a well accepted measure of central tendency, its effectiveness is restricted to situations where the group of numbers has an evenly distributed nature. For skewed data sets, the median would not be a very good measure of central tendency. Thus, if my group of numbers is: 3, 5, 6, 88, 113. My median would be 6 and as you can yourself understand, 6 is not a good measure of central tendency here. Hence, in real life estimations one should use the median with some caution and only for appropriate situations.

---

3. **Mode:** This is the third measure of central tendency and is defined as the maximum occurring number in a group of numbers. For instance, if we are looking at a situation where we are taking several readings of the time-period of a pendulum – we might be interested at which is the reading that is happening most commonly. Thus, if the readings in seconds were 7, 7.1, 7.1, 7.3, 7.5, 7.1, 7.2, 6.9, 7, 6.8, 7.4; in this situation the most commonly occurring reading is 7.1 since it has occurred three times. Hence, the mode of this group would be 7.1.

   Again as you can visualise, the effectiveness of the mode as a measure of central tendency for a group of numbers is limited – and you should only use it for situations where it might be logically relevant to use the mode.

   All said and done, the arithmetic mean is the most effective measure of central tendency and hence also the most commonly and widely used one in real-life statistical situations.

Let us get our focus back on this again now:

Simple Averages versus Weighted Averages:

If you have to find the average of three numbers, say 20,30 and 70, you can find the average using sum of the numbers divided by 3. So, the average would be $\frac{20+30+70}{3} = 40$.

However, consider the following situations:

(a) You go to a shop and purchase three varieties of rice 1 kg @`20 kg, 2 kgs @`30 kg and 7 kgs @`70 kg. What would be the average price for a kilogram of rice you purchased?

(b) You drive your car for 1 hour @20 kmph, 2 hours @30 km/h and 7 hours @ 70 km/h. What would be your average speed?

(c) You mix three varieties of milk – water mixtures as follows: 1 litre containing 20% milk, 2 litres containing 30% milk and 7 litres containing 70% milk. What would be your percentage concentration of milk in the mixture?

(d) You make three investments that yield a different return: 1 lac with a return of 20%, 2 lacs with a return of 30% and 7 lacs with a return of 70%. What would be the average return on the total investment?

For each of these cases, the simple average calculation of $\frac{20+30+70}{3}$ would be incorrect. The reason is that in each of these cases, the correct logic to apply would be the logic of the weighted average. Let's first take a look at weighted averages:

When we have two or more groups whose individual averages are known, then to find the combined average of all the elements of all the groups, we use weighted average. Thus, if we have k groups with averages A_1, A_2 ... A_k and having n_1, n_2 ... n_k elements then the weighted average is given by the formula:

$$\text{Aw} = \frac{n_1 A_1 + n_2 A_2 + n_3 A_3 + \ldots + n_k A_k}{n_1 + n_2 + n_3 + \ldots + n_k}$$

Thus, for each of the above cases, the average we are looking for would be given by:

$$Average = \frac{1\times20+2\times30+7\times70}{10} = \frac{570}{10} = 57$$

An important point to note: Suppose you bought 37 kgs of rice @ 50 ₹/kg and 74 kgs of rice @ 80 ₹/kg. In such a case, the weighted average would be calculated normally as:

$$\text{Average} = \frac{37\times50+74\times80}{37+74} = 70.$$ However, a much simpler way to do this would be:

$$\text{Average} = \frac{1\times50+2\times80}{1+2} = 70.$$

What have we done here and how is the answer the same? Well, we have replaced 37 and 74 by 1 and 2, i.e. we have replaced the weights with the ratio of the weights.

So, one should realise that in the formula for weighted averages, we have to use the ratio of the weights and not the actual weights. Always keep an eye open for this, whenever you are solving any weighted average question.

Another Meaning of Average The average [also known as *arithmetic mean* (AM)] of a set of numbers can also be defined as the number by which we can replace each and every number of the set without changing the total of the set of numbers.

Property 1: The average of 4 numbers 12, 13, 17 and 18 is:

Solution: Required average = (12 + 13 + 17 + 18)/4 = 60/4 = 15

This means that if each of the 4 numbers of the set were replaced by 15 each, there would be no change in the total.

This is an important way to look at averages. In fact, whenever you come across any situation where the average of a group of 'n' numbers is given, you should visualise that there are 'n' numbers, each of whose value is the average of the group. This view is a very important way to visualise averages.

This can be visualised as

$$\begin{array}{c} 12 \rightarrow +3 \rightarrow 15 \\ 13 \rightarrow +2 \rightarrow 15 \\ 17 \rightarrow -2 \rightarrow 15 \\ 18 \rightarrow -3 \rightarrow 15 \\ \hline 60 \rightarrow +0 \rightarrow 60 \\ \hline \end{array}$$

Property 2: In Example 1, visualise addition of a fifth number, which increases the average by 1.

$$\begin{array}{c} 15+1=16 \\ 15+1=16 \\ 15+1=16 \\ 15+1=16 \end{array}$$

The +1 appearing 4 times is due to the fifth number, which is able to maintain the average of 16 first and then 'give one' to each of the first 4.

Hence, the fifth number in this case is 20.

Property 3: The average always lies above the lowest number of the set and below the highest number of the set. The only situation where this is not obeyed is when all the numbers of the set of numbers are the same. For instance, the average of 7, 7, 7, 7, 7 is 7.

Property 4: The net deficit due to the numbers below the average always equals the net surplus due to the numbers above the average.

Property 5: *Ages and averages:* If the average age of a group of persons is x years today then after n years their average age will be $(x + n)$.

Also, n years ago their average age would have been $(x - n)$. This happens due to the fact that for a group of people, 1 year is added to each person's age every year.

WORKED-OUT PROBLEMS

Problem 3.1: The average of a batsman after 25 innings was 56 runs per innings. If after the 26th inning, his average increased by 2 runs, then what was his score in the 26th inning?

Solution: *Normal process:*

Runs in 26th inning = Runs total after 26 innings – Runs total after 25 innings

$= 26 \times 58 - 25 \times 56$

For mental calculation use:

$$(56 + 2) \times 26 - 56 \times 25$$
$$= 2 \times 26 + (56 \times 26 - 56 \times 25)$$
$$= 52 + 56 = 108$$

Short Cut Since the average increases by 2 runs per innings it is equivalent to 2 runs being added to each score in the first 25 innings. Now, since these runs can only be added by the runs scored in the 26th inning, the score in the 26th inning must be $25 \times 2 = 50$ runs higher than the average after 26 innings (i.e. new average = 58).

Hence, runs scored in 26th inning = new average + old innings × change in average

$= 58 + 25 \times 2 = 108$

Visualise this as:

Average in first 25 innings	Average after 26 innings
56	58
56	58
56	58
…	…
…	…
25 times…	26 times…

Difference in total is two, 25 times and 58 once, that is, $58 + 25 \times 2$.

Problem 3.2: The average age of a class of 30 students and a teacher reduces by 0.5 years, if we exclude the teacher. If the initial average is 14 years, find the age of the class teacher.

Solution: *Normal process:*

Age of teacher = Total age of (students + teacher) – Total age of students

$= 31 \times 14 - 30 \times 13.5$

$= 434 - 405$

$= 29$ years

Short Cut The teacher after fulfilling the average of 14 (for the group to which he belonged) is also able to give 0.5 years to the age of each of the 30 students. Hence, he has $30 \times 0.5 \rightarrow 15$ years to give over and above maintaining his own average age of 14 years.

Age of teacher $= 14 + 30 \times 0.5 = 29$ years

Note: This problem should be viewed as change of average from 13.5 to 14 when teacher is included.

Problem 3.3: The average marks of a group of 20 students on a test is reduced by 4 when the topper who scored 90 marks is replaced by a new student. How many marks did the new student have?

Solution: *Normal process:*

Let initial average be x.

Then the initial total is $20x$

New average will be $(x - 4)$ and the new total will be $20(x - 4) = 20x - 80$.

The reduction of 80 is created by the replacement.

Hence, the new student has 80 marks less than the student he replaces. Hence, he must have scored 10 marks.

Short Cut The replacement has the effect of reducing the average marks for each of the 20 students by 4. Hence, the replacement must be $20 \times 4 = 80$ marks below the original.

Hence, answer = 10 marks.

Problem 3.4: The average marks of 3 students *A*, *B* and *C* is 48 marks. Another student *D* joins the group and the new average becomes 44 marks. If another student *E*, who has 3 marks more than *D*, joins the group, the average of the 4 students *B*, *C*, *D* and *E* becomes 43 marks. Find how many marks *A* got in the exam.

Solution: Solve while reading. The first sentence gives you a total of 144 for *A*, *B* and *C*'s marks. *Second sentence*: When *D* joins the group, the total becomes $44 \times 4 = 176$. Hence *D* must get 32 marks.

Alternatively, you can reach this point by considering the first 2 statements together as:

D's joining the group reduces the average from 48 to 44 marks (i.e., 4 marks).

This means that to maintain the average of 44 marks, *D* has to take 4 marks from *A*, 4 from *B* and 4 from $C \rightarrow$ *A* total of 12 marks. Hence, he must have got 32 marks.

From here:

The first part of the third sentence gives us information about *E* getting 3 marks more than 32. Hence, *E* gets 35 marks.

Now, it is further stated that when *A* is replaced by *E*, the average marks of the students reduces by 1 to 43.

Mathematically, this can be shown as

$A + B + C + D = 44 \times 4 = 176$ while, $B + C + D + E = 43 \times 4 = 172$

Subtracting the two equations, we get $A - E = 4$ marks. Hence, A would have obtained 39 marks.

Alternatively, you can think of this as:

The replacement of A with E results in the reduction of 1 mark from each of the 4 people who belong to the group. Hence, the difference is 4 marks. Hence, A would get 4 marks more than E i.e., A gets 39 marks.

Problem 3.5: The mean temperature of Monday to Wednesday was 27 °C and of Tuesday to Thursday was 24 °C. If the temperature on Thursday was 2/3rd of the temperature on Monday, what was the temperature on Thursday?

Solution: From the first sentence, we get that the total from Monday to Wednesday was 81 while from Tuesday to Thursday was 72. The difference is arising out of the replacement of Monday by Thursday.

This can be mathematically written as

$$\text{Mon} + \text{Tue} + \text{Wed} = 81 \quad (1)$$

$$\text{Tue} + \text{Wed} + \text{Thu} = 72 \quad (2)$$

Hence, $\text{Mon} - \text{Thu} = 9$

We have two unknown variables in the above equation. To solve for 2 unknowns, we need a new equation. Looking back at the problem, we get the equation:

$\text{Thu} = (2/3) \times \text{Mon}$

Solving the two equations we get: Thursday = 18 °C.

However, in the exam, you should avoid using equation-solving as much as possible. You should, ideally, be able to reach half way through the solution during the first reading of the question, and then meet the gap through the use of options.

The answer to this problem should be obtained by the time you finish reading the question for the first time.

Thus, suppose we have the equations:

$M - T = 9$ and $T = 2M/3$ or $T/M = 2/3$ and have the options for T as

(a) 12 (b) 15

(c) 18 (d) 27

To check which of these options is the appropriate value, we need to check one by one.

Option (a) gives $T = 12$, then we have $M = 21$. But $12/21 \neq 2/3$. Hence, this is not the correct option.

Option (b) gives $T = 15$, then $M = 24$. But again $15/24 \neq 2/3$. Hence, this is not the correct option.

Option (c) gives $T = 18$, then $M = 27$. Now $18/27 = 2/3$. Hence, this is the correct option.

So we no longer need to check for option (d).

However, if we had checked for option (d) then $T = 27$, so $M = 36$. But again $27/36 \neq 2/3$. Hence, this is not the correct option.

In the above, we used 'solving-while-reading' and 'option-based' approaches.

These two approaches are very important and by combining the two, you can reach amazing speeds in solving the question.

You are advised to practice both these approaches while solving questions, which will surely improve your efficiency and speed. You will see that, with practice, you will be able to arrive at the solution to most of the LOD I problems (given later in this chapter) even as you finish reading the questions. And since it is the LOD I level problems that appear in most examinations (like SNAP, NMAT, CUET, CLAT, CET, BANK PO, SSC, BBA/BMS entrance etc.), you will gain a significant advantage in solving these problems.

On LOD II, LOD III and CAT-type problems, you will find that using solving-while-reading and option-based approaches together would take you through anywhere between 30 and 70% of the question by the time you finish reading the question for the first time.

This will give you a tremendous time advantage over the other students appearing in the examination.

Problem 3.6: A person covers half his journey by train at 60 kmph, half of the remainder by bus at 30 km/h and the rest by cycle at 10 km/h. Find his average speed during the entire journey.

Solution: Assume the total distance to be 120 kms. Then the distances traveled by train bus and cycle are 60,30 and 30 respectively. Using the formula: Average speed = Total Distance/Total time

$$\text{we get: } \frac{120}{(1+1+3)} = \frac{120}{5} = 24 \text{ km/h.}$$

Problem 3.7: A school has only 3 classes that contain 10, 20 and 30 students, respectively. The pass percentage of these classes are 20%, 30% and 40% respectively. Find the pass percentage of the entire school.

Solution

$$\text{Using weighted average: } \frac{10 \times 0.2 + 20 \times 0.3 + 30 \times 0.4}{10 + 20 + 30}$$

$$= \frac{20}{60} = 33.33\%$$

Alternatively, we can also use solving-while-reading as Recognise that the pass percentage would be given by

$$\frac{\text{Passed students}}{\text{Total students}}$$

As soon as you get into the second line of the question, get back to the first sentence and get the total number of passed students = 2 + 6 + 12 and you are through with the problem.

LEVEL OF DIFFICULTY (I)

1. The average of the first fifteen natural numbers is
(a) 8.5 (b) 7.5
(c) 6.5 (d) 8
2. Find the average increase rate (per annum) if increase in the population in the first year is 10% and that in the second year is 20%.
(a) 11 (b) 16
(c) 20 (d) 18
3. The average of the first ten even numbers is
(a) 18 (b) 22
(c) 9 (d) 11
4. The average of 61 results is 43. If the average of the first 48 results is 36 and that of the last 12 is 49. Find the 49th result.
(a) 302 (b) 307
(c) 304 (d) 328
5. A man covers half of his journey by train at 50 km/hr, half of the remainder by bus at 25 km/h and the rest by cycle at 5 km/h. Find his average speed during the entire journey.
(a) 100/7 kmph (b) 25/3 kmph
(c) 14 kmph (d) 18 kmph
6. The average weight of 10 men is decreased by 5 kg when, one of them weighing 100 kg is replaced by another person. This new person is again replaced by another person, whose weight is 10 kg lower than the person he replaced. What is the overall change in the average due to this dual change?
(a) 5 kg (b) 6 kg
(c) 12 kg (d) 15 kg
7. The average of the first ten prime numbers, which are odd, is
(a) 12.9 (b) 13.8
(c) 17 (d) 15.8
8. The average age of 13 boys and the principal is 10 years. When the principal's age is excluded, the average age decreases by 2 year. What is the age of the principal?
(a) 34 (b) 36
(c) 38 (d) 40
9. The average weight of 3 boys *A*, *B* and *C* is 74 kg. Another boy *D* joins the group and the average now becomes 70 kg. If another boy *E*, whose weight is 3 kg more than that of *D*, replaces *A* then the average weight of *B*, *C*, *D* and *E* becomes 75 kg. The weight of *A* is
(a) 40 kg (b) 42 kg
(c) 49 kg (d) 41 kg
10. The mean temperature of Monday to Wednesday was 35 °C and of Tuesday to Thursday was 30 °C. If the temperature on Thursday was 1/2 that of Monday, the temperature on Thursday was
(a) 30 °C (b) 15 °C
(c) 20 °C (d) 25 °C
11. Five years ago, the average age of *A*, *B* and *C* was 25 years and that of *B* and *C* 10 years ago was 20 years. *A*'s present age is
(a) 30 years (b) 35 years
(c) 40 years (d) 48 years
12. Ganguly has a certain average for 4 innings. In the 5th inning, he scores 40 runs thereby increasing his average by 4 runs. His new average is
(a) 20 (b) 24
(c) 28 (d) 32
13. The average of the first six multiples of 5 is
(a) 18.50 (b) 21
(c) 28 (d) 17.50
14. There are three fractions *A*, *B* and *C*. If $A = 1/5$ and $B = 1/8$ and the average of *A*, *B* and *C* is 1/10. What is the value of *C*?
(a) –1/20 (b) – 1/60
(c) –1/30 (d) – 1/40
15. The marks obtained by Alan in Mathematics, English and Biology are respectively 90 out of 100, 70 out of 150 and 150 out of 200. Find his average score in percent.
(a) 87.83 (b) 68.88
(c) 76.33 (d) 77.33
16. The average monthly expenditure of a family was 2250 for the first 3 months, ₹2150 for the next three months and ₹ 5750 for the next three months. Find the average income of the family for the 9 months, if they save ₹500 per month.
(a) ₹3866.66 (b) ₹3883.33
(c) ₹3666.66 (d) ₹3222.66
17. The average age of a family of 5 members is 20 years. If the age of the youngest member be 5 years, what was the average age of the family at the birth of the youngest member?
(a) 15.25 (b) 18.75
(c) 21.25 (d) 12.50
18. The average age of 5 persons in a group is increased by 10 years when two men aged 30 years and 40 years are substituted by two women. Find the average age (in years) of the two women.
(a) 60 (b) 65
(c) 51 (d) 62
19. The average temperature for Wednesday, Thursday and Friday was 20 °C. The average for Thursday, Friday and Saturday was 21 °C. If the temperature on Saturday was 22 °C, what was the temperature on Wednesday?
(a) 19 °C (b) 24 °C
(c) 18 °C (d) 21 °C
20. The speed of the train in going from Kanpur to Lucknow is 60 km/hr while when coming back from

Lucknow to Kanpur, its speed is 40 km/hr. Find the average speed (in km/hr) during the whole journey.
(a) 45 (b) 48
(c) 50 (d) 46

21. The average weight of a class of 19 students is 20 kg. If the weight of the teacher be included, the average rises by 1 kg. What is the weight of the teacher?
(a) 40 kg (b) 50 kg
(c) 45 kg (d) 55 kg

22. The average of 3 numbers is 20 and that of the first two is 25. Find the third number.
(a) 15 (b) 10
(c) 20 (d) 12

23. The average weight of 29 men in a ship is increased by 5 kg when one of the men, who weighs 120 kg, is replaced by a new man. Find the weight of the new man (In kg)
(a) 265 (b) 205
(c) 245 (d) 240

24. The age of A and B is in the ratio 1: 3. After 10 years, the ratio of their ages will become 1:2. Find the average of their ages after 20 years.
(a) 22 (b) 40
(c) 37 (d) 30

25. Find the average of the first 100 natural numbers.
(a) 50.50 (b) 52.50
(c) 51.50 (d) 49

26. Find the average of all prime numbers between 20 and 50.
(a) 35.8 (b) 34.65
(c) 35.85 (d) 31.8

27. If we take four numbers, the average of the first three is 20 and that of the last three is 25. If the last number is 30, the first number is
(a) 20 (b) 21
(c) 23 (d) 15

28. The average of 15 results is 40 and that of 25 more results is 48. For all the results taken together, the average is
(a) 45 (b) 42
(c) 46 (d) 44

29. The average of 7 consecutive numbers is 21. The highest of these numbers will be
(a) 20 (b) 23
(c) 24 (d) 22

30. The average age of 8 students is 11 years. If 2 more students of age 15 and 17 years join, their average will become
(a) 13 years (b) 12 years
(c) 14 years (d) 15 years

31. The average of 9 numbers is 14. If each number is increased by 4, the new average will be
(a) 16 (b) 15
(c) 18 (d) 17

32. The average of 11 consecutive numbers is n. If the next two numbers are also included, the average will.
(a) increase by 1 (b) remain the same
(c) increase by 1.4 (d) increase by 2

33. The average of 40 numbers is 45. If two numbers, namely, 65 and 25 are discarded, the average of the remaining numbers is
(a) 35 (b) 45
(c) 40 (d) 43

34. The average of 15 numbers is 18. If each number is multiplied by 9, then the average of the new set of numbers is
(a) 162 (b) 152
(c) 144 (d) 164

35. In a family of 5 males and a few ladies, the average monthly consumption of grain per head is 9 kg. If the average monthly consumption per head be 12 kg in the case of males and 8 kg in the case of females, find the number of females in the family.
(a) 18 (b) 12
(c) 9 (d) 15

36. Average marks obtained by a student in 3 papers is 63 and in the fourth paper he obtains 67 marks. Find his new average.
(a) 54 (b) 62
(c) 64 (d) 65

37. The average earning of Srikanth for the initial three months of the calendar year 2012 is ₹2100. If his average earning (in ₹) for the second and third month is ₹2250 find his earning in the first month?
(a) 1950 (b) 1500
(c) 1700 (d) 1800

38. In a hotel where rooms are numbered from 201 to 230, each room gives an earning of ₹2000 for the first fifteen days of a month and for the latter half, ₹1000 per room. Find the average earning per room per day (in ₹) over the month. (Assume 30 day month)
(a) 1450 (b) 1500
(c) 1750 (d) 1666.66

39. The average weight of 10 men is decreased by 2 kg when, one of them weighing 140 kg is replaced by another person. Find the weight of the new person.
(a) 142 kg (b) 130 kg
(c) 138 kg (d) 120 kg

40. The average age of a group of men is increased by 6 years when a person aged 26 years is replaced by a new person of aged 56 years. How many men are there in the group?
(a) 3 (b) 4
(c) 5 (d) 6

41. The average score of a cricketer in three matches is 33 runs and in two other matches, it is 23 runs. Find the average in all the five matches.
(a) 31 (b) 26
(c) 29 (d) 28

42. The average of 15 papers is 50. The average of the first 8 papers is 48 and of the last eight papers is 54. Find the marks obtained in the 8th paper.

(a) 66 (b) 64
(c) 58 (d) 56

43. The average age of the Indian cricket team playing the Coimbatore test is 28. The average age of 5 of the players is 26 and that of another set of 5 players, totally different from the first five, is 29. If it is the captain who was not included in either of these two groups, then find the age of the captain.
(a) 35 (b) 30
(c) 33 (d) 28

44. Siddhartha has earned an average of 3200 dollars for the first eleven months of the year. If he justifies his staying on in the US on the basis of his ability to earn at least 4000 dollars per month for the entire year, how much should he earn (in dollars) in the last month to achieve his required average for the whole year?
(a) 11,800 (b) 12,800
(c) 10,800 (d) 13,800

45. A bus goes to Ranchi from Patna at the rate of 80 km per hour. Another bus leaves Ranchi for Patna at the same time as the first bus at the rate of 90 km per hour. Find the average speed for the journeys of the two buses combined if it is known that the distance from Ranchi to Patna is 720 kilometres.
(a) 84.705 kmph (b) 84 kmph
(c) 81.63 kmph (d) 82.82 kmph

46. A train travels 12 km in the first quarter of an hour, 15 km in the second quarter and 30 km in the third quarter. Find the average speed of the train per hour over the entire journey.
(a) 76 km/h (b) 72 km/h
(c) 77 km/h (d) 73 km/h

47. The average weight of 6 men is 58.5 kg. If it is known that Ram and Tram weigh 65 kg each, find the average weight of the others.
(a) 55 kg (b) 54.25 kg
(c) 54 kg (d) 55.25 kg

48. The average score of a class of 30 students is 56. What will be the average score of the rest of the students if the average score of 10 of the students is 59.
(a) 52.5 (b) 54.5
(c) 52 (d) 53

49. The average age of 60 students of IIM, Bangalore of the 1995 batch is 23 years. What will be the new average if we include the 40 faculty members whose average age is 35 years?
(a) 27 years (b) 26.5 years
(c) 27.8 years (d) 28 years

50. Out of three numbers, the first is twice the second and three times the third. The average of the three numbers is 132. The smallest number is
(a) 36 (b) 72
(c) 42 (d) 48

51. In a bag, there are 150 coins of ₹1, 50 p and 25 p denominations. If the total value of coins is ₹150, then find how many rupees can be constituted by 50 p coins.
(a) 16 (b) 20
(c) 28 (d) None of these

52. The age of two friends Aman and Baman is in the ratio 1:2. After 5 years, the ratio of their ages will become 3:5. Find the average of their ages after 10 years.

53. If we take four numbers, the average of the first three is 20 and that of the last three is 10. If the first number is 20, the last number is:

54. Sachin has a batting average of 40 runs per innings in 15 ODIs. It was found that in the 2 ODI match series against South Africa (which were part of his first 15 ODIs), his average score was 40 and not 80. His correct average is:

55. The average of temperatures at noontime from Monday to Friday is 40; the lowest one is 35. What is the possible maximum temperature at noontime on any of these days?

56. The average age of a family of 3 members is 30 years. If the age of the youngest member is 5 years, then what was the average age of the family immediately prior to the birth of the youngest member?

57. The average of 50 numbers is zero. Of them, at the most, how many may be greater than zero?

58. The average of 40 numbers is 25. If two numbers namely 40 and 50 are discarded, the average of the remaining numbers is:

59. The average of ten numbers is 60. The average of the first five numbers is 50 and that of last four numbers is 30. Then the 6th number is:

60. The average of 10 integers is found to be 10. But after the calculation, it was detected that, by mistake, the integer 20 was copied as 30, while calculating the average. After the due correction is made, the new average will be:

Space for Rough Work

LEVEL OF DIFFICULTY (II)

1. The average marks of 35 boys and 25 girls in a school was 80. When one of the boys, whose marks were 3/5th more than the average marks, and a girl whose marks were half of the average marks, were replaced with a new boy and girl, the average of the class dropped by 2 marks. What percentage of marks of the ones who were replaced is the marks of the new students?
   (a) 28.6% (b) 30%
   (c) 28.7% (d) 28.4%
2. The average weight of 24 students increases by 6 kg when four of them leave the group. If the average weight of these four students is one-fourth of the average weight of the original 24 students, then what is the average weight of the remaining 20 students, in kg?
3. 3 liters of a mixture of A & B is mixed with 15 liters of another mixture of A & B. Due to this the concentration of A in the second mixture decreases by 10 percentage points. What is the difference between the concentration percentage of B in both the mixtures?
4. If the average of n consecutive natural numbers is 8.33% less than the highest number, then what is the sum of all the terms when n is minimum?
5. The average of Alternate numbers of a set of 7 integers is 18 and average of the remaining numbers is 25. What is the difference between the maximum and minimum possible average of the whole set?
6. The average score of a group of players of the Indian cricket team decreases by 60 runs when the runs of some of the players of the India A team are also considered. If the average runs scored by players (under consideration here) of the A team is 110 less than that averaged by the players of the Indian cricket team being considered here, then what could be the total number of players in discussion?
   (a) 25 (b) 39
   (c) 44 (d) 67
7. Meenakshi earns ₹8000 per month and wants to save an average of ₹1100 per month in a year. In the first nine months, her monthly expense was ₹7000, and she foresees that her monthly expense will increase by 2/35. In order to meet her yearly savings target, her monthly earnings, for the remaining year should be.
   (a) 8400 (b) 8800
   (c) 8500 (d) 8700
8. The average weight of 30 parcels in a goods train is 60. Six of the heaviest parcels are equal in weight. Find the maximum weight of the heaviest parcel if the lowest is 35 and all weights are distinct apart from these six.
9. 5 racers took part in a 100m dash organized by Mindworkzz. The clock showing the time taken by the racers displays the average time taken by the racers who have finished the race till that instant. The clock displayed 10s, 15s, 14s, 12s, and 13s after the five racers crossed the finish line in no particular order. What was the time taken by the last racer (in seconds)?
10. The average of the marks of ten students in a test was 4.4. The test comprised ten questions, each carrying one mark, –1 for incorrect answers and 0 for unattempted questions. However, the answer to one of the question was eventually changed during evaluation, because of which the average became 3.8. At the maximum, how many had not earned any marks for the question that was removed if no one gained in this change?
11. At a science lab, a student was given 4 liters of a mixture of HCL and NaOH containing 20% NaOH. Out of curiosity, he added 1L of similar mixture containing 30% NaOH. He further added 1 liter of NaOH to the new mixture. What is the percentage of HCl in the resulting concoction?
    (a) 35% (b) 65%
    (c) 25% (d) 45%
12. There are twelve distinct natural numbers such that the average of the three smallest numbers is 17, and the average of the three largest numbers is 32. The maximum possible value of the average of these twelve numbers is.
    (a) 27 (b) 26
    (c) 34.66 (d) 25
13. There are 5 tribes on an island, tribe A through E. Two of the tribes have 16 and 64 members. What is the sum of the highest and lowest possible average of the total number of members in the five tribes if the number of members in the five tribes form an increasing GP?
14. The marks of 17 students in a class is in an AP when arranged according to their ranks. The class teacher found that the students who were ranked 5th, 7th, 9th, 11th and 17th had cheated and hence, got all of them rusticated. The average of the class changed from A to B. Which of the following would be true?
    (a) $A = B$ (b) $A > B$
    (c) $A < B$ (d) $A \leq B$
    17, 16, 15, 14, **13**, 12, **11**, 10, **9**, 8, **7**, 6, 5, 4, 3, **2**, 1
15. The heights of 4 employees of Mindworkzz are distinct integers such that the average height is 4.5 feet. The maximum possible difference in the average height (in feet) of the two tallest employees cannot exceed:

16. What is the minimum possible average of a non decreasing GP of natural numbers?

17. In a class, 60% of the students passed the mathematics exam, and the rest failed. Among the students who passed, the highest score achieved was 98, and the lowest score was 40. Among the students who failed, the highest score achieved was 35, and the lowest score was 12. Which of the following is the correct range of the average score of the class?

(a) 36 to 64 (b) 36.9 to 64.7
(b) 35.9 to 65.7 (d) 35 to 65

18. The average marks of 6 students in a test whose max marks is 100 is 72. All the students got different marks, one of the students obtained 80 marks. The lowest possible score for rest is 50. The maximum possible difference between the second highest and the second lowest marks is:

19. A drone is flying along the sides of a square area having side 30 km. It covers the first side at a speed of 10 km/h, consequently it increases its speed by 10 km/h for each consecutive side till it completes one round of the whole perimeter. The average speed of the drone was what percentage more than the initial speed?

(a) 150% (b) 92%
(c) 87.5% (d) 75%

20. The average of 20 whole numbers is 4.5. The maximum number of distinct numbers in the dataset is

21. Sanjeeta finds the average of five two digits numbers. If she reversed one of the numbers, the average increased by 7.2. If all five numbers are consecutive multiples of four, then what was the number that was reversed?

22. In a school, 50 students each took 6 subjects with max marks as 100. The students' average percentage across all subjects is 75%. Two students want to re-evaluate their scores in one subject each. If their marks don't decrease and the new overall average becomes 75.05%, what is the maximum possible score increase for either of the two students?

23. A bus travels with a speed of 10 km/h in the first 15 minutes, goes 5 km in the next 15 minutes, 15 km in the next 15, 10 km in the next 15. What is the average speed of the bus in kilometre per hour for the journey described?

(a) 45 km/h (b) 32.50 km/h
(c) 50.50 km/h (d) 40 km/h

24. In the month of January of a certain year, the average daily expenditure of an organisation was ₹60. For the first 15 days of the month, the average daily expenditure was ₹ 80 and for the last 17 days, ₹50. Find the amount spent by the organisation on the 15th of the month.

(a) 190 (b) 160
(c) 180 (d) 130

25. A batsman makes a score of 40 runs in the 5th inning and thus increases his average by 4. Find the possible value of the new average.

(a) 28 (b) 24
(c) 12 (d) 20

26. Aman can type a sheet in 10 minutes, Baman in 20 minutes and Chaman in 30 minutes. The average number of sheets typed per hour per typist for all three typists is

(a) 11/3 (b) 30/7
(c) 55/9 (d) 32/11

27. The mean of 29 observations is 211. If the first number is increased by 1, the second number is increased by 2 and so on, the new mean would be?

28. The average weight of 32 students in a class is increased by 3 kgs when 4 students, whose average weight is $\frac{1}{4}$th the average weight of the original 32 students leave the class. What is the average weight of the remaining 28 students in the class (after the 4 students leave)?

(a) 28 kgs (b) 29 kgs
(c) 30 kgs (d) 31 kgs

29. In hotel Jaysarmin, the rooms are numbered from 101 to 150 on the first floor, 201 to 240 on the second floor and 316 to 355 on the third floor. In the month of May 2022, the room occupancy was 50% on the first floor, 50% on the second floor and 30% on the third floor. If it is also known that the room charges are ₹2000, ₹1000 and ₹1500 on each of the floors, then find the average income per room (in ₹) for the month of May 2018.

(a) 676.92 (b) 880.18
(c) 783.3 (d) 650.7

30. A salesman gets a bonus according to the following structure: If he sells articles worth ₹x then he gets a bonus of ₹(x/10 – 1000). In the month of January, his sales value was ₹10000, in February it was ₹12000, from March to November it was ₹30000 for every month and in December it was ₹12000. Apart from this, he also receives a basic salary of ₹3000 per month from his employer. Find his average income per month (in ₹) during the year.

(a) 4533 (b) 4517
(c) 4532 (d) 4668

Directions for Questions 31 and 32: Based on the following information:

Ramya, based in Shanpur, took her car for a 400 km trip to Rampur. She maintained a log of the odometer readings and the amount of petrol she purchased at different petrol pumps at different prices (given below). Her car already had 10 litres of petrol at the start of the journey, and she first purchased petrol at the start of the journey, as given in table below, and she had 5 liters remaining at the end of the journey.

	Odometer Reading (Km)	Petrol purchased (Liter)	Rate of Petrol (₹/liter)
Start of journey	400	20	30
	600	15	35
	650	10	40
End of journey	800		

31. What has been the mileage (in kilometers per liter) of her car over the entire trip?
(a) 8.00 (b) 8.50
(c) 9.00 (d) 9.50

32. Her car's tank-capacity is 35 litres. Petrol costs ₹45/ liter in Rampur. What is the minimum amount of money she would need for purchasing petrol for the return trip from Rampur to Shanpur, using the same route? Assume that the mileage of the car remains unchanged throughout the route, and she did not use her car to travel around in Rampur.
(a) 1714 (b) 1724
(c) 1734 (d) 1744

33. In a country, the production of steel grew by 50 percent in a year. In the same year, it was observed that, the per capita production of steel grew by 35%. What is the closest approximation of the growth of the population of the country during the same year?
(a) 10% (b) 11%
(c) 12% (d) 15%

34. Find the average weight of four packets, if it is known that the weight of the first packet is 20 kg and the weights of the second, third and fourth packets' each is defined by $f(x) = x^2 - \frac{2}{5} \times (x^2)$ where $x = 10$.
(a) 50 kg (b) 90 kg
(c) 70 kg (d) 40 kg

35. There are five boxes in a box hold. The weight of the first box is 40 kg and the weight of the second box is 50% higher than the weight of the third box, whose weight is 25% higher than the first boxes' weight. The fourth box at 150 kg is 50% heavier than the fifth box. Find the difference in the average weight of the four heaviest boxes and the four lightest boxes.
(a) 21.5 kg (b) 25 kg
(c) 27.5 kg (d) 22.5 kg

36. For Question 35, find the difference in the average weight of the heaviest three and the lightest three.
(a) 66.66 kg (b) 25 kg
(c) 50 kg (d) 53.33 kg

37. 20 persons went to a hotel for a combined dinner party. 15 of them spent ₹ 90 each on their dinner and the rest spent ₹ 30 more than the average expenditure of all the 20. What was the total money spent (in ₹) by them?
(a) 1700 (b) 2000
(c) 2200 (d) None of these

38. There were 30 students in a hostel. Due to the admission of 20 new students, the expenses of the mess increase by ₹1600 per day while the average expenditure per head diminished by ₹8. What was the original expenditure of the mess?
(a) 3000 (b) 1600
(c) 2000 (d) 1200

39. The average price of 3 precious diamond studded platinum thrones is ₹ 97610498312. If their prices are in the ratio 4:7:9. The price of the cheapest is
(a) 5, 65, 66, 298.972 (b) 5, 85, 66, 29, 8987.2
(c) 58, 56, 62, 889.72 (d) None of these

40. The average weight of 23boxes is 3kg. If the weight of the container (in which the boxes are kept) is included, the calculated average weight per box increases by 1 kg. What is the weight of the container?
(a) 26 kg (b) 4 kg
(c) 5 kg (d) None of these

41. 3 years ago, one-fifth of Amit's age was equal to one-fourth of the age of Sumit, and the average of their age was 31.5 years. If the age of Punit is also considered, the average age of three of them declines to 28 years. What will be the average age of Amit and Punit 3 years from now?
(a) 33 years (b) 34 years
(c) 32.5 years (d) 35 years

42. Two farmers were cultivating wheat on their respective agricultural land in a village. Farmer A had an average production of 30 bushels from a hectare. Farmer B, who had 25 hectares of more land dedicated to wheat cultivation, had an output of 40 bushels of wheat from a hectare. If farmer B harvested 1120 bushels of wheat more than farmer A, how many bushels of wheat did farmer A cultivate?
(a) 480 (b) 120
(c) 360 (d) 150

43. The average salary of the entire staff in a department is ₹2000 per month. The average salary of officers is ₹ 3000 and that of non-officers is ₹ 1500. If the number of officers is 10, then find the number of non-officers in the office?
(a) 20 (b) 25
(c) 15 (d) 10

44. The average of 'n' numbers is z. If the number x is replaced by the number x^1, then the average becomes z^1. Find the relation between n, z, z^1, x and x^1.
(a) $\left[\frac{z^1 - 2}{x^1 - x} = \frac{1}{n}\right]$ (b) $\frac{x^1 - x}{z^1} = \frac{1}{n}$
(c) $\left[\frac{z - z^1}{x - x^1} = \frac{1}{n}\right]$ (d) $\left[\frac{x - x^1}{z - z^1} = \frac{1}{n}\right]$

45. A person travels three equal distances at a speed of x km/h, y km/h and z km/h respectively. What will be the average speed during the whole journey?
(a) $xyz/(xy + yz + zx)$ (b) $(xy + yz + zx)/xyz$
(c) $3xyz/(xy + yz + xz)$ (d) None of these

Directions for Questions 46 to 49: Read the following passage and answer the questions that follow.

Aman, Binod, Charan, Dharam and Ehsaan are the members of the same family. Each and everyone loves one another very much. Their birthdays are in different months and on different dates. *Aman* remembers that his birthday is between 25th and 30th, of *Binod* it is between 20th and 25th, of *Charan* it is between 10th and 20th, of *Dharam* it is between 5th and 10th and of *Ehsaan* it is between 1st to 5th of the month. The sum of the date of birth is defined as the addition of the date and the month, for example 12th January will be written as 12/1 and will add to a sum of the date of 13. (Between 25th and 30th includes both 25 and 30).

46. What may be the maximum average of their sum of the dates of birth?
(a) 24.6 (b) 15.2
(c) 28 (d) 32

47. What may be the minimum average of their sum of the dates of births?
(a) 24.6 (b) 15.2
(c) 28 (d) 32

48. If it is known that the dates of birth of three of them are even numbers then find maximum average of their sum of the dates of birth.
(a) 24.6 (b) 15.2
(c) 27.6 (d) 28

49. If the dates of birth, of four of them are prime numbers, then find the maximum average of the sum of their dates of birth.
(a) 27.2 (b) 26.4
(c) 28 (d) None of these

50. In a local shop, as part of promotional measures, the shop owner sells three different varieties of soap, one at a loss of 15 percent, another at a profit of 23 percent and the third one at a loss of 22 percent. Assuming that the shop owner sells all three varieties of soap at the same price, the approximate percentage by which average cost price is lower or higher than the selling price is
(a) 9.03% higher (b) 12.5 lower
(c) 14.5 lower (d) 8.5 higher

51. An engineering college has only four batches that contain 20, 40, 60 and 80 students respectively. The pass percentage of these classes, are 10%, 20%, 30% and 40% respectively. Find the pass percentage of the entire college.
(a) 50% (b) 70%
(c) 30% (d) 60%

52. A Pharmaceutical company produces two chemicals X and Y, such that X consists of 5% salt A and 10% salt B and Y consists of 10% salt A and 6% salt B. For producing the chemicals X and Y, the company requires at least 7 gm of Salt A and at least 7 gm of Salt B. If chemical X costs ₹10.50 per gm and chemical Y costs ₹7.80 per gm, what is the minimum cost at which the company can meet the requirement by using a combination of both types of chemicals?
(a) ₹810 (b) ₹850
(c) ₹537. (d) None of these

Directions for Questions 53 to 56: Read the following and answer the questions that follows.

During the final match of ICC championship 2000, India playing against Australia scored in the following manner:

Partnership	*Runs scored*
1st wicket	62
2nd wicket	48
3rd wicket	32
4th wicket	62
5th wicket	26
6th wicket	13

53. Find the average runs scored by the first four batsmen.
(a) 83.5 (b) 60.5
(c) 66.8 (d) Cannot be determined

54. The maximum average runs scored by the first five batsmen could be
(a) 48.6 (b) 36.8
(c) 46 (d) Cannot be determined.

55. The minimum average runs scored by the last five batsmen to get out could be
(a) 13.6 (b) 24.4
(c) 36.8 (d) 0

56. If the fifth down batsman gets out for a duck, then find the average runs scored by the first six batsmen.
(a) 27.1 (b) 33.3
(c) 28.5 (d) Cannot be determined

57. The weight of a metal piece as calculated by the average of 7 different experiments is 53.735 gm. The average of the first three experiments is 54.005 gm, of the fourth is 0.004 gm greater than the fifth, while the average of the sixth and seventh experiment was 0.010 gm less than the average of the first three. Find the weight of the body obtained by the fourth experiment.
(a) 49.353 gm (b) 51.712 gm
(c) 53.072 gm (d) 54.512 gm

58. Sumer's average expenditure for the first 4 months of the year was ₹251.25. For the next 5 months the average monthly expenditure was ₹26.27 more than what it was during the first 4 months. If the person spent ₹760 in all during the remaining 3 months of the year, find what percentage of his annual income of ₹3000 he saved in the year.
(a) 13.667% (b) –5.0866%
(c) 12.333% (d) None of these

59. A certain number of tankers were required to transport 60 lakh liters of oil from the IOCL factory in Mathura. However, it was found that since each tanker could take 50,000 liters of oil less, another 4 tankers were needed. How many tankers were initially, planned to be used?
(a) 10 (b) 15
(c) 20 (d) 25

60. One collective farm got an average harvest of 21 tons of wheat per hectare and another collective farm that had 12 acres of land less given to wheat, got 25 tons from a hectare. As a result, the second farm harvested 300 tons of wheat more than the first. How many tons of wheat did each farm harvest?
(a) 3150, 3450 (b) 3250, 3550
(c) 2150, 2450 (d) None of these

61. If the product of n positive integers is n^n, then what is the minimum value of their average for $n = 6$?

62. Anurag Mishra buys ₹24900 worth of goodies for the animals at his farm. For each dog, he gets a pack of dog food priced at ₹330 per pack, while for each cat he gets a pack of tuna fish priced at ₹290 per pack. How many packs of each type did he buy?
(a) 21, 57 (b) 57,21
(c) 37, 51 (d) 27,51

Directions for Questions 63 and 64: On January 15, 2001 there were 6 members in Binod's family and their average age was 28 years. He got married between 2001 and 2004 and on January 15, 2004 there was an addition of a child in his family. On January 15th 2006, the average age of his family is 32 years.

63. What is the present age of Binod's wife (in years) on January 15th 2006?

64. If Binod's age is greater than his wife and in 2001 his age was a prime number then what is the minimum possible value of Binod's present age? (in 2006) (in years) All dates refer to 15th January of the respective year.

65. If the average of 21, 23, x, 24, 27 lies in between 25, 28 (including both). Find the number of possible integral values of x.

66. Rozer a great tennis player has 10 boxes with him, which have an average of 25 tennis balls per box. If each box has at least 8 balls and no two boxes have an equal number of balls, then what is the maximum possible number of balls in any box?

67. If the average of five different numbers is 6, and if all the numbers are distinct postive integers then what is the largest possible value of the average of the 2 biggest numbers?

Directions for Questions 68 and 69: In CMS, Delhi students of two different sections appeared for a test. The average score of students of Class 9th is 80 and the average score of class 10th is 73. Average scores of girls and boys of class 9th are 70 and 85, respectively and that of class 10th are 70 and 74, respectively. The number of boys of class 10th is 3 times the number of girls of class 9th

68. What is the ratio of boys and girls of class 9th?

69. What is the average score of all the students of class 9th and 10th together?

70. There are four numbers w, x, y, z. If the sum of all possible distinct groups, each having two numbers from amongst w, x, y, z is 1440, then what is the average of these four numbers?

71. A shop sells bags in three sizes: small, medium and large. A large bag costs ₹1000, a medium bag costs ₹200, and a small bag costs ₹50. Three buyers, Ashish, Banti and Chintu, independently buy some numbers of these types of bags. The respective amounts spent by Ashish, Banti and Chintu are equal. Put together, the shop sells 1 large bag, 15 small bags and some medium bags to these three buyers. What is the minimum number of medium bags that the shop sells to them?

72. For the above question, if we knew that the total expense by the three of them was more than ₹10000, then the minimum value of the number of medium bags that the shop sells to them is?

High Yield Questions

Scan this QR code to access assisted problem solving videos on questions 1, 2, 9, 10 and 18 from LOD 2

Space for Rough Work

LEVEL OF DIFFICULTY (III)

1. In a class of 200 students, the ratio of boys who play cricket to those who play badminton is 4 : 3, while the ratio of girls who play cricket to those who play badminton is 2 : 7. Each student plays exactly one game. What is the average of the maximum possible number of students who play cricket and the maximum possible number of students who play badminton?
2. The average age of a family of 2 decreases by A when they adopted a new born. 5 years down the line, They adopted another new born because of which the average changes by B. If the difference between the two changes is 12, then find the average of the family before the first baby was adopted.
3. If the average marks of Pallav and Shaurya is 50, and average of Anshuman and Pulkit is 80 such that Pulkit scored more than Anshuman who scored more than Shaurya who scored more than Pallav and the marks are positive integers, then what is the difference between the maximum and minimum possible average marks of Pallav and Pulkit?
   (a) 64 (b) 62.5
   (c) 70 (d) 67.5
4. If the average of n consecutive two digit even natural numbers is 6.667% less than the highest term, then what is highest value 'n' can take?
5. 25 students of a class A is combined with another class of 75 students of Class B. The average marks of class A quadruples and that of class B decreases by 15 marks. What is the maximum marks of the test if it is known that class B averaged at 83.33% of the total marks?
6. Verghese the milkman makes two mixtures of milk, water and some more liquids. In the first mixture A, Milk is 5%, Water is 10% whereas the second mixture B has 10% milk and 6% water. The first mixture is sold at ₹105 per liter while the second mixture is sold for ₹78 per liter. What is the minimum revenue (in rupees) accruing to Verghese, if he uses at least 7 liters of Milk and 7 liters of water on that day?
7. The average score of x Batters of team India (P1, P2, P3 … Px) in non-decreasing order is 51. If the score of the first batter P1 is replaced by its quadruple, the new average becomes 102. Then, the sum of all the possible scores of P1 is:
8. The average of N natural numbers each of which is less than 100 is 60. If a_1 which is the smallest number is increased by 35, a_N which is the largest number is decreased by 15, then the resultant average is 65. If $(a_1)_{new} \leq (a_2)_{new}$, then the number of terms in the set of these N natural numbers is:
9. In an examination, the average marks of students in sections A and B are 32 and 60, respectively. The number of students in section A is 10 less than that in section B. If the average marks of all the students across both the sections combined is an integer, then the difference between the maximum and minimum possible number of students in section A is
10. Consider six distinct natural numbers such that the average of the two smallest numbers is 14, and the average of the two largest numbers is 28. Then, the difference between the maximum possible average and the minimum possible average of these six numbers is
    (a) 2.5 (b) 3
    (c) 4 (d) 3.5
11. In a group of 10 students, the mean of the lowest 9 scores is 42 while the mean of the highest 9 scores is 47. What is the difference between the highest possible average and the lowest possible average for all the 10 students?
    (a) 5 (b) 3
    (c) 4 (d) 6
12. In a group of 10 students everyone scores a distinct score. The mean of the lowest 9 scores is 42 while the mean of the highest 9 scores is 47. What is the difference between the highest possible average and the lowest possible average for all the 10 students?
13. The weight machine at a gym calculated the average weight of all the people who stood on the weighing machine. Surprisingly, the machine displayed an integer value each time. The weight of the 5 people who stood on the machine were 62, 67,71, 73 and 82 in no particular order. The weight of the last person was:
14. Indian Batting Legend, Virat Kohli played a certain number of innings in the year 2022. All his innings were completed as he was out every single time. The average runs scored by him increases by 1 if his first 10 matches are not considered, and decreases by 1 if his last 10 matches are not considered. If the average runs scored by him for the first 10 and the last 10 matches are 20 and 30, respectively, then the total number of matches Kohli played in 2022 is
15. A student wrote 6 three-digit numbers on the board. If he had written the reverse of two of the numbers A and B instead of the actual numbers, the average of the numbers would have been 115.5 less. The sum of the averages of the hundreds and the units digits of A and the hundreds and the units digits of B is 9.5. Find the sum of the hundreds digits of A and B.

(a) 12 (b) 13
(c) 18 (d) 16

16. In the PMO Office, the number of people aged 57 years and above is 30 and there are at most 39 people whose ages are below 57 years. The average age of all the people in the office is 44 years. What is the largest possible average age, in years, of the people whose ages are below 57 years?
(a) 35 (b) 36
(c) 37 (d) 34

17. Shaurya played ten games in the badminton tournament. His scores in the sixth, seventh, eighth, and ninth games were 22, 16, 14, and 20 points. His points-per-game average was higher after nine games than the average after the first five games. If his average after ten games was more than 19, then what is his minimum number of points in the tenth game?
(a) 31 (b) 30
(c) 29 (d) 28

18. Let $a_1, a_2, ..., a_{50}$ be positive integers in increasing order. The arithmetic mean of $a_1, a_2, ..., a_{50}$ is 34. If the arithmetic mean of $a_{26}, a_{27}, ..., a_{50}$ is 48. If $a_1, a_2, ..., a_{25}$ are in an arithmetic progression, then what is the sum of maximum possible values of a_{26} and a_{50}?

19. Let $a_1, a_2, ..., a_{50}$ be positive integers in increasing order. The arithmetic mean of $a_1, a_2, ..., a_{50}$ is 34. If the arithmetic mean of $a_{26}, a_{27}, ..., a_{50}$ is 48. If $a_1, a_2, ..., a_{25}$ are in an arithmetic progression, then what is the sum of minimum possible values of a_{26} and a_{50}?

20. Average of 3 numbers x, y and z is 35 where $x : z = 2 : 5$ and y is greater than x by 15. Also, z is given by the equation $z = ab - 25$ where a and b are natural numbers, then what is the difference between the maximum and minimum possible average of a and b?

21. Five students, including Shaurya, appear for an examination where the max marks is 50. The average marks for all the students is 38 with only 3 people scoring more than 32. If Shaurya scored the minimum marks among the 5 students and all scores were distinct, then the difference between the highest and lowest possible marks of Shaurya is.

22. Pallav bought a 2L bottle of milk and drank 5% of it on the first day and replaced it with coke. On the second day he drank 10% of the contents and replaced it with coke. On the third day he drank 15% and replaced it with coke. He continued in this way and drank the whole bottle on the 20th day. Find the average quantity of coke that Pallav drank per day from the bottle in these 20 days.

23. The average of 8 numbers is 75. If the smallest number is deleted, then the average of the remaining numbers is A and if the largest number is deleted, then the average of the remaining numbers is B. If A + B = 90, then what is the average of the smallest and largest numbers?
(a) 275 (b) 355
(c) 315 (d) 285

24. In the first 20 matches of IPL 2034, five players A, B, C, D, and E, had average scores of 30, 40, 35, 45, and 50 runs, respectively. In the subsequent 5 matches, A and B each scored 200 runs, while C's score exceeded D's by 50%. Following these 25 matches, if A's new average score is 4/5 that of D, what is the average score of player C?

25. There are 8 students in a group. When the heaviest student leaves the group the average weight of the new group reduces by 2 kg. When the lightest student leaves the group the average of the new group increases by 2 kg. If both of them leave the group, then the sum of the weights of the remaining students in the group was 270 kg. What is the weight (in kg) of the heaviest student in the original group?

Directions for Questions 26 to 33: Read the following:
There are 3 classes having 20, 25 and 30 students, respectively, having average marks in an examination as 20, 25 and 30, respectively. If the three classes are represented by *A*, *B* and *C* and you have the following information about the three classes, answer the questions that follow:

A → Highest score 22, Lowest score 18
B → Highest score 31, Lowest score 23
C → Highest score 33, Lowest score 26

If five students are transferred from *A* to *B*.

26. What will happen to the average score of *B*?
(a) Definitely increase (b) Definitely decrease
(c) Remain constant (d) Cannot say

27. What will happen to the average score of *A*?
(a) Definitely increase (b) Definitely decrease
(c) Remain constant (d) Cannot say

In a transfer of five students from *A* to *C*

28. What will happen to the average score of *C*?
(a) Definitely increase (b) Definitely decrease
(c) Remain constant (d) Cannot say

29. What will happen to the average score of *A*?
(a) Definitely increase (b) Definitely decrease
(c) Remain constant (d) Cannot say

In a transfer of five students from *B* to *C* (Questions 30–31)

30. What will happen to the average score of *C*?
(a) Definitely increase (b) Definitely decrease
(c) Remain constant (d) Cannot say

31. Which of these can be said about the average score of *B*?
(a) Increases if *C* decreases
(b) Decreases if *C* increases
(c) Increases if *C* decreases
(d) Decreases if *C* decreases

32. In a transfer of five students from A to B, the maximum possible average achievable for group B is
(a) 25 (b) 24.5
(c) 25.5 (d) 24

33. For the above case, the maximum possible average achieved for group A will be
(a) 20.66 (b) 21.5
(c) 20.75 (d) 20.5

34. What will be the minimum possible average of Group A if five students are transferred from A to B?
(a) 19.55 (b) 21.5
(c) 19.33 (d) 20.5

35. If five students are transferred from B to A, what will be the minimum possible average of A?
(a) 20.69 (b) 21
(c) 20.75 (d) 20.6

36. For question 35, what will be the maximum average of A?
(a) 23.2 (b) 22.2
(c) 18.75 (d) 19

Directions for Questions 37 to 42: Read the following and answer the questions that follow.

If five people are transferred from A to B and another independent set of five people are transferred back from B to A, then after this operation (Assume that the set transferred from B to A contains none from the set of students that came to B from A)

37. What will happen to B's average?
(a) Increases if A's average decreases
(b) Decrease always
(c) Cannot be said
(d) Decreases if A's average decreases

38. What can be said about A's average?
(a) Will decrease
(b) Will always increase
(c) May increase or decrease
(d) Will increase only if B's average decreases

39. At the end of the two steps mentioned above (in the *direction*), what could be the maximum value of the average of class B?
(a) 25.4 (b) 25
(c) 24.8 (d) 24.6

40. For question 39, what could be the minimum value of the average of class B?
(a) 22.4 (b) 24.2
(c) 25 (d) 23

41. What could be the maximum possible average achieved by class A at the end of the operation?
(a) 25.2 (b) 26
(c) 23.25 (d) 23.75

42. What could be the minimum possible average of class A at the end of the operation?
(a) 21.4 (b) 19.2
(c) 28.5 (d) 20.25

Directions for Questions 43 to 48: Read the following and answer the questions that follow.

If five people are transferred from C to B, further, five more people are transferred from B to A, then five are transferred from A to B and finally, five more are transferred from B to C.

43. What is the maximum possible average achieved by class C?
(a) 30.833 (b) 30
(c) 29.66 (d) 30.66

44. What is the maximum possible average of class B?
(a) 26 (b) 27
(c) 25 (d) 28

45. What is the maximum possible average value attained by class A?
(a) 22.75 (b) 23.75
(c) 23.5 (d) 24

46. The minimum possible value of the average of group C is
(a) 26.3 (b) 27.5
(c) 29.6 (d) 28

47. The minimum possible average of group B after this set of operation is
(a) 21.6 (b) 22.2
(c) 21.8 (d) 21.4

48. The minimum possible average of group A after the set of three operation is
(a) 20 (b) 20.3
(c) 20.4 (d) 19.8

49. Which of these will definitely not constitute an operation for getting the minimum possible average value for group A?
(a) Transfer of five 31s from B to A
(b) Transfer of five 26s from C to B
(c) Transfer of five 22s from A to B
(d) Transfer of five 33s from C to B

50. For getting the lowest possible value of C's average, the sequence of operations could be
(a) Transfer five 33s from C to B, five 23s from B to A, five 18s from A to B, five 18s from B to C
(b) Transfer five 33s from C to B, 31s from B to A
(c) Both (a) and (b)
(d) None of these

51. If we set the highest possible average of class C as the primary objective and want to achieve the highest possible value for class B as the secondary objective, what is the maximum value of class B's average that is attainable?
(a) 27 (b) 26
(c) 25 (d) 24

52. For Question 51, if the secondary objective is changed to achieving the minimum possible average value

of class B's average, the lowest value of class B's average that could be attained is

(a) 22.6 (b) 23
(c) 22.2 (d) 22

53. For question 52, what can be said about class A's average?

(a) Will be determined automatically at 23.25
(b) Will have a maximum possible value of 23.25
(c) Will have a minimum possible value of 22.25
(d) Will be determined automatically at 22.25

54. A team of miners planned to mine 1800 tons of ore during a certain number of days. Due to technical difficulties in one-third of the planned number of days, the team was able to achieve an output of 20 tons of ore less than the planned output. To make up for this, the team overachieved for the rest of the days by 20 tons. The end result was that the team completed the task one day ahead of time. How many tons of ore did the team initially plan to ore per day?

(a) 50 tons (b) 100 tons
(c) 150 tons (d) 200 tons

55. According to a plan, a team of woodcutters decided to harvest 216 m^3 of wheat in several days. In the first three days, the team fulfilled the daily assignment, and then it harvested 8 m^3 of wheat over and above the plan everyday. Therefore, a day before the planned date, they had already harvested 232 m^3 of wheat. How many cubic metres of wheat a day did the team have to cut according to the plan?

(a) 12 (b) 13
(c) 24 (d) 25

56. On an average, two litres of milk and one litre of water are needed to be mixed to make 1 kg of sudha shrikhand of type A, and 3 litres of milk and 2 litres of water are needed to be mixed to make 1 kg of sudha shrikhand of type B. How many kilograms of each type of shrikhand was manufactured if it is known that 130 litres of milk and 80 litres of water were used?

(a) 20 of type A and 30 of type B
(b) 30 of type A and 20 of type B
(c) 15 of type A and 30 of type B
(d) 30 of type A and 15 of type B

57. There are 500 seats in Minerva Cinema, Mumbai, placed in similar rows. After the reconstruction of the hall, the total number of seats became 10% less. The number of rows was reduced by five but each row contained five seats more than before. How many rows and how many seats in a row were there initially in the hall?

(a) 20 rows and 25 seats
(b) 20 rows and 20 seats
(c) 10 rows and 50 seats
(d) 50 rows and 10 seats

58. One fashion house has to make 810 dresses and another one 900 dresses during the same period of time. In the first house, the order was ready three days ahead of time and in the second house, six days ahead of time. How many dresses did each fashion house make a day if the second house made 21 dresses more a day than the first?

(a) 54 and 75 (b) 24 and 48
(c) 44 and 68 (d) 4 and 25

59. In a class, the number of people who scored 61 or more is 30 and there are at most 39 people who scored below 61 marks. If the average marks of the class is 48, what is the largest possible average marks of the people who scored below 61 marks?

(a) 38 (b) 35
(c) 32 (d) None of these

60. An enterprise got a bonus and decided to share it in equal parts between the exemplary workers. It turned out, however, that there were three more exemplary workers than it had been assumed. In that case, each of them would have got ₹4 less. The administration had found the possibility to increase the total sum of the bonus by ₹90 and as a result each exemplary worker received ₹25. How many people received the bonus?

(a) 9 (b) 18
(c) 8 (d) 16

Directions for Questions 61 to 64: Read the following and answer the questions that follow.

In the island of Hoola Boola Moola, the inhabitants have a strange process of calculating their average incomes and expenditures. According to an old legend prevalent on that island, the average monthly income had to be calculated on the basis of 14 months in a calendar year while the average monthly expenditure was to be calculated on the basis of 9 months per year. This would lead to people having an underestimation of their savings since there would be an underestimation of the income and an overestimation of the expenditure per month.

61. If the minister for economic affairs decided to reverse the process of calculation of average income and average expenditure, what will happen to the estimated savings of a person living on Hoola Boola Moola island?

(a) It will increase
(b) It will decrease
(c) It will remain constant
(d) Will depend on the value

62. If it is known that Mr. Magoo Hoola Boola estimates his monthly savings at 10 Moolahs and if it is further known that his actual expenditure is 288 Moolahs in a year (Moolahs, for those who are not aware, is the official currency of Hoola Boola Moola), then what will happen to his estimated savings if he suddenly calculates on the basis of a 12 month calendar year?

(a) Will increase by 5 (b) Will increase by 15
(c) Will increase by 10 (d) Will triple

63. Mr. Boogie Woogie comes back from the USA to Hoola Boola Moola and convinces his community comprising 546 families to start calculating the average income and average expenditure on the basis of 12 months per calendar year. Now if it is known that the average estimated income on the island is (according to the old system) 87 Moolahs per month, then what will be the change in the average estimated savings for the island of Hoola Boola Moola (Assume that there is no other change).

(a) 12.5 Moolahs (b) 14.5 Moolahs
(c) 14 Moolahs (d) Cannot be determined

64. Mr. Boogle Woogle comes back from the USSR and convinces his community comprising 273 families to start calculating the average income on the basis of 12 months per calendar year. Now if it is known that the average estimated income in his community is (according to the old system) 87 Moolahs per month, then what will be the change in the average estimated savings for the island of Hoola Boola Moola (Assume that there is no other change).

(a) 12.5 Moolahs (b) 14.5 Moolahs
(c) 14 Moolahs (d) Cannot be determined

65. Aman stays in Bangalore in a joint family comprising his parents, his uncle, aunt, an elder sister and a cousin two years younger than him. He graduated from IIM Bangalore in 2021, when the average age of his family was 38 years. He got married in 2023 and became a father in 2025. If the average age of his family in 2027 is the same as in 2021, and he is older to his wife by 3 years, find the age at which he graduated from IIM Bangalore. Assume, that there is no other change (person leaving/dying or person getting added to the family – than what is described here).

66. The owner of a grocery shop purchases two varieties of oil. He mixes these varieties and sells them at ₹37.5 Per litre, thus gaining a profit of 25% on his cost price. If the ratio of mixing the two varieties of oil is 2 : 3 and the price of the first variety is 2.25 times the price of the second variety, what is the price of the first variety of oil (₹ Per litre)?

67. The tax rates for various income slabs are given below.

Income Slab (₹)	Tax rate
≤500	Nil
>500 to ≤2000	5%
>2000 to ≤5000	10%
>5000 to <10000	15%

There are 15 persons working in an organisation. Out of them, 3 to 5 persons are falling in each of the income slabs mentioned above. Which of the following is the correct tax range of the 15 persons? (E.g. If one is earning ₹2000, the tax would be: $500 \times 0 + 1500 \times 0.05$)

(a) 1350 to 7350, both excluded
(b) 1350 to 9800, both included
(c) 2175 to 7350, both excluded
(d) 2175 to 9800, both included

68. The mean of six positive integers is 15. The median is 18, and the only mode of the integers is less than 18. The maximum possible value of the largest of the six integers is

(a) 26 (b) 28
(c) 30 (d) 32

69. Prof. Suman takes a number of quizzes for a course. All the quizzes are out of 100. A student can get an A grade in the course if the average of her scores is more than or equal to 90. Grade B is awarded to a student if the average of her scores is between 87 and 89 (both included). If the average is below 87, the student gets a C grade. Ramesh is preparing for the last quiz and he realises that he will need to score a minimum of 97 to get an A grade. After the quiz, he realises that he will score 70, and he will just manage a B. How many quizzes did Prof. Suman take?

(a) 6 (b) 7
(c) 8 (d) 9

70. A teacher noticed a strange distribution of marks in the exam. There were only three distinct scores: 6, 8 and 20. The mode of the distribution was 8. The sum of the scores of all the students was 504. The number of students in the most populated category was equal to the sum of the number of students with lowest score and twice the number of students with the highest score. The total number of students in the class was:

(a) 50 (b) 51
(c) 53 (d) 57

71. The median of 11 different positive integers is 15 and seven of those 11 integers are 8, 12, 20, 6, 14, 22, and 13. Statement I: The difference between the averages of four largest integers and four smallest integers is 13.25. Statement II: The average of all the 11 integers is 16. Which of the statements would be sufficient to find the largest possible integer of these numbers?

(a) Statement I only.
(b) Statement II only.
(c) Both Statement I and Statement II are required.
(d) Neither Statement I nor Statement II is sufficient
(e) Either Statement I or Statement II is sufficient.

High Yield Questions

Scan to access assisted problem solving videos on questions 1, 2, 3, 5 and 16 from LOD 3

ANSWER KEY

Level of Difficulty (I)

1. (d)	2. (b)	3. (d)	4. (b)
5. (a)	6. (b)	7. (d)	8. (b)
9. (d)	10. (b)	11. (a)	12. (b)
13. (d)	14. (d)	15. (b)	16. (b)
17. (b)	18. (a)	19. (a)	20. (b)
21. (a)	22. (b)	23. (a)	24. (b)
25. (a)	26. (c)	27. (d)	28. (a)
29. (c)	30. (b)	31. (c)	32. (a)
33. (b)	34. (a)	35. (d)	36. (c)
37. (d)	38. (b)	39. (d)	40. (c)
41. (c)	42. (a)	43. (c)	44. (b)
45. (a)	46. (a)	47. (d)	48. (b)
49. (c)	50. (b)	51. (d)	52. 25
53. –10	54. 34.66	55. 60	56. 37.50
57. 49	58. 23.94	59. 230	60. 9

Level of Difficulty (II)

1. (a)	2. 46	3. 60	4. 33
5. 1	6. (c)	7. (b)	8. 114
9. 19	10. 7	11. (b)	12. (b)
13. 1116	14. (c)	15. 2	16. 1
17. (b)	18. 48	19. (b)	20. 13
21. 48	22. 15	23. (b)	24. (a)
25. (b)	26. (a)	27. 226	28. (d)
29. (a)	30. (a)	31. (a)	32. (d)
33. (b)	34. (a)	35. (c)	36. (d)
37. (b)	38. (a)	39. (b)	40. (d)
41. (b)	42. (c)	43. (a)	44. (c)
45. (c)	46. (c)	47. (b)	48. (d)
49. (a)	50. (a)	51. (c)	52. (a)
53. (d)	54. (a)	55. (d)	56. (d)
57. (c)	58. (b)	59. (c)	60. (a)
61. 6	62. (b)	63. 56	64. 58
65. 16	66. 142	67. 12	68. 2
69. 76	70. 120	71. 7	72. 43

Level of Difficulty (III)

1. 122	2. 79.5	3. 27	4. 7
5. 90	6. 8100	7. 85	8. 4
9. 63	10. (b)	11. (c)	12. 3.2
13. 71	14. 60	15. (b)	16. (d)
17. (b)	18. 165	19. 95	20. 28
21. 20	22. 950ml	23. (d)	24. 34
25. 59	26. (b)	27. (d)	28. (b)
29. (d)	30. (d)	31. (b)	32. (b)
33. (a)	34. (c)	35. (d)	36. (b)
37. (b)	38. (b)	39. (c)	40. (a)
41. (c)	42. (d)	43. (a)	44. (b)
45. (b)	46. (b)	47. (b)	48. (a)
49. (c)	50. (a)	51. (d)	52. (c)
53. (a)	54. (b)	55. (c)	56. (a)
57. (a)	58. (a)	59. (a)	60. (b)
61. (a)	62. (b)	63. (d)	64. (b)
65. 29	66. ₹45 per litre		67. (a)
68. (d)	69. (d)	70. (e)	71. (e)

SOLUTIONS AND SHORTCUTS

Level of Difficulty (I)

1. Required average = $(1 + 2 + 3 + \ldots + 15)/15 = 120/15 = 8$. Alternately you could use the formula for sum of the first n natural numbers as $n(n + 1)/2$ with n as 15. Then average = Sum/15 = $(15 \times 16/2)/15 = 8$
2. $100 \to 110 \to 132$. Hence, $32/2 = 16$.
3. Required average = $(2 + 4 + 6 + 8 + 10 + 12 + 14 + 16 + 18 + 20)/10 = 110/10 = 11$. Alternately you could use the formula for sum of the first n even natural numbers as $n(n + 1)$ with n as 10. Then average = Sum/10 = $10 \times 11/10 = 11$.
4. $61 \times 43 = 48 \times 36 + x + 12 \times 49 \to x = 307$.
5. Let the journey be 100 km. The average speed is given by:
   Total Distance/Total time = $100/(1+1+5) = 100/7$ kmph.
6. The weight of the second man is 50 kg and that of the third is 40 kg. Hence, net result is a drop of 60 for 10 people. Hence, 6 kg is the drop in the average.
7. Required average = $(3 + 5 + 7 + 11 + 13 + 17 + 19 + 23 + 29 + 31)/10 = 158/10 = 15.8$.
8. $P = 14 \times 10 - 13 \times 8 = 140 - 104 = 36$
9. D's weight = $4 \times 70 - 3 \times 74 = 280 - 222 = 58$.
   E's weight = $58 + 3 = 61$.
   Now, we know that $A + B + C + D = 4 \times 70 = 280$ and $B + C + D + E = 75 \times 4 = 300$. Hence, A's weight is 20 kg less than E's weight. $A = 61 - 20 = 41$ kg.
10. Monday + Tuesday + Wednesday = $3 \times 35 = 105$;
    Tuesday + Wednesday + Thursday = $3 \times 30 = 90$.
    Thus, Monday – Thursday = 15 and
    Thursday = Monday/2 → Monday = 30 and Thursday = 15
11. Total present age of A, B and $C = 25 \times 3 + 15 = 75 + 15 = 90$.
    Total present age of B and $C = 20 \times 2 + 20 = 60$.
    A's age = $90 - 60 = 30$.
12. $4x + 40 = 5(x + 4) \to x = 20$ (average after 4 innings).
    Hence, new average = $20 + 4 = 24$.
13. $(5+10+15+20+25+30)/6 = 105/6 = 17.5$
14. $1/5 + 1/8 + C = 3 \times 1/10 \to C = -1/40$.
15. His total score is $90 + 70 + 150 = 310$ out of 450. This works out to a percentage score of = 68.88%
16. Average income over 9 months = $[3 \times (2250 + 500) + 3 \times (2150 + 500) + 3 \times (5750+500)]/9 = 3883.33$
17. Total age (at present) = $5 \times 20 = 100$ years. Total age of the family excluding the youngest member (for the remaining 5 people) = $100 - 5 = 95$. Average age of the other 4 people in the family = 95/4 years.
    5 years ago their average age = $95/4 - 5 = 75/4 = 18.75$ years.

18. If the average age of 5 persons has gone up by 10 years it means the total age has gone up by 50 years. Thus the total age of the two women would be: 30 + 40 + 50 = 120. Hence, their average age = 60 years.
19. $W + T + F = 60$; $T + F + S = 63 \rightarrow S - W = 3$. Hence temperature on Wednesday = 22 – 3 = 19.
20. Average speed = $\frac{2 \times 60 \times 40}{60 + 40}$ = 48 km/hr.
21. Teacher's weight = 21 × 20 – 20 × 19 = 420– 380 = 40.
22. 3 × 20 – 2 × 25 = 60 – 50 = 10.
23. The weight of the new man would be 29 × 5 kgs more than the weight of the man he replaces. New man's weight = 120 + 29 × 5 = 265 kgs.
24. Let their current ages be x and $3x$. Then their ages after 10 years would be $x + 10$ and $3x + 10$. Now it is given that $(x + 10)/(3x + 10) = 1/2 \rightarrow x = 10$ and hence their current ages are 10 years and 30 years, respectively. So their current average age is 20 years. After 20 years their average age would be 20+20 = 40 years.
25. The average would be given by the average of the first and last numbers (since the series 1, 2, 3, 4…100 is an Arithmetic Progression).
Hence, the average = (1 + 100)/2 = 50.50
26. We need the average of the numbers: 23, 29, 31, 37, 41, 43 and 47
Average = Total/number of numbers → 251/7 = 35.85
27. Let the numbers be a, b, c and d, respectively. $a + b + c = 20 \times 3 = 60$ and $b + c + d = 25 \times 3 = 75$. Also, since d-a = 15, we have 30- a = 15 or a = 15.
28. Required average = (15 × 40 + 25× 48)/40 = 1800/40 = 45.
29. The numbers would form an *AP* with common difference 1 and the middle term (also the 4th term) as 21. Thus, the numbers would be 18, 19, 20, 21, 22, 23 and 24. The highest of these numbers would be 24.
30. Required average = (8 × 11 + 15 + 17)/10 = 120/10 = 12.
31. The new average would also go up by 4. Hence, 14 + 4 = 18.
32. If the numbers are $a + 1$, $a + 2$, $a + 3$, $a + 4$, $a + 5$….a+11 the average would be $a + 6$. If we take 13 numbers as:
$a + 1$, $a + 2$, $a + 3$, $a + 4$, $a + 5$, $a + 6$…. and $a + 13$ their average would be a+7. Hence, the average increases by 1. You can also experimentally verify this by taking any 11 consecutive numbers and finding their average, then adding the next two numbers and finding the average of the 13 numbers.
33. Total of 38 numbers = 40 × 45 – 65 – 25 = 1710. Average of 38 numbers = 1710/38 = 45.
34. When we multiply each number by 9, the average would also get multiplied by 9. Hence, the new average = 18 × 9 = 162.
35. Let the number of ladies be n. Then we have $5 \times 12 + n \times 8 = (5 + n) \times (9) \rightarrow 60 + 8n = 45 + 9n \rightarrow n = 15$.
36. (3 × 63 + 67)/4 = 256/4 = 64.
37. 2100 × 3 – 2250 × 2 = 1800.
38. (2000 × 15 + 1000 × 15)/30 = (2000 + 1000)/2 = 1500.
39. The decrease in weight would be 20 kgs (10 people's average weight drops by 2 kgs). Hence, the new person's weight = 140 - 20 = 120.
40. When a person aged 26 years, is replaced by a person aged 56 years, the total age of the group goes up by 30 years. Since this leads to an increase in the average by 6 years, it means that there are 30/6 = 5 persons in the group.
41. (33 × 3 + 23 × 2)/5 = 145/5 = 29.
42. Let the number of marks in the 8th paper be M. Then the total of the first eight papers = 8 × 48 while the total of the last 8 (i.e., 8th to 15th papers) would be 8 × 54.
Total of 1st 8 + total of 8th to 15th = total of all 15 + marks in the 8th paper →
$8 \times 48 + 8 \times 54 = 15 \times 50 + M$
$816 = 750 + M \rightarrow M = 66$
(Note: We write this equation since marks in the eighth paper is counted in both the first 8 and the last 8)
43. Let the captain's age by C. Then: $11 \times 28 = 26 \times 5 + 29 \times 5 + C \rightarrow 308 = 130 + 145 + C \rightarrow C = 33$.
44. His earning in the 12th month should be: 4000 × 12 – 3200 × 11 = 48000 – 35200 = 12800.
45. Total distance divided by total time = 1440/17 = 84.705.
46. In three quarters of an hour the train has traveled 57 km. Thus, in a full hour the train would have traveled $1/3^{rd}$ more (as it gets $1/3^{rd}$ time more). Thus, the speed of the train = 57+ 1 × 57/3 = 57 + 19 = 76.
47. Total weight of all 6 = 58.5 × 6. Total weight of Ram and Tram = 65 × 2 = 130. Average weight of the 4 people excluding Ram and Tram = (58.5 × 6 – 130)/4 = 55.25 kg.
48. $10 \times 59 + 20 \times A = 30 \times 56 \rightarrow A = (1680 - 590)/20 = 1090/20 = 54.5$
49. (60 × 23 + 40 × 35)/100 = 2780/100 = 27.8
50. If we take the first number as $6n$, the second number would be $3n$ and the third would be $2n$. Sum of the three numbers = $6n + 3n + 2n = 11n = 132 \times 3 \rightarrow n = 36$. The smallest number would be $2n$ = 72.
51. For 150 coins to be of a value of ₹150, using only 25 paise, 50 paise and 1 Rupee coins, we cannot have any coins lower than the value of ₹1. Thus, the number of 50 paise coins would be 0. Option (d) is correct.
52. Let the present ages of Aman and Baman be x and $2x$ respectively.

$$\frac{x+5}{2x+5} = \frac{3}{5}$$

$5x + 25 = 6x + 15$

$x = 10$. Hence their present ages are 10 and 20. In 10 years time their ages would be 20 and 30 years respectively. The average age would be 25 years.

53. Let the numbers be a, b, c, d

$a + b + c = 3 \times 20$ .....(1)

$b + c + d = 3 \times 10$ .....(2)

Equation (1) – Equation (2)

$a - d = 30$

$d = a - 30$

$d = 20 - 30 = -10$.

54. Correct average

$$= \frac{15\times 40-2(80-40)}{15} = \frac{520}{15} = 34.66$$

55. M + T + W + Th + Fr = 40 × 5 = 200

If four of these were equal to the lowest possible, i.e. 35 each, the maximum possible temperature for the fifth day is 200 – 35× 4 = 60.

56. Present sum of ages of the family = 3 × 30 = 90

Sum of ages (5 years ago) = 90 – 3 × 5 = 75.

Required average = 75/2 = 37.50 years

57. If the Average of 50 numbers is 0, then at most 49 of them can be greater than 0 and 50th number can be such that its negative value equals to the sum of the positive values of the first 49 numbers.

58. Required average = $\frac{40.25-50-40}{38} = \frac{910}{38} = 23.94$.

59. 6th number = (10 × 60 – 5 × 50 – 4 × 30) = 230

60. New average = $\frac{10\times 10-30+20}{10} = 9$

Level of Difficulty (II)

1. Marks of the old boy = (8/5) × 80 = 128

Marks of the old girl = (1/2) × 80 = 40

Total marks = 168

Average drops by 2 marks. Therefore, we have a reduction of 60 × 2 = 120 marks

Hence, marks of new students = 168–120 = 48

Required percentage = 48/168 = 28.6%

Hence, Option (a) is the correct answer.

2. Assume the average weight of 4 students to be 'A' kg. The average weight of the entire 24 students will be 4A (given). Then, the average weight of the remaining 20 students would be 4A + 6. This situation can be represented on an alligation number line as shown in the figure– and it can be deduced that the difference between 4A and A viz: 3A = 30. Hence, A = 10, 4A = 40 and the required average of the 20 students is 4A + 6 = 46.

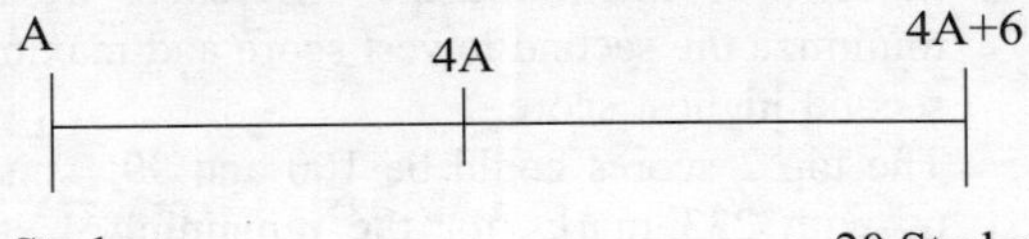

Hence, the correct answer is 46.

3. Let concentration of A in the first mixture be x and that in the second mixture be y. These two are mixed in the ratio of 1:5. Hence, their respective distances from the average will be in the ratio of 5:1. It is given that the concentration the concentration of A in the second mixture decreases by 10 percent points. This means that the concentration of A in the first will increase by 50 percent points.

Therefore, $x + 50 = y - 10$......(i)

Concentration of A in first = x

Concentration of B in first = $100 - x$

Concentration of A in second = y

Concentration of B in second = $100 - y$

Required difference = $(100 - x) - (100 - y) \rightarrow y - x$

From (i) we get $y - x = 60$. Hence, 60 is the required answer.

4. 8.33% is 1/12. This means that if the highest value is 12, then the difference between the average and the highest term would be 1. Therefore the average would be 11 and the lowest term would be 10. At this point we realize that this would also be the minimum value of n. Hence, the sum of the terms would be 10 + 11 + 12 = 33.

Hence, the correct answer is 33.

5. Let the set of 7 numbers be {$n1$, $n2$, $n3$, $n4$, $n5$, $n6$, $n7$}.

Case 1: Alternate Numbers {$n1$, $n3$, $n5$, $n7$} have an average of 18 and remaining numbers have average of 25. Hence, total sum is 72 + 75 = 147.

Average of Set: 21

Case 2: Alternate Numbers {$n2$, $n4$, $n6$} have an average of 18 and remaining numbers have average of 25. Hence, total sum is 54 + 100 = 154.

Average of the Set: 22.

Hence, difference between the maximum and the minimum averages = 1.

Hence, the correct answer is 1.

6. The net average of runs scored is 60 less than that averaged by ICT. And India A averages 110 less than ICT which means that it is 50 less than the net average. This means that the ratio of distances from the average is 5:6. Hence, number of players in the two teams are in the ratio 6:5. So total number of players needs to be a multiple of 11. Hence, Option (c) is the correct answer.

7. Since Meenakshi wanted to save ₹1100 but in the first nine months only managed to save ₹1000, She is ₹900 short of her target. She forecasts that her expenses will increase to ₹7400 (after a 2/35 increase). This means that in order to meet her monthly target she needs to earn ₹8500. She also needs to save ₹300/ month more in order to offset the shortage from the first 9 months. Hence, she needs to earn ₹8800 in

the remaining months in order to meet the target for the year. Hence, Option (b) is the correct answer.

8. Total weight of the 30 parcels = 1800. In order to maximize the top 6 weights, we need to minimize the lower 24. This can be done only if the weights are consecutive numbers from 35 till 58. Total weight accounted for = 1116. Remaining weight belongs to the top 6. So weight of the heaviest parcel = 684/6 = 114. Hence, 114 is the correct answer.
9. Since the given times are averages of the time taken by the number of racers who have crossed the finish line up till that point. The first racer will have to take 10 sec as anyone who comes after him will only increase the average. Similarly for subsequent racers the clock shows 10s, 12s, 13s,14s, 15s in that order.
   So, Racer1 = 10s
   Racer1 + Racer2 = 24s → Racer2 = 14s.
   Racer1 + Racer2 + Racer3 = 39s → Racer3 = 15s.
   Racer1 + Racer2 + Racer3 + Racer4 = 56s → Racer4 = 17s
   Racer1 + Racer2 + Racer3 + Racer4 + Racer5 = 75s → Racer5 = 19s.
   Hence, the last racer took 19s to complete the race. Hence, the correct answer is 19.
10. The total marks of the class = 44.
    New total marks = 38.
    So we have a drop of 6 marks. Each student who lost marks because of this change must have lost 2 marks. Hence, total 3 students suffered because of this. Hence, 7 is the correct answer.
11. After adding the two solutions the average concentration of NaOH in the mixture becomes 22%. When the student adds another liter of NaOH to the mixture the concentration changes to 35%. Hence, the concentration of HCl in the final mixture would be 65%. Hence, Option (b) is the correct answer.
12. Sum of lowest 3 numbers = 51
    Sum of Highest 3 numbers = 96.
    In order to maximize the average of the 12 numbers we need to maximize the remaining numbers. This is possible if the first 3 numbers are 16, 17, 18 and last three numbers are 31, 32 and 33. So the remaining 6 numbers are 25, 26, 27, 28, 29 and 30. Sum of these 6 = 165. Hence, total sum of 12 numbers = 312. Hence, maximum average = 312/12 = 26. Hence, Option (b) is the correct answer.
13. For the numbers to be an increasing GP, the common ratio has to be more than 1. In order to maximize the average we need to maximize the sum. For this we need to take the given 2 numbers as the first two terms of the GP. So the common ratio would be 4. Hence, the remaining terms would be 256, 1024 and 4096. So the maximum average = 5456/5 = 1091.2
    To minimize the average, we can fix the highest term at 64. If we make our second highest term as 16 we wont get an integral fifth value. Hence, 16 would be our third highest term. This means that the common ratio would be 2. Hence, the five terms are 4, 8, 16, 32 and 64. So the minimum average number of members = 124/5 = 24.8. Hence, the required sum is 1091.2 + 24.8 = 1116. Hence, the correct answer is 1116.
14. For this question we need to visualise the data provided to us. Since the scores are in AP, the average marks would be the 9th term. Since three of the 5 eliminated numbers are 7, 9 and 11 which are the average and numbers equidistant from the average, they wont have an effect on our average. Rank 5 would be equivalent to rank 13. If we had eliminated rank 13 along with rank 5, the average would not change. However, since we are eliminating rank 17 instead of 13th, it means that we are losing less value in terms of magnitude. Hence, the new average would be higher than the old one. Hence, option (c) is correct.
15. Total height of the employees = 4.5 × 4 = 18.
    In order to maximize the average of the two tallest employees we need to minimize the two shortest people. The lowest possible values are 1ft. and 2ft. Hence, the remaining 15 ft should be from the two tallest people. Hence, their average would be 7.5 at max. On the lower side, the 4 heights need to be 3 ft, 4 ft, 5 ft and 6 ft respectively. In this case, the average height of the two tallest employees is 5.5 ft (and this represents the minimum average height of the two tallest employees). The maximum difference is 2 feet. Hence, the correct answer is 2.
16. For a Gp to be non-decreasing the common ratio has to be more than or equal to 1. Since the Gp has only natural numbers, the minimum value for the first term is 1. So we get the minimum average when the first term is 1 and the common ratio is 1. Hence, the minimum possible average is 1. Hence, the correct answer is 1
17. To find the range of average, we need to find the max and min value for the same. Hence, we need to maximize and minimize the total sum of marks. Let us assume the total number of students be 10. Hence, 6 of them passed while 4 failed.
    Minimizing the Sum = (40 × 5 + 98) + (35 + 12 × 3) = 298 + 71 = 369. This gives us a minimum average of 369/10 = 36.9.
    Maximizing the Sum = (98 × 5 + 40) + (35 × 3 + 12) = 530 + 117 = 647. The maximum average = 647/10 = 64.7
    Hence, Option (b) is the correct answer.
18. Total marks of the class = 72 × 6 = 432
    In order to maximize the difference, we need to minimize the second lowest score and maximize the second highest score.
    The top 2 scores could be 100 and 99. This leaves us with 233 marks for the remaining 4 students.

The lowest 2 scores could be 50 and 51 and the remaining scores would be 80 and 52. Hence, the required difference is 99–51 = 48. 48 is the correct answer.

19. The speed of the drone for first side of 30km = 10km/h
The speed of the drone for second side of 30km = 20km/h
The speed of the drone for third side of 30km = 30km/h
The speed of the drone for fourth side of 30km = 40km/h
Avg speed = total distance/total time
120/(3 + 1.5 + 1 + 0.75) = 19.2
Initial speed was 10km/h. Hence, Option (b) is the correct answer.

20. Total sum of 20 numbers is 90. We know that sum of first 14 whole numbers is 91. So we need to reduce one number by 1 to get the required total. Rest of the numbers can be all different. So we can have maximum of 13 distinct whole numbers in the dataset. Hence, the correct answer is 13.

21. If the average increases by 7.2, the total has to increase by 36. Let the number be 'ab'.
So $9 \times (b - a) = 36 \rightarrow b - a = 4$. The possibilities for the original number are 04, 15, 26, 37, 48 and 59. The only 2 digit multiple of 4 in this set is 48. Hence, 48 is the correct answer.

22. As the average percentage increases by 0.05%, the total percent increase has to be 2.5%. This whole increase can be allotted to a single student. So an increase of 2.5% for a single student across 6 subjects. So 2.5% increase on a total of 600 marks is an increase of 15 marks. Hence, 15 is the correct answer.

23. Find the total distance covered in each segment of 15 minutes. You will get total distance = 32.50 kilometres in 60 minutes.

24. Standard question requiring good calculation speed. Obviously, the 15th day is being double counted. Calculations can be reduced by thinking as:
Surplus in first 15 days – Deficit in last 17 days = 15 × 20 – 17 × 10 = 300 – 170 → Net surplus of 130. This means that the sum is advancing by 130 due to the double counting of the 15th day. This can only mean that the 15th day's expenditure is 60 + 130 = 190.
(Lengthy calculations would have yielded the following calculations: 80 × 15 + 50 × 17 – 60 × 31 = 190).

25. $4x + 40 = (x + 4) \times 5$ (where x is the average of first four innings.)
On solving we get, $x = 20$. x is the old average here.
Hence, the new average $= x + 4 = 20 + 4 = 24$.

26. In one hour the total number of sheets typed will be:
60/10 + 60/20 + 60/30 = 11
Hence, the number of sheets/hour per typist is 11/3.

27. The initial total of 29 numbers is 29 × 211 = 6119. The increment in the total by the addition of 1 + 2 + 3 +... 29 = 435. The new mean would be $\frac{(6119+435)}{29} = 226$.

28. Let the average height of the 32 students be $4A$. Then, the given situation can be represented by the equation:
$32 \times 4A = 28 \times (4A + 3) + 4 \times A \rightarrow 12A = 84 \rightarrow A = 7$.
Hence, the original average of the class was $28 = 4A = 28$ kgs. The average weight of the 28 remaining students after 4 students left the class = 28 + 3 = 31 kgs.
Hence, option (d) is correct.

29. The number of rooms is 50 + 40 + 40 = 130 on the three floors respectively.
Total revenues are: 25 × 2000 + 20 × 1000 + 12 × 1500 = 88000. Hence the required average = 88000/130 = 676.92

30. Replace x with the sales value to calculate the bonus in a month.
Bonus = 0 in January, 200 in February, 2000 each from March to November and 200 in December. Hence, his Total bonus = 0 + 200 + 2000 × 9 + 200 = 18400. Salary for the year = 3000 × 12. Total annual income = 36000+18400 = 54400. Hence, the average monthly income = 4533.33. Option (a) is closest and hence is the correct answer.

31. Mileage = total distance covered/total petrol consumed = (800 – 400)/(10 + 20 + 15 + 10 – 5) = 400/50 = 8 km/liter.

32. Before starting for Shanpur, Ramya's car has 5 liters of petrol. She can fill a maximum of 30 liters petrol. But to minimize the cost of petrol on the way is ₹40 per liter and ₹35 per liter.
At first pump as well she will purchase enough petrol so that she can reach the second pump since the cost of petrol at the second pump is less.
Minimum amount required
$= \frac{[150 - (5 \times 8)]}{8} \times 45 + \frac{50}{8} \times 40 + \frac{200}{8} \times 35 \approx$ `1744.

33. Let the original steel production by $100x$ and the original population by 100p. The per capita production of steel will be given by: $\frac{100x}{100p} = \frac{x}{p}$.
Then, we have new steel production = $150x$. Also, since the per capita production of steel grows by 35%, it means that the new per capita production is $\frac{1.35x}{p}$. The population can be calculated as:
$$\frac{150x}{New\ population} = \frac{1.35x}{p} \rightarrow \text{New population}$$

$= \dfrac{150p}{1.35} = 111.11\,p$

Thus, the population has grown by approximately 11.11%. Option (b) is correct.

34. Put $x = 10$ to get the weight of the last three packets. These packets would weigh 60 kgs each. Thus the total of the four packets would be $60 \times 3 + 20 = 200$. Their average weight $200/4 = 50$ kg.
35. The weight of the boxes are 1st box → 40, 3rd box → 50 kg, 2nd box → 75 kg, 4th box → 150 and 5th box → 100 kg. Hence difference between the heaviest 4 and the lightest 4 is 110 kg. Hence, difference in the averages is 27.5 kg.
36. Difference between heaviest three and lightest three totals is: $(150 + 100) - (40 + 50) = 160$
Difference in average weights is $160/3 = 53.33$ kg.
37. Assume x is the average expenditure of 20 people. Then, $20x = 15 \times 90 + 5(x + 30)$. On solving we get $x = 100$
Total expenditure = 20×100 = ₹ 2000.
38. $30 \times A + 1600 = 50 \times (A - 8) \rightarrow 20 \times A = 2000 \rightarrow A = 100$. Total expenditure original = 100×30 = ₹ 3000.
39. The total price of the three stones would be $97610498312 \times 3 = 292831494936$. Since, this price is divided into the three stones in the ratio of 4: 7: 9, the price of the cheapest one would be = $(4 \times 2928314936/20) = 58566298987.2$.
40. The average weight per box is asked. Hence, the container does not have to be counted as the 24th item. Also, since the average for 23 boxes goes up by 1 kg, the total weight must have gone up by 23 kgs. That weight is the actual weight of the container. Hence, option (d) is correct.
41. Three years ago: $\dfrac{A}{5} = \dfrac{S}{4} \rightarrow A = 1.25S$. Also $A + S = 63$. $S = 28$ and $A = 35$. Also, given $A + S + P = 84$, we get P 21. So, 3 years from now, $A = 41$ and $P = 27$. Their average age = 34. Option (b) is correct.
42. Let the number of hectares of land be A and $A + 25$ for the two farmers. Then, the equation that gets formed based on the situation is:
$30 \times A + 1120 = 40 \times (A + 25) \rightarrow A = 12$. Hence, the number of bushels of wheat cultivated by farmer A = 360.
43. Use alligation to solve.

non officer	officer
	2000
1500	3000
3000 – 2000 = 1000	3000 – 2000 = 1000

1000:500 = 2:1

Non-officers = 20.

44. $nz - x + x^1 = nz^1 \rightarrow$ Simplify to get Option (c) correct.
45. Let the equal distances be '*d*' each. Then using the formula for the average speed as: Total distance/ total time we get: Average speed = $3d/(d/x + d/y + d/z) = 3xyz/(yx + yz + xz)$.

46–47. You have to take between 25th and 30th to mean that both these dates are also included.

46. The maximum average will occur when the maximum possible values are used. Thus:
Aman should have been born on 30th, *Binod* on 25th, *Charan* on 20th, *Dharam* on 10th and *Ehsaan* on 5th. Further, the months of births in random order will have to be between August to December to maximize the average.
Hence the maximum total will be $30 + 25 + 20 + 10 + 5 + 12 + 11 + 10 + 9 + 8 = 140$. Hence, the maximum average is 28.
47. The minimum average will be when we have $1 + 5 + 10 + 20 + 25 + 1 + 2 + 3 + 4 + 5 = 76$. Hence, average is $= 76/5 = 15.2$.
48. This does not change anything. Hence the answer is the same as the previous question.
49. The prime dates must be 29th, 23rd, 19th and 5th. This represents a reduction in the totals from 30+25+20+5 to 29+23+19+5 – a drop of 4. Hence, the maximum possible average will reduce by $4/5 = 0.8$. Hence, the answer will be 27.2.
50. Let the S.P. for each type of soap be ₹100
C.P. of soap sold at 15% loss = $\dfrac{100}{0.85} \approx 117.6$
C.P. of soap sold at 23% profit = $\dfrac{100}{1.23} \approx 81.3$
C.P. of soap sold at 22% loss = $\dfrac{100}{0.78} \approx 128.2$
Average C.P. = $\dfrac{(117.6 + 81.3 + 128.2)}{3} \approx 109.03$.
The average cost price is 9.03% higher than the average selling price.
The closest answer is option (a).
51. The number of pass candidates are = $2 + 8 + 18 + 32 = 60$ out of a total of 200. Hence, 30%.
52. Let the quantity of chemical x & y be x gm and y gm respectively. According to the question:
$0.05x + 0.1y \geq 7$
$0.1x + 0.06y \geq 7$
On solving the above two inequalities, we get $x \geq 40$, $y \geq 50$
Minimum possible cost = $40 \times 10.5 + 50 \times 7.8$ = ₹810.
Option (a) is correct.
53. You don't know who got out when. Hence, cannot be determined.
54. Since possibilities are asked about, you will have to consider all possibilities. Assume, the sixth and

seventh batsmen have scored zero. Only then will the possibility of the first 5 batsmen scoring the highest possible average arise. In this case the maximum possible average for the first 5 batsmen could be 243/5 = 48.6

55. Again it is possible that only the first batsman has scored runs. Hence, the minimum average would be 0.
56. We cannot find out the number of runs scored by the 7th batsman. Hence the answer is (d).
57. You can take 53 as the base to reduce your calculations. Otherwise the question will become highly calculation intensive. Let the fifth experiments measurement be 'x' above 53. Then you get: $0.735 \times 7 = 1.005 \times 3 + (x + 0.004) + x + 0.995 \times 2 \rightarrow 5.145 = 3.015 + 2x + 0.004 + 1.99$. On solving this you get $x = 0.068$. Hence, the weight of the fifth body is 53.068 and the weight of the fourth body is 53.072. Hence, option (c) is correct.
58. $251.25 \times 4 + 277.52 \times 5 + 760 = 3152.6$
    Required percentage
    $$= \frac{3000 - 3152.6}{3000} = -5.087\%$$
59. Solve using options. 20 is the only possible value.
60. Check through options to solve. Option (a) is correct since if the first farm harvested 3150 tons of wheat, with an average harvest of 21 tons per hectare – the number of hectares would be 3150/21 = 150. The second farm would then harvest 12 hectares less (as given in the question) - thus would harvest 138 hectares with an average output of 25 tons per hectare. The total harvest would be in this case 138 × 3450 – and is 300 tons more than the first farm as required. Hence, this answer is correct.
61. Let the numbers be $n_1, n_2, n_3, n_4, \ldots\ldots n_n$.
    $(n_1 + n_2 + n_3 + n_4, \ldots\ldots + n_n)/n \geq (n_1 \times n_2 \times n_3 \times \ldots\ldots \times n_n)^{1/n}$
    $(n_1 + n_2 + n_3 + n_4, \ldots\ldots + n_n)/n \geq n$
    For $n = 6$, the minimum value of the LHS is 6.
    Therefore, the minimum value of the average of these numbers = 6
62. Solve this one through options. If you use option (a), you get: $21 \times 330 + 57 \times 290 = 23460 \neq 24900$. Option (b) gives us: $57 \times 330 + 21 \times 290 = 24900$. Hence, Option (b) is correct
63. If present age of Binod's wife is x years.
    Then according to the question:
    $$\frac{33 \times 6 + x + 2}{8} = 32$$
    $x + 2 + 198 = 256$
    $x + 2 = 58$
    $x = 56$
    $x = 56$ years
64. Binod's wife's age in 2001 was 51 years. Therefore Binod's age in 2001 was greater than 51 and minimum possible prime number above 51 is 53. Therefore minimum possible present age of Binod = 53 + 5 = 58 years.
65. $$25 \leq \frac{21 + 23 + x + 24 + 27}{5} \leq 28$$
    $125 \leq 95 + x \leq 140$
    $30 \leq x \leq 45$
    Number of possible values of x = 16.
66. Total number of balls in all 10 boxes = 10 × 25 = 250.
    Minimum possible number of balls in 9 of these 10 boxes = 8 + 9 + 10 +11 +12 + 13 + 14 + 15 + 16 = 108.
    Maximum possible number of balls in any box = 250 – 108 = 142.
67. Sum of these five numbers = 6 × 5 = 30.
    Maximum average of the largest two numbers would occur when the three smaller numbers are as small as possible (i.e., when they are 1, 2 and 3, respectively) → Max. Average = (30 – 1 – 2 – 3)/2 = 24/2 = 12.
68. Let there be B number of boys, G number of girls in class 9th.
    $$\frac{B}{G} = \frac{80 - 70}{85 - 80} = \frac{10}{5} = 2:1$$
69. Let the number of girls and boys in class 10TH are g and b respectively.
    $$\frac{b}{g} = \frac{73 - 70}{74 - 73} = 3:1, b = 3g$$
    Number of boys of class 10th is three times the number of girls in 9th
    b = 3G
    let B = 2k, G = k, b = 3k, g = k
    Average score of all students of class 9th and 10th
    $$\frac{2k.85 + k.70 + 3k.74 + k.70}{2k + k + 3k + k} = \frac{532}{7} = 76$$
70. Total possible groups = $(w, x), (w, y), (w, z), (x, y), (x, z), (y, z)$
    According to the question = $w + x + w + y + w + z + x + y + x + z + y + z = 1440$
    $3(w + x + y + z) = 1440$. Hence, $(w + x + y + z) = 480$.
    Required average = 480/4 = 120.
71. In this question, the key logics are: i) All of them spent an equal amount of money – which means that each of them has to spend at least 1000 rupees – since someone would have bought the large bag – and he would have spent at least 1000 or more. Thus all of them have to spend a minimum amount of 1000 each. Further, the amount spent by each of them has to be a multiple of 50 or 100, since the price of the bags are all in multiples of 50 or 100. Thus, the total expense has to be a number like 1000 × 3 or 1050 × 3 or 1100 × 3

and so on. We know exactly, that 1 large and 15 small bags were sold. This means that the total cost of the bags is: $1000 \times 1 + 200 \times n + 50 \times 15 = 1750 + 200n$. (Where n is the number of medium bags sold by the shop). We can see that the first number that matches both these conditions – i.e. it should be $1750 + 200n$ as well as 1000×3 or 1050×3 or 1100×3 is the number 3150 and that occurs for a value of $n = 7$. At this value, each of them has to spend 1050 each. It can be done if one person spends $1000 \times 1 + 50 \times 1$, a second person spends $200 \times 5 + 50 \times 1$ and the third person spends $200 \times 2 + 50 \times 13$. (Note, that there will be many more such possible ways in which the second and third could create 1050 amongst them.)
Hence, the correct answer is 7.

72. For this question, the minimum spend is 3350 each. So the total spend will be part of the series of numbers:
$3350 \times 3 = 10050$; $3400 \times 3 = 10200$; $3450 \times 3 = 10350$ and so on.
The number also has to be part of the series 1750 + 200n. The first value at which these two series give the same value is at $n = 43$, when the total expense becomes 3450 for each. Hence, the correct answer is 43.

Level of Difficulty (III)

1.

	Badminton	Cricket	Total
Boys	$3x$	$4x$	$7x$
Girls	$7y$	$2y$	$9y$
Total	$3x + 7y$	$4x + 2y$	200

For Maximizing the number of players who play badminton, we need to maximize the variable with the higher coefficient which is y.
It is given that $7x + 9y = 200$. Y would be maximum when $x = 8$. Hence, $y = 16$. So maximum number of badminton palyers = 24 + 112 = 136.
For Maximizing the number of players who play cricket, we need to maximize the variable with the higher coefficient which is x.
It is given that $7x + 9y = 200$. x would be maximum when $y = 2$. Hence, $x = 26$. So maximum number of cricket players = 104 + 4 = 108.
Hence, the required average = (136 + 108)/2 = 122.
Hence, the correct answer is 122.

2. Let the initial average age of the family be x so the total age will be $2x$. When they adopt the first child, the average decreases by A. So the total age at this point will be $3(x - a)$. This will be equal to $2x$ as the baby's age will be 0. Hence, $x = 3A$.
Now it is given that 5 years after that, they adopted another child. During this time the total will increase by 15 years. Hence, total age of the family at this point will be $3(x - A) + 15$. It is given that the average changes by B. We know the the average will decrease again so average at this point will be $x - A - B$. Hence, total age will be $4(x - A - B + 5)$. It is given that the difference between A and B is 12. This means that $A - B$ or $B - A = 12$.
So, $3(x - A) + 15 = 4(x - A - B + 5)$ and $x = 3A$ $\Rightarrow 2A - 4B = -5$.
Now if $B - A = 12$, then $A = -43/2$ but this is not possible. Hence, $A - B = 12$. So combining both the equations we get, $A = 26.5$. Hence, $x = 3 \times 26.5 = 79.5$. Hence, 79.5 is the correct answer.

3. Total marks of Pallav and Shaurya = 100
Total marks of Anshuman and Pulkit = 160
It is given that Pulkit>Anshuman>Shaurya>Pallav.
The variable to be focused on is the average marks of Pallav and Pulkit.
Minimizing this means minimizing the sum of Pallav and Pulkit. Minimizing Pulkit with the constraint that Pulkit > Anshuman and Pulkit + Anshuman = 160, would occur when we take Anshuman as 79 and Pulkit as 81. With these values set, the minimisation of Pallav would occur if we maximise Shaurya's score. With Anshuman as 79, Shaurya's maximum value possible is 78 and hence, Pulkit is minimized at 22. The minimum sum of Pulkit and Pallav → 22 + 81 = 103. Hence, the minimum average is 51.5
Maximizing the average requires us to maximize the sum of Pulkit and Pallav. For this, through trial and error we can work out that Pulkit = 108, Anshuman = 52, Shaurya = 51 and Pallav = 49. (Note: If we try to take Pulkit as 109, Anshuman becomes 51 and then we cannot have a sum of 100 for Shaurya and Pallav such that Shaurya > Pallav).
Hence, the maximum total of Pulkit and Pallav → 49 + 108 = 157
Hence, Maximum average is 78.5
Required difference = 27.
Hence, the correct answer is 27.

4. 6.667% is 1/15. This means that if the highest value is 15, then the difference between the average and the highest term would be 1. But the question states that the numbers are consecutive even terms, hence, we would take 2/30, where the highest number is 30 and the difference is 2. Similarly, we can see that this is true for 4/60 and 6/90. We cannot go beyond this because of set constraints, if we want to remain in two digit numbers. So, if the highest number is 90 and its difference with the average is 6, we have a situation where we have 84 as the average of consecutive even numbers where the highest number is 90. The series can be visualized as 78, 80, 82, 84, 86, 88, 90. We can see that the total number of terms

have to be 7. Hence, 'n' can take a maximum value of 7. Hence, the correct answer is 7.

5. Let average marks of class A be x and that of class B be y. These two are combined in the ratio of 1:3. Hence, their respective distances from the average will be in the ratio of 3:1. It is given that the Average marks of A quadruples and that of B decreases by 15 marks. This means that average of A increases by 45 marks. So, $x + 45 = 4x \rightarrow x = 15 \rightarrow y = 75$. It is also given that $75 = (5/6) \times$ Max marks. Hence, Maximum marks = 90. Hence, the correct answer is 90.

6. Let the total amount of mixture A be $100x$ liters and that of mixture B be $100y$ liters.

	Mixture A ($100x$)	Mixture B ($100y$)	Total used
Milk	$5x$	$10y$	$5x + 10y \geq 7$
Water	$10x$	$6y$	$10x + 6 \geq 7$

For the minimum revenue, the value of total milk and total water used needs to be minimized at 7 liters each.

$5x + 10y = 7$

$10x + 6y = 7$

Solving the above two equations we get, $x = 0.4$, $y = 0.5$. Hence, at a minimum, the total amount of mixture A is 40 liters, mixture B is 50 liters.

The minimum revenue he gets would be: $105 \times 40 + 78 \times 50 = 8100$. Hence, the correct answer is 8100.

7. Let the score of the first batter be P1. Also, the total score of x batters initially would be $51x$. After the score of P1 is quadrupled, the new total is $102x$. This change in total has only occurred because of the increase in P1 from P1 to 4P1. Hence, $3P1 = 102x - 51x = 51x \rightarrow P1 = 17x$.

If we consider only 1 batter, this situation would not match.

At $x = 2$, we get: Total runs = 102, P1 = 34. So the runs of the second batter would be 68. This obeys the non-decreasing order of P1,P2 scores. If we quadruple P1 to 136, Total runs = 136 + 68 and average would be 102.

At $x = 3$, we get: Total runs = 153, P1 = $17x$ = 51. So the runs of the other two batters would be 102. For a non decreasing set of scores, we would need to take P2 = 51 and P3 = 51. If we quadruple P1 to 204, Total runs = 204 + 102 = 306 and average would be 102.

At $x = 4$, we get: Total runs = 204, P1 = $17x$ = 68. So the runs of the other three batters would be 136. But this is not possible since nobody can score less than 68 runs (P1's score).

Hence, the correct answer is 34 + 51 = 85.

8. Net change in the total sum = + 35 – 15 = + 20.
Net change in average = 5.
Number of terms in the set = 20/5 = 4. Hence, the correct answer is 4.

9. Given that, Average of A = 32 and B = 60. Since B has more students than A, the net average will be more than 46. We need to take care of the constraint of difference in the number of students while taking different values as averages. On checking with different values we see that this would be true if we take net average among 47, 48, 51, 53 and 56.
If Average is 47, number of students in A = 65, and in B = 75.
If Average is 48, number of students in A = 30 and in B = 40.
If Average is 51, number of students in A = 9 and in B = 19.
If Average is 53, number of students in A = 5 and in B = 15.
If Average is 56, number of students in A = 2 and in B = 12.
Hence, the difference between the maximum and minimum possible values of A = 65 – 2 = 63. Hence, the correct answer is 63.

10. In order to minimize the average of the set, we need to minimize the sum of the remaining 2 numbers. This would be possible if we minimize the value of the second term. Hence, the first two numbers are 13 and 15. So the next two terms would be 16 and 17. Hence, average of the set is (28 + 33 + 56)/6 = 19.5
In order to maximize the average of the set, we need to maximize the sum of the remaining 2 numbers. This would be possible if we maximize the value of the second last term. Hence, the last two numbers are 27 and 29. So the two terms would be 25 and 26. Hence, average of the set is (28 + 51 + 56)/6 = 22.5
Hence, the required difference is 3. Hence, Option (b) is the correct answer.

11. Let the 10 scores be $a, b, c, d, e, f, g, h, I, j$. Sum of a to $i = 9 \times 42 = 378$. Sum of b to j $= 9 \times 47 = 423$. Hence, $j - a = 45$. The total can be seen as $a + b + c + d + e + f + g + h + i + j = 378 + j = 423 + a$. Since a and j are connected to each other's values, we would get the maximum total when we maximise both of them. The value of a can be maximized only at 42 (If each of the first nine numbers are 42 each). In that case the value of j would be 42 + 45 = 87. Hence, the total would become $378 + j = 378 + 87 = 465$. The maximum average of the ten numbers would be 465/10 = 46.5. In the other case, when we want to minimize the total, we would try to minimize both a and j together. The minimization of j would occur when $j = 47$, in which case the value of a

would be 47 – 45 = 2. The total would be 423 + 2 = 425. The minimum average of the ten numbers would be 425/10 = 42.5. The difference between the maximum and minimum possible averages would be 46.5–42.5 = 4. Hence, the correct answer is 4.

12. Let the 10 scores be $a, b, c, d, e, f, g, h, I, j$. Sum of a to i = 9 × 42 = 378. Sum of b to j = 9 × 47 = 423. Hence, $j - a = 45$. The total can be seen as $a + b + c + d + e + f + g + h + i + j = 378 + j = 423 + a$. Since a and j are connected to each other's values, we would get the maximum total when we maximise both of them. To maximise a, the values of the first nine numbers (a to i) needs to be taken as 38, 39, 40, 41, 42, 43, 44, 45, 46. In this case, the value of the tenth number would be 38 + 45 = 83. The maximum total of all the numbers is 378 + 83 = 461. Likewise, in order to minimize the sum, we need to minimize the values of a and j. The minimum value of j has to be 51. (Note: It cannot be 50 for instance, since if we try to fit 9 number less than equal to 50, these numbers would be 42, 43, 44, 45, 46, 47, 48, 49, 50 which falls short of the required total of 423 for these nine numbers.). Hence, the numbers for the minimum total are 6, 43, 44, 45, 46, 47, 48, 49, 50, 51. The total of all the numbers in this case is $378 + j = 378 + 51 = 423 + a = 423 + 6 = 429$. The maximum average is 46.1. The minimum average is 42.9. The required difference is 3.2.

13. For the average to be an integer after each subsequent person gets on the machine, the numbers need to be a multiple of 2, 3, 4 and 5. But first we need to identify the weight of the first person.
If the first number is even, the second also needs to be an even number for the sum to be a multiple of 2. So sum of first two weights is 144. Since this number is already a multiple of 3, the third weight also needs to be a multiple of 3. From the remaining numbers we see that we don't have a multiple of 3. Hence, our first weight cannot be either 62 or 82. Now we have 3 possibilities for the sum of first 2 numbers (138, 140 and 144). Among the 3 numbers we see that 2 sums are multiples of 3 and can be ruled out because of the reason stated earlier. Hence, the first two numbers are 67 and 73. Next number has to be 82. Our fourth number has to be 62. So the weight of the last person will be 71. Hence, 71 is the correct answer.

14. Although this question can be solved using the algebraic approach but it would be highly time consuming.
Let the total runs be T. When first 10 are not considered, Total drops by (20 × 10) 200 and average increases by 1. When last 10 are not considered, the Total drops by (30 × 10) 300 and average decreases by 1. Net change in total runs between the two scenarios = 100. Net change in average = 2. So the number of innings = 100/2 = 50.
Hence, total number of innings = 50 + 10 (The ones which were not considered in either of the cases) = 60. Hence, the correct answer is 60.

15. Let the number A = $100x + 10y + z$
Number B = $100c + 10d + e$
Change in total because of reversing the digits = $99(x - z) + 99(c - e) = 693 \rightarrow x - z + c - e = 7$
It is given that $(x + z)/2 + (c + e)/2 = 9.5 \rightarrow x + z + c + e = 19$.
Adding both the equations we get $2(x + c) = 26 \rightarrow x + c = 13$. Hence, Option (b) is the correct answer.

16. In order to find the maximum average value of the people below 57 years, we need to minimize the higher ages. So the lowest value of the average of those people whose ages are 57 and above can be 57. Also, since there are a maximum of 39 people below 57 years of age, if we take exactly 39 people below the age of 57, we will get a ratio of number of people as 13:10 (below 57: 57 and above). In this case, the respective averages of the two groups will be at a distance (on the number line) of 10:13 from the group average. Since, the average of all the people is 44, and the minimum average of the 57 and above age group is 57, it follows that the maximum average of the people who are below 57 years of age would be 44 – 10 = 34. So the maximum possible value of the average age of the lower age group can be 34. This structure can be understood using alligations as shown:

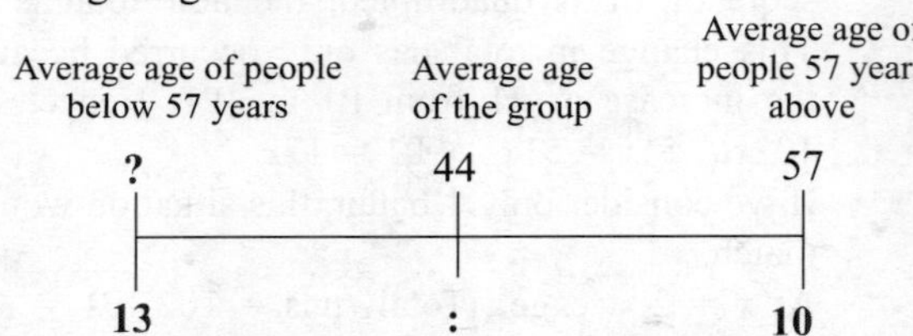

Hence, the correct answer is option (d)

17. Let the average of the first games be x. So total sum = $5x$.
Sum of 9 games = $5x + 72$.
It is given that $(5x + 72)/9 > x \rightarrow x < 18$.
Sum of first 5 games is less than 90. So maximum sum after 9 games is 161.
Also it is given that sum of 10 games is more than 190. Hence, minimum sum of 10 games is 191. Hence, minimum score of tenth game is 30. Hence, Option (b) is the correct answer.

18. The sum of a_{26} to a_{50} is 48 × 25 = 1200. Hence, the sum of a_1 to a_{25} = 50 × 34–1200 = 500. Thus, the average of a_1 to a_{25} is 20. Since the fifty numbers

are in increasing order, the objective of maximization of sum of a_{26} and a_{50}, will happen, if we use the minimum possible values for all numbers from a_{26} to a_{49} and load the maximum amount in a_{50}. There is also the constraint of keeping a_1 to a_{25} in an arithmetic progression. This can be achieved using the numbers 8, 9, 10, 11,...32 for a_1 to a_{25}. And the numbers 33 to 56 for a_{26} to a_{49}. In this case the sum of a_{26} to a_{49} comes out as 24 × (89)/2 = 12 × 89 = 1068. But the sum of a_{26} to a_{50} is 1200. This means that the value of a_{50} should be 1200–1068 = 132. Thus, the maximum possible sum of a_{26} and a_{50} is 33 + 132 = 165. Hence, the correct answer is 165.

19. The sum of a_{26} to a_{50} is 48 × 25 = 1200. Hence, the sum of a_1 to a_{25} = 50 × 34–1200 = 500. Thus, the average of a_1 to a_{25} is 20. Since the fifty numbers are in increasing order, and a_1 to a_{25} are in an Arithmetic Progression, it can only mean that they take the integers from 8 to 32 (an arithmetic progression of 25 terms with the middle term 20 and having a common difference of + 1). Thus all numbers from a_{26} to a_{50} would be 33 and above. Also, The average of a_{26} to a_{50} is 48. If we try to first fit an arithmetic progression of 25 terms for these numbers, with middle term 48 and common difference + 1, we can see that the numbers 36, 37, 38, ...59, 60 fit the situational requirements. In this case, the sum of a_{26} and a_{50} is 36 + 60 = 96. This value can be further reduced if we reduce a_{26} by 2 and increase each of a_{49} and a_{50} by 1 each. In this case a_{26} is equal to 34 and a_{50} equals 61. The sum of 34 + 61 = 95 is achieved for these two numbers. Any other reduction in a_{26} to 33, results in a subsequent increase in a_{50}, thus not giving us a smaller sum of these two values than 95. Hence, the correct answer is 95. Thus, the minimum possible sum of a_{26} and a_{50} is 34 + 61 = 33 + 62 = 95.
Hence, the correct answer is 95.

20. $X = 2m$, $z = 5m$, $y = 2m + 15$.
$X + y + z = 105 \rightarrow m = 10 \rightarrow x = 20$, $y = 35$, $z = 50$.
Given that, $ab = 75$. For maximizing the average, we need to assign values to a and b as far as possible and for minimizing as close as possible.
Maximum average = 38 ($a = 1$, $b = 75$)
Minimum Average = 10 ($a = 5$, $b = 15$)
Hence, required difference is 28. Hence, the correct answer is 28.

21. Total marks of the group = 38 × 5 = 190. In order to minimize the score of Shaurya, we need to maximize the top 3 scores. So that can be 48,49 and 50 which adds up to 147. That leaves us with 43 marks. Lowest marks obtained by Shaurya can be 11 as the fourth person can take max value of 32.
To maximize the score of Shaurya, we need to minimize the top 3. The highest possible value for second lowest score is 32 and that for Shaurya is 31. Since these 2 are 6 and 7 less than the average, the three numbers have to have a cumulative difference of + 13 from the average. This can be possible in any number of ways. Hence, 31 is an acceptable max marks for Shaurya. Hence, the difference between the maximum and minimum possible score of Shaurya is 20. Hence, the correct answer is 20.

22. Since Pallav drank the whole bottle at the end, the total amount of coke consumed would be the quantity he finished during these 20 days.
Quantity consumed on Day 1: 100ml
Quantity consumed on Day 2: 200ml
Quantity consumed on Day 3: 300ml
Quantity consumed on Day 4: 400ml
.
.
.
Quantity consumed on Day 19: 1900ml
Since the quantity consumed by him across these 19 days is 19L. On day 20, he finished the whole bottle – and hence, he would not have added any coke on that day. So the amount of coke he consumed across these 19 days has to be 19L. Hence, the required average consumption per day is 19L/20 = 950ml. Hence, the correct answer is 950 ml.

23. Let the smallest and highest number be x and y respectively. Required answer = $(x + y)/2$
It is given that $7A + x = 600$ and $7B + y = 600 \rightarrow A = (600 - x)/7$, $B = (600 - y)/7$. It is given that $A + B = 90 \rightarrow (600 - x)/7 + (600 - y)/7 = 90 \rightarrow 1200 - x - y = 630 \rightarrow x + y = 570$. Hence, 285 is the correct answer.

24. First 20 matches:
Score of A = 600
Score of B = 800
Score of C = 700
Score of D = 900
Score of E = 1000
It is given that after 25 matches, Score of A is 800 and B is 1000.
Also given that $800/25 = (4/5)(900 + x)/25$ where x is the runs scored by D in the next 5 matches.
$\rightarrow 900 + x = 1000 \rightarrow x = 100$. This means that in this period C scored 150 runs. Total score of C is 850. Hence, his average is 850/25 = 34. The correct answer is 34.

25. Let the average weight of the 8 students be x. Their total is $8x$. When the heaviest leaves the group, the total is $7(x - 2) = 7x - 14$. Thus, the weight of the heaviest student would be $8x - (7x - 14) = x + 14$ kgs. When the lightest student leaves the group, the

total weight is $7(x + 2) = 7x + 14$. Hence, weight of lightest student $= 8x - 7x - 14 = x - 14$.

When both of them leave the total weight removed is $2x$. Thus, the total weight of the six remaining people must be $6x$, which is also equal to $270 \rightarrow x = 45$. Hence, the weight of the heaviest student in the group is $x + 14 = 59$ kgs. Hence, the correct answer is 59.

26. Definitely decrease since the highest marks in Class A is less than the lowest marks in Class B.
27. Cannot say since there is no indication of the values of the numbers which are transferred.
28. It will definitely decrease since the highest possible transfer is lower than the lowest value in C.
29. The effect on A will depend on the profile of the people who are transferred. Hence, anything can happen.
30. Cannot say since there is a possibility that the numbers transferred are such that the average can either increase, decrease or remain constant.
31. If C increases, then the average of C goes up from 30. For this to happen, it is definite that the average of B should drop.
32. The maximum possible average for B will occur if all the 5 transferees from A have 22 marks.
33. The average of Group A after the transfer in Q. 7 above is:
$(400 - 18 \times 5)/15 = 310/15 = 20.66$
34. $(400 - 22 \times 5)/15 = 19.33$
35. $400 + 23 \times 5 = 515$. Average $= 515/25 = 20.6$
36. $400 + 31 \times 5 = 555$. Average $= 555/25 = 22.2$
37. Will always decrease since the net value transferred from B to A will be higher than the net value transferred from A to B.
38. Since the lowest score in Class B is 23 which is more than the highest score of any student in Class A. Hence, A's average will always increase.
39. The maximum possible value for B will happen when the A to B transfer has the maximum possible value and the reverse transfer has the minimum possible value.
40. For the minimum possible value of B, we will need the A to B transfer to be the lowest possible value while the B to A transfer must have the highest possible value. Thus, A to B transfer $\rightarrow 18 \times 5$ while B to A transfer will be 31×5. Hence, answer is 22.4.
41. The maximum value for A will happen in the case of Q. 40. Then the increment for group A is:
$31 \times 5 - 18 \times 5 = 5 \times (31 - 18) = 65$.
Thus, maximum possible value is $465/20 = 23.25$.
42. Minimum possible average will happen for the transfer we saw in Q. 39. Thus, the answer will be $405/20 = 20.25$.
43. The maximum possible value for C will be achieved when the transfer from C is of five 26's and the transfer back from B is of five 31's. Hence, difference is totals will be +25. Hence, max. average $= (900 + 25)/30 = 30.833$.
(**Note:** Here that 900 has come by 30×30)
44. For the maximum possible value of Class B, the following set of operations will have to hold:
Five 33's are transferred from C to B, whatever goes from B to A comes back from A to B, then five 23's are transferred from B to C. This leaves us with:
Increase of 50 marks $\rightarrow$ average increases by 2 to 27.
45. A will attain maximum value if five 33's come to A from C through B and five 18's leave A. In such a case the net result is going to be a change of +75. Thus, the average will go up by $75/20 = 3.75$ to 23.75.

Solutions for Questions 46 to 48:

Will be solved by the same pattern as the above questions.

(**Note:** For question 47, you need to realise that there are only a maximum of six 31's in group B.)

49. Option (c) is correct, since you need to transfer out whatever you got into A, in order to keep the value of A's average at the minimum.

Solutions for Questions 50 to 53:

Will be solved by the same pattern as above questions.

Solutions for Questions 54 to 60:

These are standard questions using the concept of averages. Hence, analyse each and every sentence by itself and link the interpretations. If you are getting stuck, the only reason is that you have not used the information in the questions fully.

59. The question tells us that there are exactly 30 people whose marks are 61 or above. Also, there are at most 39 people with marks below 61. Assume that there are 'n' people with marks below 61. Also, the average of all the people in the class is 48. Then, to maximise the average of the people whose marks are below 61, we need to minimise the average of the people whose marks are above or equal to 61. This will occur, if we assume all the people who scored 61 or more marks to have scored exactly 61 marks. Thus, we would have the equation:
$48 \times (30 + n) = 61 \times 30 + A \times n$ (where A is the average of the people who scored below 61 marks).
$\rightarrow 1440 + 48n = 1830 + A \times n \rightarrow 390 = (48 - a) \times n$.
In this equation, n has to be an integer. The maximum value of A occurs when $n = 39$ and $A = 38$. Hence, the correct answer is 38. [Note: If we try to reduce n to 30, $A = 35$, is not giving us the maximum possible value of A]
Hence, option (a) is correct.

Hint for 61 to 64:

Monthly estimates of income is reduced as the denominator is increased from 12 to 14 at the same time the monthly estimate of expenditure is increased as the denominator is reduced from 12 to 9. Hence, the savings will be underestimated.

65. In 2021, the family has 7 members, with an average age of 38. Hence, the total age of the 7 member family in 2021 would be 7 × 38 = 266 years. By 2027, these 7 members would have added a total of 42 years to their total age and hence the total age of these 7 members would be 266 + 42 = 308 years. But, it is mentioned that the average age of the family is still 38 in 2027 – as two new members have entered the family. Thus, the total age of the family in 2027 = 9 × 38 = 342. Thus, the total age of Aman's wife and his son is 342 – 308 = 34 years. We also know that his son was born in 2025, hence he is two years old. Thus, his wife is 32 years old in 2027. Aman, would be 32 + 3 = 35 years old in 2027 and hence would be 29 years old when he graduated.

66. The situation described in the question can be represented on the number line with the figure shown, where x is the price of the second oil and $2.25x$ is the price of the first oil. We will have the equation:

$$\frac{2.25x-30}{30-x} = \frac{3}{2} \to 4.5x - 60 = 90 - 3x \to = 20$$

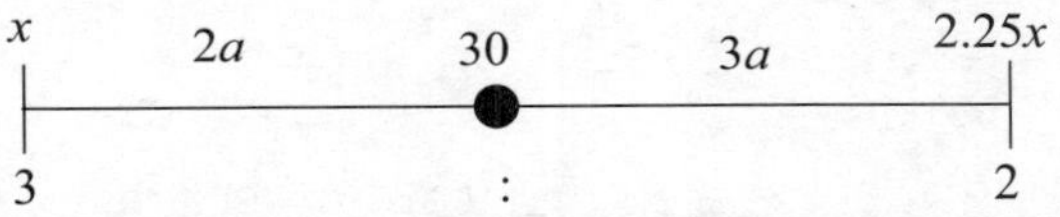

x $2a$ 30 $3a$ $2.25x$

3 : 2

Hence, the price of the first oil is $2.25x$ = ₹45 per litre.

67. The maximum tax would be if the maximum possible numbers of people were earning the maximum possible amounts. This would happen under the following situation: 5 people earn 10000 (tax = 0 + 75 + 300 + 750 each), 4 people earn 5000 (tax = 0 + 75 + 300 each) and 3 people earn 2000 (tax = 0 + 75 each) and 3 people earn 500 (tax = 0). The total tax in this case would be: 1125 × 5 + 375 × 4 + 75 × 3 = 5625 + 1500 + 225 = 7350. However, we need to note here that the value would not include 7350, because the last tax slab is only till <10000

The minimum tax would be in the case that the maximum numbers of people are earning the least amounts. Thus, we get: 3 people earn just above 5000 (tax = 0 + 75 + 300 each), 3 people earn just above 2000 (tax = 0 + 75 each) and 4 people earn just above 500 (tax = 0 each) and 5 people earn under 500 (tax = 0). The total tax in this case would be: 375 × 3 + 75 × 3 = 1125 + 225 = 1350. However, we need to note here that the value would not include 1350, since we have calculated at the extreme values that are not included in the tax slabs. Hence, the minimum and maximum taxes possible are: 1350 and 7350 respectively (both excluded). Option (a) is correct.

68. For the largest of the six numbers to be the maximum possible value, the other five numbers should be the least possible. The sum of the six numbers = 6 × 15 = 90. Visualise this as __ + __ + __ + __ + __ + __ = 90

(putting the least number on the left and the maximum number on the right. Now we know that the median of the numbers is 18—and since there are six numbers, the median would be the average of third and the fourth numbers in the list. Thus, the sum of the third and fourth numbers must be 36 (the numbers could be 17 + 19, 16 + 20, 15 + 21 etc.)

Now, the sum of the other four numbers (excluding the two numbers defining the median) would be 54. In order to make the largest number as big as possible, we would need to take the minimum possible values of the other three unknowns. This would occur under the following condition: 1 + 1 + 17 + 19 + 20 + _ = 90. Hence, the largest possible value for the highest number is 32. Hence, option (d) is correct.

69. The difference between just getting an A grade and just getting a B grade would be equal to (number of quizzes × 3). The difference between the required score to manage an A grade and the score achieved to just manage a B grade as given in the problem's information is equal to 97 – 70 = 27.

Thus, number of quizzes × 3 = 27.

Hence, number of quizzes is 9. Hence, Option (d) is correct.

70. Let the number of students scoring 6, 8 and 20 be a, b, and c respectively. So, $6a + 8b + 20c = 504$

Also, since 'The number of students in the most populated category was equal to the sum of the number of students with lowest score and twice the number of students with the highest score' we get: $a + 2c = b$. Thus, $14a + 36c = 504$.

By trying out values we get that: $c = 7$ and $a = 18$ which gives us $b = 32$. Therefore, total number of students = 18 + 32 + 7 = 57

Hence, Option (e) is the correct answer.

71. In this case, we are given 8 of the 11 numbers, which can be placed in increasing order as: 6, 8, 12, 13, 14, Median 15, 20, 22

Clearly, three numbers above the median are missing. If we use only the statement I, we will get that the sum of the 4 largest numbers should be 53 more (logic 13.25 × 4) than the sum of the four smallest numbers. This means that the sum of the four largest numbers should be 92. (53 more than 6 + 8 + 12 + 13). In order to create the largest possible number in the list we would need to make sure that both 22 and 20 are part of the four largest numbers and also that two of the missing three numbers should be 16 each. In such a case, the only missing number should be 92 – 22 – 20 – 16 – largest possible number = 34.

Thus, it is possible to find out the largest possible integer amongst these numbers using statement I alone.

Using Statement II alone, we get that the sum of the 11 numbers should be 176. We already know the sum of 8 of these numbers, while of the three missing numbers the scenario required to create the largest possible number would be that two of these numbers should be as small as possible. Since the median is 15, these two numbers should be 16 each. In this case the largest possible number can be found as: 176 – (6 + 8 + 12 + 13 + 14 + 15 + 16 + 16 + 20 + 22) = 34.

Thus, Statement I or Statement II is sufficient independently of each other.

CHAPTER

4 Percentages

Chapter Launchpad

Scan this QR code to access a video on 'Introduction to Percentages' and this chapter's importance for CAT

INTRODUCTION

Percentage is one of the three base chapters of arithmetic (Block II along with Averages, and Ratio and Proportions). The concepts of the percentages chapter are applied not only to questions that are asked in this chapter – but also are used across the chapters of this block. Thus, you will see a lot of application of percentages in the chapters of Time and Work, Time Speed and Distance and sometimes even in ratio and proportions. Besides, the chapters of Interests and Profit and Loss are completely dependent on the concepts and reactions of the percentages chapter. From the exam point of view, you would regularly find the use of percentages either through direct questions or through questions from the other arithmetic chapters, where percentages are used (as listed above). Hence, while studying this chapter, you should make sure that you grasp and naturalise for your mind the main triggers and their reactions.

Besides, the calculation skills that you can develop while going through the chapter on percentages will help you in handling Data Interpretation (DI) calculations. A closer look at that topic will yield that at least 50% of the total calculations in any DI paper is constituted of calculations on additions and percentage.

BASIC DEFINITION AND UTILITY OF PERCENTAGE

Percent literally, means 'for every 100' and is derived from the French word 'cent', which is French for 100.

The basic utility of percentage arises from the fact that it is one of the most powerful tools for comparison of numerical data and information. It is also one of the simplest tools for comparison of data.

In the context of business and economic performance, it is specifically useful for comparing data such as profits, growth rates, performance, magnitudes and so on.

Mathematical Definition of Percentage The concept of percentage mainly applies to ratios, and the percentage value of a ratio is arrived at by multiplying by 100, the decimal value of the ratio.

For example, a student scores 20 marks out of a maximum possible 30 marks. His marks can then be denoted as 20 out of 30 = (20/30) or (20/30) × 100% = 66.66%.

The process for getting this is perfectly illustrated through the unitary method:

	Marks scored	*Out of*
then,	$20 \xrightarrow{\text{out of}}$	30
	$x \xrightarrow{\text{out of}}$	100

Then the value of $x \times 30 = 20 \times 100$

$x = (20/30) \times 100 \rightarrow$ the percentage equivalent of a ratio.

Now, let us consider a classic example of the application of percentage:

Example: Student *A* scores 20 marks in an examination out of 30 while another student *B* scores 40 marks out of 70. Who has performed better?

Solution: Just by considering the marks as 20 and 40, we do not a get clear picture of the actual performance of the two students. In order to get a clearer picture, we consider the percentage of marks.

Thus, *A* gets (20/30) × 100 = 66.66%
While *B* gets (40/70) × 100 = 57.14%

Now, it is clear that the performance of *A* is better.
Consider another example:

Example: Company *A* increases its sales by 1 crore rupees while company *B* increases its sales by 10 crore rupees. Which company has grown more?

Solution: Apparently, the answer to the question seems to be company *B*. However, in this situation, growth has to be further qualified as to whether it is percentage growth or absolute growth. In terms of absolute growth, *B* has grown more since absolute growth is simply defined as the difference of the current value and the original value. Thus, *B* has an absolute growth of 10 crores, while *A* has an absolute growth of 1 crore. Thus, absolute growth of *B* > absolute growth of *A*. However, if we are interested to find the percentage growth (or growth rate or growth percentage, which is sometimes also referred to as the growth relative to the previous year), we cannot answer that question since, we do not know the base figures on which these sales have grown.

If we had further information saying that company *A* had a sales turnover of ₹1 crore in the previous year and company *B* had a sales turnover of ₹100 crore in the previous year, we can compare growth rates and say that it is company *A* that has grown by 100%. Hence, company *A* has a higher growth rate, even though in terms of absolute value increase of sales, company *B* has grown much more.

IMPORTANCE OF BASE/DENOMINATOR FOR PERCENTAGE CALCULATIONS

Mathematically, the percentage value can only be calculated for ratios that, by definition, must have a denominator. Hence, one of the most critical aspects of the percentage is the denominator, which in other words, is also called the base value of the percentage. No percentage calculation is possible without knowing the base to which the percentage is to be calculated.

Hence, whenever faced with the question 'What is the percentage ...?' always try first to find out the answer to the question 'Percentage to what base?'

CONCEPT OF PERCENTAGE CHANGE

Whenever the value of a measured quantity changes, the change can be captured through

(a) Absolute value change or

(b) Percentage change

Both these measurements have their own advantages and disadvantages.

Absolute value change: It is the actual change in the measured quantity. For instance, if sales in year one is ₹2500 crore and the sales in year two is ₹2600 crore, then the absolute value of the change is ₹100 crore.

Percentage change: It is the percentage change obtained by the formula

$$\text{Percentage change} = \frac{\text{Absolute value change}}{\text{Original quantity}} \times 100$$

$$= \frac{100}{2500} \times 100 = 4\%$$

As seen earlier, this often gives us a better picture of the effect of the change. (**Note:** In order to point you towards the percentage change calculation, you can come across a few different languages, which you should be able to decode without error and effortlessly (These are all natural for someone whose quants skills are good – but I have often found that for students who are weak at Mathematics or Quantitative thinking- they often have difficulty in reacting correctly to these language triggers)).

1. What is the percentage change of A from B? (Correct calculation: $\frac{A-B}{B} \times 100$)
2. What is the percentage change from A to B? (Correct calculation: $\frac{B-A}{A} \times 100$)
3. How much more is A relative to B? (Correct calculation: $\frac{A-B}{B} \times 100$)

Note: The base used for the sake of percentage change calculations is always the original quantity unless otherwise stated.

Example: The population of a city grew from 20 lac to 22 lac. Find the

(a) percentage change

(b) percentage change based on the final value of population

Solution: (a) percentage change = (2/20) × 100 = 10%

(b) percentage change on the final value = (2/22) × 100 = 9.09%

Difference between the Percentage Point Change and the Percentage Change

The difference between the percentage point change and the percentage change is best illustrated through an example. Consider this:

The savings rate as a percentage of the GDP was 25% in the first year and 30% in the second year. Assume that there is no change in the GDP between the two years. Then:

Percentage point change in savings rate = 30%–25% = 5 percentage points.

Percentage change in savings rate = $\frac{30-25}{25} \times 100$ = 20%.

PERCENTAGE RULE FOR CALCULATING PERCENTAGE VALUES THROUGH ADDITIONS

Illustrated below is a powerful method of calculating percentages. In my opinion, the ability to calculate percentage through this method depends on your ability to handle two digit additions. Unless you develop the skill to add two digit additions in your mind, you are always likely to face problems in calculating percentage through the method illus-trated below. In fact, trying this method without being strong at two-digit additions/subtractions (including two digits after decimal point) would prove to be a disadvantage in your attempt at calculating percentages fast.

Concept Explainer

Scan this QR code to access a conceptual video on Percentage Rule for Calculating Percentage Values Through Additions

This process, essentially being a commonsense process, is best illustrated through a few examples:

Example: What is the percentage value of the ratio: 53/81?

Solution: The process involves removing all the 100%, 50%, 10%, 1%, 0.1% and so forth of the denominator from the numerator.

Thus, 53/81 can be rewritten as: (40.5 + 12.5)/81 = 40.5/81 + 12.5/81 = 50% + 12.5/81

= 50% + (8.1 + 4.4)/81 = 50% + 10% + 4.4/81
= 60% + 4.4/81

At this stage, you know that the answer to the question lies between 60 and 70% (Since 4.4 is less than 10% of 81)

At this stage, you know that the answer to the calculation will be in the form: 6*a.bcde* ....

All you need to do is find out the value of the missing digits.

In order to do this, calculate the percentage value of 4.4/81 through the normal process of multiplying the numerator by 100.

Thus, the % value of $\frac{4.4}{81} = \frac{4.4 \times 100}{81} = \frac{440}{81}$

Note: Use the multiplication by 100, once you have the 10% range. This step reduces the decimal calculations.

Thus, $\frac{440}{81}$ = 5% with a remainder of 35.

Our answer is now refined to 65.*bcde.* (1% range)

Next, in order to find the next digit (first one after the decimal add a zero to the remainder;)

Hence, the value of '*b*' will be the quotient of

$b \rightarrow$ 350/81 = 4 remainder 26

Answer: 65.4*cde* (0.1% range)

$c \rightarrow$ 260/81 = 3 remainder 17

Answer: 65.43 (0.01% range)

and so forth.

The advantages of this process are two fold:

1. You only calculate as long as you need to in order to eliminate the options. Thus, in case there was only a single option between 60 and 70% in the above question, you could have stopped your calculations right there.
2. This process allows you to go through with the calculations as long as you need to.

However, remember what I had advised you right at the start: Strong addition skills are a primary requirement for using this method properly.

Note: The relationship between the decimal value and the percentage value of a ratio.

Every ratio has a percentage value and a decimal value and the difference between the two is just in the positioning of the decimal point.

Thus, 2/4 can be represented as 0.5 in terms of its decimal value and can be represented by 50% in terms of its percentage value. Thus, in the above calculation when you have got an answer of 65.43% for the percentage value of 53/81, you actually have the decimal value of 53/81 as 0.6543. Thus, the percentage calculation can also be used as a proxy calculation to replace your process of division. Also, in case you were finding the decimal value of 53/81, it is unlikely that in the context of any aptitude exam, you would be asked to get an answer of anything beyond the first two decimal places of the answer. In such a case, you could simply calculate the percentage value of 53/81 as 65._ _ % and conclude that the division of 53/81 would give you an answer of 0.65_ _.

To illustrate another example:

What is the percentage value of the ratio $\frac{223}{72}$?

223/72 $\rightarrow$ 300 – 310% remainder 7

700/72 = 9 +. Hence, 309 – 310%, remainder 52

520/72 $\rightarrow$ 7 Hence, 309.7, remainder 16

160/72 $\rightarrow$ 2 Hence, 309.72, remainder 16

Hence, 309.7222 (2 recurs, since we enter an infinite loop of 160/72 calculations).

Decimal interpretation: The division of 223/72 would yield you an answer of 3.097222.

In my view, percentage rule (as I call it) is one of the best ways to calculate percentages since it gives you the flexibility to calculate the percentage value up to as many digits after decimals as you are required to and at the same time allows you to stop the moment you attain the required accuracy range. It is also a very effective way to replace your division process – provided you have worked on your 2 digit additions.

Effect of a Percent Change in the Numerator on a Ratio's Value

The numerator has a direct relationship with the ratio, that is, if the numerator increases the ratio increases. The percentage increase in the ratio is the same as the percentage increase in the numerator, if the denominator is constant.

Thus, $\frac{22}{40}$ is exactly 10% more than $\frac{20}{40}$ (in terms of percentage change).

Percentage Change Graphic and its Applications

In Mathematics, there are many situations where one is required to work with percentage changes. In such situations, the following thought structure (Something I call Percentage Change Graphic) is a very useful tool.

What I call Percentage Change Graphic (PCG) is best illustrated through an example:

Suppose you have to increase the number 20 by 20%. Visualise this as follows:

$$20 \xrightarrow[=+4]{20\%\uparrow} 24$$

The PCG has six major applications listed and explained below: PCG applied to:

1. Successive changes
2. Product change application
3. Product constancy application
4. A $\rightarrow$ B$\rightarrow$A application
5. Denominator change to ratio change application
6. Use of PCG to calculate ratio changes

Application 1: PCG Applied to Successive Changes

This is a very common situation in most questions.

Suppose you have to solve a question in which a number 30 has two successive percentage increases (20% and 10% respectively).

The situation is handled in the following way using PCG:

$$30 \xrightarrow[+6]{20\%\text{ increase}} 36 \xrightarrow[+3.6]{10\%\text{ increase}} 39.6$$

Illustration

A's salary increases by 20% and then decreases by 20%. What is the net percentage change in *A*'s salary?

Solution:

$$100 \xrightarrow[+20]{20\%\text{ increase}} 120 \xrightarrow[-24]{20\%\text{ decrease}} 96$$

Hence, *A*'s salary has gone down by 4%.

Illustration

A trader gives successive discounts of 10%, 20% and 10% respectively. What is the percentage of the original cost price he will recover?

Solution:

$$100 \xrightarrow[-10]{10\%\text{ decrease}} 90 \xrightarrow[-18]{20\%\text{ decrease}} 72 \xrightarrow[-7.2]{10\%\text{ decrease}} 64.8$$

Hence, the overall discount is 35.2% and the answer is 64.8%.

Illustration

A trader marks up the price of his goods by 20%, but to a particularly haggling customer he ends up giving a discount of 10% on the marked price. What is the percentage profit he makes?

Solution:

$$100 \xrightarrow[+20]{20\%\text{ increase}} 120 \xrightarrow[-12]{10\%\text{ decrease}} 108$$

Hence, the percentage profit is 8%.

Application 2: PCG applied to Product Change

Suppose you have a product of two variables say 10 × 10.

If the first variable changes to 11 and the second variable changes to 12, what will be the percentage change in the product? (**Note:** There is a 10% increase in one part of the product and a 20% increase in the other part.)

The formula given for this situation goes as: $(a + b + ab/100)$

Hence, required % change $= 10 + 20 + \dfrac{10 \times 20}{100}$

where 10 and 20 are the respective percentage changes in the two parts of the product

(This is being taught as a shortcut at most institutes across the country currently.)

However, a much easier solution for this case can be visualised as:

$100 \xrightarrow[+20]{20\%\uparrow} 120 \xrightarrow[+12]{10\%\uparrow} 132$. Hence, the final product shows a 32% increase.

Similarly, suppose 10 × 10 × 10 becomes 11 × 12 × 13. In such a case, the following PCG will be used:

$$100 \xrightarrow[+30]{30\%\uparrow} 130 \xrightarrow[+26]{20\%\uparrow} 156 \xrightarrow[+15.6]{10\%\uparrow} 171.6$$

Hence, the final product sees a 71.6 percent increase (Since, the product changes from 100 to 171.6).

Note: You will get the same result irrespective of the order in which you use the respective percentage changes.

Also note that this process is very similar to the one used for calculating successive percentage change.

Application for DI:

Suppose you have two pie charts as follows:

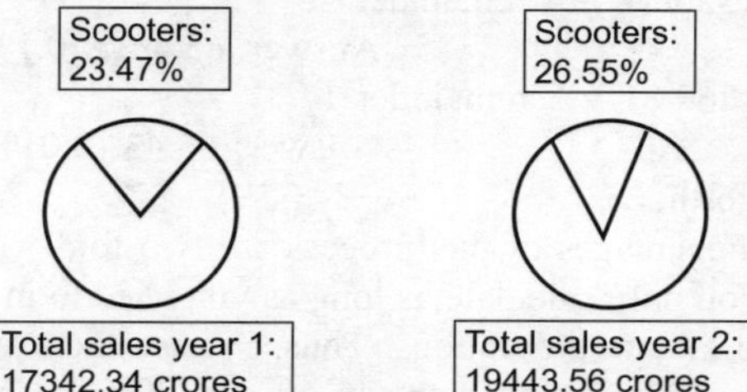

If you are asked to calculate the percentage change in the sales revenue of scooters for the company from year one to year two, what would you do?

The formula for percentage change would give us:

$$\frac{(0.2655 \times 19443.56) - (0.2347 \times 17342.34)}{(0.2347 \times 17342.34)} \times 100$$

i.e. $\dfrac{\text{New Sales Revenue} - \text{Original Sales Revenue}}{\text{Original Sales Revenue}} \times 100$

Obviously, this calculation is easier said than done.

However, the product change application of PCG allows us to execute this calculation with a lot of ease comparatively. Consider the following solution:

Product for year one is: 0.2347 × 17342.34

Product for year two is: 0.2655 × 19443.56

These can be approximated into:
234 × 173 and 265 × 194 respectively (**Note** that by moving into three digits, we do not end up losing any accuracy. We have elaborated this point in the chapter on Ratio and Proportions.)

The overall percentage change depends on two individual percentage changes:
234 increases to 265: A % change of 31/234 = 13.2 % approx. This calculation has to be done using the percentage rule for calculating the percentage value of the ratio.

173 increases to 194 — A percentage change of approximately 12%.

Thus, PCG will give the answer as follows:

$$100 \xrightarrow[+13.2]{13.2\%\uparrow} 113.2 \xrightarrow[+13.56]{12\%\uparrow} 126.76$$

Hence, 26.76 % increase in the product's value. (**Note:** the value on the calculator for the full calculation sans any approximations is 26.82 %, and given the fact that we have come extremely close to the answer—the method is good enough to solve the question with a reasonable degree of accuracy.)

Application 3: Product Constancy Application (Inverse proportionality)

Suppose you have a situation wherein the price of a commodity has gone up by 25%. In case you are required to keep the total expenditure on the commodity constant, you would obviously need to cut down on the consumption. By what percentage? Well, PCG gives you the answer as follows:

$$100 \xrightarrow[\substack{+25 \\ \text{Price effect}}]{25\%\uparrow} 125 \xrightarrow[\substack{-25 \\ \text{Consumption effect}}]{} 100$$

Hence, the percentage drop in consumption to offset the price increase is 20%.

I leave it to the student to discover the percentage drop required in the second part of the product if one part increases by 50 percent.

Note: Product constancy is just another name for inverse proportionality.

Table 4.1 gives you some standard values for this kind of a situation.

Application 4: A→B→A

Very often we are faced with a situation where we compare two numbers say A and B. In such cases, if we are given a relationship from A to B, then the reverse relationship can be determined by using PCG in much the same way as the product constancy use shown above.

Illustration

B's salary is 25% more than A's salary. By what percent is A's salary less than B's salary?

$$100(A) \xrightarrow[+25]{25\%\uparrow} 125(B) \xrightarrow[-25]{} 100(A)$$

A drop of 25 on 125 gives a 20% drop.
Hence, A's salary is 20% less than B's.

Note: The values which applied for product constancy also apply here. Hence, Table 4.1 is useful for this situation also.

Application 5: Effect of change in Denominator on the Value of the Ratio

The denominator has an inverse relationship with the value of a ratio.

Hence, the process used for product constancy (and explained above) can be used for calculating percentage change in the denominator.

For instance, suppose you have to evaluate the difference between two ratios:

Ratio 1 : 10/20
Ratio 2 : 10/25

As is evident, the denominator is increasing from 20 to 25 by 25%.

If we calculate the value of the two ratios we will get:

Ratio 1 = 0.5, Ratio 2 = 0.4

Percentage change between the two ratios = $\frac{0.1}{0.5} \times 100$ = 20% drop

This value can be obtained through PCG as:

$100 \longrightarrow 125 \longrightarrow 100$ Hence, 20% drop.

Note: This is exactly the same as product constancy and works here because the numerator is constant.

Hence, $R_1 = N/D_1$ and $R_2 = N/D_2$

i.e. $R_1 \times D_1 = N$ and $R_2 \times D_2 = N$, which is the product constancy situation.

Direct process for calculation

To find out the percentage change in the ratio due to a change in the denominator, follow the following process:

In order to find the percentage change from 10/20 to 10/25, calculate the percentage change in the denominator in the reverse fashion, i.e. the required percentage change from R_1 to R_2 will be given by calculating the percentage change in the denominators from 25 to 20 (i.e. in a reverse fashion) and not from 20 to 25.

Concept Explainer
Scan this QR code to access a conceptual video on **Table 4.1**

Table 4.1 Product Constancy Table, Inverse Proportionality Table, A → B → A table, Ratio Change to Denominator table

Product XY is constant	*X increases (%)*	*Y decreases (%)*
A → B → A	*A → B % increase*	*B → A% decrease*
X is inversely proportional to Y	*X increases (%)*	*Y decreases (%)*
Ratio change effect of denominator change	*Denominator increases (%)*	*Ratio decreases (%)*
Denominator change effect of ratio change	*Ratio increases (%)*	*As denominator decreases (%)*
Standard Value 1	5	4.76
Standard Value 2	9.09	8.33
Standard Value 3	10	9.09
Standard Value 4	11.11	10

Product XY is constant	*X increases (%)*	*Y decreases (%)*
A → B → A	*A → B % increase*	*B → A% decrease*
X is inversely proportional to Y	*X increases (%)*	*Y decreases (%)*
Ratio change effect of denominator change	*Denominator increases (%)*	*Ratio decreases (%)*
Denominator change effect of ratio change	*Ratio increases (%)*	*As denominator decreases (%)*
Standard Value 5	12.5	11.11
Standard Value 6	14.28	12.5
Standard Value 7	16.66	14.28
Standard Value 8	20	16.66
Standard Value 9	25	20
Standard Value 10	33.33	25
Standard Value 11	40	28.57
Standard Value 12	50	33.33
Standard Value 13	60	37.5
Standard Value 14	66.66	40
Standard Value 15	75	42.85
Standard Value 16	100	50

Fractional increase-decrease view of the above table:

Did you notice a consistent fractional pattern for the above table?

When the percentage increase is 9.09 (=fractional increase of 1/11); the corresponding percentage decrease is 8.33 (1/12).

Other pairs, simplify to: 1/10 increase → 1/11 decrease; 1/9 increase, 1/10 decrease; 1/8 increase, 1/9 decrease, going all the way to 1/2 increase (50%), 1/3 decrease (33.33%). This even works for the 40% and 28.57% pair in the table above – i.e. 2/5 increase, 2/7 decrease, 3/4 increase (75%), 3/7 decrease (42.85%) and so on. This is obviously much more versatile than knowing the percentage value pairs mentioned above, since you could possibly never remember in percentage terms non-standard pairs like: 3/43 increase, 3/46 decrease and infinite other such pairs. Knowing the fractional increase-decrease perspective for the above table massively enables you to create numerical patterns in your mind that you previously did not have.

However, even though the fractions are much more versatile, I would still advise you to remember the standard percentage pairs given in the table above.

Sample usage of these: Suppose you are given a situation where a shopkeeper marks up the price of his items by 25% and is now selling his items at ₹195. What is his cost price? In this situation, you should realise that if the CP is 'x', the SP is 25% more than 'x'. This means that in the reverse direction if we want to come back from 195 to 'x', we would need to reduce 195 by 20%. Thus, the value of x = 195 – 20% of 195 = 195–39 = 156. For the same situation, you could also have thought about the cost price using fractional increase-decrease pairs as follows: Going from x to 195 is an increase of 1/4, hence coming back from 195 to x, there would be a drop of 1/5 of 195. Hence, the value of x = 195 – 1/5 of 195 = 195 – 39 = 156.

Now, if I say that the shopkeeper has marked up by 3/19 to mark the price of the items at ₹506, and I ask you to find the cost price for the shopkeeper. In this situation, as you can appreciate, we cannot use a percentage increase-decrease pair since the value of the increase is a non-standard value. However, using fractional increase-decrease logic, such a situation can be very easily resolved as follows:

X → 506 (is a 3/19 increase), hence 506 → x would be a 3/22 decrease. Hence, the value of x = 506 – 3/22 of 506 = 506 – 69 = 437. I would encourage you to look for more such reactions and possibilities whenever we have a product constancy situation, an A → B → A situation or a denominator change → ratio change situation in any chapter in your QA portion.

Application 6: Use of PCG to Calculate Ratio Changes

Under normal situations, you will be faced with ratios where both numerator and denominator change. The process to handle and calculate such changes is also quite convenient if you go through PCG.

Illustration

Calculate the percentage change between the ratios.

Ratio 1 = 10/20; Ratio 2 = 15/25

The answer in this case is 0.5 → 0.6 (20% increase). However, in most cases calculating the values of the ratio will not be easy. The following PCG process can be used to get the answer:

When 10/20 changes to 15/25, the change occurs primarily due to two reasons:

1. Change in the numerator (Numerator effect)
2. Change in the denominator (Denominator effect)

By segregating the two effects and calculating the effect due to each separately, we can get the answer easily as follows:

Numerator Effect The numerator effect on the value of the ratio is the same as the change in the numerator. Hence, to calculate the numerator effect, just calculate the percentage change in the numerator.

In this case, the numerator is clearly changing from 10 to 15 (i.e. a 50% increase.) This signifies that the numerator effect is also 50%.

Denominator Effect As we have just seen above, the effect of a percentage change in the denominator on the value of the ratio is seen by calculating the denominator's percentage change in the reverse order.

In this case, the denominator is changing from 20 to 25. Hence, the denominator effect will be seen by going reverse from 25 to 20, i.e. 20% drop.

With these two values, the overall percentage change in the ratio is seen by:

$$100 \xrightarrow[\substack{+50 \\ \text{Numerator effect}}]{50\%\uparrow} 150 \xrightarrow[\substack{-30 \\ \text{Denominator effect}}]{20\%\downarrow} 120$$

This means that the ratio has increased by 20%.

I leave it to the student to practice such calculations with more complicated values for the ratios.

Implications for Data Interpretation

Percentage is perhaps one of the most critical links between QA and data interpretation.

In the chapter theory mentioned above, the percentage rule for percentage calculations and the PCG applied to product change and ratio change are the most critical.

As already shown, the use of PCG to calculate the percentage change in a product (as exhibited through the pie chart example above) as well as the use of PCG to calculate ratio changes are two extremely useful applications of the concepts of percentages into DI.

Applying percentages for the special case of comparing two ratios to find the larger one.

Suppose you have two ratios to compare. Say $R_1 = N_1/D_1$ and $R_2 = N_2/D_2$

The first step is to find the ten percent ranges for each of these ratios. In case, they belong to different ranges of 10% (say R1 lies between 50 and 60 while R2 lies between 70 and 80), it becomes pretty simple to say which one will be higher.

In case, both of these values for percentage of the ratios belong to the same ten percent range, then we can use the following process.

Step 1: Calculate the percentage change in the numerator

Step 2: Calculate the percentage change in the denominator.

There could be four cases in this situation, when we move from ratio_1 to ratio_2:

Case 1: **Numerator is increasing while denominator is decreasing** → obviously the net effect of the two changes will be an increase in the ratio. Hence, R_2 will be greater.

Case 2: **Numerator is decreasing while denominator is increasing** → obviously the net effect of the two changes will be a decrease in the ratio. Hence, R_1 will be greater.

It is only in the following cases that we need to look at the respective changes in the numerator and denominator.

Case 3: Numerator and denominator are both increasing.

Calculate the percentage value of the respective increases. If the numerator is increasing more than the denominator, the ratio will go up. On the other hand, if the denominator is increasing more than the numerator, ratio_2 will be smaller than ratio_1. (**Note:** Compare in percentage values)

Case 4: **Numerator and denominator are both decreasing** →

Calculate the percentage value of the respective decreases. If the numerator is decreasing more than the denominator, the ratio will go down. On the other hand, if the denominator is decreasing more than the numerator, ratio_2 will be greater than ratio_1.

FRACTION TO PERCENTAGE CONVERSION TABLE

The following percentage values appear repeatedly over the entire area where questions can be framed on the topic of percentage. Further, it would be of great help to you if you are able to recognise these values separately from values that do not appear in the Table 4.2.

Some Utilisations of the Table

- The values that appear in the table are all percentage values. These can be converted into decimals by just shifting the decimal point by two places to the left. Thus, 83.33% = 0.8333 in decimal value.
- A second learning from this table is in the process of division by any of the numbers such as 2, 3, 4, 5, 6, 7, 8, 9, 11, 12, 15, 16, 24 and so on; students normally face problems in calculating the decimal values of these divisions. However, if one gets used to the decimal values that appear in the **Table 5.2**, calculation of decimals in divisions will become very simple. For instance, when an integer is divided by 7, the decimal values can only be 0.14, 0.28, 0.42, 0.57, 0.71, 0.85 or 0.00. (These are approximate values)
- This also means that the difference between two ratios like $\frac{x}{6} - \frac{x}{7}$ can be integral if and only if x is divisible by both 6 and 7.

This principle is very useful as an advanced short cut for option-based solution of some questions. I leave it to the student to discover applications of this principle.

Calculation of Multiplication by Numbers like 1.21, 0.83 and so on

Table 4.2 Percentage Conversion Table

	1	*2*	*3*	*4*	*5*	*6*	*7*	*8*	*9*	*10*	*11*	*12*
1	100											
2	50	100										
3	33.33	66.66	100									
4	25	50	75	100								
5	20	40	60	80	100							
6	16.66	33.33	50	66.66	83.33	100						
7	14.28	28.57	42.85	57.14	71.42	85.71	100					
8	12.5	25	37.5	50	62.5	75	87.5	100				
9	11.11	22.22	33.33	44.44	55.55	66.66	77.77	88.88	100			
10	10	20	30	40	50	60	70	80	90	100		
11	9.09	18.18	27.27	36.36	45.45	54.54	63.63	72.72	81.81	90.90	100	
12	8.33	16.66	25	33.33	41.66	50	58.33	66.66	75	83.33	91.66	100
15	6.66	13.33	20	26.66	33.33	40						
16	6.25	12.5	18.75	25								
20	5	10	15	20	25							
24	4.166	8.33	12.5	16.66	20.83	25						
25	4	8	12	16	20	24	28	32	26	40		
30	3.33	6.66	10	13.33	16.66	20						
40	2.5	5	7.5	10	12.5	15	17.5	20				
60	1.66	3.33	5	6.66	8.33	10						

Formula for any cell = Column value ¥ 100/Row value

In my opinion, the calculation of multiplication of any number by a number of the form 0.*xy* or of the form 1.*ab* should be viewed as a subtraction/addition situation and not as a multiplication situation. This can be explained as follows.

Example: Calculate 1.23 × 473.

Solution: If we try to calculate this by multiplying, we will end up going through a very time-taking process, which will yield the final value at the end but nothing before that (i.e. you will have no clue about the answer's range till you reach the end of the calculation).

Instead, one should view this multiplication as an addition of 23% to the original number. This means, the answer can be obtained by adding 23% of the number to itself.

Thus, $473 \times 1.23 = 473 + 23\%$ of $473 = 473 + 94.6 + 3\%$ of $473 = 567.6 + 14.19 = 581.79$.

(The percentage rule can be used to calculate the addition and get the answer.)

The similar process can be utilised for the calculation of multiplication by a number such as 0.87.

(Answer can be obtained by subtracting 13% of the number from itself and this calculation can again be done by percentage rule.)

Hence, the student is advised to become thorough with the percentage rules. Percentage calculation and additions of 2 and 3 digit numbers.

Space for Notes

WORKED-OUT PROBLEMS

Problem 4.1: *A* sells his goods 30% cheaper than *B* and 30% dearer than *C*. By what percentage is the cost of *C*'s goods cheaper than *B*'s goods?

Solution: There are two alternative processes for solving this question:

1. Assume the price of *C*'s goods as *p*.: Then *A*'s goods are at 1.3 p and *B*'s goods are such that *A*'s goods are 30% cheaper than *B*'s goods, i.e. *A*'s goods are priced at 70% of *B*'s goods.

$$\text{Hence, } 1.3\,p \to 70$$
$$B\text{'s price} \to 100$$
$$B\text{'s price} = 130\,p/70 = 1.8571\,p$$

Then, the percentage by which *C*'s price is cheaper than *B*'s price

$$(1.8571\,p - p) \times 100/(1.8571\,p) = 600/13 = 46.15\%$$

Learning task for student Could you answer the question: Why did we assume *C*'s price as a variable *p* and then work out the problem on its basis. What would happen if we assumed *B*'s price as *p* or if we assumed *A*'s price as *p*?

2. Instead of assuming the price of one of the three as *p*, assume the price as 100.

Let *B* = 100. Then *A* = 70, which is 30% more than *C*. Hence, *C* = 23.07% less than *A* (from Table 4.1) = approx. 53.84. Hence, answer is 46.15% approximately.

(This calculation can be done mentally if you are able to work through the calculations by the use of percentage rule. The students are advised to try to assume the value of 100 for each of the variables *A*, *B* and *C* and see what happens to the calculations involved in the problem. Since the value of 100 is assumed for a variable to minimise the requirements of calculations to solve the problems, we should ensure that the variable assumed as 100 should have the maximum calculations associated with it.)

Note: In fact this question and the ones that follow contain some of the most basic operations in the chapter of percentages. The questions at the first level of difficulty would appear in examinations like CET Maharashtra, Bank P.O., CUET, IPMAT, MAT, NMAT, SNAP, CLAT and most other aptitude exams. Hence, if you are able to do the operations illustrated here mentally, you would be able to solve LOD I questions easily and gain a significant time advantage over your competitors.

However, for a serious CAT aspirant, the logic used for LOD I questions would normally be used as a part of the entire logic. You would be able to see this in the questions of the second and the third level of difficulties in the exercises later in the chapter. Hence, developing the process for solving questions of the LOD I level mentally would help you gain an improved speed for the CAT level questions.

Also remember that since percentages are the basis for most of the commercial Mathematics as well as for calculation and the data interpretation section, developing skills for calculation and problem solving illustrated here would go a long way towards helping you clear aptitude exams.

Problem 4.2: The length and the breadth of a rectangle are changed by +20% and by –10%, respectively. What is the percentage change in the area of the rectangle?

Solution: The area of a rectangle is given by: length × breadth. If we represent these by:

Area = $L \times B = LB \to$ then we will get the changed area as

$$\text{Area}_{(\text{NEW})} = 1.2\,L \times 0.9\,B = 1.08\,LB$$

Hence, the change in area is 8% increase.

Note: You can solve (and in fact, finish the problem) during your first reading by using percentage change graphic as follows:

$100 \xrightarrow{+20\%} 120 \xrightarrow{-10\%} 108$. Hence, the percentage change is 8%.

Problem 4.3: Due to a 25% price hike in the price of rice, a person is able to purchase 20 kg less of rice for ₹400. Find the initial price.

Solution: Since price is rising by 25%, consumption has to decrease by 20%. But there is an actual reduction in the consumption by 20 kg. Thus, 20% decrease in consumption is equal to a 20 kg drop in consumption.

Hence, original consumption is: 100 kg of rice.

Money spent being ₹400, the original price of rice is ₹4 per kg.

(There, you see the benefit of internalising the product constancy table! It is left to the student to analyse why and how the product constancy table applies here.)

Problem 4.4: *A*'s salary is 20% lower than *B*'s salary, which is 15% lower than *C*'s salary. By how much percent is *C*'s salary more than *A*'s salary?

Solution: The equation approach here would be

$$A = 0.8\,B$$
$$B = 0.85\,C$$

Then $A = 0.8 \times 0.85\,C$

$A = 0.68\ C$ (Use percentage change graphic to calculate the value of 0.68)

Thus, A's salary is 68 % of C's salary.

If A's salary is 68, C's salary is 100.

Using percentage change graphic

$$68 \xrightarrow[+32]{(3200/68)\%} 100$$

Students are advised to refrain from using equations to solve questions of this nature. In fact, you can adopt the following process, which can be used while you are reading the problem, to get the result faster.

Assume one of the values as 100. (Remember, selection of the right variable that has to take the value of 100 may make a major difference to your solving time and effort required). The thumb rule for selecting the variable whose value is to be taken as 100 is based on three principal considerations:

Select as 100, the variable

1. With the maximum number of percentage calculations associated with it
2. Select as 100, the variable with the most difficult calculation associated with it
3. Select as 100, the variable at the start of the problem solving chain

The student will have to develop his own judgement in applying these principles in specific cases.

Here I would take C as 100, getting B as 85 and A as 68.

Hence, the answer is (32 × 100/68).

Problem 4.5: The cost of manufacture of an article is made up of four components A, B, C and D which have a ratio of 3 : 4 : 5 : 6, respectively. If there are respective changes in the cost of +10%, –20%, –30% and +40%, then what would be the percentage change in the cost?

Solution: Assume the cost components to be valued at 30, 40, 50 and 60 as you read the question. Then we can get changed costs by affecting the appropriate changes in each of the four components.

Thus, we get the new cost as 33, 32, 35 and 84 respectively.

The original total cost was 180; the new one is 184. The percent change is 4/180 = 2.22%.

Problem 4.6: Harsh receives an inheritance of a certain amount from his grandfather. Of this, he loses 32.5% in his effort to produce a film. From the balance, a taxi driver stole the sum of ₹1,00,000 that he used to keep in his pocket. Of the rest, he donated 20% to a charity. Further, he purchases a flat in Ganga Apartment for ₹7.5 lac. He then realises that he is left with only ₹2.5 lac cash of his inheritance. What was the value of his inheritance?

Solution: These sort of problems should either be solved through the reverse process or through options.

Reverse process for this problem He is left with ₹2.5 lac after spending ₹7.5 lac on the apartment.

Therefore, before the apartment purchase he has ₹10 lac. But this is after the 20% reduction in his net value due to his donation to charity. Hence, he must have given ₹2.5 lac to charity (20% decrease corresponds to a 25% increase). As such, he had 12.5 lac before the charity. Further, he must have had ₹13.5 lac, before the taxi driver stole the sum. From 13.5 lac you can reach the answer by trial and error trying whole number values. You will get that if he had 20 lac and lost 32.5% of it, he would be left with the required 13.5 lac.

Hence, the answer is ₹20 lac.

This process can be done mentally by: 2.5 + 7.5 = 10 lac → +25% → 12.5 lac → + 1 lac → 13.5 lac.

From this point, move by trial and error. You should try to find the value of the inheritance, which on reduction by 32.5%, would leave 13.5 lac. A little experience with numbers leaves you with ₹20 lac as the answer. This process should be started as soon as you finish reading the first time.

Through options Suppose the options were:

(a) 25 lac (b) 22.5 lac

(c) 20 lac (d) 18 lac

Start with any of the middle options. Then keep performing the mathematical operation in the order given in the problem. The final value that he is left with should be ₹2.5 lac. The option that gives this, will be the answer. If the final value yielded is higher than ₹2.5 lac in this case, start with a value lower than the option checked. In case it is the opposite, start with the option higher than the one used.

As a thumb rule, start with the most convenient option—the middle one. This would lead us to start with ₹20 lac here.

However, if we had started with ₹25 lac, the following would have occurred.

25 lac –32.5% → 16.875 lac –1 lac → 15.875 lac –20% – 7.5 lac, should equal 2.5 lac → (Prior to doing this calculation, you should see that there is no way the answer will yield a nice whole number like 2.5 lac. Hence, you can abandon the process here and move to the next option).

Trying with 20 lac, 20 –32.5% → 13.5 lac – 1 lac. → 12.5 lac –20% → 10 lac – 7.5 lac = 2.5 lac → Required answer.

LEVEL OF DIFFICULTY (I)

1. If we express 12(4/15)% as a fraction, then it is equal to
(a) 46/375 (b) 46/125
(c) 23/250 (d) None of these.

2. What is 10% of 20% of 25% of 100?
(a) 0.5 (b) 0.75
(c) 0.25 (d) 1.0

3. Which of the following is the largest number?
(a) 40% of 400 (b) 5% of 800
(c) 1000% of 4 (d) 200% of 9

4. If 30% of a number is 300, then 50% of that number is:
(a) 400 (b) 125
(c) 150 (d) 500

5. If 25% of x = 30% of y, then find the value of x if $y = 5000$.
(a) 2000 (b) 3000
(c) 4000 (d) 6000

6. 30% of a% of b is 25% of b% of c. Which of the following is c?
(a) $1.5a$ (b) $0.667a$
(c) $0.5a$ (d) 1.20a

7. 20% of a number when subtracted from 108, gives the number itself. Find the number.
(a) 50 (b) 80
(c) 70 (d) 90

8. When 40% of a number A is added to another number B, B becomes 125% of its previous value. Then which of the following is true regarding the values of A and B?
(a) $A > B$
(b) $B > A$
(c) $B = A$
(d) Either (a) or (b) can be true depending upon the values of A and B

9. Two students appeared at an examination. One of them secured 10 marks more than the other and his marks was 60% of the sum of their marks. The marks obtained by the better student are:

10. Two numbers A and B are such that the sum of 5% of A and 10% of B is 1/2 of the sum of 20% of A and 10% of B. Find the ratio of A:B?

11. Mr. Ram is worried about the balance of his monthly budget. The price of petrol has increased by 50%. By what percent should he reduce the consumption of petrol so that he is able to balance his budget?
(a) 33.33 (b) 28.56
(c) 25 (d) 14.28

12. In Question 11, if Mr. Ram wanted to limit the increase in his expenditure to 20% on his basic expenditure on petrol then what should be the corresponding decrease in consumption?
(a) 33.33 (b) 12.50
(c) 25 (d) 20

13. Ashok sells his goods 50% dearer than Shankar and 20% dearer than Bishnu. How much percentage is Bishnu's goods dearer than Shankar's?
(a) 33.33% (b) 25%
(c) 66.66% (d) 40%

14. In an election between 2 candidates, Chaman gets 80% of the total valid votes. If the total votes were 12000, what is the number of valid votes that the other candidate Dhande gets if 15% of the total votes were declared invalid?
(a) 1645 (b) 1545
(c) 1675 (d) 2040

15. In a physical measurement, by mistake Shyam gave his height as 25% more than normal. In the interview panel, he clarified that his height was 5 feet 5 inches. Find the percentage correction made by the candidate from his stated height to his actual height.
(a) 20 (b) 28.56
(c) 25 (d) 16.66

16. Raunak generally wears his father's coat. Unfortunately, his cousin Vikas told him one day that he was wearing a coat of length more than his height by 15%. If the length of Raunak's father's coat is 345 cm then find the actual length (in cm) of his coat.
(a) 110 (b) 345
(c) 300 (d) 105

17. A number is mistakenly divided by 2 instead of being multiplied by 2. Find the percentage change in the result due to this mistake.
(a) 100% (b) 125%
(c) 200% (d) 75%

18. Sachin wanted to subtract 10 from a number. Unfortunately, he added 10 instead of subtracting. Find the percentage change in the result.
(a) 300% (b) 66.66%
(c) 50% (d) Cannot be determined

19. In a mixture of 100 litres of milk and water, 25% of the mixture is milk. How much water should be added to the mixture so that milk becomes 20% of the mixture?
(a) 25 litres (b) 15 litres
(c) 20 litres (d) 24 litres

20. A landowner increased the length and the breadth of a rectangular plot by 20% and 30% respectively. Find the percentage change in the cost of the plot assuming land prices are uniform throughout his plot.

(a) 23% (b) 52%
(c) 56% (d) None of these

21. The height of a triangle is increased by 30%. What can be the maximum percentage increase in length of the base so that the increase in area is restricted to a maximum of 90%?
(a) 33.33% (b) 20.67%
(c) 46.15% (d) 25.34%

22. The length, breadth and height of a room in the shape of a cuboid are increased by 10%, 20% and 50%, respectively. Find the percentage change in the volume of the cuboid.
(a) 47.20% (b) 55.33%
(c) 48% (d) 98%

23. The salary of Ajay is 10% more than that of Vivek. Find by what percentage is the salary of Vivek less than that of Ajay?
(a) 16.12% (b) 13.07%
(c) 11.23% (d) 9.09%

24. The price of salt is reduced by 50% but, inspite of the decrease, Aayush ends up increasing his expenditure on salt by 50%. What is the percentage change in his monthly consumption of salt?
(a) +60% (b) –100%
(c) +25% (d) 200%

25. The price of wheat falls by 20%. How much wheat can be bought now with the money that was sufficient to buy 100 kg of rice previously?
(a) 105 kg (b) 115 kg
(c) 125 kg (d) 130 kg

26. At an election, the candidate who got 60% of the votes cast won by 200 votes. Find the total number of voters on the voting list if 66.67% people cast their vote and there were no invalid votes.
(a) 3000 (b) 2400
(c) 1800 (d) 1500

27. The population of a town is 5,00,000. The rate of increase is 20% per annum. Find the population at the start of the third year.
(a) 6,20,000 (b) 7,20,000
(c) 8,30,000 (d) None of these.

28. The population of the city of Gotham is 50,000 at this moment. It increases by 20% in the first year. However, in the second year, due to immigration, the population drops by 10%. Find the population at the end of the third year if in the third year the population increases by 30%.
(a) 82,340 (b) 70,200
(c) 62,540 (d) 52,340

29. Shyam invests ₹ 40,000 in some shares in the ratio 1 : 4 : 5 which pay dividends of 10%, 15% and 25% (on his investment) for that year respectively. Find his dividend income.
(a) 5900 (b) 2000
(c) 8800 (d) 7800

30. In an examination, Madan obtained 20% more than Sahir but 40% less than Ravi. If the marks obtained by Sahir is 80, find the percentage marks obtained by Ravi if the full marks is 200.
(a) 80% (b) 70%
(c) 78.33% (d) 71.11%

31. In a class, 20% of the students were absent for an exam. 10% failed by 10 marks and 20% just passed because of grace marks of 5. Find the average score of the class if the remaining students scored an average of 50 marks and the pass marks are 30 (counting the final scores of the candidates).
(a) 41.25 (b) 37
(c) 38 (d) 33

32. Sharad spends 20% of his monthly income on his household expenditure, 30% of the rest on food, 10% of the rest on clothes and saves the rest. On counting, he comes to know that he has finally saved ₹10080. Find his monthly income (in ₹).
(a) 10000 (b) 15000
(c) 20000 (d) 12000

33. Harish and Bhuvan have salaries that jointly amount to ₹ 10,000 per month. They spend the same amount monthly and then it is found that the ratio of their savings is 6 : 1. Which of the following can be Harish's salary?
(a) ₹ 6000 (b) ₹ 5000
(c) ₹ 4000 (d) ₹ 3000

34. The population of a town is 6000. If the number of males increases by 10% and the number of females increases by 20%, then the population becomes 6800. Find the population of females in the town.
(a) 2500 (b) 3000
(c) 2000 (d) 3500

35. Raju sells his goods 20% cheaper than Bharat and 20% dearer than Charan. How much percentage Charan's goods cheaper/dearer than Bharat's?
(a) 33.33% cheaper (b) 50% dearer
(c) 42.85% dearer (d) None of these

36. In an election contested by two parties, Party SJP secured 12 percentage points of the total votes more than Party SJD. If party SJD got 132,000 votes and there are no invalid votes, by how many votes did it lose the election?
(a) 18,000 (b) 25,000
(c) 24,000 (d) 36,000

37. During winters, an athlete can run 'x' metres on one bottle of energy drink. But in the summer, he can only run 0.2 x metres on one bottle of energy drink. How many bottles of energy drink are required to run 1000 metres during summer?
(a) $1000/x$ (b) $5000/x$
(c) $2000/x$ (d) $4500/x$

38. Vinay's salary is 75% more than Ashok's. Vinay got a raise of 40% on his salary while Ashok got a raise

of 25% on his salary. By what percent is Vinay's salary more than Ashok's?
(a) 96% (b) 51.1%
(c) 90% (d) 52.1%

39. On a morning prayer all the students of a school stand in three rows, the first row has 20% more students than the second row and the third row contains 20% less students than the second row. If the total number of students in all the rows is 300, then find the number of students in the first row.
(a) 120 (b) 125
(c) 100 (d) None of these.

40. An ore contains 20% of an alloy that has 50% copper. Other than this, in the remaining 80% of the ore, there is no copper. How many kilograms of the ore are needed to obtain 10 kg of pure copper?
(a) 100 kg (b) 125 kg
(c) 80 kg (d) 75 kg

41. Last year, the Australian Football team played 80 football matches out of which they managed to win only 20%. This year, so far it has played some matches, which has made it mandatory for it to win 80% of the remaining matches to maintain its existing winning percentage. Find the number of matches played by Australia so far this year.
(a) 30 (b) 25
(c) 28 (d) Insufficient Information

42. The population of a village is 4,00,000. Increase rate per annum is 20%. Find the population at the starting of the 4th year.
(a) 691400 (b) 591200
(c) 691200 (d) None of these

43. In a conference, out of 200 men, 100 women, 400 children present inside the building premises, 10% of the men, 20% of the women and 30% of the children were Indians. Find the percentage of people who were not Indian.
(a) 73% (b) 77%
(c) 79% (d) 83%

44. A table and a chair are priced at ₹3000 and ₹1000 respectively. If the price of the table and that of the chair is increased by 10% and 20% respectively, then the price of 10 tables and 20 chairs is:
(a) 52,000 (b) 57,000
(c) 54,000 (d) None of these

45. Out of the total production of Aluminum from Bauxite, an ore of Aluminum, 30% of the ore gets wasted, and out of the remaining ore, only 30% is pure Aluminum. If the pure Aluminum obtained in a year from a mine of Bauxite was 42,000 kg, then the quantity of Bauxite mined from that mine in the year is
(a) 3,00,000 kg (b) 2,00,000 kg
(c) 2,50,000 kg (d) None of these

46. Ramesh buys a house for ₹ 2,00,000. The annual repair cost comes to 6.0% of the price of purchase. Besides, he has to pay an annual tax of ₹ 12000. At what monthly rent must he rent out the house to get a return of 20% on his net investment (in ₹) of the first year?
(a) ₹ 3867.67 (b) ₹ 3733.33
(c) ₹ 3000 (d) ₹ 3212.50

47. Recently, while shopping in Meena Market in Lucknow, I came across two new trousers selling at a discount. I decided to buy one of them for my little boy Sherry. The shopkeeper offered me the first trouser for ₹ 42 and said that it usually sold for 8/7 of that price. He then offered me the other trouser for ₹ 36 and said that it usually sold for 7/6th of that price. Of the two trousers which one do you think is a better bargain and what is the percentage discount on it?
(a) first trouser, 12.5%
(b) second trouser, 14.28%
(c) Both are same
(d) None of these

48. 4/5 th of the voters in Kanpur promised to vote for Modi and the rest promised to vote for Advani. Of these voters, 10% of the voters who had promised to vote for Modi, did not vote on the election day, while 20% of the voters who had promised to vote for Advani did not vote on the election day. What is the total number of votes polled if Modi got 216000 votes?
(a) 200000 (b) 300000
(c) 264000 (d) 100000

49. In an examination, 80% students passed in Physics, 70% in Chemistry while 15% failed in both the subjects. If 3250 students passed in both the subjects. Find the total number of students who appeared in the examination.
(a) 7500 (b) 8,000
(c) 3000 (d) 5,000

50. Sudhir spends 25% of his salary on house rent, 20% of the rest he spends on his children's education and 10% of the total salary he spends on clothes. After his expenditure, he is left with ₹ 20,000. What is Sudhir's salary?
(a) ₹ 40,000 (b) ₹ 20,000
(c) ₹ 25,000 (d) ₹ 35,000

51. The entrance ticket at the Imagica in Mumbai is worth ₹ 1000. When the price of the ticket was lowered, the sale of tickets increased by 25% while the collections recorded a decrease of 20%. Find the deduction in the ticket price.
(a) ₹ 240 (b) ₹ 360
(c) ₹ 105 (d) ₹ 120

52. Raman's monthly salary is *A* rupees. Of this, he spends *X* rupees. The next month he has an increase

of C% in his salary and D% in his expenditure. The new amount saved is:
(a) $A(1 + C/100) - X(1 + D/100)$
(b) $(A/100)(C - (D) X (1 + D/100)$
(c) $X(C - (D)/100$
(d) $X(C + D)/100$

53. In the year 2010, the luxury bike industry had two bike manufacturers—Splendor and Passion with market shares of 30% and 70%, respectively. In 2011, the overall market for the product increased by 20% and a new player Yamaha also entered the market and captured 10% of the market share. If we know that the market share of Splendor increased to 40% in the second year, the share of Passion in that year was:

54. Ranjan buys goods worth ₹ 10,000. He gets a rebate of 20% on it. After getting the rebate, he pays sales tax @ 10%. Find the amount he will have to pay for the goods.

55. A number is mistakenly divided by 5 instead of being multiplied by 5. What is the percentage error in the result?

56. The salary of Anuj is 20% lower than Bhuwan's salary and the salary of Chauhan is 56.25% greater than Anuj's salary. By how much percent the salary of Bhuwan is less than the salary of Chauhan.
(a) 20% (b) 25%
(c) 40% (d) 15%

57. The length and breadth of a rectangle are changed by +20% and −50%. What is the percentage change in area of rectangle?

58. I recently got a promotion accompanied by 23% hike in salary but due to recession my company reduced my salary by 32%. What was the net change in my salary?

59. A number when reversed becomes 45% greater than the original. By how much percentage is the units place digit greater than the tens' place digit?

60. A batsman scored 100 runs which included 4 boundaries and 6 sixes. What percent of his total score did he make by running between the wickets?

Space for Rough Work

LEVEL OF DIFFICULTY (II)

1. Due to a 25% hike in the price of rice per kilogram, a person is able to purchase 5 kg less for ₹200. Find the increased price of rice per kilogram.
   (a) ₹5 (b) ₹6
   (c) ₹10 (d) ₹4
2. A fraction is such that if the double of the numerator and the triple of the denominator is changed by +10% and –30% respectively then we get 33% of 16/21. Find the fraction.
   (a) $\frac{4}{25}$ (b) $\frac{8}{11}$
   (c) $\frac{3}{25}$ (d) None of these
3. After receiving two successive hikes, Karun's salary became equal to 15/8 times of his initial salary. By how much percent was the salary raised the first time if the second raise was twice as high (in percent) as the first?
   (a) 15% (b) 20%
   (c) 25% (d) 30%
4. After three successive equal percentage rise in the salary the sum of 1000 rupees turned into 1331 rupees. Find the percentage rise in the salary.
   (a) 10% (b) 22%
   (c) 66% (d) 82%
5. Sudhir, a very clever businessman, started off a business with very little capital. In the first year, he earned a profit of 50% and donated 50% of the total capital (initial capital + profit) to a charitable organisation. The same course was followed in the 2nd and 3rd years also. If at the end of three years, he is left with ₹ 33,750, then find the amount donated by him at the end of the 2nd year.
   (a) ₹90,000 (b) ₹25,000
   (c) ₹45,000 (d) ₹40,000
6. In an examination, 48% students failed in Physics and 32% students in Chemistry, 20% students failed in both the subjects. If the number of students who passed the examination was 880 (by passing both the subjects), how many students appeared in the examination if the examination consisted only of these two subjects?
   (a) 2000 (b) 2200
   (c) 2500 (d) 1800
7. A machine depreciates in value each year at the rate of 10% of its previous value. However, every second year there is some maintenance work so that in that particular year, depreciation is only 5% of its previous value. If at the end of the fourth year, the value of the machine stands at ₹ 1,46,205, then find the value of machine at the start of the first year.
   (a) ₹1,90,000 (b) ₹2,00,000
   (c) ₹1,95,000 (d) ₹2,10,000
8. Kaku's project report consists of 25 pages each of 60 lines with 75 characters on each line. In case the number of lines is reduced to 55 but the number of characters is increased to 90 per line, what is the percentage change in the number of pages. (Assume the number of pages to be a whole number.)
   (a) +10% (b) +5%
   (c) –8% (d) –10%
9. The price of soap is collectively decided by five factors: raw materials, research, labour, advertisements and transportation. Assume that the functional relationship is
   Price of soap = (k' × Raw material costs × Research costs × Labour costs × Advertising cost × Transportation cost).
   If there are respective changes of 20%, 20%, –20%, 25% and 10% in the five factors, then find the percentage change in the price of soap.
   (a) +58.40% (b) 54.40%
   (c) 48.50% (d) 56%
10. The ratio of Jim's salary for October to his salary for November was 9: 8 and the ratio of the salary for November to that for December was 3: 4. The worker got 40 rupees more for December than for October and received a bonus constituting 40 per cent of the salary for three months. Find the bonus. (Assume that the number of workdays is the same in every month.)
11. Praveen goes to a shop to buy a sofa set costing ₹ 13,080. The rate of sales tax is 10%. She tells the shopkeeper to reduce the price of the sofa set to such an extent that she has to pay ₹13080 inclusive of sales tax. Find the percentage reduction needed in the price of the sofa set to just satisfy her requirement.
    (a) 8.33% (b) 9.09%
    (c) 9% (d) 8.5%
12. The price of a certain product was raised by 20% in India. The consumption of the same article was increased from 400 tons to 440 tons. By how much percent will the expenditure on the article rise in the Indian economy?
    (a) 32% (b) 25%
    (c) 27% (d) 26%
13. In the university examination last year, Samanyu scored 65% in English and 82% in History. What is the minimum percent he should score in Sociology, which is out of 50 marks (if English and History were for 100 marks each), if he aims at getting 78% overall?

(a) 94% (b) 92%
(c) 98% (d) 96%

14. King Dashratha, at his eleventh hour, called his three queens and distributed his gold in the following way: He gave 50% of his wealth to his first wife, 50% of the rest to his second wife and again 50% of the rest to his third wife. If their combined share is worth 1,30,900 kilograms of gold, find the quantity of gold King Dashratha was having initially?
(a) 1,50,000 kg (b) 1,49,600 kg
(c) 1,51,600 kg (d) 1,52,600 kg

15. The population of Swansea increases with a uniform rate of 8% per annum, but due to immigration, there is a further increase of population by 1% (however, this 1% increase in population is to be calculated on the population after the 8% increase and not on the previous years population). Find what will be the percentage increase in population after 2 years.
(a) 18.984 (b) 18.081
(c) 18.24 (d) 17.91

16. 10% of Mexico's population migrated to South Asia, 10% of the remaining migrated to America and 10% of the rest migrated to Australia. If the female population, which was left in Mexico, remained only 3,64,500, find the population of Mexico City before the migration and its effects if it is given that before the migration the female population was half the male population and this ratio did not change after the migration?
(a) 10,00,000 (b) 12,00,000
(c) 15,00,000 (d) 16,00,000

17. Malti has ₹*M* with her and her friend Chinki has ₹*C* with her. Malti spends 12% of her money and Chinki also spends the same amount as Malti did. What percentage of her money did Chinki spend?

(a) $\frac{18M}{C}$ (b) $\frac{18C}{M}$

(c) $\frac{12M}{C}$ (d) $\frac{12C}{M}$

18. In a village consisting of p persons, x% can read and write. Of the males alone y%, and of the females alone z% can read and write. Find the number of males in the village in terms of p, x, y and z if $z < y$.

(a) $\frac{[p(x-z)]}{[y+x-z]}$ (b) $\frac{[p(x-z)]}{[y+x-2z]}$

(c) $\frac{[p(x-z)]}{[x-z]}$ (d) $\frac{[p(x-z)]}{[y-z]}$

19. According to a recent survey report issued by the Commerce Ministry, Government of India, 30% of the total FDI goes to Gujarat and 20% of this goes to rural areas. If the FDI in Gujarat, which goes to urban areas, is \$72 m, then find the size of FDI in rural Andhra Pradesh, which attracts 50% of the FDI that comes to Andhra Pradesh, which accounts for 20% of the total FDI?
(a) \$30 m (b) \$9 m
(c) \$60 m (d) \$40 m

20. If in the previous question, the growth in the size of FDI for the next year with respect to the previous year is 20%, then find the share of urban Maharashtra next year if 12% of the total FDI going to Maharashtra went to urban areas (provided Maharashtra attracted only 10% of the total share for both years).
(a) \$36 m (b) \$4.32 m
(c) \$3 m (d) \$5 m

21. The cost of food accounted for 25% of the income of a particular family. If the income gets raised by 20%, then what should be the percentage point decrease in the food expenditure as a percentage of the total income to keep the food expenditure unchanged between the two years?
(a) 3.5 (b) 8.33
(c) 4.16 (d) 5

22. If the length, breadth and height of a cube are decreased, decreased and increased by 5%, 5% and 20%, respectively, then what will be the impact on the surface area of the cube (in percentage terms)?
(a) 7.25% (b) 5%
(c) 8.33% (d) 6.0833%

23. *Aman*'s salary is first increased by 25% and then decreased by 20%. The result is the same as *Baman*'s salary increased by 20% and then reduced by 25%. Find the ratio of *Baman*'s initial salary to that of *Aman*'s initial salary.
(a) 4 : 3 (b) 11 : 10
(c) 10 : 9 (d) 12 : 11

24. The minimum quantity of Kerosene in liters (in whole number) that should be mixed in a mixture of 60 liters in which the initial ratio of Kerosene to water is 1:4, so that the resulting mixture has 15% Kerosene is
(a) 3 (b) 4
(c) 5 (d) This is not possible

25. A person saves 5% of his income. Two years later, his income shoots up by 20% but his savings remain the same. Find the hike in his expenditure.
(a) 25.95% (b) 24.07%
(c) 21.05%. (d) 15.5%

26. *P* is 50% more than *Q*, *R* is 2/3 of *P* and *S* is 60% more than *R*. Now, each of *P*, *Q*, *R* and *S* is increased by 10%. Find what per cent of *Q* is *S*(after the increase)?
(a) 150% (b) 160%
(c) 175% (d) 176%

27. *Alok* and *Bimal* have, between them, ₹ 12000. *Alok* spends 12% of his money while *Bimal* spends 20% of his money. They are then left with a sum that

constitutes 85% of the whole sum. Find what amount is left with *Alok*.
(a) ₹ 7500 (b) ₹ 8000
(c) ₹ 7000 (d) ₹ 6600

28. In order to maximise his gain, a theatre owner decides to reduce the price of tickets by 20% and as a result of this, the sales of tickets increase by 40%. If, as a result of these changes, he is able to increase his weekly collection by 1,68,000, find by what value did the gross collection increase per day.
(a) 14,000 (b) 18,000
(c) 24,000 (d) 20,000

29. In a town consisting of three localities *A*, *B* and *C*, the population of the three localities *A*, *B* and *C* are in the ratio 9:8:3. In locality *A*, 80% of the people are literate, in locality *B*, 30% of the people are illiterate. If 90% people in locality *C* are literate, find the percentage literacy in that town.
(a) 61.5% (b) 78%
(c) 75% (d) None of these

30. To pass an examination, 30% marks are essential. *A* obtains 20% marks less than the pass marks and *B* obtains 50% marks less than *A*. What percent less than the sum of *A*'s and *B*'s marks should *C* obtain to pass the exam?
(a) 40% (b) 41(3/17)%
(c) 28% (d) None of these

Directions for Questions 31 to 33: Read the following passage and answer the questions.

In a recent youth fete organised by Mindworkzz, the entry tickets were sold out according to the following scheme:

Tickets bought in one lot	6	12	18
Percentage discount	10%	20%	25%

Original price per ticket: ₹40

This offer could have been availed only when tickets were bought in a fixed lot according to the scheme and any additional ticket was available at its original price.

31. If a person has to buy 25 tickets, then what will be the minimum price per ticket?
(a) Equal to ₹32 (b) ₹32.32
(c) ₹31.84 (d) Cannot be determined.

32. In the above question, what will be the approximate possible maximum price per ticket (if discounts have been availed for 24 tickets)?
(a) ₹30 (b) ₹32
(c) ₹36 (d) ₹36.16

33. On the last day of the fete, with the objective of maximising participation, the number of tickets sold in a lot was halved with the same discount offer. Mr. *X* is in a fix regarding the number of tickets he can buy with ₹ 532. The maximum number of tickets he can purchase with this money is
(a) 14 (b) 15
(c) 16 (d) 17

34. 800 people were supposed to vote on a resolution, but 1/3rd of the people who had decided to vote for the motion were abducted. However, the opponents of the motion, through some means managed to increase their strength by 100%. The motion was then rejected by a majority, which was 50% of that by which it would have been passed if none of these changes would have occurred. How many people finally voted for the motion and against the motion?
(a) 200 (for), 400 (against)
(b) 100 (for) and 200 (against)
(c) 150 (for), 300 (against)
(d) 200 (for) and 300 (against)

35. At IIM Bangalore, 60% of the students are boys and the rest are girls. Further 15% of the boys and 7.5% of the girls are getting a fee waiver. If the number of those getting a fee waiver is 90, find the total number of students getting 50% concession if it is given that 50% of those not getting a fee waiver are eligible to get half fee concession?

36. A watch gains by 2% per hour when the temperature is in the range of 40°C–50°C and it loses at the same rate when the temperature is in the range of 20°C–30°C. However, the watch owner is fortunate since it runs on time in all other temperature ranges. On a sunny day, the temperature started soaring up from 8 a.m. in the morning at the uniform rate of 2°C per hour and sometime during the afternoon it started coming down at the same rate. Find what time will it be by the watch at 7 pm, if at 8 am the temperature was 32°C and at 4 pm, it was 40°C.
(a) 6 : 55 p.m. (b) 6 : 55 : 12 p.m.
(c) 6 : 55 : 24 p.m. (d) None of these

37. There were '*a*' 10 ₹ Notes and '*b*' 100 ₹ Notes. If there had been '*a*' ₹ 100 notes and '*b*' ₹ 10 notes the amount would have been 200% more.
Find the minimum possible value of *a* If $1 \leq b \leq 20$

38. In a garment shop there are four types of shirts namely *w*, *x*, *y*, *z*. There are 20% more shirts of type '*x*' than type '*w*'. 20% less shirts of type '*x*' than type '*y*' and there are 30% more shirts of type '*z*' than type '*x*'. If there are 156 shirts of type '*z*', then find the total number of shirts.

39. Of the adult population in Nagpur, 45% of men and 25% of women are married. What percentage of the total population of adults is married (assume that no man marries more than one woman and vice versa)?

40. The weight of a bucket increases by 33.33% when filled with water to 50% of its capacity. Which of these may be 50% of the weight of the bucket when it is filled with water (assume the weight of bucket and its capacity in kg to be integers)?
(a) 7 kg (b) 6 kg
(c) 5 kg (d) 8 kg

41. Pakistan scored a total of x runs in 20 overs. India tied the scores in 10% less overs. If India's average run-rate had been 50% higher the scores would have been tied 5 overs earlier. Find how many runs were scored by Pakistan.
(a) 60 (b) 20
(c) 80 (d) Cannot be determined

42. Ashish, a salesman is appointed on the basic salary of ₹ 1200 per month and the condition that for every sales of ₹ 10,000 above ₹ 10,000, he will get 50% of basic salary and 10% of the sales as a reward. This incentive scheme does not operate for the first ₹10000 of sales. What should be the value of sales if he wants to earn ₹7600 in a particular month?
(a) ₹ 60,000 (b) ₹ 50,000
(c) ₹ 40,000 (d) None of these

43. In the previous question, which of the following income cannot be achieved in a month?
(a) ₹6000
(b) ₹ 9000
(c) Both a and b
(d) Any income can be achieved

44. An organization gives its' sales staff incentives based on the value of their sales. In a particular year, despite a 5 percentage point increment on the commission from 20%, the total commission for a sales organization remained unaltered. Find the change in the volume of the sales.
(a) –10% (b) –16%
(c) –25% (d) –20%

45. In a Local election at Kanpur, the total turnout was 80% out of which 16% of the total voters on the voting list were declared invalid. Find which of the following can be the percentage votes got by the winner of the election if the candidate who came second got 20% of the total voters on the voting list. (There were only three contestants, only one winner and the total number of voters on the voters list was 20000.)
(a) 44.8% (b) 46.6%
(c) 48% (d) None of these

46. The hourly wages of Rahim are increased by 10%, whereas the weekly working hours are reduced by 10%. Find the percentage change in the weekly wages if she was getting ₹ 1000 per week for 50 hours previously.
(a) 1% (b) 4%
(c) 2% (d) None of these

47. Two numbers A and B are 20% and 28% less than a third number C. Find by what percentage is the number B less than the number A.
(a) 8% (b) 12%
(c) 10% (d) 9%

48. Price of a commodity is first increased by x% and then decreased by x%. If the new price is $K/100$, find the original price.
(a) $(x - 100)100/K$ (b) $(x^2 - 100^2)100/K$
(c) $(100 - x)100/K$ (d) $100K/(100^2 - x^2)$

49. The salary of Sahir is increased by ₹ 4800 and the rate of tax is decreased by 2% from 12% to 10%. The effect is such that he is now paying the same tax as before. If in both the cases, the standard tax deduction is fixed at 20% of the total income, find the increased salary?
(a) ₹ 32,800 (b) ₹ 36,800
(c) ₹ 28,000 (d) None of these

50. Seema goes to a shop to buy a radio costing ₹ 2568. The rate of sales tax is 7% and the final value is rounded off to the next higher integer. She tells the shopkeeper to reduce the price of the radio so that she has to pay ₹2568 inclusive of sales tax. Find the discount she is asking for.
(a) ₹ 180 (b) ₹ 210
(c) ₹ 168 (d) None of these

Questions 51 and 52: Study the following table and answer the questions that follow.

Beverages	*% of Vitamin*	*% of Minerals*	*% of Micronutrients*	*Cost per 250 gram (In ₹)*
7up	12	18	30	8
Dew	15	20	10	10
Sprite	20	10	40	7

51. Which of the following beverages contains the maximum amount of vitamins?
(a) 7up worth ₹ 16
(b) Dew worth ₹ 15
(c) Sprite worth ₹ 8
(d) All the three worth ₹ 12.5 (125 grams of each)

52. Which of these is the cheapest?
(a) 200 grams of 7up + 200 grams of Dew
(b) 300 grams of Dew +100 grams of 7up
(c) 100 grams of Dew + 100 grams of 7up + 100 grams of Sprite
(d) 300 grams of Dew +100 grams of Sprite

Directions for questions 53 to 54: Three great gamblers Ajay, Biru, Chetan were playing a game of Teen-Patti (3 card flush). At the beginning of the game Ajay and Biru together had as much money as Chetan had and Ajay and Chetan together had 100% more money than Biru. At the end of the game Ajay and Biru together had 100% more money than Chetan. Also, Ajay and Chetan together had 200% more money than Biru. If at the end of the game Biru had ₹1500 then answer the following questions.

53. How many persons have suffered a loss?

54. The percentage change of money for Ajay is:

Directions for questions 55 to 57: Mindworkzz has two offices, one in Delhi and the other in Lucknow. This year the number of employees in the Lucknow office remained the same as the previous year but the ratio of male to female employees has changed. In the Delhi office, this year the number of employees grew by 25% to 2500. Last year the ratio of male to female employees in the Delhi office was 3:1. The number of female employees in the Delhi office grew by 20% from the last year to this. The number of male employees in the Lucknow office last year equals the number of female employees in Delhi this year. The total number of employees in both the company offices grew to 3500 this year. The number of female employees in Lucknow grew up by 25% from last year to this year. Based on this information, answer the following questions.

55. What is the number of females in the Delhi office this year?

56. The percentage growth of the number of men from last year to this year in the Delhi office is

57. The difference between number of male employees and number of female employees in Lucknow and Delhi office together this year.

58. A company has '*n*' employees in 2011. In 2012, 20% of the employees left the company while no one was hired. In 2013 and 2014, the number of employees again grew by 50% and 15% respectively. In 2015 the company fired 280 employees and at the end of 2015 the percentage increase in the number of employees from 2011 was found to be 10%. Find the number of employees at the end of the year 2015:

(a) 1200 (b) 1300
(c) 1100 (d) None of these.

Directions for Questions 59 to 60: The Food and Beverage unit of Pepsi-co India produces 1,00,000 chips packets per annum. If each packet is being sold at ₹10 and the cost of raw material is ₹ 1 per packet, the cost of manufacturing and labour is ₹ 2 per packet. The maintenance and marketing cost is ₹ 1 per packet. 10% taxes are being paid on selling price of the packet. Based on this information, answer the following questions.

59. What is the percentage profit of the company at the end of the year?

(a) 25% (b) 50%
(c) 33% (d) None of these.

60. If government increased taxes from 10% to 20% and cost of raw material also increased by 100%, then the percentage increase in selling price per packet of chips to maintain the same profit would be.

High Yield Questions

Scan this QR code to access assisted problem solving videos on questions 3, 11, 16, 19 and 20 from LOD 2

Space for Rough Work

LEVEL OF DIFFICULTY (III)

1. The price of raw materials has gone up by 15%, labour cost has also increased from 25% of the cost of raw material to 30% of the cost of raw material. By how much percentage approximately should there be a reduction in the usage of raw materials so as to keep the cost same?
   (a) 17% (b) 24%
   (c) 28% (d) 25%
2. Mr. A is a computer programmer. He is assigned three jobs for which time allotted is in the ratio of 5 : 4 : 2 (jobs are needed to be done individually). But due to some technical snag, 10% of the time allotted for each job gets wasted. Thereafter, owing to the lack of interest, he invests only 40%, 30% and 20% of the hours of what was actually allotted to do the three jobs individually. Find how much percentage of the total time allotted is the time invested by A.
   (a) 38.33% (b) 39.4545%
   (c) 32.72% (d) 36.66%
3. In the Mock CAT paper at Mindworkzz, questions were asked in five sections. Out of the total students, 5% candidates cleared the cut-off in all the sections and 5% cleared none. Of the rest, 25% cleared only one section and 20% cleared four sections. If 24.5% of the entire candidates cleared two sections and 300 candidates cleared three sections, find out how many candidates appeared at the Mock CAT at Mindworkzz?
   (a) 1000 (b) 1200
   (c) 1500 (d) 2000
4. There are three galleries in a coal mine. On the first day, two galleries are operative and after some time, the third gallery is made operative. With this, the output of the mine became half as large again. What is the capacity of the second gallery as a percentage of the first, if it is given that a four-month output of the first and the third galleries was the same as the annual output of the second gallery?
   (a) 70% (b) 64%
   (c) 60% (d) 65%
5. 10% of salty sea water contained in a flask was poured out into a beaker. After this, a part of the water contained in the beaker was vapourised by heating and due to this, the percentage of salt in the beaker increased M times. If it is known that after the content of the beaker was poured into the flask, the percentage of salt in the flask increased by x%. Find the original quantity of sea water in the flask.
   (a) $\frac{9M+1\%}{M-1}$ (b) $\frac{(9M+1)x\%}{M-1}$
   (c) $\frac{9M-1x\%}{M+1}$ (d) $\frac{9M+x\%}{M+1}$
6. In an election of 3 candidates A, B and C, A gets 50% more votes than B. A also beats C by 1,80,00 votes. If it is known that B gets 5 percentage point more votes than C, find the number of voters on the voting list (given 90% of the voters on the voting list voted and no votes were illegal)
   (a) 72,000 (b) 81,000
   (c) 90,000 (d) 1,00,000
7. A clock is set right at 12 noon on Monday. It loses 1/2% on the correct time in the first week but gains 1/4% on the true time during the second week. The time shown on Monday after two weeks will be
   (a) 12 : 25 : 12 (b) 11 : 34 : 48
   (c) 12 : 50 : 24 (d) 12 : 24 : 16
8. The petrol prices shot up by 7% as a result of the hike in the price of crudes. The price of petrol before the hike was ₹ 28 per litre. Vawal travels 2400 kilometres every month and his car gives a mileage of 18 kilometres to a litre. Find the increase in the expenditure that Vawal has to incur due to the increase in the price of petrol (to the nearest rupee)?
   (a) ₹ 270 (b) ₹ 262
   (c) ₹ 276 (d) ₹ 272
9. For Question 8, by how many kilometres should Vawal reduce his travel if he wants to maintain his expenditure at the previous level (prior to the price increase)?
   (a) 157 km (b) 137 km
   (c) 168 km (d) 180 km
10. In Question 8, if Vawal wants to limit the increase in expenditure to ₹ 200, what strategy should he adopt with respect to his travel?
    (a) Reduce travel to 2350 kilometres
    (b) Reduce travel to 2340 kilometres
    (c) Reduce travel to 2360 kilometres
    (d) None of these
11. A shopkeeper announces a discount scheme as follows: for every purchase of ₹ 3000 to ₹ 6000, the customer gets a 15% discount or a ticket that entitles him to get a 7% discount on a further purchase of goods costing more than ₹ 6000. The customer, however, would have the option of reselling his right to the shopkeeper at 4% of his

initial purchase value (as per the right refers to the 7% discount ticket). In an enthusiastic response to the scheme, 10 people purchase goods worth ₹ 4000 each. Find the maximum. Possible revenue for the shopkeeper.

(a) ₹ 38,400 (b) ₹ 38,000
(c) ₹ 39,400 (d) ₹ 39,000

12. For question 11, find the maximum possible discount that the shopkeeper would have to offer to the customer.

(a) ₹ 1600 (b) ₹ 2000
(c) ₹ 6000 (d) ₹ 4000

Directions for Questions 13 to 16: Read the following and answer the questions that follow.

Two friends Shayam and Kailash own two versions of a car. Shayam owns the diesel version of the car, while Kailash owns the petrol version.

Kailash's car gives an average that is 20% higher than Shayam's (in terms of litres per kilometre). It is known that petrol costs 60% of its price higher than diesel.

13. The ratio of the cost per kilometre of Kailash's car to Shayam's car is

(a) 3 : 1 (b) 1 : 3
(c) 1.92 : 1 (d) 2 : 1

14. If Shayam's car gives an average of 20 km per litre, then the difference in the cost of travel per kilometre between the two cars is

(a) ₹ 4.3 (b) ₹ 3.5
(c) ₹ 2.5 (d) Cannot be determined

15. For Question 14, the ratio of the cost per kilometre of Shayam's travel to Kailash's travel is

(a) 3 : 1 (b) 1 : 3
(c) 1 : 1.92 (d) 2 : 1

16. If diesel costs ₹ 12.5 per litre, then the difference in the cost of travel per kilometre between Kailash's and Shayam's is (assume an average of 20 km per litre for Shayam's car and also assume that petrol is 50% of its own price higher than diesel)

(a) ₹ 1.75 (b) ₹ 0.875
(c) ₹ 1.25 (d) ₹ 1.125

Directions for Questions 17 to 23: Read the following and answer the questions that follow.

In the island of Hoola Boola Moola, the inhabitants have a strange process of calculating their average incomes and expenditures. According to an old legend prevalent on that island, the average monthly income had to be calculated on the basis of 14 months in a calendar year while the average monthly expenditure was to be calculated on the basis of 9 months per year. This would lead to people having an underestimation of their savings since there would be an underestimation of the income and an overestimation of the expenditure per month.

17. Mr. Boogle Woogle comes back from the USSR and convinces his community comprising 273 families to start calculating the average income and the average expenditure on the basis of 12 months per calendars year. Now if it is known that the average estimated income in his community is (according to the old system) 87 moolahs per month, then what will be the percentage change in the savings of the community of Mr. Boogle Woogle (assume that there is no other change)?

(a) 12.33% (b) 22.22%
(c) 31.31% (d) Cannot be determined

18. For Question 17, if it is known that the average estimated monthly expenditure is 19 moolahs per month for the island of Hoola Boola Moola, then what will be the percentage change in the estimated savings of the community?

(a) 32.42% (b) 38.05%
(c) 25.23% (d) Cannot be determined

19. For Question 18, if it is known that the average estimated monthly expenditure was 22 moolahs per month for the community of Boogle Woogle (having 273 families), then what will be the percentage change in the estimated savings of the community?

(a) 30.77% (b) 28.18%
(c) 25.23% (d) 25.73%

20. For Question 19, what will be the percentage change in the estimated average income of the community (calculated on the basis of the new estimated average)?

(a) 14.28% increase (b) 14.28% decrease
(c) 16.66% increase (d) 16.66% decrease

21. If the finance minister of the island Mr. Bhola Ram declares that henceforth the average monthly income has to be estimated on the basis of 12 months per year while the average monthly expenditure is to be estimated on the basis of 11 months to the year, what will happen to the savings in the economy of Hoola Boola Moola?

(a) Increase (b) Decrease
(c) Remain constant (d) Either (b) or (c)

22. For Question 21, what will be the percentage change in savings?

(a) 3.1% (b) 1.52%
(c) 2.5% (d) Cannot be determined

23. For Question 22, what will be the percentage change in the estimated monthly expenditure?

(a) 22.22% decrease (b) 22.22% increase
(c) 18.18% decrease (d) 18.18% increase

24. Abhimanyu Banerjee has 72% vision in his left eye and 68% vision in his right eye. On corrective therapy, he starts wearing contact lenses, which augment his vision by 15% in the left eye and 11% in the right eye. Find out the percentage of normal vision that he possesses after corrective therapy. (Assume that a person's eyesight is a multiplicative construct of the eyesight's of his left and right eyes)

(a) 52.5% (b) 62.5%
(c) 72.5% (d) 68.6%

25. A shopkeeper gives 3 consecutive discounts of 10%, 15% and 15% after which he sells his goods at a percentage profit of 30.05% on the C.P. Find the value of the percentage profit that the shopkeeper would have earned if he had given discounts of 10% and 15% only.

(a) 53% (b) 62.5%
(c) 72.5% (d) 68.6%

26. If the third discount in Question 25 was ₹ 2,29,50, then find the original marked price of the item.

(a) ₹ 1,00,000 (b) ₹ 1,25,000
(c) ₹ 2,00,000 (d) ₹ 2,50,000

27. Krishna Iyer, a motorist uses 24% of his fuel in covering the first 20% of his total journey (in city driving conditions). If he knows that he has to cover another 25% of his total journey in city driving conditions, what should be the minimum percentage increase in the fuel efficiency for non-city driving over the city driving fuel efficiency, so that he is just able to cover his entire journey without having to refuel? (Approximately)

(a) 39.2% (b) 43.5%
(c) 45.6% (d) 41.2%

Directions for Questions 28 to 30: Read the following and answer the questions that follow the BSNL announced a cut in the STD rates on 27 December 2011. The new rates and slabs are given in the table below and are to be implemented from 14 January 2012.

Slab Details

Distance	*Rates (₹/min)*			
	Peak Rates		*Off Peak*	
	Old	*New*	*Old*	*New*
50–200	4.8	2.4	1.2	1.2
200–500	11.6	4.8	3.0	2.4
500–1000	17.56	9.00	4.5	4.5
1000+	17.56	9.00	6.0	4.5

28. The maximum percentage reduction in costs will be experienced for calls over which of the following distances?

(a) 50–200 (b) 500–1000
(c) 1000+ (d) 200–500

29. The percentage difference in the cost of a set of telephone calls made on the 13th and 14th January having durations of 4 minutes over a distance of 350 km, 3 minutes for a distance of 700 km and 3 minutes for a distance of 1050 km is (if all the three calls are made in peak times)

(a) 51.2% (b) 51.76%
(c) 59.8 % (d) cannot be determined

30. If one of the three calls in Question 29 were made in an off peak time on both days, then the percentage reduction in the total cost of the calls between 13th and 14th January will

(a) definitely reduce
(b) definitely increase
(c) will depend on which particular call was made in an off peak time
(d) cannot be determined

Directions for Questions 31 to 35: Read the following caselet and answer the questions that follow.

The circulation of the *Deccan Emerald* newspaper is 3,73,000 copies, while its closest competitors are *The Times of Hindustan* and *India's Times,* which sell 2,47,000 and 20% more than that respectively (rounded off to the higher thousand). All the newspapers cost ₹ 2 each. The hawker's commissions offered by the three papers are 20%, 20% and 30%, respectively (these commissions are calculated on the sale price of the newspaper). Also, it is known that newspapers earn primarily through sales and advertising.

31. Taking the base as the net revenue of *Deccan Emerald*, the percentage difference of the net revenue (revenues — commission disbursed to hawkers) between *Deccan Emerald* and *India's Times* is

(a) 24.62% (b) 30.32%
(c) 26.28% (d) None of these

32. The ratio of the percentage difference in the total net revenue between *Deccan Emerald* and *India's Times* to the percentage difference in the total revenue between *Deccan Emerald* and *India's Times* is

(a) 1.488 (b) 0.3727
(c) 0.6720 (d) Cannot be determined

33. If the cost of printing the newspaper is ₹ 8, 7.5 and 7, respectively per day for *Deccan Emerald*, *Times of Hindustan* and *India's Times* respectively and on any day the available advertising space in the *Deccan Emerald* newspaper is 800 cc (column centimetres) and the advertising rate for *Deccan Emerald* is ₹ 3000 per cc then the percentage of the advertising space that must be utilised to ensure the full recovery of the day's cost for *Deccan Emerald* is

(a) 95.83% (b) 99.46%
(c) 97.28% (d) Cannot be determined

34. Based on the data in the previous question and the additional information that the space availability in *India's Times* is 1000 cc and that in the *Times of Hindustan* is 1100 cc, find the percentage point difference in the percentage of advertising space to be utilised in *India's Times* and that which must be utilised in *Times of Hindustan* so that both newspapers just break even.

(a) 4.5 (b) 5.2
(c) 10 (d) Cannot be determined

35. For the data in Questions 33 and 34 if it is known that the advertising rate in *Times of Hindustan* is ₹ 1800 per cc and that in the *India's Times* is ₹ 2100 per cc, then what is the percentage point difference in the percentage of advertising space to be utilised by *Times of Hindustan* and *India's Times* so that both of them are just able to break even?

(a) 4.18 (b) 5.6
(c) 4.09 (d) Cannot be determined

36. On a train journey, there are 5 kinds of tickets AC I, AC II, AC III, 3-tier, and general. The relationship between the rates of the tickets for the Eurail is: AC II is 20% higher than AC III and AC I is 70% of AC III's value higher than the AC II ticket's value. The 3-tier ticket is 25% of the AC I's ticket cost and the general ticket is 1/3 the price of the AC II ticket. The AC II ticket costs 780 euros between London and Paris. The difference in the rates of 3 tier and general ticket is

(a) 41.25 euros (b) 55.8 euros
(c) 48.75 euros (d) 52.75 euros

37. For the above question, the total cost of one ticket of each class will be

(a) 3233.75 (b) 3533.75
(c) 4233.75 (d) 3733.75

Directions for Questions 38 to 40: Read the following and answer the questions that follow.

A Eurailexpress train has 2 AC I bogeys having 24 berths each, 3 AC II bogeys having 45 berths each, 2 AC III bogeys having 64 berths each and 12 3-tier bogeys having 64 berths each. There are no general bogeys in the train. If 200 euros is the cost of an AC 3-tier berth from London to Glasgow, answer the following questions:

38. The value of the maximum revenues possible from the Eurailexpress between Glasgow to London and back is

(a) 3,15,600 (b) 2,44,800
(c) 2,98,400 (d) 2,96,760

39. For a Eurailexpress journey from London to Glasgow, 80% of the train was uniformly booked across classes. What percentage of the total revenues came out of the sales of 3-tier tickets?

(a) 44.23% (b) 52.18%
(c) 39.23% (d) 48.9%

40. If bookings for the above question was 40% in AC I, 70% in AC II, 60% in AC III and 55% in 3-tier, then what will happen to the percentage contribution of 3-tier to the total revenues on the train journey?

(a) Decrease (b) Increase
(c) Remain constant (d) Cannot be determined

41. A 14.4 kg gas cylinder runs for 104 hours when the smaller burner on the gas stove is fully opened while it runs for 80 hours when the larger burner on the gas stove is fully opened. Which of these values are the closest to the percentage difference in the usage of gas per hour, between the smaller and the larger burner?

(a) 26.23% (b) 30%
(c) 32.23% (d) 23.07%

42. For Question 41, assume that the rate of gas dispersal is directly proportional to the degree of opening of the aperture of the gas. If we are given that the smaller burner is open to 60% of its maximum and the larger burner is open to 50% of its maximum, the percentage decrease in the percentage difference between the smaller burner and the larger burner (in terms of hours per kg) is

(a) 72.22% (b) 73.33%
(c) 66.66% (d) None of these

43. Hursh Sarma has a salary of ₹10,800 per month. In the first month of the year, he spends 40% of his income on food, 50% on clothing and saves 11.11% of what he has spent. In the next two months, he saves 9.09% of what he has spent (spending 38.33% of his income on food). In the fourth month, he gets an increment of 11.11% on his salary and spends every single paise on celebrating his raise. But from the fifth month onwards good sense prevails on him and he saves 12.5%, 15%, 20%, 10%, 8.33%, 12.5%, 15% and 20% on his new income per month. The ratio between the sum of the savings for the two months having the highest savings to the sum of the savings for the two months having the lowest savings is

(a) 2.6666 (b) 5.3333
(c) 8 (d) None of these

44. In an economy, the rate of savings has a relation to the investment in industry for that year and the following three years. The relation is such that a percentage point change in investment in industry for that year has a relation to the total production output in the next 4 years. A 2 percentage point increase in the savings rate in a year, increases the investment in the industry of the economy by 1%. Further, the rate of investment also goes up by 0.5% in the next year, by 0.25% in the second year and again by 0.25% in the third year. Also assume that the investment in an economy is only dependent on the patterns of savings in the previous 3 years in the economy. Also, the percentage change in the investment in a particular year is got by adding the effect of the previous three years savings pattern.

In fiscal 2008–09, the rate of savings in the Indian economy is 25% while that in the Pakistani economy, is 20%. This has remained constant since 2003. In 2009–10 the savings rate in the Indian economy suddenly rises by 5 percentage points to 30% while that in the Pakistani economy rises by 2 percentage points to 22%. It is further known that the value of the investment in the industry in the 2 countries was 2 million dollars and 1.8 million dollars respectively (for the previous year). The percentage difference between the investment in the Pakistani economy to the investment in the Indian economy in 2010–11 will be (if it is known that there is no change in the savings rate in 2010–11):

(a) 13.6% (b) 15.12%
(c) 11.18% (d) 12.2%

Directions for Questions 45 to 48: In an economy the rate of savings has a relation to the investment in industry for that year and for the following three years and the investment in industry for that year has a relation to the total production output in the next 4 years.

45. For Question 44, if there is no additional change in the savings rate until 2011–12, then the percentage difference in the value of the investment in India to the investment in Pakistan in 2011–12 (as a percentage of the investment in India) is

(a) 11.28% (b) 14.18%
(c) 14.02% (d) None of these

46. If the change in production is directly related to the change in investment in the previous year, and if the data of the savings rate change for the previous 2 questions are to be assumed true, then for which year did the difference between the production in the Indian economy and the production in the Pakistani economy show the maximum percentage change?

(a) 2010–11 (b) 2011–12
(c) 2012–13 (d) Cannot be determined

47. For Question 44, it is known that the percentage change in investment in a year leads to a corresponding equal percentage increase in the manufacturing production in the next year. Further, if the growth rate of manufacturing production is 27% of the GDP growth rate of the country, then what is the GDP growth rate of India in 2010–11?

(a) 8.52% (b) 7.28%
(c) 9.26% (d) None of these

48. The Euro was ushered in on the Ist January 2002 and the old currencies of the European economies were exchanged into Euros. In France, 4 Francs were exchanged for 1 Euro while in Germany 5 Deutsche Marks were exchanged for 1 Euro and in Italy 3 Liras were exchanged for 1 Euro. The exchange rate for Moolahs, the official currency of Hoola Boola Moola, was set at 185 Moolahs per Euro. Dr. Krishna Iyer, an NRI doctor based in Europe, had a practice across each of these three countries and he sends back money orders to his native island of Hoola Boola Moola. The existing exchange rate of Moolahs with the above-mentioned currencies was 51 moolahs per Franc, 36 Moolahs per Deutsche Mark and 70 moolahs per Lira. If Dr. Iyer has this information, then what should he do with his currency holdings in these three currencies on the 31st December 2001 so that he maximises his moolah value on the Ist of January 2002. (Assume no arbitrage possibilities between the three currencies)

(a) Change to Francs
(b) Change to Deutsche Marks
(c) Change to Liras
(d) Remain indifferent

49. For the above questions, the exchange rates for the three currencies with respect to a dollar was: 2$ per Lira, 1.5$ per Franc and 1.4 dollar per Deutshce Mark. If Dr. Iyer has 100 liras, 100 Deutsche Marks and 100 Francs on 31st December 2001, the maximum percentage change he can achieve in his net holding in terms of dollars due to the arbitrage created by the Euro conversion could be

(a) 17.23%
(b) 7.33%
(c) 11.2%
(d) Cannot be determined

50. For Question 48, which one of the following will allow the calculation of all possibilities of percentage change in terms of moolah value of Dr. Iyer's portfolio? (That is possible through currency conversions.)

(a) Dr. Iyer's money holding in all three currencies
(b) Dr. Iyer's monthly earnings in all three currencies
(c) The inter-currency conversion rates between Liras, Deutsche Mark and Francs
(d) Both (a) and (c)

High Yield Questions

Scan to access assisted problem solving videos on questions 1, 3 and 17 to 23 from LOD 3

ANSWER KEY

Level of Difficulty (I)

1. (a)	2. (a)	3. (a)	4. (d)
5. (d)	6. (d)	7. (d)	8. (d)
9. 30	10. 1 : 1	11. (a)	12. (d)
13. (b)	14. (d)	15. (a)	16. (c)
17. (d)	18. (d)	19. (a)	20. (c)
21. (c)	22. (d)	23. (d)	24. (d)
25. (c)	26. (d)	27. (b)	28. (b)
29. (d)	30. (a)	31. (a)	32. (c)
33. (a)	34. (c)	35. (a)	36. (d)
37. (b)	38. (a)	39. (a)	40. (a)
41. (d)	42. (c)	43. (b)	44. (b)
45. (b)	46. (b)	47. (b)	48. (c)
49. (d)	50. (a)	51. (b)	52. (a)
53. 50%	54. 8800	55. 96%	56. (a)
57. –40%	58. –16.36%	59. 57.89%	60. 48%

Level of Difficulty (II)

1. (c)	2. (d)	3. (c)	4. (a)
5. (c)	6. (b)	7. (b)	8. (c)
9. (a)	10. 265.6	11. (b)	12. (a)
13. (d)	14. (b)	15. (a)	16. (c)
17. (c)	18. (d)	19. (a)	20. (b)
21. (c)	22. (d)	23. (c)	24. (d)
25. (c)	26. (b)	27. (d)	28. (c)
29. (d)	30. (d)	31. (c)	32. (d)
33. (c)	34. (a)	35. 330	36. (d)
37. 29	38. 526	39. 32.14	40. (c)
41. (d)	42. (b)	43. (b)	44. (d)
45. (d)	46. (a)	47. (c)	48. (d)
49. (d)	50. (a)	51. (a)	52. (c)
53. 2	54. 150	55. 600	
56. 26.67%	57. 1300	58. (c)	59. (b)
60. 25%			

Level of Difficulty (III)

1. (a)	2. (c)	3. (b)	4. (c)
5. (b)	6. (d)	7. (a)	8. (b)
9. (a)	10. (d)	11. (a)	12. (c)
13. (a)	14. (d)	15. (a)	16. (b)
17. (d)	18. (d)	19. (a)	20. (c)
21. (a)	22. (d)	23. (c)	24. (b)
25. (a)	26. (c)	27. (b)	28. (d)
29. (b)	30. (a)	31. (b)	32. (a)
33. (b)	34. (c)	35. (b)	36. (c)
37. (a)	38. (c)	39. (a)	40. (a)
41. (b)	42. (a)	43. (b)	44. (a)
45. (c)	46. (d)	47. (c)	48. (b)
49. (d)	50. (d)		

SOLUTIONS AND SHORTCUTS

Level of Difficulty (I)

1. 12(4/15)% = 184/15%. As a fraction, the value = 184/(15 × 100) = 46/375
2. 10% of 20% of 25% of 100 = $\frac{10}{100} \times \frac{20}{100} \times \frac{25}{100} \times 100 = 0.50$
3. It can be clearly seen that 40% of 400 = 160 is the highest number.
4. $0.30N = 300 => 1000$. Thus, $0.50 \times 1000 = 500$.
5. 25% of x = 30% of 5000 or $0.25x = 1500 = 6000$
6. $(30/100) \times (a/100) \times (b) = (25/100) \times (b/100) \times (c) = 30a = 25c$, $c = 1.2a$
7. Check the options. If you check with Option d = 90, you get → 108 – 20% of 90 = 108 – 18 = 90. This matches the given requirement and hence Option (d) is the correct answer.
8. B + 40% of A = 125% of B

   40% of A = 25% of B.

   i.e. $0.4A = 0.25B$

   $A/B = 5/8$

   Apparently it seems that B is bigger, but if you consider A and B to be negative the opposite would be true.

   Hence, option (d) is correct.
9. Let their marks be $(x + 10)$ and x.

   Then $\frac{x+10}{2x+10} \times 100 = 60$

   $x = 20$

   Hence $(x + 10) = 30$.
10. $0.05A + 0.1B = \frac{1}{2}(0.2A + 0.1B)$

    $0.05A = 0.05B$

    $A:B = 1:1$
11. The following PCG will give the answer:

    $100 \xrightarrow{50\%} 150 \xrightarrow{33.33\%} 100$

    Hence, the percentage reduction required is 33.33% (50/150).
12. 100 ------ → 150 ------- →120.

    The reduction from 150 to 120 is 20% and hence, it means that he needs to reduce his consumption by 20%.
13. Shankar (100) $\xrightarrow{\text{50\% more}}$ Ashok (150) $\xrightarrow{\text{20\% more}}$ Bishnu (125)

    Required percentage = $\frac{25}{100} \times 100 = 25\%$
14. Total votes = 12000. Valid votes = 85% of 12000 = 10200. Chaman gets 80% of 10200 votes = 8160 votes and Dhande would get 10200 – 8160 = 2040 Votes.
15. If Shyam has inadvertently increased his height by 25% the correction he would need to make to go back to his original height would be to reduce the stated height by 20%.

16. Let Raunak's height be H. Then, $H \times 1.15 = 345$, $H = 345/1.15 = 300$.
17. Let the number be *100*. Then, 200 should be the correct outcome. But instead the value got is 50. Change in value = 200 – 50 = 150. The percentage change in the value = 150 × 100/200 = 75%. Alternately, you could think of this as the number being 'x' and the required result being 2x and the derived result being 0.5x. Hence, the percentage change in the result is 1.5x × 100/2x. Clearly, the value would be 75%. (Note: In this case, the percentage change in the answer does not depend on the value of 'x').
18. The percentage difference would be given by thinking of the percentage change between two numbers: $(x - 10)$ to $(x + 10)$ ['What he wanted to get' to 'what he got by mistake'].
The value of the percentage difference in this case depends on the value of x. Hence, this cannot be answered. Option (d) is correct.
19. From the first statement we get that out of 100 litres of the mixture, 25 litres must be milk. Since, we are adding water to this and keeping the milk constant, it is quite evident that 25 litres of milk should correspond to 20% of the total mixture. Thus, the amount in the total mixture must be 125, which means we need to add 25 litres of water to make 100 litres of the mixture.
20. Let the area of the land is 100 square units. On increasing the length of the land by 20% the area will get increased by 20%. Similarly on increasing the breadth by 30% the area would get increased by 30%. The answer can be thought on the following percentage change graphic (PCG):

$$100 \xrightarrow[\substack{+20 \\ \text{Effect of length increase}}]{\text{20\% increases}} 120 \xrightarrow[\substack{+36 \\ \text{Effect of breadth increase}}]{\text{30\% increases}} 156$$

Hence, the required answer is 56%
21. The area of a triangle depends on the product: base × height.
Since, the height increases by 30% and the area has to increase by 90% overall, the following PCG will give the answer. Let 100 be the original area.

$$100 \xrightarrow[\substack{+30 \\ \text{Effect of increase in base}}]{\text{30\% increases}} 130 \xrightarrow[\text{Effect of increase in height}]{} 190$$

The required answer will be $\frac{60}{130} \times 100 = 46.15\%$
22. The volume goes up by:

$$100 \xrightarrow[\substack{+10 \\ \text{Effect of increase in length}}]{} 110 \xrightarrow[\substack{+22 \\ \text{Effect of increase in breadth}}]{}$$

$$132 \xrightarrow[\substack{+66 \\ \text{Effect of increase in height}}]{} 198$$

Hence, 98%.
23. Let the salary of Vivek and Ajay be ₹ 100 and ₹ 110 respectively.

Required percentage = $\frac{110 - 100}{110} \times 100 = 9.09\%$
24. $100 \xrightarrow[\text{Effect of price}]{\text{50\% drop}} 50 \xrightarrow[\text{+100 Effect of consumption}]{} 150$

We have assumed initial expenditure to be 100, in the above figure. Then the final expenditure is 150. The percentage change in consumption can be seen to be $\frac{150 - 50}{50} \times 100 = 200\%$
25. If the price of wheat has fallen by 20% the quantity would be increased by 25% (if we keep the expenditure constant.)
This means that 100 kgs would increase by 25% to 125 kgs.
26. The winning candidate gets 60% of the votes cast and the losing candidate gets 40% of the votes cast. Thus, the gap between the two is 20% of the votes cast = 200 votes. Thus, the votes cast = 1000. Since, this is 66.67% of the number of voters on the voting list, the number of people on the voting list = 1500.
27. $500000 \xrightarrow{\text{20\% increase}} 600000 \xrightarrow{\text{20\% increase}} 720000$
28. $50{,}000 \xrightarrow{\text{20\% increase}} 60{,}000 \xrightarrow{\text{10\% decrease}} 54{,}000 \xrightarrow{\text{30\% increase}} 70{,}200$
29. His investments are 4000, 16,000 and 20,000 respectively. His dividends are: 400, 2400 and 5000, which means that his total dividend = ₹7800.
30. Sahir obtained 80 marks, hence Madan obtained = 80 × 1.2 = 96. Ravi = 96/0.6 = 160. 160 out of 200 means a percentage of 80%.
31. 10% students got a final score of 20. 20% students got a final score of 30 (inclusive of grace marks.) 50 % students got a final score of 50.
Hence, average score of the class (Note: For the class average, we would not take into account the students who were absent)

$$= \frac{10 \times 20 + 20 \times 30 + 50 \times 50}{80} = 41.25$$
32. If his income is 100, his household expenditure is 20, expenditure on food is 24, on clothes it is 5.6. Thus he saves: 100 – 20 – 24 – 5.6 = 50.4% of his income. Since, this is given to us as 10080, the total income would be: $\frac{100}{50.4} \times 10080 = 20000$
33. The only logic for this question is that Harish's salary would be more than Bhuvan's salary. Thus, only option (a) is possible for Harish's salary.
34. By using options, you can easily see that option (c) satisfies.
2000 females and 4000 males.
Increase = 2000 × 0.2 + 4000 × 0.1 = 800

35. If we take Raju as 100, we will get Bharat as 125 and Charan as 83.33. This means Charan's goods are priced at 2/3rd Bharat's and hence he sells his goods 33.33% cheaper than Bharat.
36. Let the percentage of the total votes secured by Party SJP be x% Then the percentage of total votes secured by Party SJD = (x – 12)% As there are only two parties contesting in the election, the sum total of the votes secured by the two parties should total up to 100%, i.e., $x + x - 12 = 100 \rightarrow 2x - 12 = 100$ or $2x = 112$ or $x = 56\%$. If Party SJP got 56% of the votes, then Party SJD got (56 – 12) = 44% of the total votes. 44% of the total votes = 132,000, i.e.,

$$\frac{44}{100} \times T = 132{,}000$$

$$T = \frac{132{,}000}{44} \times 100 = 300{,}000$$

The margin by which Party SJD lost the election = 12% of the total votes = 12% of 300,000 = 36,000.
37. 1 Bottle = 0.2x metres
? Bottles = 1000 metres
Using unitary method, we get the number of bottles = 1000/0.2x = 5000/x Bottles.
38. If Ashok's salary = 100, then Vinay's salary = 175. Ashok's new salary = 125, Vinay's new salary = 175 × 1.4 = 245. Percentage difference between Vinay's salary and Ashok's salary now = 120 × 100/125 = 96%.
39. Let the second row has 100 students. Then, the first row would contain 120 students and the third row would contain 80 students. The total number of students would be 100 + 120 + 80 = 300. But this number is given as 300. Thus, the first row would contain 120 students.
40. Since the only copper contained in the ore is 50% of 20%, the net copper percentage would be 10%. Thus, 10 kg should be 10% of the ore = 10/0.1 = 100 kg.
41. The data is insufficient since the number of matches to be played by Australia this year is not given. (You cannot assume that they will play 80 matches.)
42. Start of the 4th year, means end of the third year too. The following PCG diagram gives us the answer:

$$400000 \xrightarrow{\text{20\% increase}} 4800000 \xrightarrow{\text{20\% increase}}$$
$$576000 \xrightarrow{\text{20\% increase}} 691200$$

43. Total people present = 200 + 100 + 400 = 700. Indians = 0.1 × 200 + 0.2 × 100 + 0.3 × 400 = 160 = 22.85% of the population. Thus, 77.15 % or 77% of the people were not Indians.
44. Price of a table after increase 10% = 3000+ 300 = 3300. Price of a chair after 20% increase = 1000+ 20% of 1000 = 1200. Cost of 10 tables and 20 chairs = 10 × 3300 + 20 × 1200 = ₹57000.
45. (100 × 0.7 × 0.3)% = 42,000 kg
21% = 42,000 kg. Thus, the total quantity of hematite mined = 2,00,000 kg.
46. The total cost for a year = 2,00,000 + 6% of 2,00,000 + 12000 = 2,00,000 + 24000 = 2,24,000
To get a return of 20% he must earn: 2,24,000 × 0.20 = 44,800 in twelve months.
Hence, the monthly rent should be 44800/12 = 3733.33.
47. The sales price of the first trousers is $\frac{8}{7} \times 42 =$ ₹48.
Hence, I am being offered a discount of ₹ 6 on a price of ₹ 48 → a 12.5% discount.
The sales price of the second trousers is 7/6 × 36 = ₹ 42.
Hence, I am being offered a discount of ₹ 6 on ₹ 42 → a 14.28% discount. Hence, the second trouser is a better bargain.
48. 72% must have voted for Modi and 16% for Advani. Since, Modi got 216000 votes, 72% = 216000.1% = 3000. Hence, total number of votes 88 × 3000 = 264000.
49. The following Venn diagram would solve this problem:
20% failed in Physics, 30% failed in Chemistry and 15% failed in both.

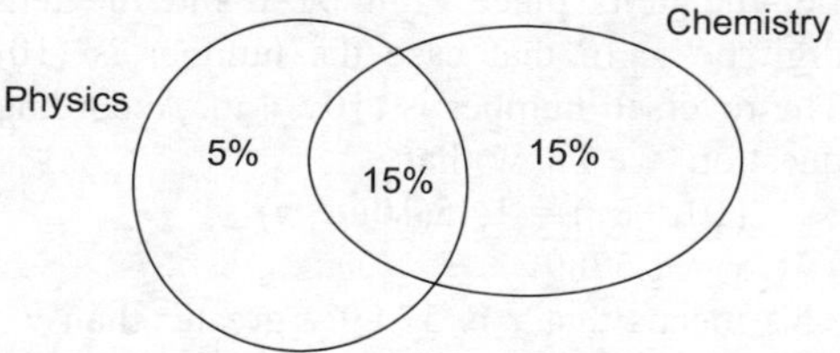

We can clearly see from the above figure that 35% of the people failed in at least one subject or 65% passed in both subjects. Since this value is given as 3250, we get that the total number of students who appeared for the exam is 5,000.
50. Out of 100, he spends 25 on house rent, 15 on children's education and 10 on clothes. Thus, he is left with 100 – 25 – 15 – 10 = 50% of his income. Since, he is left with ₹ 20000, his income must be ₹40000.
51. $\xrightarrow[\text{Effect of increases in sales of tickets}]{\text{25\% increase}} 125 \xrightarrow[\text{Effect of reduction in ticket price}]{} 80$

From the PCG figure, we get that the deduction in the ticket price = $\frac{125-80}{125} \times 100 = \frac{45}{125} \times 100 = 36\%$

Thus there is a drop of 36% of 1000 = ₹ 360
52. A C % increase in income means the new income is A (1 + C/100) while a D% increase in expenditure means

that the new expenditure would be $X(1 + D/100)$. Thus, the new savings $= A(1 + C/100) - X(1 + D/100)$

53. In 2001, YAHAMA = 10%, Spendor = 40% and hence Passion = 50%
54. Rebate = 20% of 10,000 = 2000;
Sales tax = 10% of (10000 – 2000) = 800;
Amount to be paid = 8000 + 800 = 8800.
55. The actual number should be $5x$ but it is $x/5$. So the percentage error $\frac{5x - \frac{x}{5}}{5x} \times 100 = 96\%$
56. Let the salary of Bhuwan = ₹ 100
Salary of Anuj = ₹ 80
Salary of Chauhan $= \frac{80 \times 156.25}{100} = 125$
So the required percentage $= \frac{125 - 100}{125} \times 100 =$ 20%
57. $100 \xrightarrow[\text{Effect of increase in length}]{\text{20\% increase}} 120 \xrightarrow[\text{Effect of decrease in breadth}]{\text{50\% decrease}}$
From the PCG we can make out that there must have been a 40% decrease.
58. $100 \xrightarrow[\text{+23 Effect of increase}]{\text{23\% increase}} 123 \xrightarrow[\text{39.36 Effect of decrease}]{\text{32\% increase}} 83.64$
16.36% decrease or –16.36%.
59. Let the units place digit be x and the tens place digit be y. In that case the number is $(10y + x)$. The reversed number is $(10x + y)$. According to the question, we know that:
$(10x + y) = 1.45(10y + x)$
$x = 1.5789y$
This means that x is 57.89% greater than y.
60. Number of runs made by running
$= 100 - (4 \times 4 + 6 \times 6)$
$= 100 - (52)$
$= 48$
Required percentage = 48%.

Level of Difficulty (II)

1. The expenditure is constant. Thus, the drop of 5 kg, in what he can buy, is equivalent to 20% of the original consumption. Hence, the original consumption should be 25 kg and the new consumption should be 20 kg. The increased price of rice would be 200/20 = ₹ 10.
Income of the salesman = 1200 + (1600x)
2. None of the options fit. Hence, the correct answer is option (d).
3. The total raise of salary is 87.5% (That is what 15/8 means here).
Using the options and PCG, you get option (c) as the correct answer. You will see the following PCG if you try with 25% being the first raise.
$100 \xrightarrow[+25]{\text{25\% increase}} 125 \xrightarrow[+62.5]{\text{50\% increase}} 187.5$
4. Solve through trial and error using the options. 10% (option a) is the only value that fits the situation.
5. You can make the following table to see the flow of his capital:

Year	*Capital at the beginning*	*Capital after profit*	*Capital after donation*
1	100	150	75
2	75	112.5	56.25
3	56.25	84.375	42.1875

Since, this value is given to us as: 33750, we get 42.1875% = 33750 → 1% = 800. Hence, donation at the end of the 2nd year = 56.25 × 800 = 45000.
6. The following figure shows the percentage of failures:

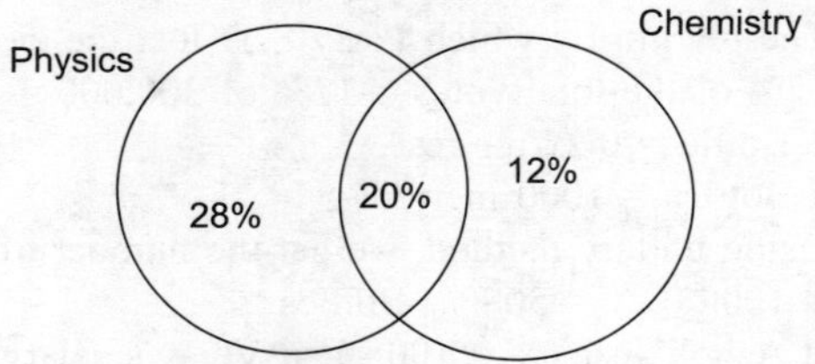

From the figure it is clear that 60% of the people have failed in at least one subject, which means that 40% of the students would have passed in both subjects. This value is given as 880 people. Hence, there would be 880/0.4 = 2200 students who would appear in the examination.
7. Solve using options. Checking for option (b), gives us:
200000 → 180000 → 171000 → 153900 → 146205 (by consecutively decreasing 200000 by 10% and 5% alternately)
8. Total characters in her report = 25 × 60 × 75.
Let the new number of pages be n.
Then:
$n \times 55 \times 90 = 25 \times 60 \times 75$
$n = 22.72$
This means that her report would require 23 pages. A drop of 8% in terms of the pages.
9. The following percentage change thinking would give us the value of the percentage increase as 58.4%
$100 \xrightarrow{+20\%} 120 \xrightarrow{+20\%} 144 \xrightarrow{-20\%}$
$115.2 \xrightarrow{+25\%} 144 \xrightarrow{+10\%} 158.4$
10. October: November: December = 9:8:10.666 since, he got ₹40 more in December than October, we can conclude that 1.666 = 40 → 1 = 24.

Thus, total Bonus for the three months is:

$0.4 \times 27.666 \times 24 = 265.6$

11. 10% increase is offset by 9.09% decrease. Hence, option (b) is correct.
12. The expenditure increase can be calculated using PCG as:

$$100 \xrightarrow{+20\%} 120 \xrightarrow{+20\%} 132$$

A 32% increase.

13. Samanyu's scores in each area is 65 and 82 respectively out of 100 each. Since, the exam is of a total of 250 marks (100 + 100 + 50) he needs a total of 195 marks in order to get his target of 78% overall. Thus, he should score 195 – 65 – 82 = 195 – 147 = 48 marks in Sociology, which would mean 96%.
14. The total wealth given would be 50% + 25% (which is got by 50% of the remaining 50%) + 12.5% (which is got by 50% of the remaining 25%). Thus, the total wealth given by him would be equivalent to 87.5% of the total. Since, this is equal to 130900 kilograms of gold, the total gold would be:

    $130900 \times 8/7 = 149600$.
15. Population at the start = 100.
    Population after 2 years = $100 \times 1.08 \times 1.01 \times 1.08 \times 1.01 = 118.984$
    Thus, the required percentage increase = 18.984%
16. After the migrations, 72.9% of the people would remain in the country. This would comprise females and males in the ratio of 1:2 (as given) and hence, the women's population left would be 1/3rd of 72.9% = 24.3% which is given as being equal to 364500. Thus, the total population would be

    $364500 \times 100/24.3 = 1500000$
17. Chinki would have spent 12% of Malti.
    Thus, her percentage of expenditure would be $0.12 \text{ M} \times 100/\text{C} = 12 \text{ M/C}$
18. Option (d) is correct and can be verified experimentally by using values for x, y, z and p.
19. 24% of the total goes to urban Gujarat = \$72 m
    1% = \$ 3 million.
    The required value for Rural AP
    = 50% of 20% = 10%
    Hence, required answer = \$ 30 mn
20. In the previous question, the total FDI was \$ 300 mn.
    A growth of 20% this year means a total FDI of \$360 mn.
    The required answer is 12% of 10% of 360 mn
    = 1.2% of 360 = \$4.32 mn.
21. The income goes to 120. Food expenditure has to be maintained at 25. (i.e. 20.833%)
    Hence, percentage point drop from 25 to 20.833 is 4.16%
22. Assume the initial surface area as 100 on each side. A total of 6 such surfaces would give a total surface area of 600. Two surface areas would be impacted by the combined effect of length and breadth, two would be affected by length and height and two would be affected by breadth and height. Thus, the respective surface areas would be (90.25 twice, 114 twice and 114 twice) Thus, new surface area = 180.5 + 456 = 636.5. A percentage increase of 6.0833%. Option (d) is correct.
23. Option (c) fits the situation as if the ratio is 10:9, the value of Baman's salary would first go up from 10 to 12 and then come down from 12 to 9 (after a 25% decrease). On the other hand, the value of Aman's salary would go up from 9 to 11.25 and then come back to 9 (Note that a 25% increase followed by a 20% decrease gets one back to the starting value.)
24. Initial quantity of Kerosene and water = 12 and 48 litres respectively. Since, this is already containing 20% Kerosene, adding more Kerosene to the mixture cannot make the mixture reach 15% Kerosene. Hence, it is not possible.
25. On 100 he saves ₹ 5. On 120 he still saves 5. Thus, his expenditure goes up from 95 to 115- a percentage increase of 20 on 95 = 21.05%.
26. $Q = 100$, $P = 150$, $R = 100$, $S = 160$. S is 160% of Q. Note that this does not change if all the values are incremented by the same percentage value.
27. Think about this problem through alligation. Since, *Alok* spends 12% of his money and *Bimal* spends 20% of his money and together they spend 15% of their money- we can conclude that the ratio of the money Alok had to the money Bimal had would be 5:3. Hence, Total money with *Alok* = 5/8 of 12000 = $5 \times 12000/8 = 7500$.
    Money spent by *Alok* = 12% of 7500 = 900.
    Money left with *Alok* = 7500 – 900 = 6600.
28. The weekly change is equal to ₹ 1,68,000.
    Hence, the daily collection will go up by 1,68,000/7 = 24,000.
29. The total population of the town can be taken as 9 + 8 + 3 = 20.
    The number of literates would be:
    80% of 9 + 70% of 8 + 90% of 3 = 7.2 + 5.6 + 2.7 = 15.5
    15.5 out of 20 represents a 77.5% literacy rate.
30. Let the exam be of 100 marks. *A* obtains 24 marks while *B* obtains 12 marks (50% less than *A*). The sum of *A* and *B*'s marks are 24+ 12 = 36. To pass *C* can obtain 6 marks less than 36. This is a percentage of 16.67%. Thus, option (d) is correct.
31. The minimum price occurs at:

    $18 \times 30 + 6 \times 36 + 1 \times 40$

    Hence, the average price = 796/25 = 31.84

32. For the maximum price, discounts should be availed only at the minimum rate of discount. Thus, if one buys 4 lots of six tickets each at a discount of 10%, the condition required would be fulfilled. The total cost of 25 tickets = 36 × 24 + 40 × 1 = 904
Required average price per ticket = 904/25 = 36.16.
33. If the ticket lots are halved, the maximum discount will be available for 9 tickets (25%). A maximum number of 16 tickets can be bought in ₹532 as: 9 tickets for ₹30 each, 6 tickets for ₹32 each and 1 ticket for ₹40 would use up ₹502 of the amount available. The remaining ₹30 cannot be used to purchase another ticket since the price of the ticket is greater than that.
34. Solve using options.
Checking for option (a) will go as: According to this option 400 people have voted against the motion. Hence, originally 200 people must have favoured the motion. (Since, there is a 100% increase in the opponents)
This means that 200 people who were for the motion initially went against it.
This leaves us with 400 people who were for the motion initially (after the abduction.)
1/3rd of the original having been abducted, they should amount to half what is left.
This means that 600 (for) and 200 (against) were the original distribution of 800.
This option fits perfectly (given all the constraints) and hence is the correct answer.
35. The thought process would go like:
If we assume 100 students
Total : 60 boys and 40 girls.
Fee waiver : 9 boys and 3 girls.
This means that a total of 12 people are getting a fee waiver. (But this figure is given as 90.)
Hence, 1 corresponds to 7.5.
Now, number of students not getting a fee waiver = 51 boys and 37 girls
Students getting a 50% concession = 25.5 boys and 18.5 girls (i.e. a total of 44.)
Hence, the required answer = 44 × 7.5 = 330.
36. At 12 noon, the watch would show the correct time (since till then the temperature range was below 40°C). The watch would gain 2% every hour between 12 and 4. An hour having 3600 seconds, it would gain 72 seconds in each of these hours. Thus, at 7 pm it would be 72 × 4 = 288 seconds ahead. The time exhibited would be 7: 04: 48.
37. $3 \times (10a + 100b) = 100a + 10b$

$290b = 70a \rightarrow a = 29b/7$

a will be an integer when $b = 7 \rightarrow a = 29$.
38. According to the last statement

$1.3x = z = 156 \rightarrow x = 120.$

$1.2w = x = 120 \rightarrow w = 100$

$0.8y = x = 120 \rightarrow y = 150.$

Therefore total number of shirts = 156 + 120 + 100 + 150 = 526
39. 1 man is married to 1 woman.
Hence, 45% of men = 25% of women.
i.e. $0.45\ M = 0.25\ W$

Hence $\frac{0.25}{0.45} = \frac{W}{M}$

Women to men ratio of 9:5
Using alligation, the required answer is 32.14
40. The required weight of the bucket to the water when full is 3:2. (Note: This is the interpretation of the first statement of the question – 'The weight of a bucket increases by 33.33% when filled with water to 50% of its capacity.')
If both the weights (bucket and water) are integers, then the total weight must be a multiple of 5.
Only option (c) shows this characteristic.
41. We do not have sufficient information to solve the question.
42. For every ₹10000 increase in sales, his income would increment by 600+1000 = ₹1600.
If x is the number of ₹10000 sales he achieves over the initial ₹10000, we would have:

$1200 + 1600\,x = 7600$

We get $x = 4$.
This means that the sales value must be ₹50000.
43. An income value of ₹ 9000 cannot be achieved, since his basic salary is 1200 and his increments are only in quantum of 1600 for every 10000 rupees of sales. 9000 would not be a term of the arithmetic progression 1200, 2800, 4400, 6000, 7600, 9200.... Hence, option (b) is the correct answer.
44. This question is based on a product constancy situation. A 25% increment in the commission (How?? Note: When the commission goes up by 5 percentage points from 20 to 25, there is a 25% increment in the commission) would get offset by a 20% drop in the volume of the transaction. Option (d) is correct.
45. Out of a total of 100% votes; 80% voted. 16% were invalid and 20% went to the second placed candidate. This means that the maximum the winner can get is 44%. Options a, b and c are greater them 44% and hence cannot be correct. Hence, none of these.
46. Let the old wage = 1000 ₹ per week for 50 hours. The wages per hour would increase by 10% and the number of hours would decrease by 10%. Using PCG you can see that there would be a 1% decrease in the weekly wages.
47. If $C = 100$, $A = 80$ and $B = 72$.
Thus, B is less then A by 10%
48. Assume values of $x\% = 10\%$ and the original price as 100, then the final price $= K/100 = 99 \rightarrow K = 9900$.

(Note: After an increase of 10% followed by a decrease of 10% a price of 100 would become 99). Put these values of x, and K in the options. The option that gives a value of 100 for the original price should be the correct answer.
Option (d) is correct.

49. The correct answer should satisfy the following condition: If 'x' is the increased salary
$x \times 0.8 \times 0.1 = (x - 4800) \times 0.8 \times 0.12.$
None of the first 3 options satisfies this.
In fact, solving for x we get $x = 28800$.
Option (d) is correct.
50. A sales tax of 7% on a price of 2568 would amount to a tax amount of 179.76. Since, the price is rounded off to the next higher integer, the tax would be rounded off to ₹180. This would also be the amount of discount (or reduction in price) that Seema is asking for.
51. 7up worth ₹16 would be containing 60 grams of vitamins would contain the maximum vitamin amongst the three.
52. Option (a) would cost: 6.4 + 8 = 14.8
Option (b) would cost: 12 + 3.2 = 15.2
Option (c) would cost: 4 + 3.2 + 2.8 = 10
Option (d) would cost: 12 + 2.8 = 14.8
Option (c) is the cheapest.

Solutions to questions 53 and 54: Let initially Ajay, Biru. Chetan had A, B and$C$ rupees, respectively.

$$A + B = C \quad (1)$$
$$A + C = 2B \quad (2)$$

By solving equation (1) and (2) we get
$A : B = 1 : 2$, $B:C = 2:3$
$A : B : C = 1 : 2 : 3$

At the end of the game If they have a, b and c rupees respectively then:

$$a + b = 2c \quad (3)$$
$$a + c = 3b \quad (4)$$

By solving equation (3), (4) we get
$a : b = 5 : 3$, $b : c = 3 : 4$
$a : b : c = 5 : 3 : 4$
$b = 1500$. So $a = 2500$ and $c = 2000$. So, $a + b + c = 6000$.
Since the total amount of money at the start and at the end is equal we can say that: $A + B + C = 6000$. With a ratio of 1:2:3, the respective values of A, B and C would be $A = 1000$, $B = 2000$, $C = 3000$.

53. Chetan and Biru had suffered a loss. So two people had suffered a loss.
54. Percentage change in money of Ajay = 150% (since the value for A has gone from 1000 to 2500).

Solutions 55 to 57: You will get the following table by using the information in the question

	DELHI OFFICE			LUCKNOW OFFICE		
	MALES	FEMALES	TOTAL	MALES	FEMALES	TOTAL
LAST YEAR	1500	500	2000	600	400	1000
THIS YEAR	1900	600	2500	500	500	1000

Logic for the table:
Statement: In the Delhi office, this year the number of employees grew by 25% to 2500 → last years total employees in Delhi = 2000 and this years total number of employees in Delhi is 2500.
Statements: Last year the ratio of male to female employees in the Delhi office was 3:1. The number of female employees in the Delhi office grew by 20% from the last year to this. → Delhi Male employees last year = 1500; Delhi female employees last year = 500; Delhi Female employees this year = 600. Hence, Delhi male employees this year = 2500 – 600 = 1900.
Statement: The total number of employees in both the company offices grew to 3500 this year and this year the number of employees in the Lucknow office remained the same as the previous year → Lucknow total employees in each of the two years is equal to 1000 each.
Consequently, we can complete the number of employees (male and female) for Lucknow for both the years.

The answers are:

55. 600
56. % of growth = $\dfrac{1900 - 1500}{1500} \times 100 = 26.67\%$
57. Required difference = (1900 + 500) – (600 + 500) = 1300
58. As per the question →

$$\left(1-\frac{20}{100}\right)\left(1+\frac{50}{100}\right)\left(1+\frac{15}{100}\right)n - 280 = 1.1n$$

$n \times 0.8 \times 1.5 \times 1.15 - 1.1\,n = 280$
$n = 1000$
$1.1n = 1100$

59. Per packet cost = $1 + 2 + 1 + 10 \times \dfrac{10}{100}$ = ₹5
Per packet profit = 10 – 5 = ₹5
% profit per packet = $\dfrac{5}{10} \times 100 = 50\%$
This will be the percentage profit of the company at the end of the year.

60. New cost per packet = $\left[1+\frac{100}{100}\right]+2+1+0.2\left(\frac{x}{100}\right)$

$= 5 + 0.2\,x$

(where x is the new selling price)

$x - (5 + 0.2x) = 5$ (Note: The profit needs to be maintained at ₹5 per packet, in order to maintain the same profit)

$0.8x = 10$ or $x = 12.5$.

Required percentage increase in selling price = $\frac{2.5}{10} \times 100 = 25\%$

Level of Difficulty (III)

1. Let the initial price of raw materials be 100. The new cost of the same raw material would be 115.
   The initial cost of labour would be 25 and the new cost would be 30% of 115 = 34.5
   The total cost initially would be ₹125.
   The total cost for the same usage of raw material would now be: 115 + 34.5 = 149.5
   This cost has to be reduced to 125. The percentage reduction will be given by 24.5/149.5 = 17 % approx.
2. Let the initial times allotted be: 50, 40 and 20 hours.
   Then, the time used in each activity is
   20, 12 and 4 hours. Thus, 36 hours out of 110 are used in all.
   Hence, the answer is 36/110 = 32.72 %
3. The following structure would follow:
   Passed all: 5%
   Passed 4: 20% of 90% =18%
   Passed 1: 25% of 90% = 22.5%
   Passed 2: 24.5%
   Passed None: 5%
   Passed 3: Rest (100 – 5 – 18 – 22.5 – 24.5 – 5 = 25%)
   But it is given that 300 people passed 3. Hence, 25% = 300.
   Hence, 1200 students must have appeared in the test.
4. The third gallery making the capacity 'half as large again' means: an increase of 50%.
   Further, it is given that : 4(first + third) = 12 (second)
   In order to get to the correct answer, try to fit in the options into this situation.
   (Note here that the question is asking you to find the capacity of the second gallery as a percentage of the first.)
   If we assume option (a) as correct – 70% the following solution follows:
   If second is 70, then first is 100 and first + second is 170. Then third will be 85 (50% of first + second).
   Then the equation:
   $4 \times (100 + 85)$ should be equal to 12×70
   But this is not true.
   Through trial and error, you can see that the third option fits correctly.
   $4 \times (100 + 80) = 12 \times 60$.
   Hence, it is the correct answer.
5. Let the initial percentage of salt be 10% in 100 litres of sea water in the flask.
   10% of this is poured out (i.e.,10 litres are poured out) and the water heated so as to increase the percentage of salt in the beaker 5 times (we have assumed M as 5 here.)
   This means that there will be 30% salt in the beaker.
   Since, the salt concentration is increased by only evaporating water, the amount of salt remains the same.
   Initially the salt was 10% of 10 litres (= worth 1 litre).
   Hence, the water must have been worth 9 litres.
   Now, since this amount of salt becomes worth 50% of the total solution, the amount of water left after evaporation would have been 1 litre and the total would be 2 litres.
   When the 2 litres are mixed back again: The new concentration of salt in sea water would go up. In this specific case by alligation we would get the following alligation situation:
   Mix 90 litres of 10% salted sea water with 2 litres of 50% salted sea water.
   The result using alligation will be: [10 + 40/46] % concentration of salted sea water. The value of the increase percentage will be 400/46. (this will be the value of x)
   Now, try to use the given options in order to match the fact that originally the flask contained 100 litres of sea water.
   Use $M = 5, x = 400/46$,
   Only option (b) matches the situation.
   $$\frac{(9\times5+1)400/46}{(5-1)} = 100$$
6. The only values that fit this situation are C 25%, B 30%, and A 45%. These are the percentage of votes polled. (*Note*: these values can be got either through trial and error or through solving $c + c + 5 + 1.5\,(c + 5) = 100\%$
   Then, 20% is 18000 (the difference between A & C.)
   Hence, 90000 people must have voted and 100000 people must have been on the voter's list.
7. The net time lost over two weeks would be 0.25% of a week's time (since in the first week the clock loses 1/2% and in the second week the clock gains 1/4% on the true time.)
   A week contains 168 hours. Hence, the clock loses 0.42 hours.i.e. 25.2 minutes or 25 minutes 12 seconds.
   Hence, the correct time would be 12:25:12.
8. Traveling for 2400 kms at 18 kmph, Vawal will use 133.33 litres of petrol every month. The increase in expenditure for Vawal will be $133.33 \times 0.7 \times 28$ = ₹ 262 (approx).

9. The required answer will be given by: (7/107) × 2400 = 157 km
10. The original expenditure is 28 × 133.333 = ₹ 3733.333
The new expenditure will be given by 28 × 1.07 × n/18 where n = the no. of kilometres to travel.
Since the new expenditure should increase by ₹ 200, its value has to be equal to ₹ 3933.333
This gives us n = 2363.15
Hence, the answer is (d).
11. The shopkeeper would get the maximum revenue when everybody opts for a 4% resale of the right. In such a case, the revenue for the shopkeeper from each customer would be: 96% of 4000 = 4000 – 160 = 3840. hence, total revenue is 38400.
12. Similarly, the highest discount would be if everybody opts for the 15% discount. In such a case, the total discount would be: 600 × 10 = 6000.
13. Average in litre per kilometre multiplied by the Cost of fuel in ₹/litre will give the required cost per kilometre.
14. Shyam's car gives 20 km/litre means 0.05 litres per kilometre then Kailash's car gives 0.06 litre/km. However, since we do not know the price of petrol or diesel we cannot find out the difference in the cost of travel.
15. This question is the opposite of question 13.
16. Cost of petrol is ₹25 per litre. Cost per kilometre for Shyam = 12.5 × 0.05
Also, cost per kilometre for Kailash = 25 × 0.06
17. The value will depend on the values of annual expenditure which is not available.
18. Average estimated monthly expenditure is given for the island of Hoola Boola Moola and not for Mr. Boogle Woogle's community.
19. Original estimated savings = 87 – 22 = 65 Moolahs.
New estimated savings = 1218/12 – 198/12 = 85.
20. x/14 = 87. Hence, annual income = 1218.
New income = 1218/12 = 101.5
Change in estimated income due to the change in process of average calculation = 14.5/87 → 16.66% increase.
21. Estimated monthly income would go up, while the estimated monthly expenditure would go down. Hence, Savings (estimated) would increase.
22. Cannot be determined since the percentage change would depend on the actual values which are not available for this question.
23. The estimated monthly expenditure would change from: x/9 to x/11. Hence, percentage drop in the ratio will be 2/11 → 18.18%
24. 0.72 × 1.15 × 0.68 × 1.11.
25. Solve through options: A 15% reduction on the correct answer will give a profit of 30.05%.
Option (a) is correct.
26. The last discount being 22,950, it means that the value prior to this 15% discount must have been 1,53,000 checking with options:

$$200{,}000 \xrightarrow{15\%\downarrow} 17{,}000 \xrightarrow{10\%\downarrow} 1{,}53{,}000.$$

Hence option (c) is correct.
27. For 45% of the journey in city driving conditions, 54% of the fuel is consumed.
Hence, for the remaining 55% journey, 46% fuel is left.
Required increase in fuel efficiency

$$= \frac{\frac{55}{46} - \frac{45}{54}}{\frac{45}{54}} \times 100.$$

28. The maximum percentage reduction in peak rates is for the 200 – 500 category.
29. $$\frac{(4\times11.6+3\times17.56+3\times17.56)-(4\times4.8+3\times9+3\times9)}{4\times11.6+3\times17.56+3\times17.56}$$

31-34. The following table will give a clearer picture of the situation:

Newspaper	*Circulation (in 000)*	*Revenues*	*Commission*	*Net Revenues*
Deccan Emerald	373	746	20%	596.8
Times of Hindustan	247	494	20%	395.2
India's Times	297	594	30%	415.8

31. Reduction of $\frac{181\times100}{596.8}$ = 30.32%
32. The percentage difference between the revenues is: (746–594) × 100/746 = 20.37
Hence, the required value is 30.32/20.37 = 1.488
33. The day's cost of printing 373000 copies of Deccan Emerald is: 373000 × 8 = 2984000
Out of this, the paper recovers 596800. The remaining cost to be recovered would be: 2387200.
At ₹ 3000 per cc, 795.733 cc will have to be booked on any given day in order to obtain the cost. This represents 99.46% of the total value.
35. Times of Hindustan:
Total cost = 2,47,000 × 7.5 = 18,52,500
Net revenues from newspaper sales is 3,95,200
Cost to be covered through advertising = 18,52,500 – 3,95,200 = 14,57,300.
At an ad rate of ₹1800 per cc, they would have to sell 809.61 cc i.e.73.6%
Similar calculations for India's Times will give 79.2%.
Hence, the percentage point difference = 5.6

36. If AC 3rd costs 100, AC 2nd would cost 120 and AC 1st would cost 190. 3 Tier ticket would cost : 47.5 and general ticket would cost 40.

AC 2nd $\rightarrow$ 780 = 120

Then the difference between 3 Tier and general ticket would be: $7.5 \times 780 = 48.75$

37. Total cost $\rightarrow 100 + 120 + 190 + 47.5 + 40 = 497.5$
This gives $(497.5/120) \times 780 = 3233.75$.

43. Hursh Sarma's savings:

Month	Salary	Savings
1	10800	1080
2	10800	900
3	10800	900
4	10800	0
5	12000	1500
6	12000	1800
7	12000	2400
8	12000	1200
9	12000	1000
10	12000	1500
11	12000	1800
12	12000	2400

Required Ratio = 4800/900 = 5.333

48. Assume he has 1200 francs, 1200 DM and 1200 Liras. If he converts everything to francs, the result will be:
1200 DM will convert to 240 Euros which will convert to 960 francs. But 51 Moolas = 1 Franc. Thus the value of 1200 DM in terms of Moolas goes up from $1200 \times 36 = 43200$ to $960 \times 51 = 48960$. This increase in value has occurred only because of the change of currency. Hence, he should convert all his DM into Francs. However, before concluding on this you also will need to consider the effect of Liras.
It is evident that 1200 DM will yield 240 Euros, which would yield 720 Liras (since 1 euro is 3 lira), which in turn would yield $720 \times 70 = 5040$ Moolas. Thus, it is evident that by converting DM into Liras the increase in value is higher than that achieved by converting DM into Francs.
Similarly, converting Francs to Liras also increases the value of the Francs.
1200×51 becomes equivalent to 900×70.
Note: The thought process goes like this: 1200 Francs = 300 Euros (since 1 euro = 4 francs). Further 300 Euros equals 900 liras which equal 900×70 Moolas.

49. Cannot be determined since the conversion from dollar to Euro is not given, neither is the inter currency exchange rate between Lira, Francs and DMs.

50. Obviously, both a and c are required in order to answer this question.

CHAPTER 5

Ratio, Proportion and Variation

Chapter Launchpad

Scan this QR code to access a video on 'Introduction to Ratio, Proportion and Variation' and this chapter's importance for CAT

INTRODUCTION

The concept of ratio, proportion and variation is one of the most important and widely used concept in arithmetic as well as other areas of quantitative aptitude. The importance of the concepts of this chapter are two-fold: (a) questions from this chapter are regularly asked in all aptitude exams; (b) concepts and reactions that you should learn from this chapter, would be not limited to just questions that arise from this chapter, but also comes from Questions based on this chapter have been regularly asked in the CAT exam (direct or application based). In fact, questions based on this concept regularly appear in all aptitude tests (XLRI, CMAT, NMAT, SNAP, IPMAT, CUET, Banking, SSC and all other aptitude exams.)

Besides, this concept is very important in the area of Data Interpretation, where questions involving ratio change and ratio comparisons are very popular.

RATIO

When comparing any two numbers, sometimes, it is necessary to find out how many times one number is of than the other. In other words, we often need to express one number as a fraction of the other.

In general, the ratio of a number x to a number y is defined as the quotient of the numbers x and y.

The numbers that form the ratio are called the terms of the ratio. The numerator of the ratio is called the *antecedent* and the denominator is called the *consequent* of the ratio.

The ratio may be taken for homogenous quantities or for heterogeneous quantities. In the first case, the ratio has no unit (or is unitless), while in the second case, the unit of the ratio is based on the units of the numerator and that of the denominator.

Calculation of a ratio:

Percentage and decimal values

The value of every ratio can be expressed either as a decimal value or a percentage value. Thus, for instance, the value of the ratio 4/5 = 0.8 (when it is expressed as a decimal), also the value of the ratio 4/5 = 80% (when it is expressed as a percentage). [**Note:** To express the value of a ratio as a percentage, we multiply the ratio by 100. Thus, in effect, the difference between the decimal value of a ratio and its percentage value is just in the positioning of its decimal point. In order to convert a decimal value of a ratio to its percentage value we shift the decimal point to the right by two places (the effect of multiplying the ratio by 100), and likewise if we want to convert the percentage value of a ratio to the decimal, we do so by shifting the decimals by two places to the left. This property has a huge application as a calculation short cut. In the chapter on Percentages, we have already seen the percentage rule (as I call it), which allows us to calculate the value of a percentage mentally. I hope, that you have practiced the process for 2-digit by 2-digit percentage calculations as well as for 3-digit by 3-digit percentage calculations. The calculation convenience I am talking about here is that, if you have practiced percentage calculations mentioned in the previous sentence, then you need not do any other calculation practice for divisions separately. Whenever, you are forced to do a division, just calculate the percentage value and shift the decimal point by two places to the left to get the correct answer. So, if you can calculate that a ratio like 34/73 has a percentage value of 46.57%, you would know that the decimal value would be 0.4657 (refer back to the percentage chapter for details of how to do this calculation and revise it, if necessary). What is important is that, in the case of a normal division, an answer till two digits after the decimal place would be sufficient. Hence, even if you can just calculate the answer of 34/73 to 46.ab%, you would know that the decimal value would be 0.46 (and this would suffice in most cases)].

Some Important Properties of Ratios

1. If we multiply the numerator and the denominator of a ratio by the same number, the ratio remains unchanged.

   That is, $$\frac{a}{b} = \frac{ma}{mb}$$

2. If we divide the numerator and the denominator of a ratio by the same number, the ratio remains unchanged. Thus,

   $$a/b = \frac{(a/d)}{(b/d)}$$

3. Denominator equation method:
   The magnitudes of two ratios can be compared by equating the denominators of the two ratios and then checking for the value of the numerator.

Thus, if we have to check for

$8/3$ vs $11/4$

We can compare $\frac{(8 \times 1.33)}{(3 \times 1.33)}$ vs $\frac{11}{4}$

That is, $\frac{10.66}{4} < \frac{11}{4}$

In fact, the value of a ratio has a direct relationship with the value of the numerator of the ratio. At the same time, it has an inverse relationship with the denominator of the ratio. Since the denominator has an inverse relationship with the ratio's value, it involves an unnecessary inversion in the minds of the reader. Hence, in my opinion, we should look at maintaining constancy in the denominator and work all the requisite calculations on the numerator's basis.

The reader should recall here the Product Constancy Table (or the denominator change to ratio change table) explained in the chapter of percentages to understand the mechanics of how a change in the denominator affects the value of the ratio. A clear understanding of these dynamics will help the student become much faster in solving the problems based on ratios.

4. The ratio of two fractions can be expressed as a ratio of two integers. Thus, the ratio:

$$a/b : c/d = \frac{(a/b)}{(c/d)} = \frac{ad}{bc}$$

5. If either or both the terms of a ratio are a surd quantity, then the ratio will never evolve into integral numbers unless the surd quantities are equal. Use this principle to spot options in questions having surds.

Example: $\frac{\sqrt{3}}{\sqrt{2}}$ can never be represented by integers.

This principle can also be understood in other words as follows:

Suppose while solving a question, you come across a situation where $\sqrt{3}$ appears as a part of the process. In such a case, it would be safe to assume that $\sqrt{3}$ will also be part of the answer. Since the only way the $\sqrt{3}$ can be removed from the answer is by multiplying or dividing the expression by $\sqrt{3}$. Thus for instance, the formula for the area of an equilateral triangle is $(\sqrt{3}/4)a^2$.

Hence, you can safely assume that the area of any equilateral triangle will have $\sqrt{3}$ in its answer. The only case when this gets negated would be when the value of the side has a component which has the fourth root of three.

6. The multiplication of the ratios $\frac{a}{b}$ and $\frac{c}{d}$ yields:

$$a/b \times c/d = \frac{ac}{bd}$$

7. When the ratio a/b is compounded with itself, the resulting ratio is a^2/b^2 and is called the duplicate ratio. Similarly, a^3/b^3 is the triplicate ratio and $a^{0.5}/b^{0.5}$ is the sub-duplicate ratio of a/b.

8. If $a/b = c/d = e/f = g/h = k$ then

$$k = \frac{(a+c+e+g)}{(b+d+f+h)}$$

9. If $a_1/b_1, a_2/b_2, a_3/b_3 \ldots a_n/b_n$ are unequal fractions Then the ratio.

$$\frac{(a_1 + a_2 + a_3 + \ldots + a_n)}{(b_1 + b_2 + b_3 + \ldots b_n)}$$

lies between the lowest and the highest of these fractions.

10. If we have two equations containing three unknowns as

$$a_1x + b_1y + c_1z = 0 \quad (1)$$

and $$a_2x + b_2y + c_2z = 0 \quad (2)$$

Then, the value of x, y and z cannot be resolved without having a third equation.

However, in the absence of a third equation, we can find the proportion $x:y:z$. This will be given by $b_1c_2 - b_2c_1 : c_1a_2 - c_2a_1 : a_1b_2 - a_2b_1$.

This can be remembered by writing as follows:

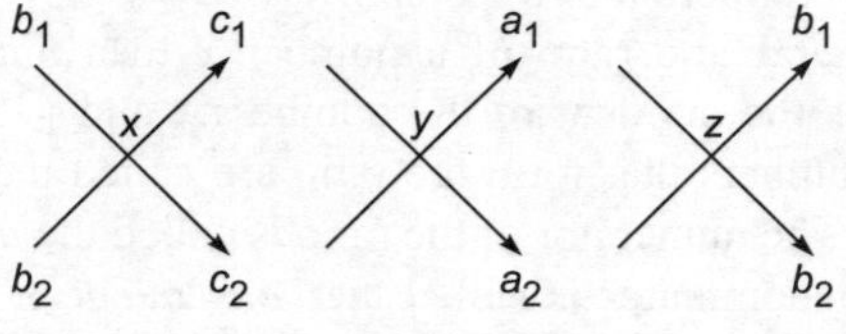

Fig. 8.1

Multiply the coefficients across the arrow indicated always taking a multiplication as positive if the arrow points downwards and taking it as negative if the arrow points upwards.

Thus, x corresponds to $b_1c_2 - b_2c_1$ and so on.

11. If the ratio $a/b > 1$ (called a ratio of greater inequality) and if k is a positive number:

$(a+k)/(b+k) < a/b$ and $(a-k)/(b-k) > a/b$

Similarly if $a/b < 1$ then

$(a+k)/(b+k) > a/b$ and $(a-k)/(b-k) < a/b$

[The student should try assuming certain values and check the results.]

12. Maintenance of equality when numbers are added in both the numerators and the denominators.

This is best illustrated through an example:

$$20/30 = (20 + 2)/(30 + 3)$$

i.e., $a/b = (a + c)/(b + d)$ if and only if $c/d = a/b$. In other words, the ratio of the additions should be equal to the original ratio to maintain equality of ratios when two different numbers are added in the numerator and denominator.

Consequently, if $c/d > a/b$ then $(a + c)/(b + d) > a/b$
and if $c/d < a/b$ then $(a + c)/(b + d) < a/b$

The practical applications of (11) and (12) is of immense importance for all aptitude exams.

MATHEMATICAL USES OF RATIOS

Use 1

As a bridge between 3 or more quantities: Case of chain ratios:

Suppose you have a ratio relationship given between the salaries of two individuals *A* and *B*. Further, if there is another ratio relationship between *B* and *C*. Then, by combining the two ratios, you can come up with a single consolidated ratio between *A*, *B* and *C*. This ratio will give you the relationship between *A* and *C*.

Illustration

The ratio of *A*'s salary to *B*'s salary is 2:3. The ratio of *B*'s salary to *C*'s salary is 4:5. What is the ratio of *A*'s salary to C's salary?

Using the conventional process in this case:

Take the LCM of 3 and 4 (the two values representing *B*'s amount). The LCM is 12.

Then, convert *B*'s value in each ratio to 12.

Thus, Ratio 1 = 8/12 and Ratio 2 = 12/15

Thus, *A*:*B*:*C* = 8:12:15

Hence, *A*:*C* = 8:15

Further, if it were given that *A*'s salary was 800, you could derive the values of *C*'s salary (as 1500).

SHORTCUT for this process:

The LCM process gets very cumbersome especially if you are trying to create a bridge between more than three quantities.

Suppose, you have the ratio train as follows:

A:*B* = 2:3
B:*C* = 4:5
C:*D* = 6:11
D:*E* = 12:17

In order to create one consolidated ratio for this situation, using the LCM process becomes too long.

The short cut goes as follows:

A:*B*:*C*:*D*:*E* can be written directly as:

$2 \times 4 \times 6 \times 12 : 3 \times 4 \times 6 \times 12 : 3 \times 5 \times 6 \times 12 : 3 \times 5 \times 11 \times 12 : 3 \times 5 \times 11 \times 17$

Thought algorithm for this case goes as:

To get the consolidated ratio *A*:*B*:*C*:*D*:*E*, *A* will correspond to the product of all numerators ($2 \times 4 \times 6 \times 12$) while *B* will take the first denominator and the last 3 numerators ($3 \times 4 \times 6 \times 12$). *C*, on the other hand, takes the first two denominators and the last 2 numerators ($3 \times 5 \times 6 \times 12$), *D* takes the first three denominators and the last numerator ($3 \times 5 \times 11 \times 12$) and *E* takes all the four denominators ($3 \times 5 \times 11 \times 17$).

In mathematical terms, this can be written as:

If $a/b = N_1/D_1$, $b/c = N_2/D_2$, $c/d = N_3/D_3$ and $d/e = N_4/D_4$ then $a : b : c : d : e = N_1N_2N_3N_4 : D_1N_2N_3N_4 : D_1D_2N_3N_4 : D_1D_2D_3N_4 : D_1D_2D_3D_4$

Use 2

Ratio as a multiplier

This is the most common use of ratios:

If *A*:*B* is 3:1, then the value of *B* has to be multiplied by 3 to get the value of *A*.

CALCULATION METHODS related to RATIOS

(A) Calculation methods for ratio comparisons:

The ratio comparison situation is one of the most common calculations situations in Mathematics as well as in Data Interpretation. Hence, equipping yourself for improving your ratio comparison calculation is an important imperative. There could be four broad cases when you might be required to do ratio comparisons:

The table below clearly illustrates these:

	Numerator	*Denominator*	*Ratio*	*Calculations*
Case 1	Increases	Decreases	Increase	Not required
Case 2	Increases	Increases	May increase or decrease	Required
Case 3	Decreases	Increases	Decreases	Not required
Case 4	Decreases	Decreases	May increase or decrease	Required

In case 2 and 4 in the table, calculations will be necessitated. In such a situation, the following process can be used for ratio comparisons.

1. The Cross Multiplication Method

Two ratios can be compared using the cross multiplication method as follows. Suppose you have to compare

12/17 with 15/19

Then, to test which ratio is higher, cross multiply and compare 12×19 and 15×17.

If 12 × 19 is bigger the ratio 12/17 will be bigger. If 15 × 17 is higher, the ratio 15/19 will be higher.

In this case, 15 × 17 being higher, the ratio 15/19 is higher.

Note: In real time usage (especially in D.I.), this method is highly impractical and calculating the product might be more cumbersome than calculating the percentage values.

Thus, this method will not be able to tell you the answer if you have to compare $\frac{3743}{5624}$ with $\frac{3821}{5783}$.

2. Percentage Value Comparison Method

Suppose you have to compare: $\frac{173}{212}$ with $\frac{181}{241}$

In such a case, just by estimating the 10% ranges for each ratio you can clearly see that —
the first ratio is > 80% while the second ratio is < 80%.

Hence, the first ratio is obviously greater.

This method is extremely convenient if the two ratios have their values in different 10% ranges.

However, this problem will become slightly more difficult, if the two ratios fall in the same 10% range. Thus, if you had to compare $^{173}/_{212}$ with $^{181}/_{225}$, both the values would give values between 80 and 90%. The next step would be to calculate the 1% range.

The first ratio here is 81 – 82% while the second ratio lies between 80 and 81%

Hence, the first ratio is the larger of the two.

Note: For this method to be effective for you, you will first need to master the percentage rule method for calculating the percentage value of a ratio. Hence, if you cannot see that 169.6 is 80% of 212 or for that matter that 81% of 212 is 171.72 and 82% is 173.84 you will not be able to use this method effectively. (This is also true for the next method.) However, once you can calculate percentage values of 3-digit ratios to 1% range, there is not much that can stop you in comparing ratios. The CAT and all other aptitude exams normally do not challenge you to calculate further than the 1% range when you are looking at ratio comparisons.

3. Numerator Denominator Percentage Change Method

There is another way in which you can compare close ratios like 173/212 and 181/225. For this method, you need to calculate the percentage changes in the numerator and the denominator.

Thus:

173 → 181 is a % increase of 4 – 5%.

While 212 → 225 is a % increase of 6 – 7%.

In this case, since the denominator is increasing more than the numerator, the second ratio is smaller.

This method is a powerful method for comparing ratios. As you could yourself see in the given example, we had taken two ratios whose values were very close to each other. Yet, using this method, we could resolve, which one is larger using a 10% range calculation - comparing 60+% to 80+%. I would encouage you to try this method with more examples that you can set for yourself.

4. Ratio of the Changes Method

However, the best method to compare ratios is to compare the ratio of the increases with the original ratio. This method can be understood as follows: Suppose you are asked to compare: 181/225 and 173/212 to find out which one is larger.

Step 1: place them in the order such that there are increases in both the numerator and the denominator. Thus, view them as: 173/212 (first ratio) and 181/225 (second ratio).

Step 2: Instead of comparing 173/212 with 181/225, first find out the ratio of the increases in the numerator and denominator. In this case, we can see that the numerator is going from 173 to 181 (an increase of 8); the denominator is increasing from 212 to 225 (an increase of 13). Thus, we get the ratio of increases in the numerator and denominator as 8/13.

Third Step: Compare the first ratio with the ratio of the increases. In this case, we will compare 173/212 with 8/13. The following cases might happen in general:

Case 1: The ratio of increases is larger than the first ratio → Conclusion: The second ratio is larger.

Case 2: The ratio of increases is equal to the first ratio → Conclusion: The first and second ratios are equal.

Case 3: The ratio of increases is smaller than the first ratio → Conclusion: The second ratio is smaller.

In this case, 8/13 (just larger than 60%) is smaller than 173/212 (definitely over 80%). Hence, the second ratio is smaller. We conclude: 173/212 > 181/225.

(B) Method for calculating the value of a percentage change in the ratio

PCG (Percentage Change Graphic) gives us a convenient method to calculate the value of the percentage change in a ratio.

Suppose, you have to calculate the percentage change between two ratios. This has to be done in two stages as:

$$\text{Original Ratio} \xrightarrow[\text{numerator}]{\text{Effect of}} \text{Intermediate Ratio}$$

$$\xrightarrow[\text{Denominator}]{\text{Effect of}} \text{Final Ratio}$$

Thus, if 20/40 becomes 22/50.

Effect of numerator = 20 → 22(10% increase)

Effect of denominator = 50 → 40(20% decrease) (reverse fashion)

Overall effect on the ratio:

$$100 \xrightarrow[\substack{\text{Numerator}\\\text{Effect}}]{10\%\uparrow} 110 \xrightarrow[\substack{\text{Denominator}\\\text{Effect}}]{20\%\downarrow} 88$$

Hence, overall effect = 12% decrease.

PROPORTION

When two ratios are equal, the four quantities composing them are said to be proportionals. Thus, if $a/b = c/d$, then a, b, c, d are proportionals. This is expressed by saying that a is to b as c is to d, and the proportion is written as

$$a : b :: c : d$$

or

$$a : b = c : d$$

- The terms a and d are called the extremes while the terms b and c are called the means.
- **If four quantities are in proportion, the product of the extremes is equal to the product of the means.**

  Let a, b, c, d be the proportionals.

  Then by definition $a/b = c/d$

  $\therefore \quad ad = bc$

  Hence, if any three terms of proportion are given, the fourth may be found. Thus, if a, c, d are given, then $b = ad/c$.
- **If three quantities a, b and c are in continued proportion, then $a : b = b : c$.**

  $\therefore \quad ac = b^2$

  In this case, b is said to be a *mean proportional* between a and c; and c is said to be a *third proportional* to a and b.
- **If three quantities are proportionals, the first is to the third is the duplicate ratio of the first to the second.**

  That is: for $a : b :: b : c$

  $$a : c = a^2 : b^2$$
- If four quantities a, b, c and d form a proportion, many other proportions may be deduced by the properties of fractions. The results of these operations are very useful. These operations are

  1. Invertendo: If $a/b = c/d$ then $b/a = d/c$
  2. Alternando: If $a/b = c/d$, then $a/c = b/d$
  3. Componendo: If $a/b = c/d$, then $\left(\dfrac{a+b}{b}\right) = \left(\dfrac{c+d}{d}\right)$
  4. Dividendo: If $a/b = c/d$, then $\left(\dfrac{a-b}{b}\right) = \left(\dfrac{c-d}{d}\right)$
  5. Componendo **and Dividendo:** If $a/b = c/d$, then $(a + b)/(a - b) = (c + d)/(c - d)$

VARIATION

Essentially there are two kinds of proportions that two variables can be related by:

(1) Direct Proportion

When it is said that A varies directly as B, you should understand the following implications:

(a) Logical **implication:** When A increases, B increases

(b) Calculation **implication:** If A increases by 10%, B will also increase by 10%.

(c) Graphical **implications:** The following graph is representative of this situation.

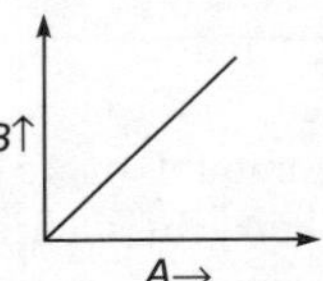

(d) Equation **implication:** The ratio A/B is constant.

(2) Inverse Proportion

When A varies inversely as B, the following implications arise.

(a) **Logical implication:** When A increases, B decreases.

(b) Calculation **implication:** If A decreases by 9.09%, B will increase by 10%.

(c) Graphical **implication:** The following graph is representative of this situation.

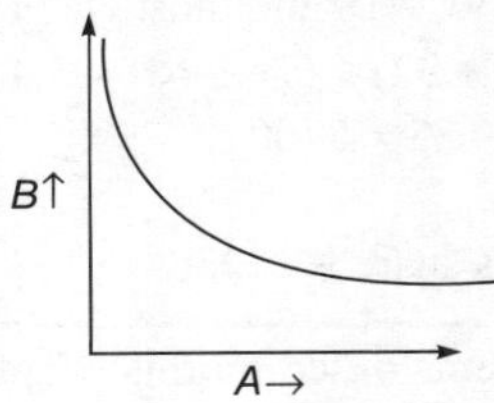

(d) Equation **implication:** The product $A \times B$ is constant.

A quantity 'A' is said to vary directly as another 'B' when the two quantities depend upon each other in such a manner that if B is changed, A is changed in the same ratio.

Note: The word directly is often omitted, and A is said to vary as B.

The symbol $\propto$ is used to denote variation. Thus, $A \propto B$ is read "A varies as B".

If $A \propto B$ then, $A = KB$ where K is any constant.

Thus, to find $K = A/B$, we need one value of A and a corresponding value of B.

where $K = 3/12 = 1/4 \Rightarrow A = B \times (1/4)$.

A quantity A is said to vary inversely as another B when A varies directly as the reciprocal of B. Thus, if A varies inversely as B, $A = m/B$, where m is constant.

A quantity is said to vary jointly as a number of others when it varies directly as their product. Thus, A varies jointly as B and C, when $A = mBC$.

If A varies as B when C is constant, and A varies as C when B is constant, then A will vary as BC when both B and C vary.

The variation of A depends partly on that of B and partly on that of C. Assume that each letter variation takes place separately, each in its turn producing its own effect on A.

WORKED-OUT PROBLEMS

Problem 5.1: The amount of ₹5783 is divided among Sherry, Berry, and Cherry in such a way that if ₹28, ₹37 and ₹18 be deducted from their respective shares, they have money in the ratio 4:6:9. Find Sherry's share.

(a) ₹1256 (b) ₹1228
(c) ₹1456 (d) ₹1084

Solution: The problem clearly states that when we reduce 28, 37 and 18 rupees, respectively from Sherry's, Berry's and Cherry's shares, the resultant ratio is: 4:6:9.

Thus, if we assume the reduced values as

$4x$, $6x$ and $9x$, we will have →

Sherry's share → $4x + 28$, Berry's share → $6x + 37$ and Cherry's share → $9x + 18$ and thus, we have

$(4x + 28) + (6x + 37) + (9x + 18) = 5783$

$\rightarrow 19x = 5783 - 83 = 5700$

Hence, $x = 300$.

Hence, Sherry's share is ₹1228.

Note: For problems based on this chapter, we are always confronted with ratios and proportions between different number of variables. For the above problem, we had three variables which were in the ratio of 4:6:9. When we have such a situation, we normally assume the values in the same proportion, using one unknown 'x' only (in this example, we could take the three values as $4x$, 6x and $9x$, respectively).

Then, the total value is represented by the addition of the three giving rise to a linear equation, which on solution, will result in the answer to the value of the unknown 'x'.

However, the student should realise that most of the time this unknown 'x' is not needed to solve the problem. This is illustrated through the following alternate approach to solving the above problem:

Assume the three values as 4, 6 and 9.

Then we have

(**4** + 28) + (**6** + 37) + (**9** + 18) = 5783

→ **19** = 5783–83 = 5700 → **1** = 300

Hence, **4** + 28 = 1228.

While adopting this approach, the student should be careful in being able to distinguish the numbers in bold as pointing out the unknown variable.

Problem 5.2: Two numbers are in the ratio $P:Q$. When 1 is added to both the numerator and the denominator, the ratio gets changed to R/S. Again, when 1 is added to both the numerator and the denominator, it becomes 1/2. Find the sum of P and Q.

(a) 3 (b) 4
(c) 5 (d) 6

Solution: The normal process of solving this problem would be through the writing of equations.

Approach 1: We have: Final ratio is $x/2x$.

Then, $\dfrac{x-2}{2x-2} = P/Q$

Then, $Qx - 2Q = 2Px - 2P$

$2(P - Q) = x(2P - Q)$ (At this stage, we see that the solution is a complex one)

Approach 2: $\dfrac{R+1}{S+1} = \dfrac{1}{2}$

$$2R + 2 = S + 1 \rightarrow R = \frac{S-1}{2}$$

Now, $\dfrac{P+1}{Q+1} = \dfrac{R}{S} = \dfrac{S-1}{2S}$ (At this time, we realise that we are getting stuck)

Start from front:

$\dfrac{P+2}{Q+2} = 1/2 \rightarrow 2P + 4 = Q + 2$ (Again the solution is not visible and we are likely to get stuck)

Note: Such problems should never be attempted by writing the equations since this process takes more time than is necessary to solve the problem and is impractical in the exam situation due to the amount of time required in writing.

Besides, in complex problems where the final solution is not visible to the student while starting off, many a times the student has to finally abort the problem midway. This results in an unnecessary wastage of time, if the student has attempted to write equations.

In fact, the student should realise that selecting the correct questions to solve in aptitude exams like the CAT is more important than being aware of how all the problems are solved.

The following process will illustrate the option, based solution process.

Option A: It has $P + Q = 3$. The possible values of P/Q are 1/2 or 2/1.

Using 1/2, we see that on adding 2 to both the numerator and the denominator we get 3/4 (Not the required value.)

Similarly, we see that 2/1 will also not give the answer. We should also realise that the numerator has to be lower than the denominator to have the final value of 1/2.

Next we try **Option B,** where we have 1/3 as the only possible ratio.

Then we get the final value as 3/5 (Not equal to 1/2) Hence, we reject option B.

Next we try **Option C,** where we have 1/4 or 2/3

Checking for 1/4, we get 3/6 = 1/2. Hence, the option is correct.

Problem 5.3: If 10 persons can clean 10 floors by 10 mops in 10 days, in how many days can 8 persons clean 8 floors by 8 mops?

(a) 12 ½ days (b) 8 days
(c) 10 days (d) 8 ⅓ days

Solution: Do not get confused by the distractions given in the problem. Ten men and 10 days means 100 man-days are required to clean 10 floors.

That is, 1 floor requires 10 man-days to get cleaned. Hence, 8 floors will require 80 man-days to clean.

Therefore, 10 days are required to clean 8 floors.

Problem 5.4: Three quantities A, B, C are such that $AB = KC$, where K is a constant. When A is kept constant, B varies directly as C; when B is kept constant, A varies directly C and when C is kept constant, A varies inversely as B.

Initially, A was at 5 and $A{:}B{:}C$ was 1:3:5. Find the value of A when B equals 9 at constant C.

(a) 8 (b) 8.33
(c) 9 (d) 9.5

Solution: Initial values are 5, 15 and 25.

Thus, we have $5 \times 15 = K \times 25$.

Hence, $K = 3$.

Thus, the equation is $AB = 3C$.

For the problem, keep C constant at 25. Then, $A \times 9 = 3 \times 25$.

i.e. $A = 75/9 = 8.33$

Problem 5.5: If $x/y = 3/4$, then find the value of the expression, $(5x - 3y)/(7x + 2y)$.

(a) 3/21 (b) 5/29
(c) 3/29 (d) 5/33

Solution: Assume the values as $x = 3$ and $y = 4$.

Then we have

$$\frac{(15-12)}{(21+8)} = 3/29$$

Problem 5.6: The amount, ₹3650 is divided among four engineers, three MBAs and five CAs such that three CAs get as much as two MBAs and three engineers as much as two CAs. Find the share of an MBA.

(a) 300 (b) 450
(c) 475 (d) None of these

Solution:

$$4E + 3M + 5C = 3650$$

Also, $3C = 2M$, that is, $M = 1.5\,C$

and $3E = 2C$ that is, $E = 0.66C$

Thus, $4 \times 0.66C + 3 \times 1.5\,C + 5C = 3650$

$$C = 3650/12.166$$

That is, $C = 300$

Hence, $M = 1.5\,C = 450$

Problem 5.7: The ratio of water and milk in a 30 litre mixture is 7 : 3. Find the quantity of water to be added to the mixture in order to make this ratio 6:1.

(a) 30 (b) 32
(c) 33 (d) 35

Solution: Solve while reading → As you read the first sentence, you should have 21 litres of water and 9 litres of milk in your mind.

In order to get the final result, we keep the milk constant at 9 litres.

Then, we have 9 litres, which corresponds to 1

Hence, '?' corresponds to 6.

Solving by using unitary method we have

54 litres of water to 9 litres of milk.

Hence, we need to add 33 litres of water to the original mixture.

Alternatively, we can solve this by using options. The student should try to do the same.

Problem 5.8: Three containers A, B and C are having mixtures of milk and water in the ratio of 1:5, 3:5 and 5 : 7, respectively. If the capacities of the containers are in the ratio 5:4:5, find the ratio of milk to water, if the mixtures of all the three containers are mixed together.

Solution: Assume that there are 500, 400 and 500 litres respectively in the three containers.

Then we have, 83.33,150 and 208.33 litres of milk in each of the three containers.

Thus, the total milk is 441.66 litres. Hence, the amount of water in the mixture is

$$1400 - 441.66 = 958.33 \text{ litres}$$

Hence, the ratio of milk to water is

441.66:958.33 → 53:115 (Using division by 0.33333)

The calculation thought process should be:
$(441 \times 3 + 2) : (958 \times 3 + 1) = 1325 : 2875$
Dividing by 25 → 53 : 115

LEVEL OF DIFFICULTY (I)

1. Divide ₹1870 into three parts in such a way that half of the first part, one-third of the second part and one-sixth of the third part are equal.
(a) 241, 343, 245 (b) 400, 800, 670
(c) 470, 640, 1160 (d) None of these

2. Divide ₹500 among A, B, C and D so that A and B together get thrice as much as C and D together, B gets four times of what C gets and C gets 1.5 times as much as D. Now the value of what B gets is
(a) 300 (b) 75
(c) 125 (d) 150

3. If $\frac{a}{b+c} = \frac{b}{c+a} = \frac{c}{a+b}$, then each fraction is equal to
(a) $(a+b+c)2$ (b) 1/2
(c) 1/4 (d) 0

4. If $6x^2 + 6y^2 = 13xy$, what is the ratio of x to y?
(a) 1:4 (b) 3:2
(c) 4:5 (d) 1:2
(Hint: Use options to solve fast)

5. If $a:b = c:d$ then the value of $\frac{a^2+b^2}{c^2+d^2}$ is
(a) 1/2 (b) $\frac{a+b}{c+d}$
(c) $\frac{a-b}{c-d}$ (d) $\frac{ab}{cd}$

6. A crew can row a certain course up the stream in 84 minutes; they can row the same course down stream in 9 minutes less than they can row it in still water. How long would they take to row down with the stream?
(a) 45 or 23 minutes (b) 63 or 12 minutes
(c) 60 minutes (d) 19 minutes

7. If a, b, c, d are in continued proportion then $\frac{a-d}{b-c} \geq x$. What is the value of x?
(a) 2 (b) 3
(c) 1 (d) 0

8. If four examiners can examine a certain number of answer books in eight days by working five hours a day, for how many hours a day would two examiners have to work in order to examine twice the number of answer books in twenty days?
(a) 6 (b) 7 ½
(c) 8 (d) 9

9. If a, b, c, d are proportional, then $(a - b)(a - c)/a$ equals
(a) $a+c+d$ (b) $a+d-b-c$
(c) $a+b+c+d$ (d) $a+c-b-d$

10. In a mixture of 40 litres, the ratio of milk and water is 4:1. How much water must be added to this mixture so that the ratio of milk and water becomes 2:3?
(a) 20 litres (b) 32 litres
(c) 40 litres (d) 30 litres

11. If A varies as C, and B varies as C, then which of the following is false?
(a) $(A+B) \propto C$ (b) $(A-B) \propto 1/C$
(c) $\sqrt{AB} \propto C$ (d) $AB \propto C^2$

12. If three numbers are in the ratio of 1:2:3 and half the sum is 18, then the ratio of squares of the numbers is
(a) 6:12:13 (b) 1:2:4
(c) 36:144:324 (d) 3:5:7

13. The ratio between two numbers is 3:4 and their LCM is 180. The first number is
(a) 60 (b) 45
(c) 15 (d) 20

14. A and B are two alloys of argentum and brass prepared by mixing metals in proportions 7:2 and 7:11, respectively. If equal quantities of the two alloys are melted to form a third alloy C, the proportion of argentum and brass in C will be
(a) 5:9 (b) 5:7
(c) 7:5 (d) 9:5

15. If 30 men working seven hours a day can do a piece of work in 18 days, in how many days will 21 men working eight hours a day do the same work?
(a) 24 days (b) 22.5 days
(c) 30 days (d) 45 days

16. The incomes of A and B are in the ratio 3 : 2 and their expenditures are in the ratio 5 : 3. If each saves ₹1000, then, A's income can be
(a) ₹3000 (b) ₹4000
(c) ₹6000 (d) ₹9000

17. If the ratio of sines of angles of a triangle is 1:1: $\sqrt{2}$, then the ratio of square of the greatest side to sum of the squares of other two sides is
(a) 3:4 (b) 2:1
(c) 1:1 (d) 1:2

18. Divide ₹680 among A, B and C such that A gets 2/3rd of what B gets and B gets 1/4th of what C gets. Now the share of C is
(a) ₹480 (b) ₹300
(c) ₹420 (d) ₹360

19. A, B, C enter into a partnership. A contributes one-third of the whole capital while B contributes as much as A and C together contribute. If the profit at the end of the year is ₹84,000, how much would each receive?
(a) 24,000, 20,000, 40,000
(b) 28,000, 42,000, 14,000

(c) 28,000, 42,000, 10,000
(d) 28,000, 14,000, 42,000

20. The students in three batches at Mindworkzz are in the ratio 2:3:5. If 20 students are increased in each batch, the ratio changes to 4:5:7. The total number of students in the three batches before the increases were
(a) 10 (b) 90
(c) 100 (d) 150

21. The speeds of three cars are in the ratio 2 : 3 : 4. The ratio between the times taken by these cars to travel the same distance is
(a) 2:3:4 (b) 4:3:2
(c) 4:3:6 (d) 6:4:3

22. If *a*, *b*, *c* and *d* are proportional, then the mean proportion between $a^2 + c^2$ and $b^2 + d^2$ is
(a) ac/bd (b) $ab + cd$
(c) $a/b + d/c$ (d) $a^2/b^2 + c^2/d^2$

23. A number *z* lies between 0 and 1. Which of the following is true?
(a) $z > \sqrt{z}$ (b) $z > 1/z$
(c) $z^3 > z^2$ (d) $1/z > \sqrt{z}$

24. An Amount of ₹2250 is divided among three friends Amar, Bijoy and Chandra in such a way that 1/6th of Amar's share, 1/4th of Bijoy's share and 2/5th of Chandra's share are equal. Find Amar's share.
(a) ₹720 (b) ₹1080
(c) ₹450 (d) ₹1240

25. After an increment of 7 in both the numerator and denominator, a fraction changes to 3/4. Find the original fraction.
(a) 5/12 (b) 7/9
(c) 2/5 (d) 3/8

26. The difference between two positive numbers is 10 and the ratio between them is 5:3. Find the product of the two numbers.
(a) 375 (b) 175
(c) 275 (d) 125

27. If 30 oxen can plough 1/7th of a field in two days, how many days 18 oxen will take to do the remaining work?
(a) 30 days (b) 20 days
(c) 15 days (d) 18 days

28. A cat takes five leaps for every four leaps of a dog, but three leaps of the dog are equal to four leaps of the cat. What is the ratio of the speed of the cat to that of the dog?
(a) 11:15 (b) 15:11
(c) 16:15 (d) 15:16

29. The present ratio of ages of *A* and *B* is 4:5. Eighteen years ago, this ratio was 11:16. Find the sum total of their present ages.
(a) 90 years (b) 105 years
(c) 110 years (d) 80 years

30. Four numbers in the ratio 1:3:4:7 add up to give a sum of 105. Find the value of the biggest number.
(a) 42 (b) 35
(c) 49 (d) 63

31. Three men rent a farm for ₹7000 per annum. *A* puts 110 cows in the farm for three months, *B* puts 110 cows for six months and *C* puts 440 cows for three months. What percentage of the total expenditure should *A* pay?
(a) 20% (b) 14.28%
(c) 16.66% (d) 11.01%

32. Ten students can do a job in eight days, but on the starting day, two of them informed that they are not coming. By what fraction will the number of days required for doing the whole work get increased?
(a) 4/5 (b) 3/8
(c) 3/4 (d) 1/4

33. A dishonest milkman mixed 1 litre of water for every 3 litres of milk and thus, made up 36 litres of milk . If he now adds 15 litres of milk to the mixture, find the ratio of milk and water in the new mixture.
(a) 12:5 (b) 14:3
(c) 7:2 (d) 9:4

34. An Amount of ₹3000 is distributed among *A*, *B* and *C* such that *A* gets 2/3rd of what *B* and *C* together get and *C* gets 1/2 of what *A* and *B* together get. Find *C*'s share.
(a) ₹750 (b) ₹1000
(c) ₹800 (d) ₹1200

35. If the ratio of the ages of Maya and Chhaya is 6:5 at present, and fifteen years from now, the ratio will get changed to 9:8, then find Maya's present age.
(a) 24 years (b) 30 years
(c) 18 years (d) 33 years

36. At constant temperature, pressure of a definite mass of gas is inversely proportional to the volume. If the pressure is reduced by 20%, find the respective change in volume.
(a) –16.66% (b) +25%
(c) –25% (d) +16.66%

37. If ₹58 is divided among 150 children such that each girl and each boy gets 25 p and 50 p respectively. Then how many girls are there?
(a) 52 (b) 54
(c) 68 (d) 62

38. If 391 bananas were distributed among three monkeys in the ratio 1/2:2/3:3/4, how many bananas did the first monkey get?
(a) 102 (b) 108
(c) 112 (d) 104

39. A mixture contains milk and water in the ratio 5:1. On adding 5 litres of water, the ratio of milk to water becomes 5:2. The quantity of milk in the mixture is:
(a) 16 litres (b) 25 litres
(c) 32.5 litres (d) 22.75 litres

40. A beggar had ten paise, twenty paise and one rupee coins in the ratio 10:17:7 respectively at the end of day. If that day he earned a total of ₹57, how many twenty paise coins did he have?
(a) 114 (b) 171
(c) 95 (d) 85

41. Vijay has coins of the denomination of Re. 1, 50 p and 25 p in the ratio of 12:10:7. The total worth of the coins he has is ₹75. Find the number of 25 p coins that Vijay has.
(a) 48 (b) 72
(c) 60 (d) None of these

42. If two numbers are in the ratio of 5 : 8 and if 9 be added to each, the ratio becomes 8 : 11. Now find the lower number.
(a) 5 (b) 10
(c) 15 (d) None of these

43. What number must be taken from each term of the fraction 27/35 that it may become 2 : 3?
(a) 9 (b) 10
(c) 11 (d) None of these

44. If x varies inversely as $y^2 - 1$ and is equal to 24 when $y = 10$, find x when $y = 5$.
(a) 99 (b) 101
(c) 91 (d) 93

45. If x varies as y, and $y = 7$ when $x = 18$, find x when $y = 21$.
(a) 36 (b) 54
(c) 72 (d) 18

46. A varies jointly as B and C; and $A = 6$ when $B = 3$, $C = 2$; find A when $B = 5$, $C = 7$.
(a) 17.5 (b) 35
(c) 70 (d) 105

47. If x varies as y directly, and as z inversely, and $x = 14$ when $y = 10$; find z when $x = 49$, $y = 45$.
(a) 14/10 (b) 10
(c) 10/14 (d) Cannot be determined

48. A cask contains a mixture of 49 litres of wine and water in the proportion 5:2. How much water must be added to it so that the ratio of wine to water may be 7:4?
(a) 3.5 (b) 6
(c) 7 (d) None of these

49. A cask contains 12 gallons of mixture of wine and water in the ratio 3:1. How much of the mixture must be drawn off and water substituted, so that wine and water in the cask may become half.
(a) 3 litres (b) 5 litres
(c) 6 litres (d) None of these

50. The total number of pupils in three classes of a school is 333. The number of pupils in classes I and II are in the ratio 3:5 and those in classes II and III are in the ratio 7:11. Find the number of pupils in the class that had the highest number of pupils.
(a) 63 (b) 105
(c) 165 (d) 180

Space for Rough Work

LEVEL OF DIFFICULTY (II)

1. If the work done by p men in $(p + 2)$ days is to the work done by $(p + 4)$ men in $(p - 1)$ days is in the ratio 1: 1, then the value of p is
   (a) 2 (b) 4
   (c) 6 (d) 5
2. The duration of a railway journey varies as the distance and inversely as the velocity; the velocity varies directly as the square root of the quantity of coal used, and inversely as the number of carriages in the train. In a journey of 50 km in half an hour with 18 carriages, 100 kg of coal is required. How much coal will be consumed in a journey of 42 km in 28 minutes with 16 carriages?
   (a) 64 kg (b) 49 kg
   (c) 25 kg (d) 36 kg
3. The mass of a circular disc varies as the squares of the radius when the thickness remains the same; it also varies as the thickness when the radius remains the same. Two discs have their thicknesses in the ratio of 16:3; find the ratio of the radii if the mass of the first is thrice that of the second.
   (a) 3: 4 (b) 5:2
   (c) 2:1 (d) 1:2
4. If p and q are positive integers then $\sqrt{2}$ always lies between
   (a) $(p + q)/(p - q)$ and pq
   (b) p/q and $(p + 2q)/(p + q)$
   (c) p and q
   (d) $pq/(p + q)$ and $(p - q)/pq$
5. The cost of digging a pit was ₹2,694. How much will it cost (approximately) if the wages of workmen per day had been increased by 1/8 of the former wages and length of the working day increased by 1/20 of the former period?
   (a) ₹2886 (b) ₹2468
   (c) ₹2878 (d) ₹2000
6. A vessel contains p litres of wine, and another vessel contains q litres of water. r litres are taken out of each vessel and transferred to the other. If $r \times (p + q) = pq$. If A and B are the respective values of the amount of wine contained in the respective containers after this operation, then what can be said about the relationship between A and B?
   (a) $A = B$ (b) $\dfrac{A - C}{B - C} > 2$
   (c) $A - B = 4c$ (d) None of these
7. If sum of the roots and the product of the roots of a quadratic equation S are in the ratio of 3 : 1, then which of the following is true?
   (a) $f(S) < 0$
   (b) $(b^2 - 4ac) < 0$
   (c) S is a perfect square
   (d) None of these
8. The incomes of Rahul, Saurav, and Sachin are in the ratio of 4: 5: 6 respectively and their spending are in the ratio of 6: 7: 8 respectively. If Rahul saves one fourth his income, then the savings of Rahul, Saurav, and Sachin are in the ratio
   (a) 2 : 3: 4 (b) 5 : 6 : 9
   (c) 5 : 9 : 6 (d) 9 : 5 : 6
   (e) None of these
9. If $a:b = c:d$, and $e:f = g:h$, then $(ae + bf):(ae - bf) = ?$
   (a) $\dfrac{(e + f)}{(e - f)}$ (b) $\dfrac{(cg + dh)}{(cg - dh)}$
   (c) $\dfrac{(cg + dh)}{(cg - dh)}$ (d) $\dfrac{e - f}{e + f}$
10. X is an alloy of A and B. Y is an alloy containing 80% of A, 4 % of B and 16% of C. A fused mass of X and Y is found to contain 74% of A, 16% of B, and 10% of C. The ratio of A to B in X is
    (a) 9:16 (b) 12:17
    (c) 16:9 (d) None of these
11. Shatabdi Express without its rake can go 36 km in an hour, and the speed is diminished by a quantity that varies as the square root of the number of wagons attached. If it is known that with four wagons its speed is 24 km/h, the greatest number of wagons with which the engine can just move is
    (a) 35 (b) 40
    (c) 36 (d) 42
12. If p varies as q then $p^2 + q^2$ varies as
    (a) $p + q$ (b) $p - q$
    (c) $p^2 - q^2$ (d) None of these
13. If $f(x) = \dfrac{x+1}{x-1}$, then the ratio of x to $f(y)$ where $y = f(x)$ is
    (a) $x : y$ (b) $x^2 : y^2$
    (c) $1 : 1$ (d) $y : x$
14. Sahil employs 200 men to build a bund. They finish 5/6 of the work in ten weeks. Because of some natural calamity not only does the work remain suspended for four weeks but also half of the work already done is washed away. After the calamity, when the work is resumed, only 140 men turn up. The total time in which the contractor is able to complete the work assuming that there are no further disruptions in the schedule is
    (a) 25 weeks (b) 26 weeks
    (c) 24 weeks (d) 20 weeks
15. Rahim covers a distance of 48 km performed by train, bike and car in that order, the distance covered

by the three ways in that order are in the ratio of 8 : 1 : 3 and charges per kilometre in that order are in the ratio of 8 : 1 : 4. If the train charges being ₹24 per kilometre, the total cost of the journey is

(a) ₹924 (b) ₹1000
(c) ₹1200 (d) None of these

16. A bag contains 25 paise, 50 paise and 1 rupee coins. There are 220 coins in all and the total amount in the bag is ₹160. If there are thrice as many 1 rupee coins as there are 25 paise coins, then what is the number of 50 paise coins?

(a) 60 (b) 40
(c) 120 (d) 80

Directions for Questions 17 to 19: Read the following and answer the questions that follow.
Sahir runs in a triathlon consisting of three phases in the following manner. Running 12 km, cycling 24 km and swimming 5 km. His speeds in the three phases are in the ratio 2 : 6 : 1. He completes the race in *n* minutes. Later, he changes his strategy so that the distances he covers in each phase are constant but his speeds are now in the ratio 3 : 8 : 1. The end result is that he completes the race taking 20 minutes more than the earlier speed. It is also known that he has not changed his running speed when he changes his strategy.

17. What is his initial speed while swimming?

(a) 1/2 km/min (b) 0.05 km/min
(c) 0.15 km/min (d) None of these

18. If his speeds are in the ratio 1:3:1, with the running time remaining unchanged, what is his finishing time?

(a) 500/3 min (b) 250/3 min
(c) 200/3 min (d) 350/3 min

19. What is Sahir's original speed of running?

(a) 9 kmph (b) 18 kmph
(c) 54 kmph (d) 12 kmph

20. Concentrations of three type of milks *X*, *Y* and *Z* are 10%, 20% and 30%, respectively. They are mixed in the ratio 2 : 3 : *P* resulting in a 23% concentration solution. Find *P*.

(a) 7 (b) 6
(c) 5 (d) 4

21. The cost of an article (which is composed of raw materials and wages) was three times the value of the raw materials used. The cost of raw materials increased in the ratio 3 : 7 and wages increased in the ratio 4 : 9. Find the present cost of the article if its original cost was ₹18.

(a) ₹41 (b) ₹30
(c) ₹40 (d) ₹46

22. In a co-educational school, there are 15 more girls than boys. If the number of girls is increased by 10% and the number of boys is also increased by 16%, there would be nine more girls than boys. What is the number of students in the school?

(a) 140 (b) 125
(c) 265 (d) 255

23. At IIM Bangalore class of 1995, Sonali, a first year student has taken ten courses, earning grades *A* (worth 4 points each), *B* (worth 3 points each) and *C* (worth 2 points each). Her grade point average is 3.2, and if the course in which she get *C*'s were deleted, her GPA in the remaining courses would be 3.333. How many *A*'s, *B*'s and *C*'s did she get?

(a) 3, 1 and 6 (b) 1, 3 and 6
(c) 3, 6 and 1 (d) 1, 6 and 3

24. Total expenses of running the hostel at Harvard Business School are partly fixed and partly varying linearly with the number of boarders. The average expense per boarder is $70 when there are 25 boarders and $60 when there are 50 boarders. What is the average expense per boarder when there are 100 boarders?

(a) 55 (b) 56
(c) 54 (d) 50

25. The speed of the engine of Gondwana Express is 42 km/h when no compartment is attached, and the reduction in speed is directly proportional to the square root of the number of compartments attached. If the speed of the train carried by this engine is 24 km/h when nine compartments are attached, the maximum number of compartments that can be carried by the engine is

(a) 49 (b) 48
(c) 46 (d) 47

Directions for Questions 26 to 28: Three drunkards agree to pool their vodka and decided to share it with a fourth drunkard (who had no vodka) at a price equal to 5 roubles a litre. The first drunkard contributed 1 litre more than the second and the second contributed a litre more than the third. Then all four of them divided the vodka equally and drank it. The fourth drunkard paid money, which was divided in the ratio of each drunkard's contribution towards his portion. It was found that the first drunkard should get twice as much money as the second. Based on this information answer the questions 26–28. (Assume that all shares are integral).

26. How much money did the second drunkard get (in roubles)?

(a) 8 (b) 10
(c) 5 (d) Data insufficient

27. How many litres of vodka was consumed in all by the four of them?

(a) 12 (b) 16
(c) 10 (d) None of these

28. What proportion of the fourth drunkard's drink did the second drunkard contribute?

(a) 1/3 (b) 2/3
(c) 1/2 (d) None of these

29. In Ramnagar Colony, the ratio of school going children to non-school going children is 5 : 4. If in the next year, the number of non-school going children is increased by 20%, making it 35,400, what is the new ratio of school going children to non-school going children?

(a) 4 : 5 (b) 3 : 2
(c) 25 : 24 (d) None of these

30. A precious stone weighing 35 grams worth ₹12,250 is accidentally dropped and gets broken into two pieces having weights in the ratio of 2 : 5. If the price varies as the square of the weight, then find the loss incurred.

(a) ₹5750 (b) ₹6000
(c) ₹5500 (d) ₹5000

31. On his deathbed, Mr. Kalu called upon his three sons and told them to distribute all his assets worth ₹5,25,000 in the ratio of 1/15 : 1/21 : 1/35 amongst themselves. Find the biggest share amongst the three portions.

(a) 17,500 (b) 2,45,000
(c) 10,500 (d) 13,250

32. Three jackals—Paar, Maar and Taar together have 675 loaves of bread. Paar has got three times as much as Maar but 25 loaves more than Taar. How many does Taar have?

(a) 175 (b) 275
(c) 375 (d) None of these

33. King Sheru had ordered the distribution of apples according to the following plan : for every 20 apples the elephant gets, the zebra should get 13 apples and the deer should get 8 apples. Now his servant Shambha jackal is in a fix. Can you help him by telling how much should he give to the elephant if there were 820 apples in total?

(a) 140 (b) 160
(c) 200 (d) 400

34. In the famous Bhojpur island, there are four men for every three women and five children for every three men. How many children are there in the island if it has 531 women?

(a) 454 (b) 1180
(c) 1070 (d) 389

35. Which of the following will have the maximum change in their values if 5 is added to both the numerator and denominator of all the fractions?

(a) 3/4 (b) 2/3
(c) 4/7 (d) 5/7

36. Forty men could have finished the whole project in 28 days but due to the inclusion of a few more men, work got done in 3/4 of the time. Find out how many more men were included (in whole numbers).

(a) 12 (b) 13
(c) 14 (d) None of these

37. Mr. *AM*, the magnanimous cashier at *XYZ* Ltd., while distributing salary, adds whatever money is needed to make the sum a multiple of 50. He adds ₹10 and ₹40 to *A*'s and *B*'s salary respectively and then he realises that the salaries of *A*, *B* and *C* are now in the ratio 4 : 5 : 7. The salary of *C* could be

(a) ₹2300 (b) ₹2150
(c) ₹1800 (d) ₹2100

38. A mother divided an amount of ₹61,000 between her two daughters aged 18 years and 16 years respectively and deposited their shares in a bond. If the interest rate is 20% compounded annually and if each received the same amount as the other when she attained the age of 20 years, their shares are

(a) ₹35,600 and ₹25,400
(b) ₹30,500 each
(c) ₹24,000 and ₹37000
(d) None of these

Directions for Questions 39 to 41: Read the passage below and answer the questions that follow:

Anshu gave Bobby and Chandana as many pens as each one of them already had. Then Chandana gave Anshu and Bobby as many pens as each already had. Now each had an equal number of pens.The total number of pens is 72.

39. How many pens did Bobby have initially?

(a) 24 (b) 18
(c) 12 (d) 6

40. How many pens did Chandana have initially?

(a) 24 (b) 18
(c) 12 (d) 6

41. How many pens did Anshu have initially?

(a) 30 (b) 36
(c) 42 (d) 48

42. The volume of a pyramid varies jointly as its height and the area of its base; and when the area of the base is 60 square dm and the height 14 dm, the volume is 280 cubic dm. What is the area of the base of a pyramid whose volume is 390 cubic dm and whose height is 26 dm?

(a) 40 (b) 45
(c) 50 (d) None of these

43. The expenses of an all-boys' institute are partly constant and partly vary as the number of boys. The expenses were ₹10,000 for 150 boys and ₹8400 for 120 boys. What will the expenses be when there are 330 boys?

(a) 18,000 (b) 19,600
(c) 22,400 (d) None of these

44. The distance of the horizon at sea varies as the square root of the height of the eye above sea-level. When the distance is 14.4 km, the height of the eye is 18 metres. Find, in kilometres, the distance when the height of the eye is 8 metres.

(a) 4.8 km (b) 7.2 km
(c) 9.6 km (d) 12 km

45. A mixture of cement, sand and gravel in the ratio of 1:2:4 by volume is required. A person wishes to measure out quantities by weight. He finds that the weight of one cubic foot of cement is 94 kg, of sand 100 kg and gravel 110 kg. What should be the ratio of cement, sand and gravel by weight in order to give a proper mixture?

(a) 47:100:220 (b) 94:100:220
(c) 47:200:440 (d) None of these

Directions for Questions 46 and 47: Read the passage below and answer the questions that follow:

The sum of three numbers x, y, z is 5000. If we reduce the first number by 50, the second number by 100, and the third number by 150, then the new ratio of x and y = 4: 5 and the new ratio of y and z =3: 4. Answer the following questions

46. $x + y = ?$

47. If we reduce x by a and y by b such that the new ratio of x and y is 1: 1 if $b = 2.4a$ then find the value of $|(a - b)|$.

Directions for Questions 48 and 49: Read the passage below and answer the questions that follow:

There are three containers x, y, z. In container x, the ratio of milk and water is 2: 1, in container y the ratio of water and milk is 2: a. If container x and y are mixed in the ratio of 2: 3, to get 100 litres of a mixture having milk and water in the ratio 3: 1.

48. Then a = ?

49. If after inspection, it was found that the milk we are using in container x, is actually a mixture of milk and water in the 1:2 ratio, then the ratio of milk and water in the final mixture will be?

Directions for Questions 50 to 52: Read the passage below and answer the questions that follow:

The average temperature of Delhi and Lucknow was in the ratio 3:5 in July and 2: 3 in August. The percentage increase in temperature from August to September is twice as from July to August for Delhi and same as for July to August for Lucknow. If the ratio of the sum of the temperatures of these two cities in August and July was 5: 4, then answer the following questions.

50. What was the percentage increase in temperature of Lucknow from July to August?

51. What was the value of the ratio (temperature of Lucknow in September/temperature of Delhi in September)?

52. If temperature of Delhi in August was 20°C, then what was the sum of the temperatures of these two cities in September?

53. In 2006, Raveendra was allotted 650 shares of Sun Systems Ltd in the initial public offer, at the face value of ₹10 per share. In 2007, Sun Systems declared a bonus at the rate of 3:13. In 2008, the company again declared a bonus at the rate of 2:4. In 2009, the company declared a dividend of 12.5%. What is the ratio of the dividend and the initial investment of Raveendra in 2009?

54. The ratio of 'metal 1' and 'metal 2' in Alloy '*A*' is 3: 4. In Alloy '*B*' same metals are mixed in the ratio 5: 8. If 26 kg of Alloy '*B*' and 14 kg of Alloy '*A*' are mixed then find out the ratio of 'metal 1' and 'metal 2' in the new Alloy.

55. Karam purchased four varieties of paint at the rate of 0.10 litres per rupee, 0.20 litres per rupee, 0.30 litres per rupee and 0.40 litre per rupee. If he mixes all the four varieties of paints in the ratio of 1: 2: 3: 4 in the given order, then find the price (in rupee/litre) at which Karam should sell the mixture to make a profit of 10% on his entire stock.

High Yield Questions

Scan this QR code to access assisted problem solving videos on 33, 42, 43, 45, 53 and 55 from LOD 2

Space for Rough Work

LEVEL OF DIFFICULTY (III)

1. An alloy of gold and silver is taken in the ratio of 1:2, and another alloy of the same metals is taken in the ratio of 2:3. How many parts of the two alloys must be taken to obtain a new alloy consisting of gold and silver that are in the ratio 3:5?
   (a) 3 and 5 (b) 2 and 9
   (c) 2 and 5 (d) 1 and 5
2. There are two quantities of oil, with the masses differing by 2 kg. The same quantity of heat, equal to 96 kcal, was imparted to each mass, and the larger mass of oil was found to be 4 degrees cooler than the smaller mass. Find the mass of oil in each of the two quantities.
   (a) 6 and 8 (b) 4 and 6
   (c) 2 and 9 (d) 4 and 9
3. There are two alloys of gold and silver. In the first alloy, there is twice as much gold as silver, and in the second alloy there is five times less gold than silver. How many times more must we take of the second alloy than the first in order to obtain a new alloy in which there would be twice as much silver as gold?
   (a) Two times (b) Three times
   (c) Four times (d) Ten times
4. Calculate the weight and the percentage of zinc in the zinc–copper alloy being given that the latter's alloy with 3 kg of pure zinc contains 90 per cent of zinc and with 2 kg of 90% zinc alloy contains 84% of zinc.
   (a) 3 kg or 80% (b) 1.4 kg or 88%
   (c) 3.4 kg or 60% (d) 7.4 kg or 18%
5. Two solutions, the first of which contains 0.8 kg and the second 0.6 kg of salt, were poured together and 10 kg of a new salt solution was obtained. Find the weight of the first and of the second solution in the mixture if the first solution is known to contain 10 per cent more of salt than the second.
   (a) 4 kg, 6 kg (b) 3 kg, 7 kg
   (c) 4 kg, 9 kg (d) 5 kg, 9 kg
6. From a full barrel containing 729 litres of honey, we pour off '*a*' litre and add water to fill up the barrel. After stirring the solution thoroughly, we pour off '*a*' litre of the solution and again add water to fill up the barrel. After the procedure is repeated six times, the solution in the barrel contains 64 litres of honey. Find *a*.
   (a) 243 litres (b) 81 litres
   (c) 2.7 litres (d) 3 litres
7. In two alloys, the ratios of nickel to tin are 5:2 and 3:4 (by weight). How many kilogram of the first alloy and of the second alloy should be alloyed together to obtain 28 kg of a new alloy with equal contents of nickel and tin?
   (a) 9 kg of the first alloy and 22 kg of the second
   (b) 17 kg of the first alloy and 11 kg of the second
   (c) 7 kg of the first alloy and 21 kg of the second
   (d) 8 kg and 20 kg respectively
8. In two alloys, aluminium and iron are in the ratios of 4:1 and 1:3. After alloying together 10 kg of the first alloy, 16 kg of the second and several kilograms of pure aluminium, an alloy was obtained in which the ratio of aluminium to iron was 3:2. Find the weight of the new alloy.
   (a) 15 (b) 35
   (c) 65 (d) 95
9. There are two alloys of gold, silver and platinum. The first alloy is known to contain 40 per cent of platinum and the second alloy 26 per cent of silver. The percentage of gold is the same in both alloys. Having alloyed 150 kg of the first alloy and 250 kg of the second, we get a new alloy that contains 30 per cent of gold. How many kilogram of platinum is there in the new alloy?
   (a) 170 kg (b) 175 kg
   (c) 160 kg (d) 165 kg
10. Two alloys of iron have different percentage of iron in them. The first one weighs 6 kg and second one weighs 12 kg. One piece each of equal weight was cut off from both the alloys and the first piece was alloyed with the second alloy and the second piece alloyed with the first one. As a result, the percentage of iron became the same in the resulting two new alloys. What was the weight of each cut-off piece?
    (a) 4 kg (b) 2 kg
    (c) 3 kg (d) 5 kg
11. Two litres of a mixture of wine and water contain 12% water. They are added to 3 litres of another mixture containing 7% water, and half a litre of water is then added to whole. What is the percentage of water in resulting concoction?
    (a) 17(2/7)% (b) 15 (7/11)%
    (c) 17(3/11)% (d) 16 (2/3)%
12. Three vessels having volumes in the ratio of 1:2:3 are full of a mixture of coke and soda. In the first vessel, ratio of coke and soda is 2:3, in second, 3:7 and in third, 1:4. If the liquids in all the three vessels were mixed in a bigger container, what is the resulting ratio of coke and soda?

(a) 4:11 (b) 5:7
(c) 7:11 (d) 7:5

13. Two types of tea are mixed in the ratio of 3:5 to produce the first quality and if they are mixed in the ratio of 2:3, the second quality is obtained. How many kilograms of the first quality has to be mixed with 10 kg of the second quality so that a third quality having the two varieties in the ratio of 7:11 may be produced?

(a) 5 kg (b) 10 kg
(c) 8 kg (d) 9 kg

14. A toy weighing 24 grams of an alloy of two metals is worth ₹174, but if the weights of metals in alloy be interchanged, the toy would be worth ₹162. If the price of one metal be ₹8 per gram, find the price of the other metal in the alloy used to make the toy.

(a) ₹10 per gram (b) ₹6 per gram
(c) ₹4 per gram (d) ₹5 per gram

15. The weight of three heaps of gold are in the ratio 5:6:7. By what fractions of themselves must the first two be increased so that the ratio of the weights may be changed to 7:6:5?

(a) $\frac{24}{25}, \frac{2}{5}$ (b) $\frac{48}{50}, \frac{4}{5}$

(c) $\frac{48}{50}, \frac{3}{5}$ (d) $\frac{24}{25}, \frac{3}{7}$

16. An alloy of gold, silver and bronze contains 90% bronze, 7% gold and 3% silver. A second alloy of bronze and silver only is melted with the first and the mixture contains 85% of bronze, 5% of gold and 10% of silver. Find the percentage of bronze in the second alloy.

(a) 75% (b) 72.5%
(c) 70% (d) 67.5%

17. Gunpowder can be prepared by saltpetre and nitrous oxide. Price of saltpetre is thrice the price of nitrous oxide. Notorious gangster Kallu Bhai sells the gunpowder at ₹2160 per 10 g, thereby making a profit of 20%. If the ratio of saltpetre and nitrous oxide in the mixture be 2:3, find the cost price of saltpetre.

(a) ₹210/g (b) ₹300/g
(c) ₹120/g (d) None of these

18. Two boxes A and B were filled with a mixture of rice and dal—in A in the ratio of 5:3, and in B in the ratio of 7:3. What quantity must be taken from the first to form a mixture that shall contain 8 kg of rice and 3 kg of dal?

(a) 4 kg
(b) 5 kg
(c) 6 kg
(d) This cannot be achieved

19. A person buys 18 local tickets for ₹110. Each first class ticket costs ₹10 and each second class ticket costs ₹3. What will another lot of 18 tickets in which the number of first class and second class tickets are interchanged cost?

(a) 112 (b) 118
(c) 121 (d) 124

20. Two jars having a capacity of 3 and 5 litres respectively are filled with mixtures of milk and water. In the smaller jar, 25% of the mixture is milk and in the larger 25% of the mixture is water. The jars are emptied into a 10 litre cask whose remaining capacity is filled up with water. Find the percentage of milk in the cask.

(a) 55% (b) 50%
(c) 45% (d) None of these

21. Two cubes of bronze have their total weight equivalent to 60 kg. The first piece contains 10 kg of pure zinc and the second piece contains 8 kg of pure zinc. What is the percentage of zinc in the first piece of bronze if the second piece contains 15 per cent more zinc than the first?

(a) 15% (b) 25%
(c) 55% (d) 24%

22. Sonu gets a jewellery made of an alloy of copper and silver. The alloy with a weight of 8 kg contains p per cent of copper. What piece of the alloy must be alloyed with another silver-copper alloy, containing 40% silver in order to obtain a new alloy with the minimum percentage of copper if the weight of the second piece is 2 kg?

(a) 2 kg for $p > 60$, a kg, where $a \in [0, 2]$, for $p = 60$, 0 kg for $0 < p < 60$
(b) 0 kg for $p > 60$, a kg, where $a \in [0, 8]$, for $p = 60$, 8 kg for $0 < p < 60$
(c) 0 kg for $p > 60$, a kg, where $a \in [0, 3]$, for $p = 70$, 0 kg for $0 < p < 70$
(d) None of these

23. From a vessel filled up with pure spirit to the brim, two litres of spirit was removed and two litres of water were added. After the solution was mixed, two litres of the mixture was poured off and again two litres of water was added. The solution was stirred again and two litres of the mixture was removed and two litres of water was added. As a result of the above operations, the volume of water in the vessel increased by three litres than the volume of spirit remaining in it. How many litres of spirit and water were there in the vessel after the above procedure was carried out?

(a) 0.7 litre of spirit and 3.7 litres of water
(b) 1.5 litres of spirit and 4.5 litres of water
(c) 8.5 litre of spirit and 11.5 litres of water
(d) 0.5 litre of spirit and 3.5 litres of water

24. There are two qualities of milk—Amul and Sudha having different prices per litre, their volumes being 130 litres and 180 litres, respectively. After equal amounts of milk was removed from both, the milk removed from Amul was added to Sudha and vice-versa. The resulting two types of milk now have the same price. Find the amount of milk drawn out from each type of milk.

(a) 58.66 (b) 75.48
(c) 81.23 (d) None of these

25. Assume that the rate of consumption of coal by a locomotive varies as the square of the speed and is 1000 kg per hour when the speed is 60 km per hour. If the coal costs the railway company ₹15 per 100 kg and if the other expenses of the train be ₹12 per hour, find a formula for the cost in paise per kilometre when the speed is S km per hour.

(a) $1200 + \frac{5S^2}{18}$ (b) $1200 + \frac{75S^2}{18}$

(c) $\frac{1200}{S} + \frac{75S^2}{18}$ (d) None of these

High Yield Questions

Scan to access assisted problem solving videos on questions 3, 4, 5, 9 and 24 from LOD 3

Space for Rough Work

ANSWER KEY

Level of Difficulty (I)

1. (d)	2. (a)	3. (b)	4. (b)
5. (d)	6. (b)	7. (b)	8. (c)
9. (b)	10. (c)	11. (b)	12. (c)
13. (b)	14. (c)	15. (b)	16. (c)
17. (c)	18. (a)	19. (b)	20. (c)
21. (d)	22. (b)	23. (d)	24. (b)
25. (c)	26. (a)	27. (b)	28. (d)
29. (a)	30. (c)	31. (b)	32. (d)
33. (b)	34. (b)	35. (b)	36. (b)
37. (c)	38. (a)	39. (b)	40. (d)
41. (d)	42. (c)	43. (c)	44. (a)
45. (b)	46. (b)	47. (d)	48. (b)
49. (d)	50. (c)		

Level of Difficulty (II)

1. (b)	2. (a)	3. (a)	4. (b)
5. (a)	6. (d)	7. (d)	8. (a)
9. (b)	10. (c)	11. (a)	12. (c)
13. (c)	14. (c)	15. (a)	16. (a)
17. (c)	18. (b)	19. (b)	20. (c)
21. (a)	22. (c)	23. (c)	24. (a)
25. (b)	26. (c)	27. (a)	28. (a)
29. (c)	30. (d)	31. (b)	32. (b)
33. (d)	34. (b)	35. (b)	36. (c)
37. (d)	38. (d)	39. (d)	40. (a)
41. (c)	42. (b)	43. (b)	44. (c)
45. (a)	46. 2850	47. 350	48. 8.28
49. 37:23	50. 20	51. 1.08	52. 69.33
53. 0.23	54. 0.67	55. 4.4	

Level of Difficulty (III)

1. (a)	2. (a)	3. (a)	4. (a)
5. (a)	6. (a)	7. (c)	8. (b)
9. (a)	10. (a)	11. (c)	12. (a)
13. (c)	14. (b)	15. (a)	16. (b)
17. (b)	18. (d)	19. (d)	20. (c)
21. (b)	22. (b)	23. (d)	24. (b)
25. (c)			

SOLUTIONS AND SHORTCUTS

Level of Difficulty (I)

1. Solve this question using options. 1/2 of the first part should be equal to 1/3rd of the second part and 1/6 of the third part. This means that the first part should be divisible by 2, the second one by 3, and the third one by 6. Looking at the options, none of the first three options has its third number divisible by 6. Thus, option (d) is correct.
2. $(A + B) = 3(C + D) \rightarrow A + B = 375$ and $C + D = 125$

   Also, since C gets 1.5 times D we have $C = 75$ and $D = 50$, and $B = 4$, $C = 300$.
3. The given condition has a, b and c symmetrically placed. Thus, if we use $a = b = c = 2$ (say) we get each fraction as 1/2.
4. Solve using options. Since $x > y > 0$, it is clear that a ratio of $x{:}y$ as 3:2 fits the equation.
5. $1 : 2 = 3 : 6$. So, $(a^2 + b^2)/(c^2 + d^2) = 5/45 = 1/9$

   From the given options, only ab/cd gives us this value.
6. If you try to solve this question through equations, the process becomes too long and almost inconclusive. The best way to approach this question is by trying to use options.

   The question asks us to find the time in which the boat can move downstream.

   The basic situation in this question is:

   Percentage increase over still water speed while going downstream = Percentage decrease over still water speed while going upstream.

   (Since: $S_{downstream} = S_{boat} + S_{stream}$ and $S_{upstream} = S_{boat} - S_{stream}$)

   Hence, the percentage increase in time while going upstream should match the percentage decrease in time while going downstream in such a way that the percentage change in the speed is same in both the cases.

   Testing for option (a):

   $Time_{upstream}$ = 84 minutes (given)

   $Time_{downstream}$ = 45 minutes (first value from the option)

   $Time_{stillwater}$ = 54 minutes (45 + 9)

   % increase in time when going upstream = 30/54

   (Note: The percentage increase should be written as 30 × 100/54. However, as I have repeatedly pointed out right from the chapter of percentages, you need to be able to look at % values of ratios directly by using the Percentage rule for calculations)

   % decrease in time when going downstream = 9/54 =16.66%

   Since, the % decrease is 16.66%, this should correspond to a % increase in speed by 20% (Since, product speed × time is constant).

   This means that the speed should drop by 20% while going upstream and hence the time should increase by 25% while going upstream. But, 30/54 does not give us a value of 25% increase. Hence, this option is incorrect.

   Testing for option (b):

   $Time_{upstream}$ = 84 minutes (given)

   $Time_{downstream}$ = 63 minutes (first value from the option)

   $Time_{stillwater}$ = 72 minutes (63 + 9)

   % increase in time when going upstream = 12/72 = 16.66%

   % decrease in time when going downstream = 9/72 =12.5%

Since, the % decrease is 12.5%, this should correspond to a % increase in speed by 14.28% (Since, product speed × time is constant).
This means that the speed should drop by 14.28% while going upstream and hence the time should increase by 16.66% while going upstream. This is actually occurring. Hence, this option is correct.
Options (c) and (d) can be seen to be incorrect in this context.

7. Experimentally if you were to take the value of a, b, c, and d as 1 : 2 : 4 : 8, you get the value of the expression as 3.5. If you try other values for a, b, c and d experimentally, you can see that while you can approach 3, you cannot get below that.
For instance,
1 : 1.1 : : 1.21 : 1.331
Gives us: – 0.331/–0.11 which is slightly greater than 3.
8. 4 × 8 × 5 = 160 man-hours are required for 'x' number of answer sheets. So, for '$2x$' answer sheets, we would require 320 man-hours = 2 × 20 × n → n = 8 hours a day.
9. Assume a set of values for a, b, c, d such that they are proportional, i.e. $a/b = c/d$. Suppose we take a:b as 1:4 and c:d as 3:12, we get the given expression: $(a - b)(a - c)/a = -3 \times -2/1 = 6$. This value is also given by $a + d - b - c$ and hence, option (b) is correct.
10. In 40 litres, milk = 32 and water = 8. We want to create 2 : 3 milk to water mixture, for this we would need: 32 milk and 48 water. (Since milk is not increasing). Thus, we need to add 40 litres of water.
11. Option (b) is not true.
12. 1 : 2 : 3 → x, $2x$ and $3x$ add up to 36.
So the numbers are: 6, 12 and 18.
Ratio of squares = 36 : 144 : 324.
13. The numbers would be $3x$ and $4x$ and their LCM would be $12x$. This gives us the values as 45 and 60. The first number is 45.
14. Since equal quantities are being mixed, assume that both alloys have 18 kg (18 being a number which is the LCM of 9 and 18).
The third alloy will get 14 kg of argentum from the first alloy and 7 kg of argentum from the second alloy. Hence, the required ratio: 21:15 = 7:5.
15. The total number of manhours required = 30 × 7 × 18 = 3780
21 × 8 × number of days → 3780/168 = 22.5 days
Note, you could have done this directly by: (30 × 7 × 18)/(21 × 8).
16. Solve using options. Option (c) fits the situation as if you take A's income as ₹6,000, B's income will become ₹4,000 and if they each save ₹1,000, their expenditures would be ₹5,000, ₹3,000 respectively. This gives the required 5: 3 ratio.
17. The given ratio for sines would only be true for a 45-45-90 triangle. The sides of such a triangle are in the ratio $1{:}1{:}\sqrt{2}$. The square of the longest side is 2 while the sum of the squares of the other two sides is also 2. Hence, the required ratio is 1:1.
18. Solve by options. Option (a) C = 480 fits perfectly because if C = 480, B = 120 and A = 80.
19. A's contribution = 33.33%
B's contribution = 50%
C's contribution = 16.66%
Ratio of profit sharing = Ratio of contribution
= 2 : 3 : 1
Thus, profit would be shared as : 28000 : 42000 : 14000.
20. $2x + 20 : 3x + 20 : 5x + 20 = 4 : 5 : 7 \rightarrow x = 10$ and initially the number of students would be 20, 30 and 50 → a total of 100.
21. The ratio of time would be such that speed × time would be constant for all three. Thus, if you take the speeds as $2x$, $3x$ and $4x$ respectively, the times would be $6y$, $4y$ and $3y$ respectively.
22. Again in order to solve this question, try to assume values for a, b, c and d such that $a{:}b = c{:}d$ (i.e. a, b, c and d are proportional). Let us say, we assume a = 1, b = 4, c = 3 and d = 12 we get:
$a^2 + c^2 = 10$ and $b^2 + d^2 = 160$. The mean proportional between 10 and 160 is 40. $ab + cd$ gives us this value and can be checked by taking another set of values to see that it still works.
23. Option (d) is true since $1/z$ will be greater than 1 and $\sqrt{z}$ would be less then 1.
24. Amar's share should be divisible by 6. Option (d) gets rejected by this logic.
Further: $A + B + C = 2250$. If Amar's share is 720, (according to option (a)) Bijoy's share should be 480 and Chandra's share should be 300. (Gives us a total of 720 + 480 + 300 = 1500).
But the required total is 2250 (50% more than 1500). Since all relationships are linear, 1500 will increase to 2250, if we increase all values by 50%. Hence, Amar's share should be 1080.
25. Trial and error would give us 2/5 as the original fraction.
26. Their ratio being 5:3, the difference according to the ratio is 2. But this difference is 10. To get the values, expand the ratio 5 times. This gives 25 and 15 as the required values. Hence, the product is 375.
27. 60 oxen days = 1/7 of the field → 420 oxen days are required to plough the field. Thus, the remaining work would be 360 oxen days. With 18 oxen, it would take 20 days.
28. Assume that 1 cat leap is equal to 3 metres and 1 dog leap is equal to 4 metres.
Then the speed of the cat in one unit time = 3 × 5 = 15 metres.

Also, the speed of the dog in one unit time = 4 × 4 = 16 metres.
The required ratio is 15 : 16.

29. $4x$ and $5x$ are their current ages. According to the problem, $4x - 18 : 5x - 18 = 11 : 16 \rightarrow x = 10$ and hence the sum total of their present ages is 90 years (40 + 50).
30. $x + 3x + 4x + 7x = 105 \rightarrow x = 7$
Thus, $7x = 49$.
31. The share of the rent is on the basis of the ratio of the number of cow months. *A* uses 330 cow months (110 × 3), *B* uses 660(110 × 6) and *C* uses 1320 cow months (440 × 3).
Hence, the required ratio is: 330:660:1320 = 1:2:4.
32. 10 × 8 = 80 man days is required for the job. If only 8 students turn up, they would require 10 days to complete the task. The number of days is increasing by 1/4.
33. The initial amount of water is 9 litres and milk is 27 litres. By adding 15 litres of milk, the mixture becomes 42 milk and 9 water → 14:3. the required ratio.
34. From the first statement $A = 1200$ and $B + C = 1800$. From the second statement $C = 1000$ and $A + B = 2000$.
35. $6x + 15 : 5x + 15 = 9 : 8$
$\rightarrow 45x + 135 = 48x + 120$
$3x = 15 \rightarrow x = 5$
Maya's present age = $6x$ = 30
36. Since pressure and volume are inversely proportional, we get that if one is reduced by 20% the other would grow by 25%. Option (b) is correct.
37. Solve using options.
For option (c), 68 girls. Hence, 82 boys
Amount with girls = 68 × 0.25 = 17
Amount with boys = 82 × 0.5 = 41.
Total of ₹58.
Thus, option (c) fits the conditions.
38. The ratio : 1/2 : 2/3 : 3/4
Converts to 6 : 8 : 9 (on multiplying by 12)
Thus, the first monkey would get (391/23) × 6 = 102 bananas.
39. Let the values of milk and water be $5x$ and x, respectively. Then when we add 5 litres of water to this mixture, water would become $x + 5$.
Now: $5x/(x + 5) = 5:2 \rightarrow x = 5$. Thus, $5x$ is 25.
40. The ratio of the values of the three coins are:
10 × 10 : 17 × 20 : 7 × 100 = 100:340:700
= 5:17:35 is the ratio of division of value of coins.
Thus, 20 paise coins correspond to ₹17. Hence, there will be 85 coins.
41. Ratio of number of coins = 12 : 10 : 7
Ratio of individual values of coins = 1 : 0.5 : 0.25
Ratio of gross value of coins = 12 : 5 : 1.75
= 48 : 20 : 7 → ₹75
Thus, he has ₹7 in 25 paisa coins which means that he would have 28 such coins.
42. Solve using options. 15/24 becomes 24/33 → 8/11
43. $\frac{27-11}{35-11}$ = 16/24 = 2/3.
Thus, option (c) is correct.
44. $x = k/(y^2-1)$. This gives $k = 24 \times 99 = 2376$.
The equation becomes $x = 2376/(24) = 99$.
45. $x = ky \rightarrow 18 = 7k \rightarrow k = 18/7$
Hence, $x = 18/7 \times y$
When $y = 21$, $x = 54$.
46. $A = K \times B \times C \rightarrow$ It is known that when $A = 6$, $B = 3$ and $C = 2$. Thus, we get $6 = 6K \rightarrow K = 1$.
Thus, our relationship between *A*, *B* and *C* becomes $A = B \times C$. Thus, when $B = 5$ and $C = 7$ we get $A = 35$.
47. $x = ky/z$
We cannot determine the value of *k* from the given information and hence, cannot answer the question.
48. Initial wine = 35 litres
Initial water = 14 litres
Since, we want to create 7 : 4 mixture of wine and water by adding only water, it means that the amount of wine is constant at 35 litres. Thus, 7 : 4 = 35 : 20. So, we need 6 litres of water.
49. If we were to draw out 4 litres of wine and substitute it with plain water, the ratio of wine to water would become 1:1. Hence, option (d) is correct.
50. The overall ratio is: 21:35:55. Dividing 333 in 111 parts (21 + 35 + 55), each part will be 3 and Class III will have the highest number of pupils → 55 × 3 = 165.

Level of Difficulty (II)

1. By taking the value of $p = 4$ from option (b), the required ratio of 1: 1 is achieved.
2. $T = KD/V$. Also $V = (K_1\sqrt{Q})/N$ where K and K_1 are constants, T is the time duration of the journey, Q is the quantity of coal used and N is the number of carriages.
Thus, $T = (KDN)/(K_1\sqrt{Q})$ or $T = (K_2DN)/(\sqrt{Q}) \rightarrow$ if we take K/K_1 as K_2.
From the information provided in the question: $30 = (K_2 \times 50 \times 18)/10 \rightarrow K_2 = 1/3$
Thus, the equation becomes: $T = (DN)/(3\sqrt{Q})$. Then, when $D = 42$, $T = 28$, and $N = 16$ we get:
$$28 = 42 \times 16/(3\sqrt{Q}) \rightarrow Q = 64$$
3. $3w/w = 16r_1^2/3r_2^2$
Thus, $r_1/r_2 = 3:4$
4. Suppose you take $p = 3$ and $q = 2$. It can be clearly seen that the square root of 2 does not lie between 2 and 3. Hence, option (c) is incorrect.

Further with these values for p and q, option (a) also can be ruled out since it means that the value should lie between 5 and 6 which it obviously does not. Also, option (d) gives 6/5 and 1/6. This means that the value should lie between 0.1666 and 1.2 (which it obviously does not). Hence, option (b) is correct.

5. Since there is a 12.5% increase in the wages, the cost of digging the pit would get increase by 12.5% - due to the increase in wages. However, since now the workers are working for 5% longer time, you can divide the increased wages by 1.05 to get the required answer. Thus, the answer would be: New cost = $2694 \times \frac{1.125}{1.05}$ = 2886 (approximately)

6. The constraint given to us for the values of p, q, and r is $r \times (p + q) = pq$.
So, if we take $p = 6$, $q = 3$ and $r = 2$, we have 18 = 18 and a feasible set of values for p, q and r respectively. With this set of values, we can complete the operation as defined and see what happens.
Wine left in the vessel A = 4 = (6 – 2)
Wine in the vessel B = 2
With these values, none of the first three options matches. Thus, option (d) is correct.

7. The only information available here is that – b/c should be equal to 3/1. This is not sufficient to make any of the first three options as conclusions. Hence, option (d) is correct.

8. Let the incomes be $4x$, $5x$, $6x$
And the spending be $6y$, $7y$, $8y$
And savings are $(4x – 6y)$, $(5x – 7y)$ and $(6x – 8y)$
Rahul saves 1/4th of his income.
Therefore, $4x – 6y = 4x/4$
$4x – 6y = x$
$3x = 6y$
$x/y = 2$
Therefore $y = x/2$
Ratio of Rahul's Saurav's and Sachin's savings
$= 4x – 6y : 5x – 7y : 6x – 8y$
$= x: 5x – 7y: 6x – 8y$
$= x: 5x – 7x/2: 6x – 8x/2$
$= x: 3x/2: 2x$
$= 2:3:4$

9. Solve by taking values of a, b, c, d and e, f, g, and h independently of each other
$a = 1$, $b = 2$, $c = 3$, $d = 6$
and $e = 3$, $f = 9$, $g = 4$
and $h = 12$
gives $(ae + bf) : (ae – bf) = 21: – 15 = – 7/5$
Option (b) $(cg + dh)/(cg – dh) = 84/ – 60 = – 7/5$.
This would be the answer, since no other option gives us the same value.

10. Since X has 0% C and Y has 16% C, the ratio of mixing in the fused mass must be 3:5. Using alligation as follows:

10		6
0% C	10% C	16% C
X	Fused mass	Y

Hence, 6:10 or 3:5

Then, percentage of A in X can be got as follows:

x	74	80
X	Fused mass	Y
3		5

x = 64%

Required ratio = 64:(100 – 64) = 64: 36 = 16:9

11. Speed = $36 – k\sqrt{N}$.
Putting value of $N = 4$ we get:
$24 = 36 – 2k$. Hence, $k = 6$.
Thus, the equation is: $S = 36 – 6\sqrt{N}$
This means that when $N = 36$, the speed will become zero. Hence, the train can just move when 35 wagons are attached.

12. p varies as $q \rightarrow p = kq$
$p^2 + q^2 = k^2q^2 + q^2 = q^2(k^2 + 1)$ (1)
Also, $p^2 – q^2 = q^2(k^2 – 1)$ (2)
Thus, we have
$$p^2 + q^2 = (p^2 - q^2)\times\frac{k^2+1}{k^2-1} \rightarrow (p^2 - q^2) \times Constant$$
Hence, option (c) is correct.

13. Let $x = 5$
Then $y = f(x) = 6/4 = 1.5$
And $f(y) = 2.5/0.5 = 5$.
Thus, the ratio of $x : f(y) = 1 : 1$
(Note: Even if you take some other value of y, you would still get the same answer.)

14. In 2000 man-weeks before the calamity, 5/6th of the work is completed. Hence, 2400 man-weeks will be the total amount of work. However, due to the calamity half the work gets washed off → This means that 1000 man-weeks worth of work must have got washed off. This leaves 1400 man-weeks of work to be completed by the 140 men. They will take 10 more weeks and hence the total time required is 24 weeks.

15. Total distances covered under each mode = 32, 4 and 12 km respectively.
Total charges = 32 × 24 + 4 × 3 + 12 × 12 = ₹924.

16. Let the number of coins of ₹1, 50 p, 25 p be A, B and C respectively.
$A + B + C = 220$ (1)
$A = 3C$ (2)
$A + 0.5B + 0.25C = 160$ (3)
We have a situation with three equations and three unknowns. We can solve for

A (number of 1 rupee coins),
B (number of 50 paise coins),
and *C* (number of 25 paise coins)
However, a much smarter approach would be to go through the options. If we check option (a) – number of 50 paise coins = 60 we would get the number of 1 rupee coins as 120 and the number of 25 paise coins as 40.

$120 \times 1 + 60 \times 0.5 + 40 \times 0.25 = 160$

This fits the conditions perfectly and is hence the correct answer.

Solutions for Questions 17 to 19:

In order to solve this question, if you try going through equation and expressions, it would lead you in to a very long drawn solution.

Thus: $12/2x + 24/6x + 5/x = n/60$

and $12/3y + 24/8y + 5/y = n + 20/60$

We also know that $3y = 2x$.

In order to handle this expression, you can try be substituting the values of the speeds. Also, we know that his running speed (initially) is twice his swimming speed.

Question 17 is asking us his swimming speed, while 19 is asking us his running speed. So the answer of the two questions should be in the ratio 1 : 2.

However, a scrutiny of the options shows us that only the third option (values) in question 17 has a value which is half the values provided for in 19. [you would need to check for this after converting the values into kmph – you would see that for 18 kmph in question 19, you have a corresponding swimming speed of 9 kmph in question 17's option (c)].

So, we can start by checking the option (b) from question 19.

Checking for it we have:

Scenario 1:12/18 + 24/54 + 5/9 = 40 minutes + 1 hour = 1 hour 40 minutes.

Scenario 2:12/18 + 24/48 + 5/6 = 40 minutes + 30 minutes + 50 minutes = 2 hours.

This matches the condition of 20 minutes extra, and hence is the correct answer pair. His running speed is 18 kmph and swimming speed is 9 kmph or 0.15 km/minute.

Answers are:

17. (c)
18. (b) $(12/18 + 24/54 + 5/18 = \dfrac{36+24+15}{54} = \dfrac{75}{54}$ hours
    = 83.33 minutes. (**Note:** Here we took the running speed as 18 kmph because that was the answer for the speed of running that we got when we solved question 19 and question 17 as a pair.)
19. (b)
20. $(20 + 60 + 30P)/(2 + 3 + P) = 23 \rightarrow 80 + 30P = 115 + 23P$ or $P = 5$
21. Assume raw materials cost as 150 and total cost as 450. (Thus, wages cost is 300).
    Since, the cost of raw materials goes up in the ratio of 3:7, the new raw material cost would become 350 and the new wages cost would become in the ratio 4:9 as 675.
    The new cost would become 1025.
    Since 450 becomes 1025 (change in total cost), unitary method calculation would give us that 18 would become ₹41.
22. Solve using options. For option (c), we will get that initially there are 125 boys and 140 girls. After the given increases, the number of boys would be 145 and the number of girls would become 154 which gives a difference of 9 as required.
23. From the question, it is evident that after leaving out the *C* courses, Sonali's GPA goes to 3.33. This means that the number of subjects, she must have had after leaving out the *C*'s must be a multiple of 3. This only occurs in option (c). Hence, that is the answer.
24. When there are 25 boarders, the total expenses are \$1750. When there are 50 boarders, the total expenses are \$ 3000. The change in expense due to the coming in of 25 boarders is \$ 1250. Hence, expense per boarder is equal to \$50. This also means that when there are 25 boarders, the variable cost would be 25 × 50 = \$1250. Hence, \$500 must be the fixed expenses.
    So for 100 boarders, the total cost would be: \$ 500 (fixed) + \$ 5000 = \$5500
25. $S = 42 - k\sqrt{n}$
    $$24 = 42 - k \times 3 \rightarrow k = 6$$
    So, $S = 42 - 6\sqrt{n}$
    For 49 compartments, the train would not move. Hence, it would move for 48 compartments.

Solutions for Questions 26 to 28:

Let the third drunkard get in *x* litres. Then the second will contribute $x + 1$ and the first will contribute $x + 2$ litres. Thus, in all they have $3x + 3$ litres of the drink. Using option (a) in question 27, this value is 12, giving *x* as 3.

Also, each drunkard will drink 3 litres.

Thus, the first drunkard brings 5 litres and the second 4 litres. Their contribution to the fourth drunkard will be in the ratio 2:1 and hence their share of money would be also in the ratio 2:1. Hence, this option is correct for question 27.

Hence, for question 26, the second drunkard will get 5 roubles (for his contribution of 1 litre to the fourth) and for question 28, the answer would be 1:3.

29. $5 : 4 \rightarrow 5 : 4.8 \rightarrow 25 : 24$.
    Option (c) is correct.

30. $P = K \times W^2 \rightarrow 12250 = K \times 35^2 \rightarrow K = 10$.
Thus, our price and weight relationship is: $P = 10W^2$.
When the two pieces are in the ratio 2:5 (weight-wise) then we know that their weights must be 10 grams and 25 grams, respectively. Their values would be:
10 gram piece: 10×10^2 = ₹1000;
25 gram piece: 10×25^2 = ₹6250.
Total price = 1000 + 62450 = 7250. From an initial value of 12250, this represents a loss of ₹5000.

31. The ratio of distribution should be:
$21 \times 35 : 15 \times 35 : 15 \times 21 \rightarrow 147 : 105:63 \rightarrow 7:5:3$
The biggest share will be worth: $7 \times 525000/15$ = 245000.

32. $P + M + T = 675 \rightarrow 3M + M + 3M - 25 = 675 \rightarrow 7M = 700$. Hence, $M = 100$, $P = 300$ and $T = 275$.

33. Ratio of distribution = 20 : 13 : 8
So the elephant should get $(20/41) \times 820 = 400$.

34. Women : Men = 3 : 4
Men : Children = 3 : 5
$\rightarrow$ Women : Men : children = 9 : 12 : 20
In the ratio, $9 \rightarrow 531$ women
Thus, $20 \rightarrow 1180$ children.

35. 2/3 becomes 7/8, change from 0.666 to 0.875 while the other changes are smaller than this. For instance, 4/7 becomes 9/12, a change from 0.5714 to 0.75 which is smaller than the change in 2/3. Similarly, the other options can be checked and rejected.

36. Since, the work gets done in 25% less time there must have been an addition of 33.33% men.
This would mean 13.33 men extra $\rightarrow$ which would mean 14 extra men (in whole numbers).

37. From the given options, we just need to look for a multiple of 7. 2100 is the only option which is a multiple of 7 and is hence, the correct answer.

38. This is a simple question if you can catch hold of the logic of the question, i.e., the younger daughter's share must be such after adding a CI of 20% for two years, she should get the same value as her elder sister.
None of the options meets this requirement. Hence, none of these is correct.

Solutions for Questions 39 to 41:

You should realise that when Anshu gives her pens to Bobby and Chandana, the number of pens for both Bobby and Chandana should double. Also, the number of pens for Anshu and Bobby should also double when Chandana gives off her pens. Further the final condition is that each of them has 24 pens. The following table will emerge on the basis of this logic.

	Anshu	*Bobby*	*Chandana*
Final	24	24	24
Second round	12	12	48
Initial	42	6	24

42. $V = k\,AH \rightarrow 280 = k \times 60 \times 14 \rightarrow 280 = 840k$.
Thus, $k = 1/3$ and the equation becomes:
$V = AH/3$ and $390 = 26A/3 \rightarrow A = 45$.

43. Expenses for 120 boys = 8400
Expenses for 150 boys = 10000
Thus, variable expenses are ₹1600 for 30 boys.
If we add 180 more boys to make it 330 boys, we will get an additional expense of 1600×6 = ₹9600.
Total expenses are ₹19600.

44. Let the distance be d. Then, $d/14.4 = \sqrt{8}/\sqrt{18} \rightarrow d = 9.6$

45. 47 : 100: 220 would give: 0.5 cubic feet of Cement, 1 cubic feet of sand and 2 cubic feet of gravel. Required ratio 1 : 2 : 4 is satisfied.

46. If new values of x, y, z are x', y' and z', and respectively then $x': y' = 4:5$, $y': z' = 3:4$
$x': y': z' = 12:15:20$
$x + y + z = 5000$
$x' + 50 + y' + 100 + z' + 150 = 5000$
$x' + y' + z' = 4700$
$12k + 15k + 20k = 4700$
$k = 100$
$x = 1200 + 50 = 1250$
$y = 1500 + 100 = 1600$
$z = 2000 + 150 = 2150$
$x + y = 1250 + 1600 = 2850$

47. $\dfrac{x-a}{y-2.4a} = 1$
$x - a = y - 2.4a$
$x - y = -1.4a$
$1.4a = y - x = 1600 - 1250 = 350$. Hence:
$a = \dfrac{350}{14} = 250$
The required value of $|a - b|$ would be given by $|250 - 2.4 \times 250| = 350$

48. Quantity of x in the container of 100 litres = 40 litres.
Quantity of y in the container of 100 litres = 60 litres.
Quantity of milk in final mixture = $100 \times \dfrac{3}{4} = 75$ litres.
Quantity of water in final mixture = 100 − 75 = 25 litres.
Quantity of milk and water in 40 litres of the mixture
$x = 40 \times \dfrac{2}{3}, 40 \times \dfrac{1}{3} = \dfrac{80}{3}, \dfrac{40}{3}$ (in litres)
Quantity of milk and water in 60 litres of mixture
$y = \dfrac{60 \times a}{(a+2)}, \dfrac{60 \times 2}{(a+2)} = \dfrac{60 \times a}{(a+2)}, \dfrac{120}{(a+2)}$

$\frac{80}{3}+\frac{60a}{a+2}=75$

$\frac{60a}{a+2}=\frac{225-80}{3}=\frac{145}{3}$

$180a = 145a + 290$

$\rightarrow a=\frac{290}{35}=8.28$

49. In container x, is actually a mixture of milk and water in the ratio 1 : 2.
Thus, the quantity of milk in 40 litres of the mixture x would be = $\frac{40}{3}$ litres.
Therefore, in the final mixture, the quantity of milk will get reduced by $\frac{40}{3}$ litres and quantity of water will be increased by $\frac{40}{3}$ litres. This would mean that the required ratios would be:

$$\frac{75-\frac{40}{3}}{25+\frac{40}{3}}=\frac{185}{115}=\frac{37}{23}$$

Solutions for Questions 50 to 52:

Let the temperatures of Delhi and Lucknow in July be $3x$ and $5x$, respectively.
Let the temperatures of Delhi and Lucknow in August be $2y$ and $3y$, respectively.
It is given to us that (the ratio of the sum of the temperatures of these two cities in August and July was 5: 4) which essentially means that:

$\frac{5y}{8x}=\frac{5}{4}$

i.e. $y = 2x \rightarrow$ Temperature in Delhi and Lucknow in August would be $4x$ and $6x$, respectively.

50. The percentage increase in temperature of Lucknow from July to August = $\frac{3\times 2x-5x}{5x}\times 100=20\%$.

51. The percentage increase in temperature of Delhi from July to August= $\frac{4x-3x}{3x}\times 100=33.33\%$.
Hence, the percentage increase in temperature of Delhi from August to September = 2 × 33.33% = 66.66%.
Temperature of Lucknow in September = $3y\left(1+\frac{20}{100}\right)=3.6y$
Temperature of Delhi in September = $2y\left(1+\frac{66.66}{100}\right)=\frac{10y}{3}$

Required ratio = $\frac{3.6y}{\frac{10}{3}y}=\frac{10.8}{10}=1.08$

52. $2y = 20°C$
$y = 10°C$
Required sum (x) = $3.6y+\frac{10}{3}y$
= 36 + 33.33
= 69.33°C

53. In 2007, total number of shares = $650+650\times\frac{3}{13}$
= 800
In 2008, total number of shares = $800+800\times\frac{2}{4}$
= 1200.
The dividend being 12.5%, he would get ₹1.25 per share as the dividend (calculated as 12.5% of the face value of the share). Hence, his total dividend in 2009, would be ₹1500. Also, his total initial investment is ₹6500 (650 shares at ₹10 per share).
Hence, the required ratio = 1500/6500 = 3/13 = 0.23

$$\frac{\text{Dividend}}{\text{Initial investment}}=\frac{12.5}{100}\times\frac{1200}{650}$$
$$=0.23$$

54. Quantity of metal 1 in mixture = $14\times\frac{3}{7}+26\times\frac{5}{13}$
=16 kg.
$\therefore$ Required ratio $=\frac{16}{40-16}=\frac{16}{24}=0.67$

55. Price of all four varieties =10 ₹/litre, 5 ₹/litre.
$\frac{10}{3}$ ₹/litre, $\frac{10}{4}$ ₹/litre.
Let the cost price of mixture be X then using the concept of weighted averages, we get that:

$$X=\frac{1}{(1+2+3+4)}\left(10\times 1+5\times 2+\frac{10}{3}\times 3+\frac{10}{4}\times 4\right)=\frac{40}{10}.$$

$\rightarrow X = 4$ ₹/litre.
Hence, the selling price to make a 10% profit would need an increment of 10% on ₹4 per litre. Thus, the required selling price would be ₹4.4 per litre.

Level of Difficulty (III)

1. You can use alligation between 33.33% and 40% to get 37.5%. Hence, the ratio of mixing would be 2.5:4.16 → 3:5.
6. Check each of the options as follows:
Suppose you are checking option (b) which gives the value of a as 81 litres.
Then, it is clear that when you are pouring out 81 litres, you are leaving 8/9 of the honey in the barrel.
Thus, the amount of honey contained after 6 such operations will be given by:
$729 \times (8/9)^6$. If this answer has to be correct, this value must be equal to 64 (which it clearly is not since the value will be in the form of a fraction).
Hence, this is not the correct option. You can similarly rule-out the other options.
7. It is clear that if 7 kg of the first is mixed with 21 kg of the second, you will get 5 + 9 = 14 kg of

nickel and 14 kg of tin. You do not need to check the other options, since they will go into fractions.

10. The piece that is cut off should be such that the fraction of the first to the second alloy in each of the two new alloys formed should be equal.
    If you cut off 4 kg, the respective ratios will be:
    First alloy: 2 kg of first alloy and 4 kg of second alloy
    Second alloy: 4 kg of first alloy and 8 kg of the second alloy. It can easily be seen that the ratios are equal to 1:2 in each case.
13. This is again the typical alligation situation.
    The required ratio will be given by (7/18 – 3/8) : (2/5 – 7/18)
    Alternately, you can also look at it through options. It can be easily seen that if you take 8 kg of the first with 10 kg of the second, you will get the required 7:11 ratio.
17. The cost of making one gram of gun powder would be ₹180. This will contain 0.4 g of saltpetre and 0.6 g of nitrous oxide. Check through options.
    At the rate of saltpetre of 300/g, the nitrous oxide will cost ₹100/g. The total cost of 0.4 grams of saltpetre will be 120 and 0.6 grams of nitrous oxide will be ₹60 giving the total cost as 180.
20. There will be a total of 4.5 litres of milk (25% of 3 + 75% of 5) giving a total of 4.5. Hence, 45%.
23. Go through the options as follows:
    According to option (d), if the initial quantity of spirit is 4 litres, half the spirit is taken out when 2 litres are drawn out. Thus the spirit after three times of the operation would be:
    $4 \times (1/2)^2 = 0.5$ litres. This matches with the option.
    You can check for yourself that the first three options will not work.

CHAPTER 6

Alligations and Mixtures

Chapter Launchpad

Scan this QR code to access a video on 'Introduction to Alligations and Mixtures' and this chapter's importance for CAT

INTRODUCTION

In the chapter of Averages, we have seen in detail about the situation of averages and weighted averages. To recollect, whenever one faces situation where one needs to find the average of a few groups of readings, the simple average formula no longer works. In such situations, we move to dealing with the situation using the approach of weighted averages.

However, before we move there, I am sure you are wondering why I am talking about weighted averages in the introduction of the chapter on Alligations. Well, as you are about to see, Alligations is nothing but a smarter and visual way of solving weighted average questions (and dealing with weighted average situations), when two groups are involved. We will be eventually moving to discussing those situations, but to start off, let us first recollect what weighted averages was.

To recollect, the weighted average is used when a number of smaller groups are mixed together to form one larger group.

If the average of the measured quantity was

A_1 for group	1	containing	n_1	elements
A_2 for group	2	containing	n_2	elements
A_3 for group	3	containing	n_3	elements
A_k for group	k	containing	n_k	elements

We say that the weighted average, Aw is given by:

$Aw = (n_1A_1 + n_2 A_2 + n_3 A_3 + \ldots\ldots + n_kA_k)/ (n_1 + n_2 + n_3 \ldots + n_k)$

That is, the weighted average

$$= \frac{\text{Sum total of all groups}}{\text{Total number of elements in all groups together}}$$

In this formula, we have also seen in the theory of the averages chapter, that we do not specifically require to use the values of n_1, n_2, etc. But we actually just need to use the ratios of the values of n_1, n_2 etc. Thus, if you purchase 12kg of rice @ ₹40/kg and 18kgs of rice @ ₹70/kg, we can calculate the average price, by assuming that you have purchased only 2kg @ ₹40/kg and 3kg @ ₹70/kg and the required answer would be obtained by using: $\frac{2\times40+3\times70}{5}$ = ₹58/kg, rather than doing: $\frac{12\times40+18\times70}{5}$ = ₹58/kg.

Let us now move to understand how the same situation can also be handled using Alligations (since in this situation, we are dealing with weighted average of two groups).

THEORY

In the case of the situation where just two groups are being mixed, we can write the weighted average formula as:

$$Aw = (n_1A_1 + n_2 A_2)/(n_1 + n_2)$$

Rewriting this equation we get: $(n_1 + n_2) Aw = n_1A_1 + n_2A_2$

$$n_1(Aw - A_1) = n_2 (A_2 - Aw)$$

or $n_1/n_2 = (A_2 - Aw)/(Aw - A_1) \rightarrow$ the alligation equation.

This equation can be read in language and logical terms as: The difference between A_2 and A_w is proportional to n_1 (the weight on A_1) and the difference between A_w and A_1 is proportional to n_2 (the weight on A_2). In other words, there is a cross proportionality between the difference of the averages and the weights on the individual averages.

Alligation Situation: Consider the Following Situations:

Two groups of elements are mixed together to form a third group containing the elements of both the groups.

If the average of the first group is A_1 and the number of elements is n_1 and the average of the second group is A_2 and the number of elements is n_2, then to find the average of the new group formed, we can use either the weighted average equation or the alligation equation.

As a convenient convention, we take $A_1 < A_2$. Then, by the principal of averages, we get $A_1 < Aw < A_2$.

Illustration 1

Weighted Average is Unknown:

Two varieties of rice at ₹10 per kg and ₹12 per kg are mixed together in the ratio 1 : 2. Find the average price of the resulting mixture.

Solution using Alligation: $1/2 = (12 - A_w)/(A_w - 10) \rightarrow$
$A_w - 10 = 24 - 2A_w$

$\Rightarrow 3Aw = 34 \qquad \Rightarrow Aw =$ ₹11.33/kg.

Solution using weighted averages:

$\frac{1\times10+2\times12}{3}$ = ₹11.33/kg.

Illustration 2

Ratio of the Weights is Unknown:

On combining two groups of students having 30 and 40 marks respectively in an exam, the resultant group has an average score of 34. Find the ratio of the number of students in the first group to the number of students in the second group.

Solution using alligations $n_1/n_2 = (40 - 34)/(34 - 30) = 6/4 = 3/2$

Note: In this situation, though you can still solve this using the weighted averages approach, as you can yourself imagine, it would take quite a bit of writing and time to get to the same answer.

Thus, the solution would start with: $\dfrac{n_1 \times 30 + n_2 \times 40}{n_1 + n_2} = 34$.

After a few transformations, you would be able to identify the ratio of n_1/n_2.

Illustration 3

Average of One of the Smaller Groups is Unknown:

In a class containing girls and boys in the ratio 2:3, during a test, the girls scored 40 marks on average, while the overall average of the class was 52 marks. How much did the boys score on average?

Solution using alligations: $n_1/n_2 = 2/3 = (x - 52)/(52 - 40) \rightarrow$ On solving, we get $x = 60$.

Solution using weighted averages: $\dfrac{2 \times 40 + 3 \times x}{5} = 52$ $\rightarrow x = 60$.

As you can see for yourself, each of the alligation situations illustrated above can be solved using the weighted average formula. So, why does one need to equip oneself with the alligations thought? Well the answer to that will emerge out of the following discussion – where we are discussing the graphical methods to solve each of the above situations using a graphical (or visual) approach to viewing the alligation equation that we have derived above. There are essentially two methods to think visually about the components of the alligation equation. These are:

(i) the cross method and
(ii) The straight line method (or the number line method).

Graphical Representation of Alligation

The formula illustrated above can be represented by the following cross diagram:

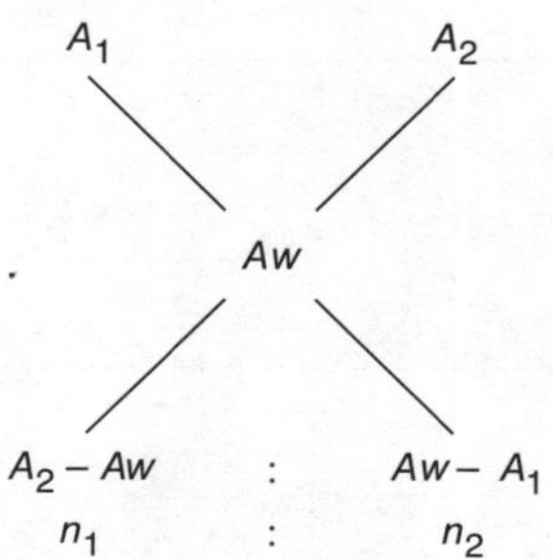

Note: The cross method yields nothing but the alligation equation. Hence, the cross method is nothing but a graphical representation of the alligation equation.

As we have seen, there are five variables embedded inside the alligation equation. These being:

the three averages $\rightarrow A_1$, A_2 and Aw
and the two weights $\rightarrow n_1$ and n_2

Based on the problem situation, one of the following cases may occur with respect to the knowns and the unknown in the problem.

Case	*Known*	*Unknown*
1	A_1, A_2, n_1, n_2	Aw
2	A_1, A_2, Aw	$n_1 : n_2$
3	A_1, Aw, n_1, n_2	A_2 (**Note:** In this situation, you could also know A_2 and need to find A_1.)

Now, let us try to evaluate the effectiveness of the cross method for each of the three cases illustrated above:

Case 1: A_1, A_2, n_1 and n_2 are known, Aw is in known.

Illustration 4

Four kg of rice at ₹5 per kg is mixed with 8kg of rice at ₹6 per kg. Find the average price of the mixture.

Solution

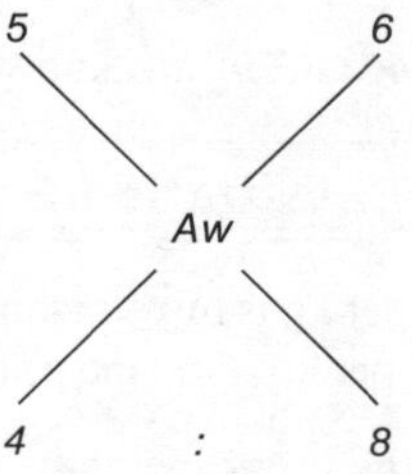

$$= (6 - Aw) : (Aw - 5)$$

$$\Rightarrow \quad (6 - Aw)/(Aw - 5) = 4/8 \rightarrow 12 - 2\,Aw = Aw - 5$$

$$3\,Aw = 17$$

$$\therefore \quad Aw = 5.66 \text{ ₹/kg}$$

Task for students: Solve through the alligation formula approach and through the weighted average approach to get the solution. Notice, the amount of time required in doing the same.

Note: The cross method becomes quite cumbersome in this case, as this method results in the formula being written. Hence, there seems to be no logic in using the cross method in this case.

Case 2: A_1, A_2, Aw are known; may be one of n_1 and n_2 is unknown.

To find: $n_1 : n_2$ and n_2 if n_1 is known OR n_1 if n_2 is known.

Let us illustrate through an example:

Illustration 5

On mixing two classes of students having average marks 25 and 40 respectively, the overall average obtained is 30 marks. Find

(a) The ratio of students in the classes

(b) The number of students in the first class if the second class had 30 students.

Solution

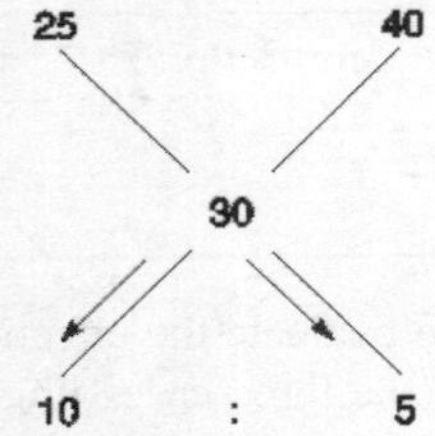

(a) Hence, solution is 2 : 1.

(b) If the ratio is 2 : 1 and the second class has 30 students, then the first class has 60 students.

Note: The cross method becomes pretty effective in this situation when all the three averages are known and the ratio is to be found out.

Case 3: A_1, Aw, n_1 and n_2 are known; A_2 is unknown.

Illustration 6

Five kg of rice at ₹6 per kg is mixed with four kg of rice to get a mixture costing ₹7 per kg. Find the price of the costlier rice.

Solution: Using the cross method:

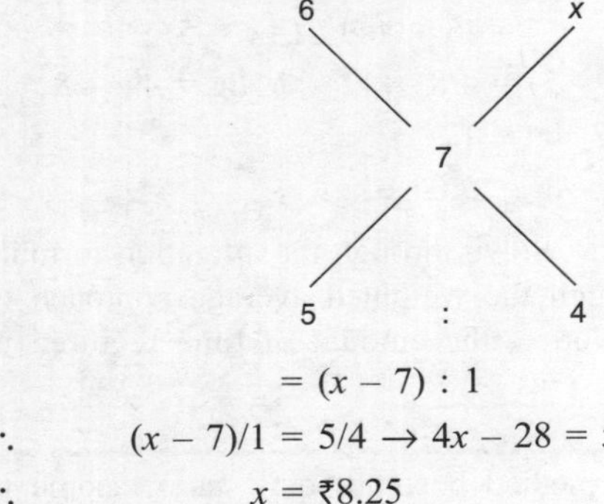

$= (x - 7) : 1$

$\therefore \quad (x - 7)/1 = 5/4 \rightarrow 4x - 28 = 5$

$\therefore \quad x = ₹8.25$

Task for student: Solve through the alligation formula approach and through the weighted average approach to get the solution. Notice the amount of time required in doing the same.

Note: The cross method becomes quite cumbersome in this case since this method results in the formula being written. Hence, there seems to be no logic in using the cross method in this case.

However, if we look at the straight line method or the number line method, we will see that the question and its' solution becomes visually solvable with little or no writing:

Straight Line Method (or the number line method)

As we have seen, the cross method becomes quite cumbersome in **Case 1 and 3**. We will now proceed to modify the cross method so that the question can be solved graphically in all the three cases.

Consider the following diagram, which results from closing the cross like a pair of scissors. Then the positions of A_1, A_2, Aw, n_1 and n_2 are as shown.

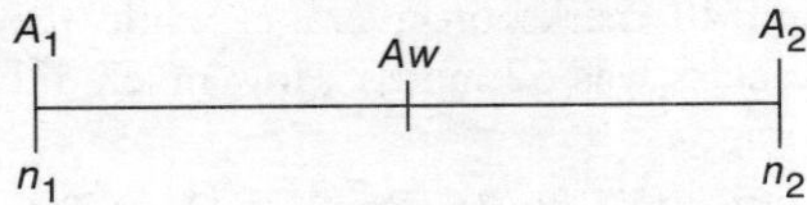

Visualise this as a fragment of the number line with points A_1, Aw and A_2 in that order from left to right. Then,

(a) n_2 is responsible for the distance between A_1 and Aw or n_2 corresponds to $Aw - A_1$

(b) n_1 is responsible for the distance between Aw and A_2 or n_1 corresponds to $A_2 - Aw$

(c) $(n_1 + n_2)$ is responsible for the distance between A_1 and A_2 or $(n_1 + n_2)$ corresponds to $A_2 - A_1$

The processes for the three cases illustrated above can then be illustrated below:

Case 1: A_1, A_2, n_1 and n_2 are known; Aw is unknown.

Illustration 7

Four kg of rice at ₹5 per kg is mixed with eight kg of rice at ₹6 per kg. Find the average price of the mixture.

Solution

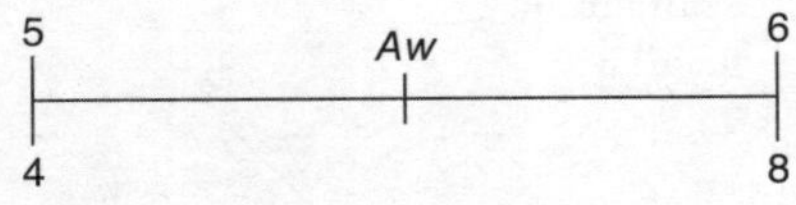

is the same as

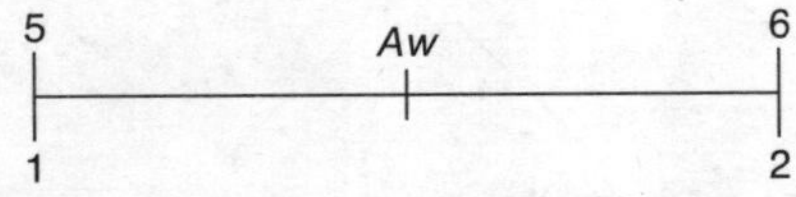

Then, by unitary method:

$n_1 + n_2$ corresponds to $A_2 - A_1$
$\rightarrow 1 + 2$ corresponds to $6 - 5$

That is, 3 corresponds to 1
$\therefore$ 2 will correspond to 0.66.
Hence, the required answer is 5 + 0.66 = 5.66.

Note: In this case, the problem associated with the cross method is overcome and the solution becomes graphical.

Illustration 8

On mixing two classes of students having average marks 25 and 40 respectively, the overall average obtained is 30 marks. Find

(a) the ratio in which the classes were mixed
(b) the number of students in the first class if the second class had 30 students

Solution

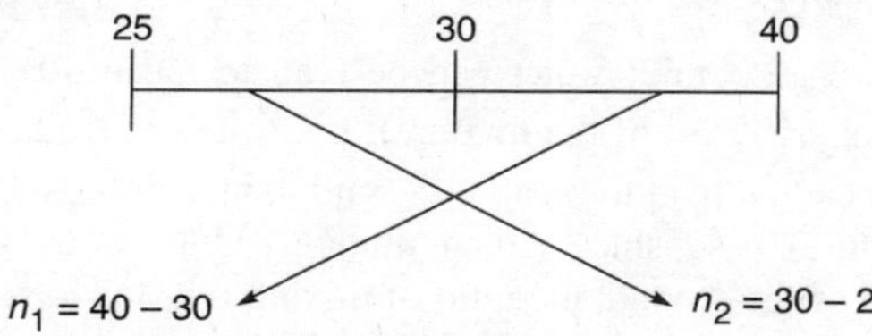

Hence, ratio is 2 : 1, and the second class has 60 students (if the first class has 30).

Case 3: A_1, Aw, n_1 and n_2 are known; A_2 is unknown.

Illustration 9

Five kg of rice at ₹6 per kg is mixed with four kg of rice to get a mixture costing ₹7 per kg. Find the price of the costlier rice.

Using straight line method:

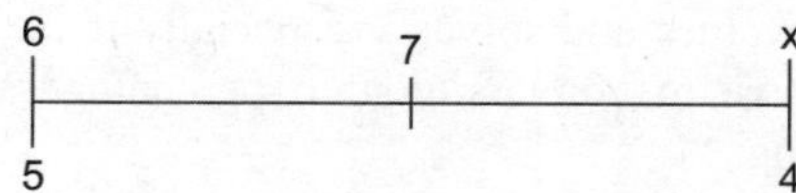

4 corresponds to 7 – 6 and 5 corresponds to $x - 7$.

The thought process should go like:

$4 \rightarrow 1$
$\therefore$ $5 \rightarrow 1.25$
Hence, $x - 7 = 1.25$
and $x = 8.25$

SOME TYPICAL SITUATIONS WHERE ALLIGATIONS CAN BE USED

Given below are typical alligation situations, which students should be able to recognise. This will help them improve upon the time required in solving questions. Although in this chapter, we have illustrated problems based on alligation at level 1 only. Alligation is used in more complex problems where the weighted average is an intermediate step in the solution process.

The following situations should help the student identify alligation problems better as well as spot the way A_1, A_2, n_1 and n_2 and Aw are mentioned in a problem.

In each of the following problems, the following magnitudes represent these variables:

$A_1 = 20, \quad A_2 = 30, \quad n_1 = 40, \quad n_2 = 60$

Each of these problems will yield an answer of 26 as the value of Aw.

1. A man buys 40kg of rice at ₹20/kg and 60kg of rice at ₹30/kg. Find his average price. (26/kg)
2. Pradeep mixes two mixtures of milk and water. He mixes 40 litres of the first containing 20% water and 60 litres of the second containing 30% water. Find the percentage of water in the final mixture. (26%)
3. Two classes are combined to form a larger class. The first class having 40 students scored an average of 20 marks on a test while the second having 60 students scored an average of 30 marks on the same test. What was the average score of the combined class on the test? (26 marks)
4. A trader earns a profit of 20% on 40% of his goods sold, while he earns a profit of 30% on 60% of his goods sold. Find his percentage profit on the whole. (26%)
5. A car travels at 20 km/h for 40 minutes and at 30 km/h for 60 minutes. Find the average speed of the car for the journey. (26 km/hr)
6. Forty percent of the revenues of a school came from the junior classes while 60% of the revenues of the school came from the senior classes. If the school raises its fees by 20% for the junior classes and by 30% for the senior classes, find the percentage increase in the revenues of the school. (26%)
7. A man sells a chair and a table at a profit of 20% and 30% respectively. If the ratio of the cost price of the table and the chair is 2:3, then what is the percentage profit for the man in the overall transaction? (26%)

Some keys to spot A_1, A_2 and Aw and differentiate these from n_1 and n_2

1. Normally, there are 3 averages mentioned in the problem, while there are only 2 quantities. This is not foolproof though, since at times the question might confuse the student by giving 3 values for quantities representing n_1, n_2 and $n_1 + n_2$ respectively.
2. A_1, A_2 and Aw are always rate units, while n_1 and n_2 are quantity units.
3. The denominator of the average unit corresponds to the quantity unit (i.e. unit for n_1 and n_2).
4. All percentage values represent the average values.

Can Alligations be Applied to Three Groups:

By definition, alligations is only applicable to two groups. However, in order to deal with the three group situation, we can use alligation twice – first to merge two groups into one larger group; then merging this larger group with the third group to get the answer for the entire problem. This process can be understood by considering the following situation;

In a test, 30 students of Section 1, scored an average of 42 marks, while 20 students of Section 2 scored an average of 52 marks. Also, 100 students of Section 3, scored an average of score of 76 marks. What is the average score of all three sections taken together?

In this situation, the first step can be to find the average score of Sections 1 and 2. Using alligation, you should be able to work out that the average score of a total of 50 students of sections 1 and 2 would be 46 marks (average of 42 and 52 in the ratio 3:2). Now, we have reached a situation in the problem where we have this combined group of 50 students with an average of 46 and we have 100 students of section 3, with an average score of 76 marks. Applying alligation again, on these two averages (46 and 76) in the ratio of 50:100, i.e. 1:2 (for the number of students), we would get the final average of 66.

This would appear as follows: First alligation between Sections 1 and 2:

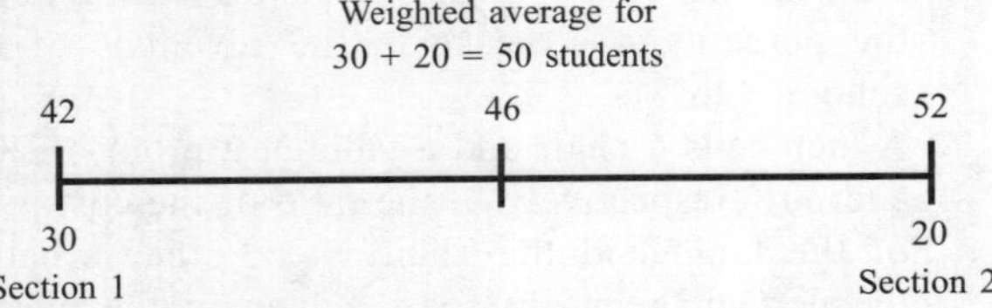

Second alligation between the combined sections 1 and 2, with section 3:

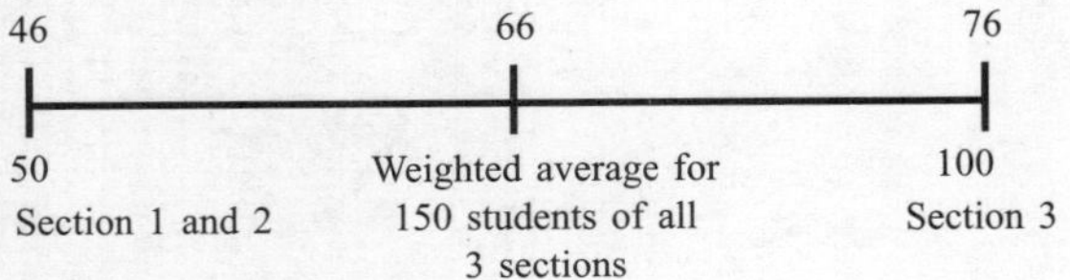

Application of Alligations to Questions Based on Mixtures:

Questions based on mixtures is one of the favorite question types of the CAT and all other aptitude exams. Alligation also provides us a view into how to solve questions based on mixtures. Let us now look at how this can be used through a couple of examples:

Note: A detailed discussion on mixtures problems can be found in the chapter of Ratio, Proportions and Variations. In this discussion, we are dealing with only viewing how these questions can be solved using alligations. For the other methods, that one has I would encourage you to also refer to that discussion in the Ratio Proportion and Variations chapter of this book.

Illustration 10

Vessel A contains 10 litres of milk and water in the ratio 2:3, while vessel B contains 30 litres of milk and water in the ratio 3:2. Find the ratio of milk and water if the contents of vessel A and B are mixed together.

Solution: 2:3 milk water can be read to mean 40% milk (since milk is 2/5th of the mixture). Likewise, 3:2 milk water mixture can be read to mean 60% milk (since milk is 3/5th of the mixture). Also, since you are mixing 10 litres of the first to 30 litres of the second, the ratio of mixing is 1:3. The following alligation solution would yield you the percentage of milk:

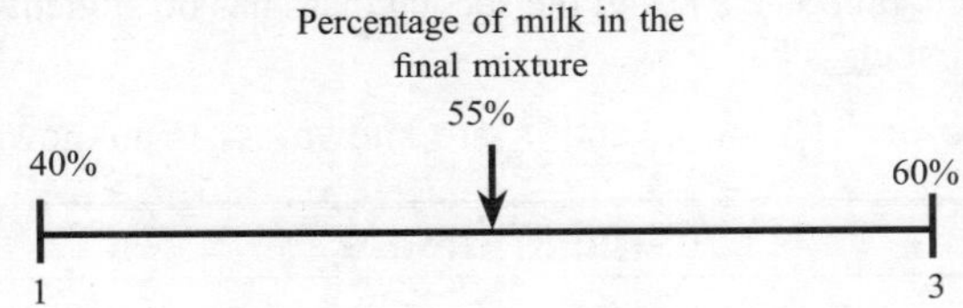

Thus, we get 55% milk and 45% water in the final mixture, which essentially converts to a ratio of 11:9 between milk and water.

However, all such questions cannot be converted into percentage values and solved – especially if the ratios are not conducive to conversion into percentages. Consider the following:

Illustration 11

Vessel A contains 10 litres of milk and water in the ratio 3:8, while vessel B contains 30 litres of milk and water in the ratio 5:9. Find the ratio of milk and water if the contents of vessel A and B are mixed together.

Solution: As you can see in this case, it is not feasible to work with milk percentages. Yet we can still solve this problem using alligation as follows: We first check, which vessel has a higher proportion of milk to understand which fraction we want to keep for A_2, in our Alligation figure

(Remember, we always use $A_1 < A_2$ as a convention) The first vessel has 3/11 milk, while the second vessel has 5/14 milk.

Since, 3/11 is smaller than 5/14, our alligation figure would be:

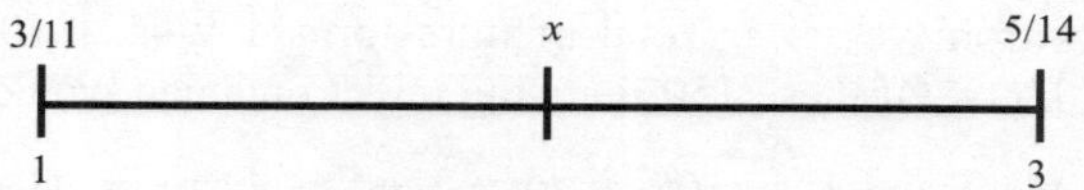

The solution of this, to solve for x would be:

$$\frac{\frac{5}{14}-x}{x-\frac{3}{11}}=\frac{1}{3} \rightarrow \frac{(5-14x)\times 3}{14}=\frac{11x-3}{11} \rightarrow 165 - 462x$$

$$= 154x - 42 \rightarrow 616x = 207$$

$$\therefore \quad x = \frac{207}{616}$$

Hence, the final mixture has 207/616 milk, which means that the milk-water ratio in the final mixture is 207:409 and this would be the required answer.

A typical problem

A typical problem related to the topic of alligation goes as follows:

Math Simplified

Scan this QR code to access a video on how to think about a typical alligation problem

Four litres of wine are drawn from a cask containing 40 litres of wine. It is replaced by water. The process is repeated three times.

(a) What is the final quantity of wine left in the cask?

(b) What is the ratio of wine to water finally?

If we try to chart out the process, we get: Out of 40 litres of wine, 4 are drawn out.

This leaves 36 litres wine and 4 litres water. (Ratio of 9 : 1)

Now, when 4 litres are drawn out of this mixture, we will get 3.6 litres of wine and 0.4 litres of water (as the ratio is 9 : 1). Thus, at the end of the second step we get: 32.4 litres of wine and 7.6 litres of water. Further, the process is repeated, drawing out 3.24 litres wine and 0.76 litres water leaving 29.16 litres of wine and 10.84 litres of water.

This gives the final values and the ratio required.

A closer look at the process will yield that we can get the amount of wine left by:

$$40 \times 36/40 \times 36/40 \times 36/40 = 40 \times (36/40)^3$$
$$\Rightarrow 40 \times (1 - 4/40)^3$$

This yields the formula:

Wine left : Capacity × (1 – fraction of wine withdrawn)^n for n operations.

Thus, you could have multiplied:

$40 \times (0.9)^3$ to get the answer

That is, reduce 40 by 10% successively thrice to get the required answer.

Thus, the thought process could be:

40 – 10% → 36 – 10% → 32.4 – 10% → 29.16

A note about mixtures:

Questions on mixtures are very common in CAT and all other aptitude exams. We have done a few such questions, in the Ratio Proportion & Variation chapter, but the importance of questions on mixtures is so high that we need to develop a proper understanding of the same. These questions require you to use the concepts of ratios, averages, weighted averages & alligations under various situations. Because of the application of so many diverse concepts, often there are many methods to solve individual questions in mixtures. It's best to look at the thought pattern of questions in mixtures through a few examples.

(a) A vessel contains milk and water in the ratio 2 : 3. Another vessel contains milk and water in the ratio 2 : 1. If equal quantities of liquid from both the vessels are mixed together, what is the ratio of milk and water in the final mixture?

As stated above, this question can be solved in various ways. Let's look at them one by one:

Solution using Ratios and Algebra: The milk water ratios given to us are 2 : 3 and 2 : 1. Assume, that the equal quantities taken from the vessel are x liters each. In such a case, the total mixture created is 2x. Then the amount of milk in this 2x mixture will be $\frac{2x}{5}$ & $\frac{2x}{3}$. Total milk = $\frac{2x}{5}+\frac{2x}{3}=\frac{16x}{15}$.

Since, the total mixture would be 2x or $\frac{30x}{15}$, and the milk inside it is $\frac{16x}{15}$, we can work out that the water will be $\frac{14x}{15}$.

Thus, the ratio of milk and water will be 16 : 14 = 8 : 7.

Solution using LCMs (most efficient method): Assume that the equal quantity mixed from both the vessels is 15 liters each (LCM of 2 + 3 = 5 & 2 + 1 = 3). Total mixture formed = 30 liters. Of these 30 liters the milk contained would be $\frac{2}{5}\times 15 = 6$ & $\frac{2}{3}\times 15 = 10$. A total of 16 liters. Hence, water will be 14 liters. Required ratio is 16 : 14 = 8 : 7.

Solution using Percentages and Alligations: The first vessel has 40% milk, while the second vessel has 66.66% milk. Since the mixing is in the ratio 1 : 1, the milk percentage in the final mixture would be the simple average of 40 and 66.66, which would become = 53.33%. Hence, water = 100 – 53.33 = 46.66%. Ratio of milk and water = 53.33 : 46.66 = 53.33 × 3 : 46.66 × 3 = 160 : 140 = 8 : 7.

The alligation picture in this can be visualised as shown

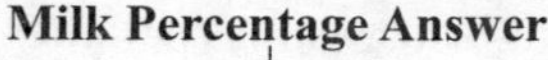

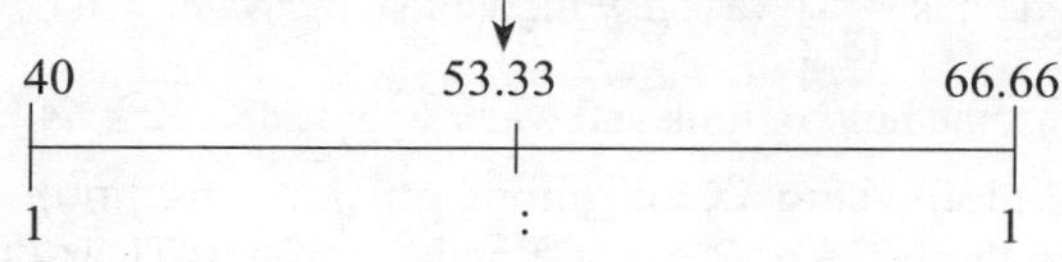

Of course you could also solve this using Water percentages – as the first vessel has 60% water and the second has 33.33% water.

Solution using Ratios and Alligations: **Note:** You might need to use this instead of the percentage approach, in case the numbers for the milk percentages are not convenient values.

The first vessel has a proportion of milk that is $\frac{2}{5}$, while the second vessel has a proportion of milk that is $\frac{2}{3}$. Since the mixing is in the ratio 1 : 1, we can first find the milk component of the mixture as shown:

Milk Proportion

2/5 x 2/3

1 : 1

The value of x can be worked out using:

$$\frac{\frac{2}{3}-x}{x-\frac{2}{5}}=\frac{1}{1} \rightarrow \frac{2}{3}-x=x-\frac{2}{5} \rightarrow x=\frac{8}{15}$$

Hence, water will be $\frac{7}{15}$ and the ratio is 8 : 7.

As, I mentioned earlier, in case the percentage values are convenient (as in ratios like 2 : 3 and 2 : 1 used in this question). However, when the ratios become difficult to convert to percentage values, and if you are thinking through alligations, you would need to solve using this method.

What do you do if the quantities mixed of the two mixtures are not equal?

(b) A vessel contains milk and water in the ratio 2 : 3. Another vessel contains milk and water in the ratio 2 : 1. If quantities from the two vessels are mixed in the ratio 3 : 7, what will be the ratio of milk and water in the final ratio.

Solution using Ratios and algebra: The milk water ratios given to us are 2 : 3 and 2 : 1. Assume, that the quantities taken from the vessels are $3x$ and $7x$ liters each. In such a case, the total mixture created is $10x$. Then the amount of milk in this 10x mixture will be $\frac{2\times 3x}{5}$ and $\frac{2\times 7x}{3}$.

The total milk in the mixture is: $\frac{6x}{5}+\frac{14x}{3}=\frac{88x}{15}$.

Since, the total mixture would be $10x$ or $\frac{150x}{15}$, and the milk inside it is $\frac{88x}{15}$, we can work out that the water will be $\frac{62x}{15}$.

Thus, the ratio of milk and water will be 88 : 62 = 44 : 31.

Solution using LCMs (most efficient method): First take the LCM of 2 + 3 = 5 and 2 + 1 = 3. Their LCM is 15. In this case, we cannot assume 15 liters of each, since the two mixtures are mixed in the ratio of 3 : 7. In order, to manage this twist in the question, assume that you are mixing 15 × 3 = 45 liters from vessel 1 and 15 × 7 = 105 liters from vessel 2. Total mixture formed = 45 + 105 = 150 liters. Of these 150 liters the milk contained would be $\frac{2}{5}\times 45=18$ and $\frac{2}{3}\times 105=70$. A total of 88 liters. Hence, water will be 150 – 88 = 62 liters. Required ratio is 88 : 62 = 44 : 31.

Solution using Percentages and Alligations: The first vessel has 40% milk, while the second vessel has 66.66% milk. Since the mixing is in the ratio 3 : 7, the milk percentage in the final mixture would be got by splitting the number line between 40 and 66.66 in the ratio 7 : 3.

The alligation picture in this can be visualised as shown

Milk Percentage

40 66.66

3 : 7

The answer can be worked out as: $40+7\times 2.66=58.66\%$. Hence, the water would be 41.33%. The required ratio would be 58.66 × 3 : 41.33 × 3 = 176 : 124, 44 : 31.

Task: Try to solve this using water percentages.

Solution using Ratios and Alligations: **Note:** You might need to use this instead of the percentage approach, in case the numbers for the milk percentages are not convenient values.

The first vessel has a proportion of milk that is $\frac{2}{5}$, while the second vessel has a proportion of milk that is $\frac{2}{3}$. Since the mixing is in the ratio 3 : 7, we can first find the milk component of the mixture as shown:

Milk Percentage

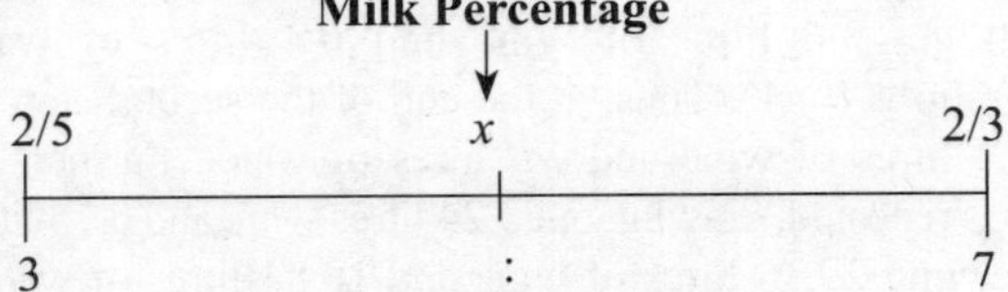

The value of x can be worked out using:

$$\frac{\frac{2}{3}-x}{x-\frac{2}{5}}=\frac{3}{7} \rightarrow \left(\frac{2}{3}-x\right)\times 7=\left(x-\frac{2}{5}\right)\times 3 \rightarrow x=\frac{8.8}{15}$$

Hence, water will be $\frac{6.2}{15}$ and the ratio is 44 : 31.

KNOWLEDGE ENRICHMENT CORNER

Scan this QR code to access a video on three 'must know' questions before heading into the LOD exercises

LEVEL OF DIFFICULTY (I)

1. A bonus of ₹1,00,000 was divided among 500 workers of a factory. Each male worker gets 500 rupees and each female worker gets 100 rupees. Find the number of male workers in the factory.
(a) 250 (b) 375
(c) 290 (d) 125

2. A mixture worth ₹80 a kg is formed by mixing two types of flour, one costing 50 per kg while the other 110 per kg. In what proportion must they have been mixed?
(a) 1 : 1 (b) 1 : 2
(c) 2: 1 (d) 1 : 3

3. In what ratio should two qualities of tea having the rates of ₹40 per kg and ₹30 per kg be mixed in order to get a mixture that would have a rate ofRs 35per kg?
(a) 1 : 2 (b) 1 : 1
(c) 1 : 3 (d) 3 : 1

4. A tank contains 500 liters of wine. 50 liters of wine is taken out of it and replaced by water. The process is repeated again. Find the proportion of water and wine in the resulting mixture.
(a) 1 : 4 (b) 41 : 50
(c) 19 : 81 (d) 81 : 19

5. A sum of ₹4 is made up of 20 coins that are either 10 paise coins or 60 paise coins. Find out how many 10 paise coins are there in the total amount.
(a) 10 (b) 13
(c) 16 (d) 15

6. A mixture of 75 liters of alcohol and water contains 20% of water. How much water must be added to the above mixture to make the water 25% of the resulting mixture?
(a) 5 liters (b) 1.5 litre
(c) 2 liters (d) 2.5 liters

7. A mixture of 40 liters of milk and water contains 10% water. How much water should be added to it to increase the percentage of water to 25%?
(a) 5 liters (b) 6 liters
(c) 2.5 liters (d) 8 liters

8. Two solutions of 80% and 87% purity are mixed resulting in 35 liters of mixture of 84% purity. How much is the quantity of the first solution in the resulting mixture?
(a) 15 liters (b) 12 liters
(c) 9 liters (d) 6 liters

9. A milkman stole milk from a can that contained 50% of milk and he replaced what he had stolen with milk having 20% milk. The bottle then contained only 25% milk. How much of the bottle did he steal?
(a) 80% (b) 83.33%
(c) 85.71% (d) 88.88%

10. A person purchased a pen and a pencil for ₹15. He sold the pen at a profit of 20% and the pencil at a profit of 30%. If his total profit was 24%, find the cost price of the pen.
(a) ₹10.50 (b) ₹12
(c) ₹9 (d) ₹10

11. A 10 percent gain is made by selling the mixture of two types of milk at ₹48 per kg. If the type costing ₹61 per kg was mixed with 100 kg of the other, how many kilograms of the former was mixed?
(a) 38 kg (b) 30.5 kg
(c) 19 kg (d) Cannot be determined

12. A mixture of 160 gallons of wine and water contains 25% water. How much water must be added to the mixture in order to increase the percentage of water to 40% of the new mixture?
(a) 40 gals (b) 50 gals
(c) 80 gals (d) 33 gals

13. If 10 kg of sugar costing ₹15/kg and 20 kg of salt costing ₹10/kg are mixed, find the average cost of the mixture in ₹per kilogram.
(a) 11.67 (b) 12.33
(c) 12.67 (d) 11.33

14. Ashok purchased two qualities of grains at the rate of ₹100 per quintal and ₹160 per quintal. In 50 quintals of the second quality, how much grain of the first quality should be mixed so that by selling the resulting mixture at ₹195 per quintal, he gains a profit of 30%?
(a) 10 quintals (b) 14 quintals
(c) 20 quintals (d) None of these

15. How many kilograms of salt worth ₹360 per kg should be mixed with 10 kg of salt worth ₹420 per kg, such that by selling the mixture at ₹480 per kg, there may be a gain of 20%?
(a) 5 kg (b) 3 kg
(c) 2 kg (d) 4 kg

16. 800 students took the CAT exam in Delhi. 50% of the boys and 90% of the girls cleared the cut off in the examination. If the total percentage of qualifying students is 60%, how many girls appeared in the examination?
(a) 100 (b) 120
(c) 150 (d) 200

17. Kiran lends ₹1000 on simple interest to Harsh for a period of 5 years. She lends a part of the amount at 2% interest and the rest at 8% and receives ₹300 as the amount of interest. How much money (in ₹) did she lend on 2% interest rate?
(a) 333.33 (b) 666.67
(c) 400 (d) 500

18. What will be the ratio of honey and water in the final solution formed by mixing honey and water that are present in three vessels of equal capacity in the ratios 4:1, 5:2 and 6:1 respectively?
(a) 166 : 22 (b) 83 : 22
(c) 83 : 44 (d) None of these

19. Two types of milk having the rates of ₹8/kg and ₹10/kg respectively are mixed in order to produce a mixture having the rate of ₹9.20/kg. What should be the amount of the second type of milk if the amount of the first type of milk in the mixture is 20 kg?
(a) 25 kg (b) 30 kg
(c) 40 kg (d) 20 kg

20. The average salary per head of all workers (Grade A and Grade B) of a company is ₹400. The average salary of 100 grade A workers is ₹1000. If the average salary per head of the rest of the Grade B workers is ₹300, find the total number of workers in the company.
(a) 1000 (b) 800
(c) 500 (d) 700

21. In what proportion must water be mixed with honey so as to gain 10% by selling the mixture at the cost price of the honey? (Assume that water is freely available)
(a) 1 : 4 (b) 1 : 5
(c) 1 : 6 (d) 1 : 10

22. A man purchased a table and a chair for ₹2000. He sold the table at a profit of 20% and the chair at a profit of 40%. In this way, his total profit was 25%. Find the cost price (in ₹) of the table.
(a) 1500 (b) 900
(c) 1000 (d) 800

23. A dishonest shopkeeper purchased milk at ₹100 per litre and mixed 10 liters of water in it. By selling the mixture at the rate of ₹100 per litre he earns a profit of 25%. The quantity of the amount of the mixture that he had was:
(a) 50 liters (b) 40 liters
(c) 25 liters (d) 60 liters

24. A tank has a capacity of 10 gallons and is full of alcohol. 2 gallons of alcohol are drawn out and the tank is again filled with water. This process is repeated 5 times. Find out how much alcohol is left in the resulting mixture finally?
(a) 2048/625 gallons (b) 3346/625 gallons
(c) 2048/3125 gallons (d) 625 gallons

25. Shruti possessing ₹10,000, lent a part of it at 5% simple interest and the remaining at 20% simple interest. Her total income after 5 years was ₹7500. Find the sum lent at 20% rate.
(a) ₹1666.67 (b) ₹6666.67
(c) ₹3333.33 (d) None of these

26. In what ratio should water be mixed with soda costing ₹12 per litre so as to make a profit of 50% by selling the diluted liquid at ₹15 per litre?
(a) 10 : 1 (b) 5 : 1
(c) 1: 5 (d) 6: 1

27. Pinku a dishonest grocer professes to sell pure butter at cost price, but he mixes it with adulterated fat and thereby gains 25%. Find the percentage of adulterated fat in the mixture assuming that adulterated fat is freely available.
(a) 20% (b) 25%
(c) 33.33% (d) 40%

28. A container is full of a mixture of kerosene and petrol in which there is 18% kerosene. Eight liters are drawn off and then the vessel is filled with petrol. If the kerosene is now 15%, how much does the container hold?
(a) 40 liters (b) 32 liters
(c) 36 liters (d) 48 liters

29. A vessel is full of milk 1/4 of the milk is taken out and the vessel is filled with water. If the process is repeated 4 times and 100 liters of milk is finally left in the vessel, what is the capacity of the vessel?
(a) 25600/243 liters (b) $\frac{2461}{81}$ liters
(c) 25600/81 liters (d) 30 liters

30. The price of a table and a chair is ₹3000. The table was sold at a 20% profit and the chair at a 10% loss. If in the transaction a man gains ₹300, how much is cost price (in ₹) of the table?
(a) 1000 (b) 2500
(c) 2000 (d) None of these

31. Two buckets of equal capacity are full of a mixture of milk and water. In the first, the ratio of milk to water is 1 : 7 and in the second it is 3 : 8. Now both the mixtures are mixed in a bigger container. What is the resulting ratio of milk to water?
(a) 35 : 141 (b) 42 : 49
(c) 43 : 41 (d) 41 : 53

32. Raman steals four gallons of liquid soap kept in a train compartment's bathroom from a container that is full of liquid soap. He then fills it with water to avoid detection. Unable to resist the temptation he steals 4 gallons of the mixture again, and fills it with water. When the liquid soap is checked at a station it is found that the ratio of the liquid soap now left in the container to that of the water in it is 36: 13. What was the initial amount of the liquid soap in the container if it is known that the liquid soap is neither used nor augmented by anybody else during the entire period?
(a) 7 gallons (b) 14 gallons
(c) 21 gallons (d) 28 gallons

33. Two vessels contain a mixture of spirit and water. In the first vessel the ratio of spirit to water is 8 : 3 and in the second vessel the ratio is 5 : 1. A 35 litre cask is filled from these vessels so as to contain a mixture of spirit and water in the ratio of 4 :1. How many liters are taken from the first vessel?
(a) 11 liters (b) 22 liters
(c) 16.5 liters (d) 17.5 liters

34. There are two kinds of alloys of silver and copper. The first alloy contains silver and copper such that 93.33% of it is silver. In the second alloy there is 86.66% silver. What weight of the first alloy should be mixed with some weight of the second alloy so as to make a 100 kg mass containing 90% of silver?
(a) 55 kg (b) 50 kg
(c) 70 kg (d) 25 kg

35. In the Delhi zoo, there are lions and there are hens. If the heads are counted, there are 180, while the legs are 448. What will be the number of lions in the zoo?
(a) 36 (b) 88
(c) 44 (d) 136

36. A man buys milk at ₹85 per liter and dilutes it with water. He sells the mixture at the same rate and thus gains 11.11%. Find the quantity of water mixed by him in every liter of milk.
(a) 0.111 liters (b) 0.909 liters
(c) 0.1 litre (d) 0.125 liters

37. Two vessels contain spirit and water mixed respectively in the ratio of 1: 4 and 4: 1 Find the ratio in which these are to be mixed to get a new mixture in which the ratio of spirit to water is 1: 3.
(a) 11 : 1 (b) 13 : 1
(c) 11 : 2 (d) 11 : 3

38. A bag contains a total of 105 coins of ₹1, 50 p and 25 p denominations. Find the total number of coins of ₹1 if there are a total of 50.5 rupees in the bag and it is known that the number of 25 paise coins are 133.33% more than the number of 1 rupee coins.
(a) 56 (b) 25
(c) 24 (d) None of these

39. There are two mixtures of milk and water, the quantity of milk in them being 20% and 80% of the mixture. If 2 liters of the first are mixed with three liters of the second, what will be the ratio of milk to water in the new mixture?
(a) 11 : 12 (b) 11 : 9
(c) 19 : 11 (d) 14 : 11

40. Sharman decides to travel 100 kilometres in 8 hours partly by foot and partly on a bicycle, his speed on foot being 10 km/h and that on bicycle being 20 km/h, what distance would he travel on foot?
(a) 20 km (b) 30 km
(c) 50 km (d) 60 km

Space for Rough Work

LEVEL OF DIFFICULTY (II)

1. Three batches at Mindworkzz take a mock test. In the mock test, the average score of batch 1 is 108 marks, the average score of batch 2 is 101 marks, while the average score of batch 3 is 110 marks. The average score of all students of batches 1 and 2 together is 104, while the average score of all students in batches 2 and 3 is 106. What is the average score of all the students of batches 1 and 3 taken together?

Directions for Questions 2 and 3: Snehal Shah is planning to invest the surplus cash he has for a month. He wishes to guarantee maximum returns on his investment. Bharat Popli, his investment manager offers him three choices, which can be utilized fully, partially or in conjunction with each other.

Option A: Invest in a scheme offered by SBI, where he will get a return of +0.4%.

Option B: Invest in mutual funds of ASK Limited. A rise in the stock market will give him +20% returns, while a fall will give him –12% returns.

Option C: Invest in a Contra fund. A rise in the stock market will give a –10% return, while a fall will give a return of +16%.

2. Bharat offers 4 alternate options to Snehal in terms of how to divide his investment in the three options. Which of the following strategies will maximise the guaranteed return to Snehal?
   (a) 100% in option A
   (b) 36% in option B and 64% in option C
   (c) 64% in option B and 36% in option C
   (d) One third in each of the options
3. The maximum guaranteed return that Snehal can expect from the options provided by Bharat is?

Directions for Questions 4 and 5: The following table presents the sweetness of different forms relative to sucrose, whose sweetness is taken to be 1.00.

Lactose 0.16
Maltose 0.32
Glucose 0.74
Sucrose 1.00
Fructose 1.70
Saccharin 675.00

4. What is the maximum amount of sucrose (to the nearest gram) that can be added to one-gram of saccharin to make a mixture that will be at least 100 times as sweet as glucose?
   (a) 7 (b) 8
   (c) 9 (d) 100
5. Approximately how many times sweeter than sucrose is a mixture consisting of glucose, sucrose and fructose in the ratio of 1 : 2 : 3?
   (a) 1.3 (b) 1
   (c) 0.6 (d) 2.3
6. The average marks of a class of 33 students, increases by 3, when three of them leave the group. If the average marks of these three students is $\frac{1}{4}^{th}$ the average marks of the original 33, then the average marks of the remaining 30 students is?
7. There are 3 mixtures. The first has water and Kerosene in the ratio 2 : 3. The second has water and petrol in the ratio 1 : 3. The third has water and diesel in the ratio 2 : 1. The three mixtures are mixed in the proportion of 5 : 4 : 3. Then the resulting mixture has:
   (a) Same amount of water and the first mixture
   (b) Same amount of water and the second mixture
   (c) The same amount of kerosene and petrol
   (d) More than one of the above
8. Sameer Contractor's distribution company, a subsidiary of a major FMCG goods marketer Maxlon, is forecasting the zonal sales for the next year. Zone I with current yearly sales of ₹213.6 lac is expected to achieve a sales growth of 8.25%; Zone II with current sales of ₹88.8 lac is expected to grow by 11.2%; and Zone III with sales of ₹70.5 lac is expected to increase sales by –3.2%. What is the expected sales growth for the next year?
   (a) 7.46% (b) 6.78%
   (c) 7.88% (d) 6.41%
9. In March 2011, EF Public Library purchased a total of 15 new books published in 2010 with a total expenditure of ₹4500. Of these books, 13 books were purchased from MN Distributors, while the remaining two were purchased from UV Publishers. It is observed that one-sixth of the average price of all the 15 books purchased is equal to one-fifth of the average price of the 13 books obtained from MN Distributors. Of the two books obtained from UV Publishers, if one-third of the price of one volume is equal to one-half of the price of the other, then the price of the two books are:
   (a) ₹900 and ₹600 (b) ₹600 and ₹400
   (c) ₹750 and ₹500 (d) None of the above
10. Sunil Mishra invested ₹50000 in two fixed deposits offered by SBI and Citibank, offering compound interest @6% per annum and 8% per annum respectively. If the total amount of interest accrued in two years through both fixed deposit schemes is ₹7036, the amount invested in Citibank is?
11. Two alloys of aluminium have different percentages of aluminium in them. The first one weighs 16 kg

and the second one weighs 32 kg. One piece each of equal weight was cut off from both the alloys and the first piece was alloyed with the second alloy and the second piece alloyed with the first one. As a result, the percentage of aluminium became the same in the resulting two new alloys. What was the weight of each cut-off piece?

12. X and Y are the two alloys which were made by mixing Zinc, Copper and Gold in the ratio 6 : 9 : 15 and 7 : 11 : 14 respectively. If 40 grams of alloy X and 60 grams of alloy Y are melted and mixed to form another alloy Z, what is the ratio of Zinc and Copper in the new

13. There are two alloys P and Q made up of silver, copper and aluminum. Alloy P contains 45% silver and rest aluminum. Alloy Q contains 30% silver, 35% copper and rest aluminum. Alloys P and Q are mixed in the ratio of 1 : 4.5. The approximate percentages of silver and copper in the newly formed alloy is:
(a) 33% and 29% (b) 29% and 26%
(c) 34% and 31% (d) None of the Above.

14. Gauri Pharmaceuticals produces two chemicals X and Y, such that X consists of 5% salt A and 10% salt B and Y consists of 10% salt A and 6% salt B. For producing the chemicals X and Y, the company requires at least 14 gm of Salt A and at least 14 gm of Salt B. If chemical X costs ₹12.5 per gm and chemical Y costs ₹8.80 per gm, what is the minimum cost at which the company can meet the requirement by using a combination of both types of chemicals?
(a) ₹1880 (b) ₹1440
(c) ₹1850 (d) None of these

15. The Drizzle Pvt. Ltd., a squash company has 2 cans of juice. The first contains 25% water and the rest is fruit pulp. The second contains 50% water and rest is fruit pulp. How much juice should be mixed from the first can to some juice of the second can, so as to get 12 liters of juice such that the ratio of water to fruit pulp is 2 : 3?

16. A 10 liter cylinder contains a mixture of water and sugar, the volume of sugar being 15% of total volume. A few liters of the mixture is released and an equal amount of water is added. Then the same amount of the mixture as before is released and replaced with water for a second time. As a result, the sugar content becomes 10% of total volume. What is the approximate quantity of mixture released each time?
(a) 1 liter (b) 1.2 liters
(c) 1.5 liters (d) 2 liters

17. A manufacturer has 400 liters of acid solution, which has 25% acid content. How many liters of acid solution with 40% acid content may be added so that acid content in the resulting mixture will be more than 30% but less than 35%?
(a) More than 200 liters but less than 600 liters
(b) More than240 liters but less than 480 liters
(c) More than 200 liters but less than 800 liters
(d) More than 240 liters but less than 600 liters

18. Product M is produced by mixing chemical X and chemical Y in the ratio of 5 : 4. Chemical X is prepared by mixing two raw materials, A and B, in the ratio of 1 : 3. Chemical Y is prepared by mixing raw materials, B and C, in the ratio of 2 : 1. Then the final mixture is prepared by mixing 864 units of product M with water. If the concentration of the raw material B in the final mixture is 40%, how much water had been added to product M?
(a) 328 units (b) 368 units
(c) 1540 units (d) 676 units

19. Prof. Pitabas Mohanty takes a number of quizzes for a course. All the quizzes are out of 100. A student can get an A grade in the course if the average of her scores is more than 85. Grade B is awarded to a student if the average of her scores is between 82 and 85 (both included). If the average is below 82, the student gets a C grade. Randhir Mishra is preparing for the last quiz and he realises that he will need to score a minimum of 97 to get an A grade. After the quiz, he realises that he will score 70, and he will just manage a B. How many quizzes did Prof. Mohanty take?
(a) 6 (b) 7
(c) 8 (d) 9

20. The strength of a salt solution is n%, if 100 grams of the solution contains n grams of salt. If three solutions X, Y, Z are mixed in the proportion 2 : 3 : 4, then the resulting solution has strength of 30%. If instead the proportion is 4 : 3 : 2, the solution has a strength of 40%. A fourth solution M is produced by mixing Y & Z in the ratio 3 : 10. The ratio of the strength of M to X is
(a) 2 : 3 (b) 4 : 13
(c) 3 : 5 (d) Cannot be determined

21. A petrol-diesel solution, containing 40% petrol is mixed with another solution M, of unknown concentration in the ratio 2 : 3 by volume. This mixture is then mixed with a double quantity of another 40% petrol solution, to obtain the final mixture. The final mixture has a petrol concentration of 45%. What is the petrol concentration in the solution M?

22. There are two drums, drum 1 and drum 2. In the first drum A, B and C are in the ratio 12 : 6 : 7. Contents from drum 1 and drum 2 are mixed together in the ratio 2 : 3, giving a final concentration of A, B and C as 11 : 5 : 4. What is the ratio of A : B : C in the drum 2.
(a) 157 : 66 : 33 (b) 171 : 77 : 33
(c) 157 : 66 : 44 (d) 179 : 77 : 44

23. A jar contains a mixture of 275 ml of water and 900 ml of alcohol. Sameer Contractor takes out 20% of the mixture and substitutes it with water. He repeats the process two more times. What is the percentage of water in the mixture now (approximate to the nearest percentage)?
(a) 71% (b) 61%
(c) 66% (d) None of these

24. Two types of rice, *A* and *B*, are mixed and then sold at ₹60 per kg. The profit is 10% if *A* and *B* are mixed in the ratio 3 : 4, and 5% if this ratio is 4 : 3. The cost prices, per kg, of *A* and *B* are in the ratio
(a) 25 : 18 (b) 18 : 25
(c) 9 : 25 (d) 25 : 9

25. A student at a reputed management institution appears for a certain number of tests. His average score increases by 2 if the first 10 tests are not considered, and decreases by 2 if the last 10 tests are not considered. If his average scores for the first 10 and the last 10 tests are 30 and 50, respectively, then his average score across all the tests was?

26. For the above question, the number of tests the student appeared for was?

27. A trader sells 10 litres of a mixture of paints *X* and *Y*, where the amount of *Y* in the mixture does not exceed that of *X*. The cost of paint *X* per litre is ₹30 more than that of paint *Y*. If the trader sells the entire mixture for ₹320 and makes a profit of 25%, then the highest possible cost of paint *Y*, in ₹ per litre, is

28. The strength of a salt solution is *p*% if 100 ml of the solution contains *p* grams of salt. Each of three vessels *A*, *B*, *C* contains 800 ml of salt solution of strengths 20%, 24%, and 32%, respectively. Now, 200 ml of the solution in vessel *A* is transferred to vessel *B*. Then, 200 ml of the solution in vessel *B* is transferred to vessel *C*. Finally, 200 ml of the solution in vessel C is transferred to vessel *A*. The strength, in percentage, of the resulting solution in vessel A is
(a) 21.88 (b) 22.88
(c) 22.22 (d) 22.56

29. Abhijit and Amartya are among 12 students who write an examination. Abhijit scores 80.5. The average score of the 11 students other than Amartya is 73. The average score of all the 12 students is one more than the average score of the 11 students other than Abhijit. The score of Amartya is

30. A mixture comprises water and liquids *A* and *B*. The volume of water is $\frac{1}{3}$rd of the total mixture and the volume of liquids *A* and *B* are in the ratio 5 : 3. To remove the water, the mixture is passed through a porous medium which completely absorbs the water and partially absorbs liquid *A*. Altogether this porous medium absorbs 400 ml of the initial mixture. If the ratio of volume of liquids *A* and *B* in the residual concentrated mixture becomes 7 : 9 then find the volume of water absorbed by the porous medium.

High Yield Questions

Scan this QR code to access assisted problem solving videos on questions 1, 7, 9, 14 and 20 from LOD 2

Space for Rough Work

ANSWER KEY

Level of Difficulty (I)

1. (d)	2. (a)	3. (b)	4. (c)
5. (c)	6. (a)	7. (d)	8. (a)
9. (b)	10. (c)	11. (d)	12. (a)
13. (a)	14. (a)	15. (a)	16. (d)
17. (a)	18. (b)	19. (b)	20. (d)
21. (d)	22. (a)	23. (a)	24. (a)
25. (b)	26. (c)	27. (a)	28. (d)
29. (c)	30. (c)	31. (a)	32. (d)
33. (a)	34. (b)	35. (c)	36. (a)
37. (a)	38. (c)	39. (d)	40. (d)

Level of Difficulty (II)

1. 109.25	2. (d)	3. 1.466%	4. (b)
5. (a)	6. 43	7. (d)	8. (b)
9. (c)	10. 30000	11. 10.666	
12. 169:261:370		13. (a)	14. (a)
15. 4.8 liters	16. (d)	17. (c)	18. (d)
19. (d)	20. (b)	21. 65	22. (d)
23. 61%	24. (a)	25. 40	26. 60
27. 10.6	28. (d)	29. 31	30. 240

SOLUTIONS AND SHORTCUTS

Level of Difficulty (I)

1. Average bonus per worker = 100000/500 = 200.

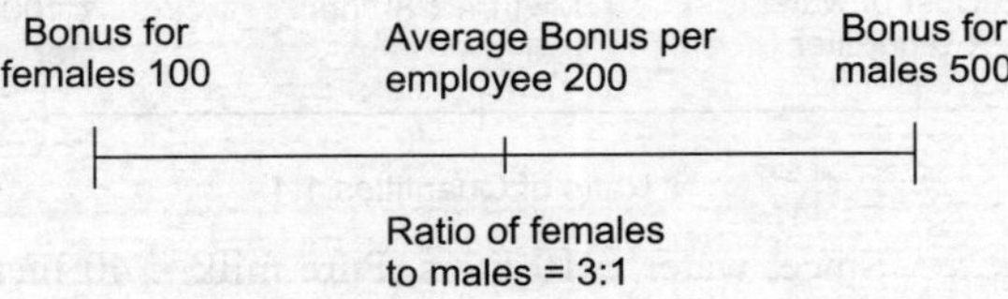

Total male workers = $500 \times \frac{1}{4} = 125$.

2. The required ratio would be 1:1 as we are mixing flour of ₹50 per kg with flour of ₹110 per kg to get flour of ₹80 per kg.
3. The ratio would be 1:1 as seen from the figure:

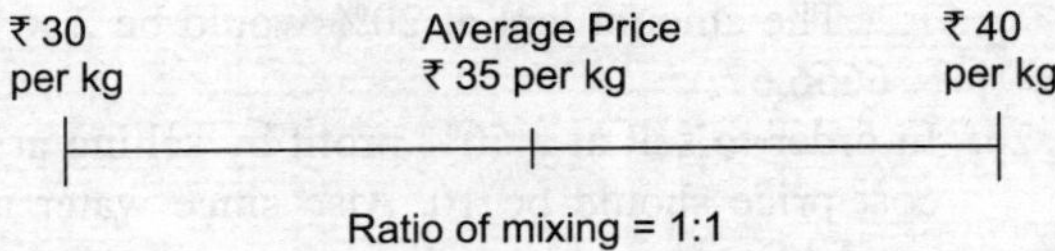

4. Amount of wine left = 500 × 9/10 × 9/10 = 405 liters. Hence, water = 95 liters. Ratio of water and wine = 19:81. Option (c) is correct.
5. The average value of a coin is 20 paise and there are only 10 paise and 60 paise coins in the sum. Hence, the ratio of the number of 10 paise coins to 60 paise coins would be 4: 1.

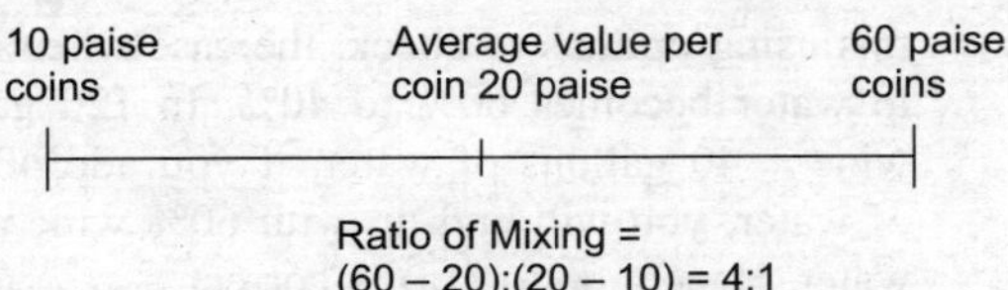

Since there are a total of 20 coins, the number of 10 paise coins would be 4 × 20/5 = 16 coins.

6. 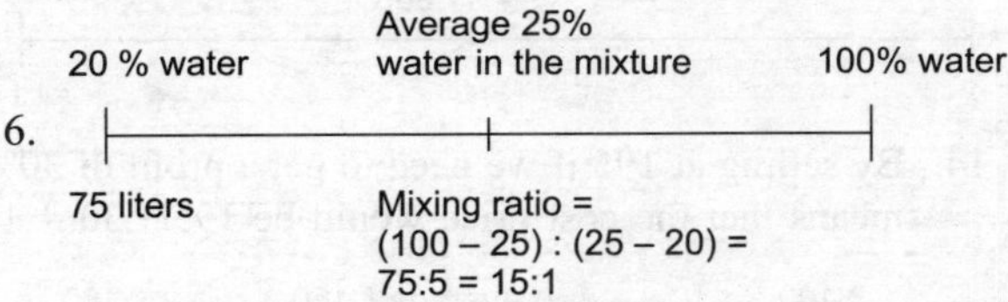

In the 15:1 ratio since, 15 corresponds to 75 liters, 1 would correspond to 5 liters. We should mix 5 liters of water.

7. In 40 liters there is 4 liters water and 36 liters milk. If we mix 8 liters of water to this (from option d); we would get a mixture containing 36 liters milk and 12 liters water – giving us the required 75% milk in the mixture. Hence, option (d) is correct.
8. 80% and 87% mixed to form 84% means that the mixing ratio is 3:4. The first solution would be $\frac{3}{7} \times 35 = 15$ liters.
9. 20% milk is mixed with 50% milk to get 25% milk. The ratio of mixing would be 5:1. This means he stole 5/6th of the bottle or 83.33% of the bottle.
10. The following alligation visualization would help us solve the problem:

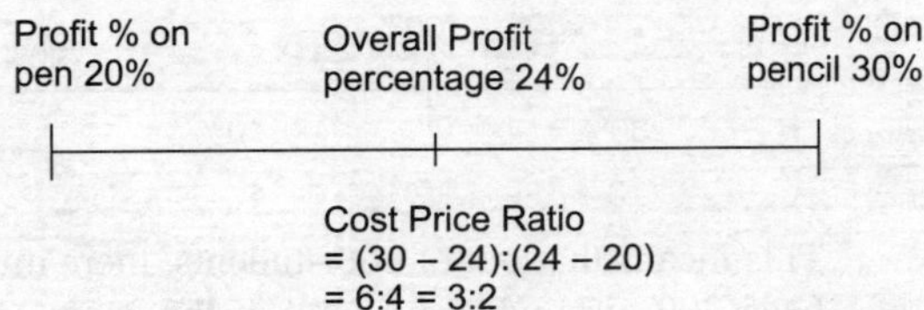

Cost of pen = 3/5 of the total cost price = $\frac{3}{5} \times 15$ = ₹9.

11. We cannot determine the answer to this question as we do not know the price per kg of the other type of milk. Hence, we cannot find the ratio of mixing which would be required in order to move further in this question.
12. There are multiple ways of solving this question. In 160 gallons since we have 25% water, the composition would be 120 gallons of wine and 40 gallons of water. After adding more water to this, the water would become 40 + w, while the wine would remain at 120 gallons. This 120 gallons of wine would correspond to 60% wine in the final mixture. Since, 120 = 60%, 200 = 100%. So we need to add, 40 gallons of water. Alternately, you can solve

this using options to check, the case when the wine to water becomes 60% to 40%. In 120 gallons of wine + 40 gallons of water, if you add 40 gallons of water, you will end up with 60% wine and 40% water. Hence, option (a) is correct.

13. Solving the following alligation figure:

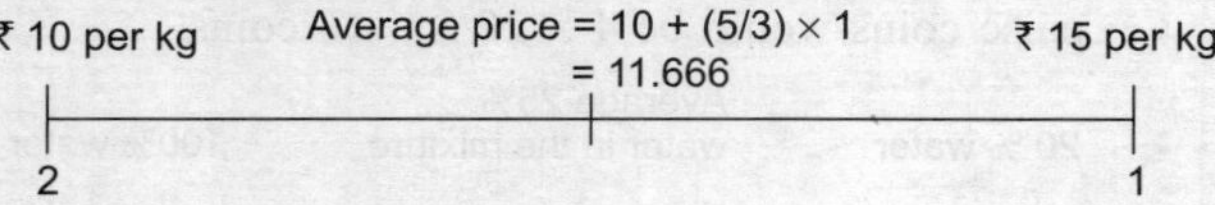

14. By selling at 195 if we need to get a profit of 30% it means that the cost price would be 195/1.30 = 150.

From the alligation figure, you can see that the ratio of the quantities of the two pulses would be 1:5. Since, we have 50 quintals of the second quality, we must have 10 quintals of the first. Hence, option (a) is correct.

15. Since by selling at ₹480 we want a profit of 20%, it means that the average cost required is ₹400 per kg. Mixing salt worth ₹360/kg and ₹420/kg to get ₹400/kg means a mixture ratio of 1:2. Thus, to 10 kg of the second variety we need to add 5 kg of the first variety to get the required cost price.

16. The ratio of boys and girls appearing for the exam can be seen to be 3:1 using the following alligation figure.

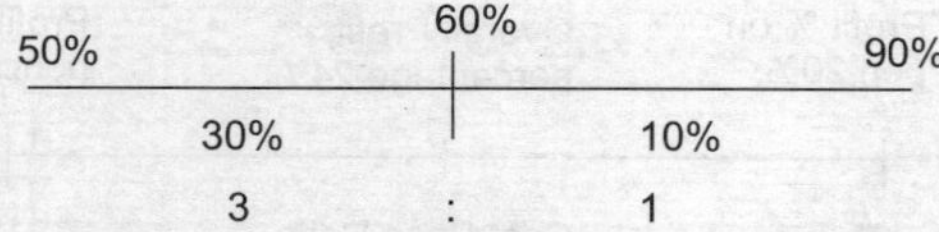

This means that out of 800 students, there must have been 200 girls who appeared in the exam.

17. Since Kiran earns ₹300 in 5 years, it means that she earns an interest of 300/5 = ₹60 per year. On an investment of 1000, an annual interest of 60 represents an average interest rate of 6%.
Then using the alligation figure below:

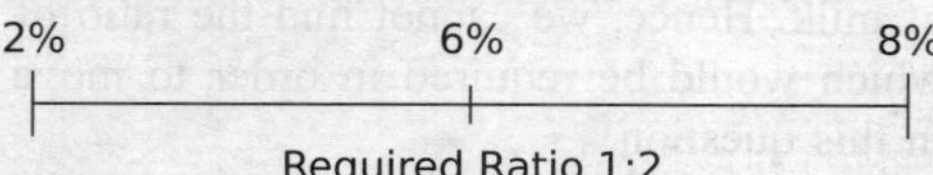

We get the ratio of investments as 1:2. Hence, she lent one third of the amount i.e. 1 × 1000/3 = 333.33 at 2% per annum.

18. In order to solve this we need to assume a value for the amounts in the vessels. If we assume 35 liters (LCM of 5, 7 and 7) as the quantities in all the three vessels we will get:
28 liters + 25 liters + 30 liters = 83 liters of honey and 22 liters of water in 105 liters of the mixture. The required ratio is 83:22.

19. Mixing ₹8/kg and ₹10/kg to get ₹9.20 per kg we get that the ratio of mixing is (10 – 9.2): (9.2 – 8) = 2:3. If the first milk is 20 kg, the second would be 30 kg.

20.

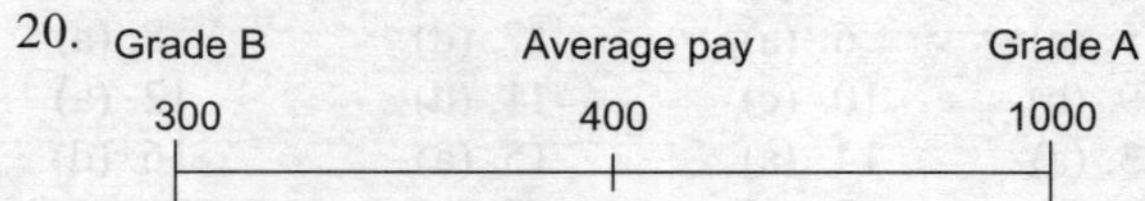

From the figure we can see that the ratio of Grade A and Grade B workers is 1: 6. Since, there are 100 grade A workers, there would be 600 Grade B workers. Hence, total number of grade B workers = 600.
Total workers in the company = 100 + 600 = 700.

21. To gain 10% by selling at cost price, water should comprise 10 out of a total of 110. The ratio of mixing that achieves this is 1:10.

22. The ratio of the cost of the table and the chair would be (40 – 25):(25 – 20) or 3:1 as can be seen from the following alligation figure:

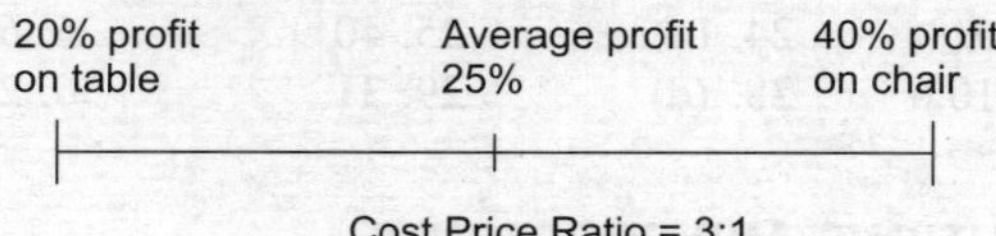

Thus, the cost of the table would be ₹1500.

23. Cost price of the mixture = ₹80 per liter

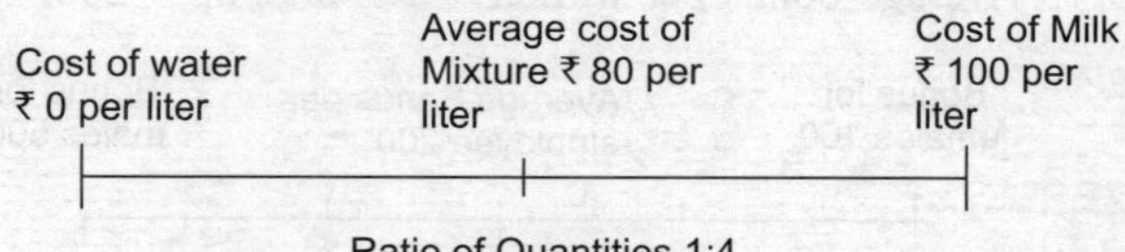

Since, water = 10 liters, Pure milk = 40 liters
Total quantity of the mixture = 40+ 10 = 50 liters.

24. The amount of alcohol left = 10 × 4/5 × 4/5 × 4/5 × 4/5 × 4/5 = 10240/3125 = 2048/625

25. Annual interest income = 7500 /5 = 1500. Interest of ₹1500 on a lending of ₹10000 implies a 15% average rate of interest. This 15% is generated by mixing the two loans @ 5% and 20% respectively. The ratio in which the two loans should be allocated would be 1:2. The amount lent at 20% would be 2 × 10000/3 = 6666.67.

26. In order to sell at a 50% profit by selling at ₹15 the cost price should be 10. Also since water is freely available, we can say that the ratio of water and soda must be 1:5 as can be seen from the alligation figure.

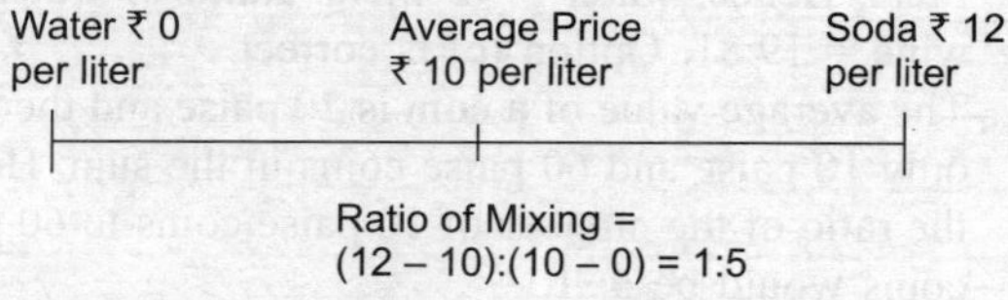

Hence, option (c) is correct.

27. The ratio of mixing would be 1:4 which means that the percentage of adulterated fat would be 20%.
28. The following visualization would help:

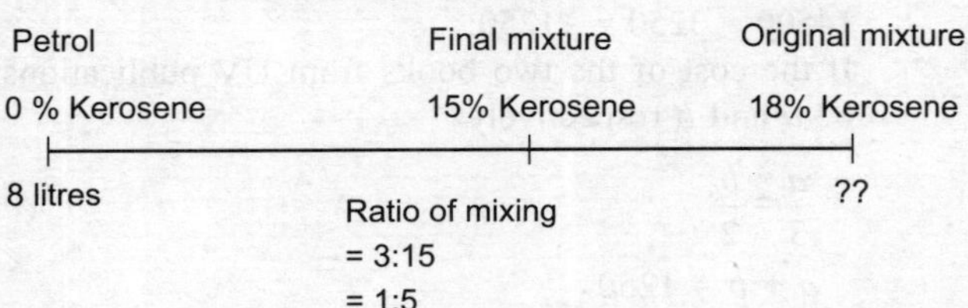

From the figure we can see that the original mixture would be 40 liters and the petrol being mixed is 8 liters. Thus, the container capacity is 48 liters.
29. Let the quantity of milk initially be Q. Then we have $Q \times 3/4 \times 3/4 \times 3/4 \times 3/4 = 100 \rightarrow Q = 25600/81$ liters.
30. Solve using options as that would be the best way to tackle this question. Option (c) fits the situation perfectly as if we take the price of the table as ₹2000, the cost of the chair would be ₹1000. The profit in selling the table would be ₹400 while the loss in selling the chair would be ₹100. The total profit would be ₹300 as stipulated by the problem.
31. Assume the capacity of the two containers is 88 liters each. When we mix 88 liters of the first and 88 liters of the second, the amount of milk would be: 88 × 1/8 + 88 × 3/11 = 11 + 24 = 35 liters. Consequently the amount of water would be 2 × 88 – 35 = 176 – 35 = 141 liters. Required ratio = 35: 141. Option (a) is correct.
32. It can be seen from the ratio 36:13 that the proportion of liquid soap to water is 36/49 after two mixings. This means that $6/7^{th}$ of the liquid soap must have been allowed to remain in the container and hence $1/7^{th}$ of the container's original liquid soap, would have been drawn out by the thief. Since he takes out 4 gallons every time, there must have been 28 gallons in the container. (as 4 is $1/7^{th}$ of 28).
33. Solving through options is the best way to tackle this question. Option (a) fits the conditions of the problem as if there are 11 liters in the first vessel, there would be 8 liters of spirit. Also it means that we would be taking 24 liters from the second vessel out of which there would be 20 liters of spirit. Thus, total spirit would be 28 out of 35 liters giving us 7 liters of water. This matches our requirement of a final ratio of 4:1 of spirit and water in the cask.
34. In order to mix two tin alloys containing 86.66% silver and 93.33% silver to get 90% silver, the ratio of mixing should be 1:1. Thus, each variety should be 50 kgs each.
35. If all the animals were hens we would have 180 heads and 360 legs. If we reduce the number of hens by 1 to 179 and increase the number of lions by 1 to 1, we would get an incremental 2 legs.

Since, the number of legs we need to increment is 88 i.e. (448 – 360 = 88), we need to have 44 lions and 136 hens.
36. The requisite 11.11% profit can be got by mixing 0.111 liters of water in 1 liter of milk. In such a case the total milk quantity would be 1.111 liters and the cost price would be for 1 liter only. The profit would be 0.111/1 = 11.11%.
37. The first vessel contains 20% spirit while the second vessel contains 80% spirit. To get a 1:3 ratio we need 25% spirit in the mixture. The ratio of mixing can be seen using the following alligation figure:

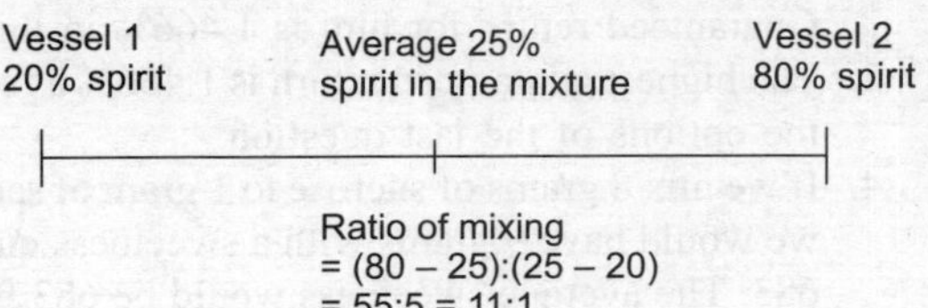

38. $O + F + T = 105$
$O + 0.5F + 0.25T = 50.5$
$T = 2.333\ O.$
Solving we get: 24 coins of ₹1.
39. The percentage of milk in the new mixture would be:
(2 × 20 + 3 × 80)/5 = 280/5 = 56%. The ratio of milk to water in the new mixture would be 56:44 = 14:11.
40. Solve using options. If he travels 60 km on foot he would take 6 hours on foot. Also, in this case he would travel 40 km on bicycle @ 20 kmph – which would take him 2 hours. Thus a total of 8 hours. Option (d) satisfies the conditions of the question.

Level of Difficulty (II)

1. Since the combined average of batch 1 and 2 is 104, with the average of batches 1 and 2 respectively being 108 and 101 marks, we can make out that the ratio of students between batches 1 and 2 are 3 : 4. Likewise, we can make out that the average of the batches 2 and 3 being 106, with individual averages of 101 and 110, the ratio of number of students between batch 2 and 3 is 4 : 5. Thus, the ratio of the number of students across batches is 3 : 4 : 5. The average of batch 1 and 3 would be $\frac{3\times108+5\times110}{8}=109.25$.
2. The following scenarios emerge for the given options:
(a) Guaranteed return is 0.4%
(b) If the stock market rises, return = 20% × 0.36 + (–10)% × 0.64 = 7.2 – 6.4 = 0.8%
If the stock market falls, return = –12% × 0.36 + (+16)% × 0.64 = –4.32 + 10.24 = 5.92%
This will give us a minimum guaranteed return of 0.8%. Hence, this is a better strategy than the one in option (a)

(c) If the stock market rises, return = 20% × 0.64 + (–10)% × 0.36 = 12.8 – 3.6 = 9.2%
If the stock market falls, return = –12% × 0.64 + (+16)% × 0.36 = –7.68 + 5.76 = –1.92%
The guaranteed return for him is negative in this case.

(d) The expected return if the market falls:
0.33 × 0.4% + 0.33 × (–12%) + 0.33 × (16%) = 1.466%
If the market rises:
0.33 × 0.4% + 0.33 × (20%) + 0.33 × (–10%) = 3.466%
Guaranteed return for him is 1.466% in this case.

3. The highest guaranteed return is 1.466% as seen from the options of the last question.
4. If we mix 8 grams of sucrose to 1 gram of saccharine, we would have 9 grams with a sweetness quotient of 683. The average sweetness would be 683/9 = 75.88 which is greater than 100 times the sweetness of sucrose. If we mix 9 grams of sucrose to 1 gram of saccharine, the average would be below 74. Hence, option (b) is the required answer.
5. The average sweetness of the mixture as defined would be: (1 × 0.74 + 2 × 1 + 3 × 1.7)/6 = 7.84/6 = 1.306. Thus, option (a) is correct.
6. Let the average of the 33 students be $4x$. Then the average of 3 students who left, is x. In this scenario, the following allegation picture will emerge:

x	$4x$	$4x + 3$
3	:	30

From this scenario, we can see that the difference between x and $4x$ has to be 30. This will give us that $x = 10$, $4x = 40$. The average marks of the remaining 30 students, after the removal of 3 students = $4x + 3$ = 43.
7. The sum of the components of the ratio are: 5, 4 and 3 respectively. Their LCM is 60. Assume, you are mixing, 60 × 5; 60 × 4 & 60 × 3 = 300 liters, 240 liters and 180 liters respectively of the three mixtures. In such a case, the total water will be: 120 + 60 + 120 = 300 liters. The total kerosene will be: 180, the total petrol will be 180 and the total diesel will be 60 liters. Hence, both options (a) and (c) are correct. Hence, option (d) is correct.
8. The required growth rate will be given by:
$$\frac{213.6\times 8.25+88.8\times 11.2+70.5\times(-3.2)}{213.6+88.8+70.5} = 6.78\%$$
9. Let the average price of the 13 books purchased from MN distributors be x.
$$\frac{\frac{4500}{15}}{6} = \frac{x}{5} \text{ or } x = 250.$$
Total price of books purchased by 13 books = 13 × 250 = ₹3250
Price of books purchased from UV publications = ₹4500 – 3250 = ₹1250.
If the cost of the two books from UV publications be a and b respectively.
$$\frac{a}{3} = \frac{b}{2}$$
$$a + b = 1250$$
On solving the above two equations, we get: a = ₹750 and b = ₹500.
10. Let the amount invested in SBI, be A. Then the amount invested in Citibank = 50000 – A. At 6% CI, A will become 1.1236A & the amount in Citibank becomes (50000 – A) × 1.1664. The interest earned in SBI is 0.1236A (12.36% of A) , while the interest earned in Citibank would be 16.64% of (50000 – A). We have: 0.1236A + (50000 – A) × 0.1664 = 7036
8320 – 0.0428A = 7036 → A = 30000.
11. The main focus in this problem should be on understanding that the cut-off piece's weight should be such that the alloyed pieces that are created should have the same ratio weight-wise for each of the two alloys.
Thus, if the weight of the cut off pieces is 'w' each, then: $\frac{(16-w)}{w} = \frac{w}{(32-w)} \to w^2 = 512 - 48w + w^2$
$\to w = 10.666$.
12. The ratios are 2 : 3 : 5 and 7 : 11 : 14. Take the LCM of 10 and 32 (sums of the components of the ratios) – Their LCM is 160. The alloys are mixed with 40 grams of the first and 60 grams of the second – which means a mixing ratio of 2 : 3. Assume, you mixed 320 grams of the first alloy, with 480 grams of the second alloy. The Zinc, copper and gold respectively from each alloy would be: 64, 96, 160 grams from first alloy; 105, 165 & 210 grams from the second alloy. The total Zinc: Copper: Gold = 169 : 261 : 370.
13. 1kg P contains = 0.45 kg Silver, 0.55 kg Aluminium.
4.5 kg Q contains = 1.35 kg Silver, 1.575 kg Aluminium, 1.575 kg Copper.
Thus newly formed 5.5 kg of alloy contains 1.8 kg Silver & 1.575 kg copper.
Percentage of Silver = $\frac{1.8}{5.5} \approx 33\%$
Percentage of Copper = $\frac{1.575\times 100}{5.5} \approx 29\%$
Option (a) is correct.
14. Let the quantity of chemical x & y be x gm and y gm respectively.
According to the question:
$0.05x + 0.1y \geq 14$

$0.1x + 0.06y \geq 14$

On solving the above two inequalities, we get

$x \geq 80$, $y \geq 100$

Minimum possible cost = 80 × 12.5 + 100 × 8.8 = 1880.

Option (a) is correct.

15. In this question, we can see that we are mixing a 25% water solution, with a 50% water solution to obtain a 40% water solution (2 : 3). The ratio of mixing has to be 2 : 3 (using alligation). Thus, in 12 liters of mixture, we need 4.8 liters from the first can and 7.2 liters from the second can.
    Hence, the correct answer is 4.8 liters.
16. Solving through options, we can check as follows: Total sugar in 10 liters to start with = 1.5 liters. Total sugar to end with in 10 liters = 1 liter. Hence, total sugar released = 1.5 – 1 = 0.5 liters.
    Option (a)—If 1 liter is released each time: First iteration, amount of reduction in sugar = 15% of 1 = 0.15 liters.
    The mixture would now contain 8.65 water and 1.35 sugar.
    Releasing 1 liter again would release less than 0.15 liters (and hence the total release cannot add up to 0.5 liters). Hence, we reject this option.
    Option (d) is the easiest to check after Option (a). Hence, we move to Option (d) next: Option (d)—If 2 liter is released each time: First iteration, amount of reduction in sugar = 15% of 2 = 0.3 liters. The mixture would now contain 8.8 water and 1.2 liters sugar. Releasing 2 liter again would release 12% sugar = 0.24. Hence, total sugar released is 0.54—giving us approximately 10% sugar in the mixture. This is the closest option & hence option (d) is correct.
17. To 400 liters of 25% acid solution, if we add 40% acid solution the resultant will be 30% if we mix the 25% and 40% acid solution in the ratio 2 : 1. Hence, for 30% acid solution, we need to mix 200 liters to 400 liters of the 25% acid solution.
    To 400 liters of 25% acid solution, if we add 40% acid solution the resultant will be 35% if we mix the 25% and 40% acid solution in the ratio 1 : 2. Hence, for 30% acid solution, we need to mix 800 liters to 400 liters of the 25% acid solution. Option (c) is correct.
18. Since the final quantity of Product M used to prepare the final mixture is 864 units, the quantity of chemical X in the mixture would be $\left(\frac{5}{9}\right) \times 864 = 5 \times 96 = 480$.
    Out of this 480 units, the amount of raw material B would be $\frac{3}{4}$ of 480 = 360 units.
    Also, the quantity of chemical Y used in the final mixture would be 864 – 480 = 384. Out of this $\frac{2}{3}$rd would be raw material B. Thus, total raw material B in the final mixture would be 360 + 256 = 616 units. This should be equal to 40% of the final mixture. Thus, the final mixture prepared would be 2.5 × 616 = 1540. The amount of water in this mixture would be 1540 – 864 = 676 units. Option (d) is correct.
19. The difference between just getting an A grade and just getting a B grade would be equal to (number of quizzes × 3). The difference between the required score to manage an A grade and the score achieved to just manage a B grade as given in the problem's information is equal to 97 – 70 = 27.
    Thus, number of quizzes × 3 = 27.
    Hence, professor Mohanty must have taken a total of 9 quizzes. Option (d) is correct.
20. Let the solutions X, Y and Z have concentrations of x, y and z% each. Then, we have:
    $2x + 3y + 4z = 9 \times 30 = 270$
    $4x + 3y + 2z = 9 \times 40 = 360$
    We have a situation, where there are two equations and three unknowns. The relationship between x and z can be established by eliminating y. We have: $2x - 2z = 90$ or $x - z = 45 \rightarrow z = x - 45$
    Putting this value in the two equations, we get: $2x + 3y + 4x - 180 = 270 \rightarrow 6x + 3y = 450 \rightarrow 2x + y = 150$. or $y = 150 - 2x$.
    The strength of $M = \frac{(3y+10z)}{13}$
    $= \frac{3(150-2x)+10(x-45)}{13} = \frac{4x}{13}$
    Thus, the ratio of the strengths of M to X is: $\frac{\frac{4x}{13}}{x} = \frac{4}{13}$
    Option (b) is correct.
21. Assume, you mixed 2 liters of the 40% petrol solution with 3 liters of M in the first case. Then, you will have 5 liters of this mixture. It is then mixed with double quantity of another 40% petrol solution – which means that you are adding 10 liters to this 5-liter mixture. However, since the 10 liters added is also of 40% concentration, you can solve this question on the basis of one mixing – i.e. 12 liters of 40% petrol with 3 liters of M. Thus, the ratio of mixing between 40% petrol and M is 12 : 3 or 4 : 1. Alligation will solve this situation as shown giving us M = 65%.

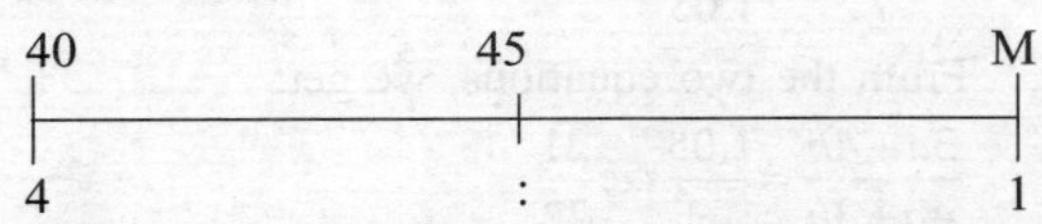

22. There are various methods of solving this question and I would encourage you to try to solve this question, using equations too. Here, I am showing

you the shortest path to solve this question.

The interpretation of the ratio of 12 : 6 : 7 can be that the first drum contains *A*, *B* and *C* in percentages 48%, 24% and 28% respectively.

Also, the final mixture has a percentage of 55, 25 and 20 respectively for *A*, *B* and *C*.

Concentration of A

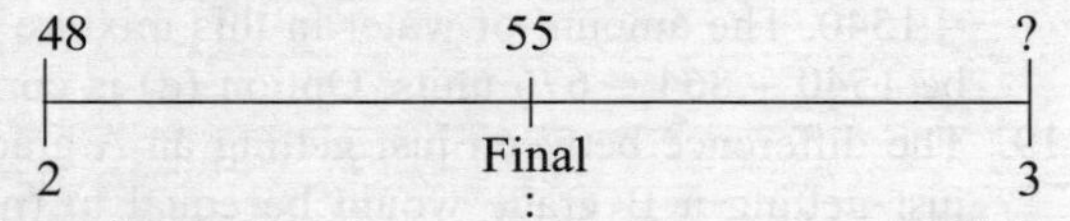

Concentration of B

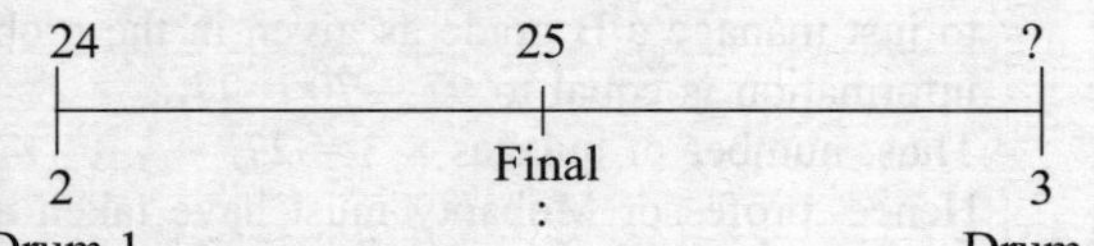

Concentration of C

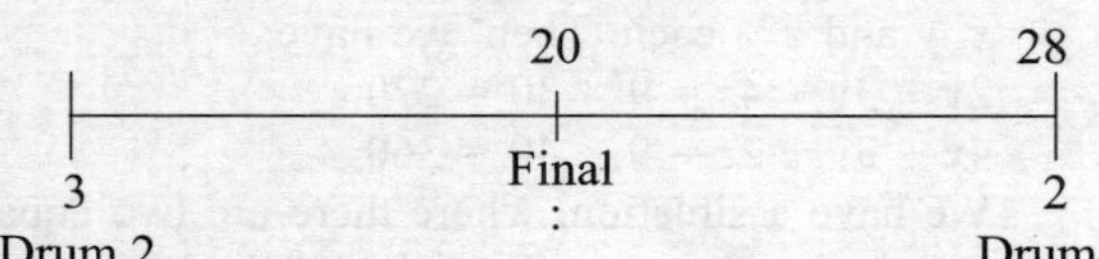

Using Alligation thrice as shown, we can find the respective percentage concentrations of *A*, *B* and *C* in drum 2 as: 59.66, 25.66 and 14.66 respectively. The ratio of A : B : C = 179 : 77 : 44. Option (d) is correct.

23. The withdrawals of 20% thrice are going to have the effect of reducing the alcohol by 20% each time. So, the series of numbers representing the alcohol in the mixture will be:

900 → 720 (after first iteration) → 576 (after second iteration) → 460.8. The total mixture is still 900 + 275 ml = 1175 ml. Hence, the water would be: 1175 – 460.8 = 714.2. Water percentage in the mixture = $\frac{714.2}{1175} \approx 61\%$

24. Let the cost of the two types of rice be *a* and *b* per kg respectively. From the first condition, we have the equation:

$$\frac{3a+4b}{7} = \frac{60}{1.1}$$

From the second condition, we have the equation:

$$\frac{4a+3b}{7} = \frac{60}{1.05}$$

From the two equations, we get:

$$\frac{3a+4b}{4a+3b} = \frac{1.05}{1.1} \text{ i.e. } \frac{21}{22}$$

$$\rightarrow 66a + 88b = 84a + 63b \rightarrow 18a = 25b \rightarrow \frac{a}{b} = \frac{25}{18}$$

Option (a) is correct.

Solutions for Questions 25 and 26:

Let the number of tests he has appeared for, be '*n*' and his average score for '*n*' tests be '*x*'. According to the question:

$$\frac{nx - 30\times 10}{n-10} = x + 2 \rightarrow nx - 300 = nx + 2n - 10x - 20 \rightarrow 10x - 2n = 280$$

Also,

$$\frac{nx - 50\times 10}{n-10} = x - 2 \rightarrow nx - 500 = nx - 2n - 10x + 20 \rightarrow 10x + 2n = 520$$

Solving, we get $x = 40$ and $n = 60$.

Hence, the answers are: 25.40; 26.60.

27. In this question, we can think of two paints *X* and *Y* being mixed in a certain proportion to get the saleable mixture of 10 liters. The cost price of this saleable mixture of 10 liters is ₹256 (since, he will only earn a profit of 25% by selling the mixture at 320, if the Cost of the mixture is 256 – derived by $\frac{320}{1.25}$ or 320 reduced by 20%.)

Thus, the average cost per liter of the mixture is ₹25.6. The alligation picture emerges as shown and since we know that there is lesser quantity of *Y* than *X* in the mixture, the maximum value of the price of *Y*, would occur if the ratio of quantities of *Y* : *X* is taken as 1 : 1.

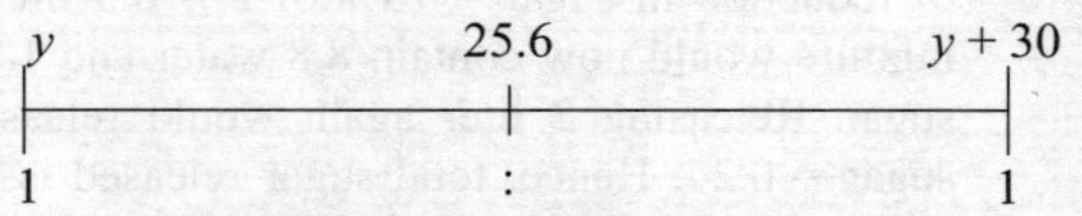

To maximise *y* take the ratio as 1 : 1

In this scenario the maximum value of *Y* emerges as ₹10.6 per liter.

28. Each of three vessels *A*, *B*, *C* contains 800 ml of salt solution of strengths 20%, 24%, and 32%, respectively.

The amount of salt in vessels *A*, *B*, *C* = 160 gm, 192 gm, 256 gm respectively.

The amount of water in vessels *A*, *B*, *C* = 640 ml, 608 ml, 544 ml respectively.

Now, 200 ml of the solution in vessel *A* is transferred to vessel *B*. In this 200 ml of the solution, 40 gm salt and 160 ml water will be transferred. After this, there will be 232 gm salt and 768 ml water in vessel *B*. Then, when 200 ml of the solution in vessel B is transferred to vessel C, there would be 46.4 gm salt and 153.6 ml water going to vessel C. Vessel C's new condition would become: 302.4 gm salt and 697.6 ml water, i.e. it would contain 30.24% salt. Finally, when 200 ml is taken back to vessel *A* (which would have 600 ml solution containing 120 gm salt and 480 ml water), there would be an addition of

60.48 gm of salt and 139.52 ml of water. Thus, at the end of the transfers there would be 180.48 gm salt and 619.52 ml water in 800 ml of the solution in vessel *A*. This means 22.56% of salt concentration. Hence, option (d) is correct.

29. Since the average score of the 11 students other than Amartya is 73, it means that the sum of their scores is 11 × 73 = 803. Of this, Abhijit has scored 80.5, hence the remaining 10 students have scored 722.5. Let the score of Amartya be A. From the second condition:

$$\frac{722.5+A}{11}+1=\frac{803+A}{12}\rightarrow A = 803 \times 11 - 733.5 \times 12 = 31.$$

30. Let the total mixture be 6*x* ml. Out of this 2*x* ml is water and *A* and *B* are 2.5*x* and 1.5*x*, respectively. After 400 ml of the total 6*x* mixture is absorbed – the 5 : 3 ratio between *A* and *B*, becomes 7 : 9. In other words, the 15 : 9 ratio of *A* and *B* becomes 7 : 9. This has happened because the medium has absorbed *A*, while leaving *B* intact. At this stage it makes sense multiply all our assumptions by 6. So, assume starting mixture is 36*x*, out of which 12*x* is water and 15*x* and 9*x* are liquids *A* and *B*. At the end of the absorption, *B* remains at 9*x*, so *A* would have come down to 7*x*. i.e. Total amount absorbed is 12*x* water and 8*x* of liquid *A* – a total of 20*x*. It is given to us that the total mixture absorbed by the medium is 400 ml. So, 20*x* = 400 → *x* = 20. This means that the water absorbed is 12*x* = 12 × 20 = 240 ml.

CHAPTER 7

Profit, Loss and Discount

Chapter Launchpad

Scan this QR code to access a video on 'Introduction to Profit, Loss and Discount' and this chapter's importance for CAT

INTRODUCTION

Profit, Loss and Discount has always been an important chapter for CAT. Besides, all other management entrance exams like XAT, SNAP, NMAT, CMAT, MAT as well as Bank P.O. exams extensively use questions from this chapter.

Besides, you will regularly find questions from this chapter in all other aptitude exams, like CUET, IPMAT, Placement Papers, SSC CGSL, SSC CHSL etc.

THEORY

Profit & Loss are part-and-parcel of every commercial transaction. In fact, the entire economy and the concept of capitalism is based on the so called "Profit Motive". Let us start to look at the basic theory of this chapter by first understanding the typical terminology of this chapter.

Key Terms and Standard Language in Profit and Loss:

Cost Price (CP): It is the price at which a seller has bought an item. It can also be seen to be the cost at which a unit of the product has been produced (in case, it is being produced).

Marked Price (MP): It is the price at which the item is marked for sale.

Percentage Mark Up: The relation between the cost price and the marked price is defined by the 'Percentage Mark Up'. A typical statement involving percentage mark-up would read as follows: 'A shopkeeper marks up his items by 30%.' The interpretation of this statement would be that if the Cost Price is taken as 100, then the Marked Price would be 130. Alternately, you could think of this algebraically also as, if the Cost Price is 'x', then the Marked Price is $1.3x$. Sometimes, you might also be provided with the value of the Cost Price along with the percentage mark up. In such cases, the Marked Price would be obtained by raising the given cost price by the percentage mark up. For instance, given: 'A shopkeeper buys a shirt for ₹400 and marks up the price by 30%' would lead to a reaction of CP = 400, MP = 400 × 1.3 = 520.

Mark Up: Sometimes, the mark-up may be given in terms of a number of Rupees (or currency). So, if the seller marks up the price of his items by ₹10 for items he purchases for ₹40, the marked price would be ₹40 + 10 = ₹50.

The operative relationships are:

CP + Mark up = Marked Price

or CP + % Mark up on CP = Marked Price

Selling Price (SP): The Selling Price is the price at which an item is actually sold for. The Selling Price might be equal to or smaller than the Marked Price. Whether it is equal or lower, depends on whether the seller is giving a discount on the Marked Price. In the case of no discount, the SP = MP. However, if there is a discount offered then the SP < MP.

Discount: Discounts are offered by sellers to attract the buyer to purchase the item/s. Discounts are reductions in the marked price that is made by the seller to sell the item below the marked price. Discounts can be offered in two forms viz:

1. **Absolute Discount:** An absolute discount is a direct value reduction in the Marked Price of an item. Thus, when a seller gives an absolute discount of ₹100 on an item marked at 1200, the SP would be 1200 – 100 = 1100.
2. **Percentage Discount:** When the discount is offered as a percentage of the Marked Price, it is referred to as a percentage discount. Consider the following statement to understand this: 'A shopkeeper offers a discount of 20% on an item marked at ₹1200.' In this case, the MP is given to us as 1200. The SP would be obtained after a 20% reduction on the MP. Thus, the SP = 1200 – 20% of 1200 = 1200 – 240 = 960.

Profit: It is the difference between the Selling Price and the Cost Price, when the SP > CP. Profit = SP – CP.

The operative relationship between CP and SP through mark ups and discounts is:

CP + Mark-up = Marked Price

Marked Price – Discount = Selling Price

Loss: If the CP> SP, then the seller is making a loss on the item. Loss = CP-SP.

Successive Mark Ups: This is best explained by looking at this statement: 'A shopkeeper successively marks up the price of his items by 20% and 10%. What would be the single equivalent mark up?' In this case, if the CP is 100, after a mark-up by 20%, the MP would become 120. However, this is not the final MP, since we will need to increase 120 by 10% again to get the effect of successive markups. We can see that 120 increase by 10%, becomes 132. Hence, the single equivalent mark-up would be 32%. Thus, in effect successive mark ups have to be thought about using the successive change use of the Percentage Change Graphic (PCG) that we have seen extensively in the chapter on percentages.

Successive Discounts: Very much like successive mark-ups, successive discounts are also, solved using the successive percentage change use of the PCG. So, the reaction to a shopkeeper giving two successive discounts of 20% and 10% would be that if the MP be 100, then after a discount of 20%, the MP would become 80. Further, a 10% discount on 80 would make it 72. Thus, successive discounts of 20% and 10% are equivalent to a single discount of 28%.

Percentage Profit: It is defined as Percentage Profit = $\frac{\text{Profit}}{\text{Cost Price}} \times 100$. (**Note:** For percentage loss, the same formula would apply, i.e. Percentage Loss = $\frac{\text{Loss}}{\text{Cost Price}} \times 100$.)

The above situation (although it is the basic building block of Profit, Loss and Discount) is not the normal situation where we face profit and loss problems. In fact, there is a wide application of profit and loss in day-to-day business and economic transactions. It is in these situations that we normally have to work out profit and loss problems.

Having investigated the basic concept of profit and loss for an individual transaction of selling and buying one unit of a product, let us now look at the concept of profit and loss applied to day-to-day business and commercial transactions.

Profit and Loss as Applied to Business and Commercial Transactions

Profit and Loss when Multiple Units of a Product are Being Bought and Sold The basic concept of profit and loss remains unchanged for this situation. However, a common mistake in this type of problem can be avoided if the following basic principle is adopted.

Profit or loss in terms of money can only be calculated when the number of items bought and sold are equal.

That is, profit or loss in money terms cannot be calculated unless we equate the number of products bought and sold.

This is normally achieved by equating the number of items bought and sold at 1 or 100 or some other convenient figure as per the problem asked.

Overlooking of this basic fact is one of the most common mistakes that students are prone to making in the solving of profit and loss problems.

Types of Costs In any business dealing, there is a situation of selling and buying of products and services. From the sellers point of view, his principle interest, apart from maximising the sales price of a product/service, is to minimise the costs associated with the selling of that product/service. The costs that a businessman/trader faces in the process of day-to-day business transaction can be subdivided into three basic categories:

1. **Direct Costs or Variable Costs** This is the cost associated with direct selling of product/service. In other words, this is the cost that varies with every unit of the product sold. Hence, if the variable cost in selling a pen for ₹20 is ₹5, then the variable cost for selling 10 units of the same pen is 10 × 5 = ₹50. As is clear from the above example, that part of the cost that varies directly for every additional unit of the product sold is called as direct or variable cost. *Typical examples of direct costs are:* raw material used in producing one unit of the product, wages to labour in producing one unit of the product when the wages are given on a piece rate basis, and so on. In the case of traders, the cost price per unit bought is also a direct cost (i.e. every such expense that can be tied down to every additional unit of the product sold is a direct cost).
2. **Indirect Costs (Overhead Costs) or Fixed Costs** There are some types of costs that have to be incurred irrespective of the number of items sold and are called as fixed or indirect costs. For example, irrespective of the number of units of a product sold, the rent of the corporate office is fixed. Now, whether the company sells 10 units or 100 units, this rent is fixed and is hence a fixed cost.
   Other examples of indirect or fixed costs: Salary to executives and managers, rent for office, office telephone charges, office electricity charges.
   Apportionment of indirect (or fixed) costs: fixed costs are apportioned equally among each unit of the product sold. Thus, if n units of a product are sold, then the fixed cost to be apportioned to each unit sold is given by
   $$\frac{\text{Fixed costs}}{n}$$
3. **Semi-Variable Costs** Some costs are such that they behave as fixed costs under normal circumstances but have to be increased when a certain level of sales figure is reached. For instance, if the sales increase to such an extent that the company needs to take up an additional office space to accommodate the increase in work due to the increase in sales than the rent for the office space becomes a part of the semi-variable cost.

Concept of Margin or Contribution per Unit The difference between the value of the selling price and the variable cost for a product is known as the margin or the contribution of the product. This margin goes towards the recovery of the fixed costs incurred in selling the product/service.

Concept of the Break-even Point The break-even point is defined as the volume of sale at which there is no profit or no loss. In other words, the sales value in terms of the number of units sold at which the company breaks even is called the break-even point. This point is also called the break-even sales.

Since for every unit of the product, the contribution goes towards recovering the fixed costs, as soon as a company sells more than the break-even sales, the company starts earning a profit. Conversely, when the sales value in terms of the number of units is below the break-even sales, the company makes losses.

The entire scenario is best described through the following example.

Let us suppose that a *pen* shop has to pay a rent of ₹1000 per month and salaries of ₹4000 to the assistants.

Also suppose that this *pen* shop sells only one variety of *pen* for ₹5 each. Further, the direct cost (variable cost) in buying one pen is ₹2.50 per *pen*, then the margin is ₹(5 – 2.50) = ₹2.50 per *pen*.

Now, break-even sales will be given by:

Break-even-sales = Fixed costs/Margin per unit = 5000/2.5 = 2000 *pens*.

Hence, the *pen* shop breaks-even on a monthly basis by selling 2000 *pens*.

Selling every additional *pen* after the 2000th *pen* goes towards increasing the profit of the shop. Also, in the case of the shop incurring a loss, the number of *pens* that are left to be sold to break-even will determine the quantum of the loss.

Note the following formulae:

Profit = (Actual sales – Break-even sales) × Contribution per unit

Also in the case of a loss:

Loss = (Break-even sales – Actual sales) × Contribution per unit

Space for Notes

Also, if the break-even sales equals the actual sales, then we reach the point of no-profit no-loss, which is also the technical definition of the break-even point.

Note: That the break-even point can be calculated on the basis of any time period (but is normally done annually or monthly

Profit Calculation on the Basis of Equating the Amount Spent and the Amount Earned

We have already seen that profit can only be calculated in the case of the number of items being bought and sold being equal. In such a case, we take the difference of the money received and the money given to get the calculation of the profit or the loss in the transaction.

There is another possibility, however, of calculating the profit. This is done by equating the money received and the money spent. In such a case, the profit can be represented by the amount of goods left. This is so because in terms of money, the person going through the transaction has got back all the money that he has spent, but has ended up with some amount of goods leftover after the transaction. These leftover items can then be viewed as the profit or gain for the individual in consideration.

Hence, profit when money is equated is given by goods left. Also, cost in this case is represented by goods sold and

hence percentage profit = $\frac{\text{Goods left}}{\text{Goods sold}} \times 100$.

Example: A fruit vendor recovers the cost of 25 mangoes by selling 20 mangoes. Find his percentage profit.

Solution: Since the money spent is equal to the money earned the percentage profit is given by:

$$\% \text{ Profit} = \frac{\text{Goods left}}{\text{Goods sold}} \times 100 = 5 \times 100/20 = 25\%$$

WORKED-OUT PROBLEMS

Before we get into the problems based on profit and loss, the reader should realise that there are essentially four phases of a profit and loss problem. These are connected together to get higher degrees of difficulty.

These are clues for (a) Cost calculations (b) Marked price calculations (c) Selling price calculations (d) Overheads/fixed costs calculations.

It is left to the reader to understand the interrelationships between *a*, *b*, *c* and *d* above. (These have already been stated in the earlier part of this chapter.)

Problem 7.1: A shopkeeper sold goods for ₹2000 at a profit of 50%. Find the cost price for the shopkeeper.

Solution: The shopkeeper sells his items at a profit of 50%. This means that the selling price is 150% of cost price (Since CP + % Profit = SP)

For short, you should view this as SP = 1.5 CP.

The problem with this calculation is that we know what 150% of the cost price is but we do not know what the cost price itself is. Hence, we have difficulty in directly working out this problem. The calculation will become easier if we know the percentage calculation to be done on the basis of the selling price of the goods.

Hence, look at the equation from the angle → CP = SP/1.5.

Considering the SP as SP/1, we have to find CP as SP/1.5. This means that the denominator is increasing by 50%. But from the table of denominator-change to ratio-change of the chapter of percentages, we can see that when the denominator increases by 50% the ratio decreases by 33.33%.

Interpret this as the CP can be obtanied from the SP by reducing the SP by 33.33%. Hence, the answer is 2000 – (1/3) × 2000 = ₹1333.33.

Also, this question can also be solved through options by going from CP (assumed from the value of the option) to the SP by increasing the assumed CP by 50% to check whether the SP comes out to 2000. If a 50% increase in the assumed CP does not make the SP equal 2000, it means that the assumed CP is incorrect. Hence, you should move to the next option. Use logic to understand whether you go for the higher options or the lower options based on your rejection of the assumed option.

Note: The above question will never appear as a full question in the examination but might appear as a part of a more complex question. If you are able to interpret this statement through the denominator-change to ratio-change table, the time requirement will reduce significantly and you will gain a significant time advantage over this statement.

Problem 7.2: A man buys a shirt and trousers for ₹371. If the trouser costs 12% more than the shirt, find the cost of the shirt.

Solution: Here, we can write the equation:
$s + 1.12s = 371 \rightarrow s = 371/2.12$ (however, this calculation is not very easily done)

An alternate approach will be to go through options. Suppose the options are

(a) ₹125	(b) ₹150
(c) ₹175	(d) ₹200

Checking for, say, ₹150, the thought process should go like:

Let s = cost of a shirt

If $s = 150$, $1.12s$ will be obtained by increasing it by 12%, i.e. 12% of 150 = 18. Hence, the value of $1.12s$ = 150 + 18 = 168 and $s + 1.12s$ = 318 is not equal to 371. Hence, check the next higher option.

If $s = 175$, $1.12s = s + 12\%$ of s = 175 + 21 = 196, i.e. $2.12\ s = 371$.

Hence, option (c) is correct.

Problem 7.3: A shopkeeper sells two items at the same price. If he sells one of them at a profit of 10% and the other at a loss of 10%, find the percentage profit/loss.

Generic question: A shopkeeper sells two items at the same price. If he sells one of them at a profit of x% and the other at a loss of x%, find the percentage profit/loss.

Solution: The result will always be a loss of $[x/10]^2\%$. Hence, the answer here is $[10/10]^2\%$ = 1% loss.

Problem 7.4: For Problem 7.3, find the value of the loss incurred by the shopkeeper, if the price of selling each item is ₹160.

Solution: When there is a loss of 10% → 160 = 90% of CP_1. ∴ $CP_1 = 177.77$

When there is a profit of 10% → 160 = 110% of CP_2
∴ $CP_2 = 145.45$

Hence, total cost price = 177.77 + 145.45 = 323.23 while the net realisation is ₹320.

Hence, loss is ₹3.23.

Short cut for calculation: Since by selling the two items for ₹320, the shopkeeper gets a loss of 1% (from the previous problem), we can say that ₹320 is 99% of the value of the cost price of the two items. Hence, the total cost is given by 320/0.99 (solution of this calculation can be approximately done on the percentage change graphic).

Problem 7.5: If by selling two items for ₹180 each, the shopkeeper gains 20% on one and loses 20% on the other, find the value of the loss.

Solution: The percentage loss in this case will always be $(20/10)^2 = 4\%$ loss.

We can see this directly as 360 → 96% of the CP → CP = 360/0.96. Hence, by percentage change graphic, 360 has to be increased by 4.166 % = 360 + 4.166% of 360 = 360 + 14.4 + 0.6 = ₹375.

Hence, the loss is ₹15.

Problem 7.6: By selling 15 mangoes, a fruit vendor recovers the cost price of 20 mangoes. Find the profit percentage.

Solution: Here since the expenditure and the revenue are equated, we can use percentage profit = (goods left × 100)/ goods sold = 5 × 100/15 = 33.33%.

Problem 7.7: A dishonest shopkeeper uses a 900 gram weight instead of 1 kilogram weight. Find his profit percent, if he sells per kilogram at the same price as he buys a kilogram.

Solution: Here again the money spent and the money received are equal. Hence, the percentage profit is received by goods left × 100/goods sold.

This gives us 11.11%.

Problem 7.8: A manufacturer makes a profit of 15% by selling a colour TV for ₹6900. If the cost of manufacturing increases by 30% and the price paid by the retailer is increased by 20%, find the profit percent made by the manufacturer.

Solution: For this problem, the first line gives us that the cost price of the TV for the manufacturer is ₹6000.

(By question stem analysis, you should be able to solve this part of the problem in the first reading and reach at the figure of 6000 as cost, before you read further. This can be achieved advantageously if your percentage rule calculations are strong. Hence, work on it. The better you can get at it, the more it will benefit you. In fact, one of the principal reasons I get through the CAT every year is the strength in percentage calculation. Besides, percentage calculation will also go a long way in improving your scores in data interpretation.)

Further, if you have reached to the 6000 figure by the end of the first line, reading further you can increase this advantage by calculating while reading as follows:

Manufacturing cost increase by 30% → New manufacturing cost = 7800 and new selling price is 6900 + 20% of 6900 = 6900 + 1380 = 8280.

Hence, profit = 8280 – 7800 = 480 and profit percent = 480 × 100/7800 = 6.15%.

Problem 7.9: Find a single discount to equal three consecutive discounts of 10%, 12% and 5%.

Solution: Using percentage change graphic, starting from 100: we get 100 → 88 → 83.6 → 75.24 (**Note:** we can change percentages in any order).

Hence, the single discount is 24.76%.

Problem 7.10: A reduction in the price of petrol by 10% enables a motorist to buy five gallons more for $180. Find the original price of petrol.

Solution: 10% reduction in price → 11.11% increase in consumption.

But 11.11% increase in consumption is equal to five gallons. Hence, original consumption is equal to 45 gallons for $180. Hence, original price = 4$ per gallon.

Problem 7.11: Ashok bought an article and spent ₹110 on its repairs. He then sold it to Bhushan at a profit of 20%. Bhushan sold it to Charan at a loss of 10%. Charan finally sold it for ₹1188 at a profit of 10%. How much did Ashok pay for the article?

(a) ₹890 (b) ₹1000
(c) ₹780 (d) ₹840

Solution: Solve through options using percentage rule and keep checking options as you read. Try to finish the first option-check before you finish reading the question for the first time. Also, as a thumb rule always start with the middle, most convenient option. This way you are likely to be required lesser number of options, on an average. Option (a) is correct.

Also note that LOD II and LOD III questions will always essentially use the same sentences as used in LOD I questions. The only requirement that you need to have to handle LOD II and III questions is the ability to string together a set of statements and interconnect them.

Problem 7.12: A dishonest businessman professes to sell his articles at cost price but he uses false weights with which he cheats by 10% while buying and by 10% while selling. Find his percentage profit.

Solution: Assume that the businessman buys and sells 1 kg of items. While buying, he cheats by 10%, which means that when he buys 1 kg, he actually takes 1100 gm. Similarly, he cheats by 10% while selling, that is, he gives only 900 g when he sells a kilogram. Also, it must be understood that since he purportedly buys and sells the same amount of goods and he is trading at the same price while buying and selling, money is already equated in this case. Hence, we can directly use: % Profit = (Goods left × 100/Goods sold) = 200 × 100/900 = 22.22% (**Note** that you should not need to do this calculation since this value comes from the fraction to percentage conversion table).

If you are looking at 70% plus net score in quantitative ability you should be able to come to the solution in about 25 seconds inclusive of problem reading time. And the calculation should go like this:

Money is equated → % profit = 2/9 = 22.22%

The longer process of calculation in this case would be involving the use of equating the amount of goods bought and sold and the money value of the profit. However, if you try to do this, you will easily see that it requires a much higher degree of calculations and the process will tend to get messy.

The options for doing this problem by equating goods would point to comparing the price per gram bought or sold. Alternatively, we could use the price per kilogram bought and sold (which would be preferable to equating on a per gram basis for this problem).

Here the thought process would be:

Assume price per kilogram = ₹1000. Therefore, he buys 1100 g while purchasing and sells 900 g while selling. To equate the two, use the following process:

	Money paid	Amount of goods	
Buying	₹1000	1100	gram (Reduce this by 10%)
After reduction	₹900	990	gram
Selling	₹1000	900	gram (Increase this by 10%)
After increase	₹1100	990	

Problem 7.13: RFO Tripathi bought some oranges in Nagpur for ₹32. He has to sell it off in Yeotmal. He is able to sell off all the oranges in Yeotmal and on reflection finds that he has made a profit equal to the cost price of 40 oranges. How many oranges did RFO Tripathi buy?

Solution: Suppose we take the number of oranges bought as x. Then, the cost price per orange would be ₹$32/x$, and his profit would by $40 \times 32/x = 1280/x$.

To solve for x, we need to equate this value with some value on the other side of the equation. But, we have no information provided here to find out the value of the variable x. Hence, we cannot solve this equation.

Problem 7.14: By selling five articles for ₹15, a man makes a profit of 20%. Find his gain or loss percentage if he sells eight articles for ₹18.4.

Solution: Questions of this type normally appear as part of a more complex problem in an exam like the CAT.

Remember, such a question should be solved by you as soon as you finish reading the question by solving-while-reading process, as follows.

By selling five articles for ₹15, a man makes a profit of 20% → SP = 3. He nce, CP = 2.5, if he sells eight articles for ₹18.4 → SP = 2.3. Hence percentage loss = 8%. For solving this question, through this method with speed, you need to develop the skill and ability to calculate percentage changes through the percentage change graphic. For this purpose, you should not be required to use a pencil and a paper.

Problem 7.15: Oranges are bought at 12 for a rupee and are sold at 10 for a rupee. Find the percentage profit or loss.

Solution: Since money spent and received are equated, use the formula for profit calculation in terms of goods left/goods sold.

This will give you percentage profit = 2/10 = 20%.

Alternatively, you can also equate the goods and calculate the percentage profit on the basis of money as

CP of 1 orange = 8.33 paise

SP of 1 orange = 10 paise

8.33 paise → 10 paise (corresponds to a percentage increase of 20% on CP)

Problem 7.16: In order to maximise its profits, Mindworkzz Corporate defines a function. Its unit sales price is ₹700 and the function representing the cost of production = 300 + $2p^2$, where p is the total units produced or sold. Find the most profitable production level. Assume that everything produced is necessarily sold.

Solution: The function for profit is a combination of revenue and costs. It is given by Profit = Revenue – Costs = $700p - (300 + 2p^2) = -2p^2 + 700p - 300$.

In order to find the maxima or minima of any quadratic function, we differentiate it and equate the differentiated equation to zero.

Thus, the differentiated profit function is $-4p + 700 = 0 \rightarrow p = 175$. This value of production will yield the maximum profits in this case.

Note: Whether a quadratic function is maximum or minimum, is decided by redifferentiating the differentiated equation. We then look at the sign of the constant term to determine whether the value got by equating the differentiated equation to zero corresponds to the maximum or the minimum. In the case of the constant term, left being negative, we say that the function is a maxima function and hence the solution point got would be a maximum point. In the event that the final constant term is positive, it is a minimum function.

Short Cut: Just look at the coefficient of x^2 in the function. If it is positive, equating the first differentiation to zero would yield the minimum point, and if the coefficient of x^2 is negative, the function is a maximum function.

Problem 7.17: For Problem 6.16, what is the value of the maximum profits for Mindworkzz Corporate?

Solution: For this, continuing from the previous question's solution, we just put the value of $p = 175$ in the equation for profit. Thus, substitute $p = 175$ in the equation. Profit $= -2p^2 + 700p - 300$ and get the answer.

Problem 7.18: A shopkeeper allows a rebate of 25% to the buyer. He sells only smuggled goods and as a bribe, he pays 10% of the cost of the article. If his cost price is ₹2500, then find what should be the marked price if he desires to make a profit of 9.09%.

Solution: Use solving-while-reading as follows: Cost price (= 2500) + Bribe (= 10% cost of article = 250) = Total cost to the shopkeeper (2500 + 250 = 2750).

He wants a profit of 9.09 percent on this value → Using fraction to percentage change table, we get 2750 + 9.09% of 2750 = 2750 + 250 = ₹3000.

But this ₹3000 is obtained after a rebate of 25%. Since we do not have the value of the marked price on which 25% rebate is to be calculated, it would be a good idea to work reverse through the percentage change graphic.

Going from the marked price to ₹3000 requires a 25% rebate. Hence, the reverse process will be obtained by increasing ₹3000 by 33.33% and getting ₹4000.

Note: The use of percentage change graphic in general and the product constancy table in particular in solving this question]

Problem 7.19: A man sells three articles, one at a loss of 10%, another at a profit of 20% and the third one at a loss of 25%. If the selling price of all the three is the same, find by how much percent is their average CP lower than or higher than their SP.

Solution:

Note: It is always convenient to solve questions involving percentages by using the number 100. The reason for this is that it reduces the amount of effort required in calculating the solution. Hence, it goes without saying that the variable to be fixed at 100 should be the one with the highest number of calculations associated with it. Another thumb rule for this is that the variable to be fixed at 100 should be the one with which the most difficult calculation set is associated.

We have to calculate: (average CP – average SP)/average SP.

Here, the selling price is equal in all three cases. Since the maximum number of calculations are associated with the SP, we assume it to be 100. This gives us an average SP of 100 for the three articles. Then, the first article will cost 111.11, the second 83.33 and the third 133.33. (The student is advised to be fluent at these calculations) Further, the CP of the three articles is 111.11 + 83.33 + 133.33 = 327.77.

The average CP of the three articles is 327.77/3 = 109.2566.

Hence, (average CP – average SP)/average SP = 9.2566%.

Any other process adopted for this problem is likely to require much more effort and time.

Note: This process will be feasible if you have worked well with the percentage calculation techniques of the previous chapter.

Space for Rough Work

LEVEL OF DIFFICULTY (I)

1. By selling a watch for ₹560, a shopkeeper incurs a loss of 20%. Find the cost price of the watch for the shopkeeper.
(a) ₹600 (b) ₹700
(c) ₹610 (d) ₹640
2. By selling a cap for ₹29.75, a man gains 6.25%. What will be the CP of the cap?
(a) ₹26 (b) ₹27.5
(c) ₹28 (d) ₹27.80
3. A cellular phone when sold for ₹3808 fetches a profit of 12%. Find the cost price of the cellular phone.
(a) ₹3190 (b) ₹3400
(c) ₹3260 (d) ₹3560
4. A machine costs ₹1025. If it is sold at a loss of 25%, what will be its cost price as a percentage of its selling price?
(a) 125% (b) 116.67%
(c) 120% (d) 133.33%
5. A shopkeeper sold goods for ₹1800 and made a profit of 20% in the process. Find his profit per cent if he had sold his goods for ₹1687.5.
(a) 11.5% (b) 10.5%
(c) 12.5% (d) 6.25%
6. A tablet is sold for ₹6612.5 at a profit of 15%. What would have been the actual profit or loss on it, if it had been sold for ₹5380?
(a) ₹370 (b) ₹410
(c) ₹480 (d) ₹340
7. A marble table when sold for ₹6400 gives a loss of 11.11% to the merchant who sells it. Calculate his loss or gain per cent, if he sells it for ₹7812.
(a) Loss of 8.625% (b) Profit of 8.5%
(c) Loss of 8% (d) Profit of 7.5%
8. By selling bouquets for ₹69, a florist gains 15%. At what price should he sell the bouquets to gain 20% on the cost price?
(a) ₹72 (b) ₹75
(c) ₹66 (d) ₹78
9. A shopkeeper bought 480 chocolates at ₹6 per dozen. If he sold all of them at ₹0.75 each, what was his profit per cent?
(a) 50% (b) 33(1/3)%
(c) 75% (d) 20%
10. A feeding bottle is sold for ₹150. Sales tax accounts for one-fifth of this and profit one-third of the remainder. Find the cost price of the feeding bottle.
(a) ₹72 (b) ₹80
(c) ₹90 (d) ₹76
11. An iron merchant makes a profit of 30% by selling iron at ₹26 per quintal. If he sells the iron at ₹22.50 per quintal, what is his profit per cent on the whole investment?
(a) 12.5% (b) 6.66%
(c) 7.5% (d) 8%
12. The cost price of a shirt and a pair of trousers is ₹473. If the shirt costs 15% more than the trousers, find the cost price of the trouser.
(a) ₹243 (b) ₹253
(c) ₹210 (d) ₹220
13. A pet shop owner sells two puppies at the same price. On one he makes a profit of 25% and on the other he suffers a loss of 25%. Find his loss or gain per cent on the whole transaction.
(a) Gain of 6.25% (b) No profit no loss
(c) Loss of 12.5% (d) Loss of 6.25%
14. The marked price of a table is ₹1200, which is 20% above the cost price. It is sold at a discount of 10% on the marked price. Find the profit per cent.
(a) 10% (b) 8%
(c) 7.5% (d) 6%
15. 125 toffees cost ₹75. Find the cost of one million toffees if there is a discount of 40% on the selling price for this quantity.
(a) ₹3,00,000 (b) ₹3,20,000
(c) ₹3,60,000 (d) ₹4,00,000
16. A shopkeeper marks the price of an article at ₹250. Find the cost price if after allowing a discount of 20% he still gains 25% on the cost price.
(a) 210 (b) 160
(c) 200 (d) 180
17. In Question 16, what will be the selling price of the article if he allows two successive discounts of 10% each?
(a) 202.5 (b) 225
(c) 200 (d) 197.5
18. A dozen pairs of gloves quoted at ₹120 are available at a discount of 20%. Find how many pairs of gloves can be bought for ₹16.
(a) 2 (b) 3
(c) 4 (d) 6
19. Find a single discount equivalent to the discount series of 25%, 20%, 10%.
(a) 66% (b) 46%
(c) 54% (d) 34%
20. The printed price of a calculator is ₹225. A retailer pays ₹148.5 for it by getting successive discounts of 20% and another rate which is illegible. What is the second discount rate?
(a) 17% (b) 18.5%
(c) 16% (d) 17.5%

21. How much percent more than the cost price should a shopkeeper mark his goods, so that after allowing a discount of 6.25% he should have a gain of 25% on his outlay?
(a) 33.33% (b) 16.66%
(c) 25% (d) 20%

22. In order to maintain the price line, a trader allows a discount of 20% on the marked price of goods in his shop. However, he still makes a gross profit of 12% on the cost price. Find the profit per cent he would have made on the selling price had he sold at the marked price.
(a) 35.67% (b) 40.67%
(c) 40% (d) 35%

23. A whole-seller allows a discount of 25% on the list price to a retailer. The retailer sells at 10% discount on the list price. If the customer paid ₹54 for an article, what is the profit by the retailer?
(a) 12 (b) 9
(c) 5 (d) 8

24. In Question 23, also find the retailer's percentage profit on his cost giving your answer correct to two decimal places.
(a) 33.33% (b) 16.66%
(c) 20% (d) 25%

25. The cost of production of a cordless phone set in 2016 is ₹1100, divided between material, labour and overheads in the ratio 4 : 5 : 2. If the cordless phone set is marked at a price that gives a 10% profit on the component of price accounted for by labour, what is the marked price of the set?
(a) ₹1140 (b) ₹1210
(c) ₹1120 (d) ₹1150

26. For Question 25, if subsequently in 2017, the cost of material, labour and overheads increased by 20%, 30% and 10% respectively, calculate the cost of manufacturing in 2017.
(a) ₹1350 (b) ₹1150
(c) ₹1250 (d) ₹1450

27. What should be the new marked price if the criteria for profit is to remain the same as for Question 25 above?
(a) ₹1420 (b) ₹1405
(c) ₹1415 (d) None of these

28. By selling a casserole for ₹820, a man incurs a loss of 18%. At what price should he sell the casserole to gain 28%?
(a) ₹1180 (b) ₹1280
(c) ₹1220 (d) None of these

29. A man sells 5 articles for ₹15 and makes a profit of 20%. Find his gain or loss percent if he sells 8 such articles for ₹18.40.
(a) 2.22% profit (b) 2.22% loss
(c) 8% loss (d) 8% profit

30. The cost price of 40 Oranges is equal to the selling price of 30 Oranges. Find the percentage profit.
(a) 20% (b) 25%
(c) 33.33% (d) None of these

31. P owns a house worth ₹20,000. He sells it to Q at a profit of 25%. After some time, Q sells it back to P at 25% loss. Find P's loss or gain percent.
(a) 25% gain (b) 6.25% gain
(c) 31.56% gain (d) 31.25% gain

32. A shopkeeper bought locks at the rate of 8 locks for ₹34 and sold them at the rate of 12 locks for ₹57. Calculate his gain percent.
(a) 9.33% (b) 12.5%
(c) 11.11% (d) 11.76%

33. Vikas bought an article at ₹150 and sold it at a profit of 20%. What would have been the increase in the profit percent if it was sold for ₹195?
(a) 10% (b) 5%
(c) 15% (d) None of these

34. A makes an article for ₹250 and sells it to B at a profit of 20%. B sells it to C who sells it for ₹386.4, making a profit of 15%. What profit percent did B make?
(a) 20% (b) 12%
(c) 16.66% (d) 33.33%

35. A reduction of 20% in the price of sugar enables a housewife to buy 5.4 kg. more for ₹432. Find the reduced price per kilogram
(a) ₹20 (b) ₹16
(c) ₹18 (d) None of these

36. A man buys 50 kg of oil at ₹10 per kilogram and another 40 kg of oil at ₹12 kilogram and mixes them. He sells the mixture at the rate of ₹11 per kilogram. What will be his gain percent if he is able to sell the whole lot?
(a) 100/98% (b) 100(10/49)%
(c) 10(1/49)% (d) None of these

37. If the cost price of 25 articles is equal to the selling price of 15 articles, find the profit percent.
(a) 33.33% (b) 20%
(c) 66.67% (d) 50%

38. A shopkeeper sells sugar in such a way that the selling price of 850 gm is the same as the cost price of one kilogram. Find his gain percent.
(a) 150/17% (b) 100/17%
(c) 17(11/17)% (d) 1/17%

39. A dealer buys eggs at ₹72 per gross. He sells the eggs at a profit of 6.25% on the cost price. What is the selling price per egg (approximately)?
(a) 53 paise (b) 50 paise
(c) 49 paise (d) 52 paise

40. P sold a table to Q at a profit of 25%. Q sold the same table to R for ₹90 thereby making a profit of 20%. Find the price at which P bought the table from Z if it is known that Z gained 25% in the transaction.

(a) ₹80 (b) ₹75
(c) ₹90 (d) ₹60

41. *A* sold a table to *B* at a profit of 15%. Later on, *B* sold it back to *A* at a profit of 20%, thereby gaining ₹69. How much did *A* pay for the table originally?
(a) ₹300 (b) ₹320
(c) ₹345 (d) ₹350

42. A dealer sold two TV sets for ₹9600 each, gaining 20% on one and losing 20% on the other set. Find his net gain or net loss.
(a) ₹400 loss (b) ₹800 loss
(c) ₹400 gain (d) ₹800 gain

43. On selling tea at ₹20 per kg a loss of 10% is incurred. Calculate the amount of tea (in kg) sold if the total loss incurred is ₹60.
(a) 27 kg (b) 21 kg
(c) 15 kg (d) 30 kg

44. A colour TV and a VCP were sold for ₹19,800 each. The TV was sold at a loss of 10% whereas the VCP was sold at a gain of 10%. Find gain or loss in the whole transaction.
(a) ₹400 loss (b) ₹1000 loss
(c) ₹960 loss (d) ₹1040 loss
(*Note:* In this case there will always be a loss)

45. A man sells a TV set for ₹33000 and makes a profit of 10%. He sells another TV at a loss of 20%. If on the whole, he neither gains nor loses, find the selling price of the second TV set.
(a) ₹15,000 (b) ₹12,000
(c) ₹30,000 (d) ₹27,000

46. A man sells an article at 10% above its cost price. If he had bought it at 15% less than what he paid for it and sold it for ₹33 less, he would have gained 10%. Find the cost price of the article.
(a) ₹400 (b) ₹260
(c) ₹325 (d) ₹200

47. A briefcase was sold at a profit of 5%. If its cost price was 5% less and it was sold for ₹63 more, the gain would have been 20%. Find the cost price of the briefcase.
(a) ₹800 (b) ₹900
(c) ₹700 (d) ₹960

48. A man sells a plot of land at 8% profit. If he had sold it at 15% profit, he would have received ₹630 more. What is the selling price of the land?
(a) ₹9320 (b) ₹9600
(c) ₹9820 (d) ₹9720

49. Ashok bought an article and spent ₹110 on its repairs. He then sold it to Bhushan at a profit of 20%. Bhushan sold it to Charan at a loss of 10%. Charan finally sold it for ₹1188 at a profit of 10%. How much did Ashok pay for the article?
(a) ₹890 (b) ₹1000
(c) ₹780 (d) ₹840

50. A man buys two cycles for a total cost of ₹900. By selling one for 4/5 of its cost and other for 5/4 of its cost, he makes a profit of ₹90 on the whole transaction. Find the cost price of lower priced cycle.
(a) ₹360 (b) ₹250
(c) ₹300 (d) ₹420

51. A merchant bought two transistors, which together cost him ₹480. He sold one of them at a loss of 15% and other at a gain of 19%. If the selling price of both the transistors are equal, find the cost of the lower priced transistor.
(a) ₹300 (b) ₹180
(c) ₹200 (d) ₹280

52. A manufacturer makes a profit of 15% by selling a colour TV for ₹5750. If the cost of manufacturing increases by 30% and the price paid by the retailer is increased by 20%, find the profit percent made by the manufacturer.
(a) 6(2/13)% (b) 4 (8/13)%
(c) 6(1/13)% (d) 7(4/13)%

53. The cost of manufacturing an article is made up of materials, labour and overheads in the ratio 6 : 7 : 2. If the cost of labour is ₹350, find the profit percent if the article is sold for ₹900.
(a) 30% (b) 33.33%
(c) 20% (d) 25%

54. Two dealers *P* and *Q* selling the same model of TV set mark them under the same selling prices. *P* gives successive discounts of 20% and 15% and *Q* gives successive discounts of 18% and 17%. From whom is it more profitable to purchase the TV set?
(a) From *P*
(b) From *Q*
(c) Indifferent between the two
(d) Cannot be determined

55. A sells a car priced at ₹1,80,000. He gives a discount of 5% on the first ₹1,00,000 and 12.5% on the remaining ₹80,000. His competitor *B* sells a car on the same marked priced at ₹1,80,000. If he wants to be competitive what percent discount should *B* offer on the marked price.
(a) 3.33% (b) 15.67%
(c) 8.33% (d) 6.67%

56. An article costs ₹1400 to a manufacturer who lists its price at ₹1600. He sells it to a trader at a discount of 5%. The trader gets a further discount of 5% on his net payment for paying in cash. Calculate the amount that the trader pays to the manufacturer.
(a) ₹1444 (b) ₹1420
(c) ₹1434 (d) None of these

57. In Question 56, find the profit percent that the manufacturer makes on the sale.
(a) 20/7% (b) 22/7%
(c) 15/7% (d) None of these

58. A firm dealing in furniture allows 5% discount on the marked price of each item. What price must be marked on a dining table that cost ₹2000 to assemble, so as to make a profit of 14%?
(a) ₹3800 (b) ₹2700
(c) ₹2500 (d) ₹2400

59. A shopkeeper allows a discount of 10% on the marked price of a certain article and makes a profit of 12.5%. If the article cost the shopkeeper ₹360, what price must be marked on the article?
(a) ₹410 (b) ₹450
(c) ₹480 (d) None of these

60. A Camera shop allows a discount of 15% on the advertised price of a camera. What price must be marked on the camera, that costs him ₹600, so that he makes a profit of 19%?
(a) ₹840 (b) ₹820
(c) ₹750 (d) ₹880

61. A watch dealer pays 20% custom duty on a watch that costs ₹450 abroad. For how much should he mark it, if he desires to make a profit of 25% after giving a discount of 20% to the buyer?
(a) ₹800 (b) ₹843.75
(c) ₹810 (d) ₹840.75

62. A shopkeeper buys an article for ₹1200 and marks it for sale at a price that gives him 60% profit on his cost. He, however, gives a 35% discount on the marked price to his customer. Calculate the actual percentage profit made by the shopkeeper.
(a) 2% (b) 4%
(c) 3% (d) 56%

63. In the land of the famous milkman Merghese Durian, a milkman sells his buffalo for ₹15400 at some profit. Had he sold his buffalo at ₹8200, the quantum of the loss incurred would have been double that of the profit earned. What is the cost price?
(a) ₹13200 (b) ₹12900
(c) ₹13500 (d) None of these

64. A trader purchases apples at ₹70 per hundred. He spends 10% on the transportation. What should be the selling price per 100 to earn a profit of 30%?
(a) ₹101.1 (b) ₹100.1
(c) ₹90.1 (d) ₹99.1

65. A dishonest dealer professes to sell at cost price but uses a 800 gram weight instead of a 1 kilogram weight. Find the percent profit to the dealer.
(a) 25% (b) 20%
(c) 12.5% (d) None of these

Space for Rough Work

LEVEL OF DIFFICULTY (II)

1. Amit makes 250 articles at a cost of 80 paise per article. He fixes the selling price such that if only 200 articles are sold, he would have made a profit of 20% on the total outlay. However, 20 articles got spoilt and he was able to sell 230 articles at this price. Find his actual profit percent as the percentage of total outlay assuming that the unsold articles are useless.
(a) 32% (b) 33%
(c) 38% (d) 36%
2. Sudhir estimates that on inspection, 20% of the articles he produces will be rejected. He accepts an order to supply 10,000 articles at ₹1.5 each. He estimates the profit on his outlay including the manufacturing of rejected articles, to be 20%. Find the cost of manufacturing each article.
(a) ₹1 (b) ₹0.50
(c) ₹1.5 (d) ₹2.50
3. Kavita fixed the selling price of her goods at 30% above the cost price. She sells 60% of the stock at this price, 30% of her stock at a discount of 20% on the original selling price and rest at a discount of 50% on the original selling price. Find the gain percent altogether.
(a) 14.75% (b) 15.70%
(c) 15.75% (d) 16.75%
4. A tradesman marks an article at ₹150 more than the cost price. He allows a discount of 20% on the marked price. Find the profit percent if the cost price is ₹x.
(a) $(12000 - 10x)/x$ (b) $(12000 - 20x)/x$
(c) $(12000 - 30x)/x$ (d) $(12000 + 40x)/x$
5. Daniella goes to a shop to purchase a TV priced at ₹80,000. She is offered four discount options by the shopkeeper. Which of these options should she opt for to gain maximum advantage of the discount offered?
(a) Single discount of 40%
(b) Two successive discounts of 20% each
(c) Two successive discounts of 30% and 10%
(d) Two successive discounts of 28% and 12%
6. Ashok marks up the price of his goods by 40% and gives a discount of 20% to the customer. He also uses a 800 g weight instead of a 1 kg weight. Find his percentage profit due to these maneuvers.
(a) 35.89 % (b) 40%
(c) 30% (d) 36%
7. A dishonest dealer marks up the price of his goods by 30% and gives a discount of 20% to the customer. Besides, he also cheats both his supplier and his buyer by 100 grams while buying or selling 1 kilogram. Find the percentage profit earned by the shopkeeper.
(a) 28.12% (b) 25.54%
(c) 23.12% (d) 27.11%
8. For Question 7, if it is known that the shopkeeper takes a discount of 10% from his supplier and he disregards this discount while marking up (i.e. he marks up at the undiscounted price), find the percentage profit for the shopkeeper, if there is no other change from the previous problem.
(a) 42.67% (b) 46.66%
(c) 40.33% (d) 41.23%
9. Ashok bought some pens at 2 per rupee and an equal number at 3 per rupee. He then sold the entire quantity at 6 for 2 rupees. What is his percentage profit or loss?
(a) 11.23% loss (b) 20% loss
(c) 8.888% profit (d) No profit no loss
10. A watch seller sells watches at ₹6000 per watch. However, he is forced to give two successive discounts of 15% and 10% respectively. However, he recovers the sales tax on the net sale price from the customer at 10% of the net price. What price does a customer have to pay him to buy the watch?
(a) ₹5390 (b) ₹5049
(c) ₹5380 (d) ₹5490
11. Satnam bought 50 kg of rice for ₹1000 and sold it at a loss of as much money as he received for 10 kg rice. At what price did he sell the rice?
(a) ₹16.67 per kg (b) ₹12.16 per kg
(c) ₹12.5 per kg (d) ₹12.33 per kg
12. A carpenter wants to sell 40 chairs. If he sells them at ₹156 per chair, he would be able to sell all the chairs. But for every ₹6 increase in price, he will be left with one additional unsold chair. At what selling price would he be able to maximise his profits (assuming unsold chairs remain with him)?
(a) 198 (b) 192
(c) 204 (d) 210
13. The cost of setting up the type of a magazine is ₹1000. The cost of running the printing machine is ₹120 per 100 copies. The cost of paper, ink and so on is 60 paise per copy. The magazines are sold at ₹2.75 each. Nine hundred copies are printed, but only 784 copies are sold. What is the sum to be obtained from advertisements to give a profit of 10% on the cost? (Assume no other source of revenues apart from sales and advertising)
(a) ₹730 (b) ₹720
(c) ₹726 (d) ₹736

14. A shopkeeper makes a profit of x% by selling an object for ₹50. Had the cost price and selling price been interchanged, it would have led to a loss of 0.8x%. With the latter cost price, what should be the new selling price to get a profit of x%?
(a) ₹50 (b) ₹55
(c) ₹62.5 (d) ₹58.4

15. Find the change in the percentage profit for a fruit vendor who, after finding 30% of the fruits rotten, increased his selling price by 20% over and above 25% that he was already charging?
(a) –20 (b) +10.5
(c) –15 (d) –10.5

Directions for Questions 16 and 17: Read the following and answer the questions that follow.

A and *B* decided to sell their bikes each at ₹36,000. While *A* decided to give a discount of 8% on the first ₹8000, 5% on next ₹12,000 and 3% on the rest to buyer *C*, *B* decided to give a discount of 7% on the first 12,000, 6% on the next 8,000 and 5% on the rest to buyer *D*. These discounts were, however, subject to the buyers making the payment on time failing which the discount gets reduced by 1% for every delay of a week. In each case, the selling price of 36,000 was arrived at by increasing the cost price by 25%.

16. If each of them got the payments on time, what is the approximate percentage profit of the person getting the higher profit?
(a) 19% (b) 21%
(c) 25% (d) 17%

17. If *C* defaults by 1 and 2 weeks in the second and third payments respectively, what would be the profit of *A* in the sale of the car?
(a) ₹5920 (b) ₹6240
(c) ₹5860 (d) ₹5980

18. What would be the difference in the profits if both the buyers default in each payment by a week?
(a) ₹200 (b) ₹300
(c) ₹400 (d) ₹500

19. Find the selling price of goods if two salesmen claim to make 20% profit each, one calculating it on cost price while another on the selling price, the difference in the profits earned being ₹500 and selling price being the same in both the cases.
(a) ₹15,000 (b) ₹16,000
(c) ₹12,000 (d) ₹25,000

20. Ashok calculates percentage profit on the buying price and Baman on the selling price. What will be their difference in profits if both claim a profit of 10% on goods sold for ₹6000?
(a) ₹68.33 (b) ₹54.44
(c) ₹36.67 (d) ₹70

21. A pen company made 5000 pens at a cost of ₹9600. The company gave away 1000 pens to stationary shopkeepers as free samples. A discount of 10% was allowed on the printed price. Find the ratio of profit if the marked price is raised from ₹3.00 to ₹4.00 per pen and if at the latter price, samples to shopkeeper were done away with. (New profit/old profit) Assuming all other things as constant.
(a) 1: 3 (b) 2:5
(c) 1: 7 (d) 7: 1

22. Saurav makes a profit of 10% by selling an article. What would be the percentage change in the profit percent had he paid 10% less for it and the customer paid 10% more for it?
(a) 244.44% (b) 125%
(c) 133.33% (d) 122.22%

23. A pen costs ₹10 and was marked 20% above the cost price. After two successive discounts of the same percentage, the customer now pays ₹9.48. What would be the change in profit had the price been increased by the same percentage twice successively instead of reducing it?
(a) ₹5.04 (b) ₹5.60
(c) ₹5.10 (d) ₹5.06

24. Aman goes to buy fruits and after a lot of bargaining is able to get the price of a dozen bananas reduced by ₹1 from the initial price, thereby enabling him to get 1 banana extra for every rupee saved. (Getting no discount on the extra bananas). What is the initial price of a dozen banana?
(a) ₹12 (b) ₹16
(c) ₹14 (d) ₹30

25. The balance sheet of a company shows sales of ₹12,600. The primary cost is 35% of sales and trading cost accounts for 25% of the gross profit. Gross profit is arrived at by excluding the primary cost plus the cost of advertising expenses of ₹1400, director's salary of ₹650 per annum plus 2% of annual sales as miscellaneous costs. Find the percentage profit (approx.) on a capital investment of ₹14,000.
(a) 35% (b) 31%
(c) 28% (d) Cannot be determined

26. Aman has two chairs and one table. The table is worth ₹9000. If he sells the table along with the first chair, he has an amount double that of the value of the second chair. But if he decides to sell the table along with the second chair, the amount received would be more than the value of first chair by ₹3000. What is the value of second chair?
(a) ₹9000 (b) ₹6000
(c) ₹15,000 (d) None of these

Directions for Questions 27 and 28: Read the following and answer the questions that follow.

Doctors have advised Renu, a chocolate freak, not to take more than 20 chocolates in one day. When she went to the market to buy her daily quota, she found that if she buys chocolates from the market complex, she would have to pay ₹3 more for the same number of chocolates than she would have to pay had she bought them from her uncle Scrooge's shop, getting two chocolates less per rupee. She finally decided to get them from Uncle Scrooge's shop paying only in one rupee coins.

27. How many chocolates did she buy?
(a) 12 (b) 9
(c) 18 (d) 15

28. How much would she have spent at the market complex?
(a) ₹6 (b) ₹12
(c) ₹9 (d) ₹5

29. *A* sells his bike to *B* at a loss of 10% who subsequently sells it to *C* at a profit of 20%. *C*, after finding some defect in the bike, returns it to *B* but could recover only ₹4.00 for every ₹5 he had paid. Find the amount of *C*'s loss if *A* had paid ₹2 lakh for the bike.
(a) ₹44,800 (b) ₹43,200
(c) ₹27,200 (d) None of these

30. Ashok is a dishonest shopkeeper, and at the time of selling and purchasing, weighs 20% less and 10% more per kilogram respectively. Find the percentage profit earned by treachery. (Assuming he sells at cost price)
(a) 30% (b) 37.50%
(c) 25% (d) 33.33%

31. A dealer marks articles at a price that gives him a profit of 40%. Twenty percent of the consignment of goods was lost in a fire in his premises, 20% was soiled and had to be sold at half the cost price. If the remainder was sold at the marked price, what percentage profit or loss did the dealer make on that consignment?
(a) 4% (b) 2.5%
(c) 3% (d) 6.0%

32. A pen was sold for a certain sum and there was a loss of 20%. Had it been sold for ₹10 more, there would have been a loss of 10%. What would be the profit if the pen were sold for ₹20 more than what it was sold for?
(a) 15% (b) 20%
(c) 10% (d) No profit, no loss

Directions for Questions 33 to 36: Use the following data:

33. A group of 3000 people bought the shares of Mindworkzz of which 65% were male and the rest were female. The male population earned a profit of 10% and the female population earned 5% on an investment of ₹500 each. Find the change in the percentage profit of the group, if the ratio of male to female gets reversed the next year, population and profit percentages for the respective groups remaining the same.
(a) Drop of 1.5 percentage points
(b) Increase of 2 percentage points
(c) Increase of 0.45 percentage points
(d) Drop of 2.5 percentage points

34. In Question 33, find the change in the percentage profit of the group if the total number of people increases by 20%. (Assume the ratio remains the same)
(a) Increase of 12% (b) Increase of 11.11%
(c) No change (d) Cannot be determined

35. For Question 34, find the percentage change in the profit.
(a) Increase of 20% (b) Increase of 11.11%
(c) No change (d) Cannot be determined

36. For Question 33, what would be the change in the percentage profit, if along with the reversal of the ratio of males to females, the profit also increases by 5% for both males and females?
(a) Drop of 3.0 percentage points
(b) Increase of 3.5 percentage points
(c) Increase of 0.8 percentage points
(d) None of these

37. Two flats were bought by two friends *A* and *B* respectively at prices of ₹4 lakh and ₹4.2 lakh. The price of the first flat rises by 20 percent every year and that of second flat by 10% every year. After two years, they decide to exchange their flats. What is percentage gain of the gainer?
(a) 37.14% (b) 16.36%
(c) 24.39% (d) None of these

38. Ajay is a driver of a cab. He makes a profit of 10% on every trip when he carries 4 passengers and the price of petrol is ₹60 per litre. Find the percentage profit for the same journey if he goes for five passengers per trip and the price of petrol reduces to ₹45 per litre. (Assume that revenue per passenger is the same in both the cases and there is negligible change in the fuel efficiency of the cab when an extra passenger sits in the cab.)
(a) 83.33% (b) 65.66
(c) 100% (d) Data inadequate

39. Mithilesh buys 30 pens for ₹4725. Of these, 8 are of type A and the rest are type B. At what price must he sell the pens of type A so that if he sells the type B at 3/4th of this price, he makes a profit of 40% on his outlay?
(a) ₹180 (b) ₹270
(c) ₹360 (d) ₹450

40. *A*man, Baman and Chaman invested in a company. Aman invests half of Chaman expecting a return of 10%. Baman invests three-fourths of Chaman, expecting a return of 15% on it. Chaman invests ₹3000 and the profit of the firm is 25% of the total investment. How much would Baman's share of profit be more than that of Aman's share if Baman gets an additional 8% for managing the business? (Assume that their expectations with respect to returns on capital invested are met before profit is divided in the ratio of capitals invested).

(a) 20% (b) 18%
(c) 15% (d) Cannot be determined

41. Raghav bought 25 washing machines and microwave ovens for ₹2,05,000. He sold 80% of the washing machines and 12 microwave ovens for a profit of ₹40,000. Each washing machine was marked up by 20% over cost and each microwave oven was sold at a profit of ₹2,000. The remaining washing machines and three microwave ovens could not be sold. What is Raghav's overall profit/loss?
(a) ₹1000 profit (b) ₹2500 loss
(c) ₹1000 loss (d) Cannot be determined

42. After selling a watch, Shyam found that he had made a loss of 10%. He also found that had he sold it for ₹27 more, he would have made a profit of 5%. The actual initial loss was what percentage of the profit earned, had he sold the watch for a 5% profit?
(a) 23% (b) 150%
(c) 200% (b) 180%

43. Sambhu buys rice at ₹10/kg and puts a price tag on it so as to earn a profit of 20%. However, his faulty balance shows 1000 g when it is actually 800 g. What is his actual gain percentage?
(a) 50% (b) 40%
(c) 18% (d) 10%

44. The profit earned when an article is sold for ₹800 is 20 times the loss incurred when it is sold for ₹275. At what price should the article be sold if it is desired to make a profit of 25%?
(a) ₹300 (b) ₹350
(c) ₹375 (d) ₹400

45. *A* sells to *B* goods at five-thirds the rate of profit at which *B* has decided to sell it to *C*. *C*, on other hand, sells it to *D* at one-third the rate of profit at which *B* sold it to *C*. If *D* gives ₹2145 to *C* at 10% profit, how much did *A* buy it for?
(a) ₹1000 (b) ₹2000
(c) ₹1500 (d) ₹1800

46. In the town of Andher Nagari Chaupat Raja, shopkeepers have to buy and sell goods in the range of ₹500 to ₹999. A shopkeeper in such a town decides not to buy or sell goods for amounts that contain the digit 9 or for amounts that add up to 13 or are a multiple of 13. What is the maximum possible profit he can earn?
(a) ₹388 (b) ₹389
(c) ₹488 (d) None of these

47. Manish bought a combined total of 25 monitors and printers. He marked up the monitors by 20% on the cost price, while each printer was marked up by ₹2000. He was able to sell 75% of the monitors and two printers and make a profit of ₹49,000. The remaining monitors and three printers could not be sold by him. Find his overall profit or loss if he gets no return on unsold items and it is known that a printer costs 50% of a monitor.
(a) Loss of ₹48,500 (b) Loss of 21,000
(c) Loss of ₹41,000 (d) Inadequate data

48. For Question 47, Manish's approximate percentage profit or loss is
(a) 14.37% loss (b) 16.5% loss
(c) 12.14% loss (d) Insufficient information

49. An orange vendor makes a profit of 20% by selling oranges at a certain price. If he charges ₹1.2 higher per orange he would gain 40%. Find the original price at which he sold an orange.
(a) ₹5 (b) ₹4.8
(c) ₹6 (d) None of these

50. The Mindworkzz prints 5000 copies of a magazine for ₹5,00,000 every month. In the July issue of the magazine, Mindworkzz distributed 500 copies free. Besides, it was able to sell 2/3 of the remaining magazines at 20% discount. Besides, the remaining magazines were sold at the printed price of the magazine (which was ₹200). Find the percentage profit of Mindworkzz in the magazine venture in the month of July (assume a uniform 20% of the sale price as the vendor's discount and also assume that Mindworkzz earns no income from advertising for the issue).
(a) 56% (b) 24.8%
(c) 28.5% (d) 22.6%

51. In a market, the price of good quality apples is three times the price of medium quality apples. A man buys 120 Kgs of good quality apples and 40 kgs of medium quality apples. He then sells the whole lot at a price that is 10% higher than the price at which he purchased the good quality mangoes. His Overall profit percentage is how much?

52. A library purchased 15 books for ₹9000. 13 of these books were purchased from Amazon and 2 were purchased directly from McGraw-Hill. It is observed that one-sixth of the average price of all the 15 books purchased is equal to one-fifth of the average price of the 13 books obtained from Amazon. Of the two books obtained from McGraw-Hill. if one-third of the price of one volume is equal to one-half of the price of the other, then the price of the two books are:

53. An inkjet printer costs ₹9000 and the cost of printing a page on it is ₹1.5 per page. A laser printer costs ₹15000 and the cost of printing a page on it is ₹1.2 per page. At how many pages printed would the cost of the two options become equal?

54. A salesman sells two kinds of trousers: cotton and woollen. A pair of cotton trousers are sold at 30% profit and a pair of woollen trousers is sold at 50% profit. The salesman has calculated that if he sells 100% more woollen trousers than cotton trousers, his overall profit will be 45%. However he ends up selling 50% more cotton trousers than woollen trousers. What will be his overall profit?

55. City Bus Corporation runs two buses from terminus A to terminus B, and B to A respectively, each bus making 5 round trips in a day. There are no stops in between. These buses ply back and forth on the same route at different but uniform speeds. Each morning the buses start at 7 AM from the respective terminuses. They meet for the first time at a distance of 7 km from terminus A. Their next meeting is at a distance of 4 km from terminus B, while travelling in opposite directions. Assuming that the time taken by the buses at the terminuses is negligibly small, and the cost of running a bus is ₹20 per km, find the daily cost of running the buses (in ₹).

(a) 3200 (b) 4000
(c) 6400 (d) 6800
(e) None of the above

56. Rani bought more apples than oranges. She sells apples at ₹23 apiece and makes 15% profit. She sells oranges at ₹10 apiece and makes 25% profit. If she gets ₹653 after selling all the apples and oranges, find her profit percentage.

(a) 16.8% (b 17.4%
(c) 17.9% (d) 18.5%
(e) 19.1%

57. Mindworkzz and Taxplan want to run financial education courses together. The capital investment of ₹200000 is made by Mindworkzz, while Taxplan bears the running cost per student of ₹400. The price at which the courses sell are ₹2000 each. The internal agreement is that the profits will be shared in the ratio 11:9. Also, Mindworkzz wants to recover it's initial investment during the first year itself. What is the minimum enrolment required for Mindworkzz to recover it's investment during the first year only?

58. A shop sells garments all marked at the same price. However, there is a special scheme this Diwali, where they offer the fourth garment for ₹100, if you buy three garments. Abdullah uses this scheme to the maximum benefit and ends up purchasing 20 garments for ₹14000. What is the marked price of each garment?

59. A wholesaler bought apples and mangoes – the price of mangoes being 4 times the price of apples. He then sold 32 kg of apples at a profit of 20% and 64 kgs of mangoes at 40% profit to Kallu, the fruit seller. However, Kallu found that 20 kgs of mangoes and 12 kgs of apples were rotten and had to be discarded. He then sold his entire lot at a price of ₹248 per kg, gaining a profit of 25% overall. At what price in Rupees per kg did the wholesaler buy the mangoes?

60. A man sells two goats procured at the same price P, to Arun and Ravi at a profit of 20% and a loss of 30%. Arun sells his goat to Ramaiya at a profit of 30%, while Ravi sells his goat to Kanhaiya at a loss of 20%. If the amounts paid by Ramaiya and Kanhaiya are a and b respectively, what is the ratio of $(a–b)$: P.

61. On selling a Pen at 5% loss and a Book at 15% gain, Abhinav gains 7% on the total cost of the two items. If he sells the pen at 5% gain and the book at 10% gain, he gains ₹13. What is the cost price of the book in rupees?

Directions for Questions no. 62 to 64: On the basis of the following information.

KK, an aspiring entrepreneur wanted to set up a pen drive manufacturing unit. Since technology was changing very fast, he wanted to carefully gauge the demand and the likely profits before investing. Market survey indicated that he would be able to sell 1 lac units before customers shifted to different gadgets. KK realized that he had to incur two kinds of costs – fixed costs (the costs which do not change, irrespective of number of units of pen drives produced) and variable costs (= variable cost per unit multiplied by number of units). KK expected fixed cost to be ₹40 lac and variable cost to be ₹100 per unit. He expected each pen drive to be sold at ₹200.

62. What would be the break-even point (defined as no profit, no loss situation) for KK's factory, in term of sales?

(a) ₹80 lac
(b) ₹100 lac
(c) ₹120 lac
(d) Cannot be found with the given data.

63. KK was skeptical that per unit variable cost might increase by 10% though the demand might remain same. What will be the expected changes in profit in such a case?

(a) Profit would decrease by 10.33%
(b) Profit will increase will by 15.75%
(c) Profit would decrease by 15.75%
(d) Profit will increase by 16.67%

64. He discussed his business plan with a chartered accountant. KK informed that he was contemplating a loan of ₹20 lac at simple interest of 10% per annum for starting the business. The chartered accountant informed him that in such a case KK has to pay interest, followed by 30% tax. By how much does KK's earning change with 20% growth in sales vis-à-vis the original sales volume, in both cases considering tax and interest on loan?

(a) 20% (b) 16.7%
(c) 25.6% (d) 34.5%

65. Ram and Shyam form a partnership (with Shyam as working partner) and start a business by Investing ₹4000 and ₹6000 respectively. The conditions of partnership were as follows:

- In case of profits till ₹200,000 per annum, profits would be shared in the ratio of the invested capital.
- Profits from ₹200,001 till ₹400,000 Shyam would take 20% out of the profit, before the division of

remaining profits, which will then be based on ratio of invested capital.

- Profits in excess of ₹400,000, Shyam would take 35% out of the profits beyond ₹400,000, before the division of remaining profits, which will then be based on ratio of invested capital.

If Shyam's share in a particular year was ₹367000, which option indicates the total business profit (in ₹) for that year?

(a) 520,000 (b) 530,000
(c) 540,000 (d) 550,000

66. The Maximum Retail Price (MRP) of a product is 55% above its manufacturing cost. The product is sold through a retailer, who earns 23% profit on his purchase price. What is the profit percentage (expressed in nearest integer) for the manufacturer who sells his product to the retailer? The retailer gives 10% discount on MRP.

(a) 31% (b) 22%
(c) 15% (d) 13%

67. A Techno company has 14 machines of equal efficiency in its factory. The annual manufacturing costs are ₹42,000 and establishment charges are ₹12,000. The annual output of the company is ₹70,000. The annual output and manufacturing costs are directly proportional to the number of machines. The share holders get 12.5% profit, which is directly proportional to the annual output of the company. If 7.14% machines remain closed throughout the year, then the percentage decrease in the amount of profit of the share holders would be:

(a) 12% (b) 12.5%
(c) 13.0% (d) None of these

68. A Metro train from Mehrauli to Gurgaon has capacity to board 900 people. The fare charged (in ₹) is defined by the function $f = \left(54 - \frac{x}{32}\right)^2$ where 'x' is the number of the people per trip. How many people per trip will make the marginal revenue equal to zero?

(a) 1728 (b) 576
(c) 484 (d) 364

69. Reliance Manufacturing company manufactures mobile phones by importing components from South East Asian countries. The Production cost involves the cost of three components viz: A,B and C plus the cost of production at the factory. In 2075, it was found that the components A,B and C respectively cost 10%, 20% and 30% of the total production costs. It sells the mobile phone at a profit of 50% on the production cost. The next year, the cost of A, B and C respectively went up by 20%,40% and 60%, all other costs remaining constant. To compensate for the increased component costs, the company raised its' selling price by 20%. Find the new percentage profit the company would be making on selling the mobile phones.

(a) 28.88 (b) 29.11%
(c) 27.77% (d) 25.55%

70. Three friends Sunil, Amitesh and Amritesh started a business last year. Sunil was operating as a full time director of the company and hence had a profit share of 10% of the total profit. The remaining profit was divided in the ratio of the equivalent capitals invested by the three of them (i.e. the product of capital invested and the time invested for). Sunil invested 40000 rupees for 6 months, Amitesh invested 100000 rupees for 12 months, while Amritesh invested 80000 rupees for 9 months. If the total profit at the end of the year was ₹900000, then find the profit earned by Amritesh.

71. Ramu bought 20 pens and 30 pencils. He marked-up the pens by 25% on the cost price of each, and the pencils by ₹50 on the cost price each. He sold 75% of the pens and 25 pencils and made a profit of ₹1625. If the cost of a pencil is 75% the cost of a pen and he got no return on unsold items, what was his overall profit or loss?

(a) Loss of ₹750 (b) Profit of ₹750
(c) Profit of ₹500 (d) Cannot be determined.

72. As a strategy towards retention of customers, the service centre of a split AC machine manufacturer offers discount as per the following rule: for the second service in a year, the customer can avail of a 10% discount; for the third and fourth servicing within a year, the customer can avail of 11% and 12% discounts respectively of the previous amount paid, Finally, if a customer gets more than four services within a year, he has to pay just 55% of the original servicing charges. If Rohan has availed 5 services from the same service centre in a given year, the total percentage discount availed by him is approximately:

(a) 16.52 (b) 20.88
(c) 22.33 (d) 24.08

73. In a local art shop, the shop owner sells three paintings for the same price. On the first he makes a loss of 12%, on the second a profit of 27% and the third at a loss of 18%. The approximate percentage by which the average cost price is lower or higher than the average selling price is:

(a) 4.8% lower (b) 9.6% lower
(c) 9.6% higher (d) 4.8% higher

74. A publishing company published 10000 copies of a book by Arun Sharma. 800 copies were given away as promotional handouts to teachers and professors at various institutes and colleges across the country. $\frac{4}{5}$ th of the remaining were sold at a discount of 25% on the printed price, while the remaining were sold at the printed price of ₹500. Assuming Vendors discount at a uniform rate of 30% on the total revenue, find the approximate percentage profit of the publishing house (to the nearest integer), if the cost of printing the 10000 copies worked out to 220 per unit, including all the overhead costs.

Directions for Questions 75 to 78: The charges of a taxi journey are decided on the basis of the distance covered and the amount of the waiting time during a journey. Distance wise, for the first 2 kilometres (or any part thereof) of a journey, the metre reading is fixed at ₹10 (if there is no waiting). Also, if a taxi is boarded and it does not move, then the metre reading is again fixed at ₹10 for the first ten minutes of waiting. For every additional kilometre, the metre reading changes by ₹5 (with changes in the metre reading being in multiples of ₹1 for every 200 metres travelled). For every additional minute of waiting, the metre reading changes by ₹1. (no account is taken of a fraction of a minute waited for or of a distance less than 200 metres travelled). The net metre reading is a function of the amount of time waited for and the distance travelled.

The cost of running a taxi depends on the fuel efficiency (in terms of mileage/litre), depreciation (straight line over 10 years) and the driver's salary (not taken into account if the taxi is self owned).

Depreciation is ₹100 per day everyday of the first 10 years. This depreciation has to be added equally to the cost for every customer while calculating the profit for a particular trip. Similarly, the driver's daily salary is also apportioned equally across the customers of the particular day. Assume, for simplicity, that there are 50 customers every day (unless otherwise mentioned). The cost of fuel is ₹15 per litre (unless otherwise stated).

The customer has to pay 20% over the metre reading while settling his bill. Also assume that there is no fuel cost for waiting time (unless otherwise stated).

Based on the above facts, answer the following:

75. If Sardar Preetpal Singh's taxi is 14 years old and has a fuel efficiency of 12 km/litre of fuel, find his profit in a run from Howrah Station to Park Street (a distance of 7 km), if the stoppage time is 8 minutes. (Assume he owns the taxi)

(a) ₹32.25 (b) ₹40.85
(c) ₹34.25 (d) ₹42.85

76. For Question 75, Sardar Preetpal Singh's percentage profit is

(a) 391.42% (b) 380%
(c) 489.71% (d) 438.23%

77. For the same journey as in question 75, if on another day, with heavier traffic, the waiting time increases to 13 minutes, find the percentage change in the profit.

(a) 12% (b) 14%
(c) 13% (d) 16%

78. For Question 77, if Sardar Preetpal Singh idled his taxi for 7 minutes and if the fuel consumption during idling is 50 mL per minute, find the percentage decrease in the profits.

(a) 10.74% (b) 11.21%
(c) 10.87% (d) 9.94%

79. A newspaper vendor sells three kinds of periodicals-dailies, weeklies and monthlies.

The weeklies sell for ₹12 at a profit of 20%, the monthlies sell for ₹50 at a profit of 25%, while the dailies sell at ₹3 at a profit of 50%. If there is a government restriction on the total number of periodicals that one particular news vendor, can sell, and Kalu a newspaper vendor, has sufficient demand for all the three types of periodicals, what should he do to maximise profits?

(a) Sell maximum weeklies
(b) Sell maximum monthlies
(c) Sell maximum dailies
(d) Cannot be determined

80. Without the restriction mentioned in the problem above, what should the newspaper vendor do to maximise his profits if his capital is limited?

(a) Sell maximum weeklies
(b) Sell maximum monthlies
(c) Sell maximum dailies
(d) Cannot be determined

81. A fruit vendor buys fruits from the fruit market at wholesale prices and sells them at his shop at retail prices. He operates his shop 30 days a month, as a rule. He buys in multiples of 100 fruits and sells them in multiples of a dozen fruits. He purchases mangoes for ₹425 per hundred and sells at ₹65 per dozen, he buys apples at ₹150 per hundred and sells at ₹30 per dozen, he buys watermelons (always of equal size) at ₹1800 per hundred and sells at ₹360 per dozen. Which of the three fruits yields him the maximum percentage profit?

(a) Mangoes (b) Apples
(c) Watermelons (d) Both (b) and (c)

82. For Question 81, if he adds oranges, which he buys at ₹180 per hundred and sells at ₹33 per dozen, what can be his maximum profit on a particular day if he invests ₹1800 in purchasing fruits everyday and he sells everything that he buys?

(a) ₹1200 (b) ₹1180
(c) ₹1260 (d) ₹1320

83. For Questions 81 and 82, if the fruit vendor hires you as a consultant and pays you 20% of his profit in the month of July 2006 as a service charge, what can be the maximum fees that you will get for your consultancy charges?

(a) ₹7200 (b) ₹14,400
(c) ₹7440 (d) Cannot be determined

84. A newspaper costs ₹11 to print on a daily basis. Its sale price (printed) is ₹3. The newspaper gives a sales incentive of 40% on the printed price, to the newspaper vendors. The newspaper makes up for the loss through advertisements, which are charged on the basis of per column centimetre rates. The advertisement rates of the newspaper are ₹300 per cc (column centimetre). It has to give an incentive of 15% on the advertising bill to the advertising agency. If the newspaper has a circulation of 12,000 copies, what is the approximate minimum advertising booking required if the newspaper has to break-even on a particular day? (Assume there is no wastage)

(a) 300 cc (b) 350 cc
(c) 435 cc (d) 450 cc

85. For Question 84, if it is known that the newspaper house is unable to recover 20% of its dues, what would be the approximate advertising booking target on a particular day in order to ensure the break-even point?

(a) 375 cc (b) 438 cc
(c) 544 cc (d) 562.5 cc

High Yield Questions

Scan this QR code to access assisted problem solving videos on questions 3, 12, 41, 56, 66 and 70 from LOD 2

Space for Rough Work

ANSWER KEY

Level of Difficulty (I)

1. (b)	2. (c)	3. (b)	4. (d)
5. (c)	6. (a)	7. (b)	8. (a)
9. (a)	10. (b)	11. (a)	12. (d)
13. (d)	14. (b)	15. (c)	16. (b)
17. (a)	18. (a)	19. (b)	20. (d)
21. (a)	22. (c)	23. (b)	24. (c)
25. (d)	26. (a)	27. (c)	28. (b)
29. (c)	30. (c)	31. (d)	32. (d)
33. (a)	34. (b)	35. (b)	36. (a)
37. (c)	38. (c)	39. (a)	40. (d)
41. (a)	42. (b)	43. (a)	44. (a)
45. (b)	46. (d)	47. (c)	48. (d)
49. (a)	50. (c)	51. (c)	52. (a)
53. (c)	54. (a)	55. (c)	56. (a)
57. (b)	58. (d)	59. (b)	60. (a)
61. (b)	62. (b)	63. (d)	64. (b)
65. (a)			

Level of Difficulty (II)

1. (c)	2. (a)	3. (b)	4. (b)
5. (a)	6. (b)	7. (d)	8. (d)
9. (b)	10. (b)	11. (a)	12. (a)
13. (c)	14. (c)	15. (a)	16. (a)
17. (a)	18. (c)	19. (a)	20. (b)
21. (d)	22. (a)	23. (a)	24. (a)
25. (b)	26. (c)	27. (a)	28. (a)
29. (b)	30. (b)	31. (d)	32. (d)
33. (a)	34. (c)	35. (a)	36. (b)
37. (d)	38. (a)	39. (b)	40. (d)
41. (c)	42. (c)	43. (a)	44. (c)
45. (a)	46. (a)	47. (a)	48. (a)
49. (d)	50. (b)	51. 32%	
52. ₹1500 and ₹1000		53. 20000	54. 40%
55. (d)	56. (b)	57. 125	58. ₹900
59. 128	60. 1:1	61. 97.5	62. (a)
63. (d)	64. (d)	65. (d)	66. (d)
67. (b)	68. (b)	69. (a)	
70. 270000	71. (b)	72. (b)	73. (d)
74. 17%	75. (d)	76. (c)	77. (b)
78. (a)	79. (b)	80. (c)	81. (d)
82. (a)	83. (a)	84. (c)	85. (c)

SOLUTIONS AND SHORTCUTS

Level of Difficulty (I)

1. $0.8 \times$ Price = 560 → Price 700.
2. The SP = 106.25% of the CP. Thus, CP = 29.75/1.0625 = ₹28.
3. $1.12 \times$ Price = 3808 → Price = 3400.
4. A loss of 25% means a cost price of 100 corresponding to a selling price of 75. CP as a percentage of the SP would then be 133.33%
5. $1800 = 1.2 \times$ cost price → Cost price = 1500
   Profit at 1687.5 = ₹187.5
   Percentage profit = $(187.5/1500) \times 100 = 12.5\%$
6. CP = 6612.5/1.15 = 5750. Selling this at 5380 would mean a loss of ₹370 on a CP of ₹5750.
7. The CP will be ₹7200 (got by 6400×1.125). Hence at an S.P. of 7812 the percentage profit will be 8.5%
8. CP = 69/1.15 = 60. Thus, the required SP for 20% profit = $1.2 \times 60 = 72$.
9. The buying price is ₹6 per dozen, while the sales price is ₹$0.75 \times 12 = 9$ per dozen – a profit of 50%
10. Sales tax = 150/5 = 30. Thus, the SP contains ₹30 component of sales tax. Of the remainder (150 – 30 = 120) 1/3rd is the profit. Thus, the profit = 120/3 = 40. Cost price = 120 – 40 = 80.
11. C.P $\times$ 1.3 = 26 → CP = 20
    At a selling price of ₹22.5, the profit percent 2.5/20 = 12.5%
12. Solve using options. Option (d) gives you ₹220 as the cost of the trouser. Hence, the shirt will cost 15% more i.e. 220 + 22 + 11 = 253.
    This satisfies the total cost requirement of ₹473.
13. The formula that satisfies this condition is:
    Loss of $a^2/100\%$ (Where a is the common profit and loss percentage). Hence, in this case 625/100 = 6.25% loss.
14. Cost price = ₹1000, selling price = 0.9 of 1200 = 1080.
    Hence, 8% is the correct answer.
15. The cost per toffee = 75/125 = ₹0.6 = 60 paise. Cost of 1 million toffees = 600000. But there is a discount of 40% offered on this quantity. Thus, the total cost for 1 million toffees is 60% of 600000 = 360000.
16. On a marked price of ₹250, a discount of 20% would mean a selling price of ₹200. Since this represents a 25% profit we get:
    $1.25 \times$ CP = 200 → CP = 160.
17. The thought process in this question would go as follows:
    250 – 10% of 250 = 225 (after the first discount).
    225 – 10% of 225 = 225 – 22.5 = 202.5 (after the second discount). You could do this on the PCG.
18. For ₹96, we can buy a dozen pair of gloves. Hence, for ₹16 we can buy 2 pairs of gloves.
19. 100 → 75 (after 25% discount) → 60 (after 20% discount) → 54 (after 10% discount).
    Thus, the single discount which would be equivalent would be 46%.
20. $225 \times 0.8 \times x = 148.5 \rightarrow x = 0.825$
    Which means a 17.5% discount.
21. If you assume the cost price to be 100 and we check from the options, we will see that for Option (a) the marked price will be 133.33 and giving a discount of 6.25% would leave the shopkeeper with a 25% profit.

22. Solve by trial and error using the options. If he marks his goods 40% above the cost price he would be able to generate a 12% profit inspite of giving a 20% discount.
23. The customer pays ₹54 after a discount of 10%. Hence, the list price must be ₹60.
This also means that at a 25% discount, the retailer buys the item at ₹45.
Hence, the profit for the retailer will be ₹9 (54 – 45).
24. The profit would be given by the percentage value of the ratio 9/45 = 20%.
25. The labour price accounts for ₹500. Since the profit percentage gives a 10% profit on this component i.e. 50.
Hence, the marked price is 1150.
26. The costs in 2016 were 400, 500 and 200 respectively. An increase of 20% in material → increase of 80. An increase of 30% in labor → increase of 150. Increase of 10% in overheads → increase of 20.
Total increase = 80 + 150 + 20 = 250. New cost = 1100 + 250 = 1350
27. For a 10% profit on labour cost, he should mark his goods at 1350 + 10% of 650 = 1415. Note, 650 is the new cost of labour after a 30% increase as described in Question 26.
28. SP = 820 = 0.82 × CP → CP = 1000. To gain a profit of 28%, the marked price should be 128% of 1000 = 1280.
29. The SP per article = ₹3. This represents a profit of 20%. Thus, CP = 3/1.2 = 2.5. 8 articles would cost ₹20 and hence selling at 18.40 would represent a loss of ₹1.6, which would mean an 8% loss on ₹20.
30. The percentage profit = $\dfrac{\text{Goods left}}{\text{Goods Sold}} \times 100.$

$$= 10/30 \times 100 = 33.33\%$$

(Note: This formula can be used if the money got and money spent is equated.)
31. In the question, *P*'s investment has to be considered as ₹20,000 (the house he puts up for sale).
He sells at ₹25000 and buys back at ₹18750. Hence his profit is ₹6250.
Required answer = (6250 × 100/20000) = 31.25%
32. For 12 locks, he would have paid ₹51, and sold them at ₹57. This would mean a profit percentage of 11.76%
33. 195/150 = 1.3 → the profit percentage would be 30% if sold at 195. Thus, the increase in profit percent = 30% – 20% = 10%.
34. A's selling price = 1.2 × 250 = 300. C's Cost price = B's selling price = 386.4/1.15 = 336. Thus, B's profit = ₹36 and his profit percent = 36 × 100/300 = 12%.
35. A 20% reduction in price increases the consumption by 25% (Refer Table 4.1). But the increase in consumption is 5.4 kg.
Hence, the consumption (original) will be 5.4 × 4 = 21.6 kg.
Hence, original price = 432/21.6 = ₹20.
Hence, reduced price = ₹16
36. Total cost = 50 × 10 + 40 × 12 = 980. Total revenue = 90 × 11 = 990. Gain percent = (10 × 100)/980 = 100/98 %.
37. Percentage profit = $\dfrac{\text{Goods left}}{\text{Goods Sold}} \times 100$

$$= 10/15 \times 100 = 66.67\%$$

38. The profit percent would be equal to 150 × 100 /850 = 15000/850 = 300/17% = 17 (11/17)%
39. A gross means 144 eggs. Thus, the cost price per egg = 50 paise and the selling price after a 6.25% profit = 53 paise (approximately).
40. Q sold the table at 20% profit at ₹90. Thus cost price would be given by: $CP_Q \times 1.2 = 90$
Q's Cost price = ₹75.
We also know that P sold it to Q at 25% profit. Thus,
P's Cost price × 1.25 = 75
→ P's cost price = 60.
41. From the options, checking option (a): 300 (*A* buys at this value) → 345 (sells it to *B* at a profit of 15%) → 414 (*B* sells it back to *A* at a profit of 20% gaining ₹69 in the process). Thus, *A*'s original cost = ₹300.
42. Net loss = $(20/10)^2$ = 4% of cost price. Thus, 19200 (total money realized) represents 96% of the value. Thus, the cost price would be ₹20,000 and the loss would be ₹800.
43. CP × 0.9 = 20 → CP = ₹22.222, Loss per kg = ₹2.222. To incur a loss of ₹60, we need to sell 60/2.22 = 27 kgs of tea.
44. The CP of the TV → $CP_{TV} \times 0.9 = 19{,}800 \rightarrow CP_{TV} = 22{,}000$
The CP of the VCP → $CP_{VCP} \times 1.1 = 19{,}800 \rightarrow CP_{VCP} = 18{,}000$.
Total sales value = 19,800 × 2 = 39,600.
Total cost price = 22000 + 18000 = 40,000. Loss = 40,000 – 39,600 = 400.
45. The profit of 10% amounts to ₹3000. This should also be the actual loss on the second TV.
Thus, the actual loss = ₹3000 (20% of C.P.)
Hence, the CP of the second set = ₹15000. SP of the second TV set = 15000 – 3000 = 12000.
46. Solve using options. The correct option (d) would work as follows: If CP = 200, the man sells at 220 (after 10% profit). If he bought for 15% less, he would have bought it at 0.85 × 200 = 170. Also, selling for ₹33 less than 220, means he would have sold at 220 – 33 = 187. This represents the required profit of 10% on his new cost price of 170. Hence, this option is correct. (Note: For the wrong options, the last percentage profit would not match the required 10% profit).

47. Let the cost price be P. Then, $P \times 0.95 \times 1.2 = P \times 1.05 + 63 \rightarrow P = 700$. Alternately, you could have solved this using options, as shown in the previous question.
48. 7% of the cost price = ₹630.
Thus, cost price = ₹9000
and selling price @ 8% profit = ₹9720.
49. From the last statement we have: Charan's cost price = 1188/1.1 = 1080 = Bhushan's selling price. Then, Bhushan's CP would be given by the equation: CP × 0.9 = 1080 → CP for Bhushan = 1200 = SP for Ashok.
Also, Ashok gains 20%. Hence, CP for Ashok → CP × 1.2 = 1200 → CP for Ashok = 1000.
This includes ₹110 component of repairs. Thus, the purchase price for Ashok would be 1000 – 110 = 890.
50. Solve through the values given in the options. Option (c) is correct because at 4/5 × 300 + 5/4 × 600 we see that the profit earned = ₹90.
51. Solve this question using the options. The first thing you should realize is that the cost of the lower priced item should be less than 240. Thus, we can reject options (a) and (d). Checking option (c) we can see that if the lower priced item is priced at 200, the higher priced item would be priced at ₹280. Then: 1.19 × 200 = 238 and 0.85 × 280 = 238. It can be seen that in this condition the values of the selling price of both the items would be equal (as required by the conditions given in the problem). Thus, option (c) is the correct answer.
52. Original Cost Price = ₹5000
New Cost Price = 1.3 × 5000 = ₹6500
Price paid by retailer = 1.2 × 5750 = ₹6900
Profit percentage = (400/6500) × 100 = 6 (2/13)%
53. The total manufacturing cost of the article = 300 + 350 + 100 = 750. SP = 900. Thus, profit = ₹150.
Profit Percent = 150 × 100/750 = 20%
54. Assume marked price for both to be 100.
P's selling price = 100 × 0.8 × 0.85 = 68
Q's selling price = 100 × 0.82 × 0.83 = 68.06.
Buying from 'P' is more profitable.
55. The total discount offered by A = 5% on 1,00,000 + 12.5% on 80,000 = 5,000 + 10,000 = 15,000.
If B wants to be as competitive, he should also offer a discount of ₹15,000 on 1,80,000. Discount percentage = 15000 × 100/1,80,000 = 8.33% discount.
56. The trader pays 1600 × 0.95 × 0.95 = ₹1444
57. Manufacturer's profit percentage = (44/1400) × 100 = (22/7)%
58. For a cost price of ₹2000, he needs a selling price of 2280 for a 14% profit. This selling price is arrived at after a discount of 5% on the marked price. Hence, the marked price MP = 2280/0.95 = 2400.
59. Solve using options. Option (b) fits the situation as a 10% discount on 450 would mean a discount of 45. This would leave us with a selling price of 405, which represents a profit percent of 12.5% on ₹360.
60. If he marks the camera at 840, a 15% discount would still allow him to sell at 714 – a profit of 19%.
Alternately: Marked Price × 0.85 = 600 × 1.19 → Marked Price = 840
61. Cost price to the watch dealer
= 450 + 20% of 450 = ₹540
Desired selling price for 25% profit
= 1.25 × 540 = 675
But 675 is the price after 20% discount on the marked price.
Thus,
Marked price × 0.8 = 675 → MP = 843.75
Hence, he should mark the item at ₹843.75.
62. If the cost price is 100, a mark up of 60% means a marked price of 160. Further a 35% discount on the marked price would be given by:
160 – 35% of 160 = 160 – 56 = 104. Thus, the percentage profit is 4%.
63. A cost price of ₹13000 would meet the conditions in the problem as it would give us a loss of 4800 (if sold at 8200) and a profit of 2400 (when sold at 15400). You can think of this as: If you take the loss as $2x$, the profit is x. Then, $3x$ = 15400 – 8200 = 7200 x = 2400. Thus, the profit is 2400 when he sells at 15400. Hence, the cost price must be 15400 – 2400 = 13000.
64. Cost per 100 apples = 70 + 10% of 70 = ₹77.
Selling price @ 30% profit = 1.3 × 77 = ₹100.1
65. Profit percent = (200/800) × 100 = 25%

Level of Difficulty (II)

1. Total outlay (initial investment) = 250 × 0.8 = ₹200.
By selling 200, he should make a 20% profit on the outlay. This means that the selling price for 200 articles must be 1.2 × 200 → ₹240
Thus, selling price per article = 240/200= 1.2. Since, he sells only 230 articles at this price, his total recovery = 1.2 × 230 = 276.
Profit percent (actual) = (76/200) × 100 = 38%
2. As only 8000 articles will be accepted so the total revenue would be ₹1.5 × 8000 = ₹12000.
After selling the article at ₹12000, he earns a 20% profit, so the cost price of 10000 articles must be ₹12000/1.2 = ₹10000.
Cost of manufacturing of each article = 10000/10000 = ₹1. Hence, option (a) is correct.
3. Assume that she sells 100 articles and the cost price of each article is ₹1 and the selling price of each article is ₹1.30
Recovered amount = 60 × 1.3 + 30 × (1.3 – 20% of 1.3) + 10 × (1.3 – 50% of 1.3)

= 78 + 31.20 + 6.5 = 115.70

Hence, profit percent = 15.70%

4. Cost price = x

Marked Price = $x + 150$

Selling Price = $0.8x + 120$

Profit = $(0.8x + 120) - x = 120 - 0.2x$.

Percentage Profit = $(120 - 0.2x) \times$ ₹$100/x = (12000 - 20x)/x$

5. She should opt for a straight discount of 40% as that gives her the maximum benefit.

6. If you assume that his cost price is ₹1 per gram, his cost for 1000 grams would be ₹1000. For supposed 1 kg sale, he would charge a price of ₹1120 (after an increase of 40% followed by a decrease of 20%). But, since he gives away only 800 grams, the cost for him would be ₹800.

Thus, he is buying at 800 and selling at 1120 – a profit percentage of 40%

7. While buying:

He buys 1100 gram instead of 1000 gram (due to his cheating).

Suppose he bought 1100 gram for ₹1000

While selling:

He sells only 900 gram when he takes the money for 1 kg.

Now according to the problem, he sells at a 4% profit (30% mark up and 20% discount).

Hence, his selling price is ₹1040 for 900 gram.

To calculate profit percentage, we either equate the goods or the money.

In this case, let us equate the money as follows:

Buying;

1100 gram for ₹1000

Hence 1144 gram for ₹1040

Selling: 900 gram for ₹1040

Hence, profit% = $\frac{244}{900} \times 100 = 27.11\%$

(using goods left by goods sold formula)

8. The new situation is

Buying: 1100 gram for ₹900

Hence, for ₹1040, he would buy: $1100 \times \frac{1040}{900} =$ 11440/9 = 1271.11 gram (using Unitary method)

Selling: 900 gram for ₹1040

Profit % = 371.11/9 = 41.23%

9. Assume he bought 30 pens each. Net investment ⇒ ₹15 + ₹10 = ₹25 for 60 pens. He would sell 60 pens @ (60 × 2)/6 = ₹20 → Loss of ₹5 or 20% loss on ₹25 investment.

10. 6000 – 15% of 6000 = 5100. 5100 – 10% of 5100 = 4590. 4590 + 10% of 4590 = ₹5049

11. The problem is structured in such a way that you should be able to interpret that if he had sold 60 kg of rice he would recover the investment on 50 kg of rice.

$$\text{\% Loss/Profit} = \frac{\text{Goods left}}{\text{Goods sold}} \times 100$$

(–10/60) × 100 = 16.66% loss.

Since, cost price for Satnam is ₹20; selling price per kg would be ₹16.67. (Using 20 – 16.67% of 20)

12. Comparisons have to be made between:

192 × 34, 198 × 33, 204 × 32 and 210 × 31 for the highest product amongst them.

The highest value of revenue is seen at a price of ₹198.

13. The total cost to print 900 copies would be given by:

Cost for setting up the type + cost of running the printing machine + cost of paper/ink etc.

= 1000 + 120 × 9 + 900 × 0.6 = 1000 +1080 + 540 = 2620.

A 10% profit on this cost amounts to ₹262. Hence, the total amount to be recovered is ₹2882.

Out of this, 784 copies are sold for ₹2.75 each to recover ₹2156.

The remaining money has to be recovered through advertising.

Hence, the money to be recovered through advertising = 2882 – 2156 = ₹726. Option (c) is correct.

14. Cost price $(1 + x/100) = 50$

$$\text{Cost price} = \frac{5000}{100+x}$$

$$50\left(1-\frac{0.8x}{100}\right)=\frac{5000}{100+x}$$

On solving the above equation, we get $x = 25$

Latter cost price = ₹50

New selling price must be 50 × 1.25 = ₹62.5

15. Assume the price of 1 kg as 100. He initially sells 1 kg at 125. (As his original profit is 25%.)

His new profit percentage = 50% (As he marks up successively by 25% and then 20%).

When he is able to sell only 70% of his items: his new revenue would be given by 70 × 1.5 = 105 on a cost of 100. Profit percentage = 5%

Change in profit percent = –20 (It drops from 25 to 5). Hence, option (a) is correct.

16. A's total discount:

8% on 8000 = ₹640

5% on 12000 = ₹600

3% on 16000 = ₹480

Total = ₹1720 on ₹36000.

Hence, realised value for A = 34280.

B's Discounts:

7% on 12000 = ₹840

6% on 8000 = ₹480

5% on 16000 = ₹800

₹2120 on ₹36000

Hence, realised value = 33880.

The higher profit is for A.

Also, the CP has a mark-up of 25% for the marked price. Thus, the CP must have been 28800 (This is got by 36000 – 20% of 36000 = 28800 → PCG thinking)
Thus, the profit percentage for *A* would be: (5480 × 100)/28800 → 19% approx.

17. In the case of the given defaults, the discount for *A* would have gone down to:
4% on 12000 (the second payment) and the second discount would thus, have been ₹480 meaning that the sale price would have risen by ₹120 (since there is a ₹120 drop in the discount)
1% on 16000 → *A* reduction of 2% of 16000 in the discount → a reduction of ₹320.
Hence, *A*'s profit would have gone up by ₹440 in all and would yield his new profit as:
5480 + 440 = ₹5920.

18. The following working would show the answer:
A's discounts
7% on 8000 = ₹560
4% on 12000 = ₹480
2% on 16000 = ₹320
Total = ₹1360 on ₹36,000.
B's discounts:
6% on 12000 = ₹720
5% on 8000 = ₹400
4% on 16000 = ₹640
₹1760 on ₹36000
Thus, their profits would vary by ₹400 (since their cost price is the same).

19. Let the cost price is ₹100.
Selling price (when percent profit is calculated on cost-price) = ₹120.
Profit = 120 – 100 = ₹20
Selling price (when percent profit is calculated on selling-price) = ₹120 (**Note**: we have to take this as 120, as the problem tells us that the selling price is the same in both the cases). The given percentage profit for this case is seen as: 20% of the selling price = 24. Thus, in this case the CP would be 120 – 24 = 96.
Profit = 120 – 96 = ₹24
Difference in profit = ₹4 which is equivalent to ₹500.
₹120 is equivalent to $\frac{120}{4}\times 500 =$ ₹15,000. Hence, option (a) is correct.

20. **Ashok:**
SP – CP = 10% of CP
1.1CP = 6000
CP = ₹6000/1.1 = ₹60000/11 = ₹5454.54
Profit = 6000 – 5454.54 = ₹545.46
Baman:
(SP – CP)/SP = 0.1
SP – CP = 0.1SP
0.9SP = CP
CP = ₹5400
Profit = 6000 – 5400 = ₹600.
Difference in profit = 600 – 545.56 = ₹54.44

21. Find out the total revenue realisation for both the cases:
Case 1: (Old) Total sales revenue = 4000 × 3.00 × 0.9 = 10800
Profit_{old} = 10800 – 9600 = ₹1200
Case 2: (New) Total sales revenue = 5000 × 4.00 × 0.9
Profit_{new} = 18000 – 9600 = ₹8400
The ratio of profit will be given 8400/1200 = 7 : 1.

22. Let the cost price of the article = ₹100
Selling price of the article = ₹110
New cost price = 100 – 10% of 100 = ₹90
New selling price = 110 + 10% of 110 = 121
New profit percentage = $\frac{121-90}{90}\times 100 = 34.44\%$
Change in percentage profit =
$\frac{34.44-10}{10}\times 100 = 244.44\%$

23. Cost price = ₹10
Marked price = ₹12
Selling price = 9.48
Discount = (12-9.48)/12 = 21% (which is equivalent to two successive 10% discounts.)
New selling price, if these had been successive increases = 12 + 21% of 12 = ₹14.52
Required change = 14.52 – 9.48 = ₹5.04

24. From the options, you can work out that if the original price was ₹12 per dozen, the cost per banana would be ₹1.
If he is able to get a dozen bananas at a reduced price (reduction of ₹1 per dozen), he would be able to purchase 1 extra banana for the 1 Rupee he saved.
Thus, option (a) is correct.

25. The following calculations will show the respective costs:
Primary cost: 35% of 12600 = 4410
Miscellaneous costs = 2% of 12600 = 252
Gross profit = 12600 – 4410 – 1400 – 650 – 252 = 5888
Trading cost = 0.25 × 5888 = 1472
Hence, net profit = 4416.
Percentage profit = 4416/14000 = 31.54%

26. Let the values of the first chair and second chair are ₹*x* and ₹*y* respectively.
According to the question:
$x + 9000 = 2y$ (1)
$y + 9000 = x + 3000$ (2)
On solving equation 1 and equation 2, we get: *y* = ₹15000. Hence, option (c) is correct.

Solutions for Questions 27 and 28:

Using options from question 28. Suppose she had spent ₹6 at the market complex, she would spend ₹3 at her uncle's shop. The other condition (that she gets two chocolates less per rupee at the market complex) gets satisfied in this scenario if she had bought 12 chocolates overall. In such a case, her buying would have been 2 per Rupee at the market and 4 per rupee at Uncle Scrooge's shop.

Trial and error will show that this condition is not satisfied for any other option combination.

29. A (100) → B (90) → C (108) → B (86.4)
C's loss corresponds to ₹21.6 when A buys the bike for ₹100.
Hence, B's loss would be ₹43200 when A buys the bike for ₹2,00,000.

30. While purchasing he would take 1100 gram for the price of 1000 gram.
While selling he would sell 800 gram for the price of 1000 gram.
Since CP = SP, the profit earned is through the weight manipulations. It will be given by:
Goods left/goods sold = 300 × 100/800 = 37.50%

31. Assume that for 100 items, the cost price is ₹100, then the selling price is ₹140. Since 20 is sold at half the price, he would recover 20 × 1/2 = ₹10 (since it is sold at half the cost price)
The remaining 60 would be sold at 60 × 1.4 = ₹84.
Total revenue = 84 + 10 = 94 → a LOSS of 6% (on a cost of 100).

32. An increase in the price by ₹10 will correspond to 10% of the CP.
Hence, the CP is ₹100 and initially the book was being sold at ₹80. Hence, if there is an increment of ₹20 in the selling price, there would be no profit or loss.

33. In the first year, the profit percentage would be:
Number of males = 3000 × 0.65 = 1950
Number of females = 3000 × 0.35 = 1050
Old Profit Percentage =
$$\frac{0.65\times10\%+0.35\times5\%}{1}=8.25\%$$
New Profit Percentage =
$$\frac{0.35\times10\%+0.65\times5\%}{1}=6.75\%$$
Drop of 1.5% points.

34. Since the ratio remains unchanged, the percentage profit of the group will remain unchanged too.

35. The profit would increase by 20% as there is an increase of 20% in the number of people, with no change in the percentage profit.

36. New Profit Percentage =
$$\frac{0.35\times15\%+0.65\times10\%}{1}=11.75\%$$
Hence, we can see an increase of 3.5% percentage points (from 8.25% profit percentage to 11.75% profit percentage). Hence, option (b) is correct.

37. After two years, the first flat would be worth ₹57,6000, while the second flat would be worth ₹508200. B would be the gainer and the profit percentage of the gainer would be given by:
$$\left(\frac{67800}{508200}\right)\times100=13.34\%$$
Hence, option (d) is correct.

38. The cost of the trip would be proportional to the price of petrol. So, if initially the cost is 100, the new cost would be 75 (because of 25% reduction in petrol price). Also, initially since his profit is 10%, his revenue would be 110. When he takes 5 passengers instead of 4, his revenue would go up by 25% to 1101.25 = 137.5 – and his profit would become 83.33% (cost 75 and revenue 137.5).

39. Let the selling price of type A pens be p. The price of type B pens would be $0.75p$.
Then, we would get: $p \times 8 + 0.75p \times 22 = 1.4 \times 4725 \rightarrow x = 270$.
Alternately, we can also think through this question as follows:
On an investment of ₹4725, a profit of 40% means a profit of 1890.
Hence, the targeted sales realisation is ₹6615.
The required equation would be:
$8p + 22\,(3p)/4 = 6615$
$\rightarrow 8p + 33p/2 = 6615$
In this expression for LHS to be equal to RHS, we need $33p/2$ to be an odd number. This can only happen when p is not a multiple of 4 (why?? Apply your mind). Hence, options a and c get eliminated automatically. Also, it is quite evident that a value of p as 450 would be too large to fit the situation. Hence, you can identify the correct option as 270.

40. Let the amounts invested by Aman, Baman and Chaman be A, B and C respectively.
The total investment will be $A + B + C$.
C being 3000, B will be 2250 and A will be 1500.
The total investment is: 6750.
Returns to be given on their expectations:
A = 150, B = 337.5. However, we can see that Chaman's expectations are not known. We are also not given clearly what Baman's share of 8% for managing the business is referring to – it could mean an additional 8% of the profit, or it could mean that Baman is getting an additional 8% over the amount he got. Due to these issues, you cannot answer the question asked.
Hence option (d) is correct.

41. Total number of microwave ovens = 15
Hence, washing machines = 10
Thus, he sells 80% of both at a profit of ₹40,000.

Cost of 80% of the goods = 0.8 × 2,05,000 = 1,64,000.

Total amount recovered = 1,64,000 + 40,000 = 2,04,000

Hence, loss = ₹1000

42. Since the actual initial loss was 10% and it is to be compared to a profit of 5%, it is 200% of the profit. Option (c) is correct.

43. He would be selling 800 gram for ₹12. Since a kg costs ₹10,800 gram would cost ₹8.

Hence, his profit percentage is 50%.

44. The interpretation of the first statement is that if the loss at 275 is L, the profit at 800 is 20L.

Thus, 21L = 800 – 275 = 525 → L = 25.

Thus, the cost price of the item is ₹300.

To get a profit of 25%, the selling price should be 1.25 × 300 = 375.

45. *C*'s purchase price = 2145 × 10/11 = 1950

B's rate of profit is 3 times *C*'s rate of profit. Hence, *B* sells to *C* at 30% profit.

B's price + 30% profit = 1950 (*C*'s price).

Hence, *B*'s price = 1500.

Further, since *A*'s profit rate is 5/3rd the rate of profit of *B*, *A*'s profit percent would be 30 × 5/3 = 50%.

Thus, *A*'s price + 50% profit = 1500 (*B*'s price)

Thus, *A*'s price = 1000

46. He would buy at 500 and sell at 888 to get a profit of 388.

47. There were five printers (2 + 3) and 20 monitors. He sells two printers for a profit of ₹2000 each. Hence, profit from printer sales = ₹4000.

Then, profit from monitor sales = ₹45000

Thus, profit per monitor = $\frac{45000}{15}$ = ₹3000

(Since, 15 monitors were sold in all.)

Hence, C.P. of monitor = ₹15000

And C.P. of Printer = ₹7500

Total cost = 15000 × 20 + 7500 × 5 = 3,37,500

Total revenues = 18000 × 15 + 9500 × 2 = 289000

Hence, loss of ₹48,500

48. Loss% = $\frac{48,500}{3,37,500}$ × 100 = 14.37%

49. By charging ₹1.2 more his profit should double to 40%. This means that his profit of 40% should be equal to ₹2.4. Thus, his cost price must be ₹6 and his original selling price should be 7.2. Hence, option (d) is correct.

50. Total cost = 5 lacs

Total revenue = 3000 × 160 + 1500 × 200 – vendors discount of 20% of revenues

= 7.8 lacs – 1.56 lacs = 6.24 lacs.

Profit percent = (1.24 × 100)/5 = 24.8%

51. Let the price of medium quality apples be ₹1 per kg. Then the price of good quality apples would be ₹3 per kg. The total purchase price of the apples would be:

120 × 3 + 40 × 1 = 400. Sold at ₹3.3 per kg, the total revenue while selling would be 160 × 3.3 = ₹528. The percentage profit = $\frac{128}{400}$ = 32%.

52. The average price of a book (for all 15 books) is ₹600. If we assume the average price of the 13 books from Amazon to be '*A*', then from the second statement, we can see that:

$\frac{1}{6}\times 600 = \frac{1}{5}A \rightarrow A = 500.$

So, the total price of the 13 books from Amazon would be 13 × 500 = 6500. This means that, the total price of two books from McGraw-Hill is ₹2500. If the price of these two books are *X* and *Y* respectively, we get:

$X + Y = 2500$ & $\frac{X}{3} = \frac{Y}{2} \rightarrow X = 1.5Y$. Solving, we get $X = 1500$ and $Y = 1000$.

53. The ink-jet printer costs ₹6000 less, but costs an extra 30 paise per page printed. Thus, for every page printed on both the printers, the gap of ₹6000 reduces by 30 paise. To make the costs equal, the number of pages required to be printed = $\frac{6000}{0.3}$ = 20000.

54. Let the cost price of a cotton trouser be *X* and a woollen trouser be *Y*. Then, their respective selling prices will be 1.3*X* and 1.5*Y*. In the first case, if we assume that he sells 1 cotton trouser and 2 woollen trousers, he gains a profit of 45%. This gives us the equation:

$1.3X + 2 \times 1.5Y = 1.45(X + 2Y) \rightarrow 0.1Y = 0.15X$ or $Y = 1.5X$.

In the second case, if he has sold 2 woollen trousers, he has sold 3 cotton trousers. The total cost would be: $3X + 2Y = 6X$ (since $Y = 1.5X$).

The total revenue would be: $3 \times 1.3X + 2 \times 1.5Y = 3.9X + 3Y = 3.9X + 4.5X = 8.4X$.

The profit percentage can then be worked out using 6*X* as cost and 8.4*X* as revenue. The percentage profit is 40%.

55. Let M be the point of first meeting and N be the point of second meeting. Let the distance MN = *d* km.

A ←— 7 km —→|←— *d* km —→|←— 4 km —→ B
(M, N marked at the two meeting points)

Total distance covered by both the buses together before first meet = (11 + *d*) km.

Total distance travelled by both the buses together from first to second meeting point = 2 × (11 + *d*) km.

To cover this double distance each bus will take double the time and hence distance traveled by each bus from first to second meeting point will be double of what each of the buses travelled till first meeting. Bus from terminus A travels 7 km before first meeting and $(d + 8)$ km between the first and second meeting. Hence $d + 8 = 2 \times 7 = 14$

$d = 6$ km

Hence, total distance between A and B $= (7 + d + 4)$ km $= (7 + 6 + 4)$ km $= 17$ km.

Hence, cost of running both the buses $= 2 \times (17 \times 20 \times 2 \times 5) =$ ₹6,800

56. Cost price of an apple = ₹20
Cost price of an orange = ₹8
If she sells 'x' apples and 'y' oranges. Then, according to the question : $23x + 10y = 653$ & $x > y$.
Possible value of $(x, y) = (21, 17)$
For (21, 17) the cost price $= 21 \times 20 + 17 \times 8 =$ ₹556
$\%\ profit = \frac{653 - 556}{556} \times 100 = 17.4\%$

57. The key here is that the profit sharing ratio is not relevant in this question – since profits will only occur after the break even point. The break even point can be calculated as:
$200000 + 400n = 2000n \rightarrow n = \frac{200000}{1600} = 125.$

58. He would have purchased 5 units of 4 garments each, in order to purchase 20 garments. Thus, each set of 4 garments would have cost $\frac{14000}{5} = 2800.$
This price $= 3P + 100 \rightarrow P = 900$

59. The shopkeeper bought 32 kgs apples and 64 kgs mangoes. Let the price to the wholesaler be: ₹N per kg for apples and $4N$ for mangoes. The total cost to the shopkeeper will be:
$32 \times 1.2N + 64 \times 5.6N = 396.8N.$
For an overall profit of 25% on this amount, he has to sell the entire quantity for $1.25 \times 396.8N = 496N$.
Since 20 kgs of mangoes and 12 kgs of apples were rotten, he is left with 44 kgs of mangoes and 20 kgs of apples – so he has a net weight of 64 kgs of fruit to be sold.
$496N = 248 \times 64 \rightarrow N = 32$ and hence the price of mangoes for the wholesaler was $4N = 128$.

60. Ramaiya's purchase price $(a) = 1.56P$, Kanhaiya's purchase price $(b) = 0.56P$. $(a - b) : P = 1 : 1$

61. Let the cost price of the book be B and the pen be P.
We have: $0.95P + 1.15B = 1.07(P + B) \rightarrow 0.12P = 0.08B \rightarrow B = 1.5P$
We are also given:
$1.05P + 1.1B = P + B + 13$
$\rightarrow 2.7P = 2.5P + 13$ (Using $B = 1.5P$)
$P = 65, B = 97.5.$

62. Fix cost of 1 lac units = 40 lac
Let the breakeven point be attained on the sale of 'x' units.
Therefore, 40 lac + $100x = 200x$
or $x = 40000$
Hence the total sales $= 40000 \times 200 =$ ₹80 lac.

63. Total cost when variable cost increases by 10% then total cost = 40 lac + 100 × 1.1 lac = ₹150 lac
Initial Profit = 200 lac – 140 lac = ₹60 lac
New Profit = ₹200 lac – ₹150 lac = ₹50 lac
$\%\ decrease\ in\ the\ profit = \left(\frac{10}{60}\right) \times 100 = 16.67\%$

64. Initial profit = (200 lac – 140 lac) = ₹60 lac
Interest paid by KK on 20 lac = 10% of 20 lac = ₹2 lac
Profit after interest + taxes = 70% of (60 – 2) lac = ₹40.6 lac
After 20% growth in sales, he sells 1.2 lac units
New profit = (200 × 1.2) lac – (40 + 100 × 1.2) lac = ₹80 lac
Interest paid = 10% of 20 lac = ₹2 lac
Profit after interest and taxes = 70% of (80 – 2) lac = ₹54.6 lac
$\%\ change\ in\ earning = \frac{54.6 - 40.6}{40.6} \times 100 = 34.5\%$

65. Let the profit (in ₹) for the year be ₹p. Then according to the question
$\frac{3}{5} \times 200000 + \left(0.20 + \frac{3}{5} \times 0.8\right) \times 200000 + \left(0.35 + \frac{3}{5} \times 0.65\right) \times (p - 400000) = 367000$
$256000 + 0.74 \times (p - 400000) = 367000$
By solving the above equation we get $p =$ ₹5,50,000.

66. As the retailer sells the item at a 10% discount, if we assume that the cost of manufacturing was 100, the MRP would be 155 – we would get that the retailer sells at a 10% discount on 155. This means that the retailer would be selling the item at 0.9 × 155 = 139.5. Since the retailer sells at a 23% profit on his purchase price, his purchase price has to be such that if we add the effect of a 23% increase in the purchase price to the purchase price, we would get a selling price of 139.5 (approximately). Checking from the options, if we check the middle option of 15% – as the profit percentage for the manufacturer, we would get that the manufacturer sells at 115. However, adding 23% of 115 to 115, we would get 115 + 23% of 115 = 115 + 26.45 = 141.45. This is clearly above the required 139.5, and hence the manufacturer's profit would be below 15%. Checking Option (d) of 13% we get: Cost = 100, Manufacturer's selling price = retailer's purchase price = 113. Retailers' selling price = 113 + 23% of 113 ≈ 139.
This will clearly give us the closest answer to the question asked. Hence, Option (d) is correct

67. Profit = 70000 – 54000 = ₹16,000
Now, 7.14 % out of 14 machines are not working it means 7.14% of 14 ≈ 1 out of 14 machines is not working.
Total cost $= 42000 \times \frac{13}{14} + 12000 =$ ₹51,000

Annual output = $\frac{70000}{14}$ × 13 = ₹65,000

Profit = 65000 – 51000 = ₹14,000

Percentage decrease in profit = $\frac{2000}{16000}$ × 100 = 12.5%

68. Revenue $r(x)$ = Total number of people × revenue per person = $x\left(54 - \frac{x}{32}\right)^2$
Checking the options, we can see that at 575 to 576 units the revenue increases, but increasing the number of people from 576 to 577 reduces the revenue. Hence, option (b) is correct.

69. Let the production cost of the mobiles be 100. Then the 100 is composed of:
Cost of A + Cost of B + Cost of C + Factory Production costs = 10 + 20 + 30 + 40 = 100.
The selling price = 1.5 × 100 = 150.
In the next year after the increased price of the components, the total cost = 12 + 28 + 48 + 40 = 128. Selling price = 150 × 1.2 = 180. Profit percentage is given by the ratio $\frac{52}{180}$ = 28.88%. Option (a) is correct.

70. The profit share is in the ratio of: 40000 ×6 : 100000 × 12 : 80000 × 9 = 1 : 5 : 3. The total profit available for distribution is 90% of 900000 = 810000. Amritesh will get $\frac{3}{9}$ or $\frac{1}{3}$ of this profit. Hence, Amritesh gets 270000.

71. Ramu sold 15 pens and 25 pencils. His profit per pencil is ₹50. Hence, his total profit while selling the pencils is 25 × 50 = 1250. This means that 15 pens gave him a profit of 1625 – 1250 = 375. Thus, the profit per pen is $\frac{375}{15}$ = 25. Also, since the profit percentage on pens is 25%, it means the cost price of a pen is ₹100. A pencil costs ₹75.
Total loss incurred on the unsold items = 5 × 100 + 5 × 75 = 875. So his net profit is 1625 – 875 = 750. Hence, option (b) is correct.

72. Let the original service charge be ₹100
Rohan has paid 100, 90, 90 × 0.89 = 80.1,80.1 × 0.88 = 70.48 and 55 rupees for the five services
Total payment done by Rohan = 100 + 90 + 80.1 + 70.48 + 55 = ₹395.58
Total discount availed by Rohan = 500 – 395.60 = ₹104.42
Percentage discount = 104.42 × 100/500 = 20.88% (approx.)

73. Assume that the selling price of each painting is 100. Then, the cost price of the three paintings will be: $\frac{100}{0.88}$ = 113.63; $\frac{100}{1.27}$ = 78.74 and $\frac{100}{0.82}$ = 121.95.
Average cost price = $\frac{(113.63+78.74+121.95)}{3}$ = 104.77. Hence, option (d) is correct.

74. The total revenue of the publishing house was: 1840 × 500 + 7360 × 375 = 3680000. The vendors discount on this would be 30% of the revenue. Hence, net revenue = 0.7 × 3680000 = 2576000. This revenue is earned on the basis of a total cost of 2200000. Hence, the profit percentage will be $\frac{376000}{2200000}$ = 17.1%. The closest integer approximation is 17%.

Solutions to Questions 75 to 78: The key variables to consider here are the revenue he earns from the customer and the cost incurred in servicing the customer. The cost consists of 3 major components – Depreciation ($\frac{100}{50}$ = 2 rupees per customer for the first 10 years of a vehicle); Cost of fuel = fuel used × 15 per litre + cost of driver's salary. In the case of the questions asked, since Preetpal is driving his own taxi, there is no driver's salary to be paid and there is no depreciation to be considered since his taxi is 14 years old – hence fully depreciated.

75. His taxi meter for the customer will show 10 + 5 × 5 + 8 × 1 = ₹43. The customer pays him 1.2 × 43 = ₹51.6. His cost will be: kms traveled × cost per kilometer = 7 × 1.25 = 8.75. Profit = 51.6 – 8.75 = 42.85. Option (d) is correct.

76. Percentage profit = $\frac{\text{profit} \times 100}{\text{cost}} = \frac{42.85 \times 100}{8.75}$ = 489.71%. Option (c) is correct.

77. For an extra 5 minute waiting time, the meter reading will go up by ₹5 to 48. The customer will pay him 48 × 1.2 = 57.6. New profit = 457.6 – 8.75 = 48.85.
Percentage change in profit = $\frac{6}{42.85} \approx 14\%$. Option (b) is correct.

78. If the taxi is idled for 7 minutes for the above journey, the fuel required will be 0.35 liters and the cost for the same will be 0.35 × 15 = ₹5.25.
Profits will come down from 48.85 (previous question) by ₹5.25. That is a percentage drop of 10.74%. Option (a) is correct.

79. The respective costs, SP and margins will be as seen in the table below:

Periodical type	SP	CP	Margin (in ₹)
Weekly	12	10	2
Monthly	50	40	10
Daily	3	2	1

If the number of periodicals is restricted, he should sell only monthlies as he gets maximum margin per periodical in monthlies. Option (b) is correct.

80. If the capital is limited, he should go for the periodical giving him the maximum profit percentage. The profit percentage is maximum in selling dailies and hence option (c) is correct.

Solutions for Questions 81 to 83: The following table shows the cost price per fruit, the cost price per dozen, the SP per dozen and the profit percentage in selling each fruit – considering the information provided in questions 81 and 82 for mangoes, apples, watermelons and oranges.

Fruit Name	Price per piece	Price per dozen = Price per piece × 12	Margin per dozen (based on SP per dozen provided in question)	Percentage profit
Mango	4.25	51	65 – 51 = 14	$\frac{14}{51} = 27.45\%$
Apple	1.5	18	30 – 18 = 12	$\frac{12}{18} = 66.66\%$
Water-melon	18	216	360 – 216 = 144	$\frac{144}{216} = 66.66\%$
Oranges	1.8	21.6	33 – 21.6 = 11.4	$\frac{11.4}{21.6} = 52.77\%$

81. Comparing apples, mangoes and oranges, we see that the percentage profit is greatest in apples and watermelons. Hence, option (d) is correct.

82. At an investment of 1800, his profit will be maximised if he sells either only apples or only watermelons or a mixture of both. In any of the cases, the percentage profit would be 16.66% and the profit value would be ₹1200. Option (a) is correct.

83. Your maximum fees would be: 20% of maximum profit for the month. = 30 × 1200 × 0.2 = 7200.

84. The newspaper sells at ₹3, but after vendor commission, the company will only receive ₹1.8 per unit sold. Hence, there is a loss of 11 – 1.8 = ₹9.2 per newspaper sold. Total loss = 9.2 × 12000. This has to be recovered by selling advertising space @255 per column centimeter (**Note:** again here though advertising space is 300 per column centimeter, there is an agency commission of 15% and hence, the company will only receive ₹255 for every cc sold). Total column centimeter required to be sold = $\frac{9.2 \times 12000}{255}$ = 432.94. The closest answer is option (c).

85. If the company is not able to recover 20% of it's dues, it means that it needs to sell 25% more space. Hence, the correct answer is 433 × 1.25 = 541.25. However if we consider the same number after rounding off 433 to 435, we get 435 × 1.25 = 544. Option (c) is correct.

CHAPTER 8

Simple and Compound Interest

Chapter Launchpad

Scan this QR code to access a video on 'Introduction to Simple and Compound Interest and this chapter's importance for CAT

INTRODUCTION

The chapter on interest forms an important topic from the CAT's point of view. Questions from this chapter are a regular feature of *QA* section of the Online *CAT*. Besides, this chapter also has the additional importance of being a core chapter for Data Interpretation, especially with the statistical concept of the Compounded Annual Growth Rate (referred to as CAGR), being numerically akin to the compound interest situation that you would study in this chapter.

Prior to studying this chapter however, you are required to ensure that you have a clear understanding of percentages and percentage calculation. The faster you are at percentage calculations, the faster you will be in solving questions of interests.

Apart from *CAT*, questions on interest are also important for exams like *XAT, SNAP, NMAT, CUET, IPMAT*, Banking and *SSC* exams – apart from other aptitude exams. Hence, if you are planning to appear for the entire spectrum of management and aptitude exams—this chapter retains its importance for all these exams.

CONCEPT OF TIME VALUE OF MONEY

The value of money is not constant. This is one of the principal facts on which the entire economic world is based. A rupee today will not be equal to a rupee tomorrow. Hence, a rupee borrowed today cannot be repaid by a rupee tomorrow. This is the basic need for the concept of interest. The rate of interest is used to determine the difference between what is borrowed and what is repaid.

There are two bases on which interests are calculated:

Simple Interest It is calculated on the basis of a basic amount borrowed for the entire period at a particular rate of interest. The amount borrowed is the principal for the entire period of borrowing.

Compound Interest The interest of the previous year/s is/are added to the principal for the calculation of the compound interest.

This difference will be clear from the following illustration:

A sum of ₹1000 at 10% per annum will have

Simple interest		Compound interest
₹100	First year	₹100
₹100	Second year	₹110
₹100	Third year	₹121
₹100	Fourth year	₹133.1

Note: The previous years' interests are added to the original sum of ₹1000 to calculate the interest to be paid in the case of compound interest from the second year onwards.

Terminology Pertaining to Interest

- The man who lends money is the **Creditor** and the man who borrows money is the **Debtor**.
- The amount of money that is initially borrowed is called the **Capital** or **Principal** money.
- The period for which money is deposited or borrowed is called **Time**.
- The extra money that will be paid or received for the use of the principal after a certain period is called the **Total interest** on the capital.
- The sum of the principal and the interest at the end of any time is called the **Amount**.
  So, **Amount = Principal + Total Interest**
- **Rate of Interest** is the rate at which the interest is calculated and is always specified in percentage terms.

SIMPLE INTEREST(SI)

The interest of one year for every ₹100 is called the Interest rate per annum. If we say "the rate of interest per annum is r%", we mean that ₹r is the interest on a principal of ₹100 for one year.

Relation among Principal, Time, Rate Percent of Interest per Annum and Total Interest

Suppose, Principal = ₹P, Time = t years, Rate of interest per annum = r% and Total interest = ₹I

Then $$I = \frac{P \times t \times r}{100}$$

i.e. Total interest =

$$\frac{\text{Principal} \times \text{Time} \times \text{Rate of interest per annum}}{100}$$

Amount = Principal + Total interest, we can write

Note: The rate of interest is normally specified in terms of annual rate of interest. In such a case, we take the time t in years.

However, if the rate of interest is specified in terms of six-monthly rate, we take time in terms of six months.

Also, the half-yearly rate of interest is half the annual rate of interest. That is, if the interest is 10% per annum to be charged six-monthly, we have to add interest every six months @ 5%.

Logical Understanding of Simple Interest: The students must have got through the understanding of the mathematical formulae pertaining to Simple Interests above. Before we move onto a discussion of compound interest however, let's revisit Simple Interest logically. We can do this through a few examples.

Suppose a man invests ₹100 @ 8% simple interest. He would be paid an interest of ₹8 per year (simply because 8% of ₹100 is ₹8). Further, going forward, if it is mentioned to us that 'the man kept earning 8% simple interest for five years on an investment of ₹100', the straight forward logical reaction is: He earns ₹8 interest per year for five years. Hence, his interest is ₹40. It is a straight logical thought and you would never fail to see it in any *QA* problem. Hence, there is absolutely no reason for you to remember the mathematical formulae of simple interests. Just treat every simple interest question like a percentage calculation situation and you would be logically able to work out all the reactions that you need to have for every kind of problem situation on percentages. In order to strengthen these logical structures, let us take a look at various standard statements and situations that you would regularly face in the percentages chapter.

1	Statement: *A* man invests ₹200 at 8% SI for 3 years.	**Reaction:** Each year's interest is ₹16 (@8% of 200). In 3 years, the interest would be 16 × 3 = 48.
2	A man invests a certain amount at 5% per annum simple interest for 8 years	**Reaction:** Since SI every year would be 5% of the principal, the SI for 8 years would be 5 × 8 = 40% of the principal.
3	A man invests a certain amount at 5% per annum simple interest for 8 years and earns an interest of ₹4000.	**Reaction:** Since the total SI would be 40% of the principal, it means that 40% of the principal = 4000 → the principal would be 10000.
4	On an investment of a certain amount at a certain rate of interest, a man earns an interest of ₹200 every year. After a certain period of time, he has earned ₹1000 as interest. What is the time period?	**Reaction:** ₹200 per year being the SI, the time period would be: 1000/200 = 5 years.
5	₹10000 is invested @10% per annum simple interest, where the interest is paid half-yearly. Find the interest after 30 months. Also, find the amount after 30 months.	Since, the interest is paid half-yearly, the effective half-yearly rate of interest would be 10/2 = 5%. Interest would be earned @5% per 6 months. In 30 months, a total interest of 5 × 5 = 25% would be earned. Hence, the total interest earned would be 25% of 10000 = 2500. The amount would be 10000 + 2500 = 12500.

Another crucial structural point about Simple Interest- The relationship between an SI situation and Arithmetic Progressions: In chapter 2 of this book, we have worked on the thought structures around Arithmetic Progressions (APs). You might remember the basic structures of an AP. Now let us see the relationship between an AP and SI. Consider a situation where a person invests ₹1000 @ 10% per annum SI. As the years go by, the principal of ₹1000 would grow by ₹100 every year. The following series would represent the amount after various years under this SI problem situation:

Original Amount	Amount after 1 year	Amount after 2 years	Amount after 3 years	Amount after 4 years	Amount after 5 years	Amount after 6 years	Amount after 7 years	Amount after 8 years	Amount after 9 years
1000	1100	1200	1300	1400	1500	1600	1700	1800	1900
1st term of the AP	2nd term of the AP	3rd term of the AP	4th term of the AP	5th term of the AP	6th term of the AP	7th term of the AP	8th term of the AP	9th term of the AP	10th term of AP

As you can see from the table above, the numerical structure for the amounts after any period of time in a *SI*-based question, would be obeying an arithmetic progression with the principal as the first term and the annual interest amount as the common difference. Thus, if we want the amount after seven years, in this case, we can simply think about finding the 8th term of the *AP* whose first term is 1000 (principal) and common difference is 100 (interest per time period).

So for example, for a principal of 200, @8% *SI* per annum paid half-yearly, the *AP* would go as:

200, 208, 216, 224, 232©

Here the amount is 208 (after 6 months), 216 (after 12 months), and 224 (after 18 months) and so on.

If you want to find the amount after 42 months, simply find the 8th term of the AP using: 200 + 7 × 8 = 256.

COMPOUND INTEREST

Math Simplified

Scan this QR code to access a video that explains the logical thought structures available for Compound Interest and Simple Interest.

In monetary transactions, often, the borrower and the lender, in order to settle an account, agree on a certain amount of interest to be paid to the lender on the basis of specified unit of time. This may be yearly or half-yearly or quarterly, with the condition that the interest accrued to the principal at a certain interval of time be added to the principal so that the total amount at the end of an interval becomes the principal for the next interval. Thus, it is different from simple interest.

In such cases, the interest for the first interval is added to the principal and this amount becomes the principal for the second interval, and so on.

The difference between the amount and the money borrowed is called the *compound interest* for the given interval.

Formulae

Case 1: Let principal = P, time = n years and rate = r% per annum and let A be the total amount at the end of n years, then

$$A = P\left[1+\frac{r}{100}\right]^n$$

Case 2: When compound interest is reckoned half-yearly

If the annual rate is r% per annum and is to be calculated for n years,

Then in this case, rate = $(r/2)$% half-yearly and time = $(2n)$ half-years.

∴ from the above, we get

$$A = P\left[1+\frac{r/2}{100}\right]^{2n}$$

Case 3: When compound interest is reckoned quarterly

In this case, rate = $(r/4)$ % quarterly and time = $(4n)$ quarter years.

∴ as before,

$$A = P\left[1+\frac{r/4}{100}\right]^{4n}$$

Note: The difference between the compound interest and the simple interest over two years is given by

$$Pr^2/100^2 \quad \text{or} \quad P\left(\frac{r}{100}\right)^2$$

DEPRECIATION OF VALUE

The value of a machine or any other article subject to wear-and-tear, decreases with time.

This decrease is called its *depreciation*.

Thus, if V_0 is the value at a certain time and r% per annum is the rate of depreciation per year, then the value V_1 at the end of t years is

$$V_1 = V_0\left[1-\frac{r}{100}\right]^t$$

POPULATION

The problems on population change are similar to the problems on compound interest. The formulae applicable to the problems on compound interest also apply to those on population. The only difference is that in the application of formulae, the annual rate of change of population replaces the rate of compound interest.

However, unlike in compound interest where the rate is always positive, the population can decrease. In such a case, we have to treat population change as we treated depreciation of value illustrated above.

The above formulae provide us with the mathematical structures in CI. Let us now proceed to have a logical discussion around compound interests:

While discussing SI, we had seen that the structure of an AP fits the SI situation perfectly. Similarly, in the numerical structure of CI, the other progression (geometric) fits perfectly. If you remember, a geometric progression was one where a starting number was consistently multiplied repetitively by a number referred to as the common ratio (r). Exactly the same thing occurs in a CI series. Consider the case, where ₹100 is invested @10% per annum CI for five years. What would be the growth pattern for this amount?

Well, after one year, 100 becomes 110. The next year, 110 increases to 121. In the third year, 121 increases to 133.1, followed by a fourth year, the end value of 146.41 and after five years, it would become: 161.051. If you notice, this series is nothing but the series defined by:

100, 100 × 1.1 = 110; 100 × 1.1 × 1.1 = 121 and so on. Thus, a GP with first term as 100 (the principal) and a common ratio of 1.1 (in the case of 10%) would give you the series of numbers that would fit the CI situation. To illustrate a few more instances, if the interest rate is 12%, use a common ratio of 1.12, if CI rate is 8%; use a common ratio of 1.08. Use the common ratio as many times as the number of time-periods.

Notice, also that the depreciation and the population concepts discussed also fit the same structures. Thus, if a machine depreciates by 8% every year, its value would get multiplied by 0.92. If it depreciates by 10%, by 0.9 and by 12%, then multiply the amount by 0.88 and so on.

Note: The advantage of thinking this way is that you bypass the need for thinking through the formulae in these situations. You can think of all these problems as *GP* situations where the principal is taken as the first term of the ratio and the value of 'r' is created based on the thought structure explained above.

However, the biggest advantage of moving out of the formulae thinking for CI is to be able to use the successive percentage change use of the PCG (Percentage Change Graphic) for all CI, Population and Depreciation questions.

In fact, it is felt that the formulae on compound interest (CI) unnecessarily make a very simple topic overly-mathematical. Besides, the CI formulae are the most unusable formulae available in this level of mathematics since it is virtually impossible for the student to calculate a number like 1.08 raised to the power 3, 4, 5 or more without the help of a calculator.

Instead, in my opinion, you should view CI problems simply as an extension of the concept of successive percentage increases and tackle the calculations required through approximations and through the use of the percentage rule of calculations.

Thus, the calculation: 4 years increase at 6% pa CI on ₹120 would yield an expression: 120×1.06^4. It would be impossible for an average student to attempt such a question and even if one uses advanced techniques of calculations, one will end up using more time than one has. Instead, if you have to solve this problem, you should look at it from the following percentage change graphic perspective:

$$120 \xrightarrow[=7.2]{+6\%} 127.2 \xrightarrow[6+1.62]{+6\%}$$

$$134.82 \xrightarrow[6+2.1]{+6\%} 142.92 \xrightarrow[6+2.58]{+6\%} 151.5\text{ (approx.)}$$

If you try to check the answer on a calculator, you will discover that you have a very close approximation. Besides, given the fact that you would be working with options and given sufficiently comfortable options, you need not calculate so closely; instead, save time through the use of approximations.

The following illustrations would clear this for you:

₹1000 is invested @ 8% per annum for 5 years	**Reaction through GPs:** We need to find the sixth term of the GP with r = 1.08 and first term as 1000.	**Reaction through PCG:** 1000 →→→→→ (increased by 8% for 5 times.)
₹8000 is invested @12% per annum CI compounded quarterly. What would it amount to after 21 months?	**Reaction through GPs:** Since there is quarterly compounding, 12% per annum translates to 12/4 = 3% per quarter. We need to find the eighth term of the GP with r = 1.03 and first term as 8000.	**Reaction through PCG:** 8000 →→→→→ →→ (increased by 3% for 7 times.)
A machine costing 100000, depreciates by 8% every year for 3 successive years.	**Reaction through GPs:** Find the fourth term of the GP with first term as 100000, and common ratio 0.92.	**Reaction through PCG:** Reduce 100000 successively 3 times by 8%.

APPLICATIONS OF INTEREST IN D.I. AND HANDLING MORE COMPLICATED CALCULATION SITUATIONS AROUND COMPOUNDING

The difference between Simple Annual Growth Rate and Compound Annual Growth Rate:

The measurement of growth rates is a prime concern in business and Economics. While a manager might be interested in calculating the growth rates in the sales of his product, an economist might be interested in finding out the rate of growth of the GDP of an economy.

In mathematical terms, there are basically two ways in which growth rates are calculated. To familiarise you with this, consider the following example.

The sales of a brand of scooters increase from 100 to 120 units in a particular city. What does this mean to you? Simply, that there is a percentage increase of 20% in the sales of the scooters. Now read further:

What if the sales move from 120 to 140 in the next year and 140 to 160 in the third year? Obviously, there is a constant and uniform growth from 100 to 120 to 160 – i.e. a growth of exactly 20 units per year. In terms of the overall growth in the value of the sales over three years, it can be easily seen that the sale has grown by 60 on 100, i.e. 60% growth.

In this case, what does 20% represent? If you look at this situation as a plain problem of interests, 20% represents the simple interest that will make 100 grow to 160.

In the context of D.I., this value of 20% interest is also called the Simple Annual Growth Rate (SAGR).

The process for calculating SAGR is simply the same as that for calculating simple interest.

Suppose a value grows from 100 to 200 in 10 years – the SAGR is obtained by the simple calculation 100%/10 = 10%

What is Compound Annual Growth Rate (CAGR)?

Let us consider a simple situation. Let us go back to the scooter company.

Suppose, the company increases its sales by 20% in the first year, and then again increases its sales by 20% in the second year and also the third year. In such a situation, the sales (taking 100 as a starting value) trend can be easily tracked as below:

$$100 \xrightarrow[+20]{20\%\uparrow} 120 \xrightarrow[+24]{20\%\uparrow} 144 \xrightarrow[+28.8]{20\%\uparrow} 172.8$$

As you must have realised, this calculation is pretty similar to the calculation of compound interests. In the above case, 20% is the rate of compound interest which will change 100 to 172.8 in three years.

This 20% is also called as the Compound Annual Growth Rate (CAGR) in the context of data interpretation.

Obviously, the calculation of the CAGR is much more difficult than the calculation of the SAGR and the compound interest formula is essentially a waste of time for anything more than three years.

(Up to three years, if you know your squares and the methods for the cubes, you can still feasibly work things out – but beyond three years, it becomes pretty much infeasible to calculate the compound interest).

So is there an alternative? Yes there is and the alternative largely depends on your ability to add well. Hence, before trying out what I am about to tell you, I would recommend you should strengthen yourself at addition.

Suppose you have to calculate the C.I. on ₹100 at the rate of 10% per annum for a period of 10 years.

You can combine a mixture of PCG used for successive changes with guess estimation to get a pretty accurate value.

In this case, since the percentage increase is exactly 10% (which is perhaps the easiest percentage to calculate), we can use PCG all the way as follows:

$$100 \xrightarrow[+10]{10\%\uparrow} 110 \xrightarrow[+11]{10\%\uparrow} 121 \xrightarrow[+12.1]{10\%\uparrow} 133.1$$

$$\xrightarrow[+13.31]{10\%\uparrow} 146.4$$

$$\xrightarrow[14.64]{10\%\uparrow} 161.04 \xrightarrow[16.10]{10\%\uparrow} 177.14 \xrightarrow[17.71]{10\%\uparrow} 194.8$$

$$\xrightarrow[19.48]{10\%\uparrow} \ldots$$

$$214.3 \xrightarrow[21.43]{10\%\uparrow} 235.7 \xrightarrow[23.57]{10\%\uparrow} 259.2$$

Thus, the percentage increase after 10 years @ 10% will be 159.2 (approx).

However, this was the easy part. What would you do if you had to calculate 12% CI for 10 years? The percentage calculations would obviously become much more difficult and infeasible. How can we tackle this situation?

$$100 \xrightarrow[+12]{12\%\uparrow} 112 \xrightarrow[?]{12\%\uparrow} ?$$

In order to understand how to tackle the second percentage increase in the above PCG, let's try to evaluate where we are in the question.

We have to calculate 12% of 112, which is the same as 12% of 100 + 12% of 12.

But we have already calculated 12% of 100 as 12 for the first arrow of the PCG. Hence, we now have to calculate 12% of 12 and add it to 12% of 100.

Hence, the addition has to be:

$$12 + 1.44 = 13.44$$

Take note of the addition of 1.44 in this step. It will be significant later. The PCG will now look like:

$$100 \longrightarrow 112 \longrightarrow 125.44 \xrightarrow[?]{12\%\uparrow} ?$$

We are now faced with a situation of calculating 12% of 125.44. Obviously, if you try to do this directly, you will have great difficulty in calculations. We can sidestep this as follows:

12% of 125.44 = 12% of 112 + 12% of 13.44

But we have already calculated 12% of 112 as 13.44 in the previous step.

Hence, our calculation changes to:

12% of 112 + 12% of 13.44 = 13.44 + 12% of 13.44

But, 12% of 13.44 = 12% of 12 + 12% of 1.44. We have already calculated 12% of 12 as 1.44 in the previous step.

Hence, 12% of 13.44 = 1.44 + 12% of 1.44

= 1.44 + 0.17 = 1.61 (approx.)

Hence, the overall addition is

$$13.44 + 1.61 = 15.05$$

Now, your PCG looks like:

$$100 \xrightarrow{+12} 112 \xrightarrow{+13.44} 125.44 \xrightarrow{+15.05} 140.49$$

$$\xrightarrow{+?} ?$$

You are again at the same point—faced with calculating the rather intimidating looking 12% of 140.49

12% of 140.49 = 12% of 125.44 + 12% of 15.05

Already calculated

Compare this to the previous calculation:

12% of 125.44 = 12% of 112 + 12% of 13.44

Already calculated

The only calculation that has changed is that you have to calculate 12% of 15.05 instead of 12% of 13.44. (which was approximately 1.61). In this case, it will be approximately 1.8. Hence, you shall now add 16.85 and the PCG will look as:

$$100 \xrightarrow{+12} 112 \xrightarrow{+13.44} 125.44 \xrightarrow{+15.05} 140.49$$

$$\xrightarrow{+16.85} 166.34$$

If you evaluate the change in the value added at every arrow in the PCG above, you will see a trend—

The additions were:

+12, +13.44 (change in addition = 1.44), +15.05(change in addition = 1.61), +16.85 (change in addition = 1.8)

If you now evaluate the change in the change in addition, you will realise that the values are 0.17, 0.19. This will be a slightly increasing series (and can be easily approximated).

Thus, the following table (on the next page) shows the approximate calculation of 12% CI for 10 years with an initial value of 100.

Thus, 100 becomes 309.78.

(a percentage increase of 209.78%)

Similarly, in the case of every other compound interest calculation, you can simply find the trend that the first 2 – 3 years interest is going to follow and continue that trend to get a close approximate value of the overall percentage increase.

Thus, for instance 7% growth for 7 years at C.I. would mean:

$$100 \xrightarrow{+7} 107 \xrightarrow{+7.49} 114.49 \xrightarrow{+8.01} 122.5$$

$$\xrightarrow{+8.55} 131.05$$

$$\xrightarrow{+9.11} 140.16 \xrightarrow{+9.75} 149.91 \xrightarrow{+10.42} 160.33$$

At the end of	*Principal (approx.)*	*Interest for the year*	*Change in Addition*	*Change in change in Addition*
year 0	100	+12		
			1.44	
year 1	112	+13.44		0.17
			1.61	
year 2	125.44	+15.05		0.19
			1.8	
year 3	140.49	+16.85		0.21
			2.01	
year 4	157.36	+18.86		
			2.25	0.24
year 5	176.2	21.11		
			2.51	0.28
year 6	197.3	23.62		
			2.79	
year 7	220.92	26.41		0.31
year 8	247.33	29.5	3.1	
				0.35
year 9	276.83	32.95	3.45	
year 10	309.78			

This series is approximated giving all values in this table.

An approximate growth of 60.33%

The actual value (on a calculation) is around 60.57% – Hence, as you can see we have a pretty decent approximation for the answer.

Note: The increase in the addition will need to be increased at a greater rate than as an A.P. Thus, in this case if we had considered the increase to be an A.P. the respective addition would have been:

+7, +7.49, +8.01, +8.55, +9.11, +9.69, +10.29

However +7, +7.49, +8.01, +8.55, +9.11, +9.75, +10.42 are the actual addition used. Notice that using 9.75 instead of 9.69 is a deliberate adjustment, since while using C.I., the impact on the addition due to the interest on the interest shows an ever-increasing behaviour.

Space for Rough Work

WORKED-OUT PROBLEMS

Problem 8.1: The SI on a sum of money is 25% of the principal, and the rate per annum is equal to the number of years. Find the rate percent.

(a) 4.5% (b) 6%
(c) 5% (d) 8%

Solution:

Let principal = x, time = t years

Then interest = $x/4$, rate = t%

Now, using the SI formula, we get

Interest = (Principal × Rate × Time)/100

$\Rightarrow \quad x/4 = (x \times t \times t)/100$

$\Rightarrow \quad t^2 = 25$

$\Rightarrow \quad t = 5\%$

Alternatively, you can also solve this by using the options, wherein you should check that when you divide 25 by the value of the option, you get the option's value as the answer.

Thus, 25/4.5 ≠ 4.5. Hence, option (a) is incorrect.

Also, 25/6 ≠ 6. Hence, option (b) is incorrect.

Checking for option (c) we get, 25/5 = 5. Hence, (c) is the right answer.

Problem 8.2: The rate of interest for first three years is 6% per annum, for the next four years, 7 % per annum and for the period beyond seven years, 7.5 % per annum. If a man lent out ₹1200 for eleven years, find the total interest earned by him?

(a) ₹1002 (b) ₹912
(c) ₹864 (d) ₹948

Solution:

Whenever it is not mentioned whether we have to assume SI or CI, we should assume SI.

For any amount, interest for the first three years @ 6% SI will be equal to 6 × 3 = 18%.

Again, interest for next four years will be equal to 7 × 4 = 28%.

And interest for next four years (till 11 years) –7.5 × 4 = 30%

So, total interest = 18 + 28 + 30 = 76%.

So, total interest earned by him = 76% of the amount

$$= \frac{(76 \times 1200)}{100} = ₹912$$

This calculation can be done very conveniently using the percentage rule as 75% + 1% = 900 + 12 = 912.

Problem 8.3: A sum of money doubles itself in 12 years. Find the rate percentage per annum.

(a) 12.5% (b) 8.33%
(c) 10% (d) 7.51%

Solution: Let principal = x, then interest = x, time = 12 years.

Using the formula, Rate = (Interest × 100)/Principal × Time

= (x × 100)/(x × 12) = 8.33%

Alternatively: It is obvious that in 12 years, 100% of the amount is added as interest.

So, in 1 year = (100/12) % of the amount is added.

Hence, every year there is an addition of 8.33% (which is the rate of simple interest required).

Alternatively, you can also use the formula.

If a sum of money gets doubled in x years, then rate of interest = (100/x) %.

Problem 8.4: A certain sum of money amounts to ₹704 in two years and ₹800 in five years. Find the principal.

(a) ₹580 (b) ₹600
(c) ₹660 (d) ₹640

Solution: Let the principal be ₹x and rate = r%.

Then, difference in between the interest of five years and of two years equals to

₹800 – ₹704 = ₹96

So, interest for 3 years = ₹96

Hence, interest/year = ₹96/3 = ₹32

So, interest for 2 years → 2 × ₹32 = ₹64

So, the principal = ₹704 – ₹64 = ₹640

Thought-process here should be

₹96 interest in 3 years → ₹32 interest every year.

Hence, principal = 704 – 64 = 640.

Problem 8.5: A sum of money was invested at SI at a certain rate for three years. Had it been invested at a 4% higher rate, it would have fetched ₹480 more. Find the principal.

(a) ₹4000 (b) ₹4400
(c) ₹5000 (d) ₹3500

Solution: Let the rate be y% and principal be ₹x and the time be three years.

Then according to the question = $(x(y + 4) \times 3)/100 - (xy \times 3)/100 = 480$

$\Rightarrow \quad xy + 4x - xy = 160 \times 100$

$\Rightarrow \quad x = (160 \times 100)/4 = ₹4000$

Alternatively: Excess money obtained = 3 years @ 4% per annum

= 12% of whole money

So, according to the question, 12% = ₹480.

So, 100% = ₹4000 (answer arrived at by using unitary method.)

Problem 8.6: A certain sum of money trebles itself in eight years. In how many years it will be five times?

(a) 22 years (b) 16 years
(c) 20 years (d) 24 years

Solution: It trebles itself in eight years, which makes interest equal to 200% of principal.

So, 200% is added in eight years.

Hence, 400%, which makes the whole amount equal to five times of the principal, which will be added in 16 years.

Problem 8.7: If CI is charged on a certain sum for two years at 10% the amount becomes 605. Find the principal.

(a) ₹550 (b) ₹450
(c) ₹480 (d) ₹500

Solution: Using the formula, amount = Principal $(1 + \text{rate}/100)^{\text{time}}$

$605 = p(1 + 10/100)^2 = p(11/10)^2$

$p = 605(100/121) = ₹500$

Alternatively: Checking the options,

Option (a) ₹550

First year's interest = ₹55, which gives the total amount ₹605 at the end of first year. So it is not a valid option.

Option (b) ₹450

First year's interest = ₹45

Second year's interest = ₹45 + 10% of ₹45 = 49.5

So, amount at the end of two years = 450 + 94.5 = 544.5

So, it is also not valid.

Hence, the answer has to lie between 450 and 550 (since 450 yields a shortfall on ₹605 while 550 yields an excess).

Option (c) ₹480

First year's interest = ₹48

Second year's interest = ₹48 + 10% of ₹48 = 52.8

So, amount at the end of two years = 580.8 × 605

Option (d) ₹500

First year's interest = ₹50

Second year's interest = ₹50 + 10% of ₹50
= ₹55

∴ Amount = 605

Note: In general, while solving through options, the student should use the principal of starting with the middle (in terms of value); more convenient option. This will often reduce the number of options to be checked by the student, thus, reducing the time required for problem solving drastically. In fact, this thumb rule should be used not only for the chapter of interests but for all other chapters in Maths.

Furthermore, a look at the past question papers of exams like lower level MBA exams and bank PO exams will yield that by solving through options and starting with the middle more convenient option, there will be significant time savings for these exams where the questions are essentially asked from the LOD I level.

Problem 8.8: If the difference between the CI and SI on a certain sum of money is ₹72 at 12 per cent per annum for 2 years, then find the amount.

(a) ₹6000 (b) ₹5000
(c) ₹5500 (d) ₹6500

Solution: Let the principal = x

Simple interest = $(x \times 12 \times 2)/100$

Compound interest = $x[1 + 12/100]^2 - x$

So, $x[112/100]^2 - x - 24x/100 = 72$

$x[112^2/100^2 - 1 - 24/100] = 72 \Rightarrow x[12544/10000 - 1 - 24/100] = 72$

$\Rightarrow x = 72 \times 10000/144 = ₹5000$

Alternatively: Simple interest and compound interest for the first year on any amount is the same.

Difference in the second year's interest is due to the fact that compound interest is calculated over the first year's interest also.

Hence, we can say that ₹72 = interest on first year's interest → 12% on first year's interest = ₹72.

Hence, first year's interest = ₹600 which should be 12% of the original capital. Hence, original capital = ₹5000 (this whole process can be done mentally).

You can also try to solve the question through the use of options as follows.

Option (a) ₹6000

First year's CI/SI = ₹720

Difference between second year's CI and SI = 12% of ₹720 ≠ ₹72

Hence, it is not correct.

Option (b) ₹5000

First year's CI/SI = 12% of ₹5000 = ₹600

Difference between second year's CI and SI = 12% of 600 = 72 year's CI and SI = 12% of 600 = ₹72

Hence, option (b) is the correct answer.

Therefore, we need not check any other options.

Problem 8.9: The population of Jhumri Tilaiya increases by 10% in the first year; increases by 20% in the second year and due to mass exodus, it decreases by 5% in the third year. What will be its population after three years, if today it is 10,000?

(a) 11,540 (b) 13,860
(c) 12,860 (d) 12,540

Solution: Population at the end of first year will be → 10,000 + 10% of 10,000 = 11,000.

At the end of second year, it will be 11,000 + 20% of 11,000 = 13,200.

At the end of third year, it will be 13,200-5% of 13,200 = 12,540.

Problem 8.10: Seth Ankoosh Gawdekar borrows a sum of ₹1200 at the beginning of a year. After four months,

₹1800 more is borrowed at a rate of interest double the previous one. At the end of the year, the sum of interest on both the loans is ₹216. What is the first rate of interest per annum?

(a) 9% (b) 6%
(c) 8% (d) 12%

Solution: Let the rate of interest be = r%

Then, interest earned from ₹1200 at the end of year = (1200r)/100 = ₹12r

Again, interest earned from ₹1800 at the end of year = (1800/100) × (8/12) × 2r = ₹24r

So, total interest earned = 36r, which equals 216.

⇒ r = 216/36 = 6%

Alternatively: Checking the options.

Option (a) 9%

Interest from ₹1200 = 9% of 1200 = 108

Interest from ₹1800 = two-thirds of 18% on ₹1800 = 12% on ₹1800 = ₹216

Total interest = ₹324

Option (b) 6%

Interest earned from ₹1200 = 6% on 1200 = ₹72

Interest earned from ₹1800 = two-thirds of 12% on ₹1800 = ₹144

(We were able to calculate the interest over second part very easily after observing in option (a) that interest earned over second part is double the interest earned over first part.)

Total interest = ₹216

We need not check any other option now.

Problem 8.11: Rajiv lend out ₹9 to Anni on condition that the amount is payable in ten months by ten equal instalments of ₹1 each payable at the start of every month. What is the rate of interest per annum if the first instalment has to be paid one month from the date the loan is availed?

Solution: Money coming in: ₹9 todayMoney going out: ₹1 one month later + ₹1, 2 months later … + ₹1, 10 months later

The value of the money coming in should equal the value of the money going out for the loan to be completely paid off.

In the present case, for this to happen, the following equation has to hold:

₹9 + interest on ₹9 for 10 months = (₹1 + interest on ₹1 for 9 months) + (₹1 + interest on ₹1 for 8 months)

+ (₹1 + interest on ₹1 for 7 months) + (₹1 + interest on ₹1 for 6 months)

+ (₹1 + interest on ₹1 for 5 months) + (₹1 + interest on ₹1 for 4 months)

+ (₹1 + interest on ₹1 for 3 months) + (₹1 + interest on ₹1 for 2 months)

+ (₹1 + interest on ₹1 for 1 months) + (₹1)

₹9 + Interest on ₹1 for 90 months = ₹10 + interest on₹10 for 45 months.

→ Interest on ₹1 for 90 months – interest on ₹1 for 45 months = ₹10 – ₹9

→ Interest on ₹1 for 45 months = ₹1 (i.e. money would double in 45 months.)

Hence, the rate of interest = $\frac{100\%}{45}$ = 2.222% per month.

So, the annual rate of interest = 26.66% per annum.

Note: The starting equation used to solve this problem comes from crediting the borrower with the interest due to early payment for each of his first nine instalments.

Space for Rough Work

LEVEL OF DIFFICULTY (I)

1. After how many years will a sum of ₹12,500 become ₹17,500 at the rate of 10% per annum?
(a) 2 years (b) 3 years
(c) 4 years (d) 5 years

2. Interest obtained on a sum of ₹2000 for three years is ₹300. Find the rate per cent.
(a) 7% (b) 6%
(c) 5% (d) 10%

3. Find the rate of interest if the amount after 2 years of simple interest on a capital of ₹1200 is ₹1440.
(a) 8% (b) 9%
(c) 10% (d) 11%

4. Find the compound interest on ₹3000 at the rate of 12% per annum for 12 months when interest is compounded half-yearly.
(a) ₹370.8 (b) ₹331
(c) ₹310.80 (d) ₹308

5. The SBI lent ₹1331 to the Tata group at a compound interest and got ₹1728 after three years. What is the rate of interest charged if the interest is compounded annually?
(a) 11% (b) 9.09%
(c) 12% (d) 8.33%

6. ₹2100 is lent at compound interest of 5% per annum for 2 years. Find the amount after two years.
(a) ₹2300 (b) ₹2315.25
(c) ₹2310 (d) ₹2320

7. ₹1200 is lent out at 5% per annum simple interest for 3 years. Find the amount after 3 years.
(a) ₹1380 (b) ₹1290
(c) ₹1470 (d) ₹1200

8. The difference between the simple interest on a certain sum at the rate of 10% p.a. for two years and compound interest at the same rate, which is compounded every six months, is ₹124.05. What is the principal sum?
(a) ₹6000 (b) ₹8000
(c) ₹10,000 (d) ₹12,000

9. Vinay deposited ₹8000 in ICICI Bank, which pays him 12% interest per annum compounded quarterly. What is the amount that he receives after 15 months?
(a) ₹9274.2 (b) ₹9228.8
(c) ₹9314.3 (d) ₹9338.8

10. Find the principal if compound interest is charged on the principal at the rate of $16\frac{2}{3}\%$ per annum for two years and the sum becomes ₹196.
(a) ₹140 (b) ₹154
(c) ₹150 (d) ₹144

11. What is the rate of simple interest for the first 4 years if the sum of ₹360 becomes ₹540 in 9 years and the rate of interest for the last 5 years is 6%?
(a) 4% (b) 5%
(c) 3% (d) 6%

12. Find the principal if the interest compounded at the rate of 10% per annum for two years is ₹420.
(a) ₹2000 (b) ₹2200
(c) ₹1000 (d) ₹1100

13. The simple interest on a certain sum of money for three years at 8% per annum is half the compound interest on ₹4000 for two years at 10% per annum. The sum placed on simple interest is
(a) ₹1550 (b) ₹1650
(c) ₹1750 (d) ₹2000

14. The compound interest on a sum of money for two years is ₹3328 and the simple interest on the same sum for the same period is ₹3200. The difference of the compound interest and the simple interest for three years will be
(a) ₹394.24 (b) ₹392.24
(c) ₹398.56 (d) None of these

15. Raju lent ₹400 to Ajay for 2 years, and ₹100 to Manoj for 4 years and received together from both ₹60 as interest. Find the rate of interest, simple interest being calculated.
(a) 5% (b) 6%
(c) 8% (d) 9%

16. The difference between the simple interest on a certain amount at the rate of 20% per annum, for 1.5 years and compound interest which is compounded every six months is ₹155. What is the principal sum?
(a) ₹4000 (b) ₹5000
(c) ₹6000 (d) None of these

17. If the difference between the simple interest and compound interest on some principal amount at 20% per annum for 3 years is ₹48, then the principle amount must be
(a) ₹550 (b) ₹500
(c) ₹375 (d) ₹400

18. Shashikant derives an annual income of ₹688.25 from ₹10,000 invested partly at 8% p.a. and partly at 5% p.a. simple interest. How much of his money is invested at 5% ?
(a) ₹5000 (b) ₹4225
(c) ₹4800 (d) ₹3725

19. In what time will the simple interest on ₹1750 at 9% per annum be the same as that on ₹2500 at 10.5% per annum in 4 years?
(a) 6 years and 8 months
(b) 7 years and 3 months
(c) 6 years
(d) 7 years and 6 months

20. In what time will ₹5000 amount to ₹21,000 at 4% per annum? (simple interest being reckoned)
(a) 80 years (b) 50 years
(c) 110 years (d) 160 years

21. A difference between the interest received from two different banks on ₹400 for 2 years is ₹4. What is the difference between their rates?
(a) 0.5% (b) 0.2%
(c) 0.23% (d) 0.52%

22. A sum of money becomes seven times at simple interest in 15 years. What is the rate of interest?
(a) 10% (b) 20%
(c) 30% (d) 40%

23. A sum of money doubles itself in 5 years. In how many years will it become four fold (if interest is compounded)?
(a) 15 (b) 10
(c) 20 (d) 12

24. What annual payment will discharge a debt of ₹808 due in 2 years at 2% per annum?
(**Note:** The debt of 808, is the amount due after 2 years in this case.)
(a) ₹200 (b) ₹300
(c) ₹400 (d) ₹350

25. Sanjay borrowed ₹900 at 4% p.a. and ₹1100 at 5% p.a. for the same duration. He had to pay ₹364 in all as interest. What is the time period in years?
(a) 5 years (b) 3 years
(c) 2 years (d) 4 years

26. A sum of money becomes 7/4 of itself in 6 years at a certain rate of simple interest. Find the rate of interest.
(a) 12% (b) 12.5%
(c) 8% (d) 14%

27. Divide ₹1000 into two parts so that simple interest on the first part for two years at 10% p.a. may be equal to the simple interest on the second part for five years at 1% p.a.
(a) ₹400, ₹600 (b) ₹800, ₹200
(c) ₹200, ₹800 (d) None of these

28. Divide ₹3903 between Amar and Akbar such that Amar's share at the end of 7 years is equal to Akbar's share at the end of 9 years at 4% p.a. rate of compound interest.
(a) Amar = ₹2028, Akbar = ₹1875
(b) Amar = ₹2008, Akbar = ₹1000
(c) Amar = ₹2902, Akbar = ₹1001
(d) Amar = ₹2600, Akbar = ₹1303

29. If the compound interest on a certain sum for 2 years is ₹21. What could be the simple interest?
(a) ₹20 (b) ₹16
(c) ₹18 (d) ₹20.5

30. A sum of money placed at compound interest doubles itself in 3 years. In how many years will it amount to 8 times itself?
(a) 9 years (b) 8 years
(c) 27 years (d) 7 years

31. A sum of ₹600 amounts to ₹720 in 4 years at Simple Interest. What will it amount to if the rate of interest is increased by 2%?
(a) ₹648 (b) ₹768
(c) ₹726 (d) ₹792

32. What is the amount of equal instalment, if a sum of ₹1428 due 2 years hence has to be completely repaid in 2 equal annual instalments starting next year.
(a) 700 (b) 800
(c) 650 (d) Cannot be determined

33. Three persons Amar, Akbar and Anthony invested different amounts in a fixed deposit scheme for one year at the rate of 12% per annum and earned a total interest of ₹3,240 at the end of the year. If the amount invested by Akbar is ₹5000 more than the amount invested by Amar and the amount invested by Anthony is ₹2000 more than the amount invested by Akbar, what is the amount invested by Akbar?
(a) ₹12,000 (b) ₹10,000
(c) ₹7000 (d) ₹5000

34. If the difference between compound and simple interest on a certain sum of money for 3 years at 2% p.a. is ₹604, what is the sum?
(a) 5,00,000 (b) 4,50,000
(c) 5,10,000 (d) None of these

35. What is the amount of equal instalment, if a sum of ₹17800 due two years hence, has to be completely repaid in two equal annual instalments starting next year.
(a) 8900 (b) 9000
(c) 8500 (d) Cannot be determined

Space for Rough Work

LEVEL OF DIFFICULTY (II)

1. Pallav invested equal amounts in two schemes at a bank at 10% rate of interest for both schemes. If the difference between the amounts received at the end of 3 years is ₹5890, then what was the total amount invested by Pallav in the two schemes?
(a) 1.9 L (b) 3.8 L
(c) 4.2 L (d) 2.1 L
2. Amitabh invested some money in two parts in the ratio of 3 : 4 at compound interest for two years, one at 15% and the other at 20% respectively. If he swaps the interest rates, he'll get ₹1,410 less in interest than the earlier interest. Find the total money invested.
3. Bank A offers 12% interest rate per annum compounded half yearly. Bank B and Bank C offer simple interest but the annual interest rate offered by Bank C is twice that of Bank B. Shaurya invests a certain amount in Bank B for a certain period and Pallav invests 10000 in Bank C for twice that period. The interest that would be given to Shaurya during that period is equal to the interest that would have accrued had he invested the same amount in Bank A for one year. What is the interest given to Pallav?
4. Sumika invests ₹X in a scheme and earns a monthly interest of ₹3500 at 20% per annum at simple interest. Ritika invests ₹Y in another scheme at compound interest compounded semi-annually and she earns the same annual interest as Sumika. If rate of interest is same for both the schemes, then the difference (in ₹) between X and Y is
5. Alankrit invests ₹2.4 lakh in a scheme that pays 9% interest, compounded annually, and ₹2 lakh in another scheme that pays 10% interest, compounded semi-annually. Vilom invests some money in a different scheme that pays interest at the rate of 8% simple interest per annum. If both received the same amount of interest in the first year, then how much did Vilom invest?
6. Mona invested half her savings in a bond that paid simple interest for 2 years, receiving ₹5,500 as interest. The remaining amount was invested in another bond that paid compound interest for 2 years at the same rate, yielding ₹6050 as interest. What was the initial value of Mona's savings?
7. Bran had a capital of ₹1,60,000. He invested half of it in a business and the other half in a bank at a 10% p.a. compound interest for two years. In the business, Bran made a profit of 30% which he reinvested. He incurred a loss of 10% in the subsequent year and deducted it from the capital. What is the difference between the returns from the two investments?
(a) 1600 (b) 3000
(c) 3200 (d) 3400
8. Tingu gives ₹2,50,000 to Mingu at 12% p.a. compound interest for two years. Mingu gives 80% of this money to Chingu at 20% p.a. interest, compounded half-yearly for two years. Two years hence, when he receives his due amount from Chingu, Mingu clears his dues. What is the amount left with him?
9. A sum of money invested compounds to ₹2.5 lakh after 2 years and ₹3 lakh after 5 years. If compounding is done annually, the compound interest earned in 9 years as a percentage of the Principal invested at the outset, is:
(a) 20% (b) 44%
(c) 72.8% (d) 80%
10. A sum of money is kept in a bank at 8% interest compounded annually. Had the interest been 12% per annum compounded semi-annually, the amount after 1 year would have been ₹218 more. What was the principal amount (in ₹) kept in the bank?
11. Amit decides to invest a certain amount of money in a savings account of a bank that pays 20% compound interest per annum for a period of two years. In return Amit wanted payments of ₹250 at the end of first year and ₹420 at the end of second year from the bank, to fully and finally settle all dues. What is the sum of money that should be invested by Amit to achieve this?
12. Bahadur Singh left an amount of ₹340000 to be divided between his sons aged 10 years and 12 years such that both of them would get an equal amount when each attains 18 years of age. What is the share of the elder brother if the whole amount was invested at 10% simple interest?
13. A certain sum of money increased to 219.7% of its value at a certain rate of compound interest, compounded annually, in 3 years. If the same sum is lent at simple interest at the same rate of interest, in how many years would it become seven times itself?
14. Amit lent ₹50000 to Rina at a compound interest rate of 20% per annum, compounded annually. Rina had to repay the loan in three annual installments, forming an arithmetic progression. She paid a total of ₹66000. Determine the approximate amount she paid in the final year.
15. Ritika borrowed ₹63000 from Baniya ji at 20% per annum compound interest, compounded annually. At the end of the first year, she cleared a certain part of the borrowed amount and at the end of the second year, she repaid thrice the amount she repaid at the end of the first year and cleared the entire loan. What is the amount she paid at the end of the first year?

16. A person started a business with a capital of 60000. In the first year, he made a profit of 20% and added it to the capital. In the second year, he made a profit of 10% and again added it to the capital. In the third year, he incurred a loss of 10% and he set off the loss from the capital. Had he invested the money in a bank that pays 10% per annum compound interest, instead of in the business, how much more he would have received?

17. Rahul gave some money to Simran and 1.5 times that amount to Kajol for 2 years compounded annually. The rate of interest for Simran for the first year was 4% and then 10% on the total amount due for the second year. The rate of interest for Kajol for the first year was 2% and then 8% on the total amount due for the second year. Simran had paid 70000 and 37400 in two years respectively and Kajol had paid 90000 at the end of the first year. How much more interest did Kajol pay than Simran?

18. Aman borrowed a sum from Baman at 6% p.a. simple interest and thrice of that sum from Chaman at 10% p.a. simple interest. He added some more money of his own and lent the whole sum to Daman at 15% p.a. simple interest. At the end of a year, Aman gained ₹6600. If Aman lent ₹80000 to Daman, then how much money did he borrow from Chaman?

19. The difference between the simple interest for 3 years at 8.333% p.a. on a certain sum and the compound interest for 3 years at 12.5% p.a. on the same sum compounded annually is ₹5340. Find the sum to the nearest 100.

20. Mr. Sharma invests equal amounts of money in two schemes, one at simple interest and the other at compound interest. Initially, both the schemes were paying an equal interest rate of 10%. But after 2 years, the interest rate of the second scheme changes such that the total interest received by both the schemes in 3 years is equal. Find the new interest rate in the second scheme.

(a) 6.24% (b) 7.44%
(c) 8.56% (d) 9.66%

21. Sanju deposited 15,000 in a bank at the rate of 20% p.a. with interest being compounded annually. At the end of the first year, he added ₹K along with the matured amount and kept in the bank for 1 more year. At the time of maturity of the same, he deposited ₹2K along with the matured sum and kept for one more year. If doing this, at the end of 3 years, he ended up getting 13/5 times the initial amount, then what is the approximate value of K?

(a) 3100 (b) 3200
(c) 3300 (d) 3400

22. If the difference between compound interest and simple interest for the third year is ₹14832, where the rate of interest for both is 6% and compounding is done annually, then find the compound interest for 3 years (approximately).

(a) 332032 (b) 382032
(c) 352032 (d) 432032

23. Anil deposited 18,000 in a bank at the rate of 12% compounded annually. At the end of the first year, he added ₹x along with the matured amount and kept it in the bank for one more year. At the time of maturity of the same, he deposited $2x$ along with the matured sum and kept it for one more year. If by doing this, he ended up getting 5 times of his initial deposit after 3 years, what is the value of x to the nearest 100?

24. Sumika borrowed ₹30000 from Shaurya at 10% compound interest compounded annually. She had to repay the loan in three annual instalments that were in arithmetic progression. She paid ₹36000 in total. Find the amount she paid in the first year.

25. Rahim borrowed a certain sum of money at a certain rate of simple interest. If instead the sum was borrowed at the same rate of compound interest with interest being compounded annually, the total interest for the first 2 years would have increased by ₹120, while the total interest for the first 3 years would have increased by ₹375, find the sum.

26. A part of ₹38,800 is lent out at 6% per six months. The rest of the amount is lent out at 5% per annum after one year. The ratio of interest after 3 years from the time when first amount was lent out is 5 : 4. Find the second part that was lent out at 5%.

(a) ₹26,600 (b) ₹28,800
(c) ₹27,500 (d) ₹28,000

27. The RBI lends a certain amount to the SBI on simple interest for two years at 20% per annum. The SBI gives this entire amount to Bharti Telecom on compound interest for two years at the same rate annually. Find the percentage earning of the SBI at the end of two years on the entire amount.

(a) 4% (b) 3(1/7)%
(c) 3(2/7)% (d) 3(6/7)%

28. A sum of ₹1000 after 3 years at compound interest becomes a certain amount that is equal to the amount that is the result of a 3 year depreciation from ₹1728. Find the difference between the rates of CI and depreciation. (Given CI is 10% p.a.). (Approximately)

(a) 3.33% (b) 0.66%
(c) 3% (d) 1.67%

29. A certain sum of money was lent under the following repayment scheme based on Simple Interest:
8% per annum for the initial 2 years
9.5% per annum for the next 4 years
11% per annum for the next 2 years
12% per annum after the first 8 years

Find the amount which a sum of ₹9000 taken for 12 years becomes at the end of 12 years.
(a) 20,200 (b) 19,800
(c) 20,000 (d) 20,160

30. If ₹1100 is obtained after lending out ₹x at 5% per annum for 2 years and ₹1800 is obtained after lending out ₹y at 10% per annum for 2 years, find $x + y$.
(a) ₹2500 (b) ₹3000
(c) ₹2000 (d) ₹2200

31. Mr. X, a very industrious person, wants to establish his own unit. For this he needs an instant loan of ₹5,00,000 and, every five years he requires an additional loan of ₹100,000. If he had to clear all his outstandings in 20 years, and he repays the principal of the first loan equally over the 20 years, find what amount he would have to pay as interest on his initial borrowing if the rate of interest is 10% p.a. Simple Interest.
(a) ₹560,000 (b) ₹540,000
(c) ₹525,000 (d) ₹500,000

32. According to the 2011 census, the population growth rate of Lucknow is going to be an increasing AP with first year's rate as 5% and common difference as 5%, but simultaneously the migration, rate is an increasing GP with first term as 1% and common ratio of 2. If the population on 31 December 2010 is 1 million, then find in which year will Lucknow witness its first fall in population?
(a) 2015 (b) 2016
(c) 2017 (d) 2018

33. In order to buy a car, a man borrowed ₹180,000 on the condition that he had to pay 7.5% interest every year. He also agreed to repay the principal in equal annual instalments over 21 years. After a certain number of years, however, the rate of interest has been reduced to 7%. It is also known that at the end of the agreed period, he will have paid in all ₹270,900 in interest. For how many years does he pay at the reduced interest rate?
(a) 7 years (b) 12 years
(c) 14 years (d) 16 years

34. Gopal borrows ₹X from Ankit at 8% annual interest. He then adds ₹Y of his own money and lends ₹$X + Y$ to Ishan at 10% annual interest. At the end of the year, after returning Ankit's dues, the net interest retained by Gopal is the same as that accrued to Ankit. On the other hand, had Gopal lent ₹$X + 2Y$ to Ishan at 10%, and then the net interest retained by him would have increased by ₹150. If all interests are compounded annually, then find the value of $X + Y$ (IN ₹)
(a) 3000 (b) 2000
(c) 4000 (d) 5000

35. The difference between CI and SI on a certain sum of money at 10% per annum for 3 years is ₹620. Find the principal if it is known that the interest is compounded annually.
(a) ₹200,000 (b) ₹20,000
(c) ₹10,000 (d) ₹100,000

36. The population of Mangalore was 1283575 on 1 January 2011 and the growth rate of population was 10% in the last year and 5% in the years prior to it, the only exception being 2009 when because of a huge exodus there was a decline of 20% in population. What was the population on January 1, 2005?
(a) 1,000,000 (b) 1,200,000
(c) 1,250,000 (d) 1,500,000

37. Find the compound interest on ₹64,000 for 1 year at the rate of 10% per annum compounded quarterly (to the nearest integer).
(a) ₹8215 (b) ₹8205
(c) ₹8185 (d) None of these

38. Hans Kumar borrows ₹7000 at simple interest from the village moneylender. At the end of 3 years, he again borrows ₹3000 and closes his account after paying ₹4615 as interest after 8 years from the time he made the first borrowing. Find the rate of interest.
(a) 3.5% (b) 4.5%
(c) 5.5% (d) 6.5%

39. If a principal P becomes Q in 2 years when interest R% is compounded half-yearly. And if the same principal P becomes Q in 2 years when interest S% is compound annually, then which of the following is true?
(a) $R > S$ (b) $R = S$
(c) $R < S$ (d) $R \leq S$

40. An amount of ₹12820 due 3 years hence, is fully repaid in three annual instalments starting after 1 year. The first instalment is 1/2 the second instalment and the second instalment is 2/3 of the third instalment. If the rate of interest is 10% per annum, find the first instalment (assume compound interest for calculations).
(a) ₹2400 (b) ₹1800
(c) ₹2000 (d) ₹2500

41. A sum is divided between A and B in the ratio of 1 : 2. A purchased a car from his part, which depreciates $14\frac{2}{7}$% per annum and B deposited his amount in a bank, which pays him 20% interest per annum compounded annually. By what percentage will the total sum of money increase after two years due to this investment pattern (approximately)?
(a) 20% (b) 26.66%
(c) 30% (d) 25%

42. Some amount was lent at 6% per annum simple interest. After one year, ₹6800 of the principal is repaid and the rest of the amount is repaid at 5% per annum. If the second year's interest is half of the first year's interest, find what amount of money was lent out.
(a) ₹17,000 (b) ₹16,800
(c) ₹16,500 (d) ₹17,500

43. Michael Bolton has $90,000 with him. He purchases a car, a laptop and a flat for $15,000, $13,000 and $35,000 respectively and puts the remaining money in a bank deposit that pays compound interest @15% per annum. After 2 years, he sells off the three items at 80% of their original price and also withdraws his entire money from the bank by closing the account. What is the total change in his asset?
(a) −4.5% (b) +3.5%
(c) −4.32% (d) +5.5%

44. Mohit Anand borrows a certain sum of money from the Mindworkzz Bank at 10% per annum at compound interest. The entire debt is discharged in full by Mohit Anand on payment of two equal amounts of ₹1000 each, one at the end of the first year and the other at the end of the second year. What is the approximate value of the amount borrowed by him?
(a) ₹1852 (b) ₹1736
(c) ₹1694 (d) ₹1792

45. A sum of ₹8000 is borrowed at 5% p.a. compound interest and paid back in 3 equal annual instalments. What is the amount of each instalment?
(a) ₹2937.67 (b) ₹3000
(c) ₹2037.67 (d) ₹2739.76

Directions for Questions 46 and 47: Read the following and answer the questions that follow.

The leading Indian bank ISBI, in the aftermath of the Kargil episode, announced a loan scheme for the Indian Army. Under this scheme; the following options were available.

	Loans upto	*Soft loan*	*Interest (normal)*
Scheme 1	₹50,000	50% of total	8%
Scheme 2	₹75,000	40% of total	10%
Scheme 3	₹100,000	30% of total	12%
Scheme 4	₹200,000	20% of total	14%

Soft loan is a part of the total loan and the interest on this loan is half the normal rate of interest charged.

46. Start-up *A* took some loan under scheme 1, start-up *B* under scheme 2, start-up *C* under scheme 3 and start-up *D* under scheme 4. If they get the maximum loan under their respective schemes for one year, find which loan is MUL (MUL—Maximum Utility Loan, is defined as the loan with the lowest ratio of interest paid to the total loan.)
(a) *A* (b) *B*
(c) *C* (d) *D*

47. Extending this plan, *ISBI* further announced that start-ups which are operating from last six months only can get the loans in which the proportion of soft loan will be double. This increase in the proportion of the soft loan component is only applicable for the first year. For all subsequent years, the soft loan component applicable on the loan follows the values provided in the table. A start-up takes ₹40,000 under scheme 1 in one account for one year and ₹60,000 under scheme 2 for two years. Find the total interest paid by it over the two year period.
(a) ₹11600 (b) ₹10000
(c) ₹8800 (d) None of these

48. Three amounts *x*, *y* and *z* are such that *y* is the simple interest on *x* and *z* is the simple interest on *y*. If in all the three cases, rate of interest per annum and the time for which interest is calculated is the same, then find the relation between *x*, *y* and *z*.
(a) $xyz = 1$ (b) $x^2 = yz$
(c) $z = x^2y$ (d) $y^2 = xz$

49. A person bought a motorbike under the following scheme: Down payment of ₹15,000 and the rest amount at 8% per annum for 2 years. In this way, he paid ₹28,920 in total. Find the actual price of the motorbike. (Assume simple interest).
(a) ₹26,000 (b) ₹27,000
(c) ₹27,200 (d) ₹26,500

50. A certain amount grows at an annual interest rate of 12%, compounded monthly. Which of the following equations can be solved to find the number of years, y, which it would take for the investment to increase by a factor of 64?
(a) $64 = (1.01)^{12y}$ (b) $\frac{1}{64} = (1.04)12y$
(c) $64 = 1.04(12y)$ (d) $8 = 1.01(6y)$

51. Amit borrowed ₹168000 at 10% per annum, compounded annually. He repaid the loan in two equal annual instalments, the first after one year and the other after another year. The first instalment was used to pay the interest of the first year and part of the principal, while the second instalment squared off the loan. What was the value of each instalment?

52. Amitabh invests ₹20000 at 8% interest compounded annually and ₹10000 at 6% interest compounded semi-annually. Rajesh invests his whole capital at 7.5% simple interest for one year. At the end of the year it was found that Rajesh earned an interest that was 2 rupees higher than what Amitabh earned. Then the amount invested by Rajesh is equal to

53. A man invests a total of 17 lac rupees. A part of it is invested in a fixed deposit earning him 6% annual interest. The remaining amount is invested in the ratio

3 : 1 in two banks, that give him 5% interest and 4% interest per annum, respectively. If the total interest earned is 92000, what was the amount invested in the fixed deposit that yielded 6% rate of interest?

54. Abhijit invested ₹20000 at 6% simple annual interest, while Amartya invested ₹18000 at 10 per cent simple annual interest, 5 years after Abhijit's investment. After how many years from Abhijit's investment will Amartya's balance be greater than him?

55. For the same principal amount, the compound interest at 6% per annum for two years exceeds the simple interest at 4% per annum for 3 years by ₹18000. Then the principal amount is

56. An amount of money invested at 10% annual interest compounded half-yearly, becomes equal to ₹13891.5 after eighteen months. What is the sum of money invested?

57. Mr. S. Vinay invested a sum of ₹2025 through a crypto trading app available on his mobile. The invested amount appreciated at 20% per annum compound rate of appreciation. This appreciated amount after 2 years is equal to the amount that is the result of 3 years depreciation by a certain compound rate of depreciation from ₹4000. Find the difference between the compound rate of appreciation and depreciation:

(a) 8.5% (b) 5.0%
(c) 10.0% (d) 12%%

58. Kaalia took a loan at 15% per annum simple interest for 2 years. He then loaned out half the loan amount to his friend Mallya at a rate of 16% compounded half-yearly for 2 years. The remainder of the amount he loaned out to his friend Jaalia at 15% per annum compounded annually for 2 years. What was the approximate earning as a percentage of the loan amount at the end of 2 years?

(a) 5.2% (b) 4.1%
(c) 6.6% (d) 3.5%

59. Attavar borrows 12 lacs for his startup business venture at a certain rate (say n%) on 1st April 2025. On 1st August of the same year he borrows an additional 9 lacs loan. This time being a repeat customer, he is able to bargain for a 10% reduction in the rate of interest – and thus has to pay only 0.9n% as his rate of interest. At the end of the financial year, while maintaining the books, his accountant tells him that the startup had to pay a total amount of 139200 as the interest for the year on both the loans together. Can you find out the value of n (the rate of interest on the first loan)?

60. A computer is sold either for ₹38400 cash or for ₹9600 cash down payment together with five equal monthly instalments. If the rate of interest charged is 12% per annum, then the amount of each instalment (nearest to a rupee) is:

(a) ₹5720 (b) ₹5930
(c) ₹6032 (d) ₹5980

61. Professor Kalyani Gandhi has two equal investments. One at 10% per annum compounded annually, the other at 12% per annum simple interest. Till how many years is the second plan better than the first in terms of the interest she earns?

62. Mr. Mehra is planning for higher education expenses of his two sons Arjit and Shaurya aged 15 and 12. He plans to divide ₹20 lacs in two equal parts and invest in two different plans such that his sons may have access to ₹25 lacs each when they reach the age of 21. He is looking for a plan that will give him a simple interest per annum. The rates of interest of the plans for his two sons are:

63. Kishore Suratkal is planning for higher education expenses of his two sons Arjit and Shaurya aged 15 and 12. He plans to divide ₹20 lacs in two parts and invest in two different plans such that each son gets the same amount when they reach the age of 21. If the rate of interest offered to him by his financial advisor is 12% per annum compounded annually, then how much should he set aside for his younger son (approximately).

(a) 801125 (b) 831625
(c) 901125 (d) 931615

64. You borrow a sum of money at 12% simple interest per annum and the same amount at 10% simple interest, both for the same time period. You cleared the first loan 6 months before the due date and paid the second loan at the end of the scheduled period. If the amount paid in each case is ₹92625, then how much money was borrowed and what was the time period?

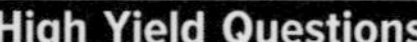

Scan this QR code to access assisted problem solving videos on questions 8, 43, 44, 56, 57 and 64 from LOD 2

Space for Rough Work

ANSWER KEY

Level of Difficulty (I)

1. (c)	2. (c)	3. (c)	4. (a)
5. (b)	6. (b)	7. (a)	8. (b)
9. (a)	10. (d)	11. (b)	12. (a)
13. (c)	14. (a)	15. (a)	16. (b)
17. (c)	18. (d)	19. (a)	20. (a)
21. (a)	22. (d)	23. (b)	24. (c)
25. (d)	26. (b)	27. (c)	28. (a)
29. (a)	30. (a)	31. (b)	32. (d)
33. (b)	34. (a)	35. (d)	

Level of Difficulty (II)

1. (b)	2. 84000	3. 4944	4. 10000
5. 526250	6. 27500	7. (c)	8. 29220
9. (c)	10. 5000	11. 500	
12. 180000	13. 20 years	14. 7636	15. 21600
16. 8580	17. 640	18. 45000	19. 30700
20. (b)	21. (d)	22. (b)	23. 18500
24. 13000	25. 7680	26. (b)	27. (a)
28. (d)	29. (d)	30. (a)	31. (c)
32. (b)	33. (c)	34. (c)	35. (b)
36. (b)	37. (d)	38. (d)	39. (c)
40. (c)	41. (a)	42. (a)	43. (c)
44. (b)	45. (a)	46. (a)	47. (b)
48. (d)	49. (b)	50. (a)	51. 96800
52. 29480	53. 9 lacs	54. 14	
55. 50 lacs	56. ₹12000	57. (c)	58. (b)
59. 8%	60. 5930	61. 4 years	
62. 25 & 16.66%		63. (b)	
64. 71250, 3 years			

SOLUTIONS AND SHORTCUTS

Level of Difficulty (I)

1. 12500 @ 10% simple interest would give an interest of ₹1250 per annum. For a total interest of ₹5000, it would take 4 years.
2. The interest earned per year would be 300/3=100. This represents a 5% rate of interest on an amount of ₹2000.
3. Interest in 2 years = ₹240

   Interest per year = ₹120

   Rate of interest = 10%
4. 3000 -----(6% increase) ----→ 3000 + 180 = ₹3180

   3180 ------ (6% increase) --- →3180 +190.80 = ₹3370.80

   Compound interest = ₹370.80
5. 1331 × 1.090909 × 1.090909 × 1.090909 = 1331 × 12/11 × 12/11 × 12/11 = 1728. Hence, the rate of compound interest is 9.09%.
6. 2100 + 5% of 2100 = 2100 + 105 = 2205 (after 1 year). Next year it would become:

   2205 + 5% of 2205 = 2205 +110.25 = 2315.25
7. The annual interest would be ₹60. After 3 years the total value would be 1200 + 60 × 3 = 1380
8. Let the sum be ₹P. Then

$$p\left[\left(1+\frac{5}{100}\right)^4-1\right]-\frac{p\times10\times2}{100}=124.05$$

$$\Rightarrow p\left[\left(\frac{21}{20}\right)^4-1-\frac{1}{5}\right]=124.05\Rightarrow p\left[\frac{194481}{160000}-\frac{6}{5}\right]=\frac{12405}{100}$$

$$\Rightarrow p\left[\frac{194481-19200}{160000}\right]=\frac{12405}{100}\Rightarrow p=\left(\frac{12405}{100}\times\frac{160000}{2481}\right)$$

   = 8000

   An easier method to solve this question would be by using options. If we try with 8000, we would get: SI for 2 years @10% = 20% of 8000 = 1600. CI @10% annually compounded half-yearly means an effective CI rate of 5% per 6 months. This can be calculated by increasing 8000 by 5% successively four times. We would get: 8000 → 8400 → 8820 → 9261 → 9724.05. The required difference in CI and SI in this case can be seen to be the same (124.05) as given in the problem. Hence, option (b) is correct.
9. 12% per annum compounded quarterly means that the amount would grow by 3% every 3 months.

   Thus, 8000 → 8000 + 3% of 8000 = 8240 after 3 months → 8240 + 3% of 8240 = 8487.2 after 6 months and so on till five 3 month time periods get over. It can be seen that the value would turn out to be 9274.2.
10. $P \times 7/6 \times 7/6 = 196 \rightarrow P = (196 \times 6 \times 6)/7 \times 7 = 144$.
11. For the last 5 years, the interest earned would be: 30% of 360 = 108. Thus, interest earned in the first 4 years would be ₹72 → ₹18 every year on an amount of ₹360, which means that the rate of interest is 5%
12. Solve using options. Thinking about option (a): 2000 → 2200 (after 1 year) → 2420 (after 2 years) which gives us an interest of ₹420 as required in the problem. Hence, this is the correct answer.
13. Let ₹x be the sum for simple interest then according to the question:

$$x\times3\times\frac{8}{100}=\frac{1}{2}\left(4000\left[1+\frac{10}{100}\right]^2-4000\right)$$

$$\frac{24x}{100}=\frac{840}{2}$$

x = ₹1750

14. Difference between CI and SI for 2 years = ₹(3328 – 3200) = ₹128
SI for 1 year = ₹1600
SI on ₹1600 for 1 year = ₹128
Interest rate = $\left(100 \times \frac{128}{1600}\right)$
Difference between CI and SI for 3rd year = 8% of (3200 + 128) = ₹266.24
Required difference = ₹(266.24 + 128) = ₹394.24
15. Total effective amount lent for 1 year
$= ₹400 \times 2 + ₹100 \times 4 = ₹1200$
Interest being ₹60, Rate of interest 5%
16. We can solve this problem by checking the options:
Simple interest for ₹5000 = $5000 \times \frac{20}{100} \times \frac{3}{2}$ = ₹1500
Compound interest for ₹5000
$= 5000\left(1+\frac{10}{100}\right)^3 - 5000$ = ₹1655
Required difference = ₹(1655 – 1500) = ₹155. Hence this option is correct.
17. Solve using options. If we try 500 (option b) for convenience, we can see that the difference between the two is ₹64 (as the SI would amount to 300 and CI would amount to 100 + 120 + 144 = 364).
Since, we need a difference of only ₹48 we can realize that the value should be 3/4th of 500. Hence, 375 is correct.
18. The average Rate of interest is 6.8825%. The ratio of investments would be 1.1175: 1.8825 (@5% is to 8%). The required answer = 10000 × 1.1175/3 = 3725.
19. 42% on 2500 = ₹1050. The required answer would be: 1050/157.5 = 6 years and 8 months.
20. The value would increase by 4% per year or ₹200 per year. Hence, required time = $\frac{21000-5000}{200} = \frac{16000}{200}$ = 80 years.
21. The difference in Simple interest represents 1% of the amount invested. Since this difference has occurred in 2 years, annually the difference would be 0.5%.
22. The sum becomes seven times means that there is a 600% increase in the sum. This would be the interest earned (600% of the original amount in 15 years). It means that the yearly interest must be 40%.
23. It would take another 5 years to double again. Thus, a total of 10 years to become four fold.
24. $A \times (1.02) + A = 808 \rightarrow A = 400$
25. The interest he pays per year would be 36 + 55 = 91. Thus, in 4 years the interest would amount to ₹364.
26. The total interest in 6 years = 75%
Thus per year = SI = 12.5%
27. 20% of x = 5% of $(1000 - x) \rightarrow x$ = ₹200.
Thus, the two parts should be ₹200 and ₹800.
28. Akbars' share should be such that at 4% p.a. compound interest it should become equal to Amar's share in 2 years. Checking thorugh the options it is clear that option (a) fits perfectly as 1875 would become 2028 in 2 years @4% p.a. compound interest.
29. If we take the principal as 100, the CI @ 10% Rate of interest would be ₹21. In such a case, the SI would be ₹20.
30. If it doubles in 3 years, it would become 4 times in 6 year and 8 times in 9 years.
31. 600 becomes 720 in 4 years SI → SI per year = ₹30 and hence the SI rate is 5%.
At 7% rate of interest the value of 600 would become 768 in 4 years. (600 + 28% of 600)
32. The rate of interest is not defined.
Hence, option (d) is correct.
33. 12% Rate of interest on the amount invested gives an interest of ₹3240. This means that 0.12 A = 3240 → A = ₹27000. The sum of the investments should be ₹27000. If Akbar invests x, Amar invests x – 5000 and Anthony invests x + 2000. Thus:
$x + x - 5000 + x + 2000 = 27000 \rightarrow x = 10000.$
34. Solve through trial and error using the values of the options. Option (a) 500000 fits the situation perfectly as the SI = ₹30000 while the CI = 30604.
35. The rate of interest is not defined.
Hence, option (d) is correct.

Level of Difficulty (II)

1. Since the rate of interest and principal amount are equal and yet there is a difference in amount received after 3 years, one scheme has to be at simple interest and other at compound interest.
Net amount after 3 years at simple interest = 1.3 P
Net amount after 3 years at compound interest = $(1.1)^3$ P → 1.331 P
Difference between the two = 0.031 P = 5890 → P = 1.9 L. Hence, total amount invested = 3.8 L. Hence, Option (b) is the correct answer.
2. Net compound interest for 2 years would be 32.25% and 44%. Let the amounts be $3x$ and $4x$. So according to question, 32.25% of $3x$ + 44% of $4x$ = 1410 + 44% of $3x$ + 32.25% of $4x$.
→ 11.75% of $4x$ = 1410 + 11.75% of $3x$ → $0.1175x$ = 1410 → x = 12000. So total amount invested = 84000. 84000 is the correct answer.
3. Bank A has a rate of interest of 12% and compounds half yearly. This is the same as having a 6% interest rate per half-year. So, the net interest rate for the year would be 12.36%. So based on the information given, Shaurya would get 12.36% interest for time t, from Bank B. Hence, for Pallav from Bank C, he

would earn 24.72% interest for time t and hence, 49.44% interest for time time $2t$. So, for Pallav, the net interest would be 0.4944 × 10000 = 4944. This is the correct answer.

4. Total interest earned by Sumika in a year = 3500 × 12 = 42000. This is 20% of the principal amount. So value of X would be 210000. Since the interest earned for both the schemes is same and the interest is compounded semi-annually for scheme Y, the net interest rate for the year would be 21%. So, 0.21 Y = 42000 → Y = 200000. So, the correct answer is 210000 – 200000 = 10000.
5. Interest earned by Alankrit from 1st scheme = 0.09 × 240000 = 21600
Interest earned by Alankrit from 2nd scheme = 0.1025 × 200000 = 20500
So the interest earned by Vilom would be 42100. Since this interest was earned at 8% simple interest, the invested amount for Vilom would be 42100/0.08 = 526250. The correct answer is 526250.
6. Since 5500 is calculated as simple interest for 2 years, the interest for each year would be 2750. In case of compound interest, the interest would be same for the first year. So the interest break up for the two years would be 2750 and 3300. Second year has an excess of 550 from first year. This is because we are charged an interest on the interest of first year. So rate of interest would be 550/2750 = 20%. So the net interest earned for 2 years would be 44%. So 0.44 P = 6050 → P = 13750. So her total savings was 13750 × 2 = 27500 (correct answer).
7. Net interest rate from the bank = 21%. So total interest earned = 16800.
From the amount invested in the business, Profit earned in first year = 24000. So new capital would be 104000. In the second year, the loss incurred would be 10400. So net profit = 24000 – 10400 = 13600. So the required difference would be 16800 – 13600 = 3200. Hence, Option (c) is the correct answer.
8. Amount Mingu owes to Tingu = 1.12 × 1.12 × 250000 = 313600.
Amount given to Chingu = 200000.
Net amount received by Mingu = 1.1^4 × 200000 = 292820
Total amount with Mingu = 292820 + 50000 = 342820
Hence, the amount left with Mingu after clearing his dues = 342820 – 313600 = 29220 (correct answer)
9. Let the compounding multiplier be x and principal amount be P. So according to the question, x^2P = 250000 and x^5P = 300000. On dividing the two equations we get, $x^3 = 1.2$. So required value = x^9P/P. From the above equation $(x^3)^3 = 1.2^3 = 1.728$. Hence, the interest percentage would be 72.8%. Hence, Option (c) is the correct answer.
10. Net rate of interest if it is compounded semi-annually at 12% per annum = 12.36%.
Difference in interest rate in both cases = 4.36%. This will be the difference in the amount received from both the cases. So, it is given that 4.36% of P = 218 → P = 5000.
11. This can be interpreted as an installment question wherein the bank pays Amit in two installments. If P is the amount invested, so 1.2 × (1.2(P) – 250) = 420 → 1.2 P – 250 = 350 → P = 500. Hence, the amount to be invested by Amit is 500.
12. Let the amount given to the elder son be P. So younger son would get 340000 – P.
Amount received by elder son in the next 6 years would be 1.6 × P. For the younger son, the time would be 8 years. So the amount received by him would be 1.8 × (340000 – P). It is given that 1.8 × (340000 – P) = 1.6 P → 3.4 P = 1.8 × 340000 → P = 180000. Hence, the share of the elder brother would be 180000 (answer).
13. It is given that $(1 + x/100)^3 = 2.197 \rightarrow x = 30\%$. Seven times of itself would require a net interest of 600%. So if the rate of interest is 30%, it will amount to 600% in 600/30 = 20 years.
14. Let the first instalment be x and common difference of AP be d. So Installment for second year would be $x + d$ and for third year would be $x + 2d$.
According to question,
$1.2 \times (1.2 \times (1.2 \times 50000 - x) - x - d) = x + 2d$.
Since, the three instalments are in Arithmetic Progression, it means that the second instalment would be 66000/3 = 22000 = $x + d$. Which means the other two instalments would be 44000 (= $x + x + 2d$).
$1.2 \times (1.2 \times (60000 - x) - 22000) = x + d + d \rightarrow$
$1.2 \times (1.2 \times (60000 - x) - 22000) = 22000 + d \rightarrow$
$1.2 \times (50000 - 1.2x) = 22000 + d \rightarrow 60000 - 1.44x = 22000 + d \rightarrow 38000 = 1.44x + d$
Since, $x + d = 22000$, $0.44x = 16000 \rightarrow x = 36363.63$, $d = -14363.63$. Hence, instalment paid in 3rd year = $x + 2d$ = 36363.63 – 2 × 14363.63 ≈ 7636. The correct answer is 7636.
15. Let the first installment be x. So according to the given information, $1.2 \times (1.2 \times (63000) - x) = 3x \rightarrow 1.2 \times 63000 - x = 2.5x \rightarrow 3.5x = 1.2 \times 63000 \rightarrow x = 21600$ (correct answer).
16. Profit in first year = 12000
New capital = 72000
Profit in second year = 7200
New capital = 79200
Loss in second year = 7920
Net Profit/Loss = 12000 + 7200 – 7920 = +11280
Total amount in 3 year had it been invested in a bank = 1.1 × 1.1 × 1.1 × 60000 = 79860. Hence, the required difference is 19860 – 11280 = 8580 (correct answer).

17. Let the amount for Simran be $2x$, So amount for Kajol would be $3x$. It is given that $1.1 \times (1.04 \times (2x) - 70000) = 37400 \rightarrow 2.08x - 70000 = 34000 \rightarrow x = 50000$. So amount lent to Simran would be 100000. Hence, amount for Kajol would be 150000. Now, According to the question, amount for Kajol for the second year would be $1.08 \times (1.02 \times (150000) - 90000) = 68040$. So total amount given by Kajol would be 158040. Hence, interest paid would be 8040. The interest paid by Simran would be 7400. Hence, the required difference is 640, which is the correct answer.
18. Let the amount borrowed from Baman be x. So amount borrowed from Chaman be $3x$. So the amount to be paid by Aman at the end of year would be $1.06 \times x + 1.1 \times 3x = 4.36x$. So interest paid by Aman would be $0.36x$. Let the amount added by Aman be y. So the interest gained by Aman would be $0.6x + 0.15y$. So the amount gained would be $0.24x + 0.15y$. This is given as 6600. Also it is given that $4x + y = 80000$.
$0.24x + 0.15y = 6600$
$4x + y = 80000$
On solving the two equations we get $x = 15000$. So, the amount borrowed from Chaman would be 45000.
19. Let the amount be P. So according to the question, $|0.25P - (1.125^3 - 1) \times P| = 5340$. On solving the equation, we get a value of P = 30720. So, the required value of P is 30700.
20. Net interest rate for 3 years in SI = 30%
Net interest rate for 2 years in CI = 21%.
CI interest rate for the 3rd year would be x.
Since the amount in both schemes is equal, it is irrelevant to our calculation. Hence, we can ignore the principal amount. It is given that $0.3 = 0.21 + x \times 1.21 \rightarrow x = 0.07438 \rightarrow x = 7.44\%$. Hence, Option (b) is the correct answer.
21. Amount at the end of first year = 1.2 × 15000 + K = 18000 + K
Amount at the end of second year = 1.2 × (18000 + K) + 2K = 21600 + 3.2K
Amount at the end of third year = 1.2 × (21600 + 3.2K) = 25920 + 3.84K
According to the question, 25920 + 3.84K = 2.6 × 15000 → 25920 + 3.84K = 39000 → 3.84K = 13080 → K = 3406.25. Hence, Option (d) is the correct answer.
22. At 6% rate of interest on principal P, SI for year 1 = CI for year 1 = 6%. SI for year 2 = 6%, CI for year 2 = 6.36%. SI for year 3 = 6%; CI for year 3 = 6.7416%. Difference between SI and CI for third year = 0.007416P = 14832 → P = 2000000. CI = 2000000 × 1.06 × 1.06 × 1.06 – 2000000 = 382032. Option (b) is correct.
23. Amount at the end of first year = $1.12 \times 18000 + x = 20160 + x$
Amount at the end of second year = $1.12 \times (20160 + x) + 2x = 22579.2 + 3.12x$
Amount at the end of third year = $1.12 \times (22579.2 + 3.12x) \approx 25288 + 3.5x$
According to question, $25288 + 3.5x = 5 \times 18000 \rightarrow 3.5x = 64712 \rightarrow x \approx 18489$. Hence, the correct answer is 18500.
24. Let the first instalment be x and common difference of AP be d. So, Installment for second year would be $x + d$ and for third year would be $x + 2d$.
According to the question,
$1.1 \times (1.1 \times (1.1 \times 30000 - x) - x - d) = x + 2d$.
Since, the three instalments are in Arithmetic Progression, it means that the second instalment would be $36000/3 = 12000 = x + d$. Which means the other two instalments would be $24000 (= x + x + 2d)$.
$1.1 \times (1.1 \times (33000 - x) - 12000) = x + d + d \rightarrow$
$1.1 \times (1.1 \times (33000 - x) - 12000) = 12000 + d \rightarrow$
$1.1 \times (24300 - 1.1x) = 12000 + d \rightarrow$
$26730 - 1.21x = 12000 + d \rightarrow 14730 = 1.21x + d$
Since, $x + d = 12000$, $0.21x = 2730 \rightarrow x = 13000$.
The correct answer is 13000.
25. Let the interest rate be r and interest amount for first year be x. So first year interest would be same for SI and CI. The difference in amount for second year would be because of the interest paid on the interest of the first year. So $\frac{xr}{100} = 120$ and $\frac{2xr}{100} + \frac{r^2x}{100^2} = 375 \rightarrow \frac{r^2x}{100^2} = 135$

$$\frac{r}{100} \times \frac{rx}{100} = 135 \rightarrow \frac{r}{100} = \frac{135}{120} = 1.125$$

So the rate of interest would be 12.5%. So, from the first equation, we get $x = 960$. Since x was the interest amount, the principal amount would be $\frac{960}{0.125} = 7680$. This is the correct answer.
26. $$\frac{F \times (0.06) \times 6}{(38800 - F) \times 0.05 \times 2} = 5/4$$
where F is the first part.

$$1.44F = 19400 - 0.5F$$
$$F = 19400/1.94 = 10000.$$

Thus, the second part = 38800 – 10000 = 28800
27. SBI would be paying 40% on the capital as interest over two years and it would be getting 44% of the capital as interest from Bharti Telecom. Hence, it earns 4%.
28. The amount @ 10% CI could become ₹1331. Also, ₹1728 depreciated at $R\%$ has to become ₹ 1331.
We also can see that
1728 × 11/12 × 11/12 × 11/12 = 1331. Hence, the rate of depreciation is 8.33%. Thus, the required difference is 1.67%.

29. 9000 + 720 + 720 + 855 + 855 + 855 + 855 + 990 + 990 + 1080 + 1080 + 1080 + 1080
= 9000 + 720 × 2 + 855 × 4 + 990 × 2 + 1080 × 4
= 20160
30. x = ₹1000 (As 1000 @ 5% for 2 years = 1100).
Similarly y = ₹1500.
$x + y = 2500$.
31. The simple interest would be defined on the basis of the sum of the AP.
50000 + 47500 + 45000 + … + 2500 = 525000.
32. Population growth rate according to the problem:
Year 1 = 5%, year 2 = 10%, year 3 = 15%
Year 4 = 20%, year 5 = 25%, year 6 = 30%.
Population decrease due to migration:
Year 1 = 1%, year 2 = 2%, year 3 = 4%
Year 4 = 8%, year 5 = 16%, year 6 = 32%.
Thus, the first fall would happen in 2016.
33. Solve this one through options. Option (c) reduced rate for 14 years fits the conditions.
34. Net interest earned by Ankit = $\frac{8x}{100}$
Net interest earned by Gopal after paying Ankit's dues = $\frac{(x+y)10}{100} - \frac{8x}{100} = \frac{2x+10y}{100}$
According to the question:
$$\frac{8x}{100} = \frac{2x+10y}{100}$$
$$\frac{6x}{100} = \frac{10y}{100}$$
Or $x : y = 5 : 3$.
According to the question:
$0.1y = 150$ or y = ₹1500
As $x : y = 5 : 3$
x = ₹2500.
Hence, $x + y$ = 2500 + 1500 = ₹4000.
Hence, option (c) is correct.
35. Go through trial and error of the options. You will get:
20000 × (1.3) = 26000 (@ simple interest)
20000 × 1.1 × 1.1 × 1.1 = 26620 @ compound interest.
Thus, 20000 is the correct answer.
36. Solve through options to see that the value of 1200000 fits the given situation.
37. $64000 \times (1.025)^4 = 70644.025$.
Interest 6644.025
Option (d). None of these is correct.
38. The interest would be paid on
7000 for 3 years + 10000 for 5 years.
@ 6.5% the total interest for 8 years
= 1365 + 3250
= ₹4615
39. Since the interest is compounded half yearly at R% per annum, the value of R would be lesser than the value of S. (Remember, half yearly compounding is always profitable for the depositor).
40. Solve using options. Option (c) fits the situation as:
12820 = 2000 + 2 years interest on 2000 + 4000 + 1 years interest on 4000 + 6000 (use 10% compound interest for calculation of interest) →
12820 = 2000 + 420 + 4000 + 400 + 6000.
Thus, option (c) fits the situation perfectly.
41. Let the amounts be ₹100 and ₹200 respectively. The value of the 100 would become 100 × 6/7 × 6/7 = 3600/49 = 73.46
The other person's investment of 200 would become 200 × 1.2 × 1.2 = 288
The total value would become 288 + 73.46 = 361.46
This represents approximately a 20% increase in the value of the amount after 2 year. Hence, option (a) is correct.
42. It can be seen that for 17000, the first year interest would be 1020, while the second year interest after a repayment of 6800 would be on 10200 @ 5% per annum. The interest in the second year would thus be ₹510 which is exactly half the interest of the first year. Thus, option (a) is correct.
43. The final value would be:
0.8 × 63000 + 27000 × 1.15 × 1.15 = 86107.5.
→ Drop in value = 4.32%
44. P + 2 years interest on P = 1000 + 1 years interest on 1000 + 1000
→ 1.21P = 2100 → P = 1736 (approx).
45. Let the repayment annually be X. Then:
8000 + 3 years interest on 8000 (on compound interest of 5%) = X + 2 years interest on X + X + 1 years interest on X + X → X = 2937.67
46. Interest for A = 6% of 50000.
Interest for B, C and D would respectively be 8, 10.2 and 12.6.
Thus, A's loan is MUL.
47. Interest the start-up would pay under scheme 1:
Year 1, the entire loan would be @ 4% – hence interest on 40000 = ₹1600.
Total interest = 1600
Interest on loan 2:
In year 1: 80% of the loan (i.e. 48000) would be on 5%, 12000 would be @10% – hence total interest = 3600
Year 2: 40% of the loan (24000) would be on 5%, while the remaining loan would be on 10% – hence total interest = 4800
Thus, total interest on the two loans would be 1600 + 3600 + 4800 = 10000.
48. You can think about this situation by taking some values. Let $x = 100$, $y = 10$ and $z = 1$ (at an interest rate of 10%). We can see that $10^2 = 100 \rightarrow y^2 = xz$
49. Solve using options. If the price is 27000, the interest on 12000 (after subtracting the down payment) would be 16% of 12000 = 1920. Hence, the total amount paid would be 28920.

50. Rate of interest =12% per annum or 1% per month.
Time = $12y$ month.
$64 = 1\left(1 + \frac{1}{100}\right)^{12y} = 1.01^{12y}$. Hence, option (a) is correct.

51. Let the instalment be equal to x.
After 1 year the balance amount would be: (168000 + 10% 0f 168000 – x).
In the second year's payment, he would have to return this principal + 10% on this principal (equal to the second year's interest).
Thus, we have: $1.1 \times (1.1 \times 168000 - x) = x \rightarrow x = 96800$

52. If Rajesh invested R, then 0.075R = 1600 + 300 + 309 + 2 → R = 29480.

53. The total interest earned is 92000 on an investment of 17 lacs. That is an average return of $5\left(\frac{7}{17}\right)$%.
Then, using the concept of weighted averages we have:
$\frac{n \times 6 + 3 \times 5 + 1 \times 4}{(n+3+1)} = 5\frac{7}{17} = \frac{92}{17} \rightarrow 102n + 323$
$= 92n + 368 \rightarrow n = 4.5$
Thus, the ratio of investment is 4.5 : 3 : 1. 17 lacs divided in this ratio would give us a 9 lac investment at 6% annual interest.

54. Abhijit's balance at the time of Amartya's investment will be 20000 + 30% of 20000 = 26000. At this time, Amartya invests 18000 @10% simple interest per annum. Abhijit has ₹8000 balance more than Amartya. Amartya, will start getting an interest amount of 1800 per year, while Abhijit will continue receiving 1200 per year. Thus, Amartya is getting 600 rupees more of interest than Abhijit. Amartya will take $\frac{8000}{600} = 13.33$ years to get equal to Abhijit and hence, after 14 years Amartya's balance would be greater than Abhijit's.

55. Let the amount be A. Then the Compound interest for 2 years will be given by:
1.06 × 1.06 × A – A = 0.1236A. This means that the CI is 12.36% of A. Also, the SI for 3 years at 4% per annum would be 12% of A. The difference would be 0.36% of A = 18000 → A = 50 lacs.

56. If the sum invested is A, then we have: $\frac{13891.5}{1.05^3} =$ 12000. Hence, the correct answer is 12000.

57. $1.44 \times 2025 = 4000 \times (n)^3 \rightarrow n = 0.9$, which means a rate of depreciation of 10%.

58. Assume that the loan taken is 200. Then, he has to pay an interest of 30% of the loan amount for keeping the loan for 2 years. Hence, he has to repay 260. From Mallya, he will get an amount equal to 100 × 1.08 × 1.08 × 1.08 × 1.08 = 100 × 1.1664 × 1.1664 ≈ 136, while from Jaalia, he will get an amount of 100 × 1.15 × 1.15 = 132.25. Thus, her earning was 268.25 – 260 = 8.25, on a loan of 200, which works out to around 4.1% approximately. Option (b) is correct.

59. The net interest payable would be n% of 1200000 for the full year borrowing of the first loan and 2/3rds of $0.9n$% of 900000 for the second loan – which was availed only for 8 months. This will be represented by the equation:
$12000 \times n \times 1 + 9000 \times 0.9n \times \frac{8}{12} = 139200 \rightarrow$
Solving this, we get $n = 8\%$.

60. The given situation can be written into an equation based on the time value of money as shown:
38400 + 5% of 38400 = 9600 + 5% of 9600 + X + 4% of X + X + 3% of X + X + 2% of X + X + 1% of X + X → 40320 = 10080 + 5X + 10% of X → 30240 = 5.1X → X = 5930.

61. If we assume 100 as the investment in each, the simple interest would be at a flat rate of 12%, hence ₹12 per year. The amount in compound interest would follow the geometric progression of 100 × 1.1 × 1.1 × 1.1... It can be seen that the amount at Compound interest would follow the series: 100, 110, 121, 133.1, 146.41, 160 + (5th year value). By this time, the amount on simple interest would only reach 160. Hence, the second plan is better till 4 years after the investment.

62. 10 lacs invested for his elder son has to become 25 lacs in 6 years – an interest that amounts to 15 lacs = 150%. Interest. Hence, the rate of interest for the elder son is $\frac{150}{6}$ = 25%. For the younger son, he needs 10 lacs to become 25 lacs in 9 years. Hence, the rate of interest is $\frac{150}{9}$ = 16.66%.

63. Let the amounts be divided as A and S for Arjit and Shaurya. For them to get the same amount when they turn 21, Shaurya's amount S, should become equal to A in 3 years of compound interest @12% compounded annually. We get two equations:
A + S = 20; $(1.12)^3 \times S = A$. Solving, we get S ≈ 831625 and A ≈ 1168375.
(**Note:** In the exam, you can solve this equation using the on-screen calculator (in CAT). For other exams, where there is no on-screen calculator, you can do this by approximating using the options.)

64. The key in this question, is to understand that the interest earned in each case will be equal – since the same amount was borrowed and the same amount of 92625 is being paid in order to discharge the loan. If the time period is 't' years, then the interest percentage charged is: $12 \times (t - 0.5) = 10 \times t \rightarrow t = 3$ years. Thus, you paid 30% interest in each case.
The amount can be calculated as: $\frac{92625}{1.3} = 71250$.

CHAPTER

9

Time and Work

Chapter Launchpad

Scan this QR code to access a video on 'Introduction to Time and Work' and this chapter's importance for CAT

INTRODUCTION

The concept of time and work is another important topic for aptitude examinations. Over the past five years, questions based on time and work have been regularly asked in CAT too. Besides, questions on this chapter have been appearing regularly over the past few decades in all aptitude exams.

Theory

The basic concepts and theory in this chapter hinge around the following concepts and thought structures:

If A does a work in a days, then in one day A does $\rightarrow \frac{1}{a}$ of the work.

If B does a work in b days, then in one day B does $\rightarrow \frac{1}{b}$ of the work.

Then, in one day, if A and B work together, then their combined work is $\frac{1}{a} + \frac{1}{b}$.

or $$\frac{a+b}{ab}$$

In the above case, we take the total work to be done as "1 unit of work". Hence, the work will be completed when 1 unit of work is completed.

For example, if A can do a work in 10 days and B can do the same work in 12 days, then the work will be completed in how many days.

One day's work = 1/10 + 1/12 = (12 + 10)/120
[Taking LCM of the denominators]
= 22/120

Then the number of days required to complete the work is 120/22.

Note: This is a reciprocal of the fraction of work done in one day. This is a benefit associated with solving time and work through fractions. It can be stated as—the number of time periods required to complete the full work will be the reciprocal of the fraction of the work done in one time period.

ALTERNATIVE APPROACHES

Percentage Approach

Instead of taking the value of the total work as 1 unit of work, we can also look at the total work as 100 per cent work. In such a case, the following rule applies:

If A does a work in a days, then in one day A does $\rightarrow \frac{100}{a}$% of the work.

If B does a work in b days, then in one day B does $\rightarrow \frac{100}{b}$% of the work.

Then, in one day, if A and B work together, then their combined work is
$$\frac{100}{a} + \frac{100}{b}$$

This is often a very useful approach to look at the concept of time and work because thinking in terms of percentages gives a direct and clear picture of the actual quantum of work done.

What I mean to say is that even though we can think in either a percentage or a fractional value to solve the problem, there will be a thought process difference between the two.

Thinking about work done as a percentage value gives us a linear picture of the quantum of the work that has been done and the quantum of the work that is to be done. On the other hand, if we think of the work done as a fractional value, the thought process will have to be slightly longer to get a full understanding of the work done.

For instance, we can think of work done as 7/9 or 77.77%. The percentage value makes it clear as to how much quantum is left – as we will be measuring the total work to be done as 100%. The percentage value can be visualised on the number line, while the fractional value requires a mental inversion to fully understand the quantum.

An additional advantage of the percentage method of solving time and work problems would be the elimination of the need to perform cumbersome fraction additions involving LCMs of denominators.

However, you should realise that this would work only if you are able to handle basic percentage calculations involving standard decimal values. If you have really internalised the techniques of percentage calculations given in the chapter of percentages, then you can reap the benefits for this chapter.

The benefit of using this concept will become abundantly clear by solving through percentages the same example that was solved above using fractions.

Example: If A can do a work in 10 days and B can do the same work in 12 days, then the work will be completed in how many days?

Solution: One day's work = 10% + 8.33% = 18.33% (**Note**: No LCMs required here)

Hence, to do 100% work, it will require: 100/18.33.

This can be solved by adding 18.33 mentally to get between 5–6 days. Then on you can go through options and mark the closest answer.

The process of solving through percentages will yield rich dividends, if and only if, you have adequate practice on adding standard percentage values. Thus, $18.33 \times 5 = 91.66$ should not give you any headaches and should be done while reading for the first time.

Thus, a thought process chart for this question should look like this.

If A can do a work in 10 days (→ means 10% work) and B can do the same work in 12 days (→ 8.33% work → 18.33% work in a day in 5 days, 91.66% work → leaves 8.33% work to be done → which can be done in 8.33/18.33 of a day = 5/11 of a day (which can be obtained by multiplying both the numerator and the denominator by 3 to get 8.33/18.33 = 25/55=5/11). Thus, the work will be completed in $5\frac{5}{11}$ days. The entire process can be done mentally.

However, the percentage method has some basic limitations – firstly it requires you to be really good at handling the decimal values of the percentages and secondly it works well only with standard denominators. For instance in the above illustration, if A could do the work in 13 days and B in 17 days, and if it is asked to you to find out how many days A and B would take together to complete the work, it would not be possible to solve using percentages – as we would not be aware of the percentage values of 1/13 and of 1/17 (and even if you were somehow aware of these numbers, it would not be possible to mentally add the difficult decimals that 1/13 and 1/17 throw up). All these problems get sorted out through the third method of thinking in these situations, which I now move onto.

LCM METHOD: The Best Approach

This is by far the best method of solving Time and Work Questions. The process is best explained through an example. Suppose, A can do a piece of work in 10 days and B can do it in 12 days. In how many days can A and B together do the work?

Solution using the LCM Method

Assume the total work to be 60 (LCM of 10 and 12). Then, since A can do the total work in 10 days, he would do 6 units of work per day (60/10). Likewise, B would do 5 units of work per day (since he does the total work of 60 units in 12 days). Thus, A and B's work in 1 day would be 6 + 5 = 11. Hence, total number of days taken to do the work = 60/11 = $5\frac{5}{11}$ days.

Concept of Negative Work

Suppose, that A and B are working to build a wall while C is working to break the wall. In such a case, the wall is being built by A and B while it is being broken by C. Here, if we consider the work as the building of the wall, we can say that C is doing negative work.

Example: A can build a wall in 10 days and B can build it in 5 days, while C can completely destroy the wall in 20 days. If they start working at the same time, in how many days will the work be completed.

Using Percentages: The net combined work per day here is:

A's work + B's work – C's work = 10% + 20% – 5% = 25% work in one day.

Hence, the work will get completed (100% work) in 4 days.

Using LCM

The LCM of 10, 20 and 5 is 20. Hence, we assume the total work as 20 units. A can do +2 units of work each day. B can do +4 units of work per day, while C can do –1 units of work each day. Thus, total work done per day = + 2 + 4 – 1 = 5 units of work per day. Thus, 20 units of work would be done in 20/5 = 4 days.

The concept of negative work commonly appears as a problem based on pipes and cisterns, where there are inlet pipes and outlet pipes/leaks which are working against each other.

If we consider the work to be filling a tank, the inlet pipe does positive work while the outlet pipe/leak does negative work.

Application of Product Constancy Table to Time and Work

The equation that applies to time and work problems is

$$\text{Work rate} \times \text{Time} = \text{Work done}$$

This equation means that if the work done is constant, then → work rate is inversely proportional to time. Hence, the product constancy table will be directly applicable to time and work questions.

Note: The parallelism between this formula and the formula of time speed and distance, where again there is product constancy between speed and time if the distance is constant.

Time is usually in days or hours, although any standard unit of time can be used. The unit of time that has to be used in a question is usually decided by the denominator of the unit of work rate.

Here, there are two ways of defining the work rate.

1. In the context of situations where individual working efficiencies or individual time requirements are given in the problem, the work rate is defined by the unit: work done per unit time.

In this case, the total work to be done is normally considered to be 1 (if we solve through fractions) or 100% (if we solve through percentages).

Thus, in the solved problem above, when we calculated that A and B together do 18.33% work in a day, this was essentially a statement of the rate of work of A and B together.

Then the solution proceeded as:

18.33% work per day × number of days required = 100% work

Giving us: the number of days required = 100/18.33 = $5\frac{5}{11}$

2. In certain types of problems (typically those involving projects that are to be completed), where a certain category of worker has the same rate of working, the work rate will be defined as the number of workers of a particular category working on the project.

For instance, questions where all men work at a certain rate, the work rate when two men are working together will be double the work rate when one man is working alone. Similarly, the work rate when ten men are working together will be ten times the work rate when one man is working alone.

In such cases, the work to be done is taken as the number of man-days required to finish the work.

Note: For future reference, that the work to be done can also be measured in terms of the volume of work defined in the context of day-to-day life.

For example, the volume of a wall to be built, the number of people to be interviewed, the number of chapter is to be made and so on.

WORK EQUIVALENCE METHOD (To Solve Time and Work Problems)

The work equivalence method is nothing but an application of the formula:

Work rate × Time = Work done (or work to be done)

Thus, if the work to be done is doubled, the product of *work rate × time* also has to be doubled. Similarly, if the work to be done increases by 20%, the product of *work rate × time* also has to be increased by 20% and so on.

This method is best explained by an example:

A contractor estimates that he will finish the road construction project in 100 days by employing 50 men.

However, at the end of the 50th day, when as per his estimation half the work should have been completed, he finds that only 40 per cent of his work is done.

(a) How many more days will be required to complete the work?

(b) How many more men should he employ in order to complete the work in time?

Solution:

(a) The contactor has completed 40 per cent of the work in 50 days.

If the number of men working on the project remains constant, the rate of work also remains constant. Hence, to complete 100 per cent work, he will have to complete the remaining 60 per cent of the work.

For this, he would require 75 more days. (This calculation is done using the unitary method.)

(b) In order to complete the work on time, it is obvious that he will have to increase the number of men working on the project.

This can be solved as:

50 men working for 50 days → 50 × 50 = 2500 man-days.

2500 man-days has resulted in 40 per cent work completion. Hence, the total work to be done in terms of the number of man-days is obtained by using unitary method:

Work left = 60% = 2500 × 1.5 = 3750 man-days

This has to be completed in 50 days. Hence, the number of men required per day is 3750/50 = 75 men.

Since, 50 men are already working on the project, the contractor needs to hire 25 more men.

Note: This can be done using the percentage change graphic for product change. Since, the number of days is constant at 50, the 50 per cent increase in work from 40 per cent to 60 per cent is solely to be met by increasing the number of men. Hence, the number of men to be increased is 50 per cent of the original number of men = 25 men.

Specific Case of Building a Wall (Work as Volume of Work)

As already mentioned, in certain cases, the unit of work can also be considered to be in terms of the volume of work. For example, building of a wall of a certain length, breadth and height.

In such cases, the following formula applies:

$$\frac{L_1 B_1 H_1}{L_2 B_2 H_2} = \frac{m_1 t_1 d_1}{m_2 t_2 d_2}$$

where L, B and H are respectively the length, breadth and height of the wall to be built, while m, t and d are respectively the number of men, the amount of time per day and the number of days. Further, the suffix 1 is for the first work situation, while the suffix 2 is for the second work situation.

Consider the following problem:

Example: Twenty men working eight hours a day can completely build a wall of length 200 metres, breadth 10 metres and height 20 metres in ten days. How many days will 25 men working 12 hours a day require to build a wall of length 400 metres, breadth 10 metres and height of 15 metres?

Solution: This question can be solved directly by using the formula above

$$\frac{L_1 B_1 H_1}{L_2 B_2 H_2} = \frac{m_1 t_1 d_1}{m_2 t_2 d_2}$$

Here, L_1 is 200 metres L_2 is 400 metres
B_1 is 10 metres B_2 is 10 metres
H_1 is 20 metres H_2 is 15 metres
while m_1 is 20 men m_2 is 25 men
d_1 is 10 days d_2 is unknown
and t_1 is 8 hours a day t_2 is 12 hours a day

Then we get $(200 \times 10 \times 20)/(400 \times 10 \times 15) = (20 \times 8 \times 10)/(25 \times 12 \times d_2)$

$$\therefore \quad d_2 = 5.333/0.6666 = 8 \text{ days}$$

Alternatively, you can also directly write the equation as follows:

$d_2 = 10 \times (400/200) \times (10/10) \times (15/20) \times (20/25) \times (8/12)$

This can be done by thinking of the problem as follows:

The number of days have to be found out in the second case. Hence, on the LHS of the equation, write down the unknown and on the RHS of the equation, write down the corresponding knowns.

$$d_2 = 10 \times ....$$

Then, the length of the wall has to be factored in. There are only two options for doing so, viz,

multiplying by 200/400 (< 1, which will reduce the number of days) or multiplying by 400/200 (>1, which will increase the number of days).

The decision of which one of these is to be done is made on the basis of the fact that when the length of the wall is increasing, the number of days required will also increase.

Hence, we take the value of the fraction greater than 1 to get

$$d_2 = 10 \times (400/200)$$

We continue in the same way to get

No change in the breadth of the wall → hence, multiply by 10/10 (no change in d_2)

Height of the wall is decreasing → hence, multiply by 15/20 (< 1 to reduce d_2).

Number of men working is increasing → hence, multiply by 20/25 (< 1 to reduce d_2).

Number of hours per day is increasing → hence, multiply by 8/12 (< 1 to reduce the number of days).

Concept of Efficiency

The concept of efficiency is closely related to the concept of work rate.

When we make a statement saying *A* is twice as efficient as *B*, we mean to say that *A* does twice the work as *B* in the same time. In other words, we can also understand this as *A* will require half the time required by *B* to do the same work.

In the context of efficiency, another statement that you might come across is: *A* is two times more efficient than *B*. This is the same as: *A* is thrice as efficient as *B* or *A* does the same work as *B* in 1/3rd of the time.

Equating Men, Women and Children This is directly derived from the concept of efficiencies.

Example: Eight men can do a work in 12 days while twenty women can do it in 10 days. In how many days can 12 men and 15 women complete the same work?

Solution: Total work to be done = 8 × 12 = 96 man-days.

or total work to be done = 20 × 10 = 200 woman-days.

Since, the work is the same, we can equate 96 man-days = 200 woman-days.

Hence, 1 man-day = 2.08333 woman-days.

Now, if 12 men and 15 women are working on the work we get

12 men are equal to 12 × 2.08333 = 25 women

Hence, the work done per day is equivalent to 25 + 15 women working per day.

That is, 40 women working per day.

Hence, 40 × number of days = 200 woman days

Number of days = 5 days.

Going Beyond the Book

Scan this QR code for a video on a detailed discussion of Pipes and Cisterns.

Space for Notes

WORKED-OUT PROBLEMS

Problem 9.1: A can do a piece of work in 10 days and B in 12 days. Find how much time they will take to complete the work under the following conditions:

(a) Working together
(b) Working alternately starting with A
(c) Working alternately starting with B
(d) If B leaves two days before the actual completion of the work
(e) If B leaves two days before the scheduled completion of the work
(f) If another person C who does negative work (i.e. works against A and B and can completely destroy the work in 20 days) joins them and they work together all the time.

Solution:

(a) One day's work for A is 1/10 and one day's work for B is 1/12.

Then, working together, the work in one day is equal to:

$\frac{1}{10}+\frac{1}{12}=\frac{11}{60}$ of the work. Thus, working together they need 60/11 days to complete the work → 5.45 days.

Alternately, you can use percentage values to solve the above question:

A's work =10%, B's work = 8.33%. Hence, A + B = 18.33% of the work in one day.

Hence, to complete 100% work, we get the number of days required = 100/18.33 → 5.55 days.

This can be calculated as

@ 18.33% per day in 5 days, they will cover 18.33 × 5 = 91.66%. (The decimal value 0.33 is not difficult to handle if you have internalised the fraction to percentage conversion table of the chapter of percentages).

Work left on the sixth day is: 8.33%, which will require: 8.33/18.33 of the sixth day.

Since, both these numbers are divisible by 1.66, we get 5/11 of the sixth day will be used → 0.45 of the sixth day is used.

Hence, 5.45 days are required to finish the work.

However, as already stated earlier, the best method is to solve this using the LCM method: Assume total work as 60 units, A's work will be 6 units, B's work will be 5 units. The work would be done in 60/11 = $5\frac{5}{11}$ days.

(b) Working alternately starting with A: When two people are working alternately, the question has to be solved by taking two days as a unit of time instead of one day.

So in (a) above, the work done in one day will be covered in two days here.

Thus, in two days the work done will be 18.33%. In ten days, it will be 91.66%. On the eleventh day, A works by himself.

But A's work in one day is 10 per cent. Therefore, he will require 5/6 of the eleventh day to finish the work.

Using the LCM method, this question can be thought through as follows:

Total work = 60. First day: A works alone and does 6 units of work; Second day: B works alone and does 5 units of work. In two days, work done = 6 + 5 = 11 units. Using unitary method, in ten days, work done is 55 units. On the eleventh day, A works alone and since 5 units of work is left and A does 6 units of work in the whole day, it means that he would take 5/6 of the day to complete the work. Hence, total days required = $10\frac{5}{6}$ days.

(c) Working alternately starting with B: Here, there will be no difference in work completed by the tenth day. On the eleventh day, B works alone and does 8.33% of the work (which was required to complete the work). Hence, the whole of the eleventh day will get used.

Using the LCM method, this question can be thought through as follows:

Total work = 60. First day: B works alone and does 5 units of work; Second day: A works alone and does 6 units of work. In two days, work done = 5 + 6 = 11 units. Using unitary method, in ten days, work done is 55 units. On the eleventh day, B works alone and since 5 units of work is left and B does 6 units of work in the whole day, it means that he would take the whole day to complete the work. Hence, total days required = 11 days.

(d) If B leaves two days before the actual completion of the work: In this case, the actual completion of the work is after two days of B's leaving. This means, that A has worked alone for the last two days to complete the work. But A does, 10% work in a day. Hence, A and B must have done 80% of the work together (@18.33% per day). Then, the answer can be found by

80/18.33 + 20/10 days.

Note: For calculation of 80/18.33, we can use the fact that the decimal value is a convenient one. If they worked together, they would complete 73.33% of the work in four days and the work that they would have done on the fifth day would be 6.66%.

At the rate of 18.33% work per day while working together, they would work together for 6.66/18.33 of the fifth day. Since both the numerator and denominator are divisible by 1.66, the above ratio is converted into 4/11 = 0.3636.

Hence, they work together for 4.3636 days after which B leaves and then A completes the work in two more days. Hence, the time required to finish the work would be = 6.3636 days.

Using the LCM method would be very convenient comparatively in this question. The following thought process would be used:

Total work = 60. A's work in 1 day = 6 units, B's work in 1 day = 5 units. Since, B's leaves two days before actual completion of work the interpretation of this would be that for the last two days A has worked alone and finished the work alone. On the last two days, A would do 6 + 6 = 12 units of work. Thus, A and B together would do 60 – 12 = 48 units of work. They would take $48/11 = 4\frac{4}{11}$ days.

Thus, the total number of days required would be $2 + 4\frac{4}{11} = 6\frac{4}{11}$ days.

(e) If B leaves two days before the scheduled completion of the work: Completion of the work would have been scheduled assuming that A and B both worked together for completing the work (say, this is x days). Then, the problem has to be viewed as: $x - 2$ days was the time for which A and B worked together. The residual amount of work left (which will be obtained by two days work of A and B together) would be done by A alone at his own pace of work.

Thus, we can get the solution by:

Number of days required to complete the work = $[(100/18.33) - 2] + \frac{36.66}{10}$

Using the LCM method: Total work = 60 units. B leaves two days before the scheduled completion of the work means that when B leaves, two scheduled days of work was left. Since, as per schedule A and B were working together, they would do 11 units of work per day. Hence, scheduled work for last 2 days = 2 × 11 = 22 units. This work would be done along by A (@ 6 units of work per day), while the other 38 units of work would be done by A and B together (@11 units of work per day). Total number of days required = $\frac{38}{11} + \frac{22}{6} = \frac{470}{66} = \frac{235}{33}$ days.

Again as you can see, the LCM method reduces your calculations and hence, the time you take to get through the question.

(f) If C joins the group and does negative work, we can see that one day's work of the three together would be

A's work + B's work – C's work = 10% + 8.33% – 5% = 13.33%

Hence, the work will be completed in (100/13.33) days.

Note: This can be calculated by 13.33 × 7 = 13 × 7 + 0.33 × 7 = 93.33.

Then, work left = 6.66, which will require half a day more at the rate of 13.33% per day. Thus, the total time required would be 7.5 days.

Using the LCM method: Total work = 60 (LCM of 10,12 and 20). $A = +6$, $B = +5$, $C = -3$. Total work done per day = + 6 + 5 – 3 = 8 units. Time required = 60/8 = 7.5 days.

Advantage of solving problems on time and work through LCM: You should realise from the above examples, that the LCM method is the best way to solve the typical questions on time and work. Once, you identify the LCM of the number of days each person requires to do the work, the LCM method reduces calculations for the solving process.

Problem 9.2: A contractor undertakes to build a wall in 50 days. He employs 50 people for the same. However, after 25 days, he finds that the work is only 40% complete. How many more men need to be employed to:

(a) complete the work in time?

Solution: In order to complete the work in time, the contractor has to finish the remaining 60% of the work in 25 days.

Now, in the first 25 days the work done = 50 × 25 =1250 man-days → 40% of the work.

Hence, work left = 60% of the work = 1875 man-days.

Since, 25 days are left to complete the task, the number of people required is 1875/25 = 75 men.

Since, 50 men are already working, 25 more men are needed to complete the work.

Thought process should go like: 1250 → 40% of work. Hence, 1875 man-days required to complete the work. Since there are only 25 days left, we need 1875/25 = 75 men to complete the work.

(b) Complete the work ten days before time?

Solution: For this purpose, we have to do 1875 man-days of work in 15 days. Hence, men = 1875/15 = 125 men. Hence, he would need to hire 75 more men.

Problem 9.3: For the previous problem, if the contractor continues with the same workforce:

(a) How many days behind schedule will the work be finished?

Solution: He has completed 40% work in 25 days. Hence, to complete the remaining 60% of the work, he would require 50% more days (i.e. 37.5 days) (Since, 60% is 1.5 times of 40%)

Hence, the work would be done 12.5 days behind schedule.

(b) How much increase in efficiency is required from the work force to complete the work in time?

Solution: If the number of men working is kept constant, the only way to finish the work in time is by increasing the efficiency so that more work is done every man-day.

This should be mathematically looked at as follows: Suppose, that one man-day takes care of 1 unit of work. Then, in the first 25 days, work done = 25 (days) × 50 (men) × 1 (work unit per man-day) = 1250 units of work. Now, this 1250 units of work is just 40% of the work. Hence, work left = 1875 units of work.

Then, 25 (days) × 50 (men) × z (work units per man-day) = 1875 → $z = 1.5$

Thus, the work done per man-day has to rise from 1 to 1.5, that is, by 50%. Hence, the efficiency of work has to rise by 50%.

Problem 9.4: A is twice as efficient as B. If they complete a work in 30 days, find the times required by each to complete the work individually.

Solution: When we say that A is twice as efficient as B, it means that A takes half the time that B takes to complete the same work.

Thus, if we denote A's one day's work as A and B's one day's work as B, we have

$A = 2B$

Then, using the information in the problem, we have:

$30A + 30B = 100\%$ work

That is, $90B = 100\%$ work → $B = 1.11\%$ (is the work done by B in one day) → B requires 90 days to complete the work alone.

Since, $A = 2B$ → we have $A = 2.22\%$ → A requires 45 days to do the work alone.

You should be able to solve this mentally with the following thought-process while reading for the first time:

$\frac{100}{30} = 3.33\%$. $\frac{3.33}{3} = 1.11\%$. Hence, work done is 1.11% per day and 2.22% per day → 90 and 45 days.

Problem 9.5: A is two times more efficient than B. If they complete a work in 30 days, then find the times required by each to complete the work individually.

Solution: Interpret the first sentence as $A = 3B$ and solve according to the process of the previous problem to get the answers. (You should get that A takes 40 days and B takes 120 days.)

Space for Rough Work

LEVEL OF DIFFICULTY (I)

1. Aruna can complete a piece of work in 5 days. A takes double the time taken by Aruna, B takes double that of A, and C takes double that of B to complete the same task. They are paired in groups of two each. One pair takes two-thirds the time needed by the second pair to complete the work. Which is the first pair?
   (a) Aruna and B
   (b) Aruna and C
   (c) A and C
   (d) Such a pairing is not possible.
2. Four small pumps and a large pump are filling a tank. Each of the three small pumps works at $\frac{3}{4}$th the rate of the large pump. If all four pumps work at the same time, they should fill the tank in what fraction of the time that it would have taken the large pump alone?
3. A tank has an inlet pipe and an outlet pipe. If the outlet pipe is closed then the inlet pipe fills the empty tank in 10 hours. If the outlet pipe is open then the inlet pipe fills the empty tank in 12 hours. If only the outlet pipe is open then in how many hours the full tank becomes a quarter full?
4. A can complete a job in 12 days and B can do it in 8 days. If they are joined by C and the work is completed in 4 days, then what should C's share be in a total payment of ₹5400 for the work?
5. Partha alone can do a job in 12 days, while Sunil alone can do it in 24 days. Partha starts the job, and after three days, Sunil joins him. Again, after a few more days, Varun joins them and they together finish the job. If Varun has done 25% of the job, then in how many days was the job done?
6. Eleven dogs and eight cats can finish a job in two-thirds the time taken by five cats and eight dogs to finish the same job. If two cats can finish the job in 13 days, then how many dogs can finish the job in 13 days?
7. Aditya, Vedus and Yuvraj alone can do a job in 6 weeks, 9 weeks and 12 weeks respectively. They work together for 2 weeks. Then Aditya leaves the job. Vedus leaves the job a week earlier than the completion of the work. The job would be completed in:
8. Amir, Abdullah and Ashok can complete a task in 45, 60 and 75 days respectively. They started the work together but Ashok left after 10 days of the start and Abdullah left 2 days before the completion of the work. In how many days will the work be completed?
9. 15 men can complete a work in ten days. 20 women can complete the same work in fifteen days. 8 men and 4 women started working and after nine days, 10 more women joined them. How many days will they now take to complete the remaining work?
10. Three workmen A, B and C are entrusted with a project. A can do the job in 50 days. If B is 32% more efficient than A and C is 50% more efficient than B, then B and C together can finish the job in approximately:
    (a) 11 days (b) 16 days
    (c) 13 days (d) 17 days
11. Raju can do 25% of a piece of work in 5 days. How many days will he take to complete the work ten times?
    (a) 150 days (b) 250 days
    (c) 200 days (d) 180 days
12. 6 men can do a piece of work in 12 days. How many men are needed to do the work in 18 days.
    (a) 3 men (b) 6 men
    (c) 4 men (d) 2 men
13. *A* can do a piece of work in 20 days and *B* can do it in 15 days. How long will they take if both work together?
    (a) $8\left(\frac{6}{7}\right)$ days (b) $8\left(\frac{4}{7}\right)$ days
    (c) $9\left(\frac{3}{7}\right)$ days (d) $9\left(\frac{4}{7}\right)$ days
14. Raman can do a work in 10 days & Rahul in 15 days. Charan, who can finish the same work in 20 days, joins them, then how long will they take to complete the work?
    (a) 5.12 days (b) 4.62 days
    (c) 5.67 days (d) 4.82 days
15. *A* and *B* can do a piece of work in eight days and *B* alone can do it in 16 days. In how many days, can *A* do it alone?
    (a) 12 days (b) 13 days
    (c) 18 days (d) 16 days
16. Baba alone can do a piece of work in 10 days. Anshu alone can do it in 15 days. If the total wages for the work is ₹50. How much should Baba be paid if they work together for the entire duration of the work?
    (a) ₹30 (b) ₹20
    (c) ₹50 (d) ₹40

17. 4 men and 3 women finish a job in 6 days, and 5 men and 7 women can do the same job in 4 days. How long will 1 man and 1 woman take to do the work?
(a) $22\left(\frac{2}{7}\right)$ days (b) $25\left(\frac{1}{2}\right)$ days
(c) $5\left(\frac{1}{7}\right)$ days (d) $12\left(\frac{7}{22}\right)$ days

18. If 8 boys and 12 women can do a piece of work in 25 days, in how many days can the work be done by 6 boys and 11 women working together?
(a) 15 days (b) 10 days
(c) 12 days (d) Cannot be determined

19. *A* can do a piece of work in 10 days and *B* can do the same work in 20 days. With the help of *C*, they finish the work in 5 days. How long will it take for *C* alone to finish the work?
(a) 20 days (b) 10 days
(c) 35 days (d) 15 days

20. Ashok can do a piece of work in ten days. He works at it for 5 days and then Saheb finishes it in ten more days. In how many days will Saheb alone finish the whole work?
(a) 8 days (b) 10 days
(c) 12 days (d) 20 days

21. In the previous question in how much time will Ashok and Saheb finish the whole work together?
(a) 6 days (b) 6.66 days
(c) 5.33 days (d) 1.66 days

22. *A* and *B* undertake to do a piece of work for ₹1000. *A* can do it in ten days and *B* can do it in twenty days. With the help of *C*, they finish it in five days. How much should *C* be paid for his contribution?
(a) ₹400 (b) ₹250
(c) ₹150 (d) ₹350

23. Arun and Vinay together can do a piece of work in 7 days. If Arun does twice as much work as Vinay in a given time, how long will Arun alone take to do the work.
(a) 6.33 days (b) 10.5 days
(c) 11 days (d) 72 days

24. Subhash can copy 50 pages in 10 hours; Subhash and Prakash together can copy 300 pages in 40 hours. In how much time can Prakash copy 30 pages?
(a) 13 h (b) 12 h
(c) 11 h (d) 9 h

25. '*x*' number of men can finish a piece of work in ten days. If there were five men more, the work could be finished in five days. What is the original number of men?
(a) 5 (b) 10
(c) 7 (d) 15

26. An engineer undertakes a project to build a road 15 km long in 300 days and employs 45 men for the purpose. After 100 days, he finds only 2.5 km of the road has been completed. Find the (approx.) number of extra men he must employ to finish the work in time.
(a) 43 (b) 45
(c) 55 (d) 68

27. Ashok and Mohan can do a piece of work in 12 days. Mohan and Binod together do it in 15 days. If Ashok is twice as good a workman as Binod. In how much time will Mohan alone can do the work?
(a) 15 days (b) 20 days
(c) 25 days (d) 35 days

28. Sambhu can do 1/2 of the work in 8 days while Kalu can do 1/3 of the work in 6 days. How long will it take for both of them to finish the work?
(a) $\frac{88}{17}$ days (b) $\frac{144}{17}$ days
(c) $\frac{72}{17}$ days (d) 8 days

29. *A* can do a work in 10 days and *B* can do the same work in 20 days. They work together for 5 days and then *A* goes away. In how many more days will *B* finish the work?
(a) 5 days (b) 6.5 days
(c) 10 days (d) $8\frac{1}{3}$ days

30. A cistern is normally filled in 5 hours. However, it takes 6 hours when there is leak in its bottom. If the cistern is full, in what time shall the leak empty it?
(a) 6 h (b) 5 h
(c) 30 h (d) 15 h

31. Apurva can do a piece of work in 12 days. Apurva and Amit complete the work together and were paid ₹54 and ₹81 respectively. How many days must they have taken to complete the work together?
(a) 4 days (b) 4.5 days
(c) 4.8 days (d) 5 days

32. *A* takes 5 days more than *B* to do a certain job and 9 days more than *C*; *A* and *B* together can do the job in the same time as *C*. How many days *A* would take to do it?
(a) 16 days (b) 10 days
(c) 15 days (d) 20 days

33. In a company XYZ Ltd. a certain number of engineers can develop a design in 40 days. If there were 5 more engineers, it could be finished in 10 days less. How many engineers were there in the beginning?
(a) 18 (b) 20
(c) 25 (d) 15

34. If three taps are open together, a tank is filled in 10 h. One of the taps can fill in 5 h and another in 10 h. At what rate does the 3rd pipe work?
(a) Waste pipe emptying the tank is 10 h
(b) Waste pipe emptying the tank is 20 h
(c) Waste pipe emptying the tank is 5 h
(d) Fills the tank in 10 h

35. Ajay, Vijay and Sanjay are employed to do a piece of work for ₹529. Ajay and Vijay together are supposed to do 19/23 of the work and Vijay and Sanjay together 8/23 of the work. How much should Ajay be paid?
(a) ₹245 (b) ₹295
(c) ₹300 (d) ₹345

36. 30 men working 5 h a day can do a work in 16 days. In how many days will 20 men working 6 h a day do the same work?
(a) $22\frac{1}{2}$ days (b) 20 days
(c) 21 days (d) None of these

37. A, B and C can do some work in 36 days. A and B together do twice as much work as C alone and A and C together can do thrice as much work as B alone. Find the time taken by C to do the whole work.
(a) 72 days (b) 96 days
(c) 108 days (d) 120 days

38. 15 men could finish a piece of work in 210 days. But at the end of 100 days, 15 additional men are employed. In how many more days will the work be complete?
(a) 80 days (b) 60 days
(c) 55 days (d) 50 days

39. Manoj takes twice as much time as Anjay and thrice as much as Vijay to finish a piece of work. Together they finish the work in 1 day. What is the time taken by Manoj to finish the work?
(a) 6 days (b) 3 days
(c) 2 days (d) 4 days

40. Anmol is thrice as good a workman as Vinay and therefore is able to finish the job in 60 days less than Vinay. In how many days will they finish the job working together?
(a) $22\left(\frac{1}{2}\right)$ days (b) $11\left(\frac{3}{2}\right)$ days
(c) 15 days (d) 20 days

41. In a fort there was sufficient food for 200 soldiers for 31 days. After 27 days 120 soldiers left the fort. For how many extra days will the rest of the food last for the remaining soldiers?
(a) 12 days (b) 10 days
(c) 8 days (d) 6 days

42. 36 men take 18 days to complete a piece of work. They worked for a period of 8 days. After that, they were joined by 4 more men. How many more days will be taken by them to complete the remaining work?

43. There are three Taps A, B and C in a tank. They can fill the tank in 10 hrs, 20 hrs and 25 hrs, respectively. At first, all of them are opened simultaneously. Then after 2 hours, tap C is closed and A and B are kept running. After the 4th hour, tap B is also closed. The remaining work is done by Tap A alone. Find the percentage of the work done by Tap A by itself.
(a) 32% (b) 52%
(c) 75% (d) None of these

44. Raju can do a piece of work in 10 days, Vicky in 12 days and Tinku in 15 days. They all start the work together, but Raju leaves after 2 days and Vicky leaves 3 days before the work is completed. In how many days is the work completed?
(a) 5 days (b) 6 days
(c) 7 days (d) 8 days

45. Ajay and Vijay together can do a piece of work in 6 days. Ajay alone does it in 10 days. What time does Vijay require to do it alone?
(a) 20 days (b) 15 days
(c) 25 days (d) 30 days

46. Sashi can do a piece of work in 25 days and Rishi can do it in 20 days. They work for 5 days and then Sashi goes away. In how many more days will Rishi finish the work?
(a) 10 days (b) 12 days
(c) 14 days (d) None of these

47. Pipe A and B running together can fill a cistern in 6 minutes. If B takes 5 minutes more than A to fill the cistern, then the time in A and B will fill the cistern separately what time?
(a) 15 min, 20 min (b) 15 min, 10 min
(c) 10 min, 15 min (d) 25 min, 20 min

48. A certain number of men complete a piece of work in 60 days. If there were 8 men more the work could be finished in 10 days less. How many men were originally there?

49. 24 men working 8 h a day can finish a work in 10 days. Working at a rate of 10 h a day, the number of men required to finish the work in 6 days is
(a) 30 (b) 32
(c) 34 (d) 36

50. The wages of 8 men and 4 women amount to ₹3500 per week and the wages of 5 men and 3 women to ₹2275 per week . Find the daily wages of a man (in rupees, assuming that the wages for a week are paid on the basis of 7 day weeks):

LEVEL OF DIFFICULTY (II)

1. Anshuman, Shaurya and Pallav together make a total of 8 DILR Sets in one day. Together, they were assigned the job of making a total of 80 Sets. Initially, Anshuman started the work, without Shaurya and Pallav joining him. After a few days, Anshuman quit, and Shaurya and Pallav took over and together they completed the job after a few more days. If it took a total of 20 days to complete the entire work and Anshuman makes at least 5 Sets per day, and Shaurya and Pallav make at least 1 set per day & everybody makes an integral number of sets per day how many days did he work on the job?
   (a) 9 (b) 10
   (c) 11 (d) 12
2. Ritika takes twice the time taken by Kavita to complete a job. Kavita takes twice the time taken by Fatima to complete the job. Fatima takes twice the time taken by Sanjeeta to complete the job. Two of the four when working together take 50% or less of the time taken by the other two together to complete the job. Find these two.
   (a) Ritika, Sanjeeta
   (b) Sanjeeta, Kavita
   (c) Kavita, Fatima
   (d) None of these
3. Aman takes x times the time taken by Baman and Chaman to complete a job. Baman takes x times the time taken by Aman and Chaman to complete the job. Chaman takes x times the time taken by Aman and Baman to complete the job. What is the value of x?
   (a) 1 (b) 2
   (c) 3 (d) 4
4. Akshak and Bhakshak can complete a piece of work in 48 and 72 days, respectively. Akshak worked for the first 20 days and then left, and then Bhakshak continued for the next 24 days and left. The remaining work is completed by Chakshak. If Chakshak received ₹18,000 for the work done by him, then what was the amount received by Akshak?
5. A, B and C started work together and after completing one fifth of the work C left, A and B worked for 30 more days. C then took over from A and B and completed the remaining work in 12 days. If C alone takes 40 days to complete the entire work, in how many days can B alone complete the entire work given that A's rate of doing work is twice that of B?
   (a) 90 (b) 120
   (c) 180 (d) 140
6. Two taps A and B can fill a tank in 20 minutes and 25 minutes respectively. The two taps are opened together. After how much time should tap B be closed so that the tank is full in exactly 14 minutes?
   (a) 7 minutes (b) 6(½) minutes
   (c) 7(½) minutes (d) 6 minutes
7. At the Darba farm, twenty cows and forty sheep can be kept for 10 days for ₹480. What would be the cost of keeping 40 cows and 50 sheep for 12 days, if the daily cost of keeping 5 sheep is the same as the daily cost of keeping 2 cows?
   (a) ₹880 (b) ₹900
   (c) ₹960 (d) ₹920
8. The rates at which Pallav and Shaurya work are in the ratio 5 : 4. They work on alternate days to complete a job. Shaurya started the job and he worked on the last day. The job was completed in 1 day more than the time Pallav alone would take to complete it. Find the time taken (in days) by them working together to complete the job.
   (a) $4\frac{1}{9}$ (b) $3\frac{1}{3}$
   (c) $4\frac{1}{3}$ (d) $4\frac{4}{9}$
9. Clegane, Mountain and Danaerys are three workers responsible for completing a wall. Clegane and Mountain build the wall in 10 and 15 hours respectively and Danaerys destroys the wall in 12 hours. If all three start working in that order for 2 hours each till the wall gets built, then how many hours will they take?
10. Sanjeeta can design the complete schedule for Mindworkzz in 30 days. After working for six days she took a break and resumed the work after 3 days but with half of her original efficiency. She completed the task in another 12 days with the help of Sumika who joined her when she came back after her leave. In how many days can Sumika design the schedule alone?
11. A tank was to be completely filled by 25 inlet pipes (Say P_1, P_2.. P_{25}), each of which fills water in the tank at the same rate. At the start of filling the empty tank, two pipes were opened for an hour (Say P_1, P_2). At the end of every hour a different pair of pipes was opened. The process was continued till all the possible pairs of pipes were opened or exactly 1 hour each. The operator Amartya realized that there was still some capacity left in the tank even after all the pairs were exhausted. Amartya opened all the 25 pipes for 4

more hours and observed that the tank got completely filled after that. How many hours it would have taken had Amartya opened all the 25 pipes at the start?

12. There are two pipes, having circular cross sections are used to fill a tank. The radius of one of the pipes is three times more than that of the other. If the smaller pipe takes 510 mins to fill the tank, then find the time taken (in minutes) by both the pipes together to fill the tank.

13. Ten floors of a building in Mumbai had already been constructed and 10 more floors were to be built by the team in the next 20 days. After 12 days of work BMC destroyed half of the building citing non-compliance reasons. How much more time (in days) will it take to complete the construction now?

14. Palak, Qutub, and Ritika are three employees who can complete a task in 4, 5 and 15 hours respectively. All the three are assigned simultaneously to the task but Palak works half heartedly for the first 2 hours and Qutub works at $1/4^{th}$ his normal efficiency for the first 4 hours. In how many hours will the task be completed (closest approximate time)?
(a) 4 hours 25 minutes
(b) 4 hours 40 minutes
(c) 3 hours 34 minutes
(d) 3 hours 25 minutes

15. Cersei, Jamie and Tyrion working alone can do a piece of work in 20, 30 and 60 hours respectively. All three of them start the work together, but after x hours Cersei leaves and then after y more hours Jamie also leaves and Tyrion completes the remaining work. Had Jamie not left, Jamie and Tyrion would have completed the remaining work in $(y + 6)$ hours after Cersei had left. If both of them had stayed, the work would have been completed in $(x + 6)$ hours. What is the total number of hours taken to complete the work?

16. A, B and C start working on a project. Both B and C can individually complete the project in 6 hours. A, being a notorious person, starts destroying the project when it is half done and can completely destroy the project in 12 hours. If all three start working simultaneously, then in how much time will the project get completed?

17. Amla and Bimla undertake a project for ₹48,000. They take 24 days and 40 days respectively to complete the project while working alone. If the work is completed in 10 days with the help of Kamla, then what is the amount received by Kamla?

18. Three friends P, Q and R are assigned a job. R can do 60% of the job in 15 days. The efficiency of Q is 25% more than that of R. Both Q and R started working together and left the work after eight days. P completed the remaining work in 7 days. The efficiency of P is what percent more or less than that of Q?
(a) 25%
(b) 15%
(c) 20%
(d) 24%

19. 58 robots take a total of 141 days to complete building the wall. On the first day one robot starts the work. Then on each day starting from the second day, one more robot joins the team of robots. If the nth robot is twice as efficient as the $(n - 1)^{th}$ robot, then on which day will the job get completed?

20. Two pipes A and B have the ability to both fill and drain a tank. For both the pipes the rate of filling is same as the rate of draining (though different from each other). A can fill the complete tank in 33.33% more time than it takes to fill the tank using both the pipes. If the tank is empty and pipe A is used to fill the tank while B is used to empty it, then what percent of the tank will be empty after '$t/5$' minutes, where 't' is the amount of time taken by both the tanks to fill the tank when both the pipes are being used as fill pipes.?

21. Shri, Hari, Ram, and Chandra have taken the task to make several wooden chairs.
Shri alone can make a chair in 12 hours. Hari is 20% more efficient than Shri, whereas Ram is 25% more efficient than Hari. Chandra is one-third as efficient as Ram. One day, they together had to make a chair. Initially, for 15 minutes all four worked on the chair. Then, Shri and Hari left and the remaining two of them worked on the chair for another 4 hours. Then, Chandra finished the remaining work alone. For how much time did Chandra work alone?

22. Thirty workers all working with the same efficiency started a job and worked on it for 30 days. From day 31 onwards, a new worker with the same efficiency as previous workers joined them every day till the job was finished. It took a total of 38 days to complete the entire work. Now, the same job has to be done, starting with the minimum possible number of workers when it is known that exactly one worker will quit the job at the end of each day after the first day. How many days will it take to finish the job in such a manner?

23. A buffalo can graze as much in 6 days as a goat can in 10 days. A cow can graze as much in 8 days as a buffalo can in 5 days. The goat and the cow together take 89 days to graze a certain field. How much time (in days) does it take for all three to graze the same field?

24. Tingu and Mingu can finish a piece of work in 12 and 15 days, respectively. They started the work at the same time. After 2 days,Tingu left work and Ringu joined Mingu. For 1 day Mingu worked with 1.5 times his efficiency and left after that. The rest of the work is finished by Ringu in 2 more days. In how many days Ringu alone can finish that piece of work?

25. A tank has three taps attached to it. While the first tap alone can fill the tank in 18 hours, the time taken by the second tap alone to fill the tank is two and a half times that of the first one. A third tap is attached to the tank, emptying it in 36 hours. Now, one day, to fill the tank, Rohan opens the first tap and after 3 hours opens the second tap as well. However, at the end of the 8th hour, he realises that the third tap has been kept open right from the beginning and promptly closes it. What would be the total time required to fill the tank?

26. A worker can build a wall in 16 days when working alone without taking any energy drink or other substance. He takes an energy drink which can double his work output on any day. He does not take the drink for 3 days consecutively as it can damage his liver. What is the minimum number of days he needs to finish the wall?

27. A tank is filled with water. There are four pipes attached to the tank from which pipe A and pipe B are outlet pipes that can empty the tank in 10 hours and 30 hours, respectively, working alone. Pipe C and D are inlet pipes and can fill the empty tank in 20 hours and 15 hours, respectively, working alone. Pipe A is opened on Monday at 3 pm, at 5 pm pipe B is opened, at 6 pm pipe C is opened, and pipe D is also opened at 7 pm. At what time the filled tank will be empty?
(a) 7 pm, Tuesday
(b) 7 pm, Wednesday
(c) 6 am, Wednesday
(d) Tank will never be empty

28. A lot of work needs to be done while planning a party – even after all the stuff is purchased from the market, you still need to organise the cooking, the setting of the table as well as making the guest list and informing everyone about it. Arun, Mini and Sherry work together to arrange a party. The time it takes them to do the work together is two and half hours hours less than Arun would have taken working alone, $\frac{5}{6}^{th}$ of an hour less than what Mini would have taken alone. Also, Sherry takes double the time that Mini takes to do the work. How long did it take them to do these chores working together?
(a) 20 minutes (b) 30 minutes
(c) 40 minutes (d) 50 minutes

29. It takes seven workers a total of ten hours to complete a painting task. The contractor entrusted with the job hired eight workers to do the job at 10 AM. He added one extra worker per hour starting at 3.00 PM. At what time will the painting job be completed?

30. A paint manufacturer produces two kinds of paints, standard and deluxe. The profit margin is ₹200 on a litre of standard paint and ₹300 on a litre of deluxe paint. Every litre of paint must be processed on machines X and Y. The processing time per litre on the two machines are as follows: (Time required (Hours/litre)

	Standard Paint	Deluxe Paint
Machine A	8	10
Machine B	12	20

The total time available on machine A is 1400 hours and on machine B is 2500 hours in the month of July. Among the following production plans, which one meets the machine availability constraints and maximises the profit?
(a) Standard 75 litres, Deluxe 80 litres
(b) Standard 100 litres Deluxe 60 litres
(c) Standard 50 litres, Deluxe 100 litres
(d) Standard 60 litres, Deluxe 90 litres

31. A chemical plant has four tanks (A, B, C and D), each containing 1600 liters of a chemical. The chemical is being pumped from one tank to another as follows
From A to B @ 20 liters/minute
From C to A @ 90 liters/minute
From A to D @ 10 liters/minute
From C to D @ 50 liters/minute
From B to C @ 100 liters/minute
From D to B @ 110 liters/minute
Which tank gets emptied first, and how long does it take (in minutes) to get empty after pumping starts?
(a) A, 26.66 minutes (b) D, 32
(c) C, 40 (d) D, 20

32. In a shoes and laces factory, one machine produces only shoes at the rate of 200 shoes per minute and needs to be cleaned for 5 minutes after production of every 1400 units. Another machine produces only laces at the rate of 150 laces per minute and needs to be cleaned for 10 minutes after the production of every 1500 laces. If both the machines start production at the same time, how many minutes more will the laces machine require after the shoes machine – if both of them have to produce 15000 units of their products.
(a) 90 minutes (b) 75 minutes
(c) 65 minutes (d) 125 minutes

33. A group of men was employed to shift 545 crates. Every day after the first, 6 more men than the previous day were put on the job. Also, every day after the first, each man working, shifted 5 fewer crates than the number of crates moved by each man the previous day. The result was that during the latter part of the period, the number of crates shifted per day began to go down. 5 days were required to finish the work. What was the number of crates shifted on the third day?

(a) 137 (b) 169
(c) 26 (d) 152

34. A piece of work is done by Men and Women. All men work at the same rate, while all women work at the same rate. The work gets completed in 30 days if 10 men and 45 women work together and in 60 days if 8 men and 18 women work together. In how many days will the work be done completely if 20 Men and 18 women work together?

35. Murali and Conti can together complete a work in 32 days. After 14 days of working together, Murali got sick and his efficiency fell by 30%. As a result, they completed the work in 34 days instead of 32 days. If Conti had worked alone after Murali fell sick, how many days more would have been required to complete the task?

36. The cooking work for cooking dinner in Mr Upadhyay's kitchen always starts at a fixed time point every day. Either Cook Kishan or Cook Shatrughan cook the meal. On 27th March, Kishan alone completed the work at 9 PM, on 28th March Shatrughan alone completed the cooking at 7 PM. On 29th March, Kishan alone worked till 6 PM and then Shatrughan worked alone and completed the work at 8 PM. At what time will the work get completed if on 30th March, both Kishan and Shatrughan work together?

37. Men and women can both perform a job but at different efficiencies. Fifteen men and five women working together take thirty hours to finish the job, whereas five men and fifteen women working together take sixty hours to finish it. How many hours will fifteen men working together take to finish the same job?

38. At their usual efficiency levels, *A* and *B* together finish a task in 15 days. If *A* had worked one third as efficiently as he usually does, and *B* had worked four times as efficiently as he usually does, the task would have been completed in 12 days. How many days would A take to finish the task if he works alone at his usual efficiency?

39. Hurshi can do a work in the same time as Rishi and Sherry together can. Rishi can do the work ten hours faster than Sherry and 8 hours slower than Hurshi. The time taken by Hurshi to do the work working alone would be?

(a) 9 hours (b) 18 hours
(c) 12 hours (d) 20 hours

40. At the annual forest party the work is entrusted to the rabbits and the deers. However, not much enthusiasm is shown by either group in doing the work. The deers don't turn up at all, while on the first day only 1 rabbit shows up to do the work. On the second day 2 new rabbits join the first one, the next day 3 new rabbits join the previous day's rabbits and so on – only rabbits being added every day. In this manner, the work gets completed in 23 days. If a deer is twice as efficient as a rabbit, in how many days would the work have got completed if 23 deer had worked on it from start to finish?

41. A tank has two inlet pipes over it that pour water into it. It also has an outlet pipe which can be used to drain off water. The inlet pipes can fill an empty tank in 24 hours and 16 hours respectively. The outlet pipe can empty a full tank in 24 hours by itself. Ayesha, had to go out one day and estimated that she would be back after a certain time. So she opened the inlet pipes together and set the outlet pipe to open when 75% of the tank was full, so that she the tank would be full just when she returned. However, due to some defect, the outlet pipe opened at a time, when only 50% of the tank was filled. What percent of the tank would still be empty when Ayesha comes back?

42. Three Professors Dr. Gupta, Dr Sharma and Dr. Singh are evaluating answer scripts of a subject. Dr. Gupta is 40% more efficient than Dr. Sharma, who is 20% more efficient than Dr. Singh. Dr. Gupta takes 10 days less than Dr. Sharma to complete the evaluation work. Dr. Gupta starts the evaluation work and works for 10 days and then Dr. Sharma takes over. Dr. Sharma evaluates for next 15 days and then stops. In how many days, Dr. Singh can complete the remaining evaluation work.

43. Four pipes A, B, C and D are connected to a tank. They can fill the empty tank in 8, 12, 16 and 24 hours respectively. They are all opened together when the tank is empty. For the first two hours, the first two pipes A and B work at $\frac{3}{5}^{th}$ of their capacity. A and B then start working at normal capacity. C and D work at $\frac{2}{5}^{th}$ of their capacity for the first three hours, after which normal flow is restored in those pipes. In how many hours (from the start) will the tank be completely filled?

44. In Azmatpur village, 18 men and 24 boys completed the construction of a local school in 60 days, by working for 7.5 hours a day. Residents of the local township of Biddipur, also decided to set up a similar school, only they wanted it to be thrice the size of the Azmatpur school – to reflect the larger population of Biddipur. If a man is able to perform the work equal to the same done by 2 boys, then how many boys will be required to help 27 men to complete the work in Biddipur in 50 days, working 9 hours a day?

45. A road construction project is to be completed in 72 days and 120 men are set to work, each working 8 hours a day. After 40 days, $\frac{2}{5}$th of the work is finished. How many additional men may be employed so that work may be completed on time, each man now working 9 hours per day?

(a) 80 men (b) 64 men
(c) 50 men (d) None of the above

46. A tank is connected with both inlet pipes and outlet pipes. Individually, an inlet pipe can fill the tank in 7 hours and an outlet pipe can empty it in 5 hours. If all the pipes are kept open, it takes exactly 7 hours for a completely filled-in tank to empty. If the total number of pipes connected to the tank is 11, how many of these are inlet pipes?

47. Kishan, Shatrughan and Ram Lagan have to cook chapatis for a dinner party at Radha Niwas Patna. They are entrusted to make a total of 156 chapatis. Kishan can cook a chapati in 4 minutes, Shatrughan can do it in 6 minutes, and Ram Lagan can do it in 8 minutes. The work is divided into 3 parts by Radha Devi, in such a manner that each of them takes the same amount of time to cook their portion of chapatis. How many chapatis should Shatrughan make?

48. Ramesh bought a total of 6 fruits (apples and oranges) from the market. He found that he required one orange less to extract the same quantity of juice as extracted from the apples. If Ramesh had used the same number of apples and oranges to make the blend, then which of the following correctly a possible value for the percentage of apple juice in the blend?

(a) 25% (b) 60%
(c) 33.3% (d) 60.6%

49. A water tank has M inlet pipes and N outlet pipes. An inlet pipe can fill the tank in 8 hours while an outlet pipe can empty the full tank in 12 hours. If all pipes are left open simultaneously, it takes 6 hours to fill the empty tank. What is the relationship between M & N?

(a) 1 : 1 (b) M : N = 3 : 2
(c) 2 : 1 (d) Cannot be determined

50. Four two-way pipes A, B, C and D can either fill an empty tank or drain the full tank in 3, 10, 12 and 15 minutes respectively. All four pipes were opened simultaneously when the tank is empty. Under which of the following conditions the tank would be half-filled after 6 minutes?

(a) Pipe A filled and pipes B, C and D drained
(b) Pipe A drained and pipes B, C and D filled
(c) Pipes A and D drained and pipes B and C filled
(d) Pipes A and D filled and pipes B and C drained

51. Three pipes are connected to an inverted cone, with its base at the top. Two inlet pipes, A and B, are connected to the top of the cone and can fill the empty cone in 8 hours and 12 hours, respectively. The outlet pipe C, connected to the bottom, can empty a filled cone in 4 hours. When the cone is completely filled with water, all three pipes are opened. Two of the three pipes remain open for 20 hours continuously and the third pipe remains open for a lesser time. As a result, the height of the water inside the cone comes down to 50%. Which of the following options would be possible?

(a) Pipe A was open for 19 hours.
(b) Pipe A was open for 19 hours 30 minutes.
(c) Pipe B was open for 19 hours 30 minutes.
(d) Pipe C was open for 19 hours 50 minutes.

52. Arun takes thrice as much time as Amitabh to finish a job. Amitabh and Aruna take one fourth of the time to finish the job as Arun takes to do it alone. Moreover, to finish the work, Arun working alone takes 4 days more than the three of them together. In how many days will Aruna finish the job working alone.

53. Three diggers dug a ditch of 324 m deep in six days working simultaneously. During one shift, the third digger digs as many metres more than the second as the second digs more than the first. The third digger's work in 10 days is equal to the first digger's work in 14 days. How many metres does the first digger dig per shift?

(a) 15 m (b) 18 m
(c) 21 m (d) 27 m

54. According to a plan, a drilling team had to drill to a depth of 270 metres below the ground level. For the first three days the team drilled as per the plan. However, subsequently finding that their resources were getting underutilised according to the plan, it started to drill 8 metres more than the plan every day. Therefore, a day before the planned date they had drilled to a depth of 280 metres. How many metres of drilling was the plan for each day.

(a) 38 metres (b) 30 metres
(c) 27 metres (d) 28 metres

55. A pipe can fill a tank in a hours and another can empty it in b hours. If the tank is $1/4^{th}$ full initially, then the number of hours in which they will together fill in the tank

(a) $\frac{3ab}{5(b-a)}$ (b) $\frac{3ab}{4(b-a)}$

(c) $\frac{4ab}{3(b-a)}$ (d) $\frac{4ab}{3(b-a)}$

56. Three students Alok, Baman and Charu were working on a project. Alok is 25% more efficient than Baman, who is 20% more efficient than Charu. Alok takes 10 days less than Baman to complete the project. Alok starts the project and works for 10 days and then Baman takes over. Baman works on the project for the next 14 days and then stops the work, handing it over to Charu to complete it. In how many days, would Charu complete the remaining project?

57. A finishes 6/7th of the work in 2z hours, B works twice as fast and finishes the remaining work. For how long did B work?

(a) $\left(\frac{2}{3}\right)z$ (b) $\left(\frac{6}{7}\right)z$

(c) $\left(\frac{6}{49}\right)z$ (d) $\left(\frac{3}{18}\right)z$

Directions for Questions 58 to 62: Read the following and answer the questions that follow.

A set of 10 pipes (set X) can fill 70% of a tank in 7 minutes. Another set of 5 pipes (set Y) fills 3/8 of the tank in 3 minutes. A third set of 8 pipes (set Z) can empty 5/10 of the tank in 10 minutes.

58. How many minutes will it take to fill the tank if all the 23 pipes are opened at the same time?

(a) 5 minutes (b) $5\frac{5}{7}$ minutes

(c) 6 minutes (d) $6\frac{5}{7}$ minutes

59. If only half the pipes of set X are closed and only half the pipes of set Y are open and all other pipes are open, how long will it take to fill 49% of the tank?

(a) 16 minutes (b) 13 minutes

(c) 7 minutes (d) None of these

60. If 4 pipes are closed in set Z, and all others remain open, how long will it take to fill the tank?

(a) 5 minutes (b) 6 minutes

(c) 7 minutes (d) 7.5 minutes

61. If the tank is half full and set X and set Y are closed, how many minutes will it take for set Z to empty the tank if alternate taps of set Z are closed.

(a) 12 minutes (b) 20 minutes

(c) 40 minutes (d) 16 minutes

62. If one pipe is added for set X and set Y and set Z's capacity is increased by 20% on its original value and all the taps are opened at 2.58 p.m., then at what time does the tank get filled? (If it is initially empty.)

(a) 3.05 p.m. (b) 3.04 p.m.

(c) 3.10 p.m. (d) 3.03 p.m.

63. Aman can do as much work in 12 days as Balbir can do in 24 days and Balbir can do as much in 4 days as Dilbeer in 5 days. A piece of work takes 10 days if all work together. How long would Balbir take to do all the work by himself?

(a) 38 days (b) 24 days

(c) 36 days (d) 40 days

64. The Bubna dam has four inlets. Through the first three inlets, the dam can be filled in 12 minutes; through the second, the third and the fourth inlet, it can be filled in 15 minutes; and through the first and the fourth inlet, in 20 minutes. How much time will it take all the four inets to fill up the dam?

(a) 8 min (b) 10 min

(c) 12 min (d) None of these

65. A tank holds 100 gallons of water. Its inlet is 7 inches in diametre and fills the tank at 5 gallons/min. The outlet of the tank is twice the diameter of the inlet. How many minutes will it take to empty the tank if the inlet is shut off, when the tank is full and the outlet is opened? (*Hint:* Rate of filling or emptying is directly proportional to the diameter)

(a) 7.14 min (b) 10.0 min

(c) 0.7 min (d) 5.0 min

66. A tank of 3600 cu m capacity is being filled with water. The delivery of the pump discharging the tank is 20% more than the delivery of the pump filling the same tank. As a result, twelve minutes more time is needed to fill the tank than to discharge it. Determine the delivery of the pump discharging the tank.

(a) 40 m^3/min (b) 50 m^3/min

(c) 60 m^3/min (d) 80 m^3/min

67. X takes 3 days to complete 50% of a job, Y takes 1 day to complete 1/4th of the same work and Z takes 2 days to complete 66.67% of the job. If all of them work together for 1 day and X and Z quit, how long will it take for Y to complete the remaining work done?

(a) 0.5 days (b) 1.25 days

(c) 5/3 days (d) 1 day

68. A completes 2/3 of a certain job in 6 days. B can complete 1/3 of the same job in 8 days and C can complete 3/4 of the work in 12 days. All of them work together for 4 days and then A and C quit. How long will it take for B to complete the remaining work alone?

(a) 3.8 days (b) 3.33 days

(c) 2.22 days (d) 4.3 days

69. Two forest officials in their respective divisions were involved in the harvesting of *tendu* leaves. One division had an average output of 21 tons from a hectare and the other division, which had 12 hectares of land less, dedicated to *tendu* leaves, got 25 tons of *tendu* from a hectare. As a result, the second division harvested 300 tons of *tendu* leaves more than the first. How many tons of *tendu* leaves did the first division harvest?

(a) 3150 (b) 3450

(c) 3500 (d) 3600

70. A, B and C working together completed a job in 10 days. However, C only worked for the first three days when 37/100 of the job was done. Also, the work done by A in 5 days is equal to the work done by B in 4 days. How many days would be required by the fastest worker to complete the entire work?

(a) 20 days (b) 25 days
(c) 30 days (d) 40 days

71. Dev and Tukku can do a piece of work in 45 and 40 days respectively. They began the work together, but Dev leaves after some days and Tukku finished the remaining work in 23 days. After how many days did Dev leave

(a) 7 days (b) 8 days
(c) 9 days (d) 11 days

72. Two persons can do a typing job in 7.5 minutes if they work together. If the first person typed alone for nine minutes and then the second person typed alone for five minutes, they would do 3/4 of the whole work. How many minutes would it take the first person to complete the job working alone?

(a) 30 minutes (b) 48 minutes
(c) 36 minutes (d) 40 minutes

73. Two men and a woman are entrusted with a task. The second man needs three hours more to cope with the job than the first man and the woman would need working together. The first man, working alone, would need as much time as the second man and the woman working together. The first man, working alone, would spend eight hours less than the double period of time the second man would spend working alone. How much time would the two men and the woman need to complete the task if they all worked together?

(a) 2 hours (b) 3 hours
(c) 4 hours (d) 5 hours

74. It takes ten days for four men and three women working together to complete a work. Two men would do the same work twenty-five days sooner than three women. How many times does the output of a man exceed that of a woman?

(a) 3 times (b) 4 times
(c) 5 times (d) 6 times

75. Each of A, B and C need a certain unique time to do a certain work. C needs 1 hour less than A to complete the work. Working together, they require 30 minutes to complete 50% of the job. The work also gets completed if A and B start working together and A leaves after 1 hour and B works for a further 3 hours. How much work does C do per hour?

(a) 16.66% (b) 33.33%
(c) 50% (d) 66.66%

76. Two women Renu and Ushi are working on an embroidery design. If Ushi worked alone, she would need eight hours more to complete the design than if they both worked together. Now if Renu worked alone, she would need 4.5 hours more to complete the design than they both working together. What time would it take Renu alone to complete the design?

(a) 10.5 hours (b) 12.5 hours
(c) 14.5 hours (d) 18.5 hours

77. A and B are quiz masters preparing for a quiz. In five hours, A makes 30 questions more than B. If both of them make two questions less per hour each, then in ten hours they would make 140 questions overall. How many questions does A make in five hours?

(a) 60 (b) 30
(c) 45 (d) 50

78. A tank of capacity 1000 litres has an inlet and an outlet tap. If both are opened simultaneously, the tank is filled in 25 minutes. But if the outlet flow rate is tripled and taps opened the tank never gets filled up while it also never gets emptied. Which of the following can be outlet flow rate in litres/min?

(a) 20 (b) 60
(c) 10 (d) 30

79. Two pipes A and B can fill up a half full tank in 1.2 hours. The tank was initially empty. Pipe B was kept open for half the time required by pipe A to fill the tank by itself. Then, pipe A was kept open for as much time as was required by pipe B to fill up 1/3 of the tank by itself. It was then found that the tank was 5/6 full. The least time in which any of the pipes can fill the tank fully is

(a) 4.8 hours (b) 4 hours
(c) 3.6 hours (d) 6 hours

80. A tank of 425 litres capacity has been filled with water through two pipes, the first pipe having been opened five hours longer than the second. If the first pipe were open as long as the second, and the second pipe was open as long as the first pipe was open, then the first pipe would deliver half the amount of water delivered by the second pipe; if the two pipes were open simultaneously, the tank would be filled up in 17 hours. How long was the second pipe open?

(a) 10 hours (b) 12 hours
(c) 15 hours (d) 18 hours

81. Three cooks have to make 80 idlis. They are known to make 20 pieces every minute working together. The first cook began working alone and made 20 pieces having worked for sometime more than three minutes. The remaining part of the work was done by the second and the third cook working together. It took a total of 8 minutes to complete the 80 idlis. How many minutes would it take the first cook alone to cook 160 idlis for a marriage party the next day?

(a) 16 minutes (b) 24 minutes
(c) 32 minutes (d) 40 minutes

82. Two pipes can fill a cistern in 12 and 18 hours respectively. The pipes are opened simultaneously and it is found that due to leakage in the bottom of the cistern, it takes 48 minutes extra for the cistern to be filled up. When the cistern is full, in what time will the leak empty it?

(a) 110 hours (b) 72 hours
(c) 90 hours (d) 80 hours

Directions for Questions 83 and 84:
Dipen Loomba builds an overhead tank in his house, which has three taps attached to it. While the first tap can fill the tank in 12 hours, the second one takes one and a half times the first one to fill it completely. A third tap is attached to the tank, which empties it in 36 hours. Now, one day, in order to fill the tank, Dipen opens the first tap and after an hour opens the second tap as well. However, at the end of the fourth hour, he realises that the third tap has been kept open right from the beginning and promptly closes it.

83. What is the ratio of volume occupied by water to volume of remaining part of the tank after 6 hours?

84. What will be the total time required to fill the tank (in minutes)?

Directions for Questions 85 and 86:

85. In the ancient city of Portheus, the emperor has installed an overhead tank that is filled by two pumps — X and Y. X can fill the tank in 12 hours while Y can fill the tank in 15 hours. There is a pipe Z which can empty the tank in 10 hours. Both the pumps are opened simultaneously. The supervisor of the tank, before going out on a work, asks his assistant to open Z when the tank is exactly 40% filled so that tank is exactly filled up by the time he is back. If he starts X and Y at exactly 11:00 AM and he comes back at A:B. Then find the value of A + B.

86. Due to a miscalculation by the assistant, he opens Z when the tank is one fourth filled. If the supervisor comes back as per the plan what percent of the tank is still empty?

87. Ashu and Ben completed a work together in ten days. Had Ashu worked at 2/3 of his speed and Ben at 1.5 times of his speed, it would have taken them ten days to complete the job. How much time would it take for Ashu alone to do the work, if he works at his normal pace?

(a) 30 days (b) 20 days
(c) 25 days (d) 50/3days

Directions for Questions 88 and 89:
Three water pipes, A, B and C are all used to full a container. These pipes can fill the container individually in 6 minutes, 12 minutes and 18 minutes, respectively. All the three pipes were opened simultaneously. However, it was observed that pipes A and B were supplying water at $2/3^{rd}$ of their normal rates for the first minute after which they supplied water at the normal rate. Pipe C supplied water at half of its normal rate for first 3 minutes, after which it supplied water at its normal rate. Now answer the following questions:

88. What fraction of the tank is empty after 2 minutes?

89. In how much time (in minutes and to the closest second), would the container be filled?

90. A project is to be completed in 60 days and 90 men are set to work, each working 6 hours a day. After 20 days, only $1/5^{th}$ of the work is finished. How many additional men need to be employed so that the work may be completed on time. (If each man is now working 8 hours per day)?

91. *A*, *B* and *C* can complete a work in 6, 8 and 12 hours, respectively. At the most, only one person can work in each hour and nobody can work for two consecutive hours. Find the minimum number of hours that they will take to finish the work.

92. The rate at which tap *X* fills a tank is 50% more than that of tap *Y*. If both the taps are opened simultaneously, they take 40 hours to fill the tank. The time taken by *Y* alone to fill the tank is (in hours)

High Yield Questions

Scan this QR code to access assisted problem solving videos on questions 1, 2, 8, 10 and 44 from LOD 2

Space for Rough Work

ANSWER KEY

Level of Difficulty (I)

1. (b)	2. $\frac{1}{4}^{th}$	3. 45 hours	4. ₹900
5. 7 days	6. 4 dogs	7. 4 weeks	
8. $23\frac{1}{7}$ day	9. 4	10. (b)	
11. (c)	12. (c)	13. (b)	14. (b)
15. (d)	16. (a)	17. (a)	18. (d)
19. (a)	20. (d)	21. (b)	22. (b)
23. (b)	24. (b)	25. (a)	26. (d)
27. (b)	28. (b)	29. (a)	30. (c)
31. (c)	32. (c)	33. (d)	34. (c)
35. (d)	36. (b)	37. (c)	38. (c)
39. (a)	40. (a)	41. (d)	42. 9
43. (d)	44. (c)	45. (b)	46. (d)
47. (c)	48. 40	49. (b)	50. 50

Level of Difficulty (II)

1. (b)	2. (b)	3. (b)	
4. ₹30000	5. (a)	6. (c)	7. (c)
8. (d)	9. 28	10. 20	11. 28
12. 30	13. 24	14. (d)	15. 28
16. 3.5	17. 16000	18. (c)	19. 12
20. 90%	21. 5.9	22. 48	23. 49
24. 5 days	25. 16.57 hours		
26. 9.5 days	27. (c)	28. (d)	29. 6 PM
30. (a)	31. (b)	32. (c)	33. (b)
34. 37.5	35. 27 days	36. 5:24 PM	
37. 32 hours	38. 20 days	39. (c)	
40. 50 days	41. 10%	42. 7.2 days	
43. 4.33 hours		44. 126	45. 80
46. 6	47. 48	48. (c)	49. (d)
50. (a)	51. (c)	52. 5 days	53. (a)
54. (b)	55. (b)	56. 28.20	57. (d)
58. (b)	59. (d)	60. (a)	61. (b)
62. (d)	63. (a)	64. (b)	65. (b)
66. (c)	67. (d)	68. (b)	69. (a)
70. (a)	71. (c)	72. (b)	73. (a)
74. (c)	75. (c)	76. (a)	77. (a)
78. (a)	79. (b)	80. (c)	81. (c)
82. (b)	83. 2 : 1	84. 504	85. 41
86. 10	87. (d)	88. 19/36	
89. 3 minutes 49 seconds		90. 45	91. 6.75
92. 100			

SOLUTIONS AND SHORTCUTS

Level of Difficulty (I)

1. If Aruna does the work in 5 days, A would take 10 days, B would take 20 and C would take 40 days. Let the total work be 40 units. Work rates are 8, 4, 2 and 1. It can be seen that if we pair Aruna and C, their total work would be 1.5 times the work of A and B. If the work is 1.5 times i.e. $\frac{3}{2}$ times, then the time required would be $\frac{2}{3}^{rd}$ as stated in the question. Hence, option (b) is correct.
2. Let the work of the large pump be 4 units, then the work of the smaller pumps are 3 units each. The total work of the 4 small pumps and 1 large pump together would be $1 \times 4 + 4 \times 3 = 16$ units. If only the large pump is working, then the work done would only be 4 units in the same time. Thus, the large pump does $\frac{1}{4}^{th}$ of the work all pumps together would do.
3. Let the capacity of the tank be 60 liters. Efficiency of the inlet pipe $= \frac{60}{10} = 6$ l/hr.

   Efficiency of the outlet + inlet $= \frac{60}{12} = 5$ l/hr

   Efficiency of the outlet pipe $= -1$ l/hr.

   Thus, to empty $\frac{3}{4}^{th}$ of the tank, it requires to empty 45 liters, which will take it 45 hours
4. Let the total work be 24 units. A's work rate = 2 units per day, B's work rate = 3 units per day while together the work rate of A,B and C $= \frac{24}{4} = 6$ units per day. Thus, C's work per day $= 6 - 2 - 3 = 1$ unit per day. The fraction of work C would do would be $\frac{1}{6}^{th}$ of the total. Hence, C should be paid $\frac{5400}{6} =$ ₹900.
5. Let the total work be 24 units. Partha = 2 units per day; Sunil = 1 unit per day. Also, Varun has done 25% of the work. Hence, he would have done 6 units of the work. Partha works alone for the first 3 days to complete 6 units of work. The remaining 12 units of work Partha and Sunil would do in a further $\frac{12}{3}$ = 4 days. Thus, the total time required is 7 days.
6. $22D + 16C = 24D + 15C \rightarrow 1C = 2D$. Since 2 cats can finish the job in 13 days, it means that the total work is equal to 26 cat days = 52 dog days. Hence, the number of dogs required to finish the job in 13 days $= \frac{52}{13} = 4$ dogs.
7. Let the total work be 108 units. Work rates would be A = 18, V = 12 and Y = 9. In first two weeks, before Aditya leaves, work done $= 39 \times 2 = 78$. Work done in the last week by Yuvraj alone = 9. Hence, the work done when only Vedus and Yuvraj are working is 21 units – which will take just 1 week for them. Thus, the total work would take $2 + 1 + 1 = 4$ weeks.

8. Let the total work be 900 units. Their work rates would be: 20, 15 and 12 units per day respectively. Ashok has worked for 10 days, hence he would have done 120 units of work. Also, Amir completes the work on the last 2 days by working alone – in those days he would have done 40 units of work. The remaining 740 units of work would be done by Amir and Abdullah, together. They would take: $\frac{740}{35} = 21\frac{1}{7}$ days. Thus, the total number of days required would be $21\frac{1}{7} + 2 = 23\frac{1}{7}$ days.
9. The work is equal to 150 man-days and is also equal to 300 woman-days. This means that 1 man-day = 2 woman-days. 8 men and 4 women are effectively equal to 10 men. The work done in 9 days would be 90 man-days of work. Work left would be equal to 60 man-days. 10 more women joining after nine days, means that effectively we have 5 new men joining – giving us 15 men working. They will do the remaining 60 man-days of work in 4 more days.
10. Let the work rates of the three be N, 1.32 N and 1.98 N. The total work would be 50 × N, which would get done by B and C, in $\frac{50N}{3.3N} = 15.15$ days. Option (b) is correct.
11. He will complete the work in 20 days. Hence, he will complete ten times the work in 200 days.
12. 6 men for 12 days means 72 mandays. This would be equal to 4 men for 18 days.
13. *A*'s one day work will be 5%, while *B* will do 6.66 % of the work in one day. Hence, their total work will be 11.66% in a day.

    In 8 days they will complete → 11.66 × 8 = 93.33% This will leave 6.66% of the work. This will correspond to 4/7 of the ninth day since in 6.66/11.66 both the numerator and the denominator are divisible by 1.66.
14. Total work = LCM of 10,15 and 20 = 60 Units. Raman does 6 units per day, Rahul does 4 units per day while Charan does 3 units of work per day. Total work together per day = 6 + 4 + 3 = 13 units of work. Total time required = $\frac{60}{13} = 4.62$ days.
15. Let the total work be 16. *A* and *B*'s one day work would be 16/8 = 2 units of work. *B*'s 1 day work would be 16/16 = 1 unit per day. Thus, *A* would do (2 – 1 = 1 unit of work) per day. He would take 16/1 = 16 days.
16. The ratio of the wages will be the inverse of the ratio of the number of days required by each to do the work. Hence, the correct answer will be 3:2 → ₹30
17. 24 man days + 18 women days = 20 man days + 28 woman days

    → 4 man days = 10 woman days.

    → 1 man day = 2.5 woman days

    Total work = 24 man days + 18 woman days = 60 woman days + 18 woman days = 78 woman days.

    Hence, 1 man + 1 woman = 3.5 women can do it in 78/3.5 = 156/7 = 22(2/7) days.
18. The data is insufficient, since we only know that the work gets completed in 200 boy days and 300 women days.
19. A = 10%, B = 5% and Combined work is 20%. Hence, *C*'s work is 5% and will require 20 days.
20. In 5 days, Ashok would do 50% of the work. Since, Saheb finishes the remaining 50% work in 10 days, Saheb would complete the 100% work in 20 days. Hence, option (d) is correct.
21. Let the total work be 20 units. Efficiency of Ashok = 20/10 = 2 units. Efficiency of Saheb = 20/20 = 1 unit per day.

    Hence, the required time = 20/(2 + 1) = 6.66 days. Hence, option (b) is correct.
22. Let the total work be 20 units. Efficiency of A = 2 units per day.

    Efficiency of B = 1 unit per day

    Combined efficiency of A, B and C = 20/5 = 4 units.

    Efficiency of C = 4 – (1 + 2) = 1 unit per day.

    Hence, the required answer = $1000 \times \frac{1}{1+2+1} = ₹250$.
23. Let the time taken by Arun be 't' days. Then, time taken by Vinay = $2t$ days.

    $1/t + 1/2t = 1/7 \rightarrow t = 10.5$
24. Subhash can copy 200 pages in 40 hours (reaction to the first sentence). Hence, Prakash can copy 100 pages in 40 hours. Thus, he can copy 30 pages in 30% of the time, i.e., 12 hours.
25. $10x = (x + 5)5$

    $10x = 5x + 25$ or $x = 5$
26. After 100 days and 4500 man days, only 1/6th of the work has been completed. You can use the product change algorithm of PCG to solve this question. 100 × 45 = 16.66% of the work. After this you have 200 days (i.e., 100% increase in the time available) while the product 200 × number of men should correspond to five times times the original product.

    $$100 \xrightarrow[+100]{\text{TIME}\ 100\%\ \text{increase}} 200 \xrightarrow[+300\ \text{required}]{?} 500$$

    This will be got by increasing the no. of men by 150% (300/200).
27. $A + M = 8.33$, $M + B = 6.66$ and $A = 2B \rightarrow$ *A*'s 1 days work = 3.33%, *M*'s = 5% and *B*'s = 1.66%. Thus, Mohan would require 100/5 = 20 days to complete the work if he works alone.

28. Sambhu requires 16 days to do the work while Kalu requires 18 days to do the work.

$(1/16 + 1/18) \times n = 1$

$\rightarrow n = 288/34 = 144/17$

29. *A*'s rate of working is 10 per cent per day while *B*'s rate of working is 5 per cent per day. In 5 days they will complete 75 per cent work. Thus the last 25 per cent would be done by *B* alone. Working at the rate of 5 per cent per day, *B* would do the work in 5 days.

30. The rate of filling will be 20% and the net rate of filling (including the leak) is 16.66%. Hence, the leak accounts for 3.33% per hour, i.e., it will take 30 hours to empty the tank.

31. Since the ratio of money given to Apurva and Amit is 2:3, their work done would also be in the same ratio. Thus, their time ratio would be 3:2 (inverse of 2:3). So, if Apurva takes 12 days, Amit would take 8 days and the total number of days required (t) would be given by the equation:

$(1/12 + 1/8)t = 1 \rightarrow t = 24/5 = 4.8$ days

32. $(A + B)$'s work = C's work.

Also if A takes 'a' days

B would take '$a - 5$' days

and C would take '$a - 9$' days.

Solving through options, option '*c*' fits.

A (15 days) $\rightarrow$ A's work = 6.66%

B (10 days) $\rightarrow$ B's work = 10%

C (6 days) $\rightarrow$ C's work = 16.66%

33. $40n = 30\ (n + 5) \rightarrow n = 15$

34. Since the net work of the three taps is 10% and the first and second do 20% + 10% = 30%. Hence, the third pipe must be a waste pipe emptying at the rate of 20% per hour. Hence, the waste pipe will take a total of 5 hours to empty the tank.

35.
$$A + V + S = 1 \quad (1)$$
$$A + V = 19/23$$
$$V + S = 8/23$$
$$\rightarrow A + 2V + S = 27/23 \quad (2)$$

(2)–(1) gives us: $V = 4/23$.

36. Work equivalence method:

$30 \times 5 \times 16 = 20 \times 6 \times n$

Gives the value of n as 20 days

37. $(A + B) = 2C$.

Also, $(A + C) = 3B$

$36(A + B + C) = 1$

Solving for C, we get:

$36\ (2C + C) = 1 \rightarrow 108C = 1$

$C = 1/108$

Hence, C takes 108 days.

38. Total work = 15 × 210 = 3150 mandays.

After 100 days, work done = 15 × 100 = 1500 mandays.

Work left = 3150 – 1500 = 1650 mandays.

This work has to be done with 30 men working each day.

The number of days (more) required = 1650/30 = 55 days.

39. Let Anjay take $3t$ days, Vijay take $2t$ days and Manoj take $6t$ days in order to complete the work. Then we get:

$1/3t + 1/2t + 1/6t = 1 \rightarrow t = 1$. Thus, Manoj would take $6t$ = 6 days to complete the work.

40. Interpret the starting statement as: Anmol takes 30 days and Vinay takes 90 days. Hence, the answer will be got by:

$(1/30 + 1/90) \times n = 1$

Alternatively, you can also solve using percentages as: 3.33 + 1.11 = 4.44% is the daily work. Hence, the no. of days required is 100/4.44 = 22.5 days.

41. After 27 days, food left = 4 × 200 = 800 soldier days worth of food. Since, now there are only 80 soldiers, this food would last for 800/80 = 10 days. Number of extra days for which the food lasts = 10 – 4 = 6 days.

42. If they take 'x' more days to complete the work then:

$36 \times 18 - (36 \times 8) = (36 + 4)x$

By solving we get x = 9 days

43. $A + B + C$ = 19%. In the first two hours they will do 38 % of the work. Further, for the next two hours work will be done at the rate of 15% per hour. Hence, after 4 hours 68% of the work will be completed, when tap B is also closed. The last 32% of the work will be done by A alone. Hence, A does 40% (first 4 days) + 32% = 72% of the work.

44. Raju = 10%, Vicky = 8.33% and Tinku = 6.66%. Hence, total work for a day if all three work = 25%.

In 2 days they will complete, 50% work. On the third day onwards Raju doesn't work. The rate of work will become 15%. Also, since Vicky leaves 3 days before the actual completion of the work, Tinku works alone for the last 3 days (and must have done the last 6.66 × 3 = 20% work alone). This would mean that Vicky leaves after 80% work is done. Thus, Vicky and Tinku must be doing 30% work together over two days.

Hence, total time required = 2 days (all three) + 2 days (Vicky and Tinku) + 3 days (Tinku alone)

45. $A + V$ = 16.66% and A = 10% $\rightarrow$ V = 6.66%. Consequently, Vijay would require 100/6.66 = 15 days to do it alone.

46. Sashi = 4%, Rishi = 5%. In five days, they do a total of 45% work. Rishi will finish the remaining 55% work in 11 more days.

47. $A + B$ = 16.66%. From here solve this one using the options. Option (c) fits the situation as it gives us A's

work = 10%, *B*'s work = 6.66% as also that *B* takes 5 minutes more than *A* (as stipulated in the problem).

48. If there were 'x' men originally then according to the question :
$x \times 60 = (x + 8)(60 - 10)$
$60x = 50x + 400$
$x = 40$
49. $24 \times 8 \times 10 = N \times 10 \times 6 \rightarrow N = 32$
50. $8m + 4w = 3500$ (1)
$5m + 3w = 2275$ (2)
By solving equations 1 and 2 we get :
m = ₹350/week or ₹50/day.

Level of Difficulty (II)

1. Let the efficiency of Anshuman, Shaurya and Pallav be A, S and P respectively and number of days worked by Anshuman be x. So according to question, A + S + P = 8 and A ≥ 5. The value of A cannot exceed 6 as S, P ≥ 1. It is given that, $Ax + (8 - A)(20 - x) = 80$. At A = 6, we get a negative value of x which is not possible. Hence, A = 5 & hence, x = 10. Hence, Option (b) is the correct answer.
2. Since time taken is inversely proportional to efficiency, so if efficiency of Sanjeeta is 8 units, then efficiency of Fatima, Kavita and Ritika will be 4, 2 and 1 respectively. So the combined efficiency of the 4 people will be 15. Since the time taken by one pair is 50% less than the time taken by other pair, the efficiency has to be more than or equal to twice the combined efficiency of the second pair. This means that the efficiency of the first pair has to be at 2/3rd of the total efficiency. Hence, the required efficiency has to be equal to or more than 10 units.
Option (a): 8 + 1 = 9
Option (b): 8 + 2 = 10 – correct answer.
Option (c): 2 + 4 = 6
Hence, option (b) is correct.
3. Let efficiency Aman, Baman and Chaman be A, B and C respectively. According to the question, $\frac{1}{A} = \frac{x}{(B+C)}$; $\frac{1}{B} = \frac{x}{(A+C)}$; $\frac{1}{C} = \frac{x}{(A+B)}$, which means $A = \frac{(B+C)}{x}$; $B = \frac{(A+C)}{x}$ & $C = \frac{(A+B)}{x}$
$A+B+C = \frac{2(A+B+C)}{x} \rightarrow x = 2.$
Hence, Option (b) is the correct answer.
4. Let the total work done be 144 units. So efficiency of A = 3, B = 2
So according to question, $60 + 48 + C = 144 \rightarrow C = 36$. The total work done by A, B and C is in the ratio 5 : 4 : 3. Hence, the amount will also be distributed in this ratio. So if Chakshak gets 18000 for the his part of work, Akshak will get 30000. Hence, ₹30000 is the correct answer.
5. Let efficiency of B = 1, So A = 2. Now it is given that Total Work = 40C. Since A,B and C already completed 1/5th of the total work before C quit, the remaining work will be 4/5th of the total work and this is equal to 32C. So, 90 + 12C = 32C → 20C = 90 → C = 4.5. So total work = 180. Hence, the required answer is 90.
6. Let the capacity of the tank be 100 units. So efficiency of tap A = 5 and B = 4.
Let the time for which both taps are opened together be x. So $9x + 5(14 - x) = 100 \rightarrow x = 7.5$. Hence, Option (c) is the correct answer.
7. It is given that 5S = 2C → S : C = 2 : 5. Now, 10 × (20C + 40S) = 480 → 20C + 40S = 48. 36C = 48 → C = 4/3, S = 8/15. So, the required value is 12 × (40C + 50S). So, putting the values of C and S, we get our value as 960. Hence, Option (c) is the correct answer.
8. Let the work done per unit time for Pallav and Shaurya be 5 and 4 units respectively. Let Pallav work for x days. Since Shaurya started the job and ended it as well, he would work 1 day more than Pallav. So total work done would be $5x + 4(x + 1)$. It is given that they took 1 day more than Pallav to complete the work. So $9x + 4$ should be a multiple of 5. We see that this is only possible at $x = 4$. At $x = 4$ only we also have a difference of 1 day. So total work done would be 40 units. So, the required answer is $\frac{40}{9} = 4\frac{4}{9}$. Hence, option (d) is the correct answer.
9. Let the total work done be 60 units. Efficiency of C, M and D is 6, 4 and –5 respectively. In the first 6 hours, total work done would be 10 units. In the next 18 hours, work done be 30 units. So total work done in 24 hrs is 40 units. C and M would complete 20 units in the next 4 hours. Hence, the wall would be built before Danaerys gets a chance to destroy the wall. Hence, the work gets completed in 24 + 4 = 28 hours. Hence, the correct answer is 28.
10. Let the efficiency of Sanjeeta be 2. So the total work done will be 60 units. In the first 6 days, total 12 units of work will be done. In the next 3 days 0 units of work will be done. That leaves us with 48 units to be done in the next 12 days. This means that 4 units will be done everyday. Since Sanjeeta will be contributing only 1 unit daily because of reduced efficiency, Sumika will contribute 3 units. This means that she can complete the whole task in 60/3 = 20 days. Hence, the correct answer is 20.
11. Let each pipe contribute 1 liter per hour. So, the total number of pairs for 25 pipes is $^{25}C_2 = 300$. A total of 300 × 2 = 600 liters of water would get filled in this time. Since, Amartya had to open all the pipes for an additional 4 hours, they would have contributed 100L more. So the total amount of water

in the tank is 300 + 100 = 700L. So, all 25 pipes when opened together will take 700/25 = 28 hours. 28 is the correct answer.

12. Since the radius of one pipe is three times more = 4 times the other, its efficiency will be 16 times the other pipe. So, if Efficiency of smaller pipe is 1 unit, then larger pipe will have 16 units. So total efficiency will be 17 units. Hence, the required time will be 510/17 = 30 minutes. Correct answer: 30.
13. Since an extra 20 days were required for 10 more floors, this means that 1 floor will be done in 2 days. This means that in 12 days, 6 floors were constructed. So a total of 16 floors were constructed. This means that the BMC destroyed 8 floors. So out of the 20 floors to be constructed, 12 were still left. This means that the team will require another 24 days to complete the task. The correct answer is 24.
14. Let 60 Units be the total work to be done. So efficiency of P = 15, Q = 12 and R = 4.
Work done in first 2 hrs = 15 + 6 + 8 = 29
Work done in next 2 hrs = 30 + 6 + 8 = 44. Since the total exceeds our total work to be done, lets look at only 1 hr. So, 15 + 3 + 4 = 22. Total work done in 3 hrs = 51. Since they contribute 22 units in 1 hour, So 9/22 of the fourth hour will be required. This is close to 25 mins. Hence, Option (d) is the correct answer.
15. Let total work done be 60 units. Hence, efficiencies of Cersei, Jamie and Tyrion are 3, 2 and 1 units respectively. Work done in x hours would be $6x$. Work in next y hours would be $3y$. Let Tyrion work alone for z hours, so work done in that period would be z. So, total work done would be $6x + 3y + z$. According to the information given in the question, Total work would be $6x + 3(y + 6)$. For the second situation, total work done would be $6(x + 6)$. From the first part, $6x + 3y + z = 6x + 3(y + 6) \rightarrow z = 18$. From the second part we get, $6x + 3y + 18 = 6(x + 6) \rightarrow y = 6$. It is given that $60 = 6 \times (x + 6) \rightarrow x = 4$. So total time taken to complete the work is $x + y + z = 4 + 6 + 18 = 28$ hours. The correct answer is 28.
16. Total work done = 12 units
Efficiency of A = –1, B = 2, C = 2
Since A will only start when half the work is done, 6 units will be completed by B and C in 1.5 hours. After that the net efficiency will be 3 units. The remaining 6 units will take 2 more hours to complete. Hence, a total of 3.5 hours. The correct answer is 3.5.
17. Let the Total work done = 120 units.
Efficiency of A = 5, B = 3
Since they complete the work in 10 days, daily efficiency should be 12. This means that Kamla contributed 4 units daily. So, contributions by Amla, Bimla and Kamla are 50, 30 and 40. Hence, the amount will be divided in the ratio 5 : 3 : 4. So the amount received by Kamla will be 16000.The correct answer is 16000.
18. Since R can do 60% of a job in 15 days, he can complete the whole work in 25 days. Let the total work done be 100 units. Efficiency of R = 4, So efficiency of Q = 5. Since they worked together for eight days, total 72 units of work was done. This means that P completed remaining 28 units in 7 days, which means that the efficiency of P is 4. So, P is 20% less than that of Q. Hence, Option (c) is the correct answer.
19. Let the efficiency of the robot on the first day be 1. The total work to be done is 58 × 141 = 8178 units.
Work done on the first day = 1
Work done on the Second day = 1 + 2 = 3
Work done on the Third day = 1 + 2 + 4 = 7
Work done on the Fourth day = 1 + 2 + 4 + 8 = 15
The series thus formed is 1 + 3 + 7 + 15 + 31….
This has to add up to 8178. We see that n^{th} term is $2^n - 1$. So the sum of the series is $2^{(n+1)} - (2 + n) = 8178 \rightarrow 2^{(n+1)} - n = 8180$. We see that the closest power of 2 to 8180 is 8192 at $n = 12$. So on the 12th day the work would get completed. The correct answer is 12.
20. Let us assume the time taken by both the pipes to fill the tank as 30 minutes. So, A would fill it in 33.33% more time i.e. 40 mins.
We know that $1/A + 1/B = 1/(A + B) \rightarrow 1/B = 1/30 - 1/40 \rightarrow B = 120$ mins. Let total work done be 120 units. So, efficiency of A = 3 units and B = 1. According to the given situation, the time worked for is $t/5$ minutes, which will be 6 minutes as per our assumption. Net efficiency is 3 – 1 = 2 units (since pipe B is being used as a drain pipe). So, work done in 6 mins is 12 units. Hence, in $t/5$ mins, 10% of the tank is filled. So, 90% of the tank would remain empty. The correct answer is 90%.
21. Let the work done for one wooden chair be 60 units. So efficiency of Shri = 5 → Hari = 6 → Ram = 7.5 → Chandra = 2.5. Since all efficiencies are in units per hour, in 15 mins they'll do 21/4 = 5.25. In the next 4 hours, 4 × 10 = 40 units of work will be done. So we have a total of 45.25 units of work done. Remaining 14.75 will be done by Chandra. So he took 14.75/2.5 = 5.9 hours working alone. The correct answer is 5.9.
22. 30 workers working for 30 days will do 900 units of work. These 30 workers worked for additional 8 days. So a total of 1140 units of work. Additionally, 1 worker joined everyday for 8 days. So extra work done in these 8 days would be 1 + 2 + 3 + 4… + 8 = 36. So total units of work to be done is 1176. Now since, everyday 1 worker would quit from first day,

the total work done would be equal to $n(n + 1)/2$ = 1176. We achieve this at n = 48. Hence, it would take 48 workers on first day to complete the work in the given manner, and the work pattern would be 48 workers on first day, 47 workers on second day and so on till we have 1 worker on the 48th day. Hence, the work gets completed in 48 days. The correct answer is 48.

23. Since the time taken by buffalo and goat is in the ratio 3 : 5, their efficiency would be in the ratio 5 : 3. For cow and buffalo, this ratio would be 5 : 8. The combined ratio for buffalo, goat and cow would be 40 : 24 : 25. It is given that the total work done would be 89 × 49. Hence, the required answer would be $\frac{89 \times 49}{(40+24+25)}$ = 49. The correct answer is 49.

24. Let total work to be done be 60 units. Hence, Efficiency of T = 5, M = 4 and R = x
Work done in 2 days = 2 × 9 = 18. Work left = 42 units.
Work done the next day = 6 + x
Work done by R alone = $2x$. So according to the situation, $6 + x + 2x = 42 \rightarrow x = 12$. Hence, the required answer is 60/12 = 5 days.

25. Let Pipes be A, B and C. It is given that time taken by A = 18 hours, B = 2.5 × 18 = 45 hours and C = 36 hours. Let the total work done be 180 units. So efficiency of A = 10, B = 4 and C = –5.
Work done in first 3 hours = 30.
Next 5 hours = 5 × 14 = 70.
Since the 3rd pipe was open since the start, work done by this pipe would be –40. Hence, total work done in first 8 hours = 70 + 30 – 40 = 60 units. Remaining work would be done in 120/14 = 8.57 hours. Hence, total time taken is 16.57 hours is the correct answer.

26. Let the total work to build the wall be 16 units. Hence, the worker's efficiency would be 1 unit. Since he cannot drink on 3 consecutive days, every third day his efficiency would be 1 unit and on rest days it'll be 2 units. So in 3 days we get total work of 5 units, In this way 15 units of work will get completed in 9 days. On the 10th day, his work rate will be double (2 units) but he has to do only 1 unit of work. Hence, he will take half the 10th day. The correct answer is 9.5 days.

27. Let the total work done be 60 units. So efficiency of A = –6, B = –2, C = 3 and D = 4. When Pipe A is opened, Work done in 2 hours = –12. Work done in next 1 hour = –8. Work done between 6 and 7 = –5. Work to be done is 60 – 25 = 35. Work done per hour after 7 pm = –1. So the tank will get empty in the next 35 hours which is Wednesday 6 am. Hence, Option (c) is the correct answer.

28. The best approach to solve such questions is through options. If we check with option (d) 50 minutes, we get that Arun would take 200 minutes, Sherry would take 200 minutes and Mini would take 100 minutes to do the same work. If we take the total work to be 1000, then Arun's work in 1 minute would be 5, Sherry's would also be 5 and Mini's work would be 10. Their work working together would be 20, which would mean that the complete work would get completed in 50 minutes. This is a complete circle, that matches the requirements of the question. Hence, Option (d) is correct.

29. The total work is 10 × 7 = 70 manhours. From 10 AM to 3 PM, the work done would be 8 × 5 = 40 manhours. From 3 to 4, 9 manhours would get done. From 4 to 5, 10 manhours would get done, while from 5 to 6 11 manhours would get done. Thus, 50 + 9 + 10 + 11 = 70 and the job would get completed at 6 PM.

30. The third and fourth options do not match the production constraints on machine *B*. Option (a) gives a profit of 75 × 200 + 80 × 300 = 39000, while option (b) gives a profit of 100 × 200 + 60 × 30 = 38000. Hence, option (a) is correct.

31. You can work out the net inflow/outflow of each tank as follows:
A: Total outflow = 30, Total inflow = 90. Thus, net inflow is 60 liters per minute.
B: Net inflow = 30 liters per minute.
C: Net outflow = 40 liters per minute.
D: Net outflow = 50 liters per minute
Thus, D would empty first in 32 minutes. Option (b) is correct.

32. The shoes factory will take 7 minutes to produce 1400 units and then be cleaned for 5 minutes – thus a total block of 12 minutes. It would take 10 such blocks of 12 minutes each to produce 14000 shoes. In the next block of 12 minutes, it would produce 1000 more units in 5 minutes more. Thus, 15000 shoes would get produced in 120 + 5 = 125 minutes. On the laces machine, we have, 1500 laces produced in every block of 10 + 10 = 20 minutes. It would produce 13500 laces, in 180 minutes (9 blocks of 20 minutes each) and then take an additional 10 minutes more to produce the last 1500 laces. Thus, total time taken is 190 minutes. The difference in times is 65 minutes. Option (c) is correct.

33. If you solve using options, Option (b) seems attractive to check first – since 13 men shifting 13 crates each would give us 169 crates shifted. This would lead to a pattern of: First day: 1 man, 23 crates; Second day: 7 men, 18 crates each = 126 crates; third day 169 crates; 4th day: 19 men, 8 crates each = 152 crates; Fifth day: 25 men, 3 crates each = 75 crates. In 5 days total crates shifted = 23 + 126 + 169 + 152 + 75 = 545 crates. Also, the condition of the number of crates going down in the latter part of the time period is true in this case. Hence, option (b) is correct.

34. Equation 1: (10M + 45W) × 30 = (8M + 18W) × 60 → 10M + 45W = 16M + 36W. → 1M = 1.5W. Also, the total work = (10M + 45W) × 30 = (15W + 45W) × 30 = 1800 Women days. 20 Men and 18 women = 30 Women + 18 Women = 48 women working together. They will take $\frac{1800}{48}$ = 37.5 days to complete the work.

35. Assume M and C as 1 days' work for Murali and Conti. The total task left after 14 days of working together would be 18M + 18C (18 days' work for each). This work is also equal to: 20C + 20 × 0.7 × M. Thus, we have: 18M + 18C = 20C + 14 M → 2C = 4M → M = $\frac{C}{2}$. Total work left after 14 days = 18M + 18C = 9C + 18C = 27C. Thus, Conti will take 27 days to complete the task.

36. From the information of 27th, 28th and 29th March, you can infer (a) Kishan takes 2 hours more than Shatrughan to complete the job. (b) 3 hours of Kishan's work is equal to 2 hours of Shatrughan's work (since on 29th March when Kishan leaves at 6 PM, the work that would be left would be 3 hours of work at Kishan's pace & Shatrughan is able to finish that work in 2 hours). Thus, we can infer that their rates of working are 3 : 2 (Shatrughan to Kishan). Thus, their time taken for the same work would be in the ratio of 2 : 3. Since, Kishan takes 2 hours extra, it means that they take 4 and 6 hours respectively to do the work. So, the fixed time of starting would be 3 PM. If we assume total work as 12 units, then Shatrughan would do 3 units of work per hour and Kishan's work rate would be 2 units per hour. Together they would take $\frac{12}{5} = 2.4$ hours to complete the work. Thus, starting at 3 PM, they would finish the work at 5 : 24 PM.

37. (15M + 5W) × 30 = (5M + 15W) × 60 → 15M + 5W = 10M + 30W → 1M = 5W. Also, the total work = (15M + 5W) × 30 = 16M × 30 Hours = 480 Man hours. 15 Men would complete it in $\frac{480}{15} = 32$ hours.

38. 15A + 15B = 4A + 48B → 11A = 33B → A = 3B. Total work = 15A + 15B = 15A + 5A = 20A. Thus, A alone would do the work in 20 days.

39. Let Hurshi take t hours, then Rishi would take $t + 8$ and Sherry would take $t + 18$ hours.
We have from the first statement that:
$\frac{1}{t} = \frac{1}{t+8} + \frac{1}{t+18} \rightarrow t = 12$

40. Assume a rabbit does 1 unit of work a day and a deer does 2 units of work a day. The work pattern is: 1 + 3 + 6 + 10 + 15 +... 210 + 231 + 253 + 276 units of work on the 23 days. The total work is 2300 units of work. 23 deer working together would do 46 units of work every day. Hence, they would require $\frac{2300}{46} = 50$ days to complete the work.

41. Let the tank capacity be 48 units. The two inlet pipes would fill $2\left(\frac{48}{24} = 2\right)$ and $3\left(\frac{48}{16} = 3\right)$ units per hour, while the outlet pipe would empty the tank at the rate of 2 units per hour $\left(\frac{48}{24} = 2\right)$. Work rates when only the inlet pipes are open = 5 units per hour. Work rates when all pipes are open = 3 units per hour.
According to the original plan, we have: 75% of the tank = 36 units need to be filled before the outlet pipe is opened. The remaining 12 units will get filled at the rate of 3 units per hour in 4 hours. This means that Ayesha has gone out for $\left(\frac{36}{5}\right) + 4 = 11.2$ hours.
However, since the outlet pipe gets opened when only half the tank was full, it means that the outlet pipe was opened at $\frac{24}{5} = 4.8$ hours, when 24 units of the tank's capacity was completed. The remaining 11.2 – 4.8 = 6.4 hours, the tank would be filled at a net rate of 3 units per hour – thus filling 19.2 units more. Thus, total water in the tank, when Ayesha comes back = 24 + 19.2 = 43.2. Tank capacity empty = 48 – 43.2 = 4.8 = 10% of the tank.

42. From the second statement we see that the work efficiency of Dr. Singh: Dr. Sharma: Dr. Gupta would be 1 : 1.2 : 1.68 = 10 : 12 : 16.8 = 50 : 60 : 84. Now, since we are given that Gupta takes 10 days less than Sharma to complete the work – we need to find out the work quantum. This is where LCM thinking sets in: The LCM of 60 and 84 would be 840. If the work amount was 840, Sharma would take 14 days $\left(\frac{840}{60}\right)$ and Gupta would take 10 days $\left(\frac{840}{84}\right)$ – a difference of only 4 days. But since the difference in time is 10 days, the work quantum needs to be multiplied by 2.5 to get total work = 840 × 2.5 = 2100. Thus, when Gupta works for 10 days and Sharma works for 15 days, the total work done would be: 84 × 10 + 60 × 15 = 1740. The work left would be 2100 – 1740 = 360, which would need to be done by Singh. Since, Singh works at the rate of 50 units per day, he would require $\frac{360}{50}$ = 7.2 days.

43. Assume that the total tank capacity is 96 units. Then, the work rates of each are: A = 12 units per hour, B = 8 units per hour, C = 6 units per hour and D = 4 units per hour. Work done per hour can be seen as: First two hours $2\times\left[\frac{3}{5}\times(12+8)+\frac{2}{5}(6+4)\right] = 32$.

Third hour = $\left[20+\frac{2}{5}(6+4)\right]$ = 24. This would leave 40 units to be filled, and the rate of filling from the 4th hour onwards would be 30 units per hour. Additional time required = $\frac{40}{30}$ = 1.33 hours. Total time required = 2 + 1 + 1.33 = 4.33 hours.

44. The total work in Azmatpur, can be defined as 18 × 7.5 × 60 = 8100 manhours and 24 × 7.5 × 60 = 10800 boy-hours.
Since 1 manhour = 2 boy hours, we know that the total work in Azmatpur is $8100+\frac{10800}{2}$ = 13500 manhours.
Thus, In Biddupur, the total work would be 13500 × 3 = 40500 manhours. 27 men working 9 hours a day for 50 hours, will give us a total of 12150 manhours work done. The remaining work of 40500 – 12150 = 28350 manhours = 28350 × 2 = 56700 boy-hours has to be done by the boys. In 50 days, working 9 hours per day, the number of boys required would be: $\frac{56700}{450}=126$.

45. Using the work equivalence approach, we see that 120 men working 8 hours a day for 40 days give us a total work output of 120 × 8 × 40 = 38400 Manhours of work. This is only $\frac{2}{5}^{th}$ of the work. Hence, the remaining work would be 38400 × 1.5 = 57600 manhours. This has to be done in 32 days, with each man working 9 hours a day. If we take the total number of men as M, we get: M × 32 × 9 = 57600 → M =200. Since, 120 people are already working on the project, we need an additional 80 people to work.

46. Let the tank capacity be 35 units. The inlet pipe would be filling the tank at 5 units per hour, while the outlet pipe empties the tank at 7 units per hour. Since the filled tank is emptied in 7 hours, it means that the per hour emptying rate is effectively $\frac{35}{7}$ = 5. If we use 6 inlet pipes and 5 outlet pipes, the net effect will be an emptying rate of 5 units per hour. Hence, the answer is 6.

47. If you assume the number of chapatis for each as K, S and R respectively as per their names, then we have K + S + R = 156 and K × 4 = S × 6 = R × 8. Solving this system of equations, we get:
K = 72, S = 48 and R = 36. Hence, the correct answer is 48.

48. Since the question tells us that the juice taken out of the apples is equal to the juice taken out by using 1 orange less than the number of apples, we should be able to see two scenarios here:
Case 1: Number of apples = 2 and number of oranges = 4.
In this case, the juice taken out of 2 apples = juice of 1 orange. Let us say that the quantity of juice in an apple is x, then the quantity of juice in 1 orange is $2x$. So, if he uses the same number of apples and oranges, he would get: Total juice = juice from 2 apples + juice from two oranges = $2x + 4x = 6x$. The percentage of apple juice in this blend would be: 33.33%.
Case 2: Number of apples bought = 3 and number of oranges bought = 3.
In this case, the juice taken out of 3 apples = juice of 2 oranges. Let us say that the quantity of juice in an apple is x, then the quantity of juice in 1 orange is $1.5x$. So, if he uses the same number of apples and oranges, he would get:
Total juice = juice from 3 apples + juice from 3 oranges = $3x + 4.5x = 7.5x$. The percentage of apple juice in this blend would be: 40%. The value of 33.33% from Case I is the only possible value given in the options. Hence, option (c) is the correct answer.

49. Let the capacity of the tank be 24 liters.
Efficiency of inlet pipe = $\frac{24}{8}$ = 3
Efficiency of outlet pipe = $\frac{24}{12}$ = 2. Since, the tank gets filled in 6 hours if all pipes are open, it follows that the net work per hour must be $\frac{24}{6}$ = 4 units/hour. With M = 4 and N = 4, we get the requisite match for this situation. However, this can also be achieved using M = 2 and N = 1. Hence, the correct answer would be option (d).

50. Let the total capacity of the tank be 60 liters. Efficiencies of pipes A, B, C and D are $\frac{60}{3},\frac{60}{10},\frac{60}{12},\frac{60}{15}$ or 20, 6, 5, 4 per minute respectively.
As tank would be half-filled after 6 minutes. So, the combined efficiencies of all pipes must be +5 per minute. Going by the options, we see that option a satisfies the given condition as 20 – (6 + 5 + 4) = 5. Hence, option (a) is correct.

51. Let the capacity of the inverted cone be 120 liters. The filling and emptying rates for A, B, C respectively would be $\frac{120}{8}$ = 15, $\frac{120}{12}$ = 10 and $\frac{120}{4}$ = 30 liters per hour. Also, the interpretation of the height of the water inside the cone coming down to 50%, is that the volume of the water in the tank would come down to $\frac{1}{8}^{th}$ of its original volume. This means, that

only 15 liters of water are left after the three pipes are opened i.e. 105 liters of water should be drained out.

Using a trial and error with the options, we see that if we open pipes A and C for 20 hours each and B for 19.5 hours, we see that the volume of water drained would be $20 \times 30 - 20 \times 15 - 19.5 \times 10 = 600 - 300 - 195 = 105$ liters drained. Hence, option (c) is correct.

52. Let Arun's work rate be x units per day. Amitabh's work rate would be $3x$ units per day. Also, Amitabh and Aruna's work rate, working together would be $4x$, which means that Aruna's work rate is also x. Also, the total work rate of the three of them would be $5x$. Since, Arun takes 4 days extra to do this work, we have: $\frac{W}{x} - \frac{W}{5x} = 4 \rightarrow W = 5x$. Hence, Aruna would take $\frac{5x}{x} = 5$ days to complete the job, if she is working alone.

53. The per day digging of all three combined is 54 metres. Hence, their average should be 18. This means that the first should be $18 - x$, the second, 18 & the third $18 + x$.

The required conditions are met if we take the values as 15, 18 and 21 metres for the first, second and third diggers, respectively. Hence, (a) is the correct answer.

54. Let n be the number of metres planned per day. Start from the options to find the number of planned days. In the options the 2 feasible values are 30 metres and 27 metres (as these divide 270). Suppose we check for 30 metres per day, the work would have got completed in 9 days as per the original plan. In the new scenario:

$3n + 5(n + 8) = 280 \rightarrow n = 30$ too. Hence, this option is correct.

Note that if we tried with 27 metres per day the final equation would not match as we would get:

$3n + 5(n + 8) = 280 \rightarrow$ which does not give us the value of n as 27 and hence this option is rejected.

55. Time required to fill the tank $= \frac{3/4}{\frac{1}{a} - \frac{1}{b}} = \frac{3ab}{4(b-a)}$

56. Let the efficiency of Charu be 100. Baman's efficiency = 120, Alok's efficieny = 150

Let Baman takes 't' days to finish the job. Alok will take 't – 10' days to finish the work.

$120 \times t = 150 \times (t - 10)$

On solving, we get: $t = 50$.

Hence, total work = $120 \times 50 = 6000$

Work done by Alok in 10 days = 1500 units

Work done by Baman in 14 days = 1680 unit

Remaining work = 6000 – 1500 – 1680 = 2820 units.

Charu will finish the remaining work in 2820/100 = 28.20 days.

57. Since A finishes $6/7^{th}$ of the work in $2z$ hours .

B would finish 12/7 of the work in $2z$ hours.

Thus, to do $1/7^{th}$ of the work (which represents the remaining work), B would require $2z/12 = z/6$ hours. Option (d) is correct.

Solutions for Questions 58 to 62:

Set X can fill 10% in a minute. Hence, every Pipe of set X can do 1% work per minute. Set Y has a filling capacity of 12.5% per minute (or 2.5% per minute for each tap in set Y). Set Z has a capacity of emptying the tank at the rate of 5% per minute and each tap of set Z can empty at the rate of 0.625% per minute.

58. If all the 23 pipes are opened the per minute rate will be:

$10 + 12.5 - 5 = 17.5\% \rightarrow$ Option (b) is correct.

59. Set X will do 5 % per minute and Set Y will do 6.25% per minute, while set Z will do 5% per minute (negative work). Hence, Net work will be 6.25% per minute. To fill 49% it will take slightly less than eight minutes and the value will be a fraction. None of the first three options matches this requirement. Hence, the answer will be option (d).

60. If 4 of the taps of set Z are closed, the net work done by Set Z would be –2.5% while the work done by Sets X and Y would remain 10% and 12.5% respectively. Thus, the total work per minute would be 20% and hence the tank would take 5 minutes to fill up.

61. Again if we close 4 taps of set Z, the rate of emptying by set Z would be 2.5% per minute. A half filled tank would contain 50% of the capacity and hence would take 50/2.5 = 20 minutes to empty.

62. The rate per minute with the given changes (in percentage terms) would be:

Set X =11%, Set Y = 15% and Set Z = –6%.

Hence, the net rate = 11 + 15 – 6 = 20% per minute and it would take 5 minutes for the tank to fill. If all pipes are opened at 7:58, the tank would get filled at 3:03.

63. Let the efficiency of Dilbeer = 100 units per day. In five days, Dilbeer would do 500 units of work. Balbir takes four days to do the same work. Hence, the efficiency of Balbir = 500/4 = 125 units per day. Also, efficiency of Aman is twice the efficiency of Balbir = $125 \times 2 = 250$.

Total work = $10 \times (100 + 125 + 250) = 4750$ units of work.

Time taken by Balbir to do all the work himself = 4750/125 = 38 days. Hence, option (a) is correct.

64. Let the inlets be A, B, C and D.

$$A+B+C=8.33\%$$
$$B+C+D=6.66\%$$
$$A+D=5\%$$

Thus, $2A+2B+2C+2D=20\%$

and $A+B+C+D=10\%$

→ 10 minutes would be required to fill the tank completely.

65. The outlet pipe will empty the tank at a rate which is double the rate of filling (Hence, 10 gallons per minute). If the inlet is shut off, the tank will get emptied of 100 gallons of water in ten minutes.

66. Use options for this question as follows:

If discharging delivery is 40, filling delivery will be 16.66% less (this will give a decimal value right at the start and is unlikely to be the answer. Hence, put this option aside for the time being.)

Option (c) gives good values. If discharging delivery is 60, filling delivery will be 50. Also, time taken for discharge of 3600 cu m will be 60 minutes and the time taken for delivery will be 72 minutes (12 minutes more — which is the basic condition of the problem).

67. X completes the task in six days. Y takes four days to complete the task, Z takes three days to complete the task. Let the total work be 12 units. Then, their respective efficiencies are: $X = 2$ units per day; $Y = 3$ units per day and $Z = 4$ units per day. In one day, they would do 9 units of work (2 + 3 + 4). The remaining work would be 3 units. Y, at his rate of working would take one day to complete the work.

68. A takes 9 days to complete the work

B takes 24 days to complete the work

C takes 16 days to complete the work

In 4 days, work done by all three would be:

$4 \times (1/9 + 1/24 + 1/16)$

$$= 4 \times \frac{(16+6+9)}{144} = 124/144$$

$$= 31/36 \text{ of the work.}$$

Work left for B would be 5/36 of the work.

B would require: $(5/36) \times 24 = 3.33$ days.

69. $25(n - 12) = 21n + 300$. Solving this equation, $n = 150$. Hence, the first division harvest 3150 tons.

70. The equations are:

$$3(A+B+C) = 37/100 = 37\% \text{ of the work.}$$
$$7(A+B) = 63/10 \rightarrow A+B = 9/100 = 9\%$$

(Where A, B and C are 1 day's work of the three respectively).

Further, $5A = 4B$ gives us

$A = 4\%$ and $B = 5\%$ work per day.

In 3 days $(A + B + C)$ do 37% of the work.

Out of this A and B would do 27% (= 3 × 9%) of the work. So, C would do 3.33% of the work per day.

$$\frac{37-27}{3}$$

Thus, B is the fastest and he would require 20 days to complete the work.

71. $n(1/45 + 1/40) + 23/40 = 1 \rightarrow n = 9$.

72. Let the efficiency of first person be 'x' pages per minute and the efficiency of the second person be 'y' pages per minute.

$7.5 \times (x + y) =$ Total work

$9x + 5y = \frac{3}{4} \times 7.5 \times (x+y) \rightarrow 13.5 \times x = 2.5 \times y \rightarrow$

$y = 5.4 \times x$

Total work $= 7.5 \times (x + y) = 7.5 \times (x + 5.4x) = 7.5 \times 6.4x = 48x$. At x pages per minute, the first person can do the entire project of typing in $48x/x = 48$ minutes.

73. In order to solve this question, if we look at the first statement, we could think of the following scenarios:

If the time taken by the first man and the woman is 1 hour (100% work per hour) , the time taken by the second man would be 4 hours (25% work per hour). In such a case, the total time taken by all three to complete the task would be 100/125 = 0.8 hours. But this value is not there in the options. Hence, we reject this set of values.

If the time taken by the first man and the woman is 2 hours (50% work per hour) , the time taken by the second man would be 5 hours (20% work per hour). In such a case, the total time taken by all three to complete the task would be 100/70 = 10/7 hours. But this value is not there in the options. Hence, we reject this set of values.

If the time taken by the first man and the woman is 3 hours (33.33% work per hour), the time taken by the second man would be 6 hours (16.66% work per hour). In such a case, the total time taken by all three to complete the task would be 100/50 = 2 hours. Since this value is there in the options we should try to see whether this set of values meets the other conditions in the question.

In this case, it is given that the first man working alone takes as much time as the second man and the woman. Since, the work of all three is 50%, this means that the work of the first man is 25%. Consequently the work of the woman is 8.33%.

Looking at the third condition given in the problem – the time taken by the first man to do the work alone (@ 25% per hour he would take 4 hours) should be 8 hours less than double the time taken by the second man. This condition can be seen to be fulfilled here because the second man would take 6 hours to complete his work (@ 16.66% per hour) and hence, double his time would be 12 hours— which satisfies the difference of 8 hours.

Thus, the total time taken is 2 hours.

74. Let the efficiencies of one man and one woman be 'm' and 'w'.
Total work = $10 \times (4m + 3w)$
Let two men take 't' days. Then, we have $2 \times m \times t = 3w \times (t + 25) = 10 \times (4m + 3w)$
Now solve using options: If we try option (b), then we get that for $m = 3w$ for which the above equation is true. Hence, option (b) is correct.

75. $0.5(A + B + C)$ = 50% of the work.
Means → A, B and C can do the full work in 1 hour.
Thus, $(A + B + C) = 100\%$

From this point it is better to solve through options. Option (c) gives the correct answer based on the following thought process.

If c = 50% work per hour, it means C takes 2 hours to complete the work.

Consequently, A would take 3 hours and hence do 33.33% work per hour.

Since, $A + B + C = 100\%$, this gives us B's hourly work rate = 16.66%.

For this option to be correct these nos. should match the second instance and the information given there.

According to the second condition:
$A + 4B$ should be equal to 100%. Putting $A = 33.33\%$ and $B = 16.66\%$ we see that the condition is satisfied. Hence, this option is correct.

76. Option (a) is correct because: $1/10.5 + 1/14 = 1/6$ which matches all the conditions of the problem.

77. Let A make 'x' questions per hour and B make 'y' questions per hour. Then, according to the question: $5x - 5y = 30$ or $x - y = 6$. From the second condition in the question, we have that:
$10 \times (x - 2) + 10 \times (y - 2) = 140$ (1)
On solving the above two equations we get: $x = 12$ and $y = 6$ questions per hour.
A makes a total of $5 \times 12 = 60$ questions in 5 hours.

78. If the outlet flow rate is tripled and taps opened the tank never gets filled up or emptied: it means that if we triple the outlet flow rate, it would be equal to the inlet flow rate. Thus, the outlet tap flow rate is 1/3 of the inlet flow rate.
By checking the options, we get that for outlet flow rate 20 litres per minute and inlet flow rate of 60 litres per minute, the tank of 1000 litres capacity will be filled within 25 minutes.

79. The interpretation of the first statement is that A and B do 41.66 percent of the work per hour. From this point if we go through the options, option (b) fits the situation as 4 hours means 25 percent work. Consequently this means 16.66 percent for the other pipe and these conditions meet all the requirements.

80. From the last statement we know that since both the pipes would require 17 hours to fill the tank together, they would discharge $425/17 = 25$ litres per hour together.

From this point try to fit the values from the options in order to see which one satisfies all the conditions.
In the case of option (a): Second pipe open for 10 hours, first pipe open for 15 hours.
When the interchange occurs: Second pipe open for 15 hours, first pipe open for 10 hours → gives us that the respective rates of the two pipes would be 3:4 (as the first pipe delivers half the amount of the second pipe— if it delivers 3 litres per minute the second pipe would need to deliver 4 litres per minute).
Thus, if the delivery of the first pipe is $3n$ litres per minute, the delivery of the second pipe would be $4n$ litres per minute. Then, in 10 hours of the second pipe and 15 hours of the first pipe, the total water would be $85n$, which should be equal to the total water of the two pipes in 17 hours each. But in 17 hours each, the two pipes would discharge $17 \times 7n = 119n$. Thus, we reject this option.
In the case of option (c): Second pipe open for 15 hours, first pipe open for 20 hours.
When the interchange occurs: Second pipe open for 20 hours, first pipe open for 15 hours → gives us that the respective rates of the two pipes would be 2:3 (as the first pipe delivers half the amount of the second pipe- if it delivers 2 litre per minute the second pipe would need to deliver 3 litres per minute).
Thus, if the delivery of the first pipe is $2n$ litres per minute, the delivery of the second pipe would be 3n litres per minute. Then, in 15 hours of the second pipe and 20 hours of the first pipe, the total water would be $85n$, which should be equal to the total water of the two pipes in 17 hours each. In 17 hours each, the two pipes would discharge $17 \times 5n = 85n$. Thus, we realize that this is the correct option.

81. From the condition of the problem and a little bit of trial and error we can see that the first cook worked for 4 minutes and the 2nd and 3rd cooks also worked for 4 minutes. As $4(A) + 4(B + C) = 4(A + B + C)$ and we know that $A + B + C = 20$ idlis per minute.

Thus, the first cook make 20 idlis in 4 minutes. To make 160 idlis he would take 32 minutes.

82. Let the total work by equal to 72 units. The pipes do 6 and 4 units of work per hour respectively. Thus, the pipes would do 10 units of work per hour and should complete the work in 7.2 hours or 7 hours 12 minutes. However, due to the leak the time taken is 8 hours. In 8 hours, the pipes would fill $10 \times 8 = 80$ units and therefore the leak would take out 8 units. Thus, the leak is operating at 1 unit leakage per hour. It will take 72 hours to empty a full tank.

83. Short cut Solution: The best way to think in this situation is to assume the tank to have a capacity of 36 litres (LCM of 12,18 and 36). In such a case, the first tap would be filling the tank at the rate of 3 litres per hour, the second one would be filling at the rate of 2 litres per hour while the third one would be emptying the tank at the rate of 1 litre per hour. In 6 hours, the total quantity of water in the tank would be 6 × 3 + 5 × 2 – 4 × 1 = 24. Hence, the ratio of volume occupied by water to the volume that is not occupied by water is 24 : 12 = 2 : 1.

84. Based on the previous solution, we have seen that after 6 hours 24 litres of the tank are filled. To fill the remaining 12 litres, when both the inlet taps are open, we would need 12 ÷ 5 = 2.4 hours = 2 hours 24 minutes. Thus, it would take a total of 6 hours + 2 hours 24 minutes to fill the tank, i.e., 8 hours 24 minutes = 504 minutes.

85. Let the total capacity of the tank be 180 litres:
Efficiency of X = 15 l/hr.
Efficiency of Y = 12 l/hr.
Efficiency of Z = –18 l/hr.
Time taken to fill the tank to 40% of it's capacity (i.e., 72 litres) = 72/27 = 2 hours 40 minutes.
After 2 hours 40 minutes, Z starts working.
The rate at which the tank would be filled after this would be: 15 + 12 – 18 = 9 litres per hour.
The total quantity to be filled in order to fill up the tank = 180 – 72 = 108 litres.
This will take 108/9=12 hours to complete. Hence, the supervisor comes back after: 12 hours + 2 hours 40 minutes = 14 hours 40 minutes.
Hence, he is supposed to come back at: 1:40 AM (the next day).
The value of A + B = 41.

86. Z opens when the tank is filled with 45 litres of water. This means that Z opened after 45/27 = 1 hour 40 minutes. In the next 13 hours, 13 × 9 = 117 litres of water will get added to the tank. Thus, 10% of the tank would be empty when the supervisor comes back.

87. Let the efficiencies of Ashu and Ben be *A* and *B* respectively.
As there is no change in time taken to finish the job after changing the efficiencies, so: It means that when Ashu starts working slower (at 2/3 of his normal rate), the reduction in his output over ten days, is compensated by Ben working faster (at 1.5 times his normal rate). This means that:

$$\frac{A}{3} = 0.5 \times B \rightarrow B = \frac{2A}{3}$$

(**Note:** When Ashu works at 2/3rd of his rate, it means that he does 1/3rd work less than his normal rate, while when Ben works at 1.5 times his rate, he would be doing half his original work as extra work.)

Total work = 10(A + B) OR $10 \times (A + \frac{2A}{3}) = 50A/3$

Total time taken by Ashu to finish the work alone = (50A/3)/A = 50/3 days

88. Let the total capacity of the container be 108 litres. The pipes A,B and C would respectively fill the container at the rates of 18 litre per minute, 9 litres per hour and 6 litres per hour. Thus, in the first two minutes, the container would get 12 + 6 + 3 + 18 + 9 + 3 = 51 litres of water. The fraction of the tank that would be empty would be 57/108 = 19/36.

89. To fill the remaining 57 litres of the container, in the third minute: Rate of filling =18 + 9 + 3 = 30 litres. This means that at the start of the fourth minute, the container would have 27 litres unfilled. The rate of filling in the fourth minute would be 18 + 9 + 6 = 33 litres. Thus, 27/33 or 9/11 of the 4th minute would be used. Thus, the container gets filled in 3(9/11) minutes = 3 minutes 49 seconds.

90. Using the work equivalence method, we know that $1/5^{th}$ of the work = 20 × 90 × 6 man hours.
Thus, the remaining work = 4 × 20 × 90 × 6. Since, this work has to be done in the remaining 40 days by working at 8 hours per day, the number of men required would be given by: (4 × 20× 90 × 6) ÷ (40 × 8) = 135 men. This means that we would need to hire 45 additional men.

91. Let the total work be 24, therefore efficiencies of *A*, *B*, *C* are 4, 3 and 2; respectively. To complete the work in minimum time, the most efficient should start the work. So, *A* will start the work and *B* will follow him.
After two hours, total work done = 4 + 3 = 7 units.
After six hours, total work done = 3 × 7 = 21 units.
Remaining work = 24 – 21 = 3 units.
A will complete the remaining work in 3/4 hours.
Total time required to finish the work = 6 + 3/4 = 6.75 hours.

92. Let the efficiency of tap *Y* be '*a*', then the efficiency of tap *X* must be '1.5*a*'.
Capacity of the tank = 40 (*a* + 1.5*a*) = 100*a*
Time taken by tap Y to fill the tank = 100*a*/*a* = 100 hours.

CHAPTER 10

Time, Speed and Distance

Chapter Launchpad

Scan this QR code to access a video on 'Introduction to Time, Speed and Distance' and this chapter's importance for CAT

INTRODUCTION

The chapter of Time, Speed and Distance (TSD) is amongst the most important for the purpose of the quantitative aptitude section in aptitude exams. This chapter can be divided into two parts – Time, Speed and Distance & Applications of Time, Speed and Distance (comprising of questions from various situational-based problem types that include: boats and streams; clocks, races and games of skill, trains, circular motion, etc.). Besides, the basic concepts of TSD are used in solving questions based on motion in a straight line, relative motion and circular motion. In this book we have taken the approach of splitting the contents of this chapter into: Chapter 10: Time, Speed and Distance, Chapter 11: Applications of Time, Speed and Distance

Due to this diversity in the possibilities for question setting, this chapter is very important for CAT aspirants. Besides, all other exams based on aptitude - XAT, NMAT, SNAP, CMAT, MAHCET, CMAT and Banking, Clerical/ SSC, UPSC, CSAT and all other aptitude examinations regularly ask questions on Time, Speed and Distance.

Rarely do you come across a year, when questions from this chapter are missing in any of these exams. Hence, my advice to all students using this book to prepare for any of these aptitude exams including CAT - closely understand the concepts contained in this chapter to be comfortable with the problems related to this topic in the examination.

THEORY OF TSD

Concept of Motion and Mathematical Representation of Motion

Motion/movement occurs when a body of any shape or size changes its position with respect to any external stationary point. Thus, when a person travels from city A to city B, we say that he has moved from city A to city B. In general, whenever a body moves with respect to a stationary point, we say that the body has undergone a displacement/motion with respect to the starting point. Thus, for motion to have occurred there must have been some displacement with respect to a stationary point on the ground.

The mathematical model that describes motion has three variables, namely: Speed, Time and Distance. The interrelationship between these three is also the formula on which this whole chapter hinges, namely:

1. Speed × Time = Distance (equation for the description of one motion of one body). Of course, this equation has three forms, namely:
2. Distance/Time = Speed and
3. Distance/Speed = Time.

In the equations above, *speed* can be defined as the rate at which distance is covered during the motion. It is measured in terms of *distance* per unit time and may have any combination of units of distance and time in the numerator and the denominator respectively (m/s, km/hour, m/min, km/min, km/day, etc.).

When we say that the speed of a body is S km/h, we mean to say that the body moves with S km/h towards or away from a stationary point (as the case may be).

Time (t) is the time duration over which the movement/ motion occurs/has occurred. The unit used for measuring time is synchronous with the denominator of the unit used for measuring speed. Thus, if the speed is measured in terms of km/h, then time is measured in hours.

Distance (d) is the displacement of the body during the motion.

The need for maintaining consistency in the units used: The most common units used for speed are km/h or meters /second. The most common units used for measuring time are hours or seconds, while the most common units used for measuring distance are kilometers and meters. One of the basic things that you need to get correct while using this formula is to use units for the three variables such that they are in sync with each other. Thus, if speed is measured in km/h then time should be in hours and distance in kilometers.

Likewise, if the speed is measured in meters/second, then naturally we should use distance in meters and time in seconds. These conversions need to be done, in questions where non-synced units are provided for the three variables. So, for instance, in some cases speed might be provided in km/h, while time and distance might be provided in seconds and meters. In such cases, one has to convert km/h to meters/second.

The following rules apply for these conversions:
Conversion from km/h to m/s → Use a multiplying factor of 5/18. For instance, 18 km/h = $18\times\frac{5}{18}$ = 5 m/s

Conversion from m/s to km/h → Multiply by 18/5. Thus, 10 m/s = $10 \times \frac{18}{5}$ = 36 km/h.

Conversion between meters and kilometers → 1 meter = 1/1000 kilometers, 1 kilometer = 1000 meters

Conversion between seconds and hours → 1 hour = 3600 seconds, 1 second = 1/3600 hours

Converting minutes to hours: The normal process to convert a number in minutes to hours is to use a multiplier of 1/60. Thus, 1 minute = 1/60 hours; 2 minutes = 2/60 hours and so on. This conversion also has an interesting decimal implication. Consider the following:

1 minute = 0.01666 hours, 2 minutes = 0.03333 hours, 3 minutes = 0.05 hours, 4 minutes = 0.0666 hours, 5 minutes = 0.08333 hours, 6 minutes = 0.1 hours. 7 minutes = 0.11666 hours, 8 minutes = 0.1333 hours and so on. The student is advised to master these decimal values so that he/she has enabled two-way conversions in the mind. Thus, 47 minutes = 42 + 5 = 0.7 + 0.0833 hours = 0.78333 hours. Conversely, 0.7833 hours would be converted to minutes as follows: 0.7 hours = 7 × 6 = 42 minutes + 0.0833 hours = 5 minutes.

Hence, 0.7833 hours = 42 + 5 = 47 minutes.

Basic Uses of the Time, Speed and Distance Equation: The first three reactions that you should organise in your mind, with respect to this chapter are the reactions that involve being given two of these in order to help finding the third. Thus, these three reactions play out as follows:

1. 'A car travels at 100 km/h for 3 hours: Reaction: $S \times t$ = distance → 100 × 3 = 300 km/s
2. A man travels from Delhi to Jaipur a distance of 250 km in 5 hours: Reaction: Distance/time = Speed → 250/5 = 50 km/h.
3. A bus covers a distance of 200 km from Mumbai to Pune at a speed of 40 km/h: Reaction: Distance/Speed = time → 200/40 = 5 hours.

The above relationships are the mathematical descriptions of the movement of a body and as can be seen, are essentially the relationships between the three variables. This is the only formula on which the whole chapter of time, speed and distance, as well as the applications of this chapter hinge. Yet, in spite of the whole chapter being dependent on only one formula, some of the toughest and most complex questions in Arithmetic come from this chapter! This would be contrary to what one would expect from a chapter with only one formula. So, how are these complications created? A little bit of analysis will show you that an individual time-speed-distance question is normally a mix of multiple motions- and the formula needs to be applied multiple times in order to solve an individual question. This is one of the main reasons that I see students struggling with solving questions based on time, speed and distance.

Hence, one of your first focuses of trying to get a grip of this chapter has to be centred on improving your ability to identify the number of motions that are happening and described in an individual question. The moment, you improve that ability, your ability to create equations and hence solve them to solve complex questions in time, speed and distance would improve drastically.

Proportionalities Implicit in the Time-Speed-Distance Equation

The above equation has three implicit proportionality dimensions each of which has its own critical bearing on the solving of time, speed and distance problems.

1. Direct proportionality between time and distance (when the speed is constant); time ∝ distance:

Note: Speed is constant here means that – between two motions described either explicitly or implicitly in the problem, the speed should be the same.

Illustration

A car moves for two hours at a speed of 25 km/h and another car moves for three hours at the same speed. Find the ratio of distances covered by the two cars.

Solution: Since, the speed is constant, we can directly conclude that time ∝ distance.

Hence, $\frac{t_A}{t_B} = \frac{d_A}{d_B}$

Since, the times of travel are two and three hours, respectively, the ratio of distances covered is also 2/3.

Note: This proportionality is basic common sense. However, if you were to work on questions of this chapter, you would find that this is the least important of the three proportionalities in this chapter. The other two proportionalities are much more important, hence let's take a look at those now.

2. Direct proportionality between speed and distance (when the time is constant); speed ∝ distance:

Note: This proportionality is one of the important proportionalities of this chapter and is usable when the time of travel in two motions is the same. The same time of travel can be indicated to you through multiple ways – both explicit and implicit. Consider the following cases, where you should be able to sport time constancy and hence, be able to use this proportionality.

Explicit ways in which time constancy is communicated:

(a) *A body travels at S_1 km/h for the first two hours and then travels at S_2 km/h for the next two hours.* Here two motions of one body are being described and between these two motions, the time is constant hence, speed will be proportional to the distance travelled.

(b) *A car travels for half the time @ 30 km/h and the other half of the time @ 50 km/h.* (Here, since time is divided into two halves, you should be able to identify that there are two journeys described here, whose times are constant).

Implicit Ways of Communicating Time Constancy

(a) *Two cars start simultaneously from A and B respectively towards each other with speeds of S_1 km/h and S_2 km/h. They meet at a point C.* You should be able to see that in this situation, even though they have not explicitly mentioned that the time is same, it is implied as a part of the situation – since, the two cars have started together and they are meeting at a point (obviously again the time is the same). Thus, the time of the two movements, are the same.

(b) Often in situations involving to-and-fro motions, moving bodies start at the same time and meet at a point and after the meeting; they keep travelling to-and-fro between the same points, turning back when they hit the ends. Questions based on such situations are very common in this chapter. In such situations, the bodies meet multiple times and time constancy is implied when we consider the movement of two bodies between one meeting point and another.

Example: Two people travel to-and-fro between Calcutta and Kharagpur, starting from opposite ends and reversing directions when they reach their destinations. They keep doing so and hence, meet multiple times. Define M_1 as their first meeting point, M_2 as the second, and M_3 as the third and so on.

In such a case, the movement of the first person between M_1 and M_2, and the movement of the second person between M_1 and M_2, would involve the same time. Likewise, their movements between M_2 and M_3 would also involve a time constancy situation.

(c) A similar situation occurs when two or more people run multiple times around a circle (either in same or in opposite direction). In such a situation, these people would be meeting multiple times and these meeting points can again be defined as M_1, M_2, and M_3 and so on.

The analysis in this case would be similar to the one discussed in the to-and-fro situation above. The movement of the first person between M_1 and M_2, and the movement of the second person between M_1 and M_2, would involve the same time. Likewise, their movements between M_2 and M_3 would also involve a time constancy situation.

When time is constant, the following ratios and thought-processes are valid: Assume that there are two motions M_1 and M_2. Let S_1, S_2 and d_1, d_2 be the speeds and distances of the two motions, respectively.

Thought 1: $S_1/S_2 = d_1/d_2$. (This can also be thought of as the direct transfer of the speed ratio to the distance ratio and vice versa.)

Thought 2: If speed from S_1 to S_2 grows by 20% percent, then the distance d_2, would also be larger than d_1 by 20%. (The same percentage change in distance as in speed and vice versa)

Thought 3: If the speed is multiplied by 6/5, going from S_1 to S_2, then the distance would also be multiplied by 6/5 going from d_1 to d_2. (The same multiplication ratio is to be used in distance as in speed and vice versa.)

Thought 4: If the speed increases by 1/5, going from S_1 to S_2, then the distance would also increase by 1/5, going from d_1 to d_2. (The same fractional change is to be used in distance as in speed and vice versa.)

Illustration

(i) A car travels at 30 km/h for the first two hours of a journey and then travels at 40 km/h for the next two hours of the journey. Find the ratio of the distances travelled at the two speeds.

Solution: Since time is constant between the two motions described, we can use the proportionality between speed and distance.

Hence, $d_1/d_2 = s_1/s_2 = 3/4$

Alternatively, you can also think in terms of percentage: d_2 will be 33.33% higher than d_1 since S_2 is 33.33% higher than S_1 and time is constant. You could also have thought of it as since speed is getting multiplied by 4/3, distance would also get multiplied by 4/3.

(ii) Two cars leave simultaneously from points *A* and *B* on a straight line towards each other. The distance between *A* and *B* is 100 km. They meet at a point 40 km from *A*. Find the ratio of their speeds.

Solution: Since time is the same for both the motions described, we have ratio of speed = ratio of distance.

$$S_A/S_B = d_A/d_b = 40/60 = 2/3$$

(iii) Two cars move simultaneously from points *A* and *B* towards each other. The speeds of the two cars are 20 m/s and 25 m/s respectively. Find the meeting point if the distance between them is 900 km.

Solution: For the bodies to meet, the time of travel is constant (since the two cars have started to move simultaneously).

Hence, speed ratio = distance ratio
$\rightarrow$ 4/5 = distance ratio

Hence, the meeting point will be 400 km from *A* and 500 km from *B*.

3. Inverse proportionality between speed and time (when the distance is constant); speed ∝ 1/time

Math Simplified

Scan this QR code to access a video on how to think in distance constancy situations

Note: This proportionality is also seen in a lot of questions and hence, quite important for you to understand. Between two motions described, if the distance covered is the same, then the speed would be inversely proportional to time. This situation too can be described in explicit and implicit ways. Some of the common descriptions you would see in the questions are provided below.

Explicit ways of communicating distance constancy in problems:

(a) *A body travels at S_1 km/h for the first half of the journey and then travels at S_2 km/h for the second half of the journey.*

(b) *A car travels at 50 km/h for 100 km and 80 km/h for the next 100 km.*

(c) Two people Ram and Shyam cover the same distance at speeds of 6 km/h and 7.5 km/h, respectively.

In each of the above cases, the situation described should show you two things – i) That there are two motions described. ii) Between the two motions, the distance travelled is constant – hence the speeds of the two motions would be inversely proportional to time travelled for in the two motions.

Implicit ways of communicating distance constancy in problems:

(a) Two cars start simultaneously from A and B, respectively towards each other at speeds of S_1 and S_2 km/h, respectively. They meet at a point C and reach their respective destinations B and A in t_1 and t_2 hours, respectively.

(b) A man goes to office and comes back. (Any motion describing going and coming back over the same distance is actually a description of two motions).

(c) A man walks at 3/4th of his normal speed and is late to reach office by twelve minutes. (This situation is again describing two motions of the man – going to his office at different speeds on different days).

(d) Travelling at 12 km/h, a man is ten minutes late in reaching his office. The next day, he travels at 15 km/h and is now late by only four minutes. (Two motions are described over the same distance).

(e) Rohit covers the distance from Delhi to Jaipur at 80km/h, while his friend Sushil covers the same journey at 100 km/h.

(f) Two runners A and B are running around a circle. A can cover the circle in twelve minutes, while B covers the circle in fifteen minutes. (In this case, since the movements are described with respect to the covering of the entire circumference of the circle for both the people, we should be able to see that the distance is constant in both cases).

In each of the above cases, there are two motions described such that their distances are same. Hence, speed is inversely proportional to time. The following reactions are valid in such a situation:

1. Inverse transfer of the speed ratio to the time ratio and vice versa. Mathematically, this means that if there are two motions M_1 and M_2 with their distances being the same, and respective speeds and times as S_1, S_2 and t_1, t_2 respectively, then $S_1/S_2 = t_2/t_1$, i.e. if the speed ratio between motion 1 and 2 is 2:3, the time ratio between the two motions would be 3:2.
2. Inverse proportionality between speed and time also means that the product of speed and time is constant. This means that all the percentage increase-decrease pairs that we have studied in the percentage chapter would apply in such situations. Thus, for two motions, if you can spot that the distance is constant, and if the speed goes up by 25%, the time would come down by 20%. (It is advisable to revise all the pairs provided in the product constancy table of the percentage chapter in this book.
3. The situation can also be dealt with by thinking about fractional increase-decrease situation. Thus, for instance, if the speed increases by 1/4th, time would decrease by 1/5th; if the speed increased by 3/13, time would decrease by 3/16 and so on.
4. Using a multiplier also works in such cases: if speed is getting multiplied by 16/13, time would get multiplied by 13/16.

Illustration

(i) This is best looked at through this CAT 2017 example.

A man travels at 12 km/h and reaches the railway station ten minutes after the train has gone. The next day, he travels at 15 km/h and reaches the railway station ten minutes before the train leaves. What is the distance to the railway station?

Solution: Our normal solution that we had thought about in school for this was: If we assume the distance as d, then we have:

$$\frac{d}{12} - \frac{d}{15} = \frac{20}{60} \rightarrow d = 20$$

However, there are many more ways to solve this using the inverse proportionality of speed and time. Let us look at multiple ways in which this question can be thought about using inverse proportionality.

1. In this situation, since two journeys are described over the same distance, the distance is constant. Here, S_1 is 12 km/h and S_2 is 15 km/h, which means

that there is a 25% increase in the speed. This means that the time would be dropping by 20%. Also, from the problem we can see that the time has dropped by 20 minutes (from 10 minutes late to 10 minutes early). This means that the original time (at a speed of 12 km/h) must have been 100 minutes. Hence, the distance = $12\times\frac{100}{60}$ = 20 km.

2. An increase of speed from 12 to 15 means a 1/4th increase in speed. Time would come down by 1/5th. Since, the time is coming down by 20 minutes it means that 1/5th of the original time (for the first motion) would be 20 minutes. Hence, the original time = 100 minutes. Hence, the distance = $12\times\frac{100}{60}$ = 20 km.
3. Alternately, since speed is getting multiplied by 5/4 ($12\times\frac{5}{4}=15$). Hence, $t_1\times\frac{4}{5}=t_2$. Also, since $t_1 - t_2$= 20, we get t_1 = 100.
4. The ratio of speeds S_1/S_2 is 4/5. Hence, the ratio of times t_1/t_2 = 5/4 (inverted transfer of the speed ratio to the time ratio). Also, since $t_1 - t_2$ = 20, we get t_1 = 100.

Illustration

(i) A train meets with an accident and moves at 3/4 its original speed. Due to this, it is twenty minutes late. Find the original time for the journey beyond the point of accident.

Solution: Speed becomes 3/4 (time becomes 4/3)

Extra time = 1/3 of normal time = 20 minutes

Normal time = 60 minutes

Alternatively, from the table on product constancy in the chapter of percentages, we get that a 25% reduction in speed leads to a 33.33% increase in time.

But, 33.33% increase in time is equal to 20 minutes increase in time.

Hence, total time (original) = 60 minutes.

(ii) A body travels half the journey at 20 km/h and the other half at 30 km/h. Find the average speed.

Solution: Since the distance is constant, the time ratio is 3:2 (inverse of the speed ratio). Using alligation, then we can get that the average speed is 24 km/h. (Good time to revise the Alligation chapter, if you did not get that!)

Relative Speed: Same Direction and Opposite Direction

Concept Explainer

Scan this QR code to access a conceptual video on Relative Speed.

Normally, when we talk about the movement of a body, we mean the movement of the body with respect to a stationary point. However, there are times when we need to determine the movement and its relationships with respect to a moving point/body. In such instances, we have to take into account the movement of the body/point with respect to which we are trying to determine relative motion.

Relative movement, therefore, can be viewed as the movement of one body relative to another moving body.

The following formulae apply for the relative speed of two independent bodies with respect to each other:

Case 1: Two bodies are moving in opposite directions at speeds S_1 and S_2 respectively.
The relative speed is defined as $S_1 + S_2$.

Case 2: Two bodies are moving in the same direction.
The relative speed is defined as:
(a) $S_1 - S_2$ when S_1 is greater than S_2.
(b) $S_2 - S_1$ when S_1 is lesser than S_2.

In other words, the relative speed can also be defined as the positive value of the difference between the two speeds, that is, $| S_1 - S_2 |$.

Motion in a Straight Line

Problems on situations of motion in a straight line are one of the most commonly asked questions in the CAT and other aptitude exams. Hence a proper understanding of the following concepts and their application to problem solving will be extremely important for the student.

Motion in a straight line is governed by the rules of relative speed enumerated above.

***A.* Two or more bodies starting from the same point and moving in the same direction: Their relative speed is $S_1 - S_2$.**

(a) *In the case of the bodies moving to-and-fro between two points A and B:* The faster body will reach the end first and will meet the second body on its way back. The relative speed $S_1 - S_2$ will apply till the point of reversal of the faster body and after that the two bodies will start to move in the opposite directions at a relative speed of $S_1 + S_2$. The relative speed governing the movement of the two bodies will alternate between $S_1 - S_2$ and $S_1 + S_2$ every time any one of the bodies reverses directions. However, if both the bodies reverse their direction at the same instant, there will be no change in the relative speed equation. In this case, the description of the motion of the two bodies between two consecutive meetings will also be governed by the proportionality between speed and distance (since the time of movement between any two meetings will be constant).

Distances covered in this case: For every meeting, the total distance covered by the two bodies will be $2D$ (where D is the distance between the extreme points). However, notice that the value of $2D$ would be applicable only if both the bodies reverse the direction between two meetings. In case only one body has reversed direction, the total distance would need to be calculated on a case-by-case basis. The respective coverage of the distance is in the ratio of the individual speeds.

Thus, for the ninth meeting (if both bodies have reversed direction between every two meetings), the total distance covered will be $9 \times 2D = 18D$.

This will be useful for solving problems that require the calculation of a meeting point.

(b) *In the case of the bodies continuing to move in the same direction without coming to an end point and reversing directions:* The faster body will take a lead and will keep increasing the lead and the movement of the two bodies will be governed by the relative speed equation: $S_1 - S_2$.

Here again, if the two bodies start simultaneously, their movement will be governed by the direct proportionality between speed and distance (as the time would be constant).

***B.* Moving in the opposite direction: Their relative speed will be initially given by $S_1 + S_2$.**

(a) *In the case of the bodies moving to-and-fro between two points A and B starting from opposite ends of the path:* The two bodies will move towards each other, meet at a point in between A and B, then move apart away from each other. The faster body will reach its extreme point first, followed by the slower body reaching its extreme point next. Relative speed will change every time; one of the bodies reverses the direction.

The position of the meeting point will be determined by the ratio of the speeds of the bodies (since the two movements can be described as having the time constant between them).

Distances covered in the above case: For the first meeting, the total distance covered by the two bodies will be D (the distance between the extreme points). The coverage of the distance is in the ratio of the individual speeds.

Thereafter, as the bodies separate and start coming together, the combined distance to be covered is $2D$. (**Note:** If only one body is reversing direction between two meetings, this would not be the case and you will have to work it out.)

Thus, for the tenth meeting (if both bodies have reverse direction between every two meetings), the total distance covered will be $D + 9 \times 2D = 19D$.

This will be useful for solving the problems that require the calculation of a meeting point.

Illustration

(i) Two bodies A and B start from opposite ends P and Q of a straight road. They meet at a point $0.6D$ from P. Find the point of their fourth meeting.

Solution: Since time is constant, we have ratio of speeds as 3 : 2.

Also, total distance to be covered by the two together for the fourth meeting is $7D$. This distance is divided in a ratio of 3: 2 and thus, we have that A will cover $4.2D$ and B will cover $2.8D$.

The fourth meeting point can then be found out by tracking either A or B's movement. A, having moved a distance of $4.2D$, will be at a point $0.2D$ from P. This is the required answer.

(ii) A starts walking from a place at a uniform speed of 2 km/h in a particular direction. After half an hour, B starts from the same place and walks in the same direction as A at a uniform speed and overtakes A after 1 hour 48 minutes. Calculate the speed of B.

Solution: Start solving as you read the question. From the first two sentences, you see that A is 1 km ahead of B when B starts moving.

This distance of 1 km is covered by B in 9/5 hours [1 hour 48 minutes = 1(4/5) = 9/5 hours].

The equation operational here $(S_B - S_A) \times T$ = initial distance

$$(S_B - 2) \times 9/5 = 1$$

Solving, we get $S_B = 23/9$ km/h.

(b) *In the case of the bodies continuing to move in the same direction without coming to an end-point and reversing directions:* The bodies will meet and following their meeting they will start separating and going away from each other. The relative speed will be given by $S_1 + S_2$ initially while approaching each other and, thereafter, it will be $S_1 + S_2$ while moving away from each other.

> ***Important:*** The student is advised to take a closer look and get a closer understanding of these concepts by taking a few examples with absolute values of speed, time and distance. Try to visualise how two bodies separate and then come together. Also, clearly understand the three proportionalities in the equation $s \times t = d$, since these are very important tools for problem solving.

Concept of Acceleration

Acceleration is defined as the rate of change of speed.

Acceleration can be positive (speed increases) or negative (speed decreases → also known as deceleration).

The unit of acceleration is speed per unit time (e.g. m/s^2).

For instance, if a body has an initial speed of 5 m/s and a deceleration of 0.1 m/s^2, it will take 50 seconds to come to rest.

Final speed = Initial speed + Acceleration × Time

Some more examples:

(i) Water flows into a cylindrical beaker at a constant rate. The base area of the beaker is 24 cm^2. The water level rises by 10 cm every second. How quickly will the water level rise in a beaker with a base area of 30 cm^2?

Solution: The flow of water in the beaker is 24 cm^2 × 10 cm/s = 240 cm^3/s.

If the base area is 30 cm^2, then the rate of water level rise will be 240/30 = 8 cm/s.

Note: In case of confusion, in such questions, the student is advised to use dimensional analysis to understand what to multiply and what to divide.

(ii) A two-kilowatt heater can boil a given amount of water in ten minutes. How long will it take for

(a) A less powerful heater of 1.2 kilowatts to boil the same amount of water?

(b) A less powerful heater of 1.2 kilowatts to boil double the amount of water?

Solution:

(a) The heating required to boil the amount of water is 2 × 10 = 20 kilowatt minutes. At the rate of 1.2 kilowatt, this heat will be generated in 20/1.2 minutes = 16.66 minutes.

(b) When the water is doubled, the heating required is also doubled. Hence, heating required = 40 kilowatt minutes. At the rate of 1.2 kilowatt, this heat will be generated in 40/1.2 = 33.33 minutes.

Space for Rough Work

LEVEL OF DIFFICULTY (I)

1. The Calcutta Mail left Mumbai at 9 PM sharp. Two hours later, the Geetanjali Express started from Mumbai in the same direction. The Geetanjali Express overtook the Calcutta Mail at 5 AM on the next morning. Find the average speed of the two trains over this journey, if the sum of their average speeds is 140 km/h.
(a) 68.57 km/h (b) 70 km/h
(c) 75 km/h (d) 6km/h
2. Two trains, Calcutta Mail and Bombay Mail, start at the same time from stations Kolkata and Mumbai respectively towards each other. After passing each other, they take 12 hours and 3 hours to reach Mumbai and Kolkata respectively. If the Calcutta Mail is moving at the speed of 48 km/h, the speed of the Bombay Mail is
(a) 24 km/h (b) 22 km/h
(c) 21 km/h (d) 96 km/h
3. Bharat walks to a viewpoint and returns to the starting point by his car and thus, takes a total time of 8 hours 45 minutes. He would have gained 2 hours by driving both ways. How long would it have taken for him to walk both ways?
(a) 10 h 45 min (b) 7 h 45 min
(c) 5 h 45 min (d) 6 h 45 min
4. A train is running at 7/11 of its speed and reached a place in 22 h. How much time could be saved, if the train runs at its speed?
(a) 7 h (b) 8 h
(c) 14 h (d) 16 h
5. Rajdhani Express travels 650 km in 5 h and another 940 km in 10 h. What is the average speed of train?
(a) 1590 km/h (b) 168 km/h
(c) 106 km/h (d) 126 km/h
6. Vandana goes to office at a speed of 6 km/h and returns to her home at a speed of 4 km/h. If she takes ten hours in all, what is the distance between her office and her home?
(a) 24 km (b) 12 km
(c) 10 km (d) 30 km
7. A railway passenger counts the telegraph poles on the rail-road as he passes them. The telegraph poles are at a distance of 50 meters. What will be his count in 4 hours, if the speed of the train is 45 km per hour?
(a) 600 (b) 2500
(c) 3600 (d) 5000
8. Harsh and Vijay move towards Hosur starting from IIM, Bangalore, at a speed of 40 km/h and 60 km/h, respectively. If Vijay reaches Hosur 200 minutes earlier then Harsh, what is the distance between IIM, Bangalore, and Hosur?
(a) 600 km (b) 400 km
(c) 900 km (d) 200 km
9. A man cycles with a speed of 10 km/h and reaches his office at 1 PM. However, when he cycles with a speed of 15 km/h, he reaches his office at 11 AM. At what speed should he cycle so that he reaches his office at 12 noon?
(a) 12 km/h (b) 12.5 km/h
(c) 18 km/h (d) None of these
10. A man moves from A to B at the rate of 4 km/h. Had he moved at the rate of 11/3 km/h, he would have taken 3 hours more to reach the destination. What is the distance between A and B?
(a) 66 km (b) 132 km
(c) 27 km (d) None of these
11. A plane left half-an-hour later than the scheduled time and in order to reach its destination 1500 kilometers away in time, it had to increase its speed by 50% over its usual speed. Find its increased speed.
(a) 500 km/h (b) 1000 km/h
(c) 750 km/h (d) 1500 km/h
12. A car travels 1/3 of the distance on a straight road with a speed of 10 km/h, the next 1/3 with a speed of 20 km/h and the last 1/3 with a speed of 60 km/h. What is the average speed of the car for the whole journey?
(a) 18 km/h (b) 10 km/h
(c) 20 km/h (d) 15 km/h
13. Ajay covers 910 km by car, bike and cycle in the ratio 4:3:6 respectively. The speeds at which the journey was covered by Ajay were in the ratio 4:3:6 respectively. The total time taken to cover entire distance was 89 hours. Find the ratio between time taken by Ajay while travelling by car, bike and cycle.
(a) 3:4:2 (b) 1:1:1
(c) 6:3:4 (d) 4:3:6
14. Two trains for Patna leave Delhi at 6 AM and 6:45 AM and travel at 98 km/h and 136 km/h, respectively. How many kilometers from Delhi (approximately) will the two trains meet?
(a) 263.05 km (b) 260 km
(c) 200 km (d) None of these
15. Rahul travels 600 km to his home partly by bus and partly by car. He takes eight hours if he travels 120 km by bus and the rest by car. He takes twenty minutes more if he travels 200 km by bus and the rest by car. Find the speed of the bus in km/h.
(a) 45 (b) 60
(c) 75 (d) None of these
16. Walking at 3/4 of his normal speed, Abhishek is 60 minutes late in reaching his office. The usual time

taken by him to cover the distance between his home and his office is
(a) 180 minutes (b) 120 minutes
(c) 150 minutes (d) 144 minutes

17. Shyam's house, his office and his gym are all equidistant from each other. The distance between any two of them is 4 km. Shyam starts walking from his gym in a direction parallel to the road connecting his office and his house and stops when he reaches a point directly East of his office. He then reverses direction and walks till he reaches a point directly South of his office. The total distance walked by Shyam is
(a) 6 km (b) 9 km
(c) 16 km (d) 12 km

18. A starts from a point that is on the circumference of a circle, moves 600 meter in the North direction and then again moves 800 meter East and reaches a point diametrically opposite the starting point. Find the diameter of the circle.
(a) 1000 m (b) 500 m
(c) 800 m (d) 900 m

19. *Ramesh* and *Barkat* travel the same distance at the rates of 16 kilometers and 20 kilometers an hour respectively. If Ramesh takes thirty minutes longer than Barkat, the distance travelled by Barkat is
(a) 12 km (b) 20 km
(c) 32 km (d) 40 km

20. Two cars started simultaneously toward each other from town *A* and *B*, which are 480 km apart. It took eight hours by the first car in travelling from *A* to *B* to cover the distance and twelve hours by the second car in travelling from *B* to *A*. Determine at what distance from A the two cars meet.
(a) 288 km (b) 200 km
(c) 300 km (d) 196 km

21. Two cars start at the same time from *A* and *B* and proceed towards *B* and *A* at 36 km/h and 42 km/h respectively. When they meet, it is found that one car has moved 48 km more than the other. What is the distance between *A* and *B* (in km)?
(a) 624 (b) 636
(c) 544 (d) 460

22. A train moves at a constant speed of 120 km/h for one kilometer and at 40 km/h for the next one kilometer. What is the average speed of the train?
(a) 48 km/h (b) 50 km/h
(c) 80 km/h (d) 60 km/h

23. A journey of 192 km takes two hours less by a fast train than by a slow train. If the average speed of the slow train be 16 km/h less than that of fast train, what is the average speed of the faster train?
(a) 32 km/h (b) 16 km/h
(c) 12 km/h (d) 48 km/h

24. Two trains *A* and *B* start simultaneously in the opposite direction from two points *A* and *B* and arrive at their destinations nine and four hours, respectively after their meeting each other. At what rate does the second train *B* travel if the first train travels at 80 km per hour?
(a) 60 km/h (b) 100 km/h
(c) 120 km/h (d) 80 km/h

25. A motor car does a journey in 17.5 hours, covering the first half at 30 km/h and the second half at 40 km/h. Find the distance of the journey.
(a) 684 km (b) 600 km
(c) 120 km (d) 540 km

26. A man walked 12 km at a certain rate, and then 6 km farther at a rate of 1/2 km/h faster. If he had walked the whole distance at the faster rate, his time would have been 20 minutes less. How long did it really take him to walk the distance of 18 km?
(a) 4h (b) 4.33h
(c) 4.66h (d) 5h

27. Anish, during his journey, travels for 20 minutes at a speed of 30 km/h, another 30 minutes at a speed of 50 km/h, and 1 hour at a speed of 50 km/h and 1 hour at a speed of 60 km/h. What is the average speed?
(a) 51.18 km/h (b) 63 km/h
(c) 39 km/h (d) 48 km/h

28. Sambhu beats Kalu by 30 meters or 10 seconds. How much time was taken by Sambhu to complete a race 1200 meters?
(a) 6 min 30 s (b) 3 min 15 s
(c) 12 min 10 s (d) 2 min 5 s

29. Shaurya's new Mercedes travelling at 70 km/h uses 30% more diesel to travel a certain distance than it does when it travels at a speed of 50 km/h. If the car can travel 19.5 km/L of diesel at 50 km/h, how far can the car travel on 10 litres of diesel at a speed of 70 km/h?
(a) 130 km (b) 140km
(c) 150 km (d) 175 km

30. Ram and Bharat travel the same distance at the rate of 6 km per hour and 10 km per hour respectively. If Ram takes 30 minutes longer than Bharat, the distance travelled by each is
(a) 6 km (b) 10 km
(c) 7.5 km (d) 20 km

31. Lonavala and Khandala are two stations 600 km apart. A train starts from Lonavala and moves towards Khandala at the rate of 25 km/h. After two hours, another train starts from Khandala at the rate of 35 km/h. How far from Lonavala will they cross each other?
(a) 250 km (b) 300 km
(c) 279.166 km (d) 475 km

32. What is the time taken by Chandu to cover a distance of 360 km by a motorcycle moving at a speed of 10 m/s?
(a) 10 h (b) 5 h
(c) 8 h (d) 6 h

33. A car travels from A to B at V_1 km/h, travels back from B to A at V_2 km/h and again goes back from A to B at V_2 km/h. The average speed of the car is

(a) $\frac{2V_1V_2}{V_1+2V_2}$ (b) $\frac{2V_1V_2}{V_2+2V_1}$

(c) $\frac{3V_1V_2}{V_2+2V_1}$ (d) $\frac{3V_1V_2}{V_1+2V_2}$

34. It takes four hours to go from Kolkata to Kharagpur. A truck of Durga Transport leaves Kolkata for Kharagpur every thirty minutes starting at 6:00 AM. If you start from Kharagpur for Kolkata at 10:30 AM and travel at the speed of the trucks, how many such trucks would you meet till you reach Kolkata?

(a) 8 (b) 9
(c) 16 (d) 17

35. Arjit covers a distance in 120 minutes if he drives at a speed of 90 kilometers per hour on an average. Find the speed at which he must drive at to reduce the time of the journey by 25%.

(a) 100 km/h (b) 105 km/h
(c) 150 km/h (d) 120 km/h

36. Vinay fires two bullets from the same place at an interval of 12 minutes but Raju sitting in a train approaching the place hears the second report 11 minutes 30 seconds after the first. What is the approximate speed of train (if sound travels at the speed of 330 meter per second)?

(a) 660/23 m/s (b) 220/7 m/s
(c) 330/23 m/s (d) 110/23 m/s

37. A passenger train takes two hours less for a journey of 300 kilometers if its speed is increased by 5 km/h over its usual speed. Find the usual speed.

(a) 10 km/h (b) 12 km/h
(c) 20 km/h (d) 25 km/h

38. A cyclist moving on a circular track of radius 200 meters completes one revolution in four minutes. What is the average speed of cyclist (approximately)?

(a) 314 m/minute (b) 200 m/minute
(c) 300 m/minute (d) 900 m/minute

39. A man leaves office daily at 7 PM. A driver with car comes from his home to pick him from office and bring back home. One day he gets free at 5:30 PM and instead of waiting for driver he starts walking towards home. On the way, he meets the car and returns home on car. He reaches home 20 minutes earlier than usual. In how much time does the man reach home usually?

(a) 1h 20min (b) 1 h
(c) 2 h 10 min (d) Cannot be determined

40. X and Y are two stations 600 km apart. A train starts from X and moves towards Y at the rate of 25 km/h. Another train starts from Y at the rate of 35 km/h. How far from X they will cross each other?

(a) 250 km (b) 300 km
(c) 450 km (d) 475 km

41. A person travelled a distance of 200 kilometers between Lucknow and Allahabad by a car covering the first quarter of the journey at a constant speed of 40 km/h and the remaining three quarters at a constant speed of x km/h. If the average speed of the person for the entire journey was 53.33 km/h, what is the value of x?

(a) 55 km/h (b) 60 km/h
(c) 70 km/h (d) 80 km/h

42. If Arun had walked 1 km/h faster, he would have taken 10 minutes less to walk 2 kilometers. What is Arun's speed of walking?

(a) 1 km/h (b) 2 km/h
(c) 3 km/h (d) 6 km/h

43. A car driver, driving in a fog, passes a pedestrian who was walking at the rate of 2 km/h in the same direction. The pedestrian could see the car for six minutes and it was visible to him up to a distance of 0.6 km. What was the speed of the car?

(a) 30 km/h (b) 15 km/h
(c) 20 km/h (d) 8 km/h

44. Manish travels a certain distance by car at the rate of 12 km/h and walks back at the rate of 3 km/h. The whole journey took five hours. What is the distance he covered on the car?

(a) 12 km (b) 30 km
(c) 15 km (d) 6 km

45. Two trains for Mumbai leave Delhi at 6:00 AM and 6:45 AM and travel at 100 km/h and 136 km/h respectively. How many kilometers from Delhi will the two trains be together?

(a) 262.4 km (b) 260 km
(c) 283.33 km (d) 275 km

46. Ishan left his home by car at 7:00 AM for Durgapur. At 7:30 AM, he overtook a truck also travelling towards Durgapur. He reached Durgapur and started his journey back home after two hours. One hour after leaving Durgapur he crossed the same truck. Find the ratio of speed of Ishan's car and the truck, if he crossed the truck for the second time at 1:00 PM (assume truck did not halt during the journey and both the car and truck travelled with constant speeds).

(a) 9:4 (b) 11:3
(c) 13:7 (d) 5:3

47. Walking at 3/4 of his normal speed, a man takes 2(1/2) hours more than the normal time. Find the normal time.

(a) 7.5 h (b) 6 h
(c) 8 h (d) 12 h

48. Without stoppage, a train travels a certain distance with an average speed of 60 km/h, and with stoppage, it covers the same distance with an average speed of 40 km/h. On an average, how many minutes per hour does the train stop during the journey?

(a) 20 min/h (b) 15 min/h
(c) 10 min/h (d) 10 min/h

49. Narayan Murthy walking at a speed of 20 km/h reaches his college ten minutes late. Next time he increases his speed by 5 km/h, but finds that he is still late by four minutes. What is the distance of his college from his house?

(a) 20 km (b) 6 km
(c) 12 km (d) None of these

50. Two trains start at same time, one from Chandigarh and second from Delhi running in opposite directions towards each other with uniform speed. They can complete their journey in 42 minutes and 56 minutes respectively. They will meet after

(a) 21 minutes (b) 22 minutes
(c) 24 minutes (d) 28 minutes

Space for Rough Work

LEVEL OF DIFFICULTY (II)

1. The J&K Express from Delhi to Srinagar was delayed by snowfall for 16 minutes and made up for the delay on a section of 80 km travelling with a speed 10 km per hour higher than its normal speed. Find the original speed of the J&K Express (according to the schedule)

(a) 60 km/h (b) 66.66 km/h
(c) 50 km/h (d) 40 km/h

2. Ayrton Senna had to cover a distance of 60 km. However, he started 6 minutes later than his scheduled time and raced at a speed 1 km/h higher than his originally planned speed and reached the finish at the time he would reach it if he began to race strictly at the appointed time and raced with the assumed speed. Find the speed at which he travelled during the journey described.

(a) 25 km/h (b) 15 km/h
(c) 10 km/h (d) 6 km/h

3. Amitabh covered a distance of 96 km two hours faster than he had planned to. This he achieved by travelling 1 km more every hour than he intended to cover every 1 hour 15 minutes. What was the speed at which Amitabh travelled during the journey?

(a) 16 km/h (b) 26 km/h
(c) 36 km/h (d) 30 km/h

4. An urgent message had to be delivered from the house of the Peshwas in Pune to Shivaji who was camping in Bangalore. A horse rider travels on horse back from Pune to Bangalore at a constant speed. If the horse increased its speed by 6 km/h, it would take the rider 4 hours less to cover that distance. And travelling with a speed 6 km/h lower than the initial speed, it would take him 10 hours more than the time he would have taken had he travelled at a speed 6 kmph higher than the initial speed. Find the distance between Pune and Bangalore.

(a) 120 km (b) 600 km
(c) 720 km (d) 750 km

5. A pedestrian and a cyclist start simultaneously towards each other from Aurangabad and Paithan which are 40 km apart and meet 2 hours after the start. Then they resumed their trips and the cyclist arrives at Aurangabad 7 hours 30 minutes earlier than the pedestrian arrives at Paithan. Which of these could be the speed of the pedestrian?

(a) 4 km/h (b) 5 km/h
(c) 3 km/h (d) 6 km/h

6. Two motorists met at 10 a.m. at the Dadar railway station. After their meeting, one of them proceeded in the East direction while the other proceeded in the North direction. Exactly at noon, they were 60 km apart. Find the speed of the slower motorist if the difference of their speeds is 6 km/h.

(a) 28 km/h (b) 18 km/h
(c) 9 km/h (d) 19 km/h

7. Two cyclists start simultaneously towards each other from Aurangabad and Ellora, which are 28 km apart. An hour later they meet and keep pedalling with the same speed without stopping. The second cyclist arrives at Ellora 35 minutes later than the first arrives at Aurangabad. Find the speed of the cyclist who started from Ellora.

(a) 12 km/h (b) 16 km/h
(c) 15 km/h (d) 10 km/h

8. Two ants start simultaneously from two ant holes towards each other. The first ant coveres 8% of the distance between the two ant holes in 3 hours, the second ant covered $\frac{7}{120}$ of the distance in 2 hours 30 minutes. Find the speed (feet/h) of the second ant if the first ant travelled 800 feet to the meeting point.

(a) 15 feet/h (b) 25 feet/h
(c) 45 feet/h (d) 35 feet/h

9. A bus left point X for point Y. Two hours later a car left point X for Y and arrived at Y at the same time as the bus. If the car and the bus left simultaneously from the opposite ends X and Y towards each other, they would meet 1.33 hours after the start. How much time did it take the bus to travel from X to Y?

(a) 2 h (b) 4 h
(c) 6 h (d) 8 h

10. A racetrack is in the form of the legs of a right triangle. The longer of the legs of the track is 2 km more than the shorter of the legs (both these legs being on a highway). The start and end points are also connected to each other through a side road. The escort vehicle for the race took the side road and rode with a speed of 30 km/h and then covered the two intervals along the highway during the same time with a speed of 42 km/h. Find the length of the racetrack.

(a) 14 km (b) 10 km
(c) 24 km (d) 36 km

11. Two planes move along a circle of circumference 1.2 km with constant speeds. When they move in different directions, they meet every 15 seconds and when they move in the same direction, one plane overtakes the other every 60 seconds. Find the speed of the slower plane.

(a) 0.04 km/s (b) 0.03 km/s
(c) 0.05 km/s (d) 0.02 km/s

12. Karim, a tourist leaves Ellora on a bicycle. Having travelled for 1.5 h at 16 km/h, he makes a stop for 1.5 h and then pedals on with the same speed. Four hours after Karim started, his friend and local guide Rahim leaves Ellora on a motorcycle and rides with a speed of 28 km/h in the same direction as Karim had gone. What distance will they cover before Rahim overtakes Karim?

(a) 88 km (b) 90.33 km
(c) 93.33 km (d) 96.66 km

13. A tourist covered a journey partly by foot and partly by tonga. He walked for 90 km and rode the tonga for 10 km. He spent 4 h less on the tonga than on walking. If the tourist had reversed the times he travelled by foot and on tonga, the distances travelled on each part of the journey would be equal. How long did he ride the tonga?

(a) He rode for 6 hours (b) He rode for 4 hours
(c) He rode for 2 hours (d) He rode for 5 hours

14. Two Indian tourists in the US cycled towards each other, one from point *A* and the other from point *B*. The first tourist left point *A* 6 hrs later than the second left point *B*, and it turned out on their meeting that he had travelled 12 km less than the second tourist. After their meeting, they kept cycling with the same speed, and the first tourist arrived at *B* 8 hours later and the second arrived at *A* 9 hours later. Find the speed of the faster tourist.

(a) 4 km/h (b) 6 km/h
(c) 9 km/h (d) 2 km/h

15. Two joggers left Delhi for Noida simultaneously. The first jogger stopped 42 min later when he was 1 km short of Noida and the other one stopped 52 min later when he was 2 km short of Noida. If the first jogger jogged as many kilometres as the second and the second as many kilometres as the first, the first one would need 17 min less than the second. Find the distance between Delhi and Noida.

(a) 5 km (b) 15 km
(c) 25 km (d) 35 km

16. A tank of 4800 m^3 capacity is full of water. The discharging capacity of the pump is 10 m^3/min higher than its filling capacity. As a result the pump needs 16 min less to discharge the fuel than to fill up the tank. Find the filling capacity of the pump.

(a) 50 m^3/min (b) 25 m^3/min
(c) 55 m^3/min (d) 24 m^3/min

17. An ant climbing up a vertical pole ascends 12 meters and slips down 5 meters in every alternate hour. If the pole is 63 meters high how long will it take it to reach the top?

(a) 18 hours
(b) 17 hours
(c) 16 hours 35 minutes
(d) 16 hours 40 minutes

18. Two ports *A* and *B* are 300 km apart. Two ships leave *A* for *B* such that the second leaves 8 hours after the first. The ships arrive at *B* simultaneously. Find the time the slower ship spent on the trip if the speed of one of them is 10 km/h higher than that of the other.

(a) 25 hours (b) 15 hours
(c) 10 hours (d) 20 hours

19. An ant moved for several seconds and covered 3 mm in the first second and 4 mm more in each successive second than in its predecessor. If the ant had covered 1 mm in the first second and 8 mm more in each successive second, then the difference between the path it would cover during the same time and the actual path would be more than 6 mm but less than 30 mm. Find the time for which the ant moved (in seconds).

(a) 5 s (b) 4 s
(c) 6 s (d) 2 s

20. The Sabarmati Express left Ahmedabad for Mumbai. Having travelled 300 km, which constitutes 66.666 per cent of the distance between Ahmedabad and Mumbai, the train was stopped by a red signal. Half an hour later, the track was cleared and the engine-driver, having increased the speed by 15 km per hour, arrived at Mumbai on time. Find the initial speed of the Sabarmati Express.

(a) 50 kmph (b) 60 kmph
(c) 75 kmph (d) 40 kmph

21. Two swimmers started simultaneously from the beach, one to the north and the other to the east. Two hours later, the distance between them turned out to be 100 km. Find the speed of the faster swimmer, knowing that the speed of one of them was 75% of the speed of the other.

(a) 30 kmph (b) 40 kmph
(c) 45 kmph (d) 60 kmph

22. A motorcyclist left point *A* for point *B*. Two hours later, another motorcyclist left *A* for *B* and arrived at *B* at the same time as the first motorcyclist. Had both the motorcyclists started simultaneously from *A* and *B* travelling towards each other, they would have met in 80 minutes. How much time did it take the faster motorcyclist to travel from *A* to *B*?

(a) 6 hours (b) 3 hours
(c) 2 hours (d) 4 hours

23. Two horses started simultaneously towards each other and meet each other 3 h 20 min later. How much time will it take the slower horse to cover the whole distance if the first arrived at the place of departure of the second 5 hours later than the second arrived at the point of departure of the first?

(a) 10 hours (b) 5 hours
(c) 15 hours (d) 6 hours

24. The difference between the times taken by two buses to travel a distance of 350 km is 2 hours 20 minutes. If the difference between their speeds is 5 kmph, find the slower speed.

(a) 35 kmph (b) 30 kmph
(c) 25 kmph (d) 20 kmph

25. One bad day, at 7 a.m. I started on my bike at a speed of 36 kmph to meet one of my relatives. After I had travelled some distance, my bike went out of order and I had to stop. After resting for 35 minutes, I returned home on foot at a speed of 14 kmph and reached home at 1 p.m. Find the distance from my house at which my bike broke down.

(a) 54 km (b) 63 km
(c) 72 km (d) None of these

Direction for Questions 26 to 30: Read the following data and answer the questions that follow.

Three brothers, Ram, Shyam and Mohan, travelled by road. They all left the college at the same time—12 noon. The description of the motions of the three are detailed below:

Name	*Ram*	*Shyam*	*Mohan*
Phase I	Bus for 2 hours @ 10 mph	Bike for @ 1 hours 30 mph	Foot for 3 hours @ 3.33 mph
Phase II	Bike for 1.5 hours @ 40 mph	Foot for 3 hours @ 3.33 mph	Bus for 3 hours @ 10 mph
Phase III	Foot for 3 hours @ 3.33 mph	Bus for 4 hours @ 10 mph	Bike for 2 hours @ 30 mph

26. When did Ram overtake Shyam?

(a) 3:15 p.m. (b) 2:22 p.m.
(c) 2:30 p.m. (d) 2:20 p.m.

27. At what distance from the start does Mohan overtake Shyam?

(a) 40 miles (b) 57 miles
(c) 70 miles (d) 80 miles

28. If Ram travelled by bike instead of foot in the last leg of his journey (for the same distance as he had covered by foot), what is the difference in the times of Ram and Mohan to cover 90 miles?

(a) 6 h 50 minutes (b) 10 h 40 minutes
(c) 3 hrs 55 minutes (d) 4 hrs 10 minutes

29. If all of them travelled a distance of 100 miles, who reached first and at what time (assume the last leg time increases to cover 100 miles)?

(a) Mohan at 6 p.m. (b) Ram at 8 p.m.
(c) Shyam at 6 p.m. (d) Mohan at 8 p.m.

30. In the above question, who reached last and at what time?

(a) Ram at 9:30 p.m. (b) Ram at 10 p.m.
(c) Shyam at 9:30 p.m. (d) Shyam at 10 p.m.

31. A motorcyclist rode the first half of his way at a constant speed. Then he was delayed for 5 minutes and, therefore, to make up for the lost time he increased his speed by 10 km/h. Find the initial speed of the motorcyclist if the total path covered by him is equal to 50 km.

(a) 36 km/h (b) 48 km/h
(c) 50 km/h (d) 62 km/h

32. Ram Singh and Priyadarshan start together from the same point on a circular path and walk around, each at his own pace, until both arrive together at the starting point. If Ram Singh performs the circuit in 3 minutes 44 seconds and Priyadarshan in 6 minutes 4 seconds, how many times does Ram Singh go around the path?

(a) 8 (b) 13
(c) 15 (d) Cannot be determined

33. Ravi, who lives in the countryside, caught a train for home earlier than usual yesterday. His wife normally drives to the station to meet him. But yesterday he set out on foot from the station to meet his wife on the way. He reached home 12 minutes earlier than he would have done had he waited at the station for his wife. The car travels at a uniform speed, which is 5 times Ravi's speed on foot. Ravi reached home at exactly 6 O'clock. At what time would he have reached home if his wife, forewarned of his plan, had met him at the station?

(a) 5 : 48 (b) 5 : 24
(c) 5 : 00 (d) 5 : 36

34. Hemant and Ajay start a two-length swimming race at the same moment but from opposite ends of the pool. They swim in lane and at uniform speeds, but Hemant is faster than Ajay. They first pass at a point 18.5 m from the deep end and having completed one length, each one is allowed to rest on the edge for exactly 45 seconds. After setting off on the return length, the swimmers pass for the second time just 10.5 m from the shallow end. How long is the pool?

(a) 55.5 m (b) 45 m
(c) 66 m (d) 49 m

35. Rahim sets out to cross a forest. On the first day, he completes 1/10th of the journey. On the second day, he covers 2/3rd of the distance travelled the first day. He continues in this manner, alternating the days in which he travels 1/10th of the distance still to be covered, with days on which he travels 2/3 of the total distance already covered. At the end of seventh day, he finds that $22\frac{1}{2}$ km more will see the end of his journey. How wide is the forest?

(a) $66\frac{2}{3}$ km (b) 100 km
(c) 120 km (d) 150 km

36. The metro service has a train going from Mumbai to Pune and Pune to Mumbai every hour, the first one at 6 a.m. The trip from one city to other takes $4\frac{1}{2}$ hours, and all trains travel at the same speed. How many trains will you pass while going from Mumbai to Pune if you start at 12 noon?
(a) 8 (b) 10
(c) 9 (d) 13

37. The distance between two towns is x km. A car travelling between the towns covers the first k km at an average speed of y km/h and the remaining distance at z km/h. The time taken for the journey is
(a) $\frac{k}{y} + \frac{(x-k)}{z}$ (b) $ky + \frac{(k-x)}{z}$
(c) $\frac{k}{y} + \frac{(k-x)}{z}$ (d) $ky + z(x-k)$

38. Two rifles are fired from the same place at a difference of 11 minutes 45 seconds. But a man who is coming towards the place in a train hears the second sound after 11 minutes. Find the speed of the train.
(a) 72 km/h (b) 36 km/h
(c) 81 km/h (d) 108 km/h

Directions for Questions 39 and 40: Read the following and answer the questions that follow.

The Kalinga Express started from Patna to Tata at 7 p.m. at a speed of 60 km/h. Another train, Rajdhani Express, started from Tata to Patna at 4 a.m. next morning at a speed of 90 km/h. The distance between Patna to Tata is 800 km.

39. How far from Tata will the two trains meet?
(a) 164 km (b) 156 km
(c) 132 km (d) 128 km

40. At what time will the two trains meet?
(a) 5 : 32 a.m. (b) 5 : 28 a.m.
(c) 5 : 36 a.m. (d) 5 : 44 a.m.

Directions for Questions 41 to 43: Read the following and answer the question that follow.

A naughty bird is sitting on top of a car. It sees another car approaching it at a distance of 12 km. The speed of the two cars is 60 kmph each. The bird starts flying from the first car and moves towards the second car, reaches the second car and comes back to the first car and so on. If the speed at which the bird flies is 120 kmph then answer the following questions. Assume that the two cars have a crash.

41. The total distance travelled by the bird before the crash is
(a) 6 km (b) 12 km
(c) 18 km (d) None of these

42. The total distance travelled by the bird before it reaches the second car for the second time is
(a) 10.55 km (b) 11.55 km
(c) 12.33 km (d) None of these

43. The total number of times that the bird reaches the bonnet of the second car is (theoretically):
(a) 12 times (b) 18 times
(c) Infinite times (d) Cannot be determined

44. A dog sees a cat. It estimates that the cat is 25 leaps away. The cat sees the dog and starts running with the dog in hot pursuit. If in every minute, the dog makes 5 leaps and the cat makes 6 leaps and one leap of the dog is equal to 2 leaps of the cat. Find the time in which the cat is caught by the dog (assume an open field with no trees)
(a) 12 minutes (b) 15 minutes
(c) 12.5 minutes (d) None of these

45. Two people A and B start from P and Q (distance = D) at the same time towards each other. They meet at a point R, which is at a distance $0.4D$ from P. They continue to move to and fro between the two points. Find the distance from point P at which the fourth meeting takes place.
(a) $0.8D$ (b) $0.6D$
(c) $0.3D$ (d) $0.4D$

46. A wall clock gains 2 minutes in 12 hours, while a table clock loses 2 minutes in 36 hours; both are set right at noon on Tuesday. The correct time when they both show the same time next would be
(a) 12:30 night (b) 12 noon
(c) 1:30 night (d) 12 night

47. Two points A and B are located 48 km apart on the riverfront. A motorboat must go from A to B and return to A as soon as possible. The river flows at 6 km/h. What must be the least speed of the motorboat in still water for the trip from A to B and back again to be completed in not more than six hours (assume that the motorboat does not stop at B)?
(a) 18 km/h (b) 16 km/h
(c) 25 km/h (d) 46 km/h

48. Two *ghats* are located on a riverbank and are 21 km apart. Leaving one of the ghats for the other, a motorboat returns to the first *ghat* in 270 minutes, spending 40 min of that time in taking the passengers at the second *ghat*. Find the speed of the boat in still water if the speed of the river flow is 2.5 km/h?
(a) 10.4 km/h (b) 12.5 km/h
(c) 22.5 km/h (d) 11.5 km/h

49. A train leaves Muzaffarpur for Hazipur at 2:15 p.m. and travels at the rate of 50 kmph. Another train leaves Hazipur for Muzaffarpur at 1:35 p.m. and travels at the rate of 60 kmph. If the distance between

Hazipur and Muzaffarpur is 590 km at what distance from Muzaffarpur will the two trains meet?

(a) 200 km (b) 300 km
(c) 250 km (d) 225 km

50. A dog after travelling 50 km meets a *swami* who counsels him to go slower. He then proceeds at 3/4 of his former speed and arrives at his destination 35 minutes late. Had the meeting occurred 24 km further the dog would have reached its destination 25 minutes late. The speed of the dog is

(a) 48 km/h (b) 36 km/h
(c) 54 km/h (d) 58 km/h

51. Ajay and Vijay start running simultaneously from the same point on a circular track in the same direction. If Ajay is running with a uniform speed of 'a' kmph and Vijay is running with 'b' kmph, they meet for the first time when Ajay is in his 4th round and Vijay is in his 3rd round. Which of the following can be value of $a : b$ (If $a > b$)?

(a) 1.4 (b) 1.46
(c) 1.35

Type (1) If only one option is correct.
Type (2) If two options are correct.
Type (3) If all the options are correct.
Type (4) If no option is correct.

52. Ozair starts for Pune from Mumbai at 2 PM, after reaching Pune he takes 2 hours to finish his work. After finishing his work he starts his return journey at $4/5^{th}$ of his previous speed. He reached Mumbai at 8:30 PM on the same day. If the distance between Pune and Mumbai is 100 kilometers, then find the speed (in km/hr) with which he returns back to Mumbai?

Directions for questions 53 and 54:

Dhoni and Kohli start running simultaneously from opposite ends on a race-track of length 100 m with speeds of 10 m/s and 4 m/s respectively. If both of them keep running continuously from one end to the other end (to and fro) then answer the following questions.

53. After how much time (in seconds) would they meet for the third time?

54. When they meet for the third time what will be the distance of Dhoni (in meters) from his starting point?

Directions for Questions 55 and 56:

Two places A and B are 120 feet apart. Ramesh starts travelling from A to B and at the same time Akhilesh starts travelling from B to A. Ramesh travels $1/3^{rd}$ of the total journey at a speed of 8 feet/minute, half of the remaining distance at 10 feet/minute and the rest at 16 feet/minute. Akhilesh completes the whole journey by travelling at 8 feet/minute, 10 feet/minute and 12 feet/minute, respectively, for equal intervals of time. Based on the above information answer questions 55 and 56:

55. The distance between Ramesh and Akhilesh after 5 minutes of the start of the journey was found to be 'x' meters. Find the value of x.

56. After how much time (in seconds) of the starting of the journey will they cross each other?

57. Bhola and Vijay start running simultaneously on a circular track from the same points in the same direction. How many times Bhola meets Vijay before they meet at the starting point for the first time (Ratio of speeds of Bhola and Vijay is 6:1)?

Directions for Questions 58 and 59:

Two trains — A and B simultaneously started from Delhi to Agra and Agra to Delhi respectively. After reaching their respective destinations, they turned back towards their starting points and finished their journeys after reaching their starting stations. They met for the first time at a distance of 80 km away from the Delhi station and they met for the second time 40 km away from the Agra station. It is further known that during both the meetings they were travelling in the opposite direction. Answer the following questions:

58. What is the distance (in km) between Delhi and Agra?

59. What is the ratio of the speeds of trains B and A?

60. Anand Pagare entered a bar between 12 AM to 1 AM when the angle between the minute hand and the hour hand of the clock was at 30°. If he spent exactly 1 hour 20 minutes in the bar and came out, and he came out at a time represented by A : B : C where A represents hours, B represents minutes and C represents seconds. Then, find the value of A + B + C.

Note: Take C as a whole number only.

61. A *tonga* started travelling at 10:00 in the morning at a speed of 24 km/hr from Chandigarh towards Delhi. A car started on the same route from Chandigarh at 12:15 PM at a speed of 60 km/hr and in the same direction. After half an hour, it had a puncture and needed 45 minutes to repair it. At what distance from Chandigarh, do the two meet?

(a) 90 km (b) 120 km
(c) 150 km (d) 180 km

62. If the ratio of speeds of three sprinters is 3 : 4 : 5 find the ratio of time taken by the three to cover 100 meters.

(a) 3 : 4 : 5 (b) 5 : 4 : 3
(c) 1 : 1 : 1 (d) 20 : 15 : 12

63. P and Q travel from D to A and break journey at M in between. Somewhere between D and M, P asks "How far have we travelled?" Q replies, "Half as far as the distance from here to M". Somewhere between M and A, exactly 300 km from the point where P asks the first question, "How far have we to go?" Q replies, "Half as far as the distance from M to here". The distance between D and A is

(a) 250 km (b) 350 km
(c) 450 km (d) 500 km

64. A, B and C start simultaneously from X to Y. A reaches Y, turns back and meets B at a distance of 11 km from Y. B reaches Y, turns back and meets C at a distance of 9 km from Y. If the ratio of the speeds of A and C is 3:2, what is the distance between X and Y?

(a) 99 km (b) 100 km
(c) 120 km (d) 142 km

65. Laila drives to the station each day to pick up her husband Majnu, who usually arrives on a train at 6 o'clock. Last Monday, Majnu finished work earlier, caught an earlier train and arrived at the station at 5 'o clock. He started to walk home and eventually met Laila who drove him the rest of the way, getting home 20 minutes earlier than usual. On Tuesday, he again finished early and found himself at the station at 5:30 PM. Again he began to walk home, again he met Laila on the way, and she drove him home the rest of the way, Assume constant speed throughout with no wasted time for waiting, backing of the car, etc. How earlier than the usual time were they home on Tuesday?

(a) 6 minutes (b) 8 minutes
(c) 10 minutes (d) 12 minutes

High Yield Questions

Scan this QR code to access assisted problem solving videos on questions 1, 2, 3 and 33 from LOD 2

Space for Rough Work

LEVEL OF DIFFICULTY (III)

1. Two people started simultaneously towards each other from Siliguri and Darjeeling, which are 60 km apart. They met five hours later. After their meeting, the first person, who travelled from Siliguri to Darjeeling, decreased his speed by 1.5 km/h and the other person, who travelled from Darjeeling to Siliguri, increased his speed by 1.5 km/h. The first person is known to arrive at Darjeeling 2.5 hours earlier than the second person arrived at Siliguri. Find the initial speed of the first person.
(a) 4.5 km/h (b) 6 km/h
(c) 7.5 km/h (d) 9 km/h
2. Two friends Arun and Nishit, on their last day in college, decided to meet after 20 years on a river. Arun had to sail 42 km to the meeting place and Nishit had to sail 35 5/7 per cent less. To arrive at the meeting place at the same time as his friend Nishit, Arun started at the same time as Nishit and sailed with the speed exceeding by 5 km/h, the speed of Nishit. Find the speed of Arun.
(a) 10 km/h (b) 14 km/h
(c) 9 km/h (d) Both (b) and (c)
3. Three cars leave Patna for Ranchi after equal time intervals. They reach Ranchi simultaneously and then leave for Vizag, which is 120 km from Ranchi. The first car arrives there an hour after the second car, and the third car, having reached Vizag, immediately reverses the direction and 40 km from Vizag meets the first car. Find the speed of the first car.
(a) 30 km/h (b) 19 km/h
(c) 32 km/h (d) 22 km/h
4. Two sea trawlers left a sea port simultaneously in two mutually perpendicular directions. Half an hour later, the shortest distance between them was 17 km, and another 15 min later, one sea trawler was 10.5 km farther from the origin than the other. Find the speed of each sea trawler.
(a) 16 km/h, 30 km/h (b) 18 km/h, 24 km/h
(c) 20 km/h, 22 km/h (d) 18 km/h, 36 km/h
5. Shaurya and Arjit take a straight route to the same terminal point and travel with constant speeds. At the initial moment, the positions of the two and the terminal point form an equilateral triangle. When Arjit covered a distance of 80 km, the triangle becomes right- angled. When Arjit was at a distance of 120 km from the terminal point, then Shaurya arrived at the point. Find the distance between them at the initial moment assuming that there are integral distances throughout the movements described.
(a) 300 km (b) 240 km
(c) 200 km (d) 225 km
6. Mrinalini and Neha travel to Connaught Place along two straight roads with constant speeds. At the initial moment, the positions of Mrinalini, Neha, and Connaught Place form a right triangle. After Mrinalini travelled 30 km, the triangle between the points became equilateral. Find the distance between Mrinalini and Neha at the initial moment, if at the time Mrinalini arrived at Connaught Place, Neha had to cover 6.66 km to reach Connaught Place.
(a) $10\sqrt{3}$ km (b) $12\sqrt{3}$ km
(c) $30\sqrt{5}$ km (d) None of these
7. Three cars started simultaneously from Ajmer to Benaras along the same highway. The second car travelled with a speed that was 10 km/h higher than the first car's speed and arrived at Benaras one hour earlier than the first car. The third car arrived at Benaras 33.33 minutes earlier than the first car, travelling half the time at the speed of the first car and the other half at the speed of the second car. Find the total distance covered by these three cars during their journey between Ajmer and Benaras.
(a) 360 km (b) 600 km
(c) 540 km (d) 840 km
8. Three sprinters A, B, and C had to sprint from points P to Q and back again (starting in that order). The time interval between the starting times of the three sprinters A, B and C was five seconds each. Thus, C started ten seconds after A, while B started five seconds after A. The three sprinters passed a certain point R, which is somewhere between P and Q, simultaneously (none of them having reached point Q yet). Having reached Q and reversed the direction, the third sprinter met the second one 9 meters short of Q and met the first sprinter 15 meters short of Q. Find the speed of the first sprinter if the distance between PQ is equal to 55 meters.
(a) 4 m/s (b) 3 m/s
(c) 2 m/s (d) 1 m/s
9. Two trains start from the same point simultaneously and in the same direction. The first train travels at 40 km/h, and the speed of the second train is 25 per cent more than the speed of the first train. Thirty minutes later, a third train starts from the same point and in the same direction. It overtakes the second train 90 minutes later than it overtook the first train. What is the speed of the third train?
(a) 20 km/h (b) 40 km/h
(c) 60 km/h (d) 80 km/h
10. A passenger train left town Alpha for town Beta. At the same time, a goods train left Beta for Alpha. The speed of each train is constant throughout the whole

trip. Two hours after the trains met, they were 450 km apart. The passenger train arrived at the place of destination 16 hours after their meeting and the goods train, 25 hours after the meeting. How long did it take the passenger train to make the whole trip?

(a) 21 hours (b) 28 hours
(c) 14 hours (d) None of these

11. Two ducks move along the circumference of a circular pond in the same direction and come alongside each other every 54 minutes. If they moved with the same speeds in the opposite directions, they would meet every nine minutes. It is known that when the ducks moved along the circumference in opposite directions, the distance between them decreased from 54 to 14 feet every 48 seconds. What is the speed of the slower duck?

(a) 20 feet/min (b) 15 feet/min
(c) 30 feet/min (d) 20.83 feet/min

12. Dev and Nishit started simultaneously from opposite points X and Y on a straight road, at constant speeds. When Dev had covered 40% of the distance from X to Y, Nishit was 4 km away from Dev after having crossed Dev. When Nishit had covered half the way, Dev was 10 km short of the midpoint. Find a possible time it took Dev to cover the distance from X to Y to the time it took Nishit to cover the same distance.

(a) $\left[\frac{1+\sqrt{3}}{2}\right]$ (b) $\frac{3\sqrt{2}+4}{2\sqrt{2}+2}$
(c) Either (a) or (b) (d) None of these

13. For Question 12, which of these is a possible value of the distance between the points X and Y?

(a) $20(2+\sqrt{3})$ (b) $20(1+\sqrt{2})$
(c) 60 km (d) Both (a) and (b)

14. Two ships sail in a fog towards each other with the same speed. When they are 4 km apart, the captains decelerate the engines for four minutes with a deceleration rate of 0.1 m/s^2, and then the ships continue sailing with the speeds attained. For what range of values of the initial speed V_0 will the ships avoid collision?

(a) $0 < V_0 < 10$ m/s (b) $0 < V_0 < 24$ m/s
(c) $0 < V_0 < 30$ m/s (d) None of these

15. Three points A, B and C are located at the vertices of an equilateral triangle with sides equal to 168 meters. A donkey called Dinky starts from A to B at 60 meters/hour and at the same time a cow called Moo starts from B to C at 30 meters/hour. In what time after their departure will the distance between the donkey and the cow be the least?

(a) 2 hours (b) 3 hours
(c) 0.5 hours (d) 8 hours

16. A train has to travel the distance between Aurangabad and Daulatabad, equal to 20 km, at a constant speed. It travelled half the way with the specified speed and stopped for three minutes, to arrive at Daulatabad on time, it had to increase its speed by 10 km/h for the rest of the way. Next time, the train stopped half-way for five minutes. By what speed must it increase its speed for the remaining half of the distance to arrive at Daulatabad as per the schedule?

(a) 10 km/h (b) 20 km/h
(c) 15 km/h (d) 16 km/h

17. Nishit travels from Patna to Kolkata, a distance of 200 km at the speed of 40 km/h. At the same time, Ravi starts from Kolkata at a speed of 20 km/h along a road, which is perpendicular to the road on which Nishit is travelling. When will Nishit and Ravi be closest to each other?

(a) In 1.5 hours (b) In 4 hours
(c) In 3.33 hours (d) In 5 hours

18. Two towns are at a distance of 240 km from each other. A motorist takes 8 hours to cover the distance if he travels at a speed of V_0 km/h from town A to an intermediate town C, and then continues on his way with an acceleration of x km/hr^2. He needs the same time to cover the whole distance if he travels from A to C at V_0 km/h and from C to B at V_1 km/h or from A to C at V_1 km/h and from C to B at V_0 km/h. Find V_0 if the acceleration 'x' is double V_0 in magnitude and $V_0 \neq V_1$.

(a) 15 km/h (b) 10 km/h
(c) 20 km/h (d) 8 km/h

19. Jaideep travels from Alaska, which is on a highway, to Burgen, which is 16 km from the highway. The distance between Alaska and Burgen along a straight line is 34 km. At what point should Jaideep turn from the highway to reach Burgen in the shortest possible time, if his speed along the highway is 10 km/h and 6 km/h otherwise.

(a) 30 km away from Alaska
(b) 20 km away from Alaska
(c) 18 km away from Alaska
(d) 15 km away from Alaska

20. An object begins moving at time moment $t = 0$ and 4 s after the beginning of the motion, attains the acceleration of 3 m/s^2. Find the speed of the object 6 s after the beginning of motion if it is known that the speed of the body varies accordingly to the law $v(t) = (t^2 + 2b.t + 4)$ m/s and the object moves along a straight line.

(a) 22 m/s (b) 10 m/s
(c) 30 m/s (d) 15 m/s

21. For question 20, find the distance covered by the object in the first seven seconds if we assume that the speed of the object in a particular second is the speed it attains at the start of the second.

(a) 15 meters (b) 14 meters
(c) 10 meters (d) 5 meters

22. Three *ghats* X, Y and Z on the Yamuna in Delhi are located on the river bank. The speed of the river flow is 8 km/h in the direction of its flow, *Ghat* Y being located midway between X and Z. A raft and a launch leave Y at the same time, the raft travelling down the river to Z and the launch travelling to X. The speed of the launch in still water is V km/h. Having reached X, the launch reverses its direction and starts to Z. Find the range of values of V for which the launch arrives at Z later than the raft.
(a) $8 < V < 24$ km/h (b) $8 < V < 16$ km/h
(c) $8 < V < 20$ km/h (d) $12 < V < 24$ km/h

23. A pedestrian left point A for a walk, going with the speed of V km/h. When the pedestrian was at a distance of 6 km from A, a cyclist followed him, starting from A and cycling at a speed 9 km/h higher than that of the pedestrian. When the cyclist overtook the pedestrian, they turned back and returned to A together, at the speed of 4 km/h. At what V will the time spent by the pedestrian on his total journey from A to A be the least?
(a) 5 km/h (b) 6 km/h
(c) 6.1 km/h (d) 5.5 km/h

24. A cyclist left point A for point B and travelled at the constant speed of 25 km/h. When he covered the distance of 8.33 km, he was overtaken by a car that left point A twelve minutes after the cyclist and travelled at a constant speed too. When the cyclist travelled another 30 km, he encountered the car returning from B. Assume that the car did not stop at point B. Find the distance between A and B.
(a) 39.5833 km (b) 41.0833 km
(c) 60.833 km (d) 43.33 km

25. A robot began moving from point A in a straight line at 6 PM with an initial speed of 3 m/s. One second later, the speed of the robot became equal to 4 m/s. Find the acceleration of the robot at the end of the 2nd second if its speed is governed by the law $s(t) = (at^2 + 2t + (b))$.
(a) 1 m/s^2 (b) −1 m/s^2
(c) 0 m/s^2 (d) 2 m/s^2

26. For Question 25, the distance of the robot from point A after 6 seconds will be (assuming that for every second, the robot travels at a constant speed equal to its starting speed for that second and any acceleration occurs at the start of the next second)
(a) 45 meters (b) 36 meters
(c) 10 meters (d) 7 meters

27. Two friends Amit and Akshay began moving simultaneously from point A along a straight line in the same direction. Amit started moving at the speed of 5 m/s and moved with a uniform acceleration of 4 m/s^2, while his friend Akshay moved at a uniform speed. The limits for Akshay's speed (S) so that he should first leave Amit behind and then get overtaken by Amit at a distance of less than 27 m
(a) $5 < S < 9$ (b) $3 < S < 5$
(c) $4 < S < 8$ (d) None of these

28. On the banks of the river Ganges, there are two bathing points in Varanasi and Patna. A *diya* left in the river at Varanasi reaches Patna in 24 hours. However, a motorboat covers the whole way to-and-fro in exactly ten hours. If the speed of the motorboat in still water is increased by 40%, then it takes the motorboat seven hours to cover the same way (from Varanasi to Patna and back again). Find the time necessary for the motorboat to sail from Varanasi to Patna when its speed in still water is not increased.
(a) 3 hours (b) 4 hours
(c) 4.8 hours (d) None of these

29. Two friends started walking simultaneously from points A and B towards each other. The distance between them 144 minutes later was 20% of the original distance. How many hours does it take the faster walker to cover the distance AB if he needs eight hours less to travel the distance than his friend (assume all times to be in whole numbers and in hours)?
(a) 3 hours (b) 6 hours
(c) 12 hours (d) 4 hours

30. Two cars left points A and B simultaneously, travelling towards each other. Nine hours after their meeting, the car travelling from A arrived at B, and sixteen hours after their meeting, the car travelling from B arrived at A. How many hours did it take the slower car to cover the whole distance?
(a) 36 hours (b) 21 hours
(c) 25 hours (d) 28 hours

31. A pedestrian and a cyclist left Nagpur for Buti Bori at the same time. Having reached Buti Bori, the cyclist turned back and met the pedestrian an hour after the start. After their meeting, the pedestrian continued his trip to Buti Bori and the cyclist turned back and also headed for Buti Bori. Having reached Buti Bori, the cyclist turned back again and met the pedestrian 30 minutes after their first meeting. Determine what time it takes the pedestrian to cover the distance between Nagpur and Buti Bori.
(a) 1 hour (b) 2 hours
(c) 2.5 hours (d) 3 hours

32. Points A, B and C are at the distances of 120, 104.66 and 112 km from point M respectively. Three people left these points for point M simultaneously: the first person started from point A, the second from B and the third from C. The first person covered the whole way at a constant speed and arrived at M an hour before the second and the third persons (who arrived simultaneously). The third person covered the whole way at a constant speed. The second person, having

travelled 72 km at the same speed as the first, stopped for two hours. The rest of the way he travelled at a speed that is less than the speed of the third person by the same amount as the speed of the third is less than that of the first. Determine the speed of the first person.

(a) 6 km/h (b) 5 km/h
(c) 4 km/h (d) 3 km/h

33. Two people started simultaneously from points A and B towards each other. At the moment, the person who started from A had covered two-thirds of the way; the other person had covered 2 km less than half the total distance. If it is known that when the person who started from B had covered 1/4 of the way, the other person was 3 km short of the midpoint. Find the distance between A and B. The speeds of the two people were constant.

(a) $(15 - 3\sqrt{17})$ km (b) $(15 + 3\sqrt{17})$ km
(c) Both (a) and (b) (d) $3\sqrt{17} - 5$ km

34. Sohan and Lallan left their house simultaneously. Thirty six minutes later, Sohan met his uncle travelling to their house, while Lallan met the uncle twelve minutes after Sohan. Twenty-four minutes after his meeting with Lallan, the uncle rang the door bell at Sohan and Lallan's house. Assume each person travels at a constant speed. Find the ratio of the speeds of Sohan to Lallan to the uncle.

(a) 1:2:2 (b) 1:3:2
(c) 3:1:3 (d) 2:1:2

35. The distance between two towns—Aurangabad and Jalna is 80 km. A bus left Aurangabad and travelled at a constant speed towards Jalna. Thirty minutes later, Deepak Jhunjhunwala left Aurangabad in his car towards Jalna. He overtook the bus in thirty minutes and continued on his way to Jalna. After a 15 minute stop at Jalna, he turned back and again encountered the bus 80 minutes after he had left Aurangabad. Determine the speed of the bus.

(a) 40 km/h (b) 45 km/h
(c) 50 km/h (d) None of these

36. Rohit left Mahabaleshwar for Nashik at 6 AM An hour and a half later Vimal, whose speed was 5 km/h higher than that of Rohit left Mahabaleshwar. At 10:30 PM of the same day, the distance between the two friends was 21 km. Find the speed of Vimal.

(a) 40 km/h (b) 29 km/h
(c) 69 km/h (d) Either (b) or (c)

37. Aurangzeb and Babar with their troops left from Delhi and Daulatabad towards each other simultaneously. Each of them marched at a constant speed and, having arrived at their respective points of destination, went back at once. Their first meeting was 14 km from Daulatabad, and the second meeting, eight hours after the first meeting was at a distance of 2 km from Delhi. Find the distance between the Delhi and Daulatabad.

(a) 30 km (b) 25 km
(c) 35 km (d) Cannot be determined

38. Two tourists left simultaneously point A for point B; the first tourist covers each kilometer two minutes faster than the second. After travelling 30 per cent of the way, the first tourist returned to A, stopped there for 102 minutes and again started for B. The two tourists arrived at B simultaneously. What is the distance between A and B if the second tourist covered it in 2.5 hours?

(a) 60 km (b) 70 km
(c) 45 km (d) None of these

39. Amar and Akbar left Bhubaneshwar simultaneously and travelled towards Cuttack. Amar's speed was 15 km/h and that of Akbar was 12 km/h. Half-an-hour later, Anthony left Bhubaneshwar and travelled in the same direction. Sometime later, he overtook Akbar and 90 minutes further on, he overtook Amar. Find Anthony's speed.

(a) 18 km/h (b) 24 km/h
(c) 20 km/h (d) 16 km/h

40. Two bodies, moving along a circle in the same direction, meet every 49 minutes. Had they moved at the same speeds in the opposite directions, they would meet every seven minutes. If, moving in the opposite directions, the bodies are at the distance of 40 meters from each other along the arc at time $t = 0$, then at $t = 24$ seconds, their distance will be 26 meters (the bodies do not meet during those 24 seconds). Find the speed of the faster body in meters per minute.

(a) 15 (b) 20
(c) 25 (d) None of these

41. The distance between Varanasi and Lucknow is 220 km. Two buses start from these towns towards each other. They can meet halfway if the first bus leaves two hours earlier than the second. If they start simultaneously, they will meet in four hours. Find the speeds of the buses.

(a) $17.5(3 + \sqrt{5})$ km/h, $17.5(1 + \sqrt{5})$ km/h
(b) $27.5(3 + \sqrt{5})$ km/h, $27.5(1 + \sqrt{5})$ km/h
(c) $27.5(3 - \sqrt{5})$ km/h, $27.5(\sqrt{5} - 1)$ km/h
(d) None of these

42. A road passes through the towns Sangamner and Yeotmal. A cyclist started from Sangamner in the direction of Yeotmal. At the same time, two pedestrians started from Yeotmal travelling at the same speed, the first of them towards Sangamner and the other in the opposite direction. The cyclist covered the distance between the towns in half an hour and, continued ahead in the same direction. He overtook the second pedestrian, 1.2 hours after he met the first pedestrian. Determine the time the cyclist spent travelling from Sangamner to the point of the meeting with the first pedestrian (assuming the speeds of the cyclist and the pedestrians to be constant).

(a) 24 min (b) 18 min
(c) 30 min (d) Cannot be determined

43. Two people A and B start moving from P and Q that are 200 km apart, towards each other A is on a moped and B on foot. They meet at a point R when A gives B a lift to P and returns to his original path to reach Q. On reaching Q he finds that he has taken 2.6 times his normal time. B on the other hand realises that he has saved 40 minutes over his normal travel time. Find the ratio of their speeds.

(a) 3 : 2 (b) 4 : 3
(c) 3 : 1 (d) None of these

44. For Question 43, find the speed of the moped.

(a) 160 km/h (b) 180 km/h
(c) 200 km/h (d) None of these

45. Three friends A, B and C start from P to Q that are 100 km apart. A is on a moped while B is riding pillion and C walks on. A takes B to a point R and returns to pick up C on the way and takes him to point Q. B, on the other hand, walks to Q from point R (R is the mid-point between P and Q).

If the ratio of speeds of the three people is 5: 2: 2, find where will the last person be when the first person reaches Q.

(a) 12.85 km from Q (b) 12.75 km from Q
(c) 16.66 km from Q (d) 83.33 km from P

46. A motorboat moves from point A to point B and back again, both points being located on the river-bank. If the speed of the boat in still water is doubled, then the trip from A to B and back again would take 20% of the time that the motorboat usually spends in the journey. How many times is the actual speed of the launch higher than the speed of the river flow?

(a) $\frac{3}{5}$ (b) $\frac{5}{3}$
(c) $\frac{2}{3}$ (d) None of these

47. A watch loses 2/3% time during the first week and gains 1/3% time during the next week. If on a Sunday noon, it showed the right time, what time will it show at noon on the Sunday after the next?

(a) 11: 26: 24 AM (b) 10: 52: 18 AM.
(c) 10: 52: 48 AM (d) 11: 36: 24 AM

48. Clocks A, B and C strike every hour. B slows down and takes two minutes longer than A per hour while C becomes faster and takes two minutes less than A per hour. If they strike together at 12 midnight, when will they strike together again?

(a) 10 AM (b) 11 AM
(c) 9 PM (d) 12 noon

49. A boat went down the river for a distance of 20 km. It then turned back and returned to its starting point, having travelled a total of seven hours. On its return trip, at a distance of 12 km from the starting point, it encountered a log, which had passed the starting point at the moment at which the boat had started downstream. The downstream speed of the boat is

(a) 7 km/h (b) 13 km/h
(c) 16 km/h (d) 10 km/h

50. Two boats go downstream from point X to point Y. The faster boat covers the distance from X to Y 1.5 times as fast as the slower boat. It is known that for every hour, the slower boat lags behind the faster boat by 8 km. However, if they go upstream, then the faster boat covers the distance from Y to X in half the time as the slower boat. Find the speed of the faster boat in still water.

(a) 12 km/h (b) 20 km/h
(c) 24 km/h (d) 25 km/h

High Yield Questions

Scan to access assisted problem solving videos on questions 1, 2, 5 and 9 from LOD 3

Space for Rough Work

ANSWER KEY

Level of Difficulty (I)

1. (a)	2. (d)	3. (a)	4. (b)
5. (c)	6. (a)	7. (c)	8. (b)
9. (a)	10. (b)	11. (d)	12. (a)
13. (b)	14. (a)	15. (b)	16. (a)
17. (d)	18. (a)	19. (d)	20. (a)
21. (a)	22. (d)	23. (d)	24. (c)
25. (b)	26. (b)	27. (a)	28. (a)
29. (c)	30. (c)	31. (c)	32. (a)
33. (c)	34. (d)	35. (d)	36. (c)
37. (d)	38. (a)	39. (d)	40. (a)
41. (b)	42. (c)	43. (d)	44. (a)
45. (c)	46. (b)	47. (a)	48. (a)
49. (d)	50. (c)		

Level of Difficulty (II)

1. (c)	2. (a)	3. (a)	4. (c)
5. (a)	6. (b)	7. (b)	8. (d)
9. (b)	10. (a)	11. (b)	12. (c)
13. (c)	14. (b)	15. (b)	16. (a)
17. (c)	18. (d)	19. (b)	20. (b)
21. (b)	22. (c)	23. (a)	24. (c)
25. (d)	26. (b)	27. (c)	28. (c)
29. (d)	30. (d)	31. (c)	32. (b)
33. (d)	34. (b)	35. (c)	36. (c)
37. (a)	38. (c)	39. (b)	40. (d)
41. (b)	42. (b)	43. (c)	44. (c)
45. (a)	46. (b)	47. (a)	48. (d)
49. (c)	50. (a)	51. 3	52. 40
53. 21.42	54. 14.28	55. 38	56. 414
57. 5	58. 200	59. 1.5	60. 53
61. (b)	62. (d)	63. (c)	64. (a)
65. (c)			

Level of Difficulty (III)

1. (c)	2. (b)	3. (a)	4. (a)
5. (b)	6. (d)	7. (b)	8. (d)
9. (c)	10. (d)	11. (d)	12. (b)
13. (b)	14. (b)	15. (a)	16. (b)
17. (b)	18. (c)	19. (c)	20. (b)
21. (b)	22. (a)	23. (b)	24. (c)
25. (b)	26. (d)	27. (a)	28. (b)
29. (d)	30. (d)	31. (b)	32. (a)
33. (c)	34. (d)	35. (a)	36. (b)
37. (d)	38. (a)	39. (a)	40. (b)
41. (d)	42. (b)	43. (d)	44. (d)
45. (a)	46. (d)	47. (c)	48. (d)
49. (d)	50. (b)		

SOLUTIONS AND SHORTCUTS

Level of Difficulty (I)

1. In this question, the distance travelled by both the trains is equal. Hence, the ratio of time for the travel being 4:3 (Geetanjali to Calcutta Mail), the ratio of speeds would be 3:4. Since, the sum of their average speeds is 140 km/h, their respective speeds would be 60 and 80 km/h respectively. Use alligation (or total distance/total time formula) to get the answer as 68.57 km/h.
2. If you assume that the initial stretch of track is covered by the two trains in time t each, the following figure will give you a clearer picture.

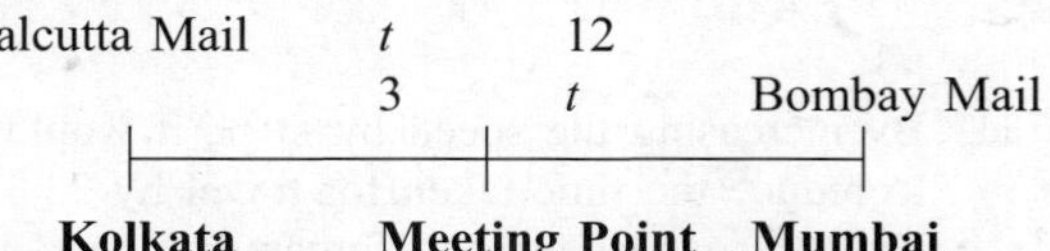

From the above figure, we can deduce that, $t/3 = 12/t$.
Hence, $t^2 = 36$, gives us $t = 6$.
Hence, the distance between Kolkata to the starting point is covered by the Calcutta Mail in six hours, while the same distance is covered by the Bombay Mail in three hours.
Hence, the ratio of their speeds would be 1:2. Hence, the Bombay Mail would travel at 96 km/h.
3. Since he gains two hours by driving both ways (instead of walking one way), the time taken for driving would be two hours less than the time taken for walking. Hence, he stands to lose another two hours by walking both ways. Hence, his total time should be 10 hrs 45 minutes.
4. Assume the original speed of the train to be '*s*'. According to the question, the train is running at $\frac{7}{11} \times s$.
The total distance would be $\frac{7}{11} \times s \times 22 = 14s$. At its original speed of '*s*', it would take $14s/s = 14$ hours to do the same journey. Hence, it would end up saving eight hours.
5. Total distance/Total time = 1590/15 = 106 km/h.
6. Assume the distance to be *d*. Then, $d/6 + d/4 = 10 \rightarrow d = 24$ km.
7. In four hours, the train will travel 180 km (180,000 meters). The number of poles would be 180,000/50 = 3600.
8. At 40 km/h, Harsh would cover (200/60) × 40 km. = 400/3 km = 133.33 km
This represents the distance by which Vijay would be ahead of Harsh, when Vijay reaches the endpoint means in essence that Vijay must have travelled for 133.33/20 hours → 6.66 hours.
Hence, the distance is 60 × 6.66 = 400 km.

9. The key for this question is to understand that when he increases his speed by 50%, his time would go down by 33.33% (since the motions are described on the same distance). In this particular case, when he is increasing his speed from 10 km/h to 15 km/h (50% increase in speed), his time is dropping by two hours. This two-hour drop in time is also equal to a 33.33% drop in time. Hence, at10km/h, his original time would have been six hours. Hence, he leaves home at 7 AM and the distance travelled is 10 × 6 = 60 km. If he has to reach the same point by 12 noon, he should cover the distance in five hours. His speed would be 60/5 = 12 km/h.

10. $\frac{d}{\frac{11}{3}} - \frac{d}{4} = 3 \rightarrow \frac{3d}{11} - \frac{d}{4} = 3 \rightarrow d = 132.$

11. By increasing the speed by 50%, it would be able to reduce the time taken for travel by 33.33%. But since this is just able to overcome a time delay of 30 minutes, 30 minutes must be equivalent to 33.33% of the time originally taken. Hence, the original time must have been 1.5 hours and the original speed would be 1000 km/h. Hence, the new speed would be 1500 km/h.

    Alternately, $\frac{1500}{s} - \frac{1500}{1.5s} = 0.5 \rightarrow s = 1000$ and $1.5s = 1500$.

12. Assume a distance of 60 km in each stretch. Get the average speed by the formula. Total distance/ Total time = 180/10 = 18 km/h.

13. Since the distance ratio is 4:3:6 and speed ratio is also 4:3:6, we get the time ratio by dividing the distance ratio by the speed ratio → Hence, the time ratio = 4/4:3/3:6/6 = 1:1:1.

    (Note: Theory point: This logic comes from the chapter on ratios, where we know that if there are two variables that have a division relationship between them to give an outcome variable; you can simply divide the ratios of the first two variables to get the ratio of the outcome variable. For example, expenditure ratio of three families on rice: 4:3:5; consumption ratio of rice: 4:3:5 → price ratio of rice purchased = 1:1:1.)

14. At 6:45, the first train would have taken a lead of $\frac{3}{4} \times 98 = 73.5$ km. The relative speed being 38 km/h, the time taken to catch up for the second train would be $\frac{73.5}{38}$. Hence, distance from the starting point = $\frac{73.5}{38} \times 136 \approx 263.05$.

15. Solve this one by assuming the speed of the bus from the options. For option (b) 60, we get: In the first case, distance travelled by bus being 120 km, he would take two hours. Remaining distance = 480 km, in six hours would mean that the speed of the car would be 80 km/h. If he goes 200 km by bus, and 400 km by car, he would take 3 hours 20 minutes by bus and 5 hours by car = a total of 8 hours 20 minutes. This matches the information given in the question – of 20 minutes extra. Hence, this option is correct.

16. When speed goes down to three-fourth (i.e. 75%), time will go up to 4/3rd (or 133.33%) of the original time. Since, the extra time required is 60 minutes; it should be equated to 1/3rd of the normal time. Hence, the usual time required will be 180 minutes.

17. 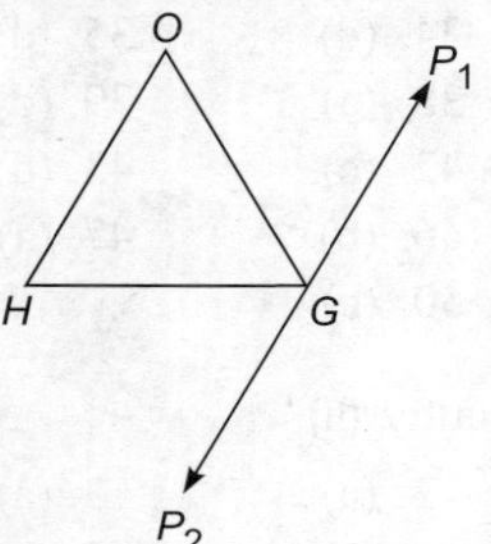

    From the figure above, we see that Shyam would have walked a distance of 4 + 4 + 4 = 12 km (G to P_1, P_1 to G and G to P_2).

18. The diameter of the circle would be given by the hypotenuse of the right triangle with legs 600 and 800, respectively. Hence, the required diameter = 1000 meters.

19. Solve using options. The value in option (d) fits the situation as 40/16 – 40/20 = 2.5 – 2 = 0.5 hours = 30 minutes.

20. The speed of the first car would be 60 km/h while the speed of the second car would be 40 km/h. The relative speed of the two cars would be 100 km/h. To cover 480 km, they would take 480/100 = 4.8 hours → In 4.8 hours, the car travelling from A to B would have travelled 4.8 × 60 = 288 km.

21. Since the faster car has moved 48 km more than the slower one, it can be deduced that the total travel must have been for eight hours. Also, since they are travelling in opposite direction, their relative speed would be 42 + 36 = 78 km/h. The total distance would be: 78 × 8 = 624 km.

22. Since, the distance is same; we can assume any distance to calculate the average speed. In this case, if we take the distance equal to 120 km, then using the formula $\frac{\text{total distance}}{\text{total time}}$, the average speed would be given by: $\frac{120+120}{4} = 60$ km/h.

23. Solve this question using the values given in the options. Option (d) can be seen to fit the situation given by the problem as it gives us the following chain of thought:

If the average speed of the faster train is 48 km/h, the average speed of the slower train would be 32 km/h. In this case, the time taken by the faster train [option (d) is 192/48 = 4 hours] is 2 hours lesser than the time taken by the slower train (192/32 = 6 hours). This satisfies the condition given in the problem and hence, is correct.

24. Refer to the solution of question 2 of this exercise.
25. If the car does half the journey at30 km/h and the other half at 40 km/h, its average speed can be estimated using weighted averages.
Since, the distance travelled in each part of the journey is equal; the ratio of time for which the car would travel will be inverse to the ratio of speeds. Since, the speed ratio is 3:4, the time ratio for the two halves of the journey would be 4:3. The average speed of the car would be:
(30 × 4 + 40 × 3)/7 = 240/7 km/h
It is further known that the car travelled for 17.5 hours (which is also equal to 35/2 hours).
Thus, total distance = average speed × total time = (240 × 35)/ (2 × 7) = 120 × 5 = 600 km.
26. The basic equation in this question would be:
$$\frac{12}{s}+\frac{6}{s+0.5}=\frac{18}{s+0.5}+\frac{1}{3}\rightarrow\frac{12}{s+0.5}=\frac{12}{s}-\frac{1}{3}\rightarrow s=4$$
$$\text{and } s+0.5=4.5\text{ km/h}$$
The total time taken by him would be $\frac{12}{4}+\frac{6}{4.5}=4.33$ km/h hours.
27. The distance covered in the various phases of his travel would be:
10 km + 25 km + 50 km + 60 km.
Thus, the total distance covered = 145 km in 2 hours 50 minutes → 145 km in 2.8333 hours → 51.18 km/h
28. Kalu's speed = 3 m/s.
For 1200 meters, Kalu would take 400 seconds and Sambhu would take 10 seconds less. Hence, 390 seconds.
29. Since, the fuel efficiency of the car is 19.5 km/litre at a speed of 50 km/h, its fuel efficiency at a speed of 70 km/h can be worked out as: Since, the car uses 30% more diesel, it means that for travelling 19.5 km at 70 km/h, the car would take 1.3 litres of diesel. Hence, its fuel efficiency at 70 km/h = 19.5/1.3 = 15 kmpl. In ten litres, it can travel 10 × 15 = 150 km.
30. Since the ratio of speeds is 3:5, the ratio of times would be 5:3. The difference in the times would be 2 (if looked at in the 5:3 ratio contexts). Further, since Ram takes 30 minutes longer, 2 corresponds to 30. Hence, using unitary method, 5 will correspond to 75 and 3 will correspond to 45 minutes. Hence at 10 km/h, Bharat would travel 7.5 km.
31. When the train from Khandala starts off, the train from Lonavala will already have covered 50 km. Hence, 550 km at a relative speed of 60 km/h will take 550/60 hrs. From this, you can get the answer as:
50 + (550/60) × 25 = 279.166 km
32. Since Chandu is moving at a speed of 10 m/s and he has to cover 360 km or 360000 meters, the time taken would be given by 360000/10 seconds = 36000 seconds = 36000/60 minutes = 600 minutes = 10 hours.
33. The average speed would be given by:
$$\frac{3d}{\frac{d}{v_1}+\frac{d}{v_2}+\frac{d}{v_2}}=\frac{3v_1v_2}{2v_1+v_2}$$
34. Since you are starting at 10:30, the first truck you would encounter would be the truck that started at 6:30 from Kolkata. Also, when you reach Kolkata, you will encounter the truck starting from Kolkata at 2:30 PM. Thus, you would encounter all the trucks that started from Kolkata between 6:30 AM to 2:30 PM. This would be a total of seventeen trucks.
35. To reduce the time of the journey by 25%, he should increase his speed by 33.33% or 1/3rd. Thus, required speed = 120 km/h.
36. G B A

In the above figure, the train travels from A to B in 11:30 minutes.
Suppose, you denote the time at which the first gunshot is heard as t = 0. Also, if you consider the travel of the sound of the second, the gunshot is heard at point B at t = 11:30 minutes. Also, the second gunshot should reach point B at t = 12 minutes. Hence, the sound of the second gunshot would take 30 seconds to travel from B to A.
Thus, $\frac{S_{train}}{S_{sound}}=\frac{t_{sound}}{t_{train}}$
$S_{train}=330\times\frac{30}{690}=\frac{330}{23}$ m/s
37. The required speed s would be satisfying the equation:
$$300/s - 300/(s+5) = 2$$
Solving for s from the options it is clear that s = 25.
38. The length of the circular track would be equal to the circumference of the circle. In four minutes thus, the cyclist covers 3.14 × 400 = 1256 meters (using the formula for the circumference of a circle).
Thus, the cyclist's speed would be 1256/4 = 314 meters/minute.
39. We do not have any information about the ratio of the speeds of the car and the walking speed of the man. Hence, we cannot determine the usual time of travel.
40. The distance would get divided in the ratio of speeds (since time is constant). Thus, the distance ratio would be 5: 7 and required distance = 5/12 × 600 = 250 km.

41. The total time taken by the motorist would be 200/53.333 = 200 × 3/160 = 3.75 hours = 3 hours 45 minutes. In the first half of the journey, the motorist covers $1/4^{th}$ the distance at 40km/h. This means that he takes 50/40 = 1.25 hours = 1 hour 15 minutes in covering the first 50 km. This also means that he covers the remaining distance of 150 km in 2 hours 30 minutes → a speed of 60 km/h. Hence, option (b) is correct.
42. Solve through options using trial-and-error. For usual speed 3 km/h (option c), we have:
    Normal time → 2/3 hours = 40 minutes
    At 4 km/h, the time would be 30 minutes. This gives us a reduction of ten minutes. Hence, option (c) is correct.
43. In six minutes, the car goes ahead by 0.6 km. Hence, the relative speed of the car with respect to the pedestrian is equal to 6 km/h. Since, the pedestrian is walking at 2 km/h, hence, the speed of the car is 8 km/h.
44. You can solve this question using the options. Option (a) fits the given situation best as if we take the distance as 12 km, he would have taken one hour to go by car and four hours to come back walking—a total of five hours as given in the problem.
45. The train that leaves at 6 AM would be 75 km ahead of the other train when it starts. Also, the relative speed being 36 km/h, the distance from Mumbai would be:
    (75/36) × 136 = 283.33 km
46. Let the distance between his home and Durgapur be 'd'. It can be inferred from the travel of Ishan, that he reaches Durgapur at 10 AM and leaves back at 12 noon. Thus, the total distance Ishan has travelled for is 1.33 × d in four hours of travel. Next, when he meets the truck on his outward journey at 7:30 AM, the distance from his home would be $d/6$. When they meet at 1 PM, the distance from Durgapur would be $d/3$. Hence, the truck travels $(d - d/3) - d/6 = 0.5d$ in five-and-a-half hours (from 7:30AM to 1 PM).
    $$\text{Speed ratio} = \frac{\frac{1.33d}{4}}{\frac{0.5d}{5.5}} = \frac{5.5}{1.5} = 11:3$$
47. When his speed becomes $3/4^{th}$, his time would increase by $1/3^{rd}$. Thus, the normal time = 7.5 hrs (since increase in time = 2.5 hrs).
48. Since the train travels at 60 km/h, its speed per minute is 1 km per minute. Hence, if its speed with stoppages is 40 km/h, it will travel 40 minutes per hour. Consequently, it would stop for 20 minutes per hour.
49. By increasing his speed by 25%, he will reduce his time by 20%. (This corresponds to a six-minute drop in his time for travel—since he goes from being ten minutes late to only four minutes late.) Hence, his time originally must have been 30 minutes. Hence, the required distance is 20 km/h × 0.5 hours = 10 km.
50. Assume that the total distance is 168 km. Then the respective speeds of the two would be 4 km/minute and 3 km/minute. Their relative speed would be 7 km/minute and hence to cover a distance of 168 km, they would take 168/7 = 24 minutes.

Level of Difficulty (II)

1. By travelling at 10 kmph higher than the original speed, the train is able to make up 16 minutes while traveling 80 km.
   This condition is only satisfied at an initial speed of 50 (and a new speed of 60 kmph).
2. Solve this question through options. For instance, if he travelled at 25 kmph, his original speed would have been 24 kmph.
   The time difference can be seen to be 6 minutes in this case:
   60/24 – 60/25 = 0.1 hrs = 6 mins. Thus, this is the correct answer.
3. In 1 hours 15 minutes an individual will be able to cover 25% more than his speed per hour. The relationship between the original speed and the new speed is best represented as below:
   Original speed $\xrightarrow{\text{25\% increase}}$ speed per 75 minutes $\xrightarrow{\text{+1 increase}}$ New speed.
   Thus, to go from the new speed to the original speed the process would be:
   New speed $\xrightarrow{-1}$ Speed per 75 minutes $\xrightarrow{20\%\downarrow}$ Original speed.
   We need to use this process to check the option. Only the first option satisfies this condition. (at 16 kmph it would take 6 hours while at 12 kmph it would take 8 hours).
4. The question's structure (and solving) have to be done on the basis of integers. The following equations emerge:
   $$\frac{d}{s} - \frac{d}{(s+6)} = 4 \text{ and } \frac{d}{(S-6)} - \frac{d}{(S+6)} = 10$$
   Solving these expressions through normal solving would take a huge amount of time. Instead this question has to be solved using the logic that integral difference in ratios in such a situation can only occur in all the three ratios (d/s), $d/(s + 6)$ and $d/(s - 6)$) are integers.
   Hence, d should have three divisors which are 6 units apart from each other.
5. The relative speed is 20 kmph. Also, the pedestrian should take 7:30 hours more than the cyclist. Using option (a) the speeds of the two people are 4km/hr

and 16 km/hr respectively. At this speed, the respective times would be 10 hrs and 2:30 hours, giving the required answer.

6. 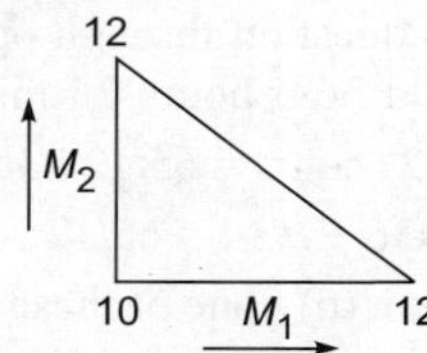

The distance between the motorists will be shown on the hypotenuse. Using the 3, 4, 5 Pythagoras triplet and the condition that the two speeds are 6 kmph different from each other, you will get the triplet as: 18, 24, 30. Hence, the slower motorist travelled at 18 kmph.

7. Since the two motorists meet after an hour, their relative speed is 28 kmph. Use options to check out the values. Since the speed of the faster cyclist is asked for it has to be greater than 14 kmph. Hence only check options > 14 kmph.

8. Since the second ant covers 7/120 of the distance in 2 hours 30 minutes, we can infer that is covers 8.4/120 = 7% of the distance in 3 hours. Thus, in 3 hours both ants together cover 15% of the distance → 5% per hour → they will meet in 20 hours.

   Also, ratio of speeds = 8 : 7.

   So, the second ant would cover 700 ft to the meeting point in 20 hours and its speed would be 35 feet/hr.

9. In this question consider the total distance as 100%. Hence the sum of their speeds will be 75% per hour. Checking option (c).

   If the bus took 6 hours, it would cover 16.66% distance per hour and the car would cover 25% distance per hour. (as it takes 2 hours less than the bus.)

   This gives an addition of only 41.66%. Hence, the answer is not correct.

   Option (b) is the correct answer.

10. The requisite conditions are met on a Pythagoras triplet 6,8,10. Since the racetrack only consists of the legs of the right triangle the length must be 6 + 8 = 14 km.

11. The sum of speeds would be 0.08 km/s (relative speed in opposite direction). Also if we go by option (b), the speeds will be 0.03 and 0.05 km/s respectively. At this speed the overlapping would occur every 60 seconds.

12. When Rahim starts, Karim would have covered 40 km. Also, their relative speed is 12 kmph and the distance between the two would get to 0 in 40/12 = 3.33 hours.

    Distance covered = 28 × 3.33 = 93.33 km.

13. Solve this question through options.

    For option (c), the conditions match since: If he rode for 2 hours (speed = 5 kmph), he would have walked for 6 hours (4 hours more) and his walking speed would be 15 kmph.

    If we interchange the times, we get 15 × 2 = 5 × 6.

14. This is a complex trial and error based question and the way you would have to think in this is:

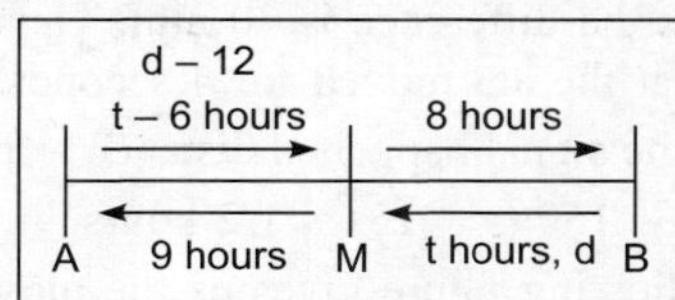

From the figure above, it is clear that A is faster as he takes only $t + 2$ hours while B has taken $t + 9$ hours to complete the journey.

Then, we get: $(t - 6)/9 = 8/t$

Solving for t, we get $t = -6$ (not possible)

Or $t = 12$. Putting this value of t in the figure it changes to:

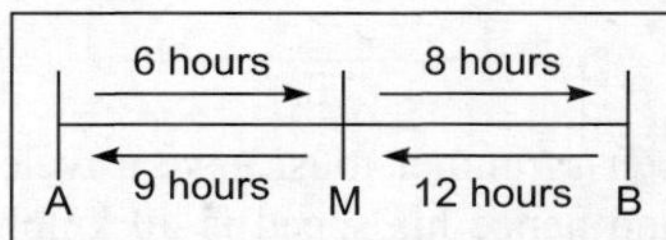

We also get ratio of speeds = 3 : 2 (inverse of ratio of times)

The next part of the puzzle is to think of the 12 km less traveled by the first person till the meeting point.

If the speed of the faster person is $3s$, that of the slower person = $2s$.

Further

$$12 \times 2s - 6 \times 3s = 12 \text{ km}$$

$$s = 2 \text{ kmph.}$$

The speed of the faster tourist is 3 × 2 = 6 kmph

15. Solve using options. The first option you would check for (given the values in the questions) would be option (b). This would give that the first jogger would run at 3 min per km, while the second jogger would run at 4 min per km. In the new condition, the first jogger would jog for 13 km while the second jogger would jog for 14 km and their respective times would be 39 mins and 56 minutes. This is consistent with the condition in the question which talks about a difference of 17 minutes in their respective times.

16. Solve this through options as: For option (a)

    4800/50 – 4800/60 = 16 minutes

17. The ant would cover 7 × 8 = 56 meters in 16 hours. Further, it would require 7/12 of the 17th hour to reach the top. Thus time required = 16 hours 35 minutes

18. If the slower ship took 20 hours (option d) the faster ship would take 12 hours and their respective speeds would be 15 and 25 kmph. This satisfies the basic condition in the question.
19. The movement of the ant in the two cases would be 3, 7, 11, 15, 19, 23 and 1, 9, 17, 25, 33, 41. It can be seen that after 3 seconds the difference is 6mm, after 4 seconds, the difference is 16mm and after 5 seconds the difference is 30 mm. Thus, it is clearly seen that the ant moved for 4 seconds.
20. When the signal happened distance left was 150 km. $150/(s) - 150/(s + 15) = 1/2$ hours $\rightarrow s = 60$.
21. The following figure gives us the movement of the two swimmers:

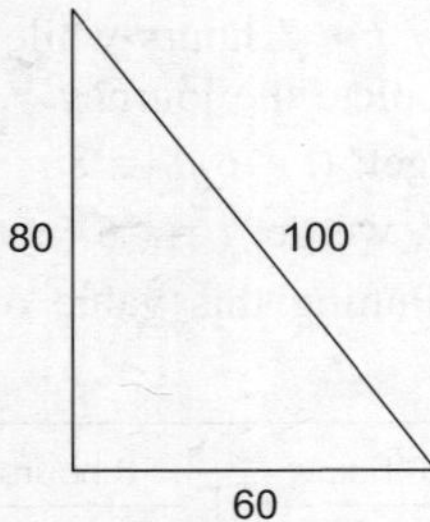

The faster swimmer must have traveled 80 km in 2 hours and hence his speed is 40 kmph.
22. Since they cover the distance in 80 minutes traveling in opposite directions we infer 100% distance is covered in 80 minutes → 1.25% per minute → 75% per hour.
i.e. their combined distance coverage is 75% per hour.
Since we are asked for the time the faster motorcyclist takes, we can pick up this time from the options.

Options	*Time for faster motorcyclist*	*Faster's % coverage per hour*	*Slower's % coverage per hour*
a	6 hours	16.66	58.33
b	3 hours	33.33	41.66
c	2 hours	50	25
d	4 hours	25	50

It is clear that options *a*, *b*, and *d* are not feasible as it is making the faster motorcyclist slower.
Thus option (c) has to be correct.
(**Note:** You can use the values in option (c) to check the other condition in the problem and see that it works.)
23. Since the two horses meet after 200 minutes, they cover 0.5% of the distance per minute (combined) or 30% per hour. This condition is satisfied only if the slower rider takes 10 hours (thereby covering 10% per hour) and the faster rider takes 5 hours (thereby covering 20% per hour).
24. Solve through options the equation: $350/s - 350/(s + 5) = 2.33$ hours.
$\rightarrow s = 25$.
25. Solve this question through options. The total travel time should be 5 hours 25 minutes.
or 5(5/12) hours = 65/12 hours
$d/36 + d/14 = 65/12 \rightarrow d = 54.6$ km.
Thus, option (d) none of these is correct.

26–28. You can make the following table to chart out the motions of the three.

Hour	Ram	Shyam	Mohan
1	10	30	3.33
2	20	33.33	6.66
3	60	36.66	10
4	81.66	40	20
5	85	50	30
6	88.33	60	40
	90(6.5)	70(7)	70(7)
		80(8)	100(8)

26. It is evident that Ram would overtake Shyam between 2 and 3. At 2, Shyam is ahead by 13.33 km.
Relative speed between 2 – 3 = 36.66 kmph.
Time required = 13.33/36.66 of the hour
= 4/11 of the hour
= 2 : 22. (approx)
27. Mohan would overtake Shyam after 70 miles.
28. Ram would cover 90 miles in 3 hours 45 minutes. Mohan would cover 90 miles in 7 hours 40 minutes.
Time difference = 3 hours 55 minutes.
29. Mohan at 8 pm (each of the others would reach later).
30. Ram would reach at 9:30 p.m., while Shyam would reach at 10:00 p.m.
31. $25/s - 25/(s + 10) = 1/12$
$S = 50$ km/hr.
32. The respective times are 224 seconds and 364 seconds. They will meet at the starting point in the LCM of these times, i.e., 224 × 13. Hence, Ram Singh will cover the circle 13 times.
33. The wife drives for 12 minutes less than her driving on normal days.
Thus, she would have saved 6 minutes each way. Hence, Ravi would have walked for 30 minutes (since his speed is 1/5th of the car's speed).
In effect, Ravi spends 24 minutes extra on the walking (rather than if he had traveled the same distance by car).
Thus, if Ravi had got the car at the station only, he would have saved 24 minutes more and reached at 5:36.

34. The following figure represents the travel of the two:

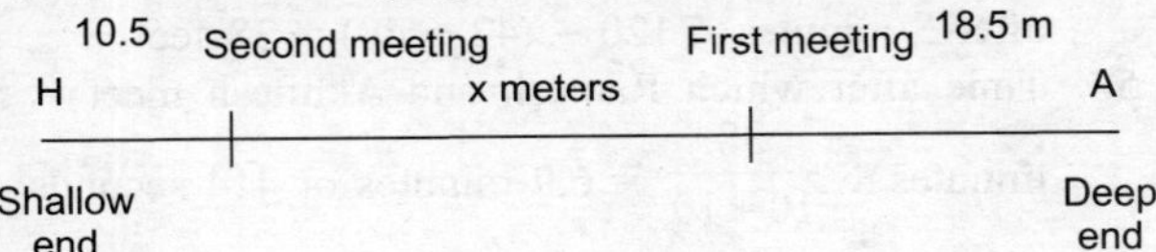

Once, you can visualise this figure, try to extract the value of x by taking the length as given in the options. For option (a) length of pool is 55.5 meters, the ratio of speeds of Ajay to Hemant on the basis of the first meeting = 18.5/37. The ratio of speeds on the basis of the second meeting = Ajay's travel to Hemant's travel = 47.5/ 63.5. The two ratios are not the same- which they should have been as both these ratios represent the speed ratio between Ajay and Hemant.

For option (b), length of pool is 45 meters, the ratio of speeds of Ajay to Hemant on the basis of the first meeting = 18.5/26.5. The ratio of speeds on the basis of the second meeting = Ajay's travel to Hemant's travel = 37/ 53. The two ratios are the same — which they should have been as both these ratios represent the speed ratio between Ajay and Hemant. Hence, this is the correct answer.

35. The distances covered in percentage would be, 10% + 6.66% + 8.33% + 16.66% + 5.833% + 31.666 + 2.0833 = 81.25%

(22.5/18.75) × 100 = 120 km

36. If you start at 12 noon, you would reach at 4:30 PM. You would be able to meet the train which left Mumbai at 8 AM, 9 AM, 10 AM, 11 AM, 12 Noon, 1 PM, 2 PM, 3 PM and 4 PM – a total of 9 trains.

37. The total time = time in the first part of the journey + time for the second part of the journey= $k/y + (x - k)/z$. Option (a) is correct.

38. If we assume the speed of the sound as 330 m/s, we can see that the distance traveled by the sound in 45 seconds is the distance traveled by the train in 11 minutes.

$330 \times 45 = 660 \times s \rightarrow s = 22.5$ m/s = 81 kmph

39–40. In 9 hours, (7 pm to 4 pm) the Kalinga Express would cover 540 kms.

Remaining distance = 260 kms

Relative speed = 150 kmph.

Time required = 260/150 =1.733 hours

= 104 minutes.

39. 1.733 × 90 = 156 km.

40. 4 A.M. + 1 hr 44 minutes = 5 : 44 A.M.

41. The total distance the bird would travel would be dependent on the time that the cars crash with each other. Also, the speed of the bird is the same as the relative speed of the cars. Hence, the answer to question 41 will be 12 km.

42. The bird would travel at 120 kmph for 4 + 4/3 + 4/9 minutes, i.e., 5.77 minutes. Hence, the answer is (5.77/60) × 120 = 11.55 km.

43. The bird would be able to theoretically reach the bonnet of the second car an infinite number of times.

44. Initial distance = 25 dog leaps.

Per minute → dog makes 5 dog leaps

Per minute → Cat makes 6 cat leaps = 3 dog leaps.

Relative speed = 2 dog leaps/minutes.

An initial distance of 25 dog leaps would get covered in 12.5 minutes.

45. Refer to the following figure which helps us understand that the ratio of speeds of A to B would be 2:3.

P Q

0.4 D means ratio of speeds = 2:3

The 4th meeting would occur after a combined movement of $D + 6D = 7D$. 2/5th of this distance would be covered by A and 3/5th of this distance would be the distance covered by B. Thus, distance covered by A would be 2/5th of $7D$, i.e., distance covered by $A = 2.8D$ – which means that the 4th meeting occurs at a distance of $0.8D$ from P.

46. In 36 hours, there would be a gap of 8 minutes. The two watches would show the same time when the gap would be exactly 12 hours or 720 minutes.

The no. of 36 hour time frames required to create this gap = 720/8 = 90.

Total time = 90 × 36 = 3240 hours. Since this is divisible by 24, the watches would show 12 noon.

47. Solve through options. At 18 kmph the motorboat would take exactly 6 hours.

48. Check through options. Option (d) will give us 14 kmph and 9 kmph as the down stream and up stream speeds. This would mean that the total travel time would be 1.5 hours and 2.33 hours down stream and up stream respectively.

49. At 2:15 PM the distance between the two trains would be 550 km as the train from Hazipur to Muzaffarpur would already have travelled for 40 minutes. After that they would take 550/110 = 5 hours to meet. Thus, the train from Muzaffarpur would have traveled 250 kms before meeting. Option (c) is correct.

50. The dog loses 1/3rd of his normal time from the meeting point. (Thus normal time = 35 × 3 = 105 minutes)

If the meeting occurred 24 km further, the dog loses 25 minutes.

This means that the normal time for the new distance would be 75 minutes. Thus, normally the dog would cover this distance of 24 km in 30 minutes. Thus, normal speed = 48 km/hr.

51. Let the length of circular track be 'x' meters. If they met at 'y' meters away from the starting point.

$$\frac{a}{b}=\frac{3x+y}{2x+y}=1+\frac{x}{2x+y}$$

Here 'y' must be greater than 0 but less than 'x'. This gives us that the lower limit of the answer would be 1.33 (if you take the higher extreme value of y as 1) and the upper limit would be 1.5 (If we take the lower extreme value of y as 0).

All the given options lie within this range, hence the correct answer is 3.

52. Since he reduces his speed to 4/5th his going out speed, his time would increase to 5/4th of his normal time. Thus, the total travel time (if we assume that the time going out is t, the time coming back would be 1.25t) Thus, the total time would be 2.25t, which is also equal to 4 hours 30 minutes. This gives us t = 2 hours and the returning time = 2 hours 30 minutes. The return speed would be 100/2.5 =40 kmph.

53.

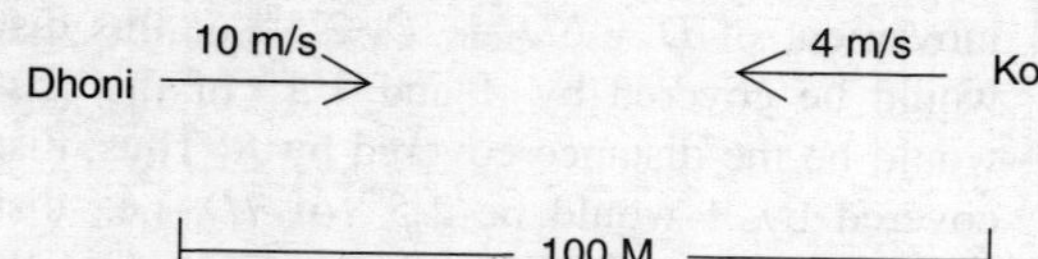

Dhoni will cover two laps in 20 seconds (as he runs at a speed of 10 m/s and the track is 100 meters).

In the same time: Kohli will cover 4 × 20 = 80 meters.

Therefore, during the first 20 seconds they would meet twice.

Also, after covering the track twice, Dhoni would be back to his original position. At that time, the distance between them would be 20 meters (distance left for Kohli to finish his first lap). Also, they would be moving in opposite directions and hence their relative speed would be 14 m/s.

Therefore, they will meet after $\frac{20}{(10+4)}=\frac{10}{7}$ seconds.

So total time taken will be $= 10 + 10 + \frac{10}{7}=\frac{150}{7}$ = 21.42 seconds

54. At their third meeting, Dhoni will be at $10\times\frac{10}{7}=\frac{100}{7}$ = 14.28 meters from his starting point.

55. If Akhilesh travels at 8 feet/minute, 10 feet /minute and 12 feet/minute for 't' minutes then according to the conditions in the problem: $8t + 10t + 12t = 120$ → t =4 minutes

Distance travelled by Akhilesh in 5 minutes = 8 × 4 + 10 × 1 = 42 feet.

Time taken by Ramesh to travel 1/3rd of the distance $=\frac{120}{3\times 8}$ = 5 minutes.

Therefore, distance between Ramesh and Akhilesh after 5 minutes = 120 – (42 + 40) = 38 feet

56. Time after which Ramesh and Akhilesh meet = 5 minutes + $\frac{38}{10+10}$ = 6.9 minutes or 414 seconds

57. Since their ratio of speeds is 6:1, they will meet for the first time at the starting point when Vijay completes his first round. At that time, since Bhola too would have been running for the entire time, Bhola would have covered six times the distance which would mean that Bhola would have covered the track for the sixth time — thus it would be their sixth meeting. Hence, he would have met Vijay 5 times before they meet at the starting point.

58. Let the distance travelled by train B before the first meeting be 'd' km.

Distance travelled by train A before 2nd and after first meeting = $(40 + d)$ km.

Distance travelled by train B before 2nd and after 1st meeting = 80 + 80 + d – 40 = (120 + d) km.

Since, their speeds are constant, the ratio of distances covered would be constant too (for both the time periods). This gives us the equation:

$$\frac{80}{d}=\frac{40+d}{120+d}\rightarrow d=120.$$

Hence, the distance between Agra and Delhi = 80 + 120 = 200 km.

59. Required ratio $=\frac{120}{80}=\frac{3}{2}=1.5$

60. Let Anand entered the bar at 'x' minutes past 12 A.M.

Speed of minute hand $=\frac{360}{60}$ degree/minute

Speed of hour hand $=\frac{30}{60}$ degree/minute

$$\therefore (360^\circ-30^\circ)\frac{x}{60}=30^\circ$$

$$x=\frac{30\times 60}{330}=\frac{60}{11}=5\frac{5}{11}$$ or 5.455 minutes or 5 minutes 27.27 seconds

Therefore, Anand entered the bar at 00:05:27 AM

He came out the bar at 00:05:27 AM + 1:20:00 = 1:25:27 AM.

∴ A = 1; B =25 and C = 27. Sum of the three = 53.

61. Effectively, the car starts at 1 PM, thus giving a head start of three hours to the *tonga*. This would mean that the *tonga* has a lead of 72 km, when the car starts. Since, the relative speed is 60 – 24 = 36 km/h, the car would catch up in 72/36 = 2 hours. The distance from Chandigarh would be 60 × 2 = 120 km.

62. The normal reaction is to invert the speed ratio to get the time ratio, since the distance is constant. That

reaction would work for two speeds (for instance, if the speed ratio of two cars over the same distance is 2:3, their time ratio would be 3:2). But for the given ratio of three speeds, 3:4:5 as speed ratio does not become 5:4:3 as the time ratio. The process in this situation is to assume the distance of 60 (LCM of 3, 4 and 5). Then, the time ratio would be 60/3:60/4:60/5 = 20:15:12. Hence, option (d) is correct.

63. The following figure represents the situation. The distance between Q1 and Q2 is 300 km = $2x + 2y$. Hence, $x + y = 150$. Also, total distance = $3x + 3y = 3(x + y) = 450$.

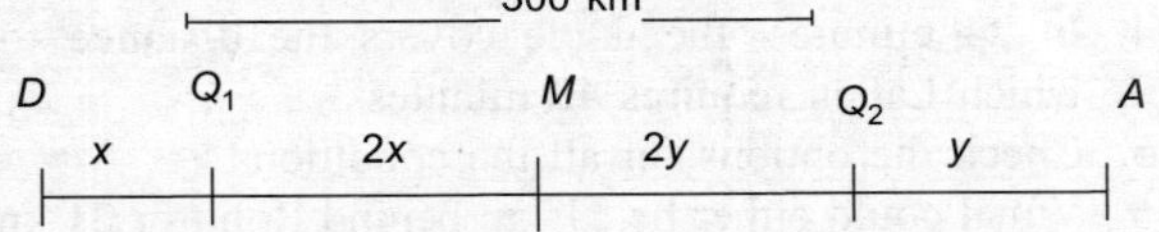

64. Solve this one using the options. If we check option (a), the meeting of A and B can be perceived as A does 110 km when B does 88 km. This gives us a ratio of 10:8 (or 5:4) for the speeds of A and B. Likewise, the meeting of B and C can be interpreted as: When B does 108 km, C does 90. So their ratio of speeds would be 6:5. Thus, we have A: B = 5:4, while B: C = 6:5 → A: B:C = 30:24:20 = 15:12:10. The ratio of A and C's speed is 15:10, which is the same as 3:2. Hence, this option fits the given situation perfectly and is the correct answer.
(Note: If you were to try this using a different option, the numbers would not match to get us 3:2 as the ratio of A and C.)

65. Laila's normal journey on a normal day would be from home to station and back. From the figure of Monday, we can see that Laila saved 20 minutes because she did not travel her normal journey to the station and back. We can infer that this would mean that she would have saved 10 minutes because she did not travel from $M1$ to the station and 10 minutes since she did not travel back from the station to $M1$. Hence, we can also infer that since she would normally reach the station at 6 PM, she must have met him 10 minutes before that at 5:50 PM. Thus, her husband must have taken 50 minutes to walk from the station to $M1$ (5 PM to 5:50 PM). So, the speed ratio of the car to the walking speed would be 5:1. Now if we consider the deductions from Tuesday, we see that they met at $M2$. The time taken by Laila to drive from $M2$ to the station would be 1/5th the time taken by her husband to walk from the station to $M2$. Since, the husband starts at 5:30 that day from the station, if we split the 30 minutes between 5:30 to 6 in the ratio of 5:1, we would be able to get the times taken by her husband and Laila to travel the distance from $M2$ to the station. The 5:1 split of 30 minutes gives us 25 minutes travel time for the husband and 5 minutes travel time for Laila. This means that she meets him at 5:55 and saves five minutes going and five minutes coming back. Thus, they would reach ten minutes early on that day. Thus, option (c) is correct.

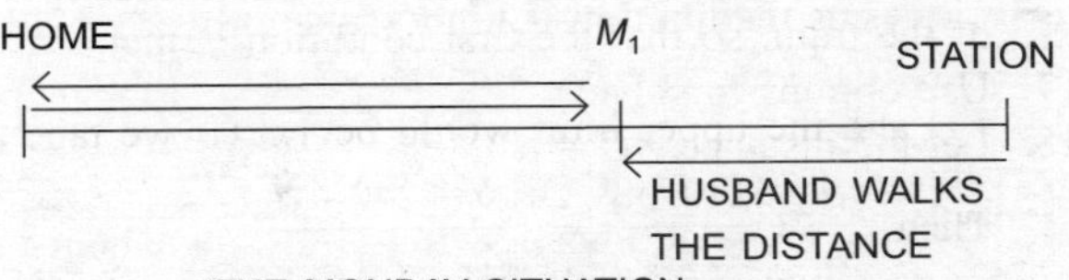

THE MONDAY SITUATION

HOME M_2 STATION

HUSBAND WALKS THE DISTANCE

THE TUESDAY SITUATION

Level of Difficulty (III)

1. The first person who travels from Siliguri to Darjeeling is obviously faster than the second. Hence, reject options (a) and (b). Then, check all the conditions with options (c) and (d) and select the one which satisfies the conditions.
2. Since distance to be travelled by Nishit is $35\frac{5}{7}$ % less, his speed will also be $35\frac{5}{7}$ % less than Arun's speed. Check the options with the conditions that Arun's speed is 5 km/h higher than that of Nishit.
3. Let S_1, S_2 and S_3 be the speeds of the three cars.

   Then: $\frac{120}{S_1} - \frac{120}{S_2} = 1$ hour (1)

   It is also known that the speed of the third car is double the speed of the first car.

   With these realisations, check for factors of 120 which can satisfy the equation above.

   (**Note**: In equations like (1) above, normally the respective values of S_1 and S_2 will be factors of 120.)
5. If the side of the initial equilateral triangle is S, then when Arjit covers (S – 120) km, Shaurya covers S kilometers. Also, when Arjit covers a distance of 80 kilometers, Shaurya covers a distance such that the resultant triangle is right-angled.

   Check these conditions through options.
6. Solve through a process similar to the previous question.
7. If S_1 is the speed of the first car, then (S_1 + 10) will be the second car's speed. If t_1 hours is the time required for the first car, then (t_1 – 1) hours is the time required for the second car in covering the same distance, while that of the third car is $\left(t_1 - \frac{33.33}{60}\right)$ hours.

   Check these conditions through options.
10. The relative speed is 225 km/h.

11. The sum of the speeds of the ducks is 50 feet/min. Hence, circumference = 9 × 50 = 450 feet and difference of speeds = $\frac{450}{54}$ = 8.33.
15. Use options to solve.
16. Through trial-and-error, try to find the initial speed of the train, so that the first condition is met.
17. Use options to solve.
18. Let the distance $AC = d$

Then, $\frac{d}{V_0} + \frac{240-d}{V_1} = \frac{d}{V_1} + \frac{240-d}{V_0}$

If $V_0 \neq V_1$, then the above condition will be satisfied only if $d = 120$ km.

19. The time required will be represented by

$$\frac{\text{Distance travelled on highway}}{10} + \frac{\text{Distance travelled on side roads}}{6}$$

This has to be minimised, check the options.

Solutions for Questions 20 and 21:

Acceleration is $\frac{dv}{dt} = 2t + 2b$

At $t = 4$, the acceleration is given to be 3.

Hence, $b = \frac{-5}{2}$

Hence, the velocity equation becomes

$V_{(t)} = t^2 - 5t + 4$

29. Total time taken to cover the entire distance together $= 144 \times \frac{5}{4} = 180$ minutes = 3 hours.

Hence, distance covered per hour = 33.33% of the total by both of them combined.

Check this condition for all the options.

31. Suppose A and B are the points where the first and the second meetings took place.

The total distance covered by the pedestrian and the cyclist before the first meeting = Twice the distance between Nagpur and Buti Bori

Total time taken is 1 hour.

Total distance covered by the pedestrian and the cyclist between the two meetings = Twice the distance between A and Buti Bori. and time taken is half an hour.

Hence, A is the mid-point. This will result in a GP.

32. Solve through options by checking all the conditions given in the question.
33. If $2d$ is the distance between A and B, then

$$\frac{\frac{2}{3} \times 2d}{d-2} = \frac{d-3}{2d \times \frac{1}{4}}$$

34. In 24 minutes, the uncle covers the distance for which Lallan requires 48 minutes.
35. Check the options for all the conditions.
36. Vimal could either be 21 km behind Rohit or 21 km ahead of Rohit.
37. If d is the distance between Delhi and Daulatabad, then you will get the following equation.

$$\frac{d-14}{14} = \frac{28+(d-16)}{(d-14)+2}$$

38. Check the conditions through the options.
47. The net time loss is 1/3% of 168 hours.
49. In the time taken by the boat in travelling $d + (d - 12)$ km, the log travels 12 km. Let, S_B be the speed of the boat in still water and, S_S be the speed of the stream.

Then

$$\frac{12}{S_S} = \frac{20}{(S_S + S_B)} + \frac{8}{(S_B - S_S)} \quad (1)$$

It is also known that,

$$\frac{20}{(S_S + S_B)} + \frac{20}{(S_B - S_S)} = 7 \text{ hours} \quad (2)$$

50. Solve using the options.

CHAPTER 11

Applications of Time, Speed and Distance

Chapter Launchpad

Scan this QR code to access a video on 'Introduction to Applications of Time, Speed and Distance' and this chapter's importance for CAT

CIRCULAR MOTION

Questions on circular motion are just an extension to the questions on time, speed and distance. Therefore, the concepts we studied in the time, speed and distance chapter will all come in handy when we are solving questions on circular motion. You would find that questions on circular motion are regularly asked in all aptitude tests and examinations.

Concept Explainer

Scan this QR code to access a conceptual video on Circular Motion

In the context of circular motion, you need to understand the following points:

(a) Variables involved and kinds of questions that emerge, when two people/bodies start running/moving around a circle/circular path in the opposite direction

(b) Variables involved and kinds of questions that emerge, when two people/bodies start running/moving around a circle/circular path in the same direction

(c) Meetings around the circle.

(a) Variables involved and kinds of questions that emerge, when two people/bodies start running/moving around a circle/circular path in the opposite direction

In such cases, they will meet each other at regular intervals of time at different points on the circle/circular path. Since, they would be moving in the opposite direction, their relative speed would be the addition of their individual speeds.

Suppose, the two people start moving at speeds of x metres/sec and y metres/sec, respectively.

(i) Their relative speed would be given by $(x + y)$.

(ii) The combined distance they will cover from one meeting to another would be equal to the circumference of the circle/circular path.

(iii) Hence, the regular time periods at which they would meet would be given by the formula:

$$\text{Time interval between meetings} = \frac{\text{Distance}}{\text{Speed}} = \frac{\text{Circumference of the circular track}}{(x+y)}$$

Example 1: Two runners A and B start running from the same point on a circular path in the opposite direction. A runs at a speed of 20 metres/sec, B runs at a speed of 30 metres/sec. The circumference of the circle is 1000 metres. At what regular time intervals would they meet?

Solution: The relative speed of the two would be given by 20 + 30 = 50 metres/sec.

They would meet at intervals of

$$\frac{\text{Circumference of the circular track}}{(x + y)} = \frac{1000}{50} = 20 \text{ seconds.}$$

Example 2: Two runners A and B start running from the same point on a circular path in the opposite direction. A can complete one round in 50 seconds, while B can complete one round in 40 seconds. At what regular time intervals would they meet, if they continue running in this way infinitely?

Solution: In this question, we are not given the speed in terms of metres/sec or kmph or any standard units of speed. Further, we are not provided with the circumference too. However, in such situations, there is a way to tackle the problem, without getting any more information. The following thought process needs to be applied here:

Assume the length of the circumference to be 100%.

Since A can run around the circular path in 50 seconds, A would be covering 2% of the total circumference per second.

Likewise, B's speed can be interpreted as 2.5% of the total per second.

Thus, their relative speed is 4.5% per second.

Hence, to cover 100% circumference, they would require 100/4.5 = 200/9 seconds.

(b) Variables involved and kinds of questions that emerge, when two people/bodies start running/moving around a circle/circular path in the same direction

In such cases, they will meet each other at regular intervals of time at different points on the circular path. In order to meet the faster runner would need to completely overlap the slower runner, i.e., by completing one round more than the slower runner.

Since, they would be moving in the same direction, their relative speed would be the difference of their individual speeds and would be found by subtracting the slower speed from the faster speed.

Suppose, the two people start moving at speeds of x and y metres/sec respectively, where $x > y$. Then,

(i) Their relative speed would be given by $(x - y)$.

(ii) The relative distance they will cover from one meeting to another would be equal to the circumference of the circular path.

(iii) Hence, the regular time periods at which they would meet would be given by the formula:

$$\text{Time Interval between meetings} = \frac{\text{Distance}}{\text{Speed}}$$

$$= \frac{\text{Circumference of the circular track}}{(x - y)}$$

Example 3: Two runners A and B start running from the same point on a circle in the same direction. A runs at a speed of 20 meters/sec, B runs at a speed of 30 meters/sec. The circumference of the circle is 1000 meters. At what regular time intervals would they meet?

Solution: The relative speed of the two would be given by 30 – 20 = 10 meters/sec. They would meet at intervals of:

$$\frac{\text{Circumference of the circular track}}{(x - y)} = \frac{1000}{10}$$

$$= 100 \text{ seconds.}$$

Example 4: Two runners A and B start running from the same point on a circle in the same direction. A can complete 1 round in 50 seconds, while B can complete a round in 40 seconds. At what regular time intervals would they meet, if they continue running in this fashion infinitely?

Solution: Again, in this question, we are neither given the speeds nor the distance in standard units of speed or distance. In order to tackle this problem, we can take the same percentage approach explained earlier for a similar problem, when we were discussing movement in opposite directions.

The following thought-process needs to be applied here:

Assume the circumference to be 100% length. Thus, for overlapping to occur, the faster runner has to overcome the slower runner by running exactly 100% of the circumference more than what the slower runner has run.

Since A can run around the circle in 50 seconds, A's speed would be 2% of the total circumference per second.

Likewise, B's speed can be interpreted as 2.5% of the total circumference per second. Thus, their relative speed is 2.5 – 2 = 0.5% per second. This means, that the faster runner gains a lead of 0.5% per second over the slower runner. Hence, to gain a lead of 100%, the faster runner would take 100/0.5 = 200 seconds. Thus, the two runners would keep meeting every 200 seconds (or in other words, B would be overlapping A, every 200 seconds).

(c) Meetings around the circle

As you must have already realised, if we know the speed of the bodies and the circumference, we also get to know the amount of time required by a body to cover the circle. Very often in circular motion questions, we come across situations, where the time to cover a circle is given for various people/bodies moving around the circular track. We have already seen a couple of instances of such a case, where we took the distance as 100% to tackle the problem.

In such situations, you should also know the following:

Suppose, you have three runners running around a circle in the same direction. Let T_A, T_B and T_C be the times taken by the three respectively to complete one round of the circular track.

In such a case, you should be able to work out the following:

First meeting at starting point of the circle: It will occur after a time that is equal to the LCM of T_A, T_B and T_C.

First meeting at any point of the circle: In order to find the time for this, you would first need to work out the times in which the fastest runner overlaps each of the slower runners. Let C, be the fastest. Then, you can find the times T_{CA} (the time taken by C to overlap A) and T_{CB} (the time taken by C to overlap B). Then their first meeting at any point of the circle, would occur after a time period that is the LCM of T_{CA} and T_{CB}.

The question that would obviously arise out of this, is how does one find these overlapping times? For that I would like to remind you of the problem, we just solved above.

Practice Exercise

1. A and B are running on a circular track of length 500 m. Speed of A is 20 m/s and speed of B is 10 m/s. They start from the same point at the same time in the same direction. After how much time will they meet again for the first time?
   (a) 40 seconds (b) 50 seconds
   (c) 60 seconds (d) None of these
2. Alok and Bhoomi are running on a circular track of length 500 m. Speed of Alok is 20 m/s and speed of Bhoomi is 30 m/s. They start from the same point at the same time in the opposite direction. After how much time will they meet again for the first time?
   (a) 40 seconds (b) 50 seconds
   (c) 60 seconds (d) None of these
3. A and B are running on a circular track of length 500 m. Speed of A is 30 m/s and speed of B is 20 m/s. They start from the same point at the same time in the same direction. After how much time will they meet for the 3rd time?
   (a) 400 seconds (b) 150 seconds
   (c) 160 seconds (d) None of these
4. A and B are running on a circular track of length 1400 m. Speed of A is 40 m/s and speed of B is 30 m/s. They start from the same point at the same time in the opposite direction. After how much time will they meet for the 2nd time?
   (a) 40 seconds (b) 30 seconds
   (c) 60 seconds (d) None of these

5. A and B are running on a circular track of length 600 m. Speed of A is 30 m/s and speed of B is 20 m/s. They start from the same point at the same time in the same direction. After how much time will they meet at the starting point?

(a) 40 seconds (b) 15 seconds
(c) 60 seconds (d) None of these

Direction for Questions 6 to 8: Ajay and Biru are running on a circular track of length 1000 m. Speed of Ajay is 50 m/s and speed of Biru is 25 m/s. If they start from the same point at the same time in the opposite direction, then answer the following questions:

6. After how much time will they meet at the starting point?

(a) 40 seconds (b) 25 seconds
(c) 50 seconds (d) None of these

7. What will the absolute difference of the distance covered by them before meeting at the starting point for the second time?

(a) 1 km (b) 1.5 km
(c) 2 km (d) None of these

8. If they are running in the same direction then after how much time they will meet at the starting point again?

(a) 40 seconds (b) 15 seconds
(c) 60 seconds (d) None of these

Direction for Questions 9 and 10: A, B and C run on a circular path at a speed of 5 m/s, 10 m/s, 25 m/s respectively in the same direction. The circumference of the path is 3 km. answer the following questions:

9. If they start from the same point at the same time then when will they be together again for the 1st time?

(a) 150 seconds (b) 200 seconds
(c) 300 seconds (d) 600 seconds

10. When will they be together again for the 1st time at the starting point?

(a) 150 seconds (b) 200 seconds
(c) 300 seconds (d) 600 seconds

Direction for Questions 11 to 13: A, B and C and D run on a circular path at a speed of 5 m/s, 10 m/s, 25 m/s, 30 m/s respectively. A, B & C are running in the clockwise direction while D is running in the anticlockwise direction. The circumference of the path is 7 km. Answer the following questions:

11. If they start from the same point at the same time then when will they be together again for the 1st time?

(a) 1500 seconds (b) 2000 seconds
(c) 1400 seconds (d) 600 seconds

12. When will they be together again for the 1st time at the starting point?

(a) 1500 seconds (b) 2000 seconds
(c) 1400 seconds (d) 600 seconds

13. What is the ratio of distances covered by A, B, C & D when will they meet for the first time?

(a) 1 : 2 : 3 : 6 (b) 1 : 2 : 5 : 6
(c) 1 : 3 : 5 : 6 (d) None of these

ANSWER KEY

1. (b)	2. (d)	3. (b)	4. (a)
5. (c)	6. (a)	7. (c)	8. (a)
9. (d)	10. (d)	11. (c)	12. (c)
13. (b)			

SOLUTIONS AND SHORTCUTS

1. Time taken by A and B to meet first time
= Length of circular track/Relative speed
= 500/(20 – 10) = 500/10 = 50 seconds
2. Time taken by Alok and Bhoomi to meet first time
= Length of circular track/Relative speed
= 500/(30 + 20) = 500/50 = 10 seconds
3. Time taken by A and B to meet for the third time = 3 × (Length of circular track/Relative speed)
= 3 × 500/(30 – 20) = 1500/10 = 150 seconds
4. Time taken by A and B to meet first time = Length of circular track/Relative speed
= 1400/(40 + 30) = 1400/70 = 20 seconds
Hence, they will meet again for the 2nd time after 2 × 20 = 40s seconds
5. Time taken by A to complete one round = 600/30 = 20 seconds
Time taken by B to complete one round = 600/20 = 30 seconds
First meeting at the starting point will happen after LCM of 20 and 30 = 60 seconds.
Hence, they will meet after 60 seconds.
6. Time taken by Ajay to complete one round = 1000/50 = 20 seconds
Time taken by Biru to complete one round = 1000/25 = 40 seconds
First meeting at the starting point will happen after = LCM of 20 and 40 = 40 seconds.
Hence, they will meet at the starting point for the first time after 40 seconds of the start of their journey.
7. Time taken by them to meet at the starting point for the 2nd time = 2 × 40 = 80 seconds.
The absolute difference of the distance covered by Ajay and Biru = $80\times(50-25) = 2000$ m or 2 km.
8. In circular motion the time at which two bodies meet each other at the starting point is independent to the direction of motion of the bodies. Hence, if they move in the same direction they will meet again at the starting point after 40 seconds.
9. C meets B after every
$$= \frac{3000}{25-10} = 200 \text{ seconds}$$

C meets A after every $= \frac{3000}{25-5} = 150$ seconds

Therefore they will meet each other for the 1st time after = LCM (150, 200) = 600 seconds

10. Time taken by A to complete one round $= \frac{3000}{5} = 600$ seconds

Time taken by B to complete one round

$= \frac{3000}{10} = 300$ seconds

Time taken by C to complete one round

$= \frac{3000}{25} = 150$ seconds

So, they will be together again for the 1st time at the starting point after: LCM (150, 300 and 600) = 600 seconds

11. D meets A after every

$= \frac{7000}{30+5} = \frac{7000}{35}$ seconds

D meets B after every

$= \frac{7000}{30+10} = \frac{7000}{40}$ seconds

D meets C after every

$= \frac{7000}{30+25} = \frac{7000}{55}$ seconds

Hence, they meet each other for the 1st time at LCM of (7000/35, 7000/40, 7000/55) = LCM of (200, 175, 1400/11) = 1400 seconds.

12. To complete the circle:
A takes = 7000/5 = 1400 seconds
B takes = 7000/10 = 700 seconds
C takes = 7000/25 = 280 seconds
D takes = 7000/30 = 700/3 seconds
LCM of (1400, 700, 280, 700/3) = 1400 seconds

13. Ratio of distances covered by A, B, C & D when they meet first time
= Ratio of their speeds = 5 : 10 : 25 : 30
= 1 : 2 : 5 : 6

TRAINS

Questions related to movement and crossing of trains also inherently use the same concepts of relative speed, that we have discussed in details in the chapter Time, Speed and Distance. However, these questions have appeared very frequently in aptitude tests. Also, the questions on trains require specific thought processes, and hence, I have chosen to deal with this in a separate chapter so that you can teach yoruself to deal with questions on trains as a block.

(a) *Understanding distance travelled when a train crosses an object*

(b) *Understanding speed as the relative speed of the train and the object being crossed*

We all have seen and travelled in trains. When a train starts moving and starts crossing objects during its movement, it gives rise to some interesting problems with regards to the train's crossing of the object.

The basic formula that applies to train's crossing of the objects is the same as the time, speed and distance formula, viz:,

$$\text{Speed} \times \text{Time} = \text{Distance}$$

However, you need to understand how to identify the speed and the distance in these problems.

Understanding Distance Travelled when a Train Crosses an Object

A train is said to start crossing the object, when its engine comes in line with the object. The train is said to have completely crossed the object, when its tail-end bogey has come in line with the object. Thus, in case the object has no length (such situations occur when a train crosses a tree, a car, a man, an electric pole, etc), the train would have to traverse a distance equal to its own length in order to cross the object.

However, in situations where the train crosses an object whose length cannot be neglected (for instance, a train crossing a bridge, another train, etc.), the distance that the train would need to cover in order to cross the object completely would be equal to the length of the train + the length of the object.

Let L_t is the length of the train and L_o is the length of the object. Then:

The distance for objects without length would be L_t

Or the distance for objects with length

$$L_t + L_o$$

Understanding Speed as the Relative Speed of the Train and the Object being Crossed

When you want to consider the speed of the crossing, you need to look out for:

(i) Whether the object being crossed by the train is moving or is stationary.
(ii) If it is a moving object and is moving, whether it is moving in the same direction as the train or in the opoosite direction to the direction of the train.

Since we consider speed as relative speed, if the object is stationary, the speed of the crossing would be S_t (where S_t is the speed of the train)

For objects moving in the opposite direction to the train, the speed of the crossing would be $S_t + S_o$ (where S_o is the speed of the object).

For objects moving in the same direction as the train, the speed of the crossing would be $S_t - S_o$.

The various dimensions of these questions give rise to following 6 basic situations as tabulated here:

Situation #	Movement of the Object	Length of the Object	Formula
1	Stationary	Zero	$S_t \times T = L_t$
2	Stationary	L_o	$S_t \times T = (L_t + L_o)$
3	Moving (same direction)	Zero	$(S_t - S_o) \times T = (L_t)$
4	Moving (same direction)	L_o	$(S_t - S_o) \times T = (L_t + L_o)$
5	Moving (opposite direction)	Zero	$(S_t + S_o) \times T = (L_t)$
6	Moving (opposite direction)	L_o	$(S_t + S_o) \times T = (L_t + L_o)$

where T is time taken to cross.

Note In many train problems, speeds would be given in kmph, while the lengths of the train and the objects would be given in metres. In such cases, one needs to often use a conversion from kmph to metres/sec. The conversion from kmph to m/sec is done by multiplying the kmph by 5/18. Similarly, the conversion from m/sec to kmph is done by multiplying the m/sec value by 18/5 to get to kmph.

Solved Examples

1. A train, 300 m long, passed a man, walking along the line in the same direction at the rate of 3 kmph in 33 seconds. The speed of the train is:

(a) 30 kmph (b) 32 kmph

(c) $32\frac{8}{11}$ kmph (d) $35\frac{8}{11}$ kmph

Solution: If the speed of the train is s kmph, the relative speed = $(s - 3)$ kmph

or $(s-3) \times \frac{5}{18}$ m/sec

$\therefore \quad \frac{300}{(s-3) \times \frac{5}{18}} = 33$

or $5400 = 33 \times 5(s-3)$

or $11s - 33 = 360$

or $s = \frac{393}{11} = 35\frac{8}{11}$ kmph

2. A train 100 m long meets a man going in the opposite direction at 5 kmph and passes him in $7\frac{1}{5}$ seconds. What is the speed of the train in kmph?

(a) 45 kmph (b) 60 kmph

(c) 55 kmph (d) 50 kmph

Solution: Speed of train = x kmph

Relative speed = $(x + 5)$ kmph

Length of train = 100 m = 0.1 km.

$\therefore \quad \frac{0.1}{x+5} = \frac{36}{5 \times 60 \times 60}$

or $\frac{1}{(x+5)} = \frac{1}{50}$

or $x + 5 = 50$

or $x = 45$ km/hr.

3. A train, 120 m long, takes 6 seconds to pass a telegraph post. The speed of the train is:

(a) 72 kmph (b) 62 kmph

(c) 55 kmph (d) 85 kmph

Solution: Speed of the train

$= \frac{\text{Length of train}}{\text{Time taken in crossing the pole}}$

$= \frac{120}{6} = 20$ m/s

$= 20 \times \frac{18}{5}$ kmph

$= 72$ kmph.

4. A train 125 m long passes a man, running at 5 kmph in the same direction in which the train is going, in 10 seconds. The speed of the train is:

(a) 35 kmph (b) 50 kmph

(c) 70 kmph (d) 65 kmph

Solution: Speed of the train relative to man

$= \left(\frac{125}{10}\right)$ m/s

$= \left(\frac{25}{2}\right)$ m/s

$= \left(\frac{25}{2} \times \frac{18}{5}\right)$ kmph

$= 45$ kmph

Let the speed of the train be s kmph. Then, relative speed = $(s - 5)$ kmph

$\therefore \quad s - 5 = 45$

or $s = 50$ kmph.

5. A train goes from Hosur to Sealdah at an average speed of 20 kmph and comes back at an average speed of 30 kmph. The average speed of the train for the whole journey is:

(a) 27 kmph (b) 26 kmph

(c) 25 kmph (d) 24 kmph

Solution: Required average speed

$= 2S_1S_2/(S_1 + S_2) = \frac{2 \times 30 \times 20}{30 + 20} = 24$ kmph.

Note You could also solve this by assuming the distance as 60 km, and then using the formula:

$$\text{Average speed} = \frac{\text{Total Distance}}{\text{Total time}} = \frac{60+60}{3+2} = 24 \text{ kmph}$$

6. Two trains 108 m and 112 m in length are running towards each other on parallel lines at a speed of 45 kmph and 54 kmph, respectively. To cross each other after they meet, it will take?
(a) 12 seconds (b) 9 seconds
(c) 8 seconds (d) 10 seconds

Solution: Relative speed = 45 + 54

$$= 99 \text{ kmph} = \left(99 \times \frac{5}{18}\right) \text{m/s or } \frac{55}{2} \text{ m/s}$$

$\therefore$ Required time =

$$\frac{108+112}{\frac{55}{2}} = \frac{220 \times 2}{55} = 8 \text{ seconds}.$$

7. Two trains, each 100 m long, moving in opposite directions, cross each other in 8 seconds. If one is moving twice as fast the other, the speed of the faster train is:
(a) 50 kmph (b) 55 kmph
(c) 60 kmph (d) 65 kmph

Solution: Let the speed of the slower train be x m/s. Then, the speed of the faster train will be $2x$ m/s. Relative speed of both the trains

$$= (x + 2x) \text{ m/s} = 3x \text{ m/s}.$$

Now according to the question,

$$\frac{100+100}{8} = 3x$$

or $24x = 200$

or $x = \frac{25}{3}$ m/s

So, the speed of the faster train = $\frac{2 \times 25}{3}$ m/s

or $\left(\frac{50}{3} \times \frac{18}{5}\right)$ kmph = 60 kmph.

8. A train travels at a certain average speed for a distance of 63 km and then travels a distance of 72 km at an average speed of 6 kmph more than its original speed. If it takes 3 hours to complete the total journey, what is the original speed of the train (in kmph)?
(a) 24 (b) 33
(c) 42 (d) 66

Solution: The following equation can be formed from the equation,

$$\frac{63}{s} + \frac{72}{s+6} = 3$$

or $s = 42$ kmph

9. A train requires 7 seconds to pass a pole while it requires 25 seconds to cross a stationary train which is 378 m long. Find the speed of the train.
(a) 75.6 kmph (b) 75.4 kmph
(c) 76.2 kmph (d) 21 kmph

Solution: If you assume the length of the train to be L, you would get two equations:

$$S \times 7 = L \text{ and } S \times 25 = (L + 378).$$

This means that the train takes 18 seconds extra to cover 378 m. Hence, the speed of the train is 378/18 = 21 m/s = 75.6 kmph.

10. Two trains pass each other on parallel lines. Each train is 100 m long. When they are going in the same direction, the faster one takes 60 seconds to pass the other completely. If they are going in opposite direction, they pass each other completely in 10 seconds. Find the speed of the slower train in kmph.
(a) 30 kmph (b) 42 kmph
(c) 48 kmph (d) 60 kmph

Solution: Let the speeds of the two trains be x m/s and y m/s, respectively. From the conditions given in the question, we have

$(x + y) \times 10 = 200$

or $(x + y) = 20$

and $(x - y) \times 60 = 200$

or $(x - y) = 3.33$

This gives us, $x = 11.66$ m/s and $y = 8.33$ m/s.
The speed of the slower train = 8.33 = 25/3 m/s.
Hence, speed in kmph = (25/3) × (18/5) = 30 kmph

Practice Exercise

1. A train travels 700 km in 5 hours and another 800 km in 10 hours. What is the average speed of train?
(a) 100 kmph (b) 80 kmph
(c) 140 kmph (d) 110 kmph
2. A 100 m long train crosses a stationary man in 10 seconds. What is the speed of the train?
(a) 10 kmph (b) 24 kmph
(c) 48 kmph (d) 36 kmph
3. A train 350 m long passes a pole in 35 seconds. How long (in seconds) will it take to pass a platform 450 m long?
(a) 50 (b) 80
(c) 20 (d) 30

4. A train running at the speed of 90 kmph crosses a pole in 9 seconds. What is the length of the train (in m)?
(a) 225 (b) 146
(c) 144 (d) 166

5. A train 200 m long passes a man, running at 5 kmph in the same direction in which the train is going, in 10 seconds. The speed of the train (in kmph) is:
(a) 45 (b) 54
(c) 77 (d) 60

6. The length of the bridge (in metres), which a train 225 m long and travelling at 45 kmph can cross in 30 seconds, is:
(a) 150 (b) 500
(c) 250 (d) 300

7. A train passes a station platform in 40 seconds and a man standing on the platform in 20 seconds. If the speed of the train is 72 kmph, what is the length of the platform (in m)?
(a) 450 (b) 540
(c) 770 (d) 400

8. A train 260 m long is running at a speed of 10 kmph. In what time (in seconds) will it pass a 240 m long bridge?
(a) 450 (b) 540
(c) 700 (d) 180

9. A goods train runs at the speed of 30 m/s and crosses a 200 m long platform in 20 seconds. What is the length (in metres) of the goods train?
(a) 500 (b) 480
(c) 520 (d) 400

10. If a Shatabdi Express train running at 72 kmph crosses a boy standing by the side of the track in 7 seconds, the length of the train is:
(a) 137 m (b) 157 m
(c) 140 m (d) 166 m

11. Two trains 170 m and 130 m long run at the speed of 20 m/s and 40 m/s, respectively in opposite direction on parallel tracks. The time (in seconds), which they take to cross each other, is:
(a) 5 (b) 2.5
(c) 7 (d) 8

12. A 600 m long train crosses a platform in 36 seconds while it crosses a signal pole in 18 seconds. What is the length (in metres) of the platform?
(a) 500 (b) 800
(c) 1200 (d) 600

13. Two trains are moving in opposite direction at speed of 70 kmph and 80 kmph, respectively. Their lengths are 1.20 km and 0.8 km, respectively. The time (in seconds) taken by the slower train to cross the faster train in seconds is:
(a) 50 (b) 48
(c) 52 (d) 53

14. In what time will a train Rajdhani Express 140 m long travelling at 90 kmph cross another train of length 160 m moving in the opposite direction at 72 kmph?
(a) 3 s (b) 1 s
(c) 6.67 s (d) 5 s

15. A 250 m long train running at the speed of 110 kmph crosses another train running in opposite direction at the speed of 90 kmph in 9 seconds. What is the length (in metres) of the other train?
(a) 450 (b) 250
(c) 700 (d) 280

16. A 500 m long train is running at a speed of 20 m/s. If it crosses a tunnel in 1 minute, the length of the tunnel (in metres) is:
(a) 500 (b) 270
(c) 700 (d) 800

17. Mumbai and Pune are two cities with their stations at a distance of 298 km. A train starts from Mumbai and moves towards Pune at a speed of 45 kmph. After 2 hours, another train starts from Pune at the rate of 35 kmph. How far from Mumbai will they will cross each other?
(a) 217 km (b) 117 km
(c) 207 km (d) 200 km

18. Two trains running in opposite direction cross a man standing on the platform in 26 seconds and 21 seconds, respectively and they cross each other in 24 seconds. The ratio of their speeds is:
(a) 1 : 3 (b) 3 : 2
(c) 3 : 4 (d) 4 : 1

19. A jogger running at 18 kmph alongside a railway track is 200 m ahead of the engine of a 160 m long train running at 54 kmph in the same direction. In how much time (in seconds) will the train pass the jogger?
(a) 25 (b) 3.6
(c) 40 (d) 36

20. A 150 m long train crosses a milestone in 15 seconds and crosses another train of the same length travelling in the opposite direction in 12 seconds. The speed of the second train (in kmph) is:
(a) 52 (b) 56
(c) 54 (d) 58

21. Two trains, each of length 125 m, are running on parallel tracks in opposite direction. One train is running at a speed 65 kmph and they cross each other in 6 seconds. The speed of the other train is:
(a) 75 kmph (b) 85 kmph
(c) 95 kmph (d) 105 kmph

22. A train travelling at a speed of 75 kmph enters a 1.75 km long tunnel. The train is 0.75 km long. How long (in minutes) does it take for the train to pass through the tunnel from the moment the front enters to the moment the rear emerges?

(a) 2 (b) 3
(c) 4 (d) 6

23. A train travels between two stations P and Q. First it goes from P to Q at X kmph, then travels from Q to P at Y kmph, and again goes back from P to Q at Y kmph. What is the average speed of the train?

(a) $\frac{XY}{X+Y}$ (b) $\frac{2XY}{X+2Y}$
(c) $\frac{3XY}{2X+Y}$ (d) $\frac{3XY}{X+2Y}$

24. Two trains start simultaneously in the opposite direction from two points X and Y and arrive at their destinations 16 and 9 hours, respectively, after they meet each other. What is the speed of train from Y if the speed of train from X is 90 kmph?

(a) 80 kmph (b) 100 kmph
(c) 120 kmph (d) None of these

25. Rajdhani Express crosses a pole in 15 seconds and a platform 100 m long in 30 seconds. Find the length of Rajdhani Express (in metres)?

(a) 235 (b) 335
(c) 100 (d) 555

26. Two trains of equal length are running on parallel lines in the same direction at 56 kmph and 46 kmph. The faster train passes the slower train in 54 seconds. The length of each train (in metres) is:

(a) 25 (b) 35
(c) 40 (d) 75

27. There are two parallel tracks on which trains are moving in the same direction at speeds of 80 kmph and 40 kmph, respectively. The faster train crosses a passenger in the slower train in 72 seconds. The length of the faster train is:

(a) 720 m (b) 800 m
(c) 400 m (d) 880 m

28. Two trains Rajdhani Express and Shatabdi Express start at the same time from Mumbai and Delhi and proceed towards each other at the rate of 45 kmph and 50 kmph, respectively. When they meet, it is found that one of the trains has travelled 120 km more than the other. Find the distance between the 2 stations?

(a) 2235 km (b) 2260 km
(c) 2275 km (d) 2280 km

29. A metro train starts from Rajauri station at 7 a.m. at 60 kmph towards Rajiv Chowk. At 1 p.m. another train starts from Rajiv Chowk towards Rajauri at 80 kmph. When do the above trains meet, if the distance between Rajauri and Rajiv Chowk is 1200 km?

(a) 7:15 p.m. (b) 8:20 p.m.
(c) 7:20 p.m. (d) 7 p.m.

30. A train approaches a tunnel X – Y. Inside the tunnel a cow is located at a point, i.e. at 2/7 of the distance X – Y measured from the entrance X. When the train whistles the cow runs. If the cow moves to the exit Y, the train catches the cow exactly at the exit and if the cow moves to entrance X, the train catches the cow exactly at the entrance X. Find the ratio of the speeds of the train and the cow.

(a) 7 : 3 (b) 14 : 3
(c) 13 : 7 (d) None of these

ANSWER KEY

1. (a)	2. (d)	3. (b)	4. (a)
5. (c)	6. (a)	7. (d)	8. (d)
9. (d)	10. (c)	11. (a)	12. (d)
13. (b)	14. (c)	15. (b)	16. (c)
17. (c)	18. (b)	19. (d)	20. (c)
21. (b)	22. (a)	23. (c)	24. (c)
25. (c)	26. (d)	27. (b)	28. (d)
29. (d)	30. (a)		

SOLUTIONS AND SHORTCUTS

1. Average speed = (Total distance/Total time)
= (700 + 800)/(5 + 10)
= 1500/15 = 100 kmph.

2. Speed = $\frac{\text{Distance}}{\text{Time}}$, and distance = 100 m,
Time = 10 seconds
Speed = $\frac{100}{10}$ = 10 m/s
= $10 \times \frac{18}{5}$ = 36 kmph.

3. Speed = (350/35) = 10 m/s
Required time = (350 + 450)/10 = 80 s.

4. Speed (in m/s) = 90 × 5/18 = 25
Length of the train = 25 × 9 = 225 m.

5. Relative speed of train with respect to man is 200/10 = 20 m/s = 20 × (18/5) = 72 kmph
Let the speed of the train be x kmph.
Then the relative speed = (x – 5) kmph
Hence, x – 5 = 72
or x = 77 kmph.

6. Speed = 45 × (5/18)
= (25/2) m/s; Time = 30 s;
Let the length of the bridge be x m. Then
(225 + x)/30 = (25/2)
or x = 150 m.

7. In passing the man, the train has to cover only its own length. Also, the speed of the train
= (72) × (5/18) = 20 m/s
Length of the train = Speed of the train × time it takes to cross the man
= 20 × 20 = 400 m
We also know that the train crosses the platform in 40 seconds. At a speed of 20 m/s, it would cover a total distance of 40 × 20 = 800 m.

This distance would be equal to the length of the train + the length of the platform.

Since, the length of the train is 400 m, the length of the platform would be 400.

8. Speed = (10) × (5/18) = 25/9 m/s

Total distance to be covered = 260 + 240 = 500 m.

Required Time = (500)/(25/9) =180 s.

9. Speed = 30 m/s

Time = 20 s

Let the length of the train be x m

Then $(x + 200)/20 = 30$

or $x = 400$ m.

10. Speed of the train = 72 × (5/18)

= 20 m/s

Time = 7 s

Distance = Speed × Time = 20 × 7 = 140 m.

11. Relative speed = (20 + 40) m/s

= 60 m/s

Distance covered = 170 + 130 = 300 m

Required Time = (300)/60 = 5 s.

12. Speed = (600/18) m/s = 100/3 m/s

Let the length of the platform be x m

Then $(x + 600)/36 = 100/3$

or $x = 600$ m.

13. Relative speed = (70 + 80) = 150 kmph

= (125/3) m/s

Distance covered =1.2 + 0.8 = 2 km

Required time = 2000/(125/3) = 48 s.

14. Relative speed = (72 + 90) = 162 kmph

= 45 m/s

Distance covered =140 + 160 = 300 m

Required time = 300/45 = 20/3 s = 6.67 s.

15. Relative speed = (110 + 90) kmph;

= 200 × (5/18)

= (500/9) m/s

Let the length of the train be x m

$(x + 250)/9 = 500/9$

$x = 250$ m.

16. Speed = 20 m/s

Time = 1 min = 60 s

Let the length of the tunnel be x m

Then $(x + 500)/60 = 20$

or $x = 700$ m.

17. In 2 hours, the first train travels 45 × 2 = 90 km.

Now the distance between them = 208 km

and relative speed = 45 + 35 = 80 kmph

Time for them to meet = $\frac{208}{80}$ hours.

In this time train from Mumbai travels a distance =

$\frac{208}{80} \times 45$ = 117 km

Total distance from Mumbai = 90 + 117

= 207 km.

18. Let the speeds of the two trains be x m/s and y m/s, respectively.

Then, the length of the first train = $26x$ m,

And the length of the second train = $21y$ m

or $[(26x + 21y)/(x + y)] = 24$

or $26x + 21y = 24x + 24y$

or $2x = 3y$

or $x : y = 3 : 2$.

19. The speed of the train relative to jogger

= (54 – 18) kmph = 36 kmph

= (36 × 5/18) = 10 m/s

Distance to be covered = (200 + 160) m

= 360 m.

Time taken = (360/10) = 36 s.

20. Speed of the first train = $\frac{150}{15} = 10$ m/sec

$$\text{Time} = \frac{\text{Length of both trains}}{\text{Relative speed}}$$

$$12 = \frac{2 \times 150}{10 + x}$$

(where x is the speed of the second train in m/s)

or $120 + 12x = 300$

or $x = \frac{180}{12} = 15$ m/sec

$= \frac{15 \times 18}{5} = 54$ kmph.

21. Length of both trains = 250 m

Speed of the second train = x kmph

Relative speed = $(65 + x) \times \frac{5}{18}$ m/s

$$\therefore \quad \text{Time} = \frac{\text{Sum of lengths of trains}}{\text{Relative speed}}$$

or ⇒ $6 = 250/(65 + x) \times \frac{5}{18}$

or $6 \times \frac{5}{18} \times (65 + x) = 250$

or $65 + x = \frac{250 \times 3}{5}$

or $65 + x = 150$

or $x = 150 - 65 = 85$

22. Total distance covered = 1.75 + 0.75

= 2.5 km

Time taken = (2.5)/75 = (1/30) hour

= 2 minutes.

23. Average speed = (Total distance/Total time)

Total distance = $3d$, where d is the distance between P and Q.

Total time is the sum of times taken for 3 journeys, i.e.

$$\frac{d}{X} + \frac{d}{Y} + \frac{d}{Y} = \frac{d}{X} + \frac{2d}{Y} = \frac{d(Y + 2X)}{XY}.$$

On dividing total distance by total time, we get

$$\text{Average speed} = \frac{3XY}{2X+Y}.$$

24. After meeting,

$$S_2/S_1 = \sqrt{t_1/t_2}$$

or $S_2 \quad = S_1 \times \sqrt{t_1/t_2}$

$$= 90 \times \sqrt{16/9} = 120 \text{ kmph.}$$

25. Let the speed of train = S m/s and its length = L m. When it passes a pole only train's length is considered whereas when it crosses the platform, the sum of lengths of the train and the platform is considered. So
L/S = 15 and $(L + 100)/S$ = 30.
Solving, we get
S = (100/15) m/s and L = 100 m.
26. Let the length of each train be x m
Then, the distance covered = $2x$ m
Relative speed = (56 – 46) kmph
Relative speed (in m/s) = 10 × (5/18) = 25/9
Hence, $(2x/54)$ = 25/9
Solving, we get
x = 75 m.
27. Relative speed of the trains = 80 – 40

$$= 40 \text{ kmph} = 40 \times \frac{5}{18} = \frac{100}{9} \text{ m/s}.$$

Let the length of the faster train = L m.

$$\text{Time taken} = L \div \left(\frac{100}{9}\right) = 72\text{s}.$$

(Note: The length of the second train doesn't matter as the situation is of the train crossing a man in the other train.)
Solving, we get

$$L = 72 \times \frac{100}{9} = 800 \text{ m}.$$

28. Let the distance between Mumbai and Delhi = d km. From the information given in the question, we can infer that the two trains must have travelled for 120/5 = 24 hours before they meet each other.
This can be thought of as : For 1 hour of movement, the faster train would travel 5 km more than the slower train.
Hence, it would travel 120 km extra in 24 hours.
Hence, the distance between Mumbai and Delhi = 24 × (45 + 50) = 2280 km.
29. Till 1 p.m., the train from Rajauri travels a distance of 6 × 60 = 360 km.
So now the distance left = 1200 – 360
= 840 km.
Relative speed = 60 + 80 = 140 kmph.
Time after which the trains will meet
= (840/140)
= 6 hours.
Hence, the time at which they meet is 1 p.m. + 6 hours = 7 p.m.
30. Solve this through options. Assume the tunnel has a length of 7 units. So, the distance of the cow from entrance X is 2 units and from exit Y is 5 units. If we check for option (a), which gives us the speed ratio of 7:3 and match it for the meeting at the entrance and the exits we see the following: When the cow moves to the entrance he would move 2 units. In the same time, the train would move 7 × 2/3 = 14/3 units of distance. This means that the train is at a distance of 14/3 units away from the tunnel's entrance. Next, when we compare the meeting points at the exit Y, we see that, the train would have moved 14/3 + 7 = 35/3 units, while the cow would move 5 units to the meeting point at the exit Y. The ratio of distances traveled would be 7:3, which matches the ratio we started with. If you try to do the same steps with a ratio of 13 : 7, the final ratio would not match. Hence, option (a) is correct.

BOATS AND STREAMS

The chapter on boats and streams is an important topic for aptitude examinations. You can expect some questions from this topic in most aptitude examinations. Since, this topic is clearly drawn from the time, speed and distance concept, the same equation (Speed × Time = Distance) works in this topic too.

A boat moving in a stream has its own speed. This speed is called as the *speed of the boat* in still water. However, if the boat is moving in a stream that is not still but moving, the effective speed of the boat increases if the boat is going along with the stream (downstream), while the effective speed of the boat reduces if it is traveling against the stream (upstream). If the speed of the boat in still water is S_B, and the speed of the stream is S_S, then:

Speed downstream, $S_D = S_B + S_S$
Speed upstream, $S_U = S_B - S_S$.

Note: If you are given the speed of the boat upstream and the speed of the boat downstream (S_U and S_D), the speed of the boat in still water S_B is the average of S_U and S_D.

Example 1: A boat travels 12 kmph while going downstream and 8 kmph while going upstream. What is the speed of the boat in still water and what is the speed of the stream?

Solution: It is given that

S_U = 8 kmph and S_D = 12 kmph, Then
S_B = Average of 8 and 12 = 10 kmph
and S_S = Difference between S_B and S_U = 2 kmph

Solved Examples

1. A boat sails downstream from point A to point B, which is 10 km from A, and then returns to A. If the actual speed of the boat (in still water) is 3 km/h, the trip from A to B takes 8 hours less than that from B to A. What must the actual speed of the boat for the trip from A to B to take exactly 100 minutes?
(a) 1 kmph (b) 2 kmph
(c) 3 kmph (d) 4 kmph

Solution: In order to solve this, you first need to think of the speed of the river flow (if the speed of the boat in still water is 3 kmph).

Let the speed of the river flow = s kmph and the speed of the boat be x kmph.
Then the downstream speed = $(3 + s)$ kmph
and the upstream speed = $(3 - s)$ kmph.
Clearly,
$10/(3 - s) - 10/(3 + s) = 8$
or $s = 2$ kmph.
This is the speed of the river flow. Next we need to solve the equation

$$10/(x + 2) = 1.66$$

or $x = 4$ kmph

2. A boat sails down the river for 10 km and then up the river for 6 km. The speed of the river flow is 1 kmph. What should be the minimum speed of the boat for the trip to take a maximum of 4 hours?
(a) 2 kmph (b) 3 kmph
(c) 4 kmph (d) 5 kmph

Solution: Solve through options.
For option (c), At 4 kmph, the boat would take exactly 4 hours to cover the distance.

3. A man rows 6 kmph in still water. If the river is running at 3 kmph, it takes him 45 minutes to row to a place and back. How far is the place?
(a) 1.12 km (b) 1.25 km
(c) 1.6875 km (d) 2.5 km

Solution: Let the distance be x km. Then

$$(x/9) + (x/3) = 3/4$$

or $4x/9 = 3/4$

or $x = 27/16$

$= 1.6875$ km.

4. A boat goes 40 km upstream in 8 hours and a distance of 49 km downstream in 7 hours. The speed of the boat in still water is
(a) 5 kmph (b) 5.5 kmph
(c) 6 kmph (d) 6.5 kmph

Solution: Upstream speed = 40/8 = 5 kmph.
Downstream speed = 49/7 = 7 kmph.
Speed in still water = Average of the upstream speed and the downstream speed = (7 + 5)/2 = 6 kmph.

5. In a stream, B lies in between A and C such that it is equidistant from both A and C. A boat can go from A to B and back in 6 hours 30 minutes while it goes from A to C in 9 hours. How long would it take to go from C to A?
(a) 3.75 h (b) 4 h
(c) 4.25 h (d) 4.5 h

Solution: Since A to C is double the distance of A to B, it is evident that the time taken for A to C and back would be double the time taken from A to B and back (i.e. double of 6.5 hours = 13 hours). Since going from A to C takes 9 hours, coming back from C to A would take 4 hours (as 9 + 4 = 13 h).

6. A boat goes 15 km upstream in 80 minutes. The speed of the stream is 5 kmph. The speed of the boat in still water is
(a) 16.25 kmph (b) 16 kmph
(c) 15 kmph (d) 17 kmph

Solution: 15 km upstream in 80 minutes, i.e. the speed of the boat 15/1.33 = 11.25 kmph (Upstream speed of the boat).

Thus, still water speed of the boat = 11.25 + 5 = 16.25 kmph.

7. A motorboat went downstream for 28 km and immediately returned. It took the boat twice as long to make the return trip. If the speed of the river flow were twice as high, the trip downstream and back would take 672 minutes. Find the speed of the boat in still water and the speed of the river flow.
(a) 9 kmph, 3 kmph
(b) 9 kmph, 6 kmph
(c) 8 kmph, 2 kmph
(d) 12 kmph, 3 kmph

Solution: From the situation described in the first condition itself, we can see that the speed of coming back has to be double the speed of going downstream.
Checking the options, only the Option (a) fits this condition, i.e
Downstream speed = 2 × Upstream speed
Hence, the option (a) is correct.

8. A motorboat whose speed in still water is 10 kmph went 91 km downstream and then returned to its starting point. Calculate the speed of the river flow if the round trip took a total of 20 hours.
(a) 3 kmph (b) 4 kmph
(c) 6 kmph (d) 8 kmph

Solution: Look for the solution by thinking of the factors of 91. It can be seen that 91/13 + 91/7 = 7 + 13 =20 hours.
It means that the speed of the boat in still water is 10 kmph and the speed of the water flow would be 3 kmph.
Hence, the Option (a) is correct.

9. A motorboat went down the river for 14 km and then up the river for 9 km. It took a total of 5 hours for the entire journey. Find the speed of the river flow if the speed of the boat in still water is 5 kmph

(a) 1 kmph (b) 1.5 kmph
(c) 2 kmph (d) 3 kmph

Solution: We have the equation,

$$14/(5 + x) + 9/(5 - x) = 5$$

or $$x = 2 \text{ kmph}$$

Practice Exercise

1. A boat goes downstream 18 km is 4 hours and upstream in 12 hours. The rate of current (in kmph)
(a) 1 (b) 1.75
(c) 1.5 (d) 3

2. In one hour, a boat goes 10 km along the stream and 2 km against the stream. The speed of the boat in still water (in kmph) is
(a) 5 (b) 6
(c) 7 (d) 8

3. A man can row downstream at 12 kmph and upstream at 6 kmph. The speed of the stream (in kmph) is:
(a) 2 (b) 3
(c) 4 (d) 5

4. A man rows downstream 18 km and 12 km upstream. If he takes 3 hours to cover each distance, the velocity (in kmph) of the current is:
(a) 0.25 (b) 0.5
(c) 0.75 (d) 1

5. The speed of a swimmer itself is 20 kmph and the rate of flow of the river is 4 kmph. Moving with the stream the swimmer went 120 km. What distance will the swimmer cover during the same time going against the stream?
(a) 75 km (b) 80 km
(c) 90 km (d) None of these

6. A boat running downstream covers a distance of 16 km in 2 hours while for covering the same distance upstream, it takes 4 hours. What is the speed of the boat is still water?
(a) 2 kmph (b) 6 kmph
(c) 4 kmph (d) Data inadequate

7. A man can row three-quarters of a kilometer against the stream in $11\frac{1}{4}$ minutes. The speed (in kmph) of the man in still water is:
(a) 2 (b) 3
(c) 4 (d) Data Insufficient

8. A boat covers a certain distance downstream in 1 hour, while it comes back in $1\frac{1}{2}$ hours. If the speed of the stream is 3 kmph, what is the speed of the boat in still water?
(a) 10 kmph (b) 23 kmph
(c) 14 kmph (d) 15 kmph

9. Samar can swim 3 kmph in still water. If the velocity of the stream is 2 kmph, the time taken by him to swim to a place 10 km upstream and back is:
(a) 10 hours (b) 12 hours
(c) 8.33 hours (d) 9.33 hours

10. Surya takes thrice as long to row a distance against the stream as to row the same distance with the stream. The ratio of the speed of stream and speed of the boat (in still water) is:
(a) 1 : 2 (b) 1 : 3
(c) 2 : 5 (d) None of these

11. If a boat goes 100 km down stream in 600 minutes and the speed of the stream is 5 kmph, the speed of the boat (in kmph) in still water is:
(a) 5 (b) 10
(c) 15 (d) 20

12. A man covers 12 km upstream and 18 km downstream in 3 hours, while he covers 36km upstream and 24 km downstream in 6.5 hours. What is the speed of the current (in kmph):
(a) 1 (b) 1.5
(c) 2 (d) 2.5

13. Supriya can swim in still water at a speed of 10 kmph. If speed of the current would have been 5 kmph, then she could swim 60 km:
(a) Upstream in 4 hours
(b) Downstream in 12 hours
(c) Upstream in 6 hours
(d) Downstream in 4 hours

14. Speed of a man in still water is 10 kmph and the speed of the water is 4 kmph. A man rows to a place at a distance of 84 km and comes back to the starting point. The total time taken (in hours) by him is:
(a) 7 (b) 14
(c) 20 (d) 24

15. A boat moves with a speed of 5 kmph in still water. When the river flows at 1 kmph, the boat takes 80 minutes to go from a point A to B and come back. What is the distance between the two points?
(a) 3 km (b) 2.4 km
(c) 3.2 km (d) 2.8 km

16. Arjun can swim at 10 kmph in still water. If the velocity of water is 4 kmph and it takes him 10 hours to swim to a place and come back, how far is the place?
(a) 24 km (b) 32 km
(c) 42 km (d) None of these

17. A boat goes 6 km in one hour in still water, but takes thrice as much time in going the same distance against the current. The speed of current (in kmph) is:
(a) 2 (b) 3
(c) 4 (d) 5

18. Shravan takes 18 hours for travelling upstream from point X to point Y and coming back to a point Z midway between X and Y. If the velocity of the river is 6 kmph and the speed of Shravan in still water is

10 kmph. What is the distance (in km) between X and Z?

(a) 30 (b) 32
(c) 64 (d) None of these

19. The ratio of speed of a boat to that of the current of water is 36 : 5. The boat goes along with the current in 5 hours 10 minutes. It will come back in:

(a) 5 hours 20 minutes
(b) 6 hours 10 minutes
(c) 6 hours 50 minutes
(d) 7 hours 10 minutes

20. At his usual rowing rate, a man can travel 60 km downstream in a certain river in 2 hours less than it takes him to travel the same distance upstream. But if he doubles his usual travelling speed for his 120 km round trip, the downstream 60 km then take only 200/7 minutes less than the upstream 60 km. What is the speed of the current in kmph?

(a) 4 (b) 6
(c) 8 (d) None of these

ANSWER KEY

1. (c)	2. (b)	3. (b)	4. (d)
5. (b)	6. (b)	7. (d)	8. (d)
9. (b)	10. (a)	11. (a)	12. (c)
13. (d)	14. (c)	15. (c)	16. (c)
17. (c)	18. (b)	19. (c)	20. (a)

SOLUTIONS AND SHORTCUTS

1. From the first statement, we get that the speed downstream is 4.5 kmph, while the speed upstream is 1.5 kmph (18/4 and 18/12 respectively).
Since we know that the speed of the boat in still water, is the average of the speed downstream and the speed upstream, the speed of the boat would be 3 kmph and the speed of the stream then would be: 4.5 – 3 = 1.5 kmph.
Alternate method
The solution gets significantly more time consuming as you can see if you use the mathematical approach
Let the speed of boat and current be x and y (in kmph), respectively.
According to the question,
$$(x+y)4=18 \text{ or } x=\frac{9}{2}-y \quad \text{(i)}$$
$$(x-y)12=18 \text{ or } x=\frac{3}{2}+y \quad \text{(ii)}$$
Solving, we get
$$\frac{9}{2}-y=\frac{3}{2}+y$$
or $2y=3$
$y=1.5$ kmph

2. **Mathematical solution**
Let the speed of boat and current be x kmph and y kmph (in kmph), respectively.
According to the question,
$(x+y)1=10$
or $x+y=10$ (i)
$(x-y)1=2$
or $x-y=2$ (ii)
Solving, we get
x = 6 kmph and y = 4 kmph
Hence, the speed of the boat in still water = 6 kmph
Logical reactive solution
Since the speed downstream is given as 10 kmph, and the speed upstream is 2 kmph, the speed of the boat in still water would be the average of these two, i.e. 6 kmph.

3. **Mathematical solution**
Let the speed of boat and of the current be x kmph and y kmph, respectively.
According to the question,
$(x+y)=12$ (i)
$(x-y)=6$ (ii)
Solving, we get
x = 9 kmph and y = 3 kmph.
Logical solution
Speed of boat = Average of 12 and 6 = 9 kmph.
Hence, the speed of stream = 3 kmph.

4. **Mathematical solution**
Let the speed of boat and current be x kmph and y kmph, respectively.
According to the question,
$(x+y)3=18$ or $x+y=6$ (i)
$(x-y)3=12$ or $x-y=4$ (ii)
Solving, we get
x = 5 kmph and y = 1 kmph.
Logical solution
Speed downstream = 18/3 = 6 kmph
Speed upstream = 12/3 = 4 kmph.
Therefore, the average of 4 and 6 = 6 kmph is, the speed of the boat in still water.
Hence, the speed of the stream = 1kmph.

5. Let the distance to be covered by the swimmer when it is travelling against the stream be x kmph.
The swimmer goes down the river at a speed of 20 + 4 = 24 kmph
and up the river at a speed of 20 – 4 = 16 kmph.
Since the time taken is same the time taken downstream = 120/24 = 5 hours.
In 5 hours at a speed of 16 kmph, the swimmer would be able to cover 16 × 5 = 80 km.

6. Speed of boat at downstream = $\left(\frac{16}{2}\right)$ kmph = 8 kmph

Speed of boat at upstream = $\left(\frac{16}{4}\right)$ kmph = 4 kmph

Speed of boat in still water = $\frac{1}{2}(8+4)$ kmph = 6 kmph

7. In the question, no information is given about the speed of current, Hence, we cannot find the speed of man in still water. Data insufficient.

8. Let the speed of the boat in still water be v kmph. Then,

Speed of boat downstream = $(v + 3)$ kmph

Speed of boat upstream = $(v - 3)$ kmph

$\therefore (v+3)\times 1 = (v-3)\times\frac{3}{2}$

or $2v+6=3v-9$

or $v = 15$ kmph.

Alternate method

You could also have solved these using options.

If you test Option (d), i.e. 15 kmph, the speed downstream = 18 kmph and therefore, the boat would cover 18 km in 1 hour, while the speed upstream would be 12 kmph and the boat would cover the same distance of 18 km in 1.5 hours.

Hence, Option (d) is the correct answer.

9. Time taken to swim 10 km upstream

$= \frac{10}{3+2} = 2$ hours

Time taken to swim 10 km downstream

$= \frac{10}{3-2} = 10$ hours

Total time = 2 + 10 = 12 hours.

10. Let the speed of Surya (in still water) and current be x kmph and y kmph, respectively. If he takes t hours to cover d km downstream, then according to the question,

$(x+y)t = d$ or $x+y = d/t$ (i)

$(x-y)3t = d$ or $x-y = d/3t$ (ii)

Solving, we get

$\frac{x+y}{x-y} = 3$

or $x+y=3x-3y$

or $2x = 4y$

or $x:y=2:1$

or $y:x=1:2$

A better way to solve this would again be through options. If we take the first option, we will see that if the speed of Surya in still water is $2x$ kmph, the speed of the stream is x kmph. This would give us $3x$ kmph and x kmph as the downstream and upstream speeds, respectively.

This means that Surya would take thrice as long to row a distance against the stream as to row the same distance with the stream (as given in the problem). Hence, the Option (a) is the correct option.

11. Let the speed of boat in still water be v kmph.

As per the question,

$(5+v)\left(\frac{600}{60}\right) = 100$

or $5+v=10$

or $v = 5$ kmph.

12. Let the speed of boat and current be x kmph and y kmph, respectively.

According to the question,

$$\frac{12}{x-y}+\frac{18}{x+y}=3 \quad \text{(i)}$$

$$\frac{36}{x-y}+\frac{24}{x+y}=6.5 \quad \text{(ii)}$$

Solving, we get

$$\frac{36}{x-y}+\frac{24}{x+y}-\left(\frac{12}{x-y}+\frac{18}{x+y}\right)3 = 6.5-9$$

$$= -2.5$$

or $$-\frac{30}{x+y} = -2.5$$

or $$(x+y)=12 \quad \text{(iii)}$$

Similarly multiply Eq. (i) by 4/3 and subtracting from Eq. (ii), we get:

$$\frac{20}{x-y}=2.5$$

or $$x-y=8 \quad \text{(iv)}$$

Solving Eqs. (iii) and (iv), we get

$x = 10$ kmph and $y = 2$ kmph.

Hence, the speed of the current = 2 kmph.

13. Time taken to travel 60 km downstream = $\frac{60}{10+5} = 4$ hours.

Time taken to travel 60 km upstream

$= \frac{60}{10-5} = 12$ hours.

Hence, the Option (d) is correct.

14. Time taken to travel 84 km downstream

$= \frac{84}{10+4} = 6$ hours.

Time taken to travel 84 km upstream

$= \frac{84}{10-4} = 14$ hours.

Total time taken = 6 + 14 = 20 hours.

15. Since the distance is constant, so the speed is inversely proportional to the time taken.

Downstream speed = (5 + 1) kmph = 6 kmph
Upstream speed = (5 – 1) kmph = 4 kmph
Ratio of Downstream speed : Upstream speed = 6 : 4
Therefore, the time taken in Downstream journey : Upstream journey = 4 : 6
So, the time taken in Downstream journey = (4/10) × 80 = 32 minutes
Hence, the distance = (32/60) × 6 = 3.2 km.

16. Let the place is d km away from the original position of Arjun. According to the question,

$$\frac{d}{10+4}+\frac{d}{10-4}=10$$

or $\frac{d}{14}+\frac{d}{6}=10$

Now by putting the options in the above equation or by solving the above equation, we get d = 42 km.

17. Solve this problem by checking the options for time to become 3 times when it goes upstream.
For time to become 3 times, the speed should become 1/3rd of the normal speed. Since, it is given to us that the speed of the boat in still water is 6 kmph, it is obvious that the speed of the stream would be 4 kmph, since only then do we get the speed of the boat upstream as 1/3rd the speed of the boat in still water.

18. Let the distance between point X and Y be d km. Then according to the question,

$$\frac{d}{10-6}+\frac{d/2}{10+6}=18$$

or $(d/4) + (d/32) = 18$

Solving, we get

d = 64 km

Hence, the distance between X and Z = $d/2$ = 64/2 = 32 km

19. Let the speed of the boat and of the current be $36v$ and $5v$ (in km per minutes), respectively.
Total distance covered by the boat in downstream = $41v \times 310$ km
Let the boat takes t minutes to come back, then

$$41v \times 310 = (36v - 5v)t$$

t = 410 minutes = 6 hours 50 minutes.

20. Let the speed of the boat and of the current be x kmph and y kmph, respectively.
According to the question,

$$\frac{60}{x-y}-\frac{60}{x+y}=2$$

or $\frac{1}{x-y}-\frac{1}{x+y}=1/30$

or $60y = x^2 - y^2$

or $x^2 = y^2 + 60y$ (i)

After doubling his travelling speed,

$$\frac{60}{2x-y}-\frac{60}{2x+y}=\frac{200}{420}=\frac{10}{21}$$

or $\frac{1}{2x-y}-\frac{1}{2x+y}=\frac{1}{126}$

or $\frac{2x+y-2x+y}{4x^2-y^2}=\frac{1}{126}$

or $4x^2 - y^2 = 252y$ (ii)

By putting x^2 from Eq. (i) in Eq. (ii), we get

or $4(y^2 + 60y) - y^2 = 252y$

or $3y^2 = 12y$

or y = 4 kmph.

RACES AND GAMES OF SKILL

Problems on races and games of skill are peculiar problem types that are regularly present in a lot of aptitude tests. In the case of races, these questions talk about the speeds at which different runners are running on a race-track, and ask us to find things like by how much time/distance the faster runner beats the slower runner/s.

Understand the Language of and the Thinking required to Handle Problems on Races

Since, races are essentially an offshoot of time speed and distance, the essential formula to be used here would again be

Speed × Time = Distance

For further discussions of how to handle these questions, we can look at the following examples:

You should know the following statements and their reactions with regards to problems on races.

Example 1: In a 100 m race, A beats B by 10 m or 2 seconds. Find the speeds of A and B.

Solution: Since A beats B by 10 m in terms of distance and by 2 seconds in terms of time, it means that the speed of B is 10/2 = 5 m/s. Thus, B would run the 100 m race in 100/5 = 20 seconds. Since A beats him by 2 seconds, A would take 20 – 2 = 18 seconds for 100 m. The speed of A is 100/18 = 50/9 m/s.

Example 2: In a 1000 m race, Aman beats Raman by 100 m, while Raman beats Samanyu by 100 m in a 600-m race. By how many metres would Aman beat Samanyu in a 1500 m race?

Solution: Raman is the common point between Aman and Samanyu and we would need to compare the two only by going through Raman.

From the first statement we have learned that when Aman does 1000, Raman does 900. Also, we are given that when Raman does 600, Samanyu does 500.

Therefore, when Raman would run 900, Samanyu would run 750 (using unitary method). At this point, we have a direct relation between Aman and Samanyu, i.e. when Aman does 1000, Samanyu does 750.

So, when Aman would do 1500, Samanyu would do

$$1500 \times 750 \div 1000 = 1125 \text{ m}.$$

Thus, Raman would beat Samanyu by 375 m in a 1500 m race.

Note: From the point in the problem, where we have that when Aman does 1000, Samanyu does 750, we can also think that in a 1000 m race Aman beats Samanyu by 250 m.

Hence, in a 1500-m race Aman would beat Samanyu by $250 \times 1500 \div 1000 = 250 \times 1.5 = 375$ m.

Understand the Language of and the Thinking Required to Handle Problems on Games of Skill

In problems on games of skill, relative rates of scoring of points in a game are given for different people. It is best to understand how these problems work, by looking at an example for the same.

Example 3: A can give B 10 points in 50, while B can give 6 points in 30 to C. How many points can A give C in a game of 100 points?

Solution: 'A can give B '10 points in 50' means that when A scores 50 points, B scores 40. Similarly, when B scores 30 points, C scores 24. So when B scores 40 points, C would score 32. This means that when A would score 50, C would score 32.

Therefore, when A scores 100, C would score 64.

Hence, A can give 36 points in 100 to C.

Solved Examples

1. In a race of 600 m, Ajay beats Vijay by 60 m and in a race of 500 m Vijay beats Anjay by 25 m. By how many metres will Ajay beat Anjay in a 400 m race?

   (a) 48 m (b) 52 m
   (c) 56 m (d) 58 m

Solution: When Ajay does 600 m, Anjay does 540 m. When Vijay does 500 m, Anjay does 475 m. Therefore, when Vijay would do 540 m, Anjay would do $475 \times 540 \div 500 = 513$ m

Thus, Ajay : Vijay : Anjay = 600 : 540 : 513. This means that in a 600-m race, Ajay beats Anjay by 87 m.

Hence, Ajay would beat Anjay by $(87 \times 2/3) = 58$ m in a 400 m race.

2. In a 100 m race, Shyam runs at 1.66 m/s. If Shyam gives Sujit a start of 4 m and still beats him by 12 seconds, what is Sujit's speed?

   (a) 1.11 m/s (b) 0.75 m/s
   (c) 1.33 m/s (d) 1 km/h

Solution: Solve using options 1.33 m/s fits perfectly. The thought process would go as follows:

Shyam would run a 100 m race in $100 \div 1.66 = 60$ seconds. Sujit runs 96 m in $60 + 12 = 72$ seconds. Hence, Sujit's speed $= 96 \div 72 = 1.33$ m/sec.

3. Vinay runs 100 m in 20 seconds and Ajay runs the same distance in 25 seconds. By what distance will Vinay beat Ajay in a 100 m race?

   (a) 10m (b) 20m
   (c) 25m (d) 12m

Solution: Speed of Vinay = 5 m/s, Speed of Ajay = 4m/s. In a 100-m race, Vinay would take 20 seconds to complete and in this time Ajay would only cover 80 m. Hence, Vinay beats Ajay by 20 m in a 100-m race.

4. At a game of billiards, A can give B 15 points in 60 and A can give C 20 in 60. How many points can B give C in a game of 90?

Solution: When A scores 60 points, B scores 45 and C scores 40. Thus, when B scores 90, C would score 80. B can give C 10 points in 90.

5. Ram and Shyam run a race of 2000 m. First, Ram gives Shyam a start of 200 m and beats him by 30 s. Next, Ram gives Shyam a start of 3 minutes and is beaten by 1000 m. Find the time in minutes in which Ram and Shyam can run the race separately.

   (a) 8, 10 (b) 4, 5
   (c) 5, 9 (d) 6, 9

Solution: Let the speed of Shyam be s m/s.

When Ram runs 2000 m, Shyam runs $(1800 - 30s)$

When Ram runs 1000 m, Shyam runs $(2000 - 180s)$.

Then,

$2000/1000 = (1800 - 30s)/(2000 - 180s)$

Solving, we get

$s = 6.66$ m/s

Thus, Shyam's speed = 400 m/minute and he would take 5 minutes to cover the distance. Hence, the Option (b) is the correct answer.

Practice Exercise

1. In a 200 m race, P completes the race in 20 seconds and Q in 25 seconds. In this race P beats Q by:

   (a) 10 m (b) 20 m
   (c) 30 m (d) 40 m

2. In a 300 m race Anuj beats Bimal by 15 m or 5 seconds. Time taken by Bimal to complete the race is:

(a) 100 s (b) 125 s
(c) 115 s (d) None of these

3. In the previous question, the speed of Anuj in m/s is:
(a) 60/19 (b) 25
(c) 15 (d) None of these

4. P can run 2 m in the same time that Q runs 2.5 m. In a 2-km race, Q beats P by:
(a) 200 m (b) 300 m
(c) 250 m (d) 400 m

5. In a game of 100 points, P can give Q 10 points and R, 20 points. Then, Q can give R:
(a) 10 points (b) 11.11 points
(c) 20 points (d) 40 points

6. In a game, A can give B 5 points in 90 and A can give C 10 points. How many points can B give C in a game of 170?
(a) 10 points (b) 7.5 points
(c) 5 points (d) 6 points

7. In a 100 m race, Ajay can give Bhuvi a 20 m start and Chaya a 30 m start. How many metres start can Bhuvi give to Chaya in a 500 m race?
(a) 100 m (b) 67.5 m
(c) 62.5 m (d) None of these

8. In a 150 m race, P wins over Q by 35 m and in the same race R can give a start of 25 m to Q. By how much distance can P give a start to R, so that P beats R by 5 m?
(a) 5 m (b) 7 m
(c) 8 m (d) None of these

9. In a 600 m race, M gave N a head start of 5 seconds and still won the race by 20 seconds. The ratio of speeds of M and N are 2 : 1. How long will N take to cover a 1000 m race
(a) 40.66 s (b) 41.66 s
(c) 43.66 s (d) None of these

Directions for Questions 10 and 11: In a 100 m race, Aman wins over Bharat by 8 m or by 1 second. Bharat can give a start of 10 m to Chirag in a 100 m race. Now answer the following questions:

10. Find the ratio of speeds of Aman, Bharat and Chirag.
(a) 1000 : 920 : 828 (b) 1000 : 900 : 828
(c) 1000 : 920 : 818 (d) None of these

11. By how much time Aman will win over Chirag in a 1 km race?
(a) 20.5 s (b) 21.5 s
(c) 22 s (d) None of these

12. If the ratio of speeds of A and B is 3 : 5 and A loses the race by 50 m, what is the length of the race track?
(a) 100 m (b) 125 m
(c) 150 m (d) 175 m

13. The ratio of time taken by A and B to run a certain distance is 1 : 3 and A wins the race by 100 m. Then the length of the race track is:
(a) 100 m (b) 125 m
(c) 150 m (d) 175 m

Directions for Question 14 and 15: In a 1 km race, the speeds of A and B are in the ratio of 5 : 3 and A wins by 10 seconds. Now answer the following questions:

14. What is the time taken by B to finish the race?
(a) 40 s (b) 41.66 s
(c) 42.66 s (d) None of these

15. What is the per cent of the total distance, B covers when A finishes the race?
(a) 50 (b) 56.66
(c) 60 (d) None of these

16. In a 500 m race, P runs at 10 m/s. If P gives Q a start of 50 m and still wins the race by 5 seconds, find the speed of Q.
(a) 8 m/s (b) 8.18 m/s
(c) 9.01 m/s (d) 9.19m/s

ANSWER KEY

1. (d)	2. (a)	3. (a)	4. (d)
5. (b)	6. (a)	7. (c)	8. (b)
9. (d)	10. (a)	11. (d)	12. (b)
13. (c)	14. (d)	15. (c)	16. (b)

SOLUTIONS AND SHORTCUTS

1. Distance covered by Q in 20 seconds

$= 200 \times \frac{20}{25} = 160$ m.

P beats Q by 200 – 160 = 40 m.

2. Bimal runs 15 m in 5 seconds.

Therefore, Bimal's speed $= \frac{15}{5} = 3$ m/s

Hence, the time taken by Bimal to complete the race

$= \frac{300}{3} = 100$ s

3. Anuj beats Bimal by 5 s.
Therefore, time taken by Anuj to complete the race = 95 s

Hence, the required speed $= \frac{300}{95} = \frac{60}{19}$.

4. In 2.5 m race, Q beats P by 2.5 – 2 = 0.5 m.
In 2 km race Q beats P by

$\frac{0.5}{2.5} \times 2000 = 400$ m.

5. When P scores 100 points, Q scores 90 and R scores 80.
Therefore, when Q scores 100 points, R would score 88.88 points.
Hence, Q can give 11.11 points to R in 100 points.

6. It is given that, when A scores 90, B scores 85 and C scores 80 points. In a game of 170 points, when B scores 170 points, C would score 160 points. Hence, B can give C 10 points in a game of 170 points.
7. Ratio of speeds of Ajay and Bhuvi
$= 100:(100-20) = 5:4$
Ratio of speeds of Ajay and Chaya
$= 100:(100-30) = 10:7$
Ratio of speeds of Bhuvi and Chaya
$= 80:70 = 8:7$
Since, when Bhuvi moves 8 m, Chaya moves 7 m. Therefore when Bhuvi moves 500 m, Chaya moves
$= 500 \times \frac{7}{8} = 437.5$ m.
Hence, Bhuvi can give Chaya a start of $500 - 437.5 = 62.5$ m.
8. Ratio of speeds of P and Q
$= 150:(150-35) = 150:115$
Ratio of speeds of Q and R
$= (150-25):150 = 125:150$
Ratio of speeds of P, Q and R $= 150:115:138$.
So, it is clear that when P moves 150 m, R moves 138 m.
Thus, R moves 12 m less than P.
Hence, P can give = 12 – 5 = 7 m start to R and still beat him by 5 m.
9. M gave N a head start of 5 seconds and still won the race by 20 seconds. It means that M completes the race in 5 + 20 = 25 seconds before N.
Let N takes t seconds to cover the 600-m race,
Therefore, M takes (t – 25) seconds. Then
$$2:1 = t:(t-25)$$
or, $t = 50$ s
So, speed of N = 600/50 = 12 m/s
Hence, N will take 1000/12 = 83.33 s to cover a race of 1000 m.
10. Ratio of speeds of Aman and Bharat
$= 100:(100-8) = 100:92$
Ratio of speeds of Bharat and Chirag
$= 100:(100-10) = 100:90$
Hence, the ratio of speeds of Aman, Bharat, Chirag
$= 1000:920:828$.
11. Ratio of speeds of Aman : Chirag $= 1000:828$
So in a 1 km race, Aman will win by 172 m.
Also, the speed of Bharat = $\frac{8}{1} = 8$ m/s
So, Speed of Chirag = 0.9 × 8 = 7.2 m/s
Hence, Aman will win over Chirag by $\frac{172}{7.2}$ = 23.88 secs.
12. In a 5 m race, the ratio of speeds of A and B is 3 : 5, so B will win the race by 2 m.
Hence, if B will win the race by 50 m, the length of race track = $50 \times \frac{5}{2}$ = 125 m.
13. Ratio of the speeds of A and B is 3 : 1, so in a 3-m race A wins by 2 m. So when A wins by 100 m, the length of the race track would be = $100 \times \frac{3}{2} = 150$ m.
14. A wins a 5 m race by 2 m. So, in a 1-km race, A wins by
$1000 \times \frac{2}{5} = 400$ m.
Since, A wins by 10 seconds, it means that B would cover 400 m in 10 s, i.e. giving us the speed of B as 40 m per second.
Hence, time taken by B to finish the race = $\frac{1000}{40} = 25$ s.
15. When A finishes the race, B covers total $1000 - 400 = 600$ m.
So, B covers $\frac{600}{1000} \times 100 = 60\%$ of the total distance.
16. P takes $\frac{500}{10} = 50$ s to complete the journey.
P gives Q a start of 50 m and still wins the race by 5 s, Q covered a total of 450 m in 50 + 5 = 55 s.
So, speed of Q = $\frac{450}{55} = \frac{90}{11} = 8.18$ m/s.

Going Beyond the Book

Scan this QR code to access a conceptual video on clock questions

Space for Rough Work

LEVEL OF DIFFICULTY (I)

1. A bullock cart has to cover a distance of 120 km in 15 hours. If it covers half of the journey in 3/5th time, the speed to cover the remaining distance in the time left has to be:
   (a) 6.4 kmph (b) 6.67 kmph
   (c) 10 kmph (d) 15 kmph
2. A man rides at the rate of 18 kmph, but stops for 6 minutes to change horses at the end of every 7th km. The time that he will take to cover a distance of 90 km is:
   (a) 6 hours (b) 6 hours 12 minutes
   (c) 6 hours 18 minutes (d) 6 hours 24 minutes
3. P travels for 6 hours at the rate of 5 kmph and for 3 hours at the rate of 6 kmph. The average speed of the journey (in kmph) is:
   (a) $3\frac{1}{5}$ kmph (b) $5\frac{1}{3}$ kmph
   (c) $1\frac{2}{9}$ kmph (d) $2\frac{2}{5}$ kmph
4. On a journey across Kolkata, a taxi averages 50 km/hr for 50% of the distance, 40 kmph for 40% of it and 20 kmph for the remaining. The average speed (in kmph) for the whole journey is:
   (a) 42 kmph (b) 40 kmph
   (c) 35 kmph (d) 45 kmph

Direction for Questions 5 and 6: The distance between the office and the home of John is 80 km. One day he was late by 1 hour than the normal time to leave for the office, so he increased his speed by 4 kmph and thus reached his office in time. Now answer the following questions:

5. What is the final speed of John?
   (a) 16 kmph (b) 20 kmph
   (c) 10 kmph (d) None of these
6. What is the percentage increase in the speed of John?
   (a) 10% (b) 15%
   (c) 20% (d) 25%
7. Trisha goes to office at 10 kmph and reaches the office 2 minutes late. If she goes at 15 kmph she reaches the office 2 minutes earlier than the scheduled time. What is the distance of her office?
   (a) 3 km (b) 2 km
   (c) 4 km (d) 2.5 km

Direction for Questions 8 to 11: The distance between two cities A and B is 100 km and speed of Ram and Anuj are 15 kmph and 25 kmph, respectively. Initially both are at A and start moving toward B. If they move between A and B to and fro, answer the following questions:

8. Find the time required for the first meeting?
   (a) 3 hours (b) 4 hours
   (c) 5 hours (d) None of these
9. What is the distance covered by Anuj before the first meeting?
   (a) 125 km (b) 150 km
   (c) 250 km (d) None of these
10. The ratio of distances covered by Anuj and Ram when they meet for the fourth time is?
    (a) 2 : 3 (b) 3 : 5
    (c) 2 : 5 (d) None of these
11. The distance between A and the place of their 5th meeting is?
    (a) 15 km (b) 50 km
    (c) 25 km (d) None of these
12. A train approaches a tunnel XY. Inside the tunnel a cow is standing at a point, i.e. at 2/7 of the distance XY measured from the entrance X. When the train whistles the cow runs. If the cow moves to the exit Y, the train catches the cow exactly at the exit and if the cow moves to entrance X, the train catches the cow exactly at the entrance X. Find the ratio of speeds of the train and the cow?
    (a) 7 : 3 (b) 14 : 3
    (c) 13 : 7 (d) None of these
13. Location of B is north of A and location of C is west of A. The distances AB and AC are 5 km and 12 km, respectively. The shortest distance (in km) between the locations B and C is:
    (a) 60 (b) 13
    (c) 17 (d) 7
14. A thief running at 8 kmph. is chased by a policeman whose speed is 10 kmph. If the thief is 100 m ahead of the policeman, the time required for the policeman to catch the thief will be:
    (a) 2 min (b) 3 min
    (c) 4 min (d) 6 min
15. Johnny Scottish walked 12 km to reach the station from his house, then he boarded a train whose average speed was 120 kmph and thus he reached his destination. In this way, he took a total of 8 hours. If the average speed of the entire journey was 99 kmp/h the average speed of walking is:
    (a) 8 kmph (b) 12 kmph
    (c) 9 kmph (d) 6 kmph

Direction for Questions 16 and 17: Two trains leave Lucknow for Pune, which are 600 Km apart. They leave 4 hours after each other. The first train leaves at 10 am at

30 kmph and the faster train leaves later at 70 kmph in the same direction.

16. When the faster train will overtake the slower train?

(a) 4 p.m. (b) 7 p.m.
(c) 5 p.m. (d) 6:30 p.m.

17. What is the distance from Lucknow, where the faster train would overtake the slower train?

(a) 180 km (b) 270 km
(c) 255 km (d) 210 km

18. Mr Kumar drives to work at an average speed of 48 kmph. The time taken to cover the first 60% of the distance is 10 minutes more than the time taken to cover the remaining distance. How far is his office?

(a) 30 km (b) 40 km
(c) 45 km (d) 48 km

Direction for Questions 19 and 20: Two places A and B are 120 metres apart. Ramesh starts travelling from A to B and at the same time Sachin starts travelling from B to A. Ramesh travels 1/3rd of the total journey at a speed of 8 m/minute, half of the remaining distance at 10 m/minute and the rest at 12 m/minute. Sachin completes the whole journey by travelling at 8 m/minute, 10 m/minute and 12 m/minute, respectively for equal intervals of time. Answer the following questions:

19. Distance between Ramesh and Sachin, after 5 minutes of the start of the journey is x metres. The value of $x = ?$

(a) 28 m (b) 38 m
(c) 35 m (d) 32 m

20. After how much time (in seconds) of the starting of the journey, will both cross each other?

(a) 428 seconds (b) 414 seconds
(c) 435 seconds (d) 432 seconds

Space for Rough Work

LEVEL OF DIFFICULTY (II)

1. At the ancient Athens Olympic Games, in a duel between two runners, Portheus and Morpheus, they were made to start running in opposite direction from diametrically opposite ends of a circular racetrack of length (circumference) 2 km. The first time they met was after 24 minutes. If the distance between them exactly 'n' minutes after they start is equal to a quarter of the length of the track, which of the following is a possible value of 'n'?
   (a) 124 (b) 184
   (c) 160 (d) 204
2. Aman and Biman started a walkathon around a circular track starting from the same point on the track in opposite directions. They met for the first after time't'. Had they walked in the same direction with their speeds intact, they would have met after a time '$7t$'. It was also observed that Aman was slower than Biman, and Aman's speed was measured at 12 km/h. Find the speed of Biman.
   (a) 4 m/s (b) 5 m/s
   (c) 6 m/s (d) None of these
3. Abhishek and Aishwarya start from two opposite ends of a tunnel AB, which is 182 meters in length. Abhishek starts from A and Aishwarya starts from B. After they meet, they continue moving in their respective directions, till one of them reaches his end point and immediately reverses direction and starts walking back towards the other end. The ratio of their speeds is 7:6. At what distance (in meters) from A, will they meet when Abhishek is in his eight round?
   (a) 105 (b) 130
   (c) 125 (d) They will not meet
4. For the above question, at what distance (in meters) from A will they meet when Abhishek is in his twelfth round?
   (a) 126 (b) 118
   (c) 91 (d) They will not meet
5. Two runners Portheus and Zeus, are running around a circular track at different speeds such that they meet after regular time intervals. The length of the track (circumference) is 1600 meters. If they run in opposite directions, they meet at eight different points while if they run in the same direction, it is observed that they meet at two distinct points on the circular track. If they meet at intervals of 1.33 minutes when they run in the same direction, how much time does the faster runner (Portheus) take to complete one round?
   (a) 80 s (b) 32 s
   (c) 120 s (d) None of these
6. At the Vijayantkhand Mini Stadium, there are two circular racetracks — A with radius 40 meters and B with radius 80 meters, respectively such that they touch each other at a point X. The coach Vijay Sir has a particular ritual with his best athletes Mridul and Odeon. Mridul runs at a speed of 80π m/min on racetrack A and Odeon runs at a speed of 40π m/min along the racetrack B. Both of them start from the point X and run multiple rounds. If Mridul gives Odeon a start of 4 minutes exactly before he starts running himself, after how much time (in minutes) will the straight line distance between the two be exactly 240 meters?
   (a) 6 (b) 10
   (c) 12.5 (d) Never
7. Bolt and Milkha, start running around a racetrack simultaneously. Bolt runs at a speed of 's' km/h, while Milkha runs at a speed of 'm' km/h. They meet for the first time when Bolt is in his third round. Which of the following can be the value of s: m?
   (a) 11 : 6 (b) 11 : 5
   (c) 17 : 8 (d) 9 : 4
8. Amar, Abhijit and Arun start running on a circular racetrack (from the same point). Amar and Abhijit run in a clockwise fashion while Arun runs anticlockwise. When Amar and Arun meet for the first time, Abhijit is at a distance which is equal to half of the circumference of the circular racetrack. It is also known that Amar runs faster than Arun. The ratio of speeds of Amar, Arun and Abhijit cannot be
   (a) 5 : 1 : 2 (b) 3 : 1 : 1
   (c) 4 : 2 : 1 (d) 3 : 2 : 1
9. At what time between 6 and 7 o'clock is the minute-hand of a clock 4 minutes ahead of the hour-hand?
   (a) $34\frac{1}{11}$ minutes past 6
   (b) $36\frac{5}{11}$ minutes past 6
   (c) $37\frac{1}{11}$ minutes past 6
   (d) None of these
10. The minute-hand of a clock overtakes the hour-hand at intervals of 66 minutes of the correct time. How much time does the clock gain or lose in four hours?
   (a) $1\frac{119}{121}$ minutes (b) $1\frac{114}{121}$ minutes
   (c) 2 minutes (d) None of these
11. Robin Varkey's watch always runs faster than the actual time and gains time uniformly. He sets the watch to be ten minutes behind time at 12 noon on a Sunday. He observes that the watch is 5 minutes

48 seconds faster the following Sunday at 12 noon. At what exact time would the watch be correct?

(a) $\frac{26}{79}$ Hours past 10 PM on Thursday

(b) $\frac{13}{79}$ Hours past 8 PM on Thursday

(c) $\frac{26}{79}$ Hours past 6 PM on Thursday

(d) None of these

12. Prawin Tiwari sets his clock right at 10 AM on Monday. However, being a defective piece (the clock); it loses 32 minutes every day. He has to get up on Friday at exactly 4 AM to catch his flight to Lebuana. At what time on Friday morning should he set the alarm on his watch in order for the watch to ring at exactly 4 AM?

(a) 3 AM (b) 2 AM
(c) 5 AM (d) None of these

13. At what time, in minutes, between 4 o'clock and 5 o'clock, would both the hands of a clock coincide with each other?

(a) $22\frac{1}{11}$ (b) $21\frac{9}{11}$
(c) $22\frac{4}{11}$ (d) $21\frac{7}{11}$

14. At what time between 8 PM to 9 PM will the hands of a clock be in the same straight line pointing away from each other?

(a) $10\frac{8}{11}$ Minutes past 8

(b) $10\frac{10}{11}$ Minutes past 8

(c) $10\frac{3}{11}$ Minutes past 8

(d) $9\frac{10}{11}$ Minutes past 8

15. A watch which gains five seconds in three minutes was set right at 7 AM. In the afternoon of the same day, when it indicated quarter past 4 o'clock, the true time is

(a) $59\frac{7}{12}$ Minutes past 3

(b) 4 PM

(c) $58\frac{7}{11}$ Minutes past 3

(d) $2\frac{3}{11}$ Minutes past 4

16. In a 2000 meters race between Portheus and Cassius, Portheus gives Cassius a head start of a minute but still beats him by 200 meters. When, he increases the head start to 80 seconds, the race ends in a dead heat. Find the speed of Portheus.

(a) 25 m/s (b) 18 m/s
(c) 13.33 m/s (d) 16.66 m/s

17. How many right angles would be formed between the minute and the hour hand of a watch in a day?

(a) 48 (b) 46
(c) 45 (d) 44

18. How many times between 2 PM and 4 PM does the minutes hand coincide with the second's hand?

(a) 118 (b) 119
(c) 120 (d) 121

19. A man enters his house at some time between 6 to 7 PM. When he leaves his house sometime between 7 to 8 PM, he observes that the minute-hand and the hour-hand have interchanged positions. At what exact time did the man enter the house?

(a) $38\frac{82}{121}$ Minutes past 6

(b) $37\frac{42}{121}$ Minutes past 6

(c) $37\frac{82}{121}$ Minutes past 6

(d) $37\frac{62}{121}$ Minutes past 6

20. How many straight lines would be formed between the minute and the hour-hand of a watch in a day?

(a) 48 (b) 46
(c) 45 (d) 44

21. Two friends started simultaneously from Kanpur towards Lucknow in the same direction along a straight road. The faster friend Raveesh was on a bike while Prakash was in an auto. The ratio of their speeds was 1 : 5 respectively. Two hours later, Raveesh parked his bike and started running back towards Prakash's auto. His speed dropped by 80% as a result of this. They meet at a point which is 15 km from Kanpur. What was the speed of the auto?

(a) 2 kmph (b) 2.5 kmph
(c) 3 kmph (d) None of these

22. Two brothers came to know about their sister's wedding at the last minute. The wedding was to be held at a location which was 800 km away from Mumbai where both of them lived. The elder brother Kanhaiya came to know about the wedding at 6 PM and left immediately in his car. His younger brother Ramaiyya came to know about the wedding at 9:30 PM and left in his car immediately at a speed which was 15 km/h higher than the speed of his elder brother. At 4:30 AM, it was found that the two cars were 70 km apart. If the cars had travelled continuously without taking any rest, find the speed (in km/hr) of Kanhaiya's car.

(a) 40 (b) 50
(c) 60 (d) Cannot be determined

23. Ranatunga once challenged Bolt to a race. The distance of the race was set at 2 km. They start at the same time and the ratio of their speeds is seen to be 4:1 (obviously Bolt would be faster). After sometime passes, Bolt realises that he is far ahead and calculates that even if he stops for a snack and a nap for 'n' minutes, he would still reach his destination and beat Ranatunga by 13 minutes. Hence, he plans to take a break of 'n' minutes. Ranatunga keeps walking during this whole time. However, when Bolt wakes up, he realises that he has stopped for a total of (n + 15) minutes. He redoubles his efforts by increasing his speed to double his original speed. The race eventually ended in a dead heat. If it is known that Bolt overstayed his stop by $6n/5$ mins, how long did Ranatunga take to complete the race?

(a) 32 minutes (b) 34 minutes
(c) 25 minutes (d) None of these

24. A and B run a 300 meters race where the initial speed of B is double the speed of A. After some time, going on these speeds, A realises that he would be losing the race and redoubled his effort and increased his speed to four times his initial speed. As a result, they reached the end point at the same time and the race resulted in a dead heat. What was the distance travelled by B, when A quadrupled his speed?

(a) 100 m (b) 200 m
(c) 150 m (d) None of these

25. Amit and Bimal start running in opposite directions around a circular track of circumference 4200 meters. Their respective speeds are 15m/s and 3 m/s. Their fourteenth meeting occurs at point P and their twenty-second meeting occurs at the point Q. Find the longer distance (along the circumference) between points P and Q.

(a) 2800 (b) 1400
(c) 3500 (d) 3150

26. In a 2 km race, Ravi beats Sandeep by 45 seconds and beats Tarun by a further 75 seconds. In the same race, Ravi beats Tarun by 400 meters. Find the time in which Ravi can run the race (in seconds).

(a) 240 (b) 300
(c) 360 (d) 480

High Yield Questions

Scan this QR code to access assisted problem solving videos on questions 1, 2, 3, 7 and 9 from LOD 2

Space for Rough Work

ANSWER KEY

Level of Difficulty (I)

1. (c)	2. (b)	3. (b)	4. (b)
5. (b)	6. (d)	7. (b)	8. (c)
9. (a)	10. (d)	11. (c)	12. (a)
13. (b)	14. (b)	15. (a)	16. (c)
17. (d)	18. (b)	19. (b)	20. (b)

Level of Difficulty (II)

1. (d)	2. (d)	3. (d)	4. (a)
5. (b)	6. (d)	7. (a)	8. (d)
9. (c)	10. (a)	11. (a)	12. (b)
13. (b)	14. (b)	15. (b)	16. (d)
17. (d)	18. (d)	19. (a)	20. (c)
21. (b)	22. (b)	23. (b)	24. (b)
25. (a)	26. (d)		

SOLUTIONS AND SHORTCUTS

Level of Difficulty (I)

1. Remaining time

$$= \left(1-\frac{3}{5}\right)\times 15 = \frac{2}{5}\times 15 = 6 \text{ hours}$$

Remaining distance to be covered = 60 km.

$\therefore$ Required speed $= \frac{60}{6} = 10$ kmph

2. Number of stoppages $= \left[\frac{90}{7}\right] = 12$

(where [ ] represents greatest integer function.)

Total time = Time consumed during motion + Time taken in changing the horses

$\therefore$ Total time $= \left(\frac{90}{18}\right)$ hours $+ \frac{12\times 6}{60}$ hours

= 6 hours 12 minutes.

3. Total distance

$= 5\times 6 + 3\times 6$

= 30 + 18 = 48 km

Total time = 9 hours

$\therefore$ Average speed $= \frac{48}{9} = \frac{16}{3} = 5\frac{1}{3}$ kmph

4. Let the total distance be 100 km.

Total time $= \frac{50}{50}+\frac{40}{40}+\frac{10}{20} = 1+1+\frac{1}{2} = \frac{5}{2}$ hours

$\therefore$ Average speed $= \frac{100\times 2}{5}$

= 40 kmph

Solution for Questions 5 and 6: Let us assume the initial speed of John is x kmph.

Now after increasing his speed by 4 kmph his final speed $= x + 4$ kmph.

According to the question,

$$\frac{80}{x} - \frac{80}{x+4} = 1$$

From this point you can try to put the options from question 5, as the value of $x + 4$ to check for the value of x. $x + 4 = 20$ satisfies the equation. Hence, the Option (b) is correct.

5. Final speed of John = 16 + 4 = 20 kmph.

6. % change in speed $= \frac{20-16}{16}\times 100 = 25\%$

7. If the original time is t minutes. Then

$$10\times\frac{(t+2)}{60} = 15\times\frac{(t-2)}{60}$$

or $5t = 50$

or $t = 10$ minutes.

So the distance to her office

$$= 10\times\frac{10+2}{60} = 2 \text{ km.}$$

8. The total distance covered by Anuj and Ram for the first meeting = 200 km.

Combined speed of Anuj and Ram

= 15 kmph + 25 kmph = 40kmph

Time required for the first meeting = 200/40 = 5 hours

9. Distance covered by Anuj before the first meeting = 25 × 5 = 125 km.

10. Ratio of distance covered by Ram and Anuj is always in the ratio of their speeds. So the required ratio = 15 : 25 = 3 : 5

11. The total distance covered by Anuj and Ram before their fifth meeting = 1000 km.

Combined speed of Anuj and Ram

= 15 kmph + 25 kmph = 40 kmph

Time of fifth meeting = 1000/40 = 25 hours

Distance covered by Anuj at the fifth meeting = $25\times 25 = 625 \text{ km} = (600+25)$ km

So distance between A and the meeting point = 25 km.

12.

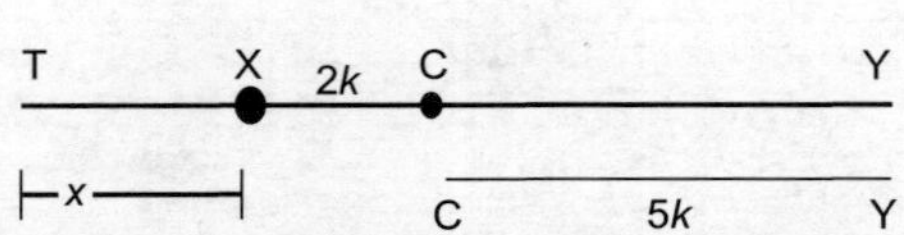

Let the train is at T when the train whistles. If the speed of train and cow are t and c respectively. If TX $= x$ and XC $= 2k$, CY $= 5k$, then

$$\frac{t}{c} = \frac{x+7k}{5k} = \frac{x}{2k}$$

or $\frac{x}{k} = \frac{14}{3}$

Hence, $\frac{t}{c} = \frac{x}{2k} = \frac{14}{2 \times 3} = 7:3$

13. The following figure explains the situation.

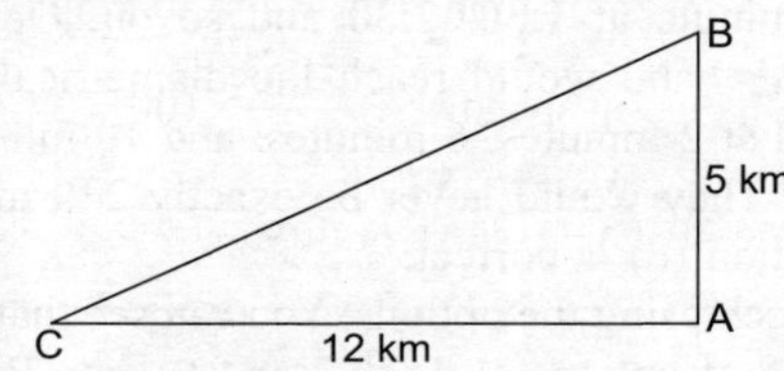

The distance can be found by using the Pythagoras Theorem

$AC^2 + AB^2 = CB^2$

or $12^2 + 5^2 = CB^2$

or $CB^2 = 169$

or $CB = 13$

14. Speed of thief = 8 kmph = $\frac{20}{9}$ m/sec

Speed of policeman = 10 kmph = $\frac{25}{9}$ m/sec

Relative speed = $\frac{25}{9} - \frac{20}{9} = \frac{5}{9}$ m/sec

Time required to catch the thief = 100/ (5/9) = 180 sec = 3 minutes

15. The total distance traveled by Johnny Scottish is 99 × 8 = 792 km out of which 12 km is in walking.

So the distance traveled by him by train is 780 km, which will take 780/120 = 6.5 hours.

Total time taken for the journey is 8 hours.

So he spent remaining 1.5 hour in walking.

So the speed of walking was 12/1.5 = 8 kmph.

16. As the first train leaves at 10 a.m., the faster train will leave at 2 p.m. after a gap of 4 hours.

Let T_1 be the time taken by train 1 and T_2 be the time taken by the train 2 to meet at the same point.

Since the distance is constant, so

$S_1/S_2 = T_2/T_1$

or $30/70 = (T_2)/(T_2 + 4)$

So, $T_2 = 3$

So the faster train will catch the slower train 3 hours after the former departs.

Thus the faster train will meet the slower train at 5 p.m.

17. Required distance = Distance covered by the faster train in 3 hours.

= 3 × 70 = 210 km from Lucknow.

18. Let Mr Kumar take t minutes to cover 40% of the distance.

Hence, he takes t + 10 minutes to cover 60% of the distance. Here, the average speed is constant.

Hence, we have,

$$\frac{t+10}{t} = \frac{3}{2}$$

(since, Ratio of times = Ratio of distances)

Solving, t = 20 minutes

Hence, time required to complete the journey = $2t$ + 10 = 50

Hence, total distance travelled is

$\frac{50}{60} \times 48 = 40$ km

19. If Sachin travels at 8 m/minute, 10 m/minute,12 m/minute for 't' minutes, then

$8t + 10t + 12t = 120$

$t = 4$ minutes.

Distance travelled by Sachin in 5 minutes = 8 × 4 + 10 × 1 = 42 metres.

Time taken by Ramesh to travel 1/3rd of the distance

$= \frac{120}{3 \times 8} = 5$ minutes.

Therefore, distance between Ramesh and Sachin after 5 minutes = 120 − (42 + 40)

= 38 metres

20. Time after which Ramesh and Sachin meet

$= 5 + \frac{38}{10+10}$

= 6.9 minutes or 414 seconds

Level of Difficulty (II)

1. They would first meet after 24 minutes (after covering 50% of the distance represented by the circumference of the circle). The next time they would meet will be at 72 minutes, then 120 minutes, then 168 minutes, 216 minutes and so on.

Every time they meet, they will be together and after the meeting point they continue running in opposite directions till they meet again. Between two meeting points, the distance between them would be 25% of the length of the circle's circumference in two cases: first when they are going away from each other after meeting (this would occur at a time of 12 minutes after the meeting point) and second when they are approaching each other before their next meeting

(this would occur at a time of 12 minutes before the next meeting point).
The meeting times 24, 72, 120, 168, 216, and 264, etc.; the times at which the distance would be 25% of the circumference:
$(24 - 12 = 12)$; $(24 + 12 = 36)$; $(72 - 12 = 60)$;
$(72 + 12 = 84)$; $(120 - 12 = 108)$; $(120 + 12 = 132)$;
$(168 - 12 = 156)$; $(168 + 12 = 180)$;
$(216 - 12 = 204)$
Only option (d) is possible and hence is the correct answer.

2. The ratio of their speeds can be worked out to be 4:3. Hence, Biman's speed (*b*) would be 16 km/h. b = 16 km/h = 16 × 5 ÷ 18 = 80 ÷ 18 m/s = 4.44 m/s. Option (d) is the correct answer.
3. When Abhishek would complete seven rounds, Aishwarya would have completed: 7 × 6 ÷ 7 = 6 rounds.
This means that both of them would be at the point B at this time. Since Abhishek is faster than Aishwarya, during his eighth round; there would be no meeting with Aishwarya. Hence, option (d) is correct.
4. When Abhishek would complete eleven rounds, Aishwarya would have completed: 11 × 6 ÷ 7 rounds $= 9\frac{3}{7}$ rounds.
This means that Aishwarya would be at a distance of 3/7 from *A*, while Abhishek would be at *B* at this point of time. The distance between them would be 4/7 of the total distance between *A* and *B*. Aishwarya would further cover a distance of 4/7 × 6/13 in order to meet Abhishek. Thus, the total distance from *A* is (3/7 + 24/91) × 182 = 63 × 182 ÷ 91 = 126 meters from *A* and 56 meters from *B*. Option (a) is correct.
5. Let the ratio of speeds be *P*: *Z* (where *P*>*Z*).
Since they meet at eight distinct points on the circle when they move in opposite directions, it automatically means that the sum of $P + Z = 8$. (I would like to encourage you to discover this piece of logic through trial-and-error.)
Similar logic gives us that $P - Z = 2$ (since they meet at two distinct points when travelling in the same direction).
Using these two equations, we can determine that if $P = 5$, $Z = 3$. Let the speeds of *P* be 5*x* and *Z* be 3*x* (in m/s). Then we have: $1600/2x = 80$ seconds $\rightarrow x = 10$ and hence, the speeds are $P = 50$ m/s and $Z = 30$ m/s.
P would take 1600 ÷ 50 = 32 seconds to complete one round.
Option (b) will be the correct answer.
6. Since the radii of the circles are 40 meters and 80 meters respectively, the circumference would be 80π and 160π meters respectively. Since Odeon's speed is 40π m/min, he would take four minutes to cover a round. This also means that when Mridul starts running, they would both be at point *X*, since Odeon would have covered one round exactly in four minutes. Also, for the straight line distance to be 240 meters, they should be at the diametrically opposite ends from the point *X* (of their respective circles). Mridul reaches the diametrically opposite end (from *X*) of his circle for the first time in 30 seconds and after that he would reach the same point every 1 minute at 1:30, 2:30 and so on. Odeon on the other hand would reach the diametrically opposite end at 2 minutes, 6 minutes, and 10 minutes and so on. They would never be exactly 240 meters apart. Option (d) is correct.
7. Check using the options. You can see that only in the case of option (a) do they meet when Bolt is in his third round. For all other options, Bolt would cross Milkha when Bolt is in his second round.
8. Checking the options, it can be seen that the condition of diametrically opposite is satisfied in each of the first three options. It is only in option (d) that it is not satisfied. Hence, option (d) is correct.
9. At 6 o'clock, the minute-hand is 30 minutes behind the hour-hand.
From this position, we need to reach a position, where the minute-hand is four minutes ahead of the hour-hand. For this to occur, the minute-hand has to gain (30 + 4) = 34 minute spaces on the hour-hand. In one hour, the minute-hand moves 60 minutes while the hour-hand moves 5 minute spaces on the clock. Hence, the minute-hand gains 55 minutes on the hour-hand in an hour.
Hence, to gain 34 minutes, the minute-hand would take $\left(\frac{60}{55}\times 34\right) = 37\frac{1}{11}$ minutes.
The required answer would be $37\frac{1}{11}$ minutes past 6. Option (c) is correct.
10. Assume the clock to be a circular race track of 60 km with each minute denoting 1 km. Also imagine two runners Mr. Minute and Mr. Hour running on this track. Normally, in a correct clock, Mr. Minute would cover 55 km more than Mr. Hour every hour. This means that they would be together (meaning Mr. Minute would overtake Mr. Hour) every $\left(\frac{60}{55}\times 60\right)$ minutes. $= 65\frac{5}{11}$ minutes. If they meet at longer time intervals than this, it means that the clock is slow. If the time intervals are shorter, it would mean that the clock is fast.
In this problem, they are together after 66 minutes. Thus, the clock loses time.
Loss in 66 minutes $\left(66 - 65\frac{5}{11}\right) = \frac{6}{11}$ minutes.
Using unitary method, we get loss in 4 hours = $\left(\frac{6}{11}\times\frac{60\times 4}{66}\right)$ minutes $= 1\frac{119}{121}$ minutes.

11. In one week, the time elapsed is exactly 168 hours. Robin's watch gains 15 minutes 48 seconds in 168 hours. In other words, it gains $\left(10+5\frac{4}{5}\right)$ minutes or $\frac{79}{5}$ minutes in 168 hrs.
To be showing the exact time, the watch should have gained exactly 10 minutes.
Using unitary method, it can be seen that ten minutes would be gained by the watch in: $\left(168\times\frac{5}{79}\times10\right)$ hrs. = $106\frac{26}{79}$ hours.
$\therefore$ Watch is correct at $\frac{26}{79}$ hours past 10 PM on Thursday. Hence, option (a) is the correct answer.
12. Time from 10 AM on Monday to 2 AM on Friday = 88 hours.
Now 23 hrs 28 minutes of this clock = 24 hours of correct clock.
$\therefore$ $\frac{352}{15}$ hrs of this clock = 24 hours of correct clock
88 hrs of this clock = $\left(24\times\frac{15}{352}\times88\right)$ hrs of correct clock.
= 90 hrs of correct clock. This means that at 4 AM on Friday, his clock would show 2 AM. Hence, if he needs to wake up at 4 AM, he should set his clock's alarm at 2 AM.
Hence, option (b) is the correct answer.
13. Assume the clock to be a circular race track of 60 km with each minute denoting 1 km. Also imagine two runners Mr. Minute and Mr. Hour running on this track. Normally, in a correct clock, Mr. Minute would cover 55 km more than Mr. Hour every hour. At 4 o'clock, the minute-hand is 20 km behind the hour-hand.
It would hence, need to gain 20 km to coincide with the hour-hand.
In 60 minutes, it gains 55 km.
In t minutes, it gains 20 km.
$t = \left(\frac{60}{55}\times20\right)$ minutes = $21\frac{9}{11}$ minutes
14. Thinking as in the previous question, we can think that at 8 PM, the minute-hand is 40 km behind the hour-hand. For it to become 30 km behind the hour-hand, we would need it to cover 10 km over the hour-hand.
In 60 minutes, it gains 55 km.
In t minutes, it gains 10 km.
$t = \left(\frac{60}{55}\times10\right)$ minutes = $10\frac{10}{11}$ minutes
Option (b) is correct.
15. Time from 7 AM to 4:15 PM = 9 hrs 15min = $\frac{37}{4}$ hrs
3 min 5 sec of this clock = 3 min of the correct clock
$\Rightarrow$ $\frac{37}{720}$ hrs of this clock = $\frac{1}{20}$ hrs of the clock
$\Rightarrow$ $\frac{37}{4}$ hrs of this clock = $\left(\frac{1}{20}\times\frac{720}{37}\times\frac{37}{4}\right)$ hrs of the correct clock
= 9 hrs of the correct clock
The correct time is 9 hrs after 7 AM, i.e. 4 PM.
16. Since Cassius is able to get a dead heat when he gets a head start of 80 seconds, it means that he would cover 200 meters in 20 seconds. Hence, his speed is 10m/s.
Let the time taken by Portheus to finish the race be t seconds. Then tracking the movement of Cassius we get:
$t \times 10 + 60 \times 10 = 2000 - 200.$
So t = 120 seconds.
Hence, the speed of Portheus would be = 2000/120 = 250/15 = 50/3 = 16.666 m/s. Option (d) is correct.
17. There are two right angles that are formed every hour between the hands of a watch. Hence, in 24 hours, we would expect 48 right angles. However, between 2 to 4 AM and 2 to 4 PM the number of right angles formed is only 3, because the right angle formed at 3 O'Clock (both AM and PM) is the second right angle for the hour between 2 O'Clock and 3 O'Clock. It is also the first right angle between 3 O'Clock and 4 O'Clock. This makes the clock lose two of its 48 expected right angles. Similarly, two right angles are lost when the clock passes through 8 O'Clock to 10 O'Clock. Hence, there would be a total of 44 right angles formed. Option (d) is correct.
18. In two hours, the minute-hand completes two rounds around the circumference of the clock's dial. In the same time, the seconds-hand covers 120 rounds. If we count 2 PM coincidence as the first one, the 4 PM coincidence would be the last one. There would be a total of 121 coincidences in two hours. Option (d) is correct.
19. Assume the clock to be a circular race track of 60 km with each minute denoting 1 km. Also imagine two runners Mr. Minute and Mr. Hour running on this track. Normally, in a correct clock, Mr. Minute would cover 55 km more than Mr. Hour every hour. For the conditions given in the problem, when the man enters the house, the time would be somewhere between 6:35 to 6:40 while when he leaves the time would be somewhere between 7:30 to 7:35.
Let, the distance between the two is equal to x km. When the hands interchange positions, the hour-hand would have travelled x km and the minute-hand would have travelled $(60 - x)$ km.
Using unitary method, we get:
When the minute-hand travels 60 km, the hour-hand travels 5 km.
When the minute-hand travels '60 – x' km, the hour-hand travels 'x' km.
$60x = 300 - 5x \rightarrow x = \frac{300}{55} = 5\frac{5}{11}$ minutes.

This means that when he comes home, the minute-hand is $5\frac{5}{11}$ minutes ahead of the hour-hand.

In order to find the exact time at which this happens between 6 and 7, we know that at 6, the minute-hand is 30 km behind the hour-hand. For the minute-hand to move $5\frac{5}{11}$ minutes ahead of the hour-hand, we would need the minute- hand to cover $35\frac{5}{11}$ km.

In 60 minutes, the minute-hand covers 55 km.

In t minutes, the minute-hand covers $35\frac{5}{11}$ minutes.

$t = 60 \times 35\frac{5}{11} \div 55 = \frac{12}{11} \times \frac{390}{11}$ minutes = 4680 ÷ 121 = $38\frac{82}{121}$ minutes.

He comes home at 38 minutes past 6.

20. There are two times that the hands of a watch form straight lines every hour. Hence, in 24 hours, we would expect 48 straight lines. However, between 11 and 1 and between 5 and 7, we would 'lose' one straight line as the 12 o'clock straight line and the 6 o'clock straight lines are double counted. Hence, the number of straight lines = 48 – 1 (for 5 AM to 7AM) – 1 (for 11 AM to 1 PM) – 1 (for 5 PM to 7 PM). Hence, there would be a total of 45 straight lines formed in a day. Hence, option (c) is correct.

21. Solve this through options. Option (b) matches the conditions of the problem and is hence, the correct answer.

The thought-process for this goes as follows:

If the auto's speed is 2.5, the bike's speed would be 12.5. Naturally two hours later, Raveesh would be at 25 km while Prakash would be at 5 km: a distance of 20 km. When Raveesh starts back, his speed would be 2.5 km/h and hence, the total speed at which they would approach each other would be 5 km/h. They would meet six hours after starting — and in this time Prakash would have covered 15 km and hence they would meet at 15 km from Kanpur. (This last bit would not match for the other options.)

For example, if we check option (a):

The thought-process for this goes as follows:

If the auto's speed is 2, the bike's speed would be 10. Naturally two hours later, Raveesh would be at 20 km while Prakash would be at 4 km:a distance of 16 km. When Raveesh starts back, his speed would be 2 km/h and hence, the total speed at which they would approach each other would be 4 km/h. They would meet six hours after starting — and in this time Prakash would have covered 12 km and hence, they would meet at 12 km from Kanpur which does not match the information in the problem.

22. Solve using options. For option (b), at 4:30 AM, the elder brother has travelled for 10:30 hours and hence, must have covered 525 km. The younger brother has travelled only for seven hours and at a speed of 65 kmph, the distance travelled would be 455 km. This would mean that the distance between them would be 70 km (as given). Hence, this option works correctly. The other options do not work and can be tested in a similar way. For instance, for option (a), 40 kmph does not work because $10.5 \times 40 - 7 \times 55 \neq 70$.

Similarly, option (c) can be rejected because $10.5 \times 60 - 7 \times 75 \neq 70$.

23. Since Bolt outstretched his time by $6n/5$ minutes and this is also equal to 15 minutes. Solving, we get: n = 12.5 minutes.

Let their original speeds be '$4s$' and 's' km/h respectively.

Had Bolt not overstretched his nap, he would have beaten Ranatunga by 13 minutes.

$\therefore \frac{2000}{4s} + 12.5 + 13 = \frac{2000}{s} \Rightarrow s = 1000/17$

Hence, the time taken by Ranatunga to complete the race = 2000 × 17 ÷ 1000 = 34 minutes.

Hence, option (b) is correct.

24. The distance travelled by B in the initial phase of the race will be double the distance travelled by A during the same time. Likewise, in the second phase of the race, the distance travelled by A will be double the distance travelled by B. Also the total distance travelled by A and B would be 300 meters. The only value which creates this symmetrical situation is if the initial phase is such that B travels 200 meter and A travels 100 meter. Hence, option (b) is correct.

25. Imagine the circle to be a clock with 12 divisions on the circumference — each division equal to a distance of 4200 ÷ 12 = 350 meters. (Imagine these are representing 1 o'clock to 12 o'clock for ease of understanding). Since they travel at a ratio of speed as 5:1, imagine Amit travels clockwise and Bimal travels anti clockwise. Their first meeting would occur at the point representing 10 o'clock, the next at 8 o'clock, then 6 o'clock and so on. It can be seen that the 14th meeting would occur at 8 o'clock and the 22nd meeting at 4 o'clock. The longer distance between them would be equal to eight markings on the clock. This distance would be 8 × 350 = 2800 meters. Option (a) is correct.

26. Ravi beats Tarun by 120 seconds or 400 meters. Hence, Tarun's speed is 400 ÷ 2 = 200 meters/minute. Also, when Ravi does 2000 meters, Tarun does 1600 meters — which he would do in eight minutes. Thus, Ravi takes 8 minutes = 480 seconds to complete the race. Hence, option (d) is correct

TASTE OF THE EXAMS—BLOCK II

CAT

1. In a 10 km race, A, B, and C, each running at uniform speed, get the gold, silver, and bronze medals, respectively. If A beats B by 1 km and B beats C by 1 km, then by how many metres does A beat C? **(CAT 2017)**

2. Bottle 1 contains a mixture of milk and water in 7 : 2 ratio and Bottle 2 contains a mixture of milk and water in 9 : 4 ratio. In what ratio of volumes should the liquids in Bottle 1 and Bottle 2 be combined to obtain a mixture of milk and water in 3 : 1 ratio? **(CAT 2017)**
(a) 27 : 14 (b) 27 : 13
(c) 27 : 16 (d) 27 : 18

3. Arun drove from home to his hostel at 60 miles per hour. While returning home he drove half way along the same route at a speed of 25 miles per hour and then took a bypass road which increased his driving distance by 5 miles, but allowed him to drive at 50 miles per hour along this bypass road. If his return journey took 30 minutes more than his onward journey, then the total distance traveled by him is: **(CAT 2017)**
(a) 55 miles (b) 60 miles
(c) 65 miles (d) 70 miles

4. Out of the shirts produced in a factory, 15% are defective, while 20% of the rest are sold in the domestic market. If the remaining 8840 shirts are left for export, then the number of shirts produced in the factory is **(CAT 2017)**
(a) 13600 (b) 13000
(c) 13400 (d) 14000

5. The average height of 22 toddlers increases by 2 inches when two of them leave this group. If the average height of these two toddlers is one-third the average height of the original 22, then the average height, in inches, of the remaining 20 toddlers is **(CAT 2017)**
(a) 30 (b) 28
(c) 32 (d) 26

6. The manufacturer of a table sells it to a wholesale dealer at a profit of 10%. The wholesale dealer sells the table to a retailer at a profit of 30%. Finally, the retailer sells it to a customer at a profit of 50%. If the customer pays ₹4290 for the table, then its manufacturing cost (in ₹) is **(CAT 2017)**
(a) 1500 (b) 2000
(c) 2500 (d) 3000

7. A tank has an inlet pipe and an outlet pipe. If the outlet pipe is closed then the inlet pipe fills the empty tank in 8 hours. If the outlet pipe is open then the inlet pipe fills the empty tank in 10 hours. If only the outlet pipe is open then in how many hours the full tank becomes half-full? **(CAT 2017)**
(a) 20 (b) 30
(c) 40 (d) 45

8. Mayank buys some candies for ₹15 a dozen and an equal number of different candies for ₹12 a dozen. He sells all for ₹16.50 a dozen and makes a profit of ₹150. How many dozens of candies did he buy altogether? **(CAT 2017)**
(a) 50 (b) 30
(c) 25 (d) 45

9. In a village, the production of food grains increased by 40% and the per capita production of food grains increased by 27% during a certain period. The percentage by which the population of the village increased during the same period is nearest to **(CAT 2017)**
(a) 16 (b) 13
(c) 10 (d) 7

10. If a, b, c are three positive integers such that a and b are in the ratio 3 : 4 while b and c are in the ratio 2 : 1, then which one of the following is a possible value of $(a + b + c)$? **(CAT 2017)**
(a) 201 (b) 205
(c) 207 (d) 210

11. A motorbike leaves point A at 1 pm and moves towards point B at a uniform speed. A car leaves point B at 2 pm and moves towards point A at a uniform speed, which is double that of the motorbike. They meet at 3:40 pm at a point, which is 168 km away from A. What is the distance, in km, between A and B? **(CAT 2017)**
(a) 364 (b) 378
(c) 380 (d) 388

12. Amal can complete a job in 10 days and Bimal can complete it in 8 days. Amal, Bimal and Kamal together complete the job in 4 days and are paid a total amount of ₹1000 as remuneration. If this amount is shared by them in proportion to their work, then Kamal's share, in rupees, is **(CAT 2017)**
(a) 100 (b) 200
(c) 300 (d) None of these

13. Consider three mixtures – the first having water and liquid A in the ratio 1 : 2, the second having water and liquid B in the ratio 1 : 3, and the third having water and liquid C in the ratio 1 : 4. These three mixtures of A, B, and C, respectively, are further

mixed in the proportion 4 : 3 : 2. Then the resulting mixture has (CAT 2017)

(a) The same amount of water and liquid B
(b) The same amount of liquids B and C
(c) More water than liquid B
(d) More water than liquid A

14. Arun's present age in years is 40% of Barun's. In another few years, Arun's age will be half of Barun's. By what percentage will Barun's age increase during this period? **(CAT 2017)**

15. A person can complete a job in 120 days. He works alone on Day 1. On Day 2, he is joined by another person who also can complete the job in exactly 120 days. On Day 3, they are joined by another person of equal efficiency. Like this, everyday a new person with the same efficiency joins the work. How many days are required to complete the job? **(CAT 2017)**

16. An elevator has a weight limit of 630 kg. It is carrying a group of people of whom the heaviest weighs 57 kg and the lightest weighs 53 kg. What is the maximum possible number of people in the group? **(CAT 2017)**

17. A man leaves his home and walks at a speed of 12 km per hour, reaching the railway station 10 minutes after the train had departed. If instead he had walked at a speed of 15 km per hour, he would have reached the station 10 minutes before the train's departure. The distance (in km) from his home to the railway station is **(CAT 2017)**

18. Ravi invests 50% of his monthly savings in fixed deposits. Thirty percent of the rest of his savings is invested in stocks and the rest goes into Ravi's savings bank account. If the total amount deposited by him in the bank (for savings account and fixed deposits) is ₹59500, then Ravi's total monthly savings (in ₹) is? **(CAT 2017)**

19. If a seller gives a discount of 15% on retail price, she still makes a profit of 2%. Which of the following ensures that she makes a profit of 20%? **(CAT 2017)**

(a) Give a discount of 5% on retail price
(b) Give a discount of 2% on retail price
(c) Increase the retail price by 2%
(d) Sell at retail price

20. A man travels by a motor boat down a river to his office and back. With the speed of the river unchanged, if he doubles the speed of his motor boat, then his total travel time gets reduced by 75%. The ratio of the original speed of the motor boat to the speed of the river is? **(CAT 2017)**

(a) $\sqrt{6} : \sqrt{2}$ (b) $\sqrt{7} : 2$
(c) $2\sqrt{5} : 3$ (d) $3 : 2$

21. Suppose $C1$, $C2$, $C3$, $C4$, and $C5$ are five companies. The profits made by $C1$, $C2$, and $C3$ are in the ratio 9 : 10 : 8 while the profits made by $C2$, $C4$, and $C5$ are in the ratio 18 : 19 : 20. If $C5$ has made a profit of ₹19 crore more than $C1$, then the total profit (in ₹) made by all five companies is: **(CAT 2017)**

(a) 438 crore (b) 435 crore
(c) 348 crore (d) 345 crore

22. The number of girls appearing for an admission test is twice the number of boys. If 30% of the girls and 45% of the boys get admission, the percentage of candidates who do not get admission is: **(CAT 2017)**

(a) 35 (b) 50
(c) 60 (d) 65

23. A stall sells popcorn and chips in packets of three sizes: large, super, and jumbo. The numbers of large, super, and jumbo packets in its stock are in the ratio 7 : 17 : 16 for popcorn and 6 : 15 : 14 for chips. If the total number of popcorn packets in its stock is the same as that of chips packets, then the numbers of jumbo popcorn packets and jumbo chips packets are in the ratio **(CAT 2017)**

(a) 1 : 1 (b) 8 : 7
(c) 4 : 3 (d) 6 : 5

24. In a market, the price of medium quality mangoes is half that of good mangoes. A shopkeeper buys 80 kg good mangoes and 40 kg medium quality mangoes from the market and then sells all these at a common price which is 10% less than the price at which he bought the good ones. His overall profit is: **(CAT 2017)**

(a) 6% (b) 8%
(c) 10% (d) 12%

25. If Fatima sells 60 identical toys at a 40% discount on the printed price, then she makes 20% profit. Ten of these toys are destroyed in fire. While selling the rest, how much discount should be given on the printed price so that she can make the same amount of profit? **(CAT 2017)**

(a) 30% (b) 25%
(c) 24% (d) 28%

26. A water tank has inlets of two types A and B. All inlets of type A when open bring in water at the same rate. All inlets of type B, when open, bring in water at the same rate. The empty tank is completely filled in 30 minutes if 10 inlets of type A and 45 inlets of type B are open and in 1 hour if 8 inlets of type A and 18 inlets of type B are open. In how many minutes will the empty tank get completely filled if 7 inlets of type A and 27 inlets of type B are open? **(CAT 2018)**

27. Points A, P, Q and B lie on the same line such that P, Q and B are, respectively, 100 km, 200 km and 300 km away from A. Cars 1 and 2 leave A at the same time and move towards B. Simultaneously, car 3 leaves B and moves towards A. Car 3 meets car 1 at Q, and car 2 at P. If each car is moving in uniform speed then the ratio of the speed of car 2 to that of car 1 is **(CAT 2018)**

(a) 2 : 7 (b) 2 : 9
(c) 1 : 4 (d) 1 : 2

28. Gopal borrows ₹X from Ankit at 8% annual interest. He then adds ₹Y of his own money and lends ₹$X + Y$ to Ishan at 10% annual interest. At the end of the year, after returning Ankit's dues, the net interest retained by Gopal is the same as that accrued to Ankit. On the other hand, had Gopal lent ₹$X + 2Y$ to Ishan at 10%, and then the net interest retained by him would have increased by ₹150. If all interests are compounded annually, then find the value of $X + Y$. **(CAT 2018)**

29. The scores of Amal and Bimal in an examination are in the ratio 11 : 14. After an appeal, their scores increase by the same amount and their new scores are in the ratio 47 : 56. The ratio of Bimal's new score to that of his original score is **(CAT 2018)**

(a) 8 : 5 (b) 3 : 2
(c) 4 : 3 (d) 5 : 4

30. The strength of a salt solution is p% if 100 ml of the solution contains p grams of salt. If three salt solutions A, B, C are mixed in the proportion 1: 2: 3, then the resulting solution has strength 20%. If instead the proportion is 3 : 2 : 1, then the resulting solution has strength 30%. A fourth solution, D, is produced by mixing B and C in the ratio 2 : 7. The ratio of the strength of D to that of A is **(CAT 2018)**

(a) 1 : 3 (b) 2 : 5
(c) 1 : 4 (d) 3 : 10

31. A 20% ethanol solution is mixed with another ethanol solution, say, S of unknown concentration in the proportion 1 : 3 by volume. This mixture is then mixed with an equal volume of 20% ethanol solution. If the resultant mixture is a 31.25% ethanol solution, then the unknown concentration of S is **(CAT 2018)**

(a) 55% (b) 52%
(c) 48% (d) 50%

32. There are two drums, each containing a mixture of paints A and B. In drum 1, A and B are in the ratio 18 : 7. The mixtures from drums 1 and 2 are mixed in the ratio 3 : 4 and in this final mixture, A and B are in the ratio 13 : 7. In drum 2, then A and B were in the ratio **(CAT 2018)**

(a) 239 : 161 (b) 220 : 149
(c) 229 : 141 (d) 251 : 163

33. Ramesh and Ganesh can together complete a work in 16 days. After seven days of working together, Ramesh got sick and his efficiency fell by 30%. As a result, they completed the work in 17 days instead of 16 days. If Ganesh had worked alone after Ramesh got sick, in how many days would he have completed the remaining work? **(CAT 2018)**

(a) 14.5 (b) 13.5
(c) 11 (d) 12

34. On a long stretch of east-west road, A and B are two points such that B is 350 km west of A. One car starts from A and another from B at the same time. If they move towards each other, then they meet after one hour. If they both move towards east, then they meet in seven hrs. The difference between their speeds, in km per hour, is **(CAT 2018)**

35. A jar contains a mixture of 175 ml water and 700 ml alcohol. Gopal takes out 10% of the mixture and substitutes it by water of the same amount. The process is repeated once again. The percentage of water in the mixture is now **(CAT 2018)**

(a) 20.5 (b) 30.3
(c) 25.4 (d) 35.2

36. The arithmetic mean of x, y and z is 80, and that of x, y, z, u and v is 75, where $u = (x + y)/2$ and $v = (y + z)/2$. If $x \geq z$, then the minimum possible value of x is **(CAT 2018)**

37. A tank is emptied everyday at a fixed time point. Immediately, thereafter, either pump A or pump B or both start working until the tank is full. On Monday, A alone completed filling the tank at 8 PM. On Tuesday, B alone completed filling the tank at 6 PM. On Wednesday, A alone worked till 5 PM, and then B worked alone from 5 PM to 7 PM, to fill the tank. At what time was the tank filled on Thursday if both pumps were used simultaneously all along? **(CAT 2018)**

(a) 4 : 12 PM (b) 4 : 24 PM
(c) 4 : 48 PM (d) 4 : 36 PM

38. Points A and B are 150 km apart. Cars 1 and 2 travel from A to B, but car 2 starts from A when car 1 is already 20 km away from A. Each car travels at a speed of 100 kmph for the first 50 km, at 50 kmph for the next 50 km, and at 25 kmph for the last 50 km. The distance, in km, between car 2 and B when car 1 reaches B is **(CAT 2018)**

39. Train T leaves station X for station Y at 3 PM. Train S, travelling at three quarters of the speed of T, leaves Y for X at 4 PM. The two trains pass each other at a station Z, where the distance between X and Z is three-fifths of that between X and Y. How many hours does train T take for its journey from X to Y? **(CAT 2018)**

40. Two types of tea, A and B, are mixed and then sold at ₹40 per kg. The profit is 10% if A and B are mixed in the ratio 3: 2, and 5% if this ratio is 2: 3. The cost prices, per kg, of A and B are in the ratio **(CAT 2018)**

(a) 18 : 25 (b) 17 : 25
(c) 21 : 25 (d) 19 : 24

41. A CAT aspirant appears for a certain number of tests. His average score increases by 1 if the first 10 tests are not considered, and decreases by 1 if the last 10 tests are not considered. If his average scores for the first 10 and the last 10 tests are 20 and 30, respectively, then the total number of tests taken by him is **(CAT 2018)**

42. Point P lies between points A and B such that the length of BP is thrice that of AP. Car 1 starts from A and moves towards B. Simultaneously, car 2 starts from B and moves towards A. Car 2 reaches P one hour after car 1 reaches P. If the speed of car 2 is half that of car 1, then the time, in minutes, taken by car 1 in reaching P from A is **(CAT 2018)**

43. John borrowed ₹2,10,000 from a bank at an interest rate of 10% per annum, compounded annually. The loan was repaid in two equal instalments, the first after one year and the second after another year. The first instalment was interest of one year plus part of the principal amount, while the second was the rest of the principal amount plus due interest thereon. Then each instalment, in ₹ is **(CAT 2018)**

44. In an examination, the maximum possible score is N while the pass mark is 45% of N. A candidate obtains 36 marks, but falls short of the pass mark by 68%. Which one of the following is correct? **(CAT 2018)**

(a) $N \leq 200$ (b) $243 \leq N \leq 252$
(c) $N \geq 253$ (d) $201 \leq N \leq 242$

45. In an apartment complex, the number of people aged 51 years and above is 30 and there are at most 39 people whose ages are below 51 years. The average age of all the people in the apartment complex is 38 years. What is the largest possible average age, in years, of the people whose ages are below 51 years? **(CAT 2018)**

(a) 25 (b) 26
(c) 27 (d) 28

46. The distance from A to B is 60 km. Partha and Narayan start from A at the same time and move towards B. Partha takes four hours more than Narayan to reach B. Moreover, Partha reaches the mid-point of A and B two hours before Narayan reaches B. The speed of Partha, in km per hour, is **(CAT 2018)**

(a) 5 (b) 3
(c) 4 (d) 6

47. Humans and robots can both perform a job but at different efficiencies. Fifteen humans and five robots working together take thirty days to finish the job, whereas five humans and fifteen robots working together take sixty days to finish it. How many days will fifteen humans working together (without any robot) take to finish it? **(CAT 2018)**

(a) 36 (b) 40
(c) 45 (d) 32

48. A trader sells 10 litres of a mixture of paints A and B, where the amount of B in the mixture does not exceed that of A. The cost of paint A per litre is ₹8 more than that of paint B. If the trader sells the entire mixture for ₹264 and makes a profit of 10%, then the highest possible cost of paint B, in ₹ per litre, is **(CAT 2018)**

(a) 26 (b) 22
(c) 20 (d) 16

49. Raju and Lalitha originally had marbles in the ratio 4 : 9. Then Lalitha gave some of her marbles to Raju. As a result, the ratio of the number of marbles with Raju to that with Lalitha became 5 : 6. What fraction of her original number of marbles was given by Lalitha to Raju? **(CAT 2018)**

(a) 6/19 (b) 7/33
(c) 1/5 (d) 1/4

50. A wholesaler bought walnuts and peanuts; the price of walnut per kg being thrice that of peanut per kg. He then sold 8 kg of peanuts at a profit of 10% and 16 kg of walnuts at a profit of 20% to a shopkeeper. However, the shopkeeper lost 5 kg of walnuts and 3 kg of peanuts in transit. He then mixed the remaining nuts and sold the mixture at ₹166 per kg, thus making an overall profit of 25%. At what price, in ₹ per kg, did the wholesaler buy the walnuts? **(CAT 2018)**

(a) 84 (b) 96
(c) 86 (d) 98

51. The average of 30 integers is 5. Among these 30 integers, there are exactly 20 which do not exceed 5. What is the highest possible value of the average of these 20 integers? **(CAT 2019)**

(a) 3.5 (b) 5
(c) 4.5 (d) 4

52. Amal invests 12000 at 8% interest, compounded annually, and 10000 at 6% interest, compounded semi-annually, both investments being for one year. Bimal invests his money at 7.5% simple interest for one year. If Amal and Bimal get the same amount of interest, then the amount, in Rupees, invested by Bimal is **(CAT 2019)**

53. Two ants A and B start from a point P on a circle at the same time, with A moving clock-wise and B moving anti-clockwise. They meet for the first time at 10:00 AM when A has covered 60% of the track. If A returns to P at 10:12 AM, then *B* returns to *P* at **(CAT 2019)**

(a) 10:25 AM (b) 10:45 AM
(c) 10:18 AM (d) 10:27 AM

54. The strength of a salt solution is *p*% if 100 ml of the solution contains *p* grams of salt. Each of three vessels *A*, *B*, *C* contains 500 ml of salt solution of strengths 10%, 22%, and 32%, respectively. Now, 100 ml of the solution in vessel *A* is transferred to vessel *B*. Then, 100 ml of the solution in vessel *B* is transferred to vessel *C*. Finally, 100 ml of the solution in vessel *C* is transferred to vessel *A*. The strength, in percentage, of the resulting solution in vessel *A* is **(CAT 2019)**

(a) 15 (b) 13
(c) 12 (d) 14

55. A cyclist leaves *A* at 10 AM and reaches *B* at 11 AM. Starting from 10:01 AM, every minute a motorcycle leaves *A* and moves towards *B*. Forty-five such motorcycles reach *B* by 11 AM. All motorcycles have the same speed. If the cyclist had doubled his speed, how many motorcycles would have reached *B* by the time the cyclist reached *B*? **(CAT 2019)**

(a) 22 (b) 23
(c) 15 (d) 20

56. John jogs on track *A* at 6 kmph and Mary jogs on track *B* at 7.5 kmph. The total length of tracks *A* and *B* is 325 metres. While John makes nine rounds of track *A*, Mary makes five rounds of track *B*. In how many seconds will Mary make one round of track *A*? **(CAT 2019)**

57. In 2010, a library contained a total of 11500 books in two categories - fiction and nonfiction. In 2015, the library contained a total of 12760 books in these two categories. During this period, there was 10% increase in the fiction category while there was 12% increase in the non-fiction category. How many fiction books were in the library in 2015? **(CAT 2019)**

(a) 6160 (b) 6600
(c) 6000 (d) 5500

58. A shopkeeper sells two tables, each procured at cost price *p*, to Amal and Asim at a profit of 20% and at a loss of 20%, respectively. Amal sells his table to Bimal at a profit of 30%, while Asim sells his table to Barun at a loss of 30%. If the amounts paid by Bimal and Barun are *x* and *y*, respectively, then $(x - y)/p$ equals **(CAT 2019)**

(a) 1 (b) 1.2
(c) 0.50 (d) 0.7

59. Mukesh purchased ten bicycles in 2017, all at the same price. He sold six of these at a profit of 25% and the remaining four at a loss of 25%. If he made a total profit of 2000, then his purchase price of a bicycle, in Rupees, was **(CAT 2019)**

(a) 6000 (b) 8000
(c) 4000 (d) 2000

60. In an examination, the score of *A* was 10% less than that of *B*, the score of *B* was 25% more than that of *C*, and the score of *C* was 20% less than that of *D*. If *A* scored 72, then the score of *D* was **(CAT 2019)**

61. The salaries of Ramesh, Ganesh and Rajesh were in the ratio 6:5:7 in 2010, and in the ratio 3 : 4 : 3 in 2015. If Ramesh's salary increased by 25% during 2010–2015, then the percentage increase in Rajesh's salary during this period is closest to **(CAT 2019)**

(a) 10 (b) 7
(c) 9 (d) 8

62. Anil alone can do a job in twenty days while Sunil alone can do it in forty days. Anil starts the job, and after three days, Sunil joins him. Again, after a few more days, Bimal joins them and they together finish the job. If Bimal has done 10% of the job, then in how many days was the job done? **(CAT 2019)**

(a) 12 (b) 13
(c) 14 (d) 15

63. In an examination, Rama's score was one-twelfth of the sum of the scores of Mohan and Anjali. After a review, the score of each of them increased by 6. The revised scores of Anjali, Mohan, and Rama were in the ratio 11 : 10 : 3. Then Anjali's score exceeded Rama's score by **(CAT 2019)**

(a) 26 (b) 32
(c) 35 (d) 24

64. Two cars travel the same distance starting at 10:00 AM and 11:00 AM, respectively, on the same day. They reach their common destination at the same point of time. If the first car travelled for at least six hours, then the highest possible value of the percentage by which the speed of the second car could exceed that of the first car is **(CAT 2019)**

(a) 20 (b) 30
(c) 25 (d) 10

65. The income of Amala is 20% more than that of Bimala and 20% less than that of Kamala. If Kamala's income goes down by 4% and Bimala's goes up by 10%, then the percentage by which Kamala's income would exceed Bimala's is nearest to **(CAT 2019)**

(a) 31 (b) 29
(c) 28 (d) 32

66. In a race of three horses, the first beats the second by 11 metres and the third by 90 metres. If the second beats the third by 80 metres, what was the length, in metres, of the racecourse? **(CAT 2019)**

67. Amala, Bina, and Gouri invest money in the ratio 3 : 4 : 5 in fixed deposits having respective annual interest rates in the ratio 6 : 5 : 4. What is their total interest income (in rupees) after an year, if Bina's interest income exceeds Amala's by 250? **(CAT 2019)**

(a) 6350 (b) 6000
(c) 7000 (d) 7250

68. One can use three different transports which move at 10, 20, and 30 km/h, respectively. To reach from *A* to *B*, Amal took each mode of transport 1/3 of his total journey time, while Bimal took each mode of transport 1/3 of the total distance. The percentage by which Bimal's travel time exceeds Amal's travel time is nearest to **(CAT 2019)**

(a) 22 (b) 20
(c) 19 (d) 21

69. Meena scores 40% in an examination and after review, even though her score is increased by 50%, she fails by 35 marks. If her post-review score is increased by 20%, she will have 7 marks more than the passing score. The percentage score needed for passing the examination is **(CAT 2019)**

(a) 60 (b) 80
(c) 70 (d) 75

70. A person invested a total amount of 15 lakhs. A part of it was invested in a fixed deposit earning 6% annual interest, and the remaining amount was invested in two other deposits in the ratio 2 : 1, earning annual interest at the rates of 4% and 3%, respectively. If the total annual interest income is 76000, then the amount (in lakh) invested in the fixed deposit was **(CAT 2019)**

71. At their usual efficiency levels, *A* and *B* together finish a task in 12 days. If *A* had worked half as efficiently as she usually does, and *B* had worked thrice as efficiently as he usually does, the task would have been completed in 9 days. How many days would A take to finish the task if she works alone at her usual efficiency? **(CAT 2019)**

(a) 36 (b) 24
(c) 18 (d) 12

72. In a class, 60% of the students are girls and the rest are boys. There are 30 more girls than boys. If 68% of the students, including 30 boys, pass an examination, the percentage of the girls who do not pass is **(CAT 2019)**

73. On selling a pen at 5% loss and a book at 15% gain, Karim gains ₹7. If he sells the pen at 5% gain and the book at 10% gain, he gains ₹13. What is the cost price of the book in Rupees? **(CAT 2019)**

(a) 95 (b) 85
(c) 80 (d) 100

74. A chemist mixes two liquids 1 and 2. One litre of liquid 1 weighs 1 kg and one litre of liquid 2 weighs 800 g. If half litre of the mixture weighs 480 g, then the percentage of liquid 1 in the mixture, in terms of volume, is **(CAT 2019)**

(a) 80 (b) 70
(c) 85 (d) 75

75. Ramesh and Gautam are among 22 students who write an examination. Ramesh scores 82.5. The average score of the 21 students other than Gautam is 62. The average score of all the 22 students is one more than the average score of the 21 students other than Ramesh. The score of Gautam is **(CAT 2019)**

(a) 53 (b) 51
(c) 48 (d) 49

76. Three men and eight machines can finish a job in half the time taken by three machines and eight men to finish the same job. If two machines can finish the job in 13 days, then how many men can finish the job in 13 days? **(CAT 2019)**

77. Let A, B and C be three positive integers such that the sum of A and the mean of B and C is 5. In addition, the sum of B and the mean of A and C is 7. Then the sum of A and B is **(CAT 2020)**

(a) 5 (b) 4
(c) 7 (d) 6

78. A straight road connects points A and B. Car 1 travels from A to B and Car 2 travels from B to A, both leaving at the same time. After meeting each other, they take 45 minutes and 20 minutes, respectively, to complete their journeys. If Car 1 travels at the speed of 60 km/hr, then the speed of Car 2, in km/hr, is **(CAT 2020)**

(a) 100 (b) 80
(c) 70 (d) 90

79. Leaving home at the same time, Amal reaches office at 10:15 am if he travels at 8 km/hr, and at 9:40 am if he travels at 15 km/hr. Leaving home at 9:10 am, at what speed, in km/hr, must he travel so as to reach office exactly at 10 am? **(CAT 2020)**

(a) 11 (b) 12
(c) 14 (d) 13

80. Veeru invested ₹10000 at 5% simple annual interest, and exactly after two years, Joy invested ₹8000 at 10% simple annual interest. How many years after Veeru's investment, will their balances, i.e., principal plus accumulated interest, be equal? **(CAT 2020)**

81. A solution, of volume 40 litres, has dye and water in the proportion 2 : 3. Water is added to the solution to change this proportion to 2 : 5. If one–fourths of this diluted solution is taken out, how many litres of dye must be added to the remaining solution to bring the proportion back to 2 : 3? **(CAT 2020)**

82. Two persons are walking beside a railway track at respective speeds of 2 and 4 km per hour in the same direction. A train came from behind them and crossed them in 90 and 100 seconds, respectively. The time, in seconds, taken by the train to cross an electric post is nearest to **(CAT 2020)**

(a) 82 (b) 87
(c) 78 (d) 75

83. A train travelled at one-thirds of its usual speed, and hence reached the destination 30 minutes after the scheduled time. On its return journey, the train initially travelled at its usual speed for 5 minutes but then stopped for 4 minutes for an emergency. The percentage by which the train must now increase its usual speed so as to reach the destination at the scheduled time, is nearest to **(CAT 2020)**

(a) 67 (b) 61
(c) 50 (d) 58

84. A person spent ₹50000 to purchase a desktop computer and a laptop computer. He sold the desktop at 20% profit and the laptop at 10% loss. If overall he made a 2% profit then the purchase price, in rupees, of the desktop is **(CAT 2020)**

85. In a car race, car A beats car B by 45 km, Car B beats Car C by 50 kms and car A beats car C by 90 km. The distance (in km) over which the race has been conducted is **(CAT 2020)**

(a) 500 (b) 450
(c) 475 (d) 550

86. The distance from B to C is thrice that from A to B. Two trains travel from A to C via B. The speed of train 2 is double that of train 1 while traveling from A to B and their speeds are interchanged while traveling from B to C. The ratio of the time taken by train 1 to that taken by train 2 in travelling from A to C is **(CAT 2020)**

(a) 4:1 (b) 5:7
(c) 7:5 (d) 1:4

87. John takes twice as much time as Jack to finish a job. Jack and Jim together take one–thirds of the time to finish the job than John takes working alone. Moreover, in order to finish the job, John takes three days more than that taken by three of them working together. In how many days will Jim finish the job working alone? **(CAT 2020)**

88. A and B are two points on a straight line. Ram runs from A to B while Rahim runs from B to A. After crossing each other, Ram and Rahim reach their destinations in one minute and four minutes, respectively. If they start at the same time, then the ratio of Ram's speed to Rahim's speed is **(CAT 2020)**

(a) $\sqrt{2}$ (b) $2\sqrt{2}$
(c) $\frac{1}{2}$ (d) 2

89. In a group of 10 students, the mean of the lowest 9 scores is 42 while the mean of the highest 9 scores is 47. For the entire group of 10 students, the maximum possible mean exceeds the minimum possible mean by **(CAT 2020)**

(a) 3 (b) 6
(c) 4 (d) 5

90. Anil buys 12 toys and labels each with the same selling price. He sells 8 toys initially at 20% discount on the labeled price. Then he sells the remaining 4 toys at an additional 25% discount on the discounted price. Thus, he gets a total of ₹2112, and makes a 10% profit. With no discounts, his percentage of profit would have been **(CAT 2020)**

(a) 60 (b) 55
(c) 50 (d) 54

91. For the same principal amount, the compound interest for two years at 5% per annum exceeds the simple interest for three years at 3% per annum by ₹1125. Then the principal amount in rupees is **(CAT 2020)**

92. A sum of money is split among Amal, Sunil and Mita so that the ratio of the shares of Amal and Sunil is 3 : 2, while the ratio of the shares of Sunil and Mita is 4 : 5. If the difference between the largest and the smallest of these three shares is ₹400, then Sunil's share, in rupees, is **(CAT 2020)**

93. Two circular tracks T1 and T2 of radii 100 m and 20 m, respectively touch at a point A. Starting from A at the same time, Ram and Rahim are walking on track T1 and track T2 at speeds 15 km/hr and 5 km/hr respectively. The number of full rounds that Ram will make before he meets Rahim again for the first time is **(CAT 2020)**

(a) 2 (b) 5
(c) 3 (d) 4

94. In May, John bought the same amount of rice and the same amount of wheat as he had bought in April, but spent ₹150 more due to price increase of rice and wheat by 20% and 12%, respectively. If John had spent ₹450 on rice in April, then how much did he spend on wheat in May? **(CAT 2020)**

(a) ₹580 (b) ₹590
(c) ₹560 (d) ₹570

95. Anil, Sunil, and Ravi run along a circular path of length 3 km, starting from the same point at the same time, and going in the clockwise direction. If they run at speeds of 15 km/hr, 10 km/hr, and 8 km/hr, respectively, how much distance in km will Ravi have run when Anil and Sunil meet again for the first time at the starting point? **(CAT 2020)**

(a) 4.6 (b) 5.2
(c) 4.8 (d) 4.2

96. A and B are two railway stations 90 km apart. A train leaves A at 9:00 am, heading towards B at a speed of 40 km/hr. Another train leaves B at 10:30 am, heading towards A at a speed of 20 km/hr. The trains meet each other at **(CAT 2020)**

(a) 11:20 am (b) 11:00 am
(c) 10:45 am (d) 11:45 am

97. A man buys 35 kg of sugar and sets a marked price in order to make a 20% profit. He sells 5 kg at this price, and 15 kg at a 10% discount. Accidentally, 3 kg of sugar is wasted. He sells the remaining sugar by raising the marked price by p percent so as to make an overall profit of 15%. Then p is nearest to **(CAT 2020)**

(a) 35 (b) 25
(c) 31 (d) 22

98. A person invested a certain amount of money at 10% annual interest, compounded half-yearly. After one and a half years, the interest and principal together became ₹18522. The amount, in rupees, that the person had invested is **(CAT 2020)**

99. Dick is thrice as old as Tom and Harry is twice as old as Dick. If Dick's age is 1 year less than the average age of all three, then Harry's age, in years, is **(CAT 2020)**

100. Vimla starts for office every day at 9 am and reaches exactly on time if she drives at her usual speed of 40 km/hr. She is late by 6 minutes if she drives at 35 km/hr. One day, she covers two-thirds of her distance to office in one-thirds of her usual time to reach office, and then stops for 8 minutes. The speed, in km/hr, at which she should drive the remaining distance to reach office exactly on time is **(CAT 2020)**

(a) 26 (b) 27
(c) 28 (d) 29

101. In the final examination, Bishnu scored 52% and Asha scored 64%. The marks obtained by Bishnu is 23 less, and that by Asha is 34 more than the marks obtained by Ramesh. The marks obtained by Geeta, who scored 84%, is **(CAT 2020)**

(a) 417 (b) 399
(c) 439 (d) 357

102. A contractor agreed to construct a 6 km road in 200 days. He employed 140 persons for the work. After 60 days, he realized that only 1.5 km road has been completed. How many additional people would he need to employ in order to finish the work exactly on time? **(CAT 2020)**

103. Two alcohol solutions, A and B, are mixed in the proportion 1 : 3 by volume. The volume of the mixture is then doubled by adding solution A such that the resulting mixture has 72% alcohol. If solution A has 60% alcohol, then the percentage of alcohol in solution B is **(CAT 2020)**

(a) 92% (b) 94%
(c) 90% (d) 89%

104. A batsman played $n + 2$ innings and got out on all occasions. His average score in these $n + 2$ innings was 29 runs and he scored 38 and 15 runs in the last two innings. The batsman scored less than 38 runs in each of the first n innings. In these n innings, his average score was 30 runs and lowest score was x runs. The smallest possible value of x is **(CAT 2020)**

(a) 1 (b) 4
(c) 2 (d) 3

105. A basket of 2 apples, 4 oranges and 6 mangoes costs the same as a basket of 1 apple, 4 oranges and 8 mangoes, or a basket of 8 oranges and 7 mangoes. Then the number of mangoes in a basket of mangoes that has the same cost as the other baskets is **(CAT 2021)**

(a) 13 (b) 10
(c) 12 (d) 11

106. Anil invests some money at a fixed rate of interest, compounded annually. If the interests accrued during the second and third year are ₹806.25 and ₹866.72, respectively, the interest accrued, in INR, during the fourth year is nearest to **(CAT 2021)**

(a) 934.65 (b) 929.48
(c) 931.72 (d) 926.84

107. Amal purchases some pens at ₹8 each. To sell these, he hires an employee at a fixed wage. He sells 100 of these pens at ₹12 each. If the remaining pens are sold at ₹11 each, then he makes a net profit of ₹300, while he makes a net loss of ₹300 if the remaining pens are sold at ₹9 each. The wage of the employee, in INR, is **(CAT 2021)**

108. The amount Neeta and Geeta together earn in a day equals what Sita alone earns in 6 days. The amount Sita and Neeta together earn in a day equals what Geeta alone earns in 2 days. The ratio of the daily earnings of the one who earns the most to that of the one who earns the least is **(CAT 2021)**

(a) 7 : 3 (b) 3 : 2
(c) 11 : 7 (d) 11 : 3

109. Amar, Akbar and Anthony are working on a project. Working together Amar and Akbar can complete the project in 1 year, Akbar and Anthony can complete in 16 months, Anthony and Amar can complete in 2 years. If the person who is neither the fastest nor the slowest works alone, the time in months he will take to complete the project is **(CAT 2021)**

110. Anu, Vinu and Manu can complete a work alone in 15 days, 12 days and 20 days, respectively. Vinu works everyday. Anu works only on alternate days starting from the first day while Manu works only on alternate days starting from the second day. Then, the number of days needed to complete the work is **(CAT 2021)**

(a) 7 (b) 6
(c) 8 (d) 5

111. Suppose hospital A admitted 21 less Covid infected patients than hospital B, and all eventually recovered. The sum of recovery days for patients in hospitals A and B were 200 and 152, respectively. If the average recovery days for patients admitted in hospital A was 3 more than the average in hospital B then the number admitted in hospital A was **(CAT 2021)**

112. Onion is sold for 5 consecutive months at the rate of ₹10, 20, 25, 25, and 50 per kg, respectively. A family spends a fixed amount of money on onion for each of the first three months, and then spends half that amount on onion for each of the next two months. The average expense for onion, in rupees per kg, for the family over these 5 months is closest to **(CAT 2021)**
(a) 20 (b) 26
(c) 16 (d) 18

113. Identical chocolate pieces are sold in boxes of two sizes, small and large. The large box is sold for twice the price of the small box. If the selling price per gram of chocolate in the large box is 12% less than that in the small box, then the percentage by which the weight of chocolate in the large box exceeds that in the small box is nearest to **(CAT 2021)**
(a) 127 (b) 135
(c) 124 (d) 144

114. Two trains cross each other in 14 seconds when running in opposite directions along parallel tracks. The faster train is 160 m long and crosses a lamp post in 12 seconds. If the speed of the other train is 6 km/hr less than the faster one, its length, in m, is **(CAT 2021)**
(a) 180 (b) 184
(c) 192 (d) 190

115. The strength of an indigo solution in percentage is equal to the amount of indigo in grams per 100 cc of water. Two 800 cc bottles are filled with indigo solutions of strengths 33% and 17%, respectively. A part of the solution from the first bottle is thrown away and replaced by an equal volume of the solution from the second bottle. If the strength of the indigo solution in the first bottle has now changed to 21% then the volume, in cc, of the solution left in the second bottle is **(CAT 2021)**

116. A box has 450 balls, each either white or black, there being as many metallic white balls as metallic black balls. If 40% of the white balls and 50% of the black balls are metallic, then the number of non-metallic balls in the box is **(CAT 2021)**

117. A person buys tea of three different qualities at ₹800, ₹500, and ₹300 per kg, respectively, and the amounts bought are in the proportion 2 : 3 : 5. She mixes all the tea and sells one-sixth of the mixture at ₹700 per kg. The price, in INR per kg, at which she should sell the remaining tea, to make an overall profit of 50%, is **(CAT 2021)**
(a) 692 (b) 653
(c) 675 (d) 688

118. In a football tournament, a player has played a certain number of matches and 10 more matches are to be played. If he scores a total of one goal over the next 10 matches, his overall average will be 0.15 goals per match. On the other hand, if he scores a total of two goals over the next 10 matches, his overall average will be 0.2 goals per match. The number of matches he has played is **(CAT 2021)**

119. From a container filled with milk, 9 litres of milk are drawn and replaced with water. Next, from the same container, 9 litres are drawn and again replaced with water. If the volumes of milk and water in the container are now in the ratio of 16 : 9, then the capacity of the container, in litres, is **(CAT 2021)**

120. Anil can paint a house in 60 days while Bimal can paint it in 84 days. Anil starts painting and after 10 days, Bimal and Charu join him. Together, they complete the painting in 14 more days. If they are paid a total of ₹21000 for the job, then the share of Charu, in INR, proportionate to the work done by him, is **(CAT 2021)**
(a) 9150 (b) 9200
(c) 9000 (d) 9100

121. Two pipes A and B are attached to an empty water tank. Pipe A fills the tank while pipe B drains it. If pipe A is opened at 2 pm and pipe B is opened at 3 pm, then the tank becomes full at 10 pm. Instead, if pipe A is opened at 2 pm and pipe B is opened at 4 pm, then the tank becomes full at 6 pm. If pipe B is not opened at all, then the time, in minutes, taken to fill the tank is **(CAT 2021)**
(a) 264 (b) 144
(c) 120 (d) 140

122. Anil, Bobby and Chintu jointly invest in a business and agree to share the overall profit in proportion to their investments. Anil's share of investment is 70%. His share of profit decreases by 420 if the overall profit goes down from 18% to 15%. Chintu 's share of profit increases by ₹80 if the overall profit goes up from 15% to 17%. The amount, in INR, invested by Bobby is **(CAT 2021)**
(a) 2400 (b) 1800
(c) 2200 (d) 2000

123. Raj invested ₹10000 in a fund. At the end of first year, he incurred a loss but his balance was more than, ₹5000. This balance, when invested for another year, grew and the percentage of growth in the second year was five times the percentage of loss in the first year. If the gain of Raj from the initial investment over the two year period is 35%, then the percentage of loss in the first year is **(CAT 2021)**

(a) 10 (b) 5
(c) 70 (d) 15

124. Two trains A and B were moving in opposite directions, their speeds being in the ratio 5 : 3. The front end of A crossed the rear end of B 46 seconds after the front ends of the trains had crossed each other. It took another 69 seconds for the rear ends of the trains to cross each other. The ratio of length of train A to that of train B is **(CAT 2021)**
(a) 2 : 3 (b) 2 : 1
(c) 5 : 3 (d) 3 : 2

125. A tea shop offers tea in cups of three different sizes. The product of the prices, in INR, of three different sizes is equal to 800. The prices of the smallest size and the medium size are in the ratio 2 : 5. If the shop owner decides to increase the prices of the smallest and the medium ones by INR 6 keeping the price of the largest size unchanged, the product then changes to 3200. The sum of the original prices of three different sizes, in INR, is **(CAT 2021)**

126. A shop owner bought a total of 64 shirts from a wholesale market that came in two sizes, small and large. The price of a small shirt was INR 50 less than that of a large shirt. She paid a total of INR 5000 for the large shirts, and a total of INR 1800 for the small shirts. Then, the price of a large shirt and a small shirt together, in INR, is **(CAT 2021)**
(a) 150 (b) 200
(c) 175 (d) 225

127. One part of a hostel's monthly expenses is fixed, and the other part is proportional to the number of its boarders. The hostel collects ₹1600 per month from each boarder. When the number of boarders is 50, the profit of the hostel is ₹200 per boarder, and when the number of boarders is 75, the profit of the hostel is ₹250 per boarder. When the number of boarders is 80, the total profit of the hostel, in INR, will be **(CAT 2021)**
(a) 20200 (b) 20000
(c) 20500 (d) 20800

128. In a tournament, a team has played 40 matches so far and won 30% of them. If they win 60% of the remaining matches, their overall win percentage will be 50%. Suppose they win 90% of the remaining matches, then the total number of matches won by the team in the tournament will be **(CAT 2021)**
(a) 84 (b) 80
(c) 86 (d) 78

129. The total of male and female populations in a city increased by 25% from 1970 to 1980. During the same period, the male population increased by 40% while the female population increased by 20%. From 1980 to 1990, the female population increased by 25%. In 1990, if the female population is twice the male population, then the percentage increase in the total of male and female populations in the city from 1970 to 1990 is **(CAT 2021)**
(a) 68.50 (b) 69.25
(c) 68.25 (d) 68.75

130. Mira and Amal walk along a circular track, starting from the same point at the same time. If they walk in the same direction, then in 45 minutes, Amal completes exactly 3 more rounds than Mira. If they walk in opposite directions, then they meet for the first time exactly after 3 minutes. The number of rounds Mira walks in one hour is **(CAT 2021)**

131. If a certain weight of an alloy of silver and copper is mixed with 3 kg of pure silver, the resulting alloy will have 90% silver by weight. If the same weight of the initial alloy is mixed with 2 kg of another alloy which has 90% silver by weight, the resulting alloy will have 84% silver by weight. Then, the weight of the initial alloy, in kg, is **(CAT 2021)**
(a) 3 (b) 3.5
(c) 4 (d) 2.5

132. Anil can paint a house in 12 days while Barun can paint it in 16 days. Anil, Barun, and Chandu undertake to paint the house for ₹24000 and the three of them together complete the painting in 6 days. If Chandu is paid in proportion to the work done by him, then the amount in INR received by him is **(CAT 2021)**

133. One day, Rahul started a work at 9 AM and Gautam joined him two hours later. They then worked together and completed the work at 5 PM the same day. If both had started at 9 AM and worked together, the work would have been completed 30 minutes earlier. Working alone, the time Rahul would have taken, in hours, to complete the work is **(CAT 2021)**
(a) 11.5 (b) 12
(c) 12.5 (d) 10

134. The arithmetic mean of scores of 25 students in an examination is 50. Five of these students top the examination with the same score. If the scores of the other students are distinct integers with the lowest being 30, then the maximum possible score of the toppers is **(CAT 2021)**

135. Bank A offers 6% interest rate per annum compounded half yearly. Bank B and Bank C offer simple interest but the annual interest rate offered by Bank C is twice that of Bank B. Raju invests a certain amount in Bank B for a certain period and Rupa invests ₹10,000 in Bank C for twice that period. The interest that would accrue to Raju during that period is equal to the interest that would have accrued had he invested the same amount in Bank A for one year. The interest accrued, in INR, to Rupa is **(CAT 2021)**
(a) 2346 (b) 3436
(c) 1436 (d) 2436

136. The average weight of students in a class increases by 600 gm when some new students join the class. If the average weight of the new students is 3 kg more than the average weight of the original students, then the ratio of the number of original students to the number of new students is **(CAT 2022)**

(a) 1 : 4 (b) 3 : 1
(c) 4 : 1 (d) 1 : 2

137. Trains A and B start traveling at the same time towards each other with constant speeds from stations X and Y, respectively. Train A reaches station Y in 10 minutes while train B takes 9 minutes to reach station X after meeting train A. Then the total time taken, in minutes, by train B to travel from station Y to station X is **(CAT 2022)**

(a) 10 (b) 15
(c) 6 (d) 12

138. Amal buys 110 kg of syrup and 120 kg of juice, syrup being 20% less costly than juice, per kg. He sells 10 kg of syrup at 10% profit and 20 kg of juice at 20% profit. Mixing the remaining juice and syrup, Amal sells the mixture at ₹308.32 per kg and makes an overall profit of 64%. Then, Amal's cost price for syrup, in rupees per kg, is? **(CAT 2022)**

139. In a village, the ratio of number of males to females is 5 : 4. The ratio of number of literate males to literate females is 2 : 3. The ratio of the number of illiterate males to illiterate females is 4 : 3. If 3600 males in the village are literate, then the total number of females in the village is? **(CAT 2022)**

140. Ankita buys 4 kg cashews, 14 kg peanuts and 6 kg almonds when the cost of 7 kg cashews is the same as that of 30 kg peanuts or 9 kg almonds. She mixes all the three nuts and marks a price for the mixture in order to make a profit of ₹1752. She sells 4 kg of the mixture at this marked price and the remaining at a 20% discount on the marked price, thus making a total profit of ₹744. Then the amount, in rupees, that she had spent in buying almonds is **(CAT 2022)**

(a) 1176 (b) 1440
(c) 1680 (d) 2520

141. Alex invested his savings in two parts. The simple interest earned on the first part at 15% per annum for 4 years is the same as the simple interest earned on the second part at 12% per annum for 3 years. Then, the percentage of his savings invested in the first part is **(CAT 2022)**

(a) 37.5% (b) 60%
(c) 40% (d) 62.5%

142. The average of three integers is 13. When a natural number n is included, the average of these four integers remains an odd integer. The minimum possible value of n is **(CAT 2022)**

(a) 1 (b) 3
(c) 4 (d) 5

143. A mixture contains lemon juice and sugar syrup in equal proportion. If a new mixture is created by adding this mixture and sugar syrup in the ratio 1 : 3, then the ratio of lemon juice and sugar syrup in the new mixture is **(CAT 2022)**

(a) 1 : 7 (b) 1 : 5
(c) 1 : 6 (d) 1 : 4

144. Mr. Pinto invests one-fifth of his capital at 6%, one-third at 10% and the remaining at 1%, each rate being simple interest per annum. Then, the minimum number of years required for the cumulative interest income from these investments to equal or exceed his initial capital is? **(CAT 2022)**

145. Five students, including Amit, appear for an examination in which possible marks are integers between 0 and 50, both inclusive. The average marks for all the students is 38 and exactly three students got more than 32. If no two students got the same marks and Amit got the least marks among the five students, then the difference between the highest and lowest possible marks of Amit is **(CAT 2022)**

(a) 21 (b) 24
(c) 20 (d) 22

146. Working alone, the times taken by Anu, Tanu and Manu to complete any job are in the ratio 5 : 8 : 10. They accept a job which they can finish in 4 days if they all work together for 8 hours per day. However, Anu and Tanu work together for the first 6 days, working 6 hours 40 minutes per day. Then, the number of hours that Manu will take to complete the remaining job working alone is? **(CAT 2022)**

147. In an election, there were four candidates and 80% of the registered voters casted their votes. One of the candidates received 30% of the casted votes while the other three candidates received the remaining casted votes in the proportion 1 : 2 : 3. If the winner of the election received 2512 votes more than the candidate with the second highest votes, then the number of registered voters was **(CAT 2022)**

(a) 60288 (b) 62800
(c) 40192 (d) 50240

148. If a and b are non-negative real numbers such that $a + 2b = 6$, then the average of the maximum and minimum possible values of $(a + b)$ is **(CAT 2022)**

(a) 3 (b) 3.5
(c) 4 (d) 4.5

149. Two ships meet mid-ocean, and then, one ship goes south and the other ship goes west, both travelling at constant speeds. Two hours later, they are 60 km apart. If the speed of one of the ships is 6 km per hour more than the other one, then the speed, in km per hour, of the slower ship is **(CAT 2022)**

(a) 24 (b) 12
(c) 20 (d) 18

150. There are two containers of the same volume, first container half-filled with sugar syrup and the second container half-filled with milk. Half the content of the first container is transferred to the second container, and then the half of this mixture is transferred back to the first container. Next, half the content of the first container is transferred back to the second container. Then the ratio of sugar syrup and milk in the second container is **(CAT 2022)**
(a) 6 : 5 (b) 4 : 5
(c) 5 : 6 (d) 5 : 4

151. Manu earns ₹4000 per month and wants to save an average of ₹550 per month in a year. In the first nine months, his monthly expense was ₹3500, and he foresees that, tenth month onward, his monthly expense will increase to ₹3700. In order to meet his yearly savings target, his monthly earnings, in rupees, from the tenth month onward should be **(CAT 2022)**
(a) 4200 (b) 4300
(c) 4350 (d) 4400

152. A glass contains 500 cc of milk and a cup contains 500 cc of water. From the glass, 150 cc of milk is transferred to the cup and mixed thoroughly. Next, 150 cc of this mixture is transferred from the cup to the glass. Now, the amount of water in the glass and the amount of milk in the cup are in the ratio **(CAT 2022)**
(a) 10 : 13 (b) 3 : 10
(c) 1 : 1 (d) 10 : 3

153. Moody takes 30 seconds to finish riding an escalator if he walks on it at his normal speed in the same direction. He takes 20 seconds to finish riding the escalator if he walks at twice his normal speed in the same direction. If Moody decides to stand still on the escalator, then the time, in seconds, needed to finish riding the escalator is? **(CAT 2022)**

154. Bob can finish a job in 40 days, if he works alone. Alex is twice as fast as Bob and thrice as fast as Cole in the same job. Suppose Alex and Bob work together on the first day, Bob and Cole work together on the second day, Cole and Alex work together on the third day, and then, they continue the work by repeating this three-day roster, with Alex and Bob working together on the fourth day, and so on. Then, the total number of days Alex would have worked when the job gets finished, is? **(CAT 2022)**

155. Two cars travel from different locations at constant speeds. To meet each other after starting at the same time, they take 1.5 hours if they travel towards each other, but 10.5 hours if they travel in the same direction. If the speed of the slower car is 60 km/hr, then the distance traveled, in km, by the slower car when it meets the other car while traveling towards each other, is **(CAT 2022)**
(a) 120 (b) 100
(c) 150 (d) 90

156. In an examination, the average marks of students in sections A and B are 32 and 60, respectively. The number of students in section A is 10 less than that in section B. If the average marks of all the students across both the sections combined is an integer, then the difference between the maximum and minimum possible number of students in section A is? **(CAT 2022)**

157. A donation box can receive only cheques of ₹100, ₹250, and ₹500. On one good day, the donation box was found to contain exactly 100 cheques amounting to a total sum of ₹15250. Then, the maximum possible number of cheques of ₹500 that the donation box may have contained, is? **(CAT 2022)**

158. Nitu has an initial capital of ₹20,000. Out of this, she invests ₹8,000 at 5.5% in bank A, ₹5,000 at 5.6% in bank B and the remaining amount at x% in bank C, each rate being simple interest per annum. Her combined annual interest income from these investments is equal to 5% of the initial capital. If she had invested her entire initial capital in bank C alone, then her annual interest income, in rupees, would have been **(CAT 2022)**
(a) 700 (b) 800
(c) 1000 (d) 900

159. Consider six distinct natural numbers such that the average of the two smallest numbers is 14, and the average of the two largest numbers is 28. Then, the maximum possible value of the average of these six numbers is **(CAT 2022)**
(a) 23.5 (b) 23
(c) 24 (d) 22.5

160. A group of N people worked on a project. They finished 35% of the project by working 7 hours a day for 10 days. Thereafter, 10 people left the group and the remaining people finished the rest of the project in 14 days by working 10 hours a day. Then the value of N is **(CAT 2022)**
(a) 140 (b) 23
(c) 36 (d) 150

ANSWER KEY

1. 1900	2. (b)	3. (c)	4. (b)
5. (c)	6. (b)	7. (a)	8. (a)
9. (c)	10. (c)	11. (b)	12. (a)
13. (c)	14. 20	15. 15	16. 11
17. 20	18. 70,000	19. (d)	20. (b)
21. (a)	22. (d)	23. (a)	24. (b)
25. (d)	26. 48 min	27. (c)	28. 4000
29. (c)	30. (a)	31. (d)	32. (a)
33. (b)	34. 50kmph	35. (d)	36. 105
37. (b)	38. 5 km	39. 15 h	40. (d)
41. 60	42. 12 min	43. 121000	44. (b)
45. (d)	46. (a)	47. (d)	48. (c)
49. (b)	50. (b)	51. (c)	
52. (20,920)	53. (10.27 AM)		54. (d)
55. (c)	56. 48 seconds		57. (b)
58. (a)	59. (c)	60. 80	61. (b)
62. (b)	63. (b)	64. (a)	65. (a)
66. 880	67. (d)	68. (a)	69. (c)
70. 9	71. (c)	72. 20	73. (c)
74. (a)	75. (b)	76. 13 men	77. (d)
78. (d)	79. (b)	80. 12 Years	81. 8
82. (a)	83. (a)	84. 20000	85. (b)
86. (b)	87. 4	88. (d)	89. (c)
90. (c)	91. 90000	92. 800	93. (c)
94. (c)	95. (c)	96. (b)	97. (b)
98. 16000	99. 18 Years	100. (c)	101. (b)
102. 40 Men		103. (a)	104. (c)
105. (a)	106. (c)	107. 1000	108. (d)
109. 32	110. (a)	111. 35	112. (d)
113. (a)	114. (d)	115. 200	116. 250
117. (d)	118. 10	119. 45	120. (d)
121. (b)	122. (d)	123. (a)	124. (d)
125. 34	126. (b)	127. (c)	128. (a)
129. (d)	130. 8	131. (a)	132. 3000
133. (d)	134. 92	135. (d)	136. (c)
137. (b)	138. 160	139. 43200	140. (c)
141. (a)	142. (d)	143. (a)	144. 20
145. (c)	146. 6	147. (b)	148. (d)
149. (d)	150. (c)	151. (d)	152. (c)
153. 60	154. 11	155. (d)	156. 63
157. 12	158. (b)	159. (d)	160. (a)

SOLUTIONS AND SHORTCUTS

1. Ratio of speeds of A and $B = 10 : 9$

   Ratio of speeds of B and $C = 10 : 9$

   Ratio of speeds of A, B and $C = 100 : 90 : 81$

   In 100 meters race A beats C by $100 - 81 = 19$ m. Therefore, in a 10 km race A beats C by 1900 m.

2. 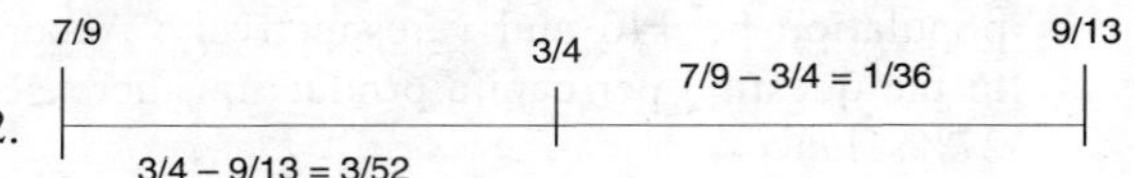

   3/52: 1/36 = 108: 52 = 27: 13

3. Check the options: If he travels total 65 miles then he travelled 30 miles in his onward journey and 35 miles in his return journey.

   For option (c) time taken in onward journey = 30/60 = 30 minutes

   Time taken in the return journey

   $$= \frac{15}{25} + \frac{20}{50} = \frac{50}{50} = 1 \text{ hour}$$

   Hence, this option is correct.

4. If we take the total number of shirts produced as 100, 15 would be defective and another 17 would be sold in the domestic market.

   Hence 68 of the 100 shirts are exported– this number is given to us as 8840. Hence, total shirts produced is 13000.

5. Let the average height of the 22 toddlers be x inches. When the 2 toddlers are excluded, the average of the group increases by 2, i.e. it becomes $x + 2$. Also, given, that the average height of the 2 toddlers is one-third of the average height of the 22 toddlers or $x/3$.

   $$\frac{\left[20(x+2) + 2 \cdot \frac{x}{3}\right]}{22} = x$$

   $$22x = 20x + 40 + \frac{2x}{3}$$

   $$\frac{4x}{3} = 40$$

   Upon solving, $x = 30$ inches.

   Average height of remaining 20 toddlers $= x + 2 = 30 + 2 = 32$ inches.

6. 100---------110---------143---------143 + 71.5 = 214.50% = 4290

   100% = 2000

7. Let the capacity of the tank be 40 liters. Efficiency of the inlet pipe = 40/8 = 5 l/hr.

   Efficiency of the outlet + inlet = 40/10 = 4 l/hr

   Efficiency of the outlet pipe = 5 – 4 = 1 l/hr

   Required time = (40/2)/1 = 20 hours.

8. Let him buy 'x' dozens of each type of candies. Then according to the question:

   $$16.50 \times 2x - 15x - 12x = 150$$

   $$x = 25$$

   $2x = 50$ dozens.

9. Let initial production and population be 100, x respectively and the final production and

population be 140 and y respectively. According to the question per capita production increases by 27%. Hence,

$$\frac{140}{y} = 1.27 \text{ of } \frac{100}{x}$$

$$\frac{y}{x} = \frac{140}{127} \approx 1.10$$

Required percentage = 10%.

10. $a : b : c = 3 \times 2 : 4 \times 2 : 4 \times 1 = 6 : 8 : 4 = 3 : 4 : 2$
$3x + 4x + 2x = 9x$. Hence, the sum must be multiple of 9. Only option (c) is a multiple of 9. Hence, this option is correct.

11. Let the speeds of the motorbike at A and car at B be 'v' and '$2v$' respectively and the distance between A and B is 'd'. In the first hour between 1 to 2, the bike would cover 'v' km.

d km
At 1 pm At 2 pm
A ---------------- B
v (d – v) km

After 2 PM, Relative speed = $v + 2v = 3v$ kmph.

Total time required to meet = $\frac{d-v}{3v} = 1\frac{2}{3} = \frac{5}{3}$

$\frac{d-v}{v} = 5$ or $d = 6v$ or $v = d/6$.

Total distance travelled by bike = $\left(1\frac{2}{3} + 1\right) \times v = \frac{8v}{3}$
= 168

$v = 63$ kmph

Total distance travelled by car = $1\frac{2}{3} \times 2v = \frac{10v}{3}$
= 210 km

Total distance between A and B = 168 + 210
= 378 km.

12. Let the total work be 40 units. Let the efficiencies of Amal, Bimal and Kamal be a, b and c respectively. Then, $a = 40/10 = 4$, $b = 40/8 = 5$, $a + b + c = 40/4 = 10$
On solving we get, $c = 1$.

Kamal's share = $\frac{1}{1+4+5} \times 1000 =$ ₹100

13. 4 liters of mixture A would have $\frac{4}{3}$ liters of water and $\frac{8}{3}$ liters of liquid A.

3 liters of mixture B would have $\frac{3}{4}$ liters of water and $\frac{9}{4}$ liters of liquid B.

2 liters of mixture C would have $\frac{2}{5}$ liters of water and $\frac{8}{5}$ liters of liquid C.

Total amount of water = $\frac{4}{3} + \frac{3}{4} + \frac{2}{5} = \frac{149}{60}$ Liters.

Only option (c) is correct.

14. Let the ages of Arun and Barun be 4 and 10 years respectively. After 2 years Arun age will be half of the Barun's age. The required percentage = $\frac{2}{10} \times 100$ = 20%.

15. Let the total work = 120 units
Efficiency of each person = 120/120 = 1unit per day
Total work done on day 1 = 1
Total work done on day 2 = 1 + 1 = 2
Total work done on day n = 1 + 1 + 1….n times = n
(Let the total work is finished in 'n' days)

$$1 + 2 + 3 + \ldots + n = 120$$

$$\frac{n(n+1)}{2} = 120$$

$n(n + 1) = 240$ or $n = 15$ days.

16. Let the maximum possible number of people is 'n'. To maximise the value of n we assume that only one person weighs 57 kg and rest of the persons weigh 53 kg.
$57 + (n - 1)53 = 630$ or $(n - 1)$

$$= \frac{630 - 57}{53} = \frac{573}{53} = 10.81$$

Therefore maximum possible value of $n - 1 = 10$ or n = 11 persons.

17. Let's assume if the man travels at a speed of 'v' kmph and reaches station in time (in t minutes). Let the distance between station and home is 'd' km.
According to the question:

$$\frac{d}{12} = \frac{d}{v} + \frac{10}{60} \quad (1)$$

$$\frac{d}{15} = \frac{d}{v} - \frac{10}{60} \quad (2)$$

$$\frac{d}{12} - \frac{d}{15} = \frac{10}{60} + \frac{10}{60} = \frac{20}{60}$$

On solving we get: $d = 20$ km
Alternate method: The speed of walking is increasing by 25%, hence the time reduction would be 20% (as the distance is constant). This time reduction is 20 minutes and hence, the original time would be 100 minutes. The distance would be $12 \times \frac{100}{60} = 20$ km.

18. Of every 100 saving, Ravi would deposit 50 in an FD, 15 in stocks and 35 in his bank account. Hence, the total savings deposited in bank would be 85%, which is given to us as 59500.

Total monthly savings = $\frac{59500}{85} \times 100 = 70,000$

19. Using the *PCG* logic, it is quite clear that if the cost price is 100 and the retail price is 120, giving a discount of 15% would mean selling at 102 – and this would give a profit of 2%.

    Thus, to get a profit of 20%, he must sell at retail price.

20. Let the speed of the river be v and the speed of the boat be u and the distance between the home of the man and his office be 'd' km and 't' is the initial time taken.

$$t = \frac{d}{u-v} + \frac{d}{u+v} \quad (1)$$

$$\frac{t}{4} = \frac{d}{2u-v} + \frac{d}{2u+v} \quad (2)$$

From equations (1) and (2) we get:

$$\frac{2u}{u^2 - v^2} = \frac{16u}{4u^2 - v^2}$$

$$4u^2 - v^2 = 8u^2 - 8v^2$$

$$4u^2 = 7v^2$$

$$\frac{u^2}{v^2} = \frac{7}{4} \text{ or } \frac{u}{v} = \sqrt{7} : 2$$

21. C1 : C2 : C3 = 9 : 10 : 8 = 162 : 180 : 144

    C2 : C4 : C5 = 18 : 19 : 20 = 180 : 190 : 200

    C1 : C2 : C3 : C4 : C5 = 162 : 180 : 144 : 190 : 200

    If 200 – 162 = 38 → 19 crore

    Then, (162 + 180 + 144 + 190 + 200 = 876) → $\frac{19}{38} \times$ 876 = 438 crore.

22. Let 200 girls and 100 boys be appearing for the admission test. 60 girls and 45 boys get admission.

    Total candidates who do not get admission = 200 + 100 – 60 – 45 = 195.

    Required percentage = $\frac{195}{300} \times 100 = 65\%$.

23. Let the number of large, super, and jumbo packets of popcorn in its stock are $7x$, $17x$, $16x$ and the number of large, super, and jumbo packets of chips in its stock are $6y$, $15y$, $14y$.

$$7x + 17x + 16x = 6y + 15y + 14y$$

$$40x = 35y$$

$$x : y = 7 : 8$$

Required ratio = $16x$: $14y$ = $\frac{16}{14} \times \frac{7}{8} = 1 : 1$.

24. Let the price of good mangoes be ₹100 per kg.

    Cost price = $80 \times 100 + 40 \times \frac{100}{2} = 10,000$

    Selling price = $120 \times 90 = 10800$

    Percentage profit = $\frac{800}{10,000} \times 100 = 8\%$.

25. If we take the Cost price of the 60 toys as 100, the marked price should be such that after a 40% discount on the marked price, the selling price of the items should be 120. A little bit of Percentage change graphic thinking explained in the chapter of percentages, would easily give you that the marked price should be 200. Since, 10 toys are destroyed, it means that 1/6th of the toys are destroyed. Thus, the marked price of the toys on sale would be: 166.6666. To sell these at 120, we can find out what percent of 166.6666 is 120: Since: 120/166.666 = 360/500 = 0.72, this means that she should give a discount of 28%.

    Alternately, you could also solve this question going through mathematical equations as follows – but this would take significantly more time:

    Let the marked price of one toy be ₹X and the cost price be ₹Y.

    According to the question:

$$0.6X = 1.2Y$$

$$X = 2Y$$

Cost price of 60 toys = $60Y$

After destruction of 10 toys only 50 are remaining.

(If 'p' is the offered discount), then:

Then, $X(1 - p) \times 50 = 72Y$

$$1 - p = 0.72 \text{ or } p = 28\%.$$

26. Let the efficiency of inlet of type A and inlet of type B be 'a' and 'b', respectively and the capacity of tank be 'c'.

    According to the question:

$$(10a + 45b) \times \frac{1}{2} = 8a + 18b \rightarrow$$

$$a = 1.5b.$$

Thus, the total work in terms of 'b' would be $8a + 18b$ = $12b + 18b = 30b$.

If seven inlets of A and 27 inlets of B are open, it means that effectively 10.5 inlets of B and 27 inlets of B are open → 37.5 inlets of B are open.

To fill a tank requiring $30b$ to fill, with $37.5b$ as the filling rate one would take: 30/37.5 = 4/5 hours = 48 minutes.

27. CAR 1, CAR2 (at A) —— P —— Q —— B (CAR3)

    AP = 100 km, PQ = 100 km, QB = 100 km

    Let the speed of car 1, car 2 and car 3 be V_1, V_2 and V_3 respectively.

    According to the question:

    $200/V_1 = 100/V_3 \rightarrow V_1 : V_3 = 2 : 1$ and

    $100/V_2 = 200/V_3 \rightarrow V_2 : V_3 = 1 : 2$

Thus, $V_1 : V_2 : V_3 = 4 : 1 : 2$

Hence, $V_2 : V_1 = 1 : 4$

Hence, option (c) is correct.

28. The net interest retained by Gopal in the original case = 2% of X + 10% of Y. This is given to be the same as the interest earned by Ankit = 8% of X. Equating we get:

2% of X + 10% of Y = 8% of $X \rightarrow$ 6% of X = 10% of $Y \rightarrow 0.06 \times X = 0.1 \times Y \rightarrow \frac{X}{Y} = \frac{5}{3}$.

In the second case, it is given to us that the net interest retained by Gopal = (2% of X + 20% of Y) and this value is 150 greater than the net interest retained by Gopal in the first situation, i.e. (2% of X + 10% of Y). Thus, $(0.02X + 0.2Y) - (0.02X + 0.1Y) = 150 \rightarrow Y = 1500$ and since X: Y = 5:3, X = 2500. Hence, $X + Y = 4000$.

29. Let the initial scores of Amal and Bimal be $11x$ and $14x$ respectively. If their scores were increased by a, then, according to the question:

$\frac{(11x+a)}{14x+a} = 47 : 56$

$616x + 56a = 658x + 47a$

$9a = 42x \rightarrow a = 14x/3$

Bimal's new score: his old score $= \frac{(14x + \frac{14x}{3})}{14x} = \frac{56x}{42x}$ = 4:3. Hence, option (c) is correct.

30. Let the strength of A, B and C be a, b and c respectively. Let us take 100 ml, 200 ml and 300 ml of A, B and C.

According to the question: $a + 2b + 3c$ = 20% of (100 + 200 + 300)

$a + 2b + 3c = 120$ (1)

$3a + 2b + c$ = 30% of (100 + 200 + 300)

$3a + 2b + c = 180$ (2)

Eq. (2) Eq. (1) = $a - c = 30$ or $c = a - 30$.

$a + 2b + 3(a - 30) = 120$ or $4a$

$= 210 - 2b$ or $b = 105 - 2a$

Concentration of $D = \frac{2b+7c}{9} = \frac{2\times(105-2a)+7(a-30)}{9}$

$\frac{3a}{9} = \frac{a}{3}$

Hence, the required ratio = $d : a = 1 : 3$. Hence, option (a) is correct.

31. Let the concentration of the unknown concentration solution is s%.

Let us take 100 ml of first and 300 ml of the second solution and this mixture is mixed with 400 ml of 20% solution.

According to the question:

(20% of 100 + s% of 300 + 20% of 400) = 31.25% of (100 + 300 + 400)

$20 + 3s + 80 = 250$ or $s = 50$. Hence, option (d) is correct.

32. Think of the mixtures in terms of percentage concentrations. Drum 1 has 72% of paint A, drum 2 has an unknown percentage, while combined in the ratio 3 : 4 the mixture has a 65% of paint A. This can be seen on an alligation picture as follows:

X —— 65% —— 72%
4 ———————— 3

In the figure: 4 → 7 (i.e. 72 – 65). Hence, 3 → 5.25 and hence, $X = 65 - 5.25 = 59.75$ (using alligation).

59.75% of paint A, means 40.25% of paint B. The required ratio = 59.75:40.25 = 239:161. Hence, option (a) is correct.

33. Let the efficiencies of Ramesh and Ganesh be R and G respectively. Let the total work = W units.

According to the question:

$W = 16 \times (R + G)$ and $W = 7 \times (R + G) + 10 \times (0.7R + G) = 14R + 17G$. Since the work is equal, we get:

$16 \times (R + G) = 14R + 17G$

$2R = G$ OR R:G = 1 : 2. Hence, Ramesh is half as efficient as Ganesh.

Let the efficiencies of Ramesh and Ganesh be one unit per day and two units per day respectively.

$W = 16 \times (1 + 2) = 48$ units

Total work done in seven days = $7 \times (1 + 2) = 21$ units.

Remaining work = 48 – 21 = 27 units.

Required time to finish the remaining work = 27/2 = 13.5 days. Hence, option (b) is correct.

34. Let the speed of the car which starts from point A is a kmph and the car which starts from point B is b kmph.

According to the question:

$350 = 1 \times (a + b)$ and $350 = 7 \times (a - b)$

On solving the above two equations, we get $a = 200$ kmph and $b = 150$ kmph.

Hence, the required difference = 200 – 150 = 50 kmph.

35. Final quantity of alcohol in the mixture

$= 700 \times \left(1 - \frac{10}{100}\right)^2 = 567$ ml.

Final amount of water in the mixture = 700 + 175 – 567 = 308 ml.

Required percentage = $\frac{308}{875} = 35.2\%$

Hence, option (d) is correct.

36. $\frac{x+y+z}{3} = 80, x + y + z = 240$ (1)

$\frac{x+y+z+u+v}{5} = 75, x + y + z + u + v = 375$ (2)

From equations (1) and (2), we get $u + v = 135$.

$$u+v=\frac{(x+y)}{2}+\frac{(y+z)}{2}$$

$u+v = 120 + y/2 = 135$ or $y = 30$.

Put $y = 30$ in equation (1), we get:

$x+z=210$

As $x \geq z$, then minimum possible value of x will occur when we take $x = z$. This value would be 105 for x and z each. Hence, minimum value of $x = 105$.

37. From the starting information, it should be clear to you that pump *B* takes two hours less than pump *A* to empty the tank. This gives rise to various possibilities for how many hours each pump takes to empty the tank, as well as when the pumps are opened originally. For instance, if you assume the values of four hours (for pump *A* to empty) and two hours for pump *B* to empty, it would mean that the emptying of the tank is started every day at 4 PM. Also, *A* empties 25% per hour, while *B* empties 50% per hour. We need to check whether this condition is fulfilled for Wednesday. We are told that *A* alone worked till 5 PM and *B* worked from 5 to 7 PM. But in two hours, *B* would empty the tank completely by itself. Hence, this cannot be the correct scenario.

    Checking with three hours for *B* and five hours for *A*, we get 33.33% work per hour for *B* and 20% per hour for *A*. Also, the normal time for opening the pumps is 3 PM. For Wednesday, pump *A* is open for two hours (3 PM to 5PM) and pump *B* is open for two hours (5 PM to 7 PM). We can see that: $2 \times 33.33 + 2\times 20 \neq 100$. Hence, this scenario is also not true.

    Checking with four hours for *B* and six hours for *A*, we get 25% work per hour for *B* and 16.66% per hour for *A*. Also, the normal time for opening the pumps is 2 PM. For Wednesday, pump *A* is open for three hours (3 PM to 5 PM) and pump *B* is open for two hours (5 PM to 7 PM). We can see that: $3\times16.666 + 2 \times 25 = 100$. Hence, this scenario is true.

    Thus, their combined work together = 25 + 16.66 = 41.66% per hour. To do 100% of the work, they would take 100/41.66 = 300/125 = 2.4 hours or 2 hours 24 minutes. Starting from 2 PM, they would empty the tank completely at 4:24 PM. Hence, option (b) is correct.

38. Total time taken by car 1 to reach at *B* = $\frac{50}{100}+\frac{50}{50}+\frac{50}{25}=3.5$ hours or 3 hours 30 minutes.

    Time taken by car 1 to travel 20 km = 20/100 = 0.2 hours or 12 minutes. This means that car 2 is 12 minutes behind car 1. Since, their speeds are equal in all phases; car 2 would also take a total of 3.5 hours to reach *B*. The last part of the journey by both the cars is done at 25 kmph and the last 12 minutes would be spent in the last part of the journey only, we can deduce that after car 1 reaches *B*, car 2 would take 12 minutes @ 25kmph, to reach *B*. Thus, the distance from *B* for car 2 = 25 kmph × 0.2 = 5 km.

39. T at 3 PM S at 4 PM

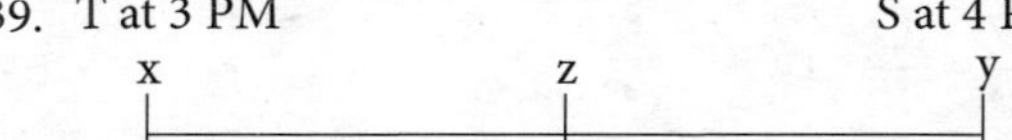

    The speeds of *T* and *S* are '*V*' and '3*V*/4' respectively.

    Let $XY = d$.

$$XZ=\frac{3d}{5},\ ZY=\frac{2d}{5}$$

    According to the question:

$$\frac{\frac{3d}{5}}{V}=\frac{\frac{2d}{5}}{\frac{3v}{4}}+1$$

$$\frac{3d}{5V}=\frac{8d}{15V}+1$$

    On solving the above equation, we get: $d/V = 15$ hours.

40. Let the cost price of *A* and *B* are ₹*a* per kg and ₹*b* per kg, respectively. When *A* and *B* are mixed in 3: 2, then the cost price of the mixture would be:

$$\frac{3a+2b}{3+2}=\frac{40}{1.1} \quad (1)$$

    When A and B are mixed in 2: 3 then:

$$\frac{2a+3b}{2+3}=\frac{40}{1.05} \quad (2)$$

    Equation (1)/ equation (2):

$$\frac{3a+2b}{2a+3b}=\frac{1.05}{1.1}$$

    On solving the above equation, we get: $a : b = 19 : 24$. Hence, option (d) is correct.

41. Let the number of tests he has appeared for, be '*n*' and his average score for '*n*' tests be '*x*'.

    According to the question:

$$\frac{[nx-20\times10]}{n-10}=x+1$$

$$nx - 200 = nx - 10x + n - 10$$

$$10x - n = 190 \quad (1)$$

$$\frac{[nx-30\times10]}{n-10}=x-1$$

$$nx - 300 = nx - 10x - n + 10$$

$$10x + n = 310 \quad (2)$$

    On solving equation (1) and (2), we get: $x = 25$, $n = 60$. Hence, 60 is the correct answer.

42. Let $AB = 4d$

    $AP = d$ and $BP = 3d$

    Let the speed of car 1 be '*V*' kmph and the speed of car 2 be *V*/2 kmph.

    According to the question:

$$\frac{d}{V}=\frac{\frac{3d}{V}}{2}-1$$

$$\frac{d}{V}=\frac{6d}{V}-1$$

$$\frac{5d}{V}=1$$

$\frac{d}{V}=\frac{1}{5}$ hour or 12 minutes is the time taken by car 1 to reach P from A.

43. Let 'p' be the instalments.

After one year, the net amount = 210000 + 10% of 210000 – p

At the end of the second year, net amount to be paid = 210000 + 10% of 210000 – p + 10% of (210000 + 10% of 210000 – p) = p

$210000 + 21000 - p + 23100 - 0.1p = p$

$2.1p = 254100$ or p = ₹121000

Hence, each instalment is equal to ₹121000.

44. According to the question:

$0.45N = 36 + 68\%$ of $0.45N$

32% of $0.45N = 36$

$$N=\frac{36}{0.32\times0.45}=250$$

$243 \le N \le 252$. Hence, option (b) is correct.

45. To maximise the largest possible age of those who are below 51 years, we need to minimise the total age of the persons whose ages are not below 51. So, to maximise the largest possible age of those persons who are below 51 years, the age of rest of the persons must be 51 years.

According to the question:

$51 \times 30 + 39a = 69 \times 38$ (where 'a' is the largest possible average age of all those people who are below 51 years).

Or a = 28 years. Hence, option (d) is correct.

46. Check the options:

Option (a): If the speed of Partha = 5 kmph

Time taken by Partha to reach at B = 60/5 = 12 hrs.

Time taken by Narayan to reach at B = 12 – 4 = 8 hrs.

Speed of Narayan = 60/8 = 7.5 kmph.

Time taken by Partha to travel 30 km = 30/5 = 6 hours.

Time taken by Narayan to travel 60 km = 8 hours

Time difference = 8 – 6 = 2 hours, thus, meeting the requirement of the question.

Hence, option (a) is correct.

47. Let the efficiencies of human and robot are 'h' and 'r' respectively. Let the total work = W

According to the question: $30 \times (15h + 5r) = W$ (1)

$60 \times (5h + 15r) = W$ (2)

$30 \times (15h + 5r) = 60 \times (5h + 15r)$

$15h + 5r = 10h + 30r$

$5h = 25r \rightarrow r = h/5$

$$W = 30 \times (15h + 5r) = 30 \times \left(15h+\frac{5h}{5}\right) = 480 \times h$$

Required time to finish the job by 15 humans = $\frac{480h}{15h}$ 32 days. Hence, option (d) is correct.

48. Let the amounts of paints A and B are 'a' litres and 'b' litres respectively.

Let the cost of paints B is ₹'x' per litre and cost of paint A is ₹'$x + 8$' per litre.

Cost of the ten litres mixture = 264/1.1 = ₹240

$$\frac{[a(x+8)+bx]}{a+b}=\frac{240}{10}$$

$$x+\frac{8a}{a+b}=24$$

To minimise the value of x, $a = b$.

$$x+\frac{8a}{a+a}=24$$

x = 20 per litre.

Hence, option (c) is correct.

49. Let Raju and Lalitha originally had $4n$ and $9n$ marbles respectively and Lalitha gave 'x' marbles to Raju.

$\frac{4n+x}{9n-x}=\frac{5}{6}$ or $24n + 6x = 45n - 5x \rightarrow 11x = 21n$

or $\frac{x}{n}=\frac{21}{11}$

We need to find the value of $\frac{x}{9n}=\frac{21}{9\times11}=\frac{7}{33}$

Hence, option (b) is correct.

50. The question should be looked at from the shopkeeper's perspective. Let the purchase price of the wholesaler be 3 and 1 respectively, for the walnuts and the peanuts. Then, the shopkeeper would have purchased his items for: $8 \times 1.1 + 16 \times 3.6 = 66.4$. While selling he had only 11 kg of walnuts and 5 kg of peanuts with him. Since he mixes them, he is selling 16 kg overall. For an overall cost of 66.4, a profit of 25% means that the revenue generated by the shopkeeper would be $1.25 \times 66.4 = 83$. This, revenue in actual terms is $166 \times 16 = 2656$. Thus, in our assumptions, $83 \rightarrow 2656$. Hence, 1 = 32 and 3 = 96. The price of walnuts would be ₹96.

51. The sum of the 30 integers would be 150. Exactly 20 numbers do not exceed 5, means that 10 numbers would definitely exceed 5. For maximising the average of the 20 numbers, the averages of the 10 numbers that exceed 5 have to be minimised. This would be done if we take all these 10 numbers to be as small as possible, i.e. 6 each. Thus, the total of these 10 numbers would be 60. Consequently, the total of the remaining 20 numbers would be 150 – 60 = 90 and hence, their

average would be 90/20 = 4.5 (maximum possible average of the 20 numbers). Option (c) is correct.

52. Let 'x' be the amount invested by Bimal.

$$8\% \text{ of } 12000 + 10000 \times \left(1+\frac{3}{100}\right)^2 - 10000 = 7.5\% \text{ of } x$$

$960 + 609 = 0.075 \times x$

$x = 1569/0.075 =$ ₹20,920

53. According to the question, A covered 40% of the track in 12 minutes. Hence, A covered 100% track in 30 minutes. It means both A and B started their journey at 9:42 AM.

A and B met first time at 10:00 AM and A covered 60% of the track which means by 10:00 AM, B covered 40% of the distance. Hence, B covered 40% of the track in 18 minutes or it covered 100% distance in 45 minutes. Hence, B returns to P at 10:27 AM. Option (d) is correct.

54. Each of three vessels A, B, C contains 500 ml of salt solution of strengths 10%, 22%, and 32%, respectively.

The amount of salt in vessels A, B, C = 50g, 110g, 160g respectively.

The amount of water in vessels A, B, C = 450 ml, 390 ml, 340 ml respectively.

Now, 100 ml of the solution in vessel A is transferred to vessel B. In this 100 ml of the solution, 10 g salt and 90 mls water will be transferred. After this, there will be 120 g salt and 480 g water in vessel B. Then, when 100 ml of the solution in vessel B is transferred to vessel C, there would be 20 g salt and 80 ml water going to vessel C. Vessel C's new condition would become: 180 g salt and 420 ml water, i.e. it would contain 30% salt. Finally, when 100 ml is taken back to vessel A (which would have 400 ml solution containing 40 g salt and 360 ml water), there would be an addition of 30 g of salt and 70 ml of water. Thus, at the end of the transfers there would be 70 g salt and 430 ml water in 500 ml of the solution in vessel A. This means 14% of salt concentration. Hence, option (d) is correct.

55. From the events described in the problem, we can see that the last motorcyclist will leave point A at 10:45 AM and the last motorcyclist reaches B at 11:00 AM. Hence, it will take 15 minutes to complete the journey. If A doubles his speed then it will reach B at 10: 30 AM.

By 10:30, exactly 15 motorcyclists will reach at B (the last motorcyclist that would reach point B would be the motorcyclist that left at 10:15 AM).

Hence, option (c) is correct.

56. Let the track lengths of A and B are 'a' and 'b' respectively.

According to the question: $a + b = 325$ (1)

$(9a/6) = (5b/7.5) \rightarrow a : b = 4 : 9$ (2)

On solving, we get: $a = 100$ m, $b = 225$ m

$$\text{Required time} = \frac{100}{7.5\times\frac{5}{18}} = 48 \text{ s}$$

57. Let there were 'a' fiction and 'b' nonfiction books in the library in 2010.

$a + b = 11500$ (1)

$1.1a + 1.12b = 12760$ (2)

On solving, we get $a = 6000$, $b = 5500$

Hence, there were total $1.1 \times 6000 = 6600$ fiction books in the library in 2015.

58. Let the CP be 100 each. Then the shopkeeper sells to Amal at 120 and sells to Asim at 80. Amal sells at a profit of 30% to Bimal – hence, Bimal purchases at 156. Likewise, Asim sells to Barun at a loss of 30%, hence Barun purchases at 56. $(x - y)/p = (156 - 56)/100 = 1$.

Hence, option (a) is correct.

59. Let the cost of each cycle be 100. Then the cost of ten cycles is 1000. Selling price of six bicycles would be 125 each, while the selling price of four bicycles would be 75 each. Hence, total revenue is $125 \times 6 + 75 \times 4 = 1050$. The profit is 50, which is on the basis of an assumption of 1000 for the total cost of ten bicycles. This profit is actually given to us as 2000 – which means that if $50 \rightarrow 2000$, then $100 \rightarrow 4000$. Option (c) is correct.

Alternately, you could also do this by assuming $100x$ as the cost price of one bicycle. According to the question: $6 \times 125x + 4 \times 75x - 10 \times 100x = 2000$

$50x = 2000$ or $100x =$ ₹4000

Hence, option (c) is correct.

60. Let the score of D was $100x$.

Score of $C = 100x - 20\%$ of $100x = 80x$

Score of $B = 80x + 25\%$ of $80x = 100x$

Score of $A = 100x - 10\%$ of $100x = 90x$

$90x = 72$ or $100x = 80$

61. Let the salaries of Ramesh, Ganesh and Rajesh in 2010 be, 6, 5 and 7, respectively. Then, since it is known that Ramesh's salary increased by 25%, his salary would be 7.5 in 2015. Also, in 2015, the ratio of the salaries of the three was 3 : 4 : 3. Hence, the salary of Rajesh would also be 7.5 in 2015. Thus, Rajesh's salary has increased from 7 to 7.5 – an increase of around 7%. Hence, option (b) is correct.

62. Let the total work be 40 units.

Efficiency of Anil = 40/20 = 2 units per day.

Efficiency of Sunil = 40/40 = 1 unit per day.

Bimal has done 10% of 40 units = 4 units of work.

Work done by Anil in the first 3 days = 6 units.

Thus, the rest of the 40 – 4 – 6 = 30 units of work

would be done by Anil and Bimal together.

Total time taken by Anil and Bimal together to finish the job = 30/ (2 + 1) = 10 days.

Hence, it would take total 10 + 3 = 13 days to complete the job. Hence, option (b) is correct.

63. Let the scores of Rama, Mohan and Anjali be 'r', 'm' and 'a' respectively.

$r=\frac{1}{12}\times(m+a)$. After the review, their scores would be $a + 6$, $m + 6$ and $r + 6$ for Anjali, Mohan and Rama respectively. Thus, $(a + 6) : (m + 6) : (r + 6) = 11 : 10 : 3$

Let $a + 6 = 11x$, $m + 6 = 10x$ and $r + 6 = 3x$

Or $a = 11x - 6$, $m = 10x - 6$, $r = 3x - 6$

$$3x-6=\frac{1}{12}\times(11x-6+10x-6)$$

On solving the above equation, we get $x = 4$. Their respective scores would be: Anjali = $11x - 6 = 38$, Mohan = $10x - 6 = 34$; Rama = $3x - 6 = 6$. Difference between Anjali and Rama is 38 – 6 = 32. Hence, option (b) is correct.

64. The highest possible percentage value by which the speed of the second car would exceed the first car, will occur when both the cars take the least amount of time. Thus, we would need to consider the travel times for both to the least possible. Since, the first car travels at least six hours then the second car would travel at least five hours. Thus, their time ratio would be 6:5. Since, the distance is constant; their speed ratio would be in the ratio of 5:6. Thus, the second car's speed would exceed the first car's speed by a maximum of 20%. Hence, option (a) is correct.

65. Let the income of Bimala be ₹100.

Income of Amala = ₹120

Income of Kamala = ₹150

After 4% reduction, Kamala's income = 150 – 6 = 144.

After 10% increment of Bimala's income = 100 + 10 =110. Thus, Kamala's income is greater than Bimala's income by: $\frac{144-110}{110}\times100\approx31\%$

Hence, option (a) is correct.

66. Let the length of the racecourse = x metres

Race of speeds of 1st, 2nd and 3rd horses = $x: x - 11: x - 90$

Ratio of speeds of 2nd and 3rd horses = $x: x - 80$

Hence, $\frac{x-11}{x-90}=\frac{x}{x-80}$

On solving the above equation, we get $x = 880$ m.

67. Let the investments of Amala, Bina and Gouri are $3x$, $4x$ and $5x$ respectively, and their interest rates are $6y$, $5y$ and $4y$ respectively.

According to the question: $\left(4x\times\frac{5y}{100}\right)-\left(3x\times\frac{6y}{100}\right)$ = 250

$\frac{2xy}{100}=250$ or $\frac{xy}{100}=125$

Total interest = $3x\times\frac{6y}{100}+4x\times\frac{5y}{100}+5x\times\frac{4y}{100}=\frac{58xy}{100}$

= 58 × 125 = ₹7250

Hence, option (d) is correct.

68. Assume that Amal travelled for three hours at each speed. He would take a total of nine hours. He would cover 30 + 60 + 90 = 180 km and that would be the total distance to be covered by Bimal. Bimal would, thus, cover 60 km at each speed. He would take: 60/10 + 60/20 + 60/30 = 6 + 3 + 2 = 11 hours. Bimal's travel time exceeds Amal's by 2/9 = 22.22%. Hence, option (a) is correct.

69. Let the maximum marks in the exam was 100 x.

Meena scored $40x$ and after the review, her score became $40x$ + 50% of $40x = 60x$.

Passing marks = $60x + 35$ (1)

When her post review score is increased by 20%, she would score: $60x$ + 20% of $60x = 72x$

$72x$ = passing marks + 7 (2)

On solving equation (1) and (2), we get: $x = 3.5$. Hence, the passing marks = $60x + 35 = 245$ and the total marks = 350.

Passing percentage = $\frac{245}{350}\times100$. Hence, option (c) is correct.

70. Let the amount invested in fixed deposit was ₹x.

6% of x + 4% of $\frac{(15,00,000-x)\times2}{3}$ + 3% of $\frac{(15,00,000-x)\times1}{3}=76000$

On solving the above equation, we get: x = ₹9,00,000 = 9 lakh.

Hence, the correct answer must be 9.

71. Let the efficiencies of A and B is '$2a$' and 'b' respectively.

Total work = $12 \times (2a + b) = 24a + 12b$

Total work = $9 \times (a + 3b) = 9a + 27b$

Equating, we get: $15a = 15b \rightarrow a = b$. Thus, the total work would be: $24a + 12a = 36a$. If A works at her normal speed of $2a$, she would take $36a/2a$ = 18 days.

Hence, option (c) is correct.

72. Since there are 60% girls, there would be 40% boys. Also, since there are 30 girls more than boys, it means that 20% = 30 → 100% = 150, i.e. there are a total of 150 students in the class, with 60% (90 girls) and 40% boys (60 boys). If 68% pass, it means that

68 × 1.5 = 102 pass, out of which 30 being boys, means that there are 72 girls who pass. Out of 90, 72 gives us 80% pass percentage. Hence, 20% of the girls do not pass.

73. Let the cost prices of 1 pen and 1 book are $100x$ and $100y$ respectively.

$95x + 115y - (100x + 100y) = 7$

$15y - 5x = 7$ (1)

$(105x + 110y) - 100x - 100y = 5x + 10y = 13$ (2)

On solving equation (1) and (2), we get: $x = 1, y = 0.8$

Cost price of book = $100y$ = ₹80.

74. Weight/volume for liquid 1 = 1000/1000 = 1 kg/litre

Weight/volume for liquid 2 = 800/1000 = 0.8 kg/litre. The average weight/volume of the mixture is 0.96 (480 g in 500 ml). Hence, the ratio of mixing would be 4:1 for the first and second liquids. Thus, liquid 1 would be 80% of the mixture.

Hence, option (a) is correct.

75. Let the average score of 20 students other than Gautam and Ramesh is x.

$20x + 82.5 = 21 \times 62$

$20x = 1219.50$

$x = 60.975$

Let Gautam scores 'p' marks in the test.

According to the question:

$$\frac{20x+p}{21}+1=\frac{20x+p+82.5}{22}$$

On solving the above equation, we get: $p = 51$. Hence, option (b) is correct.

76. Let the efficiencies of one man and one machine be 'a' and 'b' respectively.

According to the question: $(3a + 8b) = 2 \times (3b + 8a)$

$3a + 8b = 6b + 16a$

$13a = 2b$ or $a{:}b = 2{:}13$

It means that one machine is 13/2 = 6.5 times as efficient as one man. Thus, the work that is done by one machine can be done by 6.5 men in the same time. Hence, the work done by two machines in 13 days would be equal to the work done by 13 men in 13 days.

77. It is given to us that:

$$A+\frac{B+C}{2}=5 \Rightarrow 2A+B+C=10$$

Also, $2B + A + C = 14$

Thus, we get: B – A = 4 and also 3A + 3B + 2C = 24. Checking the options, if we choose A + B = 6 from option (d), we get: 2C = 6 ⇒ C = 3. Also, since B – A = 4, we get B = 5 and A = 1. These values satisfy all the equations. Hence, this is the correct option. If we try to use a wrong option (say A + B = 7 from option (c)), we get: 2C = 3 ⇒ C = 1.5, which is not possible, since A,B,C are integers. Option (a) also gets rejected, since we get C as a decimal value, which is not possible. If we tried option (b), A + B = 4, we get C = 6. This gives us B = 4 and A = 0, which is again not possible, since A,B,C are positive integers. Hence, option (d) is correct.

78. Since the speeds of the cars are constant we have from the A to M journey: $\frac{\text{Speed of car 1}}{\text{Speed of car 2}}=\frac{20}{t}$

From the M to B journey, we have:

$$\frac{\text{Speed of car 1}}{\text{Speed of car 2}}=\frac{t}{45}$$

Hence, $\frac{\text{Speed of car 1}}{\text{Speed of car 2}}=\frac{20}{t}=\frac{t}{45}$

⇒ t = 30 mins.

Hence, the ratio of $\frac{\text{Speed of car 1}}{\text{Speed of car 2}}=\frac{2}{3}$. Hence, if Car 1 travels at 60 kmph, Car 2 travels at 90 kmph. Option (d) is correct.

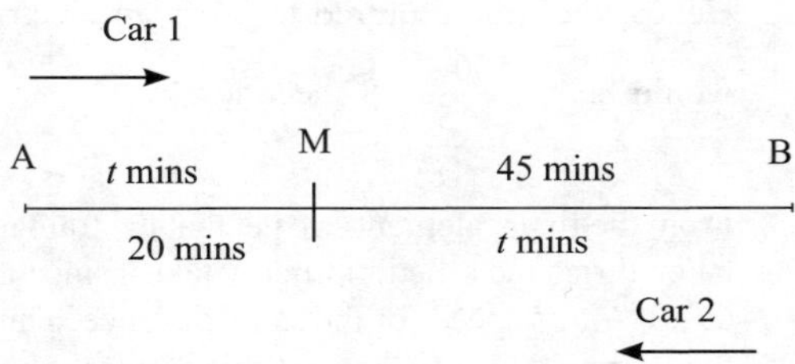

79. From a speed of 8 kmph, to 15 kmph, Amal, has increased his speed by $\frac{7}{8}$. This means that his time will go down by $\frac{7}{15}$ (since the distance is constant). The time actually has gone down by 35 minutes. Hence, if the original time required is t mins, then $\frac{7}{15}\times t=35 \Rightarrow t$ = 75 mins. Hence, since he reaches office at 10:15, it follows that he must have left home at 9 AM. Thus, the distance = 8 × 1.25 = 10 kms. If he leaves at 9:10 and has to reach at 10 AM, he has to reach in 50 minutes or $\frac{5}{6}$ of an hour. The speed required should be such that: $s\times\frac{5}{6}=10 \Rightarrow s = 12$ kmph.

Option (b) is correct.

80. After 2 years, Veeru's amount would be 10000 + 1000 = 11000. Further his interest earned per year will continue to be 5% of 10000 = 500 (since, it is simple interest). Joy, invests 8000 and 10% pa simple interest. This means that he would earn 800 per year simple interest. Thus, Joy would catch up with Veeru's amount at the rate of 300 rupees a year. He will take

10 years to catch up. Hence, the total time required to catch up after Veeru's investment would be $2 + 10 = 12$ years.

81. Initially the solution has 16 dye and 24 water. To this we have to add 16 water to make the dye to water equal a ratio of 2 : 5. At this stage there will be 16 dye and 40 water, a total of 56 liters. When one fourth of this diluted mixture is withdrawn, 14 liters would be withdrawn out of the 56 liters of mixture. Dye and water will come out in the same proportion (i.e. 2 : 5). Thus, dye withdrawn = 4 and water withdrawn = 10. Dye left = 16 – 4 = 12, water left = 40 – 10 = 30. We would need to add 8 liters of dye to make its dye and water ratio as 20 : 30 = 2 : 3. Hence, the correct answer is 8.

82. Let the speed of the train be S kmph. Then, according to the condition given in the question we have:
$(S - 2) \times 90 = (S - 4) \times 100$
$\Rightarrow S = 22$ kmph
Total length of train $= (22 - 2) \times \frac{5}{18} \times 90$
= 500 meters.
Hence, the time required to cross an electric post would be: $\frac{500}{22 \times \frac{5}{18}} \approx 82$ seconds.

83. From the first statement, we get that the train must have taken thrice the time it normally takes, since it traveled at 1/3rd of its speed for the same distance. Thus, if 't' is the original time it takes, on this day it took time '$3t$'.
Extra time taken $= 3t - t = 2t = 30$ minutes
$\Rightarrow$ Normal time = 15 minutes.
On the return journey, in 5 minutes at normal speed, the train would cover 1/3rd the distance. It would be left with a journey of 10 minutes at normal speed. However, it has to cover this distance in 6 minutes $\Rightarrow$ since it stopped for 4 minutes. This entails a 40% decrease in time taken for the same distance – which, means a 66.66% increase in speed would be required. Option (a) is correct.
Note: Alternately, we could have thought of this as: drop in time: $\frac{2}{5}$;
Hence, increase in speed $= \frac{2}{3}$.

84. Using the concept of alligation, you can work out that the ratio of the price of the desktop to the laptop is 2:3. Note: In the case of profit and loss situations, the average profit percentage created on the sale of two items of different costs, is the weighted average of the individual profits on the two items. The weights to be used in such a case would be the ratio of the costs of the two items. In this question, we are given that he makes a profit of 20% and a loss of 10% on the desktop and laptop respectively. Also that he makes an overall profit of 2% $\Rightarrow$ which is what gives us that the ratio of the price of the desktop to the laptop is 2:3. Hence, the price of the desktop is 20000.

85. Let the race be for a distance of 'd'. Then according to the question, we have $\frac{d}{d-50} = \frac{d-45}{d-90}$
Inserting values for d from the options, we see that d = 450, satisfies this equation. Hence, option (b) is correct.

86. Let the distance from A to B be 50 km and from B to C be 150 km. Let the initial speeds of the two trains be 25 and 50 kmph. Train 1 will cover the distance in: $\frac{50}{25} + \frac{150}{50} = 5$ hours; Train 2 will cover the distance in: $\frac{50}{50} + \frac{150}{25} = 7$ hours. Required ratio of time taken is 5:7. Option (b) is correct.

87. If John takes time $2t$, then Jack takes time t for the same work. This means that the work ratio of John and Jack are in the ratio 1:2. Also, it is given to us that Jack and Jim finish the work in one third the time that John takes to finish the work. This means that the work rate of Jack and Jim (combined) is thrice the work rate of John alone. Hence, the ratio of work rates of John, Jack and Jim is 1:2:1. If the total work is taken as 4 units, and their individual rates of work are taken as 1 unit, 2 units and 1 unit per day, we get that together they will take 1 day, while John will take 4 days (i.e. 3 days more than they take together). This satisfies the given condition and hence, Jim will finish the work in $\frac{4}{1} = 4$ days. The correct answer is 4.

88. A B

t 1 min

4 min t

Distance is constant, So ratio of their time taken is same
$\frac{t}{4} = \frac{1}{t}$.
$t^2 = 4$
$t = 2$
Ram takes 3 minutes and Rahim takes 6 minutes
So Ratio of Ram's speed : Rahim's speed
= 2 : 1 = 2
Option (d) is correct.

89. Let the numbers be a, b, c, d, e, f, g, h, i and j, such that a is the smallest number and j the largest. The average of the first 9 numbers is given as 42, hence the sum of the first 9 numbers (a to i) would be 42 × 9 = 378. Likewise, the sum of the last 9 numbers

(b to j) would be $47 \times 9 = 423$. Thus, $j - a = 45$. The instance of the maximum average would be if we take a to i as 42 each and j as 87. In such a case, the sum of the 10 numbers is $378 + 87 = 465$ and their average is 46.5. The other extreme is the minimum average, this would occur when the values of $a = 2$ and b to j is 47 each. In this case, the total is $423 + 2 = 425$ and the minimum average is 42.5.
(Note: we cannot take $a = 0$ and $i = 45$ as in such a case, there will be at least 1 number greater than j to achieve an average of 47 for the last 9 numbers).
The required difference of averages is
$46.5 - 42.5 = 4$
Option (c) is correct.

90. Assume, he buys each toy and labels at ₹1 each. Thus, the labeled price of 12 toys would be a total of rupees 12. He sells, 8 toys at 0.8 and 4 toys at 0.6. Hence, he recovers a total of $6.4 + 2.4 =$ ₹8.8. This represents a profit of 10% on his cost, which means that his cost is $\frac{8.8}{1.1} = 8$ rupees. If he were able to sell all his toys at the labeled price, he would have recovered ₹12 on a cost of 8 rupees. This would mean a profit percentage of 50%.
Option (c) is correct.

91. $P(1.05)^2 - P = CI$
$P = \frac{3 \times 3}{100} = SI$
$CI = 0.1025\ P$
$SI = 0.09P$
$CI - SI = 0.0125P = \left(\frac{125}{10000}\right)\ P = 1125$
$P = 90000$

92. The ratio of money split between Amal, Sunil and Mita will be 6:4:5 or $6x$, $4x$ and $5x$. The difference between the largest and the smallest, i.e. $6x$ and $4x$ is given as 400.
Hence, $2x = 400$
$\Rightarrow x = 200$ and hence, Sunil will get ₹800.

93. $R_1 = 100$ m and $R_2 = 20$m
Speed of Ram = 15 km/hr and
Rahim's speed = 5 km/hr
Time taken by Ram = $2\pi\frac{(100)}{15}$
Time taken by Rahim = $2\pi\frac{(20)}{5}$
Ratio of the time taken by Ram : Rahim to cover the round = 5 : 3. Thus, when after 15 units of time, Ram and Rahim would be at the starting point again. In this situation, Ram would have done 3 rounds and Rahim would have done 5 rounds. Option (c) is correct.

94. Expense of Rice in April = 450 (given)
Increase in 20% in expense of rice = + 90
Since 150 more is the amount he spent in May, + 60 should be the extra expense on wheat.
So 12% of amount spent on Wheat in April is = ₹60
Hence, amount spent on wheat in April = 500
So amount spent on Wheat in May = 500 + 60 = 560.

95. Anil will take 12 minutes to cover a round, while Sunil will take 18 minutes to do so. Hence, they will first meet at the starting point after 36 minutes = 0.6 hours. In this time, distance covered by Ravi will be $8 \times 0.6 = 4.8$ kms.
Option (c) is correct.

96. By 10:30 AM, the train from A, would have already covered 60 km. Thus, the distance between the two trains would be 30 km. Since, they are traveling towards each other, with speeds of 40 and 20 kmph respectively, it means that they would be approaching each other with a relative speed of 60 kmph. At that speed they would take half an hour more to meet. Hence, the time at which they would meet would be 11 AM. Option (b) is correct.

97. Assume that he bought the sugar at ₹1 per kg. Hence, his total purchase price is ₹35. His marked price will be 1.2. According to the conditions in the problem, he sells 5 kg at the marked price and 15 kgs at a 10% discount on the marked price. He also loses 3 kgs as wastage. Hence, his total recovery for these $5 + 15 + 3$
$= 23$ kgs would be:
$5 \times 1.2 + 15 \times 1.08 + 3 \times 0 = 22.2$.
In order to gain an overall 15%, he needs to recover a total of $35 \times 1.15 = 40.25$.
Thus, he has to sell the remaining 12 kgs for $40.25 - 22.2 =$ ₹18.05. The selling price has to be approximately 1.5. From a marked price of 1.2, he needs approximately a 25% markup to get to a selling price of 1.5. Hence, option (b) is correct.

98. The correct answer can be simply derived using:
$$\frac{18522}{1.05 \times 1.05 \times 1.05} = 16000.$$
(**Note:** You are advised to do such calculations on the calculator in the CAT.)

99. Let Tom = t, Dick = $3t$ and Harry = $6t$. Average age = $10t/3 = 3.33t$.
Difference between average age and Dick's age = $0.33t = 1$year $\Rightarrow t = 3$.
Hence, the age of Harry is 18 years.

100. This problem has to be solved in two parts.
First part: When, Vimla reduces her speed by $1/8^{th}$, her time would go up by $1/7^{th}$ (since distance traveled is constant). It is given to us that her time increases by 6 minutes. Thus, 6 minutes is $1/7^{th}$ of the time she normally takes to reach her office. Hence, at 40 kmph, she would take 42 minutes (or

0.7 hours). Hence, the distance to her office is 40 × 0.7 = 28 kms.

Second part: It is given to us that: 'she covers two – thirds of her distance to office in one – thirds of her usual time to reach office, and then stops for 8 minutes.' This essentially means that she has covered 2/3rd of 28 kms = 18.66 kms and has consumed 14 + 8 = 22 mins to do so. She has 20 more minutes to reach office on time and in that time she has to cover 9.33 kms more. Her speed in kmph = 28 kmph in order to cover 9.33 km in 20 minutes (use unitary method thinking here). Option (c) is correct.

101. The difference between Bishnu's and Asha's percentage score is 12%. This difference is also given to us as 23 + 34 = 57 (Interpretation of the second line of the question). Hence, we can deduce that since 12% is 57, 100% will be 475. (using unitary method). Geeta's score would be 84% of 475 = 399. Option (b) is correct.

102. The contractor finishes 1.5 km in 60 days with 140 people.
That means, he finishes, 0.5 km in 20 days with 140 people.
He has 200 – 60 = 140 days left to finish the job.
Also, since he has to do a total of 6 km, he needs to do triple the work already done. The work already done was 140 × 60 (number of men × number of days).
Work to be done in next 140 days = 3 × 140 × 60 = 180 × 140. Since the number of days left is 140, the number of men required is 180. He has to hire 180 – 140 = 40 men.

103. Initially the ratio of A:B is 1:3. Then, if the mixture is doubled by adding A, it means that we are adding 4 of A, to make the effective A:B ratio as: 5:3. The percentage of alcohol in solution B can be worked out using alligations as shown:

60% 72% ?
A B
5 3

The value of B works out to 92%. Option (a) is correct.

104. The average score of the last 2 innings

$$=\frac{(38+15)}{2}=26.5$$

The average of the first n innings = 30
The average of all the n + 2 innings = 29.
29 × (n + 2) = n × 30 + 2 × 26.5
n = 5
The average of the first 5 innings = 30 and in none of the innings did the batsman score 38 or above. The minimum score for an innings will happen if we maximise the scores of the first 4 innings at 37 each. Hence, the minimum possible score in any one inning = 150 – 37 × 4 = 150 – 148 = 2.

105. 2A + 4O + 6M = 1A + 4O + 8M → A = 2M. Thus, 1A + 4O + 8M = 10M + 4O. Also, we have that 8O + 7M also costs the same. Thus, 10M + 4O = 8O + 7M → 4O = 3M.
For the same amount of money he can purchase 8O + 7M = 6M + 7M = 13 mangoes.

106. There is an increase of 60.47 rupees in the interest in the third year – over the interest on the second year. This represents the extra interest Anil must have got in the third year due to the interest he has earned during the second year. Thus, the rate of interest can be found out using the percentage value of $\frac{60.47}{806.25}$ = 7.5%.
In the fourth year his interest will again grow by 7.5%, which means that his fourth year interest is 866.72 × 1.075 = 931.72 (**Note:** You should use the on–screen calculator in the CAT for these calculations)

107. Let Amal purchase 100 + n pens. Then, his total revenue is 100 × 12 + n × 11 in the first case. If the wages of the employee is W, we have the equation:
100 × 12 + n × 11 – 300 = (100 + n) × 8 + W (1)
From the second situation, we get:
100 × 12 + n × 9 + 300 = (100 + n) × 8 + W (2)
Equating the LHS of the two equations (since the RHS is the same in both), we get:
2n = 600 → n = 300. We can get the value of W = 1000, by inserting this value of n into either of the two equations.

108. If we assume, N, G and S as their respective daily incomes, we have:
N + G = 6S & S + N = 2G. From here, use the options to try to fit in the values. It is intuitively evident from these equations that Sita's earnings are quite low compared to the other two.
If we take the ratio between the highest and lowest earners as 11 : 3 (from the fourth option), and we freeze the least income for Seeta, we can try to check for G = 11 or N = 11. If we insert G = 11 and S = 3 in the first equation, we get N = 7. These numbers do not satisfy the second equation.
If we try to reverse, N = 11, S = 3, we get G = 7. These numbers fit the second equation perfectly and hence this option is the correct one.

109. Let the work rates of Amar, Akbar and Anthony be a, b, c respectively. Also, let the total work be 48 units of work. The a + b = 4 (units of work per month); b + c = 3 and a + c = 2. Thus, 2a + 2b + 2c = 9 & a + b + c = 4.5. Thus, c = 4.5 – 4 = 0.5 units of work per month. Thus, b = 2.5 units of work per month and a = 1.5 units of work per month. We

are asked for how long the medium paced worker would take to finish the job. The answer can be got by identifying that we need to find the number of months for B to complete the job. Answer = 48/1.5 = 32.

110. Let the total work be 60 units. Then, A = 4 units, B = 5 units and C = 3 units of work per day (60/15; 60/12 and 60/3 respectively).
Also, their rates of combined work is (5 + 4) = 9 on odd days and 5 + 3 = 8 on even days. Thus, in 2 days, total work done would be 9 + 8 = 17. In 6 days the work done would be 17 × 3 = 51. On the 7th day Anu and Vinu would work and complete the remaining 9 units of work on that day. They require 7 days to finish the work. Thus, option (a) is correct.

111. Let hospital A admit $n - 21$ patients. Then, hospital B would admit n patients. The average recovery days in hospital A= $200/(n - 21)$ and for hospital B= $152/n$. According to the question: $(152/n) + 3 = 200/(n–21)$. This, would lead to a quadratic equation, yielding $n = 56$ and $n - 21 = 35$. Hence, the number of patients admitted in hospital A = 35.

112. For the first 3 months, take the total spending to be $300x$. Then, the consumption for the first three months are $30x$, $15x$ and $12x$ respectively. The total spending in the last two months being half that of the first three months, the total spending would be: $150x$. Hence, the consumption of onions would be 6x and $3x$ respectively for months 4 and 5. Thus, the ratio of consumption for the five months is 10 : 5 : 4 : 2 : 1. Using weighted average, the average price will be given by:

$$\frac{10\times10+5\times20+4\times25+2\times25+1\times50}{22}=\frac{400}{22}.$$

Thus, the closest answer is 18. Option (d) is correct.

113. Let the smaller box contain 100 grams and let the average selling price of the chocolate in the smaller box be P rupees per gram. The total cost of the smaller box would be 100P. The larger box would be priced at 0.88P per gram and the total price would be 200P. The contents in the larger box would be equal to 200P/0.88P = 227.27 grams. This means that against the weight of the smaller box, the larger box has 127% extra. Hence, option (a) is correct.

114. From the information that the faster train crosses a pole in 12 seconds, we can see that it has a speed of (160/12 =13.33 m/s). The slower train has a speed of $13.33-6\times\frac{5}{18}=10.666$ m/s. Thus, their relative speed while crossing each other = 13.333+10.666=25 m/s. In 14 seconds total distance traveled would be 350 meters. This would also equal the sum of the lengths of the two trains. Hence, the length of the slower train = 350 – 160 = 190 meters. Option (d) is correct.

115. This is a classic alligation situation. When you are mixing a 33% solution from the first bottle with a 17% solution from the second bottle, you are ending up with a 21% solution overall. This means, that the ratio of mixing is 1:3 (first bottle to second bottle). Also, you need to understand that after the mixing the first bottle is completely full (viz: 800 ml) with the 1:3 mixture from the first and second bottles respectively. Thus, 600 ml must have been taken out from the second bottle and transferred to the first. The residual amount of solution left in the second bottle would be 800 – 600 = 200.

116. Let the number of White balls be W and the number of black balls be B. Then, we have: 0.4W (Metallic White balls) = 0.5B (Metallic Black Balls) → W : B = 5 : 4. Thus, there are a total of 250 White balls and 200 Black Balls. The number of metallic balls = 0.4W + 0.5B = 100 + 100 = 200. Hence, the number of non-metallic balls = 450 – 200 = 250.

117. Let the person buy 2 kgs, 3 kgs and 5 kgs of the three varieties of teas respectively. The average cost can be worked out as:

$$\frac{2\times800+3\times500+5\times300}{10}=460.$$

His total cost would be 4600 for 10 kgs. Also, since he is selling one-sixth of his tea at 700, it might be a good idea to increase the amounts bought by a multiple of 6. Thus, assume that he bought 12, 18 and 30 kgs of the three teas for a total of 460 × 60 = 27600. For a 50% profit, he needs a revenue of 27600 × 1.5 = 41400. Of this he gets a revenue of 700 × 10 = 7000 by selling 10 kgs. He has to generate, 34400 by selling 50 kgs. Price in INR = 688. Option (d) is correct.

118. If the player has played n matches till date and scored g goals, we get the equations: $g + 1 = 0.15 \times (n + 10)$ & $g + 2 = 0.2 \times (n + 10)$. $g = 2$ and $n = 10$ would be the respective values. The question has asked us for the value of n, which is 10. Hence, the correct answer is 10.

119. The final ratio of 16 : 9, means that there is 64% milk and 36% water in the mixture. This is after 2 iterations. This can only occur if we are taking out 20% of the mixture every time (Think successive percentage decrease of 20% twice on the PCG). Thus, 9 liters being drawn off represents 20% of the total mixture. Hence, the total mixture is 45 liters.

120. Let the total work be 420 units. In such a case, Anil's one day's work = 7 units and Bimal does 5 units per day. Anil works for 10 days and will do 70 units of work in 10 days. Work left = 350. Work done per day by Anil, Bimal and Charu = $\frac{350}{14}$ = 25 units.

So Charu does a total of 13 units of work per day (25 – 7 – 5). In 14 days, Charu will do 14 × 13 = 182 units of work. His share of the payment would be:

$$\frac{182}{420} \times 21000 = 9100$$

Option (d) is correct.

121. Let the filling rate of pipe A be *a*% per hour and the draining rate of Pipe B be *b*% per hour. Then from the given conditions in the problem, we can make the equations: $8a - 7b = 100$ and $4a - 2b = 100 \rightarrow$ b = 33.33% and a = 41.66%. Time required to fill the tank if only A is opened = $\frac{100}{41.666} = \frac{300}{125} = 2.4$ hours = 144 minutes. Option (b) is correct.

122. When the profit percent of the business goes down from 18 to 15%, it means that the profit would drop by $\frac{1}{6}^{\text{th}}$ and that would also be the drop in the profit share of Anil. Thus, Anil's profit share for 18% profit in the business is 2520, while, his profit becomes 2100 when the business makes 15% profit. Also, from the statement about Chintu, we see that Chintu's profit at 15% rate of profit must have been 600. (To work this out, use the following thought – When profit percentage increases from 15 to 17, Chintu's profit increases by ₹80. Thus, using Unitary method, we can see that Chintu's profit at 15% profit percentage would be 600. Now, we know that when the profit percentage is 15%, Anil gets 2100 (70% of the profit) and Chintu gets 600 (20% of the profit). Thus, the total profit would be 3000 and Bobby would get 10% of the total profit – meaning he has invested 10% of the total amount. Further, this 3000 profit represents a percentage profit of 15% on the total investment. Thus, the total investment must be 20000. Bobby's investment being 10% of this would be 2000. Option (d) is correct.

123. Let the loss percentage be *n*%. Then the profit percentage in the second year on the residual capital, would be 5*n*%. In such a case, the net profit on the initial investment is 35% at the end of 2 years. Thus, 10000 would have become 13500 in 2 years. From this point, do a trial and error with the options. If we try to use option (a), we get 10% loss in the first year → Balance amount after loss = 9000. Profit in second year = 50% on 9000 = 4500. Thus, the amount at the end of the second year = 13500, which matches the condition of the problem. Hence, option (a) is correct.

124. Let the speeds of trains A and B be 5s and 3s in meters/second respectively. Their relative speed while crossing each other would be 5s + 3s = 8s. By the statement, 'The front end of A crossed the rear end of B, 46 seconds after the front ends of the trains had crossed each other' we should interpret that the length of Train B = 46 × 8s meters. From the other condition of the question, we can understand that the length of Train A = 69 × 8s meters. The ratio of lengths of Train A and B would be 69 : 46 = 3 : 2. Option (d) is correct.

125. Let the price of the smallest and medium-sized cups be 2*p* and 5*p* respectively. If the price of the largest cup is L, we have $10 \times p^2 \times L = 800 \rightarrow p^2L = 80$. Also, we have: $(2p + 6) \times (5p + 6) \times (L) = 3200$ Trying to fit in numbers to match these equations, rather than solving these two equations algebraically will be a better strategy to get to the answers faster. You can spot that: If $p = 2$, L = 20 form the first equation. In that case the second equation becomes 10 × 16 × 20 = 3200 and matches the requirements. Hence, the sum of original prices of the three would be $2p + 5p + L = 4 + 10 + 20 = 34$.

126. If he bought S, small shirts and L large shirts, we have from the first statement that S + L = 64. Also, if the price of a small shirt is P, the price of the large shirt is (P + 50). From the payments mentioned, we get the equations L × (P + 50) = 5000 & S × P = 1800. Use the options to proceed from this point. If the price of the large shirt and small shirt together is 200, (as given in option (b)) it means that P = 75 and P + 50 = 125. L = $\frac{5000}{125}$ = 40 & S= $\frac{1800}{75}$ = 24. These numbers match S + L = 64. Hence, this option is correct. You can check the other options to confirm that for any other value of the sum of prices of the small and large shirts the numbers for L and S would not match the given conditions. Option (b) is correct.

127. The total cost of the hostel can be seen as F + 50V for 50 boarders, F + 75V at 75 boarders and F + 80V at 80 boarders. Also, revenues would be 50 × 1600 = 80000 for 50 boarders, 75 × 1600 = 120000 for 75 boarders and 80 × 1600 = 128000 for 80 boarders. Profit at 50 boarders = 50 × 200 = 10000 can also be written as: 80000 – (F + 50V) = 10000 & at 75 boarders the profit can be written as 120000 – (F + 75V) = 75 × 250 = 18750. Solving we get V = 1250 & F = 7500. For 80 boarders, the total cost would be 80 × 1250 + 7500 = 107500. Profit = 1600 × 80 – 107500 = 20500. Option (c) is correct.

128. The team would have won 12 matches out of 40. Using, alligation, since win rate of 30% and win rate of 60% combines to form a net win rate of 50% in all the matches played, we get the ratio of number of matches already played to the number of matches to be played would be 1:2. Hence, the team is going to play another 80 matches. If it wins 90% of it's remaining 80 matches, the team would be winning another 72 matches, in the tournament.

Thus, the total number of wins for the team would be 84. Option (a) is correct.

129. From 1970 to 1980, the female population grew by 20%, while the male population grew by 40%. In the same time the overall population grew by 25%. This means that the ratio of the male to female population in the city is 1 : 3. The numbers can be visualized as shown in the table:

	1970	1980	1990
Female population	300n	360n	450n
Male population	100n	140n	225n
Overall Population	400n	500n	675n

The total population has increased from 400n to 675n from 1970 to 1990. This is a percentage growth given by the ratio of $\frac{275}{400}$ → 68.75%. Option (d) is correct.

130. In opposite directions, total distance covered by Amal and Mira in 45 minutes = 15 rounds (since they cover a round in 3 minutes together). This means, that when they were walking in the same direction, their respective coverage in 45 minutes would be 9 rounds and 6 rounds (since 9 + 6 = 15 & further it is known that Amal completes exactly 3 rounds more than Mira in 45 minutes. Thus, Mira walks 1 round in $\frac{45}{6}$ = 7.5 minutes & hence she would cover 8 rounds in an hour.

131. Check through the options. If from option (a), we take the desired weight of the initial alloy to be 3 kgs, then from the first situation we can work out that the percentage concentration of silver would be 80%. You can visualize 3 kg of 80% alloy and 2 kg of 90% silver giving you exactly 84% silver alloy in the second case. Hence, this option is correct.

132. Let the total work be 48 units of work. Anil = 4 units per day, Barun = 3 units per day. With Chandu, they complete the work in 6 days. Thus, one day's work of A, B and C = A + B + C = $\frac{48}{6}$ = 8 units. This means C = 8 – 4 – 3 = 1. Thus, Chandu, would do $\frac{6}{48}$ of the work in 6 days and would get paid $\frac{1}{8}$th of the amount. Hence, the correct answer is $\frac{24000}{8}$ = 3000.

133. Let Rahul's work in an hour be R and Gautam's work in an hour be G. From the first scenario, the total work = 8R + 6G. From the second scenario, the total work = 7.5R + 7.5G. Equating the two, we get: 0.5R = 1.5G → R = 3G. Hence, the total work = 8R + 6G = 8R + 2R = 10R. Thus, Rahul would complete the work alone in 10 hours. Option (d) is correct.

134. The total score of 25 students = 25 × 50 = 1250. Scores of the lowest 20 students = 30 + 31 + 32 +... + 49 = 20 × 39.5 = 790. The total score of the five top students would be 1250 – 790 = 460. Since, they have each got the same marks, it means that each of them scores $\frac{460}{5}$ = 92 marks.

135. Let Raju have invested an amount equal to P. Raju would receive 6.09 percent interest on his amount in Bank A after a year → 3% compounded twice. Since, in Bank B he has earned the same amount of interest for a Principal P at a rate of interest r for a time period t (at simple interest), it means that the principal P at rate of interest r for time period t would yield an interest of 6.09% of the principal in Bank B. In Bank C, if Rupa had invested the same principal for double the period, she would have earned an interest rate of 2r (since the interest rate in Bank C is twice the interest rate offered in Bank B). For a Principal P, Time period 2t and interest 2r, the interest earned would be 4 times the interest on the same principal for time period t and interest r. We have already worked the latter out to be 6.09% from our analysis of Raju's interest earning. Hence, Rupa would get an interest equal to 6.09 × 4 = 24.36% on her principal of 10000. Hence, the interest accrued to Rupa would be 2436. Option (d) is correct.

136.

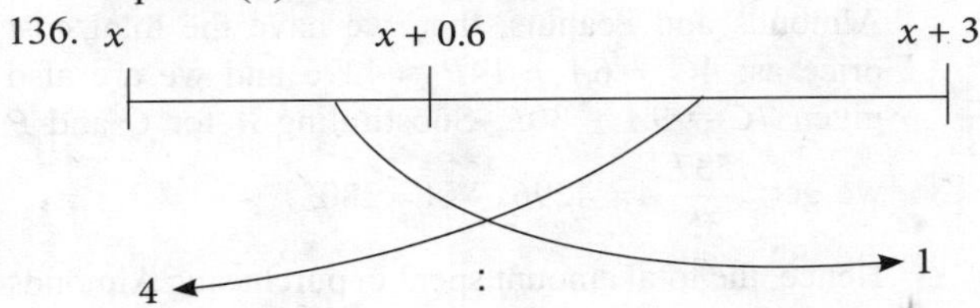

137. The situation can be represented as shown (where t is the amount of time taken by each of them to reach their meeting point):

X —A→ t | (10 – t) Y; 9, t ←B

Solving for t, we get t = 6. Hence, the total time taken by Train A would be 15 minutes. Option (b) is correct.

138. Assume the cost price of Juice as 10x and that of syrup as 8x. His total cost price would be $110 \times 8x + 120 \times 10x = 2080x$. His revenue from 10 and 20 kg sale of syrup and juice = $10 \times 8.8x + 20 \times 12x = 328x$. After selling the entire contents his revenue = $2080x \times 1.64 = 3411.2x$. Thus, he gets a revenue of $3411.2x - 328x = 3083.2x$ when he sells 200 kgs. Thus, his per kg price while selling

is $\frac{3083.2x}{200} = 15.416x = 308.32 \rightarrow x = 20$. Thus, the required price of syrup is $8x = 160$. 160 is the correct answer.

139. The ratio of illiterate males to females is given as 4 : 3. Let their numbers be $4n$ and $3n$ respectively. Also, since the number of literate males is given as 3600, the literate females would be 5400 (since these are given as a ratio of 2 : 3 in the problem). Then from the overall 5 : 4 ratio we have: $\frac{3600+4n}{5400+3n} = \frac{5}{4} \rightarrow n = 12600$. Hence, the total number of females is: $12600 \times 3 + 5400 = 43200$

140. The key to this question is understanding that she has 24 kgs of the mixture, of which he sells 4 kgs at the marked price and the remaining 20 kgs at a 20% discounted price. The effect on his profit because of the discount is a drop of 1008. From this it can be inferred that the marked price of 20 kgs (which she sold at a discount) would have been 1008 × 5 = ₹5040. Also, the marked price of the entire lot would be $5040 \times \frac{6}{5} = 6048$. We can also infer that her cost price must have been 6048 – 1752 = 4296. (as 1752 is the profit he would have earned if she had sold everything at the marked price)
Now, if C, A and P are the cost prices of Cashews, Almonds and Peanuts, then we have the total cost price as: $4C + 6A + 14P = 4296$ and we are also given $7C = 9A = 30P$. Substituting A for C and P we get: $\frac{537}{35}A = 4296 \rightarrow A = 280$.

Hence, the total amount spent in purchasing Almonds is 280 × 6 = 1680. Option (c) is correct.

141. We can infer that if A is the amount of the first investment and B is the amount of the second investment then 60% of A = 36% of B. Hence, A/B = 3/5. The first investment accounts for 37.5% of his total investment. Option (a) is correct.

142. The sum of the three integers is 39. If 5 is added, the average becomes 11. It can be easily seen that it does not happen if 1, 2, 3 or 4 are added. Hence, n's minimum value being 5, option (d) is correct.

143. Assume, we add 100 ml of the mixture to 300 ml of sugar syrup. The total lemon juice in the mixture would be 50 and sugar syrup would be 50 + 300 = 350. The required ratio would be 1 : 7. Option (a) is correct.

144. If we assume that his total investment is 300, then his three investments would be: 60, 100 and 140 respectively. His yearly interest income would be 60@6% = 3.6; 100@10% = 10; 140@1% = 1.4. Thus, his annual total simple interest would be 15, which he would earn every year. In order to earn 300 or more as his interest income, he would take a minimum of $\frac{300}{15} = 20\ years$

145. The total marks of the 5 students would be 5 × 38 = 190. At one extreme the top 3 students can score 50, 49 and 48 marks. The fourth student can score a maximum of 32 marks. This situation will give us the minimum marks for Amit as 190 – 50 – 49 – 48 – 32 = 11.
The maximum marks for Amit will be when he scores 31 and the next person scores 32, while the three top students can score a total of 190 – 31 – 32 = 127 marks in a variety of combinations. Hence, the difference between maximum and minimum marks for Amit would be 31 – 11 = 20.

146. Since the times taken by them to complete the job is in the ratio of 5 : 8 : 10, if we assume a job as 80 units, we get their work rates as 16 : 10 : 8. Let us assume that Anu, Tanu and Manu do 16 units, 10 units and 8 units of work per hour. Then the total work for the job described would be (16 + 10 + 8) × 4 × 8 = 1088 units. Anu and Tanu, working 6 hours 40 minutes per day, would do 40 hours of work and hence would complete 40 × (16 + 10) = 1040 units of work. The remaining 48 units of work can be done by Manu is 48/8 = 6 hours.

147. Let the total number of voters who voted by $300n$. The vote distribution amongst the candidates was: $90n$, $35n$, $70n$ and $105n$. Thus, the difference between the top two candidates is $15n = 2512 \rightarrow 300n = 2512$ × 20 = 50240. This is 80% of the registered voters. Hence, the total voters = $50240 \times \frac{5}{4} = 62800$.

148. Since, a and b are non-negative real numbers and $a + 2b = 6$, we have $a = 0$, $b = 3$ as one extreme value of a, b; If we start to increase a upwards from 0 and decrease b from 3, we see that the value of $a + b$ starts to increase (for instance at $a = 0.1$, $b = 2.95$; $a + b = 3.05$). Hence, we reach the other extreme when we reach $b = 0$ at $a = 6$. Hence, the other extreme is $a = 6$, $b = 0$. The average of the minimum and maximum possible value of $a + b$ = $\frac{3+6}{2} = 4.5$.

149. The right angled triangle formed has a hypotenuse of 60 kms. Since, the speeds of the boats differ by 6, the difference in the lengths of the legs of the right triangle would be 6 × 2 = 12 kms. The triangle formed is a 36 – 48 – 60 right triangle. This means the slower ship has traveled 36 kms in 2 hours and hence has a speed of 18 kmph. Option (d) is correct.

150. Let the two containers have capacities of 100 ml each. There are a total of 3 transfers.

After the first transfer: First container: Sugar syrup 25; Second container: Sugar syrup: 25, Milk: 50.
After the second transfer: First container: Sugar syrup: 25 + 12.5 = 37.5; Milk = 0 + 25; Second container: Sugar Syrup: 25 – 12.5 = 12.5; Milk = 50 – 25 = 25.
After the third transfer: Second container: Sugar syrup: 12.5 + 18.75 = 31.25; Milk: 25 + 12.5 = 37.5.
Ratio of sugar syrup to milk in second container = 31.25 : 37.5 = 5 : 6. Option (c) is correct.

151. Since his target savings are 550 per month, it means that he is targeting a total saving of 550 × 12 = 6600 for the year. In the first 9 months he would have saved 9 × (4000 – 3500) = 4500. He needs to save 6600 – 4500 = 2100 in the last 3 months i.e. 700 per month. Hence, his income from the 10th month onwards would need to be 3700 + 700 = 4400. Option (d) is correct.

152.

	Glass	*Cup*
Initial	500 milk	500 water
After first transfer	350 milk	500 water + 150 milk
After second transfer	$350 + \frac{3}{13} \times 150$ milk & $\frac{10}{13} \times 150$ water	$500 - \frac{10}{13} \times 150$ water; $150 - \frac{3}{13} \times 150$ milk

Required ratio = $\dfrac{\frac{10}{13} \times 150}{\frac{1500}{13}} = 1:1$

Option (c) is correct.

153. Let the speed of the escalator be x steps per second and Moody's walking speed be y steps per second. Then we have from the information:
$30x + 30y = 20\,x + 20 \times 2y \rightarrow x = y$. Hence, the total distance on the escalator is $30x + 30y = 60x$. At a speed of x steps per second, the escalator would cover a distance of $60x$ steps in 60 seconds.

154. Let the total work be 600, then the work rate of Alex would be 30, Bob 15 and Cole 10.
The 3 day pattern of work would be 45 $(A + B)$ + 25 $(B + C)$ + 40$(A + C)$ = 110. There would be 5 completed sets of this 3 day work pattern adding up to 550 units of work. On the 16th day A & B would do 45 units of work and the work will get completed in 1/5th of the 17th day (with B & C working). Hence, Alex would work for 5 × 2 + 1 = 11 days.

155. This is a straight question. The speed of the slower car is given as 60 kmph and it is given that the two cars need to travel for 1.5 hours when they are approaching each other, in order to meet each other. Thus, the distance traveled by the slower car before meeting would be 1.5 × 60 = 90.

156. The average of both sections together would be larger than 46, since the number of students in Section B is larger than those in Section A. Also, depending on the average of the total we can try to work out the number of students in each section and see if the difference of 10 can be maintained. For instance, we can see that an average of 59 is not possible to be achieved, since if the overall average is 59, the ratio of number of students in Section A: Section B = 1 : 27 i.e. if there are k students in Section A, there will be $27k$ students in section B. Their difference of $26k$ cannot be equal to 10, if the number of students is an integer and hence we can reject this as a possible scenario. A trial and error approach will give us that at an overall average of 56, the ratio of Section A : Section B students = 4 : 24 = 1 : 6. Also, since the difference between the two is 10, we get 2 and 12 as the minimum number of students for Section A and B. For maximizing the number of students in Section A, we can try an average of 47. In this case, the ratio of Section A : Section B students = 13 : 15, gives us 65 students in section A and 75 in section B.
The required difference = 65 – 2 = 63.

157. If we try to use only 100 and 250 rupee cheques to make 15250, we can use 150 hundred rupee cheques and 1 two-fifty rupee cheque to make the amount. If we keep the number of 250 rupee cheques constant at 1, the remaining 15000 can be made using 100 and 500 cheques in multiple combinations like: 150, 0; 145, 1; 140, 2; 135, 3 and so on. Since we are trying to reduce the total number of cheques to 100, we get close to 100 at 85 hundred rupee and 13 five-hundred rupee cheques. Thus, we get a combination of 85 – 1 – 13 of the three types of cheques to get a value of 15250. However, in this case, we have used only 99 cheques, which goes against the problem's conditions. Thus, 13 cheques of 500 rupees are not possible. This can also be confirmed by the thought that if one has 13 cheques of 500, the total amount becomes 6500. The balance amount is 8750, in 87 cheques, which is not possible by using 100 and 250-rupee cheques. For twelve 500 rupee cheques, total amount would become 6000. Balance 9250 in 88 cheques is possible using 85 and 3 of hundred and 250 rupee cheques. Hence, the correct answer is 12.

158. Her combined annual total interest being 5% of capital, should be ₹1000. She earns 5.5% on 8000 = 440; 5.6% on 5000 = 280. So she earns (1000 – 440 – 280 = 280) on the balance 7000, which means that the rate of interest x% mentioned in the question is equal to 4%. If she had invested the entire 20000 @4%, her annual interest income would have been ₹800. Option (b) is correct.

159. Let the numbers be a, b, c, d, e, f. The sum of the two smallest would be 28 (say $a + b$), the sum of the two largest would be 56 (say $e + f$). Thus, $a + b + e + f = 84$. The largest possible values of the two middle numbers c, d would be 25 and 26 (as e and f can at best be taken as 27, 29 to leave scope for c, d to be maximized). In this case, the total of all the six numbers is 84 + 25 + 26 = 135. The average of these six numbers is $\frac{135}{6} = 22.5$. Option (d) is correct.

160. $N \times 7 \times 10 = 0.35J$ (where J = the total job); $(N-10)10 \times 14 = 140N - 1400 = 0.65J$.

Thus, we have:

$$\frac{70N}{140N-1400} = \frac{7}{13} \rightarrow 910N = 980N - 9800$$

$\rightarrow 70N = 9800 \therefore N = 140$.

Option (a) is correct.

BLOCK STARTER

Scan this QR code to access a video on this block's chapters, the time needed to cover them, and their weightage in the examination.

BLOCK

GEOMETRY

BACK TO SCHOOL...

The word GEOMETRY is derived from two words—GEO meaning earth and METRY meaning measurement. Hence, it is quite evident that geometry as a mathematical science developed mainly due to the human need of measuring land masses and distances. The major developments in the fields of geometry and mensuration are mainly credited to the ancient Egyptian and Greek civilisations. (In fact, this is one of the reasons why all formulae and theorems primarily carry Greek names.)

Key Geometrical Concepts

Point: The point should be visualised as a singular dot. In physical terms, a point can be defined as a single dot that can be created on a plain paper by a very sharp pencil. It could also be visualised as a singular prick on a piece of paper by a very sharp nail or pin.

Line: Mathematically, lines are defined as a group of points which are straight one after another. All lines are supposed to extend infinitely in two directions.

Segment of a Line

If a part of a line is cut out, we get a segment of a line.

Physically, the closest representations of a segment of a line would be a tight thread or the straight crease of a piece of paper.

Plane: The surface of a smooth wall or a table top is the closest representation of a portion of a plane.

Some Geometrical Properties

1. Lines Between Points: Let us take two distinct points in a plane. You can easily verify that an infinite number of lines can be drawn in the plane passing through any one of these two points. However, if you wanted to draw a line which passes through both the points, you will be able to draw only one line. This is an important result in geometry.

Property: Given any two distinct points in a plane, there exists one and only one line containing both the points. Alternately, we can state that two distinct points in a plane determine a unique line.

2. Collinearity of Points: Collinear or non-collinear points are only defined in the context of three or more points.

Consider the situation of three points. There can only be two cases with respect to three points:

(a) All the points lie on the same line. (Here, the points are said to be collinear).

(b) All the three points do not lie on the same line (In this case, the points are said to be non-collinear).

(Note: It is quite evident that we will discuss collinear or non-collinear points only if the number of points is more than two. Obviously, if there are only two points they would always lie on one line.)

3. Points in Common between Distinct Lines: In the case of distinct lines, there can only be two cases:

(a) There is one point in common: In such a case, the common point is called the point of intersection, and the two lines are called as intersecting lines.

(b) There is no point in common: In such a case, the two lines are non-intersecting and are also called as parallel lines.

The property can, thus, be stated as:

Property: Two distinct lines in a plane cannot have more than one point in common.

4. Lines and Points:

Property: Given a line and a point in the same plane, such that the point is not on the line, there is one and only one line which passes through the point and is parallel to the given line.

5. Lines:

Property: Two intersecting lines cannot be parallel to the same line.

6. Multiple Lines: There can be four distinct possibilities in such a case.

(a) No two lines intersect each other
(b) Some lines intersect
(c) Every line intersects all other lines, but their respective points of intersection are different from each other.
(d) Every pair of lines is intersecting and all the points of intersection coincide

The reader is required to visualise the figures for each of these situations.

The remaining formulae and results for geometry have been given within the chapter. You are required to move to the respective formulae. However, an important note while you are doing this.

Important Note

One of the least understood issues with respect to this block is:

How does a person move from:

"Cannot Solve Geometry and Mensuration!" to "Can Solve Geometry and Mensuration!"?

In fact, this transition should be your sole aim while studying and solving this block of chapters.

As you are already aware, mere knowledge of formulae does not guarantee this movement. Then in that case what should a person do if he/she has to engineer this transition of abilities?

Well, the answer is really quite simple and for understanding the same, you need to move out of conventional mathematical study processes. In your mind you need to create an awareness of how to think while solving a geometry/mensuration question. Here are a few tips that will help you through this transition:

1. Some Formulae are More Important than Others: For the CAT (and indeed, all other MBA and aptitude examinations) your concentration should not be on memorising complex formulae. A close study of the past trends for questions from this block will show you that the formulae themselves can be graded into the important and the not so important formulae. In fact, if you study over 200 questions from this block that have been asked in the CAT in the past decade or more, you will realise that over 98% of the questions are simply based on a small subset of geometrical formulae and results. This important set of formulae is listed below for your convenience:

Lines: Properties related to intersecting lines and angles formed

Polygons: Basic properties of regular polygons

Triangles: Pythagoras theorem, 30-60-90 triangle, 45-45-90 triangle, Sine rule, properties of exterior angles of a triangle, equilateral triangle, isosceles triangle

Quadrilaterals: Areas, perimeters, diagonals and angles between diagonals for all standard quadrilaterals.

Hexagon: A hexagon can be divided into six equal triangles.

2. Length/Area/Volume Measuring Formulae versus Angle Measuring Formulae: In your mind, divide the formulae into length/area/volume measuring formulae on the one hand and angle measuring formulae on the other hand. This will be very helpful, since most questions in this block can be clearly segregated as length or angle measuring questions. In such a scenario, in case you have a question requiring angle measurements, you will only require to think of angle measuring formulae.

(**Note:** There are very few formulae that connect lengths with angles. (for example, Sine rule and Cosine rule in the context of triangles).

---

3. Use of Reverse Flowcharting for Solving Questions: All questions in geometry and mensuration ask you to find a particular value. Very often, it makes the question much more convenient to solve if instead of trying to find what is asked, you try to find a value which is related to the required value.

Thus, for example, if in a triangle ABC angle A is given to be 40° and angle B is asked for and you are not getting a clear strategy for getting the value of angle B, then it might be wise to try to derive the value of angle C. If you can get C, then B will be obtained by 140-C.

This process is called as reverse flowcharting and is an extremely crucial process for solving questions in geometry.

In other words, it can also be seen to be a deflection of the original question into a more convenient question.

(**Note:** You are advised to concentrate on the special note for solving CAT questions provided prior to the LOD I Questions while studying this block.)

CHAPTER 12

Geometry and Mensuration

Chapter Launchpad

Scan this QR code to access a video on 'Introduction to Geometry and Mensuration' and this chapter's importance for CAT

The chapters on geometry and mensuration have their own share of questions in the CAT and other MBA entrance examinations. For doing well in questions based on this chapter, the student should familiarise themselves with the basic formulae and visualisations of the various shapes of solids and two-dimensional figures based on this chapter.

The following is a comprehensive collection of formulae based on two-dimensional and three-dimensional figures:

For the purpose of this chapter, we have divided the theory in two parts:

- Part I consists of geometry and mensuration of two-dimensional figures
- Part II consists of mensuration of three-dimensional figures

PART I: GEOMETRY

INTRODUCTION

Geometry and Mensuration are important areas in the CAT examination. In the Online CAT, the Quantitative Aptitude section has consisted of an average of 15–20% questions from these chapters. Besides, questions from these chapters appear prominently in all major aptitude based exams for MBAs, Bank POs, etc.

Hence, the student is advised to ensure that they study this chapter completely and thoroughly. Skills to be developed while studying and practising this chapter will be based on the application of formula and visualisation of figures and solids.

The principal skill required for doing well in this chapter is the ability to apply the formulae and theorems.

The following is a comprehensive collection of formulae based on two-dimensional figures. The student is advised to remember the formulae in this chapter so that he/she is able to solve all the questions based on this chapter.

THEORY

Basic Conversions

A. 1 m = 100 cm = 1000 mm
1 km = 1000 m
= 0.621 miles
1 inch = 2.54 cm

B. 1 m = 39.37 inches
1 mile = 1760 yd
= 6076 ft
1 nautical mile (knot)
= 6080 ft

C. 100 kg = 1 quintal
10 quintal = 1 tonne
= 1000 kg
1 kg = 2.2 pounds
(approx.)

D. 1 litre = 1000 cc
1 acre = 4046.86 sq m
1 hectare = 10000 sq m

TYPES OF ANGLES

Basic Definitions

Acute angle: An angle whose measure is less than 90 degrees. The following is an acute angle.

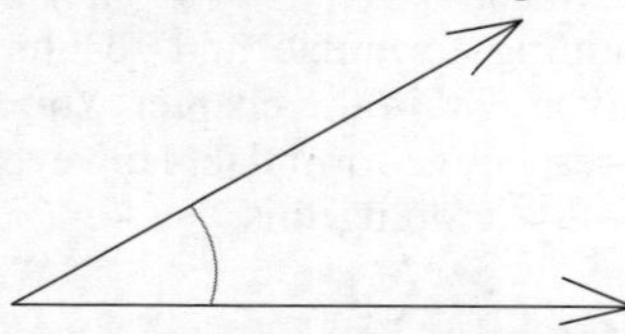

Right angle: An angle whose measure is 90 degrees. The following is a right angle.

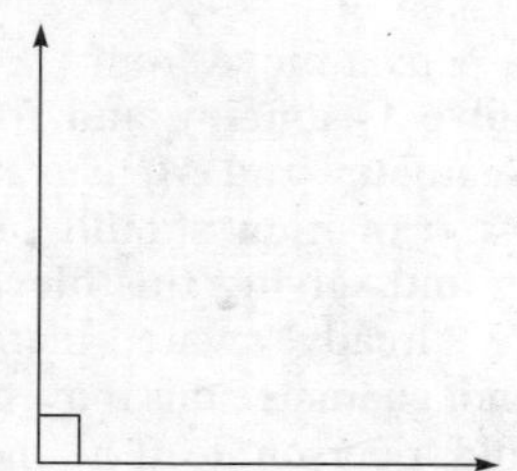

Obtuse angle: An angle whose measure is bigger than 90 degrees but less than 180 degrees. Thus, it is between 90 degrees and 180 degrees. The following is an obtuse angle.

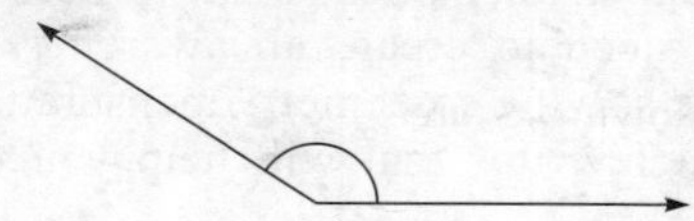

Straight angle: It is an angle whose measure is 180 degrees.

Reflex angle: An angle whose measure is more than 180 degrees but less than 360 degrees. The following is a reflex angle.

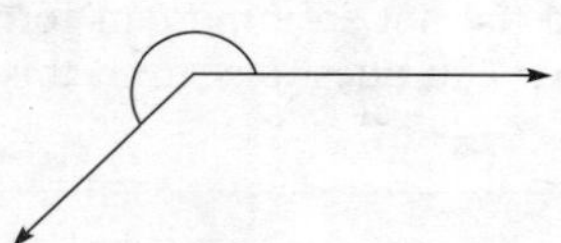

Adjacent angles: Angles with a common vertex and one common side. In the figure below, $\angle 1$ and $\angle 2$ are adjacent angles.

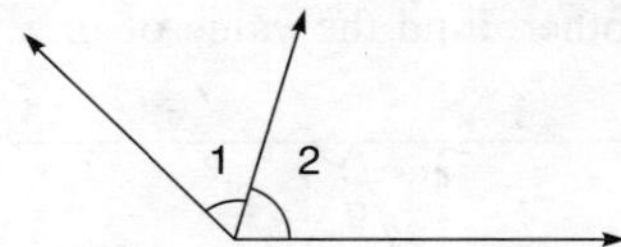

Complementary angles: Two angles whose measures add to 90 degrees $\angle 1$ and $\angle 2$ are complementary angles because together they form a right angle.

However, one thing that you should note is that, even though in the figure given here, the two angles are shown as adjacent, they need not be so to be called complementary. As long as two angles add up to 90 degrees, they will be called complementary (even if they are not adjacent to each other).

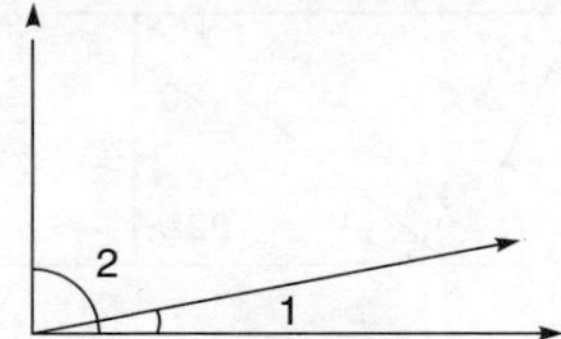

Supplementary angles: Two angles whose measures add up to 180 degrees. The following angles $\angle 1$ and $\angle 2$ are supplementary angles. However, supplementary angles do not need to be adjacent to be called supplementary (quite like complementary angles). The only condition for two angles to be called supplementary is if they are adding up to 180 degrees.

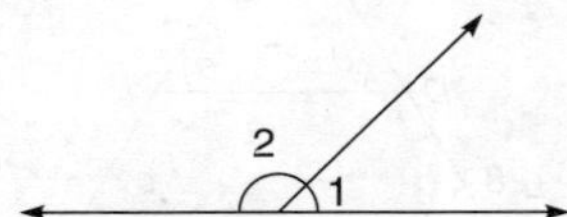

Vertical angles: Angles that have a common vertex and whose sides are formed by the same lines. The following ($\angle 1$ and $\angle 2$) are vertical angles.

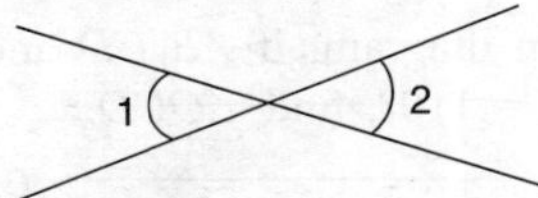

Angles formed when two parallel lines, are crossed by a transversal: When two parallel lines are crossed by a third line, (transversal), eight angles are formed. Take a look at the following figure:

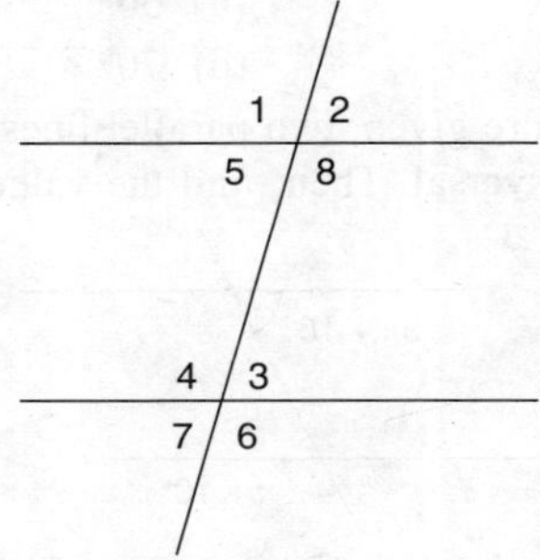

Angles 3,4,5,8 are interior angles.
Angles 1,2,6,7 are exterior angles.

Alternate interior angles: Pairs of interior angles on opposite sides of the transversal.

For instance, angle 3 and angle 5 are alternate interior angles. Angle 4 and angle 8 are also alternate interior angles. Both the angles in a pair of alternate interior angles are equal. Hence, in the figure we have: angle 3 = angle 5; also angle 4 = angle 8.

Alternate exterior angles: Pairs of exterior angles on opposite sides of the transversal.

Angle 2 and angle 7 are alternate exterior angles. Angles 1 and 6 are also alternate exterior angles. Both the angles in a pair of alternate exterior angles are equal. Thus, in the figure angle 2 = angle 7 and angle 1 = angle 6.

Co-interior angles: When two lines are cut by a third line (transversal), co-interior angles are between the pair of lines on the same side of the transversal. If the lines that are being cut by the transversal are parallel to each other, the co-interior angles are supplementary (add up to 180 degrees). In the given figure, angles 3 and 8 are co-interior angles. Also, angles 4 and 5 are co-interior angles, since, the lines being cut are parallel in this case, $\angle 3 + \angle 8 = 180$. Also, $\angle 4 + \angle 5 = 180$.

Corresponding angles: Are pairs of angles that are in similar positions when two parallel lines are intersected by a transversal.

Angle 3 and angle 2 are corresponding angles. Similarly, the pairs of angles 1 and 4; 5 and 7; 6 and 8 are corresponding angles. Corresponding angles are equal. Thus, in the figure- $\angle 1 = \angle 4$; $\angle 5 = \angle 7$; $\angle 2 = \angle 3$ and $\angle 6 = \angle 8$.

Linear pair: $\angle XOY$ and $\angle YOZ$ are linear pair angles. One side must be common (e.g. OY) and these two angles must be supplementary.

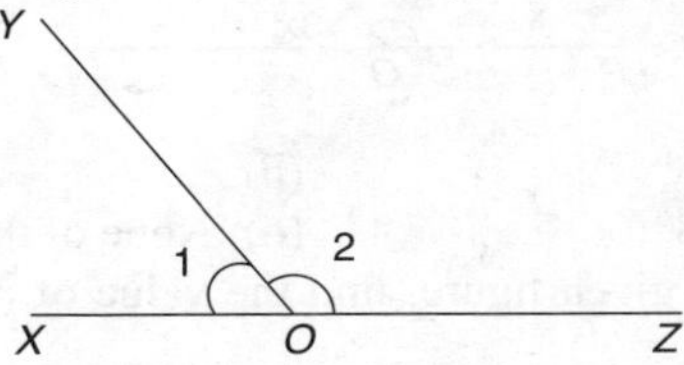

Angles on one side of a line: $\angle 1 + \angle 2 + \angle 3 = 180°$

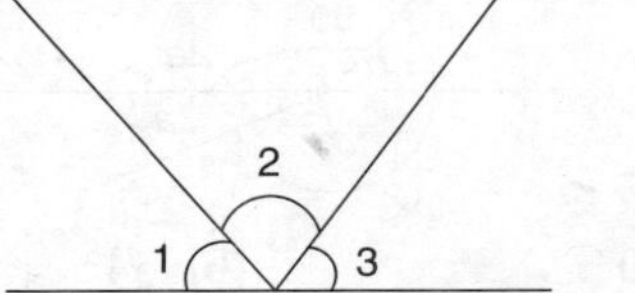

Angles around the point: $\angle 1 + \angle 2 + \angle 3 + \angle 4 + \angle 5 = 360°$

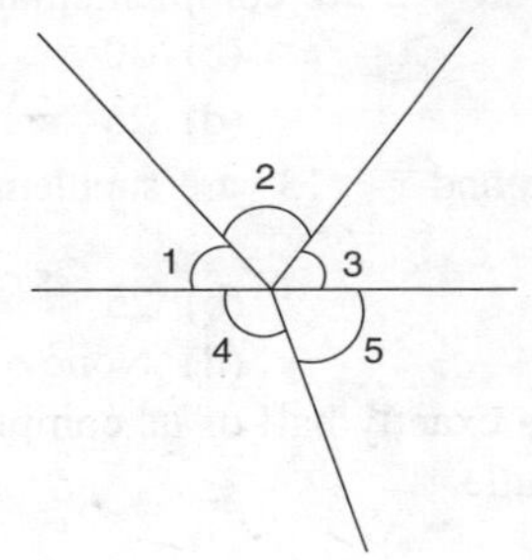

Angle bisector: OY is the angle bisector for the ∠XOZ.

i.e. $\angle XOY = \angle ZOY = \frac{1}{2}\angle XOZ$

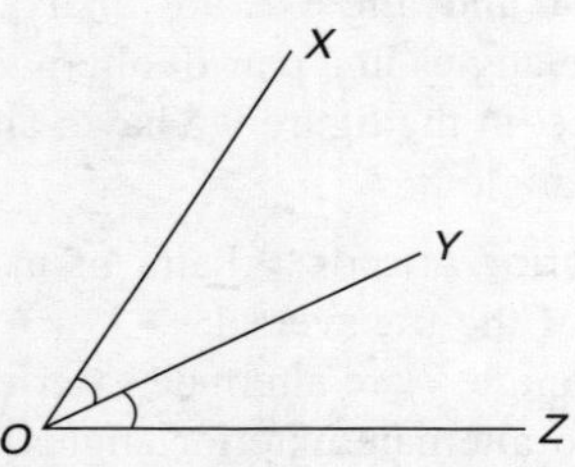

When a line segment divides an angle equally into two parts, then it is said to be the angle bisector (*OY*).

(Angle bisector is equidistant from the two sides of the angle.)

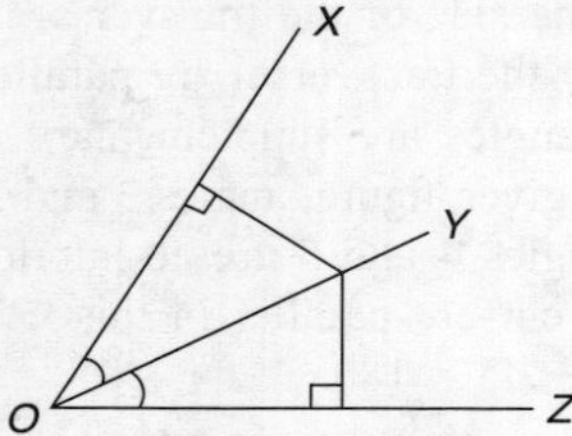

The distance between the lines *OX* and *OY* and the lines *OY* and *OZ* are equal to each other.

Practice Exercise

1. What is the value of *x* in the given figure?

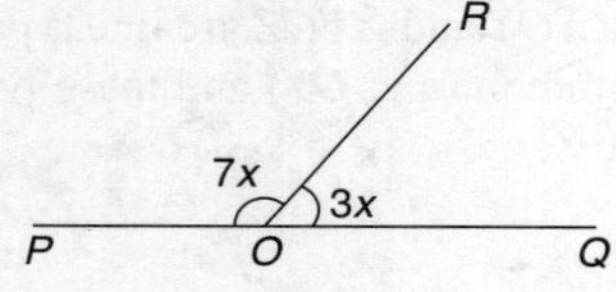

(a) 18° (b) 20°
(c) 28° (d) None of these

2. In the given figure, find the value of $(a + b)$

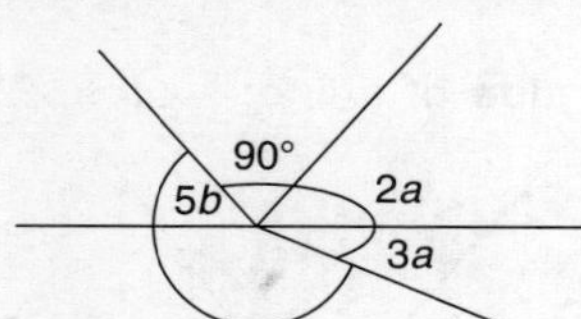

(a) 50° (b) 54°
(c) 60° (d) None of these

3. If $2a + 3$, $3a + 2$ are complementary, then find *a*,
(a) 17° (b) 20°
(c) 23° (d) 26°

4. If $5x + 17°$ and $x + 13°$ are supplementary, then find *x*,
(a) 20° (b) 25°
(c) 30° (d) None of these

5. An angle is exactly half of its complementary angle; find the angle.
(a) 30° (b) 40°
(c) 50° (d) 60°

6. In the following figure, lines L1 and L2 are parallel to each other. Find the value of *q*.

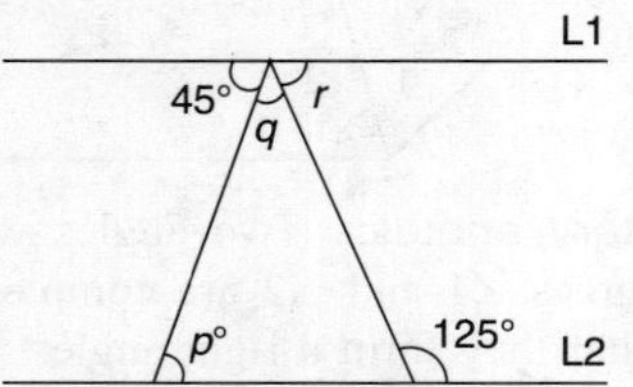

(a) 60° (b) 80°
(c) 90° (d) 85°

7. In the given figure if $L_1 \| L_2$, then values of *x*, *y*, *z* are:

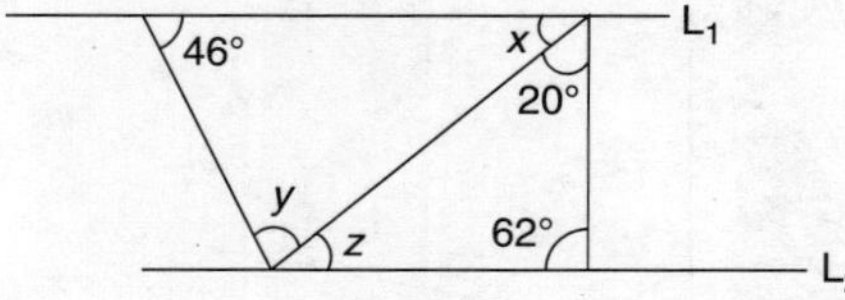

(a) 98°, 98°,36° (b) 98°, 36°, 98°
(c) 36°,98°,36° (d) None of these

8. In the given diagram if $BC \| ED$ and $\angle BAC = 70°$, then find the value of *d* and *c*.

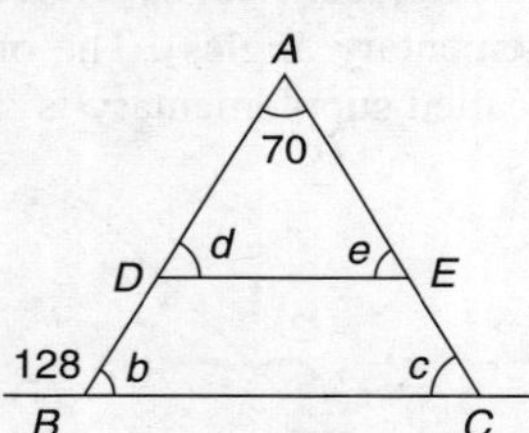

(a) 52°, 58° (b) 58°, 52°
(c) 44°, 36° (d) 36°, 44°

9. In the given diagram, if $AB \| CD$ and $\angle ABO = 60°$ and $\angle BOC = 110°$, find $\angle OCD$.

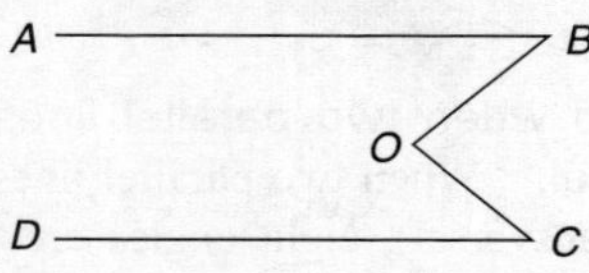

(a) 40° (b) 50°
(c) 60° (d) 70°

10. In the figure given, two parallel lines are intersected by a transversal. Then, find the value of *x*.

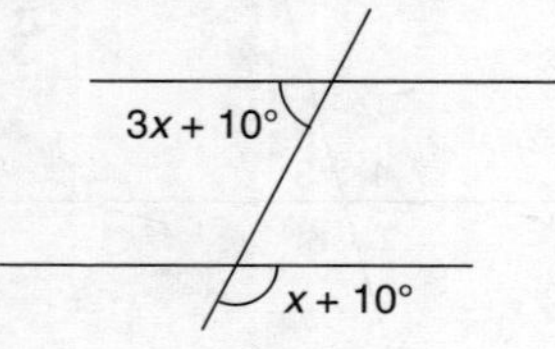

(a) 40° (b) 50°
(c) 55° (d) 65°

11. Maximum number of points of intersection of five lines on a plane is

(a) 6 (b) 8
(c) 10 (d) 12

12. If $PQ \| RS$, then find the value of x.

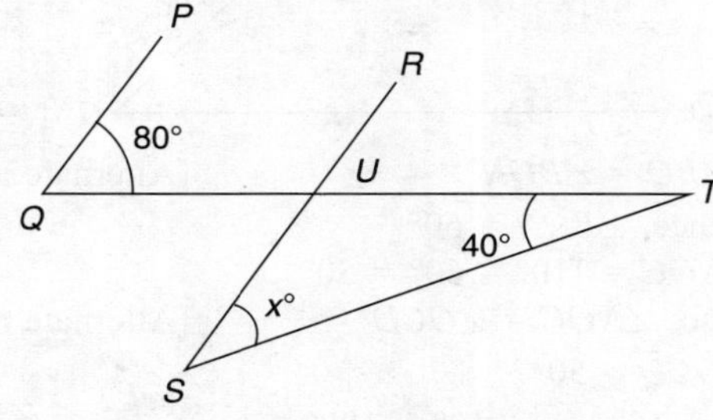

(a) 40° (b) 60°
(c) 70° (d) 80°

13. If $AB \| CD$ and $AF \| BE$, then the value of x is

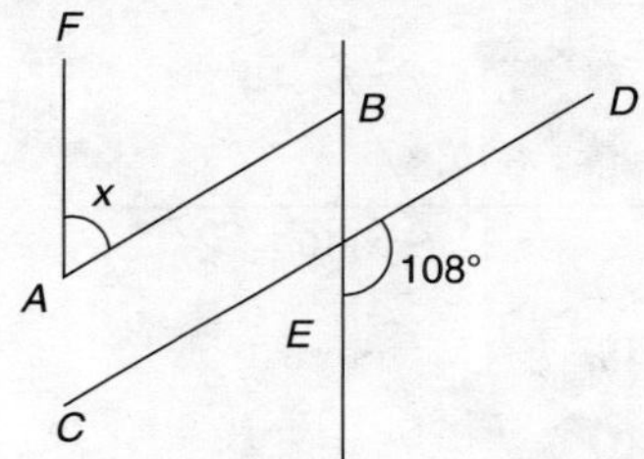

(a) 108° (b) 72°
(c) 88° (d) 82°

14. In the figure if $PQ \| SR$ and $ST \| QR$, then find x.

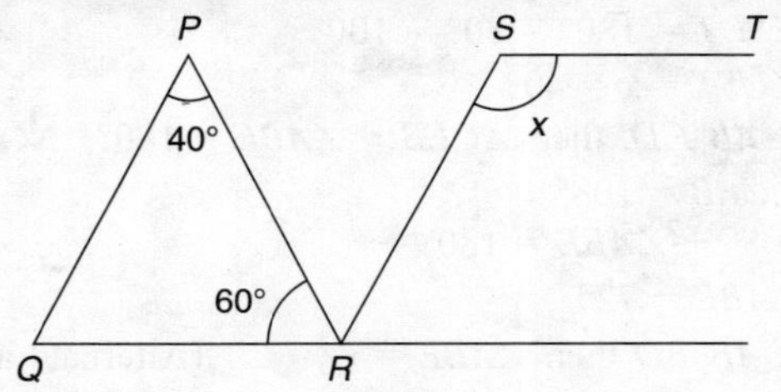

(a) 70° (b) 80°
(c) 90° (d) 100°

15. In the given figure, if $AB \| CD$ then find the value of x.

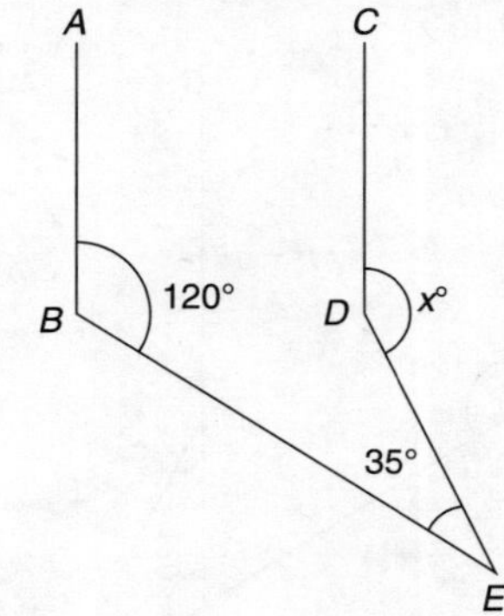

(a) 135° (b) 145°
(c) 155° (d) None of these

16. If $PQ \| RS$ and $QT \| SU$, then find the value of $x + y$.

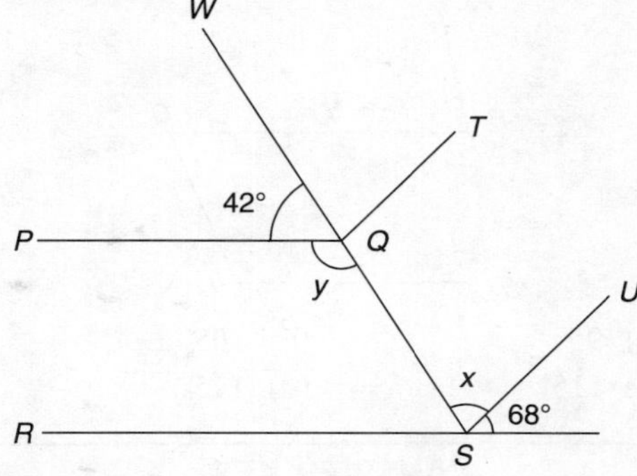

(a) 188° (b) 202°
(c) 208° (d) 212°

17. If $PQ \| RS$ and AC is angle bisector of $\angle PAB$, BC is angle bisector of $\angle RBA$. Then find $\angle ACB$.

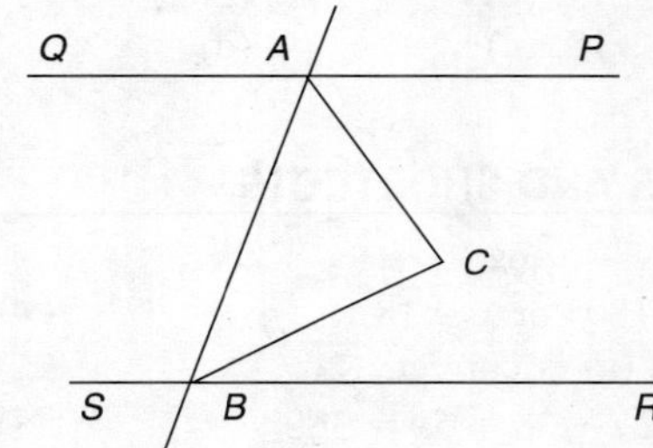

(a) 45° (b) 75°
(c) 90° (d) 110°

18. In the given figure, if $AB \| CD$ then find $x + y$.

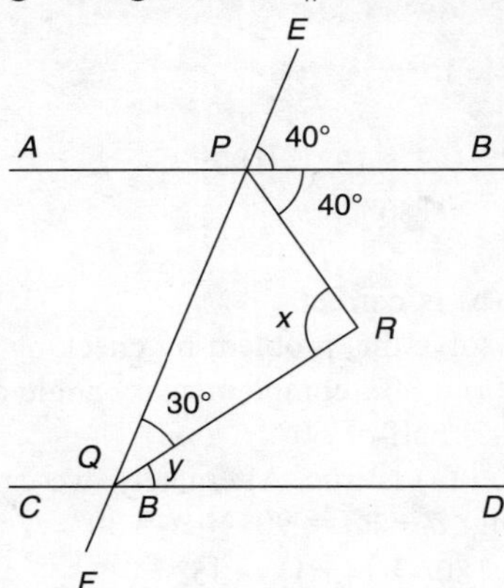

(a) 100° (b) 110°
(c) 60° (d) 125°

19. In the figure, if $CD \| EF \| AB$ then, find the value of x.

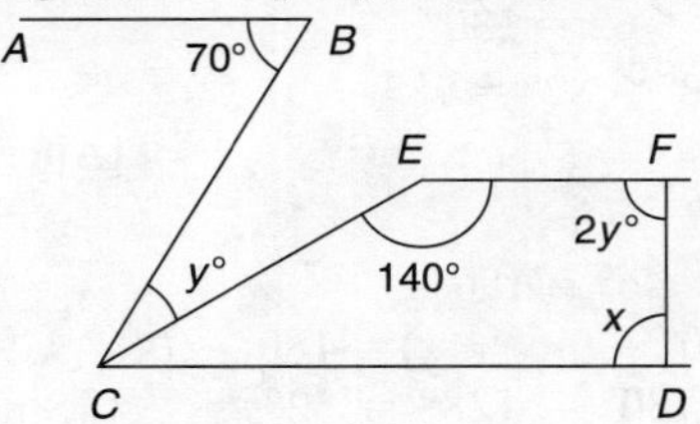

(a) 70° (b) 90°
(c) 110° (d) 120°

20. If in the given figure, $AB \| CD$ and $BC \| DE$, then find x.

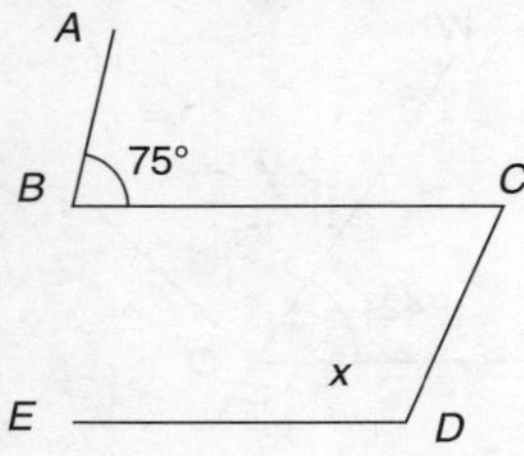

(a) 95° (b) 105°
(c) 115° (d) 125°

ANSWER KEY

1. (a)	2. (b)	3. (a)	4. (b)
5. (a)	6. (b)	7. (b)	8. (a)
9. (b)	10. (a)	11. (c)	12. (a)
13. (b)	14. (d)	15. (c)	16. (c)
17. (c)	18. (c)	19. (d)	20. (b)

SOLUTIONS AND SHORTCUTS

1. $7x + 3x = 180°$
   $10x = 180°$ or $x = 18°$
   Option (a) is correct.
2. $90° + 2a + 3a + 5b = 360°$
   $5a + 5b = 270°$
   $a + b = 54°$
3. $2a + 3 + 3a + 2 = 90°$
   $5a + 5 = 90°$
   $a = \frac{85°}{5} = 17°$
4. $5x + 17° + x + 13° = 180°$
   $6x + 30° = 180°$
   $x = 25°$
   Option (b) is correct.
5. We can solve this problem by checking the options. Option (a) = 30°, complementary angle of 30° is 60° and 30° is half of 60°.
   So option (a) is true. Alternately, we can also solve this using: $a + 2a = 90 \rightarrow a = 30°$.
6. $q + r = 180° - (45°) = 135°$
   $r + 125° = 180° \Rightarrow r = 55°$
   $q + 55° = 135°$
   $q = 80°$
7. $x + 20 + 62 = 180°$
   $x = 180° - 82° = 98°$
   $x = z$ [Alternate angles]
   $z = 98°$
   $x + y + 46° = 180°$
   $y = 180° - (46° + x) = 180° - (46° + 98°) = 36°$
8. $\angle b = 180° - 128° = 52° = \angle d$ (Since they are corresponding angles)
   $\angle c = 180° - (70° + 52°) = 58°$
9. Draw line $MON \| AB \| CD$

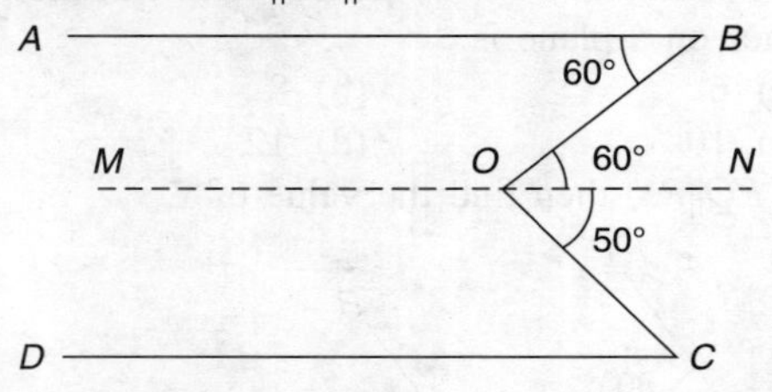

$\angle ABO = \angle BON$ [Alternate angles]
Hence, $\angle BON = 60°$
$\angle NOC = 110° - 60° = 50°$
Also, $\angle NOC = \angle OCD$ [Alternate angles]
$\angle OCD = 50°$

10. $3x + 10° + x + 10° = 180°$

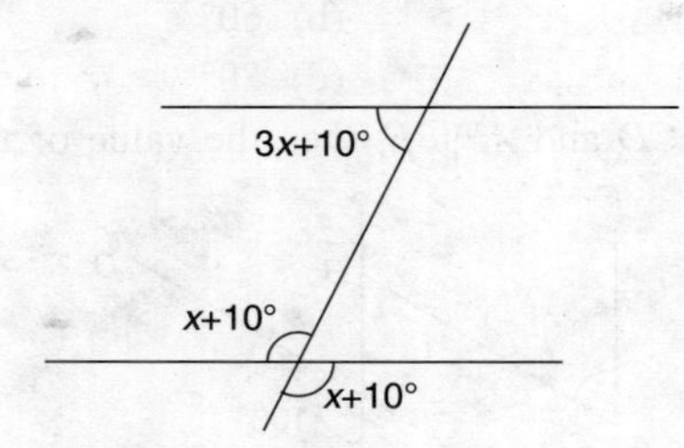

$4x = 160°$
$x = 40°$

11. ${}^5C_2 = \frac{5!}{2! \times 3!} = 10$
    Option (c) is correct.
12. $\angle PQU = \angle SUQ = 80°$ [Alternate angles]
    $\angle SUT = 180° - 80° = 100°$
    $\angle UST = x = 40°$
13. If $AB \| CD$, then $\angle CEB + \angle ABE = 180°$
    $\angle CEB = 108°$
    $108° + \angle ABE = 180°$
    $\angle ABE = 72°$
    If $AB \| BD$ then $\angle ABE = x$ [Alternate angles]
    $x = 72°$
14. $\angle QPR = \angle SRP = 40°$ [Alternative angles]
    $x = \angle SRQ = \angle SRP + \angle PRQ$ [Alternative angles]
    $x = 60° + 40° = 100°$
15. Extend CD to x

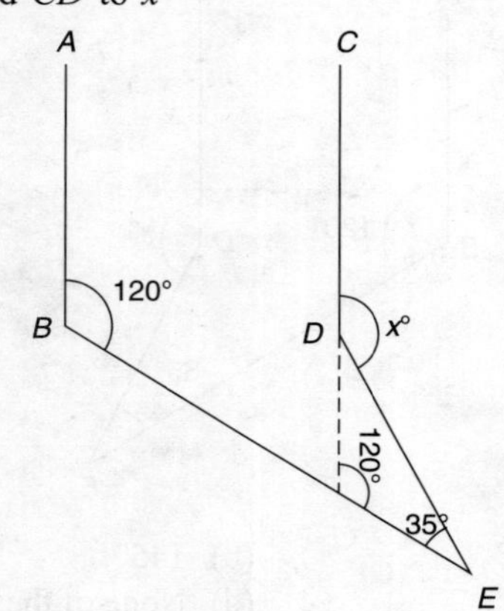

$\angle ABX = \angle CXE = 120°$

$x = 120° + 35°$ [x is exterior angle of ΔDXE)

$x = 155°$

16. $y = 180° - 42 = 138°$

$\angle PQW = \angle RSQ = 42°$

$42° + x + 68° = 180°$

$x = 70°$

$x + y = 70° + 138° = 208°$

17. $\angle ACB = 180° - (\angle CAB + \angle CBA)$

$\angle PAB + \angle RBA = 180°$

$$\frac{\angle PAB}{2} + \frac{\angle RBA}{2} = 90°$$

$\angle CAB + \angle CBA = 90°$

$\angle ACB = 180° - (90°) = 90°$

18. $\angle RPQ = 180° - (40° + 40°) = 100°$

$x = 180° - (100° + 30°) = 50°$

$30° + y = 40°$

($\angle BPQ$ and $\angle DQP$ are corresponding angles).

$y = 10°$

$x + y = 50° + 10° = 60°$

19. $\angle ABC = \angle BCD = 70°$ [Alternate angles]

$\angle ECD = 180° - 140° = 40°$

[As angles FEC and ECD are co-interior angles]

$40° + y = 70°$

$y = 30°$

$EF \parallel CD$ then $2y + x = 180°$

$x = 180° - 2y = 180° - 60° = 120°$

20. Extend AB to E

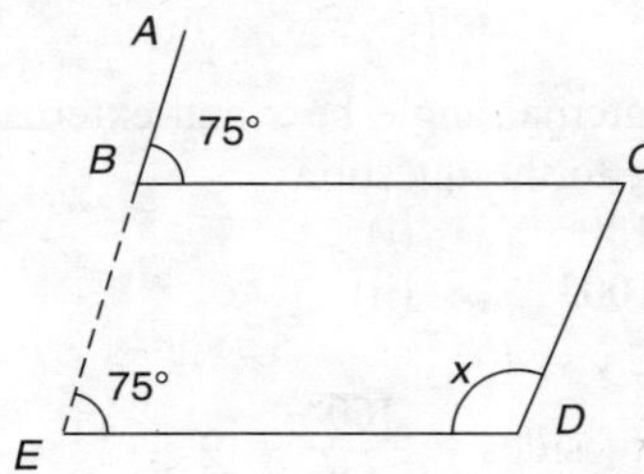

$BC \parallel DE$, so $\angle ABC = \angle AFD = 75°$

$CD \parallel BE$, hence $x + 75° = 180°$

$x = 105°$

POLYGONS

Polygons are plane figures formed by a closed series of rectilinear (straight) segments. The following are examples of polygons:

triangle, rectangle, pentagon, hexagon, heptagon, octagon, nonagon (9-sided), decagon, undecagon or hendecagon (11-sided), dodecagon (12-sided), triskaidecagon or tridecagon (13-sided). Subsequent polygons are named as per the table below:

Number of sides	*Name of the Polygon*
14	Tetradecagon, Terakaidecagon
15	Pentadecagon, Pentakaidecagon
16	Hexadecagon, Hexakaidecagon
17	Heptadecagon, Heptakaidecagon
18	Octadecagon, Octakaidecagon
19	Enneadecagon, Enneakaidecagon
20	Icosagon
30	Triacontagon
40	Tetracontagon
50	Pentacontagon
60	Hexacontagon
70	Heptacontagon
80	Ontacontagon
90	Enneacontagon
100	Hectogon, Hecatontagon
1000	Chiliagon
10000	Myriagon

Polygons can broadly be divided into two types:

(a) *Regular polygons:* Polygons with all the sides and angles equal

(b) *Irregular polygons:* Polygons in which all the sides or angles are not of the same measure.

Polygons can also be divided as *concave* or *convex polygons*.

Convex polygons are the polygons in which all the diagonals lie inside the figure otherwise its a concave polygon

Polygons can also be divided on the basis of the number of sides they have.

Number of sides	*Name of the polygon*	*Sum of all the angles*
3	Triangle	180°
4	Quadrilateral	360°
5	Pentagon	540°
6	Hexagon	720°
7	Heptagon	900°
8	Octagon	1080°
9	Nonagon	1260°
10	Decagon	1440°

Properties

1. Sum of all the angles of a polygon with n sides $= (2n - 4)\pi/2$ or $(n - 2)\pi$ Radians $= (n - 2)$ 180° degrees
2. Sum of all exterior angles = 360°
i.e. in the figure below:
$\theta_1 + \theta_2 + ... + \theta_6 = 360°$
In general, $\theta_1 + \theta_2 + ... + \theta_n = 360°$

3. Number of sides = 360°/exterior angle.

Note: This property is true only for regular polygons.

4. Area = $(ns^2/4) \times \cot(180/n)$; where s = length of side, n = number of sides.

Note: This property is true only for regular polygons.

5. Perimeter = $n \times s$

Note: This property is true only for regular polygons.

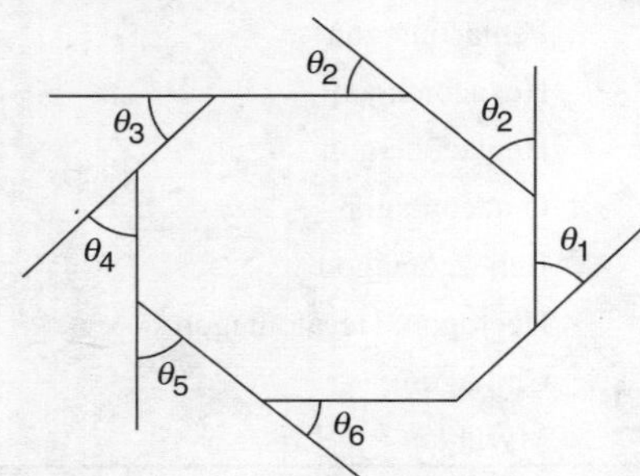

Practice Exercise

1. Each interior angle of a regular polygon is 140°. Then the number of sides is
   (a) 6 (b) 8
   (c) 9 (d) 12
2. Each interior angle of a regular octagon is
   (a) 90° (b) 115°
   (c) 125° (d) 135°
3. The sum of the interior angles of a polygon is 1440°. The number of sides of the polygon is
   (a) 8 (b) 10
   (c) 12 (d) 14
4. Difference between interior and exterior angles of a polygon is 100°. Then the number of sides in the polygon is
   (a) 8 (b) 9
   (c) 10 (d) 11
5. If the ratio of interior and exterior angles of a regular polygon is 2:1, then find the number of sides of the polygon.
   (a) 6 (b) 8
   (c) 10 (d) 12
6. The ratio of the measure of an angle of a regular octagon to the measure of its exterior angle is:
   (a) 2:1 (b) 1:3
   (c) 3:1 (d) 1:1
7. Ratio between, the numbers of sides of two regular polygons is 2:3 and the ratio between their interior angles is 3:4. The number of sides of these polygons respectively is
   (a) 4, 6 (b) 6, 9
   (c) 8, 12 (d) None of these
8. Number of diagonals of a six-sided polygon is
   (a) 6 (b) 9
   (c) 12 (d) 15
9. Find the sum of all internal angles of a five-point star.
   (a) 160° (b) 180°
   (c) 240° (d) 300°
10. If the length of each side of a hexagon is 6 cm, then the area of the hexagon is
   (a) 54 cm^2 (b) $54\sqrt{3}$ cm^2
   (c) 68 cm^2 (d) None of these

ANSWER KEY

1. (c)	2. (d)	3. (b)	4. (b)
5. (a)	6. (c)	7. (a)	8. (b)
9. (b)	10. (b)		

SOLUTIONS AND SHORTCUTS

1. Exterior angle of given polygon = 180° – 140° = 40°
   Number of sides = 360°/40° = 9. (Since the sum of all exterior angles of a polygon is 360°)
   Option (c) is correct.
2. Total number of sides in octagon = 8
   Each interior angle = $\frac{(8-2)\times180°}{8} = \frac{6\times180°}{8} = 135°$
3. Let the number of sides be x.
   Then according to the question
   $(x - 2) \times 180° = 1440°$
   $x - 2 = 8$
   $x = 10$.
4. Let the internal angle be x and external angle be y, according to the question
   $x + y = 180°$ (i)
   $x - y = 100°$ (ii)
   $x = 140°, y = 40°$
   Number of sides = $\frac{360°}{40°} = 9$
5. If interior angle be '$2x$' and exterior angle be x
   Then $2x + x = 180°$
   $3x = 180°$
   $x = 60°$
   Number of sides = 360°/60° = 6
6. Interior angle of a regular octagon = 135°
   Exterior angle of a regular octagon = 45°
   Required ratio = $\frac{135°}{45°} = 3:1$
7. We can solve this problem by checking the options.
   Option (a) 4, 6
   Interior angle of a four-sided polygon = 90°
   Interior angle of a six-sided polygon = 120°

So the ratio of interior angles = 90° : 120° = 3 : 4
Hence, this option is correct.

8. Number of diagonals = $^6C_2 - 6$

$$= \frac{6!}{2!4!} - 6 \Rightarrow 15 - 6 = 9$$

9. Sum of the angles of an x-pointed star = $(x - 4) \times \pi$
So the required sum = $(5 - 4) \times \pi = 180°$

10. Required area = $6 \times \frac{\sqrt{3}}{4} \times 6^2$

$$= 54\sqrt{3} \text{ cm}^2$$

TRIANGLES (Δ)

A triangle is a polygon having three sides. Sum of all the angles of a triangle = 180°.

Types

1. *Acute angle triangle:* Triangles with all three angles acute (less than 90°).
2. *Obtuse angle triangle:* Triangles with one of the angles obtuse (more than 90°).

Note: We cannot have more than one obtuse angle in a triangle.

3. *Right angle triangle:* Triangle with one of the angles equal to 90°.
4. *Equilateral triangle:* Triangle with all sides equal. All the angles in such a triangle measure 60°.
5. *Isosceles triangle:* Triangle with two of its sides equal and consequently the angles opposite the equal sides are also equal.
6. *Scalene triangle:* Triangle with none of the sides equal to any other side.

Properties (General)

- Sum of the length of any two sides of a triangle has to be always greater than the third side.
- Difference between the lengths of any two sides of a triangle has to be always lesser than the third side.
- Side opposite to the greatest angle will be the greatest and the side opposite to the smallest angle the smallest.
- *The sine rule:* $a/\sin A = b/\sin B = c/\sin C = 2R$ (where R = circum-radius.)
- *The cosine rule:* $a^2 = b^2 + c^2 - 2bc \cos A$
This is true for all sides and respective angles.

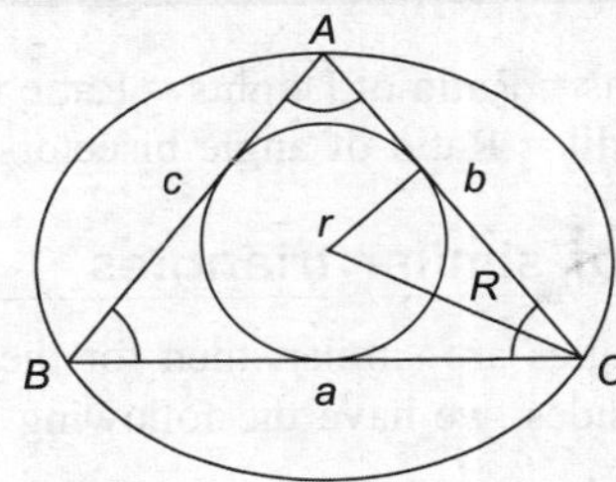

In case of a right triangle, the formula reduces to
$a^2 = b^2 + c^2$
Since cos 90° = 0

- The exterior angle is equal to the sum of two interior angles not adjacent to it.

$$\angle ACD = \angle BCE = \angle A + \angle B$$

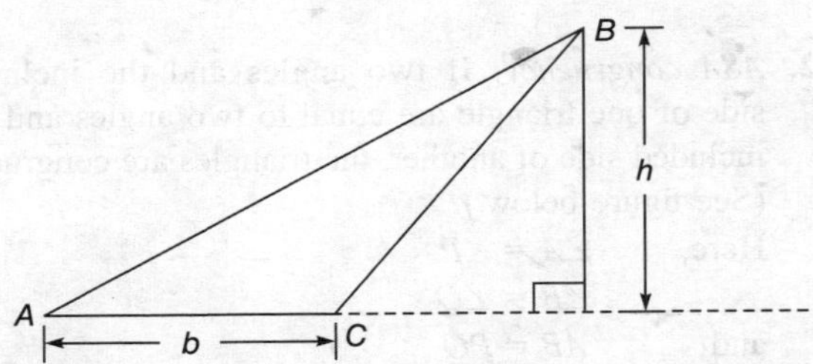

Area

1. Area = 1/2 base × height or 1/2 bh
Height = Perpendicular distance between the base and vertex opposite to it
2. Area = $\sqrt{s(s-a)(s-b)(s-c)}$ (Heron's formula)
where $s = \frac{a+b+c}{2}$ (a, b and c being the length of the sides)
3. Area = rs (where r is **inradius**)
4. Area = 1/2 × product of two sides × sine of the included angle
= 1/2 ac sin B
= 1/2 ab sin C
= 1/2 bc sin A

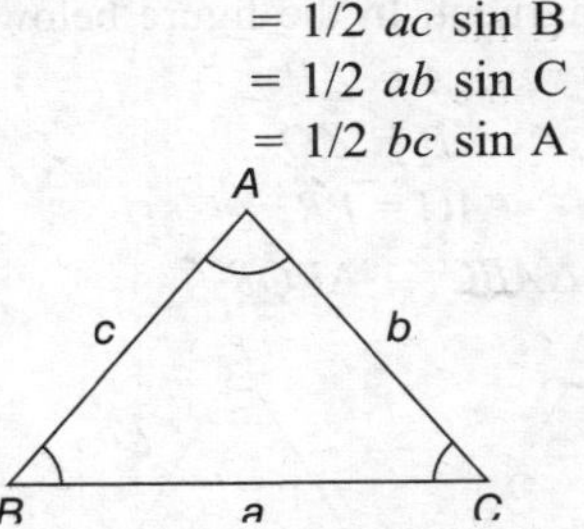

5. Area = $abc/4R$
where R = **circumradius**

Congruency of Triangles Two triangles are congruent if all the sides of one are equal to the corresponding sides of another. It follows that all the angles of one are equal to the corresponding angles of another. The notation for congruency is (≅).

Conditions for Congruency

1. *SAS congruency*: If two sides and an included angle of one triangle are equal to two sides and an included

angle of another, the two triangles are congruent. (See figure below.)

Here, $AB = PQ$

$BC = QR$

and $\angle B = \angle Q$

So, $\Delta ABC \cong \Delta PQR$

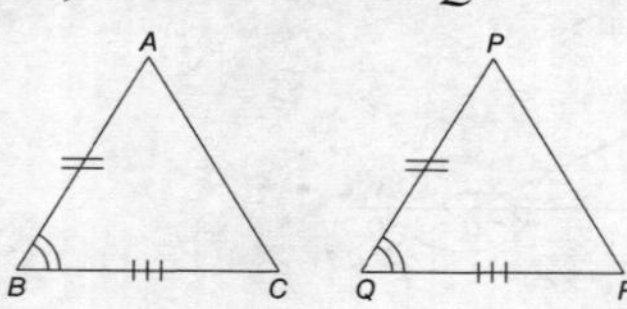

2. *ASA congruency*: If two angles and the included side of one triangle are equal to two angles and the included side of another, the triangles are congruent. (See figure below.)

Here, $\angle A = \angle P$

$\angle B = \angle Q$

and $AB = PQ$

So, $\Delta ABC \cong \Delta PQR$

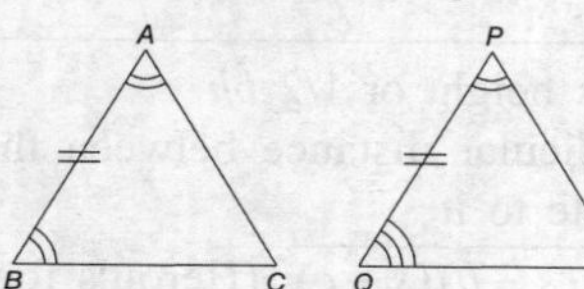

3. *AAS congruency*: If two angles and side opposite to one of the angles are equal to the corresponding angles and the side of another triangle, the triangles are congruent. In the figure below:

$\angle A = \angle P$

$\angle B = \angle Q$

and $AC = PR$

So, $\Delta ABC \cong \Delta PQR$

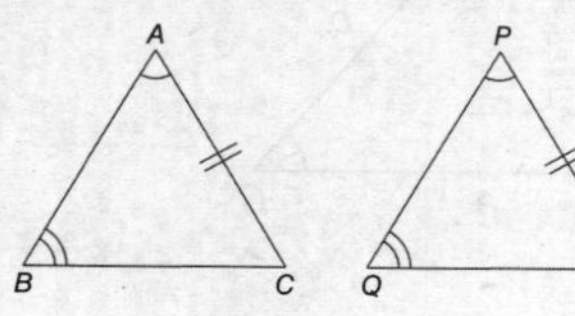

4. *SSS congruency*: If three sides of one triangle are equal to three sides of another triangle, the two triangles are congruent. In the figure below:

$AB = PQ$

$BC = QR$

$AC = PR$

$\therefore \quad \Delta ABC \cong \Delta PQR$

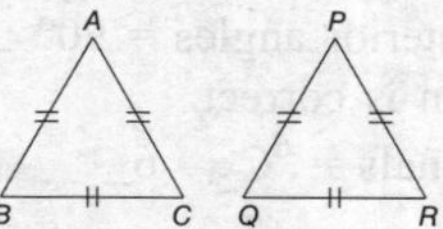

5. *SSA congruency*: If two sides and the angle opposite the greater side of one triangle are equal to the two sides and the angle opposite to the greater side of another triangle, then the triangles are congruent. The congruency does not hold if the equal angles lie opposite the shorter side. In the figure below, if

$AB = PQ$

$AC = PR$

$\angle B = \angle Q$

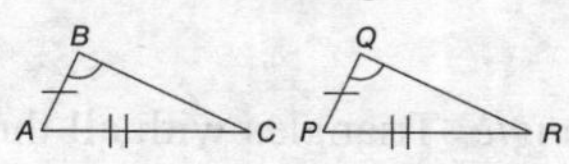

then the triangles are congruent.

i.e. $\Delta ABC \cong \Delta PQR$.

Similarity of triangles It is a special case where if either of the conditions of similarity of polygons holds, the other will hold automatically.

Types of Similarity

1. *AAA similarity:* If in two triangles, corresponding angles are equal, that is, the two triangles are equiangular then the triangles are similar.
   Corollary (*AA similarity*): If two angles of one triangle are respectively equal to two angles of another triangle then the two triangles are similar. The reason being, the third angle becomes equal automatically.
2. *SSS similarity:* If the corresponding sides of two triangles are proportional then they are similar. For ΔABC to be similar to ΔPQR, $AB/PQ = BC/QR = AC/PR$, must hold true.
3. *SAS similarity:* If in two triangles, one pair of corresponding sides are proportional and the included angles are equal then the two triangles are similar.

$\Delta ABC \sim \Delta PQR$

If $AB/BC = PQ/QR$ then $\angle B = \angle Q$

Note: In similar triangles; the following identity holds:

Ratio of medians = Ratio of heights = Ratio of circumradii = Ratio of inradii = Ratio of angle bisectors

Properties of similar triangles

If the two triangles are similar, then for the proportional/ corresponding sides, we have the following results.

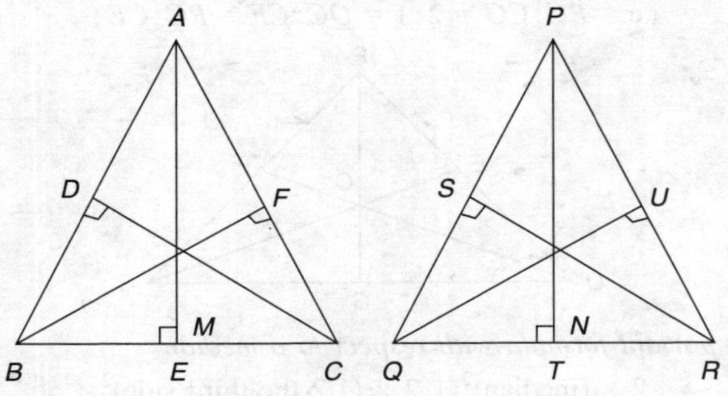

1. Ratio of sides = Ratio of heights (altitudes)
   = Ratio of medians
   = Ratio of angle bisectors
   = Ratio of inradii
   = Ratio of circumradii
2. Ratio of areas = Ratio of square of corresponding sides.

   i.e., if $\Delta ABC \sim \Delta PQR$, then

$$\frac{A(\Delta ABC)}{A(\Delta PQR)} = \frac{(AB)^2}{(PQ)^2} = \frac{(BC)^2}{(QR)^2} = \frac{(AC)^2}{(PR)^2}$$

While there are a lot of methods through which we see similarity of triangles, the one thing that all our Maths teachers forgot to tell us about similarity is the basic real life concept of similarity, i.e. **two things are similar if they look similar!!**

If you have been to a toy shop lately, you would have come across models of cars or bikes which are made so that they look like the original—but are made in a different size from the original. Thus, you might have seen a toy Maruti car which is built in a ratio of 1:25 of the original car. The result of this is that the toy car would look very much like the original car (of course, if it is built well!!). Thus, if you have ever seen a father and son looking exactly like each other, you have experienced similarity!!

You should use this principle to identify similar triangles. In a figure, two triangles would be similar simply if they look like one another.

Thus, in the figure below if you were to draw the radii OB and O′A, the two triangles MOB and MO′A will be similar to each other. Simply, because they look similar. Of course, the option of using the different rules of similarity of triangles still remains with you.

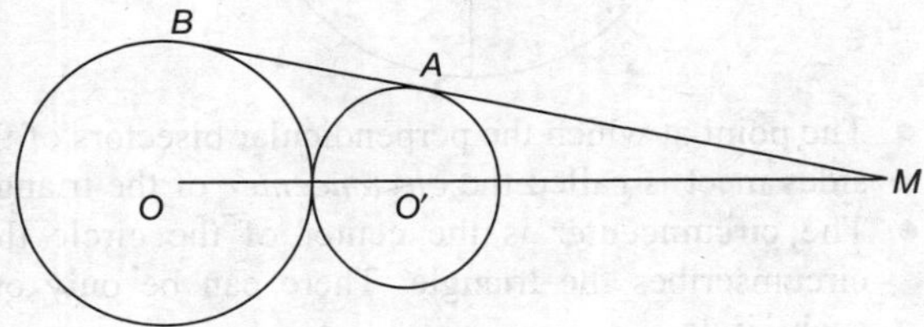

Equilateral Triangles (of side a):

1. ($\because$ sin 60 = $\sqrt{3}/2 = h$/side)

$$h = \frac{a\sqrt{3}}{2}$$

2. Area = 1/2 (base) × (height) = $\frac{1}{2} \times a \times \frac{a\sqrt{3}}{2} = \frac{\sqrt{3}}{4}a^2$

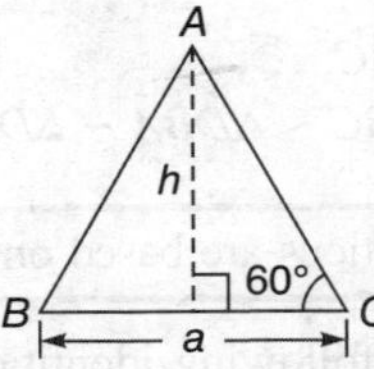

3. R (circumradius) = $\frac{2h}{3} = \frac{a}{\sqrt{3}}$

4. r (inradius) = $\frac{h}{3} = \frac{a}{2\sqrt{3}}$

Properties

1. The in-center and circum-center lies at a point that divides the height in the ratio 2: 1.
2. The circum radius is always twice the inradius [$R = 2r$].
3. Among all the triangles that can be formed with a given perimeter, the equilateral triangle will have the maximum area.
4. An equilateral triangle in a circle will have the maximum area compared to other triangles inside the same circle.

Isosceles Triangle

Area = $\frac{b}{4}\sqrt{4a^2 - b^2}$

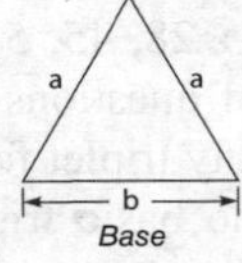

In an isosceles triangle, the angles opposite to the equal sides are equal.

Right-Angled Triangle

Pythagoras Theorem In the case of a right angled triangle, the square of the hypotenuse is equal to the sum of the squares of the other two sides. In the figure below, for triangle ABC, $a^2 = b^2 + c^2$.

Area = 1/2 (product of perpendicular sides)

$$R\text{(circum radius)} = \frac{\text{hypotenuse}}{2}$$

Area = rs

(where r = **inradius** and $s = (a + b + c)/2$ where a, b and c are sides of the triangle)

$\Rightarrow$ $1/2\ bc = r(a + b + c)/2$

$\Rightarrow$ $r = (bc)/(a + b + c)$

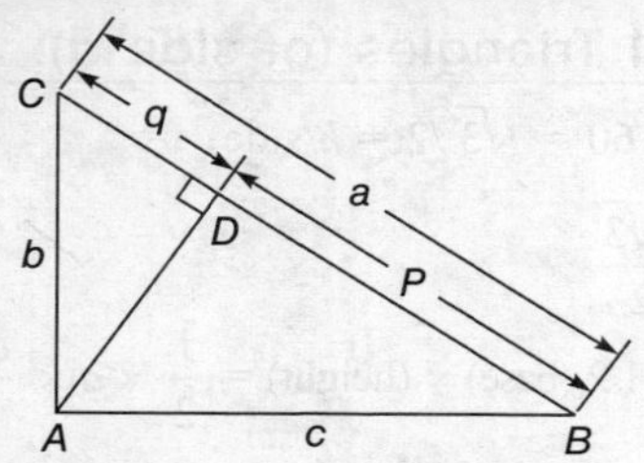

In the triangle ABC,

$$\Delta ABC \sim \Delta DBA \sim \Delta DAC$$

Note: A lot of questions are based on this figure.

Further, we find the following identities:

1. $\Delta ABC \sim \Delta DBA$

$\therefore \quad AB/BC = DB/BA$

$\Rightarrow \quad AB^2 = DB \times BC$

$\Rightarrow \quad c^2 = pa$

2. $\Delta ABC \sim \Delta DAC$

$AC/BC = DC/AC$

$\Rightarrow \quad AC^2 = DC \times BC$

$\Rightarrow \quad b^2 = qa$

3. $\Delta DBA \sim \Delta DAC$

$DA/DB = DC/DA$

$DA^2 = DB \times DC$

$\Rightarrow \quad AD^2 = pq$

Basic Pythagorean Triplets

→ 3, 4, 5 → 5, 12, 13 → 7, 24, 25 → 8, 15, 17 → 9, 40, 41 → 11, 60, 61 → 12, 35, 37 → 16, 63, 65 → 20, 21, 29 → 28, 45, 53 These triplets are very important since a lot of questions are based on them.

Any triplet formed by either multiplying or dividing one of the basic triplets by any positive real number will be another Pythagorean triplet.

Thus, since 3, 4, 5 form a triplet so also will 6, 8 and 10 as also 3.3, 4.4 and 5.5.

Similarity of Right Triangles Two right triangles are similar if the hypotenuse and side of one is proportional to hypotenuse and side of another (RHS–similarity–Right angle hypotenuse side).

Important Terms with Respect to a Triangle

1. Median A line joining the mid-point of a side of a triangle to the opposite vertex is called a median. In the figure, the three medians are PG, QF and RE where G, E and F are mid-points of their respective sides.

- A median divides a triangle into two parts of equal area.
- The point where the three medians of a triangle meet is called the *centroid* of the triangle.
- The centroid of a triangle divides each median in the ratio 2: 1.

i.e. $PC : CG = 2 : 1 = QC : CF = RC : CE$

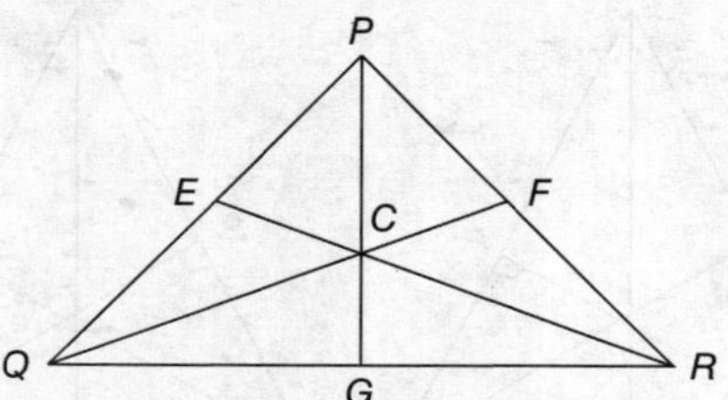

Important formula with respect to a median

→ $2 \times (\text{median})^2 + 2 \times (1/2 \text{ the third side})^2$

= Sum of the squares of other two sides

$$\Rightarrow 2(PG)^2 + 2 \times \left(\frac{QR}{2}\right)^2 = (PQ)^2 + (PR)^2$$

2. Altitude/Height A perpendicular drawn from any vertex to the opposite side is called the *altitude*. (In the figure, AD, BF and CE are the altitudes of the triangles).

- All the altitudes of a triangle meet at a point called the *orthocenter* of the triangle.
- The angle made by any side at the orthocenter and the vertical angle make a supplementary pair (i.e. they both add up to 180°). In the figure below: $\angle A + \angle BOC = 180° = \angle C + \angle AOB$

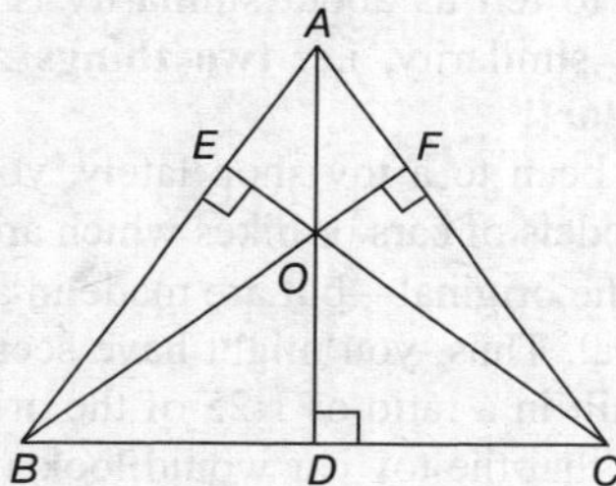

3. Perpendicular Bisectors A line that is a perpendicular to a side and bisects it is the perpendicular bisector of the side.

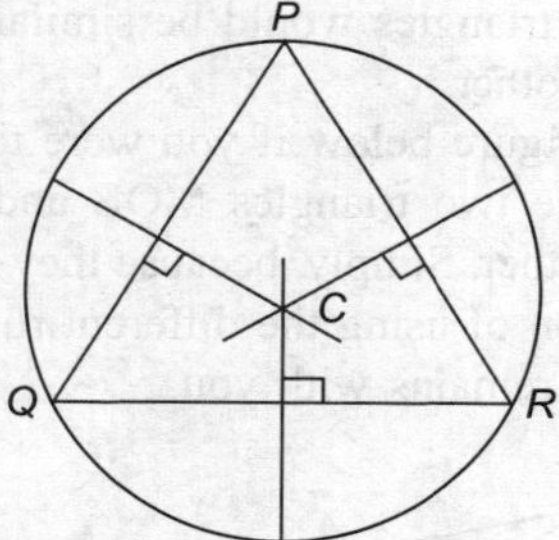

- The point at which the perpendicular bisectors of the sides meet is called the *circumcenter* of the triangle
- The circumcenter is the center of the circle that circumscribes the triangle. There can be only one such circle.
- Angle formed by any side at the circumcenter is two times the vertical angle opposite to the side. This is the property of the circle whereby angles formed

by an arc at the center are twice that of the angle formed by the same arc in the opposite arc. Here we can view this as:

$\angle QCR = 2\ \angle QPR$ (when we consider arc QR and its opposite arc QPR)

4. In-center

- The lines bisecting the interior angles of a triangle are the angle bisectors of that triangle.
- The angle bisectors meet at a point called the *in-center* of the triangle.
- The in-center is equidistant from all the sides of the triangle.

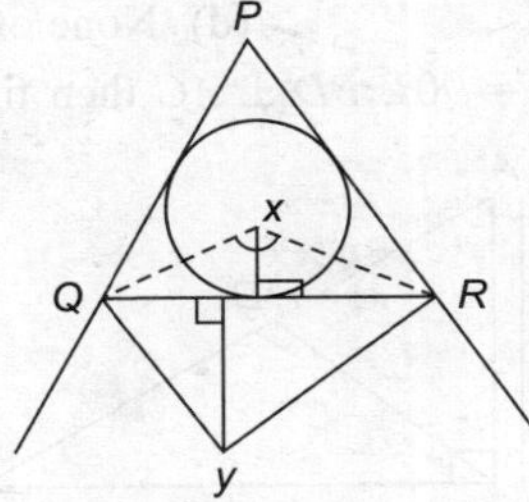

- From the in-center with a perpendicular drawn to any of the sides as the radius, a circle can be drawn touching all the three sides. This is called the *in-circle* of the triangle. The radius of the incircle is known as *in-radius*.
- The angle formed by any side at the in-center is always a right angle more than half the angle opposite to the side.

  This can be illustrated as $\angle QXR = 90 + \frac{1}{2}\angle P$.
- If QY and RY are the angle bisectors of the exterior angles at Q and R, then:

  $\angle QYR = 90 - \frac{1}{2}\angle P$

Mid-Point Theorem

The line segment joining the mid-points of two sides of a triangle is parallel to the third side and equal to half the third side.

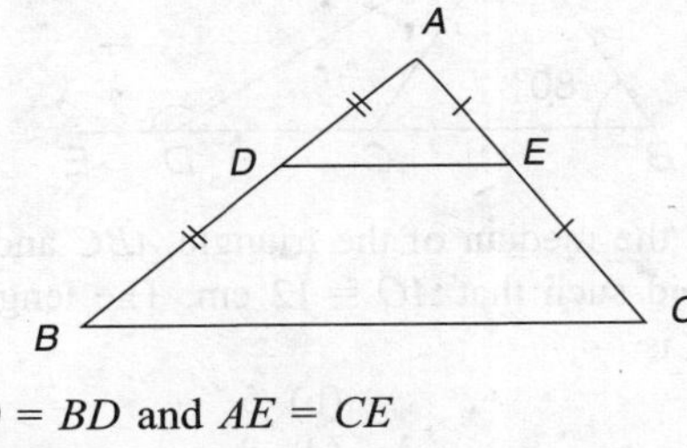

$AD = BD$ and $AE = CE$

$DE \parallel BC$

Apollonius' theorem

"The sum of the squares of any two sides of any triangle equals twice the square on half the third side plus twice the square of the median bisecting the third side".

Specifically, in any triangle ABC, if AD is a median, then

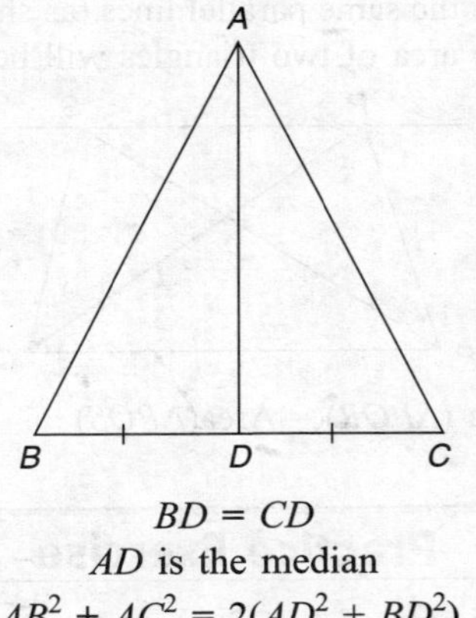

$BD = CD$

AD is the median

$AB^2 + AC^2 = 2(AD^2 + BD^2)$.

Angle-bisector theorem

In a triangle, the angle bisector of an angle divides the opposite side, to the angle in the ratio of the remaining two sides, i.e. $\frac{BD}{CD} = \frac{AB}{AC}$ and $BD \times AC - CD \times AB = AD^2$.

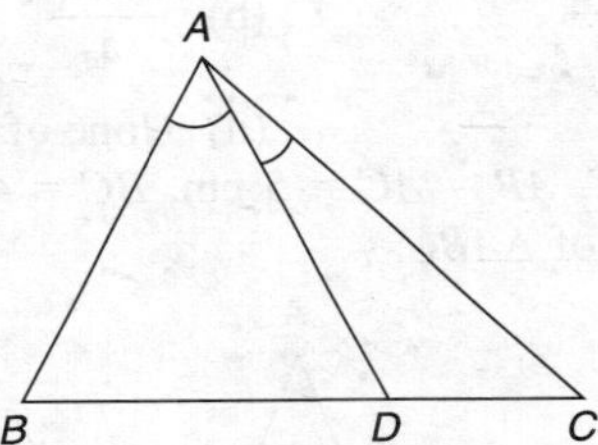

Exterior angle bisector theorem

In a triangle, the angle bisector (represented by CE in the figure) of any exterior angle of a triangle divides the side opposite to the external angle in the ratio of the remaining two sides i.e, $\frac{BE}{AE} = \frac{BC}{AC}$.

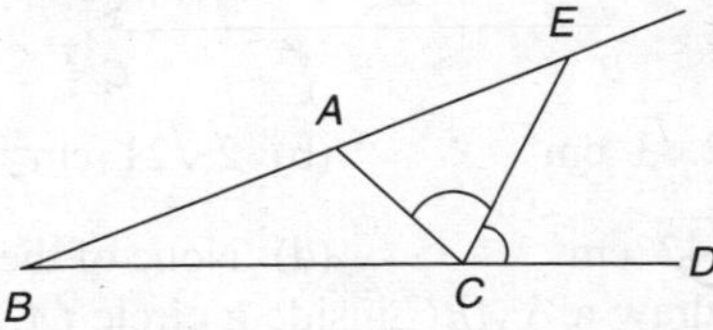

Few important results:

1. In a triangle AE, CD and BF are the medians then $3(AB^2 + BC^2 + AC^2) = 4(CD^2 + BF^2 + AE^2)$

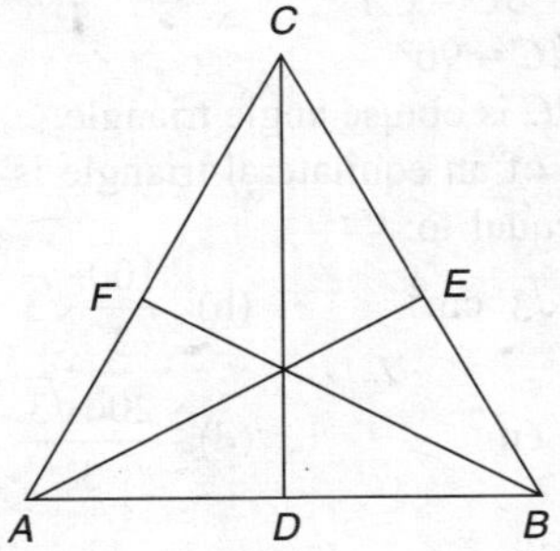

2. If the two triangles have the same base and lie between the same parallel lines (as shown in figure), then the area of two triangles will be equal.

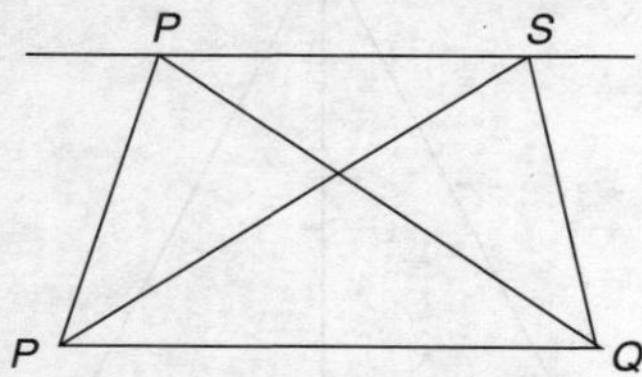

i.e. Area (ΔPQR) = Area(ΔPQS)

Practice Exercise

1. Find the area of ΔPQR.

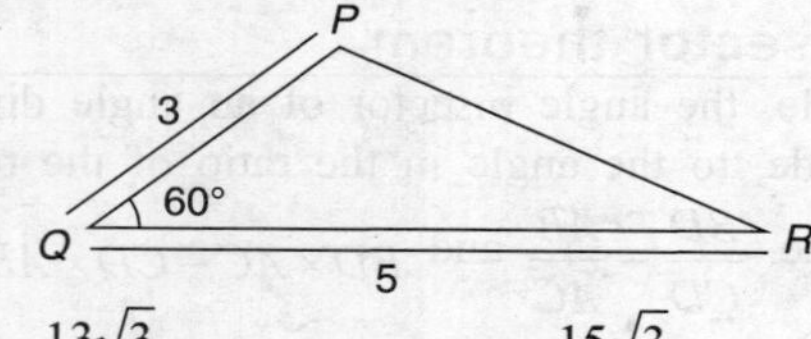

(a) $\frac{13\sqrt{3}}{4}$ (b) $\frac{15\sqrt{3}}{4}$

(c) $5\sqrt{3}$ (d) None of these

2. In ΔABC, $AB = AC = 5$ cm, $BC = 4$ cm, then find the area of ΔABC.

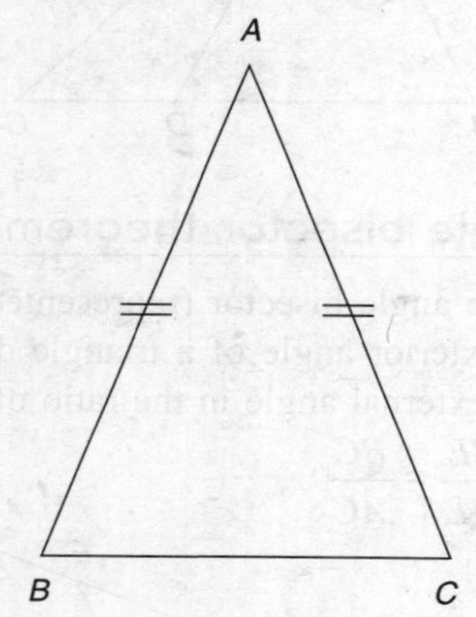

(a) $12\sqrt{3}$ cm^2 (b) $2\sqrt{21}$ cm^2

(c) $\sqrt{42}$ cm^2 (d) None of these

3. If we draw a Δ ABC inside a circle (A, B, C are on the circumference of a circle), then area of the ΔABC is maximum when:
(a) $AB = BC \neq AC$
(b) $AB = BC = CA$
(c) $\angle BAC = 90°$
(d) ΔABC is obtuse angle triangle

4. If height of an equilateral triangle is 10 cm, its area will be equal to:

(a) $100\sqrt{3}$ cm^2 (b) $\frac{100}{3}\sqrt{3}$ cm^2

(c) $\frac{100}{3}$ cm^2 (d) $\frac{200\sqrt{3}}{3}$ cm^2

5. Find the area of a triangle whose sides are 11, 60, 61.
(a) 210 (b) 330
(c) 315 (d) 275

6. If AD, BE, CF are medians of a ΔABC and O is the centroid of ΔABC. If area of ΔAOF is 36 cm^2, then find the area of ΔOFB + area of ΔOEC.
(a) 36 cm^2 (b) 54 cm^2
(c) 72 cm^2 (d) None of these

7. If three sides of a triangle are 5, 12, 13, then the circum-radius of the triangle is
(a) 6cm (b) 2.5cm
(c) 6.5cm (d) None of these

8. ΔABC, $\angle B = 90°$, $BD \perp AC$ then find BD.

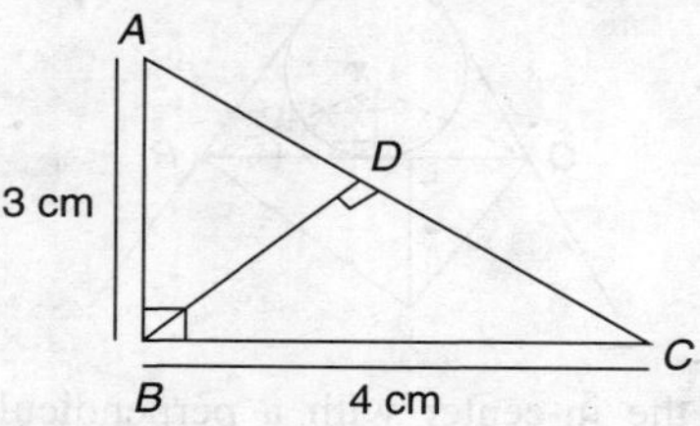

(a) 2.2 cm (b) 2.4 cm
(c) 2.6 cm (d) None of these

9. If $\angle A = 90°$, then the in-radius of ΔABC is

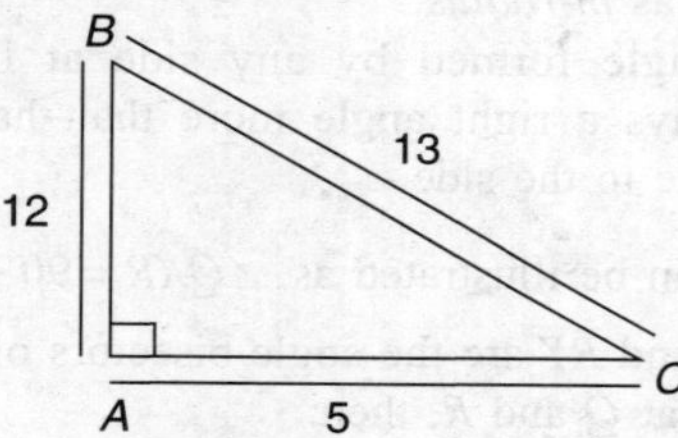

(a) 2 cm (b) 4 cm
(c) 6 cm (d) 8 cm

10. In ΔABC $AB = AC$, $\angle B = 80°$, $\angle BAD = 90°$, find $\angle ADE$.

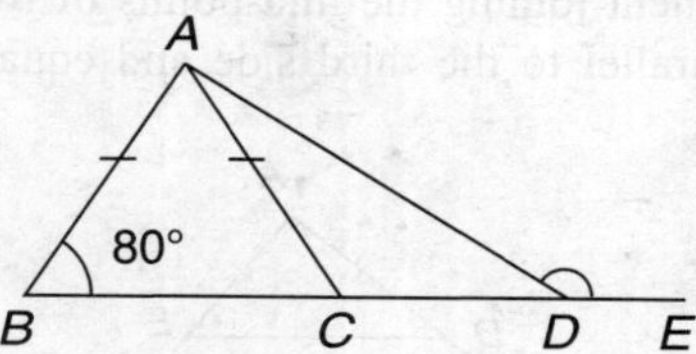

11. AD is the median of the triangle ABC and O is the centroid such that $AO = 12$ cm. The length of OD in cm is
(a) 4 (b) 5
(c) 6 (d) 8

12. If ΔABC is an isosceles triangle with $\angle C = 90°$ and $AC = 7$ cm, then AB is
(a) 8.5 cm (b) 8.2 cm
(c) $7\sqrt{2}$ cm (d) 7.5 cm

13. In $\Delta\ ABC$, $AB = AC$, $\angle BAC = 50°$, now CB is extended to D, then the external angle at $\angle DBA$ is

(a) 90° (b) 70°
(c) 115° (d) 80°

14. The sides of a triangle are in the ratio 4:5:6. The triangle is

(a) Acute-angled
(b) Right-angled
(c) Obtuse-angled
(d) Either acute-angled or right angled

15. The sum of three altitudes of a triangle is

(a) Equal to the sum of three sides
(b) Less than the sum of sides
(c) $1/\sqrt{2}$ times of the sum of sides
(d) Half the sum of sides

16. Two medians PS and RT of ΔPQR intersect at G at right angles. If $PS = 9$ cm and $RT = 6$ cm, then the length of RS in cm is

(a) 10 (b) 6
(c) 5 (d) 3

17. Two triangles ABC and PQR are similar to each other in which $AB = 5$ cm, $PQ = 4$ cm. Then the ratio of the areas of triangles ABC and PQR is

(a) 4:5 (b) 25:16
(c) 64:125 (d) 4:7

18. In ΔABC, the internal bisectors of $\angle ACB$ and $\angle ABC$ meet at X and $\angle BAC = 30°$. The measure of $\angle BXC$ is

(a) 95° (b) 105°
(c) 125° (d) 130°

19. The area of an equilateral triangle is $900\sqrt{3}$ sq m. Its perimeter is

(a) 120 m (b) 150 m
(c) 180 m (d) 135 m

20. The sides of a triangle are 3 cm, 4 cm and 5 cm. The area (in cm^2) of the triangle formed by joining the mid points of this triangle is

(a) 6 (b) 3
(c) 3/2 (d) 3/4

ANSWER KEY

1. (b)	2. (b)	3. (b)	4. (b)
5. (b)	6. (c)	7. (c)	8. (b)
9. (a)	10. 170^0	11. (c)	12. (c)
13. (c)	14. (a)	15. (b)	16. (c)
17. (b)	18. (b)	19. (c)	20. (c)

SOLUTIONS AND SHORTCUTS

1. Area $= \frac{1}{2} \times 3 \times 5 \times \sin 60^o = \frac{15}{2} \times \frac{\sqrt{3}}{2} = \frac{15\sqrt{3}}{4}$

2. Area $= \frac{b}{4}\sqrt{4a^2 - b^2}$

$= \frac{4}{4}\sqrt{4 \times 25 - 16} = \sqrt{84} = 2\sqrt{21}$ cm^2

3. An equilateral triangle will have the maximum area compared to other triangles inside the same circle. So $AB = BC = CA$.

4. $h = 10$ cm

$h = \frac{a\sqrt{3}}{2} \Rightarrow a = \frac{10 \times 2}{\sqrt{3}} = \frac{20}{\sqrt{3}}$ cm

Area $= \frac{1}{2} \times \frac{20}{\sqrt{3}} \times 10 = \frac{100}{\sqrt{3}}$ cm^2 or $\frac{100\sqrt{3}}{3}$ cm^2

5. 11, 60, 61 form a Pythagoras triplet. Hence, the triangle is a right-angled triangle.

Area $= \frac{1}{2} \times 11 \times 60 = 330$

6. 'O' is the centroid of ΔABC
Then area of ΔAOF = area ΔOFB = area of ΔOEC
Area (ΔOFB) + Area(ΔOEC) = 36 + 36 = 72 cm^2

7. 5, 12, 13 form a Pythagoras triplet.
Circum-radius = 13/2 = 6.5 cm

8. $\frac{1}{BD^2} = \frac{1}{4^2} + \frac{1}{3^2} = \frac{25}{144}$

$BD = \left(\frac{144}{25}\right)^{\frac{1}{2}} = \frac{12}{5} = 2.4$ cm

9. In-radius $= \frac{12 \times 5}{12 + 5 + 13} = \frac{60}{30} = 2$ cm

10. $\angle B = \angle ACB = 80°$

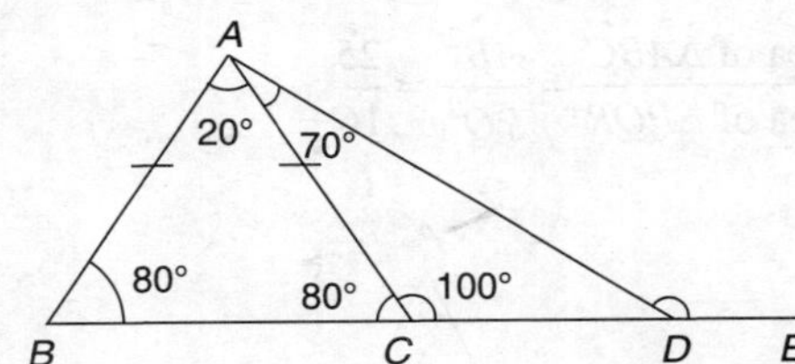

$\angle BAC = 180° - (80° + 80°) = 20°$
$\angle ADE = \angle CAD + \angle ACD = 70° + 100° = 170°$

11. D, is the mid-point of side BC.
Centroid 'O' divides AD in the ratio 2:1

$\therefore OD = \frac{12}{2} = 6$ cm

12. $AC = BC = 7$ cm

$\therefore AB = \sqrt{AC^2 + BC^2} = \sqrt{7^2 + 7^2} = \sqrt{98} = 7\sqrt{2}$ cm

13.

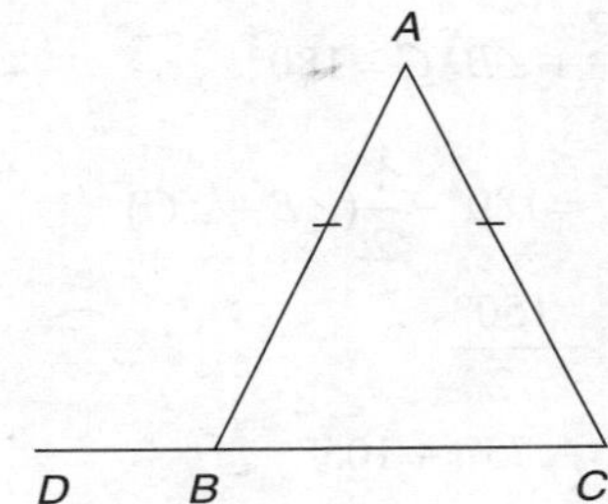

$\angle ABC = \angle ACB$

$\angle BAC = 50°$

$\therefore \angle ABC + \angle ACB = 130°$

$\angle ABC = 65°$

$\therefore \angle ABD = 180° - 65° = 115°$

14. Let the sides of the triangle be 3x, 4x and 6x units.

Clearly, $(4x)^2 + (5x)^2 > (6x)^2$

$\therefore$ the triangle will be acute-angled.

15. For a triangle *PQR*, let the altitudes be *AP*, *BR* and *CQ* respectively. Then:

$AP < PR$

$BR < RQ$

$CQ < PQ$

$\therefore AP + BR + CQ < PQ + QR + PR$

16. $PS = 9$ cm

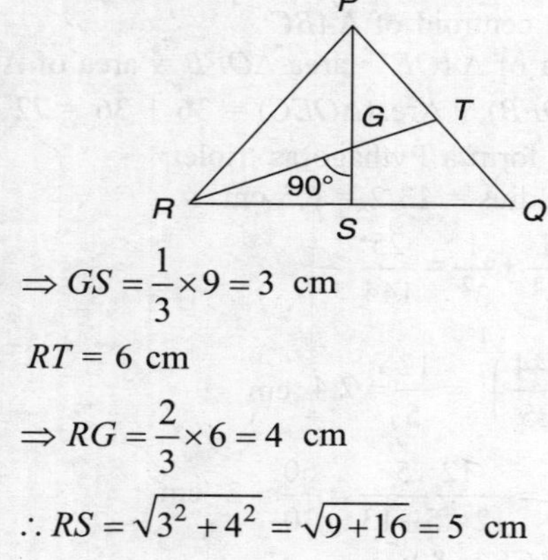

$\Rightarrow GS = \frac{1}{3} \times 9 = 3$ cm

$RT = 6$ cm

$\Rightarrow RG = \frac{2}{3} \times 6 = 4$ cm

$\therefore RS = \sqrt{3^2 + 4^2} = \sqrt{9+16} = 5$ cm

17. $\frac{\text{area of } \Delta ABC}{\text{area of } \Delta PQR} = \frac{AB^2}{PQ^2} = \frac{25}{16}$

18.

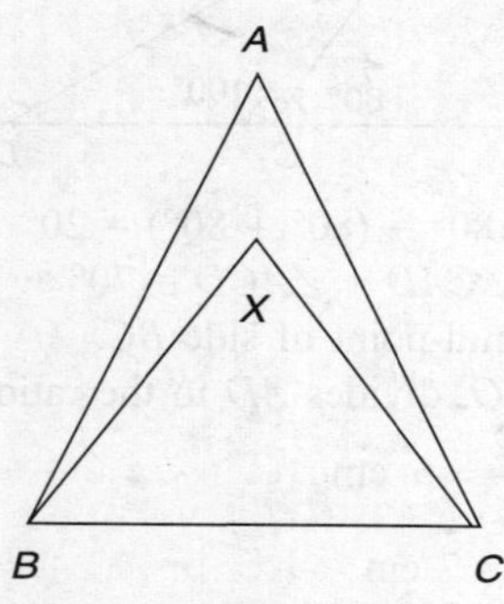

$\angle B + \angle C = 180° - 30° = 150°$

In ΔBXC,

$\frac{\angle B}{2} + \frac{\angle C}{2} + \angle BXC = 180°$

$\Rightarrow \angle BXC = 180° - \frac{1}{2}(\angle B + \angle C)$

$= 180° - \frac{150°}{2}$

$= 180° - 75° = 105°$

19. Let the side of the equilateral triangle be *X* cm. Area of equilateral triangle

$= \frac{\sqrt{3}}{4} \times (X)^2$

$\Rightarrow \frac{\sqrt{3}}{4} \times (X)^2 = 900\sqrt{3}$

$\Rightarrow (X)^2 = \frac{900\sqrt{3} \times 4}{\sqrt{3}}$

$\therefore X = \sqrt{4 \times 900} = 60$ meters

$\therefore$ Perimeter $= 3 \times X = 3 \times 60 = 180$ meters

20. The area of the triangle formed by joining the midpoint of the triangle is 1/4th of the area of the original triangle.

Area of the original triangle $= \frac{1}{2} \times 3 \times 4 = 6$ cm^2

$\therefore$ Required area $= \frac{1}{4} \times 6 = \frac{3}{2}$ cm^2

QUADRILATERALS

Area

(a) Area = 1/2 (product of diagonals) × (sine of the angle between them)

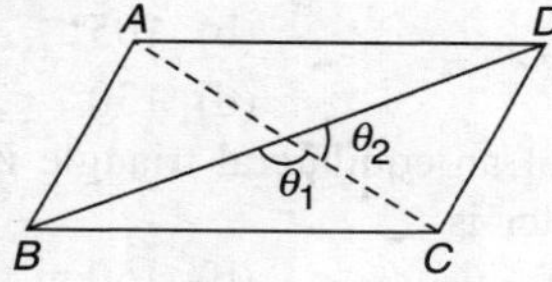

If θ_1 and θ_2 are the two angles made between themselves by the two diagonals, we have by the property of intersecting lines $\rightarrow \theta_1 + \theta_2 = 180°$.

Then, the area of the quadrilateral $= \frac{1}{2} d_1 d_2 \sin \theta_1$

$= \frac{1}{2} d_1 d_2 \sin \theta_2$.

(b) Area = 1/2 × diagonal × sum of the perpendiculars to it from opposite vertices $= \frac{d(h_1 + h_2)}{2}$.

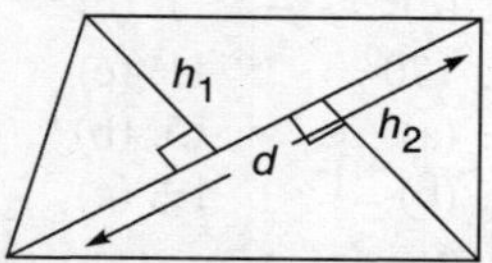

(c) Area of a circumscribed quadrilateral

$A = \sqrt{(S-a)(S-b)(S-c)(S-d)}$

where $S = \frac{a+b+c+d}{2}$

(where *a*, *b*, *c* and *d* are the lengths of the sides)

Properties

1. In a convex quadrilateral inscribed in a circle, the product of the diagonals is equal to the sum of the products of the opposite sides. For example, in the figure below:
$(a \times c) + (b \times d) = AC \times BD$

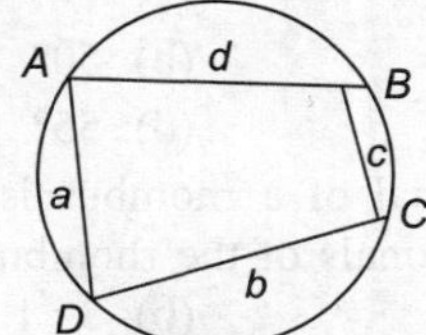

2. Sum of all the angles of a quadrilateral = 360°.

TYPES OF QUADRILATERALS

1. Parallelogram (|| gm)

A parallelogram is a quadrilateral with opposite sides parallel (as shown in the figure).

(a) Area = Base (b) × Height (h)
$= bh$

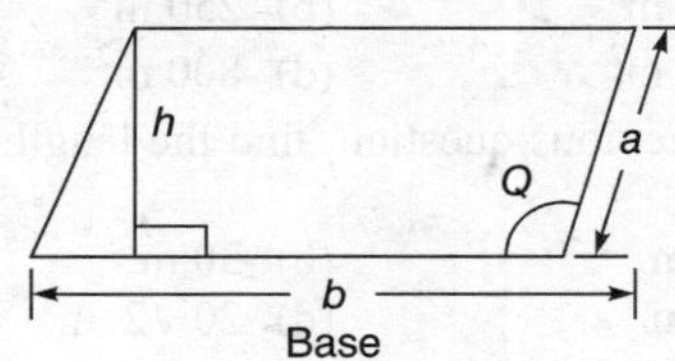

(b) Area = product of any two adjacent sides × sine of the included angle
$= ab \sin Q$

(c) Perimeter = $2(a + b)$
where, a and b are any two adjacent sides.

Properties

(a) Diagonals of a parallelogram bisect each other
(b) Bisectors of the angles of a parallelogram form a rectangle
(c) A parallelogram inscribed in a circle is a rectangle
(d) A parallelogram circumscribed about a circle is a rhombus
(e) The opposite angles in a parallelogram are equal
(f) The sum of the squares of the diagonals is equal to the sum of the squares of the four sides. In the figure,
$AC^2 + BD^2 = AB^2 + BC^2 + CD^2 + AD^2$
$= 2(AB^2 + BC^2)$

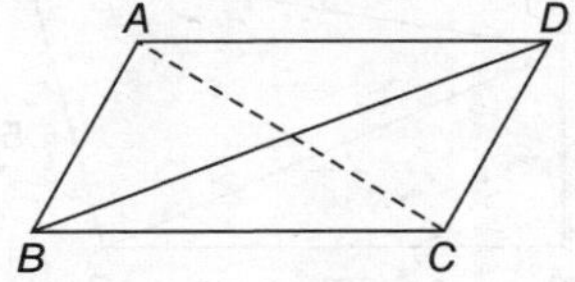

2. Rectangles

A rectangle is a parallelogram with all angles 90°.

(a) Area = Base × Height = $b \times h$

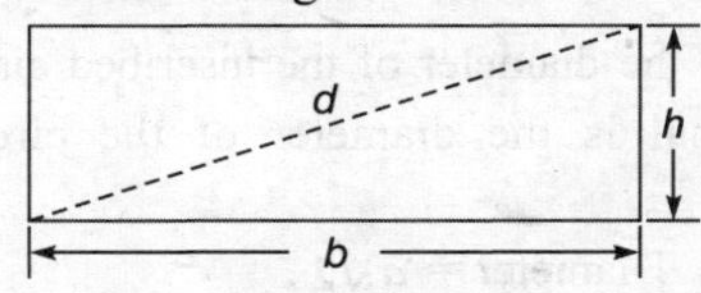

Note: Base and height are also referred to as the length and the breadth in a rectangle.

(b) Diagonal (d) = $\sqrt{b^2 + h^2}$ (by Pythagoras theorem)

Properties of a Rectangle

(a) Diagonals are equal and bisect each other
(b) Bisectors of the angles of a rectangle (a parallelogram) form another rectangle
(c) All rectangles are parallelograms but the reverse is not true

3. Rhombus

A parallelogram having all the sides equal is a rhombus.

(a) Area = 1/2 × product of diagonals × sine of the angle between them
$= 1/2 \times d_1 \times d_2 \sin 90°$ (Diagonals in a rhombus intersect at right angles)
$= 1/2 \times d_1 d_2$ (since $\sin 90° = 1$)

(b) Area = product of adjacent sides × sine of the angle between them

Properties

(a) Diagonals bisect each other at right angles
(b) All rhombuses are parallelograms but the reverse is not true
(c) A rhombus may or may not be a square but all squares are rhombuses

4. Square

A square is a rectangle with adjacent sides equal or a rhombus with each angle 90°.

(a) Area = base × height = a^2
(b) Area = 1/2 (diagonal)^2 = $1/2\, d^2$ (square is a rhombus too)
(c) Perimeter = $4a$ (a = side of the square)
(d) Diagonal = $a\sqrt{2}$
(e) Inradius = $\dfrac{a}{2}$

d
a
Height
a
Base

Properties

(a) Diagonals are equal and bisect each other at right angles
(b) Side is the diameter of the inscribed circle
(c) Diagonal is the diameter of the circumscribing circle

$\Rightarrow$ Diameter = $a\sqrt{2}$.

Circum-radius = $a/\sqrt{2}$

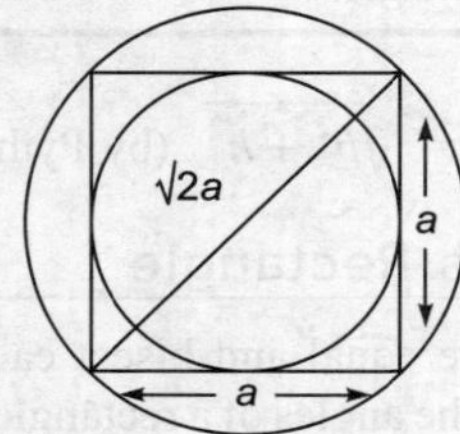

5. Trapezium

A trapezium is a quadrilateral with only two sides parallel to each other.

(a) Area = 1/2 × sum of parallel sides × height = 1/2 $(AB + DC) \times h$—for the figure below.
(b) Median = 1/2 × sum of the parallel sides (median is the line equidistant from the parallel sides)
For any line *EF* parallel to *AB*:

$$EF = \frac{\{[P \times (AB)] + [Q \times (DC)]\}}{AD}$$

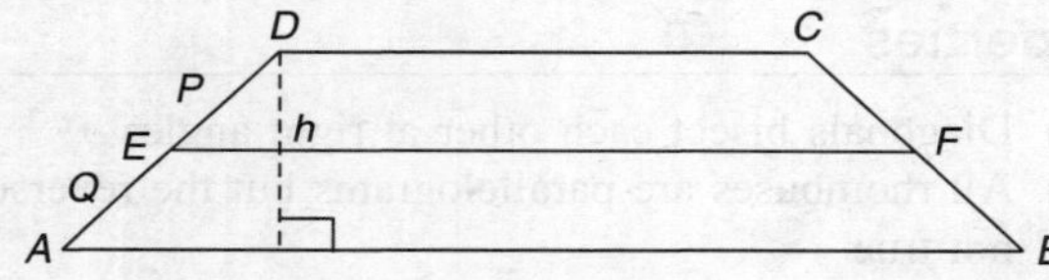

Properties

(a) If the non-parallel sides are equal then diagonals will be equal too.

Practice Exercise

1. Find the smallest angle of a quadrilateral if the measure of its interior angles is in the ratio of 1:2:3:4.
(a) 18° (b) 36°
(c) 54° (d) 72°

2. In a parallelogram *PQRS* if bisectors of *P* and *Q* meet at *X*, then the value of *PXQ* is
(a) 45° (b) 90°
(c) 75° (d) 60°

3. In a parallelogram *PQRS*, if S = 105° and *PRQ* = 25° then find *QPR*.

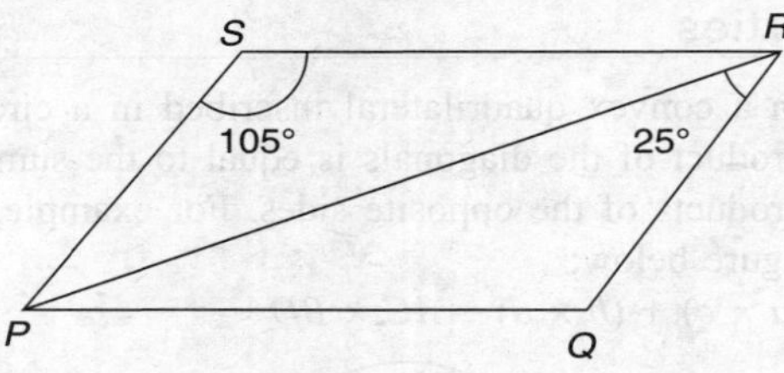

(a) 40° (b) 50°
(c) 60° (d) 55°

4. If one diagonal of a rhombus is equal to its side, then the diagonals of the rhombus are in the ratio.
(a) $\sqrt{3}:1$ (b) 3 : 1
(c) 2 : 1 (d) None of these

5. A triangle and a parallelogram are constructed on the same base such that their areas are equal. If the altitude of the parallelogram is 100 m, then the altitude of the triangle is
(a) 50 m (b) 100 m
(c) 200 m (d) None of these

6. In a square *PQRS*, *A* is the midpoint of *PQ* and *B* is the midpoint of *QR*, if area of ΔAQB is 100 m^2 then find the area of the square *PQRS*.
(a) 400 m^2 (b) 250 m^2
(c) 600 m^2 (d) 800 m^2

7. In the previous question, find the length of diagonal *PR*.
(a) 20 m (b) 30 m
(c) 40 m (d) $20\sqrt{2}$ m

8. If a triangle with area *x*, rectangle with area *y*, parallelogram with area *z* were all constructed on the same base and all have the same altitude, then which of the following options is true?
(a) $x = y = z$ (b) $x = y/2 = z$
(c) $2x = y = z$ (d) $2x = 2y = z$

9. □*ABCD* is a parallelogram; *AC*, *BD* are the diagonals and intersect at point *O*. *X* and *Y* are the centroids of ΔADC and ΔABC respectively. If *BY* = 6 cm, then find *OX*.
(a) 2 cm (b) 3 cm
(c) 4 cm (d) 6 cm

10. If area of a rectangle with sides *x* and *y* is *X* and that of a parallelogram (which is strictly not a rectangle) with sides *x* and *y* is *Y*, then
(a) $X = Y$ (b) $X \leq Y$
(c) $X < Y$ (d) $X > Y$

11. In □*ABCD*, A = 90°, *BC* = *CD* = 5 cm, *AD* = 3 cm, *BA* = 4 cm. Find the value of $\angle BCD$.

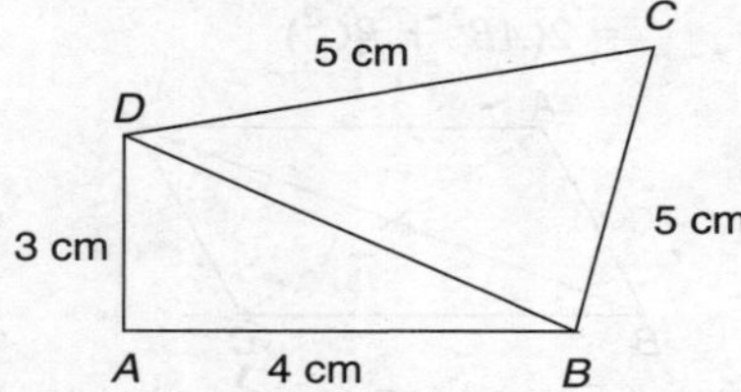

(a) 45° (b) 60°
(c) 75° (d) 85°

12. In the above question, what will be the area of □ABCD?
(a) 16.83 cm^2 (b) 15.36 cm^2
(c) 14.72 cm^2 (d) 13.76 cm^2

13. □*PQRS* is a parallelogram. '*O*' is a point within it and area of parallelogram *PQRS* is 50 cm^2. Find the sum of areas of ΔOPQ and ΔOSR (in cm^2).
(a) 15 (b) 20
(c) 25 (d) 30

14. *ABCD* is a rhombus, such that *AB* = 5cm *AC* = 8 cm. Find the area of □*ABCD*

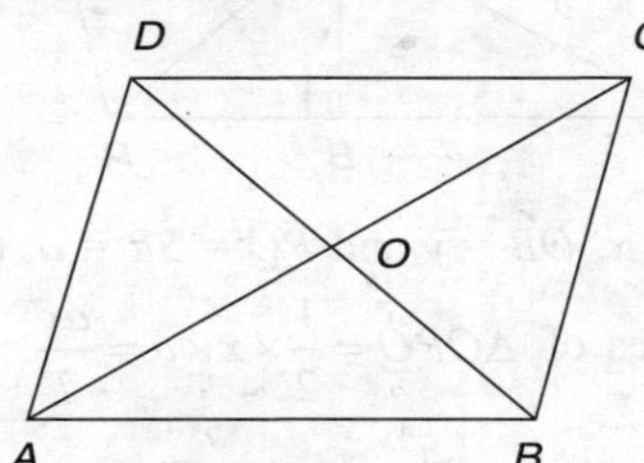

(a) 12 cm^2 (b) 18 cm^2
(c) 24 cm^2 (d) 36 cm^2

15. If *ABCD* is a trapezium, then find the value of *x*.

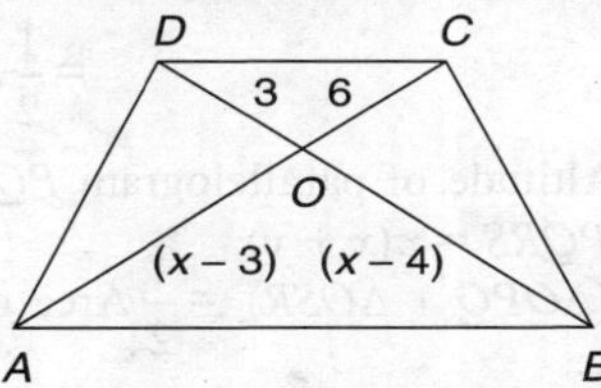

(a) 3 (b) 4
(c) 5 (d) 6

16. A square and a rhombus have the same base and the rhombus is inclined at 45° then what will be the ratio of area of the square to the area of the rhombus?
(a) 2:1 (b) $\sqrt{2}:1$
(c) $1:\sqrt{2}$ (d) $\sqrt{3}:1$

17. *PQRS* is a quadrilateral and *PQ* || *RS*. *T* is the midpoint of *PQ*. *ST* || *RQ*. If area of the triangle ΔPST is 50 cm^2 then area of □*PQRS* is

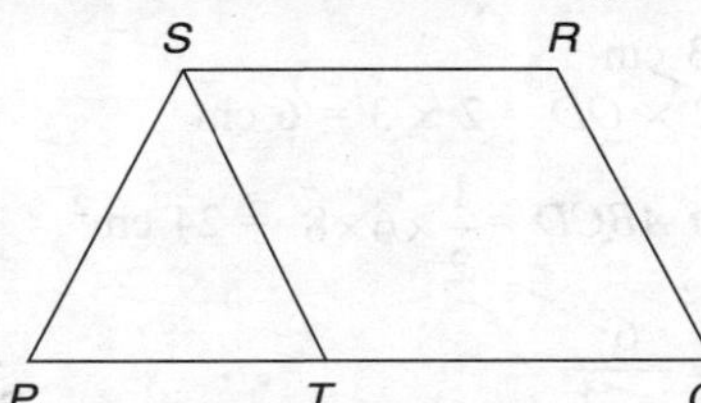

(a) 100 cm^2 (b) 125 cm^2
(c) 150 cm^2 (d) 175 cm^2

18. In □*ABCD*, *AB* = *BC*, *AD* = *CD*. *BD* and *AC* are diagonals of □*ABCD*, such that *BD* = 10 cm, *AC* = 5 cm. Find area of □ABCD.

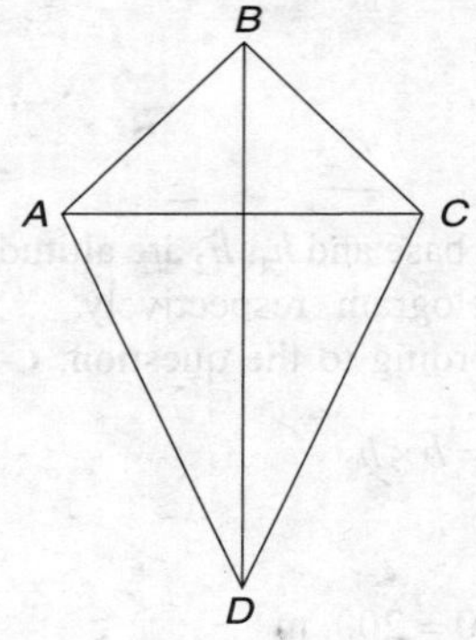

ANSWER KEY

1. (b)	2. (b)	3. (b)	4. (a)
5. (c)	6. (d)	7. (c)	8. (c)
9. (b)	10. (d)	11. (b)	12. (a)
13. (c)	14. (c)	15. (c)	16. (b)
17. (c)	18. 25 cm^2		

SOLUTIONS AND SHORTCUTS

1. Let the angles be *x*, 2*x*, 3*x*, 4*x*, respectively
According to the question:
$x + 2x + 3x + 4x = 360°$
$10x = 360°$
$x = 36°$
Smallest angle = 36°

2. $P + Q = 180°$
$$\frac{\angle P}{2} + \frac{\angle Q}{2} = 90°$$
$$\angle PXQ = 180^o - \left[\frac{\angle P}{2} + \frac{\angle Q}{2}\right] = 180^o - 90^o = 90^o$$

3. $PQR = PSR = 105°$
$RPQ = 180° - (105° + 25°) = 50°$

4. Let $AB = BD = DC = a$, $AC = b$

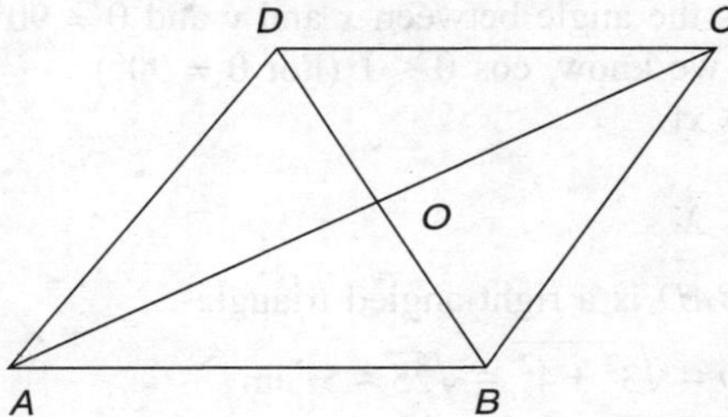

In ΔCOD: $(CD)^2 = (OC)^2 + (OD)^2$
$$a^2 = \left(\frac{b}{2}\right)^2 + \left(\frac{a}{2}\right)^2$$
$$\frac{3a^2}{4} = \frac{b^2}{4}$$

$b = a\sqrt{3}$

$\frac{b}{a} = \frac{\sqrt{3}}{1}$

5. If 'b' is the base and h_1, h_2 are altitudes of the triangle and parallelogram, respectively.
Then, according to the question,

$\frac{1}{2} \times b \times h_1 = b \times h_2$

$h_1 = 2h_2$

$h_1 = 2 \times 100 = 200$ m

6. Area of ΔAQB = $\frac{1}{2} \times AQ \times BQ$ = 100 = 100

$\frac{1}{2} \times \frac{PQ}{2} \times \frac{QR}{2} = 100$

$PQ \times QR = 2 \times 2 \times 2 \times 100 = 800$ m^2

7. $PQ.QR$ = 800 m^2
$PQ = QR$ (□$PQRS$ is a square)
$(PQ)^2 = 800$
$PQ = 20\sqrt{2}$ m
Length of the diagonal = $PQ\sqrt{2} = 20\sqrt{2} \times \sqrt{2}$ = 40 m.

8. Area of triangle = $\frac{1}{2}$ × Area of Parallelogram
$x = z/2$
Area of parallelogram = Area of rectangle
$y = z$
$2x = y = z$

9. ΔABC and ΔADC are congruent to each other.
So $OD = OB$

$\frac{OD}{3} = \frac{OB}{3}$

$OX = OY$

$OX = \frac{BY}{2} = \frac{6}{2} = 3$ cm

10. Area of rectangle $ABCD = X = xy$
Area of parallelogram $PQRS = Y = x.y \cos\theta$ (where θ is the angle between x and y and $\theta \neq 90°$)
As we know, $\cos\theta < 1$ (For $\theta \neq 90°$)
$Y < xy$
or
$Y < X$

11. Δ BAD is a right-angled triangle

$BD = \sqrt{3^2 + 4^2} = \sqrt{25} = 5$ cm

In ΔBCD, all the sides are equal to each other, so ΔBCD is an equilateral triangle.
∴ BCD = 60°

12. Area of □$ABCD$ = Area of ΔABC + Area of ΔBCD

$= \frac{1}{2} \times 3 \times 4 + \frac{\sqrt{3}}{4}(5)^2$ cm^2

$= 6 + \frac{25\sqrt{3}}{4}$ cm^2

$= (6 + 6.25\sqrt{3})$ cm^2

$= 16.83$ cm^2

13. Draw $OA \perp PQ$ and $OB \perp SR$.

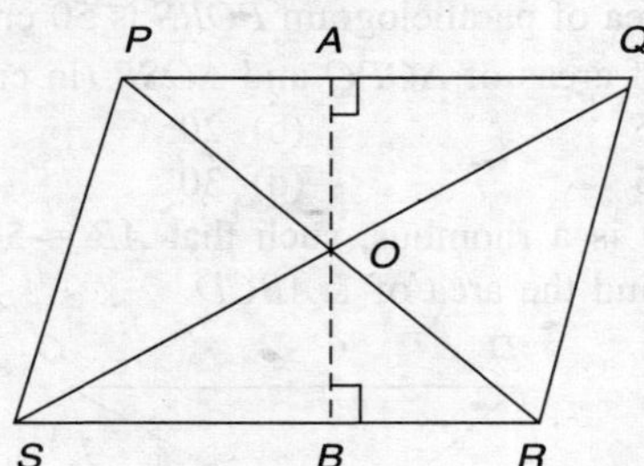

If $OA = x$, $OB = y$ and $PQ = SR = a$, $QR = PS = b$

Then area of $\Delta OPQ = \frac{1}{2} \times x \times a = \frac{ax}{2}$

Area of $\Delta OSR = \frac{1}{2} \times y \times a = \frac{ay}{2}$

Area of ΔOPQ + Area of $\Delta OSR = \frac{ax}{2} + \frac{ay}{2}$

$= \frac{1}{2}a(x + y)$

$x + y$ = Altitude of parallelogram $PQRS$
Area of $PQRS = a(x + y)$
Area of (ΔOPQ + ΔOSR) $= \frac{1}{2}$ Area of □$PQRS$

$= \frac{1}{2} \times 50 = 25$ cm^2

14. $OC = \frac{AC}{2} = \frac{8}{2} = 4$ cm

$\because \angle DOC = 90°$

$\therefore OD^2 + OC^2 = CD^2$

$OD^2 + 4^2 = 5^2$

$OD^2 = 9$

OD = 3 cm
$BD = 2 \times OD = 2 \times 3 = 6$ cm

Area of $ABCD = \frac{1}{2} \times 6 \times 8$ = 24 cm^2

15. $\frac{3}{x-4} = \frac{6}{x-3}$

$3(x - 3) = 6(x - 4)$
$x - 3 = 2(x - 4)$
$x - 3 = 2x - 8$
$x = 5$

16. Let the length of base be 'x' units. Area of square = x^2

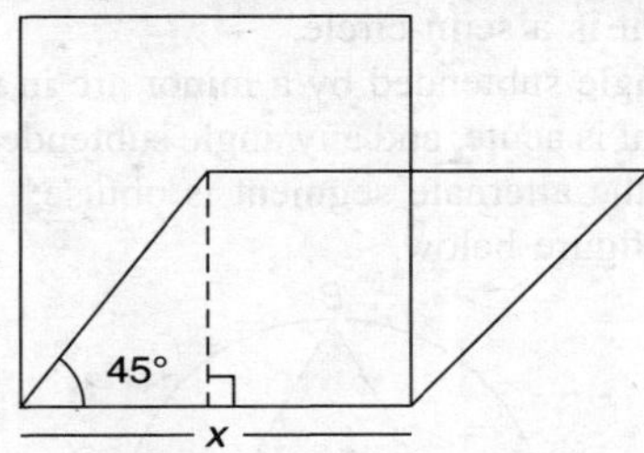

Area of rhombus = $x^2 \times \sin 45°$

$$= x \times \frac{x}{\sqrt{2}} = \frac{x^2}{\sqrt{2}}$$

Required ratio $= x^2 : \frac{x^2}{\sqrt{2}}$

$$= 1 : \frac{1}{\sqrt{2}}$$

$$= \sqrt{2} : 1$$

17. T is the midpoint of PQ

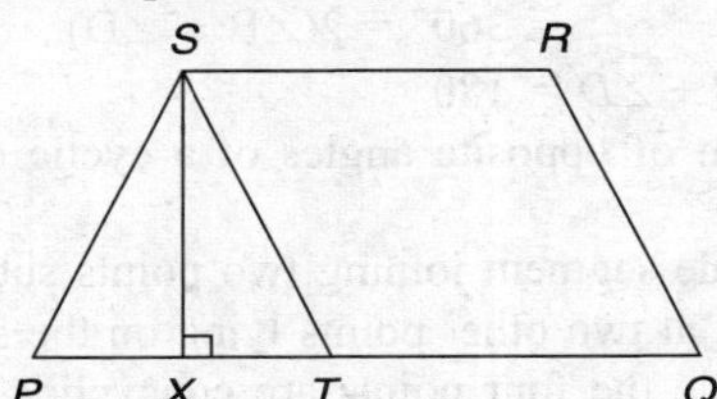

$PT = TQ$

Draw $SX \perp PQ$, if $SX = h$ and $PT = TQ = a$

Area of $\Delta PST = \frac{1}{2} \times a \times h = \frac{ah}{2}$

Area of $\square PQRS$ = Area of ΔPST + Area of $\square STQR$

$$= \frac{ah}{2} + ah$$

$$= \frac{3ah}{2}$$

$$= 3[50] = 150 \text{ cm}^2$$

18. $\square ABCD$ has a kite like structure, so it's diagonals intersect each other perpendicularly

Area = $\frac{1}{2}$ × (product of diagonals)

$$= \frac{1}{2} \times 10 \times 5 = 25 \text{ cm}^2$$

REGULAR HEXAGON

(a) Area = $[(3\sqrt{3})/2]$ (side)^2

$$= \frac{3\sqrt{3} \times a^2}{2}$$

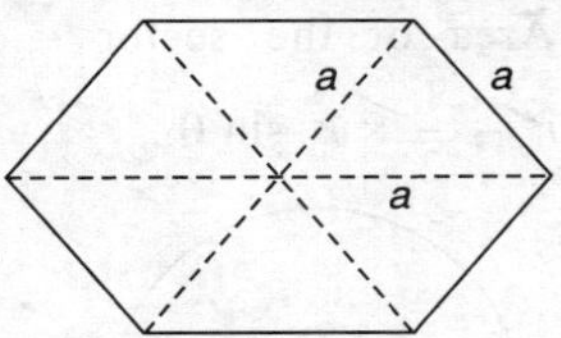

(b) A regular hexagon is actually a combination of six equilateral triangles all of side 'a'. Hence, the area is also given by: 6 × area of an equilateral triangle having the same side as the side of the hexagon = $6 \times \frac{\sqrt{3}}{4} a^2$

(c) If you look at the figure closely, it will not be difficult to realise that circumradius (R) = a; i.e. the side of the hexagon is equal to the circum-radius of the same.

CIRCLES

(a) Area = πr^2

(b) Circumference = $2\pi r$ = (r = radius)

(c) Area = 1/2 × circumference × r

Arc: It is a part of the circumference of the circle. The bigger one is called the *major arc* and the smaller one the *minor arc*.

(d) Length (Arc XY) = $\frac{\theta}{360} \times 2\pi r$

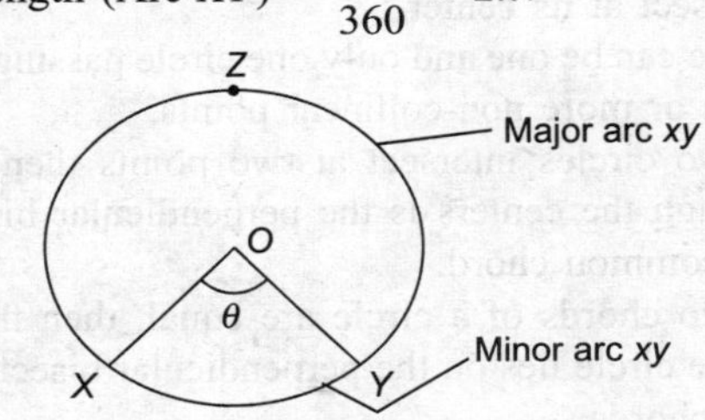

(e) **Sector of a circle** is a part of the area of a circle between two radii.

(f) Area of a sector = $\frac{\theta}{360} \times \pi r^2$

(where θ is the angle between two radii)

= $(1/2) r$ × length (arc xy)

($\because \pi r\theta/180$ = length arc xy)

$$= \frac{1}{2} \times r \times \frac{\pi r \theta}{360}$$

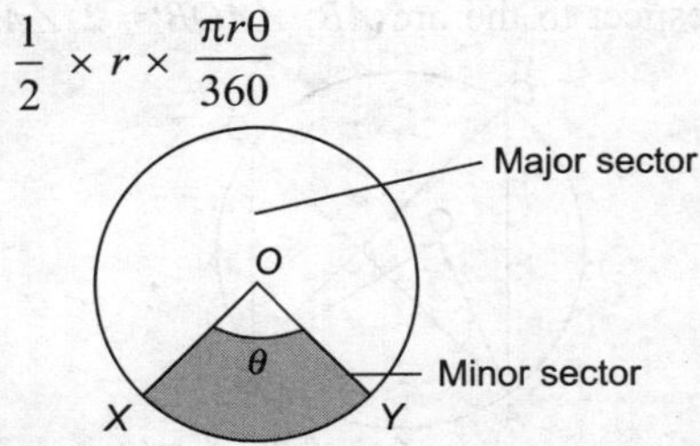

(g) **Segment:** A sector minus the triangle formed by the two radii is called the segment of the circle.

(h) Area = Area of the sector − Area ΔOAB = $\frac{\theta}{360} \times \pi r^2 - \frac{1}{2} \times r^2 \sin\theta$

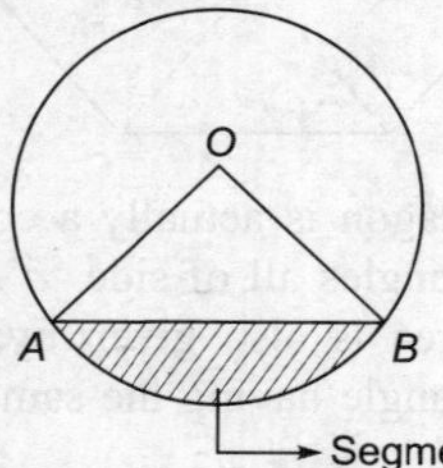

(i) Perimeter of segment = length of the arc + length of segment AB

$$= \frac{\theta}{360} \times 2\pi r + 2r\sin\left(\frac{\theta}{2}\right)$$

$$= \frac{\pi r\theta}{180} + 2r\sin\left(\frac{\theta}{2}\right)$$

(j) **Congruency:** Two circles can be congruent if and only if they have equal radii.

Properties

(a) The perpendicular from the center of a circle to a chord bisects the chord. The converse is also true.

(b) The perpendicular bisectors of two chords of a circle intersect at its center.

(c) There can be one and only one circle passing through three or more non-collinear points.

(d) If two circles intersect at two points then the line through the centers is the perpendicular bisector of the common chord.

(e) If two chords of a circle are equal, then the center of the circle lies on the perpendicular bisector of the two chords.

(f) Equal chords of a circle or congruent circles are equidistant from the center.

(g) Equidistant chords from the center of a circle are equal to each other in terms of their length.

(h) The degree measure of an arc of a circle is twice the angle subtended by it at any point on the alternate segment of the circle. This can be clearly seen in the following figure:
With respect to the arc AB, $\angle AOB = 2\,\angle ACB$.

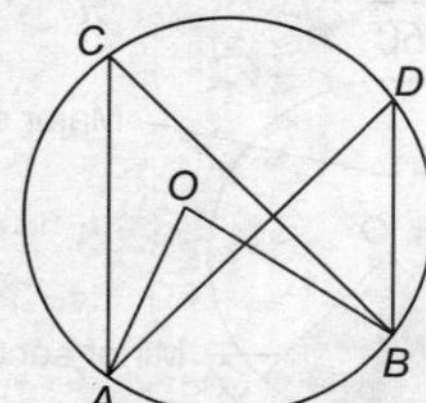

(i) Any two angles in the same segment are equal. Thus, $\angle ACB = \angle ADB$.

(j) The angle subtended by a semi-circle is a right angle. Conversely, the arc of a circle subtending a right angle at any point of the circle in its alternate segment is a semi-circle.

(k) Any angle subtended by a minor arc in the alternate segment is acute, and any angle subtended by a major arc in the alternate segment is obtuse.
In the figure below.

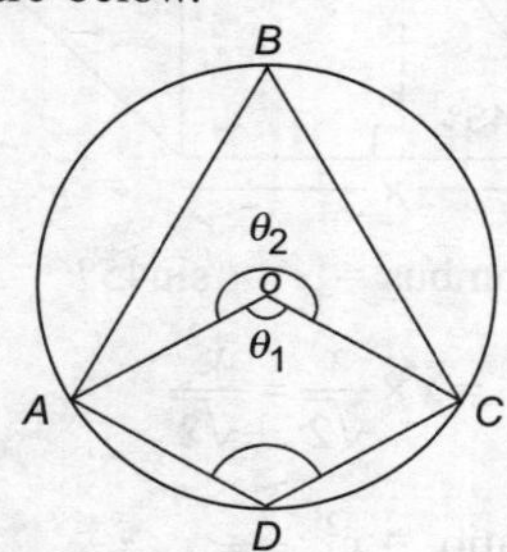

$\angle ABC$ is acute and

$\angle ADC$ = obtuse

Also $\theta_1 = 2\,\angle B$

And $\theta_2 = 2\,\angle D$

$\therefore \theta_1 + \theta_2 = 2(\angle B + \angle D)$

$= 360° = 2(\angle B + \angle D)$

or $\angle B + \angle D = 180°$

or sum of opposite angles of a cyclic quadrilateral is 180°.

(l) If a line segment joining two points subtends equal angles at two other points lying on the same side of the line, the four points are concyclic. Thus, in the following figure:
If, $\theta_1 = \theta_2$
then $ABCD$ are concyclic, that is, they lie on the same circle.

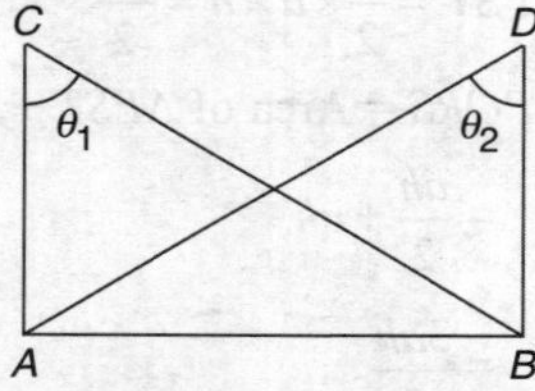

(m) Equal chords of a circle (or of congruent circles) subtend equal angles at the center (at the corresponding centers.) The converse is also true.

(n) If the sum of the opposite angles of a quadrilateral is 180°, then the quadrilateral is cyclic.
Secant: A line that intersects a circle at two points
Tangent: A line that touches a circle at exactly one point

(o) If a circle touches all the four sides of a quadrilateral then the sum of the two opposite sides is equal to the sum of other two.

$$AB + DC = AD + BC$$

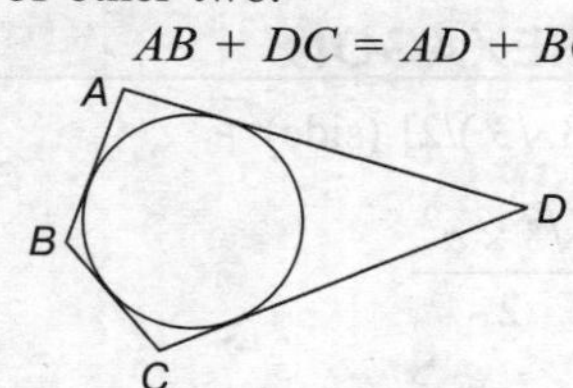

(p) In two concentric circles, the chord of the larger circle that is tangent to the smaller circle is bisected at the point of contact.

Tangents

- Length of direct common tangents is

$= \sqrt{(\text{Distance between their centres})^2 - (r_1 - r_2)^2}$

where, r_1 and r_2 are the radii of the circles

$= \sqrt{(OO')^2 - (r_1 - r_2)^2}$

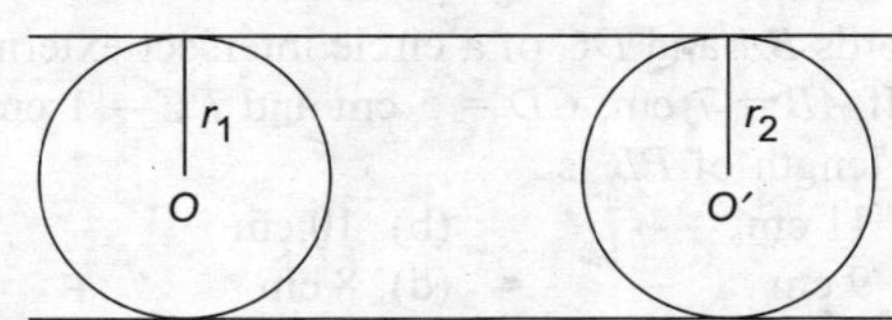

- Length of transverse common tangents is

$= \sqrt{(\text{distance between their centres})^2 - (r_1 + r_2)^2}$

$= \sqrt{(OO')^2 - (r_1 + r_2)^2}$

ELLIPSE

- Perimeter = $\pi (a + b)$
- Area = πab

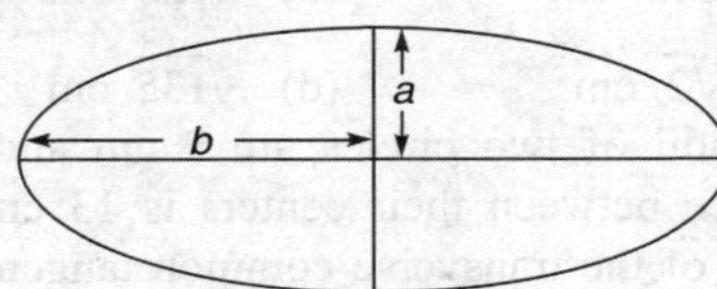

Practice Exercise

1. Find the area of a circle of radius 5cm.
   (a) 25π (b) 20π
   (c) 22π (d) None of these
2. Find the circumference of the circle in the previous question:
   (a) 10π (b) 5π
   (c) 7π (d) None of these
3. If O is the center of the circle and $OC \perp AB$ and $AC = x + 6$, $BC = 2x - 4$, then find AB.

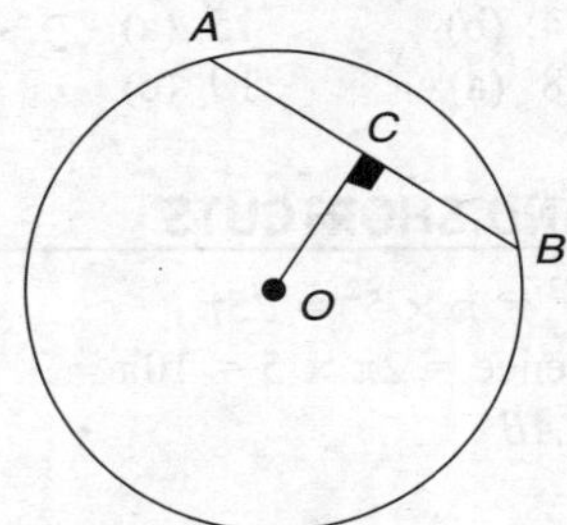

   (a) 22 (b) 31
   (c) 32 (d) 26
4. If $\overline{AB} = \overline{CD}$ and AB = 12 cm and 'O' is the center of the circle, OD = 8 cm, $OE \perp CD$, then length of OE is

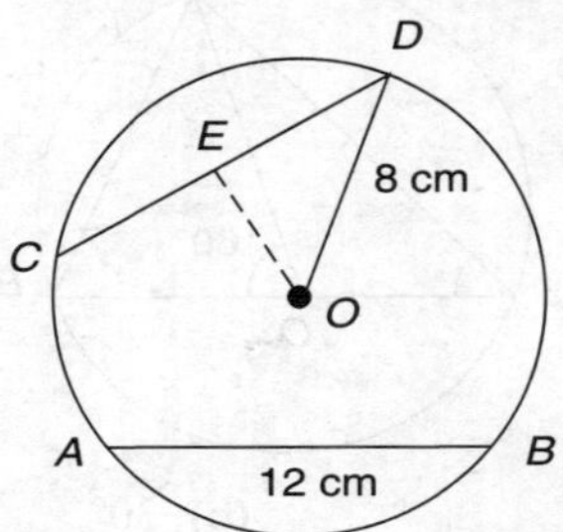

   (a) 2 cm (b) $2\sqrt{7}$ cm
   (c) $2\sqrt{11}$ cm (d) None of these
5. In the given figure, O is the center of the circle. $ABO = 45°$. Find the value of ACB

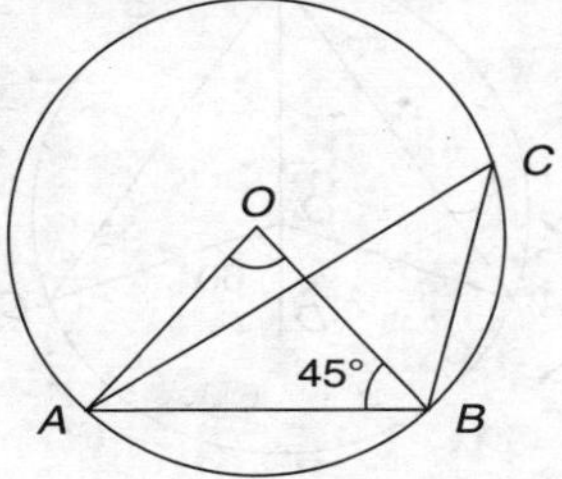

   (a) 60° (b) 75°
   (c) 90° (d) None of these
6. In the given figure, AOC = 130°, where O is the center. Find $\angle CBE$

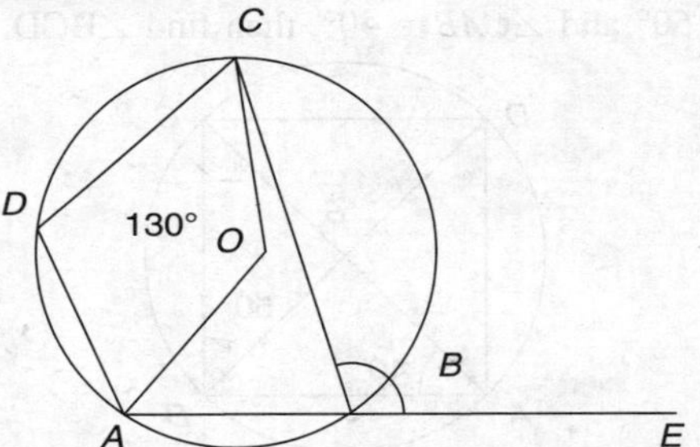

   (a) 100° (b) 70°
   (c) 115° (d) 130°
7. In the given figure, ΔABC is an equilateral triangle. Find $\angle BEC$

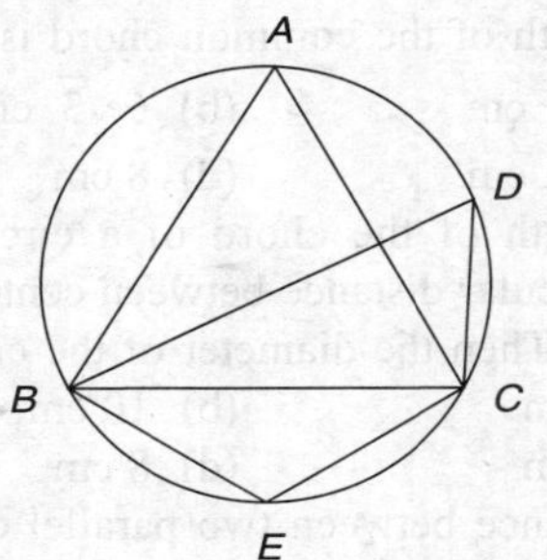

   (a) 120° (b) 60°
   (c) 80° (d) None of these

8. In the given figure, $COB = 60°$, AB is the diameter of the circle. Find $\angle ACO$

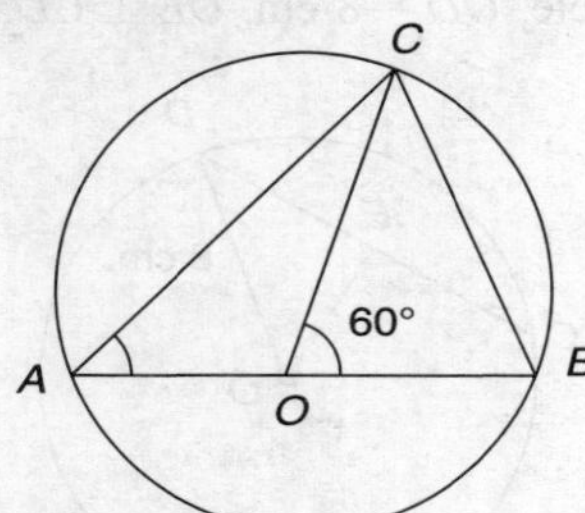

(a) 20° (b) 30°
(c) 35° (d) 40°

9. O is the center of the circle; line segment BOD is the angle bisector of $\angle AOC$, and $\angle COD = 60°$. Find $\angle ABC$.

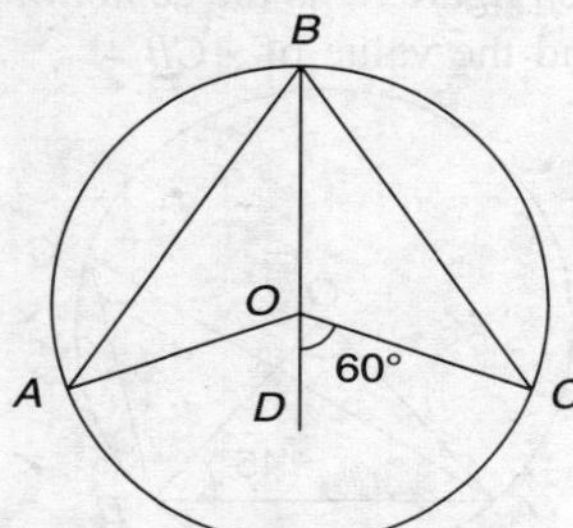

(a) 30° (b) 40°
(c) 50° (d) 60°

10. In the given figure, $ABCD$ is a cyclic quadrilateral and the diagonals bisect each other at P. If $\angle CBD = 50°$ and $\angle CAB = 40°$, then find $\angle BCD$.

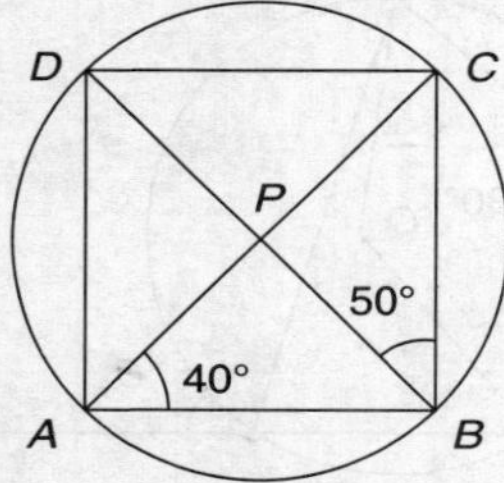

(a) 60° (b) 75°
(c) 90° (d) 105°

11. Two equal circles of radius 6 cm intersect each other such that each passes through the center of the other. The length of the common chord is:
(a) $2\sqrt{3}$ cm (b) $6\sqrt{3}$ cm
(c) $2\sqrt{2}$ cm (d) 8 cm

12. The length of the chord of a circle is 6 cm and perpendicular distance between center and the chord is 4 cm. Then the diameter of the circle is equal to:
(a) 12 cm (b) 10 cm
(c) 16 cm (d) 8 cm

13. The distance between two parallel chords of length 6 cm each in a circle of diameter 10 cm is
(a) 8 cm (b) 7 cm
(c) 6 cm (d) 5.5 cm

14. The length of the common chord of two intersecting circles is 24. If the diameters of the circles are 30 cm and 26 cm, then the distance between the centers of the circles (in cm) is
(a) 13 (b) 14
(c) 15 (d) 16

15. If two equal circles whose centers are O and O', intersect each other at the points A and B. $OO' = 6$ cm and $AB = 8$ cm, then the radius of the circles is
(a) 5 cm (b) 8 cm
(c) 12 cm (d) 14 cm

16. Chords BA and DC of a circle intersect externally at P. If $AB = 7$ cm, $CD = 5$ cm and $PC = 1$ cm, then the length of PB is
(a) 11 cm (b) 10 cm
(c) 9 cm (d) 8 cm

17. Two circles touch each other internally. Their radii are 3 cm and 4 cm. The biggest chord of the greater circle which is outside the inner circle is of length
(a) $2\sqrt{3}$ cm (b) $3\sqrt{2}$ cm
(c) $4\sqrt{3}$ cm (d) $4\sqrt{2}$ cm

18. If the radii of two circles are 8 cm and 4 cm and the length of the transverse common tangent is 13 cm, then the distance between the two centers is
(a) $\sqrt{313}$ cm (b) $\sqrt{125}$ cm
(c) $5\sqrt{2}$ cm (d) $\sqrt{135}$ cm

19. The radii of two circles are 9 cm and 4 cm, the distance between their centers is 13 cm. Then the length of the transverse common tangent is
(a) 12 cm (c) $12\sqrt{2}$ cm
(c) 5 cm (d) 15 cm

20. The radii of two circles are 9cm and 4cm, the distance between their centers is 13cm. Then the length of the direct common tangent is
(a) 12 cm (b) $12\sqrt{2}$ cm
(c) 5 cm (d) 15 cm

ANSWER KEY

1. (a)	2. (a)	3. (c)	4. (b)
5. (d)	6. (c)	7. (a)	8. (b)
9. (d)	10. (c)	11. (b)	12. (b)
13. (a)	14. (b)	15. (a)	16. (b)
17. (c)	18. (a)	19. (c)	20. (a)

SOLUTIONS AND SHORTCUTS

1. Area $= \pi r^2 = \pi \times 5^2 = 25\pi$
2. Circumference $= 2\pi \times 5 = 10\pi$
3. As $OC \perp AB$
$AC = BC$
$x + 6 = 2x - 4$
$x = 10$
$AB = x + 6 + 2x - 4 = 3x + 2 = 30 + 2 = 32$

4. If $\overline{AB} = \overline{CD}$

Then $AB = CD = 12$ cm

If $CD = 12$, then $CE = DE = 6$cm

$OE = \sqrt{8^2 - 6^2} = \sqrt{28} = 2\sqrt{7}$ cm

5. $AO = BO$

$ABO = BAO = 45°$

$AOB = 180° - (45° + 45°) = 90°$

$\angle ACB = \dfrac{\angle AOB}{2} = \dfrac{90°}{2} = 45°$

6. $\angle ABC = \dfrac{130°}{2} = 65°$ $\angle CBE = 180° - 65° = 115°$

7. $BAC = 60°$

$\angle BEC = 180° - \angle BAC = 180° - 60° = 120°$

8. $\angle COB = 60°$

$\angle AOC = 180° - 60° = 120°$

$\angle CAO = \dfrac{60°}{2} = 30°$

$\angle ACO = 180° - (120° + 30°) = 180° - 150° = 30°$

9. $\angle COD = 60°$

$\angle AOC = 2 \times 60° = 120°$

$\angle ABC = \dfrac{120°}{2} = 60°$

10. $\angle CDB = \angle CAB = 40°$

In $\Delta BDC = \angle BCD + 50° + 40° = 180°$

$\angle BCD = 90°$

11. $OO' = 6$ cm

$OC = 3$ cm

$OA = 6$ cm

$\therefore AC = \sqrt{6^2 - 3^2} = \sqrt{36 - 9} = \sqrt{27} = 3\sqrt{3}$ cm

$\therefore AB = 6\sqrt{3}$ cm

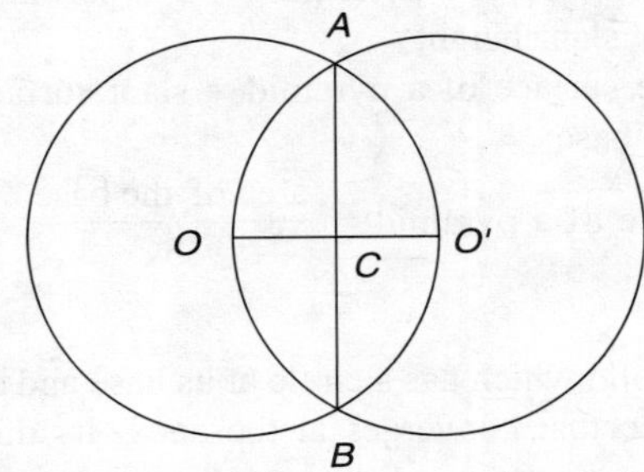

12. $AC = CB = 3$ cm

$OC = 4$ cm

$\therefore OA = \sqrt{OC^2 + CA^2}$

$= \sqrt{4^2 + 3^2}$

$= \sqrt{16 + 9} = \sqrt{25} = 5$ cm

Diameter = 10 cm

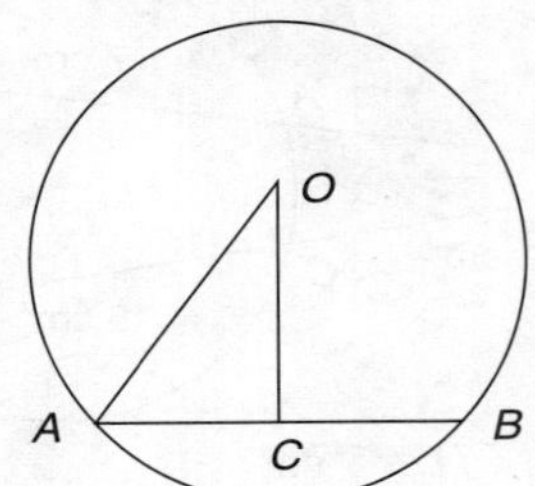

13.

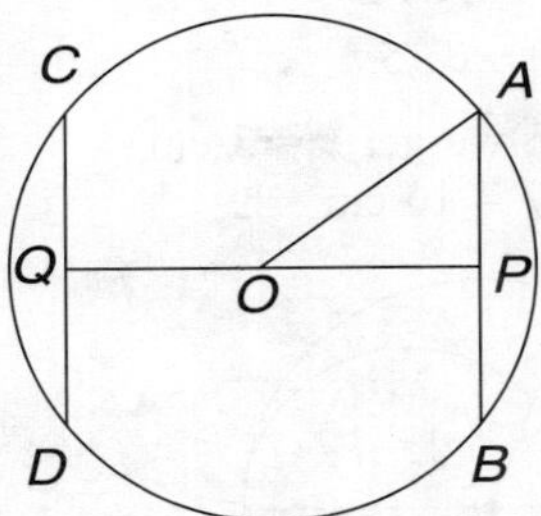

$AB = CD$

$OP = OQ$

From ΔOAP

$OP = \sqrt{OA^2 - AP^2} = \sqrt{5^2 - 3^2} = \sqrt{25 - 9} = \sqrt{16}$

$= 4$cm

$\therefore QP = 2 \times OP = 8$ cm

14. $AC = CB = 12$ cm

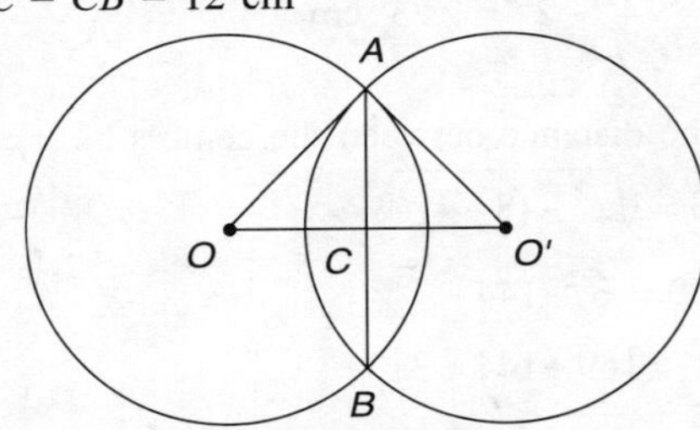

$OC = \sqrt{15^2 - 12^2} = \sqrt{225 - 144} = \sqrt{81} = 9$ cm

$O'C = \sqrt{13^2 - 12^2} = \sqrt{169 - 144} = \sqrt{25} = 5$ cm

$\therefore OO' = 9 + 5 = 14$ cm

15.

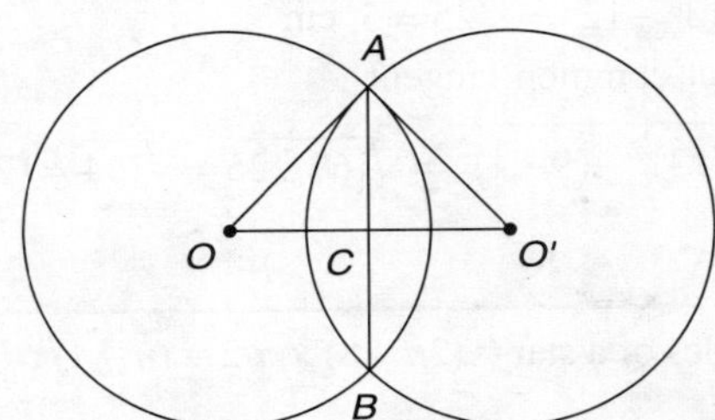

$AB = 8$ cm

$AC = BC = 4$ cm

$OC = CO' = 3$ cm

$\therefore OA = \sqrt{OC^2 + CA^2} = \sqrt{3^2 + 4^2} = \sqrt{9 + 16} = \sqrt{25} = 5$ **cm**

16.

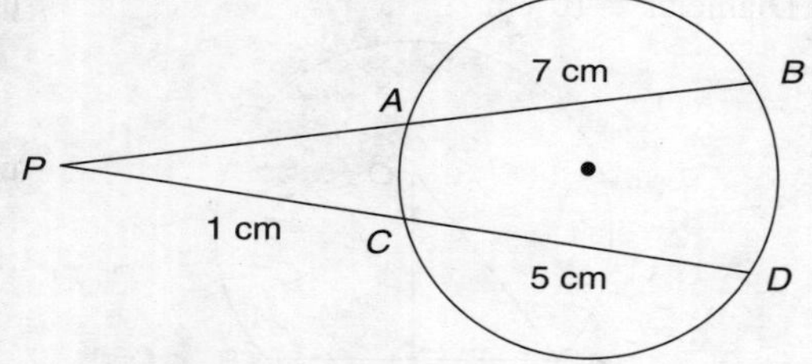

$AB = 7$ cm, $CD = 5$ cm
$PC = 1$ cm, $PA = x$ cm
$PA \times PB = PC \times PD$
$\Rightarrow x(x+7) = 6 \times 5$

By solving, we get $x = 3$ cm
$PB = 3 + 7 = 10$ cm

17.

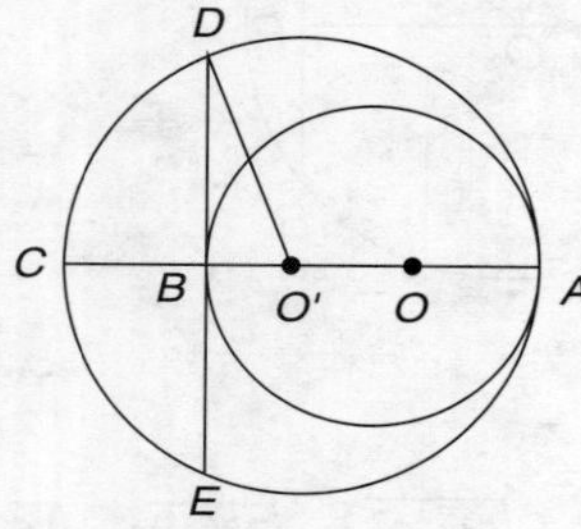

$O'A = 4$ cm
$AB = 6$ cm
$O'B = AB - O'A = 6 - 4 = 2$ cm

$BD = \sqrt{4^2 - 2^2} = 2\sqrt{3}$ cm

$DE = 4\sqrt{3}$ cm

18. Let the distance between the centers be x cm.

$\Rightarrow 13 = \sqrt{x^2 - (8+4)^2}$

$\Rightarrow 169 = x^2 - 144$

$\Rightarrow x^2 = 169 + 144 = 313$

$\Rightarrow x = \sqrt{313}$ cm

19. Transverse common tangent

$= \sqrt{(\text{Distance between centres})^2 - (r_1 + r_2)^2}$

$= \sqrt{13^2 - 12^2} = \sqrt{25} = 5$ cm

20. Direct common tangent

$= \sqrt{(13)^2 - (9-4)^2} = \sqrt{169 - 25} = \sqrt{144} = 12$ cm

STAR

Sum of angles of a star = $(2n - 8) \times \pi/2 = (n - 4)\pi$

PART II: MENSURATION

The following formulae hold true in the area of mensuration:

1. Cuboid

A cuboid is a three-dimensional box. It is defined by the virtue of its length l, breadth b and height h. It can be visualised as a room which has its length, breadth and height different from each other.

(a) Total surface area of a cuboid = $2(lb + bh + lh)$
(b) Volume of the cuboid = lbh

2. Cube of side s

A cube is a cuboid which has all its edges equal i.e. length = breadth = height = s.

(a) Total surface area of a cube = $6s^2$.
(b) Volume of the cube = s^3.

3. Prism

A prism is a solid which can have any polygon at both its ends. Its dimensions are defined by the dimensions of the polygon at its ends and its height.

(a) Lateral surface area of a right prism = perimeter of base × height
(b) Volume of a right prism = area of base × height
(c) Whole surface of a right prism = lateral surface of the prism + the area of the two plane ends

4. Cylinder

A cylinder is a solid which has both its ends in the form of a circle. Its dimensions are defined in the form of the radius of the base (r) and the height h. A gas cylinder is a close approximation of a cylinder.

(a) Curved surface of a right cylinder = $2\pi rh$, where r is the radius of the base and h the height.
(b) Whole surface of a right circular cylinder = $2\pi rh + 2\pi r^2$
(c) Volume of a right circular cylinder = $\pi r^2 h$

5. Pyramid

A pyramid is a solid which can have any polygon as its base and its edges converge to a single apex. Its dimensions are defined by the dimensions of the polygon at its base and the length of its lateral edges which lead to the apex. The Egyptian pyramids are examples of pyramids.

(a) Slant surface of a pyramid = 1/2 × perimeter of the base × slant height
(b) Whole surface of a pyramid = slant surface + area of the base
(c) Volume of a pyramid = $\frac{\text{area of the base}}{3} \times$ height

6. Cone

A cone is a solid which has a circle at its base and a slanting lateral surface that converges at the apex. Its dimensions are defined by the radius of the base (r), the height (h) and the slant height (l). A structure similar to a cone is used in ice-cream cones.

(a) Curved surface of a cone = πrl where l is the slant height
(b) Whole surface of a cone = $\pi rl + \pi r^2$
(c) Volume of a cone = $\frac{\pi r^2 h}{3}$

7. Sphere

A sphere is a solid in the form of a ball with radius r.

(a) Surface area of a sphere = $4\pi r^2$

(b) Volume of a sphere = $\frac{4}{3}\pi r^3$

8. Frustum of a pyramid

When a pyramid is cut, the left-over part is called the frustum of the pyramid.

(a) Slant surface of the frustum of a pyramid = 1/2 × sum of perimeters of end × slant height

(b) Volume of the frustum of a pyramid = $\frac{k}{3}[E_1 + (E_1, E_2)^{1/2} + E_2]$, where k is the height of the frustum and E_1, E_2 the areas of the ends

9. Frustum of a cone

When a cone is cut, the left-over part is called the frustum of the cone.

(a) Slant surface of the frustum of a cone = $\pi(r_1 + r_2)l$ where l, is the slant height

(b) Volume of the frustum of a cone = $\frac{\pi}{3}\ k(r_1^2 + r_1 r_2 + r_2^2)$

Where 'k' is the height of the frustum.

Space for Rough Work

WORKED-OUT PROBLEMS

Problem 12.1: A right triangle with hypotenuse 10 inches and other two sides of variable length is rotated about its longest side thus giving rise to a solid. Find the maximum possible volume of such a solid.

(a) $(250/3)\pi \text{in}^3$ (b) $(160/3)\pi \text{in}^3$
(c) $325/3\pi \text{in}^3$ (d) None of these

Solution: Most of the questions like this that are asked in the CAT will not have figures accompanying them. Drawing a figure takes time, so it is always better to strengthen our imagination. The beginners can start off by trying to imagine the figure first and trying to solve the problem. They can draw the figure only when they do not arrive at the right answer and then find out where exactly they went wrong. The key is to spend as much time with the problem as possible trying to understand it fully and analysing the different aspects of the same without investing too much time on it.

Let's now look into this problem. The key here lies in how quickly you are able to visualise the figure and are able to see that

(i) the triangle has to be an isosceles triangle,
(ii) the solid, thus, formed is actually a combination of two cones,
(iii) the radius of the base has to be the altitude of the triangle to the hypotenuse.

After you have visualised, this comes the calculation aspect of the problem. This is one aspect where you can score over others.

In this question, the figure will be somewhat like this (as shown alongside) with triangles ABC and ADC representing the cones and AC being the hypotenuse around which the triangle ABC revolves. Now that the area has to be maximum with AC as the hypotenuse, we must realise that ADB has to be an isosceles triangle, which automatically makes BCD an isosceles triangle too.

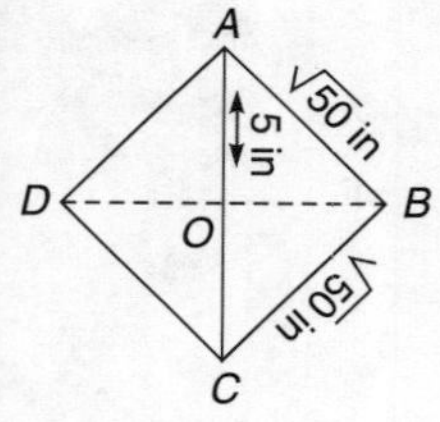

The next step is to calculate the radius of the base, which is essentially the height of the triangle ABC. To find that, we have to first find AB. We know

$$AC^2 = AB^2 + BC^2$$

For triangle to be one with the greatest possible area, AB must be equal to BC, that is, $AB = BC = \sqrt{50}$, since $AO = 1/2AC = 5$ inches.

Now take the right angle triangle ABO, BO being the altitude of triangle AOC. By Pythagoras theorem, $AB^2 = AO^2 + BO^2$, so $BO^2 = 25$ inches.

The next step is to find the volume of the cone ABD and multiply it with two to get the volume of the whole solid.

Volume of the cone $ADB = \frac{\pi}{3} \times BO^2 \times AO = \frac{125\pi}{3}$.

Therefore volume of the solid $ABCD = 2 \times \frac{125\pi}{3} = \frac{250\pi}{3}$.

Problem 12.2: A right circular cylinder is to be made out of a metal sheet such that the sum of its height and radius does not exceed 9 cm can have a maximum volume of

(a) $54\ \pi\ \text{cm}^3$ (b) $108\ \pi\ \text{cm}^3$
(c) $81\ \pi\ \text{cm}^3$ (d) None of these

Solution: Solving this question requires the knowledge of ratio and proportion also. To solve this question, one must know that for $a^2b^3c^4$ to have the maximum value when $(a + b + c)$ is constant, a, b and c must be in the ratio 1:2:3.

Now let's look at this problem.

Volume of a cylinder $= \pi r^2 h$.

If you analyse this formula closely, you will find that r and h are the only variable term. So for volume of the cylinder to be maximum, r^2h has to be maximum under the condition that $r + h = 9$. By the information given above, this is possible only when $r{:}h = 2{:}1$, that is, $r = 6$, $h = 3$. So,

Volume of the cylinder $= \pi r^2 h$
$= \pi \times 6^2 \times 3$
$= \mathbf{108\pi}$

Problem 12.3: There are five concentric squares. If the area of the circle inside the smallest square is 77 square units and the distance between the corresponding corners of consecutive squares is 1.5 units, find the difference in the areas of the outermost and innermost squares.

Solution: Here again the ability to visualise the diagram would be the key. Once you gain expertise in this aspect, you will be able to see that the diameter of the circle is equal to the side of the innermost square, that is

$$\pi r^2 = 77$$

or $$r = 3.5\sqrt{2}$$

or $$2r = 7\sqrt{2}$$

Then the diagonal of the square is 14 units which means the diagonal of the fifth square would be 14 + 12 units = 26

Which means the side of the fifth square would be $13\sqrt{2}$.

Therefore, the area of the fifth square = 338 sq units.

Area of the first square = 98 sq units.

Hence, the difference would be 240 sq. units.

Problem 12.4: A spherical pear of radius 4 cm is to be divided into eight equal parts by cutting

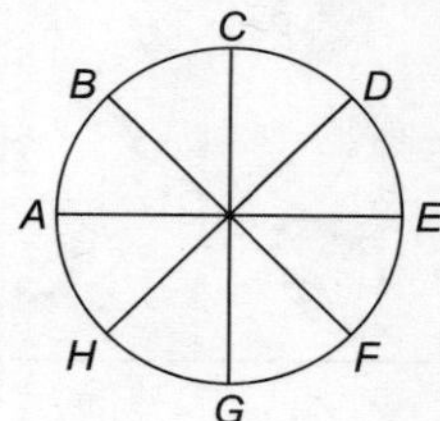

it in halves along the same axis. Find the surface area of each of the final piece.

(a) 20 π (b) 25 π
(c) 24 π (d) 19 π

Solution: The pear after being cut will have eight parts each of same volume and surface area. The figure will be somewhat like the above figure if seen from the top before cutting. After cutting, it looks something like the figure given below.

Now the surface area of each piece = Area *ACBD* + 2 (Area *CODB*).

The darkened surface is nothing but the arc *AB* from side glance which means its surface area is one eighth the area of the sphere, that is, $1/8 \times 4\pi r^2 = (1/2)\pi r^2$.

Now *CODB* can be seen as a semicircle with radius 4 cm.

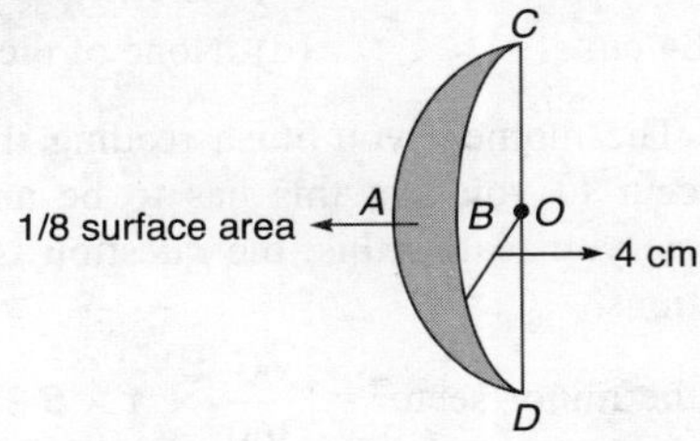

Therefore, 2 (Area *CODB*) = $2[(1/2)]\ \pi r^2 = \pi r^2$

$\Rightarrow$ surface area of each piece = $(1/2)\ \pi r^2 + \pi r^2$

$= (3/2)\ \pi r^2$

$= 24\pi$

Problem 12.5: A solid metal sphere is melted and smaller spheres of equal radii are formed. Ten percent of the volume of the sphere is lost in the process. The smaller spheres have a radius, that is $1/9^{th}$ the larger sphere. If ten litres of paint were needed to paint the larger sphere, how many litres are needed to paint all the smaller spheres?

(a) 90 (b) 81
(c) 900 (d) 810

Solution: questions like this require, along with your knowledge of formulae, your ability to form equations. Stepwise, it will be something like this;

Step 1: Assume values

Step 2: Find out the volume left

Step 3: Find out the number of small spheres possible

Step 4: Find out the total surface area of each small spheres as a ratio of the original sphere

Step 5: Multiply it by 10

Step 1: Let radius of the larger sphere be *R* and that of smaller ones be *r*.

Then, volume = $\frac{4}{3}\pi R^3$ and $\frac{4}{3}\pi r^3 = \frac{4}{3}\pi (R/9)^3$, respectively for the larger and smaller spheres.

Step 2: Volume lost due to melting = $\frac{4}{3}\pi R^3 \times \frac{10}{100} = \frac{4\pi R^3}{30}$

Volume left = $\frac{4}{3}\pi R^3 \times \frac{90}{100} = \frac{4\pi R^3 \times 0.9}{3}$

Step 3: Number of small spheres possible = volume left/ volume of the smaller sphere

$$= \frac{\frac{4}{3}\pi R^3 \times 0.9}{\frac{4}{3}\pi \times (R/9)^3} = 9^3 \times 0.9$$

Step 4: Surface area of larger sphere = $4\pi R^2$

Surface area of smaller sphere = $4\pi r^2 = 4\pi\ (R/9)^2 = \frac{4\pi R^2}{81}$

Surface area of all smaller spheres = number of small spheres × surface area of smaller sphere

$= (9^3 \times .9) \times (4\pi R^2)/81$

$= 8.1 \times (4\pi R^2)$

Therefore, ratio of the surface area is $\frac{[8.1 \times (4\pi R^2)]}{4\pi R^2} = 8.1$

Step 5:

8.1 × number of litres = 8.1 × 10 = 81

Problem 12.6: A solid wooden toy in the shape of a right circular cone is mounted on a hemisphere. If the radius of the hemisphere is 4.2 cm and the total height of the toy is 10.2 cm, find the volume of the wooden toy.

(a) 104 cm^3 (b) 162 cm^3
(c) 427 cm^3 (d) 266 cm^2

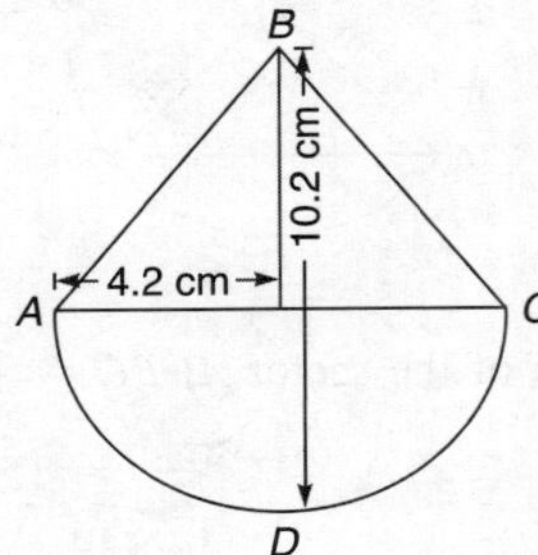

Solution: Volume of the cone is given by –1/3 ¥ pr^2h

Here, $r = 4.2$ cm; $h = 10.2 - r = 6$ cm

Therefore, the volume of the cone = $1/3\ \pi \times (4.2)^2 \times 6$

$= 110.88\ cm^3$

Volume of the hemisphere = $\frac{1}{2} \times \frac{4}{3}\ \pi r^3 = 155.23$

Total volume = 110.88 + 155.232 = 266.112

Problem 12.7: A vessel is in the form of an inverted cone. Its depth is 8 cm and the diameter of its top, which is open, is 10 cm. It is filled with water up to the brim. When bullets, each of which is a sphere of radius 0.5 cm, are dropped into the vessel 1/4 of the water flows out. Find the number of bullets dropped in the vessel.

(a) 50 (b) 100 (c) 150 (d) 200

Solution: In these types of questions, it is just your calculation skills that are being tested. You just need to take care that while trying to be fast you do not end up making mistakes like taking the diameter to be the radius and so forth. The best way to avoid such mistakes is to proceed systematically. For example, in this problem we can proceed, thus:

Volume of the cone = $\frac{1}{3}\pi r^2 h = \frac{200}{3}\pi$ cm^3

Volume of all the lead shots = Volume of water that spilled out = $\frac{50}{3}\pi$ cm^3

Volume of each lead shot = $\frac{4}{3}\pi r^3 = \frac{\pi}{6}$ cm^3

Number of lead shots = (volume of water that spilled out)/(volume of each lead shot)

$$= \frac{\frac{50}{3}\pi}{\frac{\pi}{6}} = \frac{50}{3} \times 6 = 100$$

Problem 12.8: *AB* is a chord of a circle of radius 14 cm. The chord subtends a right angle at the center of the circle. Find the area of the minor segment.

(a) 98 sq cm (b) 56 sq cm
(c) 112 sq cm (d) None of these

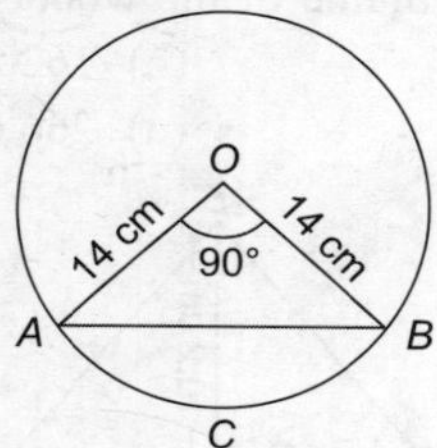

Solution: Area of the sector *ACBO* = $\frac{90\pi \times 14^2}{360}$ = 154 sq cm

Area of the triangle *AOB* = $\frac{14 \times 14}{2}$ = 98 sq cm

Area of the segment *ACB* = Area sector *ACBO* – Area of the triangle *AOB* = 56 sq cm

Problem 12.9: A sphere of diameter 12.6 cm is melted and cast into a right circular cone of height 25.2 cm. Find the diameter of the base of the cone.

(a) 158.76 cm (b) 79.38 cm
(c) 39.64 cm (d) None of these

Solution: In questions like this, do not go for complete calculations. As far as possible, try to cancel out values in the resulting equations.

Volume of the sphere = $\frac{4}{3}\pi r^3 = \frac{4}{3}\pi(6.3)^3$

Volume of the cone = $\frac{1}{3}\pi r^2 h = \frac{\pi}{3}r^2(25.2)$

Now, volume of the cone = volume of the sphere

Therefore, *r* (radius of the cone) = 6.3 cm

Hence the diameter = 12.6 cm

Problem 12.10 A chord *AB* of a circle of radius 5.25 cm makes an angle of 60° at the center of the circle. Find the area of the major and minor segments. (Take π = 3.14)

(a) 168 cm^2 (b) 42 cm^2
(c) 84 cm^2 (d) None of these

Solution: The moment you finish reading this question, it should occur to you that this has to be an equilateral triangle. Once you realise this, the question is reduced to just calculations.

Area of the minor sector = $\frac{60}{360} \times \pi \times 5.25^2$ = 14.4375 cm^2

Area of the triangle = $\frac{\sqrt{3}}{4} \times 5.25^2$ = 11.93 cm^2

Area of the minor segment = Area of the minor sector – Area of the triangle = 2.5 cm^2

Area of the major segment = Area of the circle – Area of the minor segment.

= 86.625 cm^2 – 2.5 cm^2 = 84.125 cm^2

Problem 12.11 A cone and a hemisphere have equal bases and equal volumes. Find the ratio of their heights.

(a) 1:2 (b) 2:1
(c) 3:1 (d) None of these

Solution: Questions of this type should be solved without the use of pen and paper. A good authority over formulae will make things easier.

Volume of the cone = $\frac{\pi r^2 h}{3}$ = Volume of a hemisphere = $\frac{2}{3}\pi r^3$,

Height of a hemisphere = Radius of its base

So the question is effectively asking us to find out *h*/*r*.

By the formula above we can easily see that *h*/*r* = 2/1.

GEOMETRY

LEVEL OF DIFFICULTY (I)

1. $ABCD$ is a quadrilateral. The diagonals of $ABCD$ intersect at the point P. The area of the triangles APD and BPC are 27 and 12, respectively. If the areas of the triangles APB and CPD are equal then the area of triangle APB is
(a) 12 (b) 15
(c) 16 (d) 18
2. In a right angle triangle BAC given below, AD is the altitude of the hypotenuse BC. The figure is followed by three possible inferences.

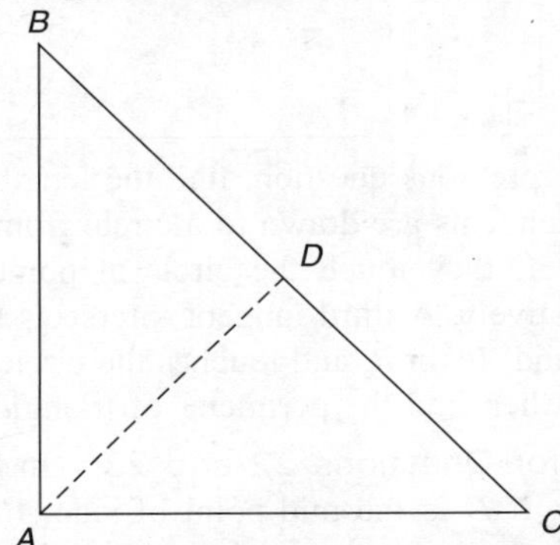

1. Triangle ABD and triangle CAD are similar
2. Triangle ADB and triangle CDA are congruent
3. Triangle ADB and triangle CAB are similar

Mark the correct option.
(a) 1 and 2 are correct
(b) 1 and 3 are correct
(c) Only 3 is correct
(d) All three are correct
3. The area of an isosceles triangle is 12 cm^2. If one of the equal sides is 5 cm long, mark the option which can give the length of the base.
(a) 4 cm (b) 6 cm
(c) 10 cm (d) 9cm
4. An arc AB of a circle subtends an angle 'x' radian at the center O of the circle. If the area of the sector AOB is equal to the square of the length of the arc AB, then find x.
5. What is the value of c^2 in the given figure, where the radius of the circle is 'a' units?

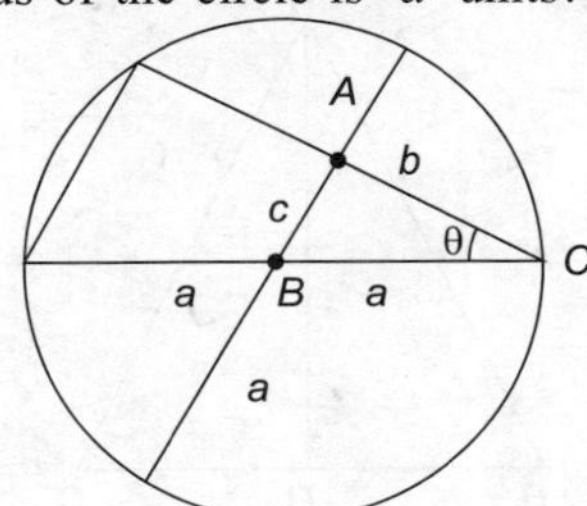

(a) $c^2 = a^2 + b^2 - 2\,ab\cos\theta$
(b) $c^2 = a^2 + b^2 - 2ab\sin\theta$
(c) $c^2 = a^2 - b^2 + 2ab\cos\theta$
(d) None of these
6. In a circle, the height of an arc is 21 cm and the diameter is 84 cm. Find the chord of 'half of the arc'.
7. The perimeter of a right-angled triangle measures 234 m and the hypotenuse measures 97 m. Then the other two sides of the triangle are measured as
(a) 100 m and 37 m (b) 72 m and 65 m
(c) 80 m and 57 m (d) None of these
8. A 25 feet long ladder is placed against the wall with its base 7 feet from the wall. The base of the ladder is drawn out so that the top comes down by half the distance that the base is drawn out. This distance is in the range
(a) (2, 7) (b) (5, 8)
(c) (9, 10) (d) None of these
9. In KyaKya Island, there is a circular park. There are four points of entry into the park, namely – P, Q, R and S. The king of the island His Excellency Mr. Honolulu got three paths constructed which connected the points PQ, RS, and PS. The length of the path PQ is 10 units, and the length of the path RS is 7 units. Later, the municipal corporation extended the paths PQ and RS past Q and R respectively, and they meet at a point T on the main road outside the park. The path from Q to T measures 8 units, and it was found that the $\angle PTS$ is 60°. Find the area (in square units) enclosed by the paths PT, TS, and PS.

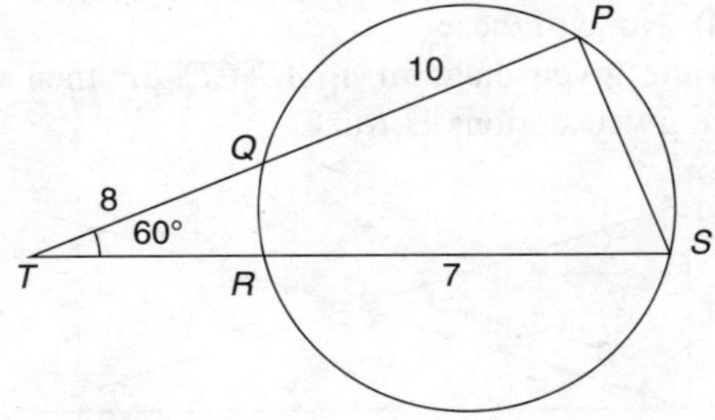

(a) $36\sqrt{3}$ (b) $54\sqrt{3}$
(c) $72\sqrt{3}$ (d) $90\sqrt{3}$
10. There are two circles C_1, and C_2 of radii 3 and 8 units respectively. The common internal tangent T touches the circles at points P and Q respectively. The line joining the centers of the circles intersects T at X. The distance of X from the center of the smaller circle is 5 units. What is the length of the line segment PQ?

(a) ≤ 13 (b) >13 and ≤ 14
(c) > 14 and < 15 (d) >15 and ≤ 16

11. If ΔABC is a right-angled triangle such that $\angle B = 90°$, $(AB + BC) - AC = 20$ cm and perimeter of $\Delta ABC = 60$ cm, then find the area of the triangle (in cm^2).

12. Find the sum of the squares of the medians of a triangle whose sides are 6 cm, 7 cm, and 8 cm.

13. In the diagram given below, $RT \perp PQ$ S is a point on QR such that
$\angle QPS = 40°$, $\angle TRQ = 30°$, then find $\angle PSQ$.

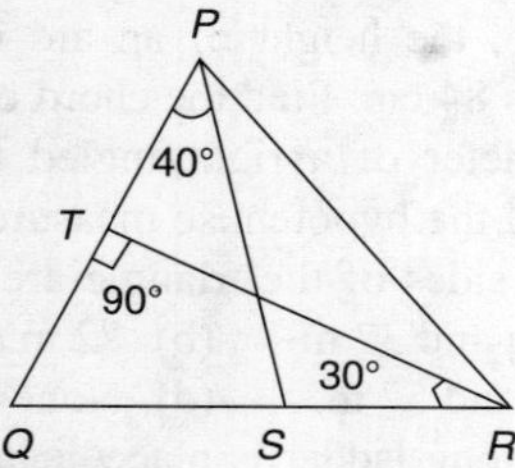

14. In the given diagram, PQ touches the circle at R. T, S, U are the points on the circle. If $\angle SRQ = 60°$ then find $\angle SUR$.

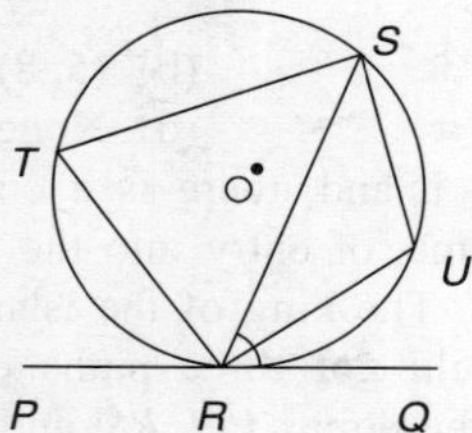

15. In a right-angled triangle ΔPQR, $\angle Q = 90°$, if A and B are points on the sides PQ and QR respectively then:
(a) $AR^2 + PB^2 = 2(PR^2 + AB^2)$
(b) $AR^2 + PB^2 = PR^2 + AB^2$
(c) $AR^2 + RB^2 = 0.5(PR^2 + AB^2)$
(d) None of these

16. In the given diagram, if $AB||CD||EF$ then which of the given options is true?

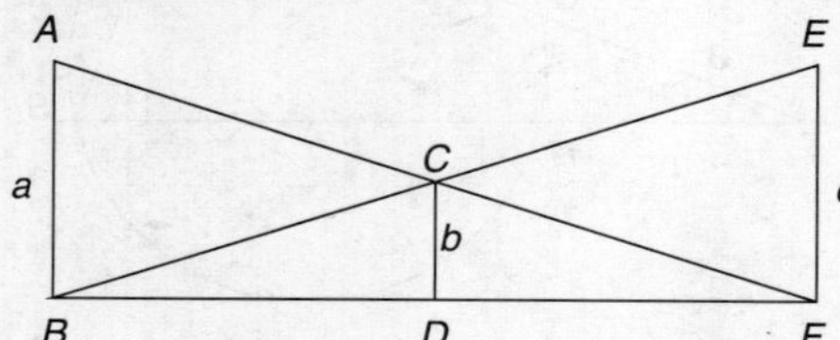

(a) $\frac{1}{a} - \frac{1}{c} = \frac{1}{b}$ (b) $\frac{1}{a} + \frac{1}{b} = \frac{1}{c}$

(c) $\frac{1}{b} - \frac{1}{a} = \frac{1}{c}$ (d) $\frac{1}{c} - \frac{1}{b} = \frac{1}{a}$

17. In the given figure, $PR = QR = PS$, $\angle PSR = x$, $\angle TPS = 90°$ then find x.

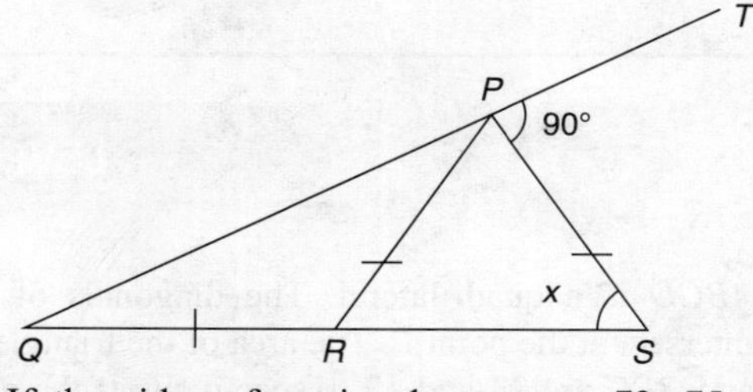

18. If the sides of a triangle measure 72, 75 and 21. What is the measure of its in-radius?

19. $ABCD$ has area equals to 28. BC is parallel to AD. BA is perpendicular to AD. If BC is 6 and AD is 8, then what is AB?

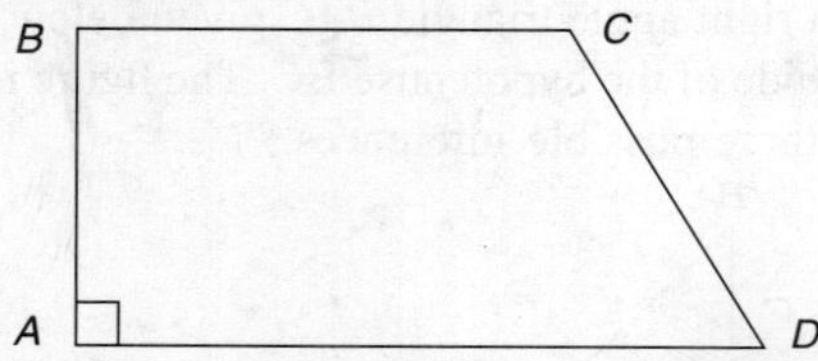

20. In the previous question, find the length of CD..

21. Two tangents are drawn to a circle from an exterior point A; they touch the circle at points B and C, respectively. A third tangent intersects segment AB in P and AC in R, and touches the circle at Q. If $AB = 20$, then find the perimeter of triangle APR.

Directions for Questions 22 and 23: In the diagram given below, if D is the mid-point of side AC and $DB = AD = DC$, then answer the following questions:

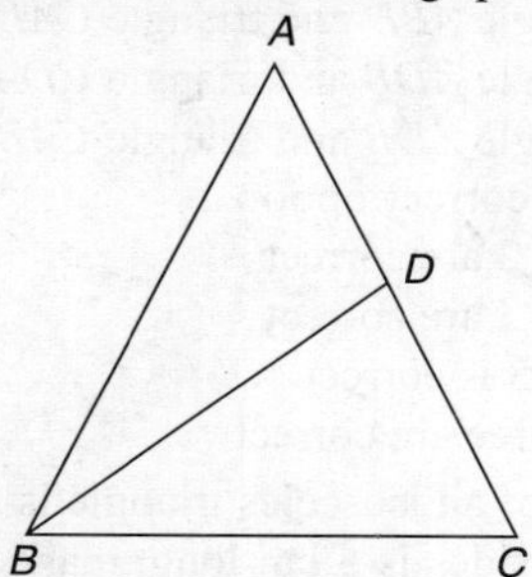

22. ΔABC is a
(a) Right-angled triangle
(b) Equilateral triangle
(c) Acute-angled triangle
(d) Obtuse-angled triangle

23. If ΔABC is an isosceles triangle then find $\angle BDC$.

24. In the diagram given below, if $AB = AC$ and $\angle ADC = 2\angle ABD$, $\angle DAC = 30°$ then find $\angle BAD$.

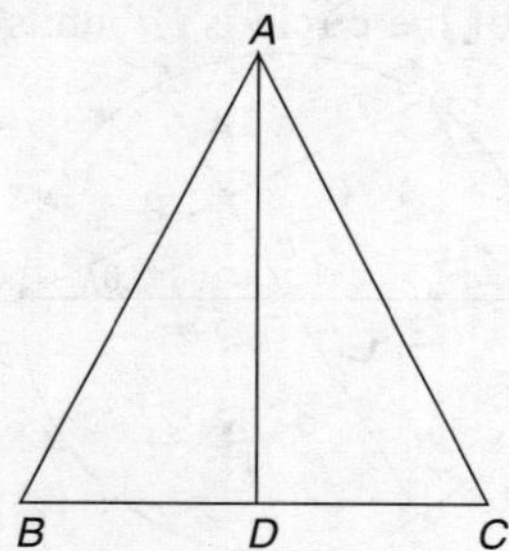

25. In the figure given below, 'O' is the center of the circle. If PQ and QR are chords of the circle, find the measure of $\angle POR$.

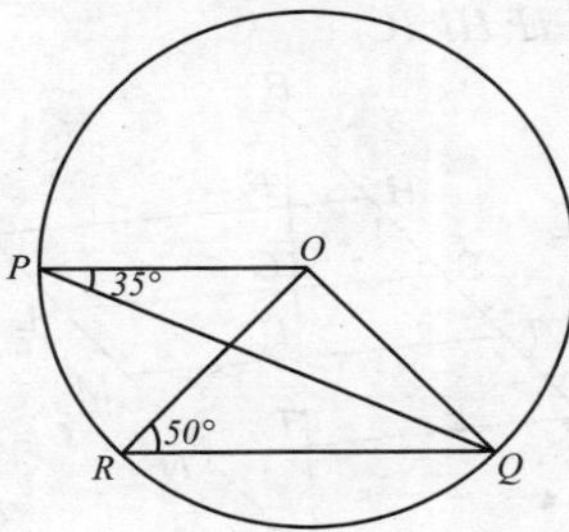

(a) 15° (b) 30°
(c) 45° (d) 60°

26. If the interior angle of a regular polygon is 120°, find the number of diagonals of the polygon.

27. The internal angle of a regular polygon exceeds the internal angle of another regular polygon by 18°. If the second polygon has half the number of sides as the first, then find the number of sides in the first polygon.

28. The sum of the interior angles of a regular polygon is 40 times the exterior angle. Find the number of sides of the polygon.

29. In the given diagram, O is the center of the circle and $\angle AOC = 140°$. If $AB = BC$ then find $\angle BCA$.

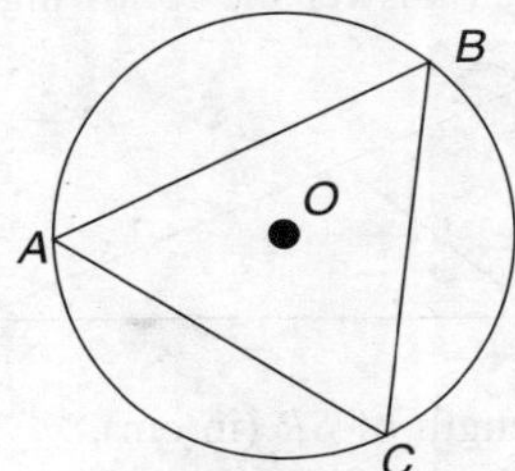

30. In the given diagram, if 'O' is the center of the circle, chord PR and SQ intersect each other at O, and $\angle POQ = 80°$, then find $\angle QSR$.

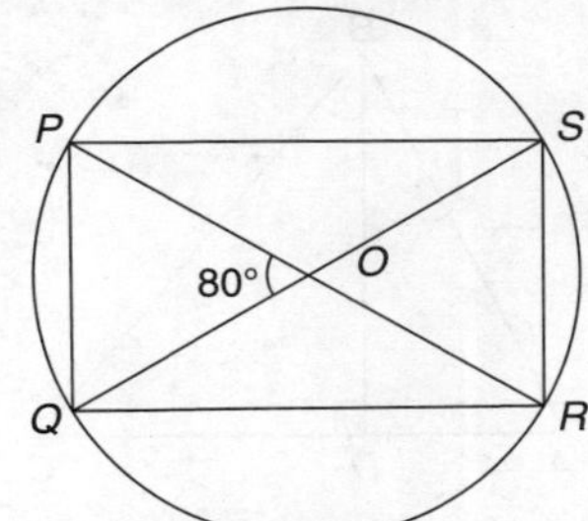

31. Find the value of x in the figure, if it is given that AC and BD are diameters of the circle.

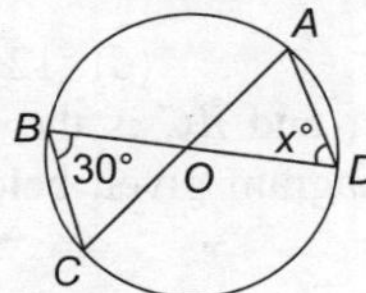

(a) 60° (b) 45°
(c) 15° (d) 30°

32. Find the value of x in the given figure.

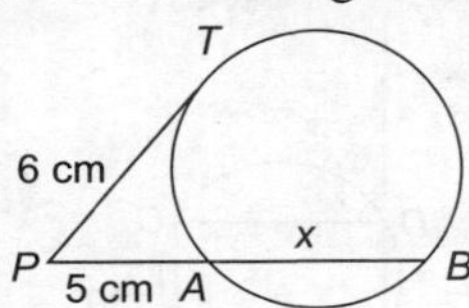

(a) 2.2 cm (b) 1.6 cm
(c) 3 cm (d) 2.6 cm

Directions for Questions 33 and 34: P is a point outside a circle with center O and radius 6 units, such that $OP = 10$ units. Tangents are drawn from P to the circle touching it at M and N (see the figure given below). The line segment OP cuts the circle at point C and the tangent drawn to the circle at C meets PM and PN at points A and B, respectively.

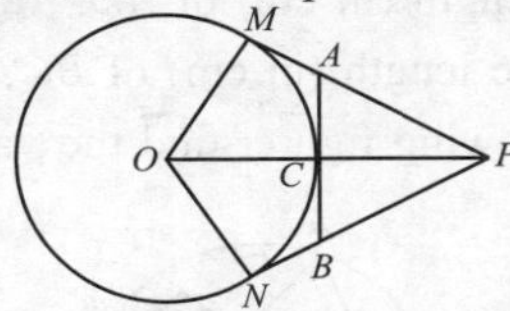

33. What is the length of AP (in cm)?

34. What is the length (in cm) of in-radius of triangle APB?

35. ABC is a right angled triangle with $BC = 6$ cm and $AB = 8$ cm. A circle with center O and radius x has been inscribed in ΔABC. What is the value of x?

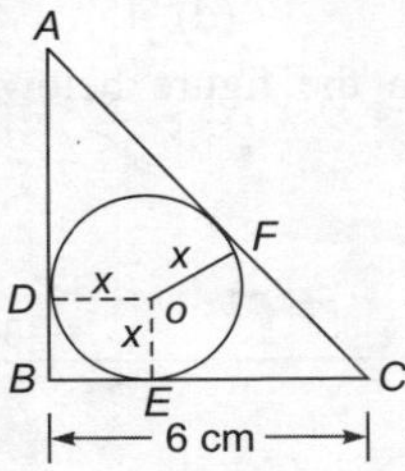

(a) 2.4 cm (b) 2 cm
(c) 3.6 cm (d) 4 cm

36. In the given figure, AB is the diameter of the circle and $\angle PAB = 25°$. Find $\angle TPA$.

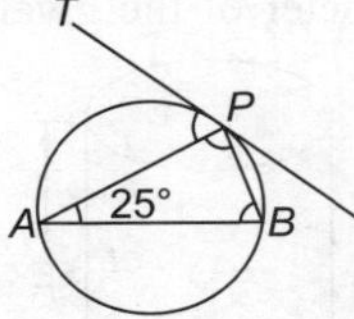

(a) 50° (b) 65°
(c) 70° (d) 45°

Directions for Questions 37 and 38: There are two concentric circles of radii 7 cm and 8 cm. PQ, a diameter of the larger circle, cuts the smaller circle at S and T. A tangent drawn from Q touches the inner circle at R.

37. What is the length of QR (in cm)?

38. What is the length of PR (in cm)?

39. In the following figure A, B, C and D are the concyclic points. Find the value of x.

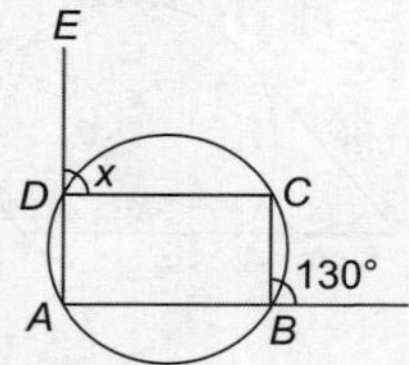

(a) 130° (b) 50°
(c) 60° (d) 30°

Directions for Questions 40 and 41: In ΔABC, $AB = 16$ cm and $AC = 9$ cm. AD is the perpendicular drawn from the vertex A to the side BC and the circum-radius of the triangle is 9 cm.

40. Find the length (in cm) of AD.

41. What is the length (in cm) of BC?

42. In the following figure, find the value of x

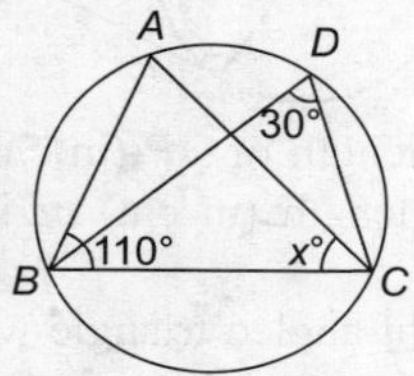

(a) 40° (b) 25°
(c) 30° (d) 45°

43. If $L_1 \parallel L_2$ in the figure below, what is the value of x?

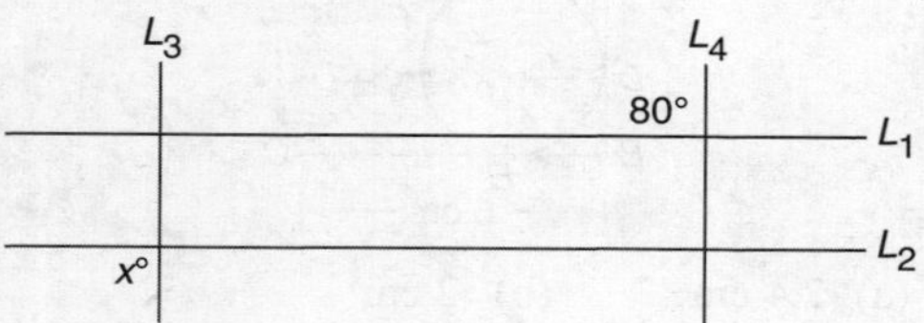

(a) 80° (b) 100°
(c) 40° (d) Cannot be determined

44. Find the perimeter of the given figure.

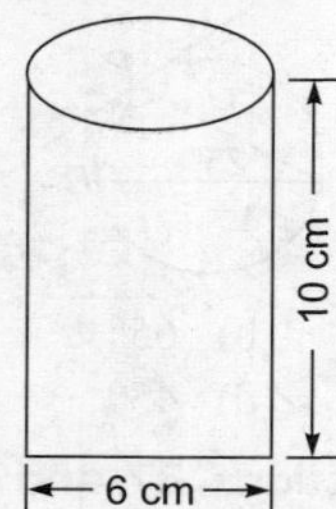

(a) $(32 + 3\pi)$ cm (b) $(36 + 6\pi)$ cm
(c) $(46 + 3\pi)$ cm (d) $(26 + 6\pi)$ cm

45. In the figure, AB is parallel to CD and $RD \parallel SL \parallel TM \parallel AN$, and $BR{:}RS{:}ST{:}TA = 3{:}5{:}2{:}7$. If it is known that $CN = 1.333\ BR$. Find the ratio of $BF{:}FG{:}GH{:}HI{:}IC$.

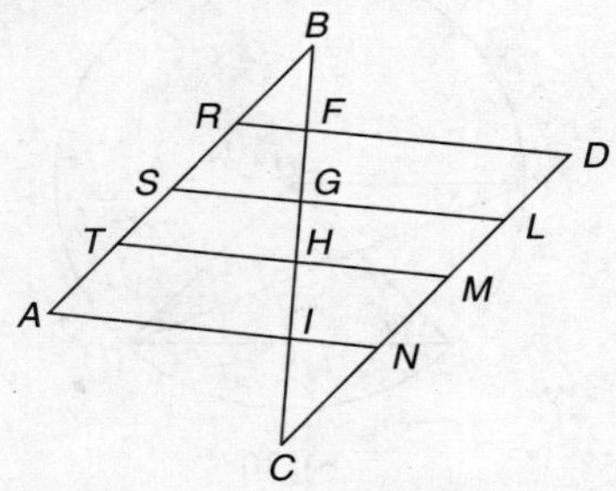

(a) 3:7:2:5:4 (b) 3:5:2:7:4
(c) 4:7:2:5:3 (d) 4:5:2:7:3

46. In a regular polygon, the number of diagonals is 'k' times the number of sides. If the interior angle of the polygon is x, then the value of k is

(a) $\dfrac{3x-\pi}{2(\pi-x)}$ (b) $\dfrac{3x+\pi}{2(\pi-x)}$

(c) $\dfrac{3x-\pi}{2(\pi+x)}$ (d) None of these

Directions for Questions 47 and 48: ΔPQR is a right-angled triangle and $\angle Q = 90°$, $PQ = 15$ cm, $QR = 20$ cm and $QS \perp PR$, then answer the following questions.

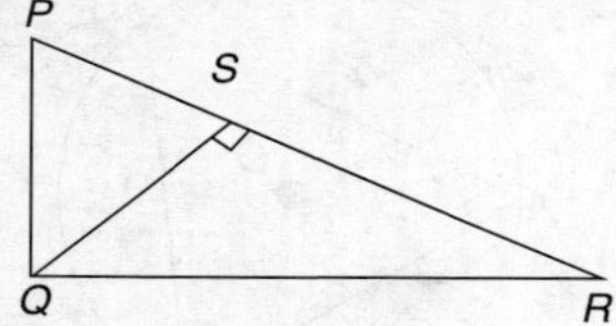

47. Find the length of SR (in cm).

48. Find the length of SQ (in cm).

49. In the given diagram ΔABC is a right-angled triangle, $\angle ABC = 90°$, $BD \perp AC$. If $AB{:}AC = 3{:}5$ and area of ΔABD is 90 cm^2, then the area of ΔABC (in cm^2) is

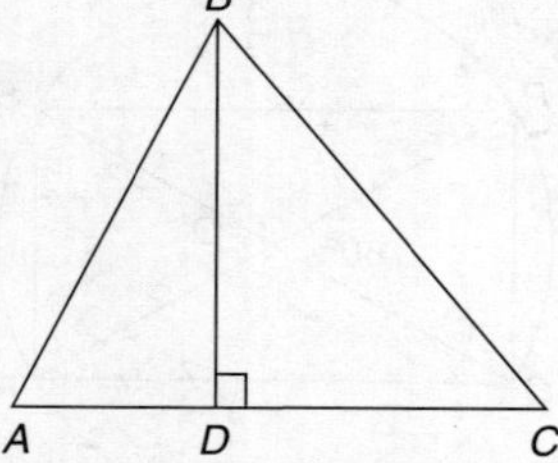

50. If the inradius of an equilateral triangle is $\sqrt{3}$ cm, then its area is

(a) $7\sqrt{3}$ cm^2 (b) $9\sqrt{3}$ cm^2

(c) $10\sqrt{3}$ cm^2 (d) $12\sqrt{3}$ cm^2

51. O is the center and AC is the tangent of the circle at B. In the diagram given below, if $\angle OBE = 70°$, find $\angle BOE$.

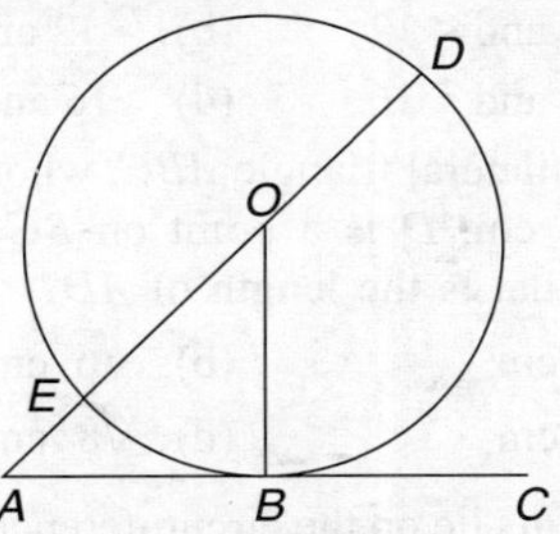

52. In the previous question, find $\angle BAO$.

Directions for Questions 53 and 54: Two circles having equal radius intersect each other at A and B as shown in the diagram below. The diameters AC and AD intersect at A. If C, B, D are collinear and $\angle ACB = 30°$, then answer the following questions:

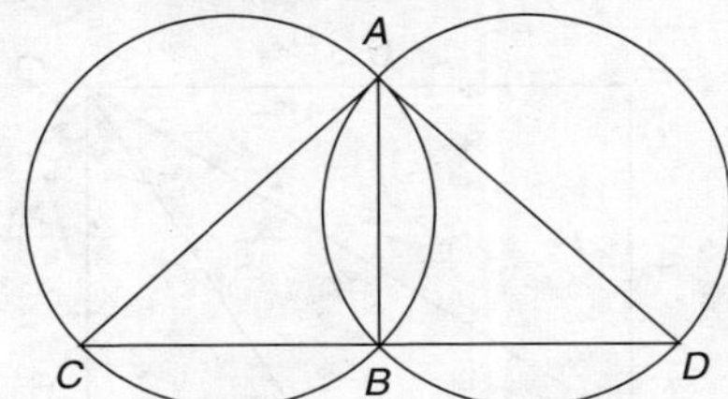

53. Find $\angle CAD$.

54. If $BC = 2$ cm, then AD (in cm) is
(a) 4 (b) $4/\sqrt{2}$
(c) 3 (d) None of these

55. In the diagram O is the center of the circle. PS is the tangent of the circle at S and $\angle OSQ = 50°$. Find $\angle SPR$.

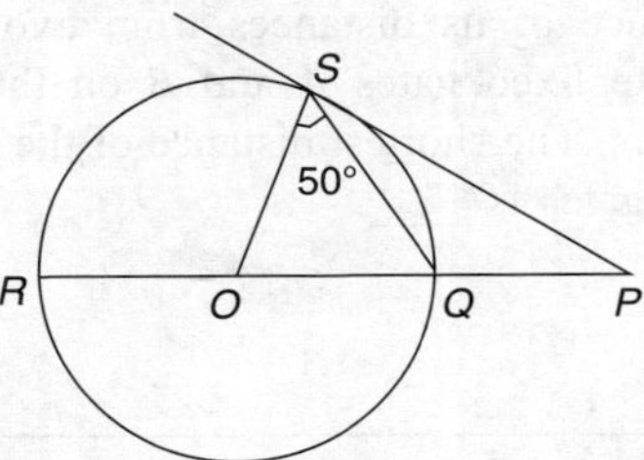

56. Lines joining midpoint of a quadrilateral form a
(a) Square (b) Parallelogram
(c) Rectangle (d) None of these

57. In the given diagram, □$ABCD$ is a trapezium. If $AB = 4$ cm, $CD = 6$ cm and $OB = 5$ cm, then BD = ____cm.

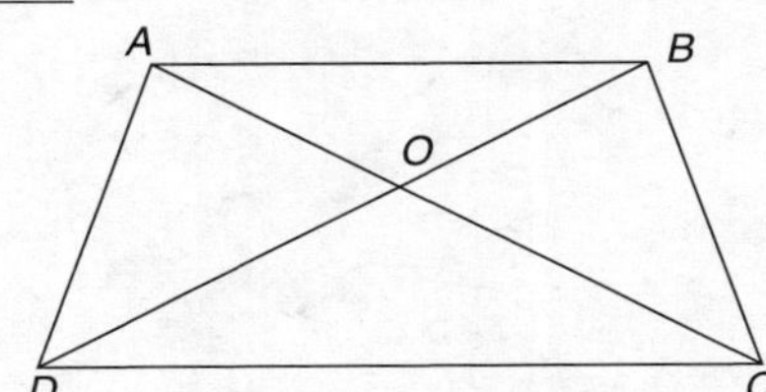

Directions for Questions 58 to 59: In the given diagram, $PQRS$ is a trapezium and SR = $4\sqrt{6}$ cm and $\angle SQR = 60$, °$\angle QSR = 45°$. Answer the following questions:

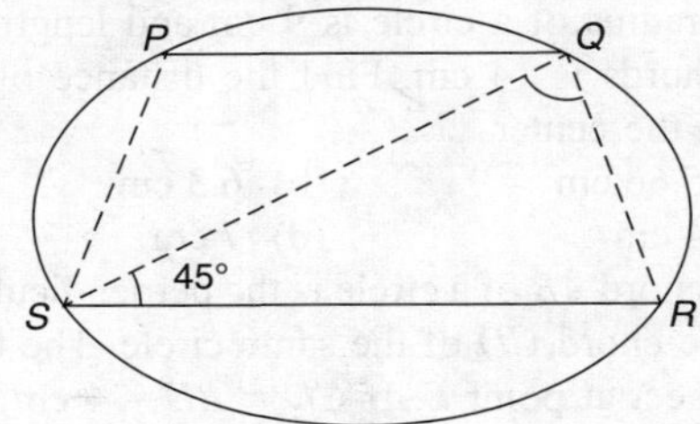

58. Length of QR is ___cm.

59. $PS + QR =$ ___cm.

60. $ABCD$ is a rectangle with $AD = 10$. P is a point on BC such that $\angle APD = 90°$. If $DP = 8$, then the length of BP is.

61. A vertical stick 20 m long casts a shadow 10 m long on the ground. At the same time, a tower casts the shadow 50 m long on the ground. Find the height of the tower.
(a) 100 m (b) 120 m
(c) 25 m (d) 200 m

62. In the figure, ΔABC is similar to ΔEDC.

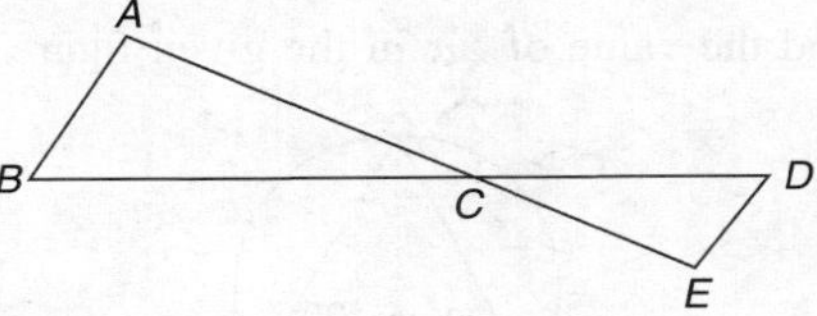

If we have $AB = 4$ cm, $ED = 3$ cm, $CE = 4.2$ and $CD = 4.8$ cm, find the value of CA and CB.
(a) 6 cm, 6.4 cm (b) 4.8 cm, 6.4 cm
(c) 5.4 cm, 7.2 cm (d) 5.6 cm, 6.4 cm

63. The area of similar triangles, ABC and DEF are 144 cm^2 and 81 cm^2 respectively. If the longest side of larger ΔABC be 36 cm, then the longest side of smaller ΔDEF is
(a) 20 cm (b) 26 cm
(c) 27 cm (d) 30 cm

64. Two isosceles triangles have equal angles and their areas are in the ratio 16:25. Find the ratio of their corresponding heights.
(a) 4/5 (b) 5/4
(c) 3/2 (d) 5/7

65. $ABCD$ is a quadrilateral inscribed in a acircle.

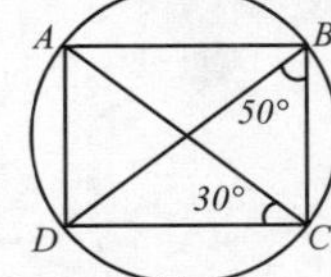

$\angle BDC$ is thrice of $\angle BCA$. Find the value of $\angle BAC$.

66. Two poles of height 6 m and 11 m respectively stand vertically upright on a plane ground. If the distance between their feet is 12 m, find the distance between their tops.
(a) 12 m (b) 14 m
(c) 13 m (d) 11 m

67. The radius of a circle is 9 cm and length of one of its chords is 14 cm. Find the distance of the chord from the center.

(a) 5.66 cm (b) 6.3 cm
(c) 4 cm (d) 7 cm

68. The chord *AB* of a circle is the perpendicular bisector of the chord *CD* of the same circle. The two chords intersect at point *E*. If *CD* = *BE* = 4 cm, then what is the diameter of the circle?

(a) 4 cm (b) 5 cm
(c) 6 cm (d) 8 cm

69. If *O* is the center of circle, find ∠*x*.

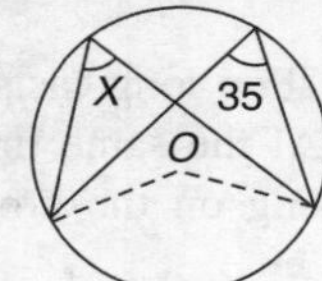

(a) 35° (b) 30°
(c) 39° (d) 40°

70. Find the value of ∠*x* in the given figure.

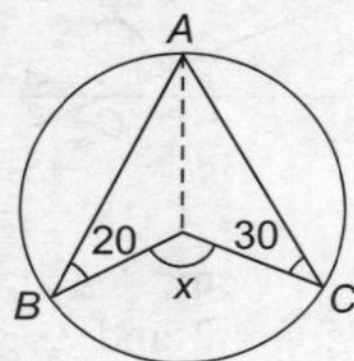

(a) 120° (b) 130°
(c) 110° (d) 100°

71. In quadrilateral *PQRS*, *PQ* = 5 units, *QR* = 17 units, *RS* = 5 units, and *PS* = 9 units. The length of the diagonal *QS* can be

(a) > 10 and < 12 (b) > 12 and < 14
(c) > 14 and < 16 (d) >16 and <18

72. In an equilateral triangle *ABC*, whose length of each side is 3 cm, *D* is a point on *BC* such that *BD* = *CD*/2. What is the length of *AD*?

(a) $\sqrt{5}$ cm (b) $\sqrt{6}$ cm
(c) $\sqrt{7}$ cm (d) $\sqrt{8}$ cm

73. Eight points lie on the circumference of a circle. Find the difference between the number of triangles and the number of quadrilaterals that can be formed by connecting these points.

74. In a square *PQRS*, *A* and *B* are two points on *PS* and *SR* such that *PA* = 2*AS*, and *RB* = 2*BS*. If *PQ* = 6, the area of the triangle *ABQ* is

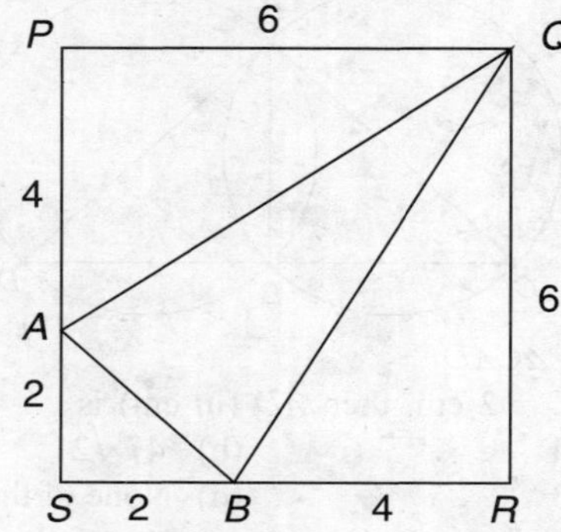

75. A pole has to be erected on the boundary of a circular park of diameter 13 meters in such a way that the difference of its distances from two diametrically opposite fixed gates *A* and *B* on the boundary is 7 meters. The shortest distance of the pole from one of the gates is ____.

Space for Notes

LEVEL OF DIFFICULTY (II)

1. If D is the midpoint of side BC of a triangle ABC and AD is perpendicular to AC then

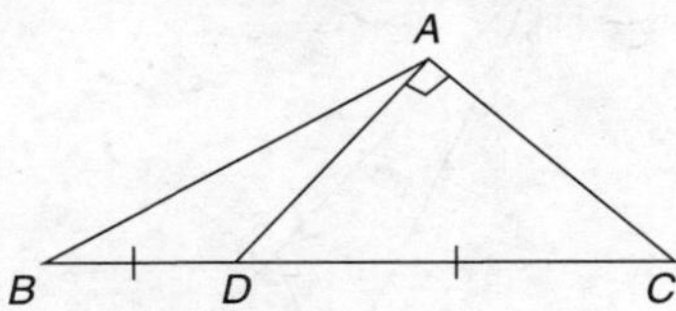

(a) $3AC^2 = BC^2 - AB^2$
(b) $3BC^2 = AC^2 - 3AB^2$
(c) $5AB^2 = BC^2 + AC^2$
(d) None of these

2. In a triangle ABC, the length of side BC is 295. If the length of side AB is a perfect square, then the length of side AC is a power of 2, and the length of side AC is twice the length of side AB. Determine the perimeter of the triangle.

3. There is a triangular building (ABC) located in the heart of Aurangabad, the city of Aurangzeb. The length of the one wall in the East (BC) direction is 397 feet. If the length of South wall (AB) is a perfect cube, the length of the Southwest wall (AC) is a power of three, and the length of wall in Southwest (AC) is thrice the length of side AB, determine the perimeter of this triangular building.
(a) 3609 feet (b) 3813 feet
(c) 3773 feet (d) 3313 feet

4. In a circular field, AOB and COD are two mutually perpendicular diameters having length of 4 meters. X is the mid-point of OA. Y is a point on the circumference such that $\angle YOD = 30°$. Which of the following correctly gives the relation among the three alternate paths from X to Y?

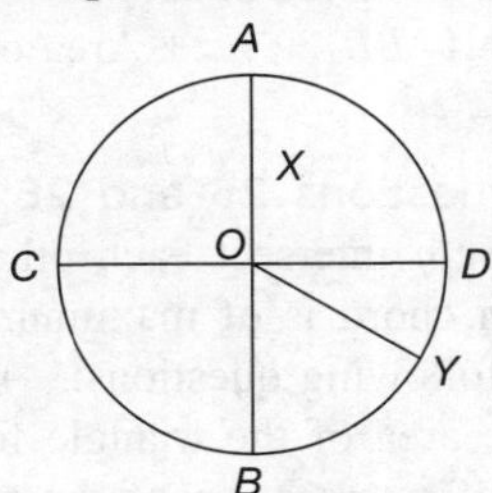

(a) $XOBY$: $XODY$: $XADY$: 5.15: 4.50: 5.06
(b) $XADY$: $XODY$: $XOBY$: 6.25: 5.34: 4.24
(c) $XODY$: $XOBY$: $XADY$: 4.04: 5.35: 5.25
(d) $XADY$: $XOBY$: $XODY$: 5.19: 5.09: 4.04

5. $ABCD$ is a parallelogram with $\angle ABC = 60°$. If the longer diagonal is of length 7 cm and the area of the parallelogram $ABCD$ is $15\frac{\sqrt{3}}{2}$ cm^2, then find the perimeter of the parallelogram (in cm).

6. The center of a circle inside a triangle is at a distance of 625 cm, from each of the vertices of the triangle. If the diameter of the circle is 350 cm and the circle is touching only two sides of the triangle, find the area of the triangle.
(a) 240000 (b) 387072
(c) 480000 (d) 506447

7. Two poles, of height 2 meters and 3 meters, are 5 meters apart. The height of the point of intersection of the lines joining the top of each pole to the foot of the opposite pole is
(a) 1.2 meters (b) 1.0 meters
(c) 5.0 meters (d) 3.0 meters

8. There are two squares S_1 and S_2 with areas 8 and 9 units, respectively. S_1 is inscribed within S_2, with one corner of S_1 on each side S_2. The corners of the smaller square divides the sides of the bigger square into two segments, one of length 'a' and the other of length 'b', where, $b > a$.
A possible value of 'b/a', is
(a) ≥5 and <8
(b) ≥8 and <11
(c) ≥11 and <14
(d) ≥14 and <17

9. In ΔABC, $\frac{\angle A}{\angle B} = 1 - \frac{\angle C}{\angle B}$, then which of the following statement is true?
(a) Δ ABC is always an acute-angled triangle
(b) $\angle > 90°$
(c) $AB^2 + BC^2 = AC^2$
(d) None of these

10. A city has a park which is shaped as a right-angled triangle. The length of the longest side of this park is 80 m. The Mayor of the city wants to construct three paths from the corner point opposite to the longest side such that these three paths divide the longest side into four equal segments. Determine the sum of the squares of the lengths of the three paths (in m^2).

11. The angles of a convex nonagon are in an arithmetic progression. Then, which of the following can never be the value of any of its angles?
(a) 900 (b) 1100
(c) 1200 (d) None of these

Directions for Questions 12 to 15: A circle with center at O is shown in the figure given below. PQ is a chord of the circle having length 16 cm. OR = 6 cm and is perpendicular to the chord PQ. RO when extended intersects the circumference of the circle at U. T is the mid-point of QU. TO, when extended, intersects QP extended at the point V.

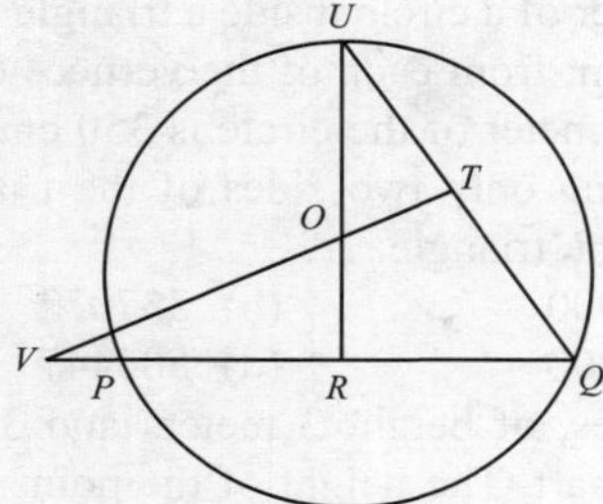

12. What is the length of chord QU (in cm)?
13. What is the length of VT (in cm)?
14. What is the length of VP (in cm)?
15. What is the area of triangle VOQ (in cm^2)?
16. The area of a regular polygon of side 'a' cm is '$25a$' square cm. If the length of the radius of the in-circle is an integer then, how many such polygons will be there?
17. Each exterior angle of an n-sided regular polygon is an integer. If n is an odd number, then how many values are possible for n?
18. Each exterior angle of an n-sided regular polygon is an integer. If n is an odd number, then find the maximum possible value of n.
19. Each exterior angle of an n-sided regular polygon is an integer. If n is an odd number, then find the maximum possible value of interior angle of n.
20. In the right-angled ΔPQR (see figure), PR = 25 units and PQ = 7 units. It is given that QT: TR = 1: 3. Find the approximate length of QS.

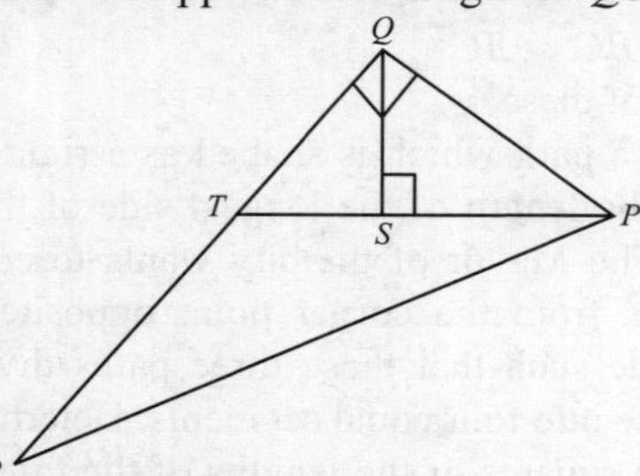

21. Triangle ABC is a right-angled triangle. D and E are mid points of AB and BC respectively. Read the following statements.
    I. $AE = 19$
    II. $CD = 22$
    III. Angle B is a right angle
    Which of the following statements would be sufficient to determine the length of AC?
    (a) Statements I and II
    (b) Statements I and III
    (c) Statements II and III
    (d) All three statements
22. In Δ RPQ, $\angle P$ = 120° angle bisector of $\angle P$ meets RQ at S and PQ = 9 cm, PS = 6 cm. Then the value of PR (in cm) is

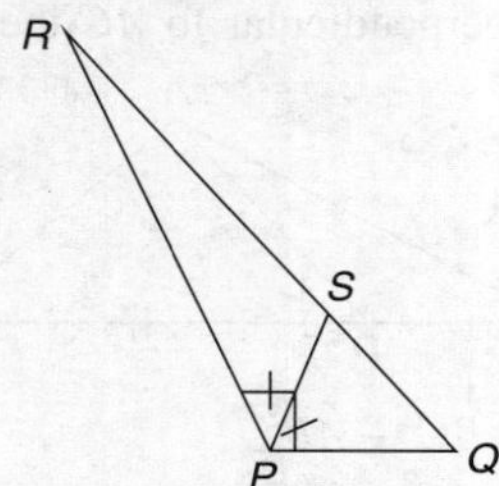

Directions for Questions 23 and 24: In the diagram given below in ΔABC in which AB = 5 cm, BC = 12 cm, AC = 13 cm. Sides AB and BC are divided in n-equal parts by n – 1 equally spaced points as shown in the diagram. A_1 joined to B_1, A_2 joined to B_2 and so on, then answer the following questions:

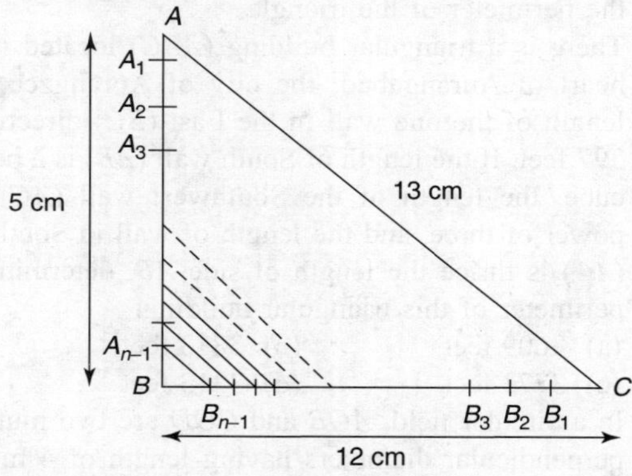

23. Find the value of 'n' for which $A_{n-1}B_{n-1} + A_{n-2}B_{n-2} + A_{n-3}B_{n-3} + \ldots + AC$ = 130 cm.
24. What will be the value of n for which:
    Area of ΔABC + Area of $\Delta A_1 BB_1$ + Area of ΔA_2BB_2 + Area of $\Delta A_3 BB_3$ + ... + Area of $\Delta A_{n-1} BB_{(n-1)}$ = 66 cm^2

Directions for Questions 25 and 26: Two circles of radii 3 cm and 6 cm intersect each other in such a way that their common chord is of maximum possible length. Then answer the following questions:

25. What is the area of the triangle formed by joining the points of intersection of the two circles to the center of the bigger circle?
    (a) $7\sqrt{3}$ cm^2 (b) $9\sqrt{3}$ cm^2
    (c) $10\sqrt{3}$ cm^2 (d) $12\sqrt{3}$ cm^2
26. What is the area of the region that is common to the two circles (in cm^2)?
    (a) $\left[\frac{21}{2}\pi + 9\sqrt{3}\right]$ (b) $\left[\frac{21}{2}\pi - 9\sqrt{3}\right]$
    (c) $\left[\frac{11}{2} + 9\sqrt{3}\right]$ (d) $\left[\frac{11}{2} - 9\sqrt{3}\right]$

Directions for Questions 27 and 28: In the given diagram, *PQR* is an isosceles right-angled triangle with the center *O* touching the side *QR* at *W*, *PR* at *X* and *PQ* at *Y*. If $PR = 3\sqrt{2}$ cm, then answer the following questions:

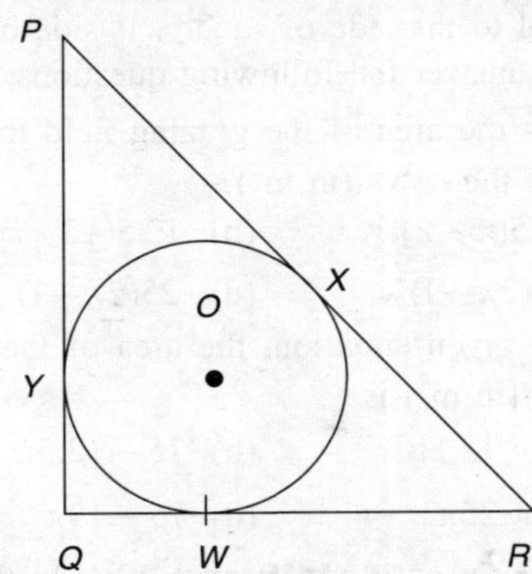

27. The ratio *PX*: *QW*: *PY* is:

(a) $1:(\sqrt{2}-1):1$ (b) $1:\left(1-\frac{1}{\sqrt{2}}\right):1$

(c) $1:\left(\sqrt{2}-\frac{1}{2}\right):1$ (d) None of these

28. The area of quadrilateral *PYOX* is:

(a) $9(\sqrt{2}+1)$ cm^2 (b) $9(\sqrt{2}-1)$ cm^2

(c) $\frac{9}{2}(\sqrt{2}+1)$cm^2 (d) $\frac{9}{2}(\sqrt{2}-1)$cm^2

29. In the given figure, ΔABC is an equilateral triangle and $BP \perp AC$, and $PR \perp AB$, and $PQ \perp BC$. The ratio of area of ΔPRB and ΔPQC is

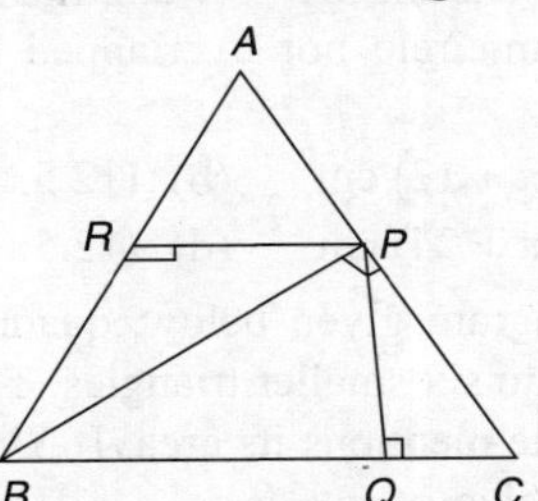

(a) 4:1 (b) 3:1

(c) 2:1 (d) None of these

30. In the previous question, if length of side of equilateral triangle is 4 cm, then area of ΔRPQ is

(a) $\frac{3\sqrt{3}}{2}$cm^2 (b) $\frac{3\sqrt{3}}{4}$cm^2

(c) $\frac{\sqrt{3}}{2}$cm^2 (d) None of these

31. In an isosceles triangle *PQR PQ* = *PR*; *A* and *B* are points on *PR* and *PQ* respectively such that *AB*||*QR*. *C* and *D* are the points on *QR* such that *AC*||*PD*. If *PQ* = 10 cm, *PA*: *AR* = 2:3 and $\angle APD = \angle BAC$, then find the length of *DC* (in cm)

32. In a ΔPQR, *X*, *Y*, *Z* are points on sides *PQ*, *QR*, *PR* such that *PX*: *XQ* = 1:1, *PZ*: *ZR* = 1:2, and *QY*: *YR* = 2:3. What is the ratio of the area of quadrilateral *XYRZ* to that of ΔPXZ?

Directions for Questions 33 and 34: In the diagram given below, *ED* is a tangent to the circle and line *AE* intersects the circle at point *C*. *B* is a point on *AC* such that *DB* is angle bisector of $\angle ADC$. If $\angle ADB = 30°$ and $\angle EDC : \angle ECD = 2:5$, then answer the following questions:

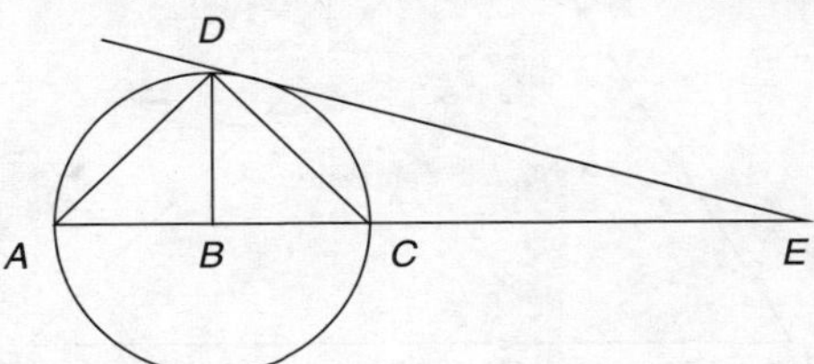

33. Find $\angle DEC$ (in degrees).

34. If *AB*: *AC* = 1:3 and *DC* = 6 cm, then find *AD* (in cm).

35. In a regular polygon, the number of sides is '*P*' times the number of diagonals. If the interior angle of the polygon is *x*, then *x* is

(a) $\frac{2\pi(P+1)}{3P+2}$ (b) $\frac{\pi(2+P)}{3P+2}$

(c) $\frac{3\pi(P+2)}{3P+2}$ (d) None of these

Directions for Questions 36 and 37: In the diagram given below, ΔPQR, and ΔQTR are right-angled triangles with $\angle PQR = \angle QTR = 90°$, *PR* = 25 cm, *PQ* = 15 cm, *QS* = 12 cm, *RT* = 16 cm. Then answer the following questions:

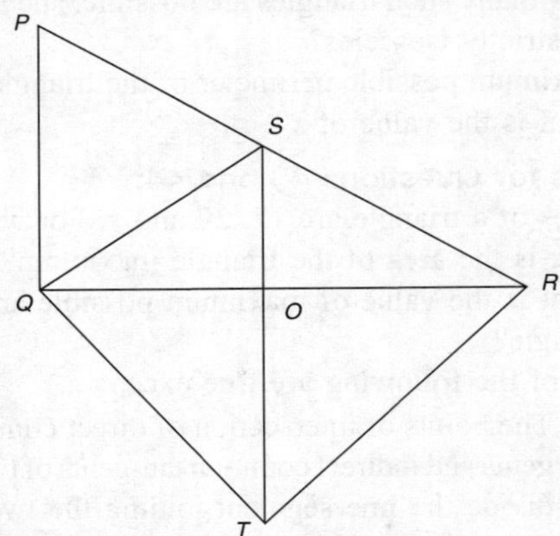

36. Find the ratio of *RO*:*OQ*.

(a) 3: 4 (b) 5: 4

(c) 16: 9 (d) 25: 16

37. If *ST* = *x* cm, then find *x*.

(a) 18.20 (b) 18.60

(c) 19.20 (d) 19.60

38. In a triangle *ABC*, *AB* = 3, *BC* = 4 and *CA* = 5. Point *D* is the midpoint of *AB*, point *E* is on the segment *AC* and point *F* is on the segment *BC*. If *AE* = 1.5 and *BF* = 0.5, then find $\angle DEF$.

(a) 30° (b) 60°

(c) 45° (d) 75°

39. In a ΔPQR, three points X, Y, Z lie on PQ, QR, PR respectively and if $PX: QZ = 1:2$, $QX: QZ = 3:2$ and $PY: YR = 1:3$, then which of the following options is true?

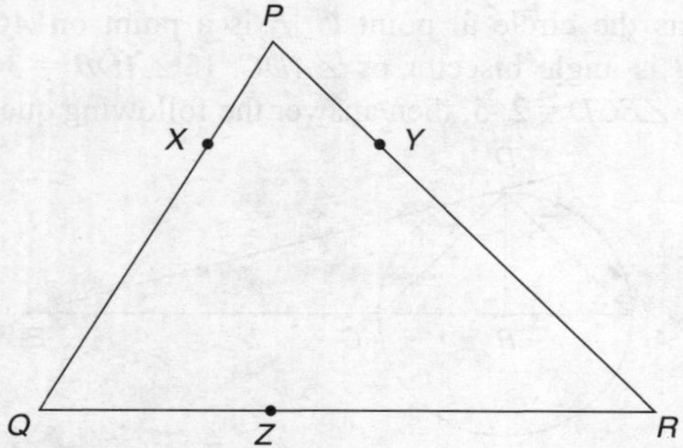

(a) Area of ΔXYZ is maximum when $QZ: QR = 1:2$
(b) Area of ΔXYZ is minimum when $QZ: QR = 2:3$
(c) Area of ΔXYZ is maximum when $QZ: QR = 2:3$
(d) Area of ΔXYZ will be same for any value of $QZ : QR$.

40. $ABCD$ is a square with sides of length 10 units. OCD is an isosceles triangle with base CD. OC cuts AB at point Q and OD cuts AB at point P. The area of trapezoid $PQCD$ is 80 square units. Find the altitude from O of the triangle OPQ.

Directions for Questions 41 and 42: Sum of two sides of an isosceles triangle is 10 cm and the length of each side is a positive integer.

41. How many such triangles are possible, such that they are strictly isosceles?

42. Maximum possible perimeter of the triangle = x cm. What is the value of x?

Directions for Questions 43 and 44:

43. Sides of a triangle are 12, 20 and x. For what value of x, is the area of the triangle maximum?

44. What is the value of maximum possible area of the triangle?

45. All of the following are true except:

(a) The points of intersection of direct common tan-gents and indirect common tan-gents of two circles divide the line segment joining the two centers respectively externally and internally in the ratio of their radii.
(b) In a cyclic quadrilateral $ABCD$, if the diagonal CA bisects the angle C, then diagonal BD is parallel to the tangent at A to the circle through A, B, C, D.
(c) If TA, TB are tangent segments to a circle $C(O, r)$ from an external point T and OT intersects the circle in P, then AP bisects the angle TAB.
(d) If in a right triangle ABC, BD is the perpendicular on the hypotenuse AC, then
(i) $AC|AD = AB^2$ and
(ii) $AC \cdot AD = BC^2$

Directions for Questions 46 and 47: Two cows are tethered at the mid-points of two adjacent sides of a square field. Each of them is tied with a rope in such a way that grazing area of each cow is a semicircular region of diameter equal to the side of square. If side of the square is 10 m, then answer the following questions:

46. What is the area of the grazing field that is grazed by both the cows (in m^2)?

(a) $12.5(\pi + 2)$
(b) $12.5(-2 + \pi)$
(c) $25(2\pi + 1)$
(d) $25(2\pi - 1)$

47. For the given situation, the area of the non-grazed regions (in m^2) is

(a) $75 + 12.5\pi$
(b) $75 - 12.5\pi$
(c) $75 + 25\pi$
(d) $75 - 13\pi$

Directions for Questions 48 and 49: In the rectangle $PQRS$, M and N are two points on SR and PQ respectively such that MN bisects SQ perpendicularly at O. If $SR = 4$ cm, $RQ = 3$ cm.

48. What will be the value of MO/SO?

(a) 0.8
(b) 0.75
(c) 0.65
(d) None of these

49. Find the area of quadrilateral $SONP$.

(a) 3.65 cm^2
(b) 4.66 cm^2
(c) 2.66 cm^2
(d) None of these

50. A rectangle $PQRS$ is inscribed in a semicircle of center O and diameter MN. M, S, R, N are collinear. If $RN = 2$ cm and $QR = 4$ cm, then what is the area of the semicircle not overlapped by the rectangle $PQRS$?

(a) $(12.5\pi + 12)$ cm^2
(b) $(12.5\pi - 12)$ cm^2
(c) $(12.5\pi + 24)$ cm^2
(d) $(12.5\pi - 24)$ cm^2

51. In the diagram given below, quadrilateral $PQRS$ is divided into six smaller triangles. The number inside the triangle mentions its area. If $SN/NR = 1.25$, then find the value of $a + b$.

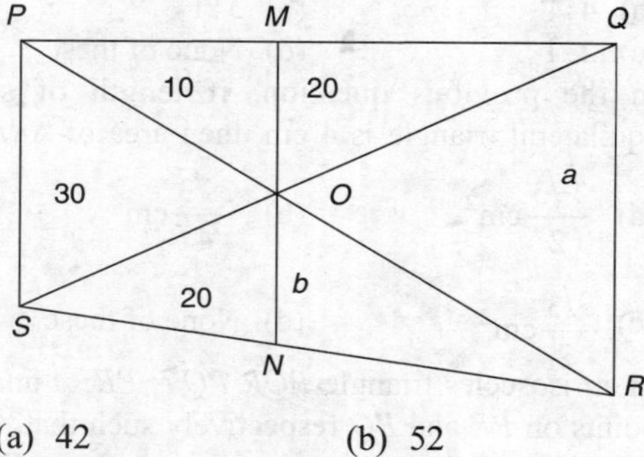

(a) 42
(b) 52
(c) 54
(d) 60

Directions for Questions 52 and 53: In the figure given below: QM, PN, RT are the altitudes of an isosceles triangle and $PQ = QR = 15$ cm and $PR = 18$ cm. Answer the following questions:

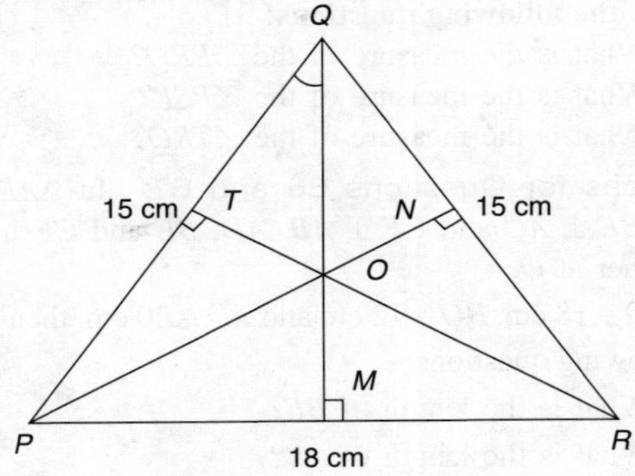

52. Find the ratio of QT/QO.

(a) 0.8 (b) 0.6
(c) 0.7 (d) 0.9

53. The value of OT is

(a) 3.15 cm (b) 3.35 cm
(c) 3.05 cm (d) 3.55 cm

54. In the figure given below ΔPQR is a right angled triangle with $\angle P = 90°$. The center of the incircle of the given triangle is O. Circles with centers O_1 and O_2 touch the circle and two sides as shown in the figure. If the radius of the incircle of ΔPQR is 1 cm and BR: BQ = 2:3, then find the value of r_1: r_2 (where r_1 is the radius of circle with center O_1 and r_2 is the radius of circle with center O_2).

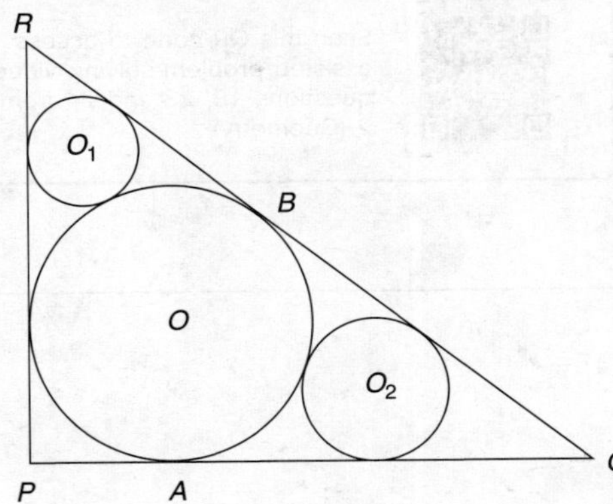

(a) $(33-11\sqrt{5}-6\sqrt{10}+10\sqrt{2})/18$

(b) $(33+11\sqrt{5}-6\sqrt{10}-10\sqrt{2})/18$

(c) $(33-11\sqrt{5}+6\sqrt{10}-10\sqrt{2})/18$

(d) $(33+11\sqrt{5}-6\sqrt{10}-10\sqrt{2})/18$

Directions for Questions 55 and 56: A circle is inscribed in a triangle PQR. It touches side PQ at point X. If $\angle P = 60°$, PX = 3 cm, QX = 5 cm, then answer the following questions:

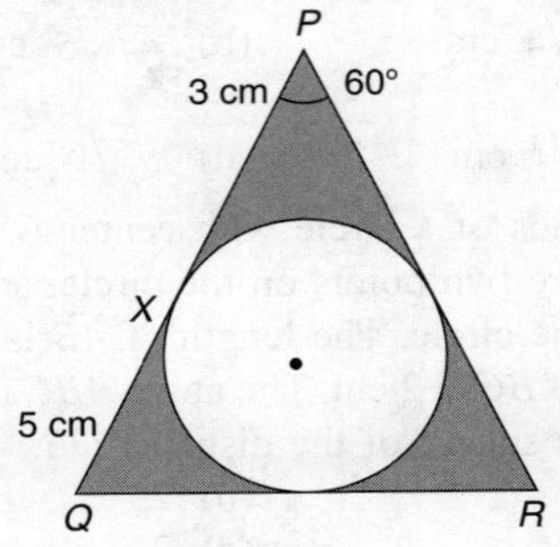

55. Find the radius of the circle.

(a) $3\sqrt{\frac{5}{7}}$ (b) $\frac{5}{7}\sqrt{3}$

(c) $3\sqrt{\frac{5}{17}}$ (d) None of these

56. Find the area of the shaded portion.

(a) $10\sqrt{3}-3\pi$ cm^2 (b) $10\sqrt{3}-13\pi$ cm^2

(c) $10\sqrt{3}-2\pi$cm^2 (d) None of these

Directions for Questions 57 and 58: In quadrilateral $PQRS$, $PQ||SR$ and $PS||QR$. $TU||SR$ and TU passes through the point of intersection of PR and WS. If the ratio of the area of ΔPOW to ΔSOR is 9:25, then answer the following questions:

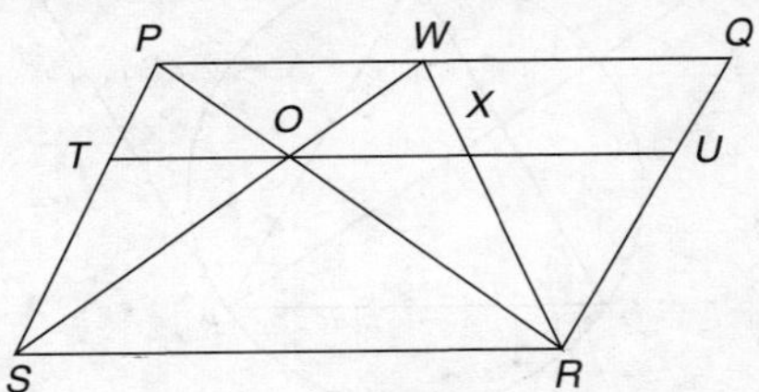

57. Find the ratio of area of quadrilateral $WQUX$ and ΔXUR.

(a) 38:25 (b) 39:25
(c) 41:25 (d) None of these

58. If WQ = 2 cm, then find $TX \times XU$.

(a) 25/4 cm^2 (b) 75/16 cm^2
(c) 50/33 cm^2 (d) 100/67 cm^2

59. In the given figure, PQ and PR are tangents of a semicircle. Centre 'O' of this semicircle lies on QR. If QO = 2 cm, OR = 4 cm, and $\angle P = 90°$, then radius of the semicircle is

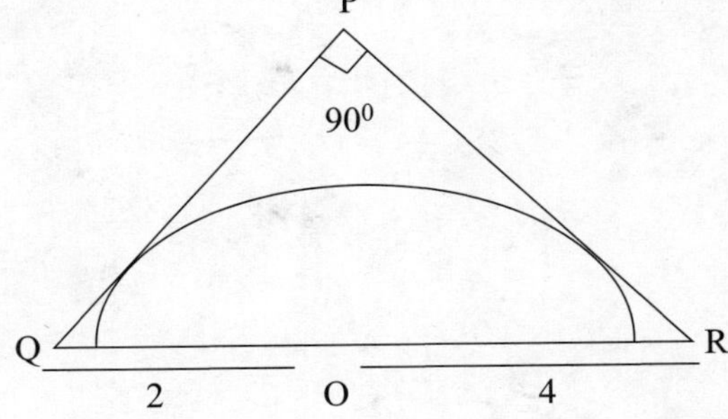

(a) $\sqrt{5}/4$ cm (b) $4/\sqrt{5}$ cm

(c) $\sqrt{5}/3$ cm (d) $\sqrt{5}/6$ cm

60. The radius of a circle with center O is $\sqrt{50}$ cm. A and C are two points on the circle, and B is a point inside the circle. The length of AB is 6 cm, and the length of BC is 2 cm. The angle ABC is a right angle. Find the square of the distance OB.

(a) 26 (b) 25
(c) 24 (d) 23

Directions for Questions 61 and 62: A circle is drawn with the center at O and radius as OA, where OA is one of the sides of a parallelogram $ABCO$. The circle cuts CO and BA at Q and P respectively. If the area of the circle is 36π and $BP = 2$ cm, $PA = 8$ cm, then answer the following questions:

61. What is the area of the triangle POA (in cm^2)?
62. What is the length of PQ (in cm)?

Directions for Questions 63 to 65: In the figure ΔPQR is an equilateral triangle. ST is a tangent to the circle at P. If $\angle PRS = 40°$ and $\angle PSR = 4 \times \angle RTS$ and $\angle TPQ = 60°$

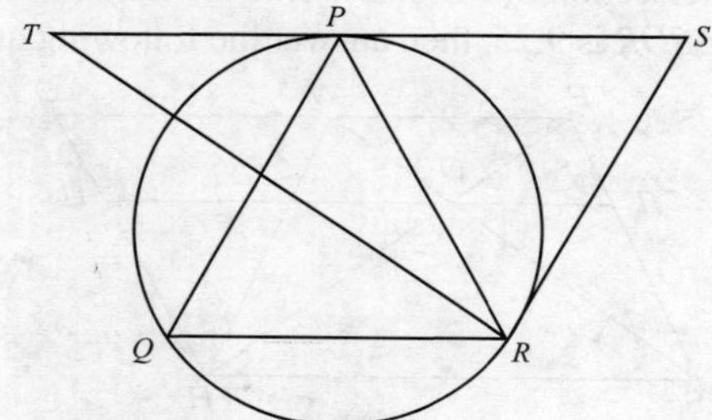

Answer the following questions:

63. What is the measure of the $\angle PRQ$?
64. What is the measure of the $\angle PSR$?
65. What is the measure of the $\angle TRQ$?

Directions for Questions 66 and 67: In ΔABC, $AD \perp BC$, $BE \perp AC$ and $CF \perp AB$. AD, BE and CF intersect each other at O.

If $AO = 18$ cm, $BO = 12$ cm and $AD = 20$ cm, then answer the following questions:

66. What is the length of BE?
67. What is the length of AB?

Directions for Questions 68 to 70: In an obtuse-angled triangle ABC, $AB = a$, $BC = b$, $AC = c$, where a, b and c are integers.

It is given that $a \times b = 9$. Based on this information, answer the following questions:

68. How many such triangles are possible?
69. Find the maximum possible value of c.
70. Find the maximum area of the ABC.

71. In a rectangle $PQRS$, $PQ = 14$ cm, X is a point on SR such that SX: XR = 4:3 and $QX = 10$ cm. If $\angle PXQ = a$, $\angle XPQ = b$, $\angle XQP = c$, then which of the following is correct?

(a) $a > b > c$ (b) $b > c > a$
(c) $a > c > b$ (d) $c > b > a$

High Yield Questions

Scan this QR code to access assisted problem solving videos on questions 10, 23 and 24 from LOD 2 (Geometry)

Space for Notes

MENSURATION

LEVEL OF DIFFICULTY (I)

1. The volume of a right circular cone is 100π cm^3 and its height is 12 cm. Find its slant height.
(a) 13 cm (b) 16 cm
(c) 9 cm (d) 26 cm
2. The short and the long hands of a clock are 4 cm and 6 cm long respectively. What will be sum of distances travelled by their tips in 4 days? (Take $\pi = 3.14$)
(a) 954.56 cm (b) 3818.24 cm
(c) 2909.12 cm (d) 2703.56 cm
3. The surface areas of two spheres are in the ratio of 1:4. Find the ratio of their volumes.
(a) 1:2 (b) 1:8
(c) 1:4 (d) 2:1
4. The outer and inner diameters of a spherical shell are 10 cm and 9 cm respectively. Find the volume of the metal contained in the shell. (Use $\pi = 22/7$)
(a) 6956 cm^3 (b) 141.95 cm^3
(c) 283.9 cm^3 (d) 478.3 cm^3
5. The radii of two spheres are in the ratio of 1 : 2. Find the ratio of their surface areas.
(a) 1:3 (b) 2:3
(c) 1:4 (d) 3:4
6. A sphere of radius r has the same volume as that of a cone with a circular base of radius r. Find the height of cone.
(a) $2r$ (b) $r/3$
(c) $4r$ (d) $(2/3)r$
7. Find the number of bricks, each measuring 25 cm × 12.5 cm × 7.5 cm, required to construct a wall 12 meters long, 5 meters high and 0.25 meters thick, while the sand and cement mixture occupies 5% of the total volume of wall.
(a) 6080 (b) 3040
(c) 1520 (d) 12160
8. A road that is 7 m wide surrounds a circular path whose circumference is 352 m. What will be the area of the road?
(a) 2618 meters^2 (b) 654.5 meters^2
(c) 1309 meters^2 (d) 5236 meters^2
9. In a shower, 10 cm of rain falls. What will be the volume of water that falls on 1 hectare area of ground?
(a) 500 meters^3 (b) 650 meters^3
(c) 1000 meters^3 (d) 750 meters^3
10. Seven equal cubes each of side 5 cm are joined end to end. Find the surface area of the resulting cuboid.
(a) 750 cm^2 (b) 1500 cm^2
(c) 2250 cm^2 (d) 700 cm^2
11. A rectangular piece of paper is 22 cm long and 10 cm wide. A cylinder is formed by rolling the paper along its length. Find the volume of the cylinder.
12. Consider the volumes of the following objects and arrange them in **decreasing** order of their volumes:
   1. A parallelepiped of length 5 cm, breadth 3 cm and height 4 cm
   2. A cube of each side 4 cm
   3. A cylinder of radius 3 cm and length 3 cm
   4. A sphere of radius 3 cm

(a) 4, 3, 2, 1 (b) 4, 2, 3, 1
(c) 4, 3, 1, 2 (d) None of these
13. A hemispherical bowl is filled with hot water to the brim. The contents of the bowl are transferred into a cylindrical vessel whose radius is 50% more than its height. If diameter of the bowl is the same as that of the vessel and the volume of the hot water in the cylindrical vessel is x% of the volume of the cylindrical vessel then x =?
14. In a circular field, there is a rectangular tank of length 130 m and breadth 110 m. If the area of the land portion of the field is 20350 m^2, then find the radius of the field.
15. A tank internally measuring 150 cm × 120 cm × 100 cm has 1281600 cm^3 water in it. Porous bricks are placed in the water until the tank is full up to its brim. Each brick absorbs one tenth of its volume of water. How many bricks, of 20 cm × 6 cm × 4 cm, can be put in the tank without spilling over the water?
16. A spherical metal ball of radius 10 cm is molten and made into 1000 smaller spheres of equal sizes. In this process the surface area of the metal is increased by n %. Then n =?
17. Suresh, who runs a bakery, uses a conical-shaped equipment to write decorative labels (e.g., Happy Birthday etc.) using cream. The height of this equipment is 7 cm and the diameter of the base is 5 mm. A full charge of the equipment will write 330 words on an average. How many words can be written using two fifth of a litre of cream?
18. Your friend's cap is in the shape of a right circular cone of base radius 14 cm and height 26.5 cm. Find

the approximate area of the sheet required to make seven such caps.

19. In an engineering college there is a rectangular garden of dimensions 34 m by 21 m. Two mutually perpendicular walking corridors of 4 m width have been made in the central part and flowers have been grown in the rest of the garden. Find the area under the flowers.

20. A right circular cone is enveloping a right circular cylinder that rests on the base of the cone. If the radius and the height of the cone is 4 cm and 10 cm respectively, and the radius of the cylinder is 'r' cm, the largest possible curved surface area of the cylinder is '$a\pi r(b-r)$' then $a \times b = ?$

21. In a right-angled triangle, find the hypotenuse if base and perpendicular are respectively 36015 cm and 48020 cm.

(a) 69125 cm (b) 60025 cm
(c) 391025 cm (d) 60125 cm

22. The perimeter of an equilateral triangle is $72\sqrt{3}$ m. Find its height.

(a) 63 meters (b) 24 meters
(c) 18 meters (d) 36 meters

23. The inner circumference of a circular track is 440 cm. The track is 14 cm wide. Find the diameter of the outer circle of the track.

(a) 84 cm (b) 168 cm
(c) 336 cm (d) 77 cm

24. A race track is in the form of a ring whose inner and outer circumferences are 352 meter and 396 meter respectively. Find the width of the track.

(a) 7 meters (b) 14 meters
(c) 14π meters (d) 7π meters

25. The outer circumference of a circular track is 220 meter. The track is 7 meter wide everywhere. Calculate the cost of levelling the track at the rate of 50 paisa per square meter.

(a) ₹1556.5 (b) ₹3113
(c) ₹593 (d) ₹693

26. Find the area of a quadrant of a circle whose circumference is 44 cm.

(a) 77 cm^2 (b) 38.5 cm^2
(c) 19.25 cm^2 (d) 19.25π cm^2

27. A pit 7.5 meters long, 6 meters wide and 1.5 meters deep is dug in a field. Find the volume of soil removed in cubic meters.

(a) 135 $meters^3$ (b) 101.25 $meters^3$
(c) 50.625 $meters^3$ (d) 67.5 $meters^3$

28. Find the length of the longest pole that can be placed in an indoor stadium 24 meters long, 18 meters wide and 16 meters high.

(a) 30 meters (b) 25 meters
(c) 34 meters (d) $\sqrt{580}$ meters

29. The length, breadth and height of a room are in the ratio of 3:2:1. If its volume be 1296 m^3, find its breadth

(a) 18 meters (b) 6 meters
(c) 16 meters (d) 12 meters

30. The volume of a cube is 216 cm^3. Part of this cube is then melted to form a cylinder of length 8 cm. Find the volume of the cylinder.

(a) 342 cm^3 (b) 216 cm^3
(c) 36 cm^3 (d) Data inadequate

31. If x units are added to the length of the radius of a circle, what is the number of units by which the area of the circle is increased?

32. A man walks diagonally across a square plot. Approximately, what is the percentage reduction in the total distance that he walked vis-à-vis the distance he would have walked had he walked along the edges? (To the closest 1%)

33. The radius of circle is so increased that its circumference is increased by 5%. The area of the circle then increases by

(a) 12.5% (b) 10.25%
(c) 10.5% (d) 11.25%

34. The biggest possible cube is taken out of a right solid cylinder of radius 15 cm and height 20 cm respectively. What will be the volume of the cube?

35. How many cuboids of different dimensions can be assembled with 100 identical cubes?

36. What is the least number of square tiles required to pave the floor of a room 1517 cm long and 902 cm broad?

37. A wire, if bent into *a* square, encloses an area of 484 cm^2. This wire is cut into two pieces with the bigger piece having *a* length three-fourth of the original wire's length. Now, if *a* circle and *a* square are formed with the bigger and the smaller piece respectively, what would be the area enclosed by the two pieces?

38. A spiral staircase is made up of 13 successive semicircles, with center alternately at A and B, starting with center at A. The radii of semicircles, thus developed, are 0.5 cm, 1.0 cm, 1.5 cm, and 2.0 cm and so on. Find the total length of the spiral. Use $\pi = \frac{22}{7}$

39. A cylinder, a hemisphere and a cone stand on the same base and have the same heights. The ratio of the areas of their curved surface is

(a) 2: 2: 1 (b) $\sqrt{2}:\sqrt{2}:1$
(c) $2:\sqrt{2}:1$ (d) None of these

40. The radius of a spherical balloon, of radii 30 cm, increases at the rate of 2 cm per second. Then by how much does its curved surface area increases?

41. The whole surface of a rectangular block is 8788 square cm. If length, breadth and height are in the ratio of 4:3:2, find length.

(a) 26 cm (b) 52 cm
(c) 104 cm (d) 13 cm

42. Three metal cubes with edges 6 cm, 8 cm and 10 cm respectively are melted together and formed into a single cube. Find the side of the resulting cube.

(a) 11 cm (b) 12 cm
(c) 13 cm (d) 24 cm

43. Find curved and total surface area of a conical flask of radius 6 cm and height 8 cm.

(a) 60π, 96π (b) 20π, 96π
(c) 60π, 48π (d) 30π, 48π

44. The volume of a right circular cone is 100π cm^3 and its height is 12 cm. Find its curved surface area.

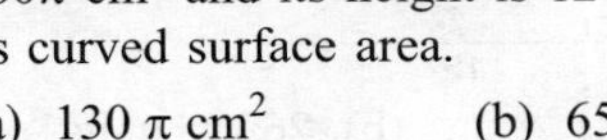

(a) $130\ \pi$ cm^2 (b) $65\ \pi$ cm^2
(c) $204\ \pi$ cm^2 (d) 65 cm^2

45. The diameters of two cones are equal. If their slant height be in the ratio 5:7, find the ratio of their curved surface areas.

(a) 25:7 (b) 25:49
(c) 5:49 (d) 5:7

46. The curved surface area of a cone is 2376 square cm and its slant height is 18 cm. Find the diameter.

(a) 6 cm (b) 18 cm
(c) 84 cm (d) 12 cm

47. The ratio of radii of a cylinder to a cone is 1:2. If their heights are equal, find the ratio of their volumes.

(a) 1:3 (b) 2:3
(c) 3:4 (d) 3 : 1

48. A silver wire when bent in the form of a square encloses an area of 484 cm^2. Now if the same wire is bent to form a circle, the area enclosed by it would be

(a) 308 cm^2 (b) 196 cm^2
(c) 616 cm^2 (d) 88 cm^2

49. The circumference of a circle exceeds its diameter by 16.8 cm. Find the circumference of the circle.

(a) 12.32 cm (b) 49.28 cm
(c) 58.64 cm (d) 24.64 cm

50. A bicycle wheel makes 5000 revolutions in moving 11 km. What is the radius of the wheel?

(a) 70 cm (b) 135 cm
(c) 17.5 cm (d) 35 cm

51. In a swimming pool measuring 90 meters by 40 meters, 150 men take a dip. If the average displacement of water by a man is 8 cubic meters, what will be the rise in the water level?

(a) 30 cm (b) 50 cm
(c) 20 cm (d) 33.33 cm

52. How many meters of cloth 5 meters wide will be required to make a conical tent, the radius of whose base is 7 meters and height is 24 meters?

(a) 55 meters (b) 330 meters
(c) 220 meters (d) 110 meters

53. Two cones have their heights in the ratio 1:2 and the diameters of their bases are in the ratio 2:1. What will be the ratio of their volumes?

(a) 4:1 (b) 2:1
(c) 3:2 (d) 1:1

54. A conical tent is to accommodate ten persons. Each person must have 6 meters^2 space to sit and 30 meters^3 of air to breathe. What will be the height of the cone?

(a) 37.5 meters (b) 150 meters
(c) 75 meters (d) None of these

55. A closed wooden box measures externally 10 cm long, 8 cm broad and 6 cm high. Thickness of wood is 0.5 cm. Find the volume of wood used.

(a) 230 cubic cm (b) 165 cubic cm
(c) 330 cubic cm (d) 300 cubic cm.

56. A cuboid of dimension 24 cm × 9 cm × 8 cm is melted and smaller cubes of side 3 cm are formed. Find how many such cubes can be formed.

(a) 27 (b) 64
(c) 54 (d) 32

57. Three cubes each of volume of 216 meters^3 are joined end to end. Find the surface area of the resulting figure.

(a) 504 meters^2 (b) 216 meters^2
(c) 432 meters^2 (d) 480 meters^2

58. A hollow spherical shell is made of a metal of density 4.9 g/cm^3. If its internal and external radii are 10 cm and 12 cm respectively, find the weight of the shell. (Take $\pi = \frac{22}{7}$)

(a) 5016 g (b) 1416.8 g
(c) 14948.26 g (d) 5667.1 g

59. The largest cone is formed at the base of a cube of side measuring 7 cm. Find the ratio of volume of cone to cube.

(a) 20:21 (b) 22:21
(c) 21:22 (d) 11:42

60. A spherical cannon ball, 28 cm in diameter, is melted and cast into a right circular conical mould the base of which is 35 cm in diameter. Find the height of the cone correct up to two places of decimals.

(a) 8.96 cm (b) 35.84 cm
(c) 5.97 cm (d) 17.92 cm

61. Find the area of the circle circumscribed about a square each side of which is 10 cm.

(a) 314.28 cm^2 (b) 157.14 cm^2
(c) 150.38 cm^2 (d) 78.57 cm^2

62. Find the radius of the circle inscribed in a triangle whose sides are 8 cm, 15 cm and 17 cm.

(a) 4 cm (b) 5 cm
(c) 3 cm (d) $2\sqrt{2}$ cm

63. In the given diagram, a rope is wound around the outside of a circular drum whose diameter is 70 cm and a bucket is tied to the other end of the rope. Find the number of revolutions made by the drum if the bucket is raised by 11 m.

(a) 10 (b) 2.5
(c) 5 (d) 5.5

64. A cube whose edge is 20 cm long has circles on each of its faces painted black. What is the total area of the unpainted surface of the cube if the circles are of the largest area possible?

(a) 85.71 cm^2 (b) 257.14 cm^2
(c) 514.28 cm^2 (d) 331.33 cm^2

65. The areas of three adjacent faces of a cuboid are x, y, z. If the volume is V, then V^2 will be equal to

(a) xy/z (b) yz/x^2
(c) x^2y^2/z^2 (d) xyz

66. In the adjacent figure, find the area of the shaded region. (Use $\pi = 22/7$)

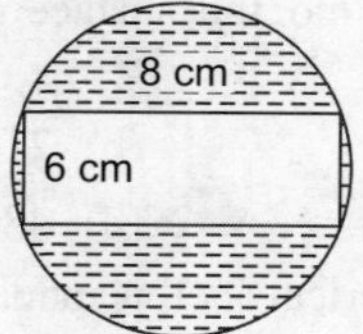

(a) 15.28 cm^2 (b) 61.14 cm^2
(c) 30.57 cm^2 (d) 40.76 cm^2

67. The diagram represents the area swept by the wiper of a car. With the dimensions given in the figure, calculate the shaded area swept by the wiper.

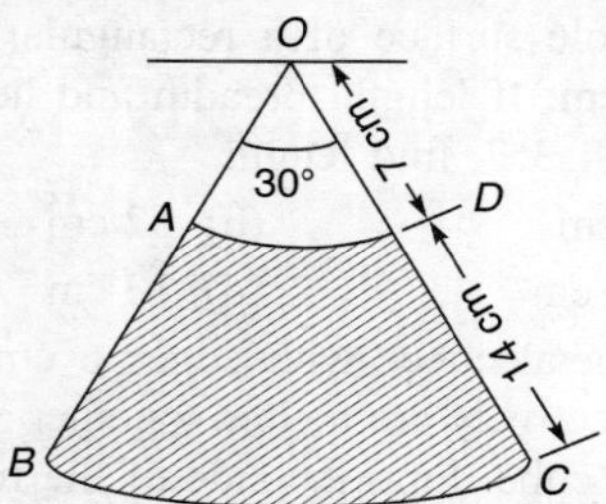

(a) 102.67 cm^2 (b) 205.34 cm^2
(c) 51.33 cm^2 (d) 208.16 cm^2

68. Find the area of the quadrilateral $ABCD$. (Given, $\sqrt{3} = 1.73$)

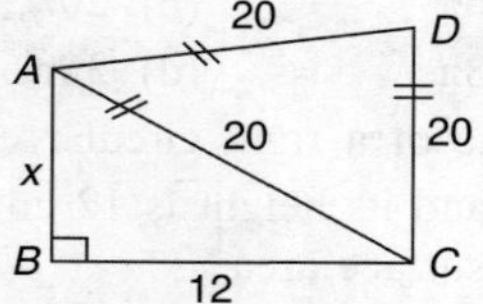

(a) 452 sq units (b) 269 sq units
(c) 134.5 sq units (d) 1445 g cm

69. The base of a pyramid is a rectangle of sides 18 m × 26 m and its slant height to the shorter side of the base is 24 m. Find its volume.

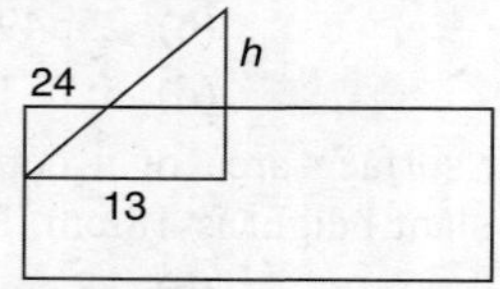

(a) $156\sqrt{407}$
(b) $78\sqrt{407}$
(c) $312\sqrt{407}$
(d) $234\sqrt{407}$

70. A wire is looped in the form of a circle of radius 28 cm. It is bent again into a square form. What will be the length of the diagonal of the largest square possible thus?

(a) 44 (b) $44\sqrt{2}$
(c) $176/2\sqrt{2}$ (d) $88\sqrt{2}$

Space for Notes

LEVEL OF DIFFICULTY (II)

1. A solid is in the form of a right circular cylinder with a hemisphere at one end and a cone at the other end. Their common diameter is 3.5 cm and the heights of conical and cylindrical portions are respectively 6 cm and 10 cm. Find the volume of the solid. **(Use π = 3.14)**
   (a) 117 cm^3 (b) 234 cm^3
   (c) 58.5 cm^3 (d) None of these
2. In the adjoining figure, *AOBCA* represents a quadrant of a circle of radius 3.5 cm with center *O*. Calculate the area of the shaded portion. (Use π = 22/7)
   (a) 35 cm^2 (b) 7.875 cm^2
   (c) 9.625 cm^2 (d) 6.125 cm^2

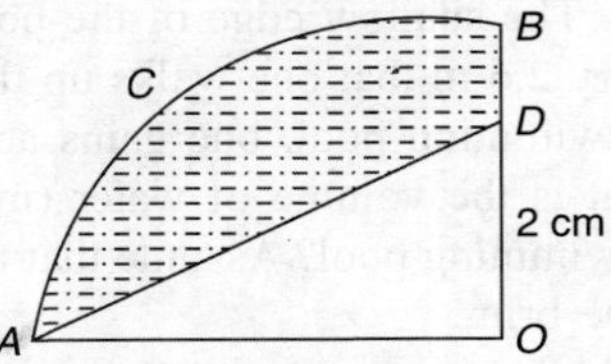

3. Find the area of the shaded region if the radius of each of the circles is 1 cm.

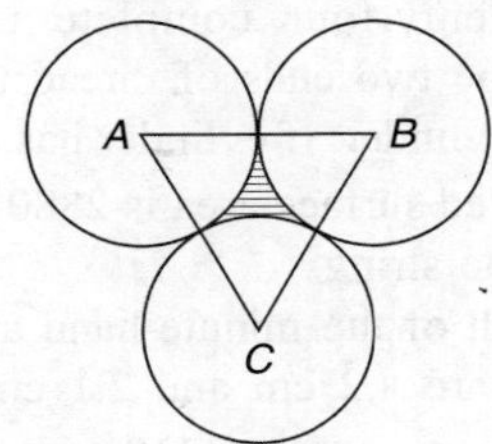

   (a) $2-\frac{\pi}{3}$ (b) $\sqrt{3}-\pi$
   (c) $\sqrt{3}-\frac{\pi}{2}$ (d) $\sqrt{3}-\pi/4$
4. A right elliptical cylinder full of petrol has its widest elliptical side 2.4 m and the shortest 1.6 m. Its height is 7 m. Find the time required to empty half the tank through a hose of diameter 4 cm if the rate of flow of petrol is 120 m/min
   (a) 60 min (b) 90 min
   (c) 75 min (d) 70 min
5. Find the area of the trapezium *ABCD*.

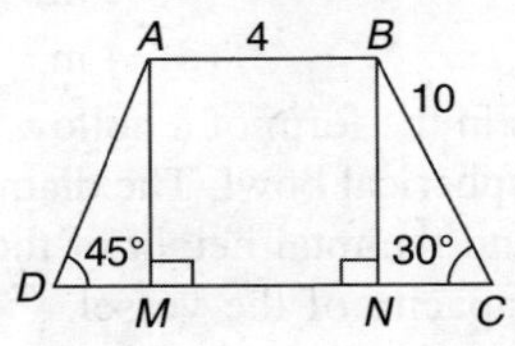

   (a) $5/2(13+2\sqrt{3})$ (b) $\frac{5\sqrt{3}(13+5\sqrt{3})}{2}$
   (c) $13(13+2\sqrt{3})$ (d) None of these
6. *PQRS* is the diameter of a circle of radius 6 cm. The lengths *PQ*, *QR* and *RS* are equal. Semi-circles are drawn with *PQ* and *QS* as diameters as shown in the figure alongside. Find the ratio of the area of the shaded region to that of the un-shaded region.

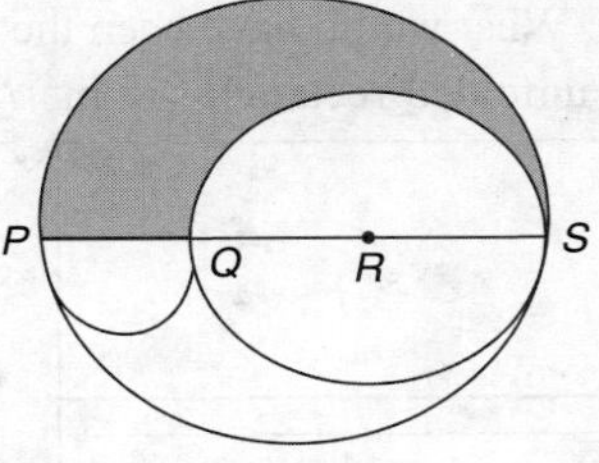

   (a) 1:2 (b) 25:121
   (c) 5:18 (d) 5:13
7. In the right-angled triangle *PQR*, find *Rx*.

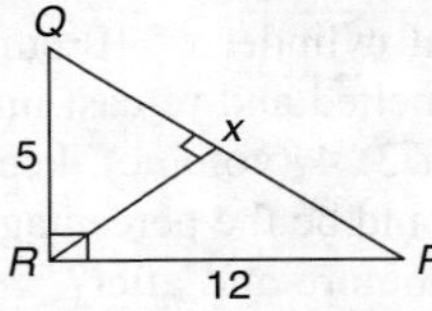

   (a) 13/60 (b) 13/45
   (c) 60/13 (d) 23/29
8. The radius of a right circular cylinder is increased by 50%. Find the percentage increase in volume
   (a) 120% (b) 75%
   (c) 150% (d) 125%
9. Two persons start walking on a road that diverges at an angle of 120°. If they walk at the rate of 3 km/h and 2 km/h repectively, find the distance between them after four hours.

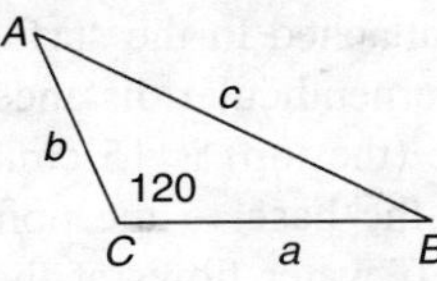

   (a) $4\sqrt{19}$ km (b) 5 km
   (c) 7 km (d) $8\sqrt{19}$ km
10. Water flows out at the rate of 10 m/min from a cylindrical pipe of diameter 5 mm. Find the time taken to fill a conical tank whose diameter at the surface is 40 cm and depth 24 cm.
   (a) 50 min (b) 102.4 min
   (c) 51.2 min (d) 25.6 min

11. At the center of a city's municipal park there is a large circular pool. A fish is released in the water at the edge of the pool. The fish swims north for 30 meters before it hits the edge of the pool. It then turns east and swims for 40 meters before it hits the edge of the pool. If the area of the pool is $X\pi$ m^2 then X is

(a) 625 (b) 125
(c) 250 (d) 500

12. The figure below has been obtained by folding a rectangle. The total area of the figure (as visible) is 144 square meters. Had the rectangle not been folded, the current overlapping part would have been a square. What would have been the total area of the original unfolded rectangle (in m^2)?

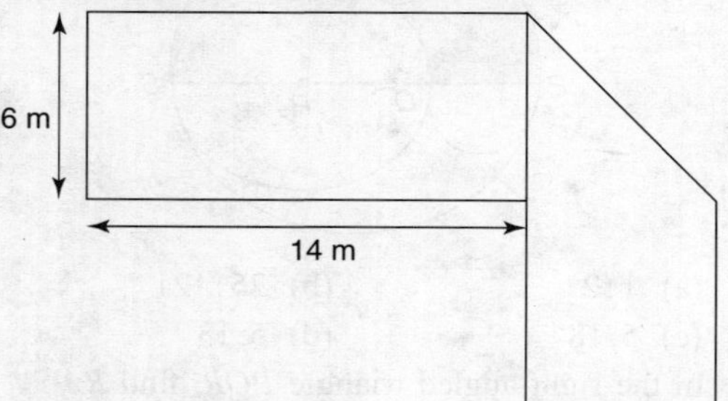

13. A solid metal cylinder of 10 cm height and 14 cm diameter is melted and re-cast into two cones in the proportion of 3: 4 (volume), keeping the height 10 cm. What would be the percentage change in the flat surface area before and after?

(a) 9% (b) 16%
(c) 25% (d) 50%

14. A circular road is constructed outside a square field. The perimeter of the square field is 200 ft. If the width of the road is $7\sqrt{2}$ ft. and cost of construction is ₹100 per sq. ft, find the lowest possible cost to construct 50% of the total road.

(a) ₹70,400 (b) ₹125,400
(c) ₹140,800 (d) ₹235,400

15. Diameter of the base of a water-filled inverted right circular cone is 26 cm. A cylindrical pipe, 5 mm inradius, is attached to the surface of the cone at a point. The perpendicular distance between the point and the base (the top) is 15 cm. The distance from the edge of the base to the point is 17 cm, along the surface. If water flows at the rate of 10 meters per minute through the pipe, how much time would elapse before water stops coming out of the pipe?

(a) $\geq$ 5.2 minutes
(b) $\geq$ 4.5 minutes but $<$ 4.8 minutes
(c) $\geq$ 4.8 minutes but $<$ 5 minutes
(d) $\geq$ 5 minutes but $<$ 5.2 minutes

16. Consider a rectangle *ABCD* of area 90 units. The points *P* and *Q* trisect *AB*, and *R* bisects *CD*. The diagonal *AC* intersects the line segments *PR* and *QR* at *M* and *N* respectively. What is the area of the quadrilateral *PQNM*?

(a) $>$ 9.5 and $\leq$ 10 (b) $>$ 10 and $\leq$ 10.5
(c) $>$ 10.5 and $\leq$ 11 (d) $>$ 11 and $\leq$ 11.5

17. The central park of the city is 40 meters long and 30 meters wide. The Mayor wants to construct two roads of equal width in the park such that the roads intersect each other at right angles and the diagonals of the park are also the diagonals of the small rectangle formed at the intersection of the two roads. Further, the mayor wants that the area of the two roads to be equal to the remaining area of the park. What should be the width of the roads?

(a) 10 meters (b) 12.5 meters
(c) 14 meters (d) 15 meters

18. A rectangular swimming pool is 48 m long and 20 m wide. The shallow edge of the pool is 1 m deep. For every 2.6 m that one walks up the inclined base of the swimming pool, one gains an elevation of 1 m. What is the volume of water (in cubic meters), in the swimming pool? Assume that the pool is filled up to the brim.

(a) 528 (b) 960
(c) 6790 (d) 10560

19. A thread is wound on a cylinder such that it makes exactly twenty-four complete turns around the cylinder. The two ends of thread touch the top and bottom of cylinder. If cylinder has a radius of 15 cm and its curved surface area is 2880 cm^2 then find the length of the string.

20. If the length of the minute-hand and the hour-hand of a clock are 4.2 cm and 2.1 cm and the minute hand covers an area of 110.88 cm^2, then find the area covered by hour hand during the same period. **[take π = 22/7]**

21. The perimeter of a sector of a circle of radius 5.7 m is 27.2 m. Find the area of the sector.

(a) 90.06 cm^2 (b) 135.09 cm^2
(c) 45 cm^2 (d) None of these

22. The dimensions of a field are 20 m by 9 m. A pit 10 m long, 4.5 m wide and 3 m deep is dug in one corner of the field and the earth removed has been evenly spread over the remaining area of the field. What will be the rise in the height of field as a result of this operation?

(a) 1 m (b) 2 m
(c) 3 m (d) 4 m

23. A vessel is in the form of a hollow cylinder mounted on a hemispherical bowl. The diameter of the sphere is 14 cm and the total height of the vessel is 13 cm. Find the capacity of the vessel. (Take π = 22/7)

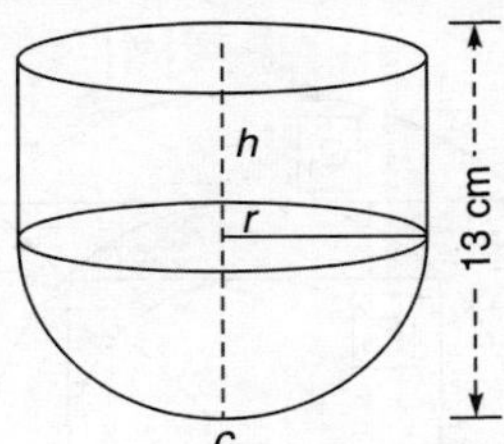

(a) 321.33 cm^3 (b) 1642.67 cm^3
(c) 1232 cm^3 (d) 1632.33 cm^3

24. The sides of a triangle are 21, 20 and 13 cm. Find the area of the larger triangle into which the given triangle is divided by the perpendicular upon the longest side from the opposite vertex.
(a) 72 cm^2 (b) 96 cm^2
(c) 168 cm^2 (d) 144 cm^2

25. A circular tent is cylindrical to a height of 3 meters and conical above it. If its diameter is 105 m and the slant height of the conical portion is 53 m, calculate the length of the canvas 5 m wide to make the required tent.
(a) 3894 m (b) 973.5 m
(c) 1947 m (d) 1800 m

26. A steel sphere of radius 4 cm is drawn into a wire of diameter 4 mm. Find the length of wire.
(a) 10,665 mm (b) 42,660 mm
(c) 21,333 mm (d) 14,220 mm

27. A cylinder and a cone having equal diameter of their bases are placed in the Qutab Minar one on the other, with the cylinder placed in the bottom. If their curved surface area are in the ratio of 8: 5, find the ratio of their heights. Assume the height of the cylinder to be equal to the radius of Qutab Minar. (Assume Qutab Minar to be having same radius throughout.)
(a) 1:4 (b) 3:4
(c) 4:3 (d) 2:3

28. If the curved surface area of a cone is thrice that of another cone and slant height of the second cone is thrice that of the first, find the ratio of the area of their base.
(a) 81:1 (b) 9:1
(c) 3:1 (d) 27:1

29. A solid sphere of radius 6 cm is melted into a hollow cylinder of uniform thickness. If the external radius of the base of the cylinder is 5 cm and its height is 32 cm, find the uniform thickness of the cylinder.
(a) 2 cm (b) 3 cm
(c) 1 cm (d) 3.5 cm

30. A hollow sphere of external and internal diameters 6 cm and 4 cm respectively is melted into a cone of base diameter 8 cm. Find the height of the cone.
(a) 4.75 cm (b) 9.5 cm
(c) 19 cm (d) 38 cm

31. Find the ratio of the diameter of the circles inscribed in and circumscribing an equilateral triangle to its height.
(a) 1:2:1 (b) 2:4:3
(c) 1:3:4 (d) 3:2:1

32. Find the sum of the areas of the shaded sectors given that *ABCDFE* is any hexagon and all the circles are of same radius *r* with different vertices of the hexagon as their centers as shown in the figure.

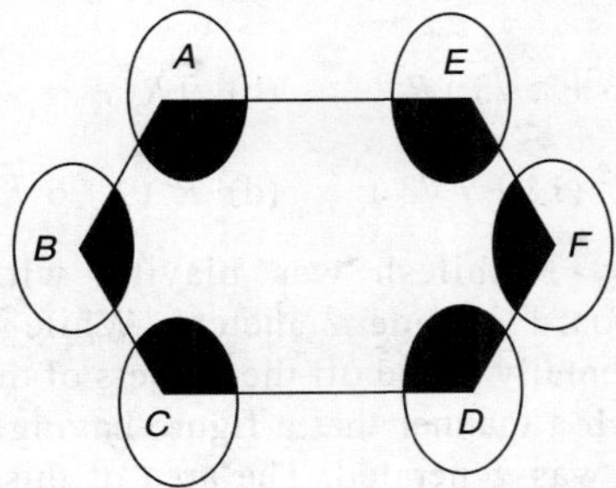

(a) πr^2 (b) $2\pi r^2$
(c) $5\pi r^2/4$ (d) $3\pi r^2/2$

33. Circles are drawn with four vertices as the center and radius equal to the side of a square. If the square is formed by joining the mid-points of another square of side $2\sqrt{6}$, find the area common to all the four circles.
(a) $[(\sqrt{3}-1)/2)]\,6\pi$ (b) $4\pi - 3\sqrt{3}$
(c) $1/2\,(\pi - 3\sqrt{3})$ (d) $4\pi - 12(\sqrt{3}-1)$

34. *ABDC* is a circle and circles are drawn with *AO*, *CO*, *DO* and *OB* as diameters. Areas *E* and *F* are shaded. *E*/*F* is equal to

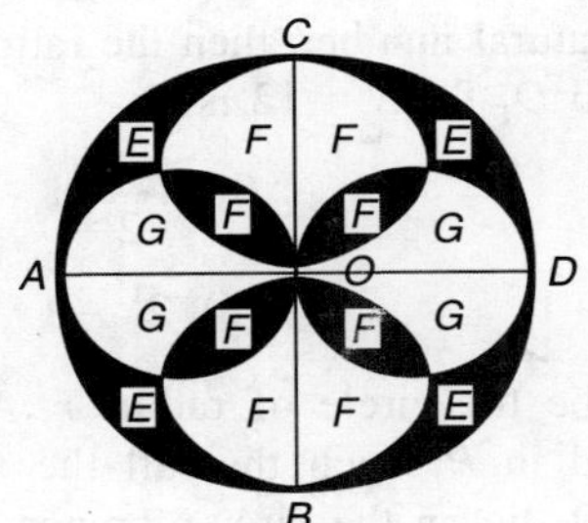

(a) 1 (b) 1/2
(c) 1/2 (d) $\pi/4$

35. The diagram shows six equal circles inscribed in an equilateral triangle *ABC*. The circles touch externally among themselves and also touch the sides of the triangle. If the radius of each circle is *R*, then area of the triangle is

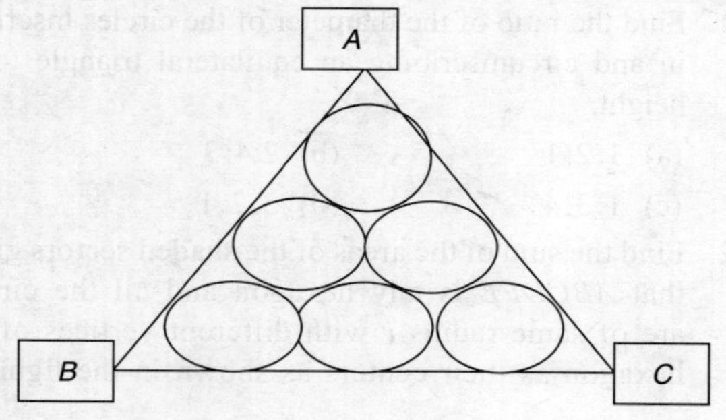

(a) $(6 + \pi\sqrt{3})R^2$ (b) $9R^2$

(c) $R^2(12 + 7\sqrt{3})$ (d) $R^2(9 + 6\sqrt{3})$

36. A boy Mithilesh was playing with a square cardboard of side 2 meters. While playing, he accidentally sliced off the corners of the cardboard in such a manner that a figure having all its sides equal was generated. The area of this eight-sided figure is

(a) $\frac{4\sqrt{2}}{\sqrt{2}+1}$ (b) $\frac{4}{\sqrt{2}+1}$

(c) $\frac{2\sqrt{2}}{\sqrt{2}+1}$ (d) $\frac{8}{\sqrt{2}+1}$

37. In a painting competition, students were asked to draw alternate squares and circles, circumscribing each other. The first student drew A_1 a square whose side is '*a*' meters. The second student drew circle C_1 circumscribing the square A_1 such that all its vertices are on C_1. Subsequent students drew square A_2 circumscribing C_1, circle C_2 circumscribing A_2 and A_3 circumscribing C_2, and so on. If D_N is the area between the square A_N and the circle C_N, where N is a natural number, then the ratio of the sum of all D_N to D_1 for $N = 12$ is

(a) 1 (b) $\frac{\pi}{2} - 1$

(c) $2^{12} - 1$ (d) $2^{11} - 1$

38. Let P_1 be the circle of radius r. A square Q_1 is inscribed in P_1 such that all the vertices of the square Q_1 lie on the circumference of P_1. Another circle P_2 is inscribed in Q_1. Another square Q_2 is inscribed in the circle P_2. Circle P_3 is inscribed in the square Q_2 and so on. S_N is the area between Q_N and P_{N+1} where N represents the set of natural numbers. If the ratio of sum of all such S_N to that of the area of the square Q_1 is $\frac{a-\pi}{b}$ then $a + b$ =?

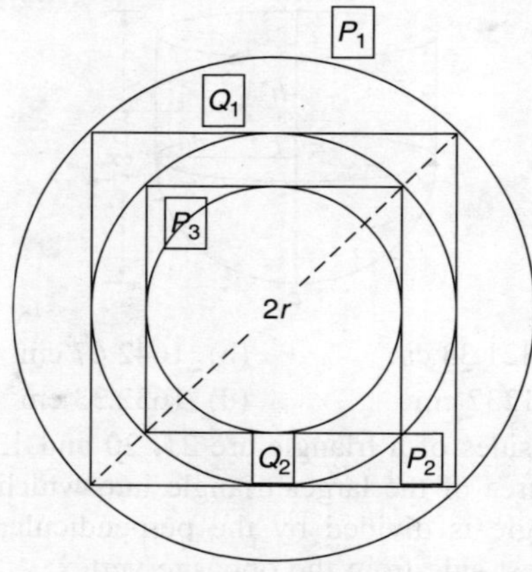

39. In the figure, *ABCDEF* is a regular hexagon and *PQR* is an equilateral triangle of side '*a*'. The area of the shaded portion is $23\sqrt{3}$ cm² and *CD*: *PQ*:: 2 : 1. If the area of the circle circumscribing the hexagon is $X\pi$ cm², then X =?

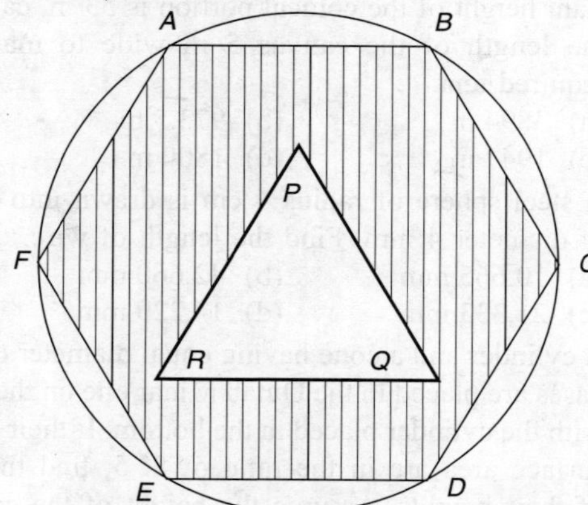

40. Let S_1, S_2, ...be the squares such that for each $n \geq 1$, the length of the diagonal of S_n is equal to the length of the side of S_{n+1}. If the length of the side of S_3 is 4 cm, what is the area of the square S_{11} ?

41. Three equal cubes are placed adjacently in a row. Find the ratio of total surface area of the new cuboid to that of the sum of the surface areas of the three cubes.

(a) 7:9 (b) 49:81

(c) 9:7 (d) 27:23

42. If V be the volume of a cuboid of dimension x, y, z and A is its surface, then A/V will be equal to

(a) $x^2y^2z^2$ (b) $1/2\,(1/xy + 1/xz + 1/yz)$

(c) $2\left(\frac{1}{x} + \frac{1}{y} + \frac{1}{z}\right)$ (d) $1/xyz$

43. The minute hand of a clock is 10 cm long. Find the area of the face of the clock described by the minute-hand between 9 AM and 9: 35 AM

(a) 183.3 cm² (b) 366.6 cm²

(c) 244.4 cm² (d) 188.39 cm²

44. Two circles touch internally. The sum of their areas is 116π cm^2 and distance between their centers is 6 cm. Find the radii of the circles.
(a) 10 cm, 4 cm (b) 11 cm, 4 cm
(c) 9 cm, 5 cm (d) 10 cm, 5 cm

45. A toy is in the shape of a right circular cylinder with a hemisphere on one end and a cone on the other. The height and radius of the cylindrical part are 13 cm and 5 cm respectively. The radii of the hemispherical and conical parts are the same as that of the cylindrical part. Calculate the surface area of the toy if the height of conical part is 12 cm.
(a) 1440 cm^2 (b) 385 cm^2
(c) 1580 cm^2 (d) 770 cm^2

46. A solid wooden toy is in the form of a cone mounted on a hemisphere. If the radius of the hemisphere is 4.2 cm and the total height of the toy is 10.2 cm, find the volume of wood used in the toy.
(a) 343.72 cm^3 (b) 266.11 cm^3
(c) 532.22 cm^3 (d) 133.55 cm^3

47. A cylindrical container whose diameter is 12 cm and height is 15 cm, is filled with ice cream. The whole ice-cream is distributed to ten children in equal cones having hemispherical tops. If the height of the conical portion is twice the diameter of its base, find the diameter of the ice-cream cone.
(a) 6 cm (b) 12 cm
(c) 3 cm (d) 18 cm

48. A solid is in the form of a cylinder with hemispherical ends. The total height of the solid is 19 cm and the diameter of the cylinder is 7 cm. Find the total surface area of the solid. (Use $\pi = 22/7$)

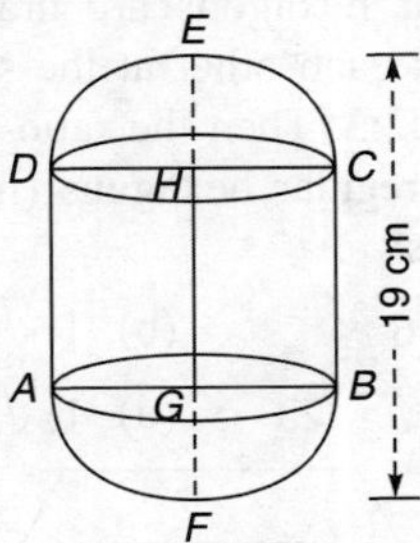

(a) 398.75 cm^2 (b) 418 cm^2
(c) 444 cm^2 (d) 412 cm^2

49. A cone, a hemisphere and a cylinder stand on equal bases and have the same height. What is the ratio of their volumes?
(a) 2:1:3 (b) 2.5:1:3
(c) 1:2:3 (d) 1.5:2:3

50. The internal and external diameters of a hollow hemispherical vessel are 24 cm and 25 cm respectively. The cost of painting 1 cm^2 of the surface is ₹0.05. Find the total cost of painting the vessel all over. (Take $\pi = 22/7$)
(a) ₹97.65 (b) ₹86.4
(c) ₹184 (d) ₹96.28

51. The section of a solid right circular cone by a plane containing vertex and perpendicular to base is an equilateral triangle of side 12 cm. Find the volume of the cone.
(a) 72 cc (b) 144 cc
(c) $72\sqrt{2}\,\pi$ cc (d) $72\sqrt{3}\,\pi$ cc

52. Iron weighs eight times the weight of oak. Find the diameter of an iron ball whose weight is equal to that of a ball of oak 18 cm in diameter.
(a) 4.5 cm (b) 9 cm
(c) 12 cm (d) 15 cm

53. In the figure, ABC is a right-angled triangle with $\angle B = 90°$, $BC = 21$ cm and $AB = 28$ cm. With AC as diameter of a semicircle and with BC as radius, a quarter circle is drawn. Find the area of the shaded portion correct to two decimal places.

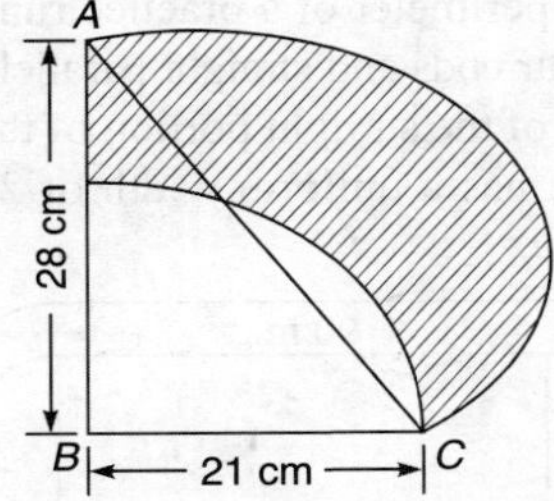

(a) 428.75 cm^2 (b) 857.50 cm^2
(c) 214.37 cm^2 (d) 371.56 cm^2

54. Find the perimeter and area of the shaded portion of the adjoining diagram:

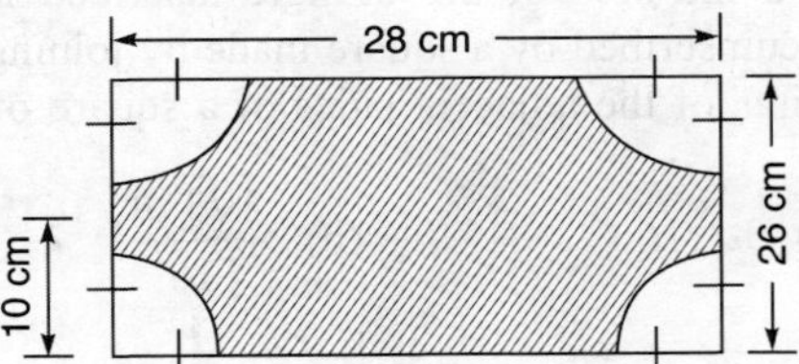

(a) 90.8 cm, 414 cm^2 (b) 181.6 cm, 423.7 cm^2
(c) 90.8 cm, 827.4 cm^2 (d) 181.6 cm, 827.4 cm^2

55. In the adjoining figure, a circle is inscribed in the quadrilateral $ABCD$. Given that $BC = 38$ cm, $AB = 27$ cm and $DC = 25$ cm, and that AD is perpendicular to DC. Find the maximum limit of the radius and the area of the circle.

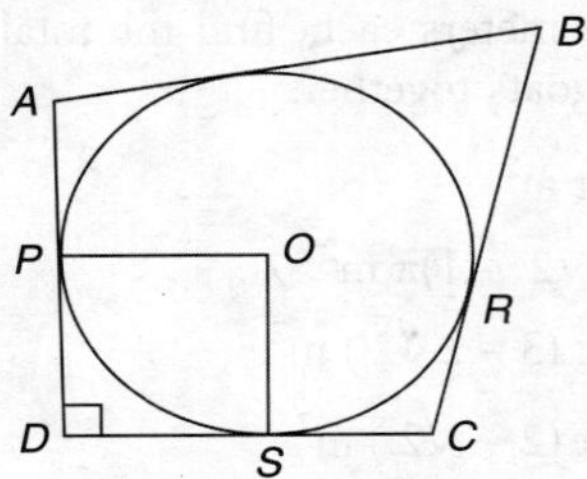

(a) 10 cm; 226 cm^2 (b) 14 cm; 616 cm^2
(c) 14 cm; 216 cm^2 (d) 28 cm; 616 cm^2

56. From a piece of cardboard, in the shape of a trapezium $ABCD$ and $AB \parallel DC$ and $\angle BCD = 90°$, a quarter circle ($BFEC$) with C as its center is removed. Given $AB = BC = 3.5$ cm and $DE = 2$ cm, calculate the area of the remaining piece of the cardboard. (Take $\pi = 22/7$)

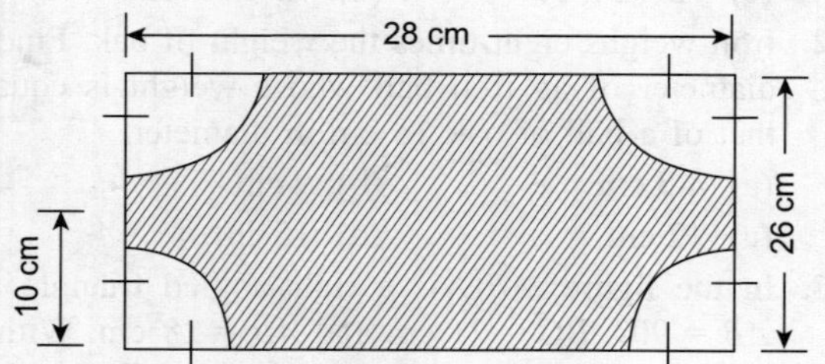

(a) 3.325 cm^2 (b) 3.125 cm^2
(c) 6.075 cm^2 (d) 12.25 cm^2

57. The inside perimeter of a practice running track with semi-circular ends and straight parallel sides is 312 m. The length of the straight portion of the track is 90 m. If the track has a uniform width of 2 m throughout, find its area.

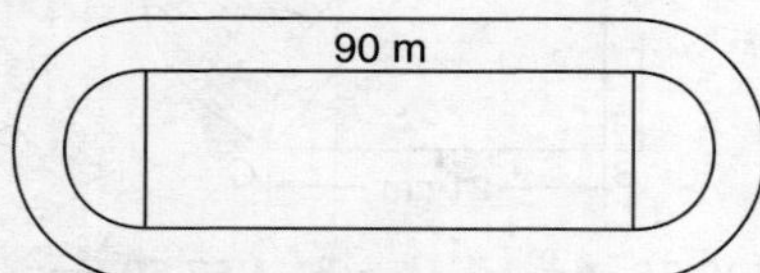

(a) 5166 m^2 (b) 5802.57 m^2
(c) 636.57 m^2 (d) 1273.14 m^2

58. Find the area of the triangle inscribed in a circle circumscribed by a square made by joining the mid-points of the adjacent sides of a square of side a.

(a) $3a^2/16$ (b) $\frac{3\sqrt{3}\,a^2}{16}$

(c) $3/4\, a^2(\pi - 1/2)$ (d) $\frac{3\sqrt{3}\,a^2}{32}$

59. Two goats are tethered to the diagonally opposite vertices of a square field formed by joining the mid-points of the adjacent sides of another square field of side $20\sqrt{2}$ meters. The inner square field is fenced on all sides and the goats are allowed to graze only inside the inner field. If their grazing ropes are of a length of $10\sqrt{2}$ meters each, find the total area grazed by the two goats together.

(a) 100π m^2
(b) $50(\sqrt{2} - 1)\pi$ m^2
(c) $100\pi(3 - 2\sqrt{2})$ m^2
(d) $200\pi(2 - \sqrt{2})$ m^2

60. The area of the circle circumscribing three circles of unit radius touching each other is

(a) $(\pi/3)(2 + \sqrt{3})^2$ (b) $6\pi(2 + \sqrt{3})^2$
(c) $3\pi(2 + \sqrt{3})^2$ (d) $\left(\frac{\pi}{6}\right)(2 + \sqrt{3})^2$

61. Hiru has a rhombus-shaped farm $ABCD$. This farm is surrounded, by a path of width 2 m, as shown in the diagram. If $\angle ADC = 30°$, $AD = 10$ m. Then find the area of the path.

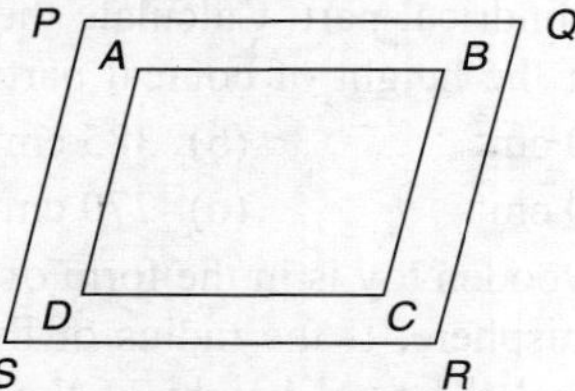

62. A series of infinite concentric squares are drawn as shown below. Starting with the first square $ABCD$, subsequent squares drawn are $PQRS$, $XYZW$ and so on as shown in the diagram. If areas of the squares $ABCD$, $PQRS$, $XYZW$, …. are 1, 3/2, 7/4, 15/8… and so on, then find the area of the diagram when the infinite number square is drawn.

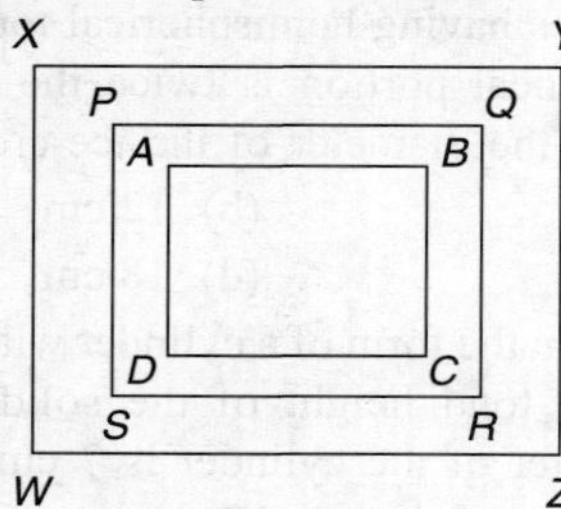

63. Three regular hexagons are drawn such that their diagonals cut each other at the same point and area $A_1:A_2:A_3 = 1:2:3$. Then the ratio of the length of the sides of the regular hexagons (from the smallest to the largest) is:

(a) $1:\sqrt{2}:\sqrt{6}$ (b) $1:\sqrt{2}:\sqrt{3}$
(c) $1:\sqrt{3}:2\sqrt{2}$ (d) $1:\sqrt{3}:\sqrt{6}$

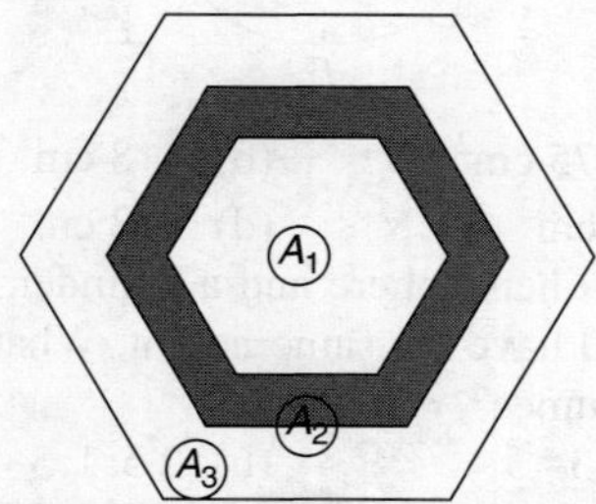

High Yield Questions

Scan this QR code to access assisted problem solving videos on questions 1, 12, 18 and 23 from LOD 2 (Mensuration)

ANSWER KEY

GEOMETRY

Level of Difficulty (I)

1. (d)	2. (b)	3. b	4. 0.5
5. (a)	6. 42 cm	7. (b)	8. (d)
9. (c)	10. (c)	11. 300	12. 111.75
13. 80	14. 120	15. (b)	16. (c)
17. 60°	18. 9	19. 4 cm	20. $\sqrt{20}$cm
21. 40	22. (a)	23. 90°	24. 50°
25. 30°	26. 9	27. 20	28. 10
29. 55°	30. 50°	31. (d)	32. (a)
33. 5	34. 1.5	35. (b)	36. (b)
37. $\sqrt{15}$ cm	38. $\sqrt{211}$ cm	39. (b)	40. 8
41. 17.97	42. (a)	43. (d)	44. (d)
45. (b)	46. (a)	47. 16 cm	48. 12 cm
49. 250 cm^2	50. (b)	51. 40°	52. 50°
53. 120°	54. (d)	55. 10°	56. (b)
57. 12.5 cm	58. 8 cm	59. 16 cm	60. 3.6
61. (a)	62. (d)	63. (c)	64. (a)
65. 75°	66. (c)	67. (a)	68. (b)
69. (a)	70. (d)	71. (b)	72. (c)
73. 14	74. 10	75. 5 m	

Level of Difficulty (II)

1. (a)	2. 1063	3. (d)	4. (d)
5. 16	6. (b)	7. (a)	8. (d)
9. (c)	10. 5600	11 (a)	
12. $\sqrt{320}$ cm	13. $8\sqrt{5}$ cm	14. 4	15. 60 cm^2
16. 4	17. 5	18. 45°	19. 172°
20. 4.56 cm	21. (d)	22. 18	23. 19
24. 5	25. (b)	26. (b)	27. (a)
28. (d)	29. (b)	30. (b)	31. 4cm
32. 19:5	33. 40°	34. 3	35. (b)
36. 16:9	37. (c)	38. (c)	39. (d)
40. 15	41. 13	42. 19	
43. $\sqrt{544}$ cm	44. 120	45. (d)	46. (b)
47. (b)	48. (b)	49. (a)	50. (d)
51. (b)	52. (a)	53. (a)	54. (c)
55. (d)	56. (a)	57. (b)	58. (b)
59. (b)	60. (a)	61. $8\sqrt{5}$ cm^2	62. $2\sqrt{6}$cm
63. 60°	64. 80°	65. 20°	66. 15 cm
67. $\sqrt{540}$cm	68. 1	69. 5	70. $\frac{3}{4}\times\sqrt{11}$
71. (c)			

MENSURATION

Level of Difficulty (I)

1. (a)	2. (b)	3. (b)	4. (b)
5. (c)	6. (c)	7. (a)	8. (a)
9. (c)	10. (a)	11. 385 cm^3	12. (a)
13. 100	14. 105 m	15. 1200	16. 900
17. 288000	18. 9240 cm^2	19. 510 sq. m.	20. 20
21. (b)	22. (d)	23. (b)	24. (a)
25. (d)	26. (b)	27. (d)	28. (c)
29. (d)	30. (d)	31. $\pi x(2r + x)$	32. 29%
33. (b)	34. 8000	35. 8	36. 814
37. 376.75 cm^2		38. 143 cm	39. (b)
40. 480 π	41. (b)	42. (b)	43. (a)
44. (b)	45. (d)	46. (c)	47. (c)
48. (c)	49. (d)	50. (d)	51. (d)
52. (d)	53. (b)	54. (d)	55. (b)
56. (b)	57. (a)	58. (c)	59. (d)
60. (b)	61. (b)	62. (c)	63. (c)
64. (c)	65. (d)	66. (c)	67. (a)
68. (b)	69. (a)	70. (b)	

Level of Difficulty (II)

1. (d)	2. (d)	3. (c)	4. (d)
5. (d)	6. (d)	7. (c)	8. (d)
9. (a)	10. (c)	11. (a)	12. 162 m^2
13. (d)	14. (b)	15. (d)	16. (d)
17. (a)	18. (d)	19. 408 cm	20. 2.31
21. (d)	22. (a)	23. (b)	24. (b)
25. (c)	26. (c)	27. (b)	28. (a)
29. (c)	30. (d)	31. (b)	32. (b)
33. (d)	34. (a)	35. (c)	36. (d)
37. (c)	38. 6	39. 16	
40. 4096 cm^2		41. (a)	42. (c)
43. (a)	44. (a)	45. (d)	46. (b)
47. (a)	48. (b)	49. (c)	50. (d)
51. (d)	52. (b)	53. (a)	54. (a)
55. (b)	56. (c)	57. (c)	58. (d)
59. (a)	60. (a)	61. 112 m^2	62. 2
63. (d)			

SOLUTIONS AND SHORTCUTS

GEOMETRY

Level of Difficulty (I)

1.

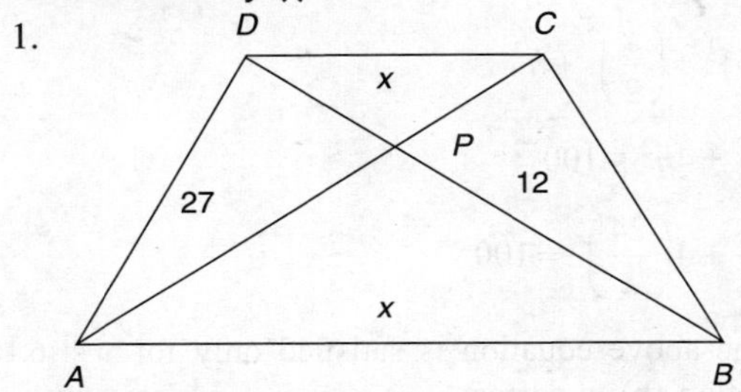

Let the area of ΔABP and ΔDPC is x.

$27\times12 = x\times x$

$x^2 = 27\times12$

$x = 18$

2. 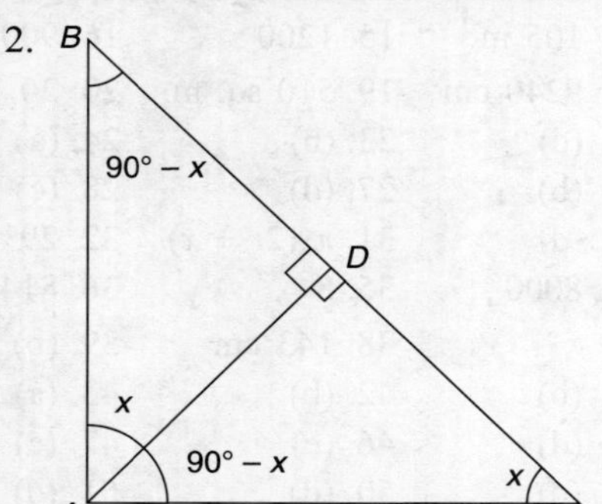

All the corresponding angles of ΔABD and in ΔCAD are equal, so ΔABD and ΔCAD are similar to each other.

So, the first statement is correct.

$\Delta ADB \sim \Delta CDA$. But it is not necessary that both triangles are congruent.

So, the second statement is incorrect.

In ΔADB and ΔCAB:

$\angle BAC = \angle ADB$

$\angle ABC = \angle ABD$

$\angle BCA = \angle BAD$

So $\Delta ADB \sim \Delta CAB$

So, third statement is also correct. Hence option (b) is correct.

3. 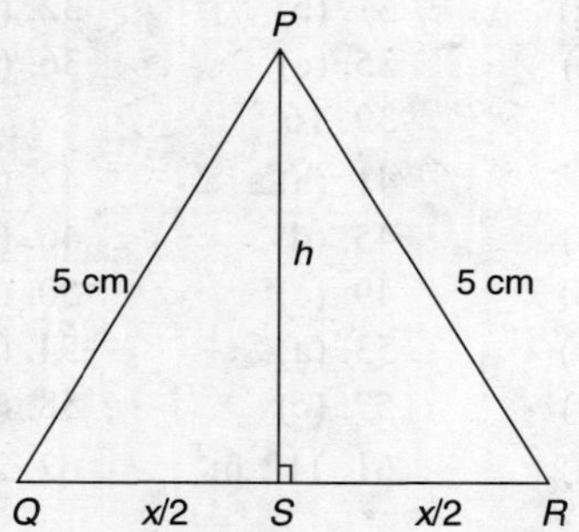

Area of $\Delta PQR = \frac{1}{2} \times x \times h = 12 \text{ cm}^2$

$xh = 24 \text{ cm}^2$

Also in the right angle ΔPQS,

$$(5)^2 = \left(\frac{x}{2}\right)^2 + h^2$$

$$x^2 + 4h^2 = 100$$

$$x^2 + 4\left(\frac{24}{x}\right)^2 = 100$$

The above equation is satisfied only for $x = 6$. So option (b) is correct.

4. Let the radius of the circle be 'l'.

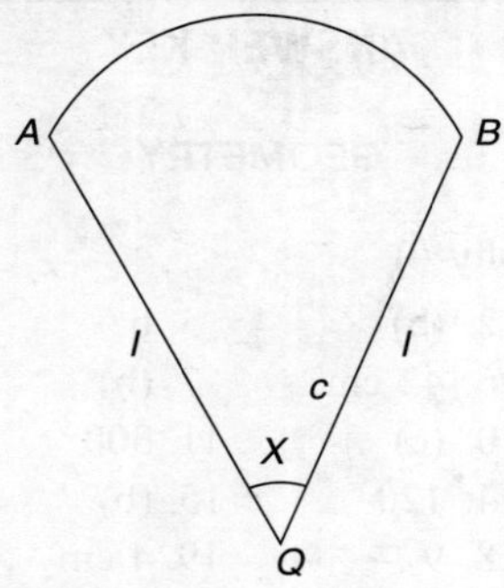

Length of $arc = lx$

Area of the sector $= \frac{x}{2\pi} \times \pi l^2 = \frac{xl^2}{2}$

According to the question: $\frac{xl^2}{2} = (lx)^2$ or $x = 0.5$.

5. By applying cosine formula in ΔABC, we get:

$$cos\theta = \frac{a^2 + b^2 - c^2}{2ab} \text{ or } a^2 + b^2 - 2abcos\theta = c^2$$

6. Here PQ is the chord. Height of chord $= RS = 21$ cm

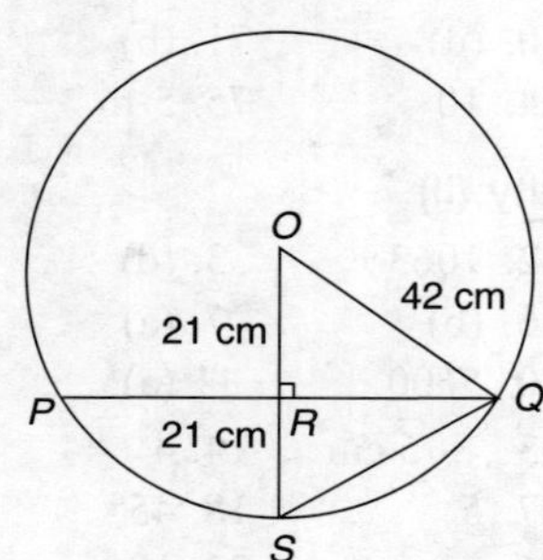

Here we need to find the length of chord (QS) of half arc QS.

$RO = 42 - 21 = 21$ cm.

In ΔORQ and ΔSRQ : $OR = RS$, $QR = QR$, $\angle ORQ = \angle SRQ = 90^0$

So both the triangles are congruent.

So $OQ = SQ = 42$ cm.

7. Let the other sides of the right angle triangle be x and y respectively.

Then according to the question: $\sqrt{x^2 + y^2} = 97$, $x + y = 234 - 97 = 137$

Now by checking the options we can see that only option (b) satisfies both the equations.

So, option (b) is correct.

8. Let the base of the ladder is drawn out by x feet.

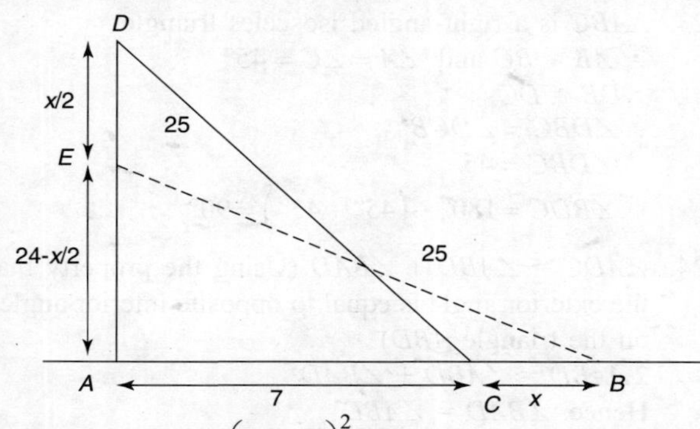

In ΔEAB: $\left(24-\frac{x}{2}\right)^2+(7+x)^2=25^2$ (Using the Pythagoras theorem)

By solving the above quadratic equation, we get x = 0, 8. So, option (d) is correct.

9. $TQ\times TP = TR\times TS$

$8 \times 18 = TR\ (TR + 7)$

$TR = 9$ units

Area of the $\Delta PTS = \frac{1}{2}\times 16\times 18\times \sin 60^0 = 72\sqrt{3}$ sq. units

10.

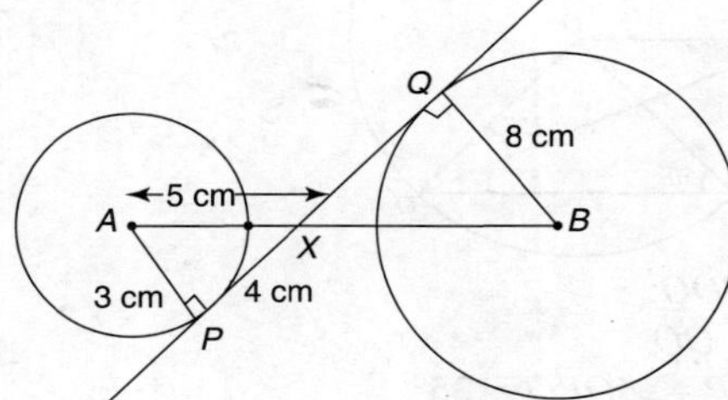

Let A and B are centers of circles. $PX=\sqrt{5^2-3^2}=4$ cm

ΔAPX and ΔBQX are similar to each other as their three angles are equal.

$\frac{AP}{BQ}=\frac{PX}{QX}$

$QX = 8\times\frac{4}{3}=10.66$ cm

$PQ = PX + XQ = 4+10.66=14.66$ cm

11. In-radius of $\Delta ABC = \frac{(AB+BC)-AC}{2}=\frac{20}{2}=10$ cm

(Formula for inradius)

Semi-perimeter $= s = \frac{60}{2}=30$ cm

$r=\frac{\text{Area}}{s}$

Area $= r\times s$ (formula for area of any triangle using the semi-perimeter and inradius)

$=10\times 30=300\text{ cm}^2$

12. 3 × (Sum of squares of the sides of a triangle) = 4 × (Sum of squares of the medians of the triangle)

$\frac{3}{4}\left(6^2+7^2+8^2\right)=$ Sum of square of medians

$=\frac{3}{4}[149]=111.75\text{ cm}^2$

13. In ΔQTR: $\angle TOR = 180° - (90° + 30°) = 180° - 120° = 60°$ (angles of a triangle add up to 180)

In $\Delta QPS : \angle PSQ = 180^o - (60^o + 40^o) = 80^o$

14. According to the Alternate Segment Theorem:

$\angle SRQ = \angle STR = 60°$

□ $TSUR$ is a cyclic quadrilateral. Therefore $\angle STR + \angle SUR = 180°$

$\angle SUR = 180° - 60° = 120°$

15. $AR^2=AQ^2 + RQ^2$ (Using Pythagoras Theorem)

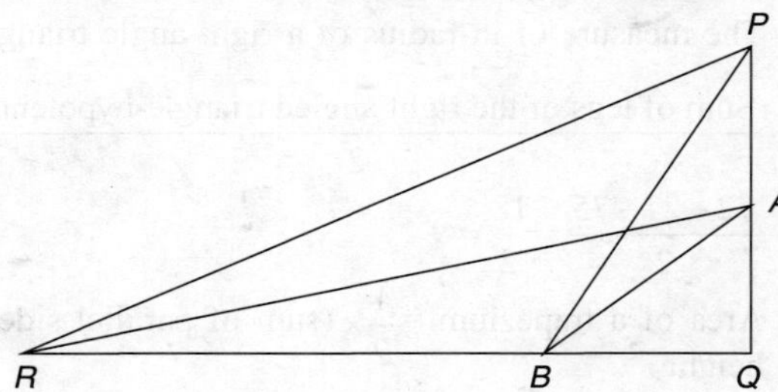

$PB^2 = PQ^2+BQ^2$ (Pythagoras Theorem)

$AR^2 + PB^2 = (PQ^2 + RQ^2) + (AQ^2 + BQ^2)$

$=PR^2 + AB^2$

16. $AB \parallel CD$ therefore ΔABF and ΔCDF are similar to each other.

$$\frac{DF}{BF}=\frac{b}{a} \qquad (1)$$

Similarly ΔBCD and ΔBEF are similar each other:

$$\frac{BD}{BF}=\frac{b}{c} \qquad (2)$$

By adding (1) and (2), we get

$\frac{BD+DF}{BF}=\frac{b}{a}+\frac{b}{c}$

$\frac{BF}{BF}=\frac{b}{a}+\frac{b}{c}=1$

$\frac{1}{b}=\frac{1}{a}+\frac{1}{c}$

$\frac{1}{b}-\frac{1}{a}=\frac{1}{c}$

17. $PR = PS$

$\angle PRS = \angle PSR$ (angles opposite equal sides are equal in an isosceles triangle)

$\angle PRS = x$

Let $\angle RPQ = y$

$PR = QR$

$\angle RPQ = \angle PQR = y$(angles opposite equal sides are equal in an isosceles triangle)

$\angle PRQ = 180° - 2y = 180^o - x$

$x = 2y \; or \; y = \frac{x}{2}$

$\angle RPS = 180° - 2x$

$\angle QPR + \angle RPS + 90° = 180°$

$\frac{x}{2} + 180^o - 2x + 90^o = 180^o$

$90^o = \frac{3x}{2}$

$x = 60^o$

18. 72, 21, 75 form a Pythagorean triplet. The triangle is a right-angled triangle.
The measure of in-radius of a right angle triangle =

$\frac{\text{Sum of legs of the right angled triangle-hypotenuse}}{2}$

$\frac{72+21-75}{2} = \frac{18}{2} = 9$

19. Area of a trapezium $= \frac{1}{2} \times$ (sum of parallel sides) × height

$28 = \frac{1}{2}(6+8)\,AB$

$AB = 4$ cm

20.

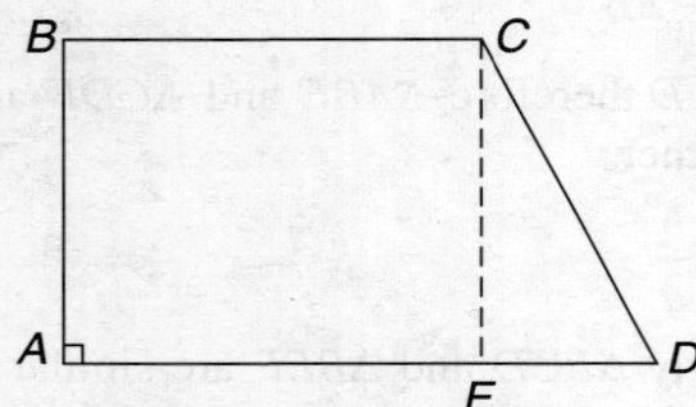

Draw $CE \perp AD$.

$DE = 8 - 6 = 2$ cm

$CE = AB = 4$ cm

$CD = \sqrt{(4)^2 + (2)^2} = \sqrt{20}$ cm

(Using Pythagoras theorem)

21. If $BP = x$, $CR = y$ then $PQ = BP = x$, $RC = QR = y$ (The two tangents to a circle from an external point are equal in length)

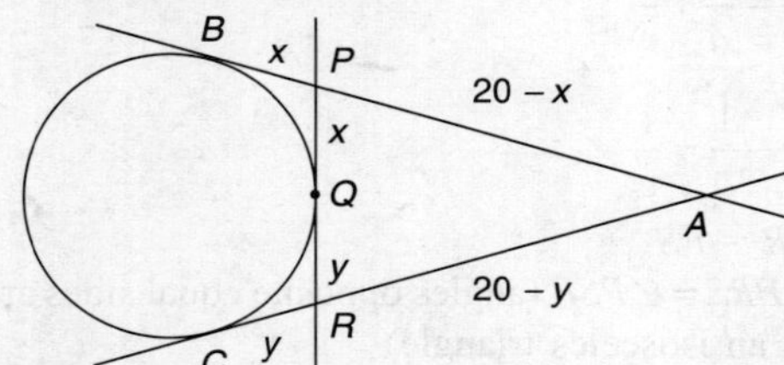

Perimeter of $\Delta APR = AP + PR + AR$

$= 20 - x + x + y + 20 - y$

$= 40$ units

22. BD is the median of the triangle ABC and $AD = DC = BD$. therefore ΔABC is a right-angled triangle. Option (a) is correct.

23. ΔABC is a right-angled isosceles triangle.

$\therefore AB = BC$ and $\angle A = \angle C = 45°$

$\therefore DB = DC$

$\therefore \angle DBC = \angle DCB$

$\angle DBC = 45°$

$\angle BDC = 180^o - (45^o + 45^o) = 90°$

24. $\angle ADC = \angle ABD + \angle BAD$ (Using the property that the exterior angle is equal to opposite interior angles on the triangle ABD)

$2\angle ABD = \angle ABD + \angle BAD$

Hence, $\angle BAD = \angle ABD$

Let $\angle ABD = \angle BAD = \angle ACB = x$ (**Note:** $\angle ACB$ and $\angle ABC$ are equal as the triangle ABC is an isosceles triangle)

Then in $\Delta ABC \Rightarrow 30° + x + x + x = 180°$

$3x = 150°$

$x = 50° = \angle BAD$

25.

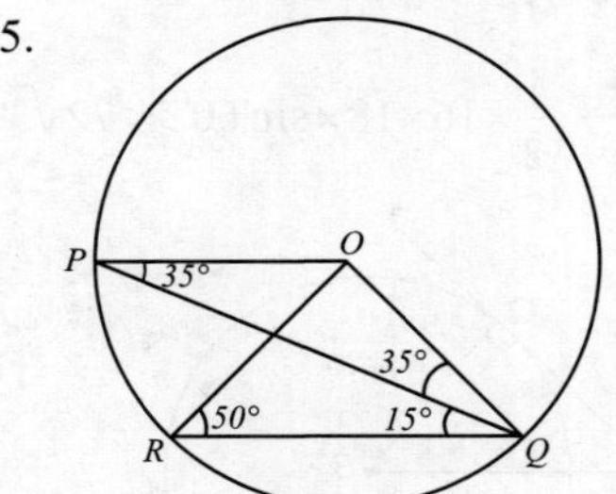

In ΔPOQ:

$OP = OQ$

$\angle OQP = \angle OPQ = 35°$

In ΔORQ:

$\angle OQR = \angle ORQ = 50°$

$\angle PQR = \angle OQR - \angle OQP = 50° - 35° = 15°$

Hence, $\angle POR = 2\angle PQR = 2 \times 15° = 30°$ (Since, POR is an angle subtended by the minor arc PR at the center, while the angle PQR is an angle subtended by the same arc at a point on the circumference of a circle).

26. $\frac{(2n-4)90^{\circ}}{n} = 120°$ (Formula for interior angle of a regular polygon)

$\frac{n-2}{n} = \frac{120^o}{180^o} = \frac{2}{3}$

$3n - 6 = 2n$

$n = 6$

Number of diagonals $= {}^6C_2 - 6 = 9$ (Number of diagonals of any n sided polygon is given by the formula ${}^nC_2 - n$)

27. Let the number of sides of the polygons be $2n$ and n respectively.

As per the question:

$18 = \frac{2n-2}{2n} \times 180° - \frac{n-2}{n} \times 180°$ (formula for interior angle of a regular polygon applied to both the polygons)

$$18 = \left[\frac{n-1}{n} - \frac{n-2}{n}\right]180°$$

$$18 = \frac{1}{n}\times 180°$$

$\Rightarrow n = 10$ or $2n = 20$

28. Let the number of sides in the polygon be n as per the question:

$$(n-2)180° = 40\left(180° - \left[\frac{n-2}{n}\right]180°\right)$$

$$(n-2)180° = 40\left\{\frac{n-n+2}{n}\right\}180°$$

$$\frac{2}{n} = \frac{(n-2)}{40}$$

$n = 10$

29. $\angle ABC = \frac{\angle AOC}{2} = \frac{140°}{2} = 70°$ (Using the logic that the angle subtended by an arc at the center of a circle is twice the angle subtended by the same arc at any point on the circle).

$AB = BC$

$\angle BAC = \angle BCA$

$2\angle BCA + \angle ABC = 180°$

$2\angle BCA = 180° - \angle ABC = 180° - 70° = 110°$

$\angle BCA = \frac{110°}{2} = 55°$

30. $\angle QOR = 180° - \angle POQ = 180° - 80° = 100°$

$\angle QSR = \frac{\angle QOR}{2} = 50°$ (Using the logic that the angle subtended by an arc at the center of a circle is twice the angle subtended by the same arc at any point on the circle)

31. The triangle BOC is an isosceles triangle with sides OB and OC both being equal as they are the radii of the circle. Hence, the angle OBC = angle OCB = 30°. Hence, the third angle of the triangle BOC viz: angle BOC would be equal to 120°. Also, BOC = AOD = 120°. Hence, in the isosceles triangle DOA, angle ODA = angle DAO = x = 30°.

32. By the rule of tangents, we know:

$6^2 = (5 + x)5 \Rightarrow 36 = 25 + 5x \Rightarrow 11 = 5x \Rightarrow x = 2.2$ cm

Solutions for Questions 33 and 34:

33. $MP = \sqrt{OP^2 - OM^2} = \sqrt{10^2 - 6^2} = 8$ cm

Triangle OMP and triangle ACP are similar.

$OP/MP = AP/CP$

$$AP = CP \times \frac{OP}{MP} = 4 \times \frac{10}{8} = 5 \text{ cm}$$

34. Similarly, $AC = 3$ cm, $AB = 6$ cm

In-radius of triangle ABP =

$$\frac{\frac{1}{2}\times 4\times 6}{\frac{1}{2}(6+5+5)} = \frac{24}{16} = 1.5 \text{ cm}$$

35. Use the formula: In-radius = Area/ Semi-perimeter = 24/12 = 2 cm

36. $\angle APB = 90°$ (angle in a semicircle = 90°)

$\angle PBA = 180 - (90 + 25) = 65°$

$\angle TPA = \angle PBA$ (the angle that a chord makes with the tangent, is subtended by the chord on the circumference in the alternate segment)

= 65°

(Note: This is also called as the Alternate Segment Theorem.)

37.

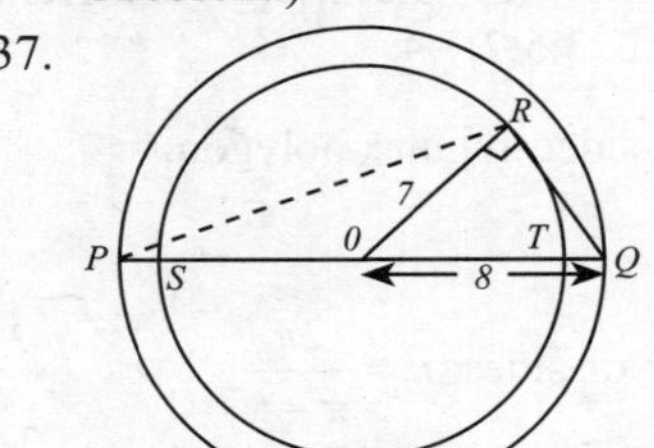

RQ is a tangent of inner circle.

$RQ = \sqrt{8^2 - 7^2} = \sqrt{15}$ cm

38. In triangle PQR, apply Apollonius theorem:

$PR^2 + RQ^2 = 2(OR^2 + OQ^2)$

$PR^2 = 2(7^2 + 8^2) - 15 = \sqrt{211}$

39. $\angle ABC = 180° - 130° = 50°$

($\therefore$ sum of angles on a line = 180°)

$\angle ADC = 180° - \angle ABC = 130°$

($\because$ opposite angles of a cyclic quadrilateral are supplementary)

$\angle x = 180° - 130° = 50°$

($\therefore$ sum of angles on a line = 180°)

Solutions for Questions 40 and 41:

40.

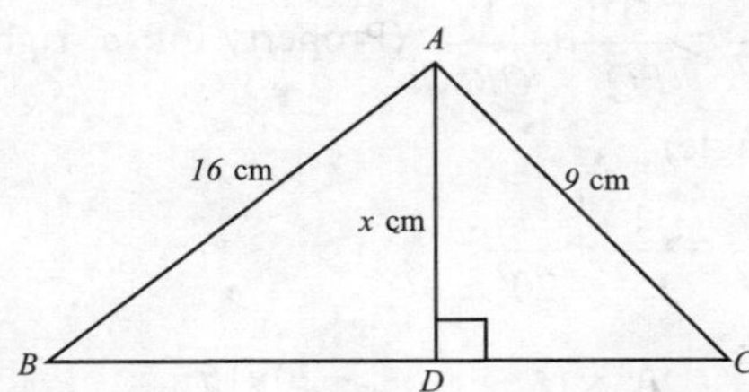

Area of the triangle = $\frac{1}{2}\times BC \times x = \frac{16\times 9\times BC}{4\times 9}$

$x = 8$ cm

41. $BD = \sqrt{16^2 - 8^2} = 13.85$ cm

$DC = \sqrt{9^2 - 8^2} = 4.12$

$BC = BD + DC = 13.85 + 4.12 = 17.97$ cm

42. $\angle BAC = 30°$ ($\because$ angles subtended by an arc anywhere on the circumference in the same segment are equal)
In ΔBAC; $\angle x = 180° - (110° + 30°) = 40°$
($\because$ sum of angles of a triangle = 180°)

43. As L_4 and L_3 are not parallel lines, so there cannot be any relation between 80° and x°.
Hence, the answer cannot be determined.

44. Perimeter of the figure = 10 + 10 + 6 + 6π = 26 + 6π

45. Since the lines *AB* and *CD* are parallel to each other, and the lines *RD* and *AN* are parallel, it means that the triangles *RBF* and *NCI* are similar to each other. Since the ratio of *CN*: *BR* = 1.333, if we take *BR* as 3, we will get *CN* as 4. This means that the ratio of *BF*: *CI* will also be 3:4. Also, the ratio of *BR*: *RS*: *ST*: *TA* = *BF*: *FG*: *GH*: *HI* = 3:5:2:7 (given). Hence, the correct answer is 3:5:2:7:4.

46. Interior angle of *n*-sided regular polygon =
$\frac{n-2}{n} \times \pi = x$
Hence, the number of sides, $n = \frac{2\pi}{\pi - x}$
The number of diagonals in an *n*-sided polygon = $^nC_2 - n = k \times n$ (given)
$\frac{n(n-1)}{2} - n = kn$ or $k = \frac{n-3}{2}$
Hence, $k = \frac{\frac{2\pi}{\pi - x} - 3}{2} = \frac{3x - \pi}{2(\pi - x)}$. Option (a) is correct.

47. $PR = \sqrt{PQ^2 + QR^2}$ (Using Pythagoras Theorem)
$= \sqrt{15^2 + 20^2} = \sqrt{625} = 25$ cm
$SR = \frac{QR^2}{PR} = \frac{20^2}{25} = 16$ cm
(Property of a right-angled triangle)

48. $\frac{1}{SQ^2} = \frac{1}{PQ^2} + \frac{1}{QR^2}$ (Property of *a* right-angled triangle)
$\frac{1}{SQ^2} = \frac{1}{15^2} + \frac{1}{20^2}$
$SQ^2 = \frac{20^2 \times 15^2}{20^2 + 15^2} \rightarrow SQ = \frac{20 \times 15}{25} = 12$ cm

49. $\Delta ABD \sim \Delta ACB$
$\frac{\text{area of } \Delta\, ABC}{\text{area of } \Delta\, ADB} = \frac{AC^2}{AB^2} = \left(\frac{5}{3}\right)^2 = \frac{25}{9}$
(Using the property that in similar figures, area ratios are squared off the side ratios)
Area of ΔABC $= 90 \times \frac{25}{9} = 250$ cm^2

50. Inradius of an equilateral triangle = $\frac{side}{2\sqrt{3}}$ (formula for in-radius)
Side = $2\sqrt{3} \times \sqrt{3} = 6$ cm
Required area $= \frac{\sqrt{3}}{4} \times 6^2 = 9\sqrt{3}$ cm^2 (Using the formula that the area of an equilateral triangle of side *a* is given by the formula: $\frac{\sqrt{3}}{4} \times a^2$.

51. *OE* = *OB* = radius of the circle
$\angle OEB = \angle OBE$ (angles opposite equal sides of an isosceles triangle are equal)
In $\Delta OEB : \angle OEB + \angle OBE + \angle BOE = 180°$
$2\angle OEB + \angle BOE = 180°$
$\angle BOE = 180° - 2\angle OEB = 180° - 2 \times 70°$
$= 40°$

52. In $\Delta OBA \Rightarrow \angle BAO + 90° + \angle AOB = 180°$
$\angle BAO = 180° - (90° + \angle AOB)$
$= 180° - (90° + 40°)$ (Since we have already found the angle *AOB* as 40^0 in the previous question) = 50°

53. In $\Delta ACD : AC = AD$
$\angle ACD = \angle ADC = 30°$ (Angles opposite equal sides on an isosceles triangle are equal)
$\angle CAD = 180^o - (\angle ACD + \angle ADC)$
$= 180° - (30° + 30°) = 120°$

54. In ΔABC & ΔABD
$\angle ACB = \angle ADB$
$\angle ABC = \angle ABD = 90°$
$AC = AD$
$\Delta ABC \cong \Delta ABD$
$\therefore BC = BD$
$\therefore CD = 4$ cm
In $\Delta CAD = \frac{CD}{\sin 120°} = \frac{AD}{\sin 30°}$ (Using the sine rule and values of sin 30 = 1/2 and value of sin 120 = $\frac{\sqrt{3}}{2}$)
$AD = \frac{4}{\sqrt{3}} \times 2 \times \frac{1}{2} = \frac{4}{\sqrt{3}}$ cm

55. $OS = OQ$
$\angle OSQ = \angle OQS = 50°$
$\angle SOQ = 180° - 100° = 80°$ (Angles of a triangle add up to 180)
In ΔOSP:
$80^o + 90^o + \angle SPR = 180^o$ (Angles of a triangle add up to 180)
$\angle SPR = 180° - (80° + 90°) = 10°$

56. Lines joining midpoint of a quadrilateral form a parallelogram.

57. Diagonals of trapezium intersect each other proportionally in the ratio of length of parallel sides. Therefore,

$$\frac{AB}{CD} = \frac{OB}{OD}$$

$$OD = \frac{OB \times CD}{AB} = \frac{5 \times 6}{4} = 7.5 \text{ cm}$$

Length of diagonal $BD = 5 + 7.5 = 12.5$ cm

58. Using the sine rule we get: $\frac{QR}{\sin 45°} = \frac{SR}{\sin 60°}$

$$QR = 4\sqrt{6} \times \frac{1}{\sqrt{2}} \times \frac{2}{\sqrt{3}}$$

$QR = 8$ cm

59. If a trapezium is inscribed in a circle then it is an isosceles trapezium with equal oblique sides.

$PS = QR = 8$ cm

$PS + QR = 8 + 8 = 16$ cm

60.

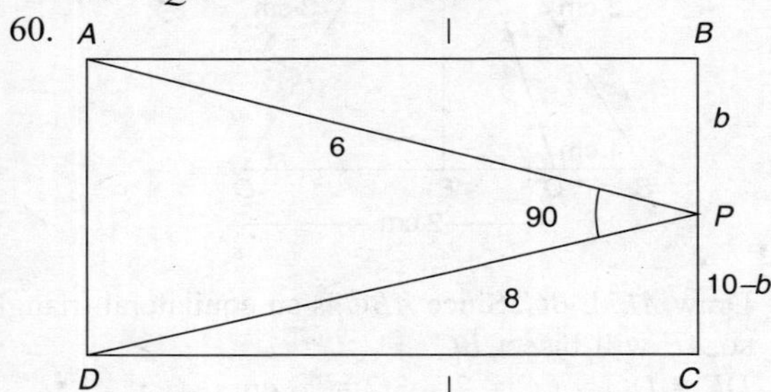

In ΔAPD: $AP = \sqrt{10^2 - 8^2} = \sqrt{36} = 6$

Let $AB = l$, $BP = b$

Now using the Pythagoras theorem on the triangles ABP and PCD we get two equations between l and b as follows:

In $\Delta ABP: l^2 + b^2 = 6^2$ (1)

In $\Delta PCD: l^2 + (10-b)^2 = 8^2$ (2)

From equation (2) – (1), we get

$$-b^2 + (10-b)^2 = -6^2 + 8^2$$

$$100 - 20b = 28$$

$b = 3.6$

61. When the length of stick = 20 m, then length of shadow = 10 m, i.e. in this case, length = 2 × shadow. With the same angle of inclination of the sun, the length of tower that casts a shadow of 50 m ⇒ 2 × 50 m = 100 m.

Therefore, height of tower = 100 m

62. $\Delta ABC \sim \Delta EDC$

Then $\frac{AC}{EC} = \frac{BC}{DC} = \frac{AB}{ED}$

Then $\frac{AC}{4.2} = \frac{4}{3} = AC = 5.6$ cm and

$\frac{BC}{4.8} = \frac{4}{3} = BC = 6.4$ cm

63. For similar triangles ⇒ (Ratio of sides)^2 = Ratio of areas

Then as per question = $\left(\frac{36}{x}\right)^2 = \frac{144}{81}$

{Let the longest side of $\Delta DEF = x$}

$\Rightarrow \frac{36}{x} = \frac{12}{9} \Rightarrow x = 27$ cm

64. (Ratio of corresponding sides)^2 = Ratio of area of similar triangles

∴ Ratio of corresponding sides in this question

$= \sqrt{\frac{16}{25}} = \frac{4}{5}$. This will also be their height ratio.

65. Let $\angle BCA = x$, $\angle BDC = 3x$

$x + 3x + 30° + 50° = 180°$ or $x = 25°$

$\angle BDC = 3x = 75°$

$\angle BAC = \angle BDC = 75°$

66.

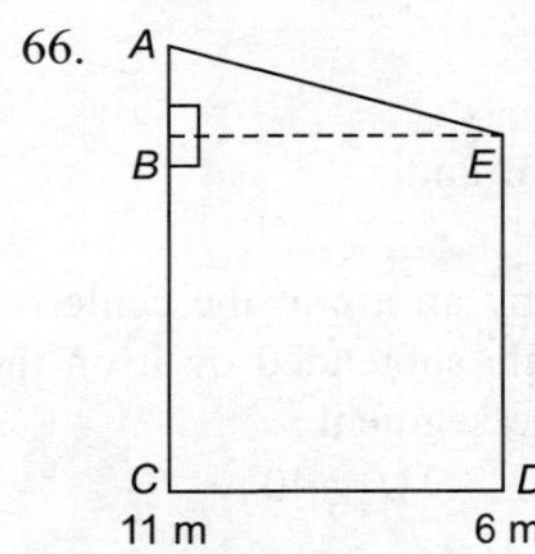

$BC = ED = 6$ m

So $AB = AC - BC = 11 - 6 = 5$ m

$CD = BE = 12$ m

Then by Pythagoras theorem:

$AE^2 = AB^2 + BE^2 \Rightarrow AE = 13$ m

67.

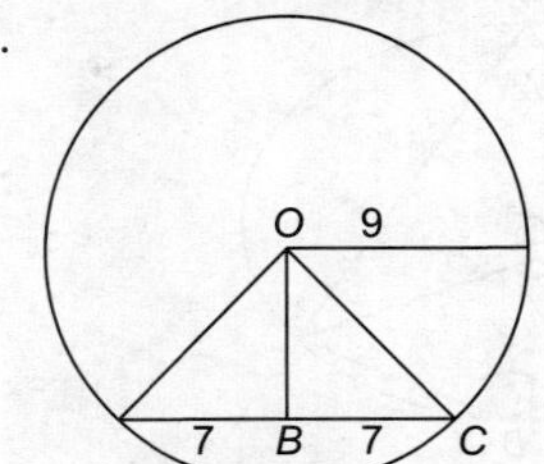

In the ΔOBC; $BC = 7$ cm and $OC = 9$ cm, then using Pythagoras theorem

$OB^2 = OC^2 - BC^2$

$OB = \sqrt{32} = 5.66$ cm (approx.)

68. $AE \times BE = CE \times DE$

$AE \times 4 = 2 \times 2$

$AE = 1$ cm

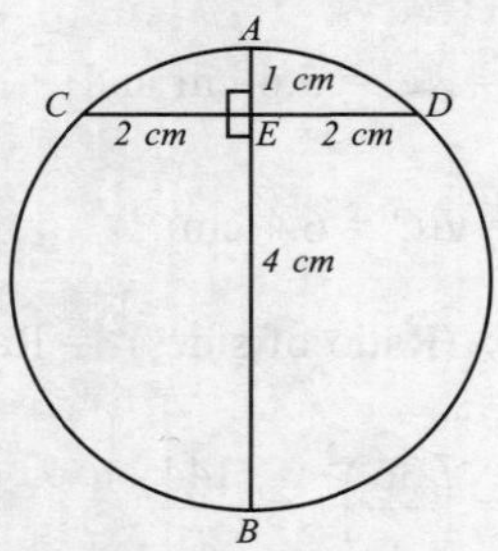

Chord AB of the circle is the perpendicular bisector of the chord CD. Hence, AB is the diameter of the circle.

$AB = AE + EB = 1 + 4 = 5$ cm. Hence, option (b) is correct.

69. $\angle x = 35°$; because angles subtended by an arc, anywhere on the circumference are equal.

70.

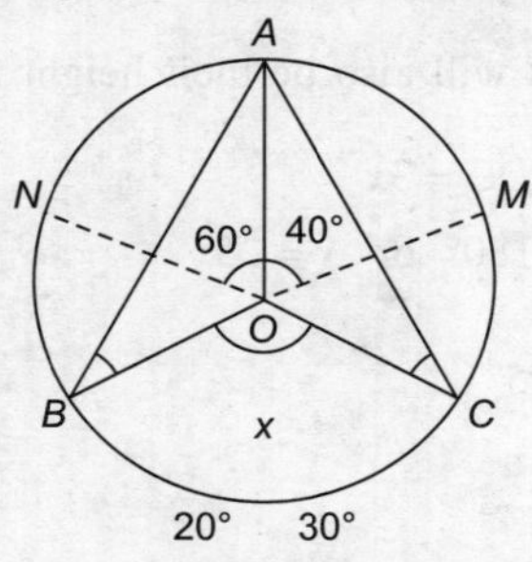

$$\angle AOM = 2\angle ABM \text{ and}$$
$$\angle AON = 2\angle ACN$$

because angle subtended by an arc at the center of the circle is twice the angle subtended by it on the circumference on the same segment.

$$\angle AON = 60° \quad \text{and} \quad \angle AOM = 40°$$
$$\angle X = \angle AON + \angle AOM$$
(∵ vertically opposite angles).
$$\angle X = 100°$$

Alternately, you could also solve this using the following process:

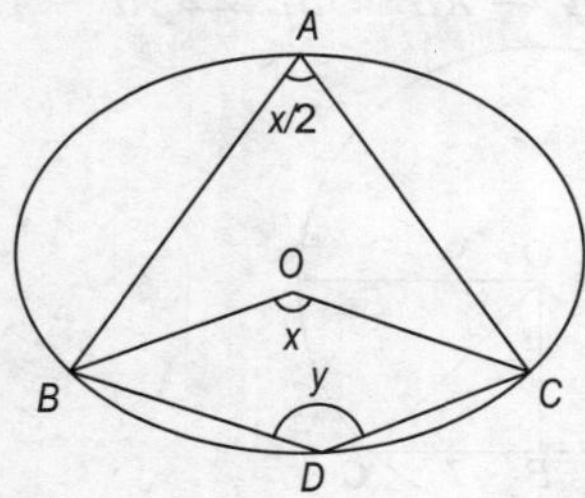

In the given figure, join the points BD and CD. Then, in the cyclic quadrilateral $ABDC$, the sum of angles $x/2$ and y would be 180°. Hence, $y = 180 - x/2$. Also, the sum of the angles $OBD + OCD = 180 - 20 - 30 = 130°$. Therefore, $x + y = 230$ (as the sum of the angles of the quadrilateral $OBDC$ is 360). Solving, the two equations, we get $x = 100$.

71. In a triangle the sum of any two sides > third side.

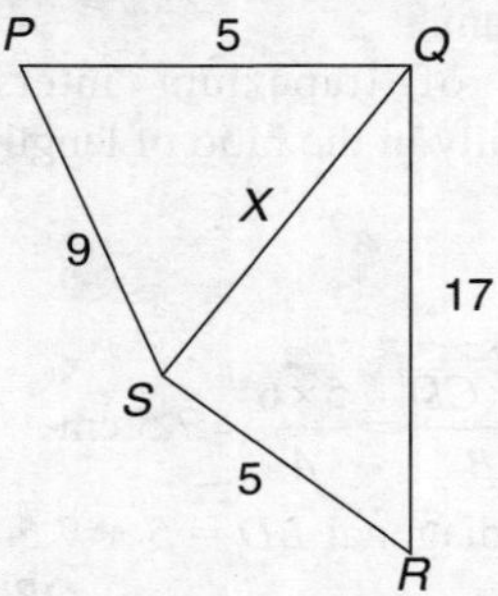

In ΔPQS $5 + 9 > x$; $x < 14$

In ΔRQS $x + 5 > 17$; $x > 12$

$14 > x > 12$

72.

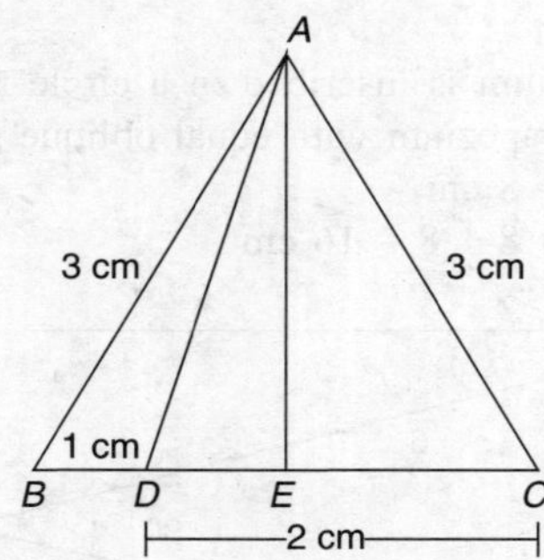

Draw $AE \perp BC$. Since ABC is an equilateral triangle so AE will bisect BC.

$DE = DC - EC = 2 - 3/2 = ½$ cm

$$AE = \sqrt{3^2 - 1.5^2} = \frac{3}{2}\sqrt{3} \text{ cm}$$

$$AD = \sqrt{\left(\frac{3}{2}\sqrt{3}\right)^2 + \left(\frac{1}{2}\right)^2} = \sqrt{7} \text{ cm}$$

73. Number of quadrilaterals that can be formed = $^8C_4$ = 70.

Number of triangles that can be formed = $^8C_3 = 56$.

Required difference = 70 – 56 = 14

74. According to the figure, the area of the triangle QAB = area of square $PQRS$ – area of Δ ABS – area of ΔPAQ – area of ΔQBR

= 36 – 2 – 12 – 12 = 10

75.

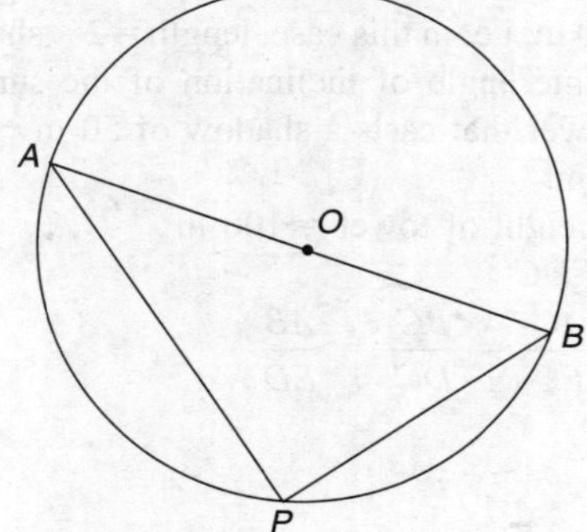

Let 'p' be the position of pole and A and B are the gates referred to in the question. We are given that $AP - BP = 7$;

AB is the diameter. Therefore ΔAPB is a right-angled triangle:

$$AB^2 = AP^2 + BP^2$$

$$13^2 = (7 + BP)^2 + BP^2$$

By solving we get $BP = 5$ m and $AP = 12$ m.

Required shortest distance = 5 m.

Level of Difficulty (II)

1. In $\Delta\ CAD : AD^2 + CA^2 = CD^2$

Using Apollonius theorem we get : $AB^2 + AC^2 = 2(AD^2 + CD^2)$

$AB^2 + AC^2 = 2AD^2 + BC^2/2$

$AB^2 + AC^2 = 2(CD^2 - AC^2) + BC^2/2$

$AB^2 + AC^2 = 2(BC^2/4 - AC^2) + BC^2/2$

$3AC^2 = BC^2 - AB^2$

Theory Note: Apollonius' theorem I relating the length of a median of a triangle to the lengths of its side is a theorem: *t* states that the sum of the squares of any two sides of any triangle equals twice the square on half the third side, together with twice the square on the median bisecting the third side" Specifically, in any triangle ABC, if AD then, is a median.

$$AB^2 + AC^2 = 2(AD^2 + BD^2)$$

2. Let $AC = 2^a$, where $a \in N$

$$AB = AC/2 = \frac{2^a}{2} = 2^{a-1}$$

According to the question AB is a perfect square. So a – 1 should be even or 'a' should be odd.

$AB + AC > BC$

$3AB > 295$

$AB > 98.33$

$2^{a-1} > 98.33$ (1)

$AC - AB < BC$

$2^a - 2^{a-1} < 295$ or $2^{a-1} < 295$ (2)

Only a = 9 satisfies equation (1) and (2).

$\therefore\ AB = 2^8 = 256,\ AC = 2^9 = 512$

$\therefore$ Perimeter of the triangle = 256 + 512 + 295 = 1063

3. Let $AB = a^3$, $AC = 3^n$ according to the question : $3^n = 3.a^3$ or $a^3 = 3^{n-1}$

Perimeter $P = 397 + 3^n + 3^{n-1}$

$P - 397 = 3^{n-1}\ [3 + 1] = 4.3^{n-1}$

Thus P- 397 should be a multiple of both 3 and 4, only option (d) $p = 3313$ feet satisfies this condition, so option (d), is correct.

4.

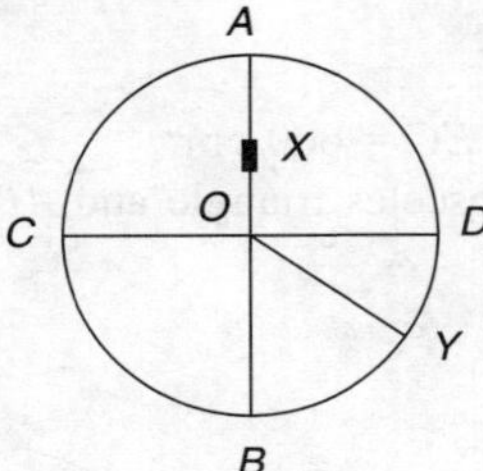

$$XADY = 1 + 4\pi\times\frac{120^\circ}{360^\circ} = 1 + \frac{4\pi}{3} = 5.19$$

$$XOBY = 1 + 2 + 4\pi\times\frac{60^\circ}{360^\circ} = 3 + \frac{4\pi}{6} = 5.09$$

$$XODY = 1 + 2 + 4\pi\times\frac{30^\circ}{360^\circ} = 4.04$$

$XADY : XOBY : XODY$ :: 5.19 : 5.09 : 4.04

5.

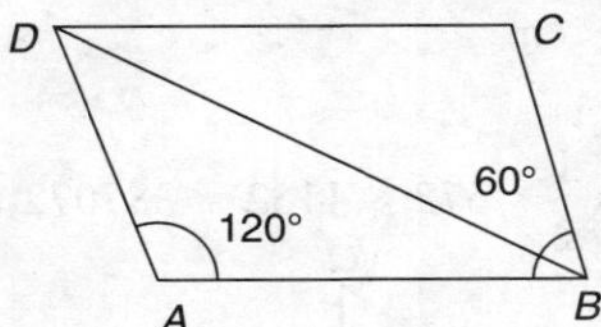

Let $AB = a$ and $AD = b$

Area of parallelogram = $ab\sin 60° = ab\frac{\sqrt{3}}{2} = 15\frac{\sqrt{3}}{2}$

$ab = 15$ .....(1)

By applying cosine rule in $\Delta\ ABD$:

$$\cos 120^o = \frac{a^2 + b^2 - 49}{2ab} = -\frac{1}{2} \text{ or } a^2 + b^2 = 34$$

$$a^2 + \frac{225}{a^2} = 34$$

By solving the above equation we get $a^2 = 9$ or 25

$a = 3$ or 5

$ab = 15$ so $b = 5$ or 3

Perimeter = $2(a + b) = 2(5 + 3)$ or $2(3 + 5) = 16$ cm

6. Let ABC is the triangle and the circle touches AB, AC at D, E respectively as shown in the diagram.

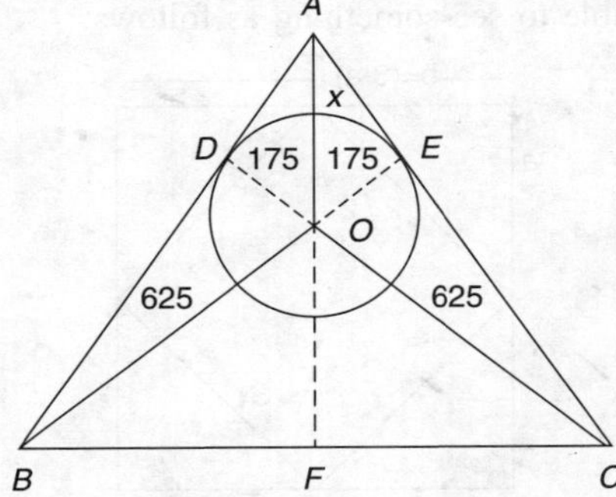

$OD \perp AB$ and $OE \perp AC$

$OA = OB = OC = 625$ cm (Given)

In ΔODB, $BD^2 + OD^2 = OB^2$ (Using Pythagoras theorem)

$BD^2 + 175^2 = 625^2$
$\Rightarrow BD = 600$ cm.
Similarly, $AD = AE = EC = 600$ cm
Hence, ΔABC is an isosceles triangle and $AB = AC = 1200$ cm
So, $AF \perp BC$
In ΔAEO and ΔAFC :
$\angle OAE = \angle CAF$
$\angle AEO = \angle AFC = 90^0$
So, $\Delta AEO \sim \Delta AFC$

$$\frac{AE}{AF} = \frac{OE}{CF} = \frac{OA}{AC}$$

$$\frac{600}{AF} = \frac{175}{CF} = \frac{625}{1200}$$

So, $AF = 1200 \times \frac{600}{625} = 1152$ cm and $CF = 1200 \times \frac{175}{625} = 336$ cm
$CB = 672$ cm
Area of $\Delta ABC = \frac{1}{2} \times 672 \times 1152 = 387072 \text{ cm}^2$

7.

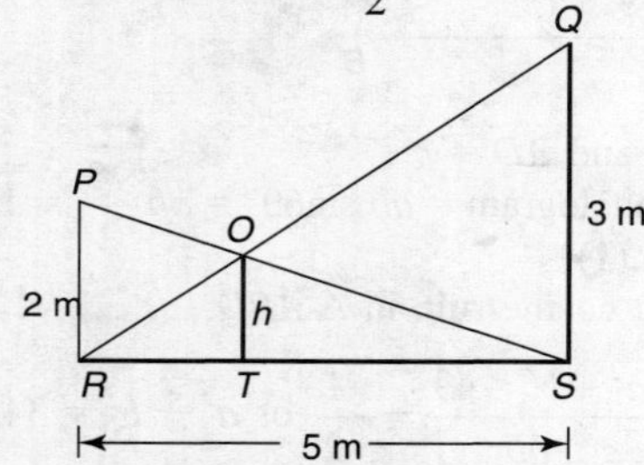

ΔROT and ΔRQS are similar to each other:
$OT/QS = RT/RS$
$RT/RS = h/3$ .....(1)
ΔSOT and ΔSPR are similar to each other:
$ST/SR = h/2$ ......(2)
Adding (1) and (2), we get:
$(RT + ST)/ RS = RS/ RS = 1 = h/2 + h/3$
$h = 1.2$ m

8. If we visualise a figure for this situation, you would be able to see something as follows:

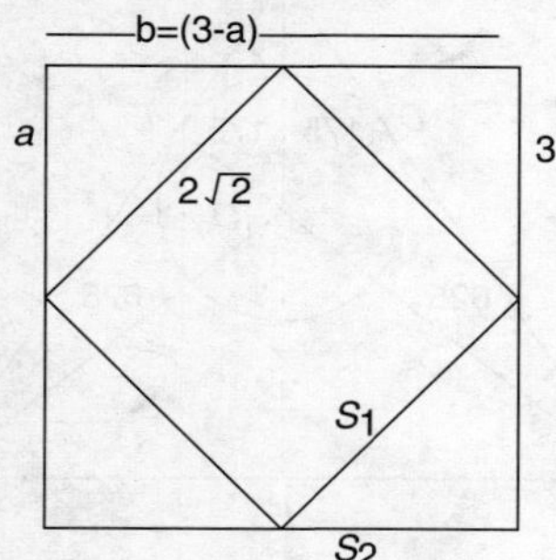

Solving through Pythagoras theorem, we will get $a = 0.18$ and $b = 3 - 0.18 = 2.82$.
Hence, the value of $b/a = 2.82/0.18 = 15.666$.

9. $\frac{\angle A}{\angle B} = 1 - \frac{\angle C}{\angle B}$
$\angle A = \angle B - \angle C$
$\angle A + \angle C = \angle B$
In ΔABC: $\angle A + \angle B + C = 180°$
$2\angle B = 180°$
$\angle B = 90°$
$\therefore AB^2 + BC^2 = AC^2$

10.

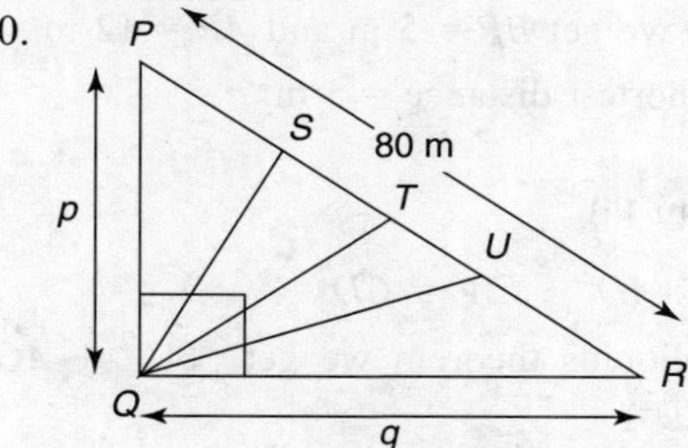

$PR = 80$ m, $PS = ST = TU = UR = 20$m
T is the midpoint of PR(hypotenuse) so $PT = TR = QT = 40$m
Applying Apollonius theorem in ΔPQT,
$p^2 + 40^2 = 2(QS^2 + 20^2)$ .....(1)
Again applying Apollonius theorem in ΔQRT,
$q^2 + 40^2 = 2(QU^2 + 20^2)$ .....(2)
By adding equation 1 and 2 we get:
$p^2 + q^2 + 2$
$40^2 = 2 (QS^2 + QU^2) + 40^2$
$QS^2 + QU^2 = (p^2 + q^2 + 40^2)/2 = (80^2 + 40^2)/2 = 4000 \text{ m}^2$
$QS^2 + QU^2 + QT^2 = 4000 \text{ m}^2 + 40^2 \text{ m}^2 = 5600 \text{ m}^2$

11. Let the angles of the convex nonagon be $x - 4y$, $x - 3y$, $x - 2y$, $x - y$, x, $x + y$, $x + 2y$, $x + 3y$, $x + 4y$. (assuming 9 numbers in an arithmetic progression)
Sum of all the angles of the nonagon $= (9 - 2) \times 180° = 1260°$.
Sum of all the angles of the nonagon $= 9x$
According to the question: $9x = 1260°$ or $x = 140°$.
The smallest and the largest angles are $x - 4y$ and $x + 4y$. As this is a convex polygon, so $x + 4y < 180°$
$140° + 4y < 180°$
$y < 10°$.
The smallest angle must be greater than $140° - 40° = 100°$. Hence, option (a) is correct.

Solutions for Questions 12 to 15:

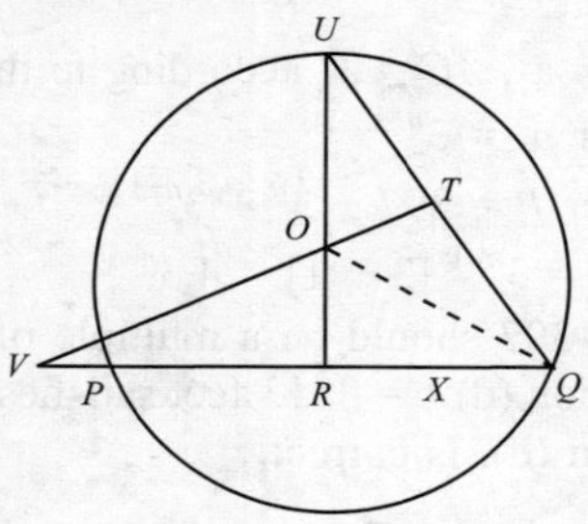

12. Connect points Q and O.
$OR = 6$ cm, $QR = PQ/2 = 16/2 = 8$ cm
$OQ = \sqrt{6^2+8^2} = 10$ cm (and this is the radius of the circle)
$UR = UO + OR = 10 + 6 = 16$ cm
ΔURQ is a right-angle triangle. $UQ =$
$\sqrt{UR^2+RQ^2} = \sqrt{16^2+8^2} = \sqrt{320}$ cm

13. As $OT \perp UQ$, triangles URQ and VTQ are similar to each other. Hence,
$$\frac{UR}{VT} = \frac{RQ}{TQ} \rightarrow VT = UR \times \frac{TQ}{RQ} = \frac{16 \times 80^{0.5}}{8} = 8\sqrt{5} \text{ cm}$$

14. $VP = VQ - PQ = 20 - 16 = 4$ cm

15. Area of triangle $VOQ =$
$$\frac{1}{2} \times VQ \times OR = \frac{1}{2} \times 20 \times 6 = 60 \text{ cm}^2$$

16. Area of the polygon = semi-perimeter of the polygon × in-radius
$25a = \frac{na}{2} \times r$ (Let the polygon has 'n' sides).
$n \times r = 50$
As n and r both are positive integers, possible values of (n, r) are (50, 1), (25, 2), (10, 5), (5, 10). Hence, four such polygons are possible.

17. Every exterior angle of an n-sided polygon is 360°/n. 360°/n must be an integer and n must be an odd number and $n > 2$.
$360 = 2^3 \times 3^2 \times 5$
Number of odd factors of 360 = (2 + 1) (1 + 1) = 6.
out of these six odd factors, one factor is 1, so total five values are possible for n.

18. Every exterior angle of an n-sided polygon is 360°/n. 360°/n must be an integer and n must be an odd number and $n > 2$.
$360 = 2^3 \times 3^2 \times 5$
The largest odd factor of 360 = $3^2 \times 5 = 45$. Hence, maximum possible value of $n = 45$.

19. Every exterior angle of an n-sided polygon is 360°/n. 360°/n must be an integer and n must be an odd number and $n > 2$.
$360 = 2^3 \times 3^2 \times 5$
Largest odd factor of 360 = $3^2 \times 5 = 45$. Hence, maximum possible value of $n = 45$.
The sum of every pair of interior and exterior angles in a polygon is always equal to 180. Hence, the maximum possible value of the interior angle =
$$180^\circ - \frac{360^\circ}{45} = 180^\circ - 8^\circ = 172^\circ.$$

20. $QR = \sqrt{25^2 - 7^2} = 24$ cm
$$QT = \frac{1}{1+3} \times 24 = 6 \text{ cm}$$
$$\frac{1}{QS^2} = \frac{1}{QT^2} + \frac{1}{PQ^2} = \frac{1}{6^2} + \frac{1}{7^2} = \frac{85}{42^2}.\ QS \approx \frac{42}{9.21} \approx 4.56 \text{ cm}$$

21. First-things-first, while solving this. If we do not include Statement III, we do not know which angle is a right angle and hence cannot uniquely calculate the value of the side AC.
Also, Statement III alone does not give us anything. Hence, we can reject options (a). Option (b) and (c) gives us similar set of information – i.e. the value of one median and the fact that B is the right angle in the triangle. This is also clearly not sufficient to answer the question.
For option (d): We have two medians of a right-angled triangle, and we know B is the right angle. Hence, we can find AC.
Hence, option (d) is the correct answer.

22. Area of $\Delta RPQ = \frac{1}{2} \times PR \times PQ \times \sin 120°$
Area of $\Delta PSR = \frac{1}{2} \times PS \times PR \times \sin 60^\circ$
Area of $\Delta PSQ = \frac{1}{2} \times PS \times PQ \times \sin 60°$
$$\frac{1}{2} \times PQ \times PR \times \sin 120^\circ = \frac{1}{2} \times PS \times PR \times \sin 60^\circ + \frac{1}{2} \times PS \times PQ \times \sin 60^\circ$$
$$\frac{9\sqrt{3}}{2} \times PR = 6 \times PR \times \frac{\sqrt{3}}{2} + 6 \times 9 \times \frac{\sqrt{3}}{2}$$
$9PR = 6PR + 54$
$$PR = \frac{54}{3} = 18 \text{ cm}$$

23. 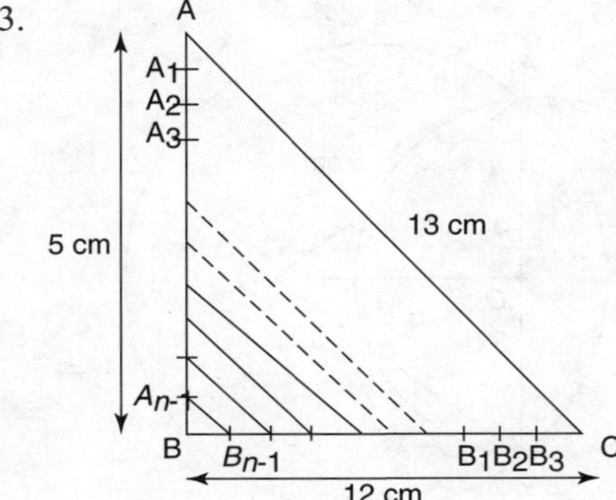

$AB = 5$cm
$$A_{n-1}B = \frac{5}{n}$$
$$A_{n-2}B = \frac{10}{n},\ A_{n-3}B = \frac{15}{n},\ \ldots$$

Similarly $BB_{n-1} = \frac{12}{n}, BB_{n-2} = \frac{24}{n}, BB_{n-3} = \frac{36}{n}, \ldots$

$$A_{n-1}B_{n-1} = \sqrt{\left(\frac{5}{n}\right)^2 + \left(\frac{12}{n}\right)^2} = \frac{13}{n}$$

$$A_{n-2}B_{n-2} = \sqrt{\left(\frac{10}{n}\right)^2 + \left(\frac{24}{n}\right)^2} = \frac{26}{n}$$

And so on…

$A_{n-1}B_{n-1} + A_{n-2}B_{n-2} + A_{n-3}B_{n-3} + \ldots +$

$$AC = \frac{13}{n} + \frac{26}{n} + \frac{39}{n} + \ldots n \text{ terms } =$$

$$\frac{13}{n}[1+2+3+\ldots+n] = 130$$

$$\frac{13}{n} \times \frac{n}{2}(n+1) = 130$$

$(n + 1) = 20$

$n = 19$

24. *Area of* $\Delta A_{n-1}\ BB_{n-1}$ + *Area of* $\Delta A_{n-2}\ BB_{(n-2)}$ + *Area of* $\Delta A_{n-3}BB_{(n-3)}$ + … + *Area of* ΔABC = 66 cm^2
Area of $\Delta A_{n-1}\ BB_{n-1}$ + *Area of* $\Delta A_{n-2}\ BB_{(n-2)}$ + *Area of* $\Delta A_{n-3}BB_{(n-3)}$ + … + *Area of* ΔABC = 66 cm^2

$$\Rightarrow \frac{1}{2} \times \frac{5}{n} \times \frac{12}{n} + \frac{1}{2} \times \frac{10}{n} \times \frac{24}{n} + \frac{1}{2} \times \frac{15}{n} \times \frac{36}{n} + \ldots + \frac{1}{2} \times 5 \times 12 = 66$$

$$\Rightarrow \frac{60}{2n^2}\left[1^2 + 2^2 + 3^2 + \ldots + n^2\right] = 66$$

$$\Rightarrow \frac{30}{n^2} \times \frac{n(n+1)(2n+1)}{6} = 66$$

$$\Rightarrow \frac{5}{n}(n+1)(2n+1) = 66$$

$\Rightarrow n = 5$

25.

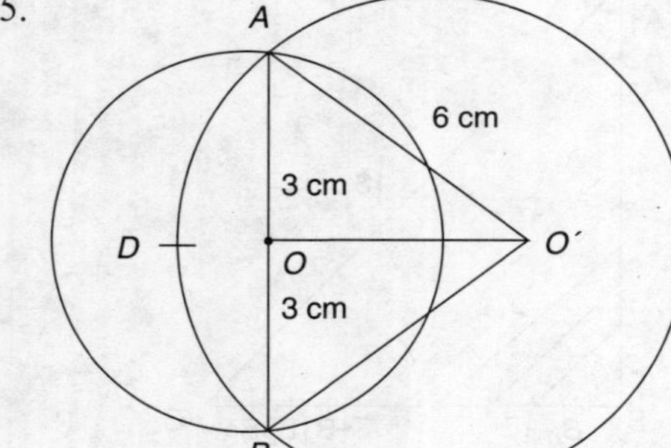

Let the center of the smaller and the bigger circle be O, O' respectively (as shown in the diagram above). And A, B are the points of intersection of the circles.

The common chord will be of maximum length, if it is the diameter of the smaller circle. (**Note:** You cannot make the common chord longer than the diameter of the smaller circle.)

$AB = 3 \times 2 = 6$ cm

$O'A = O'B = 6$cm

This means that the $\Delta ABO'$ is an equilateral triangle having side 6 cm.

So area of $\Delta ABO' = \frac{\sqrt{3}}{4}(6)^2 = 9\sqrt{3}$ cm^2.

26. Area of intersection of the two circles = Area of smaller circle/2 + Area of segment ABD

$$= \frac{\pi(3)^2}{2} + (\text{area of segment } ADBO' - \text{area of } \Delta ABO')$$

$$= \frac{\pi}{2}(3)^2 + \left(\pi(6)^2 \times \frac{60^\circ}{360^\circ} - 9\sqrt{3}\right)$$

$$= \frac{9\pi}{2} + 6\pi - 9\sqrt{3}$$

$$= \left[\frac{21}{2}\pi - 9\sqrt{3}\right] \text{cm}^2$$

27.

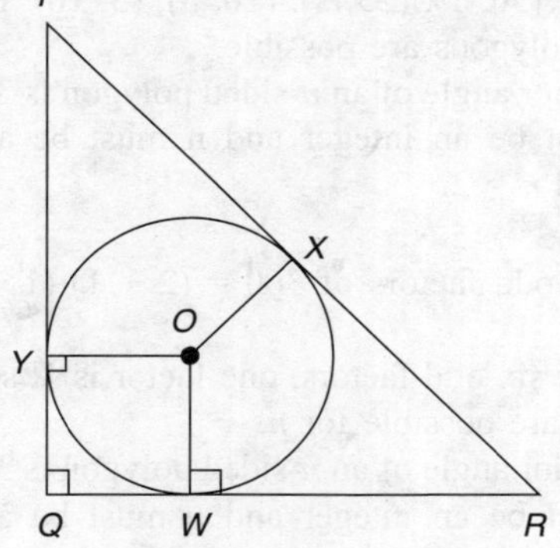

$PR = 3\sqrt{2}$ cm

$PQ = QR = 3$ cm

In-circle of an isosceles right angle triangle touches the hypotenuse at its mid-point.

So, $PX = XR = 1.5\sqrt{2}$ cm

and $WR = XR = 1.5\sqrt{2}$ cm

$QW = QR - WR = (3 - 1.5\sqrt{2})$cm

So the required ratio is:

$1.5\sqrt{2} : 3 - 1.5\sqrt{2} : 1.5\sqrt{2}$

$1 : (\sqrt{2} - 1) : 1$

28. $\angle XOY = 180° - \angle YPX$
$= 180° - 45° = 135°$

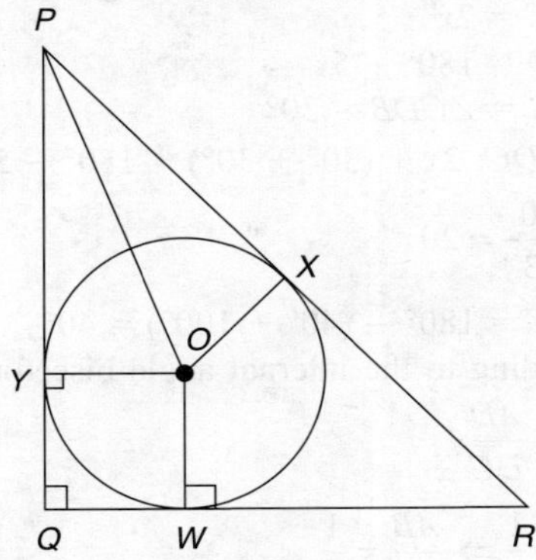

Radius of in-circle $= OY = QW = \left[3 - \frac{3}{2}\sqrt{2}\right]$ cm

Area of $PYOX$ = *area of* ΔPYO + *area of* PXO = 2 (*area of* ΔPYO)

$= \frac{1}{2} \times \left[3 - \frac{3}{2}\sqrt{2}\right] \times \frac{3}{2}\sqrt{2} \times 2$

$= \frac{9}{2}\sqrt{2} - \frac{9}{4} \times 2 = \frac{9}{2}\sqrt{2} - \frac{9}{2} = \frac{9}{2}\left(\sqrt{2} - 1\right)\text{ cm}^2$

29. $BP \perp AC$, ΔABC is an equilateral triangle so $AP = PC$ and if side of ΔABC is a. Then $BP = \frac{a\sqrt{3}}{2}$ (Altitude of an equilateral triangle). In order to find the area of ΔPQC we would need to find the base QC and the height PQ. Also, in order to find the area of the ΔPRB, we would need to find the base BR and the height PR of the triangle.

In ΔPQC:

$$\sin 60^\circ = \frac{PQ}{PC} = \frac{\sqrt{3}}{2} \Rightarrow \frac{\sqrt{3}}{2} = \frac{PQ}{\frac{a}{2}} \Rightarrow PQ = \frac{\sqrt{3}}{4}a$$

$$\cos 60^\circ = \frac{QC}{PC} = \frac{1}{2} \Rightarrow QC = \frac{a}{4}$$

$$\text{Area of } \Delta PQC = \frac{1}{2} \times \frac{a}{4} \times \frac{a\sqrt{3}}{4} = \frac{a^2\sqrt{3}}{32}\text{ cm}^2$$

In ΔARP

$$\sin \angle RAP = \frac{RP}{AP} = \frac{RP}{\frac{a}{2}} \Rightarrow \sin 60^\circ = \frac{2RP}{a}$$

$$RP = \frac{a\sqrt{3}}{4}\text{ cm}$$

$\angle PBR = 30°$

$$BR = PB\cos 30° = \frac{a\sqrt{3}}{2} \times \frac{\sqrt{3}}{2} = a \times \frac{3}{4}$$

$$\text{Area of } \Delta PRB = \frac{1}{2} \times RB \times PR = \frac{1}{2} \times \frac{3a}{4} \times \frac{a\sqrt{3}}{4}$$

$$= \frac{3a^2\sqrt{3}}{32}$$

So the required ratio $= \dfrac{\frac{3a^2\sqrt{3}}{32}}{\frac{a^2\sqrt{3}}{32}} = 3:1$

30.

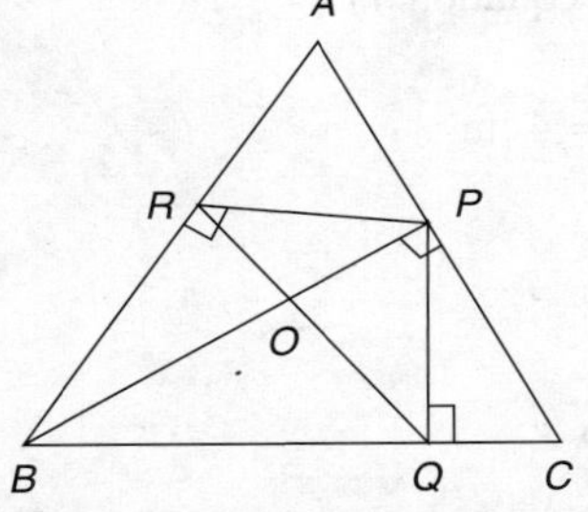

We have already seen $AR = QC = a/4$

$\Rightarrow RQ \parallel AC$

$\Rightarrow \Delta BRQ \sim \Delta BAC$

$$\frac{RQ}{AC} = \frac{BO}{BP} = \frac{BR}{AB} = \frac{AB - AR}{AB} = \frac{\frac{3a}{4}}{a} = \frac{3}{4}$$

$$\frac{RQ}{AC} = \frac{3}{4}$$

$$RQ = \frac{3a}{4}\text{ cm}$$

$$BO = \frac{3}{4} \times \frac{a\sqrt{3}}{2} = \frac{3a\sqrt{3}}{8}$$

$$OP = BP - BO = \frac{a\sqrt{3}}{2} - \frac{3a\sqrt{3}}{8}$$

$$= \frac{a\sqrt{3}}{8}\text{ cm}$$

$$\text{Area of } \Delta PRQ = \frac{1}{2} \times \frac{3a}{4} \times \frac{a\sqrt{3}}{8}$$

$$= \frac{1}{2} \times \frac{3 \times 4}{4} \times \frac{4\sqrt{3}}{8} = \frac{3\sqrt{3}}{4}\text{cm}^2$$

31.

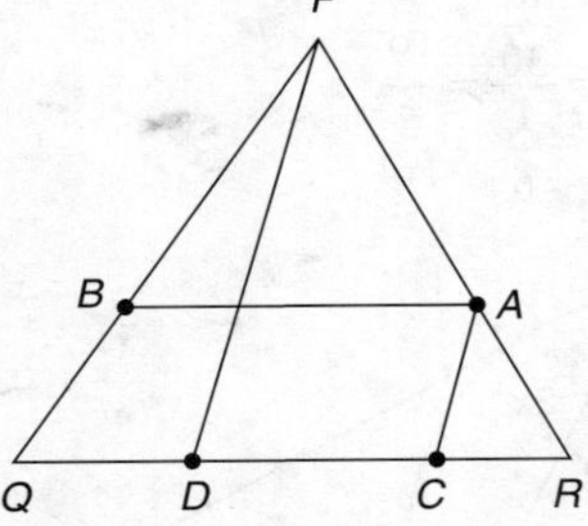

$PQ = PR = 10$ cm.

$PA : AR = 2 : 3$

$\Rightarrow PA = 10 \times \frac{2}{2+3} = 4\text{ cm}$, AR $= 10 \times \frac{3}{2+3} = 6$ cm

In ΔPRD & ΔACR : $AC \parallel PD$

$\Rightarrow \Delta ACR \sim \Delta PRD$

$$\frac{PA}{AR} = \frac{DC}{CR} = \frac{2}{3} \quad (1)$$

$AB \parallel DC$ and $AC \parallel PD$

$\Rightarrow \angle PDC = \angle BAC$

$\angle APD = \angle BAC$ (given)

$\Rightarrow \angle PDC = \angle APD$ or $PR = RD = 10$cm.

$\frac{DC}{CR} = \frac{2}{3}$ (From equation 1)

$DC = 10 \times \frac{2}{2+3} = 4\,\text{cm}$

32.

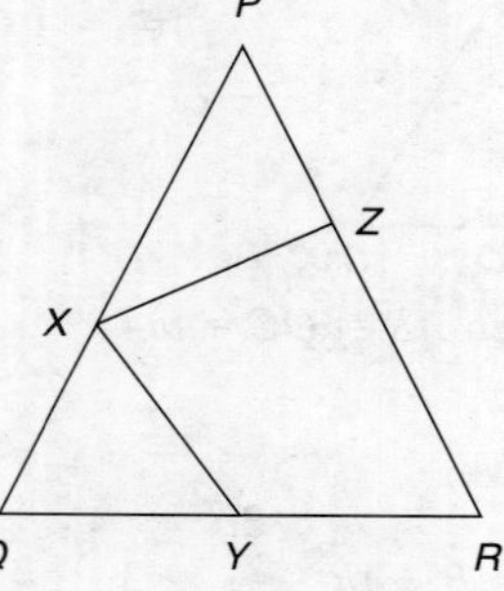

$$\frac{\text{Area of}\Delta PXZ}{\text{Area of}\Delta PQR} = \frac{\frac{1}{2} \times PX.PZ.\sin P}{\frac{1}{2} \times PQ.PR.\sin P}$$

$$= \left(\frac{PX}{PQ} \times \frac{PZ}{PR}\right) = \left(\frac{1}{2} \times \frac{1}{3}\right) = \frac{1}{6}$$

$$\frac{\text{Area of } \Delta QXY}{\text{Area of } \Delta PQR} = \frac{\frac{1}{2} QX.QY.\sin Q}{\frac{1}{2} .PQ.QR.\sin Q}$$

$$= \frac{QX}{PQ} \times \frac{QY}{QR} = \frac{1}{2} \times \frac{2}{5} = \frac{2}{10}$$

$$\frac{\text{Area of } \square XYRZ}{\text{Area of}\Delta PQR} = \frac{1 - \left(\frac{1}{6} + \frac{2}{10}\right)}{1} = \frac{19}{30}$$

$$\frac{\text{Area of } \square XYRZ}{\text{Area of}\Delta PXZ} = \frac{\frac{19}{30}}{\frac{1}{6}} = \frac{19}{5}$$

33.

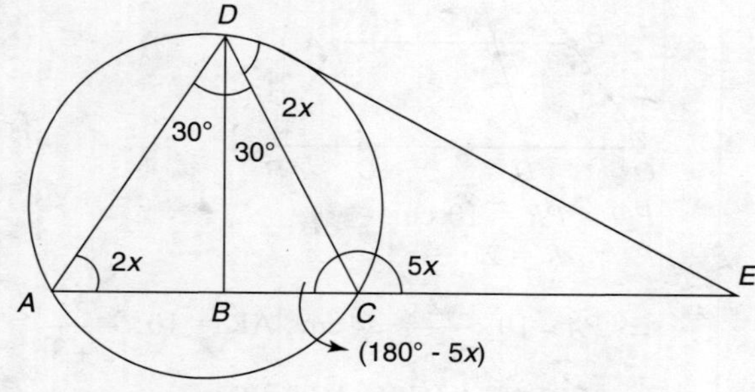

Let $\angle EDC = 2x$ and $\angle ECD = 5x$

According to alternate segment theorem:

$\angle EDC = \angle DAC$

$\angle DAC = 2x$

$\angle BCD = 180° - 5x$

$\angle ADB = \angle CDB = 30°$

In ΔADC: $2x + (30° + 30°) + 180° - 5x = 180°$

$x = \frac{60°}{3} = 20°$

$\angle DEC = 180° - (40° + 100°) = 40°$

34. According to the internal angle bisector theorem:

$\frac{AB}{BC} = \frac{AD}{DC}$

$\frac{AB}{AC} = \frac{1}{3} \Rightarrow \frac{AB}{BC} = \frac{1}{2}$

$\Rightarrow \frac{AD}{DC} = \frac{1}{2}$

$AD = \frac{DC}{2} = \frac{6}{2} = 3\,\text{cm}$

35. In an n-sided regular polygon number of diagonals $= {}^nC_2 - n$

$= \frac{n(n-3)}{2}$

$p\left[\frac{n(n-3)}{2}\right] = n$

$p(n - 3) = 2 \Rightarrow \frac{2}{n-3} = p$

Internal angle $x = \frac{(n-2)\pi}{n}$. On transformation, we get $n = \frac{2\pi}{\pi - x}$.

Hence, P =

$$\frac{2}{n-3} = \frac{2}{\left[\frac{2\pi}{\pi - x}\right] - 3} = \frac{2(\pi - x)}{2\pi - 3\pi + 3x} = \frac{2(\pi - x)}{3x - \pi}$$

$p = \frac{2(\pi - x)}{3x - \pi}$

$3xp - \pi p = 2\pi - 2x$

$x(3p + 2) = 2\pi + \pi p$

$x = \frac{\pi(2+P)}{(3P+2)}$

Alternative method:

Let the polygon is a square then $n = 4$, $p = 2$ and $x = 90°$

Only option (b) satisfies these conditions. Hence, it is the correct option.

36. ΔPQR is a right-angle triangle.

$PQ = 15$cm, $PR = 25$cm

$QR = \sqrt{PR^2 - PQ^2} = \sqrt{25^2 - 15^2} = \sqrt{400} = 20\,\text{cm}$

Since $PQ \times QR = 20 \times 15 = 300$ and $QS \times PR = 12 \times 25 = 300$, therefore $QS \perp PR$ (**Note:** This is a property of right-angled triangles that you should know).

$SR = \sqrt{(20)^2 - 12^2} = 16\,\text{cm}$

In ΔQTR: QT = $\sqrt{QR^2 - RT^2} = \sqrt{20^2 - 16^2} = 12\,\text{cm}$

ΔQTR and ΔQSR are congruent to each other therefore $\angle SOQ = \angle TOQ = 90°$

It is obvious that $ST \perp QR$.

Hence, $\Delta ROS \sim RQP$

$\frac{RO}{RQ} = \frac{RS}{RP} = \frac{16}{25}$

$\Rightarrow \frac{RO}{OQ} = \frac{16}{9}$

37. Area of quadrilateral $SQTR$ = Area of ΔSQR + Area of ΔQTR. We know that the area of a quadrilateral is given by product of diagonals ÷ 2. Hence, we get:

$\frac{ST \times 20}{2} = \frac{1}{2} \times 12 \times 16 + \frac{1}{2} \times 12 \times 16$ (Using the lengths of SQ, QR, QT and TR which we know from the previous question and the given information)

Hence, ST = 19.20 cm

38.

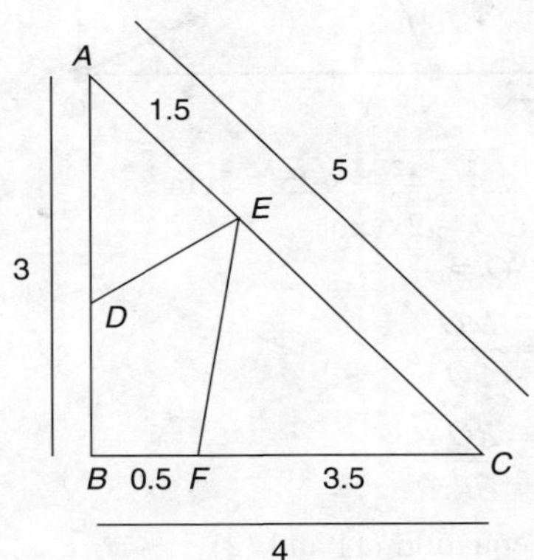

ΔABC is right angle triangle and $\angle B = 90°$

Let $\angle BAC = A$

$\Rightarrow \angle BCA = 90° - A$

In ΔADE: $AD = AE = 1.5$

$\Rightarrow \angle ADE = \angle AED = \frac{180° - A}{2} = 90° - \frac{A}{2}$

In ΔEFC: $EC = FC = 3.5$ cm

$\angle CEF = \angle CFE = \frac{180° - (90° - A)}{2} = 45° + \frac{A}{2}$

$\angle AED + \angle DEF + \angle FEC = 180°$

$90° - \frac{A}{2} + \angle DEF + 45° + \frac{A}{2} = 180°$

$\angle DEF = 45°$

39. $\frac{PX}{QZ} = \frac{1}{2}$ and $\frac{QX}{QZ} = \frac{3}{2}$

$\therefore PX: XQ = 1: 3$

$\Rightarrow \frac{PX}{XQ} = \frac{PY}{YR} = \frac{1}{3}$

$\therefore XY \parallel QR$

If $XY \parallel QR$, then for any point Z on the line QR, ΔXYZ will have the same area as the base and the height of the triangle would be constant irrespective of where Z is placed. So area of ΔXYZ will be same for any value of QZ: QR.

40.

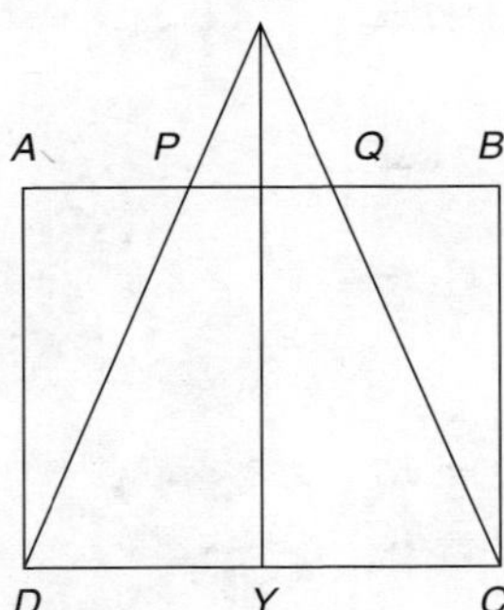

Let the altitude from O of ΔOPQ is OX and $OY \perp DC$.

Area of $\square PQCD = \frac{1}{2}(PQ + DC)BC = 80$ sq units

$\Rightarrow \frac{1}{2}(PQ + 10)10 = 80$

PQ = 6 units

ΔOPQ and ΔODC are similar triangles.

$\frac{OX}{OY} = \frac{PQ}{DC} = \frac{6}{10}$

$\frac{OX}{OX + 10} = \frac{6}{10}$

$10\,OX = 6\,OX + 60$

$OX = \frac{60}{4} = 15$ units

Solutions for Questions 41 to 42:

41. **Case 1:** Two equal sides could add up to 10.
Let the sides are a, a and c.
$a + a = 10$ or $a = 5$
Possible combinations: (5, 5, 1), (5, 5, 2), (5, 5, 3), (5, 5, 4), (5, 5, 6), (5, 5, 7), (5, 5, 8), (5, 5, 9)
There are eight possible triangles. (**Note:** we exclude the triangle (5, 5, 5) because it would become an equilateral triangle.)
Case 2: $a + c = 10$
Possible values of (a, c) are (4, 6), (6, 4), (7, 3), (8, 2), (9, 1)
There are five possible triangles.
Hence, total 8 + 5 = 13 triangles are possible.

42. Maximum possible perimeter = 5 + 5 + 9 = 19 cm.
$x = 19$

Solutions for Questions 43 and 44:

43. Let the angle between 12 and 20 be '*i*'.

$\frac{1}{2} \times 12 \times 20 \times \sin A = \text{Area}$

To maximise the area value of sin *A* must be 1.

Maximum possible area = $\frac{1}{2} \times 12 \times 20 = 120$ square units.

In this case: $x = \sqrt{12^2 + 20^2} = \sqrt{544}$ cm.

44. 120 square cm

45.

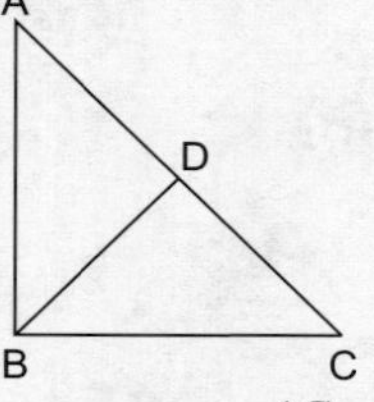

$$AC \cdot AD = AB^2$$
$$AC \cdot AD = BC^2$$

$\Delta ABC \approx \Delta ADB$

$\therefore \frac{AC}{AB} = \frac{AB}{AD}$

(Corresponding sides of similar triangle are proportional)

$$AC \cdot AD = AB^2 \quad (1)$$

Also, $\Delta ABC\ N\ \Delta BDC \Rightarrow \frac{AC}{BC} = \frac{BC}{CD}$

$$AC \cdot CD = BC^2 \quad (2)$$

Both conditions of option (d) are found; therefore (d) is the answer.

46.

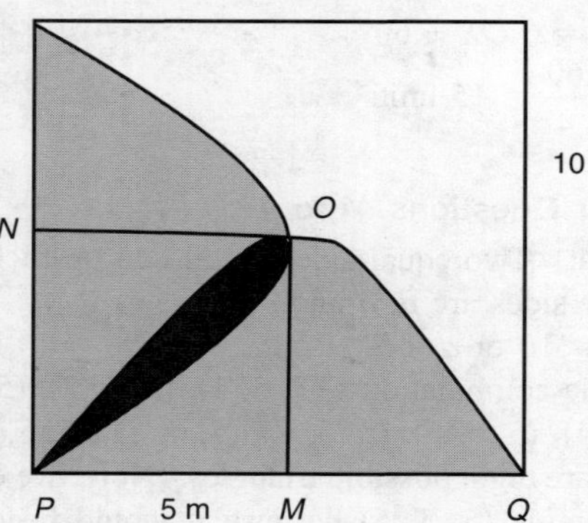

Let *PQRS* be the square grazing field and *M*, *N* are the points at which cows are tethered.

Area grazed by both cows = [Area of quadrant *POM* + Area of quadrant *NOP*] − [Area of square *PMON*]

$= \frac{\pi}{4}(5)^2 \times 2 - 5 \times 5$

$= \frac{50}{4} \times \pi - 25$

$= \frac{25\pi}{2} - 25$

$= \frac{25\pi - 50}{2}$

$= \frac{25}{2}[\pi - 2] = 12.5(\pi - 2)\text{m}^2$

47. Area of grazed region = Area of *OMPN* + Area of *OMQ* + Area of *OSN*

$= 5^2 + \frac{\pi}{4}(5)^2 \times 2$

$= 25 + \frac{25\pi}{2} = \frac{25}{2}[\pi + 2] = 12.5(\pi + 2)$

Area of non-grazed region = 10 × 10 − 12.5π − 25 = 75 − 12.5π m^2

48.

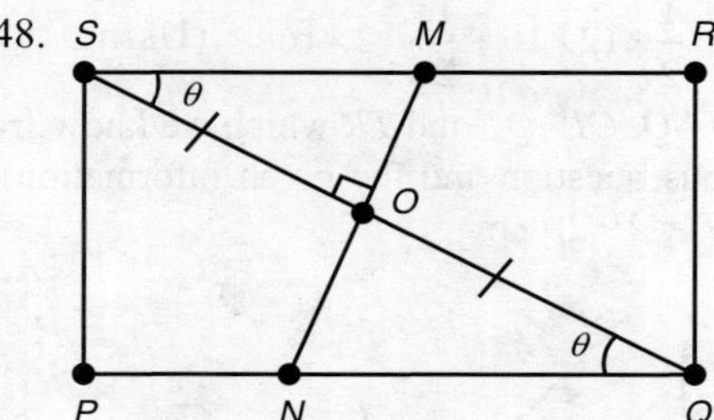

$SQ = \sqrt{3^2 + 4^2} = \sqrt{25} = 5\text{cm}$

$SO = OQ = 2.5\text{cm}$

If $\angle RSQ =$

$$\tan\theta = \frac{MO}{SO} \quad (1)$$

$$\tan\theta = \frac{RQ}{SR} \quad (2)$$

From equation (1) and (2)

$\frac{MO}{SO} = \frac{RQ}{SR} = \frac{3}{4}$

$\frac{MO}{SO} = 0.75$

49. $OQ = 2.5\text{cm}$

$\tan\theta = \frac{ON}{OQ}$

$ON = OQ \tan\theta$

Area of $\Delta QNO = \frac{1}{2} \times OQ \times ON = \frac{1}{2} \times OQ \times OQ \tan\theta$

$= \frac{1}{2}(OQ)^2 \tan\theta$

$= \frac{1}{2} \times \left(\frac{5}{2}\right)^2 \times \frac{3}{4} = \frac{75}{32}$

Area of $SONP = \frac{1}{2} \times 4 \times 3 - \frac{75}{32}$

$= 6 - \frac{75}{32} = \frac{192-75}{32} = \frac{117}{32} cm^2 = 3.65 cm^2$

50. Let 'r' be the radius of the semicircle.

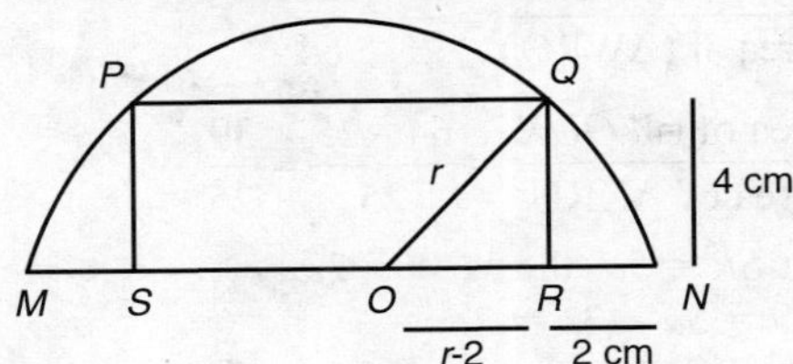

In ΔORQ: $r^2 = (r-2)^2 + 4^2$

$r^2 = r^2 + 4 - 4r + 16$

$4r = 20$

$r = 5$ cm

Area of rectangle PQRS $= 2(r-2) \times 4$

$= 2(5-2) \times 4 = 24$ cm^2

Required area = Area of the semi-circle – Area of rectangle $PQRS = \frac{\pi}{2}(5)^2 - 24$

$= (12.5\pi - 24)$ cm^2

51. $\frac{\text{Area of } \Delta SNO}{\text{Area of } \Delta RNO} = \frac{20}{b} = \frac{SN}{NR} = 1.25$

$b = \frac{20}{1.25} = 16$

Area of $\Delta POS \times$ Area of ΔQOR = Area of ΔPOQ $\times$ Area of ΔSOR {Property of the diagonals of a quadrilateral]

$30 \times a = 30 \times 36$

$a = 36$

$a + b = 36 + 16 = 52$

52. In $\Delta PMQ: QM = \sqrt{(PQ)^2 - (PM)^2}$

$QM = \sqrt{(15)^2 - 9^2} = 12$ cm

In ΔQTO and ΔQMP:

$\angle QTO = \angle QMP = 90°$

$\angle PQM = \angle TQO$[They are angles between the same lines]

Hence, $\Delta QTO \sim \Delta QMP$

$\frac{QT}{QO} = \frac{QM}{QP} = \frac{12}{15} = \frac{4}{5} = 0.8$

53. $TR^2 = QR^2 - QT^2 = PR^2 - PT^2$

$15^2 - QT^2 = 182 - (15 - QT)^2$

$15^2 - QT^2 = 18^2 - 15^2 - QT^2 + 30QT$

$30QT = 450 - 324$

$QT = \frac{126}{30} = 4.2$ cm

ΔQTO and ΔQMP are similar to each other, then:

$\frac{QT}{OT} = \frac{QM}{PM}$

$OT = QT \times \frac{PM}{QM} = 4.2 \times \frac{9}{12}$

$= 3.15$ cm

54.

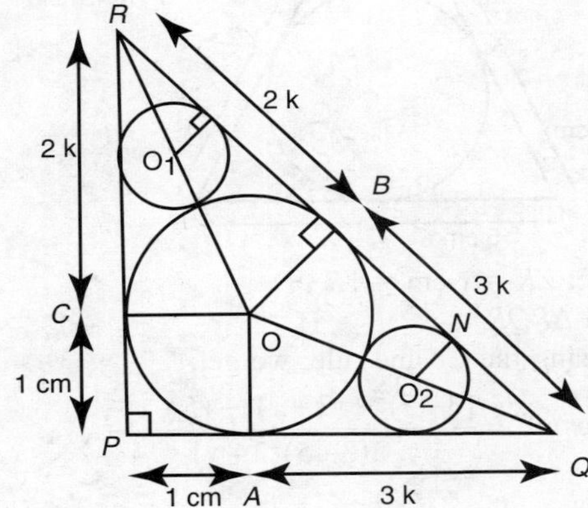

Let $RB = RC = 2k$

$BQ = AQ = 3k$

In ΔPQR, $(2k+1)^2 + (3k+1)^2 = (2k+3k)^2$

By solving, we get $k = 1$

So $RB = RC = 2$ cm

$BQ = AQ = 3$ cm

$PQ = 1 + 3 = 4$ cm, $PR = 1 + 2 = 3$ cm, $RQ = 2 + 3 = 5$ cm

$OQ = \sqrt{3^2 + 1^2} = \sqrt{10}$ cm

$OR = \sqrt{2^2 + 1^2} = \sqrt{5}$ cm

In the solution figure mark point M, where the perpendicular from O_1 cuts RB.

$O_1M \perp RB$, $O_2N \perp BQ$

In ΔOBR and O_1MR:

$\frac{O_1M}{OB} = \frac{O_1R}{OR}$

$\frac{r_1}{1} = \frac{OR - (r_1 + 1)}{OR}$

$r_1 = \frac{\sqrt{5} - (r_1 + 1)}{\sqrt{5}}$

By solving, we get $r_1 = \frac{\sqrt{5} - 1}{\sqrt{5} + 1}$

Similarly $r_2 = \frac{\sqrt{10} - 1}{\sqrt{10} + 1}$

$\frac{r_1}{r_2} = \frac{\sqrt{5}-1}{\sqrt{5}+1} \times \frac{\sqrt{10}+1}{\sqrt{10}-1} = \frac{(\sqrt{5}-1)^2}{4} \times \frac{(\sqrt{10}+1)^2}{9}$

$= (33 - 11\sqrt{5} + 6\sqrt{10} - 10\sqrt{2})/18$

55.

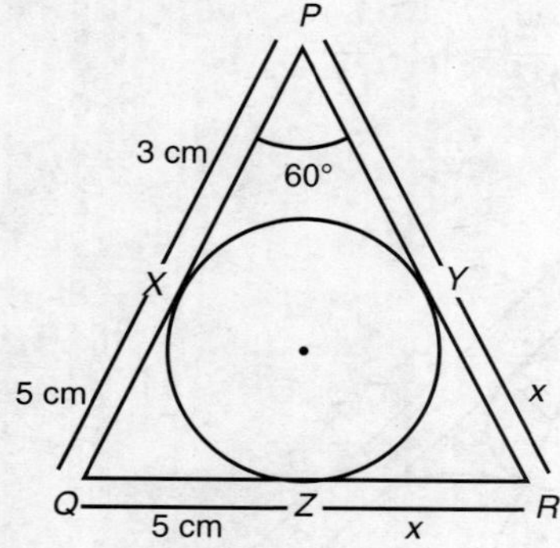

Let $ZR = x$ cm $= YR$

In ΔPQR:

Using the Cosine rule, we get:

$$\cos 60^o = \frac{(3+5)^2+(3+x)^2-(5+x)^2}{2(3+5)(3+x)}$$

$8(3 + x) = 64 + 9 + x^2 + 6x - 25 - x^2 - 10x$

$24 + 8x = 64 - 16 - 4x$

$12x = 24$

$x = 2$ cm

Sides of the ΔPQR: $PQ = 8$ cm

$RQ = 7$ cm

$PR = 5$ cm

Semi-perimeters $= \frac{8+7+5}{2} = 10\,\text{cm}$

Area of $\Delta PQR == \sqrt{s(s-a)(s-b)(s-c)}$

$= \sqrt{10(2)(3)(5)}$

$= 10\sqrt{3}$ cm^2

Radius of in-circle $= \frac{10\sqrt{3}}{10} = \sqrt{3}$ cm (Since area of a triangle is given by $s \times r$)

56. Area of the shaded portion =

$10\sqrt{3} - \pi\left(\sqrt{3}\right)^2 = 10\sqrt{3} - 3\pi$ cm^2

57. ΔPOW and ΔROS are similar to each other,

$$\frac{PO}{OR} = \frac{OW}{OS} = \frac{PW}{SR} = \sqrt{\frac{\text{area of}(\Delta POW)}{\text{area of}(\Delta SOR)}} = \sqrt{\frac{9}{25}} = \frac{3}{5}$$

$PQ \| TU \| SR$.

According to the basic proportionality theorem:

$$\frac{PT}{TS} = \frac{PO}{OR} = \frac{WO}{OS} = \frac{WX}{XR} = \frac{QU}{UR} = \frac{3}{5}$$

ΔWRQ *and* ΔXRU are similar and

$$\frac{XU}{WQ} = \frac{RX}{RW}$$

$$\frac{WX}{XR} = \frac{3}{5} \Rightarrow \frac{WX}{XR} + 1 = \frac{3}{5} + 1$$

$$\frac{WX + XR}{XR} = \frac{8}{5}$$

$$\frac{WR}{XR} = \frac{8}{5}$$

$$\frac{XR}{WR} = \frac{5}{8}$$

$$\frac{\text{Area of}(\Delta\text{XRU})}{\text{Area of}(\Delta\text{WRQ})} = \frac{5^2}{8^2} = \frac{25}{64}$$

$$\frac{\text{area of } \square WQUX}{\text{area of } \Delta\text{XRU}} = \frac{64-25}{25} = \frac{39}{25}$$

58. Let $SR = 5a$, then $PW = 3a$

$WQ = 5a - 3a = 2a$

But $WQ = 2$ cm

$2a = 2$ cm

$a = 1$ cm

$$\frac{WQ}{XU} = \frac{WR}{XR} = \frac{3+5}{5} = \frac{8}{5}$$

$$XU = 2 \times \frac{5}{8} = \frac{5}{4}\text{cm}$$

$$TX = 5 - \frac{5}{4} = \frac{15}{4}\text{cm}$$

$$TX \times XU = \frac{15}{4} \times \frac{5}{4} = \frac{75}{16}\ \text{cm}^2$$

59.

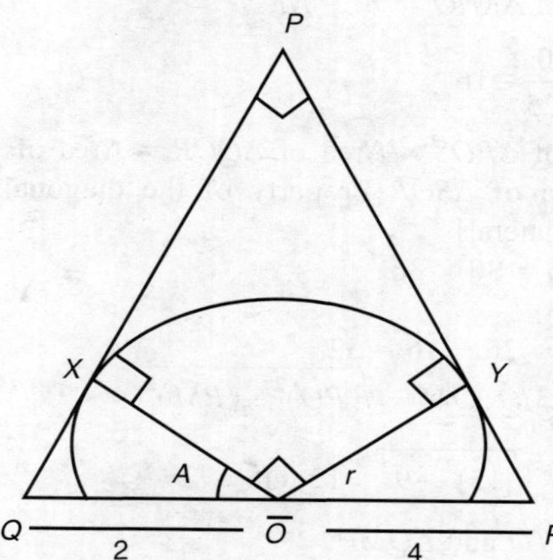

Let PQ and PR touches the semicircle at X and Y respectively.

$OX \perp PQ$, $OY \perp PR$

$\square PXOY$ is a square, $\angle XOY = 90°$

Let the radius of the semicircle be r.

Let $\angle XOQ = A$, then in ΔOXQ:

$$\cos A = \frac{r}{2} \quad (1)$$

Similarly in ΔOYR:

$$\cos\left(90^o - A\right) = \frac{r}{4} \quad (\angle YOR = 180° - A - 90° - A)$$

$$\sin A = \frac{r}{4} \quad (2)$$

Squaring and adding equation (1) and (2), we get

$$\cos^2 A + \sin^2 A = \left(\frac{r}{2}\right)^2 + \left(\frac{r}{4}\right)^2$$

$$1 = \frac{r^2}{4} + \frac{r^2}{16}$$

$$\frac{5r^2}{16} = 1$$

$$r^2 = 16/5$$

$$r = \frac{4}{\sqrt{5}} \text{ cm}$$

60.

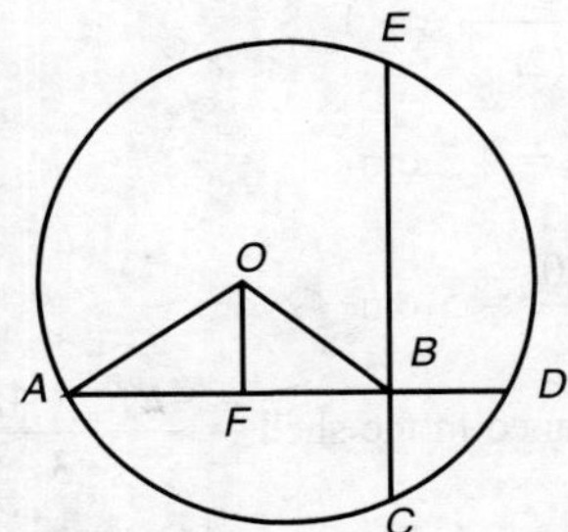

In this figure, our objective is to find the value of OB.

Obviously, the value of OB depends on the values of OF and FB. Hence, we would need to think of a way in which we can work out the values of OF and FB respectively.

If we were to take the values of BD as x and BE as y respectively, then using the intersecting chord theorem (for chords intersecting at right angles), we get:

$AB \times BD = BE \times BC$

$\rightarrow 6x = 2y \rightarrow y = 3x$

Now, $OF = \dfrac{3x - 2}{2}$ and $AF = \dfrac{6+x}{2}$. Solving for x, using Pythagoras theorem, we get x as 4.

Then, in right angled triangle OFA, we have $OA^2 = OF^2 + AF^2$

$$OF^2 = 50 - \frac{(6+x)^2}{4} = 41 - 3x - \frac{x^2}{4}$$

Hence, $OF = 5$ and $BF = AB - AF = 1$.

Then, in the right-angled triangle OFB, we get $OB^2 = OF^2 + FB^2 = 25 + 1 = 26$.

Hence, option (a) is correct.

61. 

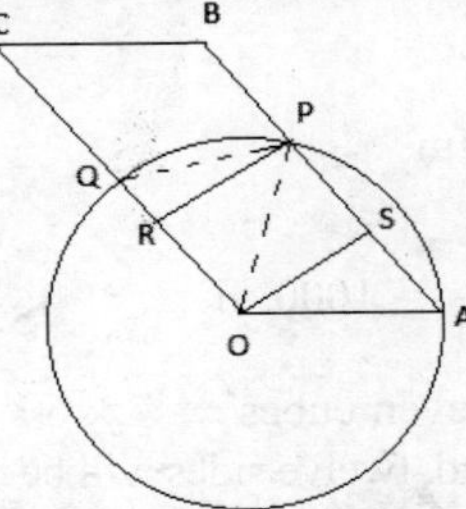

Radius of the circle $= \left(\dfrac{36\pi}{\pi}\right)^{\frac{1}{2}} = 6$ cm.

Join OP, triangle OPA is an isosceles triangle since $OP = OA = 6$ (radii). Also, $AP = 8$ (given). So the area of the triangle is $=$

$\sqrt{s(s-a)(s-b)(s-c)} = \sqrt{10 \times 4 \times 4 \times 2} = 8\sqrt{5}$ cm^2.

62. Construct OS and PR, such that OS is perpendicular of AB and PR is perpendicular to OC. Since, the area of the triangle POA is as found in the previous question, we can use for triangle POA, area $=$

$\frac{1}{2} \times OS \times AP = 8\sqrt{5} \rightarrow OS = 2\sqrt{5}$ cm $= PR$. Also, RO

$= PS = \sqrt{6^2 - \left(2\sqrt{5}\right)^2} = 4$ cm

Side QR of the triangle PQR, $QR = OQ - OR = 6 - 4 = 2$ cm

$PQ = \sqrt{PR^2 + QR^2} = \sqrt{2\sqrt{5}^2 + 2^2} = 2\sqrt{6}$ cm

Solutions for Questions 63 to 65:

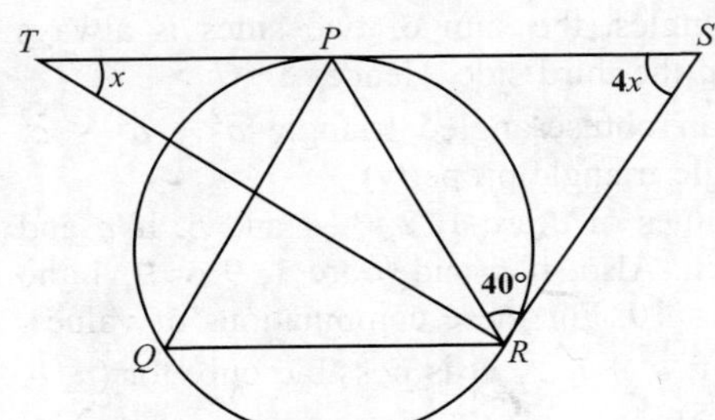

$\angle TPQ = \angle PRQ = 60^\circ = \angle SPR$

ST || QR

$\angle PTR = \angle TRQ = x$

$\angle PSR = 4x$

In ΔPSR:

$\angle SPR + 40° + 4x = 180°$

Or $60° + 40° + 4x = 180°$ or $x = 20°$

$\angle TRQ = \angle PTR = 20°$

$\angle PSR = 80°$

63. $\angle PRQ = 60°$

64. $\angle PSR = 80°$

65. $\angle TRQ = 20°$

Solutions for Questions 66 and 67:

66.

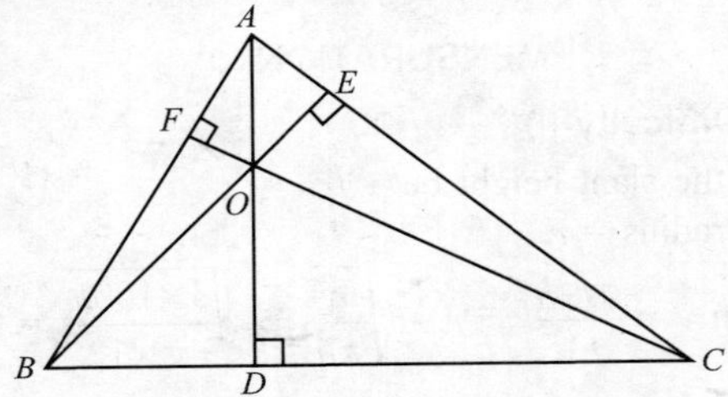

ΔBOD and ΔAOE are similar.

$$\frac{BO}{AO} = \frac{OD}{OE}$$

$BO \times OE = AO \times OD$

$BO \times (BE - BO) = AO \times (AD - AO)$

$12 \times (BE - 12) = 18 \times (20 - 18)$
$BE = 15$ cm

67. $AB = \sqrt{AE^2 + BE^2}$. From the solution to the previous question, we know that $BE = 15$. So, we need to focus on finding AE. $OD = AD - AO = 20 - 18 = 2$ cm.
ΔAOE and ΔBOD are similar to each other.
$$\frac{OE}{OD} = \frac{AO}{BO}$$
$$OE = \frac{AO \times DO}{BO} = \frac{18 \times 2}{12} = 3\text{cm}$$
$$AE = \sqrt{18^2 - 3^2} = 3\sqrt{35}$$
Hence, $AB = \sqrt{AE^2 + BE^2} = \sqrt{315 + 225} = \sqrt{540}$ cm

Solutions for Questions 68 to 70:

$a \times b = 9$
$(a, b) = (3, 3)$ or $(1, 9)$ or $(9, 1)$
For all triangles, the sum of two sides is always greater than the third side. Hence, $a + b > c$.
Also, for an obtuse-angled triangle $a^2 + b^2 < c^2$ (obtuse-angle triangle property)
Possible values of c are 1, 2, 3, 4 and 5, if a and b are 3 each. Also, if a and b are 1, 9 or 9, 1 the value of $c < 10$. For these combinations of values, the value of: $a^2 + b^2 < c^2$ is possible only for $(a, b, c) = (3, 3, 5)$.

68. One
69. The maximum possible value of $c = 5$.
70. Area of $\Delta ABC = \frac{5}{2} \times \sqrt{3^2 - \left(\frac{5}{2}\right)^2} = \frac{5}{4} \times \sqrt{11}$.
71. $PQ = SR = 14$ cm
$SX : XR = 4 : 3$
$SX = 8$cm, $XR = 6$cm
$QR = \sqrt{10^2 - 6^2} = 8$cm
$PS = 8$cm
$PX = \sqrt{8^2 + 8^2} = 8\sqrt{2}$ cm
In ΔPXQ: $PQ = 14$cm, $PX = 8\sqrt{2}$ cm, $QX = 10$cm
$\therefore a > c > b$

MENSURATION

Level of Difficulty (I)

1. Let the slant height be $= l$
Let radius $= r$
Then $v = \frac{\pi r^2 h}{3} \Rightarrow r = \sqrt{\frac{3v}{\pi h}} \Rightarrow \sqrt{\frac{3 \times 100\pi}{\pi \times 12}} = 5$ cm
$$l = \sqrt{h^2 + r^2} = \sqrt{12^2 + 5^2} = 13 \text{ cm}$$
2. In four days the short-hand will cover the circumference 4×2 = 8 times, while the long-hand will cover its circumference 4×24 = 96 times.
Then, the total distance they will cover would be:
$(2 \times \pi \times 4)8 + (2 \times \pi \times 6)96 = 3818.24$ cm
3. Let the radius of the smaller sphere $= r$
Then, the radius of the bigger sphere $= R$
Let the surface area of the smaller sphere = 1
Then, the surface area of the bigger sphere = 4
Then, as per question
$$\Rightarrow \frac{4\pi r^2}{4\pi R^2} = \frac{1}{4} \Rightarrow \frac{r}{R} = \frac{1}{2} \Rightarrow R = 2r$$
Ratio of their volumes
$$= \frac{4\pi r^3}{3} \times \frac{3}{4\pi (2r)^3} \Rightarrow 1:8$$
4. Inner radius $(r) = \frac{9}{2} = 4.5$ cm
Outer radius $(R) = \frac{10}{2} = 5$ cm
Volume of metal contained in the shell $= \frac{4\pi R^3 - 4\pi r^3}{3}$
$\Rightarrow \frac{4\pi}{3}(R^3 - r^3)$
$\Rightarrow 141.9$ cm^3
5. Let smaller radius $(r) = 1$
Then bigger radius $(R) = 2$
Then, as per question
$$\Rightarrow \frac{4\pi r^2}{4\pi R^2} = \left(\frac{r}{R}\right)^2 \Rightarrow \left(\frac{1}{2}\right)^2 = 1:4$$
6. As per question $\Rightarrow \frac{4\pi r^3}{3} = \frac{\pi r^2 h}{3} \Rightarrow h = 4r$
7. Volume of wall = 1200 × 500 × 25 = 15000000 cm^3
Volume of cement = 5% of 15000000 = 750000 cm^3
Remaining volume = 15000000 – 750000
= 14250000 cm^3
Volume of a brick = 25 × 12.5 × 7.5 = 2343.75 cm^3
Number of bricks used $= \frac{14250000}{2343.75} = 6080$
8. Let the inner radius $= r$
Then, $2\pi r = 352$ m. Then $r = 56$
Then, outer radius $= r + 7 = 63 = R$
Now, $\pi R^2 - \pi r^2 =$ area of road
$\Rightarrow \pi(R^2 - r^2) = 2618$ m^2
9. 1 hectare = 10000 m^2
Height = 10 cm $= \frac{1}{10}$ m
Volume $= 10000 \times \frac{1}{10} = 1000$ m^3
10. Total surface area of seven cubes $\Rightarrow 7 \times 6a^2 = 1050$
But on joining end to end, twelve sides will be covered.
So, their area $= 12 \times a^2 \Rightarrow 12 \times 25 = 300$
So, the surface area of the resulting figure = 1050 – 300 = 750

11. Circumference of the base of the cylinder = 22
Let the radius of base of cylinder r.
$2\pi r = 22$ or $r = \frac{11}{\pi}$
Height of the cylinder = 10 cm
Volume of the cylinder = $\pi\left(\frac{11}{\pi}\right)^2 10 = 385 \text{ cm}^3$

12. Volume of parallelepiped = $3\times4\times5 = 60 \text{ cm}^3$
Volume of cube = $4\times4\times4 = 64 \text{ cm}^3$
Volume of the cylinder = $\pi(3)^2 3 = 27\pi \text{ cm}^3$
Volume of sphere = $\frac{4}{3}\pi(3)^3 = 36\pi \text{ cm}^3$
Therefore 4 > 3 > 2> 1

13. If radius of the hemispherical bowl is 'r' then its volume would be $\frac{2}{3}\pi r^3$
Radius of cylinder = r and height = 2/3 r
Volume of cylinder = $\pi r^2.\frac{2}{3}r = \frac{2}{3}\pi r^3$
It means that the volume of the hot water in the cylindrical vessel is 100% of the cylindrical vessel, therefore x= 100

14. Let the radius of the field be 'r' meters. According to the question
$\pi r^2 - (130\times110) = 20350$
$\pi r^2 = 20350 + 14300 = 34650$
$r^2 = 34650\times\frac{7}{22} = 11025$ or r = 105 m

15. Let n bricks can be put in the tank without spilling over the water. According to the question, the volume of the tank should be totally occupied by the available water and the bricks. Also, since the question tells us that each brick absorbs 10% of its' own volume of water, the additional volume added to the current water by each brick added to the tank would only by 90% of the brick's own volume. Let the number of bricks required by n. Then:
$150\times120\times100 = n\times20\times6\times4\left(1-\frac{10}{100}\right)+1281600$
$150\times120\times100 - 1281600 = n\times20\times6\times4\times0.9$
$n = \frac{518400}{20\times6\times4\times0.9} = 1200$

16. Let radius of smaller sphere be 'r cm'.
$\frac{4}{3}\times\pi\times(10)^3 = 1000\times\frac{4}{3}\times\pi\times(r)^3$
$r = 1\text{ cm}$
Surface area of the larger sphere = $4\pi(10)^2 = 400\pi$
Total surface area of 1000 smaller spheres = 1000 $4\pi(1)^2$= 4000π
Increase in the surface area = 4000π – 400π = 3600π
Hence, surface area of the metal is increased by 900%. Therefore, n = 900.

17. Volume of the conical writing equipment = $\frac{1}{3}\pi\left(2.5\times10^{-1}\right)^2\times7 = \frac{11}{24}\text{ cm}^3$
11/24 cm^3 cream can be used to write 330 words.
Number of words that can be written with 1 cm^3 cream = $330\times\frac{24}{11} = 720$
Since 1 litre is 1000 cm^3, 2/5 litres = $\frac{2}{5}\times1000 = 400$ cm^3.
Therefore, number of words that can be written with $\frac{2}{5}$ litre or 400 cm^3 = 400 × 720 = 288000.

18. The surface area of the sheet required to make the cap will be equal to the lateral surface area of the cap, which is given by the formula $\pi\times r\times l$ Since the base radius is 14cm and height is 26.5cm, the value of 'l' can be calculated using $r^2 + h^2 = l^2 \rightarrow l = 29.97 \approx 30$.
Thus, seven caps would require 7 × π × 14 × 30 = 9240 cm^2.

19. The area of the garden is $34\times21 = 714$ sq. m. Out of this the area covered by the paths = $4\times34+4\times21-4\times4 = 204$ sq. m. The remaining area being covered by flowers will be equal to: 714 – 204 = 510 sq. m.

20. Surface area of the cylinder will be largest when the cylinder touches as shown in the diagram given below:

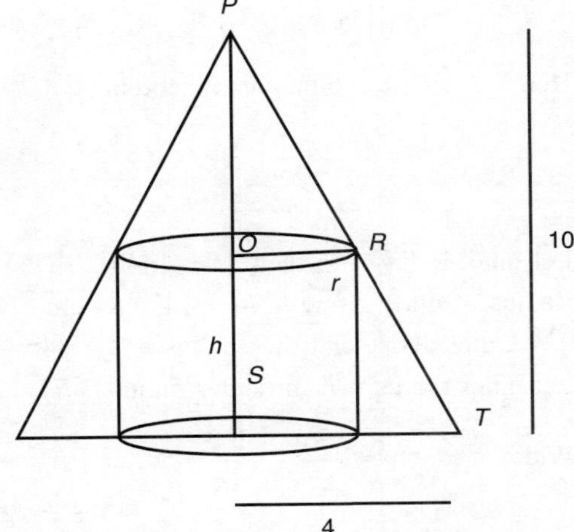

If ST and PS are the radius and height of the right circular cone respectively and h is the height of the cylinder.
ΔPOR and ΔPST are similar to each other.
$\frac{PO}{PS} = \frac{OR}{ST}$

$$\frac{10-h}{10} = \frac{r}{4}$$

$$h = \frac{20-5r}{2}$$

Curved surface area of the cylinder = $2\pi rh$

$$2\pi r\left(\frac{20-5r}{2}\right)$$

$$5\pi r(4-r)$$

By comparison we get $a = 5, b = 4$

$a \times b = 5 \times 4 = 20$

21.

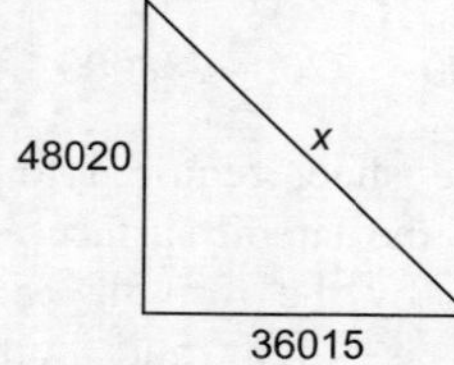

Let hypotenuse = x cm

Then, by Pythagoras theorem:

$$x^2 = (48020)^2 + (36015)^2$$

$$x \Rightarrow 60025 \text{ cm}$$

22.

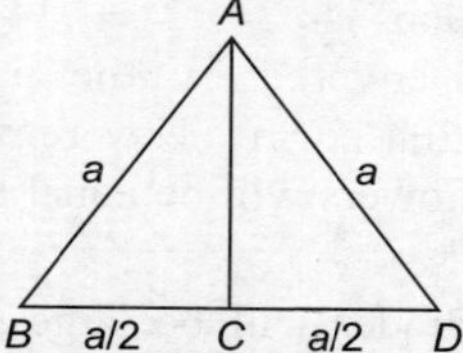

Let one side of the Δ be = a

Perimeter of equilateral triangle = $3a$

$\therefore \quad 3a = 72\sqrt{3} \rightarrow a = 24\sqrt{3}$ m

Height = AC; by Pythagoras theorem

$$AC^2 = a^2 - \left(\frac{a}{2}\right)^2$$

$$AC = 36 \text{ m}$$

23. Let inner radius = r; then $2\pi r = 440 \quad \therefore r = 70$

Radius of outer circle = 70 + 14 = 84 cm

$\therefore$ Outer diameter = 2 × radius = 2 × 84 = 168

24. Let inner radius = r and outer radius = R

$$\text{Width} = R - r = \frac{396}{2\pi} - \frac{352}{2\pi}$$

$$\Rightarrow \quad (R - r) = \frac{44}{2\pi} = 7 \text{ meters}$$

25. Let outer radius = R; then inner radius = $r = R - 7$

$2\pi R = 220 \Rightarrow R = 35$ m;

$r = 35 - 7 = 28$ m

Area of track = $\pi R^2 - \pi r^2 \Rightarrow \pi(R^2 - r^2) = 1386 \text{ m}^2$

Cost of levelling it = $1386 \times \frac{1}{2}$ = ₹693

26. Circumference of circle = $2\pi r = 44$

$= r = 7$ cm

Area of a quadrant = $\frac{\pi r^2}{4} = 38.5 \text{ cm}^2$

27. Volume of soil removed = $l \times b \times h$

$= 7.5 \times 6 \times 1.5 = 67.5 \text{ m}^3$

28. The longest pole can be placed diagonally (three-dimensional).

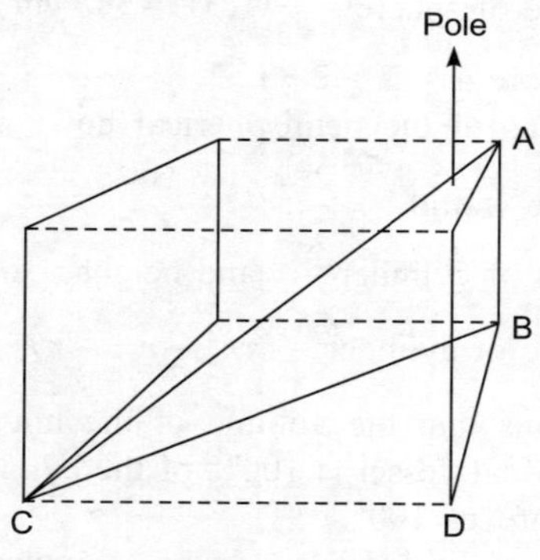

$$BC = \sqrt{18^2 + 24^2} = 30$$

$$AC = \sqrt{30^2 + 16^2} = 34 \text{ m}$$

29. Let the common ratio be = x

Then; length = $3x$, breadth = $2x$ and height = x

Then; as per question $3x \cdot 2x \cdot x = 1296 \Rightarrow 6x^3 = 1296$

$\Rightarrow x = 6$ m

Breadth = $2x$ = 12 m

30. Data is inadequate as it is not mentioned that what part of the cube is melted to form cylinder.

31. Let the initial radius of the circle = r

Area = πr^2

New radius = $(r + x)$

New area = $\pi(r + x)^2$

So the area increased by $\pi(r + x)^2 - r^2 = \pi x (2r + x)$

32. Let the side of square $PQRS$ be x meters.

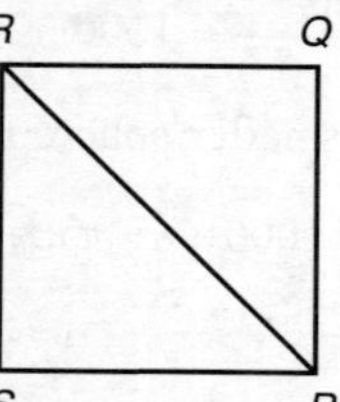

$PR = x\sqrt{2}$ meters or $1.414x$ meters

$PQ + QR = x + x = 2x$ m

Total saving = $2x - 1.41x = 0.586\,x$ meters

% saving $= \frac{0.586x}{2x} \times 100 = 29.3\% \approx 29\%$

33. Two circles will be similar to each other. When you increase the length measures of a figure by a certain percentage, the effect is the multiplication of the length measure by a certain value. (Thus a 5% increase is the same as a multiplication of the original length by 1.05). In such a case the area measures, for a similar figure, get multtplied twice (by the same multiplier). Thus, the new area = original area × 1.05 × 1.05 → 10.25% increase.
This can also be understood as below:
Circumference of a circle= $2\pi r$, where r is the radius.
Circumference α radius
As the circumference increases by 5%, the radius also increases by 5%
∴ New radius = $1.05r$
∴ As area α(radius)^2
∴ New area = $(1.05)^2$ × old area= 1.1025 ×old area
∴ Percentage increase in area = 10.25%

34. Side of the biggest possible cube in given cylinder = 20 cm
Volume of cube = $(20)^3$ = 8000

35. Only possible values are: 1 × 1 × 100; 1 × 2 × 50; 1 × 4 × 25; 1 × 5 × 20; 1 × 10 × 10; 2 × 2 × 25; 2 × 5 × 10 and 4 × 5 ×5.
Hence, there are total eight possibilities:

36. Length of largest tile = H.C.F. of 1517 cm and 902 cm = 41 cm.
Area = $(41 \times 41)\text{cm}^2$
Required number of tiles $= \frac{1517 \times 902}{41 \times 41} = 814$

37. Side of square $= \sqrt{484} = 22$ cm
So length of the wire $= 4 \times 22 = 88$ cm
Longer part $= 88 \times \frac{3}{4} = 66$ cm. So the radius of the circle will be $\frac{66}{2\pi}$.
Shorter part $= 88 \times \frac{1}{4} = 22$ cm. So the length of the side of the square will be $= \frac{11}{2}$.
Area of circle formed by longer part =
$\pi\left(\frac{66}{2\pi}\right)^2 = \frac{693}{2}\text{cm}^2 (\text{Using}\,\pi = \frac{22}{7}).$
Area of square $= \left(\frac{11}{2}\right)^2 = \frac{121}{4}\text{cm}^2$
Therefore, the total area of both the pieces =
$\left(\frac{693}{2} + \frac{121}{4}\right)\text{cm}^2 = 376.75\ \text{cm}^2$

38. There are thirteen successive semicircles with radii 0.5 cm, 1.0 cm, 1.5 cm, and so on.
Total length of the spiral = π × 0.5 + π ×1.0 + ...+ π × 6.5 = π (0.5 + 1.0 + ... + 6.5) = 143 cm.

39. Let the three solids have base radius of r units. Height of hemisphere = r = height of cylinder = height of cone. The curved surface areas of the three solids are:
The curved surface area of the cylinder = $2\pi r \times r = 2\pi r^2$
The curved surface area of the hemisphere: $2\pi r^2$
The curved surface area of the cone = $\pi r\sqrt{r^2 + r^2} = \sqrt{2}\pi r^2$
So the required ratio $= 2\pi r^2 : 2\pi r^2 : \sqrt{2}\pi r^2 = \sqrt{2} : \sqrt{2} : 1$.

40. The curved surface area of sphere, $S = 4\pi r^2$
The rate of change of the radius per unit time can be represented mathematically using:
dr/dt =+ 2 cm per second and r =30 cm
The rate of change of the surface area (s) will then be given by: $ds/dt = d(4\pi r^2)/dt = 4\pi \times 2r \times dr/dt$ = 8 π × 30 × 2 = 480 π.

41. Let the common ratio be = x
Then, length = $4x$, breadth = $3x$ and height = $2x$
As per question;
$2(4x \cdot 3x + 3x \cdot 2x + 2x \cdot 4x) = 8788$
$2(12x^2 + 6x^2 + 8x^2) = 8788 \Rightarrow 52x^2 = 8788$
$\Rightarrow x = 13$
Length = $4x$ = 52 cm

42. The total volume will remain the same, let the side of the resulting cube be = a. Then,
$$6^3 + 8^3 + 10^3 = a^3 \Rightarrow a = \sqrt[3]{1728} = 12 \text{ cm}$$

43. Slant length $= l = \sqrt{6^2 + 8^2} = 10$ cm
Then curved surface area = $\pi rl = \pi \times 6 \times 10 \Rightarrow 60\pi$
And total surface area = $\pi rl + \pi r^2 \Rightarrow \pi((6 \times 10) + 6^2)$ = $96\pi\ \text{cm}^2$

44. Volume of a cone $= \frac{\pi r^2 h}{3}$
Then, $100\pi = \frac{\pi r^2 \cdot 12}{3} \Rightarrow r = 5$ cm
Curved surface area = πrl
$$l = \sqrt{h^2 + r^2} \Rightarrow \sqrt{12^2 + 5^2} = 13$$
Then, $\pi rl = \pi \times 13 \times 5 = 65\pi\ \text{cm}^2$

45. Let the radius of the two cones be = x cm
Let slant height of first cone = 5 cm and
Slant height of second cone = 7 cm
Then, ratio of covered surface area $= \frac{\pi \times 5}{\pi \times 7}$ = 5: 7

46. Radius $= \frac{\pi rl}{\pi l} = \frac{2376}{3.14 \times 18} = 42$ cm
Diameter = 2 × Radius = 2 × 42 = 84 cm

47. Let the radius of cylinder = 1(r)
Then the radius of cone be = 2(R)

Then, as per question = $\dfrac{\pi r^2 h}{\dfrac{\pi R^2 h}{3}} \Rightarrow \dfrac{3\pi r^2 h}{\pi R^2 h}$

$\Rightarrow \dfrac{3r^2}{R^2} \Rightarrow 3: 4$

48. The perimeter will remain the same in any case.
Let one side of a square be = a cm
Then, $a^2 = 484 \Rightarrow a = 22$ cm $\therefore$ perimeter $= 4a = 88$ cm
Let the radius of the circle be = r cm
Then, $2\pi r = 88 \Rightarrow r = 14$ cm
Then, area = $\pi r^2 = 616$ cm^2

49. Let the radius of the circle be = r
Then, $2\pi r - 2r = 16.8 \Rightarrow r = 3.92$ cm
Then, $2\pi r = 24.64$ cm

50. Let the radius of the wheel be = r
Then $5000 \times 2\pi r = 1100000$ cm $\Rightarrow r = 35$ cm

51. Let the rise in height be = h
Then, as per the question, the volume of water should be equal in both the cases.
Now, $90 \times 40 \times h = 150 \times 8$

$$h = \frac{150 \times 8}{90 \times 40} = \frac{1}{3} \text{ m} = \frac{100}{3} \text{ cm}$$
$= 33.33$ cm

52. Slant height (l) = $\sqrt{7^2 + 24^2} = 25$ m
Area of cloth required = curved surface area of cone
$= \pi rl = \dfrac{22}{7} \times 7 \times 25 = 550$ m^2

Amount of cloth required = $\dfrac{550}{5} = 110$ m

53. If the ratio of their diameters = 2 : 1, then the ratio of their radii will also be = 2 : 1
Let the radii of the broader cone = 2 and height be = 1
Then the radii of the smaller cone = 1 and height be = 2

Ratio of volumes = $\dfrac{\pi 2^2 \cdot 1}{3} \div \dfrac{\pi 1^2 \cdot 2}{3}$

$\dfrac{4\pi}{3} \times \dfrac{3}{2\pi} \Rightarrow 2: 1$

54. Area of base = $6 \times 10 = 60$ m^2
Volume of tent = $30 \times 10 = 300$ m^3
Let the radius be = r, height = h, slant height = l
$\pi r^2 = 60 \Rightarrow r = \sqrt{\dfrac{60}{\pi}}$

$300 = \dfrac{\pi r^2 h}{3} \Rightarrow 900 = \pi \cdot \dfrac{60}{\pi} \cdot h \Rightarrow h = 15$ m

55. Volume of wood used = External volume – Internal volume
$\Rightarrow (10 \times 8 \times 6) - (10 - 1) \times (8 - 1) \times (6 - 1)$
$\Rightarrow 480 - (9 \times 7 \times 5) = 165$ cubic cm.

56. Total volume in both the objects will be equal. Let the number of smaller cubes = x

$x \cdot 3^3 = 24 \times 9 \times 8 \Rightarrow x = \dfrac{24 \times 72}{27} = 64$

57. Let one side of the cube = a
Then, $a^3 = 216 \Rightarrow a = 6$ m
Area of the resultant figure
= Area of all three cubes – Area of covered figure
$\Rightarrow 216 \times 3 - (4 \times a^2) \Rightarrow 648 - 144 \Rightarrow 504$ m^2

58. Volume of metal used = $\dfrac{4\pi R^3}{3} - \dfrac{4\pi r^3}{3}$
$= \dfrac{4\pi}{3}(12^3 - 10^3)$
$= 3050.66$ cm^3
Weight = volume × density $\Rightarrow 4.9 \times 3050.66$
$\Rightarrow 14948.26$

59. Volume of cube = $7^3 = 343$ cm^3
Radius of cone = $\dfrac{7}{2} = 3.5$ cm
Height of cone = 7 cm

Ratio of volumes = $\dfrac{\dfrac{\pi r^2 h}{3}}{343} = \dfrac{22 \times 3.5 \times 3.5 \times 7}{7 \times 3 \times 343}$

$\Rightarrow 11:42$

60. The volume in both the cases will be equal. Let the height of cone be = h

$$4 \times \frac{22}{7} \times (14)^3 \times \frac{1}{3} = \frac{22}{7} \times \left(\frac{35}{2}\right)^2 \times \frac{h}{3}$$

$$\Rightarrow \quad 4(14)^3 = h\left(\frac{35}{2}\right)^2 = h$$

$$= \frac{4 \times 14 \times 14 \times 14 \times 2 \times 2}{35 \times 35}$$

$= h = 35.84$ cm

61. Diameter of circle = diagonal of square
$= \sqrt{10^2 + 10^2} = \sqrt{200} = 10\sqrt{2}$

$\therefore$ Radius = $\dfrac{10\sqrt{2}}{2} = 5\sqrt{2}$

Area of circle = $\pi r^2 \Rightarrow 50\pi = 157.14$ cm^2

62. Area of triangle = rS; where r = in-radius

$S = \dfrac{15 + 8 + 17}{2} = 20$ cm

$\Delta = \sqrt{S(S-a)(S-b)(S-c)}$

$\Rightarrow \Delta \sqrt{20(20-15)(20-8)(20-17)}$

$\Delta = \sqrt{20 \times 5 \times 12 \times 3} = 60$ cm^2

$r = \dfrac{\Delta}{S} = \dfrac{60}{20} = 3$ cm

63. Circumference of the circular face of the cylinder
$= 2\pi r$

$\Rightarrow 2 \times \frac{22}{7} \times \frac{35}{100} = 2.2$ m

Number of revolutions required to lift the bucket by $11\,\text{m} = \frac{11}{2.2} = 5$

64. Surface area of the cube $= 6a^2 = 6 \times (20)^2$
$= 2400$

Area of six circles of radius 10 cm $= 6\pi r^2$
$= 6 \times \pi \times 100$
$= 1885.71$

Remaining area $= 2400 - 1885.71 = 514.28$

65. $x \cdot y \cdot z \quad = lb \times bh \times lh = (lbh)^2$
(V) Volume of a cuboid $= lbh$
So, $\quad V^2 = (lbh)^2 = xyz$

66. Diameter of the circle = diagonal of rectangle
$= \sqrt{8^2+6^2} = 10$ cm

Radius $= \frac{10}{2} = 5$ cm

Area of shaded portion $= \pi r^2 - lb$
$= (22/7) \times 5^2 - 8 \times 6$
$= 30.57$ cm^2

67. Larger radius (R) = 14 + 7 = 21 cm
Smaller radius (r) = 7 cm

Area of shaded portion $\pi R^2 \frac{\theta}{360} - \frac{\pi r^2\theta}{360}$

$\Rightarrow \frac{\pi\theta}{360}(21^2 - 7^2) \Rightarrow 102.67$ cm

68. Area of quadrilateral = Area of right angled triangle + Area of equilateral triangle $x = \sqrt{20^2 - 12^2} = 16$

Area of quadrilateral $= \left(\frac{1}{2}\times 16 \times 12\right) + \frac{\sqrt{3}}{4} \times 20 \times 20$

$= 269$ units^2

69. Height $= \sqrt{24^2 - 13^2} = \sqrt{407}$

Volume $= \frac{\text{Area of base} \times \text{height}}{3} \Rightarrow \frac{18 \times 26 \times \sqrt{407}}{3}$

$\Rightarrow 156\sqrt{407}$

70. The perimeter will remain the same in both cases.

Circumference of circle $= 2\pi r = 2 \times \frac{22}{7} \times 28 = 176$ cm
Perimeter of square = 176

Greatest side possible $= \frac{176}{4} = 44$ cm

Length of diagonal $= \sqrt{44^2 + 44^2}$

$= \frac{88}{2} \cdot \sqrt{2} = 44\sqrt{2}$

Level of Difficulty (II)

1. Radius $= \frac{3.5}{2} = 1.75$ cm

Volume of solid $= \pi r^2 h + \frac{\pi r^2 h}{3} + \frac{2\pi r^3}{3}$

$\Rightarrow \pi r^2\left(h + \frac{h}{3} + \frac{r}{3}\right)$

$\Rightarrow 3.14 \times (1.75)^2 \times \left(10 + \frac{6}{3} + \frac{1.75}{3}\right)$

$\Rightarrow 121$ cm^3

2. Area of shaded portion = area of quadrant – area of triangle

$\Rightarrow \frac{\pi r^2}{4} - \frac{1}{2} \times 3.5 \times 2 = \frac{3.14 \times (3.5)^2}{4} - 3.5$

$\Rightarrow 6.125$ cm^2

3. ABC is an equilateral triangle with sides = 2 cm
Area of shaded portion = Area of equilateral triangle –Area of three quadrants

$\Rightarrow$ i.e. $\frac{\sqrt{3}}{4}a^2 - 3\left(\pi r^2 \frac{\theta}{360}\right)$; $\theta = 60°$ (Since ΔABC is an equilateral triangle)

$\Rightarrow \frac{\sqrt{3}}{4} \times 2^2 - 3\left(3.14 \times 1 \times \frac{60}{360}\right)$

$\Rightarrow \sqrt{3} - \frac{3.14}{2} = \sqrt{3} - \frac{\pi}{2}$

4. Volume of elliptical cylinder =
$\pi\left(\frac{2.4}{2}\right)\left(\frac{1.6}{2}\right).7 = 21.12$ m^3

Amount of water emptied per minute =
$\pi\left(\frac{2}{100}\right)^2 120$ m^3

Time required to empty half the tank =
$$\frac{\frac{21.12}{2}}{\pi\left(\frac{2}{100}\right)^2 120} = 70 \text{ min}$$

5. 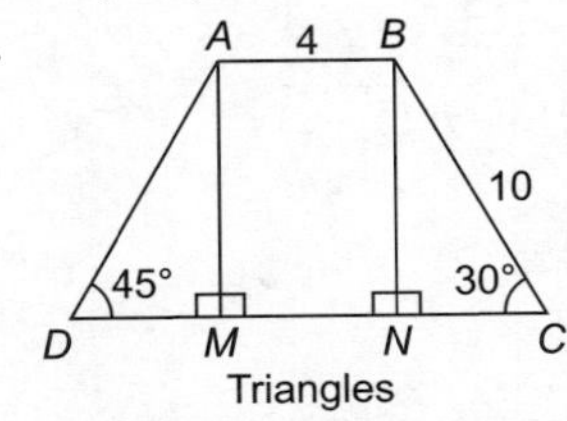

Triangles

AB and DC are the parallel sides
Height $= AM = BN$
$AB = MN = 4$

ΔBNC and ΔAMD are right-angled triangles

In $\Delta BNC \Rightarrow \sin 30 = \frac{BN}{10} \Rightarrow BN = 5$

Using Pythagoras theorem, $NC = \sqrt{10^2 - 5^2} = 5\sqrt{3}$

In ΔADM; $AM = 5$; $\tan 45 = \frac{AM}{DM} = 1 = \frac{5}{DM}$

$\Rightarrow \quad DM = 5$

Area of trapezium $\Rightarrow \frac{1}{2}$ (Sum of parallel sides) × height

$\Rightarrow \frac{1}{2}(4 + 4 + 5\sqrt{3} + 5) \times 5 = \frac{5(13+5\sqrt{3})}{2}$

6. $PQ = QR = RS = \frac{12}{3} = 4$ cm

Area of unshaded region $\Rightarrow \frac{\pi 6^2}{2} + \frac{\pi 4^2}{2}$

$\Rightarrow 18\pi + 8\pi \Rightarrow 26\pi$

Area of shaded region $\Rightarrow \frac{\pi 6^2}{2} - \frac{\pi 4^2}{2}$

$\Rightarrow 18\pi - 8\pi = 10\pi$

Ratio $= \frac{10\pi}{26\pi} \Rightarrow \frac{5}{13} \Rightarrow 5: 13$

7. $QP = \sqrt{5^2 + 12^2} = 13$

Area of the triangle $= \frac{1}{2} \times b \times h = 30$

$\Rightarrow$ As Rx is $a \perp$ drawn to the hypotenuse

So $Rx = \frac{2 \times \text{Area}}{\text{Hypotenuse}} = \frac{60}{13}$

8. A fifty-percent increase in the radius without increasing the height will mean a multiplication of the radius by 1.5. This would mean that the volume would get multiplied by 1.5 × 1.5 (since the volume formula is $\pi r^2 h$).

9. Distance after four hours = $AB = C$

$a = 3 \times 4 = 12$; $b = 2 \times 4 = 8$

and $\frac{a+b+c}{2} \Rightarrow \frac{12+8+C}{2} \Rightarrow \left(10+\frac{C}{2}\right)$

Area $= \sqrt{S(S-a)(S-b)(S-c)}$

Area $= \frac{1}{2}ab \sin 120°$

Area $\Rightarrow 48 \times \frac{\sqrt{3}}{2} = 24\sqrt{3}$

As per question:

$24\sqrt{3} = \sqrt{\left(10+\frac{c}{2}\right)\left(\frac{c}{2}-2\right)\left(2+\frac{c}{2}\right)\left(10-\frac{c}{2}\right)}$

On solving, we get $c = 4\sqrt{19}$ km

10. Volume of the cone =

$\frac{\pi r^2 h}{3} = \frac{22 \times 20 \times 20 \times 24}{3 \times 7} = 10057.14 \text{ cm}^3$

Diameter of the pipe = 5 mm = 0.5 cm.

Volume of water flowing out of the pipe per minute (in cm^3) =

$1000 \times 0.25 \times 0.25 \times \pi = 196.42 \text{ cm}^3$

Hence, the time taken to fill the tank = 10057.14 ÷ 196.42 = 51.2 minutes.

11.

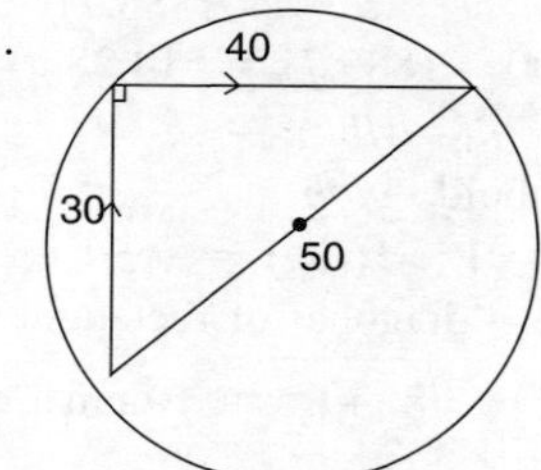

Radius of the circle $= \frac{1}{2}\left(\sqrt{(30^2 + 40^2}\right) = 25$ m

Area of the pool $= \pi (25)^2 = 625\ \pi\text{m}^2 = X\pi$

Therefore, $X = 625$

12.

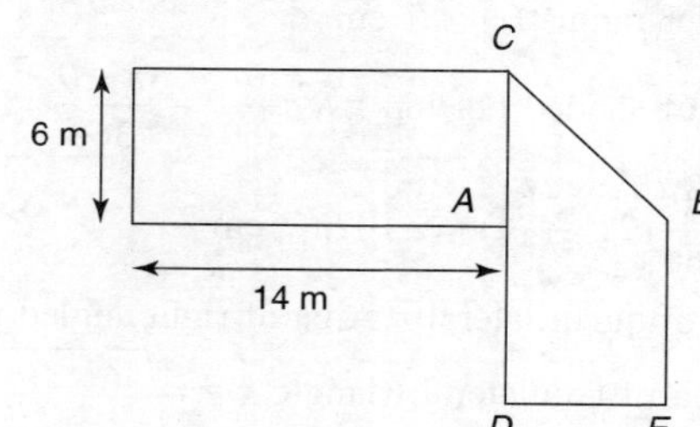

It can be seen from the diagram that actual area = folded area + area of triangular portion (ABC).

Area of triangular portion (ABC) $= \frac{1}{2} \times 6 \times 6 = 18 \text{ m}^2$

So, there is an increase of 18 m^2. Total area of the unfolded rectangle = 144 m^2 + 18 m^2 = 162 m^2.

13. Volume of cylinder= $\pi r^2 h = \pi \times 7^2 \times 10 = 1540 \text{ cm}^3$

Flat surface area of cylinder = $2\pi \times 7^2 = 308 \text{ cm}^2$

Cone 1: Volume= (3/7) × 1540 = 660 cm^3

Volume of cone = (1/3) $\pi r^2 h = 660$

$\Rightarrow (1/3)\pi r^2\ 10 = 660 \Rightarrow \pi r^2 = 66 \times 3 = 198 \text{ cm}^2$

Flat surface area= $\pi r^2 = 198 \text{ cm}^2$

Cone 2: Volume= (4/7) × 1540 = 880 cm^3

Volume of cone = (1/3) $\pi r^2 h = 880$

$\Rightarrow (1/3)\pi r^2\ 10 = 880 \Rightarrow \pi r^2 = 88 \times 3 = 264 \text{ cm}^2$

Final flat surface area = 198 + 264 cm^2 = 462 cm^2

Increase in flat surface area = 462 – 308 = 154 cm^2

Percentage increase = (154/308) × 100 = 50%

14. The following image explains the construction.

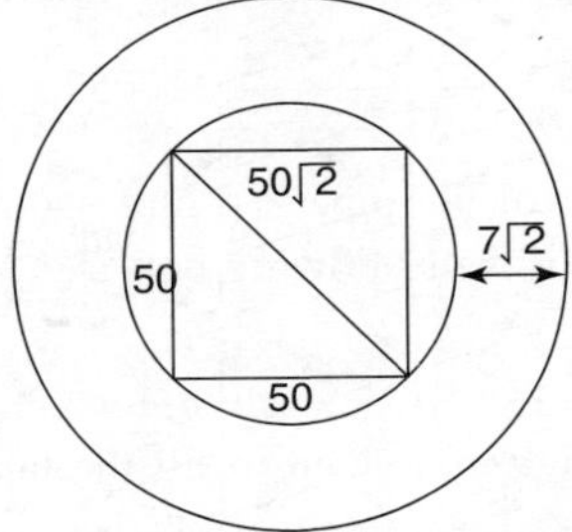

Radius of inner circle= (1/2) × 50 $\sqrt{2}$ ft. = 25 $\sqrt{2}$ ft.

Radius of outer circle = 32 $\sqrt{2}$ ft.

Area of the path = π × [(32 $\sqrt{2}$ ft.)^2 – (25 $\sqrt{2}$ ft.)^2] = 2508 ft^2

Total cost = 2508 × 100 = ₹250800

50% of this = ₹125400

15. The following figure would exemplify the situation, with the pipe attached at a height of h from the apex (bottom) of the cone.

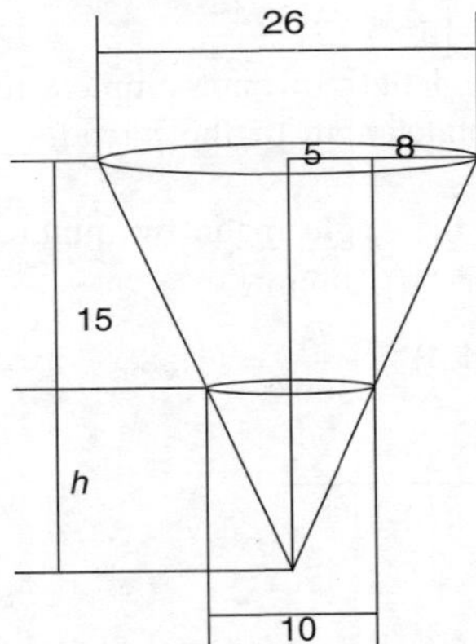

In the above figure, the cones with height h and the cone with height h + 15 are similar to each other. Hence, using similarity, we will get:

$$\frac{10}{26} = \frac{h}{h+15}$$

$\rightarrow 10h + 150 = 26h \rightarrow 16h = 150 \rightarrow h = 9.375$ cm

Based on this information, we can then calculate the volume of water that would flow out from the pipe as: total volume of the cone with height (h + 15) – volume of cone of height h.

$$= \frac{1}{3}\pi[(13^2 \times (15 + 9.375) - (5^2 \times 9.375)]$$

Calculating this, we get the volume of water that overflows = 1295 π cm^3.

Further, the rate at which the water flows out of the hole per minute is given by:

$\pi \times (0.5^2 \times 1000)$ cm^3

Hence, the required time can be given as,

$$\frac{1295\pi}{\pi \times (0.5^2 \times 1000)} = 5.18 \text{ minutes}$$

16. The given situation can be visualised based on the following figure:

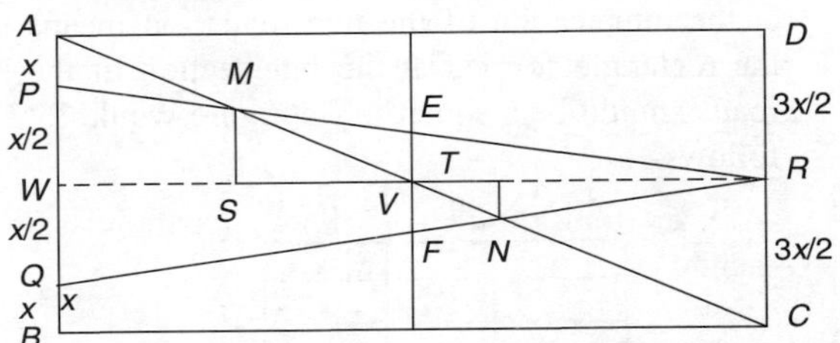

The area of the quadrilateral $PQNM$ = area of $PQFE$ – area triangle MVE + area triangle VFN.

So our focus to find the area of the required quadrilateral should shift to the area of the three individual components on the right-hand side of the above equation.

Finding the area of quadrilateral $PQFE$:

Being a parallelogram, the required area would be given by:

$\frac{1}{2} \times$ sum of parallel sides ×

perpendicular distance between the parallel sides.

In the figure, let side AB = $3x$ and side BC = y. Then, for the quadrilateral $PQFE$, the perpendicular distance between the parallel side will be $y/2$. Further, the sum of parallel sides would be equal to

$$PQ + EF = x + \frac{x}{2} = \frac{3x}{2}$$

Area of $PQFE$ = $\frac{1}{2} \times \frac{3x}{2} \times \frac{y}{2}$

We know that the area of the rectangle is $3x \times y$ = 90.

Hence, area of $PQFE$ = 90 ÷ 8 = 11.25.

Finding the area of the triangle MEV:

$$\frac{1}{2} \times \text{base} \times \text{height} = \frac{1}{2} \times EV \times \text{height}$$

Using similarity between APM and VEM, we can see that since $AP = x$ and $EV = x/4$, the ratios of the lengths of APM and VEM will be 4:1.

Thus, if the height of $APM = 4h$, the height of VEM = h and also $4h + h = y/2 \rightarrow h$ = height of VEM with base $VE = y/10$

Hence, area triangle MEV = $\frac{1}{2} \times EV \times \text{height}$ = $\frac{xy}{80}$ = 0.375

Similarly, the area of $\Delta VFN \approx 0.27$.

Thus, the required area = 11.25 – 0.375 + 0.27 ≈ 11.145.

17. Think of this question as follows:

The entire park is 1200 square meters. Out of this, the area of the road formed has to be 600 meters (based on the condition that 'the Mayor wants that the area of the two roads to be equal to the remaining area of the park'). Also, the width of all the roads should be equal (since, the diagonals of the parks have to be diagonals of the small rectangle formed at the intersection of the two roads - it means that the rectangle formed at the intersection of the two roads should be a square). The figure would look as follows:

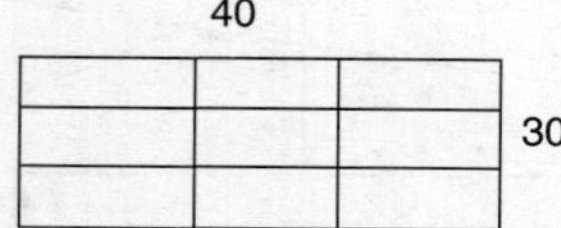

Using the options, we can see that if the road width is 10 meters, the areas covered by the roads will be 10 × 40 + 10 × 30 – 10 × 10 = 600, which will mean that exactly half the area of the park will be covered by roads.
Hence, option (a) is correct.

18. For every 2.6m that one walks along the slant part of the pool, there is a height of 1 m that is gained. Also, since the length of the pool is 48 m, we get the following dimensions of the pool.

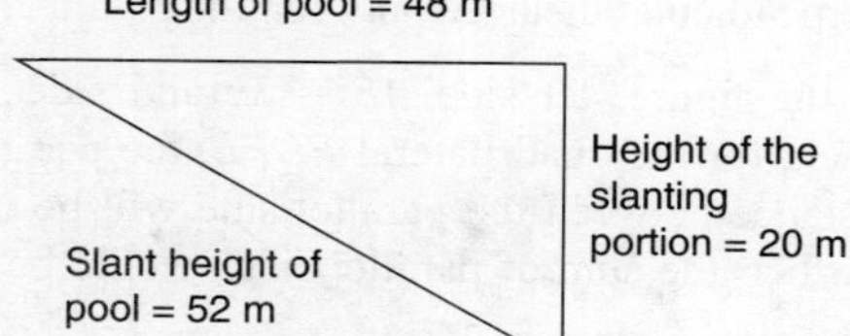

The pool would look as given in the figure below:

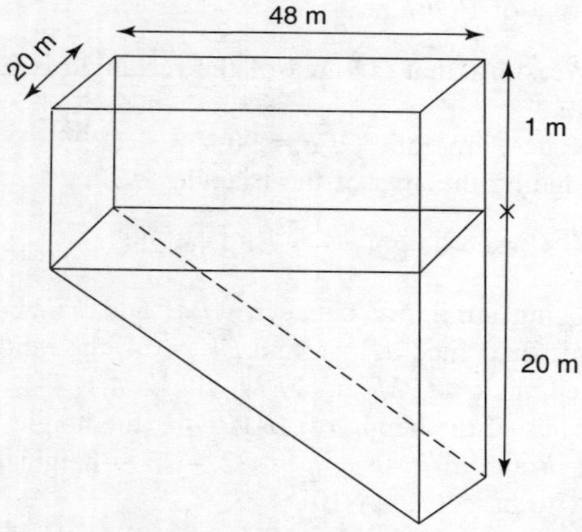

The volume of water in the pool = volume of the upper part + volume of the standard triangular vessel

$$=\left(\frac{1}{2}\times 48\times 20\right)\times 20+(48\times 20\times 1)$$

$$\Rightarrow 48\times 20\times 11 \Rightarrow 10560 \text{ m}^3$$

Hence, option (d) is the correct answer.

19.

2800 cm²

192/24 = 8

8

15

$$h=\frac{2\pi rh}{2\pi r}=\frac{2880}{15}=192 \text{ cm}$$

$$I=\sqrt{8^2+15^2}=17 \text{ cm}$$

Therefore, length of one complete turn = 17 cm
Hence, total length of the thread = 17 × 24 = 408 cm

20. Let θ be the angle made by minute-hand to cover an area of 110.88 cm^2.

$$\Rightarrow \frac{22}{7}\times(4.2)^2\times\frac{\theta}{360^\circ}=110.88$$

$$\theta=\frac{110.88\times 360^\circ\times 7}{22\times(4.2)^2}$$

$$\theta=720^\circ$$

As we know that speed of hour-hand is $\frac{1}{12}$ of the speed of minute-hand, therefore, angle covered by hour-hand during this period is $\frac{720^\circ}{12}=60^\circ$.

Area covered by hour-hand $=\pi(2.1)^2\times\frac{60^\circ}{360^\circ}$.

$$=\frac{22}{7}\times 2.1\times 2.1\times\frac{1}{6}$$

$$= 2.31 \text{ cm}^2$$

21. Let the angle subtended by the sector at the center be = θ.
Then,

$$5.7 + 5.7 + (2\pi)\times 5.7\times\frac{\theta}{360}=27.2$$

$$11.4+\frac{11.4\times 3.14\times\theta}{360}=27.2$$

$$\Rightarrow \frac{\theta}{360}=0.44$$

Area of the sector $= \pi r^2 \frac{\theta}{360} \Rightarrow (22/7) \times (5.7)^2 \times 0.44$

$= 44.92$ (approx.)

22. Volume of mud dug out $= 10 \times 4.5 \times 3 = 135 \text{ m}^3$
Let the remaining ground rise by $= h$ m
Then, $\{(20 \times 9) - (10 \times 4.5)\}h = 135$
$135h = 135 \Rightarrow h = 1$ m

23. Height of the cylinder $= 13 - 7 = 6$ cm
Radius of the cylinder and the hemisphere $= 7$ cm
Volume of the vessel = volume of cylinder + volume of hemisphere

$\Rightarrow \pi r^2 h + \frac{4\pi r^3}{3\times 2} \Rightarrow 3.14 \times (7)^2 \times 6 + \frac{4\times 3.14\times (7)^3}{3\times 2}$

$\Rightarrow 1642.6 \text{ cm}^3$

24.

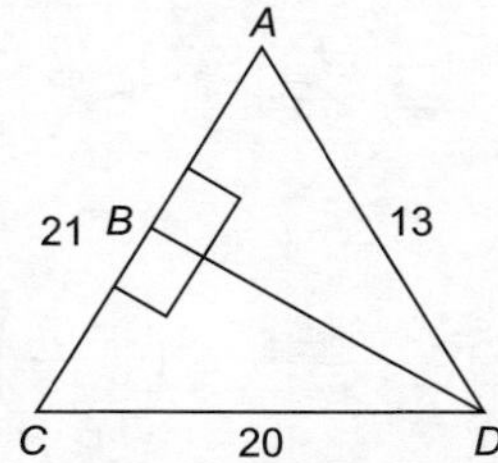

Let the original triangle be $= ACD$
Longest side $= AC = 21$cm
In the right angled ΔABD, by Pythagorean triplets, we get $AB = 5$ and $BD = 12$.
Then, $BC = 21 - 5 = 16$
By Pythagoras theorem,

$BD^2 = CD^2 - BC^2 \Rightarrow BD = 12$ cm

Thus, our assumption is correct.

Area of the larger $\Delta BDC = \frac{1}{2} \times 16 \times 12 \Rightarrow 96 \text{ cm}^2$

25. Radius = 52.5 m
Area of the entire canvas, used for the tent
= Surface area of cylinder + Surface area of cone
$= 2\pi rh + \pi rl$

$= -2 \times \frac{22}{7} \times 52.5 \times 3 + \frac{22}{7} \times 52.5 \times 53$

This surface area has to be equal to $5w \times$.

Thus, we have $5w = 2\times\frac{22}{7}\times 52.5\times 3+\frac{22}{7}\times 52.5\times 53$
$\rightarrow$ w = 1947

26. The volume in both the cases will be the same.

Therefore $= \frac{4\pi r^3}{3} = \pi r^2 h$

$\frac{4\times 3.14\times (4\times 10)^3}{3} = 3.14 \times 2^2 \times h$

$\Rightarrow \quad h = \frac{64000}{3} = 21333.33$ mm

27. As the cylinder and cone have equal diameters. So they have equal area. Let cone's height be h_2 and as per question, cylinder's height be h_1.

$$\frac{2\pi r h_1}{\pi r\sqrt{h_2^2 + r^2}} = \frac{8}{5}$$

On solving, we get the desired ratio as 4: 3

28. Let the slant height of first cone $= L$
Then the slant height of second cone $= 3L$
Let the radius of first cone $= r_1$
And let the radius of second cone $= r_2$
Then, $\quad \pi r_1 L = 3 \times \pi r_2 \times 3L$
$\Rightarrow \quad \pi r_1 L = 9\pi r_2 L \Rightarrow r_1 = 9r_2$
Ratio of area of the base

$$\frac{\pi r_1^2}{\pi r_2^2} \Rightarrow \left(\frac{r_1}{r_2}\right)^2 = \left(\frac{9}{1}\right)^2 \Rightarrow 81: 1$$

29. Let the internal radius of the cylinder $= r$
Then, the volume of sphere = volume of cylinder

$\Rightarrow \quad \frac{4\pi \cdot 6^3}{3} = \pi h(5^2 - r^2)$

$\Rightarrow \quad \frac{864\pi}{3} = 32\pi(25 - r^2)$

$\Rightarrow \quad r^2 = 16 \Rightarrow r = 4$ cm

So thickness of the cylinder $= 5 - 4 = 1$ cm

30. The volume in both the cases will be the same.
Let the height of the cone $= h$
Then, external radius $= 6$ cm
Internal radius $= 4$ cm

$\Rightarrow \quad \frac{4\pi(6^3 - 4^3)}{3} = \frac{\pi \cdot 4^2 \cdot h}{3}$

$\Rightarrow \quad h = \frac{6^3 - 4^3}{4} \Rightarrow h = \frac{216 - 64}{4} = 38$ cm

31.

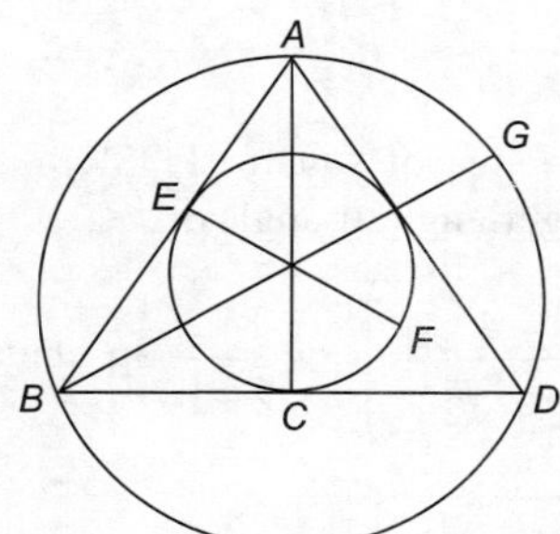

Let side of equilateral triangle $= a$

Then height $= \frac{a\sqrt{3}}{2}$

Area $= \frac{\sqrt{3}}{4}a^2$; $S = \frac{a+a+a}{2} = \frac{3a}{2}$

Diameter of inner circle $= \frac{2\times \text{Area}}{S}$

$$= \frac{\sqrt{3}}{2}a^2 \times \frac{2}{3a} = \frac{a}{\sqrt{3}}$$

$$\text{Diameter of outer circle} = \frac{a^3}{2 \times \text{Area}} = a^3 \times \frac{2}{\sqrt{3}a^2}$$

$$\Rightarrow \frac{2a}{\sqrt{3}}$$

$$\text{Ratio} = \frac{a}{\sqrt{3}} : \frac{2a}{\sqrt{3}} : \frac{a\sqrt{3}}{2} \Rightarrow \text{Ratio} = 2 : 4 : 3$$

32. Sum of interior angles of a hexagon = 720°
six sectors with same radius r = two full circles of same radius
So area of shaded region $\Rightarrow 2\pi r^2$

34. $AO = CO = DO = OB$ = radius of bigger circle = r(let)

Then area of $(G + F) = \frac{\pi r^2}{2}$

Area of $2(G + F) = \pi r^2$. Also area of $2G + F + E = \pi r^2$

i.e. $2G + F + F = 2G + F + E \Rightarrow F = E$

So the ratio of areas E and F = 1: 1

36. If Mithilesh cuts the cardboard as shown in the diagram below:

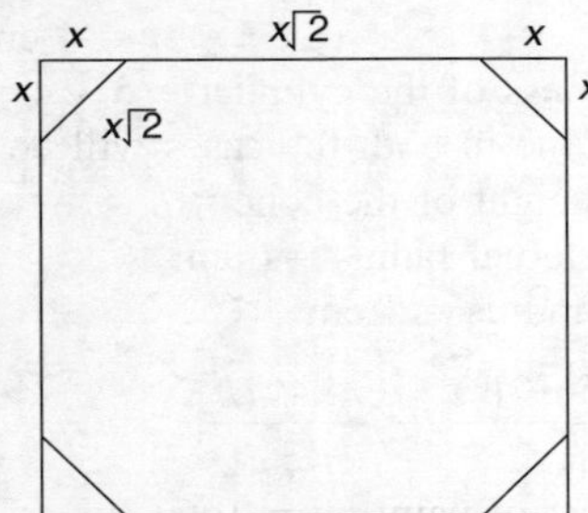

Length of the side of the square =

$$x\sqrt{2} + x + x = 2x + x\sqrt{2} = 2$$

$$x = \frac{2}{2+\sqrt{2}}$$

Reduced area = area of square (PQSR) – (sum of areas of four right-angle triangles)

$$= 4 - \left(4 \times \frac{1}{2} \times \frac{4}{(2+\sqrt{2})^2}\right) = \frac{8}{\sqrt{2}+1} \text{ Sq. units}$$

37.

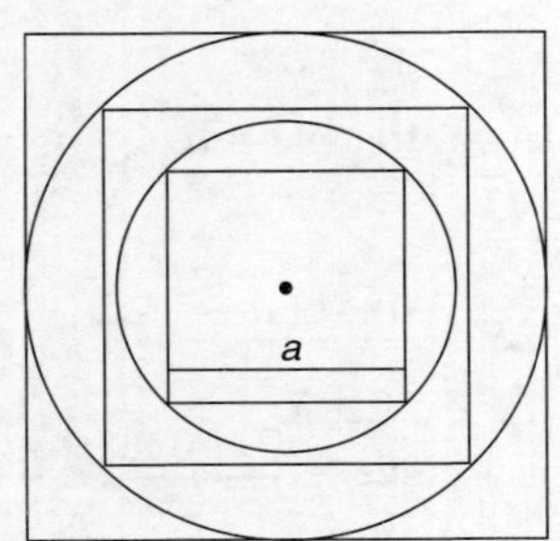

Let the radius of the circle be x, then according to the question:

$$x^2 + x^2 = a^2 \text{ or } x = \frac{a}{\sqrt{2}}$$

$$D_1 = \frac{\pi a^2}{2} - a^2$$

For A_2 and C_2:

$C_2 = \pi a^2$ and $A_2 = 2a^2$

$$D_2 = \pi a^2 - 2a^2 = 2\left(\frac{\pi}{2}a^2\right) = 2D_1$$

Similarly $D_3 = 4D_1$ and so on. Hence, $D_N = 2^{N-1}D_1$
Required ratio = $(D_1 + D_2 + D_3 + D_4 + \ldots D_N)/D_1$
$= (1 + 2 + 4 + \ldots + 2^{(N-1)})D_1/D_1 = (2^N - 1)/(2 - 1)$
$= (2^{12} - 1)$ (for $N = 12$).

38. $S_1 = Q_1 - P_2 = \frac{1}{2}(2r)^2 - \pi\left(\frac{r}{\sqrt{2}}\right)^2 = 2r^2 - \frac{\pi r^2}{2} = r^2\left(\frac{4-\pi}{2}\right)$

$$S_2 = Q_2 - P_3 = \frac{1}{2}(\sqrt{2}r)^2 - \frac{\pi r^2}{4} = r^2\left(\frac{4-\pi}{4}\right)$$

Required sum, $S_n = S_1 + S_2 + S_3 \ldots$
i.e. Sum of infinite GP having common ratio 1/2

$$S_n = \left(\frac{r^2\frac{(4-\pi)}{2}}{1-\frac{1}{2}}\right) = 2r^2\left(\frac{4-\pi}{2}\right) = r^2(4-\pi)$$

$$\text{Required ratio} = \frac{S_n}{Q_1} = \left(\frac{r^2(4-\pi)}{2r^2}\right) = \frac{4-\pi}{2}$$

By comparing we get $a = 4$, $b = 2$, therefore $a + b = 4 + 2 = 6$

39. Area of hexagon = area of six equilateral triangles having their side equal to the side of the hexagon

$$= 6 \times \frac{\sqrt{3}}{4} \times (2a)^2 = 6\sqrt{3}a^2$$

$$\text{Area of } PQR = \frac{\sqrt{3}}{4} \times a^2 = \frac{\sqrt{3}}{4}a^2$$

$$\text{Difference} = \sqrt{3}a^2\left(6 - \frac{1}{4}\right) = \frac{23}{4}\sqrt{3}a^2 = 23\sqrt{3}$$

$$\Rightarrow a^2 = \frac{4 \times 23\sqrt{3}}{23\sqrt{3}} \Rightarrow a^2 = 4$$

Now, we know for such circles circumscribed around a regular hexagon, the radius of the circle is equal to the side of the hexagon. Hence, the radius of the circle is $2a$.

Area of circle $= \pi r^2 = \pi(2a)^2 = 4\pi a^2 = 4\pi \times 4 = 16\pi$ cm^2 $\because a^2 = 4$.

Therefore, $X = 16$.

40. Side of the square S_3 = diagonal of the square S_2 = 4 cm
Side of a square is $\frac{1}{\sqrt{2}}$ times of its diagonal. So side of square $S_2 = \frac{4}{\sqrt{2}}$ cm $= 2\sqrt{2}$ cm

Similarly side of square $S_1 = \frac{2\sqrt{2}}{\sqrt{2}}$ = 2 cm. This means that the sides of the consecutive squares form a geometric progression, with common ratio = $\sqrt{2}$ cm.
So side of $S_n = 2\left(\sqrt{2}\right)^{n-1} = 2^{\frac{n+1}{2}}$ cm

Side of $S_{11} = 2^{\frac{11+1}{2}} = 2^6 = 64$ cm

Area of the square = 64^2 = 4096 cm^2

41. Let the side of the cube be = a units
Total surface area of three cubes = $3 \times 6a^2$
$= 18a^2$
Total surface area of cuboid = $18a^2 - 4a^2 = 14a^2$

Ratio = $\frac{14a^2}{18a^2}$ = 7: 9

42. $A = 2(xy + yz + zx)$
$V = xyz$

$A/V = \frac{2(xy+yz+zx)}{xyz} = \frac{2}{z} + \frac{2}{x} + \frac{2}{y}$

$\Rightarrow 2\left(\frac{1}{x}+\frac{1}{y}+\frac{1}{z}\right)$

43. The entire dial of the clock $=360^0$
In 35 minutes, the hand would traverse 210^0 on the dial.
Hence, the required area $= \frac{210}{360} \times \pi \times 10 \times 10 = 183.33$ cm^2.

44. Let the radius of the bigger circle = R
Let the radius of the smaller circle = r
Then as per question; $R - r = 6$
Solving through options; only option (a) satisfies this condition.

45. Radius of cylinder, hemisphere and cone = 5 cm
Height of cylinder = 13 cm
Height of cone = 12 cm

Surface area of toy = $2\pi rh + \frac{4\pi r^2}{2} + \pi rL$

$L = \sqrt{h^2+r^2} = \sqrt{12^2+5^2} = 13$

Then $\Rightarrow$ (2 × 3.14 × 5 × 13) + (2 × 3.14 × 25) + (3.14 × 5 × 13) $\Rightarrow$ 770 cm^2

46. Height of cone = 10.2 – 4.2 = 6 cm

Volume of wood = $\frac{\pi r^2 h}{3} + \frac{4\pi r^3}{3\times 2}$

$\Rightarrow \frac{3.14\times(4.2)^2\times 6}{3} + \frac{4\times 3.14\times(4.2)^3}{3\times 2}$

$\Rightarrow$ 266 cm^3

47. Volume of cylindrical container= $\pi(6)^2 15$
Volume of one cone= volume of the cone + volume of hemispherical top = $\frac{1}{3}\pi r^2 4r + \frac{2}{3}\pi r^3 = 2\pi r^3$
(Where 'r' is the radius of the cone).
According to the question:

$10 \times 2\pi r^3 = \pi(6)^2 15$ or $r^3 = 27 \Rightarrow 2r = 2(27)^{\frac{1}{3}} = 6$ cm

Thus, option (a) is true.

48. Radius of cylinder and hemispheres = $\frac{7}{2}$ = 3.5 cm
Height of cylinder = 19 – (3.5 × 2) = 12 cm
Total surface area of solid = $2\pi rh + 4\pi r^2$
$\Rightarrow$ 2 × 3.14 × 3.5 × 12 + 4 × 3.14 × $(3.5)^2$
$\Rightarrow$ 418 cm^2

49. As they stand on the same base so their radius is also same.

Then; volume of cone = $\frac{\pi r^2 h}{3}$

Volume of hemisphere = $\frac{2\pi r^3}{3}$

Volume of cylinder = $\pi r^2 h$

Ratio = $\frac{\pi r^2 h}{3} : \frac{2\pi r^3}{3} : \pi r^2 h$

$\Rightarrow \frac{h}{3} : \frac{2r}{3} : h$

$\Rightarrow h : 2r : 3h$
Radius of a hemisphere = its height
So h: $2h$: $3h \Rightarrow$ 1 : 2 : 3

50. Total cost of painting = Total surface to be painted × 0.05 = {External Surface Area + Internal Surface area + Area of ring} ×0.05
= $\{2\pi R^2 + 2\pi r^2 + \pi(R^2 - r^2)\}$ × 0.05 = ₹96.28

51. One side of the equilateral triangle = diameter of cone.
Therefore radius of cone = $\frac{12}{2}$ = 6
Height of cone = height of equilateral triangle
Height of cone = $6\sqrt{3}$

Volume of cone = $\frac{\pi r^2 h}{3}$

$\Rightarrow \frac{\pi \times 6^2 \times 6\sqrt{3}}{3} = 72\sqrt{3}\pi$ cm^3

52. Let the radius of the iron ball = r_1;
Let the radius of the oak ball = r_0;
Since, the weight of iron is eight times the weight of oak the volume of the oak ball would need to be

eight times the volume of the iron ball for the same weight of the two balls.

Thus, we have:

$\frac{4\pi r_0^3}{3} = \frac{8 \times 4\pi r_1^3}{3} \rightarrow r_0 = 2r_1$

Hence, the diameter of the iron ball is half the diameter of the oak ball.

53.

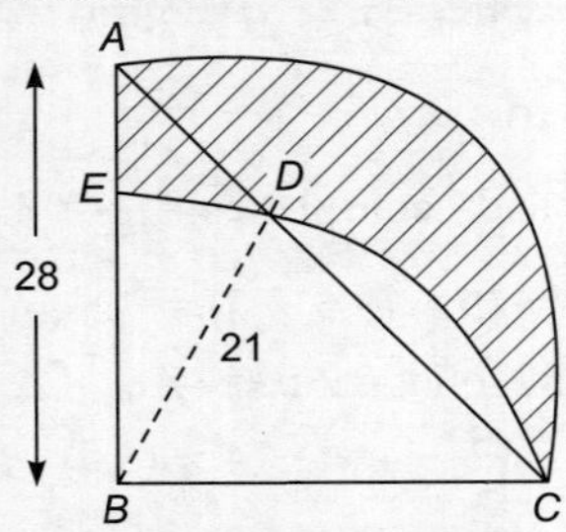

Area of shaded portion = area of ADC – area of sector DC + area of ΔADB – sector BED

$\Rightarrow$ Area of $ADC = \pi \times (17.5)^2 \times \frac{1}{2} = 481$ cm^2

$\frac{\angle DBC}{\angle ABC} = \frac{21}{28} \Rightarrow \angle DBC = 67.5$ and $\angle DBA = 22.5$

$\Rightarrow$ Area of sector $DC = \left(\pi \times 21^2 \times \frac{67.5}{360}\right)$

$- \left(\frac{1}{2} \times 21^2 \times \sin 67.5\right) = 56$ cm^2

$\Rightarrow$ Area of $ADE = \left(\frac{1}{2} \times 28 \times 21\right)$

$- \left(204 + \frac{1}{2} \times 21^2 \times \sin 22.5\right) = 5.6$ cm^2

Thus, area of shaded portion = 480 – 56 + 5.6 = 429 cm^2

54.

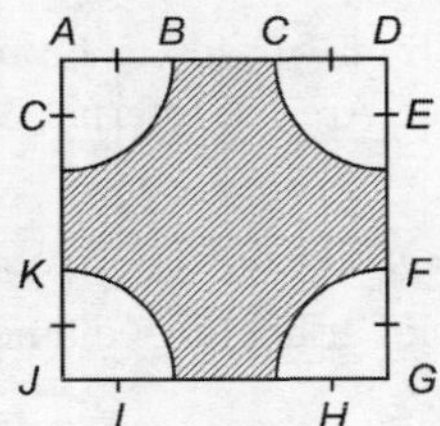

KJ = radius of semicircles = 10 cm

Four quadrants of equal radius = 1 circle of that radius

Area of shaded portion $\Rightarrow$ area of rectangle – area of circle

$\Rightarrow (28 \times 26) - (3.14 \times 10^2) \Rightarrow 414$ cm^2

$BC = 28 - (10 + 10) = 8$ and $EF = 26 - (10 + 10) = 6$

Perimeter of shaded portion = 28 cm + $2\pi r$

Answer $\Rightarrow$ 414 cm^2 = area and

perimeter = 90.8 cm

55. Go through the option

Only option (b) is correct as it's area matches with the radius.

56. Area of remaining cardboard = area of trapezium – area of quadrant

$\Rightarrow$ Area of trapezium = $\frac{1}{2}$(sum of parallel sides) × height

$= \frac{1}{2} \times (AB + DC) \times BC$

$\Rightarrow \frac{1}{2} \times (3.5 + 5.5) \times 3.5$

$= 4.5 \times 3.5 = 15.75$ cm^2

Area of quadrant = $\frac{\pi r^2}{4} \Rightarrow \frac{3.14 \times 3.5 \times 3.5}{4} = 9.625$

$\Rightarrow$ Area of remaining cardboard = 15.7 – 9.6 = 6.075 cm^2

57. Circumference of the two semicircles = 312 – (90 + 90) = 132

Two semicircles = one circle with equal radius

So $2\pi r = 132 \Rightarrow 2r = \frac{132}{3.14} \Rightarrow 42$ m diameter

Area of track = Area within external border – Area within internal border

$\Rightarrow \pi(23^2 - 21^2) + 90 \times 46 - 90 \times 42$

$\Rightarrow 88\pi + 360 \Rightarrow 636.57$ m^2

58.

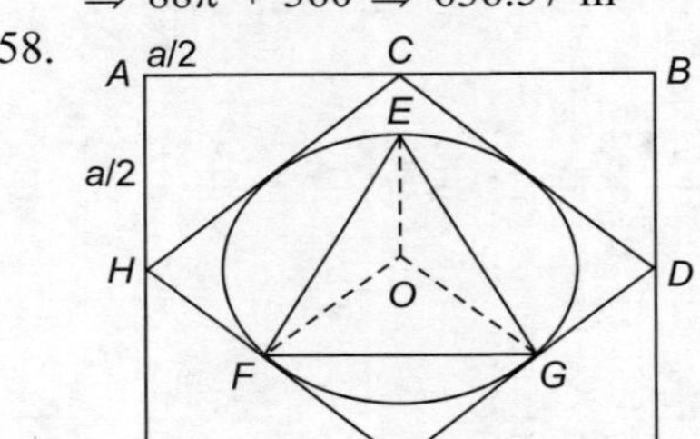

AB = side of the outermost square = a

$AC = CB = a/2$

$HC = \sqrt{\frac{a^2}{4} + \frac{a^2}{4}} = \frac{a}{\sqrt{2}}$

Diameter of circle = $\frac{a}{\sqrt{2}}$; radius = $\frac{a}{2\sqrt{2}}$

O is the center of the circle. Then $\angle EOF = 120°$

Then area of $\Delta EOF = \frac{1}{2} EO \cdot OF \cdot \sin 120°$

$\Rightarrow \quad \frac{1}{2} \times \frac{a^2}{8} \times \frac{\sqrt{3}}{2} = \frac{\sqrt{3}a^2}{32}$

Then, area of $\Delta EFG = \frac{3\sqrt{3}a^2}{32}$

59.

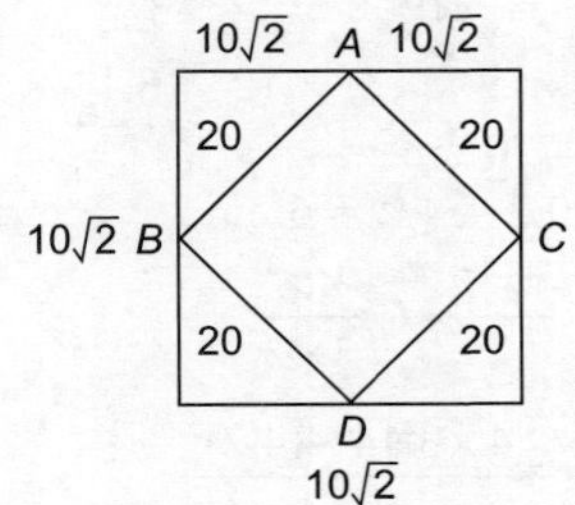

The length of rope of goat = $10\sqrt{2}$ m.
Then the two goats will graze an area = area of a semicircle with radius $10\sqrt{2}$ m.

So total area grazed = $\frac{\pi r^2}{2} \Rightarrow 100\pi$ m^2

60.

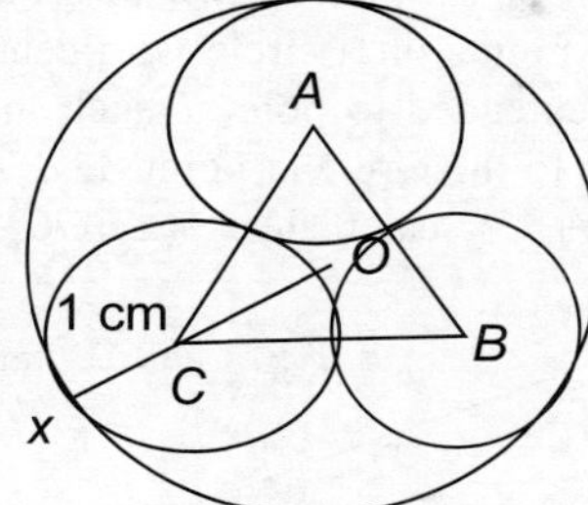

Let A, B, C be centers of circles having radius 1 cm and O is the center of the circle circumscribing these three circles.

$AC = AB = BC = 2$ cm

By using the formula of the circum-radius, we can calculate OC.

$$OC = \frac{2 \times 2 \times 2}{4 \times \frac{\sqrt{3}}{4}(2)^2} = 2/\sqrt{3}$$

$$OX = OC + CX = \frac{2}{\sqrt{3}} + 1\text{ cm}$$

Required area= $\pi\left(\frac{2}{\sqrt{3}}+1\right)^2 = \frac{\pi}{3}\left(2+\sqrt{3}\right)^2$ cm^2.

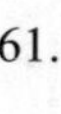

61.

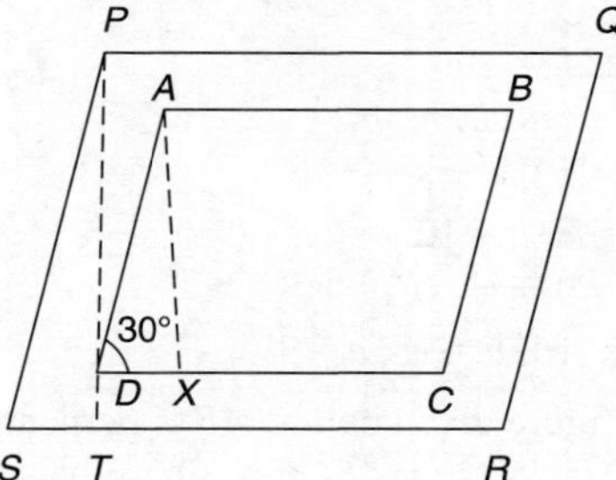

Draw $AX \perp DC$

$AX = 10 \sin 30° = 5$ m

If $PT \perp SR$

$PT = 5 + 2 + 2 = 9$ m

$$PS = \frac{PT}{\sin 30°} = \frac{9}{1/2} = 18 \text{ m}$$

Area of the path = area of $PQRS$ – area of $ABCD$

(Using area of rhombus = base × height)

= 18 × 9 – (10 × 5)

= 162 – 50 = 112 m^2

62. Area of $\square ABCD = 1$

Area of portion between $ABCD$ and $PQRS$ = $\frac{3}{2} - 1$

$= \frac{1}{2}$

Area of the next portion (between $PQRS$ and $XYZW$)

$= \frac{7}{4} - \frac{3}{2} = \frac{1}{4}$

Area of the next portion = $\frac{15}{8} - \frac{7}{4} = \frac{1}{8}$

So the required area is the sum of the infinite geometric progression represented by: $1 + \frac{1}{2} + \frac{1}{4} + \frac{1}{8} + \ldots$

$$= \frac{1}{1 - \frac{1}{2}} = 2$$

63. If side of the smallest hexagon is 'a' and the side of the second largest and largest hexagons are b and c respectively. Then according to the question:

$$\frac{3\sqrt{3}}{2}a^2 = A_1$$

$$\frac{3\sqrt{3}}{2}b^2 = A_1 + A_2 = 3A_1$$

$$\frac{3\sqrt{3}}{2}c^2 = A_1 + A_2 + A_3 = 6A_1$$

$$a^2 : b^2 : c^2 = 1 : 3 : 6$$

$$a : b : c = 1 : \sqrt{3} : \sqrt{6}$$

Space for Rough Work

EXTRA PRACTICE EXERCISE ON GEOMETRY AND MENSURATION

1. In the figure given what is the measure of $\angle ACD$?

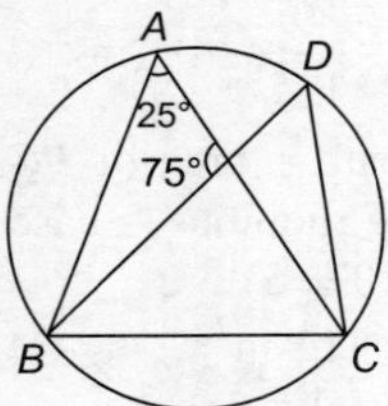

(a) 75° (b) 80°
(c) 90° (d) 105°

2. Two circles C_1 and C_2 of radius 2 and 3 respectively touch each other as shown in the figure. If AD and BD are tangents then the length of BD is

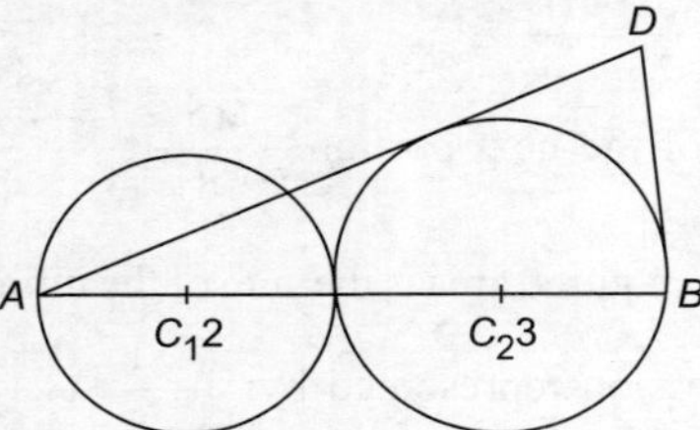

(a) $3\sqrt{6}$ (b) $5\sqrt{6}$
(c) $(3\sqrt{10})/2$ (d) 6

3. If the sides of a triangle measure 13, 14, 15 cm respectively, what is the height of the triangle for the base side 14?
(a) 10 (b) 12
(c) 14 (d) 13

4. A right-angled triangle is drawn on a plane such that sides adjacent to right angle are 3 cm and 4 cm. Now three semi-circles are drawn taking all three sides of the triangle as diameters respectively (as shown in the figure). What is the area of the shaded regions $A_1 + A_2$?

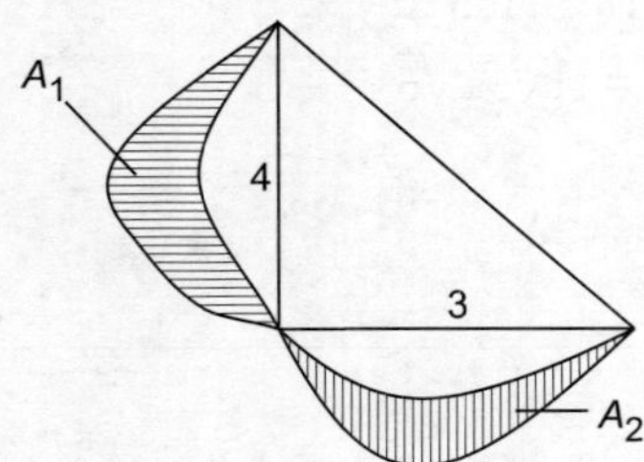

(a) 3π (b) 4π
(c) 5π (d) None of these

5. A lateral side of an isosceles triangle is 15 cm and the altitude is 8 cm. What is the radius of the circumscribed circle?
(a) 9.625 (b) 9.375
(c) 9.5 (d) 9.125

6. Let a, b, c be the length of the sides of triangle ABC. Given $(a + b + c)(b + c - a) = \alpha bc$. Then the value of α will lie in between
(a) -1 and 1 (b) 0 and 4
(c) 0 and 1 (d) 0 and 2

7. In the figure given below (not drawn to scale). A, B and C are three points on a circle with center O. The chord BC is extended to point T such that AT becomes a tangent to the circle at point A. If $\angle CTA = 35°$ and $\angle CAT = 45°$. calculate $x°$ ($\angle BOC$).

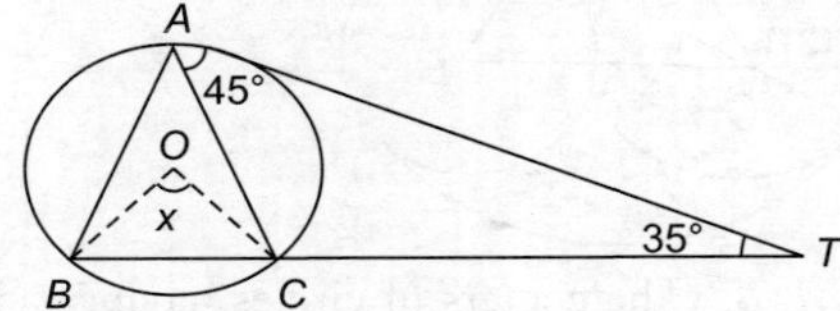

(a) 100° (b) 90°
(c) 110° (d) 65°

8. In the given figure.

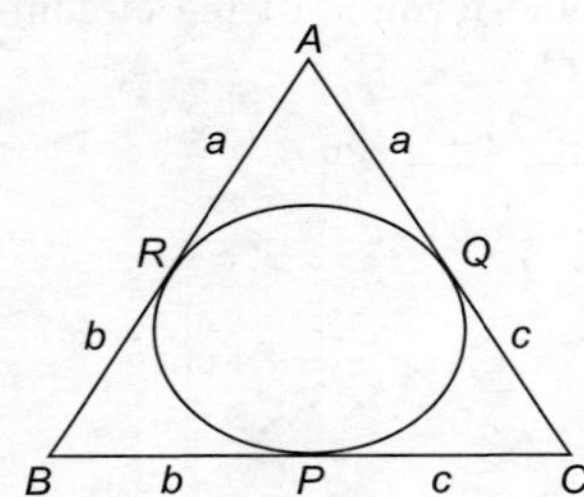

$AB = 20$
$BC = 15$
$CA = 19$

Calculate a, b, c.
(a) $a = 12, b = 8, c = 7$
(b) $a = 8, b = 12, c = 7$
(c) $a = 9, b = 10, c = 15$
(d) $a = 10, b = 15, c = 9$

9. In the figure given below, AB is perpendicular to ED. $\angle CED = 75°$ and $\angle ECF = 30°$. What is the measure of $\angle ABC$?

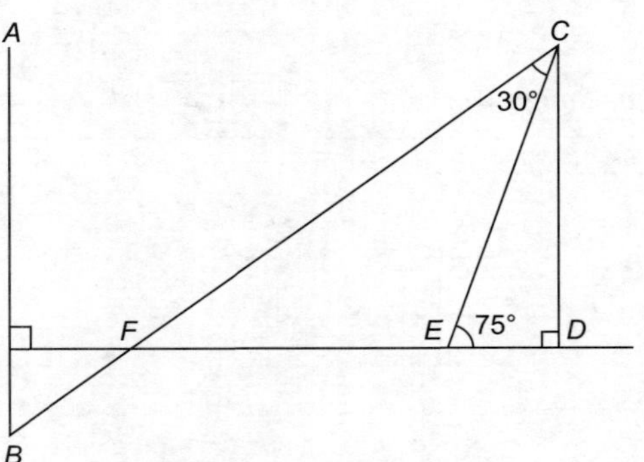

(a) 60° (b) 45°
(c) 55° (d) 30°

10. The angle between lines L and M measures 35° degrees. If line M. is rotated 45° degrees counter clockwise about point P to line M^1 what is the angle in degrees between lines L and M^1?

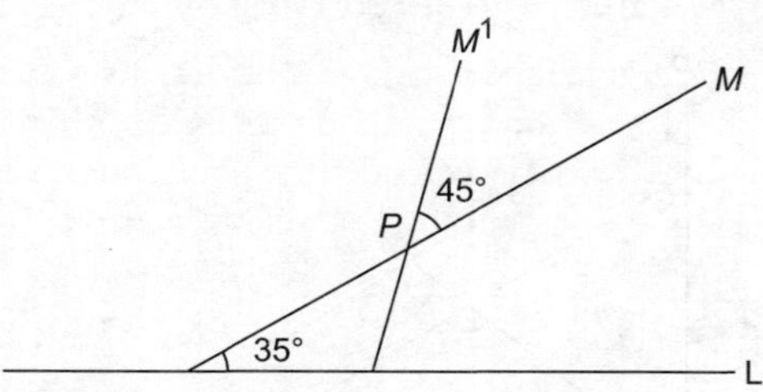

(a) 90° (b) 80°
(c) 75° (d) 60°

11. In the figure given below, XYZ is a right-angled triangle in which $\angle Y = 45°$ and $\angle X = 90°$. $ABCD$ is a square inscribed in it whose area is 64 cm^2. What is the area of triangle XYZ?

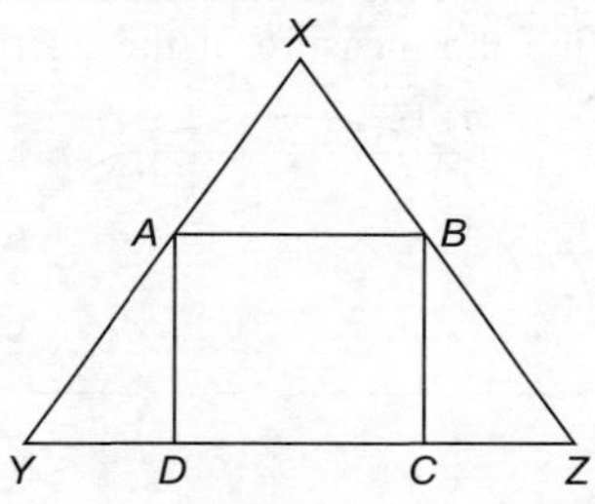

(a) 100 (b) 64
(c) 144 (d) 81

12. The area of circle circumscribed about a regular hexagon is 144π. What is the area of hexagon?
(a) $300\sqrt{3}$ (b) $216\sqrt{3}$
(c) 256 (d) 225

13. Find the area of the shaded portion.

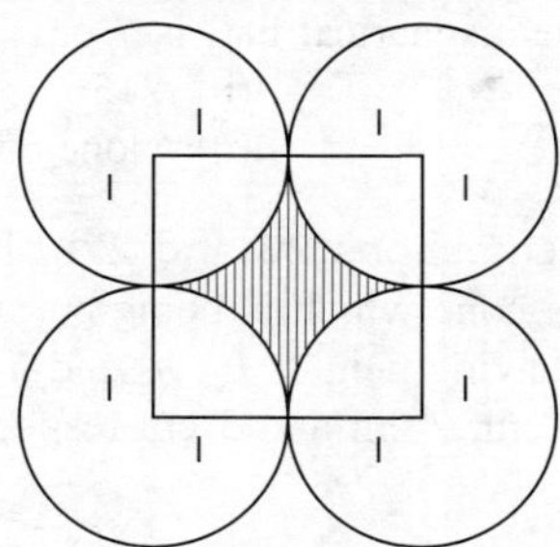

(a) $4 - \pi$ (b) $6 - \pi$
(c) $5 - \pi$ (d) π

14. The numerical value of the product of the three sides (which are integers when measured in cm) of a right-angled triangle having a perimeter of 56 cm is 4200. Find the length of the hypotenuse.
(a) 24 (b) 25
(c) 15 (d) 30

15. In the figure, $ABDC$ is a cyclic quadrilateral with O as center of the circle. Find $\angle BDC$.

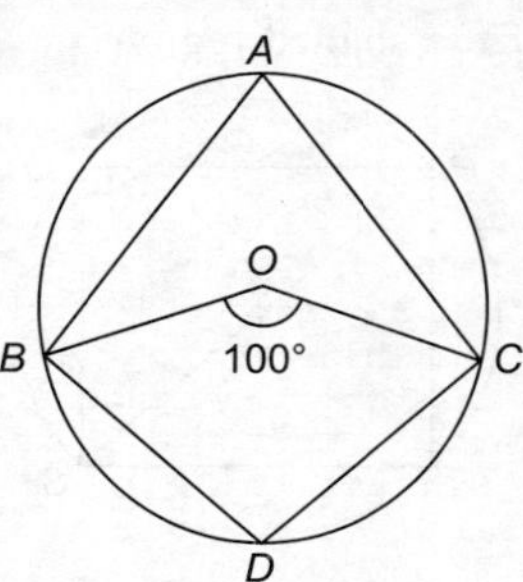

(a) 105° (b) 120°
(c) 130° (d) 95°

16. B, O, and P are centers of semicircles AXC, AYB and BZC respectively and AC = 12 cm. Find the area of the shaded region.

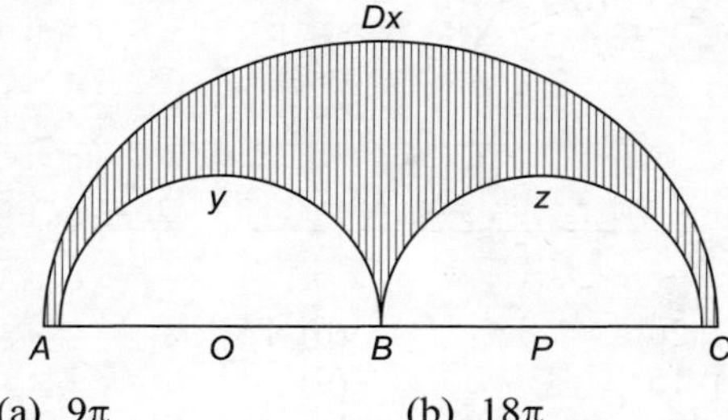

(a) 9π (b) 18π
(c) 20π (d) 25π

17. O is the center of the circle. OP = 5 and OT = 4, and AB = 8. The line PT is a tangent to the circle. Find PB.

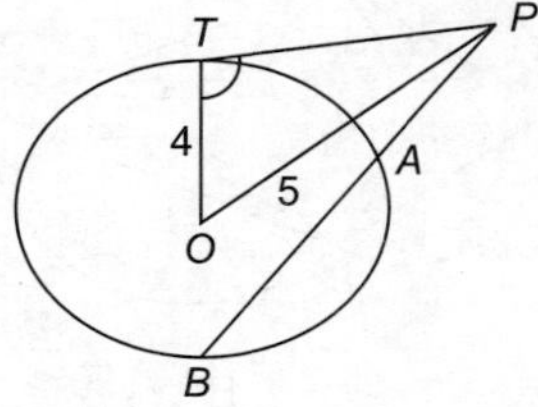

(a) 9 cm (b) 10 cm
(c) 7 cm (d) 8 cm

18. In the figure given below, AB = 16, CD = 12 and OM = 6. Calculate ON.

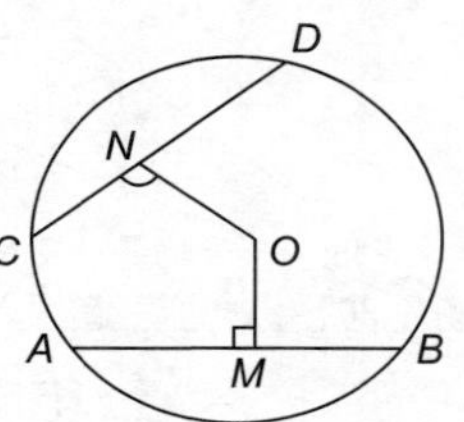

(a) 8 (b) 10
(c) 12 (d) 14

19. In the figure, M is the center of the circle. $L(QS) = 10\sqrt{2}$, $L(PR) = L(RS)$ and PR is parallel to QS. Find the area of the shaded region.

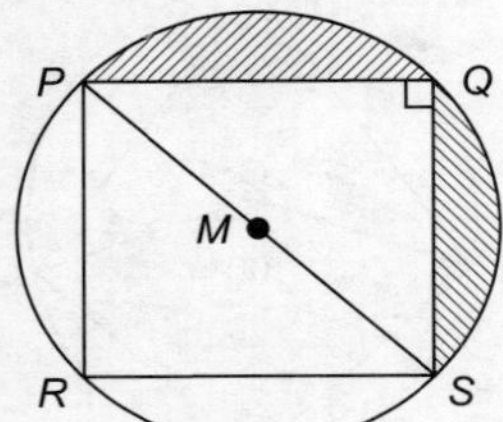

(a) $90\pi - 90$ (b) $50\pi - 100$
(c) $150\pi - 150$ (d) $125\pi - 125$

20. In the given figure PBC and PKH are straight lines. If $AH = AK$, $b = 70°$, $c = 40°$, the value of d is

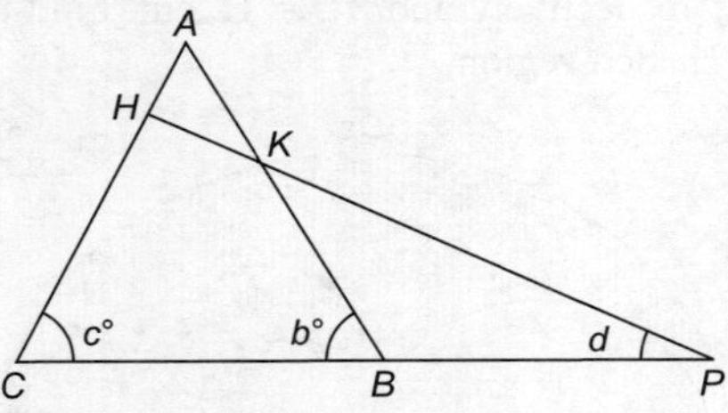

(a) 20° (b) 25°
(c) 15° (d) 35°

21. In the given figure, circle AXB passes through 'O', the center of circle AYB. AX and BX and AY and BY are tangents to the circles AYB and AXB respectively. The value of $y°$ is

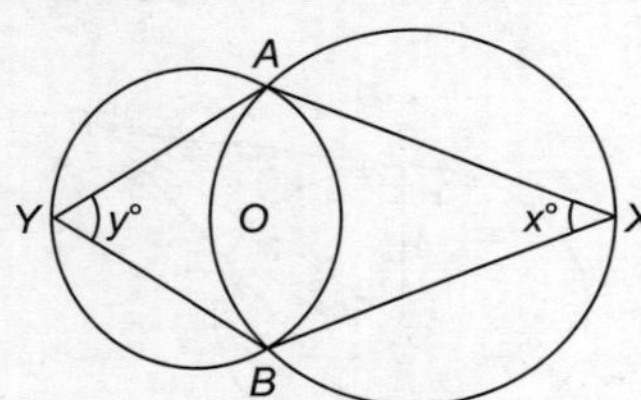

(a) $180° - x°$, (b) $180° - 2x°$
(c) ½ $(90° - x°)$ (d) $90° - (x°/2)$

22. In the figure, $AB = x$
Calculate the area of triangle ADC ($\angle B = 90°$).

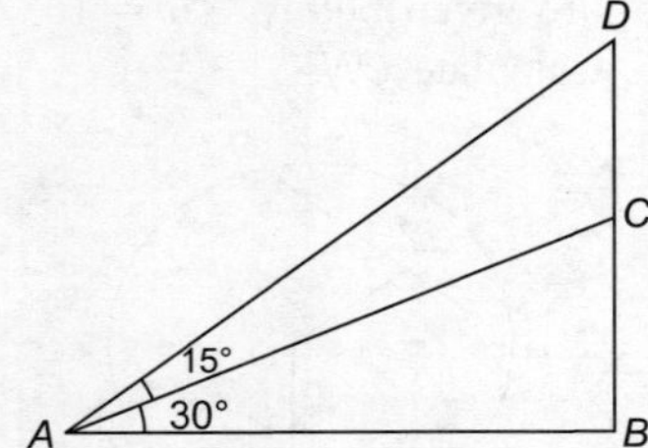

(a) $\frac{1}{2}x^2 \sin 30°$ (b) $\frac{1}{2}x^2 \cos 30°$

(c) $\frac{1}{2}x^2 \tan 30°$ (d) $\frac{1}{2}x^2(\tan 45° - \tan 30°)$

23. In the given figure. $SQ = TR = a$, $QT = b$, $QM \perp PR$, ST is parallel to PR.
$m \angle STQ = 30°$
$m \angle SQT = 90°$

Find QM.

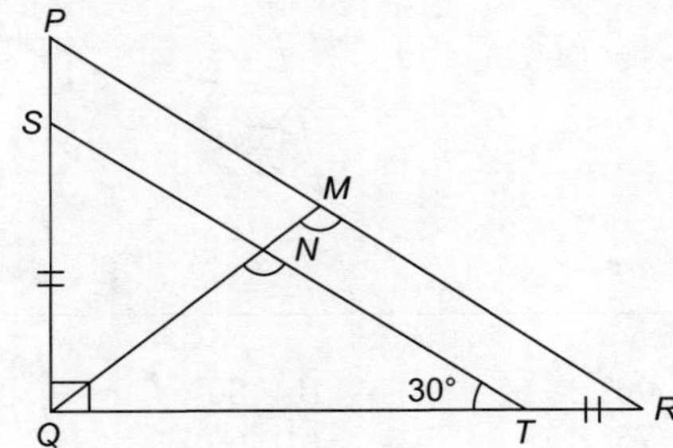

(a) $(a + b)/2$ (b) $2(a + b)$
(c) $(2a + b)/2$ (d) $(a + 2b)/2$

24. In the figure given, AB is a diameter of the circle and C and D are on the circumference such that $\angle CAD = 40°$. Find the measure of the $\angle ACD$

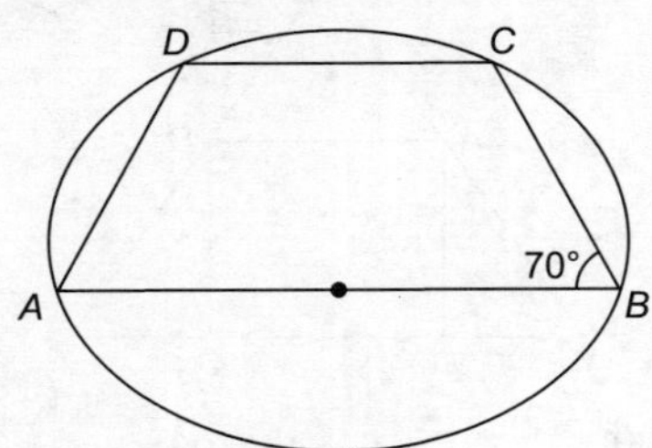

(a) 40° (b) 50°
(c) 60° (d) None of these

25. Six solid hemispherical balls have to be arranged one upon the other vertically. Find the minimum total surface area of the cylinder in which the hemispherical balls can be arranged, if the radius of each hemispherical ball is 7 cm.
(a) 2056 (b) 2156
(c) 1232 (d) None of these

Directions for Questions 26 and 27: In the following figure, there is a cone which is being cut and extracted in three segments having heights h_1, h_2 and h_3 and the radius of their bases 1 cm, 2 cm and 3 cm respectively, then

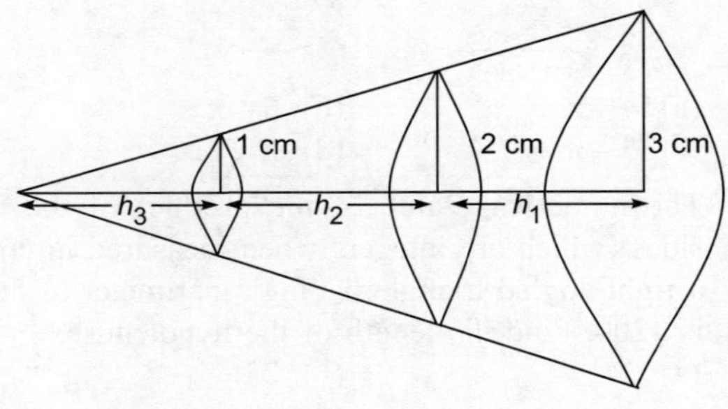

26. The ratio of the volumes of the smallest segment to that of the largest segment is
(a) 1 : 27 (b) 27 : 1
(c) 1: 19 (d) None of these

27. The ratio of the curved surface area of the second largest segment to that of the full cone is:
(a) 1 : 3 (b) 4 : 9
(c) Cannot be determined
(d) None of these

28. On a semicircle with diameter *AD*, chord *BC* is parallel to the diameter. Further each of the chords *AB* and *CD* has length 2 cm while *AD* has length 8 cm. Find the length of *BC*.
(a) 7.5 cm (b) 7 cm
(c) 7.75 cm (d) Cannot be determined

29. In the given figure, *B* and *C* are points on the diameter *AD* of the circle such that *AB* = *BC* = *CD*. Then find the ratio of area of the shaded portion to that of the whole circle.

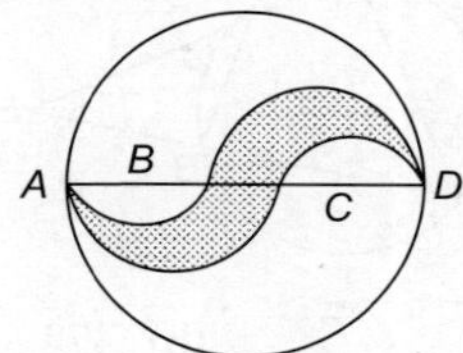

(a) 1 : 3 (b) 2 : 3
(c) 1 : 2 (d) None of these

30. In the given figure, *ABC* is a triangle in which *AD* and *DE* are medians to *BC* and *AB* respectively, then the ratio of the area of Δ*BED* to that of Δ*ABC* is

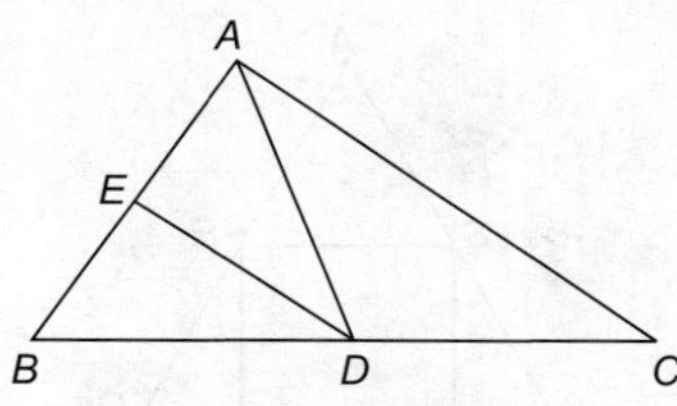

(a) 1 : 4 (b) 1 : 16
(c) Data inadequate (d) None of these

31. Two identical circles intersect so that their centers, and the points at which they intersect, form a square of side 1 cm. The area in square cm of the portion that is common to the two circles is
(a) $\pi/4$ (b) $\pi/2 - 1$
(c) $\pi/5$ (d) $\sqrt{2} - 1$

32. If the height of a cone is trebled and its base diameter is doubled, then the ratio of the volume of the resultant cone to that of the original cone is
(a) 9 : 1 (b) 9 : 2
(c) 12 : 1 (d) 6 : 1

33. If two cylinders of equal volume have their heights in the ratio 2: 3, then the ratio of their radii is
(a) $\sqrt{3} : \sqrt{2}$ (b) 2 : 3
(c) $\sqrt{5} : \sqrt{3}$ (d) $\sqrt{6} : \sqrt{3}$

34. Through three given non-collinear points, how many circles can pass?
(a) 2 (b) 3
(c) Both 1 and 2 (d) None of these

35. The area of the rectangle *ABCD* is 2 and *BD* = *DE*. Find the area of the shaded region.

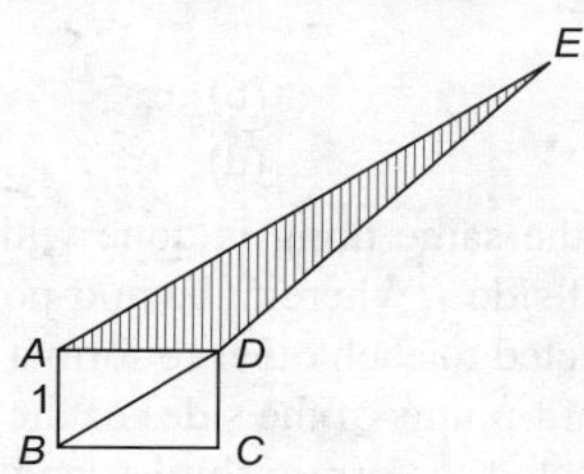

(a) $\sqrt{5}$ (b) $2\sqrt{5}$
(c) $\sqrt{(5/2)}$ (d) 1

36. In a right-angled triangle, the square of the hypotenuse is equal to twice the product of the other two sides. The acute angles of the triangle are
(a) 30° and 30° (b) 30° and 60°
(c) 15° and 75° (d) 45° and 45°

37. Find ∠*ALC* if *AB* || *CD*.

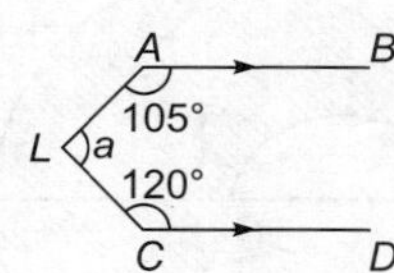

(a) 75 (b) 135
(c) 110 (d) 145

38. If the sides of a triangle are in the ratio of 1/2 : 1/3: 1/4 , the perimeter is 52 cm, then the length of the smallest side is
(a) 12 cm (b) 11 cm
(c) 8 cm (d) None of these

39. The number of distinct triangles with integral valued sides and perimeter as 14 is
(a) 2 (b) 3
(c) 4 (d) 5

40. A polygon has 65 diagonals. Then, what is the number of sides of the same polygon?
(a) 11 (b) 12
(c) 14 (d) None of these

41. *PQRS* is a square drawn inside square *ABCD* of side 2*x* units by joining the mid-points of the sides *AB*, *BC*, *CD*, and *DA*. The square *TUVW* is drawn inside *PQRS*, where *T*, *U*, *V*, *W* are the mid-points of SP, PQ, QR and RS. If the process is repeated an infinite number of times the sum of the areas of all the squares will be equal to

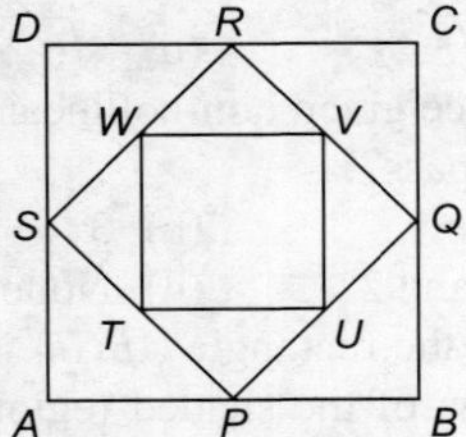

(a) $8x^2$ (b) $6x^2$
(c) $16x^2$ (d) $6x^2/2$

42. Suppose the same thing is done with an equilateral triangle of side x, wherein the mid-points of the sides are connected to each other to form a second triangle and the mid-points of the sides of the second triangle are connected to form a third triangle and so on an infinite number of times—then the sum of the areas of all such equilateral triangles would be
(a) $3x^2$ (b) $6x^2$
(c) $12x^2$ (d) None of these

43. If in the figure given below $OP = PQ = 28$ cm and OQ, PQ and OP are all joined by semicircles, then the perimeter of the figure (shaded area) is equal to

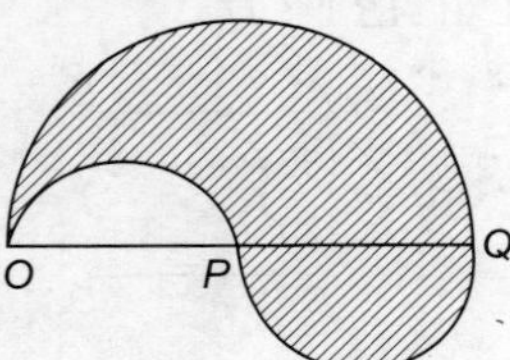

(a) 352 cm (b) 264 cm
(c) 176 cm (d) 88 cm

44. For the question above, what is the shaded area?
(a) 1352 sq. cm (b) 1264 sq. cm
(c) 1232 sq. cm (d) 1188 sq. cm

45. What is the area of the shaded portion? It is given that $ZV \| XY$, $WZ = ZX$, $ZV = 2a$ and $ZX = 2b$.

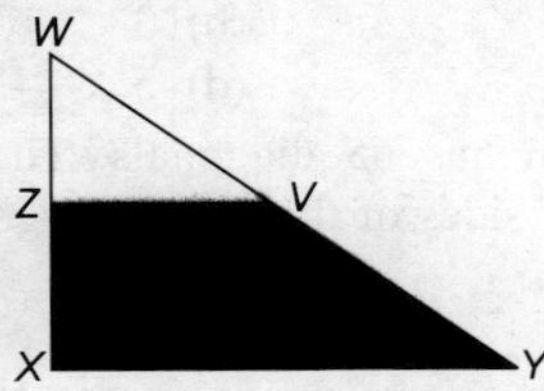

(a) $\dfrac{4ab}{2}$ (b) $\dfrac{8ab}{3}$
(c) $6ab$ (d) $3ab$

46. In the given figure, there is an isosceles triangle ABC with angle A = angle C = 50°. $ABDE$ and $BCFG$ are two rectangles drawn on the sides AB and BC respectively, such that $BD = BG = AE = CF$.

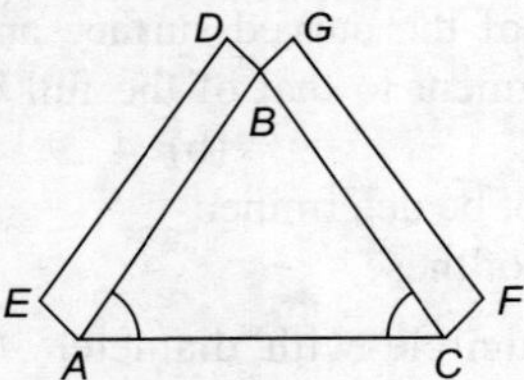

Find the value of the angle DBG.
(a) 80° (b) 120°
(c) 100° (d) 140°

47. In the figure, ABE, DCE, BCF and ADF are straight lines. If $E = 50°$, $F = 56°$, find $\angle A$.

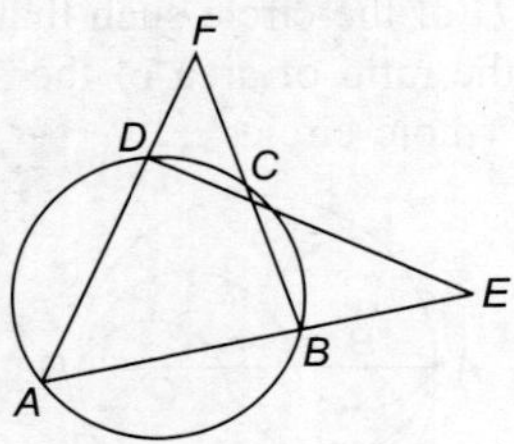

(a) 47° (b) 37°
(c) 40° (d) 42°

48. ABC is an equilateral triangle. $PQRS$ is a square inscribed in it. Therefore.
(a) $AR^2 = RC^2$ (b) $2AR^2 = RC^2$
(c) $3AR^2 = 4RC^2$ (d) $4AR^2 = 3RC^2$

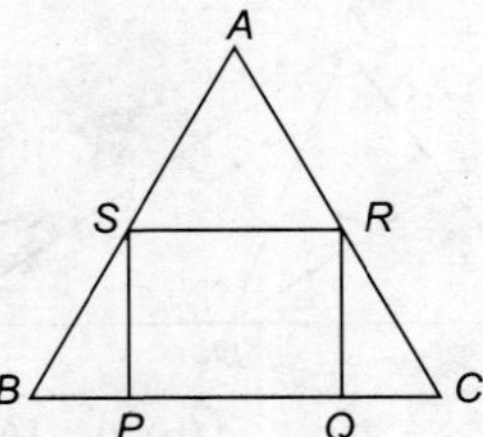

49. Consider the five points comprising the vertices of a square and the intersection point of its diagonals. How many triangles can be formed using these points?
(a) 4 (b) 6
(c) 8 (d) 10

50. In a triangle ABC, the internal bisector of the angle A meets BC at D. If $AB = 4$, $AC = 3$ and $\angle A = 60°$. Then, the length of AD is
(a) $2\sqrt{3}$ (b) $(12\sqrt{3})/7$
(c) $(15\sqrt{3})/8$ (d) $(6\sqrt{3})/7$

Directions for Questions 51 and 52: Answer the questions based on the following information.

A rectangle *PRSU*, is divided into two smaller rectangles *PQTU* and *QRST* by the line *QT*. *PQ* = 40 cm. *QR* = 20 cm, and *RS* = 40cm. Points *A*, *B*, *F* are within rectangle *PQTU*, and points *C*, *D*, *E* are within the rectangle *QRST*. The closest pair of points among the pairs (*A*, *C*), (*A*, *D*), (*A*, *E*), (*F*, *C*), (*F*, *D*), (*F*, *E*), (*B*, *C*), (*B*, *D*), (*B*, *E*) are $40\sqrt{3}$ cm apart.

51. Which of the following statements is necessarily true?
   (a) The closest pair of points among the six given points cannot be (*F*, *C*).
   (b) Distance between *A* and *B* is greater than that between *F* and *C*.
   (c) The closest pair of points among the six given points is (*C*, *D*), (*D*, *E*) or (*C*, *E*).
   (d) None of these.

52. $AB > AF > BF$; $CD > DE > CE$; and $BF = 24\sqrt{5}$ cm. Which is the closest pair of points among all the six given points?
   (a) *B*, *F* (b) *C*, *D*
   (c) *A*, *B* (d) None of these

53. If *ABCD* is a square and *CDE* is an equilateral triangle, what is the measure of $\angle DEB$?

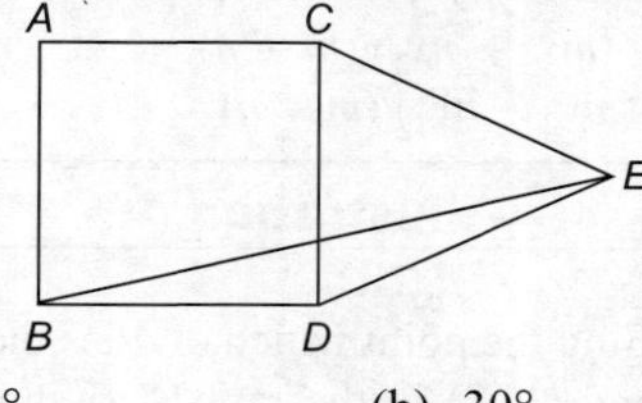

   (a) 15° (b) 30°
   (c) 20° (d) 45°

54. $AB \perp BC$, $BD \perp AC$ and *CE* bisects $\angle C$, $\angle A = 30°$. Then, what is $\angle CED$?

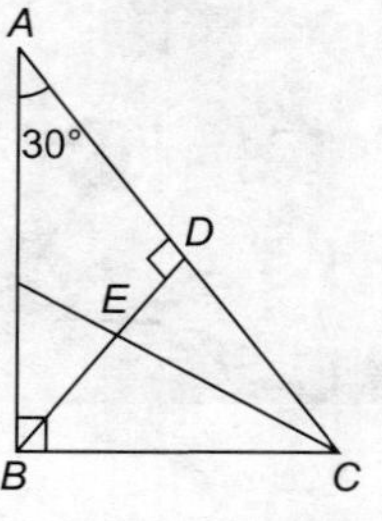

   (a) 30° (b) 60°
   (c) 45° (d) 65°

55. Instead of walking along two adjacent sides of a rectangular field, a boy took a short cut along the diagonal and saved a distance equal to half the longer side. Then, the ratio of the shorter side to the longer side is
   (a) 1/2 (b) 2/3
   (c) 1/4 (d) 3/4

ANSWER KEY

1. (b)	2. (c)	3. (b)	4. (d)
5. (b)	6. (b)	7. (c)	8. (a)
9. (b)	10. (b)	11. (c)	12. (b)
13. (a)	14. (b)	15. (c)	16. (a)
17. (a)	18. (a)	19. (b)	20. (c)
21. (d)	22. (d)	23. (a)	24. (d)
25. (b)	26. (c)	27. (a)	28. (b)
29. (a)	30. (a)	31. (b)	32. (c)
33. (a)	34. (d)	35. (d)	36. (d)
37. (b)	38. (a)	39. (c)	40. (d)
41. (a)	42. (d)	43. (c)	44. (c)
45. (c)	46. (c)	47. (b)	48. (d)
49. (c)	50. (b)	51. (d)	52. (d)
53. (a)	54. (b)	55. (d)	

CHAPTER 13

Coordinate Geometry

Chapter Launchpad

Scan this QR code to access a video on 'Introduction to Coordinate Geometry' and this chapter's importance for CAT

From the CAT examinations, point of view, Coordinate Geometry by itself is not a very significant chapter. Basically, applied questions are asked in the form of tabular representation or regarding the shape of the structure formed. However, it is advised to go through the basics and important formulae to have a feel-good effect as also to be prepared for surprises, if any, in the examination. Logical questions might be asked based on the formulae and concepts contained in this chapter. Besides, the student will have an improved understanding of the graphical representation of functions if he/she has gone through coordinate geometry.

CARTESIAN COORDINATE SYSTEM

Rectangular Coordinate Axes

Let $X'OX$ and $Y'OY$ be two mutually perpendicular lines through any point O in the plane of the paper. Point O is known as the origin. The line $X'OX$ is called the x-axis or axis of x; the line $Y'OY$ is known as the y-axis or axis of y; and the two lines taken together are called the coordinate axes or the axes of coordinates.

II Quadrant (–, +)
I Quadrant (+, +)
III Quadrant (–, –)
IV Quadrant (+, –)

Any point can be represented on the plane described by the coordinate axes by specifying its x and y coordinates. The x coordinate of the point is also known as the abscissa while the y coordinate is also known as the ordinate.

1. Distance Formula: If two points p and Q are such that they are represented by the points (x_1, y_1) and (x_2, y_2) on the x-y plane (Cartesian plane), then the distance between the points p and $Q = \sqrt{(x_1 - x_2)^2 + (y_1 - y_2)^2}$.

Illustration

Problem 1: Find the distance between the points (5, 2) and (3, 4).

Solution : Distance $= \sqrt{(5-3)^2 + (2-4)^2}$

$\left[\text{Using the formula } \sqrt{(x_1 - x_2)^2 + (y_1 - y_2)^2}\right]$

$= 2\sqrt{2}$ units

2. Section Formula: If any point (x, y) divides the line segment joining the points (x_1, y_1) and (x_2, y_2) in the ratio $m : n$ internally,

then $x = (mx_2 + nx_1)/(m + n)$

$y = (my_2 + ny_1)/(m + n)$ (see figure)

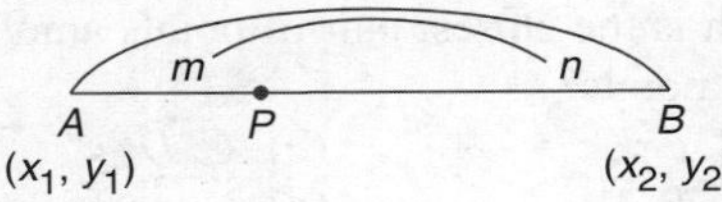

If any point (x, y) divides the line segment joining the points (x_1, y_1) and (x_2, y_2) in the ratio $m: n$ externally,

then $x = (mx_2 - nx_1)/(m - n)$

$y = (my_2 - ny_1)/(m - n)$

Illustration

Problem 2: Find the point which divides the line segment joining (2, 5) and (1, 2) in the ratio 2 : 1 internally.

Solution: $X = (2.1 + 1.2)/(1 + 2) = 4/3$

$Y = (2.2 + 1.5)/(2 + 1) = 9/3 = 3$

3. Area of a Triangle: The area of a triangle whose vertices are $A (x_1, y_1)$, $B (x_2, y_2)$ and $C (x_3, y_3)$ is given by

$$\left[\frac{\{x_1 (y_2 - y_3) + x_2 (y_3 - y_1) + x_3 (y_1 - y_2)\}}{2}\right]$$

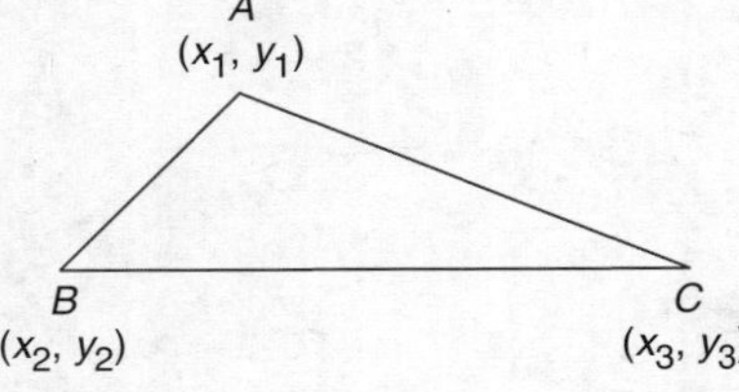

Note: Since the area cannot be negative, we have to take the modulus value given by the above equation.

Corollary: If one of the vertices of the triangle is at the origin and the other two vertices are $A (x_1, y_1)$, $B (x_2, y_2)$, then the area of triangle is $\left|\frac{(x_1 y_2 - x_2 y_1)}{2}\right|$.

Illustration

Problem 3: Find the area of the triangle (0, 4), (3, 6) and (–8, –2).

Solution: Area of triangle = |1/2 {0 (6– (–2)) + 3 ((–2) –4) + (–8) (4–6)}|
= |1/2 {(0) + 3 (–6) + (–8) (–2)}|
= |1/2 (–2)| = |–1| = 1 square unit

4. Center of gravity or centroid of a triangle: The centroid of a triangle is the point of intersection of its medians (the line joining the vertex to the middle point of the opposite side). Centroid divides the medians in the ratio 2 : 1. In other words, the *CG* or the centroid can be viewed as a point at which the whole weight of the triangle is concentrated.

Formula: If $A\ (x_1, y_1)$, $B\ (x_2, y_2)$ and $C\ (x_3, y_3)$ are the coordinates of the vertices of a triangle, then the coordinates of the centroid G of that triangle are

$$x = (x_1 + x_2 + x_3)/3 \text{ and } y = (y_1 + y_2 + y_3)/3$$

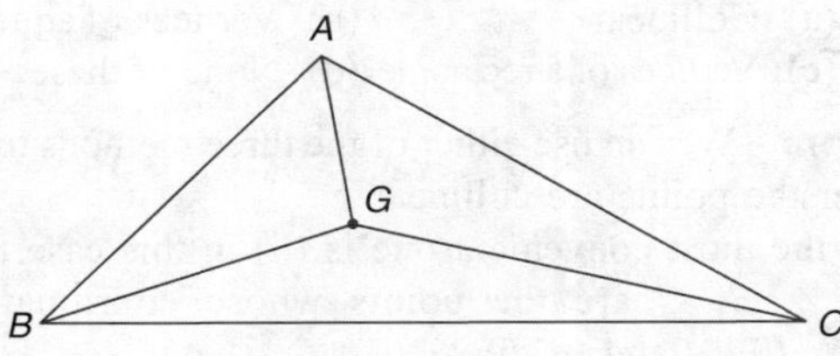

Illustration

Problem 4: Find the centroid of the triangle whose vertices are (5, 3), (4, 6) and (8, 2).

Solution: *X* coordinate = (5 + 4 + 8)/3 = 17/3
Y coordinate = (3 + 6 + 2)/3 = 11/3

5. In-center of a triangle: The center of the circle that touches the sides of a triangle is called its in-center. In other words, if the three sides of the triangle are tangential to the circle then the center of that circle represents the in-center of the triangle.

The in-center is also the point of intersection of the internal bisectors of the angles of the triangle. The distance of the in-center from the sides of the triangle is the same and this distance is called the in-radius of the triangle.

If $A\ (x_1, y_1)$, $B\ (x_2, y_2)$ and $C\ (x_3, y_3)$ are the coordinates of the vertices of a triangle, then the coordinates of its in-center are

$$x = \frac{(ax_1 + bx_2 + cx_3)}{(a+b+c)} \quad \text{and} \quad y = \frac{(ay_1 + by_2 + cy_3)}{(a+b+c)}$$

where, $BC = a$, $AB = c$ and $AC = b$.

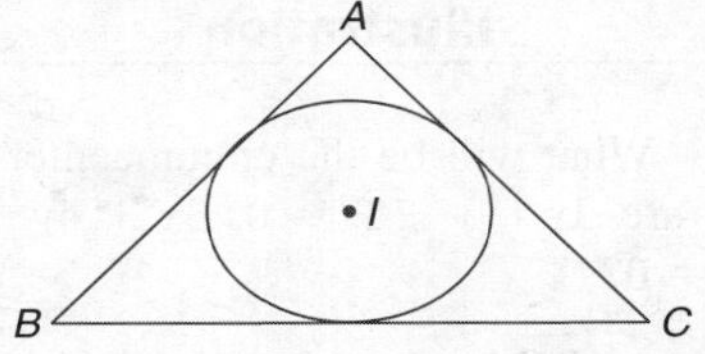

Illustration

Problem 5: Find the in-center of the right-angled isosceles triangle having one vertex at the origin and having the other two vertices at (6, 0) and (0, 6).

Solution: Obviously, the length of the two sides *AB* and *BC* of the triangle is 6 units and the length of the third side is (62 + 62)1/2.

Hence, $a = c = 6,\ b = 6\sqrt{2}$.

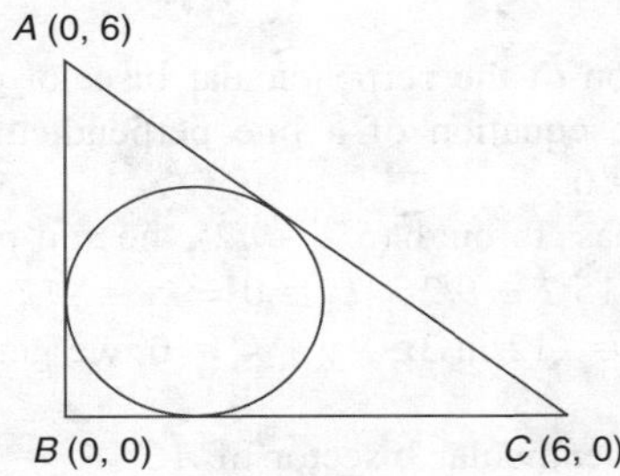

In-center will be at

$$\frac{(6.0 + 6\sqrt{2}.0 + 6.6)}{(6+6+6\sqrt{2})}, \frac{(6.6 + 6\sqrt{2}.0 + 6.0)}{(6+6+6\sqrt{2})}$$

$$= \frac{36}{12 + 6\sqrt{2}}, \frac{36}{12 + 6\sqrt{2}}$$

6. Circumcenter of a triangle The point of intersection of the perpendicular bisectors of the sides of a triangle is called its circumcenter. It is equidistant from the vertices of the triangle. It is also known as the center of the circle which passes through the three vertices of a triangle (or the center of the circle that circumscribes the triangle.)

Let *ABC* be a triangle. If *O* is the circumcenter of the triangle *ABC*, then *OA* = *OB* = *OC* and each of these three represent the circum radius.

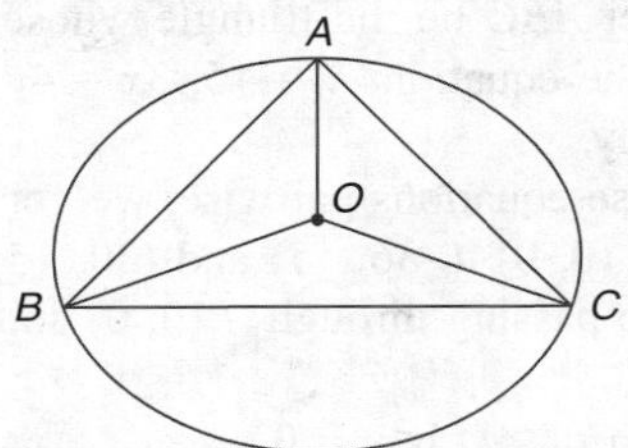

Illustration

Problem 6: What will be the circumcenter of a triangle whose sides are $3x - y + 3 = 0$, $3x + 4y + 3 = 0$ and $x + 3y + 11 = 0$?

Solution: Let ABC be the triangle whose sides AB, BC and CA have the equations $3x - y + 3 = 0$, $3x + 4y + 3 = 0$ and $x + 3y + 11 = 0$ respectively.

Solving the equations, we get the points A, B and C as (–2, –3), (–1, 0) and (7, – 6), respectively.

The equation of a line perpendicular to BC is $4x - 3y + k = 0$.

[For students unaware of this formula, read the section on straight lines later in the chapter.]

This will pass through (3, –3), the mid-point of BC, if $12 + 9 + k = 0 \Rightarrow k = -21$.

putting $k_1 = -21$ in $4x - 3y + k = 0$, we get $4x - 3y - 21 = 0$ (1)

as the equation of the perpendicular bisector of BC.

Again, the equation of a line perpendicular to CA is $3x - y + k_1 = 0$.

This will pass through (5/2, –9/2), the mid-point of AC if

$$15/2 + 9/2 + k_1 = 0 \Rightarrow k_1 = -12$$

putting $k_1 = -12$ in $3x - y + k_1 = 0$, we get $3x - y - 12 = 0$ (2)

as the perpendicular bisector of AC.

Solving (1) and (2), we get $x = 3$, $y = -3$.

Hence, the coordinates of the circumcenter of ΔABC are (3, –3).

7. Orthocenter of a triangle: The orthocenter of a triangle is the point of intersection of the perpendiculars drawn from the vertices to the opposite sides of the triangle.

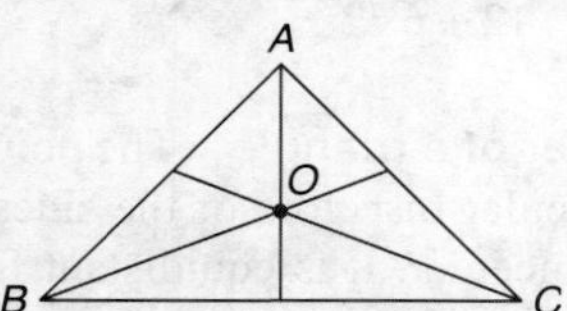

Illustration

Problem 7: Find the orthocenter of the triangle whose sides have the equations $y = 15$, $3x = 4y$, and $5x + 12y = 0$.

Solution: Let ABC be the triangle whose sides BC, CA and AB have the equations $y = 15$, $3x = 4y$, and $5x + 12y = 0$ respectively.

Solving these equations pairwise, we get coordinates of A, B and C as (0, 0), (–36, 15) and (20, 15), respectively.

AD is a line passing through A (0, 0) and perpendicular to $y = 15$.

So, equation of AD is $x = 0$.

The equation of any line perpendicular to $3x - 4y = 0$ is represented by $4x + 3y + k = 0$.

This line will pass through (–36, 15) if $-144 + 45 + k = 0 \Rightarrow k = 99$.

So the equation of BE is $4x + 3y + 99 = 0$.

Solving the equations of AD and BE, we get $x = 0$, $y = -33$.

Hence, the coordinates of the orthocenter are (0, –33).

8. Collinearity of three points: Three given points A, B and C are said to be collinear, that is, lie on the same straight line, if any of the following conditions occur:

(i) Area of triangle formed by these three points is zero
(ii) Slope of AB = Slope of AC
(iii) Any one of the three points (say C) lies on the straight line joining the other two points (here A and B).

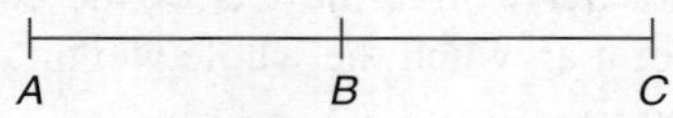

Illustration

Problem 8: Select the right option the points $(-a, -b)$, (0, 0) and (a, b) are

(a) Collinear (b) Vertices of square
(c) Vertices of a rectangle (d) None of these

Solution: We can use either of the three methods to check whether the points are collinear.

But the most convenient one is (ii) in this case.

Let A, B, C are the points whose coordinates are $(-a, -b)$, (0, 0) and (a, b).

Slope of $BC = b/a$

Slope of $AB = b/a$

So, the straight line made by points A, B and C is collinear.

Hence, (a) is the answer.

[If you have not understood this here, you are requested to read the following section on straight lines and their slopes and then re-read this solution]

Alternative: Draw the points on paper assuming the paper to be a graph paper. This will give you an indication regarding the nature of points. In the above question, point (a, b) is in first quadrant for $a > 0$, $b > 0$ and point $(-a, -b)$ is directly opposite to the point (a, b) in the third quadrant with the third point (0, 0) in the middle of the straight line joining the points A and B.

You can check this by assuming any value for 'a' and 'b'.

Also, you can use this method for solving any problem involving points and diagrams made by those points. However, you should be fast enough to trace the points on paper. A little practice of tracing points might help you.

9. Slope of a line: The slope of a line joining two points A (x_1, y_1) and B (x_2, y_2) is denoted by m and is given by $m = (y_2 - y_1)/(x_2 - x_1) = \tan q$, where q is the angle that the line makes with the positive direction of x-axis. This angle q is taken positive when it is measured in the anti-clockwise direction from the positive direction of the axis of x.

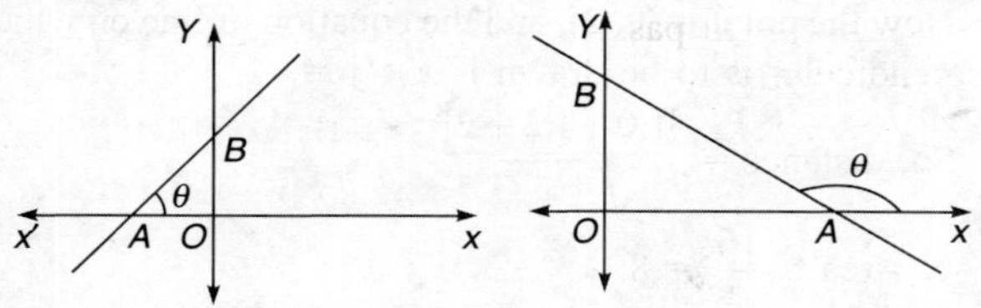

Illustration

Problem 9: Find the equation of a straight line passing through (2, –3) and having a slope of 1 unit.

Solution: Here slope = 1

And point given is (2, –3).

So, we will use point-slope formula for finding the equation of straight line. This formula is given by:

$$(y - y_1) = m\,(x - x_1)$$

So, equation of the line will be $y - (-3) = 1\,(x - 2)$

$$\Rightarrow \quad y + 3 = x - 2$$

$$\Rightarrow \quad y - x + 5 = 0$$

10. Different Forms of the Equations of a Straight Line:

(a) General Form: The general form of the equation of a straight line is $ax + by + c = 0$.

First degree equation in x and y, Where a, b and c are real constants and a, b are not simultaneously equal to zero.

In this equation, slope of the line is given by $\frac{-a}{b}$.

The general form is also given by $y = mx + c$; where m is the slope and c is, the intercept on y-axis.

In this equation, slope of the line is given by m.

(b) Line parallel to the X-axis: The equation of a straight line parallel to the x-axis and at a distance b from it, is given by $y = b$.

Obviously, the equation of the x-axis is $y = 0$.

(c) Line parallel to Y-axis: The equation of a straight line parallel to the y-axis and at a distance a from it, is given by $x = a$.

Obviously, the equation of y-axis is $x = 0$.

(d) Slope Intercept Form: The equation of a straight line passing through the point $A\,(x_1, y_1)$ and having a slope m is given by

$$(y - y_1) = m\,(x - x_1)$$

(e) Two points Form: The equation of a straight line passing through two points $A\,(x_1, y_1)$ and $B\,(x_2, y_2)$ is given by

$$(y - y_1) = \frac{(y_2 - y_1)\,(x - x_1)}{(x_2 - x_1)}$$

Its slope $= \left(\frac{y_2 - y_1}{x_2 - x_1}\right)$

(f) Intercept Form: The equation of a straight line making intercepts a and b on the axes of x and y respectively is given by

$$x/a + y/b = 1$$

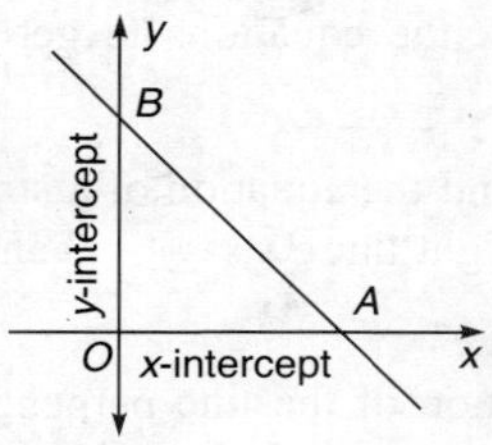

If a straight line cuts x-axis at A and the y-axis at B then OA and OB are known as the intercepts of the line on x-axis and y-axis respectively.

11. Perpendicularity and Parallellism:

Condition for two lines to be parallel: Two lines are said to be parallel, if their slopes are equal.

For this to happen, ratio of coefficient of x and y in both the lines should be equal.

In a general form, this can be stated as: line parallel to $ax + by + c = 0$ is $ax + by + k = 0$ or $dx + ey + k = 0$ if $a/d = b/e$ where k is a constant.

Illustration

Problem 10: Which of the lines represented by the following equations are parallel to each other?

1. $x + 2y = 5$ 2. $2x - 4y = 6$
3. $x - 2y = 4$ 4. $2x + 6y = 8$

(a) 1 and 2 (b) 2 and 4 (c) 2 and 3 (d) 1 and 4

Solution: Go through the options and check which of the two lines given will satisfy the criteria for two lines to be parallel. It will be obvious that option (c) is correct, that is, the line $2x - 4y = 6$ is parallel to the line $x - 2y = 4$.

Problem 11: Find the equation of a straight line parallel to the straight line $3x + 4y = 7$ and passing through the point (3, –3).

Solution: Equation of the line parallel to $3x + 4y = 7$ will be of the form $3x + 4y = k$.

This line passes through (3, –3), so this point will satisfy the equation of straight line $3x + 4y = k$. So, $3.3 + 4.(-3) = k \Rightarrow k = -3$.

Hence, equation of the required straight line will be $3x + 4y + 3 = 0$.

Condition for two lines to be perpendicular: Two lines are said to be perpendicular if product of the slopes of the lines is equal to –1.

For this to happen, the product of the coefficients of x + the product of the coefficients of y should be equal to zero.

Illustration

Problem 12: Which of the following two lines are perpendicular?

1. $x + 2y = 5$ 2. $2x - 4y = 6$
3. $2x + 3y = 4$ 4. $2x - y = 4$

(a) 1 and 2 (b) 2 and 4 (c) 2 and 3 (d) 1 and 4

Solution: Check the equations to get option (d) as the correct answer.

Problem 13: Find the equation of a straight line perpendicular to the straight line $3x + 4y = 7$ and passing through the point $(3, -3)$.

Solution: Equation of the line perpendicular to $3x + 4y = 7$ will be of the form $4x - 3y = K$.

This line passes through $(3, -3)$, so this point will satisfy the equation of straight line $4x - 3y = K$. So, $4.3 - 3.-3 \Rightarrow K = 21$.

Hence, equation of required straight line will be $4x - 3y = 21$.

12. Length of Perpendicular or Distance of a Point from a line: The length of perpendicular from a given point (x_1, y_1) to a line $ax + by + c = 0$ is

$$\frac{|ax_1 + by_1 + c|}{\sqrt{a^2 + b^2}}$$

Corollary:

(a) Distance between two parallel lines.

If two lines are parallel, the distance between them will always be the same.

When two straight lines are parallel whose equations are $ax + by + c = 0$ and $ax + by + c_1 = 0$, then the distance between them is given by $\frac{|c - c_1|}{\sqrt{a^2 + b^2}}$.

(b) The length of the perpendicular from the origin to the line $ax + by + c = 0$ is given by $\frac{|c|}{\sqrt{a^2 + b^2}}$.

Illustration

Problem 14: Two sides of a square lie on the lines $x + y = 2$ and $x + y = -2$. Find the area of the square formed in this way.

Solution: Obviously, the difference between the parallel lines will be the side of the square.

To convert it into the form of finding the distance of a point from a line, we will have to find out a point at which any one of these two lines cut the axes and then we will draw a perpendicular from that point to the other line, and this distance will be the side of the square.

To find the point at which the equation of the line $x + y = 2$ cut the axes, we will put once $x = 0$ and then again $y = 0$.

When $x = 0$, $y = 2$, so the coordinates of the point where it cuts y-axis is $(0, 2)$.

Now the point is $(0, 2)$, and the equation of line on which perpendicular is to be drawn is $x + y = -2$.

So, distance $= \frac{|1.0 + 1.2 + 2|}{\sqrt{1^2 + 1^2}} = \frac{4}{\sqrt{2}}$.

$\therefore$ Area $= \frac{16}{2} = 8$.

Alternatively: Draw the points on the paper and you will get the length of diagonal as 4 units; so, length of side will be $2\sqrt{2}$ and, therefore, the area will be 8 sq units.

Alternatively: You can also use the formula for the distance between two parallel lines as

$$\frac{|2 + 2|}{\sqrt{1^2 + 1^2}} = \frac{4}{\sqrt{2}}$$

13. Change of axes: If origin $(0, 0)$ is shifted to (h, k) then the coordinates of the point (x, y) referred to the old axes and (X, Y) referred to the new axes can be related with the relation $x = X + h$ and $y = Y + k$.

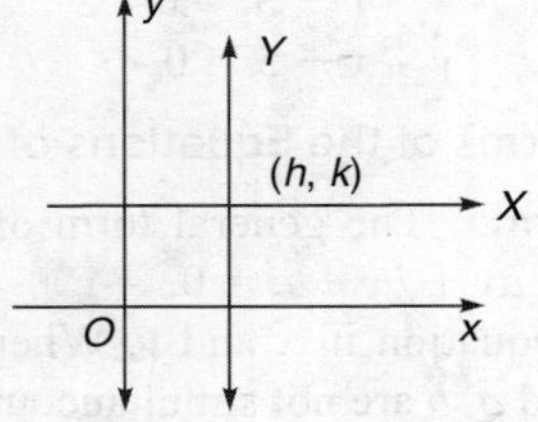

Illustration

Problem 15: If origin $(0, 0)$ is shifted to $(5, 2)$, what will be the coordinates of the point in the new axis which was represented by $(1, 2)$ in the old axis?

Solution: Let (X, Y) be the coordinates of the point in the new axis.

Then, $1 = X + 5 \quad \therefore X = -4$

$2 = Y + 2 \quad \therefore Y = 0$

So, the new coordinates of the point will be $(-4, 0)$.

14. Point of intersection of two lines: Point of intersection of two lines can be obtained by solving the equations as simultaneous equations.

An Important Result

If all the three vertices of a triangle have integral co-ordinates, then that triangle cannot be an equilateral triangle.

Space for Rough Work

LEVEL OF DIFFICULTY (I)

1. Find the distance between the points (3, 4) and (8, –6).
(a) $\sqrt{5}$ (b) $5\sqrt{5}$
(c) $2\sqrt{5}$ (d) $4\sqrt{5}$

2. Find the distance between the points (5, 2) and (0, 0).
(a) $\sqrt{27}$ (b) $\sqrt{21}$
(c) $\sqrt{29}$ (d) $\sqrt{31}$

3. Find the value of π if the distance between the points (8, π) and (4, 3) is 5.
(a) 6 (b) 0
(c) Both (a) and (b) (d) None of these

4. Find the value of c if the distance between the point (c, 4) and the origin is 5 units.
(a) 3 (b) –3
(c) Both (a) and (b) (d) None of these

5. Find the mid-point of the line segment made by joining the points (3, 2) and (6, 4).
(a) $\left(\frac{9}{2}, 3\right)$ (b) $\left(\frac{-3}{2}, -1\right)$
(c) $\left(\frac{9}{2}, -\frac{3}{2}\right)$ (d) $\left(\frac{3}{-1}\right)$

6. If the origin is the mid-point of the line segment joined by the points (2, 3) and (x, y), find the value of (x, y).
(a) (2, 3) (b) (–2, 3)
(c) (–2, –3) (d) (2, –3)

7. Find the points that divide the line segment joining (2, 5) and (–1, 2) in the ratio 2 : 1 internally.
(a) (1, 2) (b) (–3, 2)
(c) (3, 1) (d) (0, 3)

8. In what ratio does the x-axis divide the line segment joining the points (2, –3) and (5, 6)?
(a) 2 : 1 (b) 1 : 2
(c) 3 : 4 (d) 2 : 3

9. How many squares are possible if two of the vertices of a quadrilateral are (1, 0) and (2, 0)?
(a) 1 (b) 2
(c) 3 (d) 4

10. If the point R (1, –8) divides externally the line segment joining p (2, 5) and Q in the ratio 3 : 4, what will be the coordinates of Q?
(a) (–3, 6) (b) (2, –4)
(c) (7/3, 28/3) (d) (1, 2)

11. Find the coordinates of the points that trisect the line segment joining (1, –2) and (–3, 4).
(a) $\left(\frac{-1}{3}, 0\right)$ (b) $\left(\frac{-5}{3}, 2\right)$
(c) Both (a) and (b) (d) None of these

12. Find the coordinates of the point that divides the line segment joining the points (6, 3) and (–4, 5) in the ratio 3: 2 internally.
(a) $\left(0, \frac{-21}{5}\right)$ (b) $\left(0, \frac{21}{5}\right)$
(c) $\left(\frac{11}{2}, \frac{14}{3}\right)$ (d) $\left(\frac{-11}{2}, \frac{-14}{3}\right)$

13. In Question 12 , find the coordinates of the point if it divides the points externally.
(a) (24, –9) (b) (3, –5)
(c) (–24, 9) (d) (5, –3)

14. In what ratio is the line segment joining (–1, 3) and (4, –7) divided at the point (2, –3)?
(a) 3 : 2 (b) 2 : 3
(c) 3 : 5 (d) 5 : 3

15. In question 14, find the nature of division.
(a) Internal (b) External
(c) Cannot be said (d) All of these

16. In what ratio is the line segment made by the points (7, 3) and (–4, 5) divided by the y-axis?
(a) 2 : 3 (b) 4 : 7
(c) 3 : 5 (d) 7 : 4

17. What is the nature of the division in the above question?
(a) External (b) Internal
(c) Cannot be said (d) All of these

18. If the coordinates of the mid-point of the line segment joining the points (2, 1) and (1, –3) is (x, y) then the relation between x and y can be best described by
(a) $3x + 2y = 5$ (b) $6x + y = 8$
(c) $5x - 2y = 4$ (d) $2x - 5y = 4$

19. Points (6, 8), (3, 7), (–2, –2) and (1, –1) are joined to form a quadrilateral. What will be this structure?
(a) Rhombus (b) parallelogram
(c) Square (d) Rectangle

20. Points (4, –1), (6, 0), (7, 2) and (5, 1) are joined to be a vertex of a quadrilateral. What will be the structure?
(a) Rhombus (b) Parallelogram
(c) Square (d) Rectangle

21. What will be the centroid of a triangle whose vertices are (2, 4), (6, 4) and (2, 0)?
(a) $\left(\frac{7}{2}, \frac{5}{2}\right)$ (b) (3, 5)
(c) $\left(\frac{10}{3}, \frac{8}{3}\right)$ (d) (1, 4)

22. The distance between the lines $4x + 3y = 11$ and $8x + 6y = 15$ is
(a) 4 (b) $\frac{7}{10}$
(c) $\frac{5}{7}$ (d) 26

23. If the mid-point of the line joining (3, 4) and (π, 7) is (x, y) and $2x + 2y + 1 = 0$, then what will be the value of π?
(a) 15 (b) $\frac{-17}{2}$
(c) –15 (d) $\frac{17}{2}$

24. Find the third vertex of the triangle whose two vertices are (–3, 1) and (0, –2) and the centroid is the origin.
(a) (2, 3) (b) $\left(\frac{-4}{3}, \frac{14}{3}\right)$
(c) (3, 1) (d) (6, 4)

25. Find the area of the triangle whose vertices are (1, 3), (–7, 6) and (5, –1).
(a) 20 (b) 10
(c) 18 (d) 24

26. Find the area of the triangle whose vertices are $(a, b + c)$, $(a, b - c)$ and $(-a, c)$.
(a) $2ac$ (b) $2bc$
(c) $b(a + c)$ (d) $c(a - b)$

27. The number of lines that are parallel to $2x + 6y + 7 = 0$ and have an intercept of length 10 between the coordinate axes is
(a) 0 (b) 1
(c) 2 (d) Infinite

28. Which of the following three points represent a straight line?
(a) $\left(\frac{-1}{2}, 3\right)$, (–5, 6) and (– 8, 8)
(b) $\left(\frac{-1}{2}, 3\right)$, (5, 6) and (– 8, 8)
(c) $\left(\frac{1}{2}, 3\right)$, (–5, 6) and (– 8, 8)
(d) $\left(\frac{-1}{2}, 3\right)$, $\left(\frac{5}{6}\right)$ and (8, 8)

29. Which of the following will be the equation of a straight line that is parallel to the y-axis at a distance 11 units from it?
(a) $x = +11, x = -11$ (b) $y = 11, y = -11$
(c) $y = 0$ (d) None of these

30. Which of the following will be the equation of a straight line parallel to the y-axis at a distance of 9 units to the left?
(a) $x = -9$ (b) $x = 9$
(c) $y = 9$ (d) $y = -9$

31. What can be said about the equation of the straight line $x = 7$?
(a) It is the equation of a straight line at a distance of 7 units towards the right of the y-axis.
(b) It is the equation of a straight line at a distance of 7 units towards the left of the y-axis.
(c) It is the equation of a straight line at a distance of 7 units below the x-axis.
(d) It is the equation of a straight line at a distance of 7 units above the x-axis.

32. What can be said about the equation of the straight line $y = -8$?
(a) It is the equation of a straight line at a distance of 8 units below the x-axis.
(b) It is the equation of a straight line at a distance of 8 units above the x-axis.
(c) It is the equation of a straight line at a distance of 8 units towards the right of the y-axis.
(d) It is the equation of a straight line at a distance of 8 units towards the left of the y-axis.

33. Which of the following straight lines passes through the origin?
(a) $x + y = 4$ (b) $x + y = -6$
(c) $x + y = 5$ (d) $x = 4y$

34. What will be the point of intersection of the equation of lines $2x + 5y = 6$ and $3x + 4y = 7$?
(a) $\left(\frac{11}{7}, \frac{4}{7}\right)$ (b) $\left(\frac{-11}{7}, 4\right)$
(c) $\left(3, \frac{-2}{7}\right)$ (d) $\left(4, \frac{-2}{5}\right)$

35. If P (6, 7), Q (2, 3) and R (4, –2) be the vertices of a triangle, then which of the following is not a point contained in this triangle?
(a) (4, 3) (b) (3, 3)
(c) (4, 2) (d) (6, 1)

36. What will be the reflection of the point (4, 5) in the second quadrant?
(a) (– 4, – 5) (b) (– 4, 5)
(c) (4, – 5) (d) None of these

37. What will be the reflection of the point (4, 5) in the third quadrant?
(a) (– 4, – 5) (b) (– 4, 5)
(c) (4, – 5) (d) None of these

38. What will be the reflection of the point (4, 5) in the fourth quadrant?
(a) (– 4, – 5) (b) (– 4, 5)
(c) (4, –5) (d) None of these

39. If the origin gets shifted to (2, 2) then what will be the new coordinates of the point (4, –2)?
(a) (– 2, 4) (b) (2, 4)
(c) (4, 2) (d) (2, – 4)

40. What will be the length of the perpendicular drawn from the point (4, 5), upon the straight line $3x + 4y = 10$?
(a) $\frac{12}{5}$ (b) $\frac{32}{5}$
(c) $\frac{22}{5}$ (d) $\frac{42}{5}$

ANSWER KEY

Level of Difficulty (I)

1. (b)	2. (c)	3. (c)	4. (c)
5. (a)	6. (c)	7. (d)	8. (b)
9. (c)	10. (c)	11. (c)	12. (b)
13. (c)	14. (a)	15. (a)	16. (d)
17. (b)	18. (b)	19. (b)	20. (a)
21. (c)	22. (b)	23. (c)	24. (c)
25. (b)	26. (a)	27. (c)	28. (a)
29. (a)	30. (a)	31. (a)	32. (a)
33. (d)	34. (a)	35. (d)	36. (b)
37. (a)	38. (c)	39. (d)	40. (c)

TASTE OF THE EXAMS—BLOCK III

CAT

1. From a triangle ABC with sides of lengths 40 ft, 25 ft and 35 ft, a triangular portion GBC is cut off where G is the centroid of ABC. The area, in sq.ft, of the remaining portion of triangle ABC is **(CAT 2017)**
(a) $225\sqrt{3}$ (b) $500/\sqrt{3}$
(c) $275/\sqrt{3}$ (d) $250/\sqrt{3}$

2. Let ABC be a right-angled isosceles triangle with hypotenuse BC. Let BQC be a semi-circle, away from A, with diameter BC. Let BPC be an arc of a circle centered at A and lying between BC and BQC. If AB has length 6 cm then the area, in sq cm, of the region enclosed by BPC and BQC is **(CAT 2017)**
(a) $9\pi - 18$ (b) 18
(c) 9π (d) 9

3. A solid metallic cube is melted to form five solid cubes whose volumes are in the ratio 1:1:8:27:27. The percentage by which the sum of the surface areas of these five cubes exceeds the surface area of the original cube is nearest to **(CAT 2017)**
(a) 10 (b) 50
(c) 60 (d) 20

4. A ball of diameter 4 cm is kept on top of a hollow cylinder standing vertically. The height of the cylinder is 3 cm, while its volume is 9π cm^3. Then the vertical distance, in cm, of the topmost point of the ball from the base of the cylinder is **(CAT 2017)**

5. Let ABC be a right-angled triangle with BC as the hypotenuse. Lengths of AB and AC are 15 km and 20 km, respectively. The minimum possible time, in minutes, required to reach the hypotenuse from A at a speed of 30 km per hour is **(CAT 2017)**

6. The shortest distance of the point $\left(\frac{1}{2}, 1\right)$ from the curve $y = |x - 1| + |x + 1|$ is **(CAT 2017)**
(a) 1 (b) 0
(c) $\sqrt{2}$ (d) $\sqrt{3}/2$

7. Let $ABCDEF$ be a regular hexagon with each side of length 1 cm. The area (in sq cm) of a square with AC as one side is **(CAT 2017)**
(a) $3\sqrt{2}$ (b) 3
(c) 4 (d) $\sqrt{3}$

8. The base of a vertical pillar with uniform cross section is a trapezium whose parallel sides are of lengths 10 cm and 20 cm while the other two sides are of equal length. The perpendicular distance between the parallel sides of the trapezium is 12 cm. If the height of the pillar is 20 cm, then the total area, in square cm, of all six surfaces of the pillar is **(CAT 2017)**
(a) 1300 (b) 1340
(c) 1480 (d) 1520

9. If three sides of a rectangular park have a total length 400 ft, then the area of the park is maximum when the length (in ft) of its longer side is **(CAT 2017)**

10. $ABCD$ is a quadrilateral inscribed in a circle with centre O. If $\angle COD = 120$ degrees and $\angle BAC = 30$ degrees, then the value of $\angle BCD$ (in degrees) is **(CAT 2017)**

11. Let P be an interior point of a right-angled isosceles triangle ABC with hypotenuse AB. If the perpendicular distance of P from each of AB, BC, and CA is $4(\sqrt{2} - 1)$ cm, then the area, in sq cm, of the triangle ABC is **(CAT 2017)**

12. The points (2, 5) and (6, 3) are two end points of a diagonal of a rectangle. If the other diagonal has the equation $y = 3x + c$, then c is **(CAT 2017)**
(a) –5 (b) –6
(c) –7 (d) –8

13. A right circular cone, of height 12 ft, stands on its base which has diameter 8 ft. The tip of the cone is cut off with a plane which is parallel to the base and 9 ft from the base. With $\pi = 22/7$, the volume, in cubic ft, of the remaining part of the cone is **(CAT 2018)**

14. In a circle, two parallel chords on the same side of a diameter have lengths 4 cm and 6 cm. If the distance between these chords is 1 cm, than the radius of the circle, in cm, is **(CAT 2018)**
(a) $\sqrt{11}$ (b) $\sqrt{13}$
(c) $\sqrt{12}$ (d) $\sqrt{14}$

15. Points E, F, G, and H lie on the sides AB, BC, CD, and DA, respectively, of a square $ABCD$. If $EFGH$ is also a square whose area is 62.5% of that of $ABCD$ and CG is longer than EB, then the ratio of length of EB to that of CG is **(CAT 2018)**
(a) 2 : 5 (b) 4 : 9
(c) 3 : 8 (d) 1 : 3

16. In a circle with centre O and radius 1 cm, an arc AB makes an angle 60 degrees at O. Let R be the region bounded by the radii OA, OB and the arc AB. If C and D are two points on OA and OB, respectively, such that $OC = OD$ and the area of triangle OCD is half that of R, then the length of OC, in cm, is **(CAT 2018)**

(a) $\left(\frac{\pi}{4}\right)$ (b) $\left(\frac{\pi}{6}\right)^{\frac{1}{2}}$

(c) $\left(\frac{\pi}{4\sqrt{3}}\right)^{\frac{1}{2}}$ (d) $\left(\frac{\pi}{3\sqrt{3}}\right)^{\frac{1}{2}}$

17. Given an equilateral triangle *T*1 with side 24 cm, a second triangle *T*2 is formed by joining the midpoints of the sides of *T*1. Then a third triangle *T*3 is formed by joining the midpoints of the sides of *T*2. If this process of forming triangles is continued, the sum of the areas, in sq cm, of infinitely many such triangles *T*1, *T*2, *T*3,... will be **(CAT 2018)**

(a) $192\sqrt{3}$ (b) $164\sqrt{3}$
(c) $248\sqrt{3}$ (d) $188\sqrt{3}$

18. Let *ABCD* be a rectangle inscribed in a circle of radius 13 cm. Which one of the following pairs can represent, in cm, the possible length and breadth of *ABCD*? **(CAT 2018)**

(a) 25, 10 (b) 24, 12
(c) 25, 9 (d) 24, 10

19. In a parallelogram *ABCD* of area 72 sq cm, the sides *CD* and *AD* have lengths 9 cm and 16 cm, respectively. Let *P* be a point on *CD* such that *AP* is perpendicular to *CD*. Then the area, in sq cm, of triangle *APD* is **(CAT 2018)**

(a) $18\sqrt{3}$ (b) $24\sqrt{3}$
(c) $32\sqrt{3}$ (d) $12\sqrt{3}$

20. From a rectangle *ABCD* of area 768 sq cm, a semicircular part with diameter *AB* and area 72π sq. cm is removed. The perimeter of the leftover portion, in cm, is **(CAT 2018)**

(a) $82 + 24\pi$ (b) $88 + 12\pi$
(c) $80 + 16\pi$ (d) $86 + 8\pi$

21. On a triangle *ABC*, a circle with diameter *BC* is drawn, intersecting *AB* and *AC* at points *P* and *Q*, respectively. If the lengths of *AB*, *AC*, and *CP* are 30 cm, 25 cm, and 20 cm respectively, then the length of *BQ*, in cm, is **(CAT 2018)**

22. A chord of length 5 cm subtends an angle of 60° at the centre of a circle. The length, in cm, of a chord that subtends an angle of 120° at the centre of the same circle is **(CAT 2018)**

(a) $6\sqrt{2}$ (b) 8
(c) 2π (d) $5\sqrt{3}$

23. A triangle *ABC* has area 32 sq units and its side *BC*, of length 8 units, lies on the line *x* = 4. Then the shortest possible distance between *A* and the point (0, 0) is **(CAT 2018)**

(a) $4\sqrt{2}$ units (b) 8 units
(c) 4 units (d) $2\sqrt{2}$ units

24. A parallelogram *ABCD* has area 48 sq cm. If the length of *CD* is 8 cm and that of *AD* is s cm, then which one of the following is necessarily true? **(CAT 2018)**

(a) $5 \leq s \leq 7$ (b) $s \leq 6$
(c) $s \geq 6$ (d) $s \neq 6$

25. The area of a rectangle and the square of its perimeter are in the ratio 1 : 25. Then the lengths of the shorter and longer sides of the rectangle are in the ratio **(CAT 2018)**

(a) 1 : 3 (b) 3 : 8
(c) 2 : 9 (d) 1 : 4

26. With rectangular axes of coordinates, the number of paths from (1, 1) to (8, 10) via (4, 6), where each step from any point (x, y) is either to (*x*, *y* + 1) or to (*x* + 1, *y*), is **(CAT 2019)**

27. Let *T* be the triangle formed by the straight line $3x + 5y - 45 = 0$ and the coordinate axes. Let the circumcircle of *T* have radius of length *L*, measured in the same unit as the coordinate axes. Then, the integer closest to *L* is **(CAT 2019)**

28. If the rectangular faces of a brick have their diagonals in the ratio 3: $2\sqrt{3} : \sqrt{15}$, then the ratio of the length of the shortest edge of the brick to that of its longest edge is **(CAT 2019)**

(a) $\sqrt{3}:2$ (b) $1:\sqrt{3}$
(c) $2:\sqrt{5}$ (d) $\sqrt{2}:\sqrt{3}$

29. In a circle of radius 11 cm, *CD* is a diameter and *AB* is a chord of length 20.5 cm. If *AB* and *CD* intersect at a point *E* inside the circle and *CE* has length 7 cm, then the difference of the lengths of *BE* and *AE*, in cm, is **(CAT 2019)**

(a) 1.5 (b) 3.5
(c) 0.5 (d) 2.5

30. *AB* is a diameter of a circle of radius 5 cm. Let *P* and *Q* be two points on the circle so that the length of *PB* is 6 cm, and the length of *AP* is twice that of *AQ*. Then the length, in cm, of *QB* is nearest to **(CAT 2019)**

(a) 8.5 (b) 9.3
(c) 9.1 (d) 7.8

31. Let *S* be the set of all points (*x*, *y*) in the *x*-*y* plane such $|x| + |y| \leq 2$ and $|x| \geq 1$. Then, the area, in square units, of the region represented by *S* equals [TITA] **(CAT 2019)**

32. Corners are cut off from an equilateral triangle *T* to produce a regular hexagon *H*. Then, the ratio of the area of *H* to the area of *T* is **(CAT 2019)**

(a) 5 : 6 (b) 3 : 4
(c) 2 : 3 (d) 4 : 5

33. In a triangle *ABC*, medians *AD* and *BE* are perpendicular to each other, and have lengths 12 cm and 9 cm, respectively. Then, the area of triangle *ABC*, in sq cm, is **(CAT 2019)**

(a) 80 (b) 68
(c) 72 (d) 78

34. Two circles, each of radius 4 cm, touch externally. Each of these two circles is touched externally by a third circle. If these three circles have a common tangent, then the radius of the third circle, in cm, is **(CAT 2019)**

(a) $\frac{1}{3}$ (b) 1

(c) $\frac{1}{\sqrt{2}}$ (d) $\sqrt{2}$

35. Let *ABC* be a right angled triangle with hypotenuse *BC* of length 20cm. If *AP* is perpendicular on *BC*, then the maximum possible length of *AP*, in cm, is **(CAT 2019)**

(a) 10 (b) $8\sqrt{2}$

(c) $6\sqrt{2}$ (d) 5

36. A man makes complete use of 405 cc of iron, 783 cc of aluminium, and 351 cc of copper to make a number of solid right circular cylinders of each type of metal. These cylinders have the same volume and each of these has radius 3 cm. If the total number of cylinders are to be kept at a minimum, then the total surface area of all these cylinders, in sq cm, is **(CAT 2019)**

(a) $1026(1 + \pi)$ (b) 8464π

(c) 928π (d) $1044(4 + \pi)$

37. The base of a regular pyramid is a square and each of the other four sides is an equilateral triangle, length of each side being 20 cm. The vertical height of the pyramid, in cm, is **(CAT 2019)**

(a) $10\sqrt{2}$ (b) $8\sqrt{3}$

(c) 12 (d) $5\sqrt{5}$

38. Let *A* and *B* be two regular polygons having *a* and *b* sides, respectively. If $b = 2a$ and each interior angle of *B* is 3/2 times each interior angle of *A*, then each interior angle, in degrees, of a regular polygon with $a + b$ sides is **(CAT 2019)**

39. A circle is inscribed in a rhombus with diagonals 12 cm and 16 cm. The ratio of the area of circle to the area of rhombus is **(CAT 2020)**

(a) $\frac{2\pi}{15}$ (b) $\frac{5\pi}{18}$

(c) $\frac{3\pi}{25}$ (d) $\frac{6\pi}{25}$

40. A solid right circular cone of height 27 cm is cut into two piece along a plane parallel to its base a height of 18 cm from the base. If the difference in volume of the two pieces is 225 cc, the volume, in cc, of the original cone is **(CAT 2020)**

(a) 256 (b) 232

(c) 243 (d) 264

41. On a rectangular metal sheet of area 135 sq in, a circle is painted such that the circle touches two opposite sides. If the area of the sheet left unpainted is two–thirds of the painted area then the perimeter of the rectangle in inches is **(CAT 2020)**

(a) $3\sqrt{\pi}\left(5+\frac{12}{\pi}\right)$ (b) $5\sqrt{\pi}\left(3+\frac{9}{\pi}\right)$

(c) $3\sqrt{\pi}\left(\frac{5}{2}+\frac{6}{\pi}\right)$ (d) $4\sqrt{\pi}\left(3+\frac{9}{\pi}\right)$

42. Let C be a circle of radius 5 meters having center at O. Let PQ be a chord of C that passes through points A and B where A is located 4 meters north of O and B is located 3 meters east of O. Then, the length of PQ, in meters, is nearest tois **(CAT 2020)**

(a) 7.8 (b) 7.2

(c) 8.8 (d) 6.6

43. The sum of the perimeters of an equilateral triangle and a rectangle is 90 cm. The area, T, of the triangle and the area, R, of the rectangle, both in sq cm, satisfy the relationship $R = T^2$. If the sides of the rectangle are in the ratio 1:3, then the length, in cm, of the longer side of the rectangle isis **(CAT 2020)**

(a) 18 (b) 24

(c) 21 (d) 27

44. Let C1 and C2 be concentric circles such that the diameter of C1 is 2 cm longer than that of C2. If a chord of C1 has length 6cm and is tangent to C2, then the diameter, in cm, of C1 is **(CAT 2020)**

45. From an interior point of an equilateral, triangle, perpendiculars are drawn on all three sides. The sum of the lengths of the three perpendiculars is *s*. Then the area of the triangle is **(CAT 2020)**

(a) $\frac{2s^2}{\sqrt{3}}$ (b) $\frac{s^2}{\sqrt{3}}$

(c) $\frac{s^2}{2\sqrt{3}}$ (d) $\frac{\sqrt{3}s^2}{2}$

46. In a trapezium *ABCD*, *AB* is parallel to *DC*, *BC* is perpendicular to *DC* and $\angle BAD = 45°$, If *DC* = 5 cm, *BC* = 4 *cm*, the area of the trapezium in sq cm is **(CAT 2020)**

47. The points (2, 1) and (–3, –4) are opposite vertices of a parallelogram. If the other two vertices lie on the line $x + 9y + c = 0$ then *c* is **(CAT 2020)**

(a) 13 *(b) 14*

(c) 12 *(d) 15*

48. If the area of a regular hexagon is equal to the area of an equilateral triangle of side 12 cm, then the length, in cm, of each side of the hexagon is **(CAT 2021)**

(a) $\sqrt{6}$ (b) $6\sqrt{6}$

(c) $2\sqrt{6}$ (d) $4\sqrt{6}$

49. Suppose the length of each side of a regular hexagon ABCDEF is 2 cm. If T is the midpoint of CD, then the length of AT, in cm, is **(CAT 2021)**

(a) $\sqrt{15}$ (b) $\sqrt{12}$
(c) $\sqrt{14}$ (d) $\sqrt{13}$

50. A circle of diameter 8 inches is inscribed in a triangle ABC where ∠ABC = 90°. If BC = 10 inches then the area of the triangle in square inches is **(CAT 2021)**

51. Let D and E be points on sides AB and AC, respectively, of a triangle ABC, such that AD : BD = 2 : 1 and AE : CE = 2 : 3. If the area of the triangle ADE is 8 sq cm, then the area of the triangle ABC, in sq cm, is **(CAT 2021)**

52. If a rhombus has area 12 sq cm and side length 5 cm, then the length, in cm, of its longer diagonal is **(CAT 2021)**

(a) $\frac{\sqrt{37}+\sqrt{13}}{2}$ (b) $\frac{\sqrt{13}+\sqrt{12}}{2}$
(c) $\sqrt{(13)}+\sqrt{(12)}$ (d) $\sqrt{(37)}+\sqrt{(13)}$

53. The sides AB and CD of a trapezium ABCD are parallel, with AB being the smaller side. P is the midpoint of CD and ABPD is a parallelogram. If the difference between the areas of the parallelogram ABPD and the triangle BPC is 10 sq cm, then the area, in sq cm, of the trapezium ABCD is **(CAT 2021)**

(a) 20 (b) 30
(c) 25 (d) 40

54. A park is shaped like a rhombus and has area 96 sq m. If 40 m of fencing is needed to enclose the park, the cost, in INR, of laying electric wires along its two diagonals, at the rate of ₹125 per m, is **(CAT 2021)**

55. The cost of fencing a rectangular plot is ₹200 per ft along one side, and ₹100 per ft along the three other sides. If the area of the rectangular plot is 60000 sq. ft, then the lowest possible cost of fencing all four sides, in INR, is **(CAT 2021)**

(a) 100000 (b) 160000
(c) 120000 (d) 90000

56. Let ABCD be a parallelogram. The lengths of the side AD and the diagonal AC are 10 cm and 20 cm, respectively. If the angle ∠ADC is equal to 30° then the area of the parallelogram, in sq. cm, is **(CAT 2021)**

(a) $\frac{25\left(\sqrt{5}+\sqrt{15}\right)}{2}$ (b) $25\left(\sqrt{3}+\sqrt{15}\right)$
(c) $25\left(\sqrt{5}+\sqrt{15}\right)$ (d) $\frac{25\left(\sqrt{3}+\sqrt{15}\right)}{2}$

57. In a triangle ABC, ∠BCA = 50°. D and E are points on AB and AC, respectively, such that AD = DE. If F is a point on BC such that BD = DF, then ∠FDE, in degrees, is equal to **(CAT 2021)**

(a) 72 (b) 80
(c) 100 (d) 96

58. A trapezium *ABCD* has side *AD* parallel to *BC*, ∠*BAD* = 90°, *BC* = 3 cm and *AD* = 8 cm. If the perimeter of this trapezium is 36 cm, then its area, in sq. cm, is? **(CAT 2022)**

59. Let *ABCD* be a parallelogram such that the coordinates of its three vertices *A*, *B*, *C* are (1, 1), (3, 4) and (–2, 8), respectively. Then, the coordinates of the vertex *D* are **(CAT 2022)**

(a) (–3, 4) (b) (–4, 5)
(c) (0, 11) (d) (4, 5)

60. All the vertices of a rectangle lie on a circle of radius *R*. If the perimeter of the rectangle is *P*, then the area of the rectangle is **(CAT 2022)**

(a) $\frac{P^2}{8}-2R^2$ (b) $\frac{P^2}{8}-\frac{R^2}{2}$
(c) $\frac{P^2}{2}-2PR$ (d) $\frac{P^2}{16}-R^2$

61. The length of each side of an equilateral triangle *ABC* is 3 cm. Let *D* be a point on *BC* such that the area of triangle *ADC* is half the area of triangle *ABD*. Then the length of *AD*. in cm, is **(CAT 2022)**

(a) $\sqrt{5}$ (b) $\sqrt{6}$
(c) $\sqrt{8}$ (d) $\sqrt{7}$

62. Regular polygons *A* and *B* have number of sides in the ratio 1 : 2 and interior angles in the ratio 3 : 4. Then the number of sides of *B* equals? **(CAT 2022)**

63. In triangle *ABC*, altitudes *AD* and *BE* are drawn to the corresponding bases. If ∠*BAC* = 45° and ∠*ABC* = *θ*, then $\frac{AD}{BE}$ equals **(CAT 2022)**

(a) $\frac{(\sin\theta+\cos\theta)}{\sqrt{2}}$ (b) $\sqrt{2}\sin\theta$
(c) $\sqrt{2}\cos\theta$ (d) 1

64. Two ships are approaching a port along straight routes at constant speeds. Initially, the two ships and the port formed an equilateral triangle with sides of length 24 km. When the slower ship travelled 8 km, the triangle formed by the new positions of the two ships and the port became right-angled. When the faster ship reaches the port, the distance, in km, between the other ship and the port will be **(CAT 2022)**

(a) 6 (b) 12
(c) 8 (d) 4

65. In a triangle *ABC*, *AB* = *AC* = 8 cm. A cirde drawn with *BC* as diameter passes through *A*. Another circle drawn with center at *A* passes through *B* and *C*. Then the area, in sq. cm, of the overlapping region between the two circles is **(CAT 2022)**

(a) 16π (b) 16 (π – 1)
(c) 32 (π – 1) (d) 32 π

66. The lengths of all four sides of a quadrilateral are integer valued. If three of its sides are of length 1 cm, 2 cm and 4 cm, then the total number of possible lengths of the fourth side is **(CAT 2022)**

(a) 6 (b) 4

(c) 5 (d) 3

67. Suppose the medians *BD* and *CE* of a triangle *ABC* intersect at a point *O*. If area of triangle *ABC* is 108 sq. cm., then, the area of the triangle *EOD*, in sq. cm., is? **(CAT 2022)**

High Yield Questions

Scan this QR code to access assisted problem solving videos on questions 4, 13, 19 and 53

ANSWER KEY

1. (b)	2. (b)	3. (b)	4. 6
5. 24	6. (a)	7. (b)	8. (c)
9. 200	10. 90	11. 16	12. (d)
13. 198 cm^3	14. (b)	15. (d)	16. (d)
17. (a)	18. (d)	19. (c)	20. (b)
21. 24 cm	22. (d)	23. (c)	24. (c)
25. (d)	26. 3920	27. 9	28. (b)
29. (c)	30. (c)	31. 2 units	32. (c)
33. (c)	34. (b)	35. (a)	36. (a)
37. (a)	38. 150 degrees		39. (d)
40. (c)	41. (a)	42. (c)	43. (d)
44. 10	45. (b)	46. 28	47. (b)
48. (c)	49. (d)	50. 120	51. 30
52. (d)	53. (b)	54. 3500	55. (c)
56. (b)	57. (b)	58. 66	59. (b)
60. (a)	61. (d)	62. 10	63. (b)
64. (b)	65. (c)	66. (c)	67. 9

SOLUTIONS AND SHORTCUTS

1. Area of triangle ABC = $\sqrt{S(S-a)(S-b)(S-c)}$

where $S = \dfrac{40+25+35}{2} = 50$

$= \sqrt{50(50-40)(50-35)(50-25)}$

$= \sqrt{50.10.15.25} = 250\sqrt{3}$

Let *E* is the mid-point of *BC*.

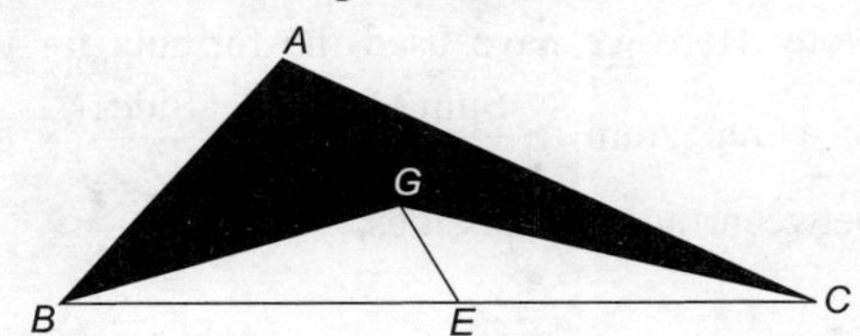

Area of ΔBGE = Area of $\Delta CGE = \dfrac{1}{6}$Area of ΔABC

Area of the remaining portion (after cutoff of triangle *BGC*)

$= \dfrac{4}{6}(\text{Area of }\Delta ABC) = \dfrac{4}{6}\times 250\sqrt{3} = \dfrac{500}{\sqrt{3}}$ sq. ft

2.

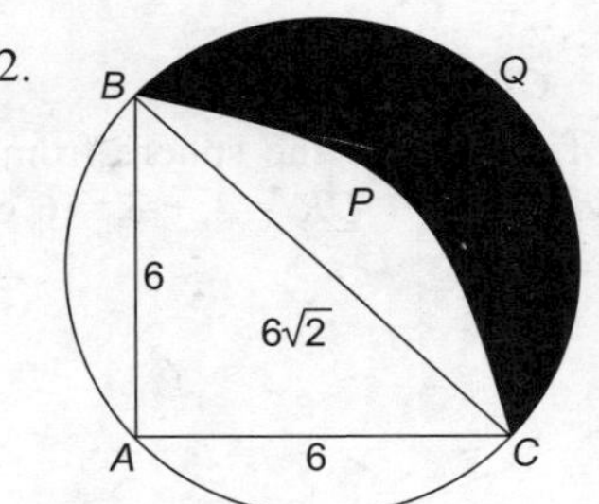

Area of arc *BPC* = Area of circular segment *ABPC* – Area of ΔABC

$= \dfrac{1}{4}\pi(6)^2 - \dfrac{1}{2}\times 6\times 6$

$= 9\pi - 18$

Area of semicircle $BQC = \dfrac{\pi}{2}\times r^2 = \dfrac{\pi\times 3\sqrt{2}^2}{2} = 9\pi$

Area of shaded portion = Area of semi circle *BQC* – Area of arc *BPC* = 9π – (9π – 18) = 18 sq. cm

3. Let the side of five cubes are 1 cm, 1 cm, 2 cm, 3 cm, 3 cm respectively.

Sum of surface areas of the cubes = $6[1^2 + 1^2 + 2^2 + 3^2 + 3^2]$ = 144 sq. cm.

Volume of the five cubes = $1^3 + 1^3 + 2^3 + 3^3 + 3^3$ = 64 cm^3

Side length of the original cube = $(64\ )^{1/3}$ = 4 cm.

Surface area of the original cube = $6(4)^2$ = 96 sq. cm.

Required percentage increase from 96 to 144 sq. cm is 50%.

4. Let the radius of the cylinder is '*r*' cm

$\pi r^2 h = V = 9\pi$ (given). Since, $h = 3$ cm (given), $r = \sqrt{3}$.

As the radius of the cylinder is not equal to the radius of the sphere so the sphere would be at the top of the cylinder as shown in the following diagram.

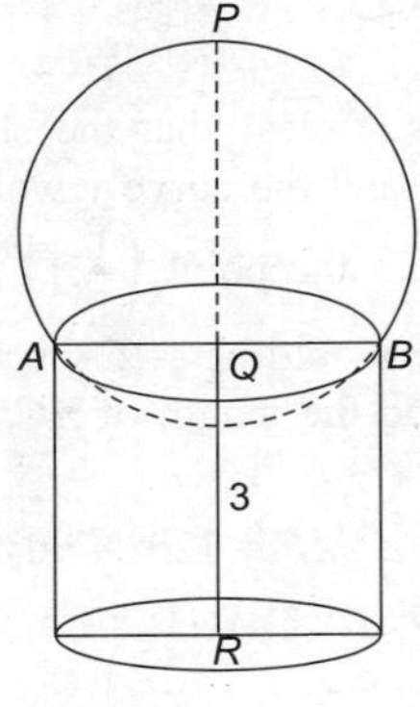

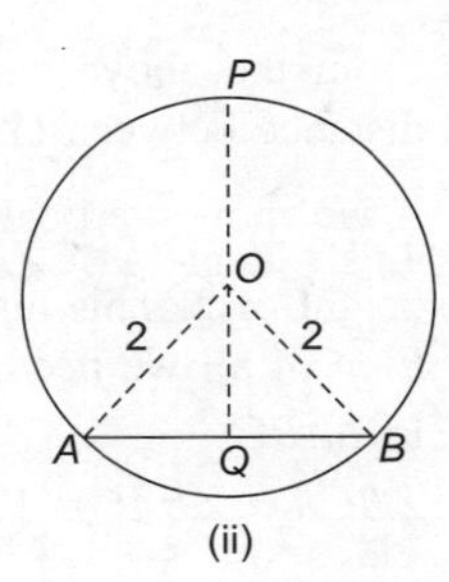

(ii)

Distance of the top of the sphere from bottom of the cylinder = $PQ + QR = PQ + 3$

In diagram II:

In $\Delta AOQ \rightarrow AQ = AB/2$ = Radius of the cylinder $= \sqrt{3}$.

AO = Radius of the sphere = 2

$$OQ = \sqrt{AO^2 - AQ^2} = 1$$

Hence, $PQ = PO + OQ = 2 + 1 = 3$ cm

Thus, the height of the top of the sphere from the base of the cylinder = $PQ + QR = 3 + 3 = 6$ cm.

5. 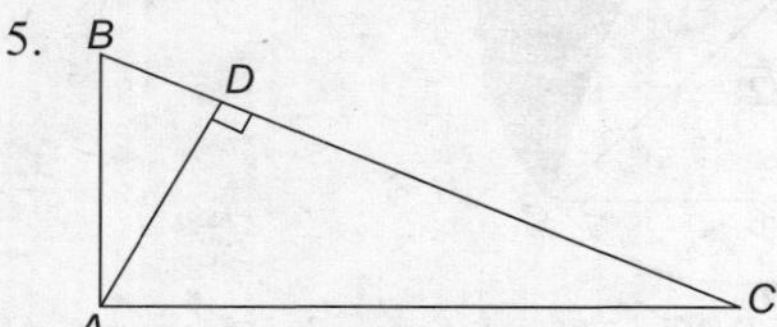

To reach at the hypotenuse BC in minimum time we have to follow the shortest possible path which is AD, where $AD \perp BC$.

As we know that, $\frac{1}{AD^2} = \frac{1}{AB^2} + \frac{1}{AC^2} = \frac{1}{15^2} + \frac{1}{20^2}$

By solving the above equation we get, AD = 12 km.

Required time to reach at $BC = \frac{12}{30}$ h or $\frac{12}{30} \times 60$ = 24 min

6. $y = |x - 1| + |x + 1|$

For $x < -1$

$y = -(x - 1) - (x + 1) = -2x$

For $-1 < x < 1$

$y = -x + 1 + x + 1 = 2$

For $x > 1$

$y = x - 1 + x + 1 = 2x$.

Thus, the graph of the function, $y = |x - 1| + |x + 1|$ can be drawn as follows:

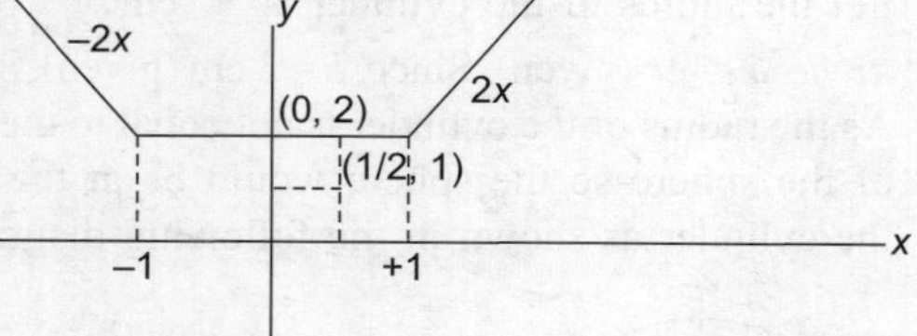

From the above curve it is clear that the shortest distance between (1/2, 1) and the curve y would be if we move vertically from the point $\left(\frac{1}{2}, 1\right)$ to the height of 2. This distance would be = 2 – 1 = 1.

7. First of all we need to find the length of AC.

In ΔABC:

$\angle BCA = \angle BAC = 120° - \angle CAF = 120° - 90° = 30°$

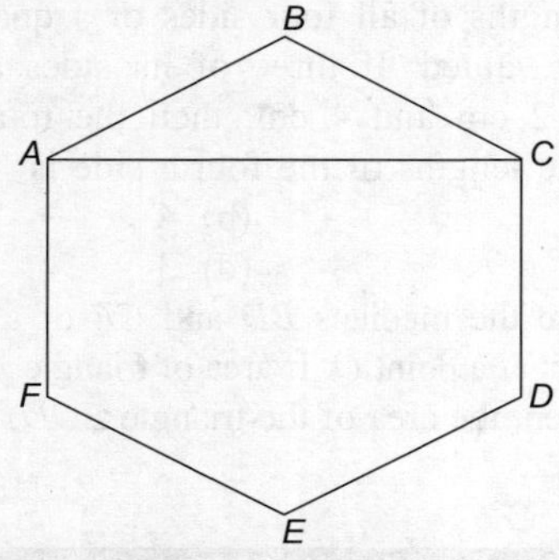

Apply sine rule in triangle ABC:

$$\frac{AB}{\sin 30°} = \frac{AC}{\sin 120°}$$

$$\frac{1}{\sin 30°} = \frac{AC}{\sin 120°}$$

$$AC = \frac{1}{\sin 30°} \cdot \sin 120° = \sqrt{3} \text{ cm}$$

$\left(\text{Using } \sin 30 = \frac{1}{2} \text{ and } \sin 120 = \frac{\sqrt{3}}{2}\right)$.

Area of the square with side $AC = \sqrt{3}^2 = 3$ sq. cm

8. 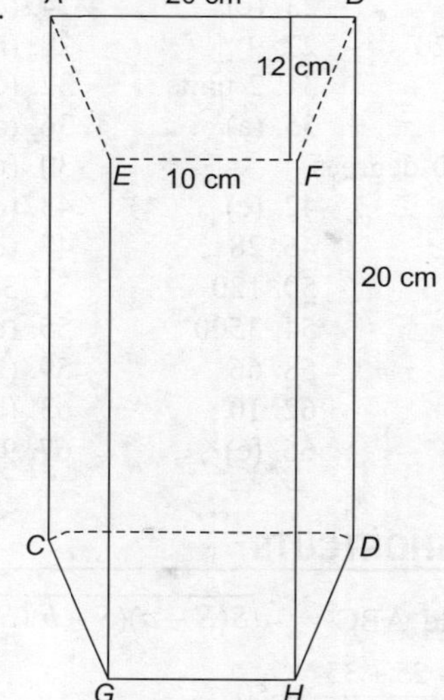

Top and bottom surfaces are trapeziums and the rest are rectangular in shape.

Sum of areas of top and the bottom surfaces = 2(Area of $ABFE$) $= 2\left[\frac{10 + 20}{2} \cdot 12\right]$ = 360 square cm.

Note: Here we have used the formula for the area of a trapezium = $\frac{\text{Sum of parallel Sides}}{2}$ × distance between the parallel sides.

The areas of the lateral sides of the pillar would be equal and both would be rectangles. To find the area of $AEGC$, we need the length of AE.

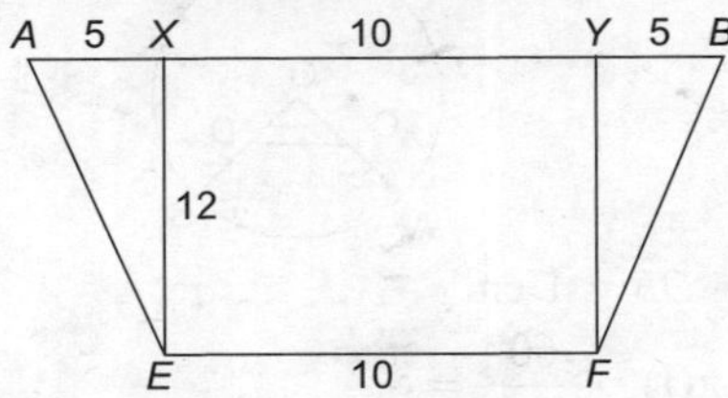

$$AE = \sqrt{12^2 + 5^2} = \sqrt{169} = 13 \text{ cm}$$

Sum of areas of $AEGC$ and $BFHD$ = 2(Area of $AEGC$) = 2(13 × 20) = 520 sq. cm

Area of $ABCD$ = 20 × 20 = 400 sq. cm.

Area of $EFHG$ = 10 × 20 = 200 sq. cm.

Sum of all the six surfaces of the pillar = 360 + 520 + 400 + 200 = 1480 sq. cm.

9. Let the length and breadth of the rectangular park are L and B respectively.

Case I: If we are given the sum of the two lengths and one breadth of the rectangle: as 400:

We have: $2L + B = 400$

$B = 400 - 2L$

Area = $L \times B = L \times (400 - 2L) = 400L - 2L^2$

The area is maximum when the differentiation of this expression is 0:

Thus: d(area)/dL = $400 - 4L = 0$

$L = 100\text{m} \rightarrow B = 200$ m.

Case II: If we are given the sum of the two shorter sides and one longer side as 400:

We have: $2B + L = 400$

$L = 400 - 2B$

Area = $L \times B = B \times (400 - 2B) = 400B - 2B^2$

Differentiating, the area is maximum when: $400 - 4B = 0 \rightarrow B = 100$, which means that L = 200. (Since $L + 2B = 400$).

Hence longer side must be 200 m (in both the cases).

10.

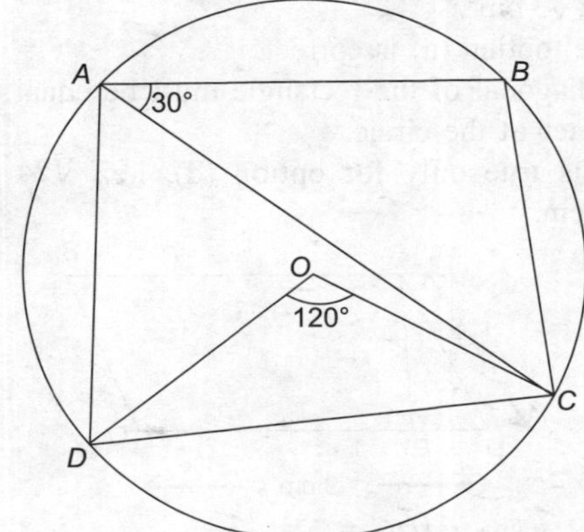

$$\angle CAD = \frac{\angle COD}{2} = \frac{120°}{2} = 60°$$

$$\angle BAD = \angle CAD + \angle BAC = 60° + 30° = 90°$$

Since, the Quadrilateral is a cyclic quadrilateral, the sum of the opposite angles would be 180. Hence, $\angle BCD = 90°$

11. As the distance of P from all the three sides AB, BC and CA are equal so it means 'P' is the in-centre of the triangle ABC.

Let $AC = BC = a$

$$\therefore \quad r = \frac{\Delta}{s} = \left(\frac{\frac{1}{2} \times a \times a}{\frac{a + a + a\sqrt{2}}{2}}\right)$$

$$= \frac{a}{\sqrt{2}}(\sqrt{2} - 1) = 4(\sqrt{2} - 1)$$

$$a = 4\sqrt{2} \text{ cm.}$$

Area of the triangle = $\frac{1}{2} \times 4\sqrt{2} \times 4\sqrt{2}$ sq cm.

12. Diagonals of the rectangle bisects each other it means point $\left(\frac{2+6}{2}, \frac{3+5}{2}\right) = (4, 4)$ lies on the other diagonal $y = 3x + c$.

Therefore, $4 = 3.4 + c$ or $c = 4 - 12 = -8$.

13. When you cut off the tip of the cone, it creates a frustum of the cone at the bottom. However, the part of the cone that is cut off at the top is similar to the original cone. This thought is crucial to solve this question quickly and gives us the solution thinking in the following manner. Since, the cut is made at a height of 9 ft from the base; it is made at a height of 3 ft from the top. Thus, the cut off part of the cone would be a cone with height 3. The original cone, being a cone of height 12, it means that the new cut-off cone has a height as $1/4^{th}$ of the original cone. Using the concept of similarity and the concept, that if the lengths are made as $1/4^{th}$ the original in two similar objects, the volumes would be $1/64^{th}$, we can easily solve this question as:

Now, the volume of the original cone = $\frac{1}{3} \times \pi \times r^2 \times h = 64\pi$. Volume of the cut off cone $= \frac{1}{64} \times 64\pi = \pi$. Thus, the volume of the frustum of the cone = $64\pi - \pi = 63\pi = 63 \times \frac{22}{7} = 198 \text{ cm}^3$.

14. Let O be the centre of the circle and CE and DF are the parallel chords of lengths 6 cm and 4 cm respectively.

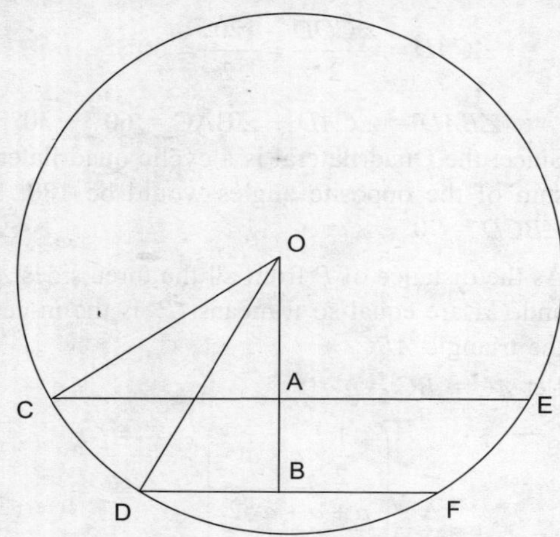

Draw $OB \perp DF$ which cuts CE at A.

As CE and DF are parallel so, $OA \perp CE$.

$CA=CE/2=3$. $DB= DF/2= 2$ cm

Let 'r' be the radius of the circle. $OC = OD = r$

In Δ OAC:

$OA= \sqrt{r^2-3^2} = \sqrt{r^2-9}$

In Δ ODB:

$OB= \sqrt{r^2-2^2} = \sqrt{r^2-4}$

It is given to us that: $AB = 1 = OB - OA = \sqrt{r^2-4} - \sqrt{r^2-9}$

Now check the options: The above equation satisfies for $r = \sqrt{13}$ cm.

Hence, option (b) is correct.

15.

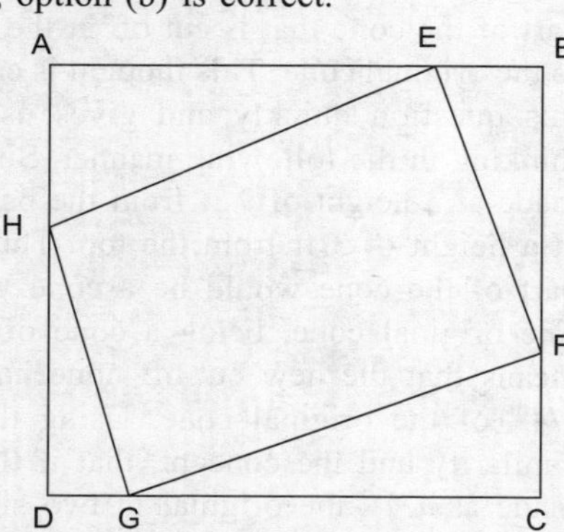

Let $AB = a$

Area of $ABCD = a^2$

Area of $EFGH$ = 62.5% of $a^2 = 0.625\ a^2$

As $EFGH$ is a square, then $EF = FG = GH = HE$. This is possible only when $AE = BF = GC = DH$ and $EB = FC = DG = AH$.

Now check the options:

Option (d): $EB : CG = 1 : 3$

$EB = k$, $CG = 3k$

$AB = AE + EB = k + 3k = 4k$. So the area of $ABCD = 16k^2$

$EH = \sqrt{k^2+(3k)^2} = k\sqrt{10}$ cm

Area of $EFGH = 10k^2$

In this case, area of $EFGH$ is 62.5% of $ABCD$. Hence, option (d) is correct.

16.

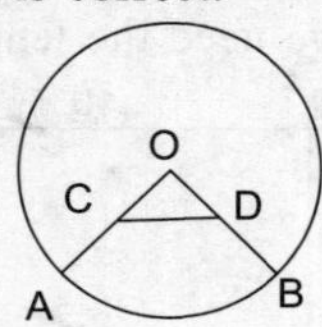

$OA = OB = 1$ cm

$$R = \pi(1)^2 \times \frac{60^\circ}{360^\circ} = \frac{\pi}{6}$$

$$\text{Area of } \Delta\ OCD = \frac{\sqrt{3}}{4}(OC)^2 = \frac{\pi}{12}$$

$$\sqrt{3}(OC)^2 = \frac{\pi}{3}$$

$$OC = \left[\frac{\pi}{3\sqrt{3}}\right]^{1/2}$$

Hence, option (d) is correct.

17. Let ABC is the equilateral triangle $T1$. After meeting the mid-points of AB and AC, a second triangle ADE is formed which is also an equilateral triangle. Similarly $T3$, $T4$, ... are equilateral triangles. AB = 24 cm, each side of $T2$ must be 12 cm, each side of $T3$ = 6 cm and so on.

$$\text{Area of } T1 = \frac{\sqrt{3}}{4}(24)^2 \text{ cm}^2$$

$$\text{Area of } T2 = \frac{\sqrt{3}}{4}(12)^2 \text{ cm}^2$$

$$\text{Area of } T3 = \frac{\sqrt{3}}{4}(6)^2 \text{ cm}^2$$

Required sum $= \frac{\sqrt{3}}{4}(24)^2 + \frac{\sqrt{3}}{4}(12)^2 + \frac{\sqrt{3}}{4}(6)^2$ + ... would be the sum of this infinite geometric progression.

$$= \frac{\sqrt{3}}{4}\left[24^2 + \frac{(24)^2}{4} + \frac{24^2}{16} + \ldots\right] = \frac{\sqrt{3}}{4}\left[\frac{24^2}{1-\frac{1}{4}}\right]$$

$= 192\sqrt{3}$ cm^2.

Hence, option (a) is correct.

18. The diagonal of the rectangle must be equal to the diameter of the circle.

This is true only for option (d), i.e., $\sqrt{24^2+10^2}$ = 26 cm.

19.

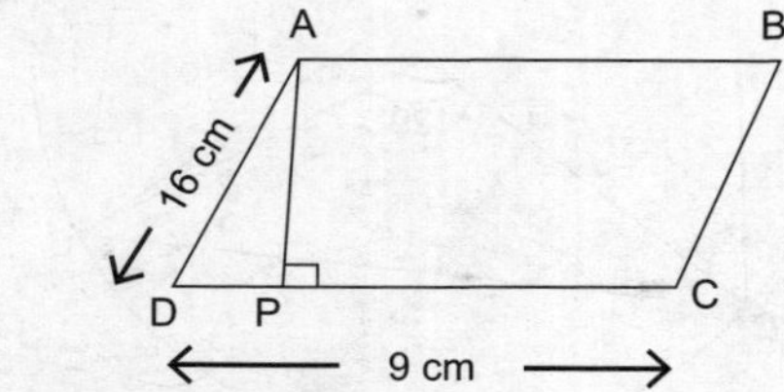

$16 \times 9 \times \sin \angle ADC = 72$

$\sin \angle ADC = 1/2$

$\angle ADC = 30^\circ$

$DP = 16 \cos 30^\circ = 8\sqrt{3}$ cm.

Area of $\Delta APD = \frac{1}{2} \times 16 \times 8\sqrt{3} \times \sin \angle ADP$

$= \frac{1}{2} \times 16 \times 8\sqrt{3} \times \frac{1}{2} = 32\sqrt{3}$ cm^2

Hence, option (c) is correct.

20. 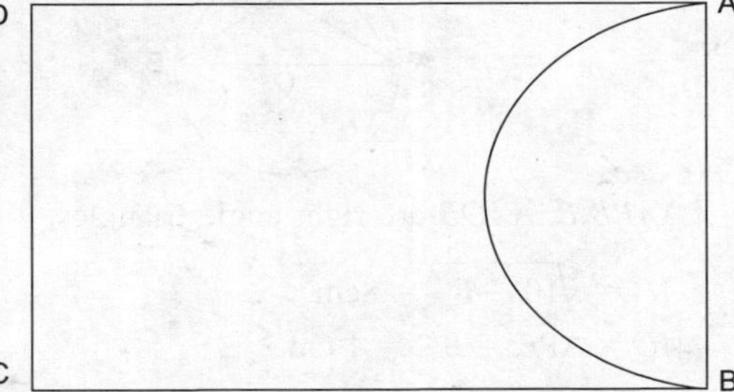

Area of semicircular portion $AB = 72\pi$

$\pi\left(\frac{AB}{2}\right)^2 \times \frac{1}{2} = 72\pi$

$AB = 24$ *cm*

$AB \times AD = 768$

$AD = 768/AB = \frac{768}{24} = 32$ cm

Perimeter of semicircular portion $AB = \pi\left(\frac{AB}{2}\right) = \frac{\pi(24)}{2}$ $= 12\pi$ cm

Perimeter of the leftover portion $= AD + DC + BC +$ Perimeter of semicircular portion $AB = 32 + 24 + 32 + 12\pi = 88 + 12\pi$ cm. Hence, option (b) is correct.

21. 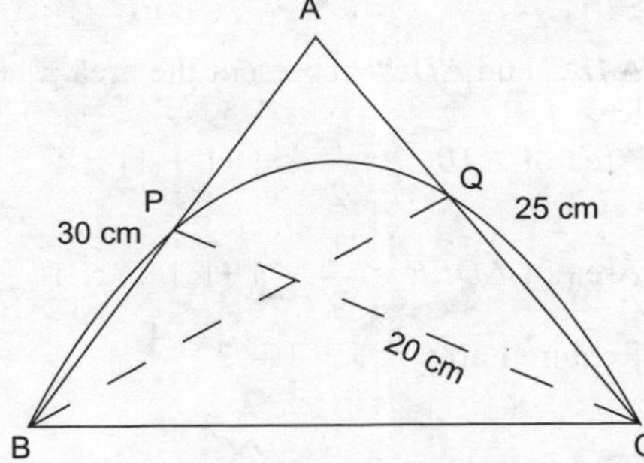

In triangle ABC: $\angle BPC = \angle BQC = 90^\circ$, $BQ \perp AC$, $CP \perp AB$

Area of triangle $= \frac{1}{2} \times AB \times CP = \frac{1}{2} \times AC \times BQ$

$BQ = \frac{AB \times CP}{AC} = \frac{30 \times 20}{25} = 24$ cm

22. Let the centre of the circle be '*O*'. Chord *AB* subtends 60° at the centre of the circle and chord *CD* subtends 120° at the centre of the circle. Draw a perpendicular *OP* from the centre to *CD*, The figure for these would be as shown below.

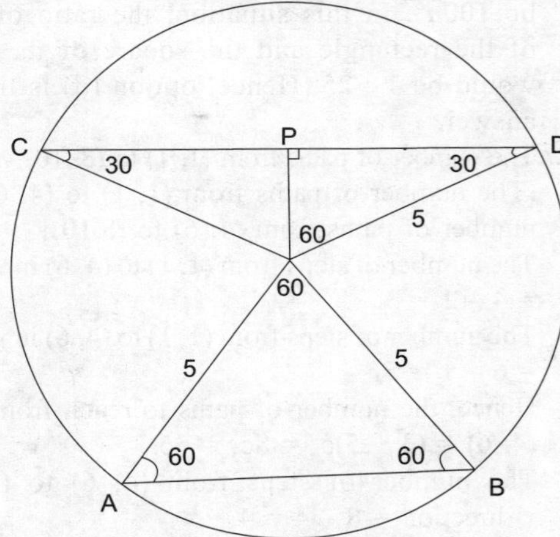

In the triangle *DOP*, which is a 30 – 60 – 90 triangle, we can see that the side opposite the 90° angle is 5. Hence, the side opposite the 60° angle, i.e. $PD = 2.5\sqrt{3}$.

Also, $CD = 2PD = 5\sqrt{3}$.

23. 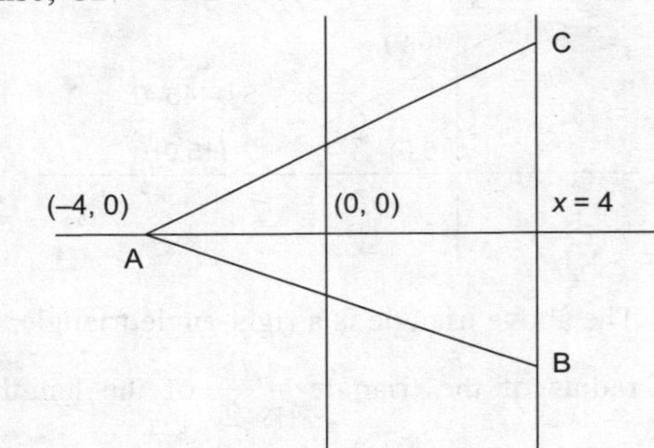

The distance between *A* and (0, 0) is minimum possible when *A* lies on the *X*-axis.

In this case, the minimum possible distance = 4. Hence, option (c) is correct.

24. 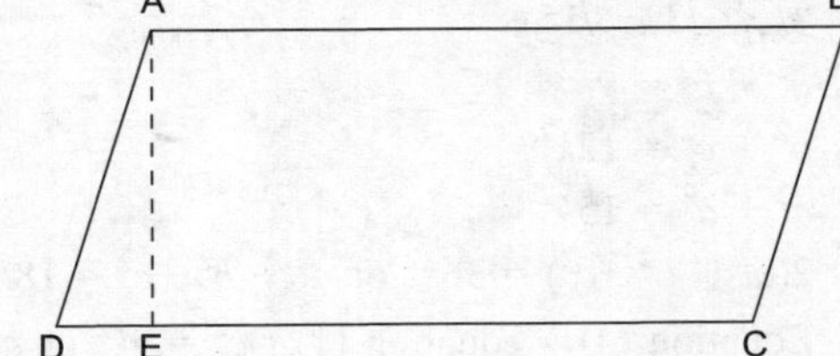

Draw $AE \perp CD$.

According to the question:

$AE \times CD = 48$ OR $AE \times 8 = 48$ OR $AE = 6$ cm

As, $AD \geq AE$ OR $AD \geq 6$ cm. Hence, option (c) is correct.

25. Solve this question using the options.

For option (d), if we assume the sides of the rectangle as '*n*' and '4*n*' respectively, we get:

Area of the rectangle $= 4n^2$ and its perimeter as $10n$. Hence, the square of the perimeter would

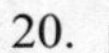

be $100n^2$. In this situation, the ratio of the area of the rectangle and the square of its perimeter would be 1 : 25. Hence, option (d) is the correct answer.

26. The number of paths from (1, 1) to (8, 10) via (4, 6) = [The number of paths from (1, 1) to (4, 6)] × [The number of paths from (4, 6) to (8,10)]
The number of steps from (1, 1) to (4, 6) in x-direction = 4 – 1 = 3.
The number of steps from (1, 1) to (4, 6) in y-direction = 6 – 1 = 5
Hence, the number of paths to reach from (1, 1) to (4, 6) = $(3 + 5)c_3 = 8c_3 = 56$.
The number of steps from (4, 6) to (8, 10) in x-direction = 8 – 4 = 4.
The number of steps from (4, 6) to (8, 10) in y-direction = 10 – 6 = 4.
Hence, the number of paths to reach from (4, 6) to (8, 10) = $(4 + 4)c_4 = 8c_4 = 70$.
The number of paths from (1, 1) to (8, 10) = 56 × 70 = 3920

27.

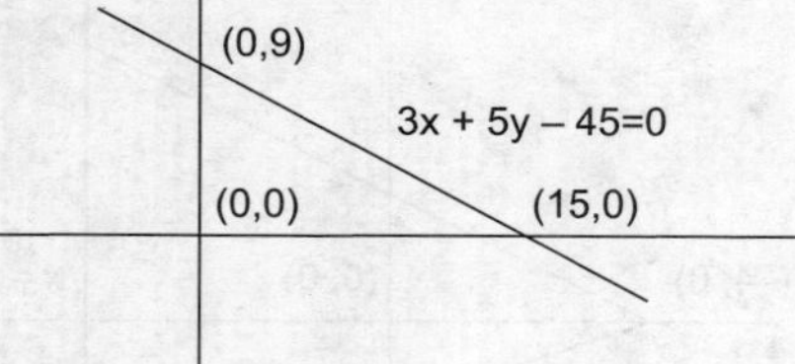

The above triangle is a right-angle triangle. Circum-radius of the triangle = $\frac{1}{2}$ of the length of the hypotenuse = $\frac{1}{2} \times \sqrt{9^2 + 15^2} = 8.5+$

Hence, the integer closest to $L = 9$.

28. Assuming the dimensions of the brick is a, b and c. Let the lengths of the diagonals be
$3k$: $2\sqrt{3}k$: $\sqrt{15}k$

$a^2 + b^2 = 9k^2$ (1)

$b^2 + c^2 = 12k^2$ (2)

$c^2 + a^2 = 15k^2$ (3)

$2(a^2 + b^2 + c^2) = 36k^2$ or $a^2 + b^2 + c^2 = 18k^2$ (4)

Equation (4) – equation (1) : $c^2 = 9k^2$ or $c = 3k$

Equation (4) – equation (2) : $a^2 = 6k^2$ or $a = k\sqrt{6}$

Equation (4) – equation (3) : $b^2 = 3k^2$ or $b = k\sqrt{3}$

Hence, the required answer: $b : c = \sqrt{3} : 3 = 1 : \sqrt{3}$

Hence, option (b) is correct.

29.

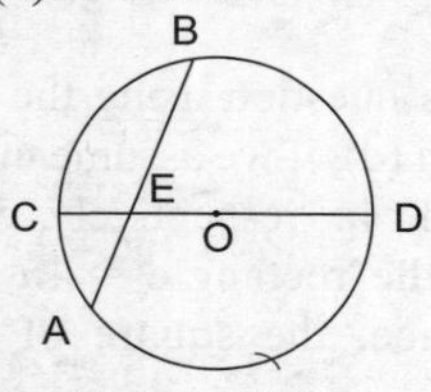

$AE \times BE = CE \times DE$

$AE (20.5 – AE) = 7 \times 15$

$AE (20.5 – AE) = 105$

On solving we get: $AE = 10$ or 10.5

Required difference = 10.5 – 10 = 0.5 cm

Hence, option (c) is correct.

30.

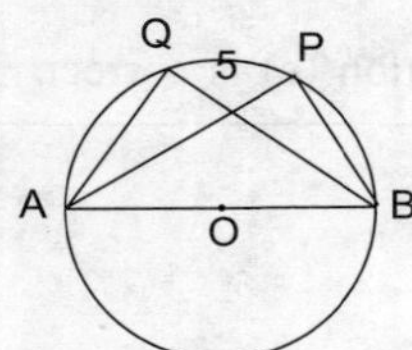

ΔAPB & ΔAQB are right angle triangles.

$AP = \sqrt{10^2 - 6^2} = 8$cm.

AQ = AP/2 = 8/2 = 4 cm.

$BQ = \sqrt{10^2 - 4^2} = 9.1$ cm.

Hence, option (c) is correct.

31.

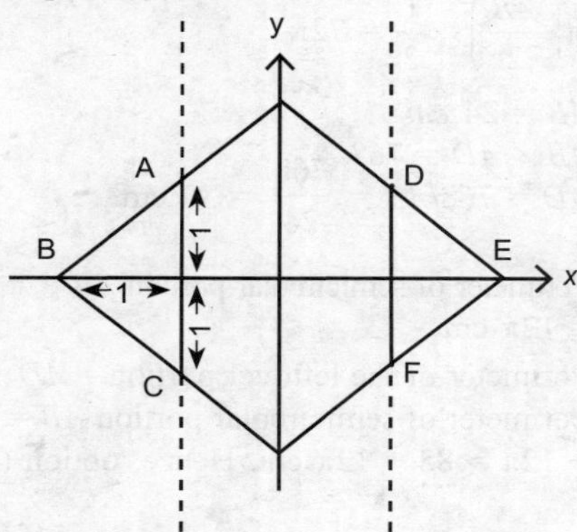

ΔABC and ΔDEF represent the area $|x| + |y| \le 2$ and $|x| \ge 1$.

Area of $\Delta ABC = \frac{1}{2} \times 1 (1 + 1) = 1$

Area of $\Delta DEF = \frac{1}{2} \times 1 (1 + 1) = 1$

Required area = 1 + 1 = 2

32.

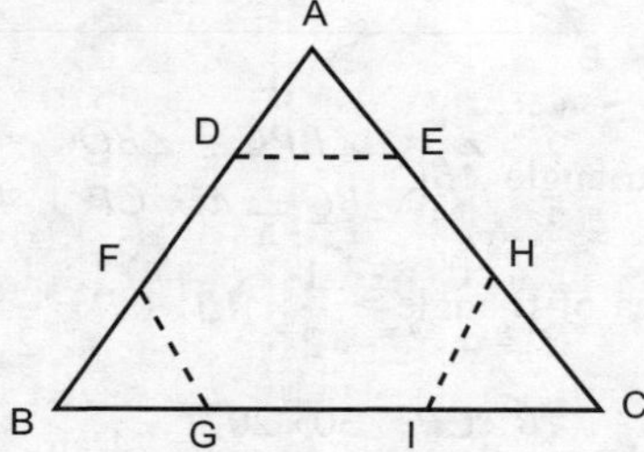

Let ABC be an equilateral triangle, with $AB = BC = AC = 6a$. If we connect the points D, E, H, I, G and F on this so as to make the hexagon $DEHIGF$ into a regular hexagon, we would need: $AD = BF = BG = IC = CH = AE = 2a$. This means that the side of the hexagon would be $2a$.

The area of the triangle =

$$\frac{\sqrt{3}}{4}(side)^2 = \frac{\sqrt{3}}{4}(6a)^2 = 9\sqrt{3}a^2$$

The area of the regular hexagon is given by: $\frac{6\times\sqrt{3}}{4}(side)^2 = \frac{6\times\sqrt{3}}{4}(2a)^2 = 6\sqrt{3}a^2$

The required ratio of $H : T = 2 : 3$. Hence, option (c) is correct.

33.

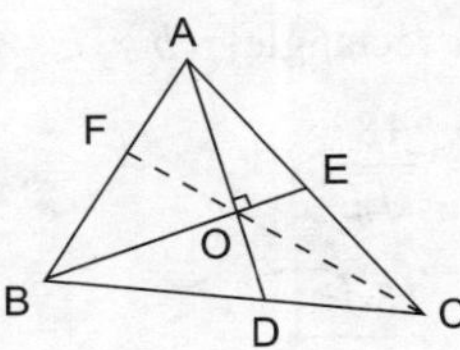

AREA of ΔABC = 6[Area of ΔAOE]

$AD = 12$ cm, $AO = \frac{2}{3} \times 12 = 8$ cm.

$BE = 9$ cm, $OE = \frac{1}{3} \times 9 = 3$ cm.

Area of $\Delta AOE = \frac{1}{2} \times 8 \times 3 = 12$ cm^2.

Area of $\Delta ABC = 6 \times 12 = 72$ cm^2.

Hence, option (c) is correct.

34.

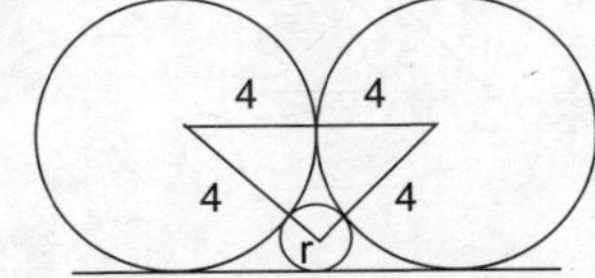

Let the centres of the three circles be A, B and C (for the smaller circle). Also, assume the radius of the smaller circle to be r. Then, the semi-perimeter of the triangle ABC would be $(8 + 8 + 2r)/2 = 8 + r$. Using the formula: $\sqrt{s\times(s-a)(s-b)(s-c)}$, for the area of the triangle, we get the area equal to: $\sqrt{(8+r)\times(r)(4)(4)}$.

But the same area can also be derived using base of the triangle as 8 (AB) and height as $(4 - r)$.

Thus, we have: $\sqrt{(8+r)\times(r)(4)(4)} = \frac{1}{2} \times 8 \times (4-r)$

Solving this, we get $r = 1$ cm.

Hence, option (b) is correct.

35. Length of the perpendicular is maximum, if the length of rest of the two sides is equal.

In this case, the length of the perpendicular = 20/2 = 10. Hence, option (a) is correct.

36. As the number of cylinders is to be kept minimum, the volume of each cylinder would be the *HCF* of 405, 783 and 351 = 27 cc

Number of cylinders = $\frac{405}{27} + \frac{783}{27} + \frac{351}{27} = 15 + 29 + 13 = 57$

Since, the volume of each cylinder is 27 cc and the radius is 3 cm, we can get the height of the cylinders as: $\pi r^2 h = \pi \times 3^2 \times h = 27 \rightarrow h = 3/\pi$

Total surface area of the 57 cylinders = 57 × (Curved surface area + area of the flat sides) = $57 \times (2\pi rh + 2\pi r^2) = 114\pi \times \left(\frac{9}{\pi} + 9\right) = 1026(1 + \pi)$ cc

Hence, option (a) is correct.

37.

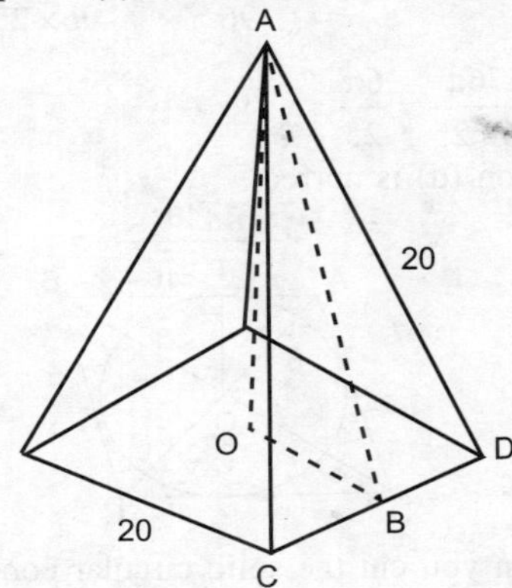

$AB = \frac{20\sqrt{3}}{2} = 10\sqrt{3}$ (As it is the median of the equilateral triangle ACD.)

$OB = 20/2 = 10$ cm

$AO = \sqrt{(AB^2 - OB^2)} = \sqrt{(300-100)} = 10\sqrt{2}$ cm

Hence, option (a) is correct.

38. Interior angle of a 'n' sided polygon = $(n - 2) \times \pi$

According to the question:

$$\frac{(a-2)\pi}{a} \times \frac{3}{2} = \frac{(b-2)\pi}{b}$$

$\frac{(b-2)}{b} = \frac{3}{2} \times \frac{(a-2)}{a}$. Putting $b = 2a$ in this equation, we get:

$$\frac{2a-2}{2a} = \frac{3}{2} \times \frac{a-2}{a}$$

$2a - 2 = 3a - 6$

$a = 4$ and $b = 8$

Interior angle of a polygon with $a + b$ sides =

$$\frac{(a+b-2)\times\pi}{a+b} = \frac{(12-2)\times\pi}{12} = 150°$$

39. In the figure, AB = 10, since it is the hypotenuse of the right triangle AOB, with AO = 6 and OB = 8. (Note: AO = 6, since AC = 12, while OB = 8, since BD = 16). Let, OT = r = radius of the inscribed circle.

In right triangle OTB, $r^2 + (10 - x)^2 = 8^2$, while in right triangle AOT, $x^2 + r^2 = 36$. Subtracting the second equation from the first we get

$20x = 72$ and hence, $x = 3.6$. Consequently, from the second equation, we have $r^2 = 36 - x^2 = 36 - (3.6)^2$

$= 23.04$. Also, the area of the rhombus is given by: $\frac{1}{2} \times$ product of diagonals

$= \frac{1}{2} \times 192 = 96.$

Required ratio $= \dfrac{23.04\pi}{96} = \dfrac{23.04\pi \times 25}{96 \times 25}$

$= \dfrac{576\pi}{96 \times 25} = \dfrac{6\pi}{25}$

Option (d) is correct.

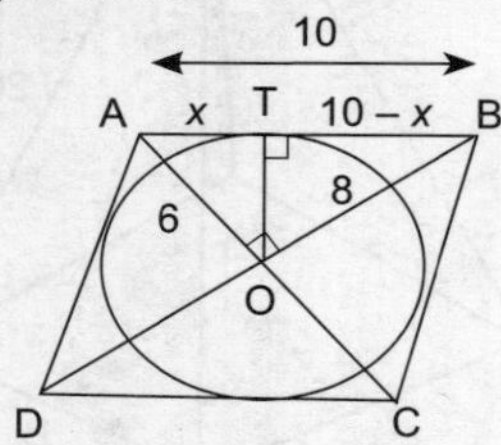

40. When you cut the solid circular cone at a height of 18 from the base, it means you are cutting it at a height of 9 from the top. Since, the height of the new cone thus formed is 1/3rd the height of the original cone, the volume of the new cone will be $\frac{1}{27}$ of the volume of the original cone and the volume of the frustum of the cone formed, would be $\frac{26}{27}$ of the original cone. Assume the volume of the original cone is 27V, then the volume of the frustum would be 26V and the volume of the new cone (smaller one with height 9), would be V. The difference between 26V and V = 25V is given to us as 225.

Hence, $V = \frac{225}{25} = 9$. Thus, the volume of the original cone = 27V = 279 = 243.

Option (c) is correct.

41. The given sheet of metal will look as shown in the figure.

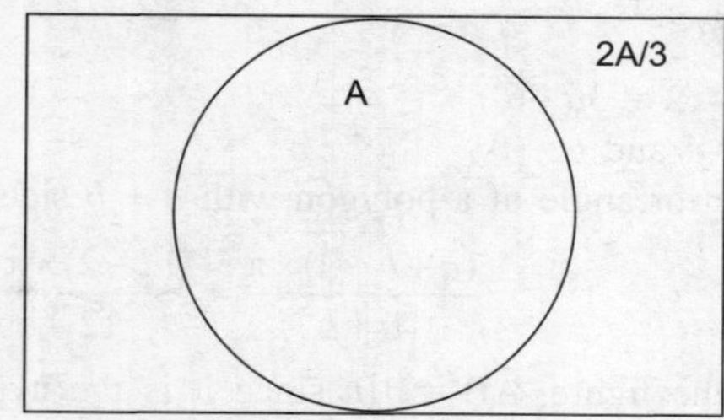

Since, the total area of the rectangular sheet is 135, we get that the area of the circle A = 81 and $\frac{2A}{3} = 54$. We can calculate the radius of the circle and consequently find the height of the rectangle by doubling the radius (since the height of the rectangular sheet would be equal to the diameter of the circle). $\pi \times r^2 = 81$

$\Rightarrow r = \dfrac{9}{\sqrt{\pi}}$

Hence, the height of the rectangle

= diameter of the circle $= \dfrac{18}{\sqrt{\pi}}$.

We are also given the area of the rectangular sheet as 135. Using:

Area of a rectangle $= b \times h$

$\Rightarrow 135 = \dfrac{18}{\sqrt{\pi}} \times b$

$\Rightarrow \quad b = \dfrac{15\sqrt{\pi}}{2}$.

The perimeter of the rectangle would be:

$2 \times \dfrac{18}{\sqrt{\pi}} + 2 \times \dfrac{15\sqrt{\pi}}{2}$

$= \dfrac{36}{\sqrt{\pi}} + 15\sqrt{\pi} = 3\sqrt{\pi}\left(5 + \dfrac{12}{\pi}\right)$

Hence, option (a) is correct.

42.

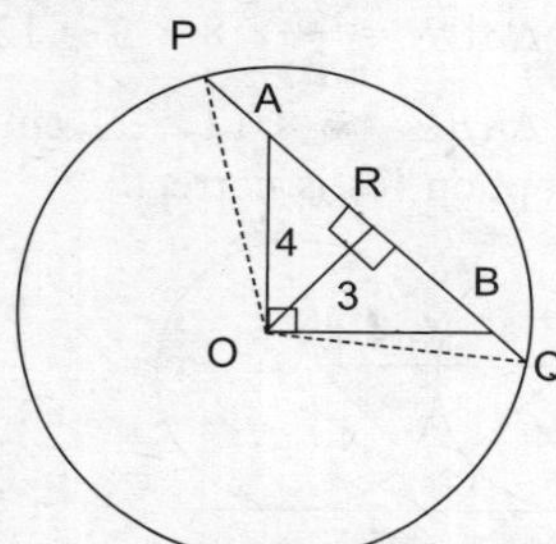

O is the center of the circle and the radius of the circle = 5

In triangle AOB, AB = 5 (Pythagoras theorem).

Drop a perpendicular from O to R as shown. Using the property of right angled triangles,

$OR = \dfrac{3 \times 4}{5} = 2.4$. OR being dropped from the centre as a perpendicular to the chord, means that it bisects the chord. Thus, we can find the length of PR and double it to get PQ.

In triangle ORP, $OP^2 = OR^2 + PR^2$, we get: $PR^2 = 19.24$, $PR = \sqrt{19.24} \approx 4.4$.

Hence, $PQ \approx 8.8$. Option (c) is correct.

43. Let the lengths of the sides of the rectangle be 'l' and '$3l$' respectively. The area of the rectangle $R = 3l^2 = T^2 \Rightarrow T = l\sqrt{3}$ = area of the triangle.

Also, area of an equilateral triangle having area 'a' is given by: $\dfrac{\sqrt{3}}{4}a^2 = l\sqrt{3} \Rightarrow a = 2\sqrt{l}$

The sum of the perimeters

$= 6\sqrt{l} + 8l = 90 \Rightarrow l = 9$

Hence, the length of the longer side of the rectangle = 27.

Option (d) is correct.

44. We can visualise the 3-4-5 Pythagoras triplet as shown in the figure. Hence, the radius of C_1 = 5 and it's diameter is 10.

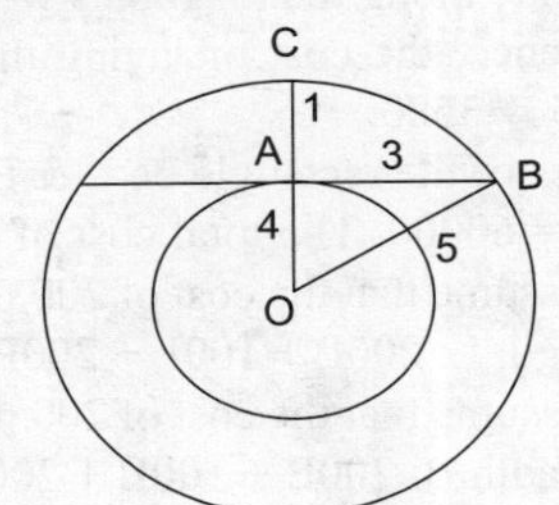

45.

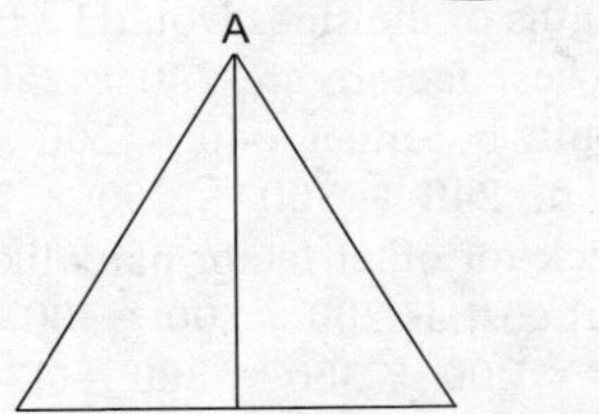

From any point on an equilateral triangle, if we draw three perpendiculars on other sides those three perpendiculars will add up to the Altitude of the equilateral triangle. We know that the value of the altitude of an equilateral triangle with side 'a' is $\frac{\sqrt{3}}{2}a$

Hence, $s = \frac{\sqrt{3}}{2}a$

$\Rightarrow \quad a = \frac{2s}{\sqrt{3}}$.

Thus, the area of the triangle

$= \frac{\sqrt{3}}{4} a \times a = \frac{\sqrt{3}}{4} \times \frac{2s}{\sqrt{3}} \times \frac{2s}{\sqrt{3}} \rightarrow \frac{s^2}{\sqrt{3}}$.

Hence, option (b) is correct.

46. We can make the following figure for the given trapezium:

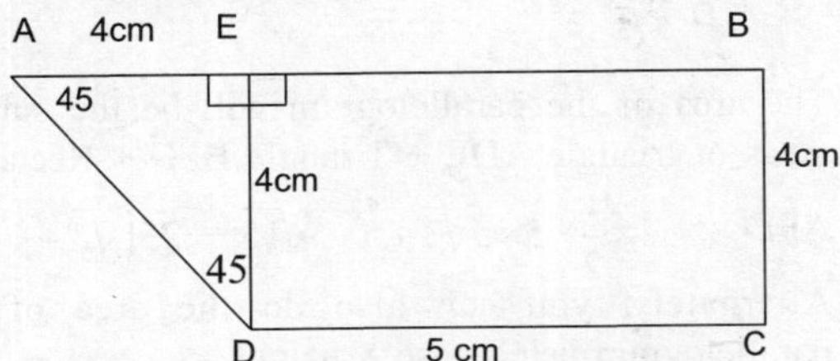

The required area would be Area of rectangle BCDE + Area of Triangle ADE = 20 + 8 = 28.

47. The diagonals of a parallelogram bisect each other. Hence, the midpoint of the diagonal across the given vertices, should also lie on the other diagonal, which is given to us as $x + 9y + c = 0$. The mid – point of the line connecting (2, 1) and (–3, –4) would be given by: x coordinate $= \frac{2-3}{2} = -0.5$;

y coordinate $= \frac{1-4}{2} = -1.5$

$x = -0.5$ and $y = -1.5$ should equate LHS and RHS in the equation $x + 9y + c = 0$. Inserting these values, we get:

$-0.5 - 13.5 + c = 0 \Rightarrow c = 14$.

Option (b) is correct.

48. $\frac{3 \times \sqrt{3}a^2}{2} = \frac{\sqrt{3}}{4} \times 144 \rightarrow$ a $= 2\sqrt{6}$. Option (c) is correct.

49.

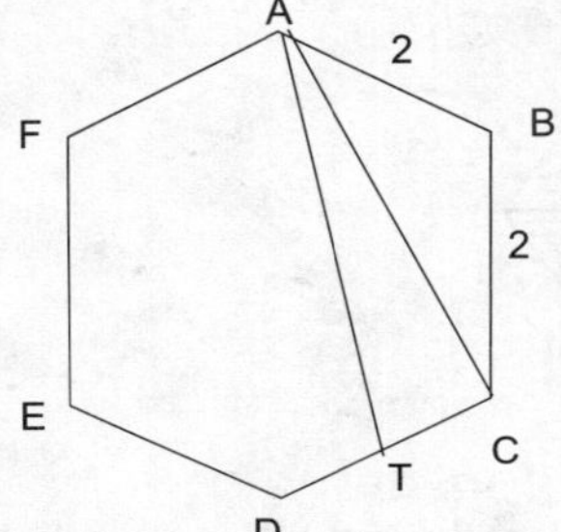

In a regular hexagon, each internal angle is equal to 120°.

From isosceles triangle ABC, we know the length of two sides and included angle. Using Pythagoras theorem, the length of AC can be found to be $2\sqrt{3}$ cm.

Given that, T is the midpoint.

So, CT = 1 cm.

From the right–angled ΔACT, $AC^2 + CT^2 = AT^2$

$AT^2 = (2\sqrt{3})^2$

$AT = \sqrt{13}$

50.

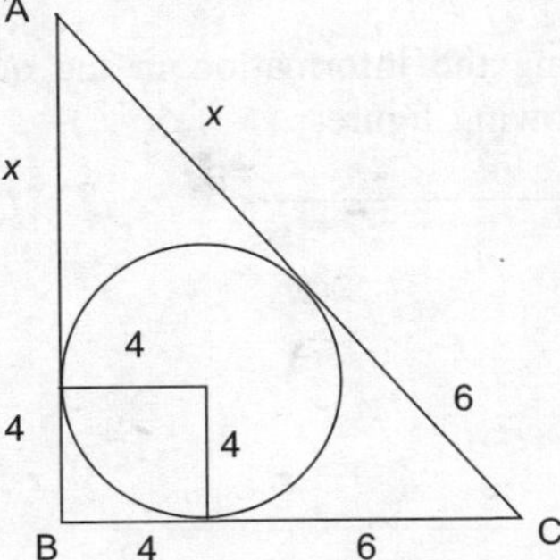

Using the Pythagoras theorem, we have:

$(x + 4)^2 + 10^2 = (x + 6)^2$

We will get $x = 20$. Thus, the triangle has a base of 10 and a height of 24.

The area of the triangle $= \frac{1}{2} \times b \times h = 120$ sq inches

51.

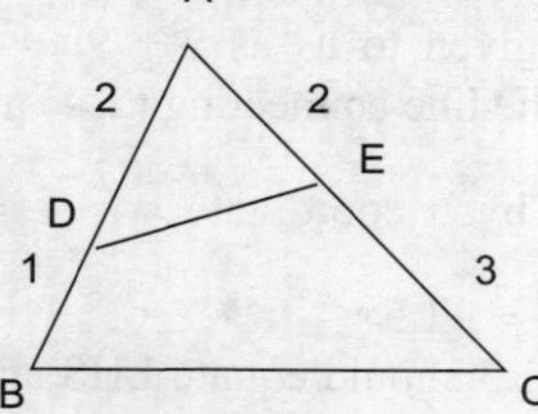

$$\frac{\text{Area of } \Delta ADE}{\text{Area of } \Delta ABC} = \frac{AD}{AB} \times \frac{AE}{AC}$$

$\rightarrow 8 = \frac{2}{3} \times \frac{2}{5} \times$ Area of ΔABC

$\rightarrow$ Area of $\Delta ABC = 30\text{cm}^2$

52.

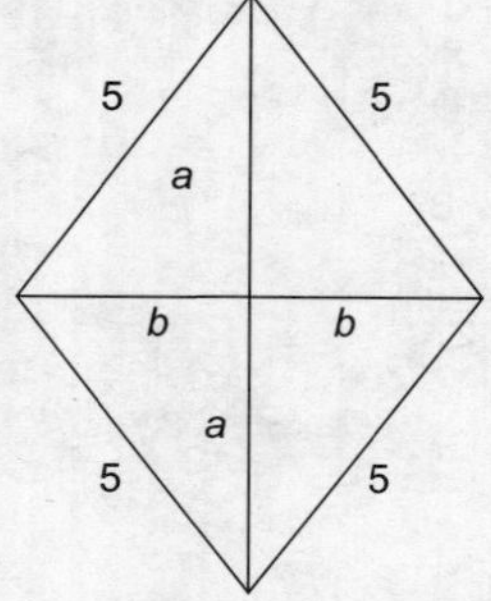

Let's consider the length of the longer and shorter diagonal of the rhombus to be '$2a$' and '$2b$' respectively.

The area of the rhombus = 12 sq cm

$\frac{1}{2} \times 2a \times 2b = 12 \rightarrow ab = 6.$

The side of the rhombus = 5 cm.

So, $a^2 + b^2 = 25.$

$(a + b)^2 = 25 + 2(6) = 37$

$a + b = \sqrt{37}$ (1)

$(a - b)^2 = a^2 + b^2 - 2ab$

$(a - b)^2 = 25 - 2(6) = 13$

$a - b = \sqrt{13}$ (2)

We get: $2a = \sqrt{37} + \sqrt{13}$

53. After considering the information in the question, we get the following figure:

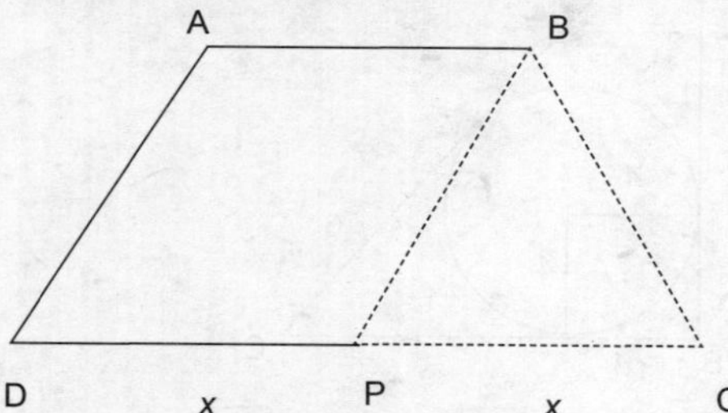

In this figure, the area of triangle PBC = 10 = Area of triangle PAB = Area of Triangle APD. (Three triangles having the same base and the same height). Hence, the required area = 30 sq cm. Hence, option (b) is correct.

54. If the diagonals of the rhombus are d_1 and d_2, we can see that area of the rhombus would be given by $\frac{1}{2} \times d_1d_2 = 96 \rightarrow$ Product of the diagonals = 192. The length of the side would be 10 Also, for a rhombus, the diagonals bisect each other at right angles. Hence, the larger diagonal would be 16 and the smaller one would be 12. The total wire length required to lay along the diagonals would be 16 + 12 = 28 m. Hence, the cost of laying the electric wire = 28 × 125 = 3500.

55. Let the sides of the rectangle be L & B. we are given that L × B = 60000. The total cost of fencing can be

(i) If we assume that the cost of 200 per feet is along the length L: 200L + 100L + 200B or

(ii) If we assume that the cost of 200 per feet is along the breadth B: 200B + 100B + 200L.

Also, possible lengths of the sides would be factors of 60000. The closest factors are 240 × 250. For this, the cost would be either 240 × 200 + 250 × 300 = 123000 or 240 × 300 + 250 × 200 = 122000. If we check for other factor pairs like 200 × 300, we get total cost as 200 × 300 + 300 × 200 = 120000 or 200 × 200 + 300 × 300 = 130000. Since, we are trying to minimize the value of the possible total cost, we will consider 120000 as the value from these two trials. Trying for other factors like 150 × 400 or 120 × 500 would end up raising costs above 120000. Hence, we can see that we are not able to reduce costs below 120000. Option (c) is correct.

56. The following figure can be drawn by dropping perpendiculars to E and F from A and C respectively. Since AD = 10, AE would be 5 and DE would be $5\sqrt{3}$ (Using the property of a 30 – 60 – 90 triangle). Also, CE = $\sqrt{20^2 - 5^2} = \sqrt{375} = 5\sqrt{15}$

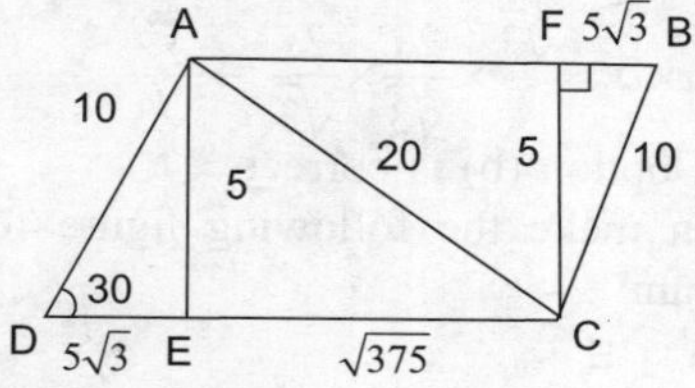

The area of the parallelogram will be the sum of areas of triangle ADE + Triangle BFC + Rectangle AFEC = $2 \times \frac{1}{2} \times 5 \times 5\sqrt{3} + 5 \times 5\sqrt{15} = 25\left(\sqrt{3} + \sqrt{15}\right)$.

Alternately, you can also do the area of the parallelogram using base × height

$= 5 \times 5\left(\sqrt{3} + \sqrt{15}\right) = 25\left(\sqrt{3} + \sqrt{15}\right)$

Hence, option (b) is correct.

57. The following figure can be drawn based on the given information:

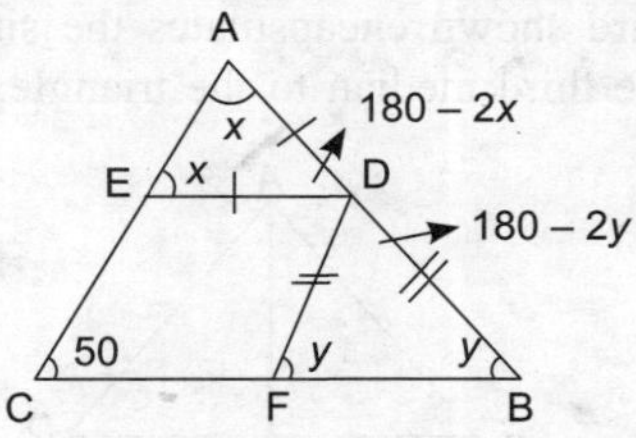

From the figure, we have: $x + y + 50 = 180 \rightarrow x + y = 130$. Also, Angle FDE = $180 - (180 - 2x) - (180 - 2y) = 2(x + y) - 180 = 80$. Option (b) is correct.

58. We can identify that there will be a 5 – 12 – 13 pythagoras triplet that fits the situation. Hence, the required area = $3 \times 12 + \frac{1}{2}\times 5\times 12 = 66$.

59. Since the sides BC and AD are parallel to each other, $B_x - C_x = A_x - D_x$, where B_x is the x coordinate of B and so on. So, $3 - (-2) = 1 - D_x \rightarrow D_x = -4$. Likewise, $4 - 8 = 1 - D_y \rightarrow D_y = 5$. The coordinates of D are $(-4, 5)$. Option (b) is correct.

60. We can solve this using mathematical induction, by taking the rectangle to have sides 6 and 8. In this case, the length of the diagonal would be 10, which would also be the diameter of the circle. Thus, the circle has a radius $R = 5$. The area of the rectangle would be $6 \times 8 = 48$, while $P = 6 + 6 + 8 + 8 = 28$. With these values of P and R, if we check the options, to see which ones give us a value of 48 as the area, we can see that only option (a) fits the situation.

61.

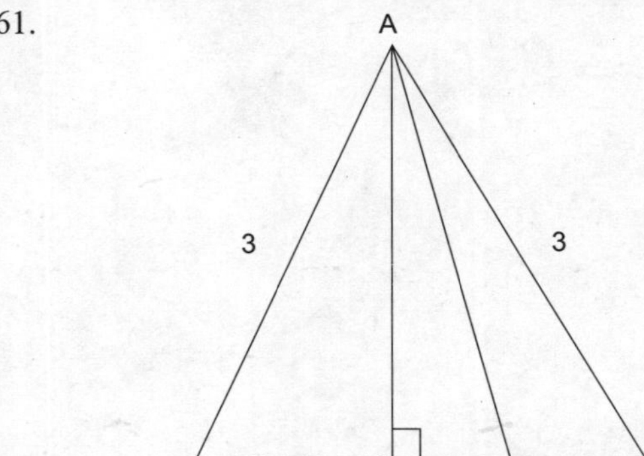

In triangle AEC, $AE = \sqrt{\frac{27}{4}} = \frac{3\sqrt{3}}{2}$. Hence, in triangle $ADE \rightarrow AD = \sqrt{\frac{27}{4} + \frac{1}{4}} = \sqrt{7}$

62. The given situation can be expressed using the following equation, where n is the number of sides of the polygon A and $2n$ is the number of sides of the polygon B:

$$\frac{\frac{(n-2)\times 180}{n}}{\frac{(2n-2)\times 180}{2n}} = \frac{3}{4} \rightarrow n = 5.$$

63. The figure for the given question looks as follows:

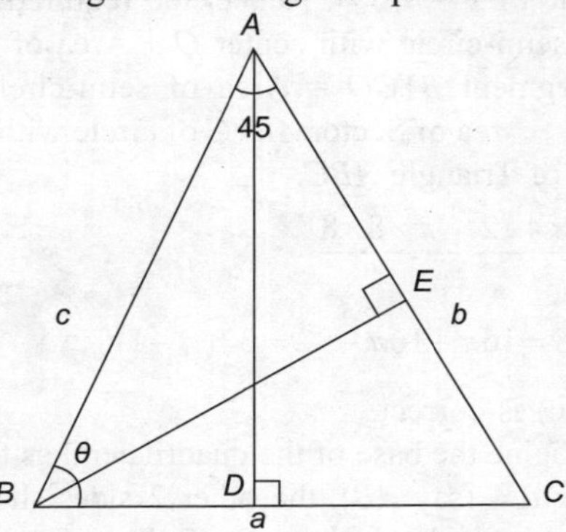

In the figure, the area of the triangle is given by $\frac{1}{2}\times a\times c\times Sin\theta = \frac{1}{2}\times b\times c\times Sin 45 \rightarrow \frac{a}{b} = \frac{1}{\sqrt{2}\times Sin\theta}$.

Also, the area of the triangle

$= \frac{1}{2}\times a\times AD = \frac{1}{2}\times b\times BE \rightarrow \frac{AD}{BE} = \frac{b}{a} = \sqrt{2}\times Sin\theta$.

Option (b) is correct.

64.

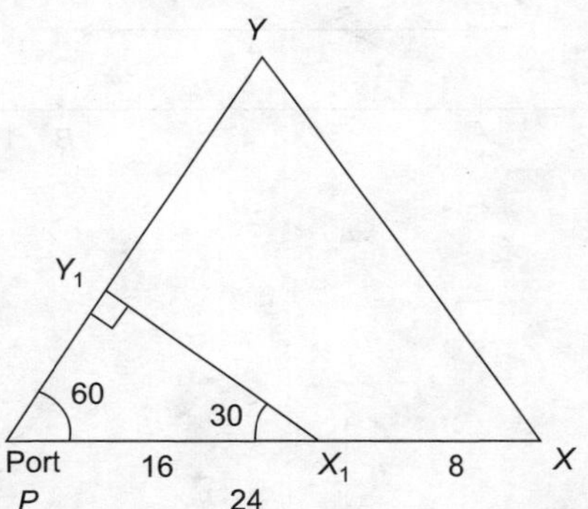

Let X and Y be the initial positions of the slow and fast ships. The angle YPX is 60 degrees and will remain 60 degrees throughout the journey. The triangle formed by $PY_1 X_1$ will be a 30-60-90 triangle. Hence, the side PY_1 will be half $PX_1 = 8$. This means that the faster boat has traveled 16 km while the slower one has traveled 8 i.e. their speed ratio is 2 : 1. When the faster reaches the port, the slower will be 12 kms away. Hence, option (b) is correct.

65. The given situation can be best encapsulated by the figure:

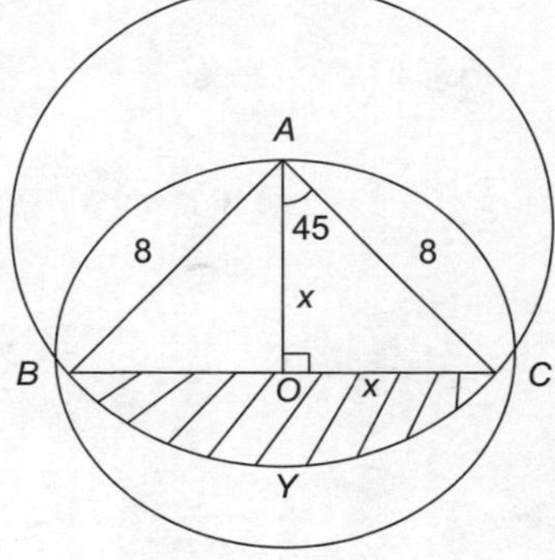

The value of $x = 4\sqrt{2}$. Hence, the required area = Area of semi-circle with center O + Area of shaded minor segment $BYCO$ = Area of semi-circle with center O + Area of Sector $ABYC$ of circle with center A -Area of Triangle ABC.

$$\frac{\pi\times4\sqrt{2}\times4\sqrt{2}}{2}+\frac{\pi\times8\times8}{4}$$

$$-\frac{1}{2}\times8\times8=16\pi+16\pi-32=32(\pi-1)$$

Option (c) is correct.

66. If we imagine the base of the quadrilateral as the side with length 4 (say AB), the other 2 sides should be such that there should be a feasibility of creating a quadrilateral. From the figure we can see that in case, the fourth side is 7 or larger we will not be able to close the figure and the same thing occurs if the fourth sides is 1 or smaller. Hence, the only possible integral values of the 4th side are 2, 3, 4, 5, 6. Hence, a total of 5 values are possible. Option (c) is correct.

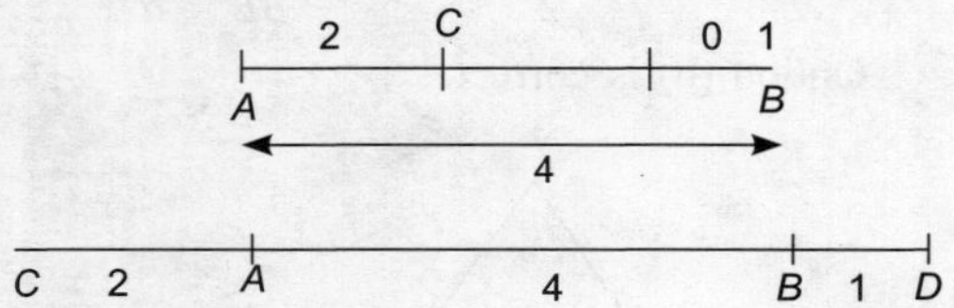

67. The figure shown encapsulates the situation where AF is the third median to the triangle.

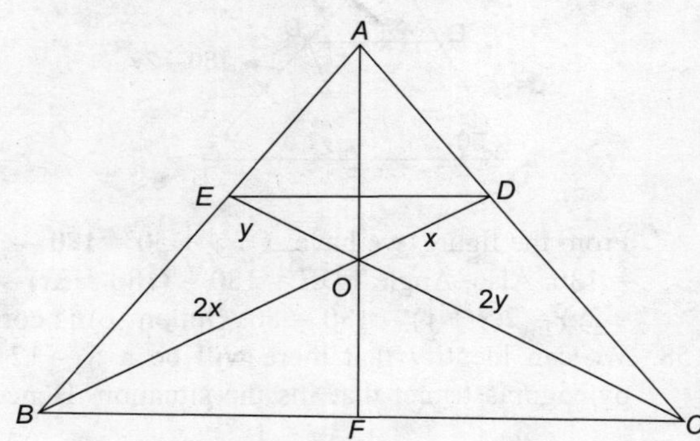

The triangles BOC and EOD are similar to each other and their sides are in the ratio 2 : 1, since the medians of a triangle cut each other in that ratio. Hence, the ratio of areas of BOC to EOD would be 4 : 1. Also, the three medians of any triangle divide the area of the triangle in six equal areas (in this case of 18 sq. cm each). Hence, the area of the triangle BOC would be 2 × 18 = 36. Thus, the area of EOD would be $\frac{1}{4}\times36=9$.

BLOCK STARTER

Scan this QR code to access a video on this block's chapters, the time needed to cover them, and their weightage in the examination.

BLOCK IV

ALGEBRA

BACK TO SCHOOL...

This block of chapters (consisting of Functions, Inequalities, Quadratic and other Equations and Logarithms) has always been a source of discomfort for students who have had negative experiences with mathematics. At the same time, students who have had a positive experience throughout their school, junior college and college years find these chapters extremely easy.

Throughout my experience in training students preparing for the CAT examination and other aptitude exams like CMAT, SNAP, IIFT, MAT, XAT, etc., I have always critically tried to understand the key mental representations that differentiate the two categories of students I have mentioned above—how is it that two students who are basically similarly talented with similar IQs be so different when it comes to higher mathematics?

The reason I am talking about this issue is that Block IV consists of some of the most critical areas of the entire QA Section for the CAT examination. Besides the XLRI entrance test, XAT also has a very high focus on this block of chapters. Hence, this is one area where you simply cannot allow yourselves to remain in the '*I cannot solve Block V questions*' category if you want to seriously take a crack at the CAT examination. However, to enable students who are weak at mathematics to move from the 'I cannot' to the 'I can' category in this block of chapters, you will first have to believe that this can happen.

And the good news is that in my experience of having trained and mentored lakhs of students for aptitude examinations, I have seen a lot of mediocre students in mathematics transit from being initially poor at the chapters of this block to becoming strong in the same.

If you belong to such a category of students, what you first need to understand is that the reason for your inability in Higher mathematics lies in the way you have approached it up to now. There is simply no reason that a better approach will not help you.

WHAT DO YOU NEED TO DO?

To put it simply—rather than trying to study these higher mathematics chapters in so called mathematical language, you need to study the same in plain logical language (with as little mathematics as possible). The following write-up is an attempt at the same. My attempt in the following part of this section is to give you in as simple language as possible some of the missing reactions that makes you consider yourself weak in mathematics (especially this block of chapters).

The following is a list of start-up issues you need to resolve in your mind in order to make yourself comfortable with this block of chapters.

ISSUE 1: The $X - Y$ Plot
ISSUE 2: Locus of Points
ISSUE 3: What is an Equation?
ISSUE 4: Equations and Functions
ISSUE 5: How Inequalities Relate to Graphs of Functions?

Let us now start to look at these issues one by one

ISSUE 1: The X – Y Plot: The need for an $X - Y$ plot essentially arises out of the need to measure anything which cannot be measured in a single dimension.

For instance, any object that can be represented on a straight line (like a rope, a tape, etc.) could be easily represented on the number line itself. However, when you are required to represent any two-dimensional figures (like table top, a book, etc.), simply one-dimensional representations (which can be done on the number line only) are not sufficient.

You are required to be able to represent things in two dimensions.

For this purpose, a vertical line is drawn from point '0' of the number line. This line is perpendicular to the number line and is called the *Y*-axis (which in plain language terms can be understood as the axis which provides the vital second dimension of measurement which helps us describe plain figures better.)

In this situation, the horizontal line (which we know as the number line) is called the *X*-axis and the diagram which emerges represents what is known as the $X - Y$ plane and is also called as the $X - Y$ plot.

The number line (*X*-axis) has a positive measurement direction on the right side of zero (and keeps going to a mathematically defined, in reality non-existent point called infinity). On the left side of zero, the *X*-axis shows negative measurements and keeps going to negative infinity.

In a similar manner, the *Y*-axis starts from 0 and moves upwards to positive infinity and moves downwards to negative infinity.

The following figures illustrate this point

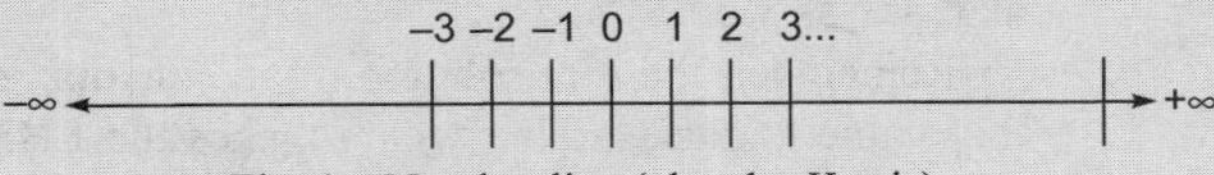

Fig. 1 Number line (also the *X*-axis)

As can be seen the $X - Y$ plot divides the plane into four4 parts (quadrants). The origin is the point where both *X* and *Y* are zero.

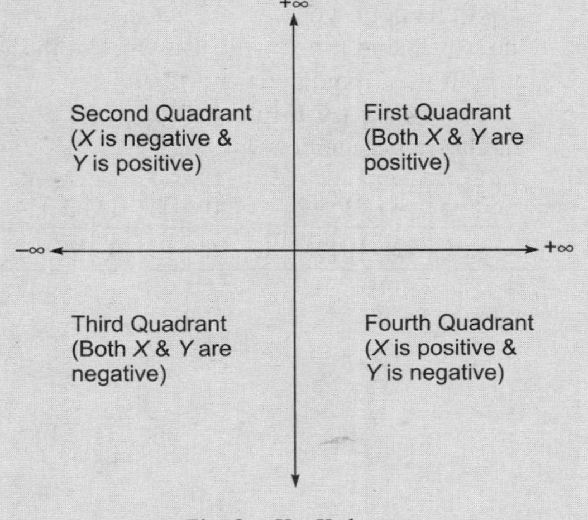

Fig. 2 $X - Y$ plot

Plotting a Point on the X – Y Plot

Suppose, we have to plot the point (2, 3) on the $X - Y$ plot. In order to do so, we first need to understand what $x = 2$ means on the $X - Y$ chart. On the $X - Y$ plot, if you start from the $x = 2$ point on the *X*-axis and draw a line parallel to the *Y*-axis, you will get a set of points which represent a constant value of x (=2). Similarly for $y = 3$, draw a line parallel to the *X*-axis from the $y = 3$ point on the *Y*-axis.

In this situation, the point of intersection between these two lines will be the point (2, 3).

The readers are encouraged to try to draw the figure as described above.

ISSUE 2: Locus of Points In the above situation we have come across a set of points which represents $x = 2$. In mathematics lingo, a set of points is also referred to as a locus of points.

ISSUE 3: What is an Equation? Consider the following:

(a) $2x + 3 = 0$

(b) $x^2 - 5x + 6 = 0$

(c) $4x^3 - 3x^2 - 11x - 18 = 0$

In each of the above cases, we have a situation where there is equality between what is written on the left side of the equality sign and the right side of the equality sign, i.e. LHS = RHS (Left Hand Side = Right Hand Side).

This is the basic definition of an equation.

All Equations have Solutions

Consider the first equation above:

Here you have: $2x + 3 = 0 \rightarrow 2x = -3 \rightarrow x = -3/2$

i.e. $x = -1.5$

This means that at the value $x = -1.5$, the condition of the equation (i.e. LHS = RHS) is satisfied. This value of x is called the 'solution' or the 'root' of the equation.

(Note: The equation we have just seen had a highest power of 'x' as 1. Such equations are called as linear equations. [We shall come to this issue of why they are called as linear equations shortly.] What you need to remember at this stage is that linear equations have only one solution. (or root as mathematicians prefer to call it)

ISSUE 4: Equations and Functions: Before we move ahead into the second and third equations given above, let us first try to connect equations and functions.

If you remember, we studied in school a chapter called as the "Equation of a Straight Line". For instance, parallel to the equation $2x + 3 = 0$, we have $y = 2x + 3$ (which was defined as the equation of a straight line – hence $2x + 3 = 0$ is called a linear equation).

In $y = 2x + 3$, we have a consistent relationship between the values of x and the corresponding values of y that we could get.

Thus, for $y = 2x + 3$, we can create the following table giving us the specific points which satisfy the equation as below:

x	–3	–2	–1	0	1	2
y	–3	–1	+1	3	5	7

If you plot these points on the $X – Y$ plane, you will get the following figure.

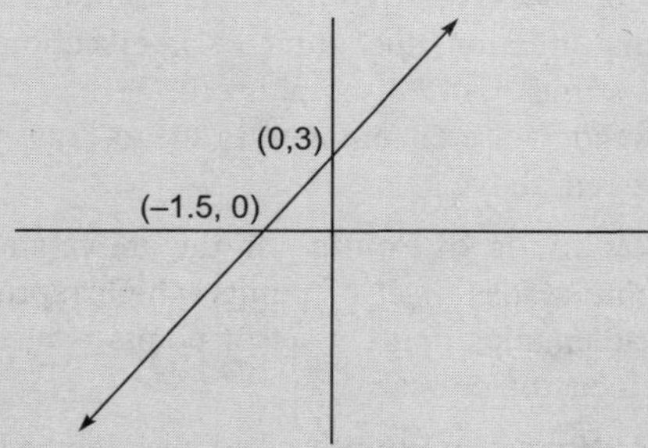

All the points in the table above will lie on this line. The locus of points which are commonly represented by $y = 2x + 3$ is represented by the line above.

In higher mathematics instead of calling expressions like $y = 2x + 3$ as linear equations, they are called as linear functions. (Perhaps the reason for this is that in higher mathematics, we are interested in identifying relationships and behaviours of interdependent variables especially how a change in one variable changes the other variables. Hence, while equations which are of the form $f(x) = 0$ deal with only one variable x, functions represent relationships between two or more variables. They are denoted in mathematics as $y = f(x)$ [Reads as: y is a function of x] or $y = f(a, b)$ [Read as: y is function of a and b].

In general, whenever we have any expression in x (denoted by $f(x)$) we can use it either as

$y = f(x)$ [which is what a function is !!]

$f(x) = 0$ [an equation]

Other Principles Related to Functions and Equations

(a) Every function of the form $y = f(x)$ can be plotted on the $X – Y$ plane.

For instance, consider what we did with the function $y = 2x + 3$. [This form of writing a function is called as its analytical representation, while the graph plotted is called as the graphical representation of the function.]

We first created a table where we started putting values of x and getting the respective value for y. Thus, we got a locus of points (as shown in the table above) which represented the function $y = 2x + 3$. This representation of the function is called as the analytical representation of the function.

Further, the line representing $y = 2x + 3$ was plotted on the $X – Y$ plane. This is called as the graphical representation of the function.

(b) The point/points where the graph of the function $y = f(x)$ cuts the x-axis, represents the solution of the equation $f(x) = 0$.

Thus, if you noticed $y = 2x + 3$ cuts the x axis at $x = –1.5$. At the same time the root or solution of the equation $2x + 3 = 0$ is $x = – 1.5$.

This is not accidental but will happen in each and every case. Thus, in general you can state that the point where the graph of a function $y = f(x)$ cuts the x-axis is the solution of the equation $f(x) = 0$. (**Note:** This will be true for every expression in x-irrespective of the highest power of 'x' in the expression.)

It is a consequence of this logic, that linear functions will cut the x-axis only once (since linear equations have only one solution.)

(c) **Quadratic Equations and Quadratic Functions:** Let us now pick up the equation: $x^2 – 5x + 6 = 0$.

If you solve this equation you will get the solution of this equation at two values of x. viz. at $x = 2$ as well as at $x = 3$.

[Remember, the root/solution of an equation is that value of the variable which makes the LHS = RHS in the equation. You can easily see that at both $x = 2$ and $x = 3$ the expression $x^2 – 5x + 6$ yields a value of 0.

At $x = 2$, $x^2 – 5x + 6 \to 2^2 – 5 \times 2 + 6 = 0$

At $x = 3$, $x^2 – 5x + 6 \to 3^2 – 5 \times 3 + 6 = 0$

At this point you can predict that the graph of the expression $y = x^2 – 5x + 6$ will cut the x axis at both these points viz. $x = 2$ and $x = 3$.

If you now try to plot $y = x^2 – 5x + 6$, your tabular representation will be:

x	–5	–4	–3	–2	–1	0	1	2	3	4	5
y	56	42	30	20	12	6	2	0	0	2	6

This locus of points will look like the figure below:

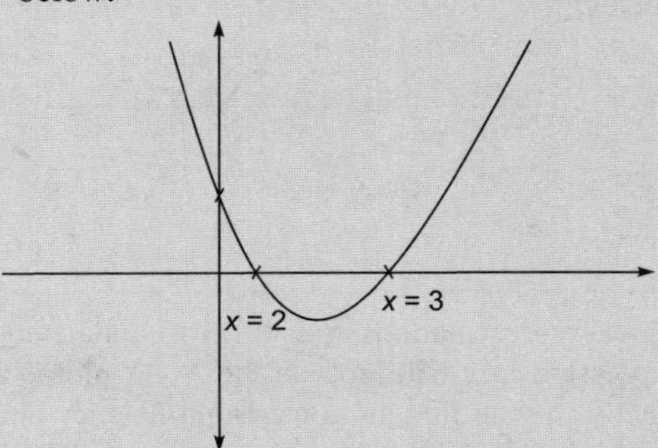

Naturally, the graph cuts the x axis at $x = 2$ and $x = 3$.

Special Note on Quadratic Equations

Since all quadratic equations have two solutions, graph of the function for the same expression should cut the x-axis at two points.

However, this might not always be true.

For instance, look at the following graphs.

Case 1:

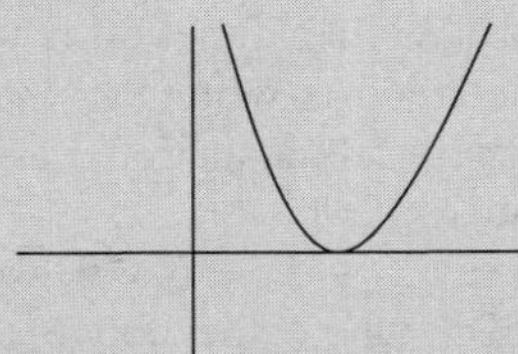

In this case the roots are said to be real and equal.

Case 2:

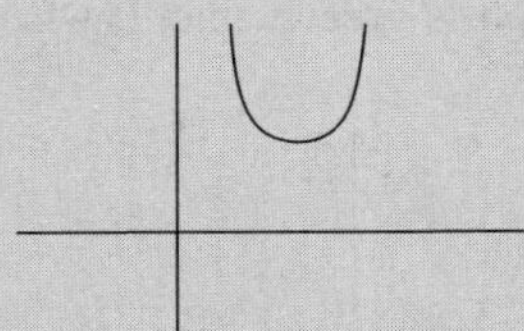

In this case the roots of the quadratic equation are imaginary with respect to the x-axis.

(**Note:** You also need to know that quadratic functions can also look inverted as shown below. This occurs when the coefficient of x^2 is negative.)

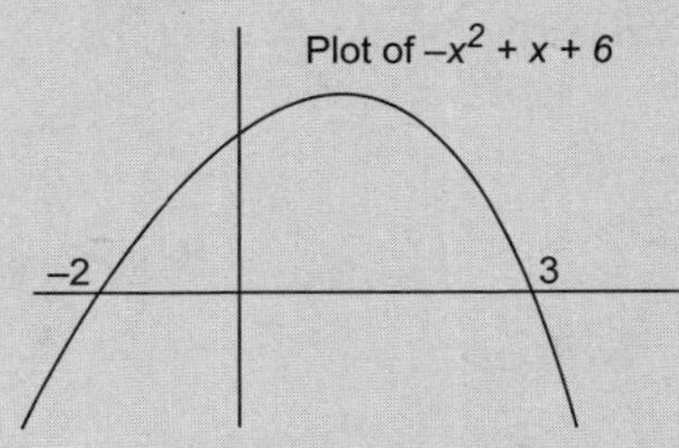

In general, quadratic equations then can take any of six shapes (with respect to the x-axis).

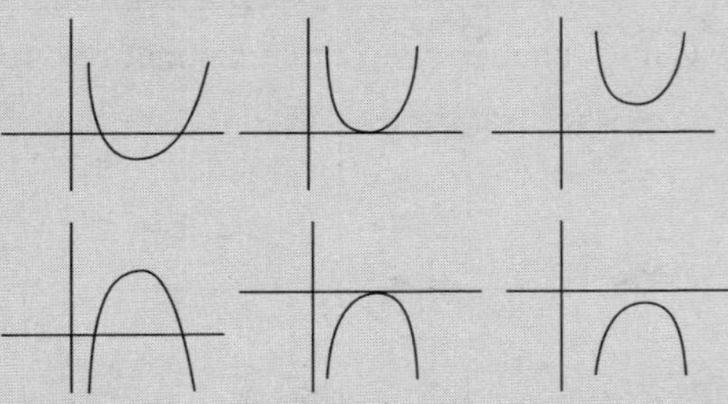

(d) How cubic functions look: Cubic functions have x^3 as their highest powers of x. Cubic equations have three solutions and hence cubic functions will cut the x-axis thrice.

They can look like:

CASE 1: When the Coefficient of x^3 is Positive

(a) Cubic functions with three distinct real roots (e.g. $y = x^3 - 6x^2 + 11x - 6$)

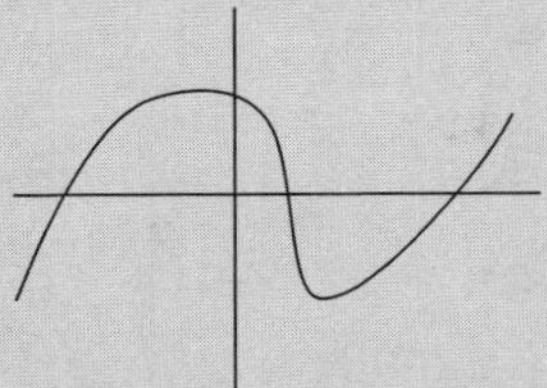

(b) Cubic function with three real and equal roots. (e.g.: $y = (x - 1)^3$)

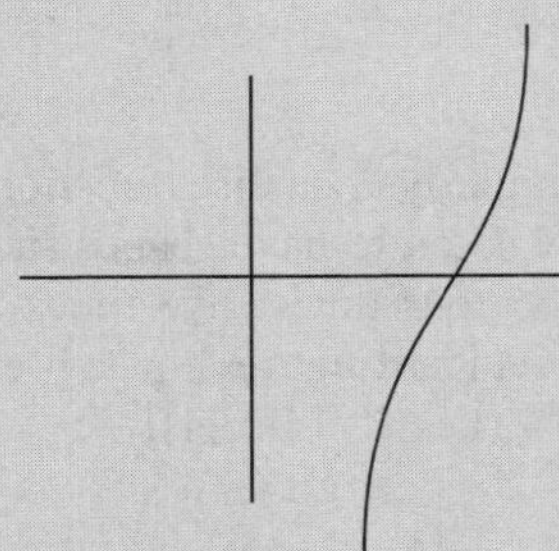

(c) Cubic function with one real and two imaginary roots

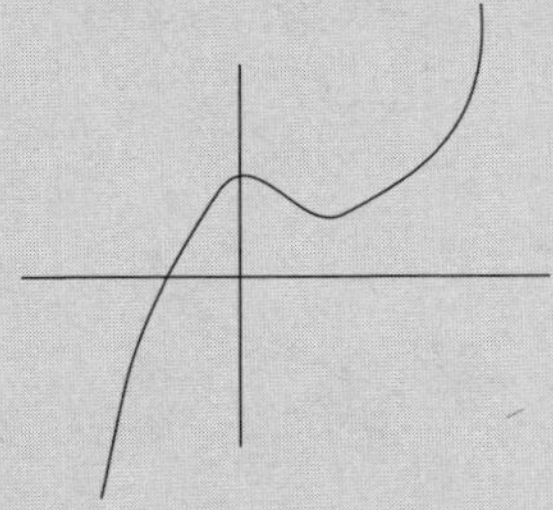

CASE 2: When the Coefficient of x^3 is Negative

(a) Cubic function with three distinct real roots

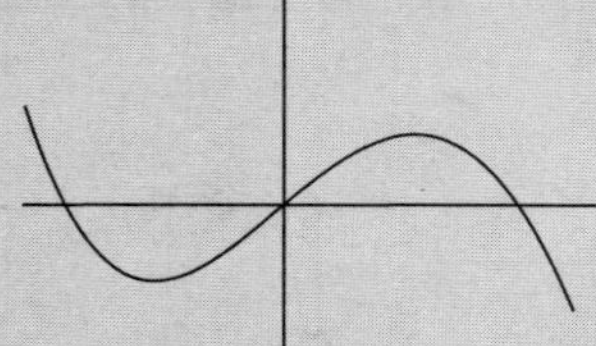

(b) Cubic function with three real and equal roots

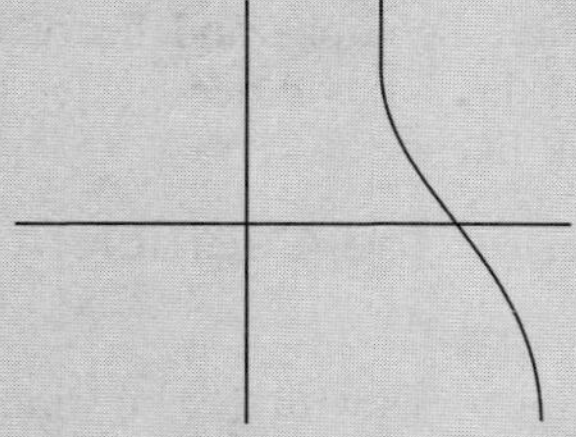

(c) Cubic function with one real and two imaginary roots

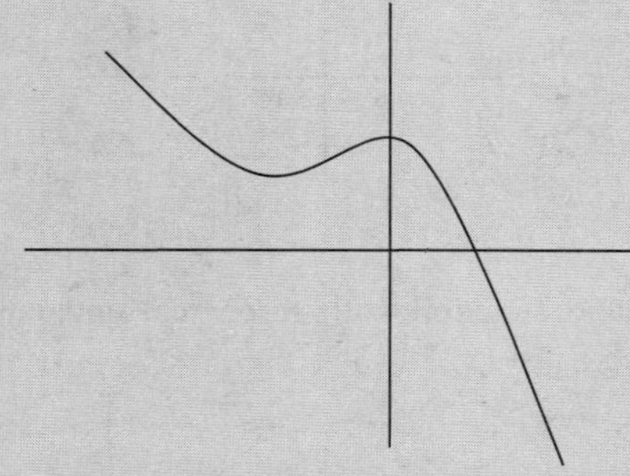

You can similarly visualise functions with highest power 4, 5 and so on to have shapes such that they can cut the x – axis four times, five times and so on. The following are standard figures for expressions with

(a) Degree 4 (i.e. x^4) [4 roots]

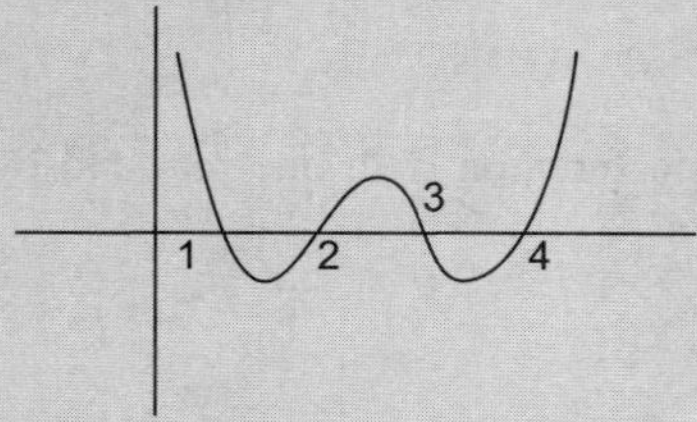

(b) Degree 5 [5 roots]

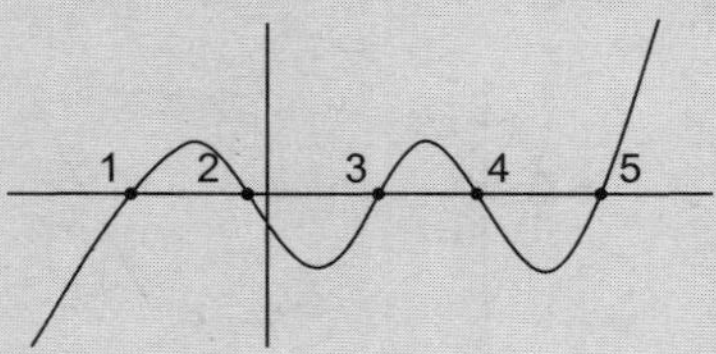

Key Note

Graphical representations and ability to understand how an expression in x will look on the $X - Y$ plot is a very key factor in your moving towards proficiency and self-dependence in this crucial block of chapters. Hence, it is encouraged to try to plot the graphs of as many $y = f(x)$ functions as one can imagine. To give you a target, it is recommended a minimum of 100 graphs to be plotted by you. Only then would you be able to move to a level of comfort in visualising graphs.

ISSUE 5: How Inequalities Relate to Graphs of Functions?

We have just seen the relationship between a function and an equation. While a function is written in the $y = f(x)$ form, an equation is written in the $f(x) = 0$ form.

An inequality (or an inequation) can be written in the form $f(x) > 0$ or $f(x) \geq 0$.

Thus, if we say $x^2 - 5x + 6 > 0$, we are looking for those values of x where the above expression yields values above 0.

Going back to the graph for $x^2 - 5x + 6$, it is obvious that the function is greater than 0 when $x > 3$ or $x < 2$.

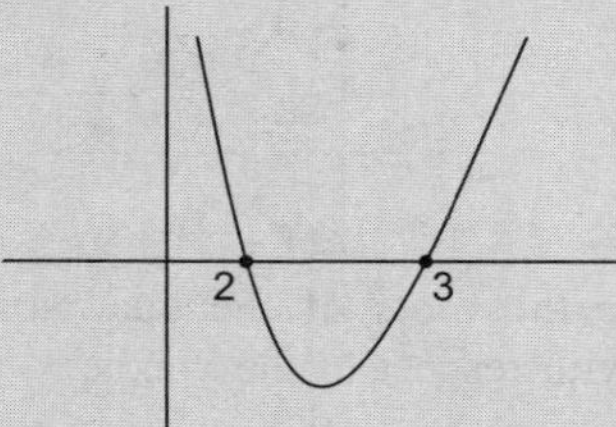

In such a case, the solution of the inequality $x^2 - 5x + 6 > 0$ becomes $x > 3$ or $x < 2$.

Understand here that when we are solving an inequality all we are bothered about is to see at what values of x does the inequality hold true.

CHAPTER 14

Functions

Chapter Launchpad

Scan this QR code to access a video on 'Introduction to Functions' and this chapter's importance for CAT

Quantities of various characters such as length, area, mass, temperature and volume either have constant values or they vary based on the values of other quantities. Such quantities are called constant and variable, respectively.

Function is a concept of mathematics that studies the dependence between variable quantities in the process of their change. For instance, with a change in the side of a square, the area of the square also varies. The question of how the change in the side of the square affects the area is answered by a mathematical relationship between the area of the square and the side of the square.

Let the variable *x* take on numerical values from the set *D*.

A function is a rule that attributes to every number x from D one definite number y where y belongs to the set of real numbers.

Here, x is called the independent variable and y is called the dependent variable.

The set D is referred to as the *domain of definition* of the function and the set of all values attained by the variable y is called the *range of the function*.

In other words, a variable y is said to be the value of function of a variable x in the domain of definition D if to each value of x belonging to this domain there corresponds a definite value of the variable y.

This is symbolised as $y = f(x)$, where f denotes the rule by which y varies with x.

BASIC METHODS OF REPRESENTING FUNCTIONS

Analytical Representation

This is essentially representation through a formula.

This representation could be a uniform formula in the entire domain, for example, $y = 3x^2$

Or

By several formulae which are different for different parts of the domain.

Example: $y = 3x^2$ if $x < 0$
and $y = x^2$ if $x > 0$

In analytical representations, the domain of the function is generally understood as the set of values for which the equation makes sense.

For instance, if $y = x^2$ represents the area of a square then we get that the domain of the function is $x > 0$.

Problems based on the analytical representation of functions have been a favourite for the XLRI exam and have also become very common in the CAT over the past few years. Other exams are also moving towards asking questions based on this representation of functions.

Tabular Representation of Functions

For representing functions through a table, we simply write down a sequence of values of the independent variable x and then write down the corresponding values of the dependent variable y. Thus, we have tables of logarithms, trigonometric values and so forth, which are essentially tabular representations of functions.

The types of problems that appear based on tabular representation have been restricted to questions that give a table and then ask the student to trace the appropriate analytical representation or graph of the function based on the table.

Graphical Representation of Functions

This is a very important way to represent functions. The process is: on the coordinate xy-plane for every value of x from the domain D of the function, a point $P(x, y)$ is constructed whose abscissa is x and whose ordinate y is obtained by putting the particular value of x in the formula representing the function.

For example, for plotting the function $y = x^2$, we first decide on the values of x for which we need to plot the graph.

Thus, we can take $x = 0$ and get $y = 0$ (means the point (0, 0) is on the graph).

Then for $x = 1$, $y = 1$; for $x = 2$, $y = 4$; for $x = 3$, $y = 9$ and for $x = -1$, $y = 1$; for $x = -2$, $y = 4$, and so on.

EVEN AND ODD FUNCTIONS

Even Functions

Let a function $y = f(x)$ be given in a certain interval. The function is said to be even if for any value of x

$$\rightarrow \quad f(x) = f(-x)$$

Properties of even functions:

(a) The sum, difference, product and quotient of an even function are also even functions.

(b) The graph of an even function is symmetrical about the y-axis.

Concept Explainer

Scan this QR code to access a conceptual video on **Even and Odd Functions**

However, when y is the independent variable, it is symmetrical about the x-axis. In other words, if $x = f(y)$ is an even function, then the graph of this function will be symmetrical about the x-axis. Example: $x = y^2$.

Examples of even functions: $y = x^2$, $y = x^4$, $y = -3x^8$, $y = x^2 + 3$, $y = x^4/5$, $y = |x|$ are all even functions.

The symmetry about the y-axis of an even function is illustrated below.

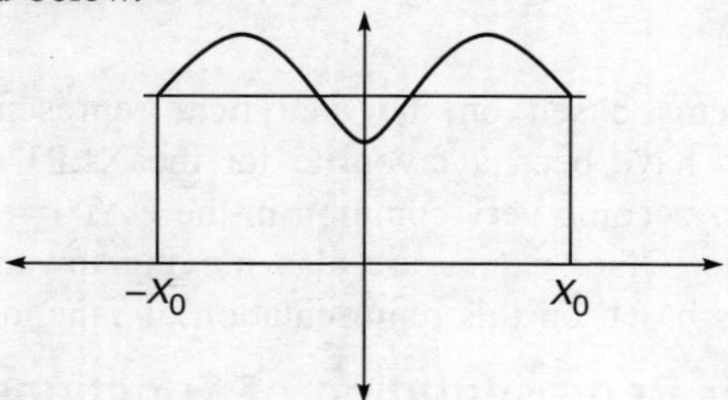

Odd Functions

Let a function $y = f(x)$ be given in a certain interval. The function is said to be odd, if for any value of x

$$f(x) = -f(-x)$$

Properties of odd functions:

(a) The sum and difference of an odd function is an odd function.

(b) The product and quotient of an odd function is an even function.

(c) The graph of an odd function is symmetrical about the origin.

The symmetry about the origin of an odd function is illustrated below.

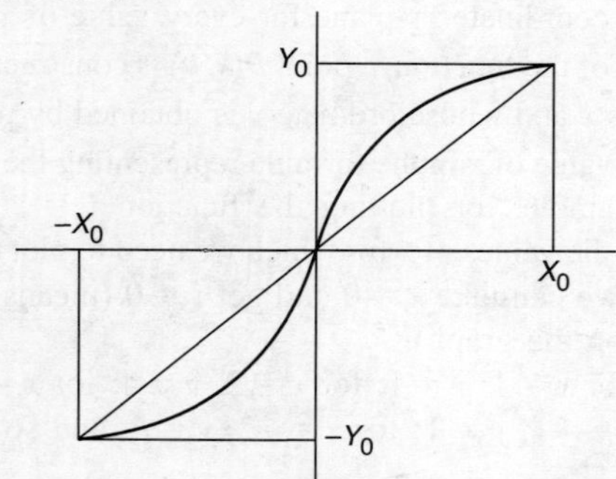

Examples of odd functions $y = x^3$, $y = x^5$, $y = x^3 + x$, $y = x/(x^2 + 1)$.

Not all functions need to be even or odd. However, every function can be represented as the sum of even functions and odd functions.

Inverse of a Function

Let there be a function $y = f(x)$, which is defined for the domain D and has a range R.

Then, by definition, for every value of the independent variable x in the domain D, there exists a certain value of the dependent variable y. In certain cases, the same value of the dependent variable y can be obtained for different values of x. For example, if $y = x^2$, then for $x = 2$ and $x = -2$ give the value of y as 4.

In such a case, the inverse function of the function $y = f(x)$ *does not exist.*

However, if a function $y = f(x)$ is such that for every value of y (from the range of the function R), there corresponds one and only one value of x from the domain D, then the inverse function of $y = f(x)$ exists and is given by $x = g(y)$. Here it can be noticed that x becomes the dependent variable and y becomes the independent variable. Hence, this function has a domain R and a range D.

Under the above situation, the graph of $y = f(x)$ and $x = g(y)$ are one and the same.

However, when denoting the inverse of the function, we normally denote the independent variable by y and, hence, the inverse function of $y = f(x)$ is denoted by $y = g(x)$ and not by $x = g(y)$.

The graphs of two inverse functions, when this change is used are symmetrical about the line $y = x$ (which is the bisector of the first and the third quadrants).

Graphs of Some Simple Functions The student is advised to familiarise himself/herself with the following figures.

Graphs of $y = b$, $y = kx$, $y = kx + b$, $y = kx - b$

Note the shifting of the line when a positive number b is added and subtracted to the function's equation.

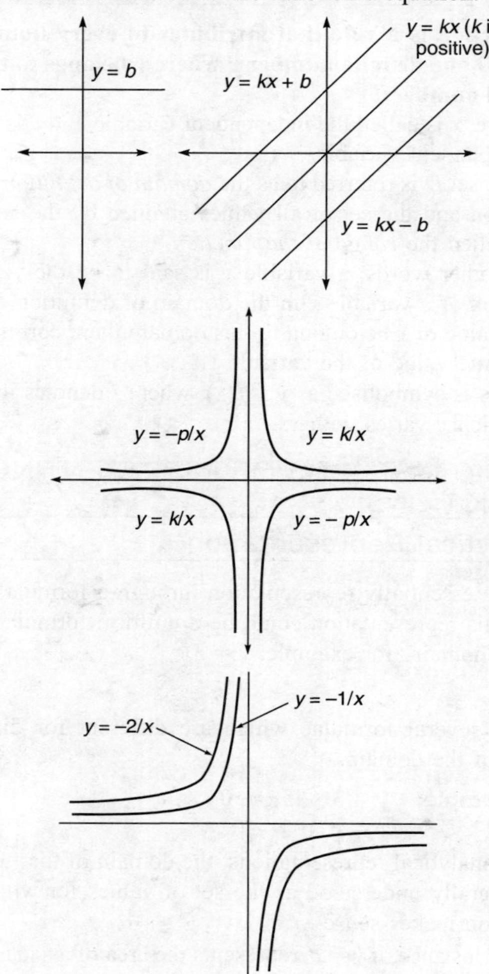

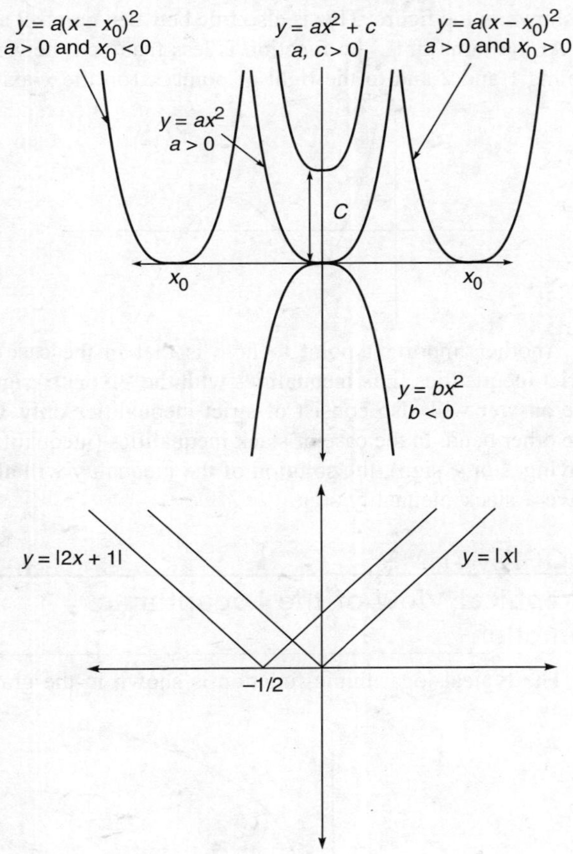

SHIFTING OF GRAPHS

The ability to visualise how graphs shift when the basic analytical expression is changed is a very important skill. For instance, if you knew how to visualise the graph of $(x + 2)^2 - 5$, it will definitely add a lot of value to your ability to solve questions of functions and all related chapters of block V graphically.

In order to be able to do so, you first need to understand the following points clearly:

1. **Relationship between the graph of $y = f(x)$ and $y = f(x) + c$ (where c represents a positive constant.):** The shape of the graph of $y = f(x) + c$ will be the same as that of the $y = f(x)$ graph. The only difference would be in terms of the fact that $f(x) + c$ is shifted c units up on the $x - y$ plot.

   The following figure will make it clear for you:

Example: Relationship between $y = x^2$ and $y = x^2 + 2$

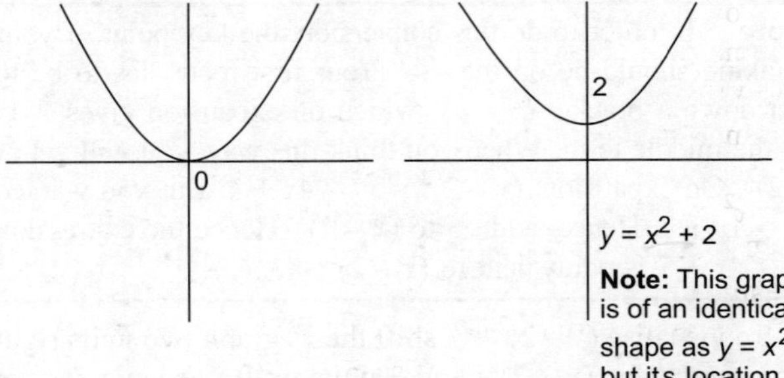

Note: This graph is of an identical shape as $y = x^2$, but its location is shifted 2 units up.

2. **Relationship between $y = f(x)$ and $y = f(x) - c$:** In this case, while the shape remains the same, the position of the graph gets shifted c units down.

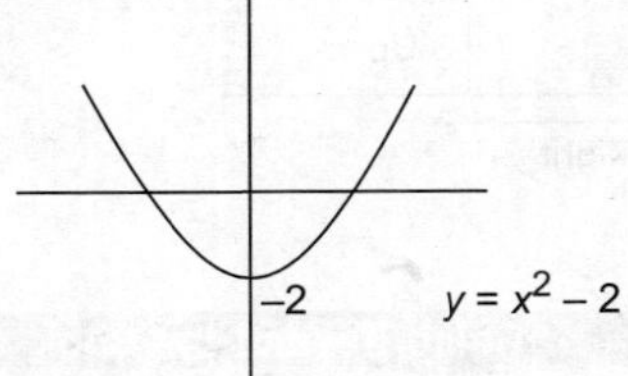

3. **Relationship between $y = f(x)$ and $y = f(x + c)$:** In this case, the graph will get shifted c units to the left. (Remember, c is a positive constant)

Example:

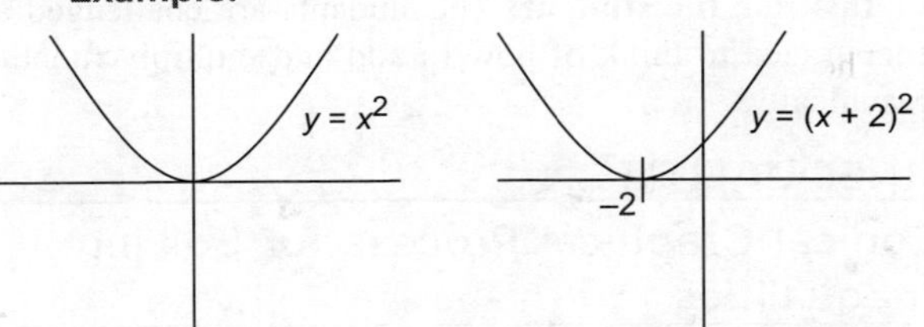

4. **Relationship between $y = f(x)$ and $y = f(x - c)$:** In this case, the graph will get shifted c units to the right on the $x - y$ plane.

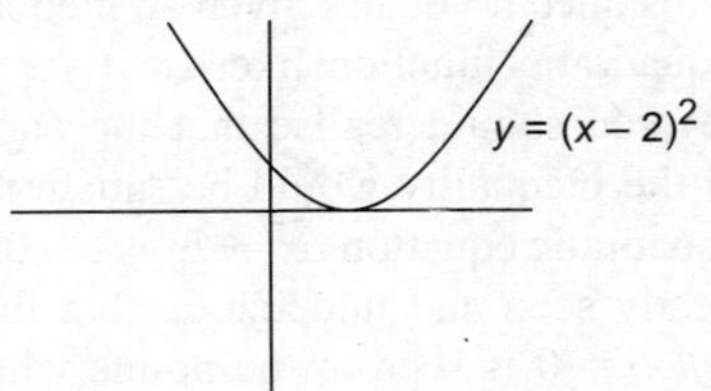

COMBINING MOVEMENTS

It is best understood through an example:

Visualising a graph for a function like $x^2 - 4x + 7$

First convert $x^2 - 4x + 7$ into $(x - 2)^2 + 3$

Note: In order to do this conversion, the key point of your thinking should be on the $-4x$. Your first focus has to be to put down a bracket $(x - a)^2$ which on expansion gives $-4x$ as the middle term. When you think this way, you will get $(x - 2)^2$. On expansion, $(x - 2)^2 = x^2 - 4x + 4$. But you wanted $x^2 - 4x + 7$. Hence, add +3 to $(x - 2)^2$. Hence the expression $x^2 - 4x + 7$ is equivalent to $(x - 2)^2 + 3$.

To visualise $(x - 2)^2 + 3$ shift the x^2 graph two units right [to account for $(x - 2)^2$] and 3 units up [to account for the +3] on the $x - y$ plot. This will give you the required plot.

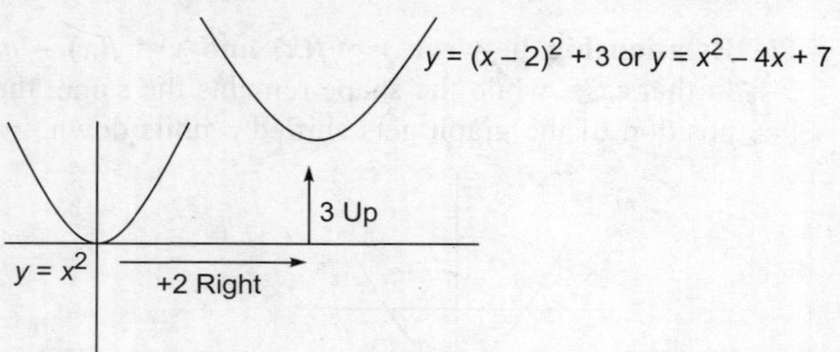

Going Beyond the Book

Scan this QR code to access a video on how to visualise Graphical Transformations

Task for the student: The students are challenged and encouraged to think of how to add and multiply functions graphically.

INEQUALITIES

Logical Graphical Process for Solving Inequalities

Your knowledge of the standard graphs of functions and how these shift can help you immensely while solving inequalities.

Thus, for instance if you are given an inequality question based on a quadratic function like $ax^2 + bx + c < 0$ (and a is positive) you should realise that the curve will be U shaped. And the inequality would be satisfied between the roots of the quadratic equation $ax^2 + bx + c = 0$. [Remember, we have already seen and understood that the solution of an equation $f(x) = 0$ is seen at the points where the graph of $y = f(x)$ cuts the x axis.]

Similarly, for a cubic curve like the one shown below, you should realise that it is greater than 0 to the left of the point 1 shown in the figure. This is also true between points 2 and 3. At the same time, the function is less than zero between points 1 and 2 and to the right of point 3. (on the x-axis).

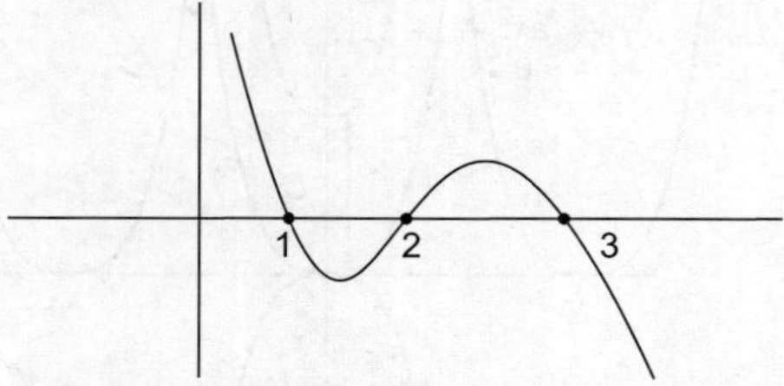

Another important point to note is that in the case of strict inequalities (i.e., inequalities with the ‘$<$’ or ‘$>$’ sign), the answer will also consist of strict inequalities only. On the other hand, in the case of slack inequalities (inequalities having $\leq$ or $\geq$ sign), the solution of the inequality will also have a slack inequality sign.

LOGARITHMS

Graphical View of the Logarithmic Function

The typical logarithmic function is shown in the graph below:

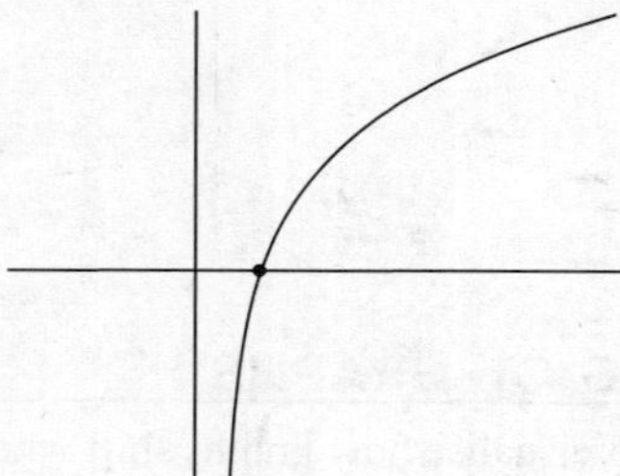

Note the following points about the logarithmic function, $y = \log x$.

1. It is only defined for positive values of x.
2. For values of x below 1, the logarithmic function is negative. At the same time for $x = 1$, the logarithmic function has a value of 0. (Irrespective of the base)
3. The value of $\log x$ becomes 2, when the value of x becomes equal to the square of the base.
4. As we go further right on the x-axis, the graph keeps increasing. However, this increase becomes more and more gradual and hence, the shape of the graph becomes increasingly flatter as we move further on the x-axis.

Space for Notes

WORKED-OUT PROBLEMS

Problem 14.1: Find the domain of the definition of the function $y = 1/(x^2 - 2x)^{1/2}$

(a) $(-\infty, -2)$ (b) $(-\infty, +\infty)$ except $[0, 2]$
(c) $(2, +\infty)$ (d) $(-\infty, 0)$

Solution: For the function to be defined, the expression under the square root should be non-negative and the denominator should not be equal to zero.

So, $x^2 - 2x > 0$ and $(x^2 - 2x) \neq 0$
or, $x(x-2) > 0$ or $(x^2 - 2x) \neq 0$

So, x will not lie in between 0 and 2 and $x \neq 0$, $x \neq 2$.

So, x will be $x\ (-\infty, +\infty)$ excluding the range $0 \le x$ to ≤ 2.

In exam situations, to solve the above problem, you should check the options as below.

In fact, for solving all questions on functions, the student should explore the option-based approach.

Often you will find that going through the option-based approach will help you save a significant amount of time. The student should try to improve his/her selection of values through practice so that he/she is able to eliminate the maximum number of options on the basis of every check. The student should develop a knack for disproving three options so that the fourth automatically becomes the answer. It should also be noted that if an option cannot be disproved, it means that it is the correct option.

The meaning of what has been said will be clear from the following solution process.

For this question, if we check at $x = 3$, the function is defined. However, $x = 3$ is outside the ambit of options *a* and *d*. Hence, *a* and *d* are rejected on the basis of just one value check, and *b* or *c* has to be the answer.

Alternately, you can try to disprove each and every option one by one.

Problem 14.2: Which of the following is an even function?

(a) $|x^2| - 5x$ (b) $x^4 + x^5$
(c) $e^{2x} + e^{-2x}$ (d) $|x|^2/x$

Solution: Use options for solving.

If a function is even, it should satisfy the equation $f(x) = f(-x)$.

We now check the four options to see which of them represents an even function.

Checking option (a): $f(x) = |x^2| - 5x$

Putting $(-x)$ in the place of x.

$$f(x) = |(-x)^2| - 5(-x)$$
$$= |x^2| + 5(x) \neq f(x)$$

Checking option (b) $f(x) = x^4 + x^5$

Putting $(-x)$ in the place of x,

$$f(-x) = (-x)^4 + (-x)^5 = x^4 - x^5 \neq f(x)$$

Checking option (c): $f(x) = e^{2x} + e^{-2x}$

Putting $(-x)$ in the place of x.

$$f(-x) = e^{-2x} + e^{-(-2x)} = e^{-2x} + e^{2x} = f(x)$$

So (c) is the answer.

You do not need to go further to check for (d). However, if you had checked, you would have been able to disprove it as follows:

Checking option (d): $f(x) = |x|^2/x$

Putting $f(-x)$ in the place of x,

$$f(-x) = |-x|^2/-x = |x|^2/-x \neq f(x)$$

Directions for Problem 14.3 to 14.6:

Mark (a), if $f(-x) = f(x)$
Mark (b), if $f(-x) = -f(x)$
Mark (c), if neither (a) nor (b)

Problem 14.3:

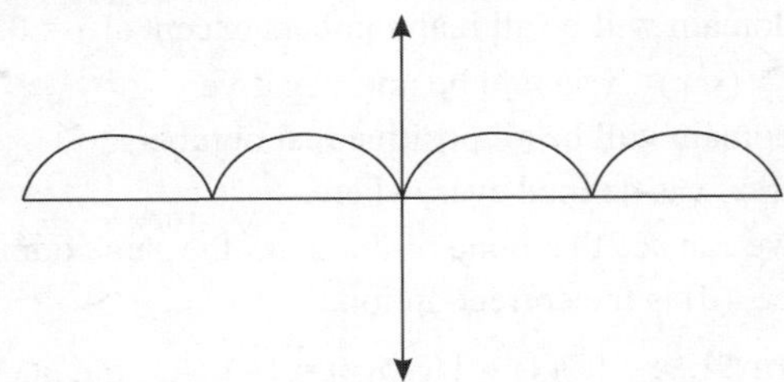

Solution: The graph is symmetrical about the y-axis. This is the definition of an even function. So (a) is the answer.

Problem 14.4:

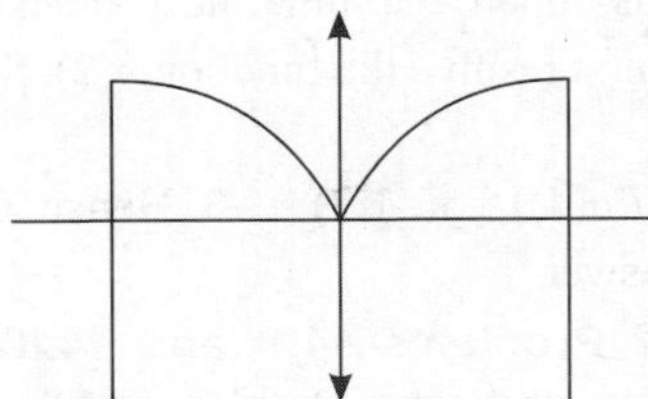

Solution: The graph is symmetrical about the y-axis. This is the definition of an even function. So (a) is the answer.

Problem 14.5:

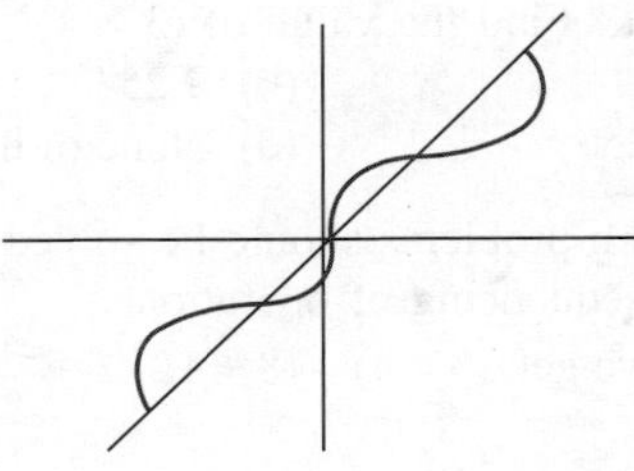

Solution: The graph is symmetrical about origin. This is the definition of an odd function. So (b) is the answer.

Problem 14.6:

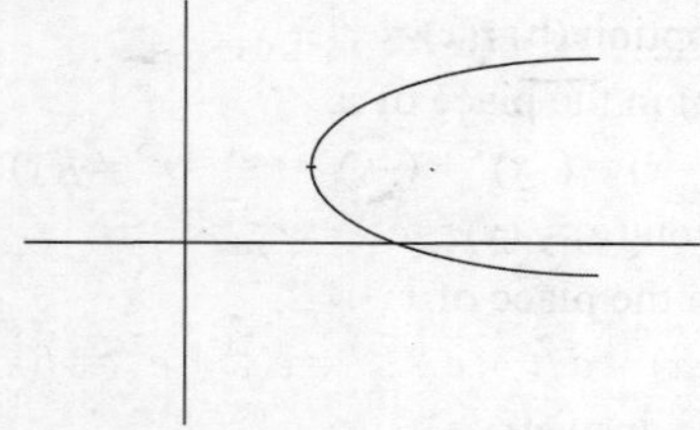

Solution: The graph is neither symmetrical about the y-axis nor about origin. So (c) is the answer.

Problem 14.7: Which of the following two functions are identical?

(a) $f(x) = x^2/x$ (b) $g(x) = (\sqrt{x})^2$
(c) $h(x) = x$
(i) (a) and (b) (ii) (b) and (c)
(iii) (a) and (c) (iv) None of these

Solution: For two functions to be identical, their domains should be equal.

Checking the domains of $f(x)$, $g(x)$ and $h(x)$,

$f(x) = x^2/x$, x should not be equal to zero.

So, domain will be all real numbers except at $x = 0$.

$g(x) = (\sqrt{x})^2$, x should be non-negative.

So, domain will be all positive real numbers.

$h(x) = x$, x is defined everywhere.

So, we can see that none of them has the same domain.

Hence, (d) is the correct option.

Problem 14.8: If $f(x) = 1/x$, $g(x) = 1/(1 - x)$ and $h(x) = x^2$, then find *fogoh* (2).

(a) –1 (b) 1
(c) 1/2 (d) None of these

Solution: *fogoh* (2) is the same as $f(g(h(2)))$

To solve this, open the innermost bracket first. This means that, we first resolve the function $h(2)$. Since $h(2) = 4$, we will get

$f(g(h(2))) = f(g(4)) = f(-1/3) = -3$. Hence, the option (d) is the correct answer.

Directions for Problems 14.9 and 14.10: Read the instructions below and solve Problems 14.9 and 14.10.

$A \times B = A^3 - B^3$

$A + B = A - B$

$A - B = A/B$

Problem 14.9: Find the value of (3 × 4) – (8 + 12).

(a) 9 (b) 9.25
(c) –9.25 (d) None of these

Solution: Such problems should be solved by the BODMAS rule for sequencing of operations.

Solving, thus, we get: (3 × 4) – (8 + 12)

= –37 – (–4). (**Note:** The '–' sign between –37 and –4 is the operation defined above.)

= 37/4 = 9.25

Problem 14.10: Which of the following operation will give the sum of the reciprocals of x and y and unity?

(a) $(x + y) \times (x - y)$
(b) $[(x \times y) - x] - y$
(c) $(x + y) - (x - y)$
(d) None of these

For solving questions containing a function in the question as well as a function in the options (where values are absent), the safest process and most effective is to assume certain convenient values of the variables in the expression and checking for the correct option that gives us equality with the expression in the question. The advantage of this process of solution is that there is very little scope for making mistakes. Besides, if the expression is not simple and directly visible, this process takes far less time as compared to simplifying the expression from one form to another.

This process will be clear after perusing the following solution to the above problem.

Solution: The problem statement above defines the expression: $(1/x) + (1/y) + 1$ and asks us to find out which of the four options is equal to this expression. If we try to simplify, we can start from the problem expression and rewrite it to get the correct option. However, in the above case this will become extremely complicated since the symbols are indirect. Hence, if we have to solve through simplifying, we should start from the options one-by-one and try to get the problem expression. However, this is easier said than done and for this particular problem, going through this approach will take you at least two minutes plus.

Hence, consider the following approach:

Take the values of x and y as 1 each. Then,

$$(1/x) + (1/y) + 1 = 3.$$

Put the value of x and y as 1 each in each of the four options that we have to consider.

Option (a) will give a value of $-1 \neq 3$. Hence, option (a) is incorrect.

Option (b) will give a value of 0: $0 \neq 3$. Hence, option (b) is incorrect.

Option (c) gives an answer of 0: $0 \neq 3$. Hence, option (c) is incorrect.

Now since options (a), (b) and (c) are incorrect and option (d) is the only possibility left, it has to be the answer.

Problem 14.11: For any real number x, the function $I(x)$ denotes the integer part of x – i.e. the largest integer less than or equal to x. At the same time, the function $D(x)$ denotes the fractional part of x. For arbitrary real numbers x, y and z, only one of the following statements is correct. Which one is it?

(a) $I(x+y) = I(x) + I(y)$
(b) $I(x+y+z) = I(x+y) + I(z) = I(x) + I(y+z) = I(x+z) + I(y)$
(c) $I(x+y+z) = I(x+y) + I(z + D(y+x))$
(d) $D(x+y+z) = y + z - I(y+z) + D(x)$

Solution: There are three principle, themes you need to understand in order to answer such questions.

1. **Thinking in language**: The above question is garnished with a plethora of mathematical symbols. Unless you are able to convert each of the situations given in the options into clear logical language, your mind cannot make sense of what is written in the options. The best mathematical brains work this way. Absolutely nobody has the mathematical vision to solve such problems by simply reading the notations in the problem and/or the options.
2. While thinking in language terms in the case of a question such as this, in order to understand and grasp the mathematical situation confronting us, the best thing to do is to put values into the situation. This is very critical in such problems because as you can yourself see – if you are thinking about say $I(x + y + z)$ and you keep the same notation to think through the problem, you would need to carry $I(x + y + z)$ throughout the thinking inside the problem. On the other hand, if you replace the $I(x + y + z)$ situation by replacing values for x, y and z, the expression would change to a single number. Thus, if you take $I(4.3 + 2.8 + 5.3) = I(12.4) = 12$. Obviously thinking further in the next steps with 12, as the handle, would be much easier than trying to think with $I(x + y + z)$.
3. Since the question here is asking us to identify the correct option which always gives us LHS = RHS, we can proceed further in the problem using the options given to us. While doing this, when you are testing an option, the approach has to be to try to think of values for the variables such that the option is rejected, i.e. we need to think of values such that LHS $\neq$ RHS. In this fashion, the idea is to eliminate three options and identify the one option that cannot be eliminated because it cannot be disproved.

Keeping these principles in mind, if we try to look at the options in this problem, we have to look for the one correct statement.

Let us check option (a) to begin with:

The LHS can be interpreted as: $I(x + y)$ means the integer part of $x + y$. Suppose we use x as 4.3 and y as 4.2, we would get $I(x + y) = I(4.3 + 4.2) = I(8.5) = 8$.

The RHS in this case would be $I(4.3) + I(4.2) = 4 + 4 = 8$. This gives us LHS = RHS.

However, if you use $x = 4.3$ and $y = 4.8$, you would see that LHS $= I(4.3 + 4.8) = I(9.1) = 9$, while the RHS would be $I(4.3) + I(4.8) = 4 + 4 = 8$. This would clearly give us LHS $\neq$ RHS and hence, this option is incorrect.

The point to note here is that whenever you are solving a function-based question through the rejection of the options route, the vision about what kind of numbers would reject the case becomes critical. It is advisable that as you start solving questions through this route, you would need to improve your vision of what values to assume while rejecting an option. This is one key skill that differentiates the minds and the capacities of the top people from the average aspirants. Hence, if you want to compete against the best, you should develop this numerical vision. To illustrate what is meant by numerical vision, think of a situation where you are faced with the expression $(a + b) > (a \times b)$. Normally this does not happen, except when you are multiplying with numbers between 0 and 1.

Moving on with our problem. Let us look at Option (b).
$I(x + y + z) = I(x + y) + I(z) = I(x) + I(y + z) = I(x + z) + I(y)]$

In order to reject this option, the following values would be used:

$x = 4.3$, $y = 5.1$, and $z = 6.7$

LHS $= I(4.3 + 5.1 + 6.7) = I(16.1) = 16$

When we try to see whether the first expression on the RHS satisfies this, we can clearly see it does not because:

$I(x + y) + I(z)$ would give us $I(4.3 + 5.1) + I(6.7) = I(9.4) + I(6.7) = 9 + 6 = 15$ in this case.

Thus, $I(x + y + z) = I(x + y) + I(z)$ is disproved and this option can be rejected at this point.

We, thus, move onto option (c), which states:

$I(x + y + z) = I(x + y) + I(z + D(y + x))$

Let us try this in the case of the values we previously took, i.e. $x = 4.3$, $y = 5.1$, and $z = 6.7$.

We get:

$I(4.3 + 5.1 + 6.7) = I(4.3 + 5.1) + I(6.7 + D(4.3 + 5.1))$
$\rightarrow I(16.1) = I(9.4) + I(6.7 + D(9.4))$
$\rightarrow I(16.1) = I(9.4) + I(6.7 + 0.4)$
$\rightarrow I(16.1) = I(9.4) + I(7.1)$
$\rightarrow 16 = 9 + 7$

Suppose we try 4.3, 4.9 and 5.9, we get:

$I(4.3 + 4.9 + 5.9) = I(4.3 + 4.9) + I(5.9 + D(4.3 + 4.9)$
$\rightarrow I(15.1) = I(9.2) + I(5.9 + D(9.2))$
$\rightarrow I(15.1) = I(9.4) + I(5.9 + 0.2)$
$\rightarrow I(15.1) = I(9.4) + I(6.1)$
$\rightarrow 15 = 9 + 6$

We can see that this option is proving to be difficult to shake off as a possible answer. However, this logic is not enough to select this as the correct answer. In order to make sure that you never err when you solve a question this way, you would need to either do one of two things at this point in the problem-solving approach.

Approach 1: Try to understand and explain to yourself the mathematical reason as to why this option should be correct.

Approach 2: Try to eliminate the remaining option/s at this point of time.

Amongst these, it is recommended to opt for approach 2 because that is likely to be easier than approach 1. Approach 1 is only to be used in case you have seen and understood during your checking of the option as to why the particular option is always guaranteed to be true. In case, you have not seen the mathematical logic for the same during your checking of the option, you typically should not try to search for the logic while trying to solve the problem. The quicker way to the correct answer would be to eliminate the remaining option/s.

(Of course, once you are done with solving the question, during your review of the question, you should ideally try to explain to yourself as to why one particular option worked – because that might become critical mathematical logic inside your mind for the next time you face a similar mathematical situation.)

In this case, let us try to do both. To freeze option (c) as the correct answer, you would need to look at option (d) and try to reject it.

Option (d) says:

$D(x + y + z) = y + z - I(y + z) + D(x)$

Say we take $x = 4.3$, $y = 5.1$ and $z = 6.7$, we can see that:

$D(4.3 + 5.1 + 6.7) = 5.1 + 6.7 - \text{I}(5.1 + 6.7) + D(4.3) \rightarrow$

$D(16.1) = 11.8 - \text{I}(11.8) + D(4.3) \rightarrow$

$0.1 = 11.8 - 11 + 0.3 \rightarrow$

$0.1 = 1.1$; this is clearly incorrect.

Hence, option (c) is the correct answer.

If we were to look at the mathematical logic for option (c) (for our future reference), we can think of why option (c) would always be true as follows:

One of the problems in these greatest integer problems is what can be described as the loss of value due to the greatest integer function.

Thus, $I\,(4.3 + 4.8) > I(4.3) + I\,(4.8)$ since the LHS is 9 and the RHS is only 8. What happens here is that the LHS gains by 1 unit because the 0.3 and the 0.8 in the two numbers add up to 1.1 and help the sum of the two numbers to cross 9. On the other hand, if you were to look at the RHS in this situation, you would realise that the decimal values of 4.3 and 4.8 are individually both lost.

In this context, when you look at the LHS of the equation given in option (c), you see that the value of the LHS would retain the integer values of x, y and z while the sum of the decimal values of x, y and z would get aggregated and combined into 1 number. This gives us three cases:

Case 1: When the addition of the decimal values of x, y and z is less than 1;

Case 2: When the addition of the decimal values of x, y and z is more than 1 but less than 2;

Case 3: When the addition of the decimal values of x, y and z is more than 2 but less than 3.

Each of these three cases would be further having a two-way fork – viz:

Case A: When the addition of the decimal values of x and y add up to less than 1;

Case B: When the addition of the decimal values of x and y add up to more than 1 but less than 2.

The readers are encouraged to take this case from this point and move it to a point where they can explore each of these six situations and see that for all these situations, the value of the LHS of the expression is equal to the value of the RHS of the equation.

Problem 14.12: During the reign of the great government in the country of Riposta, the government forms committees of ministers whenever it is faced with a problem. One particular year, there are x ministers in the government and they are organised into four committees such that:

(i) Each minister belongs to exactly two committees

(ii) Each pair of committees has exactly one minister in common

Then

(a) $x = 4$

(b) $x = 6$

(c) $x = 8$

(d) x cannot be determined from the given information

Solution: In order to think about this situation, you need to think of the number of unique people you need in order to make up the committees as defined in the problem. However, before you start to do this, a problem you need to solve is—how many members do you put in each committee?

Given the options for x, when we look at the options, it is clear that the number is unlikely to be larger than 4. Hence, suppose we try to think of committees with four members, we will get the following thought process:

First, we create the first two committees with exactly one member common between the two committees. We would get the following table at this point of time:

Committee 1	*Committee 2*	*Committee 3*	*Committee 4*
1	4		
2	5		
3	6		
4	7		

Here we have taken the individual members of the committees as 1, 2, 3, 4, 5, 6 and 7. We have obeyed the second rule for committee formation (i.e. each pair of committees has exactly one member in common) by taking only the member 4 as the common member.

From this point in the table, we need to try to fill in the remaining committees obeying the twin rules given in the problem.

So, each member should belong to exactly two committees and each pair of committees should have only 1 member in common.

When we try to do that in this table we reach the following point.

Committee 1	Committee 2	Committee 3	Committee 4
1	**4**	**7**	
2	5	**1**	
3	6	8	
4	**7**	9	

Here we have taken 7 common between the committees 2 and 3, while 1 is common between committees 1 and 3. This point freezes the individuals 1, 4 and 7 as they have been used twice (as required). However, this leaves us with 2, 3, 5, 6, 8 and 9 to be used once more and only committee 4 is left to fill in into the table. This is obviously impossible to do and hence, we are sure that each committee would not have had four members.

Obviously, if four members are too many, we cannot move to trying five members per committee. Thus, we should move trying to form committees with three members each.

When we do so, the following thought-process unfolds:

We first fill-in the first two committees by keeping exactly one person common between these committees. By taking the person '3' as a common member between committees 1 and 2, we reach the following table:

Committee 1	Committee 2	Committee 3	Committee 4
1	3		
2	4		
3	5		

We now need to fill in committee 3 with exactly one member from committee 1 and exactly one member from committee 2. Also, we cannot use the member number '3' as that has already been used twice. Thus, by repeating '5' from committee 2 and '1' from committee 1, we can reach the following table.

Committee 1	Committee 2	Committee 3	Committee 4
1	3	5	
2	4	1	
3	5		

Since the remaining person in committee 3 would have to be unique from members of committees 1 and 2, we would need to introduce a new member (say 6) in order to complete committee 3. Thus, our table evolves to the following situation.

Committee 1	Committee 2	Committee 3	Committee 4
1	**3**	**5**	
2	4	**1**	
3	**5**	6	

At this point, the members 2, 4 and 6 have not been used a second time. Also, the committee 4 has to have its three members filled such that it has exactly one member common with committees 1, 2 and 3 respectively.

This is easily achieved using the following structure.

Committee 1	Committee 2	Committee 3	Committee 4
1	**3**	**5**	2
2	4	**1**	4
3	**5**	6	6

Hence, we can clearly see that the value of x is 6, i.e. the government had six ministers.

Problem 14.13: During the IPL Season 14, the Mumbai Indians captained by a certain Sachin Tendulkar who emerged out of retirement, played 60 games in the season. The team never lost three games consecutively and never won five games consecutively in that season. If N is the number of games the team won in that season, then N satisfies

(a) $24 \le N \le 48$ (b) $20 \le N \le 48$
(c) $12 \le N \le 48$ (d) $20 \le N \le 42$

Solution: In order to solve this question, we need to see the limit of the minimum and maximum number of matches that the team could have won. Let us first think about the maximum number of matches the team could have won. Since the team 'never won five games consecutively' during that season, we would get the value for the maximum number of wins by trying to make the team win four games consecutively—as many times as we can. This can be thought of as follows:

WWWWLWWWWLWWWWL ... and so on

From the above sequence, we can clearly see that with four wins consecutively, we are forming a block of five matches in which the team has won 4 and lost 1. Since, there are a total of 60 matches in all; there would be 12 such blocks of five matches each. The total number of wins in this case would amount to $12 \times 4 = 48$ (this is the highest number possible).

This eliminates option (d) as the possible answer.

If we think about the minimum number of wins, we would need to maximise the number of losses. In order to do so, we get the following thought-process:

Since the team never lost three games consecutively; for the maximum number of losses the pattern followed would be–

LLWLLWLLWLLW… and so on

Thus, there are two losses and one win in every block of three matches. Since, there would be a total of 20 such blocks; it would mean that there would be a total of $20 \times 1 = 20$ wins. This number would represent the minimum possible number of wins for the team.

Thus, N has to be between 20 and 48. Thus, option (b) is correct.

Problem 14.14: How many pairs of positive integers m, n satisfy $1/m + 4/n = 1/12$ where n is an odd integer less than 60?

(a) 7 (b) 5
(c) 3 (d) 6
(e) 4

Thought-process:

Deduction 1: Since two positive fractions on the LHS equals 1/12 on the right hand side; the value of both these fractions must be less than 1/12. Hence, n can take only the values 49, 51, 53, 55, 57 and 59.

Deduction 2: We now need to check which of the possible values of n would give us an integral value of m.

The equation can be transformed to: $1/12 - 4/n = 1/m \rightarrow (n - 48)/12n = 1/m$. On reading this equation, you should realise that for m to be an integer, the LHS must be able to give you a ratio in the form of $1/x$. It can be easily seen that this occurs for $n = 49$, $n = 51$ and $n = 57$. Hence, there are only three pairs.

Problem 14.15: The price of Darjeeling tea (in rupees per kilogram) is $100 + 0.1\ n$, on the nth day of 2007 (n = 1, 2, ..., 100), and then remains constant. On the other hand, the price of Ooty tea (in rupees per kilogram) is $89 + 0.15n$, on the nth day of 2007 (n = 1, 2, .,., 365). On which date in 2007, will the prices of these two varieties of tea be equal?

(a) May 21 (b) April 11
(c) May 20 (d) April 10
(e) June 30

The gap between the two prices initially is of ₹11 or 1100 paisa. The rate at which the gap closes down is 5 paisa per day for the first hundred days. (The gap covered would be 500 paisa which would leave a residual gap of 600 paisa.) Then the price of Darjeeling tea stops rising and that of Ooty tea rises at 15 paisa per day. Hence, the gap of 600 paisa would get closed out in another 40 days. Hence, the prices of the two varieties would become equal on the 140th day of the year. 31 + 28 + 31 + 30 + 20 = 140, means May 20th is the answer.

Problem 14.16: The number of ordered pairs of integers (x, y) satisfying the equation $x^2 + 6x + 2y^2 = 4 + y^2$ is

(a) 12 (b) 8
(c) 10 (d) 14

These kinds of questions and thinking are very common in examinations and hence, you need to understand how to solve such questions.

In order to think of such questions, you need to first 'read' the equation given. What does it mean by 'reading' the equation? Let us illustrate:

The first thing we do is to simplify the equation by putting all the variables on the LHS. This would give us the equation $x^2 + 6x + y^2$. When we have an equation like $x^2 + 6x + y^2 = 4$, we should realise that the value on the RHS is fixed at 4. Also, if we take a look at the LHS of the equation, we realise that the terms x^2 and y^2 would always be positive integers or 0 (given that x and y are integers). $6x$, on the other hand, could be positive, zero or negative depending on the value of x (if x is positive, $6x$ is also positive; if x is negative, $6x$ would be negative and if x is 0, $6x$ would also be zero).

Thus, we can think of the following structures to build a value of 4 on the LHS for the equation to get satisfied:

	Value of x^2	*Value of 6x*	*Value of y^2*
Case 1	0	0	+
Case 2	+	+	+
Case 3	+	–	+
Case 4	+	–	0

Once you have these basic structures in place, you can think of the cases one-by-one. Thinking in this structured fashion makes sure that you do not miss out on any possible solutions — and that, as you should realise, is critical for any situation where you have to count the number of solutions. You simply cannot get these questions correct without identifying each possible situation. Trying to do such questions without first structuring your thought-process this way would lead to disastrous results in such questions!! Hence, this thinking is very critical for your development of quantitative thinking.

Let us look at **Case 1:** In case 1, since the value of the first two components on the LHS is 0, it must mean that we are talking about the case of $x = 0$. Obviously, in this case the entire value of 4 for the LHS has to be created by using the term y^2.

Thus, to make $y^2 = 4$, we can take $y = +2$ or $y = -2$. This gives us two possible solutions: (0, 2) and (0, –2)

Case 2: The minimum positive value for $6x$ would be when $x = 1$. This value for $6x$ turns out to be 6– which has already made the LHS larger than 4. To this, if we were to add two more positive integers for the values of x^2 and y^2, it would simply take the LHS further up from +6. Hence, in case 2, there are no solutions.

Case 3: In this case the value of x has to be negative and y can be either positive or negative. Possible negative values of x as –1, –2, –3, –4, –5, etc., give us values for $6x$ as –6, –12, –18, –24, –30, etc.

We then need to fill-in the values of x^2 and y^2 and see whether it is possible to add an exact value to any of these and get + 4 as the final value of the LHS.

This thinking would go the following way:

<u>If $6x = -6$:</u> x must be –1 and hence, $x^2 = 1$. Thus, $x^2 + 6x = -5$, which means for $x^2 + 6x + y^2 = 4$, we would need $-5 + y^2 = 4 \rightarrow y^2 = 9 \rightarrow y = +3$ and $y = -3$

Thus, we have identified two more solutions as (–1, 3) and (–1, –3).

<u>If $6x = -12$:</u> x must be –2 and hence, $x^2 = 4$. Thus, $x^2 + 6x = -8$, which means for $x^2 + 6x + y^2 = 4$, we would need $-8 + y^2 = 4 \rightarrow y^2 = 12 \rightarrow y$ is not an integer in this case and hence, we get no new solutions for this case.

<u>If $6x = -18$:</u> x must be –3 and hence, $x^2 = 9$. Thus, $x^2 + 6x = -9$, which means for $x^2 + 6x + y^2 = 4$, we would need $-9 + y^2 = 4 \rightarrow y^2 = 13 \rightarrow y$ is not an integer in this case and hence, we get no new solutions for this case.

<u>If $6x = -24$:</u> x must be -4 and hence, $x^2 = 16$. Thus, $x^2 + 6x = -8$, which means for $x^2 + 6x + y^2 = 4$, we would need $-8 + y^2 = 4 \rightarrow y^2 = 12 \rightarrow y$ is not an integer in this case and hence, we get no new solutions for this case.

<u>If $6x = -30$:</u> x must be -5 and hence, $x^2 = 25$. Thus, $x^2 + 6x = -5$, which means for $x^2 + 6x + y^2 = 4$, we would need $-5 + y^2 = 4 \rightarrow y^2 = 9 \rightarrow y = +3$ and $y = -3$

Thus we have identified two more solutions as $(-5, 3)$ and $(-5, -3)$.

<u>If $6x = -36$:</u> x must be -6 and hence, $x^2 = 36$. Thus, $x^2 + 6x = 0$, which means for $x^2 + 6x + y^2 = 4$, we would need $0 + y^2 = 4 \rightarrow y^2 = 4 \rightarrow y = +2$ and $y = -2$.

Thus, we have identified two more solutions as $(-6, 2)$ and $(-6, -2)$.

<u>If $6x = -42$:</u> x must be -7 and hence, $x^2 = 49$. Thus, $x^2 + 6x = 7$, which means that $x^2 + 6x$ itself is crossing the value of 4 for the LHS. There is no scope to add any value of y^2 as a positive integer to get the LHS of the equation equal to 4. Thus, we can stop at this point.

Notice that we did not need to check for the case 4 because if there were a solution for case 4, we would have been able to identify it while checking for case 3 itself.

Thus, the equation has eight solutions.

Problem 14.17: Consider the equation of the form $x^2 + bx + c = 0$. The number of such equations that have real roots and have coefficients b and c in the set $\{1, 2, 3, 4, 5, 6, 7\}$, is

(a) 20 (b) 25
(c) 27 (d) 29

We know, that in order to have the roots of an equation to be real, we should have the values of the discriminant of the quadratic equation (defined as the value $b^2 - 4ac$ for a standard quadratic equation $ax^2 + bx + c = 0$) to be non-negative.

In the context of the given equation in this problem, since the value of the coefficient of x^2 is 1, it means that we need to have $b^2 - 4c$ to be positive or 0.

The only thing to be done from this point is to look for possible values of a and b which fit this requirement. In order to do this, assume a value for 'b' from the set $\{1, 2, 3, 4, 5, 6$, and $7\}$ and try to see which values of b and c satisfy $b^2 - 4c \geq 0$.

When $b = 1$, c can take none of the values between 1 and 6, since "$b^2 - 4c$" would end up being negative.

When $b = 2$, c can be 1;

When $b = 3$, c can be 1 or 2;

When $b = 4$, c can be 1 or 2 or 3 or 4;

When $b = 5$, c can take any value between 1 and 6;

When $b = 6$, c can take any value between 1 and 7;

When $b = 7$, c can take any value between 1 and 7.

Thus, there are a total of 27 such equations with real roots.

Problem 14.18: Let $x_1, x_2, \ldots\ldots, x_{40}$ be forty non-zero numbers such that $x_i + x_{i+1} = k$ for all i, $1 \leq i \leq \infty$. If $x_{14} = a$, $x_{27} = b$, then $x_{30} + x_{39}$ equals

(a) $3(a + b) - 2k$
(b) $k + a$
(c) $k + b$
(d) None of the foregoing expressions

Since, $x_{14} = a$, x_{15} would equal $(k - a)$ [we get this by equating $x_{14} + x_{15} = k \rightarrow a + x_{15} = k \rightarrow x_{15} = (k - a)$]. By using the same logic on the equation $x_{15} + x_{16} = k$, we will get $x_{16} = a$. Consequently, $x_{17} = k - a$, $x_{18} = a$, $x_{19} = k - a$, $x_{20} = a$. Thus, we see that every odd term is equal to '$k - a$' and every even term is equal to 'a'. Further, we can develop a similar logic for x_i in the context of 'b'. Since, $x_{27} = b$, $x_{28} = k - b$, $x_{29} = b$ and so on. This series also follows a similar logic with x_i being equal to b, when 'i' is odd and being equal to $k - b$, when 'i' is even.

Thus, for every value of x_i, we have two ways of looking at its value—viz. either in terms of a or in terms of b. Thus, for any x_{even}, we have for instance $x_{20} = a = k - b$.

Solving $a = k - b$, we get $a + b = k$.

Further, when we look at trying to solve for the specific value of what the question has asked us, i.e. the value of $x_{30} + x_{39}$, we realise that we can either solve it in terms of 'a' or in terms of 'b'. If we try to solve it in terms of 'a', we would see the following happening:

$X_{30} + x_{39} = a + k - a = k$

Similarly, in terms of 'b', $x_{30} + x_{39} = k - b + b = k$. Since we know that $k = a + b$ (deduced above), we can conclude $x_{30} + x_{39} = a + b$. However, if we look at the options, none of the options is directly saying that.

Options (b) and (c) can be rejected because their values are not equal to $a + b$. A closer inspection of option (a), gives us an expression: $3(a + b) - 2k$. This expression can be expressed as $3(a + b) - 2(a + b) = (a + b)$ and hence, this is the correct answer.

Directions for Problems 19 to 21: Answer the questions based on the following information.

For three distinct positive real numbers x, y and z, let

$f(x, y, z) = \text{Min}(\text{Max}(x, y), \text{Max}(y, z), \text{Max}(z, x))$
$g(x, y, z) = \text{Max}(\text{Min}(x, y), \text{Min}(y, z), \text{Min}(z, x))$
$h(x, y, z) = \text{Max}(\text{Max}(x, y), \text{Max}(y, z), \text{Max}(z, x))$
$j(x, y, z) = \text{Min}(\text{Min}(x, y), \text{Min}(y, z), \text{Min}(z, x))$
$m(x, y, z) = \text{Max}(x, y, z)$
$n(x, y, z) = \text{Min}(x, y, z)$

Solutions for Problems 19 to 21: A closer reading of the given functions tells us that the function:

$f(x, y, z) = \text{Min}(\text{Max}(x, y), \text{Max}(y, z), \text{Max}(z, x))$ gives us the second highest value of the three numbers x, y, z;

$g(x, y, z) = \text{Max}(\text{Min}(x, y), \text{Min}(y, z), \text{Min}(z, x))$ gives us the second highest value of the three numbers x, y, z;

$h(x, y, z) = \text{Max}(\text{Max}(x, y), \text{Max}(y, z), \text{Max}(z, x))$ gives us the highest value of the three numbers x, y, z;

$j(x, y, z) = \text{Min}(\text{Min}(x, y), \text{Min}(y, z), \text{Min}(z, x))$ gives us the minimum value of the three numbers x, y, z;

$m(x, y, z) = \text{Max}(x, y, z)$gives us the highest value of the three numbers x, y, z;

$n(x, y, z) = \text{Min}(x, y, z)$ gives us the minimum value of the three numbers x, y, z;

Thus, we have: $f(x, y, z) = g(x, y, z)$; $h(x, y, z) = m(x, y, z)$ and $j(x, y, z) = n(x, y, z)$.

With this starting understanding if we move into the questions, the solving of the questions would be much easier than by blindly substituting values in the options and checking to see which answer is correct.

Problem 14.19 Which of the following is necessarily greater than 1?

(a) $[h(x, y, z) - f(x, y, z)] / j(x, y, z)$
(b) $j(x, y, z) / h(x, y, z)$
(c) $f(x, y, z) / g(x, y, z)$
(d) $[f(x, y, z) + h(x, y, z) - g(x, y, z)] / j(x, y, z)$

Solution: Since we are looking at a value 'necessarily greater than 1' it means we are looking for the numerator to be greater than the denominator. When we look at the first option, we see that: $(h - f)/j$ = (highest - second highest)/ lowest → Can be more than or less than one depending on the values we choose for x, y and z;

Option (b) j/h = minimum/maximum would necessarily be less than 1;

Option (c) f/g = (second highest)/(second highest) = 1;

Option (d) $[f + h - g]/j = h/j$ (since f and g are same) = maximum/minimum → necessarily greater than 1.

Problem 14.20: Which of the following expressions is necessarily equal to 1?

(a) $[f(x, y, z) - m(x, y, z)] / [g(x, y, z) - h(x, y, z)]$
(b) $[m(x, y, z) - f(x, y, z)] / [g(x, y, z) - n(x, y, z)]$
(c) $[j(x, y, z) - g(x, y, z)] / h(x, y, z)$
(d) $[f(x, y, z) - h(x, y, z)] / f(x, y, z)$

Solution: Option (a) is [second highest - highest]/[second highest - highest] = 1. Hence, option (a) is correct.

Problem 14.21: Which of the following expressions is indeterminate?

(a) $[f(x, y, z) - h(x, y, z)] / [g(x, y, z) - j(x, y, z)]$
(b) $[f(x, y, z) + h(x, y, z) + g(x, y, z) + j(x, y, z)] / [j(x, y, z) + h(x, y, z) - m(x, y, z) - n(x, y, z)]$
(c) $[g(x, y, z) - j(x, y, z)] / [f(x, y, z) - h(x, y, z)]$
(d) $[h(x, y, z) - f(x, y, z)] / [n(x, y, z) - g(x, y, z)]$

Solution: For an indeterminate expression, we need the denominator to be zero. This would occur only when the components of the denominator cancel out. Checking the options, the first option has a denominator of $g - h$ = second highest - highest $\neq 0$. Hence, option (a) is not indeterminate. In option (b), we see that the denominator is $j + h - m - n$ = minimum + maximum – maximum – minimum = 0. Hence, the denominator is 0 and hence option (b) is indeterminate.

Directions for Problems 22 and 23: Answer the questions based on the following information.

For a real number x, let **(CAT 2000)**

$$f(x) = \frac{1}{1+x} \quad \text{if } x \text{ is non-negative}$$
$$= 1 + x \quad \text{if } x \text{ is negative}$$
$$f^n(x) = f(f^{n-1}(x)),\ n = 2, 3, \ldots$$

Problem 14.22: What is the value of the product $f(2)\, f^2(2)\, f^3(2)\, f^4(2)\, f^5(2)$?

(a) 1/3 (b) 3
(c) 1/18 (d) None of these

Solution: $f(2) = \frac{1}{1+2} = \frac{1}{3},\ f^2(2) = f\left(\frac{1}{3}\right) = \frac{1}{1+\frac{1}{3}} = \frac{3}{4},$

$$f^3(2) = f\left(\frac{3}{4}\right) = \frac{4}{7},\ f^4(2) = f\left(\frac{4}{7}\right) = \frac{7}{11},$$

$$f^5(2) = f\left(\frac{7}{11}\right) = \frac{11}{18}$$

$$f(2) f^2(2) f^3(2) f^4(2) f^5(2) = \frac{1}{3} \times \frac{3}{4} \times \frac{4}{7} \times \frac{7}{11} \times \frac{11}{18} = \frac{1}{18}$$

Problem 14.23: r is an integer ≥ 2. Then what is the value of

$f^{r-1}(-r) + f^r(-r) + f^{r+1}(-r)$?

(a) –1 (b) 0
(c) 1 (d) None of these

Solution: Let $r = 2$

$f(-2) = 1 - 2 = -1$
$f^2(-2) = f(-1) = 1 - 1 = 0$
$f^3(-2) = 1/1 + 0 = 1$
$f^{r-1}(-r) + f^r(-r) + f^{r+1}(-r) = -1 + 0 + 1 = 0$

Problem 14.24: The set of all positive integers is the union of two disjoint subsets: **(CAT 2000)**

$\{f(1), f(2), \ldots, f(n), \ldots\}$ and $\{g(1), g(2), \ldots, g(n), \ldots\}$, where

$f(1) < f(2) < \ldots < f(n) \ldots$, and $g(1) < g(2) < \ldots < g(n) \ldots$, and

$g(n) = f(f(n)) + 1$ for all $n \geq 1$.

What is the value of $g(1)$?

(a) 0 (b) 2
(c) 1 (d) Cannot be determined

Solution: In the question, $f(n)$ represents the series of all odd numbers 1, 3, 5, 7, 9… and $g(n)$ represents the series of all even numbers 2, 4, 6, 8, 10. Hence, $g(1) = 2$.

Problem 14.25: Let x, y be two positive numbers such that $x + y = 1$. Then, the minimum value of $(x + 1/x)^2 + (y + 1/y)^2$ is… **(CAT 2001)**

(a) 12 (b) 20
(c) 12.5 (d) 13.3

Solution: The required minimum value would occur when both x and y are taken as 1/2. Then the required sum

$$= \left(\frac{1}{2^2}+2^2\right)+\left(\frac{1}{2^2}+2^2\right) = 6.25 + 6.25 = 12.5$$

Problem 14.26: The number of real roots of the equation $\frac{A^2}{x}+\frac{B^2}{x^{-1}}=1$ where A and B are real numbers not equal to zero simultaneously, is **(CAT 2002)**

(a) 1 (b) 2
(c) 1 or 2 (d) None of these

Solution: The given would have only one real root if either A or B is equal to 0 (as both can never be zero simultaneously).

When both A and B are non-zero then, it would be a quadratic equation so in this case there would be two real roots, or zero real roots, depending on the value of A and B.

So, option (d) is correct.

Problem 14.27: Suppose for any real number x, $[x]$ denotes the greatest integer less than or equal to x. Let $L(x, y) = [x] + [y] + [x + y]$ and $R(x, y) = [2x] + [2y]$. Then it is impossible to find any two positive real numbers x and y for which **(CAT 2002)**

(a) $L(x, y) = R(x, y)$
(b) $L(x, y) \neq R(x, y)$
(c) $L(x, y) < R(x, y)$
(d) $L(x, y) > R(x, y)$

Solution: We can solve this problem just by inserting values for x and y in the given expressions. Put $x = 2.2$ and $y = 1.7$ $L(x, y) = 6$ & $R(x, y) = 7$ so we can eliminate option (b), (c).

Now put $x = y = 1$ then $L(x, y) = R(x, y)$. So we can eliminate option (a).

So, option (d) is the correct option.

Problem 14.28: If both a and b belong to the set {1, 2, 3, 4}, then the number of equations of the form $ax^2 + bx + 1 = 0$ having real roots is **(CAT 2002)**

(a) 10 (b) 7
(c) 6 (d) 12

Solution: $ax^2 + bx + 1 = 0$

For real roots

$b^2 - 4ac \geq 0$

$\therefore\ b^2 - 4a(1) \geq 0$

$\therefore\ b^2 \geq 4a$

For $a = 1$, possible values of b are 2, 3, 4.

$a = 2$, $4a = 8$, possible values of b are 3, 4.

$a = 3$, $4a = 12$, possible value of b is 4.

$a = 4$, $4a = 16$, possible value of b is 4.

$\therefore$ Number of equations possible = 7.

KNOWLEDGE ENRICHMENT CORNER

Scan this QR code to access a video on 'must know' questions before heading into the LOD exercises

Space for Rough Work

LEVEL OF DIFFICULTY (I)

1. If $f(x) = (7x + 4)/(4x - 7)$ and $g(x) = x^2 - 3x - 7$ be two functions, then what is the value of $g(f(g(f(g(f(3))))))$.
2. If $f_1(x) = 2x^2 + 10x + n$ and $f_2(x) = 2x$, how many 2-digit positive values of 'n' exist for which the equation $f_1(x) = f_2(x)$ is never negative?
3. Let $f(x) = 4x + 4$ and $g(x) = 2 - 4x$. For what values of x does $|f(x) + g(x)| = |f(x)| + |g(x)|$ hold true?
   (a) $-1 \le x \le 1/2$ (b) $x < -1$
   (c) $x > 1/2$ (d) All x
4. Let $f(x)$ be a function such that $f(x + y) = f(x) \times f(y)$ for all natural numbers. If $f(1) = 4$ and $f(1) + f(2) + f(3) + ... + f(n) = 1364$, then the value of n is
   (a) 4 (b) 5
   (c) 6 (d) 7
5. If $f(x) = 2[x] + 3$ and $g(x) = 2[x - 2] + 5$. Then for all integer values of x, $f(x) - g(x)$ is equal to:
   Note: $[x]$ is the greatest integer function of x.
   (a) –4 (b) 4
   (c) –2 (d) 2
6. If $f(a,b,c) = \min\{\min(a,b),\min(b,c),\min(c,a)\}$
   $g(a,b,c) = \max\{\max(a,b),\max(a,c),\max(b,c)\}$
   Find $f(a,b,c) - g(a,b,c)$, if a, b and c are in an AP with a common difference of 2?
   (a) –4 or 4 (b) 4
   (c) –4 (d) None of these

Directions for Questions 7 and 8: In these questions, the following functions are defined: Min (p, q) = least of p, q
Max (p, q) = larger of p, q
G(p, q) = GCD of p, q
L(p, q) = LCM of p, q
P(p, q) = product of p, q

7. What will be the maximum value of the expression $L(1, P(3,\max(3, p)))$ and for what value (or value range) of p would it occur?
   (a) $-\infty$ when $p > 39$ (b) $3p$, when $p > 3$
   (c) 0 when $p = 0$ (d) None of these
8. $P(9, \max(4, \min(L(12, 9), P(5, 3))))$. The value of above expression is
   (a) 120 (b) 105
   (c) 135 (d) 115
9. Let $f(x) = ax/(x + 1)$, *x not equal to –1*. Find the value of a for which $f(f(x)) = x$.
   (a) $20^{.5}$ (b) $-20^{.5}$
   (c) 1 (d) –1
10. If $f(x) = 2x^2 + 7x - 9$ and $g(x) = 2x + 3$, then find the value of $g(f(x))$ at $x = 3$.
    (a) 63 (b) 46
    (c) 57 (d) 49
11. Find the range of x, for which the function $y = (169 - x^2)^{1/2}$ is defined.
    (a) $0 \le x \le 13$ (b) $(-\infty, -13]$ U $[13, \infty)$
    (c) $-13 \le x$ (d) $-13 \le x \le 13$
12. Which of the following is an even function?
    (a) x^{12}
    (b) $(x - 3)^2$
    (c) $(x + 3)^4$
    (d) More than one of the above
13. Find the inverse of the function $f(x) = 1/(x - 1)$.
    (a) $(x - 1)$ (b) $(x + 1)$
    (c) $1/(1 - x)$ (d) $(1 + x)/x$
14. Consider $f(x) = f(x - 1) + f(x - 2)$, x is a positive integer.
    $f(1) = 2$, $f(2) = 3$
    Now, find the value of $f(6)$.
    (a) 21 (b) 13
    (c) 19 (d) None of these
15. A function $F(n)$ is defined as $F(n - 1) = \frac{1}{(2 - F(n))}$ for all natural numbers 'n'. If $F(1) = 3$, then what is the value of $[F(1)] + [F(2)] + ... + [F(1000)]$? (Here, $[x]$ is equal to the greatest integer less than or equal to 'x')
    (a) 1001 (b) 1002
    (c) 3003 (d) None of these
16. For the above question, find the value of the expression: $F(1) \times F(2) \times F(3) \times F(4) \times .... F(1000)$.
    (a) 2001 (b) 1999
    (c) 2004 (d) 1997
17. A function $f(x)$ is defined for all real values of x as $f(x) = ax^2 + bx + c$. If $f(3) = f(-3) = 18$, $f(0) = 15$, then what is the value of $f(12)$?
    (a) 63 (b) 159
    (c) 102 (d) None of these
18. Two operations, for real numbers x and y, are defined as given below.
    (i) $M(x\ \theta\ y) = (x + y)^2$
    (ii) $f(x\ \psi\ y) = (x - y)^2$
    If $M(x^2\,\theta\,y^2) = 361$ and $M(x^2\,\psi\,y^2) = 49$, then what is the value of the square root of $((x^2 y^2) + 3)$?
    (a) ±81 (b) ±9
    (c) ±7 (d) ±11
19. The function $\Psi(m) = [m]$, where $[m]$ represents the greatest integer less than or equal to m. Two real numbers x and y are such that $\Psi(4x + 5) = 5y + 3$ and $\Psi(3y+7) = x + 4$, then find the value of $x^2 \times y^2$.
    (a) 1 (b) 2
    (c) 4 (d) None of these
20. A certain function always obeys the rule: If $f(x.y) = f(x).f(y)$, where x and y are positive real numbers. A certain Mr. Mogambo found that the value of $f(128) = 4$, then find the value of the variable $M = f(0.5).f(1).f(2).f(4).f(8).f(16).f(32).f(64).f(128).f(256)$.

(a) 128 (b) 256
(c) 512 (d) 1024

21. x and y are non-negative integers such that $4x + 6y = 20$, and $x^2 \leq M/y^{2/3}$ for all values of x, y. What is the minimum value of M?
(a) $2^{2/3}$ (b) $2^{1/3}$
(c) $2^{8/3}$ (d) $4^{2/3}$

22. Let $\Psi(x) = \dfrac{x+3}{2}$ and $\theta(x) = 3x^2 + 2$. Find the value of $\theta(\Psi(-7))$.
(a) 12 (b) 14
(c) 50 (d) 42

23. If $F(a + b) = F(a). F(b) \div 2$, where $F(b) \neq 0$ and $F(a) \neq 0$, then what is the value of $F(12b)$?
(a) $(F(b))^{12}$ (b) $F(b))^{12} \div 2$
(c) $(F(b))^{12} \div 2^{12}$ (d) $(F(b))^{12} \div 2^{11}$

24. A function $a = \theta(b)$ is said to be reflexive if $b = \theta(a)$. Which of the following is/are reflexive functions?
(i) $\dfrac{3b+5}{4b-3}$ (ii) $\dfrac{3b+5}{5b-2}$
(iii) $\dfrac{2b+12}{12b-2}$
(a) All of these are reflexive
(b) Only (i) and (ii) are reflexive
(c) Only (i) and (iii) are reflexive
(d) None of these are reflexive

25. The points of intersection of the graphs of the functions $f(x) = 2x^2 - 1$ and $g(x) = 1 - 3x$ are
(a) {2, –1/2} (b) {–2, ½}
(c) {1, 2} (d) {–2, –1/2}

26. If $f(x) = 1/x$, $g(x) = 1/(1 - x)$ and $h(x) = x^2$, then find fogoh (2).
(a) –1 (b) 1
(c) 1/2 (d) None of these

27. Which of the following is not an odd function?
(a) $(x + 1)^3$ (b) x^{23}
(c) x^{53} (d) x^{77}

Directions for Questions 28 to 30: Read the instructions below and solve.
$f(x) = f(x - 2) - f(x - 1)$, where x is a natural number
$f(1) = 0$, $f(2) = 1$

28. The value of $f(8)$ is
(a) 0 (b) 13
(c) –5 (d) –9

29. The value of $f(7) + f(4)$ is
(a) 11 (b) –6
(c) –12 (d) 12

30. What will be the value of $\sum_{n=1}^{9} f(n)$?
(a) –12 (b) –15
(c) –14 (d) –13

31. What will be the domain of the definition of the function $f(x) = {}^{8-x}C_{5-x}$ for positive values of x?
(a) {1, 2, 3} (b) {1, 2, 3, 4, 5}
(c) {0, 1, 2, 3, 4, 5} (d) {1, 2, 3, 4, 5, 6, 7, 8}

Directions for Questions 32 to 34
Mark a, if $f(-x) = f(x)$
Mark b, if $f(-x) = -f(x)$
Mark c, if neither a nor b is true
Mark d, if $f(x)$ does not exist at least one point of the domain

32.

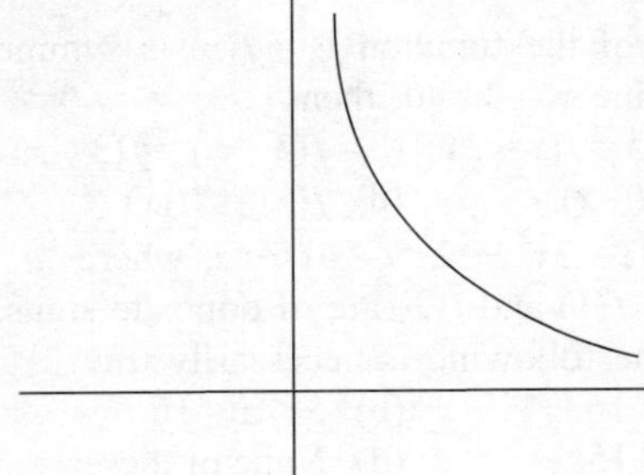

33.

34.

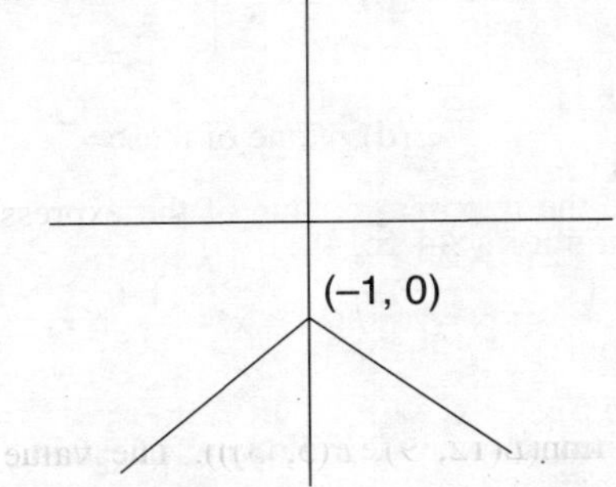

35. If $f(x) = 2x + 5$ and $h(x) = (x - 5)/2$, the value of $foh(x) = hof(x)$. What is the value of hofofohohof(x) × fohofoh(x)?
(a) $x - 5$ (b) $(2x + 5)/x + 5$
(c) x (d) x^2

36. For the above question, what is the value of $fo(foh)o(hof)(x)$?
(a) $2x + 5$ (b) x
(c) $x - 5$ (d) $x - 2$

37. Let $f(x) = |x - 4| + |x - 5| + |x - 6|$ and $A(x) = f(x + 1)$. Then
(a) $A(x)$ is an even function
(b) $A(x)$ is an odd function
(c) $A(x)$ is neither even or odd
(d) None of these

38. The inverse function of the function $f(x) = (e^x - e^{-x})/(e^x + e^{-x})$ is

(a) $y = ½ \log_e \frac{x+1}{1-x}$ (b) $y = ½ \log_e \frac{x+2}{2-x}$

(c) $y = ½ \log_e \frac{1-x}{1+x}$ (d) $½ \log_e x$

39. The graph of the function $y = f(x)$ is symmetrical about the line $x - 3 = 0$, then

(a) $f(x+3) = f(x-3)$ (b) $f(3+x) = f(3-x)$

(c) $f(x) = f(-x)$ (d) $f(x) = 2f(x)$

40. If $f(x) = x^5 - 3x^4 + 2x^2 - 4x + a$, where '$a$' is an integer and $f(1)$ and $f(2)$ are of opposite signs, then which of the following is necessarily true?

(a) $5 < a < 16$ (b) $5 \le a \le 16$

(c) $5 \le a \le 15$ (d) None of these

41. Find the sum of the coefficients of the polynomial $(1 + x - 3x^2)^{2163}$.

(a) –2 (b) –1

(c) 0 (d) 1

42. If $f(x) = |x - 2|$, then

(a) $f(x^2) = [f(x)]^2$

(b) $f(|x|) = f(x)$

(c) $f(x+y) = f(x) + f(y)$

(d) None of these

43. $f(x) = \frac{1}{x}, g(x) = |3x-2|$

Then $f(g(x)) = ?$

(a) $\frac{1}{|3x-2|}$ (b) $\left|\frac{1}{3x} - 2\right|$

(c) $\frac{1}{|3x|} - 2$ (d) None of these

Directions for Questions 44 to 48:

$f(x) = x^2 + \frac{1}{x^2}, g(x) = |x|, h(x) = x^3 - \frac{1}{x^3}, t(x),$

$= x^2 - \frac{1}{x^2}$, then answer the following questions:

44. $f(g(x))$ is an:

(a) Even function (b) Odd function

(c) Neither even nor odd

45. Which of the following options is true?

(a) $f(x) = g(x) + (g(x))^2$

(b) $f(x) = -f(g(x))$

(c) $f(g(x)) = g(f(x))$

(d) None of these

46. Out of $f(x)$, $g(x)$, $h(x)$, $t(x)$ how many are even functions?

47. Is $h(f(x))$ an even function or odd function? Type 1 if it is even; Type 2 if it is odd; Type 3 if it is neither even nor odd.

48. Is $h(t(x))$ an even function or an odd function or neither even nor odd? Type 1 if it is even; Type 2 if it is odd; Type 3 if it is neither even nor odd.

49. If $f(x) = \frac{x^2+1}{x-1}$, then- $f(f(f(2))) = 2$?

Directions for Questions 50 and 51:

$S(x, y) = x + y$
$P(x, y) = x \times y$
$D(x, y) = x/y$
$t(x, y) = |x - y|$

50. Find the value of $P(S(2,(D(3, 4)), 5)$.

51. $S(S(P(2,3), D(4,2)), t(1, 5)) = ?$

Directions for Questions 52 to 54: Define the following functions as:

$$xPy = \begin{cases} |x-y|, \text{if } x < y \\ xQy, \text{otherwise} \end{cases}$$

$$xQy = \begin{cases} \frac{x}{y}, \text{if } x > y \\ xRy, \text{otherwise} \end{cases}$$

$$xRy = \begin{cases} x \times y, \text{if } x \le y \\ xSy, \text{otherwise} \end{cases}$$

$$xSy = \begin{cases} \frac{1}{xy}, \text{if } x > y \\ xPy, \text{otherwise} \end{cases}$$

Here x & y are real numbers. Solve the following questions based on these definitions of the above functions.

52. Find the value of $[(5P6)Q(4Q2)]S(3S1)$.

53. Which of the following is true?

(a) $(4P2) \ne (2P4)$ (b) $(4Q2) = (2R4)$

(c) $(6Q3) = (2S(0.5))$ (d) None of these

54. If $(5P3)Q(4S2) = 20K1.5$. What is the correct operator to replace the 'K'?

Type 1 if your answer is 'P'; Type 2 if your answer is 'Q'; Type 3 if your answer is 'R'; Type 4 if your answer is 'S'

Directions for Questions 55 to 57:

$[x]$ is defined as the greatest integer less than equal to x.

$\{x\}$ is defined as the least integer greater than or equal to x

The functions f, g, h and i are defined as follows:

$f(a,b) = [a] + \{b\}$

$g(a,b) = [b] - \{a\}$

$h(a,b) = [a \div b]$

$i(a,b) = \{-a + b\}$

55. Find the value of $i(f(3,4))$, $g(3.5, 4.5))$.

(a) 2 (b) 1

(c) –1 (d) None of these

56. If $a^3 = 64, b^2 = 16$ and $8 + f(a,b) = -g(a,b)$ then $a - b = ?$

57. If $f(1.2,-2.3) + g(-1.2,2.3) = i(a,-1.3)$, then which of the following values can a take?
(a) –4.3 (b) –5.3
(c) 5.6 (d) –2.4

Directions of Questions 58 and 59:

Define the functions: $xPy = \dfrac{1}{1+\dfrac{y}{x}}, xQy = 1 + \dfrac{x}{y}$

58. Which of the following equals to $\dfrac{x}{y}$?
(a) $(xPy) + (xQy)$ (b) $(xPy) - (xQy)$
(c) $(xPy) \times (xQy)$ (d) $(xPy) \div (xQy)$

59. If the functions $S(x, y) = (xPy)P(xQy)$ is defined, then find the value of $S(2, 3)$ (correct to two decimal points)?

Directions for Questions 60 to 62:

Define the functions:

$aAb = |a - b|$

$aBb = [a \div b]$

$aCb = |a \times b|$

$$\min(x, y) = \begin{cases} y, \text{when } x > y \\ x, \text{when } y > x \\ 0, \text{when } x = y \end{cases}$$

$$\max(x, y) = \begin{cases} x^2, \text{when } x \geq y \\ y^2, \text{when } y \geq x \end{cases}$$

Here $a, b, x, y \in R$.

60. Find the value of (1 + min(2A3, 1C2))B[max(1A2, 1C1)].

61. The value of max(7A3, 16B2) will be equal to the value of which of the following options?
(a) (32B16)C(max(4,8))
(b) (32B2)C(min(4,8))
(c) (16B2)C((min(4,8))
(d) None of these

62. max(3,4) ÷ min(8, 4) = ?
(a) 8A2 (b) 28B7
(c) 4C2 (d) None of these

Directions for Questions 63 to 67:

$f(a_1, a_2, a_3,\ldots,a_n)$ = minimum of $(a_1, a_2,\ldots a_n)$ and
$g(a_1, a_2, a_3,\ldots a_n)$ = maximum of $(a_1, a_2, a_3\ldots a_n)$
$h(x, y) = [x/y]$, where $[a]$ represents the greatest integer less than or equal to a.

$t(a_1, a_2, a_3, \ldots, a_n) = a_1 \times a_2 \times a_3 \times \ldots \times a_n$

$i(a_1, a_2, a_3, \ldots, a_n) = a_1 + a_2 + a_3 + \ldots + a_n$

63. If $f(1,3,5,7) + g(2,4,6,8) = h(aK, K)$
Where a, K are both positive integers, then find the value of a.

64. The value of $f(t(1,2,3,4), i(1,2,3,4)) = ?$

65. The value of $h(f(5,6,7,8), i(1,2,3,4)) = ?$

66. If $P = f(2,3,4,6)$, $Q = g(1,2,3,4)$, $R = h(8,4)$, $S = t(1,2,3,4)$, $T = i(4,5,6)$ then which of the following options is true?
(a) $P < R = Q < S < T$ (b) $P = R < Q < S < T$
(c) $P = R < Q < T < S$ (d) $P = R < Q = T < S$

67. $f(f(1,2,3), g(2,3,4), f(0,1,2), g(-3,-2)) = ?$
(a) –3 (b) –2
(c) 1 (d) 0

68. Which of the following curves correctly represents $y = |x - 2|$?

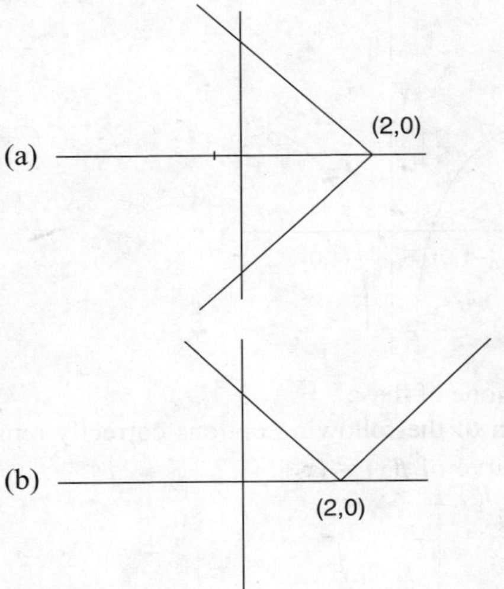

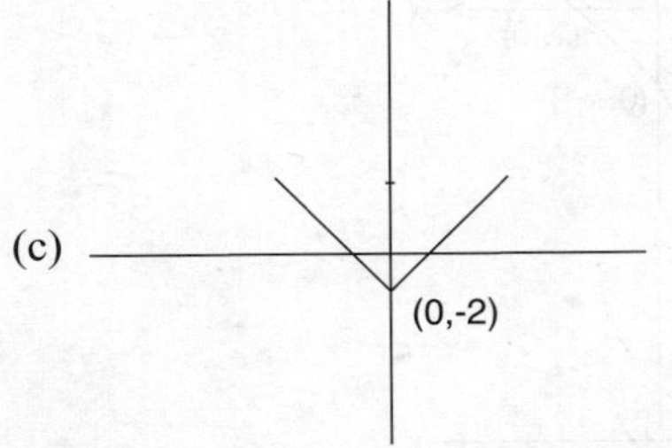

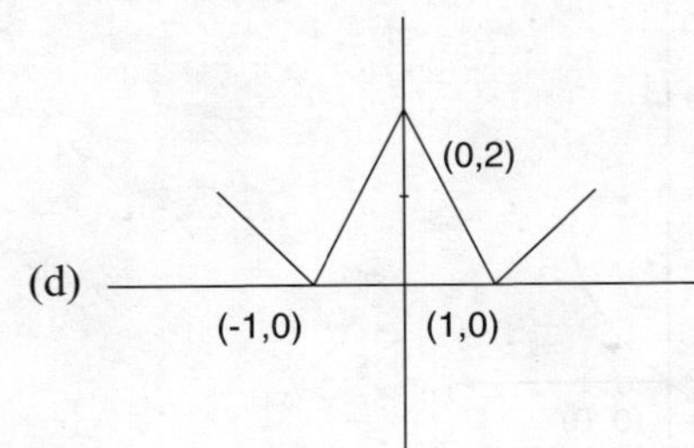

69. Which of the following represents the curve of $y = \log|x|$?

(a) 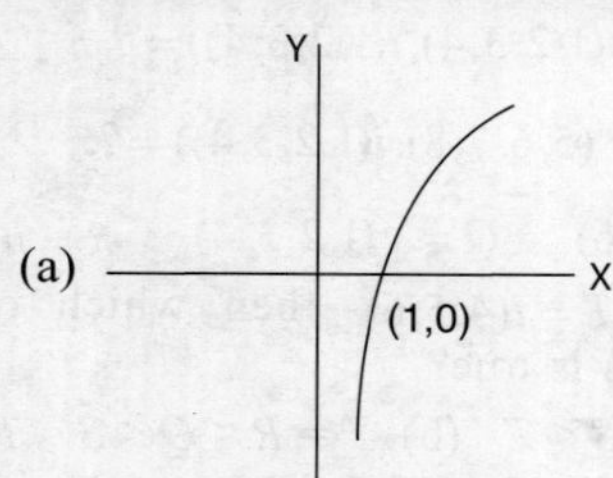

(b) 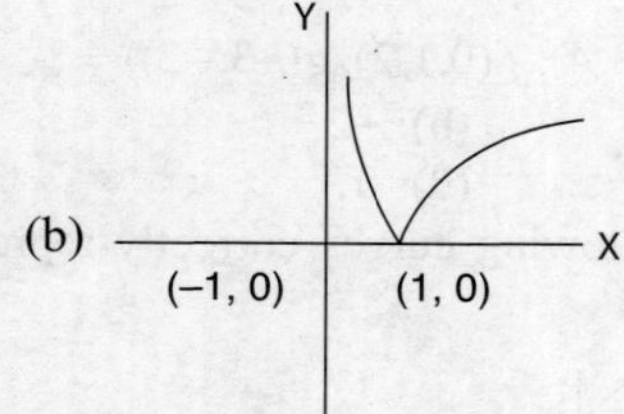

(c) 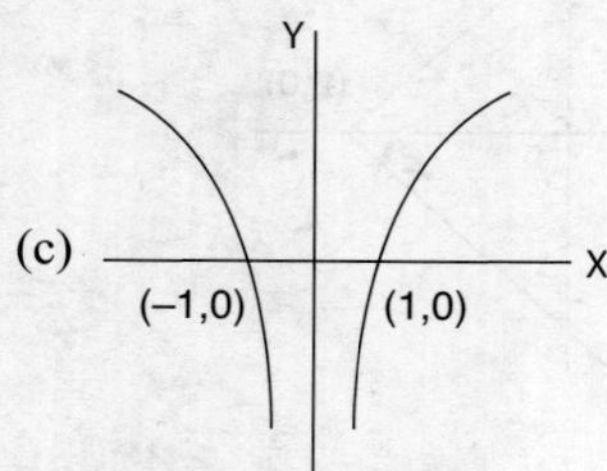

(d) None of these

70. Which of the following options correctly represents the curve of $f(x) = (x - 1)^3$?

(a) 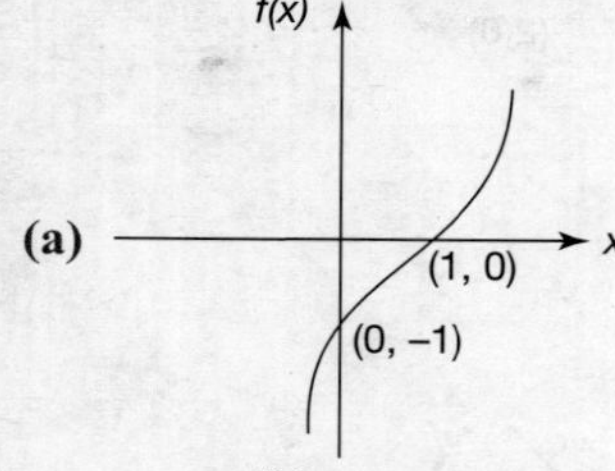

(b) 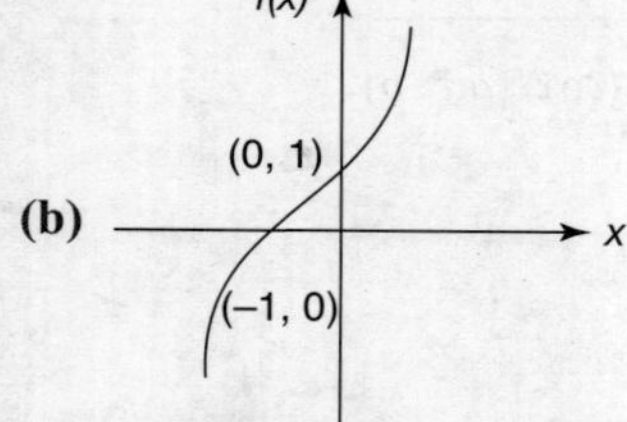

(c) 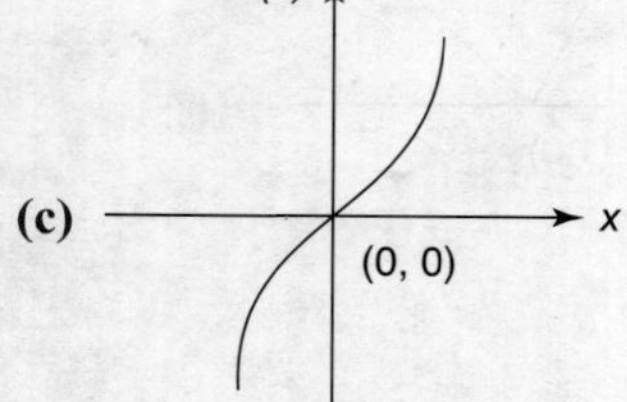

(d) None of these

71. Which of the following options correctly represents the curve $f(x) = \dfrac{e^{|x|}}{2}$?

(a) 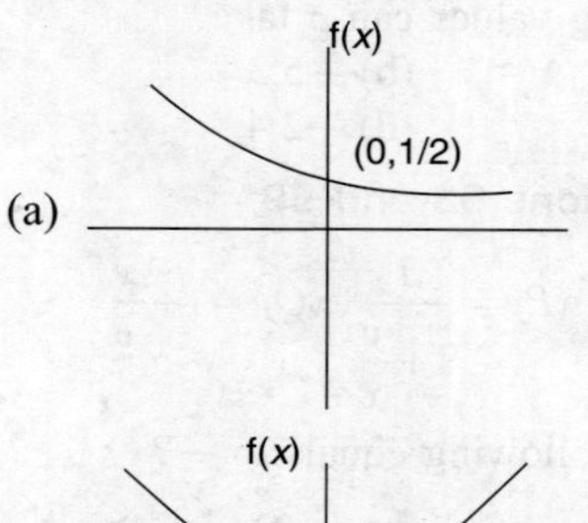

(b) 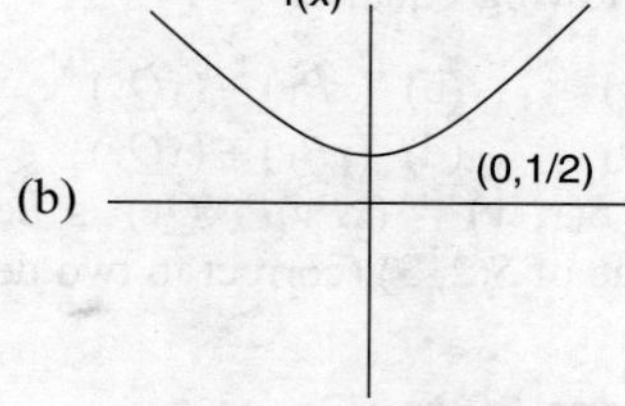

(c) 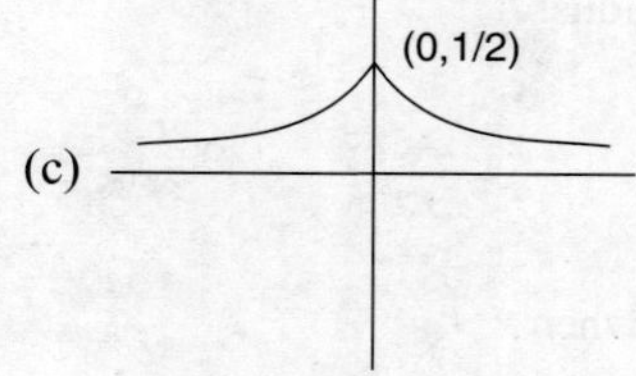

(d) None of these

72. Which of the following options correctly represents the curve of $f(x) = \max(x, x^2)$?

(a) 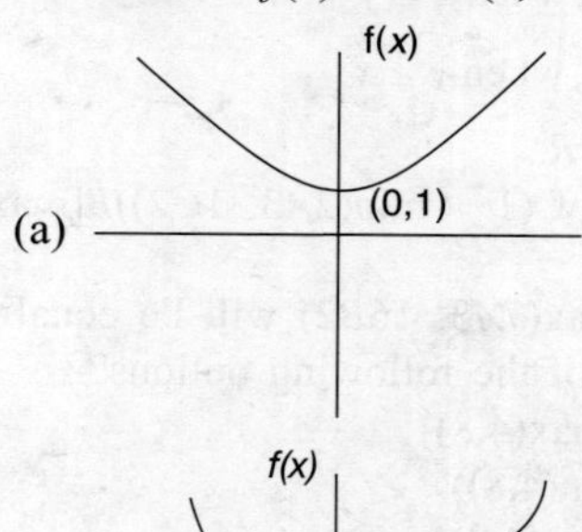

(b) 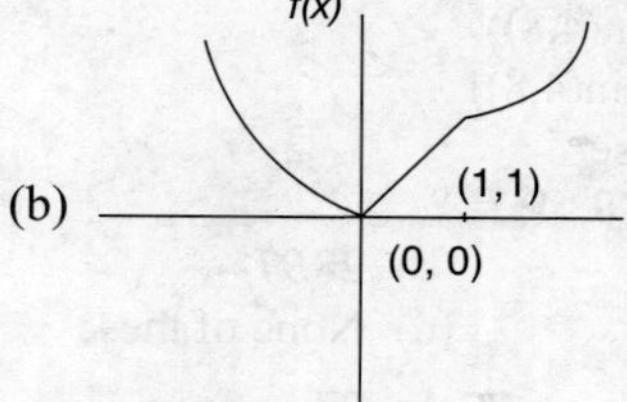

(c) 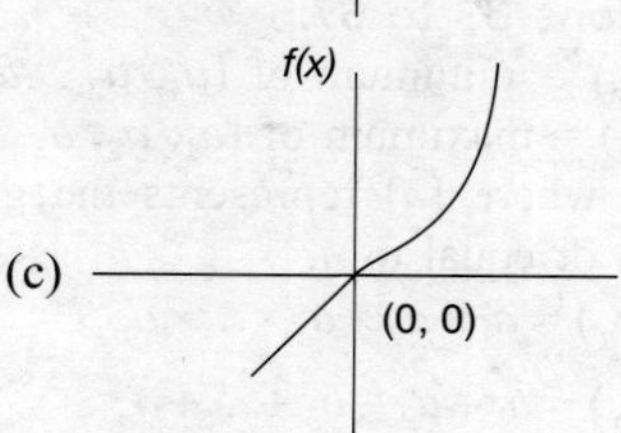

(d) None of these

Directions for Questions 73 to 77: Following functions are defined:

$x \$ y = x^2 + y^2$ $\quad x \% y = (x - 1)(y - 1)$

$x \& y = (x + 1)(y + 1)$

73. Find the value of $(a \$ b)\%(a \& b)$, when it is given that $a = 2$, $b = 3$.
(a) 42 (b) 123
(c) 132 (d) None of these

74. What is the value of [(4\$3)%6]&[5\$(2%7)] ?
(a) 7502 (b) 7320
(c) 7140 (d) None of these

75. Which of the following operation will yield 3 as the result for $p = 2$ and $q = 4$?
(a) $p\$q$
(b) $p\%q$
(c) $p\&q$
(d) More than one of the above

76. For what values of a and b will $a\$b$ give 100 as the result?
(a) $a = 101, b = 2$
(b) $a = 99, b = 0$
(c) $a = 8, b = 6$
(d) More than one of the above

77. Which of the following will always be true for all real values of x and y?
(a) $x \$ y \geq 0$ (b) $x\% y \geq 0$
(c) $x \& y \geq 0$ (d) None of these

78. Find the maximum value of the function $1/(x^2 - 3x + 2)$.
(a) 11/4 (b) 1/4
(c) 0 (d) None of these

79. Find the minimum value of the function $f(x) = \log_2 (x^2 - 2x + 5)$.
(a) –4 (b) 2
(c) 4 (d) –2

Directions for Questions 80 to 83: Define the following functions:

(i) $a @ b = \dfrac{a+b}{2}$

(ii) $a \# b = a^2 - b^2$

(iii) $(a ! b) = \dfrac{a-b}{2}$

80. Find the value of {[(3@4)!(3#2)] @ [(4!3)@(2#3)]}.
(a) –0.75 (b) –1
(c) –1.5 (d) –2.25

81. Which of the following has a value of 0.25 for $a = 0$ and $b = 0.5$?
(a) $a @ b$ (b) $a \# b$
(c) Either a or b (d) Cannot be determined

82. Which of the following expressions has a value of 4 for $a = 5$ and $b = 3$?
(a) $\dfrac{(a!b)}{(a\#b)}$ (b) (a!b)(a@b)
(c) $\dfrac{(a\#b)}{(a!b)(a@b)}$ (d) Both (b) and (c)

83. If we define $a\$b$ as $a^3 - b^3$, then for integers $a, b > 2$ and $a > b$ which of the following will always be true?
(a) $(a@b) > (a!b)$ (b) $(a@b) \geq (a!b)$
(c) $(a\#b) < (a\$b)$ (d) Both (*a*) and (*c*)

Directions for Questions 84 to 87: Define the following functions:

(a) $(a\,M\,b) = a - b$ (b) $(a\,D\,b) = a + b$
(c) $(a\,H\,b) = (ab)$ (d) $(a\,P\,b) = a/b$

84. Which of the following functions will represent $a^2 - b^2$?
(a) $(a\,M\,b)\,H\,(a\,D\,b)$ (b) $(a\,H\,b)\,M\,(a\,P\,b)$
(c) $(a\,D\,b)/(a\,M\,b)$ (d) None of these

85. Which of the following represents a^2?
(a) $(a\,M\,b)\,H\,(a\,D\,b) + b^2$
(b) $(a\,H\,b)\,M\,(a\,P\,b) + b^2$
(c) $\dfrac{(a\,M\,b)}{(a\,P\,b)}$
(d) Both (a) and (c)

86. Which of the four functions defined has the maximum value?
(a) $(a\,M\,b)$ (b) $(a\,D\,b)$
(c) $(a\,P\,b)$ (d) Cannot be determined

87. Which of the four functions defined has the minimum value?
(a) $(a\,M\,b)$ (b) $(a\,D\,b)$
(c) $(a\,H\,b)$ (d) Cannot be determined

88. If $0 < a < 1$ and $0 < b < 1$ and $a > b$, which of the four expressions will take the highest value?
(a) $(a\,M\,b)$ (b) $(a\,D\,b)$
(c) $(a\,P\,b)$ (d) Cannot be determined

89. If $0 < a < 1$ and $0 < b < 1$ and if $a < b$, which of the following expressions will have the highest value?
(a) $(a\,M\,b)$ (b) $(a\,D\,b)$
(c) $(a\,P\,b)$ (d) Cannot be determined

Directions for Questions 90 and 91:

If $f(x) = x^3 - x^2 - 6x$ for all $x \in R$, then answer the following questions:

90. For how many values of x, is $f(x) = 0$?

91. If $f(x)$ is defined only for interval (–2, 3), then $f(x)$ will attain its minima in the interval
(a) (–2, 0) (b) (–2, –1)
(c) (0, 3) (d) None of these

92. If for all $x \in R, f(x) \in R$, then which of the following options correctly represents $f(x)$?

(a) $f(x) = log x$ (b) $f(x) = 1/|x|$
(c) $f(x) = log(x^4+7)$ (d) $f(x) = 1/x$

93. Which of the following statements is true?
(a) If $f(x)$ and $g(x)$ are odd functions then their sum is an even function.
(b) If $f(x)$ and $g(x)$ are even functions then their sum is an odd function.
(c) If $f(x)$ and $g(x)$ are odd functions then their product is an even function
(d) None of these

94. If $f(x)$ is an even function, $g(x)$ is an odd function, then which of the following options is true?
(a) $f(g(x))$ is an odd function, $g(f(x))$ is an even function.
(b) $f(g(x))$, $g(f(x))$ are odd functions
(c) $f(g(x))$, $g(f(x))$ are even functions
(d) $g(f(x))$ is an odd function, $f(g(x))$ is an even function

Space for Rough Work

LEVEL OF DIFFICULTY (II)

1. For natural numbers $x \geq 2$, $f(1) + 2f(2) + 3f(3) + ... + xf(x) = x(x + 1) f(x)$ and $f(1) = 1$. Then find the value of $f(1024)/f(2048)$.
(a) 1/2 (b) 2
(c) 4 (d) 1024
2. If $f(x) = x^2 \times (1 - x)^2$, then what is the value of $f(1/2025) - f(2/2025) + f(3/2025) - ... + f(2023/2025) - f(2024/2025)$.
3. The function f is defined as $f(1) = 2$ and $f(n) = 1/f(n - 1)$ for all $n > 1$. If $g(n) = n - 1/f(n)$, then for the lowest value of n for which $g(1) + g(2) + g(3) + ... + g(n) > 100$ is
(a) 15 (b) 7
(c) 8 (d) 16
4. If $f(x - 3) = 2x^3 + p - qx$ and $f(x^2 - 4) = x^2 - 8q + 6p$, then what is the value of $p - q$?
(a) 5 (b) 10
(c) 6 (d) Cannot be determined
5. Let $f(x) = ax^2 + bx + c$ be a quadratic polynomial in x such that $f(x) \geq 0$ for all real numbers x.
If $f(3) = 0$ and $f(6) = 9$, then what is the value of $f(-1) - f(-3)$?
(a) 52 (b) –20
(c) –24 (d) 36
6. Let $f(x) = |x| + |x - 3| + |x - 6| + |x - 9| + ... + |x - 3a|$, where x is an integer and a is an even positive integer, that is less than 5. Find the minimum value of $f(x)$.
(a) $a^2 + 2$ (b) $-a(a + 1)/2$
(c) $(a + 1)/2$ (d) $a(a + 1)$
7. If $f(x) = \max\{1, 6x - 8x^2\}$, then what is the minimum value of $f(x)$?
8. Consider the function $g(x) = \min\{-4, 2x - 6x^2\}$. What is the difference between the max value of this function and the value at which it is achieved?
(a) 5 (b) –14/3
(c) –5 (d) Cannot be Determined
9. If $f(x) = 2^x - 2^{-x}$, then what is the value of $2f(x) - 5f(x - 1) + 2f(x - 2)$?
10. Let $f(x) \times f(y) = f(x + y) + f(x - y)$, where x and y are non-negative integers. If $f(0) = 0$ and $f(1) = 2$, then find the unit digit of $f(1) f(2) f(3)... f(2023)$.
11. For a function $f(x)$, $f(1) + f(2) + f(3) + ... + f(n) = n^2 \times f(n)$. The value of $f(200)/f(201)$ is:
(a) 101 (b) 100!
(c) 1.01 (d) 10.1
12. If $2|a| + 3|b| = 12$ and $|a| - [a] = 10$, then which of the following is a possible value of 'b'?
(a) –1/3
(b) 4/3
(c) –2/3
(d) None of these
13. Let $f(x) + f(2x) + f(1 + x) + f(2 - x) = 2x$ for all x, Then, the value of $f(0)$ is:
(a) 0 (b) –1/2
(c) –1 (d) 1
14. Suppose $f(x,y)$ is a real-valued function such that $f(7x - 5y, 3x + 7y) = 64x$, for all real numbers x and y. What is the value of x for which $f(2x, 5x) = 78$?

Directions for Questions 15 to 18: If $f(x)$ is represented by the graph below.

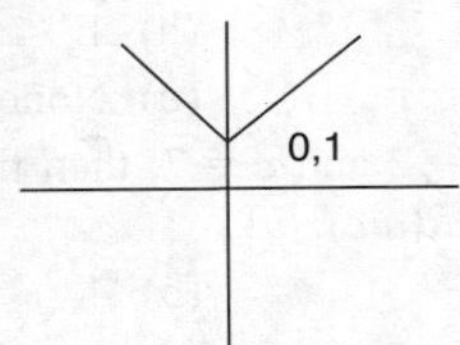

15. Which of the following will represent the function $-f(x)$?
16. Which of the following will represent the function $-f(x) + 1$?
17. Which of the following will represent the function $f(x) - 1$?
18. Which of the following will represent the function $f(x) + 1$?

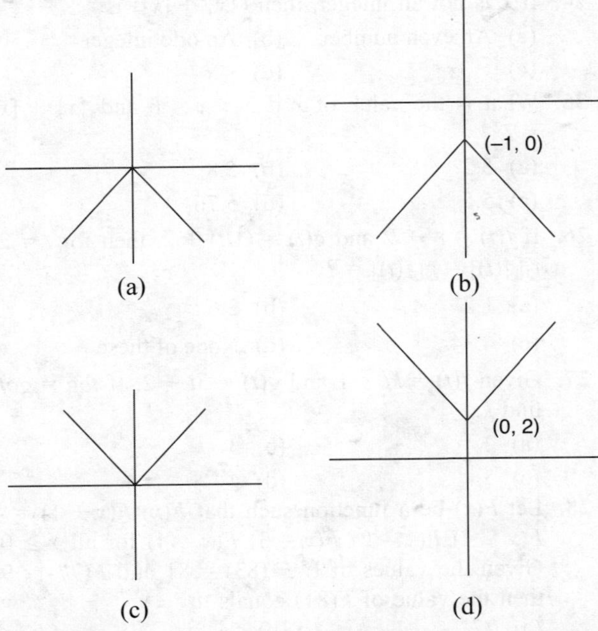

19. If $f(x) = 1/g(x)$, then the minimum value of $f(x) + g(x)$, $f(x) > 0$ and $g(x) > 0$, will be
(a) 0
(b) 2
(c) Depends upon the value of $f(x)$ and $g(x)$
(d) None of these

Directions for Questions 20 to 22: If $R(a/b)$ = Remainder when a is divided by b;

$Q(a/b)$ = Quotient obtained when a is divided by b;

$SQ(a)$ = Smallest integer just bigger than the positive square root of a.

20. If $a = 12$, $b = 5$, then find the value of $SQ[R\ \{(a + b)/b\}]$.
(a) 0 (b) 1
(c) 2 (d) 3

21. If $a = 9$, $b = 7$, then the value of $Q\ [[SQ(ab)+b]/a]$ will be
(a) 0 (b) 1
(c) 2 (d) None of these

22. If $a = 18$, $b = 2$ and $c = 7$, then find the value of $Q\ [\{SQ(ab) + R(a/c)\}/b]$.
(a) 3 (b) 4
(c) 5 (d) 6

Directions for Questions 23 to 25: Read the following passage and try to answer questions based on them.

$[x]$ = Greatest integer less than or equal to x

$\{x\}$ = Smallest integer greater than or equal to x.

23. If x is not an integer, what is the value of $([x] - \{x\})$?
(a) 0 (b) 1
(c) –1 (d) 2

24. If x is not an integer, then $(\{x\} + [x])$ is
(a) An even number (b) An odd integer
(c) $> 3x$ (d) $< x$

25. What is the value of x if $5 < x < 6$ and $\{x\} + [x] = 2x$?
(a) 5.2 (b) 5.8
(c) 5.5 (d) 5.76

26. If $f(t) = t^2 + 2$ and $g(t) = (1/t) + 2$, then for $t = 2$, $f[g(t)] - g[f(t)] = ?$
(a) 1.2 (b) 2.6
(c) 4.34 (d) None of these

27. Given $f(t) = kt + 1$ and $g(t) = 3t + 2$. If $fog = gof$, find k.
(a) 2 (b) 3
(c) 5 (d) 4

28. Let $F(x)$ be a function such that $F(x)\ F(x + 1) = -F(x - 1)\ F(x - 2)\ F(x - 3)\ F(x - 4)$ for all $x \geq 0$. Given the values of If $F(83) = 81$ and $F(77) = 9$, then the value of $F(81)$ equals to
(a) 27 (b) 54
(c) 729 (d) Data insufficient

29. Let $f(x) = 121 - x^2$, $g(x) = |x - 8| + |x + 8|$ and $h(x) = \min\ \{f(x), g(x)\}$. What is the number of integer values of x for which $h(x)$ is equal to a positive integral value?
(a) 17 (b) 19
(c) 21 (d) 23

30. If the function $R(x) = \max\ (x^2 - 8, 3x, 8)$, then what is the max value of $R(x)$?
(a) 4 (b) $\frac{1+\sqrt{5}}{2}$
(c) ∞ (d) 0

31. If the function $R(x) = \min\ (x^2 - 8, 3x, 8)$, what is the maximum value of $R(x)$?
(a) 4 (b) 8
(c) ∞ (d) None of these

32. The minimum value of $ax^2 + bx + c$ is 7/8 at $x = 5/4$. Find the value of the expression at $x = 5$, if the value of the expression at $x = 1$ is 1.
(a) 75 (b) 29
(c) 121 (d) 129

33. Find the range of the function $f(x) = (x + 4)(5 - x)(x + 1)$.
(a) $[-2, 3]$ (b) $(-\infty, 20]$
(c) $(-\infty, +\infty)$ (d) $[-20, \infty)$

34. The function $f(x)$ is defined for positive integers and is defined as:

$f(x) = 6^x - 3$, if x is a number in the form $2n$.

$= 6^x + 4$, if x is a number in the form $2n + 1$.

What is the remainder when $f(1) + f(2) + f(3) + ... + f(1001)$ is divided by 2?
(a) 1 (b) 0
(c) –1 (d) None of these

35. p, q and r are three non-negative integers such that $p + q + r = 10$. The maximum value of $pq + qr + pr + pqr$ is
(a) ≥ 40 and < 50 (b) ≥ 50 and < 60
(c) ≥ 60 and < 70 (d) ≥ 70 and < 80

36. A function $\alpha(x)$ is defined for x as $3\alpha(x) + 2\alpha(2 - x) = (x + 3)^2$. What is the value of $[\alpha(-5)]$ where $[x]$ represents the greatest integer less than or equal to x?
(a) 37 (b) –38
(c) –37 (d) Cannot be determined

37. For a positive integer x, $f(x + 2) = 3 + f(x)$, when x is even and $f(x + 2) = x + f(x)$, when x is odd. If $f(1) = 6$ and $f(2) = 4$, then find $f(f(f(f(1)))) \times f(f(f(f(2))))$.
(a) 1375 (b) 1425
(c) 1275 (d) None of these

38. If $x > 0$, the minimum value of $\dfrac{\left(x+\frac{1}{x}\right)^6 - \left(x^6+\frac{1}{x^6}\right) - 2}{\left(x+\frac{1}{x}\right)^3 + \left(x^3+\frac{1}{x^3}\right)}$ is ______?
(a) 3 (b) 1
(c) 2 (d) 6

39. If $[x]$ denotes the greatest integer $\leq x$, then $\left[\frac{1}{3}\right]+\left[\frac{1}{3}+\frac{1}{99}\right]+\left[\frac{1}{3}+\frac{2}{99}\right]+...\left[\frac{1}{3}+\frac{98}{99}\right] = ?$

(a) 98 (b) 33
(c) 67 (d) 66

40. If x and y are real numbers, then the minimum value of $x^2 + 4xy + 6y^2 - 4y + 4$ is
(a) -4 (b) 0
(c) 2 (d) 4

41. What is the maximum possible value of (21 sin X + 72 cos X)?
(a) 21 (b) 57
(c) 63 (d) 75

42. The sum of the possible values of X in the equation $|x + 7| + |x - 8| = 16$ is
(a) 0 (b) 1
(c) 2 (d) 3

43. If $|3x+4| \leq 5$ and a and b are the minimum and maximum values of x respectively, then $a + b$ = ?

44. For how many positive integer values of x, is $x^3 - 16x + x^2 + 20 \leq 0$?

45. $3f(x)+2f\left(\frac{4x+5}{x-4}\right) = 7(x+3)$. where $x \in R$ and $x \neq 4$. What is the value of $f(11)$?

Directions for Questions 46 and 47: If $q = p \times [p]$ and 'q' is an integer such that $7 < q < 17$. Then answer the following questions:

46. Find the number of positive real values of 'p'.

47. Find the product of all possible values of p.

48. If $f(1) = -1$, $f(2x) = 4f(x) + 9$, $f(x + 2) = f(x) + 8(x + 1)$, find the value of $f(24) - f(7)$.

49. In the previous question, find the value of $f(1000)$

50. $f(x) = (x^2 + [x]^2 - 2x[x])^{1/2}$, where x is real and $[x]$ denotes the greatest integer less than or equal to x. Find the value of $f(10.08) - f(100.08)$.

51. Find the sum of coefficients of the polynomial $(x - 4)^7 (x - 3)^4 (x - 5)^2$.
(a) $2^8 3^7$ (b) $-2^6.3^8$
(c) $-2^8.3^7$ (d) $2^6.3^8$

52. A function $f(x)$ is defined as $f(x) = x - \frac{1}{9-3x} - 3$. If $x > 3$, then find the minimum possible value of $f(x)$.
(a) $3 - \frac{1}{\sqrt{3}}$ (b) $\frac{1}{\sqrt{3}}$
(c) $\sqrt{3} - \frac{1}{3}$ (d) $\sqrt{3} + \frac{1}{3}$

53. The graph of $h(x)$ and $g(x)$ are given below. Then which of the following defines the relation between $h(x)$ and $g(x)$?

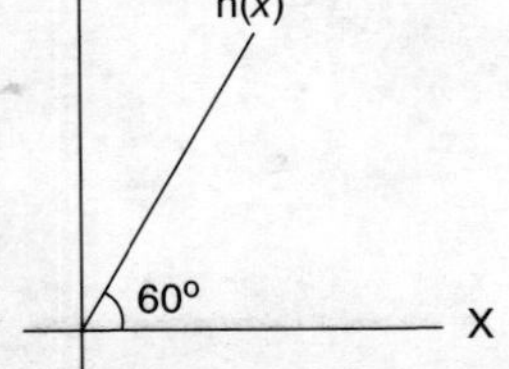

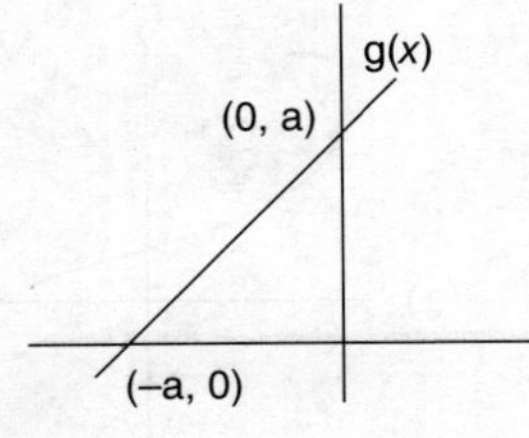

(a) $\sqrt{3}g(x) - h(x) = a\sqrt{3}$
(b) $\sqrt{3}g(x) + h(x) = a\sqrt{3}$
(c) $g(x) + h(x)\sqrt{3} = \frac{a}{\sqrt{3}}$
(d) None of these

54. Consider a function 'f' is such that $\frac{f(xy)}{f(x+y)} = 1$ for all real values of x, y. If $f(6) = 7$, then find the value of $f(-10) + f(10)$.

55. A function $f(x)$ is defined such that
$$f\left(\frac{x}{y}\right) = \frac{f(x)}{f(y)}$$
If $f(3) = 5$, then $f(81)$ = ?

56. Find the sum of all the coefficients of the polynomial $(x - 4)^3 (x - 2)^{10} (x - 3)^3$.

57. $f(x) = \begin{cases} 3^x \text{ when } x \text{ is an odd number.} \\ 3^x + 4 \text{ when } x \text{ is an even number.} \end{cases}$

What is the value of
$\frac{1}{4}[f(1) + f(2) + f(3) + f(4) + \ldots + f(n)]$ if $n = 72$?
(a) $\frac{3}{8}(3^{72} - 1) + 36$ (b) $\frac{3}{8}(3^{72} + 1) + 36$
(c) $\frac{3}{8}(3^{72}) + 36$ (d) None of these

58. $f(x + y) = f(x \cdot y)$, where x and y are real numbers and 'f' is a real function.
If $f(10) = 12$, then $[f(7)]^{143} - [f(11)]^{143} + f(5)$ = ?

59. Which of the following represents the curve of $|e^{-|x|}|$?

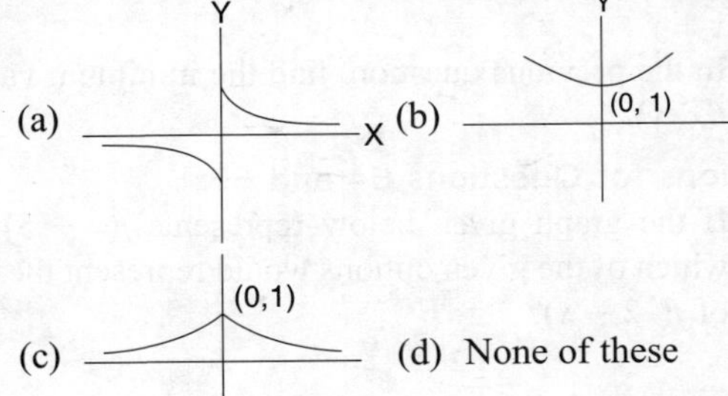

60. Which of the following function correctly represents the curve of $|e^{-x} - 3|$?

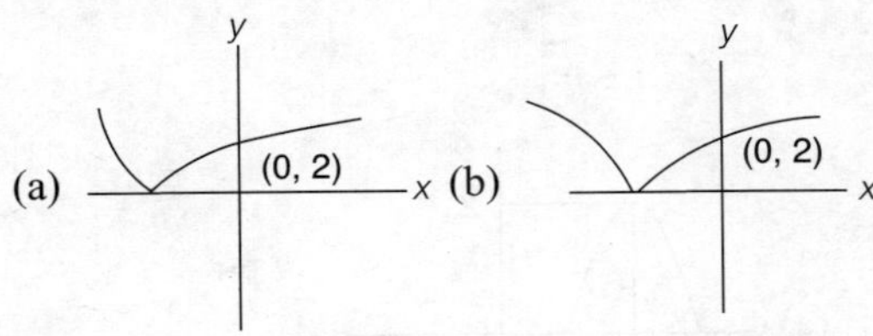

(c) 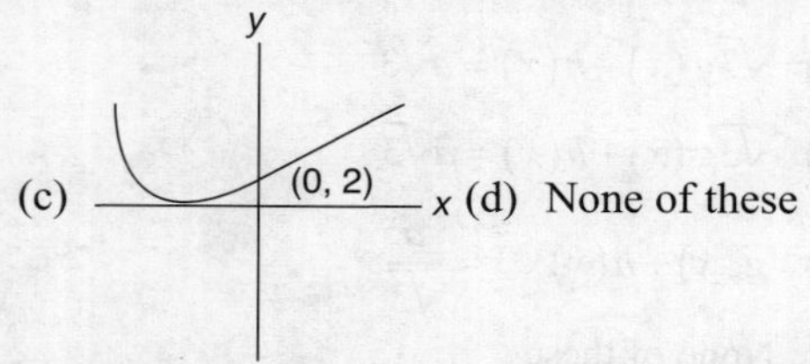

(d) None of these

61. Which of the following represents the curve of |log|x – 3||?

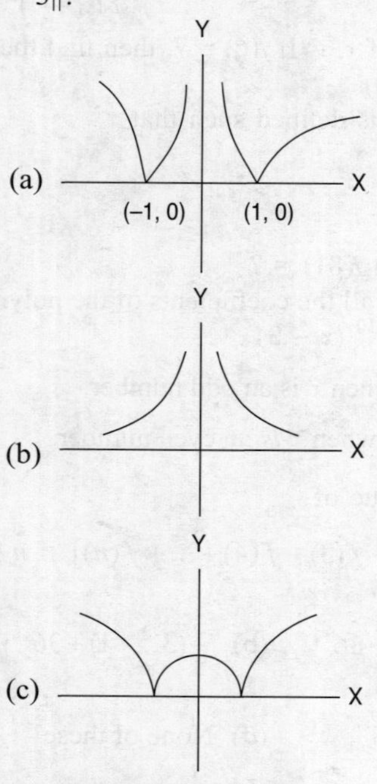

(d) None of these

62. $f(x, y) = x^2 + y^2 - x - \frac{3y}{2} + 1$

When $f(x, y)$ is minimum, then find the value of $x + y$.

63. In the previous question, find the minimum value of $f(x, y)$.

Directions for Questions 64 and 65:

64. If the graph given below represents $f(x + 5)$, then which of the given options would represent the graph of $f(-2 - x)$?

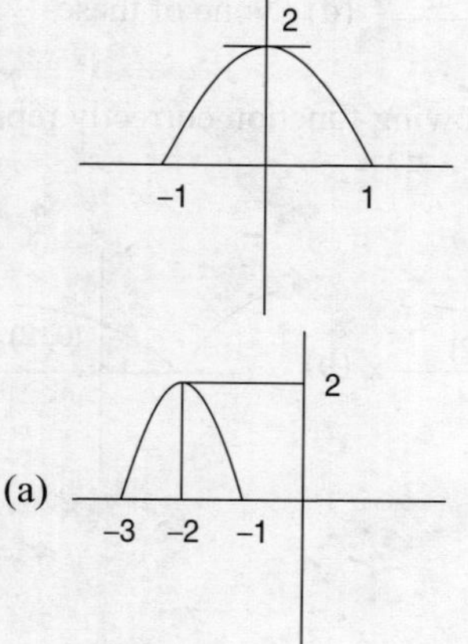

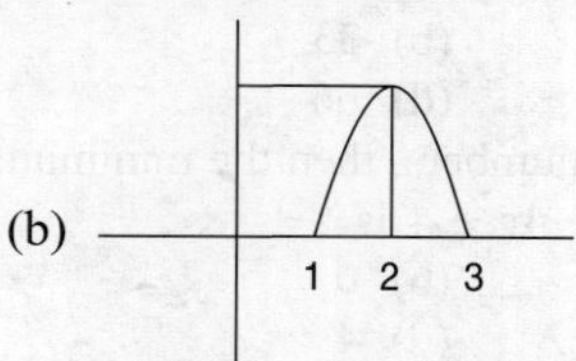

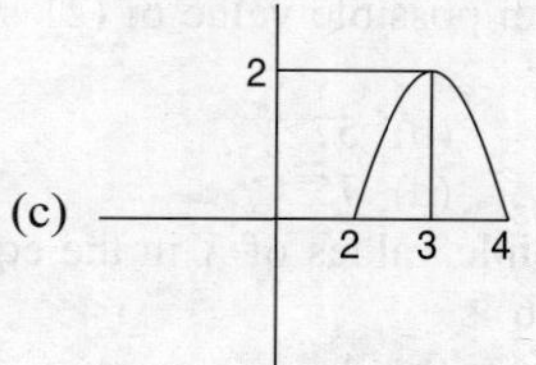

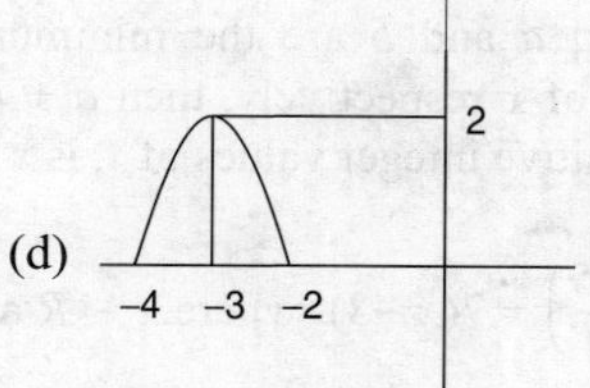

65. Which of the following options represents curve of $f(-2x)$?

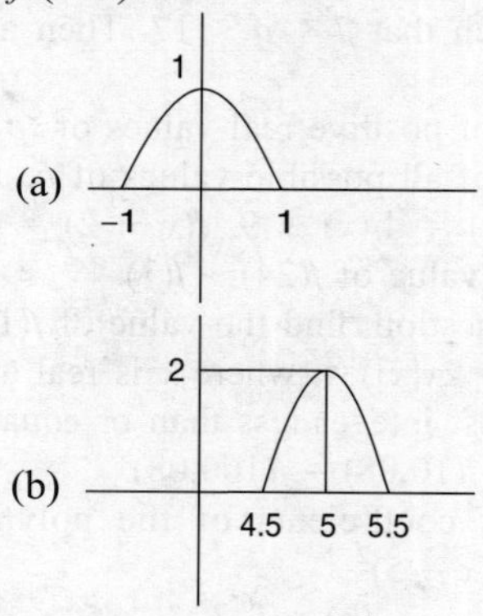

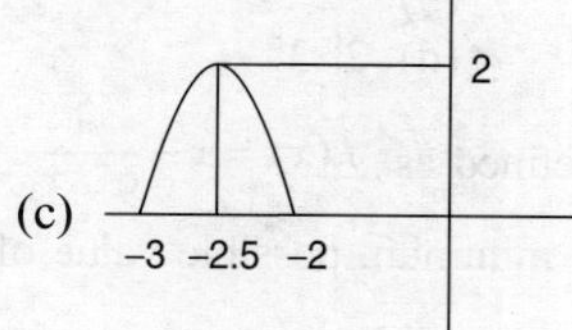

(d) None of these

66. If x, y are real numbers and function $g(x)$ satisfies $\frac{(g(x+y)+g(x-y))}{2} = g(x)g(y)$ and $g(0)$ is a positive real number, then which of the following options may represent graph of $g(x)$?

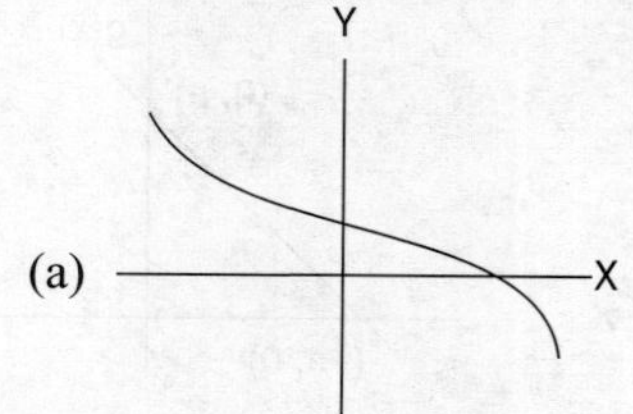

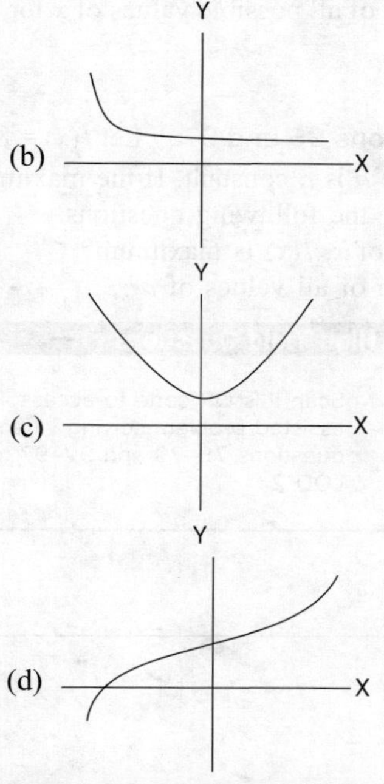

Directions for Questions 67 to 69: A function $f(x)$ is defined for all natural numbers $x > 1$ as $f(x) = \left(1-\frac{1}{x}\right)$ $f(x-1)$. Based on this information, answer the following questions:

67. Find the value of $f(1)$, if $f(3) = 10$.

68. Find the value of $f(1000)$. If $f(1) = 10$.

69. Find the value of $\frac{1}{f(1)}+\frac{1}{f(2)}+\frac{1}{f(3)}+\ldots+\frac{1}{f(9)}$.

It is given that $f(1) = 12$.

Directions for Questions 70 and 71: Let $f(x)=\sqrt{f(x-1)\,f(x+1)}$ & $f(0) = 1$, $f(1) = ½$

70. What is the value of $f(3)$?

71. What is the value of $f(1) + f(2) + f(3) + f(4) + \ldots.. f(\infty)$?

72. $f(x) = \frac{(x+3)}{2x^2+18+12x}$. x is a non-negative integer.

Find the maximum possible value of $f(x)$.

Directions for Questions 73 and 74:

A cubic polynomial $f(x)$ yields a remainder of 3 when divided by $(x - 2)$ and remainder of 2 when divided by $(x - 3)$. Answer the following questions based on the above information.

73. Find the value of $f(3)$.

74. Find the remainder when we divide $f(x)$ by $(x - 2)(x - 3)$.

(a) $x + 5$ (b) $5 - x$
(c) 5 (d) None of these

Directions for Questions 75 to 77:

Let x be a real number that always satisfies the equation: $\left[\frac{x}{7}\right]=\left[\frac{x}{9}\right]$, where [] is the greatest integer function.

75. Find the number of integral solutions of the above equation.

76. Find the sum of integral solutions of the above equation.

77. Find the maximum value of x.

Directions for Questions 78 and 79:

$$f(x)=(x^2-7x+13)^{2x+5}$$

78. For how many values of x, is $f(x) = 1$?

79. Find the sum of values of x, for which $f(x) = 1$.

80. Let $f(x)=|x-3|+|x-4|+|x-5|$, $f(x+2)$ is minimum at $x = k$. Find the value of k.

Directions for Questions 81 and 82:

$f(x) = 2 - 1/f(x - 1)$ for all natural number values of 'x'. If $f(2) = 3/2$, then answer the following questions:

81. Find the value of $f(500)$.

82. What is the value of $[f(100001)]$, where '[]' represents greatest integer function.?

83. If $[x]$ denotes the greatest integer less than or equal to x, then the solution set of the in-equation $\frac{[x]-2}{4-[x]} > 0$, is

(a) (2, 3] (b) [3, 4)
(c) [2, 3] (d) [3, 4]

Directions for Questions 84 and 85:

$f(x)$ is an integer valued function, that satisfies the following conditions:

$f(xy) = f(x)\,f(y)$

If $f(x) > f(y)$, then $x > y$, where x and y are natural numbers.

It is also known that $f(2) = 2$.

Answer the following questions based on the above information:

84. Find the value of $f(3)$.

85. Find the value of $f(2001)$.

86. If $n^2 f(n)+f(1-n)=2n-n^4$, where n is a real number, then what is the value of $f(2) \times f(5)$?

87. Find the coefficient of x^{203} in the expansion of the following expression. $(x - 2)(x(x + 1)(x + 2)(x + 3)(x + 4) \ldots..(x + 202))$

88. Find the maximum value of $f(x) = (x + 5)(36 - 12x)$

89. Let $f(x) = [x]$, where $[x]$ denotes the greatest integer less than or equal to x. If 'a' and 'b' are two real numbers such that $f(b - 2) = 3a + 4$ and $f(a - 4) = b - 12$. Find the product of a and b, assuming 'a' and 'b' are integers.

90. $f(x) = x^{[x]}$ and $g(x)=\frac{x^2}{9}$, where $[x]$ denotes greatest integer less than or equal to 'x' and $x \neq 0$. What is the minimum value of $f(g(x))$, if x cannot be 0?

91. If $f(x) = ax^2 + bx + c$ and $g(x) = px^2 + qx$ with $g(1) = f(1)$, $g(2) - f(2) = 1$, $g(3) - f(3) = 4$, then $g(4) - f(4)$ is

(a) 0 (b) 5

(c) 6 (d) None of these

Directions for Questions 92 to 95: A function $f(x)$ is defined for all real values of x as:

$5f(x) + 2f(1/x) = 4x + 2.$

Answer the following questions based on the above information:

92. If s is the sum of all the values of x for which $f(x) = 70$, then find the value of s.

93. What is the value of $f(2)$?

94. Find the sum of all values of x for which $f(x) = \frac{18}{21}$.

95. Find the product of all possible values of x for which $f(x) = \frac{18}{21}$.

Directions for Questions 96 and 97: Let $f(x) = 8a^2 - 8 + 8(x - 1) - x^2$, where a is a constant. If the maximum of $f(x)$ is 72, then answer the following questions.

96. For what value of x, $f(x)$ is maximum?

97. What is the sum of all values of a?

High Yield Questions

Scan this QR code to access assisted problem solving videos on questions 75–79 and 92–97 from LOD 2

Space for Rough Work

LEVEL OF DIFFICULTY (III)

1. Let $f(x) = |x - a| + |x - 20| + |x - a - 20|$, where $0 < a < 20$. What is the minimum value of $f(x)$ for x in the interval $a \leq x \leq 20$?
2. Let $f(x) = |x - b| + |x - 15| + |x - b - 15|$, where $0 < b < 15$. Determine the minimum value of $f(x)$ for x in the interval $b \leq x \leq 15$.
3. Consider the function $f(x) = |x - c| + |x - 18| + |x - c - 18|$, where $0 < c < 18$. Find the maximum value of $f(x)$ over the interval $c \leq x \leq 18$.
4. Let $f(x + y) = f(x) \times f(y)$ be a function where x, y are natural numbers, and $f(1) = 3$. If $f(k + 1) + f(k + 2) + f(k + 3) + ... + f(k + n + 1) = 243 \times (3^n - 1)/2$, then what is the value of 'k'?
   (a) 2 (b) 3
   (c) 4 (d) 5
5. The sum of all values of x that satisfy the equation $3[x] = 4x - 2$, when $[x]$ is the greatest integer function, is:
   (a) 1 (b) 1.25
   (c) 1.75 (d) 3.5
6. Let $f(x)$ be a function such that $f(1) = f(2) = 1$ and $f(x) = f(x - 1) - f(x - 2) + x$ for all integers $x \geq 3$. Find the value of $f(2024)$.
   (a) 2025 (b) 2024
   (c) 2023 (d) 2022
7. Let x, y be such that $f(x) f(y) = f(x + y) + f(x - y)$. If $f(0) \neq 0$ and $f(1) = 5$, then the value of $f(7)$ is:
   (a) 57965 (b) 57975
   (c) 57955 (d) 75965
8. Let $f(x) = 2x^3 + px^2 + qx - 4$ and $f(2) = 0$, where p and q are non-zero. If a, b, and c be three integral roots of $f(x) = 0$ such that $a = b$, then find the value of $q - p$.
   (a) –2 (b) 2
   (c) 10 (d) 21
9. A function $f(n)$ is defined as $f(n) = f(n - 2) + n(n - 2)$ for all the integer values of 'n'. If $f(1) = -f(6)$, then what is the value of $f(2) + f(3) + f(4) + f(5)$?
   (a) –35 (b) –20
   (c) 0 (d) 10
10. The functions $f(x)$ and $g(x)$ are defined as: $f(x) = f(x - 1) + x$ and $g(x) = g(x - 1) + f(x)$, where integer $x \geq 1$. If $f(0) = 0$, then the value of $g(10) - g(8)$ is:
11. Given $f(x + y) = f(x) f(y)$ for all x, y, $f(4) = 3$ what is $f(-8)$?
    (a) 1/3 (b) 1/9
    (c) 9 (d) 6
12. Which of the following is not an even function?
    (a) $f(x) = e^x + e^{-x}$ (b) $f(x) = e^x - e^{-x}$
    (c) $f(x) = e^{2x} + e^{-2x}$ (d) None of these
13. If $f(x)$ is a function satisfying $f(x).f(1/x) = f(x) + f(1/x)$ and $f(4) = 65$, what will be the value of $f(6)$?
    (a) 37 (b) 217
    (c) 64 (d) None of these

Directions for Questions 14 to 19: Define the functions:

$A(x, y, z)$ = Max (max (x, y), min (y, z) min (x, z))
$B(x, y, z)$ = Max (max (x, y), min (y, z) max (x, z))
$C(x, y, z)$ = Max (min (x, y), min (y, z) min (x, z))
$D(x, y, z)$ = Min (max (x, y), max (y, z) max (x, z))
Max (x, y, z) = Maximum of x, y and z
Min (x, y, z) = Minimum of x, y and z

Assume that x, y and z are distinct integers.

14. For what condition will $A(x, y, z)$ be equal to Max (x, y, z)?
    (a) When x is maximum (b) When y is maximum
    (c) When z is maximum (d) Either (a) or (b)
15. For what condition will $B(x, y, z)$ be equal to Min (x, y, z)?
    (a) When y is minimum (b) When z is minimum
    (c) Either (a) or (b) (d) Never
16. For what condition will $A(x, y, z)$ not be equal to $B(x, y, z)$?
    (a) $x > y > z$ (b) $y > z > x$
    (c) $z > y > x$ (d) None of these
17. Under what condition will $C(x, y, z)$ be equal to $B(x, y, z)$?
    (a) $x > y > z$ (b) $z > y > x$
    (c) Both (*a*) and (*b*) (d) Never
18. Which of the following will always be true?
    (I) $A(x, y, z)$ will always be greater than Min (x, y, z)
    (II) $B(x, y, z)$ will always be lower than Max (x, y, z)
    (III) $A(x, y, z)$ will never be greater than $B(x, y, z)$
    (a) I only (b) III only
    (c) Both (*a*) and (*b*) (d) All the three
19. The highest value amongst the following will be
    (a) Max/Min (b) A/B
    (c) C/D (d) Cannot be determined

Directions for Questions 20 and 21:

If $f(x) = \frac{x^2}{4}$ and $g(x) = 2x^{[3x]} + 2$, where $[x]$ is the greatest integer less than or equal to 'x', then answer the following questions:

20. Which of the following statement is true about $g(f(x))$?
    (a) $g(f(x))$ is neither even nor odd
    (b) $g(f(x))$ is maximum for $x = 11$

(c) $g(f(x))$ will have its minimum for a value of x that obeys $\frac{3x^2}{4} \le 1$

(d) None of these

21. Which of the following is the value of $g(f(x))$ at $x = 2$?

(a) 66 (b) 34
(c) 18 (d) 64

22. The area bounded between $|x + y| = 2$ and $|x - y| = 2$ is

(a) 2 (b) 4
(c) 6 (d) 8

Directions for Questions 23 to 25:

If $f(x) = |x| + |x + 4| + |x + 8| + |x + 12| + \ldots + |x + 4n|$, where x is an integer and n is a positive integer.

23. If $n = 8$, what is the minimum value of $f(x)$?

24. If $n = 7$, then for how many values of x, $f(x)$ is minimum?

25. For $n = 9$, which of the following statements is true?

(a) $f(x)$ will be minimum for a total 5 values of x
(b) $f(-17) = f(-19)$
(c) Minimum value of $f(x)$ is 100
(d) All of these

26. Find the area enclosed by the graph $|x| + |y| = 3$.

27. Find the area enclosed by curve $|x - 2| + |y - 3| = 3$.

Directions for Questions 28 and 29:

$8\{x\} = x + 2[x]$

$\{x\}$ denotes the fractional part of x

$[x]$ denotes the greatest integer less than or equals to x

28. For how many positive values of x, is the given equation true?

29. Find the difference of the greatest and the least value of x for which the given equation is true? (Till two digits after the decimal point)

Directions for Questions 30 and 31:

If $f(x) = \frac{4^{x-1}}{4^{x-1}+1}$ and $g(x) = 2x$, then answer the following questions.

30. $fog\left(\frac{1}{4}\right) + fog\left(\frac{3}{4}\right) = ?$

31. $fog\left(\frac{1}{2}\right) + fog\left(\frac{1}{4}\right) + fog\left(\frac{1}{8}\right) + f\left(\frac{1}{16}\right) + f\left(\frac{3}{4}\right) + fog\left(\frac{7}{8}\right) + fog\left(\frac{15}{16}\right) = ?$

Directions for Questions 32 to 35:

If for a positive integer x, $f(x + 2) = f(x) + 2(x + 1)$, when x is even and $f(x + 2) = f(x) + 1$, when x is odd. If $f(1) = 1$ and $f(2) = 5$, then answer the following questions.

32. $f(24) = ?$

33. $\left[\frac{f(14)}{f(11)}\right] = ?$, where [ ] denotes the greatest integer function

34. Which of the following statement is true?

(a) For even value of x value of $f(x)$ is also even
(b) For odd value of x, value of $f(x)$ is odd
(c) For even value of x, value of $f(x)$ is odd
(d) None of these

35. Value of $f(f(f(f(3)))) + f(f(f(2))) = ?$

Directions for Questions 36 and 37:

$F(x)$ is a 6th degree polynomial of x. It is given that $F(0) = 0$, $F(1) = 1$, $F(2) = 2$, $F(3) = 3$, $F(4) = 4$, $F(5) = 5$, $F(6) = 7$

36. Find the value of $F(8)$.

37. If x is a negative integer then find the maximum value of $F(x)$.

38. If $g(x + y) = g(x).g(y)$ and $g(1) = 5$, then find the value of $g(1) + g(2) + g(3) + g(4) + g(5)$.

39. In the previous question, if

$$\sum_{p=1}^{n} g(q+p) = \frac{1}{4}\left(5^{p+3} - 125\right)$$

where 'p' is a positive integer then find q.

40. If $3f(x+2) + 4f\left(\frac{1}{x+2}\right) = 4x$, $x \neq -2$, then $f(4) = ?$

(a) 7 (b) $-52/7$
(c) 8 (d) None of these

41. The figure below shows the graph of a function f(x). How many solutions does the equation $f(f(x)) = 15$ have for the span of the graph shown?

(a) 5 (b) 6
(c) 7 (d) 8

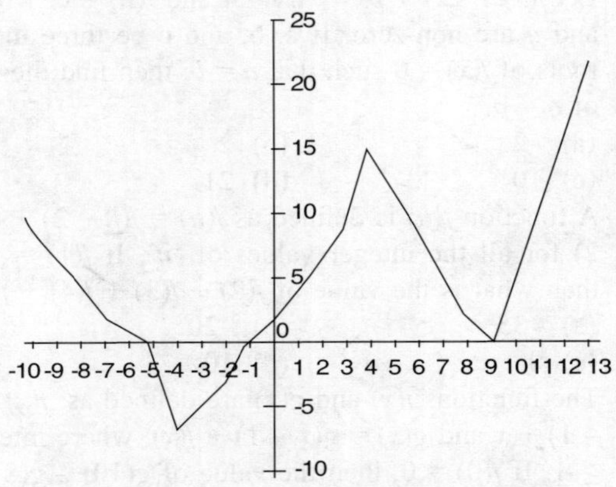

42. If $f(x) = (x-6), g(x) = \frac{(x-9)(x-1)}{(x-7)(x-3)}$, how many real values of x satisfy the equation $[f(x)]^{g(x)} = 1$?

43. A continuous function $f(x)$ is defined for all real values of x, such that $f(x) = 0$, only for two distinct real values of x. It is also known that $f(4) + f(6) = 0$, $f(5).f(7) > 0$, $f(4).f(8) < 0$, $f(1) > 0$ & $f(2) < 0$ Which of the following statement must be true?

(a) $f(1)f(2)f(4) < 0$ (b) $f(5)f(6)f(7) < 0$
(c) $f(1)f(3)f(4) > 0$ (d) None of these

44. $f(x) = 7[x] + 4\{x\}$
where $[x]$ = greatest integer less than or equals to x.
$\{x\} = x - [x]$
How many real values of x satisfy the equation?
$f(x) = 12 + x$
(a) 0 (b) 1
(c) 2 (d) None of these

45. How many non-negative integer solutions (x, y) are possible for the equation $x^2 - xy + y^2 = x + y$ such that $x \geq y$?
(a) 1 (b) 2
(c) 3 (d) 4

46. A function 'g' is defined for all natural numbers $n \geq 2$ as $\frac{g(n-1)}{g(n)} = \frac{n}{n-1}$.

If $g(1) = 2$ then what is the value of

$$\frac{\left[\frac{1}{g(1)} \times \frac{1}{g(2)} \times \frac{1}{g(3)} \times \ldots \frac{1}{g(8)}\right]}{\left[\frac{1}{g(1)} + \frac{1}{g(2)} + \frac{1}{g(3)} + \ldots \frac{1}{g(8)}\right]}?$$

(a) $8!/2^8$ (b) $8!/(2^8.18)$
(c) $8!/18.2^7$ (d) $8!/3^7.24$

47. $f(x)$ is a polynomial of degree 77 which when divided by $(x - 1)$, $(x - 2)$, $(x - 3)$, $(x - 4)$,..., $(x - 77)$, leaves 1, 2, 3, ..., 77 respectively as the remainders. Find the value of $f(0) + f(78)$.
(a) 77 (b) 78
(c) −77 (d) 78!

48. A function $f(n)$ is defined as $f(n - 1)\,[2 - f(n)] = 1$ for all natural numbers 'n'. If $f(1) = 3$, then find the value of $f(21)$.
(a) 42/41 (b) 45/43
(c) 43/41 (d) 47/45

Directions for Questions 49 and 50: If $f(x) = 10[x] + 22\{x\}$, where $[x]$ denotes the largest integer less than or equal to x and $\{x\} = x - [x]$, (i.e. the fractional part of x), then answer the following questions.

49. How many solutions does the equation $f(x) = 250$ have?
(a) 0 (b) 1
(c) 2 (d) 3

50. What is the sum of all possible values of x?

51. If $f(x + 1) = f(x) - f(x-1)$ and $f(5) = 6$ and $f(17) = 2f(16)$, then $f(17) = ?$
(a) 5 (b) 6
(c) 16 (d) 18

52. If $h(x)$ is a positive valued function and $\frac{h(x)}{h(x-1)} = \frac{h(x-2)}{h(x+1)}$ for all $x \geq 0$

If $h(56) = 16$ and $h(52) = 4$ then $h(54) = ?$

53. $f(x) = 1 - \frac{2}{(x+1)}$

If $f^2(x) = f(f(x))$, $f^3(x) = f(f(f(x)))$, $f^4(x) = f(f(f(f(x))))$ and so on, then find $f^{802}(x)$ at $x = -1/2$.

Directions for Questions 54 and 55: If $\log_3(x + y) + \log_3(x - y) = 3$, where x and y are positive integers then answer the following questions:

54. If $y > 0$, then how many different pairs of (x, y) are possible?

55. The maximum value of $x + y$ = ____?

Directions for Questions 56 and 57:
$f(x) = |x + 2|$
$g(x) = x^2 - 7x + 10$
$h(x) = \min(f(x), g(x))$

56. For how many positive integer values of x, is $h(x) \leq 0$?

57. Find the sum of all integer values of x for which $h(x) < 0$.

58. If $[x]$ denotes the greatest integer less than or equal to x, if p and q are two distinct real numbers and $[2p - 3] = q + 7$, $[3q + 1] = p + 6$, then find the value of $p^2 \times q^2$.

59. If $f(a) = 3^a$ and $f(a + 1) = 3^{(a+1)} + 4$, where 'a' is an odd number, what is the value of

$\frac{1}{4}[f(1) + f(2) + f(3) + f(4) + \ldots + f(72)]$?

(a) $\frac{3}{8}(3^{72} - 1) + 36$
(b) $\frac{3}{8}(3^{72} - 1) - 36$
(c) $\frac{3}{8}(3^{72} + 1) + 36\frac{3}{8}(3^{72} + 1) + 36$
(d) None of these

Directions for Questions 60 to 68: Suppose x and y are real numbers. Let $f(x, y) = |x + y|$ $F(f(x, y)) = -f(x, y)$ and $G(f(x, y)) = -F(f(x, y))$

60. Which one of the following is true?
(a) $F(f(x, y)).G(f(x, y)) = -F(f(x, y)).\ G.(f(x, y))$
(b) $F(f(x, y)).G(f(x, y)) \leq -F(f(x, y)).\ G.(f(x, y))$
(c) $G(f(x, y)).f(x, y) = F(f(x, y)).\ (f(x, y)$
(d) $G(f(x, y)).F(f(x, y)) = f(x, y).\ f(x, y)$

61. Which of the following has a^2 as the result?
(a) $F(f(a, -a)), G(f(a, -a))$
(b) $-F(f(a, a), G(f(a, a))/4$
(c) $F(f(a, a)), G(f(a, a))/2^2$
(d) $f(a, a), f(a, a)$

62. Find the value of the expression.

$$\frac{G(f(3, 2)) + F(f(-1, 2))}{f(2, -3) + G(f(1, 2)} \ldots$$

(a) 3/2 (b) 2/3
(c) 1 (d) 2

63. Which of the following is equal to

$$\frac{G(f(32,13)) + F(f(15,-5))}{f(2,3) + G(f(1.5,0.5))}?$$

(a) $\frac{2G(f(1,2)) + (f(-3,1))}{G(f(2,6) + F(f(-8,2))}$

(b) $\frac{3.G(f(3,4)) + F(f(1,0))}{f(1,1) + G(f(2,0))}$

(c) $\frac{(f(3,4)) + F(f(1,2))}{G(f(1,1))}$

(d) None of these

Now if $A(f(x, y) = f(x, y)$
$B(f(x, y) = -f(x, y)$
$C(f(x, y) = f(x, y)$
$D(f(x, y) = -f(x, y)$ and similarly
$Z(f(x, y) = -f(x, y)$

Now, solve the following:

64. Find the value of $A(f(0, 1)) + B(f(1, 2)) + C(f(2, 3)) + \ldots + Z(f(25, 26))$.
(a) –50 (b) –52
(c) –26 (d) None of these

65. Which of the following is true?
(i) $A(f(0, 1)) < B(f(1, 2)) < C(f(2, 3)\ldots$
(ii) $A(f(0, 1)).\ B(f(1, 2)) > B(f(1, 2)).C(f(2, 3)) > C(f(2, 3)).\ D(f(3, 4))$
(iii) $A(f(0, 0)) = B(f(0, 0)) = C(f(0, 0)) = \ldots = Z(f(0, 0))$
(a) Only (i) and (ii) (b) Only (ii) and (iii)
(c) Only (ii) (d) Only (i)

66. If max (x, y, z) = maximum of x, y and z
Min (x, y, z) = minimum of x, y and z
$f(x, y) = |x + y|$
$F(f(x, y)) = -f(x, y)$
$G(f(x, y) = -F(f(x, y))$
Then find the value of the following expression:
Min (max $[f(2, 3), F(f(3, 4)), G(f(4, 5))]$, min $[f(1, 2), F(f(-1, 2)), G(f(1, -2))]$, max $[f(-3\ -4), f(-5\ -1), G(f(-4, -6))]$)
(a) –1 (b) –7
(c) –6 (d) –10

67. Which of the following is the value of Max. $[f(a, b), F(f(b, c), G(f(c, d))]$ for all $a > b > c > d$?
(a) Anything but positive
(b) Anything but negative
(c) Negative or positive
(d) Any real value

68. If another function is defined as $P(x, y) = \frac{F(f(x, y))}{(x.y)}$, which of the following is second lowest in value?
(a) Value of $P(x, y)$ for $x = 2$ and $y = 1$
(b) Value of $P(x, y)$ for $x = 3$ and $y = 4$
(c) Value of $P(x, y)$ for $x = 3$ and $y = 5$
(d) Value of $P(x, y)$ for $x = 3$ and $y = 2$

69. If $f(s) = (b^s + b^{-s})/2$, where $b > 0$, find $f(s + t) + f(s - t)$.
(a) $f(s) - f(t)$ (b) $2 f(s).f(t)$
(c) $4 f(s).f(t)$ (d) $f(s) + f(t)$

Directions for Questions 70 to 79 are all actual questions from the XAT exam.

70. $A_0, A_1, A_2,\ldots$ is a sequence of numbers with $A_0 = 1$, $A_1 = 3$, and $A_t = (t + 1)A_{(t-1)} - tA_{(t-2)}$, where $t = 2,3,4\ldots$
Conclusion I. $A_8 = 77$
Conclusion II. $A_{10} = 121$
Conclusion III. $A_{12} = 145$
(a) Using the given statement, only Conclusion I can be derived.
(b) Only Conclusion II can be derived, using the given statement
(c) Only Conclusion III can be derived, using the given statement
(d) Conclusion, Using the given statement I, II and III can be derived.
(e) None of the three Conclusions, Using the given statement I, II and III can be derived.

71. A, B, C be real numbers satisfying $A < B < C$, $A + B + C = 6$ and $AB + BC + CA = 9$
Conclusion I. $1 < B < 3$
Conclusion II. $2 < A < 3$
Conclusion III. $0 < C < 1$
(a) Using the given statement, only Conclusion I can be derived.
(b) Using the given statement, only Conclusion II can be derived.
(c) Using the given statement, only Conclusion III can be derived.
(d) Using the given statement, Conclusion I, II and III can be derived.
(e) Using the given statement, none of the three Conclusions I, II and III can be derived.

72. If $F(x, n)$ be the number of ways of distributing 'x' toys to 'n' children so that each child receives at the most two toys, then $F(4, 3)$ = ___?
(a) 2 (b) 6
(c) 3 (d) 4
(e) 5

73. The figure below shows the graph of a function $f(x)$. How many solutions does the equation $f(f(x)) = 15$ have?

(a) 5 (b) 6
(c) 7 (d) 8
(e) Cannot be determined from the given graph

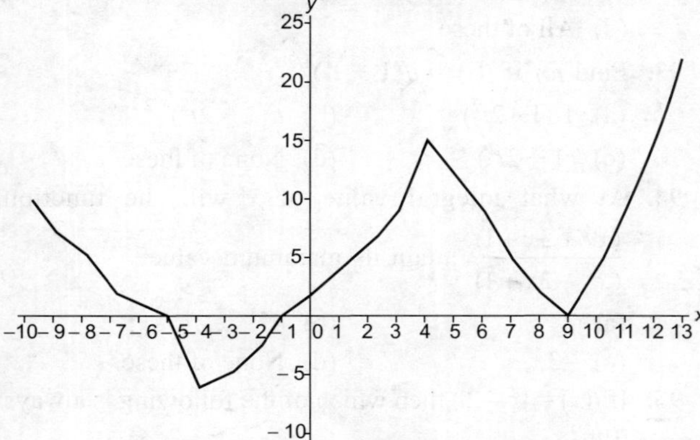

74. The following question is followed by two statements. Mark your answer as:

(a) If the question can be answered by the first statement alone but cannot be answered by the second statement alone;
(b) If the question can be answered by the second statement alone but cannot be answered by the first statement alone;
(c) If the question can be answered by both the statements together but cannot be answered by any one of the statements alone;
(d) If the question can be answered by the first statement alone as well as by the second statement alone;
(e) If the question cannot be answered even by using both the statements together.

A sequence of positive integers is defined as $A_{n+1} = A_n^2 + 1$ for each $n \geq 1$. What is the value of the Greatest Common Divisor of A_{900} and A_{1000}?

I. $A_0 = 1$ II. $A_1 = 2$

75. A manufacturer produces two types of products— A and B, which are subjected to two types of operations, viz., grinding and polishing. Each unit of product A takes two hours of grinding and three hours of polishing whereas product B takes three hours of grinding and two hours of polishing. The manufacturer has ten grinders and fifteen polishers. Each grinder operates for 12 hours/day and each polisher 10 hours/day. The profit margin per unit of A and B are ₹5 and ₹7 respectively. If the manufacturer utilises all his resources for producing these two types of items, what is the maximum profit that the manufacturer can earn?

(a) ₹280 (b) ₹294
(c) ₹515 (d) ₹550
(e) None of these

76. Consider a function $f(x) = x^4 + x^3 + x^2 + x + 1$, where x is a positive integer greater than 1. What will be the remainder if $f(x^5)$ is divided by $f(x)$?

(a) 1 (b) 4
(c) 5 (d) A monomial in x
(e) A polynomial in x

77. For all real numbers x, except $x = 0$ and $x = 1$, the function F is defined by $F\left(\frac{x}{x-1}\right) = \frac{1}{x}$.

If $0 < \alpha < 90°$ then $F((\text{cosec}\ \alpha)^2) = ?$

(a) $(\sin \alpha)^2$ (b) $(\cos \alpha)^2$
(c) $(\tan \alpha)^2$ (d) $(\cot \alpha)^2$
(e) $(\sec \alpha)^2$

78. $F(x)$ is a fourth order polynomial with integer coefficients and with no common factor. The roots of $F(x)$ are –2, –1, 1, 2. If p is a prime number greater than 97, then the largest integer that divides $F(p)$ for all values of p is

(a) 72 (b) 120
(c) 240 (d) 360
(e) None of these

79. If $x = (9 + 4\sqrt{5})^{48} = [x] + f$, where $[x]$ is defined as integral part of x and f is a fraction, then $x(1 - f)$ equals

(a) 1 (b) Less than 1
(c) More than 1 (d) Between 1 and 2
(e) None of these

80. Find the domain of the definition of the function $y = 1/(x - |x|)^{1/2}$.

(a) $-\infty < x < \infty$ (b) $-\infty < x < 0$
(c) $0 < x < \infty$ (d) Nowhere

81. Find the domain of the definition of the function $y = (x - 1)^{1/2} + 2(1 - x)^{1/2} + (x^2 + 3)^{1/2}$.

(a) $x = 0$ (b) $[1, \infty)$
(c) $[-1, 1]$ (d) $x = 1$

82. Find the domain of the definition of the function $y = \log_{10} [(x - 5)/(x^2 - 10x + 24)] - (x + 4)^{1/2}$.

(a) $x > 6$ (b) $4 < x < 5$
(c) Both (*a*) and (*b*) (d) None of these

83. Find the domain of the definition of the function $y = [(x - 3)/(x + 3)]^{1/2} + [(1 - x)/(1 + x)]^{1/2}$.

(a) $x > 3$ (b) $x < -3$
(c) $-3 \leq x \leq 3$ (d) Nowhere

84. Find the domain of the definition of the function $y = (2x^2 + x + 1)^{-3/4}$.

(a) $x \geq 0$ (b) All x except $x = 0$
(c) $-3 \leq x \leq 3$ (d) Everywhere

85. Find the domain of the definition of the function $y = (x^2 - 2x - 3)^{1/2} - 1/(-2 + 3x - x^2)^{1/2}$.

(a) $x > 0$ (b) $-1 < x < 0$
(c) x^2 (d) None of these

86. Find the domain of the definition of the function $y = \log_{10} [1 - \log_{10}(x^2 - 5x + 16)]$.

(a) (2, 3] (b) [2, 3)
(c) [2, 3] (d) None of these

87. If $f(t) = (t - 1)/(t + 1)$, then $f(f(t))$ will be equal to

(a) $1/t$ (b) $-1/t$
(c) t (d) $-t$

88. If $f(x) = e^x$ and $g(x) = \log_e x$ then value of *fog* will be

(a) x (b) 0
(c) 1 (d) e

89. In the above question, find the value of *gof*.

(a) x (b) 0
(c) 1 (d) e

90. The function $y = 1/x$ shifted 1 unit down and 1 unit right is given by

(a) $y - 1 = 1/(x + 1)$ (b) $y - 1 = 1/(x - 1)$
(c) $y + 1 = 1/(x - 1)$ (d) $y + 1 = 1/(x + 1)$

91. Which of the following functions is an even function?

(a) $f(t) = (a^t + a^{-t})/(a^t - a^{-t})$
(b) $f(t) = (a^t + 1)/(a^t - 1)$
(c) $f(t) = t.\,(a^t - 1)/(a^t + 1)$
(d) None of these

92. Which of the following functions is not an odd function?

(a) $f(t) = \log_2(t + \sqrt{t^2} + 1)$
(b) $f(t) = (a^t + a^{-t})/(a^t - a^{-t})$
(c) $f(t) = (a^t + 1)/(a^t - 1)$
(d) All of these

93. Find *fof* if $f(t) = t/(1 + t^2)^{1/2}$.

(a) $1/(1+2t^2)^{1/2}$ (b) $t/(1 + 2t^2)^{1/2}$
(c) $(1 + 2t^2)$ (d) None of these

94. At what integral value of x will the function $\dfrac{(x^2 + 3x + 1)}{(x^2 - 3x + 1)}$ attain its maximum value?

(a) 3 (b) 4
(c) −3 (d) None of these

95. If $f(x) = |x - 2|$, then which of the following is always true?

(a) $f(x) = (f(x))^2$ (b) $f(x) = f(-x)$
(c) $f(x) = x - 2$ (d) None of these

High Yield Questions

Scan to access assisted problem solving videos on questions 54–55, 73, 74 and 76 from LOD 3

Space for Rough Work

ANSWER KEY

Level of Difficulty (I)

1. 3	2. 90	3. (a)	4. (c)
5. (d)	6. (c)	7. (b)	8. (c)
9. (d)	10. (a)	11. (d)	12. (a)
13. (d)	14. (a)	15. (b)	16. (a)
17. (a)	18. (b)	19. (d)	20. (d)
21. (c)	22. (b)	23. (d)	24. (c)
25. (b)	26. (d)	27. (a)	28. (b)
29. (b)	30. (a)	31. (c)	32. (c)
33. (d)	34. (a)	35. (d)	36. (a)
37. (c)	38. (a)	39. (b)	40. (c)
41. (b)	42. (d)	43. (a)	44. (a)
45. (c)	46. 3	47. 1	48. 1
49. 7.86	50. 13.75	51. 12	52. 1.5
53. (d)	54. 2	55. (d)	56. 8
57. (d)	58. (c)	59. 0.14	60. 2
61. (b)	62. (b)	63. 9	64. 10
65. 0	66. (c)	67. –2	68. (b)
69. (c)	70. (a)	71. (b)	72. (b)
73. (c)	74. (a)	75. (b)	76. (c)
77. (a)	78. (d)	79. (b)	80. (c)
81. (a)	82. (d)	83. (d)	84. (a)
85. (a)	86. (d)	87. (d)	88. (d)
89. (d)	90. 3	91. (c)	92. (c)
93. (c)	94. (c)		

Level of Difficulty (II)

1. (b)	2. 0	3. (a)	4. (b)
5. (b)	6. (a)	7. 1	8. (d)
9. 0	10. 0	11. (c)	12. (c)
13. (b)	14. $x = 2$	15. (b)	16. (a)
17. (c)	18. (d)	19. (b)	20. (c)
21. (b)	22. (c)	23. (c)	24. (b)
25. (c)	26. (d)	27. (a)	28. (a)
29. (c)	30. (c)	31. (b)	32. (b)
33. (c)	34. (b)	35. (c)	36. (b)
37. (a)	38. (d)	39. (b)	40. (c)
41. (d)	42. (b)	43. –8/3	44. 1
45. 30.8	46. 4	47. 440/3	48. 1054
49. 1999997	50. 0	51. (c)	52. (b)
53. (a)	54. 14	55. 625	56. 216
57. (a)	58. 12	59. (c)	60. (a)
61. (d)	62. 1.25	63. 3/16	64. (d)
65. (c)	66. (c)	67. 30	68. 0.01
69. 3	70. 1/8	71. 1	72. 1/6
73. 2	74. (b)	75. 32	76. –16
77. 27	78. 3	79. 4.5	80. 2
81. 501/500	82. 1	83. (b)	84. 3
85. 2001	86. 72	87. 20501	88. 192
89. 9	90. 1	91. (d)	92. 707/10
93. 2	94. 3/5	95. –0.4	96. 4
97. 0			

Level of Difficulty (III)

1. 20	2. 15	3. 36	4. (c)
5. (c)	6. (c)	7. (a)	8. (d)
9. (a)	10. 100	11. (b)	12. (b)
13. (b)	14. (d)	15. (d)	16. (c)
17. (d)	18. (c)	19. (d)	20. (c)
21. (b)	22. (d)	23. 80	24. 5
25. (d)	26. 18	27. 18	28. 2
29. 2.86	30. 1	31. 3.5	32. 291
33. 16	34. (c)	35. 4	36. 36
37. 0	38. 3905	39. 2	40. (b)
41. (c)	42. 3	43. (c)	44. (b)
45. (d)	46. (b)	47. (b)	48. (c)
49. (d)	50. 73.36	51. (b)	52. 8
53. 2	54. 2	55. 27	56. 4
57. 7	58. 784	59. (a)	60. (b)
61. (b)	62. (c)	63. (b)	64. (c)
65. (b)	66. (a)	67. (b)	68. (d)
69. (b)	70. (e)	71. (a)	72. (b)
73. (e)	74. (d)	75. (b)	76. (c)
77. (b)	78. (d)	79. (a)	80. (d)
81. (d)	82. (c)	83. (d)	84. (d)
85. (d)	86. (d)	87. (b)	88. (a)
89. (a)	90. (c)	91. (c)	92. (a)
93. (b)	94. (a)	95. (d)	

SOLUTIONS AND SHORTCUTS

Level of Difficulty (I)

1. Putting 3 in $f(x)$, we get $f(3) = 5$. Putting this value in $g(x)$. We get $g(5) = 3$. We see that this pattern will continue for $f(x)$ and $g(x)$. Hence, on solving the expression, we get 3 as our answer.
2. Given, $f_1(x) = f_2(x) \rightarrow 2x^2 + 10x + n = 2x \rightarrow 2x^2 + 8x + n = 0$. For this to always return a positive value, the graph needs to lie only in the positive y axis which means the roots are imaginary. Hence, the discriminant needs to be less than 0. So $64 - 8n < 0 \rightarrow n > 8$. Hence, we have a total of 90 two digit values of n, that would make the equation never negative.
3. For this question, we can check through options. At $x = 0$, the equation would be satisfied and hence, we can eliminate Options (b) & (c). At $x = -2$, the equation will not be satisfied. Hence, we can eliminate option (d). Hence, Option (a) is the correct answer. Alternately, we can think of this as the LHS would be equal to the RHS if and only if each of $f(x)$ and $g(x)$ is non-negative. $f(x) > 0$, when $x \geq -1$ and $g(x) \geq 0$, when $x \leq 1/2$. Combining these two ranges, we can see that the correct range for the given equality would be $-1 \leq x \leq 1/2$.
4. The given function can be rewritten as $f(x) = 4^x$ $1 + 4 + 4^2 + 4^3 + 4^4 + \ldots + 4^n$ can be expressed as the sum of gp with common ratio of 4 and first term as 1. Sum $= (4^n - 1)/3 = 1365 \rightarrow 4^n = 4096$. Hence, $n = 6$. Hence, Option (c) is the correct answer.

5. We can test for random numbers for this question as the question suggests we would get a specific value for different values of x. At $x = 5$, we get $f(x) - g(x) = 2$. At $x = 10$, we get $f(x) - g(x) = 2$. Hence, we can deduce that Option (d) is the correct answer.
6. Since a, b, c are in AP with a common difference of 2, it means that the difference between the greatest value and the smallest value between a, b and c would always be 4. The functions given to us $f(a,b,c)$ and $g(a,b,c)$ represent the minimum and the maximum value between a, b, and c, respectively. Hence $f(a,b,c) - g(a,b,c) = -4$. Hence, option (c) is correct.
7. When $p < 3$, max $(p, 3) = 3$
   Expression = 9
   When $p > 3$, max $(p, 3) = p$
   Expression = $3p$ (as $p > 3$)
   Hence, option (b) is correct.
8. $P(5, 3) = 15$
   $L(12, 9) = 36$
   Min (36, 15) = 15
   Max (4, 15) = 15
   $P(9, 15) = 135$
   Hence, option (c) is correct.
9. $f(x) = \dfrac{ax}{x+1}$. $f(f(x)) = f\left(\dfrac{ax}{x+1}\right) = \dfrac{a \times \dfrac{ax}{x+1}}{\dfrac{ax}{x+1}+1} = \dfrac{a^2x}{ax+x+1}$

   According to the question, we also have: $\dfrac{a^2x}{ax+x+1} = x$

   This, would occur at $a = -1$. Hence, option (d) is correct.
10. $f(3) = 2 \times (3)^2 + 7 \times (3) - 9 = 30$
    $g(30) = 2 \times 30 + 3 = 63$
    Hence, option (a) is correct.
11. This function will be defined only when the base of the exponent (1/2) is non-negative.
    Thus, for the domain,
    $(169 - x^2) \geq 0$
    Or $(13 - x)(13 + x) \geq 0$
    This gives $-13 \leq x \leq 13$
    Hence, (d) is the correct option.
12. Considering the definition of an even function, i.e. $f(x) = f(-x)$,
    It is clear that only x^{12} satisfies this condition.
    For option (b), $f(-x) = (-x - 3)^2$ which is not same as $f(x)$.
    For option (c), $f(-x) = (-x + 3)^4$ which is again not equal to $f(x)$.
    Hence, (a) is the correct option.
13. Putting $y = 1/(x - 1)$, we get: $x - 1 = 1/y \rightarrow x = 1 + 1/y$
    Or $x = (1 + y)/y$.
    Now we will replace y with x and x with y to get the inverse function as $y = (1 + x)/x$.
    Hence, (d) is the correct option.
14. $f(1) = 2, f(2) = 3, f(3) = f(2) + f(1) = 5; f(4) = f(3) + f(2) = 8; f(5) = f(4) + f(3) = 13; f(6) = f(5) + f(4) = 21$
    Hence, (a) is the correct option.
15. Given that $F(n - 1) = \dfrac{1}{(2 - F(n))}$, we can rewrite the expression as $F(n) = (2F(n-1) - 1)/((F(n-1))$.
    For $n = 2$: $F(2) = \dfrac{6-1}{3} \Rightarrow F(2) = \dfrac{5}{3}$.
    The value of $F(3)$ will come out as 7/5 and $F(4)$ comes out as 9/7 and so on. What we realise is that for each value of n, after and including $n = 2$, the value of $F(n) = \dfrac{2n+1}{2n-1}$.
    This means that the greatest integral value of $F(n)$ will always be 1 for $n = 2$ to $n = 1000$.
    Thus, the value of the given expression will turn out to be:
    $3 + 1 \times 999 = 1002$. Hence, option (b) is the correct answer.
16. From the solution to the previous question, we already know how the value of the given functions at $n = 1, 2, 3$ and so on would behave.
    Thus, we can try to see what happens when we write down the first few terms of the expression:
    $F(1) \times F(2) \times F(3) \times F(4) \times \ldots. F(1000)$
    $= 3 \times \dfrac{5}{3} \times \dfrac{7}{5} \times \dfrac{9}{7} \times \cdots \times \dfrac{2001}{1999} = 2001$
17. Since $f(0) = 15$, we get $c = 15$.
    Next, we have $f(3) = f(-3) = 18$. Using this information, we get:
    $9a + 3b + c = 9a - 3b + c \rightarrow 3b = -3b$
    $\therefore \quad 6b = 0 \rightarrow b = 0$.
    Also, since
    $f(3) = 9a + 3b + c = 18 \rightarrow$ we get: $9a + 15 = 18 \rightarrow a = 1/3$
    The quadratic function becomes $f(x) = x^2/3 + 15$.
    $f(12) = 144/3 + 15 = 63$.
18. What you need to understand about $M(x^2 \theta y^2)$ is that it is the square of the sum of two squares. Since $M(x^2 \theta y^2) = 361$, we get $(x^2 + y^2)^2 = 361$, which means that the sum of the sqaures of x and y, viz. $x^2 + y^2 = 19$. (**Note:** It cannot be -19 as we are talking about the sum of two squares, which cannot be negative under any circumstance).
    Also, from $M(x^2 \psi y^2) = 49$,we get $(x^2 - y^2)^2 = 49$, $\rightarrow (x^2 - y^2) = \pm 7$.
    Based on these two values, we can solve for two distinct situations:
    (a) When $x^2 + y^2 = 19$ and $x^2 - y^2 = 7$, we get $x^2 = 13$ and $y^2 = 6$
    (b) When $x^2 + y^2 = 19$ and $x^2 - y^2 = -7$, we get $x^2 = 6$ and $y^2 = 13$
    In both cases, we can see that the value of: $((x^2 y^2) + 3)$ will come out as $13 \times 6 + 3 = 81$ and the square root of its value will turn out to ± 9. Hence option (b) is correct.

19. The first thing you need to understand while solving this question is that, since $[m]$ will always be integral, hence $\Psi(4x + 5)$ will also be integral. Since $\Psi(4x + 5) = 5y + 3$, naturally, the value of $5y + 3$ will also be integral. By a similar logic, the value of x will also be an integer considering the second equation: $\Psi(3y + 7) = x + 4$.
Using, this logic we know that $\Psi(4x+5) = 4x+5$ (because, whenever m is an integer the value of $[m] = m$).
This leads us to two linear equations as follows:
$4x + 5 = 5y + 3$ (1)
$3y + 7 = x + 4$ (2)
Solving simultaneously, we will get: $x = -3$ and $y = -2$.
Thus, $x^2 \times y^2 = 9 \times 4 = 36$.
20. Since $f(128) = 4$, we can see that the product of $f(256).f(0.5) = f(256 \times 0.5) = f(128) = 4$.
Similarly, the products $f(1).f(128) = f(2).f(64) = f(4).f(32) = f(8).f(16) = 4$.
Thus, $M = 4\times4\times4\times4\times4 = 1024$.
Hence, option (d) is the correct answer.
21. The only values of x and y that satisfy the equation $4x + 6y = 20$ are $x = 2$ and $y = 2$ (since, x, y are non-negative integers). This gives us: $4 \le M/2^{2/3}$. M has to be greater than $2^{8/3}$ for this expression to be satisfied. Hence, option (c) is correct.
22. $\theta(\Psi(-7)) = \theta(-2) = 14$. Hence, option (b) is correct.
23. $F(2b) = F(b + b) = F(b).F(b) \div 2 = (F(b))^2 \div 2$.
Similarly, $F(3b) = F(b + b + b) = F(b + b).F(b) \div 2 = \{F(b)^2 \div 2\}.\{F(b)\} \div 2 = (F(b))^3 \div 2^2$.
Similarly, $F(4b) = (F(b))^4 \div 2^3$.
Hence, $F(12b) = (F(b))^{12} \div 2^{11}$. Option (d) is correct.
24. To test for a reflexive function as defined in the problem, use the following steps:
Step 1: To start with, assume a value of 'b' and derive a value for 'a' using the given function.
Step 2: Then, insert the value, you got for 'a' in the first step into the value of 'b' and get a new value of 'a'. This value of 'a' should be equal to the first value of 'b' that you used in the first step. If this occurs, the function would be reflexive. Else it is not reflexive.
Checking for the expression in (i), if we take $b = 1$, we get:
$a = 8/1 = 8$. Inserting, $b = 8$ in the function gives us $a = 29/29 = 1$. Hence, the function given in (i) is reflexive.
Similarly checking the other two functions, we get that the function in (ii) is not reflexive while the function in (iii) is reflexive.
Thus, option (c) is the correct answer.
25. $2x^2 - 1 = 1 - 3x$
$2x^2 + 3x - 2 = 0 \Rightarrow (2x - 1)(x + 2) = 0 \Rightarrow x = -2, 1/2$.
26. $fogoh(2) = f(g(h(2)))$
$h(2) = 4$
$f(g(h(2))) = f(g(4)) = f(-1/3) = -3$. Hence, the option (d) is correct answer.
27. $(x+1)^3$ is not odd as $f(x) \neq -f(-x)$. Hence, option (a) is correct.

Solutions for Questions 28 to 30:

$f(1) = 0, f(2) = 1$
$f(x) = f(x - 2) - f(x - 1)$
$f(3) = f(1) - f(2) = -1$
$f(4) = f(2) - f(3) = 2$
$f(5) = f(3) - f(4) = -3$
$f(6) = f(4) - f(5) = 5$
$f(7) = f(5) - f(6) = -8$
$f(8) = f(6) - f(7) = 13$
$f(9) = f(7) - f(8) = -21$

28. 13. Hence, option (b) is correct.
29. $f(7) + f(4) = -8 + 2 = -6$. Hence, option (b) is correct.
30. $0 + 1 - 1 + 2 - 3 + 5 - 8 + 13 - 21 = -12$. Hence, option (a) is correct.
31. For any ${}^nC_r$, n should be positive and $r \ge 0$.
Thus, for positive x, $5 - x \ge 0$
$\Rightarrow x = 0, 1, 2, 3, 4, 5$. Hence, option (c) is correct.
32. (c)
33. (d)
34. (a)
35. $foh(x) = hof(x) = x$
You will realise that if were to form a chain of these functions for even number of times, you would still end up getting x. For example, $Fohofoh(x) = foho(x) = x$
Since both the parts of the multiplication of the two functions, have the functions h and f repeated for even number of times; each of their values will be x and their product will be x^2.
Hence, option (d) is correct.
36. $fo(foh)o(hof)(x)$
$= fo(foh)(x)$
$= f(x) = 2x + 5$
Hence, option (a) is correct.
37. $A(x) = f(x + 1) \Rightarrow |x - 4 + 1| + |x - 5 + 1| + |x - 6 + 1|$
$A(x) \Rightarrow |x - 3| + |x - 4| + |x - 5|$
Obviously, this is neither odd or nor even alternatively, we know the graph of this function will neither be symmetrical to axis or origin.
Hence, option (c) is correct.
38. Let $f(x) = y$
Then $y = \dfrac{e^x - e^{-x}}{e^x - e^{-x}} = \dfrac{e^{2x} - 1}{e^{2x} + 1}$
Now find the value x in terms of y.
$\Rightarrow \dfrac{y+1}{y-1} = -e^{2x}$ [Applying componendo-dividendo]

$\Rightarrow \frac{y+1}{1-y} = e^{2x} \Rightarrow x = ½ \log_e \frac{y+1}{1-y}$

Then put y in place of x and x in place of y.

Thus, we will get inverse function of $f(x)$ as: y = 1/2 $\log_e \frac{x+1}{1-x}$

$\Rightarrow$ Option (a) is correct.

39. If $f(x) = f(-x)$, i.e. $f(0 + x) = f(0 - x)$, the graph is symmetrical about $x = 0$.
Therefore, the graph is symmetrical about $x = 3$ if $f(3 + x) = f(3 - x)$
Hence, option (b) is correct.

40. $f(1) = 1^5 - 3 \times (1)^4 + 2 \times (1)^2 - 4 \times (1) + a = a - 4$
$f(2) = 32 - 48 + 8 - 8 + a$
$= a - 16$.
Once we have these expressions for $f(1)$ and $f(2)$, we need to use the information of $f(1)$ and $f(2)$ being of opposite signs. Applying a bit of common sense here, we can see that it is not possible for $f(2)$ to be positive, if $f(1)$ is negative, since $f(2) < f(1)$. Hence, the only situation where the condition of opposite signs will be true would be if $f(1)$ is positive and $f(2)$ is negative. $f(1)$ will be positive if $a > 4$, and $f(2)$ will be negative for values of a up to and including 15. Hence, the correct answer will be option (c).

41. Sum of coefficients can be found by putting $x = 1$.
$(1 + 1 - 3)^{2163} = -1$
Hence, option (b) is correct.

42. Let $x = -2$ and check the options one by one:
(a) $f(-2^2) = |(-2^2) - 2| = 2$ and $f(x) = 4$
$[f(x)]^2 = 16$. We do not get the equality of the two values. Hence, option (a) is not correct.
(b) $f(|-2|) = 0$ and $f(-2) = 4$. Hence, option (b) is not correct.
(c) Let $x = -2$ and $y = 3$
$f(-2 + 3) = |1 - 2| = 1$ and $f(-2) = 4$ and $f(3) = 1$
Hence, option (c) is not correct.
Thus, option (d) is correct.

43. $f(g(x)) = f(|3x-2|) = \frac{1}{|3x-2|}$
Hence, option (*a*) is correct.

44. $f(g(x)) = f(|x|) = |x|^2 + \frac{1}{|x|^2}$. This function would take the same values when you try to use a positive value or a negative value of x. For instance, if you were to put x as 2, you would get the same answer as if you were to use x as -2. Hence, $f(g(x))$ is an even function.

45. For this question, you would have to go through each of the options checking them for their correctness in order to identify the correct answer. Thus,
For option (a): $g(x) + (g(x))^2 = |x| + |x|^2$
$\Rightarrow f(x) \neq g(x) + (g(x))^2$. Hence, option (a) is not correct.
For option (b): $f(x) = x^2 + \frac{1}{x^2}, f(g(x)) = |x|^2 + \frac{1}{|x|^2}$
$f(x) \neq -f(g(x))$. Hence, option (b) is not correct.
For option (c): $g(f(x)) = \left|x^2 + \frac{1}{x^2}\right|$
$f(g(x)) = |x|^2 + \frac{1}{|x|^2}$ which is the same as $\left|x^2 + \frac{1}{x^2}\right|$.
Hence, $f(g(x)) = g(f(x))$
$\because$ Hence, option (c) is correct.

46. $f(x) = f(-x)$
$g(x) = g(-x)$
$h(x) = -h(-x)$
$t(x) = t(-x)$
Therefore three functions are even.

47. $f(x) = f(-x)$
$\Rightarrow h(f(x)) = h(f(-x))$
$\Rightarrow$ Hence, $h(f(x))$ is an even function. So the correct answer is 1.

48. $t(x) = t(-x)$
Hence, $h(t(x)) = h(t(-x))$
$\Rightarrow h(t(x))$ is an even function. Thus, correct answer is 1.

49. $f(2) = \frac{2^2+1}{2-1} = 5$
$f(f(2)) = f(5) = \frac{5^2+1}{5-1} = \frac{26}{4}$
$f(f(f(2))) = f\left(\frac{26}{4}\right) = \frac{\left(\frac{26}{4}\right)^2+1}{\frac{26}{4}-1} = \frac{\frac{676+16}{16}}{\frac{22}{4}}$
$= \frac{692}{16} \times \frac{4}{22} = 7.86$

50. $D(3,4) = \frac{3}{4} = 0.75$
$S(2, D(3,4)) = S(2, 0.75) = 2.75$
$P(S(2, D(3,4)), 5) = P(2.75, 5) = 2.75 \times 5 = 13.75$

51. $P(2, 3) = 2 \times 3 = 6$
$D(4, 2) = 4 \div 2 = 2$
$S(P(2,3), D(4,2)) = S(6,2) = 8$
$t(1,5) = |1-5| = 4$
$S(8,4) = 8 + 4 = 12$

Solutions for Questions 52 to 54:

52. [(5 P 6)Q(4 Q 2)]S (3 S 1)
$= [(|5-6|)Q\ (4/2)]S\ (1/3)$
$= [1\ Q\ 2]S\left(\frac{1}{3}\right)$
$= [1\ R\ 2]S\left(\frac{1}{3}\right)$
$= [1 \times 2)S\left(\frac{1}{3}\right)$
$= 2\ S\ \frac{1}{3}$
$= \left(\frac{1}{2\times\frac{1}{3}}\right) = \frac{3}{2} = 1.5$

53. For this Question, we would need to check each option and select the one that is true.
Checking option (a) we can see that:
(4P2) = (4Q2) = 4/2 = 2, (2P4) = |2– 4| = 2
So, option (a), is incorrect.
Checking option (b) we get:
(4Q2) = 4/2 = 2, 2R4 = 2 × 4 = 8
Hence, option (b), is incorrect.
Checking option (c) we get:
(6Q3)= 6/3= 2
2 S (0.5) = 1/(2 × 0.5)= 1
Hence, option (c) is incorrect.
Hence, option (d) is correct.

54. (5P3)Q(4S2) = (5 Q 3)$Q\left(\frac{1}{4.2}\right)$
$= \frac{5}{3}Q\frac{1}{8}$
$= \frac{40}{3}$

20Q1.5 = 20 ÷ 1.5 = $\frac{40}{3}$, therefore, the operator Q should replace 'K' in the equation.

Solutions for Questions 55 to 57:

55. $f(3,4) = [3] + \{4\} = 3 + 4 = 7$
$g(3.5, 4.5) = [4.5] - \{3.5\} = 4 - 4 = 0$
$i(f(3,4), g(3.5,4.5)) = i(7,0) = -7$
Hence, option (d) is correct.

56. $a^3 = 64 \Rightarrow a = 4$
$b^2 = 16 \Rightarrow b = 4 or -4$
When a = 4, b = 4
$f(4,4) = [4] + \{4\} = 4 + 4 = 8$
$g(4,4) = [4] - \{4\} = 4 - 4 = 0$
But these values do not satisfy the condition in the problem that $8 + f(a,b) = -g(a,b)$. Hence, we will try to use a = 4 and b = –4, to see whether that gives us the right set of values for the conditions to be matched.
When a = 4, b = –4
$f(4,-4) = [4] + \{-4\} = 4 - 4 = 0$
$g(4,-4) = [-4] - \{4\} = -4 - 4 = -8$
The given condition is satisfied here. Hence, a = 4 and b = –4. Therefore, a – b = 4 – (–4) = 8.

57. $f(1.2,-2.3) + g(-1.2, 2.3)$
$= [1.2] + \{-2.3\} + [2.3] - \{-1.2\}$
$= 1 - 2 + 2 + 1$
$= 2$
$= i(a,-1.3) = \{-a - 1.3\}$
For $a = -2.4 \Rightarrow i(-2.4,-1.3) = \{2.4 - 1.3\} = \{1.1\} = 2$
Hence, option (d) is correct.

Solutions for Questions 58 and 59:

58. Given: $xPy = \frac{1}{1+\frac{y}{x}} = \frac{x}{x+y}$ and $xQy = 1 + \frac{x}{y} = \frac{x+y}{y}$.
From this point you would need to read the options and check the one that gives you a value of $\frac{x}{y}$. It is easily evident here that:
$(xPy)\times(xQy) = \frac{x}{x+y}\times\frac{x+y}{y} = \frac{x}{y}$
Hence, Option (c) is correct.

59. $S(2,3) = (2P3)P(2Q3)$
$= \left(\frac{2}{2+3}\right)P\left(\frac{2+3}{3}\right)$
$= \frac{2}{5}P\frac{5}{3} = \frac{\frac{2}{5}}{\frac{2}{5}+\frac{5}{3}} = 0.19$

Solutions for Questions 60 to 62:

60. (1 + min(2A3, 1C2))B(max(1A2), 1C1)
=[1 + min(1, 2)]B max(1, 1)
(1 + 1)B(1^2) = 2B1 = [2 ÷ 1] = 2

61. max(7A3, 16B2) = max(4, 8) = 8^2 = 64
Now by checking the options we get only option (b) that gives us the correct value.
(32B2)C(min(4, 8))
|[32 ÷ 2] × 4| = |16 × 4| = 64
Hence, option (b) is correct.

62. max (3, 4) ÷ min (8, 4) = 4^2 ÷ 4 = 4. Checking the options we see:
Option (a): 8A2 = |8 – 2| = 6
Option (b): 28B7 = 28 ÷ 7 = 4
Option (c): 4C2 = |4 × 2| = 8
Hence option (*b*) is correct.

Solutions for Questions 63 to 67:

63. $f(1,3,5,7)+g(2,4,6,8)=1+8=9$

$h[aK,K]=\left[\frac{aK}{K}\right]=[a]=a,[a\in I]$

$\Rightarrow a=9$

64. $t(1,2,3,4)=1\times2\times3\times4=24$

$i(1,2,3,4)=1+2+3+4=10$

$f(t(1,2,3,4),i(1,2,3,4))=f(24,10)=10$

65. $f(5,6,7,8) = 5$, $i(1,2,3,4,) = 1 + 2 + 3 + 4 = 10$

$h(5,10)=\left[\frac{5}{10}\right]=[0.5]=0$

66. $P = f(2,3,4,6) = 2$

$Q = g(1,2,3,4) = 4$

$R=h(8,4)=\left[\frac{8}{4}\right]=2$

$S = t(1, 2, 3, 4) = 1 \times 2 \times 3 \times 4 = 24$

$T = i(4,5,6) = 4 + 5 + 6 = 15$

$\therefore P = R < Q < T < S.$

Hence, option (*c*) is correct

67. $f(1,2,3)=1, g(2,3,4)=4, f(0,1,2)$

$=0, g(-3,-2)=-2$

$f(1,4,0,-2)=-2.$

68. $|x|$

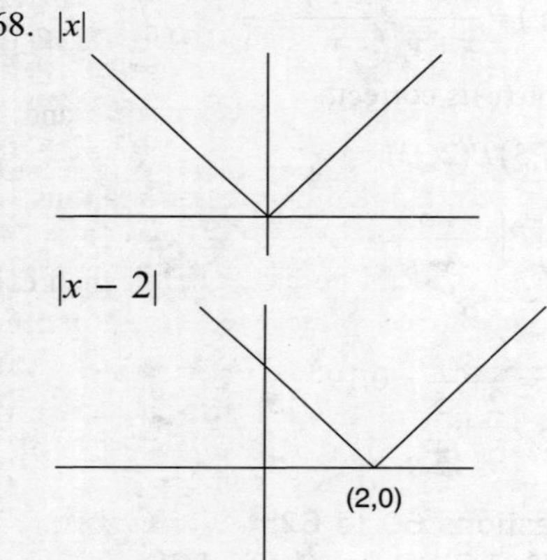

$|x - 2|$

69. $\log x$

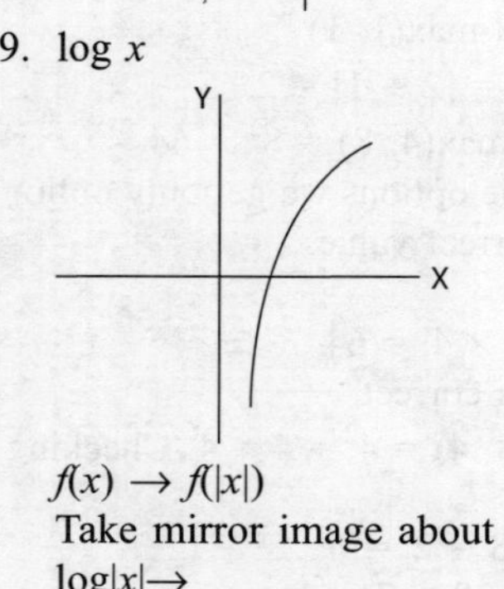

$f(x) \to f(|x|)$

Take mirror image about *y*-axis

$\log|x| \to$

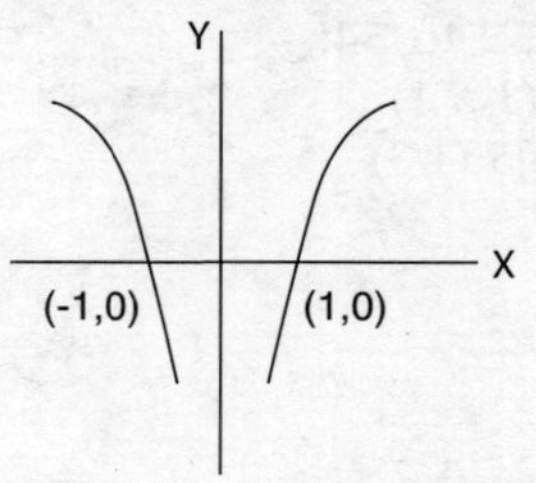

70. $x^3 \to$

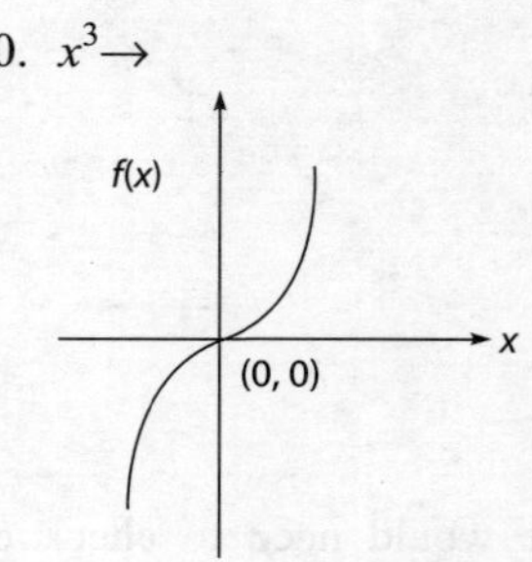

$(x-1)^3 \to$

[Shift curve one unit right]

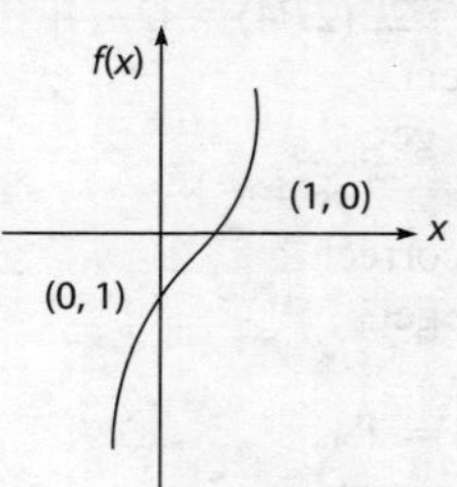

Hence, option (a) is correct.

71. $e^x \to$

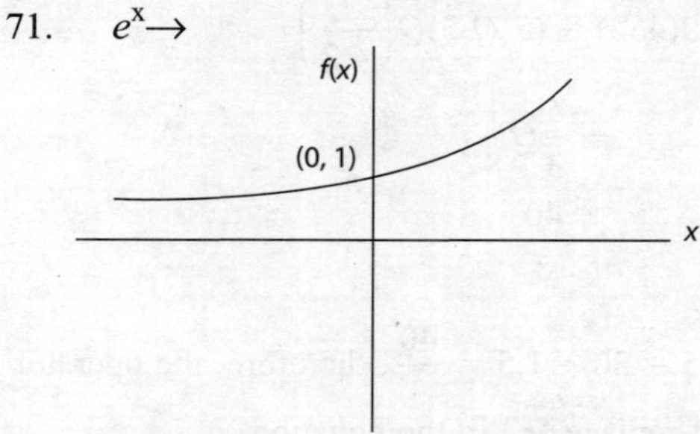

$e^{|x|} \to$

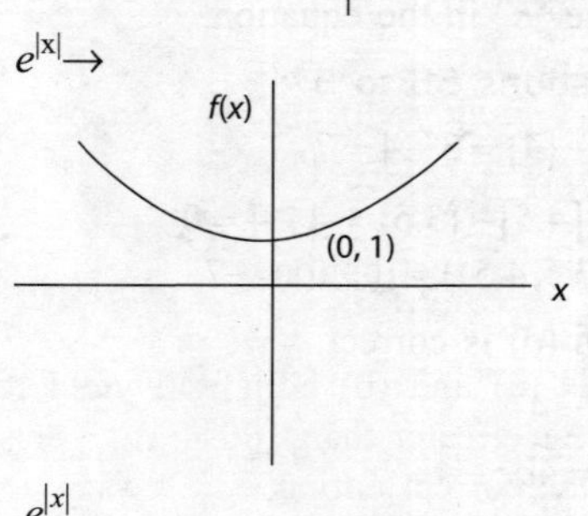

$\frac{e^{|x|}}{2} \to$

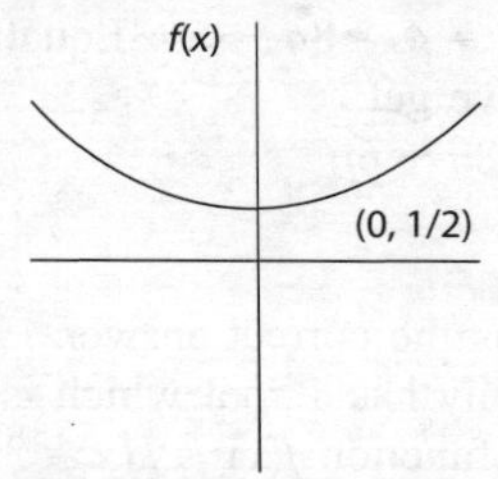

Hence, option (b) is correct.

72. $\max\left(x, x^2\right) = \begin{cases} x^2, \text{for} -\infty < x \le 0 \\ x, \text{for } 0 \le x \le 1 \\ x^2, \text{for } x > 1 \end{cases}$

$\Rightarrow f(x) = \max(x, x^2) \Rightarrow ?$

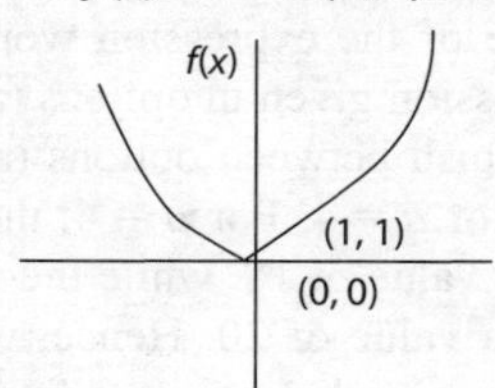

Hence, option (b) is correct.

73. $a\$b = 2\$3 = 4 + 9 = 13$
$a\&b = 2\&3 = 3 \times 4 = 12$
$13\%12 = (13 - 1)(12 - 1)$
$= 12 \times 11$
$= 132$
Hence, option (c) is correct.

74. Solving the left hand side expression of sign '&' first,
$4\$3 = 4^2 + 3^2 = 25$
$25\%6 = (25 - 1)(6 - 1) = 120.$
Solving the right bracket of the expression (after the sign '&'),
$2\%7 = (2 - 1)(7 - 1) = 6$
$5\$6 = 5^2 + 6^2 = 61$
$120\&61 = (120 + 1)(61 + 1) = 7502$
Hence, (a) is the correct option.

75. Going by the options,
Gives $(2\$4) = 2^2 + 4^2 = 20$
Gives $(2\%4) = (2 - 1)(4 - 1) = 3$
Gives $(2\&4) = (2 + 1)(4 + 1) = 15$
Hence, (b) is the correct option.

76. As $a\$b = a^2 + b^2$
Clearly options (a) and (b) both will yield results which will be far greater than 100.
Hence, (c) is the correct option.

77. As square of any number is always non negative, other expressions can give any value.
Hence, (a) is the correct option.

78. Since the denominator $x^2 - 3x + 2$ has real roots, the maximum value would be infinity.

79. The minimum value of the function would occur at the minimum value of $(x^2 - 2x + 5)$ as this quadratic function has imaginary roots.
For $y = x^2 - 2x + 5$
$dy/dx = 2x - 2 = 0 \Rightarrow x = 1$
$\Rightarrow x^2 - 2x + 5 = 4$
Thus, minimum value of the argument of the log is 4.
So, minimum value of the function is $\log_2 4 = 2$.

80. {[(3@4)! (3 #2)] @ [(4!3) @ (2 # 3)]}
{[(3.5) ! (5)] @ [(0.5) @ (–5)]}.
{[–0.75] @ [–2.25]} = –1.5

81. 0 @ 0.5 = 0.25. Thus, (a) is the correct option.

82. *Option (b) gives us:* (1) (4) = 4.
Option (c) gives us: $\frac{(16)}{(1)(4)}$
$16/4 = 4$
Hence, both (b) and (c) are correct.

83. (a) will always be true because $(a + b)/2$ would always be greater than $(a - b)/2$ for the given value range.
Further, $a^2 - b^2$ would always be less than $a^3 - b^3$.
Thus, option (d) is correct.

Solutions for Questions 84 to 87.

84. Option (a) = $(a - b)(a + b) = a^2 - b^2$
85. Option (a) = $(a^2 - b^2) + b^2 = a^2$.
86. The maximum will depend on the values of a and b. Thus, cannot be determined.
87. The minimum will depend on the values of a and b. Thus, cannot be determined.
88. Any of $(a + b)$ or a/b could be greater and thus, we cannot determine this.
89. Again $(a + b)$ or a/b can both be greater than each other depending on the values, we take for a and b.
E.g. for $a = 0.9$ and $b = 0.91$, $a + b > a/b$
For $a = 0.1$ and $b = 0.11$, $a + b < a/b$

90. $f(x) = x^3 - x^2 - 6x$
$= (x + 2)\, x\, (x - 3)$
$\Rightarrow f(x) = 0$
$\Rightarrow (x + 2)\, x\, (x - 3) = 0$
$X = 0, 3, -2$. There are three such values.

91. Curve of $f(x)$ will look like this:

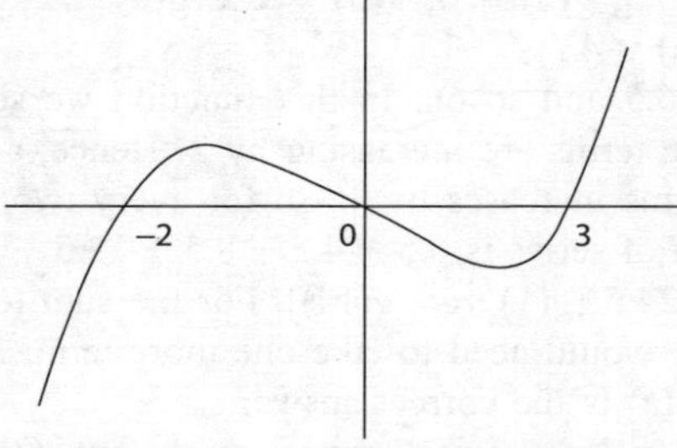

For interval (–2, 3), $f(x)$ will attain its minima in the interval (0, 3).

92. Options (a), (b), (d) are undefined for $x = 0$.
As $x^4 + 7$ is always positive for $x \in R$, therefore, $\log(x^4 + 7) \in R$ for all $x \in R$. Hence, option (c) is true. Each of the other options has at least one value where $f(x)$ does not remain real.

93. When $f(x)$ and $g(x)$ both are odd, then $S(x) = f(x) + g(x)$
$S(-x) = f(-x) + g(-x) = -[f(x) + g(x)]$, $S(x)$ is an odd function. This conclusion rejects option (a).
Their product $P(x) = f(x).g(x)$.
$P(-x) = f(-x).g(-x) = [-f(x)][-g(x)] = f(x)g(x)$. $P(x)$ is an even function. This is what is being said by the option (c). Hence, it is the correct answer.
If we check for option (b) we can see that: when $f(x)$ and $g(x)$ both are even then $S(x) = f(x) + g(x)$
$S(-x) = f(-x) + g(-x) = [f(x) + g(x)]$, $S(x)$ is an even function.
Hence, only option (c) is true.

94. $f(g(-x)) = f(-g(x)) = f(g(x))$
$\therefore f(g(x))$ is an even function.
$g(f(x)) = g(f(-x)) = g(f(x))$
$\therefore g(f(x))$ is an even function.
Hence, option (c) is true.

Level of Difficulty (II)

1. Given, $f(1) = 1$. Putting $x = 2$, we get, $f(1) + 2f(2) = 6f(2) \rightarrow 4f(2) = 1 \rightarrow f(2) = 1/4$.
For $x = 3$, we get, $f(1) + 2f(2) + 3f(3) = 12f(3) \rightarrow 3/2 = 9f(3) \rightarrow f(3) = 1/6$
For $x = 4$, we get, $f(1) + 2f(2) + 3f(3) + 4f(4) = 20f(4) \rightarrow 2 = 16f(4) \rightarrow f(4) = 1/8$.
From this we see that, different terms would be equal to $1/(2x)$.
So $f(1024) = 1/2048$ & $f(2048) = 1/4096$
Hence, required answer is 2. Option (b) is the correct answer.

2. Putting $x = 1 - x$ in $f(x)$, we see that $f(x) = f(1 - x)$. So $f(1/2025) = f(2024/2025)$. Hence, the corresponding terms will total up to 0 for all pairs of $f(x)$ and $f(1 - x)$. Hence, the answer would be 0.

3. For the function f, we get
$f(1) = 2$; $f(2) = 1/2$; $f(3) = 2$; $f(4) = 1/2$ and so on. Thus, $f(x)$ is an alternating series between 2 values.
For function g, we get the terms as follows:
$g(1) = 0.5$; $g(2) = 0$; $g(3) = 2.5$; $g(4) = 2$; $g(5) = 4.5$; $g(6) = 4$
$g(7) = 6.5$ and so on. In this function we see that alternate terms are increasing by 2. Hence, a group of 2 terms increases by 4. So for every two terms, the sum of series is 0.5 + 4.5 + 8.5 + 12.5 + 16.5 + 20.5 + 24.5 [$g(1) + \ldots g(14)$]. For the sum to cross 100, we would need to take one more term. Hence, Option (a) is the correct answer.

4. $f(x - 3) = 2x^3 + p - qx$. Let $x = 3$, then $f(0) = 54 + p - 3q$
$f(x^2 - 4) = x^2 - 8q + 6p$
At $x = 2$, then $f(0) = 4 - 8q + 6p$. Equating these two values of $f(0)$ we get:
$54 + p - 3q = 4 - 8q + 6p$
$50 = 5p - 5q$
$p - q = 10$
Hence, Option (b) is the correct answer.

5. Since $f(x) \geq 0$, it only has 1 root which is equal to 3. Hence, required function $f(x) = k(x - 3)^2 \rightarrow f(x) = k(x^2 - 6x + 9)$.
And $f(6) = 9 \rightarrow 9k = 9 \rightarrow k = 1$.
$f(-1) - f(-3) \rightarrow 16 - 36 = -20$. Hence, Option (b) is the correct answer.

6. Since, a is an even positive integer, the first expression we get is when $a = 2$. The expression would be $|x| + |x - 3| + |x - 6|$. This gets minimized when $x = 3$. The value of the expression would be 6. This fits in the expression given in options (a) and (d). In order to distinguish between options (a) and (d) we need to check for $a = 4$. For $a = 4$, the first option would give us a value of 18, while the fourth option would give us a value of 20. Hence, we are sure to be able to distinguish between the two once we find a value for the expression. The expression would be: $|x| + |x - 3| + |x - 6| + |x - 9| + |x - 12|$. This is minimized at $x = 6$ and the value turns out to be 18. This matches the expression in option (a) and hence, we can reject option (d) and select option (a) as the answer. Hence, Option (a) is the correct answer.

7. The function will attain a minimum value when $6x - 8x^2$ is equal to 1.
$6x - 8x^2 = 1 \rightarrow 8x^2 - 6x + 1 = 0 \rightarrow x = 1/2, 1/4$. For both these values we get our answer as 1. Hence, 1 is the correct answer.

8. The function will attain a maximum value when both the given terms are equal to each other.
$2x - 6x^2 = -4 \rightarrow 6x^2 - 2x - 4 = 0 \rightarrow 3x^2 - x - 2 = 0 \rightarrow x = 1, -2/3$. For both these values we get our answer as -4. Since we get 2 values of x, the difference between the minimum value of the function and the value of x at which it is achieved cannot be determined distinctly. Hence, Option (d) is the correct answer.

9. The given expression whose value has to be evaluated has three values for the argument of $f()$ – viz: x, $x - 1$ and $x - 2$. So, we will need to work out at least three values of $f(x)$ in order to make out a value of the given expression. Using the expression: $f(x) = 2^x - 2^{-x}$ we get:
$f(0) = 0$; $f(1) = 3/2$; $f(2) = 15/4$.
Putting $x = 2$ in the expression given, we get $2f(2) - 5f(1) + 2f(0)$. Putting the respective values, we get $15/2 - 15/2 + 0 = 0$. To confirm this answer, we can also try to find out the value of the expression at $x = 3$. $f(3) = 55/8$. So, $2f(3) - 5(f(2) + 2(f(1)) =$

$63/4 - 75/4 + 3 = 0$. This confirms the value of the given expression will always be 0. Hence, 0 is the correct answer.

10. $f(1)^2 = f(2) + f(0) \rightarrow f(2) = 4$;
$f(2)\,f(1) = f(3) + f(1) \rightarrow f(3) = 6$;
$f(3)\,f(1) = f(4) + f(2) \rightarrow f(4) = 8$;
$f(4)\,f(1) = f(5) + f(3) \rightarrow f(5) = 10$
We get $f(5) = 10$, which means the given product will have units digit as 0.
11. $f(1) + f(2) = 4f(2) \rightarrow f(2) = f(1)/3$
$f(1) + f(2) + f(3) = 9f(3) \rightarrow f(3) = f(2)/2 \rightarrow f(3) = f(1)/6$
$f(1) + f(2) + f(3) + f(4) = 16f(4) \rightarrow f(4) = f(1)/10$
From the above example we see that $f(n) = 2f(1)/n(n + 1)$
$f(200) = 2f(1)/(200 \times 201)$
$f(201) = 2f(1)/(201 \times 202)$
$f(200)/f(201) = 202/200 \rightarrow 1.01$. Hence, Option (c) is the correct answer.
12. Let's try putting values from the given options. Using option (a), which gives us a value of $b = -1/3$, this gives us:
$|a| = 5.5 \rightarrow a = \pm 5.5$
This gives us two values of $|a| - [a] = 0.5$ or 11.5. But, the problem tells us $|a| - [a] = 10$, which is not satisfied by this option. Hence, we can reject option (a).
Going through option (b), $b = 4/3$, gives us $|a| = 4 \rightarrow a = \pm 4 \rightarrow |a| - [a] = 0$ or 8, which again helps us reject option (b) for us.
Going through option (c), we get: $b = -2/3 \rightarrow |a| = 5 \rightarrow a = \pm 5$
$|a| - [a] = 0$ or 10. This matches the information given in the question. Hence, option (c) is correct.
13. Putting $x = 1 \rightarrow f(1) + f(2) + f(2) + f(1) = 2 \rightarrow f(1) + f(2) = 1$
Putting $x = 0 \rightarrow 2f(0) + f(1) + f(2) = 0$.
From the first equation, we get $f(0) = -1/2$. Hence, Option (b) is the correct answer.
14. Let $7x - 5y = a$ and $3x + 7y = b \rightarrow 7a + 5b = 64x \rightarrow f(a, b) = 7a + 5b$
$f(2x, 5x) = 14x + 25x = 39x = 78$. Hence, $x = 2$ is the correct answer.
15. $-f(x)$ will be the mirror image of the function, about the x-axis which is seen in option (b).
16. $-f(x) + 1$ will be mirror image about the x-axis and then shifted up by 1. Option (a) satisfies this.
17. $f(x) - 1$ will shift down by 1 unit. Thus option (c) is correct.
18. $f(x) + 1$ will shift up by 1 unit. Thus, option (d) is correct.
19. The required minimum value will occur at $f(x) = g(x) = 1$.
20. $SQ\,[R[(a + b)/b]] = SQ\,[R[17/5]] \Rightarrow SQ\,[2] = 2$
21. $Q\,[[SQ(63) + 7\,]/9] = Q\,[[\,8 + 7]/9] = Q\,[15/9] = 1$
22. $Q\,[[SA\,(36) + R\,(18/7)]/2] = Q\,[(7 + 4)/2] = Q\,[11/2] = 5$
23. $[x] - \{x\} = -1$
24. $[x] + \{x\}$ will always be odd as the values are consecutive integers.
25. At $x = 5.5$, the given equation can be seen to be satisfied as: $6 + 5 = 2 \times 5.5 = 11$.
26. $f(g(t)) - g(f(t)) = f(2.5) - g(6) = 8.25 - 2.166 = 6.0833$
27. fog $= f(3t + 2) = k(3t + 2) + 1$
gof $= g\,(kt + 1) = 3(\,kt + 1) + 2$
$$k(\,3t + 2) + 1 = 3\,(kt + 1) + 2$$
$$\Rightarrow \quad 2\,k + 1 = 5$$
$$\Rightarrow \quad k = 2$$
28. When the value of $x = 81$ and 82 is substituted in the given expression, we get,
$F(81)\,F(82) = -\,F(80)\,F(79)\,F(78)\,F(77)$ (1)
$F(82)\,F(83) = -\,F(81)\,F(80)\,F(79)\,F(78)$ (2)
On dividing (1) by (2), we get
$$\frac{F(81)}{F(83)} = \frac{F(77)}{F(81)} \rightarrow F(81) \times F(81) = 81 \times 9$$
$F(81) = 27$
Hence, option (a) is the correct answer.
29. In order to understand this question, you first need to develop your thought-process about what the value of $h(x)$ is in various cases. A little bit of trial-and-error will show you that the value of $h(x)$ since it depends on the minimum of $f(x)$ and $g(x)$, would definitely be dependent on the value of $f(x)$; once x becomes greater than +11 or less than –11. Also, the value of $g(x)$ is fixed as an integer at 16, whenever x is between –8 to +8. Also, at $x = 9$, $x = 10$ and $x = -9$ and $x = -10$, the value of $h(x)$ would still be an integer.
With this thought, when you look at the expression of $f(x) = 121 - x^2$, you realise that the value of x can be –10, –9, –8, –7, …0, 1, 2, 3,….8, 9, 10, i.e. 21 values of x when $h(x) = g(x)$. When we use $x = 11$ or $x = -11$, the value of $f(x) = 0$ and is not a positive integral value.
Hence, the correct answer is option (c).
30. Since, $R(x)$ is the maximum amongst the three given functions, its value will always be equal to the highest amongst the three. It is easy to imagine that $x^2 - 8$ and $3x$ are increasing functions, therefore, the value of the function is continuously increasing as you increase the value of x. Similarly $x^2 - 8$ would be increasing continuously as you go farther and farther down on the negative side of the x-axis. Hence, the maximum value of $R(x)$ would be infinity. Thus,

option (c) is the correct answer.

31. In this case, the value of the function, is the minimum of the three values. If you visualise the graphs of the three functions (viz: $y = x^2 - 8$, $y = 3x$ and $y = 8$), you realise that the function $y = 3x$ (being a straight line) will keep going to negative infinity as you move to the left of zero on the negative side of the x-axis. Hence, the minimum value of the function $R(x)$ after a certain point (when x is negative) would get dictated by the value of $3x$. This point will be the intersection of the line $y = 3x$ and the function $y = x^2 - 8$, when x is negative.
The two intersection points of the line ($3x$) and the quadratic curve ($x^2 - 8$) will be obtained by equating $3x = x^2 - 8$. Solving this equation tells us that the intersection points are:
$\frac{3-\sqrt{41}}{2}$ and $\frac{3+\sqrt{41}}{2}$.
$R(x)$ would depend on the following structures based on the value of x:
(i) When x is smaller than $\frac{3-\sqrt{41}}{2}$, the value of the function $R(x)$ will be given by the value of $3x$.
(ii) When x is between $\frac{3-\sqrt{41}}{2}$ and 4 is the value of the function $R(x)$ will be given by the value of $x^2 - 8$, since that would be the least amongst the three functions.
(iii) After $x = 4$, on the positive side of the x-axis, the value of the function will be defined by the third function, viz: $y = 8$.
A close look at these three ranges will give you that amongst these three ranges, the third range would yield the highest value of $R(x)$. Hence, the maximum possible value of $R(x) = 8$. Thus, option (b) is correct.

32. The expression is $2x^2 - 5x + 4$, and its value at $x = 5$ will be equal to $50 - 25 + 4 = 29$. Thus, option (b) is correct.

33. At $x = 0$, the value of the function is 20 and this value rejects the first option. Taking some higher values of x, we realise that on the positive side, the value of the function will become negative when we take x greater than 5, since the value of $(5 - x)$ would be negative. Also, the value of $f(x)$ would start tending to $-\infty$, as we take bigger values of x.
Similarly, on the negative side, when we take the value of x lower than -4, $f(x)$ becomes positive and when we take it farther away from 0 on the negative side, the value of $f(x)$ would continue tending to $+\infty$. Hence, option (c) is the correct answer.

34. The remainder when $6^x + 4$ is divided by 2 would be 0 in every case (when x is odd).
Also, when x is even, we would get $6^x - 3$ as an odd number. In every case, the remainder would be 1 (when it is divided by 2).
Between $f(2)$, $f(4)$, $f(6)$,….$f(1000)$, there are 500 instances when x is even. In each of these instances, the remainder would be 1 and hence, the remainder would be 0 (in total). Thus, option (b) is correct.

35. The product of p, q and r will be maximum, if p, q and r are as symmetrical as possible. Therefore, the possible combination is (4, 3, 3).
Hence, maximum value of $pq + qr + pr + pqr = 4 \times 3 + 4 \times 3 + 3 \times 3 + 4 \times 3 \times 3 = 69$.
Hence, option (c) is correct.

36. The equation given in the question is: $3\alpha(x) + 2\alpha(2-x) = (x + 3)^2$ (1)
Replacing x by $(2-x)$ in the above equation, we get
$3\alpha(2-x) + 2\alpha(x) = (5-x)^2$
Solving the above pairs of equation, we get
$5\alpha(x) = 3(x + 3)^2 - 2(5 - x)^2 = 3(x^2 + 6x + 9) - 2(25 - 10x + x^2) = 3x^2 + 18x + 27 - 50 + 20x - 2x^2 = x^2 + 38x - 23$
Thus, $\alpha(x) = (x^2 + 38x - 23)/5$
Thus, $\alpha(-5) = -188/5 = -37.6$. The value of $[-37.6] = -38$. Hence, option (b) is the correct answer.

37. The first thing you do in this question is to create the chain of values of $f(x)$ for $x = 1, 2, 3$ and so on. The chain of values will look something like this:

When x is odd			*When x is even*		
$f(1)$	Value is given	6	$f(2)$	Value is given	4
$f(3)$	$= 1 + f(1)$	7	$f(4)$	$= 3 + f(2)$	7
$f(5)$	$= 3 + f(3)$	10	$f(6)$	$= 3 + f(4)$	10
$f(7)$	$= 5 + f(5)$	15	$f(8)$	$= 3 + f(6)$	13
$f(9)$	$= 7 + f(7)$	22	$f(10)$	$= 3 + f(8)$	16
$f(11)$	$= 9 + f(9)$	31			

In order to evaluate the value of the embedded function represented by $(f(f(f(f(1)))))$, we can use the above values and think as follows:
$f(f(f(f(1)))) = f(f(f(6))) = f(f(10)) = f(16) = 25$
Also, $f(f(f(f(2)))) = f(f(f(4))) = f(f(7)) = f(15) = 55$
Hence, the product of the two values is $25 \times 55 = 1375$.
Thus, option (a) is correct.

38. For $x > 0$, $x+\frac{1}{x}$ has a minimum value of 2, when x is taken as 1. Why we would need to minimise $x+\frac{1}{x}$ is because it is raised to the power 6 in the numerator, so allowing $x+\frac{1}{x}$ to become greater than its minimum will increase the value of the

expression. Also, the value of any expression of the form $x^n + \frac{1}{x^n}$ will also give us a value of 2. Hence, the value of the expression would be:

$$\frac{\left(x+\frac{1}{x}\right)^6 - \left(x^6+\frac{1}{x^6}\right) - 2}{\left(x+\frac{1}{x}\right)^3 + \left(x^3+\frac{1}{x^3}\right)} = \frac{2^6-2-2}{2^3+2} = 6$$

Hence, (d) is the correct choice.

39. $\left[\frac{1}{3}\right]+\left[\frac{1}{3}+\frac{1}{99}\right]+\left[\frac{1}{3}+\frac{2}{99}\right]+\left[\frac{1}{3}+\frac{65}{99}\right] = 0$

$\left[\frac{1}{3}+\frac{66}{99}\right]+\left[\frac{1}{3}+\frac{2}{99}\right]+\ldots+\left[\frac{1}{3}+\frac{98}{99}\right] = 33$

$\left[\frac{1}{3}\right]+\left[\frac{1}{3}+\frac{1}{99}\right]+\left[\frac{1}{3}+\frac{2}{99}\right]$

$+\ldots\left[\frac{1}{3}+\frac{98}{99}\right] = 0 + 33 = 33$

Hence, option (b) is correct.

40. $x^2 + 4xy + 6y^2 - 4y + 4$
$= x^2 + 4y^2 + 4xy + 2y^2 - 4y + 2 + 2$
$= (x + 2y)^2 + 2(y^2 - 2y + 1) + 2$
The above expression is minimum for $y = 1$, $x = -2$.
So minimum value of the given expression
$= 0 + 0 + 2 = 2.$

Hence, option (c) is correct.

41. Let $f(X) = 21 \sin X + 72 \cos X$
$\Rightarrow f'(X) = 21 \cos X - 72 \sin X$
If $f'(X) = 0$, $21 \cos X = 72 \sin X$
$\therefore \tan X = 21/72$ therefore, $\sin X = 21/75$, $\cos X = 72/75$ (Since, from the value of tan X, we can think of a right-angled triangle with the legs as 21 and 72, respectively. This would give us the hypotenuse length of the triangle as 75 – using the Pythagoras theorem.)
Since $f''(x) = -21 \sin X - 72 \cos X < 0$, therefore, $f(X)$ has a maximum at $f'(X) = 0$. Thus, we can use the values of $\sin X = 21/75$ and $\cos X = 72/75$.
$\therefore$ Maximum value of

$$f(x) = \frac{21.21}{75} + \frac{72.72}{75} = \frac{75^2}{75} = 75$$

Thus, option (d) is correct.

42. For $x < -7$
$|x + 7| + |x - 8| = -(x + 7) - (x - 8)$
$-(x + 7) - (x - 8) = 16$
$-2x + 1 = 16$
$x = -7.5$
For $-7 \le x \le 8$
$|x + 7| + |x - 8| = x + 7 - x + 8 = 15 \ne 16$
Therefore the given equation has no solution in this range.
For $x \ge 8$
$|x + 7| + |x - 8| = x + 7 + x - 8 = 2x - 1$
$2x - 1 = 16$
$\Rightarrow x = \frac{17}{2} = 8.5$
So the required sum $= -7.5 + 8.5 = 1$
Hence option (b) is correct.

43. $|3x + 4| \le 5$
$-5 \le 3x + 4 \le 5$
$-3 \le x \le 1/3$
$a = -3$, $b = 1/3$
$a + b = -3 + \frac{1}{3}$
$= -\frac{8}{3}$

44. $x^3 - 16x + x^2 + 20 \le 0 = (x + 5)(x - 2)^2 \le 0$
For any positive integer, the given expression can never be less than 0. Therefore, $x = 2$, is the only positive integer value of x for which the given inequality holds true. Alternately, you can also solve this question using trial-and-error, where you can start with $x = 1$ and then try to see the value of the expression at $x = 2$. At $x = 1$, the expression is positive, at $x = 2$ it is 0, while at $x = 3$, it again becomes positive. Once, x crosses 3, the term x^3 by itself will become so large that it would not be possible to pull the value of the expression into the non-positive territory because the magnitude of the negative term in the expression, viz. $16x$, would not be large enough to make the expression ≤ 0.

45. Putting $x = 7$ in the given equation, we get:
$3f(7) + 2f(11) = 70$ (1)
Similarly by putting $x = 11$ in the given equation, we get:
$3f(11) + 2f(7) = 98$ (2)
Solving equation (1) and (2) we get
$f(11) = \frac{154}{5} = 30.8$

46. $q = p \times [p]$
When you start to think about the values of q from 8 onwards to 16, the first solution is quite evident at $q = 9$ and $p = 3$. At $q = 10$, p can be taken to be 10/3 to give us the expression of $p \times [p]$ equal to 10. Similarly.
For $q = 11$, $p = 11/3$.
For $q = 16$, $p = 4$
So the required number of positive real values of $p = 4$.

47. Required product is $= 3 \times \frac{10}{3} \times \frac{11}{3} \times 4 = \frac{440}{3}$

48. $f(3) = f(1) + 8(1 + 1)$
$= -1 + 16 = 15$
$f(5) = f(3) + 8(3 + 1)$
$= (15 + 32)$
$= 47$

$f(10) = 4.f(5) + 9$
$= 4 \times 47 + 9$
$= 197$
$f(20) = 4 \times 197 + 9$
$= 797$
$f(22) = f(20) + 8(20 + 1)$
$= 797 + 168$
$= 965$
$f(24) = 965 + 8(22 + 1) = 1149$
$f(7) = f(5) + 8(5 + 1) = 47 + 48 = 95$
Hence, $f(24) - f(7) = 1149 - 95 = 1054$

49. If we observe values of $f(x)$ for different values of x, then we can see that $f(x) = 2x^2 - 3$.
Hence, $f(1000) = 2(1000)^2 - 3$
$= 1999{,}997$

50. $f(x) = (x^2 + [x]^2 - 2x[x])^{1/2} = \left[(x-[x])^2\right]^{\frac{1}{2}} = x - [x]$
$f(x) = x - [x]$ represents the fractional part of x.
Hence, $f(10.08) = 0.08$
$f(100.08) = 0.08$
$f(10.08) - f(100.08) = 0.08 - 0.08 = 0$

51. Let $f(x) = (x - 4)^7 (x - 3)^4 (x - 5)^2$
$f(1) = (1 - 4)^7 (1 - 3)^4 (1 - 5)^2$
$= (-3)^7 (-2)^4 (-4)^2$
$= -2^8.3^7$
Hence, option (c) is correct.

52. $f(x) = x - \frac{1}{3(3-x)} - 3 = (x-3) + \frac{1}{3(x-3)} \geq \left[(x-3)\times\frac{1}{3(x-3)}\right]^{\frac{1}{2}}$. Hence, $(x-3)+\frac{1}{3(x-3)} \geq \frac{1}{\sqrt{3}}$
Hence, option (b) is correct.

53.

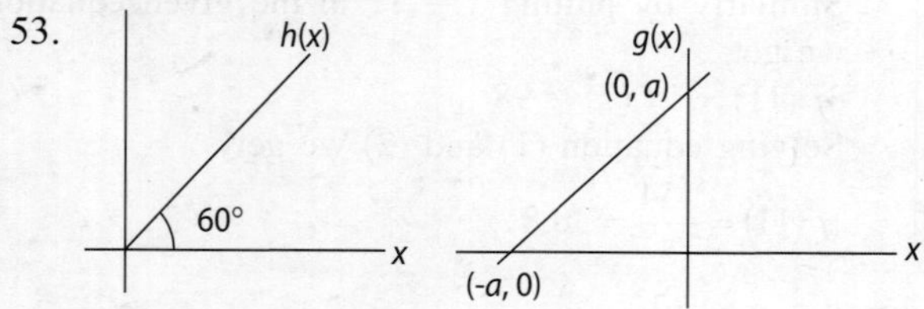

$h(x) = x\tan 60^\circ = x\sqrt{3}$

$x = \frac{h(x)}{\sqrt{3}}$

$\frac{x}{-a} + \frac{g(x)}{a} = 1$

$g(x) = \left[1 + \frac{x}{a}\right]a = a + x = a + \frac{h(x)}{\sqrt{3}}$

$\sqrt{3}g(x) = a\sqrt{3} + h(x)$

$\sqrt{3}g(x) - h(x) = a\sqrt{3}$

Hence, option (a) is correct.
Alternately, you can also solve this by looking at the values of the graphs. At $x = 0$, $h(x) = 0$ and $g(x) = a$. At $x = 1$, $h(x) = \sqrt{3}$ (This can be visualised, since the triangle that is formed by the graph of $h(x)$ with the x-axis is a 30-60,90 triangle. Hence, if we take the side opposite the 30° angle as 1, the height (side opposite the 60° angle) would be $\sqrt{3}$. Also, the value of $g(x)$ would be $a + 1$ (since the gradient of the $g(x)$ slope is 45°). The first option satisfies both these pairs of values. Hence, it is the correct answer.

54. $\frac{f(xy)}{f(x+y)} = 1$ or $f(xy) = f(x + y)$
Put $x = 0$: $f(0.y) = f(0 + y) \Rightarrow f(y) = f(0)$
Put $y = 0$: $f(x.0) = f(x + 0) \Rightarrow f(x) = f(0)$
Therefore, function 'f' is a constant function. (This can also be interpreted since the function reads that the value of f when you put an argument equal to the product of x and y is the same as the value of f when you put the argument of the function as $x + y$).
$f(-10) = f(10) = f(6) = 7$
$f(-10) + f(10) = 7 + 7 = 14$

55. Putting $x = 9$, $y = 3$, in the above equation we get

$f\left(\frac{9}{3}\right) = \frac{f(9)}{f(3)}$

$f(3) = \frac{f(9)}{f(3)}$

$f(9) = [f(3)]^2 = 5^2 = 25$

Similarly, $x = 81$, $y = 9$

$f\left(\frac{81}{9}\right) = \frac{f(81)}{f(9)}$

$f(9) = \frac{f(81)}{f(9)}$

$f(81) = [f(9)]^2 = 25^2 = 625$

56. We can find the sum of all coefficients of a polynomial by putting each of the variables equals to 1:
Therefore, the required sum $= (1 - 4)^3 (1 - 2)^{10} (1 - 3)^3$
$= -3^3 \times 1 \times (-2)^3$
$= 27 \times 8 = 216$

57. $f(a) = 3^a$ (If a is an odd number)
$f(a + 1) = 3^{a+1} + 4 = 3.3^a + 4$

$\frac{1}{4}[f(a) + f(a+1)] = \frac{3^a + 3.3^a + 4}{4}$

$= \frac{3^a.4 + 4}{4} = 3^a + 1$

$\Rightarrow \frac{1}{4}[f(1) + f(2)] + (f(3) + f(4))$
$+ \ldots + f(71) + f(72)]$

$= \frac{f(1)+f(2)}{4} + \frac{f(3)+f(4)}{4}$
$+ \ldots + \frac{f(71)+f(72)}{4}$

$= 3^1 + 1 + 3^3 + 1 + \ldots + 3^{71} + 1$
$= (3^1 + 3^3 + \ldots + 3^{71}) + 36$

$$= \frac{3\left(\left(3^2\right)^{36} - 1\right)}{3^2 - 1} + 36$$

(Using the formula for the sum of a geometric progression, since the series containing the powers of 3 is essentially a geometric progression).

$$= \frac{3}{8}\left(3^{72} - 1\right) + 36$$

58. Put $x = 0$, then $f(0 + y) = f(0) \to f(y) = p$
Put $y = 0$, then $f(x + 0) = f(0) \to f(x) = p$
Therefore, 'f' is a constant function.
$f(7) = f(10) = f(5) = 12$
$[f(7)]^{143} - [f(11)]^{143} + f(5) = 12^{143} - 12^{143} + 12 = 12$

59. 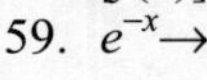

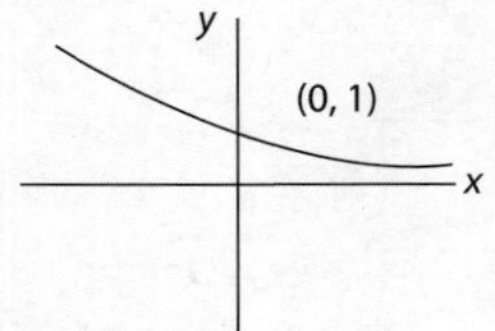

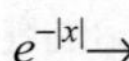

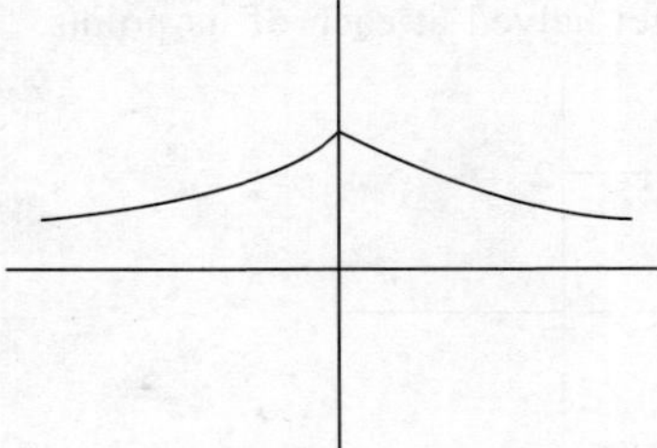

$|e^{-|x|}| \to$

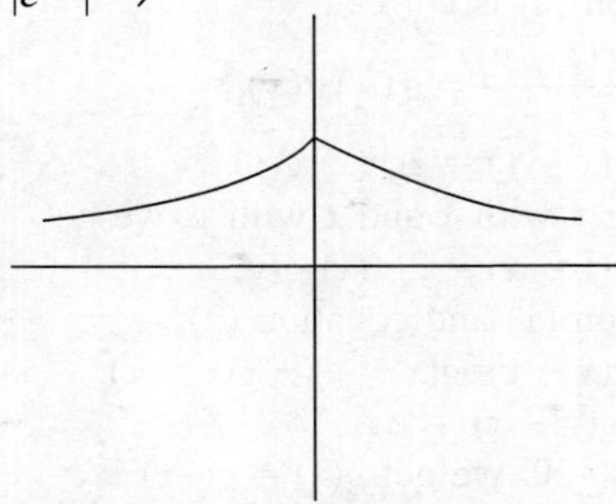

Hence, option (c) is correct.

60. $e^{-x} \to$

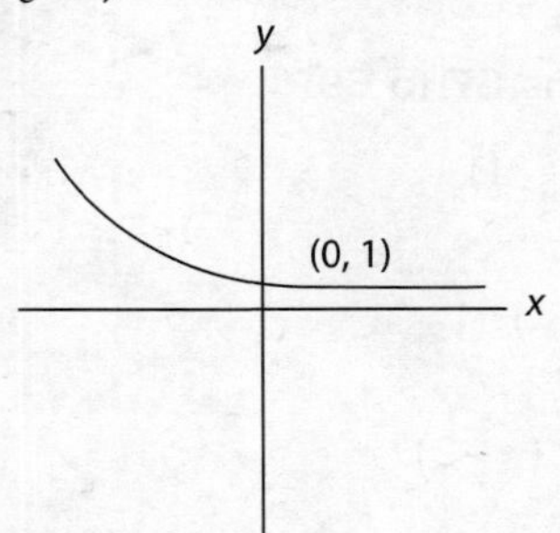

$e^{-x} - 3 \to$

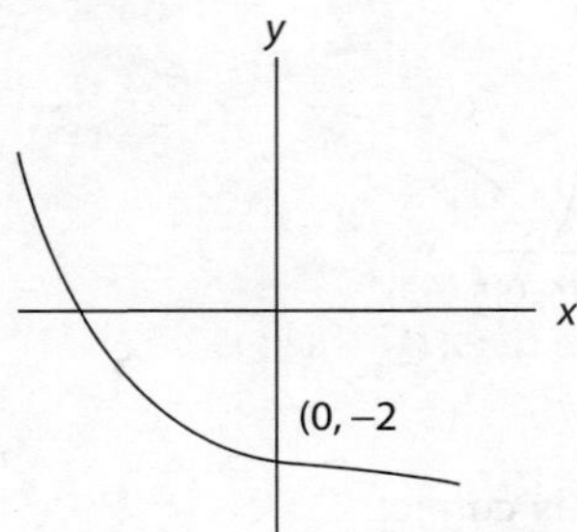

$|e^{-x} - 3| \to$

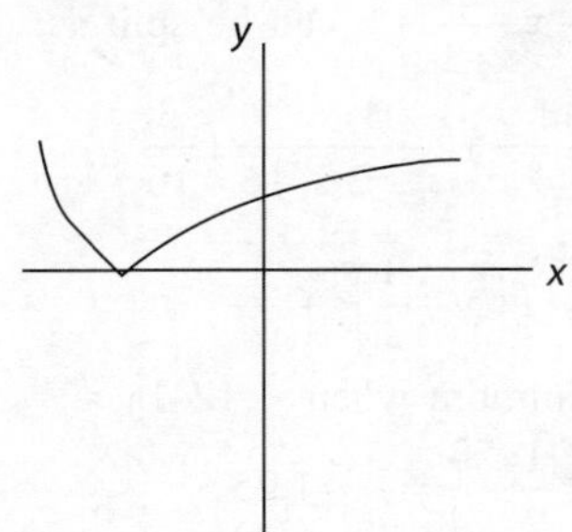

Hence, option (a) is correct.

61. Log $x \to$

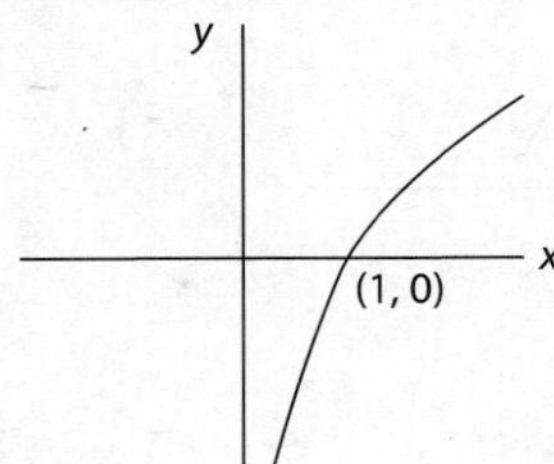

$\log|x| \to$

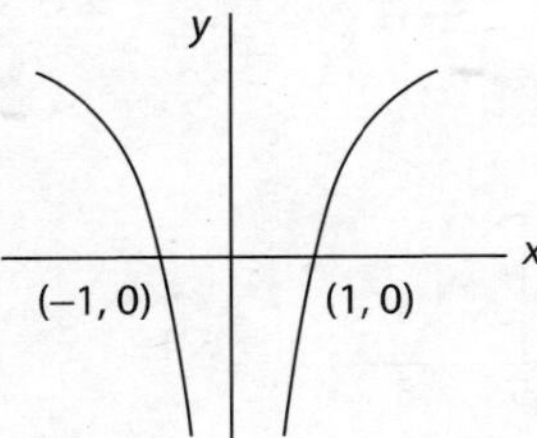

$\log|x-3| \to$

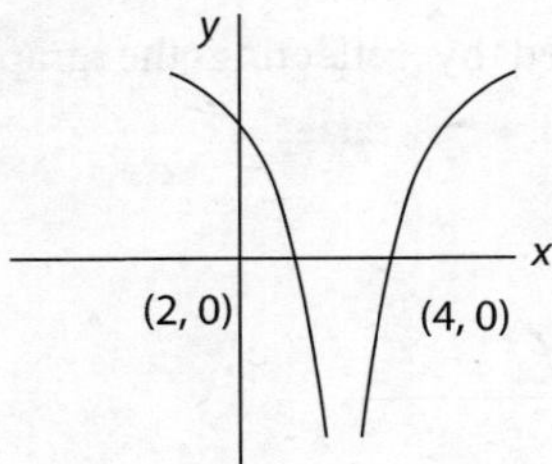

$||\log|x-3|| \rightarrow$

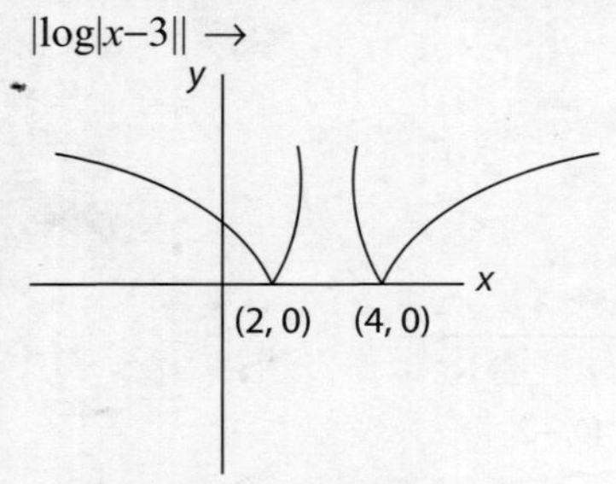

Hence, option (d) is correct.

62. $f(x, y) = x^2 + y^2 - x - \frac{3y}{2} + 1$ can be split as:

$$= x^2 - x + \frac{1}{4} + y^2 - \frac{3y}{2} + \frac{9}{16} + \frac{3}{16}$$

$$= \left(x - \frac{1}{2}\right)^2 + \left(y - \frac{3}{4}\right)^2 + \frac{3}{16}$$

$f(x, y)$ will be minimum when $x = ½$, $y = ¾$

Therefore, $x + y = \frac{1}{2} + \frac{3}{4} = \frac{5}{4} = 1.25$

63. $f(x, y)$ min = 3/16

64. $f(x + 5)$

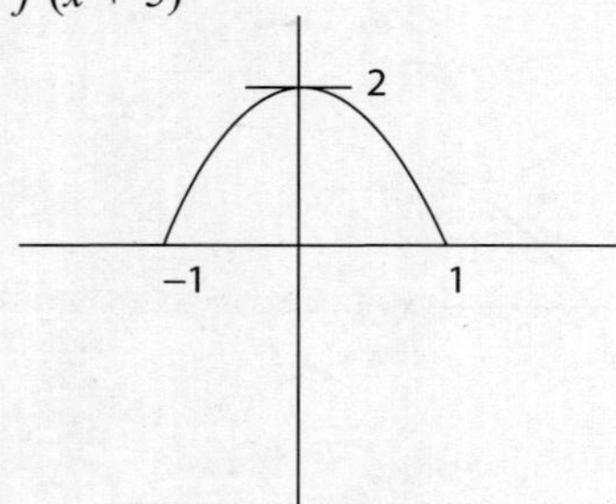

$f(x)$ can be obtained by shifting $f(x + 5)$ right by 5 units.

$f(x) \Rightarrow$

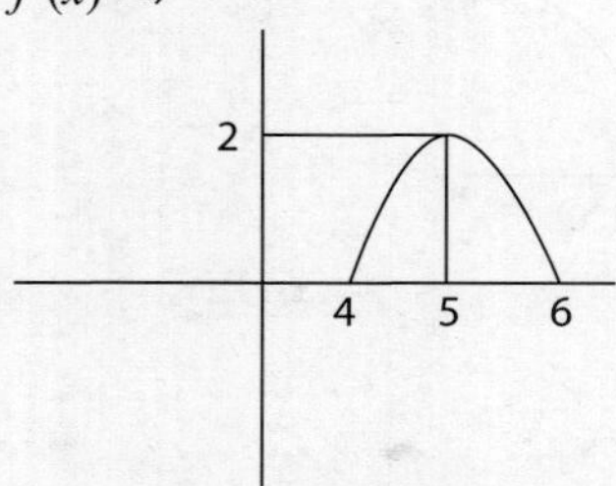

$f(-x)$can be obtained by reflecting the graph $f(x)$ about the y – axis

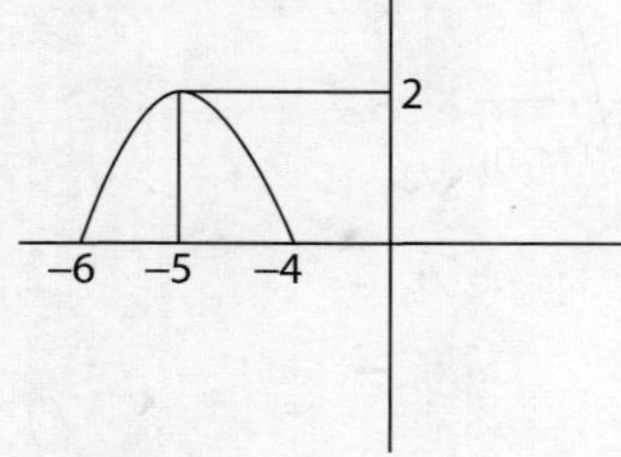

$f(-x - 2)$ can be obtained by shifting curve of $f(-x)$ to the right by 2 units

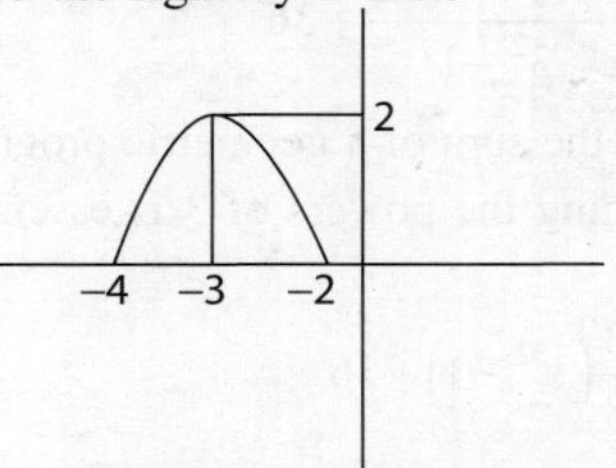

Hence, option (d) is correct.

65. From our discussion of the previous question, we know that $f(-x)$ will look as below:

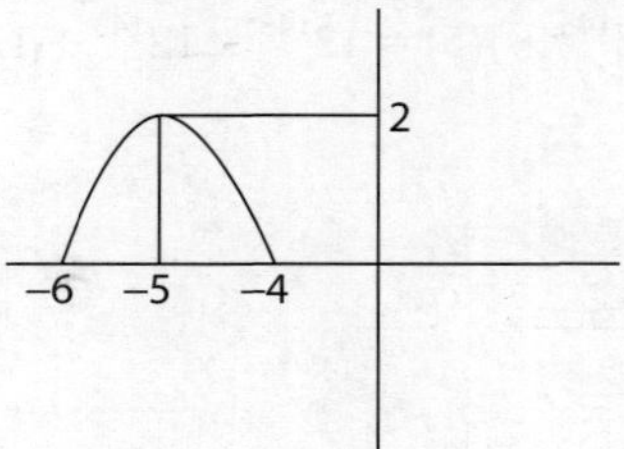

$f(-2x)$ would mean that the graph's value on the x-axis, will get halved at each of its points.

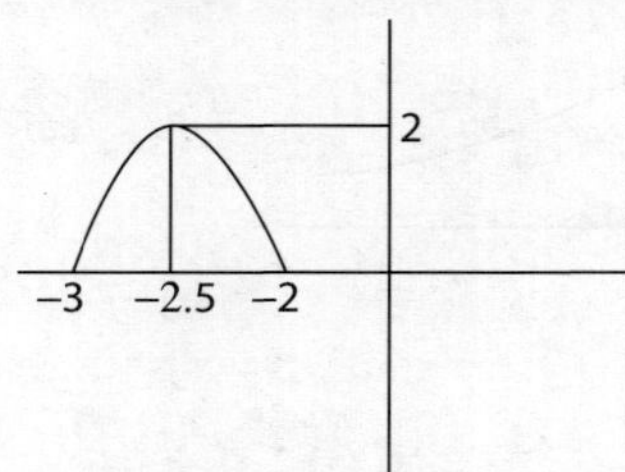

Hence, option (c) is correct.

66. $\frac{g(x+y)+g(x-y)}{2} = g(x)g(y)$

$g(x + y) + g(x - y) = 2g(x)\, g(y)$ (1)

By replacing y with x and x with y, we get

$g(x + y) + g(y - x) = 2g(x)\, g(y)$ (2)

From equation (1) and equation (2),

$g(x + y) + g(x - y) = g(x + y) + g(y - x)$

$g(x - y) = g(y - x)$

By putting $y = 0$, we get $g(x) = g(-x)$

Therefore, $g(x)$ must be an even function: therefore only option (c) satisfies because it also represents an even function.

Solutions for Questions 67 to 69:

$f(x) = (1 - \frac{1}{x})\, f(x - 1)$

$f(x) = \frac{x-1}{x} f(x-1)$

$f(x - 1) = \frac{x-2}{x-1} f(x-2)$

$f(x-2) = \frac{x-3}{x-2} f(x-3)$ and so on till $f(1)$

In the value of $f(x)$, if we replace the value of $f(x-1)$ with $\frac{x-2}{x-1} f(x-2)$ and then subsequently replace $f(x-2)$ with $f(x-2) = \frac{x-3}{x-2} f(x-3)$, we will end with a chain that would end with $f(1)$. After doing so, we will get the following equation:

$f(x) = \frac{x-1}{x} \times \frac{x-2}{x-1} \times \frac{x-3}{x-2} \times \ldots f(1)$

Thus, we get the expression: $f(x) = f(1)/x$.

67. According to the question, $f(3) = 10$.
$f(3) = f(1)/3 = 10$. Thus, $f(1) = 30$.

68. $f(1000) = f(1)/1000 = 10/1000 = 0.01$

69. $\frac{1}{f(1)} + \frac{1}{f(2)} + \frac{1}{f(3)} + \ldots + \frac{1}{f(9)} = \frac{1}{f(1)} + \frac{2}{f(1)} + \frac{3}{f(1)} + \ldots + \frac{8}{f(1)} = \frac{36}{f(1)} = \frac{36}{12} = 3$

Solutions for Questions 70 and 71:

70. $f(x) = \sqrt{f(x-1) f(x+1)}$. Squaring both the sides, we get: $f(x+1) = \frac{[f(x)]^2}{f(x-1)}$

Since, we are given the values of $f(0)$ and $f(1)$, we get:

$f(2) = \frac{[f(1)]^2}{f(0)} = \frac{1}{4}$

$f(3) = \frac{[f(2)]^2}{f(1)} = \frac{\frac{1}{16}}{\frac{1}{2}} = \frac{1}{8}$

71. Similarly, $f(4) = \frac{1}{16}, f(5) = \frac{1}{32}$

$f(1) + f(2) + f(3) + \ldots f(\infty) =$

$\frac{1}{2} + \frac{1}{4} + \frac{1}{8} + \frac{1}{16} + \ldots = \frac{\frac{1}{2}}{1 - \frac{1}{2}} = 1$

(Using the formula for the sum of an infinite geometric progression.)

72. $f(x) = \frac{x+3}{2 \times (x^2 + 6x + 9)} = \frac{x+3}{2(x+3)^2} = \frac{1}{2(x+3)}$

As x is non-negative integer so the maximum possible value of $f(x)$ would occur, when $x = 0$. We get the maximum possible value of $f(x) = \frac{1}{2 \times (0+3)} = \frac{1}{6}$.

Solutions for Questions 73 and 74:

Assume that the original polynomial is: $f(x) = Q[(x)(x-2)(x-3)] + px + q$, where p and q are constants.

(**Note:** We make this assumption, in order to solve the question through the process that follows. In this assumption.)

The remainder when a polynomial in x, is divided by $(x - a)$, is obtained by inserting the value of $x = a$, in the polynomial. Using this logic, we can see that:

For $x = 2$, $f(2) \rightarrow 2p + q = 3$

For $x = 3$, $f(3) \rightarrow 3p + q = 2$

On solving, we get: $p = -1$ and $q = 5$

Hence, the correct polynomial would be

$f(x) = Q[(x)(x-2)(x-3)] + (5 - x)$

73. $f(3) = 2$

74. When we divide $f(x)$ by $(x-2)(x-3)$, then the remainder is $5 - x$. Hence, option (b) is correct.

Solutions for Questions 75 to 77:

75. $\left[\frac{x}{7}\right] = \left[\frac{x}{9}\right]$

For $0 \le x \le 6$, both LHS and RHS are equal to 0. (7 solutions)

For $9 \le x \le 13$, both LHS and RHS are equal to 1. (5 solutions)

For $18 \le x \le 20$ both LHS and RHS are equal to 2. (3 solutions)

For $x = 27$, both LHS and RHS are equal to 3. (1 solution)

After $x = 27$, there would be no value at which the LHS and RHS give the same answer.

Hence, the number of non-negative integral solutions is 7 + 5 + 3 + 1 = 16 solutions.

For $-7 \le x \le -1$, both LHS and RHS is equal to –1. (7 solutions)

For $-14 \le x \le -10$ both LHS and RHS is equal to –2. (5 solutions)

For $-21 \le x \le -19$ both LHS and RHS is equal to –3. (3 solutions)

For $x = -28$, both LHS and RHS is equal to –4. (1 solution)

Hence, the number of non-negative integral solutions is 7 + 5 + 3 + 1 = 16 solutions.

Total number of integral solutions = 16 + 16 = 32 solutions.

76. Required sum = 0 + 1 + 2 + 3 + …. + 6 + 9 + 10 + … + 13 + 18 + 19 + 20 + 27 – (1 + 2 + …. + 7 + 10 + … + 14 + 19 + 20 + 21 + 28) = (0 – 7 + 9 – 14 + 18 – 21 + 27 – 28) = –16

77. Maximum value of $x = 27$

Solutions for Questions 78 and 79:

78. $(x^2 - 7x + 13)^{2x+5} = 1$

The above equation is possible when $2x + 5 = 0$ or When $2x + 5 = 0$, then $x = -5/2$.

When $x^2 - 7x + 13 = 1$, then $x = 3$ or 4.

Hence, for three values of x, $f(x) = 1$.

79. Required sum = $3 + 4 - 5/2 = 4.5$

80. $f(x + 2) = |x-1|+|x-2|+|x-3|$

It can be seen that this would reach its minimum value when $x = 2$. Since, the question tells us that $f(x + 2)$ is minimum at $x = k$, we get: $k = 2$.

Solutions for Questions 81 and 82:

81. $f(x) = 2 - 1/f(x - 1)$

For $x = 2$, $f(2) = 2 - 1/f(1)$ or $f(1) = 2$.

Similarly, $f(3) = 4/3$, $f(4) = 5/4$ and so on. We can observe that, $f(n) = (n + 1)/n$

$f(500) = 501/500$

82. $f(n) = (n + 1)/n = 1 + 1/n$

$[f(n)] = [1 + 1/n] = 1$. Hence, $[f(100001)] = 1$

83. $\dfrac{[x]-2}{4-[x]} > 0$ when $[x] < 4$ and $[x] > 2$

It is only possible when $[x] = 3 \Rightarrow x \in [3,4)$. Hence, option (b) is correct.

Solutions for Questions 84 and 85:

84. $f(xy) = f(x) \times f(y)$

$f(4) = f(2) \times f(2) = [f(2)]^2 = 2^2 = 4$

$f(2) < f(3) < f(4)$

f(x) is an integer valued function. $f(3)$ must be an integer. Hence, $f(3) = 3$.

85. From the above analysis, we can say that $f(n) = n$. Hence, $f(2001) = 2001$.

86. $n^2 f(n) + f(1-n) = 2n - n^4$

On putting $n = -1$, we get:

$f(-1) + f(2) = 2(-1) - (-1)^4 = -3$ (1)

On putting $n = 2$, we get:

$4f(2) + f(-1) = 2(2) - (2)^4 = -12$ (2)

On solving equation (1) and (2), we get $f(2) = -3$

On putting $n = 5$, we get:

$25f(5) + f(-4) = -615$ (3)

On putting $n = -4$, we get:

$16f(-4) + f(5) = -264$ (4)

On solving equation (3) and (4), we get: $f(5) = -24$

Hence, $f(2)\,f(5) = -3 \times -24 = 72$.

87. $(x-2)(x(x+1)(x+2)(x+3)(x+4).....(x+202))$

$= (x-2)(x(x+1)(x+2)(x+3)(x+4).....(x+202))$

$= (x-2)(x^{203} + x^{202}(1+2+3+\ldots+202)+..)$

Coefficient of x^{203} is $= -2+(1+2+3+\ldots 202) = -2+202\times\dfrac{203}{2} = -2+20503 = 20501$

88. $f(x) = (x + 5) \times (36 - 12x) = 12 \times (3 - x)(x + 5)$

The value of $f(x)$ is maximum when $3 - x = x + 5$ or $x = -1$.

Maximum value of $f(x) = 12 \times (3 + 1) \times (-1 + 5) = 192$.

89. '$3a + 4$' and '$b - 12$' must be integers. Also, it is given to us that a and b must be integers. Therefore, $b - 2$ and $a - 4$ must be integers.

$f(b - 2) = b - 2 = 3a + 4$ or $b - 3a = 6$

$f(a - 4) = b - 12$ or $a - 4 = b - 12$ or $a - b = -8$

On solving the above two equations, we get: $a = 1$, $b = 9$

Product of a and $b = 1 \times 9 = 9$.

90. $f(g(x)) = \left[\dfrac{x^2}{9}\right]^{\left[\frac{x^2}{9}\right]}$

The value of $f(g(x))$ will be minimum when value of x is as low as possible. Since, x cannot be 0; the values of the expression would get minimised if $0 < g(x) < 1$. $f(g(x)) = 1$; this will be the minimum possible value of $f(g(x))$.

91. $g(x) - f(x) = (p-a)x^2 + (q-b)x - c$ for all x

$\therefore g(1) = f(1), g(2) - f(2) = 1 and g(3) - f(3) = 4$

$g(1) - f(1) = (p-a) + (q-b) - c = 0$ (1)

$g(2) - f(2) = 4(p-a) + 2(q-b) - c = 1$ (2)

$g(3) - f(3) = 9(p-a) + 3(q-b) - c = 4$ (3)

By solving equations 1, 2, 3, we get $p - a = 1$, $q - b = -2$ and $c = -1$

$\therefore g(4) - f(4) = 16(p-a) + 4(q-b) - c$

$= 16\times1 + 4\times-2 + 1 = 9$

Solutions for Questions 92 to 95:

$5f(x) + 2f\left(\dfrac{1}{x}\right) = 4x + 2$

$5f\left(\dfrac{1}{x}\right) + 2f(x) = \dfrac{4}{x} + 2$ (Replacing x by $1/x$)

On solving the above two equations for $f(x)$, we get:

$f(x) = \dfrac{1}{21}\left[\dfrac{20x}{} - \dfrac{8}{x} + \dfrac{6}{}\right]$

92. Putting $f(x) = 70$, gives us a quadratic equation whose sum of roots is 707/10

93. $f(2) = \dfrac{1}{21}\left(\dfrac{40}{} - \dfrac{8}{2} + \dfrac{6}{}\right) = \dfrac{84}{42} = 2$

94. $f(x) = \dfrac{1}{21}\left[\dfrac{20x}{} - \dfrac{8}{x} + \dfrac{6}{}\right] = \dfrac{18}{21} \rightarrow 20x^2 - 12x - 8 = 0$

$5x^2 - 3x - 2 = 0$

Sum of all values of x for which $f(x) = \dfrac{18}{21}$ is $(-b/a) = 3/5$

95. Product of roots= $c/a = -2/5 = -0.4$

Solutions for Questions 96 and 97:

96. $f(x) = 8a^2 - 8 + 8(x-1) - x^2 = 8a^2 - (x^2 - 8x + 16)$

$= 8a^2 - (x-4)^2$

Hence, $f(x)$ is maximum for $x = 4$.

97. $8a^2 = 72 \text{ or } a = 3 \text{ or } -3$

Required Sum = –3 + 3 = 0

Level of Difficulty (III)

1. The trigger points for this would be a, 20 and a + 20 in that order. It is given that x lies in the range [a, 20]. There will be three cases for the expression's value depending on relative values of a and x.
Case 1: If $x = a$. Then $f(x) = 40 - a$.
Case 2: If $x = 20$. Then $f(x) = 20$
Case 3: If x = anywhere between a and 20. Then $f(x) = 40 - x$. (Note: This happens since the value of $|x - a|$ would be $x - a$; $|x - 20|$ would be $20 - x$ and the value of $|x - a - 20|$ would be $20 - x + a$. Thus, the overall expression would be $x - a + 20 - x + 20 - x + a = 40 - x$.
In order to minimize the value of $f(x)$, we need to maximize the value of either x or a. 'a' can take a maximum value of 19 and 'x' can take 20. In either case the lowest total we achieve is 20.
Hence, 20 is the correct answer.
2. The trigger points for this would be for values of x as: b, 15 and b + 15 in that order. It is given that x lies in the range [b, 15]. For these three cases,
Case 1: If $x = b$. Then $f(x) = 30 - b$.
Case 2: If $x = 15$. Then $f(x) = 15$
Case 3: If x = anywhere between b and 15. Then $= |x - b| + |x - 15| + |x - b - 15| = x - b + 15 - x + 15 - x + b = f(x) = 30 - x$.
In order to minimize the value of $f(x)$, we need to maximize the value of either x or b. 'b' can get max value of 14 and 'x' can take 15. In either case the lowest total we achieve is 15. Hence, 15 is the correct answer.
3. It is given that x lies in the range [c, 18]. Let us assume,
$x = c$. Then $f(x) = 36 - c$.
$x = 18$. Then $f(x) = 18$
x = anywhere between c and 18. Then $f(x) = 36 - x$.
In order to maximize the value of $f(x)$, we need to minimize the value of either x or c. 'c' and 'x' can get a min value of 0. In either case the highest total we achieve is 36. Hence, 36 is the correct answer.
4. Since the value of $f(1) = 3$ and $f(x + y) = f(x) \times f(y)$, Value of $f(2) = f(1 + 1) = f(1) \times f(1) = 3^2$. Likewise, $f(3) = (f(2 + 1) = f(2) \times f(1) = 3^3$ and so on. Hence, $f(x) = 3^x$
RHS = $3^5(3^n - 1)/2$.
We know that $1 + 3 + 3^2 + 3^3 + .. + 3^n = (3^n - 1)/2$
So if we put $k = 4$, we get $f(5) + f(6) + \ldots + f(5 + n) = 3^5 + 3^6 + 3^7 + 3^8 + \ldots + 3^{5+n} = 3^5(3^n - 1)/2$
Taking 3^5 common we see that LHS = RHS.
Hence, Option (c) is the correct answer.
5. x can be written as $[x] + \{x\}$ where $\{x\}$ is the fractional part of x.
$3[x] = 4[x] + 4\{x\} - 2$.
$-4\{x\} = [x] - 2$
Integer – Integer = integer.
So LHS has to be an integer. For this to be possible, $\{x\} = 1/2$ or $1/4$.
If $\{x\} = 1/2$
$[x] - 2 = -2 \rightarrow [x] = 0 \rightarrow x = 0.5$
If $\{x\} = 1/4$
$[x] - 2 = -1 \rightarrow [x] = 1 \rightarrow x = 1.25$
Sum of all values of $x = 1.75$. Hence, Option (c) is the correct answer.
6. Lets find values for different x.
$f(1) = 1$
$f(2) = 1$
$f(3) = 3$
$f(4) = 6$
$f(5) = 8$
$f(6) = 8$
$f(7) = 7$
$f(8) = 7$
$f(9) = 9$
$f(10) = 12$
$f(11) = 14$
$f(12) = 14$
From the above sequence we see that it follows a six value pattern for the expression $f(x) - x$. These six values from $f(1)$ to $f(6)$ are: $f(x) - x = 0, -1, 0, +2, +3, +2$. The same values are repeated for $f(7) - 7$ to $f(12) - 12$. Now we form groups of 6 and $f(2024)$ will be the second term in the sequence. Hence, $f(2024) - 2024 = -1$. $\rightarrow f(2024) = 2023$. Hence, the answer is option (c).
7. Putting x & $y = 0$, we get $f(0)^2 = 2f(0) \rightarrow f(0) = 2$ (since $f(0) \neq 0$).
Putting x and y as 1 each, $f(1)^2 = f(2) + f(0) \rightarrow f(2) = 23$
$f(2)\, f(1) = f(3) + f(1) \rightarrow f(3) = 110$.
$f(3)\, f(1) = f(4) + f(2) \rightarrow f(4) = 527$.
We can generalise this to be $f(n + 1) = f(n) \times 5 - f(n - 1)$.
$f(5) = 2525$
$f(6) = 12098$
$f(7) = 57965$
Hence, Option (a) is the correct answer.
8. Putting $x = 2$, we get $12 + 4p + 2q = 0 \rightarrow 2p + q = -6$.
Since the product of roots is 2 and we already have a 2 as our root, the other two roots would be reciprocal of each other. And since two of the roots are equal, this is only possible when both of them are 2. Hence, the third root is 1/2. Using the sum of roots as $-p/2 = 9/2$ we get $p = -9$. Likewise, using the pairwise product of roots we get $q/2 = 6$, which gives us $q = 12$. Hence, the value of $q - p = 21$. Hence, Option (d) is the correct answer.

9. The problem in this question is that there is no value for any $f(x)$ given to us. Hence, the only way to solve this would be to create a workaround for that. We are given: $f(n) = f(n-2) + n(n-2)$; If we put the value of n as 2, we get: $f(2) = f(0)$.
For $n = 3$, we get: $f(3) = f(1) + 3$. At this point, it is natural to think about where this is leading us? Looking at the question, we should think of proceeding to $f(6)$ to be able to use $f(1) = -f(6)$ or $f(1) + f(6) = 0$. Hence, we continue to find:
$f(4) = f(2) + 8$; $f(5) = f(3) + 15$ & $f(6) = f(4) + 24$
Then, we have: $f(1) + f(6) = 0 \rightarrow f(3) - 3 + f(4) + 24 = 0 \rightarrow f(3) + f(4) = -21$
Now, since $f(3) + f(4) = -21$; using the values for $f(3)$ and $f(4)$ in terms of $f(5)$ and $f(2)$ we get:
$f(5) - 15 + f(2) + 8 = -21 \rightarrow f(2) + f(5) = -14$
So, $f(2) + f(3) + f(4) + f(5) = -35$. Hence, Option (a) is the correct answer.
10. $f(1) = f(0) + 1 \rightarrow f(1) = 1$;
$f(2) = f(1) + 2 \rightarrow f(2) = 3$;
$f(3) = f(2) + 3 \rightarrow f(3) = 6$;
$f(4) = f(3) + 4 \rightarrow f(4) = 10$;
$f(5) = f(4) + 5 \rightarrow f(5) = 15$;
$f(6) = f(5) + 6 \rightarrow f(6) = 21$;
This can be generalised as $f(x)$ = sum of 1 to x
$g(9) = g(8) + f(9)$
$g(10) = g(9) + f(10)$
$g(10) = g(8) + f(9) + f(10)$
$g(10) - g(8) = f(9) + f(10) \rightarrow 45 + 55 = 100$. Hence, 100 is the correct answer.
11. $f(1 + 0) = f(1) \times f(0) \rightarrow f(0) = 1$
$f(4 + -4) = f(0)$
$f(4 + -4) = f(4) \times f(-4)$
$1 = 3 \times f(-4) \rightarrow f(-4) = 1/3$
$f(-8) = f(-4 + (-4)) = f(-4) \times f(-4) = 1/9$. Hence, Option (b) is the correct answer.
12. Option (b) is not even since $e^x - e^{-x} \neq e^{-x} - e^x$.
13. We have $f(x) \cdot f(1/x) = f(x) + f(1/x)$
$\Rightarrow f(1/x)\,[f(x) - 1] = f(x)$
For $x = 4$, we have $f(1/4)\,[f(4) - 1] = f(4)$
$\Rightarrow f(1/4)\,[64] = 65$
$\Rightarrow f(1/4) = 65/64 = 1/64 + 1$
This means $f(x) = x^3 + 1$
For $f(6)$ we have $f(6) = 216 + 1 = 217$.

Solutions for Questions 14 to 19:

In order to solve this set of questions first analyse each of the functions:

$A(x, y, z)$ = will always return the value of the highest between x and y.

$B(x, y, z)$ will return the value of the maximum amongst x, y and z.

$C(x, y, z)$ and $D(x, y, z)$ will return the second highest values in all cases while max (x, y, z) and min(x, y, z) would return the maximum and minimum values amongst x, y, and z respectively.

14. When either x or y is maximum
15. This would never happen.
16. When z is maximum, A and B would give different values. Thus, option (c) is correct.
17. Never
18. I and III are always true
19. We cannot determine this because it would depend on whether the integers x, y, and z are positive or negative.
20. $g(f(x)) = 2.\dfrac{x^{2\left[\frac{3x^2}{4}\right]}}{4} + 2$
$= \dfrac{x^{2\left[\frac{3x^2}{4}\right]}}{2} + 2$
$g(f(x))$ is an even function, so option (a) is incorrect. As we increase the value of x, value of $g(f(x))$ will get increased. Therefore, it will attain its maxima at ∞. So option (b) is also incorrect.
$\dfrac{x^{2\left[\frac{3x^2}{4}\right]}}{2} + 2$ will attain its minima when $0 \le \dfrac{3x^2}{4} \le 1$.
Since, the expression $\dfrac{3x^2}{4}$ is always going to be positive, hence, we can say that the only constraint we need to match for the minima of the function is $\dfrac{3x^2}{4} \le 1$. Therefore, option(c) is true.
21. $\dfrac{x^{2\left[\frac{3x^2}{4}\right]}}{2} + 2 = 2^5 + 2 = 34$. Hence, option (b) is correct.
22.

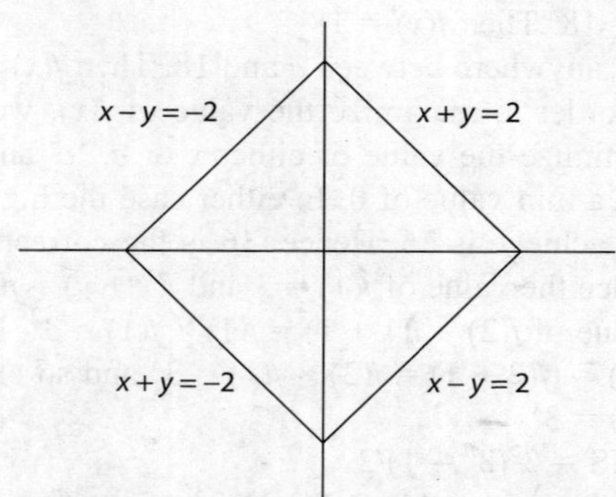

As shown in the above diagram, the region bounded by $|x + y| = 2$ and $|x - y| = 2$ is a square of side $\sqrt{2^2 + 2^2} = 2\sqrt{2}$.

Required area = $(2\sqrt{2})^2 = 8$

23. For $n = 8$
$f(x) = |x| + |x + 4| + |x + 8| + \ldots + |x + 32|$
The minimum value of $f(x)$ will be when $x = -16$ when the middle term of this expression, viz. $|x + 16|$ becomes 0. (i.e. it is minimised)
We have: $f(-16) = |-16| + |-12| + |-8| + |-4| + 0 + |4| + |8| + |12| + |16| = 80$.

24. For $n = 7$, $f(x) = |x| + |x + 4| + |x + 8| + \ldots + |x + 28|$. In this case there would be two middle terms in the expression, viz. $|x + 12|$ and $|x + 16|$. The value of the expression would be minimised when the value of the sum of the middle terms is minimised.
We can see that $|x + 12| + |x + 16|$ gets minimised at $-16 \le x \le -12$. (Note that the values of the sum of the remaining six terms of the expression would remain constant whenever we take the values of x between -12 and -16.)
Thus, we have a total of five values at which the expression is minimised for $n = 7$.

25. For $n = 9$, $f(x) = |x| + |x + 4| + |x + 8| + \ldots + |x + 36|$. The middle terms of this expression are $|x + 16|$ and $|x + 20|$. Hence, this expression would attain its minimum value when
$-20 \le x \le -16$
Therefore $f(x)$ is minimum for a total of five values of x.
Minimum value of $f(x)$ can be seen at $x = -16 \rightarrow$ $f(-16) = |-16| + |-16 + 4| + | + |-16 + 8| + |-16 + 12| + |-16 + 16| + |-16 + 20| + |-16 + 24| + |-16 + 28| + |-16 + 32| + |-16 + 36|$
$= 16 + 12 + 8 + 4 + 0 + 4 + 8 + 12 + 16 + 20$
$= 100$
For $n = 9$, $f(x)$ will be minimum for $x = -16$ to -20
$\therefore f(-17) = f(-19) = 100$ minimum value of $f(x)$
Hence, option (d) is correct.

26. The curve of $|x| + |y| = 3$ is shown below.

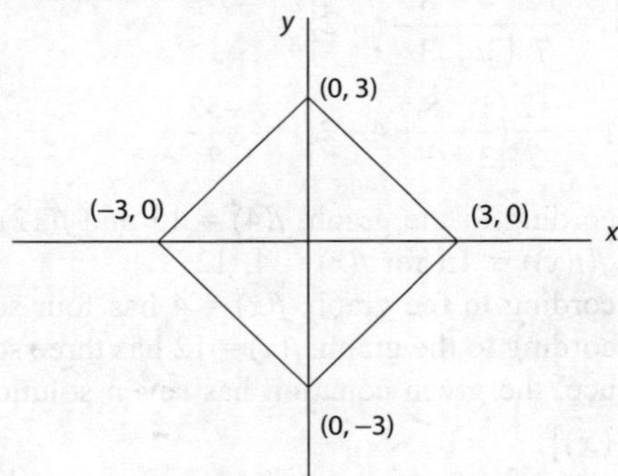

The curve is a square of side of length $3\sqrt{2}$ units.
Therefore, required area $= (3\sqrt{2})^2 = 18$ square units.

27. In the previous question, we found the area of curve $|x| + |y| = 3$.
$|x - a| + |y - b| = 3$ also has the same graph with the same shape and size only its center shifted to a new point (a, b). (Previous centre was (0, 0)).
Hence, area enclosed by curve $|x - 2| + |y - 3| = 3$ is same as area enclosed by curve $|x| + |y| = 3 = 18$ square units.

28. $8\{x\} = x + 2[x] \rightarrow 8\{x\} = [x] + \{x\} + 2[x] \rightarrow 7\{x\} = 3[x] \rightarrow [x] = \frac{7}{3}\{x\}$. This gives us the relationship between $[x]$ and $\{x\}$ and can also be expressed as $\{x\} = \frac{3}{7}[x]$.
Further, since $\{x\}$ is a fraction between 0 and 1, we get: $0 \le \frac{3}{7}[x] < 1 \rightarrow 0 \le 3[x] < 7 \rightarrow 0 \le [x] < \frac{7}{3}$
Thus, $[x] = 0, 1, 2$ (we obtained three possible values between the limits).
Then using the relationship between $\{x\}$ and $[x]$, we get the possible values of $\{x\} = 0, \frac{3}{7}, \frac{6}{7}$ when $[x]$ is 0,1 and 2 respectively.
Since $x = [x] + \{x\}$ we get $x = 0, \frac{10}{7}, \frac{20}{7}$.
Therefore, there are two positive values of x for which the given equation is true.

29. Difference between the greatest and least value of $x = \frac{20}{7} - 0 = \frac{20}{7} = 2.85$

30. $f(x) = \frac{4^{x-1}}{4^{x-1} + 1} = \frac{4^x}{4^x + 4}$

$$fog(x) = \frac{4^{2x}}{4^{2x} + 4}$$

$$fog(1 - x) = \frac{4^{2(1-x)}}{4^{2(1-x)} + 4}$$

$$= \frac{4^2.4^{-2x}}{4^2.4^{-2x} + 4}$$

$$= \frac{4^2}{4^2 + 4.4^{2x}}$$

$$= \frac{4}{4 + 4^{2x}}$$

$$fog(x) + fog(1 - x) = \frac{4^{2x}}{4^{2x} + 4} + \frac{4}{4 + 4^{2x}}$$

$$= \frac{4^{2x} + 4}{4^{2x} + 4} = 1$$

put $x = \frac{1}{4}$

we get $fog\left(\frac{1}{4}\right) + fog\left(1 - \frac{1}{4}\right) = fog\left(\frac{1}{4}\right) + fog\left(\frac{3}{4}\right) = 1$

$$\Rightarrow fog\left(\frac{1}{4}\right) + fog\left(\frac{3}{4}\right) = 1$$

31. Put $x = ½$

$$fog\left(\frac{1}{2}\right) + fog\left(1-\frac{1}{2}\right) = 1$$

$$2\,fog\left(\frac{1}{2}\right) = 1 \Rightarrow fog\left(\frac{1}{2}\right) = \frac{1}{2}$$

$$fog\left(\frac{1}{2}\right) + fog\left(\frac{1}{4}\right) + fog\left(\frac{3}{4}\right) + fog\left(\frac{1}{8}\right)$$

$$+ fog\left(\frac{7}{8}\right) + fog\left(\frac{1}{16}\right) + fog\left(\frac{15}{16}\right)$$

$$= \frac{1}{2} + 1 + 1 + 1 = 3\frac{1}{2} = 3.5$$

32. $f(x + 2) = f(x) + 2(x + 1)$ when x is even.

$f(2) = 5$

$f(4) = f(2) + 2(2 + 1) = 5 + 6 = 11$

$f(6) = f(4) + 2(4 + 1) = 11 + 10 = 21$

Therefore, for even values of x, $f(x) = \frac{x^2}{2} + 3$

$f(1) = 1$

$f(3) = 1 + 1 = 2$

$f(5) = 2 + 1 = 3$

$\Rightarrow$ For odd value of x, $f(x) = \frac{x+1}{2}$

$$f(24) = \frac{(24)^2}{2} + 3$$

$= 291$

33. $f(14) = \frac{(14)^2}{2} + 3 = 101$

$$f(11) = \frac{11+1}{2} = 6$$

$$\left[\frac{f(14)}{f(11)}\right] = \left[\frac{101}{6}\right] = [16.83] = 16$$

34. From the solution of question 32, it is clear that only option (c) is correct.

35. $f(f(f(f(3)))) + f(f(f(2)))$

$= f(f(f(2))) + f(f(5))$

$= f(f(5)) + f(3)$

$= f(3) + 2$

$= 2 + 2$

$= 4$

36. From the given information we can assume $F(x)$ as a sum of $P(x)$ and x, where

$P(x) = kx\,(x - 1)\,(x - 2)\,(x - 3)\,(x - 4)\,(x - 5)$, k is a constant.

$F(x) = kx\,(x - 1)\,(x - 2)\,(x - 3)\,(x - 4)\,(x - 5) + x$

$F(6) = k \times 6 \times 5 \times 4 \times 3 \times 2 \times 1 + 6$

It is given $F(6) = 7$

$\therefore\ k \times 6! + 6 = 7$

$k \times 6! = 1$

Hence, $k = \frac{1}{6!}$.

Thus, $F(x) = \frac{x(x-1)(x-2)(x-3)(x-4)(x-5)}{6!} + x$.

$$F(8) = \frac{8 \times 7 \times 6 \times 5 \times 4 \times 3}{6!} + 8$$

$= 28 + 8 = 36$

37. By putting negative values of x, we can see that $F(x)$ is a decreasing function for negative integer values of x, therefore, $F(x)$ will be maximum for $x = -1$

$$\text{Maximum value of } f(x) = \frac{-1 \times -2 \times -3 \times -4 \times -5 \times -6}{6!} - 1$$

$\Rightarrow 1 - 1 = 0$

38. $g(x + y) = g(x)\,g(y)$

$g(1 + 1) = g(1)\,.g(1) = g(1)^2 = 5^2 = 25$

$g(2) = 5^2$

Similarly, $g(3) = 5^3$, $g(4) = 5^4$, $g(5) = 5^5$

$g(1) + g(2) + g(3) + g(4) + g(5) = 5 + 25 + 125 + 625 + 3125 = 3905$

39. $g(x) = 5^x$

If we put $n = 1$ in the given summation then

$$g(q+1) = \frac{1}{4}(5^4 - 125) = \frac{500}{4} = 125$$

$5^{q+1} = 125 \Rightarrow q + 1 = 3$ or $q = 2$

40. $3f(x + 2) + 4f\left(\frac{1}{x+2}\right) = 4x$

Let $x + 2 = t$

$3f(t) + 4f\left(\frac{1}{t}\right) = 4t - 8$ or $\frac{3}{4}f(t) + f\left(\frac{1}{t}\right) = t - 2$ **(1)**

Now replacing t with $\frac{1}{t}$ in the above equation, we get

$3f\left(\frac{1}{t}\right) + 4f(t) = \frac{4}{t} - 8$ or $f\left(\frac{1}{t}\right) + \frac{4}{3}f(t) = \frac{4}{3t} - \frac{8}{3}$ **(2)**

From (1) and (2).

$$f(t) = \frac{12}{7}\left\{\frac{4}{3t} - \frac{8}{3} - t + 2\right\}$$

$$f(4) = \frac{12}{7}\left\{\frac{1}{3} - \frac{8}{3} - 4 + 2\right\} = \frac{-52}{7}$$

41. According to the graph, $f(4) = 15$ and $f(12) = 15$.

So $f(f(x)) = 15$ for $f(x) = 4, 12$.

According to the graph, $f(x) = 4$ has four solutions.

According to the graph, $f(x) = 12$ has three solutions.

Hence, the given equation has seven solutions.

42. $[f(x)]^{g(x)} = 1$

Now three cases are possible:

Case I: $f(x) = 1$ and $g(x)$ may be anything.

$x - 6 = 1$ or $x = 7$

But for $x = 7, g(x)$ is not defined.

Case II: $f(x) = -1$ and $g(x)$ is an even exponent

$x - 6 = -1$

$x = 5$

For $x = 5$

$$g(x)=\frac{(5-9)(5-1)}{(5-7)(5-3)}=\frac{-4\times 4}{-2\times 2}=4$$

So for $x = 5$, $g(x)$ is even, which satisfies the given equation.

Case III: $g(x) = 0$ and $f(x) \neq 0$

$$\frac{(x-9)(x-1)}{(x-7)(x-3)}=0 \text{ for } x = 1, 9$$

For $x = 1$ and 9 $f(x) \neq 0$. So both of these values of x satisfy the given equation.

So the given equation is satisfied for three values of x.

43. $f(4) + f(6) = 0$ implies that $f(4)$ and $f(6)$ are of opposite sign but same absolute value. Hence one root of the equation lies between 4 and 6.
$f(1) > 0$ and $f(2)<0$ implies that another root lies between 1 and 2.
$f(5).f(7) > 0$ implies that $f(5)$ and $f(7)$ are of same sign, so $f(4)$ and $f(5)$ must be of opposite sign. So the second root of $f(x) = 0$ must lie between $x = 4$ and $x = 5$.
So $f(x)$ would look like:

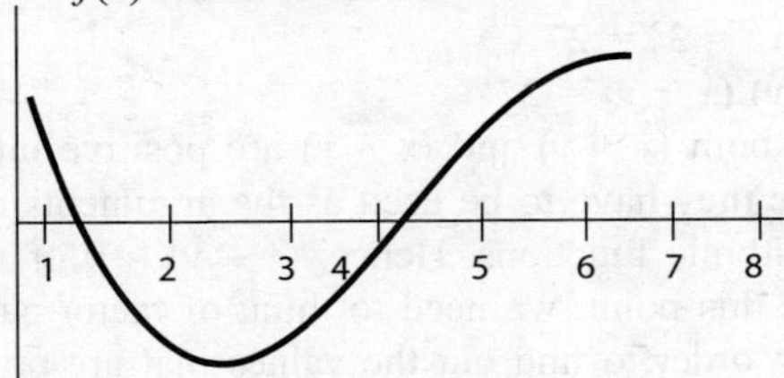

As $f(1) > 0$ & $f(2)$ & $f(4) < 0$
So $f(1)\, f(2)\, f(4) > 0$. Option (a) is incorrect.
As $f(5)$, $f(6)$ & $f(7)$ are greater than 0.
So $f(5)\, f(6)\, f(7) > 0$. So option (b) is wrong.
As $f(1) > 0$ & $f(3)$ & $f(4) < 0$. So $f(1)\, f(3)\, f(4) > 0$
So option (c) is true.

44. $f(x) = 12 + x$
$7[x] + 4\{x\} = 12 + x$
$3[x] + 4[[x] + \{x\}] = 12 + x$
$3[x] + 4x = 12 + x$
$3[x] + 3x = 12$
$[x] + x = 4$
Since 4 and $[x]$ are both integers, in the above equations x must also be an integer. This means that the value of $[x] = x$. So:
$2x = 4$
$x = 2$
Therefore, only one value of x satisfies the given equation.

45. $x^2 - xy + y^2 = x + y$
Multiplying both sides by 2, we get:
$2x^2 - 2xy + 2y^2 = 2x + 2y$
$x^2 - 2xy + y^2 + x^2 - 2x + 1 + y^2 - 2y + 1 = 2$
$(x - y)^2 + (x - 1)^2 + (y - 1)^2 = 2$
In the question, we are interested to find non-negative integer solutions, therefore, three cases are possible.
Case I: $x - y = 0$, $(x - 1)^2 = 1$, $(y - 1)^2 = 1$
Possible solutions (0, 0) and (2, 2)
Case II: $(x - y)^2 = 1$, $(x - 1)^2 = 1$, $(y - 1)^2 = 0$
Possible solutions: (2, 1), (0, 1).
Case III: $(x - y)^2 = 1$, $(y - 1)^2 = 1$, $(x - 1)^2 = 0$
Possible solutions: (1, 2) and (1, 0)
Possible solutions (x, y) such that $x \geq y$ are (0, 0), (2, 2), (1, 0), (2, 1). There are four such solutions.

46. $g(n)=\dfrac{n-1}{n}g(n-1)$

$$g(2)=\frac{1}{2}g(1)$$

$$g(3)=\frac{2}{3}g(2)=\frac{2}{3}\times\frac{1}{2}g(1)=\frac{1}{3}g(1).$$

Similarly:

$$g(4)=\frac{1}{4}g(1);g(5)=\frac{1}{5}g(1);$$

$$g(6)=\frac{1}{6}g(1);g(7)=\frac{1}{7}g(1);g(8)=\frac{1}{8}g(1)$$

Since $g(1) = 2$, the given expression will become:

$$\frac{\left[\frac{1}{2}\times\frac{2}{2}\times\frac{3}{2}\times\ldots\frac{8}{2}\right]}{\left[\frac{1}{2}+\frac{2}{2}+\frac{3}{2}+\ldots\frac{8}{2}\right]}$$

Required answer is $\dfrac{8!}{2^8}\times\dfrac{1}{18}$.

47. Let $f(x) = a(x - 1)(x - 2)(x - 3)\ldots(x - 77) + x$ where 'a' is any constant.
Now putting $x = 78$ in the above equation, we get
$f(78) = a.77.76.75.74\ldots1 + 78 = a.77! + 78$
Similarly, $f(0) = a.(-1)(-2)(-3)\ldots(-77) + 0$
$f(0) = a(-1)^{77}77! = -a.77!$
$f(78) + f(0) = a.77! + 78 - a.77! = 78$

48. $f(n - 1)\,(2 - f(n)) = 1$

$$2-f(n)=\frac{1}{f(n-1)}$$

$$f(n)=2-\frac{1}{f(n-1)}$$

$$f(2)=2-\frac{1}{f(1)}=2-\frac{1}{3}=\frac{5}{3}$$

$$f(3)=2-\frac{1}{f(2)}=2-\frac{3}{5}=\frac{7}{5}$$

$$f(4)=2-\frac{1}{f(3)}=2-\frac{5}{7}=\frac{9}{7}$$

Observing this pattern, we can see that:

$$f(n)=\frac{2n+1}{2n-1}$$

$$f(21)=\frac{2\times 21+1}{2\times 21-1}=\frac{43}{41}$$

49. Since: $0 \le \{x\} < 1$

The expression: $10[x] + 22\{x\} = 250$ gives us the inequality: $228 < 10[x] \le 250$

$22.8 < [x] \le 25$

Possible values of $[x] = 23, 24, 25$

For $[x] = 23$, $\{x\} = \frac{250-230}{22} = \frac{20}{22} = \frac{10}{11}$

For $[x] = 24$, $\{x\} = \frac{250-240}{22} = \frac{10}{22} = \frac{5}{11}$

For $[x] = 25$, $\{x\} = 0$

So the possible values of x are $23\frac{10}{11}, 24\frac{5}{11}, 25$.

So there are three possible values of x.

50. $23\frac{10}{11} + 24\frac{5}{11} + 25 = 73\frac{4}{11} \approx 73.36$

51. $f(x+1) = f(x) - f(x-1)$

$f(x) = f(x+1) + f(x-1)$

$f(17) = f(18) + f(16)$

$2f(16) = f(18) + f(16)$

$f(16) = f(18)$

Let $f(16) = f(18) = x$

$f(17) = 2x$

$f(16) = f(15) + f(17) \rightarrow f(15) = -x;$

$f(15) = f(14) + f(16) \rightarrow f(14) = -2x;$

$f(14) = f(13) + f(15) \rightarrow f(13) = -x;$

$f(13) = f(12) + f(14) \rightarrow f(12) = x$

$f(12) = f(11) + f(13) \rightarrow f(11) = 2x$

$f(11) = f(10) + f(12) \rightarrow f(10) = x$

$f(10) = f(9) + (f(11) \rightarrow f(9) = -x$

If we observe the above pattern of values that we are getting, we can observe that $f(18) = f(12)$; $f(17) = f(11)$; $f(16) = f(10)$ and $f(15) = f(9)$. Here we can easily observe that values repeat for every six terms. So $f(5) = f(11) = f(17) = 6$

Thus, option (b) is correct.

52. $\frac{h(x)}{h(x-1)} = \frac{h(x-2)}{h(x+1)}$

On putting $x = 54$, we get:

$$\frac{h(54)}{h(53)} = \frac{h(52)}{h(55)} \quad (1)$$

On putting $x = 55$, we get:

$$\frac{h(55)}{h(54)} = \frac{h(53)}{h(56)} \quad (2)$$

Equation (1) ÷ Equation (2)

$$\frac{[h(54)]^2}{h(53)\times h(55)} = \frac{h(52)\times h(56)}{h(55)\times h(53)}$$

$[h(54)]^2 = 4 \times 16$

$h(54) = 8$

53. $f(x) = 1 - \frac{2}{x+1} = \frac{x+1-2}{x+1} = \frac{x-1}{x+1}$

$$f^2(x) = f(f(x)) = \frac{\frac{x-1}{x+1} - 1}{\frac{x-1}{x+1} + 1} = -\frac{1}{x}$$

$$f^3(x) = f(f(f(x))) = -\frac{x+1}{x-1}$$

$$f^4(x) = f(f(f(f(x)))) = x$$

$$f^5(x) = f(x) = \frac{x-1}{x+1}$$

Here we can see that $f(x) = f^5(x)$, so the given function has a cyclicity of 4, therefore:

$f^n(x) = f^{n+4k}(x)$, where k is a whole number

$$f^{802} = f^{2+4\times 200}(x) = f^2(x) = -\frac{1}{x}$$

$$f^{802}(x)\, at\; x = -\frac{1}{2} = -\frac{1}{-\frac{1}{2}} = 2$$

54. $\log_3(x+y) + \log_3(x-y) = 3$

$\log_3(x^2 - y^2) = 3$

$x^2 - y^2 = 3^3 = 27$

$(x-y)(x+y) = 27$

Here both $(x+y)$ and $(x-y)$ are positive integers (since they have to be used as the arguments of the logarithmic functions. Hence, $(x-y) > 0$ or $x > y$. From this point, we need to think of factor pairs of 27, in order to find out the values that are possible for x and y.

Case 1: $x + y = 9$, $x - y = 3$ or $x = 6$, $y = 3$

Case 2: when $x + y = 27$, $x - y = 1$ or $x = 14$, $y = 13$

Two pairs of (x, y) are possible.

55. The maximum value of $x + y = 14 + 13 = 27$.

56. In the following figure, the bold portion shows the graph of $h(x)$.

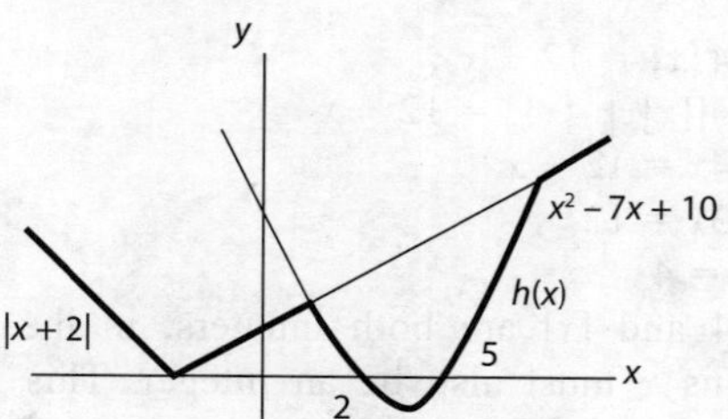

Therefore, $h(x) \le 0$ for $x = 2, 3, 4, 5$. There are four such values.

57. We can observe from the graph that $h(x) < 0$ only for two integer values (3, 4) of x. So the required sum = 3 + 4 = 7.

58. $[2p - 3]$ is an integer. Hence, $q + 7$ is also an integer or q must be an integer.

Similarly p is also an integer (since $[3q + 1]$ is an integer, hence $p + 6$ should also be an integer.)

$\Rightarrow [2p - 3] = 2p - 3 = q + 7$

$2p - q = 10$ (1)

$\Rightarrow 3q + 1 = p + 6$

$3q - p = 5$ (2)

By solving equations (1) and (2), we get the values of p and q as:

$p = 7, q = 4$

The required answer is then given by $7^2 \times 4^2 = 784$.

59. $f(a) = 3^a$ (If a is an odd number)

$f(a + 1) = 3^{(a+1)} + 4 = 3.3^a + 4$

$$\frac{1}{4}[f(a) + f(a+1)] = \frac{3^a + 3.3^a + 4}{4} = \frac{3^a.4 + 4}{4} = 3^a + 1$$

$$\Rightarrow \frac{1}{4}[f(1) + f(2) + (f(3) + f(4)) + \ldots + f(71) + f(72)]$$

$$= \frac{f(1)+f(2)}{4} + \frac{f(3)+f(4)}{4} + \ldots + \frac{f(71)+f(72)}{4}$$

$= 3^1 + 1 + 3^3 + 1 + \ldots + 3^{71} + 1$

$= (3^1 + 3^3 + \ldots + 3^{71}) + 36$

$$= \frac{3((3^2)^{36} - 1)}{3^2 - 1} + 36$$

$$= \frac{3}{8}(3^{72} - 1) + 36$$

Solutions for Questions 60 to 63:

$f(x, y)$ is always positive or zero

$F(f(x, y)$ is always negative or zero

$G(f(x, y)$ is always positive or zero

60. $F \times G$ will always be negative while $- F \times G$ will always be positive except when they are both equal to zero.

Hence, option (b), i.e. $F \times G \le - F \times G$ is correct.

61. Option (b) can be seen to give us $4a^2/4 = a^2$.

62. $(5 - 1)/(1 + 3) = 4/4 = 1$

63. The given expression $= (45 - 10)/(5 + 2) = 35/7 = 5$. Option (b) $= 20/4 = 5$.

Solutions for Questions 64 to 68:

Do the following analysis:

$A(f(x, y))$ is positive

$B(f(x, y))$ is negative

$C(f(x, y))$ is positive

$D(f(x, y))$ is negative

$E(f(x, y))$ is positive and so on

64. $1 - 3 + 5 - 7 + 9 - 11 + \ldots - 51$

$= (1 + 5 + 9 + 13 + \ldots 49) - (3 + 7 + 11 \ldots + 51)$

$= -26$

65. Verify each statement to see that (ii) and (iii) are true.

66. The given expression becomes:

Min (max [5, – 7, 9], min [3, – 1 , 1], max [7, 6, 10])

= Min [9, – 1, 10]

= – 1

67. The given expression becomes:

Max $[|a + b|, -|b + c|, |c + d|]$

This will never be negative.

68. The respective values are:

$-3/2, -7/12, -8/15$, and $-5/6$

Option (d) is second lowest.

69. Let $s = 1$, $t = 2$ and $b = 3$

Then, $f(s + t) + f(s - t)$

$= f(3) + f(-1) = (3^3 + 3^{-3})/2 + (3^{-1} + 3^1)/2$

$= [(27 + (1/27)]/2 + [3 + (1/3)]/2$

$= 730/54 + 10/6$

$= 820/54 = 410/27$

Option (b), i.e. $2 f(s) \times f(t)$ gives the same value.

70. This question is based on the logic of a chain function. Given the relationship

$A_t = (t + 1)A_{(t-1)} - tA_{(t-2)}$

We can clearly see that the value of A_2 would depend on the values of A_0 and A_1. Putting $t = 2$ in the expression, we get:

$A_2 = 3A_1 - 2A_0 = 7$; $A_3 = 19$; $A_4 = 67$ and $A_5 = 307$.

Clearly, $A6$ onwards will be larger than 307 and hence none of the three conclusions are true. Hence, option (e) is the correct answer.

71. In order to solve this question, we would need to check each of the value ranges given in the conclusions:

Checking whether Conclusion I is possible

For $B = 2$, we get $A + C = 4$ (since $A + B + C = 6$). This transforms the second equation $AB + BC + CA = 9$ to:

$2(A + C) + CA = 9 \rightarrow CA = 1$.

Solving $CA = 1$ and $A + C = 4$ we get: $(4 - A)A = 1 \rightarrow A^2 - 4A + 1 = 0 \rightarrow A = 2 + 3^{1/2}$ and $C = 2 - 3^{1/2}$. Both these numbers are real and it satisfies $A < B < C$ and hence, Conclusion I is true.

Checking Conclusion II: If we chose $A = 2.5$, the condition is not satisfied since we get the other two variables as $(3.5 + 11.25^{1/2}) \div 2 \approx 3.4$ and $(3.5 - 11.25^{1/2}) \div 2 \approx 0.1$. In this case, A is no longer the least value and hence Conclusion II is rejected.

Checking Conclusion III we can see that $0 < C < 1$ cannot be possible since C being the largest of the three values has to be greater than 3 (the largest amongst A, B, and C would be greater than the average of A, B, C).

Thus, option (a) is correct.

72. The number of ways of distributing n identical things to r people such that any person can get any number of things including 0 is always given by ${}^{n+r-1}C_{r-1}$. In the case of $F(4,3)$, the value of $n = 4$ and $r = 3$ and hence, the total number of ways without any constraints would be given by ${}^{4+3-1}C_{3-1} = {}^6C_2 = 15$. However, out of these 15 ways of distributing the toys, we cannot count any way in which more than 2 toys are given to any one child. Hence, we need to reduce as follows:

The distribution of 4 toys as (3, 1 and 0) amongst three children A, B and C can be done in $3! = 6$ ways.

Also, the distribution of 4 toys as (4, 0 and 0) amongst three children *A*, *B* and *C* can be done in 3 ways.

Hence, the value of $F(4, 3) = 15 - 6 - 3 = 6$.

Thus, option (b) is correct.

73. $f(f(x)) = 15$, when $f(x) = 4$ or $f(x) = 12$ in the given function. The graph given in the figure becomes equal to 4 at 4 points and it becomes equal to 12 at 3 points in the figure. This gives us 7 points in the given figure when $f(f(x)) = 15$. However, the given function is continuous beyond the part of it which is shown between –10 and +13 in the figure. Hence, we do not know how many more solutions to $f(f(x)) = 15$ will be there. Hence, option (e) is the correct answer.

74. The given function is a chain function where the value of A_{n+1} depends on the value A_n.

Thus for $n = 0$, $A_1 = A_0^2 + 1$.

For $n = 1$, $A_2 = A_1^2 + 1$ and so on.

In such functions, if you know the value of the function at any one point, the value of the function can be calculated for any value till infinity.

Hence, statement I is sufficient by itself to find the value of the GCD of A_{900} and A_{1000}.

So also, the statement II is sufficient by itself to find the value of the GCD of A_{900} and A_{1000}.

Hence, option (d) is correct.

75. This question can be solved by first putting up the information in the form of a table as follows:

	Product A	*Product B*	*Number of machines available*	*Number of hours/day per machine.*	*Total hours per day available for each activity*
Grinding	2 hr	3 hr	10	12	120
Polishing	3 hr	2 hr	15	10	150
Profit	₹5	₹7			

On the surface, the profit of Product B being higher, we can think about maximising the number of units of Product B. Grinding would be the constraint when we maximise Product B production and we can produce a maximum of $120 \div 3 = 40$ units of Product B to get a profit of ₹280. The clue that this is not the correct answer comes from the fact that there is a lot of 'polishing' time left in this situation. In order to try to increase the profit, we can check that if we reduce production of Product *B* and try to increase the production of Product *A*, does the profit go up? When we reduce the production of Product *B* by 2 units, the production of Product *A* goes up by 3 units and the profit goes up by +1 ($-2 \times 7 + 3 \times 5$ gives a net effect of +1). In this case, the grinding time remains the same (as there is a reduction of 2 units × 3 hours/unit = 6 hours in grinding time due to the reduction in Product *B*'s production, but there is also a simultaneous increase of 6 hours in the use of the grinders in producing 3 units of Product *A*). Given that a reduction in the production of Product *B*, with a simultaneous maximum possible increase in the production of Product *A*, results in an increase in the profit, we would like to do this as much as possible. To think about it from this point, this situation can be tabulated as under for better understanding:

	Product A Production (A)	*Product B Production (B)*	*Grinding Machine Usage = 3A + 2B*	*Polishing Machine Usage = 2A + 3B*	*Time Left on Grinding Machine*	*Time Left on Polishing Machine*	*Profit = 7A+5B*
Case 1	40	0	120	80	0	70	280
Case 2	38	3	120	85	0	65	281
Case 3	36	6	120	90	0	60	282

The limiting case would occur when we reduce the time left on the polishing machine to 0. That would happen in the following case:

Optimal case	12	42	120	150	0	0	294

Hence, the answer would be 294.

76. The value of $f(x)$ as given is: $f(x) = x^4 + x^3 + x^2 + x + 1 = 1 + x + x^2 + x^3 + x^4$. This can be visualised as a geometric progression with 5 terms with the first term 1 and common ratio *x*. The sum of the

$$GP = f(x) = \frac{x^5 - 1}{x - 1}.$$

The value of $f(x^5) = x^{20} + x^{15} + x^{10} + x^5 + 1$ and this can be rewritten as:

$F(x^5) = (x^{20}-1) + (x^{15}-1) + (x^{10}-1) + (x^5-1) + 5$. When this expression is divided by $f(x) = \frac{x^5-1}{x-1}$, we get each of the first four terms of the expression will be divisible by it, i.e. $(x^{20}-1)$ will be divisible by $f(x) = \frac{x^5-1}{x-1}$, and would leave no remainder (because $x^{20}-1$ can be rewritten in the form $(x^5-1)\times(x^{15}+x^{10}+x^5+1)$ and when you divide this expression by $\left(\frac{x^5-1}{x-1}\right)$, we get the remainder as 0.)

A similar logic will also hold for the terms $(x^{15}-1)$, $(x^{10}-1)$ and (x^5-1). The only term that will leave a remainder would be 5 when it is divided by $\left(\frac{x^5-1}{x-1}\right)$

Also, for $x \geq 2$, we can see the value of $\left(\frac{x^5-1}{x-1}\right)$ will be more than 5. Hence, the remainder will always be 5 and option (c) is the correct answer.

77. Start by putting $\frac{x}{x-1} = (\text{cosec } \alpha)^2$ in the given expression.

$$F\left(\frac{x}{x-1}\right) = \frac{1}{x}$$

Now for $0 < \alpha < 90°$

$$\frac{x}{x-1} = (\text{cosec } \alpha)^2,\ x = \frac{1}{1-\sin^2\alpha} \Rightarrow \frac{1}{x} = \cos^2\alpha$$

Hence, option (b) is correct.

78. Given that the roots of the equation $F(x) = 0$ are -2, -1, 1 and 2 respectively, and the $F(x)$ is a polynomial with the highest power of x as x^4, we can create the value of

$F(x) = (x + 2)(x + 1)(x - 1)(x - 2)$

Hence, $F(p) = (P + 2)(P + 1)(P - 1)(P - 2)$.

It is given to us that P is a prime number greater than 97. Hence, p would always be of the form $6n \pm 1$ where n is a natural number greater than or equal to 17.

Thus, we get two cases for $F(p)$.

Case 1: If $p = 6n + 1$

$F(6n + 1) = (6n + 3)(6n + 2)(6n)(6n - 1)$

$= 3(2n + 1)\cdot 2(3n + 1)(6n)(6n - 1)$

$= (36)(2n + 1)(3n + 1)(n)(6n - 1)$ (1)

If you try to look for divisibility of this expression by numbers given in the options for various values of $n \geq 17$, we see that for $n = 17$ and 18, both 360 divides the value of $F(p)$. However at $n = 19$, none of the values in the four options divides $36 \times 39 \times 58 \times 19 \times 113$. In this case, however, at $n = 19$, $6n + 1$ is not a prime number hence, this case is not to be considered. Whenever we put a value of n as a value greater than 17, such that $6n+1$ becomes a prime number, we also see that the value of $F(p)$ is divisible by 360. This divisibility by 360 happens since the expression $(2n + 1)(3n + 1)(n)(6n - 1)$ ... is always divisible by 10 in all such cases. A similar logic can be worked out when we take $p = 6n-1$. Hence, the option (d) is the correct answer.

79. In order to solve this question, we start from the value of $x = (9 + 4\sqrt{5})^{48}$.

Let the value of $x(1-f) = xy$. (We are assuming $(1-f) = y$, which means that y is between 0 to 1). The value of $x = (9 + 4\sqrt{5})^{48}$ can be rewritten as $[{}^{48}C_0\, 9^{48} + {}^{48}C_1\, 9^{47}(4\sqrt{5}) + {}^{48}C_2\, 9^{46}(4\sqrt{5})^2 + \ldots + {}^{48}C_{47}(9)(4\sqrt{5})^{47} + {}^{48}C_{48}\,(4\sqrt{5})^{48}]$ using the binary theorem.

In this value, it is going to be all the odd powers of the $(4\sqrt{5})$ which would account for the value of 'f' in the value of x. Thus, for instance it can be seen that the terms ${}^{48}C_0\, 9^{48}$, ${}^{48}C_2\, 9^{46}(4\sqrt{5})^2$, ... ${}^{48}C_{48}\,(4\sqrt{5})^{48}$ would all be integers. It is only the terms: ${}^{48}C_1 9^{47}(4\sqrt{5})$, ${}^{48}C_3\, 9^{45}(4\sqrt{5})^3$,... ${}^{48}C_{47}\,(9)(4\sqrt{5})^{47}$ which would give us the value of 'f' in the value of x.

Hence, $x(1-f) = x\,[1 - {}^{48}C_1\, 9^{47}\,(4\sqrt{5}) - {}^{48}C_3\, 9^{45}(4\sqrt{5})^3 - \ldots - {}^{48}C_{47}\,(9)(4\sqrt{5})^{47}]$

In order to think further from this point, you would need the following thought. Let $y = (9-4\sqrt{5})^{48}$.

Also, $x+y = \{{}^{48}C_0 9^{48} + {}^{48}C_1 9^{47}(4\sqrt{5}) + {}^{48}C_2 9^{46}(4\sqrt{5})^2 + \ldots + {}^{48}C_{47}\,(9)(4\sqrt{5})^{47} + {}^{48}C_{48}\,(4\sqrt{5})^{48}\} + \{{}^{48}C_0\, 9^{48} - {}^{48}C_1\, 9^{47}\,(4\sqrt{5}) + {}^{48}C_2\, 9^{46}\,(4\sqrt{5})^2 + \ldots - {}^{48}C_{47}\,(9)\,(4\sqrt{5})^{47} + {}^{48}C_{48}\,(4\sqrt{5})^{48}\} = 2\{{}^{48}C_0\, 9^{48} + {}^{48}C_2\, 9^{46}\,(4\sqrt{5})^2 + \ldots {}^{48}C_{48}\,(4\sqrt{5})^{48}\}$ – the bracket in this expression has only retained the even terms which are integral. Hence, the value of $x+y$ is an integer. Further, $x + y = [x] + f + y$ and hence, if $x+y$ is an integer, $[x] + f + y$ would also be an integer. This automatically means that $f+y$ must be an integer (as $[x]$ is an integer).

Now, the value of y is between 0 and 1 and hence, when we add the fractional part of x, i.e. 'f' to y, and we need to make it an integer, the only possible integer that $f + y$ can be equal to 1.

Thus, if $f + y = 1 \rightarrow y = (1 - f)$.

In order to find the value of $x(1 - f)$, we can find the value of $x \times y$.

Then, $x(1-f) = x \times y = (9 + 4\sqrt{5})^{48} \times (9 - 4\sqrt{5})^{48}$

$= (81-80)^{48} = 1$

$x(1 - f) = 1$

80. $x - |x|$ is either negative for $x < 0$ or 0 for $x \geq 0$. Thus, option (d) is correct.

81. The domain should simultaneously satisfy:

$$x - 1 \geq 0,\ (1 - x) \geq 0 \text{ and } (x^2 + 3) \geq 0.$$

Gives us: $x \geq 1$ and $x \leq 1$

The only value that satisfies these two simultaneously is $x = 1$.

82. For the function to exist, the argument of the logarithmic function should be positive. Also, $(x + 4) \geq 0$ should be obeyed simultaneously.

For $\frac{(x-5)}{(x^2-10x+24)}$ to be positive, both numerator and denominator should have the same sign. Considering all this, we get:

$$4 < x < 5 \text{ and } x > 6$$

Hence, option (c) is correct.

83. Both the brackets should be non-negative and neither $(x + 3)$ nor $(1+ x)$ should be 0.

For $(x - 3)/(x + 3)$ to be non negative, we have $x > 3$ or $x < -3$.

Also for $(1- x)/(1+ x)$ to be non-negative, $-1 < x < 1$. Since there is no interference in the two ranges, option (d) will be correct.

87. $f(f(t)) = f((t-1)/(t+1))$

$$= \left[\left(\frac{t-1}{t+1}\right)-1\right] \Big/ \left[\left(\frac{t-1}{t+1}\right)+1\right] = \frac{t-1-t-1}{t-1+t+1}$$

$$= -2/2t = -1/t$$

88. $fog = f(\log_e x) = e^{\log_e x} = x$

89. $gof = g(e^x) = \log_e e^x = x$

90. Looking at the options, one unit right means x is replaced by $(x - 1)$. Also, 1 unit down means -1 on the RHS.

Thus, $(y + 1) = 1/(x - 1)$.

91. For option (c), we can see that $f(t) = f(-t)$. Hence, option (c) is correct.

92. Option (b) is odd because:

$$\frac{a^{-t}+a^t}{a^t-a^{-t}} = -1 \times \left(\frac{a^{-t}+a^t}{a^{-t}-a^t}\right)$$

Similarly option (c) is also representing an odd function. The function in option (a) is not odd.

93. $f(f(t)) = f[t/(1+t^2)^{1/2}] = t/(1+2t^2)^{1/2}$

94. By trial-and-error, it is clear that at $x = 3$, the value of the function is 19. At other values of 'x', the value of the function is less than 19.

95. Take different values of x to check each option. All the options, i.e. (a), (b) and (c) can be ruled out. Hence, option (d) is correct.

CHAPTER

15

Inequalities

Chapter Launchpad

Scan this QR code to access a video on 'Introduction to Inequalities' and this chapter's importance for CAT

This chapter will seem highly mathematical to you while you read the theory and have look at the solved examples in the chapter. For students who are weak in mathematics, there is no need to be disheartened about the seemingly high mathematical content. It is advised to go through this chapter and internalise the concepts. However, keep in mind the fact that in an aptitude test, the questions will have options, and with options all you will need to do is to check the validity of the inequality for the different options. Even with the advent of the TITA questions in CAT, having no options; questions on inequalities have always been asked in an option-based format.

However, while you would need to master how to solve inequalities using options, at the base level, it would also be a good idea to review and strengthen your mathematical bases for this chapter – as even while solving questions purely through options, knowing what to look for inside the options would help you to speed up your solving capability. This understanding of what to look for inside the options is where your mathematical understanding and would help you.

Two real numbers or two algebraic expressions related by the symbol > ("Greater Than") or < ("Less Than") (and also by the signs ≥ or ≤) form an inequality.

$A < B$, $A > B$ (are plain inequalities)

$A \geq B$, $A \leq B$ (are called as inequations)

The inequality consists of two sides—the left-hand side, A and the right-hand side, B. A and B can be algebraic expressions or they can be numbers.

An inequality with the < or > sign is called a *strict inequality* while an inequality having ≥ or ≤ sign is called a *slack inequality*. The expressions A and B have to be considered on the set where A and B have sense simultaneously. This set is called the set of permissible values of the inequality. If the terms on the LHS and the RHS are algebraic equations/identities, then the inequality may or may not hold true for a particular value of the variable/set of variables assumed.

For two real numbers a and b:

The inequality $a > b$ means that the difference $a - b$ is positive.

The inequality $a < b$ means that the difference $a - b$ is negative.

Properties of Inequalities

For any two real numbers, a and b, only one of the following restrictions can hold true:

$$a = b,\ a > b \text{ or } a < b$$

Definitions of Slack Inequalities

The inequality $a \geq b$ means that $a > b$ or $a = b$, that is, a is not less than b.

The inequality $a \leq b$ means that $a < b$ or $a = b$, that is, a is not greater than b.

We can also have the following double inequalities for simultaneous situations:

$$a < b < c,\ a < b \leq c,\ a \leq b < c,\ a \leq b \leq c$$

A. Mathematical transformations while solving inequalities:

Whenever you face an inequality situation like: LHS >RHS, you can do all the normal operations on both the LHS and RHS, without changing the sense of the inequality. Thus, the following operations hold true: (**Note:** in the following examples, I am exhibiting the valid operations on the inequality LHS>RHS, but would like the student to realise that these hold equally true for LHS<RHS or for that matter for the slack inequalities: LHS ≥ RHS or LHS ≤ RHS):

1. LHS + Constant > RHS + Same Constant
2. LHS – Constant > RHS – Same Constant
3. LHS × Positive constant > RHS × Same Positive constant
4. LHS ÷ Positive constant > RHS ÷ Same Positive constant

   The only thing you need to be careful about is that, if you are multiplying or dividing both the sides of the inequality by the same negative constant, then you have to reverse the sign of the inequality. Thus, if LHS>RHS, then:

5. LHS × Negative constant < RHS × Same Negative constant
6. LHS ÷ Negative constant < RHS ÷ Same Negative constant

Contd.

Some other important properties of inequalities:

1. If $a > b$ then $b < a$ and vice versa.
2. If $a > b$ and $b > c$ then $a > c$. Example: $5 > 3$ and $3 > 0$. Hence, $5 > 0$.
3. If $a > b$ and $c > d$ then $a + c > b + d$. Example: $5 > 3$ and $2 > 0$. Hence, $(5 + 2) > (3 + 0)$.
4. If $a > b$ and $c < d$ then $a - c > b - d$. Example: $5 > 3$ and $0 < 2$. Hence, $5 - 0 > 3 - 2$.
5. If a, b, c, d are non-negative numbers such that $a > b$ and $c > d$ then $ac > bd$. Example: $5 > 3$ and $3 > 0$. Hence, $15>0$.
6. If a and b are positive numbers where $a > b$, then $a^n > b^n$ for any natural n.
7. If a and b are positive numbers where $a > b$ then $a^{1/n} > b^{1/n}$ for any natural $n \geq 2$.
8. $1/a^n < 1/b^n$; that is $a^{-n} < b^{-n}$
9. The square of every real quantity is positive, and therefore, greater than zero. Thus, $(a - b)^2$ is positive.
10. Let a and b be two positive quantities, S their sum and P their product. Then from the identity
    $4ab = (a + b)^2 - (a - b)^2$
    we have $4P = S^2 - (a - b)^2$, and $S^2 = 4P + (a - b)^2$
    Hence, if S is given, P is greatest when $a = b$; and if P is given, S is least when $a = b$;
    That is, if the sum of two positive quantities is given, their product is greatest when they are equal; and if the product of two positive quantities is given, their sum is least when they are equal. This is a very important property, which is used many times in questions.
11. If $a_1>b_1, a_2>b_2, a_3>b_3,\ldots a_m>b_m$, it is clear that $a_1 + a_2 + a_3 + \ldots + a_m > b_1 + b_2 + b_3 + \ldots + b_m$; and In case the numbers are non-negative then, $a_1a_2a_3\ldots a_m > b_1b_2b_3\ldots b_m$.

The readers are encouraged to work on these points with a few numerical examples so that they get comfortable with all these moves.

Certain Important Inequalities (know these well, as a lot of questions are based on these)

1. $a^2 + b^2 \geq 2ab$ (Equality for $a = b$)
2. $|a + b| \leq |a| + |b|$ (Equality reached if both a and b are of the same sign or if one of them is zero.)
   This can be generalised as $|a_1 + a_2 + a_3 + \ldots + a_n| \leq |a_1| + |a_2| + |a_3| + \ldots\ldots |a_n|$
3. $|a - b| \geq |a| - |b|$
4. $ax^2 + bx + c \geq 0$ if $a > 0$ and $D = b^2 - 4ac \leq 0$. The equality is achieved only if $D = 0$ and $x = -b/2a$.

Contd.

5. Arithmetic mean $\geq$ Geometric mean. That is, $\frac{(a+b)}{2} \geq \sqrt{ab}$
6. $a/b + b/a \geq 2$ if $a > 0$ and $b > 0$ or if $a < 0$ and $b < 0$, that is, both a and b have the same sign.
7. $a^3 + b^3 \geq ab(a + b)$ if $a > 0$ and $b > 0$, the equality being obtained only when $a = b$.
8. $a^2 + b^2 + c^2 \geq ab + ac + bc$
9. $(a + b)(b + c)(a + c) \geq 8abc$, if $a \geq 0$, $b \geq 0$ and $c \geq 0$, the equation being obtained when $a = b = c$.
10. For any four numbers x_1, x_2, y_1, y_2, satisfying the conditions
    $$x_1^2 + x_2^2 = 1$$
    $$y_1^2 + y_2^2 = 1$$
    the inequality $|x_1y_1 + x_2y_2| \leq 1$ is true.
11. $\frac{a}{b^{1/2}} + \frac{b}{a^{1/2}} \geq a^{1/2} + b^{1/2}$, where $a \geq 0$ and $b \geq 0$
12. If $a + b = 2$, then $a^4 + b^4 \geq 2$
13. The inequality $|x| \leq a$, means that
    $$-a \leq x \leq a \text{ for } a > 0$$
14. $2^n > n^2$ for $n \geq 5$

To Find the Greatest Value of a Product, the Sum of whose Factors is Constant

Let there be n factors $a, b, c,\ldots n$, of a composite number and suppose that their sum is constant and equal to S.

Consider the product $abc\ldots.n$, and suppose that a and b are any two unequal factors. If we replace the two unequal factors a and b by the two equal factors $(a + b)/2$, and $(a + b)/2$, the product is increased while the sum remains unaltered. Hence, so *long as the product contains two unequal factors, it can be increased without altering the sum of the factors; therefore, the product is greatest when all the factors are equal.* In this case, the value of each of the n factors is S/n, and the greatest value of the product is $(S/n)^n$.

This will be clearer with an example.

Let us define a number as $a \times b = c$ such that we restrict $a + b = 100$ (maximum) where a, b are non-negative.

Then, the maximum value of the product will be achieved if we take the value of a and b as 50 each.

Thus, $50 \times 50 = 2500$ will be the highest number achieved for the restriction $a + b \leq 100$.

Further, you can also say that $50 \times 50 > 51 \times 49 > 52 \times 48 > 53 \times 47 > 54 \times 46 > \ldots > 98 \times 2 > 99 \times 1$.

Thus, if we have a larger multiplication as $4 \times 6 \times 7 \times 8$; this will always be less than $5 \times 5 \times 7 \times 8$ [it holds true only for positive numbers].

Corollary If $a, b, c \ldots k$, are unequal, $\{(a + b + c + \ldots + k)/n\}^n > abc \ldots k$; that is , $(a + b + c + , \ldots + k)/n > (abc \ldots k)^{1/n}$.

By an extension of the meaning of the arithmetic and geometric means, this result is usually quoted as follows: *The arithmetic mean of any number of positive quantities is greater than the geometric mean.*

Solution of an Inequality

The solutions of an inequality will always be in the form of a range of values of the unknown variable, at which the inequality is satisfied. In other words, the solution of an inequality $f(x)>0$, will always be in the form of a range of values of x at which the inequality would be satisfied.

An inequality has no solution if there is no such value for which the given inequality is true.

Notation of Ranges

1. Ranges where the Ends are Excluded If the value of x is denoted as (1, 2), it means $1 < x < 2$, i.e. x is greater than 1 but smaller than 2.

Similarly, if we denote the range of values of x as $-(7, -2)\ U(3, 21)$, this means that the value of x can be denoted as $-7 < x < -2$ and $3 < x < 21$. This would mean that the inequality is satisfied between the two ranges and is not satisfied outside these two ranges.

Based on this notation, write the ranges of x for the following representations:

$$(1, +\infty)\ U(-\infty, -7)$$
$$(-\infty, 0)\ U(4, +\infty), (-\infty, 50)\ U(-50, +\infty)$$

2. Ranges where the Ends are Included

$[2, 5]$ means $2 \le x \le 5$

3. Mixed Ranges

$(3, 21]$ means $3 < x \le 21$

Solving Linear Inequalities in one Unknown

Type 1: Linear Inequalities in one Unknown

A linear inequality is defined as an inequality of the form

$$ax + b\ I\ 0$$

where the symbol 'I' represents any of the inequalities $<, >, \ge, \le$.

For instance, if $ax + b \le 0$, then $ax \le -b$.
$\rightarrow x \le -b/a$ if $a > 0$ and $x \ge -b/a$ if $a < 0$

Example: Solve the inequality $2(x - 3) - 1 > 3(x - 2) - 4(x + 1)$.

$\rightarrow 2x - 7 > 3x - 6 - 4x - 4 \rightarrow 3x > -3.$
Hence, $x > -1$

This can be represented in mathematical terms as $(-1, +\infty)$.

Example: Solve the inequality $2(x - 1) + 1 > 3 - (1 - 2x)$ $\rightarrow 2x - 1 > 2 + 2x \rightarrow 0.x > 3 \rightarrow$ This can never happen. Hence, this inequality has no solution.

Example: Solve the inequality $2(x - 1) + 1 < 3 - (1 - 2x)$.
Gives: $0.x < 3$
This is true for all values of x.

Example: Solve the inequality $ax > a$.

This inequality has the parameter a that needs to be investigated further.

If $a > 0$, then $x > 1$
If $a < 0$, then $x < 1$

Type 2: Quadratic Inequalities

A quadratic inequality is defined as an inequality of the form:

$$ax^2 + bx + c\ I\ 0\ (a \ne 0)$$

where, the symbol I represents any of the inequalities $<, >, \ge, \le$.

For a quadratic expression of the form $ax^2 + bx + c$, $(b^2 - 4ac)$ is defined as the discriminant of the expression and is often denoted as D, i.e. $D = b^2 - 4ac$

The following cases are possible for the value of the quadratic expression. For each of these cases, it would be best to visualise the graph of the quadratic function that is part of the inequality, in order to understand the various reactions you need to have.

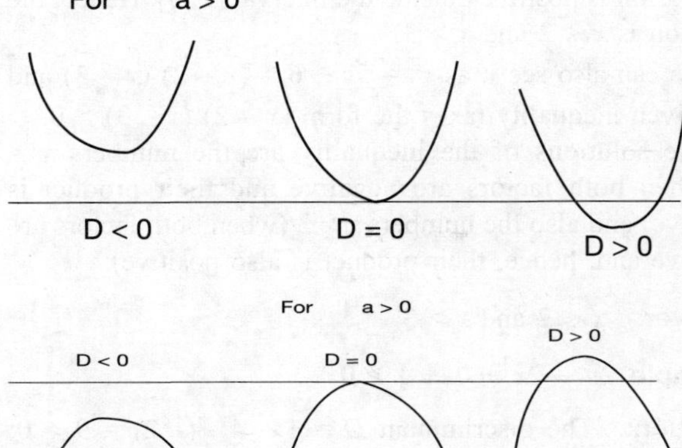

These cases can be paraphrased as follows:

Case 1: If $D < 0$

1. If $a < 0$, then $ax^2 + bx + c < 0$ for all x. In other words, in such situations, the quadratic expression would be negative for all values of x, or always negative.
2. If $a > 0$, then $ax^2 + bx + c > 0$ for all x. In other words, in such situations, the quadratic expression would be positive for all values of x, or always positive.

Case 2: $D = 0$

If the discriminant of a quadratic expression is equal to zero, then the value of the quadratic expression takes the same sign as that of the coefficient of x^2 (except when $x = -b/2a$, at which point the value of the quadratic expression becomes 0).

Case 3: $D > 0$

If x_1 and x_2 are the roots of the quadratic expression, then it can be said that:

1. For $a > 0$, $ax^2 + bx + c$ is positive for all values of x outside the interval $[x_1, x_2]$ and is negative for all values of x within the interval (x_1, x_2). Besides for values of $x = x_1$ or $x = x_2$, the value of the quadratic expression becomes zero (by definition of the root).
2. For $a < 0$, $ax^2 + bx + c$ is negative for all values of x outside the interval $[x_1, x_2]$ and is positive for all values of x within the interval (x_1, x_2). Besides for values of $x = x_1$ or $x = x_2$, the value of the quadratic expression becomes zero (by definition of the root).

Solve the following inequalities.

Example 1: $x^2 - 5x + 6 > 0$

Solution: (a) The discriminant $D = 25 - 4 \times 6 > 0$, and a is positive (+1); the roots of the quadratic expression are real and distinct: $x_1 = 2$ and $x_2 = 3$.

By the property of quadratic inequalities, we get that the expression is positive outside the interval [2, 3]. Hence, the solution is $x < 2$ and $x > 3$.

We can also see it as $x^2 - 5x + 6 = (x - 2)(x - 3)$ and the given inequality takes the form $(x - 2)(x - 3) > 0$.

The solutions of the inequality are the numbers $x < 2$ (when both factors are negative and their product is positive) and also the numbers $x > 3$ (when both factors are positive and, hence, their product is also positive).

Answer: $x < 2$ and $x > 3$.

Example 2: $-2x^2 + x + 1 \geq 0$

Solution: The discriminant $D = 1 - 4 \cdot (-2) = 9 > 0$; the roots of the quadratic expression are real and distinct:

$$x_{1,2} = \frac{-1 \pm \sqrt{9}}{2 \cdot (-2)} = \frac{-1 \pm 3}{-4}$$

Hence, $x_1 = -1/2$ and $x_2 = 1$, and consequently, $-2x^2 + x + 1 = -2(x + 1/2) \times (x - 1)$. We have

$$-2(x + 1/2)(x - 1) \geq 0 \text{ or } (x + 1/2)(x - 1) \leq 0$$

(When dividing both sides of an inequality by a negative number, the sense of the inequality is reversed). The inequality is satisfied by all numbers from the interval

$$[-1/2, 1]$$

Please note that this can also be concluded from the property of quadratic expressions when $D > 0$ and a is negative.

Answer: $-1/2 \leq x \leq 1$.

Example 3: $-2x^2 + x - 1 < 0$

Solution: $D = 1 - 4 \cdot (-2) \cdot (-1) < 0$, the coefficient of x^2 is negative. By the property of the quadratic expression when $D < 0$ and a is negative $-2x^2 + x - 1$ attains only negative, values.

Answer: x can take any value.

Example 4: $3x^2 - 4x + 5 < 0$

Solution: $D = 16 - 4 \times 3 \times 5 < 0$, the coefficient of x^2 is positive. The quadratic expression $3x^2 - 4x + 5$, takes only positive values.

Answer: There is no solution.

Example 5: $4x^2 + 4x + 1 > 0$

Solution: $D = 16 - 4 \times 4 = 0$. The quadratic expression $4x^2 + 4x + 1$ is the square $(2x + 1)^2$, and the given inequality takes the form $(2x + 1)^2 > 0$. It follows that all real numbers x, except for $x = -1/2$, are solutions of the inequality.

Answer: $x \neq -1/2$.

Example 6: $(a - 2)x^2 - x - 1 \geq 0$

Solution: Here, the value of the determinant $D = 1 - 4(-1)(a - 2) = 1 + 4(a - 2) = 4a - 7$.

There can then be three cases:

Case 1: $D < 0 \rightarrow a < 7/4$

Then the coefficient of $x^2 \rightarrow a - 2$ is negative.

Hence, the inequality has no solution.

Case 2: $D = 0$

$a = 7/4$. Put $a = 7/4$ in the expression and then the inequality becomes

$-(x - 2)^2 \geq 0$. This can only happen when $x = 2$.

Case 3: $D > 0$

Then $a > 7/4$ and $a \neq 2$, then we find the roots x_1 and x_2 of the quadratic expression:

$$x_1 = \frac{1 + \sqrt{4a - 7}}{2(a - 2)} \quad \text{and} \quad x_2 = \frac{1 - \sqrt{4a - 7}}{2(a - 2)}$$

Using the property of quadratic expression's values for $D > 0$, we get

If $a - 2 < 0$, the quadratic expression takes negative values outside the interval $[x_1, x_2]$. Hence, it will take positive values inside the interval (x_1, x_2).

If $a - 2 > 0$, the quadratic expression takes positive values outside the interval $[x_1, x_2]$ and becomes zero for x_1 and x_2.

If $a - 2 = 0$, then we get a straight linear equation: $-x - 1 \geq 0 \rightarrow x \leq -1$.

Other types of inequalities get formed, when the expression $f(x)$ is cubic (leading to cubic inequalities); logarithmic (leading to logarithmic inequalities);

System of Inequalities in One Unknown

Let there be given several inequalities in one unknown. If it is required to find the number that will be the solution of all the given equalities, then the set of these inequalities is called a *system of inequalities*.

The solution of a system of inequalities in one unknown is defined as the value of the unknown for which all the inequalities of the system reduce to true numerical inequalities.

To solve a system of inequalities means to find all the solutions of the system or to establish that there is none.

Example 1: Solve the system of inequalities:

$$3x - 4 < 8x + 6$$
$$2x - 1 > 5x - 4$$
$$11x - 9 \leq 15x + 3$$

Solution: We solve the first inequality:

$$3x - 4 < 8x + 6$$
$$-5x < 10$$
$$x > -2$$

It is fulfilled for $x > -2$.

Then we solve the second inequality

$$2x - 1 > 5x - 4$$
$$-3x > -3$$
$$x < 1$$

It is fulfilled for $x < 1$.

And, finally, we solve the third inequality:

$$11x - 9 \leq 15x + 3$$
$$-4x \leq 12$$
$$x \geq -3$$

It is fulfilled for $x \geq -3$. The solution for the system of inequalities will be the range of values of x, at which all the inequalities are satisfied. In this case, All the given inequalities are true for $-2 < x < 1$.

Answer: $-2 < x < 1$.

Example 2: Solve the inequality $\frac{2x-1}{x+1} < 1$

Solution: We have $\frac{2x-1}{x+1} - 1 < 0 \rightarrow \frac{x-2}{x+1} < 0$

This means that the fraction above has to be negative. A fraction is negative only when the numerator and the denominator have opposite signs.

Hence, the above inequality is equivalent to the following set of two inequalities:

$x - 2 > 0$ and $x + 1 < 0$ OR $x - 2 < 0$ and $x + 1 > 0$

From the first system of inequalities, we get

$x > 2$ or $x < -1$. This cannot happen simultaneously since these are inconsistent.

From the second system of inequalities, we get

$$x < 2 \text{ and } x > -1, \text{ i.e } -1 < x < 2$$

Inequalities Containing a Modulus

Result:

$|x| \leq a$, where $a > 0$ means the same as the double inequality

$$-a \leq x \leq a$$

This result is used in solving inequalities containing a modulus.

Example 1: $|2x - 3| \leq 5$

This is equivalent to $-5 \leq 2x - 3 \leq 5$.

i.e. $2x - 3 \geq -5$ and $2x - 3 \leq 5$

$2x \geq -2$ $\quad$ $x \leq 4$

$x \geq -1$

The solution is

$$-1 \leq x \leq 4$$

Example 2: $|1 - x| > 3$

$$|1 - x| = |x - 1|$$

Hence, $|x - 1| > 3 \rightarrow x - 1 > 3$ i.e $x > 4$

or $x - 1 < -3$ or $x < -2$

Solution: $x > 4$ or $x < -2$.

Space for Notes

WORKED-OUT PROBLEMS

Problem 15.1: Solve the inequality $\frac{1}{x} < 1$.

Solution: $\frac{1}{x} < 1 \Leftrightarrow \frac{1}{x} - 1 < 0 \Leftrightarrow \frac{1-x}{x} < 0 \Leftrightarrow \frac{x-1}{x} > 0.$

This can happen only when both the numerator and denominator take the same sign (Why?)

Case 1: Both are positive: $x - 1 > 0$ and $x > 0$ i.e. $x > 1$.

Case 2: Both are negative: $x - 1 < 0$ and $x < 0$ i.e. $x < 0$.

Answer: $(-\infty, 0)$ U $(1, +\infty)$

Problem 15.2: Solve the inequality $\frac{x}{x+2} \le \frac{1}{x}$.

Solution: $\frac{x}{x+2} \le \frac{1}{x} \Leftrightarrow \frac{x}{x+2} - \frac{1}{x} \le 0 \Leftrightarrow \frac{x^2 - x - 2}{x(x+2)}$

$\le 0 \Leftrightarrow \frac{(x-2)(x+1)}{x(x+2)} \le 0$

The function $f(x) = \frac{(x-2)(x+1)}{x(x+2)}$ becomes negative when numerator and denominator are of opposite sign.

Case 1: Numerator positive and denominator negative: This occurs only between $-2 < x < -1$.

Case 2: Numerator negative and denominator positive: Numerator is negative when $(x - 2)$ and $(x + 1)$ take opposite signs. This can be obtained for:

Case A: $x - 2 < 0$ and $x + 1 > 0$, i.e. $x < 2$ and $x > -1$

Case B: $x - 2 > 0$ and $x + 1 < 0$, i.e. $x > 2$ and $x < -1$.

Thus, this cannot happen.

Hence, the answer is $-2 < x < 2$.

Problem 15.3: Solve the inequality $\frac{x}{x-3} \le \frac{1}{x}$.

Solution: $\frac{x}{x-3} \le \frac{1}{x} \Leftrightarrow \frac{x}{x-3} - \frac{1}{x} \ge 0 \Leftrightarrow \frac{x^2 - x + 3}{x(x-3)}$

≤ 0. The function $f(x) = \frac{x^2 - x + 3}{x(x-3)}$.

The numerator being a quadratic equation with $D < 0$ and $a > 0$, we can see that it will always be positive for all values of x. (from the property of quadratic inequalities).

Further, for the expression to be negative, the denominator should be negative.

That is, $x^2 - 3x < 0$. This will occur when $x < 3$ and x is positive.

Answer: (0, 3)

Problem 15.4: Solve the inequality $(x - 1)^2 (x + 1)^3 (x - 4) < 0$.

Solution: The above inequality is valid for

Case 1: $x + 1 < 0$ and $x - 4 > 0$

That is, $x < -1$ and $x > 4$ simultaneously. This cannot happen together.

Case 2: $x + 1 > 0$ and $x - 4 < 0$

That is, $x > -1$ or $x < 4$, i.e. $-1 < x < 4$ is the answer.

Problem 15.5: Solve the inequality $\frac{(x-1)^2(x+1)^3}{x^4(x-2)}$ £ 0.

Solution: The above expression becomes negative when the numerator and the denominator take opposite signs.

That means that the numerator is positive and the denominator is negative or vice versa.

Case 1: Numerator positive and denominator negative: The sign of the numerator is determined by the value of $x + 1$ and that of the denominator is determined by $x - 2$.

This condition happens when $x < 2$ and $x > -1$ simultaneously.

Case 2: Numerator negative and denominator positive: This happens when $x < -1$ and $x > 2$ simultaneously. This will never happen.

Hence, the answer is $-1 \le x < 2$.

Space for Notes

LEVEL OF DIFFICULTY (I)

Evaluate x in the following inequalities:

1. $4x^2 + 3x + 5 < 0$
(a) For all x (b) $x > 0$
(c) $x < 0$ (d) None of these

2. $2x^2 - x + 6 < 0$
(a) $x < 3$ (b) $x > 4$
(c) $3 < x < 4$ (d) None of these

3. $2x^2 - x - 6 < 0$
(a) $x < -\frac{3}{2}$
(b) $x > 2$
(c) $-\frac{3}{2} < x < 2$
(d) None of these $-\sqrt{2} < x < \sqrt{2}$

4. $x^2 - 2 < 0$
(a) $x < \sqrt{2}$ (b) $x > \sqrt{2}$
(c) $-\sqrt{2} < x < \sqrt{2}$ (d) None of these

5. $|x^2 + 5x| < 12x$
(a) $0 < x < 7$ (b) $x < -17$
(c) $x > 0$ (d) All of these

6. $|x^2 - 3x + 6| < 4x - 6$
(a) $3 < x < 4$ (b) $x < -1, x > 0$
(c) Both (a) and (b) (d) None of these

7. $|x^2 - 5x - 6| + 4x - 5 < 0$
(a) $x < \frac{1}{2}\left[9 - \sqrt{65}\right]$
(b) $x < \frac{1}{2}\left[9 + \sqrt{65}\right]$
(c) $-2 < x < \frac{1}{2}\left[9 - \sqrt{65}\right]$
(d) None of these

8. $x^2 - 6x + 9 < |x - 3|$
(a) $2 < x < 3$ (b) $3 < x < 4$
(c) Both (a) and (b) (d) None of these

9. $x^2 - |2x - 6| - x < 3$
(a) $x > \frac{1}{2}\left[-1 - \sqrt{37}\right]$
(b) $x < 3$
(c) $\frac{1}{2}\left[-1 + \sqrt{37}\right] < x < 3$
(d) None of these

10. $|2 - 2x| > x^2 - 3x + 4$
(a) $x < 1$ (b) $x > 3$
(c) $2 < x < 3$ (d) Both (b) and (c)

11. $|2 - 2x| < x^2 - 3x + 4$
(a) $x > 1$ (b) $x<2$ and $x>3$
(c) $1<x<3$ (d) All of these

12. $|x - 3| \le 3x^2 - 7x + 2$
(a) $x > 3$ (b) $x \le \frac{1}{2}\left[6 - 4\sqrt{3}\right]$
(c) Both (a) and (b) (d) None of these

13. $2x^2 - |x - 5| > 10x - 15$
(a) $x \ge 5$ (b) $x < 2$
(c) $5/2 < x < 5$ (d) All of these

14. $x^2 - |5x + 50| > 0$
(a) $-10 \le x < -5, x > 10$ (b) $x \le -10$
(c) Both (a) and (b) (d) None of these

15. $6|x - 2| + x^2 - 28 > 0$
(a) $x > 4$ (b) $x < -2$
(c) Both (a) and (b) (d) None of these

16. $|x - 7| > |x^2 - 7x + 15|$
(a) $2 < x < 4$ (b) $x > 7$
(c) Both (a) and (b) (d) None of these

17. $(|x - 5| - 2)(|x + 3| - 1) < 0$
(a) $-4 < x < -3$
(b) $-3 < x < -2, 3 < x < 5$
(c) $-4 < x < -2$ and $3 < x < 7$
(d) All of these

18. $|x^2 - 6x + 36| > 6x$
(a) $x \ge 6$ (b) $x \le 6$
(c) $x \le -6$ (d) All x except $x = 6$

19. $(x-3)\sqrt{x^2 - 10x + 21} \ge 0$
(a) $x > -3$ (b) $x < -3$
(c) $x \ge 0$ (d) None of these

20. $(x-2)\sqrt{x^2 - 9x + 20} > 0$
(a) $x \ge 5$ (b) $x > 0$
(c) $2 < x \le 4$ (d) Both (a) and (c)

21. $\sqrt{\dfrac{x-5}{1-x}} > 0$
(a) $x > 5$ (b) $1 < x < 5$
(c) $x < 1$ (d) Both (a) and (c)

22. $\sqrt{\dfrac{4x-5}{1-2x}} > 0$

(a) $1 < x < 1.25$ (b) $\frac{1}{2} < x < 1.25$
(c) Both (a) and (b) (d) None of these

23. $\sqrt{2x-5} > \sqrt{7-x}$
(a) $x \geq \frac{5}{2}$ (b) $4 < x \leq 7$
(c) $x \leq \frac{5}{2}$ (d) All of these

24. $\sqrt{x^2-1} < 1$
(a) $-\sqrt{2} < x \leq -1$ (b) $-\sqrt{2} < x < \sqrt{2}$
(c) $1 \leq x < \sqrt{2}$ (d) Both (a) and (c)

25. $2\sqrt{2x-4} < x$
(a) $x \geq 2$ (b) $x > 2$
(c) $x < 2$ (d) $x \geq 2, x \neq 4$

26. $2\sqrt{x+7} < 1-x$
(a) $x < -3$ (b) $x > 9$
(c) $7 \leq x$ (d) $-7 \leq x < -3$ and $x > 9$

27. $x > \sqrt{20-x}$
(a) $x < -5, x > 4$ (b) $x < -5$
(c) $4 < x \leq 20$ (d) Both (b) and (c)

28. $\sqrt{14x-48} < x$
(a) $x \geq \frac{24}{7}$ (b) $x < 6$
(c) $\frac{24}{7} \leq x < 6, x > 8$ (d) None of these

29. $\sqrt{x+6} < x$
(a) $-6 \leq x < -2$ (b) $x > 3$
(c) Both (a) and (b) (d) None of these

30. The solution set of the in-equation $|x - 1| \geq |x - 3|$, is
(a) $[-\infty, 2]$ (b) $[2, \infty]$
(c) $[1, 3]$ (d) None of these

31. The solution of the set of the in-equation $|[x|x|-7]| -5 < 0$ is ([.] denotes the greatest integer function)
(a) [3, 12) (b) (–12, –3]
(c) (–12, 12) (d) Both (a) and (b)

32. If $[x]$ denotes the greatest integer less than or equal to x, then the solution set of the inequation $\frac{[x]-2}{4-[x]} > 0$, is
(a) (2, 3] (b) [3, 4)
(c) [2, 3] (d) [3, 4]

Directions for Questions 33 to 39: Evaluate x in the following inequalities:

33. $|x - 3| \geq 0$
(a) $x - 3 < 0$ (b) $x \geq 3$
(c) $x \geq 9$ (d) None of these

34. $\frac{x}{x-3} > 0$
(a) $x > 3$ (b) $x > 0$
(c) $x < 2$ (d) $x > 3$ and $x < 0$

35. $x^2 - 3x + 2 > 0$
(a) $x > 3$ (b) $x > 0$
(c) $x < 2$ (d) None of these

36. $\frac{x^2-4}{x+3} > 0$
(a) $x > 2$ (b) $-3 < x < -2$
(c) Both (a) and (b) (d) None of these

37. $\frac{x+3}{x-3} > 0$
(a) $x > 3$ (b) $x > 0$
(c) $x < -3$ (d) Both (a) and (c)

38. $|x^2 - 4| > 0$
(a) $x > 3$ (b) $x > 0$
(c) $x < -3$ (d) All except $x = 2$ or -2

39. $\left|\frac{x^2-9}{x-2}\right| \geq 0$
(a) All values of x
(b) All values of x except $x = 2$
(c) $x < -2$
(d) None of these

40. If for all 'x', $x^2 + 2ax + 10 - 3a > 0$, find the interval in which 'a' lies.
(a) (–5, 2) (b) $a < -5$
(c) $a > 5$ (d) $2 < a < 5$

Directions for Questions 41 and 42:

$$\frac{x^2-7|x|+10}{x^2-8x+16} < 0$$

41. For how many negative integral values of x, is the above inequality true?

42. Find the sum of all integer values for which the above inequality is true.

Directions for Questions 43 and 44:

$$f(x) = \frac{x^2-4x-5}{x^2+7x+12}$$

43. For how many positive integer values of x is $f(x) \leq 0$?

44. For how many negative integer values of x is $f(x) \leq 0$?

45. If $f(x) = x^2 + 2|x| + 1$, then for how many real values of x is: $f(x) \leq 0$?

46. If $\frac{1}{|x|-2} > \frac{1}{3}$, then the least positive integer value of x, for which this inequality is true?

Directions for Questions 47 and 48: If $f(x) = |2x - 4|$ and x is an integer, then answer the following questions:

47. Find the maximum value of x for which $f(x) \leq 5$.
48. Find minimum value of x for which $f(x) \leq 5$.
49. For how many integer values of x, is the expression? $(x - 1)(4 - x)(x - 2)^2 > 0$

Directions for Questions 50 and 51:

If $\dfrac{x^2 - 5x + 6}{|x| + 5} \leq 0$

50. Find the minimum value of x, for which the above inequality is true.
51. For how many integer values of x, the above inequality is true?
52. Find the minimum value of x for which $\dfrac{1}{x - 0.5} < 2$ where $x \in I^+$.
53. For how many integer values of x is: $\dfrac{x^2 + 6x - 7}{x^2 + 1} > 2$
54. Maximum value of x, for which $\dfrac{x^2 - 9}{x^2 + x + 1} \leq 0$
55. Find the maximum value of x for which $\dfrac{x+2}{x} \geq x$.

Space for Rough Work

LEVEL OF DIFFICULTY (II)

1. Let $f(x) = (x^2 - 6x + 5)/(x^2 - 5x + 6)$. If $x > 5$, then which of the following is true?
   (a) $0 < f(x) < 1$ (b) $f(x) < 0$
   (c) $f(x) > 0$ (d) $f(x) < 1$
2. If $(|x + 3| + x)/(x + 2) > 1$, then x lies in the range
   (a) $(-5, -2) \cup (-1, \infty)$ (b) $(-5, -2) \cup (1, \infty)$
   (c) $(-5, -2)$ (d) $(-1, \infty)$
3. The area enclosed by the graphs of $(x^2 - 5x + 6) > 0$ and $y < 3$ will definitely be more than
   (a) 13 (b) $35\sqrt{13}/2$
   (c) $1.5(\sqrt{13} + 1)$ (d) Cannot be determined
4. If $n^3(n - 4)^4 (n + 6)^7 (n + 11) > 0$, where $n < 4$ is an integer. Then how many values can n take?
5. For how many values of $n \geq 0$ does the expression $f(n - 3) + 2f(n + 1) \leq 50$ hold true if it known that $f(x) = \max\{x, 0\}$?
   (a) 17 (b) 18
   (c) 19 (d) 20
6. The set of values of x which would satisfy the inequality $(0.8)^{(3x^2 - 8x + 7)} < 0.512$?
   (a) $(⅔, 2)$ (b) $(⅔, \infty)$
   (c) $(-\infty, ⅔) \cup (2, \infty)$ (d) $(-\infty, 3/2) \cup (2, \infty)$
7. If n and m are two positive integers, the inequality $2^n \times 5^m < 4500$ holds true and $n + 2m$ is an odd number, then how many pairs of (n, m) are there?
8. What is the maximum value of x for which $\frac{2x-1}{3} \geq \frac{3x-2}{4} - \frac{2-x}{5}$?
9. For how many integral values of x, is the inequality $\frac{4-|x|}{5-|x|} \geq 0$ not satisfied.
10. For how many integers x, will the inequality $(x - 9)(x - 12) - 6(x - 3) \leq 0$ be satisfied?
    (a) 14 (b) 15
    (c) 16 (d) 17
11. How many integer values of x satisfy $|x - 1| + |x + 4| + |6 - x| + |x - 9| \leq 20$?
12. If $3|x| + 5|y| = 21$ and $|x| - 4|y| = 6$ such that $x - 2y > 3$, then the maximum number of such possible pairs of (x, y) is:
13. For two integers x and y if $x - 2y = 0$ and $x + 2y \leq 6$ & $y - 3x \leq 3$, then which of these can be the value of $x + y$?
    (a) 0 (b) -3
    (c) 6 (d) 4
14. How many solutions does $|x^2 + x - 6| - 3x + 7 < 0$ have if $|x| < 20$?
15. What are the number of integral solutions for the inequality $|3x - 6| + |x + 5| + |7 - x| + |x - 4| \leq 25$
16. Find the number of integral values of x for which $|2x + 4| + |x - 1| + |5 - x| < 15$.
17. Determine the number of integer solutions to $|4x - 12| + |x + 2| + |9 - x| \leq 30$.
18. Solve the inequality $|2x - 8| + |x + 6| + |8 - x| + |x - 5| > 18$.
19. Solve the inequality $|2x - 8| + |x + 6| - |8 - x| + |x - 5| > 18$.
20. Find the values of x for which $|x + 1| + |x - 4| + |6 - x| + |3x - 9| \geq 22$
21. For how many positive integral values, the inequality $\log_{0.6}\left[\log_6 \frac{x^2+x}{x+4}\right] < 0$ does not hold true?
22. How many positive integer x are there such that $(x - 3)^{3/2} - 5(x - 3) < 0$ holds true?
23. What will be the solution set for the function $(x!)^2 - x! - 552 \geq 0$, where x is a natural number?
    A. $x \leq 23$ B. $[0, 5]$
    C. $[0, 4]$ D. $[4, \infty)$
24. What will be the sum of the positive solution set of the inequality $(x!)^2 - x! - 552 \geq 0$, if x is an even number less than 100.
25. For how many integral values of 'x', the inequalities $|x| - 1 - |x| + |2x| + 3 \geq 2x + 4$ and $|x| < 10$ holds?
26. How many integer solutions exist if $|x + 6| + |x - 10| \leq 16$?
27. The area enclosed by the equation $(2x^2 - 8x + 8) < 0$ and $y > -3$ will be
28. How many integral solutions exist for the equation $|x - 105| + |y - 103| \leq 2$
29. If $|x^2 - 30x + 221| > x^2 - 30x + 221$, then what is the difference between the highest and lowest possible value of x?
30. Find the area of the region bounded by $y \geq -|x| + 5$, $y \leq |x| + 5$ and $-5 \leq x \leq 5$.
31. What is the maximum value of $3x + 8y$, if $3x + 5y \leq 30$, $5x + 2y \leq 12$, where x and y are whole numbers?
32. If x satisfies the inequality $|x - 1| + |x - 2| + |x - 3| \geq 6$, then
    (a) $0 \leq x \leq 4$ (b) $x \leq 0$ or $x \geq 4$
    (c) $x \leq -2$ or $x \geq 3$ (d) $x \geq 3$

Direction for Questions 33 and 34: If $f(x) = |x + 4| - |x - 4|$ and $|f(x)| < 8$, then answer the following questions:

33. How many integer values of x satisfy the above inequality?
    (a) 6 (b) 7
    (c) 8 (d) 9
34. What is the sum of all positive integer values of x satisfying the above inequality?
    (a) 5 (b) 6
    (c) 8 (d) 10

Directions for Questions 35 and 36: If $x > -6$ and $\frac{1}{x-5}+\frac{1}{x+3}<0$, then answer the following questions:

35. Find the number of positive integer values of x, which satisfy the given inequality.

36. Find the sum of all positive integer values of x which satisfy the given inequality.

Directions for Questions 37 and 38: $|4x - 3| \le 8$ and $|3y + 4| \le 17$, then answer the following questions:

37. Minimum value of $|x|+|y| =$

38. Maximum value of $|x| - |y| =$

39. If $f(x)=\frac{x}{2x^2+5x+8}$ for all $x > 0$ what is the greatest value of $f(x)$?

(a) 1/4 (b) 1/8
(c) 1/13 (d) 1/5

40. The shaded portion of which of the following options represents $y \ge x^2$, $y \le 3$?

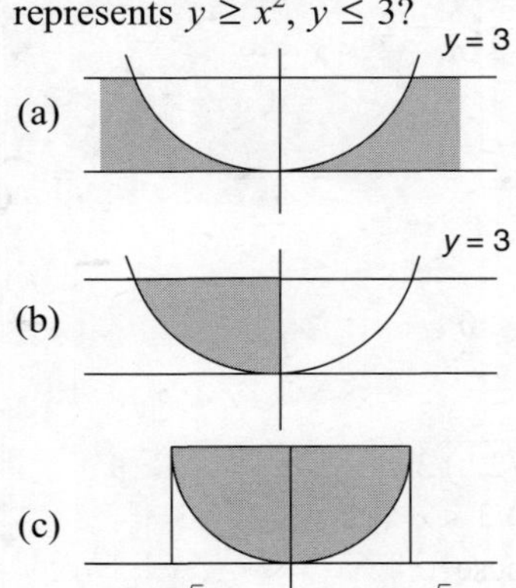

(d) None of these

41. Find the range of values of x for which $x^4 + 8x < 8x^3 + x^2$.

(a) $(-1,0) \cup (1,8)$ (b) $(0,1) \cup (8,\infty)$
(c) $(-\infty,-8) \cup (1, 8)$ (d) $(-1, 0) \cup (8, \infty)$

42. If $\frac{45}{25x^{14}-8x^7+1} \le p$, then find the minimum value of p,

43. If $0 \le x \le 13$ for how many integer values of x, $7^{x-1} + 11^{x-1} > 170$?

44. If $f(x) = \min(3x + 4, 6 - 2x)$ and $f(x) < p$ where p is an integer then the minimum possible value of p = ?

45. For how many non-negative integer values of 'x' is $||||||x - 1| - 2| - 3| - 4| - 5| - 6| - 7| < 9$?

(a) 35 (b) 36
(c) 37 (d) 38

46. $x^2 - 5|x| + 6 < 0$

(a) $-3 < x < -2$ (b) $2 < x < 3$
(c) Both (a) and (b) (d) $-3 < x < 3$

47. $x^2 - |x| - 2 \ge 0$

(a) $-2 < x < 2$ (b) $x \le -2$ or $x \ge 2$
(c) $x < -2$ or $x > 1$ (d) $-2 < x < 1$

Directions for Questions 48 to 55: Solve the following polynomial inequalities

48. $(x - 1)(3 - x)(x - 2)^2 > 0$

(a) $1 < x < 2$ (b) $-1 < x < 3$
(c) $-3 < x < -1$ (d) $1 < x < 3, x \ne 2$

49. $\frac{0.5}{x-x^2-1} < 0$

(a) $x > 0$ (b) $x \le 0$
(c) $x \ge 0$ (d) For all real x

50. $\frac{x^2-5x+6}{x^2+x+1} < 0$

(a) $x < 2$ (b) $x > 3$
(c) $2 < x < 3$ (d) $x < 2$ or $x > 3$

51. $\frac{x^2+2x-3}{x^2+1} < 0$

(a) $x < -3$ (b) $-7 < x < -3$
(c) $-3 < x < 1$ (d) $-7 < x < 1$

52. $\frac{(x-1)(x+2)^2}{-1-x} < 0$

(a) $x < -1$
(b) $x < -1$ or $x > 1$
(c) $x < -1$ and $x \ne 2$
(d) $x < -1$ or $x > 1$ and $x \ne -2$

53. $\frac{x^2+4x+4}{2x^2-x-1} > 0$

(a) $x < -2$ (b) $x > 1$
(c) $x \ne 2$ (d) None of these

54. $x^4 - 5x^2 + 4 < 0$

(a) $-2 < x < 1$
(b) $-2 < x < 2$
(c) $-2 < x < -1$ or $1 < x < 2$
(d) $1 < x < 2$

55. $x^4 - 2x^2 - 63 \le 0$

(a) $x \le -3$ or $x \ge 3$ (b) $-3 \le x \le 0$
(c) $0 \le x \le 3$ (d) $-3 \le x \le 3$

Directions for Questions 56 to 91: Solve the following polynomial and quadratic inequalities

56. $\frac{5x-1}{x^2+3} < 1$

(a) $x < 4$ (b) $1 < x < 4$
(c) $x < 1$ or $x > 4$ (d) $1 < x < 3$

57. $\frac{x-2}{x^2+1} < -\frac{1}{2}$

(a) $-3 < x < 3$ (b) $x < -3$
(c) $-3 < x < 6$ (d) $-3 < x < 1$

58. $\frac{x+1}{(x-1)^2} < 1$

(a) $x > 3$ or x is negative
(b) $x > 3$
(c) $x > 3$ or $-23 < x < 0$
(d) x is negative and $x > 2$

59. $\frac{x^2-7x+12}{2x^2+4x+5} > 0$

(a) $x < 3$ or $x > 4$ (b) $3 < x < 4$
(c) $4 < x < 24$ (d) $0 < x < 3$

60. $\frac{x^2+6x-7}{x^2+1} \le 2$

(a) x is negative (b) $x \ge 0$
(c) $x > 0$ or $x < 0$ (d) Always

61. $\frac{x^4+x^2+1}{x^2-4x-5} < 0$

(a) $x < -1$ or $x > 5$ (b) $-1 < x < 5$
(c) $x > 5$ (d) $-5 < x < -1$

62. $\frac{1+3x^2}{2x^2-21x+40} < 0$

(a) $0 < x < 8$ (b) $2.5 < x < 8$
(c) $-8 < x < 8$ (d) $3 < x < 8$

63. $\frac{1+x^2}{x^2-5x+6} < 0$

(a) $x < 2$ (b) $x > 3$
(c) Both (a) and (b) (d) $2 < x < 3$

64. $\frac{x^4+x^2+1}{x^2-4x-5} > 0$

(a) $-1 < x < 5$ (b) $x < -1$ or $x > 5$
(c) $x \le -1$ or $x > 5$ (d) $-1 < x < 1$

65. $\frac{1-2x-3x^2}{3x-x^2-5} > 0$

(a) $x < -1$ or $x > 1/3$ (b) $x < -1$ or $x = 1/3$
(c) $-1 < x < 1/3$ (d) $x < 1/3$

66. $\frac{x^2-5x+7}{-2x^2+3x+2} > 0$

(a) $x > 0.5$ (b) $x > -0.5$
(c) $-0.5 < x < 5$ (d) $-0.5 < x < 2$

67. $\frac{2x^2-3x-459}{x^2+1} > 1$

(a) $x > -20$ (b) $x < 0$
(c) $x < -20$ (d) $-20 < x < 20$

68. $\frac{x^2-1}{x^2+x+1} < 1$

(a) $x > -2$ (b) $x > 2$
(c) $-2 < x < 2$ (d) $x < 2$

69. $\frac{1-2x-3x^2}{3x-x^2-5} > 0$

(a) $1 < x < 3$ (b) $1 < x < 7$
(c) $-3 < x < 3$ (d) None of these

70. $\frac{x}{x^2-3x-4} > 0$

(a) $-1 < x < 0$ (b) $4 < x$
(c) Both (a) and (b) (d) $-1 < x < 4$

71. $\frac{x^2+7x+10}{x+2/3} > 0$

(a) $-5 < x < -2$ or $\frac{-2}{3} < x < \infty$
(b) $-5 < x < 8$
(c) $x < -2$
(d) $x > -2$

72. $\frac{3x^2-4x-6}{2x-5} < 0$

(a) $x < (2-\sqrt{22})/3$
(b) $x > (2+\sqrt{22})/3$
(c) $(2-\sqrt{22})/3 < x < (2+\sqrt{22})/3$
(d) None of these

73. $\frac{17-15x-2x^2}{x+3} < 0$

(a) $-8.5 < x \le -3$
(b) $-17 < x < -3$
(c) $-8.5 < x < -3$ or $x > 1$
(d) $-8.5 < x < 1$

74. $\frac{x^2-9}{3x-x^2-24} < 0$

(a) $-3 < x < 3$ (b) $x < -3$ or $x > 3$
(c) $x < -5$ or $x > 5$ (d) $x < -7$ or $x > 7$

75. $\frac{x+7}{x-5} + \frac{3x+1}{2} \ge 0$

(a) $1 < x < 5$ (b) $-1 < x < 5$
(c) $1 \le x \le 3$ or $x > 5$ (d) $-1 < x < 3$

76. $2x^2 + \frac{1}{x} > 0$

(a) $x > 0$ (b) $x < -1/2$
(c) Both (a) and (b) (d) None of these

77. $\dfrac{x^2 - x - 6}{x^2 + 6x} \geq 0$

(a) $x < -6$ (b) $-2 \leq x < 0$
(c) $x > 3$ (d) All of these

78. $\dfrac{x^2 - 5x + 6}{x^2 - 11x + 30} < 0$

(a) $x < 3$ or $x > 5$
(b) $2 < x < 4$ or $5 < x < 7$
(c) $2 < x < 3$ or $5 < x < 6$
(d) $2 < x < 3$ or $5 < x < 7$

79. $\dfrac{x^2 - 8x + 7}{4x^2 - 4x + 1} < 0$

(a) $x < 1$ or $x > 7$ (b) $1 < x < 7$
(c) $-7 < x < 1$ (d) $-7 < x < 7$

80. $\dfrac{x^2 - 36}{x^2 - 9x + 18} < 0$

(a) $-6 < x < 3$ (b) $-6 < x < 6$
(c) $x < -6$ or $x > 3$ (d) $-3 < x < 3$

81. $\dfrac{x^2 - 6x + 9}{5 - 4x - x^2} \geq 0$

(a) $-5 < x < 1$ or $x = 3$ (b) $-5 \leq x < 1$ or $x = 3$
(c) $-5 < x \leq 1$ or $x = 3$ (d) $-5 \leq x \leq -1$

82. $\dfrac{x - 1}{x + 1} < x$

(a) $x < -1$ (b) $x > -1$
(c) $-1 < x < 1$ (d) For all real values of x

83. $\dfrac{14x}{x + 1} - \dfrac{9x - 30}{x - 4} < 0$

(a) $-1 < x < 1$ or $4 < x < 6$
(b) $-1 < x < 4$, $5 < x < 7$
(c) $1 < x < 4$ or $5 < x < 7$
(d) $-1 < x < 1$ or $5 < x < 7$

84. $\dfrac{5x^2 - 2}{4x^2 - x + 3} < 1$

(a) $x < 1$
(b) $-2 < x < 2$
(c) $-2.7 < x < 1.75$
(d) $(-(1 + \sqrt{21})/2 < x < (\sqrt{21} - 1)/2$

85. $\dfrac{x^2 - 5x + 12}{x^2 - 4x + 5} > 3$

(a) $x > 0.5$ (b) $1/2 < x < 3$
(c) $x < 0.5, x > 3$ (d) $1 < x < 3$

86. $\dfrac{x^2 - 3x + 24}{x^2 - 3x + 3} < 4$

(a) $x < -1$ (b) $4 < x < 8$
(c) $x < 4$ or $x > 8$ (d) None of these

87. $\dfrac{x^2 - 1}{2x + 5} < 3$

(a) $x < -2.5$ or $-2 < x < 8$
(b) $-2.5 < x < -2$
(c) $-2.5 < x < 8$
(d) Both (a) and (b)

88. $\dfrac{x^2 + 1}{4x - 3} > 2$

(a) $x > 7$ (b) $x > 7, x < 87$
(c) $0.75 < x < 1, x > 7$ (d) $0.25 < x < 1, x > 7$

89. $\dfrac{x^2 + 2}{x^2 - 1} < -2$

(a) $-1 < x < 2$
(b) $-1 < x < 1,$
(c) $-1 < x < 0, 0 < x < 1$
(d) $-2 < x < 2$

90. $\dfrac{3x - 5}{x^2 + 4x - 5} > \dfrac{1}{2}$

(a) $x < -5$ (b) $x > 1$
(c) $-5 < x < 1$ (d) $-5 < x < 5$

91. $\dfrac{2x + 3}{x^2 + x - 12} \leq \dfrac{1}{2}$

(a) $-4 < x < -3, 3 < x < 6$
(b) $-4 < x < -3, 0 < x < 6$
(c) $x < -4, -3 \leq x < 3, x > 6$
(d) $x < -4, x > 6$

Directions for Questions 92 to 116: Solve inequalities based on modulus.

92. $|x^3 - 1| \geq 1 - x$

(a) $-1 < x < 0$ (b) $x < -1$
(c) $0 < x$ (d) Always except (a)

93. $\dfrac{x^2 - 5x + 6}{|x| + 7} < 0$

(a) $2 \leq x \leq 3$ (b) $2 < x$
(c) $1 < x < 3$ (d) $2 < x < 3$

94. $\dfrac{x^2 + 6x - 7}{|x + 4|} < 0$

(a) $-7 < x < -5$ and $-4 < x < 1$
(b) $-7 < x < -5$ and $-4 < x < 0$
(c) $-7 < x < -4$ and $-4 < x < 1$
(d) None of these

95. $\dfrac{|x - 2|}{x - 2} > 0$

(a) $2 < x < 10$ (b) $3 \leq x$
(c) $2 \leq x$ (d) $2 < x$

96. $\left|\frac{2}{x-4}\right| > 1$

(a) $2 < x < 4; 4 \le x \le 5$ (b) $2 < x \le 4; 4 \le x \le 5$
(c) $2 < x < 4; 4 < x < 6$ (d) $2 < x < 4; 4 \le x \le 6$

97. $\left|\frac{2x-1}{x-1}\right| > 2$

(a) $2 < x$ (b) $1 < x$
(c) $3/4 < x < 1$ (d) Both (b) and (c)

98. $\left|\frac{x^2-3x-1}{x^2+x+1}\right| < 3$

(a) $x < -2$ (b) $-1 < x$
(c) Always except (b) (d) Both (a) and (b)

99. $\frac{x^2-7|x|+10}{x^2-6x+9} < 0$

(a) $-5 \le x \le -2; 2 < x < 5$
(b) $-5 < x < -2; 2 < x < 5$
(c) $-5 < x < -2; 2 < x < 3; 3 < x < 5$
(d) $-5 < x < -2; 3 < x < 5$

100. $\frac{|x+3|+x}{x+2} > 1$

(a) $-5 < x \le -2$ (b) $-2 \le x \le -1$
(c) $-1 < x$ (d) Always except (b)

101. $\frac{|x-1|}{x+2} < 1$

(a) $-8 < x \le -3$
(b) $-3 < x \le -2$
(c) Always except $x = -2$
(d) Both (a) and (b)

102. $\frac{|x+2|-x}{x} < 2$

(a) $-5 \le x < 0$ (b) $0 \le x \le 1$
(c) Both (a) and (b) (d) Always except (b)

103. $\frac{1}{|x|-3} < \frac{1}{2}$

(a) $x < -5$ and $-3 < x < 3$
(b) $3 \le x \le 5$
(c) $-5 \le x \le -3$
(d) Always except (b) and (c)

104. $\left|\frac{3x}{x^2-4}\right| \le 1$

(a) $x \le -4$ and $-1 \le x \le 1$
(b) $4 \le x$
(c) Both of these
(d) None of these

105. $\left|\frac{x^2-5x+4}{x^2-4}\right| \le 1$

(a) $[0 < x < 8/5]\ U\ [5/2 < x < +\infty]$
(b) $[0, 5/2]\ U\ [16/5, +\infty]$
(c) $[0, 8/5]\ U\ [5/2, +\infty]$
(d) $[0, 8/5]\ U\ [5/2, +\infty]$

106. $\frac{|x-3|}{x^2-5x+6} \ge 2$

(a) [3/2, 1] (b) [1, 2]
(c) [1.5, 2] (d) None of these

107. $\frac{x^2-|x|-12}{x-3} \ge 2x$

(a) $-101 < x < 25$ (b) $[-\infty, 3]$
(c) $x \le 3$ (d) $x < 3$

108. $|x| < \frac{9}{x}$

(a) $x < -1$ (b) $0 < x < 3$
(c) $1 < x < 3; x < -1$ (d) $-\infty < x < 3$

109. $1 + \frac{12}{x^2} < \frac{7}{x}$

(a) $x < -2; 2 < x < 3$ (b) $3 \le x < 4$
(c) Both (a) and (b) (d) None of these

110. $\frac{(x^2-4x+5)}{(x^2+5x+6)} \ge 0$

(a) $-\infty < x < \infty$ (b) $x < -3$
(c) $x > -2$ (d) Both (b) and (c)

111. $\frac{x+1}{x-1} \ge \frac{x+5}{x+1}$

(a) $x < -1$ (b) $0 < x < 3$
(c) $1 < x \le 3, x < -1$ (d) $-\infty < x < 3$

112. $\frac{x-1}{x^2-x-12} \le 0$

(a) $x < -3; 2 < x < 3$ (b) $3 \le x < 4$
(c) Both (a) and (b) (d) None of these

113. $1 < (3x^2 - 7x + 8)/(x^2 + 1) \le 2$

(a) $1 < x < 6$ (b) $1 \le x < 6$
(c) $1 < x \le 6$ (d) $1 \le x \le 6$

114. If $f'(x) \ge g(x)$, where $f(x) = 5 - 3x + \frac{5}{2}x^2 - \frac{x^3}{3}$, $g(x) = 3x - 7$

(a) [2, 3] (b) [2, 4]
(c) $x = 2.5$ (d) None of these

115. $f'(x) \ge g'(x)$, if $f(x) = 10x^3 - 13x^2 + 7x$, $g(x) = 11x^3 - 15x^2 - 3$

(a) [–1, 7/3] (b) [–1, 3.5]
(c) [–1, 9/3] (d) [1, 7/3]

116. $\dfrac{1}{x-2} - \dfrac{1}{x} \le \dfrac{2}{x+2}$

(a) $(-2, -1)\ U\ (2, +\infty)$
(b) $-2 < x < 1$
(c) Both (a) and (b)
(d) None of these

Directions for Questions 117 to 119: Solve the following irrational inequalities.

117. $(x-1)\sqrt{x^2 - x - 2} \ge 0$

(a) $x < 2$
(b) $3 \le x < \infty$
(c) Always except (a)
(d) Both (a) and (b)

118. $(x^2 - 1)\sqrt{x^2 - x - 2} \ge 0$

(a) $x < -1$ (b) $2 \le x$
(c) Both (a) and (b) (d) None of these

119. $\dfrac{\sqrt{x-3}}{x-2} > 0$

(a) $0 \le x < 2$ (b) $x > 3$
(c) $0 < x < 1$ (d) Both (b) and (c)

High Yield Questions

Scan this QR code to access assisted problem solving videos on questions 16, 35, 36, 92, 94 and 117 from LOD 2

Space for Rough Work

ANSWER KEY

Level of Difficulty (I)

1. (d)	2. (d)	3. (c)	4. (c)
5. (a)	6. (a)	7. (d)	8. (c)
9. (d)	10. (c)	11. (b)	12. (c)
13. (d)	14. (c)	15. (c)	16. (c)
17. (c)	18. (d)	19. (d)	20. (d)
21. (b)	22. (b)	23. (b)	24. (d)
25. (d)	26. (d)	27. (d)	28. (c)
29. (c)	30. (d)	31. (d)	32. (b)
33. (d)	34. (d)	35. (d)	36. (c)
37. (d)	38. (d)	39. (b)	40. (a)
41. 2	42. –4	43. 5	44. 1
45. 0	46. 3	47. 4	48. 0
49. 1	50. 2	51. 2	52. 2
53. 0	54. 3	55. 2	

Level of Difficulty (II)

1. (a)	2. (a)	3. (c)	4. 7
5. (b)	6. (a)	7. 13	8. 2
9. 2	10. (c)	11. 8	12. 2
13. (a)	14. 30	15. 5	16. 3
17. 9	18. $(-\infty, 3) \cup (5.66, \infty)$		
19. $(-\infty, -6.33) \cup (6.66, \infty)$			
20. $(-\infty, 0.5] \cup [6.66, \infty)$			
21. 7	22. 26	23. (d)	24. 2448
25. 9	26. 17	27. 0	28. 12
29. 2	30. 50	31. 48	32. (b)
33. (b)	34. (b)	35. (3)	36. 9
37. 0	38. 2.75	39. (c)	40. (c)
41. (a)	42. 125	43. 10	44. 6
45. (c)	46. (c)	47. (b)	48. (d)
49. (d)	50. (c)	51. (c)	52. (d)
53. (d)	54. (c)	55. (d)	56. (c)
57. (d)	58. (a)	59. (a)	60. (d)
61. (b)	62. (b)	63. (d)	64. (b)
65. (a)	66. (d)	67. (c)	68. (a)
69. (d)	70. (c)	71. (a)	72. (d)
73. (c)	74. (b)	75. (c)	76. (d)
77. (d)	78. (c)	79. (b)	80. (a)
81. (a)	82. (b)	83. (a)	84. (d)
85. (b)	86. (d)	87. (a)	88. (c)
89. (c)	90. (c)	91. (c)	92. (d)
93. (d)	94. (c)	95. (d)	96. (c)
97. (d)	98. (d)	99. (c)	100. (d)
101. (c)	102. (d)	103. (d)	104. (c)
105. (a)	106. (d)	107. (d)	108. (b)
109. (b)	110. (d)	111. (c)	112. (d)
113. (d)	114. (d)	115. (a)	116. (d)
117. (c)	118. (c)	119. (b)	

SOLUTIONS AND SHORTCUTS

While practically solving inequalities, remember the following:

1. The answer to an inequality question is always in the form of a range and represents the range of values where the inequality is satisfied.
2. In the cases of all continuous functions, the point at which the range of the correct answer will start will always be a solution of the same function if written as an equation.

   This rule is only broken for non-continuous functions.

   Hence, if you judge that a function is continuous always check the options for LHS = RHS at the starting point of the option.
3. The correct range has to have two essential properties if it has to be the correct answer:
   (a) The inequality should be satisfied for each and every value of the range.
   (b) There should be no value satisfying the inequality outside the range of the correct option.

   Questions on inequalities are always solved using options and based on (3) (a) and (3) (b) above; we would reject an option as the correct answer if:
   (i) We find even a single value not satisfying the inequality within the range of a single option.
   (ii) We can reject given option, even if we find a single value satisfying the inequality but not lying within the range of the option under check.

   I will now show you certain solved questions on this pattern of thinking.

Level of Difficulty (I)

1. $4x^2 + 3x + 5 < 0$
   Here discriminant of this equation is < 0.
   So this will always be either positive or always negative.
   But since a, i.e. 4 > 0.
   This will always be positive.
   Hence, (d) is the correct option.
2. Here discriminant of this equation is < 0.
   So this will always be either positive or always negative.
   But since a i.e. 2 > 0.
   This will always be positive.
   Hence, (d) is the correct option
3. $2x^2 - x - 6 < 0$
   Or $(x - 2)(2x + 3) < 0$
   Or $-\frac{3}{2} < x < 2$
   Hence, option (c) is the correct option.
4. $x^2 - 2 < 0$
   Or $\left(x-\sqrt{2}\right)\left(x+\sqrt{2}\right)<0$

Or $-\sqrt{2} < x < \sqrt{2}$

Hence, option (c) is the correct option.

5. Here $|x^2 + 5x| = x^2 + 5x$ if $x^2 + 5x > 0$
$= -5x - x^2$ if $x^2 + 5x < 0$
Or $|x^2 + 5x| = x^2 + 5x$ if $x < -5, x > 0$
$= -5x - x^2$ if $-5 < x < 0$
Thus, the given equation implies the following cases:
Case 1: $x < -5, x > 0$
$x^2 + 5x < 12x$
$x^2 - 7x < 0$
Or $x(x-7) < 0$
Or $0 < x < 7$
Case 2: $-5 < x < 0$
$-5x - x^2 < 12x$
Or $x^2 + 17x > 0$
$x(x+17) > 0$
So, $x < -17, x > 0$ (but they do not lie in $-5 < x < 0$)
Hence, there is no solution for this case
Hence, (a) is the correct option.

6. Here $|x^2 - 3x + 6| = x^2 - 3x + 6$ if $x^2 - 3x + 6 > 0$
$= -x^2 + 3x - 6$ if $x^2 - 3x + 6 < 0$
But $(x^2 - 3x + 6)$ is always greater than 0. ($D < 0$, $a > 0$)
So, $|x^2 - 3x + 6| = x^2 - 3x + 6$.
Thus, $x^2 - 3x + 6 < 4x - 6$
Or $x^2 - 7x + 12 < 0$
Or $(x-3)(x-4) < 0$
Or $3 < x < 4$
Hence, option (a) is the correct option.

7. Here $|x^2 - 5x - 6| = x^2 - 5x - 6$ if $x^2 - 5x - 6 > 0$
$= 6 + 5x - x^2$ if $x^2 - 5x - 6 < 0$
Or $|x^2 - 5x - 6| = x^2 - 5x - 6$ if $x < -1, x > 6$
$= 6 + 5x - x^2$ if $-1 < x < 6$
Thus, the given equation implies the following cases:
Case 1: $x < -1, x > 6$
$x^2 - 5x - 6 + 4x - 5 < 0$
$x^2 - x - 11 < 0$
Or $\frac{1}{2}\left[1-3\sqrt{5}\right] < x < \frac{1}{2}\left[1+3\sqrt{5}\right]$
So $\frac{1}{2}\left[1-3\sqrt{5}\right] < x < -1$
Case 2: $-1 < x < 6$
$6 + 5x - x^2 + 4x - 5 < 0$
Or $x^2 - 9x - 1 > 0$
$x < \frac{1}{2}\left[9-\sqrt{85}\right], x > \frac{1}{2}\left[9+\sqrt{85}\right]$
So, $-1 < x < \frac{1}{2}\left[9-\sqrt{85}\right]$
Hence, (d) is the correct option.

8. Here $|x - 3| = x - 3$ if $x - 3 > 0$
$= 3 - x$ if $x - 3 < 0$
Or $|x - 3| = x - 3$ if $x > 3$
$= 3 - x$ if $x < 3$
Thus, the given equation implies the following cases:
Case 1: $x > 3$
$x^2 - 6x + 9 < x - 3$
$x^2 - 7x + 12 < 0$
Or $(x-3)(x-4) < 0$
So $3 < x < 4$
Case 2: $x < 3$
$x^2 - 6x + 9 < 3 - x$
Or $x^2 - 5x + 6 < 0$
$(x-2)(x-3) < 0$
So $2 < x < 3$
Hence, (c) is the correct option.

9. Here $|2x - 6| = 2x - 6$ if $2x - 6 > 0$
$= 6 - 2x$ if $2x - 6 < 0$
Or $|2x - 6| = 2x - 6$ if $x > 3$
$= 6 - 2x$ if $x < 3$
Thus, the given equation implies the following cases:
Case 1: $x > 3$
$x^2 - 2x + 6 - x < 3$
$x^2 - 3x + 3 < 0$
The LHS is always positive, so no solution for this case.
Case 2: $x < 3$
$x^2 - 6 + 2x - x < 3$
Or $x^2 + x - 9 < 0$
So $x > \frac{1}{2}\left[-1-\sqrt{37}\right], x < \frac{1}{2}\left[-1+\sqrt{37}\right]$
Hence, option (d) is the correct option.

10. Here $|2 - 2x| = 2 - 2x$ if $2 - 2x > 0$
$= 2x - 2$ if $2 - 2x < 0$
Or $|2 - 2x| = 2 - 2x$ if $x < 1$
$= 2x - 2$ if $x > 1$
Thus, the given equation implies the following cases:
Case 1: If $x < 1$
$2 - 2x > x^2 - 3x + 4$.
$x^2 - x + 2 < 0$
This is always positive, so no solution for this case.
Case 2: $x > 1$
$2x - 2 > x^2 - 3x + 4$
Or $x^2 - 5x + 6 < 0$
$(x-2)(x-3) < 0$
So $2 < x < 3$
Hence, option (c) is the correct option.

11. Here $|2 - 2x| = 2 - 2x$ if $2 - 2x > 0$
$= 2x - 2$ if $2 - 2x < 0$
Or $|2 - 2x| = 2 - 2x$ if $x < 1$
$= 2x - 2$ if $x > 1$
Thus, the given equation implies the following cases:

Case 1: $x < 1$

$2 - 2x < x^2 - 3x + 4 \qquad x^2 - x + 2 > 0$

The above polynomial is always positive for all the real values of x. Hence, for this case, the answer would be when $x < 1$.

Case 2: $x > 1$

$2x - 2 < x^2 - 3x + 4$

Or $\quad x^2 - 5x + 6 > 0$

$(x - 2)(x - 3) > 0$

So, $x < 2$ and $x > 3$. In this case, the solution would be $1 < x < 2$ and $x > 3$.

Combining the ranges for the two case, we can see that the correct answer would be $x < 2$ and $x > 3$.

Hence, option (b) is the correct option.

12. Here $|x - 3| = x - 3 \quad$ if $x - 3 > 0$
$= 3 - x \quad$ if $x - 3 < 0$
Or $\quad |x - 3| = x - 3 \quad$ if $x > 3$
$= 3 - x \quad$ if $x < 3$

Thus, the given equation implies the following cases:

Case 1: $x > 3$

$x - 3 \leq 3x^2 - 7x + 2$

Or $\quad 3x^2 - 8x + 5 \geq 0$

$(x - 1)(3x - 5) \geq 0$

$x \leq 1, x \geq \frac{5}{3}$

But since $x > 3$

So $x > 3$ is the solution for this case.

Case 2: $x < 3$

$3 - x \leq 3x^2 - 7x + 2$

Or $\quad 3x^2 - 6x - 1 \geq 0$

So $\quad x \leq \frac{1}{2}\left[6 - 4\sqrt{3}\right], x \geq \frac{1}{2}\left[6 + 4\sqrt{3}\right]$

But since $x < 3$

Hence, $x \leq \frac{1}{2}\left[6 - 4\sqrt{3}\right]$ is the solution for this case.

Hence, option (c) is the correct option.

13. Here $|x - 5| = x - 5 \quad$ if $x - 5 > 0$
$= 5 - x \quad$ if $x - 5 < 0$
Or $\quad |x - 5| = x - 5 \quad$ if $x > 5$
$= 5 - x \quad$ if $x < 5$

Thus, the given equation implies the following cases:

Case 1: $x > 5$

$2x^2 - x + 5 > 10x - 15$

Or $\quad 2x^2 - 11x + 20 > 0$

This expression will always be positive, i.e. greater than 0.

But since $x > 5$

So, $x > 5$ is the solution for this case.

Case 2: $x < 5$

$2x^2 - 5 + x > 10x - 15$

Or $\quad 2x^2 - 9x + 10 > 0$

So $\quad (x - 2)(2x - 5) > 0$

$x < 2, x > \frac{5}{2}$

But since $x < 5$

Hence, $x < 2, \frac{5}{2} < x < 5$ is the solution for this case.

Also, at $x = 5$, we can see that the inequality is satisfied.

Hence, (d) is the correct option

14. Here $|5x + 50| = 5x + 50 \quad$ if $5x + 50 > 0$
$= -5x - 50 \quad$ if $5x + 50 < 0$
Or $\quad |5x + 50| = 5x + 50 \quad$ if $x > -10$
$= -5x - 50 \quad$ if $x < -10$

Thus, the given equation implies the following cases:

Case 1: $x > -10$

$x^2 - 5x - 50 > 0$

Or $\quad (x - 10)(x + 5) > 0$

Or $\quad x < -5, x > 10$

But $x > -10$

So $-10 < x < -5$ and $x > 10$ is the solution for this case.

Case 2: $x < -10$

$x^2 + 5x + 50 > 0$

This expression is always positive.

But since $x < -10$

Hence, $x < -10$ is the solution for this case.

Hence, option (c) is the correct option.

15. Here $|x - 2| = x - 2 \quad$ if $x - 2 > 0$
$= 2 - x \quad$ if $x - 2 < 0$
Or $\quad |x - 2| = x - 2 \quad$ if $x > 2$
$= 2 - x \quad$ if $x < 2$

Thus, the given equation implies the following cases:

Case 1: $x > 2$

$x^2 + 6x - 40 > 0$

Or $\quad (x + 10)(x - 4) > 0$

Or $\quad x < -10, x > 4$

But $x > 2$

So, $x > 4$ is the solution for this case.

Case 2: $x < 2$

$x^2 - 6x - 16 > 0$

$(x - 8)(x + 2) > 0$

$x < -2, x > 8$

Since, $x < 2$

Hence, $x < -2$ is the solution for this case.

Hence, option (c) is the correct option.

16. Since $x^2 - 7x + 15$ is always positive,
Hence, $|x^2 - 7x + 15| = x^2 - 7x + 15$.
Thus, the question becomes $|x - 7| > x^2 - 7x + 15$.
Here $|x - 7| = x - 7 \quad$ if $x - 7 > 0$
$= 7 - x \quad$ if $x - 7 < 0$
Or $\quad |x - 7| = x - 7 \quad$ if $x > 7$
$= 7 - x \quad$ if $x < 7$

Thus, the given equation implies the following cases:

Case 1: If $x > 7$

$x - 7 > x^2 - 7x + 15$

Or $\quad x^2 - 8x + 22 > 0$

As this expression is always positive, $x > 7$ is the solution.

Case 2: $x < 7$

$7 - x > x^2 - 7x + 15$

$x^2 - 6x + 8 < 0$

$(x - 4)(x - 2) < 0$

$2 < x < 4$

And this is in accordance with $x < 7$.

Hence, option (c) is the correct option.

17. This is to be solved considering the following three cases:

Case 1: $x < -3$

For this, $|x - 5| = 5 - x$

$|x + 3| = -x - 3$

So the equation becomes

$(5 - x - 2)(-x - 3 - 1) < 0$

Or $(3 - x)(-x - 4) < 0$

Or $(x - 3)(x + 4) < 0$

Or $-4 < x < 3$

But $x < -3$,

Thus, $-4 < x < -3$ is the solution for this case.

Case 2: $-3 < x < 5$

For this, $|x - 5| = 5 - x$

$|x + 3| = x + 3$

So the equation becomes

$(5 - x - 2)(x + 3 - 1) < 0$

Or $(3 - x)(x + 2) < 0$

Or $(x - 3)(x + 2) > 0$

Or $x < -2, x > 3$

But $-3 < x < 5$,

Thus, $-3 < x < -2, 3 < x < 5$ is the solution for this case.

Case 3: $x > 5$

For this, $|x - 5| = x - 5$

$|x + 3| = x + 3$

So the equation becomes

$(x - 5 - 2)(x + 3 - 1) < 0$

Or $(x - 7)(x + 2) < 0$

Or $-2 < x < 7$

But since $x > 5$

Thus, $5 < x < 7$ is the solution for this case.

Also, we can check that at $x = -3$ and at $x = 5$, the inequality is satisfied.

Thus, (c) is the correct option.

18. $x^2 - 6x + 36$ is always positive.

$|x^2 - 6x + 36| = x^2 - 6x + 36$

For this, the equation becomes $x^2 - 6x + 36 > 6x$.

Or $x^2 - 12x + 36 > 0$

Or $(x - 6)^2 > 0$

This is true for all except $x = 6$.

Hence, option (d) is the correct option.

19. The given equation is defined only if $x^2 - 10x + 21 \geq 0$

Or $(x - 3)(x - 7) \geq 0$

Or $x \leq 3, x \geq 7$

But none of the given options satisfies this.

Hence, option (d) is the correct option.

20. Firstly, $x^2 - 9x + 20 \geq 0$

Or $(x - 4)(x - 5) \geq 0$

$x \leq 4, x \geq 5$

Also $x - 2 > 0$

Or $x > 2$

Thus, $2 < x \leq 4$ and $x \geq 5$ is the solution.

Hence, option (d) is the correct option.

21. For the given fraction to be defined either numerator and denominator, both should be positive or both should be negative.

If it is defined then it will always be greater than 0.

Thus, $x - 5 > 0$ and $1 - x > 0$ Or $x > 5$ and $x < 1$

But this is not possible.

So, $x - 5 < 0$ and $1 - x < 0$

$x < 5$ and $x > 1$

Thus, $1 < x < 5$.

Hence, option (b) is the correct option.

22. Here again either

$4x - 5 > 0$ and $1 - 2x > 0 \rightarrow x > \frac{5}{4}$ and $x < \frac{1}{2}$

But this is not possible at the same time.

Now, if both the numerator and denominator are negative, then:

$4x - 5 < 0$ and $1 - 2x < 0 \rightarrow x < \frac{5}{4}$ or $x > \frac{1}{2}$

Hence, option (b) is the correct option.

23. Firstly, $2x - 5 \geq 0 \rightarrow x \geq 2.5$

Also, $7 - x \geq 0 \rightarrow x \leq 7$. Thus, the expression is defined for $2.5 \leq x \leq 7$.

Again $2x - 5 > 7 - x \rightarrow 3x > 12$ Or $x > 4$.

So, $4 < x \leq 7$

Hence, option (b) is the correct option.

24. Firstly, $x^2 - 1 \geq 0$.

Or $(x + 1)(x - 1) \geq 0$

Or $x \leq -1, x \geq 1$

Also $x^2 - 1 < 1$

Or $x^2 - 2 < 0$

Or $-\sqrt{2} < x < \sqrt{2}$

Considering all this, $-\sqrt{2} < x \leq -1$ and $1 \leq x < \sqrt{2}$

Hence, option (d) is the correct option.

25. Firstly, $2x - 4 \geq 0$

Or $x \geq 2$

Since $x \geq 2$

Also, $4(2x - 4) < x^2$

Or $x^2 - 8x + 16 > 0$

Or $(x - 4)^2 > 0$

This is true for all x except $x = 4$.

Hence, option (d) is the correct option.

26. Firstly, $x + 7 \geq 0$

Or $x \geq -7$

Squaring both sides, we get: $x^2 - 2x + 1 > 4(x + 7)$.

Or $x^2 - 6x - 27 > 0$

Or $(x - 9)(x + 3) > 0$

Or $x < -3, x > 9$
So, $-7 \le x < -3$ and $x > 9$
Hence, option (d) is the correct option.

27. First of all, for the RHS to be defined, we have $20 - x \ge 0 \to x \le 20$.
Also $x^2 > 20 - x$
Or $x^2 + x - 20 > 0$
Or $(x + 5)(x - 4) > 0$
Or $x < -5, x > 4$
So, $x < -5$ and $4 < x \le 20$
Hence, option (d) is the correct option.

28. First of all for the LHS to be defined, we have $14x - 48 \ge 0$.
Or $x \ge \frac{24}{7}$
Also $14x - 48 < x^2$
Or $x^2 - 14x + 48 > 0$
$(x - 8)(x - 6) > 0$
$x < 6, x > 8$
Thus, $\frac{24}{7} \le x < 6, x > 8$
Hence, option (c) is the correct option.

29. Firstly, $x + 6 \ge 0$
Or $x \ge -6$
Also, squaring both sides, we have $x + 6 < x^2$.
$x^2 - x - 6 > 0$
$(x - 3)(x + 2) > 0$
Or $x < -2, x > 3$
So, $-6 \le x < -2, x > 3$
Hence, option (c) is the correct option.

30. Here, $x = 1$ and $x = 3$ are two critical points which divide the real line into three parts, namely, $x < 1$, $1 \le x < 3$ and $x \ge 3$. So, we discuss the following cases:
Case 1: When $x < 1$
$|x - 1| = -(x - 1)$ and $|x - 3| = -(x - 3)$
$\therefore |x - 1| \ge |x - 3|$
$\Rightarrow -(x - 1) \ge -(x - 3) \Rightarrow 1 \ge 3$, which is not possible.
So, the inequality has no solution for $x < 1$.
Case 2: When $1 \le x < 3$
In this case, we have
$|x - 1| = x - 1$ and $|x - 3| = -(x - 3)$
$\therefore |x - 1| \ge |x - 3|$
$\Rightarrow x - 1 \ge -(x - 3) \Rightarrow 2x - 4 \ge 0 \Rightarrow x \ge 2$
But, $1 \le x < 3$ and $x \ge 2 \Rightarrow x \in [2,3)$
Case 3: When $x \ge 3$
In this case, we have
$|x - 1| = x - 1$ and $|x - 3| = x - 3$
$\therefore |x - 1| \ge |x - 3|$
$\Rightarrow x - 1 \ge x - 3 \Rightarrow -1 \ge -3$, which is correct.
Hence, the solution set of the given inequality is $[2, \infty)$.

31. $|[x|x| - 7]| - 5 < 0$
$|[x|x| - 7]| < 5$
$\Rightarrow -5 < [|x| - 7] < 5$. Check the options, you can reject option (c).
Hence, option (d) is correct.

32. $\frac{[x]-2}{4-[x]} > 0$ when $[x] < 4$ or > 2
It is only possible when $[x] = 3 \Rightarrow x \in [3,4)$.. Thus, option (b) is correct.

33. $|x - 3| > 0$
$|x - 3|$ is greater than or equal to 0 for all the possible values of $(x - 3)$. Hence, option (d) would be the correct answer.

34. The inequality would be positive in two cases: If both the numerator and denominator are positive, or if both of them are negative.
For both positive: $x > 0$ and $x - 3 > 0$, i.e. $x > 3$. Combining both, we see that $x > 3$, would satisfy this requirement.
For both negative: $x < 0$ and $x - 3 < 0$, i.e. $x < 3$. Combining both, we see that $x < 0$, would satisfy this requirement.
Hence, $\frac{x}{x-3}$ is greater than 0 for $x > 3$ and $x < 0$.
Hence, option (d) is correct.

35. $x^2 - 3x + 2 > 0$ *or* $(x - 2)(x - 1) > 0$
$x > 2$ will make both the components positive. At the same time, $x < 1$ would also make both the components negative, giving us a positive product.
Hence, option (d) is correct.

36. $\frac{x^2-4}{x+3} > 0$
$-3 < x < -2$ and $x > 2$
Hence, option (c) is correct.

37. $\frac{x+3}{x-3} > 0$ for $x > 3$ or $x < -3$.
Hence, option (d) is correct.

38. $|x^2 - 4| = 0$, only if the modulus is 0. This works only when $x = 2$ or -2. Hence, option (d) is correct.

39. $\left|\frac{x^2-9}{x-2}\right| \ge 0$ for all values of x except $x = 2$. Hence, option (b) is correct.

40. For the quadratic function to be positive, $D < 0$.
$4a^2 - 40 + 12a < 0$
$a^2 + 3a - 10 < 0$. The values of a, for equality to 0, $= -5$ and 2. Also, since the coefficient of a^2 is positive, the value of $a^2 + 3a - 10$ will be negative between -5 and 2, i.e. $-5 < a < 2$.
Hence, option (a) is correct.

Solutions for Questions 41 and 42:

$$\frac{(|x|)^2 - 7|x| + 10}{x^2 - 2\times 4\times x + 4^2} < 0$$

$\frac{(|x|-5)(|x|-2)}{(x-4)^2} < 0$

$\Rightarrow 2 < |x| < 5$, but $x \neq 4$

The upper limit defines the range of x as: $-5 < x < 5$

The lower limit defines the range of x as: $x < -2$, $x > 2$

To obey both the limits, we will get: $-5 < x < -2$, $2 < x < 5$ & $x \neq 4$.

41. The above inequality is true for $x = -4, -3$. Therefore, for two negative integral values of x, the given inequality is true.
42. Required sum $= -4 - 3 + 3 = -4$

Solutions for Questions 43 and 44:

43. $\frac{x^2 - 4x - 5}{x^2 + 7x + 12} \leq 0$

$\frac{(x-5)(x+1)}{(x+4)(x+3)} \leq 0$

$-4 < x < -3$ and $-1 \leq x \leq 5$

Therefore, $f(x) \leq 0$ is true for a total of five positive integer values of x (1, 2, 3, 4 and 5).

44. $f(x) \leq 0$ is true for only one negative integer value of x (at $x = -1$).
45. $x^2 + 2|x| + 1 \leq 0$

$|x|^2 + 2|x| + 1 \leq 0$

$(|x| + 1)^2 \leq 0$

This is not possible for any real value of x.

46. $\frac{1}{|x|-2} - \frac{1}{3} > 0$

$\frac{(3-|x|+2)}{3(|x|-2)} > 0$

$\frac{5-|x|}{|x|-2} > 0$

$x \in (-5, -2) \cup (2, 5)$

Therefore, the least positive integer value of $x = 3$.

Solutions for Questions 47 and 48:

x is an integer.

$|2x - 4| \leq 5$

$-5 \leq 2x - 4 \leq 5$

$-1 \leq 2x \leq 9$

$-\frac{1}{2} < x \leq \frac{9}{2}$.

47. Maximum value of $x = 4$.
48. Minimum value of $x = 0$.
49. $(x - 1)(4 - x)(x - 2)^2 > 0$

As $(x - 2)^2$ is always non-negative.

This means that the product of the first two brackets would be positive. This also means that$(x - 1)(x - 4) < 0$.

$\Rightarrow 1 < x < 4$

x has two integer values 2 and 3 between 1 and 4.

But for $x = 2$, $(x - 1)(4 - x)(x - 2)^2 = 0$.

$\Rightarrow$ Therefore, the given inequality is true only for one integer value of x.

Solutions for Questions 50 and 51:

$\frac{x^2 - 5x + 6}{|x| + 5} \leq 0$

$\frac{(x-2)(x-3)}{|x|+5} \leq 0$

Case 1: $x > 0$

In this case, the expression will become:

$\Rightarrow \frac{(x-2)(x-3)}{x+5} \leq 0$

$\Rightarrow 2 \leq x \leq 3$

Case 2: $x < 0$

In this case, the expression will become:

$\frac{(x-2)(x-3)}{-x+5} \leq 0$

$\frac{(x-2)(x-3)}{x-5} \geq 0$

The above inequality is not satisfied for any negative value of x.

Therefore, solution of the above inequality $\rightarrow 2 \leq x \leq 3$

50. Minimum value of $x = 2$
51. The above inequality is true for two integral values of x.
52. $x \in I^+$ means x is a positive integer.

Now we can check the above inequality by putting positive integer values of x.

For $x = 1$, $\frac{1}{1-0.5} = 2$, so $x = 1$ is not a solution.

For $x = 2$, $\frac{1}{2-0.5} = \frac{1}{1.5} < 2$, therefore $x = 2$ is a solution.

The correct answer is $x = 2$.

53. $\frac{x^2 + 6x - 7}{x^2 + 1} - 2 > 0$

$\frac{-x^2 + 6x - 9}{x^2 + 1} > 0$

$\frac{(x-3)^2}{x^2+1} < 0$

$(x - 3)^2 > 0$, $x^2 + 1 > 0$

So, the above inequality is not true for any real value of x.

54. $x^2 + x + 1 > 0$ (It is a quadratic equation with negative discriminant)

Hence, for the expression to be non-positive, the numerator has to be non-positive, *i.e.* $x^2 - 9 \leq 0$.

$(x - 3)(x + 3) \leq 0$

$\Rightarrow -3 \leq x \leq 3$

Required maximum value of $x = 3$

55. $\frac{x+2}{x} - x \geq 0$

$\frac{x+2-x^2}{x} \geq 0$

$\frac{x^2-x-2}{x} \leq 0$

$\frac{(x-2)(x+1)}{x} \leq 0$

Case 1: $(x - 2)(x + 1) \geq 0$ and $x < 0$

This occurs only for $x \leq -1$.

Case 2: $(x - 2)(x + 1) \leq 0$ and x are positive.

This occurs when $0 < x \leq 2$.

Therefore, maximum value of x which satisfies the condition is at $x = 2$.

Level of Difficulty (II)

1. We can write the expression as $f(x) = (x - 5)(x - 1)/(x - 3)(x - 2)$. If $x > 5$, the expression would return a positive value, hence, we can eliminate options (b) and (d). For finding whether the expression would give us a value more than 1, we need to find the range for x that would satisfy this condition. Hence, $x^2 - 6x + 5 > x^2 - 5x + 6$. On solving this we get $x < -1$. The expression would give a value of more than 1 only if $x < -1$ but it is given that $x > 5$. Hence, we can eliminate option (c). Hence, Option (a) is the correct answer.
2. For questions related to inequalities, we can get to our answer by using the options we have. To increase our efficiency and speed, we need to check with those values which would help us eliminate the maximum number of options. If we test for 0, we find that the inequality is satisfied. Hence, we can eliminate Options (b) & (c). On checking with –3, we get that the inequality is still satisfied. So we can eliminate option (d). Hence, Option (a) is the correct answer.
3. The graph will cut the x-axis on 2 & 3 i.e. on the points represented by (2, 0) and (3, 0). Let us think of these points as A and B respectively. Since the area representing $y < 3$, will be bounded by the line $y = 3$. This line will intersect the graph of $x^2 - 5x + 6$ at two points where the value of the graph becomes equal to 3. These points can be found by solving the equation: $x^2 - 5x + 6 = 3$.

   Solving, we get $x = (5 \pm \sqrt{13})/2$. Thus, these two points would be represented by the points having coordinates as: $\{(5 + \sqrt{13})/2, 3\}$ & $\{(5 - \sqrt{13})/2, 3\}$. Let us think of these points as C and D respectively.

   The straight lines connecting A, B, C, D will form a trapezium and the area of the graph will be more than that of the trapezium (since the curve $(x^2 - 5x + 6)$ will lie outside the trapezium thus formed). The distance between the points C and D will be $\sqrt{13}$. This will be the length of one of the bases of the trapezium ABCD. Length of the other base would be the distance between A and B, which is 1. Also, the height of the trapezium is 3. Hence, the area of the trapezium would be $=$ Height $\times \frac{\text{Sum of Parallel sides}}{2}$

   $= \frac{3(\sqrt{13}+1)}{2}$. Hence, Option (c) is the correct answer.
4. Since $(n - 4)^4$ will always give a positive value, We need to find the positive range for other terms. Different trigger points would be 0, –6, –11. These are the numbers which indicate a change in sign for a specific term. Between 0 and –6 the expression will be negative. Between –6 & –11, the expression will be positive. The expression will be negative for numbers less than –11. The required range would be $(-6, -11) \cup (0, 4)$. Hence, there are a total of 7 values.
5. Given $f(x) = \max(x, 0)$

   First, we need to find the different values we'll get for n. We see that for $n \leq 3$, we get 0 as our answer for $f(n - 3)$. For $f(n + 1)$, we'll get $n + 1$ as our answer as n is positive.

   So, for $n \leq 3$, the expression can be rewritten as $2(n + 1)$

   for $n > 3$, the expression can be rewritten as $n - 3 + 2(n + 1) \rightarrow 3n - 1$

   Case 1: $n \leq 3$

   $2(n + 1) \leq 50$

   $n \leq 24$

   So, the total number of values satisfying both the ranges is 4.

   Case 2: $n > 3$

   $3n - 1 \leq 50$

   $n \leq 17$

   We have a total of 14 values that satisfy both the ranges. Hence, we have a total of 14 + 4 = 18 values. Hence, Option (b) is the correct answer.
6. To solve this, we first need to bring both the terms to the same base. This expression can be rewritten as $\left(\frac{8}{10}\right)^{3x^2-8x+7} < \left(\frac{8}{10}\right)^3$. This will be satisfied if $(3x^2 - 8x + 7) < 3 \rightarrow 3x^2 - 8x + 4 < 0$. This range is given in Option (a). Hence, Option (a) is the correct answer.
7. Since $n + 2m$ is odd, n must be an odd number and m can be both even and odd.

   n can take values 1, 3, 5, 7 and 9 as for $n = 10$, the minimum value of the expression would be 5120 (when m is taken as 1).

So, for $n = 1$, m will take values from 1 to 4 (4 pairs)
for $n = 3$, m will take values from 1 to 3 (3 pairs)
for $n = 5$, m will take values 1, 2 and 3 (3 pairs)
for $n = 7$, m will be 1 and 2. (2 pairs)
for $n = 9$, m will be 1 (1 pair)
Hence, we have a total of 13 pairs that satisfy the condition.

8. The given expression is $\frac{2x-1}{3} \geq \frac{3x-2}{4} - \frac{2-x}{5}$. On simplifying we get, $20(2x-1) \geq 3(19x-18)$. On further solving we get that $x \leq 2$. So the maximum value of x is 2. Hence, 2 is the correct answer.
9. The inequality will be satisfied if both the numerator and denominator are either positive or negative. This range would not include values in the range [–5, –4) ∪ (4, 5]. The only integral values in this range are –5 & 5. Hence, 2 is the correct answer.
10. This expression can be rewritten as $x^2 - 27x + 126 \leq 0$. This would give non-positive values in the range of [6, 21]. Hence, we have a total of 16 values. Hence, Option (c) is the correct answer.
11. The trigger points for the given inequality are –4, 1, 6 and 9 and the minimum value for this expression would be 18. We would need to check the values of the expression in these ranges to find out how the expression works for different values of x.
For $x = -5$, we get the value as 32. Not satisfying the inequality. For values below this we'll get a higher sum. Hence, going in that direction would not be valid. At $x = -4, -3, -2, -1$ we can again see that the value of the expression is greater than 20.
At $x = -4$ we get a value of 28 and at $x = -2$ we get 24. We notice that as we move towards the positive side our value decreases. At $x = 0$ we get the value as 20. We get our minimum value of 18 for any value between 1 and 6 and sum as 20 at $x = 7$. Hence, the values satisfying the inequality would lie in the range 0 to 7 (both included). Hence, we have a total of 8 integer values.
12. $3|x| + 5|y| - 3|x| + 12|y| = 21 - 18 \rightarrow 17|y| = 3 \rightarrow |y| = 3/17$. Consequently, $|x| = 114/17$. i.e. y = either 3/17 or –3/17, x = 114/17 or –114/17. The condition $x - 2y > 3$ is obeyed in two cases, (114/17, 3/17) or (114/17, –3/17). Hence, there are 2 pairs (x, y). The correct answer is 2.
13. From the first equation, we get $x = 2y$. Putting this in the inequalities we get $4y \leq 6$ and $-5y \leq 3$. This translates to $y \leq 1.5$ and $y \geq -3/5$.
Our required value is $3y$ which is in the range $-9/5 \leq 3y \leq 4.5$. Amongst the given options only option (a) is in the given range. Hence, the correct answer is Option (a).
14. On removing the mod sign we get $\pm (x^2 + x - 6) < 3x - 7$.
    1. $x^2 + x - 6 < 3x - 7 \rightarrow (x-1)^2 < 0$. There are no values of x which would satisfy this as the expression will always give a non-negative value.
    2. $-x^2 - x + 6 < 3x - 7 \rightarrow x^2 + 4x - 13 > 0$. The equation will give positive values in the range $(-\infty, -2 - \sqrt{17}) \cup (-2 + \sqrt{17}, \infty)$. This gives us an approx value of $(-\infty, -6.12) \cup (2.12, \infty)$. Also, since $|x|$ is less than 20,the values of that will satisfy are –7 to –19 and 3 to 19. A total of 13 + 17 = 30 values.

    Hence, the number of values satisfying the conditions is 30.
15. The trigger points for the given inequality are –5, 2, 7 and 4 and the minimum value for this expression would be 14. Lets check for different ranges.
For $x = -6$, we get the value as 48. Not satisfying the inequality. For values below this we'll get a higher sum.
At $x = -4$ we get a value of 38 and at $x = -1$ we get 26. We notice that as we move towards the positive side our value decreases. At $x = 0$ we get the value as 22 and with every integer shift to the right, we reduce our sum by 4. So at different integers from $x = 0$, we get our sum as 22, 18, 14, 18, 22 (since 14 is our minimum value and our sum will increase after that) Hence, we have a total of 5 values.
16. The given inequality gets satisfied at x=-3,-2,...x=3. Hence, we get a total of 7 values.
17. The value of $|x + 2| + |9 - x|$ would be equal to 11 for all values between –2 and 9. After than on increasing the value of x beyond 9 to 10, 11 and so on, there would be an increase of +2 in the value of $|x + 2| + |9 - x|$ for every integral change in x. However, the value of $|4x - 12|$ would be quite large when x is 10 or more or –3 or less. Hence, we need to keep the value of x, between –2 to 9 to check for the LHS to be below 30. In this range, the LHS value would be $11 + |4x - 12|$. Thus, the value of $|4x - 12|$ would need to be ≤19. x can be –1 to 7 for this to happen.
Hence, we would have 9 integer values satisfying this inequality.
18. The value of $|x + 6| + |8 - x|$ would be equal to 14 for any value of x between –6 to 8. At $x = 9$ and at $x = -7$, it's value would be 16 and at $x = 10$ and $x = -8$ it's value would be 18. Hence, for values after $x = 10$ and $x = -8$, the expression on the LHS would definitely be above 18. In order to solve the inequality, we need to check the value of the expression $|2x - 8| + |x - 5|$, between –8 to 10, and we need it to be below a value of 4, for the inequality to not be satisfied. At $x = 3$, the value of this expression would be 4, at $x = 4$ it would be 1 and at $x = 5$, it would be 2. At $x = 6$, it's value would

be 5. Thus, the inequality is not satisfied at values of x at 3, 4 and 5. Also, $|2x - 8| + |x - 5| \le 4$ for $3 \le x \le 5.66$. Hence, the solution of the inequality is: $(-\infty, 3) \cup (5.66, \infty)$.

19. The trigger points for the LHS expression are –6, 4, 5 and 8. Let us first analyse the expression and it's values for non-negative values of x. At $x = 0$, the value of the LHS is 11. At $x = 1$ it is 10, $x = 2$ it is 9, at $x = 3$ it is 8; at $x = 4$ it is 7. At $x = 5$ it goes up to 10. A $x = 6$ it is 15; At $x = 7$ it becomes 20. At $x = 8$ it becomes 25 (Note: The behaviour keeps changing at different trigger points). After $x = 8$, the value of the expression would go up by + 2 + 1 – 1 + 1 (i.e. by a net value of 3 for every unit increment in x). Hence, at $x = 9$, 10, 11 the respective values of the expression would be 28, 31, 34 and so on. Observing these values, we can see that the LHS value crosses 18 between $x = 6$ and 7 & we also observe that within trigger points the value moves in Arithmetic Progression. At $x = 6$, the LHS was 15, while at $x = 7$ it was 20. Hence, intrapolating we can see that at $x = 6.6$, the value of the LHS would be exactly 18. Hence, on the positive side of the x axis, the inequality would be satisfied at $x > 6.6$.

   To solve the inequality completely, we would also need to check the value of the LHS for negative values of x. At $x = 0$ we know the value of the LHS to be 11. As we reduce x by unit increments to $x = -1, -2$ and so on we can anticipate a change of + 2 – 1 – 1 + 1, i.e. a net change of +1 going all the way to the trigger point of $x = -6$. Thus, the values of the LHS would increase to 12, 13, 14, 15, 16 and 17 as we move from $x = -1$ to $x = -6$. After reaching the trigger point of –6, going further to the left on the x axis, we can see that the behaviour of the LHS would be modified according to + 2 + 1 – 1 + 1 → a net change of +3. Thus at $x = -7$, we can see that the value of the expression becomes 20. Hence, the LHS crosses the value of 18 somewhere between –6 to –7. Also, since all movements are straight lines, we can intrapolate the value of x to $x = -6.33$ for the LHS to be exactly equal to 18. Hence, the values of $x < -6.33$ would satisfy the inequality.

   Hence, the correct answer for the solution of the inequality would be $(-\infty, -6.33) \cup (6.66, \infty)$.

20 Think similarly as the solution to the previous question. You can see that the trigger points in this expression are –1, 3, 4 and 6. At $x = 6$, the value of the expression is 18 and at $x = 7$ it becomes 24. Thus, at $x = 6.66$, it would be 22. Also, at $x = 0$, the expression has a value of 20. At $x = -1$, the value becomes 24. Hence, at $x = -0.5$, the expression of the LHS would give a value of exactly 22. Hence, the correct answer is: $(-\infty, 0.5] \cup [6.66, \infty)$.

21. In order to solve this question, we need to know how to plot the graph of logs with fraction base. What we need to know is that the log to a fractional base is always negative, if the argument is greater than 1. Thus, we determine that for the inequality in the question to be possible $\left[\log_6 \dfrac{x^2+x}{x+4}\right] > 1$. This means that $\dfrac{x^2+x}{x+4} > 6$. $x^2 - 5x - 24 > 0$. This inequality will not be satisfied in the range (–3, 8). Hence, we'll have 7 positive integers not satisfying the above inequality.

22. This expression can be simplified to $(x-3)(\sqrt{x-3}-5) \le 0$. For this to be satisfied $3 \le x \le 28$. Hence, there are 26 values.

23. Let $x! = a$. The expression becomes $a^2 - a - 552 \ge 0$. $(a - 24)(a + 23) \ge 0$. Since a can only be positive, the range would be $a \ge 24 \Rightarrow x! \ge 24$. Hence, Option (d) is the correct answer.

24. From the above solution we can determine that the x will take even numbers from 4 to 98. Hence, the sum can be found out by using formula for sum of AP = 48 × 51 = 2448.

25. Case 1: $x > 0$

   The expression would be $x - 1 - x + 2x + 3 \ge 2x + 4 \rightarrow 2 \ge 4$. This is not true. Hence, we wont have a solution for this case.

   Case 2: $x < 0$

   The expression would be $-x - 1 + x - 2x + 3 \ge 2x + 4 \rightarrow 4x \le -2 \rightarrow x \le -0.5$. Since $|x| < 10$, the values satisfying this would lie in the range $-10 < x \le -0.5$. Hence, we'll have 9 integral values in this range.

   Hence, we have a total of 9 values.

26. The minimum value of the LHS of the expression would be 16, between $x = -6$ and $x = 10$. Hence, we have a total of 17 values that satisfy the given condition.

27. For this question we need to understand how to plot the graph for the first inequality.

   $(2x^2 - 8x + 8) < 0 \Rightarrow 2(x^2 - 4x + 4) < 0 \Rightarrow 2(x - 2)^2 < 0$. Since a perfect square will always return a positive value, no portion of the graph will be below the x axis. Hence, the area enclosed will be 0.

28. For this to be possible, there are only two values possible 1 and 2 as both the terms are under mod and would return positive values.

   1. For 1: Possible pairs include (106, 103) (104, 103) (105, 102) (105, 104)
   2. For 2: Similarly we'll have 8 pairs in this case.

   Hence, we have a total of 12 pairs that satisfy the given inequality.

29. In order to solve this we need to understand that mod of a number will be greater than the number itself if and only if the value inside the mod is a negative number. This means that $x^2 - 30x + 221 <$

$0 \rightarrow (x - 13)(x - 17) < 0$. If the above expression is to be valid then x has to lie between 13 & 17. Hence, the maximum and minimum possible value of x is 16 and 14 respectively. Hence, 2 is correct answer.

30. The graph would be a double triangle with same area. The height of the triangle would be 5 units and the length of the base would be equal to 10 units. Hence, the area enclosed by the figure would be 2 × 25 = 50 sq. units.

31. From the second part of the question we can determine that when y increases, x decreases for a given sum. So if we want to maximise $3x + 8y$, y should be maximum as coefficient of y is higher as compared with x.
From given inequalities maximum value of y is 6 and then the value of x will be 0. These two values satisfy the second inequality as well.
Hence, the maximum of $3x + 8y = 3 \times 0 + 8 \times 6 = 48$. Hence, 48 is the correct answer.

32. If we put $x = 3$,
Then $|3 - 1| + |3 - 2| + |3 - 3| = 3 \leq 6$.
Therefore, options (a), (c), (d) are not correct.
Hence only option (b) is correct.

33. $|f(x)| < 8$
$$||x+4|-|x-4|| < 8$$
$$-8 < |x + 4| - |x - 4| < 8$$
Case 1: when $x \leq -4$
$\Rightarrow |x + 4| - |x - 4| = -x - 4 + x - 4 = -8$, therefore the above inequality is not true for any $x \leq -4$.
Case 2: when $x \geq 4$:
$|x + 4| - |x - 4| = x + 4 - x + 4 = 8$, therefore the above inequality is not true for any $x \geq 4$.
Case 3: when $-4 < x < 4$
$|x + 4| - |x - 4| = x + 4 + x - 4 = 2x$
$\Rightarrow x = \{-3, -2, -1, 0, +1, +2, +3\}$
So, the inequality $|f(x)| < 8$ is true for seven integer values of x.

34. Required sum = 1 + 2 + 3 = 6

35. $$\frac{1}{x-5} + \frac{1}{x+3} < 0$$
$$\frac{x+3+x-5}{(x+3)(x-5)} < 0$$
$$\frac{2x-2}{(x+3)(x-5)} < 0$$
$$\frac{x-1}{(x+3)(x-5)} < 0$$
$\frac{(x-1)^2}{(x-1)(x+3)(x-5)} < 0$. The numerator of this expression will always be positive.
Hence, we need: $(x - 1)(x + 3)(x - 5) < 0$.
$x < -3$ or $1 < x < 5$, therefore, the given inequality is true for three positive integer values of x, i.e. x = 2, 3 or 4.

36. Required sum = 2 + 3 + 4= 9

37. $-8 \leq 4x - 3 \leq 8$ $\quad$ $|3y + 4| \leq 17$
$-5 \leq 4x \leq 11$ $\quad$ $-17 \leq 3y + 4 \leq 17$
$-\frac{5}{4} \leq x \leq \frac{11}{4}$ $\quad$ $-7 \leq y \leq \frac{13}{3}$
x and y both can be zero, therefore, minimum value of $|x| + |y| = 0 + 0 = 0$.

38. $|x| - |y|$ will be maximum, when $|x|$ is maximum and $|y|$ is minimum.
$$(|x| - |y|)_{max} = |x|_{max} - |y|_{min}$$
$$= \frac{11}{4} - 0$$
$$= \frac{11}{4} = 2.75$$

39. $$f(x) = \frac{x}{2x^2 + 5x + 8} = \frac{1}{2x + \frac{8}{x} + 5}$$
$f(x)$ is maximum where denominator is minimum
$$\frac{\left(2x + \frac{8}{x}\right)}{2} \geq \sqrt{2x \times \frac{8}{x}}$$
$$2x + \frac{8}{x} \geq 8$$
$$\left(2x + \frac{8}{x}\right)_{\min} = 8$$
$$(f(x))_{\max} = \frac{1}{8+5} = \frac{1}{13}$$

40. Solution: $y \geq x^2$

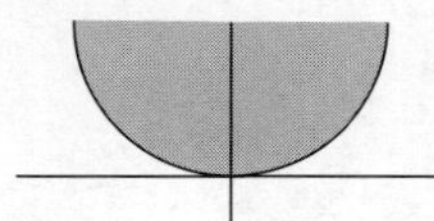

$y \leq 3$

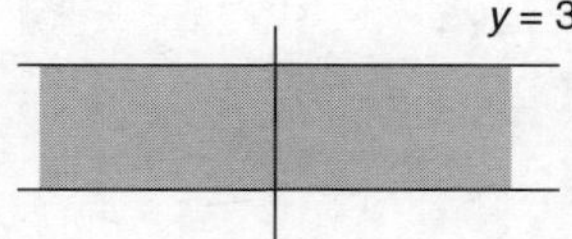

By combining the above graphs, we get

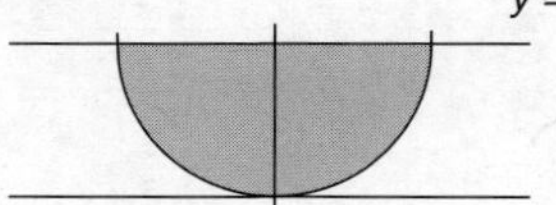

Hence, option (c) is correct.

41. $x^4 - 8x^3 - x^2 + 8x < 0$

$x^3(x - 8) - x(x - 8) < 0$

$(x^3 - x)(x - 8) < 0$

$x(x - 1)(x + 1)(x - 8) < 0$

This expression would be alternately positive and negative in various ranges of x as shown below:

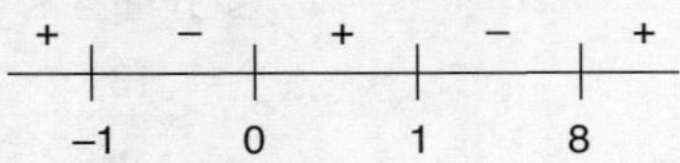

$x \in (-1, 0) \cup (1, 8)$

Hence, option (a) is correct.

42. $$\frac{45}{(5x^7)^2 - 2\times 5x^7 \times \frac{4}{5} + \frac{16}{25} - \frac{16}{25} + 1} = \frac{45}{\left(5x^7 - \frac{4}{5}\right)^2 + \frac{9}{25}}$$

Minimum value of p is the maximum value of $\frac{45}{25x^{14} - 8x^7 + 1}$

Minimum value of $\left(5x^7 - \frac{4}{5}\right)^2 = 0$

$$(p)_{\min} = \frac{45}{\frac{9}{25}} = 5 \times 25 = 125$$

43. For $x = 3$, $7^{3-1} + 11^{3-1} = 7^2 + 11^2 = 170$

$7^{x-1} + 11^{x-1}$ is an increasing function, so for $x > 3$, $7^{x-1} + 11^{x-1} > 170$

$\therefore$ $7^{x-1} + 11^{x-1} > 170$, for a total $13 - 3 = 10$ values of x

44. $3x + 4$ is an increasing while $6 - 2x$ is a decreasing function.

Graph of min $(3x + 4, 6 - 2x)$

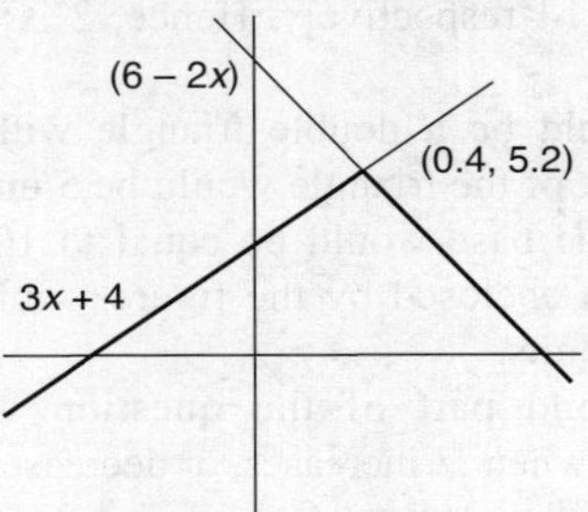

From the graph, it is clear that maximum value of $f(x) = 5.2$, which occurs at $x = 0.4$.

$f(x) < p$ (where p is an integer)

Least value of p must be 6.

45. For maximum possible values of x which satisfy the above inequality, all the modulus open with a positive sign, i.e.

$|x - 1| > 0$, $||x - 1|-2| > 0$, $|||x - 1|-2|-3| > 0$, etc.

Hence, for $x = x_{max}$, the given inequality will be

$x - 1 - 2 - 3 - 4 - 5 - 6 - 7 < 9$

$x_{max} < 37$

Hence, a total for 37 non-negative integers (0 to 36) are possible. Thus, option (c) is correct.

Solutions for Questions 46 to 119:

Try to use options based approach to check for the correct option.

CHAPTER 16

Quadratic and Other Equations

Chapter Launchpad

Scan this QR code to access a video on 'Introduction to Quadratic and Other Equations' and this chapter's importance for CAT

We have already seen in the *Back to School* part of this block the key interrelationship between functions, equations and inequalities. In this chapter we are specifically looking at questions based on equations—with an emphasis on quadratic equations. Questions based on equations are an important component of the CAT and XAT examinations and hence your ability to formulate and solve equations is a key skill in the development of your thought process for QA.

As you go through with this chapter, focus on understanding the core concepts and also look to create a framework in your mind which would account for the typical processes that are used for solving questions based on equations.

THEORY OF EQUATIONS

Equations in One Variable

An equation is any expression in the form $f(x) = 0$; the type of equation we are talking about depends on the expression that is represented by $f(x)$. The expression $f(x)$ can be linear, quadratic, and cubic or might have a higher power and accordingly the equation can be referred to as linear equations, quadratic equations, cubic equations, etc. Let us look at each of these cases one by one.

Linear Equations

$2x + 4$; we have the expression for $f(x)$ as a linear expression in x. Consequently, the equation $2x+4 = 0$ would be characterised as a linear equation. This equation has exactly one root (solution) and can be seen by solving $2x+4 = 0 \rightarrow x = -2$, which is the root of the equation. Note that the root or solution of the equation is the value of 'x' which would make the LHS of the equation equals the RHS of the equation. In other words, the equation is satisfied when the value of x becomes equal to the root of the equation.

The linear function $f(x)$ when drawn would give us a straight line and this line will be intersecting with the x-axis at the point where the value of x equals the root (solution) of the equation.

Quadratic Equations

An equation of the form: $2x^2 - 5x + 4 = 0$; we have the expression for $f(x)$ as a quadratic expression in x. Consequently, the equation $2x^2 - 5x + 4 = 0$ would be characterised as a quadratic equation. This equation has exactly two roots (solutions) and leads to the following cases with respect to whether these roots are real/imaginary or equal/unequal.

Case 1: Both the roots are real and equal;

Case 2: Both the roots are real and unequal;

Case 3: Both the roots are imaginary.

A detailed discussion of quadratic equations and the analytical formula based approach to identify which of the above three cases prevails, follows later in this chapter.

The graph of a quadratic function is always U-shaped and will just touch the X-axis in the first case above; will cut the X-axis twice in the second case above and will not touch the X-axis at all in the third case above.

Note that the roots or solutions of the equation are the values of 'x' which would make the LHS of the equation equal the RHS of the equation. In other words, the equation is satisfied when the value of x becomes equal to the root of the equation.

Going Beyond the Book

Scan this QR code to access a conceptual video on Cubic Equations

Cubic Equations

An equation of the form: $x^3 + 2x^2 - 5x + 4 = 0$ where the expression $f(x)$ is a cubic expression in x. Consequently, the expression will have three roots or solutions.

Depending on whether the roots are real or imaginary, we can have the following two cases in this situation:

Case 1: All three roots are real; (Graph might touch/cut the x-axis once, twice or thrice.)

In this case, depending on the equality or inequality of the roots, we might have the following cases:

Case (i): All three roots are equal; (The graph of the function would touch the X-axis only once as all the three roots of the equation coincide.)

Case (ii): Two roots are equal and one root is distinct; (In this case the graph cuts the X-axis at one point and touches the X-axis at another point where the other two roots coincide.)

Case (iii): All three roots are distinct from each other. (In this case the graph of the function cuts the x-axis at three distinct points.)

Case 2: One root is real and two roots are imaginary. (Graph would cut the X-axis only once.)

The shapes of the graph that a cubic function can take have already been discussed as a part of *Back to School* write up of this block.

Note: For a cubic equation $ax^3 + bx^2 + cx + d = 0$ with roots as l, m and n:

The product of its three roots viz: $l \times m \times n = -d/a$;

The sum of its three roots viz: $l + m + n = -b/a$

The pair wise sum of its roots taken two at a time viz: $lm + ln + mn = c/a$.

THEORY OF QUADRATIC EQUATIONS

An equation of the form

$$ax^2 + bx + c = 0 \quad (1)$$

where a, b and c are all real and a is not equal to 0, is a quadratic equation. Then,

$D = (b^2 - 4ac)$ is the discriminant of the quadratic equation.

If $D < 0$ (i.e. the discriminant is negative) then the equation has no real roots.

If $D > 0$, (i.e. the discriminant is positive) then the equation has two distinct roots, namely,

$x_1 = (-b + \sqrt{D})/2a$, and $x_2 = (-b - \sqrt{D})/2a$

and then $\quad ax^2 + bx + c = a(x - x_1)(x - x_2) \quad (2)$

If $D = 0$, then the quadratic equation has equal roots given by

$$x_1 = x_2 = -b/2a$$

and then $\quad ax^2 + bx + c = a(x - x_1)^2 \quad (3)$

To represent the quadratic $ax^2 + bx + c$ in form (2) or (3) is to expand it into linear factors.

Properties of Quadratic Equations and Their Roots

1. If D is a *perfect square* then the roots are *rational* and in case, it is not a perfect square then the roots are *irrational*.
2. In the case of imaginary roots ($D < 0$) and if $p + iq$ is one root of the quadratic equation, then the other must be the conjugate $p - iq$ and vice versa (where p and q are real and $i = \sqrt{-1}$).
3. If $p + \sqrt{q}$ is one root of a quadratic equation, then the other must be the conjugate $p - \sqrt{q}$ and vice versa, (where p is rational and $\sqrt{q}$ is a surd).
4. If $a = 1$, b, $c \in I$ and the roots are rational numbers, then the root must be an integer.

Sign of a Quadratic Expression

Let $f(x) = y = ax^2 + bx + c$ where a, b, c are real and $a \neq 0$, then $y = f(x)$ represents a parabola whose axis is parallel to y-axis. For some values of x, $f(x)$ may be positive, negative or zero. Also, if $a > 0$, the parabola opens upwards and for $a < 0$, the parabola opens downwards. This gives the following cases:

(i) $a > 0$ and $D < 0$ (The roots are imaginary)

The function $f(x)$ will always be positive for all real values of x. So $f(x) > 0 \ \forall \ x \in R$. Naturally the graph as shown in the figure does not cut the X-axis.

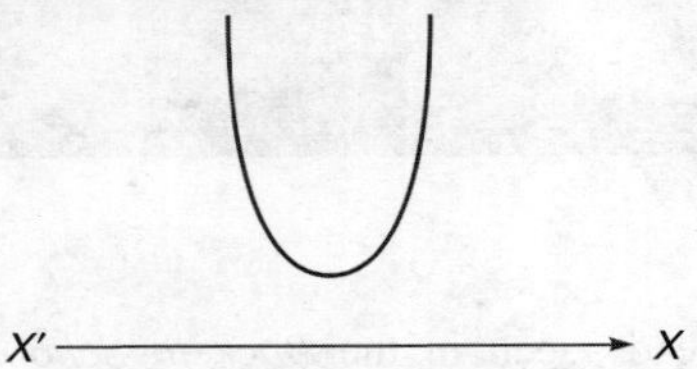

(ii) When $a > 0$ and $D = 0$ (The roots are real and identical)

$f(x)$ will be positive for all values of x except at the vertex where $f(x) = 0$.

So, $f(x) \geq 0 \ \forall \ x \in R$. Naturally, the graph touches the X-axis once.

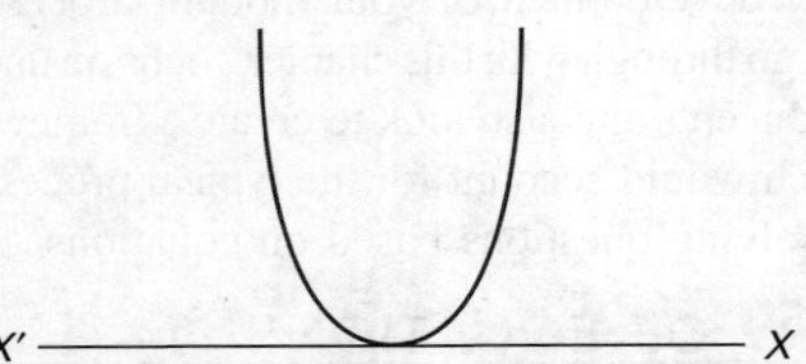

(iii) When $a > 0$ and $D > 0$ (The roots are real and distinct)

Let $f(x) = 0$ have two real roots α and β ($\alpha < \beta$) then $f(x)$ will be positive for all real values of x which are lower than α or higher than β; $f(x)$ will be equal to zero when x is equal to either of α or β.

When x lies between α and β, then, $f(x)$ will be negative. Mathematically, this can be represented as $f(x) > 0 \ \forall \ x \in (-\infty, \alpha) \cup (\beta, \infty)$ and $f(x) < 0 \ \forall \ x \in (\alpha, \beta)$ (Naturally, the graph cuts the X-axis twice)

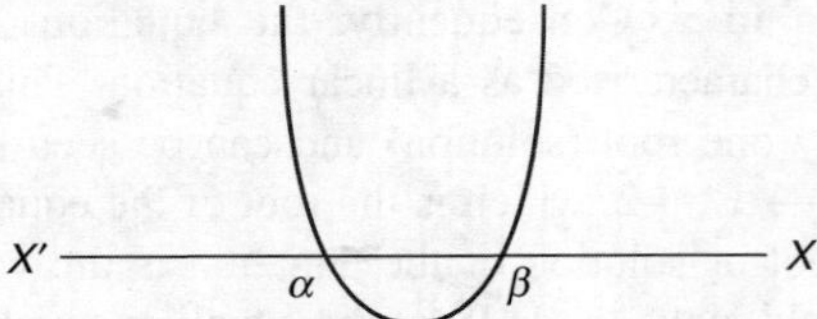

(iv) When $a < 0$ and $D < 0$ (Roots are imaginary)

$f(x)$ is negative for all values of x. Mathematically, we can write $f(x) < 0 \ \forall \ x \in R$. (The graph will not cut or touch the X-axis.)

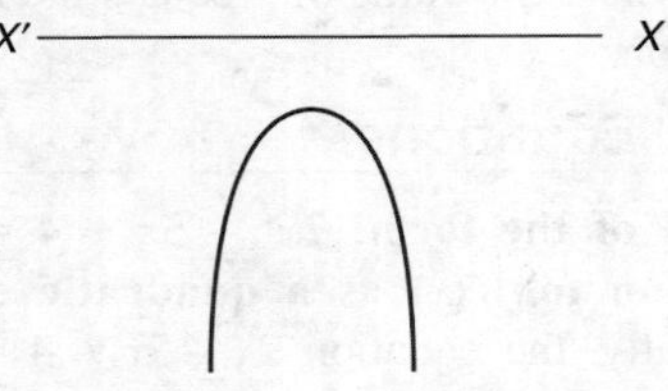

(v) When $a < 0$ and $D = 0$ (Roots are real and equal)

$f(x)$ is negative for all values of x except at the vertex where $f(x) = 0$, i.e., $f(x) \leq 0 \ \forall \ x \in R$ (The graph touches the X-axis once.)

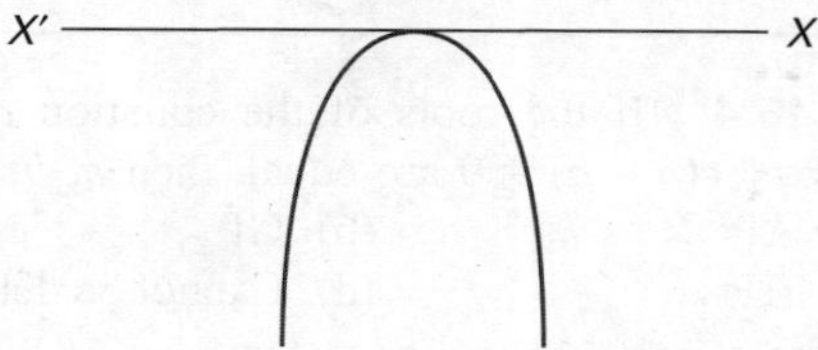

(vi) When $a < 0$ and $D > 0$

Let $f(x) = 0$ have two roots α and β ($\alpha < \beta$) then $f(x)$ will be negative for all real values of x that are lower than α or higher than β. $f(x)$ will be equal to zero when x is equal to either of α or β. The graph cuts the X-axis twice.

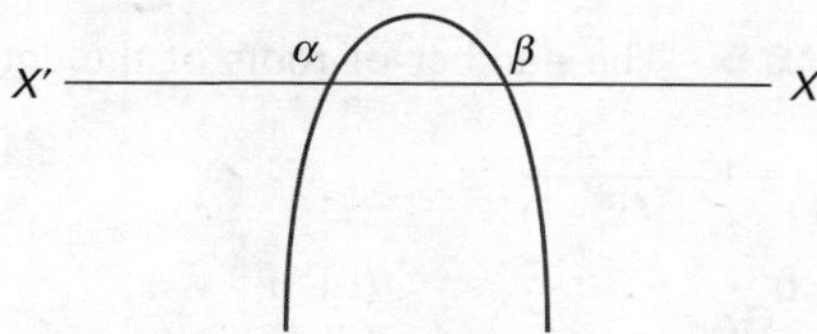

When x lies between α and β, then $f(x)$ will be positive.

Mathematically, this can be written as $f(x) < 0 \ \forall \ x \in (-\infty, \alpha) \cup (\beta, \infty)$ and $f(x) > 0 \ \forall \ x \in (\alpha, \beta)$.

Sum of the roots of a quadratic equation $= -b/a$.

Product of the roots of a quadratic equation $= c/a$

Equations in More than One Variable

Sometimes, an equation might contain not just one variable but more than one variable. In the context of an aptitude examination like the CAT, multiple variable equations may be limited to two or three variables. Consider this question from a past CAT examination which required the student to understand the interrelationship between the values of x and y.

The question was as follows:

$4x - 17y = 1$ where x and y are integers with $x,y > 0$ and $x, y < 1000$. How many pairs of values of (x, y) exist such that the equation is satisfied?

In order to solve this equation, you need to consider the fact that $4x$ in this equation should be looked upon as a multiple of 4 while $17y$ should be looked upon as a multiple of 17. A scan of values which exist such that a multiple of 4 is 1 more than a multiple of 17 starts from $52 - 51 = 1$, in which case the value of $x = 13$ and $y = 3$. This represents the first set of values for (x, y) that satisfies the equation.

The next pair of values in this case would happen if you increase x from 13 to 30 (increase by 17 which is the coefficient of y); at the same time increase y from 3 to 7 (increase by 4 which is the coefficient of x). The effect this has on $4x$ is to increase it by 68 while $17y$ would also increase by 68 keeping the value of $4x$ exactly 1 more than $17y$. In other words, at $x = 30$ and $y = 7$, the equation would give us $120–119 = 1$. Going further, you should realise that the same increases need to be repeated to again identify the pair of x, y values. ($x = 47$ and $y = 11$ gives us $188–187 = 1$).

Once you realise this, the next part of the visualisation in solving this question has to be on creating the series of values which would give us our desired outcomes every time.

This series can be viewed as

(13, 3); (30, 7); (47, 11); (64, 15)....and the series would basically be two arithmetic progressions running parallel to each other (viz: 13, 30, 47, 64, 81,....) and (3, 7, 11, 15, 19,...) and obviously the number of such pairs would depend on the number of terms in the first of these arithmetic progressions (since that AP would cross the upper limit of 1000 first).

You would need to identify the last term of the series below 1000. The series can be visualised as 13, 30, 47, 64,… 999 and the number of terms in this series is $986/17 + 1 = 59$ terms. [Refer to the chapter on Arithmetic Progressions for developing the thinking that helps us do these last two steps.]

Space for Rough Work

WORKED-OUT PROBLEMS

Problem 16.1: Find the value of $\sqrt{6+\sqrt{6+\sqrt{6+...}}}$

(a) 4 (b) 3
(c) 3.5 (d) 2.5

Solution: Let $y = \sqrt{6+\sqrt{6+\sqrt{6+...}}}$

Then, $y = \sqrt{6+y} \Rightarrow$ or $y^2 - y - 6 = 0$

Or, $(y+2)(y-3) = 0 \Rightarrow y = -2, 3$

$y = -2$ is not admissible

Hence $y = \mathbf{3}$

Alternative: Going through options:

Option (a): For 4 to be the solution, value of the whole expression should be equal to 16. Looking into the expression, it cannot be equal to 16. So, option (a) cannot be the answer. Option (b): For 3 to be the solution, the value of the expression should be 9.

So, the expression is = $\sqrt{6+\sqrt{6+\sqrt{6+...}}}$

But $\sqrt{6} \approx 2.4$, hence = $\sqrt{6+\sqrt{8.4}} \cong \sqrt{8.9+\cdots} \cong \mathbf{3}$

(Since, the remaining part is negligible in value)

Problem 16.2: One of the two students, while solving a quadratic equation in x, copied the constant term incorrectly and got the roots 3 and 2. The other copied the constant term and coefficient of x correctly and got his roots as –6 and 1 respectively. The correct roots are

(a) 3, –2 (b) –3, 2
(c) –6, –1 (d) 6, –1

Solution: Let a, b be the roots of the equation. Then $\alpha + \beta = 5$ and $\alpha\beta = -6$. So, a possible equation is $x^2 - 5x - 6 = 0$. The roots of the equation are 6 and –1.

Problem 16.3: If p and q are the roots of the equation x2 + px + q = 0 then we can conclude that:

(a) $p = 1$ (b) $p = 1$ or 0 or $-\frac{1}{2}$
(c) $p = -2$ (d) $p = -2$ or 0

Solution: Since p and q are roots of the equation x^2 + px + q = 0,

$$p^2 + p^2 + q = 0 \text{ and } q^2 + pq + q = 0$$
$$\Rightarrow 2p^2 + q = 0 \text{ and } q(q+p+1) = 0$$
$$\Rightarrow 2p^2 + q = 0 \text{ and } q = 0 \text{ or } q = -p - 1$$

When we use, $q = 0$ and $2p^2 + q = 0$

We get $p = 0$.

Or when we use $q = -p - 1$ and $2p^2 + q = 0$

We get $2p^2 - p - 1 = 0 \rightarrow$ which gives us

$p = 1$ or $p = -1/2$

Hence, there can be three values for p

i.e. $p = 1, p = 0$, or $p = -\frac{1}{2}$

Problem 16.4: If the roots of the equation $a(b-c)x^2 + b(c-a)x + c(a-b) = 0$ are equal, then a, b, c are in

(a) AP (b) GP
(c) HP (d) Cannot be determined

Solution: Since roots of the equation $a(b-c)x^2 + b(c-a)x + c(a-b) = 0$ are equal

$$\Rightarrow b^2(c-a)^2 - 4ac(b-c)(a-b) = 0$$
$$\Rightarrow b^2(c+a)^2 - 4abc(a+c) + 4a^2c^2 = 0$$
$$\Rightarrow [b(c+a) - 2ac]^2 = 0 \Rightarrow b(c+a) - 2ac = 0$$
$$\Rightarrow b = (2ac)/(a+c) \Rightarrow a, b, c, \text{ are in HP}$$

Problem 16.5 The number of roots of the equation

$x - \frac{2}{(x-1)} = 1 - \frac{2}{(x-1)}$ is

(a) 0 (b) 1
(c) 2 (d) Infinite

Solution: The equation gives x = 1.

But $x = 1$ is not admissible because it gives $x - 1 = 0$ which, in turn, makes the whole expression like this: x–2/0 = 1–2/0. But 2/0 is not defined. Hence, no solution is possible.

Problem 16.6: If the roots of the equation $x^2 - bx + c = 0$ differ by 2, then which of the following is true?

(a) $c^2 = 4(c+1)$ (b) $b^2 = 4c + 4$
(c) $c^2 = b + 4$ (d) $b^2 = 4(c+2)$

Solution: Let the roots be a and a + 2.

Then $\alpha + \alpha + 2 = b \Rightarrow \alpha = (b-2)/2$ (1)

and $\alpha(\alpha+2) = c \Rightarrow \alpha^2 + 2\alpha = c$ (2)

Putting the value of α from (1) in (2).

$$((b-2)/2)^2 + 2(b-2)/2) = c$$
$$\Rightarrow (b^2 + 4 - 4b)/4 + b - 2 = c$$
$$\Rightarrow b^2 + 4 - 8 = 4c$$
$$\Rightarrow b^2 = 4c + 4$$

$\therefore$ Hence, option (b) is the correct answer.

Problem 16.7: What is the condition for one root of the quadratic equation $ax^2 + bx + c = 0$ to be twice the other?

(a) $b^2 = 4ac$ (b) $2b^2 = 9ac$
(c) $c^2 = 4a + b^2$ (d) $c^2 = 9a - b^2$

Solution:

$$\therefore \alpha + 2\alpha = -(b/a) \text{ and } \alpha \times 2\alpha = c/a$$
$$\Rightarrow 3\alpha = -(b/a) \Rightarrow \alpha = -b/3a$$
$$\text{and } 2\alpha^2 = c/a \Rightarrow 2(-b/3a)^2 = c/a$$
$$\Rightarrow 2b^2/9a^2 = c/a \Rightarrow 2b^2 = 9ac$$

Hence, the required condition is $2b^2 = 9ac$.

Alternative: Assume any equation having two roots as 2 and 4 or any equation having two roots one of which is twice the other.

When roots are 2 and 4, then equation will be $(x - 2)(x - 4) = x^2 - 6x + 8 = 0$.

Now, check the options one by one and you will find only **(b)** as a suitable option.

Problem 16.8: Solve the system of equations

$$\begin{cases} 1/x + 1/y = 3/2, \\ 1/x^2 + 1/y^2 = 5/4 \end{cases}$$

Solution: Let 1/x = u and 1/y = v. We then obtain

$$\begin{cases} u + v = 3/2, \\ u^2 + v^2 = 5/4 \end{cases}$$

From the first equation, we find $v = (3/2) - u$ and substitute this expression into the second equation

$$u^2 + ((3/2) - u)^2 = 5/4 \text{ or } 2u^2 - 3u + 1 = 0$$

when $u_1 = 1$ and $u_2 = 1/2$; consequently, $v_1 = 1/2$ and $v_2 = 1$. Therefore, $x_1 = 1$,

$$y_1 = 2 \quad \text{and} \quad x_2 = 2, y_2 = 1$$

Answer: (1, 2) and (2, 1).

Problem 16.9: The product of the roots of the equation mx2 + 6x + (2m – 1) = 0 is – 1. Then m is

(a) 1 (b) 1/3
(c) –1 (d) –1/3

Solution: We have (2m – 1)/m = –1 fi m = 1/3

Problem 16.10: If $13x + 17y = 643$, where x and y are natural numbers, what is the value of two times the product of x and y? Assume x, y are both >10.

(a) 744 (b) 844
(c) 924 (d) 884

Solution: The solution of this question depends on your visualisation of the multiples of 13 and 17 which would satisfy this equation. (Note: Your reaction to $13x$ should be to look at it as a multiple of 13 while $17y$ should be looked at as a multiple of 17). A scan of multiples of 13 and 17 gives us the solution at 286 + 357 which would mean 13 × 22 and 17 × 21 giving us x as 22 and y as 21. The value of $2xy$ would be 2 × 22 × 21 = 2 × 462 = 924.

Problem 16.11: If $[x]$ denotes the greatest integer $\le x$, then

$$\left[\frac{1}{3}\right] + \left[\frac{1}{3} + \frac{1}{99}\right] + \left[\frac{1}{3} + \frac{2}{99}\right] + \cdots \left[\frac{1}{3} + \frac{198}{99}\right] = \boxed{}$$

(a) 99 (b) 66
(c) 132 (d) 167

Solution: When the value of the sum of the terms inside the function is less than 1, the value of its greatest integer function would be 0. In the above sequence of values, the value inside the bracket would become equal to 1 or more from the value $\left[\frac{1}{3} + \frac{66}{99}\right]$.

Further, this value would remain between 1 and 2 up till the term $\left[\frac{1}{3} + \frac{164}{99}\right]$.

There would be 99 terms each with a value of 1 between 66/99 to 164/99. Hence, this part of the expression would each yield a value of 1 giving us:

$$\left[\frac{1}{3} + \frac{66}{99}\right] + \left[\frac{1}{3} + \frac{67}{99}\right] + \cdots \left[\frac{1}{3} + \frac{164}{99}\right] = 99$$

Further, from $\left[\frac{1}{3} + \frac{165}{99}\right] + \left[\frac{1}{3} + \frac{167}{99}\right] + \cdots \left[\frac{1}{3} + \frac{198}{99}\right]$

$= 2 \times 34 = 68$

This gives us a total value of 99 + 68 = 167 which means that option (d) is the correct answer.

Space for Rough Work

LEVEL OF DIFFICULTY (I)

1. If the roots of the equation $x^2 + kx + 504 = 0$ are positive even integers, then the number of possible values of 'k' is:
(a) 8 (b) 6
(c) 16 (d) 18

2. Find the value of k, if the equation $2x^2 - 7x + k = 0$ has one root which is twice the reciprocal of the other.

3. What should be the value of m such that the roots of the quadratic equation $mx^2 - 8x + 8 = 0$ are real and equal?

4. Find all the values of b for which the equation $x^2 - bx + 1 = 0$ does not possess real roots.
(a) $-1 < b < 1$ (b) $0 < b < 2$
(c) $-2 < b < 2$ (d) $-1.9 < b < 1.9$

5. Find the value of the expression
$(\sqrt{x + (\sqrt{x + (\sqrt{x \cdots +}))}})$.
(a) $\frac{1}{2}\left[2\sqrt{(2x-1)}+1\right]$ (b) $\frac{1}{2}\left[\sqrt{(4x+1)}+1\right]$
(c) $\frac{1}{2}\left[2\sqrt{(2x-1)}-1\right]$ (d) $\frac{1}{2}\left[\sqrt{(4x-1)}-1\right]$

6. If a and b are the roots of the equation $ax^2 + bx + c = 0$, then the equation whose roots are $a + \frac{1}{\beta}$ and $b + \frac{1}{\alpha}$ is
(a) $abx^2 + b(c + a)x + (c + a)^2 = 0$
(b) $(c + a)x^2 + b(c + a)x + ac = 0$
(c) $cax^2 + b(c + a)x + (c + a)^2 = 0$
(d) $cax^2 + b(c + a)x + c(c + a)^2 = 0$

7. If $a = \sqrt{(7 + 4\sqrt{3})}$, what will be the value of $\left(a + \frac{1}{a}\right)$?
(a) 7 (b) 4
(c) 3 (d) 2

8. If the roots of the equation $(a^2 + b^2)x^2 - 2(ac + bd)x + (c^2 + d^2) = 0$ are equal then which of the following is true?
(a) $ab = cd$ (b) $ad = bc$
(c) $ad = \sqrt{bc}$ (d) $ab = \sqrt{cd}$

9. If $x^2 + ax + b$ leaves the same remainder 5 when divided by $x - 1$ or $x + 1$, then the values of a and b are respectively
(a) 0 and 4 (b) 3 and 0
(c) 0 and 3 (d) 4 and 0

10. If the product of roots of the equation $x^2 - 3(2a + 4)x + a^2 + 18a + 81 = 0$ is unity, then a can take the values as
(a) 3, – 6 (b) 10, – 8
(c) –10, –8 (d) –10, – 6

11. If a and b are the roots of the quadratic equation $5y^2 - 7y + 1 = 0$. then find the value of $\frac{1}{\alpha} + \frac{1}{\beta}$.
(a) $\frac{7}{25}$ (b) –7
(c) $\frac{-7}{25}$ (d) 7

12. Find the maximum value of the expression $(x^2 + 8x + 20)$.
(a) 4 (b) 2
(c) 29 (d) None of these

13. If the roots of the equation $x^2 + bx + c = 0$ differ by 2, then which of the following is true?
(a) $a^2c^2 = 4(1 + c)$ (b) $4b + c = 1$
(c) $c^2 = 4 + b$ (d) $b^2 = 4(c + 1)$

14. Two numbers a and b are such that the quadratic equation $ax^2 + 3x + 2b = 0$ has – 6 as the sum and the product of the roots. Find $a + b$.
(a) 2 (b) –1
(c) 1 (d) –2

15. If equation $x^2 + bx + 12 = 0$ gives 2 as its one of the roots and $x^2 + bx + q = 0$ gives equal roots then the value of b is
(a) $\frac{49}{4}$ (b) – 8
(c) 4 (d) $\frac{25}{2}$

16. Find the minimum value of the expression $(p + 1/p)$; $p > 0$.
(a) 1 (b) 0
(c) 2
(d) Depends upon the value of p

17. For what value of c the quadratic equation $x^2 - (c + 6)x + 2(2c - 1) = 0$ has sum of the roots as half of their product?
(a) 5 (b) – 4
(c) 7 (d) 3

18. If $f(x) = (x + 2)$ and $g(x) = (4x + 5)$, and $h(x)$ is defined as $h(x) = f(x) \cdot g(x)$, then sum of roots of $h(x)$ will be
(a) $\frac{3}{4}$ (b) $\frac{13}{4}$
(c) $\frac{-13}{4}$ (d) $\frac{-3}{4}$

19. For the equation $2^{a+3} = 4^{a+2} - 48$, the value of a will be
(a) $\frac{-3}{2}$ (b) –3
(c) –2 (d) 1

20. Find the maximum value of the expression

$$\frac{1}{x^2+5x+10}.$$

(a) $\frac{15}{2}$ (b) 1

(c) $\frac{4}{15}$ (d) $\frac{1}{3}$

Directions for Questions 21 to 24: If graph of $y = f(x)$ is shown in the diagram below, then answer the following questions

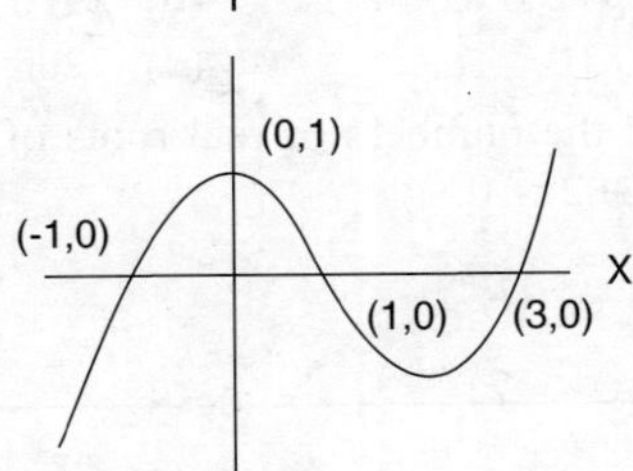

21. If $f(x) = 0$ has 'n' real roots then $n =$

22. Sum of all roots of $f(x) = 0$ is

23. Total number of roots of $f(x) = 2$ is

24. Total number of roots of $f(|x|) = 0$ is

25. For how many real values of x is $3^{x^2-2x-1} = 9$?

26. If a and b are roots of the equation $x^2 + ax + b = 0$ then

(a) $a = 1, b = -2$ (b) $a = 0, b = -2$

(c) $a = 1, b = 0$ (d) None of these

27. Find the number of real roots of the equation $|x|^2 - 2|x| - 3 = 0$.

Directions for Questions 28 and 29: $f(x) = -x^2 + x - 4$, then answer the following questions.

28. If $x \in R$, then which of the following statements is true about $f(x)$ if $f(x) = 0$ has no real root?

(a) The graph of $f(x) = -x^2 + x - 4$ opens upward and $f(x) = 0$ has no real root.

(b) Graph of $f(x) = -x^2 + x - 4$ opens downward and $f(x) = 0$ has two real roots that are equal.

(c) Graph of $f(x) = -x^2 + x - 4$ opens downward and $f(x) = 0$ has no real root.

(d) None of these

29. If a, b are two positive integers and both a and b are greater than 1000 then $f(a).f(b)$ is

(a) > 0 (b) < 0

(c) $= 0$ (d) ≤ 0

30. If m, n are the roots of the equation $x^2 - 6x - 3 = 0$, then the equation whose roots are m^2, n^2 could be

(a) $x^2 - 36x + 9 = 0$ (b) $x^2 - 18x - 6 = 0$

(c) $x^2 - 42x + 9 = 0$ (d) None of these

31. If m, n are the roots of the equation $x^2 + ax + b = 0$ and m, n, a, b all are real numbers then which of the following options can never be a value for (a, b)?

(a) (1, 1) (b) (3, 2)

(c) (4, 4) (d) (7, 3)

32. If m, n are the roots of the equation $px^2 + qx + r = 0$ and km, kn are the roots of the equation $ax^2 + bx + c = 0$, then k is

(a) $\sqrt{\frac{cp}{ar}}$ (b) $\sqrt{\frac{cr}{ap}}$

(c) $\sqrt{\frac{ap}{cr}}$ (d) None of these

33. For how many real values of x, is $x^2 = |x|$?

34. The numbers of real solutions of the equation $3^{2x^2+3x+1} = 0$

35. The number of real roots of the equation $x^2 + (x + 1)^2 + (x - 2)^2 = 0$

36. For how many values of k, the absolute value of the difference between the roots of the equation $x^2 + kx + 15 = 0$ is 2?

37. If $f(x) = x^2 - 8x + 12$, then for how many integer values of x is $f(x) \leq 0$?

38. In the above question for what value of x, does $f(x)$ attain its minimum value?

39. For how many different values of p, does the equation $16x^2 + px + 9 = 0$ have equal roots?

40. If m, n are the roots of $px^2 + qx + r = 0$ and $m + k$, $n + k$ are the roots of the equation $ax^2 + bx + c = 0$ then $k = ?$

(a) $\frac{1}{2}\left[\frac{b}{a}-\frac{q}{p}\right]$ (b) $\frac{1}{2}\left[\frac{q}{p}-\frac{b}{a}\right]$

(c) $\frac{1}{2}\left[\frac{q}{p}+\frac{b}{a}\right]$ (d) None of these

41. The variables p, q, r and s are correlated with each other with the following relationship: $s^{0.5}/p = q/r^2$. The ranges of values for p, q and r are respectively: $-0.04 \leq p \leq -0.03$, $-0.25 \leq q \leq -0.09$, $1 \leq r \leq 7$ Determine the difference between the maximum and minimum value of s.

(a) -0.2 (b) 0.02

(c) 0.1 (d) None of these

Directions for Questions 42 to 45: Read the data given below and solve the questions that follow.

If a and b are roots of the equation $x^2 + x - 7 = 0$, then

42. Find $a^2 + b^2$.

(a) 10 (b) 15

(c) 5 (d) 18

43. Find $a^3 + b^3$.

(a) 22 (b) -22

(c) 44 (d) 36

44. For what values of c in the equation $2x^2 - (c^3 + 8c - 1)x + c^2 - 4c = 0$ the roots of the equation would be opposite in signs?

(a) $c \in (0, 4)$ (b) $c \in (-4, 0)$
(c) $c \in (0, 3)$ (d) $c \in (-4, 4)$

45. For what values of k, the expression $x^2 + kx + 9$ becomes positive (given that x is real)?
(a) $k < 6$ (b) $k > 6$
(c) $|k| < 6$ (d) $|k| \leq 6$

46. The number of positive integral values of x that satisfies $x^3 - 32x - 5x^2 + 64 \leq 0$ is/are
(a) 4 (b) 5
(c) 6 (d) More than 6

47. Find the positive integral value of x that satisfies the equation $x^3 - 32x - 5x^2 + 64 = 0$.
(a) 5 (b) 6
(c) 7 (d) 8

48. Find the number of solutions of $a^3 + 2^{a+1} = a^4$.
(a) 0 (b) 1
(c) 2 (d) 3

49. If a, b, c are positive integers, such that $\frac{1}{a}+\frac{1}{b}+\frac{1}{c} = \frac{29}{72}$, how many sets of (a, b, c) exist?
(a) 3 (b) 4
(c) 5 (d) 6

50. If $9^{a-2} \div 3^{a+4} = 81^{a-11}$, then find the value of $3^{a-8} + 3^{a-6}$.
(a) 972 (b) 2916
(c) 810 (d) 2268

51. Find the numbers of real roots of the equation $x^2 + 3|x| + 2 = 0$.

Space for Rough Work

LEVEL OF DIFFICULTY (II)

1. Given an equation, $a^2 - 8|a - 1| + |b| = 0$ has real roots. Then how many non-negative integer values can 'b' take?
2. For how many values of a, will $(a + 2)(a + 3)(a + 4)(a + 5) + 1992$ achieve its minimum possible value?
3. What is the difference between the possible values of p for which the equation $16x^2 + 2px + 20x + 36 = 0$ has only one solution for x?
4. If $a + b = 4$ and $4^a + 4^b = 40$, then the value of $24a - 3 + 24b - 3$ is equal to
   (a) 80 (b) 100
   (c) 72 (d) 90
5. Find the sum of all possible values of 'a' if $x^2 + ax + 4a = 0$ has only 1 root.
6. If 'k' is a positive integer, then what is the sum of all values of k such that $2x(kx - 4.5) - x^2 + 6 = 0$ has real roots?
   (a) 1 (b) 2
   (c) 3 (d) 4
7. If p & q are integral roots of $ax^2 + 4x + 6 = 0$ and $2x^2 - 7x + 3 = 0$ respectively and $p = q^2$, then what is the value of 'a'?
   1) -112 2) $-5/9$
   3) $14/27$ 4) $-14/27$
8. Which of the following could be the value of $n - m$, if $x^2 - 2x - (15 + nm) = x(x + n + m)$?
   (a) 8 (b) 4
   (c) 2 (d) -2
9. The number of integral values of k, for which one root of the equation $x^2 - 11x + k = 0$ lies in the interval (3, 5) and its other root lies in the interval (6, 8), is
   (a) 4 (b) 5
   (c) 6 (d) 7
10. If both roots of the equation $x^2 - 2kx + k^2 - 4 = 0$ are greater than -4 but less than 5, and if the value of k^2 is less than 30, then k lies in the interval
    (a) $-2 < k < 4$ (b) $k > 3$
    (c) $-1 < k < 3$ (d) $-2 < k < 3$
11. Let x and y be integers such that $x > y$. If $x^2 - xy + x = 24$ and $y^2 - xy - y = 32$, then the value of $(5x - 6y)$ is
12. If the equation $|x + (1 + c)| + |x - 2| = 4$ has infinite number of solutions, then the max real value of 'c' is
    (a) 1 (b) -7
    (c) -3 (d) 5
13. If one root of the equation $x^2 - 4ax + a + f(b) = 0$ is three times of the other root, then minimum value of $f(b)$ will be when a is equal to:
    (a) 1/6 (b) $-1/6$
    (c) $-1/10$ (d) $-1/12$
14. What is the lowest integer value of a, for which the equation $x^2 - 2x(a + 4) + 8 + a^2 = 0$ has real roots?
    (a) -1 (b) 0
    (c) 1 (d) 2
15. In the Maths Olympiad of 2020 at Animal Planet, two representatives from the donkey's side, while solving a quadratic equation, committed the following mistakes:
    (i) One of them made a mistake in the constant term and got the roots as 5 and 9.
    (ii) Another one committed an error in the coefficient of x and he got the roots as 12 and 4.
    But in the meantime, they realised that they are wrong and they managed to get it right jointly. Which of the following could be the quadratic equation?
    (a) $x^2 + 4x + 14 = 0$
    (b) $2x^2 + 7x - 24 = 0$
    (c) $x^2 - 14x + 48 = 0$
    (d) $3x^2 - 17x + 52 = 0$
16. The number of distinct points at which the curve $y^3 - 4y^2 + x^2 - 5x + 3y = 0$ intersects either the y-axis or the x-axis is.
17. If $f(x) = px^2 + qx + r$ and $g(x) = rx^2 + qx + p$.If one root of $f(x) = 0$ is 2 and one root of $g(x) = 0$ is 1/4, then find the sum of the roots of $f(x)$ and $g(x)$.
18. If the sum of the roots of the quadratic equation $px^2 + qx + r = 0$ is equal to the sum of the square of their reciprocals, mark all the correct statements.
    (a) r/p, p/q and q/r are in A. P.
    (b) p/r, q/p and r/q are in G. P.
    (c) p/r, q/p and r/q are in H. P.
    (d) Both (*a*) and (*c*).

Directions for Questions 19 and 20: The equation $x^4 - 594 = ax^3 + bx^2 + cx$ has exactly three distinct integral roots. If a, b and c are real numbers, then answer the following questions:

19. Find the largest value of 'b'.
20. Find the minimum possible value of a.

Directions for Questions 21 and 22: If the roots of the equation $x^3 - 5x^2 + qx + r = 0$ represent the length of the sides of a triangle PQR and the length of the sides are perfect integers, then answer the following questions:

21. Find the maximum possible value of r.
22. Find the minimum possible value of the product of in radius and circum-radius of the triangle.
23. How many common roots do the equations
    $1000x^2 + 1001x + 1 = 0$ and $x^2 + 1001x + 1000 = 0$
    have?

24. How many integer values of 'p' are there such that the inequality $x^2 + 4px + (p + 3) > 0$ is true for all values of x?

25. If $g(x) = x^3 - px^2 - \frac{qx}{2} - r$ can be factorised as $(x - p)(x - q)(x - r)$, then $g(4) = ?$

26. Find the product of the roots of the equation $x^2 + 10x + 19 = 2\sqrt{x^2 + 10x + 22}$.

27. The cost of ten pears, eight grapes and six mangoes is ₹44. The cost of five pears, four grapes and three mangoes is ₹22. Find the cost of four mangoes and three grapes, if the cost of each of the items, in rupees, is a natural number and the cost of no two items is the same.

(a) ₹17 (b) ₹18
(c) ₹14 (d) Cannot be determined

28. If the roots of the equation $px^3 - 20x^2 + 4x - 5 = 0$, where $p \neq 0$, are l, m and n, then what is the value of $\frac{1}{lm} + \frac{1}{mn} + \frac{1}{ln}$?

(a) 5 (b) –4
(c) 4 (d) 8

29. If one of the roots of the equation $ax^2 + bx + c = 0$ is less than –3 and other is greater than 3, where $a > 0$, then $4a - 2b + c$ is

(a) >0 (b) <0
(c) $=0$ (d) Cannot be determined

30. In the previous question, $9a + 3|b| + c$ is

(a) >0 (b) <0
(c) $=0$ (d) Cannot be determined

31. The sum of roots of the equation $px^2 + qx + r = 0$ is equal to sum of squares of their reciprocals. If p, q and r are real numbers and $p \neq 0$, then pq^2, rp^2, qr^2 are in

(a) A.P. (b) G.P.
(c) H.P. (d) None of these

32. If 'x' is a real number then what is the number of solutions for the equation: $(x^8 + 12)^{1/2} = x^4 - 2$?

(a) 0 (b) 1
(c) 2 (d) Cannot be determined

Directions for Questions 33 and 34:

33. Find the number of integral solutions of the equation, $x^2 - 4xy + 3y = 0$ where x and y are non-zero real numbers.

34. In the above question what would be the maximum possible value of $x + y$?

35. If the equation $ax^2 + bx + a = 0 (a > 0)$ has real and positive roots then which of the following is always true?

(a) $b < 2a$ (b) $b < 0$
(c) $b \leq -2a$ (d) All the options are true

36. If $f(x) = x^3 - 3x^2 + 2x + 5$ and $g(x) = x^3 + x^2 + 7x + 6$ then what is the number of common roots of $f(x) = 0$ and $g(x) = 0$?

37. The graph of $ax^2 + bx + c$ is shown below. Then which of the following is true?

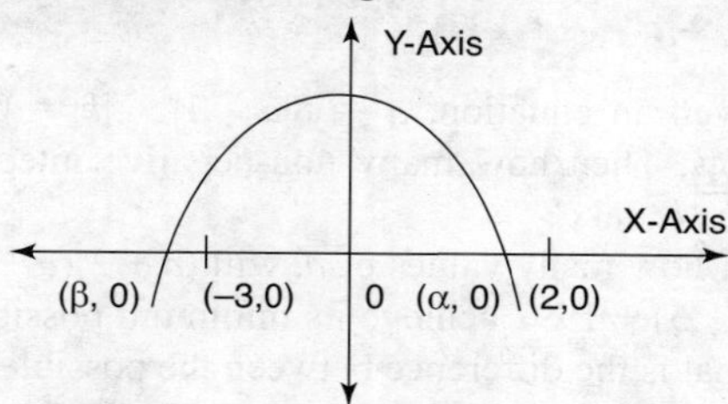

(a) $a < 0, b < 0, c > 0$ (b) $a < 0, b < 0, c < 0$
(c) $a < 0, b > 0, c > 0$ (d) $a < 0, b > 0, c < 0$

38. $f(x) = px^3 - 2x + c$
$f(1) = -5$ and $f(4) = 52$. For how many values of x, $f(x) = 0$?

39. Find the number of real roots of the equation $4^{-x} + 2x = 5$.

40. $Q_1(x)$ and $Q_2(x)$ are quadratic functions such that $Q_1(10) = Q_2(8) = 0$. If the corresponding equations $Q_1(x) = 0$ and $Q_2(x) = 0$ have a common root and $Q_1(4) \times Q_2(5) = 36$, what is the value of the common root?

(a) 10 (b) 6
(c) Either 9 or 6 (d) Cannot be determined

41. For the above question, if it is known that the coefficient of x^2 for $Q_1(x) = 0$ is 1/15 and that of $Q_2(x) = 0$ is 1, then which of the following options is a possible value of the sum of the roots of $Q_2(x) = 0$?

(a) 18 (b) 36
(c) 25 (d) 11

42. If the roots of the equation $x^3 - ax^2 + bx - 1080 = 0$ are in the ratio 2 : 4 : 5, then find the value of the coefficient of x^2.

(a) 33 (b) 66
(c) –33 (d) 99

43. If $f(x)$ is a quadratic polynomial, such that $f(5) = 75$ and $f(-5) = 45$, and $f(p) = f(q) = 0$, then find $p \times q$, given that the value of the constant term in the polynomial is 10.

(a) 2 (b) –3
(c) 5 (d) Cannot be determined

44. Find the sum of values of x that satisfies the equation $\left(x^2 - 4x - 4\right)^{x^2 - 16} - 1 = 0$ is:

45. If $|a| + a + b = 75$ and $a + |b| - b = 150$, then what is the value of $|a| + |b|$?

(a) 105 (b) 60
(c) 90 (d) Cannot be determined

46. If the equations $5x + 9y + 17z = a$, $4x + 8y + 12z = b$ and $2x + 3y + 8z = c$ have at least one solution for x, y and z and a, b, and $c \neq 0$, then which of the following is true?

(a) $4a - 3b - 3c = 0$ (b) $3a - 4b - 3c = 0$
(c) $4a - 3b - 4c = 0$ (d) Nothing can be said

47. If the roots of the equation $x^3 + qx^2 + rx + s = 0$ are in *GP*, then which of the following is true?
(a) $r^2 = q^2 s$ (b) $r^3 = q^3 s$
(c) $r = qs^2$ (d) $r = qs^3$

48. The 9-to-9 supermarket purchases *x* litres of fruit juice from the Fruit Garden Inc for a total price of \$ $4x^2$ and sells the entire *x* litres at a total price of \$ $10 \times (15 + 16x)$. Find the maximum amount of profit that the 9-to-9 supermarket makes in the process.
(a) 1700 (b) 1,000
(c) 1,750 (d) 1,300

49. $x - y = 6$ and $P = 7x^2 - 12y^2$, where $x, y > 0$. What is the maximum possible value of *P*?
(a) Infinite (b) 352.8
(c) 957.6 (d) 604.8

50. If α, β are the roots of the quadratic equation $x^2 + mx + 1 = 0$ and γ, δ are the roots of the equation $x^2 + nx + 1 = 0$, then the value of $(\alpha - \gamma)(\beta - \gamma)(\alpha + \delta)(\beta + \delta)$ is equal to
(a) $n^2 - m^2$ (b) $m^2 - n^2$
(c) $2m^2 - n^2$ (d) None of these

51. If $f(x) = px^2 + qx + r$ and $f(x)$ is exactly divisible by $(x + 2)$ and $(x + 3)$ but leaves remainder of 7 when divided by $(x - 1)$, find the approximate value of *q*.

52. If $f(x) = 4x - 7\sqrt{x}$, which of the following statements is true about the roots of the equation $f(x) = 2$?
(a) It has only one real root which is not an integer
(b) It has no real root
(c) It has one real root which is a positive integer
(d) It has two real roots

53. $f(x) = (x - 2)(x^2 + 2x + 5)$
If *a*, *b*, *c* are the roots of $f(x) = 0$, then find the value of $a^3 + b^3 + c^3$.

54. $f(x) = x^3 - qx^2 - p^2 x + 288$. If *p*, *q* and -12 are the roots of the equation $f(x) = 0$, then find the value of $f(2)$.

55. If $x^3 - mx^2 + nx - p = 0$ has three roots α, β, γ. If we add 3 in each of the roots of $x^3 - mx^2 + nx - p = 0$, then we get the roots of the equation $x^3 - ax^2 + bx - 27 = 0$. What is the value of $p + 9m + 3n$?
(a) 0 (b) 1
(c) −54 (d) 54

56. If *p*, *q*, *r* are real and $(x - p)(x - q)+(x - q)(x - r)+(x - r)(x - p)=0$ if $p \neq q \neq r$ then which of the following options is true?
(a) Roots of the given equations are imaginary.
(b) Roots of the given equation are real.
(c) Roots of the given equation are equal.
(d) None of these

57. Which of the following could be a possible value of '*x*' for which, each of the fractions is in its simplest form, where $[x]$ stands for the greatest integer less than or equal to '*x*'?

$$\frac{[x]+7}{10}, \frac{[x]+18}{11}, \frac{[x]+31}{12}, \frac{[x]+46}{13}, \ldots, \frac{[x]+1138}{39} \text{ and } \frac{[x]+1207}{40}$$

(a) 95.71 (b) 93.71
(c) 94.71 (d) 92.71

58. The sum of the reciprocals of the roots of the equation $px^2 + qx + r = 0$ is 7/23 and the product of the roots of the equation $rx^2 + qx + p = 0$ is 1/23, find the sum of the roots of the equation $qx^2 + px + r = 0$
(a) 1/7 (b) −7
(c) −1/7 (d) −7

59. The roots of $x^3 - px^2 + qx - r = 0$ are *a*, *b*, *c* while the roots of $x^3 + wx^2 + yz - 47 = 0$ are $a + 2$, $b + 2$, $c + 2$, then the value of $4p + 2q + r = ?$

Directions for Questions 60 and 61: One of the roots of the equation $x^2 + bx + 3b = 0$ ($b \in R$) is thrice the other root, then answer the following questions.

60. What is the value of 3*b*?

61. Which of the following options correctly represents roots of the equation $x^2 - 33x + 17b = 0$?
(a) $b, b + 1$ (b) $b - 1, b$
(c) $b - 1, b + 1$ (d) None of these

62. A polynomial $ax^3 + bx^2 + cx + d$ intersects the *x*−axis at 1 and −1, and *y*-axis at 2. The value of *b* is
(a) −2 (b) 0
(c) 1 (d) 2

63. If $3^{|2x+1|} = 9^{(4x-5)}$, then find the product of all possible values of *x*.

64. The number of positive integral solutions to the system of equations $a_1 + a_2 + a_3 + a_4 + a_5 = 47$ and $a_1 + a_2 = 37$ is
(a) 2376 (b) 2246
(c) 2024 (d) 1296

65. If *x* is real, the smallest value of the expression $3x^2 - 4x + 7$ is
(a) 2/3 (b) 3/4
(c) 7/9 (d) None of these

66. If $0 < p < 1$ then the roots of the equation $(1 - p)x^2 + 4x + p = 0$ are ___?
(a) Real and of opposite sign
(b) Real and both negative
(c) Imaginary
(d) Real and both positive

67. If $[x]$ represents the greatest integer less than or equal to *x*, then the value of $\left[315^{\frac{1}{3}}\right] + \left[316^{\frac{1}{3}}\right] + \left[317^{\frac{1}{3}}\right] + \ldots + \left[515^{\frac{1}{3}}\right]$ is
(a) 1383 (b) 1379
(c) 1183 (d) 1351

68. The roots of $x^2 + 5x + a = 0$ are p and q while the roots of $x^2 + 23x + b = 0$ are q and r. If p, q, r are in an arithmetic progression then the value of $|a \times b| = ?$

69. One day each of Neha's friends consumed some cold drink and some orange squash. Though the quantities of cold drink and orange squash varied for the friends, the total consumption of the two liquids was exactly nine litres for each friend. If Neha had one-ninth of the total cold drink consumed and one-eleventh of the total orange squash consumed, find the ratio of the quantity of cold drink to that of orange squash consumed by Neha on that day?

(a) 3 : 2 (b) 5 : 4
(c) 2 : 1 (d) 1 : 1

70. If $x^2 + 3x - 10$ is a factor of $3x^4 + 2x^3 - ax^2 + bx - a + b - 4$, then the closest approximate values of a and b are

(a) 25, 43 (b) 52, 43
(c) 52, 67 (d) None of these

71. a, b, c, d and e are five consecutive integers $a < b < c < d < e$ and $a^2 + b^2 + c^2 = d^2 + e^2$. What is/are the possible value(s) of d?

(a) –2 and 10
(b) –1 and 11
(c) 0 and 12
(d) None of these

Directions for Questions 72 to 74: $f(x) = ax^3 + bx^2 + cx + d$ where a, b, c and d are natural numbers. When $f(x)$ is divided by x, the remainder is k^4, where 'k' is a prime number. The square root of the remainder when $f(x)$ is divided by $(x - k)$ is the perfect cube of a natural number. If a, b, c and d are in increasing geometric progression, then answer the following questions.

72. Find the value of 'k'.

73. What is the value of a?

74. $f(4) = ?$

75. $f(x) = x^8 - 4$ and $f(k) = 0$. The value of $(k - 1)(k^{12} + k^{13} + k^{14} + k^{15} + ... + k^{51}) = ?$

High Yield Questions

Scan this QR code to access assisted problem solving videos on questions 1, 10, 15, 21 and 22 from LOD 2

Space for Rough Work

LEVEL OF DIFFICULTY (III)

1. How many solutions does $3|x| (x^2 + 8/3) = 10x^2$ have?
2. If x and y are distinct integers and $m^2 + xm + y = 0$ and $m^2 + ym + x = 0$ both have real roots. If the sum of the squares of the roots of both the equations are equal, then find what will be the absolute value of the sum of x & y.
3. If both roots of the quadratic equation $x^2 - 52x + a = 0$ are prime numbers, then the number of possible values of 'a' is
   (a) 1 (b) 2
   (c) 3 (d) 4
4. Let p, q and $p + q$ be three roots of the equation $x^3 - 4x^2 + 2x + a = 0$, where a is a real number, then what can be the value of $p - q + a$?
   (a) $4 + 2\sqrt{3}$ (b) $2 + 2\sqrt{3}$
   (c) $4 - 2\sqrt{3}$ (d) Both (a) and (c)
5. Let $f(x) = x^2 - px + q$ be a quadratic function of real values, where p and q are real numbers. If $f(1) \times f(2) < 0$, then which of the following CANNOT be the value of $f(0)$?
   (a) –3 (b) 1
   (c) 0 (d) 2
6. What is the product of the real roots of the equation $x^2 + 5x + 12 = 2\sqrt{x^2 + 5x + 20}$
7. If $x < 0$ and $9x^2 + 1/x^2 = 3$, then $27x^3 + 1/x^3$ is equal to?
   (a) 18 (b) –18
   (c) 36 (d) –36
8. Let p and q be the roots of the quadratic equation $x^2 + 2bx + b = 2$. The smallest possible value of $(p - q)^2$?
   (a) 0 (b) 3
   (c) 4 (d) 7
9. Let the equation $x^2 + 2nx + ab = 0$ have distinct real roots, then how many real roots does equation $x^2 - 2(a + b)x + a^2 + b^2 + 2n^2 = 0$ has?
10. What is the minimum integral value of $(3x^2 - 12x + 27)/(x^2 + 4x + 9)$?
    (a) 10 (b) 1
    (c) 15 (d) 2
11. The work done by Anish is directly proportional to the square of the number of days spent by Dhruv. The work done by Bimal is directly proportional to time spent on the job by Dhruv and Charu takes 5 days to complete a 5 unit task. If only Anish, Bimal, and Charu work on the job, then find the amount of work done in a day if the time taken to complete it is maximum. It was found that Anish completed 16 units of work in 1 day for which Dhruv took 4 days and Bimal completed 4 units of work in a day for which Dhruv took 4 days.
12. The productivity of an outlet pipe A is directly proportional to the square of the number of hours taken by Pipe D to fill the tank. The productivity of an inlet pipe B is directly proportional to the time spent by Pipe D, and Pipe C takes 4 days to complete a 12 unit task. Find the work done in a day if Pipe A, B and C are opened and take the minimum possible time. It was found that Pipe A removed 9 units in 1 Hr from a tank which was filled by Pipe D in 3Hrs and Pipe B took 1 hr to fill a 10 unit tank which was filled by Pipe D in 2 Hrs.
    (a) –13/4 (b) 37/4
    (c) 5/2 (d) –5/2
13. If the difference between the corresponding roots of quadratic equations $2x^2 + 3bx + c = 0$ and $2x^2 + 3cx + b = 0$ is equal and $b \neq c$, then $6(b + c)$ is
    (a) –8 (b) –16/3
    (c) –8/3 (d) –16
14. If a is an integer such that $2x^2 + ax + 8 = 0$ has no real roots and $x^2 + (a - 3)x + 3 = 0$ has two distinct real roots, then how many values of a are there?
    (a) 2 (b) 10
    (c) 8 (d) 40
15. $f(x) = x^3 - (5 + k)x^2 + (6 + 5k)x - 6k$, where '$k$' is an odd prime number and $k > 3$. What is the range of values of x for which $f(x) < 0$?
    (a) $2 < x < 3$ or $x > k$ (b) $x < 2, 3 < x < k$
    (c) $x < 3, x > k$ (d) None of these
16. $f(x) = [x]^2 - 11[x] + 30$, where $[x]$ represents the largest integer less than or equal to x, then what is the sum of all integer solutions of the equation $f(x) = 0$?
17. $f(x, p) = a(x - p)^2 + b(x - p) + c$, where a, b, c are constants and $a < 0$ and 'p' is a natural number. It is given that the roots of the equation $ax^2 + bx + c = 0$ are 3, 4. Then,the value of x at which $f(x, 5)$ attains its maximum value is
    (a) 9 (b) 8.5
    (c) 7.5 (d) 5.5

Directions for Questions 18 and 19:
If $f(x) = x^3 - px^2 - 2qx + r$ and
$g(x) = (x - p)(x - q)(x - r)$,
answer the following questions.

18. Find the value of $p + q$ for which $f(x) = g(x)$,
19. Find the value of $f(4)$, if $f(x) = g(x)$,

Directions for Questions 20 to 22: $f(x) = ax^2 - 150x + 5b$ where a and b are two positive integers. Then answer the following questions

20. For how many ordered pairs (a, b) will $(x - 3)$ be a factor of $f(x)$?
21. Find the maximum possible value of $a + b$ for which $(x - 3)$ is a factor of $f(x)$.

22. If a and b are integers then for how many ordered pairs (a, b) will $(x - 3)$ be a factor of $f(x)$?
(a) 9 (b) 18
(c) 180 (d) None of these

Directions for Questions 23 and 24: If all the roots of $(x - k)^3 (x - 7) - 27 = 0$ are integers then answer the following questions:

23. How many integer values can k have?

24. Find the difference between the maximum and minimum possible values of k.

25. Find all values of 'a', such that 4 lies somewhere between the roots of the equation $3x^2 + 4ax + (a + 3) = 0$ for all values of x.
(a) $a < -3$ (b) $a < -2$
(c) $a > 3$ (d) $a > 2$

26. $f(x) = ax^2 + bx + c$ & $a < 0$.
The equation $f(x) = 0$ has two distinct roots which is from the set $\{-2, -1, 0, 1, 2\}$. How many different pairs of roots of $f(x)$ are possible such that $f(0)$ is greater than or equals to 0?.
(a) 4 (b) 6
(c) 8 (d) 10

27. If $f(x) = x^2, g(x) = x^3 - 2^x$, where x is a positive integer then for how many values of x, is $f(x) = g(x)$?

Directions for Question 28 and 29: If $h(x)$ is a quadratic function which attains its maximum value of 10 at $x = 4$. If $t(x)$ is a function such that $3h(x) + 5t(x) = 0$, then answer the following questions:

28. Which of the following option is true?
(a) $h(x)$ and $t(x)$ have roots of opposite sign
(b) Sum of roots of $h(x)$ and $t(x)$ is 0
(c) Sum of roots of $h(x)$ is equal to the sum of roots of $t(x)$
(d) None of these

29. Find the minimum value of $t(x)$.

30. Find the number of real solutions of equation $\left|\left||x|-1\right|-2\right| = \left(\frac{1}{2}\right)^x$.
where 'p' is a positive integer then find q.

31. $px^2 + qx + r = 0$ has one root greater than 3 and other root less than 1. Which of the following is necessarily true?
(a) $p(4p + 2q + r) < 0$ (b) $p(4p + 2q + r) > 0$
(c) $p(4p - 2q + r) < 0$ (d) $p(9p - 3q + r) < 0$

32. If all the three roots of the equation $x^3 - 12x^2 + px - 42 = 0$ are unequal and prime. Then find p.

Direction for Question 33: If 'd' is a root of the equation $ax^2 + bx + c = 0$ and 'c' is a root of the equation $ax^2 + bx + d = 0$ and if $c \neq d$ then answer the following questions:

33. Find the value of $c + d$
(a) $a(b - 1)$ (b) $\frac{b-1}{a}$
(c) $\frac{1-b}{a}$ (d) None of these

34. If $f(x) = max(|x^2 - 4|, 2x + 4)$ then find the number of solutions of the equation $f(x) = \frac{5}{2}$.

35. The values of a quadratic function $f(x)$ is a positive for all values of x, except for $x = 4$. If $f(0) = 10$, find the value of $f(-4)$.

36. The curve shown below can possibly represent which of the following equation (assume the curve does not exist at $x = 0$).

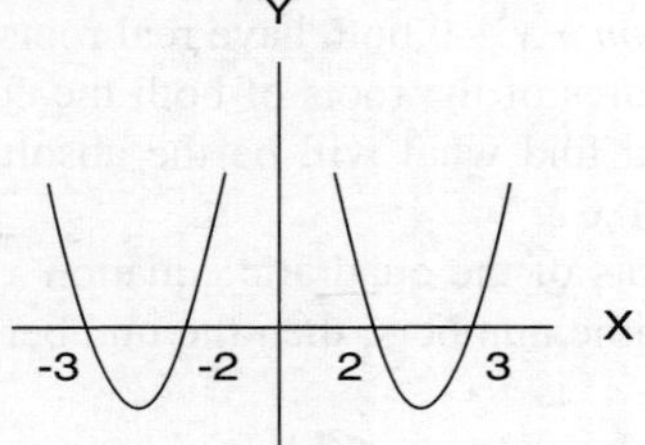

(a) $\frac{6}{|x|} = 5 + |x|$ (b) $-\frac{6}{|x|} = 5 - |x|$
(c) $\frac{6}{|x|} = 5 - |x|$ (d) None of these

37. Find the number of real solutions of the equation $||x| - 1| = e^x$.

38. If $f(x, y) = 4^{x^y} + x^{4^y}$ then what is the total number of solutions for the equation $f(x, y) = 5$.
(a) 0 (b) 1
(c) 2 (d) More than 2

39. If $f(x) = (b - 1)x^2 + (c + d)x + e$ and $a:b = 1:2$, $b:c = 2:3$, $c:d = 3:4$, $d:e = 4:5$, then find the square of difference of the roots of the equation $f(x) = 0$.

40. $\log_3 x \times \log_3 y + \log_3 z \times \log_3 xy = 11$, where x, y, z all are real numbers.
If $(\log_3 x)^2 + (\log_3 y)^2 = 14 - (\log_3 z)^2$ and $xyz = k_1^2 = k_2^3$ then $k_1 + k_2 = ?$

41. Find the value of p for which the sum of the square of the roots of the equation $x^2 - (p - 3)x + (p - 4) = 0$ is minimum.

Directions for Questions 42 and 43: If $f(x) = x^3 - 12x^2 + 47x - 60$. then answer the following questions:

42. How many quadratic equations of the form $x^2 + bx + c = 0$, can be formed such that both the roots of the quadratic equation are common with the roots of $f(x) = 0$?
(a) 3 (b) 5
(c) 6 (d) None of these

43. If the product of all the roots of the quadratic equations of the form $x^2 + bx + c = 0$, that can be formed such that both roots of the quadratic equation are common with the roots of $f(x) = 0$ is p then find $p^{1/4}$.
(a) 30 (b) 40
(c) 50 (d) 60

High Yield Questions

Scan this QR code to access assisted problem solving videos on questions 18, 19, 23, 24, 42 and 43 from LOD 3

ANSWER KEY

Level of Difficulty (I)

1. (b)	2. 4	3. 2	4. (c)
5. (b)	6. (c)	7. (b)	8. (b)
9. (a)	10. (c)	11. (d)	12. (d)
13. (d)	14. (b)	15. (b)	16. (c)
17. (c)	18. (c)	19. (d)	20. (c)
21. 3	22. 3	23. 1	24. 4
25. 2	26. (a)	27. 2	28. (c)
29. (a)	30. (c)	31. (a)	32. (a)
33. 3	34. 0	35. 0	36. 2
37. 5	38. 4	39. 2	40. (b)
41. (d)	42. (b)	43. (b)	44. (a)
45. (c)	46. (d)	47. (d)	48. (b)
49. (d)	50. (c)	51. 0	

Level of Difficulty (II)

1. 25	2. 2	3. 48	4. (d)
5. 16	6. (c)	7. (d)	8. (a)
9. (b)	10. (d)	11. 39	12. (a)
13. (a)	14. (a)	15. (c)	16. 4
17. 6.75	18. (d)	19. 1183	20. –294
21. –4	22. 0.4	23. 1	24. 1
25. 31.5	26. 13	27. (b)	28. (c)
29. (b)	30. (b)	31. (a)	32. (a)
33. 2	34. 4	35. (d)	36. 0
37. (a)	38. 1	39. 2	40. (d)
41. (a)	42. (c)	43. (c)	44. 4
45. (a)	46. (c)	47. (b)	48. (c)
49. (d)	50. (a)	51. 2.92	52. (c)
53. 30	54. 0	55. (a)	56. (b)
57. (c)	58. (a)	59. 39	60. 48
61. (a)	62. (a)	63. 1.65	64. (d)
65. (d)	66. (b)	67. (a)	68. 1568
69. (d)	70. (c)	71. (d)	72. 2
73. 2	74. 240	75. 8184	

Level of Difficulty (III)

1. 4	2. 2	3. (c)	4. (d)
5. (d)	6. 4	7. (b)	8. (d)
9. 0	10. (b)	11. 3/4	12. (b)
13. (b)	14. (c)	15. (b)	16. 11
17. (b)	18. 3/2	19. 54	20. 9
21. 86	22. (d)	23. 4	24. 52
25. (a)	26. (c)	27. 1	28. (c)
29. –6	30. 5	31. (a)	32. 41
33. (c)	34. 2	35. 40	36. (c)
37. 3	38. (d)	39. 29	40. 36
41. 4	42. (c)	43. (d)	

SOLUTIONS AND SHORTCUTS

Level of Difficulty (I)

1. The pair of even factors of 504 are: (2, 252), (4, 126), (6, 84), (14, 36), (18, 28), (12, 42).
   For all these pairs, we'll get a different value of k as $-k$ represents the sum of the roots.
   Hence, 6 values of 'k' are possible. Hence, option (b) is correct.
2. If one of the roots of the given equation is a, then the other root would be $2/a$. The product of the roots would be 2. For the given equation, the product of the roots can be determined by $k/2$. As $k/2 = 2$, Value of k would be 4. Hence, the correct answer is 4.
3. The nature of the roots are determined by the value of the determinant of the given equation.
   For roots to be real and equal, $(b^2 - 4ac) = 0$.
   $(8)^2 - 4(m)(8) = 0 \Rightarrow 32m = 64$. Hence, $m = 2$.
   Hence, the correct answer is 2.
4. $b^2 - 4 < 0 \Rightarrow -2 < b < 2$
5. $y = \sqrt{x + \sqrt{x + \sqrt{x + \cdots}}}$
   $\Rightarrow y = \sqrt{x + y}$
   $\Rightarrow y^2 = x + y$
   $y^2 - y - x = 0$
   Solving quadratically, we have option (b) as the root of this equation.
6. Assume any equation:
   Say $x^2 - 5x + 6 = 0$
   The roots are 2, and 3.
   We are now looking for the equation, whose roots are:
   $(2 + 1/3) = 2.33$ and $(3 + 1/2) = 3.5$
   Also $a = 1$, $b = -5$ and $c = 6$.
   Put these values in each option to see which gives 2.33 and 3.5 as its roots.
7. The approximate value of $a = \sqrt{13.92} = 3.6$ (approx.)
   $a + 1/a = 3.6 + 1/3.6$ is closest to 4.
8. Solve this by assuming each option to be true and then check whether the given expression has equal roots for the option under check.
   Thus, if we check for option (b),
   $ad = bc$,
   We assume $a = 6$, $d = 4$, $b = 12$, $c = 2$ (any set of values that satisfies $ad = bc$).
   Then $(a^2 + b^2)x^2 - 2(ac + bc)x + (c^2 + d^2) = 0$
   $180x^2 - 120x + 20 = 0$
   We can see that this has equal roots. Thus, option (b) is a possible answer. The same way if we check for a, c and d, we see that none of them gives us equal roots and can be rejected.
9. Remainder when $x^2 + ax + b$ is divided by $x - 1$ is obtained by putting $x = 1$ in the expression. Thus, we get.

$a + b + 1 = 5$ and
$b - a + 1 = 5$
$\Rightarrow \quad b = 4$ and $a = 0$

10. The product of the roots is given by: $(a^2 + 18a + 81)/1$.
Since product is unity, we get: $a^2 + 18a + 81 = 1$.
Thus, $a^2 + 18a + 80 = 0$
Solving, we get: $a = -10$ and $a = -8$.
11. $1/\alpha + 1/\beta = (\alpha + \beta)/\alpha\beta$
$= (7/5)/(1/5) = 7$
12. Has no maximum.
13. To solve this, take any expression whose roots differ by 2.
Thus, $(x - 3)(x - 5) = 0$
$\Rightarrow \quad x^2 - 8x + 15 = 0$
In this case, $a = 1$, $b = -8$ and $c = 15$.
We can see that $b^2 = 4(c + 1)$.
14. $-3/a = -6 \Rightarrow a = 1/2$,
$2b/a = -6$ and $a = 1/2$
Gives us $\quad b = -1.5$
$a + b = -1$
15. $x^2 + bx + 12 = 0$ has 2 as a root.
Thus, $b = -8$.
16. The minimum value of $(p + 1/p)$ is at $p = 1$. The value is 2.
17. $(c + 6) = 1/2 \times 2(2c - 1) \Rightarrow c + 6 = 2c - 1 \Rightarrow c = 7$
18. $h(x) = 4x^2 + 13x + 10$.
Sum of roots – 13/4.
19. Solve through options. LHS = RHS for $a = 1$.
20. For the given expression to be a maximum, the denominator should be minimised. (Since, the function in the denominator has imaginary roots and is always positive). $x^2 + 5x + 10$ will be minimised at $x = -2.5$ and its minimum values at $x = -2.5$ is 3.75.
Hence, required answer = 1/3.75 = 4/15.
21. Graph of $f(x) = 0$ cuts x-axis at three distinct points. Therefore, $f(x) = 0$ has three roots.
22. Sum of roots of $f(x) = 0$ is $-1 + 1 + 3 = 3$.
23.

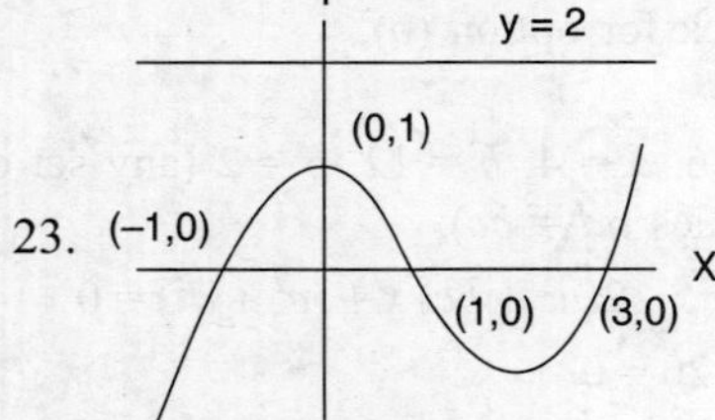

The $y = 2$ line intersects the curve $y = f(x)$ at only one point, hence total number of roots of $f(x) = 2$ is 1.
24. Process to draw graph $f(|x|)$, if graph of $f(x)$ is given: First erase the negative x portion of $f(x)$ then take a mirror image of positive X portion. Curve of $y = f(|x|)$ is shown below.

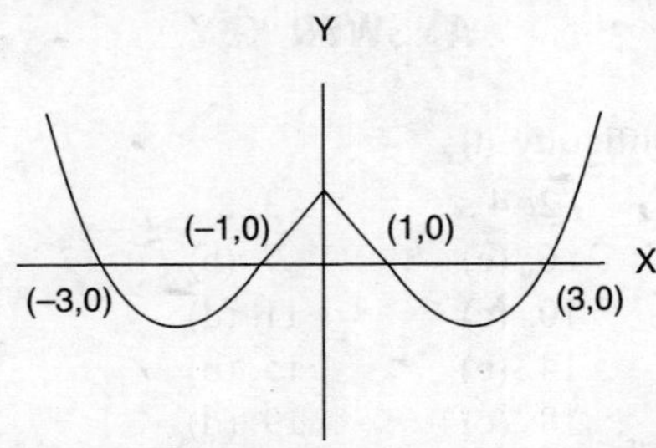

Here we can see that the curve of $y = f(|x|)$ cuts the x-axis at four distinct points, hence $y = f(|x|)$ has four real roots.
25. $3^{x^2-2x-1} = 9 = 3^2$
$\Rightarrow x^2 - 2x - 1 = 2$
$\Rightarrow x^2 - 2x - 3 = 0$
$\Rightarrow (x - 3)(x + 1) = 0$
$\Rightarrow x = 3, -1$
The given equation has two solutions. Hence, there are two values of x at which the equation is satisfied.
26. $a + b = -a$, $ab = b$
$\Rightarrow ab = b$
$\Rightarrow ab - b = 0$
$\Rightarrow (a - 1)b = 0$
This gives us two possibilities: $b = 0$ or $a = 1$
For $b = 0$, $a + 0 = -a$, $\Rightarrow a = 0$
For $a = 1$, $1 + b = -1 \Rightarrow b = -2$
Option (a) is correct.
27. $|x|^2 - 2|x| - 3 = 0$
$\Rightarrow (|x| - 3)(|x| + 1) = 0$
$\Rightarrow |x| = 3, -1$
$|x| = -1$ is not possible
$\Rightarrow |x| = 3$
$\Rightarrow x = \pm 3$
Therefore, for the given equation only two real roots are possible.
28. $f(x) = -x^2 + x - 4$
The discriminant of the equation $f(x) = 0$ is less than zero. Therefore, $f(x) = 0$ has no real root and the coefficient of x^2 is less than 0. Therefore, $f(x) = -x^2 + x - 4$ opens downward. Hence, option (c) is correct.
29. $f(x)$ is less than 0 for all real values of x (As $D < 0$, $a < 0$).
Therefore, $f(a) < 0$, $f(b) < 0$
$f(a).f(b) > 0$
Hence, option (a) is correct.
30. $m + n = 6$, $mn = -3$
$(m + n)^2 = m^2 + n^2 + 2mn$
$36 = m^2 + n^2 - 6$
$m^2 + n^2 = 42$ (Sum of roots of the required equation)
Also, since $mn = -3$, the value of $m^2n^2 = 9$ (product of roots of the required equation)
Therefore the equation must be $x^2 - 42x + 9 = 0$..
Hence, option (c) is correct.

31. Checking from the options, if we put $a = 1$ and $b = 1$ (from option (a). then we get the equation, $x^2 + x + 1 = 0$, and this equation does not have any real roots.) So, this option is correct.

32. $mn = \frac{r}{p}$ (1)

$(mk)(nk) = mnk^2 = \frac{c}{a}$ (2)

Equation (2) ÷ equation (1)

$k^2 = \frac{c}{a} \times \frac{p}{r}$

$k = \sqrt{\frac{cp}{ar}}$

Thus, option (a) is correct.

33. For $x \geq 0 : x^2 = x$

$\Rightarrow x^2 - x = 0$

$\Rightarrow x(x - 1) = 0$

$\Rightarrow x = 0, 1$

For $x < 0 : x^2 = -x$

$\Rightarrow x^2 + x = 0$

$\Rightarrow x(x + 1) = 0$

$\Rightarrow x = 0, -1$

Therefore, for three real values of x, we will get $x^2 = |x|$.

34. a^x can never be equal to 0 for any real value of x. Therefore, 3^{2x^2+3x+1} can never be equal to 0 for any real value of x. So the given equation has no real solution.

35. $x^2 + (x + 1)^2 + (x - 2)^2 = 0$

It is possible when $x = 0$, $x + 1 = 0$, $x - 2 = 0$ (Since each of the terms within the brackets in the given expression is non-negative).

Thus, we get the required values of $x = 0$, $x = -1$, $x = 2$ all at the same time. It is not possible that a variable would have the same. Therefore, the given equation has no real root.

36. Let the roots of the equation $x^2 + kx + 15 = 0$ be m, n.

$m + n = -k$, $mn = 15$, $m - n = 2$

$(m + n)^2 - 4mn = (m - n)^2$

$k^2 - 60 = 4$

$k^2 = 64$

$k = +8, -8$

The correct answer is 2.

37. $f(x) = x^2 - 8x + 12 = (x - 2)(x - 6)$

2 3 4 5 6

$\therefore f(x) \leq 0$ for $x = 2, 3, 4, 5$ and 6

$\therefore$ the correct answer is 5.

38. $f(x) = 0$ has two roots 2, 6 and curve of $f(x)$ opens upwards. So $f(x)$ is minimum for $f'(x) = 0$. This gives us $2x - 8 = 0$. Thus, the function would attain its minimum at $x = 4$.

Therefore, $f(x)$ is minimum for $x = 4$.

39. $16x^2 + px + 9 = 0$

For equal roots, the discriminant of the above equation must be zero.

$p^2 - 4 \times 16 \times 9 = 0$

$p^2 = 4 \times 16 \times 9$

$p = \pm(2 \times 4 \times 3) = \pm 24$

Therefore for two different values of p, $16x^2 + px + 9 = 0$, has equal roots.

40. $m + n = -\frac{q}{p}$ (1)

$(m + k) + (n + k) = -\frac{b}{a}$

$m + n + 2k = -\frac{b}{a}$ (2)

Subtract equation (1) from equation (2):

$2k = -\frac{b}{a} + \frac{q}{p}$

$k = \frac{1}{2}\left[\frac{q}{p} - \frac{b}{a}\right]$

Option (b) is correct.

41. The equation can be rewritten as $s^{0.5} = \frac{pq}{r^2}$ or $s = \frac{(pq)^2}{r^4}$

The maximum value of s will happen when pq is maximum and r is minimum. pq is maximum when $p = -0.04$ and $q = -0.25$ and $r = 1$ similarly s will be minimum when $p = -0.03$ and $q = -0.09$ and $r = 7$.

$s_{max} = \frac{(-0.04 \times -0.25)^2}{1}$ $s_{min} = \frac{(-0.03 \times -0.09)^2}{7^4}$

$s_{max} - s_{min} = \frac{(-0.04 \times -0.25)^2}{1} - \frac{(-0.03 \times -0.09)^2}{7^4}$

≈ 0.0001

42. $(a^2 + b^2) = (a + b)^2 - 2ab$

$= (-1)^2 - 2 \times (-7) = 15$

43. $(a^3 + b^3) = (a + b)^3 - 3ab(a + b)$

$= (-1)^3 - 3 \times (-7)(-1)$

$= -1 - 21 = -22$

44. For the roots to be opposite in sign, the product should be negative.

$(c^2 - 4c)/2 < 0 \Rightarrow 0 < c < 4$

45. The roots should be imaginary for the expression to be positive

i.e. $k^2 - 36 < 0$

thus, $-6 < k < 6$ or $|k| < 6$.

46. The values of x, where the above expression turns out to be negative or 0 are $x = 2, 3, 4, 5, 6, 7$ or 8. Hence, option (d) is correct.

47. The value of the LHS will become 512 – 256 – 320 + 64 = 0 when $x = 8$.
48. In order to think of this situation, you need to think of the fact that "the cube of a number + a power of two" (LHS of the equation) should add up to the fourth power of the same number.
The only situation in which this happens is for 8 + 8 = 16 where $a = 2$ giving us $2^3 + 2^3 = 2^4$.
Hence, option (b) is the correct answer.
49. The above equation gets satisfied at $a = 9$, $b = 8$ and $c = 6$. (In order to visualise this, look for sets of 3 numbers with an LCM of 72). All different arrangements of (9, 8, and 6) will be possible values of (a, b, c). Possible arrangements of (a, b, c) are (9, 8, 6), (8, 9, 6), (6, 8, 9), (8, 6, 9), (6, 9, 8), (9, 6, 8). Thus, there are a total of six such sets possible. Hence, option (d) is correct.
50. Simplifying the equation $9^{a-2} \div 3^{a+4} = 81^{a-11}$, we will get: $3^{2a-4} \div 3^{a+4} = 3^{4a-44}$. This gives us:
$2a–4 – a – 4 = 4a–44 \rightarrow a–8 = 4a–44 \rightarrow 3a = 36$
$\rightarrow a = 12$
Hence, we have to evaluate the value of $3^4 + 3^6$ = 81 + 729 = 810. Hence, option (c) is correct.
51. For $x > 0$
$\Rightarrow x^2 + 3x + 2 = 0$
$\Rightarrow x^2 + 2x + x + 2 = 0$
$\Rightarrow (x + 2)(x + 1) = 0$
$\Rightarrow x = -1$ or -2
But here $x > 0$, so these values of x are not possible in this case.
For $x < 0$.
$\Rightarrow x^2 - 3x + 2 = 0$
$\Rightarrow (x - 2)(x - 1) = 0$
$\Rightarrow x = 1$ or 2
But here $x < 0$, so these values of x are not possible in this case.
Therefore, the given equation has no real root.

Level of Difficulty (II)

1. Case 1: $a - 1 > 0$
$a^2 - 8|a - 1| + |b| = 0$
$a^2 - 8a + 8 + |b| = 0$
Since the roots are real, $64 - 4(8 + |b|) \geq 0 \Rightarrow |b| \leq 8$
$-8 \leq b \leq 8$
Case 2: $a - 1 < 0$
$a^2 - 8|a - 1| + |b| = 0$
$a^2 + 8a - 8 + |b| = 0$
Since the roots are real, $64 - 4(-8 + |b|) \geq 0 \Rightarrow |b| \leq 24$
$-24 \leq b \leq 24$
Hence, there are 25 non-negative integer values of b. The correct answer is 25.
2. In order to find the minimum value of the expression, we need to minimize the variable part of the expression which is $(a + 2)(a + 3)(a + 4)(a + 5)$. This can be written as $[(a + 2)(a + 5)][(a + 4)(a + 3)]$
$[(a^2 + 7a + 11) - 1][(a^2 + 7a + 11) + 1]$
$[(a^2 + 7a + 11)^2 - 1^2]$
Since a perfect square would always give a non negative value, the expression gets minimised when $(a^2 + 7a + 11)^2 = 0$.
So the roots of this will be $[(-7) \pm \sqrt{5}]/2$. For either of these two values, we'll achieve a minimum possible value for our expression. Hence, 2 is the correct answer.
3. An equation will have only one root if and only if it is a perfect square. On comparing the structure of $(mx + n)^2$, We see that $m^2 = 16$ and $n^2 = 36$. $m = \pm 4$ and $n = \pm 6$.
In the given expression, $2p + 20 = 2mn \Rightarrow p + 10 = \pm 24$. Hence, the possible values for p are 14 and –34. Hence, the difference between the values is 48. The correct answer is 48.
4. $4^a + 4^b = 40$
$2^{2a} + 2^{2b} = 40$
On trial and error based solving we find that the only value of $2a$ & $2b$ which satisfy the given condition is 5 and 3. Hence, a & b will be 5/2 and 3/2. Putting the value in the required equation we get 90 as our answer. Hence, option (d) is the correct answer.
5. Since the given equation has only 1 root, it is a perfect square. Let us assume that:
$x^2 + ax + 4a = (x + y)^2$
From this we get $2y = a$ and $y^2 = 4a$. On solving the two we get $a = 0, 16$. Hence, the sum of all possible values of a is 16. The correct answer is 16.
6. The given expression can be simplified as $(2k - 1)x^2 - 9x + 6 = 0$
For the equation to have real roots, the discriminant should be more than or equal to 0.
$81 - 4 \times 6 \times (2k - 1) \geq 0$
$81 - 48k + 24 \geq 0$
$48k \leq 105$
$k \leq (35/16)$
So k can take 1 and 2 as values. Hence, option (c) is the correct answer.
7. The second equation can be written as
$2x^2 - 6x - x + 3 = 0$
$(2x - 1)(x - 3) = 0$
$x = 3, ½$
Hence, $q = 3$. Now $p = 9$. Since p is a root of the first equation, $a \times 81 + 4 \times 9 + 6 = 0$
$81a + 42 = 0$
$a = -42/81 \Rightarrow a = -14/27$
Hence, Option (d) is the correct answer.
8. The given equation can be written as $x^2 - 2x - (15 + nm) = x^2 + x(n + m)$. On comparing the corresponding terms, we get that $m + n = -2$ and $mn = -15$. The values of m & n satisfying the given relationship are –5 and 3, in any order. Hence, $n - m$ can take either 8 or –8. Hence, option (a) is the correct answer.

9. Since the root lies in the range (3, 5), On one value extreme of the interval the equation would give positive value and on the other it will give a negative value. Hence, $f(3) \times f(5) < 0$.
$\Rightarrow (k - 24) \times (k - 30) < 0 \rightarrow 24 < k < 30$
Similarly in the second interval, we get $(k - 30) \times (k - 24) < 0$
Hence, $24 < k < 30$. Values of k which satisfy both the conditions lie in $25 \le k \le 29$. Hence, we have a total of 5 integral values of k.
Hence, Option (b) is the correct answer.

10. If both the roots of the equation lie between –4 and 5, then the product $f(-4) \times f(5)$ will be positive.
$(k^2 + 8k + 12) \times (k^2 - 10k + 21) > 0$
$(k + 6) \times (k + 2) \times (k - 3) \times (k - 7) > 0$
From the given options we can see that only Option (d) satisfies the given condition. Hence, Option (d) is the correct answer.

11. On adding the two equations we get, $(x - y)^2 + (x - y) = 56 \Rightarrow (x - y)(x - y + 1) = 56$. From this we can deduce that 56 is a product of two consecutive integers. Therefore, $x - y = 7$ ....(i)
Now subtracting the first equation from the second we get $(x + y)(y - x - 1) = 8$. Since $x - y = 7$, it means $y - x - 1 = -8$. Hence, we get $x + y = -1$....(ii)
From (i) and (ii) we get, $x = 3$ and $y = -4$. So, the required value of $5x - 6y = 15 + 24 = 39$. Hence, 39 is the correct answer.

12. As we have learnt that modulus represents the distance between 2 points. These two points are $-(1 + c)$ and 2. The total distance between them is given as 4. This is possible if the other point is either –2 or 6.
If $-(1 + c) = -2 \Rightarrow c = 1$
If $-(1 + c) = 6 \Rightarrow c = -7$
Hence, Option (a) is the correct answer.

13. Let the roots be k and $3k$.
Sum of the roots $= 4k = 4a \Rightarrow k = a$.
So the roots are a and $3a$.
Product of roots are $3a^2 = a + f(b)$
$f(b) = 3a^2 - a$
The minimum value of $f(b)$ will be achieved at $a = 1/6$. Hence, Option (a) is the correct answer.

14. $x^2 - 2x(a + 4) + (8 + a^2) = 0$
For real roots,
$4(a + 4)^2 - 4(8 + a^2) \ge 0$
$4a^2 + 32a + 64 - 32 - 4a^2 \ge 0$
$32a + 32 \ge 0$
$a \ge -1$
Hence, lowest integer value for a is –1. Hence, Option (a) is the correct answer.

15. From (1), we have sum of roots = 14 and from (2) we have product of roots = 48. Checking the options, for option (c) we have that the sum of roots is 14 and the product of the roots is 48. Hence, option (c) is correct.

16. When the curve intersects the x–axis, then $y = 0$
$\Rightarrow x^2 - 5x = 0$
$\Rightarrow (x)(x - 5) = 0$ or $x = 0, 5$
When the curve intersects the y–axis then $x = 0$
$y^3 - 4y^2 + 3y = 0$
$y(y^2 - 4y + 3) = 0$
$y(y - 3)(y - 1) = 0$
$y = 0, 1, 3$
But the points $x = 0$ and $y = 0$ would coincide at the origin. So there are a total of 4 points.
These are (0, 0), (0, 1), (0, 3), (5, 0).

17. $f\left(\frac{1}{x}\right) = p\left(\frac{1}{x}\right)^2 + q\left(\frac{1}{x}\right) + r$
$= rx^2 + qx + p = g(x)$
Therefore, the roots of $g(x)$ and $f(x)$ are the inverse of each other.
$\therefore$ The roots of $f(x) = 0$ are 2 and 4.
The roots of $g(x) = 0$ are $\frac{1}{2}, \frac{1}{4}$
$\text{Required sum} = 2 + 4 + \frac{1}{2} + \frac{1}{4} = 6.75$

18. Let x and y be the roots of the given equation. Then,
$x + y = \frac{-q}{p}$ and $x \times y = \frac{r}{p}$
Now, $\frac{1}{x^2} + \frac{1}{y^2} = \frac{x^2 + y^2}{(xy)^2} = \frac{(x + y)^2 - 2xy}{(xy)^2}$
$$= \frac{\left(\frac{-q}{p}\right)^2 - 2\left(\frac{r}{p}\right)}{\left(\frac{r}{p}\right)^2}$$
As per the question:
$$\frac{-q}{p} = \frac{\left(\frac{-q}{p}\right)^2 - 2\left(\frac{r}{p}\right)}{\left(\frac{r}{p}\right)^2}$$
$\Rightarrow 2p^2r = pq^2 + qr^2$
$\Rightarrow \frac{2p^2r}{pqr} = \frac{pq^2}{pqr} + \frac{qr^2}{pqr}$ (dividing by pqr)
$\Rightarrow \frac{2p}{q} = \frac{q}{r} + \frac{r}{p}$ (1)
From equation (1) it is clear that $\frac{r}{p}$, $\frac{p}{q}$ and $\frac{q}{r}$ are in arithmetic progression so option (a) is correct.
As $\frac{q^2}{p^2} \ne \frac{p}{r} \times \frac{r}{q} = \frac{p}{q}$, so option (b) is incorrect.

Option (c): As $\frac{r}{p}$, $\frac{p}{q}$ and $\frac{q}{r}$ are in arithmetic progression; their reciprocals are in harmonic progression. Therefore this option is also correct.
Hence option (d) is correct.

Solutions for Questions 19 and 20:

Let the roots of the equation $x^4 - 594 - ax^3 - bx^2 - cx = 0$ are p, p, q and r.

$pq + qr + pr + p.p + pq + pr = -b$ and $p \times p \times q \times r = -594$

b will be maximum when $pq + qr + pr + p.p + pq + pr$ is minimum. For this to be minimum, $p = 1$, $q = 2$ and $r = -297$.

Hence, the maximum possible value of $b =$
$-(1\times1 + 1\times2 + 1\times(-297) + 1\times2 + 1\times(-297) + 2\times(-297))$
$= 1183$.

For an equation with the highest power of x being the power 4, we have:

Generic Form: $ax^4 + bx^3 + cx^2 + dx + e = 0$. Let the roots be: p, q, r, s.

Then: $p + q + r + s = -b/a$; $pq + pr + ps + qr + qs + rs = c/a$; $pqr + pqs + prs + qrs = -d/a$; and $pqrs = e/a$

20. $p + p + q + r = a$ or $2p + q + r = a$. a will be minimum when $2p + q + r$ is minimum. For this to be minimum, $p = 1$, $q = 2$ and $r = -297$.
$a = 2p + q + r = -294$

Solutions for Questions 21 and 22:

21. Let the roots of the equation be a, b and c.
$a + b + c = 5$ as a, b and c are the sides of a triangle.
& $a + b > c$
The only possible values of (a, b, c) are $(1, 2, 2)$.
Product of the roots $= -r = 1\times2\times2 \rightarrow r = -4$

22. In-radius $= \frac{\Delta}{s}$

Circum-radius $= abc/4\Delta$
Product of in-radius and circum-radius $=$

$$\frac{\Delta}{s} \times \frac{abc}{4\Delta} = \frac{abc}{2(a+b+c)} = \frac{4}{10}$$

Hence, the product of in-radius and circum-radius $= 0.4$.

23. Let's first find the intersection points of the two functions underlying the equations.
$1000x^2 + 1001x + 1 = x^2 + 1001x + 1000 \rightarrow$
$999x^2 = 999 \rightarrow x = \pm 1$
Of these two values of x, we can see that +1 is not a root of the equations, while –1 is a root for both the equations. Hence, the two equations have only 1 common root.

24. For the inequality to be true for all values of x, the quadratic expression $x^2 + 4px + (p + 3)$ should have imaginary roots. Using the discriminant < 0, we get:
$16p^2 - 4(p + 3) < 0$
$16p^2 - 4p - 12 < 0$
$4p^2 - p - 3 < 0$
$4p^2 - 4p + 3p - 3 < 0$
$4p(p - 1) + 3(p - 1) < 0$
$(4p + 3)(p - 1) < 0$
$p \in (-3/4, 1)$
Only possible integer value of p in this range would be at $p = 0$.
Hence, there is only one integer value of p that satisfies the condition.

25. $g(x) = x^3 - px^2 - \frac{q}{2}x - r = (x - p)(x - q)(x - r)$
$p + q + r = p$
$q + r = 0$ (1)
$pq + qr + pr = -\frac{q}{2} \Rightarrow p(q + r) + qr = -\frac{q}{2} \Rightarrow r = -\frac{1}{2}$
$q = \frac{1}{2}$
$pqr = r$
$pq = 1$
$p = 2$
$g(4) = (4)^3 - 2(4)^2 - \frac{1}{4}(4) + \frac{1}{2}$
$= 64 - 32 - 1 + \frac{1}{2}$
$= 31.5$

26. Let: $\sqrt{x^2 + 10x + 22} = u$. Then, $x^2 + 10x + 19 = u^2 - 3$
Thus, the equation becomes: $u^2 - 3 = 2u$
$u^2 - 2u - 3 = 0$
$(u - 3)(u + 1) = 0$
$u = 3$ and by definition $u \neq -1$ (as a value inside a square root cannot be negative). The equation we have is:
$x^2 + 10x + 19 = 2\sqrt{x^2 + 10x + 22} \rightarrow$
$x^2 + 10x + 19 = 2\times3$
$x^2 + 10x + 13 = 0$
Product of the roots $= c/a = 13$.

27. When you look at this question, it seems that there are two equations with three unknowns. However, a closer look of the second equation shows us that the second equation is the same as the first equation.
i.e. $10p + 8g + 6m = 44$ and $5p + 4g + 3m = 22$ are nothing but one and the same equation. Hence, you have only one equation with three unknowns. However, before you jump to the 'cannot be determined' answer, consider this thought-process. The cost of ten pears would be a multiple of 10 (since all costs are natural numbers). Similarly, the cost of eight grapes would be a multiple of 8

while the cost of six mangoes would be a multiple of 6.

Thus, the first equation can be numerically thought of as follows:

By fixing the cost of ten pears as a multiple of 10 and the cost of 8 grapes as a multiple of 8, we can see whether the cost of six mangoes turns out to be a multiple of 6.

Total cost	*Total cost of 10 pears*	*Total cost of 8 grapes*	*Total cost of 6 mangoes*	
44	10	16	18	Possible
44	10	24	10	Not possible
44	10	32	2	Not possible
44	20	8	16	Not possible
44	20	24	0	Not possible
44	30	8	6	Not possible, since both the cost of mangoes and grapes turns out to be ₹ 1 per unit (They have to be distinct.)

Thus, there is only one possibility that fits into the situation. The cost per pear = ₹ 1. The cost per grape = ₹ 2 per unit and the cost per mango = ₹ 3 per unit. Hence, the total cost of 4 mangoes + 3 grapes = 12 + 6 = ₹ 18.

Option (b) is correct.

28. The value of the expression $\frac{1}{lm}+\frac{1}{mn}+\frac{1}{ln}=lmn$ $(l + m + n)/l^2m^2n^2 = (l + m + n)/lmn$. For any cubic equation of the form $ax^3 + bx^2 + cx + d = 0$, the sum of the roots is given by $-b/a$; while the product of the roots is given by $-d/a$. The ratio $(l + m + n)/lmn$ $= b/d = -20/-5 = 4$. Option (c) is correct.

29. The graph of $ax^2+bx+c=0$ would look like:

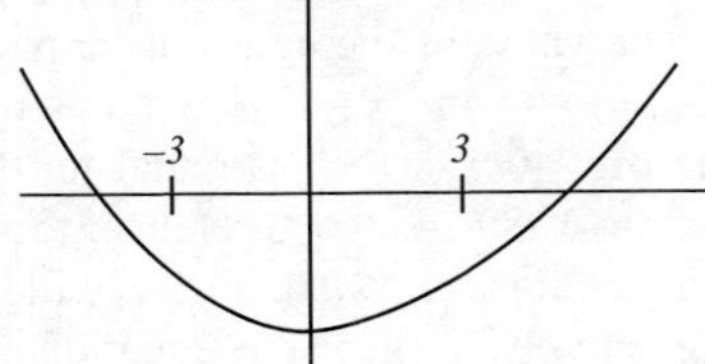

So, at $x = -3$ and $+3$, the value of the given function must be negative for all values between (–3, 3). At $x = -2$, we have

$a(-2)^2+b(-2)+c<0$ or $4a-2b+c<0$

Hence, option (b) is correct.

30. $f(3)=9a+3b+c<0, f(-3)=9a-3b+c<0$

$9a+3|b|+c<0$

Hence, option (b) is correct.

31. Let the roots of the equation be a and b. According to the question:

$$a+b=\frac{1}{a^2}+\frac{1}{b^2}$$

$$a+b=\frac{a^2+b^2}{a^2b^2}$$

$$a+b=\frac{(a+b)^2-2ab}{a^2b^2}$$

$$-\frac{q}{p}=\frac{\left(-\frac{q}{p}\right)^2-\frac{2r}{p}}{\left(\frac{r}{p}\right)^2} \Rightarrow 2rp^2=pq^2+qr^2$$

pq^2, rp^2, and qr^2, are in *A.P.*

32. $x^8 + 12$ is always greater than x^8.

So $(x^8 + 12)^{1/2}$ will always be greater than $(x^8)^{1/2} = x^4$

x^4 will always be greater than $x^4 - 2$

so $(x^8 + 12)^{1/2}$ will always be greater than $x^4 - 2$. Hence, the LHS and the RHS of the given equation can never be equal to each other. This means that there are no solutions for the given equation. Hence, option (a) is correct.

33. $x^2-4xy+3y=0$. This is a quadratic equation in the variable x. Using the formula for the roots of a quadratic equation, we have:

$x=2y\pm\sqrt{4y^2-3y}$

For x to be an integer $4y^2-3y$ must be the perfect square of an integer.

$4y^2-3y=k^2$ or $y=\frac{[3\pm\sqrt{9+16k^2}]}{8}$, where k is an integer. Again, for y to be an integer, $16k^2 + 9$ should be an integer.

Thus, the only possible value of k for which y is an integer is $k = 1$.

$\Rightarrow y=\frac{3+5}{8}=1$ and $x=2\pm\sqrt{1}=1$ and 3.

Hence, there are two possible integer pairs which are (1, 1) and (3, 1).

34. Maximum possible value of $x + y = 3 + 1 = 4$.

35. $b^2-4a^2\geq 0$ (roots are real)

$(b - 2a)(b + 2a) \geq 0$

Both the roots are positive, therefore, the sum of the roots must be greater than 0.

$-\frac{b}{a}>0$

But $a > 0$, so b must be less than 0

$\therefore\ b - 2a < 0$ or $b < 2a$ & $b + 2a \le 0$ or $b \le -2a$

Therefore, all the options are true.

36. $x^3 - 3x^2 + 2x + 5 = x^3 + x^2 + 7x + 6$

$$4x^2 + 5x + 1 = 0$$

$$x = -1 \ or -1/4$$

None of the two values satisfies the given equations. Hence, the two equations do not have any common roots. Hence, correct answer is 0.

37. Graph opens downwards, so $a < 0$

As we can see that, $\alpha < 2$, $\beta < -3$

So sum of roots of $ax^2 + bx + c$ is less than 0 or

$$-\frac{b}{a} < 0$$

$$\text{or} \frac{b}{a} > 0$$

As $a < 0$, so $b < 0$

Product of the roots is also less than 0.

$$\alpha\beta = \frac{c}{a} < 0$$

As $a < 0$, so $c > 0$

Hence, option (a) is correct.

38. $f(1) = p - 2 + c = -5$

$p + c = -3$ (1)

$f(4) = 64p - 8 + c = 52$

$64p + c = 60$ (2)

Solving equations (1) and (2), we get: $p = 1$, $c = -4$.

$$f(x) = x^3 - 2x - 4$$

There is only one real root for $f(x) = 0$. Hence, the correct answer is 1.

39. $4^{-x} = 5 - 2x$

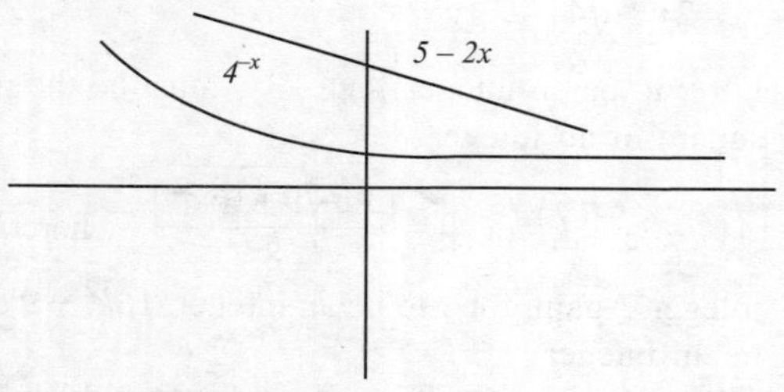

The graphs of 4^{-x} and $5 - 2x$ are shown above. There are exactly two intersection points of 4^{-x} and $5 - 2x$. Hence, the correct answer is 2.

40. Let the common root be 'm'. Since we know that $Q_1(10) = 0$, it means that 10 would be one of the roots of Q_1. By the same logic it is given to us that 8 is one of the roots of Q_2. Using this information, we have:

$Q_1 = c_1 \times (x - 10) \times (x - m)$

and $Q_2 = c_2 \times (x - 8) \times (x - m)$. (**Note:** c_1 and c_2 are constants (each not equal to 0)).

The only information we have beyond this is that the product $Q_1(4) \times Q_2(5) = 36$. However, it is evident that by replacing $x = 4$ and $x = 5$ in the expressions for Q_1 and Q_2 respectively, we would not get any conclusive value for m since the value of m will depend on the values of c_1 and c_2. You can see this happening here:

$c_1 \times -6 \times (4 - m) \times c_2 \times -3 \times (5 - m) = 36$

$c_1 \times c_2 \times (20 - 9m + m^2) = 2$

In this equation, it can be clearly seen that the value of the common root 'm' would be dependent on the values of c_1 and c_2 and hence we cannot determine the answer to the question. Option (d) becomes the correct answer.

41. Since we got: $c_1 \times c_2 \times (20 - 9m + m^2) = 2$ as the equation in the previous solution, we can see that if we insert $c_1 = 1/15$ and $c_2 = 1$ in this equation we will get:

$m^2 - 9m + 20 = 30 \rightarrow m^2 - 9m - 10 = 0 \rightarrow (m-10)(m+1) = 0 \rightarrow m = 10$ or $m = -1$. i.e., the common roots for the two equations could either be 10 or –1 giving rise to two cases for the quadratic equation $Q_2 = 0$:

Case 1: When the common root is 10; Q_2 will become $\rightarrow (x - 8)(x - 10) = x^2 - 18x + 80$. The sum of roots for $Q_2(x) = 0$ in this case will be 18.

Case 2: When the common root is –1; Q_2 will become $\rightarrow (x - 8)(x + 1) = x^2 - 7x - 8$. The sum of roots for $Q_1(x) = 0$ in this case will be 7.

Option (a) gives us a possible sum of roots as 18 and hence, is the correct answer.

42. The equation can be thought of as $(x - 2m)(x - 4m)(x - 5m) = 0$. The value of the constant term would be given by $(-2m) \times (-4m) \times (-5m)$ which will give us an outcome of $-40m^3$ which is equal to -1080. Solving $-40m^3 = -1080 \rightarrow m = 3$. Hence, the roots of the equation being $2m$, $4m$ and $5m$ will be 6, 12 and 15 respectively. Hence, the equation would become $(x - 6)(x - 12)(x - 15) = 0$. The coefficient of x^2 will be $(-15x^2 - 6x^2 - 12x^2) = -33x^2$. Hence, the value of '$a$' will be +33. Hence, option (c) will be the correct answer.

43. Let the polynomial be $f(x) = ax^2 + bx + 10$. The value of $f(5)$ in this case, would be:

$f(5) = 25a + 5b + 10 = 75$

$f(-5) = 25a - 5b + 10 = 45$

$f(5) - f(-5) = 10b = 30 \rightarrow b = 3$. The polynomial expression is: $ax^2 + 3x + 10$.

Further, if we put the value of $b = 3$ in the equation for $f(5)$, we would get: $25a + 15 + 10 = 75 \rightarrow 25a = 50 \rightarrow a = 2$.

Since $f(p)$ and $f(q)$ are both equal to zero, it means that p and q are the roots of the equation $2x^2 + 3x + 10 = 0$. Finding $p \times q$ would mean that we have to find the product of the roots of the equation. The product of the roots will be equal to $10/2 = 5$. Option (c) is the correct answer.

44. $\left(x^2-4x-4\right)^{x^2-16}-1=0$ *or* $\left(x^2-4x-4\right)^{x^2-16}=1$

This is possible when $x^2-4x-4=1$ *or* $x^2-16=0$
For: $x^2-4x-4=1$ → we get: $x = 5$ or -1
For: $x^2-16=0$ → we get $x = -4$ or $+4$.
Sum of all possible roots of the equation = $-1 + 5 - 4 + 4 = 4$.

45. The various possibilities for the values of a and b (in terms of their being positive or negative) will be as follows:
Possibility 1: a positive and b positive;
Possibility 2: a positive and b negative;
Possibility 3: a negative and b positive;
Possibility 4: a negative and b negative.
Let us look at each of these possibilities one-by-one and check out which one of them is possible.
Possibility 1: If a and b are both positive the second equation becomes $a = 150$ (since the value of $|b| - b$ would be equal to zero if b is positive). However, this value of 'a' does not fit the first equation since the value of the LHS would easily exceed 75 if we use $a = 150$ in the first equation. Hence, the possibility of both a and b being positive is not feasible and can be rejected.
Through similar thinking the possibilities 3 and 4 are also rejected. Consider this:
For possibility 3: a negative and b positive: the second equation will give us $a = 150$ which contradicts the presupposition that a is negative. Hence, this possibility can be eliminated.
For possibility 4: a negative and b negative: the first equation would give us $b = 75$ (since the value of $|a| + a$ will be equal to zero if a is negative) which contradicts the presupposition that b is negative. Hence, this possibility can be eliminated.
The only possibility that remains is possibility 2: a positive and b negative. In this case, the equations will transform as follows:
$|a| + a + b = 75$ will become $2a + b = 75$;
$a + |b| - b = 150$ will become $a - 2b = 150$.
Solving the two equations simultaneously, we will get the value of $a = 60$ and $b = -45$.
The sum of $|a| + |b| = 60 + 45 = 105$.
Option (a) is the correct answer.

46. Only in the case of option (c) do we get the LHS of the equation $4a - 3b - 4c = 0$ such that all the x, y and z cancel each other out. Hence, option (c) is the sole correct answer.

47. Using mathematical induction, let us assume the roots to be 1, 2, and 4.
The sum of the roots = $1 + 2 + 4 = -q \rightarrow q = -7$
The product of the roots = $1.2.4 = -s \rightarrow s = -8$
The pair-wise product of the roots, $r = 1 \times 2 + 2 \times 4 + 4 \times 1 \Rightarrow r = 14$
Only option (b) satisfies for $r = 14$, $q = -7$, $s = -8$
So, option (b) is correct.

48. The profit of the 9-to-9 supermarket would be:
Total sales price – Total cost price
$= 10 \times (15 + 16x) - 4x^2$
$= -4x^2 + 160x + 150$
The maximum value of this function can be traced by differentiating it with respect to x and equating to 0. We get:
$-8x + 160 = 0 \rightarrow x = 20$. The maximum value of profit will occur at $x = 20$.
The maximum profit will be $= -4 \times 20^2 + 160 \times 20 + 150 = -1600 + 3200 + 150 = 1750$.
Option (c) is the correct answer.

49. $x - y = 6 \rightarrow x = 6 + y$. Substituting this value of x in the expression for the value of P, we get:
$P = 7(6 + y)^2 - 12y^2$
$P = 252 + 7y^2 + 84y - 12y^2 = 84y - 5y^2 + 252$
Differentiating P with respect to y and equating to zero we get:
$84 - 10y = 0 \rightarrow y = 8.4$
The maximum value of P will be obtained by inserting $y = 8.4$ in the expression. It gives us:
$84 \times 8.4 - 5 \times 8.4^2 + 252 = 705.6 - 5 \times 70.56 + 252 = 957.6 - 352.8 = 604.8$

50 $\alpha + \beta = -m$ and $\alpha\beta = 1$
$\Rightarrow \gamma + \delta = -n$ and $\gamma\delta = 1$
$(\alpha - \gamma)(\beta - \gamma)(\alpha + \delta)(\beta + \delta) = (\alpha - \gamma)(\beta + \delta)(\beta - \gamma)(\alpha + \delta)$
$= [\alpha\beta + \alpha\delta - \gamma\beta - \gamma\delta][\alpha\beta + \beta\delta - \alpha\gamma - \gamma\delta]$
$=[1 + \alpha\delta - \gamma\beta - 1][1 + \beta\delta - \gamma\alpha - 1]$
$=(\alpha\delta - \gamma\beta)(\beta\delta - \gamma\alpha)$
$= 1.\delta^2 - \alpha^2.1 - \beta^2.1 + \gamma^2.1 = (\delta^2 + \gamma^2) - (\alpha^2 + \beta^2)$
$= [(\delta + \gamma)^2 - 2\delta\gamma] - [(\alpha + \beta)^2 - 2\alpha\beta]$
$= [(-n)^2 - 2.1] - [(-m)^2 - 2.1] = n^2 - m^2$
Option (*a*) is correct.

51. $f(x)$ is exactly divisible by $(x + 2)$, $(x + 3)$
Therefore, $f(-2) = f(-3) = 0$
$4p - 2q + r = 0$ (1)
$9p - 3q + r = 0$ (2)
Also, since the remainder of $f(x)$ when divided by $(x - 1)$ is 7, we can use $f(1) = 7$, which in turn gives us that:
$p + q + r = 7$ (3)
By solving equations (1), (2), (3) we get $q \approx 2.92$

52. $f(x) = 4x - 7\sqrt{x} = 2$

Let $t = \sqrt{x}$
$\Rightarrow 4t^2 - 7t = 2$
$\Rightarrow 4t^2 - 7t - 2 = 0$
$\Rightarrow 4t(t - 2) + 1(t - 2) = 0$
$\Rightarrow t = -\frac{1}{4}, 2$
$\Rightarrow \sqrt{x} = -\frac{1}{4}$ or 2. (However, the value of $\sqrt{x} = -\frac{1}{4}$ is not possible)

$\sqrt{x} = 2 \rightarrow x = 4$

$\therefore$ Only option (c) is correct.

53. $f(x) = (x - 2)(x^2 + 2x + 5) = x^3 - 2x^2 + 2x^2 + 5x - 4x - 10$
$= x^3 + x - 10$
$a + b + c = 0 \qquad abc = 10$
If $a + b + c = 0$, then
$a^3 + b^3 + c^3 = 3abc = 3 \times (10) = 30$

54. The sum of the roots of a cubic equation $ax^3 + bx^2 + cx + d = 0$ are given by: $-b/a$.
Hence, $p + q - 12 = q$ or $p = 12$
Also, using the product of roots, we get: $p \times q \times (-12) = -288$. Using $p = 12$, we get, $q = 2$.
Hence, $= f(x) = x^3 - 2x^2 - 144x + 288$
$$f(2) = 2^3 - 2 \times 2^2 - 144 \times 2 + 288 = 0$$
Hence, $f(2) = 0$.

55. $(\alpha + 3)(\beta + 3)(\gamma + 3) = 27$
$\alpha\beta\gamma + 9(\alpha + \beta + \gamma) + 3(\alpha\beta + \beta\gamma + \gamma\alpha) + 27 = 27$
$P + 9m + 3n = 0$ (**Note:** the product of the roots of the equation $x^3 - mx^2 + nx - p = 0$ will be equal to p; the sum of the roots would be equal to m; the pair-wise product of the roots will be equal to n.)

56. $(x - p)(x - q) + (x - q)(x - r) + (x - r)(x - p) = 0$
$\Rightarrow x^2 - (p + q)x + pq + x^2 - (q + r)x + qr + x^2 - (p + r)x + pr = 0$
$3x^2 - 2(p + q + r)x + pq + qr + pr = 0$
Discriminant of the above equation $= 4(p + q + r)^2 - 12(pq + qr + pr)$
$= 4[p^2 + q^2 + r^2 + 2pq + 2pr + 2qr - 3pq - 3pr - 3qr]$
$= 4[p^2 + q^2 + r^2 - pr - qr - pr]$
$$= \frac{4}{2}\left[(p-q)^2 + (q-r)^2 + (p-r)^2\right]$$
$= 2[(p - q)^2 + (q - r)^2 + (p - r)^2]$
As p, q, r are not equal to each other, so the discriminant of the given equation is always greater than 0, therefore the roots are real.
Thus, option (b) is true.

57. In order to solve this question, the first thing we need to do is to identify the pattern of the numbers in the expression. The series 7, 18, 31, 46, etc., can be identified as 7, 7 + 11 × 1; 7 + 12 × 2; 7 + 13 × 3 and so on. Thus, the logic of the term when 39 is in the denominator is 7 + 39 × 29 = 1138 and the last term is 7 + 40 × 30 = 1207.
The series can be rewritten as:
$$\frac{[x]+7}{10}, 1+\frac{[x]+7}{11}, 2+\frac{[x]+7}{12}, 3+\frac{[x]+7}{13} \cdots 29+\frac{[x]+7}{39}$$
and $30 + \dfrac{[x]+7}{40}$
For each of these to be in their simplest forms, the value of $[x]$ should be such that $[x] + 7$ is co-prime to each of the 31 denominators (from 10 to 40). From amongst the options, option (c) gives us a value such that $[x] + 7 = 101$ which is a prime number and would automatically be co-prime with the other values.

58. Let the roots of the equation $px^2 + qx + r = 0$ are a and b.
$$\frac{1}{a} + \frac{1}{b} = \frac{a+b}{ab} = \frac{\left(-\frac{q}{p}\right)}{\frac{r}{p}} = -\frac{q}{r} = 7/23 \qquad (1)$$
$$\frac{p}{r} = \frac{1}{23} \qquad (2)$$
Equation 1/ equation 2:: $\dfrac{-\frac{q}{r}}{\frac{p}{r}} = \dfrac{\frac{7}{23}}{\frac{1}{23}}$ or $-\dfrac{q}{p} = 7$
Sum of the roots of $qx^2 + px + r = 0$ is $-\dfrac{p}{q}$ which would be equal to 1/7 in this case.
Hence, option (a) is correct.

59. $(a + 2)(b + 2)(c + 2) = 47$
$abc + 4(a + b + c) + 2(ab + bc + ca) + 8 = 47$
$4p + 2q + r = 39$

60. Let the roots of $x^2 + bx + 3b = 0$ are a and $3a$.
$a + 3a = -b \Rightarrow 4a = -b \qquad (1)$
$3a^2 = 3b \Rightarrow a^2 = b \qquad (2)$
By solving equation (1) and (2), we get
$a = -4$, $b = 16$
Value of $3b = 3 \times 16 = 48$

61. The given equation is $x^2 - 33x + 17 \times 16 = 0$
$x^2 - 33x - 272 = 0$
Roots of the equation are 16, 17 or b, $b + 1$. Hence, option (a) is correct.

62. We are given that the expression $ax^3 + bx^2 + cx + d$ intersects the x-axis at 1 and –1. It means that at $x = 1$ and -1 the value of the given polynomial is equal to 0.
$\therefore \quad a + b + c + d = 0$ and $-a + b - c + d = 0$
$\therefore \quad 2(b + d) = 0$
$\therefore \quad b + d = 0 \qquad (1)$
We are also given that; $ax^3 + bx^2 + cx + d$ intersects the y–axis at 2. This means that at $x = 0$, the value of the given polynomial is equal to 2.
$0 + d = 2$
$\therefore \quad d = 2 \qquad (2)$
From equations (1) and (2), $b = -2$

63. $f(x) = 0$
$3^{|2x+1|} = 9^{4x-5}$ or $3^{|2x+1|} = 3^{2(4x-5)}$
or $|2x+1| = 2\times(4x-5)$
This gives us two scenarios: $2x+1 = 2\times(4x-5)$ or $2x+1 = -2\times(4x-5)$
When, $2x+1 = 2\times(4x-5)$
$2x+1 = 8x-10$ or $6x = 11$ or $x = 11/6$

When, we use: $2x+1=-2\times(4x-5)$ or $10x = 9$ or $x = 9/10$

Product of the possible values of $x = \frac{11}{6}\times\frac{9}{10} = 33/20$ = 1.65.

64. There are 36 ways of distributing the sum of 37 between a_1 and a_2 such that both a_1 and a_2 are positive and integral. (From 1, 36; 2, 35; 3, 34; 4, 33…; 36, 1)
Similarly, there are ${}^9C_2$ (= 36) ways of distributing the residual value of 10 amongst a_3, a_4 and a_5. Thus, there are a total of 36 × 36 = 1296 ways of distributing the values amongst the five variables such that each of them is positive and integral. Option (d) is the correct answer.

65. Let $f(x) = 3x^2 - 4x + 7$
$f'(x) = 6x - 4 = 0$ or $x = 2/3$
The minimum value of $f(x)$ will then be given by:
$3(2/3)^2 - 4(2/3) + 7 = 17/3$

66. Discriminant of the given equation is $16 - 4(1 - p)p$ or $16 - 4p(1 - p) > 0$ for $0 < p < 1$.

Sum of roots $\left(\frac{-4}{(1-p)}\right) < 0$ for $0 < p < 1$

Product of roots $\left(\frac{p}{1-p}\right) > 0$, for $0 < p < 1$

Therefore, roots of the given equation are real and negative.

67. The value of the expression will be dependent on the individual values of each of the terms in the expression. $[315^{1/3}]$ will give us a value of 6 and so would all the terms upto $[342^{1/3}]$. (as $6^3 = 216$ and $7^3 = 343$). Hence, the value of the expression from $[315^{1/3}] + [316^{1/3}] + \ldots + [342^{1/3}] = 28 \times 6 = 168$.
Similarly, the value of the expression from $[343^{1/3}] + [344^{1/3}] + \ldots + [511^{1/3}] = 169 \times 7 = 1183$.
Also, the value of the expression from $[512^{1/3}] + [513^{1/3}] + \ldots + [515^{1/3}] = 4 \times 8 = 32$.
Thus, the answer = 168 + 1183 + 32 = 1383. Option (a) is correct.

68. $p + q = -5$
$q + r = -23$
$p + 2q + r = -28$ or $(p + r) + 2q = -28$ (1).
Since, p, q and r are in arithmetic progression, the value of $(p + r) = 2q$. Using this in equation (1), we get:
$4q = -28$ or $q = -7$. Using the logic of the Arithmetic Progression, we can get the values of p and r respectively, as:
$p = 2, r = -16$
$|a \times b| = |pq \times qr| = |pq^2r| = |2 \times -7^2 \times -16| = 1568$

69. Let there be 'n' friends of Neha which would mean that the amount of total liquids consumed by the group would be $9n$. Further let the total amount (in litres) of cold drink consumed by Neha and her friends be 'x' litres. Then, the amount of orange squash consumed by the friends will be $9n–x$. As per the given information, we know that Neha has consumed one-ninth of the total cold drink (i.e. $x/9$) and also that she has consumed one-eleventh of the total orange squash $(9n–x)/11$. Also, since Neha has consumed a total of 9 litres of the liquids, we will get:
$$\frac{x}{9}+\frac{(9n-x)}{11} = 9$$
$11x + 81n - 9x = 891$
$\rightarrow 2x + 81n = 891 \rightarrow x = (891 - 81n) \div 2$
In this equation, n is an integer and x should be less than $9n$. This gives rise to the inequality:
$0 < x < 9n \rightarrow 0 < (891–81n)/2 < 9n \rightarrow 0 < 891 - 81n < 18n$
The only value of n that satisfies this inequality is at $n = 10$.
This means that there were ten friends in the group and the amount of liquids consumed in total would have been 90 litres (9 litres each). Putting this value in the equation, we get: $2x + 810 = 891 \rightarrow x = 40.5$. This would mean that Neha consumes 40.5/9 = 4.5 litres of cold drink and hence, she would consume 4.5 litres of orange squash. The required ratio would be 1:1.

70. $(x^2 + 3x - 10) = 0$
$(x - 2)(x + 5) = 0$ or $x = 2, -5$
Therefore, for $x = +2$ and $x = -5$
$3x^4 + 2x^3 - ax^2 + bx - a + b - 4 = 0$
For $x = 2 \rightarrow 3(2)^4 + 2(2)^3 - 4a + 2b - a + b - 4 = 0$
$48 + 16 - 4a + 2b - a + b - 4 = 0$
$5a - 3b = 60$ (1)
For $x = -5$,
$3 \times (-5)^4 + 2 \times (-5)^3 - a \times (-5)^2 + b\times(-5) - a + b - 4 = 0$
$1875 - 250 - 25a - 5b - a + b - 4 = 0$
$26a + 4b = 1621$ (2)
By solving equation (1) and (2) we get:
$a \approx 52, b \approx 67$

71. The five consecutive integers can be represented by: $(c - 2)$; $(c - 1)$; c; $(c + 1)$ and $(c + 2)$.
Then we have $a^2 + b^2 + c^2 = d^2 + e^2$, giving us:
$(c - 2)^2 + (c - 1)^2 + c^2 = (c + 1)^2 + (c + 2)^2 \rightarrow$
$3c^2 - 6c + 5 = 2c^2 + 6c + 5 \rightarrow$
$c^2 - 12c = 0 \rightarrow$
$c = 0$ or $c = 12$
Hence, the possible values of $d = c + 1$ would be 1 or 13. Option (d) is correct.

72. When, $f(x)$ is divided by x, the remainder will be $f(0) = d = k^4$.
Now, 'k' is prime number and a, b, c and d, form an increasing G.P.
$a = k$, $b = k^2$, $c = k^3$, $d = k^4$, and subsequently the expression is: $f(x) = kx^3 + k^2x^2 + k^3x + k^4$.
So the remainder when $f(x)$ is divided by $(x - k)$, which is derived by putting $x = k$ in $f(x)$, i.e. $f(k) = 4k^4$

So square root of $f(k) = 2k^2$.

$f(k)$ is a perfect cube only when $k = 2$.

73. $a = 2$

74. $f(4) =$

$2\times4^3+2^2\times4^2+2^3\times4+2^4=128+64+32+16=240$

75. $f(k)=k^8-4=0 or k^4=2$

$(k-1)(k^{12}+k^{13}+k^{14}+k^{15}+.....+k^{51})$

$=(k-1)\times k^{12}\times(1+k+k^2+...+k^{39})$

At this point, we can replace: $(1+k+k^2+...+k^{39})$,

with: $\frac{(k^{40}-1)}{k-1}$. Thus, we get:

$\frac{(k-1)k^{12}(k^{40}-1)}{k-1}=k^{12}(k^{40}-1)=(8)\times(2^{10}-1)$

$=1023\times8=8184$

Level of Difficulty (III)

1. For $x > 0$

$3x(x^2 + 8/3) = 10x^2 \Rightarrow 3(x^2 + 8/3) = 10x \Rightarrow 3x^2 - 10x + 8 = 0 \Rightarrow (x - 2)(3x - 4) = 0 \Rightarrow x = 2, 4/3$. Since both values of x are positive, we'll count them in our solution.

For $x < 0$

$-3x(x^2 + 8/3) = 10x^2 \Rightarrow -3(x^2 + 8/3) = 10x \Rightarrow 3x^2 + 10x + 8 = 0 \Rightarrow (3x - 2)(x + 4) = 0 \Rightarrow x = -4/3, -2$. Both these solutions being negative, we can count them both. Hence, we have a total of 4 solutions. The correct answer is 4.

2. Sum of the squares of the roots can be expressed ass (Sum of roots)^2 – 2 × Product of roots.

Sum of roots for first equation = $-x$

Product of roots for first equation = y

Sum of roots for second equation = $-y$

Product of roots for second equation = x

According to question,

$(-x)^2 - 2y = (-y)^2 - 2x \rightarrow x^2 - 2y = y^2 - 2x \rightarrow x^2 - y^2 - 2y + 2x \rightarrow (x + y)(x - y) + 2(x - y) = 0 \rightarrow$

The expression can be written as: $(x + y + 2)(x - y) = 0$

Since x and y are distinct, $x - y$ cannot be 0

Hence, $(x + y + 2) = 0$

So the absolute value of the sum would be 2

Hence, 2 is the correct answer.

3. For the given equation, sum of the roots is 52. Also, the product of the roots is 'a'. The prime numbers between 1 & 52 are 2, 3, 5, 7, 11, 13, 17, 19, 23, 29, 31, 37, 41, 43 and 47. Out of these only 3 combinations (5,47 / 11,41 / 23,29) satisfy the given constraint. This gives us three possible products of the roots. Hence, the number of values possible for a would be 3. The correct answer is 3.

4. For a cubic equation $ax^3 + bx^2 + cx + d = 0$, the sum of roots is given by $-b/a$, sum of the pairwise product of roots is given by c/a and the product of the roots is given by $-d/a$. Using these formulae we get the following reactions:

Sum of the roots of the equation will be $p + q + p + q = 4 \Rightarrow p + q = 2$ ....(i)

Pair wise product of the roots will be $pq + q(p + q) + (p + q)p = 2 \rightarrow$

$pq + (p + q)^2 = 2 \rightarrow pq = -2$ **........(ii)**

Product of the roots will be $pq(p + q) = -a$ **.......(iii)**

Putting values of (i) & (ii) in (iii) we get $a = 4$

On solving (i) & (ii) we get the value of p and q as $1 + \sqrt{3}$ and $1 - \sqrt{3}$ in any order.

Now, $p - q = -2\sqrt{3}$ or $2\sqrt{3}$

Hence, $p - q + a = 4 - 2\sqrt{3}$ or $4 + 2\sqrt{3}$. Hence, Option (d) is the correct answer.

5. Putting the value 0 in $f(x)$, we get $f(0) = q$. Hence, according to the question we need to find the value of q. Now, $f(1) \times f(2) < 0 \Rightarrow (1 - p + q)(4 - 2p + q) < 0$

Now we can use the options to check which one satisfies the given equation.

At $q = -3$

$f(1) \times f(2) = (-p - 2)(1 - 2p) < 0$, the inequality satisfies for $p < 1/2$.

For $q = 1$

$f(1) \times f(2) = (2 - p)(5 - 2p) < 0$, the inequality satisfies for $2 < p < 5/2$.

For $q = 0$

$f(1) \times f(2) = (1 - p)(4 - 2p) < 0$, the expression will be less than zero for $1 < p < 2$.

For $q = 2$

$f(1) \times f(2) = (3 - p)^2 < 0$, Since a square always gives a positive value, the expression cannot be negative. Hence, q cannot take 2 as its value. Thus, option (d) is correct.

6. We can substitute the value of $x^2 + 5x + 12$ in LHS and RHS. So, $a = 2\sqrt{a+8}$

Squaring both sides, we get $a^2 = 4(a + 8) \Rightarrow a^2 - 4a - 32 = 0$. Value of a would be 8 and –4.

   1. $x^2+5x+12=8 \Rightarrow x^2+5x+4=0 \Rightarrow$ roots $=-4, -1$
   2. $x^2 + 5x + 12 = -4 \Rightarrow x^2 + 5x + 16 = 0 \Rightarrow$ roots = no real roots.

Hence, the product of roots for the given expression is 4. Hence, 4 is the correct answer.

7. $9x^2 + 1/x^2 = 3$ can be modified to $9x^2 + 1/x^2 + 6 - 6 = 3$

This becomes $(3x + 1/x)^2 = 9$

$3x + 1/x = -3$, since x is negative.

Raising both side to power of 3, we get $27x^3 + 1/x^3 + 3(3x + 1/x) = -27$

$27x^3 + 1/x^3 + 3(-3) = -27$

$27x^3 + 1/x^3 = -18$. Hence, option (b) is correct.

8. First lets simplify the question $(p - q)^2 = p^2 + q^2 - 2pq$

$p^2 + q^2 = (p + q)^2 - 2pq$

$(p - q)^2 = (p + q)^2 - 2pq - 2pq$

$(p - q)^2 =$ (Sum of roots)^2 – 4 × (product of roots)

Now,
Sum of roots for the given equation: $-2b$
Product of roots: $b - 2$
So $(p - q)^2 = (-2b)^2 - 4(b - 2) \Rightarrow 4b^2 - 4b + 8$.
In order to minimize our answer, we need to find the minimum value of the resultant equation. This is achieved at b = ½ (differentiating the equation and equating with 0)
Hence, at $b = ½$, value of $(p - q)^2 = 1 - 2 + 8 = 7$.
Hence, option (d) is the correct answer.

9. For $x^2 + 2nx + ab = 0$ to have distinct real roots, the discriminant needs to be more than 0.
Hence, $(4n^2 - 4ab) > 0$
Now, $x^2 - 2(a + b)x + a^2 + b^2 + 2n^2 = 0$ can have 0, 1 or 2 real roots depending on the nature of the discriminant.
For the given equation, discriminant= $(4(a + b)^2 - 4(a^2 + b^2 + 2n^2))$
This can be further simplified as $(-8(n^2 - ab)) \Rightarrow -2(4n^2 - 4ab)$. This term will always be negative as $4n^2 - 4ab$ is greater than 0. Hence, the given equation will have no real roots. Hence, the answer is 0.

10. Let $y = (3x^2 - 12x + 27)/(x^2 + 4x + 9)$
$yx^2 + 4yx + 9y = 3x^2 - 12x + 27$
$(y - 3)x^2 + 4(y + 3)x + 9(y - 3) = 0$
This is a quadratic equation in x. Now, for x to be real, the discriminant needs to be more than or equal to 0
$16(y + 3)^2 - 36(y - 3)^2 \geq 0 \rightarrow -20y^2 + 312y - 180 \geq 0$. On dividing both sides by -4, we get:
$5y^2 - 78y + 45 \leq 0$
$(y - 15)(5y - 3) \leq 0$
$3/5 \leq y \leq 15$
Hence, the least integral value of the expression is 1. Hence, the correct answer is option (b)

11. For Anish's case: Let the number of days taken by Dhruv be x
Work done by Anish in a day = kx^2 where k is the proportionality constant.
Work done by Bimal in a day = mx where m is the proportionality constant.
From the last statement of the question, we can determine that the values of k and m would be 1.
Work done by Charu in a day = 1
Hence, total work done by Anish, Bimal and Charu in a day = $x^2 + x + 1$
In order to maximize the time taken to complete the task, we need to minimize the work done in a day. This is achieved at $x = -½$ (This means that Dhruv is doing negative work). Hence, The minimum work done in a day is ¾ units.

12. Let the number of Hours taken by Pipe D to fill the tank be x
Work done by Pipe A in a day = $-kx^2$ where k is the proportionality constant. We have used a negative sign because it is an outlet pipe.
Work done by Pipe B in a day = mx where m is the proportionality constant.
From the last statement of the question, we can determine that the values of k and m would be 1 and 5 respectively.
Work done by Pipe C in a day = 3
Hence, total work done by A, B and C in a day = $-x^2 + 5x + 3$
In order to minimize the time taken to complete the task, we need to maximize the work done in a day. This is achieved at $x = 5/2$. Hence, The maximum work done in a day is 37/4 units.
Hence, Option (b) is the correct answer.

13. Difference of roots =
$$\sqrt{Sum\ of\ roots^2 - 4 \times product\ of\ roots}$$
For equation 1, the square of the difference of roots would be given as: $(-3b/2)^2 - 4(c/2)$;
For equation 2, $(-3c/2)^2 - 4(b/2)$
Equating these we get:
From i and ii
$9b^2/4 - 2c = 9c^2/4 - 2b \rightarrow$
$$\frac{9}{4}(b+c)(b-c)+2(b-c)=$$
$$0 \rightarrow (b-c)\left(\frac{9}{4}(b+c)+2\right)=0$$
Since, $b - c$ cannot be 0, it means that $\left(\frac{9}{4}(b+c)+2\right) = 0$.
Solving we get $b + c = -8/9$. Hence, $6(b + c) = -16/3$
Hence, Option (b) is the correct answer.

14. For an equation to have imaginary roots, the discriminant should be less than 0.
$a^2 - 64 < 0 \Rightarrow a^2 < 64 \Rightarrow -7 \leq a \leq 7$
For an equation to have distinct real roots, the discriminant should be more than 0.
$(a - 3)^2 - 12 > 0 \Rightarrow (a - 3)^2 > 12 \Rightarrow a - 3 \leq -4$ or $a - 3 \geq 4 \Rightarrow a \leq -1$ or $a \geq 7$. Combining the possible values of 'a' from the two inequalities, we see that the values of a possible are from -7 to -1 and 7 – a total of 8 values.
Hence, Option (c) is the correct answer.

15. $f(x) = x^3 - (5 + k)x^2 + (6 + 5k)x - 6k$
Let $k = 5$
$f(x) = x^3 - 10x^2 + 31x - 30$
By factorisation, we get:
$f(x) = (x - 2)(x - 3)(x - 5)$
$f(x) < 0$ for $x < 2$, $3 < x < 5$
Similarly, we can put few other values of x and confirm that $f(x) < 0$ for $x < 2$ and for $3 < x < k$.

16. $[x]^2 - 11[x] + 30 = 0$
$[x]^2 - 5[x] - 6[x] + 30 = 0$
$([x] - 5)([x] - 6) = 0$
$[x] = 5, 6$

The integer solutions of x are at $x = 5$ and 6

So the required sum = 5 + 6 = 11.

17. $f(x, 5) = a(x - 5)^2 + b(x - 5) + c$

$ax^2 + bx + c$ has roots 3, 4. Then roots of $f(x, 5)$ are $5 + 3, 5 + 4 = 8, 9$.

$f(x, 5)$ attains its maximum value at $\frac{8+9}{2} = \frac{17}{2} = 8.5$

∴ option (b) is correct.

18. $f(x) = g(x)$

$x^3 - px^2 - 2qx + r = (x - p)(x - q)(x - r)$

$p + q + r = p \Rightarrow q + r = 0$ (1)

$pq + qr + pr = -2q$

$p(q + r) + qr = -2q$

As $q + r = 0$ from equation (1), therefore, $qr = -2q$

$r = -2$

$q = +2$

$pqr = -r$

$pq = -1$

$p = -1/2$

So the required value of $p+q = -\frac{1}{2}+2 = \frac{3}{2}$

19. $f(x) = g(x)$

$f(x) = g(x) = (x - p)(x - q)(x - r)$

$f(4) = \left(4+\frac{1}{2}\right)(4-2)(4+2)$

$= \frac{9}{2} \times 2 \times 6$

$= 54$

20. $(x - 3)$ is a factor of $f(x)$ then $f(3) = 0$

$9a - 150 \times 3 + 5b = 0$

$9a - 450 + 5b = 0$

$a = 50 - \frac{5}{9}b$

a and b are positive integers, therefore, b must be a multiple of 9.

For $b = 9$, $a = 45$

$b = 18$, $a = 40$

$b = 27$, $a = 35$

$b = 36$, $a = 30$

$b = 45$, $a = 25$

$b = 54$, $a = 20$

$b = 63$, $a = 15$

$b = 72$, $a = 10$

$b = 81$, $a = 5$

Therefore, total possible ordered pairs of (a, b) is 9.

21. Maximum possible value of $a + b = 81 + 5 = 86$.

22. If a and b are integers then a and b both can be negative then there are infinite pairs of (a, b) for which $(x - 3)$ is a factor of $f(x)$.

Hence, option (d) is correct.

23. $(x - k)^3 (x - 7) - 27 = 0$

$(x - k)^3(x - 7) = 27$

Roots of the equations are integers, which mean that x is an integer. Now the following four cases are possible:

Case 1: $(x - k)^3 = 27$, $x - 7 = 1$

Case 2: $(x - k)^3 = 1$, $x - 7 = 27$

Case 3: $(x - k)^3 = -27$, $x - 7 = -1$

Case 4: $(x - k)^3 = -1$, $x - 7 = -27$

Case 1: $x - 7 = 1 \Rightarrow x = 8$

$(8 - k)^3 = 27$

$8 - k = 3$

$k = 5$

Case 2: $(x - 7) = 27 \Rightarrow x = 34$

$(x - k)^3 = 1 \Rightarrow 34 - k = 1$

$k = 33$

Case 3: $(x - k)^3 = -27$, $x - 7 = -1$

Therefore, $x = 6$

$x - k = -3$

$k = 9$

Case 4: $x - 7 = -27$, $x = -20$

$x - k = -1$ or $k = x + 1 = -20 + 1 = -19$

Therefore, four values are possible for k.

24. Required difference = 33 – (–19) =52

25. 4 lies in between roots of the equations, so:

$3(4)^2 + 4a(4) + a + 3 < 0$

$48 + 16a + a + 3 < 0$

$17a + 51 < 0$

$a < -3$

∴ option (a) is correct.

26. $f(0)$ is greater than or equals to 0 means that the value of $c \geq 0$. Also, since 'a' is negative as given in the question, the product of the roots given by $\frac{c}{a}$ will be negative or zero. So, the roots of $f(x) = 0$ are of opposite sign or their product is zero.

So the possibilities for the two roots from the given values are: (0, 2), (0, 1), (1, –2), (0, –1), (0, –2), (–1, 2), (–2, 2), (–1, 1). Therefore a total of eight different sets are possible for the roots of $f(x) = 0$.

∴ option (c) is correct.

27. $f(x) = g(x)$

$x^2 = x^3 - 2^x$

$x^3 - x^2 = 2^x$

$x^2(x - 1) = 2^x$

for $x = 2$; $x^2(x - 1) = 2^x$

For $x > 2$, either x^2 or $(x - 1)$ is odd and hence, $x^2(x - 1)$ cannot be equal to 2^x. Therefore, $f(x) = g(x)$ only for one value of x.

28. $3h(x) + 5t(x) = 0$

$t(x) = -\frac{3}{5}h(x)$

If $h(x) = -(x - p)(x - q)$ then $t(x) = \frac{3}{5}(x-p)(x-q)$

Therefore, roots of $t(x)$ and $h(x)$ are same, so their sums are also equal. Option (c) is correct.

29. If $h(x)$ is maximum at $x = 4$ then $t(x)$ will be minimum at $t = 4$ and its minimum value will be $-\frac{3}{5}$ times of the maximum value of $h(x)$.

$t(x)|_{\min} = -\frac{3}{5}h(x)|_{\max} = -\frac{3}{5} \times 10 = -6$

30. $||x|-1|$ would look like the figure shown below:

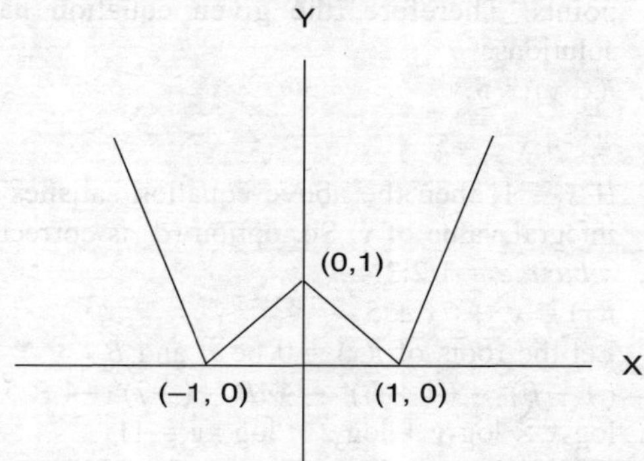

$||x| - 1| - 2$ will look like the figure shown below:

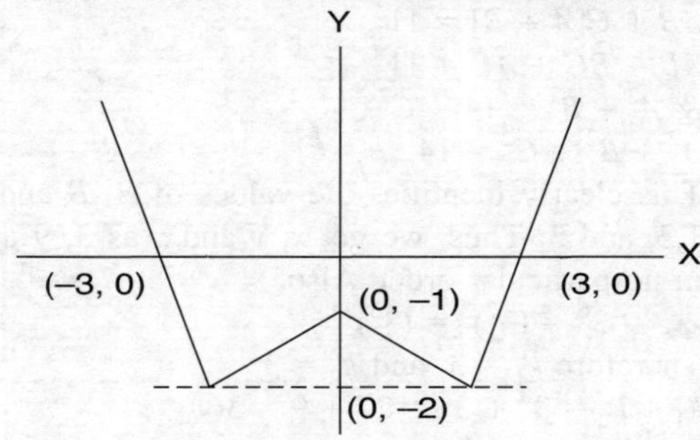

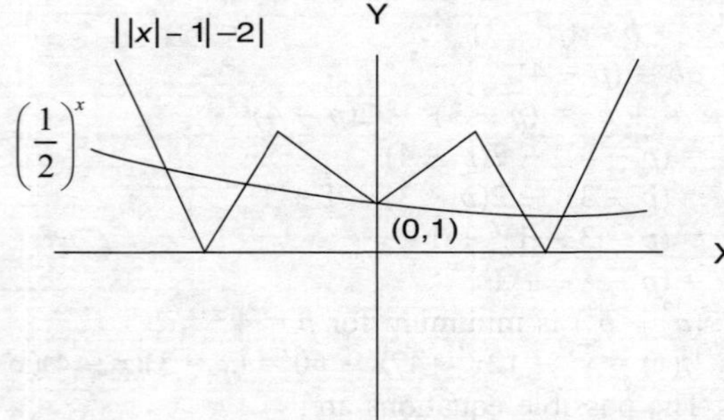

The graph of $(1/2)^x$ cuts the graph of $|||x| - 1| - 2|$ at five distinct points. Therefore the given equation has five solutions.

31. Let $f(x) = px^2 + qx + r$

$px^2 + qx + r = 0$. Here, two cases are possible:

Case 1: $p > 0$

When $p > 0$ then $px^2 + qx + r$ will open upwards and $p \times f(2) < 0$ will give us that $p(4p + 2q + r) < 0$. This is the same value as option (a). Hence, option (a) is correct. Option (b) is automatically rejected since it is the opposite of option (a).

(Note: Option (c) is rejected because In this case whether $p \times f(-2)$ [Which will give us $p(4p - 2q + r]$ is greater than or less than zero depends upon the location of the other root which is less than 1.Similarly, Option (d) is rejected as it is asking you to commit about the value of $p \times f(-3) < 0$. Whether this value is greater than or less than zero depends upon the location of the other root of $f(x) = 0$ (which is less than 1)).

So option (b), (c), and (d) are not necessarily true.

Case 2: $p < 0$

When $p < 0$ then $p\,f(2) < 0$ [because $f(x)$ will open downwards].

In this case whether $p\,f(-2)$, $p\,f(-3)$ will be greater than or less than zero depends upon the location of the other root of $f(x) = 0$. So only option (a) is correct in this case too.

32. If the three roots are x, y, z

$\Rightarrow x + y + z = 12$

Only one combination of $(x, y, z) = (2, 3, 7)$ is possible.

Product of the roots $= 2 \times 3 \times 7 = 42$.

So the chosen values are correct.

$p = 2 \times 3 + 3 \times 7 + 2 \times 7 = 6 + 21 + 14 = 41$

33. d is a root of the equation $ax^2 + bx + c = 0$

$\therefore\ ad^2 + bd + c = 0$ (1)

c is a root of the equation $ax^2 + bx + d = 0$

$\therefore\ ac^2 + bc + d = 0$ (2)

Equation (2) – equation (1):

$a(c^2 - d^2) + b(c - d) + (d - c) = 0$

$a(c - d)(c + d) + b(c - d) - (c - d) = 0$

$(c - d)[a(c + d) + b - 1] = 0$. In this expression, the value of $[a(c + d) + b - 1]$ has to be zero because it is given that $c \neq d$.

Solving: $[a(c+d)+b-1]=0$, we get $(c+d)=\dfrac{1-b}{a}$

$\therefore$ option (c) is correct.

34. $f(x) = max(|x^2 - 4|, 2x + 4)$

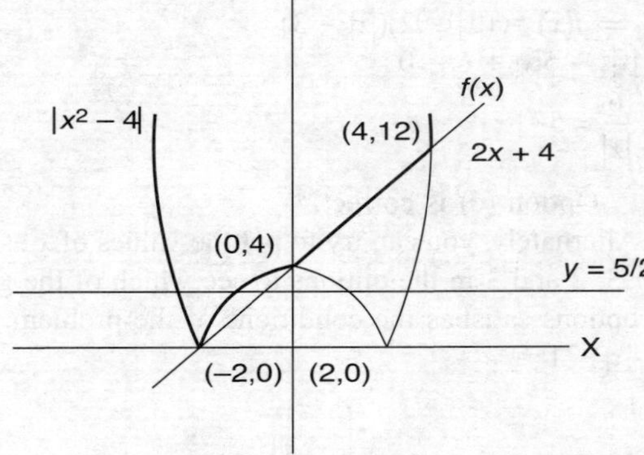

As we can see in the diagram shown above that $y=\dfrac{5}{2}$ intercepts $f(x)$ at two different points, therefore, the given equation has two solutions.

35. Let $f(x) = ax^2 + bx + c$

$f(4) = 16a + 4b + c = 0$ [$At\ x = 4\ f(x) = 0$]

$f(0) = c = 10$

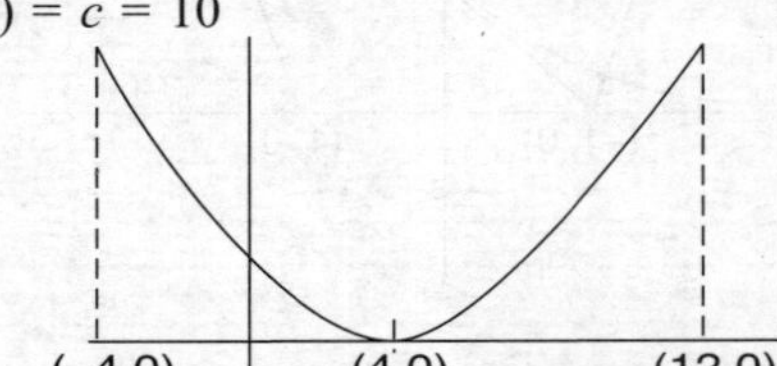

$f(x)$ is symmetric about $x = 4$.
$f(3) = f(5)$
$9a + 3b + c = 25a + 5b + c$
$16a + 2b = 0$
$8a + b = 0$
$b = -8a$
$f(4) = 0$
$16a + 4b + 10 = 0$
$16a - 32a + 10 = 0$

$$a = \frac{10}{16} = \frac{5}{8}$$

$f(-4) = 16a - 4b + 10$

$$= 16 \times \frac{5}{8} - 4 \times (-8) \times \frac{5}{8} + 10$$

$= 10 + 20 + 10 = 40$

Alternative method: the minimum value of $f(x)$ must be 0 and this minima occurs at $x = 4$.
Let $f(x) = a(x - 4)^2$
$f(0) = 16a = 10$

$$a = \frac{5}{8}$$

Hence, $f(x) = \frac{5}{8}(x-4)^2$

$$f(-4) = \frac{5}{8} \times (-8)^2 = 40$$

36. If we see the graph carefully, then we get:
For $x < 0$ $f(x) = (x - (-3))(x - (-2)) = (x + 2)(x + 3)$
For $x > 0$ $f(x) = (x - 2)(x - 3)$
$\Rightarrow f(x) = (|x| - 2)(|x| - 3)$
$|x|^2 - 5|x| + 6 = 0$

$$\frac{6}{|x|} = 5 - |x|$$

∴ Option (c) is correct.
Alternately, you can try to put the values of x as -2, -3, 2 and 3 in the options to see which of the given options satisfies the conditions of the problem.

37. $||x| - 1| = e^x$

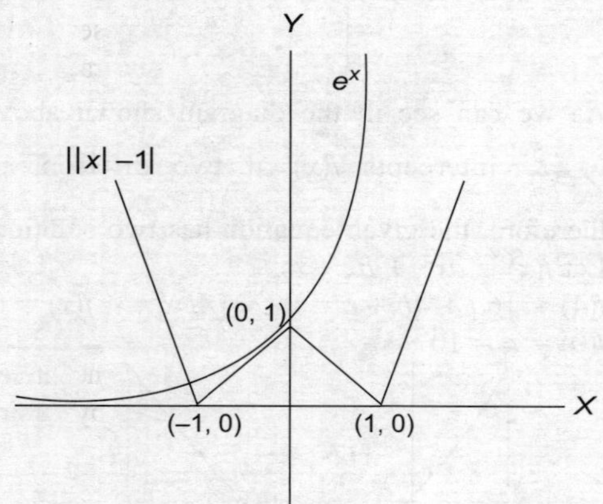

The curve of e^x cuts the curve of $||x| - 1|$ at three points. Therefore, the given equation has three solutions.

38. $f(x, y) = 5$

$$4^{x^y} + x^{4^y} = 5$$

If $x = 1$, then the above equation satisfies for any integral value of y. So, option (d) is correct.

39. $a:b:c:d:e = 1:2:3:4:5$
$f(x) = x^2 + 7x + 5$
Let the roots of $f(x) = 0$ be A and B
$(A - B)^2 = (A + B)^2 - 4AB = (-7)^2 - 4 \times 5 = 29$

40. $\log_3 x \times \log_3 y + \log_3 z \times \log_3 xy = 11$
$\log_3 x \times \log_3 y + \log_3 z\,[\log_3 x + \log_3 y] = 11$
Let $\log_3 x = A, \log_3 y = B, \log_3 z = C$
$AB + C[A + B] = 11$
$AB + BC + AC = 11$
& $A^2 + B^2 = 14 - C^2$
$A^2 + B^2 + C^2 = 14$
This clearly identifies the values of A, B and C as 1,2, and 3. Thus, we get x, y and z as 3, 9 and 27 in no particular order. Also,
$xyz = 3^6 = (3^2)^3 = (3^3)^2$
Therefore $k_1 = 3^3$ and $k_2 = 3^2$
$k_1 + k_2 = 3^3 + 3^2 = 27 + 9 = 36$

41. Let the roots of the quadratic equation be a, b.
$a + b = (p - 3)$
$ab = (p - 4)$
$a^2 + b^2 = (p - 3)^2 - 2(p - 4)$
$= (p - 3)^2 - 2(p - 4)$
$= (p - 3)^2 - 2(p - 3) + 1 + 1$
$= (p - 3 - 1)^2 + 1$
$= (p - 4)^2 + 1$
$(a^2 + b^2)$ is minimum for $p = 4$

42. $f(x) = x^3 - 12x^2 + 47x - 60 = (x - 3)(x - 4)(x - 5)$
The possible equations are:
$(x - 3)^2, (x - 4)^2, (x - 5)^2, (x - 3)(x - 4), (x - 4)(x - 5), (x - 3)(x - 5)$. We get a total of six such equations.
Hence, option (c) is correct.

43. Required product $= 3^2 \times 4^2 \times 5^2 \times 4 \times 5 \times 3 \times 5 \times 3 \times 4$
$p = 3^4 \times 4^4 \times 5^4$
$p^{1/4} = 3 \times 4 \times 5 = 60$
Option (d) is correct.

CHAPTER

17

Logarithms

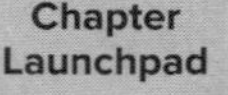

Scan this QR code to access a video on 'Introduction to Logarithms' and this chapter's importance for CAT

INTRODUCTION

Logarithms is an important chapter with questions being frequently asked in all important management entrance exams from this chapter. In examinations, most problems that have used the concept of logs have been of an applied nature. However, the aspirants should know the basic concepts of logarithms to ensure there are no surprises in the paper.

In the Online CAT especially, questions on logarithms have been a constant presence across the last decade. Hence, do not undermine the need to study this chapter well.

While studying this chapter, the student should pay particular attention to the basic rules of logarithms as well as develop an understanding of situations where these rules apply.

THEORY

Let a be a positive real number, $a \neq 1$ and $a^x = m$. Then x is called the logarithm of m to the base a and is written as $\log_a m$, and conversely, if $\log_a m = x$, then $a^x = m$.

Note: Logarithm to a negative base is not defined.

Also, logarithm of a negative number is not defined. Hence, in the above logarithmic equation, $\log_a m = x$, and we can say that $m > 0$ and $a > 0$.

Thus, $a^x = m \Rightarrow x = \log_a m$ and $\log_a m = x \Rightarrow a^x = m$.

In short, $a^x = m \Rightarrow x = \log_a m$.

$x = \log_a m$ is called the logarithmic form and $a^x = m$ is called the exponential form of the equation connecting a, x and m.

Two Properties of Logarithms

1. $\log_a 1 = 0$ for all $a > 0, a \neq 1$

That is, log 1 to any base is zero.

Let $\log_a 1 = x$. Then by definition, $a^x = 1$.

But $a^0 = 1 \therefore a^x = a^0 \Leftrightarrow x = 0$.

Hence, $\log_a 1 = 0$ for all $a > 0, a \neq 1$.

2. $\log_a a = 1$ for all $a > 0, a \neq 1$

That is, log of a number to the same base is 1.

Let $\log_a a = x$. Then by definition, $a^x = a$.

But $a^1 = a \therefore a^x = a^1 \Rightarrow x = 1$.

Hence, $\log_a a = 1$ for all $a > 0, a \neq 1$.

Laws of Logarithms

First law: $\log_a (mn) = \log_a m + \log_a n$

That is, log of product = sum of logs

Second law: $\log_a (m/n) = \log_a m - \log_a n$

That is, log of quotient = difference of logs

Note: The first theorem converts a problem of multiplication into a problem of addition and the second theorem converts a problem of division into a problem of subtraction, which are far easier to perform than multiplication or division. That is why, logarithms are so useful in all numerical calculations.

Third Law: $\log_a m^n = n \log_a m$

Generalisation

1. $\log (mnp) = \log m + \log n + \log p$
2. $\log (a_1 a_2 a_3 \ldots a_k) = \log a_1 + \log a_2 + \ldots + \log a_k$

Note: *Common logarithms*: We shall assume that the base $a = 10$ whenever it is not indicated. Therefore, we shall denote $\log_{10} m$ by $\log m$ only. The logarithms calculated to base 10 are called common logarithms.

Characteristic and Mantissa of a Logarithm

The logarithm of a number consists of two parts: the *integral* part and the *decimal* part. The integral part is known as the *characteristic* and the decimal part is called the *mantissa*.

For example,

In $\log 3257 = 3.5128$, the integral part is 3 and the decimal part is 0.5128; therefore, characteristic = 3 and mantissa = 0.5128.

It should be remembered that the mantissa is always written as positive.

Rule: To make the mantissa positive (in case the value of the logarithm of a number is negative), subtract 1 from the integral part and add 1 to the decimal part.

Thus, $-3.4328 = -(3 + .4328) = -3 - 0.4328$

$= (-3 - 1) + (1 - 0.4328)$

$= -4 + 0.5672$

So the mantissa is = 0.5672.

Note: The characteristic may be positive or negative. When the characteristic is negative, it is represented by putting a bar on the number.

Thus, instead of -4, we write $\bar{4}$.

Hence, we may write $-4 + .5672$ as $\bar{4}.5672$.

Base Change Rule

Up till now all rules and theorems you have studied in logarithms have been related to operations on logs with the same bases. However, there are a lot of situations in logarithm problems where you have to operate on logs which have different bases. The base change rule is used in such situations.

This rule states that

(i) $\log_a (b) = \log_c (b)/\log_c (a)$
It is one of the most important rules for solving logarithms.
A corollary of this rule is:

(ii) $\log_a (b) = 1/\log_b (a)$

(iii) log c to the base a^b is equal to $\frac{\log_a c}{b}$

Results on Logarithmic Inequalities

(a) If $a > 1$ and $\log_a x_1 > \log_a x_2$ then $x_1 > x_2$
(b) If $a < 1$ and $\log_a x_1 > \log_a x_2$ then $x_1 < x_2$

Applied conclusions for logarithms

1. The characteristic of common logarithms of any positive number less than 1 is negative.
2. The characteristic of common logarithm of any number greater than 1 is positive.
3. If the logarithm to any base a gives the characteristic n, then we can say that the number of integers possible is given by $a^{n+1} - a^n$.

Example: $\log_{10} x = 2.bcde...$, then the number of integral values that x can take is given by: $10^{2+1} - 10^2 = 900$. This can be physically verified as follows.
Log to the base 10 gives a characteristic of 2 for all three digit numbers with the lowest being 100 and the highest being 999. Hence, there are 900 integral values possible for x.

4. If $-n$ is the characteristic of $\log_{10} y$, then the number of zeros between the decimal and the first significant number after the decimal is $n - 1$.
Thus, if the log of a number has a characteristic of -3, then the first two decimal places after the decimal point will be zeros.
Thus, the value will be $-3.00ab...$

Space for Notes

WORKED-OUT PROBLEMS

Problem 17.1: Find the value of x in $3^{|3x-4|} = 9^{2x-2}$.
(a) 8/7 (b) 7/8
(c) 7/4 (d) 16/7

Solution: Take the log of both sides, then we get,

$$|3x-4| \log 3 = (2x-2) \log 9$$
$$= (2x-2) \log 3^2$$
$$= (4x-4) \log 3$$

Dividing both sides by log 3, we get

$$|3x-4| = (4x-4) \quad (1)$$

Now, $|3x-4| = 3x-4$ if $x > 4/3$
so if $x > 4/3$
$3x-4 = 4x-4$
or $3x = 4x$
or $3 = 4$
But this is not possible.
Let's take the case of $x < 4/3$
Then $|3x-4| = 4-3x$
Therefore, $4-3x = 4x-4$ from (1)
or $7x = 8$
or $x = 8/7$

Problem 17.2 Solve for x.

$$\log_{10}x - \log_{10}\sqrt{x} = 2\log_x 10$$

Solution: Now, $\log_{10}\sqrt{x} = \frac{1}{2} \times \log_{10}x$

Therefore, the equation becomes

$$\log_{10}x - \frac{1}{2}\log_{10}x = 2\log_x 10$$

or $\frac{1}{2}\log_{10}x = 2\log_x 10 \quad (1)$

Using base change rule ($\log_b a = 1/\log_a b$)
Therefore, equation (1) becomes

$$\frac{1}{2}\log_{10}x = 2/\log_{10}x$$

$\Rightarrow$ $(\log_{10}x)^2 = 4$
or $\log_{10}x = 2$
Therefore, $x = 100$

Problem 17.3: If $7^{x+1} - 7^{x-1} = 48$, find x.

Solution: Take 7^{x-1} as the common term. The equation then reduces to

$$7^{x-1}(7^2-1) = 48$$
or $7^{x-1} = 1$
or $x-1 = 0$ or $x = 1$

Problem 17.4: Calculate: $\log_2 (2/3) + \log_4 (9/4)$.
$= \log_2 (2/3) + (\log_2 (9/4) / \log_2 4$
$= \log_2 (2/3) + 1/2 \log_2 (9/4)$
$= \log_2 (2/3) + 1/2 (2\log_2 3/2)$
$= \log_2 2/3 + \log_2 3/2 = \log_2 1 = 0$

Problem 17.5: Find the value of the expression

$1/\log_3 2 + 2/\log_9 4 - 3/\log_{27} 8$
Passing to base 2.
we get

$$\log_2 3 + 2\log_2 29 - 3\log_2 327$$
$$= \log_2 3 + \frac{4\log_2 3}{2} - \frac{9\log_2 3}{3}$$
$$= 3\log_2 3 - 3\log_2 3$$
$$= 0$$

Problem 17.6: Solve the inequality.

(a) $\log_2 (x+3) < 2$
$\Rightarrow$ $2^2 > x+3$
$\Rightarrow$ $4 > x+3$
$1 > x$
or $x < 1$
But log of negative number is not possible.
Therefore, $x + 3 \geq 0$
That is, $x \geq -3$
Therefore, $-3 \leq x < 1$

(b) $\log_2 (x^2 - 5x + 5) > 0$
$= x^2 - 5x + 5 > 1$
$\to x^2 - 5x + 4 > 0$
$\to (x-4)(x-1) > 0$

Therefore, the value of x will lie outside 1 and 4.
That is, $x > 4$ or $x < 1$.

Space for Rough Work

LEVEL OF DIFFICULTY (I)

1. log 32700 = ?
(a) log 3.27 + 4 (b) log 3.27 + 2
(c) 2 log 327 (d) 100 × log 327
2. log 0.0867 = ?
(a) log 8.67 + 2 (b) log 8.67 – 2
(c) $\frac{\log 867}{1000}$ (d) –2 log 8.67
3. If $\log_{10}2 = 0.301$, find $\log_{10}125$.
(a) 2.097 (b) 2.301
(c) 2.10 (d) 2.087
4. $\log_{32} 8$ = ?
(a) 2/5 (b) 5/3
(c) 3/5 (d) 4/5

Find the value of x in equations 5–6.

5. $\log_{0.5}x = 25$
(a) 2^{-25} (b) 2^{25}
(c) 2^{-24} (d) 2^{24}
6. $\log_3 x = \frac{1}{2}$
(a) 3 (b) $\sqrt{3}$
(c) $\frac{3}{2}$ (d) $\frac{2}{3}$
7. $\log_{15}3375 \times \log_4 1024$ = ?
(a) 16 (b) 18
(c) 12 (d) 15
8. $\log_a 4 + \log_a 16 + \log_a 64 + \log_a 256 = 10$. Then, a = ?
(a) 4 (b) 2
(c) 8 (d) 5
9. $\log_{625} \sqrt{5}$ = ?
(a) 4 (b) 8
(c) 1/8 (d) 1/4
10. If log x + log (x + 3) = 1, then the value(s) of x will be, the solution of the equation
(a) $x + x + 3 = 1$ (b) $x + x + 3 = 10$
(c) $x(x + 3) = 10$ (d) $x(x + 3) = 1$
11. If $\log_{10}a = b$, find the value of 10^{3b} in terms of a.
(a) a^3 (b) $3a$
(c) $a \times 1000$ (d) $a \times 100$
12. 3 log 5 + 2 log 4 – log 2 = ?
(a) 4 (b) 3
(c) 200 (d) 1000

Solve equations 13–25 for the value of x.

13. log (3x – 2) = 1
(a) 3 (b) 2
(c) 4 (d) 6
14. log (2x – 3) = 2
(a) 103 (b) 51.5
(c) 25.75 (d) 26
15. log (12 – x) = –1
(a) 11.6 (b) 12.1
(c) 11 (d) 11.9
16. log (x^2 – 6x + 6) = 0
(a) 5 (b) 1
(c) Both (a) and (b) (d) 3 and 2
17. log 2^x = 3
(a) 9.87 (b) 3 log 2
(c) 3/log 2 (d) 9.31
18. $3^x = 7$
(a) 1/ $\log_7 3$ (b) $\log_7 3$
(c) 1/$\log_3 7$ (d) $\log_3 7$
19. $5^x = 10$
(a) log 5 (b) log 10/log 2
(c) log 2 (d) 1/log 5
20. Find x, if $0.01^x = 2$.
(a) log 2/2 (b) 2/log 2
(c) –2/log 2 (d) –log 2/2
21. Find x, if log x = log 7.2 – log 2.4.
(a) 1 (b) 2
(c) 3 (d) 4
22. Find x, if log x = log 1.5 + log 12.
(a) 12 (b) 8
(c) 18 (d) 15
23. Find x, if log x = 2 log 5 + 3 log 2.
(a) 50 (b) 100
(c) 150 (d) 200
24. log (x – 13) + 3 log 2 = log (3x + 1)
(a) 20 (b) 21
(c) 22 (d) 24
25. log (2x – 2) – log (11.66 – x) = 1 + log 3
(a) 452/32 (b) 350/32
(c) 11 (d) 11.33

Space for Rough Work

LEVEL OF DIFFICULTY (II)

1. If x and y are positive real numbers such that $\log_x(x^2+12)=4$ and $3\log_y(x)=1$, then $x+y$ equals
(a) 20 (b) 11
(c) 68 (d) 10

2. For some positive real number x, if $\log_{\sqrt{3}}(x)+\frac{\log_x 25}{\log_x 0.008}=\frac{16}{3}$, then the value of $\log_3(3x^2)$ is

3. Given that $a > 1$ and $x > 1$ satisfy the equations $\log_z 2x+\log_z 3x=10$ and $\log_z x^2=8$, then how many factors does x^3 have?
(a) 7 (b) 49
(c) 8 (d) 16

4. Find the value of $(2x - 3y - 2z)$, if
$$5\log\frac{49}{32}+3\log\frac{125}{98}+2\log\frac{128}{25}+\log\frac{2^x}{7^y\times 5^z}=0$$

5. For how many positive integers M is the expression $\log_{10}(M - 30) + \log_{10}(50 - M) < 2$ not satisfied?

6. Let $\log_2(\log_3(\log_4(x))) = \log_3(\log_4(\log_2 y)) = \log_4(\log_2(\log_3 z)) = 0$ and $m \times x \times y \times z)$ is a perfect cube. If 'a' is a natural number, then what is the minimum possible value of 'm'?

7. If $\log_8(x) + \log_4(y^2) = 7$ and $\log_8(y) + \log_4(x^2) = 5$, then the value of $(y/x)^3$ is:

8. How many roots does the equation $x + 2\log(x - 1) = 1 + \frac{2}{\log_{x-1} 10}$ have?
(a) No root (b) One root
(c) Two roots (d) Infinite many roots

9. The inequality $\log_3[(5x - 1)/(3 - x)] < 1$ holds true for:
(a) $x \in (-\infty, 5/4)$
(b) $x \in (-\infty, 1/5)$
(c) $x \in (1/5, 5/4)$
(d) $x \in (-\infty, 5/4); x \neq 1/5$

10. If $a, b, c > 1$ and N is a positive number such that $\log_a N = 48$, $\log_b N = 80$ and $\log_{abc} N = 24$, then what is the value of $\log_c N$?

11. If x, y and z are distinct positive real numbers and not equal to 1 such that $(\log_y x \times \log_z x - 1) + (\log_x y \times \log_z y - 1) + (\log_x z \times \log_y z - 1) = 0$. Then what is the value of $3xyz$?

12. How many roots does the equation $(x + 1)\log_2(x + 1) = 4(x + 1)$ has?
(a) 2 (b) 0
(c) 1 (d) 3

13. For a natural number N, $\frac{1}{10}\times \log_5 1024 - \log_5 N + \frac{1}{5}\times \log_5 3125 = 0$. What is the value of N?
(a) 50 (b) 25
(c) 10 (d) 5

14. If $\log_2(\log_3(\log_5 a)) = \log_3(\log_5(\log_2 b)) = \log_5(\log_2(\log_3 c)) = 0$, then $a + 2b + 3c$ is:

15. If $(2/\log_p 8) + (4/\log_q 64) + (6/\log_r 512) \geq 2$. Then find the minimum possible value of $(p^2 \times q + q^2 \times r + r^2 \times p)$.

16. If $\log_7 \log_3 \log_5 (n^2 - 12n + 17) = 0$, then what is the sum of the sum and the product of the values of n that will satisfy the given equation?

17. If $\log_5(x - 2) = 2\log_{25}(2x - 4)$. How many values of x will satisfy the given equation?

18. If a, b, m, n are positive numbers and $m\log a + n\log b = 170\log 225$, Then find the minimum possible value of $m + n$.

19. If $\log(2^{x^2} + 2^{2x+30}) = (x^2 + \frac{x}{2} + 8)\log 4$, then find the product of all the possible values of x.

20. If $\log_x a$, $a^{x/2}$ and $\log_b x$ are in geometric progression, then the value of x is
(a) $\log_a(\log_b a)$ (b) $\log_b(\log_a b)$
(c) $\log_b a$ (d) $a^{(\log b\, a)}$

21. Express $\log\frac{\sqrt[3]{a^2}}{b^5\sqrt{c}}$ or $\frac{a^{2/3}}{b^5\sqrt{c}}$ in terms of log a, log b and log c.
(a) $\frac{3}{2}\log a + 5\log b - 2\log c$
(b) $\frac{2}{3}\log a - 5\log b - \frac{1}{2}\log c$
(c) $\frac{2}{3}\log a - 5\log b + \frac{1}{2}\log c$
(d) $\frac{3}{2}\log a + 5\log b - \frac{1}{2}\log c$

22. If $\log 3 = 0.4771$, find $\log(.81)^2 \times \log\left(\frac{27}{10}\right)^{\frac{2}{3}} \div \log 9$.
(a) 2.689 (b) – 0.0552
(c) 2.2402 (d) 2.702

23. If $\log 2 = 0.301$, $\log 3 = 0.477$, find the number of digits in $(108)^{10}$.
(a) 21 (b) 27
(c) 20 (d) 18

24. If $\log 2 = 0.301$, find the number of digits in $(125)^{25}$.
(a) 53 (b) 50
(c) 25 (d) 63

25. Which of the following options represents the value of log $\sqrt{128}$ to the base 0.625?

(a) $\frac{2+\log_8 2}{\log_8 5-1}$ (b) $\frac{\log_8 128}{2\log_8 0.625}$

(c) $\frac{2+\log_8 2}{2(\log_8 5-1)}$ (d) Both (b) and (c)

26-28. Solve for x:

$\log\frac{75}{35}+2\log\frac{7}{5}-\log\frac{105}{x}-\log\frac{13}{25}=0.$

(a) 90 (b) 65
(c) 13 (d) 45

27. $2\log\frac{4}{3}-\log\frac{x}{10}+\log\frac{63}{160}=0$

(a) 7 (b) 14
(c) 9 (d) 3

28. $\log\frac{12}{13}-\log\frac{7}{25}+\log\frac{91}{3}=x$

(a) 0 (b) 1
(c) 2 (d) 3

Directions for Questions 29 to 31: Which one of the following is true?

29. (a) $\log_{17}275=\log_{19}375$ (b) $\log_{17}275<\log_{19}375$
(c) $\log_{17}275>\log_{19}375$ (d) Cannot be determined

30. (a) $\log_{11}1650>\log_{13}1950$
(b) $\log_{11}1650<\log_{13}1950$
(c) $\log_{11}1650=\log_{13}1950$
(d) None of these

31. (a) $\frac{\log_2 4096}{3}=\log_8 4096$

(b) $\frac{\log_2 4096}{3}<\log_8 4096$

(c) $\frac{\log_2 4096}{3}>\log_8 4096$

(d) Cannot be determined

32. $\log\frac{16}{15}+5\log\frac{25}{24}+3\log\frac{81}{80}=\log x,\ x=?$

(a) 2 (b) 3
(c) 0 (d) None of these

If log 2 = 0.301 and log 3 = 0.4771, then find the number of digits in the following.

33. 60^{12}
(a) 25 (b) 22
(c) 23 (d) 24

34. 72^{9}
(a) 17 (b) 20
(c) 18 (d) 15

35. 27^{25}
(a) 38 (b) 37
(c) 36 (d) 35

Directions for Questions 36 to 38: Find the value of the logarithmic expression in the questions below.

36. $\frac{\log\sqrt{27}+\log 8-\log\sqrt{1000}}{\log 1.2}$

where, $\log_{10}2=0.30103$, $\log_{10}3=0.4771213$

(a) 1.77 (b) 1.37
(c) 2.33 (d) 1.49

37. $\frac{1}{\log_{xy}(xyz)}+\frac{1}{\log_{yz}(xyz)}+\frac{1}{\log_{zx}(xyz)}=?$

(a) 1 (b) 2
(c) 3 (d) 4

38. $\log a^n/b^n+\log b^n/c^n+\log c^n/a^n=?$

(a) 1 (b) n
(c) 0 (d) 2

39. $\log_{10}x-\log_{10}\sqrt{x}=2\log_x 10$, then $x=?$

(a) 50 (b) 100
(c) 150 (d) 200

40. $\left(\frac{21}{10}\right)^x=2.$ Then $x=?$

(a) $\frac{\log 2}{\log 3+\log 7-1}$ (b) $\frac{\log 2}{\log 3+\log 7+1}$

(c) $\frac{\log 3}{\log 2+\log 7-1}$ (d) $\frac{\log 2}{\log 3-\log 7+1}$

41. $\log(x^3+5)=3\log(x+2)$, then $x=?$

(a) $\frac{-2+\sqrt{2}}{2}$ (b) $\frac{-2-\sqrt{2}}{2}$

(c) Both (a) and (b) (d) None of these

42. $(a^4-2a^2b^2+b^4)^{x-1}=(a-b)^{-2}(a+b)^{-2}$, then $x=?$

(a) 1 (b) 0
(c) None of these (d) 2

43. If $\log_{10}242=a$, $\log_{10}80=b$ and $\log_{10}45=c$, express $\log_{10}36$ in terms of a, b and c.

(a) $\frac{(c-1)(3c+b-4)}{2}$ (b) $\frac{(c-1)(3c+b-4)}{3}$

(c) $\frac{(c-1)(3c-b-4)}{2}$ (d) None of these

44. For the above problem, express $\log_{10}66$ in terms of a, b and c.

(a) $\frac{(c-1)(3c+b-4)}{8}$ (b) $\frac{3(a+c)+(2b+-5)}{6}$

(c) $\frac{3(a+c)+(2b-5)}{6}$ (d) $\frac{3(c-1)(3c+b-4)}{6}$

45. $\log_2 (9 - 2^x) = 10^{\log (3-x)}$. Solve for x.
(a) 0
(b) 3
(c) Both (a) and (b)
(d) 0 and 6

46. If $\dfrac{\log x}{(b-c)} = \dfrac{\log y}{(c-a)} = \dfrac{\log z}{(a-b)}$. Mark all the correct options.
(a) $xyz = 1$
(b) $x^a y^b z^c = 1$
(c) $x^{b+c} y^{c+a} z^{a+b} = 1$
(d) All the options are correct.

47. What will be the value of x, if it is given that

$$\log_x \left[\frac{1}{5}+\frac{1}{12}+\frac{1}{21}+\frac{1}{32}+\frac{1}{45}+\ldots+\infty \text{ terms}\right]^2 = 2$$

48. $(\log_4 x^2)(x\log_{27} 8)(\log_x 243)$ is equal to
(a) $2x$ (b) $5x$
(c) $3x$ (d) 1

49. For how many real values of x will the equation $\log_3 \log_6 (x^3 - 18x^2 + 108x) = \log_2 \log_4 16$ be satisfied?

50. If $n = 12\sqrt{3}$, then

$$\frac{1}{\log_2 n}+\frac{1}{\log_3 n}+\frac{1}{\log_4 n}+\frac{1}{\log_6 n}+\frac{1}{\log_8 n}+\frac{1}{\log_9 n}+\frac{1}{\log_{18} n} = ?$$

51. $(\log_2 x)^2 + 2\log_2 x - 8 = 0$, where x is a natural number. If $x^p = 64$, then what is the value of $x + p$?

Directions for 52 and 53: $A = \sum_{i=2}^{a} \log_3 (i)$, $B = \sum_{j=2}^{b} \log_3 (j)$ & $C = \sum_{k=2}^{(a-b)} \log_3 k$, where $a \geq b$. If $D = A - B - C$. then answer the following questions.

52. If $a = 10$, then for what value of b, D is minimum

53. For $a = 6$, D is maximum for $b = ?$

54. If 'p' and 'q' are integers and $\log_p (-q^2 + 6q - 8) + \log_q (-2p^2 + 20p - 48) = 0$ then $p \times q = ?$

High Yield Questions

Scan this QR code to access assisted problem solving videos on questions 1, 2, 6, 17 and 23 from LOD 2

Space for Rough Work

ANSWER KEY

Level of Difficulty (I)

1. (a)	2. (b)	3. (a)	4. (c)
5. (a)	6. (b)	7. (d)	8. (a)
9. (c)	10. (c)	11. (a)	12. (b)
13. (c)	14. (b)	15. (d)	16. (c)
17. (c)	18. (a)	19. (d)	20. (d)
21. (c)	22. (c)	23. (d)	24. (b)
25. (c)			

Level of Difficulty (II)

1. (d)	2. 7	3. (b)	4. 6
5. 1	6. 12	7. 512	8. (a)
9. (d)	10. 120	11. 3	12. (c)
13. (c)	14. 216	15. 24	16. –96
17. 0	18. 2	19. –30	20. (a)
21. (b)	22. (b)	23. (a)	24. (a)
25. (d)	26. (c)	27. (a)	28. (c)
29. (b)	30. (a)	31. (a)	32. (d)
33. (b)	34. (a)	35. (c)	36. (d)
37. (b)	38. (c)	39. (b)	40. (a)
41. (c)	42. (b)	43. (d)	44. (c)
45. (a)	46. (d)	47. 25/48	48. (b)
49. 1	50. 4	51. 7	52. 10
53. 3	54. 15		

SOLUTIONS AND SHORTCUTS

Level of Difficulty (I)

1. Log 32700 = log 3.27 + log 10000 = log 3.27 + 4
2. Log 0.0867 = log (8.67/100) = log 8.67 – log 100
   Log 8.67 – 2
3. $\log_{10} 125 = \log_{10}(1000/8) = \log 1000 - 3\log 2$
   $= 3 - 3 \times 0.301 = 2.097$
4. $\log_{32} 8 = \log 8/\log 32$ (by base change rule)
   $= 3\log 2/5\log 2 = 3/5$
5. $\log_{0.5} x = 25 \Rightarrow x = 0.5^{25} = (½)^{25} = 2^{-25}$
6. $x = 3^{1/2} = \sqrt{3}$
7. $\log_{15} 3375 \times \log_4 1024$
   $= 3 \log_{15} 15 \times 5 \log_4 4 = 3 \times 5 = 15$
8. The given expression is:
   $\log_a (4 \times 16 \times 64 \times 256) = 10$
   i.e. $\log_a 4^{10} = 10$
   Thus, $a = 4$.
9. $1/2 \log_{625} 5 = [1/(2 \times 4)] \log_5 5 = 1/8$
10. $\log x (x + 3) = 1 \Rightarrow 10^1 = x^2 + 3x$
    or $x(x + 3) = 10$
11. $\log_{10} a = b \Rightarrow 10^b = a \Rightarrow$ by definition of logs.
    Thus, $10^{3b} = (10^b)^3 = a^3$.
12. 3 log 5 + 2 log 4 – log 2
    = log 125 + log 16 – log 2
    = log (125 × 16)/2 = log 1000 = 3
13. $10^1 = 3x - 2 \Rightarrow x = 4$
14. $10^2 = 2x - 3 \Rightarrow x = 51.5$
15. $1/10 = 12 - x \Rightarrow x = 11.9$
16. $x^2 - 6x + 6 = 10^0 \Rightarrow x^2 - 6x + 6 = 1$
    $\Rightarrow x^2 - 6x + 5 = 0$
    Solving gives us $x = 5$ and 1.
17. $x \log 2 = 3$
    $\log 2 = 3/x$
    Therefore, $x = 3/\log 2$.
18. $3^x = 7 \Rightarrow \log_3 7 = x$
    Hence, $x = 1/\log_7 3$.
19. $x = \log_5 10 = 1/\log_{10} 5 = 1/\log 5$
20. $x = \log_{0.01} 2 = -\log 2/2$
21. $\log x = \log (7.2/2.4) = \log 3 \Rightarrow x = 3$
22. $\log x = \log 18 \Rightarrow x = 18$
23. $\log x = \log 25 + \log 8 = \log (25 \times 8) = \log 200$
24. $\log (x - 13) + \log 8 = \log[3x + 1]$
    $\Rightarrow \log (8x - 104) = \log (3x + 1)$
    $\Rightarrow 8x - 104 = 3x + 1$
    $5x = 105 \Rightarrow x = 21$
25. $\log (2x - 2)/(11.66 - x) = \log 30$
    $\Rightarrow (2x - 2)/(11.66 - x) = 30$
    $2x - 2 = 350 - 30x$
    Hence, $32x = 352 \Rightarrow x = 11$.

Level of Difficulty (II)

1. From the first part of the question, we can determine that $x^2 + 12 = x^4$. Since x is a positive real number, Value of x would be 2. Putting this value in the second part of the question, we get y equal to 8. Hence, $x + y$ would be 10. Hence, Option (d) is the correct answer.
2. $$\log_{\sqrt{3}}(x) + \frac{\log_x 25}{\log_x 0.008} = \frac{16}{3} \rightarrow$$
   $$\log_{\sqrt{3}}(x) + \frac{2\log_x 5}{-3\log_x 5} = \frac{16}{3}\left(\text{since } 0.008 = 5^{-3}\right) \rightarrow$$
   $$\log_{\sqrt{3}}(x) = 6 \rightarrow x = 27.$$
   We have to evaluate the value of $\log_3(3x^2) = \log_3(3^7) = 7$. Hence, the correct answer is 7.
3. $\log_z 6x^2 = 10 \rightarrow 6x^2 = z^{10}$ ---(1). From $\log_z x^2 = 8$, we have $x^2 = z^8$. Hence, $z^2 = 6$ and $x^3 = z^{12} = 6^6 = 2^6 \times 3^6$. The number of factors for this number would be 7 × 7 = 49 factors. Hence, option (b) is correct.
4. The given expression can be rewritten as $\left(\frac{49}{32}\right)^5 \times \left(\frac{125}{98}\right)^3 \times \left(\frac{128}{25}\right)^2 \times \frac{2^x}{7^y \times 5^z} = 1$.
   After cancelling all the corresponding terms, we can simplify this equation to $\frac{7^4 \times 5^5}{2^{14}} \times \frac{2^x}{7^y \times 5^z} = 1$.
   Comparing the terms in the numerator and the denominator we see that $x = 14$, $y = 4$ and $z = 5$. The value of $2x - 3y - 2z = 28 - 12 - 10 = 6$. Hence, the correct answer is 6.

5. Log_{10} (M – 30) (50 – M) < 2 log 10 → (M – 30) (50 – M) < 100 → M^2 – 80M + 1600 > 0 → $(M – 40)^2$ > 0. This will be not satisfied only at one integral value of M, viz. 40. Hence, the correct answer is 1.
6. From the first part, $\log_2 (\log_3 (\log_4 (x))) = 0$. For this to be possible $\log_3 (\log_4 (x)) = 1 \rightarrow x = 64$. Similarly, $y = 16$ and $z = 9$. For $m \times (64 \times 16 \times 9)$ to be a perfect cube, a's minimum value should be equal to 12. Hence, the correct answer is 12.
7. $\log_8 (x) + \log_4 (y^2) = 7 \rightarrow \frac{1}{3} \times \log_2 (x) + \log_2 (y) = 7 \log_2 2 \rightarrow x \times y^3 = 2^{21}$. Similarly, from the second equation, we get $y \times x^3 = 2^{15}$. On dividing the two resultant equations we get $(y/x)^2 = 2^6$. Hence, $(y/x)^3 = 2^9 = 512$. Hence, the correct answer is 512.
8. On simplifying the equations, on the RHS $1 + \frac{2}{\log_{x-1} 10}$ becomes $1 + 2 \log (x - 1)$. the terms containing logs cancel out each other and we get $x = 1$. However, at $\log(x - 1)$ becomes undefined. Hence, the expression will have no roots. Hence, option (a) is correct.
9. The inequality would be satisfied if $(5x – 1)/(3 – x) < 3$, solving we get $x < 5/4$. However, we need to be careful to eliminate the value of x, at which the expression $(5x – 1)/(3 – x)$ becomes 0, since inside a logarithm, the argument of the logarithm cannot be 0. Hence, $x \neq 1/5$. Hence, Option (d) is the correct answer.
10. From the given equations, we get $N = a^{48}$, $N = b^{80}$, $N = (abc)^{24} \rightarrow a^{24} = b^{40}$. Hence, $(abc)^{24} = (b^{64} c^{24}) = b^{80} \rightarrow c^{24} = b^{16} \rightarrow N = b^{80} = c^{120}$. So, $\log_c c^{120} = 120$. Hence, the correct answer is 120.
11. This equation can be rewritten as
$$\frac{\log x^2}{\log y \times \log z} + \frac{\log y^2}{\log x \times \log z} + \frac{\log z^2}{\log x \times \log y} = 3 \rightarrow$$
$(\log x)^3 + (\log y)^3 + (\log z)^3 = 3 \log x \log y \log z$.
Using the identity: $a^3 + b^3 + c^3 = 3abc \rightarrow a + b + c = 0$
$\text{Log } x + \log y + \log z = 0 \rightarrow xyz = 1 \rightarrow 3xyz = 3$.
Hence, the correct answer is 3.
12. $(x + 1) (\log_2 (x + 1) – 4) = 0$
Either $x = –1$ or $\log_2 (x + 1) = 4$
$x + 1 = 16 \rightarrow x = 15$
Since the term inside the log cannot be 0, we cannot take –1 as our root. Hence, it only has 1 possible root. Option (c) is correct.
13. This equation can be simplified to
$$\frac{1}{10} \times 10 \frac{\log_{10} 2}{\log_{10} 5} - \frac{\log_{10} N}{\log_{10} 5} + \frac{1}{5} \times 5 =$$
$$\frac{\log_{10} 2}{\log_{10} 5} - \frac{\log_{10} N}{\log_{10} 5} + 1 = 0 \rightarrow \log_{10} \frac{2}{N} = - \log_{10} 5 \rightarrow$$
2/N = 1/5. Hence, N = 10. Hence, the correct answer is option (c).
14. From the first part, $\log_2 (\log_3 (\log_5 a))) = 0$. For this to be possible $(\log_3 \log_5 a) = 1$, $\log_5 a = 3$, $a = 125$. Similarly, $b = 32$ and $c = 9$. Hence, $a + 2b + 3c = 216$. Hence, the correct answer is 216.
15. This can simplified to (2 log p/3 log 2) + (4 log q/ 6 log 2) + (6 log r/ 9 log 2) ≥ 2.
(⅔) × log (pqr)/log 2 ≥ 2
→ log pqr ≥ 3 log 2 → log pqr ≥ log 8
Lowest possible value for pqr is 8 and the expression would be minimized if and only if all three numbers are as close as possible. So $p = q = r = 2$. Hence, the expression would be 24. Hence, the correct answer is 24.
16. For the equation to be satisfied, $\log_3 \log_5 (n^2 – 12n + 17) = 1 \rightarrow \log_5 (n^2 – 12n + 17) = 3 \rightarrow$
$(n^2 – 12n + 17) = 125$.
Hence, $n^2 – 12n – 108 = 0$
On solving the above equation, we get n = 18, –6.
Sum of the values = 12, Product of the values = –108. Hence, the sum of the sum and Product of the possible values of n are: –96. Hence, –96 is the correct answer.
17. The expression can be rewritten as log (x – 2)/log 5 = 2 log (2x – 4)/2 log 5
In the end we get, (x – 2) = 2x – 4
x = 2. But at x = 2, we get 0 inside log which is not possible. Hence, no value of x will satisfy the given equation. The answer is 0.
18. The above equation can be converted to $\log (a^m \times b^n) = \log (225^{170})$.
So, $a^m \times b^n = 225^{170} \Rightarrow 15^{340} \Rightarrow 3^{340}5^{540})$. Both of these numbers can be represented as: $(3^{340})^1$ & $(5^{540})^1$. In this representation the values of m and n are 1 each. Hence, the minimum sum possible of m and n is 2. Hence, the correct answer is 2.
19. The above expression can be simplified to $\log (2^{x^2} + 2^{2x + 30}) = \log 2^{2x^2+x+16}$. Comparing the two expressions we get,
$2^{x^2} + 2^{2x + 30} = 2^{2x^2+x+16}$.
This expression is of the form: A Power of 2 + Another Power of 2 = Another power of 2.
If we scan the values in powers of 2, we can see that powers of 2 are 1, 2, 4, 8, 16 and so on. Two powers of 2 adding to the third power only occurs in cases like 2 + 2 = 4; 4 + 4 = 8; 8 + 8 = 16 and so on. Hence, in this case we should have: $2^{x^2} = 2^{2x + 30}$ or $x^2 = 2x + 30 \rightarrow x^2 – 2x – 30 = 0$. The product of roots of this equation is –30. Hence, the correct answer is –30.
20. Since the terms are in GP, $(a^{x/2})^2 = \log a/\log b \rightarrow a^x = \log_b a$.
Taking log on both sides we get,
$x \log a = \log (\log_b a) \rightarrow x = \log (\log_b a)/\log a \rightarrow x = \log_a (\log_b a)$. Hence, Option (a) is the correct answer.
21. 2/3 log a – 5 log b – 1/2 log c

22. 2 log (81/100) × 2/3 log (27/10) ÷ log 9
= 2 [log3^4 – log 100] × 2/3 [(log 3^3 – log10)] ÷ 2 log 3
= 2 [log3^4 – log 100] × 2/3 [(3log 3 – 1)] ÷ 2 log 3
Substitute log 3 = 0.4771 ⇒ – 0.0552.

23. Let the number be y.

$$y = 108^{10}$$

⇒ log y = 10 log 108
Log y = 10 log (27 × 4)
Log y = 10 [3log3 + 2 log 2]
Log y = 10 [1.43 + 0.602]
Hence, log y = 10[2.03] = 20.3.
Thus, y has 21 digits.

24. log y = 25 log 125
= 25 [log 1000 – 3 log 2] = 25 × (2.097)
= 52 +
Hence, 53 digits.

25. 0.5 $\log_{0.625}$ 128
= 0.5 [$\log_8$128/$\log_8$0.625]
= 1/2 [$\log_8$128/$\log_8$0.625]

$$\frac{\text{Log}_8 128}{2(\log_8 5 - \log_8 8)} = \frac{\text{Log}_8 128}{2[\log_8 5 - 1]} = \frac{2 + \log_8 2}{2(\log_8 5 - 1)}$$

26. (75/35) × (49/25) × (x/105) × (25/13) = 1
⇒ x = 13

27. (16/9) × (10/x) × (63/160) = 1
⇒ x = 7

28. Solve in similar fashion.

29. $\log_{17} 275 < \log_{19} 375$
Because the value of $\log_{17}$275 is less than 2, while $\log_{19}$375 is greater than 2.

30. $\log_{11}1650 > 3$
$\log_{13}1950 < 3$
Hence, $\log_{11}1650 > \log_{13}1950$

31. $\dfrac{\log_2 4096}{3} = \log_8 4096$

32. $x = (16/15) \times (25^5/24^5) \times (81^3/80^3)$
None of these is correct.

Solutions for Questions 33 to 35:

Solve similarly as 23 and 24.

38. log ($a^n b^n c^n / a^n b^n c^n$) = log 1 = 0

39. (1/2) log x = 2$\log_x$10
⇒ log x = 4 $\log_x$10
⇒ log x = 4/$\log_{10} x$ ⇒ $(\log x)^2 = 4$
So log x = 2 and x = 100.

40. $x = \log_{(21/10)} 2$

$$= \frac{\text{Log } 2}{\text{Log } 21 - \log 10} = \frac{\text{Log } 2}{[\text{Log } 3 + \log 7 - 1]}$$

41. $6x^2 + 12x + 3 = 0$ or $2x^2 + 4x + 1 = 0$
Solving, we get both the options (a) and (b) as correct. Hence, option (c) is the correct answer.

45. For x = 0, we have LHS
$\log_2 8 = 3$
RHS: $10^{\log 3} = 3$
We do not get LHS = RHS for either x = 3 or x = 6.
Thus, option (a) is correct.

46. $\dfrac{\log x}{b-c} = \dfrac{\log y}{c-a} = \dfrac{\log z}{a-b} = k$

⇒ $x = 10^{k(b-c)}$, $y = 10^{k(c-a)}$, $z = 10^{k(a-b)}$
∴ $xyz = 10^{k(b-c+c-a+a-b)} = 10^0 = 1$
Therefore, option (a) is correct.
$x^a y^b z^c = 10^{k[a(b-c) + b(c-a) + c(a-b)]}$
$= 10^{k(ab - ac + bc - ab + ca - bc)}$
$= 10^{k.0} = 1$
Therefore option (b) is correct.
$x^{b+c} y^{c+a} z^{a+b} = 10^{k[(b+c)(b-c) + (c+a)(c-a) + (a+b)(a-b)]}$
$= 10^{k.0} = 1$
Therefore, option (c) is also correct.
Since all the first three options are correct, we choose option (d) as the correct answer.

47. $\log_x\left[\dfrac{1}{5}+\dfrac{1}{12}+\dfrac{1}{21}+\dfrac{1}{32}+\dfrac{1}{45}+\ldots+\infty \text{ terms}\right]^2$

$= 2\log_x\left(\dfrac{1}{5}+\dfrac{1}{12}+\dfrac{1}{21}+\dfrac{1}{32}+\dfrac{1}{45}+\ldots+\infty \text{ terms}\right)$

Let $\dfrac{1}{5}+\dfrac{1}{12}+\dfrac{1}{21}+\dfrac{1}{32}+\dfrac{1}{45}+\ldots+\infty \text{ terms} = P$

$$P = \frac{1}{4}\left[\frac{4}{1\times5}+\frac{4}{2\times6}+\frac{4}{3\times7}+\frac{4}{4\times8}+\frac{4}{5\times9}+\ldots\infty\right]$$

$$4P = \left[1-\frac{1}{5}+\frac{1}{2}-\frac{1}{6}+\frac{1}{3}-\frac{1}{7}+\frac{1}{4}-\frac{1}{8}+\frac{1}{5}-\frac{1}{9}\right]$$

$$4P = \left[1+\frac{1}{2}+\frac{1}{3}+\frac{1}{4}\right]$$

$$4P = \frac{25}{12}$$

$$P = \frac{25}{48}$$

$$\log_x \frac{25}{48} = 1 \text{ or } x = 25/48$$

48. $\log_4 x^2.x\log_{27} 8.\log_x 243 = \dfrac{2\log x}{\log 4}.\dfrac{x\log 8}{\log 27}.\dfrac{\log 243}{\log x}$

$= \dfrac{\log x}{\log 2}.\dfrac{3x\log 2}{3\log 3}.\dfrac{5\log 3}{\log x} = 5x$

49. $\log_2(\log_4 16) = \log_2 \log_4 4^2 = \log_2 2 = 1$
$\log_3 \log_6 (x^3 - 18x^2 + 108x) = 1$
$\log_6(x^3 - 18x^2 + 108x) = 3$
$x^3 - 18x^2 + 108x = 6^3$
$x^3 - 18x^2 + 108x - 216 = 0$
$(x - 6)^3 = 0$

$x = 6$ is the only value for which the above equation is true.

50. $n = 12\sqrt{3} = 2^2 \times 3^{1.5}$

$\frac{1}{\log_2 n}+\frac{1}{\log_3 n}+\frac{1}{\log_4 n}+\frac{1}{\log_6 n}$

$+\frac{1}{\log_8 n}+\frac{1}{\log_9 n}+\frac{1}{\log_{18} n}$

$= \log_n 2 + \log_n 3 + \log_n 4 + \log_n 6 + \log_n 8 + \log_n 9 + \log_n 18$

$= \log_n (2 \times 3 \times 4 \times 6 \times 8 \times 9 \times 18)$

$= \log_n (2^8 \times 3^6)$

$= \log_n (2^2 \times 3^{1.5})^4$

$= 4 \log_n (2^2 \times 3^{1.5})$

$= 4\log_{2^2\times 3^{1.5}}\left(2^2\times 3^{1.5}\right) = 4$

51. $(\log_2 x)^2 + 2\log_2 x - 8 = 0$

$(\log_2 x)^2 + 4\log_2 x - 2\log_2 x - 8 = 0$

$\log_2 x\,[\log_2 x + 4] - 2\,[\log_2 x + 4] = 0$

$[\log_2 x - 2]\,[\log_2 x + 4] = 0$

Since, x is a natural number hence, $[\log_2 x + 4]$ cannot be zero. Hence, $\log_2 x - 2 = 0$.

$\log_2 x = 2$

$x = 2^2 = 4$

We are given that: $x^p = 64$. Since x is 4, this means that:

$4^p = 64$

$p = 3$

Hence, the value of $(x + p) = 4 + 3 = 7$.

52. $A=\sum_{i=2}^{a}\log_3 i=\log_3 2+\log_3 3+\log_3 4+\ldots+\log_3 a$

$= \log_3(2.3.4\ldots.a) = \log_3(a!)$

Similarly, $B = \log_3(b!)$, $C = \log_3(a - b)!$

$D = \log_3 a! - \log_3 b! - \log_3(a - b)!$

$= \log_3 \frac{a!}{b!(a-b)!}$

$= \log_3({}^aC_b)$

If $a = 10$, then D will be minimum when $b = 10$, since the smallest value of ${}^nC_r$ occurs when $n = r$.

53. If $a = 6$, then D will be maximum for $b = 3$ (since the value of ${}^nC_r$ attains its maximum when the value of r is half the value of n).

54. Both p, q must be greater than 0 as logarithms are not defined to negative bases. Now looking at the two parts of the expression, we see that both:

$-q^2 + 6q - 8 > 0$ and $-2p^2 + 20p - 48 > 0$.

This leads us to the following conclusions:

$q^2 - 6q + 8 < 0$. Hence, $(q - 2)(q - 4) < 0$. The only integer value of q that satisfies this is $q = 3$.

Likewise, $2p^2 - 20p + 48 < 0$ means $2(p - 4)(p - 6) < 0$.

Only integer value of p which satisfies the above ineq uality is $p = 5$.

$\therefore\ p \times q = 3 \times 5 = 15$

Space for Rough Work

TASTE OF THE EXAMS—BLOCK IV

CAT

1. If x is real number such that $\log_3 5 = \log_5(2 + x)$, then which of the following is true? **(CAT 2017)**
(a) $0 < x < 3$ (b) $23 < x < 30$
(c) $x > 30$ (d) $3 < x < 23$

2. Let $f(x) = x^2$ and $g(x) = 2^x$, for all real x. Then the value of $f(f(g(x)) + g(f(x)))$ at $x = 1$ is **(CAT 2017)**
(a) 16 (b) 18
(c) 36 (d) 40

3. The minimum possible value of the sum of the squares of the roots of the equation **(CAT 2017)** $x^2 + (a + 3)x - (a + 5) = 0$ is
(a) 1 (b) 2
(c) 3 (d) 4

4. If $9^{x-1/2} - 2^{2x-2} = 4^x - 3^{2x-3}$, then x is **(CAT 2017)**
(a) 3/2 (b) 2/5
(c) 3/4 (d) 4/9

5. If $\log(2^a \times 3^b \times 5^c)$ is the arithmetic mean of $\log(2^2 \times 3^3 \times 5)$, $\log(2^6 \times 3 \times 5^7)$, and $\log(2 \times 3^2 \times 5^4)$, then a equals **(CAT 2017)**

6. If $f(ab) = f(a)f(b)$ for all positive integers a and b, then the largest possible value of $f(1)$ is **(CAT 2017)**

7. Let $f(x) = 2x - 5$ and $g(x) = 7 - 2x$. Then $|f(x) + g(x)| = |f(x)| + |g(x)|$ if and only if
(a) $5/2 < x < 7/2$
(b) $x \leq 5/2$ or $x \geq 7/2$
(c) $x < 5/2$ or $x \geq 7/2$
(d) $5/2 \leq x \leq 7/2$ **(CAT 2017)**

8. The area of the closed region bounded by the equation $|x| + |y| = 2$ in the two-dimensional plane is
(a) 4π (b) 4
(c) 8 (d) 2π **(CAT 2017)**

9. Suppose, $\log_3 x = \log_{12} y = a$, where x, y are positive numbers. If G is the geometric mean of x and y, then $\log_6 G$ is equal to **(CAT 2017)**
(a) $\sqrt{a}$ (b) $2a$
(c) $a/2$ (d) a

10. If $x + 1 = x^2$ and $x > 0$, then $2x^4$ is **(CAT 2017)**
(a) $6 + 4\sqrt{5}$ (b) $3 + 5\sqrt{5}$
(c) $5 + 3\sqrt{5}$ (d) $7 + 3\sqrt{5}$

11. The value of $\log_{0.008} \sqrt{5} + \log_{\sqrt{3}} 81 - 7$ is equal to **(CAT 2017)**
(a) 1/3 (b) 2/3
(c) 5/6 (d) 7/6

12. If $9^{2x-1} - 81^{x-1} = 1944$, then x is? **(CAT 2017)**
(a) 3 (b) 9/4
(c) 4/9 (d) 1/3

13. If $f_1(x) = x^2 + 11x + n$ and $f_2(x) = x$, then the largest positive integer n for which the equation $f_1(x) = f_2(x)$ has two distinct real roots, is **(CAT 2017)**

14. If $f(x) = (5x + 2)/(3x - 5)$ and $g(x) = x^2 - 2x - 1$, then the value of $g(f(f(3)))$ is **(CAT 2017)**
(a) 2 (b) 1/3
(c) 6 (d) 2/3

15. If $f(x + 2) = f(x) + f(x + 1)$ for all positive integers x, and $f(11) = 91$, $f(15) = 617$, then $f(10)$ equals **(CAT 2018)**

16. If $\log_2 (5 + \log_3 a) = 3$ and $\log_5 (4a + 12 + \log_2 b) = 3$, then $a + b$ is equal to **(CAT 2018)**
(a) 67 (b) 40
(c) 32 (d) 59

17. If x is a positive quantity such that $2^x = 3^{\log_5 2}$, then x is equal to **(CAT 2018)**
(a) $1 + \log_3 \frac{5}{3}$ (b) $\log_5 8$
(c) $\log_5 9$ (d) $1 + \log_5 \frac{3}{5}$

18. Let $f(x) = \min\{2x^2, 52 - 5x\}$, where x is any positive real number. Then the maximum possible value of $f(x)$ is **(CAT 2018)**

19. The smallest integer n such that $n^3 - 11n^2 + 32n - 28 > 0$ is **(CAT 2018)**

20. Let $f(x) = \max\{5x, 52 - 2x^2\}$, where x is any positive real number. Then the minimum possible value of $f(x)$ is **(CAT 2018)**

21. If a and b are integers such that $2x^2 - ax + 2 > 0$ and $x^2 - bx + 8 \geq 0$ for all real numbers x, then the largest possible value of $2a - 6b$ is **(CAT 2018)**

22. If $p^3 = q^4 = r^5 = s^6$, then the value of $\log_s (pqr)$ is equal to **(CAT 2018)**
(a) 24/5 (b) 16/5
(c) 47/10 (d) 1

23. $$\frac{1}{\log_2 100} - \frac{1}{\log_4 100} + \frac{1}{\log_5 100} - \frac{1}{\log_{10} 100} + \frac{1}{\log_{20} 100} - \frac{1}{\log_{25} 100} + \frac{1}{\log_{50} 100} = ?$$ **(CAT 2018)**

24. The real root of the equation $2^{6x} + 2^{3x+2} - 21 = 0$ is **(CAT 2019)**
(a) $(\log_2 3)/3$ (b) $\log_2 9$
(c) $(\log_2 7)/3$ (d) $\log_2 27$

25. What is the largest positive integer such that $(n^2 + 7n + 12)/(n^2 - n - 12)$ is also a positive integer? **(CAT 2019)**
(a) 6 (b) 8
(c) 16 (d) 12

26. Let f be a function such that $f(m \times n) = f(m) \times f(n)$ for every positive integers m and n. If $f(1)$, $f(2)$ and $f(3)$ are positive integers, $f(1) < f(2)$, and $f(24) = 54$, then $f(18)$ equals what? **(CAT 2019)**

27. Let A be a real number. Then the roots of the equation $x^2 - 4x - \log_2 A = 0$ are real and distinct if and only if **(CAT 2019)**

(a) $A < \frac{1}{16}$ (b) $A > \frac{1}{8}$

(c) $A > \frac{1}{16}$ (d) $A < \frac{1}{8}$

28. The quadratic equation $x^2 + bx + c = 0$, has two roots $4a$ and $3a$, where 'a' is an integer. Which of the following is a possible value of $b^2 + c$? **(CAT 2019)**

(a) 3721 (b) 549

(c) 361 (d) 427

29. If $5^x - 3^y = 13438$ and $5^{x-1} + 3^{y+1} = 9686$, then $x + y$ equals [TITA] **(CAT 2019)**

30. For any positive integer n, let $f(n) = n \times (n + 1)$ if n is even, and $f(n) = n + 3$, if n is odd. If m is a positive integer such that $8 \times f(m + 1) - f(m) = 2$, then m equals **(CAT 2019)**

31. Let x and y be positive real numbers such that $\log_5(x + y) + \log_5(x - y) = 3$, and $\log_2 y - \log_2 x = 1 - \log_2 3$. Then xy equals **(CAT 2019)**

(a) 25 (b) 150

(c) 250 (d) 100

32. The number of solutions of the equation $|x|(6x^2 + 1) = 5x^2$ is **(CAT 2019)**

33. The product of the distinct roots of $|x^2 - x - 6| = x + 2$ is **(CAT 2019)**

(a) –4 (b) –16

(c) –8 (d) –24

34. Consider a funtion $f(x + y) = f(x)\, f(y)$ where x, y are positive integers, and $f(1) = 2$. if $f(a + 1) + f(a + 2) + \ldots\ldots + f(a + n) = 16(2^n - 1)$ then a is equal to: **(CAT 2019)**

35. If x is a real number, then $\sqrt{\log_e \frac{4x - x^2}{3}}$ is a real number if and only if **(CAT 2019)**

(a) $-3 \le x \le 3$ (b) $1 \le x \le 2$

(c) $1 \le x \le 3$ (d) $-1 \le x \le 3$

36. If $(5.55)^x = (0.555)^y = 1000$, then the value of $\frac{1}{x} - \frac{1}{y}$ is **(CAT 2019)**

(a) 1 (b) $\frac{1}{3}$

(c) $\frac{2}{3}$ (d) 3

37. If $f(5 + x) = f(5 - x)$ for every real x, and $f(x) = 0$ has four distinct real roots, then the sum of these roots is **(CAT 2020)**

(a) 20 (b) 0

(c) 40 (d) 10

38. The area of the region satisfying the inequalities $|x| - y \le 1, y \ge 0$ and $y \le 1$ is **(CAT 2020)**

39. Among 100 students, x_1 have birthdays in January, x_2 have birthdays in February, and so on. If $x_0 = \max(x_1, x_2, \ldots x_{12})$, then the smallest possible value of x_0 is **(CAT 2020)**

(a) 10 (b) 9

(c) 12 (d) 8

40. If y is a negative number such that $2^{y^2 \log_3 5} = 5^{\log_2 3}$, then y equals **(CAT 2020)**

(a) $-\log_2 (1/5)$ (b) $-\log_2 (1/3)$

(b) $\log_2 (1/3)$ (d) $\log_2 (1/5)$

41. The number of real-valued solutions of the equation $2^x + 2^{-x} = 2 - (x - 2)^2$ is **(CAT 2020)**

(a) 2 (b) infinite

(c) 0 (d) 1

42. If $\log_4 5 = (\log_4 y)(\log_6 \sqrt{5})$, then y equals **(CAT 2020)**

43. The number of distinct real roots of the equation $\left(x+\frac{1}{x}\right)^2 - 3\left(x+\frac{1}{x}\right) + 2 = 0$ equals **(CAT 2020)**

44. How many distinct positive integer–valued solutions exist to the equation $(x^2 - 7x + 11)^{(x^2 - 13x + 42)} = 1$? **(CAT 2020)**

(a) 6 (b) 2

(c) 8 (d) 4

45. The number of integers that satisfy the equality $(x^2 - 5x + 7)^{x+1} = 1$ is **(CAT 2020)**

(a) 3 (b) 5

(c) 2 (d) 4

46. If x and y are positive real number satisfying $x + y = 102$, then the minimum possible value of $2601\left(1+\frac{1}{x}\right)\left(1+\frac{1}{y}\right)$ is **(CAT 2020)**

47. For real x, the maximum possible value of $\frac{x}{\sqrt{1+x^4}}$ is **(CAT 2020)**

(a) $\frac{1}{\sqrt{2}}$ (b) 1

(c) $\frac{1}{\sqrt{3}}$ (d) $\frac{1}{2}$

48. The value of $\log_a\left(\frac{a}{b}\right) + \log_b\left(\frac{b}{a}\right)$, for $1 < a \le b$ cannot be equal to **(CAT 2020)**

(a) –0.5 (b) 1

(c) 0 (d) –1

49. If x and y are non–negative integers such that $x + 9 = z$, $y + 1 = z$ and $x + y < z + 5$, then the maximum possible value of $2x + y$ equals **(CAT 2020)**

50. In how many ways can a pair of integers (x, a) be chosen such that $x^2 - 2\,|\,x\,|\, + \,|\, a - 2\,| = 0$? **(CAT 2020)**

(a) 4 (b) 6

(c) 7 (d) 5

51. The number of pairs of integers (x, y) satisfying $x \ge y \ge -20$ and $2x + 5y = 99$ is **(CAT 2020)**

52. Let $f(x) = x^2 + ax + b$ and $g(x) = f(x + 1) - f(x - 1)$. If $f(x) \geq 0$ for all real x, and $g(20) = 72$ then the smallest possible value of b is **(CAT 2020)**
(a) 1 (b) 16
(c) 4 (d) 0

53. Let k be a constant. The equations $kx + y = 3$ and $4x + ky = 4$ have a unique solution if and only if **(CAT 2020)**
(a) $|k| = 2$ (b) $k \neq 2$
(c) $k = 2$ (d) $|k| \neq 2$

54. If $x_1 = -1$ and $x_m = x_{m+1} + (m + 1)$ for every positive integer m, then x_{100} equals **(CAT 2020)**
(a) –5150 (b) –5051
(c) –5050 (d) –5151

55. $\dfrac{2\times4\times8\times16}{(\log_2 4)^2(\log_4 8)^3(\log_8 16)^4}$ equals **(CAT 2020)**

56. The vertices of a triangle are (0, 0), (4, 0) and (3, 9). The area of the circle passing through these three points is **(CAT 2020)**
(a) $\dfrac{12\pi}{5}$ (b) $\dfrac{205\pi}{9}$
(c) $\dfrac{123\pi}{7}$ (d) $\dfrac{14\pi}{3}$

57. The area, in sq. units, enclosed by the lines $x = 2$, $y = |x - 2| + 4$ the x-axis and the y-axis is equal to **(CAT 2020)**
(a) 8 (b) 6
(c) 12 (d) 10

58. Let m and n be positive integers, If $x^2 + mx + 2n = 0$ and $x^2 + 2nx + m = 0$ have real roots, then the smallest possible value of $m + n$ is **(CAT 2020)**
(a) 8 (b) 7
(c) 6 (d) 5

59. If $f(x + y) = f(x) f(y)$ and $f(5) = 4$, then $f(10) - f(-10)$ is equal to **(CAT 2020)**
(a) 0 (b) 3
(c) 15.9375 (d) 14.0625

60. Let $\log_a 30 = A, \log_a \dfrac{5}{3} = -B$ and $\log_2 a = \dfrac{1}{3}$, then $\log_3 a$ equals **(CAT 2020)**
(a) $\dfrac{2}{A+B-3}$ (b) $\dfrac{A+B-3}{2}$
(c) $\dfrac{A+B}{2}-3$ (d) $\dfrac{2}{A+B}-3$

61. $f(x) = \dfrac{x^2+2x-15}{x^2-7x-18}$ is negative if and only if **(CAT 2021)**
(a) $-5 < x < -2$ or $3 < x < 9$
(b) $-2 < x < 3$ or $x < 9$
(c) $x < -5$ or $-2 < x < 3$
(d) $x < -5$ or $3 < x < 9$

62. If $x_0 = 1$, $x_1 = 2$, and $x_{n+2} = \dfrac{1+x_{n+1}}{x_n}$, $n = 0, 1, 2, 3, ...$, then x_{2021} is euqal to **(CAT 2021)**
(a) 2 (b) 1
(c) 3 (d) 4

63. If r is a constant such that $|x^2 - 4x - 13| = r$ has exactly three distinct real roots, then the value of r is **(CAT 2021)**
(a) 18 (b) 17
(c) 15 (d) 21

64. The number of integers n that satisfy the inequalities $|n - 60| < |n - 100| < |n - 20|$ is **(CAT 2021)**
(a) 20 (b) 21
(c) 19 (d) 18

65. $5-\log_{10}\sqrt{1+x}+4\log_{10}\sqrt{1-x}=\log_{10}\dfrac{1}{\sqrt{1-x^2}}$, then $100x$ equals **(CAT 2021)**

66. For a sequence of real numbers $x_1, x_2, ..., x_n$, if $x_1 - x_2 + x_3 + ... + (-1)^{n+1} x_n = n^2 + 2n$ for all natural numbers n, then the sum $x_{49} + x_{50}$ equals **(CAT 2021)**
(a) 200 (b) 2
(c) –2 (d) –200

67. For a real number x the condition $|3x - 20| + |3x - 40| = 20$ necessarily holds if **(CAT 2021)**
(a) $7 < x < 12$ (b) $9 < x < 14$
(c) $10 < x < 15$ (d) $6 < x < 11$

68. Consider the pair of equations $x^2 - xy - x = 22$ and $y^2 - xy + y = 34$. If $x > y$, then $x - y$ equal **(CAT 2021)**
(a) 4 (b) 6
(c) 8 (d) 7

69. Suppose one of the roots of the equation $ax^2 - bx + c = 0$ is $2 + \sqrt{3}$, where a, b and c are rational numbers and $a \neq 0$. If $b = c^3$ then $|a|$ equals **(CAT 2021)**
(a) 3 (b) 2
(c) 1 (d) 4

70. Three positive integers x, y and z are in arithmetic progression. If $y - x > 2$ and $xyz = 5(x + y + z)$, then $z - x$ equals **(CAT 2021)**
(a) 14 (b) 8
(c) 10 (d) 12

71. If $\log_2[3 + \log_3\{4 + \log_4(x - 1)\}] - 2 = 0$ then $4x$ equals **(CAT 2021)**

72. For all real values of x, the range of the function $f(x) = \dfrac{x^2+2x+4}{2x^2+4x+9}$ is **(CAT 2021)**

73. The number of distinct pairs of integers (m, n) satisfying $|1 + mn| < |m + n| < 5$ is **(CAT 2021)**

74. For a real number a, if $\dfrac{\log_{15} a+\log_{32} a}{(\log_{15} a)(\log_{32} a)} = 4$, then a must lie in the range **(CAT 2021)**
(a) $2 < a < 3$ (b) $4 < a < 5$
(c) $a < 5$ (d) $3 < a < 4$

75. If $f(x) = x^2 - 7x$ and $g(x) = x + 3$, then the minimum value of $f(g(x)) - 3x$ is **(CAT 2021)**
(a) –16 (b) –20
(c) –12 (d) –15

76. If $3x + 2|y| + y = 7$ and $x + |x| + 3y = 1$, then $x + 2y$ is **(CAT 2021)**
(a) 0 (b) $\frac{8}{3}$
(c) $-\frac{4}{3}$ (d) 1

77. The largest real value of a for which the equation $|x + a| + |x - 1| = 2$ has an infinite number of solutions for x is **(CAT 2022)**
(a) 0 (b) 2
(c) –1 (d) 1

78. Let a, b, c be non-zero real numbers such that $b^2 < 4ac$, and $f(x) = ax^2 + bx + c$. If the set S consists of all integers m such that $f(m) < 0$, then the set S must necessarily be **(CAT 2022)**
(a) either the empty set or the set of all integers
(b) the empty set
(c) the set of all positive integers
(d) the set of all integers

79. Let $0 \le a \le x \le 100$ and $f(x) = |x - a| + |x - 100| + |x - a - 50|$. Then the maximum value of $f(x)$ becomes 100 when a is equal to **(CAT 2022)**
(a) 50 (b) 25
(c) 0 (d) 100

80. For any real number x, let $[x]$ be the largest integer less than or equal to x. if $\sum_{n=1}^{N}\left[\frac{1}{5}+\frac{n}{25}\right] = 25$ then N is? **(CAT 2022)**

81. Let r and c be real numbers. If r and $-r$ are roots of $5x^3 + cx^2 - 10x + 9 = 0$, then c equals **(CAT 2022)**
(a) $-\frac{9}{2}$ (b) $\frac{9}{2}$
(c) 4 (d) – 4

82. Suppose for all integers x, there are two functions f and g such that $f(x) + f(x - 1) - 1 = 0$ and $g(x) = x^2$. If $f(x^2 - x) = 5$, then the value of the sum $f(g(5)) + g(f(5))$ is? **(CAT 2022)**

83. The number of distinct integer values of n satisfying $\frac{4 - \log_2 n}{3 - \log_4 n} < 0$, is? **(CAT 2022)**

84. Let $f(x)$ be a quadratic polynomial in x such that $f(x) \ge 0$ for all real numbers x. If $f(2) = 0$ and $f(4) = 6$, then $f(-2)$ is equal to **(CAT 2022)**
(a) 12 (b) 24
(c) 6 (d) 36

85. The number of integer solutions of the equation $(x^2 - 10)^{(x^2 - 3x - 10)} = 1$ is? **(CAT 2022)**

86. Suppose k is any integer such that the equation $2x^2 + kx + 5 = 0$ has no real roots and the equation $x^2 + (k - 5)x + 1 = 0$ has two distinct real roots for x. Then, the number of possible values of k is **(CAT 2022)**
(a) 7 (b) 8
(c) 13 (d) 9

87. If $c = \frac{16x}{y} + \frac{49y}{x}$ for some non-zero real numbers x and y, then c cannot take the value **(CAT 2022)**
(a) – 70 (b) 60
(c) – 60 (d) – 50

88. The minimum possible value of $\frac{x^2 - 6x + 10}{3 - x}$, for $x < 3$, is **(CAT 2022)**
(a) $\frac{1}{2}$ (b) –2
(c) $-\frac{1}{2}$ (d) 2

89. If $(3 + 2\sqrt{2})$ is a root of the equation $ax^2 + bx + c = 0$, and $(4 + 2\sqrt{3})$ is a root of the equation $ay^2 + my + n = 0$, where a, b, c, m and n are integers, then the value of $\left(\frac{b}{m} + \frac{c - 2b}{n}\right)$ is **(CAT 2022)**
(a) 3 (b) 4
(c) 1 (d) 0

90. Let r be a real number and $f(x) = \begin{cases} 2x - r & \text{if } x \ge r \\ r & \text{if } x < r \end{cases}$.
Then, the equation $f(x) = f(f(x))$ holds for all real values of x where **(CAT 2022)**
(a) $x \le r$ (b) $x \ge r$
(c) $x > r$ (d) $x \ne r$

Going Beyond the Book

Scan this QR code to access a video on 5 'must-know' questions from previous years' CAT papers (Q 3,15, 25, 58, 73)

ANSWER KEY

1. (d)	2. (c)	3. (c)	4. (a)
5. 3	6. 1	7. (d)	8. (c)
9. (d)	10. (d)	11. (c)	12. (b)
13. 24	14. (a)	15. 54	16. (d)
17. (d)	18. 32	19. 8	20. 20
21. 36	22. (c)	23. $\frac{1}{2}$	24. (a)
25. (d)	26. 12	27. (c)	28. (b)
29. 13	30. 10	31. (b)	32. 5
33. (b)	34. 3	35. (c)	36. (b)
37. (a)	38. 3	39. (b)	40. (c)
41. (c)	42. 36	43. 1	44. (a)
45. (a)	46. 2704	47. (a)	48. (b)
49. 23	50. (c)	51. 17	52. (c)
53. (d)	54. (c)	55. 24	56. (b)
57. (d)	58. (c)	59. (c)	60. (a)
61. (a)	62. (a)	63. (b)	64. (c)
65. 99	66. (c)	67. (a)	68. (c)

69. (b) 70. (a) 71. 5 72. (c)
73. 12 74. (b) 75. (a) 76. (a)
77. (d) 78. (a) 79. (a) 80. 44
81. (a) 82. 12 83. 47 84. (b)
85. 4 86. (d) 87. (d) 88. (d)
89. (b) 90. (a)

SOLUTIONS AND SHORTCUTS

1. No need to solve this question mathematically, we can solve it just by estimating the value ranges of $\log_3 5$ and then matching them with the value range of $\log_5(2+x)$ by picking up values of x from the options. The first thing we realise is that: $\log_3 9 > \log_3 5 > \log_3 3$.
$2 > \log_3 5 > 1$. Hence, we want $\log_5(2+x)$ to lie between 1 to 2. The only option that gives us the value of $\log_5(2+x)$ between 1 to 2 would be the fourth one. Going through the other options (a to c) we can reject them as follows:
   - ⇒ **Option (a):** When $0 < x < 3$ then $\log_5(2+x)$ will always less than 1 because $2 + x = 2 + 3 = 5$ and $\log_5(2+3) = \log_5 5 = 1$. This option is not correct.
   - ⇒ **Option (b):** When $23 < x < 29$, then minimum value of $\log_5(2+x) = \log_5(2+23) = \log_5 25 = 2$. So this option is also not correct. Similarly option (c) is also not correct.

   Hence, option (d) is correct.
2. $f(x) = x^2, g(x) = 2^x$
$$f(f(g(x)) + g(f(x)) = (2^{2x} + 2^{x^2})^2$$
At $x = 1$, $f(f(g(x)) + g(f(x)) = (2^{2x} + 2^{x^2})^2 = (2^{2\times 1} + 2^{1^2})^2 = (4+2)^2 = 36$. Hence, option (c) is correct.
3. Let the values of roots of the equation be p and q.
$p^2 + q^2 = (p+q)^2 - 2pq = (a+3)^2 + 2(a+5) = a^2 + 9 + 6a + 2a + 10$
$= a^2 + 8a + 16 + 3 = (a+4)^2 + 3$
Minimum possible value of $(a+4)^2 + 3$ is 3 (when we take $a = -4$). Hence, option (c) is correct.
4. By checking the options we can see that for $x = 3/2$ the LHS and RHS of the above equation are equal to each other. So, option (a) is correct.
5. Arithmetic mean $= [\log(2^2 \times 3^3 \times 5) + \log(2^6 \times 3 \times 5^7) + \log(2 \times 3^2 \times 5^4)]/3 = \log(2^9 \times 3^6 \times 5^{12})^{\frac{1}{3}} = \log(2^3 \times 3^2 \times 5^4) = \log(2^a \times 3^b \times 5^c)$
By comparing we get $a = 3$.
6. $f(ab) = f(a)f(b)$
Put $a = 1, b = 0$
$$f(0) = f(1)f(0)$$
$\rightarrow f(1) = 1$.
7. $|f(x) + g(x)| = |f(x)| + |g(x)|$
$$f(x) = 2x - 5, g(x) = 7 - 2x$$
$$|2x - 5 + 7 - 2x| = |2x - 5| + |7 - 2x|$$
$$2 = |2x - 5| + |7 - 2x|$$
By checking the options, we get that the above equation satisfies for any value of x which lies in between 5/2 and 7/2 (including both the values). So, option (d) is correct.
8. Curve of $|x| + |y| = 2$ is as shown below:

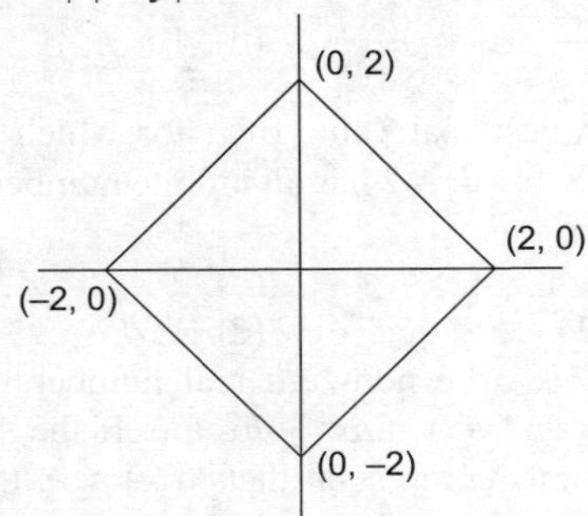

There are four triangles with base 2 and height 2 in this figure. The area of each triangle is 2. Hence, the area of the enclosed region is $2 \times 4 = 8$
9. $\log_3 x = \log_{12} y = a$
Or $x = 3^a, y = 12^a$
$$G = \sqrt{xy} = \sqrt{3^a \cdot 12^a} = \sqrt{6^{2a}} = 6^a$$
$$\log_6 G = \log_6 6^a = a$$
10. $x + 1 = x^2$
$$x^2 - x - 1 = 0$$
$$x = \frac{1 \pm \sqrt{5}}{2}$$
According to the question, $x > 0$, hence, $x = \frac{1+\sqrt{5}}{2}$
$$2x^4 = 2\left[\frac{1+\sqrt{5}}{2}\right]^4 = \frac{2}{16}[1 + 5 + 2\sqrt{5}]^2 = \frac{1}{8}[6 + 2\sqrt{5}]^2$$
$$= \frac{1}{8}[36 + 20 + 24\sqrt{5}] = \frac{1}{8}[56 + 24\sqrt{5}] = 7 + 3\sqrt{5}$$
Option (d) is correct.
Alternately, from the point where we got the value of $x = \frac{1+\sqrt{5}}{2}$, we can use the value of the square root of 5 as 2.23 and check with the options to get the correct answer.
11. $\log_{0.008}\sqrt{5} = \frac{1}{2}\log_{0.008} 5 = 1/6 \log_{0.2} 5 = 1/(6\log_5 0.2)$
$= 1/(6\log_5 1/5) = -1/6$
$$\log_{\sqrt{3}} 81 = 2\log_3 3^4 = 8.$$
Required answer $= -\frac{1}{6} + 8 - 7 = \frac{5}{6}$
12. $9^{2x-1} - 81^{x-1} = 9^{2x-1} - 9^{2x-2} = 9^{2x-2}(9-1) = 1944$
$$9^{2x-2} = 243$$
$$3^{4x-4} = 3^5 \text{ or } 4x - 4 = 5 \text{ or } x = 9/4$$

13. $f_1(x) = x^2 + 11x + n$ and $f_2(x) = x$

$x^2 + 11x + n = x$

$x^2 + 10x + n = 0$

If the above equation has two distinct real roots then $b^2 - 4ac > 0$

$10^2 - 4n > 0$

$100 - 4n > 0$ or $n < 25$

So the largest possible value of n is 24.

14. $f(3) = \dfrac{5 \times 3 + 2}{3 \times 2 - 5} = \dfrac{17}{4}$

Similarly $f(17/4) = 3$.

$g(3) = 3^2 - 3 \times 2 - 1 = 2$

15. It is obvious that $f(10) + f(11) = f(12)$ would have to be used in this question. However, the hurdle involved in getting $f(10)$ is to find the value of $f(12)$. Also, since we are given the value of $f(15)$, we can see that we would need to move from $f(11)$ towards $f(15)$. The following thought-process would give us the solution.

Given, $f(x + 2) = f(x) + f(x + 1)$

$f(11) = 91, f(15) = 617$

We get, $91 + f(12) = f(13)$

Let, $f(12) = X$

So, $91 + X = f(13)$

$f(12) + f(13) = f(14)$

$X + 91 + X = f(14)$

So, $f(14) = 2X + 91$. Also, $f(13) + f(14) = f(15) = 617$

So, $91 + X + 2X + 91 = 617$

$3X + 182 = 617$

$X = 145$

Substituting the value of X and $f(11)$, in $f(12) = f(10) + f(11)$, we get

$f(10) + 91 = 145$

$f(10) = 54$

16. $\log_2 (5 + \log_3 a) = 3 \Rightarrow 5 + \log_3 a = 2^3 \Rightarrow \log_3 a = 3$ or $a = 27$

$\log_5(4a + 12 + \log_2 b) = 3$

$4a + 12 + \log_2 b = 5^3 = 125$

$(4 \times 27) + 12 + \log_2 b = 125$

$120 + \log_2 b = 125$

$\log_2 b = 5$

$b = 2^5 = 32$

$a + b = 27 + 32 = 59$

Hence, option (d) is correct.

17. $2^x = 3^{\log_5 2}$

$\log_3 2^x = \log_3 3^{\log_5 2}$

$x\log_3 2 = \log_5 2$

$x\log_2 5 = \log_2 3$

$\log_2 5^x = \log_2 3$

$5^x = 3$

$x = \log_5 3 = 1 + \log_5\left(\dfrac{3}{5}\right)$

Hence, option (d) is correct.

18. 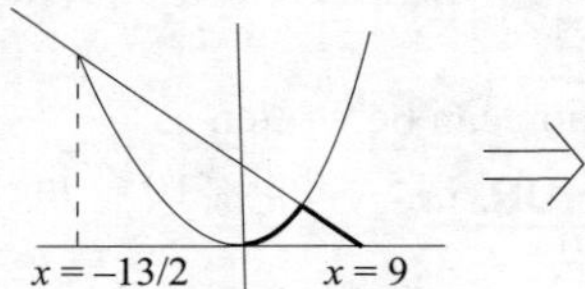

$2x^2 = 52 - 5x$

$2x^2 + 5x - 52 = 0$

$2x^2 + 13x - 8x - 52 = 0$

$x(2x + 13) - 4(2x + 13) = 0$

$x = 4$ or $-13/2$

for positive real value we should ignore the left portion of the above curve.

From the above curve it is clear that a $f(x)$ is maximum at $x = 4$.

$f(x)$ at $x = 4 = 2(4)^2 = 32$

19. $n^3 - 11n^2 + 32n - 28 > 0$

$(n - 7)(n - 2)^2 > 0$

$(n - 2)^2$ is always greater than 0. Hence, $n - 7 > 0$ or $n > 7$

So the smallest possible integer must be 8.

20. 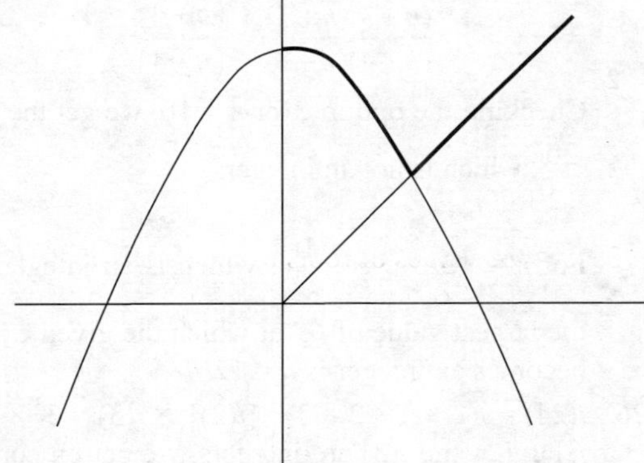

For $x > 0$, $5x$ is an increasing function and $52 - 2x^2$ is a decreasing function. So, the minimum value of $f(x)$ is the value of $f(x)$ at the intersection point of $5x$ and $52 - 2x^2$.

$5x = 52 - 2x^2$

Or $x = -13/2, 4$

At $x = 4$, value of $f(x) = 20$.

21. $2x^2 - ax + 2 > 0$, means that the roots of the equation $2x^2 - ax + 2 = 0$ must be imaginary. For that to occur: $a^2 - 16 < 0$. So, possible values of 'a' are: $-4 < a < 4$. In other words, possible values for a are: –3, –2, –1, 0, 1, 2 or 3.

Likewise, for $x^2 - bx + 8 \geq 0$, $b^2 - 32 < 0 \rightarrow$ values of 'b' should be –5, –4,…0, 1, 2, 3, 4, 5.

For $2a - 6b$ to be maximum, we have: $2 \times 3 - 6 \times (-5) = 6 + 30 = 36$.

22. Let, $p^3 = q^4 = r^5 = s^6 = k^{60}$. Thus, $p = k^{20}$, $q = k^{15}$, $r = k^{12}$ and $s = k^{10}$.
Then, $\log_s (pqr) = 47/10$. Hence, option (c) is correct.

23. The given expression can be written as:
$\log_{100}2 - \log_{100}4 + \log_{100}5 - \log_{100}10 + \log_{100}20 - \log_{100}25 + \log_{100}50$
$$= \log_{100} \frac{50\times 20\times 5\times 2}{25\times 10\times 4} = \log_{100}10 = \frac{1}{2}$$

24. Check the options:
$2^{6x} + 2^{3x+2} - 21 = 0$
$2^{6x} + 2^2 \cdot 2^{3x} - 21 = 0$
Option (a): Put $x = \frac{\log_2 3}{3}$
$$= 2^{\frac{6}{3}\times\log_2 3} + 4\bullet 2^{3\times\frac{\log_2 3}{3}} - 21$$
$$= 2^{2\log_2 3} + 4\bullet 2^{\log_2 3} - 21$$
$$= 2^{\log_2 3^2} + 4\bullet 2^{\log_2 3} - 21$$
$3^2 + 4 \cdot 3 - 21$
$9 + 12 - 21 = 0$
Hence, option (a) is correct.

25. The expression can be written as:
$$\frac{(n+3)(n+4)}{(n-4)(n+3)} = \frac{(n+4)}{(n-4)}$$
Checking the options, for $n = 16$, we get the value as $\frac{20}{12}$, which is not an integer.
For $n = 12$, we get $\frac{16}{8}$, which is an integer. Hence, the largest value of 'n' at which the given expression becomes an integer is $n = 12$.

26. $f(24) = f(2 \times 2 \times 2 \times 3) = [f(2)]^3 \times f(3) = 3^3 \times 2$. Since $f(1)$, $f(2)$ and $f(3)$ are integers, we get on comparing: $f(2) = 3$, $f(3) = 2$. The value of $f(18)$ can be obtained using $f(18) = f(3 \times 3 \times 2) = [f(3)]^2 \times f(2) = 2^2 \times 3 = 12$.

27. The roots of $x^2 - 4x - \log_2 A = 0$, will be real and distinct if an only if $16 + 4\log_2 A > 0$.
Hence, $\log_2 A > -4 \rightarrow A > 2^{-4}$. Thus, $A > 1/16$ is the correct range of A. Hence, option (c) is correct.

28. The sum of the roots would be: $4a + 3a = 7a$. This would be equal to '$-b$'. Thus, we get that $b = -7a$.
Also, the value of 'c' can be calculated using the logic of the product of the roots →
$c = 4a \times 3a = 12a^2$
$b^2 + c = 49a^2 + 12a^2 = 61a^2$
As 'a' is an integer, so a^2 will be an integer and a perfect square which is possible for option (b) only.

29. $5^x - 3^y = 13438$
$5^{x-1} + 3^{y+1} = 9686$ or $0.2 \times 5^x + 3 \times 3^y = 9686$
On solving the above two equations, we get:
$5^x = 15625 \rightarrow x = 6$
$3^y = 2187 \rightarrow y = 7$
Hence, $x + y = 6 + 7 = 13$.

30. Assuming 'm' is even:
$8 \times f(m + 1) - f(m) = 2$
$8 \times (m+ 1+ 3) - m \times (m + 1) = 2$
$8(m + 4) - m \times (m + 1) - 2 = 0$
$8m + 32 - m^2 - m - 2 = 0 \rightarrow$
$m^2 - 7m - 30 = 0 \rightarrow m = 10, -3$
Rejecting the negative value, we get $m = 10$.
If 'm' is odd on the other hand, we do not get integral values of m, and hence this case can be ignored.

31. $\log_5(x + y) + \log_5(x - y) = 3$
$\log_5(x + y)(x - y) = 3$
$(x^2 - y^2) = 5^3 = 125$ (1)
$\log_2 y - \log_2 x = 1 - \log_2 3$
$$\log_2\left[\frac{3y}{2x}\right] = 0$$
$$\frac{3y}{2x} = 1$$
$3y = 2x$ (2)
On solving equation (1) and equation (2), we get:
$x = 15, y = 10$
$xy = 150$

32. For $x \geq 0$, $x \times (6x^2 + 1) = 5x^2$
$x \times (6x^2 + 1 - 5x) = 0$.
For this situation, we have either $x = 0$ or $6x^2 - 5x + 1 = 0$. The roots of this quadratic equation are 0.33 and 0.5. Thus, for $x \geq 0$, we have three solutions for the given equation.
For $x < 0$, $-x \times (6x^2 + 1) = 5x^2$
$x \times (6x^2 + 1 + 5x) = 0$. For this to be true $6x^2 + 5x + 1 = 0$ should be satisfied (and that too only for x negative). The roots of the equation are: -0.5 and -0.33. Thus, there are five solutions to the given equation.

33. $|x^2 - x - 6| = x + 2$
For $x^2 - x - 6 >$ greater than or equal to 0.
$x^2 - x - 6 = x + 2$
$x^2 - 2x - 8 = 0$
Roots = 4, –2
For $x^2 - x - 6 < 0$
$-x^2 + x + 6 = x + 2$
$x^2 = 4$
Roots = 2, –2. But, we will take only 2 as the root that satisifes the starting condition.

Product of roots = 4 × 2 × –2 = –16

Hence, option (b) is correct.

34. $f(2) = f(1 + 1) = f(1) \cdot f(1) = 2^2$

$f(3) = f(2 + 1) = f(2) \cdot f(1) = 2^2 \cdot 2 = 2^3$

Similarly $f(n) = 2^n$

$f(a + 1) + f(a + 2) + f(a + 3) + \ldots\ldots + f(a + n) = 2^{a+1} + 2^{a+2} + \ldots\ldots + 2^{a+n} = 2^a(2 + 2^2 + 2^3 + \ldots\ldots + 2^n)$

$= 2^a[2 \cdot (2^n - 1)] = 16(2^n - 1)$. Comparing LHS and RHS, we get:

$2^{a+1} = 16 = 2^4 \rightarrow a = 3$

35. $\sqrt{\log_e \frac{4x - x^2}{3}}$ is a real number if :

$$\log_e \frac{4x - x^2}{3} \geq 0$$

$$\frac{4x - x^2}{3} \geq e^0$$

$$\frac{4x - x^2}{3} \geq 1$$

$4x - x^2 \geq 3$

$x^2 - 4x + 3 \leq 0$

$x^2 - 3x - x + 3 \leq 0$

$x(x - 3) - 1(x - 3) \leq 0$

$(x - 3)(x - 1) \leq 0$

or $1 \leq x \leq 3$

Hence, option (c) is correct.

36. We have, $(5.55)^x = (0.555)^y = 1000$

Taking log in base 10 on both sides:

$x \log_{10}5.55 = y \log_{10}0.555 = \log_{10}1000 = 3$

$$x\,[\log_{10}555 - 2] = 3 \quad (1)$$

$$y\,[\log_{10}555 - 3] = 3 \quad (2)$$

From equation (1) and equation (2)

$$\log_{10} 555 = \frac{3}{x} + 2 = \frac{3}{y} + 3$$

$$3\left[\frac{1}{x} - \frac{1}{y}\right] = 1$$

$$\frac{1}{x} - \frac{1}{y} = \frac{1}{3}$$

Hence, option (b) is correct.

37. Since the value of $f(5 + x)$ and $f(5 - x)$ are equal, it means that if a root exists at $f(6)$, it will also exist at $f(4)$. This is because the function can be thought of as $f(6) = f(4)$ when $x = 1$; $f(7) = f(3)$ when $x = 2$; $f(8) = f(4)$ when $x = 3$. Further, the function will also equate itself for decimal values of x. For instance, at $x = 1.5$, we can see that $f(6.5) = f(3.5)$. Thus, whenever we discover a root at $f(5 + x)$, there is also a root at $f(5 - x)$. This means that each pair of roots will have their arguments adding to 10. Since, there are a total of 4 roots, it means that there are two pairs of roots. Thus, the sum of the roots is 10 + 10 = 20

38. The area formed is the area shown by the shaded region ABCD in the figure. It can be calculated using Required area = (Area of triangle ADE + Area of triangle BCF + Area of rectangle ABFE) = 0.5 + 0.5 + 2 = 3. The correct answer is 3.

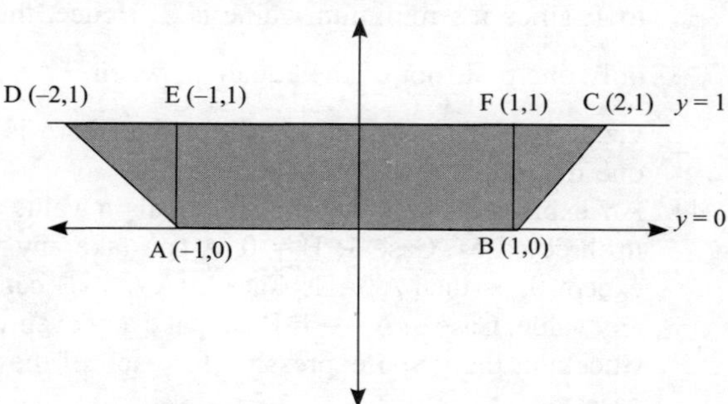

39. This question is based on the pigeon hole principle. The required answer will be derived if we equally place 8 students having birthdays in each month from January to December. This would account for the birthday of 96 children. The birthday of the remaining 4 children can be distributed as 1 each to 4 different months amongst January to December. Thus, there will be a pattern that will look like: x_0 = Max (8, 8, 8, 8, 8, 8, 8, 8, 9, 9, 9, 9). The required maximum is 9. Hence, option (b) is correct.

40. Taking logs to base 3 on both sides, we get: $y^2\log_3 5 \times \log_3 2 = \log_2 3 \times \log_3 5$

$\Rightarrow y^2 = (\log_2 3)^2$.

Thus, $y = \pm\log_2 3$. Since, it is given to us that y is a negative number, it follows that we should consider $y = -\log_2 3 = \log_2(1/3)$. Option (c) is correct.

41. The given expression on the LHS is of the form: $2^x + \frac{1}{2^x}$

The minimum value of the LHS is 2 and occurs at $x = 0$. The RHS, at $x = 0$ is 2 –(4) = –2. The RHS becomes equal to 2 only at $x = 2$, but at that value the LHS is not equal to 2. Hence, since the LHS ≥ 2 and the RHS ≤ 2, and they are not equal to 2 at the same time, it means that there is no solution where the LHS and RHS of the given equation are equal. Hence, option (c) is correct.

42. $\log_4 5 = (\log_4 y)(\log_6 \sqrt{5})$

$$\Rightarrow \log_4 5 = \frac{(\log_4 y)(\log_4 \sqrt{5})}{\log_4 6}$$

$$= \frac{1}{2} \times \frac{(\log_4 y)(\log_4 5)}{(\log_4 6)}$$

Canceling $\log_4 5$ from both sides, we get:

$\log_4 y = 2 \log_4 6$

$\Rightarrow \log_4 y = \log_4 36$.
Hence, the value of $y = 36$.

43. Think of the expression as $A^2 - 3A + 2 = 0$.
The value of $A = \dfrac{3 \pm \sqrt{9-8}}{2} = 1$ or 2.
However, an expression like $x + \dfrac{1}{x}$ cannot be equal to 1, since it's minimum value is 2. Hence, there is only one real root of the equation, when $x + \dfrac{1}{x} = 2$, viz: $x = 1$. The correct answer is that there is only one distinct real root for the equation.

44. An expression of the form A^B equals a value of 1, in three cases: Case 1: B = 0, A can take any value except 0, as then $A^0 = 1$; Case 2: A = 1, B can take any value; Case 3: A = – 1, B can take any even value. Checking the given expression for each of the three cases.
Checking for Case 1
B = 0: $x^2 - 13x + 42 = 0$
$\Rightarrow$ $x = 6,7$. Two solutions.
Checking for Case 2
A = 1 and
$B \neq 0$: $x^2 - 7x + 11 = 1$
$\Rightarrow x^2 - 7x + 10 = 0$
$\Rightarrow$ $x = 2,5$ and
we already know that B = 0 is occurring at $x = 6,7$.
Hence, we can count both these values as solutions.
Checking for Case 3
A = – 1 and B is even: $x^2 - 7x + 11 = -1$
$\Rightarrow x^2 - 7x + 12 = 0$
$\Rightarrow x = 3,4$ and
we can check at $x = 3$ and $x = 4$, the value of $x^2 - 13x + 42$ is even. Hence, we can count both these values as solutions.
Thus, there are a total of 6 solutions in this case.

45. In general the value of an expression like A^B can be equal to 1 for 3 cases. First: If B = 0, the value of A does not matter, since A^0 is always equal to 1; Second: If A = 1, the value of B does not matter since $1^B = 1$, no matter what value B takes. Also, for A = –1, B should be even for A^B to be 1. In this situation, we have: for $x = -1$, the first case takes place. For the second case to happen, $x^2 - 5x + 7 = 1 \rightarrow x^2 - 5x + 6 = 0 \rightarrow x = 2$ and 3. If we look for the third case, we want to get integer values of x, for $x^2 - 5x + 7 = -1 \rightarrow x^2 - 5x + 8 = 0$. But this equation has imaginary roots and hence the third case would not occur here. Thus there are a total of 3 integer values of x. Option (a) is correct.

46. To find the minimum possible value keep x and y as close as possible
So, $x = y = 51$
$$= 2601\left(1+\frac{1}{51}\right)\left(1+\frac{1}{51}\right) = 52 \times 52 = 2704.$$

47. Dividing both numerator and denominator by x,
$$\frac{1}{\sqrt{\dfrac{1+x^4}{x^2}}} = \frac{1}{\sqrt{\dfrac{1}{x^2}+x^2}}$$
$$\frac{1}{x^2}+x^2 \geq 2$$
$$\sqrt{\left[\frac{1}{x^2}+x^2\right]} \geq \sqrt{2}$$
$$\frac{1}{\sqrt{\dfrac{1}{x^2}+x^2}} \leq \frac{1}{\sqrt{2}}$$

48. The given expression can be written as:
$(\log_a a - \log_a b) + (\log_b b - \log_b a)$.
This simplifies to: $2 - \left\{\log_a b + \dfrac{1}{\log_a b}\right\}$.
The value of $\left(x + \dfrac{1}{x}\right)$ is always ≥ 2. Hence, the expression $2 - \left\{\log_a b + \dfrac{1}{\log_a b}\right\}$. can never be equal to 1. It can be 0 or negative.
Hence, option (b) is correct.

49. If we assume, $x = 1$, z will equal 10 and $y = 9$. In this case checking for $x + y < z + 5 \Rightarrow 10 < 15$. We are asked to find the maximum value of $2x + y$. Hence, we should look for larger values of x and y.

Value of x	Value of z	Value of y	Value of $x+y$	Value of $z+5$	Is $x+y$ $< z+5$
2	11	10	12	16	Yes
3	12	11	14	17	Yes
4	13	12	16	18	Yes
5	14	13	18	19	Yes
6	15	14	20	20	No

Hence, the maximum value of $2x + y$
$= 10 + 13 = 23$.

50. $x^2 - 2|x| + |a - 2| = 0$
For the given expression to be equal to 0, we see that for $x = 1$, $-2|x| = -2$ and hence $x^2 - 2|x| = -1$.
At $x = 2$, the value of $x^2 - 2|x| = 0$. Values of x above 2 will not work, since the expression cannot be equal to 0, if $x^2 - 2|x|$ is greater than 0. Also, the same conditions will be met for $x = -1$ and $x = -2$. Besides, at $x = 0$, we will get $x^2 - 2|x| = 0$ and there can be a solution of this expression for that value of x too.
For $x = 1$, since $x^2 - 2|x|$ is equal to –1, we get $|a - 2| = 1 \Rightarrow a = 3$ or $a = 1$;
For $x = 2$, since $x^2 - 2|x|$ is equal to 0, we get $|a - 2| = 0 \Rightarrow a = 2$;
For $x = -1$, since $x^2 - 2|x|$ is equal to –1, we get $|a - 2| = 1 \Rightarrow a = 3$ or $a = 1$;

For $x = -2$, since $x^2 - 2\,|\,x\,|$ is equal to 0, we get $|a - 2| = 0 \Rightarrow a = 2$;

For $x = 0$, since $x^2 - 2\,|\,x\,|$ is equal to 0, we get $|a - 2| = 0 \Rightarrow a = 2$

We can thus see a total of 7 solutions for the integer pair (x, a).

Hence, option (c) is correct.

51. The first set of values that comes to mind that satisfies $2x + 5y = 99$ would be $x = 2$ and $y = 19$. However, this value would not be counted since we are given that $x \geq y \geq -20$.

The next values for (x, y) would be (7, 17); (12, 15) both not counted. The first feasible pair when $x > y$ is (17, 13) followed by (22, 11); (27, 9)....(?, –19). The number of pairs can be counted using the arithmetic progression that y takes from 13, 11, 9, 7...–19. This has 17 terms and hence the correct answer would be 17.

52. $f(x + 1) = (x + 1)^2 + a(x + 1) + b$

$f(x - 1) = (x - 1)^2 + a(x - 1) + b$

$g(x) = (x + 1)^2 + a(x + 1) + b - (x - 1)^2 - a(x - 1) - b = 4x + 2a.$

Since it is given to us that $g(20) = 72$; we can use $g(x) = 4x + 2a = 72$. With $x = 20$, we get $a = -4$. Also, it is given to us that $f(x) \geq 0$, which means that for the quadratic expression $x^2 + ax + b$, the value of the discriminant viz $a^2 - 4b \leq 0$. With $a = -4$, this occurs at a minimum value of $b = 4$. Hence, option (c) is correct.

53. It can be seen that at $k = 2$, the two equations become inconsistent since, we get $2x + y = 3$ and $4x + 2y = 4$ (which essentially is $2x + y = 2$). These two equations cannot co-exist at the same time. Hence, the value of $k = 2$ is not possible.

Also, at $k = -2$, we get: $-2x + y = 3$ and $4x + -2y = 4$ (which essentially is $-2x + y = -2$). These two equations cannot co-exist at the same time. Hence, the value of $k = -2$ is not possible.

Hence, the correct answer is option (d).

54. $x_m = x_{m+1} + (m + 1)$

$\Rightarrow \quad x_{m+1} = x_m - (m + 1)$

Since it is given to us that $x_1 = -1$, we can calculate

$x_2 = x_1 - (2) = -3;$

$x_3 = x_2 - (3) = -3 - 3 = -6;$

$x_4 = x_3 - 4 = -6 - 4 = -10$ and so on.

We realise that the value of x_n in general is just the negative outcome of the addition of the first n natural numbers.

Thus, we have $x_{100} = -(1 + 2 + 3 + \ldots + 100)$.

$$x_{100} = -\frac{100 \times 101}{2} = -5050.$$

Option (c) is correct.

55. If we evaluate each component of the denominator separately, we will get:

$(\log_2 4)^2 = 2^2 = 4$; $(\log_4 8)^3 = \left(\frac{1}{2} \times 3\right)^3 = \frac{27}{8}$;

$$(\log_8 16)^4 = \left(\frac{1}{3} \times \log_2 16\right)^4 = \frac{4 \times 4 \times 4 \times 4}{3 \times 3 \times 3 \times 3}.$$

The given expression transforms to:

$$\frac{2 \times 4 \times 8 \times 16}{\frac{4 \times 27 \times 256}{8 \times 81}} = \frac{8 \times 81}{27} = 24$$

56. We are asked to find the area of this circle

We know that the area of a triangle with sides a, b and c, inscribed in a circle of radius R is given by Area = abc/4R where a, b, c are the lengths of the sides of the triangle and R is the radius of the circle.

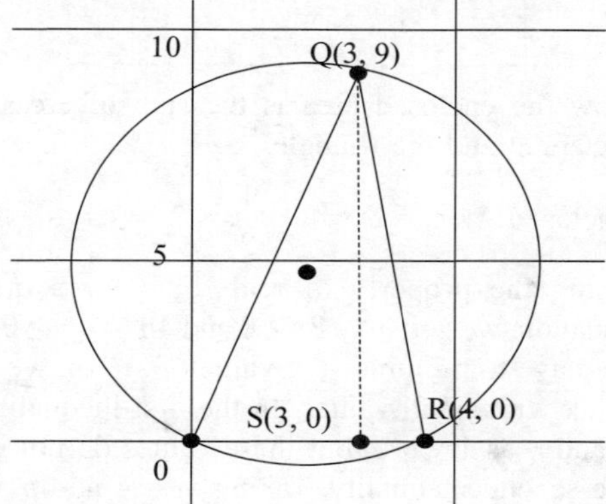

With the help of the co-ordinates of the triangle it is easy to find the height of the triangle, which is QS = 9 units.

Hence, the area of the triangle

$$A = \frac{1}{2} \times \text{base} \times \text{height}$$

$$= \frac{1}{2} \times \text{PR} \times \text{QS}$$

$$= \frac{1}{2} \times 4 \times 9 = 18 \text{ sq. units.}$$

The sides of the triangle can be calculated using the distance formula as:

a = PR = 4 units

$$b = \text{QR} = \sqrt{(4-3)^2 + (9-0)^2} = \sqrt{82}$$

$$c = \text{PQ} = \sqrt{(3-0)^2 + (9-0)^2} = \sqrt{90}$$

Thus, we have: $18 = \frac{4\sqrt{82} \times \sqrt{90}}{4R}$

$$\Rightarrow \quad R = \frac{\sqrt{205}}{3}$$

Area of the circle $= \pi \times R^2 = 205\frac{\pi}{9}$.

Hence, Option (b) is correct.

57. We can visualise the following figure for the given enclosed area.

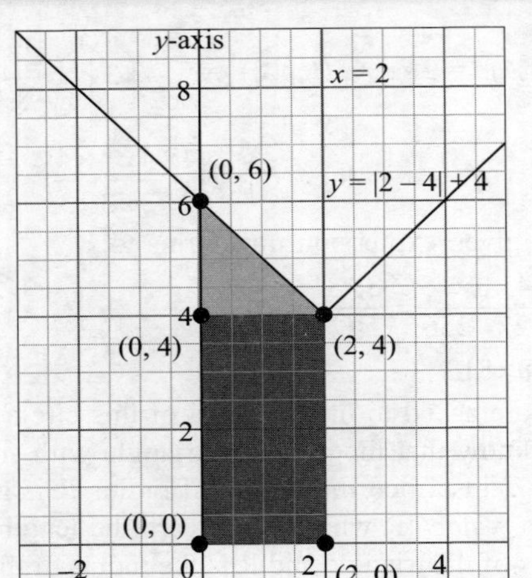

Now the enclosed area is the sum of areas of the rectangle and the triangle.

Enclosed Area = $2 \times 4 + \frac{1}{2} \times 2 \times 2 = 8 + 2 = 10$.

58. Using the property of real roots for a quadratic equation, we get: $m^2 - 8n \geq 0$ and $4n^2 - 4m \geq 0$. Since, we have to minimise the value of $m + n$, we start to think with small values. In the first inequality, m as 3 and n as 1 work, but these values do not work in the second inequality. Taking $m = 4$ and $n = 2$, we see that it works for both the inequalities. Hence, the minimum value of $m + n = 6$. Option (c) is correct.

59. We are told that $f(x + y) = f(x) \times f(y)$
$f(x) = f(x + 0) = f(x) \times f(0)$
$f(x) = f(x) \times f(0)$
Assuming that $f(x)$ is non-zero;
This implies: $f(0) = 1$
$f(5) = 4$ (Given)
$f(10) = f(5 + 5) = f(5) \times f(5) = 4 \times 4 = 16$
$f(10) = 16$
We know that $f(0) = 1$
$f(0) = f(10 - 10) = f(10 + (-10))$
$= f(10) \times f(-10) = 1$
$16 \times f(-10) = 1$
$f(-10) = \frac{1}{16} = 0.0625$
$f(10) - f(-10) = 16 - 0.0625 = 15.9375$.
Option (c) is correct.

60. Since all the options have a component of A + B, we should first look at what A + B, yields us.

$$A + B = \log_a 30 - \log_a \left(\frac{5}{3}\right)$$

$= \log_a 18 = 2 \log_a 3 + \log_a 2$.

We are told that $\log_2 a = \frac{1}{3}$

$\log_2 a = \frac{1}{3}$ implies $\log_a 2 = 3$

Hence, $A + B = 2 \log_a 3 + 3$.
Hence, $A + B - 3 = 2 \log_a 3$
Going for option (a) we see that:

$$\frac{2}{A + B - 3} = \frac{2}{2\log_a 3} = \frac{1}{\log_a 3} = \log_3 a.$$

Hence, option (a) is correct.

61. The roots of the numerator are –5 and +3, hence, the numerator would be positive for $x < -5$ and $x > 3$. The roots of the quadratic in the denominator are 9 and –2. Thus, the denominator would be positive for $x < -2$ and $x > 9$. The expression for $f(x)$ would be negative, if the numerator is positive and the denominator is negative or vice-versa. These occur between –5 to –2 (numerator negative, denominator positive) & between 3 to 9 (numerator positive and denominator negative). Hence, option (a) is correct.

62. We can work out that $X_2 = 3$; $X_3 = 2$; $X_4 = 1$; $X_5 = 1$; $X_6 = 2$. Thus, in this chain function, the values of X_5 and X_6 replicate the values of X_0 and X_1 respectively. Thus $X_1 = X_6 = X_{11} = \ldots = X_{5n+1} = X_{2021} = 2$. Option (a) is correct.

63. If we remove the modulus, we can form two quadratic equations:
If $x^2 - 4x - 13 > 0$, we get: $x^2 - 4x - 13 = r$
If $x^2 - 4x - 13 < 0$, we get: $-x^2 + 4x + 13 = r$.
The next thing is to try to fit in values of r from the options to check whether the two quadratics give exactly 3 distinct real roots. Before you start that process, you should be able to work out the logic that, this would occur in two cases – one if one of the two equations becomes a perfect square; second if each equation gives 2 distinct roots by itself, but one of the two roots for each of the two equations is the same.
With this logic, if we try to use options for the value of 'r'. we get that at $r = 17$, the second equation becomes: $-x^2 + 4x - 4 = 0$ or $x^2 - 4x + 4 = 0$, giving us coincident roots – since the equation is essentially $(x - 2)^2$. In this situation, we would still need to confirm that the first equation does give us real distinct roots. With $r = 17$, the first equation becomes: $x^2 - 4x - 30 = 0$, and it's roots are real and distinct since D > 0. Thus, we can conclude that this answer is correct.

64. $|n - 60| < |n - 100|$ for $n = 60$ to 79 (a total of 20 numbers). However, at $n = 60$, $|n - 100| < |n - 20|$ is not satisfied, as they are equal. From, $n = 61$ to 79, both the inequalities are matched. Hence, there are 19 such integers that satisfy the inequality.

65. The expression can be written as:

$$5 - \frac{\log(1+x)}{2} + 2\log(1-x) = \log 1 - \frac{1}{2}\log(1-x)(1+x)$$

$\Rightarrow 5-\frac{\log(1+x)}{2}+2\log(1-x)=0-\frac{1}{2}[\log(1-x)+\log(1+x)]$

$\Rightarrow$ 5= –2.5 log(1 – x) → log (1 – x) = –2. Since, the base is 10, we get 10^{-2} = 1 – x. So, x = 1 – 0.01 = 0.99. The value of 100x = 99.

66. The value of $X_1 = 1^2 + 2 = 3$. The value of $X_2 = 3 - (2^2 + 4) = -5$; The value of $X_3 = 3^2 + 6 - 3 - 5 = 7$. Similarly, the values of X_4, X_5, X_6 would be –9, 11, –13 respectively. The value of X_{49} = 99 and the value of X_{50} = –101. Thus, the value of X_{49} + X_{50} = –2. Option (c) is correct.

67. We can verify the values at which the equation is satisfied. At x = 6.00001, the value of the expression is not equal to 20 and hence, we can reject option (d). Also, when the value of 'x' exceeds 13.333, the LHS of the expression crosses 20 again. Thus, options (b) and (c) can both be rejected. Option (a) is the only option that stands and is hence the correct answer.

68. If we add the two equations, we get: $(x - y)^2$ + $(y - x)$ = 56. Let $x - y$ = B, the equation can be visualized as $B^2 - B$ = 56. B = 8 (since it is given to us that $x > y$, B can only take the positive square root of 64). Hence, option (c) is correct.

69. For a quadratic equation, $ax^2 - bx + c = 0$, if a, b, c are rational and if one of the roots is irrational, the other will be it's conjugate. Thus, the roots of the equation are $2+\sqrt{3}$ & $2-\sqrt{3}$. Sum of roots = $\frac{b}{a}$ = 4 & Product of roots = $\frac{c}{a}=(2+\sqrt{3})(2-\sqrt{3})$ = 1.

Thus, we get, $b = 4a$ and $c = a$. We are also given that: $b = c^3 \rightarrow 4a = a^3$

$4 = a^2$. Hence, $|a|$= 2. Option (b) is correct.

70. Since the three integers are in an Arithmetic Progression, y being the middle term would be the average of the three numbers. We also realise that since $y - x > 2$, the Arithmetic Progression is an increasing one. Thus from $xyz = 5(x + y + z)$, we get: $xyz = 5 \times 3y \rightarrow xz = 15$. If we take x = 1, z = 15, the expression gets satisfied for 3 positive integers. Hence, $z - x$ = 14.

71. $\text{Log}_2[3 + \log_3\{4 + \log_4\{x - 1)\}]$ = 2. Hence, 3 + $\log_3\{4 + \log_4\{x - 1)\}$ = 4.
Hence, $\log_3\{4 + \log_4\{x - 1)\}$ = 1. Thus, $\log_4\{x - 1)$ = –1. Using the definition of logs, we have: $x - 1 = 4^{-1} \rightarrow x$ = 1.25. Hence, the value of 4x = 5.

72. You can try to solve this question through the options, as solving algebraically is likely to take a lot of writing effort and time. If we try to see the value of the expression at various values of x, we can see that at x = 0, $f(x) = \frac{4}{9}$, at x = 1, $f(x) = \frac{7}{15}$, *at x* = 2, $f(x) = \frac{12}{25}$. As you continue to increase the value of x, the value of $f(x)$ never crosses $\frac{1}{2}$. This can be confirmed by checking at x = 100, $f(x) = \frac{10204}{20409}$, which is very close to $\frac{1}{2}$ but not quite there. Hence, we can establish that the upper limit is $\frac{1}{2}$ (and it is not included). Options (b) and (d) get rejected. On the negative side, as you reduce x to –1, you discover the value of $\frac{3}{7}$ and since you are only between options (a) and (c), the only thing you needed to identify is whether $\frac{3}{7}$ was included in the range or not. x = –1, confirms that $\frac{3}{7}$ is indeed to be included in the range for $f(x)$. Hence, option (c) is the correct answer.

73. $|m + n|$ would be less than 5 for the following pair of values:
If one of them is zero:(0, 0); (0, 1); (1, 0); (0, 2); (2, 0); (0, 3); (3,0); (0,4); (4,0). Also, at (0, –1); (–1, 0); (0, –2); (–2, 0); (0, –3); (–3, 0); (0, –4); (–4, 0).
If one of them is 1 or –1 (but none is zero): (1, 2); (1, 3); (1, –1);(1, –2); (1, –3); (1, –4); (1, –5); (–1, 2); (–1, 3); (–1, 4); (–1, 5) and vice versa.
If one of them is 2 or –2, but none of them is either 1 or –1 or 0 (since those cases have already been considered): (2, 2); (2, –3); (2, –4); (2, –5); (2, –6) or (–2, –2); (–2, 3); (–2, 4); (–2, 5); (–2, 6).
Out of these cases, in the following cases, |1 + mn| < |m + n| only in the cases where either m or n is zero. The cases are: (0, 2); (2, 0); (0, 3); (3, 0); (0, 4); (4, 0). Also, at (0, –2); (–2, 0); (0, –3); (–3, 0); (0, –4); (–4, 0).
A total of 12 cases.

74. $$\frac{\frac{1}{\log 15}+\frac{1}{\log 32}}{\frac{1}{\log 15\times\log 32}}$$
(**Note:** all logs to the base a) → $\log_a 480$ = 4. Thus, a^4 = 480. 'a' has to be a number greater than 4 and less than 5, since 4^4 = 256 & 5^4 = 625. Option (b) is correct.

75. $f(g(x) - 3x = f(x + 3) - 3x = (x + 3)^2 - 7(x + 3) - 3x = x^2 - 4x - 12$.
The minimum value of this expression would occur at $2x - 4 = 0 \rightarrow x = 2$.
The minimum value would be got by inserting the value of x as 2 in the expression $x^2 - 4x - 12 \rightarrow 2^2 - 4 \times 2 - 12 = -16$. Option (a) is correct.

76. **Case 1:** If $x \geq 0$ & $y \geq 0$, the expressions would become:
3x + 3y = 7 & 2x + 3y = 1. On solving we get x = 6 and $y = -\frac{11}{3}$, which is a contradiction that x and

y are both greater than or equal to zero. Hence, we reject this case.

Case 2: If $x > 0$ & $y < 0$, the expressions would become:

$3x - y = 7$ & $2x + 3y = 1$. On solving we get $x = 2$ and $y = -1$, which satisfies the initial assumptions about x and y. In this case $x + 2y = 2 - 2 = 0$.

We can neglect solving for **Case 3:** $x < 0, y \geq 0$ & **Case 4:** $x < 0$ & $y < 0$, because the options in the question are close-ended in nature– viz: they suggest that this question has a single answer. That means, the answer cannot be different for other cases, and if it does turn out to be different if we consider a new case, then the question itself would be wrong. Since you would be solving this question inside the exam, getting a value of 0 at this point allows you to take the decision of not checking the last two cases and marking option (a) as the correct answer.

77. The value of $|x + 1| + |x - 1|$ is minimized at when we take the value of x as any number between -1 and $+1$. Since, x is not necessarily an integer in this question, it means that the value of x can be any integer/decimal value between -1 and $+1$. There are infinite values possible for x. Hence, the largest value of a possible is $+1$. Option (d) is correct.

78. Since $b^2 < 4ac$, the quadratic expression is either entirely positive (if a is positive) or entirely negative (if a is negative). Hence, S can be the empty set if a is positive and it can be the set of all integers if a is negative. Hence, option (a) is correct.

79. From the options, when $a = 50$, the range of x is between 50 to 100. The given expression becomes $\{|x - 50| + |x - 100|\} + |x - 100|$. For the values of x between 50 and 100, we can see that the value of $\{|x - 50| + |x - 100|\}$ would be a constant at 50. The value of the other $|x - 100|$, would be a maximum of 50, when x is at 50. At $x > 50$, the value of $|x - 100| < 50$. Hence, 100 is the maximum value of the expression. We do not need to check any of the other options. Option (a) is hence the correct answer.

80. The expression $\left[\frac{1}{5}+\frac{N}{25}\right]$ has a value of 0 from $1 \leq n \leq 19$. From $n = 20, 21, 22$ etc, the value of the expression is always 1, till $N = 44$. Since, there are 25 numbers from 20 to 44, the value of the LHS equals the RHS when $N = 44$.

81. The sum of the roots is $-\frac{c}{5}$. Since, two roots are given as r and $-r$, their sum being 0, the third root should be $-\frac{c}{5}$. Also, $r\times(-r)+r\times-\frac{c}{5}+-r\times-\frac{c}{5}$ $=-r^2=-2\rightarrow r=\sqrt{2}$

Thus, from the product of the roots $-\frac{9}{5}=r\times-r\times-\frac{c}{5}=\frac{2c}{5}\rightarrow c=-\frac{9}{2}$. Option (a) is correct.

82. $f(g(5)) = f(25)$. To evaluate $f(25)$ we can think as follows.
Since, $f(x^2 - x) = 5$, if we take $x = 6$, we get $f(30) = 5$. Then from $f(x) + f(x - 1) = 1$, we get $f(29) = -4$, $f(28) = 5$; $f(27) = -4$; $f(26) = 5$; $f(25) = -4$. Thus, not only do we get a value of $f(25)$ as -4, we also see that in general f(even number) = 5 and f(odd number) = -4.
Evaluating: $f(g(5)) + g(f(5)) = f(25) + g(-4) = -4 + 16 = 12$.

83. For a ratio to be negative the possible conditions are: $\frac{+}{-}$ or $\frac{-}{+}$. We can see that 4-$\log_2 n \geq 0$, for $n \leq 16$. Hence, it becomes negative for $n > 16$.
Also, 3-$\log_4 n \geq 0$, for $n \leq 64$. Hence, it becomes negative for $n > 64$. For values on $17 \leq n \leq 63$, gives us 47 possible values of n.

84. $f(x) \geq 0$, where $f(x)$ is a quadratic polynomial, means that the roots of $f(x) = 0$ are equal. Also, since $f(2) = 0$ (given), the polynomial can be expressed as $f(x) = a \times (x - 2)^2 = a \times [x^2 - 4x + 4]$.
$f(4) = 6 \rightarrow a \times [4^2 - 4 \times 4 + 4] = 6 \rightarrow a = 1.5$.
Hence, $f(-2) = 1.5 \times [-4]^2 = 1.5 \times 16 = 24$. Hence, option (b) is correct.

85. There are three possibilities for A^B to equal 1. These are: 1^{anything}; $(-1)^{\text{Even power}}$; 0^{anything}.
Comparing the given expression $(x^2-10)^{x^2-3x-10}$ with these structures:
First structure would give us $x^2-10=1\rightarrow x^2=11$. There are no integral solutions for this structure
The Second structure would be at $x^2-10=-1\rightarrow x^2=9\rightarrow x=\pm3$. At $x = 3$, $x^2-3x-10=-10$, hence, $x = 3$ is a possible value of x. Also, at $x = -3$, $x^2-3x-10=8$, hence $x = -3$ is also a possible value of x. Thus, for the second structure there are two possible integral solutions for x.
The third structure would be at $x^2-3x-10=0\rightarrow$ $x=5,-2$. Thus, for the third structure there are two possible integral solutions for x.
Thus the correct answer is $2 + 2 = 4$.

86. From the first quadratic and it's condition of no real roots, we have $k^2 - 40 < 0$ or $k^2 < 40$. For integral k, the value of k can be $-6 \leq k \leq 6$, which gives us 13 possible values for k. From the second quadratic equation, $(k - 5)^2 - 4 > 0$, we can see that the value of k cannot be 6, 5, 4, or 3. Thus, the total number of possible values of k are $13 - 4 = 9$. Option (d) is correct.

87. If we assume $\frac{x}{y}=k$ the given expression becomes $16k+\frac{49}{k}=c \rightarrow 16k^2-ck+49=0$. For real x and y, k will also be real. Thus, $c^2-4\times16\times49>0 \rightarrow c^2-3136>0$. From the given options, c cannot take a value of –50. Option (d) is correct.

88. The given expression can be reframed as: $\frac{(x-3)^2}{(3-x)}+\frac{1}{(3-x)}=\frac{(3-x)}{1}+\frac{1}{(3-x)}$. The value of (3 – x) is positive since $x < 3$ (given).
If we assume (3 – x) as y, the expression becomes $y+\frac{1}{y}$, whose minimum value is 2 (if y is positive, which it is in this case). Option (d) is correct.

89. The first equation would have roots as: $3+2\sqrt{2}$ *and* $3-2\sqrt{2}$. *Hence,* $-\frac{b}{a}=6 \rightarrow b=-6a$. Also, $\frac{c}{a}=(3+2\sqrt{2})\times(3-2\sqrt{2})=1 \rightarrow c=a$. Thus, the first equation is $ax^2-6ax+a=0$
The second equation would have the roots as: $4+2\sqrt{3}$ *and* $4-2\sqrt{3}$. *Hence,* $-\frac{m}{a}=8 \rightarrow m=-8a$.
Also,
$\frac{n}{a}=(4+2\sqrt{3})\times(4-2\sqrt{3})=4 \rightarrow n=4a$. Thus, the second equation is $ay^2-8ay+4a=0$

$$\frac{b}{m}+\frac{c-2b}{n}=\frac{-\frac{b}{a}}{-\frac{m}{a}}+\frac{a+12a}{4a}=\frac{6}{8}+\frac{13}{4}=4.$$

90. $f(x)=2x-r$ when $x \geq r$ also means that when $x=r$, $f(x)=2r-r=r$. For $x<r$, $f(x)=r$ (given). Hence, if $x \leq r$, $f(x)=r$ and $f(f(x))=f(r)=r$. Thus, the equation is satisfied when $x \leq r$. Hence, option (a) is correct.

BLOCK STARTER

Scan this QR code to access a video on this block's chapters, the time needed to cover them, and their weightage in the examination.

BLOCK V

COUNTING

BACK TO SCHOOL...

In my experience, students can be divided into two broad categories on the basis of their ability in solving chapters of this block.

Category 1: Students who are comfortable in solving questions of this block, since they understand the underlying concepts well.

Category 2: Students who are not able to tackle questions of this block, since they are not conversant with the counting tools and methods used in this block.

If you belong to the second category, the main thing you would need to do is to familiarise yourself with the counting methods and techniques of Permutations and Combinations (P and C). Once you are through with the same, you would find yourself relatively comfortable with both the concepts, and Probability—the chapters in this block which create the maximum problems for students. Set Theory being a relatively easier chapter, the Back to School section of this block concentrates mostly on P and C, and Probability. However, before we start looking at these counting methods, right at the outset, I would want you to remove any negative experiences you might have had while trying to study (P and C), and Probability. So if you belong to the second category of students, you are advised to read on:

Look at the following table:

Suppose, I was to ask you to count the number of cells in the table above, how would you do it??

$$5 \times 5 = 25!!$$

I guess, all of you realise the fact that the number of cells in this table is given by the product of the number of rows and columns. However, if you ask a five-year old child to count the same, they would be counting the number of cells physically. In fact, when you were five-years old, you would also have required doing a physical count of the number of cells in the table. However, there must have come a point where you must have understood that in all such situations (number of cells in a table, number of students in a class, etc.) the total count is obtained by simply multiplying the number of rows and the number of columns. What I am interested in pointing out to you is that the discovery of this process for this specific counting situation surely made your counting easier!! What used to take you much longer started taking you shorter times. Not only that, in situations where the count was too large (e.g. 100 rows × 48 columns) an infeasible count became extremely easy. So why am I telling you this??

Simply because just as the rows into columns tool for counting had the effect of making your count easier, so also the tools for counting which P and C describe will also have the effect of making counting easier for you in the specific situations of counting that you will encounter. My experience of training the students shows that the only reason they have problems in this block is because it is not been explained properly to them in their +2 classes.

One must try to understand these chapters with the approach that they are not meant to complicate your life but to simplify it; you might end up finding out that there is nothing much to fear in this chapter.

TOOL BOX APPROACH TO P AND C

While studying P and C, your primary objective should be to familiarise yourself with each and every counting situation. You also need to realise that there are a limited number of counting situations which you need to tackle. You can look at this as the process of the creation of what can be described as a counting tool box.

Once this tool box is created, you would be able to understand the basic situations for counting. Then solving tough questions becomes a matter of simplifying the language of the question into the language of the answer—a matter I would come back to later.

Let us now proceed to list out the specific counting situations which you need to get a hold on. You need to know and understand the following twelve situations of counting and the tools that are used in these situations. Please take a note that these tools are explained in detail in various parts of the text on the Permutations and Combinations chapter. You are required to keep these in mind along with the specific situations in which these apply. Look at these as a kind of comprehensive list of situations in which you should know how to count using mathematical tools for your convenience.

Twelve Counting Situations and Their Tools

Tool No. 1: **The ^nC_r tool**—This tool is used for the specific situation of counting the number of ways of selecting r things out of n **distinct** things.

Example: Selecting a team of eleven cricketers out of a team of sixteen distinct players will be $^{16}C_{11}$.

Tool No. 2: The tool for counting the number of selections of r things out of n **identical** things. (Always 1)

Example: The number of ways of selecting three letters out of five A's. Note that in such cases there will only be one way of selecting them.

Tool No. 3: **The 2^n tool**—The tool for selecting any number (including 0) of things from n **distinct** things ($^nC_0 + {}^nC_1 + {}^nC_2 \ldots + {}^nC_n = 2^n$).

Example: The number of ways you can or cannot eat sweets at a party, if there are ten sweets and you have the option of eating one piece of as many sweets as you like or even of not eating any sweet. (Will be given by 2^{10}).

Corollary: **The $2^n - 1$ tool**—Used when zero selections are not allowed. For instance, in the above situation, if you are asked to eat at least one sweet and rejecting all sweets is not an option.

Tool No. 4: **The $n + 1$ tool**—The tool for selecting any number (including 0) of things from n **identical** things. For instance, if you have to select any number of letters from A, A, A, A and A, then you can do it in six ways.

Tool No. 5: **The $^{n+r-1}C_{r-1}$ tool**—The tool for distributing n identical things amongst r people/groups such that any person/group might get any number (including 0). For instance, if you have to distribute seven identical gifts amongst five children in a party then it can be done in $^{(7+5-1)}C_{(5-1)}$ ways, i.e. $^{11}C_4$ ways.

Tool No. 6: **The $^{n-1}C_{r-1}$ tool**—The tool for distributing n identical things amongst r people/groups such that any person/group might get any number (except 0).

Suppose in the above case you have to give at least one gift to each child; it can be done in: $^6C_4$ ways.

Tool No. 7: **The mnp rule tool**—The tool for counting the number of ways of doing three things when each of them has to be done and there are m ways of doing the first thing, n ways of doing the second thing and p ways of doing the last thing. Suppose you have to go from Lucknow to Varanasi to Patna to Ranchi to Jamshedpur and there are five trains from Lucknow to Varanasi and there are four trains from Varanasi to Patna, six from Patna to Ranchi and three from Ranchi to Jamshedpur, then the number of ways of going from Lucknow to Jamshedpur through Varanasi, Patna and Ranchi is $5 \times 4 \times 6 \times 3 = 360$.

Note that this tool is extremely crucial and is used to form numbers and words.

For example, how many four-digit numbers can you form using the digits 0, 1, 2, 3, 4, 5 and 6 only without repeating any digits? In this situation, the work outline is to choose a digit for the first place (=6, any one out of 1, 2, 3, 4, 5 and 6 as zero cannot be used there), then choosing a digit for the second place (=6, select any one out of 5 remaining digits plus 0), then a digit for the third place (five ways) and a digit for the fourth place (four ways).

Tool No. 8: **The $r!$ tool for arrangement**—This tool is used for counting the number of ways in which you can arrange r distinct things in r places. Notice that this can be derived out of the mnp rule tool.

Tool No. 9: **The AND rule tool**—Whenever you describe the counting situation and connect two different parts of the count by using the conjunction **'AND'**, you will always replace the **'AND'** with a multiplication sign between the two parts of the count. This is also used for solving probability questions. For instance, suppose you have to choose a vowel **'AND'**, a consonant from the letters of the word PERMIT, you can do it in $^4C_1 \times {}^2C_1$ ways.

Tool No. 10: **The OR rule tool**—Whenever you describe the counting situation and connect two different parts of the count by using the conjunction **'OR'**, you will always replace the **'OR'** with an addition sign between the two parts of the count. This is also used for solving Probability questions. For instance, suppose you have to select either two consonants or a vowel from the letters of the word PERMIT, you can do it in $^4C_2 + {}^2C_1$ ways.

Tool No. 11: **The Circular Permutation Tool [(n – 1)! Tool]**—This gives the number of ways in which n distinct things can be placed around a circle. The need to reduce the value of the factorial by 1 is due to the fact that in a circle, there is no defined starting point.

Tool No. 12: **The Circular Permutation Tool when there is no distinction between clockwise and anti-clockwise arrangements [(n – 1)!/2 tool]**—This gives the number of ways in which n distinct things can be placed around a circle when there is no distinction between clockwise and anti-clockwise arrangements. In such a case the number of circular permutations is just divided by 2.

Two More Issues

(1) What about the ^nP_r tool? The ^nP_r tool is used to arrange r things amongst n. However, my experience shows that the introduction of this tool just adds to the confusion for most students. A little bit of smart thinking gets rid of all the problems that the ^nP_r tool creates in your mind. For this let us consider the difference between the $^n\boldsymbol{P}_r$ and the $^n\boldsymbol{C}_r$ tools.

$$^n\boldsymbol{C}_r = n!/[r! \times (n-r)!] \text{ while } {}^n\boldsymbol{P}_r = n!/[(n-r)!]$$

A closer look would reveal that the relationship between the ^nP_r and the ^nC_r tools can be summarised as:

$$^n\boldsymbol{P}_r = {}^n\boldsymbol{C}_r \times r!$$

Read this as: If you have to arrange r things amongst n distinct things, then simply select r things amongst n things and use the r! tool for the arrangement of the selected r items amongst themselves. This will result in the same answer as the $^n\boldsymbol{P}_r$ tool.

In fact, for all questions involving arrangements, always solve the question in two parts—first finish the selection within the question and then arrange the selected items amongst themselves. This will remove a lot of confusions in questions of this chapter.

(2) Treat both permutations and combinations and probability as English language chapters rather than Maths chapters: One of the key discoveries in getting stronger at this block is that after knowing the basic twelve counting situations and their tools (as explained above), you need to stop treating the questions in this chapter as questions in Mathematics and rather treat them as questions in English. Thus, while solving a question in these chapters, your main concentration and effort should be on converting the question language into the answer language.

What do I mean by this?

Consider this:

Question Language: What is the number of ways of forming four-letter words from five vowels and six consonants, such that the word contains one vowel and three consonants?

To solve this question, first create the answer language in your mind.

Answer Language: Select one vowel out of five **AND** select three consonants out of six **AND** arrange the four selected letters amongst themselves.

Once you have this language, the remaining part of the answer is just a matter of using the correct tools. Thus, the answer is $^5C_1 \times {}^6C_3 \times 4!$

As you can see, the main issue in getting the solution to this question was working out the language by connecting the various parts of the solution using the conjunction AND (In this case, the conjunction OR was not required.). Once, you had the language all you had to do was use the correct tools to count.

The most difficult of questions are solved this way. This is why, I advise you to treat this chapter as a language chapter and not as a chapter in Mathematics!!

CHAPTER

18 Permutations and Combinations

Chapter Launchpad

Scan this QR code to access a video on 'Introduction to Permutations and Combinations' and this chapter's importance for CAT

STANDARD THEORY

Factorial Notation! Or $\lfloor$

$$\lfloor n = n(n-1)(n-2)\ldots 3.2.1$$

$$n! = n(n-1)(n-2)\ldots 3.2.1$$

= Product of n consecutive integers starting from 1.

1. $0! = 1$
2. Factorials of only natural numbers are defined.
3. $n!$ is defined only for $n \geq 0$
   $n!$ is not defined for $n < 0$
4. ${}^nC_r = 1$ when $n = r$.
5. Combinations (represented by ${}^nC_r$) can be defined as the number of ways in which r things at a time can be **SELECTED** from amongst n things available for selection.
   The key word here is **SELECTION**. Please understand here that the order in which the r things are selected has no importance in the counting of combinations.
   ${}^nC_r$ = Number of combinations (selections) of n things taken r at a time
   ${}^nC_r = n!/[r!\,(n-r)!]$; where $n \geq r$ (n is greater than or equal to r)

Some typical situations where selection/combination is used:

(a) Selection of people for a team, a party, a job, an office, etc. (e.g. Selection of a cricket team of eleven from sixteen members)
(b) Selection of a set of objects (like letters, hats, points pants, shirts, etc) from amongst another set available for selection

In other words, any selection in which the order of selection holds no importance is counted by using combinations.

6. Permutations (represented by ${}^nP_r$) can be defined as the number of ways in which r things at a time can be **SELECTED** and **ARRANGED** at a time from amongst n things.
   The key word here is **ARRANGEMENT**. Hence, please understand here that the order in which the r things are arranged has critical importance in the counting of permutations.
   In other words, permutations can also be referred to as an **ORDERED SELECTION**.
   ${}^nP_r$ = number of permutations (arrangements) of n things taken r at a time.
   ${}^nP_r = n!/(n-r)!$; $n \geq r$

Some typical situations where **ordered selection/permutations** are used:

(a) Making words and numbers from a set of available letters and digits respectively
(b) Filling posts with people
(c) Selection of batting order of a cricket team of eleven from sixteen members
(d) Putting distinct objects/people in distinct places, (e.g. making people sit, putting letters in envelopes, finishing order in horse race, etc.)

The exact difference between selection and arrangement can be seen through the illustration below.

Selection

Suppose we have three men A, B and C, out of which two have to be selected for two posts.

This can be done in the following ways: AB, AC or BC (these three represent the basic selections of two people out of three which are possible). Physically they can be counted as three distinct selections. This value can also be obtained by using $3C_2$.

Note here that we are counting AB and BA as one single selection. Therefore, AC and CA, and BC and CB, also are considered to be the same instances of selection since the order of selection is not important.

Arrangement

Suppose we have three men A, B and C, out of which two men have to be selected for the post of captain and vice captain of a team.

In this case, we have to take AB and BA as two different instances since the order of the arrangement makes a difference in who is the captain and who is the vice-captain.

Similarly, we have BC, and CB and AC and CA as four more instances. Thus, in all, there could be six arrangements of two things out of three.

This is given by ${}^3P_2 = 6$.

7. **Relationship between Permutation and Combination:**
   When we look at the formulae for Permutations and Combinations and compare the two we see that,
   $${}^nP_r = r! \times {}^nC_r$$
   $$= {}^nC_r \times {}^rP_r$$
   In words, this can be said as:
   The permutation or arrangement of r things out of n is nothing but the selection of r things out of n

followed by the arrangement of the r selected things amongst themselves.

8. MNP **Rule:** If there are three things to do and there are M ways of doing the first thing, N ways of doing the second thing and P ways of doing the third thing then there will be $M \times N \times P$ ways of doing all the three things together.The works are mutually inclusive.
   This is used for situations like:
   The numbers 1, 2, 3, 4 and 5 are to be used for forming three-digit numbers without repetition. In how many ways, can this be done?
   Using the MNP rule you can visualise this as: There are three things to do→ the first digit can be selected in five distinct ways, the second can be selected in four ways and the third can be selected in three different ways. Hence, the total numbers of three digit numbers that can be formed are $5 \times 4 \times 3 = 60$.
9. When the pieces of work are mutually exclusive, there are $M + N + P$ ways of doing the complete work.

Important Results

The following results are important as they help in problem solving.

1. Number of permutations (or arrangements) of n different things taken all at a time = $n!$
2. Number of permutations of n things out of which P_1 are alike and are of one type, P_2 are alike and are of a second type and P_3 are alike and are of a third type and the rest are all different = $n! / P_1! P_2! P_3!$
   Illustration: The number of words formed with the letters of the word Allahabad.

Solution: Total number of letters = 9 of which A occurs four times, L occurs twice and the rest are all different.
   Total number of words formed = 9! / (4! 2! 1!)

3. Number of permutations of n different things taken r times when repetition is allowed = $n \times n \times n \times \ldots$ (r times) = n^r.
   Illustration: In how many ways can four rings be worn in the index, ring finger and middle finger if there is no restriction of the number of rings to be worn on any finger?

Solution: Each of the four rings could be worn in three ways either on the index, ring or middle finger.
   So, four rings could be worn in $3 \times 3 \times 3 \times 3 = 3^4$ ways.

4. Number of selections of r things out of n identical things = 1
   Illustration: In how many ways, five marbles can be chosen out of hundred identical marbles?

Solution: Since, all the hundred marbles are identical, Hence, number of ways to select five marbles = 1

5. Total number of selections of zero or more things out of k identical things = $k + 1$.
   This includes the case when zero articles are selected.
6. Total number of selections of zero or more things out of n different things =
   $^nC_o + {^nC_1} + {^nC_2} + \ldots + {^nC_n} = 2^n$
   Corollary: The number of selections of 1 or more things out of n different things = $^nC_1 + {^nC_2} + \ldots + {^nC_n} = 2^n - 1$
7. Number of ways of distributing n identical things among r persons when each person may get any number of things = $^{n+r-1}C_{r-1}$
   Imagine a situation where 27 marbles have to be distributed amongst four people such that each one of them can get any number of marbles (including zero marbles). Then for this situation we have, n = 27(number of identical objects), r = 4 (number of people) and the answer of the number of ways by which this can be achieved is given by: $^{n+r-1}C_{r-1} = {^{30}C_3}$.
8. Corollary: Number of ways of dividing n non-distinct things to r distinct groups are:
   $^{n-1}C_{r-1}$ → For non-empty groups only
   Also, the number of ways in which n distinct things can be distributed to r different persons:
   $= r^n$
9. Number of ways of dividing $m + n$ different things in two groups containing m and n things respectively = $^{m+n}C_n \times {^mC_m}$ =
   $= (m + n)! / m!\ n!$
10. Number of ways of dividing $2n$ different things in two groups containing n things = $2n! / n!\ n!\ 2!$
11. $^nC_r + {^nC_{r-1}} = {^{n+1}C_r}$
12. $^nC_x = {^nC_y} \Rightarrow x = y$ or $x + y = n$
13. $^nC_r = {^nC_{n-r}}$
14. $r \cdot {^nC_r} = n \cdot {^{n-1}C_{r-1}}$
15. $^nC_r / (r + 1) = {^{n+1}C_{r+1}} / (n + 1)$
16. For ^nC_r to be greatest,
    (a) if n is even, $r = n/2$
    (b) if n is odd, $r = (n + 1)/2$ or $(n - 1)/2$
17. Number of selections of r things out of n different things
    (a) When k particular things are always included $= {^{n-k}C_{r-k}}$
    (b) When k particular things are excluded = $^{n-k}C_r$
    (c) When all the k particular things are not together in any selection
    $= {^nC_r} - {^{n-k}C_{r-k}}$

Number of ways of doing a work with given restriction = total Number of ways of doing it — Number of ways of doing the same work with opposite restriction.

18. The total number of ways in which 0 to n things can be selected out of n things such that p are of one type, q are of another type and the balance r of different types, is given by: $(p + 1)(q + 1)(2^r - 1)$.
19. Total number of ways of taking some or all out of $p + q + r$ things such that p are of one type and q are of another type and r of a third type $= (p + 1)(q + 1)(r + 1) - 1$ [Only non-empty sets]
20. $\frac{^nC_r}{^nC_{r-1}} = \frac{n-r+1}{r}$
21. Number of selections of k consecutive things out of n things in a row $= n - k + 1$

Circular Permutations

Consider two situations:

There are three A, B and C. In the first case, they are arranged linearly and in the other, around a circular table –

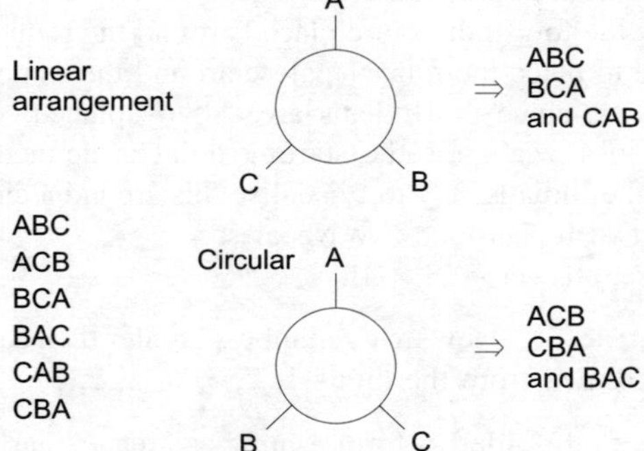

For the linear arrangement, each arrangement is a totally new way. For circular arrangements, three linear arrangements are represented by one and the same circular arrangement.

So, for six linear arrangements, there correspond only two circular arrangements. This happens because there is no concept of a starting point on a circular arrangement. (i.e., the starting point is not defined.)

Generalising the whole process, for $n!$, there corresponds to be $(1/n)\ n!$ ways.

Important Results

1. Number of ways of arranging n people on a circular track (circular arrangement) $= (n - 1)!$
2. When clockwise and anti-clockwise observations are not different then number of circular arrangements of n different things $= (n - 1)!\ /2$
   For example, the case of a necklace with different beads, the same arrangement when looked at from the opposite side becomes anti-clockwise.
3. Number of selections of k consecutive things out of n things in a circle
   $= n$ when $k < n$
   $= 1$ when $k = n$

Some More Results

1. Number of terms in $(a_1 + a_2 + \ldots + a_n)^m$ is $^{m+n-1}C_{n-1}$
   Illustration: Find the number of terms in $(a + b + c)^2$.
   Solution: n = 3, m = 2
   $^{m+n-1}C_{n-1} = {}^4C_2 = 6$
   Corollary: Number of terms in
   $(1 + x + x^2 + \ldots x^n)^m$ is $mn + 1$
2. Number of zeroes ending the number represented by $n! = [n/5] + [n/5^2] + [n/5^3] + \ldots [n/5^x]$
   [] shows greatest integer function where $5^x \le n$
   Illustration: Find the number of zeroes at the end of 1000!?
   Solution: $[1000/5] + [1000/5^2] + [1000/5^3] + [1000/5^4]$
   $200 + 40 + 8 + 1 = 249$
   Corollary: Exponent of 3 in $n! = [n/3] + [n/3^2] + [n/3^3] + \ldots [n/3^x]$ where 3^x is less than or equal to n and $[x]$ represents the greatest integer less than or equal to x.
   Illustration: Find how many exponents of three will be there in 24!.
   Solution: $[24/3] + [24/3^2] = 8 + 2 = 10$
3. Number of squares in a square of $n \times n$ side $= 1^2 + 2^2 + 3^2 + 4^2 + \ldots.\ n^2$
   Number of rectangles in a square of $n \times n$ side $= 1^3 + 2^3 + 3^3 + 4^3 + \ldots.\ n^3$ (This includes the number of squares.)
   Thus, the number of squares and rectangles in the following figure are given by:

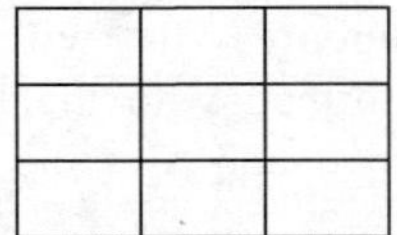

Number of squares $= 1^2 + 2^2 + 3^2 = 14 = \in n^2$

Number of rectangles $= 1^3 + 2^3 + 3^3 = 36\ (\in n)^2 = \in n^3$ for the rectangle.

A rectangle having m rows and n columns:

The number of squares is given by: $m.n + (m - 1)(n - 1) + (m - 2)(n - 2) + \ldots..$ until any of $(m - x)$ or $(n - x)$ comes to 1.

The number of rectangles is given by: $(1 + 2 + \ldots\ldots + m)(1 + 2 + \ldots\ldots + n)$

Going Beyond the Book

Scan this QR code to access a conceptual video on Counting Squares and Rectangles

WORKED-OUT PROBLEMS

In the following examples, the solution is given upto the point of writing down the formula that will apply for the particular question. The student is expected to calculate the values after understanding the solution.

Problem 18.1: In how many ways can the seven letters *M*, *N*, *O*, *P*, *Q*, *R*, *S* be arranged so that *P* and *Q* occupy continuous positions?

Solution: For arranging the seven letters keeping P and Q always together we have to view P and Q as one letter. Let this be denoted by PQ.

Then, we have to arrange the letters *M*, *N*, *O*, <u>*PQ*</u>, *R* and *S* in a linear arrangement. Here, it is like arranging six letters in six places (since two letters are counted as one). This can be done in 6! ways.

However, the solution is not complete at this point of time since in the count of 6! the internal arrangement between *P* and *Q* is neglected. This can be done in 2! ways. Hence, the required answer is $6! \times 2!$.

Task for the student: What would happen if the letters *P*, *Q* and *R* are to be together? (Answer: $5! \times 3!$)

What if *P* and *Q* are never together? (Answer will be given by the formula: Total number of ways – Number of ways they are always together)

Problem 18.2: Of the different words that can be formed from the letters of the words BEGINS, how many begin with *B* and end with *S*?

Solution: B and S are fixed at the start and the end positions. Hence, we have to arrange E, G, I and N amongst themselves. This can be done in 4! ways.

Task for the student: What will be the number of words that can be formed with the letters of the word BEGINS which have *B* and *S* at the extreme positions? (Answer: $4! \times 2!$)

Problem 18.3: In how many ways can the letters of the word VALEDICTORY be arranged, so that all the vowels are adjacent to each other?

Solution: There are four vowels and seven consonants in the word valedictory. If these vowels have to be kept together, we have to consider AEIO as one letter. Then the problem transforms itself into arranging eight letters amongst themselves (8! ways). Besides, we have to look at the internal arrangement of the four vowels amongst themselves. (4! ways)

Hence, answer = $8! \times 4!$.

Problem 18.4: If there are two kinds of hats, red and blue and at least five of each kind, in how many ways can the hats be put in each of five different boxes?

Solution: The significance of at least five hats of each kind is that while putting a hat in each box, we have the option of putting either a red or a blue hat. (If this was not given, there would have been an uncertainty in the number of possibilities of putting a hat in a box.)

Thus, in this question for every task of putting a hat in a box, we have the possibility of either putting a red hat or a blue hat. The solution can then be looked at as: there are five tasks each of which can be done in two ways. Through the MNP rule, we have the total number of ways = 2^5 (Answer).

Problem 18.5: In how many ways can four Indians and four Nepalese people be seated around a round table so that no two Indians are in adjacent positions?

Solution: If we first put four Indians around the round table, we can do this in 3! ways.

Once the four Indians are placed around the round table, we have to place the four Nepalese around the same round table. Now, since the Indians are already placed, we can do this in 4! ways (as the starting point is defined when we put the Indians. Try to visualise this around a circle for placing two Indians and two Nepalese.)

Hence, answer = $3! \times 4!$.

Problem 18.6: How many numbers greater than a million can be formed from the digits 1, 2, 3, 0, 4, 2, 3?

Solution: In order to form a number greater than a million, we should have a seven-digit number. Since we have only seven digits with us, we cannot take 0 in the starting position. View this as seven positions to fill:

_ _ _ _ _ _ _

To solve this question we first assume that the digits are all different. Then the first position can be filled in six ways (0 cannot be taken), the second in six ways (one of the six digits available for the first position was selected. Hence, we have five of those six digits available. Besides, we also have the zero as an additional digit), the third in five ways (six available for the second position – 1 taken for the second position.) and so on. Mathematically, this can be written as:

$$6 \times 6 \times 5 \times 4 \times 3 \times 2 \times 1 = 6 \times 6!$$

This would have been the answer had all the digits been distinct. But in this particular example, we have two 2's and two 3's which are identical to each other. This complication is resolved as follows to get the answer:

$$\frac{6 \times 6}{2! \times 2!}$$

Problem 18.7: In how many ways can eighteen identical white and sixteen identical black balls be arranged in a row so that no two black balls are together?

Solution: When eighteen identical white balls are put in a straight line, there will be nineteen spaces created. Thus, sixteen black balls will have nineteen places to fill in. This will give an answer of: ${}^{19}C_{16}$. (Since, the balls are identical, the arrangement is not important.)

Problem 18.8: A mother with seven children takes three at a time to a cinema. She goes with every group of three that she can form. How many times can she go to the cinema with distinct groups of three children?

Solution: She will be able to do this as many times as she can form a set of three distinct children from amongst the seven children. This essentially means that the answer is the number of selections of three people out of seven that can be done.

Hence, answer = ${}^{7}C_3$.

Problem 18.9: For the above question, how many times will an individual child go to the cinema with her before a group is repeated?

Solution: This can be viewed as: The child for whom we are trying to calculate the number of ways is already selected. Then, we have to select 2 more children from amongst the remaining 6 to complete the group. This can be done in ${}^{6}C_2$ ways.

Problem 18.10: How many different sums can be formed with the following coins:
5 rupee, 1 rupee, 50 paisa, 25 paisa, 10 paisa and 1 paisa?

Solution: A distinct sum will be formed by selecting either 1 or 2, or 3 or 4, or 5 or all 6 coins.

But from the formula we have the answer to this as: $2^6 - 1$.

[Task for the student: How many different sums can be formed with the following coins:

5 rupee, 1 rupee, 50 paisa, 25 paisa, 10 paisa, 3 paisa, 2 paisa and 1 paisa?]

[Hint: You will have to subtract some values for double counted sums.]

Problem 18.11: A train is going from Mumbai to Pune and makes five stops on the way. Three persons enter the train during the journey with three different tickets. How many different sets of tickets may they have had?

Solution: Since the three persons are entering during the journey, they could have entered at the:

1st station (from where they could have bought tickets for the 2nd, 3rd, 4th or 5th stations or for Pune → total of 5 tickets)

2nd station (from where they could have bought tickets for the 3rd, 4th or 5th stations or for Pune → total of 4 tickets)

3rd station (from where they could have bought tickets for the 4th or 5th stations or for Pune → total of 3 tickets)

4th station (from where they could have bought tickets for the 5th station or for Pune → total of 2 tickets)

5th station (from where they could have bought a ticket for Pune → total of 1 ticket)

Thus, we can see that there is a total of 5 + 4 + 3 + 2 + 1 = 15 tickets available out of which three tickets were selected. This can be done in ${}^{15}C_3$ ways (Answer).

Problem 18.12: Find the number of diagonals and triangles that can be formed using the vertices of a decagon.

Solution: A decagon has ten vertices. A line is formed by selecting any two of the ten vertices. This can be done in ${}^{10}C_2$ ways. However, these ${}^{10}C_2$ lines also count the sides of the decagon.

Thus, the number of diagonals in a decagon is given by: ${}^{10}C_2 - 10$ (Answer)

Triangles are formed by selecting any three of the ten vertices of the decagon. This can be done in ${}^{10}C_3$ ways (Answer).

Problem 18.13: Out of eighteen points in a plane, no three are in a straight line except five which are collinear. How many straight lines can be formed?

Solution: If all eighteen points were non-collinear then the answer would have been ${}^{18}C_2$. However, in this case ${}^{18}C_2$ has double counting since the five collinear points are also amongst the eighteen. These would have been counted as ${}^{5}C_2$ whereas they should have been counted as 1. Thus, to remove the double counting and get the correct answer we need to adjust by reducing the count by $({}^{5}C_2 - 1)$.

Hence, answer = ${}^{18}C_2 - ({}^{5}C_2 - 1) = {}^{18}C_2 - {}^{5}C_2 + 1$

Problem 18.14: For the above situation, how many triangles can be formed?

Solution: The triangles will be given by ${}^{18}C_3 - {}^{5}C_3$.

Problem 18.15: A question paper had ten questions. Each question could only be answered as True (T) or False (F). Each candidate answered all the questions. Yet, no two candidates wrote the answers in an identical sequence. How many different sequences of answers are possible?

(a) 20 (b) 40
(c) 512 (d) 1024

Solution: 210 = 1024 unique sequences are possible. Option (d) is correct.

Problem 18.16: When ten persons shake hands with one another, in how many ways is it possible?

(a) 20 (b) 25
(c) 40 (d) 45

Solution: For n people, there are always ${}^{n}C_2$ shake hands. Thus, for ten people shaking hands with each other the number of ways would be ${}^{10}C_2 = 45$.

Problem 18.17: Each person's performance compared with all other persons is to be done to rank them subjectively. How many comparisons are needed in all, if there are eleven persons?

(a) 66 (b) 55
(c) 54 (d) 45

Solution: There would be $^{11}C_2$ combinations of two people taken two at a time for comparison. $^{11}C_2 = 55$.

Problem 18.18: A person X has four notes of Rupee 1, 2, 5 and 10 denomination. The number of different sums of money she can form from them is

(a) 16 (b) 15
(c) 12 (d) 8

Solution: $2^4 - 1 = 15$ sums of money can be formed. Hence, option (b) is correct.

Problem 18.19: A person has four coins each of different denomination. What is the number of different sums of money the person can form (using one or more coins at a time)?

Solution: We cannot determine the answer to this question, since we do not know whether two or more coins can or cannot form the same sum.

Problem 18.20: How many three-digit numbers can be generated from 1, 2, 3, 4, 5, 6, 7, 8, 9, such that the digits are in ascending order?

(a) 80 (b) 81
(c) 83 (d) 84

Solution: Numbers starting with 12 – 7 numbers

Numbers starting with 13 – 6 numbers; 14 – 5, 15 – 4, 16 – 3, 17 – 2, 18 – 1. Thus, total number of numbers starting from 1 is given by the sum of 1 to 7 = 28.

Number of numbers starting from 2- would be given by the sum of 1 to 6 = 21

Number of numbers starting from 3 – sum of 1 to 5 = 15
Number of numbers starting from 4 – sum of 1 to 4 = 10
Number of numbers starting from 5 – sum of 1 to 3 = 6
Number of numbers starting from 6 = 1 + 2 = 3
Number of numbers starting from 7 = 1

Thus, a total of: 28 + 21 + 15 + 10 + 6 + 3 + 1 = 84 such numbers. Hence, option (d) is correct. Of course, a much easier way to think here would be that since we do not need to arrange the digits, this question is just about the selection of digits. So, using 9C3 would give us the answer directly

Problem 18.21: In a carrom board game competition, m boys and n girls ($m > n > 1$) of a school participate in a way in which every student has to play exactly one game with every other student. Out of the total games played, it was found that in 221 games one player was a boy and the other player was a girl.

Consider the following statements:

I. The total number of students that participated in the competition is 30
II. The number of games in which both players were girls is 78

Which of the statements given above is/are correct?

(a) I only (b) II only
(c) Both I and II (d) Neither I nor II.

Solution: The given condition can get achieved if we were to use 17 boys and 13 girls. In such a case both statement I and II are correct. Hence, option (c) is correct.

Problem 18.22:

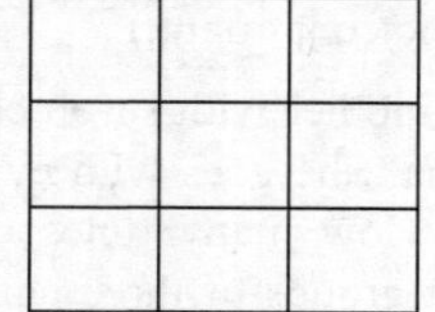

In how many different ways, can all of five identical balls be placed in the cells shown above such that each row contains at least one ball?

(a) 64 (b) 81
(c) 84 (d) 108

Solution: The placement of balls can be 3, 1, 1 and 2, 2, 1. For 3, 1, 1- If we place three balls in the top row, there would be $^3C_1$ ways of choosing a place for the ball in the second row and $^3C_1$ ways of choosing a place for the ball in the third row. Thus, $^3C_1 \times {}^3C_1 = 9$ ways. Similarly, there would be nine ways each if we were to place three balls in the second row and three balls in the third row. Thus, with the 3, 1, 1 distribution of five balls, we would get 9 + 9 + 9 = 27 ways of placing the balls.

We now need to look at the 2, 2, 1 arrangement of balls. If we place one ball in the first row, we would need to place two balls each in the second and the third rows. In such a case, the number of ways of arranging the balls would be $^3C_1 \times {}^3C_2 \times {}^3C_2 = 27$ ways. (choosing one place out of three in the first row, two places out of three in the second row and two places out of three in the third row).

Similarly, if we were to place one ball in the second row and two balls each in the first and third rows, we would get 27 ways of placing the balls and another 27 ways of placing the balls, if we place one ball in the third row and two balls each in the other two rows.

Thus, with a 2, 2, 1 distribution of the five balls, we would get 27 + 27 + 27 = 81 ways of placing the balls.

Hence, total number of ways = number of ways of placing the balls with a 3,1,1 distribution of balls + number of ways of placing the balls with a 2, 2, 1 distribution of balls = 27 + 81 = 108.

Hence, option (d) is correct.

Problem 18.23: There are six different letters and six correspondingly addressed envelopes. If the letters are randomly put in the envelopes, what is the probability that exactly five letters go into the correctly addressed envelopes?

(a) Zero (b) 1/6
(c) 1/2 (d) 5/6

Solution: If five letters go into the correct envelopes, the sixth would automatically go into its correct envelope. Thus, there is no possibility when exactly five letters are correct and one is wrong. Hence, option (a) is correct.

Problem 18.24:

There are two identical red, two identical black and two identical white balls. In how many different ways can the balls be placed in the cells (each cell to contain one ball) shown above such that balls of the same colour do not occupy any two consecutive cells?

(a) 15 (b) 18
(c) 24 (d) 30

Solution: In the first cell, we have three options of placing a ball. Suppose we were to place a red ball in the first cell- then the second cell can only be filled with either black or white – so two ways. Subsequently, there would be two ways, each of filling each of the cells (because we cannot put the colour, we have already used in the previous cell).

Thus, the required number of ways would be 3 × 2 × 2 × 2 = 24 ways.

Hence, option (c) is correct.

Problem 18.25:

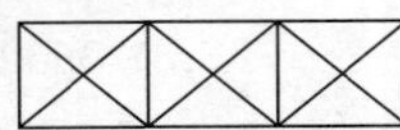

How many different triangles are there in the figure shown above?

(a) 28 (b) 24
(c) 20 (d) 16

Solution: Look for the smallest triangles first—there are 12 of them.

Then, look for the triangles which are equal to half the rectangle—there are 12 of them.

Besides, there are four bigger triangles (spanning across two rectangles).

Thus, a total of 28 triangles can be seen in the figure.

Hence, option (a) is correct.

Problem 18.26: A teacher has to choose the maximum different groups of three students from a total of six students. Of these groups, in how many groups there will be included a particular student?

(a) 6 (b) 8
(c) 10 (d) 12

Solution: If the students are A, B, C, D, E and F- we can have ${}^6C_3$ groups in all. However, if we have to count groups in which a particular student (say A) is always selected- we would get ${}^5C_2 = 10$ ways of doing it. Hence, option (c) is correct.

Problem 18.27: Three dice (each having six faces with each face having one number from 1 to 6) are rolled. What is the number of possible outcomes such that at least one dice shows the number 2?

(a) 36 (b) 81
(c) 91 (d) 116

Solution: All 3 dice have twos – one case.

Two dice have twos:

This can principally occur in three ways which can be broken into:

If the first two dice have 2- the third dice can have 1, 3, 4, 5 or 6 = 5 ways.

Similarly, if the first and third dice have two, the second dice can have five outcomes → five ways and if the second and third dice have a 2, there would be another five ways. Thus, a total of 15 outcomes are possible if two dice have a 2.

With only one dice having a two- If the first dice has 2, the other two can have 5 × 5 = 25 outcomes.

Similarly, 25 outcomes are possible if the second dice has 2 and 25 outcomes if the third dice has 2. A total of 75 outcomes are possible. Thus, a total of 1 + 15 + 75 = 91 outcomes are possible.

Hence, option (c) is correct.

Problem 18.28: All the six letters of the name SACHIN are arranged to form different words without repeating any letter in any one word. The words so formed are then arranged as in a dictionary. What will be the position of the word SACHIN in that sequence?

(a) 436 (b) 590
(c) 601 (d) 751

Solution: All words staring with A, C, H, I and N would be before words starting with *S*. So we would have 5! words (= 120 words) each starting with A, C, H, I and N. Thus, a total of 600 words would get completed before we start off with S. SACHIN would be the first word starting with S, because A, C, H, I, N in that order is the correct alphabetical sequence. Hence, Sachin would be the 601^{s}t word. Hence, option (c) is correct.

Problem 18.29: Five balls of different colours are to be placed in three different boxes such that any box contains at least one ball. What is the maximum number of different ways in which this can be done?

(a) 90 (b) 120
(c) 150 (d) 180

Solution: The arrangements can be [3 & 1 & 1 or 1 & 3 & 1 or 1 & 1 & 3] or 2 & 2 & 1 or 2 & 1 & 2 or 1 & 2 and 2.

Total number of ways = $3 \times {}^5C_3 \times {}^2C_1 \times {}^1C_1 + 3 \times {}^5C_2 \times {}^3C_2 \times {}^1C_1 = 60 + 90 = 150$ ways

Hence, option (c) is correct.

Problem 18.30: Amit has five friends: three girls and two boys. Amit's wife also has five friends : three boys and two girls. In how many maximum numbers of different ways, can they invite two boys and two girls such that two of them are Amit's friends and two are his wife's?

(a) 24 (b) 38
(c) 46 (d) 58

Solution: The selection can be done in the following ways:

Two boys from Amit's friends and two girls from his wife's friends OR one boy and one girl from Amit's friends and one boy and one girl from his wife's friends OR two girls from Amit's friends and two boys from his wife's friends.

The number of ways would be:

${}^2C_2 \times {}^2C_2 + {}^3C_1 \times {}^2C_1 \times {}^3C_1 \times {}^2C_1 + {}^3C_2 \times {}^3C_2 = 1 + 36 + 9 = 46$ ways.

Problem 18.31:

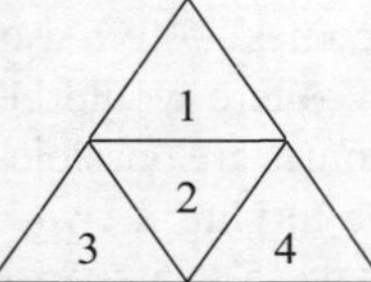

In the given figure, what is the maximum number of different ways in which eight identical balls can be placed in the small triangles 1, 2, 3 and 4 such that each triangle contains at least one ball?

(a) 32 (b) 35
(c) 44 (d) 56

Solution: The ways of placing the balls would be 5, 1, 1, 1 (4!/3! = 4 ways); 4, 2, 1 & 1 (4!/2! = 12 ways); 3, 3, 1, 1 (4!/2! × 2! = 6 ways); 3, 2, 2, 1 (4!/2! = 12 ways) and 2, 2, 2, 2 (1 way). Total number of ways = 4 + 12 + 6 + 12 + 1 = 35 ways. Hence, option (b) is correct.

Problem 18.32: Six equidistant vertical lines are drawn on a board. Six equidistant horizontal lines are also drawn on the board cutting the Six vertical lines, and the distance between any two consecutive horizontal lines is equal to that between any two consecutive vertical lines. What is the maximum number of squares thus formed?

(a) 37 (b) 55
(c) 91 (d) 225

Solution: The number of squares would be $1^2 + 2^2 + 3^2 + 4^2 + 5^2 = 55$. Hence, option (b) is correct.

Problem 18.33: Groups each containing three boys are to be formed out of five boys—*A*, *B*, *C*, *D* and *E* such that no group contains both *C* and *D* together. What is the maximum number of such different groups?

(a) 5 (b) 6
(c) 7 (d) 8

Solution: All groups – groups with *C* and *D* together = ${}^5C_3 - {}^3C_1 = 10 - 3 = 7$

Problem 18.34:

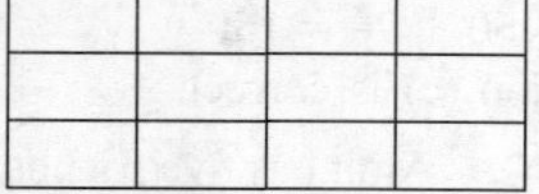

In how many maximum different ways can three identical balls be placed in the 12 squares (each ball to be placed in the exact centre of the squares and only one ball is to be placed in one square) shown in the figure given above such that they do not lie along the same straight line?

(a) 144 (b) 200
(c) 204 (d) 216

Solution: The thought-process for this question would be: All arrangements (${}^{12}C_3$) – Arrangements where all three balls are in the same row ($3 \times {}^4C_3$)– arrangements where all three balls are in the same straight line diagonally (four arrangements) – arrangements where all three balls are in the same column (four arrangements) = ${}^{12}C_3 - 3 \times {}^4C_3 - 4 - 4 = 220 - 12 - 4 - 4 = 200$ ways.

Hence, option (b) is correct.

Problem 18.35: How many numbers are there in all from 6000 to 6999 (both 6000 and 6999 included) having at least one of their digits repeated?

(a) 216 (b) 356
(c) 496 (d) 504

Solution: All numbers – numbers having no numbers repeated = 1000 – 9 × 8 × 7 = 1000 – 504 = 496 numbers. Hence, option (c) is correct.

Problem 18.36: Each of two women and three men is to occupy one chair out of eight chairs; each of which is numbered from one to eight. First, women are to occupy any two chairs from those numbered one to four; and then the three men would occupy any three chairs out of the remaining six chairs. What is the maximum number of different ways in which this can be done?

(a) 40 (b) 132
(c) 1440 (d) 3660

Solution: ${}^4C_2 \times 2! \times {}^6C_3 \times 3! = 6 \times 2 \times 20 \times 6 = 1440$. Hence, option (c) is correct.

Problem 18.37 A box contains five set of balls while there are three balls in each set. Each set of balls has one ball, whose colour is different from every other ball in that set and also from every other ball in any other set. What is the least number of balls that must be removed from the box in order to claim with certainty that a pair of balls of the same colour has been removed?

(a) 6 (b) 7
(c) 9 (d) 11

Solution: Let *C*1, *C*2, *C*3, *C*4 and *C*5 are the five distinct colours which have no repetition. For being definitely sure that we have picked up two balls of the same colour we need to consider the worst case situation.

Consider the following scenario:

Set 1	*Set 2*	*Set 3*	*Set 4*	*Set 5*
C1	C2	C3	C4	C5
C6	C8	C7	C9	C9
C7	C6	C10	C10	C8

In the above distribution of balls each set has exactly one ball which is unique in its colour while the colours of the other two balls are shared at least once in one of the other sets. In such a case, the worst scenario would be if we pick up the first ten balls and they all turn out to be of different colours. The eleventh ball has to be of a colour which has already been taken. Thus,if we were to pick out eleven balls, we would be sure of having at least two balls of the same colour. Hence, option (d) is correct.

Problem 18.38: In a question paper, there are four multiple-choice questions. Each question has five choices with only one choice as the correct answer. What is the total number of ways in which a candidate will not get all the four answers correct?

(a) 19 (b) 120
(c) 624 (d) 1024

Solution: The total number of ways in which the questions can be answered would be 5^4. Out of these, there would be only one way of getting all four correct. Thus, there would be 624 ways of not getting all answers correct.

Problem 18.39:

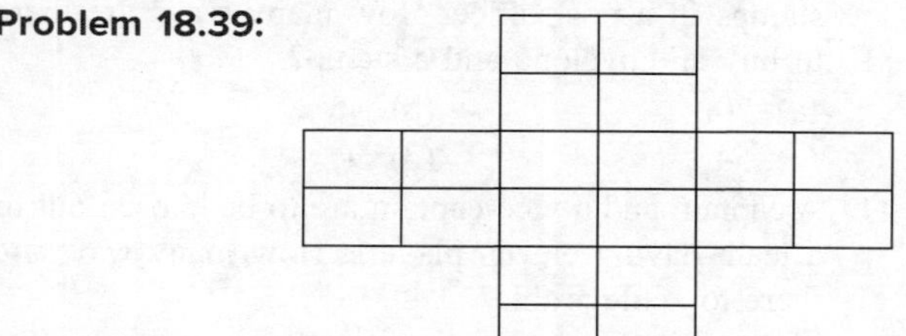

Each of eight identical balls is to be placed in the squares shown in the figure given in a horizontal direction such that one horizontal row contains six balls and the other horizontal row contains two balls. In how many maximum different ways can this be done?

(a) 38 (b) 28
(c) 16 (d) 14

Solution: The six balls must be on either of the middle rows. This can be done in two ways. Once, we put the six balls in their single horizontal row- it becomes evident that for placing the two remaining balls on a straight line, there are two principal options:

1. **Placing the two balls in one of the four rows with two squares.** In this case, the number of ways of placing the balls in any particular row would be one way (since once you were to choose one of the four rows, the balls would automatically get placed as there are only two squares in each row.) Thus, the total number of ways would be $2 \times 4 \times 1 = 8$ ways.
2. **Placing the two balls in the other row with six squares.** In this case the number of ways of placing the two balls in that row would be ${}^6C_2$. This would give us ${}^2C_1 \times 1 \times {}^6C_2 = 30$ ways. Total is $30 + 8 = 38$ ways.

Hence, option (a) is correct.

Problem 18.40: In a tournament, each of the participants was to play one match against each of the other participants. Three players fell ill after each of them had played three matches and had to leave the tournament. What was the total number of participants at the beginning, if the total number of matches played was 75?

(a) 8 (b) 10
(c) 12 (d) 15

Solution: The number of players at the start of the tournament cannot be 8, 10 or 12 because in each of these cases the total number of matches would be less than 75 (as ${}^8C_2$, ${}^{10}C_2$ and ${}^{12}C_2$ are all less than 75.) This only leaves 15 participants in the tournament as the only possibility.

Hence, option (d) is correct.

Problem 18.41: There are three parallel straight lines. Two points A and B are marked on the first line, points C and D are marked on the second line and points E and F are marked on the third line. Each of these six points can move to any position on its respective straight line.

Consider the following statements:

I. The maximum number of triangles that can be drawn by joining these points is 18.
II. The minimum number of triangles that can be drawn by joining these points is zero.

Which of the statements given above is/are correct?

(a) I only (b) II only
(c) Both I and II (d) Neither I nor II

Solution: The maximum triangles would be in case all these six points are non-collinear. In such a case, the number of triangles is ${}^6C_3 = 20$. Hence, statement I is incorrect.

Statement II is correct because if we take the position that A and B coincide on the first line, C and D coincide on the second line, E and F coincide on the third line and all these coincidences happen at three points which are on the same straight line- in such a case there would be 0 triangles formed. Hence, option (b) is correct.

Problem 18.42: A mixed-doubles tennis game is to be played between two teams (each team consists of one male and one female). There are four married couples. No team is to consist of a husband and his wife. What is the maximum number of games that can be played?

(a) 12 (b) 21
(c) 36 (d) 42

Solution: First, select the two men. This can be done in ${}^4C_2$ ways. Let us say, the men are A, B, C and D and their respective wives are a, b, c and d.

If we select A and B as the two men then while selecting the women there would be two cases as seen below:

Case 1:

A	If b is selected to partner A
B	There will be three choices for choosing B's partner – viz, a, c and d

Thus, total number of ways in this case $= {}^4C_2 \times 1 \times {}^3C_1 = 18$ ways.

Case 2:

A	If either c or d is selected to partner A
B	There will be two choices for choosing B's partner – viz, a and any one of c and d

Total number of ways of doing this $= {}^4C_2 \times 2 \times {}^2C_1 = 24$ ways.

Hence, the required answer is $18 + 24 = 42$ ways.

Hence, option (d) is correct.

LEVEL OF DIFFICULTY (I)

1. There are five routes to go from Allahabad to Patna and four ways to go from Patna to Kolkata, then how many ways are possible for going from Allahabad to Kolkata via Patna?
(a) 20 (b) 5^4
(c) 4^5 (d) $5^4 + 4^5$

2. In how many ways can the letters of the word DELHI be arranged?
(a) 119 (b) 120
(c) 60 (d) 24

3. How many straight lines can be formed from eight non-collinear points on the *X-Y* plane?
(a) 28 (b) 56
(c) 18 (d) 19860

4. There are four qualifying examinations to enter into Oxford University: RAT, BAT, SAT, and PAT. An engineer cannot go to Oxford University through BAT or SAT. A CA on the other hand can go to the Oxford University through the RAT, BAT and PAT but not through SAT. Further there are three ways to become a CA (viz., Foundation, Inter and Final). Find the ratio of number of ways in which an engineer can make it to Oxford University to the number of ways a CA can make it to Oxford University.
(a) 3:2 (b) 2:3
(c) 2:9 (d) 9:2

5. In how many ways can five prizes be distributed to eight students if each student can get any number of prizes?
(a) 40 (b) 5^8
(c) 8^5 (d) 120

6. In how many ways can seven Indians, five Pakistanis and six Dutch be seated in a row so that all persons of the same nationality sit together?
(a) 3! (b) 7!5!6!
(c) 3!.7!.5!.6! (d) 182

7. How many numbers between 2000 and 3000 can be formed with the digits 0, 1, 2, 3, 4, 5, 6, 7 (repetition of digits not allowed)?
(a) 42 (b) 210
(c) 336 (d) 440

8. In how many ways can a person send invitation cards to six of his friends if he has four servants to distribute the cards?
(a) 6^4 (b) 4^6
(c) 24 (d) 120

9. How many numbers of three-digits can be formed with the digits 1, 2, 3, 4, 5 (repetition of digits not allowed)?
(a) 125 (b) 120
(c) 60 (d) 150

10. There are five types of envelopes and four types of stamps in a post office. How many ways are there to buy an envelope and a stamp?
(a) 20 (b) 45
(c) 54 (d) 9

11. A captain and a vice-captain are to be chosen out of a team having eleven players. How many ways are there to achieve this?
(a) 10.9 (b) ${}^{11}C_2$
(c) 110 (d) 10.9!

12. In how many ways can Ram choose a vowel and a consonant from the letters of the word ALLAHABAD?
(a) 4 (b) 6
(c) 9 (d) 5

13. How many four digit numbers are possible, criteria being that all the four digits are odd?
(a) 125 (b) 625
(c) 45 (d) None of these

14. There are three rooms in a motel: one single, one double and one for four persons. How many ways are there to house seven persons in these rooms?
(a) 7!/1!2!4! (b) 7!
(c) 7!/3 (d) 7!/3!

15. In how many ways can ten identical presents be distributed among six children so that each child gets at least one present?
(a) ${}^{15}C_5$ (b) ${}^{16}C_6$
(c) ${}^{9}C_5$ (d) 6^{10}

16. How many ways are there to choose four cards of different suits and different values from a deck of 52 cards?
(a) 13.12.11.10 (b) ${}^{52}C_4$
(c) 134 (d) 52.36.22.10

17. Arjit being a party animal wants to hold as many parties as possible amongst his twenty friends. However, his father has warned him that he will be financing his parties under the following conditions only:
(a) The invitees have to be amongst his twenty best friends.
(b) He cannot call the same set of friends to a party more than once.
(c) The number of invitees to every party has to be the same.

Given these constraints. Arjit wants to hold the maximum number of parties. How many friends should he invite to each party?

(a) 11 (b) 8
(c) 10 (d) 12

18. How many new words are possible from the letters of the word PERMUTATION?
(a) 11!/2! (b) (11!/2!) – 1
(c) 11! – 1 (d) None of these

19. If the letters of the word PATNA, are used to form 5 letter words, how many words will start with *P* and end with *T*?
(a) 3 (b) 6
(c) 11 (d) 12

20. How many numbers of four digits can be formed with the digits 0, 1, 2, 3 (repetition of digits is not allowed)?
(a) 18 (b) 24
(c) 64 (d) 192

21. For the above question, how many numbers can be formed with the same digits if repetition of digits is allowed?
(a) 18 (b) 192
(c) 32 (d) 64

22. How many numbers between 200 and 1200 can be formed with the digits 0, 1, 2, 3 (repetition of digits not allowed)?
(a) 6 (b) 6
(c) 2 (d) 14

23. For the arrangements of the letters of the word PATNA, how many words would start with the letter *P*?
(a) 24 (b) 12
(c) 60 (d) 120

24. How many numbers $200 < N < 1200$ can be formed with the digits 0, 1, 2, 3 (repetition of digits being allowed)?
(a) 48 (b) 14
(c) 32 (d) 63

25. In how many ways can the letters of the word PATNA be rearranged?
(a) 60 (b) 120
(c) 119 (d) 59

26. There are eight consonants and five vowels in a word jumble. In how many ways can we form five-letter words having three consonants and two vowels?
(a) 67200 (b) 8540
(c) 720 (d) None of these

27. How many distinct words can be formed out of the word PROWLING which start with *R* and end with *W*?
(a) 8!/2! (b) 6!2!
(c) 6! (d) None of these

28. There are five blue socks, four red socks and three green socks, all different in Debu's wardrobe. He has to select four socks from this set. In how many ways can he do so?
(a) 245 (b) 120
(c) 495 (d) 60

29. How many seven-digit numbers are there having the digit 3, three times and the digit 5, four times?
(a) 7!/(3!)(5!) (b) $3^3 \times 5^5$
(c) 77 (d) 35

30. How many batting orders are possible for the Indian cricket team if there is a squad of fifteen to choose from such that Sachin Tendulkar is always chosen?
(a) 1001.11! (b) 364.11!
(c) 11! (d) 15.11!

31. How many seven-digit numbers are there having the digit 3, three times and the digit 0 four times?
(a) 15 (b) $3^3 \times 4^4$
(c) 18 (d) None of these

32. A class prefect goes to meet the principal every week. His class has thirty people apart from him. If he has to take groups of three every time he goes to the principal, in how many weeks will he be able to go to the principal without repeating the group of same three which accompanies him?
(a) ${}^{30}P_3$ (b) ${}^{30}C_3$
(c) 30!/3 (d) None of these

33. For the above question if on the very first visit, the principal appoints one of the boys accompanying him as the head boy of the school and lays down the condition that the class prefect has to be accompanied by the head boy every time he comes then for a maximum of how many weeks (including the first week) can the class prefect ensure that the principal sees a fresh group of three accompanying him?
(a) ${}^{30}C_2$ (b) ${}^{29}C_2$
(c) ${}^{29}C_3$ (d) None of these

34. From a set of three capital consonants, five small consonants and four small vowels, how many words can be made each starting with a capital consonant and containing three small consonants and two small vowels?
(a) 3600 (b) 7200
(c) 21600 (d) 28800

35. Several teams take part in a competition, each of which must play one game with all the other teams. How many teams took part in the competition if they played 45 games in all?
(a) 5 (b) 10
(c) 15 (d) 20

36. A man has three shirts, four trousers and six ties. What are the number of ways in which he can dress himself with a combination of all the three?
(a) 13 (b) 72
(c) 13!/3!.4!.6! (d) 3!.4!.6!

37. In how many ways can the letters of the word 'EQUATION' be arranged so that all the vowels come together?

(a) ${}^9C_4 \cdot {}^9C_5$ (b) 4!.5!
(c) 9!/5! (d) 9! – 4!5!

38. How many motor vehicle registration number plates can be formed with the digits 1, 2, 3, 4, 5 (No digits being repeated) if it is given that registration number can have 1 to 5 digits?

(a) 100 (b) 120
(c) 325 (d) 205

Directions for Question 39 to 41: There are 25 points on a plane of which seven are collinear. Now solve the following:

39. How many straight lines can be formed?

(a) 7 (b) 300
(c) 280 (d) None of these

40. How many triangles can be formed from these points?

(a) 453 (b) 2265
(c) 755 (d) None of these

41. How many quadrilaterals can be formed from these points?

(a) 5206 (b) 2603
(c) 13015 (d) None of these

42. How many motor vehicle registration number of four digits can be formed with the digits 0, 1, 2, 3, 4, 5? (No digit being repeated.)

(a) 1080 (b) 120
(c) 300 (d) 360

43. In how many ways can twelve papers be arranged if the best and the worst paper never come together?

(a) 12!/2! (b) 12! – 11!
(c) (12! – 11!)/2 (d) 12! – 2.11!

44. There are ten subjects in the school day at St.Vincent's High School but the sixth standard students have only five periods in a day. In how many ways can we form a time table for the day for the sixth standard students if no subject is repeated?

(a) 510 (b) 105
(c) 252 (d) 30240

45. A set of fifteen different words are given. In how many ways is it possible to choose a subset of not more than five words?

(a) 4944 (b) 4^{15}
(c) 15^4 (d) 4943

Space for Rough Work

LEVEL OF DIFFICULTY (II)

1. How many sets of two numbers are there in the set of first 20 natural numbers whose difference is at least 4?
2. If the number of rectangles formed by 6 parallel lines and x lines which are perpendicular to these parallel lines is 420, what is the value of x?
3. Three dice, each showing numbers 1 to 6, are coloured white, black and orange respectively. Each of the dice is rolled once. The total of the numbers rolled is 10. In how many different ways can this happen?
4. In how many ways can we pick 5 numbers from the set of first 50 natural numbers such that the numbers are selected in descending order?
5. How many different integer averages are possible for a set of first 10 natural numbers if selected numbers are distinct?
6. How many natural numbers can be formed using the digits 3, 4, 5, 6, 7, and 8 (with no digit being repeated)?
7. The number of integers lying between 1000 and 10000 which have at least two digits equal is
   (a) 4464 (b) 5974
   (c) 5975 (d) 4463
8. There are 12 teams of 8 members each at Mindworkzz. During the office dinner, each team member gave every other team member a watch. Every team also gives every other team a photo frame. What is the total number of watches and photo frames if none of these items are reused?
9. How many three-digit numbers are greater than 100 and increase by 297 when the three digits are arranged in the reverse order?
10. Find the number of numbers that can be formed using all the digits 1, 2, 3, 4, 3, 2, 1 only once so that the odd digits occupy odd places only.
    (a) $4!/(2!)^2$ (b) $7!/(2!)^3$
    (c) 1!.3!.5!.7! (d) None of these
11. There are eight orators A, B, C, D, E, F, G and H. In how many ways can the arrangements be made so that A always comes before B and B always comes before C?
    (a) 8!/3! (b) 8!/6!
    (c) 5!.3! (d) 8!/(5!.3!)
12. There are four letters and four envelopes. In how many ways can wrong choices be made?
    (a) 4^3 (b) $4! - 1$
    (c) 16 (d) $4^4 - 1$
13. In the question above, find the number of ways in which only one letter goes in the wrong envelope?
    (a) 4^3
    (b) ${}^4C_1 + {}^4C_2 + {}^4C_3 + {}^4C_4$
    (c) ${}^4C_0 + {}^4C_1 + {}^4C_2 + {}^4C_3$
    (d) 0
14. In question 12, find the number of ways in which only two letters go in the wrong envelopes?
    (a) 4 (b) 5
    (c) 6 (d) 3
15. If a team of four persons is to be selected from eight males and eight females, then in how many ways can the selections be made to include at least one male?
    (a) 3500 (b) 875
    (c) 1200 (d) None of these
16. In the above question, in how many ways can the selections be made if it has to contain at the maximum three women?
    (a) 1750 (b) 1200
    (c) 875 (d) None of these
17. A train is running between Patna to Howrah. Seven people enter the train somewhere between Patna and Howrah. It is given that nine stops are there in between Patna and Howrah. In how many ways can the tickets be purchased if no restriction is there with respect to the number of tickets at any station? (Two people do not buy the same ticket.)
    (a) ${}^{45}C_7$ (b) ${}^{63}C_7$
    (c) ${}^{56}C_7$ (d) ${}^{52}C_7$
18. How many six-digit numbers have all their digits either all odd or all even?
    (a) 31,250 (b) 28,125
    (c) 15,625 (d) None of these
19. On a triangle ABC, five points are marked on the side AB, six points are marked on the side BC and three points are marked on the side AC (none of the points being the vertex of the triangle). How many triangles can be made by using these points?
    (a) 90 (b) 333
    (c) 328 (d) None of these
20. How many six-digit numbers have at least one even digit?
    (a) 884375 (b) 3600
    (c) 880775 (d) 15624
21. If we have to make seven boys sit with seven girls around a round table, then the number of different relative arrangements of boys and girls that we can make so that there are no two boys or any two girls sitting next to each other is

(a) $2 \times (7!)^2$ (b) $7! \times 6!$
(c) $7! \times 7!$ (d) None of these

22. In how many ways one white and one black rook can be placed on a chessboard so that they are never in an attacking position?
(a) 64×50 (b) 64×49
(c) 63×49 (d) None of these

23. If we have to make seven boys sit alternately with seven girls around a round table which is numbered, then the number of ways in which this can be done is
(a) $2 \times (7!)^2$ (b) $7! \times 6!$
(c) $7! \times 7!$ (d) None of these

24. How many ten-digit numbers have at least two equal digits?
(a) $9 \times {}^{10}C_2 \times 8!$ (b) $9.10^9 – 9.\ 9!$
(c) $9 \times 9!$ (d) None of these

25. There are seven pairs of black shoes and five pairs of white shoes. They all are put into a box and shoes are drawn one at a time. To ensure that at least one pair of black shoes are taken out, what is the number of shoes required to be drawn out?
(a) 12 (b) 13
(c) 7 (d) 18

26. In the above question, what is the minimum number of shoes required to be drawn out to get at least one pair of correct shoes (either white or black)?
(a) 12 (b) 7
(c) 13 (d) 18

27. In the Suniti Building in Mumbai, there are twelve floors plus the ground floor. Nine people get into the lift of the building on the ground floor. The lift does not stop on the first floor. If 2, 3 and 4 people alight from the lift on its upward journey, then in how many ways can they do so? (Assume they alight on different floors.)
(a) ${}^{11}C_3 \times {}^3P_3$ (b) ${}^{11}P_3 \times {}^9C_4 \times {}^5C_3$
(c) ${}^{10}P_3 \times {}^9C_4 \times {}^5C_3$ (d) ${}^{12}C_3$

28. From four gentlemen and four ladies a committee of five is to be formed. Find the number of ways of doing so if the committee consists of a president, a vice-president and three secretaries?
(a) ${}^8P_5$ (b) 1120
(c) ${}^4C_2 \times {}^4C_3$ (d) None of these

29. In the above question, what will be the number of ways of selecting the committee with at least three women such that at least one woman holds the post of either a president or a vice-president?
(a) 420 (b) 610
(c) 256 (d) None of these

30. Find the number of ways of selecting the committee with a maximum of two women and having at the maximum one woman holding one of the two posts on the committee.
(a) 16 (b) 512
(c) 608 (d) 324

31. The crew of an eight-member rowing team is to be chosen from twelve men, of which three must row on one side only and two must row on the other side only. Find the number of ways of arranging the crew with four members on each side.
(a) 40,320 (b) 30,240
(c) 60,480 (d) None of these

32. How many four-digit numbers divisible by five can be formed with the digits 0, 1, 2, 3, 4, 5, 6 and 6?
(a) 220 (b) 249
(c) 432 (d) 288

33. There are six pups and four cats. In how many ways can they be seated in a row so that no cats sit together?
(a) 6^4 (b) 10!/(4!).(6!)
(c) $6! \times {}^7P_4$ (d) None of these

34. How many even numbers of four-digits can be formed with the digits 1, 2, 3, 4, 5, 6 (repetitions of digits are allowed)?
(a) 648 (b) 180
(c) 1296 (d) 600

35. Seven different objects must be divided among three people. In how many ways can this be done if one or two of them can get no objects?
(a) 15120 (b) 2187
(c) 3003 (d) 792

36. How many six-digit even numbers can be formed from the digits 1, 2, 3, 4, 5, 6 and 7 so that the digits should not repeat?
(a) 720 (b) 1440
(c) 2160 (d) 6480

37. How many six-digit even numbers can be formed from the digits 1, 2, 3, 4, 5, 6 and 7 so that the digits should not repeat and the second last digit is even?
(a) 720 (b) 320
(c) 2160 (d) 1440

38. How many different four-digit numbers are there which have the digits 1, 2, 3, 4, 5, 6, 7 and 8 such that the digit 1 appears exactly once?
(a) $7.\ {}^8P_4$ (b) ${}^8P_4$
(c) 4.7^3 (d) 7^3

39. How many five-digit numbers that do not contain identical digits can be written by means of the digits 1, 2, 3, 4, 5, 6, 7, 8 and 9?
(a) 6048 (b) 7560
(c) 5040 (d) 15,120

40. How many different seven-digit numbers can be written using only three digits 1, 2 and 3 such that the digit 3 occurs twice in each number?
(a) ${}^7C_2.2^5$ (b) 7!/(2!)
(c) $7!/(2!)^3$ (d) None of these

41. How many different four-digit numbers can be written using the digits 1, 2, 3, 4, 5, 6, 7 and 8 only once such that the number 2 is contained once?
(a) 360 (b) 840
(c) 760 (d) 1260

42. In how many ways can ten identical marbles be distributed among six children so that each child gets at least one marble?
(a) ${}^{15}C_5$ (b) ${}^{15}C_9$
(c) ${}^{10}C_5$ (d) ${}^9C_5$

43. In how many ways, five MBA students and six Law students can be arranged together so that no two MBA students are side by side?
(a) $\frac{7!6!}{2!}$ (b) 6!.6!
(c) 5!.6! (d) ${}^{11}C_5$

44. The latest registration number issued by the Delhi Motor Vehicle Registration Authority is DL-5S 2234. If all the numbers and alphabets before this have been used up, then find how many vehicles have a registration number starting with DL-5?
(a) 1,92,234 (b) 1,92,225
(c) 1,72,227 (d) None of these

45. There are hundred balls numbered n_1, n_2, n_3, n_4,... n_{100}. They are arranged in all possible ways. How many arrangements would be there in which n_{28} ball will always be before n_{29} ball and the two of them will be adjacent to each other?
(a) 99!/2! (b) 99!.2!
(c) 99! (d) None of these

46. Find the sum of the number of sides and number of diagonals of a hexagon.
(a) 210 (b) 15
(c) 6 (d) 9

47. The number of positive numbers of ten digits formed by using 0, 1, 2, 3 is
(a) $4^{10} - 1$ (b) 4^{10}
(c) $4^9 - 1$ (d) None of these

48. There is a number lock with four rings with each ring having digits 0 to 9. How many attempts at the maximum would have to be made before getting the right number?
(a) 10^4 (b) 255
(c) $10^4 - 1$ (d) None of these

49. In how many ways can a selection be made of five letters out of 5As, 4Bs, 3Cs, 2Ds and 1E?
(a) 70 (b) 71
(c) ${}^{15}C_5$ (d) None of these

50. Find the number of ways of selecting 'n' articles out of $3n + 1$, out of which n are identical.
(a) 2^{2n-1} (b) ${}^{3n+1}C_n/n!$
(c) ${}^{3n+1}P_n/n!$ (d) None of these

51. Mr. Shah has to divide his assets worth ₹ 30 crores in three parts to be given to three of his sons Ajay, Vijay and Arun ensuring that every son gets assets atleast worth ₹ 5 crores. In how many ways can this be done if it is given that the three sons should get their shares in multiples of ₹ 1 crore?
(a) 136 (b) 152
(c) 176 (d) 98

52. The letters of the word ALLAHABAD are rearranged to form new words and put in a dictionary. If the dictionary has only these words and one word on every page in alphabetical order then what is the page number on which the word LABADALAH comes?
(a) 6269 (b) 6268
(c) 6087 (d) 6086

53. There are N men sitting around a circular table at N distinct points. Every possible pair of men except the ones sitting adjacent to each other sings a two-minute song one pair after other. If the total time taken is 88 minutes, then what is the value of N?
(a) 8 (b) 9
(c) 10 (d) 11

54. Three variables x, y, z have a sum of 30. All three of them are non-negative integers. If any two variables do not have the same value and exactly one variable has a value less than or equal to three, then find the number of possible solutions for the variables.
(a) 98 (b) 285
(c) 68 (d) 252

55. There are nine points in a plane such that no three are collinear. Find the number of triangles that can be formed using these points as vertices.
(a) 81 (b) 90
(c) 9 (d) 84

56. In a class with boys and girls, a chess competition was played wherein every student had to play one game with every other student. It was observed that in 36 matches, both the players were boys and in 66 matches both were girls. What is the number of matches in which 1 boy and 1 girl play against each other?
(a) 108 (b) 189
(c) 210 (d) 54

57. There are nine points in a plane such that exactly three points out of them are collinear. Find the number of triangles that can be formed using these points as vertices.

(a) 81 (b) 90
(c) 9 (d) 83

58. Zada has to distribute fifteen chocolates among five of her children Sana, Ada, Jiya, Amir and Farhan. She has to make sure that Sana gets at least three and at most six chocolates. In how many ways can this be done if each child gets at least one chocolate?

(a) 495 (b) 77
(c) 417 (d) 425

59. If x, y and z can only take the values 1, 2, 3, 4, 5, 6, 7 then find the number of solutions of the equation $x + y + z = 12$.

(a) 36 (b) 37
(c) 38 (d) 31

60. If xy is a two-digit number and u, v, x, y are digits, then find the number of solutions of the equation: $(xy)^2 = u! + v$

(a) 2 (b) 3
(c) 0 (d) 5

61. For a scholarship, at the most n candidates out of $2n + 1$ can be selected. If the number of different ways of selection of at least one candidate is 63, the maximum number of candidates that can be selected for the scholarship is

(a) 3 (b) 4
(c) 2 (d) 5

62. One red flag, three white flags and two blue flags are arranged in a line such that,

(a) No two adjacent flags are of the same colour
(b) The flags at the two ends of the line are of different colours.

In how many different ways can the flags be arranged?

(a) 6 (b) 4
(c) 10 (d) 2

63. Sam has forgotten his friend's seven-digit telephone number. He remembers the following: the first three digits are either 635 or 674; the number is odd, and the number nine appears once. If Sam were to use a trial-and-error process to reach his friend, what is the minimum number of trials he has to make before he can be certain to succeed?

(a) 1000 (b) 2430
(c) 3402 (d) 3006

64. There are three cities A, B and C. Each of these cities is connected with the other two cities by at least one direct road. If a traveller wants to go from one city (origin) to another city (destination), she can do so either by traversing a road connecting the two cities directly, or by traversing two roads, the first connecting the origin to the third city and the second connecting the third city to the destination. In all there are 33 routes from A to B (including those via C). Similarly there are 23 routes from B to C (including those via A). How many roads are there from A to C directly?

(a) 6 (b) 3
(c) 5 (d) 10

65. Let n be the number of different five-digit numbers, divisible by four that can be formed with the digits 1, 2, 3, 4, 5 and 6, with no digit being repeated. What is the value of n?

(a) 144 (b) 168
(c) 192 (d) None of these

66. In how many ways is it possible to choose a white square and a black square on a chess board so that the squares must not lie in the same row or column?

(a) 56 (b) 896
(c) 60 (d) 768

67. How many numbers greater than 0 and less than a million can be formed with the digits 0, 7 and 8?

(a) 486 (b) 1086
(c) 728 (d) None of these

68. In how many ways, five chocolates can be chosen from an unlimited number of Cadbury, Five-star, and Perk chocolates?

(a) 81 (b) 243
(c) 21 (d) 31

69. In how many ways a selection can be made of at least one fruit out of five bananas, four mangoes and four almonds?

(a) 129 (b) 149
(c) 139 (d) 109

70. There are five boys of McGraw-Hill Mindworkzz and three girls of I.I.M. Lucknow who are sitting together to discuss a management problem at a round table. In how many ways can they sit around the table so that no two girls are together?

(a) 1220 (b) 1400
(c) 1420 (d) 1440

71. Amita has three library cards and seven books of her interest in the library of Mindworkzz. Of these books, she would not like to borrow the D.I. book, unless the Quants book is also borrowed. In how many ways can she take the three books to be borrowed?

(a) 15 (b) 20
(c) 25 (d) 30

72. There is a question paper consisting of fifteen questions. Each question has an internal choice of two options. In how many ways can a student attempt one or more questions of the given fifteen questions in the paper?

(a) 3^7 (b) 3^8
(c) 3^{15} (d) $3^{15} - 1$

73. From a group of twelve dancers, five have to be taken for a stage show. Among them Radha and Mohan decide either both of them would join or none of them would join. In how many ways can the five dancers be chosen?

(a) 190 (b) 210
(c) 278 (d) 372

74. How many numbers can be formed with the digits 1, 6, 7, 8, 7, 6, 1 so that the odd digits always occupy the odd places?

(a) 15 (b) 12
(c) 18 (d) 20

75. An urn contains five boxes. Each box contains five balls of different colours red, yellow, white, blue and black. Rangeela wants to pick up five balls of different colours, a different coloured ball from each box. If from the first box in the first draw, he has drawn a red ball and from the second box he has drawn a black ball, find the maximum number of trials that are needed to be made by Rangeela to accomplish his task if a ball picked is not replaced.

(a) 12 (b) 11
(c) 20 (d) 60

76. Find the number of six-digit numbers that can be formed using the digits 1, 2, 3, 4, 5, 6 once such that the six-digit number is divisible by its unit digit. (The unit digit is not 1.)

(a) 620 (b) 456
(c) 520 (d) 528

Directions for Questions 77 and 78: In a chess tournament, there were two women participating and every participant played two games with the other participants. The number of games that the men played among themselves exceeded the number of games that the men played with the women by 66.

77. The number of participants in the tournament was

(a) 12 (b) 13
(c) 15 (d) 11

78. The total number of games played in the tournament was

(a) 132 (b) 110
(c) 156 (d) 210

79. Twenty-seven persons attend a party. Which one of the following statements can never be true?

(a) There is a person in the party who is acquainted with all the twenty six others.
(b) Each person in the party has a different number of acquaintances.
(c) There is a person in the party who has an odd number of acquaintances.
(d) In the party, there is no set of three mutual acquaintances.

80. How many numbers can be formed with odd digits 1, 3, 5, 7, 9 without repetition?

(a) 275 (b) 325
(c) 375 (d) 235

81. There are six boxes numbered 1, 2, ...6. Each box is to be filled up either with a red or a green ball in such a way that at least one box contains a green ball and the boxes containing green balls are consecutively numbered. The total number of ways in which this can be done is

(a) 5 (b) 21
(c) 33 (d) 60

High Yield Questions

Scan this QR code to access assisted problem solving videos on questions 2, 6, 17 and 31 from LOD 2

Space for Rough Work

LEVEL OF DIFFICULTY (III)

1. How many even integers between 1000 and 5000 have four different digits?
2. How many whole numbers till 100 are divisible by their units digits?
3. How many 6-digit multiples of 15 are there that contain only the digits 1, 3 and 5 with 5 occurring at least twice?
4. Ten identical pens are to be distributed among five aspirants such that only two aspirants get exactly two pens each while the rest could get any number of pens. How many ways are there of doing so?
   (a) 150 (b) 180
   (c) 120 (d) 210
5. In how many ways can we choose 4 numbers from the set 1, 2, 3, ..., 40 such that the numbers are in arithmetic progression?
6. A safe at Mindworkzz requires a code of 2 letters and 3 digits out of $\{a, b, c, d, e\}$ letters and $\{1, 2, 3, 4, 5, 6, 7, 8\}$ digits. How many attempts are required to open the safe if there is a combination of two specific digits which cannot be used together in the code?
7. Shaurya randomly selects an ordered pair of two distinct numbers from the set 1—5, and Pallav randomly selects a number from the set 1—10. In how many ways can Shaurya choose his ordered pair, such that the sum of the numbers is always less than the number chosen by Pallav?
8. How many numbers are there between 1 and 10000, having at least one of their digits 9?
9. Let S = {1, 2, 3, 4, 5, 6, 7, 8, 9, 10}. If a, b are selected from U, find the number of pairs such that $a!/b!$ is divisible by 4.
10. How many three digit numbers with at least one zero are there having the sum of their digits as odd?
11. How many four-digit numbers are there using only the digits 2, 4 and 5 such that both 4 and 5 appear at least once?
12. The number of seven-digit integers, with sum of the digits equal to 10 and formed by using the digits 1, 2 and 3 only, is
    (a) 55 (b) 66
    (c) 77 (d) 88
13. If A, B, C, D are distinct natural numbers and A + B + C + D = 15, then the number of possible ordered solutions for the values of (A, B, C, D) is:
14. Let $n \geq 2$ be an integer. Take n distinct points on a circle and join each pair of points by a line segment. Colour the line segment joining every pair of adjacent points by blue and the rest by red. If the number of red and blue line segments are equal, then the value of n is
15. Six cards and six envelopes are numbered 1, 2, 3, 4, 5, 6 and cards are to be placed in envelopes so that each envelope contains exactly one card and no card is placed in the envelope bearing the same number and moreover the card numbered 1 is always placed in envelope numbered 2. Then the number of ways it can be done is
16. Let n be the number of ways in which 5 boys and 5 girls can stand in a queue in such a way that all the girls stand consecutively in the queue. Let m be the number of ways in which 5 boys and 5 girls can stand in a queue in such a way that exactly four girls stand consecutively in the queue. Then the value of $\frac{m}{n}$ is
17. A debate club consists of 6 girls and 4 boys. A team of 4 members is to be selected from this club including the selection of a captain (from among these 4 members) for the team. If the team has to include at most one boy, then the number of ways of selecting the team is
    (a) 380 (b) 320
    (c) 260 (d) 95
18. Let S = {1, 2, 3,….., 9}. For k = 1, 2,…., 5, let N_k be the number of subsets of S, each containing five elements out of which exactly k are odd. Then $N_1 + N_2 + N_3 + N_4 + N_5$ =
19. The number of 5 digit numbers that can be made from 1, 2, 3, 4, 5, 6 such that they are divisible by 4 are:
20. How many 5 digit numbers divisible by 3 can be formed using the digits 1, 2, 3, 4, 5, 6, 7 if repetition of digits is not allowed?
21. How many numbers of five digits can be made having exactly two identical digits?
22. Find the number of $2n$ digit numbers whose all digits are prime and sum of any two consecutive digits is also prime.
23. How many sets of three numbers can be formed using each and every digits (0, 1, 2, 3,…., 8) exactly once in each set. Each number in the sets is of at least two digits and the digits are in decreasing order from left to right in each number.
24. Find the number of odd integers between 30000 and 80000 in which no digit is repeated.
25. The number of ways in which four particular persons A, B, C, D and six more persons can stand in a queue so that A always stands before B, B always before C and C always before D is
    (a) $10!/4!$ (b) ${}^{10}P_4$
    (c) ${}^{10}C_4$ (d) None of these

26. The number of circles that can be drawn out of ten points of which seven are collinear is
(a) 130 (b) 85
(c) 45 (d) Cannot be determined

27. How many different nine-digit numbers can be formed from the number 223355888 by rearranging its digits so that the odd digits occupy even positions?
(a) 120 (b) $9!/(2!)^3.3!$
(c) $(4!)(2!)^3.3!$ (d) None of these

28. How many diagonals are there in an n-sided polygon ($n > 3$)?
(a) $({}^nC_2 - n)$ (b) ${}^nC_2$
(c) $n(n-1)/2$ (d) None of these

29. A polygon has 54 diagonals. Find the number of sides.
(a) 10 (b) 14
(c) 12 (d) 9

30. The number of natural numbers of two or more than two digits in which digits from left to right are in increasing order is
(a) 127 (b) 128
(c) 502 (d) 512

31. In how many ways a cricketer can score 200 runs with fours and sixes only?
(a) 13 (b) 17
(c) 19 (d) 16

32. A dice is rolled six times. One, two, three, four, five and six appears on consecutive throws of dice. How many ways are possible of having 1 before 6?
(a) 120 (b) 360
(c) 240 (d) 280

33. The number of permutations of the letters a, b, c, d, e, f, g such that neither the pattern '*beg*' nor '*acd*' occurs is
(a) 4806 (b) 420
(c) 2408 (d) None of these

34. In how many ways can the letters of the English alphabet be arranged so that there are seven letters between the letters A and B?
(a) 31!.2! (b) ${}^{24}P_7.18!.2$
(c) 36.24! (d) None of these

35. There are twenty people among whom two are sisters. Find the number of ways in which we can arrange them around a circle so that there is exactly one person between the two sisters.
(a) 18! (b) 2!.19!
(c) 19! (d) None of these

36. In an examination, the maximum marks for each of the three papers is 50 each. The maximum marks for the fourth paper is 100. Find the number of ways with which a student can score 60% marks in aggregate.
(a) 3,30,850 (b) 2,33,551
(c) 1,10,551 (d) None of these

37. How many rectangles can be formed out of a chessboard?
(a) 204 (b) 1230
(c) 1740 (d) None of these

38. On a board having 18 rows and 16 columns, find the number of squares.
(a) ${}^{18}C_2 . {}^{16}C_2$
(b) ${}^{18}P_2 . {}^{16}P_2$
(c) 18.16 + 17.15 + 16.14 + 15.13 + 14.12 +……+ 4.2 + 3.1
(d) None of these

39. In the above question, find the number of rectangles.
(a) ${}^{18}C_2 . {}^{16}C_2$ (b) ${}^{18}P_2 . {}^{16}P_2$
(c) 171.136 (d) None of these

Directions for Questions 40 and 41: Read the passage below and answer the questions.

In the famous program *Kaun Banega Crorepati*, the host shakes hand with each participant once, while he shakes hands with each qualifier (amongst participant) twice more. Besides, the participants are required to shake hands once with each other, while the winner and the host each shake hands with all the guests once.

40. How many handshakes are there if there are ten participants in all, three finalists and sixty spectators?
(a) 118 (b) 178
(c) 181 (d) 122

41. In the above question, what is the ratio of the number of handshakes involving the host to the number of handshakes not involving the host?
(a) 43 : 75 (b) 76 : 105
(c) 46 : 75 (d) None of these

42. What is the percentage increase in the total number of handshakes if all the guests are required to shake hands with each other once?
(a) 82.2% (b) 822%
(c) 97.7% (d) None of these

43. Two variants of the CAT paper are to be given to twelve students. In how many ways can the students be placed in two rows of six each so that there should be no identical variants side by side and that the students sitting one behind the other should not have the same variant?
(a) $2 \times {}^{12}C_6 \times (6!)^2$ (b) $6! \times 6!$
(c) $7! \times 7!$ (d) None of these

44. For the above question, if there are now three variants of the test to be given to the twelve students (so that each variant is used for four students) and there should be no identical variants side by side and that the students sitting one behind the other should have the same variant. Find the number of ways this can be done.

(a) $6!^2$ (b) $6 \times 6! \times 6!$
(c) $6!^3$ (d) None of these

45. Five boys and three girls are sitting in a row of eight seats. In how many ways can they be seated so that not all girls sit side by side?
(a) 36,000 (b) 45,000
(c) 24,000 (d) None of these

46. How many natural numbers are there those are smaller than 10^4 and whose decimal notation consists only of the digits 0, 1, 2, 3 and 5, which are not repeated in any of these numbers?
(a) 32 (b) 164
(c) 31 (d) 212

47. Seven different objects must be divided among three people. In how many ways can this be done if one or two of them must get no objects?
(a) 381 (b) 36
(c) 84 (d) 180

48. Seven different objects must be divided among three people. In how many ways can this be done if at least one of them gets exactly one object?
(a) 2484 (b) 1218
(c) 729 (d) None of these

49. How many natural numbers smaller than 10,000 are there in the decimal notation of which all the digits are different?
(a) 2682 (b) 4474
(c) 5274 (d) 1448

50. How many four-digit numbers are there whose decimal notation contains not more than two distinct digits?
(a) 672 (b) 576
(c) 360 (d) 448

51. How many different seven-digit numbers are there the sum of whose digits are odd?
(a) 45.10^5 (b) 24.10^5
(c) 224320 (d) None of these

52. How many 6-digit numbers contain exactly 4 different digits?
(a) 4536 (b) 2,94,840
(c) 1,91,520 (d) None of these

53. How many numbers smaller than 2.10^8 which are divisible by 3 can be written by means of the digits 0, 1 and 2 (exclude single digit and double digit numbers)?
(a) 4369 (b) 4353
(c) 4373 (d) 4351

54. Six white and six black balls of the same size are distributed among ten urns so that there is at least one ball in each urn. What is the number of different distributions of the balls?
(a) 25,000 (b) 26,250
(c) 28,250 (d) 13,125

55. A bouquet has to be formed from 18 different flowers so that it should contain not less than three flowers. How many ways are there of doing this in?
(a) 5,24,288 (b) 2,62,144
(c) 2,61,156 (d) None of these

56. How many different numbers which are smaller than 2.10^8 can be formed using the digits 1 and 2 only?
(a) 766 (b) 94
(c) 92 (d) 126

57. How many distinct six-digit numbers are there having three odd and three even digits?
(a) 55 (b) $(5.6)^3.(4.6)^3.3$
(c) 281250 (d) None of these

58. How many eight-digit numbers are there the sum of whose digits is even?
(a) 14400 (b) 4.5^5
(c) 45.10^6 (d) None of these

59. There are five bottles of sherry and each have their respective caps. If you are asked to put the correct cap to the correct bottle then how many ways are there so that not a single cap is on the correct bottle?
(a) 44 (b) $5^5 - 1$
(c) 5^5 (d) None of these

60. Amartya Banerjee has forgotten the telephone number of his best friend Abhijit Roy. All he remembers is that the number had eight-digits and ended with an odd number and had exactly one 9. How many possible numbers does Amartya have to try to be sure that he gets the correct number?
(a) 104.9^5 (b) 113.9^5
(c) 300.9^5 (d) $764.9^5.6!$

61. In Question 60, if Amartya is reminded by his friend Sharma that apart from what he remembered there was the additional fact that the last digit of the number was not repeated under any circumstance then how many possible numbers does Amartya have to try to be sure that he gets the correct number?
(a) $200.8^5 + 72.9^5$ (b) 8.9^6
(c) $36.8^5 + 7.9^6$ (d) $36.8^5 + 8.9^6$

62. How many natural numbers not more than 4300 can be formed with the digits 0,1, 2, 3, 4 (if repetitions are allowed)?
(a) 574 (b) 570
(c) 575 (d) 569

63. How many natural numbers less than 4300, can be formed with the digits 0, 1, 2, 3, 4 (if repetitions are not allowed)?
(a) 113 (b) 158
(c) 154 (d) 119

64. How many even natural numbers divisible by 5, can be formed with the digits 0, 1, 2, 3, 4, 5, 6 (if repetitions of digits not allowed)?

(a) 1957 (b) 1956
(c) 1236 (d) 1235

65. The letters of the word PASTE are written in all possible orders and these words are written out as in a dictionary. Then the rank of the word SPATE is
(a) 432 (b) 86
(c) 59 (d) 446

66. A library has twenty copies of CAGE; twelve copies each of RAGE Part1 and Part 2; five copies of PAGE Part 1, Part 2 and Part 3 and single copy of SAGE, DAGE and MAGE. In how many ways can these books be distributed?
(a) $62!/(20!)(12!)(5!)$ (b) $62!$
(c) $62!/(37)^3$ (d) $62!/(20!)(12!)^2(5!)^3$

High Yield Questions

Scan this QR code to access assisted problem solving videos on questions 6, 15, 60, 61 and 65 from LOD 3

Space for Rough Work

ANSWER KEY

Level of Difficulty (I)

1. (a)	2. (b)	3. (a)	4. (b)
5. (c)	6. (c)	7. (b)	8. (b)
9. (c)	10. (a)	11. (c)	12. (a)
13. (b)	14. (a)	15. (c)	16. (a)
17. (c)	18. (b)	19. (a)	20. (a)
21. (b)	22. (d)	23. (b)	24. (d)
25. (d)	26. (a)	27. (c)	28. (c)
29. (d)	30. (a)	31. (a)	32. (b)
33. (b)	34. (c)	35. (b)	36. (b)
37. (b)	38. (c)	39. (c)	40. (b)
41. (d)	42. (d)	43. (d)	44. (d)
45. (a)			

Level of Difficulty (II)

1. 136	2. 8	3. 27	
4. 2118760	5. 10	6. 1956	7. 4463
8. 804	9. 60	10. (d)	11. (a)
12. (b)	13. (d)	14. (c)	15. (d)
16. (a)	17. (a)	18. (b)	19. (b)
20. (a)	21. (b)	22. (b)	23. (a)
24. (b)	25. (d)	26. (c)	27. (b)
28. (b)	29. (d)	30. (b)	31. (c)
32. (b)	33. (c)	34. (a)	35. (b)
36. (c)	37. (a)	38. (c)	39. (d)
40. (a)	41. (b)	42. (d)	43. (a)
44. (d)	45. (c)	46. (b)	47. (a)
48. (c)	49. (b)	50. (d)	51. (a)
52. (a)	53. (d)	54. (d)	55. (d)
56. (a)	57. (d)	58. (d)	59. (b)
60. (b)	61. (a)	62. (a)	63. (c)
64. (a)	65. (c)	66. (d)	67. (c)
68. (b)	69. (b)	70. (d)	71. (c)
72. (d)	73. (d)	74. (c)	75. (a)
76. (d)	77. (b)	78. (c)	79. (b)
80. (b)	81. (b)		

Level of Difficulty (III)

1. 1008	2. 50	3. 50	4. 150
5. 247	6. 8400 × 5!	7. 80	8. 3439
9. 33	10. 85	11. 50	12. 77
13. 144	14. $n = 5$	15. 53 ways	16. 5
17. (a)	18. 126	19. 1944	20. 840
21. 45360	22. 2^{n+1}	23. 3696	24. 7392
25. (a)	26. (b)	27. (d)	28. (a)
29. (c)	30. (c)	31. (b)	32. (b)
33. (a)	34. (c)	35. (d)	36. (c)
37. (d)	38. (c)	39. (c)	40. (c)
41. (b)	42. (d)	43. (a)	44. (d)
45. (a)	46. (b)	47. (a)	48. (b)
49. (c)	50. (b)	51. (a)	52. (b)
53. (c)	54. (b)	55. (c)	56. (a)
57. (c)	58. (c)	59. (a)	60. (c)
61. (a)	62. (c)	63. (b)	64. (b)
65. (b)	66. (d)		

SOLUTIONS AND SHORTCUTS

Level of Difficulty (I)

1. Use the MNP rule to get the answer as $5 \times 4 = 20$.
2. There would be 5! ways of arranging the five letters. Thus, $5! = 120$ ways.
3. For a straight line, we just need to select two points out of the eight points available. ${}^8C_2$ would be the number of ways of doing this.
4. An engineer can make it through in two ways, while a CA can make it through in three ways. Required ratio is 2 : 3. Hence, option (b) is correct.
5. In this case, since nothing is mentioned about whether the prizes are identical or distinct we can take the prizes to be distinct (the most logical thought given the situation). Thus, each prize can be given in eight ways — thus a total of 8^5 ways.
6. We need to assume that the seven Indians are one person, so also for the six Dutch and the five Pakistanis. These three groups of people can be arranged amongst themselves in 3! ways. Also, within themselves the seven Indians the six Dutch and the five Pakistanis can be arranged in 7!, 6! and 5! ways respectively. Thus, the answer is $3! \times 7! \times 6! \times 5!$.
7. The first digit can only be 2 (one way), the second digit can be filled in seven ways, the third in six ways and the fourth in five ways. A total of $1 \times 7 \times 6 \times 5 = 210$ ways.
8. Each invitation card can be sent in four ways. Thus, $4 \times 4 \times 4 \times 4 \times 4 \times 4 = 4^6$.
9. The number of numbers formed would be given by $5 \times 4 \times 3$ (given that the first digit can be filled in five ways, the second in four ways and the third in three ways – MNP rule).
10. $5 \times 4 = 20$.
11. ${}^{11}C_1 \times {}^{10}C_1 = 110$. Alternately, ${}^{11}C_2 \times 2!$
12. In the letters of the word ALLAHABAD, there is only one vowel available for selection (*A*). Note that the fact that *A* is available four times has no impact on this fact. Also, there are four consonants available — viz: *L*, *H*, *B* and *D*. Thus, the number of ways of selecting a vowel and a consonant would be $1 \times {}^4C_1 = 4$.
13. For each digit, there would be five options (viz, 1, 3, 5, 7, and 9). Hence, the total number of numbers would be $5 \times 5 \times 5 \times 5 = 625$.
14. Choose one person for the single room & from the remaining choose two people for the double room & from the remaining choose four people for the four persons room $\rightarrow {}^7C_1 \times {}^6C_2 \times {}^4C_4$.
15. This is a typical case for the use of the formula ${}^{n-1}C_{r-1}$ with $n = 10$ and $r = 6$. So the answer would be given ${}^9C_5$.

16. From the first suit, there would be thirteen options of selecting a card. From the second suite, there would be twelve options; from the third suite, there would be eleven options; and from the fourth suite, there would be ten options for selecting a card. Thus, 13 × 12 × 11 × 10.
17. The maximum value of ^nC_r for a given value of n, happens when r is equal to the half of n. So if he wants to maximise the number of parties given that he has twenty friends, he should invite 10 to each party.
18. Number of eleven-letter words formed from the letters $P, E, R, M, U, T, A, T, I, O, N$ = 11!/2!.
Number of new words formed = total words –1 = 11!/2!–1.
19. P _ _ _ T. Missing letters have to be filled with A,N,A. 3!/2!.= 3 ways.
20. 3 × 3 × 2 × 1 = 18
21. 3 × 4 × 4 × 4 = 192
22. Divide the numbers into three-digit numbers and four-digit numbers—Number of three-digit numbers = 2 × 3 × 2 = 12. Number of four-digit numbers starting with 10 = 2 × 1 = 2. Total = 14 numbers.
23. We need to count words starting with P. These words would be represented by P _ _ _ _.
The letters ATNA can be arranged in 4!/2! ways in the four places, i.e. a total of twelve ways.
24. 3-digit numbers = 2 × 4 × 4 –1 = 31 (–1 is because the number 200 cannot be counted); 4-digit numbers starting with 10 = 4 × 4 = 16, Number of 4 digit numbers starting with 11 = 4 × 4 = 16. Total numbers = 31 + 16 + 16 = 63.
25. Rearrangements do not count the original arrangements. Thus, 5!/2! – 1 = 59 ways of rearranging the letters of PATNA.
26. $^8C_3 \times {^5C_2} \times 5! = 67200$
27. R _ _ _ _ _ _ W. The letters to go into the spaces are P, O, L, I, N, G. Since all these letters are distinct the number of ways of arranging them would be 6!.
28. $^{12}C_4 = 495$
29. 7!/3! × 4! = 35
30. The selection of the eleven player team can be done in $^{14}C_{10}$ ways. This results in the team of eleven players being completely chosen. The arrangements of these eleven players can be done in 11! ways.
Total batting orders = $^{14}C_{10} \times 11! = 1001 \times 11!$
(**Note:** Arrangement is required here because we are talking about forming batting orders).
31. The number has to start with a 3 and then in the remaining six digits it should have two 3's and four 0's. This can be done in 6!/2! × 4! = 15 ways.
32. $^{30}C_3$
33. $^{29}C_2$
34. $^3C_1 \times {^5C_3} \times {^4C_2} \times 5! = 21600$
35. If the number of teams is n, then $^nC_2$ should be equal to 45. Trial and error gives us the value of n as 10.
36. $^3C_1 \times {^4C_1} \times {^6C_1} = 72.$
37. The vowels EUAIO need to be considered as one letter to solve this. Thus, there would be 4! ways of arranging Q, T and N and the five vowels taken together. Also, there would be 5! ways of arranging the vowels amongst themselves. Thus, we have 4! × 5!.
38. Single-digit numbers = 5
Two-digit numbers = 5 × 4 = 20
Three-digit numbers = 5 × 4 × 3 = 60
Four-digit numbers = 5 × 4 × 3 × 2 = 120
Five-digit numbers = 5 × 4 × 3 × 2 × 1 = 120
Total = 5 + 20 + 60 + 120 + 120 = 325
39. $^{25}C_2 - {^7C_2} + 1 = 280$
40. $^{25}C_3 - {^7C_3} = 2265$
41. $^{25}C_4 - {^7C_4} - {^7C_3} \times {^{18}C_1} = 11985$
42. Four-digit Motor vehicle registration numbers can have 0 in the first digit. Thus, we have 6 × 5 × 4 × 3 = 360 ways.
43. All arrangements – arrangements with best and worst paper together = 12! – 2! × 11!.
44. $^{10}C_5 \times 5! = 30240$
45. $^{15}C_0 + {^{15}C_1} + {^{15}C_2} + {^{15}C_3} + {^{15}C_4} + {^{15}C_5} = 1 + 15 + 105 + 455 + 1365 + 3003 = 4944$

Level of Difficulty (II)

1. Among the first 20 natural numbers, the maximum difference can be 19 (1, 20). The range of differences is 4 to 19.
Difference 19 : 1 pair only {1, 20}; Difference 18 : 2 pairs {1, 19 & 2, 20}; Difference 17 : 3 pairs {1, 18; 2, 19 & 3, 20}; Difference 16 : 4 pairs {1, 17; 2, 18; 3, 19 & 4, 20}
Based on the given pattern, difference of 4 will have 16 possibilities. Hence, total number of pairs = 1 + 2 + 3 + 4 + 5.... + 16 = 136. The correct answer is 136.
2. To form a rectangle, we need to 2 parallel lines and 2 lines which are perpendicular to these lines. So $^6C_2 \times {^xC_2} = 420 \rightarrow \frac{6\times5\times x\times(x-1)}{2\times2} = 420 \rightarrow x(x-1) = 56.$
This is true if x = 8. Hence, 8 is the correct answer.
3. There are a total of 6 distinct ways of expressing 10 as sum of 3 numbers (1, 3, 6; 1, 4, 5; 2, 2, 6; 2, 3, 5; 2, 4, 4; 3, 3, 4). Since there are 3 different dice, we can have different possibilities for each die. For groups in which there is a repetition of numbers, we'll have to divide by 2!. Hence, the required number is 3 × 3! + 3 × 3!/2! = 27. The correct answer is 27.
4. From the set of 50 natural numbers we can select any 5 numbers. Each of these selections will have one specific order in which they are in descending order. So the required number is $^{50}C_5$.
This is equal to 50!/(5! × 45!) = 2118760. The correct answer is 2118760

5. For averages to be integers, the sum of different groups needs to be a multiple of the number of integers in that group. For distinct integer average values, we can just find distinct sums we'll get for different numbers. We can do this by simply looking at different multiples of each number. The highest sum possible for the given set is 55. Hence, we'll look for multiples of different numbers that are less than or equal to 55. Alternatively, we know that the average has to lie between the highest and the lowest value which is 10 and 1 respectively. Also, we haven't been given the minimum or maximum number of elements in the set, so we can say that all integers from 1 to 10 can be the average. We can visualise some of this as: The set (1, 2, 3, 4, 5) has an average of 3; The set (2, 4, 6) has an average of 4; the set (10) has an average of 10 and so on. Hence, 10 different possible integer values of averages are there. The correct answer is 10.
6. One digit number: 6
   Two digit numbers: $6 \times 5 = 30$
   Three digit numbers: $6 \times 5 \times 4 = 120$
   Four digit numbers: $6 \times 5 \times 4 \times 3 = 360$
   Five digit numbers: $6 \times 5 \times 4 \times 3 \times 2 = 720$
   Six digit numbers: $6 \times 5 \times 4 \times 3 \times 2 \times 1 = 720$
   Hence, the required answer is 1956
7. We can do this either by calculating individually or by subtracting the numbers with no digits equal from total number of possible values.
   Total numbers between 1000 and 10000 = 8999
   Total numbers with all distinct digits = $9 \times 9 \times 8 \times 7$ = 4536
   Hence, the required answer is 8999 – 4536 = 4463
8. Since, within a team, each member gives every other member a watch, for 1 team we'll require 8×7 = 56 watches. So for all the teams combined, we will require $56 \times 12 = 672$ watches. Now, each team gives every other team a photo frame. So we require a total of $12 \times 11 = 132$ photo frames. Hence, the required total is 672 + 132 = 804
9. A three digit number can be expressed as $100a + 10b + c$. Its reverse will be $100c + 10b + a$. According to question, c is more than a and $99 \times (c - a) = 297$ $\rightarrow c - a = 3$.
   If $c = 4$, $a = 1$; If $c = 5$, $a = 2$; If $c = 6$, $a = 3$; If $c = 7$, $a = 4$; If $c = 8$, $a = 5$; If $c = 9$, $a = 6$
   For each of these possibilities, we will have 10 values for b (between 0 to 9). Note that since b is the middle digit in both abc and cba, it can take any value from 0 to 9. Hence, the required answer is $10 \times 6 = 60$.
10. For odd places, the number of arrangements = $\frac{4!}{2!2!}$

    For even places, the number of arrangements = $\frac{3!}{2!}$

    Hence the total number of arrangements = $\frac{4! \times 3!}{2! \times 2! \times 2!}$
11. Select any three places for A, B and C. They need no arrangement amongst themselves as A would always come before B and B would come before C.
    The remaining five people have to be arranged in five places.
    Thus, ${}^8C_3 \times 5! = 56 \times 120 = 6720$ OR 8!/3!
12. Total number of choices = 4! out of which only one will be right.
13. At least, two letters have to interchange their places for a wrong choice.
14. Select any two letters and interchange them (${}^4C_2$).
15. $1m + 3f = {}^8C_1 \times {}^8C_3 = 8 \times 56 = 448$
    $2m + 2f = {}^8C_2 \times {}^8C_2 = 28 \times 28 = 784$
    $3m + 1f\ {}^8C_3 \times {}^8C_1 = 56 \times 8 = 448$
    $4m + 0f = {}^8C_4 \times {}^8C_0 = 70 \times 1 = 70$
    Total = 1750
16. Solve this by dividing the solution into,
    3 women and 1 man or
    2 women and 2 men or
    1 woman and 3 men or
    0 woman and 4 men
    This will give us:
    ${}^8C_3 \times {}^8C_1 + {}^8C_2 \times {}^8C_2 + {}^8C_1 \times {}^8C_3 + {}^8C_0 \times {}^8C_4$
    $= 448 + 784 + 448 + 70 = 1750$
17. ${}^{45}C_7$ (refer to solved example 18.14).
18. When all digits are odd
    $5 \times 5 \times 5 \times 5 \times 5 \times 5 = 5^6$
    When all digits are even
    $4 \times 5 \times 5 \times 5 \times 5 \times 5 = 4 \times 5^5$
    $5^6 + 4 \times 5^5 = 28125$
19. There will be two types of triangles.
    The first type will have its vertices on the three sides of the ΔABC.
    The second type will have two of its vertices on the same side and the third vertex on any of the other two sides.
    Hence, the required number of triangles
    $= 6 \times 5 \times 3 + {}^6C_2 \times 8 + {}^5C_2 \times 9 + {}^3C_2 \times 11$
    $= 90 + 120 + 90 + 33$
    $= 333$
20. All six digit numbers – Six digit numbers with only odd digits
    $= 900000 - 5 \times 5 \times 5 \times 5 \times 5 \times 5 = 884375$.
21. First step – arrange seven boys around the table according to the circular permutations rule, i.e. in 6! ways.
    Second step – now, we have seven places and have to arrange seven girls on these places. This can be done in ${}^7P_7$ ways. Hence, the total number of ways = 6! × 7!
22. The first rook can be placed in any of the 64 squares and the second rook will then have only 49 places so that they are not attacking each other.

23. $2 \times 7! \times 7!$ (**Note:** we do not need to use circular arrangements here because the seats are numbered.)

24. "Total number of all ten-digits numbers – Total number of all ten-digits numbers with no digit repeated" will give the required answer.
$= 9 \times 10^9 - 9 \times {}^9P_8$

25. For one pair of black shoes, we require one left black and one right black. Consider the worst case situation:
$7LB + 5LW + 5RW + 1RB$ or
$7RB + 5LW + 5RW + 1LB = 18$ shoes

26. For one pair of correct shoes, one of the possible combinations is $7LB + 5LW + 1R$ (B or W) $= 13$. Some other cases are also possible with at least 13 shoes.

27. We just need to select the floors and the people who get down at each floor.
The floors selection can be done in ${}^{11}C_3$ ways.
The people selection is ${}^9C_4 \times {}^5C_3$.
Also, the floors need to be arranged using 3!.
Thus, ${}^{11}C_3 \times {}^9C_4 \times {}^5C_3 \times 3!$ or ${}^{11}P_3 \times {}^9C_4 \times {}^5C_3$

28. From eight people we have to *arrange* a group of five in which three are similar $\frac{8P_5}{3!}$ or $\frac{8C_5 \times 5!}{3!}$.

29. $\frac{4C_4 \times 4C_1 \times 5!}{3!} + \frac{4C_2 \times 4C_3 \times 5!}{3!} - 4C_2 \times 4C_3 \times 2C_2 \times \mathbf{2!}$

30. Since the number of men and women in the question is the same, there is no difference in solving this question and solving the previous one as committees having a maximum of two women would mean committees having a minimum of three men and committees having at maximum one woman holding the post of either president or vice president would mean at least one man holding one of the two posts.
Thus, the answer would be:
Number of committees with four men and one woman (including all arrangements of the committees) + Number of committees with three men and two women (including all arrangements of the committees)–Number of committees with three men and two women where both the women are occupying the two posts
$= ({}^4C_4 \times {}^4C_1 \times 5!)/3! + ({}^4C_3 \times {}^4C_2 \times 5!)/3! - ({}^4C_3 \times {}^4C_2 \times {}^2C_2 \times 2!) = 80 + 480 - 48 = 512$

31. ${}^7C_1 \times {}^6C_2 \times 4! \times 4! = 60480$

32. We need to think of this as: Number with two sixes or numbers with one six or number with no six.
0, 1, 2, 3, 4, 5, 6 and 6
Numbers with two sixes:
Numbers ending in 0 $\quad {}^5C_1 \times 3!/2! = 15$
Numbers ending in 5 and
(a) Starting with 6 $\quad {}^5C_1 \times 2! = 10$
(b) Not starting with 6 $\quad {}^4C_1$ (as zero is not allowed) $= 4$
Number with one six or no sixes.
Numbers ending in 0 $\quad {}^6C_3 \times 3! = 120$
Numbers ending in 5 $\quad {}^5C_1 \times {}^5C_2 \times 2! = 100$
Thus, a total of 249 numbers.

33. First arrange six pups in six places in 6! ways. This will leave us with seven places for four cats.
Answer $= 6! \times 7p_4$.

34. Number of even numbers $= 6 \times 6 \times 6 \times 3$

35. Since it is possible to give no objects to one or two of them, we would have three choices for giving each item.
Thus, $3 \times 3 \times 3 \times 3 \times 3 \times 3 \times 3 = 2187$.

36. For an even number, the unit's digit should be either 2, 4 or 6. For the other five places we have six digits. Hence, the number of six digit numbers $= {}^6P_5 \times 3 = 2160$.

37. This number has to have the last two digits even. Thus, ${}^3C_2 \times 2!$ will fill the last two digits.
For the remaining places: ${}^5C_4 \times 4!$
Thus, we have ${}^5C_4 \times 4! \times {}^3C_2 \times 2! = 720$.

38. ${}^4C_1 \times 7 \times 7 \times 7 = {}^4C_1 \times 7^3$

39. ${}^9C_5 \times 5! = 15120$

40. Select the two positions for the two 3's. After that the remaining five places have to be filled using either 1 or 2.
Thus, ${}^7C_2 \times 2^5$.

41. ${}^4C_1 \times {}^7C_3 \times 3! = 840$

42. Give one marble to each of the six children. Then, the remaining four identical marbles can be distributed amongst the six children in ${}^{(4+6-1)}C_{(6-1)}$ ways.

43. First make the six law students sit in a row. This can be done in 6! ways. Then, there would be seven places for the MBA students. We need to select five of these seven places for five MBA students and then arrange these five students in those five places. This can be done in ${}^7C_5 \times 5!$ ways.
Thus, the answer is:
$6! \times {}^7C_5 \times 5! = 7! \times 6!/2!$

44. The required answer will be given by counting the total number of registration numbers starting with DL-5A to DL-5R and the number of registration numbers starting with DL-5S that have to be counted.

45. Out of 100 balls arrange 99 balls (except n_{28}) amongst themselves. Now put n_{28} just before n_{29} in the above arrangement.

46. ${}^6C_2 = 15$.

47. We have four options for every place including the left most.
So the total number of numbers $= 4 \times 4 \times 4 \times ... = 4^{10}$.
We have to consider only positive numbers, so we do not consider one number in which all ten digits are zeroes.

48. Total number of attempts $= 10^4$ out of which one is correct.

49. Number of ways of selecting 5 different letters $= {}^5C_5 = 1$

Number of ways of selecting 2 similar and 3 different letters = ${}^4C_1 \times {}^4C_3 = 16$
Number of ways of selecting 2 similar letters + 2 more similar letters and 1 different letter = ${}^4C_2 \times {}^3C_1 = 18$
Number of ways of selecting 3 similar letters and 2 different letters = ${}^3C_1 \times {}^4C_2 = 18$
Number of ways of selecting 3 similar letters and another 2 other similar letters = ${}^3C_1 \times {}^3C_1 = 9$
Number of ways of selecting 4 similar letters and 1 different letter = ${}^2C_1 \times {}^4C_1 = 8$
Number of ways of selecting 5 similar letters = ${}^1C_1$ = 1
Total number of ways = 1 + 16 + 18 + 18 + 9 + 8 + 1 = 71.

50. Divide $3n + 1$ articles in two groups.
(i) n identical articles and the remaining
(ii) $2n + 1$ non-identical articles
We will select articles in two steps. Some from the first group and the rest from the second group.

Number of articles from first group	*Number of articles from second group*	*Number of ways.*
0	n	$1 \times {}^{2n+1}C_n$
1	$n - 1$	$1 \times {}^{2n+1}C_{n-1}$
2	$n - 2$	$1 \times {}^{2n+1}C_{n-2}$
3	$n - 3$	$1 \times {}^{2n+1}C_{n-3}$
..	..	....
$n - 1$	1	$1 \times {}^{2n+1}C_1$
n	0	$1 \times {}^{2n+1}C_0$

Total number of ways = ${}^{2n+1}C_n + {}^{2n+1}C_{n-1} + {}^{2n+1}C_{n-2} + \ldots {}^{2n+1}C_1 + {}^{2n+1}C_0 = \frac{2^{2n+1}}{2} = 2^{2n}$.

51. Firstly, we will give 5 crores each to the three sons. That will cover 15 crores out of 30 crores leaving behind 15 crores. Now, 15 crores can be distributed in three people in 17!/15!2! ways or 136 ways.
Hence, option (a) is the answer.

52. Number of words starting with A = 8!/ 2!3! = 3360.
Number of words starting with B = 8!/ 2!4! = 840
Number of words starting with D = 8!/2!4! = 840
Number of words starting with H = 8!/2!4! = 840
Now words with L start.
Number of words starting with LAA = 6!/2! = 360
Now, LAB starts and first word starts with LABA.
Number of words starting with LABAA = 4! = 24
After this the next words will be LABADAAHL, LABADAALH, LABADAHAL, LABADAHLA and hence, option (a) is the answer.

53. Total number of pairs of men that can be selected if the adjacent ones are also selected is ${}^NC_2$. Total number of pairs of men selected if only the adjacent ones are selected is N. Hence total number of pairs of men selected if the adjacent ones are not selected is ${}^NC_2 - N$.
Since the total time taken is 88 min, hence the number of pairs is 44.
Hence, ${}^NC_2 - N = 44 \rightarrow N = 11$.
Hence, Option (d) is the answer.

54. Let $x = 3$. Then $y + z = 27$. For the conditions given in the question, number of solutions is 20.
Similarly for $x = 2$, there will be 20 solutions; for $x = 1$ there will be 22 solutions and for $x = 0$, there will be 22 solutions. Therefore, total 84 solutions are possible.
Similarly, for $y = 3$ to 0, there will be 84 solutions and for $z = 3$ to 0, there will be 84 solutions.
Hence, there will be total of 252 solutions. Hence, Option (d) is the answer.

55. As no three points are collinear, therefore, every combination of three points out of the nine points will give us a triangle. Hence, the answer is ${}^9C_3$ or 84.
Hence, option (d) is correct.

56. Let the number of boys be B. Then ${}^BC_2 = 36 \rightarrow B = 9$.
Let the number of girls be G. Then ${}^GC_2 = 66 \rightarrow G = 12$.
Therefore, total number of students in the class = 12 + 9 = 21. Hence total number of matches = ${}^{21}C_2 = 210$. Hence, number of matches between one boy and one girl = 210 – (36 + 66) = 108.
Hence, option (a) is the answer.

57. The number of combinations of three points picked from the nine given points is ${}^9C_3$ or 84. All these combinations will result in a triangle except the combination of the three collinear points. Hence number of triangles formed will be 84 – 1 = 83.
Hence, option (d) is the answer.

58. With three chocolates to Sana, the remaining 12 chocolates, would then get divided among four children, with each child getting minimum one chocolate in ${}^{11}C_3$ ways.
With four chocolates to Sana, the remaining 11 chocolates, would then get divided among four children, with each child getting minimum one chocolate in ${}^{10}C_3$ ways.
With five chocolates to Sana, the remaining 10 chocolates, would then get divided among four children, with each child getting minimum one chocolate in ${}^9C_3$ ways.
With six chocolates to Sana, the remaining 9 chocolates, would then get divided among four children, with each child getting minimum one chocolate in ${}^8C_3$ ways.
The total number of distributions = 165 + 120 + 84 + 56 = 425. Hence, option (d) is correct.

59. We will consider $x = 7$ to $x = 1$.
For $x = 7$, $y + z = 5$. Number of solutions = 4

For $x = 6$, $y + z = 6$. Number of solutions = 5
For $x = 5$, $y + z = 7$. Number of solutions = 6
For $x = 4$, $y + z = 8$. Number of solutions = 7
For $x = 3$, $y + z = 9$. Number of solutions = 6
For $x = 2$, $y + z = 10$. Number of solutions = 5
For $x = 1$, $y + z = 11$. Number of solutions = 4
Hence, number of solutions = 37
Hence, option (b) is the answer.

60. $(xy)^2 = u! + v$

Here, xy is a two-digit number and maximum value of its square is 9801. 8! is a five-digit number => u is less than 8 and 4! is 24 which when added to a single digit will never give the square of a two-digit number. Hence u is greater than 4. So, possible values of u can be 5, 6 and 7.

If $u = 5$, $u! = 120 \Rightarrow (xy)^2 = u! + v \Rightarrow (xy)^2 = 120 + v = 120 + 1 = 121 = 11^2$

If $u = 6$, $u! = 720 \Rightarrow (xy)^2 = u! + v \Rightarrow (xy)^2 = 720 + v = 720 + 9 = 729 = 27^2$

If $u = 7$, $u! = 5040 \Rightarrow (xy)^2 = u! + v \Rightarrow (xy)^2 = 5040 + v = 5040 + 1 = 5041 = 71^2$

So, there are three cases possible. Hence, three solutions exist for the given equation.

Hence, option (b) is the correct answer.

61. If we have 'n' candidates, who can be selected at the maximum, naturally, the answer to the question would also represent 'n'.

Hence, we check for the first option. If $n = 3$, then $2n + 1 = 7$ and it means that there are seven candidates to be chosen from. Since it is given that the number of ways of selection of at least one candidate is 63, we should try to see, whether selecting 1, 2 or 3 candidates from 7 indeed adds up to 63 ways. If it does this would be the correct answer.

${}^7C_1 + {}^7C_2 + {}^7C_3 = 7 + 21 + 35 = 63$. Thus, the first Option fits the situation and is hence correct.

62. This problem can be approached by putting the white flags in their possible positions. There are essentially four possibilities for placing the three white flags based on the condition that two flags of the same color cannot be together:

1, 3, 5; 1, 3, 6; 1, 4, 6 and 2, 4, 6

Out of these four possible arrangements for the three white flags we cannot use 1, 3, 6 and 1, 4, 6 as these have the same color of flag at both ends-something which is not allowed according to the question. Thus there are only two possible ways of placing the white flags— 1, 3, 5 OR 2, 4, 6. In each of these two ways, there are a further three ways of placing the one red flag and the two blue flags. Thus we get a total of six ways. Option (a) is correct.

63. The possible numbers are:

635_ _ _9	9 in the units place	$9 \times 9 \times 9 = 729$ numbers
635 _ _ _ _	9 used before the units place	$3 \times 9 \times 9 \times 4 = 972$ numbers
674_ _ _9	9 in the units place	$9 \times 9 \times 9 = 729$ numbers
674 _ _ _ _	9 used before the units place	$3 \times 9 \times 9 \times 4 = 972$ numbers
Total		3402 numbers

64. We need to go through the options and use the MNP rule tool relating to Permutations and Combinations. We can draw up the following possibilities table for the number of routes between each of the three towns. If the first option is true, i.e., there are six routes between A to C:

A-C	*Possibilities for C-B*	*Possibilities for total routes A-C-B (Say X)*	*Possibilities for total routes A–B (Y)*
6	5, 4, 3, 2, 1	30, 24, 18, 12, 6	3, 9, 15, 21, 27 **Note:** these values are derived based on the logic that $X + Y = 33$

We further know that there are 23 routes between B to C.

From the above combinations, the possibilities for the routes between B to C are:

B–A (Y in the table above)	*A–C*	*B–A–C*	*B–C*	*Total*
3	6	18	5	23
9	6	54 not possible	4	
15	6	90 not possible	3	
21	6	126 not possible	2	
27	6	162 not possible	1	

It is obvious that the first possibility in the table above satisfies all conditions of the given situation. Hence, option (a) is correct.

65. With the digits 1, 2, 3, 4, 5 and 6 the numbers divisible by 4 that can be formed are numbers ending in: 12, 16, 24, 32, 36, 52, 56 and 64.

Number of numbers ending in 12 is: $4 \times 3 \times 2 = 24$

Thus, the number of numbers is $24 \times 8 = 192$

Hence, option (c) is correct.

66. The white square can be selected in 32 ways and once the white square is selected, eight black squares become ineligible for selection. Hence, the black square can be selected in 24 ways. $32 \times 24 = 768$. Hence, option (d) is correct.

67. A million is 1000000 (i.e. the first seven digit number). So we need to find how many numbers of less than seven digits can be formed using the digits 0,7 and 8.

Number of 1-digit numbers = 2
Number of 2-digit numbers = 2 × 3 = 6
Number of 3-digit numbers = 2 × 3 × 3 = 18
Number of 4-digit numbers = 2 × 3 × 3 × 3 = 54
Number of 5-digit numbers = 2 × 3 × 3 × 3 × 3 = 162
Number of 6-digit numbers = 2 × 3 × 3 × 3 × 3 × 3 = 486
Total number of numbers = 728. Hence, option (c) is correct.

68. For each selection there are three ways of doing it. Thus, there are a total of 3 × 3 × 3 × 3 × 3 = 243. Hence, option (b) is correct.

69. From five bananas we have six choices available (0, 1, 2, 3, 4 or 5). Similarly, four mangoes and four almonds can be chosen in five ways each.
So total ways = 6 × 5 × 5 = 150 possible selections.
But in this 150, there is one selection where no fruit is chosen.
So required number of ways = 150 – 1 = 149
Hence, option (b) is correct.

70. We have no girls together, let us first arrange the five boys and after that we can arrange the girls in the spaces between the boys.
Number of ways of arranging the boys around a circle = [5 – 1]! = 24.
Number of ways of arranging the girls would be by placing them in the five spaces that are formed between the boys. This can be done in ${}^5P_3$ ways = 60 ways.
Total arrangements = 24 × 60 = 1440.
Hence, option (d) is correct.

71. Books of interest = 7, books to be borrowed = 3
Case 1: Quants book is taken. Then D.I book can also be taken.
So Amita is to take two more books out of six which she can do in ${}^6C_2$ = 15 ways.
Case 2: If Quants book has not been taken, the D.I book would also not be taken.
So Amita will take three books out of five books. This can be done in ${}^5C_3$ = 10 ways.
So total ways = 15 + 10 = 25 ways.
Hence, option (c) is correct.

72. For each question, we have three choices of answering the question (two internal choices + one non-attempt). Thus, there are a total of 3^{15} ways of answering the question paper. Out of this there is exactly one way in which the student does not answer any question. Thus there are a total of $3^{15} - 1$ ways in which at least one question is answered.
Hence, option (d) is correct.

73. We have to select 5 out of 12.
If Radha and Mohan join then we have to select only 5 – 2 = 3 dancers out of 12 – 2 = 10 which can be done in ${}^{10}C_3$ = 120 ways.
If Radha and Mohan do not join, then we have to select 5 out of 12 – 2 = 10 → ${}^{10}C_5$ = 252 ways.
Total number of ways = 120 + 252 = 372.
Hence, option (d) is correct.

74. The digits are 1, 6, 7, 8, 7, 6, and 1. In this seven-digit number. there are four odd places and three even places— OEOEOEO. The four odd digits 1, 7, 7, 1 can be arranged in four odd places in [4!/2! × 2] = 6 ways [as 1 and 7 are both occurring twice]. The even digits 6, 8, 6 can be arranged in three even places in 3!/2! = 3 ways.
Total number of ways = 6 × 3 = 18.
Hence, Option (c) is correct.

75. As we need to find the maximum number of trials, so we have to assume that the required ball in every box is picked as late as possible. So in the third box, first two balls will be red and black. Hence, third trial will give him the required ball. Similarly, in fourth box, he will get the required ball in fourth trial and in the fifth box, he will get the required ball in fifth trial. Hence, maximum total number of trials required is 3 + 4 + 5 = 12.
Hence, option (a) is the answer.

76. The unit digit can either be 2, 3, 4, 5 or 6.
When the unit digit is 2, the number would be even and hence will be divisible by 2. Hence, all numbers with unit digit 2 will be included which is equal to 5! or 120.
When the unit digit is 3, then in every case the sum of the digits of the number would be 21 which is a multiple of 3. Hence, all numbers with unit digit 3 will be divisible by 3 and hence, will be included. Total number of such numbers is 5! or 120.
Similarly, for unit digit 5 and 6, the number of required numbers is 120 each.
When the unit digit is 4, then the number would be divisible by 4 only if the ten's digit is 2 or 6. Total number of such numbers is 2 × 4! or 48.
Hence, total number of required numbers is (4 × 120) + 48 = 528.
Hence, option (d) is the answer.

77. Solve this one through options. If you pick up option (a), it gives you twelve participants in the tournament. This means that there are ten men and two women. In this case there would be 2 × ${}^{10}C_2$ = 90 matches amongst the men and 2 × ${}^{10}C_1 \times {}^2C_1$ = 40 matches between one man and one woman. The difference between number of matches where both participants are men and the number of matches where one participant is a man and one is a woman is 90 – 40 = 50 – which is not what is given in the problem.
With thirteen participants → eleven men and two women
In this case, there would be 2 × ${}^{11}C_2$ = 110 matches amongst the men and 2 × ${}^{11}C_1 \times {}^2C_1$ = 44 matches between one man and one woman. The difference between number of matches where both participants

are men and the number of matches where one participant is a man and one is a woman is 110 – 44 = 66 – which is the required value as given in the problem. Thus, option (b) is correct.

78. Based on the above thinking we get that since there are thirteen players and each player plays each of the others twice, the number of games would be $2 \times {}^{13}C_2 = 2 \times 78 = 156$.

79. Each of the first, third and fourth options can be obviously seen to be true— no mathematics needed there. Only the second option can never be true.
In order to think about this mathematically and numerically— think of a party of three persons say *A*, *B* and *C*. In order for the second condition to be possible, each person must know a different number of persons. In a party with three persons this is possible only if the numbers are 0, 1 and 2. If *A* knows, both *B* and *C* (2), *B* and *C* both would know at least one person— hence it would not be possible to create the person knowing zero people. The same can be verified with a group of four persons, i.e., Hence, option the minute you were to make one person know three persons it would not be possible for anyone in the group to know zero persons and hence you would not be able to meet the condition that every person knows a different number of persons. Hence, option (b) is correct.

80. One digit number = 5; two digit numbers = 5×4 = 20; three digit number = $5 \times 4 \times 3 = 60$; four digit number = $5 \times 4 \times 3 \times 2 = 120$; Five digit number = $5 \times 4 \times 3 \times 2 \times 1 = 120$ Total number of numbers = 325. Hence, option (b) is correct.

81. With one green ball there would be six ways of doing this. With two green balls five ways; with three green balls four ways; with four green balls three ways; with five green balls two ways and with six green balls one way. So, a total of 1 + 2 + 3 + 4 + 5 + 6 = 21 ways are possible. Hence, option (b) is correct.

Level of Difficulty (III)

1. Among the four positions available to us, we'll start with the last position as we first need to consider that our number is even, so a total of 5 possibilities (0, 2, 4, 6, 8).
Last digit 0: 4 possibilities for the first digit (1 to 4). That leaves us with 8 possibilities for the second and 7 for the third. This means that total numbers possible are $4 \times 8 \times 7 = 224$.
Last digit 2 and 4: 3 possibilities for the first digit (1, 3, 4 or 1, 2, 3). That leaves us with 8 possibilities for the second and 7 for the third. This means that total numbers possible are $3 \times 8 \times 7 \times 2 = 336$.
Last digit 6 and 8: 4 possibilities for the first digit (1 to 4). That leaves us with 8 possibilities for the second and 7 for the third. This means that total numbers possible are $4 \times 8 \times 7 \times 2 = 448$.
Hence, the required answer is 224 + 336 + 448 = 1008.

2. Single digit numbers: Since all the numbers are divisible by itself, we would consider all single digit numbers. **Hence, 9 numbers are there in single digit numbers.**
Two-digit numbers will have to be divided into what their last digit are.
For last digit 1, 2 and 5, we'll consider all numbers as they would be divisible by the units digit without any constraints. **Total 9 + 9 + 9 = 27 numbers.**
For last digit 3, sum of both the digits should be a multiple of 3. Since we already have a 3 in the units place, the tens place should also be a multiple of 3, so the tens place can be 3, 6 or 9. So, a **total of 3 numbers are possible.**
For last digit 4, the tens place can take values among 2, 4, 6 and 8. **Hence, there are 4 such numbers.**
For last digit 6, the number needs to be multiple of 2 and 3. Since the units digit is 6, our number is already a multiple of 2. For it to be a multiple of 3, the values possible for tens place are 3, 6 and 9. **Hence, there are 3 possibilities.**
For last digit 7, **There is only 1 possible value (77).**
For last digit 8, **There are only 2 possibilties (48 & 88).**
For last digit 9, sum of both the digits should be a multiple of 9. Since we already have a 9 in the units place, the tens place should also be a multiple of 9. So **only 1 number is possible.**
From the above scenarios, we can see that there a total of 9 + 27 + 3 + 4 + 3 + 1 + 2 + 1 = 50 such numbers. Hence, the correct answer is 50.

3. For a number to be a multiple of 15, it has to be multiple of both 3 and 5. This means that the units digit has to be 5. Now we need to deal with the remaining 5 digits, at least 1 of which has to be 5. Since we need 1 and 3 as well, we can have a maximum of four 5s which means 3 additional 5s.
Four 5s: Total sum = $1 + 3 + 4 \times 5 = 24$. This number will be a multiple of 3. For finding the total number of numbers which will be using this combination of digits, we need to realise that one of the 5's is fixed as the units digit. So we need to arrange 1, 3, 5, 5, 5 in five places. This can be done in $5!/3! = 20$ ways. Hence, the total numbers possible = 20.
Three 5s: For the remaining 3 numbers the sum should be a multiple of 3. This situation will not be possible because two positions will be taken by 1 and 3. No matter which number we choose for the third place, our sum wont be a multiple of 3. Hence, we don't have a number which is a multiple of 15 and has three 5s.

Two 5s: In this case, two positions are filled with 5s, one with 1 and one with 3. Total sum is 14. Last two positions can have sums among 1 + 1 = 2, 3 + 3 = 6 and 1 + 3 = 4. We get the sum as multiple of 3 if and only if the last two digits used for the number are 1 and 3. Hence, for the first 5 positions of the six digit number, we have one 5, two 1s and two 3s. So total numbers possible are 5!/2! × 2! = 30. Hence, total numbers possible are 30 + 20 = 50. The correct answer is 50.

4. Two aspirants getting 2 pens each leaves us with 6 pens for the remaining 3 aspirants. There are 7 ways of dividing 6 into three parts (6, 0, 0/5, 1, 0/4, 2, 0/4, 1, 1/3, 3, 0/3, 2, 1/2, 2, 2). But we are given that only 2 aspirants got two pens each. Hence, we can eliminate 3 of these possibilities, which involve giving 2 pens to more people. Now we are left with (6, 0, 0; 5, 1, 0; 3, 3, 0; 4, 1, 1). The detailed thought in each of these four cases can be illustrated as below:

   Case 1: Distribution 6, 0, 0, 2, 2. Select 2 people from 5 for the two 2's. Then, select 2 people from the remaining three for the two 0's. The 6 pens will automatically go to the fifth person. Hence, the number of distributions = ${}^5C_2 \times {}^3C_2$ = 30 ways.

   Case 2: Distribution 5, 1, 0, 2, 2. Select 2 people from 5 for the two 2's. Then, distribute 5, 1, 0 between the remaining three people in 3! Ways. Hence, the number of distributions = ${}^5C_2 \times 3!$ = 60 ways.

   Case 3: Distribution 3, 3, 0, 2, 2. Select 2 people from 5 for the two 2's. Then, select 2 people from the remaining three for the two 3's. The 0 pens will automatically go to the fifth person. Hence, the number of distributions = ${}^5C_2 \times {}^3C_2$ = 30 ways

   Case 4: Distribution 4, 1, 1, 2, 2. Select 2 people from 5 for the two 2's. Then, select 2 people from the remaining three for the two 1's. The 4 pens will automatically go to the fifth person. Hence, the number of distributions = ${}^5C_2 \times {}^3C_2$= 30 ways.

   Hence, the correct answer is 30 + 60 + 30 + 30 = 150.

5. The highest common difference can be 13 with the 4 numbers being 1, 14, 27 and 40. The range of common differences for the AP will be 1 to 13.

   Common Difference = 13 : 1 possibility {1, 14, 27, 40}

   Common Difference = 12 : 4 possibilities {1, 13, 25, 37/2, 14, 26, 38/3, 15, 27, 39/4, 16, 28, 40}

   Common Difference = 11 : 7 possibilities {1, 12, 23, 34...7, 18, 29, 40}

   Common Difference = 10 : 10 possibilities {1, 11, 21, 31...10, 20, 30, 40}

   We see that if we reduce the common difference by 1, the number of possibilities increases by 3. Hence, we'll have a total of 1 + 4 + 7 + 10 + 13 + 16 + 19 + 22 + 25 + 28 + 31 + 34 + 37 = 19 × 13 = 247 possibilities. The correct answer is 247.

6. Since the question talks about two specific digits which cannot be taken together, we can solve this using total arrangements - arrangements having those two specific digits used in the code.

   Total arrangements = ${}^5C_2 \times {}^8C_3 \times 5!$ – =560 × 5!.

   Let the specific digits be 1 and 2. In that case, the number of codes with these two digits included will be: ${}^5C_2 \times {}^6C_1 \times 5! = 60 \times 5!$.

   Hence, the required answer is 560 × 5! – 60 × 5! = 500 × 5!

7. Before determining the number of possibilities for Shaurya, we need to first determine the possibilities for Pallav. Since the minimum sum for Shaurya is 3, We'll have to consider numbers for Pallav from 4.

Pallav	*Shaurya*
4	1 (1, 2)
5	2 (1, 2/1, 3)
6	4 (1, 2/1, 3/1, 4/2, 3)
7	6 (1, 2/1, 3/1, 4/1, 5/2, 3/2, 4)
8	8 (1, 2/1, 3/1, 4/1, 5/2, 3/2, 4/2, 5/3, 4)
9	9 (all pairs except 4, 5)
10	10 (all pairs)

   From the above table we can see that there will be a total of 40 pairs. However for each these pairs their reverse will also be true. Hence, the required answer is 80.

8. We will have to consider numbers with different number of digits: 1 digit numbers, 2 digit numbers, 3 digit numbers and 4 digit numbers.

   1 digit number: There is only 1 number – the number 9 itself.

   2-digit numbers: 8 numbers with a single 9 such that the 9 is in the units place) + 9 numbers with a single 9 such that the 9 is in the tens place + 1 number with both digits 9 = 18 numbers

   3-digit numbers: 72 numbers with a single 9, such that the 9 is in the units place + 72 numbers with a single 9, such that the 9 is in the tens place + 81 numbers with a single 9, such that the 9 is in the hundreds place + (9 + 9 + 8) = 26 numbers of the form 99*a*; 9*a*9 and *a*99 – i.e. numbers with 2 nines + 1 number with all three 9s i.e. 999.

   The total number of numbers is 252.

4 digit numbers: 2673 (one 9 in 4 different places) + 459 (two 9s in different places) + 35 (three 9s in different places) + 1(four 9s) = 3168

Hence, required answer is 1 + 18 + 252 + 3168 = 3439.

9. For the resultant number to be a multiple of 4, $b!$ has to be less than $a!$. Hence, b has to be less than a.

By visualisation we can see that the minimum value of 'a' for which we'll get a possibility is 4.

If $a = 4$, b can values from 1–3. 3 possibilities
If $a = 5$, b can values from 1–3. 3 possibilities
If $a = 6$, b can values from 1–3. 3 possibilities
If $a = 7$, b can values from 1–3. 3 possibilities
If $a = 8$, b can values from 1–7. 7 possibilities
If $a = 9$, b can values from 1–7. 7 possibilities
If $a = 10$, b can values from 1–7. 7 possibilities

Hence, the required answer is 33.

10. We cannot have three 0s. So we have either one or two 0s. We need to consider each possibility separately.

Numbers with two 0s: Since 2 out of the 3 digits are 0, the third digit has to be odd. Each of these numbers have to necessarily end with two zeroes. Hence, we have 5 values.

Numbers with one 0:

Sum = 1: not possible; Sum = 3: (1, 2) → 4 numbers;
Sum = 5: (1, 4 or 2, 3) → 8 numbers
Sum = 7: (1, 6 or 2, 5 or 3, 4) → 12 numbers;
Sum = 9: (1, 8 or 2, 7 or 3, 6 or 4, 5) → 16 numbers
Sum = 11: (2, 9 or 3, 8 or 4, 7 or 5, 6) → 16 numbers;
Sum = 13: (4, 9 or 5, 8 or 6, 7) → 12 numbers
Sum = 15: (6, 9 or 7, 8) → 8 Numbers;
Sum = 17: (8, 9) → 4 numbers

We cannot achieve an odd sum more than 17 with two single digit numbers.

Hence, the required total is 85

11. Different possibilities are:

Case 1: Single 4 and 5. Digits used (4, 5, 2, 2). Total number of numbers = 4!/2! = 12.

Case 2: Two 4's and one 5. Digits used (4, 4, 5, 2). Total number of numbers = 4!/2! = 12.

Case 3: Two 5's and one 4. Digits used (5, 5, 4, 2). Total number of numbers = 4!/2! = 12.

Case 4: Two 4's and Two 5's. Digits used (4, 4, 5, 5). Total number of numbers = 4!/(2! × 2!) = 6.

Case 5: Three 4's and one 5. Digits used (4, 5, 4, 4). Total number of numbers = 4!/3! = 4.

Case 6: Three 5's and one 4. Digits used (4, 5, 5, 5). Total number of numbers = 4!/3! = 4.

Hence, the required answer is 50

12. There are two possible cases

Case 1: Five 1's, one 2's, one 3's

Number of numbers = $\frac{7!}{5!} = 42$

Case 2: Four 1's, three 2's

Number of numbers = $\frac{7!}{4!3!} = 35$

Hence, the total number of numbers = 42 + 35 = 77

13. We can first assume that A < B < C < D and then try to find the distinct cases by fixing values of A and B, then trying to see how many values C and D can take. Thus, with A = 1, B = 2, C + D = 12, we have 3 solutions viz: (3, 9); (4, 8); (5, 7) for (C, D).

Case 2: A, B (1, 3); C, D can be (4, 7); (5, 6) – two solutions.

Case 3: A, B (1, 4); No solution for C, D.

Case 4: A, B (2, 3); C, D (4, 6) One solution.

There are no other cases for A, B, C, D that satisfy the given condition if we have assumed A < B < C < D. Thus, for this case there are 6 solutions. Each case will have to be multiplied by 4! in order to get the total number of solutions of (A, B, C, D) such that A, B, C, D are distinct from each other. Hence, the correct answer is 6 × 4! = 144.

14.

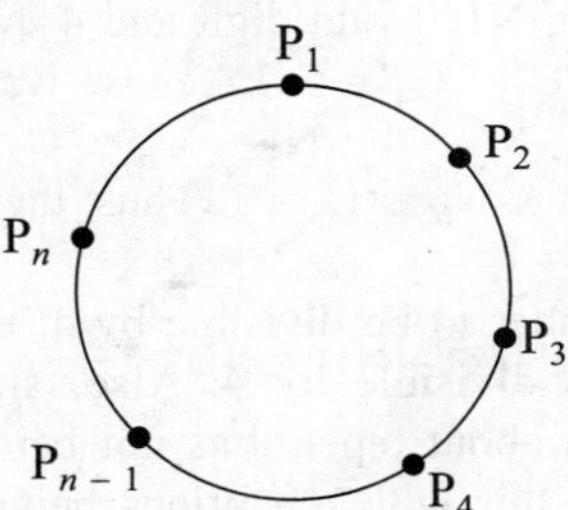

Number of adjacent lines = n

Number of line segments joining non-adjacent points is ${}^nC_2 - n$.

Now, $n = \left({}^nC_2 - n\right)$

$\Rightarrow 2n = \frac{n(n-1)}{2} \Rightarrow n = 0, 5$

But $n \geq 2$. So, $n = 5$.

15.

Cards	Envelopes
1	1
2	2
3	3
4	4
5	5
6	6

(arrow from card 1 to envelope 2)

If '2' goes in '1' then it is de-arrangement of 4 things which can be done in $4! \times \left(\frac{1}{2!} - \frac{1}{3!} + \frac{1}{4!}\right) = 9$ ways.

If '2' doesn't go in 1, it is de-arrangement of 5 things which can be done in $5! \times \left(\frac{1}{2!} - \frac{1}{3!} + \frac{1}{4!} - \frac{1}{5!}\right) = 44$.

Hence, there are a total of 9 + 44 = 53 ways.

16. Thinking about n, think of arranging 6 people in a queue (as the 5 girls can be taken as one person) & then arrange the 5 girls amongst themselves. Hence, $n = 5! \times 6!$
For m, The 5 boys can be arranged amongst themselves in 5! ways and then out of 6 places that open up for the girls we need to select 2 places and then select 4 girls to go into one of these two places, arrange them and also arrange into which place the single girl and the 4 girls go. The value of m can be visualized as: $m = 5! \times {}^6C_2 \times {}^5C_4 .2!.4!$
Hence, the required ratio of $\frac{m}{n} = \frac{5! \times 15 \times 2 \times 5!}{5! \times 6!} = 5.$

17. You can select a team with 4 girls and 0 boys & select a captain amongst them. This can be done in ${}^6C_4 \times {}^4C_1 = 60$ ways. Or you can select a team with 3 girls and 1 boy and select a captain from amongst them. This can be done in ${}^6C_3 \times {}^4C_1 \times {}^4C_1 = 320$ ways. Hence, the correct answer is 380 i.e. option (a)

18. For finding N1, 1 odd digit and 4 even digits to be selected: ${}^5C_1 \times {}^4C_4 = 5$. Likewise we can find $N_2 = {}^5C_2 \times {}^4C_3 = 40$; $N_3 = {}^5C_3 \times {}^4C_2 = 60$; $N_4 = {}^5C_4 \times {}^4C_1 = 20$ & $N_5 = {}^5C_5 = 1$. Thus, the correct answer is 126.

19. For a number to be divisible by 4, the last 2 digits should be divisible by 4. Also, since nothing is mentioned about repetitions not being allowed, we will solve this with repetitions being allowed. The cases for divisibility by 4 would be numbers ending with 12, 16, 24, 32, 36, 44, 52, 56 and 64. In each case, the first three digits can be filled in 6 ways each. Thus, the correct answer is:
$6 \times 6 \times 6 \times 9 = 1944.$

20. The sum of the seven digits is 28. For a 5 digit number to be divisible by 3, the sum of it's digits should be divisible by 3. Hence, we need to target values like 24, 21, 18 and 15 for the sum of digits of the 5 digit number. Let us look at these cases one by one.
Case 1: Sum of digits 24. Digits to be dropped are 1 and 3. So the number will get formed using 2, 4, 5, 6, 7 and there will be 5! = 120 such numbers.
Case 2: Sum of digits 21. Digits to be dropped are 1 and 6 Or 2 and 5 or 3 and 4. So the number will get formed using 2, 3, 4, 5, 7 or 1, 3, 4, 6, 7 or using 1, 2, 5, 6, 7. For each of these three situations there will be 5! = 120 such numbers. Thus, there will be 360 such numbers.
Case 3: Sum of digits 18. Digits to be dropped are 3 and 7 Or 4 and 6. So the number will get formed using 1, 2, 4, 5, 6 or 1, 2, 3, 5, 7. For each of these three situations there will be 5! = 120 such numbers. Thus, there will be 240 such numbers.
Case 4: Sum of digits 15 can be formed only using 1, 2, 3, 4, 5. A total of 5! = 120 such numbers.
Hence, the correct answer is 120 + 360 + 240 + 120 = 840.

21. **Case 1:** Two identical digits are 0, 0.
Number of ways to select 3 more digits = ${}^9C_3$
Number of arrangements of these 5 digits = $\frac{5!}{2!} - 4! = 36.$
(When 0 comes in the first-place number of numbers = 4!)
Therefore, the number of such numbers = $\frac{9 \times 8 \times 7}{3 \times 2} \times 36 = 3024.$
Case 2: Two identical digits are any one of (1, 1) or (2, 2) or ….or (9, 9)
For 1, 1, 0, Selection of 2 more = ${}^8C_2$
Arrangement of these 5 digits = $\frac{5!}{2!} - \frac{4!}{2!} = 48$
Therefore, number of such numbers = ${}^8C_2 \times 48$
For 1, 1 and no zero in the number:
Selection of 3 more (non – zero) = ${}^8C_3 \times \frac{5!}{2!} = {}^8C_3 \times 60$
So, total number of numbers in the case 2 = $9 \times \left({}^8C_2 \times 48 + {}^8C_3 \times 60\right) = 42336$
So, overall, total number of numbers = numbers in case 1 + numbers in case 2 = 3024 + 42336 = 45360.
The answer is 45360.

22. The prime digits are 2, 3, 5 and 7. As sum of two digits is also prime, this can be happen with 2, 3 and 2, 5 only. So the $2n$–digit number is comprising only these (2, 3, 5) digits and 2 occurs at every alternate place.
Now,
Case 1: The number starts with '2' and has either 3 or 5 in the second place followed by a 2 and then another 3 or 5 and so on. Since, we will have the option of using 3 or 5 in n distinct places, so the number of numbers in this case = $2 \times 2 \times 2 \times$ ……….n times = 2^n
Case 2: The number starts with 3 or 5, in such a case the first place from the left will be 3 or 5 followed by a 2, then followed by 3 or 5, then followed again by 2 and so on. we will have the option of using 3 or 5 in n distinct places, so the number of numbers in this case = $2 \times 2 \times 2 \times$ ……….n times = 2^n
So, the total number of such numbers
$= 2 \times 2^n = 2^{n+1}$

23. The required number of ways is same as the number of ways to divide the ten digits into three groups,

each group having at least two digits. The cases are:

Case 1: 2-digit, 2 digit and 5 digit number: ${}^9C_2 \times {}^7C_2 \times {}^5C_5 = 36 \times 21 = 756$.

Case 2: 2-digit, 3 digit and 4 digit number: ${}^9C_2 \times {}^7C_3 \times {}^4C_4 = 36 \times 35 = 1260$.

Case 3: 3-digit, 3-digit and 3-digit number: ${}^9C_3 \times {}^6C_3 \times {}^3C_3 = 84 \times 20 = 1680$.

Hence, the total number of ways = 756 + 1260 + 1680 = 3696.

24. Let *abcde* be the required odd integers, *a* can be chosen from 3, 4, 5, 6 and 7 and *e* can be chosen from 1, 3, 5, 7, 9. Here 3, 5 and 7 can occupy both the positions *a* and *e*.
So, let us consider the case where one of 3, 5, 7 occupies the position *a*.
Case I: If *a* gets one of the values 3, 5, 7, then there are three choices for *a*, but then *e* has just four choices as repetition is not allowed. Thus, *a* and *e* can be chosen in this case in $3 \times 4 = 12$ ways.
The 3 positions *b, c, d* can be filled from among the remaining 8 digits in $8 \times 7 \times 6$ ways. Total number of ways in this case $= 12 \times 8 \times 7 \times 6 = 4032$.
Case II: If *a* takes the values 4 or 6, then there are two choices for *a* and there are five choices for *e*. There are again eight choices altogether for the digits *b, c, d* which could be done in $8 \times 7 \times 6$ ways. Therefore in this case, the total numbers are $2 \times 5 \times 8 \times 7 \times 6 = 3360$.
Hence, total number of odd numbers between 30000 and 80000 without repetition of digits are 4032 + 3360 = 7392. Hence, the correct answer is 7392.

25. ${}^{10}C_4 \times 6! = 10!/4!$

26. For drawing a circle, we need three non collinear points. This can be done in:
$${}^3C_3 + {}^3C_2 \times {}^7C_1 + {}^3C_1 \times {}^7C_2 = 1 + 21 + 63 = 85$$

27. The odd digits have to occupy even positions. This can be done in $\frac{4!}{2!2!} = 6$ ways.
The other digits have to occupy the other positions.
This can be done in $\frac{5!}{3!2!} = 10$ ways.
Hence, total number of rearrangements possible = $6 \times 10 = 60$.

28. The number of straight lines is ${}^nC_2$ out of which there are *n* sides. Hence, the number of diagonals is ${}^nC_2 - n$.

29. ${}^nC_2 - n = 54$.

30. We cannot take '0' since the smallest digit must be placed at the left most place. We have only nine digits from which to select the numbers. First select any number of digits. Then for any selection, there is only one possible arrangement where the required condition is met. This can be done in ${}^9C_1 + {}^9C_2 + {}^9C_3 + \ldots + {}^9C_9$ ways $= 2^9 - 1 = 511$ ways.
But we cannot take numbers which have only one digit, hence the required answer is 511 – 9.

31. Two-hundred runs can be scored by scoring only fours or through a combination of fours and sixes. Possibilities are 50×4, $47 \times 4 + 2 \times 6$, $44 \times 4 + 4 \times 6$ … a total of seventeen ways.

32. Of the total arrangements possible (6!) exactly half would have 1 before 6. Thus, 6!/2 = 360.

33. Total number of permutations without any restrictions – Number of permutations having the '*acd*' pattern – Number of permutations having the '*beg*' pattern + Number of permutations having both the '*beg*' and '*acd*' patterns.

34. *A* and *B* can occupy the first and the ninth places, the second and the tenth places, the third and the eleventh place and so on... This can be done in eighteen ways.
A and *B* can be arranged in two ways.
All the other 24 alphabets can be arranged in 24! ways.
Hence, the required answer = $2 \times 18 \times 24!$

35. First arrange the two sisters around a circle in such a way that there will be one seat vacant between them. [This can be done in 2! ways since the arrangement of the sisters is not circular.]
Then, the other eighteen people can be arranged on 18 seats in 18! ways.

36. To score 60% marks out of 250, the student has to score 150 marks exactly. In other words, he loses 100 marks. Let the four papers, be A, B, C, D where D is the hundred mark paper and the number of marks lost in these papers be *a, b, c, d* respectively. Then, using distribution of identical things, if we allow each of *a, b, c, d* to take any values between 0 to 100. This can be thought of as: $a + b + c + d = 100$, and using $n = 100$, $r = 4$ in the formula for distribution of identical things we will get the number of ways as: ${}^{(100 + 4 - 1)}C_{(4 - 1)} = {}^{103}C_3 = 176851$. However, we need to reduce this answer, as *a, b* and *c* cannot cross 50. So if we check for the number of ways in which a get minimum 51. This can be done using: $a + b + c + d = 49$ and using $n = 49$ and $r = 4$, we get ${}^{52}C_3 = 22100$ as the number of cases in which the value of '*a*' goes over 50. Similarly, *b* and *c* cannot be over 50 too. Hence, we need to subtract 22100 three times.
Thus, the answer = $176851 - 22100 \times 3 = 176851 - 66300 = 110551$.

37. A chess board consists 9 parallel lines × 9 parallel lines. For a rectangle, we need to select two parallel lines and two other parallel lines that are perpendicular to the first set. Hence, ${}^9C_2 \times {}^9C_2$

Solutions for Questions 38 and 39:

Based on direct formulae.

38. This is a direct result based question. Option (c) is correct. Refer to result no. 6 in Important Results 2.
39. (1 + 2 + 3 + … + 18) (1 + 2 + 3 + … + 16)

Solutions for Questions 40 to 42:

Based on simple counting according to the conditions given in the passage

40. $^{10}C_1 + 3 \times 2 + {}^{10}C_2 + 60 + 60 = 181$
41. Handshakes involving host = 76
    Hence, the required ratio is 76: 105.
42. The guests (spectators) would shake hands $^{60}C_2$ times = 1770.
    Required percentage increase = 977.9%.
43. First select six people out of twelve for the first row. The other six automatically get selected for the second row. Arrange the two rows of people amongst themselves. Besides, the papers can be given in the pattern of 121212 or 212121. Hence the answer is $2 \times ({}^{12}C_6 \times 6! \times 6!)$.
44. The difference in this question from the previous question is the number of ways in which the papers can be distributed. This can be done by either distributing three different variants in the first three places of each row or by repeating the same variant in the first and the third places.
45. Required permutations = total permutations with no condition – permutations with the conditions which we do not have to count.
46. We have to count natural numbers which have a maximum of four digits. The required answer will be given by:
    Number of single digit numbers + Number of two digit numbers + Number of three digit numbers + Number of four digit numbers.
47. Let the three people be A, B and C.
    If one person gets no objects, the seven objects must be distributed such that each of the other two get one object at least.
    This can be done as 6 & 1, 5 & 2, 4 & 3 and their rearrangements.
    The answer would be
    $$({}^7C_6 + {}^7C_5 + {}^7C_4) \times 3! = 378$$
    Also, two people getting no objects can be done in three ways.
    Thus, the answer is 378 + 3 = 381
48. If only one gets one object
    The remaining can be distributed as: (6,0), (4, 2), (3, 3).
    $({}^7C_1 \times {}^6C_6 \times 3! + {}^7C_1 \times {}^6C_4 \times 3! + {}^7C_1 \times {}^6C_3 \times 3!/2!)$
    $= 42 + 630 + 420 = 1092$
    If two people get one object each:
    $${}^7C_1 \times {}^6C_1 \times {}^5C_5 \times 3!/2! = 126$$
    Thus, a total of 1218 is possible.
49. Number of 1 digit numbers = 9
    Number of 2 digit numbers = 81
    Number of 3 digit numbers = 9 × 9 × 8 = 648
    Number of 4 digit numbers = 9 × 9 × 8 × 7 = 4536
    Total numbers = 9 + 81 + 648 + 4536 = 5274
50. If the two digits are a and b, then four-digit numbers can be formed in the following patterns.
    aabb; *aaab* or *aaaa*.
    You will have to take two situations in each of the cases- first when the two digits are non-zero digits and second when the two digits are zero.
51. For the total of the digits to be odd one of the following has to be true:
    The number should contain 1 odd + 6 even or 3 odd + 4 even or 5 odd + 2 even or 7 odd digits. Count each case separately.
55. $^{18}C_4 + {}^{18}C_5 + {}^{18}C_6 + \ldots + {}^{18}C_{17} + {}^{18}C_{18}$
    $= [{}^{18}C_0 + {}^{18}C_4 + \ldots + {}^{18}C_{18}] - [{}^{18}C_0 + {}^{18}C_1 + {}^{18}C_2 + {}^{18}C_3]$
    $= 2^{18} - [1 + 18 + 153 + 816]$
    $= 261156$
57. Total number of six-digit numbers having three odd and three even digits (including zero in the left most place) = $5^3 \times 5^3$.
    From this subtract the number of five-digit numbers with two even digits and three odd digits (to take care of the extra counting due to zero)
58. Half the eight digit numbers = $9 \times 10^{7/2} = 45 \times 10^6$
59. This question is based on a formula: The condition is that 'n' things (each thing belonging to a particular place) have to be distributed in 'n' places such that no particular thing is arranged in its correct place.
    $n! - \frac{n!}{1!} + \frac{n!}{2!} - \frac{n!}{3!}$ sign of the terms will be alternate and the last term will be $\frac{n!}{n!}$.
    However, this can also be solved through logic.
60. The possible cases for counting are:
    Number of numbers when the units digit is nine + the number of numbers when neither the units digit nor the leftmost is nine + number of numbers when the left most digit is nine.
62. The condition is that we have to count the number of natural numbers not more than 4300.
    The total possible numbers with the given digits = 5 × 5 × 5 × 5 = 625 – 1 = 624.

Subtract form this the number of natural number greater than 4300 which can be formed from the given digits = $1 \times 2 \times 5 \times 5 - 1 = 49$.

Hence, the required number of numbers = $624 - 49 = 575$.

63. The required answer will be given by

The number of one digit natural number + number of two digit natural numbers + the number of three digit natural numbers + the number of four digit natural number starting with 1, 2, or 3 + the number of four digit natural numbers starting with 4.

65. The following words will appear before SPATE. All words starting with A + All words starting with E + All words starting with P + All words starting with SA + All words starting with SE + SPAET

66. Use the formula $\dfrac{n!}{p!q!r!}$

CHAPTER 19

Probability

Chapter Launchpad

Scan this QR code to access a video on 'Introduction to Probability' and this chapter's importance for CAT

CONCEPT AND IMPORTANCE OF PROBABILITY

Probability is one of the most important mathematical concepts that we use/come across in our day-to-day life. Particularly important in business and economic situations, probability is also used by us in our personal lives. For a lot of students who are not in touch with mathematics after their Xth/XIIth classes, this chapter along with permutations and combinations one is seen as an indication that XIIth standard mathematics appear in the MBA entrance exams. This leads to students taking negative approach while tacking/preparing for the mathematics section. Students are advised to remember that the questions based on mathematics asked in MBA entrance is mainly logical while studying the chapter.

As I set out to explain the basics of this chapter, I intend to improve your concepts of probability to such an extent that you feel in total control of this topic.

For those who are reasonably strong, my advice would be to use this chapter both for revisiting the basic concepts as well as for extensive practice.

Probability means the chance of the occurrence of an event. In layman terms, we can say that it is the likelihood that something—that is defined as the event—will or will not occur. Thus, probabilities can be estimated for each of the following events in our personal lives:

(a) The probability that an individual student of B.Com will clear the CAT
(b) The chance that a candidate chosen at random will clear an interview
(c) The chance that you will win a game of flush in cards if you have a trio of twos in a game where four people are playing
(d) The likelihood of India's winning the football World Cup in 2046
(e) The probability that a bulb will fuse in its first day of operation, and so on

The knowledge of these estimations helps individuals decide on the course of action they will take in their day-to-day life. For instance, your estimation/judgement of the probability of your chances of winning the card game in event (c) above will influence your decision about the amount of money you will be ready to invest in the stakes for the particular game. The application of probability to personal life helps in improving our decision making.

However, the use of probability is much more varied and has far reaching influence on the world of economics and business. Some instances of these are:

(a) The estimation of the probability of the success of a business project
(b) The estimation of the probability of the success of an advertising campaign in boosting the profits of a company
(c) The estimation of the probability of the death of a 25-year old man in the next ten years and that of the death of a 55-year old man in the next ten years leading to the calculation of the premiums for life insurance
(d) The estimation of the probability of the increase in the market price of the share of a company, and so on

UNDERLYING FACTORS FOR REAL-LIFE ESTIMATION OF PROBABILITY

The factors underlying an event often affect the probability of that event's occurrence. For instance, if we estimate the probability of India winning the 2027 cricket world cup as 0.14 based on certain expectations of outcomes, then this probability will definitely improve if we know that Virat Kohli will score 800 runs in that particular World Cup.

As we now move towards the mathematical aspects of the chapter, one underlying factor that recurs in every question of probability is that whenever one is asked the question, what is the probability? The immediate question that arises/should arise in one's mind is the probability of what?

The answer to this question is the probability of the EVENT.

The EVENT is the cornerstone or the bottom-line of probability. Hence, the first objective while trying to solve any question in probability is to define the event.

The event whose probability is to be found out is described in the question and the task of the student in trying to solve the problem is to define it.

In general, the student can either define the event narrowly or broadly. Narrow definitions of events are the building blocks of any probability problem and whenever there is a doubt about a problem, the student is advised to get into the narrowest form of the event definition.

The *difference* between the narrow and broad definition of event can be explained through an example:

Example: What is the probability of getting a number greater than 2, in a throw of a normal unbiased dice having six faces?

The broad definition of the event here is getting a number greater than 2 and this probability is given by 4/6. However, this event can also be broken down into its more basic definitions as:

The event is defined as getting 3 or 4 or 5 or 6. The individual probabilities of each of these are 1/6,1/6,1/6 and 1/6 respectively.

Hence, the required probability is 1/6 + 1/6 + 1/6 + 1/6 = 4/6 = 2/3.

Although in this example it seems highly trivial, the narrow event-definition approach is very effective in solving difficult problems on probability.

In general, event definition means breaking up the event to the most basic building blocks, which have to be connected together through the two English conjunctions—AND and OR.

Use of the Conjunction AND (Tool No. 9)

Refer *Back to School* section. Whenever we use AND as the natural conjunction joining two separate parts of the event definition, we replace the AND by the multiplication sign.

Thus, if A AND B have to occur, and if the probability of their occurrence are $P(A)$ and $P(B)$ respectively, then the probability that A AND B occur is obtained by connecting $P(A)$ AND $P(B)$. Replacing the AND by multiplication sign we get the required probability as:

$$P(A) \times P(B)$$

Example: If we have the probability of A hitting a target as 1/3 and that of B hitting the target as 1/2, then the probability that both hit the target if one shot is taken by both of them is obtained by

Event Definition: A hits the target AND B hits the target.

$$\rightarrow P(A) \times P(B) = 1/3 \times 1/2 = 1/6$$

Note: That since we use the conjunction AND in the definition of the event here, we multiply the individual probabilities that are connected through the conjunction AND.

Use of the Conjunction OR (Tool No. 10)

Refer *Back to School* section. Whenever we use OR as the natural conjunction joining two separate parts of the event definition, we replace the OR by the addition sign.

Thus, if A OR B have to occur, and if the probability of their occurrence are $P(A)$ and $P(B)$ respectively, then the probability that A OR B occur is obtained by connecting $P(A)$ OR $P(B)$. Replacing the OR by addition sign, we get the required probability as

$$P(A) + P(B)$$

Example: If we have the probability of A winning a race as 1/3 and that of B winning the race as 1/2, then the probability that either A or B win a race is obtained by

Event Definition: A wins OR B wins.

$$\rightarrow P(A) + P(B) = 1/3 + 1/2 = 5/6$$

Note: that since we use the conjunction OR in the definition of the event here, we add the individual probabilities that are connected through the conjunction OR.

Combination of AND and OR

If two dice are thrown, what is the chance that the sum of the numbers is not less than 10?

Event Definition: The sum of the numbers is not less than 10 if it is either 10 OR 11 OR 12.

This can be done by

(6 AND 4) OR (4 AND 6) OR (5 AND 5) OR (6 AND 5) OR (5 AND 6) OR (6 AND 6)

that is, $1/6 \times 1/6 + 1/6 \times 1/6 + 1/6 \times 1/6 + 1/6 \times 1/6 + 1/6 \times 1/6 + 1/6 \times 1/6 = 6/36 = 1/6$

The bottom-line is that no matter how complicated the problem on probability is, it can be broken up into its narrower parts, which can be connected by ANDs and ORs to get the event definition.

Once the event is defined, the probability of each narrow event within the broad event is calculated and all the narrow events are connected by multiplication (for AND) or by addition (for OR) to get the final solution.

Example: In a four-game match between Kasporov and Anand, the probability that Anand wins a particular game is 2/5 and that of Kasporov winning a game is 3/5. Assuming that there is no probability of a draw in an individual game, what is the chance that the match is drawn (Score is 2–2)?

For the match to be drawn, two games have to be won by each of the players. If A represents the event that Anand won a game and K represents the event that Kasporov won a game; the event definition for the match to end in a draw can be described as: [The student is advised to look at the use of narrow event definition.]

(A&A&K&K) OR (A&K&A&K) OR (A&K&K&A) OR (K&K&A&A) OR (K&A&K&A) OR (K&A&A&K)

This further translates into

$$(2/5)^2(3/5)^2 + (2/5)^2(3/5)^2 + (2/5)^2(3/5)^2 + (2/5)^2(3/5)^2 + (2/5)^2(3/5)^2 + (2/5)^2(3/5)^2$$

$$= (36/625) \times 6 = 216/625$$

After a little bit of practice, you can also think about this directly as:

$${}^4C_2 \times (2/5)^2 \times {}^2C_2 \times (3/5)^2 = 6 \times 1 \times 36/625 = 216/625$$

Where, $4C_2$ gives us the number of ways in which Anand can win two games and $2C_2$ gives us the number of ways in which Kasporov can win the remaining 2 games (obviously, only one).

BASIC FACTS ABOUT PROBABILITY

For every event that can be defined, there is a corresponding non-event, which is the opposite of the event. The relationship between the event and the non-event is that they are mutually exclusive, that is, if the event occurs then the non-event does not occur and vice versa.

The event is denoted by E; the number of ways in which the event can occur is defined as $n(E)$ and the probability of the occurrence of the event is $P(E)$.

The non-event is denoted by E'; the number of ways in which the non-event can occur is defined as $n(E')$ while the probability of the occurrence of the event is $P(E')$.

The following relationships hold true with respect to the event and the non-event.

$n(E) + n(E')$ = sample space representing all the possible events that can occur related to the activity.

$$P(E) + P(E') = 1$$

This means that if the event does not occur, then the non-event occurs.

$$\rightarrow P(E) = 1 - P(E')$$

This is often very useful for the calculation of probabilities of events where it is easier to describe and count the non-event rather than the event.

Illustration

The probability that you get a total more than three in a throw of two dice

Here, the event definition will be a long and tedious task, which will involve long counting. Hence, it would be more convenient to define the non-event and count the same.

Therefore, here the non-event will be defined as

A total not more than 3 $\rightarrow$ 2 or 3 $\rightarrow$ (1&1) OR (1&2) OR (2&1) = 1/36 + 1/36 + 1/36 = 3/36 = 1/12.

However, a word of caution especially for students not comfortable at Mathematics: Take care while defining the non-event. Beware of a trap like $\rightarrow$ event definition: Total > 10 in two throws of a dice does not translate into a non-event of < 10 but instead into the non-event of ≤ 10.

SOME IMPORTANT CONSIDERATIONS WHILE DEFINING EVENT

Random Experiment An experiment whose outcome has to be among a set of events that are completely known but whose exact outcome is unknown is a random experiment (e.g. throwing of a dice, tossing of a coin). Most questions on probability are based on random experiments.

Sample Space This is defined in the context of a random experiment and denotes the set representing all the possible equally likely outcomes of the random experiment. [e.g. sample space when a coin is tossed is (head, tail). Sample space when a dice is thrown is (1, 2, 3, 4, 5, 6).]

Event The set representing the desired outcome of a random experiment is called the event. Note that the event is a subset of the sample space.

Non-event The outcome that is opposite to the desired outcome is the non-event. Note that if the event occurs, the non-event does not occur and vice versa.

Impossible Event An event that can never occur is an impossible event. The probability of an impossible event is 0. (for example, probability of the occurrence of 7 when a dice with six faces numbered 1–6 is thrown).

Mutually Exclusive Events A set of events is mutually exclusive when the occurrence of any one of them means that the other events cannot occur. (If head appears on a coin, tail will not appear and vice versa.)

Equally Likely Events If two events have the same probability or chance of occurrence, they are called equally likely events. (e.g. in a throw of a dice, the chance of 1 showing on the dice is equal to 2 is equal to 3 is equal to 4 is equal to 5 is equal to 6 appearing on the dice.)

Exhaustive Set of Events A set of events that includes all the possibilities of the sample space is said to be an exhaustive set of events. (e.g. in a throw of a dice, the number is less than three or more than or equal to three.)

Independent Events An event is described as such if the occurrence of an event has no effect on the probability of the occurrence of another event. (e.g. if the first child of a couple is a boy, there is no effect on the chances of the second child being a boy.)

Conditional Probability It is the probability of the occurrence of an event A given that the event B has already occurred. This is denoted by $P(A|B)$. (e.g. the probability that in two throws of a dice, we get a total of 7 or more, given that in the first throw of the dice, the number 5 had occurred.)

Concept of Odds For and Odds Against

Sometimes, probability is also viewed in terms of *odds* for and *odds against* an event.

Odds in favour of an event E are defined as: $\dfrac{P(E)}{P(E)'}$

Odds against an event are defined as: $\dfrac{P(E)'}{P(E)}$

Expectation: The expectation of an individual is defined as Probability of winning × Reward of winning

Illustration

A man holds 20 out of the 500 tickets to a lottery. If the reward for the winning ticket is ₹1000, find the expectation of the man.

Solution: Expectation = Probability of winning × Reward of winning = $\dfrac{20}{500} \times 1000$ = ₹40.

ANOTHER APPROACH TO LOOK AT THE PROBABILITY PROBLEMS

In the cases, where all outcomes have an equal likelihood of occurring, the probability of an event is defined as:

$$\frac{\text{Number of ways in which the event occurs}}{\text{Total number of outcomes possible}}$$

This means that the probability of any event can be obtained by counting the numerator and the denominator independently.

Hence, from this approach, the concentration shifts to counting the numerator and the denominator.

Thus, for the example used above, the probability of a number > 2 appearing on a dice is:

$$\frac{\text{Number of ways in which the event occurs}}{\text{Total number of outcomes possible}} = \frac{4}{6}$$

The counting is done through any of the following:

(a) The physical counting as illustrated above
(b) The use of the concept of permutations
(c) The use of the concept of combinations
(d) The use of the MNP rule

[*Refer to the chapter on Permutations and Combinations to understand (b), (c) and (d) above.*]

Space for Notes

WORKED-OUT PROBLEMS

Problem 19.1: In a throw of two dice, find the probability of getting one prime and one composite number.

Solution: The probability of getting a prime number when a dice is thrown is 3/6 = 1/2. (This occurs when we get 2, 3 or 5 out of a possibility of getting 1, 2, 3, 4, 5 or 6.)

Similarly, in a throw of a dice, there are only two possibilities of getting composite numbers, viz: 4 or 6 and this gives a probability of 1/3 for getting a composite number.

Now, let us look at defining the event. The event is—getting one prime and one composite number.

This can be obtained as:

The first number is prime, and the second is composite OR the first number is composite and the second is prime.

$$= (1/2) \times (1/3) + (1/3) \times (1/2) = 1/3$$

Problem 19.2: Find the probability that a leap year chosen at random will have 53 Sundays.

Solution: A leap year has 366 days. Fifty-two complete weeks will have 364 days. The 365th day can be a Sunday (probability = 1/7) OR the 366th day can be a Sunday (probability = 1/7). Answer = 1/7 + 1/7 = 2/7.

Alternatively, you can think of this as: The favourable events will occur when we have Saturday and Sunday or Sunday and Monday as the 365th and 366th, days respectively. (i.e. two possibilities of the event occurring). Besides, the total number of ways that can happen are Sunday and Monday OR Monday and Tuesday … OR Friday and Saturday OR Saturday and Sunday.

Problem 19.3: There are two bags containing white and black balls. In the first bag, there are eight white and six black balls and in the second bag, there are four white and seven black balls. One ball is drawn at random from any of these two bags. Find the probability of this ball being black.

Solution: The event definition here is: first bag and black ball OR second Bag and Black Ball. The chances of picking up either the first OR the second bag are 1/2 each.

Besides, the chance of picking up a black ball from the first bag is 6/14 and the chance of picking up a black ball from the second bag is 7/11.

Thus, using these values and the ANDs and Ors, we get:

$$(1/2) \times (6/14) + (1/2) \times (7/11) = (3/14) + (7/22) = (66 + 98)/308) = 164/308 = 41/77$$

Problem 19.4: The letters of the word LUCKNOW are arranged among themselves. Find the probability of always having NOW in the word.

Solution: The required probability will be given by the equation

= Number of words having NOW/Total number of words

= 5!/7! = 1/42 [See the chapter of Permutations and Combinations to understand the logic behind these values.]

Problem 19.5: A person has three children with at least one boy. Find the probability of having at least two boys among the children.

Solution: The event is occurring under the following situations:

(a) Second is a boy and third is a girl OR
(b) Second is a girl and third is a boy OR
(c) Second is a boy and third is a boy

This will be represented by: $(1/2) \times (1/2) + (1/2) \times (1/2) + (1/2) \times (1/2) = 3/4$

Problem 19.6: Out of thirteen applicants for a job, there are five women and eight men. Two persons are to be selected for the job. The probability that at least one of the selected persons will be a woman is:

Solution: The required probability will be given by

First is a woman and second is a man OR
First is a man and second is a woman OR
First is a woman and second is a woman

i.e. $(5/13) \times (8/12) + (8/13) \times (5/12) + (5/13) \times (4/12)$
$= 100/156 = 25/39$

Alternatively, we can define the non-event as: There are two men and no women. Then, probability of the non-event is

$$(8/13) \times (7/12) = 56/156$$

Hence, $P(E) = (1 - 56/156) = 100/156 = 25/39$

Note: This is a case of probability calculation where repetition is not allowed.

Problem 19.7: The probability that A can solve the problem is 2/3 and B can solve it is 3/4. If both of them attempt the problem, then what is the probability that the problem gets solved?

Solution: The event is defined as:

A solves the problem AND B does not solve the problem

OR

A does not solve the problem AND B solves the problem

OR

A solves the problem AND B solves the problem

Numerically, this is equivalent to:

$$(2/3) \times (1/4) + (1/3) \times (3/4) + (2/3) \times (3/4) = (2/12) + (3/12) + (6/12) = 11/12$$

Problem 19.8: Six positive numbers are taken at random and are multiplied together. Then what is the probability that the product ends in an odd digit other than 5.

Solution: The event will occur when all the numbers selected are ending in 1, 3, 7 or 9.

If we take numbers between 1 to 10 (both inclusive), we will have a positive occurrence if each of the six numbers selected are 1, 3, 7 or 9.

The probability of any number selected being either of these 4 is 4/10 (four positive events out of ten possibilities).

Note: If we try to take numbers between 1 to 20, we will have a probability of 8/20 = 4/10. Hence, we can extrapolate up to infinity and say that the probability of any number selected ending in 1, 3, 7 or 9 so as to fulfil the requirement is 4/10.

Hence, answer = $(0.4)^6$

Problem 19.9: The probability that Arjit will solve a problem is 1/5. What is the probability that he solves at least one problem out of ten problems?

Solution: The non-event is defined as:

He solves no problems, i.e. he does not solve the first problem and he does not solve the second problem ... and he does not solve the tenth problem.

Probability of non-event = $(4/5)^{10}$

Hence, probability of the event is $1 - (4/5)^{10}$.

Problem 19.10: A carton contains twenty-five bulbs, eight of which are defective. What is the probability that if a sample of four bulbs is chosen, exactly two of them will be defective?

Solution: The probability that exactly two bulbs are defective and exactly two are not defective will be given by $(4C_2) \times (8/25) \times (7/24) \times (17/23) \times (16/22)$.

Problem 19.11: Out of forty consecutive integers, two are chosen at random. Find the probability that their sum is odd.

Solution: Forty consecutive integers will have twenty odd and twenty even integers. The sum of two chosen integers will be odd, only if

(a) First is even and second is odd OR

(b) First is odd and second is even

Mathematically, the probability will be given by:

P(first is even) × P(second is odd) + P(first is odd) × P(second is even)

$= (20/40) \times (20/39) + (20/40) \times (20/39)$

$= (2 \times 20^2/40 \times 39) = 20/39$

Problem 19.12: An integer is chosen at random from the first 100 integers. What is the probability that this number will not be divisible by 5 or 8?

Solution: For a number from 1 to 100 to not be divisible by 5 or 8, we need to remove all the numbers that are divisible by 5 or 8.

Thus, we remove 5, 8, 10, 15, 16, 20, 24, 25, 30, 32, 35, 40, 45, 48, 50, 55, 56, 60, 64, 65, 70, 72, 75, 80, 85, 88, 90, 95, 96, and 100.

i.e. 30 numbers from the 100 are removed.

Hence, answer is 70/100 = 7/10 (required probability).

Alternatively, we could have counted the numbers as number of numbers divisible by 5 + number of numbers divisible by 8 – number of numbers divisible by both 5 or 8.

$= 20 + 12 - 2 = 30$

Problem 19.13: From a bag containing eight green and five red balls, three are drawn one after the other. Find the probability of all three balls being green if

(a) The balls drawn are replaced before the next ball is picked

(b) The balls drawn are not replaced

Solution:

(a) When the balls drawn are replaced, we can see that the number of balls available for drawing out will be the same for every draw. This means that the probability of a green ball appearing in the first draw and a green ball appearing in the second draw as well as one appearing in the third draw are equal to each other.

Hence, answer to the question above will be:

Required probability $= \frac{8}{13} \times \frac{8}{13} \times \frac{8}{13} = (8^3/13^3)$

(b) When the balls are not replaced, the probability of drawing any colour of ball for every fresh draw changes. Hence, the answer here will be:

Required probability $= \frac{8}{13} \times \frac{7}{12} \times \frac{6}{11}$

Space for Rough Work

LEVEL OF DIFFICULTY (I)

1. In throwing a fair dice, what is the probability of getting the number '3'?

(a) $\frac{1}{3}$ (b) $\frac{1}{6}$

(c) $\frac{1}{9}$ (d) $\frac{1}{12}$

2. What is the chance of throwing a number greater than four with an ordinary dice whose faces are numbered from 1 to 6?

(a) $\frac{1}{3}$ (b) $\frac{1}{6}$

(c) $\frac{1}{9}$ (d) $\frac{1}{8}$

3. Find the chance of throwing at least one ace in a simple throw with two dice.

(a) $\frac{1}{12}$ (b) $\frac{1}{3}$

(c) $\frac{1}{4}$ (d) $\frac{11}{36}$

4. Find the chance of drawing two blue balls in succession from a bag containing five red and seven blue balls, if the balls are not being replaced.

(a) $\frac{3}{13}$ (b) $\frac{21}{64}$

(c) $\frac{7}{22}$ (d) $\frac{21}{61}$

5. From a pack of 52 cards, two are drawn at random. Find the chance that one is a knave and the other a queen.

(a) $\frac{8}{663}$ (b) $\frac{1}{6}$

(c) $\frac{1}{9}$ (d) $\frac{1}{12}$

6. If a card is picked up at random from a pack of 52 cards. Find the probability that it is

(i) A spade

(a) $\frac{1}{9}$ (b) $\frac{1}{6}$

(c) $\frac{1}{4}$ (d) $\frac{2}{9}$

(ii) A king or queen

(a) $\frac{3}{13}$ (b) $\frac{2}{13}$

(c) $\frac{7}{52}$ (d) $\frac{1}{169}$

(iii) 'A spade' or 'a king' or 'a queen'

(a) $\frac{21}{52}$ (b) $\frac{5}{13}$

(c) $\frac{19}{52}$ (d) $\frac{15}{52}$

7. Three coins are tossed. What is the probability of getting

(i) Two tails and one head?

(a) $\frac{1}{4}$ (b) $\frac{3}{8}$

(c) $\frac{2}{3}$ (d) $\frac{1}{8}$

(ii) One tail and two heads?

(a) $\frac{3}{8}$ (b) 1

(c) $\frac{2}{3}$ (d) $\frac{3}{4}$

8. Three coins are tossed. What is the probability of getting?

(i) Neither three heads nor three tails?

(a) $\frac{1}{2}$ (b) $\frac{1}{3}$

(c) $\frac{2}{3}$ (d) $\frac{3}{4}$

(ii) Three heads?

(a) $\frac{1}{8}$ (b) $\frac{1}{4}$

(c) $\frac{1}{2}$ (d) $\frac{2}{3}$

9. For the above question, the probability that there is at least one tail is

(a) $\frac{2}{3}$ (b) $\frac{7}{8}$

(c) $\frac{3}{8}$ (d) $\frac{1}{2}$

10. Two fair dice are thrown. Find the probability of getting the sum as:

(i) A number divisible by 2 or 4

(a) $\frac{1}{2}$ (b) $\frac{3}{4}$

(c) $\frac{1}{3}$ (d) $\frac{2}{3}$

(ii) A number divisible by 2 and 4

(a) $\frac{1}{3}$ (b) $\frac{1}{4}$

(c) $\frac{3}{4}$ (d) $\frac{5}{7}$

(iii) A prime number less than 8

(a) $\frac{11}{13}$ (b) $\frac{1}{13}$

(c) $\frac{1}{4}$ (d) $\frac{13}{36}$

11. A bag contains three green and seven white balls. Two balls are drawn from the bag in succession without replacement. What is the probability that

(i) Both are white?

(a) $\frac{1}{7}$ (b) $\frac{5}{11}$

(c) $\frac{7}{11}$ (d) $\frac{7}{15}$

(ii) They are of different colour?

(a) $\frac{7}{15}$ (b) $\frac{7}{9}$

(c) $\frac{5}{11}$ (d) $\frac{7}{11}$

12. One-hundred students appeared for two examinations. Sixty passed the first, fifty passed the second and thirty passed both. Find the probability that a student selected at random has failed in both the examinations.

(a) $\frac{1}{5}$ (b) $\frac{1}{7}$

(c) $\frac{5}{7}$ (d) $\frac{5}{6}$

13. What is the probability of throwing a number greater than two with a fair dice?

(a) $\frac{2}{3}$ (b) $\frac{2}{5}$

(c) 1 (d) $\frac{3}{5}$

14. Three cards numbered 2, 4 and 8 are put into a box. If a card is drawn at random, what is the probability that the card drawn is

(i) A prime number?

(a) 1 (b) $\frac{1}{3}$

(c) $\frac{4}{5}$ (d) $\frac{5}{7}$

(ii) An even number?

(a) 1 (b) $\frac{2}{3}$

(c) $\frac{1}{2}$ (d) $\frac{3}{5}$

(iii) An odd number?

(a) 1 (b) 0

(c) $\frac{1}{3}$ (d) $\frac{2}{3}$

15. Two fair coins are tossed. Find the probability of obtaining

(i) Two heads

(a) 1 (b) $\frac{2}{3}$

(c) $\frac{1}{2}$ (d) $\frac{1}{4}$

(ii) One head and one tail

(a) $\frac{1}{2}$ (b) 1

(c) $\frac{1}{3}$ (d) $\frac{2}{3}$

(iii) Two tails

(a) 1 (b) $\frac{1}{4}$

(c) $\frac{2}{3}$ (d) $\frac{1}{2}$

16. In rolling two dice, find the probability that

(i) There is at least one '6'

(a) $\frac{11}{36}$ (b) $\frac{22}{36}$

(c) $\frac{15}{36}$ (d) $\frac{29}{36}$

(ii) The sum is 5

(a) $\frac{1}{4}$ (b) $\frac{1}{9}$

(c) $\frac{1}{2}$ (d) $\frac{1}{6}$

17. From a bag containing four white and five black balls a man draws three at random. What are the odds against these being all black?

(a) $\frac{5}{37}$ (b) $\frac{37}{5}$

(c) $\frac{11}{13}$ (d) $\frac{13}{37}$

18. Amit throws three dice in a special game of Ludo. If it is known that he needs 15 or higher in this throw to win then find the chance of his winning the game.

(a) $\frac{5}{54}$ (b) $\frac{17}{216}$

(c) $\frac{13}{216}$ (d) $\frac{15}{216}$

19. Find out the probability of forming 187 or 215 with the digits 1, 2, 3, 4, 5, 6, 7, 8, 9 when only numbers of three digits are formed and when

(i) Repetitions are not allowed

(a) $\frac{12}{504}$ (b) $\frac{18}{504}$

(c) $\frac{2}{504}$ (d) $\frac{24}{504}$

(ii) Repetitions are allowed

(a) $\frac{2}{729}$ (b) $\frac{6}{729}$

(c) $\frac{11}{729}$ (d) $\frac{4}{729}$

20. In a horse race there were eighteen horses numbered 1–18. The probability that horse 1 would win is 1/6, that 2 would win is 1/10 and that 3 would win is 1/8. Assuming that a tie is impossible, find the chance that one of the three will win.

(a) $\frac{47}{120}$ (b) $\frac{119}{120}$

(c) $\frac{11}{129}$ (d) $\frac{1}{5}$

21. Two balls are to be drawn from a bag containing eight grey and three blue balls. Find the chance that they will both be blue.

(a) $\frac{1}{5}$ (b) $\frac{3}{55}$

(c) $\frac{11}{15}$ (d) $\frac{14}{45}$

22. Two fair dice are thrown. What is the probability of

(i) Throwing a double?

(a) $\frac{1}{6}$ (b) 1

(c) $\frac{2}{3}$ (d) $\frac{1}{2}$

(ii) The sum is greater than 10?

(a) $\frac{2}{3}$ (b) $\frac{2}{5}$

(c) $\frac{1}{6}$ (d) $\frac{1}{12}$

(iii) The sum is less than 10?

(a) $\frac{5}{6}$ (b) $\frac{2}{5}$

(c) $\frac{3}{5}$ (d) $\frac{2}{3}$

23. In a certain lottery the prize is one crore and 5000 tickets have been sold. What is the expectation of a man who holds ten tickets?

(a) ₹20,000 (b) ₹25,000

(c) ₹30,000 (d) ₹15,000

24. Two letters are randomly chosen from the word LIME. Find the probability that the letters are *L* and *M*.

(a) $\frac{1}{2}$ (b) $\frac{1}{4}$

(c) $\frac{1}{3}$ (d) $\frac{1}{6}$

Directions for Questions 25 to 27: Read the following passage and answer the questions based on it.

The Bangalore office of Infosys has 1200 executives. Of these, 880 subscribe to the *Time* magazine and 650 subscribe to the *Economist*. Each executive may subscribe to either the *Time* or the *Economist* or both. If an executive is picked at random, answer questions 25–27.

25. What is the probability that

(i) He has subscribed to the *Time* magazine?

(a) $\frac{11}{15}$ (b) $\frac{11}{12}$

(c) $\frac{7}{15}$ (d) $\frac{7}{11}$

(ii) He has subscribed to the *Economist*?

(a) $\frac{13}{21}$ (b) $\frac{13}{20}$

(c) $\frac{13}{24}$ (d) $\frac{12}{30}$

26. He has subscribed to both magazines?

(a) $\frac{22}{40}$ (b) $\frac{11}{40}$

(c) $\frac{12}{20}$ (d) $\frac{4}{20}$

27. If among the executives who have subscribed to the *Time* magazine, an executive is picked at random. What is the probability that he has also subscribed to the *Economist*?

(a) $\frac{3}{8}$ (b) $\frac{5}{8}$

(c) $\frac{2}{3}$ (d) $\frac{1}{8}$

28. A bag contains four black and five red balls. If three balls from the bag are chosen at random, what is the chance that they are all black?

(a) $\frac{1}{21}$ (b) $\frac{1}{20}$

(c) $\frac{2}{23}$ (d) $\frac{1}{9}$

29. If a number of two digits is formed with the digits 2, 3, 5, 7, 9 without repetition of digits, what is the probability that the number formed is 35?

(a) $\frac{1}{10}$ (b) $\frac{1}{20}$

(c) $\frac{2}{11}$ (d) $\frac{1}{11}$

30. From a pack of 52 playing cards, three cards are drawn at random. Find the probability of drawing a king, a queen and jack.

(a) $\frac{16}{5525}$ (b) $\frac{1}{13^3}$

(c) $\frac{1}{14^3}$ (d) $\frac{1}{15^3}$

31. A bag contains twenty balls marked 1 to 20. One ball is drawn at random. Find the probability that it is marked with a number multiple of 5 or 7.

(a) $\frac{3}{10}$ (b) $\frac{7}{10}$

(c) $\frac{1}{11}$ (d) $\frac{2}{3}$

32. A group of investigators took a fair sample of 1972 children from the general population and found that there are 1000 boys and 972 girls. If the investigators claim that their research is so accurate that the sex of a new born child can be predicted based on the ratio of the sample of the population, then what is the expectation in terms of the probability that a new child born will be a girl?

(a) $\frac{243}{250}$ (b) $\frac{250}{257}$

(c) $\frac{9}{10}$ (d) $\frac{243}{493}$

33. A bag contains three red, six white and seven black balls. Two balls are drawn at random. What is the probability that both are black?

(a) $\frac{1}{8}$ (b) $\frac{7}{40}$

(c) $\frac{12}{40}$ (d) $\frac{13}{40}$

34. A bag contains six red, four white and eight blue balls. If three balls are drawn at random, find the probability that

(i) All the three balls are of the same colour

(a) $\frac{17}{240}$ (b) $\frac{5}{51}$

(c) $\frac{31}{204}$ (d) None of these

(ii) All the three balls are blue

(a) $\frac{8}{51}$ (b) $\frac{50}{51}$

(c) $\frac{7}{102}$ (d) $\frac{13}{51}$

35. If $P(A) = 1/3$, $P(B) = 1/2$, $P(A \cap B) = 1/4$ then find $P(A' \cup B')$.

(a) $\frac{1}{3}$ (b) $\frac{2}{5}$

(c) $\frac{2}{3}$ (d) $\frac{3}{4}$

36. A and B are two candidates seeking admission to the IIMs. The probability that A is selected is 0.5 and the probability that both A and B are selected is at most 0.3. Is it possible that the probability of B getting selected is 0.9?

(a) No (b) Yes

(c) Either (a) or (b) (d) Cannot say

37. The probability that a student will pass in Mathematics is 3/5 and the probability that he will pass in English is 1/3. If the probability that he will pass in both Mathematics and English is 1/8, what is the probability that he will pass in at least one subject?

(a) $\frac{97}{120}$ (b) $\frac{87}{120}$

(c) $\frac{53}{120}$ (d) $\frac{120}{297}$

38. The odds in favour of standing first of three students, Amit, Vikas and Vivek appearing at an examination are 1:2. 2:5 and 1:7 respectively. What is the probability that either of them will stand first (assume that a tie for the first place is not possible)?

(a) $\frac{168}{178}$ (b) $\frac{122}{168}$

(c) $\frac{5}{168}$ (d) $\frac{125}{168}$

39. A, B, C are three mutually exclusive and exhaustive events associated with a random experiment. Find $P(A)$, if it is given that $P(B) = 3/2\ P(A)$ and $P(C) = 1/2\ P(B)$.

(a) $\frac{4}{13}$ (b) $\frac{2}{3}$

(c) $\frac{12}{13}$ (d) $\frac{1}{13}$

40. A and B are two mutually exclusive events of an experiment. If $P(A') = 0.65$, $P(A \cup B) = 0.65$ and $P(B) = p$, find the value of p.

(a) 0.25 (b) 0.3

(c) 0.1 (d) 0.2

41. A bag contains four white and two black balls. Another contains three white and five black balls. If one ball is drawn from each bag, find the probability that

(i) Both are white

(a) $\frac{1}{3}$ (b) $\frac{2}{3}$

(c) $\frac{1}{4}$ (d) $\frac{3}{4}$

(ii) Both are black

(a) $\frac{3}{24}$ (b) $\frac{1}{24}$

(c) $\frac{3}{12}$ (d) $\frac{5}{24}$

(iii) One is white and one is black

(a) $\frac{13}{24}$ (b) $\frac{15}{24}$

(c) $\frac{11}{21}$ (d) $\frac{1}{2}$

42. The odds against an event are 5:3 and the odds in favour of another independent event are 7:5. Find the probability that at least one of the two events will occur.

(a) $\frac{52}{96}$ (b) $\frac{69}{96}$

(c) $\frac{71}{96}$ (d) $\frac{13}{96}$

43. Kamal and Monica appeared for an interview for two vacancies. The probability of Kamal's selection is 1/3 and that of Monica's selection is 1/5. Find the probability that only one of them will be selected.

(a) $\frac{2}{5}$ (b) $\frac{1}{5}$

(c) $\frac{5}{9}$ (d) $\frac{2}{3}$

44. A husband and a wife appear in an interview for two vacancies for the same post. The probability of husband's selection is (1/7) and that of the wife's selection is 1/5. What is the probability that

(i) Both of them will be selected?

(a) $\frac{1}{35}$ (b) $\frac{2}{35}$

(c) $\frac{3}{35}$ (d) $\frac{1}{7}$

(ii) One of them will be selected?

(a) $\frac{1}{7}$ (b) $\frac{3}{7}$

(c) $\frac{2}{7}$ (d) $\frac{5}{7}$

(iii) None of them will be selected?

(a) $\frac{24}{35}$ (b) $\frac{20}{35}$

(c) $\frac{21}{35}$ (d) $\frac{2}{7}$

(iv) At least one of them will be selected?

(a) $\frac{12}{35}$ (b) $\frac{11}{35}$

(c) $\frac{16}{35}$ (d) $\frac{1}{5}$

Space for Rough Work

LEVEL OF DIFFICULTY (II)

1. Two fair dice are thrown. Given that the sum of the dice is less than or equal to four, find the probability that only one dice shows two.
   (a) $\frac{1}{4}$ (b) $\frac{1}{2}$
   (c) $\frac{2}{3}$ (d) $\frac{1}{3}$
2. *A* can hit the target three times in six shots, *B* two times in six shots and *C* four times in six shots. They fire a volley. What is the probability that at least two shots hit?
   (a) $\frac{1}{2}$ (b) $\frac{1}{3}$
   (c) $\frac{2}{3}$ (d) $\frac{3}{4}$
3. There are two bags, one of them contains five red and seven white balls and the other three red and twelve white balls, and a ball is to be drawn from one or the other of the two bags. Find the chance of drawing a red ball.
   (a) $\frac{37}{120}$ (b) $\frac{30}{120}$
   (c) $\frac{11}{120}$ (d) None of these
4. In two bags there are to be put altogether five red and twelve white balls, neither bag being empty. Apart from this, there is no constraint of placing the balls. Once the balls are placed, a person will draw one ball from either of the two bags. Find the probability for the following conditions to be met:
   (i) The least chance of drawing a red ball?
   (a) $\frac{3}{35}$ (b) $\frac{5}{32}$
   (c) $\frac{7}{32}$ (d) $\frac{1}{16}$
   (ii) The greatest chance of drawing a red ball?
   (a) $\frac{3}{4}$ (b) $\frac{2}{3}$
   (c) $\frac{5}{8}$ (d) $\frac{5}{7}$
5. If eight coins are tossed, what is the chance that one and only one will turn up head?
   (a) $\frac{1}{16}$ (b) $\frac{3}{35}$
   (c) $\frac{3}{32}$ (d) $\frac{1}{32}$
6. What is the chance that a leap year, selected at random, will contain 53 Sundays?
   (a) $\frac{2}{7}$ (b) $\frac{3}{7}$
   (c) $\frac{1}{7}$ (d) $\frac{5}{7}$
7. Out of all the two-digit integers between 1 to 200, a two-digit number has to be selected at random. What is the probability that the selected number is not divisible by 7?
   (a) $\frac{11}{90}$ (b) $\frac{33}{90}$
   (c) $\frac{55}{90}$ (d) $\frac{77}{90}$
8. A child is asked to pick up two balloons from a box containing ten blue and fifteen red balloons. What is the probability of the child picking, at random, two balloons of different colours?
   (a) $\frac{1}{2}$ (b) $\frac{2}{3}$
   (c) $\frac{1}{3}$ (d) $\frac{3}{5}$
9. Tom and Dick are running in the same race; the probability of their winning is 1/5 and ½ respectively. Find the probability that
   (i) Either of them will win the race
   (a) $\frac{7}{10}$ (b) $\frac{3}{10}$
   (c) $\frac{1}{5}$ (d) $\frac{7}{9}$
   (ii) Neither of them will win the race
   (a) $\frac{7}{10}$ (b) $\frac{3}{10}$
   (c) $\frac{2}{5}$ (d) $\frac{4}{5}$
10. Two dice are thrown. If the total on the faces of the two dices are six, find the probability that there are two odd numbers on the faces.
    (a) $\frac{2}{5}$ (b) $\frac{1}{5}$
    (c) $\frac{5}{9}$ (d) $\frac{3}{5}$
11. Amarnath appears in an exam that has four subjects. The chance he passes an individual subject's test is 0.8. What is the probability that he will
    (i) Pass in all the subjects?
    (a) 0.8^4 (b) 0.3^4
    (c) 0.7^3 (d) None of these

(ii) Fail in all the subjects?
(a) 0.4^2 (b) 0.2^4
(c) 0.3^4 (d) None of these
(iii) Pass in at least one of the subjects?
(a) 0.99984 (b) 0.9984
(c) 0.0016 (d) None of these

12. A box contains two tennis, three cricket and four squash balls. Three balls are drawn in succession with replacement. Find the probability that
(i) All are cricket balls
(a) $\frac{1}{27}$ (b) $\frac{2}{27}$
(c) $\frac{25}{27}$ (d) $\frac{1}{8}$
(ii) The first is a tennis ball, the second is a cricket ball, and the third is a squash ball
(a) $\frac{8}{243}$ (b) $\frac{5}{243}$
(c) $\frac{4}{243}$ (d) $\frac{11}{243}$
(iii) All three are of the same type
(a) $\frac{11}{81}$ (b) $\frac{1}{9}$
(c) $\frac{13}{81}$ (d) $\frac{17}{81}$

13. With the data in the above question, answer the questions when the balls are drawn in succession without replacement.
(i)
(a) $\frac{3}{84}$ (b) $\frac{1}{84}$
(c) $\frac{5}{84}$ (d) None of these
(ii)
(a) $\frac{2}{21}$ (b) $\frac{4}{21}$
(c) $\frac{1}{21}$ (d) $\frac{1}{9}$
(iii)
(a) $\frac{3}{84}$ (b) $\frac{1}{84}$
(c) $\frac{5}{84}$ (d) $\frac{11}{84}$

14. In the Mindworkzz library, there are eight books by Stephen Covey and one book by Vinay Singh in shelf *A*. At the same time, there are five books by Stephen Covey in shelf *B*. One book is moved from shelf *A* to shelf *B*. *A* student picks up a book from shelf *B*. Find the probability that the book by Vinay Singh
(i) Is still in shelf *A*
(a) $\frac{1}{3}$ (b) $\frac{8}{9}$
(c) $\frac{3}{4}$ (d) None of these
(ii) Is in shelf *B*
(a)· $\frac{3}{54}$ (b) $\frac{4}{54}$
(c) $\frac{5}{54}$ (d) None of these
(iii) Is taken by the student
(a) $\frac{3}{54}$ (b) $\frac{1}{54}$
(c) $\frac{2}{27}$ (d) None of these

15. The ratio of number of men and ladies in the Scorpion Squadron and in the Gunners Squadron are 3:1 and 2:5, respectively. An individual is selected to be the chairperson of their association. The chance that this individual is selected from the Scorpions is 2/3. Find the probability that the chairperson will be a man.
(a) $\frac{25}{42}$ (b) $\frac{13}{43}$
(c) $\frac{11}{43}$ (d) $\frac{7}{42}$

16. A batch of fifty transistors contains three defective ones. Two transistors are selected at random from the batch and put into a radio set. What is the probability that
(i) Both the transistors selected are defective?
(a) $\frac{4}{1225}$ (b) $\frac{3}{1225}$
(c) $\frac{124}{1224}$ (d) None of these
(ii) Only one is defective?
(a) $\frac{141}{1225}$ (b) $\frac{121}{1225}$
(c) $\frac{123}{1224}$ (d) None of these
(iii) Neither is defective?
(a) $\frac{1082}{1224}$ (b) $\frac{1081}{1225}$
(c) $\frac{1081}{1224}$ (d) None of these

17. The probability that a man will be alive in 35 years is $\frac{3}{5}$ and the probability that his wife will be alive is $\frac{3}{7}$. Find the probability that after 35 years

(i) Both will be alive

(a) $\frac{2}{35}$ (b) $\frac{9}{35}$

(c) $\frac{6}{35}$ (d) $\frac{3}{35}$

(ii) Only the man will be alive

(a) $\frac{12}{35}$ (b) $\frac{11}{35}$

(c) $\frac{13}{35}$ (d) $\frac{8}{35}$

(iii) Only the wife will be alive

(a) $\frac{2}{35}$ (b) $\frac{3}{35}$

(c) $\frac{6}{35}$ (d) $\frac{11}{35}$

(iv) At least one will be alive

(a) $\frac{27}{35}$ (b) $\frac{12}{35}$

(c) $\frac{11}{35}$ (d) $\frac{7}{35}$

18. *A* speaks the truth three out of four times, and *B* five out of six times. What is the probability that they will contradict each other in stating the same fact?

(a) $\frac{2}{3}$ (b) $\frac{1}{3}$

(c) $\frac{5}{6}$ (d) None of these

19. A party of n persons sit at a round table. Find the odds against two specified persons sitting next to each other.

(a) $\frac{n+1}{2}$ (b) $\frac{n-3}{2}$

(c) $\frac{n+3}{2}$ (d) None of these

20. If four whole numbers are taken at random and multiplied together, what is the chance that the last digit in the product is 1, 3, 7 or 9?

(a) $\frac{15}{653}$ (b) $\frac{12}{542}$

(c) $\frac{16}{625}$ (d) $\frac{17}{625}$

21. In four throws with a pair of dice, what is the chance of throwing a double twice?

(a) $\frac{11}{216}$ (b) $\frac{25}{216}$

(c) $\frac{35}{126}$ (d) $\frac{41}{216}$

22. A life insurance company insured 25,000 young boys, 14,000 young girls and 16,000 young adults. The probability of death within ten years of a young boy, young girl and a young adult are 0.02, 0.03 and 0.15 respectively. One of the insured persons dies. What is the probability that the dead person is a young boy?

(a) $\frac{36}{165}$ (b) $\frac{25}{166}$

(c) $\frac{26}{165}$ (d) $\frac{32}{165}$

23. Three groups of children consist of three girls and one boy, two girls and two boys, and one girl and two boys, respectively. One child is selected at random from each group. The probability that the three selected consist of one girl and two boys is

(a) $\frac{3}{8}$ (b) $\frac{1}{5}$

(c) $\frac{5}{8}$ (d) $\frac{3}{5}$

24. A locker at the world famous WTC building can be opened by dialling a fixed three-digit code (between 000 and 999). Don, a policeman, only knows that the number is a three-digit number and has only one six. Using this information, he tries to open the locker by dialling three digits at random. The probability that he succeeds in his endeavour is

(a) $\frac{1}{243}$ (b) $\frac{1}{900}$

(c) $\frac{1}{1000}$ (d) $\frac{3}{216}$

25. In a bag, there are twelve black and six white balls. Two balls are chosen at random and the first one is found to be black. The probability that the second one is also black is

(a) $\frac{11}{17}$ (b) $\frac{12}{17}$

(c) $\frac{13}{18}$ (d) None of these

26. In the above question, what is the probability that the second one is white?

(a) $\frac{3}{17}$ (b) $\frac{6}{17}$

(c) $\frac{5}{17}$ (d) $\frac{1}{17}$

27. A fair dice is tossed six times. Find the probability of getting a third six on the sixth throw.

(a) $\frac{^5C_2\,5^2}{6^2}$ (b) $\frac{^5C_2\,5^3}{6^6}$

(c) $\frac{^5C_3\,5^2}{6^3}$ (d) $\frac{^5C_3\,5^2}{6^6}$

28. In shuffling a pack of cards, four are accidentally dropped. Find the chance that the dropped cards should be one from each suit.

(a) $\frac{13^4}{^{52}C_4}$ (b) $\frac{12^4}{^{52}C_2}$

(c) $\frac{13^2}{^{34}C_2}$ (d) $\frac{12^2}{^{22}C_3}$

29. Three of the six vertices of a regular hexagon are chosen at random. The probability that the triangle with these vertices is equilateral is

(a) $\frac{1}{10}$ (b) $\frac{3}{10}$

(c) $\frac{1}{5}$ (d) $\frac{4}{10}$

30. There are five red shoes and four black shoes in a sale. They have got all mixed up with each other. What is the probability of getting a matched shoe if two shoes are drawn at random?

(a) $\frac{6}{9}$ (b) $\frac{4}{9}$

(c) $\frac{2}{9}$ (d) $\frac{5}{9}$

31. A person draws a card from a pack of 52, replaces it and shuffles it. He continues doing it until he draws a heart. What is the probability that he has to make three trials?

(a) $\frac{9}{64}$ (b) $\frac{3}{64}$

(c) $\frac{5}{64}$ (d) $\frac{1}{64}$

32. For the above problem, what is the probability if he does not replace the cards?

(a) $\frac{274}{1700}$ (b) $\frac{123}{1720}$

(c) $\frac{247}{1700}$ (d) $\frac{234}{1500}$

33. An event X can happen with probability P, and event Y can happen with probability P'. What is the probability that exactly one of them happens?

(a) $P + P' - 2PP'$ (b) $2PP' - P' + P$

(c) $P - P' + 2PP'$ (d) $2P'P - P' + P$

34. In the above question, what is the probability that at least one of them happens?

(a) $P + P' + PP'$ (b) $P + P' - PP'$

(c) $2PP' - P' - P$ (d) $P + P' - 2PP'$

35. Find the probability that a year chosen at random has 53 Mondays.

(a) $\frac{2}{7}$ (b) $\frac{5}{28}$

(c) $\frac{1}{28}$ (d) $\frac{3}{28}$

36. There are four machines and it is known that exactly two of them are faulty. They are tested one by one in a random order till both the faulty machines are identified. Then the probability that only two tests are needed is

(a) $\frac{2}{3}$ (b) $\frac{1}{6}$

(c) $\frac{1}{3}$ (d) $\frac{5}{6}$

37. For the above question, the probability that exactly three tests will be required to identify the two faulty machines is

(a) $\frac{1}{2}$ (b) 1

(c) $\frac{1}{3}$ (d) $\frac{2}{3}$

38. Seven white balls and three black balls are randomly placed in a row. Find the probability that no two black balls are placed adjacent to each other.

(a) $\frac{7}{15}$ (b) $\frac{2}{15}$

(c) $\frac{3}{7}$ (d) $\frac{2}{7}$

39. A fair coin is tossed repeatedly. If head appears on the first four tosses then the probability of appearance of tail on the fifth toss is

(a) $\frac{1}{7}$ (b) $\frac{1}{2}$

(c) $\frac{3}{7}$ (d) $\frac{2}{3}$

40. The letters of the word ARTICLE are arranged at random. Find the probability that the vowels may occupy the even places.

(a) $\frac{2}{35}$ (b) $\frac{1}{35}$

(c) $\frac{3}{36}$ (d) $\frac{2}{34}$

41. What is the probability that four S come consecutively in the word MISSISSIPPI?

(a) $\frac{4}{165}$ (b) $\frac{2}{165}$

(c) $\frac{3}{165}$ (d) $\frac{1}{165}$

42. Eleven books, consisting of five Engineering books, four Mathematics books and two Physics books, are arranged in a shelf at random. What is the probability that the books of each kind are all together?

(a) $\frac{5}{1155}$ (b) $\frac{2}{1155}$

(c) $\frac{3}{1155}$ (d) $\frac{1}{1155}$

43. Three students appear in an examination of mathematics. The probability of their success is 1/3,

1/4, 1/5, respectively. Find the probability of success of at least two.

(a) $\frac{1}{6}$ (b) $\frac{2}{5}$

(c) $\frac{3}{4}$ (d) $\frac{3}{5}$

44. A bag contains eight white and four red balls. Five balls are drawn at random. What is the probability that two of them are red and three are white?

(a) $\frac{12}{44}$ (b) $\frac{14}{33}$

(c) $\frac{14}{34}$ (d) $\frac{15}{34}$

45. A team of four is to be constituted out of five girls and six boys. Find the probability that the team may have three girls.

(a) $\frac{4}{11}$ (b) $\frac{3}{11}$

(c) $\frac{5}{11}$ (d) $\frac{2}{11}$

46. Twelve persons are seated around a round table. What is the probability that two particular persons sit together?

(a) $\frac{2}{11}$ (b) $\frac{1}{6}$

(c) $\frac{3}{11}$ (d) $\frac{3}{15}$

47. Six boys and six girls sit in a row randomly. Find the probability that all the six girls sit together.

(a) $\frac{3}{22}$ (b) $\frac{1}{132}$

(c) $\frac{1}{1584}$ (d) $\frac{1}{66}$

48. From a group of seven men and four women, a committee of six persons is formed. What is the probability that the committee will consist of exactly two women?

(a) $\frac{5}{11}$ (b) $\frac{3}{11}$

(c) $\frac{4}{11}$ (d) $\frac{2}{11}$

49. A bag contains five red, four green and three black balls. If three balls are drawn out of it at random, find the probability of drawing exactly two red balls.

(a) $\frac{7}{22}$ (b) $\frac{10}{33}$

(c) $\frac{7}{12}$ (d) $\frac{7}{11}$

50. A bag contains 100 tickets numbered 1, 2, 3, …, 100. If a ticket is drawn out of it at random, what is the probability that the ticket drawn has the digit 2 appearing on it?

(a) $\frac{19}{100}$ (b) $\frac{21}{100}$

(c) $\frac{32}{100}$ (d) $\frac{23}{100}$

High Yield Questions

Scan this QR code to access assisted problem solving videos on questions 6, 20, 24 and 28 from LOD 2

Space for Rough Work

ANSWER KEY

Level of Difficulty (I)

1. (b)	2. (a)	3. (d)	4. (c)
5. (a)	6(i). (c)	6(ii). (b)	6(iii). (c)
7(i). (b)	7(ii). (a)	8(i). (d)	8(ii). (a)
9. (b)	10(i). (a)	10(ii). (b)	10(iii). (d)
11(i). (d)	11(ii). (a)	12. (a)	13. (a)
14(i). (b)	14(ii). (a)	14(iii). (b)	15(i). (d)
15(ii). (a)	15(iii). (b)	16(i). (a)	16(ii). (b)
17. (b)	18. (a)	19(i). (c)	19(ii). (a)
20. (a)	21. (b)	22(i). (a)	22(ii). (d)
22(iii). (a)	23. (a)	24. (d)	25(i). (a)
25(ii). (c)	26. (b)	27. (a)	28. (a)
29. (b)	30. (a)	31. (a)	32. (d)
33. (b)	34(i). (b)	34(ii). (c)	35. (d)
36. (a)	37. (a)	38. (d)	39. (a)
40. (b)	41(i). (c)	41(ii). (d)	41(iii). (a)
42. (c)	43. (a)	44(i). (a)	44(ii). (c)
44(iii). (a)	44(iv). (b)		

Level of Difficulty (II)

1. (d)	2. (a)	3. (a)	4(i) (b)
4(ii) (c)	5. (d)	6. (a)	7. (d)
8. (a)	9(i) (a)	9(ii) (b)	10. (d)
11(i). (a)	11(ii). (b)	11(iii). (b)	12(i). (a)
12(ii).(a)	12(iii). (a)	13(i). (b)	13(ii). (c)
13(iii). (c)	14(i). (b)	14(ii). (c)	14(iii). (b)
15. (a)	16(i). (b)	16(ii). (a)	16(iii). (b)
17(i). (b)	17(ii). (a)	17(iii). (c)	17(iv). (a)
18. (b)	19. (b)	20. (c)	21. (b)
22. (b)	23. (a)	24. (a)	25. (a)
26. (b)	27. (b)	28. (a)	29. (a)
30. (b)	31. (a)	32. (c)	33. (a)
34. (b)	35. (a)	36. (b)	37. (c)
38. (a)	39. (b)	40. (b)	41. (a)
42. (d)	43. (a)	44. (b)	45. (d)
46. (a)	47. (b)	48. (a)	49. (a)
50. (a)			

SOLUTIONS AND SHORTCUTS

Level of Difficulty (I)

1. Out of a total of six occurrences, three is one possibility = 1/6.
2. 5 or 6 out of a sample space of 1, 2, 3, 4, 5 or 6 = 2/6 = 1/3
3. Event definition is:
   (1 and 1) or (1 and 2) or (1 and 3) or (1 and 4) or (1 and 5) or (1 and 6) or (2 and 1) or (3 and 1) or (4 and 1) or (5 and 1) or (6 and 1)
   Total 11 out of 36 possibilities = 11/36
4. Event definition: First is blue and second is blue = 7/12 × 6/11 = 7/22.
5. Knave and Queen or Queen and Knave →
   4/52 × 4/51 + 4/52 × 4/51 = 8/663
6. (i) 13/52 = 1/4
   (ii) Four kings and Four queens out of 52 cards. Thus, 8/52 = 2/13.
   (iii) 13 spades + 3 kings + 3 queens → 19/52
7. (i) Event definition is: T and T and H or T and H and T or H and T and T = 3 × 1/8 = 3/8.
   (ii) Same as above = 3/8
8. (i) Probability of three heads = 1/8
   Also, probability of three tails = 1/8
   Required probability = 1 – (1/8 + 1/8) = 6/8 = 3/4
   (ii) H and H and H = 1/8
9. At least one tail is the non-event for all heads.
   Thus, P (at least 1 tail) = 1 – P (all heads)
   = 1 – 1/8 = 7/8.
10. (i) Positive outcomes are 2(1 way), 4(3 ways), 6(5 ways) 8(5 ways), 10 (3 ways), 12 (1way).
    Thus, 18/36 = 1/2
    (ii) Positive outcomes are: 4, 8 and 12
    4 (3 ways), 8(5 ways) and 12(1 way)
    Gives us 9/36 = 1/4
    (iii) Positive outcomes are 2(1 way), 3(2 ways), 5(4 ways), 7(6 ways). Total of 13 positive outcomes out of 36
    Thus, 13/36
11. (i) First is white and second is white 7/10 × 6/9 = 7/15
    (ii) White and green or green and white
    7/10 × 3/9 + 3/10 × 7/9
    42/90 = 7/15
12. 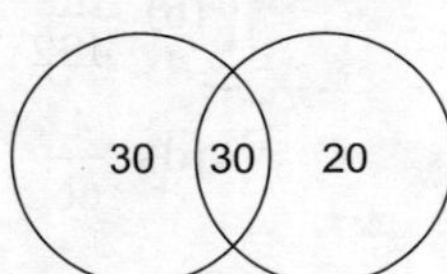

    From the figure, it is evident that 80 students passed at least one exam. Thus, twenty failed both and the required probability is 20/100 = 1/5.
13. 3 or 4 or 5 or 6 = 4/6 = 2/3
14. (i) Since 2 is the only prime number out of the three numbers, the answer would be 1/3.
    (ii) Since all the numbers are even, it is sure that the number drawn out is an even number. Hence, the required probability is 1.
    (iii) Since there are no odd numbers amongst 2, 4 and 8, the required probability is 0.
15. (i) The event would be head and head → $\frac{1}{2} \times \frac{1}{2} = \frac{1}{4}$
    (ii) The event would be head and tail OR tail and head
    $\rightarrow = \frac{1}{2} \times \frac{1}{2} + \frac{1}{2} \times \frac{1}{2} = \frac{1}{2}$

(iii) The event would be tail and tail $\rightarrow \frac{1}{2} \times \frac{1}{2} = \frac{1}{4}$

16. (i) With a six on the first dice, there are six possibilities of outcomes that can appear on the other dice (viz. 6 & 1, 6 & 2, 6 & 3, 6 & 4, 6 & 5 and 6 & 6). At the same time with 6 on the second dice, there are five more possibilities for outcomes on the first dice: (1 & 6, 2 & 6, 3 & 6, 4 & 6, 5 & 6).
Also, the total outcomes are 36. Hence, the required probability is 11/36.
(ii) Out of 36 outcomes, five can come in the following ways – 1 + 4; 2 + 3; 3 + 2 or 4 + 1 → 4/36 = 1/9.

17. Odds against an event = $\frac{p(E')}{p(E)}$
In this case, the event is: all black, i.e. first is black and second is black and third is black.
$P(E) = 5/9 \times 4/8 \times 3/7 = 60/504 = 5/42$
Odds against the event = 37/5

18. Event definition is: 15 or 16 or 17 or 18
15 can be obtained as: 5 and 5 and 5 (one way)
Or
6 and 5 and 4 (Six ways)
Or
6 and 6 and 3 (3 ways)
Total ten ways
16 can be obtained as: 6 and 6 and 4 (3 ways)
Or
6 and 5 and 5 (3 ways)
Total six ways
17 has three ways and 18 has one way of appearing.
Thus, the required probability is: (10 + 6 + 3 + 1)/216 = 20/216 = 5/54.

19. (i) Positive outcomes = 2 (187 or 215)
Total outcomes = 9 × 8 × 7
Required probability = 2/504 = 1/252
(ii) = 2/729

20. 1/6 + 1/10 + 1/8 = 47/120

21. The event definition would be given by:
First is blue and second is blue = 3/11 × 2/10 = 3/55

22. (i) There are six doubles (1, 1; 2 & 2; 3 & 3; 4 & 4; 5 & 5; 6 & 6) out of a total of 36 outcomes → 6/36 = 1/6
(ii) Sum greater than 10 means 11 or 12 → 3/36 = 1/12
(iii) Sum less than 10 is the non-event for the case sum is 10 or 11 or 12. There are three ways of getting 10, two ways of getting 11 and one way of getting a sum of 12 in the throw of two dice. Thus, the required probability would be 1 – 6/36 = 5/6.

23. Expectation = Probability of winning × Reward of winning = (10/5000) × 1 crore = (1 crore/500) = 20000.

24. $1/{}^4C_2 = 1/6$

25.
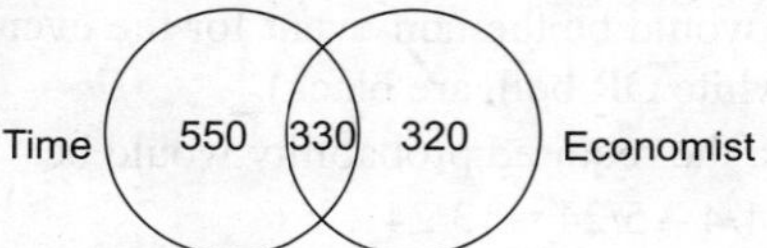

(i) 880/1200 = 11/15
(ii) 650/1200 = 13/24

26. 330/1200 = 11/40

27. 330/880 = 3/8

28. Black and black and black = 4/9 × 3/8 × 2/7 = 24/504 = 1/21

29. $1/{}^5P_2 = 1/20$

30. 6 × (4/52) × (4/51) × (4/50) = 16/5525

31. Positive outcomes are: 5, 7, 10, 14, 15 or 20
Thus, 6/20 = 3/10

32. 972/1972 = 243/493

33. Black and black = (7/16) × 6/15 = 7/40

34. (i) The required probability would be given by:
All are red OR all are white OR all are blue
= (6/18) × (5/17) × (4/16) + (4/18) × (3/17) × (2/16) + (8/18) × (7/17) × (6/16)
= 480/(18 × 17 × 16)
(ii) All blue = (8 × 7 × 6)/(18 × 17 × 16) = 7/102

35. The required value of the union of the two non-events (of *A* and *B*) would be 1 – 1/4 = ¾

36. *P* (both are selected) = *P*(*A*) × *P*(*B*)
Since *P*(*A*) = 0.5, we get
0.3 = 0.5 × 0.6
The maximum value of *P*(*B*) = 0.6
Thus, *P*(*B*) = 0.9 is not possible.

37.
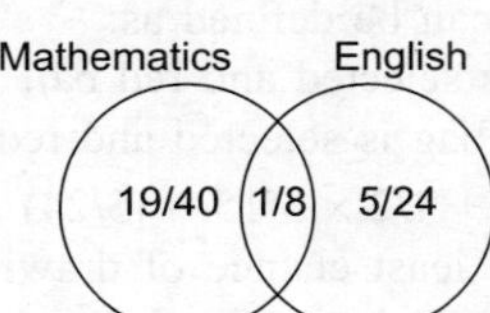

We have: 19/40 + 1/8 + 5/24 = 97/120

38. *P* (Amit) = 1/3
P (Vikas) = 2/7
P (Vivek) = 1/8
Required probability = 1/3 + 2/7 + 1/8 = 125/168

39. $P(A) + P(B) + P(C) = 1 \rightarrow 2P(B)/3 + P(B) + P(B)/2 = 1 \rightarrow 13P(B)/6 = 1 \rightarrow P(B) = 6/13$. Hence, $P(A) = 4/13$

40. *P*(*A*) = 1 – 0.65 = 0.35
Hence, *P*(*B*) = 0.65 – 0.35 = 0.3

41. (i) The required probability would be given by the event:
White from first bag and white from second bag
= (4/6) × (3/8) = $\frac{1}{4}$
(ii) The required probability would be given by the event:
Black from first bag and black from second bag
= (2/6) × (5/8) = 10/48 = 5/24

(iii) This would be the non-event for the event [both are white OR both are black).
Thus, the required probability would be:
1 – 1/4 – 5/24 = 13/24

42. $P(E_1) = 3/8$
$P(E_2) = 7/12$
Event definition is: E_1 occurs and E_2 does not occur or E_1 occurs and E_2 occurs or E_2 occurs and E_1 does not occur
(3/8) × (5/12) + (3/8) × (7/12) + (5/8) × (7/12) = 71/96

43. Kamal is selected and Monica is not selected or Kamal is not selected and Monica is selected → (1/3) × (4/5) + (2/3) × (1/5) = (6/15) = (2/5).

44. (i) 1/5 × 1/7 = 1/35
(ii) (1/5) × (6/7) + (4/5) × (1/7) = 10/35 = 2/7
(iii) (4/5) × (6/7) = 24/35
(iv) Both selected or one selected = 1/35 + 2/7 = 11/35

Level of Difficulty (II)

1. The possible outcomes are:
(1, 1); (1, 2); (2, 1), (2, 2); (3, 1); (1, 3)
Out of six cases, in two cases there is exactly one '2'.
Thus, the correct answer is 2/6 = 1/3.

2. Event definition is A hits, B hits and C hits OR any two of the three hits.
$$\frac{3}{6}\times\frac{2}{6}\times\frac{4}{6}+\frac{3}{6}\times\frac{2}{6}\times\frac{4}{6}+\frac{3}{6}\times\frac{4}{6}\times\frac{4}{6}+\frac{3}{6}\times\frac{2}{6}\times\frac{2}{6}=\frac{1}{2}$$

3. The event can be defined as:
First bag is selected and red ball is drawn.
Or second bag is selected and red ball is drawn.
1/2 × 5/12 + 1/2 × 3/15 = (5/24) + (3/30) = 37/120

4. (a) For the least chance of drawing a red ball, the distribution has to be five red + eleven white in one bag and one white in the second bag. This gives us
$$\frac{1}{2}\times\frac{5}{16}+\frac{1}{2}\times 0 = \frac{5}{32}$$
(b) For the greatest chance of drawing a red ball the distribution has to be one red in the first bag and four red + twelve white balls in the second bag. This gives us
$$\frac{1}{2}\times 1+\frac{1}{2}\times\frac{4}{16} = \frac{5}{8}$$

5. One head and seven tails would have eight positions where the head can come.
Thus, $8 \times (1/2)^8 = (1/32)$

6. A leap year has 366 days – which means 52 completed weeks and two more days. The last two days can be (Sunday, Monday) or (Monday, Tuesday) or ...... (Saturday, Sunday).
Two scenarios out of seven have a 53rd Sunday.
Thus, 2/7 is the required answer.

7. The count of the event will be given by:
The number of all two digit integers – the number of all two digit integers divisible by 7 = 90 – 13 = 77. Hence, Required probability = 77/90.

8. Blue and red or red and blue
= (10/25) × (15/24) + (15/25) × (10/24) = (1/2)

9. (i) $1/5 + \frac{1}{2} = 7/10$
(ii) 1 – (7/10) = (3/10)

10. A total of six can be made in any of the following ways (1 + 5, 2 + 4, 3 + 3, 4 + 2, 5 + 1)
Required probability = 3/5

11. The event definitions are:
(a) Passes the first AND passes the second AND passes the third AND passes the fourth
(b) Fails the first AND fails the second AND fails the third AND fails the fourth
(c) Fails all is the non-event

12. (i) First is cricket and second is cricket and third is cricket → (3/9) × (3/9) × (3/9) = (1/27)
(ii) (2/9) × (3/9) × (4/9) = (8/243)
(iii) All are cricket or all are tennis or all are squash
$(3/9)^3 + (2/9)^3 + (4/9)^3 = (99/729) = (11/81)$

13. (i) (3/9) × (2/8) × (1/7) = (1/84)
(ii) (2/9) × (3/8) × (4/7) = (1/21)
(iii) (3/9) × (2/8) × (1/7) + 0 + (4/9) × (3/8) × (2/7)
30/504 = 5/84

14. The event definitions are:
(i) The book transferred is by Stephen Covey
(ii) The book transferred is by Vinay Singh AND the book picked up is by Stephen Covey
(iii) The book transferred is by Stephen Covey AND the book picked up is by Vinay Singh

15. (2/3) × (3/4) + (1/3) × (2/7) = (1/2) + (2/21) = (25/42)

16. (i) (3/50) × (2/49) = (3/1225)
(ii) (3/50) × (47/49) + 47/50 × (3/49) = (141/1225)
(iii) (47/50) × (46/49) = (1081/1225)

17. (i) (3/5) × (3/7) = (9/35)
(ii) (3/5) × 4/7) = (12/35)
(iii) (2/5) × (3/7) = (6/35)
(iv) (3/5) × (4/7) + (2/5) × (3/7) + (3/5) × (3/7) = 27/35

18. They will contradict each other if: A is true and B is false or A is false and B is true.
(3/4) × (1/6) + (1/4) × (5/6) = 1/3

19. For the counting of the number of events, think of it as a circular arrangement with n – 1 people (by considering the two specified persons as one). This will give you $n(E) = (n - 2)! \times (2)!$
The total number of ways of them sitting without constraint = $(n - 1)!$. Hence, Probability of the event

i.e. Probability of both sitting next to each other P(E) $= (n-2)! \times 2/(n-1)!$.
Probability of the non-event P(E') = 1 – P(E).
Required odds against = P(E')/P(E) = $(n-3)/2$

20. The whole numbers selected can only be 1, 3, 7 or 9 and cannot contain 2, 4, 6, 8, 0 or 5.
Required probability = $(2/5)^4$
21. ${}^4C_2 \times (6/36)^2 \times (30/36)^2 = 6 \times (1/36) \times (25/36) =$ 25/216.
22. The required probability will be given by the expression:

$$\frac{\text{The number of young boys who will die}}{\text{The total number of people who will die}}$$

$$\frac{500}{(500+420+2400)} = \frac{25}{166}$$

23. Girl and boy and boy or boy and girl and boy
Or
Boy and boy and girl
= (3/4) × (2/4) × (2/3) + (1/4) × (2/4) × (2/3) + (1/4) × (2/4) × (1/3) = 18/48 = 3/8
24. $n(E) = 1$
$n(S) = {}^3C_1 \times 9 \times 9 = 243$
25. 11/17 (if the first one is black, there will be 11 black balls left out of 17)
26. 6/17
27. There must have been two sixes in the first five throws. Thus, the answer is given by:

$${}^5C_2 \times \frac{1}{6} \times \frac{1}{6} \times \frac{1}{6} \times \frac{5}{6} \times \frac{5}{6} \times \frac{5}{6}$$

28. $$\frac{{}^{13}C_1 \times {}^{13}C_1 \times {}^{13}C_1 \times {}^{13}C_1}{{}^{52}C_4}$$

29. There will be ${}^6C_3$ triangles formed overall. Out of these, there will be 2 equilateral triangles. Hence, the required probability is 2/20 = 1/10.
30. (5/9) × (4/8) + (4/9) × (3/8) = 32/72 = 4/9
As matched shoes means both red or both black
31. The event definition here is that first is not a heart and second is not a heart and third is a heart = (3/4) × (3/4) × (1/4) = 9/64.
32. (39/52) × (38/51) × (13/50) = 247/1700
33. The event definition will be: Event X happens and Y does not happen Or Y happens and X does not happen.
34. X happens and Y does not happen or X does not happen and Y happens or X happens and Y happens $P \times (1-P') + (1-P) \times P' + P \times P' = P + P' - PP'$
35. Same logic as question 6.
36. (2/4) × (1/3) = 1/6 (Faulty and faulty)
37. Faulty and not faulty and faulty or not faulty and faulty and faulty = (2/4) × (2/3) × (1/2) + (2/4) × (2/3) × (1/2) = 1/3
38. When you put the seven balls with a gap between them in a row, you will have eight spaces. The required probability will be: ${}^8C_3/(10!/7! \times 3!) = 7/15$
39. The appearance of head or tail on a toss is independent of previous occurrences.
Hence, 1/2.
40. $$\frac{3! \times 4!}{7!} = 1/35$$
41. $$P = \frac{\text{No. of arrangements with four S together}}{\text{Total No. of arrangements}}$$
$$= \frac{[8!/(4! \times 2!)]}{[11!/(4! \times 4! \times 2!)]}$$
$= 8! \times 4!/11! = 24/990 = 4/165$
42. $$\frac{(5! \times 4! \times 2! \times 3!)}{11!} = \frac{24 \times 2 \times 6}{11 \times 10 \times 9 \times 8 \times 7 \times 6} = 1/1155$$
43. (1/3) × (1/4) × (4/5) + (1/3) × (3/4) × (1/5) + (2/3) × (1/4) × (1/5) + (1/3) × (1/4) × (1/5)
= 10/60 = 1/6
44. ${}^5C_3 \times [\,(8/12) \times (7/11) \times (6/10) \times (4/9) \times (3/8)] =$ 14/33
45. ${}^5C_3 \times {}^6C_1/{}^{11}C_4 = 2/11$
46. $$P = \frac{\text{Total no of ways in which two people sit together}}{\text{Total No. of ways}}$$
$= (10! \times 2!)/11!$
47. Consider the six girls to be one person. Then the number of arrangements satisfying the condition is given by $n(E) = 7! \times 6!$.
48. ${}^6C_2 \times [(7/11) \times (6/10) \times (5/9) \times (4/8) \times (4/7) \times (3/6)] = 5/11.$
49. The event definition is red AND red AND not red OR red AND not red AND red OR not red AND red AND red.
50. The numbers having 2 in them are: 2, 12, 22, 32….92 and 21, 23, 24, 25….29. Hence, $n(E) = 19$.

CHAPTER 20

Set Theory

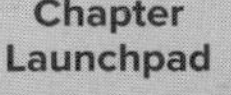

Scan this QR code to access a video on 'Introduction to Set Theory' and this chapter's importance for CAT

Set Theory is an important concept of mathematics which is often asked in aptitude exams. There are two types of questions in this chapter:

1. Numerical questions on set theory based on Venn diagrams
2. Logical questions based on set theory

Let us first take a look at some standard theoretical inputs related to set theory.

SET THEORY

Look at the following diagrams:

Figure 1: Refers to the situation where there are two attributes *A* and *B*. (Let's say *A* refers to people who passed in Physics and *B* refers to people who passed in Chemistry.) Then the shaded area shows the people who passed both in Physics and Chemistry.

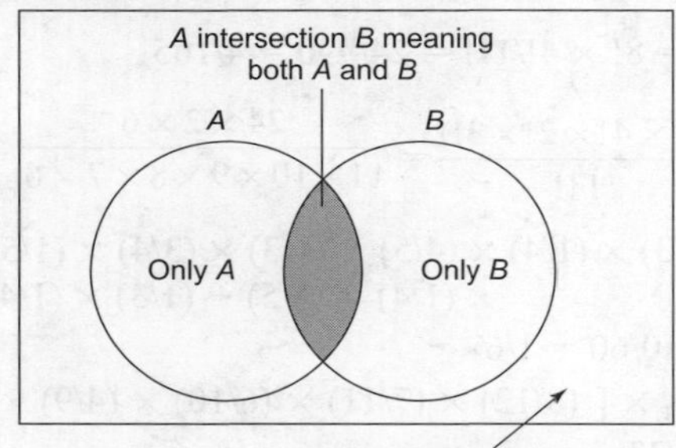

In mathematical terms, the situation is represented as:

Total number of people who passed at least one subject = $A + B - A \cap B$

Figure 2: Refers to the situation where there are three attributes being measured. In the figure below, we are talking about people who passed Physics, Chemistry and/or Mathematics.

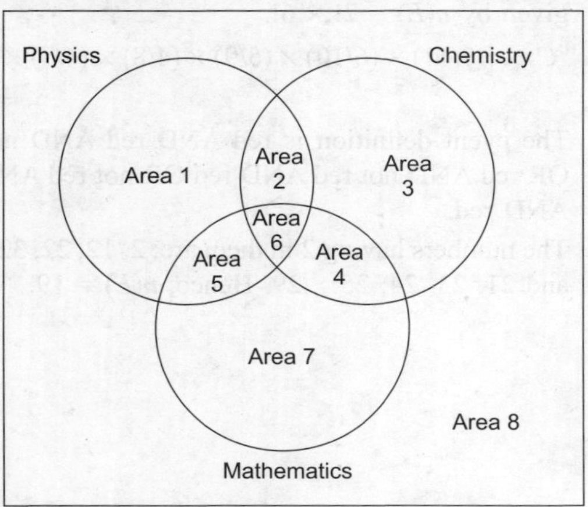

In the above figure, the following explain the respective areas:

Area 1: People who passed in Physics only

Area 2: People who passed in Physics and Chemistry only (in other words—people who passed Physics and Chemistry but not Mathematics)

Area 3: People who passed Chemistry only

Area 4: People who passed Chemistry and Mathematics only (also, can be described as people who passed Chemistry and Mathematics but not Physics)

Area 5: People who passed Physics and Mathematics only (also, can be described as people who passed Physics and Mathematics but not Chemistry)

Area 6: People who passed Physics, Chemistry and Mathematics

Area 7: People who passed Mathematics only

Area 8: People who passed in no subjects

Also take note of the following language which there is normally confusion about:

People passing Physics and Chemistry—Represented by the sum of areas 2 and 6

People passing Physics and Mathematics—Represented by the sum of areas 5 and 6

People passing Chemistry and Mathematics—Represented by the sum of areas 4 and 6

People passing Physics—Represented by the sum of the areas 1, 2, 5 and 6

In mathematical terms, this means:

Total number of people who passed at least one subject = $P + C + M - P \cap C - P \cap M - C \cap M + P \cap C \cap M$

Let us now consider the following questions and see how these figures work in terms of real-time problem-solving:

Illustration 1

At the birthday party of Sherry, a baby boy, 40 persons chose to kiss him and 25 chose to shake hands with him. Ten persons chose to both kiss him and shake hands with him. How many persons turned out at the party?

(a) 35 (b) 75
(c) 55 (d) 25

Solution: Kiss (40) Shake hands (25)

Only Kiss 30 | Both (10) | Only Shake hand 15

From the figure, it is clear that the number of people at the party were 30 + 10 + 15 = 55.

We can, of course, solve this mathematically as below:

Let $n(A)$ = Number of persons who kissed Sherry = 40

$n(B)$ = Number of persons who shake hands with Sherry = 25

and $n(A \cap B)$ = Number of persons who shook hands with Sherry and kissed him both = 10

Then using the formula, $n(A \cup B) = n(A) + n(B) - n(A \cap B)$

$n(A \cup B) = 40 + 25 - 10 = 55$

Illustration 2

Directions for Questions 1 to 4: Refer to the data below and answer the questions that follow:

In an examination 43% passed in Mathematics, 52% passed in Physics and 52% passed in Chemistry. Only 8% students passed in all the three. Fourteen per cent passed in Mathematics and Physics and 21% passed in Mathematics and Chemistry and 20% passed in Physics and Chemistry. Number of students who took the exam is 200.

1. How many students passed in Mathematics only?
   (a) 16 (b) 32
   (c) 48 (d) 80
2. Find the ratio of students passing in Mathematics only to the students passing in Chemistry only?
   (a) 16:37 (b) 29:32
   (c) 16:19 (d) 31:49
3. What is the ratio of the number of students passing in Physics only to the students passing in either Physics or Chemistry or both?
   (a) 34/46 (b) 26/84
   (c) 49/32 (d) None of these
4. A student is declared pass in the exam only if he/she clears at least two subjects. The number of students who were declared passed in this exam is?
   (a) 33 (b) 66
   (c) 39 (d) 78

Solution: Let P denote Physics, C denote Chemistry and M denote Mathematics.

% of students who passed in P and C only is given by:

% of students who passed in P and C - % of students who passed all three = 20% – 8% = 12%

% of students who passed in P and M only is given by:

% of students who passed in P and M - % of students who passed all three = 14% – 8% = 6%

% of students who passed in M and C only is given by:

% of students who passed in C and M - % of students who passed all three = 21% – 8% = 13%

So, % of students who passed in P only is given by:

Total number passing in P – Number passing in P and C only – Number passing P and M only – Number passing in all three→ 52% – 12% – 6% – 8% = 26%

% of students who passed in M only is given by:

Total number passing in M – Number passing in M and C only – Number passing P and M only – Number passing in all three→ 43% – 13% – 6% – 8%- = 16%

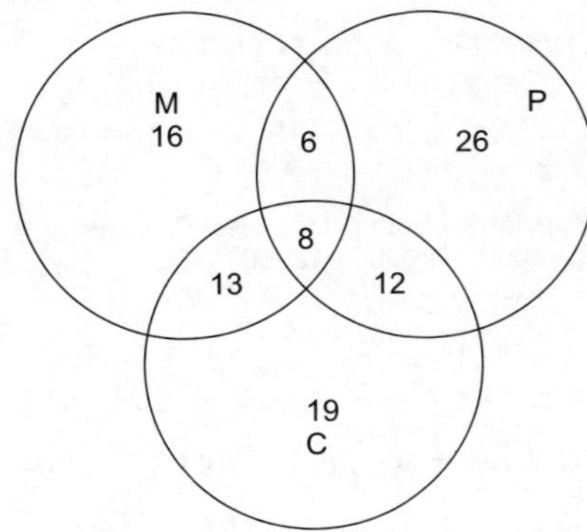

% of students who passed in Chemistry only is given by:

Total number passing in C – Number passing in P and C only – Number passing in C and M only – Number passing in all three →
52% – 12% – 13% – 8%– = 19%

The answers are:

1. Only Mathematics =16% = 32 people. Option (b) is correct.
2. Ratio of only Mathematics to only Chemistry = 16:19. Option (c) is correct.
3. 26:84 is the required ratio. Option (b) is correct.
4. 39% or 78 people. Option (d) is correct.

Illustration 3

In the Mindworkzz club, all the members participate either in the Tambola or the Fete. In the fete, 320 participate,; 350 participate in the Tambola and 220 participate in both. How many members does the club have?

(a) 410 (b) 550
(c) 440 (d) None of these

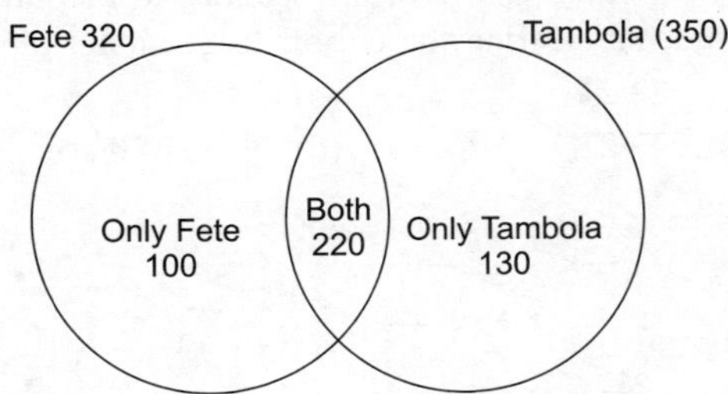

The total number of people = 100 + 220 + 130 = 450
Option (d) is correct.

Illustration 4

There are 20000 people living in Defence Colony, Gurugram. Out of them, 9000 subscribe to Star TV Network and 12000 to Zee TV Network. If 4000 subscribe to both, how many do not subscribe to any of the two?

(a) 3000 (b) 2000
(c) 1000 (d) 4000

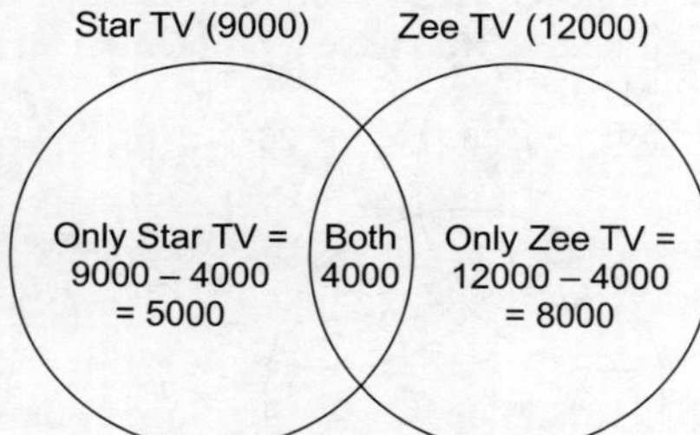

The required answer would be 20000 – 5000 – 4000 – 8000 = 3000.

Illustration 5

Directions for Questions 1 to 3: Refer to the data below and answer the questions that follow.

Last year, there were three sections in the Catalyst, a mock CAT paper. Out of them, 33 students cleared the cut-off in Section 1, 34 students cleared the cut-off in Section 2 and 32 cleared the cut-off in Section 3. Ten students cleared the cut-off in Section 1 and Section 2, nine cleared the cut-off in Section 2 and Section 3, and eight cleared the cut-off in Section 1 and Section 3. The number of people who cleared each section alone was equal and was 21 for each section.

1. How many cleared all the three sections?

(a) 3 (b) 6
(c) 5 (d) 7

2. How many cleared only one of the three sections?

(a) 21 (b) 63
(c) 42 (d) 52

3. The ratio of the number of students clearing the cut-off in one or more of the sections to the number of students clearing the cut-off in Section 1 alone is?

(a) 78/21 (b) 3
(c) 73/21 (d) None of these

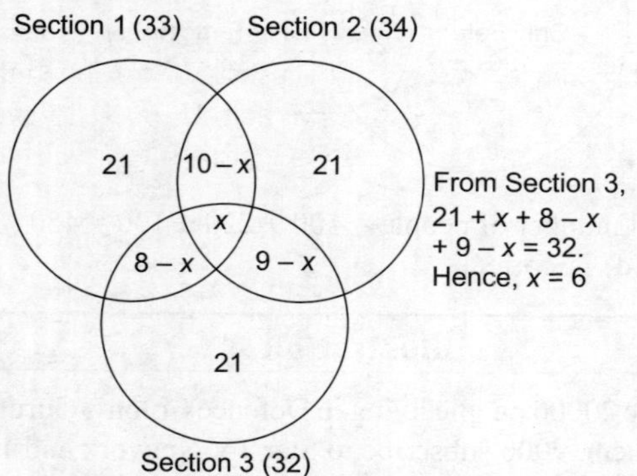

Since, x = 6, the figure becomes:

The answers would be:

1. 6. Option (b) is correct.
2. 21 + 21 + 21 = 63. Option (b) is correct.
3. (21 + 21 + 21 + 6 + 4 + 3 + 2)/21 = 78/21. Option (a) is correct.

Illustration 6

In a locality having 1500 households, 1000 watch Zee TV, 300 watch NDTV and 750 watch Star Plus. Based on this information, answer the questions that follow:

1. The minimum number of households watching Zee TV and Star Plus is:

Logic: If we try to consider each of the households watching Zee TV and Star Plus as independent of each other, we would get a total of 1000 + 750 = 1750 households. However, we have a total of only 1500 households in the locality and hence, there has to be a minimum interference of at least 250 households who would be watching both Zee TV and Star Plus. Hence, the answer to this question is 250.

2. The minimum number of households watching both Zee TV and NDTV is:

In this case, the number of households watching Zee TV and NDTV can be separate from each other since there is no interference required between the households watching Zee TV and the households watching NDTV as their individual sum (1000 + 300) is smaller than the 1500 available households in the locality. Hence, the answer in this question is 0.

3. The maximum number of households who watch none of the three channels is:

For this to occur, the following situation would give us the required solution:

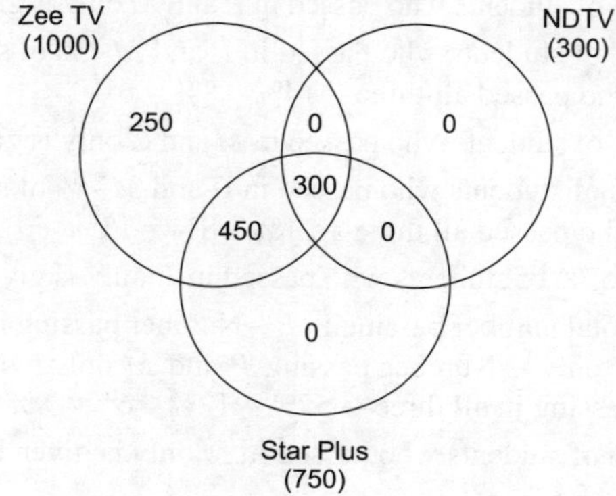

As you can clearly see from the figure, all the requirements of each category of viewers are fulfilled by the given allocation of 1000 households. In this situation, the maximum number of households who do not watch any of the three channels is visible as 1500 – 1000 = 500.

Illustration 7

1. In a school, 90% of the students faced problems in Mathematics, 80% of the students faced problems in Computers, 75% of the students faced problems in Sciences, and 70% of the students faced problems in Social Sciences. Find the minimum percent of the students who faced problems in all four subjects.

Going Beyond the Book

Scan this QR code to access a video explanation of Illustration 7

Solution: In order to think about the minimum number of students who faced problems in all four subjects you would need to think of keeping the students who did not face a problem in any of the subjects separate from each other. We know that 30% of the students did not face problems in Social Sciences, 25% of the students did not face problems in Sciences, 20% students did not face problems in Computers and 10% students did not face problems in Mathematics. If each of these were separate from each other, we would have 30 + 25 + 20 + 10 = 85% people who did not face a problem in one of the four subjects. Naturally, the remaining 15% would be students who faced problems in all four subjects. This represents the minimum percentage of students who faced problems in all the four subjects.

2. For the above question, find the maximum possible percentage of students who could have problems in all four subjects.

   In order to solve this, you need to consider the fact that 100 (%) people are counted 315 (%) times, which means that there is an extra count of 215 (%). When you put a student into the 'has problems in each of the four subjects', he is one student counted four times — an extra count of 3. Since, 215/3 = 71 (quotient), we realise that if we have 71 students who have problems in all four subjects — we will have an extra count of 213 students. The remaining extra count of 2 more can be matched by putting one student in 'has problems in three subjects' or by putting two students in 'has problems in two subjects'. Thus, from the extra count angle, we have a limit of 71% students in the 'have problems in all four categories.'

   However, in this problem there is a constraint from another angle, i.e., there are only 70% students who have a problem in Social Sciences — and hence, it is not possible for 71% students to have problems in all the four subjects. Hence, the maximum possible percentage of people who have a problem in all four subjects would be 70%.

3. In the above question if it is known that 10% of the students faced none of the above mentioned four problems, what would have been the minimum number of students who would have a problem in all four subjects?

   If there are 10% students who face none of the four problems, we realise that these 10% would be common to students who face no problems in Mathematics, students who face no problems in Sciences, students who face no problems in Computers and students who face no problems in Social Sciences.

   Now, we also know that overall there are 10% students who did not face a problem in Mathematics; 20% students who did not face a problem in Computers; 25% students who did not face a problem in Sciences and 30% students who did not face a problem in Social Sciences. The 10% students who did not face a problem in any of the subjects would be common to each of these four counts. Out of the remaining 90% students, if we want to identify the minimum number of students who had a problem in all four subjects we will take the same approach as we took in the first question of this set — i.e. we try to keep the students having problems in the individual subjects separate from each other. This would result in: 0% additional students having no problem in Mathematics; 10% additional students having no problem in Computers; 15% additional students having no problem in Sciences and 20% additional students having no problem in Social Sciences. Thus, we would get a total of 45% (0+10+15+20=45) students who would have no problem in one of the four subjects. Thus, the minimum percentage of students who had a problem in all four subjects would be 90 – 45 = 45%.

Illustration 8

In a class of 80 students, each of them studies at least one language—English, Hindi and Sanskrit. It was found that 65 studied English, 60 studied Hindi and 55 studied Sanskrit.

1. Find the maximum number of people who study all three languages.

   This question again has to be dealt with from the perspective of extra counting. In this question, 80 students in the class are counted 65 + 60 + 55 = 180 times — an extra count of 100. If we put 50 people in all the three categories as shown below, we would get the maximum number of students who study all three languages.

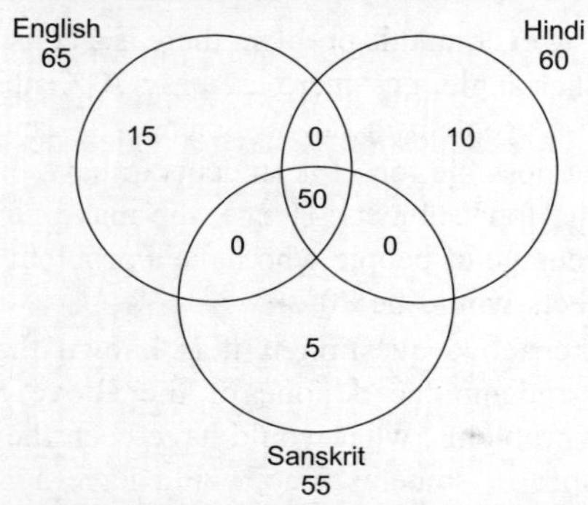

Going Beyond the Book

Scan this QR code to access a video explanation of Illustration 8

2. Find the minimum number of people who study all three languages.

In order to think about how many students are necessarily in the 'study all three languages' area of the figure (this thinking would lead us to the answer to the minimum number of people who study all three languages), we need to think about how many people we can shift out of the 'study all three category' for the previous question. When we try to do that, the following thought - process emerges:

Step 1: Let's take a random value for the all three categories (less than 50 of course) and see whether the numbers can be achieved. For this purpose we try to start with the value as 40 and see what happens. Before we move on, realise that the basic situation in the question remains the same — 80 students have been counted 180 times — which means that there is an extra count of 100 students and also realise that when you put an individual student in the all three categories, you get an extra count of 2, while at the same time when you put an individual student into the 'exactly two languages category', he/she is counted twice — hence an extra count of 1.

The starting figure we get, looks something like this:

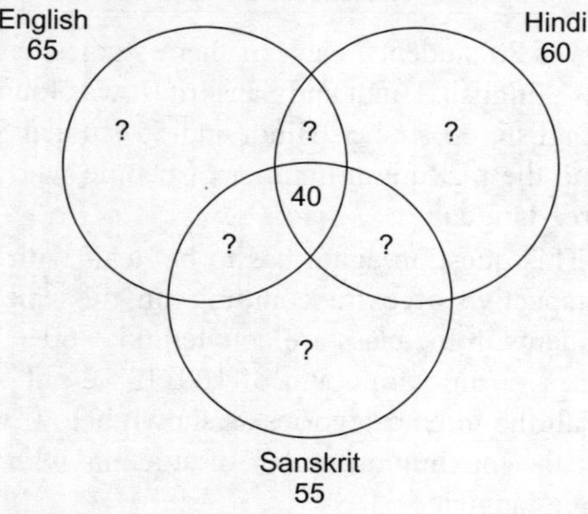

At this point, since we have placed 40 people in the all three categories, we have taken care of an extra count of $40 \times 2 = 80$. This leaves us with an extra count of 20 more to manage and as we can see in the above figure we have a lot of what can be described as 'slack' to achieve the required numbers. For instance, one solution we can think of from this point is as below:

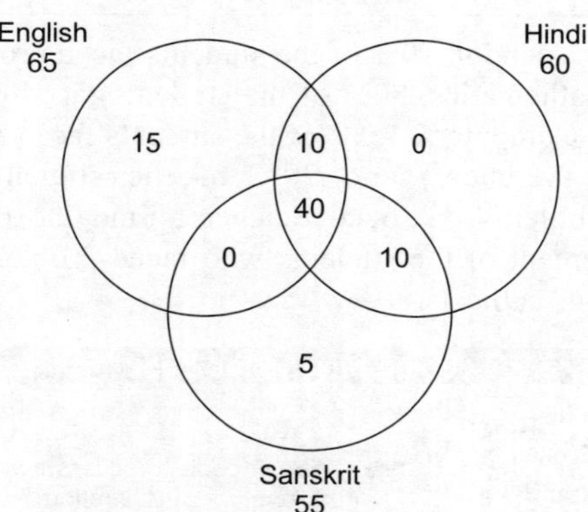

One look at this figure should tell you that the solution can be further optimised by reducing the middle value in the figure since there is still a lot of 'slack' in the figure — in the form of the number of students in the 'exactly one language category'. Also, you can easily see that there are many ways in which this solution could have been achieved with 40 in the middle. Hence, we go in search of a lower value in the middle.

So, we try to take an arbitrary value of 30 to see whether this is still achievable.

In this case we see the following as one of the possible ways to achieve this (again there is a lot of slack in this solution as the 'only Hindi' or the 'only Sanskrit' areas can be reallocated):

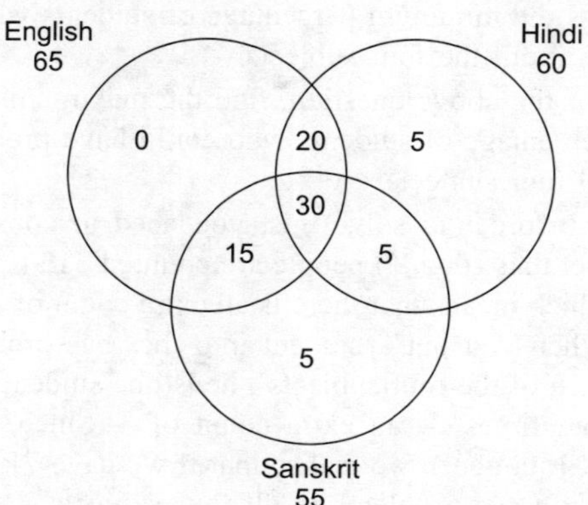

Trying the same solution for 20 in the middle, we get the optimum solution:

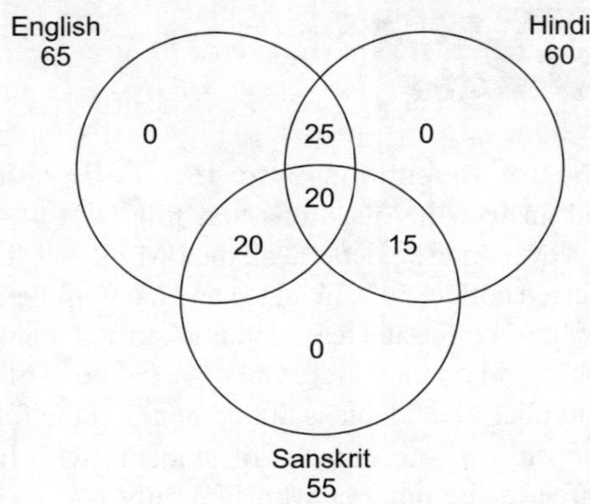

We realise that this is the optimum solution since there is no 'slack' in this solution and hence, there is no scope for re-allocating numbers from one area to another.

Author's note: You might be justifiably thinking, how do you do this kind of a random trial—and—error inside the exam! That is not the point of this question at this place. What I am trying to convey to you is that this is a critical thought structure which you need to have in your mind. Learn it here and do not worry about how you would think inside the exam — remember that in the CAT and in Aptitude tests, question setters have a responsibility to keep lengths limited and hence they would give you a question structure that is feasible to be solved within 3- 4 steps. Also, for this question, try to start by minimising the middle value as '0' and see how it works, feeling the slack and the movement in the question. I have a video description of this solution on my youtube channel – ARUN SHARMA MINDWORKZZ.

Illustration 9

In a group of 120 athletes, the number of athletes who can play Tennis, Badminton, Squash and Table Tennis is 70, 50, 60 and 30, respectively. What is the maximum number of athletes who can play none of the games?

Going Beyond the Book

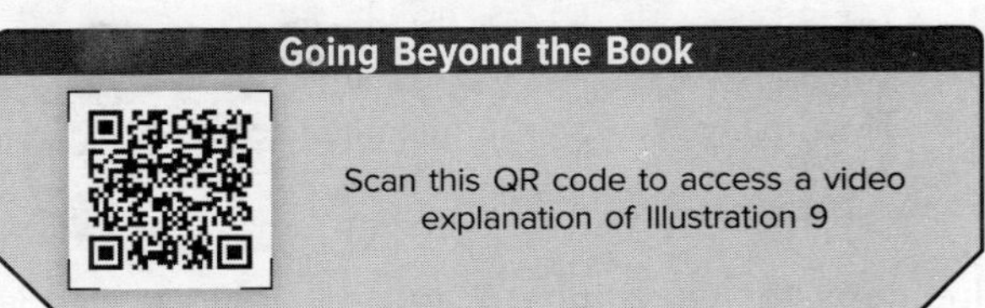

Solution: In order to think of the maximum number of athletes who can play none of the games, we can think of the fact that since there are 70 athletes who play tennis, fundamentally there are a maximum of 50 athletes who would be possibly in the 'can play none of the games'. No other constraint in the problem necessitates a reduction of this number and hence, the answer to this question is 50.

Space for Rough Work

LEVEL OF DIFFICULTY (I)

Directions for Questions 1 and 2: Refer to the data below and answer the questions that follow:

In the Indian athletic squad sent to the Olympics, 21 athletes were in the triathlon team; 26 were in the pentathlon team; and 29 were in the marathon team. Fourteen athletes can take part in triathlon and pentathlon; 12 can take part in marathon and triathlon; 15 can take part in pentathlon and marathon; and 8 can take part in all the three games.

1. How many players are there in all?
(a) 35 (b) 43
(c) 49 (d) None of these
2. How many were in the marathon team only?
(a) 10 (b) 14
(c) 18 (d) 15

Directions for Questions 3 and 4: Refer to the data below and answer the questions that follow.

In a test in which 120 students appeared, 90 passed in History, 65 passed in Sociology and 75 passed in Political Science. Thirty students passed in only one subject and 55 students in only two. Five students passed no subjects.

3. How many students passed in all the three subjects?
(a) 25 (b) 30
(c) 35 (d) Data insufficient
4. Find the number of students who passed in at least two subjects.
(a) 85 (b) 95
(c) 90 (d) Data insufficient

Directions for Questions 5 to 8: Refer to the data below and answer the questions that follow.

Five per cent of the passengers who boarded Guwahati-New Delhi Rajdhani Express on 20 February, 2022, do not like coffee, tea and ice cream and 10% like all the three. Twenty per cent like coffee and tea, 25% like ice cream and coffee and 25% like ice cream and tea. Fifty-five per cent like coffee, 50% like tea and 50 % like ice cream.

5. The number of passengers who like only coffee is greater than the passengers who like only ice cream by
(a) 50% (b) 100%
(c) 25% (d) 0
6. The percentage of passengers who like both tea and ice cream but not coffee is
(a) 15 (b) 5
(c) 10 (d) 25
7. The percentage of passengers who like at least two of the three products is
(a) 40 (b) 45
(c) 50 (d) 60
8. If the number of passengers is 180, then the number of passengers who like ice cream only is
(a) 10 (b) 18
(c) 27 (d) 36

Directions for Questions 9 to 15: Refer to the data below and answer the questions that follow.

In a survey among students at all the IIMs, it was found that 48% preferred coffee, 54% liked tea and 64% smoked. Of the total, 28% liked coffee and tea, 32% smoked and drank tea and 30% smoked and drank coffee. Only 6% did none of these. If the total number of students is 2000, then find the following.

9. The ratio of the number of students who like only coffee to the number who like only tea is
(a) 5:3 (b) 8:9
(c) 2:3 (d) 3:2
10. Number of students who like coffee and smoking but not tea is
(a) 600 (b) 240
(c) 280 (d) 360
11. The percentage of those who like coffee or tea but not smoking among those who like at least one of these is
(a) More than 30 (b) Less than 30
(c) Less than 25 (d) None of these
12. The percentage of those who like at least one of these is
(a) 100 (b) 90
(c) Nil (d) 94
13. The two items having the ratio 1:2 are
(a) Tea only and tea and smoking only.
(b) Coffee and smoking only and tea only.
(c) Coffee and tea but not smoking and smoking but not coffee and tea.
(d) None of these
14. The number of persons who like coffee and smoking only and the number who like tea only bear a ratio
(a) 1:2 (b) 1:1
(c) 5:1 (d) 2:1
15. Percentage of those who like tea and smoking but not coffee is
(a) 14 (b) 14.9
(c) Less than 14 (d) More than 15
16. Thirty monkeys went to a picnic. Twenty-five monkeys chose to irritate cows while twenty chose to irritate buffaloes. How many chose to irritate both buffaloes and cows?
(a) 10 (b) 15
(c) 5 (d) 20

Directions for Questions 17 to 20: Refer to the data below and answer the questions that follow.

In the CBSE Board Exams last year, 53% passed in Biology, 61% passed in English, 60% in Social Studies, 24% in Biology and English, 35% in English and Social Studies, 27% in Biology and Social Studies and 5% in none.

17. Percentage of passes in all subjects is
(a) Nil (b) 12
(c) 7 (d) 10

18. If the number of students in the class is 200, how many passed in only one subject?
(a) 48 (b) 46
(c) More than 50 (d) Less than 40

19. If the number of students in the class is 300, what will be the percentage change in the number of passes in only two subjects, if the original number of students is 200?
(a) More than 50% (b) Less than 50%
(c) 50% (d) None of these

20. What is the ratio of percentage of passes in Biology and Social Studies but not English in relation to the percentage of passes in Social Studies and English but not Biology?
(a) 5:7 (b) 7:5
(c) 4:5 (d) None of these

Directions for Questions 21 to 25: Refer to the data below and answer the questions that follow.

In the McGraw-Hill Mindworkzz Quiz held last year, participants were free to choose their respective areas from which they were asked questions. Out of 880 participants, 224 chose Mythology, 240 chose Science and 336 chose Sports, 64 chose both Sports and Science, 80 chose Mythology and Sports, 40 chose Mythology and Science and 24 chose all the three areas.

21. The percentage of participants who did not choose any area is
(a) 23.59% (b) 30.25%
(c) 37.46% (d) 27.27%

22. Of those participating, the percentage who choose only one area is
(a) 60% (b) More than 60%
(c) Less than 60% (d) More than 75%

23. Number of participants who chose at least two areas is
(a) 112 (b) 24
(c) 136 (d) None of these

24. Which of the following areas shows a ratio of 1:8?
(a) Mythology and Science but not Sports: Mythology only
(b) Mythology and Sports but not Science: Science only
(c) Science: Sports
(d) None of these

25. The ratio of students choosing Sports and Science but not Mythology to Science but not Mythology and Sports is
(a) 2:5 (b) 1:4
(c) 1:5 (d) 1:2

Directions for Questions 26 to 30: Refer to the data below and answer the questions that follow.

The table here gives the distribution of students according to professional courses.

Courses	STUDENTS			
	English		*Mathematics*	
	MALES	*FEMALES*	*MALES*	*FEMALES*
Part-time MBA	30	10	50	10
Full-time MBA only	150	8	16	6
CA only	90	10	37	3
Full time MBA and CA	70	2	7	1

26. The number of Mathematics students (for all courses) as a percentage of the number of English students (for all courses) is:
(a) 50.4 (b) 61.4
(c) 49.4 (d) None of these

27. The average number of females in all the courses is (count people doing full-time MBA and CA as a separate course)
(a) Less than 12 (b) Greater than 12
(c) 12 (d) None of these

28. The ratio of the number of girls to the number of boys is
(a) 5:36 (b) 1:9
(c) 1:7.2 (d) None of these

29. The percentage increase in students of full-time MBA only over CA only is
(a) Less than 20 (b) Less than 25
(c) Less than 30 (d) More than 30

30. The number of students doing full-time MBA or CA is
(a) 320 (b) 80
(c) 160 (d) None of these

Directions for Questions 31 to 34: Refer to the data below and answer the questions that follow:

A newspaper agent sells The TOI, HT and IN in equal numbers to 302 persons. Seven get HT and IN, twelve get The TOI and IN, nine get The TOI and HT and three get all the three newspapers. The details are given in the Venn diagram:

31. How many get only one paper?
(a) 280 (b) 327
(c) 109 (d) None of these

32. What percent get The TOI or The HT or both (but not The IN)? (Approximately)
(a) More than 65% (b) Less than 60%
(c) 64% (d) 72%

33. The number of persons buying The TOI and The HT only, The TOI and The IN only and The HT and The IN only are in the ratio of

(a) 6:4:9 (b) 6:9:4
(c) 4:9:6 (d) None of these

34. The difference between the number reading The HT and The IN only and HT only is

(a) 77 (b) 78
(c) 83 (d) None of these

35. A group of 78 people watch Zee TV, Star Plus or Sony. Of these, 36 watch Zee TV, 48 watch Star Plus and 32 watch Sony. If 14 people watch both Zee TV and Star Plus, 20 people watch both Star Plus and Sony, and 12 people watch both Sony and Zee TV find the ratio of the number of people who watch only Zee TV to the number of people who watch only Sony.

(a) 9:4 (b) 3:2
(c) 5:3 (d) 7:4

Directions for Questions 36 and 37: Answer the questions based on the following information.

The following data was observed from a study of car complaints received from 180 respondents at Colonel Verma's car-care workshop, viz., engine problem, transmission problem or mileage problem. Of those surveyed, there was no one who faced exactly two of these problems. There were 90 respondents who faced engine problems, 120 who faced transmission problems and 150 who faced mileage problems.

36. How many of them faced all the three problems?

(a) 45 (b) 60
(c) 90 (d) 20

37. How many of them faced either transmission problems or engine problems?

(a) 60 (b) 30
(c) 90 (d) 40

Directions for Questions 38 to 42: Given below are five diagrams one of which describes the relationship among the three classes given in each of the five questions that follow. You have to decide which of the diagrams is the most suitable for a particular set of classes.

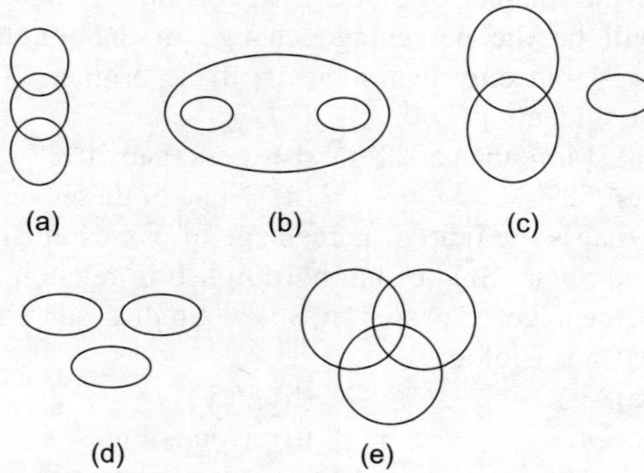

38. Elephants, Tigers, Animals

39. Administrators, Doctors, Authors

40. Platinum, Copper, Gold

41. Gold, Platinum, Ornaments

42. Television, Radio, Mediums of Entertainment

43. Seventy percent of the employees in a multinational corporation have VCD players, 75 percent have microwave ovens, 80 percent have ACs and 85 percent have washing machines. At least what percentage of employees has all four gadgets?

(a) 15 (b) 5
(c) 10 (d) Cannot be determined

Space for Rough Work

LEVEL OF DIFFICULTY (II)

1. At the Rosary Public School, there are 870 students in the senior secondary classes. The school is widely known for its Science education and there is the facility for students to do practical training in any of the four sciences – viz: Physics, Chemistry, Biology or Social Sciences. Some students in the school, however, have no interest in the sciences and hence do not undertake practical training in any of the four sciences. While considering the popularity of various choices for opting for practical training for one or more of the choices offered, Mr. Arvindaksham, the school principal noticed something quite extraordinary. He noticed that for every student in the school who opts for practical training in at least M sciences, there are exactly three students who opt for practical training in at least (M – 1) sciences, for M = 2, 3 and 4. He also found that the number of students who opt for all four sciences was half the number of students who opt for none. Can you help him with the answer to "How many students in the school opt for exactly three sciences?"
   (a) 30 (b) 60
   (c) 90 (d) None of these
2. A bakery sells three kinds of pastries—pineapple, chocolate and black forest. On a particular day, the bakery owner sold the following number of pastries: 90 pineapple, 120 chocolate and 150 black forest. If none of the customers bought more than two pastries of each type, what is the minimum number of customers that must have visited the bakery that day?
   (a) 80 (b) 75
   (c) 60 (d) 90
3. Gauri Apartment housing society organised annual games, consisting of three games – viz: snooker, badminton and tennis. In all, 510 people were members in the apartments' society and they were invited to participate in the games — each person participating in as many games as he/she feels like. While viewing the statistics of the performance, Mr Kapoor realised the following facts. The number of people who participated in at least two games was 52% more than those who participated in exactly one game. The number of people participating in 1, 2 or 3 games respectively was at least equal to 1. Being a numerically inclined person, he further noticed an interesting thing — the number of people who did not participate in any of the three games was the minimum possible integral value with these conditions. What was the maximum number of people who participated in exactly three games?
   (a) 298 (b) 300
   (c) 303 (d) 304
4. A school has 180 students in its senior section where foreign languages are offered to students as part of their syllabus. The foreign languages offered are: French, German and Chinese and the numbers of people studying each of these subjects are 80, 90 and 100 respectively. The number of students who study more than one of the three subjects is 50% more than the number of students who study all the three subjects. There are no students in the school who study none of the three subjects. Then how many students study all three foreign languages?
   (a) 18 (b) 24
   (c) 36 (d) 40

Directions for Questions 5 and 6: Answer the questions on the basis of the information given below.

In the second year, the Hampard Business School students are offered a choice of the specialisations, they wish to study from amongst only three specialisations —Marketing, Finance and HR. The number of students who have specialised in only Marketing, only Finance and only HR is all the numbers in an Arithmetic Progression— in no particular order. Similarly, the number of students specialising in exactly two of the three types of subjects are also numbers that form an Arithmetic Progression.

The number of students specialising in all three subjects is one-twentieth of the number of students specialising in only Finance which in turn is half of the number of students studying only HR. The number of students studying both Marketing and Finance is 15, whereas the number of students studying both Finance and HR is 19. The number of students studying HR is 120, which is more than the number of students studying Marketing (which is a two digit number above 50). It is known that there are exactly four students who opt for none of these specialisations and opt only for general subjects.

5. What is the total number of students in the batch?
   (a) 223 (b) 233
   (c) 237 (d) Cannot be determined
6. What is the number of students specialising in both Marketing and HR?
   (a) 11 (b) 21
   (c) 23 (d) Cannot be determined

Directions for Questions 7 to 9: In the Stafford Public School, students had an option to study none or one or more of three foreign languages, viz: French, Spanish and German. The total student strength in the school was 2116 students out of which 1320 students studied French and 408 students studied both French and Spanish. The number of people who studied German was found to be 180 higher than the number of students who studied Spanish. It was also observed that 108 students studied all three subjects.

7. What is the maximum possible number of students who did not study any of the three languages?
   (a) 890 (b) 796
   (c) 720 (d) None of these

8. What is the minimum possible number of students who did not study any of the three languages?

(a) 316 (b) 0
(c) 158 (d) None of these

9. If the number of students who used to speak only French was one more than the number of people who used to speak only German, then what could be the maximum number of people who used to speak only Spanish?

(a) 413 (b) 398
(c) 403 (d) 431

Directions for Questions 10 to 13: In the Vijayantkhand sports stadium, athletes choose from four different racquet games (apart from athletics which is compulsory for all). These are Tennis, Table Tennis, Squash and Badminton. It is known that 20% of the athletes practising there are not choosing any of the racquet sports. The four games given here are played by 460, 360, 360 and 440 students respectively. The number of athletes playing exactly two racquet games for any combination of two racquet games is 40. There are 60 athletes who play all the four games but in a strange coincidence, it was noticed that the number of people playing exactly three games was also equal to 20 for each combination of three games.

10. What is the number of athletes in the stadium?

(a) 1140 (b) 1040
(c) 1200 (d) 1300

11. What is the number of athletes in the stadium who play either only squash or only Tennis?

(a) 120 (b) 220
(c) 340 (d) 440

12. How many athletes in the stadium participate in only athletics?

(a) 160 (b) 1040
(c) 260 (d) 220

13. If all the athletes were compulsorily asked to add one game to their existing list (except those who were already playing all the four games) — then what will be the number of athletes who would be playing all four games after this change?

(a) 80 (b) 100
(c) 120 (d) 140

Directions for Questions 14 and 15: Answer the questions on the basis of the following information.

In the Pattabhiraman family, a clan of 192 individuals, each person has at least one of the three Pattabhiraman characteristics—blue eyes, blonde hair, and sharp mind. It is also known that:

(i) The number of family members who have only blue eyes is equal to the number of family members who have only sharp minds and this number is also equal to twice the number of family members who have blue eyes and sharp minds but not blonde hair.

(ii) The number of family members who have exactly two of the three features is 50.

(iii) The number of family members who have blonde hair is 62.

(iv) Among those who have blonde hair, 26 family members have at least two of the three characteristics.

14. If the number of family members who have blue eyes is the maximum amongst the three characteristics, then what is the maximum possible number of family members who have both sharp minds and blonde hair but do not have blue eyes?

(a) 11 (b) 10
(c) 12 (d) Cannot be determined

15. Which additional piece of information is required to find the exact number of family members who have blonde hair and blue eyes but not sharp minds?

(a) The number of family members who have exactly one of the three characteristics is 140

(b) Only two family members have all three characteristics.

(c) The number of family members who have sharp minds is 89.

(d) The number of family members who have only sharp minds is 52.

16. In a class of 97 students, each student plays at least one of the three games – Hockey, Cricket and Football. If 47 play Hockey, 53 play Cricket, 72 play Football and 15 play all the three games, what is the number of students who play exactly two games?

(a) 38 (b) 40
(c) 42 (d) 45

Directions for Questions 17 to 19: Answer the questions on the basis of the information given below.

In the ancient towns of Mohenjo Daro, a survey found that students were fond of three kinds of cold drinks (Pep, Cok and Thum). It was also found that there were three kinds of beverages that they liked (Tea, Cof and ColdCof).

The population of these towns was found to be 40,0000 people in all—and the survey was conducted on 10% of the population. Mr. Yadav, a data analyst observed the following things about the survey:

(i) The number of people in the survey who like exactly two cold drinks is five times the number of people who like all the three cold drinks

(ii) The sum of the number of people in the survey who like Pep and 42% of those who like Cok but not Pep is equal to the number of people who like Tea

(iii) The number of people in the survey who like Cof is equal to the sum of 3/8th of those who like Cok and ½ of those who like Thum. This number is also equal to the numbers who like ColdCof.

(iv) 18500 people surveyed like Pep

(v) 15000 like all the beverages and 3500 like all the cold drinks;

(vi) 14000 do not like Pep but like Thum

(vii) 11000 like Pep and exactly one more cold drink

(viii) 6000 like only Cok and the same number of people like Pep and Thum but not Cok

17. The number of people in the survey who do like at least one of the three cold drinks?

(a) 38,500 (b) 31,500
(c) 32,500 (d) 39,500

18. What is the maximum number of people in the survey who like none of the three beverages?

(a) 24,000 (b) 16,000
(c) 12,000 (d) Cannot be determined

19. What is the maximum number of people in the survey who like at least one of the three beverages?

(a) 7000 (b) 32,000
(c) 33,000 (d) Cannot be determined

20. In a certain class of students, the number of students who drink only tea, only coffee, both tea and coffee and neither tea nor coffee are x, $2x$, $3x$ and $4x$ respectively such that the value of x and $3x$ are both factors of 57. The number of people who drink coffee can be

(a) 5 (b) 40
(c) 95 (d) Both (a) and (c)

High Yield Questions

Scan this QR code to access assisted problem solving videos on questions 1, 5, 6, 17, 18 and 19 from LOD 2

Space for Rough Work

ANSWER KEY

Level of Difficulty (I)

1. (b)	2. (a)	3. (b)	4. (a)
5. (b)	6. (a)	7. (c)	8. (b)
9. (c)	10. (b)	11. (a)	12. (d)
13. (c)	14. (b)	15. (a)	16. (b)
17. (c)	18. (b)	19. (c)	20. (a)
21. (d)	22. (c)	23. (c)	24. (a)
25. (b)	26. (d)	27. (b)	28. (b)
29. (c)	30. (a)	31. (a)	32. (c)
33. (b)	34. (d)	35. (a)	36. (c)
37. (b)	38. (b)	39. (e)	40. (d)
41. (a)	42. (b)	43. (c)	

Level of Difficulty (II)

1. (b)	2. (b)	3. (c)	4. (c)
5. (c)	6. (c)	7. (b)	8. (b)
9. (d)	10. (d)	11. (c)	12. (c)
13. (d)	14. (a)	15. (c)	16. (d)
17. (a)	18. (b)	19. (c)	20. (d)

SOLUTIONS AND SHORTCUTS

Level of Difficulty (I)

Solutions for Questions 1 and 2:

Since there are 14 players who are in triathlon and pentathlon, and there are 8 who take part in all three games, there will be 6 who take part in only triathlon and pentathlon. Similarly, only triathlon and marathon = 12 – 8 = 4 and only Pentathlon and Marathon = 15 – 8 = 7.

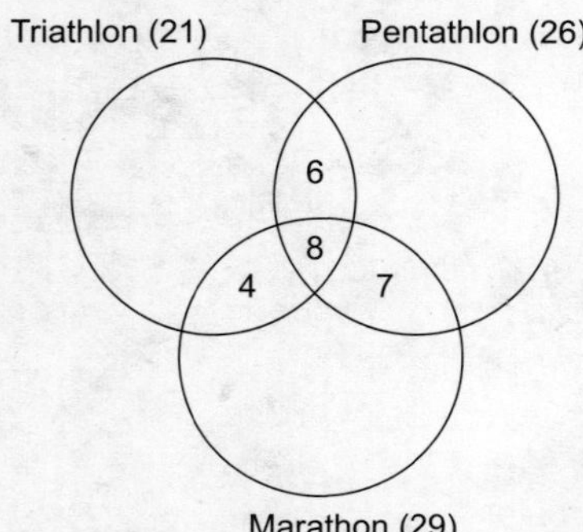

The figure above can be completed with values for each sport (only) plugged in:

The answers would be:

3 + 6 + 8 + 4 + 5 + 7 + 10 = 43. Option (b) is correct.

Option (a) is correct.

Solutions for Questions 3 and 4:

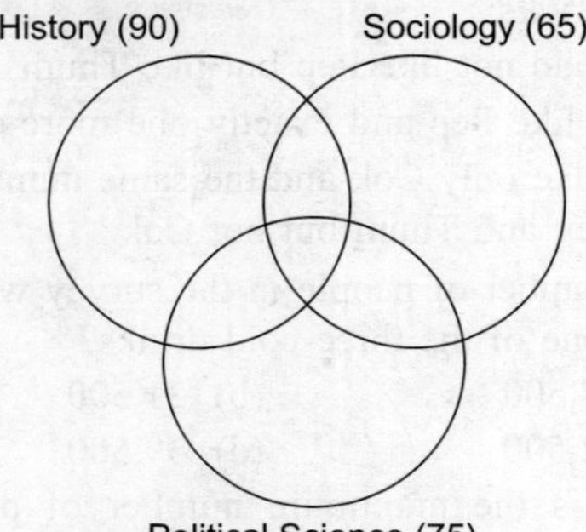

The given situation can be read as follows:

115 students are being counted 75 + 65 + 90 = 230 times. This means that there is an extra count of 115. This extra count of 115 can be created in two ways.

1. By putting people in the 'passed exactly two subjects' category. In such a case each person would get counted two times (double counted), i.e., an extra count of 1.
2. By putting people in the 'all three' category, each person put there would be triple counted. One person counted three times – meaning an extra count of two per person.

The problem tells us that there are 55 students who passed exactly two subjects. This means an extra count of 55 would be accounted for. This would leave an extra count of 115 – 55 = 60 more to be accounted for by 'passed all three' category. This can be done by using thirty people in the 'all 3' category.

Hence, the answers are:

3. Option (b)
4. Option (a)

Solutions for Questions 5 to 8:

Based on the information provided, we would get the following figure:

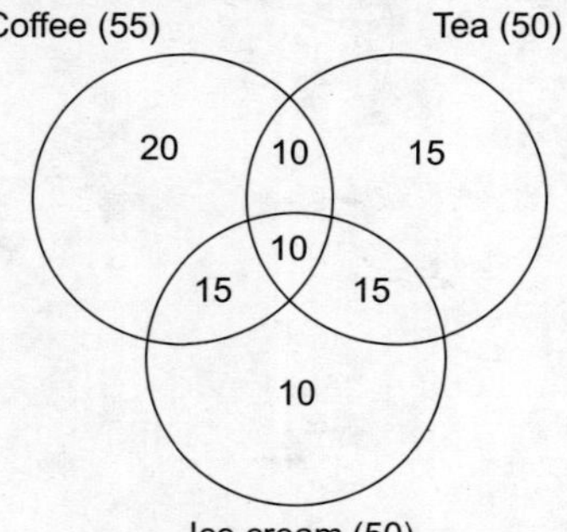

The answers could be read off the figure as:

5. [(20 – 10)/10] × 100 = 100%. Option (b) is correct.
6. 15% (from the figure). Option (a) is correct.
7. 10+10+15+15=50%. Option (c) is correct.
8. Only ice cream is 10% of the total. Hence, 10% of 180 =18. Option (b) is correct.

Solutions for Questions 9 to 15:

If you try to draw a figure for this question, the figure would be something like:

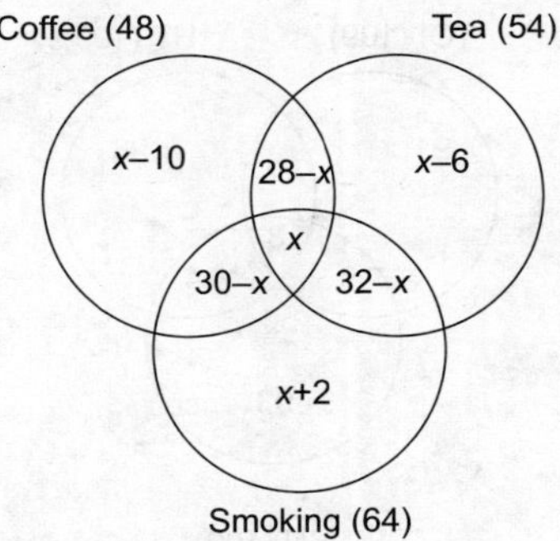

We can then solve this as:

$x - 10 + 28 - x + x + 30 - x + x + 2 + 32 - x + x - 6 = 94 \rightarrow$
$x + 76 = 94 \rightarrow x = 18.$

(Note: In this question, since all the values for the use of the set theory formula are given, we can find the missing value of students who liked all three as follows:

$94 = 48 + 54 + 64 - 28 - 32 - 30 + \text{All three} \rightarrow \text{All three} = 18$

As you can see, this is a much more convenient way of solving this question, and the learning you take away for the three circle situation is that whenever you have all the values known and the only unknown value is the centre value – it is wiser and more efficient to solve for the unknown using the formula rather than trying to solve through a Venn diagram.)

Based on this value of x, we get the diagram completed as:

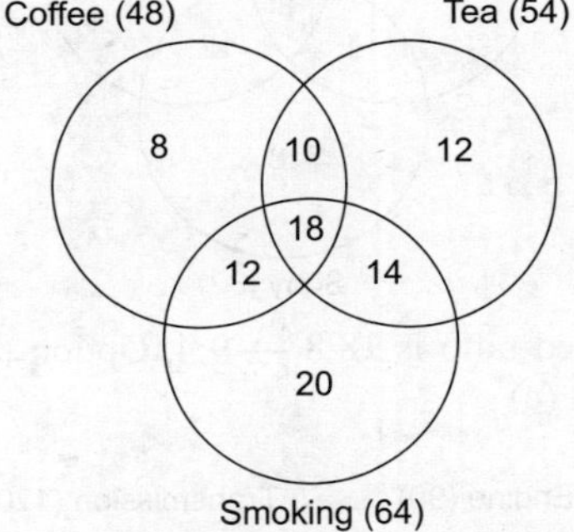

The answers then are:

9. 8:12 = 2:3 → Option (c) is correct.
10. 12 % of 2000 = 240. Option (b) is correct.
11. 30/94 → more than 30%. Option (a) is correct.
12. 94%. Option (d) is correct.
13. Option (c) is correct as the ratio turns out to be 10:20 in that case.
14. 12:12 = 1:1 → Option (b) is correct.
15. 14%. Option (a) is correct.
16. 30 = 25 + 20 – $x \rightarrow x$ = 15. Option (b) is correct.

Solutions for Questions 17 to 20:

Let people who passed all three be x. Then:

$53 + 61 + 60 - 24 - 35 - 27 + x = 95 \rightarrow x = 7.$

The Venn diagram in this case would become:

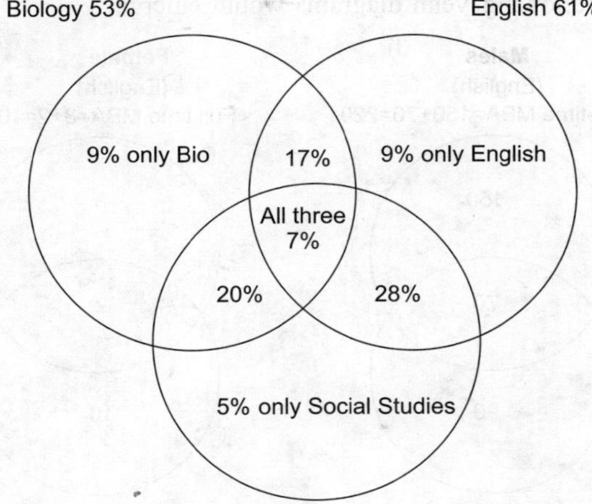

17. Option (c) is correct.
18. 23% of 200 = 46. Option (b) is correct.
19. If the number of students is increased by 50%, the number of students in each category would also be increased by 50%. Option (c) is correct.
20. 20:28 = 5:7. Option (a) is correct.

Solutions for Questions 21 to 25:

The following figure would emerge on using all the information in the question:

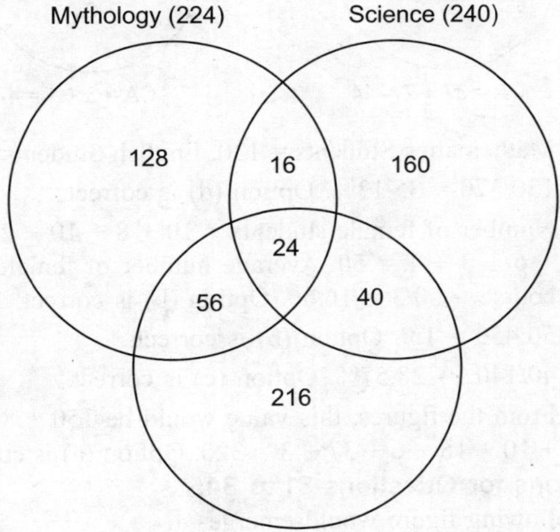

The answers would then be:

21. 240/880 = 27.27%. Option (d) is correct.
22. 504/880 = 57.27%. Hence, less than 60. Option (c) is correct.
23. 40 + 16 + 56 + 24 = 136. Option (c) is correct.
24. Option (a) gives us 16:128 = 1:8. Option (a) is hence correct.
25. 40:160 → 1:4. Option (b) is correct.

Solutions for Questions 26 to 30:

The following Venn diagrams would emerge:

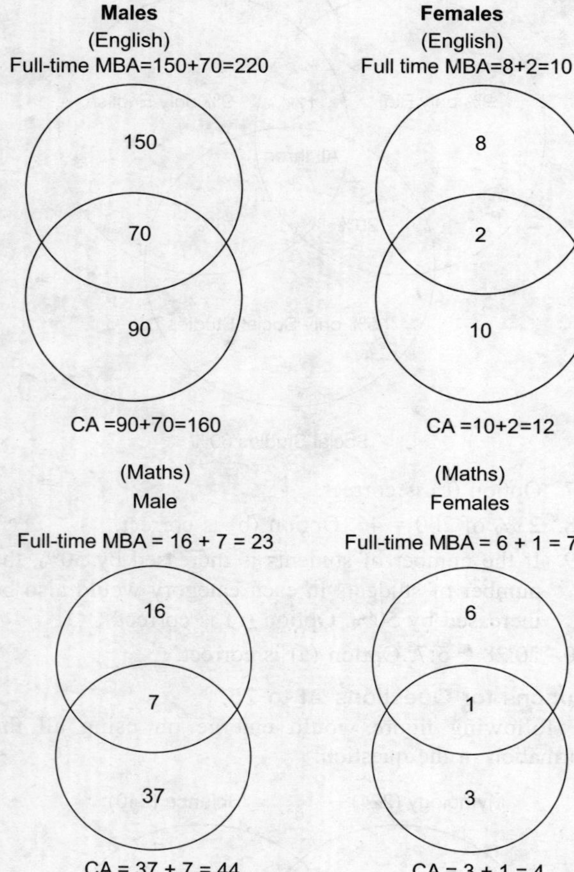

26. Mathematics Students = 130. English Students =370 130/370 = 35.13%. Option (d) is correct.
27. Number of female students = 10 + 8 + 10 + 2 + 10 + 6 + 3 + 1 = 50. Average number of females per course = 50/3 = 16.66. Option (b) is correct.
28. 50:450 = 1:9. Option (b) is correct.
29. 40/140 → 28.57%. Option (c) is correct.
30. From the figures, this value would be 150 + 8 + 90 + 10 + 16 + 6 + 37 + 3 = 320. Option (a) is correct.

Solutions for Questions 31 to 34:

The following figure would emerge-

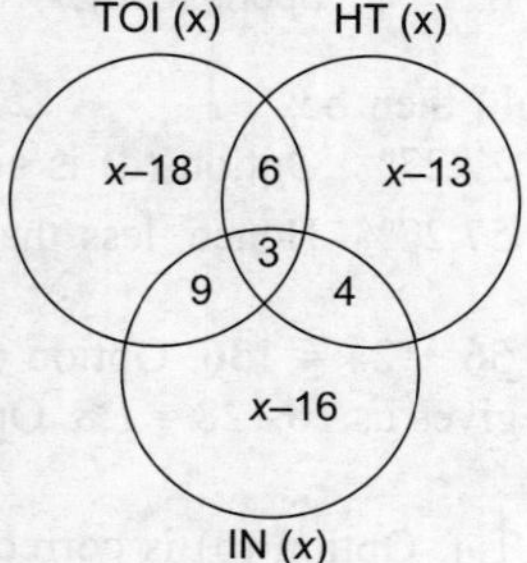

Based on this figure, we have:

$x + x - 13 + 4 + x - 16 = 302 \rightarrow 3x - 25 = 302 \rightarrow x = 109.$

Consequently, the figure becomes:

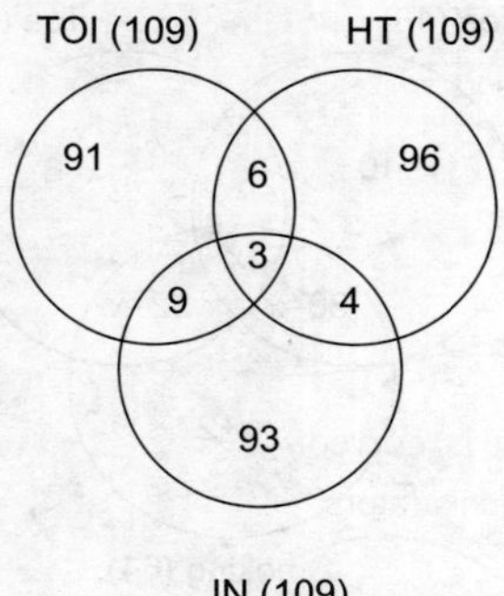

The answers are:

31. 91 + 93 + 96 = 280. Option (a) is correct.
32. 193/302 ≅ 64%
33. 6:9:4 is the required ratio. Option (b) is correct.
34. 96 – 4 = 92. Option (d) is correct.
35. $78 = 36 + 48 + 32 - 14 - 20 - 12 + x \rightarrow x = 8.$

    The figure for this question would become:

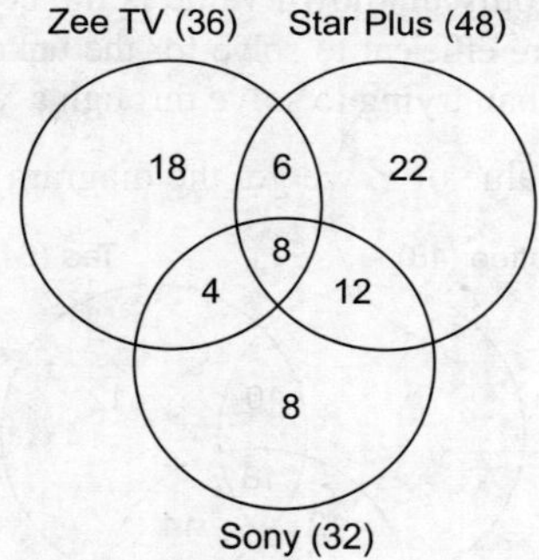

Required ratio is 18:8 → 9:4. Option (a) is correct.

36. Option (c)

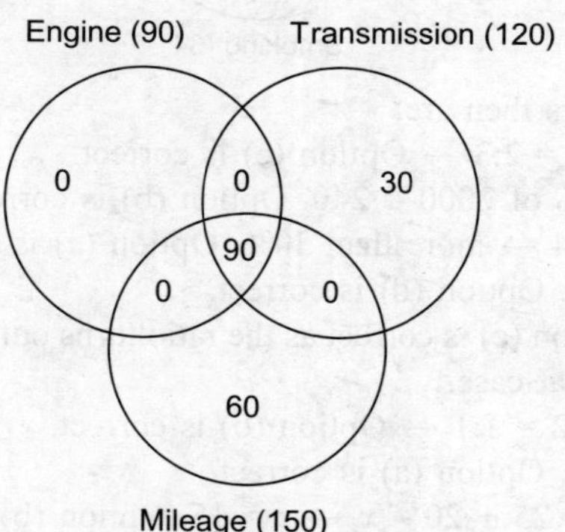

37. There are thirty such people. Option (b) is correct.

Solutions for Questions 38 to 42:

38. Option (b) is correct

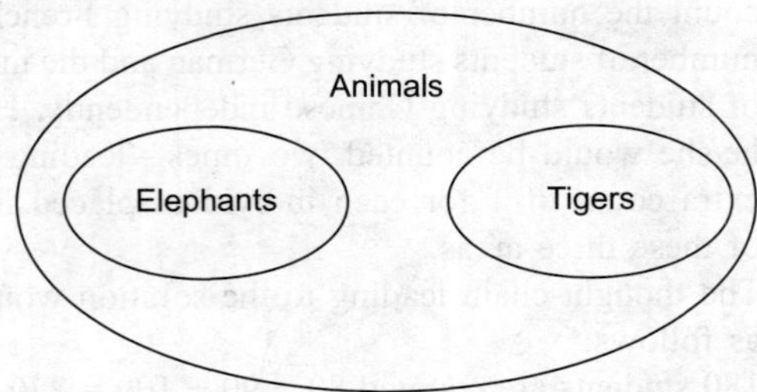

39. Option (e) is correct.

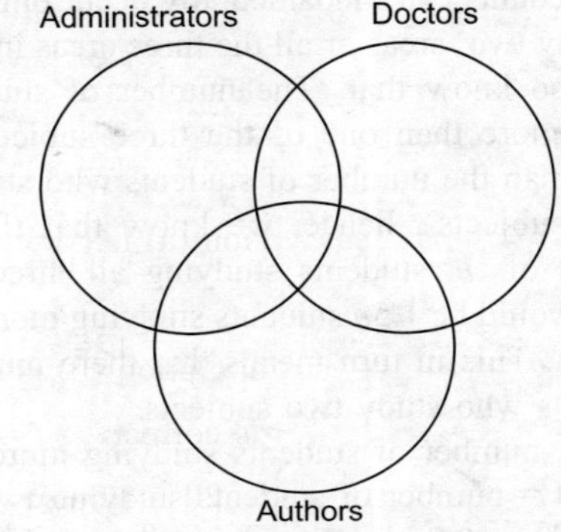

40. Option (d) is correct.

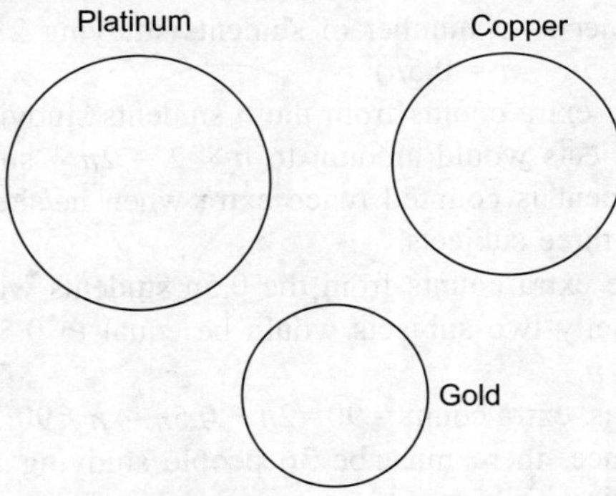

41. Option (a) is correct.

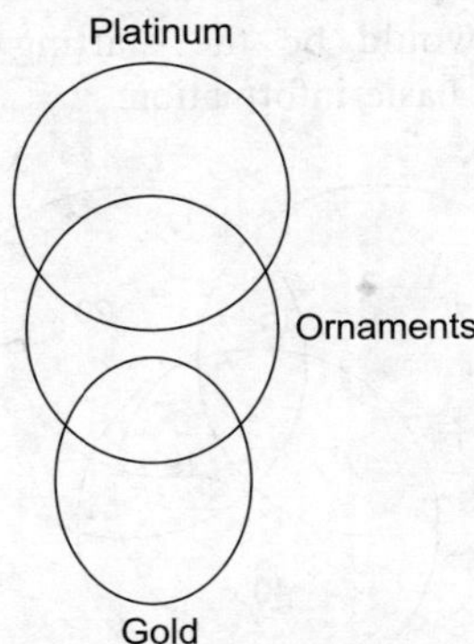

42. Option (b) is correct

Solution for Question 43:

43. The least percentage of people with all four gadgets would happen if all the employees who are not having any one of the four objects is mutually exclusive.

Thus, $100 - 30 - 25 - 20 - 15 = 10$

Option (c) is correct.

Level of Difficulty (II)

1. The key to think about this question is to understand what is meant by the statement —"for every student in the school who opts for practical training in at least M sciences, there are exactly three students who opt for practical training in at least $(M - 1)$ sciences, for $M = 2$, 3 and 4".

   What this statement means is that if there are x students who opt for practical training in all four sciences, there would be $3x$ students who would opt for practical training in at least three sciences. Since opting for at least 3 sciences includes those who opted for exactly 3 sciences and those who opted for exactly 4 sciences—we can conclude from this that:

   The number of students who opted for exactly 3 sciences = Number of students who opted for at least 3 sciences – Number of students who opted for all 4 sciences $= 3x - x = 2x$

   Thus, the number of students who opted for various number of Science practicals can be summarised as below:

	Number of students who opted for at least n subjects	Number of students who opted for exactly n subjects
$n = 4$	x	x
$n = 3$	$3x$	$2x$
$n = 2$	$9x$	$6x$
$n = 1$	$27x$	$18x$

   Also, number of students who opt for none of the sciences = twice the number of students who opt for exactly 4 sciences = $2x$.

   Based on these deductions, we can clearly identify that the number of students in the school would be: $x + 2x + 6x + 18x + 2x = 29x = 870 \rightarrow x = 30$.

   Hence, number of students who opted for exactly three sciences $= 2x = 60$

2. (b) In order to estimate the minimum number of customers we need to assume that each customer, must have bought the maximum number of pastries possible for him to purchase.

   Since, the maximum number of pastries an individual could purchase is constrained by the information that no one bought more than two pastries of any one kind—this would occur under the following situation—First 45 people would buy two pastries of all three kinds, which would completely exhaust the 90 pineapple pastries and leave the bakery with 30 chocolate and 60 black forest pastries. The next 15 people would buy two pastries each of the available kinds and after this; we would be left with 30 black forest pastries. Fifteen people would buy these pastries, each person buying two pastries each. Thus, the total number of people (minimum) would be: 45 + 15 + 15 = 75.

3. (c) Let the number of people who participated in 0, 1, 2 and 3 games is A, B, C, D respectively. Then from the information, we have:

   $C + D = 1.52 \times B$ (Number of people who participate in at least two games is 52% higher than the number of people who participate in exactly one game)

   $A + B + C + D = 510$ (Number of people invited to participate in the games is 510)

   This gives us: $A + 2.52B = 510 \rightarrow B = \frac{25}{63}(510 - A)$

   For A to be minimum, $510 - A$ should give us the largest multiple of 63. Since, $63 \times 8 = 504$, we have $A = 6$.

   Also, 2.52B = 504, so $B = 200$ and $C + D = 1.52B = 304$.

   For number of people participating in exactly three games to be maximum, the number of people participating in exactly two games has to be minimised and made equal to 1. Thus, the required answer = 304 – 1 = 303.

4. (c) In order to think about this question, the best way is to use the process of slack thinking. In this question, we have 180 students counted 270 times. This means that there is an extra count of 90 students. In a three circle Venn diagram, extra counting can occur only due to exactly two regions (where 1 individual student would be counted in two subjects leading to an extra count of 1) and the exactly three region (where 1 individual student would be counted in 3 subjects leading to an extra count of 2). This can be visualised in the figure below:

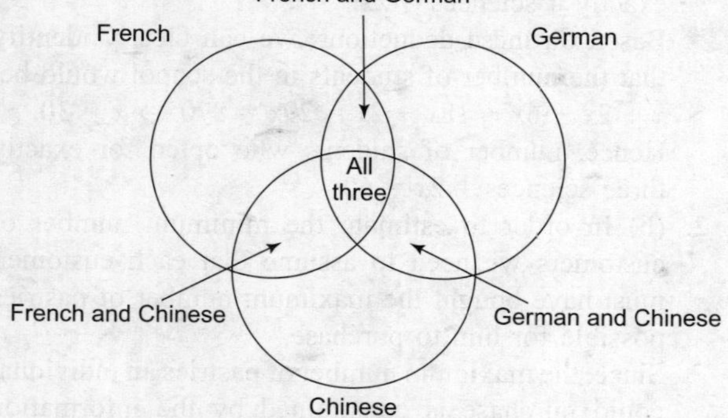

A student placed in all the three areas will be counted three times when you count the number of students studying French, the number of students studying German and the number of students studying Chinese independently. Hence, he/she would be counted three times—leading to an extra count of 2 for each individual places here.

A person placed in any of the three 'Exactly two' areas would be counted two times when we count the number of students studying French, the number of students studying German and the number of students studying Chinese independently. Hence, he/she would be counted two times—leading to an extra count of 1 for each individual placed in any of these three areas.

The thought-chain leading to the solution would go as follows:

(i) 180 students are counted 80 + 90 + 100 = 270 times

(ii) This means that there is an extra count of 90 students

(iii) Extra counts can fundamentally occur only from the 'exactly two' areas or all the three areas in the figure

(iv) We also know that 'The number of students who study more than one of the three subjects is 50% more than the number of students who study all the three subjects', hence, we know that if there are a total of 'n' students studying all three subjects, there would be $1.5n$ students studying more than one subject. This in turn means that there must be $0.5n$ students who study two subjects.

(Since, number of students studying more than one subject = number of students studying two subjects + number of students studying three subjects, i.e., $1.5n = n$ + number of students studying 2 subjects → number of students studying 2 subjects $= 1.5n - n = 0.5n$)

(v) The extra counts from the n students studying three subjects would amount to $n \times 2 = 2n$ – since each student is counted twice extra when he/she studies all three subjects.

(vi) The extra counts from the 0.5n students who study exactly two subjects would be equal to $0.5n \times 1 = 0.5\ n$.

(vii) Thus, extra count $= 90 = 2n + 0.5n \rightarrow n = 90/2.5 = 36$.

(viii) Hence, there must be 36 people studying all three subjects.

Solutions for Questions 5 and 6:

The following would be the starting Venn diagram encapsulating the basic information:

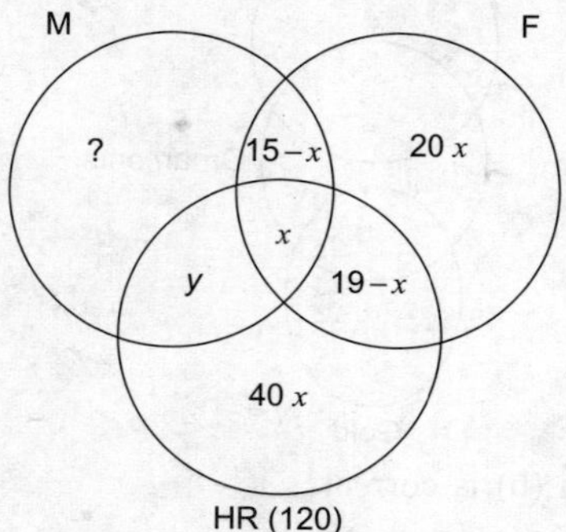

From this figure, we get the following equation: $40x + (19 - x) + x + y = 120$. This gives us $40x + y = 101$

Thinking about this equation, we can see that the value of x can be either 1 or 2. In case we put x as 1, we get $y = 61$ and then we have to also meet the additional condition that $15–x$, $19–x$ and y should form an AP which is obviously not possible (since it is not possible practically to build an AP having two positive terms below 19 and the third term being 61. Hence, this option is rejected).

Moving forward, the other possible value of x from the equation is $x = 2$ in which case we get, $y = 21$ and $15 - x = 13$ and $19 - x = 17$. Thus, we get the AP 13, 17, 21 which satisfies the given conditions. Putting $x = 2$ and $y = 21$ in the figure, the Venn diagram evolves to:

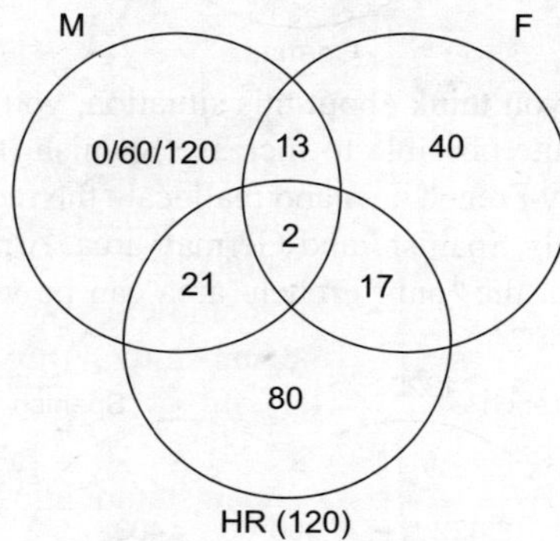

In this figure, the value that only Marketing takes can either be 0, 60 or 120 (to satisfy the AP condition). However, since the total number of students in Marketing is a two-digit number above 50; the number of people studying only marketing would be narrowed down to the only possibility which remains – viz. 60.

Thus, the number of students studying in the batch $= 120 + 40 + 60 + 13 + 4 = 237$.

The number of students specialising in both Marketing and HR is $21 + 2 = 23$.

5. (d) The total number of students is 237.
6. (c) The number of students studying both Marketing and HR is 23.

Solutions for Questions 7 to 9:

7 and 8: In order to think about the possibility of the maximum and/or the minimum number of people who could be studying none of the three languages, you need to first think of the basic information in the question. The basic information in the question can be encapsulated by the following Venn diagram:

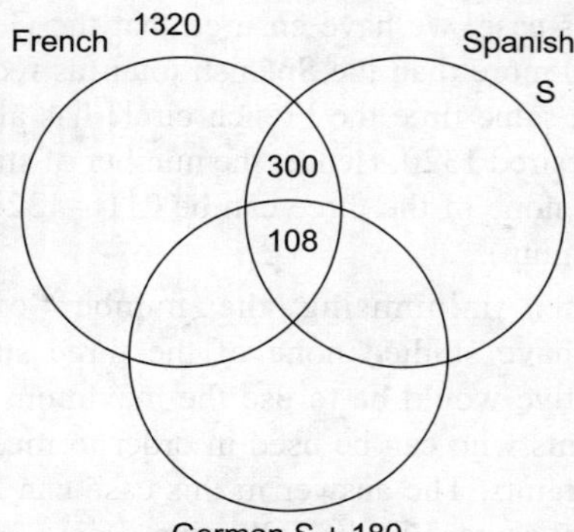

At this point, we have the flexibility to try to put the remaining numbers into this Venn diagram while maintaining the constraints the question has placed on the relative numbers in the figure. In order to do this, we need to think of the objective with which we have to fill in the remaining numbers in the figure. At this stage, you have to keep two constraints in mind while filling the remaining numbers:

(a) The remaining part of the French circle has to total $1320 - 408 = 912$;

(b) The German circle has to be 180 more than the Spanish circle.

When we try to fill in the figure for making the number of students who did not study any of the three subjects maximum:

You can think of first filling the French circle by trying to think of how you would want to distribute the remaining 912 in that circle. When we want to maximise the number of students who study none of the three, we would need to use the minimum number of people inside the three circles—while making sure that all the constraints are met.

Since we have to forcefully fit in 912 into the remaining areas of the French circle, we need to see whether while doing the same, we can also meet the second constraint.

This thinking would lead you to see the following solution possibility:

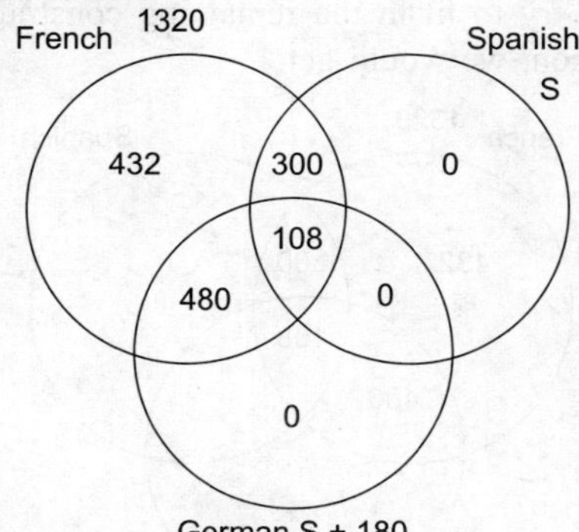

In this case, we have ensured that the German total is 180 more than the Spanish total (as required) and at the same time the French circle has also reached the desired 1320. Hence, the number of students who study none of the three can be 2116–1320 = 796 (at maximum).

When minimising the number of students who have studied none of the three subjects, the objective would be to use the maximum number of students who can be used in order to meet the basic constraints. The answer in this case can be taken to as low as zero in the following case:

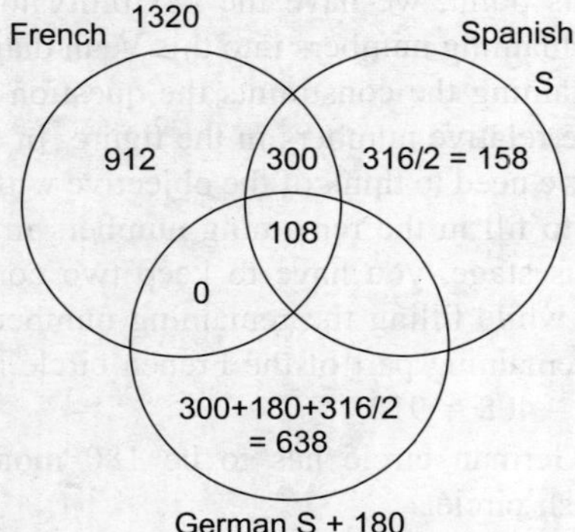

(**Note:** While thinking about the numbers in this case, we first use the 912 in the 'only French' area. At this point, we have 796 students left to be allocated. We first make the German circle 180 more than the Spanish circle (by taking the only German as 300 +180 to start with; this is accomplished). At this point, we are left with 316 more students, who can be allocated equally as 316 ÷ 2 for both the 'only German' and the 'only Spanish' areas.)

Thus, the minimum number of students who study none of the three is 0.

Solution for Question 9:

In order to think about this question, let us first see the situation we had in order to maintain all constraints.

If we try to fit in the remaining constraints in this situation, we would get:

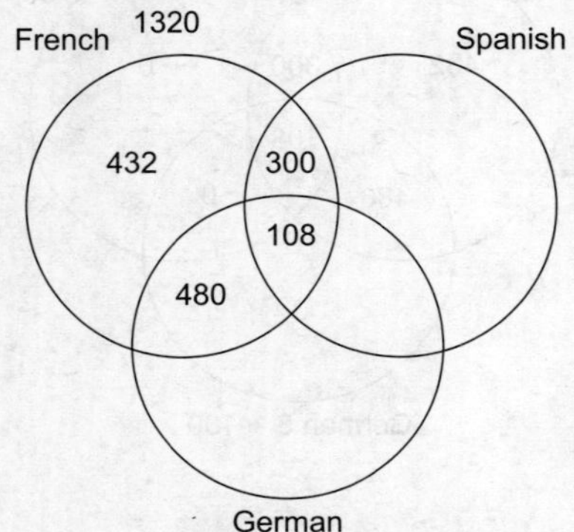

This leaves us with a slack of 796 people which would need to be divided equally since we cannot disturb the equilibrium of German being exactly 180 more than Spanish.

This gives us the following figure:

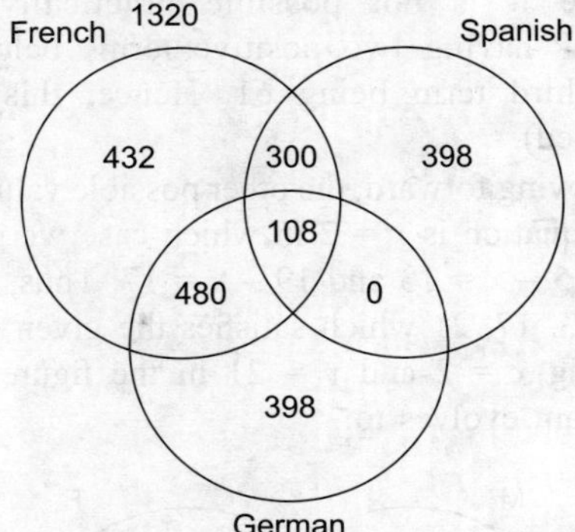

When you think about this situation, you realise that it is quite possible to increase Spanish if we reduce the only French area and reallocate the reduction into the 'only Spanish' and German area. A reduction of 10 from the 'only French' area can be visualised as follows:

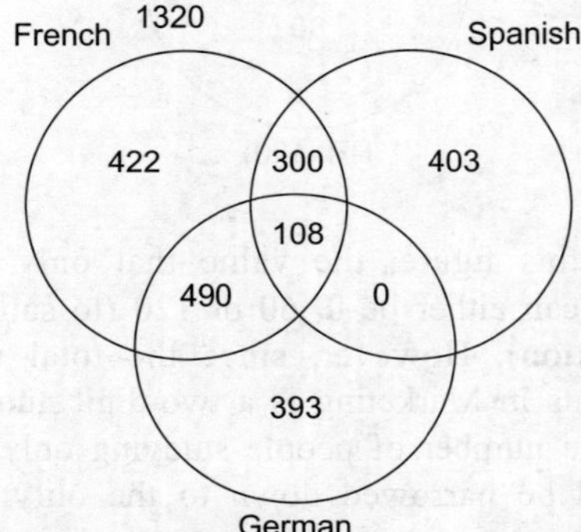

In this case, as you can see from the figure above, the number of students who study only Spanish has gone up by 5 (which is half of 10).

Since, there is still some gap between the 'only German' and the 'only French' areas in the figure; we should close that gap by reducing the 'only French' area as much as possible.

The following solution figure would emerge when we think that way:

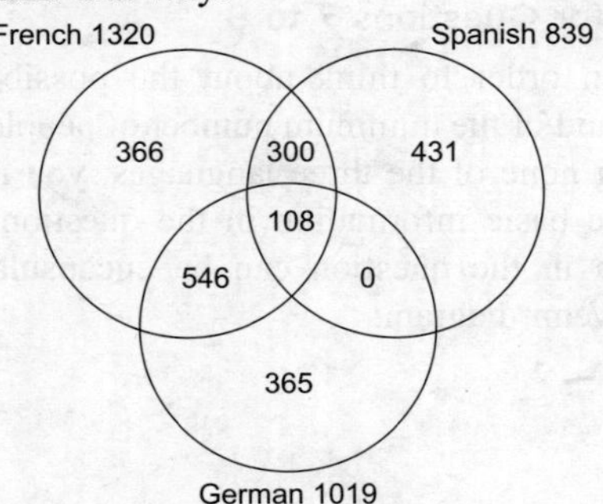

Hence, the maximum possible for the only Spanish area is 431.

Solutions for Questions 10 to 13:

The information given in the question can be encapsulated in the following way:

Game	*Only that game*	*2 games combination 1*	*2 games combination 2*	*2 games combination 3*	*3 games combination 1*	*3 games combination 2*	*3 games combination 3*	*All 4 games*
Tennis (460)	220	40	40	40	20	20	20	60
TT (360)	120	40	40	40	20	20	20	60
Squash (360)	120	40	40	40	20	20	20	60
Badminton (440)	200	40	40	40	20	20	20	60

From the above table, we can draw the following conclusions,, which can then be used to answer the questions asked.

The total number of athletes who play at least one of the four games = 220 + 120 + 120 + 200 + 40 × 6 + 20 × 4 + 60 = 1040.

(**Note**: In doing this calculation, we have used 40 × 6 for calculating how many unique people would be playing exactly two games—where 40 for each combination is given and there are $^4C_2$= 6 combinations of exactly two sports that exist. Similar logic applies to the 20 × 4 calculation for number of athletes playing exactly three sports.)

Also, since we know that the number of athletes who participate in none of these four games is 20% of the total number of athletes, we can calculate the total number of athletes who practise in the stadium as 5×1040 ÷ 4=1300.

Thus, the questions can be answered as follows:

10. The number of athletes in the stadium = 1300.
11. Only squash + only tennis = 120 + 220 = 340 (from the table)
12. Only athletics means none of the four games = total number of athletes – number of athletes who play at least one game = 1300 – 1040 = 260.
13. In case, all the three game athletes would add one more game they would become four game athletes. Hence, the number of athletes who play all four games would be: Athletes playing 3 games earlier + athletes playing all 4 games earlier = 80+60=140.

Solutions for Questions 14 and 15:

The starting figure based on the information given in the question would look something as below:

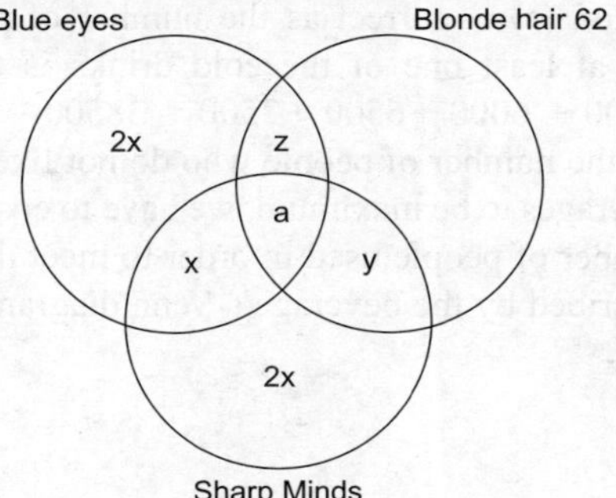

From this figure, we see a few equations:

$x + y + z = 50$; $a + y + z = 26 \rightarrow x - 24 = a$

Also, since, $5x + 62 = 192$, we get the value of x as 26. The figure would evolve as follows.

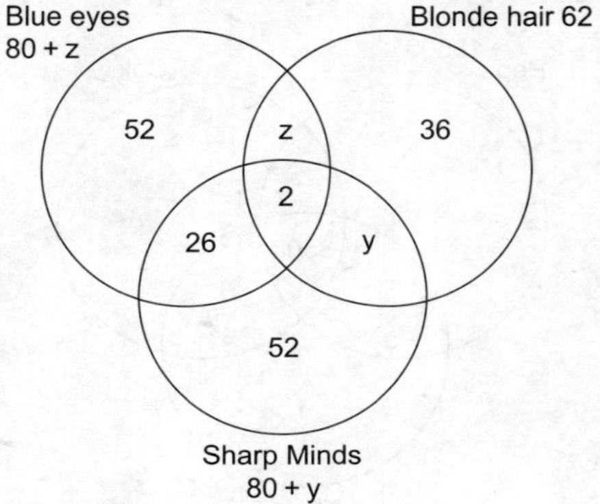

Based on this, we can deduce the answer to the two questions as:

14. For the number of family members with blue eyes to be maximum, the family members with both sharp minds and blonde hair, but not blue eyes (represented by '*y*' in the figure), would be at maximum 11 because we would need to keep $z > y$. Hence, option (a) is the correct answer.
15. If we are given the information in option (c), we know the value of y would be 9 and hence, the value of z would be determined as 15. Hence, option (c) provides us the information to determine the exact number of family members who have blonde hair and blue eyes but not sharp minds. Notice here that the information in each of the other options is already known to us.
16. Solve this again using slack thinking by using the following thought process:

    97 students are counted 47 + 53 + 72 = 172 times—which means that there is an extra count of 75 students (172–97 = 75). Now, since there are 15 students who are playing all the three games, they would be counted 45 times—hence, they take care of an extra count of 15 × 2 = 30. (**Note:** in a three circle Venn diagram

situation, any person placed in the all three areas is counted thrice—hence he/she is counted two extra times).

This leaves us with an extra count of 45 to be managed—and the only way to do so is to place people in the exactly two areas. A person placed in the 'exactly two games area' would be counted once extra. Hence, with each student who goes into the 'exactly two games' areas it would be counted once extra. Thus, to manage an extra count of 45, we need to put 45 people in the 'exactly two' area. Hence, option (d) is correct.

Solutions for Questions 17 to 19:

Once you fill in the basic information into the Venn diagram, you reach the following position:

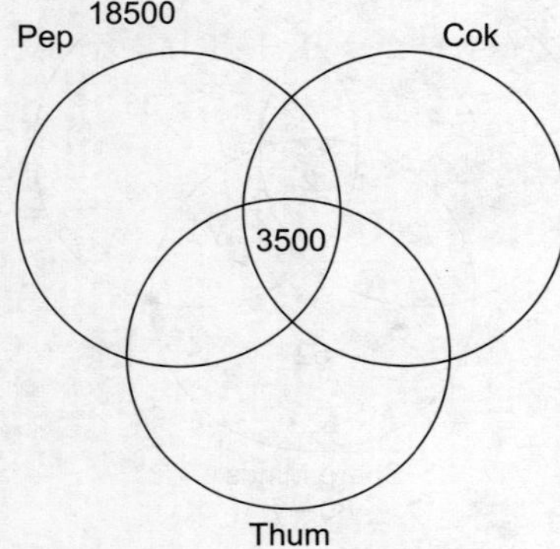

At this point, we know that since the 'all three area' is 3500, the value of the 'exactly two areas' would be 5 × 3500 = 17,500. Also, we know that "11,000 like Pep and exactly one more cold drink" which means that the area for Cok and Thum but not Pep is equal to 17,500 – 11000 = 6500. Further, when you start adding the information: "6000 like only Cok and the same number of people like Pep and Thum but not Cok,", the Venn Diagram transforms to the following:

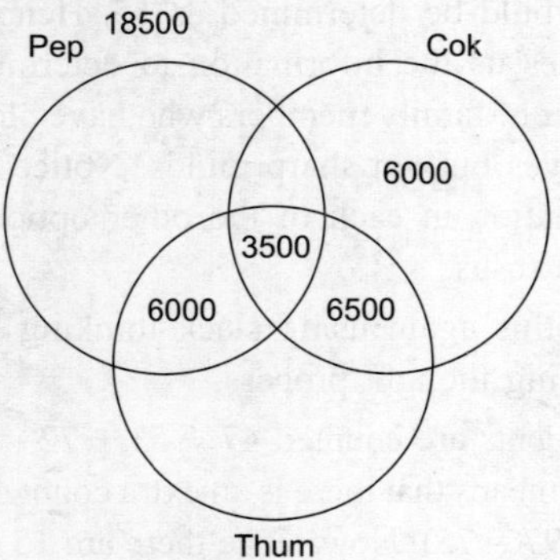

Filling in the remaining gaps in the picture, we get:

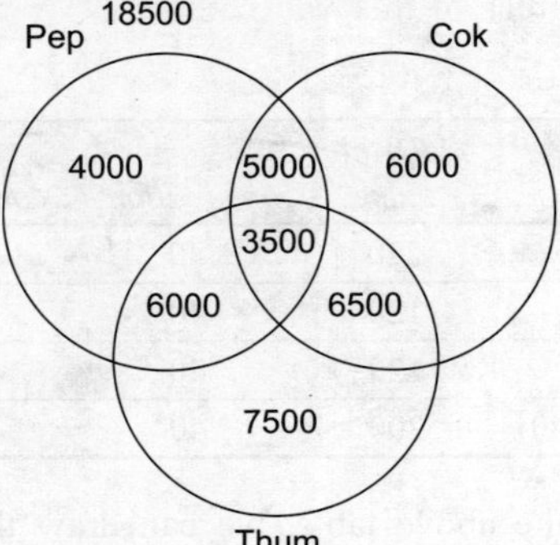

(**Note:** we have used the following info here: Thum but not Pep is 14,000 and since we already know that Thum and Cok but not Pep is 6500, the value of 'only Thum' would be 14,000 – 6500 = 7500.

We also know that the 'exactly two' areas add up to 17500 and we know that two of these three areas are 6500 and 6000 respectively. Thus, Pep and Cok but not Thum is 17500 – 6000 – 6500 = 5000. Finally, the 'only Pep' area would be 18500 – 5000 – 6000 – 3500 = 4000.

Once we have created the Venn diagram for the cold drinks, we can focus our attention to the Venn diagram for the beverages.

Based on the information provided, the following diagram can be created.)

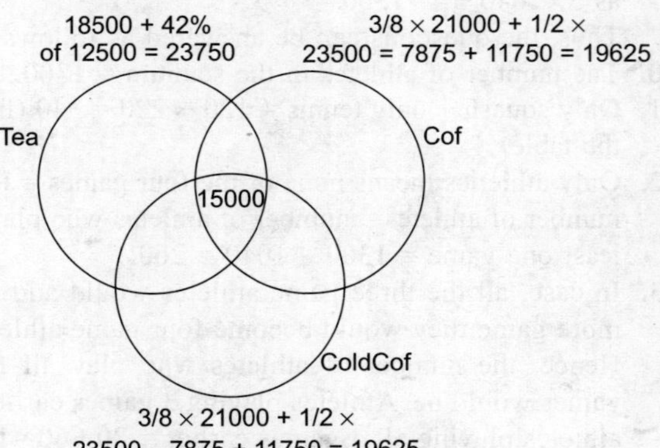

Based on these figures, the questions asked can be solved as follows:

17. Option (a) is correct as the number of people who like at least one of the cold drinks is the sum of 18500 + 6000 +6500 +7500 = 38500.
18. For the number of people who do not like any of the beverages to be maximum, we have to ensure that the number of people used in order to meet the situation described by the beverage's Venn diagram should be

minimum. This can be done by filling values in the inner areas of this Venn diagram:

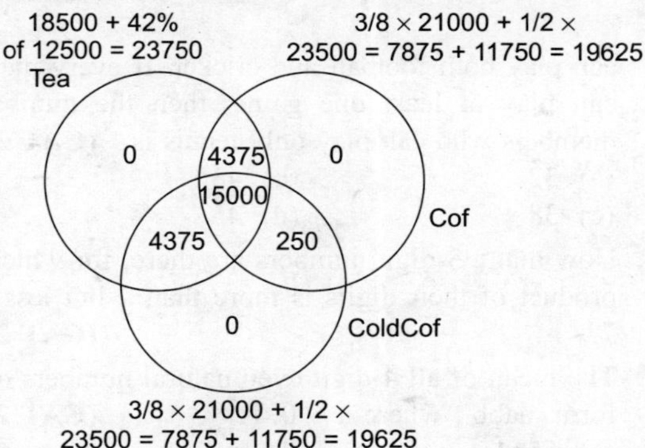

In this situation, the number of people used inside the Venn diagram to match upto all the values for this figure = 15000 + 4375 + 4375 + 250 = 24000.

Naturally, in this case the number of people who do not like any of the beverages is maximised at 40000 − 24000 = 16000. Option (b) is correct.

19. The solution for this situation would be given by the following figure:

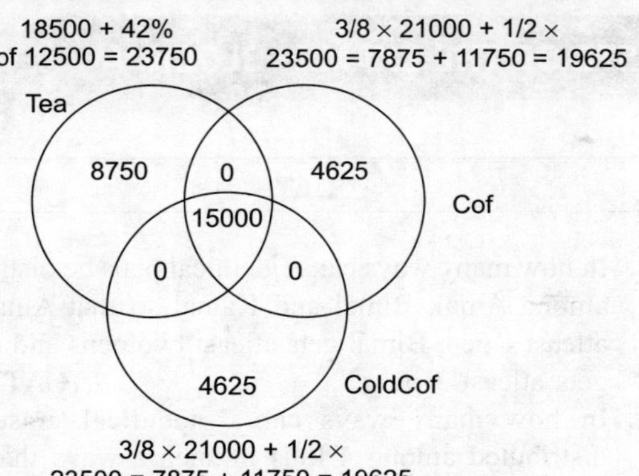

The number of people who like at least one of the three beverages is:
15000 + 8750 +4625 + 4625 = 33000. Hence, option (c) is correct.

20. The number of people cannot be a fraction in any situation. We can deduce that the values of x and $3x$ have to be factors of 57. This gives us that the values of x can only be either 1 or 19 (for both x and $3x$ to be a factor of 57).
So, the number of people who drink coffee is equal to $2x + 3x$ which can be 5 (if $x = 1$) or 95 (if $x = 19$). Hence, Option (d) is correct.

TASTE OF THE EXAMS—BLOCK V

CAT

1. In how many ways can 8 identical pens be distributed among Amal, Bimal and Kamal so that Amal gets atleast 1 pen, Bimal gets atleast two pens and Kamal gets atleast 3 pens? **(CAT 2017)**
2. In how many ways can 7 identical erasers be distributed among 4 kids in such a ways that each kid gets atleast one eraser and no kid gets more than 3 erasers? **(CAT 2017)**
3. Each of 74 students in a class studies at least one of the three subjects *H*, *E* and *P*. Ten students study all three subjects, while twenty study *H* and *E*, but not *P*. Every student who studies *P* also studies *H* or *E*, or both. If the number of students studying *H* equals that studying *E*, then the number of students studying *H* is **(CAT 2018)**
4. If among 200 students, 105 like pizza and 134 like burger, then the number of students who like only burger can possibly be **(CAT 2018)**
   (a) 26 (b) 23
   (c) 96 (d) 93
5. For two sets *A* and *B*, let $A\Delta B$ denote the set of elements which belong to *A* or *B* but not both. If $P = \{1,2,3,4\}$, $Q = \{2,3,5,6,\}$, $R = \{1,3,7,8,9\}$, $S = \{2,4,9,10\}$, then the number of elements in $(P\Delta Q)\Delta(R\Delta S)$ is **(CAT 2018)**
   (a) 7 (b) 8
   (c) 9 (d) 6
6. If $A = \{6^{2n} - 35n - 1 : n = 1,2,3,...\}$ and $B = \{35(n-1) : n = 1,2,3,...\}$ then which of the following is true? **(CAT 2018)**
   (a) Neither every member of *A* is in *B*, nor is every member of *B* in *A*
   (b) Every member of *A* is in *B* and at least one member of *B* is not in *A*
   (c) Every member of *B* is in *A*
   (d) At least one member of *A* is not in *B*
7. In a tournament, there are 43 junior-level and 51 senior-level participants. Each pair of juniors plays one match. Each pair of seniors plays one match. There is no junior versus senior match. The number of girls versus girl matches in junior level is 153, while the number of boys versus boy matches in senior level is 276. The number of matches a boy plays against a girl is **(CAT 2018)**
8. A club has 256 members of whom 144 can play football, 123 can play tennis, and 132 can play cricket. Moreover, 58 members can play both football and tennis, 25 can play both cricket and tennis, while 63 can play both football and cricket. If every member can play at least one game, then the number of members who can play only tennis is **(CAT 2019)**
   (a) 32 (b) 43
   (c) 38 (d) 45
9. How many 3-digit numbers are there, for which the product of their digits is more than 2 but less than 7? **(CAT 2020)**
10. The mean of all 4-digit even natural numbers of the form 'aabb', where $a > 0$, is **(CAT 2020)**
    (a) 5544 (b) 4466
    (c) 4864 (d) 5050
11. In a group of people, 28% of the members are young while the rest are old. If 65% of the members are literates, and 25% of the literates are young, then the percentage of old people among the illiterates is nearest to **(CAT 2020)**
    (a) 66 (b) 55
    (c) 59 (d) 62
12. Students in a college have to choose at least two subjects from chemistry, mathematics and physics. The number of students choosing all three subjects is 18, choosing mathematics as one of their subjects is 23 and choosing physics as one of their subjects is 25. The smallest possible number of students who could choose chemistry as one of their subjects is **(CAT 2020)**
    (a) 19 (b) 21
    (c) 20 (d) 22
13. How many 4-digit numbers, each greater than 1000 and each having all four digits distinct, are there with 7 coming before 3? **(CAT 2020)**
14. How many integers in the set {100, 101, 102, ..., 999} have at least one digit repeated? **(CAT 2020)**
15. The number of groups of three or more distinct numbers that can be chosen from 1, 2, 3, 4, 5, 6, 7 and 8 so that the groups always include 3 and 5, while 7 and 8 are never included together is **(CAT 2021)**
16. The number of ways of distributing 15 identical balloons, 6 identical pencils and 3 identical erasers among 3 children, such that each child gets at least four balloons and one pencil, is **(CAT 2021)**
17. A four-digit number is formed by using only the digits 1, 2 and 3 such that both 2 and 3 appear at least once. The number of all such four-digit numbers is **(CAT 2021)**
18. In a class of 100 students, 73 like coffee, 80 like tea and 52 like lemonade. It may be possible that some students do not like any of these three drinks. Then

the difference between the maximum and minimum possible number of students who like all the three drinks is **(CAT 2022)**
(a) 48 (b) 47
(c) 52 (d) 53

19. The number of ways of distributing 20 identical balloons among 4 children such that each child gets some balloons but no child gets an odd number of balloons, is? **(CAT 2022)**

20. The number of integers greater than 2000 that can be formed with the digits 0, 1, 2, 3, 4, 5, using each digit at most once, is **(CAT 2022)**
(a) 1200 (b) 1440
(c) 1480 (d) 1420

21. The arithmetic mean of all the distinct numbers that can be obtained by rearranging the digits in 1421, including itself, is **(CAT 2022)**
(a) 2222 (b) 2442
(c) 3333 (d) 2592

High Yield Questions

Scan this QR code to access assisted problem solving videos on questions 5, 14 and 17

ANSWER KEY

1. 6	2. 16	3. 52	4. (d)
5. (a)	6. (b)	7. 1098	8. (b)
9. 21	10. (a)	11. (a)	12. (c)
13. 315	14. 252	15. 47	16. 1000
17. 50	18. (b)	19. 84	20. (b)
21. (a)			

SOLUTIONS AND SHORTCUTS

1. After distributing 1, 2 and 3 pens to Amal, Bimal and Kamal we are left with only 2 pens.

   Now we can distribute 2 (n) pens among 3 (r) persons in ${}^{n+r-1}C_{r-1}$ ways. Hence, we have ${}^{4}C_{2}$ ways = 6 ways.

2. After distributing one eraser to each of the four kids we are left only with 3 erasers.

   We can distribute these 3 erasers in the following ways:

   Case 1: When one kid gets 2 erasers and one kid gets 1 eraser. We can do this in 12 ways.

   Case 2: When three kids get 1 eraser each. We can do this in 4 ways.

   Hence the required number of ways = 12 + 4 = 16.

3. From the figure, we know that only P is 0, and hence, $a+b+c+d=44$. Also, the number of students studying H equals that studying E means that: $20 + 10 + a + c = 20 + 10 + b + d \rightarrow a + c = b + d = 44/2 = 22$. Hence, number of students studying $H = 30 + a + c = 30 + 22 = 52$.

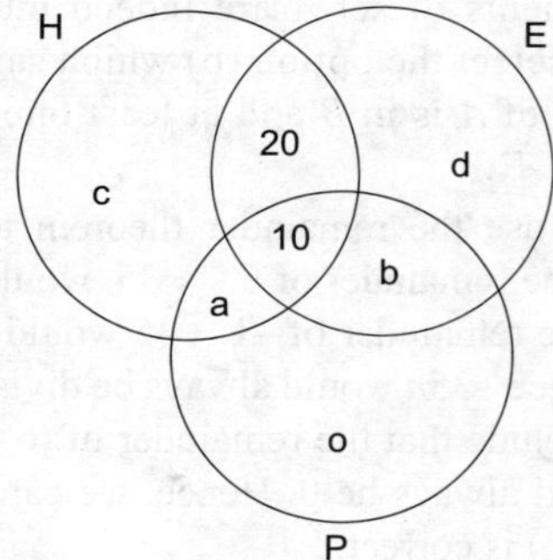

4. 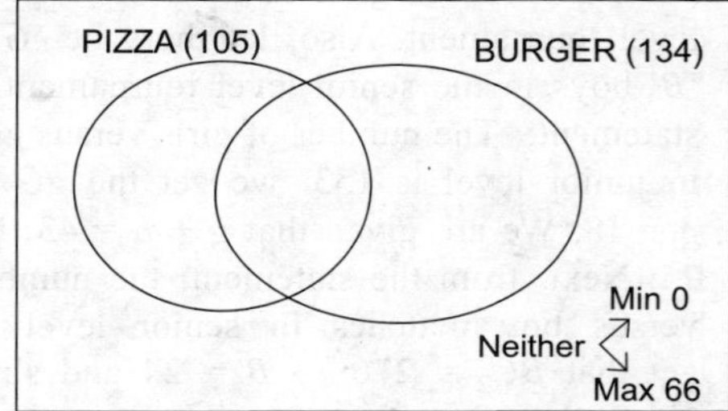

In this question, the key thought is that we do not know how many like neither. From the given circumstances, it can be seen that if 0 people like neither, then the central value x would become equal to 39. (Use the principle of double counting to get only pizza: 66, pizza and burger: 39 and only burger = 95).

The other extreme is when we maximise the number of people who like neither. From the given situation, we can see that out of 200 people, since 134 like burger, the maximum who would like neither would be 200 – 134 = 66. In such a case, we will get the following break up: Only pizza = 0, pizza and burger = 105, only burger = 29.

As we move the numbers who like neither from 0 to 66, the numbers for who like only burgers drops from 95 to 29. Hence, amongst the options, the only possible value that only burgers could have is 93. Hence, option (d) is correct.

5. $(P\Delta Q) = \{1, 4, 5, 6\}$. $(R\Delta S) = \{1, 2, 3, 4, 7, 8, 10\}$
   $(P\Delta Q)\Delta(R\Delta S) = \{1, 4, 5, 6\}\Delta\{1, 2, 3, 4, 7, 8, 10\} = \{2, 3, 5, 6, 7, 8, 10\}$. Hence, the number of elements in the given expression is 7. Option (a) is correct.

6. It can be easily seen and understood that the set B, is the set of all multiples of 35 (starting with 0 (for $n = 1$). Hence, set B {0, 35, 70, 105, 140, … and so on till infinity}.

   The first two elements of set A can be calculated using $n = 1$ and 2 respectively to get these elements as 0 and 1225. It can be observed that both these are also multiples of 35. However, the set A seems to be containing only a few multiples of 35 (and not all multiples of 35). If we can conclude that all the elements of set A are indeed multiples of 35, we can select the option (b) which says that 'Every member of A is in B and at least one member of B is not in A'.

We can use the remainder theorem to confirm the same. The remainder of $6^{2n} \div 35$, would always be 1, while the remainder of $-1 \div 35$ would always be -1. Also, since $-35n$ would always be divisible by 35, we can conclude that the remainder of $(6^{2n} - 35n - 1) \div 35$ would always be 0. Hence, we can conclude that option (b) is correct.

7. Let there be 'g' girls and 'b' boys in the junior level tournament. Also, let there be 'G' girls and 'B' boys in the senior-level tournament. From the statement: 'The number of girls versus girl matches in junior level is 153' we get the $gC_2 = 153 \rightarrow g = 18$. We are given that $g + b = 43$. Hence, $b = 25$. Next, from the statement: the number of boys versus boy matches in senior level is 276,we get that $BC_2 = 276 \rightarrow B = 24$ and since we are given that $B + G = 51$, it means that $G = 27$. The number of matches a boy plays against a girl is obtained by: Number of boy versus girl matches in the junior level + Number of boy versus girl matches in the senior level $= gC_1 \times bC_1 + GC_1 \times BC_1 = 18C_1 \times 25C_1 + 27C_1 \times 24C_1 = 450 + 648 = 1098$.

8. We can straightaway use the formula for a three-set intersection as:
$FUTUC = 256 = F + T + C - F{\cap}T - C{\cap}T - F{\cap}C + F{\cap}C{\cap}T \rightarrow 256 = 144 + 123 + 132 - 58 - 25 - 63 + F{\cap}C{\cap}T$. Solving this, we get: $F{\cap}C{\cap}T = 3$.
This leads to the following Venn diagram:

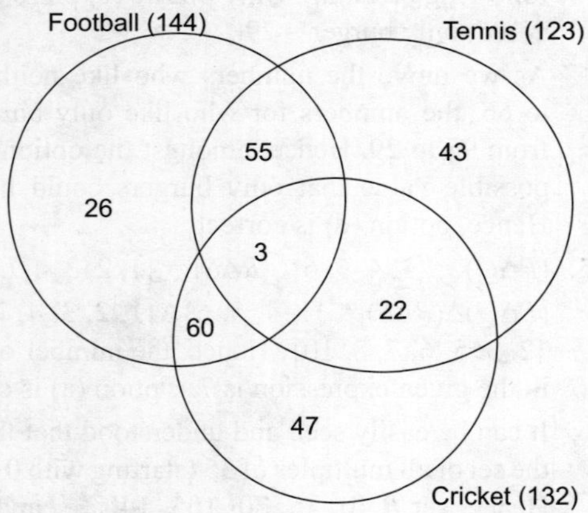

It can be seen that, the number of people with only tennis is 43. Hence, option (b) is correct.

9. We are looking for 3 digit numbers, whose product of digits is either 3,4,5 or 6. For product to be 3, the number has to be formed using the digits 1,1,3 $\Rightarrow$ 3 numbers (113,131 and 311); For product = 4, the digits used should be 2,2,1 or 4,1,1. There will be a total of 3 + 3 = 6 such numbers. For product to be 5, the number has to be formed using the digits 1,1,5 $\Rightarrow$ 3 numbers (115,151 and 511). For product = 6, the digits used should be 6,1,1 or 1,2,3. There will be a total of 3 + 6 = 9 such numbers. Total 3 + 6 + 3 + 9 = 21 numbers.

10. The numbers will be 1100, 1122, 1144, 1166, 1188, 2200, 2222, ...9988. The average value of the last two digits will be the average of 00, 22, 44, 66 and 88, which is 44 (since these numbers will appear an equal number of times in the last two digits of the numbers formed). The average of the first two digits of the number would be the average of 11,22,33,44,55,..99 $\Rightarrow$ which is 55. Hence, the correct answer is 5544. Option (a) is correct.

11. You can think of the numbers as shown here:

Young (28)		Old (72)	
Literate	Illiterate	Literate	Illiterate
16.25 (= 25% of 65)	11.75 (=28 – 16.25)		23.25 (= 35 – 11.75)

The required percentage of old people among the illiterates is $\frac{23.25}{35} \approx 66$ percent

12. 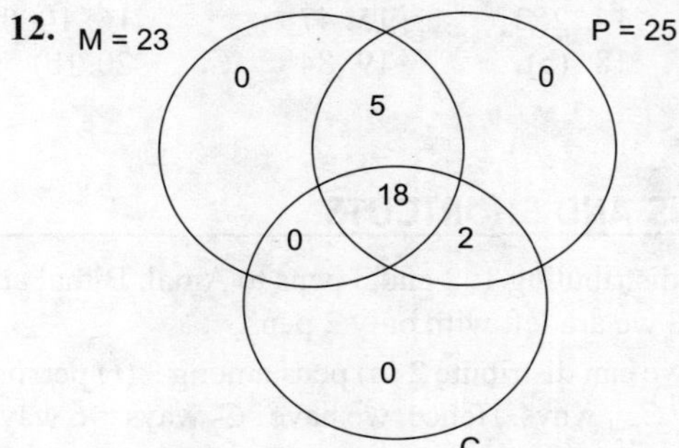

Since, we are given the value of all 3 as 18 and that to keep choosing Chemistry as minimum, it means that we need to maximise the number of people who chose Physics and Mathematics. This can be maximised at 5. Hence, the minimum number of people who chose Chemistry is 18 + 2 = 20.

13. Each of these numbers would have 7 and 3 in them. Also, the order of using 7 and 3 is fixed. Thus, there will be 6 kinds of numbers having 3 after 7 in a 4 digit number. We can think of these as:

	Thousands Place	Hundreds Place	Tens Place	Units Place	Number of cases for *a* and *b*
Case 1	7	3	a	b	8 × 7
Case 2	7	a	3	b	8 × 7
Case 3	7	a	b	3	8 × 7
Case 4	a	7	3	b	7 × 7
Case 5	a	7	b	3	7 × 7
Case 6	a	b	7	3	7 × 7
				Total cases	315

14. There will be 28 numbers with at least 1 digit repeated between 100 to 199. Some of these numbers are 100, 101, 110 to 119, 121, 122, 131, 133...191, 199. This pattern will continue from 200 to 299 and so also between 300 to 399, till 900 to 999. Thus, there will be a total of 9 sets of 28 numbers each that have the characteristic of at least 1 digit repeated. Hence, the required answer is 28 × 9 = 252.

15. You can form group of 3 to 7 numbers chosen from the 8 numbers. Note that you cannot select all 8 numbers since, both 7 and 8 cannot be taken together in any selection.

Number of numbers in the group	Compulsory selection	Remaining numbers can be selected from 1, 2, 4, 6, 7, 8
3	3 & 5	6 ways
4	3 & 5	${}^6C_2 - 1 = 14$
5	3 & 5	${}^6C_3 - 4 = 16$
6	3 & 5	${}^6C_4 - 6 = 9$
7	3 & 5	2
		Total 47 ways

16. In this situation, we have to distribute the 15 balloons & distribute the 6 pencils & distribute the 3 erasers among the three children. The given constraints for balloons is that each child gets minimum 4 balloons.

For the balloons: First give 4 balloons each to the 3 children. You would be left with 3 identical balloons to be distributed among 3 children. Using the formula for number of distribution of n identical objects among r people/groups, ${}^{n+r-1}C_{r-1} = {}^5C_2 = 10$

For the pencils: First give 1 pencil each to the 3 children. You would be left with 3 identical pencils to be distributed among 3 children. Using the formula for number of distribution of n identical objects among r people/groups, ${}^{n+r-1}C_{r-1} = {}^5C_2 = 10$

For the erasers: There is no constraint of minimum requirement for the distribution of erasers. Hence, $n = 3$ and $r = 3$, ${}^{n+r-1}C_{r-1} = {}^5C_2 = 10$.

The correct answer would be the product of 10 × 10 × 10 = 1000.

17. Numbers would be formed using the following combinations of 4 digits:

Combination 1: 2, 3, 2, 2 → $\frac{4!}{3!} = 4$ numbers;

Combination 2: 2, 3, 3, 3 → $\frac{4!}{3!} = 4$ numbers;

Combination 3: 2, 3, 2, 3 → $\frac{4!}{2! \times 2!} = 6$ numbers;

Combination 4: 2, 3, 1, 1 → $\frac{4!}{2!} = 12$ numbers;

Combination 5: 2, 3, 1, 2 → $\frac{4!}{2!} = 12$ numbers;

Combination 6: 2, 3, 1, 3 → $\frac{4!}{2!} = 12$ numbers.

Thus a total of 4 + 4 + 6 + 12 + 12 + 12 = 50 numbers are formed.

18. The solution for maximizing people who like all 3 drinks (52) is shown

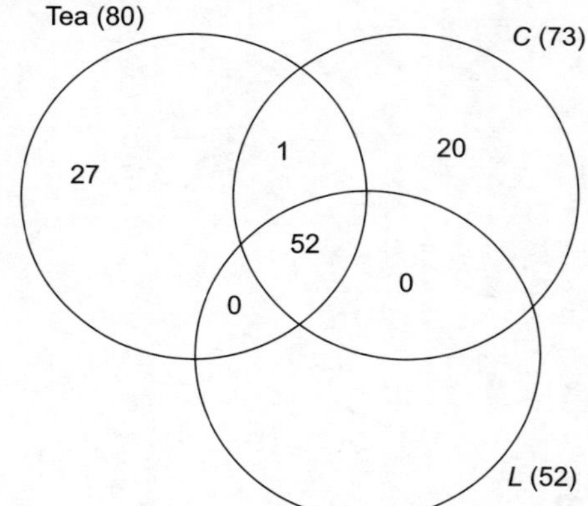

The solution for minimizing number of people who like all three (5) is shown:

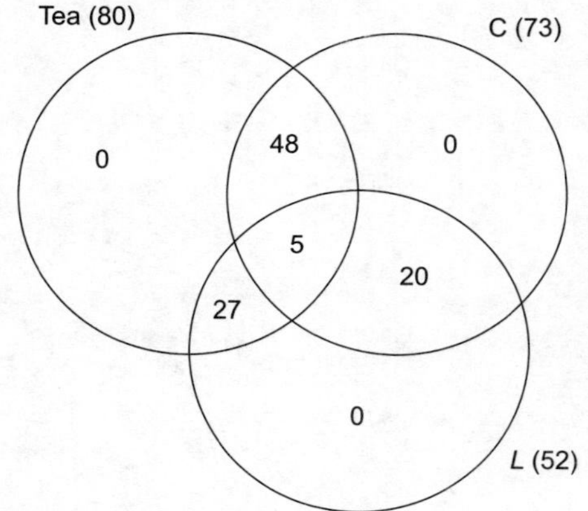

The required difference between the maximum and the minimum is 52 – 5 = 47. Option (b) is correct.

19. Think of this as distributing 10 identical objects (n) amongst 4 children (r), with 0 not allowed. The number of ways is ${}^{(n-1)}C_{(r-1)} = {}^{9}C_3 = 84$.

20. The number of 6-digit numbers = 5 × 5 × 4 × 3 × 2 × 1 = 600. The number of 5-digit numbers = 5 × 5 × 4 × 3 × 2 = 600. The number of 4-digit numbers = 4 × 5 × 4 × 3 = 240. Total number of numbers = 600 + 600 + 240 = 1440.

21. There will be a total of 4!/2 = 12 numbers formed. The digit 1 will come in the units place 3! times, the digit 4 would come in the units place 3!/2 = 3 times, the digit 2 would come in the units place 3!/2 = 3 times. The average value of the units digit would be $\frac{\text{Sum of all units digits}}{\text{Number of numbers}} = \frac{6\times1+3\times2+3\times4}{12} = 2$

Thus, the average value of each of the digits would be 2. Hence, the arithmetic mean of all the numbers would be 2222.

BLOCK STARTER

Scan this QR code to access a video explaining the logic behind The CAT Experience Test Series. Learn how to interpret your scores and correlate them with the additional preparation needed to reach your target

BLOCK

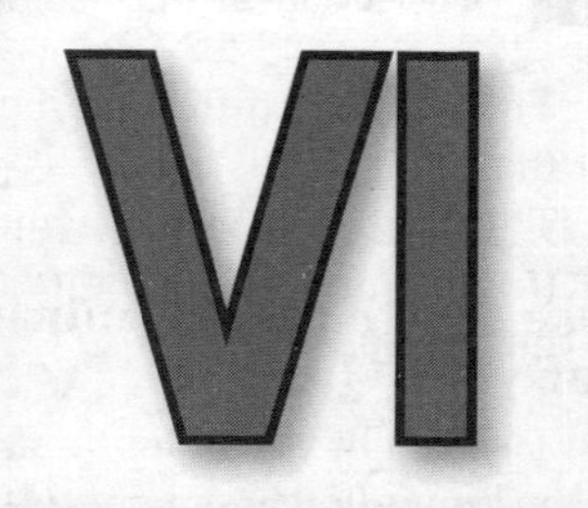

THE CAT EXPERIENCE

'THE CAT EXPERIENCE' is a series of the highest quality of mock tests based on the latest pattern and difficulty level of the CAT. It aims to provide you with comprehensive feedback in order to help you understand where you have reached in terms of your preparation levels. Keep the following points in mind while using this invaluable resource:

1. Take the first 3 of the 11 mock tests after you have finished one round of all the chapters. These should be taken under a strict 40-minute time frame. Mark yourself based on the formula [Correct answers × 3 – Wrong answers of options-based questions × 1] to check your net score. For each test, you can also find your ability level by assessing how many questions you could have solved without the time limit.
2. Do a close analysis of your performance and identify
   (i) the chapters/concepts/blocks where you need to improve your ability;
   (ii) the chapters/concepts/blocks where you need to improve your efficiency and speed.
   (iii) the chapters/concepts/blocks where you need to maintain your current level of ability and efficiency
3. Based on your analysis, revisit the chapters/blocks which you have identified under (i) above. For these, it would be a wise thing to revisit the concepts and cover the questions a second time.
   For chapters/blocks under (ii) above, revisit these with a perspective of re-solving the LOD exercises, focusing on reducing your number of readings in each problem, reducing the writing you do to solve the same and trying to discover better ways to solve the same questions.
4. Come back and take the next 3 tests and re-analyse based on (2) above. If you still find instances of (i) and (ii), revisit those topics before you come back to the remaining tests – else move on and take the remaining mocks.

Ability & Score Guide:

Use this to assess your level and how much more you need to do based on the target you have for your QA score.

Ability without time limits	*Correct answers with time limits*	*Net Score range*	*Percentile Score indicator*
19–22/22	16–18	45–52	99.9 percentile
15–18/22	12–14	33–40	99 to 99.5 percentile
12–14	8–10	24–30	97–98.5 percentile
8–11	5–7	15–20	92–96 percentile

The CAT Experience

High Yield Questions

Scan this QR Code to access video explanations for select questions from The CAT Experience tests 1 to 10

THE CAT EXPERIENCE 1

1. Let X, be the largest positive integer that divides $5^k + 6^k + 7^k + 8^k$, and Y be the largest positive integer that divides $6^k + 5 \times 6^k + 6^{k+3}$, where k is a natural number. The value of $\frac{Y}{X^2}$ is?

2. In a factory 30% of the employees are women, while the rest are men. If the total salary earned by the women is one-eighth of the total salary of all the employees in the factory, then what is the ratio of the average salary of the women to the average salary of the men?

3. Amitabh borrows ₹6 lacs at 6% per annum compounded half yearly. At the end of 1 year, he pays back ₹12270. His loan is a floating interest loan and at the end of 1 year, his bank increases his rate of interest to 8% per annum compounded half yearly. He makes no additional payments till he closes the loan outstanding by paying the entire amount due from him at the end of 3 years. What is the approximate value of the total interest paid by him on the loan?

4. The Rajdhani express leaves Kolkata for Chennai at the same time as the Coromandel express leaves Chennai for Kolkata. The Rajdhani express requires 18 hours to reach it's destination, while the Coromandel express reaches it's destination 24 hours after crossing the Rajdhani express. How much time does the Coromandel Express take for the entire journey?

5. a and b are natural numbers such that $a^3 + ab + a = 165$, while $b^3 + ab + b = 385$. The value of $3a + 2b$ is:
   (a) 18 (b) 29
   (c) 25 (d) 31

6. Let a and b be real numbers. If a and $-a$ are two roots of the equation $2x^3 - bx^2 - 40x + 15 = 0$, then what is the value of b?
   (a) 3/4 (b) –3/4
   (c) 3/8 (d) –3/8

7. Two ships X and Y are traveling towards the Singapore harbor in straight lines. Their initial positions are such that their positions form a right-angled triangle with the harbor with each ship being exactly 45 kms from the harbor. When the faster ship X, has covered two-thirds of it's distance from the harbor, the other ship Y has covered some distance such that the current distance of the ships X and Y from the harbor are in the ratio of $1:\sqrt{3}$.
   When X reaches the harbor, how much distance away from the harbor would the ship Y be?
   (a) $\frac{25\sqrt{3}-25}{3}$ (b) $\frac{45\sqrt{3}-45}{2}$
   (c) $\frac{15\sqrt{3}-15}{2}$ (d) $\frac{15\sqrt{3}-15}{4}$

8. In a triangle XYZ, $XY = XZ = 12$. A circle 'A' is drawn with YZ as diameter and it passes through X. Another circle 'B' with it's center at X and radius as XY is drawn. The area of the circle B, not intersecting the circle A is?
   (a) $72(\pi+1)$ (b) $36(\pi-1)$
   (c) $72(\pi-1)$ (d) 36π

9. The number of natural numbers less than 1000, with exactly 2 digits identical are:

10. A jar of coffee contains pure unadulterated coffee. Some part of the coffee is removed from the jar (Say Q grams) and replaced with cocoa powder to form Mixture X. Next, 1.5Q grams is removed from Mixture X and replaced with coffee powder, resulting in Mixture Y. It is found that the ratio of coffee and cocoa in mixture Y is 43 : 7. Find the ratio of cocoa in Mixture X and Mixture Y.
   (a) 5 : 11 (b) 5 : 9
   (c) 9 : 5 (d) 10 : 7

11. Arjun sells two items at the same price, making a profit of 36.36% on the first and a loss of 14.28% on the second. If he increases the selling price of each of the items, such that he continues to sell them at the same price, but gains a 30% profit on the second, what is the approximate profit percentage on the first item (round off to the closest integral percentage)?

12. Shekhar makes a mixture A of Horlicks and sugar by mixing the two in a certain proportion. He then creates a second mixture B of coffee and sugar by mixing the two ingredients in the ratio 3 : 2. He then mixes the two mixtures in the ratio 6 : 5 to make mixture C of Horlicks, coffee and Sugar. Finally, he makes a drink by Mixing Milk and Mixture C in the ratio of 3 : 11. If the resultant drink has 1/3rd sugar

as a proportion, then what is the ratio of Horlicks and Sugar in mixture A?

(a) 4 : 5 (b) 2 : 7
(c) 7 : 2 (d) 5 : 4

13. n is an integer such that $3x^2 + nx + 10 = 0$ has no real roots and the equation $x^2 + (n - 3)x + 1 = 0$ has two distinct real roots. If $|n|$ is positive, then what are the number of factors for the product of all possible values of n?

(a) 1248 (b) 896
(c) 1680 (d) 1344

14. Let $k = \frac{x}{y}$ and $m = \frac{x+5}{y-5}$. Given, $y \neq 5$, If $k < m$, then it follows that:

(a) if $y < 0$ then $-x < y$
(b) if $y > 0$, then $-x < y$
(c) if $x < 0$ then $-x < y$
(d) if $x > 0$ then $-x < y$

15. Let a and b be two positive integers, such that there are a minimum of 55 numbers between 81^a and 81^b, that can be expressed as a power of 3. What is the minimum product possible for $a \times b$.

16. An exam is conducted with 100 questions on the test. All questions are multiple choice single correct answer questions. For every correct answer, 4 marks are awarded, for every wrong answer 1 mark is deducted while for every un-attempted question 1 mark is awarded. Two friends Sameer Contractor and Sameer Deshpande attempt the paper in such a way, that both get the same net total of 133 marks. If Deshpande had 14 more correct answers than Contractor, what is the difference in the number of attempted questions by the two?

Directions for Questions 17 and 18: The following table presents the sweetness of different forms relative to sucrose, whose sweetness is taken to be 1.00.

Lactose 0.16
Maltose 0.32
Glucose 0.74
Sucrose 1.00
Fructose 1.70
Saccharin 675.00

17. What is the maximum amount of sucrose (to the nearest gram) that can be added to one-gram of saccharin to make a mixture that will be at least 100 times as sweet as glucose?

(a) 7 (b) 8
(c) 9 (d) 100

18. Approximately how many times sweeter than sucrose is a mixture consisting of glucose, sucrose and fructose in the ratio of 1 : 2 : 3?

(a) 1.3 (b) 1
(c) 0.6 (d) 2.3

19. Let $x_1, x_2, \ldots, x_{100}$ be positive integers such that $x_! + x_{!-1} + 1 = k$ for all !, where k is a constant. If $x_{10} = 1$, then the value of x_1 is

(a) k (b) $k - 2$
(c) $k + 1$ (d) 1

20. If $a_0 = 1$, $a_1 = 1$ and $a_n = a_{n-2}\, a_{n-1} + 3$ for $n > 1$, which of the following options would be true?

(a) a_{450} is odd and a_{451} is even
(b) a_{450} is odd and a_{451} is odd
(c) a_{450} is even and a_{451} is even
(d) a_{450} is even and a_{451} is odd

21. If the equation $x^3 - ax^2 + bx - a = 0$ has three real roots, then it must be the case that

(a) $b = 1$ (b) $b \neq 1$
(c) $a = 1$ (d) $a \neq 1$

22. A square tin sheet of side 12 inches is converted into a box with open top in the following steps. The sheet is placed horizontally. Then, equal-sized squares, each of side x inches, are cut from the four corners of the sheet. Finally, the four resulting sides are bent vertically upwards in the shape of a box. If x is an integer, then what value of x maximizes the volume of the box?

(a) 3 (b) 4
(c) 1 (d) 2

THE CAT EXPERIENCE 2

1. Arun is following his good friend Abhijit's car on a straight road. He is 110 meters behind Abhijit. Their common friend Amartya is driving on the same straight road but in the opposite direction. At present the distance between Amartya and Abhijit is 990 meters and they are approaching each other. If Abhijit is driving at 60 kmph and Amartya is driving at 48 kmph, then at what speed (in kmph) should Arun drive his car, so that they cross other at the same time and the same spot?

(a) 64 kmph (b) 72 kmph
(c) 60 kmph (d) 80 kmph

2. Ambujwar, Bisheshwar and Cheteshwar are working on a project together. However much to everyone's surprise (which was discovered later), Bisheshwar was actually working against the team. Ambujwar takes 1 hour more to do the complete work than Bisheshwar takes to completely destroy the work. When all the three work together, the project is completed in a total of 3 hours. On one particular day Bisheshwar and Cheteshwar worked together for an hour after which Bisheshwar had to go for an urgent meeting (thankfully). Cheteshwar completed the remaining work in 2.2 hours. If Ambujwar takes less than 5 hours for the project, how much time (in minutes) does Cheteshwar take to do the project alone?

(a) 120 minutes (b) 132 minutes
(c) 144 minutes (d) 180 minutes

3. Let n, be the largest integer such that the equation $(x - 2)^2 + 8nx + 481 = 0$ has no real roots. If m is a positive real number, then the least possible value of $\frac{(2n-1)}{22m} + 8m$ is:

4. If $\sqrt{63x+36} + \sqrt{63x-36} = 3(5+\sqrt{17})$, then find the value of $\sqrt{14x+9}$.

(a) $2\sqrt{51}$ (b) $\sqrt{51}$
(b) $2\sqrt{41}$ (d) $\sqrt{41}$

5. An isosceles triangle ABC has sides $AB = AC = 8$ and base $BC = 12$. AD is a line drawn from A to D, such that the area of ΔADB is three time the area ΔADC. What is the length of AD?

(a) $\sqrt{35}$ (b) $\sqrt{37}$
(c) $\sqrt{38}$ (d) $\sqrt{42}$

6. For any natural numbers a, b and q, if q divides $7a + 3b$ and also $15a + 6b$, then q must be a common divisor of:

(i) a and b
(ii) a and $3b$
(iii) $8a$ and $6b$

(a) Only (i) (b) Only (ii)
(c) Only (ii) and (iii) (d) All of (i), (ii) and (iii)

7. The number of numbers greater than 2000 but less than 10 million, that can be formed using the digits 0, 1, 2, 3, 4, 5 is:

(a) 279504 (b) 278604
(c) 282404 (d) 285604

8. A shopkeeper is in the business of buying and selling cloth. While buying cloth, he bargains to get 10% extra cloth length for his purchases. While selling he marks up the price of his cloth by 20%, but gives a discount of 8% to his customer. He also cheats his customers by actually giving only 90 cm of cloth for every 1 meter of cloth purchased. What is the closest estimate of his profit percentage (to the nearest integral percentage)?

9. Rajesh buys 220 kgs of katarni rice and 240 kgs of Dehradun rice, the price of Katarni rice being 30% less than Dehradun rice. He sells 10 kgs of Katarni at 10% profit and another 10 kgs at 20% profit. He also sells 40 kgs of Dehradun rice at a 30% profit. He then mixes the remaining rice and sells the remaining at ₹593.82 per kg such that overall he gets a 68% profit. What is the cost price of the 400 kgs mixture he obtained when he mixed the balance quantities of the two rice varieties (after his initial sales)?

10. If a and b are real numbers such that $a^2 + (a - 2b + 2)^4 = -4b(a + b)$, then the value of $(a^3 - b^3)$ is:

(a) $\frac{9}{8}$ (b) $-\frac{3}{8}$
(c) $-\frac{7}{8}$ (d) $-\frac{9}{8}$

11. The equation $x^3 + (r + 1)x^2 + (2r - 1)x + 4 = 0$ has -4 as one of it's roots. For how many non-negative integral values of r would the expression have only one real root?

12. In a laboratory experiment there are a total of 500 particles in a jar on day 1. On the nth day, $n \geq 2$, one out of n particles splits into exactly two particles. On the particular day when the number of particles reaches 3000, the very same day each of the particles (including the ones that had already split that day) splits into 3 particles. From the next day, the process of splitting continues with one out of n particles splitting into two particles on the nth day. On which day would the number of particles in the jar cross 20000?

13. A trapezium $ABCD$ has an area of 176 square units. If angle ADC is a right angle and $AB = 8$ units, $CD = 15$ units find the perimeter of the trapezium.

14. A man invests a certain amount in such a way that he earns 7% simple interest on 30% of his money, 12% simple interest on one third of the balance and 3% simple interest on his balance amount. Minimum how many completed years will he take to double his investment?

15. Quality A rice sells at 24 ₹/kg, while Quality B rice sells at 72 ₹/kg. Pankaj Bharadwaj on his weekly visit to the market buys some quantity of both qualities of rice (in non-zero integral kgs), such that he buys 14 kgs more of Quality B rice. When he comes back home, his wife Richa notices that the average price of rice he bought was also an integer in terms of ₹/Kg. What is the sum of the minimum quantity of quality B rice and the maximum quantity of Quality A rice that was possibly bought?

16. If a, b, c, m, n, p are natural numbers and a, b, c each is greater than 1, such that $a^m \times b^n \times c^p = 720^{200}$, then what is the difference between the maximum and the minimum possible value of $m + n + p$?

Directions for Questions 17 to 19: Answer the questions on the basis of the information given below. A city has two perfectly circular and concentric ring roads, the outer ring road (OR) being twice as long as the inner ring road (IR). There are also four (straight line) chord roads from $E1$, the east end point of OR to $N2$, the north end point of IR; from $N1$, the north end point of OR to $W2$, the west end point of IR; from $W1$, the west end point of OR, to $S2$, the south end point of IR and from $S1$, the south end point of OR to $E2$, the east end point of IR.; Traffic moves at a constant speed of 30π km/hr on the IR road, and the OR road; $15\sqrt{5}$ km/hr on all the chord roads.

17. The ratio of the sum of the lengths of all chord roads to the length of the outer ring road is
(a) $\sqrt{5}:2$ (b) $\sqrt{5}:2\pi$
(c) $\sqrt{5}:\pi$ (d) None of these

18. Amit wants to reach *N2* from *S1*. It would take him 90 minutes if he goes on minor arc *S1–E1* on OR, and then on the chord road *E1–N2*. What is the radius of the outer ring road in kms?
(a) 60 (b) 40
(c) 30 (d) 20

19. Amit wants to reach *E2* from *N1* using first the chord *N1–W2* and then the inner ring road. What will be his travel time in minutes on the basis of information given in the above question?
(a) 60 (b) 45
(c) 90 (d) 105

20. Consider two different cloth-cutting processes. In the first one, *n* circular cloth pieces are cut from a square cloth piece of side *a* in the following steps: the original square of side *a* is divided into *n* smaller squares, not necessarily of the same size, then a circle of maximum possible area is cut from each of the smaller squares. In the second process, only one circle of maximum possible area is cut from the square of side *a* and the process ends there. The cloth pieces remaining after cutting the circles are scrapped in both the processes. The ratio of the total area of scrap cloth generated in the former to that in the latter is
(a) 1 : 1 (b) $\sqrt{2}:1$
(c) $\frac{n(4-\pi)}{4n-\pi}$ (d) $\frac{4n-\pi}{n(4-\pi)}$

21. For all non-negative integers *x* and *y*, $f(x, y)$ is defined as below.
$f(0, y) = y + 1$
$f(x + 1, 0) = f(x, 1)$
$f(x + 1, y + 1) = f(x, f(x + 1, y))$
Then what is the value of $f(1, 2)$?
(a) 2 (b) 4
(c) 3 (d) Cannot be determined

22. The probability that a randomly chosen positive divisor of 10^{29} is an integer multiple of 10^{23} is: a^2/b^2, then '$b - a$' would be:
(a) 8 (b) 15
(c) 21 (d) 23

THE CAT EXPERIENCE 3

1. The sum of all possible values of *x* satisfying the equation $4^{x^2} - 2^{x^2+x+21} + 4^{x+20} = 0$ is:
(a) 2 (b) 1
(c) 1/2 (d) None of these

2. The number of positive integers less than 100, that have exactly 4 factors other than 1 and itself are?

3. The price of a precious stone is directly proportional to the square of it's weight. Amar has a precious stone weighing 26 units. The price of the original stone is 2704000. If the stone is broken into 4 pieces of integral weights, find the difference between the highest and lowest possible values of the total price of the four pieces.
(a) 960000 (b) 984000
(c) 976000 (d) 244000

4. Pulkit runs a clothing store. In one particular transaction he bought a certain number of trousers at ₹1200 and a certain number of shirts at ₹1500 (buying at least 1 of each). He then marked the price of all the clothes at 20% above the average purchase cost of each clothing item. He sold the items at 10% discount on the marked price, making a total profit of 34080. The maximum possible total number of clothing items he could have bought is?

5. For the above question what is the minimum number of shirts he sold?

6. A rectangle *ABCD* has length *AB* = 20 and *BC* = 12. *X* and *Y* are two points on *BC*, such that the areas of the triangles *ABX*; *AXY* and the quadrilateral *AYCD* are in an Arithmetic Progression. If the area of *AYCD* is seven times that of *ABX*, find the ratio of *BX* : XY : *YC*.
(a) 1 : 4 : 2 (b) 2 : 8 : 3
(c) 1 : 4 : 1 (d) 2 : 6 : 3

7. If $x^2 + y^2 - 100 = 2xy - 64 = 44 - 2xy$. Find the difference between the maximum and minimum possible values of $x^3 - y^3$.

8. For some real numbers *a* and *b*, the system of equations $x + y = 8$ and $(b^2 + 24) + (a + 8)y = 80b$ has infinitely many solutions for *x* and *y*. What is the minimum possible value of $a + b$?

9. The minimum sum of three natural numbers that have 12 factors (including 1 and itself) is:

10. At the latest Olympic Games, the ratio of European athletes to non-European athletes was 6 : 7. The ratio of female European athletes to non-European female athletes was 4 : 3, while the ratio of male European athletes to male non-European athletes was 5 : 6. If the total number of female non-European athletes was 1200, then what was the total number of athletes in the Games.

11. Amitabh buys 5 liters sunflower oil, 6 liters castor oil and 13 liters of Coconut oil. He then mixes the three oils and marks up the price of the mixture such that he gets a profit of ₹4040. He then sells 8 liters of the mixture at the marked price and gives a 30% discount on the remaining mixture. He thus earns a profit of ₹2240. If the price of 8 liters of Sunflower

oil, 10 liters of castor oil and 40 liters of coconut oil are the same, then find the total cost of his next purchase when he purchases 2 liters of sunflower oil, 3 liters of castor oil and 8 liters of coconut oil?

(a) 2400 (b) 2520
(c) 2080 (d) 2840

12. $0 \le n \le x \le 80$. If $f(x) = |x - n| + |x - 80| + |x - n - 40|$, then what is the maximum possible value of $f(x)$?

(a) 80 (b) 100
(c) 120 (d) 150

13. A number x is such that it can be expressed as $a + b + c = x$ where a, b, and c are factors of x. How many numbers below 200 have this property?

(a) 31 (b) 32
(c) 33 (d) 5

14. Two brothers Binnu and Kinnu have been challenged by their father to solve a mathematical puzzle before they are allowed to go out to play. Their father has asked them "Imagine two integers a and b, such that $1 \le b \le a \le 10$. Can you correctly find out the value of the expression $\sum ab$?" Can you help them identify the correct value of the foregoing expression?

(a) 1155 (b) 1050
(c) 1705 (d) None of these

15. For the above question, what would be the answer in case the inequality is expressed as: $1 \le b < a \le 10$?

16. Little Pika who is five-and-half years old has just learnt addition. However, he does not know how to carry. For example, he can add 14 and 5, but he does not know how to add 14 and 7. How many pairs of consecutive integers between 1000 and 2000 (both 1000 and 2000 included) can Little Pika add?

(a) 150 (b) 155
(c) 156 (d) 258

17. There is a circle of radius 1 cm. Each member of a sequence of regular polygons $S_1(n)$, $n = 4, 5, 6, \ldots$, where n is the number of sides of the polygon, is circumscribing the circle: and each member of the sequence of regular polygons $S_2(n)$, $n = 4, 5, 6, \ldots$ where n is the number of sides of the polygon, is inscribed in the circle. Let $L_1(n)$ and $L_2(n)$ denote the perimeters of the corresponding polygons of $S_1(n)$ and $S_2(n)$, then $\frac{\{L_1(13) + 2\pi\}}{L_2(17)}$ is

(a) greater than $\frac{\pi}{4}$ and less than 1
(b) greater than 2
(c) greater than 1 and less than 2
(d) less than $\frac{\pi}{4}$

18. For two positive integers a and b, define the function $h(a, b)$ as the greatest common factor (gcf) of a, b. Let A be a set of n positive integers. $G(A)$, the gcf of the elements of set A is computed by repeatedly using the function h. The minimum number of times h is required to be used to compute G is:

(a) $12n$ (b) $(n - 1)$
(c) n (d) None of these

19. The number of polynomials of the form $x^3 + ax^2 + bx + c$ which are divisible by $x^2 + 1$ and where a, b and c belong to $\{1, 2, \ldots. 8)$ is:

(a) 1 (b) 8
(c) 9 (d) 10

20. There is a square field of side 500 m length each. It has a compound wall along its perimeter. At one of its corners, a triangular area of the field is to be cordoned off by erecting a straight-line fence. The compound wall and the fence will form its borders. If the length of the fence is 100 m, what is the maximum area that can be cordoned off?

(a) 2,500 sq m (b) 10,000 sq m
(c) 5,000 sq m (d) 20,000 sq m

21. Three math classes: X, Y and Z take an algebra test.
The average score in class X is 83.
The average score in class Y is 76.
The average score in class Z is 85.
The average score of all students in classes X and Y together is 79.
The average score of all students in classes Y and Z together is 81.
What is the average for all the three classes?

(a) 81 (b) 81.5
(c) 82 (d) 84.5

22. A set of consecutive positive integers beginning with 1 is written on the blackboard. A student came along and erased one number. The average of the remaining numbers is $35\frac{7}{17}$. What was the number erased?

(a) 7 (b) 8
(c) 9 (d) None of these

THE CAT EXPERIENCE 4

1. The area of the quadrilateral bounded by the line $|x| = 7$ and the lines $|x - y| - |x - 4| = 3$ is:

2. The number of integral solutions for the expression $(x^2 - 8x + 16)^{x^2 - 25} = 1$ are?

(a) 2 (b) 3
(c) 4 (d) More than 4

3. A bottle X contains 1200 ml of Pepsi. Another bottle Y contains 1000 ml of Coca Cola. A naughty boy Viraj took 200 ml of Pepsi from the first bottle and mixed it thoroughly with the Coca Cola. He then transferred back 200 ml of this mixture from Y to X and mixed it thoroughly. The ratio of Pepsi in Bottle X to Coca Cola in Bottle Y is:

(a) 31 : 24 (b) 31 : 35
(c) 31 : 25 (d) 35 : 31

4. The number of people working in the year of inception for three companies A, B and C (which were incubated at IIM Bangalore in the same year) are in the ratio 4 : 5 : 7. In the first year the number of employees in these companies grew by 30%, 20% and 20% respectively. In the second year their number of employees grew by 50% for A and by 25% for C. If the number of employees after the growth of the second year for the three companies form an Arithmetic Progression, what is the percentage increase in the number of employees of Company B in the second year.
(a) 50% (b) 52.5%
(c) 55% (d) 57.5%

5. *ABCDEFGH* is a regular octagon. *A* and *E* are opposite vertices of the octagon. A frog starts jumping from vertex to vertex, beginning from *A*. From any vertex of the octagon except *E*, it may jump to either of the two adjacent vertices. When it reaches *E*, the frog stops and stays there. Let a_n be the number of distinct paths of exactly *n* jumps ending in *E*. Then, what is the value of a_{2n-1}?
(a) Zero
(b) Four
(c) $2n - 1$
(d) Cannot be determined

6. Find the sum of all 3 digit numbers that leave a remainder of 3 when divided by 7.
(a) 70821 (b) 60821
(c) 50521 (d) 80821

7. A square, whose side is 2 m, has its corners cut away so as to form an octagon with all sides equal. Then the length of each side of the octagon, in metres, is
(a) $\frac{\sqrt{2}}{\sqrt{2}+1}$ (b) $\frac{2}{\sqrt{2}+1}$
(c) $\frac{2}{\sqrt{2}-1}$ (d) $\frac{\sqrt{2}}{\sqrt{2}-1}$

8. In the country of Twenty, there are exactly twenty cities, and there is exactly one direct road between any two cities. No two direct roads have an overlapping road segment. After the election dates are announced, candidates from their respective cities start visiting the other cities. The following are the rules that the election commission has laid down for the candidates:

- Each candidate must visit each of the other cities exactly once.
- Each candidate must use only the direct roads between two cities for going from one city to another.
- Candidate must return to his own city at the end of the campaign.
- No direct road between two cities would be used by more than one candidate.

The maximum possible number of candidates is
(a) 6 (b) 7
(c) 8 (d) 9

9. For the circle $x^2 + 4x + y^2 - 6y - 12 = 0$, pairs of tangents with an angle between them of 60 degrees are drawn. The locus of external points of intersection for this pair of tangents is drawn. At what point does this locus intersect the line $x = 8$?
(a) 8, 4 (b) 8, 3
(c) 8, 2 (d) 8, 6

10. In a right-angled triangle *XYZ*, the height *XY* is 7 cm, while the base *YZ* is 36 cm long. There are two points *A* and *B* on *YZ*, such that the areas of the triangles *XYA*, *XYB* and *XYZ* are in geometric progression. If the area of the triangle *XYZ* is 9 times the area of the triangle *XYA*, find the length of *AB* in cm.

11. Let *n* be the smallest integer such that 240 is a factor of 810^n. If *m* is the smallest integer such that 810^n is a factor of 240^m, then the value of $m - n$ is.

12. The great mathematician Ramanujam, once was asked a puzzle in order to test his mathematical prowess. He was given two sets of numbers as follows:
Set *X* is the set of all numbers of the form: $4^n - 3n - 1$, where $n = 1, 2, 3, \ldots$
Set *Y* is the set of all numbers of the form $9n$, where $n = 0, 1, 2, 3, \ldots$
Based on these two definitions of the set, can you help Ramanujam identify the correct statement from amongst the following options?
(a) Each number in *Y* is also in *X*
(b) Each number in *X* is also in *Y*
(c) Every number in *X* is in *Y* and every number in *Y* is in *X*
(d) There are numbers in *X* that are not in *Y* and vice versa

13. If *a* and *b* are positive real numbers such that $\log_a(a^3 + 56) = 6$ and $6 \times \log_b a = 3$, then find the value of $b - 2a$.

14. The number of intersection points for the graphs of the functions $3 \times |x| \times (2x^2 + 1)$ & $19x^2$ are:

15. On a 20 km tunnel, connecting two cities *A* and *B*, there are three gutters (1, 2 and 3). The distance between gutters 1 and 2 is half the distance between gutters 2 and 3. The distance from city *A* to its nearest gutter, gutter 1, is equal to the distance of city *B* from gutter 3. On a particular day, the hospital in city *A* receives information that an accident has happened at gutter 3. The victim can be saved only if an operation is started within 40 min. An ambulance started from city *A* at 30 km/hr and crossed gutter 1 after 5 min. If the driver had doubled the speed after that, what is the maximum amount of time would the doctor get to attend the patient at the hospital. Assume 1 min is elapsed for taking the patient into and out of the ambulance?

(a) 4 min
(b) 2.5 min
(c) 1.5 min
(d) The patient died before reaching the hospital

16. Akhil went on a 10-hour trip to the beaches. At the start of the trip, the number of kilometers his car had travelled was a palindromic number i.e. a number which when reversed does not change. When he finishes his trip, the car meter reads 96969, which is again a palindromic number. If he never drove above 105 kmph during his journey, what could be the maximum average speed (in kmph) at which he drove his car during the 10-hour trip?

17. Let $x_1, x_2, \ldots\ldots, x_{40}$ be forty non-zero numbers such that $x_i + x_{i+1} = k$ for all i, $1 \le i \le \infty$. If $x_{14} = a$, $x_{27} = b$, then $x_{30} + x_{39}$ equals
(a) $3(a + b) - 2k$
(b) $k + a$
(c) $k + b$
(d) None of the foregoing expressions

18. If $\left(\sqrt{\frac{11}{7}}\right)^{2x-y} = \frac{3773}{14641}$ and $\left(\frac{12m}{3n}\right)^{4x-y} = \left(\frac{6m}{3n}\right)^{y-4x}$ then what is the sum of x & y?

19. Only a single rail track exists between stations A and B on a railway line. One hour after the northbound super fast train N leaves station A for station B, a south-bound passenger train S reaches station A from station B. The speed of the super fast train is twice that of a normal express train E, while the speed of a passenger train S is half that of E. On a particular day, N leaves for B from A, 20 min behind the normal schedule. In order to maintain the schedule, both N and S increased their speeds. If the super fast train doubles its speed, what should be the ratio (approximately) of the speeds of passenger train to that of the super fast train so that the passenger train S reaches exactly at the scheduled time at A on that day?
(a) 1 : 3 (b) 1 : 4
(c) 1 : 5 (d) 1 : 6

20. 40 identical chocolates have to be distributed amongst 5 children, such that no child gets an odd number of chocolates. The number of odd factors of the number of ways in which the distribution can be done are (if no child remains empty handed)

21. A train approaches a tunnel AB. Inside the tunnel is a cat located at a point that is 3/8 of the distance AB measured from the entrance A. When the train whistles the cat runs. If the cat moves to the entrance of the tunnel A, the train catches the cat exactly at the entrance. If the cat moves to the exit B, the train catches the cat at exactly the exit. The speed of the train is greater than the speed of the cat by what order?
(a) 3 : 1 (b) 4 : 1
(c) 5 : 1 (d) None of these

22. Two sides of a plot measure 32 m and 24 m and the angle between them is a perfect right angle. The other two sides measure 25 m each and the other three angles are not right angles.

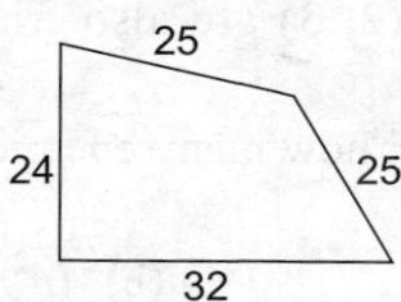

What is the area of the plot?
(a) 768 m^2 (b) 534 m^2
(c) 696.5 m^2 (d) 684 m^2

THE CAT EXPERIENCE 5

1. The number of integer solutions of the equation $2 \times |x| \times (3x^2 + 1) = 15 \times x^2$ is:

2. For any real number X, [X] represents the largest integer just below X. If $\left[\frac{1}{3}+\frac{N_1}{45}\right]+\left[\frac{1}{3}+\frac{N_2}{45}\right]+\left[\frac{1}{3}+\frac{N_3}{45}\right]+\left[\frac{1}{3}+\frac{N_4}{45}\right]\ldots+\left[\frac{1}{3}+\frac{N_x}{45}\right]<135$ then find the largest possible sum of $N_1 + N_2 + \ldots + N_x$, when the terms represented as N_a are always natural numbers.
(a) 4005 (b) 7750
(c) 8385 (d) 7140.

3. The function $f(x)$ is defined for all integers and meets the condition $f(x) + f(x - 1) - 5 = 0$. Also, it is known that $f(x^3 - x^2) = 20$. The function $g(x) = x^3$ for all integral values of x. Find the value of $f(g(12) + g(f(12))$.

4. A rectangle of the largest possible area is drawn inside a semi-circle of radius 5. What is the perimeter of the rectangle?
(a) $5\sqrt{2}$ (b) $10\sqrt{2}$
(c) $25/\sqrt{2}$ (d) $15\sqrt{2}$

5. In a class of 98 students in a school, 80 are cricket fans, 70 are football fans and 53 are tennis fans. The sum of the minimum and maximum number of students who could be fans of all three games is:

6. How many times would the digit 6 be used in numbering a book of 639 pages?
(a) 100 (b) 124
(c) 150 (d) 164

7. Ravi takes 45 seconds to walk up a moving up escalator. If he trebles his speed, he takes only 20 seconds. If his son Arjit just stands still on the same escalator, how much time would be take to reach the top?

Directions for Questions 8 and 9: Let S be the set of all pairs (i, j) where $1 \leq i < j \leq n$, and $n \geq 4$. Any two distinct members of S are called "friends", if they have one constituent of the pairs in common and "enemies" otherwise. For example, if $n = 4$, then $S = \{(1, 2), (1, 3), (1, 4), (2, 3), (2, 4), (3, 4)\}$. Here, (1, 2) and (1, 3) are friends, (1, 2) and (2, 3) are also friends, but (1, 4) and (2, 3) are enemies.

8. For general n, how many enemies will each member of S have?
   (a) $n - 3$ (b) $(n^2 - 3n - 2)/2$
   (c) $2n - 7$ (d) $(n^2 - 5n + 6)/2$
9. For general n, consider any two members of S that are friends. How many other members of S will be common friends of both these members?
   (a) $(n^2 - 5n + 8)/2$ (b) $2n - 6$
   (c) $n(n - 3)/2$ (d) $n - 2$
10. A confused bank teller transposed the rupees and paisa when he cashed a cheque for Shailaja, giving her rupees instead of paisa and paisa instead of rupees. After buying a toffee for 50 paisa, Shailaja noticed that she was left with exactly three times as much as the amount on the cheque. Which of the following is a valid statement about the cheque amount?
    (a) Over rupees 22 but less than rupees 23
    (b) Over rupees 18 but less than rupees 19
    (c) Over rupees 4 but less than rupees 5
    (d) Over rupees 13 but less than rupees 14
11. A truck travelling at 70 km/hr uses 30% more diesel to travel a certain distance than it does when it travels at a speed of 50 km/hr. If the truck can travel 19.5 km/L of diesel at 50 km/hr, how far can the truck travel on 10 L of diesel at a speed of 70 km/hr?
    (a) 130 km (b) 140 km
    (c) 150 km (d) 175 km
12. X and Y are two regular polygons with sides in the ratio 1 : 2. If their exterior angles are in the ratio 2 : 1, then the number of sides in the polygon X are?
13. Navjivan Express from Ahmedabad to Chennai leaves Ahmedabad at 6.30 a.m. and travels at 50kmph towards Baroda situated 100 km away. At 7.00 a.m. Howrah-Ahmedabad Express leaves Baroda towards Ahmedabad and travels at 40 kmph. At 7.30 a.m. Mr Shah, the traffic controller at Baroda realizes that both the trains are running on the same track. How much time does he have to avert a head-on collision between the two trains?
    (a) 15 min (b) 20 min
    (c) 25 min (d) 30 min
14. Aman Bhaiya has 100 notes in his pocket. All the notes are either of ₹10, ₹50 or ₹100 each. He notices that he has a total of ₹5620 in his pocket. If he has at least 10 notes of each value, then the maximum possible number of 100 rupee notes with him are?
15. A man bought 4 oranges and 6 apples from the market. The average price per fruit was ₹28. The price of each orange was the same, while the price of each apple was also the same. If the price of each orange was at most double the price of each apple, but at least equal to the price of each apple, how many integral values of cost are possible for a total purchase of 2 oranges and 6 apples?

Directions for Questions 16 to 18 On the basis of the information given below:

Consider three circular parks of equal size with centers at A_1, A_2 and A_3 respectively. The parks touch each other at the edge as shown in the figure (not drawn to scale). There are three paths formed by the triangles $A_1A_2A_3$, $B_1B_2B_3$ and $C_1C_2C_3$, as shown. Three sprinters A, B and C begin running from points A_1, B_2 and C_1 respectively. Each sprinter traverses her triangular path clockwise and returns to her starting point.

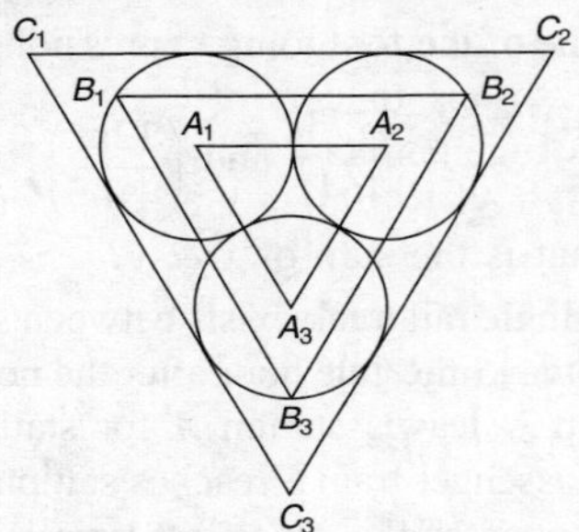

16. Let the radius of each circular park be r, and the distances to be traversed by the sprinters A, B and C be a, b and c, respectively. Which of the following is true?
    (a) $b - a = c - b = 3\sqrt{3}\,r$
    (b) $b - a = c - b = \sqrt{3}\,r$
    (c) $b = (a + c)/2 = 2(1 + \sqrt{3})\,r$
    (d) $c = 2b - a = (2 + \sqrt{3})\,r$
17. Sprinter A traverses distances A_1A_2, A_2A_3, and A_3A_1 at average speeds of 20, 30 and 15, respectively. B traverses her entire path at a uniform speed of $20 + 10\sqrt{3}$. C traverses distances C_1C_2, C_2C_3, and C_3C_1 at average speeds of $(40/3)(\sqrt{3} + 1)$, $(40/3)(\sqrt{3} + 1)$, and 120, respectively. All speeds are in the same unit. Where would B and C respectively be, when A finishes her sprint?
    (a) B_1, C_1
    (b) B_3, C_3
    (c) B_2, C_3
    (d) B_1, Somewhere between C_3 and C_1
18. Sprinters A, B and C traverse their respective paths at uniform speeds of u, v and w respectively. It is known that $u^2 : v^2 : w^2$ is equal to Area A : Area B : Area C, where Area A, Area B and Area C are the areas of

triangles $A_1A_2A_3$, $B_1B_2B_3$, and $C_1C_2C_3$, respectively. Where would A and C be when B reaches point B_3?
(a) A_2, C_3
(b) A_3, C_3
(c) A_2, C_2
(d) Somewhere between A_2 and A_3, Somewhere between C_3 and C_1.

19. If the roots of the equation $x^3 - ax^2 + bx - c = 0$ are three consecutive integers, then what is the smallest possible value of b?
(a) $-1/\sqrt{3}$ (b) -1
(c) 0 (d) 1

20. At the US Open tennis tournament, the number of spectators in the stadium on a given day was such that if divided by 8, 9, 11 or 12, the number left a remainder of 5 each time. The number was also divisible by 13. If the capacity of the stadium is less than 6000, What will be the maximum number of teams of 16 that can be formed amongst the spectators?

21. A, B and C working together can do a job in more than 8 days. A and C working together require less than 12.5 days to complete the job. They started working together and worked together for 7 days following which B alone finished the remaining job (after A and C left) in 4 days. Which of the following cannot be the value for the number of days B would require to do the job?
(i) 24 (ii) 30
(iii) 32 (iv) 28
(a) All of these (b) Only (i)
(c) Only (i) and (iii) (d) (i), (ii) and (iii)

22. Raju has 128 boxes with him. He can put a minimum of 120 oranges and a maximum of 144 in a box. Then the least number of boxes which will have the same number of oranges is:
(a) 5 (b) 103
(c) 3 (d) 6

THE CAT EXPERIENCE 6

1. Let X be a four-digit positive integer such that the unit digit of X is prime and the product of all digits of X is also prime. How many such integers are possible?
(a) 4 (b) 8
(b) 12 (d) 24

2. Three pipes, Pipe A, Pipe B, and Pipe C, can individually fill a water tank. The rates at which they fill the tank follow a harmonic progression. Pipe C takes three times as long as Pipe A to fill the tank completely. If Pipe A is opened for 6 hours and Pipe B is left running for 7 hours, Pipe C needs to operate for 18 hours to fill the remaining water in the tank. How many hours would Pipe B take to fill the tank by itself.

Directions for Questions 3 and 4: These questions are based on the situation given below.

Rajiv reaches city B from city A in 4 hours, driving at the speed of 35 km per hour for the first 2 hours and at 45 km per hour for the next two hours. Aditi follows the same route, but drives at three different speeds 30, 40 and 50 km per hour, covering an equal distance in each speed segment. The two cars are similar with petrol consumption characteristics (km per liter) shown in the figure below.

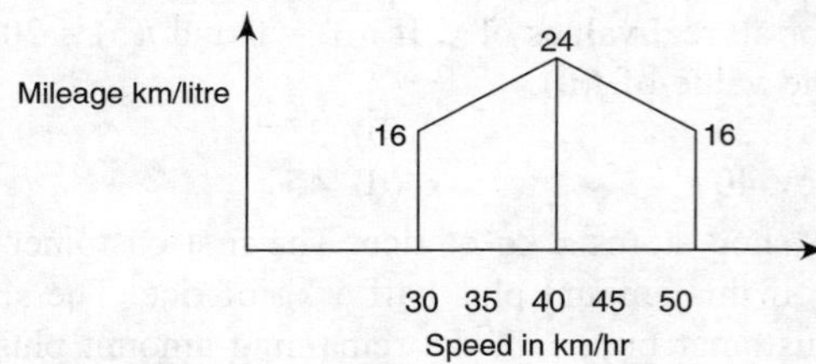

3. The amount of petrol consumed by Aditi for the journey is
(a) 8.3 liters (b) 8.6 liters
(c) 8.9 liters (d) 9.2 liters

4. Zoheb would like to drive Aditi's car over the same route from A to B and minimize the petrol consumption for the trip. The amount of petrol required by him is
(a) 6.67 liters (b) 7 liters
(c) 6.33 liters (d) None of these

5. Shyam visited Ram on vacation. In the mornings, they both would go for yoga. In the evenings they would play tennis. To have more fun, they indulge, only in one activity per day, i.e., either they went for yoga or played tennis each day. There were days when they were lazy and stayed home all day long. There were 24 mornings when they did nothing, 14 evenings when they stayed at home, and a total of 22 days when they did yoga or played tennis. For how many days did Shyam stay with Ram?
(a) 32 (b) 24
(c) 30 (d) None of these

6. Seven close friends Ritesh, Ajit, Arun, Rajiv, Bharat, Deepak and Hemendra took an exam where the marks were in integers between 0 and 50 (both inclusive). Bharat, Ritesh and Ajit were the toppers, Arun ranked fourth while Hemendra got the least marks. The average marks for all seven was 35, while exactly three of them got more than 28 marks. If no two students got the same marks, then what is the difference between the minimum marks that Arun could score and the minimum marks that Hemendra could score?

7. a, b, c, d are natural numbers such that $a \times b + a \times c + a \times d = 19$ and $d \times a + d \times b + d \times c = 51$, then the maximum possible value of $a \times b \times c \times d$ is equal to?

8. If $(2+3\sqrt{3})$ is a root of $bx^2 + cx + d = 0$ and $(3+2\sqrt{2})$ is a root of $by^2 + ey + f = 0$, then find the value of $\frac{d}{e} - \frac{c-2e}{f}$

(a) $-\frac{23}{6}$ (b) $\frac{23}{6}$
(c) $\frac{25}{6}$ (d) $-\frac{25}{6}$

9. $h(x)$ is a quadratic polynomial, such that $h(x) \geq 0$, for all real values of x. If $f(3) = 0$ and $f(5) = 20$, find the value of $f(0)$.

(a) 20 (b) 35
(c) 40 (d) 45

10. A shop stores x kg of rice. The first customer buys half this amount plus half a kg of rice. The second customer buys half the remaining amount plus half a kg of rice. Then the third customer buys half the remaining amount plus half a kg of rice. Thereafter, no rice is left in the shop. Which of the following best describes the value of x?

(a) $2 \leq x \leq 6$ (b) $5 \leq x \leq 8$
(c) $9 \leq x \leq 12$ (d) $11 \leq x \leq 14$

Directions for Questions 11 and 12: Let $f(x) = ax^2 + bx + c$, where a, b and c are certain constants and $a \neq 0$. It is known that $f(5) = -3\ f(2)$ and that 3 is a root of $f(x) = 0$.

11. What is the other root of $f(x) = 0$?

(a) -7 (b) -4
(c) 2 (d) 6

12. What is the value of $a + b + c$?

(a) 9 (b) 14
(c) 13 (d) Cannot be determined

13. Let S_1 be a square of side a. Another square S_2 is formed by joining the mid-points of the sides of S_1. The same process is applied to S_2 to form yet another square S_3, and so on. If $A_1, A_2, A_3, \ldots$ be the areas and $P_1, P_2, P_3, \ldots$ be the perimeters of $S_1, S_2, S_3, \ldots$, respectively, then the ratio $\frac{P_1 + P_2 + P_3 + \ldots}{A_1 + A_2 + A_3 + \ldots}$ equals

(a) $\frac{2(1+\sqrt{2})}{a}$ (b) $\frac{2(2-\sqrt{2})}{a}$
(c) $\frac{2(2+\sqrt{2})}{a}$ (d) $\frac{2(1+2\sqrt{2})}{a}$

14. A vessel has 50 liters of milk. 5 liters are withdrawn and replaced with water. This process of replacing 5 liters of the liquid in the container with water is repeated multiple times. What is the minimum number of times the process should be repeated for the quantity of water to be equal to or greater than twice the quantity of milk in the mixture?

15. In a bank, the account numbers are all eight-digit numbers, and they all start with the digit 2. So, an account number can be represented as $2x_1x_2x_3x_4x_5x_6x_7$. An account number is considered to be a 'magic' number if $x_1x_2x_3$ is exactly the same as $x_4x_5x_6$ or $x_5x_6x_7$ or both, x_i can take values from 0 to 9, but 2 followed by seven 0s is not a valid account number. What is the maximum possible number of customers having a 'magic' account number?

(a) 9989 (b) 19980
(c) 19989 (d) 19999

16. A piece of paper is in the shape of a right-angled triangle and is cut along a line that is parallel to the hypotenuse, leaving a smaller triangle. There was 35% reduction in the length of the hypotenuse of the triangle. If the area of the original triangle was 34 square inches before the cut, what is the area (in square inches) of the smaller triangle?

(a) 16.665 (b) 16.565
(c) 15.465 (d) 14.365

17. The triangle ABC has medians AF, BD and CE and these medians intersect at a point O inside the triangle. A line joining DE is drawn and it cuts the median AF at point X. If the area of the triangle ABC = 216, then the area of triangle OXE is:

18. For all non-negative integers x and y, $f(x, y)$ is defined as below.

$f(0, y) = y + 1$
$f(x + 1, 0) = f(x, 1)$
$f(x + 1, y + 1) = f(x, f(x + 1, y))$

Then what is the value of $f(1, 2)$?

(a) 2 (b) 4
(c) 3 (d) Cannot be determined

19. Let p and q be the roots of the quadratic equation $x^2 - (a - 2)x - (a + 1) = 0$. What is the minimum possible value of $p^2 + q^2$?

(a) 0 (b) 3
(c) 4 (d) 5

20. Both the series $a_1, a_2, a_3, \ldots$ and $b_1, b_2, b_3, \ldots$ are arithmetic progressions with common differences as prime numbers. If $a_7 = b_{11}$ and $a_{29} = b_{25}$, and if $b_3 = 10$, find the value of a_{15}.

21. If all letters of the word "CHCJL" be arranged in an English dictionary, what will be the 50th word?

(a) HCCLJ (b) LCCHJ
(c) LCCJH (d) JHCLC

22. The Investments of three friends, Anmol, Priya, and Rohan, are initially in the ratio 3 : 4 : 8, respectively. They have decided to reinvest all the returns they get on an investment. In the first year, they get a return of 15%, 10%, and 30%, respectively. In the second year, Anmol and Rohan get return of 35% and 20%, respectively, and Priya's investment becomes equal to the average investment of the three friends (investment being referred to here, being the amounts on which they earned interest during the second year). What is the approximate percentage investment return (closest integral percentage value) Priya receives in the second year?

(a) 45% (b) 42%
(c) 38% (d) 47%

THE CAT EXPERIENCE 7

1. A number written in base 3 is 10010010010010010100. What will be the value of this number in base 27?
(a) 999999 (b) 900000
(c) 989999 (d) 888888

2. How many times will the digit 6 be used when we write all the six digit numbers?
(a) 5,50,000 (b) 5,00,000
(c) 4,50,000 (d) 4,00,000

3. The largest real value of m, such that $|x + 3| + |x - m| = 6$ has infinite solutions is:

4. Let A and B be the roots of the equation $4x^2 - 24x + m = 0$. If (A + B) and A × B are the roots of the equation $x^2 + nx + n = 0$, then find the value of $7 \times (m - n)$.

5. If a certain amount of money is divided amongst n people each person receives ₹252. However, if 2 people receive ₹604 each, and the remaining money is distributed equally amongst the remaining people each of them receive ₹220 or less. The maximum possible value of n is:

6. For the above question, what is the minimum possible value of n, if the average amount of money given to the remaining $(n - 2)$ people is an integer (in terms of rupees)?

7. If $f(x) = \log\left(\frac{1+x}{1-x}\right)$, then $f(x) + f(y)$ is:
(a) $f(x + y)$ (b) $f\{(x + y)/(1 + xy)\}$
(c) $(x + y)f\{1/(1 + xy)\}$ (d) $f(x) + f(y)/(1 + xy)$

8. If both a and b belong to the set {1, 2, 3, 4}, then the number of equations of the form $ax^2 + bx + 1 = 0$ having real roots is
(a) 10 (b) 7
(c) 6 (d) 12

9. Suppose, the seed of any positive integer n is defined as follows:
Seed (n) $= n$, if $n < 10$
$=$ seed ($s(n)$), otherwise,
Where $s(n)$ indicates the sum of digits of n. For example, seed (7) = 7, seed (248) = seed (2 + 4 + 8) = seed (14) = seed (1 + 4) = seed (5) = 5 etc. How many positive integers n, such that $n < 500$, will have seed (n) = 9?
(a) 39 (b) 72
(c) 81 (d) 55

10. Find the sum of $\sqrt{1+\frac{1}{1^2}+\frac{1}{2^2}} + \sqrt{1+\frac{1}{2^2}+\frac{1}{3^2}} + \ldots\ldots + \sqrt{1+\frac{1}{2007^2}+\frac{1}{2008^2}}$
(a) $2008 - \frac{1}{2008}$ (b) $2007 - \frac{1}{2007}$
(c) $2007 - \frac{1}{2008}$ (d) $2008 - \frac{1}{2007}$

11. A shop sells two kinds of rolls—egg roll and mutton roll. Onion, tomato, carrot, chilli sauce and tomato sauce are the additional ingredients. You can have any combination of additional ingredients, or have standard rolls without any additional ingredients subject to the following constraints:
(i) You can have tomato sauce if you have an egg roll, but not if you have a mutton roll.
(ii) If you have onion or tomato or both you can have chilli sauce, but not otherwise.
How many different rolls can be ordered according to these rules?
(a) 21 (b) 33
(c) 40 (d) 42

12. In the figure (not drawn to scale) given below, P is a point on AB such that $AP : PB = 4 : 3$. PQ is parallel to AC and QD is parallel to CP. In ΔARC, $\angle ARC = 90^\circ$, and in ΔPQS, $\angle PSQ = 90^\circ$. The length of QS is 6 cm. What is the ratio of $AP : PD$?

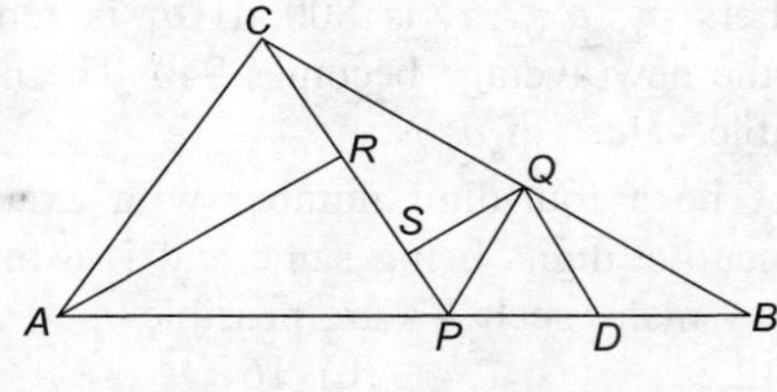

(a) 10 : 3 (b) 2 : 1
(c) 7 : 3 (d) 8 : 3

13. A car is being driven, in a straight line and at a uniform speed, towards the base of a vertical tower. The top of the tower is observed from the car and, in the process, it takes 10 min for the angle of elevation to change from 45° to 60°. After how much more time will this car reach the base of the tower?
(a) $5(\sqrt{3}+1)$ (b) $6(\sqrt{3}+\sqrt{2})$
(c) $7(\sqrt{3}-1)$ (d) $8(\sqrt{3}-2)$

14. In a survey of political preferences, 78% of those asked were in favour of at least one of the proposals: I, II and III. 50% of those asked favoured proposal I, 30% favoured proposal II and 20% favoured proposal III. If 5% of those asked favoured all three of the

proposals, what percentage of those asked favoured more than one of the three proposals?
(a) 10 (b) 12
(c) 17 (d) 22

15. In an isosceles triangle ABC, angle A is 120 degrees. Perpendiculars AD and BE are drawn from A to BC and from B to AC respectively. The ratio of AD : BE is equal to:
(a) $\frac{1}{\sqrt{3}}$ (b) $\frac{2}{\sqrt{3}}$
(c) $\sqrt{3}:1$ (d) $\sqrt{3}:2$

16. A college has raised 75% of the amount it needs for a new building by receiving an average donation of ₹600 from the people already solicited. The people already solicited represent 60% of the people the college will ask for donations. If the college is to raise exactly the amount needed for the new building, what should be the average donation from the remaining people to be solicited?
(a) ₹300 (b) ₹250
(c) ₹400 (d) ₹500

17. A shipping clerk has five boxes of different but unknown weights each weighing less than 100 kg. The clerk weighs the boxes in pairs. The weights obtained are 110, 112, 113, 114, 115, 116, 117, 118, 120 and 121 kg. What is the weight of the heaviest box?
(a) 60 kg (b) 62 kg
(c) 64 kg (d) Cannot be determined

18. The average of a non-decreasing sequence of n numbers $a_1, a_2, \ldots a_n$ is 800. If a_1 is replaced by $8a_1$, the new average becomes 940. The number of possible values of a_1 is:

19. Let X be a four-digit number with exactly three consecutive digits being same and is a multiple of 9. How many such X's are possible?
(a) 12 (b) 16
(c) 19 (d) 20

20. M men working on a project finish 30% of the work by working 12 hours per day for 7 days. The remaining job is done by 15 less men working 8 hours a day for 28 days. What is the value of M?
(a) 120 (b) 105
(c) 150 (d) 60

21. The minor angle between the minutes and hour hand of a grandfather clock was observed at 6:36 PM. The minimum time in which this angle would double would be:
(a) 24/11 (b) 36/11
(c) 48/11 (d) 60/11

22. Let h_n and j_n be two sequences such that $hn = 17 + 7(n - 1)$ and $jn = 23 + 11(n - 1)$, for all natural numbers n. The number of common terms less than 1000 in the two sequences would be:

THE CAT EXPERIENCE 8

1. For some real numbers a and b, the system of equations $x + y = 12$ and $(b^2 - 18) + (a + 8)y = 36b$ has no solutions for x and y. Which of the following can be a possible value of '$a \times b$' or $a + b$?
(a) –20 (b) 51
(c) –51 (d) 60

2. In a tournament, there are n teams $T_1, T_2, \ldots, T_n$, with $n > 5$. Each team consists of k players, $k > 3$. The following pairs of teams have one player in common:
T_1 & T_2, T_2 & T_3, …, T_{n-1} & T_n, and T_n & T_1
No other pair of teams has any player in common. How many players are participating in the tournament, considering all the n teams together?
(a) $n(k - 2)$ (b) $k(n - 2)$
(c) $(n - 1)(k - 1)$ (d) $n(k - 1)$

3. In a thrown away jar of cookies, there were 3 bacteria found on 15th January. Every subsequent day the number of bacteria were measured and were found to be 2 more than double the previous day's value on each day. On which date will the number of bacteria in the jar cross 5 lacs?
(a) 31st January (b) 1st February
(c) 2nd February (d) 30th January

4. Let us say that a natural number x, is such that $(x!)!$ divides $(50000!)$ If $x_1, x_2, \ldots x_n$ represent the set of possible values of x, then what is the number of even factors of the number $x_1 \times x_2 \times \ldots \times x_n$.

5. Let $x = 1640$, $y = 1728$ and $z = 448$. How many natural numbers are there that divide at least one amongst x, y, z?
(a) 47 (b) 48
(c) 49 (d) 50

6. Amit can do a job in 30 days, working alone. Bisheshwar can do the same job at a rate that is 3 times as fast as Amit and 6 times as fast as Charulata. They start the work with Amit and Bisheshwar working on day 1, Bisheshwar and Charulata working on day 2, Amit and Charulata working on day 3, Charulata working alone on day 4, Amit alone on day 5 and Bisheshwar alone on day 6. If they repeat this 6 day cycle to do a job that is thrice as large as the original job, for how many days would Charulata have worked in completing the job?

7. Individually Sameer Contractor, Sameer Deshpande and Sameer Shelke take times in the ratio 5 : 7 : 8 to complete any job. One particular day, the BCCI offered them a job that they could do together working 12 hours per day in 8 days. Sameer Deshpande and Sameer Shelke worked together at a leisurely pace of 7 hours per day and worked for 12 days. They then left the job half done and the BCCI had to go back

to Sameer Contractor to complete the contract, who finished it at a frenetic pace of 12 hours work per day. If Sameer (Contractor i.e.) only charges for his job done in half hour increments (charging for the next half hour even if he has only done a fraction of the work for that half hour), for how many hours work would he raise his personal bill?

(a) 88 (b) 96.5
(c) 104.5 (d) 112.5

8. Consider four digit numbers for which the first two digits are equal and the last two digits are also equal. How many such numbers are perfect squares?

(a) 4 (b) 0
(c) 1 (d) 3

9. If x is a positive real number, such that $x^8 + \left(\frac{1}{x}\right)^8 = 527$, find the value of $x^9 + \left(\frac{1}{x}\right)^9$.

(a) $424\sqrt{7}$ (b) $440\sqrt{7}$
(c) $448\sqrt{7}$ (d) $436\sqrt{7}$

10. A boy starts adding consecutive natural numbers starting with one. After reaching a total of 1000, he realises that he has made the mistake of double counting one number. Find the number double counted.

(a) 44 (b) 45
(c) 10 (d) 12

11. Ravi invested in three schemes paying out simple interest. He noticed that the amount of interest earned in the first scheme @6% Simple interest in 6 years, is the same as the amount of interest earned in the second scheme 15% for 4 years, which is also the same as the amount of interest earned @9% simple interest for 2 years. Of his total investment of 172836, what was the amount he invested in the scheme bearing 9% simple interest?

(a) 80040 (b) 88080
(c) 92060 (d) 96020

12. Amar starts from A towards B, while Bimal starts at the same time from B towards A. After crossing each other, they take 28 and 7 hours respectively to reach their destinations. If Bimal is traveling at a speed of 32 kmph, then the total distance between A and B is:

13. The sum of all the distinct numbers that can be formed by rearranging the digits of the number 13571, including the number itself is:

(a) 2244444 (b) 2255554
(c) 2266644 (d) 2266664

14. Sam has forgotten his friend's seven-digit telephone number. He remembers the following: the first three digits are either 635 or 674, the number is odd, and the number 9 appears once. If Sam were to use a trial and error process to reach his friend, what is the minimum number of trials he has to make before he can be certain to succeed?

(a) 10,000 (b) 2,430
(c) 3,402 (d) 3,006

15. Two ships A and B are crossing the ocean. They cross each other at point X while traveling at an angle of 60 degrees with respect to each other's path. After 3 hours, it is observed that Ship A is at point M, while ship B is at point N, such that the angle MNX is a right angle. If the distance between the ships at this point of time is observed as $30\sqrt{3}$, the speed of the slower ship is?

16. After the division of a number successively by 3, 4 and 7, the remainders obtained are 2, 1 and 4 respectively. What will be the remainder if 84 divides the number?

(a) 80 (b) 76
(c) 41 (d) 53

17. A quadratic function $f(x)$ attains a maximum of 3 at $x = 1$. The value of the function at $x = 0$ is 1. What is the value of $f(x)$ at $x = 10$?

(a) –119 (b) –159
(c) –110 (d) –180

18. What is the sum of 'n' terms in the series $\log m + \log\left(\frac{m^2}{n}\right) + \log\left(\frac{m^3}{n^2}\right) + \log\left(\frac{m^4}{n^3}\right) + \cdots$?

(a) $\log\left[\frac{n^{n-1}}{m^{n+1}}\right]^{n/2}$ (b) $\log\left[\frac{m^m}{n^n}\right]^{n/2}$
(c) $\log\left[\frac{m^{1-n}}{n^{1-m}}\right]^{n/2}$ (d) $\log\left[\frac{m^{n+1}}{n^{n-1}}\right]^{\frac{n}{2}}$

19. Raju has 128 boxes with him. He can put a minimum of 120 oranges and a maximum of 144 in a box. Then the least number of boxes which will have the same number of oranges is:

(a) 5 (b) 103
(c) 3 (d) 6

20. For a scholarship, at the most n candidates out of $2n + 1$ can be selected. If the number of different ways of selection of at least one candidate is 63, the maximum number of candidates that can be selected for the scholarship is

(a) 3 (b) 4
(c) 6 (d) 5

21. Amartya Banerjee earns \$5000 per month, but having a very large family he actually ends up spending \$5200 per month for the first 8 months of the year. At the start of the year he had an initial target of saving an average of \$550 per month for the year. He wants to do some serious cost cutting measures for the last 4 months of the year and estimates, that he would be able to bring down his average expenditure to \$4100 per month. What is the percentage increase (nearest integer) in income he should plan for, in the remaining months in order to achieve his target?

(a) 23% (b) 21%
(c) 18% (d) 17%

22. The lengths of the four sides of a quadrilateral are all integral. Three sides of the quadrilateral are 7, 3 and 2 respectively. What is the sum of all possible lengths of the fourth side?

THE CAT EXPERIENCE 9

1. There are 7 people in a class. If Amit joins the class, the average age of the class goes down by $2n$ years. If Ravi joins the class, the average age of the class goes up by n years. If Ravi is 12 years older than Amit, then find the value of n.

2. A fruit seller sells Mangoes, Oranges and Apples. Of the total fruit he has in his shop one particular morning, it is seen that 30% of the fruit consists of mangoes, while the remaining fruit is a mix of oranges and apples. During the day, he sells 40% of the mangoes, 80 oranges and 30% of the Apples. Thus, he sells 40% of the total number of fruits in his shop. What is the lowest possible number of fruits he had in his shop in the morning (if he only sells an integer number of fruits to each customer)?

3. For the above question, what is the second highest possible value for the number of oranges he had in his shop in the morning?

4. The average of all 4-digit terms of the series: 15, 34, 53.... is

5. In a regular polygon, each of the interior angles exceeds, each exterior angle by 108. The difference between the number of diagonals and sides of the polygon is:

6. $ABCD$ is a rhombus with the diagonals AC and BD intersecting at the origin on the $x - y$ plane. The equation of the straight line AD is $x + y = 1$. What is the equation of BC?

(a) $x+y=-1$ (b) $x-y=-1$
(c) $x+y=1$ (d) None of these

7. a and b are two real numbers such that $2a + 3b = 60$. The maximum possible value of the product $a \times b$ is:

8. Let $a_n = 30 + 7n$ and $b_n = 50 + 4n$ be two sequences with $n \leq 200$. The sum of all the terms common to both the sequences is:

9. Euclid has a triangle in mind. Its longest side has length 20 and another of its sides has length 10. Its area is 80. What is the exact length of its third side?

(a) $\sqrt{260}$ (b) $\sqrt{250}$
(c) $\sqrt{240}$ (d) $\sqrt{270}$

10. Suppose $f(a, b)$ is a real valued function such that $f(3a + 4b, 5a - 3b) = 29a$. If the value $f(a, 3a) = 60$, find the value of a.

11. Let S_n be the sum of the series 5, 17, 36, 62,.... till 60 terms. The value of $\frac{1}{40} \times S_n$ is?

(a) 6327 (b) 6427
(c) 6527 (d) 6627

12. A rich merchant had collected many gold coins. He did not want anybody to know about them. One day, his wife asked, "How many gold coins do we have?" After pausing a moment, he replied, "Well! If I divide the coins into two unequal numbers, then 48 times the difference between the two numbers equals the difference between the squares of the two numbers." The wife looked puzzled. Can you help the merchant's wife by finding out how many coins the merchant has?

(a) 96 (b) 53
(c) 43 (d) None of these

13. The length of the common chord of two circles of radii 15 cm and 20 cm, whose centres are 25 cm apart, is

(a) 24 cm (b) 25 cm
(c) 15 cm (d) 20 cm

14. A baker sells 10 litres of cupcake mixture at a bakery fair. The cupcake mixture are a mix of vanilla and chocolate, with content of chocolate being not more than that of vanilla. The cost of Only Vanilla Cupcake mixture per litre is ₹8 more than that of the chocolate mixture. If the baker sells the entire cupcake mixture for a total of ₹264 and makes a 10% profit, what is the highest possible cost, in ₹per litre, to make chocolate cupcake mixture?

15. Two types of exotic fruits, mangoes and kiwis, are mixed to create a fruit salad. The fruit salad is sold for ₹50 per kg. The vendor makes a 20% profit when mangoes and kiwis are mixed in a ratio of 5 : 3, and a 10% profit when the ratio is 3 : 5. What is the ratio of the cost prices per kg of mangoes to kiwis?

(a) 27 : 19 (b) 19 : 27
(c) 23 : 29 (d) 29 : 23

16. There are three cities: A, B and C. Each of these cities is connected with the other two cities by at least one direct road. If a traveller wants to go from one city (origin) to another city (destination), she can do so either by traversing a road connecting the two cities directly, or by traversing two roads, the first connecting the origin to the third city and the second connecting the third city to the destination. In all there are 33 routes from A to B (including those via C). Similarly, there are 23 routes from B to C (including those via A). How many roads are there from A to C directly?

(a) 6 (b) 3
(c) 5 (d) 10

17. If there are 10 positive real numbers $n_1 < n_2 < n_3 \ldots < n_{10}$. How many triplets of these numbers (n_1, n_2, n_3), (n_2, n_3, n_4), ... can be generated such that in each triplet the first number is always less than the second number, and the second number is always less than the third number?

(a) 45 (b) 90
(c) 120 (d) 180

18. 'm' is the largest positive integer such that $n > m$. Also, it is known that $n^3 - 7n^2 + 11n - 5$ is positive. Then, the largest possible value for m is:

(a) 4 (b) 5
(c) 8 (d) None of these

19. The number of non-negative real roots of $2^x - x - 1 = 0$ equals

(a) 0 (b) 1
(c) 2 (d) 3

20. If n is such that $36 < n < 72$, then

$x = \dfrac{n^2 + 2\sqrt{n}(n+4) + 16}{n + 4\sqrt{n} + 4}$ satisfies

(a) $20 < x < 54$ (b) $23 < x < 58$
(c) $25 < x < 64$ (d) $28 < x < 60$

21. Every 10 years the Indian government counts all the people living in the country. Suppose that the director of the census has reported the following data on two neighbouring villages—ChotaHazri and MotaHazri. ChotaHazri has 4,522 fewer males than MotaHazri. MotaHazri has 4,020 more females than males. ChotaHazri has twice as many females as males. ChotaHazri has 2,910 fewer females than MotaHazri. What is the total number of males in ChotaHazri?

(a) 11264 (b) 14174
(c) 5632 (d) 10154

22. In a chess tournament at the ancient Olympic Games of Reposia, it was found that the number of European participants was twice the number of non-European participants. In a round robin format, each player played every other player exactly once. The tournament rules were such that no match ended in a draw – any conventional draws in chess were resolved in favour of the player who had used up the lower time. While analysing the results of the tournament, K. Gopal, the tournament referee observed that the number of matches won by the non-European players was equal to the number of matches won by the European players. Which of the following can be the total number of matches in which a European player defeated a non-European player?

(a) 57 (b) 58
(c) 59 (d) 60

THE CAT EXPERIENCE 10

1. The number of distinct integer values satisfying $\dfrac{5 - \log_3 n}{3 - \log_5 n} < 0$, is:

2. If $b = 8 \times \dfrac{m}{n} + 12 \times \dfrac{n}{m}$, where m and n are non-zero real numbers, then b cannot take the value:

(a) –20 (b) 20
(c) –16 (d) –24

3. An intelligence agency forms a code of two distinct digits selected from 0, 1, 2, ... 9, such that the first digit of the code is not zero. The code, handwritten on a slip, can however potentially create confusion when read upside down—for example, the code 91 may appear as 16. How many codes are there for which no such confusion can arise?

(a) 80 (b) 78
(c) 71 (d) 69

4. Let D be a recurring decimal of the form, $D = 0.a_1\ a_2\ a_1\ a_2\ a_1\ a_2$ ...., where digits a_1 and a_2 lie between 0 and 9. Further, at most one of them is zero. Then which of the following numbers necessarily produces an integer, when multiplied by D.

(a) 18 (b) 108
(c) 198 (d) 288

5. Mukul and Kavita working together can finish a job in 12 days. If Mukul works at 75% of his capacity and Kavita works at 4/3rd her capacity, the job is still done on time. If A and B represent the number of days for Mukul and Kavita to do the job working alone, then find the value of (A + B).

6. Suppose for an arithmetic progression, the sum of the first n terms is given by $2n + 3n^2$. The second lowest value of n for which the nth term of the progression is divisible by 7 is?

(a) 8 (b) 11
(c) 12 (d) 13

7. The number of ordered pairs of integral solutions (m, n) which satisfy the equation $m \times n - 6(m + n) = 0$ is

(a) 5 (b) 10
(c) 14 (d) 9

8. In ΔDEF shown below, points A, B and C are taken on DE, DF and EF respectively such that $EC = AC$ and $CF = BC$. If $\angle D = 40^0$, then $\angle ACB$ =

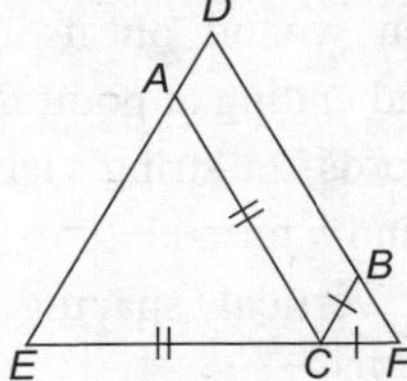

(a) 140° (b) 70°
(c) 100° (d) None of these

9. A rectangular pool of 20 m wide and 60 m long is surrounded by a walkway of uniform width. If the total area of the walkway is 516 m^2, how wide, in metres, is the walkway?
(a) 4.3 m (b) 3 m
(c) 5 m (d) 3.5 m

10. A train *X* departs from station *A* at 11.00 a.m. for station *B*, which is 180 km away. Another train *Y* departs from station *B* at the same time. Train *X* travels at an average speed of 70 km/hr and does not stop anywhere until it arrives at station *B*. Train *Y* travels at an average speed of 50 km/hr, but has to stop for 15 minutes at station *C*, which is 60 km away from station *B* enroute to station *A*. At what distance (to the closest kilometer) from *A* would they meet?
(a) 112 (b) 118
(c) 120 (d) 113

11. In the Crosswinds republic AOA committee elections, a total of four candidates filled in their nominations. It was observed that only 70% of the registered voters cast their vote and one of the candidates received 30% of the votes cast. The votes received by the other three candidates was in a Geometric progression. It was also observed that the number of votes gained by the winning candidate was 4 times the number of votes garnered by the candidate who came last. If the winning candidate got 22449 votes more than the candidate who came second, find the number of registered voters who did not vote?

12. Consider a circle with unit radius. There are seven adjacent sectors, *S*1, *S*2, *S*3, ..., *S*7, in the circle such that their total area is 1/8 of the area of the circle. Further, the area of the jth sector is twice that of the $(j-1)^{th}$ sector, for $j = 2, ..., 7$. What is the angle, in radians, subtended by the arc of *S*1 at the centre of the circle?
(a) π/508 (b) π/2040
(c) π/1016 (d) π/1524

Directions for Questions 13 and 14: Answer the questions on the basis of the information given below.

Consider a cylinder of height *h* cm and radius $r = 2/\pi$ cm as shown in the figure (not drawn to scale). A string of a certain length, when wound on its cylindrical surface, starting at point *A* and ending at point *B*, gives a maximum of *n* turns (in other words, the string's length is the minimum length required to wind *n* turns).

13. What is the vertical spacing between the two consecutive turns?

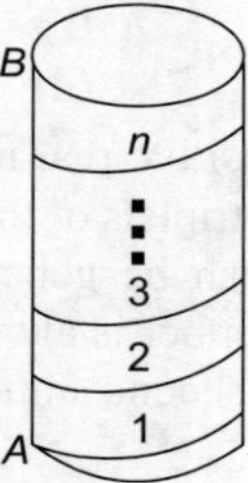

(a) $\frac{h}{n}$ cm (b) $\frac{h}{\sqrt{n}}$ cm
(c) $\frac{h}{n^2}$ cm (d) Cannot be determined

14. The same string, when wound on the exterior four walls of a cube of side *n* cm, starting at point *C* and ending at point *D*, can give exactly one turn (see figure, not drawn to scale). The length of the string is

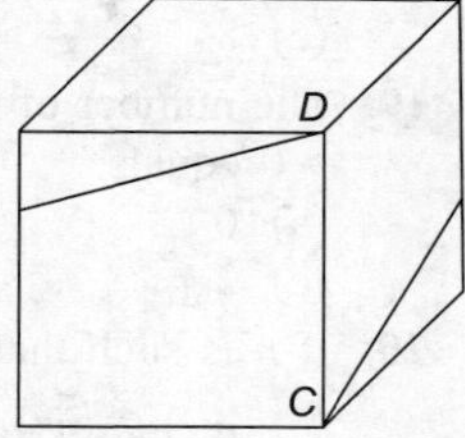

(a) $\sqrt{2}n$ cm (b) $\sqrt{17}n$ cm
(c) *n* cm (d) $\sqrt{13}n$ cm

15. A point *P* with coordinates (*x*, *y*) is such that the product of the coordinates *xy* = 144. How many possible points exist on the *X*–*Y* plane such that both *x* and *y* are integers?
(a) 15 (b) 16
(c) 30 (d) 32

Directions for Questions 16 and 17: The petrol consumption rate of a new model car 'Palto' depends on its speed and may be described by the graph below

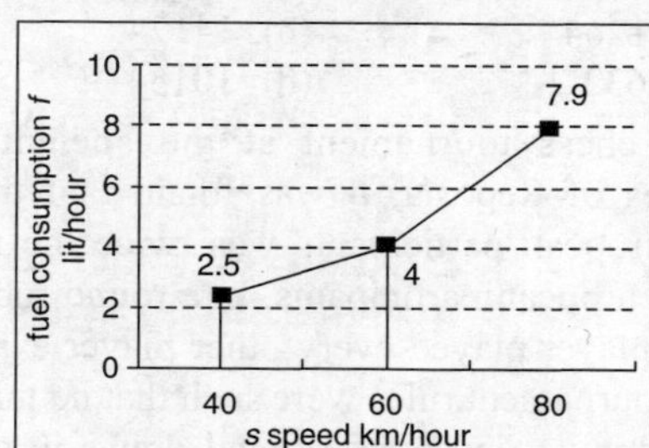

16. Manisha makes the 200 km trip from Mumbai in Pune at a steady speed of 60 km per hour. What is the amount of petrol consumed for the journey?
(a) 12.5 liters (b) 13.33 liters
(c) 16 liters (d) 19.75 liters

17. Manisha would like to minimize the fuel consumption for the trip by driving at the appropriate speed. How should she change the speed?
(a) Increase the speed
(b) Decrease the Speed

(c) Maintain the speed at 60 km/hour
(d) Cannot be determined

18. The number of acres harvested by Sachindra and Rishi per week are in the ratio 5 : 7. The total number of acres harvested by Sachindra in 3 weeks is a multiple of 7, while the total number of acres harvested by Rishi in 4 weeks is a multiple of 84. What is the second lowest possible value of the number of acres harvested by Sachindra every week?

19. The amount of work Gultu, Amit and Kanhaiya can do working alone in a day is in a harmonic progression. Kanhaiya takes thrice the time taken by Gultu to do the same work. If Gultu works for 3 days and Amit works for 11 days, Kanhaiya needs to work for 25.5 days to complete the work. How much time would Amit take to do the work, if he is working alone?

20. A man, starting from a point M in a park, takes exactly eight equal steps. Each step is in one of the four directions – East, West, North and South. What is the total number of ways in which the man ends up at point M after the eight steps?
(a) 4200 (b) 2520
(c) 4900 (d) 5120

21. In how many ways can 53 identical chocolates be distributed amongst three children– C_1, C_2 and C_3 – such that C_1 gets more chocolates than C_2, and C_2 gets more chocolates than C_3?
(a) 468 (b) 344
(c) 1404 (d) 234

22. Archana is standing in a queue just ahead of her friend Vandana. The ratio of the number of people ahead of them in the queue to those behind them in the queue is 4 : 7. If the total number of people in the queue is also multiple of 7, but is less than 300, what is the maximum possible value for the number of people ahead of them in the queue?

THE CAT EXPERIENCE 11

1. The average of 7 numbers is 17. Two numbers a and b are added to these numbers and it is observed that the average remains an odd number. What is the minimum value of $a^2 + b^2$?

2. The minimum value of the expression $\frac{x^2 - 10x + 29}{5 - x}$, if $x < 5$ is:
(a) 2 (b) –2
(c) 3.5 (d) 4

3. Bharat invests ₹33000 for 12 years in a compound interest scheme, that gives him 6% per annum compounded half yearly. Gaurav, invests some amount in the same scheme, but takes out the money after 11 years and reinvests it in another scheme giving him a 10% per annum rate of simple interest for 1 year. At the end of 12 years, both of them have the same amount. What is the amount invested by Gaurav?

4. The population of a township goes through an increase decrease cycle in successive years from 2018 to 2020 of x% and y%, both natural numbers and $x = y + 20$. The cycle is repeated in 2021 and 2022 and then again in 2023 and 2024. If it is observed that the population of the township has gone up over this 6 year period, what can be the maximum possible value of y?

5. The number of ordered pairs of integers (x, y) satisfying the equation $x^2 + 6x + 2y^2 = 4 + y^2$ is
(a) 12 (b) 8
(c) 10 (d) 14

6. If x, y and z are real numbers such that: $x + y + z = 5$ and $xy + yz + zx = 3$, what is the largest value that x can have?
(a) 5/3 (b) $\sqrt{19}$
(c) 13/3 (d) None of these

Directions for Questions 7 and 8: Answer the questions based on the following information. Each of the 11 letters $A, H, I, M, O, T, U, V, W, X$ and Z appears same when looked at in a mirror. They are called symmetric letters. Other letters in the alphabet are asymmetric letters.

7. How many four-letter computer passwords can be formed using only the symmetric letters (no repetition allowed)?
(a) 7,920 (b) 330
(c) 14,640 (d) 4,19,430

8. How many three-letter computer passwords can be formed (no repetition allowed) with at least one symmetric letter?
(a) 990 (b) 2,730
(c) 12,870 (d) 15,600

9. Based on the figure below, what is the value of x, if $y = 10$?

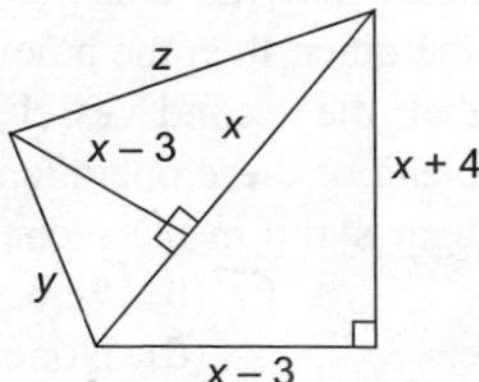

(a) 10 (b) 11
(c) 12 (d) None of these

10. Three runners A, B and C run a race, with runner A finishing 12 meters ahead of runner B and 18 meters ahead of runner C, while runner B finishes 8 meters ahead of runner C. Each runner travels the entire distance at a constant speed. What was the length of the race?

(a) 36 meters (b) 48 meters
(c) 60 meters (d) 72 meters

11. The owner of an art shop conducts his business in the following manner: every once in a while he raises his prices by X%, then a while later he reduces all the new prices by X%. After one such updown cycle, the price of a painting decreased by ₹441. After a second up-down cycle the painting was sold for ₹1,944.81. What was the original price of the painting?
(a) ₹2,756.25 (b) ₹2,256.25
(c) ₹2,500 (d) ₹2,000

12. Let n be any natural number such that it obeys $11^{n-1} < 7^{n+1}$. Then, the smallest integer value of x, such that the inequality $7^{n+1} < 5^{n+x}$, is satisfied for all possible values of n is:

13. Ten straight lines, no two of which are parallel and no three of which pass through any common point, are drawn on a plane. The total number of regions (including finite and infinite regions) into which the plane would be divided by the lines is
(a) 56 (b) 255
(c) 1024 (d) Not unique

14. Four horses are tethered at four corners of a square plot of side 14 m so that the adjacent horses can just reach one another. There is a small circular pond of area 20 m^2 at the centre. Find the ungrazed area.
(a) 22 m^2 (b) 42 m^2
(c) 84 m^2 (d) 168 m^2

15. There are two vessels of equal capacity, each filled to 60% of their capacity initially, the first vessel filled with sugar-syrup, while the second is filled with milk. A series of operations is performed on them as follows: Half the contents of the first vessel are poured into the second vessel, then half the contents in the second vessel are poured into the first vessel and finally half the contents of the first vessel are poured into the second vessel. During each of these operations, it is ensured that none of the vessels overflows (if there is an overflow happening when half the contents of one vessel are poured into the other, then the amount being poured is reduced so that, the second vessel is just filled to the brim). At the end of these operations, what is the ratio of milk to sugar syrup in the second vessel?
(a) 6 : 5 (b) 5 : 6
(c) 3 : 4 (d) None of these

16. Neeta has an initial investible capital of ₹50000. Out of this she invests ₹24000 @6.5% per annum in Scheme A, ₹12000 @7% per annum in Scheme B and the balance at x% in Scheme C (each rate being in simple interest). If her combined interest rate on her total investment is 6.2% per annum (simple interest), what would have been the gain/loss in interest income per annum if she had invested the entire amount in Scheme C.
(a) Gain 300 (b) Loss 600
(c) Gain 600 (d) Loss 300

17. Davji Shop sells samosas in boxes of different sizes. The samosas are priced at ₹2 per samosa up to 200 samosas. For every additional 20 samosas, the price of the whole lot goes down by 10 paise per samosa. What should be the maximum size of the box that would maximise the revenue?
(a) 240 (b) 300
(c) 400 (d) None of these

18. Neeraj has agreed to mow a lawn, which is a 20 m × 40 m rectangle. He mows it with 1 m wide strip. If Neeraj starts at one corner and mows around the lawn toward the centre, about how many times would he go round before he has mowed half the lawn?
(a) 2.5 (b) 3.5
(c) 3.8 (d) 4

19. In the figure (not drawn to scale) given below, if $AD = CD = BC$ and $\angle BCE = 96°$, how much is the value of DBC?

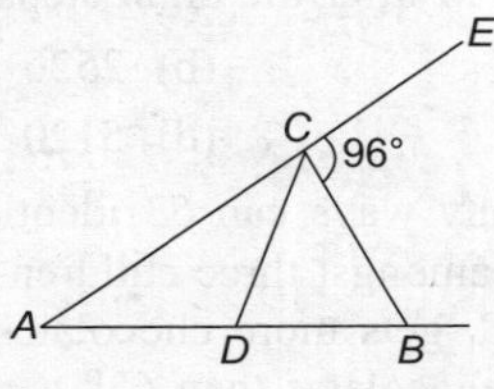

(a) 32° (b) 84°
(c) 64° (d) Cannot be determined

20. In the figure given below (not drawn to scale), A, B and C are three points on a circle with centre O. The chord BA is extended to a point T such that CT becomes a tangent to the circle at point C. If $\angle ATC = 30°$ and $\angle ACT = 50°$, then the angle $\angle BOA$ is

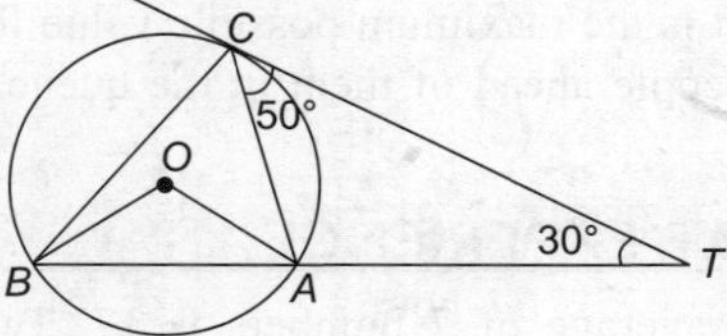

(a) 100° (b) 150°
(c) 80° (d) Cannot be determined

21. The number of real roots of the equation $\log_{2x}\left(\frac{2}{x}\right)(\log_2(x))^2 + (\log_2(x))^4 = 1$, for values of $x > 1$, is
(a) 0 (b) 1
(c) 2 (d) 27

22. The number of points at which the curve $y = x^6 + x^3 - 2$ cuts the x-axis is
(a) 1 (b) 2
(c) 4 (d) 6

ANSWER KEY

The CAT Experience 1

1. 333	2. 1 : 3	3. 70246.7	4. 36
5. (b)	6. (a)	7. (b)	8. (a)
9. 252	10. (d)	11. 107%	12. (d)
13. (d)	14. (a)	15. 15	16. 35
17. (b)	18. (a)	19. (b)	20. (b)
21. (b)	22. (d)		

The CAT Experience 2

1. (b)	2. (c)	3. 4	4. (b)
5. (b)	6. (c)	7. (a)	8. 35
9. 136000	10. (d)	11. 3	12. 26
13. 72 units	14. 16 years	15. 176	16. 1397
17. (c)	18. (c)	19. (c)	20. (a)
21. (b)	22. (d)		

The CAT Experience 3

1. (b)	2. 16	3. (c)	4. 354
5. 4	6. (c)	7. 1404	8. 36
9. 216	10. 46800	11. (a)	12. (c)
13. (c)	14. (c)	15. 1320	16. (c)
17. (b)	18. (b)	19. (b)	20. (a)
21. (b)	22. (a)		

The CAT Experience 4

1. 280	2. (b)	3. (c)	4. (b)
5. (a)	6. (a)	7. (b)	8. (d)
9. (b)	10. 8	11. 12	12. (b)
13. 0	14. 5	15. (c)	16. 101
17. (a)	18. 15	19. (d)	20. 16
21. (b)	22. (d)		

The CAT Experience 5

1. 1	2. (d)	3. 8020	4. (d)
5. 59	6. (d)	7. 120	8. (d)
9. (d)	10. (b)	11. (c)	12. 7
13. (b)	14. 46	15. 25	16. (a)
17. (c)	18. (c)	19. (b)	20. 247
21. (c)	22. (d)		

The CAT Experience 6

1. (a)	2. 31 hours	3. (c)	4. (a)
5. (c)	6. 9	7. 192	8. (d)
9. (d)	10. (b)	11. (b)	12. (d)
13. (c)	14. 11	15. (c)	16. (d)
17. 9	18. (b)	19. (d)	20. 154
21. (c)	22. (c)		

The CAT Experience 7

1. (a)	2. (a)	3. 3	4. 12
5. 24	6. 6	7. (b)	8. (b)
9. (d)	10. (a)	11. (d)	12. (c)
13. (a)	14. (c)	15. (a)	16. (a)
17. (b)	18. 39	19. (d)	20. (a)
21. (b)	22. 13		

The CAT Experience 8

1. (c)	2. (d)	3. (b)	4. 84
5. (a)	6. 20	7. (d)	8. (c)
9. (d)	10. (c)	11. (d)	12. 672
13. (c)	14. (c)	15. 10 kmph	16. (d)
17. (b)	18. (d)	19. (d)	20. (a)
21. (a)	22. 63		

The CAT Experience 9

1. 0.5	2. 350	3. 150	4. 5496.5
5. 25	6. (a)	7. 150	8. 13050
9. (a)	10. 4	11. (c)	12. (d)
13. (a)	14. 20	15. (b)	16. (a)
17. (c)	18. (b)	19. (c)	20. (d)
21. (c)	22. (d)		

The CAT Experience 10

1. 117	2. (c)	3. (b)	4. (c)
5. 49	6. (d)	7. (c)	8. (c)
9. (b)	10. (a)	11. 96210	12. (a)
13. (a)	14. (b)	15. (c)	16. (b)
17. (b)	18. 210	19. 34	20. (c)
21. (d)	22. 88		

The CAT Experience 11

1. 128	2. (d)	3. 31827	4. 35
5. (b)	6. (b)	7. (a)	8. (c)
9. (b)	10. (b)	11. (a)	12. 4
13. (a)	14. (a)	15. (a)	16. (b)
17. (b)	18. (c)	19. (c)	20. (a)
21. (b)	22. (b)		

SOLUTIONS AND SHORTCUTS

The CAT Experience 1

1. The value of $5^k + 6^k + 7^k + 8^k$ is 26 at $k = 1$ and 174 at $k = 2$. The largest common divisor of both these values is 2. Further the expression is Odd + Even + Odd + Even and hence would always be even. Thus, the value of X (the largest positive integer that divides $5^k + 6^k + 7^k + 8^k$) is 2. Next, we can see that $6^k + 5 \times 6^k + 6^{k+3} = 6^k + 5 \times 6^k + 216 \times 6^k = 222 \times 6^k$. This number will always be divisible by $222 \times 6 = 1332$, which will be the value of Y. Thus, $\frac{Y}{X^2} = \frac{1332}{4} = 333$.

2. Let the total salary of the women by $100x$, then the total salary of the factory is $800x$. The total salary of the men would be $700x$. If the number of women is $30n$, the number of men will be $70n$. The average salary of the women $= 100x/30n = 3.33x/n$; the average salary of the men $= 700x/70n = 10x/n$. The required ratio would be 3.33 : 10 = 1 : 3.

3. His loan amount of 300000 would end up becoming equal to $300000 \times 1.03 \times 1.03 = 318270$ at the end

of the first year. Thus, when he pays back 12270, the entire amount paid can be considered to be interest on the loan. Thus, his loan outstanding at the end of 1 year would be 318270 – 12270 = 306270. This amount would get charged interest at the rate of 8% per annum compounded half yearly. Thus, his loan outstanding at the end of 3 years would be equal to 306000 × 1.04 × 1.04 × 1.04 × 1.04 = ₹357976.7 (approx.). When he pays this entire amount, we can consider that ₹300000 of his payment went towards the principal and the remaining 57976.7 went towards interest. Thus, the total interest paid by Amitabh would be 57976.7 + 12270 = ₹70246.7. Hence, the correct answer is 70246.7.

4. If we assume that both of them take t hours to reach the crossing point, the situation can be represented by the figure shown. Solving for t, we get t = 12 and hence, the correct answer is 36.

R→ Kolkata t (18 – t) Chennai
24 t C ←

5. The first expression is $a \times (a^2 + b + 1) = 165$. Looking for factor pairs of 165, we get possibilities like 1 × 165; 3 × 55; 5 × 33 and 11 × 15, where the value of a can be any of 1, 3, 5, 11, 15, 33, 55 or 165. In each case, we get the value of b. When $a = 1, b = 163$ (rejected basis the second equation); $a = 3, b = 45$ (rejected basis the second equation); $a = 5, b = 7$ (fits the second equation). At this point, we also realise that at larger values of a, b would not be an integer any longer. Hence, we can freeze these values as the solution. The value of $3a + 2b$ = 3 × 5 + 2 × 7 = 29. Option (b) is correct.

6. The sum of the roots is $\frac{b}{2}$. Since, two roots are given as a and $-a$, their sum being 0, the third root should be $\frac{b}{2}$. Also, $a\times(-a)+a\times\frac{b}{2}+-a\times\frac{b}{2}=-a^2$ $=-20 \rightarrow a=\sqrt{20}=2\sqrt{5}$.

Thus, from the product of the roots

$-\frac{15}{2}=a\times-a\times\frac{b}{2}=-20\times\frac{b}{2}\rightarrow b=\frac{3}{4}$.

7. When X covers 30 kms and be 15 kms from the harbor, Y will be at a distance of $15\sqrt{3}$ kms from the destination (30-60-90 triangle). Y would have covered $(45-15\sqrt{3})$ kms. Hence, when X reaches the destination by covering an additional 15 km, Y will cover an additional $\frac{(45-15\sqrt{3})}{2}$ kms.

Thus, Y's distance from the harbor would be $15\sqrt{3}-\frac{(45-15\sqrt{3})}{2}=\frac{45\sqrt{3}-45}{2}$. Option (b) is correct.

8. 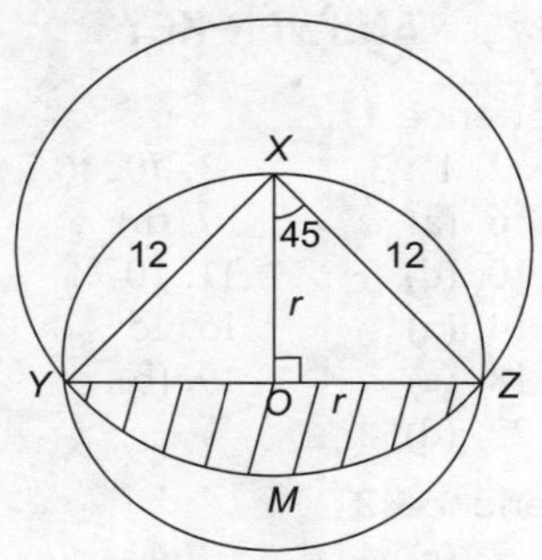

The value of $r = 6\sqrt{2}$. Hence, the required area = Area of circle with center X – [Area of semi-circle with center O – Area of shaded minor segment $YMZO$ = Area of circle with center X – [Area of semi-circle with center O + Area of Sector $YMZO$ of circle with center X – Area of Triangle XYZ].

$$144\pi-\left[\frac{\pi\times6\sqrt{2}\times6\sqrt{2}}{2}+\frac{\pi\times12\times12}{4}-\frac{1}{2}\times12\times12\right]$$
$$=[144\pi-36\pi+36\pi-72]=72(\pi+1)$$

Option (a) is correct.

9. We need to scan all two digit numbers and all 3 digit numbers systematically to get this answer. Amongst two-digit numbers, it is easy to see that there will be 9 numbers 11, 22, 33, 44, 55, ...99 that will have this property. In 3-digit numbers, with 11, there will be 24 numbers using digits 2 to 9 (3 with each, for instance with 2, we will have 211, 121 and 112). And 2 numbers 101 and 110 using 0 as the third digit. So, 11 will have a total of 26 such numbers. Likewise each of 22, 33, 44...99 will have 26 such numbers. Further there will be 9 more numbers having two zeros. Hence, the total is 9 + 26 × 9 + 9 = 252.

10. We can use the successive percentage change structure of the PCG to solve this. If a% of the coffee is drawn out and replaced with cocoa powder, 1.5a% of the mixture X would be drawn out and replaced with cocoa powder to get mixture Y. The target percentage value of coffee to cocoa in Mixture Y is 86% : 14% (converting 43 : 7 into percentages). Using a trial and error approach we can identify if a = 20%, mixture X would have 80% coffee and 20% cocoa. Next, reducing the cocoa by 30% will give us 14% cocoa in mixture Y. (Note: In the second instance, the question talks about replacing what is taken out by coffee and not by cocoa, hence the 30% reduction would work for cocoa, while coffee would drop by 24% and then increase by 30 to become 86). The ratio of cocoa in the two mixtures is 20 : 14 = 10 : 7.

11. You need to recognize that a 36.36% profit corresponds to a 4/11 profit in ratio terms. If we assume the cost price of the first item as 110, the common selling price works out to 150. Since, we have to also do a second

set of percentage calculations on the second item for this price, it makes sense to bring the common selling price down to 100. In that case, cost price of first item = 73.33 (getting it by calculating 2/3rd of 110). Next, a 14.28% loss on the second item, means that from cost price P of second item, a 14.28% drop gets us to 100. That also means that the value of P can be got by increasing 100 by 16.66%, giving us the cost price of the second item as 116.66. Thus, we have CP of first item, 73.333, Common selling price = 100 and Cost price of second item = 116.66. We can multiply the whole system by 3, to remove the decimals, so we get 220, 300 and 350 as the three values respectively. To get a 30% profit on the second item, the common selling price needs to be raised to $350 \times 1.3 = 455$. The percentage profit on the first item in that case would be $106.8\% \approx 107\%$. Hence, the correct answer is 107%.

12. In this case, we can think through options. For option (d), if we mix 900 grams of mixture A, with 750 grams of mixture B, we will get 400 + 300 = 700 grams of sugar in Mixture C out of a total of 1650 grams. Since, we are mixing mixture C and Milk in the ratio 11 : 3, it means we will add 450 units of milk to this – the drink will have 700 sugar in 2100, so giving us the required 1/3rd value. If you were to try the mixtures as stated with any other option, we would not end with sugar being 1/3rd the mixture and hence you can reject the other options.

    Hence, option (d) this is the correct answer.

13. From the first quadratic and it's condition of no real roots, we have $n^2 - 120 < 0$ or $n^2 < 120$. For integral k, the value of k can be $-10 \le k \le 10$, which gives us 21 possible values for n. From the second quadratic equation, $(n - 3)^2 - 4 > 0$, we can see that the value of k cannot be 5, 4, 3, 2 or 1. Thus, the product of all possible values of $n = 10! \times 6 \times 7 \times 8 \times 9 \times 10 = 7^2 \times 5^3 \times 3^7 \times 2^{13}$. The number of factors for this number is $3 \times 4 \times 8 \times 14 = 1344$. Option (d) is correct.

14. Thinking of option (a): If $y < 0$, for $-x < y$, the value of x, should be larger than the value of $-y$ (both of which would be positive). For instance, if $y = -5$, $x > 5$ would be the condition that would be how option (a) would be read. In such a case, the numerators of both $\frac{x}{y}$ and $\frac{x+5}{y-5}$ would be positive, while their denominators would be negative. Thus, both the fractions would lead to negative outcomes. In such a case, the absolute value of the fraction $\frac{x}{y}$, would need to be larger than the absolute value of the fraction $\frac{x+5}{y-5}$ for the condition $\frac{x}{y} < \frac{x+5}{y-5}$ to be satisfied. This would always be true if we restrict the value of $-x < y$. Hence, this option is correct. Thinking of this with values inserted would be a good way to clarify to oneself. For instance, if $y = -8$, $y - 5 = -13$, $x = 9$ (greater than $-y$, which is 8), $x + 5$ will be 14. So, in terms of absolute values we are comparing $\frac{9}{8}$ with $\frac{14}{13}$. It is guaranteed that the absolute value of the fraction $\frac{x}{y}$ is larger (since 5 is getting added to both the numerator and the denominator of $\frac{9}{8}$).

    Hence, option (a) is correct.

15. The two numbers can be viewed as 3^{4a} & 3^{4b}. At the value of a as 1 and b as 15, we will have the two numbers as 3^4 and 3^{60}. There will be exactly 55 numbers that can be expressed as powers of 3, between these two numbers. Thus $1 \times 15 = 15$, will be the lowest possible product of $a \times b$.

16. To score 133 marks, a person has to have a net loss of 267 marks from a maximum possible 400 marks in the paper. An incorrect answer loses 5 marks (–1 instead of +4), while an un-attempted question loses 3 marks (+1 instead of +4). To lose 267 marks only at the rate of 3 marks per question, one can have 89 un-attempted questions and 11 correct answers, 0 wrong answers. This would give us 133 marks. The other solutions can be visualized based on arithmetic series for each type of outcomes and can be seen in the following table:

	Corrects	*Wrongs*	*Un-Attempted*
Possibility 1	11	0	89
Possibility 2	13	3	84
Possibility 3	15	6	79
Possibility 8	25	21	54

    14 more corrects for one student over the other is possible for the pair of solutions represented by possibility 1 and possibility 8. In this case, the difference in the number of attempted questions between the two is (25 + 21) – (11 + 0) = 35.

Note: The answer remains the same if we take possibility 9 as 27, 24 and 49. Comparing to possibility 2, we see the difference in number of attempts is at 35.

17. If we mix 8 grams of sucrose to 1 gram of saccharine, we would have 9 grams with a sweetness quotient of 683. The average sweetness would be 683/9 = 75.88 which is greater than 100 times the sweetness of sucrose. If we mix 9 grams of sucrose to 1 gram of saccharine, the average would be below 74. Hence, option (b) is the required answer.

18. The average sweetness of the mixture as defined would be: $(1 \times 0.74 + 2 \times 1 + 3 \times 1.7)/6 = 7.84/6 = 1.306$. Thus, option (a) is correct.

19. Using the information in the expression which defines the function, we realise that if we use x_{10} as $x_!$, the expression gives us:
$x_{10} + x_9 + 1 = k \rightarrow x_9 = k - 2$; Further, using the value of x_9 to get the value of x_8 as follows:
$x_9 + x_8 + 1 = k \rightarrow k - 2 + x_8 + 1 = k \rightarrow x_8 = 1$;
Next: $x_8 + x_7 + 1 = k \rightarrow x_7 = k - 2$.
In this fashion, we can clearly see that x_6 would again be 1 and x_5 be $k - 2$; $x_4 = 1$ and $x_3 = k - 2$; $x_2 = 1$ and $x_1 = k - 2$. Option (b) is correct.
20. In order to solve this question, you need to think about how the initial values of a_x will behave in terms of being even and odd.
The value of $a_2 = 1 \times 1 + 3 = 4$ (this is necessarily even, since we have the construct as follows: Odd × Odd + Odd = Odd + Odd = Even.)
The value of $a_3 = 1 \times 4 + 3 = 7$ (this is necessarily odd, since we have the construct as follows: Odd × Even + Odd = Even + Odd = Odd.)
The value of $a_4 = 4 \times 7 + 3 = 31$ (this is necessarily odd, since we have the construct as follows: Odd × Even + Odd = Even + Odd = Odd.)
The value of $a_5 = 7 \times 31 + 3 = 220$ (this is necessarily even since we have the construct as follows: Odd × Odd + Odd = Odd + Odd = Even.)
The next two in the series values viz: a_6 and a_7 will be odd again since they would take the construct of Odd × Even + Odd = Even + Odd = Odd. Also, once, a_6 and a_7 turn out to be odd, it is clear that a_8 would be even and a_9 a_{10} would be odd again. Thus, we can understand that the terms a_2, a_5, a_8, a_{11}, a_{14} are even while all other terms in the series are odd. Thus, the even terms occur when we take a term whose number answers the description of a_{3n+2}. If you look at the options, all the four options in this question are asking about the value of a_{450} and a_{451}. Since, neither of these terms are in the series of a_{3n+2}, we can say that both of these are necessarily odd and hence, option (b) will be the correct answer.
21. If $b = 1$, then the factors are $(x - a)(x^2 + 1)$. This yields 2 imaginary roots. So, option (b) ($b \neq 1$) is the required answer.
22. The length and breadth of the base would be $(12 - 2x)$ and $(12 - 2x)$ respectively. The height of the box would be 'x'. Thus, the total volume would be $(12 - 2x)(12 - 2x)x$. Checking the options, it can be seen that the volume is maximized for $x = 2$.

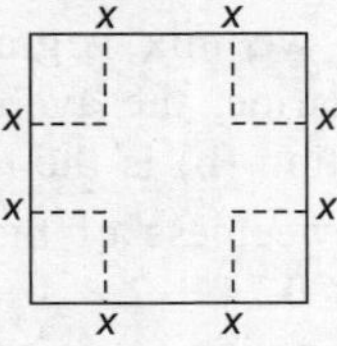

The CAT Experience 2

1. The ratio of speeds of Abhijit and Amartya is 5 : 4. Hence, they would meet at a point that splits the distance between them (990 meters) in the same ratio of 5 : 4. Thus, the meeting point of Abhijit and Amartya would be at $\frac{5}{9}990 = 550$ meters away from Abhijit. Since, Arun is 110 meters behind Abhijit, it means that Arun would have to travel a total distance of 550 + 110 = 660 meters to the meeting point. Further, we need to find out in how much time Abhijit and Amartya meet – since Arun has to reach the same point in the same time. The relative speed of Abhijit and Amartya is 60 + 48 = 108 kmph since they are moving in opposite direction i.e. $108 \times \frac{5}{18} = 30$ m/s. Thus, they would meet in 990/30 = 33 seconds. Arun has to cover the distance of 660 meters in 33 seconds. Hence, his required speed has to be 660/33 = 20 m/s, which is the same as $20 \times \frac{18}{5} = 72$ kmph. Option (b) is correct.
2. The first thing to notice in this question is that together they take 3 hours to do the work, which means that every hour their net work is 33.33% of the total project work. From the information about Bisheshwar and Cheteshwar working together, we know that Cheteshwar takes 2.2 hours (= 132 minutes) to complete the work after Bisheshwar leaves. The best approach for a question like this is to look at the options and try to fit in the conditions. If we select that Cheteshwar takes 144 minutes (= 2.4 hours from the option (c)), his work rate in percentage would be 41.66% per hour. It also means that he does 132/144 = 11/12 or 91.66% of the work alone in the last 132 minutes when he worked alone. Also, in the first hour when the two of them worked together, they would have done 100 – 91.66 = 8.33% net work. This means that the sum of B + C = 8.33% per hour. With C = 41.66, value of B would be –33.33% → Bisheshwar can destroy the work in 3 hours completely. From the given condition 'Ambujwar takes 1 hour more to do the complete work than Bisheshwar takes to completely destroy the work', Ambujwar would take 4 hours to do the work-doing 25% work per hour. In this case, we need to check with these rates of work whether their combined work of 3 hours can indeed complete the work (for which their hourly work needs to be 33.33% per hour). A + B + C = 25 – 33.33 + 41.66 = 33.33 → gives us the required value and hence is the correct answer. I would encourage you to try this approach with one of the wrong options to see how you get to values

that do not match the given conditions and hence reject those options.

Hence, option (c) is correct.

3. The quadratic equation can be written as: $x^2 + (8n - 4)x + 485 = 0 \rightarrow x^2 + 4(2n - 1)x + 485 = 0$. For the equation to have no real roots, $16 \times (2n - 1)^2 - 4 \times 1 \times 485 < 0 \rightarrow n$'s maximum integral value is + 6.

We have to evaluate the minimum possible value of $\frac{(2n-1)}{22m} + 8m \rightarrow \frac{1}{2m} + 8m$.

Differentiating this expression and equating to 0, will give us the value of m at which the minimum for this expression occurs. We get $m^2 = 1/16 \rightarrow m = 1/4$. The minimum value of the expression $\frac{(2n-1)}{22m} + 8m$, would be got if we put n as 6 and m as ¼ in the expression = 2 + 2 = 4. Hence, the correct answer is 4.

4. $\sqrt{63x+36} + \sqrt{63x-36} = 3\left(\sqrt{7x+4} + \sqrt{7x-4}\right)$ $= 3\left(5 + \sqrt{17}\right)$. Comparing the terms we can see that $\sqrt{7x+4} = 5 \rightarrow x = 3$. The value of $\sqrt{14x+9} = \sqrt{51}$.

Hence, option (b) is correct.

5.

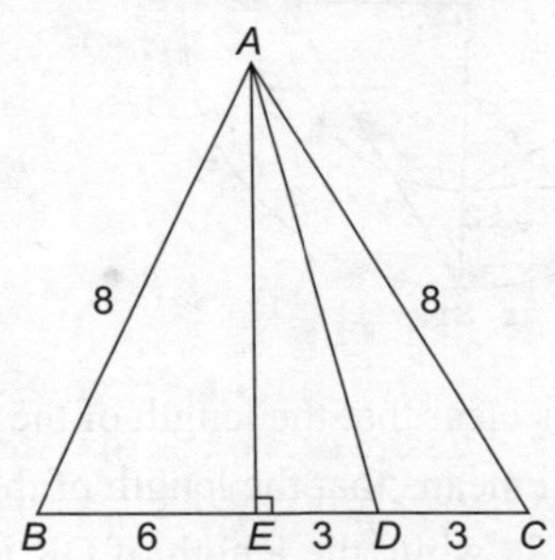

In triangle AEC, $AE = \sqrt{28} = 2\sqrt{7}$. Hence, in triangle $ADE \rightarrow AD = \sqrt{28+9} = \sqrt{37}$. Option (b) is the correct answer.

6. Since q divides $7a + 3b$ and $15a + 6b$ (given), it must also divide their difference $8a + 3b$. Hence, q would also divide $(8a + 3b) - (7a + 3b) = a$. Hence, q will also divide $7a$ and hence q will also divide $7a + 3b - 7a = 3b$. Thus, $8a + 6b$ will also be divisible by q. Hence, option (c) is correct.

7. We can have 4-digit numbers, 5 digit numbers, 6 digit numbers or 7 digit numbers (10 million being the limiting value all numbers have to be lower than or equal to 9,999,999)

Number of 4 digit numbers greater than 2000: $4 \times 6 \times 6 \times 6 = 864$. Number of 5 digit numbers = $5 \times 6 \times 6 \times 6 \times 6 = 1296 \times 5 = 6480$; Number of 6 digit numbers = $5 \times 6 \times 6 \times 6 \times 6 \times 6 = 38880$; Number of 7 digit numbers = $5 \times 6 \times 6 \times 6 \times 6 \times 6 \times 6 = 233280$. Hence, the required number of numbers = $864 + 6480 + 38880 + 233380 = 279504$. Option (a) is correct.

8. In this question, we can assume that his purchase price is 100 rupees per meter. In such a case, his selling price is $100 \times 1.2 \times 0.92 = 110.4$ rupees per meter. However, he has also purchased 110 cm of cloth for every meter bought and sold only 90 cm of cloth for every meter sold. In order to calculate the percentage profit, we can equate the money got and money spent. Then the percentage profit can be calculated using the formula $\frac{\text{Goods left}}{\text{Goods Sold}} \times 100$ (refer to the Profit and Loss chapter for this concept). The money spent by him (100) can be multiplied by 1.104 to make it equal to the money received by him. In such a case the amount of cloth he purchases would be $110 \times 1.104 = 121.44$ cm (goods bought). Goods sold = 90. Hence, his Goods left = 31.44. Required percentage profit $= \frac{\text{Goods left}}{\text{Goods Sold}} \times 100 = \frac{31.44}{90} \times 100 = 34.93\% \approx 35\%$.

Hence, the correct answer is 35.

9. Assume the cost of Dehradun rice as $10x$ and the cost of katarni rice as $7x$. The total cost incurred by Rajesh in buying the rice would be

$$220 \times 7x + 240 \times 10x = 3940x.$$

While selling his initial quantities his revenue would be:

$$10 \times 7.7x + 10 \times 8.4x + 40 \times 13x = 581x$$

Thus, he gets a revenue of $3940x \times 1.68 - 681x = 5938.2x$ when he sells the balance 400 kgs. His selling price per kg for these 400 kgs would be $\frac{5938.2x}{400} = 14.8455x = 593.82 \rightarrow x = 40$. Hence, the cost price of the 400 kgs mixture would be $200 \times 7x + 200 \times 10x = 3400x = 3400 \times 40 = 136000$.

10. The given expression can be written as $(a + 2b)^2 + (a - 2b + 2)^4 = 0$. Since, both the terms inside the brackets are raised to even powers, it follows that each of the brackets should be equal to 0. Thus, we have $a + 2b = 0 \rightarrow a = -2b$ and $a - 2b = -2 \rightarrow -4b = -2$. Hence, $b = \frac{1}{2}$, and $a = -1$. The value of $a^3 - b^3 = -1 - \frac{1}{8} = -\frac{9}{8}$. Hence, the correct answer is $-\frac{9}{8}$.

11. Let b, c be the other two roots of the equation. Using the formulae for sum, pairwise sum and product of the roots of a cubic equation $ax^3 + bx^2 + cx + d = 0$, we know that sum of roots is $-b/a$; pairwise product of roots = c/a and product of roots = $-d/a$. In this case, the product of the roots is $-4 = -4 \times b \times c \rightarrow b \times c = 1$, which means that b and c are reciprocals of each other i.e. $c = 1/b$. Using sum of roots, we

have $-4 + b + \frac{1}{b} = -(r + 1) \rightarrow b^2 - (4 - r - 1)$ $b + 1 = 0$. The roots of this would be imaginary if $(4 - r - 1)^2 - 4 < 0$. Trying out non-negative integral values of r, we see that only at $r = 2$, 3 and 4, the value of b would be imaginary. Hence, there are 3 values of r possible, if r is a non-negative integer. Hence, the correct answer is 3.

12. The series will go as: 500 + 250 (day 2 – as 1 out of every 2 particles, will add one extra particle.) = 750; 750 + 250 = 1000 (day 3 – as 1 out of every 3 particles, will add one extra particle.) 1000 + 250 = 1250 (day 4 – as 1 out of every 3 particles, will add one extra particle.) Thus, every day 250 particles getting added every day. Since 500 + 250 × 10 = 3000, it means that the number will become 3000 on day 11. So on day 11, the number of particles will become 3000 × 3 = 9000. On day 12, 1 out of every 12 particles (which means 750) will add exactly 1 particle. 9000 + 750 = 9750. Day 13, 9750 + 750 = 10500. So, we now have an arithmetic series 9000, 9750, 10500,....18000 (day 23)....19500 (day 25). Hence, the number crosses 20000 on day 26. Hence, the correct answer is 26.

13. The situation can be visualized from the figure shown.

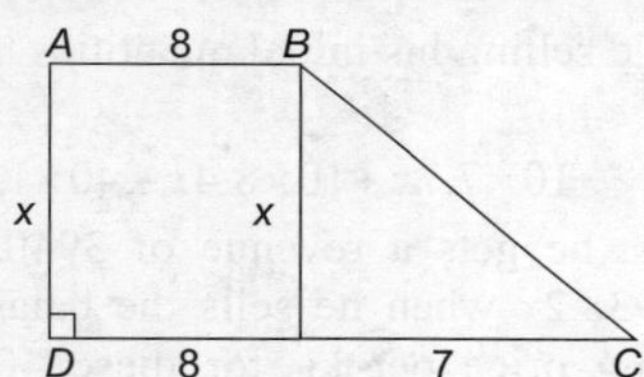

The area of the trapezium is $8x + 8x + \frac{1}{2} \times 7 \times x$ $= 11.5x = 276 \rightarrow x = 24$.

Hence, the side BC = 25 (Pythagoras triplet 7, 24, 25). The required perimeter = 8 + 15 + 24 + 25 = 72 units.

14. Let us say he invests 300. He receives interest of 6.3 (@7% on 90); 8.4 (@12% on 70) & 4.2 (@3% on 140). Hence, his total interest is 18.9 per year. To earn an interest income of 300, he will take 300/18.9 = 15.87 years. Hence, he will take 16 completed years to double his money.

15. The weighted average price of rice could be 49, 50, 51…upto 71 ₹/kg. If this average price is 71, the ratio of quantities bought of A and B would be 1 : 47, which is not possible if both quantities are integers and Quantity B is 14 kg more than Quantity A. At 70 ₹/kg, the ratio is is 1 : 23, which is again not possible. At 69 ₹/kg, the ratio is 3 : 45 or 1 : 15, which is possible if he had bought 1 kg of A and 15 kgs of B. This is the minimum quantity of B he could purchase. Also, for the maximum, we can see that at an average price of 49 ₹/kg, the ratio is 23 : 25 → with a difference of 14, the maximum quantity of A = 23 × 7 = 161. The required answer is 161 + 15 = 176.

16. The number 720, can we written in various ways as the product of powers of 3 numbers. However, the maximum value of $m + n + p$ occurs if we take $a = 2$, $b = 3$ and $p = 5$. In this case: $720^{200} = 2^{800} \times 3^{400} \times 5^{200}$. The maximum sum of $m + n + p = 1400$. However, if we take $a = 2^{800}$, $b = 3^{400}$ and $c = 5^{200}$, we end up with an expression of $(2^{800})^1 \times (3^{400})^1 \times (5^{200})^1$. In this case, we get the minimum sum of $m \times n \times p = 3$. The required difference is $1400 - 3 = 1397$. The correct answer is 1397.

Solutions for Questions 17 to 19:

The given figure would show the road network described in the question.

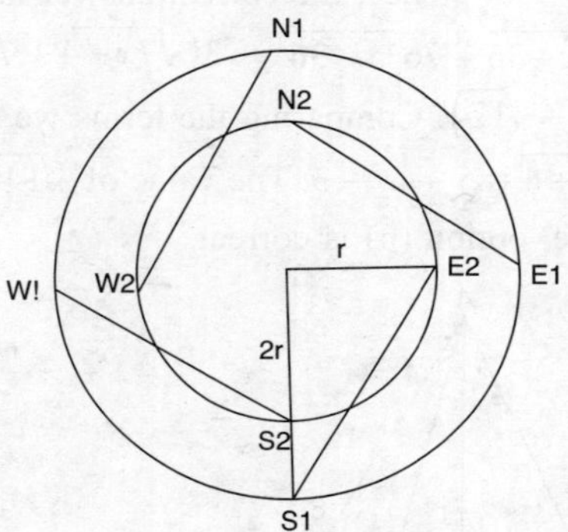

17. From the figure it is clear that the length of the chord road is $r\sqrt{5}$, which means that the length of the four chord roads is $4r\sqrt{5}$, while the length of OR is $4\pi r$. Hence, the required ratio would be $\sqrt{5}/\pi$, option (c).

18. The total distance on the chord road would be $r\sqrt{5}$, while on the OR it would be πr. If we take the value of the radius of the outer ring road as 30 (from the options, we would see that he would require 1 hour on the chord road and 30 minutes on the outer ring road—to give 90 minutes. Hence, option (c) is correct.

19. Since the value of r is 15 for the previous question, the distance covered on the chord road will be $15\sqrt{5}$ while the distance of the inner ring road would be 15π. The total time taken would be 1 hour + 30 minutes = 90 minutes, option (c).

20. Let the side of square be a.

Area of the square = a^2

Therefore, area of the largest circle which can be cut from the square = $\pi\left(\frac{a}{2}\right)^2 = \frac{\pi a^2}{4}$

$$\text{Area scrapped} = a^2 - \frac{\pi}{4}a^2 = a^2\left(1-\frac{\pi}{4}\right)$$

$$\therefore \quad \frac{\text{Area scrapped}}{\text{Area of square}} = \frac{a^2\left(1-\frac{\pi}{4}\right)}{a^2} = 1-\frac{\pi}{4}$$

As this ratio does not depend on the value of the side of the square. Therefore, whether we cut a circle from smaller square or larger square, scrapped area will be a fixed percentage of square. Therefore, the required ratio will be 1 : 1.

21. $f(0, 1) = 1 + 1 = 2$

$f(x + 1, 0) = f(x, 1)$

put $x = 0$, $f(0 + 1, 0) = f(1, 0) = f(0, 1) = 2$

$f(x + 1, y + 1) = f(x, f(x + 1, y))$

put $x = 0, y = 0$ in the above equation we get:

$f(1, 1) = f(0, f(1, 0)) = f(0, 2) = 2 + 1 = 3.$

Now put $x = 0, y = 1$ in $f(x + 1, y + 1) = f(x, f(x + 1, y))$, we get:

$f(1, 2) = f(0, f(1, 1)) = f(0, 3) = 3 + 1 = 4.$

22. The number $10^{29} = 2^{29} \times 5^{29}$.

Factors or divisors of such a number would be of the form: $2^a \times 5^b$ where the values of a and b can be represented as $0 \le a, b \le 29$, i.e. there are $30 \times 30 = 900$ possibilities when we talk about randomly selecting a positive divisor of 10^{29}.

Next, we need to think of numbers which are integral multiples of 10^{23}. Such numbers would be of the form $2^x \times 5^y$ such that $x, y \ge 23$.

Hence, the number of values possible when the chosen divisor would also be an integer multiple of 10^{23} would be when $23 \le x, y \le 29$. There would be $7 \times 7 = 49$ such combinations.

Thus, the required probability is $49 \div 900$. In the context of $a^2 \div b^2$, the values of a and b would come out as 7 and 30, respectively. The required difference between a and b is 23. Hence, option (d) is correct.

The CAT Experience 3

1. The given expression can be written as: $2^{2x^2} + 2^{2x+40} = 2^{x^2+x+21}$

This expression is of the form $2^a + 2^b = 2^c$. A little bit of numerical introspection will tell us that this sort of equation can only hold if $a = b = c - 1$. Thus, the values of x, that would satisfy the given expression should obey $2x^2 = 2x + 40 \rightarrow 2x^2 - 2x - 40 = 0$. The sum of roots for this expression is 1. Hence, the correct answer is 1. Option (b) is correct.

2. For a number to have exactly 4 factors other than 1 and itself, it should have a total of 6 factors. A number can have 6 factors if it is of the form a^5 or of the form $a^2 \times b^1$, where a and b are prime numbers. Also, since we are looking for numbers below 100, we only have to consider all numbers below 99 and trace how many can be written in either of these two forms. We can see the following cases, if we do a systematic count: 2^5; $2^2 \times 3$; $2^2 \times 5$; $2^2 \times 7$; $2^2 \times 11$; $2^2 \times 13$; $2^2 \times 17$; $2^2 \times 19$; $2^2 \times 23$; $3^2 \times 2$; $3^2 \times 5$; $3^2 \times 7$; $3^2 \times 11$; $5^2 \times 2$; $5^2 \times 3$; $7^2 \times 2$. Thus, there are a total of 16 such numbers. Hence, the correct answer is 16.

3. The total value of the 26 unit stone be $26^2 \times n = 676n = 2704000 \rightarrow n = 4000$. The lowest value of the 4 stones will occur if the weights of the four stones are 6, 6, 7 and 7 units each. In this case, the total value would be $36n + 36n + 49n + 49n = 170n$. The highest value of the stones would happen if the pieces are 20 units, 3, 2 and 1 unit each. In this case the total value would be $400n + 9n + 4n + n = 414n$. The difference between the maximum and minimum value after breakage $= 414n - 170n = 244n = 976000$. Hence, option (c) is correct.

4. The key in this question is to understand that the average cost per clothing item would vary between 1200 to 1500 (not inclusive since he buys at least one item of each). Also, his profit per item is 8% on the average cost (mark up of 20% and a discount of 10%). Thus P, his profit per item would be $96 < P < 120$. In the extreme case if he bought only trousers, his number of clothing items would have been maximized. 34080/96 = 355 trousers would be the case for him to make a profit of 34080 by only buying trousers. However, since he sells trousers as well as shirts, his total number of items would be below 355. We can work out that if he sells 350 trousers and 4 shirts his total profit would be $350 \times 96 + 4 \times 120 = 34080$. Hence, his maximum number of clothing items he could sell would be 354.

5. The minimum number of shirts he sold would have been 4 (as per the previous solution.)

6.

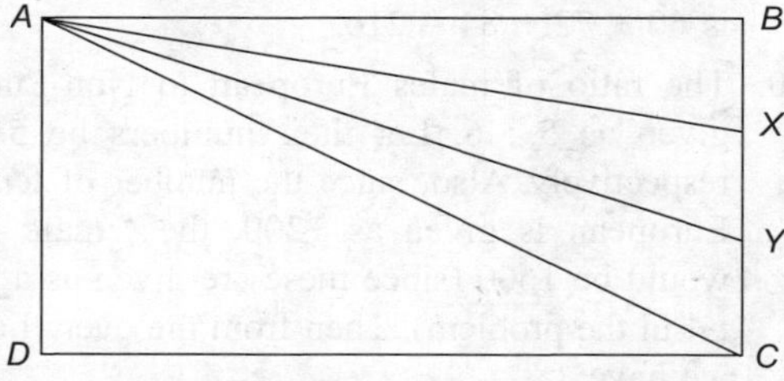

Triangles ABX, AXY; AYC and ACD are all triangles having the same heights. Also, $AYC + ACD = AYCD$. If we take area of ABX as N, area of $AYCD = 7N$ and area of $AXY = 4N$ (as the three are in arithmetic progression). Since, area AXY is 4 times the area of

ABX, it means that the length of their bases must be in the ratio 4 : 1 (as their heights are same). Thus, *BX* : *XY* = 1 : 4. Let *BX* = *L* and *XY* = 4*L*. We now need to think of the length of *YC*. Since *AYC* + *ACD* = *AYCD* = 7*N*, the net length of the bases of these two triangles has to be 7*L* (as both *AYC* and *ACD* have the same heights as *ABX* and *AXY*. If we consider *YC* as having a length of 'x', we have Base of *ACD* + Base of *AYC* = (5*L* + x) + x = 7*L* → x = *L*. Hence, the ratio of *BX* : *XY* : *YC* = 1 : 4 : 1.

Hence, option (c) is correct.

7. We have $x^2 - 2xy + y^2 = 36 \rightarrow (x - y) = \pm 6$. Also, we have $x^2 + 2xy + y^2 = 144 \rightarrow (x + y) = \pm 12$.

This gives rise to 4 cases:

Case 1: $x - y = 6$, $x + y = 12 \rightarrow x = 9$, $y = 3$. So $x^3 - y^3 = 702$ (maximum)

Case 2: $x - y = -6$, $x + y = 12 \rightarrow x = 3$, $y = 9$. So $x^3 - y^3 = -702$ (minimum)

Case 3: $x - y = 6$, $x + y = -12 \rightarrow x = -3$, $y = -9$. So $x^3 - y^3 = 702$ (maximum)

Case 1: $x - y = -6$, $x + y = -12 \rightarrow x = -9$, $y = -3$. So $x^3 - y^3 = -702$ (minimum)

So the correct answer is 1404.

8. For a system of 2 equations (with 2 unknowns) to have infinitely many solutions, the two equations should be identical to each other. This can only happen if: $b^2 + 24 = 10b = a + 8$. Solving $b^2 + 24 = 10b \rightarrow b = 4$ or 6. Using $b^2 + 24 = a + 8$, we get: $a = 32$, when $b = 4$ or $a = 52$ when $b = 6$. Minimum value of $a + b = 32 + 4 = 36$.

9. Numbers that would have 12 factors will have a standard form of representation, that would look as: $a^3 \times b^2$ OR $a^2 \times b^1 \times c^1$ OR $a^5 \times b^1$ OR a^{11}, where *a*, *b*, *c* are prime numbers. Looking for the smallest couple of values in the first three cases, we get: $2^3 \times 3^2 = 72$; $3^3 \times 2^2 = 108$; $2^2 \times 3^1 \times 5^1 = 60$; $3^2 \times 2^1 \times 5^1 = 90$; $2^2 \times 3^1 \times 7^1 = 84$; $2^5 \times 3^1 = 96$. Looking at these numbers closely, we can observe that the minimum values are 60, 72 and 84. Hence, the required answer is 60 + 72 + 84 = 216.

10. The ratio of males European to Non-European is given as 5 : 6. Let their numbers be 5*n* and 6*n* respectively. Also, since the number of female non-European is given as 1200, the female European would be 1600 (since these are given as a ratio of 3 : 4 in the problem). Then from the overall 6 : 7 ratio we have:

$\frac{1600 + 5n}{1200 + 6n} = \frac{6}{7} \rightarrow n = 4000$. Hence, the total number of athletes is:

$1600 + 20000 + 1200 + 24000 = 46800$.

11. When he sells 2/3rd of his mixture at 30% discount he loses a profit of 4040 – 2240 = 1800. Hence, the marked price of 2/3rd of his mixture should have been 6000 and the total marked price for the entire mixture would have been 9000. Hence, his total cost of purchase of the entire quantity would have been 9000 – 4040 = 4960. Also, if we assume the cost of a liter of Sunflower oil as S, Castor oil as C and Coconut oil as K, we have: 5S + 6C + 13K = 4960 and 8S = 10C = 40K. Solving for S, C and K we get their values as 400, 320 and 80 respectively. Hence, he spent 2 × 400 + 3 × 320 + 8 × 80 = 2400 rupees on his next purchase. The correct answer is option (a)

12. The value of $\{|x - n| + |x - 80|\}$ will always be equal to $80 - n$, for all values of *x* between 0 to 80. Hence, this is maximized at $n = 0$ as 80. At $n = 0$, the expression $|x - n - 40|$ becomes equal to $|x - 40|$. For the given range of *x*, the maximum value of this expression is 40 when $x = 80$ or $x = 0$. Hence, the maximum value of $f(x)$ is 120. The correct answer is 120. Option (c) is correct.

13. In order to think about this question, you need to think about whether the number can be divided by the initial numbers below the square root like 2, 3, 4, 5... and so on.

Let us say, if we think of a number that is not divisible by 2, in such a case if we take the number to be divisible by 3, 5 and 7, then the largest factors of *x* that we will get would be $\frac{x}{3}, \frac{x}{5}$ and $\frac{x}{7}$.

Even in this situation, the percentage value of these factors as a percentage of *x* would only be: for $\frac{x}{3}$ = 33.33%, $\frac{x}{5}$ = 20% and $\frac{x}{7}$ = 14.28%

Hence, if we try to think of a situation where $a = \frac{x}{3}$, $b = \frac{x}{5}$, and $c = \frac{x}{7}$ the value of $a + b + c$ would give us only (33.33% + 20% + 14.28%) = 67.61% of *x*, which is not equal to 100% of *x*.

Since the problem states that $a + b + c = x$, the value of $a + b + c$ should have added up to 100% of *x*.

The only situation, for this to occur would be if

$a = \frac{x}{2}$ = 50% of *x* $b = \frac{x}{3}$ = 33.33% of *x* and

$c = \frac{x}{6}$ = 16.66% of *x*

This means that 2, 3 and 6 should divide *x* necessarily. In other words *x* should be a multiple of 6. The multiples of 6 below 200 are 6, 12, 18 ... 198, a total of 33 numbers.

Hence, the correct answer is (c).

14. This question is again based on a pattern-recognition principle. The best way to approach the search of the pattern is to start by working-out a few values of the given expression. The following pattern would start emerging:

Value of a	*Possible values of b*	*Value of the sum of the possible products 'a × b'*	*Explanation*
1	1	1	With 'a' as 1, the only value for b is 1 itself
2	1, 2	$2 \times 1 + 2 \times 2 = 2 \times 3$	With 'a' as 2, b can take the values of 1 and 2 – and $2 \times 1 + 2 \times 2$ can be written as 2×3
3	1, 2, 3	$3 \times 1 + 3 \times 2 + 3 \times 3 = 3 \times 6$	With 'a' as 3, b can take the values of 1, 2 and 3 – and $3 \times 1 + 3 \times 2 + 3 \times 3$ can be written as 3×6
4	1, 2, 3, 4	$4 \times 1 + 4 \times 2 + 4 \times 3 + 4 \times 4 = 4 \times 10$	

At this point, you should realise that the values are following a certain pattern – the series of values for 'a' are multiplied by a series of consecutive triangular numbers (1, 3, 6, 10 and so on.) Thus, we can expect the subsequent numbers to be obtained by multiplying 5×15, 6×21, 7×28, 8×36, 9×45 and 10×55.

Hence, the answer can be obtained by:

$1 \times 1 + 2 \times 3 + 3 \times 6 + 4 \times 10 + 5 \times 15 + 6 \times 21 + 7 \times 28 + 8 \times 36 + 9 \times 45 + 10 \times 55 =$

$1 + 6 + 18 + 40 + 75 + 126 + 196 + 288 + 405 + 550 = 1705$

15. In this case, the solution will change as follows:

Value of a	*Possible values of b*	*Value of the sum of the possible products 'a × b'*	*Explanation*
1	No possible values for 'b', since b'' has to be greater than or equal to 1 but less than 'a' at the same time	0	With 'a' as 1, b has no possible values that it can take
2	1	2×1	With 'a' as 2, b can only take the value of 1
3	1, 2	$3 \times 1 + 3 \times 2 = 3 \times 3$	With 'a' as 3, b can take the values of 1 and 2 – and $3 \times 1 + 3 \times 2$ can be written as 3×3
4	1, 2, 3	$4 \times 1 + 4 \times 2 + 4 \times 3 = 4 \times 6$	With 'a' as 4, b can take the values of 1,2 and 3 – and $4 \times 1 + 4 \times 2 + 4 \times 3$ can be written as 4×6

At this point, you should realise that the values are following a certain pattern (just like in the previous question) – the series of values for 'a' are multiplied by a series of consecutive triangular numbers (1, 3, 6, 10 and so on). The only difference, in this case, is that the multiplication is what can be described as 'one removed', i.e. it starts from the value of 'a' as 2. Thus, we can expect the subsequent numbers to be obtained by multiplying 5×10, 6×15, 7×21, 8×28 and 9×36 and 10×45. Notice here that the values of 'a' can go all the way up till 10 in this case as the inequality on the rightmost side of the expression is $a \le 10$.

Hence, the answer can be obtained by:

$1 \times 0 + 2 \times 1 + 3 \times 3 + 4 \times 6 + 5 \times 10 + 6 \times 15 + 7 \times 21 + 8 \times 28 + 9 \times 36 + 10 \times 45 =$

$0 + 2 + 9 + 24 + 50 + 90 + 147 + 224 + 324 + 450 = 1320$

16. If you try to observe the situations under which the addition of two consecutive four-digit numbers between 1000 and 2000 would come through without having a carryover value in the answer you would be able to identify the following situations – each of which differs from the other due to the way it is structured with respect to the values of the individual digits.

Category 1: 1000 + 1001; 1004 +1005, 1104 + 1105 and so on. A little bit of introspection should show you that in this case, the two numbers are 1abc and 1abd where $d = c + 1$. Also, for the sum to come out without any carry-overs, the values of a, b and c should be between 0 and 4 (including both). Thus, each of a, b and c gives us five values each – giving us a total of $5 \times 5 \times 5 = 125$ such situations.

Category 2: 1009 + 1010; 1019 + 1020; 1029 + 1030; 1409 + 1410. The general form of the first number here would be 1ab 9 with the values of a and b being between 0 and 4 (including both). Thus, each of a, b gives us 5 values each – giving us a total of $5 \times 5 = 25$ such situations.

Category 3: 1099 + 1100; 1199 + 1200; 1299 + 1300; 1399 + 1400 and 1499 + 1500. There are only 5 such pairs. Note that 1599 + 1600 would not work in this case as the addition of the hundreds' digit would become more than 10 and lead to a carry-over.

Category 4: 1999 + 2000 is the only other situation where the addition would not lead to a carry-over calculation. Hence, **1 more situation is possible.**

The required answer = 125 + 25 + 5 + 1 = 156.
Option (c) is the correct answer.

17. The perimeter of any polygon circumscribed about a circle is always greater than the circumference of the circle and the perimeter of any polygon inscribed in a circle is always less than the circumference of the circle.
Hence, $L1(13) > 2\pi \cdot 1$ and $L2(17) < 2\pi$
So $\{L1(13) + 2\pi\} > 4\pi$ and hence $\frac{\{L1(13)+2\pi\}}{L2(17)}$ will be greater than 2.

18. The function $h(a, b)$ is such that it takes two values as it's input and returns one value (the GCF of the two given values). Thus, there is a reduction of one number when we use the function 'h' once. Hence, if we have to reduce the set A containing 'n' elements into one element (as defined by $G(A)$) we would need to use the function 'h' $n - 1$ times.

19. For a polynomial $P(x)$ to be divisible by another polynomial $D(x)$, there needs to be a third polynomial $Q(x)$ which would represent the quotient of the expression $P(x)/D(x)$. In other words, this also means that the product of the polynomials $D(x) \times Q(x)$ should equal the polynomial $P(x)$.
In simpler words, we are looking for polynomials that would multiply $(x^2 + 1)$ and give us a polynomial in the form of $x^3 + ax^2 + bx + c$. The key point in this situation is that the expression that would multiply $(x^2 + 1)$ to give an expression of the form $x^3 + \ldots$ will necessarily be of the form (x + constant). It is only in such a case that we would get an expanded polynomial starting with x^3. Further, the value of the constant has to be such that the product of 1 × constant will give a value for 'c' that would belong to the set {1, 2, 3, 4, 5, 6, 7, or 8). Clearly, there are only eight such values possible for the constant – viz. 1, 2, 3,...8 and hence, the required polynomials that would be divisible by $x^2 + 1$ will be obtained by the expansion of the following expressions: $(x^2 + 1)(x + 1)$; $(x^2 + 1)(x + 2)$; $(x^2 + 1)(x + 3)$;... ; $(x^2 + 1)(x + 8)$. Thus, there would be a total of eight such expressions which would be divisible by $x^2 + 1$. Hence, option (b) is the correct answer.

20. In this case, the area of the triangle would be maximum when it is an isosceles triangle.

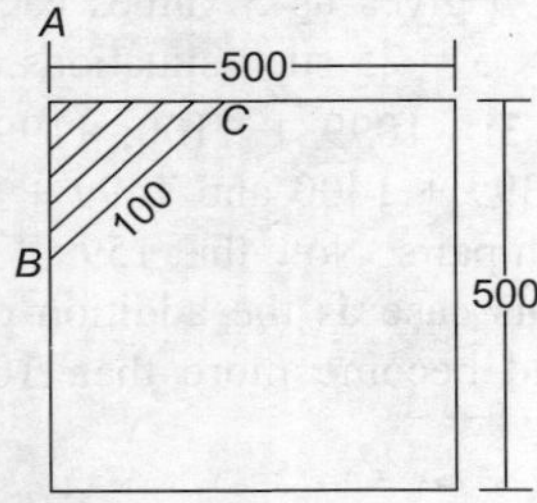

Length of $AC = \frac{100}{\sqrt{2}}$.
Area of the triangular region ABC
$$= \frac{1}{2} \times \frac{100}{\sqrt{2}} \times \frac{100}{\sqrt{2}} = 2{,}500 \text{ sq.m.}$$

21. Given that the average of X and Y is 79, the ratio of the number of students in the two classes would be 3 : 4. (Using Alligation) Also, the ratio of number of students in Y and Z would be 4 : 5. Hence, the overall average would be 3 : 4 : 5.
Using weighted average the required average
$$= \frac{3 \times 83 + 4 \times 76 + 5 \times 85}{3 + 4 + 5} = 81.5$$

22. As the value of average of remaining numbers has 17 in the denominator so the value of the number of the remaining numbers must be an integer multiple of 17 and the average of these numbers must be greater than 35. So the original number of numbers must be $17k + 1$ (18, 35, 52, 69…..)
Average of n consecutive numbers $= \frac{n+1}{2}$
For n = 18, 35, 52 the average would be 9.5, 18 and 26.5 respectively. So we can rule out these possibilities.
Now check for n = 69 the sum of total 69 numbers = $\frac{69(69+1)}{2} = 2415$.
Sum of remaining 68 numbers $= 35\frac{7}{17} \times 68 = 2408$
This gives us that the number to be erased must be 7.

The CAT Experience 4

1. The lines $|x - y| - |x - 4| = 3$ will intersect $x = 7$ at y = 1 and 13. Likewise, these lines would intersect $x = -7$ at y = 7 and –21. The enclosed figure formed will look as shown. The area would be the sum of areas of triangles DCE (42); ABF (154) and the rectangle $ABCD$ (84). The required answer is 280.

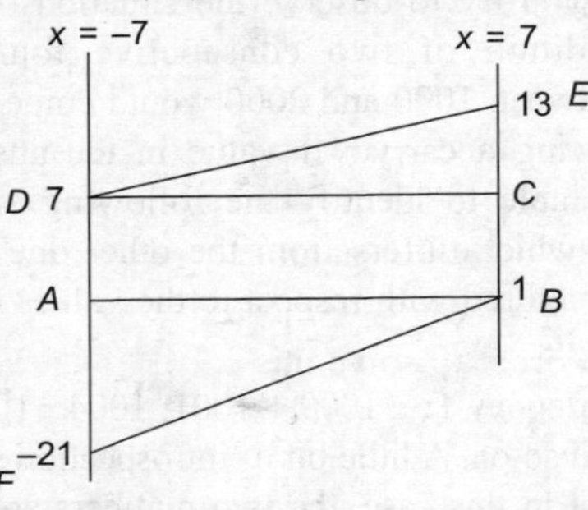

2. There are three possibilities for A^B to equal 1. These are: 1^{anything}; $(-1)^{\text{Even power}}$; 0^{anything}.
Comparing the given expression $(x^2 - 8x + 16)^{x^2-25}$ with these structures:

First structure would give us $x^2 - 8x + 16 = 1 \rightarrow x = 3$, 5. There are 2 integral solutions for this structure

The Second structure would be at $x^2 - 8x + 16 = -1 \rightarrow$. There are no integral solutions for x in this case.

The third structure would be at $x^2 - 25 = 0 \rightarrow x = \pm 5$. Thus, for the third structure there are two possible integral solutions for x. However, we need to notice that $x = 5$ is a common value under the first and third structures. Hence, we have 2 + 1 = 3 integral values of x that satisfy the expression.

Thus, the correct answer is option (b).

3.

	Bottle X	*Bottle Y*
Initial	1200 Pepsi	1000 Coca Cola
After first transfer	1000 Pepsi	1000 Coca Cola + 200 Pepsi
After second transfer	$1000 + \frac{1}{6} \times 200$ Pepsi & $\frac{5}{6} \times 200$ Coca Cola $\rightarrow$ $\frac{6200}{6}$ Pepsi, $\frac{1000}{6}$ Coca Cola	$1000 - \frac{5}{6} \times 200$ Coca Cola; $200 - \frac{1}{6} \times 200$ Pepsi $\rightarrow \frac{5000}{6}$ Coca Cola & $\frac{1000}{6}$ Pepsi

$$\text{Required ratio} = \frac{\frac{6200}{6}}{\frac{5000}{6}} = 31:25.$$

Option (c) is correct.

4. Let the number of employees working in A, B, C at inception be 400, 500 and 700. After the first year, these would become 400 × 1.3 = 520; 500 × 1.2 = 600; 700 × 1.2 = 840. After the second year, the number of employees for A would be 520 × 1.5 = 780 and for C it would be 840 × 1.25 = 1050. Thus, the number of employees for B would be the average of 780 and 1050, which is equal to 915. Hence, the percentage growth for B would be from 600 to 915 → 52.5%. Hence, the correct answer is option (b).
5. The point E is at an even number of steps away from point A. Thus, $a_{2n-1} = 0$.
6. In order to solve this question, you need to visualise the series of numbers, which satisfy this condition of the remainder 3 when divided by 7.

   The first number in 3 digits for this condition is 101 and the next will be 108, followed by 115, 122 …

   This series would have its highest value in 3 digits as 997.

   The number of terms in this series would be 129 (using the logic that for any A.P., the number of terms is given by $\frac{D}{d} + 1$).

   Also the average value of this series is the average of the first and the last term i.e. the average of 101 and 997. Hence, the required sum = 549 × 129 = 70821. Hence, the correct option is (a).
7. Let the length of the edge cut at each corner be 'a' m. After cutting away the corners we'll find a regular octagon. Each side of the regular octagon was $2 - 2a$.

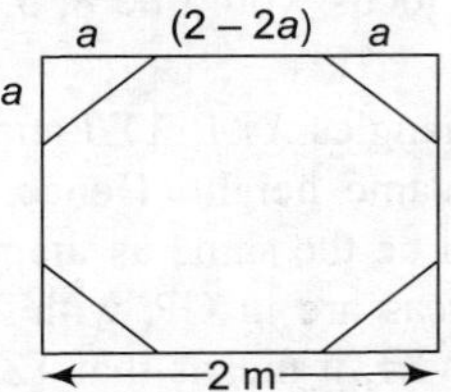

$$\therefore \quad \sqrt{a^2 + a^2} = 2 - 2a \Rightarrow a\sqrt{2} = 2 - 2a$$

$\Rightarrow \quad a\sqrt{2} \times (1 + \sqrt{2}) = 2 \Rightarrow a = \frac{\sqrt{2}}{\sqrt{2} + 1}$. Then, side of the octagon $= 2 - 2a = \frac{2}{\sqrt{2} + 1}$. Option (b) is correct.

8. The key to understanding this question is from two points.
   1. Since there is exactly one direct road between any pair of two cities – there would be a total of $20C_2$ roads = 190 roads.
   2. The other key condition in this question is the one which talks about each candidate must visit each of the other cities exactly once and 'No direct road between two cities would be used by more than one candidate.' This means two things. (i) Since each candidate visits each city exactly once, if there are 'c' candidates, there would be a total of $20c$ roads used and since no road is repeated, it means that the 20 roads Candidate A uses will be different from the 20 roads Candidate B uses and so on. Thus, the value of $20c \le 190$ should be an inequality that must be satisfied. This gives us a maximum possible value of c as 9. Hence, option (d) is correct.
9. The circle can be represented as $(x + 2)^2 + (y - 3)^2 = 25$. We, know from the standard form of the equation of a circle $(x - a)^2 + (y - b)^2 = n^2$, that the center of the circle would be (a, b) and the radius would be n. Hence, in this case, the center of the circle would be (–2, 3) and radius would be 5 as shown.

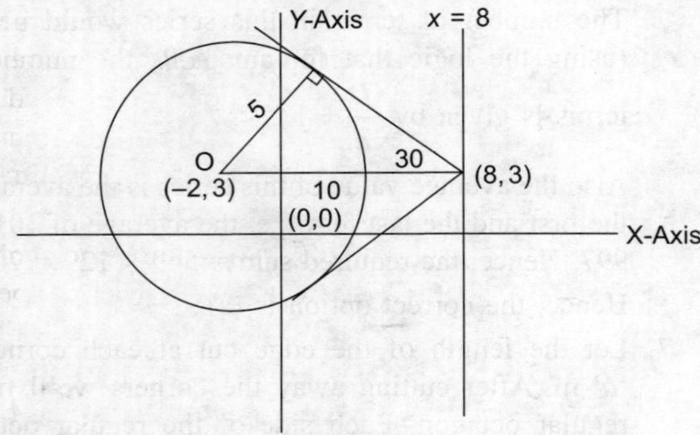

As can be seen from the figure, the intersection point of the locus would be 8, 3. Hence, option (b) is correct.

10. The three triangles *XYA*, *XYB* and *XYZ* are triangles having the same height. Hence, the ratio of their bases should be the same as the ratio of their areas. Since the areas are in GP, with *XYZ* being 9 times the area of *XYA*, it means that *YZ* should be 9 times *YA*. Also, *YB* should be 3 times *YA*. *YZ* = 36 (given), hence *YA* = 4 and *AB* = 8, satisfies *YB* = 3 × *YA*.

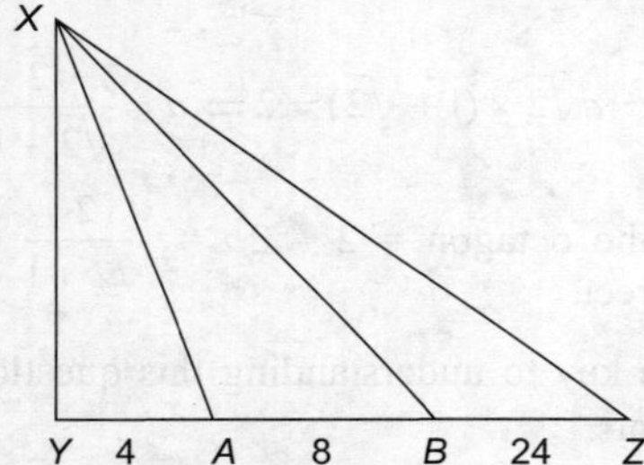

Hence, the correct answer is 8.

11. 240 = $2^4 \times 3 \times 5$; 810 = $2 \times 3^4 \times 5$. From the first condition, we have divisibility in the case of: $\frac{(2\times3^4\times5)^n}{(2^4\times3\times5)}$. '*n*' has to be at least 4, for divisibility to happen in this case. In the second case, we have divisibility for: $\frac{(2^4\times3\times5)^m}{(2\times3^4\times5)^4}$ (Note: We have already worked out that the value of *n* is 4.) The value of *m* has to be at least 16, since the denominator has a term 3^{16}. Thus, the value of $m - n = 16 - 4 = 12$. Hence, the correct answer is 12.

12. In order to solve such questions conveniently, you would need to first create a language representation for yourself with respect to the two sets.

Set *X* can be mentally thought of as:

A positive integral power of 4 – *a* multiple of 3 (with the multiplier being equal to the power of 4 used) – a constant value '1'.

Thus, the set of values in *X* can be calculated as (0, 9, 54, 243 and so on).

Similarly, Set *Y* can be thought of as multiples of 9, starting from 9 × 0 = 0.

The numbers that would belong to the set *Y* will be: (0, 9, 18, 27, 36 and pretty much all multiples of 9). It can be clearly seen that while all values in *X* are also in *Y*, the reverse is not true. Hence, the statement in option (b) is correct.

13. From $\log_a(a^3 + 56) = 6$, we have $a^6 = a^3 + 56$ (using the definition of logs) $\rightarrow a^6 - a^3 - 56 = 0 \rightarrow a^3 = 8$ or –7. Since, a is a positive real number the value of a^3 cannot be –7. Hence, $a^3 = 8 \rightarrow a = 2$. From $6 \times \log_b a = 3$, we get $6 \times \log_b 2 = 3 \rightarrow b^3 = 64$. Hence, $b = 4$. The value of $b - 2a = 4 - 2 \times 2 = 0$. Hence, the correct answer is 0.

14. It is immediately evident that at $x = 0$, the value of the two functions are both equal to 0. Hence, the two functions would definitely intersect at $x = 0$. Next, we equate: $3 \times |x| \times (2x^2 + 1) = 19x^2$ we observe that the functions on both the sides of the equation are even functions, so if we can find the number of values of *x*, for positive '*x*', we can double that number (to account for intersection points when *x* is negative) and get the answer. If $x > 0$, $3 \times |x| \times (2x^2 + 1) = 19x^2 \rightarrow 3 \times x(2x^2 + 1) = 19x^2 \rightarrow 6x^2 - 19x + 3 = 0$. This will have roots as 1/6 and 3. Hence, the graphs of the two functions intersect at –3, –1/6, 0, 1/6 and 3. Hence, we have a total of 5 intersection points for the graphs. Hence, the correct answer is 5.

15. 15 km
A | 2.5 km | X | Y | Z | 2.5 km | B

Let *X*, *Y* and *Z* be the three gutters let *XY* be *x*/2 km and *YZ* be *x* km.

According to the question $\frac{AX}{30} = \frac{5}{60}$ or *AX* = 2.5 km

$$AX + x/2 + x + BZ = 20 \text{ km}$$

$$2.5 + 3x/2 + 2.5 = 20 \text{ km}$$

$$3x/2 = 15 \text{ km}$$

After crossing the gutter 1 he doubled his speed so final speed was 60 kmph.

Time taken to cover distance *XZ* and *ZA* =

$$\frac{(15 + 17.5)\text{ km}}{2 \times 30 \text{ km/hr}} = \frac{32.5}{60} \times 60 = 32.5 \text{ minutes}$$

The patient reaches the hospital in a total of (32.5 + 5) = 37.5 minutes

Maximum time that the doctor gets to attend the patient = 40 – 37.5 – 1 = 1.5 minutes.

16. Let the average speed of his car be S kmph. Then, the total distance traveled by him would be 10S km. Thus, 96969-10S, needs to be a palindromic number. For all speeds like 10 kmph, 20 kmph, 30 kmph the starting meter reading would be 96869; 96769; 96669 and so on. Since, we are asked the maximum possible

average speed (less than 105) it follows that he could have driven a maximum of 1050 kms. Hence, his starting meter reading would ≥ 96969 – 1050 = 95919. The smallest palindromic number in the permissible range would be 95959, which would give us a total distance traveled of 1010 kms in 10 hours and hence, his greatest possible average speed for the journey would be 101 kmph. Hence, the correct answer is 101.

17. Since, $x_{14} = a$, x_{15} would equal $(k – a)$ [we get this by equating $x_{14} + x_{15} = k \rightarrow a + x_{15} = k \rightarrow x_{15} = (k – a)$]. By using the same logic on the equation $x_{15} + x_{16} = k$, we will get $x_{16} = a$. Consequently, $x_{17} = k – a$, $x_{18} = a$, $x_{19} = k – a$, $x_{20} = a$. Thus, we see that every odd term is equal to '$k – a$' and every even term is equal to 'a'. Further, we can develop a similar logic for x_i in the context of 'b'. Since, $x_{27} = b$, $x_{28} = k – b$, $x_{29} = b$ and so on. This series also follows a similar logic with x_i being equal to b, when 'i' is odd and being equal to $k – b$, when 'i' is even.

Thus, for every value of x_i, we have two ways of looking at its value—viz. either in terms of a or in terms of b. Thus, for any x_{even}, we have for instance $x_{20} = a = k – b$.

Solving $a = k – b$, we get $a + b = k$.

Further, when we look at trying to solve for the specific value of what the question has asked us, i.e. the value of $x_{30} + x_{39}$, we realise that we can either solve it in terms of 'a' or in terms of 'b'. If we try to solve it in terms of 'a', we would see the following happening:

$X_{30} + x_{39} = a + k – a = k$

Similarly, in terms of 'b', $x_{30} + x_{39} = k–b + b = k$. Since we know that $k = a + b$ (deduced above), we can conclude $x_{30} + x_{39} = a + b$. However, if we look at the options, none of the options is directly saying that.

Options (b) and (c) can be rejected because their values are not equal to $a + b$. A closer inspection of option (a), gives us an expression: $3(a + b) – 2k$. This expression can be expressed as $3(a + b) – 2(a + b) = (a + b)$ and hence, this is the correct answer.

18. $\dfrac{11^{\frac{2x-y}{2}}}{7^{\frac{2x-y}{2}}} = \dfrac{7^3}{11^3} = \dfrac{11^{-3}}{7^{-3}}$

Hence, $\dfrac{2x-y}{2} = -3 \rightarrow 2x - y = -6.$

From the powers of $3n$ in the second equation, we know $4x – y = y – 4x$ or $y = 4x$.

Hence, $x = 3$ and $y = 12$. The value of $x + y = 15$.

19. Check the options

Option (b): Speed ratio is 4 : 1. If the north bound train takes 12 min then the south bound train would take 48 minutes. As per the questions on that particular day the north bound train is late by 20 minutes, there are only 40 minutes left to complete the journey for both the trains. If the super fast doubles the speed then it would take only 6 minutes to complete the journey. So, the second train would take 40 – 6 = 34 minutes. Hence the required ratio of the speed is 6 : 34 ≈ 1 : 6.

20. The number of ways to distribute the chocolates would be $^{20}C_4 = 3 \times 5 \times 17 \times 19$. The number of factors for this number would be $(1 + 1) \times (1 + 1) \times (1 + 1) \times (1 + 1) = 16$.

21. Let the initial distance between train and point A be x and speed of train and cat be t & c respectively.

Now according to the question: $\dfrac{x}{t} = \dfrac{\frac{3d}{8}}{c}$ or

$$x = \frac{\left(\frac{3d}{8}\right)t}{c} \ldots \quad (1)$$

and $\dfrac{x+d}{t} = \dfrac{\frac{5d}{8}}{c}$ or $x + d = \dfrac{\left(\frac{5d}{8}\right)t}{c}$ (2)

By subtracting equation 1 from 2 we get $d = \dfrac{\left(\frac{2d}{8}\right)t}{c}$

or $\dfrac{t}{c} = \dfrac{4}{1}$. Option (b).

Alternate solution: Assume the distance of the tunnel to be $8x$. Initially the cat is at $3x$ from A and $5x$ from B. Now if you were to use the options, to check which option fits the situation, you would realize the following with option (b) – speed ratio is 4 : 1:

For the meeting at A: cat travels $3x$, train travels $12x$.

For the meeting at B: cat travels $5x$, train travels $12x + 8x = 20x$. This matches the given 4 : 1 ratio and hence is the correct answer.

(**Note:** If you try this with the other options, the meeting at B would not match the given ratio.)

22. $BD = \sqrt{32^2 + 24^2} = 40.$

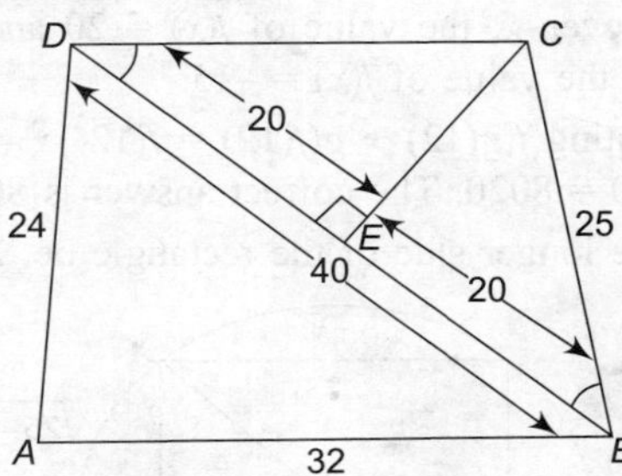

Draw $CE \perp BD$. As ΔBCD is isosceles triangle so $DE = BE$.

$CE = \sqrt{25^2 - 20^2} = 15$

So area of $\Delta ADB = \frac{1}{2} \times 32 \times 24 = 384$ sq.m

Area of $\Delta BCD = 2 \times \frac{1}{2} \times 15 \times 20 = 300$ sq.m

Hence, area of $ABCD = 384 + 300 = 684$ sq.m

The CAT Experience 5

1. It can be seen that at $x = 0$, LHS = RHS = 0. Next, notice that both the LHS and RHS of the equation are even functions. Hence, if we can find a positive integral value of x, at which the equation is satisfied, then a corresponding negative integral value of x, will also exist that would satisfy the equation. Also, the expression on the LHS is a cubic expression, while the expression on the RHS is a quadratic one. Thus, once the value of x, starts becoming larger the LHS will become larger and the two sides of the equation would never match. At $x = 1$, we have $8 < 15$. At $x = 2$, we have $52 < 60$. At $x = 3$, we have $168 > 135$. After this if we increase the value of x, the value of the LHS will never become equal to or smaller than the value of the RHS. Hence, we can conclude that there is only one integral value of x at which the equation is satisfied. Hence, the correct answer is 1.
2. The value of the term $\left[\frac{1}{3}+\frac{N}{45}\right]$ is 0 for N between 1 to 29. For $N = 30$ to 74, the value of the expression is always 1, while for N = 75 to 119, the value of the expression is 2 every time. Thus, if we start with N_1 as 1, N_2 as 2 and go till $N_x = 120$, the value of the LHS becomes equal to $0 \times 29 + 1 \times 45 + 1 \times 45 \times 2 = 135$. However, we want the LHS to be less than 135. Hence, the largest possible value of $N_x = 119$. The largest possible sum of N_1 to N_x is the sum of 1 to 119 = $\frac{119 \times 120}{2} = 7140$. Option (d) is correct.
3. Since, $f(x^3 - x^2) = 20$, it means that $f(0) = 20$ (taking $x = 1$); $f(4) = 20$ (taking $x = 2$); $f(18) = 20$ (taking $x = 3$) and so on.

   Also, $f(1) + f(0) = 5$, hence $f(1) = -15$. $f(1) + f(2) = 5 \rightarrow f(2) = 20$. Using this further we can see that for every even x, the value of $f(x) = 20$ and for every odd x, the value of $f(x) = -15$.

   Evaluating $f(g(12) + g(f(12)) = f(12^3) + g(20) = 20 + 8000 = 8020$. The correct answer is 8020.
4. Let the longer side of the rectangle be '$2a$'.

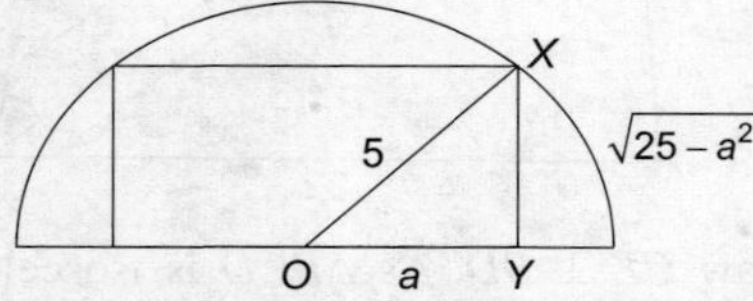

From the figure the area A of the rectangle would be $A = 2a \times \left(\sqrt{25-a^2}\right) \rightarrow A^2 = 4a^2 \times \left(25-a^2\right) =$

$-4a^4 + 100a^2 = -4\left(a^4 - 25a^2 + 156.25 - 156.25\right)$

$= 625 - 4\left(a^2 - 12.5\right)^2$

The above expression will get maximized when

$\left(a^2 - 12.5\right)^2 = 0 \rightarrow a^2 = \frac{25}{2} \rightarrow a = \frac{5}{\sqrt{2}}$

Thus, the length of the rectangle $= \frac{10}{\sqrt{2}} = 5\sqrt{2}$.

The Breadth will be $\left(\sqrt{25-a^2}\right) = \frac{5}{\sqrt{2}} = 2.5\sqrt{2}$

Hence, the perimeter of the rectangle would be $15\sqrt{2}$. Hence, the correct answer is option (d).

5. For the number of people who are fans of all three games, the maximum value is 52 while the minimum value is 7 as shown in the following figures:

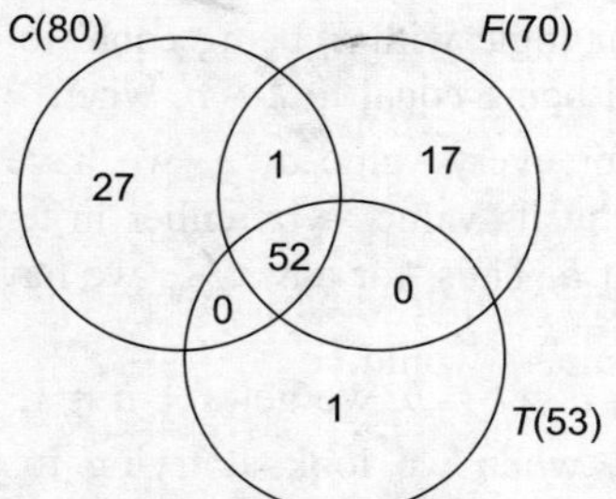

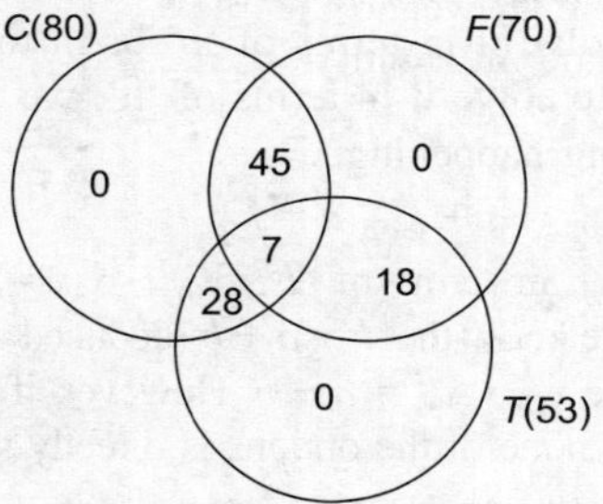

Hence, the required sum is 52 + 7 = 59.

6. In order to solve this question, you should count the digit 6 appearing in units digit, separately from the instances of the digit 6 appearing in the tens place and appearing in the hundreds place.

   When you want to find out the number of times 6 appears in the unit digit, you will have to make a series as follows: 6, 16, 26, 36 … 636.

   It should be evident to you that the above series has 64 terms because it starts from 06, 16, 26 … and continues till 636. The digit 6 will appear once in the unit digit for each of these 64 numbers.

   Next you need to look at how many times the digit 6 appears in the ten's place.

   In order to do this, we will need to look at instances when 6 appears in the tens place. These will be in 6 different ranges 60s, 160s, 260s, 360s, 460s, 560s and in each of these ranges there are 10 numbers each with exactly one instance of the digit 6 in the tens place, a total of 60 times.

Lastly, we need to look at the number of instances where 6 appears in the hundreds place. For this, we need to form the series 600, 601, 602, 603 … 639. This series will have 40 numbers each with exactly one instance of the digit 6 appearing in the hundreds place.

Therefore, the required answer would be 64 + 60 + 40 = 164.

Hence, option (d) is correct.

7. Let the speed of the escalator be x steps per second and Ravi's speed be y steps per second. Then we have from the information:

$45x + 45y = 20x + 20 \times 3y \rightarrow 25x = 15y$ or $y = \frac{5}{3}x$.

Hence, the total distance on the escalator is

$45x + 45y = 45x + 45 \times \frac{5}{3}x = 120x$. At a speed of x steps per second, the escalator would cover a distance of $120x$ steps in 120 seconds. The correct answer is 120.

8. Solve by putting values: suppose we have $n = 5$; the members would be {(1, 2), (1, 3), (1, 4), (1, 5), (2, 3), (2, 4), (2, 5), (3, 4), (3, 5), (4, 5)}.

In this case, any member can be found to have three enemies.

Thus, the answer to the above question should give us a value of 3 with $n = 5$.

Option (a): $n - 3 = 5 - 3 = 2$. Hence, cannot be the answer.

Option (b): 8/2 = 4. Hence, cannot be the answer.

Option (c): 10 – 7 = 3. To be considered.

Option (d): 6/2 = 3. To be considered.

We still need to choose one answer between options (c) and (d).

It can be seen that for $n = 6$, the values of options (c) and (d) will differ. Hence, we need to visualise how many enemies each member would have for $n = 6$.

The members would be {(1, 2), (1, 3), (1, 4), (1, 5), (1, 6), (2, 3), (2, 4), (2, 5), (2, 6), (3, 4), (3, 5), (3, 6), (4, 5), (4, 6), (5, 6)}. It can be clearly seen that the member (1, 2) will have six enemies. Option (c) gives us a value of five and hence, can be eliminated while option (d) gives us a value of six leaving it as the only possible answer.

9. Again for this question, consider the following situation where $n = 6$.

The members would be {(1, 2), (1, 3), (1, 4), (1, 5), (1, 6), (2, 3), (2, 4), (2, 5), (2, 6), (3, 4), (3, 5), (3, 6), (4, 5), (4, 6), (5, 6)}.

Suppose we consider the pair (1, 2) and (1, 3). Their common friends would be (1, 4), (1, 5), (1, 6) and (2, 3).

Thus, there are four common friends for any pair of friendly members. (You can verify this by taking any other pair of friend members.)

Thus, for $n = 6$, the answer should be 4.

Checking the options, it is clear that only option (d) gives us a value of 4.

10. **Thought-process:**

Deduction 1: Question interpretation: The solution language for this question requires you to think about what possible amount could be such that when its rupees and paisa value are interchanged, the resultant value is 50 paisa more than thrice the original amount.

Deduction 2: Option-checking process:

Armed with this logic, suppose we were to check for option (a), i.e. the value is above ₹22 but below ₹23. This essentially means that the amount must be approximately between ₹22.66 and ₹22.69. We get the paisa amount to be between 66 and 69, based on the fact that the relationship between the actual amount x and the transposed amount y is: y – 50 paisa = $3x$.

Hence, values below 22.66 and values above 22.70 are not possible.

- From this point onwards, we just have to check whether this relationship is satisfied by any of the values between ₹22.66 and ₹22.69.
- Also, realise the fact that in each of these cases the paisa value in the value of the transposed amount y would be 22. Thus, $3x$ should give us the paisa value as 72 (since we have to subtract 50 paisa from the value of 'y' in order to get the value of $3x$).
- This also means that the unit digit of the paisa value of $3x$ should be 2.
- It can be clearly seen that none of the numbers 66, 67, 68 or 69 when being multiplied by 3 give us a units digit of 2. Hence, this is not a possible answer.

Checking for option (b) in the same fashion:

You should realise that the outer limit for the range of values when the amount is between 18 and 19 is: 18.54 to 18.57. Also, the number of paisa in the value of the transposed sum 'y' would be 18. Hence, the value of $3x$ should give us a paisa value as 68 paisa. Again, using the units digit principle, it is clear that the only value where the units digit would be 8 would be for a value of 18.56.

Hence, we cheque for the check amount to be 18.56. Transposition of the rupee and paisa value would give us 56.18. When you subtract 50 paisa from this, you would get 55.68 which also happens to be thrice 18.56. Hence, the correct answer is Option (b).

Notice here that if you can work out this logic in your reactions, the time required to checking each option would be no more than 30 seconds. Hence, the net problem solving time to get the second option as correct would not be more than one minute. Add the reading time and this problem should still not require more than two minutes.

11. If the fuel efficiency at 50 km/h is 19.5 km/liter, then at 70 km/h, the fuel efficiency would be 15 km per liter (since it uses 30% more fuel when it travels at 70 km/h as compared to traveling at 50 km/h). @ 15 km/liter, the truck would travel 150 kms in 10 liters of fuel.

12. The equation for calculation of the interior angle of a regular polygon of n sides is:

$$\frac{180-\frac{(n-2)\times 180}{n}}{180-\frac{(2n-2)\times 180}{2n}}=\frac{2}{1}\rightarrow n=7.$$

13. The distance between Ahmedabad and Baroda being 100 kms, it is evident that by 7:30 am, Navjivan Express would have covered 50 kms (travelling @ 50 kmph for 1 hour), while the Howrah-Ahmedabad Express would have covered 20 kms (travelling 40 kmph for 30 minutes). Thus, the distance between the two trains would be 30 kms at 7:30 am. Since their relative speed is 90 kmph, the remaining distance of 30 kms would be covered in 1/3rd of an hour – or 20 minutes. Option (b) is correct.

14. H + F + T = 100 and 100 × H + 50 × F + 10 × T = 5620. There are two equations and 3 unknowns, which means this is a multiple possibility situation. At the first level of thought we realise that the number of 100 rupee notes has to be more than 12 (as at 12 notes of 100, would mean remaining 88 notes have to have a value of 4420, which is not possible with only 50 and 10 rupee notes. At 13, 100 rupee notes, 87 notes need to have a value of 5620 – 1300 = 4320, which is again not possible (as 87, 50 rupee notes will give a value of 4350 & 86, 50 rupee notes +1 ten rupee note would give a value of 4310). Our first feasible solutions is 14 × 100 + 84 × 50 + 2 × 10 = 5620. The next solutions would be 18, 75, 7; and we can see that each of the numbers would then move in arithmetic progressions of +4, –9 and +5 respectively. So the set of solutions is (14, 84, 2; 18, 75, 7; 22, 66, 12; 26, 57, 17; 30, 48, 22; 34, 39, 27; 38, 30, 32; 42, 21, 37; 46, 12, 42; 50, 3, 47). For each of the notes to be greater than 10, the maximum number of 100 rupee notes is 46.

15. The total price of the 10 fruits would be 10 × 28 = 280. The extreme cases for orange and apple pricing are: One extreme, when every orange had a price equal to every apple: 4 × O + 6 × A = 10 × A = 280 → A = O = ₹28.

Other extreme: When the price of each orange is equal to double the price of each apple: 4 × O + 6 × A = 8 × A + 6 × A = 14 × A = ₹280. Price of each apple = 20 and price of each orange = 40. Thus, the price of each orange varies from ₹28 to ₹40. Since, the only equation we have is 4 × O + 6 × A = 280, there are infinite possible values of A (Between 20 and 28) and O (between 28 to 40), while obeying the constraint that the price of an orange is between 1 to 2 times the price of an apple. However, we have to find number of integral values for the cost of 2 oranges and 6 apples. Thus, for O, any multiple of 0.5, between 28 to 40 should give us an integral cost of 2 oranges. We can count all these multiples like 28, 28.5, 29, 29.5…40 provided that in each case, the value of 6 × A should also be integral. Doing a small trial for O = 28.5, we get from 4 × O + 6 × A = 280, the value of A = 27.666, for O = 29, A = 27.33, for O = 29.5, A = 27 and so on. Thus, to answer this question, we need the multiple of 0.5 between 28 and 40. There will be 25 such values. Hence, the correct answer is 25.

Solutions for Questions 16 to 18:

The paths traversed by the three people can be seen to be $6r$, $6r + 3r\sqrt{3}$ and $6r + 6r\sqrt{3}$.

(**Note:** These are derived by using the properties of 30 – 60 – 90 triangles. For instance, if you connect A_2 with B_2 and make a perpendicular from A_2 to the path connecting B_2B_3, you would get a 30 – 60 – 90 triangle. You would get similar triangles at each of the corners.

16. It can be clearly seen that $b - a = c - b = 3r\sqrt{3}$. Hence, option (a) is correct.

17. Assume the value of r to be 30. Then, total time taken by the first sprinter A would be: $\frac{180}{3+2+4} = 9$ hours. In 9 hours, B would also come back to her starting point as she would cover a distance of $180 + 90\sqrt{3}$ at a speed of $20 + 10\sqrt{3}$. Hence, B would be at her starting point B_2. In the same time, C would be able to cover 2 parts of her three part journey. This can be thought of as: she has to cover a distance of $60 + 60\sqrt{3}$ on each side and her speed for the first two sides is $13.33 + 13.33\sqrt{3}$. Hence, she would take 60/13.33 = 4.5 hours per side. Thus, C would be at C_3. Hence, option (c) is correct i.e. B is at B_2 and C at C_3.

18. The ratio of squares of the speeds is given as the ratio of the areas of the respective triangles. Since all the three triangles are equilateral triangles, their areas would be proportional to the squares of the sides. Hence, $u^2 : v^2 : w^2 = 4 : (2 + \sqrt{3})^2 : 4(1 + 2\sqrt{3})^2$.

Thus, $u : v : w = 2 : (2 + \sqrt{3}) : 2(1 + 2\sqrt{3})$. Also, we know that one side of B's triangle is: $r(2 + \sqrt{3})$. So, in the time B reaches B_3 after covering one side, A would also cover one side and reach A_2, while C would reach C_2. Hence, option (c) is correct.

19. Since the question represents a cubic expression, and we want the smallest possible value of b—keeping

the constraint of their roots being three consecutive values—a little bit of guess estimation would lead you to think of –1, 0 and 1 as the three roots for minimising the value of b.

Thus, the expression would be $(x + 1)(x)(x - 1) = (x^2 + x)(x - 1) = x^3 - x$. This gives us the value of b as –1. It can be seen that changing the values of the roots from –1, 0 and 1 would result in increasing the coefficient of x–which is not what we want. Hence, the correct answer should be that the minimum value of b would be –1.

Note: For trial purposes, if you were to take the values of the three roots as 0, 1, and 2, the expressions would become $x(x - 1)(x - 2) = (x^2 - x)(x - 2)$ which would lead to the coefficient of x being 2. This would obviously increase the value of the coefficient of x above –1.

You could also go for changing the three consecutive integral roots in the other direction to –2, –1 and 0. In such a case the expression would become: $x(x + 2)(x + 1) = (x^2 + 2x)(x + 1) \rightarrow$ which would again give us the coefficient of x as + 2.

The total solving time for this question would be 30 seconds, if you were to hit on the right logic for taking the roots as –1, 0 and 1. In case you had to check for the value of b in different situations by altering the values of the roots (as explained above), the time would still be less than two minutes.

20. The number of spectators has to be such that it leaves a remainder of 5 when divided by 8, 9, 11 or 12. The LCM of 8, 9, 11 and 12 = 12 × 11 × 3 × 2 = 792. Thus, 792 + 5 = 797 is the first number that satisfies this condition. Next numbers would be 797 + 792 = 1589; 1589 + 792 = 2381; 2381 + 792 = 3173; 3173 + 792 = 3965. We can see that 3965 is a multiple of 13. Hence, there are 3965 spectators in the stadium. Since 3965/16 gives us a quotient of 247, the correct answer is 247.
21. 32 days is not possible, since, if B takes 32 days to do the job, then in the last 4 days when he works alone, he would do 1/8 of the job, which would mean that A, B, C in the first 7 days would do 7/8 of the job. This would lead to an interpretation that A, B, C can do the whole job in 8 days, which contradicts the information in the question. If we take B as taking 24 days, B's work per day would be 4.166. In the last 4 days working along B would do $1/6^{th}$ of the work (or 16.66%). Thus, in first 7 days B would do 7 × 4.1666 = 29.166% of the work. B would have done a total of 45.33% of the work. Thus, in 7 days A and C would do 54.66% of the work giving their work rate as 54.66/7 (per day) < 8% per day. This is not possible, since in this case their time to complete the work would be more than 12.5 days which contradicts the information in the question. Hence, both (i) and (iii) are not possible values for B's time to complete the job. We can check for (ii) and (iv) and see that those values adhere to both the limits mentioned in the question.

    Hence, the correct answer is option (c).
22. He has to have at least six boxes with the same number of oranges in it. The logic of this question comes from the pigeon hole principle—where we take the ratio 128/25 and take the least integer value greater than this ratio. Note, 25 comes from the different values of oranges that you can put in the boxes. Hence, we would get six as the answer.

The CAT Experience 6

1. This one is an easy question as all you need to do is understand that given the unit digit is a prime number, it would mean that the number can only be of the form *abc*2; *abc*3 or *abc*5 or *abc*7. Further, for each of these, the product of the four digits $a \times b \times c \times$ units digit has to be prime. This can occur only if $a = b = c = 1$. Thus, there are only four such numbers viz: 1112, 1113, 1115 and 1117. Hence, option (a) is correct.
2. The rates at which Pipes A, B, and C can individually fill a tank follow a harmonic progression. This means the times it takes them to fill the tank individually form an arithmetic progression (AP).

    Since Pipe C takes thrice as long as Pipe A, Pipe B's time to fill the tank falls in between A and C, similar to the middle number in an increasing sequence.

    In terms of ratios, the times taken by Pipes A, B, and C to fill the tank are in the ratio 1 : 2 : 3. This means that the work rates of A : B : C = 6 : 3 : 2. If we take A's work per hour as 6 units, B's as 3 units and C's as 2 units we can think as follows:

    We are given that 6A + 7B + 18C fills the tank. Thus, the total work is: 6 × 6 + 7 × 3 + 18 × 2 = 93 units. At the rate of 3 units per hour, B will fill the tank in 93/3 = 31 hours. The correct answer is 31 hours.
3. The distance between City *A* and City *B* would be 45 × 2 + 35 × 2 = 160 kms (as per Rajiv's movement plan). Aditi would cover this distance in three equal parts of 53.33 kms @ of 30 kmph, 40 kmph and 50 kmph respectively.

    Petrol consumed by Aditi = 53.33/16 + 53.33/24 + 53.33/16 = 160/48 + 160/72 + 160/48 = 640/72 = 8.9 liters, option (c).
4. The distance between City *A* and City *B* would be 45 × 2 + 35 × 2 = 160 kms (as per Rajiv's movement plan). Aditi would cover this distance in three equal parts of 53.33 kms @ of 30 kmph, 40 kmph and 50 kmph respectively.

In order to minimise the amount of petrol consumed, the journey should be traversed at 40 kmph (since the Highest mileage for the car is at that speed). Thus, the amount of fuel required would be 160/24 = 6.67 liters, option (a).

5. The answer would be given by 22 + 8 and is quite easy to work out. We need to understand that since there are 22 days when they play tennis or do yoga, in each of these 22 days there would be either a free morning or evening. This would account for a total of 22 free mornings/evenings. Also, the total number of free morning/evenings is 24 + 14 = 38. This means that 16 free mornings/evenings are still available—which would mean 8 days when they did nothing.

6. The total marks of the 7 students would be 7 × 35 = 245. At one extreme the top 3 students can score 50, 49 and 48 marks. The remaining 98 marks will be scored by the remaining four students. To minimize Arun's score, we can see that if we take 26, 25, 24, 23 for the 4th to the 7th student, 26 is the minimum that Arun could score – we can see that if we try to reduce Arun's score to below 26 (say 25) the sum of the four least scores cannot reach 98.

The minimization for Hemendra would happen when we maximise the other six scores as 50, 49, 48, 28, 27, 26. Hence, Hemendra (minimum) = 245 – 50 – 49 – 48 – 28 – 27 – 26 =17.

The required answer is 26 – 17 = 9.

7. From the first equation we have: $a \times (b + c + d) = 19 \rightarrow a = 1$, $(b + c + d) = 19$. From the second equation we have $d \times (a + b + c) = 51 \rightarrow$ multiple possibilities of $d = 17$ and a, b, c as 1, 1, 1 or $d = 3$ and $(a + b + c) = 17$. Exploring this further, since $a = 1$, $b + c = 16$. To maximise the value of $a \times b \times c \times d$, we can take $b = c = 8$ and the required answer is $1 \times 8 \times 8 \times 3 = 192$.

8. The roots of the first equation would be $(2+3\sqrt{3})$ and $(2-3\sqrt{3})$. Hence, sum of roots $= -\frac{c}{b} = 4 \rightarrow \frac{c}{b} = -4$. The product of roots $= \frac{d}{b} = -23$.

The roots of the second equation would be $(3+2\sqrt{2})$ and $(3-2\sqrt{2})$. Hence, sum of roots $= = -\frac{e}{b} = 6 \rightarrow \frac{e}{b} = -6$. The product of roots $= \frac{f}{b} = 1$

To evaluate the value of $\frac{d}{e} - \frac{c-2e}{f} = \frac{\frac{d}{b}}{\frac{e}{b}} - \frac{\frac{c}{b} - \frac{2e}{b}}{\frac{f}{b}}$

$= \frac{-23}{-6} - \frac{-4-2\times(-6)}{1} = \frac{23}{6} - 8 = -\frac{25}{6}$.

Option (d) is correct.

9. Since $f(3) = 0$ (given), the polynomial can be expressed as $f(x) = a \times (x - 3)^2$ $f(5) = 20 \rightarrow a \times [5 - 3]^2 = 20 \rightarrow a = 5$. Hence, $f(0) = 5 \times [0 - 3]^2 = 45$. Hence, option (d) is correct.

10. This question is based on odd numbers as only with an odd value of x you would be getting integers; if you halved the value of rice and took out another half a kg from the shop store.

From the options, let us start from the second option. (**Note**: In such questions, one should make it a rule to start from one of the middle options only as the normal realisation we would get from checking one option would have been that more than one option gets removed if we have not picked up the correct option—as we would normally know whether the correct answer needs to be increased from the value we just checked or should be decreased.)

Thus, trying for $x = 7$ according to the second option, you would get

$7 \rightarrow 3 \rightarrow 1 \rightarrow 0$ (after three customers)

This means that $5 \le x \le 8$ is a valid option for this question. Also, since the question is definitive about the correct range, there cannot be two ranges. Hence, we can conclude that option (b) is correct.

Note: The total solving time for this question should not be more than 30 seconds. Even if you are not such an experienced solver through options, and you had to check 2–3 options in order to reach the correct option, you would still need a maximum of 90 seconds.

Solutions for Questions 11 and 12:

Since, 3 is a root of the equation, we have $9a + 3b + c = 0$ (**Theory point**—A root of any equation $f(x) = 0$ has the property that if it is used to replace 'x' in every part of the equation, then the equation $f(x) = 0$ should be satisfied.)

Also $f(5) = -3f(2)$ gives us that $25a + 5b + c = -3(4a + 2b + c) \rightarrow 37a + 11b + 4c = 0$.

Combining both equations, we can see that $37a + 11b + 4c = 4(9a + 3b + c) \rightarrow a - b = 0$, i.e. $a = b$.

Now, we know that the sum of roots of a quadratic equation is given by $-b/a$. Hence, the sum of roots has to be equal to –1. Since one of the roots is 3, the other must be –4.

The answer to question 11 would be option (b).

For question 12, we need the sum of $a + b + c$. We know that $a + b = 0$. Also, product of roots is –12. One of the possible equations could be $(x - 3)(x + 4) = 0 \rightarrow x^2 + x - 12 = 0$, which gives us the value of $a + b + c$ as –10. However, –10 is not in the options. This should make us realise that there is a possibility of another equation as: $(2x - 6)(2x +$

8) = 0 → $4x^2 + 4x - 48 = 0$ in which case the value of $a + b + c$ changes. Hence, the correct answer is 'cannot be determined'.

13. Let $P_1 = P$ and $A_1 = A$. Then according to the question:

$$\frac{P_1 + P_2 + P_3 + \ldots}{A_1 + A_2 + A_3 + \ldots} = \frac{P + \frac{P}{\sqrt{2}} + \cdots \infty}{A + \frac{A}{2} + \cdots \infty} = \frac{\frac{P}{1 - \frac{1}{\sqrt{2}}}}{2A}$$

$$= \frac{P\sqrt{2}}{\sqrt{2} - 1} \times \frac{1}{2A}$$

$$= \left(\frac{\sqrt{2}P(\sqrt{2}+1)}{2A}\right)$$

$$= \frac{\sqrt{2} \times 4a(\sqrt{2}+1)}{2 \times a^2} \quad \text{(since, } P = 4a,\ A = a^2\text{)}$$

$$= \frac{\sqrt{2} \times 2(\sqrt{2}+1)}{a} = \frac{2(2+\sqrt{2})}{a}$$

14. Since we are replacing 10% of the liquid every time it means that there will be successive percentage decreases of the amount of milk by 10% each time. Thus, after 1 time, we will have $100 \times \frac{9}{10} \times \frac{9}{10} = 81\%$ milk in the mixture, and consequently 19% water. For the purpose of this problem we need $100 \times \left(\frac{9}{10}\right)^n < 33.3333$. We can see that at $n = 11$, the quantity of water becomes greater than twice the quantity of milk in the mixture. Hence, the correct answer is 11.

15. In order to solve this question, we need to think of the kinds of numbers which would qualify as magic numbers. Given the definition of a magic number in the question, a number of the form 2*mnpmnpq* would be a magic number while at the same time a number of the form 2*mnpqmnp* would also qualify as a magic number. In this situation, each of *m*, *n* and *p* can take any of the ten digit values from 0 to 9. Also, *q* would also have ten different possibilities from 0 to 9. Thus, the total number of numbers of the form 2*mnpmnpq* would be 10^4 = 10000. Similarly, the total number of numbers of the form 2*mnpqmnp* would also be 10^4 = 10000. This gives us a total of 20000 numbers. However, in this count the numbers like 21111111, 22222222, 23333333, 24444444, etc., have been counted under both the categories. Hence, we need to remove these numbers once each (a total of 9 reductions). Also, the number 20000000 is not a valid number according to the question. This number needs to be removed from both the counts.

Hence, the final answer = 20000 – 9 – 2 = 19989.

16.

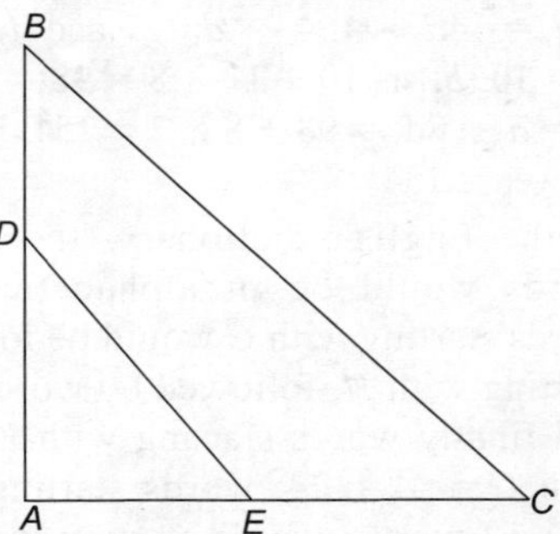

ΔDAE & ΔBAC are similar triangles and the ratio of the area of the similar triangles is the ratio of the square of the corresponding sides of the triangle. Hence, the area of the smaller triangle = 34 × 0.65 × 0.65 = 14.365

17.

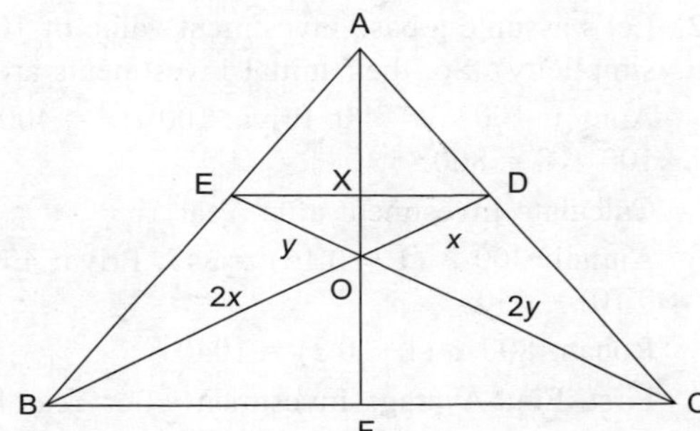

The median divides the triangle into six smaller triangles of equal area. Hence, areas of triangles BOF and COF are 36 each. So area of BOC = 36 + 36 = 72. The triangle DOE, is similar to triangle BOF and these have lengths in the ratio 1 : 2. Hence, their areas would be 1 : 2^2 = 1 : 4. Hence, Area of triangle DOE = 72/4 = 18. Thus area of OXE = 18/2 = 9.

18. $f(0, 1) = 1 + 1 = 2$

$f(x + 1, 0) = f(x, 1)$

put $x = 0$, $f(0 + 1, 0) = f(1, 0) = f(0, 1) = 2$

$f(x + 1, y + 1) = f(x, f(x + 1, y))$

put $x = 0$, $y = 0$ in the above equation we get:

$f(1, 1) = f(0, f(1, 0)) = f(0, 2) = 2 + 1 = 3.$

Now put $x = 0$, $y = 1$ in $f(x + 1, y + 1) = f(x, f(x + 1, y))$, we get:

$f(1, 2) = f(0, f(1, 1)) = f(0, 3) = 3 + 1 = 4.$

19. $(p^2 + q^2) = (p + q)^2 - 2pq = (a - 2)^2 + 2(a + 1) = a^2 - 2a + 6 = a^2 - 2a + 1 + 5 = (a - 1)^2 + 5$. This expression can be minimised at $a - 1 = 0$ and its minimum value is 5.

20. Let d_1 and d_2 be the common differences of the two given series. Since, it is given to us that $a_7 = b_{11}$ and $a_{29} = b_{25}$, we can work out that $22d_1 = 14d_2$. Since both d_1 and d_2 are prime numbers, we can work out that

$22d_1 = 14d_2 = 154 \rightarrow d_1 = 7$ and $d_2 = 11$. Also, since $b_3 = 10$, $b_{11} = 10 + 11 \times 8 = 98 = a_7$. Consequently, $a_{15} = a_7 + 8d_1 = 98 + 8 \times 7 = 154$. Hence, the correct answer is 154.

21. In the English dictionary, the ordering of the words would be in alphabetical order. Thus, words starting with *C* would be followed by words starting with *H*, followed by words starting with *J* and finally words starting with *L*. Words starting with *C* = 4! = 24; words starting with *H* = 4! ÷ 2! = 12 words; words starting with *J* = 4! ÷ 2! = 12 words. This gives us a total of 48 words. The 49th and the 50th words would start with *L*. The 49th word would be the first word starting with *L* (= *LCCHJ*) and the 50th word would be the 2nd word starting with L – which would be *LCCJH*. Option (c) is correct.

22. Let's assume a base investment value of 100 rs. for simplicity). So, their initial investments are:

Anmol: 100×3 = 300; Priya: 100 × 4 = 400; Rohan: 100 × 8 = 800

Calculate Investment after Year 1:

Anmol: 300 × (1 + 0.15) = 345; Priya: 400 × (1 + 0.10) = 440;

Rohan: 800 × (1 + 0.3) = 1040

First: Find Average Investment after Year 1:

Average Investment = $\frac{345+440+1040}{3}$ = 608.33

Solve for Priya's Return in Year 2 (unknown):

We know Priya's investment after year 2 becomes equal to the average (608.33). Let R be Priya's return in year 2

Year 1 Investment × (1 + Year 2 Return) = Average Investment

⇒ 440 × (1 + R) = 608.33

R = (612 / 440) – 1 ≈ 0.38 → Hence, she gets a 38% return in the second year.

Option (c) is correct.

The CAT Experience 7

1. The number can be visualised as:

1	0	0	1	0	0	1	0	0	1	0	0	1	0	0	1	0	0
3^{17}	3^{16}	3^{15}	3^{14}	3^{13}	3^{12}	3^{11}	3^{10}	3^9	3^8	3^7	3^6	3^5	3^4	3^3	3^2	3^1	3^0

Now in the base 27, we can visualise this number as:

—	—	—	—	—	—
27^5	27^4	27^3	27^2	27^1	27^0

When you want to write this number in base 27 the unit digit of the number will have to account for the value of 3^2 in the above number. Since the unit digit of the number in base 27 will correspond to 27^0 we would have to use 27^0, 9 times to make a value 3^2. The number would now become:

—	—	—	—	—	9
27^5	27^4	27^3	27^2	27^1	27^0

Similarly, the number of times that we will have to use 27^1 in order to make the value of 3^5 (or 243) will be $\frac{243}{27}$ = 9. Hence the second last digit of the number will also be 9.

Similarly, to make a value of 3^8 using 27^2, the number of times we will have to use 27^2 will be given by $\frac{3^8}{27^2} = \frac{3^8}{3^6}$ = 9. The number would now look as:

—	—	—	9	9	9
27^5	27^4	27^3	27^2	27^1	27^0

It can be further predicted that each of subsequent 1's in the original number will equal 9 in the number, which is being written in base 27. Since the original number in base 3 has 18 digits, the left most '1' in that number will be covered by a number corresponding to 27^5 in the new number (i.e., 3^{15}). Hence the required number will be a 6-digit number 999999. Hence, option (a) is correct.

2. When we write all 6-digit numbers, we will have to write all the numbers from 100000 to 999999, a total of 9 lac numbers in 6 digits without omitting a single number. There will be a complete symmetry and balance in the use of all the digits. However, the digit 0 is not going to be used in the leftmost place.

Using this logic, we can visualise that when we write 9 lakh, 6-digit numbers, the units place, tens place, hundreds place, thousands place, ten thousands place and lakh place — Each of these places will be written 9 lakh times. Thinking about the units place, we can think as follows: In writing, the units place 9 lakh times (once for every number) we will be using the digit 0, 1, 2, 3 … 9 an equal number of times. Hence, any particular digit like 6 would get used in the units digit a total number of 90000 times (9 lakh/10). The same logic will continue for tens, hundreds, thousands and ten thousands, i.e. the digit 6 will be used (9 lakh/10) = 90000 times in each of these places (Note here that we are dividing by 10 because we have to equally distribute 9 lakh digits amongst the ten digits 0, 1, 2, 3, 4, 5, 6, 7, 8, 9).

Finally, for the lakh place since "0" is not be used in the lakh place as it is the leftmost digit of the number, the number of times the digit 6 will be used would be 9 lakh/9 = 1 lakh. Hence, the next time you are solving the problem of this type, you should solve directly using $\frac{9\text{ lakh}}{9} + \frac{9\text{ lakh}}{10} \times 5 = 5{,}50{,}000$.

Hence, option (a) is the correct answer.

3. The value of $|x + 3| + |x - 3|$ is minimized when we take the value of x as any number between -3 and $+3$. Since, x is not necessarily an integer in this question, it means that the value of x can be any integer/decimal value between -3 and $+3$. There are infinite values possible for x. If we try to take the value of m as larger than 3, then the minimum value of the expression will become larger than 6. For instance at $m = 4$, the expression $|x + 3| + |x - 4|$ would have a minimum value of 7 (and can never be made equal to 6. Hence, the largest possible value of m possible is 3.
4. From the first equation, we have A + B = 6 and A × B = $m/4$. Thus, the roots of $x^2 + nx + n = 0$ are 6 and $m/4$. Thus, we have Sum of roots: $-n = 6 + m/4$ and Product of roots $n = 6 \times m/4$. Solving we get $m = -24/7$ and $n = -36/7$. Thus $(m - n) = 12/7$. The required value of $7 \times (m - n) = 12$. Hence, the correct answer is 12.
5. If we assume the average amount given to the $(n - 2)$ people as 220, the given situation can be expressed as a linear equation as:

   $252n - 220(n - 2) = 2 \times 604 \rightarrow 32n = 768 \rightarrow n = 24$. Note, any value of the average for $(n - 2)$ people taken below 220, will reduce the value of n.

   Hence, the maximum possible value of n is 24.
6. Since 2 people need to be given 604 each, the total amount of money has to be above ₹1208. If we take $n = 5$, we get total money $= 252 \times 5 = 1260$. After giving 604 each to 2 people, ₹52 will be shared by 3 remaining people, each getting an average of 17.33. Since, this average is referred to as an integer in the question, we will reject the value of n as 5. At $n = 6$, total money $= 252 \times 6 = 1512$. Money left for 4 people $= 1512 - 1208 = 304$. Each person gets an average amount of $304/4 = 76$. Hence, 6 is the minimum value of n.

   Hence, the correct answer is 6.
7. The best and the quickest way to solve this problem is to put $x = y$ and check the options.

   $$f(x) + f(y) = f(x) + f(x) = 2f(x) = 2\log\left(\frac{1+x}{1-x}\right)$$

   Now check the options. Option (b) gives us:

   $$F\{(x + y)/(1 + xy)\} = f\{(x + x)/(1 + x.x)\}$$

   $$= f\left(\frac{2x}{1+x^2}\right) = \log\left(\frac{1+\frac{2x}{1+x^2}}{1-\frac{2x}{1+x^2}}\right)$$

   $$= \log\left(\frac{1+2x+x^2}{1+x^2-2x}\right)$$

   $$= \log\left(\frac{1+x}{1-x}\right)^2 = 2\log\left(\frac{1+x}{1-x}\right)$$

   Hence, this is the correct answer.

   Alternately, you could also solve this question by taking $x = y = 0.5$. (**Note:** Since, there are no constraints on the values of x and y, you are free to take any value that is convenient). At $x = y = 0.5$: we get: $f(x) + f(y) = 2\log 3 = \log 9$. Only, option (b) gives us log 9 as its' outcome if we insert $x = y = 0.5$ in it. Hence, this option would be correct.
8. $ax^2 + bx + 1 = 0$

   For real roots

   $b^2 - 4ac \geq 0$

   $\therefore\ b^2 - 4a(1) \geq 0$

   $\therefore\ b^2 \geq 4a$

   For $a = 1$, possible values of b are 2, 3, 4.

   $a = 2$, $4a = 8$, possible values of b are 3, 4.

   $a = 3$, $4a = 12$, possible value of b is 4.

   $a = 4$, $4a = 16$, possible value of b is 4.

   $\therefore$ Number of equations possible = 7.
9. The first number to have a seed of 9 would be the number 9 itself.

   The next number whose seed is be 9 will be 18, then 27 and you should recognise that we are talking about numbers which are multiples of 9. Hence, the number of such numbers would be the number of numbers in the arithmetic progression:

   9, 18, 27, 36, 45, ...495 = [(495 – 9)/9] + 1 = 55 such numbers.
10. Such questions are again solved through logical processes. If you were to try this problem by going through mathematical processes you would end up with a messy solution which is not going to yield any answer in any reasonable time frame.

    Instead, look at the following process.

    1. The first thing you should notice is that the value in the answer has got something to do with the number 2008. Suppose we were to look at only the first term of the expression, by analogy the value of the sum should have something to do with the number 2.

2. Accordingly, by looking at the value obtained, we can decide on which of the options fits the given answer.

So, for the first term, we see that the value is equal to the square root of 2.25 = 1.5.

By analogy, that in this case the value of 2008 is 2, the value of 2007 would be 1 and 2009 would be 3. Replacing these values, the options become

(a) $2-\frac{1}{2}$ (b) $1-\frac{1}{1}$

(c) $1-\frac{1}{2}$ (d) $2-\frac{1}{1}$

It can be easily verified that only option (a) gives a value of 1.5. Hence, that is the only possible answer as all other values are different. In case you need greater confirmation and surety, you can solve this for the first two terms too.

11. Let the five additional ingredients onion, tomato, carrot, chilli sauce and tomato sauce are denoted by *O, T, C, CS, TS*, respectively.

Number of ways of ordering the egg roll:

For the egg roll, there are a total of 32 possibilities (with each ingredient being either present or not present – there being five ingredients, the total number of possibilities of the combinations of the egg rolls would be equal to $2 \times 2 \times 2 \times 2 \times 2 =$ 32 ways).

However, out of these 32 instances, the following combinations are not possible due to the constraint given in statement (b) which tells us that to have CS in the roll either of onion or tomato must be present (or both should be present). The combinations which are not possible are:

(CS) (CS, TS) (CS, C) (CS, C, TS)

Total number of ways, egg roll can be ordered = 32 – 4 = 28

Number of ways of ordering the mutton roll:

Total number of cases for mutton roll without any constraints = $2 \times 2 \times 2 \times 2 = 16$ ways. Cases rejected due to constraint given in statement (b): (CS); (CS, C) $\rightarrow$ 16 – 2 = 14 cases.

Total number of ways or ordering a roll = 28 + 14 = 42. Hence, option (d) is correct.

12. In ΔBAC, $AC \parallel PQ$

$$\therefore \quad \frac{CQ}{QB} = \frac{AP}{PB} = \frac{4}{3}$$

In ΔBPC, $PC \parallel DQ$

$$\therefore \quad \frac{PD}{DB} = \frac{CQ}{QB} = \frac{4}{3}$$

If $\frac{PD}{DB} = \frac{4}{3}$

$$\therefore \quad PD = \frac{4}{7}PB$$

$$\frac{AP}{PD} = \frac{AP}{\frac{4}{7}PB} = \frac{7}{4} \times \frac{AP}{PB} = \frac{7}{4} \times \frac{4}{3} = \frac{7}{3}.$$

Option (c) is correct.

13. Let $AB = H$

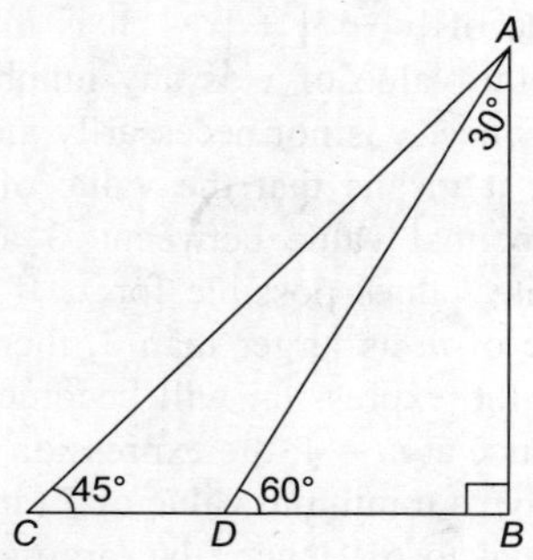

$$\therefore \quad \tan 45° = \frac{AB}{BC} \rightarrow AB = BC$$

$$\therefore \quad \tan 60° = \frac{AB}{BD} \therefore \sqrt{3} = \frac{AB}{BD},\ BD = \frac{AB}{\sqrt{3}}$$

$$\therefore \quad CD = BC - BD$$

$$= AB - \frac{AB}{\sqrt{3}}$$

As time for traveling *CD*, i.e. $AB - \frac{AB}{\sqrt{3}}$ is 10 min.

$$\therefore \text{Time required for traveling } BD = \frac{\frac{AB}{\sqrt{3}}}{AB - \frac{AB}{\sqrt{3}}} \times 10$$

$$= \frac{1}{\sqrt{3}-1} \times 10$$

$$= \frac{10}{\sqrt{3}-1}$$

$$= \left(\frac{10}{\sqrt{3}-1} \times \frac{\sqrt{3}+1}{\sqrt{3}+1}\right)$$

$$= \frac{10(\sqrt{3}+1)}{2}$$

$$= 5(\sqrt{3}+1) \text{ minutes}$$

14. 78% favoured at least one. Also, the count of the three values given for favouring I, favouring II and favouring III is 100. Thus, we have an extra count of 22, i.e., 78 people are counted 100 times, so 22 people are extra because they would be counted twice or thrice (people who favoured 2 proposals would be counted twice – so once extra; people who favoured three proposals would be counted thrice – so twice extra).

We are also given that 5% people are counted thrice (Those who favour all three proposals). Hence, they would account for 10 extra counts (5 × 2). Naturally, the remaining 12 extra counts should happen due to the people who favoured 2 proposals. Thus, we can see that 12% people were counted twice. The percentage who favoured more than one of the proposals would be 12 + 5 = 17.

Alternate solution: Formula is - Favouring I + Favouring II + Favouring III - (favoured exactly 2 proposals) – 2(favoured exactly 3 proposals) = 78

$50 + 30 + 20 - (F) - 2 \times 5 = 100$

By solving we get, $F = 12$

People who favoured more than one of the three proposals = People who favoured two proposals + People who favoured three proposals = 12 + 5 = 17%

15.

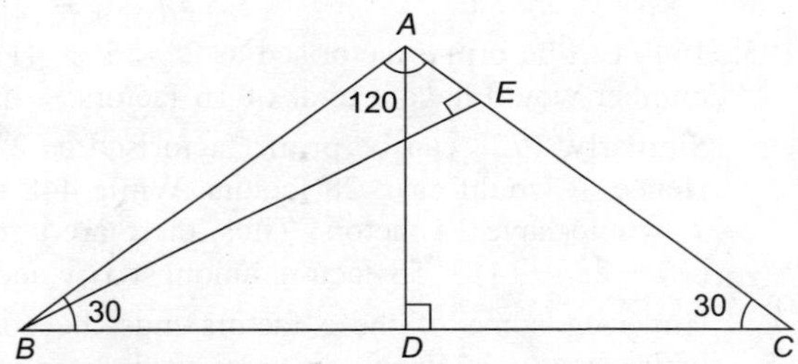

If the side opposite angles A, B and C are a, b and c respectively, we have

$$\frac{a}{\text{Sin } A} = \frac{b}{\text{Sin } B} \rightarrow \frac{a}{b} = \frac{\text{Sin}120}{\text{Sin}30} = \sqrt{3}$$

Also, the area of the triangle is $\frac{1}{2} \times a \times AD$

$= \frac{1}{2} \times b \times BE \rightarrow \frac{AD}{BE} = \frac{b}{a} = \frac{1}{\sqrt{3}}$. Option (a) is correct.

16. Let there be a total of n people the college will ask for donations.

Amount raised from the people solicited = 600 × 0.6n = 360n

Let the total amount be x then 360n = 75% of x.

Hence 25% of x = 120n.

$\therefore$ Average donation from remaining people = $\frac{120n}{0.4n}$ = 300

Alternative approach: According to the question 60% of the people have contributed 75% of the amount. Thus, each person has contributed 1.25% of the total amount.

Rest of the 40% of the people have to contribute 25% of the amount. Thus, each person has contributed 0.625 % of the total amount (against 1.25% of first 60% people). Hence, the average contribution per person = 600/2 = ₹300.

17. We can solve this problem by taking the weight of the heaviest box from the options.

Option (a): If the weight of the heaviest box is 60 kg then to arrive at 121 kg, the other box will have to weigh 61 kg so this option can never be true.

Option (c): If the weight of the heaviest box is 64 then to get a total of 121 kg, the other weight will have to be 57 and to get a total 120 kg, the next box shall have a weight 63 kg. In this case the maximum possible total weight of the two boxes would be 64 + 63 = 127, which is again not possible.

Option (b): If the weight of the heaviest box is 62 kg then second heaviest box = 121 – 62 = 59 kg.

Other possible combinations are 120 = 62 + 58, 118 = 62 + 56, 117 = 59 + 58, 116 = 62 + 54, 115 = 59 + 56, 113 = 59 + 54, 112 = 58 + 54, 110 = 56 + 54.

Thus, the weights of five boxes are 62, 59, 58, 56, 54 kg. Hence, option (b) is correct.

18. Let the number of numbers be n. Then $8a_1 - a_1 = 7a_1 = 940 \times n - 800 \times n = 140n$ OR $a_1 = 20n$. In this situation, the lowest possible value of n is 2, in which case the two terms would be a_1 and a_2 and these would be 40 and 1560 respectively to give us an average of 800 for 2 terms. At $n = 3$, $a_1 = 60$ and sum of 3 terms should be 3 × 800 = 2400, which can also be structured as a non-decreasing sequence of numbers. n = 4, 5, 6... all work as possible values of n and we need to think of the limiting case. At $n = 40$, the value of $a_1 = 800$ and a non-decreasing sequence of 40 terms with an average of 800 can only be possible if all the terms are 800 each. It can be seen that $n = 41$ is not possible, since at $n = 41$, $a_1 = 20 \times n = 820$, we cannot create a non-decreasing sequence of numbers that have an average of 800. Thus, between 2 and 40 (both inclusive) there are 39 possible values of n.

19. Since the number has to be a multiple of 9, the sum of the digits would be either 9 or 18 or 27. Also, the number would either be in the form *aaab* or *baaa*. For the sum of the digits to be 9, we would have the following cases:

$a = 1$ and $b = 6$, for the numbers 1116 and 6111;

$a = 2$ and $b = 3$, for the numbers 2223 and 3222;

$a = 3$ and $b = 0$, for the number 3330 and

$b = 9$ and $a = 0$, for the number 9000. We get a total of 6 such numbers.

Similarly for the sum of the digits to be 18, we will get: 3339, 9333; 4446, 6444; 5553, 3555; 6660; we get a total of 7 such numbers.

For the sum of the digits to be 27, we will get: 6669, 9666; 7776, 6777; 8883, 3888 and 9990; thus, we get a total of 7 such numbers. Hence, the total number of numbers is 20. Hence, option (d) is correct.

20. $M \times 12 \times 7 = 0.3J$ (where J = the total job);
$(M-15) \times 8 \times 28 = 224M - 3360 = 0.7J$.
Thus, we have: $\frac{84M}{224M - 3360} = \frac{3}{7} \to 588M = 672M - 10080 \to 84M = 10080. \therefore M = 120$.
Option (a) is correct.
21. If we consider the clock dial to have a circumference of 60 km, and the minute hand and the hour hand to be two runners running around the circumference at speeds of 60 kmph and 5 kmph respective, at 6 PM, the minute hand would be 30 kms behind the hour hand. In 60 mins, the minute hand 'covers' 55 kms over the hour hand (using the concept of relative speed). Hence, in 36 minutes, the minute hand would cover 33 minutes against the hour hand. Hence, at 6:36 PM, the minute hand would be 3 kms ahead of the hour hand. Since, we want to double the angle, we want the minute hand to further go ahead by 3 kms (to make it 6 kms ahead). In 60 minutes, coverage = 55, in ? minutes coverage = 3 → 180/55 = 36/11 minutes. Hence, option (b) is correct.
22. The sequence h_n can be recognized as an Arithmetic Progression with common difference 7, that looks like: 17, 24, 31, 38,.... Likewise j_n is also an Arithmetic Progression with common difference as 11 and can be visualized as 23, 34, 45, 56... .The series of common terms between the two sequences would also be an AP with first term 45 and a common difference of 77 (LCM of 7 and 11). The series of common terms will be 45, 122, 199,...969. The number of terms in the series would be 13.

The CAT Experience 8

1. For a system of equations to have no solutions – the x and y coefficients should match for both equations, (i.e. if there is $x + y$ in the first equation, the second equation can be $2x + 2y$ or $3x + 3y$ and so on. Also the multiplier used on the constant term in the RHS of the equation, should be different than the multiplier used on the coefficients of x and y. In this case, what we need is the following set of equations/ inequations. $b^2 - 18 = a + 8 \neq 3b$. Thus, the roots of the equation $b^2 - 3b - 18 = 0$ would not be a possible value set for b. Hence, b cannot be 6 and –3. At $b = 6$, $a = 10$ and at $b = -3$, $a = -17$. Thus ab cannot be 60 or 51 while $a + b$ cannot be 16 or –20. Hence, option (c) is correct.
2. **Thought-process:**

   If we take six teams and four players per team, we would get four players in T_1 (each one of them unique), three more players in T_2 (since one player of T_2 will be shared with T_1), three more players in T_3 (since one player of T_3 will be shared with T_2), three more players in T_4 (since one player of T_4 will be shared with T_3), three more players in T_5 (since one player of T_5 will be shared with T_4) and two more players in T_6 (since one player of T_6 will be shared with T_5 and one with T_1). Hence, there would be a total of 18 (4 + 3 + 3 + 3 + 3 + 2) players with $n = 6$ and $k = 4$. Checking from the options, we see that only option (d) gives us 18 as the solution.
3. The chain of numbers would start from 3, Day 1 8, Day 2 18, 38, 78, 158, 318,638, 1278, 2558, 5118, 10238, 20478, 40958. This will expand to the range of 81000, 162000, 324000 and cross 5 lacs on Day 17. Starting from January 16th as the first day, the 17th day would be 1st February. Hence, option (b) is correct.
4. For $(x!)!$ to divide 50000!, the value of $x!$ should be less or equal to 50000. This happens for x = 1, 2, 3, 4, 5, 6, 7 and 8. The value of
$x_1 \times x_2 \times \ldots \times x_n = 2^7 \times 3^2 \times 5^1 \times 7^1$.
The number of even factors for this number = $7 \times 3 \times 2 \times 2 = 84$.
5. 1640 can be prime factorised as $2^3 \times 5^1 \times 41^1$. This number would have a total of 16 factors.

   Similarly, 1728 can be prime factorised as $2^6 \times 3^3$. Hence, it would have 28 factors. While $448 = 2^6 \times 7^1$ would have 14 factors. Thus, there are a total of (16 + 28 + 14) = 58 factors amongst x, y and z.

   However, some of these factors must be common between x, y, z. Hence, in order to find the number of natural numbers that would divide at least one amongst x, y, z, we will need to account for double and triple counted numbers amongst these 58 numbers (by reducing the count by 2 for each triple counted number and by reducing the count by 1 for each double counted number).

   The number of cases of triple counting would be for all the common factors of (x, y, z). This number can be estimated by finding the HCF of x, y and z and counting the number of factors of the HCF. The HCF of 1640, 1728 and 448 is 8 and hence the factors of 8, i.e. 1, 2, 4 and 8 itself must have got counted in each of the 3 counts done above. Thus, each of these 4 numbers should get subtracted twice to remove the triple count. This leaves us with 58 – 4 × 2 = 50 numbers.

   We still need to eliminate numbers that have been counted twice, i.e. numbers, which belong to the factors of any two of these numbers (while counting this we need to ensure that we do not count the triple counted numbers again). This can be visualised in the following way:

   Number of common factors that are common to only 1640 and 1728 and not to 448 (x and y but not z):
   $1640 = 2^3 \times 5^1 \times 41^1$
   $1728 = 2^6 \times 3^3$

   It can be seen from these 2 standard forms of the numbers that the highest common factors of these

2 numbers is 8. Hence, there is no new number to be subtracted for double counting in this case.

The case of 1640 and 448 is similar because 1640 $= 2^3 \times 5^1 \times 41^1$ while $448 = 2^6 \times 7^1$ and HCF $= 2^3$ and hence they will not give any more numbers as common factors apart from 1, 2, 4 and 8.

Thus, there is no need of adjustment for the pair 1640 and 448.

Finally when we look for 1728 and 448, we realise that the HCF $= 2^6 = 64$ and hence, the common factors between 448 and 1728 are 1, 2, 4, 8, 16, 32, 64. But we are looking for factors which are common for 1728 and 448 but not common to 1640 to estimate the double counting error for this case. Hence, we can eliminate the number 1, 2, 4, 8 from this list and conclude that there are only 3 numbers 16, 32 and 64 that divide both 1728 and 448 but do not divide 1640.

If we subtract these numbers once each, from the 50 numbers, we will end up with 50 – 3 × 1 = 47.

The complete answer can be visualised as 16 + 28 + 14 – 4 × 2 – 3 × 1= 47.

Hence, option (a) is correct.

6. If we take the work as 100, Amit's work per day would be 3.33, Bisheshwar's work would be 10 and Charulata's work would be 1.66 per day. Multiplying the entire system by 3, we get total work as 300, Amit =10, Bisheshwar as 30 and Charulata as 5. The 6 day cycle of work would be (A + B) + (B + C) + (A + C) + C + A + B = 40 + 35 + 15 + 5 + 10 + 30 = 135 units of work. Also, since the work to be completed is 3-times the original work, the target is 900 units of work: 135 × 6 = 810 will mean 6 completed cycles of 6 days each. Work left after 36 days would be 90, which will be done as 40 + 35 + 15 = 90 (in 3 days). Thus, Charulata works for 3 × 6 + 2 = 20 days in the entire period. The correct answer is 20.

7. If we assume the total work as 280, their work rates would be 56, 40 and 35 units per hour. The total work = 12 × 8 × (56 + 40 + 35) = 12576 units. Of this, Deshpande and Shelke would do: 84 × 75 = 6300 units of work. Work left = 6276 units, which Contractor would do in 6276/56 = 112.07 hours. Hence, he would raise his bill for 112.5 hours. Option (d) is correct.

8. **Thought-process:**

If you are aware of the logic of finding squares of two digit numbers, you would realise that only three two-digit numbers after 32 have the last two digits in their squares equal (38, 62 and 88). Hence, you do not need to check any other number apart from these three. Checking these you would get the square of 88 as 7744. And hence, there is only one such number.

Note: Of course, you would ignore the values of squares with the last two digits as '00'.

9. $x^8 + \left(\frac{1}{x}\right)^8 = 527 \rightarrow \left(x^4 + \left(\frac{1}{x}\right)^4\right)^2 - 2 = 527$

$\rightarrow x^4 + \left(\frac{1}{x}\right)^4 = 23$

Repeating the above process, we get $x^2 + \left(\frac{1}{x}\right)^2 = 5$ and $x + \frac{1}{x} = \sqrt{7}$.

Cubing $x + \frac{1}{x}$ we have $x^3 + \left(\frac{1}{x}\right)^3 + 3\left(x + \frac{1}{x}\right) = 7\sqrt{7}$

$\rightarrow x^3 + \left(\frac{1}{x}\right)^3 + 3\sqrt{7} = 7\sqrt{7} \rightarrow x^3 + \left(\frac{1}{x}\right)^3 = 4\sqrt{7}$

Cubing $x^3 + \left(\frac{1}{x}\right)^3$ we get: $x^9 + \left(\frac{1}{x}\right)^9 + 3\left(x^3 + \left(\frac{1}{x}\right)^3\right)$

$= 448\sqrt{7} \rightarrow x^9 + \left(\frac{1}{x}\right)^9 = 436\sqrt{7}$. Option (d) is correct.

10. The sum of the first 10 natural numbers are 55, that of the 11th to 20th natural numbers are 155 and so on. In order to find the number added twice, we need to reach the last triangular number below 1000. This can be got by adding 55 + 155 + 255 + 355 + 41 + 42 + 43 + 44 = 990. Hence, the number added twice must be 10, i.e., option (c).

11. If A, B, C are his investments in the three schemes respectively, then we can infer that 0.36A = 0.6B = 0.18C → A : B = 5 : 3 and A : C = 1 : 2 → A : B : C = 5 : 3 : 10. Also, since A + B + C = 172836 → C = 96020. Option (d) is the correct answer.

12. If they take t hours from the starting time to the meeting point, we have:

$\frac{28}{t} = \frac{t}{7} \rightarrow t = 14.$

Thus, Bimal takes 14 + 7 = 21 hours to cover the journey. The total distance between A and B hence is: 21 × 32 = 672 kms. Hence, the correct answer is 672.

13. There will be a total of 5!/2 = 60 numbers formed. The digit 1 will come in the units place 4! times,each of the digits 3, 5, 7 would come in the units place 4!/2 = 12 times,. The average value of the units digit would be Sum of all units digits $= 24\times1 + 12\times3 + 12\times5 + 12\times7$ = 204.

This means that if we add the units digit's of all the 60 numbers, the sum would be 204. Retaining 4 as the units digit and carrying over 20 to the tens place, the sum of the tens place column would be 204 + 20 = 224 – we will keep the tens place as 4 and carry over 22 to the hundreds place (since the use of all digits would be symmetric across each of the five places in the number, the sum of each of tens, hundreds, thousands and ten thousands digit columns would be 204 each). For the hundreds place, the sum would be 204 + 22 = 226. The thousands column would again add to 204 + 22 = 226. The left most column would add up to 204 + 22 = 226. Hence, the sum of all the numbers would be 2266644.

14. There are two possible cases.

Case 1: The number 9 comes at the end.

Case 2: 9 comes at position 4, 5, or 6.

In both these cases, the blanks can be occupied by any of the available 9 digits (0, 1, 2, ..., 8).

For the first case, the number 9 can occupy the last position

Thus, total possible numbers would be $2 \times (9 \times 9 \times 9) = 1458$.

For the second case, the number 9 can occupy any of the given position 4, 5, or 6, and there shall be an odd number at position 7. Thus, the total number of ways shall be $2 \times [3 \times (9 \times 9 \times 4)] = 1944$.

Hence, total ways = 1458 + 1944 = 3402

15.

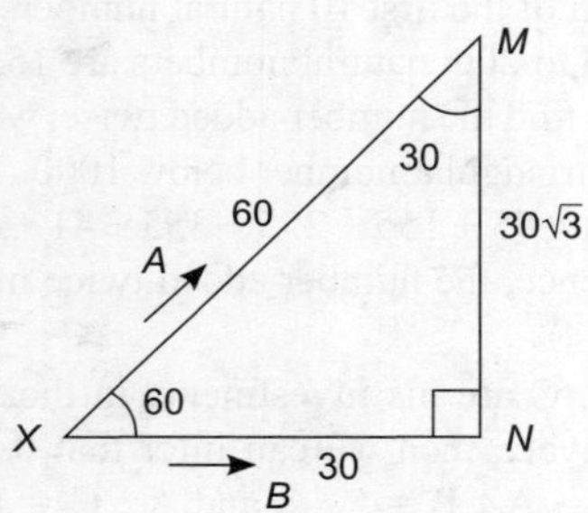

The figure gives us the situation – the angle XMN has to be 30 since the other two angles are 60 and 90. Using the 30-60-90 triangle, we see that XN = 30 and XM = 60. Thus, the speed of the slower ship is 30/3 = 10 kmph.

16. From the options, the only number which gives successive remainders as 2, 1 and 4 when divided successively by 3, 4 and 7 respectively is 53. Hence, the correct answer is 53.

17. Let the equation be $ax^2 + bx + c = 0$. If it gains the maximum at $x = 1$, it means that 'a' is negative. Also $2ax + b = 0 \rightarrow x = -b/2a$. So $-b/2a$ should be 1. So the expression has to be chosen from:

$-X^2 + 2x + c$

$-2X^2 + 4x + c$

$-3X^2 + 6x + c$ ....and so on (since we have to keep the ratio of $-b/2a$ constant at 1)

Also, it is given that the value of the function at $x = 0$ is 1. This means that $c = 1$. Putting this value of c in the possible expressions, we can see that at $x = 1$, the value of the function is equal to 3 in the case: $-2X^2 + 4x + 1$

So the expression is– $2X^2 + 4x + 1$

At $x = 10$, the value would be $-200 + 40 + 1 = -159$.

18. $\log m + \log\left(\frac{m^2}{n}\right) + \log\left(\frac{m^3}{n^2}\right) + \cdots n$ terms

$$\log \frac{m \cdot m^2 \cdot m^3 \ldots m^n}{1 \cdot n \cdot n^2 \cdot n^3 \ldots n^{n-1}} = \log m^{1+2+\ldots n} / n^{1.2\ldots n-1}$$

$$= \log \frac{m^{\frac{n(n+1)}{2}}}{n^{\frac{n(n-1)}{2}}} = \log \left[\frac{m^{n+1}}{n^{n-1}}\right]^{\frac{n}{2}}$$

19. He has to have at least six boxes with the same number of oranges in it. The logic of this question comes from the pigeon hole principle—where we take the ratio 128/25 and take the least integer value greater than this ratio. Note, 25 comes from the different values of oranges that you can put in the boxes. Hence, we would get six as the answer.

20. If we have n candidates who can be selected at the maximum, naturally, the answer to the question would also represent n. Also, we see that the options are also giving us values for n.

Hence, we check for the first option. If $n = 3$, then $2n + 1 = 7$ and it means that there are 7 candidates to be chosen from. Since it is given that the number of ways of selection of at least 1 candidate is 63, we should try to see, whether selecting 1, 2 or 3 candidates from 7 indeed adds up to 63 ways. If it does this would be the correct answer.

${}^7C_1 + {}^7C_2 + {}^7C_3 = 7 + 21 + 35 = 63$. Thus, the first option fits the situation and is correct.

21. His net savings in first eight months = $-(200 \times 8) = -1600$. His annual savings target = \$550 × 12 = \$6600. Hence, he needs to save \$6600 + \$1600 = \$8200 in the last 4 months of the year. Average savings required = 8200/4 = 2050. Hence, average income in last 4 months = \$4100 + \$2050 = \$6150. Percentage increase in income required from \$5000 is \$1150 on \$5000 which is 23%.

22. The fourth side will have to be greater than 7 – 3 – 2 i.e. 2 and less than 7 + 3 + 2 i.e. 12. Thus, integral values possible for the third side are between 3 to 11. The sum is 9 × 7 = 63.

The CAT Experience 9

1. Let the average age of the first 7 people be A. The total age of 7 people and Amit would be $8 \times (A - 2n) = 8A - 16n$. The total age of 7 people and Ravi would be $8 \times (A + n) = 8A + 8n$. The difference in totals would be the difference between the ages of Ravi and Amit. Hence, $24n = 12 \rightarrow n = 0.5$. The correct answer is 0.5.

2. The key to solving this question is to understand that since he sells 40% of his mangoes and also sells 40% of his fruit overall, it means that he must have sold 40% of his Oranges and Apples too. Let the total fruit

be $100x$. The mangoes are $30x$ and Oranges + Apples = $70x$. So he must have sold $28x$ fruits from the oranges and apples. Let the number of oranges be O and apples be A. We have O + A = $70x$ & 80 + 0.3A = $28x$ → 80 × 2.5 + 0.3A × 2.5 = $28x$ × 2.5 → 200 + 0.75A = $70x$. Equating the LHS of both the equations, we get: O + A = 200 + 0.75A → O + 0.25A = 200. Thus, the value of A must be a multiple of 4. If we take A as 4, O becomes 199 and the total number of O + A = 203 = $70x$ → $100x$ = 290. This is the least possible number of fruits in his shop from the perspective of oranges and apples, but this solution can be rejected because 40% of the mangoes will be a decimal. But we have been asked the lowest number of fruits in his shop. So, we need to look for another solution. If we take A = 8, O = 198; O + A = 206 = $70x$. In this case $100x$ turns out to be a decimal value and can be rejected. Checking for further values A = 12, O = 197 (rejected); A = 16, O = 196 (rejected); A = 20, O = 195 (rejected). We can see that at A = 32 and O = 192, $70x$ = 224 and $100x$ = 320. In this case, we get 32 Apples, 192 oranges and 96 mangoes. Again rejected because 40% of 96 is a non-integer. The next solution will be A = 60, O = 185, M = 105. Total fruit = 350. In this case, 40% of the mangoes means a total of 42 mangoes and is possible. Also, 30% of apples is 18, which is also an integer. Hence, 350 is the correct answer.

3. We need to continue our thinking from the previous question here. We have seen a pattern of solutions where (M, O, A) were (87, 199, 4); (96, 192, 32); (105, 185, 60) and so on, where we rejected the (87, 199, 4) & (96, 192, 32) cases as 40% of the mangoes or 30% of the apples was not an integer. The lowest number of fruits for Mangoes and Apples was hence 105 and 60 respectively while 185 represents the highest number of Oranges. From this point all our possible values of M, O and A will continue in their respective Arithmetic progressions. Thus, Mangoes will continue to grow by 9 each time, Oranges will continue reducing by 7 each time and Apples will continue growing by 28 each time. So the next possibilities we need to consider are (114, 178, 88) → rejected because 40% of 114 is not an integer. (123, 171, 116) and so on. We can see that at (150, 150, 200), we will get the next possible solution. At this point, we can see that 150 is the second lowest value possible for the number of mangoes. 150 is also the second highest possible value of the number of Oranges. Hence, the correct answer is 150.

4. The first four-digit term in the expression would be 1003 and the last would be 9990. In four-digits the arithmetic series would be 1003, 1022, …9990.The average of an arithmetic series is given by the average of the first and last terms → average of 1003 and 9990 = 5496.5.

5. We can work out that for a regular decagon, each interior angle is 144 degrees and the exterior angle is 36 degrees, giving us the required difference between these angles as 108. The number of diagonals in a decagon = ${}^{10}C_2$ – 10 = 35. Number of sides in a decagon = 10. Required difference = 35 – 10 = 25. Hence, the correct answer is 25.

6.

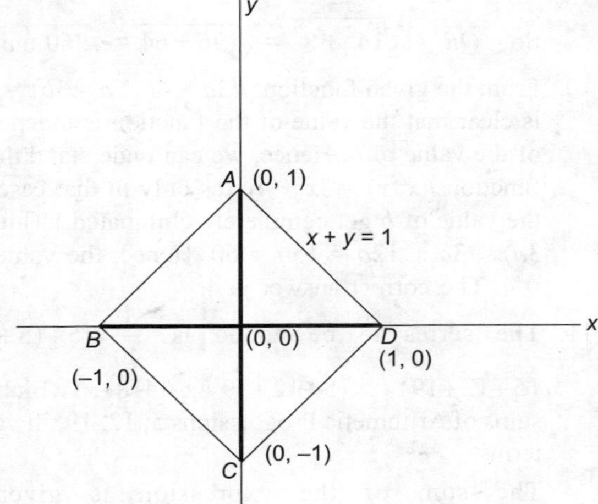

Equation of line BC is $\frac{X}{-1}+\frac{Y}{-1}=1$ OR $x + y = -1$.

7. The product $a \times b$ will have multiple values possible. To maximize it we can proceed with trying to find the value of 'a' or 'b' when $a \times b$ is maximum. Solving for the value of a, that maximises the product $a \times b$ $= a\times\frac{60-2a}{3}=20a-\frac{2a^2}{3}$

(Differentiating wrt a and equating to0) $\rightarrow 20-\frac{4a}{3}$ $=0 \rightarrow a=15$.

Thus, a = 15, b = 10, so the maximum value of the product $a \times b$ = 15 × 10 = 150. The correct answer is 150.

8. Both the sequences are arithmetic sequences, and the first common term between the two sequences 30, 37, 44, …1430 & 50, 54, 58, ….850 is 58. After 58, the next list of common terms of the two sequences will be itself in an arithmetic progression with common difference 28 (LCM of 4 and 7). Hence, the list of common terms in the two sequences can be visualized as 58, 86, 114, ...674, ...814, 842. The total of the terms in this series = (number of terms) × (Average) = 29 × 450 = 13050. The correct answer is 13050.

9. Let's assume PQ be the longest side of 20 unit and another side PR is 10 units. Hence $RS \perp PQ$.

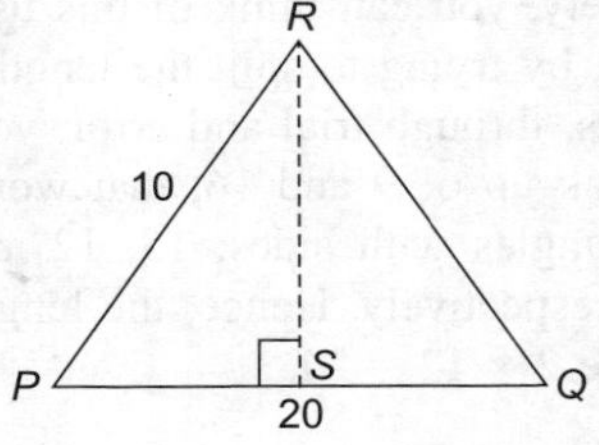

Since area of $\Delta PQR = 80 = \frac{1}{2} PQ \times RS$

So $RS = \frac{80 \times 2}{20} = 8$. In ΔPSR; $PS = \sqrt{10^2 - 8^2} = 6$

Hence $SQ = 20 - 6 = 14$

So $QR = \sqrt{14^2 + 8^2} = \sqrt{196 + 64} = \sqrt{260}$ units

10. From the given function, $f(3a + 4b, 5a - 3b) = 29a$ it is clear that the value of the function is independent of the value of b. Hence, we can understand that the function $f(x, y) = 3x + 4y$ (as only in that case does the value of b get completely eliminated.) Thus, $f(a, 3a) = 3a + 12a = 15a = 60$. Hence, the value of $a = 4$. The correct answer is 4.

11. The series to be added is $\frac{1}{40}\times[5+(5+12)+(5+12+19)+\ldots(5+12+19+..+418)]$, which are sums of Arithmetic Progressions 5, 12, 19 till various terms.

The sum of the expression is given by $\frac{1}{40}\times\sum_{1}^{60}\frac{n}{2}\times(2a+(n-1)d$

$$=\frac{1}{40}\times\sum_{1}^{60}5n+\sum_{1}^{60}3.5n\times(n-1)$$

$$=\frac{1}{40}\times1.5\times\sum_{1}^{60}n+\frac{1}{40}\times3.5\times\sum_{1}^{60}n^2$$

$$=\frac{1}{40}\times\left[1.5\times\frac{60\times61}{2}+3.5\times\frac{60\times61\times121}{6}\right]=6527$$

Option (c) is correct.

12. This question requires us to use the principle of difference of squares:

We know that $x^2 - y^2 = (x - y)(x + y)$. Hence, $x + y$ should be 48.

13. Let the length of the chord be 'a' cm.

Area of $\Delta ABC = \frac{1}{2}(15 \times 20) = \frac{1}{2} \times 25 \times \frac{a}{2}$

$\Rightarrow a = 24$ cm

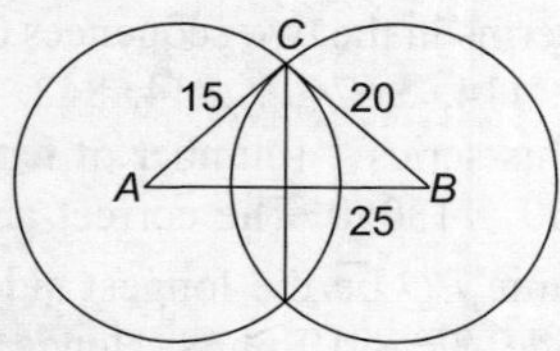

Alternately, you can think of this using Pythagoras theorem, by trying to split the length 25 of AB into two parts, through trial and error, you would arrive at a break up of 9 and 16, that would lead to two right triangles with sides: 15, 12 and 9 & 12, 16 and 20 respectively. Hence, the length of the chord would be $2 \times 12 = 24$.

14. It is given to us that Amount of Chocolate in the mixture should not exceed vanilla, at most it can be equal. Selling Price = ₹264 and Profit = 10 %. Hence, cost price for 10 liters = 240 and cost price per liter = 24. Also CP per litre of Chocolate mixture = x, then CP of vanilla Mixture = $x + 8$ to ensure that the cost of chocolate mixture is the highest, it happens only in the case when chocolate = vanilla in the mixture. To ensure the values are the same, and our average price is of ₹24 per litre and the difference between vanilla and chocolate is 8, We need to take the values of cost as 20 and 28. As any value higher than 20, will result in the ratio of Chocolate being more than that of Vanilla. For example, price of chocolate = 21 and 29 for vanilla. To ensure average price = 24, we will need to use the ratio of 5 : 3, wherein 5 units of Chocolate is used and 3 units of vanilla, which is not permitted by the question Hence the answer is 20

15. Let Mango (M) and Kiwi (K) be sold at ₹a and ₹b respectively When M and K are mixed in the ratio 5 : 3 and sold at a profit of 20% at ₹50 per Kg we get: $(5a + 3b)/8 = 50/1.2$

When M and K are mixed in the ratio 3 : 5 and sold at a profit of 10% at Rs.50 per Kg we get: $(3a + 5b)/8 = 50/1.1$

Equating both we get $1.2 \times \frac{5a+3b}{8} = 1.1\times\left(\frac{3a+5b}{8}\right)$

$= 60a+36b = 33a+55b = 27a=19b$

$=$ so $a/b = 19/27$.

Option (b) is correct.

16. We need to go through the options and use the MNP rule relating to Permutations and Combinations.

If the first option is true—i.e. there are 6 routes between A to C:

Then, the number of routes between C to B and consequently the number of routes between A to B would be given by the following possibilities:

Routes Between A–C	*C to B (possibilities)*	*Routes from A–C–B*	*Direct routes from A to B*	*Total routes from A to B*
6	5	30	3	33
	4	24	9	33
	3	18	15	33
	2	12	21	33
	1	6	27	33

We also know that there are 23 routes between B to C. If the given numbers in the first possibility of the table are true, we see that B–A–C we would have $3 \times 6 = 18$ routes and from B to C we would have 5 routes – a total of 18 + 5 as required. Hence, this option fits the situation perfectly. Option (a) is correct.

17. In this type of question, the key is to look at a systematic way of counting the number of instances. So with 1 & 2 as the first 2 numbers, we can get 8 sets (by varying the third value from 3 to 10), Similarly, with 1 & 3, we will get 7 pairs, with 1 & 4 six pairs, and so on till 1 & 9, we would get 1 pair. (A total of 1 + 2 + 3 + 4 + 5 + 6 + 7 + 8 = 36). Similarly for the first number to be starting with 2, we would get 1 + 2 + 3 + ... + 7 = 28 sets. Similarly, for sets starting with 3, there would be 21 sets, for 4, 15 sets, for sets starting with 5, 10 sets, for sets starting with 6, 6 sets, for sets starting with 7, 3 sets and for those starting with 8, 1 set. Thus, there would be a total of 36 + 28 + 21 + 15 + 10 + 6 + 3 + 1 = 120.

    Alternately, you can also solve this using Combinations. The correct answer would be $^{10}C_3$, since you only have to select 3 numbers from 10 distinct numbers. There is no arrangement to be done.

18. $n^3 - 7n^2 + 11n - 5 = (n - 1)^2(n - 5) > 0$ for $n > 5$. Hence, the largest possible value of m is 5.

19. $2^x - x - 1 = 0$

    $2^x = x + 1$

    For $x = 0$ and 1, the LHS and the RHS of the above equation are equal. So, $x = 0$ is a solution of the above equation.

    For $x = 2, 3, 4, \ldots$ $2^x > x + 1$. So the given equation has 2 solutions. Option (c) is correct.

20. $x = \dfrac{n^2 + 2\sqrt{n}\,(n+4) + 16}{n + 4\sqrt{n} + 4}$

    Put $x = 36$

    $$\therefore \quad x = \frac{(36)^2 + 2 \times 6 \times 40 + 16}{36 + 24 + 4}$$

    $$= \frac{(36)^2 + 2 \times 6 \times 40 + 16}{64}$$

    $$= \frac{81 + 30 + 1}{4} = \frac{112}{4} = 28$$

    The least value of $x = 28$, option (d) is correct.

    (**Note:** To confirm the upper end of the inequality you can try to put $x = 72$.)

21. The following table can be constructed for solving this question:

Town	*Males*	*Females*
ChotaHazri	x	$2x$
MotaHazri	$x + 4522$	$x + 4522 + 4020 = x + 8542$

    We also know that $x + 8542 - 2x = 2910$. Solving for x, we get $x = 5632$. Hence, option (c) is correct

22. If we assume the number of non-European players to be n, the number of European players would be $2n$. Then there would be three kinds of matches played –

    Matches between two Europan players – a total of $^{2n}C_2$ matches – which would yield a European winner.

    Matches between two non-European players – a total of $^{n}C_2$ matches, – which would yield a non-European winner.

    Matches, between a European and a non-European player = $2n^2$. These matches would have some European wins and some non-European wins. Let the number of European wins amongst these matches be x, then the number of non-European wins = $2n^2 - x$.

    Now, the problem clearly states that the number of European wins = Number of non-European wins

    $$\Rightarrow \quad \frac{2n(2n-1)}{2} + x = \frac{n(n-1)}{2} + 2n^2 - x$$

    $$\Rightarrow \quad n(n + 1) = 4x$$

    This means that the value of four times the number of wins for a European player over a non-European player should be a product of two consecutive natural numbers (since n has to be a natural number).

    Among the options, $x = 60$ is the only possible value as the value of $4 \times 60 = 15 \times 16$.

    Hence, option (d) is correct.

The CAT Experience 10

1. We want the expression $\dfrac{5 - \log_3 n}{3 - \log_5 n}$ to be less than 0. It happens when the numerator is positive and denominator is negative, or when the numerator is negative and denominator is positive. $5 - \log_3 n$ is positive for $n < 243$, = 0 at $n = 243$ & is negative at $n > 243$. $3 - \log_5 n$ is positive when $n < 125$, = 0 at $n = 125$ and is negative at $n > 125$. For $126 \le n \le 242$, the numerator is positive and the denominator is negative. Hence, there are 117 distinct integer values of n satisfying the inequality. The correct answer is 117.

2. If we assume $\dfrac{m}{n} = k$ the given expression becomes $8k + \dfrac{12}{k} = b \rightarrow 8k^2 - bk + 12 = 0$. For real m and n, k will also be real. Thus, $b^2 - 4 \times 12 \times 8 > 0$ $\rightarrow b^2 - 384 > 0$. From the given options, b cannot take a value of –16. Option (c) is correct.

3. The codes which will create a confusion would be: 16 and 91, 18 and 81, 19 and 61, 66 and 99, 68 and 89, 86 and 98: A total of 12 codes which will have confusion. Hence, out of 90 two-digit codes, 78 would have no confusion.

4. Numbers which have 2 digits recurring after the decimal are related to denominators which have 99 as a factor. From the options only 198 is related to 99 and is hence the correct answer.

5. Solving this through percentage of work, if M is the percentage of work done by Mukul everyday and K is the percentage of work done by Kavita everyday, we have the equations:

M + K = 8.33 & $\frac{3}{4}M + \frac{4}{3}K = 8.33$. Equating the two left hand sides, we get:

$M + K = \frac{3}{4}M + \frac{4}{3}K \rightarrow \frac{1}{4}M = \frac{1}{3}K \rightarrow 3\ M = 4\ K$ or $M = \frac{4}{3}K$

Thus, we have $\frac{7}{3}K = 8.33 \rightarrow K = \frac{25}{7}\%$. Thus, to do the work alone, Kavita would take: $\frac{100}{\frac{25}{7}} = 28$ days.

Also, since Mukul's rate of work is 4/3 times that of Kavita, he would take ¾ of her time. Hence, the number of days required by Mukul to do the work would be 21 days. Hence, $A + B = 49$. The correct answer is 49.

6. Since, the series is given as an arithmetic progression, we can find the first few terms to see what the AP looks like. $T_1 = S_1 = 5$, $T_2 = S_2 - S_1 = 11$; $T_3 = S_3 - S_2 = 33 - 16 = 17$. So, the AP is 5, 11, 17, 23, 29, **35**, 41, 47, 53, 59, 65, 71, **77.** Hence, the required value of n is 13. Option (d) is correct.

7. In order to solve a question of this nature, you again first need to 'read' the equation

The equation $m \times n - 6(m + n) = 0$ can be restructured as: $m \times n = 6(m + n)$.

When we read an equation of this form, we should be able to read this as:

The LHS is the product of two numbers, while the RHS is always going to be a multiple of 6. Further, we also know that the value of $m \times n$ would normally always be higher than the value of $m + n$. Thus, we are trying to look for situations where the product of two integers is six times their sum.

While looking for such solutions, we need to look for situations where either:

The RHS is non-negative – hence, 0, 6, 12, 18, 24, 30, 36…

The RHS is negative – hence, –6, –12, –18…

We would now need to use individual values of $m + n$ in order to check for whether $m \times n = 6(m + n)$.

For $m + n = 0$; $6(m + n) = 0$. If we use m and n both as 0, we would get 0 = 0 in the two sides of the equation. So this is obviously one solution to this equation.

For the RHS = –6, we can visualise the product of $m \times n$ as –6, if we use m as –3 and n as 2 or vice versa. Thus, we will get two solutions as (2, –3) and (–3, 2).

For the RHS = –12, $m + n = -2$, which means that m and n would take values like (–4, 2); (–5, 3); (–6, 4). If you look inside the factor pairs of –12, there is no factor pair which has an addition of –2.

For RHS = –18, $m + n = -3$. Looking into the factor pairs of 18 (viz: 1 × 18, 2 × 9, 3 × 6), we can easily see –6 and 3 as a pair of factors of –18 which would add up to –3 as required. Thus, we get two ordered solutions for (m, n), viz: (–6, 3); (3, –6)

For RHS = –24, $m + n = -4$. If we look for factors of –24, which would give us a difference of –4, we can easily see that within the factor pairs of 24 (viz: 1 × 24, 2 × 12, 3 × 8 and 4 × 6), there is no opportunity to create a sum of $m + n = -4$.

For RHS = –30, $m + n = -5 \rightarrow$ factors of 30 are 2 × 15, 5 × 6; there is no opportunity to create $m + n = -5$ and $m \times n = -30$, simultaneously. Hence, there are no solutions in this case.

For RHS = –36, $m + n = -6 \rightarrow$ factors of 36 are 2 × 18, 3 × 12, 4 × 9 and we can stop looking further; there is no opportunity to create $m + n = -6$ and $m \times n = -36$, simultaneously. Hence, there are no solutions in this case.

For RHS = –42, $m + n = -7 \rightarrow$ factors of 42 are 2 × 21, 3 × 14, 6 × 7 and we can stop looking further; there is no opportunity to create $m + n = -42$ and $m \times n = -7$, simultaneously. Hence, there are no solutions in this case.

For RHS = –48, $m + n = -8 \rightarrow$ factors of 48 are 2 × 24, 3 × 16, 4 × 12… 4 × 12 and give us the opportunity to create $m + n = -8$ and $m \times n = -48$, simultaneously. Hence, there are two solutions in this case, viz: (4, – 12) and (– 12, 4).

Note: While this process seems to be extremely long and excruciating, it is important to note that there are a lot of refinements you can make in order to do this fast. The 'searching inside the factors' shown above is itself a hugely effective short-cut in this case. Further, when you are looking for pairs of factors for any number, you need not look at the first few pairs because their difference would be very large. This point is illustrated below:

For RHS = –54, $m + n = -9 \rightarrow$ factors of 54 are 3 × 18, 6 × 9 and we can stop looking further; (notice here that we did not need to start with 1 × 54 and 2 × 27 because they are what can be called as 'too far apart' from each other). There is no opportunity to create $m + n = -6$ and $m \times n = -36$ simultaneously. Hence, there are no solutions in this case.

For RHS = –60, $m + n = -10 \rightarrow$ relevant factor search for 60 are 4 × 15, 5 × 12 and we can stop looking further; there is no opportunity to create $m + n = -10$ and $m \times n = -60$ simultaneously. Hence, there are no solutions in this case.

For RHS = –66, $m + n = -11 \rightarrow$ relevant factor search for 66 is 6 × 11 and we can stop looking further; there is no opportunity to create $m + n = -11$ and $m \times n = -66$ simultaneously. Hence, there are no solutions in this case.

Note: While solving through this route each value check should take not more than five seconds. The question that starts coming into one's mind is, how far does one need to go in order to check for values? Luckily, the answer is not too far.

As you move to the next values beyond -66, -72 (needs $m + n = -12$, while the factors of 72 do not present this opportunity), -78 (needs $m + n = -13$, which does not happen again).

To move further, you need to start working out the logic when $6(m + n)$ is positive. In such a case, the value of m and n would both need to be positive for $m \times n$ also to be positive. If $m + n = 1$, we cannot get two positive values of m and n such that their product is 6. If $m + n = 2$, $m \times n = 12$ will not happen.

A little bit of logical thought will give you the first point at which this situation would get satisfied. It would be when $6(m + n) = 144$, which means that $m + n = 24$ and for $m \times n$ to be equal to 144, the value of each of m and n would be 12 each.

(A brief note about why it is not possible to get a value before this:

If we try $6(m + n) = 132$ (for instance), we would realise that $m + n = 22$. The highest product $m \times n$ with a limit of $m + n = 22$ would occur when each of m and n is equal and hence, individually equal to 11 each. However, the value of 11 for m and n gives us a product of 121 only, which is lower than the required product of 132. This will happen in all cases where $6(m + n)$ is smaller than 144.)

Checking subsequent values of $6(m + n)$, we will get the following additional solutions to this situation:

6(m + n)	*(m + n)*	*Relevant factor pairs for the value of 6(m + n)*	*Solutions*
150	25	10,15	10,15; 15,10
156	26	None	None
162	27	9,18	9,18; 18,9
168,174	28,29	None	None
180,186	30,31	None	None
192	32	8,24	8,24; 24,8
198,204	33,34	None	None
210,216	35,36		

Break-down of the above thought-process:

(**Note:** That while checking the factor pairs for a number like 216, if you were to list the entire set of factors along with the sum of the individual factors within the pairs, you will get a list as follows:

Factor pairs for 216:

Pair	*Sum of factors in the pair*
1 × 216	217
2 × 108	110
3 × 72	75
4 × 54	58
6 × 36	42
8 × 27	35
9 × 24	33
12 × 18	30

However, a little bit of introspection in the correct direction will show you that this entire exercise was not required in order to do what we were doing in this question – i.e. trying to solve for $m + n = 36$ and $m \times n = 216$.)

The first five pairs where the larger number itself was greater than or equal to 36 were irrelevant as far as searching for the correct pair of factors is concerned for this question. When we saw the sixth pair of 8×27, we should have realised that since the sum of $8 + 27 = 35$, which is < 36, the subsequent pairs would also have a sum smaller than 36. Hence, you can stop looking for more factors for 216.

Thus, effectively to check whether a solution exists for $6(m + n) = 216$, in this question, all we needed to identify was the $8 \times 27 = 216$ pair and we can reject this value for $6(m + n)$ giving us an integral solution in this case.

This entire exercise can be completed in one 'five second thought' as follows:

If $6(m + n) = 216 \rightarrow m + n = 36$, then one factor pair is 6×36 itself whose sum obviously is more than 36. So, looking for the next factor pair where the smaller number is > 6, we see that 8×27 gives us a factor pair sum of $8 + 27 = 35 < 36$ and hence we reject this possibility.

Also, you should realise that we do not need to look further than 216 – as for values after 216, when we go to the next factor pair after $6 \times (m + n)$, we would realise that the sum of the factor pair would be lower than the required value for the immediately next factor pair.

Hence, the following solutions exist for this question: 0, 0; 2, –3; –3, 2; 3, –6 ; –6, 3; 4, –12; –12, 4; 12, 12; 15, 10; 10, 15; 9, 18; 18, 9; 8, 24; 24, 8, i.e.

a total of 14 solutions.

Author's Note: Doubtless this question is very long, but if you are able to understand the thought-process to adopt in such situations, you would do yourself a big favour in the commonly-asked questions of finding number of integral solutions.

8. Let $\angle CAE = \angle CEA = x$, $\angle CBF = \angle CFB = y$

$\angle ACE = 180 - 2x$, $\angle BCF = 180 - 2y$

In ΔDEF: $x + y + 40° = 180°$

So $x + y = 140°$

So $\angle ACB + \angle ACE + \angle BCF = 180°$

$\angle ACB = 180° - \angle ACE - \angle BCF$

$= 180° - (180° - 2x) - (180° - 2y)$

$= 2(x + y) - 180° = 2 \times 140 - 180 = 100°$

9. Let width of the path be x meters.

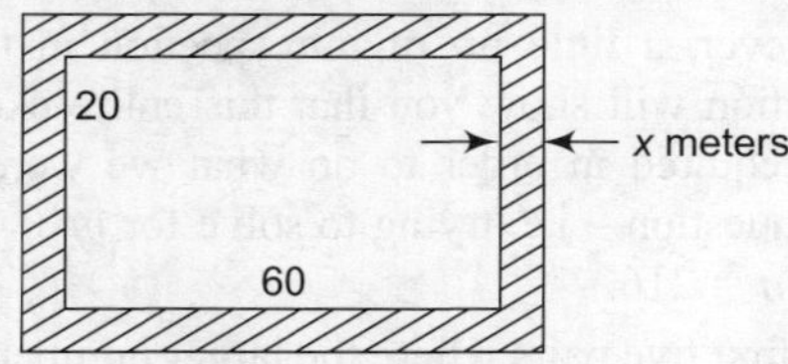

According to the question:

Area of the path = 516 m^2

$\Rightarrow (60 + 2x)(20 + 2x) - 60 \times 20 = 516 \text{ m}^2$

$\Rightarrow 1200 + 120x + 40x + 4x^2 - 1200 = 516 \text{ m}^2$

$\Rightarrow 4x^2 + 160x - 516 = 0 \Rightarrow x^2 + 40x - 129 = 0$

By solving we get $x = 3$.

Alternately, you could try to put the values of the width of the walkway from the options to check in which case do we get the value of the area of the walkway equaling 516.

For option (b) 3 m we get total area = $60 \times 3 \times 2 + 20 \times 3 \times 2 + 3 \times 3 \times 4 = 516 \text{ m}^2$.

10. It can be seen that in effect the train Y is starting at 11:15 AM. In the 15 minutes that Y is stopping, only X would be covering some distance. That distance would be equal to 17.5 km. Hence, the remaining distance of 162.5 km would have to be covered by them together at a relative speed of 120 kmph. This would take 162.5/120 hours. The distance from A would then be given by: 17.5 + (162.5/120) × 70 = 112 km approx.

11. Let the four candidates be A, B, C and D. Let A receive 30% of the total votes cast. Thus, if the total votes cast is $70n$, A receives $21n$. The balance $49n$ will get divided between B, C and D in the ratio 1 : 2 : 4. Hence, B gets $7n$ votes, C gets 14n and D gets $28n$ votes then $28n - 21n = 7n = 22449 \rightarrow n = 3207$. Hence, the total number of people who did not vote = $30n$ = 3207 × 30 = 96210.

12. Let the area of sector S_1 be A units. Then the area of the corresponding sectors shall be $2A$, $4A$, $8A$, $16A$, $32A$ and $64A$ (since every successive sector has an angle that is twice the previous one). Hence, the total area then shall be $127A$ units. This is 1/8 of the total area of the circle. Hence, the total area of the circle will be $127A \times 8 = 1016A$ units. Since, the total angle at the center of a circle is 2π, the sector S_1 should account for $\frac{1}{1016}$ of this angle. Hence, angle of sector S_1 is $\frac{\pi}{508}$.

13. The whole height of the cylinder is divided into 'n' equal parts.

So the vertical spacing between two consecutive turns = $\frac{h}{n}$.

14. If we unfold the lateral surfaces of the cube. It becomes a rectangle of sides $4n$ & n, and the string becomes the diagonal. Hence the required length = $\sqrt{(4n)^2 + n^2} = n\sqrt{17}$ cm.

15. The number of values for (x, y) such that both are integers and their product is equal to 144 is dependent on the number of factors of 144. Every factor pair would give us four possible solutions for the ordered pair (x, y). For instance, if we were to consider 1 × 144 as one ordered pair, the possible values for (x, y) would be (1, 144); (144, 1); (–1, –144); (–144, –1). This would be true for all factor pairs except the factor pair 12 × 12. In this case, the possible pairs of (x, y) would be (12, 12) and (–12, –12).

If we find out the factor pairs of 144, we will get the following list:

Factor pair	*Number of solutions for (x, y)*
1 × 144	4 solutions – as explained above
2 × 72	4 solutions
3 × 48	4 solutions
4 × 36	4 solutions
6 × 24	4 solutions
8 × 18	4 solutions
9 × 16	4 solutions
12 × 12	2 solutions

Thus, there are a total of 30 solutions in this case.

16. At 60 kmph she consumes 4 liters per hour or goes 15 km per liter. Hence, she would use 200/15 = 13.33 liters of petrol for the journey.

17. The fuel consumption at 40 km/h = $\frac{200}{40} \times 2.5$ = 12.5 L

The fuel consumption at 60 km/h = $\frac{200}{60} \times 4$ = 13.33 L

The fuel consumption at 80 km/h = $\frac{200}{80} \times 7.9$ = 19.75 L

So, Manisha has to decrease the speed.

The fuel efficiency per liter can be seen to be 15 kmpl at speeds of 60 km/h – This has to be interpreted as: In one hour she travels 60 km (@60 km/h) and consumes 4 liters of fuel. Hence, her fuel consumption is 15 kmpl. If she increases her speed from 60 km/h, the graph clearly shows that her fuel consumption goes down. However, if she reduces her speed, her fuel efficiency goes up to 16 kmpl. Hence, she should reduce her speed.

18. Let Sachindra harvest $5n$ acres per week and Rishi harvest $7n$ acres per week. In 3 weeks Sachindra harvests $15n$ acres. This has to be a multiple of 7, which means that n has to be a multiple of 7. Also, in 4 weeks Rishi will harvest $28n$ acres, which has to be a multiple of 84. Hence, n has to be a multiple of 3 too. The LCM of 3 and 7 is 21 and the second lowest value possible for $n = 42$. Hence, the answer is $5 \times 42 = 210$.

19. Since, the amount of work done by Gultu, Amit and Kanhaiya working alone is in a harmonic progression, it means that the times required by them to do the work would be in an arithmetic progression. Also, if Gultu takes t days to do the work, Kanhaiya will take $3t$ days for the same work. This also means that Amit would take $2t$ days to do the work, if he is working alone. Now from the work completion condition in the question we can write:

$$\frac{3}{t}+\frac{11}{2t}+\frac{25.5}{3t}=1 \rightarrow t=17$$

Hence, Amit takes $2t = 34$ days to complete the work. Hence, the correct answer is 34.

20. For the man to reach back to his original point, the number of steps North should be equal to the number of steps South. Similarly, the number of steps East should be equal to the number of steps West.

The following cases would exist:

4 steps North and 4 steps South = $8!/(4! \times 4!) = 70$ ways;

3 steps North, 3 steps South, 1 step East and 1 step West = $8!/(3! \times 3!) = 1120$ ways;

2 steps North, 2 steps South, 2 steps East and 2 steps West = $8!/(2! \times 2! \times 2! \times 2!) = 2520$ ways;

1 step North, 1 step South, 3 steps East and 3 steps West = $8!/(3! \times 3!) = 1120$ ways;

4 steps East and 4 steps West $=8!/(4! \times 4!) = 70$ ways;

Thus, the total number of ways $= 70 \times 2 + 1120 \times 2 + 2520 = 140 + 2240 + 2520 = 4900$ ways.

Option (c) is correct.

21. Fifty-three identical chocolates can be distributed amongst three children in ${}^{55}C_2$ ways = 1485 ways (${}^{n+r-1}C_{r-1}$ formula). Out of these ways of distributing 53 chocolates, the following distributions methods are not possible as they would have two values equal to each other– (0, 0, 53); (1, 1, 51); (2, 2, 49)….(26, 26, 1).

There are 27 such distributions, but when allocated to C_1, C_2 and C_3 respectively, each of these distributions can be allocated in three ways amongst them. Thus, $C_1 = 0$, $C_2 = 0$ and $C_3 = 53$ is counted differently from $C_1 = 0$, $C_2 = 53$ and $C_3 = 0$ and also from $C_1 = 53$, $C_2 = 0$ and $C_3 = 0$. This will remove $27 \times 3 = 81$ distributions from 1485, leaving us with 1404 distributions. These 1404 distributions are those where all three numbers are different from each other. However, whenever we have three different values allocated to three children, there can be $3! = 6$ ways of allocating the three different values amongst the three people. For instance, the distribution of 10, 15 and 48 can be seen as follows:

C_1	C_2	C_3	
48	15	10	Only case which meets the problems' requirement
48	10	15	
15	48	10	
15	10	48	
10	15	48	
10	48	15	

Hence, out of every six distributions counted in the 1404 distributions we currently have, we need to count only one. The answer can be arrived at by dividing $1404 \div 6 = 234$. Hence, option (d) is correct.

22. If $4n$ and $7n$ are the number of people ahead and behind them respectively, the total number of people in the queue is $11n + 2$ (an Arithmetic progression). The series of numbers of the form $11n + 2$, which are multiples of 7 and are below 300 are 35, 112, 189, 256. Thus, the maximum possible value of the number of people in the queue is 256. $11 \times n + 2 = 256 \rightarrow n = 22$. Hence, the required answer is $4 \times n = 88$.

The CAT Experience 11

1. The sum of the 7 numbers is 119. Also, $\frac{119+a+b}{9} = \text{H(new odd average)}$. H can take values of 15, 17 and so on. To minimize $a^2 + b^2$, we first minimize $a + b$ at H = 15. $a + b = 16$. The value of $a^2 + b^2$ will get minimized when $a = b = 8$, which gives us the value of $a^2 + b^2 = 128$.

2. The given expression can be reframed as: $\frac{(x-5)^2}{(5-x)}+\frac{4}{(5-x)}=\frac{(5-x)}{1}+\frac{4}{(5-x)}$. The value of $(5 - x)$ is positive since $x < 5$ (given).

If we assume $(5 - x)$ as y, the expression becomes $y+\frac{4}{y}$, whose minimum value we have to find. Differentiating and equating to 0, we get $1-\frac{4}{y^2} = 0 \rightarrow y = \pm 2$. At $y = 2$, $x = 3$; at $y = -2$, $x = 7$. Since $x < 5$, we reject $y = -2$. Hence, the minimum value of $y+\frac{4}{y} = 2 + 2 = 4$.

3. Let Gaurav invest a principal P. His money would amount to
$P \times (1.03)^{22} \times 1.1 = 33000 \times (1.03)^{24} \rightarrow P = 33000 \times (1.03)^2/1.1 = 31827$. Hence, the correct answer is ₹31827.
4. The key reaction in this question is that after 3 successive increase decrease cycles, the population has gone up. This can only happen if starting from 100, we increase by x% and then decrease by y% and still get an outcome more than 100. Using a trial and error approach will be the best approach from this point. If $x = 50$, $y = 30$. A population of 100 will go up to 150 and then come down to 105 after a 50% increase and a 30% decrease. Hence, we need to think of larger numbers. If $x = 55$ and y 35, the calculation $100 \times 1.55 \times 0.65 = 100.75$, gives us an increase. If $x = 56$ and $y = 36$, the calculation $100 \times 1.56 \times 0.64 = 99.84$, gives us a decrease. Thus, a value of 56 is not possible, while a value of 55 is the largest possible value of x. Consequently, the largest possible value of $y = 35$%. Hence, the correct answer is 35.
5. These kinds of questions and thinking are very common in examinations and hence, you need to understand how to solve such questions.

In order to think of such questions, you need to first 'read' the equation given. What does it mean by 'reading' the equation? Let us illustrate:

The first thing we do is to simplify the equation by putting all the variables on the LHS. This would give us the equation $x^2 + 6x + y^2$. When we have an equation like $x^2 + 6x + y^2 = 4$, we should realise that the value on the RHS is fixed at 4. Also, if we take a look at the LHS of the equation, we realise that the terms x^2 and y^2 would always be positive integers or 0 (given that x and y are integers). $6x$, on the other hand, could be positive, zero or negative depending on the value of x (if x is positive, $6x$ is also positive; if x is negative, $6x$ would be negative and if x is 0, $6x$ would also be zero).

Thus, we can think of the following structures to build a value of 4 on the LHS for the equation to get satisfied:

	Value of x^2	*Value of 6x*	*Value of y^2*
Case 1	0	0	+
Case 2	+	+	+
Case 3	+	–	+
Case 4	+	–	0

Once you have these basic structures in place, you can think of the cases one-by-one. Thinking in this structured fashion makes sure that you do not miss out on any possible solutions — and that, as you should realise, is critical for any situation where you have to count the number of solutions. You simply cannot get these questions correct without identifying each possible situation. Trying to do such questions without first structuring your thought-process this way would lead to disastrous results in such questions!! Hence, this thinking is very critical for your development of quantitative thinking.

Let us look at **Case 1:** In case 1, since the value of the first two components on the LHS is 0, it must mean that we are talking about the case of $x = 0$. Obviously, in this case the entire value of 4 for the LHS has to be created by using the term y^2.

Thus, to make $y^2 = 4$, we can take $y = +2$ or $y = -2$. This gives us two possible solutions: (0, 2) and (0, –2)

Case 2: The minimum positive value for $6x$ would be when $x = 1$. This value for $6x$ turns out to be 6– which has already made the LHS larger than 4. To this, if we were to add two more positive integers for the values of x^2 and y^2, it would simply take the LHS further up from +6. Hence, in case 2, there are no solutions.

Case 3: In this case the value of x has to be negative and y can be either positive or negative. Possible negative values of x as –1, –2, –3, –4, –5, etc., give us values for $6x$ as –6, –12, –18, –24, –30, etc.

We then need to fill-in the values of x^2 and y^2 and see whether it is possible to add an exact value to any of these and get + 4 as the final value of the LHS. This thinking would go the following way:

If $6x = -6$: x must be –1 and hence, $x^2 = 1$. Thus, $x^2 + 6x = -5$, which means for $x^2 + 6x + y^2 = 4$, we would need $-5 + y^2 = 4 \rightarrow y^2 = 9 \rightarrow y = +3$ and $y = -3$

Thus, we have identified two more solutions as (–1, 3) and (–1, –3).

If $6x = -12$: x must be –2 and hence, $x^2 = 4$. Thus, $x^2 + 6x = -8$, which means for $x^2 + 6x + y^2 = 4$, we would need $-8 + y^2 = 4 \rightarrow y^2 = 12 \rightarrow y$ is not an integer in this case and hence, we get no new solutions for this case.

If $6x = -18$: x must be –3 and hence, $x^2 = 9$. Thus, $x^2 + 6x = -9$, which means for $x^2 + 6x + y^2 = 4$, we would need $-9 + y^2 = 4 \rightarrow y^2 = 13 \rightarrow y$ is not an integer in this case and hence, we get no new solutions for this case.

If $6x = -24$: x must be –4 and hence, $x^2 = 16$. Thus, $x^2 + 6x = -8$, which means for $x^2 + 6x + y^2 = 4$, we would need $-8 + y^2 = 4 \rightarrow y^2 = 12 \rightarrow y$ is not an integer in this case and hence, we get no new solutions for this case.

If $6x = -30$: x must be –5 and hence, $x^2 = 25$. Thus, $x^2 + 6x = -5$, which means for $x^2 + 6x + y^2 = 4$, we would need $-5 + y^2 = 4 \rightarrow y^2 = 9 \rightarrow y = +3$ and $y = -3$

Thus we have identified two more solutions as (–5, 3) and (–5, –3).

If $\underline{6x = -36}$: x must be –6 and hence, $x^2 = 36$. Thus, $x^2 + 6x = 0$, which means for $x^2 + 6x + y^2 = 4$, we would need $0 + y^2 = 4 \rightarrow y^2 = 4 \rightarrow y = +2$ and $y = -2$.

Thus, we have identified two more solutions as (–6, 2) and (–6, –2).

If $\underline{6x = -42}$: x must be –7 and hence, $x^2 = 49$. Thus, $x^2 + 6x = 7$, which means that $x^2 + 6x$ itself is crossing the value of 4 for the LHS. There is no scope to add any value of y^2 as a positive integer to get the LHS of the equation equal to 4. Thus, we can stop at this point. Notice that we did not need to check for the case 4 because if there were a solution for case 4, we would have been able to identify it while checking for case 3 itself.

Thus, the equation has eight solutions.

6. $(x+y+z)^2 = x^2 + y^2 + z^2 + 2xy + 2xz + 2yz = 25 \rightarrow x^2 + y^2 + z^2 = 19 \rightarrow$ maximum value of x can be the square root of 19 if we take y^2 and z^2 both to be 0.
7. Total four-letter computer passwords that can be formed using only the symmetric letters (no repetition allowed) = 11 × 10 × 9 × 8 = 7920
8. Total possible numbers = Total number of passwords using all letters – Total number of passwords using no symmetric letters = (26 × 25 × 24) – (15 × 14 × 13) = 12870.
9. We can solve this problem just by checking the options.

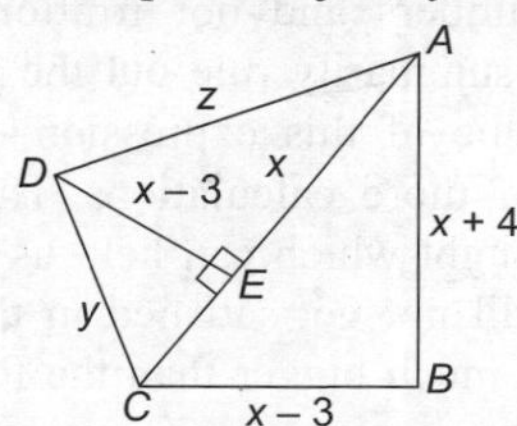

If we put $x = 11$, then in ΔABC by applying Pythagoras theorem, we get $AC = 17$ cm. and $CE = 17 - x = 17 - 11 = 6$ cm

ΔCED is a right angle triangle. For $CE = 6$ cm and $DE = 8$ cm, $y = 10$ cm

So for $x = 11$, all the conditions given in the question are satisfied.

10. Solve through options using unitary method. If the race was 36 meters long, the ratio of distances would be 36 : 24 : 18. This would not translate to a winning distance of 8 meters for B over C. For the second option, if the race was 48 meters, the ratio would be 48 : 36 : 30. This would translate into a ratio of $B : C$ as 48 : 40 giving B a win by 8 meters as required in the problem. Hence, this answer is correct.
11. In both the cases, the price of the painting would reduce by the same percentage value. Going through the options, it is evident that options (b) and (d) would not be correct since, if we start with those options, we would find that a drop of 441 itself would take the value lower than 1944.81 (which we need after 2 such drops). Even on trying to reduce 2500 consecutively in such a manner that it reduces by 441 the first time and replicating the same percentage change the second time too—our end value would be much lower than the required 1944.81. Hence, the only possible answer, which fits the situation is 2756.25, which is the correct answer.
12. If we look for the pattern of values of powers of 11 and compare them to the pattern of values of powers of 7, we see that $11^{n-1} < 7^{n+1}$ is obeyed all the way for $n = 1$ to 9. So we need 7^{10} to be surpassed by 5^{9+x}. When we use the value of x as 4, we get 5^{13} which is more than the value of 7^{10}. Hence, the minimum value of x is 4, that would satisfy the inequality for all values of n.
13. Let the number of lines be 'x'.

    The number of regions would be given by $= \frac{x(x+1)}{2} + 1$,

    Now put $x = 10$ in the above equation, we get number of regions $= \frac{10 \times 11}{2} + 1 = 56$
14. Total area of the square plot = 14 × 14 = 196 m^2

    Total area available for grazing = 196 – 20 = 176 m^2

    Grazed area $= \frac{\pi \times r^2}{4} \times 4 = \pi r^2 = 22 \times 7 (r = 7)$

    = 154 m^2

    Ungrazed area = 176 – 154 = 22 m^2
15. Let the two vessels have a capacity of 100 ml each. Thus, there will be 60 ml filled in each vessel to start with. The three operations can be summarized as shown in the table, (Sugar syrup quantities shown in brackets):

Operation #	*Vessel 1*	*Vessel 2*	*Transfer from to*	*Transfer quantity*
Starting position	(60)	60		
Operation 1	(30)	60 + (30)	Vessel 1 to 2	(30)
Operation 2	30 + (45)	30 + (15)	Vessel 2 to 1	30 + (15)
Operation 3	15 + (22.5)	45 + (37.5)	Vessel 1 to 2	15 + (22.5)

The milk to sugar syrup ratio in the second vessel is 6 : 5. Option (a) is correct.

16. Her combined annual total interest being 6.2% of capital, should be ₹3100 on 50000. She earns 6.5% on 24000 = 1560; 7% on 12000 = 840. So, she earns (3100 – 1560 – 840 = 700) on the balance 14000,

which means that the rate of interest $x\%$ mentioned in the question is equal to 5%. If she had invested the entire 50000 @5%, her annual interest income would have been ₹2500. This would amount to a loss of 600. Option (b) is correct.

17. It can be easily seen that the revenues at different values would be:

200×2, 220×1.9, 240×1.8, 260×1.7, 280×1.6, 300×1.5 and 320×1.4. The value goes up till 300×1.5 and then reduces. Hence, option (b) is correct.

18.

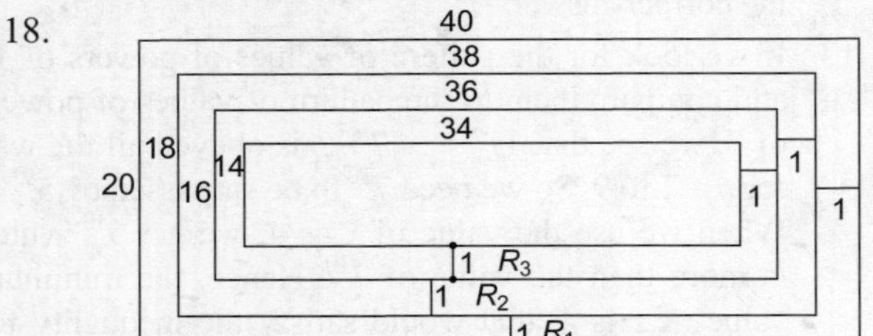

In the first round he would do 20 + 20 + 38 + 38 = 116 meters. The second round would be 18 + 18 + 36 + 36 = 108, the third round would be 100. (**Note** that the values of the area of the lawn mowed in every round would be an *AP*. So you need to calculate the total value only for the first two rounds and the remaining values you can get by considering the *AP*). Thus, in the fourth round he would do a total of 92 but to complete half the lawn he would need to do an additional of only 76 (400 – 116 – 108 – 100). This can be achieved in approximately 0.8 of the fourth round.

19. $\angle ECB$ is exterior angle of ΔACB

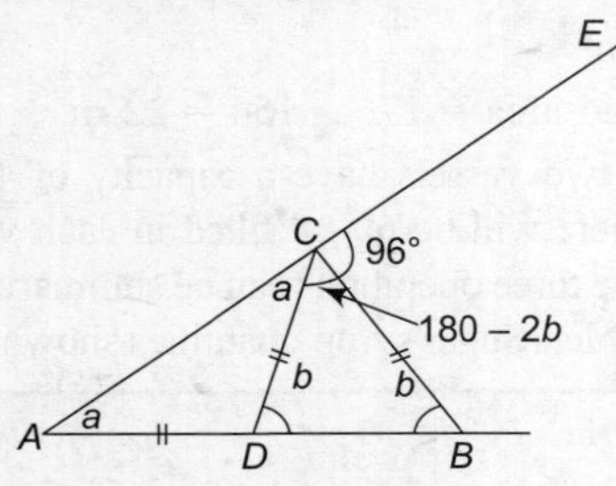

$\angle A + \angle B = \angle ECB = 96°$ (Sum of interior opposite angles).

i.e. $a + b = 96°$ (1)

Also $a + (180 - 2b) + 96° = 180°$

$\therefore \quad a - 2b + 96° = 0$

$\therefore \quad a - 2b = -96°$ (2)

Solving (1) and (2)

$b = 64°$ and $a = 32°$

$\therefore \quad \angle DBC = b = 64°$

20. We can see from the triangle *CAT* that, $\angle CAT = 100$. We can also see that $\angle OCA = 40$. Hence, $\angle OAC = 40$. Thus, $\angle OAB = \angle OBA = 40°$.

Thus, $\angle BOA = 180 - 40 - 40 = 100$.

21. The only way to handle such questions is to try to get a 'feel' of the equation by inserting a few values for x and trying to see the behaviour of the various terms in the equation.

Towards this end, let us start by trying to insert values for x in the given equation.

Because the problem tells us that $x > 1$, the first value of x which comes to mind is $x = 2$. At $x = 2$, the value of the LHS would become equal to 1. This can be thought of as follows:

LHS = $\log_{2x} (1)(\log_2(2))^2 + (\log_2(2))^4 = 0 + 1 = 1$

As we try to take higher values of x as 3, 4, and 5 and so on we realise first that for values like 3, 5, we will get terms like

$\log_6 (2/3)(\log_2 (3))^2 + (\log_2 (3))^4$ which is clearly not going to be an integral value, because terms like $\log_2 3$, $\log_6 2$ and $\log_6 3$ would have irrational decimal values by themselves. In fact, we can see that for numbers of x that are not powers of 2, we will never get an integral value to the LHS of the expression.

Thus, we need to see the behaviour of the expression only for values of x like 4, 8 and so on before we can conclude about the number of real roots of the equation.

At $x = 4$, the expression becomes:

$\log_8 (2/4)(\log_2(4))^2 + (\log_2(4))^4$

By thinking about this expression, it is again clear that there are going to be decimals in the first part of the expression—although they are going to be rational numbers and not irrational—and hence, we cannot summarily rule out the possibility of an integral value of this expression— without doing a couple of more calculations. However, there is another thought which can help us confirm that the equation will not get satisfied in this case because the LHS is much bigger than the RHS.

This thought goes as follows:

The LHS has two parts: The first part is $\log_8 (2/4)$ $(\log_2(4))^2$ while the second part is $(\log_2(4))^4$. The value of the second part is 16 while the value of the first part (though it is negative) is much smaller than the required, i.e. –15, which will make the LHS = 1.

Hence, we can reject this value.

22. By replacing $x^3 = m$, the equation given in the question, can be written in the form:

$y = m^2 + m - 2 \rightarrow$

$y = (m + 2)(m - 1) \rightarrow m = -2$ and $m = 1$

This gives $x^3 = -2$ and $x^3 = 1$. This gives us two clear values of x (these would be the roots of the equation) and hence x, the curve would cut the 'x' axis at two points exactly.

BLOCK STARTER

Scan this QR Code to access a introductory video on the CAT 2023 and CAT 2024 papers.

BLOCK

CAT 2023–24 EXAMINATION PAPERS

CAT 2023 Examination Paper

High Yield Questions

Scan this QR Code to access video solutions for High Yield Questions of the CAT 2023 Examination

CAT 2023 SLOT 1

1. If $\sqrt{5x+9}+\sqrt{5x-9}=3(2+\sqrt{2})$, then $\sqrt{10x+9}$ is equal to
(a) $2\sqrt{7}$ (b) $3\sqrt{31}$
(c) $4\sqrt{5}$ (d) $3\sqrt{7}$

2. Let n be the least positive integer such that 168 is a factor of 1134^n. If m is the least positive integer such that 1134^n is a factor of 168^m, then $m + n$ equals
(a) 12 (b) 24
(c) 9 (d) 15

3. If x and y are real numbers such that $x^2 + (x - 2y - 1)^2 = -4y(x + y)$, then the value $x - 2y$ is
(a) 0 (b) 1
(c) –1 (d) 2

4. If x and y are positive real numbers such that $\log_x (x^2 + 12) = 4$ and $3 \log_y x = 1$, then $x + y$ equals
(a) 68 (b) 20
(c) 10 (d) 11

5. The number of integer solutions of equation $2 |x| (x^2 + 1) = 5x^2$ is?

6. Let a and β be the two distinct roots of the equation $2x^2 - 6x + k = 0$, such that $(\alpha + \beta)$ and $a\beta$ are the distinct roots of the equation $x^2 + px + p = 0$. Then, the value of $8(k - p)$ is?

7. The equation $x^3 + (2r + 1)x^2 + (4r - 1)x + 2 = 0$ has –2 as one of the roots. If the other two roots are real, then the minimum possible non-negative integer value of r is?

8. A mixture P is formed by removing a certain amount of coffee from a coffee jar and replacing the same amount with cocoa powder. The same amount is again removed from mixture P and replaced with same amount of cocoa powder to form a new mixture Q. If the ratio of coffee and cocoa in the mixture Q is 16 : 9, then the ratio of cocoa in mixture P to that in mixture Q is
(a) 1 : 3 (b) 4 : 9
(c) 1 : 2 (d) 5 : 9

9. Gita sells two objects A and B at the same price such that she makes a profit of 20% on object A and a loss of 10% on object B. If she increases the selling price such that objects A and B are still sold at an equal price and a profit of 10% is made on object B, then the profit made on object A will be nearest to
(a) 45% (b) 47%
(c) 49% (d) 42%

10. The salaries of three friends Sita, Gita and Mita are initially in the ratio 5 : 6: 7, respectively. In the first year, they get salary hikes of 20%, 25% and 20%, respectively. In the second year, Sita and Mita get salary hikes of 40% and 25%, respectively, and the salary of Gita becomes equal to the mean salary of the three friends. The salary hike of Gita in the second year is
(a) 28% (b) 26%
(c) 25% (d) 30%

11. Brishti went on an 8-hour trip in a car. Before the trip, the car had travelled a total of x km till then, where x is a whole number and is palindromic, i.e., x remains unchanged when its digit are reversed. At the end of the trip, the car had travelled a total of 26862 km till then, this number again being palindromic. If Brishti never drove at more than 110 km/h, then the greatest possible average speed at which she drove during the trip, in km/h, was
(a) 80 (b) 90
(c) 100 (d) 110

12. In an examination, the average marks of 4 girls and 6 boys is 24. Each of the girls has the same marks while each of the boys has the same marks. If the marks of any girl is at most double the marks of any boy, but not less than the marks of any boy, then the number of possible distinct integer values of the total marks of 2 girls and 6 boys is
(a) 19 (b) 20
(c) 22 (d) 21

13. The minor angle between the hours hand and minutes hand of a clock was observed at 8:48 am. The minimum duration, in minutes, after 8.48 am when this angle increases by 50% is
(a) 4 (b) $\frac{36}{11}$
(c) $\frac{24}{11}$ (d) 2

14. Arvind travels from town A to town B, and Surbhi from town B to town A, both starting at the same time along the same route. After meeting each other, Arvind takes 6 hours to reach town B while Surbhi takes 24 hours to reach town A. If Arvind travelled at a speed of 54 km/h, then the distance, in km, between town A and town B is?

15. The amount of job that Amal, Sunil and Kamal can individually do in a day, are in harmonic progression. Kamal takes twice as much time as Amal to do the same amount of job. If Amal and Sunil work for 4 days and 9 days, respectively, Kamal needs to work for 16 days to finish the remaining job. Then the number of days Sunil will take to finish the job working alone, is?

16. Anil invests ₹22000 for 6 years in a certain scheme with 4% interest per annum, compounded half-yearly. Sunil invests in the same scheme for 5 years, and then reinvests the entire amount received at the end of 5 years for one year at 10% simple interest. If the amounts received by both at the end of 6 years are same, then the initial investment made by Sunil, in rupees, is?

17. Let C be the circle $x^2 + y^2 + 4x - 6y - 3 = 0$ and L be the locus of the point of intersection of a pair of tangents to C with the angle between the two tangents equal to 60°. Then, the point L touches the line $x = 6$ is
(a) (6, 6) (b) (6, 4)
(c) (6, 3) (d) (6, 8)

18. A quadrilateral $ABCD$ is inscribed in a circle such that $AB : CD = 2 : 1$ and $BC : AD = 5 : 4$. If AC and BD intersect at the point E, then $AE : CE$ equals
(a) 5 : 8 (b) 8 : 5
(c) 2 : 1 (d) 1 : 2

19. In a right-angled triangle ΔABC, the altitude AB is 5 cm, and the base BC is 12 cm. P and Q are two points on BC such that the areas of ΔABP, ΔABQ and ΔABC are in arithmetic progression. If the area of ΔABC is 1.5 times the area of ΔABP, the length of PQ, in cm, is?

20. For some positive and distinct real numbers x, y and z, if $\frac{1}{\sqrt{y}+\sqrt{z}}$ is the arithmetic mean of $\frac{1}{\sqrt{x}+\sqrt{z}}$ and $\frac{1}{\sqrt{x}+\sqrt{y}}$, then the relationship which will always hold true, is
(a) $\sqrt{x}, \sqrt{z}$ and $\sqrt{y}$ are in arithmetic progression
(b) $\sqrt{x}, \sqrt{y}$ and $\sqrt{z}$ are in arithmetic progression
(c) y, x and z are in arithmetic progression
(d) x, y and z are in arithmetic progression

21. The number of all natural numbers up to 1000 with non-repeating digits is
(a) 504 (b) 738
(c) 648 (d) 585

22. A lab experiment measures the number of organisms at 8 am every day. Starting with 2 organisms on the first day, the number of organisms on any day is equal to 3 more than twice the number on the previous day. If the number of organisms on the nth day exceeds one million, then the lowest possible value of n is?

CAT 2023 SLOT 2

1. For any natural numbers m, n, and k, such that k divides both $m + 2n$ and $3m + 4n$, k must be a common divisor of
(a) m and n (b) m and $2n$
(c) $2m$ and $3n$ (d) $2m$ and n

2. Any non-zero real numbers x, y such that $y \neq 3$ and $\frac{x}{y} < \frac{x+3}{y-3}$, will satisfy the condition
(a) If $y < 0$, then $-x < y$
(b) If $x < 0$, then $-x < y$
(c) If $y > 10$, then $-x > y$
(d) $\frac{x}{y} < \frac{y}{x}$

3. Let a, b, m and n be natural numbers such that $a > 1$ and $b > 1$. If $a^m b^n = 144^{145}$, then the largest possible value of $n - m$ is
(a) 289 (b) 579
(c) 580 (d) 290

4. The sum of all possible values of x satisfying the equation $2^{4x^2} - 2^{2x^2+x+16} + 2^{2x+30} = 0$, is
(a) $\frac{5}{2}$ (b) 3
(c) $\frac{1}{2}$ (d) $\frac{3}{2}$

5. For some positive real number x, if $\log_{\sqrt{3}}(x) + \frac{\log_x(25)}{\log_x(0.008)} = \frac{16}{3}$, then the value of $\log_3(3x^2)$ is?

6. Let k be the largest integer such that the equation $(x - 1)^2 + 2kx + 11 = 0$ has no real roots. If y is a positive real number, then the least possible value of $\frac{k}{4y} + 9y$ is?

7. The number of positive integers less than 50, having exactly two distinct factors other than 1 and itself, is?

8. In a company, 20% of the employees work in the manufacturing department. If the total salary obtained by all the manufacturing employees is one-sixth of the total salary obtained by all the employees in the company, then the ratio of the average salary obtained by the manufacturing employees to the average salary obtained by the non-manufacturing employees is
(a) 5 : 6 (b) 4 : 5
(c) 6 : 5 (d) 5 : 4

9. Anil borrows ₹2 lakhs at an interest rate of 8% per annum, compounded half-yearly. He repays ₹10320 at the end of the first year and closes the loan by paying the outstanding amount at the end of the third year. Then, the total interest, in rupees, paid over the three years is nearest to
(a) 45311 (b) 33130
(c) 51311 (d) 40991

10. Ravi is driving at a speed of 40 km/h on a road. Vijay is 54 meters behind Ravi and driving in the same direction as Ravi. Ashok is driving along the same road from the opposite direction at a speed of 50 km/h and is 225 meters away from Ravi. The speed, in km/h, at which Vijay should drive so that all the three cross each other at the same time, is
(a) 67.2 (b) 64.4
(c) 61.6 (d) 58.8

11. Pipes A and C are fill pipes while Pipe B is a drain pipe of a tank. Pipe B empties the full tank in one hour less than the time taken by Pipe A to fill the empty tank. When pipes A, B and C are turned on together, the empty tank is filled in two hours. If pipes B and C are turned on together when the tank is empty and Pipe B is turned off after one hour, then Pipe C takes another one hour and 15 minutes to fill the remaining tank. If Pipe A can fill the empty tank in less than five hours, then the time taken, in minutes, by Pipe C to fill the empty tank is
(a) 75 (b) 90
(c) 60 (d) 120

12. The price of a precious stone is directly proportional to the square of its weight. Sita has a precious stone weighing 18 units. If she breaks it into four pieces with each piece having distinct integer weight, then the difference between the highest and lowest possible values of the total price of the four pieces will be 288000. Then, the price of the original precious stone is
(a) 972000 (b) 1296000
(c) 1944000 (d) 1620000

13 Minu purchases a pair of sunglasses at ₹1000 and sells to Kanu at 20% profit. Then, Kanu sells it back to Minu at 20% loss. Finally, Minu sells the same pair of sunglasses to Tanu. If the total profit made by Minu from all her transactions is ₹500, then the percentage of profit made by Minu when she sold the pair of sunglasses to Tanu is
(a) 35.42% (b) 31.25%
(c) 52% (d) 26%

14. Jayant bought a certain number of white shirts at the rate of ₹1000 per piece and a certain number of blue shirts at the rate of ₹1125 per piece. For each shirt, he then set a fixed market price which was 25% higher than the average cost of all the shirts. He sold all the shirts at a discount of 10% and made a total profit of ₹51000. If he bought both colors of shirts, then the maximum possible total number of shirts that he could have bought is?

15. A container has 40 liters of milk. Then, 4 liters are removed from the container and replaced with 4 liters of water. This process of replacing 4 liters of the liquid in the container with an equal volume of water is continued repeatedly. The smallest number of times of doing this process, after which the volume of milk in the container becomes less than that of water, is?

16. If a certain amount of money is divided equally among n persons, each one receives ₹352. However, if two persons receive ₹506 each and the remaining amount is divided equally among the other persons, each of them receive less than or equal to ₹330. Then, the maximum possible value of n is?

17. A triangle is drawn with its vertices on the circle C such that one of its sides is a diameter of C and the other two sides have their lengths in the ratio $a : b$. If the radius of the circle is r, then the area of the triangle is
(a) $\frac{abr^2}{a^2+b^2}$ (b) $\frac{4abr^2}{a^2+b^2}$
(c) $\frac{2abr^2}{a^2+b^2}$ (d) $\frac{abr^2}{2(a^2+b^2)}$

18. In a rectangle $ABCD$, $AB = 9$ cm and $BC = 6$ cm. P and Q are two points on BC such that the areas of the figures ABP, APQ, and $AQCD$ are in geometric progression. If the area of the figure $AQCD$ is four times the area of triangle ABP, then $BP : PQ : QC$ is
(a) 2 : 4 : 1 (b) 1 : 2 : 4
(c) 1 : 1 : 2 (d) 1 : 2 : 1

19. The area of the quadrilateral bounded by the Y-axis, the line $x = 5$, and the lines $|x-y|-|x-5|=2$, is?

20. If $p^2 + q^2 - 29 = 2pq - 20 = 52 - 2pq$, then the difference between the maximum and minimum possible value of $(p^3 - q^3)$ is
(a) 486 (b) 378
(c) 189 (d) 243

21. Let both the series a_1, a_2, a_3,... and b_1 b_2 b_3... be in arithmetic progression such that the common differences of both the series are prime numbers. If $a_5 = b_9$, $a_{19} = b_{19}$ and $b_2 = 0$, then a_{11} equals
(a) 79 (b) 84
(c) 83 (d) 86

22. Let a_n and b_n be two sequences such that $a_n = 13 + 6(n-1)$ and $b_n = 15 + 7(n-1)$ for all natural numbers n. Then, the largest three digit integer that is common to both these sequences, is?

CAT 2023 SLOT 3

1. For some real numbers a and b, the system of equations $x + y = 4$ and $(a + 5)x + (b^2 - 15)y = 8b$ has infinitely many solutions for x and y. Then, the maximum possible value of ab is
(a) 33 (b) 55
(c) 15 (d) 25

2. If x is a positive real number such that $x^8 + \left(\frac{1}{x}\right)^8 = 47$, then the value of $x^9 + \left(\frac{1}{x}\right)^9$ is

(a) $34\sqrt{5}$ (b) $36\sqrt{5}$
(c) $40\sqrt{5}$ (d) $30\sqrt{5}$

3. Let n and m be two positive integers such that there are exactly 41 integers greater than 8^m and less than 8^n, which can be expressed as powers of 2. Then, the smallest possible value of $n + m$ is
(a) 44 (b) 16
(c) 42 (d) 14

4. For a real number x, if $\frac{1}{2}$, $\frac{\log_3(2^x - 9)}{\log_3 4}$, and $\frac{\log_5\left(2^x + \frac{17}{2}\right)}{\log_5 4}$ are in an arithmetic progression, then the common difference is
(a) $\log_4 7$ (b) $\log_4\left(\frac{7}{2}\right)$
(c) $\log_4\left(\frac{23}{2}\right)$ (d) $\log_4\left(\frac{3}{2}\right)$

5. The sum of the first two natural numbers, each having 15 factors (including 1 and the number itself), is?

6. A quadratic equation $x^2 + bx + c = 0$ has two real roots. If the difference between the reciprocals of the roots is $\frac{1}{3}$, and the sum of the reciprocals of the squares of the roots is $\frac{5}{9}$, then the largest possible value of $(b + c)$ is?

7. Let n be any natural number such that $5^{n-1} < 3^{n+1}$. Then, the least integer value of m that satisfies $3^{n+1} < 2^{n+m}$ for each such n, is?

8. Anil mixes cocoa with sugar in the ratio 3 : 2 to prepare mixture A, and coffee with sugar in the ratio 7 : 3 to prepare mixture B. He combines mixtures A and B in the ratio 2 : 3 to make a new mixture C. If he mixes C with an equal amount of milk to make a drink, then the percentage of sugar in this drink will be
(a) 16 (b) 24
(c) 17 (d) 21

9. Rahul, Rakshita and Gurmeet, working together, would have taken more than 7 days to finish a job. On the other hand, Rahul and Gurmeet, working together would have taken less than 15 days to finish the job. However, they all worked together for 6 days, followed by Rakshita, who worked alone for 3 more days to finish the job. If Rakshita had worked alone on the job then the number of days she would have taken the finish the job, cannot be
(a) 17 (b) 21
(c) 16 (d) 20

10. A boat takes 2 hours to travel downstream a river from port A to port B, and 3 hours to return to port A. Another boat takes a total of 6 hours to travel from port B to port A and return to port B. If the speeds of the boats and the river are constant, then the time, in hours, taken by the slower boat to travel from port A to port B is
(a) $12(\sqrt{5}-2)$ (b) $3(\sqrt{5}-1)$
(c) $3(3-\sqrt{5})$ (d) $3(3+\sqrt{5})$

11. A merchant purchases a cloth at a rate of ₹100 per meter and receives 5 cm length of cloth free for every 100 cm length of cloth purchased by him. He sells the same cloth at a rate of ₹110 per meter but cheats his customers by giving 95 cm length of cloth for every 100 cm length of cloth purchased by the customers. If the merchant provides a 5% discount, the resulting profit earned by him is
(a) 16% (b) 15.5%
(c) 9.7% (d) 4.2%

12. The population of a town in 2020 was 100000. The population decreased by y% from the year 2020 to 2021, and increased by x% from the year 2021 to 2022, where x and y are two natural numbers. If population in 2022 was greater than the population in 2020 and the difference between x and y is 10, then the lowest possible population of the town in 2021 was
(a) 74000 (b) 75000
(c) 73000 (d) 72000

13. There are three persons A, B and C in a room. If a person D joins the room, the average weight of the persons in the room reduces by x kg. Instead of D, if person E joins the room, the average weight of the persons in the room increases by $2x$ kg. If the weight of E is 12 kg more than that of D, then the value of x is
(a) 0.5 (b) 1.5
(c) 1 (d) 2

14. Gautam and Suhani, working together, can finish a job in 20 days. If Gautam does only 60% of his usual work on a day, Suhani must do 150% of her usual work on that day to exactly make up for it. Then, the number of days required by the faster worker to complete the job working alone is?

15. A fruit seller has a stock of mangoes, bananas and apples with at least one fruit of each type. At the beginning of a day, the number of mangoes make up 40% of his stock. That day, he sells half of the mangoes, 96 bananas and 40% of the apples. At the end of the day, he ends up selling 50% of the fruits. The smallest possible total number of fruits in the stock at the beginning of the day is?

16. The number of coins collected per week by two coin-collectors A and B are in the ratio 3 : 4. If the total number of coins collected by A in 5 weeks is a multiple of 7, and the total number of coins collected by B in 3 weeks is a multiple of 24, then the minimum possible number of coins collected by A in one week is?

17. A rectangle with the largest possible area is drawn inside a semicircle of radius 2 cm. Then, the ratio of the lengths of the largest to the smallest side of this rectangle is

(a) 1 : 1 (b) $\sqrt{2}:1$
(c) $\sqrt{5}:1$ (d) 2 : 1

18. Let ΔABC be an isosceles triangle such that AB and AC are of equal length. AD is the altitude from A on BC and BE is the altitude from B on AC. If AD and BE intersect at O such that $\angle AOB = 105°$, then $\frac{AD}{BE}$ equals

(a) 2 cos 15° (b) sin 15°
(c) 2 sin 15° (d) cos 15°

19. In a regular polygon, any interior angle exceeds the exterior angle by 120 degrees. Then, the number of diagonals of this polygon is?

20. Let $a_n = 46 + 8n$ and $b_n = 98 + 4n$ be two sequences for natural numbers $n \le 100$. Then, the sum of all terms common to both the sequences is

(a) 14900 (b) 14798
(c) 14602 (d) 15000

21. The value of $1+\left(1+\frac{1}{3}\right)\frac{1}{4}+\left(1+\frac{1}{3}+\frac{1}{9}\right)\frac{1}{16}+\left(1+\frac{1}{3}+\frac{1}{9}+\frac{1}{27}\right)\frac{1}{64}+\cdots$, is

(a) $\frac{15}{8}$ (b) $\frac{27}{12}$
(c) $\frac{16}{11}$ (d) $\frac{15}{13}$

22. Suppose $f(x, y)$ is a real-valued function such that $f(3x + 2y, 2x - 5y) = 19x$, for all real numbers x and y. The value of x for which $f(x, 2x) = 27$, is?

ANSWER KEY

CAT 2023 Slot 1

1. (d)	2. (d)	3. (b)	4. (c)
5. 3	6. 6	7. 2	8. (d)
9. (b)	10. (b)	11. (c)	12. (d)
13. (c)	14. 972	15. 27	16. 20808
17. (c)	18. (b)	19. 2	20. (c)
21. (b)	22. 19		

CAT 2023 Slot 2

1. (b)	2. (a)	3. (b)	4. (c)
5. 7	6. 6	7. 15	8. (b)
9. (c)	10. (c)	11. (b)	12. (b)
13. (b)	14. 407	15. 7	16. 16
17. (c)	18. (a)	19. 45	20. (b)
21. (a)	22. 967		

CAT 2023 Slot 3

1. (a)	2. (a)	3. (b)	4. (b)
5. 468	6. 9	7. 5	8. (c)
9. (b)	10. (c)	11. (b)	12. (c)
13. (c)	14. 36	15. 340	16. 42
17. (d)	18. (a)	19. 54	20. (a)
21. (c)	22. 3		

SOLUTIONS AND SHORTCUTS

CAT 2023 Slot 1

1. Based on the values in the options, we can make out that the value of $10x + 9$ are 28, 279, 80 or 63 (as per options a, b, c, d). The value of x is 1.9, 27, 7.1 and 5.4 respectively for these four options. At $x = 5.4$, we get $\sqrt{(5x+9)}+\sqrt{5x-9}=6+3\sqrt{2}=3(2+\sqrt{2})$. Hence, option (d) is correct.
2. 1134 = (2 × 3 × 3 × 3 × 3 × 7). Also, 168 is 2 × 2 × 2 × 3 × 7. For 168 to be a factor of 1134^n, the minimum value of n has to be 3 so that the three 2's in the prime factors of 168 get cancelled out completely. Thus, $n = 3$. Then $1134^n = 1134^3 = (2 \times 3 \times 3 \times 3 \times 3 \times 7)^3 = 2^3 \times 3^{12} \times 7^3$. For this to be a factor of $(2^3 \times 3^1 \times 7)^m$, the minimum value of m is 12. Thus, $m + n = 15$. Option (d) is correct.
3. The given expression can be re-written as $(x + 2y)^2 + (x - 2y - 1)^2 = 0$. An equation of this type can only give us LHS = RHS if each of the terms in the brackets is 0. For that to happen inside the second bracket, we need the value of $x - 2y$ to be equal to 1. Hence, option (b) is correct.
4. $\log_x(x^2 + 12) = 4 \rightarrow x^4 - x^2 - 12 = 0 \rightarrow x = 2$. $3 \times \log_y 2 = 1 \rightarrow y = 8$. Hence, $x + y = 10$. Option (c) is correct.
5. $2|x|(x^2 + 1) = 5x^2$ can be seen to be an even function, since it will return the same value for positive or negative x. Also, it can be clearly seen that LHS = RHS at $x = 0$ and 2. Between 0 and 2, the RHS is larger and when we take $x > 2$, we see that the LHS will become larger than the RHS and will remain so for larger values of x (since the expression on the LHS is a cubic expression, while the one on the RHS is a quadratic expression). Also, if there is a solution at $x = 2$, there will also be a solution at $x = -2$. Hence, the given equation has three integer solutions.
6. According to the question, the quadratic equation $x^2 + px + p = 0$ will have roots as 3 and $k/2$. Hence, $p = 3 \times k/2$ and $-p = 3 + k/2 \rightarrow k = -1.5$ and $p = -2.25$. Hence,
$8 \times (k - p) = 8 \times (-1.5 + 2.25) = 8 \times 0.75 = 6$.
7. The product of the roots of the cubic equation $ax^3 + bx^2 + cx + d = 0$ is given by $-d/a$. Hence, in this case, the product of the roots of the equation are -2. Since, one of the roots is already given as -2, it means that the product of the other two real

roots of the equation is 1 (in other words they are reciprocals of each other). Let the roots by n and $\frac{1}{n}$.

From formula for sum of roots, we can see that –2 + $n+\frac{1}{n} = -\frac{b}{a} = -2r - 1 \rightarrow n+\frac{1}{n} = -2r + 1$. We know that the value of $n + 1/n \leq -2$ or ≥ 2. Since, the question points us towards non-negative integral values of r, we can see that $r = 1$ is not possible – as we get $n + 1/n = -1$, which is not possible. At $r = 2$, we get $n+\frac{1}{n}=-3$, which is a possible value of the sum of two reciprocal numbers. Hence, the lowest non-negative integer value of r is 2.

8. It can be inferred after two iterations the coffee to cocoa percentages in Mixture Q is 64 and 36 respectively. Since, the same amount is being withdrawn each time, it means we are taking out 20% of the coffee the first time and 20% of the mixture P the second time and replacing with cocoa powder. Thus, in mixture P: Coffee = 80%, Cocoa = 20%. In Mixture Q Coffee = 64% and Cocoa = 36%. Since the total quantity of powder remains constant, the required ratio is 20 : 36 = 5 : 9. Option (d) is correct.
9. The key decision in this question is what same selling price to take for both objects in the first case, so that we avoid decimal calculations. *A* little bit of numerical vision can help you arrive at a number like 90, as the common selling price for both objects, which would give us cost price of A as 75 (such that 75 × 1.2 = 90) and the cost price of B as 100 (such that 100 × 0.9 = 90). In the new scenario, the selling price of both objects is kept as 100 × 1.1 = 110. Thus, the profit on Object A is 35 on a cost price of 75, which converts to a profit percentage of 46.67%. The question asks us for an approximate profit percentage, which would be 47. Option (b) is correct.
10. Let the initial salaries of Sita, Gita and Mita be 500n, 600n and 700n. After the first year, their salaries would be 600n, 750n and 840n respectively. After the second year Sita's salary = 600n × 1.4 = 840n and Mita's salary = 840n × 1.25 = 1050n. Gita's salary after the second year has to be 945n (average of Sita and Mita after 2 years). Thus, the percentage growth for Gita can be calculated from her increase from 750n to 945n, a 26% increase. Option (b) is correct.
11. Since, her number of kilometers at the end of the trip is 26862, we have the requirement of 26862 – 8 × S = Palindromic number, (where S is the average speed of her journey). It can be seen that at S = 110, we get 26862 – 880 = 25982 which is not a palindrome. At S = 100, we get 26862 – 800 = 26062 (which is a palindromic number). Hence, option (c) is correct.
12. Let the marks for each girl be G and each boy be B. Then, $4G + 6B = 240$. At $G = 2B$, we get B = 17.1428 and G = 34.2857. Also, at $G = B$, we get the other extreme of $G = B = 24$. Thus, the value of G varies from 24 to 34.2857, while the value of B varies between 17.1428 and 24. If we try to look for values at which $4G + 6B = 240$ will get satisfied after G and $B = 24$, we can see that the ratio of increase for G : decrease for B would be 3 : 2. Also, since $4G + 6B$ and also $2G + 6B$ needs to be an integer, we will need to work out the set of values of G and B, such that for G we only take values that are multiples of 0.5 and for B we only take values that are multiples of 0.1666. After 24, we can see that if we increase G to 24.5, B reduces to 23.666; G 25, gives us B as 23.33; G = 25.5, B = 23 and so on. Thus, the number of values of (G) so that 2G + 6B is an integer can be seen as G = 24, 24.5, 25, 25.5, … 34. There are 21 possible values of $2G$ + 6B. Hence, option (d) is correct.
13. If we consider the two hands of the clock as runners running around a circular track of circumference 60 kms, we can work out that their speeds are 60 kmph (minute hand) and 5 kmph (hour hand) respectively. Their relative speed would be 60 – 5 = 55 kmph. At 8 AM, the hour hand is 40 kms ahead of the minute hand on the track. At 8:48, the minute hand would 'cover' $\frac{4}{5}\times 55 = 44$ kms over the hour hand – thus it would be 4 kms ahead of the hour hand. To increase the angle by 50 degrees, it needs to go ahead by another 2 kms. The time in minutes required to do this, can be measured using unitary method as follows:

    In 60 minutes – minute hand covers 55 kms on hour hand;

    In 't' minutes – minute hand covers 2 kms on the hour hand.

    $$t = 2\times\frac{60}{55} = \frac{24}{11}\text{ hours.}$$
14. The time 't' taken by each to reach the meeting point is given by $t^2 = 24 \times 6 \rightarrow t = 12$. Hence, Arvind takes a total of 12 + 6 = 18 hours to reach his destination. Thus, the total distance = 54 × 18 = 972 kms.
15. Since the amount of job done by the three of them are in HP, it means that the number of days required to do the job by Amal, Sunil and Kamal are in an Arithmetic Progression. Also, since Kamal takes twice the time as Amal, it means that if Amal takes time t, Sunil will take 1.5t and Kamal will take 2t time to do the job. From the last piece of information in the question we get:

    $$\frac{4}{t}+\frac{9}{1.5t}+\frac{16}{2t}=1 \rightarrow \frac{24+36+48}{6t}=1 \rightarrow t=18.$$

Sunil's time required would be $1.5t = 18 \times 1.5 = 27$ days.

16. If S is the amount of investment of Sunil, we have: $22000 \times (1.02)^{12} = S \times (1.02)^{10} \times 1.1 \rightarrow$
$$S = \frac{22000 \times 1.02 \times 1.02}{1.1} = 20808$$

17. The equation of the circle is $x^2 + 4x + y^2 - 6y - 3 = 0 \rightarrow (x + 2)^2 + (y - 3)^2 = 16$. This is a circle with center at (–2, 3) and a radius of 4. The point where L will touch the line $x = 6$, can be visualized basis the 30-60-90 triangle OAB as shown in the figure:

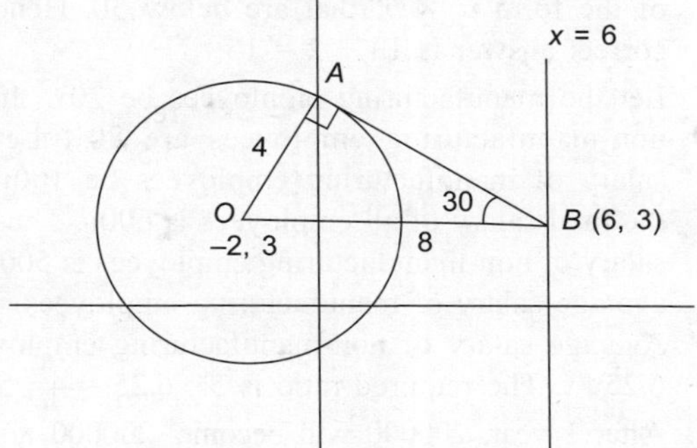

Hence, option (c) is correct.

18. The situation can be visualized as shown:

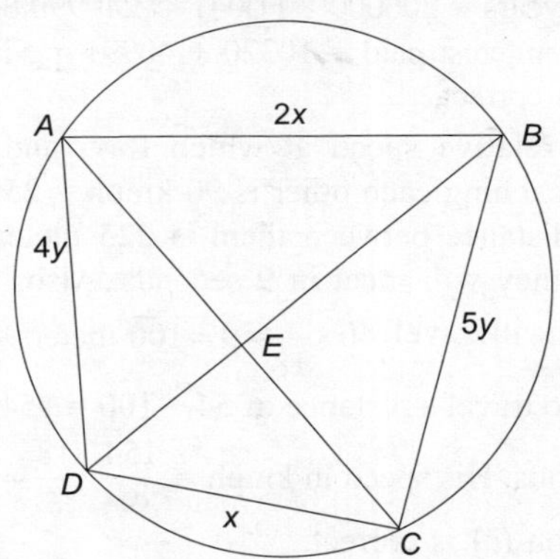

In the figure, $\Delta BEA \sim \Delta CED$. Hence, $\frac{EA}{ED} = \frac{BE}{CE} = \frac{AB}{CD} = \frac{2}{1}$.

Also, $\Delta AED \sim \Delta BEC$. Hence, $\frac{AE}{BE} = \frac{ED}{EC} = \frac{AD}{BC} = \frac{4}{5}$

Hence, $\frac{EA}{ED} \times \frac{ED}{EC} = \frac{EA}{EC} = \frac{2}{1} \times \frac{4}{5} = \frac{8}{5}$. Hence, Option (b) is correct.

19. For the areas of the triangles ABP, ABQ and ABC to be in an arithmetic progression, the lengths BP, BQ and BC should be in an arithmetic progression too – since these are three triangles with the same heights. Also, since Area $\Delta ABC = 1.5 \times$ Area ΔABP, it means that $BC = 1.5 \times BP \rightarrow 12 = 1.5 \times BP \rightarrow BP = 8$. The lengths BP, BQ and BC should be 8, 10 and 12 respectively. Hence, the length of $PQ = 10 - 8 = 2$. The correct answer is 2.

20. We are given that: $\frac{1}{\sqrt{y}+\sqrt{z}} = \frac{\frac{1}{\sqrt{x}+\sqrt{y}} + \frac{1}{\sqrt{x}+\sqrt{z}}}{2} \rightarrow$
$$\frac{2}{\sqrt{y}+\sqrt{z}} = \frac{2\sqrt{x}+\sqrt{y}+\sqrt{z}}{(\sqrt{x}+\sqrt{y})(\sqrt{x}+\sqrt{z})} \rightarrow$$
$$\frac{2x+2\sqrt{x}(\sqrt{y}+\sqrt{z})+2\sqrt{y}\sqrt{z}}{\sqrt{y}+\sqrt{z}} = 2\sqrt{x}+\sqrt{y}+\sqrt{z} \rightarrow$$
$$\frac{2x+2\sqrt{y}\sqrt{z}}{\sqrt{y}+\sqrt{z}} = \sqrt{y}+\sqrt{z} \rightarrow$$
$$2x+2\sqrt{y}\sqrt{z} = (\sqrt{y}+\sqrt{z})^2 \rightarrow 2x = y+z.$$
Hence, y, x and z are in an arithmetic progression. Option (c) is correct.

21. We can count single digit numbers, two-digit numbers and three-digit numbers separately. Single digit numbers = 9; 2-digit numbers = $9 \times 9 = 81$; 3-digit numbers = $9 \times 9 \times 8 = 648$. The total number of numbers = $9 + 81 + 648 = 738$.

22. The series of numbers would be day 1 = 2; day 2 = $2 \times 2 + 3 = 7$; day 3 = 17; day 4 = 37; day 5 = 77; day 6 = 157; day 7 = 317; day 8 = 637; day 9 = 1277. As we can see the effect of the + 3 becomes more and more negligible compared to the multiplication by 2 as we reach larger values of the numbers in the series. Hence, from this point we can roughly approximate by doubling the number.
Day 12 ≈ (Day 9 number) × 8 = 1277 × 8 ≈ 10000; Day 16 ≈ Day 12 number × 16 = 10000 × 16 ≈ 160000; Day 17 ≈ 320000; Day 18 ≈ 640000; Day 19: > 1 million. Hence, the correct answer is 19.
Note: You could also use the on screen calculator to calculate the exact values that go as: 2557; 5117; 10237; 20477; 40957; 81917; 163837; 327677; 655357 (day 18). Hence, the correct answer is 19.

CAT 2023 Slot 2

1. Since $m + 2n$ and $3m + 4n$ are divisible by k, it also means that $(3m + 4n) - (m + 2n) = 2m + 2n$ would be divisibly by k. Thus, $(2m + 2n) - (m + 2n) = m$ would also be divisible by k. Hence, $(m + 2n) - (m) = 2n$ would also be divisible by k. Thus, option (b) is correct.

2. For each of the options, we can try to eliminate by disobeying the condition in the given option and checking if we can still maintain the inequality in the question. The logic is that if the inequality can be satisfied even while disobeying a condition, that condition then cannot be a necessary condition for the given inequality to hold.
For instance, option (b) is disobeyed if we take x as –2, and y as 1. We can see that at these values

of x and y, the original inequality is still satisfied as $\frac{x}{y} < \frac{x+3}{y-3} \rightarrow \frac{-2}{1} < \frac{1}{-2}$. Thus, the condition in option (b) is not a necessary condition and this option can be rejected. You can similarly reject option (c) by values such as $y = 20$, $x = -10$ to get $\frac{-10}{20} < \frac{-7}{17}$. It is only the option (a) that cannot be rejected, since if we try to disobey it, we can see that the inequality $\frac{x}{y} < \frac{x+3}{y-3}$ gets disobeyed too. For instance, a set of values that disobey the condition in option (a) are $y = -2$, $x = 1$. $\frac{1}{-2}$ *is not* $< \frac{4}{-5}$. So we see that if we disobey the condition in option (a) the original inequality also becomes void. Hence, option (a) is the correct answer.

3. $144^{145} = 2^{580} \times 3^{290}$. To write this in the form $a^m \times b^n$ while maximizing *n-m*, we can think of this as: $2^{580} \times \left(3^{290}\right)^1$. In this case we can have $n = 580$ and $m = 1$, so the largest possible difference is 579. Option (b) is correct.
4. The given expression is of the form $2^{\text{some power}} + 2^{\text{some second power}} = 2^{\text{some third power}}$ Looking through powers of 2, we see that two powers of 2 add up to a third power of 2, only in cases like $2^1 + 2^1 = 2^2$ or $2^2 + 2^2 = 2^3$ or even $2^{10} + 2^{10} = 2^{11}$ and so on. Thus, we can use this logic in this situation by equating: $2^{4x^2} = 2^{2x+10} \rightarrow 4x^2 = 2x+10 \rightarrow 4x^2 - 2x - 10 = 0$. Sum of the roots of this equation will be the sum of all possible values of x = ½. Option (c) is correct.
5. We will first need to evaluate the expression.
$$\frac{\log_x 25}{\log_x (0.008)} = \frac{\log_{10} 25}{\log_{10}\left(\frac{2}{10}\right)^3} = \frac{2\log_{10} 5}{3\times(\log_{10} 1 - (\log_{10} 5)}$$
$$= \frac{2\log_{10} 5}{-3(\log_{10} 5)} = \frac{-2}{3}$$ Hence,
$$\log_{\sqrt{3}} x = \frac{16}{3} + \frac{2}{3} = 6 \rightarrow x = 27.$$
The value of $\log_3 3x^2 = \log_3 3^7 = 7$
6. The equation is $x^2 - 2x + 1 + 2kx + 11 = 0$, which is the same as $x^2 + 2(k-1)x + 12 = 0$. For the expression to have no real roots, $4 \times (k-1)^2 < 4 \times 1 \times 12$ or $(k-1)^2 < 12$. k's value being the largest possible value that satisfies this inequality, $k = 4$. Hence, we need to evaluate the expression $f(y) = \frac{4}{4y} + 9y = \frac{1}{y} + 9y$. Differentiating this with respect to y and equating to 0, will give us the value of y at which this is minimized. We get $f'(y) = -y^{-2} + 9 = 0 \rightarrow y = 1/3$. At $y = 1/3$, $\frac{1}{y} + 9y = 6$. This is the minimum value of the expression and is hence the correct answer.
7. The number would need to have exactly 4 factors. There are two kinds of numbers with exactly 4 factors: a^3 or $a^1 \times b^1$, where a and b are prime numbers. There are only 2 numbers of the form a^3 below 50. For numbers of the form $a^1 \times b^1$, we can see that with a as 2, b can be 3, 5, 7, 11, 13, 17, 19, 23. With a as 3, b can be 5, 7, 11, 13. With a as 5, b can only be 7. So there are a total of 13 numbers of the form $a^1 \times b^1$ that are below 50. Hence, the correct answer is 13 + 2 = 15.
8. Let the manufacturing employees be $20x$, then the non-manufacturing employees are $80x$. Let total salary of manufacturing employees be $100y$, then the total salary of all employees is $600y$. Thus, total salary of non-manufacturing employees is $500y$. The average salary of manufacturing employees = $5y/x$. Average salary of non-manufacturing employees = $6.25y/x$. The required ratio is 5 : 6.25 = 4 : 5.
9. After 1 year, 200000 will become: 200000 × 1.04 × 1.04 = 216320. After repaying 10320, he is left with a loan of 206000. The outstanding amount at the end of 3 years = 206000 × $(1.04)^4$ ≈ 240990.86 ≈ 240991. Total interest paid = 10320 + 40991 = 51311. Option (c) is correct.
10. The relative speed at which Ravi and Ashok are approaching each other is 90 kmph = 25 m/s. Since, the distance between them is 225 meters, it means that they will meet in 9 seconds. Also, in this time Ravi will travel $40 \times \frac{5}{18} \times 9 = 100$ meters. Thus, Vijay has to travel a distance of 54 + 100 = 154 meters in 9 seconds. His speed in kmph = $\frac{154}{9} \times \frac{18}{5} = 61.6$ kmph. Option (c) is correct.
11. Let Pipe A fill the tank in '$t + 1$' hours. Then Pipe B can empty it in 't' hours. Also, Pipes A, B, C together can fill the tank in 2 hours, means their combined net work per hour is 50%. Thus, if we assume A, B, C as the per hour work of the three pipes we will have $A - B + C = 50\%$. From the second condition mentioned in the problem, we have $1.25C + (C - B) = 100$. Also, the value of $A = 1/(t + 1)$, while $B = 1/t$. Substituting in the two equations we have: $\frac{100}{t+1} - \frac{100}{t} + C = 50\%$ & $C - \frac{100}{t} + 1.25C = 100\%$. From this point rather than trying to solve these equations algebraically, it is better to try to put the values for C from the options into the second equation to find different values of t and see if these values fit into the first equation. Also, it is common sense that the value of the time taken by C to fill the

tank cannot be less than 75 (and is quite unlikely to be 75 too – though possible). So, we can first check for C's time as 90 minutes. In that case, C does 66.66% of the work per hour. At this value of C, we will get $t = 2$ hours. Putting these values of t and C in the first equation, we see that we get $\frac{100}{t+1} - \frac{100}{t} + C$ = 33.33 – 50 + 66.66 = 50, which satisfies this equation. Hence, this is the correct option. Option (b) is correct.

Note: If you try to take a wrong answer for C, say 120, the value of t you would get from the second equation will not satisfy the LHS = RHS condition of the first equation.

12. She will get the highest possible value if she breaks the pieces into 12, 3, 2, 1 and the lowest possible value when she breaks the stone into pieces of 3, 4, 5, 6 units. Since the value of the stone is proportional to the square of it's weight we can assume value equation as $V = k \times W^2$. The maximum possible total value = $k \times (12^2 + 1^2 + 2^2 + 3^2) = 158k$. The minimum possible total value = $k \times (3^2 + 4^2 + 5^2 + 6^2) = 86k$. The difference = $72k = 288000 \rightarrow k = 4000$. Hence, the original value of the stone = $V = 4000 \times 18^2 = 1296000$. Option (b) is correct.

13. Minu first sells to Kanu at 1200 (a profit of 200) and buys back at 960. Hence, her cost price while selling to Tanu is 960. So she must have sold to Tanu at 960 + 300 = 1260. Her percentage of profit would be given by: $\frac{300}{960} \times 100 = \frac{5}{16} \times 100 = 31.25\%$.

14. Overall, Jayant gets a 12.5% profit (25% markup and 10% discount) per shirt on his average cost price (say C). Also 1000 < C < 1125. The extreme case in this situation to maximise the shirts would be if he bought only white shirts, in that case, his profit per shirt would be 125 and the number of shirts would be 51000/125 = 408. However, this case is not possible, since it is given to us that he has bought both white and blue shirts. This means that the maximum possible number of shirts would be 1 less than 408 = 407 (so that the average profit per shirt is more than 125). Also, we need to check whether this is a feasible solution. The profit per white shirt is 1000 × 0.125 = 125; the profit per blue shirt is 1125 × 0.125 = 140.625, hence we need to think in multiples of 8 for the number of blue shirts. At 8 blue shirts we get a profit of 8 × 140.625 = 1125. So the remaining profit has to be made on white shirts. Number of white shirts = $\frac{51000 - 1125}{125} = 399$. At 399 white shirts and 8 blue shirts we get the total profit of 51000 and hence, the number of shirts (maximum) is 399 + 8 = 407.

15. The process described is essentially taking out 10% of the milk (or mixture) and replacing with water. The effect is going to be to reduce the amount of original liquid each time by 10%. Thus, if we think in percentages, originally we have 100% milk and after 1 iteration, we will have 90% milk. After 2 iterations, it would become 81% milk. The subsequent numbers would be 72.9% (3rd); 65.61(4th); 59.049 (5th); 53.1441 (6th); 47.82 approx (7th). Hence, the correct answer is 7.
Note: The calculations can be approximate calculations to see when the milk percentage goes below 50. So tracing the numbers approximately by successively reducing the value by 10% each time as, $100 \rightarrow 90 \rightarrow 81 \rightarrow 72.9 \rightarrow 65.6 \rightarrow 59.ab \rightarrow 53.cd \rightarrow 47.xy$ would also give us the correct answer as 7.

16. If n is the number of people in the group and A is their new average the situation described in the question can be represented by:
$n \times 352 = (n - 2) \times A + 1012$ such that $A < 330$. You should recognize that we are in a single equation 2 variables situation, which means we are essentially in a multiple possibility situation. The value of n, will get maximized when $A = 330$. At $A = 330$, we get: $22 \times n = 352 \rightarrow n = 16$. Hence, the correct answer is 16.

17. Let AB be the diameter referred to and M be the third vertex of the triangle. In the triangle AMB, the angle AMB is a right angle. The area of the triangle would be

$$\frac{1}{2} \times axbx = \frac{abx^2}{2}$$

Also, from the Pythagoras theorem, we have: $(ax)^2 + (bx)^2 = 4r^2 \rightarrow (a^2 + b^2) \times x^2 = 4r^2 \rightarrow x^2 = \frac{4r^2}{(a^2 + b^2)}$

Replacing this value of x^2 in the area of the triangle we get: Area = $\frac{2abr^2}{(a^2 + b^2)}$. Option (c) is correct. Alternately, you can think of this through mathematical induction. If we take the ratio of $a : b$ as 3 : 4 and we take the diameter of the circle as 10, we get the right angled triangle 6-8-10. The area of the triangle is $\frac{1}{2} \times 6 \times 8 = 24$. With $a = 3$, $b = 4$ and $r = 5$, we get the value of the area as 24 only for option (c).

18. The area of the quadrilateral $AQCD$ will be the sum of the areas of the triangles AQM, MQD and QCD. The height of each of these triangles is the same (height = $AB = CD = 9$). Hence, the area of $AQCD$ = $\frac{1}{2} \times 9 \times (\text{AM} + \text{MD} + \text{QC}) = \frac{1}{2} \times 9(\text{BP} + \text{PQ} + 2\text{QC})$.
This can be visualized from the figure shown.

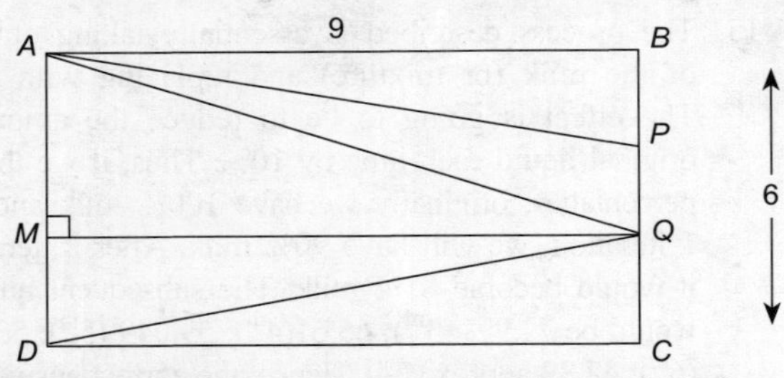

Also, the heights of the triangles ABP and APQ are also the same (i.e. 9 each). Hence, if Area ABP, Area APQ and Area $AQCD$ are in Geometric Progression, then their bases: BP, PQ and $(BP + PQ + 2QC)$ should also be in a geometric progression. Also, it is given to us that the area of $AQCD$ is 4 times the area of ABP. Hence, the area of APQ has to be 2 times the area of APQ, which essentially means that the base PQ of APQ has to be double the base BP of ABP. Looking through the options (a), (b) and (d) which satisfy this condition of PQ being double of BP, we see that the other condition of $(BP + PQ + 2QC)$ being four times the value of BP, is only satisfied for option (a). Hence, option (a) is the correct answer.

19. We first visualize the Y-Axis ($X = 0$) and the line $X = 5$ as two parallel vertical lines at a distance of 5 units from each other. Next, for identifying what the enclosed figure would look like, we can try to find points lying on $X = 5$ and $X = 0$ for the lines represented by:
$|x - y| - |x - 5| = 2$. For $x = 5$, we need $|5 - y|$ to be equal to 2. The value of y comes out as 3 (point B in the figure) or 7 (point A in the figure. For $x = 0$, we need $|x - y| = 7$ i.e. $|0 - y| = 7$. We can identify the points C (–7) and D (7) that satisfy the expression when $x = 0$. The enclosed figure will be represented by the area of the rectangle $ABEC$ and the triangle BED (shown in the figure). The required area = Area of rectangle $ABEC$ + area of triangle $BED = 5 \times 4 + \frac{1}{2} \times 5 \times 10 = 45$.

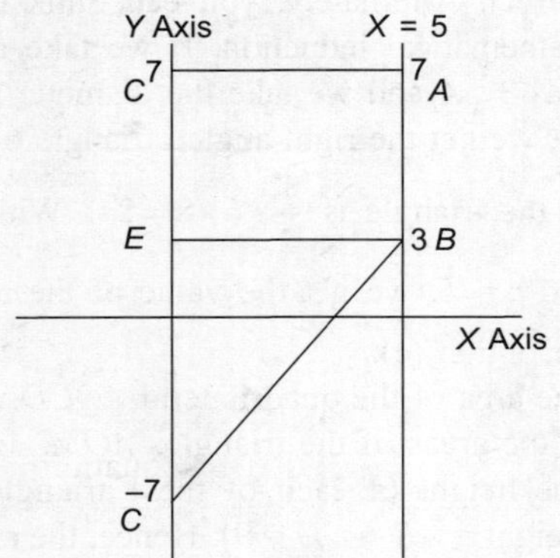

20. From $p^2 + q^2 - 29 = 2pq - 20$; we get $(p - q)^2 = 9$. Hence, $(p - q) = \pm 3$.
From $p^2 + q^2 - 29 = 52 - 2pq$ we get $(p + q)^2 = 81$. Hence, $p + q = \pm 9$
There will be four solutions to this set of values:
Case 1: $p - q = 3$; $p + q = 9 \rightarrow p = 6, q = 3$. $p^3 - q^3 = 189$.
Case 2: $p - q = 3$; $p + q = -9 \rightarrow p = -3, q = -6$. $p^3 - q^3 = 189$.
Case 3: $p - q = -3$; $p + q = 9 \rightarrow p = 3, q = 6$. $p^3 - q^3 = -189$.
Case 4: $p - q = -3$; $p + q = -9 \rightarrow p = -6, q = -3$. $p^3 - q^3 = -189$.
The difference between the maximum and minimum values of $p^3 - q^3 = 189 - (-189) = 378$.

21. Let d_a be the common difference of the series a_1, a_2, a_3 and d_b be the common difference of the series b_1, b_2, b_3. Since $a_5 = b_9$ and $a_{19} = b_{19}$, it means that $14 \times d_a = 10 \times d_b \rightarrow \frac{d_a}{d_b} = \frac{5}{7}$. Since both are prime numbers, it can only mean that $d_a = 5$ and $d_b = 7$. Also, since $b_2 = 0$, $b_9 = 0 + 7 \times 7 = 49 = a_5$. Hence, $a_{11} = 49 + 6 \times 5 = 79$. Option (a) is correct.

22. The sequence a_n is 13, 19, 25… for $n = 1, 2, 3…$ The sequence b_n is 15, 22, 29 for $n = 1, 2, 3…$ The series of common terms between the two sequences would be 43, 85, 127, … 925, 967. Hence, the largest three digit number in the series would be 967.

CAT 2023 Slot 3

1. A system of 2 equations would have infinitely many solutions, if the equations are identical. For this to happen, the second equation should be of the form $x + y = 4$ (or a common multiplication of each of the coefficients and constant terms - like $2x + 2y = 8$; $3x + 3y = 12$ and so on). This gives rise to the conditions: $(a + 5) = (b^2 - 15)$ and $8b = 4 \times (b^2 - 15)$. Solving first for b, we have: $b^2 - 2b - 15 = 0$. The roots of this quadratic equation are 5 and –3, so these are the possible values of b. Since, $(a + 5) = (b^2 - 15) \rightarrow$ we get $a = 5$ when $b = 5$ or $a = -11$ when $b = -3$. The maximum value of the product $a \times b = -11 \times -3 = 33$. Option (a) is correct.

2. $x^8 + \frac{1}{x^8} = \left(x^4 + \frac{1}{x^4}\right)^2 - 2 = 47 \rightarrow x^4 + \frac{1}{x^4} = 7 \rightarrow$

$$\left(x^2 + \frac{1}{x^2}\right)^2 - 2 = 7 \rightarrow$$

$$x^2 + \frac{1}{x^2} = 3 \rightarrow \left(x + \frac{1}{x}\right)^2 - 2 = 3 \rightarrow \left(x + \frac{1}{x}\right) = \sqrt{5}$$

Then cubing both sides we get:

$$\left(x + \frac{1}{x}\right)^3 = x^3 + \frac{1}{x^3} + 3\left(x + \frac{1}{x}\right) = 5\sqrt{5} \rightarrow x^3 + \frac{1}{x^3} + 3\sqrt{5}$$

$= 5\sqrt{5} \to x^3 + \frac{1}{x^3} = 2\sqrt{5}$

Cubing both sides, we get:

$$\left(x^3 + \frac{1}{x^3}\right)^3 = 40\sqrt{5} \to \left(x^9 + \frac{1}{x^9}\right) + 3\left(x^3 + \frac{1}{x^3}\right)$$

$$= 40\sqrt{5} \to \left(x^9 + \frac{1}{x^9}\right) = 34\sqrt{5}$$

Since, $x^3 + \frac{1}{x^3} = 2\sqrt{5}$.

Option (a) is correct.

3. $8^m = 2^{3m}$ and $8^n = 2^{3n}$. For exactly 41 powers of 2 to occur between 2^{3m} and 2^{3n}, we get the smallest value of $m + n$ if we take $m = 1$ and $n = 15$, to give us the two numbers as 2^3 and 2^{45}, that would satisfy the given condition. Hence, the correct answer is 16. Option (b) is correct.

4. The terms can be written as $\log_4 2$, $\log_4\left(2^x - 9\right)$, $\log_4\left(2^x + \frac{17}{2}\right)$. Since they are in Arithmetic progression, the second term would be the average of the first and third terms. So we have: $\log_4 2 + \log_4\left(2^x + \frac{17}{2}\right)$ $= 2\log_4\left(2^x - 9\right) \to 2\left(2^x + \frac{17}{2}\right) = \left(2^x - 9\right)^2$.

Putting 2^x as m in this equation, we get: $2m + 17 = (m - 9)^2$ or $m^2 - 20m + 64 = 0$ giving us $m = 2^x = 4$ or 16.

Thus, the value of $x = 2$ or 4. However, we reject x as 2, since in that case $2^x - 9$ would be a negative value, which is not possible. Hence, $x = 4$. Thus, the first two terms of the arithmetic progression are $\log_4 2$ & $\log_4 7$. The common difference $= \log_4 7 - \log_4 2 = \log_4\left(\frac{7}{2}\right)$

Hence, option (b) is the correct answer.

5. A number would have 15 factors in case it is of the form $a^2 \times b^4$ or a^{14}, where a, b are prime numbers. The smallest numbers in the $a^2 \times b^4$ form are $3^2 \times 2^4 = 144$ and $2^2 \times 3^4 = 324$. Their sum is $144 + 324 = 468$.

6. If the roots are m, n, we have $m + n = -b$ and $m \times n = c$. Also, it is given to us that

$$\frac{1}{m} - \frac{1}{n} = \frac{1}{3} \to \left(\frac{1}{m} - \frac{1}{n}\right)^2 = \frac{1}{9} \to \frac{1}{m^2} + \frac{1}{n^2} - \frac{2}{m \times n} = \frac{1}{9}$$

$$\to m \times n = c = \frac{9}{2} \text{ since } \frac{1}{m^2} + \frac{1}{n^2} = \frac{5}{9}.$$

Also, $\frac{1}{m^2} + \frac{1}{n^2} = \frac{5}{9}$ gives us

$$\frac{m^2 + n^2}{m^2 \times n^2} = \frac{(m+n)^2 - 2 \times m \times n}{m^2 \times n^2} = \frac{5}{9} \to \frac{(m+n)^2 - 9}{\frac{81}{4}}$$

$$= \frac{5}{9} \to (m+n)^2 = \frac{81}{4} \to m + n = -b = \mp\frac{9}{2}.$$

Hence, $b = \pm\frac{9}{2}$

So the maximum possible value of $b + c = 9$.

7. The possible values of n for $5^{n-1} < 3^{n+1}$, are 1, 2, 3, 4, 5. Thus for $3^{n+1} < 2^{n+m}$, we need to ensure a value of m, such that the inequality is satisfied for each value of n (1, 2, 3, 4, 5). At $n = 5$, we need: $3^6 < 2^{5+m}$, m's minimum value needs to be 5. This value will also ensure the inequality is satisfied at $n = 1, 2, 3$ and 4. Hence, the correct answer is 5.

8. Let's assume he mixes 200 grams of A and 300 grams of B. The sugar in the mixture C would be $80 + 90 = 170$ out of a total of 500 grams. Since he is maxing an equal amount of milk in C, the drink would have 170 grams of sugar in a drink quantity of 1000. Hence, the required percentage would be 17%.

9. Let R, K and G be the amount of job done (in percentage) by Rahul, Rakshita and Gurmeet respectively every day. Thus, we have $6R + 6K + 6G + 3K = 100$. It is given to us that all three working together require more than 7 days to complete the job. In the extreme limiting case, where if we consider that all three required 7 days to complete the job, it would mean $7R + 7K + 7G = 100$. This means $R + K + G = 3K = \frac{100}{7} \to K = \frac{100}{21}$. This means Rakshita would require 21 days to complete the job. However, this scenario is not possible since the time required by all three to do the job is more than 7 days. Hence, option (b) is correct.

10. Let x, y and z be the speeds of boat 1, boat 2 and the river respectively. Let D be the distance. Then from the information about the first boat's journey we have:

$$\frac{D}{(x+z)} = 2; \frac{D}{(x-z)} = 3 \to \frac{x-z}{x+z} = \frac{2}{3} \to x:z = 5:1.$$

Let $x = 5k$ and $z = k$, then from

$$\frac{D}{(x+z)} = 2 \text{ we get} : D = 12k.$$

Then, using the information of the second boats journey we can write the equation:

$$\frac{D}{(y+z)} + \frac{D}{(y-z)} = 6 \to \frac{12k}{(y+k)} + \frac{12k}{(y-k)} = 6 \to$$

$$24ky = 6\left(y^2 - k^2\right) \to y^2 - k^2 = 4ky \to y^2 - 4ky - k^2 = 0$$

Solving for y, we get:

$$y = \frac{4k \pm \sqrt{16k^2 + 4k^2}}{2} = 2k \pm k\sqrt{5} = k\left(2 \pm \sqrt{5}\right).$$

We can reject $k\left(2-\sqrt{5}\right)$ as it would be negative.

Hence, $y = k\left(2+\sqrt{5}\right)$

Time required to do the downstream journey from A to B, for the second boat =

$$\frac{12k}{(y+k)} = \frac{12}{3+\sqrt{5}} = \frac{12\left(3-\sqrt{5}\right)}{\left(3+\sqrt{5}\right)\left(3-\sqrt{5}\right)} = 3\left(3-\sqrt{5}\right).$$

Option (c) is correct.

Shorter process: As you can understand doing this process in the exam would be highly tedious and cumbersome and is likely to lead to a lot of heartburn during the exam. An alternate way to get the answer thinking quantitatively, is to understand that since the second boat takes 20% longer time to do the journey, than the first boat, hence, it's time going downstream would be 2+ and it's time going upstream would be 3 hours+. After we get the 5 : 1 ratio for the boat 1's speed and the river, we can assume the distance to be 12 kms. In that case, if we try a 4 : 1 ratio of the second boat's speed to the river's speed we can see that the total time taken would be $\frac{12}{5}+\frac{12}{3} = 2.4+4 = 6.4 \text{ hours}$. So the second boat's speed must be slightly higher than 4, if the first boat's speed is 5 and river's speed is 1. Thus, we can conclude that the time taken for the second boat to cover the downstream journey would be a little less than 2.4 hours. This is the value they are asking for in the question. Looking at the values of the options (if we take $\sqrt{5} \approx 2.23$, we get the values as ≈ 2.76 (option a rejected); ≈ 3.69 (option b rejected); $\approx$ 2.31 (option c); ≈ 15.69 (option d rejected). Hence, option (c) is the correct answer.

11. The merchant buys 105 cm of cloth for ₹100 and sells 95 cm of cloth for 110 × 0.95 = 104.5. In order to find the percentage profit, we can either equate the amount of cloth bought and sold or we can equate the amount of money given and got. In this case, it is easier to raise the amount spent while purchasing by 4.5% in order to equate the money. In such a case, he effectively buys 105 × 1.045 = 109.725 cm of cloth for ₹104.5 and sells 95 cm of cloth for the same price. Hence, his profit percentage

$$= \frac{\text{Goods left}}{\text{Goods Sold}} \times 100 = \frac{109.725-95}{95} \times 100 = 15.5\%.$$

Hence, option (b) is correct.

12. The best way to solve this is to think through the options. The question talks about a y% decrease followed by a $(y + 10)$% increase leading to an overall increase in the population after the second year. Note: we reject $(y - 10)$ as that would not help us get to the lowest possible value of population at the end of 2021. Since, the question asks us the population after the first year, and gives us values for it as 74000, 75000, 73000 and 720000 (options *a* to *d*) it means it is giving us options for y's value as 26%, 25%, 27% and 28% respectively. Thus, the value of $y + 10$ would be 36%, 35%, 37% and 28% respectively. Checking for option (d) first since they have asked us the lowest possible population at the end of 2021, we see that the population in 2022 would be 72000 × 1.38 = 99360. This option can hence be rejected, as the condition stated in the question, is that the population after the $(y +$ 10)% increase is above 100000. For option (c) the population at the end of 2022 would be 73000 × 1.37 = 100010, which satisfies the condition. Hence, option (c) is the correct answer.

13. If the average of 3 people A, B, C is W, the average of A, B, C, D is $(W - x)$. Their total weight is $4 \times (W - x) = 4W - 4x$. The average weight of A, B, C, E is $(W + 2x)$ and the total weight of A, B, C, E is $4 \times (W + 2x) = 4W + 8x$. The sum of weights of A, B, C, E is $12x$ more than the sum of weights of A, B, C, D. Hence, the weight of E is $12x$ more than the weight of D. This value is given to us as 12 in the problem. Hence, $12x = 12 \rightarrow x = 1$. Option (c) is correct.

14. Let G and S be the work done by Gautam and Suhani respectively per day. We have: $20 \times (G + S)$ = Total work. Also, $20 \times (0.6 \times G + 1.5 \times S)$ = Total work. Thus, $20 \times (G + S) = 20 \times (0.6 \times G + 1.5 \times S) \rightarrow 0.4 \times G = 0.5 \times S \rightarrow \frac{G}{S} = \frac{5}{4}$. So if we take Gautam's work as $5k$, Suhani's work = $4k$. Total work = $20 \times (9k)$ = $180k$. Gautam is the faster worker and he would take: $\frac{180k}{5k} = 36\,days$ to complete the job, working alone.

15. Let the number of mangoes be $40n$. The total fruit with him is $100n$. Then $(A + B) = 60n$. On that day, he sells $20n$ mangoes, and 96 bananas and $0.4 \times A$, which has to be equal to $30n$ (since he sells a total of $50n$ fruit on the day). So, $0.4 \times A + 96 = 30n$. From the two equations eliminating A, we get $96 \times 2.5 - B = 15n \rightarrow 15n + B = 240$. Also, he must have sold over 50% of his bananas, hence the number of bananas must be lower than 192. So, the value of n has to be greater than 3.2 (as at $n = 3.2$, $B = 192$, which is not possible). At $B = 191$, $n = 3.2666$; At $B = 190$, $n = 3.333$. Both these possibilities can be rejected since $100n$ would not be an integer. At B = 189, $n = 3.4$ and $100n = 340$. This would be the

value of the smallest total number of fruits he had at the start of the day.

16. Let A collect $3k$ coins per week and B collect $4k$ coins per week. In 5 weeks, A would collect a total of $15k$ coins, while B would collect a total of $12k$ coins in 3 weeks. According to the question $15k$ is a multiple of 7. Hence, k should be a multiple of 7. Also, $12k$ is a multiple of 24, hence k must be a multiple of 2. Thus, k's possible values would be common multiples of 7 and 2 → like 14, 28, 42 and so on. Since, the minimum possible value of $3k$ is asked in the question, that value would be $3 \times 14 = 42$.

17. Refer to the given figure, where we have taken the base of the rectangle as $2b$ and the height as h.

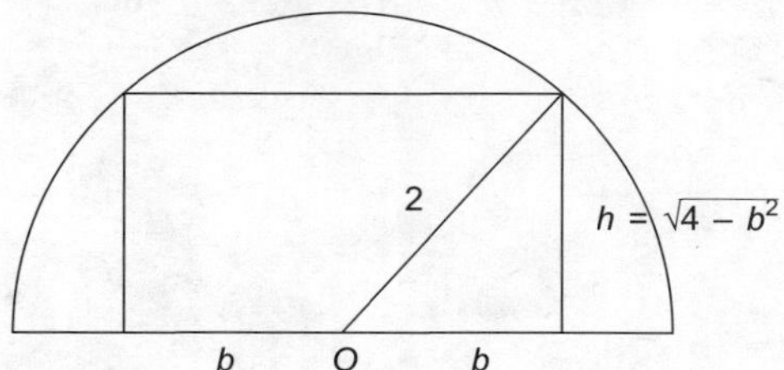

The area of the rectangle $= 2b \times h =$

$A = 2bh = 2b\sqrt{4-b^2}$ Maximising A, is the same as maximizing A^2.

So we have: $A^2 = 4b^2\left(4-b^2\right) = 16b^2 - 4b^4$.

Differentiating A^2 with respect to b and equating to 0, we get $32b - 16b^3 = 0 \rightarrow b = \sqrt{2}$

Hence, the length of the base is $2b = 2\sqrt{2}$ and the height is $\sqrt{4-b^2} = \sqrt{4-2} = \sqrt{2}$.

The ratio of lengths of longer side to shorter side = 2 : 1. Option (d) is correct.

18. We can first work out all the angles in the figure:

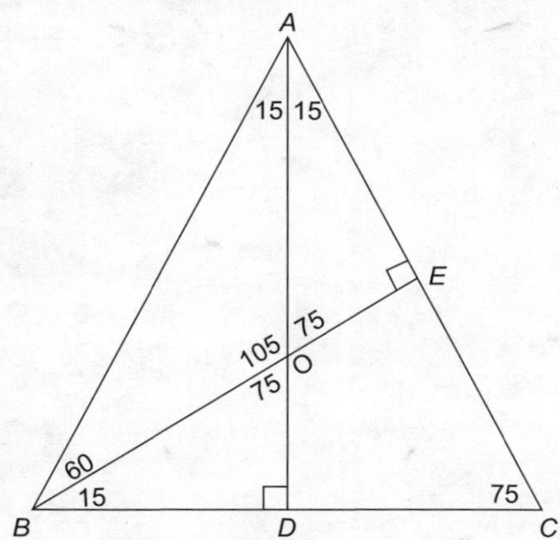

$\angle AOB = 105$, So $\angle AOE = 75 = \angle BOD$. So, $\angle OBD = 180 - 90 - 75 = 15$. Also, $\angle OAE = 180 - 75 - 90 = 15$. So $\angle ABO = 180 - 15 - 105 = 60$.

The $\Delta ADB \sim \Delta BEC$, so $\frac{AD}{BE} = \frac{AB}{BC}$, which means that to find the answer for $\frac{AD}{BE}$, we can shift our focus to finding $\frac{AB}{BC}$. $BE = AB$ Cos 60 (from ΔABE) and from ΔBEC $BE = BC$ Cos 15. Hence,

AB Cos 60 = BC Cos 15 → $\frac{AB}{BC} = \frac{Cos 15}{Cos 60} = 2Cos 15$.

Option (a) is correct.

19. The sum of internal angles of a polygon is given by $(n-2) \times 180$, where n is the number of sides. Hence, the value of the interior angle would be given by $I = \frac{(n-2)\times 180}{n}$. The sum of an exterior angle plus an interior angle is 180 for any regular polygon. So, once we calculate the interior angle we can calculate the exterior angle and see whether the difference is 120. The best process to use is a trial and error one. At $n = 10$, $I = \frac{8\times 180}{10} = 144$, which means that the exterior angle would be $180 - 144 = 36$. $I - E = 120$ is not satisfied here. At $n = 12$,

$I = \frac{(n-2)\times 180}{n} = 150$, $E = 30$. $I - E = 120$. Hence we have to find the number of diagonals for a 12 sided figure. The answer $= {}^{12}C_2 - 12 = 66 - 12 = 54$.

20. a_n is the series 46, 54, 62,...846; b_n is the arithmetic series: 98, 102, 106 ... 498. The first common term for both series is 102. The series of common terms for both series would be 102, 110, 118, .. 438, ... 494. The number of terms in this series are

$\frac{494-102}{8} + 1 = 50$.

The sum of all terms $= 50 \times \frac{494+102}{2} = 14900$.

Option (a) is correct.

21. The mathematical solution for this would go as follows:

The nth term of the series is given by

$$T_n = \left(1 + \frac{1}{3} + \frac{1}{3^2} + \ldots \frac{1}{3^n}\right) \times \frac{1}{4^{(n-1)}} = \left(\frac{1-\left(\frac{1}{3}\right)^n}{1-\frac{1}{3}}\right) \times \frac{1}{4^{(n-1)}}$$

$$= \frac{3\times(3^n - 1)}{2\times 3^n} \times \frac{1}{4^{(n-1)}}$$

$$= \frac{1}{2} \times \frac{3^n - 1}{12^{(n-1)}} = \frac{1}{2} \times \left(\frac{3}{4^{(n-1)}} - \frac{1}{12^{(n-1)}}\right)$$

$$= \left(\frac{3}{2} \times \left(\frac{1}{4}\right)^{(n-1)} - \frac{1}{2} \times \left(\frac{1}{12}\right)^{(n-1)}\right)$$

In this case, we have broken the series into two infinite series whose sum to infinity can be calculated to get us the sum of the original series.
Hence, the required answer =

$$\frac{\frac{3}{2}}{\left(1-\frac{1}{4}\right)}-\frac{\frac{1}{2}}{\left(1-\frac{1}{12}\right)}=2-\frac{6}{11}=\frac{16}{11}.$$ Hence, option (c) is correct.

As you can well imagine there will be a whole lot of challenges in executing a solution like this inside an exam like CAT.

Alternately, the same question can be solved using a value estimation through the following thought process. The value of the terms in the series are 1 + 0.33 + 0.09 + 0.02 and subsequent terms would start to become insignificant value wise. Hence, the value of the infinite series is around 1.44 to maybe 1.48. Looking at the options, the only option that has a value in this range is option (c). Hence, that is the correct answer.

22. The value of $f(3x + 2y, 2x - 5y) = 19x$ tells us that the value is independent of y. This can happen if for $f(a, b)$ the value comes out using $5 \times a + 2 \times b$. Hence, the value of $f(x, 2x) = 9x = 27 \rightarrow x = 3$ is the correct answer.

CAT 2024 Examination Paper

High Yield Questions

Scan this QR Code to access video solutions for High Yield Questions of the CAT 2024 Examination

CAT 2024 SLOT 1

1. If the equations $x^2 + mx + 9 = 0$, $x^2 + nx + 17 = 0$ and $x^2 + (m + n)x + 35 = 0$ have a common negative root, then the value of $(2m + 3n)$ is
2. In the XY-plane, the area, in sq. units, of the region defined by the inequalities $y \geq x + 4$ and $-4 \leq x^2 + y^2 + 4(x - y) \leq 0$ is
   (a) 3π (b) 4π
   (c) π (d) 2π
3. An amount of ₹10000 is deposited in bank A for a certain number of years at a simple interest of 5% per annum. On maturity, the total amount received is deposited in bank B for another 5 years at a simple interest of 6% per annum. If the interests received from bank A and bank B are in the ratio 10 :13, then the investment period, in years, in bank A is
   (a) 5 (b) 4
   (c) 3 (d) 6
4. There are four numbers such that average of first two numbers is 1 more than the first number, average of first three numbers is 2 more than average of first two numbers, and average of first four numbers is 3 more than average of first three numbers. Then, the difference between the largest and the smallest numbers, is
5. The surface area of a closed rectangular box, which is inscribed in a sphere, is 846 sq cm, and the sum of the lengths of all its edges is 144 cm. The volume, in cubic cm, of the sphere is
   (a) $750\pi\sqrt{2}$ (b) 1125π
   (c) 750π (d) $1125\pi\sqrt{2}$
6. For any natural number n, let a_n be the largest integer not exceeding $\sqrt{n}$. Then the value of $a_1 + a_2 + \ldots a_{50}$ is
7. If $(a + b\sqrt{n})$ is the positive square root of $(29 - 12\sqrt{5})$, where a and b are integers, and n is a natural number, then the maximum possible value of $(a + b + n)$ is
   (a) 4 (b) 6
   (c) 18 (d) 22
8. ABCD is a rectangle with sides AB = 56 cm and BC = 45 cm, and E is the midpoint of side CD. Then, the length, in cm, of radius of incircle of ΔADE is
9. In September, the incomes of Kamal, Amal and Vimal are in the ratio 8 : 6 : 5. They rent a house together, and Kamal pays 15%, Amal pays 12% and Vimal pays 18% of their respective incomes to cover the total house rent in that month. In October, the house rent remains unchanged while their incomes increase by 10%, 12% and 15%, respectively. In October, the percentage of their total income that will be paid as house rent, is nearest to
   (a) 15.18 (b) 13.26
   (c) 14.84 (d) 12.75
10. Suppose $x_1, x_2, x_3 \ldots, x_{100}$ are in arithmetic progression such that $x_5 = -4$ and $2x_6 + 2x_9 = x_{11} + x_{13}$. Then, x_{100} equals
    (a) 206 (b) 204
    (c) −194 (d) −196
11. A shop wants to sell a certain quantity (in kg) of grains. It sells half the quantity and an additional 3 kg of these grains to the first customer. Then, it sells half of the remaining quantity and an additional 3 kg of these grains to the second customer. Finally, when the shop sells half of the remaining quantity and an additional 3 kg of these grains to the third customer, there are no grains left. The initial quantity, in kg, of grains is
    (a) 18 (b) 36
    (c) 42 (d) 50
12. A fruit seller has a total of 187 fruits consisting of apples, mangoes and oranges. The number of apples and mangoes are in the ratio 5 : 2. After she sells 75 apples, 26 mangoes and half of the oranges, the ratio of number of unsold apples to number of unsold oranges becomes 3 : 2. The total number of unsold fruits is
13. A glass is filled with milk. Two-thirds of its content is poured out and replaced with water. If this process of pouring out two-thirds the content and replacing with water is repeated three more times, then the final ratio of milk to water in the glass, is
    (a) 1 : 27 (b) 1 : 26
    (c) 1 : 81 (d) 1 : 80
14. Two places A and B are 45 kms apart and connected by a straight road. Anil goes from A to B while Sunil goes from B to A. Starting at the same time, they cross each other in exactly 1 hour 30 minutes. If Anil reaches B exactly 1 hour 15 minutes after Sunil reaches A, the speed of Anil, in km per hour, is
    (a) 18 (b) 16
    (c) 12 (d) 14

15. The sum of all real values of k for which

$$\left(\frac{1}{8}\right)^k \times \left(\frac{1}{32768}\right)^{\frac{1}{3}} = \frac{1}{8} \times \left(\frac{1}{32768}\right)^{\frac{1}{k}}$$, is

(a) $\frac{2}{3}$ (b) $-\frac{2}{3}$

(c) $-\frac{4}{3}$ (d) $\frac{4}{3}$

16. Renu would take 15 days working 4 hours per day to complete a certain task whereas Seema would take 8 days working 5 hours per day to complete the same task. They decide to work together to complete this task. Seema agrees to work for double the number of hours per day as Renu, while Renu agrees to work for double the number of days as Seema. If Renu works 2 hours per day, then the number of days Seema will work, is

17. The selling price of a product is fixed to ensure 40% profit. If the product had cost 40% less and had been sold for 5 rupees less, then the resulting profit would have been 50%. The original selling price, in rupees, of the product is

(a) 14 (b) 15

(c) 20 (d) 10

18. If x is a positive real number such that $4 \log_{10} x + 4 \log_{100} x + 8 \log_{1000} x = 13$, then the greatest integer not exceeding x, is

19. When 10^{100} is divided by 7, the remainder is

(a) 6 (b) 4

(c) 3 (d) 1

20. Consider two sets $A = \{2, 3, 5, 7, 11, 13\}$ and $B = \{1, 8, 27\}$. Let f be a function from A to B such that for every element b in B, there is at least one element a in A such that $f(a) = b$. Then, the total number of such functions f is

(a) 667 (b) 537

(c) 665 (d) 540

21. The sum of all four-digit numbers that can be formed with the distinct non-zero digits a, b, c, and d, with each digit appearing exactly once in every number, is $153310 + n$, where n is a single digit natural number. Then, the value of $(a + b + c + d + n)$ is

22. Let x, y, and z be real numbers satisfying

$4(x^2 + y^2 + z^2) = a,$

$4(x - y - z) = 3 + a.$

Then a equals

(a) $1\frac{1}{3}$ (b) 4

(c) 1 (d) 3

CAT 2024 SLOT 2

1. The roots α, β of the equation $3x^2 + \lambda x - 1 = 0$, satisfy $\frac{1}{\alpha^2} + \frac{1}{\beta^2} = 15$. The value of $(\alpha^3 + \beta^3)^2$, is

(a) 1 (b) 16

(c) 4 (d) 9

2. P, Q, R and S are four towns. One can travel between P and Q along 3 direct paths, between Q and S along 4 direct paths, and between P and R along 4 direct paths. There is no direct path between P and S, while there are few direct paths between Q and R, and between R and S. One can travel from P to S either via Q, or via R, or via Q followed by R, respectively, in exactly 62 possible ways. One can also travel from Q to R either directly, or via P, or via S, in exactly 27 possible ways. Then, the number of direct paths between Q and R is

3. The coordinates of the three vertices of a triangle are: (1, 2), (7, 2), and (1,10). Then the radius of the incircle of the triangle is

4. Amal and Vimal together can complete a task in 150 days, while Vimal and Sunil together can complete the same task in 100 days. Amal starts working on the task and works for 75 days, then Vimal takes over and works for 135 days. Finally, Sunil takes over and completes the remaining task in 45 days. If Amal had started the task alone and worked on all days, Vimal had worked on every second day, and Sunil had worked on every third day, then the number of days required to complete the task would have been

5. The sum of the infinite series $\frac{1}{5}\left(\frac{1}{5}-\frac{1}{7}\right)+\left(\frac{1}{5}\right)^2\left(\left(\frac{1}{5}\right)^2-\left(\frac{1}{7}\right)^2\right)+\left(\frac{1}{5}\right)^3\left(\left(\frac{1}{5}\right)^3-\left(\frac{1}{7}\right)^3\right)+\cdots$ is equal to

(a) $\frac{5}{408}$ (b) $\frac{7}{816}$

(c) $\frac{7}{408}$ (d) $\frac{5}{816}$

6. A function f maps the set of natural numbers to whole numbers, such that $f(xy) = f(x)f(y) + f(x) + f(y)$ for all x, y and $f(p) = 1$ for every prime number p. Then, the value of $f(160000)$ is

(a) 8191 (b) 4095

(c) 2047 (d) 1023

7. Bina incurs 19% loss when she sells a product at ₹4860 to Shyam, who in turn sells this product to Hari. If Bina would have sold this product to Shyam at the purchase price of Hari, she would have obtained 17% profit. Then, the profit, in rupees, made by Shyam is

8. A fruit seller has a stock of mangoes, bananas and apples with at least one fruit of each type. At the beginning of a day, the number of mangoes make up 40% of his stock. That day, he sells half of the mangoes, 96 bananas and 40% of the apples. At the end of the day, he ends up selling 50% of the fruits. The smallest possible total number of fruits in the stock at the beginning of the day is

9. Three circles of equal radii touch (but not cross) each other externally. Two other circles, X and Y, are drawn such that both touch (but not cross) each of the three previous circles. If the radius of *X* is more than that of *Y*, the ratio of the radii of *X* and *Y* is

(a) $7+4\sqrt{3}:1$ (b) $4+\sqrt{3}:1$
(c) $4+2\sqrt{3}:1$ (d) $2+\sqrt{3}:1$

10. If *x* and *y* are real numbers such that $4x^2 + 4y^2 - 4xy - 6y + 3 = 0$, then the value of $(4x + 5y)$ is

11. Anil invests ₹22000 for 6 years in a scheme with 4% interest per annum, compounded half-yearly. Separately, Sunil invests a certain amount in the same scheme for 5 years, and then reinvests the entire amount he receives at the end of 5 years, for one year at 10% simple interest. If the amounts received by both at the end of 6 years are equal, then the initial investment, in rupees, made by Sunil is

(a) 20808 (b) 20860
(c) 20480 (d) 20640

12. If *x* and *y* satisfy the equations $|x| + x + y = 15$ and $x + |y| - y = 20$, then $(x - y)$ equals

(a) 20 (b) 10
(c) 15 (d) 5

13. A bus starts at 9 am and follows a fixed route every day. One day, it traveled at a constant speed of 60 km per hour and reached its destination 3.5 hours later than its scheduled arrival time. Next day, it traveled two-thirds of its route in one-third of its total scheduled travel time, and the remaining part of the route at 40 km per hour to reach just on time. The scheduled arrival time of the bus is

(a) 7 : 30 pm (b) 9 : 00 pm
(c) 10 : 30 pm (d) 7 : 00 pm

14. ABCD is a trapezium in which AB is parallel to CD. The sides AD and BC when extended, intersect at point E.
If AB = 2 cm, CD = 1 cm, and perimeter of ABCD is 6 cm, then the perimeter, in cm, of ΔAEB is

(a) 10 (b) 8
(c) 9 (d) 7

15. A vessel contained a certain amount of a solution of acid and water. When 2 litres of water was added to it, the new solution had 50% acid concentration. When 15 litres of acid was further added to this new solution, the final solution had 80% acid concentration. The ratio of water and acid in the original solution was

(a) 5 : 4 (b) 3 : 5
(c) 5 : 3 (d) 4 : 5

16. A company has 40 employees whose names are listed in a certain order. In the year 2022, the average bonus of the first 30 employees was ₹40000, of the last 30 employees was ₹60000, and of the first 10 and last 10 employees together was ₹50000. Next year, the average bonus of the first 10 employees increased by 100%, of the last 10 employees increased by 200% and of the remaining employees was unchanged. Then, the average bonus, in rupees, of all the 40 employees together in the year 2023 was

(a) 95000 (b) 90000
(c) 80000 (d) 85000

17. If *a*, *b* and *c* are positive real numbers such that $a > 10 \ge b \ge c$ and $\frac{\log_8(a+b)}{\log_2 c} + \frac{\log_{27}(a-b)}{\log_3 c} = \frac{2}{3}$, then the greatest possible integer value of *a* is

18. All the values of *x* satisfying the inequality $\frac{1}{x+5} \le \frac{1}{2x-3}$ are

(a) $x < -5$ or $\frac{3}{2} < x \le 8$

(b) $-5 < x < \frac{3}{2}$ or $x > \frac{3}{2}$

(c) $-5 < x < \frac{3}{2}$ or $\frac{3}{2} < x \le 8$

(d) $x < -5$ or $x > \frac{3}{2}$

19. If *m* and *n* are natural numbers such that $n > 1$, and $m^n = 2^{25} \times 3^{40}$, then $m - n$ equals

(a) 209947 (b) 209942
(c) 209932 (d) 209937

20. If $\left(x+6\sqrt{2}\right)^{\frac{1}{2}} - \left(x-6\sqrt{2}\right)^{\frac{1}{2}} = 2\sqrt{2}$, then *x* equals

21. When Rajesh's age was same as the present age of Garima, the ratio of their ages was 3 : 2. When Garima's age becomes the same as the present age of Rajesh, the ratio of the ages of Rajesh and Garima will become

(a) 5 : 4 (b) 4 : 3
(c) 3 : 2 (d) 2 : 1

22. When 3^{333} is divided by 11, the remainder is

(a) 10 (b) 5
(c) 1 (d) 6

CAT 2024 SLOT 3

1. For some constant real numbers *p*, *k* and *a*, consider the following system of linear equations in *x* and *y*:

$px - 4y = 2$
$3x + ky = a$

A necessary condition for the system to have no solution for (*x*, *y*), is

(a) $ap + 6 = 0$ (b) $2a + k \ne 0$
(c) $ap - 6 = 0$ (d) $kp + 12 \ne 0$

2. The midpoints of sides AB, BC, and AC in ΔABC are M, N, and P, respectively. The medians drawn from A, B, and C intersect the line segments MP, MN and NP at X, Y, and Z, respectively. If the area of ΔABC is 1440 sq cm, then the area, in sq cm, of ΔXYZ is

3. If $\left(a+b\sqrt{3}\right)^2 = 52+30\sqrt{3}$, where *a* and *b* are natural numbers, then $a + b$ equals

(a) 9 (b) 7
(c) 10 (d) 8

4. In a group of 250 students, the percentage of girls was at least 44% and at most 60%. The rest of the students were boys. Each student opted for either swimming or running or both. If 50% of the boys and 80% of the girls opted for swimming while 70% of the boys and 60% of the girls opted for running, then the minimum and maximum possible number of students who opted for both swimming and running, are
(a) 72 and 88, respectively
(b) 72 and 80, respectively
(c) 75 and 90, respectively
(d) 75 and 96, respectively

5. A certain amount of water was poured into a 300 litre container and the remaining portion of the container was filled with milk. Then an amount of this solution was taken out from the container which was twice the volume of water that was earlier poured into it, and water was poured to refill the container again. If the resulting solution contains 72% milk, then the amount of water, in litres, that was initially poured into the container was

6. A circular plot of land is divided into two regions by a chord of length $10\sqrt{3}$ meters such that the chord subtends an angle of 120° at the center. Then, the area, in square meters, of the smaller region is
(a) $25\left(\frac{4\pi}{3}-\sqrt{3}\right)$ (b) $20\left(\frac{4\pi}{3}+\sqrt{3}\right)$
(c) $20\left(\frac{4\pi}{3}-\sqrt{3}\right)$ (d) $25\left(\frac{4\pi}{3}+\sqrt{3}\right)$

7. Rajesh and Vimal own 20 hectares and 30 hectares of agricultural land, respectively, which are entirely covered by wheat and mustard crops. The cultivation area of wheat and mustard in the land owned by Vimal are in the ratio of 5 : 3. If the total cultivation area of wheat and mustard are in the ratio 11 : 9, then the ratio of cultivation area of wheat and mustard in the land owned by Rajesh is
(a) 3 : 7 (b) 4 : 3
(c) 7 : 9 (d) 1 : 1

8. For any non-zero real number x, let $f(x) + 2f\left(\frac{1}{x}\right) = 3x$. Then, the sum of all possible values of x for which $f(x) = 3$, is
(a) −2 (b) 3
(c) −3 (d) 2

9. Aman invests ₹4000 in a bank at a certain rate of interest, compounded annually. If the ratio of the value of the investment after 3 years to the value of the investment after 5 years is 25 : 36, then the minimum number of years required for the value of the investment to exceed ₹20000 is

10. If 10^{68} is divided by 13, the remainder is
(a) 9 (b) 5
(c) 8 (d) 4

11. The number of distinct integer solutions (x, y) of the equation $|x + y| + |x - y| = 2$, is

12. A regular octagon ABCDEFGH has sides of length 6 cm each. Then the area, in sq. cm, of the square ACEG is
(a) $72(1+\sqrt{2})$ (b) $36(2+\sqrt{2})$
(c) $36(1+\sqrt{2})$ (d) $72(2+\sqrt{2})$

13. A train travelled a certain distance at a uniform speed. Had the speed been 6 km per hour more, it would have needed 4 hours less. Had the speed been 6 km per hour less, it would have needed 6 hours more. The distance, in km, travelled by the train is
(a) 720 (b) 800
(c) 780 (d) 640

14. The number of all positive integers up to 500 with non-repeating digits is

15. If $3^a = 4$, $4^b = 5$, $5^c =. 6$, $6^d = 7$, $7^e = 8$ and $8^f = 9$, then the value of the product $abcdef$ is

16. The average of three distinct real numbers is 28. If the smallest number is increased by 7 and the largest number is reduced by 10, the order of the numbers remains unchanged, and the new arithmetic mean becomes 2 more than the middle number, while the difference between the largest and the smallest numbers becomes 64. Then, the largest number in the original set of three numbers is

17. The sum of all distinct real values of x that satisfy the equation $10^x + \frac{4}{10^x} = \frac{81}{2}$, is
(a) $4\log_{10} 2$ (b) $\log_{10} 2$
(c) $3\log_{10} 2$ (d) $2\log_{10} 2$

18. After two successive increments, Gopal's salary became 187.5% of his initial salary. If the percentage of salary increase in the second increment was twice of that in the first increment, then the percentage of salary increase in the first increment was
(a) 25 (b) 20
(c) 30 (d) 27.5

19. Sam can complete a job in 20 days when working alone. Mohit is twice as fast as Sam and thrice as fast as Ayna in the same job. They undertake a job with an arrangement where Sam and Mohit work together on the first day, Sam and Ayna on the second day, Mohit and Ayna on the third day, and this three-day pattern is repeated till the work gets completed. Then, the fraction of total work done by Sam is
(a) $\frac{1}{5}$ (b) $\frac{1}{20}$
(c) $\frac{3}{10}$ (d) $\frac{3}{20}$

20. Consider the sequence $t_1 = 1$, $t_2 = -1$ and $t_n = \left(\frac{n-3}{n-1}\right) t_{n-2}$ for $n \geq 3$. Then, the value of the sum $\frac{1}{t_2}+\frac{1}{t_4}+\frac{1}{t_6}+\cdots+\frac{1}{t_{2022}}+\frac{1}{t_{2024}}$, is

(a) −1026169 (b) −1022121
(c) −1024144 (d) −1023132

21. The number of distinct real values of x, satisfying the equation $\max\{x, 2\} - \min\{x, 2\} = |x + 2| - |x - 2|$, is

22. Gopi marks a price on a product in order to make 20% profit. Ravi gets 10% discount on this marked price, and thus saves ₹15. Then, the profit, in rupees, made by Gopi by selling the product to Ravi, is
(a) 15 (b) 25
(c) 10 (d) 20

ANSWER KEY

CAT 2024 Slot 1

1. 38	2. (d)	3. (d)	4. 15
5. (d)	6. 217	7. (c)	8. 10
9. (b)	10. (c)	11. (c)	12. 66
13. (d)	14. (c)	15. (b)	16. 6
17. (a)	18. 31	19. (b)	20. (d)
21. 31	22. (d)		

CAT 2024 Slot 2

1. (c)	2. 7	3. 2	4. 139
5. (a)	6. (b)	7. 2160	8. 340
9. (a)	10. 7	11. (a)	12. (c)
13. (a)	14. (b)	15. (b)	16. (a)
17. 14	18. (a)	19. (a)	20. 11
21. (a)	22. (b)		

CAT 2024 Slot 3

1. (b)	2. 90	3. (d)	4. (b)
5. 30	6. (a)	7. (c)	8. (c)
9. 9	10. (a)	11. 8	12. (b)
13. (a)	14. 378	15. 2	16. 70
17. (d)	18. (a)	19. (c)	20. (c)
21. 2	22. (c)		

SOLUTIONS AND SHORTCUTS

CAT 2024 Slot 1

1. Let the common root be 'r'. Then if we replace x by r in the equations, we should get LHS = RHS. Hence, we get three equations as:
$r^2 + mr + 9 = 0$; $r^2 + nr + 17 = 0$ and $r^2 + (mr + nr) + 35 = 0$.
Equating equations 1 and 3 we get: $nr = -26$;
Equating equations 2 and 3 we get: $mr = -18$.
The first equation then becomes: $r^2 - 9 = 0 \rightarrow r^2 = 9$. Thus, the value of $r = -3$.
Then, from $nr = -26$, we get $n = \frac{26}{3}$ and from $mr = -8$, we get $m = 6$.
The value of $2m + 3n = 2\times6+3\times\frac{26}{3} = 38$.

2. The area represented by the inequality will be the area of the X-Y plane as indicated in the figure:

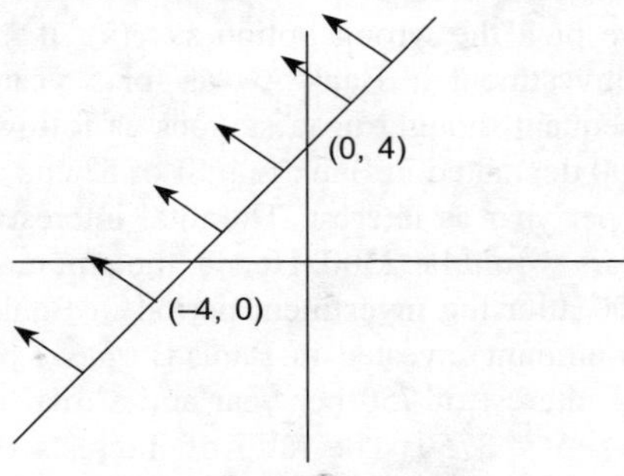

The inequality $-4 \le x^2 + y^2 + 4(x - y) \le 0$ can be rewritten as:
$-4 \le x^2 + y^2 + 4x - 4y \le 0 \rightarrow -4 \le (x + 2)^2 + (y - 2)^2 - 8 \le 0 \rightarrow 4 \le (x + 2)^2 + (y - 2)^2 \le 8$. The central part of this inequality represents a circle with center at –2, 2. Also, at it's extremes, the inequality $4 \le (x + 2)^2 + (y - 2)^2$, gives us the equality $4 = (x + 2)^2 + (y - 2)^2$, which represents the circle with center –2, 2 and a radius of 2. On the other side, thinking similarly, we get $(x + 2)^2 + (y - 2)^2 \le 8 \rightarrow$ an extremity of a circle with center (–2, 2) and a radius of $2\sqrt{2}$.

We notice that the point (–2,2) lies on the line $x + 4 = y$. Hence, the area we are looking for is as shown in the figure:

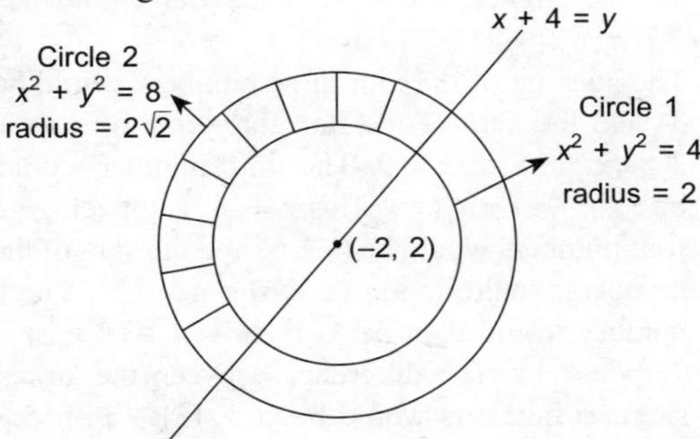

The area would be given by:

$$\frac{\pi\times\left(2\sqrt{2}\right)^2 - \pi\times2^2}{2} = 2\pi .$$

Option (d) is correct.

3. The best way to do this question is through options (since it has options available). If we pick the correct option d, it means that the investment in Bank A was for 6 years and the subsequent thought process goes as follows:
10000 deposited in Bank A @SI of 5% pa, will yield 500 per year as interest. The total interest earned in 6 years would be 3000. Hence, the amount becomes 13000 after the investment period in Bank A.
This amount invested in Bank B, @6% pa SI, will yield interest of 780 per year and a total interest of 780 × 5 = 3900. The ratio of interests earned are 3000 : 3900 = 10 : 13, which matches the given condition in the problem and hence is the correct answer.

If we pick the wrong option say (a), it means that the investment in Bank A was for 5 years and the subsequent thought process goes as follows: 10000 deposited in Bank A @SI of 5% pa, will yield 500 per year as interest. The total interest earned in 5 years would be 2500. Hence, the amount becomes 12500 after the investment period in Bank A.
This amount invested in Bank B, @6% pa SI, will yield interest of 750 per year and a total interest of 750 × 5 = 3750. The ratio of interests earned are 2500 : 3750 = 2 : 3, which does not match the given condition in the problem and hence is incorrect.
Alternately, if we assume the number of years for investment in Bank A as n, we get Interest earned in n years = 500 × n. The amount becomes 10000 + 500n. Interest earned for 5 years in Bank B @6% = (600 + 30n) × 5 = 3000 + 150n.
We are given the ratio of interests as 10:13. Hence, we get:

$$\frac{500\times n}{3000+150\times n}=\frac{10}{13}\to n=6.$$

Hence, option (d) is correct.

4. Let the first number be 'x'. Then the average of the first two numbers is (x + 1) and their sum would be 2x + 2. Hence, the second number would be 2x + 2 – x = x + 2.
The average of the first three numbers would be (x + 3) and the sum of the first three numbers would be 3 × (x + 3) = 3x + 9. The third number would then be 3x + 9 – x – (x + 2) = x + 7. The average of the four numbers would be (x + 6) and the sum of the four numbers would be 4 × (x + 6) = 4x + 24. The fourth number would then be 4x + 24 – x – (x + 2) – (x + 7) = x + 15. The difference between the largest and smallest numbers would be (x + 15) – x = 15.

5. Let l, b and h be the length breadth and height of the cuboid respectively. We are given for this question that: 2l + 2b + 2h = 846 (surface area) and 4l + 4b + 4h = 144 (sum of all the edges). Hence, l + b + h = 36. $(l + b + h)^2 = 1296 \to l^2 + b^2 + h^2 + 2l + 2b + 2h = 1296$.
Thus, $l^2 + b^2 + h^2 = 450$. For a cuboid, inscribed inside a sphere, the long diagonal of the cuboid would be equal to the diameter of the sphere.
Hence, if r is the radius of the sphere, we will have:

$$\sqrt{l^2+b^2+h^2}=2r\to 2r=\sqrt{450}\to r=\frac{15\sqrt{2}}{2}$$

The volume of the sphere would be

$$\frac{4}{3}\times\pi\times r^3=1125\pi\sqrt{2}$$

Option (d) is correct.

6. Since, the question says 'for any natural number', a_1 would represent the value of a_n, when n = 1, a_2 would represent the value of a_n, when n = 2 and so on.
The value of a_1, a_2, a_3 would be 1 each. a_4 to a_8 would each have a value of 2. a_9 to a_{15} would have a value of 3 each, a_{16} to a_{24} would have a value of 4 each, a_{25} to a_{35} would have a value of 5 each, a_{36} to a_{48} would be 6 each and a_{49} and a_{50} would be 7 each. Hence, the required answer is:
1 × 3 + 2 × 5 + 3 × 7 + 4 × 9 + 5 × 11 + 6 × 13 + 7 × 2 = 3 + 10 + 21 + 36 + 55 + 78 + 14 = 217.

7. The most natural thought in this question is to represent the condition as:

$$\left(a+b\sqrt{n}\right)^2=29-12\sqrt{5}\to a^2+b^2n+2ab\sqrt{n}$$
$$=29-12\sqrt{5}$$

Comparing this we have $a^2+b^2n=29$ and $2ab=-12$.
This leads to two possible solutions with n as 5: a = 3, b = –2 or a = –3 and b = 2.
The value of $a+b\sqrt{n}=-3+2\sqrt{5}$ (Note, we reject $3-2\sqrt{5}$ as it is a negative value which the question does not allow us to take).
Thus, if we compare $a+b\sqrt{n}=-3+2\sqrt{5}\to$ we get a = –3, b = 2 and n = 5 and a + b + n = 4. Most people got this answer while solving the exam and were surprised to see that the answer was wrong. What they had missed was the possibility of the following solution:

$$\left(a+b\sqrt{n}\right)^2=29-6\sqrt{20}\to a^2+b^2n+2ab\sqrt{n}$$
$$=29-6\sqrt{20}$$

Comparing this we have $a^2+b^2n=29$ and $2ab=-6$.
This leads to two possible solutions with n as 20: a = 3, b = –1 or a = –3 and b = 1.
The value of $a+b\sqrt{n}=-3+1\sqrt{20}$ (Note, we reject $3-1\sqrt{20}$ as it is a negative value which the question does not allow us to take).
Thus, if we compare $a+b\sqrt{n}=-3+1\sqrt{20}\to$ we get a = –3, b = 1 and n = 20 and a + b + n = 18.
This is the correct answer, since the question asks us to find the maximum possible value of a + b + n.
Correct answer = 18.

8. The figure shows the situation described.

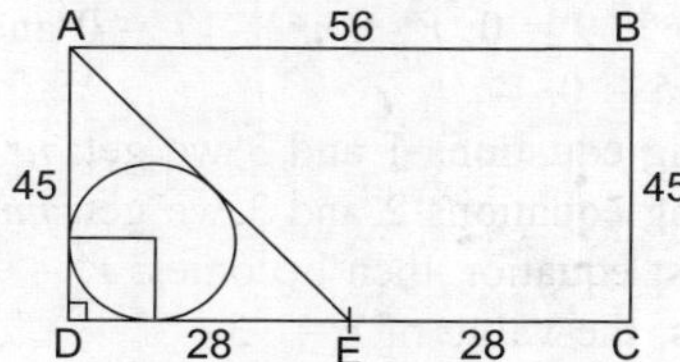

The length of AE can be calculated using the Pythagoras theorem as: $AE^2=28^2+45^2\to AE=53$.
Using the formula for inradius on a right triangle

$$=\frac{\text{base}+\text{height}-\text{hypostenuse}}{2}=\frac{28+45-53}{2}=10$$

Hence, the correct answer is 10.

9. Let Incomes of Kamal Amal and Vimal in September be $8n$, $6n$ and $5n$ respectively. Kamal will pay a rent of $0.15 \times 8n = 1.2n$; Amal will pay a rent of $0.12 \times 6n = 0.72n$; Vimal will pay a rent of $0.18 \times 5n = 0.9n$. Hence, total rent $= 2.82n$. Total income for October $= 1.1 \times 8n + 1.12 \times 6n + 1.15 \times 5n = 8.8n + 6.72n + 5.75n = 21.27n$.

Required percentage value $= \frac{2.82}{21.27} \times 100 \approx 13.26\%$.

Option (b) is correct.

10. We are given that $x_5 = a + 4d = -4$. Also, $2x_6 + 2x_9 = x_{11} + x_{13} \rightarrow 2(a + 5d) + 2(a + 8d) = (a + 10d) + (a + 12d) \rightarrow 4a + 26d = 2a + 22d \rightarrow 2a = -4d$ or $a = -2d$.

Then using $x_5 = a + 4d = -4$, we can solve for a and d. We get $a = 4$ and $d = -2$. $X_{100} = a + 99d = 4 + 99 \times (-2) = -194$. Option (c) is correct.

11. Such questions are best solved by thinking in reverse. The question tells us that the shopkeeper is selling half plus 3 to each customer and that he is left with no grains after doing so for the last customer. Reverse thinking tells us that the before the third customer the shop keeper would have 6 kgs of grain. (To get to 6, add 3 to zero and then double the number – these being the reverse steps to halving and then subtracting 3). Doing so again, will give us how much grain the shopkeeper had before he serviced the second customer – you get: $(6 + 3) \times 2 = 18$ kgs before the second customer. Further $(18 + 3) \times 2 = 42$ kgs of grain at the start. Hence, option (c) is correct.

12. Let the number of apples be $5x$, the number of mangoes be $2x$ and the number of oranges be $2n$. We are then given that the total number of all three fruits is 187. This gives us the equation $7x + 2n = 187$.

Next, he sells, 75 apples and is hence left with $5x - 75$ apples, he also sells 26 mangoes (left with $2x - 26$ mangoes) and n oranges – thus being left with n oranges. We are given that: ratio of apples left to oranges left = 3:2, which gives us the equation:

$\frac{5x-75}{n} = \frac{3}{2}$. Solving the two equations obtained we get: $x = 21$ and $n = 20$.

Thus the oranges sold = 20. Hence, total fruits sold = $75 + 26 + 20 = 121$. Fruits unsold $= 187 - 121 = 66$.

13. With every iteration, 1/3rd of the milk is left behind. Thus, if the original milk in the glass is M liters, milk left after 4 iterations will be $M \times \frac{1}{3} \times \frac{1}{3} \times \frac{1}{3} \times \frac{1}{3} = \frac{1}{81} M$

The remaining liquid in the glass would be water – hence water $= M - \frac{1}{81} M = \frac{80}{81} M$

Hence, the required ratio of Milk and water in the glass is 1 : 80. Option (d) is correct.

14. The given situation can be represented as follows:

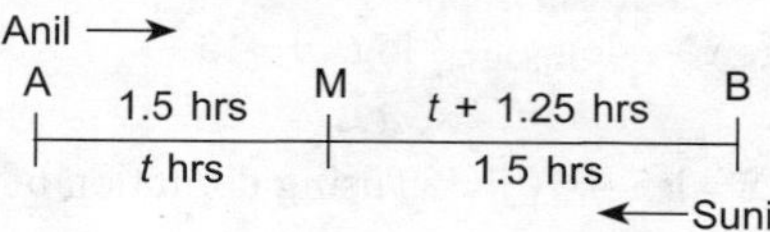

Since the ratio of speeds is inversely proportional to the times when the distance is constant, we can write the equation:

$$\frac{1.5}{t} = \frac{t+1.25}{1.5} \rightarrow t = 1$$

Hence, Anil takes $1.5 + 1 + 1.25 = 3.75$ hours to cover 45 kms. His speed would be $45/3.75 = 12$.

15. The given expression can be rewritten in terms of powers of 2 as:

$$\frac{1}{2^{3k}} \times \frac{1}{2^5} = \frac{1}{2^3} \times \frac{1}{2^{\frac{5}{k}}}$$

Taking reciprocals we get:

$$2^{3k} \times 2^5 = 2^3 \times 2^{\frac{5}{k}} \rightarrow 3k + 5 = 3 + \frac{5}{k}$$

$$\rightarrow 3k^2 + 5k - 3k - 5 = 0 \rightarrow 3k^2 + 2k - 5 = 0$$

The sum of real values of k satisfying the given expression will be equal to the sum of roots of this quadratic equation. Hence, the required answer is option (b).

16. Renu completes the work in $15 \times 4 = 60$ hours, while Seema completes the work in $8 \times 5 = 40$ hours. If the total work is taken as 120 units, Renu's work rate would be 2 units per hour and Seema's would be 3 units per hour.

Given Renu works '2' hours per day, then Seema would work '4' hours per day (according to the condition 'Seema agrees to work for double the number of hours per day as Renu').

Also, let Seema agree to work for 'd' days, then Renu would be working for 2d days (according to the condition ' Renu agrees to work for double the number of days as Seema').

Then the total work done by Renu + Seema $= 2 \times 2d \times 2 + 4 \times d \times 3 = 20d = 120$ units $\rightarrow d = 6$ days. This is the number of days Seema works for and hence is the correct answer.

17. Let the cost price be $100p$. Them the selling price is fixed at $140p$.

It is given to us that if the product cost at 40% less (means it cost $60p$) and was sold at 5 rupees less (means was sold at $140p - 5$), the profit percentage would be 50%.

This gives us the equation $1.5 \times 60p = 140p - 5 \rightarrow 50p = 5 \rightarrow p = 0.1$. Hence, the original selling price was $140 \times p = 140 \times 0.1 = 14$. Option (a) is correct.

18. The given expression is

$$4\log_{10}x + \frac{4}{2}\log_{10}x + \frac{8}{3}\log_{10}x = 13 \rightarrow$$

$$\log_{10}x = 1.5 \rightarrow 10^{\frac{3}{2}} = x(\text{using definition of logs})$$

Or $x = \sqrt{1000} \rightarrow x = 31+$

Hence, the greatest integer not exceeding $x = 31$.

19. 10^{100} divided by 7, leaves the same remainder as 3^{100} divided by 7 (using the remainder theorem). Also, 3^6 divided by 7 leaves a remainder 1. Hence, we can adopt the following thought structure:

$$\frac{3^{100}}{7} = \frac{(3^6)^{16} \times 3^4}{7} = \frac{(3^6)^{16} \times 81}{7}$$

The remainder of this expression would depend only on the remainder of 81 divided by 7, which is 4. Option (b) is correct.

20. In a round about way, the question is asking us to count the number of onto functions from the domain A to the co-domain B. Since, there are 6 elements in A and 3 elements in B, and as each element in A (say 'a') can be mapped to any of the three elements of the co-domain, we will have a total 3^6 (–729) as the total number of functions from A to B.

From this number we need to subtract cases when the function is not an onto function – i.e. cases, when there is an element in B which is not mapped to any element in A. There will be 3 functions when $f(a)$ is mapped to a single element in B. Also, there will be $2^6 \times 3 = 192$ functions when $f(a)$ is mapped to either 1 or 2 elements in B. This includes the 3 functions when $f(a)$ was mapped to a single element in B. Hence, the total number of functions that are not onto functions from A to B – are 192 – 3 = 189. The required answer = 729 – 189 = 540.

21. Since each of the digits are used equally, the average value of any of the 4 digits would be $(a + b + c + d)/4$ – lets call this M. Also, totaling each column, the total for each column would be 24 × M. The addition would look as shown:

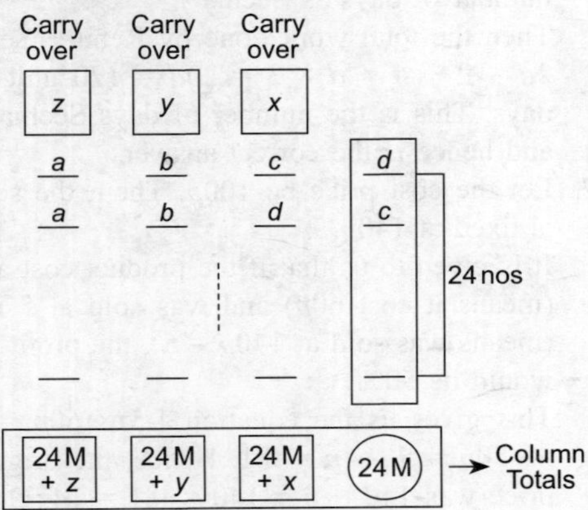

Since, the left most column total of 24 M + Z = 153, we can start to try values of M as 5.25,5.5,5.75,6 etc.

(Note: the value of M has to either be an integer or if it is a decimal it has to be either .25, .5 or .75 since M itself is $(a + b + c + d)/4$).

Using trial and error on the calculator we can see that the values work out when we take M = 5.75 as shown: (Note each column will have an inherent total of 24 × 5.75 = 138).

15	15	13		with M = 5.75
a	b	c	d	
a	b	d	c	24 nos
153	3	1	8	Column Total 138, hence carry 13 to next column
138 + 15 = 153	138 + 15 = 153	138 + 15 = 153		

Hence, the sum of a, b, c, d = 5.75 × 4 = 23 and the value of n = 8.

Thus, $a + b + c + d + n = 23 = 8 = 31$.

22. Let $y = -p$ and $z = -q$. We will have the expressions:

$$x^2 + p^2 + q^2 = \frac{a}{4} \text{ and } x + p + q = \frac{3+a}{4}$$

We also know that $x^2 + p^2 + q^2 > 2xp + 2xq + 2pq$.

Thus, the left hand side of this expression has a maximum value of $3 \times (x^2 + p^2 + q^2)$.

Thus, we get the inequality:

$$3 \times (x^2 + p^2 + q^2) \geq (x + p + q)^2 \text{ or}$$

$$3\frac{a}{4} \geq \frac{(3+a)^2}{16} \rightarrow 12a \geq (3+a)^2 \rightarrow$$

$$a^2 - 6a + 9 \leq 0 \rightarrow (a-3)^2 \leq 0$$

But, the LHS cannot be negative as it is a square. Hence, we get the expression

$$(a-3)^2 = 0 \rightarrow a = 3.$$

CAT 2024 Slot 2

1. The sum of the roots i.e.: $\alpha + \beta = -\lambda/3$ and $\alpha\beta = -1/3$

We also have:

$$\frac{\alpha^2 + \beta^2}{\alpha^2\beta^2} = 15 \rightarrow \frac{(\alpha+\beta)^2 - 2\alpha\beta}{\alpha^2\beta^2} = 15 \rightarrow \frac{\frac{\lambda^2}{9} + \frac{6}{9}}{\frac{1}{9}} = 15$$

Thus, the value of λ = +3 or –3. Sum of roots is either 1 or –1.

Now, $\alpha^3 + \beta^3 = (\alpha + \beta)^3 - 3\alpha\beta(\alpha + \beta) = 1 + 1 = 2$ or = –1 – 1 = –2

Hence, the required value is 2^2 or $-2^2 = 4$.

Option (c) is correct.

2. Number of paths PQ = 3; QS = 4; PR = 4; PS = 0; QR = n (say); RS = m (say)
The routes for PS are: P-Q-S + P-R-S + P-Q-R-S = $3 \times 4 + 4 \times m + 3 \times n \times m = 62$ routes.
This gives us: $4 \times m + 3 \times m \times n = 50 \rightarrow m \times (4 + 3 \times n) = 50$.
Possible values of m and n are 5, 2 or 2, 7.
We are also given that the paths Q-R, Q-P-R and Q-S-R add up to 27 paths. i.e. $n + 3 \times 4 + 4 \times m = 27 \rightarrow n + 4 \times m = 15$. Of the possible values we got previously, only 2, 7 works for this case. Hence, the value of number of routes between Q and R = n = 7.
Correct answer = 7.

3. We can work out that the given triangle is a right-angled triangle with a base of 6 and a height of 8. The hypotenuse hence, would be 10. The inradius of a right angled triangle is given by the formula:

$$\frac{\text{base} + \text{height} - \text{hypotenuse}}{2} = \frac{6+8-10}{2} = 2$$

Hence, the correct answer = 2

4. Let the work be equal to 300 units and the respective works per day of Amal, Vimal and Sunil be A, V and S. We have A + V = 2 and V + S = 3.
The working pattern to complete the task is: Amal 75 days, Vimal 135 days, Sunil 45 days. This can be restructured by splitting 135 days work of Vimal as 75 + 45 + 15 as: Amal + Vimal work together for 75 days; Vimal + Sunil work together for 45 days and Vimal works alone for 15 days. We get the total work as: $75 \times 2 + 45 \times 3 + 15V = 300 \rightarrow V = 1$. Hence, A = 1 and S = 2.
The work pattern given to us to complete the task is- work done in units indicated in brackets: Day 1 Amal (1); Day 2 Amal + Vimal (2); Day 3 Amal + Sunil (3); Day 4: Amal + Vimal (2); Day 5: Amal (1); Day 6 Amal + Vimal + Sunil (4). Thus, in 6 days total work done would be 13. The pattern of work would repeat for the next 6 days and so on. We can see that to complete 299 units of work in this pattern, we would required 23 complete six day periods (as $23 \times 13 = 299$). This represents $23 \times 6 = 138$ days of work. On the 139th day Amal will be working alone and complete the balance 1 unit of work.
Hence, the total number of days required = 139.

5. You can solve this question simply by value estimations of the individual terms of the expression and by comparing the approximate value we are getting with the values in the options. We can clearly see that the first term of the expression is $\frac{7-5}{5\times7\times5} = \frac{2}{175}$.

In percentage terms, this value is equal to 1.14%. Subsequent terms of the expression would start to become very small – a sample calculation with the second term will reveal this:
Value of the second term = $\frac{49-25}{25\times49\times25} = \frac{24}{625\times49}$.

We can clearly see that the value of this and subsequent terms would be very negligible. Hence, we are looking for an answer in terms of a fraction whose percentage value is slightly above 1.14%. We can reject options (b) and (d) directly as their values are below 1%. Option (c) also gets rejected as the value of 7/408 is above 1.7%, which is a value the expression can never reach. The value of the fraction in option (a) is around 1.22% and it is the only feasible option. Hence, option (a) is correct.

6. $160000 = 16 \times 100 \times 100 = 2^8 \times 5^4$.
We are given that $f(xy) = f(x) \times f(y) + f(x) + f(y)$ and also that $f(p) = 1$, whenever p is prime.
Using this, we can work out that $f(160000) = f(2^8 \times 5^4) = f(2^8) \times f(5^4) + f(2^8) + f(5^4)$. Our focus shifts to finding the values of $f(2^8)$ and $f(5^4)$.
These can be worked out as follows:
$f(5^2) = f(5) \times f(5) + f(5) + f(5) = 1 \times 1 + 1 + 1 = 3$ (since $f(5) = 1$).
$f(5^2 \times 5) = f(5^2) \times f(5) + f(5^2) + f(5) = 3 \times 1 + 3 + 1 = 7$
Hence, $f(5^3 \times 5) = f(5^4) = 7 \times 1 + 7 + 1 = 15$.
Likewise: $f(2^2) = f(2) \times f(2) + f(2) + f(2) = 1 \times 1 + 1 + 1 = 3$ (since $f(2) = 1$).
$f(2^3) = f(2^2 \times 2) = f(2^2) \times f(2) + f(2^2) + f(2) = 3 \times 1 + 3 + 1 = 7$.
Hence, $f(2^3 \times 2) = f(2^4) = 7 \times 1 + 7 + 1 = 15$.
Continuing this pattern, we see that $f(2^8) = 255$.
We then get:
$f(160000) = f(2^8 \times 5^4) = 255 \times 15 + 255 + 15 = 4095$.
Option (b) is correct.

7. If Bina's CP is P, then $0.81 \times P = 4860 \rightarrow P = 6000$. Hence, Shyam sells the product to Hari at $1.17 \times 6000 = 7020$. Profit in rupees for Shyam = 2160.

8. Let him have $100x$ total fruits. Then, he has $40x$ mangoes. This also means that he has $60x$ (bananas and Apples combined) – i.e. $B + A = 60x$. It can be inferred that 96 bananas and 0.4A equals $30x$.

Thus, we have $B + A = 60x$ and $96 + 0.4A = 30x$ $\rightarrow A = \frac{(30x-96)}{0.4}$. Then we get:

$$B + \frac{30x-96}{0.4} = 60x \rightarrow 0.4B + 30x - 96 = 24x \rightarrow 6x =$$

$$(96-0.4B) \rightarrow x = \frac{(96-0.4B)}{6} = 16 - \frac{B}{15}$$

$$100x = 1600 - \frac{100B}{15} = 1600 - 6.66B$$

Since we know that 100x has to be an integer, it means that 6.66B should be an integer. Thus, B should be a multiple of 3. Also, since it is mentioned that 96 bananas were sold, the value of B starts from 96,99 onwards. We can start to build a table for possible values of each of the variables.

The table will look as shown:

Value of B Bananas	*Value of 100x* Total fruits	*Value of 60x* Apples and Bananas	*Number of Apples*	*Number of Mangoes (40x)*	*Sells* M + B + A
96	960	576	480	384	192 + 96 + 192
99	940	564	465	376	188 + 96 + 186
102	920	552	450	368	184 + 96 + 180

After this point we should realise that all the numbers will be in arithmetic progressions, and our focus shifts to maximum value of B, so that we can minimize the value of 100x. We can see that the number of Bananas should be less than 192 – as if there had been 192 bananas, we would have been selling only 50% of the bananas and by selling 50% mangoes, 50% bananas and 40% apples, you cannot get to selling 50% of the entire fruit stock. Hence, we try to put the value of B = 189 to see, if all numbers fall into place.

189	340	204	15	136	68 + 96 + 6

Since all the numbers are indeed obeying all conditions in this case, the minimum total number of fruits is 340.

9. The visualization of the figure described will be as shown. Let y, be the radius of the smaller circle in the middle, and x be the radius of the larger outer circle. Also, let r be the radius of the three circles that are touching each other. Let P, represent the center of the inner circle Y. It will also be the center of the outer circle X.

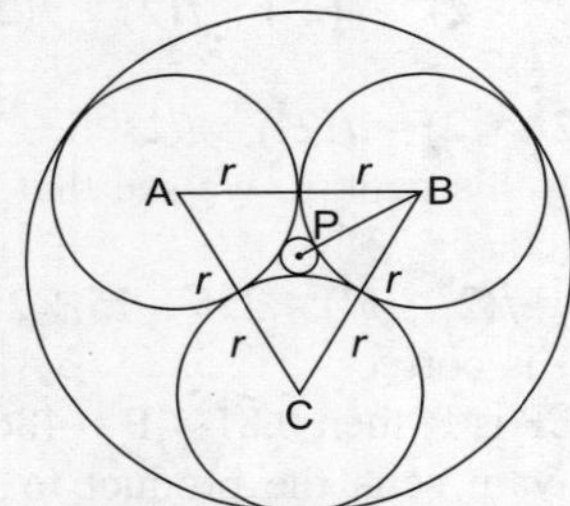

In the figure, the length of PB is

$$\frac{2r}{\sqrt{3}} = r + y \rightarrow y = \frac{2r}{\sqrt{3}} - r$$

The value of $x = 2r + y = 2r + \frac{2r}{\sqrt{3}} - r = r + \frac{2r}{\sqrt{3}}$

The required ratio is:

$$\frac{x}{y} = \frac{r + \frac{2r}{\sqrt{3}}}{\frac{2r}{\sqrt{3}} - r} = \frac{2+\sqrt{3}}{2-\sqrt{3}} = \frac{(2+\sqrt{3})\times(2+\sqrt{3})}{(2-\sqrt{3})\times(2+\sqrt{3})} = \frac{7+4\sqrt{3}}{1}$$

Hence, option (a) is correct.

10. The given expression can be rewritten as: $(2x - y)^2 + 3(y - 1)^2 = 0$. The two terms on the left hand side of this equation are both non-negative, and hence each of the terms should be 0, for equality to exist. Thus, we get $y - 1 = 0 \rightarrow y = 1$ and $2x - y = 0 \rightarrow 2x - 1 = 0$. Hence, $x = 0.5$. The value of $4x + 5y = 2 + 5 = 7$.

11. Let the amount invested by Sunil be S. The given situation can be represented by:

$$S \times 1.02^{10} \times 1.1 = 22000 \times 1.02^{12} \rightarrow S = 20808.$$

12. There are 4 cases possible here depending on x and y being positive and negative respectively:

Case 1: When x is positive and y is positive – we get the equations: $2x + y = 15$ and $x = 20$. Solving this we get $x = 20$ and $y = -25$, which is a contradiction of both x and y being positive. Hence, we reject this case.

Case 2: When x is positive and y is negative – we get the equations: $2x + y = 15$ and $x - 2y = 20$. Solving these gives us $x = 10$ and $y = -5$. This satisfies the condition in this case of x positive and y negative. The value of $(x - y) = 10 + 5 = 15$.

We can avoid checking the other cases, since the question is asking us a definitive value of $(x - y)$ and not a probable/maximum/minimum value of $(x - y)$. Hence, we conclude that the correct answer is 15.

13. Let the total distance from its starting point to the destination be 3d. Also, let his original speed be s and the original time required to reach the destination be t. Then, the situation described can be shown in the following figures:

5 → time = t, distance = 3d
Start 60 → time = t + 3.5 End

Start End
2d d
28 → time = t/3 40 →

From the last figure above:

$$\frac{t}{3} + \frac{d}{40} = t \rightarrow d = \frac{80t}{3} \rightarrow 3d = 80t.$$

Then, from the original movement of the bus, we have: $\frac{3d}{s} = t \rightarrow s = 80\,kmph.$

Once we know that the original speed of the bus was 80kmph, then from the second condition in the question, we can infer that when the bus is traveling at 60 kmph, it is dropping it's speed by 1/4th. The time required would increase by 1/3rd and become

$t + \frac{t}{3}$. It is given to us that $\frac{t}{3} = 3.5\,hours$. (Note: this represents the extra time required because the bus travels at a slower speed (of 60 kmph).

Thus, t = 10.5 hours.

Starting at 9 am, the bus would reach the destination at 7:30 PM.

Option (a) is correct.

14. The given situation is as shown in the figure. If we assume AD to be x, then DE will also be x (using similar triangles EAB and EDC, where the sides of EAB are double the sides of EDC).

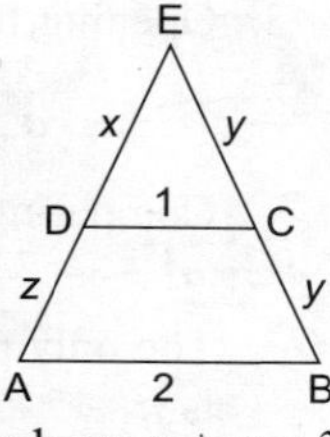

The perimeter of ABCD being 6,we have $x + y = 3$. Hence, the perimeter of the triangle AED = $2 + 2x + 2y = 2 + 2(x + y) = 8$. Option (b) is correct.

15. Let the original mixture have A liters of acid and W liters of water.

After adding 2 liters of water, water becomes $W + 2$ while acid remains at A. It is given to us that: $\frac{A}{W+2} = \frac{1}{1} \rightarrow A = W + 2$.

Next, if we add 15 liters acid to this, we get the ratio: $\frac{W+17}{W+2} = \frac{4}{1} \rightarrow W = 3$ and $A = W + 2 = 5$.

The required ratio of water to acid in the original solution was 3:5.

16. Let the employees be called E1 to E40. Sum of bonuses of E1 to E30 = 40000 × 30 = 12 lacs

Sum of bonuses of E11 to E40 = 60000 × 30 = 18 lacs.

Hence, Sum of bonuses of E1 to E10 + 2 × (E11 to E30) + E31 to E40 = 12 lacs + 18 lacs = 30 lacs.

Also, we are given separately that sum of bonuses of E1 to 10 and E31 to E40 = 20 × 50000 = 10 lacs.

Thus, (Sum of E1 to E10) + 2 × (Sum of E11 to E30) + (sum of E31 to E40) – (sum of E1 to E10) – (sum of E31 to E40) = 2 × (Sum of E11 to E30) = 30 lacs – 10 lacs = 20 lacs.

Thus, sum of bonuses of E11 to E30 = 10 lacs.

Thus, original bonus of E1 to E10 = Bonus of E1 to E30 – Bonus of E11 to E30 = 12 lacs – 10 lacs = 2 lacs.

Likewise, original bonus of E31 to E40 = Bonus of E11 to E40 – Bonus of E11 to E30 = 18 lacs – 10 lacs = 8 lacs.

In 2023, Bonus of E1 to E 10 will double to 4 lacs; E11 to E30 will remain the same at 10 lacs and E31 to E40 will triple to 3 × 8 = 24 lacs. Total bonus of 40 employees in 2023 = 4 lacs + 10 lacs + 24 lacs = 38 lacs.

Average bonus per employee in 2023 = 38 lacs/40 = 95000. Option (a) is correct.

17. The LHS of the equation can be transformed as:

$$\frac{1}{3} \times \frac{\log_2(a+b)}{\log_2 c} + \frac{1}{3} \times \frac{\log_3(a-b)}{\log_3 c} = \frac{1}{3}\left[\log_c(a+b) + \log_c(a-b)\right] = \frac{2}{3}$$

This gives is: $a^2 - b^2 = c^2$ or $a^2 = b^2 + c^2$

Since the values of b and c are limited to a maximum value of 10 each, the highest value a^2 can take is 100 + 100 = 200. For a to be an integer, it's maximum value would be 14.

18. You can simply do a question like this using the options given. The second and third options can be easily removed by checking that the inequality is not satisfied at $x = 0$ (Note: These get eliminated since we are able to identify a value in their given range where the inequality is not satisfied). To choose between the first and fourth option, we can check for a value outside the first option but inside the range of the fourth option – say $x = 10$. At $x = 10$, the inequality will read as: $\frac{1}{15} \le \frac{1}{17}$ which is clearly incorrect. Hence, we can reject the fourth option and mark option (a) as the correct answer.

19. In this question, the exponential expression can be rewritten in the m^n form writing it as: $(2^5 \times 3^8)^5$. The value of $m - n = 2^5 \times 3^8 - 5 = 209947$.

Option (a) is correct.

20. Squaring both sides of the equation, we get

$$\left(x+6\sqrt{2}\right)+\left(x-6\sqrt{2}\right)-2\sqrt{x^2-72} = 8 \rightarrow$$

$$2x - 2\sqrt{x^2-72} = 8\, or\, x - \sqrt{x^2-72} = 4 \rightarrow \sqrt{x^2-72} = (x-4)$$

From this point, we can either work out the value of x, using a small trial and error. We can see that at $x = 11$, we get $\sqrt{121-72} = 7 = (11-4) = 7$. Hence, the value of $x = 11$.

Alternately, you could also square both sides of the equation to get:

$$x^2 - 72 = x^2 - 8x + 16 \rightarrow x = 11.$$

21. Let the current age of Garima be G and Rajesh be $G + n$. It is given to us that when Rajesh was Garima's age (meaning n years ago – Rajesh's age would be G, while Garima would be 'G-n' years old); the ratio of Rajesh and Garima's age was 3:2.

This gives us the equation: $\frac{G}{G-n} = \frac{3}{2} \rightarrow G = 3n$.

Hence, Garima's age today is 3n and Rajesh is $G + n = 4n$. When Garima's age become $4n$ (n years from now), Rajesh would be at an age of $5n$. The required ratio is $5n$" $4n$ = 5 : 4. Option (a) is correct.

22. We can see that at 3^5 divided by 11, the remainder is 1. Hence, we can write:

$$\frac{3^{333}}{11} = \frac{(3^5)^{66} \times 3^3}{11}$$

The remainder of this expression would be the remainder of 3^3 when it is divided by 11 = 5. Hence, option (b) is correct.

CAT 2024 Slot 3

1. The given set of equations would have no solution if $\frac{p}{3} = \frac{-4}{k} \neq \frac{2}{a}$.

   From $\frac{-4}{k} \neq \frac{2}{a}$, we get $2a + k \neq 0$. Hence, option (b) is correct.

2. In the figure, the area of triangle MNP will be one-fourth the area of triangle ABC. Likewise, X, Y, Z will be mid points of MP, MN and NP respectively. Hence, the area of triangle XYZ will be one-fourth the area of triangle MNP. Hence, the correct answer $= 1400 \times \frac{1}{4} \times \frac{1}{4} = 90$.

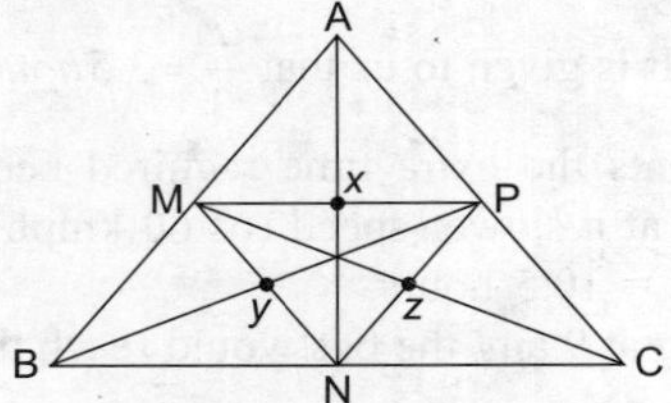

3. Opening the LHS of the expression we get:

$$a^2 + 3b^2 + 2ab\sqrt{3} = 52 + 30\sqrt{3}$$

   Comparing the two sides of this equation, we get $a^2 + 3b^2 = 52$ and $ab = 15$.

   The only pair of values that satisfies these equations is a = 5 and b = 3. Hence, option (d) is correct.

4. It is given to us that the girls are minimum 44% and maximum 60%. This means that there are between 110 to 150 girls and hence between 140-100 boys. To this deduction if we add the information that 80% of the girls and 50% of the boys opt for swimming, we realise that simultaneously the number of girls has to be a multiple of 5 (since 80% of a number is equal to 4/5th of the number), while the number of boys should be even. This gives rise to the following table:

Number of Girls (g)	110	120	130	140	150
Number of Boys (b)	140	130	120	110	100
Girls and Boys who opt for Swimming (a)	88 + 70 = 158	96 + 65 = 161	104 + 60 = 164	112 + 55 = 167	120 + 50 = 170
Girls and Boys who opt for Running (b)	66 + 98 = 164	72 + 91 = 163	78 + 84 = 162	84 + 77 = 161	90 + 70 = 160
Girls and boys who opt for both = $a + b - 250$	158 + 164 – 250 = 72	161 + 163 – 250 = 74	164 + 162 – 250 = 76	167 + 161 – 250 = 78	170 + 160 – 250 = 80

The minimum and maximum possible number of students who opted for both swimming and running are 72 and 80 respectively. Option (b) is correct.

5. Let the amount of water in the solution initially be 'n' liters. Then, the amount of milk initially is '300 – n'. This, mixture contains $\frac{n}{300} \times 100 = \frac{n}{3}\%$ water.

   At this stage in order to avoid fractions, you can change your number of liters of water in the initial solution to be $3n$. Milk = '300 – $3n$' and water percentage = n%.

   When we are taking out $6n$ liters of this solution, the remaining solution (300 – $6n$) will still have n% water. To this we are adding 6n liters of water (which is 100% water) – resulting in 72% milk i.e. 28% water. The given situation can be represented on the alligation number line as shown:

n%	28%	100%
300 – $6n$		$6n$

   The equation representing this alligation situation would give us:

$$\frac{300 - 6n}{6n} = \frac{100 - 28}{28 - n} \rightarrow n = 10$$

   Hence, $3n$ = 30. The initial solution had 30 liters of water.

6. The given situation is as shown in the figure.

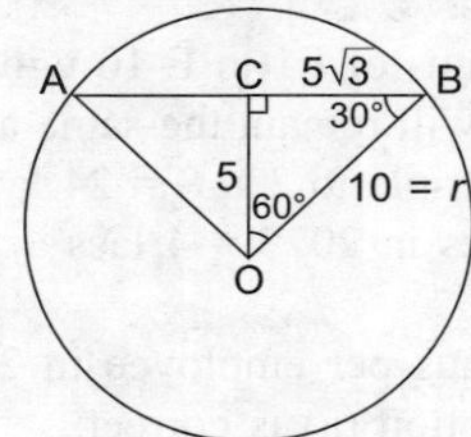